Oxford Dictionary of National Biography

Volume 33

Oxford Dictionary of National Biography

IN ASSOCIATION WITH

The British Academy

From the earliest times to the year 2000

Edited by

H. C. G. Matthew

and

Brian Harrison

Volume 33

Leared–Lister

OXFORD UNIVERSITY PRESS

OXFORD
UNIVERSITY PRESS

Great Clarendon Street, Oxford OX2 6DP

Oxford University Press is a department of the University of Oxford.
It furthers the University's objective of excellence in research, scholarship,
and education by publishing worldwide in

Oxford New York

Auckland Bangkok Buenos Aires Cape Town
Chennai Dar es Salaam Delhi Hong Kong Istanbul Karachi
Kolkata Kuala Lumpur Madrid Melbourne Mexico City Mumbai Nairobi
São Paulo Shanghai Taipei Tokyo Toronto

Oxford is a registered trade mark of Oxford University Press
in the UK and in certain other countries

Published in the United States
by Oxford University Press Inc., New York

First published 2004

British Library Cataloguing in Publication Data
Data available

Library of Congress Cataloging in Publication Data
Data available: for details see volume 1, p. iv

ISBN 0-19-861383-0 (this volume)
ISBN 0-19-861411-X (set of sixty volumes)

Text captured by Alliance Phototypesetters, Pondicherry
Illustrations reproduced and archived by
Alliance Graphics Ltd, UK
Typeset in OUP Swift by Interactive Sciences Limited, Gloucester
Printed in Great Britain on acid-free paper by
Butler and Tanner Ltd,
Frome, Somerset

LIST OF ABBREVIATIONS

1 *General abbreviations*

AB	bachelor of arts
ABC	Australian Broadcasting Corporation
ABC TV	ABC Television
act.	active
A$	Australian dollar
AD	*anno domini*
AFC	Air Force Cross
AIDS	acquired immune deficiency syndrome
AK	Alaska
AL	Alabama
A level	advanced level [examination]
ALS	associate of the Linnean Society
AM	master of arts
AMICE	associate member of the Institution of Civil Engineers
ANZAC	Australian and New Zealand Army Corps
appx *pl.* appxs	appendix(es)
AR	Arkansas
ARA	associate of the Royal Academy
ARCA	associate of the Royal College of Art
ARCM	associate of the Royal College of Music
ARCO	associate of the Royal College of Organists
ARIBA	associate of the Royal Institute of British Architects
ARP	air-raid precautions
ARRC	associate of the Royal Red Cross
ARSA	associate of the Royal Scottish Academy
art.	article / item
ASC	Army Service Corps
Asch	Austrian Schilling
ASDIC	Antisubmarine Detection Investigation Committee
ATS	Auxiliary Territorial Service
ATV	Associated Television
Aug	August
AZ	Arizona
b.	born
BA	bachelor of arts
BA (Admin.)	bachelor of arts (administration)
BAFTA	British Academy of Film and Television Arts
BAO	bachelor of arts in obstetrics
bap.	baptized
BBC	British Broadcasting Corporation / Company
BC	before Christ
BCE	before the common (*or* Christian) era
BCE	bachelor of civil engineering
BCG	bacillus of Calmette and Guérin [inoculation against tuberculosis]
BCh	bachelor of surgery
BChir	bachelor of surgery
BCL	bachelor of civil law
BCnL	bachelor of canon law
BCom	bachelor of commerce
BD	bachelor of divinity
BEd	bachelor of education
BEng	bachelor of engineering
bk *pl.* bks	book(s)
BL	bachelor of law / letters / literature
BLitt	bachelor of letters
BM	bachelor of medicine
BMus	bachelor of music
BP	before present
BP	British Petroleum
Bros.	Brothers
BS	(1) bachelor of science; (2) bachelor of surgery; (3) British standard
BSc	bachelor of science
BSc (Econ.)	bachelor of science (economics)
BSc (Eng.)	bachelor of science (engineering)
bt	baronet
BTh	bachelor of theology
bur.	buried
C.	command [identifier for published parliamentary papers]
c.	*circa*
c.	*capitulum pl. capitula*: chapter(s)
CA	California
Cantab.	Cantabrigiensis
cap.	*capitulum pl. capitula*: chapter(s)
CB	companion of the Bath
CBE	commander of the Order of the British Empire
CBS	Columbia Broadcasting System
cc	cubic centimetres
C$	Canadian dollar
CD	compact disc
Cd	command [identifier for published parliamentary papers]
CE	Common (*or* Christian) Era
cent.	century
cf.	compare
CH	Companion of Honour
chap.	chapter
ChB	bachelor of surgery
CI	Imperial Order of the Crown of India
CIA	Central Intelligence Agency
CID	Criminal Investigation Department
CIE	companion of the Order of the Indian Empire
Cie	Compagnie
CLit	companion of literature
CM	master of surgery
cm	centimetre(s)

Cmd	command [identifier for published parliamentary papers]
CMG	companion of the Order of St Michael and St George
Cmnd	command [identifier for published parliamentary papers]
CO	Colorado
Co.	company
co.	county
col. *pl.* cols.	column(s)
Corp.	corporation
CSE	certificate of secondary education
CSI	companion of the Order of the Star of India
CT	Connecticut
CVO	commander of the Royal Victorian Order
cwt	hundredweight
$	(American) dollar
d.	(1) penny (pence); (2) died
DBE	dame commander of the Order of the British Empire
DCH	diploma in child health
DCh	doctor of surgery
DCL	doctor of civil law
DCnL	doctor of canon law
DCVO	dame commander of the Royal Victorian Order
DD	doctor of divinity
DE	Delaware
Dec	December
dem.	demolished
DEng	doctor of engineering
des.	destroyed
DFC	Distinguished Flying Cross
DipEd	diploma in education
DipPsych	diploma in psychiatry
diss.	dissertation
DL	deputy lieutenant
DLitt	doctor of letters
DLittCelt	doctor of Celtic letters
DM	(1) Deutschmark; (2) doctor of medicine; (3) doctor of musical arts
DMus	doctor of music
DNA	dioxyribonucleic acid
doc.	document
DOL	doctor of oriental learning
DPH	diploma in public health
DPhil	doctor of philosophy
DPM	diploma in psychological medicine
DSC	Distinguished Service Cross
DSc	doctor of science
DSc (Econ.)	doctor of science (economics)
DSc (Eng.)	doctor of science (engineering)
DSM	Distinguished Service Medal
DSO	companion of the Distinguished Service Order
DSocSc	doctor of social science
DTech	doctor of technology
DTh	doctor of theology
DTM	diploma in tropical medicine
DTMH	diploma in tropical medicine and hygiene
DU	doctor of the university
DUniv	doctor of the university
dwt	pennyweight
EC	European Community
ed. *pl.* eds.	edited / edited by / editor(s)
Edin.	Edinburgh
edn	edition
EEC	European Economic Community
EFTA	European Free Trade Association
EICS	East India Company Service
EMI	Electrical and Musical Industries (Ltd)
Eng.	English
enl.	enlarged
ENSA	Entertainments National Service Association
ep. *pl.* epp.	*epistola(e)*
ESP	extra-sensory perception
esp.	especially
esq.	esquire
est.	estimate / estimated
EU	European Union
ex	sold by (*lit.* out of)
excl.	excludes / excluding
exh.	exhibited
exh. cat.	exhibition catalogue
f. *pl.* ff.	following [pages]
FA	Football Association
FACP	fellow of the American College of Physicians
facs.	facsimile
FANY	First Aid Nursing Yeomanry
FBA	fellow of the British Academy
FBI	Federation of British Industries
FCS	fellow of the Chemical Society
Feb	February
FEng	fellow of the Fellowship of Engineering
FFCM	fellow of the Faculty of Community Medicine
FGS	fellow of the Geological Society
fig.	figure
FIMechE	fellow of the Institution of Mechanical Engineers
FL	Florida
fl.	*floruit*
FLS	fellow of the Linnean Society
FM	frequency modulation
fol. *pl.* fols.	folio(s)
Fr	French francs
Fr.	French
FRAeS	fellow of the Royal Aeronautical Society
FRAI	fellow of the Royal Anthropological Institute
FRAM	fellow of the Royal Academy of Music
FRAS	(1) fellow of the Royal Asiatic Society; (2) fellow of the Royal Astronomical Society
FRCM	fellow of the Royal College of Music
FRCO	fellow of the Royal College of Organists
FRCOG	fellow of the Royal College of Obstetricians and Gynaecologists
FRCP(C)	fellow of the Royal College of Physicians of Canada
FRCP (Edin.)	fellow of the Royal College of Physicians of Edinburgh
FRCP (Lond.)	fellow of the Royal College of Physicians of London
FRCPath	fellow of the Royal College of Pathologists
FRCPsych	fellow of the Royal College of Psychiatrists
FRCS	fellow of the Royal College of Surgeons
FRGS	fellow of the Royal Geographical Society
FRIBA	fellow of the Royal Institute of British Architects
FRICS	fellow of the Royal Institute of Chartered Surveyors
FRS	fellow of the Royal Society
FRSA	fellow of the Royal Society of Arts

FRSCM	fellow of the Royal School of Church Music
FRSE	fellow of the Royal Society of Edinburgh
FRSL	fellow of the Royal Society of Literature
FSA	fellow of the Society of Antiquaries
ft	foot *pl.* feet
FTCL	fellow of Trinity College of Music, London
ft-lb per min.	foot-pounds per minute [unit of horsepower]
FZS	fellow of the Zoological Society
GA	Georgia
GBE	knight or dame grand cross of the Order of the British Empire
GCB	knight grand cross of the Order of the Bath
GCE	general certificate of education
GCH	knight grand cross of the Royal Guelphic Order
GCHQ	government communications headquarters
GCIE	knight grand commander of the Order of the Indian Empire
GCMG	knight or dame grand cross of the Order of St Michael and St George
GCSE	general certificate of secondary education
GCSI	knight grand commander of the Order of the Star of India
GCStJ	bailiff or dame grand cross of the order of St John of Jerusalem
GCVO	knight or dame grand cross of the Royal Victorian Order
GEC	General Electric Company
Ger.	German
GI	government (*or* general) issue
GMT	Greenwich mean time
GP	general practitioner
GPU	[Soviet special police unit]
GSO	general staff officer
Heb.	Hebrew
HEICS	Honourable East India Company Service
HI	Hawaii
HIV	human immunodeficiency virus
HK$	Hong Kong dollar
HM	his / her majesty('s)
HMAS	his / her majesty's Australian ship
HMNZS	his / her majesty's New Zealand ship
HMS	his / her majesty's ship
HMSO	His / Her Majesty's Stationery Office
HMV	His Master's Voice
Hon.	Honourable
hp	horsepower
hr	hour(s)
HRH	his / her royal highness
HTV	Harlech Television
IA	Iowa
ibid.	*ibidem*: in the same place
ICI	Imperial Chemical Industries (Ltd)
ID	Idaho
IL	Illinois
illus.	illustration
illustr.	illustrated
IN	Indiana
in.	inch(es)
Inc.	Incorporated
incl.	includes / including
IOU	I owe you
IQ	intelligence quotient
Ir£	Irish pound
IRA	Irish Republican Army
ISO	companion of the Imperial Service Order
It.	Italian
ITA	Independent Television Authority
ITV	Independent Television
Jan	January
JP	justice of the peace
jun.	junior
KB	knight of the Order of the Bath
KBE	knight commander of the Order of the British Empire
KC	king's counsel
kcal	kilocalorie
KCB	knight commander of the Order of the Bath
KCH	knight commander of the Royal Guelphic Order
KCIE	knight commander of the Order of the Indian Empire
KCMG	knight commander of the Order of St Michael and St George
KCSI	knight commander of the Order of the Star of India
KCVO	knight commander of the Royal Victorian Order
keV	kilo-electron-volt
KG	knight of the Order of the Garter
KGB	[Soviet committee of state security]
KH	knight of the Royal Guelphic Order
KLM	Koninklijke Luchtvaart Maatschappij (Royal Dutch Air Lines)
km	kilometre(s)
KP	knight of the Order of St Patrick
KS	Kansas
KT	knight of the Order of the Thistle
kt	knight
KY	Kentucky
£	pound(s) sterling
£E	Egyptian pound
L	lira *pl.* lire
l. *pl.* ll.	line(s)
LA	Lousiana
LAA	light anti-aircraft
LAH	licentiate of the Apothecaries' Hall, Dublin
Lat.	Latin
lb	pound(s), unit of weight
LDS	licence in dental surgery
lit.	literally
LittB	bachelor of letters
LittD	doctor of letters
LKQCPI	licentiate of the King and Queen's College of Physicians, Ireland
LLA	lady literate in arts
LLB	bachelor of laws
LLD	doctor of laws
LLM	master of laws
LM	licentiate in midwifery
LP	long-playing record
LRAM	licentiate of the Royal Academy of Music
LRCP	licentiate of the Royal College of Physicians
LRCPS (Glasgow)	licentiate of the Royal College of Physicians and Surgeons of Glasgow
LRCS	licentiate of the Royal College of Surgeons
LSA	licentiate of the Society of Apothecaries
LSD	lysergic acid diethylamide
LVO	lieutenant of the Royal Victorian Order
M. *pl.* MM.	Monsieur *pl.* Messieurs
m	metre(s)

m. *pl.* mm.	membrane(s)
MA	(1) Massachusetts; (2) master of arts
MAI	master of engineering
MB	bachelor of medicine
MBA	master of business administration
MBE	member of the Order of the British Empire
MC	Military Cross
MCC	Marylebone Cricket Club
MCh	master of surgery
MChir	master of surgery
MCom	master of commerce
MD	(1) doctor of medicine; (2) Maryland
MDMA	methylenedioxymethamphetamine
ME	Maine
MEd	master of education
MEng	master of engineering
MEP	member of the European parliament
MG	Morris Garages
MGM	Metro-Goldwyn-Mayer
Mgr	Monsignor
MI	(1) Michigan; (2) military intelligence
MI1c	[secret intelligence department]
MI5	[military intelligence department]
MI6	[secret intelligence department]
MI9	[secret escape service]
MICE	member of the Institution of Civil Engineers
MIEE	member of the Institution of Electrical Engineers
min.	minute(s)
Mk	mark
ML	(1) licentiate of medicine; (2) master of laws
MLitt	master of letters
Mlle	Mademoiselle
mm	millimetre(s)
Mme	Madame
MN	Minnesota
MO	Missouri
MOH	medical officer of health
MP	member of parliament
m.p.h.	miles per hour
MPhil	master of philosophy
MRCP	member of the Royal College of Physicians
MRCS	member of the Royal College of Surgeons
MRCVS	member of the Royal College of Veterinary Surgeons
MRIA	member of the Royal Irish Academy
MS	(1) master of science; (2) Mississippi
MS *pl.* MSS	manuscript(s)
MSc	master of science
MSc (Econ.)	master of science (economics)
MT	Montana
MusB	bachelor of music
MusBac	bachelor of music
MusD	doctor of music
MV	motor vessel
MVO	member of the Royal Victorian Order
n. *pl.* nn.	note(s)
NAAFI	Navy, Army, and Air Force Institutes
NASA	National Aeronautics and Space Administration
NATO	North Atlantic Treaty Organization
NBC	National Broadcasting Corporation
NC	North Carolina
NCO	non-commissioned officer
ND	North Dakota
n.d.	no date
NE	Nebraska
nem. con.	*nemine contradicente*: unanimously
new ser.	new series
NH	New Hampshire
NHS	National Health Service
NJ	New Jersey
NKVD	[Soviet people's commissariat for internal affairs]
NM	New Mexico
nm	nanometre(s)
no. *pl.* nos.	number(s)
Nov	November
n.p.	no place [of publication]
NS	new style
NV	Nevada
NY	New York
NZBS	New Zealand Broadcasting Service
OBE	officer of the Order of the British Empire
obit.	obituary
Oct	October
OCTU	officer cadets training unit
OECD	Organization for Economic Co-operation and Development
OEEC	Organization for European Economic Co-operation
OFM	order of Friars Minor [Franciscans]
OFMCap	Ordine Frati Minori Cappucini: member of the Capuchin order
OH	Ohio
OK	Oklahoma
O level	ordinary level [examination]
OM	Order of Merit
OP	order of Preachers [Dominicans]
op. *pl.* opp.	opus *pl.* opera
OPEC	Organization of Petroleum Exporting Countries
OR	Oregon
orig.	original
OS	old style
OSB	Order of St Benedict
OTC	Officers' Training Corps
OWS	Old Watercolour Society
Oxon.	Oxoniensis
p. *pl.* pp.	page(s)
PA	Pennsylvania
p.a.	per annum
para.	paragraph
PAYE	pay as you earn
pbk *pl.* pbks	paperback(s)
per.	[during the] period
PhD	doctor of philosophy
pl.	(1) plate(s); (2) plural
priv. coll.	private collection
pt *pl.* pts	part(s)
pubd	published
PVC	polyvinyl chloride
q. *pl.* qq.	(1) question(s); (2) quire(s)
QC	queen's counsel
R	rand
R.	Rex / Regina
r	recto
r.	reigned / ruled
RA	Royal Academy / Royal Academician

RAC	Royal Automobile Club
RAF	Royal Air Force
RAFVR	Royal Air Force Volunteer Reserve
RAM	[member of the] Royal Academy of Music
RAMC	Royal Army Medical Corps
RCA	Royal College of Art
RCNC	Royal Corps of Naval Constructors
RCOG	Royal College of Obstetricians and Gynaecologists
RDI	royal designer for industry
RE	Royal Engineers
repr. *pl.* reprs.	reprint(s) / reprinted
repro.	reproduced
rev.	revised / revised by / reviser / revision
Revd	Reverend
RHA	Royal Hibernian Academy
RI	(1) Rhode Island; (2) Royal Institute of Painters in Water-Colours
RIBA	Royal Institute of British Architects
RIN	Royal Indian Navy
RM	Reichsmark
RMS	Royal Mail steamer
RN	Royal Navy
RNA	ribonucleic acid
RNAS	Royal Naval Air Service
RNR	Royal Naval Reserve
RNVR	Royal Naval Volunteer Reserve
RO	Record Office
r.p.m.	revolutions per minute
RRS	royal research ship
Rs	rupees
RSA	(1) Royal Scottish Academician; (2) Royal Society of Arts
RSPCA	Royal Society for the Prevention of Cruelty to Animals
Rt Hon.	Right Honourable
Rt Revd	Right Reverend
RUC	Royal Ulster Constabulary
Russ.	Russian
RWS	Royal Watercolour Society
S4C	Sianel Pedwar Cymru
s.	shilling(s)
s.a.	*sub anno*: under the year
SABC	South African Broadcasting Corporation
SAS	Special Air Service
SC	South Carolina
ScD	doctor of science
S$	Singapore dollar
SD	South Dakota
sec.	second(s)
sel.	selected
sen.	senior
Sept	September
ser.	series
SHAPE	supreme headquarters allied powers, Europe
SIDRO	Société Internationale d'Énergie Hydro-Électrique
sig. *pl.* sigs.	signature(s)
sing.	singular
SIS	Secret Intelligence Service
SJ	Society of Jesus
Skr	Swedish krona
Span.	Spanish
SPCK	Society for Promoting Christian Knowledge
SS	(1) Santissimi; (2) Schutzstaffel; (3) steam ship
STB	bachelor of theology
STD	doctor of theology
STM	master of theology
STP	doctor of theology
supp.	supposedly
suppl. *pl.* suppls.	supplement(s)
s.v.	*sub verbo* / *sub voce*: under the word / heading
SY	steam yacht
TA	Territorial Army
TASS	[Soviet news agency]
TB	tuberculosis (*lit.* tubercle bacillus)
TD	(1) *teachtaí dála* (member of the Dáil); (2) territorial decoration
TN	Tennessee
TNT	trinitrotoluene
trans.	translated / translated by / translation / translator
TT	tourist trophy
TUC	Trades Union Congress
TX	Texas
U-boat	*Unterseeboot*: submarine
Ufa	Universum-Film AG
UMIST	University of Manchester Institute of Science and Technology
UN	United Nations
UNESCO	United Nations Educational, Scientific, and Cultural Organization
UNICEF	United Nations International Children's Emergency Fund
unpubd	unpublished
USS	United States ship
UT	Utah
v	verso
v.	versus
VA	Virginia
VAD	Voluntary Aid Detachment
VC	Victoria Cross
VE-day	victory in Europe day
Ven.	Venerable
VJ-day	victory over Japan day
vol. *pl.* vols.	volume(s)
VT	Vermont
WA	Washington [state]
WAAC	Women's Auxiliary Army Corps
WAAF	Women's Auxiliary Air Force
WEA	Workers' Educational Association
WHO	World Health Organization
WI	Wisconsin
WRAF	Women's Royal Air Force
WRNS	Women's Royal Naval Service
WV	West Virginia
WVS	Women's Voluntary Service
WY	Wyoming
¥	yen
YMCA	Young Men's Christian Association
YWCA	Young Women's Christian Association

2 Institution abbreviations

All Souls Oxf.	All Souls College, Oxford
AM Oxf.	Ashmolean Museum, Oxford
Balliol Oxf.	Balliol College, Oxford
BBC WAC	BBC Written Archives Centre, Reading
Beds. & Luton ARS	Bedfordshire and Luton Archives and Record Service, Bedford
Berks. RO	Berkshire Record Office, Reading
BFI	British Film Institute, London
BFI NFTVA	British Film Institute, London, National Film and Television Archive
BGS	British Geological Survey, Keyworth, Nottingham
Birm. CA	Birmingham Central Library, Birmingham City Archives
Birm. CL	Birmingham Central Library
BL	British Library, London
BL NSA	British Library, London, National Sound Archive
BL OIOC	British Library, London, Oriental and India Office Collections
BLPES	London School of Economics and Political Science, British Library of Political and Economic Science
BM	British Museum, London
Bodl. Oxf.	Bodleian Library, Oxford
Bodl. RH	Bodleian Library of Commonwealth and African Studies at Rhodes House, Oxford
Borth. Inst.	Borthwick Institute of Historical Research, University of York
Boston PL	Boston Public Library, Massachusetts
Bristol RO	Bristol Record Office
Bucks. RLSS	Buckinghamshire Records and Local Studies Service, Aylesbury
CAC Cam.	Churchill College, Cambridge, Churchill Archives Centre
Cambs. AS	Cambridgeshire Archive Service
CCC Cam.	Corpus Christi College, Cambridge
CCC Oxf.	Corpus Christi College, Oxford
Ches. & Chester ALSS	Cheshire and Chester Archives and Local Studies Service
Christ Church Oxf.	Christ Church, Oxford
Christies	Christies, London
City Westm. AC	City of Westminster Archives Centre, London
CKS	Centre for Kentish Studies, Maidstone
CLRO	Corporation of London Records Office
Coll. Arms	College of Arms, London
Col. U.	Columbia University, New York
Cornwall RO	Cornwall Record Office, Truro
Courtauld Inst.	Courtauld Institute of Art, London
CUL	Cambridge University Library
Cumbria AS	Cumbria Archive Service
Derbys. RO	Derbyshire Record Office, Matlock
Devon RO	Devon Record Office, Exeter
Dorset RO	Dorset Record Office, Dorchester
Duke U.	Duke University, Durham, North Carolina
Duke U., Perkins L.	Duke University, Durham, North Carolina, William R. Perkins Library
Durham Cath. CL	Durham Cathedral, chapter library
Durham RO	Durham Record Office
DWL	Dr Williams's Library, London
Essex RO	Essex Record Office
E. Sussex RO	East Sussex Record Office, Lewes
Eton	Eton College, Berkshire
FM Cam.	Fitzwilliam Museum, Cambridge
Folger	Folger Shakespeare Library, Washington, DC
Garr. Club	Garrick Club, London
Girton Cam.	Girton College, Cambridge
GL	Guildhall Library, London
Glos. RO	Gloucestershire Record Office, Gloucester
Gon. & Caius Cam.	Gonville and Caius College, Cambridge
Gov. Art Coll.	Government Art Collection
GS Lond.	Geological Society of London
Hants. RO	Hampshire Record Office, Winchester
Harris Man. Oxf.	Harris Manchester College, Oxford
Harvard TC	Harvard Theatre Collection, Harvard University, Cambridge, Massachusetts, Nathan Marsh Pusey Library
Harvard U.	Harvard University, Cambridge, Massachusetts
Harvard U., Houghton L.	Harvard University, Cambridge, Massachusetts, Houghton Library
Herefs. RO	Herefordshire Record Office, Hereford
Herts. ALS	Hertfordshire Archives and Local Studies, Hertford
Hist. Soc. Penn.	Historical Society of Pennsylvania, Philadelphia
HLRO	House of Lords Record Office, London
Hult. Arch.	Hulton Archive, London and New York
Hunt. L.	Huntington Library, San Marino, California
ICL	Imperial College, London
Inst. CE	Institution of Civil Engineers, London
Inst. EE	Institution of Electrical Engineers, London
IWM	Imperial War Museum, London
IWM FVA	Imperial War Museum, London, Film and Video Archive
IWM SA	Imperial War Museum, London, Sound Archive
JRL	John Rylands University Library of Manchester
King's AC Cam.	King's College Archives Centre, Cambridge
King's Cam.	King's College, Cambridge
King's Lond.	King's College, London
King's Lond., Liddell Hart C.	King's College, London, Liddell Hart Centre for Military Archives
Lancs. RO	Lancashire Record Office, Preston
L. Cong.	Library of Congress, Washington, DC
Leics. RO	Leicestershire, Leicester, and Rutland Record Office, Leicester
Lincs. Arch.	Lincolnshire Archives, Lincoln
Linn. Soc.	Linnean Society of London
LMA	London Metropolitan Archives
LPL	Lambeth Palace, London
Lpool RO	Liverpool Record Office and Local Studies Service
LUL	London University Library
Magd. Cam.	Magdalene College, Cambridge
Magd. Oxf.	Magdalen College, Oxford
Man. City Gall.	Manchester City Galleries
Man. CL	Manchester Central Library
Mass. Hist. Soc.	Massachusetts Historical Society, Boston
Merton Oxf.	Merton College, Oxford
MHS Oxf.	Museum of the History of Science, Oxford
Mitchell L., Glas.	Mitchell Library, Glasgow
Mitchell L., NSW	State Library of New South Wales, Sydney, Mitchell Library
Morgan L.	Pierpont Morgan Library, New York
NA Canada	National Archives of Canada, Ottawa
NA Ire.	National Archives of Ireland, Dublin
NAM	National Army Museum, London
NA Scot.	National Archives of Scotland, Edinburgh
News Int. RO	News International Record Office, London
NG Ire.	National Gallery of Ireland, Dublin

NG Scot.	National Gallery of Scotland, Edinburgh
NHM	Natural History Museum, London
NL Aus.	National Library of Australia, Canberra
NL Ire.	National Library of Ireland, Dublin
NL NZ	National Library of New Zealand, Wellington
NL NZ, Turnbull L.	National Library of New Zealand, Wellington, Alexander Turnbull Library
NL Scot.	National Library of Scotland, Edinburgh
NL Wales	National Library of Wales, Aberystwyth
NMG Wales	National Museum and Gallery of Wales, Cardiff
NMM	National Maritime Museum, London
Norfolk RO	Norfolk Record Office, Norwich
Northants. RO	Northamptonshire Record Office, Northampton
Northumbd RO	Northumberland Record Office
Notts. Arch.	Nottinghamshire Archives, Nottingham
NPG	National Portrait Gallery, London
NRA	National Archives, London, Historical Manuscripts Commission, National Register of Archives
Nuffield Oxf.	Nuffield College, Oxford
N. Yorks. CRO	North Yorkshire County Record Office, Northallerton
NYPL	New York Public Library
Oxf. UA	Oxford University Archives
Oxf. U. Mus. NH	Oxford University Museum of Natural History
Oxon. RO	Oxfordshire Record Office, Oxford
Pembroke Cam.	Pembroke College, Cambridge
PRO	National Archives, London, Public Record Office
PRO NIre.	Public Record Office for Northern Ireland, Belfast
Pusey Oxf.	Pusey House, Oxford
RA	Royal Academy of Arts, London
Ransom HRC	Harry Ransom Humanities Research Center, University of Texas, Austin
RAS	Royal Astronomical Society, London
RBG Kew	Royal Botanic Gardens, Kew, London
RCP Lond.	Royal College of Physicians of London
RCS Eng.	Royal College of Surgeons of England, London
RGS	Royal Geographical Society, London
RIBA	Royal Institute of British Architects, London
RIBA BAL	Royal Institute of British Architects, London, British Architectural Library
Royal Arch.	Royal Archives, Windsor Castle, Berkshire [by gracious permission of her majesty the queen]
Royal Irish Acad.	Royal Irish Academy, Dublin
Royal Scot. Acad.	Royal Scottish Academy, Edinburgh
RS	Royal Society, London
RSA	Royal Society of Arts, London
RS Friends, Lond.	Religious Society of Friends, London
St Ant. Oxf.	St Antony's College, Oxford
St John Cam.	St John's College, Cambridge
S. Antiquaries, Lond.	Society of Antiquaries of London
Sci. Mus.	Science Museum, London
Scot. NPG	Scottish National Portrait Gallery, Edinburgh
Scott Polar RI	University of Cambridge, Scott Polar Research Institute
Sheff. Arch.	Sheffield Archives
Shrops. RRC	Shropshire Records and Research Centre, Shrewsbury
SOAS	School of Oriental and African Studies, London
Som. ARS	Somerset Archive and Record Service, Taunton
Staffs. RO	Staffordshire Record Office, Stafford
Suffolk RO	Suffolk Record Office
Surrey HC	Surrey History Centre, Woking
TCD	Trinity College, Dublin
Trinity Cam.	Trinity College, Cambridge
U. Aberdeen	University of Aberdeen
U. Birm.	University of Birmingham
U. Birm. L.	University of Birmingham Library
U. Cal.	University of California
U. Cam.	University of Cambridge
UCL	University College, London
U. Durham	University of Durham
U. Durham L.	University of Durham Library
U. Edin.	University of Edinburgh
U. Edin., New Coll.	University of Edinburgh, New College
U. Edin., New Coll. L.	University of Edinburgh, New College Library
U. Edin. L.	University of Edinburgh Library
U. Glas.	University of Glasgow
U. Glas. L.	University of Glasgow Library
U. Hull	University of Hull
U. Hull, Brynmor Jones L.	University of Hull, Brynmor Jones Library
U. Leeds	University of Leeds
U. Leeds, Brotherton L.	University of Leeds, Brotherton Library
U. Lond.	University of London
U. Lpool	University of Liverpool
U. Lpool L.	University of Liverpool Library
U. Mich.	University of Michigan, Ann Arbor
U. Mich., Clements L.	University of Michigan, Ann Arbor, William L. Clements Library
U. Newcastle	University of Newcastle upon Tyne
U. Newcastle, Robinson L.	University of Newcastle upon Tyne, Robinson Library
U. Nott.	University of Nottingham
U. Nott. L.	University of Nottingham Library
U. Oxf.	University of Oxford
U. Reading	University of Reading
U. Reading L.	University of Reading Library
U. St Andr.	University of St Andrews
U. St Andr. L.	University of St Andrews Library
U. Southampton	University of Southampton
U. Southampton L.	University of Southampton Library
U. Sussex	University of Sussex, Brighton
U. Texas	University of Texas, Austin
U. Wales	University of Wales
U. Warwick Mod. RC	University of Warwick, Coventry, Modern Records Centre
V&A	Victoria and Albert Museum, London
V&A NAL	Victoria and Albert Museum, London, National Art Library
Warks. CRO	Warwickshire County Record Office, Warwick
Wellcome L.	Wellcome Library for the History and Understanding of Medicine, London
Westm. DA	Westminster Diocesan Archives, London
Wilts. & Swindon RO	Wiltshire and Swindon Record Office, Trowbridge
Worcs. RO	Worcestershire Record Office, Worcester
W. Sussex RO	West Sussex Record Office, Chichester
W. Yorks. AS	West Yorkshire Archive Service
Yale U.	Yale University, New Haven, Connecticut
Yale U., Beinecke L.	Yale University, New Haven, Connecticut, Beinecke Rare Book and Manuscript Library
Yale U. CBA	Yale University, New Haven, Connecticut, Yale Center for British Art

3 *Bibliographic abbreviations*

Adams, *Drama*	W. D. Adams, *A dictionary of the drama*, 1: *A–G* (1904); 2: *H–Z* (1956) [vol. 2 microfilm only]
AFM	J O'Donovan, ed. and trans., *Annala rioghachta Eireann / Annals of the kingdom of Ireland by the four masters*, 7 vols. (1848–51); 2nd edn (1856); 3rd edn (1990)
Allibone, *Dict.*	S. A. Allibone, *A critical dictionary of English literature and British and American authors*, 3 vols. (1859–71); suppl. by J. F. Kirk, 2 vols. (1891)
ANB	J. A. Garraty and M. C. Carnes, eds., *American national biography*, 24 vols. (1999)
Anderson, *Scot. nat.*	W. Anderson, *The Scottish nation, or, The surnames, families, literature, honours, and biographical history of the people of Scotland*, 3 vols. (1859–63)
Ann. mon.	H. R. Luard, ed., *Annales monastici*, 5 vols., Rolls Series, 36 (1864–9)
Ann. Ulster	S. Mac Airt and G. Mac Niocaill, eds., *Annals of Ulster (to AD 1131)* (1983)
APC	*Acts of the privy council of England*, new ser., 46 vols. (1890–1964)
APS	*The acts of the parliaments of Scotland*, 12 vols. in 13 (1814–75)
Arber, *Regs. Stationers*	F. Arber, ed., *A transcript of the registers of the Company of Stationers of London, 1554–1640 AD*, 5 vols. (1875–94)
ArchR	*Architectural Review*
ASC	D. Whitelock, D. C. Douglas, and S. I. Tucker, ed. and trans., *The Anglo-Saxon Chronicle: a revised translation* (1961)
AS chart.	P. H. Sawyer, *Anglo-Saxon charters: an annotated list and bibliography*, Royal Historical Society Guides and Handbooks (1968)
AusDB	D. Pike and others, eds., *Australian dictionary of biography*, 16 vols. (1966–2002)
Baker, *Serjeants*	J. H. Baker, *The order of serjeants at law*, SeldS, suppl. ser., 5 (1984)
Bale, *Cat.*	J. Bale, *Scriptorum illustrium Maioris Brytannie, quam nunc Angliam et Scotiam vocant: catalogus*, 2 vols. in 1 (Basel, 1557–9); facs. edn (1971)
Bale, *Index*	J. Bale, *Index Britanniae scriptorum*, ed. R. L. Poole and M. Bateson (1902); facs. edn (1990)
BBCS	*Bulletin of the Board of Celtic Studies*
BDMBR	J. O. Baylen and N. J. Gossman, eds., *Biographical dictionary of modern British radicals*, 3 vols. in 4 (1979–88)
Bede, *Hist. eccl.*	*Bede's Ecclesiastical history of the English people*, ed. and trans. B. Colgrave and R. A. B. Mynors, OMT (1969); repr. (1991)
Bénézit, *Dict.*	E. Bénézit, *Dictionnaire critique et documentaire des peintres, sculpteurs, dessinateurs et graveurs*, 3 vols. (Paris, 1911–23); new edn, 8 vols. (1948–66), repr. (1966); 3rd edn, rev. and enl., 10 vols. (1976); 4th edn, 14 vols. (1999)
BIHR	*Bulletin of the Institute of Historical Research*
Birch, *Seals*	W. de Birch, *Catalogue of seals in the department of manuscripts in the British Museum*, 6 vols. (1887–1900)
Bishop Burnet's History	*Bishop Burnet's History of his own time*, ed. M. J. Routh, 2nd edn, 6 vols. (1833)
Blackwood	*Blackwood's [Edinburgh] Magazine*, 328 vols. (1817–1980)
Blain, Clements & Grundy, *Feminist comp.*	V. Blain, P. Clements, and I. Grundy, eds., *The feminist companion to literature in English* (1990)
BL cat.	*The British Library general catalogue of printed books* [in 360 vols. with suppls., also CD-ROM and online]
BMJ	*British Medical Journal*
Boase & Courtney, *Bibl. Corn.*	G. C. Boase and W. P. Courtney, *Bibliotheca Cornubiensis: a catalogue of the writings … of Cornishmen*, 3 vols. (1874–82)
Boase, *Mod. Eng. biog.*	F. Boase, *Modern English biography: containing many thousand concise memoirs of persons who have died since the year 1850*, 6 vols. (privately printed, Truro, 1892–1921); repr. (1965)
Boswell, *Life*	*Boswell's Life of Johnson: together with Journal of a tour to the Hebrides and Johnson's Diary of a journey into north Wales*, ed. G. B. Hill, enl. edn, rev. L. F. Powell, 6 vols. (1934–50); 2nd edn (1964); repr. (1971)
Brown & Stratton, *Brit. mus.*	J. D. Brown and S. S. Stratton, *British musical biography* (1897)
Bryan, *Painters*	M. Bryan, *A biographical and critical dictionary of painters and engravers*, 2 vols. (1816); new edn, ed. G. Stanley (1849); new edn, ed. R. E. Graves and W. Armstrong, 2 vols. (1886–9); [4th edn], ed. G. C. Williamson, 5 vols. (1903–5) [various reprs.]
Burke, *Gen. GB*	J. Burke, *A genealogical and heraldic history of the commoners of Great Britain and Ireland*, 4 vols. (1833–8); new edn as *A genealogical and heraldic dictionary of the landed gentry of Great Britain and Ireland*, 3 vols. [1843–9] [many later edns]
Burke, *Gen. Ire.*	J. B. Burke, *A genealogical and heraldic history of the landed gentry of Ireland* (1899); 2nd edn (1904); 3rd edn (1912); 4th edn (1958); 5th edn as *Burke's Irish family records* (1976)
Burke, *Peerage*	J. Burke, *A general* [later edns *A genealogical*] *and heraldic dictionary of the peerage and baronetage of the United Kingdom* [later edns *the British empire*] (1829–)
Burney, *Hist. mus.*	C. Burney, *A general history of music, from the earliest ages to the present period*, 4 vols. (1776–89)
Burtchaell & Sadleir, *Alum. Dubl.*	G. D. Burtchaell and T. U. Sadleir, *Alumni Dublinenses: a register of the students, graduates, and provosts of Trinity College* (1924); [2nd edn], with suppl., in 2 pts (1935)
Calamy rev.	A. G. Matthews, *Calamy revised* (1934); repr. (1988)
CCI	*Calendar of confirmations and inventories granted and given up in the several commissariots of Scotland* (1876–)
CClR	*Calendar of the close rolls preserved in the Public Record Office*, 47 vols. (1892–1963)
CDS	J. Bain, ed., *Calendar of documents relating to Scotland*, 4 vols., PRO (1881–8); suppl. vol. 5, ed. G. G. Simpson and J. D. Galbraith [1986]
CEPR letters	W. H. Bliss, C. Johnson, and J. Twemlow, eds., *Calendar of entries in the papal registers relating to Great Britain and Ireland: papal letters* (1893–)
CGPLA	*Calendars of the grants of probate and letters of administration* [in 4 ser.: *England & Wales, Northern Ireland, Ireland*, and *Éire*]
Chambers, *Scots.*	R. Chambers, ed., *A biographical dictionary of eminent Scotsmen*, 4 vols. (1832–5)
Chancery records	chancery records pubd by the PRO
Chancery records (RC)	chancery records pubd by the Record Commissions

CIPM	*Calendar of inquisitions post mortem*, [20 vols.], PRO (1904–); also *Henry VII*, 3 vols. (1898–1955)
Clarendon, *Hist. rebellion*	E. Hyde, earl of Clarendon, *The history of the rebellion and civil wars in England*, 6 vols. (1888); repr. (1958) and (1992)
Cobbett, *Parl. hist.*	W. Cobbett and J. Wright, eds., *Cobbett's Parliamentary history of England*, 36 vols. (1806–1820)
Colvin, *Archs.*	H. Colvin, *A biographical dictionary of British architects, 1600–1840*, 3rd edn (1995)
Cooper, *Ath. Cantab.*	C. H. Cooper and T. Cooper, *Athenae Cantabrigienses*, 3 vols. (1858–1913); repr. (1967)
CPR	*Calendar of the patent rolls preserved in the Public Record Office* (1891–)
Crockford	*Crockford's Clerical Directory*
CS	Camden Society
CSP	*Calendar of state papers* [in 11 ser.: *domestic, Scotland, Scottish series, Ireland, colonial, Commonwealth, foreign, Spain* [at Simancas], *Rome, Milan*, and *Venice*]
CYS	Canterbury and York Society
DAB	*Dictionary of American biography*, 21 vols. (1928–36), repr. in 11 vols. (1964); 10 suppls. (1944–96)
DBB	D. J. Jeremy, ed., *Dictionary of business biography*, 5 vols. (1984–6)
DCB	G. W. Brown and others, *Dictionary of Canadian biography*, [14 vols.] (1966–)
Debrett's Peerage	*Debrett's Peerage* (1803–) [sometimes *Debrett's Illustrated peerage*]
Desmond, *Botanists*	R. Desmond, *Dictionary of British and Irish botanists and horticulturists* (1977); rev. edn (1994)
Dir. Brit. archs.	A. Felstead, J. Franklin, and L. Pinfield, eds., *Directory of British architects, 1834–1900* (1993); 2nd edn, ed. A. Brodie and others, 2 vols. (2001)
DLB	J. M. Bellamy and J. Saville, eds., *Dictionary of labour biography*, [10 vols.] (1972–)
DLitB	Dictionary of Literary Biography
DNB	*Dictionary of national biography*, 63 vols. (1885–1900), suppl., 3 vols. (1901); repr. in 22 vols. (1908–9); 10 further suppls. (1912–96); *Missing persons* (1993)
DNZB	W. H. Oliver and C. Orange, eds., *The dictionary of New Zealand biography*, 5 vols. (1990–2000)
DSAB	W. J. de Kock and others, eds., *Dictionary of South African biography*, 5 vols. (1968–87)
DSB	C. C. Gillispie and F. L. Holmes, eds., *Dictionary of scientific biography*, 16 vols. (1970–80); repr. in 8 vols. (1981); 2 vol. suppl. (1990)
DSBB	A. Slaven and S. Checkland, eds., *Dictionary of Scottish business biography, 1860–1960*, 2 vols. (1986–90)
DSCHT	N. M. de S. Cameron and others, eds., *Dictionary of Scottish church history and theology* (1993)
Dugdale, *Monasticon*	W. Dugdale, *Monasticon Anglicanum*, 3 vols. (1655–72); 2nd edn, 3 vols. (1661–82); new edn, ed. J. Caley, J. Ellis, and B. Bandinel, 6 vols. in 8 pts (1817–30); repr. (1846) and (1970)
DWB	J. E. Lloyd and others, eds., *Dictionary of Welsh biography down to 1940* (1959) [Eng. trans. of *Y bywgraffiadur Cymreig hyd 1940*, 2nd edn (1954)]
EdinR	*Edinburgh Review, or, Critical Journal*
EETS	Early English Text Society
Emden, *Cam.*	A. B. Emden, *A biographical register of the University of Cambridge to 1500* (1963)
Emden, *Oxf.*	A. B. Emden, *A biographical register of the University of Oxford to AD 1500*, 3 vols. (1957–9); also *A biographical register of the University of Oxford, AD 1501 to 1540* (1974)
EngHR	*English Historical Review*
Engraved Brit. ports.	F. M. O'Donoghue and H. M. Hake, *Catalogue of engraved British portraits preserved in the department of prints and drawings in the British Museum*, 6 vols. (1908–25)
ER	The English Reports, 178 vols. (1900–32)
ESTC	*English short title catalogue, 1475–1800* [CD-ROM and online]
Evelyn, *Diary*	*The diary of John Evelyn*, ed. E. S. De Beer, 6 vols. (1955); repr. (2000)
Farington, *Diary*	*The diary of Joseph Farington*, ed. K. Garlick and others, 17 vols. (1978–98)
Fasti Angl. (Hardy)	J. Le Neve, *Fasti ecclesiae Anglicanae*, ed. T. D. Hardy, 3 vols. (1854)
Fasti Angl., 1066–1300	[J. Le Neve], *Fasti ecclesiae Anglicanae, 1066–1300*, ed. D. E. Greenway and J. S. Barrow, [8 vols.] (1968–)
Fasti Angl., 1300–1541	[J. Le Neve], *Fasti ecclesiae Anglicanae, 1300–1541*, 12 vols. (1962–7)
Fasti Angl., 1541–1857	[J. Le Neve], *Fasti ecclesiae Anglicanae, 1541–1857*, ed. J. M. Horn, D. M. Smith, and D. S. Bailey, [9 vols.] (1969–)
Fasti Scot.	H. Scott, *Fasti ecclesiae Scoticanae*, 3 vols. in 6 (1871); new edn, [11 vols.] (1915–)
FO List	*Foreign Office List*
Fortescue, *Brit. army*	J. W. Fortescue, *A history of the British army*, 13 vols. (1899–1930)
Foss, *Judges*	E. Foss, *The judges of England*, 9 vols. (1848–64); repr. (1966)
Foster, *Alum. Oxon.*	J. Foster, ed., *Alumni Oxonienses: the members of the University of Oxford, 1715–1886*, 4 vols. (1887–8); later edn (1891); also *Alumni Oxonienses … 1500–1714*, 4 vols. (1891–2); 8 vol. repr. (1968) and (2000)
Fuller, *Worthies*	T. Fuller, *The history of the worthies of England*, 4 pts (1662); new edn, 2 vols., ed. J. Nichols (1811); new edn, 3 vols., ed. P. A. Nuttall (1840); repr. (1965)
GEC, *Baronetage*	G. E. Cokayne, *Complete baronetage*, 6 vols. (1900–09); repr. (1983) [microprint]
GEC, *Peerage*	G. E. C. [G. E. Cokayne], *The complete peerage of England, Scotland, Ireland, Great Britain, and the United Kingdom*, 8 vols. (1887–98); new edn, ed. V. Gibbs and others, 14 vols. in 15 (1910–98); microprint repr. (1982) and (1987)
Genest, *Eng. stage*	J. Genest, *Some account of the English stage from the Restoration in 1660 to 1830*, 10 vols. (1832); repr. [New York, 1965]
Gillow, *Lit. biog. hist.*	J. Gillow, *A literary and biographical history or bibliographical dictionary of the English Catholics, from the breach with Rome, in 1534, to the present time*, 5 vols. [1885–1902]; repr. (1961); repr. with preface by C. Gillow (1999)
Gir. Camb. opera	*Giraldi Cambrensis opera*, ed. J. S. Brewer, J. F. Dimock, and G. F. Warner, 8 vols., Rolls Series, 21 (1861–91)
GJ	*Geographical Journal*

Gladstone, *Diaries*	*The Gladstone diaries: with cabinet minutes and prime-ministerial correspondence*, ed. M. R. D. Foot and H. C. G. Matthew, 14 vols. (1968–94)
GM	*Gentleman's Magazine*
Graves, *Artists*	A. Graves, ed., *A dictionary of artists who have exhibited works in the principal London exhibitions of oil paintings from 1760 to 1880* (1884); new edn (1895); 3rd edn (1901); facs. edn (1969); repr. [1970], (1973), and (1984)
Graves, *Brit. Inst.*	A. Graves, *The British Institution, 1806–1867: a complete dictionary of contributors and their work from the foundation of the institution* (1875); facs. edn (1908); repr. (1969)
Graves, *RA exhibitors*	A. Graves, *The Royal Academy of Arts: a complete dictionary of contributors and their work from its foundation in 1769 to 1904*, 8 vols. (1905–6); repr. in 4 vols. (1970) and (1972)
Graves, *Soc. Artists*	A. Graves, *The Society of Artists of Great Britain, 1760–1791, the Free Society of Artists, 1761–1783: a complete dictionary* (1907); facs. edn (1969)
Greaves & Zaller, *BDBR*	R. L. Greaves and R. Zaller, eds., *Biographical dictionary of British radicals in the seventeenth century*, 3 vols. (1982–4)
Grove, *Dict. mus.*	G. Grove, ed., *A dictionary of music and musicians*, 5 vols. (1878–90); 2nd edn, ed. J. A. Fuller Maitland (1904–10); 3rd edn, ed. H. C. Colles (1927); 4th edn with suppl. (1940); 5th edn, ed. E. Blom, 9 vols. (1954); suppl. (1961) [see also *New Grove*]
Hall, *Dramatic ports.*	L. A. Hall, *Catalogue of dramatic portraits in the theatre collection of the Harvard College library*, 4 vols. (1930–34)
Hansard	*Hansard's parliamentary debates*, ser. 1–5 (1803–)
Highfill, Burnim & Langhans, *BDA*	P. H. Highfill, K. A. Burnim, and E. A. Langhans, *A biographical dictionary of actors, actresses, musicians, dancers, managers, and other stage personnel in London, 1660–1800*, 16 vols. (1973–93)
Hist. U. Oxf.	T. H. Aston, ed., *The history of the University of Oxford*, 8 vols. (1984–2000) [1: *The early Oxford schools*, ed. J. I. Catto (1984); 2: *Late medieval Oxford*, ed. J. I. Catto and R. Evans (1992); 3: *The collegiate university*, ed. J. McConica (1986); 4: *Seventeenth-century Oxford*, ed. N. Tyacke (1997); 5: *The eighteenth century*, ed. L. S. Sutherland and L. G. Mitchell (1986); 6–7: *Nineteenth-century Oxford*, ed. M. G. Brock and M. C. Curthoys (1997–2000); 8: *The twentieth century*, ed. B. Harrison (2000)]
HJ	*Historical Journal*
HMC	Historical Manuscripts Commission
Holdsworth, *Eng. law*	W. S. Holdsworth, *A history of English law*, ed. A. L. Goodhart and H. L. Hanbury, 17 vols. (1903–72)
HoP, *Commons*	*The history of parliament: the House of Commons* [*1386–1421*, ed. J. S. Roskell, L. Clark, and C. Rawcliffe, 4 vols. (1992); *1509–1558*, ed. S. T. Bindoff, 3 vols. (1982); *1558–1603*, ed. P. W. Hasler, 3 vols. (1981); *1660–1690*, ed. B. D. Henning, 3 vols. (1983); *1690–1715*, ed. D. W. Hayton, E. Cruickshanks, and S. Handley, 5 vols. (2002); *1715–1754*, ed. R. Sedgwick, 2 vols. (1970); *1754–1790*, ed. L. Namier and J. Brooke, 3 vols. (1964), repr. (1985); *1790–1820*, ed. R. G. Thorne, 5 vols. (1986); in draft (used with permission): *1422–1504*, *1604–1629*, *1640–1660*, and *1820–1832*]
IGI	*International Genealogical Index*, Church of Jesus Christ of the Latterday Saints
ILN	*Illustrated London News*
IMC	Irish Manuscripts Commission
Irving, *Scots.*	J. Irving, ed., *The book of Scotsmen eminent for achievements in arms and arts, church and state, law, legislation and literature, commerce, science, travel and philanthropy* (1881)
JCS	*Journal of the Chemical Society*
JHC	*Journals of the House of Commons*
JHL	*Journals of the House of Lords*
John of Worcester, *Chron.*	*The chronicle of John of Worcester*, ed. R. R. Darlington and P. McGurk, trans. J. Bray and P. McGurk, 3 vols., OMT (1995–) [vol. 1 forthcoming]
Keeler, *Long Parliament*	M. F. Keeler, *The Long Parliament, 1640–1641: a biographical study of its members* (1954)
Kelly, *Handbk*	*The upper ten thousand: an alphabetical list of all members of noble families*, 3 vols. (1875–7); continued as *Kelly's handbook of the upper ten thousand for 1878* [1879], 2 vols. (1878–9); continued as *Kelly's handbook to the titled, landed and official classes*, 94 vols. (1880–1973)
LondG	*London Gazette*
LP Henry VIII	J. S. Brewer, J. Gairdner, and R. H. Brodie, eds., *Letters and papers, foreign and domestic, of the reign of Henry VIII*, 23 vols. in 38 (1862–1932); repr. (1965)
Mallalieu, *Watercolour artists*	H. L. Mallalieu, *The dictionary of British watercolour artists up to 1820*, 3 vols. (1976–90); vol. 1, 2nd edn (1986)
Memoirs FRS	*Biographical Memoirs of Fellows of the Royal Society*
MGH	Monumenta Germaniae Historica
MT	*Musical Times*
Munk, *Roll*	W. Munk, *The roll of the Royal College of Physicians of London*, 2 vols. (1861); 2nd edn, 3 vols. (1878)
N&Q	*Notes and Queries*
New Grove	S. Sadie, ed., *The new Grove dictionary of music and musicians*, 20 vols. (1980); 2nd edn, 29 vols. (2001) [also online edn; see also Grove, *Dict. mus.*]
Nichols, *Illustrations*	J. Nichols and J. B. Nichols, *Illustrations of the literary history of the eighteenth century*, 8 vols. (1817–58)
Nichols, *Lit. anecdotes*	J. Nichols, *Literary anecdotes of the eighteenth century*, 9 vols. (1812–16); facs. edn (1966)
Obits. FRS	*Obituary Notices of Fellows of the Royal Society*
O'Byrne, *Naval biog. dict.*	W. R. O'Byrne, *A naval biographical dictionary* (1849); repr. (1990); [2nd edn], 2 vols. (1861)
OHS	Oxford Historical Society
Old Westminsters	*The record of Old Westminsters*, 1–2, ed. G. F. R. Barker and A. H. Stenning (1928); suppl. 1, ed. J. B. Whitmore and G. R. Y. Radcliffe [1938]; 3, ed. J. B. Whitmore, G. R. Y. Radcliffe, and D. C. Simpson (1963); suppl. 2, ed. F. E. Pagan (1978); 4, ed. F. E. Pagan and H. E. Pagan (1992)
OMT	Oxford Medieval Texts
Ordericus Vitalis, *Eccl. hist.*	*The ecclesiastical history of Orderic Vitalis*, ed. and trans. M. Chibnall, 6 vols., OMT (1969–80); repr. (1990)
Paris, *Chron.*	*Matthaei Parisiensis, monachi sancti Albani, chronica majora*, ed. H. R. Luard, Rolls Series, 7 vols. (1872–83)
Parl. papers	*Parliamentary papers* (1801–)
PBA	*Proceedings of the British Academy*

Pepys, *Diary*	*The diary of Samuel Pepys*, ed. R. Latham and W. Matthews, 11 vols. (1970–83); repr. (1995) and (2000)
Pevsner	N. Pevsner and others, Buildings of England series
PICE	*Proceedings of the Institution of Civil Engineers*
Pipe rolls	*The great roll of the pipe for* ..., PRSoc. (1884–)
PRO	Public Record Office
PRS	*Proceedings of the Royal Society of London*
PRSoc.	Pipe Roll Society
PTRS	*Philosophical Transactions of the Royal Society*
QR	*Quarterly Review*
RC	Record Commissions
Redgrave, *Artists*	S. Redgrave, *A dictionary of artists of the English school* (1874); rev. edn (1878); repr. (1970)
Reg. Oxf.	C. W. Boase and A. Clark, eds., *Register of the University of Oxford*, 5 vols., OHS, 1, 10–12, 14 (1885–9)
Reg. PCS	J. H. Burton and others, eds., *The register of the privy council of Scotland*, 1st ser., 14 vols. (1877–98); 2nd ser., 8 vols. (1899–1908); 3rd ser., [16 vols.] (1908–70)
Reg. RAN	H. W. C. Davis and others, eds., *Regesta regum Anglo-Normannorum, 1066–1154*, 4 vols. (1913–69)
RIBA Journal	*Journal of the Royal Institute of British Architects* [later *RIBA Journal*]
RotP	J. Strachey, ed., *Rotuli parliamentorum ut et petitiones, et placita in parliamento*, 6 vols. (1767–77)
RotS	D. Macpherson, J. Caley, and W. Illingworth, eds., *Rotuli Scotiae in Turri Londinensi et in domo capitulari Westmonasteriensi asservati*, 2 vols., RC, 14 (1814–19)
RS	Record(s) Society
Rymer, *Foedera*	T. Rymer and R. Sanderson, eds., *Foedera, conventiones, literae et cuiuscunque generis acta publica inter reges Angliae et alios quosvis imperatores, reges, pontifices, principes, vel communitates*, 20 vols. (1704–35); 2nd edn, 20 vols. (1726–35); 3rd edn, 10 vols. (1739–45), facs. edn (1967); new edn, ed. A. Clarke, J. Caley, and F. Holbrooke, 4 vols., RC, 50 (1816–30)
Sainty, *Judges*	J. Sainty, ed., *The judges of England, 1272–1990*, SeldS, suppl. ser., 10 (1993)
Sainty, *King's counsel*	J. Sainty, ed., *A list of English law officers and king's counsel*, SeldS, suppl. ser., 7 (1987)
SCH	Studies in Church History
Scots peerage	J. B. Paul, ed. *The Scots peerage, founded on Wood's edition of Sir Robert Douglas's Peerage of Scotland, containing an historical and genealogical account of the nobility of that kingdom*, 9 vols. (1904–14)
SeldS	Selden Society
SHR	*Scottish Historical Review*
State trials	T. B. Howell and T. J. Howell, eds., *Cobbett's Complete collection of state trials*, 34 vols. (1809–28)
STC, 1475–1640	A. W. Pollard, G. R. Redgrave, and others, eds., *A short-title catalogue of ... English books ... 1475–1640* (1926); 2nd edn, ed. W. A. Jackson, F. S. Ferguson, and K. F. Pantzer, 3 vols. (1976–91) [see also Wing, *STC*]
STS	Scottish Text Society
SurtS	Surtees Society
Symeon of Durham, *Opera*	*Symeonis monachi opera omnia*, ed. T. Arnold, 2 vols., Rolls Series, 75 (1882–5); repr. (1965)
Tanner, *Bibl. Brit.-Hib.*	T. Tanner, *Bibliotheca Britannico-Hibernica*, ed. D. Wilkins (1748); repr. (1963)
Thieme & Becker, *Allgemeines Lexikon*	U. Thieme, F. Becker, and H. Vollmer, eds., *Allgemeines Lexikon der bildenden Künstler von der Antike bis zur Gegenwart*, 37 vols. (Leipzig, 1907–50); repr. (1961–5), (1983), and (1992)
Thurloe, *State papers*	*A collection of the state papers of John Thurloe*, ed. T. Birch, 7 vols. (1742)
TLS	*Times Literary Supplement*
Tout, *Admin. hist.*	T. F. Tout, *Chapters in the administrative history of mediaeval England: the wardrobe, the chamber, and the small seals*, 6 vols. (1920–33); repr. (1967)
TRHS	*Transactions of the Royal Historical Society*
VCH	H. A. Doubleday and others, eds., *The Victoria history of the counties of England*, [88 vols.] (1900–)
Venn, *Alum. Cant.*	J. Venn and J. A. Venn, *Alumni Cantabrigienses: a biographical list of all known students, graduates, and holders of office at the University of Cambridge, from the earliest times to 1900*, 10 vols. (1922–54); repr. in 2 vols. (1974–8)
Vertue, *Note books*	[G. Vertue], *Note books*, ed. K. Esdaile, earl of Ilchester, and H. M. Hake, 6 vols., Walpole Society, 18, 20, 22, 24, 26, 30 (1930–55)
VF	*Vanity Fair*
Walford, *County families*	E. Walford, *The county families of the United Kingdom, or, Royal manual of the titled and untitled aristocracy of Great Britain and Ireland* (1860)
Walker rev.	A. G. Matthews, *Walker revised: being a revision of John Walker's Sufferings of the clergy during the grand rebellion, 1642–60* (1948); repr. (1988)
Walpole, *Corr.*	*The Yale edition of Horace Walpole's correspondence*, ed. W. S. Lewis, 48 vols. (1937–83)
Ward, *Men of the reign*	T. H. Ward, ed., *Men of the reign: a biographical dictionary of eminent persons of British and colonial birth who have died during the reign of Queen Victoria* (1885); repr. (Graz, 1968)
Waterhouse, *18c painters*	E. Waterhouse, *The dictionary of 18th century painters in oils and crayons* (1981); repr. as *British 18th century painters in oils and crayons* (1991), vol. 2 of *Dictionary of British art*
Watt, *Bibl. Brit.*	R. Watt, *Bibliotheca Britannica, or, A general index to British and foreign literature*, 4 vols. (1824) [many reprs.]
Wellesley index	W. E. Houghton, ed., *The Wellesley index to Victorian periodicals, 1824–1900*, 5 vols. (1966–89); new edn (1999) [CD-ROM]
Wing, *STC*	D. Wing, ed., *Short-title catalogue of ... English books ... 1641–1700*, 3 vols. (1945–51); 2nd edn (1972–88); rev. and enl. edn, ed. J. J. Morrison, C. W. Nelson, and M. Seccombe, 4 vols. (1994–8) [see also *STC, 1475–1640*]
Wisden	*John Wisden's Cricketer's Almanack*
Wood, *Ath. Oxon.*	A. Wood, *Athenae Oxonienses ... to which are added the Fasti*, 2 vols. (1691–2); 2nd edn (1721); new edn, 4 vols., ed. P. Bliss (1813–20); repr. (1967) and (1969)
Wood, *Vic. painters*	C. Wood, *Dictionary of Victorian painters* (1971); 2nd edn (1978); 3rd edn as *Victorian painters*, 2 vols. (1995), vol. 4 of *Dictionary of British art*
WW	*Who's who* (1849–)
WWBMP	M. Stenton and S. Lees, eds., *Who's who of British members of parliament*, 4 vols. (1976–81)
WWW	*Who was who* (1929–)

Leared, Arthur (1822–1879), physician and traveller, born at Wexford, Ireland, was educated at Trinity College, Dublin (BA, 1845; MB, 1847; MD, 1860), and was admitted MD *ad eundem* at Oxford on 7 February 1861. He first practised in co. Wexford, and in 1852 he established himself as a physician in London. He was admitted to the Royal College of Physicians in 1854 and became a fellow in 1871.

During the Crimean War Leared acted as physician to the British Civil Hospital at Smyrna, and he subsequently visited the Holy Land. On his return to London he became associated with the Great Northern Hospital, the Royal Infirmary for Diseases of the Chest, the Metropolitan Dispensary, and St Mark's Hospital for Fistula. He also lectured on the practice of medicine at the Grosvenor Place school of medicine. In 1862 Leared paid the first of four visits to Iceland, the last of which was in 1874. He became so proficient in Icelandic that he published a book in the vernacular, *Fatal Cystic Disease of Iceland*. In the autumn of 1870 he visited the United States. In 1872 Leared travelled to Morocco, and he revisited that country on two other occasions: in 1877, as physician to the Portuguese embassy, and in the summer of 1879. Holding a free pass received from the sultan he was able to visit the cities of Morocco, Fez, and Meknès. He likewise explored remote parts of the country, and among other minor discoveries identified the site of the Roman station of Volubilis, an account of which he communicated to *The Academy* of 29 June 1878. Leared's medical experiences in Morocco were interesting, and he brought home contributions from the native materia medica. He reported the results of his first two journeys in two books, the best-known being *Morocco and the Moors, being an account of travels with a general description of the country and its people* (1876). *A Visit to the Court of Morocco* appeared in 1879. Leared's second journey was also the subject of a paper read by him, in Dublin in 1878, at the geographical section of the British Association. Leared also acquired a piece of land north of Tangier for an intended sanatorium for consumptive patients, as he believed the climate to be more suitable than even that of southern Europe. He also invented a double stethoscope used for teaching and was an authority on cardiac diseases.

Outside medicine Leared had a large circle of literary, scientific, and artistic friends, who appreciated his many winning qualities and wide culture, and he belonged to a number of learned societies at home and abroad. He frequently contributed to professional journals, mostly on subjects connected with his main medical interests—the sounds of the heart and the disorders of digestion. He published a number of articles and short works on these subjects between 1860 and 1890; of these, *The Causes and Treatment of Imperfect Digestion* (1860), which saw seven editions, is of particular interest and contains an excellent portrait of the author.

Leared and his wife, Mary Jane, were living at 12 Old Burlington Street, London, when he died there, on 16 October 1879. She survived him.

GORDON GOODWIN, *rev.* JEFFREY S. REZNICK

Sources J. Shepherd, *The Crimean doctors: a history of the British medical services in the Crimean War*, 2 vols. (1991) · A. Leared, *Morocco and the Moors*, 2nd edn (1891) · *The Lancet* (25 Oct 1879) · *BMJ* (25 Oct 1879), 663–4 · *London and Provincial Medical Directory* (1861) · *Medical Directory* (1879) · *CGPLA Eng. & Wales* (1879)
Archives U. Edin. L., letters to James Halliwell-Phillipps
Likenesses portrait, *c*.1880–1889, repro. in A. Leared, *The causes and treatment of imperfect digestion*, 7th edn (1882) · G. Simonds, marble bust, 1881?, RCP Lond.
Wealth at death under £1500: probate, 6 Nov 1879, *CGPLA Eng. & Wales*

Learmonth, Christian (*bap.* 1718, *d.* 1762), milliner and shopkeeper, was baptized at Bo'ness, Linlithgowshire, on 21 October 1718, the daughter of John Learmonth, schoolmaster and postmaster at Bo'ness, and of his first wife, Christian Livingston (*d.* in or before 1726), third daughter of Alexander Livingston of Parkhall, near Falkirk, Stirlingshire. She had a sister and four brothers, and three stepsisters from her father's second marriage, with Ann Crawford.

Christian lived in a house in Carrubber's Close, Edinburgh, on the north side of the High Street, which she bought in 1754. Her shop was in Lyon Close, further up the High Street, also on the north side. She was already in business by 1745, when another milliner, May McCrabie, first came to know her, and she was still actively engaged in business at the time of her death. As she had had no funding from her father she probably had difficulties in keeping the business afloat but she was given £200 to help her to carry on her business by her lodger, Lady Charlotte Gordon, one of the twelve children of the second duke of Gordon. In her will, dated 20 May 1756, Christian left all her movable goods to Lady Charlotte but this was contested, after Christian's death, by her two stepsisters, Ann and Jean, who were also milliners, and a dispute ensued. In the following court case one of the witnesses, Mary (or May) McCrabie, a milliner, stated that she had heard Christian say that any of her money that was free, and thus not required to pay off debts, would be left to Lady Charlotte. Christian requested that her linen and clothes should be given to one of her stepsisters. During the court case evidence of Christian's personal and business circumstances was given by Mary McCrabie and another milliner, Ann (or Annie) Wardrope. Ann, the daughter of William Wardrope, a surgeon in Edinburgh, had been apprenticed to Christian Learmonth when she was eleven years old, Christian having found one of her own stepsisters unsatisfactory as an apprentice. Ann was later allowed to put £30 into the business and to become a partner 'in Company', and she kept the proceeds of work done for her own customers. Lady Charlotte Gordon allowed Ann to carry on business after Christian's death.

Christian Learmonth died on 12 August 1762 in Carrubber's Close, Edinburgh, in her forty-fourth year. Lady Charlotte Gordon was made her executor. Christian had requested that her cousin Alexander Learmonth should make all the necessary arrangements for her funeral. Her shop goods were rouped (auctioned) and there is therefore a detailed inventory of these in the court papers, the details of which are of interest from the point of view of both eighteenth-century shopkeeping and the fashions of the period. Like other eighteenth-century Scottish milliners Christian and her partner made up bespoke accessories, such as caps and handkerchiefs, in the shop; details of the fabrics used are usually given in bills. The inventory of the shop can be compared with that of the milliner in the English context, such as Elizabeth Brown (or Browne) in Norwich, who had a similar business, for which a similar inventory and valuation survives. Christian's customers came from the families of town merchants and craftsmen as well as those of the landed gentry. Her total inventory, with the debts due to her, was valued at £5472 12*s.* 5*d.* sterling. ELIZABETH C. SANDERSON

Sources E. C. Sanderson, *Women and work in eighteenth-century Edinburgh* (1996) • Edinburgh register of testaments, 26 Nov 1762, NA Scot., CC8/8/119/1 • Edinburgh commissary court, processes, NA Scot., CC8/4/512/1/1 (1762); CC8/4/470 (1749); CC8/4/492 (1755) • Edinburgh register of sasines, 1757, NA Scot., RS 27/Vol. 148, fol. 460 • old parish register, Bo'ness, Edinburgh Central Library, microfilm index • Learmonth, letter to Sir John Clerk, 1721, NA Scot., Clerk of Penicuik muniments, GD 18/5323/4 • P. Clabburn, 'A provincial milliner's shop in 1785', *Costume*, 11 (1977)

Wealth at death £5472 12*s.* 5*d.*: Edinburgh register of testaments, 26 Nov 1762, NA Scot. CC8/8/119/1

Learmonth, Sir James Rögnvald (1895–1967), surgeon, was born in Gatehouse of Fleet, Kirkcudbrightshire, in south-west Scotland on 23 March 1895, the eldest son of William Learmonth, headmaster of Girthon School, Gatehouse of Fleet, and his wife Katherine, *née* Craig. His father came originally from Stromness, Orkney, and it was from this viking ancestry that James was given his second forename, Rögnvald; as a schoolboy he was called Ronald. After first attending Girthon School, where his father instilled into his two sons the virtues of hard work, thorough preparation, and the correct use of words, Learmonth moved north to Kilmarnock Academy to study Greek. In 1913 he was accepted as a medical student by Glasgow University.

As with so many of his generation, Learmonth's life was profoundly affected by two world wars. In 1914 Learmonth was commissioned in the King's Own Scottish Borderers, with whom he served in France. When gas warfare started on the western front, he devised a trench anemometer to measure wind force. Later he returned to Britain as an instructor in anti-gas measures. After the war he resumed his medical studies at Glasgow University, again evincing his penchant for research by the investigations he conducted with J. M. Graham on blood transfusion. He qualified with honours in 1921, being the outstanding medical student of his year.

Between 1921 and 1922 Learmonth held house-officer appointments at the Western Infirmary, Glasgow. The next two years were spent as a research assistant to Professor Archibald Young, and led to a Rockefeller fellowship at the Mayo Clinic, Minnesota, in 1924–5. There Learmonth engaged in neurosurgical research, especially on the pathology of brain tumours. A lifelong interest in neurophysiology and the peripheral nervous system began during his year at the Mayo Clinic. There he met Charlotte Newell, daughter of F. G. Bundy, of Vermont; she was director of social services at the clinic. They were married in William Mayo's garden, on 30 June 1925. They had two children, James and Jean.

After returning to Glasgow Learmonth was an assistant to the professor of surgery, the dispensary surgeon at the Western Infirmary, from 1925 to 1928. He also published a number of papers, initially on blood transfusion. He obtained his ChM in 1927 and became FRCS (Edin.) in the following year. He was then invited to join the staff of the neurosurgical department at the Mayo Clinic. Such invitations were very rare, and indicative of the impression Learmonth had made during his first sojourn in Minnesota. During the years 1928–32 he was engaged in busy neurosurgical practice at the Mayo Clinic, but he found time to study the innervation of the bladder and blood vessels.

In 1932 the regius chair in surgery fell vacant in Aberdeen and Learmonth was appointed. His reasons for leaving a lucrative practice in America are unclear; probably the call of his native land was the deciding factor. At first his reception in Aberdeen was somewhat frosty; he was the first full-time professor and an 'outsider'. However, his administrative abilities soon won grudging admiration from senior colleagues. Of imposing, if somewhat daunting appearance, Learmonth had little time for the pompous and garrulous. All his lectures were carefully prepared and delivered in a clear and succinct fashion.

Shortly before the outbreak of the Second World War, Learmonth succeeded Sir David Wilkie in the chair of systematic surgery in Edinburgh. Wartime conditions were difficult, but he went on to establish special paediatric, neurosurgical, urological, and thoracic surgery departments. He was busily engaged in the treatment of peripheral nerve and vascular injuries, and he was visited by medical officers from all the allied armies in Britain. After the war this international exchange of ideas was strengthened, and Learmonth visited and was visited by many distinguished surgeons. Slowly he persuaded colleagues in Edinburgh to exchange ideas and to participate in an early form of surgical audit at the Saturday morning meetings which he organized. Although later he was universally respected for his surgical skill and administrative abilities, perhaps his most enduring contribution to surgery was his promotion of research. Many of the principles of bio-engineering were investigated under his guidance.

In 1946 Learmonth took over the chair of clinical surgery at Edinburgh. Late in 1948 he was called to attend King George VI, who was suffering from obliterative disease of his arteries. He operated on the king in February 1949, and was then appointed KCVO, being knighted in the king's bedroom. He had been made CBE in 1945 and was appointed a chevalier of the Légion d'honneur in 1950. Many overseas honours followed. Although committee work was not his forte, he served for many years on the Medical Research Council and the University Grants Committee.

Somewhat unexpectedly Learmonth retired in 1956 at the age of sixty-one. He went to live in the small village of

Broughton, near Biggar, in Lanarkshire. He was remembered by his students for his courtesy and kindness to patients and for the way in which he encouraged less talented students, so long as they showed effort. In retirement he practised scientific gardening and played the mandolin. Glasgow University appointed him an assessor to the university court. Early in 1967 an atypical carcinoma of the lung was diagnosed. Learmonth refused to accept his heavy smoking as a causative factor. He was treated by radiotherapy; no operation was performed. He died at his home, Ardbucho, Broughton, on 27 September 1967, and was cremated in Edinburgh. JAMES KYLE

Sources *BMJ* (7 Oct 1967), 58–9 • *The Lancet* (7 Oct 1967), 781–3 • *DNB* • private information (2004) • personal knowledge (2004)
Archives Wilkie Research Laboratory, Edinburgh | U. Glas. L., Archives and Business Records Centre, Fleming MSS
Likenesses photographs, U. Aberdeen • photographs, U. Edin.
Wealth at death £30,612 5*s*. 11*d*.: confirmation, 3 Nov 1967, *CCI*

Learoyd, Roderick Alastair Brook (1913–1996), air force officer, was born on 5 February 1913 at 15 Turketel Road, Folkestone, Kent, the son of Major Reginald Brook Learoyd, retired army officer, and his wife, Marjorie Scott, *née* Boadle. The family, of Scottish and Yorkshire descent, had been involved in the Yorkshire textile industry and his father had served in the First World War in the Highland light infantry. Rod, as his family called him, was educated at Hydreye House Preparatory School, Sussex, and Wellington College, Berkshire, before attending Chelsea College of Aeronautical and Automobile Engineering. At the conclusion of his formal education he spent two years on his uncle's fruit farm in Argentina.

In March 1936 Learoyd returned to England and took a short commission in the RAF. Following training at Hamble and at Wittering, he graduated later that year and was posted to 49 squadron at Worthy Down. In 1938 the squadron moved to Scampton where it became the first to be equipped with the new Handley Page Hampden bombers.

On the night of 12 August 1940 Acting Flight Lieutenant 'Babe' Learoyd, as he was known to his RAF colleagues because of his impressive physical size, took off with ten other Hampden bombers on a mission to destroy an old aqueduct over the River Ems, north of Münster. Having attacked the Dortmund–Ems canal on a previous sortie, he was well aware of the high risk involved. Success depended on his approaching the canal from a direction that took him through a narrow passage of carefully sited anti-aircraft batteries that were able to deliver devastating fire from point-blank range. Disregarding the loss of two other Hampden bombers, Learoyd, blinded by German searchlights directed from close range, made his attack at an altitude of 150 feet. Flying solely on instruments, with his plane almost shot to pieces, he released his bomb load on target. Despite being wounded in the raid, Learoyd brought his plane home successfully although, with the landing flaps inoperable and the undercarriage indicators out of action, he had to wait until the light of dawn before attempting to land at Scampton. This he did without injury to his crew or further damage to his aircraft. For such conspicuous gallantry, Learoyd was awarded the Victoria Cross, his citation in the *London Gazette* reading, 'The high degree of courage, skill and determination which this officer had invariably displayed on many occasions in the face of the enemy, sets an example which is unsurpassed'. The award was popular with his fellow officers at Scampton who held Babe Learoyd in the highest regard for his quiet modesty and cool unflappability. Further honours followed when in November 1940 he received the freedom of the borough of New Romney, Kent.

Following his promotion to squadron leader, Learoyd acted temporarily as personal assistant to Air Chief Marshal Sir Robert Brooke-Popham before rejoining operations in February 1941 when he was appointed officer commanding 83 squadron at Scampton. He took up a new command as wing commander at operational training unit, Cottesmore, in the following June and six months later succeeded to the command of 44 squadron at Waddington, the first Avro Lancaster unit in the RAF. From January 1943 until the end of the war, Learoyd held a number of non-operational postings with the Air Ministry and with officer training units.

In May 1945 Learoyd returned to operational flying when he joined 48 (Dakota) squadron and moved to west Africa. He returned to England in the following year and was demobilized in October 1946, transferring to the RAF reserve as wing commander. Learoyd then joined the Malayan civil aviation department where he piloted for the colony's governor. On returning to England he was employed briefly in a tractor and construction firm before joining Austin Motor Company as export sales manager. He remained with the company (later British Motor Corporation) for the rest of his working life. In the course of his work he visited the United States and later headed the company's fleet sales, particularly for government departments. His natural charm and wartime reputation led to his becoming involved in British Motor Corporation's public relations division, where he was repeatedly used as unofficial ambassador.

Learoyd was a shy, unassuming man who rarely spoke about his wartime exploits over Germany. He had a lifelong passion for cars, particularly for Aston Martins, regularly attended the Le Mans 24 hour race, and was a frequent visitor to the Silverstone circuit. Although his later years were marred by diabetes that affected his vision, Learoyd was an active member of the Victoria Cross and George Cross Association. His portrait hangs in the Imperial War Museum.

On 24 January 1996 Learoyd died suddenly at his home, 12 Fittleworth Gardens, Rustington, Sussex, from a heart attack, survived by a brother and sister. He never married. BRIAN WIMBORNE

Sources *LondG* (20 Aug 1940) • C. Bowyer, *For valour: the air VCs* (1978) • *WW* (1994) • *The Times* (26 Jan 1996) • *The Independent* (2 Feb 1996) • d. cert. • b. cert. • J. F. Turner, *V.C.s of the air* (1960), 18–23 • *The Times* (19 Aug 1940) • *CGPLA Eng. & Wales* (1996)
Likenesses portrait, IWM
Wealth at death under £145,000: administration, 1996, *CGPLA Eng. & Wales*

Leask, William (1812–1884), Congregational minister, was the second son of poor parents resident in Kirkwall, Orkney, and was born there on 4 March 1812. (Kirkwall appears in Leask's autobiography as Churchbank.) As an infant he suffered from encephalitis but somehow overcame that ailment and became a bookkeeper. He was converted at the age of sixteen and began to teach himself the biblical languages. He moved (or perhaps eloped with his intended) to Edinburgh in 1834. Though he nearly died of typhoid fever in 1835, he played some part in the same year in the events that were to lead to the Disruption of the Scottish kirk, siding with the non-intrusionist party in the hope of seeing established (as one of his pamphlets put it) 'a true theocracy where Jehovah will reign'. The rule of God was to become a dominant theme of his later ministry. He now began to preach, and in 1835 moved to Liverpool to take up first a clerical post and then one with the Christian Instruction Society. His intention to become a missionary was frustrated by the birth of a child before his marriage on 18 May 1837 to Ann Cuthbert Moir, daughter of Robert Moir, director of music at St Magnus' Cathedral, Kirkwall. At that time Leask was working as a warehouseman in Glasgow, and the marriage took place in a United Secession chapel, probably because of the irregular circumstances of their relationship. His first work, remarkable for its heady utopianism, *The Hall of Vision, a Poem to which is Added a Letter to an Infidel*, was published in Manchester in 1838.

In 1839, without any formal training, Leask embarked on his first Congregational pastorate, at Chapmanslade, Wiltshire, where he remained until 1842. From 1843 to 1844 he was at Swanscombe, Kent, and from 1844 to 1847 at the countess of Huntingdon's Zion Chapel at Dover. Here he published in 1846 a book of philosophical lectures. From 1847 to 1856 he was at Esher Street, Kennington, Surrey; from 1857 to 1865 at Ware, Hertfordshire; and from 1865 to the year of his death at Maberley Chapel, Kingsland (usually shown as Dalston), London.

A great admirer of Thomas Campbell, the 'press baron' of the denomination, Leask aspired to be in some way his successor. For a time (1853–4) he edited the *Christian Examiner*, contributed to a short-lived magazine called *The Universe*, and edited (1865–6) the *Christian Weekly News*, which in 1866 became the long-running *Christian World*. He edited the *Christian Times* (1864) and founded, and for over two years (1864–6) edited, *The Rainbow*. For these and his other literary labours he received the degree of DD from Jefferson University, in the United States. Leask's *Autobiography of a Dissenting Minister* (1864) is a particularly obscure book, with persons and places heavily disguised.

Leask wrote a number of books—some in poetry, some in prose—some of which were simple biblical or doctrinal expositions while others were of an 'improving', fictional nature. His main enthusiasms were millenarianism and the conditional immortality movement. He believed that his own time showed abundant signs that the millennium, preceded by a mass conversion of the Jews, was imminent: he called persistently and a little naïvely for his people to prepare for a theocratic utopia which was just around the corner. His other concern he dealt with mainly in the pages of *The Rainbow*, which ran long after he had ceased to edit it. For Leask conditional immortality was posited on a basis of scriptural literalism and was advocated with apocalyptic fervour. He believed that unless the churches adopted it, rejecting everlasting punishment for the doctrine of the extinction of the impenitent at death, success on the mission field would be impossible. This was the theme of his contribution to the 1876 Conditionalist Conference at the Cannon Street Hotel, London. His theological emphases are most fully expounded in his essay in the *Report of a Conference on Conditional Immortality* (1876) and *The Scripture Doctrine of a Future Life* (1877).

Somehow this busy man found time to contribute also to the YMCA and early-closing movements. Leask died at his home, 34 Sandringham Road, Dalston, on 6 November 1884, his wife having predeceased him. His funeral service was held in Maberley Chapel on the 9th. Oddly, there was no obituary in the *Congregational Year Book*.

IAN SELLERS

Sources W. Leask, *Autobiography of a dissenting minister* (1864) · *Pall Mall Gazette* (8 Nov 1884) · *Christian World* (13 Nov 1884) · G. Rowell, *Hell and the Victorians* (1974) · m. cert. · C. Surman, index, DWL
Likenesses stipple, NPG
Wealth at death £832 13*s*. 11*d*.: probate, 2 Jan 1885, *CGPLA Eng. & Wales*

Leate, Nicholas (1565/6–1631), merchant, whose parentage and apprenticeship are unknown, first appears in the records in 1590 as a party to a dispute with another English merchant in Rouen. Two years later he joined the Levant Company, and to qualify for membership he joined a livery company, in this case the Ironmongers' Company, and became a citizen of London. Commercially, he participated and invested in companies that sought new routes by which to trade to Asia. Politically, he became known for a refusal to pay a customs duty not sanctioned by parliament; and his seizure of commodities from the customs house late in his life was to prompt constitutional debate about the appropriate prerogatives of the crown.

Leate invested or participated in twelve trading companies, mainly between 1590 and 1615, more than any other contemporary merchant or member of the gentry. Among them were companies by which merchants regulated English trade to Europe, such as the Merchant Adventurers, whose members traded to Hamburg, the short-lived French and Spanish companies, and the Eastland Company, whose members traded to the Baltic ports. Looking beyond well-known horizons, Leate initially focused his interest on companies which pushed the bounds of trade further towards Asia, starting with the Russia and Levant companies. Like many charter members of the Levant Company, Leate also invested capital, in his case £200, in the 1599 subscription for the return voyage of Sir James Lancaster to India. He became a founding member of the East India Company the following year, and his fellow members elected him to the committee of directors. In this role, and perhaps because he was a member of both companies, he was one of the leaders chosen to negotiate with the Russia Company about the legal implications and financial provisions of an expedition to find the north-west passage. It was an interest that Leate continued to pursue with investments in the voyage of Henry Hudson in 1610 and in the Northwest Passage Company in 1612. In the early years of James's reign, in 1609 and 1610, he was also active in organizing colonial ventures in Ireland and Virginia.

The trading activities in which Leate engaged ranged very broadly. He used his connections in the companies to diversify the usual commercial routes, for instance trading Russian wax in the Levant; he was active in the sale of provisions to the East India Company; he owned a large ship, the *Samuel* of 280 tons, which he fitted out for a privateering voyage; and he was also a financier. There is no indication that he ever gained great wealth from these ventures, but some evidence to indicate that their sometimes speculative nature caused him at least momentary difficulties. In 1610, for instance, the common council of London intervened with his creditors to ensure their temporary forbearance.

At the centre of Leate's commercial ventures was the trade that he developed in the Levant, both in the Ottoman empire, where he traded cloth for silk, and in Zante and Cephalonia, where he traded for currants. He achieved eminence within the Levant Company and was a long-standing member of the court of assistants before serving for twelve years, between 1615 and 1627, as deputy governor. In connection with this position within the company, he moved into financial activities as a farmer of the customs. First, in 1607, with a syndicate of other prominent members, he controlled the farm on exports of tin. Second, in 1614, he was sole controller of the farm of customs and consulage for English trade to north Africa, which was later to lead him to take a central role in the problems connected with Algerian piracy. Leate interwove business with family connections, and most of his family had strong ties to the company. Leate himself married Jane, the daughter of one of the three principal founders of the company, Richard Staper; they had two sons and at least five daughters. His eldest son, Richard, served, like his father, on the court of assistants between 1629 and 1633, and his second son, Hewett, began his commercial career as their factor in Zante; two of his daughters married prominent Levant merchants of the next generation, Mabel marrying Henry Hunt, who was an assistant and the husband for nearly twenty years, and Mary marrying John Wylde, who was also briefly an assistant.

As a result of his financial commitment to the trade in north Africa, Leate conducted a series of negotiations concerning England's relations with Algiers in the years after the unsuccessful attack of Sir Robert Mansell on that port in 1620. Members of the Levant Company, led by Leate, successfully opposed a plan by the English government and the Spanish Company to levy £4500 from them in order to continue the war. In 1623, following the negotiations of Sir Thomas Roe and the adoption by the privy council of a peace treaty with Algiers, Leate worked for the appointment of the first ambassador there, James Frizell. An Algerian ambassador travelled to England in 1625 and there was a possibility for the repatriation of English slaves. Leate prevailed on the privy council to improve on the bad treatment the ambassador was receiving by according him the usual respects of a reception and presents. Leate's personal financial commitment to repatriate slaves was not, however, supported by the company, and this led to an open break between them. In July 1626 he advanced £470 to Frizell for this purpose, apparently on the understanding that the company would reimburse him. No such reimbursement was acknowledged or forthcoming, and in February 1627 Leate did not stand again for the position of deputy governor at the court of election. It took the judgment of the attorney-general the following July, when the case went to arbitration, for Leate to be paid. Roe observed that Leate's efforts to forge understanding on these matters were generally met with indifference and were 'a sad example to warn others not to serve the public at their own hazard and ruin' (Fisher, 199).

Leate's trading contacts, centred on the Levant, helped to satisfy an abiding interest in horticulture. The two well-known contemporary botanists John Gerard and John Parkinson both mention his many introductions of new flora into England. From Poland, for example, Leate obtained for the first time seeds for beets, and from the Levant he acquired more ornamental additions to English gardens, namely the Syrian double yellow rose and the Persian lily.

Leate took a more limited role in civic affairs than many of his merchant colleagues in the overseas trading companies. In 1616, 1626, and for a time after the death of William Canning in 1627 he served as the master of the Ironmongers' Company. A portrait of him, given to the company soon after his death by his sons, was prominently hung in the court hall. In the portrait he was portrayed as a successful merchant with a full, dark beard, wearing a black cape that is richly furred with a deep ruff and ruffles. Art was the object of his most ambitious civic project, and it was with the aim of furnishing statues in keeping with the intentions of Sir Thomas Gresham for the Royal Exchange that, in 1610, Leate made a proposal to the court of aldermen. Gresham had envisaged the use of thirty rooms in the exchange for this purpose, and Leate suggested that the statues, in wood with lead and oil paint overlay, should be paid for by the fines of elected aldermen who refused to take up office. The statues that were furnished by this means were burnt with the exchange during the great fire of 1666.

The one clearly political action taken by Leate touched on a constitutional issue that had become sensitive since it had first been raised in 1606. By the crown's prerogative, James had confirmed an Elizabethan imposition of 5*s.* 5*d.* per hundredweight on currants in addition to the customs levy of 1*s.* 1*d.* approved by parliament. Refusing to pay impositions, John Bate argued in a well-known case that the king thereby exceeded his prerogative because the impositions were not instruments of foreign policy or the regulation of commerce, but were intended solely for purposes of raising revenue. In 1606 his case came before the court of exchequer, but the king's prerogative was upheld. Members of the Levant Company petitioned for the imposition to be reduced by 2*s.* 2*d.*; but, whatever laxities had crept into subsequent enforcement, the privy council in February 1627 issued an order stating that no currants could clear customs until the full imposition had been paid. In September 1628 Leate and a group of twelve other merchants, including William Garway and Sir Maurice Abbot, refused to pay the full imposition and forcibly removed their currants from a customs house at Dice Quay. Leate's share was more than 5 tons. This action reignited old antagonisms about the legality of impositions, which had begun to bulk large among governmental revenues, and their legality was actively debated in parliament between the advocates of both positions, Sir Edward Coke for the parliamentary majority and Sir John Coke for the crown.

Leate died at some point between 3 June (when his will was dated) and 28 June 1631 (when it was proved). His will provided for three as yet unmarried daughters, Elizabeth, Judith, and Jane, who were each to receive 1000 marks, approximately £667. There were no philanthropic bequests. The sons, Richard and Hewett, divided the remainder of the estate.

CHARLES WELCH, *rev.* TREVOR DICKIE

Sources H. Stevens, ed., *The dawn of British trade to the East Indies as recorded in the court minutes of the East India Company, 1599–1603* (1886) • J. Nicholl, *Some account of the Worshipful Company of Ironmongers* (1851) • T. K. Rabb, *Enterprise and empire: merchant and gentry investment in the expansion of England, 1575–1630* (1967) • *CSP dom.*, 1581–1631 • PRO, SP 105/148 • will, PRO, PROB 11/160, sig. 78 • PRO, E 190/31/1, fol. 153 • R. Brenner, *Merchants and revolution: commercial change, political conflict, and London's overseas traders, 1550–1653* (1993) • A. C. Wood, *A history of the Levant Company* (1935) • R. C. Johnson and others, eds., *Proceedings in parliament, 1628*, 6 vols. (1977–83) • G. Fisher, *Barbary legend: war, trade and piracy in north Africa, 1415–1830* (1957) • *The visitation of London, anno Domini 1633, 1634, and 1635, made by Sir Henry St George*, 2, ed. J. J. Howard, Harleian Society, 17 (1883) • *DNB*

Likenesses oils, before 1631, Ironmongers' Company, Ironmongers' Hall, London • J. Payne, line engraving, BM, NPG

Wealth at death over £2000: will, PRO, PROB 11/160, sig. 78

Leatham, James (1865–1945), political activist and publisher, was born on 19 December 1865, the youngest of five children of Stephen Leatham, an army sergeant from Yorkshire, and his Scottish wife, Margaret Cattanach, a hand-loom weaver. His father died shortly after his birth and he was raised in the Rosemount area of Aberdeen by his mother and her parents in a literate, self-improving home environment where education was valued. He attended Northfield public school, where he attained dux at age ten, followed by two and a half years at Dr Brown's school, Skene Square, where he was briefly a pupil monitor. Fascinated by the world of printing and publishing, at thirteen years and eleven months he became apprentice compositor with a local firm, with whom he progressed to journeyman and then foreman until 1888, when he was sacked for leading the printers' union campaign against dilution and cheap labour. He had recently (23 December 1887) married Isabella Sinclair Duncan (1862/3–1947), a linen manufacturer's machinist, the daughter of James Duncan, a flax mill overseer, and fathered the first of their four daughters.

From his teenage years Leatham was a political activist; initially as an ardent secularist, developing and expanding his views in literary and debating societies, and, as a leading light in Aberdeen Junior Liberal Association, organizing public meetings and lecturing on radical and collectivist themes. From the mid-1880s, increasingly influenced by the socialist writings of Lawrence Gronlund, Edward Bellamy, Peter Kropotkin, and, especially, William Morris, he became a convinced socialist. An evolutionary socialist with fundamental but non-doctrinaire views, he was committed to building an open, informed, mass membership party, aiming at a maximum socialist programme of nationalization and municipal ownership, to be achieved through political representation and popular enlightenment.

Already a militant trade unionist, from 1888 until 1893 Leatham was principal standard bearer of the emerging socialist left in Aberdeen, leading the local branch of the Scottish Land and Labour League and latterly the Aberdeen Socialist Society, which merged into the Social Democratic Federation. Between 1889 and 1892 he ran a small printing and publishing co-operative, selling progressive and socialist literature, including his own very popular propagandist pamphlets, such as *The Eight Hour Day* and *The Class War*. In the winter of 1891–2 he produced *Workers Herald*, the first, though short-lived, avowedly socialist weekly paper in Scotland.

Leatham's growing reputation as a socialist propagandist and organizer created a wider demand for his political services throughout Scotland and beyond. Between 1893 and 1896 he worked in Manchester as a compositor in the large publishing firm of Heywoods, while otherwise immersing himself in lecturing, journalism, and building Lancashire branches of the Social Democratic Federation and Independent Labour Party (ILP). In Manchester he continued as a highly effective organizer of the printing trades and led the agitation that achieved shorter hours for 4000 workers. Again he was victimized, and he briefly worked full time for the Social Democratic Federation throughout the north of England.

Leatham returned to north-east Scotland in 1896 to edit-manage the struggling weekly paper *Peterhead Sentinel*, which he transformed into a lively production with a popular literary, anti-imperialist, and socialist slant. Nearby, from his Clerkhill Press, he concentrated, between 1905 and 1908, on writing, printing, and publishing a prolific output of pamphlets and longer works on literary and historical themes, always from consciously rationalist and socialist viewpoints. His talents as a socialist journalist and writer were further recognized when, in 1908, he was appointed editor–manager of the Worker Press, a group of ILP weekly newspapers in the West Riding of Yorkshire. His main charges were the *Huddersfield Worker* and the *Halifax Labour News*, and he was latterly also involved in producing the *Leeds and District Weekly Citizen* and the *Manchester Weekly Citizen*. He resigned after failing to win shareholder support to extend the specialist socialist publishing side of the firm.

Thereafter between 1912 and 1916 Leatham became a resolutely independent socialist printer and publisher, operating from his Cottingham Press in the East Riding of Yorkshire and from the Deveron Press in Turriff, Aberdeenshire, where he finally settled in 1916. From 1912 until his death Leatham's own periodical, *Gateway*, was his principal propagandist weapon, discoursing on politics, current affairs, literature, and cultural issues. Throughout a long career Leatham always made a precarious living from printing and publishing ventures. A prodigious journalist and a clear, direct prose stylist he wrote several books, including the delightful tribute *William Morris: Master of many Crafts* (1899; 4th edn, 1934), and a host of titles in pamphlet form, issued from his own presses.

Although highly critical of the record of Labour governments in 1924 and 1929–31 Leatham was elected a Labour councillor for Turriff in 1923. He also served as a leading county councillor in Aberdeenshire and as a justice of the peace. In his twelve final years he was provost of Turriff. His greatest achievements in a distinguished late career in civic life were in municipal housing, public health, and welfare provision. Leatham was appointed MBE in 1942 for his services to local government. He died at his home, 7 Hillcrest, Turriff, Aberdeenshire, on 14 December 1945 after two heart attacks, and was buried in the graveyard of St Machar's Cathedral, Aberdeen. ROBERT DUNCAN

Sources R. Duncan, *James Leatham, 1865–1945: portrait of a socialist pioneer* (1978) • J. Leatham, 'Sixty years of world mending', *Gateway*, 28/323 (April–May 1940) • J. Leatham, 'Sixty years of world mending', *Gateway*, 30/361 (Jan–Aug 1945) • U. Aberdeen, Leatham MSS, 2776/1–31 • descriptive list, 1972, U. Aberdeen, Leatham MSS, 2776/1–31 • W. Donaldson, *The language of the people* (1989) • K. Buckley, *Trade unionism in Aberdeen, 1878–1900* (1955) • E. P. Thompson, *William Morris: romantic to revolutionary*, rev. edn (1977) • d. cert. • m. cert. • St Machar's Cathedral, Aberdeen, inscription on gravestone

Archives U. Aberdeen, Special Libraries and Archives, corresp. and papers | U. Lpool L., corresp. with John Bruce Glasier and Katherine Bruce Glasier

Likenesses photograph, *c.*1943, U. Aberdeen; repro. in Duncan, *James Leatham*, back cover

Leatham, William Henry (1815–1889), poet and politician, was born at Wakefield on 6 July 1815, the second of nine children of William Leatham, banker and author of *Letters on the Currency* (1840), and his wife, Margaret, *née* Walker. One of his sisters later became the wife of the Rt Hon. John Bright, another of Joseph Gurney Barclay, the banker. Leatham's family had long been Quakers, and William Henry was educated at Bruce Grove, Tottenham, and under a classical tutor. At nineteen he entered his father's bank at Wakefield, and in the following year (1835) made a tour on the continent. On 18 February 1839 Leatham married Priscilla, the daughter of Quaker philanthropist Samuel *Gurney (1786–1856) of Upton, Essex, and they settled at Sandal, near Wakefield, the subject of Leatham's later poem 'Sandal in the Olden Time'. His first published work was a volume of poems which appeared in the year after his marriage; a few years after that Leatham and his wife formally joined the Church of England. They had nine children, seven boys and two girls, all baptized at Wakefield.

Leatham's other publications included several volumes of lectures originally delivered at literary and mechanics' institutes and printed in 1845 and 1849, and *Tales of English Life and Miscellanies* (2 vols., 1858). Many of his poems were first published in local journals, and he continued to collect and republish them throughout his life in volumes such as *The Victim: a Tale of the Lake of the Four Cantons* (1841), *Emilia Monteiro: a Ballad of the Old Hall, Heath* (1843), and *Selections from Lesser Poems* (1855).

As early as 1832 Leatham had assisted in the return of the first member—a Liberal—for Wakefield. In 1851 he purchased Hemsworth Hall (which later passed to his son Samuel Gurney Leatham), and in July 1852 he contested Wakefield as a Liberal, and was defeated. At the general election of 1859, after a contest of exceptional severity, he was returned by three votes, but was unseated on petition. Both Leatham and the defeated candidate were prosecuted for bribery, but the action was eventually dropped. In 1865 Leatham had a majority of fifty over his tory opponent, and was presented with a testimonial by 8700 non-electors. He did not stand in 1868. In 1874 he was defeated standing for the South-West Riding of Yorkshire, but in 1880 was elected for that constituency. He retired from politics in 1885. Leatham had become quite a prominent figure in his area of Yorkshire, being a JP, a deputy lieutenant, and, from 1870, deputy chairman of quarter sessions. But his political career was never substantial. He died suddenly at his home, the White House, Carleton, near Pontefract, on 14 November 1889, leaving six sons and one daughter.

CHARLOTTE FELL-SMITH, *rev.* MEGAN A. STEPHAN

Sources *WWBMP*, 1.231 • Allibone, *Dict.* • *BL cat.*, [CD-ROM] • *Wakefield Express* (16 Sept 1889) • *IGI*

Archives Wakefield Reference and Information Library, personal and business papers | U. Edin. L., letters to James Halliwell-Phillipps

Wealth at death £17,368 5*s.* 5*d.*: probate, 30 Dec 1889, *CGPLA Eng. & Wales*

Leathart, James (1820–1895), lead manufacturer and art collector, was born on 25 November 1820 at Hill House, Alston Moor, Alston, Cumberland, the son of John Leathart (*b.* 1793), mining engineer and lead miner, and Margaret Setree (1792–1870). He attended Alston grammar school until the age of fourteen when he was briefly employed by Burnett and Pattinson, an industrial chemical firm, before accepting a position as clerk at Locke, Blackett & Co. in Newcastle upon Tyne. He devoted his entire career to this firm of lead manufacturers, studying chemistry and metallurgy in his spare time in order to improve his knowledge of the industry. He was rewarded when he was placed in charge of a new smelting and refining plant at St Anthonys, Newcastle upon Tyne, in 1846. He became sole managing partner of the firm in 1857. In the following year, on 22 June, he married Maria Hedley

(1840–1899), the daughter of a Newcastle soap manufacturer, with whom he had thirteen children.

Although Leathart's salary never exceeded £600 per annum, he managed to form one of the finest collections of contemporary art in England. His early interest was in the English landscape school, represented by artists such as David Cox and John Varley. After he met the artist William Bell Scott, head of the Newcastle School of Art, his taste shifted to the more avant-garde Pre-Raphaelites. Scott's enthusiasm for advanced art impressed Leathart and he gradually sold off his earlier purchases to finance the acquisition of paintings and watercolours by artists including Dante Gabriel Rossetti, Ford Madox Brown, John Everett Millais, Edward Burne-Jones, Albert Moore, and James McNeill Whistler. His collection was distinguished by his predilection for solemn subjects, such as Millais's funereal *Autumn Leaves* (1855, Manchester City Galleries), Albert Moore's sombre *Elijah's Sacrifice* (1863, Bury Art Gallery and Museum), and Burne-Jones's compelling representations of *Sidonia von Bork* and *Clara von Bork* (both 1860, Tate collection). Leathart displayed his collection at his home in Gateshead alongside the blue and white Chinese porcelain favoured by devotees of the aesthetic movement. Fellow art lover John Hamilton Trist ranked Leathart's collection as 'one of the first in England' (J. H. Trist, 9 March 1868, Leathart MSS, University of British Columbia).

Leathart introduced Pre-Raphaelite and aesthetic art into the unusually close-knit community of Novocastrian businessmen, both in his capacity as secretary of the school of art and of the North of England Society, and as a member of the executive committees of the mechanics' institute and the Newcastle Arts Association. As a result of his proselytizing, chemical merchants Jacob Burnett and Alexander Stevenson embraced the credos of the aesthetic movement, and even more conservative collectors, such as ironmaster Sir Isaac Lowthian Bell and the armaments manufacturer Sir William Armstrong, commissioned works from Rossetti and Burne-Jones. Due to Leathart's enthusiastic but unassuming influence, Tyneside merchants and manufacturers shared artistic as well as business interests. His propensity for networking among businessmen–collectors affected his own family circle: his daughter Margaret married the son of the Liverpool banker George Rae, who was one of Rossetti's major patrons.

Despite his passion for collecting, Leathart was forced to sell a number of works of art privately after Locke, Blackett & Co. suffered financial reverses due to foreign competition, overcapacity, and the failure of new laboratory processes. Money worries weakened Leathart's constitution and brought on his death from pneumonia on 9 August 1895 at his home, Bracken Dene, Low Fell, Gateshead, co. Durham. He was buried at St John's Church, Gateshead Fell, co. Durham. His main asset was his art collection, which his heirs sold at the Goupil Gallery in June and July 1896 and at Christies on 19 July 1897; a few items remain in the family. DIANNE SACHKO MACLEOD

Sources private information (2004) [Dr Gilbert L. Leathart] · D. J. Rowe, 'Leathart, James', *DBB* · University of British Columbia Library, Vancouver, Canada, Leathart MSS · D. S. Macleod, 'The "identity" of Pre-Raphaelite patrons', *Re-framing the Pre-Raphaelites: historical and theoretical essays*, ed. E. Harding (1996), 1–26 · d. cert.
Archives NRA, priv. coll., family records · University of British Columbia Library, Vancouver, Canada, correspondence and MSS
Likenesses F. M. Brown, oils, 1863–4, repro. in Macleod, 'The "identity" of Pre-Raphaelite patrons'; priv. coll. · photographs, priv. coll.
Wealth at death £10,524 5*s.* 2*d.*: probate, 28 Sept 1895, *CGPLA Eng. & Wales*

Leather [*née* Smith], **Ella Mary** (1874–1928), folklorist, was born on 26 March 1874 at Bidney, in the parish of Dilwyn, Herefordshire, the daughter of James Smith, farmer, and his wife, Mary Ann, *née* Griffiths. She was educated at Clyde House School in Hereford and at Hereford High School for Girls. In 1893 she married Francis Leather (1864–1929), a solicitor practising in the small Herefordshire town of Weobley, where she spent the rest of her life. They had three sons: John Francis, who died in France in 1918; Geoffrey, who died in infancy; and Godfrey, who became a solicitor and died in 1943.

In 1905 Leather was persuaded by a friend and local author, the Revd Compton Reade, to contribute a chapter, 'The folk-lore of the shire', to his *Memorials of Old Herefordshire* (1905). This was followed by the publication of a selection of Herefordshire folk-tales in the first issue of the *Herefordshire Magazine* (1907). She became an ardent folklorist, conscious that the modern world was catching up with Herefordshire and that many of the old country customs of her childhood were dying out.

In 1912 Leather's *The Folk-Lore of Herefordshire* was published by Jakeman and Carver in Hereford, with an introduction by the eminent folklorist Edwin Sydney Hartland. The work was fully referenced, not only to the elderly cottagers and residents of hospitals and workhouses who contributed their recollections but also to the many archive and secondary sources consulted by the author. The book has long been considered one of the seminal texts of English folklore and continued to be regularly reprinted from 1912 until at least the 1990s.

The Folk-Lore of Herefordshire contained the lyrics and music of twenty-three traditional carols, ballads, and songs. Leather's musical skill was fairly rudimentary, but she was encouraged by Cecil Sharp and the young composer Ralph Vaughan Williams, who recognized the potential of Herefordshire as a source for new folk-music, and arranged for a phonograph to be sent to her. Sharp and Vaughan Williams made several expeditions to Weobley and accompanied Leather on her visits to local Gypsy encampments. Vaughan Williams later regarded a visit to Monkland in September 1912 where they collected a version of 'The Unquiet Grave' from the Gypsy tenor Alfred Price Jones as one of his 'most memorable musical impressions' (Jones, 53). In 1920 he collaborated with Leather in the publication of *Twelve Traditional Carols from Herefordshire*. Vaughan Williams especially admired 'The truth sent from above' and used it in the opening theme of his *Fantasia on Christmas Carols* dedicated to Sharp.

In her native county Leather had become a celebrated authority, much sought after as a speaker by visiting antiquarian societies, folklorists, and the Women's Institute, of which she was the Herefordshire president in 1928. She was especially devoted to Weobley and published a paper on its timber-framed houses in the *Transactions [of the] Woolhope Naturalists Club* for 1926. She was also personally responsible for preserving the town's old grammar school, a seventeenth-century building which she purchased and used as her study. An undated guide to the parish church was published under her name in which, rather characteristically, the loss of much of the ancient fabric of the church during the restoration of 1868 was regretted. She also planned a 'History of Weobley' in 1927, though she did not live to see it completed.

Leather was equally assiduous in the collection of folk-dances. Among other achievements she copied down the dance of the last group of Herefordshire morris men at Bromfield in 1909 and later, in 1925, established the Herefordshire branch of the Folk Dance Society. A dance called 'Haste to the wedding' collected by her was performed at the first National Festival of Folk Dance at the Albert Hall in 1926.

Ella Mary Leather died in Weobley of a heart attack on 7 June 1928 and was buried in Weobley churchyard. An obituary in the *Hereford Times* (16 June 1928, 4) regarded her death as a great loss to the nation because her musical finds had enabled Sharp and Vaughan Williams to achieve their fame. She found culture in the reputedly uncultured, and acted as a medium between the musicians of the caravan and those of the hall.

DAVID WHITEHEAD

Sources L. Jones, *A nest of singing birds* (West Midlands Folk Federation, 1978) · *Hereford Times* (16 June 1928) · *Hereford Times* (16 Nov 1929) [Francis Leather] · C. Reade, ed., *Memorials of old Herefordshire* (1904) · private information (2004) · b. cert.
Archives Hereford City Library | SOUND BBC programme, 22 Feb 1955 [brief details in *The Listener*]
Likenesses F. M. Bennett, portraits, 1928, Castle House, Weobley, Herefordshire · F. M. Bennett, portrait (posthumous), Castle House, Weobley, Herefordshire

Leathers, Frederick James, **first Viscount Leathers** **(1883–1965)**, shipping expert and government minister, was born on 21 November 1883, at 47 Bromley Street, Ratcliff, Stepney, in the East End of London, the son of Robert Leathers, carpenter, of Stowmarket, Suffolk, and his wife, Emily Seamen. His father died in Frederick's infancy, leaving the family in somewhat difficult circumstances. At fifteen he joined a company called the Steamship Owners Coal Association, which traded in coal and other commodities at Purfleet, and which was acquired by William Cory & Sons Ltd, a Thames lighterage firm, in 1913. Leathers was general manager at Purfleet at the time of acquisition. By then he was married (1 June 1907) to Emily Ethel (1882/3–1971), daughter of Henry Baxter, butcher, of Southend, Essex. They had two sons and a daughter.

Leathers's abilities were soon recognized by the Cory board and he was invited to join them. By 1917 he was joint managing director and in 1928 was appointed deputy chairman of the company. He was also a director or chairman of many other companies mainly concerned with coal or shipping auxiliary services. During the First World War he was called upon to advise the Ministry of Shipping on port problems.

During the inter-war years Leathers's main task at Cory, which for long had had a powerful position in the coal bunkering trade, was to build an equally strong position in the rapidly growing business of oil bunkers. In 1920 the firm entered into an agreement with a subsidiary of the P. & O. Line to jointly operate the Mercantile Lighterage Company. Through contacts with the chairman of P. & O., Sir James Mackay, Leathers met political figures such as Brendan Bracken and then Winston Churchill. Before long Churchill became a director of two of Cory's subsidiaries and through this came to form a high opinion of Leathers's commercial knowledge and capacities. In May 1940 Churchill arranged for the minister of shipping to appoint Leathers adviser to the ministry on all coal problems. Almost at once, when France fell, Leathers was faced with the very difficult problem of dealing with the vast quantity of coal destined for France, much of it already on the water. (Shipments of coal to France had been 1,800,000 tons in May and an even larger tonnage had been planned for June.) Leathers's intimate knowledge of the trade and the persons concerned with it enabled him to dispose of this great quantity by 'persuasion, cajolery and sometimes even stronger methods' (Jenkins, 14). No one else could have performed this task so quickly, thus freeing the ships for further service.

A year later, in May 1941, the prime minister amalgamated the ministries of Shipping and Transport and appointed Leathers minister of war transport, placing him in the House of Lords by creating him Baron Leathers. As a 'recognized authority on coal and shipping and he had exhibited gifts of organization which fully justified his appointment' (*The Times*, 20 March 1965, 14). He enjoyed the very great advantage over his predecessor that he was known to have the steady support of the prime minister; thus there was an end to the steady sniping from the ministries of Supply (which had not yet been able to work out the precise imports needed for the multifarious materials it controlled) and of Food (which consistently understated its stocks), and the co-ordination of transport and supply finally began to be greatly improved.

The shipping position was acute at the time Leathers took office; at the same time the first optimistic hopes of the American shipping aid, derived from the president's directive of 1 May, began to fade under the influence of obstruction from the American services and administrative difficulties in American government agencies. Nevertheless, lend-lease and other forms of American aid were soon giving effective help. The north Atlantic was the shortest supply route available for many of the most needed commodities but, prior to lend-lease, the shortage of hard currency prevented full advantage being taken of this short haul. In 1942 the shipping shortage grew even more acute, as the battle against Japan intensified. Leathers complained at the end of that year not only that the whole of the United States new construction was being taken for the Pacific, but that the Pacific theatre was absorbing so much that the United States could not even provide their share of naval escorts for the next convoy to northern Russia. Leathers and the British Merchant Shipping Mission in Washington sought constantly to convince the Americans of the need for a reallocation of allied shipping resources in proportion to the needs of the various military theatres, for the maintenance of areas of allied responsibility such as Africa, the Middle East, the Indian Ocean, and Australasia, and the British import programme. While this was never completely successful, by the end of 1943 this framework had been accepted in principle and great progress had been made towards implementing it in practice.

During 1943 Leathers attended the Casablanca, Washington, Quebec, and Cairo conferences which were convened to fix and co-ordinate allied strategy. Strategy had to be correlated to shipping availability. At Casablanca there was insufficient consultation on transport matters and consequently the plans made there were at risk because they were beyond the carrying resources of allied shipping. At Washington and subsequent conferences Leathers and his staff were fully consulted and operational plans brought gradually within the shipping possibilities. One of his particular aims at Washington was to secure 200 standard American war built ships on bare boat charter; previous aid had been largely on a voyage by voyage basis, the uncertainty of which prevented any precise programming. There was the further consideration that the USA had more ships than seamen whereas the British had a pool of seamen provided by the survivors of sunk ships. These 200 ships became a leitmotif and Leathers told the story of how he was quietly sipping a drink (which he did sparingly and seldom) in a New York hotel on his way back from Washington, when the street was suddenly filled with hubbub as an escorted motor cycle dispatch rider arrived to deliver a message from the president that the 200 ships would be provided.

Leathers, who was appointed CH in 1943, also accompanied the prime minister to Yalta and Potsdam, but proceedings there were more political than practical and he was not able to achieve any of his aims on transport issues.

When Churchill returned to power in 1951 he recalled Leathers to become secretary of state for the co-ordination of transport, fuel, and power, as an 'overlord' of the three departments. The experiment was neither popular nor successful. The statutory powers, the executive, and planning staffs remained with the individual departments, and Leathers found it an impossible task to achieve progress in these circumstances. He retired in 1953 and resumed his business interests, becoming first Viscount Leathers of Purfleet in the new year honours of 1954. He was an honorary LLD of the universities of Leeds (1946) and Birmingham (1951), and an honorary member of the Institution of Naval Architects. He was also an underwriting member of Lloyds, warden of the court of the Worshipful Company of Shipwrights, and president of the Institute of Chartered Shipbrokers. He died at Twyford Abbey, Ealing, London, on 19 March 1965.

FRANCIS KEENLYSIDE, *rev.* MARC BRODIE

Sources *The Times* (20 March 1965) • personal knowledge (1981) • private information (1981) • Burke, *Peerage* (1999) • b. cert. • m. cert. • M. Gilbert, *Winston S. Churchill*, 7: *Road to victory, 1941–1945* (1986) • C. Jenkins, *The Times* (26 March 1965), 14 • C. B. A. Behrens, *Merchant shipping and the demands of war* (1955) • P. Addison, *Churchill on the home front, 1900–1955* (1992) • K. E. Keenan, *The fires of London: a history of the Thames lighterage operations of William Cory & Son Ltd* (1997)

Archives PRO, private office MSS, MT 62/3–95 | FILM BFI NFTVA, news footage

Likenesses W. Stoneman, photograph, 1952, NPG • photograph, repro. in *The Times*

Wealth at death £151,515: probate, 19 May 1965, *CGPLA Eng. & Wales*

Leathes, Stanley (1830–1900), Hebrew scholar, the son of Chaloner Stanley Leathes, rector of Ellesborough, Buckinghamshire, was born in Ellesborough on 21 March 1830. He was educated privately and at Jesus College, Cambridge, where he matriculated in 1848, graduated BA in 1852, was elected first Tyrwhitt's Hebrew scholar in 1853, and proceeded MA in 1855. He was ordained deacon in 1856 and priest in 1857, and was curate successively of St Martin's, Salisbury (1856–8), St Luke's, Berwick Street, Westminster (1858), and St James's, Westminster (1858–60). On 6 July 1858 he married Matilda, daughter of John Martin Butt, the rector of East Garston, Berkshire. They had at least one child, Stanley Mordaunt *Leathes, who was born in London in 1861; he died in 1938. At St James's Leathes was appointed clerk in orders in 1860, priest and assistant in 1865, and was given the perpetual curacy of St Philip's, Regent Street, in 1869. In 1863 he was elected professor of Hebrew at King's College, London, and in 1870 he was made a member of the Old Testament Revision Company, to which he devoted much of his time until the project concluded in 1885. He was given a succession of honorary lectureships at the universities of Oxford, Cambridge, and London, being appointed Boyle lecturer from 1868 to 1870, Hulsean lecturer in 1873, Bampton lecturer in 1874, and Warburton lecturer from 1876 to 1880. These lectures, all on biblical topics, were subsequently published.

In 1876 Leathes became a prebend of St Paul's Cathedral and in 1880 was made rector of Cliffe-at-Hoo, Kent. While there he was elected honorary fellow of Jesus College, Cambridge (1885). He moved in 1889 to the more valuable benefice of Much Hadham, Hertfordshire which gave him £590 per annum, a house, and 150 acres of land. Here he died on 30 April 1900.

Leathes's theology was of a traditional Anglican variety, and was unruffled by either ritualism or liberalism. His scholarship reflected that conservatism, and his opposition to new intellectual trends in biblical criticism meant that his work was quickly superseded in his own lifetime.

Among his many published works, most consist of sermons or lectures which range in subject matter from Christian homily to Hebrew grammar, from Paul and the New Testament to the Prophets and the Old Testament, and from Judaism to ethics.

J. M. RIGG, *rev.* GERALD LAW

Sources Crockford (1899) • *Men and women of the time* (1895) • *The Times* (1 May 1900) • Venn, *Alum. Cant.* • *CGPLA Eng. & Wales* (1900)
Wealth at death £19,812 16*s.* 7*d.*: resworn probate, Nov 1900, *CGPLA Eng. & Wales*

Leathes, Sir Stanley Mordaunt (1861–1938), historian and civil service administrator, was born in London on 7 May 1861, the elder son of Stanley *Leathes (1830–1900), Hebrew scholar, and his wife, Matilda, daughter of John Martin Butt, rector of East Garston, Berkshire. He was educated at Eton College, where he was a king's scholar, from 1873 to 1880, and at Trinity College, Cambridge, of which he was also a scholar; he was awarded a first class in part one of the classical tripos of 1882 and was second chancellor's medallist in 1884. He was elected a fellow of Trinity in 1886, and was the college's lecturer in history from 1892 to 1903. As a teacher he was described by his pupils as accurate and lucid, and the same qualities appear in his writings.

With Lord Acton, Leathes helped to plan the *Cambridge Modern History*, and with A. W. Ward and G. W. Prothero edited it (1901–12). He himself wrote the chapters 'Italy and her invaders', 'France', 'Habsburg and Valois', 'Henry IV of France', 'Richelieu', 'Mazarin', 'Modern Europe', and 'Great Britain', a list which shows his own chief interests. During these years Leathes lived in college rooms (13 Nevile's Court). He took a full share in the business and social life of the college, being somewhat of a *bon vivant*. His chief recreation was riding and hunting; he was often out with the Cambridgeshire hounds on a Friday, and occasionally went by train to Huntingdon for a Cambridgeshire Tuesday or a Fitzwilliam Saturday.

In 1903 Leathes was offered and accepted the post of secretary to the civil service commission and left Cambridge. In 1907 he became a commissioner, and from 1910 to 1927 he was first commissioner. He also served as chairman of several government committees on special questions, and from January to November 1918 he was in charge of the staff and accommodation in the Ministry of Food. In 1911 he was appointed CB and in 1919 KCB.

Leathes also continued to write. In 1911 he published (under a pseudonym) *Vox clamantis*, and later (under his own name) *The People of England* (3 vols., 1915–23) and *Rhythm in English Poetry* (1935). He never married. For some time after leaving Cambridge he lived in the Temple, in London, and afterwards shared a house with the Revd J. A. Nairn, Stubbings vicarage, near Maidenhead, Berkshire. He died at Bowood House, near Gloucester, on 25 July 1938.

W. C. D. DAMPIER, *rev.* H. C. G. MATTHEW

Sources *The Times* (27 July 1938) • records, Trinity Cam. • private information (1949) • personal knowledge (1949)
Archives King's AC Cam., letters to Oscar Browning • Trinity Cam., records
Wealth at death £137 17*s.* 1*d.*: administration, 26 Aug 1938, *CGPLA Eng. & Wales*

Leavens, Elizabeth (*d.* 1665). *See under* Holme, Thomas (1626/7–1666).

Leavis, Frank Raymond (1895–1978), literary critic and university teacher, was born on 14 July 1895 at 64 Mill Road, Cambridge, the second of three children and elder son of Harry Leavis (1862–1921) and Kate Sarah Moore (1874–1929), both of whom had East Anglian rural origins. Harry Leavis was a radical and a public figure, the proprietor of a leading piano and musical instrument shop.

Early years, education, and war Leavis's home was happy, with music, reading aloud of the English classics, and affection for animals. Leavis saw himself as endowed with a 'hereditary Huguenot, ducal pride or ferocity' (MacKillop, *Life in Criticism*, 28). He was educated at Cambridge and County School and the Perse School, where he acted and was a prominent athlete—even late in life he was proud of his prowess as a runner. He gained a history scholarship to Emmanuel College, Cambridge, where he read history and English. A historical concern was lasting: he saw literature as part of a whole society, and as one index of its achievements. He took first-class honours in English in 1921 even though his father died during his final examinations.

Between his first year at Emmanuel and his graduation year lay what Leavis called the 'great hiatus' of the First World War; he served for twenty-one months, without leave, on the ambulance trains operated by the Friends' Ambulance Unit. In France he deepened his appreciation of French literature, notably the poetry of Paul Valéry; and he carried Milton in his tunic. (He had excellent French, competent Italian, and good Latin and Greek.) His health was permanently impaired by the war, of which he did not readily speak: he disliked reminiscence in the manner of (his phrase) 'Great War panache'.

Cambridge: teaching, and early publications At Cambridge the English curriculum owed much to Mansfield Forbes and Sir Arthur Quiller-Couch, for whom Leavis felt respectively admiration and affection, the greater respect afforded to Forbes. Quiller-Couch supervised his doctoral research into journalism and literature. Leavis was fascinated by publishing practice: he encouraged his pupil Gordon Fraser to found the Minority Press, which issued some of his early writings. Leavis was stimulated by I. A. Richards: he was a member of the lecture audience which submitted subjective commentaries on poetry which Richards was to analyse in *Practical Criticism* (1929). Leavis hoped to write a book about literary critical practice to complement the theories of Richards: his 'Notes on the analysis of poetry' (*Scrutiny*, 1944–52) are surviving fragments. Having been awarded his doctorate in 1924, Leavis lectured for the English faculty as a freelance known for independent-mindedness: on one occasion he was in trouble with the police and university authorities because he wanted Joyce's banned novel *Ulysses* to be available for study. In 1927 he was appointed a probationary lecturer on

Frank Raymond Leavis (1895–1978), by Paul Joyce, 1975

poetry and 'modern problems in criticism'. English literature as an academic subject gathered momentum in Britain during the 1920s, but the trend was towards the practice of criticism by men of letters, rather than academics. Leavis was unusual because he taught literature while being a regular critic of it and remaining independent of London literary journalism—'the metropolitan literary world', he would drawl, slandering its denizens as 'flank-rubbers' or 'log-rollers'. He attracted the attention of Queenie Dorothy Roth (1906–1981) [*see* Leavis, Queenie Dorothy], an undergraduate at Girton College whom he married on 16 September 1929. Leavis's career as a teacher was focused on Downing College, Cambridge. In 1931 his probationary university lectureship was terminated. In 1932 he became the director of studies in English at Downing and a fellow, rapidly establishing an envied 'English school', thought by some to rival the provision of the official English faculty. Leavis and his assistants always taught unusually long hours.

Q. D. Leavis, in the meantime, had become an outstanding doctoral student whose research, published as *Fiction and the Reading Public* (1932), was close to the historical concerns of Leavis's own doctorate and of his *Mass Civilization and Minority Culture* (1930), the argument of which she extended with verve. The marriage initiated a lifelong personal and intellectual partnership. Generations of students knew the Leavis hospitality (with ample first-class teas), their encouragement and, on occasion, painful rejection. Both partners felt slights keenly and were long-term haters.

In 1932 Leavis published *New Bearings in English Poetry* in which he argued crisply for the validity of the poets he believed truly modern: W. B. Yeats, T. S. Eliot, Ezra Pound, and G. M. Hopkins, a modern before his time. He unhesitatingly spoke up for the recent Cambridge graduate William Empson, whose literary criticism Leavis admired, for a time, intensely. Leavis's most devoted effort at literary propaganda was always reserved for T. S. Eliot's poetry, especially for its 'rhythmic life' and 'delicate play of shifting tone'. Throughout his life Leavis promoted and chided Eliot, from an early contribution in the *Cambridge Review* (1929). Leavis was also one of the first commentators on D. H. Lawrence, on whom he wrote a pamphlet (1930), but his enthusiasm was of slow growth. Only in time did Lawrence become for Leavis the touchstone for creativity.

Scrutiny, The Great Tradition, and other writings In 1932 some of Leavis's associates, regulars at a discussion group at his house in Chesterton Road, started a quarterly journal, *Scrutiny*. Leavis himself soon became the senior editor, and remained so for twenty-one years, with unremitting editorial help from Q. D. Leavis. *Scrutiny* was not a literary magazine but a general review, run from the conviction that the arts, especially those of literature, were at a human centre of the more specialist intellectual enterprise of the sciences. *Scrutiny* gained a reputation, especially in the USA, for its critical rigour, its detailed textual revaluations of a wide range of subjects, its incomparable articles on music, education, mass society, and on the practices of the cultural establishment (called on one occasion 'The Literary Racket') which was subjected, not least by Q. D. Leavis, to mordant sociological observation. *Scrutiny*, it was said, educated a generation of English teachers.

After *Scrutiny* was founded Leavis wrote copiously on, among many other authors, Swift, Bunyan, Shakespeare, Johnson, and Hopkins. With the help of Q. D. Leavis and in collaboration with his pupil Denys Thompson, he published *Culture and Environment*, an early critique of 'mass' culture, in 1933. In 1936 he was appointed as a university lecturer, when he was over forty, but only part-time. His essays on writers in the non-Spenserian Miltonic–Tennysonian tradition of English poetry (Donne, Pope, Wordsworth, Keats, Shelley) were collected in *Revaluation* (1936). The concept of cultural centrality which had occupied Leavis in *Scrutiny* was explored by him in *Education and the University* (1943) which sought for post-war reforms in the humanities curriculum and teaching method. Leavis described English studies as a central 'focus of humane consciousness, where a mature sense of values would apply itself to the problems of civilization'. The analysis was little heeded, though the proposals for the management of the curriculum were to become standard. Although Leavis's concern for the 'rhythmic life' of verse made him a natural commentator on poetry, he became increasingly absorbed by English novels, albeit as 'dramatic poems'. He wrote essays on George Eliot, Henry James, Joseph Conrad, and Dickens's *Hard Times* (as 'moral fable') which were collected into *The Great Tradition* (1948). Leavis wished to isolate a classic strain in English fiction, to define strengths in its art which equalled other arts of fiction (notably French) which had greater prestige. His determination to focus on specific authors was criticized for exclusiveness. He believed that the authors in 'his' tradition were capable of dealing subtly with ethical matters, a view which did not appeal to literary critics inclined to aestheticism. Leavis's appreciation of Dickens, as of Lawrence, was of slow growth (perhaps because he enjoyed so much the childhood readings by his father, who specialized in Mr Pickwick). Leavis's varied wartime writings were issued in 1952 as *The Common Pursuit*, a title taken from T. S. Eliot (who called literary criticism 'the common pursuit of true judgement'): it was implicitly a reproach to Eliot who had renounced some of the radicalism which inspired the young Leavis.

Leavis found it hard to maintain a team of contributors for *Scrutiny* and it suddenly ceased publication in 1953—but in 1963 the whole run was reprinted by Cambridge University Press. Leavis was finally invited to join the English faculty board in 1954. In 1955 he published *D. H. Lawrence: Novelist*, as a sequel to *The Great Tradition*. In 1959, at sixty-four, he was appointed reader. Embittered by early insecurities, he had few intimates in Cambridge, though he enjoyed a brief friendship with Ludwig Wittgenstein. Although Leavis was held responsible for narrow-minded and sanctimonious 'Leavisites', his seriousness of concern fertilized thinkers different from himself, like L. C. Knights, D. W. Harding, Marius Bewley, H. A. Mason, and Michael Tanner.

Retirement and final years In 1962 Leavis, aged sixty-seven, retired from his readership and became an honorary fellow at Downing. He had always been against quantification and materialism, including Marxist materialism. He marked his retirement with a vigorously satirical attack, in the Richmond lecture, on C. P. (later Lord) Snow's popular conception of 'two cultures'. Leavis's belief in art as central (an expression of 'the human world') was incompatible with Snow's alternating 'cultures', artistic and scientific. Leavis refused to join the campaign for the free sale of an unexpurgated *Lady Chatterley's Lover*, believing that the progressive view discredited Lawrence's powers as an artist. Leavis became a sometimes near libellous critic of what he called contemptuously 'the orthodoxy of enlightenment'. He believed that the expansion of higher education would damage the 'idea' of the university. Increasingly dubious about the policy of Downing College for English studies, he resigned his fellowship in 1964. Later he disowned a group of admirers who idealistically (and successfully) sought to endow a lectureship in his honour.

After retirement Leavis became increasingly known as a personality outside Cambridge. In 1964 he was Chichele lecturer at Oxford; in 1965 he became honorary professor at the new university at York, which he much admired; in 1968 he and his wife made their first lecturing visit to the USA. In 1967 he delivered the Clark lectures at Cambridge, published as *English Literature in our Time and the University* (1969). In 1969 and 1970 he was visiting professor and Churchill professor at Bristol University. Leavis's lecturing style remained sinewy and urgent, as he grappled with his belief that 'life is growth and growth change'. He at last argued a case for Dickens's works at large in 1970 when he published, with Q. D. Leavis, *Dickens the Novelist*. Concerned about his small pension and his wife's ill health, he published in quick succession *Nor Shall my Sword* (1972), *The Living Principle* (1975), principally an analytic study of T. S. Eliot's *Four Quartets*, and *Thought, Words and Creativity: Art and Thought in Lawrence* (1976). He was awarded honorary doctorates at Leeds, York, Queen's University (Belfast), Delhi, and Aberdeen.

Although unsparing in controversy, Leavis's prose has a romantic intensity, with its complication of personal engagement: he enjoyed being told by a relative of Henry James that he wrote 'like Uncle Henry'. In person he was courtly, especially to students, and a wit—asking 'How did Othello get away when he smote that Turk in Aleppo?' or remarking endearingly to pupils about a distasteful work of criticism, that 'to read it would be to condone it'. In appearance he was slight and weather-beaten, favouring worn but good clothes, and never a tie, except when the conventions of Cambridge academic dress required it. His spoken readings of poetry, in an East Anglian, high-pitched voice, were triumphs of sincerity.

In 1978 Leavis was appointed CH, only just in time for him to be able to appreciate the honour. He died after exhaustion and sad loss of reason in Cambridge on 14 April 1978 and was cremated there. Q. D. Leavis received many letters of condolence from distinguished admirers. Leavis was also survived by his son Ralph (musicologist), his daughter Kate (educational administrator), and his son Robin Lawrence (academic).

Posthumous reputation Leavis promoted self-reliant reading, which exhilarated educators (including self-educators). He was popular because he linked modernism with the past. His scope and decisiveness were appreciated in the United States by such diverse scholars and critics as Donald Greene, Lionel Trilling, and Marius Bewley; Eric Bentley published a collection of work by Leavis and his collaborators: *The Importance of Scrutiny* (1948). His example as teacher–critic was followed by such writers as Richard Hoggart, Raymond Williams, and Donald Davie, but Leavis's decisiveness fell out of favour. He was perceived to be restrictive, establishing an honour roll of writers, a 'canon'. The *Critical Quarterly* complained that he 'blamed Snowdon for not being Everest'.

In the 1970s continental structuralism arrived in British universities, as did fresh concerns for the politics of race, gender, and colonialism—both trends overriding Leavis's desire to analyse and judge texts on their own terms and in relation to modern poetics. The evaluative close reading known in Leavis's day as 'practical criticism' fell out of fashion. In the universities the very term 'literary criticism' became tainted with journalistic and subjective implications. Literary theory held sway, especially when the concept of the 'death of the author' gained ascendancy, contesting, in an attractively anti-authoritarian way, the Leavisian focus on individual writers. After the expansion of higher education in the 1960s, the universities gained momentum in the world of literary discussion:

there were more English departments, more academics, more specialisms, and therefore a pluralism which conflicted with the intensity of Leavis's belief in discrimination. There was more research—and Leavis, though he held one of the first British literary doctorates by research, had been wont to be suspicious of research ('the higher navvying', he called it). The post-Leavis world was not one of sensibility, nor of hierarchies of value in literature. Value was understood to be constructed rather than created, and humanism became a questionable concept. Leavis had never been happy with the avant-garde (the tradition of James Joyce against that of D. H. Lawrence). He seemed remote in the 1980s and 1990s Britain, in which avant-gardism became domesticated.

However, Leavis had always sowed seeds which grew many miles from their source. The bibliographer D. F. McKenzie confessed that he became interested in textual detail by means of Leavis's analyses, especially his widely circulated analysis study sheets. The theatre director Peter Hall believed he had more influence on the contemporary theatre than any other critic. The film critic Robin Wood said he could not have written without Leavis. Teaching method had always interested Leavis: he despised what he called 'stand-and-deliver' examinations (the three-hour examination paper), favouring the assessment of student work by means of essay or dissertation, a practice which became common. Leavis had always liked 'Life, literature and thought' courses on the Cambridge model, which enabled literature to be studied as one among many cultural artefacts (paradoxically at odds with Leavis's passion for the specific text). That such courses became standard practice in the late twentieth-century British humanities curriculum owes something to Leavis, partly through *Education and the University*, and his influence in and on the University of York. His sense of English studies was carried through into the educational world by his pupils and admirers, especially perhaps into the publication programme of Cambridge University Press, organized by Boris Ford, which paid him the great tribute in 1963 of reprinting *Scrutiny* in its entirety.

Leavis said that:

> the best way to promote profitable discussion is to be as clear as possible with oneself about what one sees and judges, to try and establish the essential discriminations in any given field of interest and to state them as clearly as one can (for disagreement, if necessary). (*The Great Tradition*, 1948, 1)

Thus he announced his procedure for criticism of the novel: he showed how writers brought imagination to bear on the moral life and he polemically fashioned a configuration of master novelists in *The Great Tradition*. He cut a pattern out of British fiction, analysing his 'hostages' (his word) in a style both responsive to nuance and mordantly clear. And the sheer cheek of his asides is still oxygenating ('It is tempting to retort there is only one Brontë' (ibid., 27). No wonder *The Great Tradition* survives.

The persistence of reference to Leavis, sometimes rueful, in the early twenty-first century shows the longevity of his passionate individualism. There were attempts at revaluation of his work in the 1990s, notably by Gary Day. There have continued to be literary critics like Terry Eagleton and Christopher Ricks who have respected Leavis. Though ostensibly different, their concerns for the aesthetic, their possession of a pragmatically wide range of concern, and their distaste for relativism echo his work.

Ian MacKillop

Sources I. MacKillop, *F. R. Leavis: a life in criticism* (1995) • W. Baker, J. Kimber, and M. Kinch, eds., *F. R. Leavis and Q. D. Leavis: an annotated bibliography* (1989) • I. MacKillop and R. Storer, *F. R. Leavis: essays and documents* (1995) • G. Singh, *F. R. Leavis: a literary biography* (1995)

Archives Downing College, Cambridge, MSS • Emmanuel College, Cambridge, corresp. • Emmanuel College, Cambridge, MSS | CUL, letters to Grattan Freyer • Ransom HRC, Bottrall, Eliot, and Leavis MSS • U. Leeds, Brotherton L., letters to Professor Walsh • U. Reading, Chatto and Windus Archive • U. Reading L., letters to Bodley Head Ltd | SOUND BL NSA, Cheltenham Festival Lecture

Likenesses R. S. Austin, pencil drawing, 1934, NPG • P. Greenham, oils, *c*.1962, Downing College, Cambridge • P. Joyce, photograph, 1975, NPG [*see illus.*] • J. Cleave, photographs, 1976, repro. in *The Times* • photographs, repro. in Mackillop, *F. R. Leavis*

Wealth at death £48,656: probate, 23 May 1978, *CGPLA Eng. & Wales*

Leavis [*née* Roth], **Queenie Dorothy** (1906–1981), literary scholar and university teacher, was born on 7 December 1906 at 79 Silver Street, Edmonton, Middlesex, the second of the three children of Morris Roth (1876–1953), hosier, and afterwards draper, and Jane Davis (1876–1940). Her parents were observant Jews. She was educated at Latymer School, Edmonton, and was a brilliant scholar, winning in 1925 a Carlisle scholarship to Girton College, Cambridge. In 1928 she was awarded a first-class degree with special distinction in the English tripos. She won the Charity Reeves prize, the Thérèse Montefiore memorial prize, the Gamble prize, and the Ottilie Hancock research fellowship at Girton. She married Frank Raymond *Leavis (1895–1978), literary scholar, editor, and university teacher, on 16 September 1929, which alienated her from her parents at having 'married out' of her faith. They had three children: Ralph, born in January 1934, Kate in September 1939, and Lawrence Robin in December 1944.

Leavis researched for the PhD (awarded in 1932), influenced by F. R. Leavis's theories of 'mass culture', but was herself an investigator of great originality, studying by questionnaire how popular writers (such as Edgar Rice Burroughs, creator of Tarzan) responded to their readership. Her dissertation was examined by E. M. Forster and published to acclaim, virtually without alteration, as *Fiction and the Reading Public* (1932). As a thesis its subtitle had been 'A study in social anthropology', appropriately because she used popular and classic fiction to analyse successive English cultures after the Elizabethan period, inspired by the historical sociology of H. M. Chadwick's 'Early literature and history' course at Cambridge in which the multifarious artefacts of ancient societies were used to detail pictures of cultural identity. Leavis did not shrink from evaluating her data, maintaining that methods of mass publication levelled down the taste of the English reading public in the modern era. Her subsequent publications were fiercely critical of the second-rate. She was awarded the Amy Mary Preston Read scholarship for further research, the first woman to receive it.

In 1932 her husband became editor of *Scrutiny*, published quarterly until 1953, and Leavis worked indefatigably at editorial business, but also made nearly fifty contributions, on fiction and the sociology of the literary world. Her taste was eclectic, with a love for the classics as well as the best in popular writing: she read Damon Runyon to her children and repeatedly sent second-hand copies of Randall Jarrell's *Pictures from an Institution* to friends and pupils. She disliked Bloomsbury and Virginia Woolf's belief that a woman must have 'a room of one's own'. Leavis thought that the management of a busy household was not inherently damaging to creativity, a belief which restricted her own career as an academic, as did scant employment opportunities in Cambridge, her commitment to *Scrutiny* and her husband's work, the demands of child rearing, and her frequent illnesses. Her decisive, scholarly, and vivid writing gained in reputation, however, especially her wartime essays on Jane Austen. When her husband delineated his definitive line of English novelists in *The Great Tradition*, he considered that his wife's work made it unnecessary to include a chapter on Austen.

In 1946 cancer was diagnosed, from which Leavis suffered in the post-war years. In the 1960s, however, her powers returned, and she was asked to teach for the English tripos at several Cambridge colleges. She visited Harvard University with her husband, which resulted in an important essay on Emily Brontë in their joint book *Lectures in America* (1969). Another collaboration, *Dickens the Novelist* (1970), followed. She was afflicted again by cancer and the burns received from radium treatment. In 1977 F. R. Leavis's health began to fail: although not strong, she nursed him at home until his death in the spring of 1978. As a widow Leavis began work on a memoir of her husband, but she also lectured widely in schools and universities on novelists in the English and other traditions. Her last lecture, for the Cheltenham festival of 1980, was 'The Englishness of the English novel'. She knew well the work of Aleksandr Solzhenitsyn, on whom she was preparing in her last weeks to lecture. She died of heart failure in Cambridge on 17 March 1981.

Q. D. Leavis was an important critic of the novel, English, American, and European, on which three posthumous volumes of essays were published. Personally she was vivacious and combative, with passionately held dislikes and likes. She had a strong visual sense, for clothes, house decoration, and book illustration. As an undergraduate she delighted in the novels of Henry James, she herself possessing some of the directness of an early James heroine. IAN MACKILLOP

Sources I. MacKillop, *F. R. Leavis: a life in criticism* (1995) • M. C. Bradbrook, 'Queenie Leavis: the dynamics of rejection', *Cambridge Review* (20 Nov 1981), 56–9 • W. Baker, J. Kimber, and M. Kinch, *F. R. Leavis and Q. D. Leavis: an annotated bibliography* (1989) • D. Thompson, *The Leavises: recollections and impressions* (1984)
Archives Girton Cam. • Palmers Green Library, London
Likenesses photographs, repro. in MacKillop, *F. R. Leavis*
Wealth at death £134,807: probate, 24 June 1981, *CGPLA Eng. & Wales*

Le Bas, Charles Webb (1779–1861), college head, was born at 20 New Bond Street, London, on 26 April 1779. He was descended from a Huguenot family at Caen, from which city his great-grandfather fled to England in 1702. His grandfather, Stephen Le Bas, was a brewer in St Giles-in-the-Fields, and his father, Charles Le Bas, a linen draper in New Bond Street. His mother was the daughter of Captain Webb of the East India Company's mercantile marine. She died when her son was only six years of age; about four years later the father settled at Bath, and afterwards at Margate. Charles was educated at Hyde Abbey School, near Winchester, where he was a contemporary of Thomas Gaisford.

In 1796 Le Bas entered Trinity College, Cambridge, where he obtained a scholarship, and was afterwards Craven scholar, members' prizeman, and senior chancellor's medallist in the university. In 1800 he graduated BA as fourth wrangler, proceeding MA in 1803. He was elected in 1801 to a fellowship of his college, which he held until 1814, when he married Sophia, daughter of Mark Hodgson of the Bow brewery, inventor of the famous India pale ale.

In 1802 Le Bas was admitted a student at Lincoln's Inn, and in 1806 was called to the bar; but deafness compelled him to abandon the legal profession. In 1808 he became tutor to the two sons of the bishop of Lincoln (Dr Pretyman, who afterwards took the name of Tomline), and took holy orders in 1809. He was presented by Pretyman to the rectory of St Paul's, Shadwell, in 1811, which he held until 1843. From 1812 until his death Le Bas was a prebendary of Lincoln Cathedral. In 1813 he was appointed mathematical professor and dean in the East India College, Haileybury, in succession to William Dealtry, a prominent evangelical. He became principal of the college in 1837 on the death of Joseph Hallet Batten (1778–1837), remaining there until increasing deafness and other infirmities led him to resign on 31 December 1843. Having responsibility for discipline over often unruly students, he was remembered by members of the college as a slightly comical figure with a high-pitched voice (Thomas, 15). But they signified their respect for his work at Haileybury by raising £1920 in 1848 to found the Le Bas essay prize at Cambridge.

Le Bas was distinguished as a preacher and as a writer. His published *Sermons on Various Occasions* (3 vols., 1822–34), chiefly delivered in the chapel of the East India College, were 'plain and practical sermons of a distinctly Anglican type' (*DNB*), indicating his influence as an 'antidote' to evangelicalism among future officers of the East India Company (Dewey, 156). He was a supporter of the Society for Promoting Christian Knowledge, for which he wrote several tracts. He was the author of the biography (2 vols., 1831) of his close friend Thomas Fanshaw Middleton, bishop of Calcutta, who shared his theological outlook, though his account omitted mention of Middleton's influence upon S. T. Coleridge. Associated with the group of high-churchmen known as the Hackney Phalanx, he belonged to the theological school that formed a link between the Caroline divines and the nonjurors and the

Oxford Movement of 1833. That school included such Cambridge men as Hugh James Rose, Christopher Wordsworth, the master of Trinity College, Professor J. J. Blunt, and W. H. Mill. Christopher Wordsworth, afterwards bishop of Lincoln, in a journal kept during his undergraduate days, frequently speaks of the large congregations that assembled in the university church to hear Le Bas preach.

Le Bas was one of the principal contributors to the *British Critic*, and wrote nearly eighty articles for it between 1827 and 1838. In the latter year John Henry Newman became editor, and, despite their theological differences, he accepted four articles by Le Bas. Le Bas also contributed to the *British Magazine* in 1831–2, which was founded and edited by Hugh James Rose for the purpose of inculcating high Anglican principles. He contributed lives of Wyclif (1831), Cranmer (1833), Jewel (1835), and Laud to the Theological Library series, edited by Rose and W. R. Lyall. In 1846 he published a biography of his friend Henry Vincent Bailey, archdeacon of Stow.

Le Bas retired to Brighton, where he died at his home, 74 Montpelier Road, on 25 January 1861. Of his large family, whose additions had necessitated extensions to the domestic accommodation at Haileybury, only one son, the Revd Henry Vincent Le Bas, survived him.

J. H. Overton, *rev.* M. C. Curthoys

Sources Boase, *Mod. Eng. biog.* • Venn, *Alum. Cant.* • I. Thomas, *Haileybury, 1806–1987* (1987) • C. Dewey, *The passing of Barchester* (1991) • P. B. Nockles, *The Oxford Movement in context: Anglican high churchmanship, 1760–1857* (1994)
Archives BL OIOC, corresp. and papers, MS Eur. D 1157 | BL OIOC, letters to H. H. Wilson, MS Eur. E 301 • LPL, corresp. with Bishop Howley • LPL, letters to Christopher Wordsworth
Likenesses portrait, repro. in Thomas, *Haileybury, 1806–1987*, 14
Wealth at death £25,000: probate, 15 Feb 1861, *CGPLA Eng. & Wales*

Le Bas, Edward (1904–1966), painter and collector, was born on 27 October 1904 in Hampstead, London, the youngest of the three children and only son of Edward Le Bas and his wife, Anna Le Grand. The Le Bas family was of Anglo-French descent, originally from Jersey, and had become wealthy through the exertions of Edward Le Bas senior in building construction and the manufacture of industrial steel products. Le Bas was educated at St Peter's preparatory school, Eastbourne, and at Harrow School (1918–22); he went up to Pembroke College, Cambridge, and graduated BA from the university architectural school in 1925. He had briefly studied painting in France in 1922 and on leaving Cambridge he attended the Royal College of Art, South Kensington, under William Rothenstein. His decision to become a painter displeased his father; his allowance was cut to £150 per annum and he lived in modest circumstances in Golden Square.

In 1933 Le Bas first exhibited at the Royal Academy (*Lady with a Siamese Cat*) and was included in group exhibitions at the Lefevre Galleries, sharing his first one-man show there with Ethel Walker in 1936. Still life, landscape, and figures in interiors were (and continued to be) his principal subjects. There were landscapes of the Hertfordshire countryside near Standon and later of the coast at Rye harbour where he had a cottage. As a boy, Le Bas had spent some summers at Le Touquet and thereafter was frequently in France, on painting expeditions to Brittany, Collioure, Nice, and Roquebrune. His preference was for tranquil landscapes and busily peopled views of harbours and seafronts (Rye, Brighton, Dieppe). More representative, however, and among his best works are genre pieces of friends in interiors, of London pubs and restaurants, very much in the tradition of the Camden Town Group. The influence of W. R. Sickert and Vuillard are especially evident in such paintings with their combination of robust portraiture and a spatial complexity brought about by his predilection for patterned surfaces, mirrors, artificial lighting, and the juxtaposing of figures and still life. Friends remember the Vuillardesque atmosphere and furnishing of the sitting-room in his flat in Bedford Square where he lived in London until taking a studio flat shortly after the war of 1939–45 in Glebe Place, Chelsea, where he lived until his death.

After the death of his father, Le Bas became financially independent, indeed wealthy, and from the later 1930s dates his extraordinary generosity in buying young painters' work as well as his discerning purchase of pictures by the masters of the modern French school—Pissarro, Cézanne, Vuillard, Bonnard (whose *Bol de lait*, *c.*1934, Le Bas left to the Tate Gallery), Derain, Braque, and Picasso. But when his collection came to be shown at the Royal Academy ('A Painter's Collection', 1963) it was seen that he had a remarkable eye for the best in modern British painting and there were groups of pictures of the highest quality by Sickert, I. C. Ginner, Sir Matthew A. B. Smith, Dame Ethel Walker, Duncan Grant, and Harold Gilman.

Le Bas did not neglect the young and unknown particularly among painters of the Euston Road School (with some of whom Le Bas shared aesthetic affinities) and those artists who emerged in the 1940s such as Robert Colquhoun and Robert MacBryde, F. John Minton, and John Craxton. Many painters were among his friends. Charles Ginner's professionalism was a continual example to Le Bas; Ginner was to be grateful for the younger painter's support at a time when his reputation had plummeted; they frequently worked together and during the war dined together in Leicester Square almost every night. Later painter friends included Vanessa Bell and Duncan Grant; Le Bas painted with them and Eardley Knollys in Asolo in 1956, at Roquebrune in 1959, and with Grant and Knollys in Spain in the early 1960s.

In 1939 Le Bas held his last one-man exhibition in England (at the Lefevre Galleries with Mark Gertler) and thereafter exhibited annually at the Royal Academy, of which he was elected an associate in 1943 and an RA in 1954. He was elected to the London Group in 1942 (with Lawrence B. Gowing, Frances M. Hodgkins, and others). In 1957 he was appointed CBE. Overcoming his distinct aversion to one-man shows, he held two successful exhibitions at the Hammer Galleries, New York, in 1956 and 1961.

Le Bas was a tall, well-built man who wore a neatly trimmed beard for most of his life. He lived comfortably, spending most of his money on travel and pictures; expensive cars were the only sign of his wealth. Although not a social man, he was extremely convivial, giving memorable if somewhat haphazard parties and suppers for his friends in Glebe Place where pictures covered the walls and were stacked against the skirting boards. Intemperate habits considerably reduced the quantity and quality of his painting during his last years though his 1964 *Lady with a Parasol* (priv. coll.) is notable for its assured composition and lyrical colour. Above all Le Bas was a colourist owing much to Bonnard and it is as a discriminating, though never slavish, descendant of the modern French school that he is best remembered. He also had something of the witty observation of Degas, Lautrec, and Sickert's London genre scenes—an amusing hat, a striking profile, or a perfectly placed little dog. And such a painting as *Interior at Long Crichel* (exh. RA, 1952) shows that he could design a contemporary conversation piece on a large scale and retain his personal sense of colour—something rare in modern British painting. Le Bas posed for the figure of Christ in Duncan Grant's *Crucifixion* (1943) at Berwick church, Sussex, and there is a small portrait by Grant (*c.*1947; priv. coll.). Good examples of work by Le Bas can be found in the Tate collection, various provincial galleries, New South Wales, America, and many private collections. Le Bas was unmarried. He died at Lymington Hospital, near Sway in the New Forest, Hampshire, on 18 November 1966.

Richard Shone, *rev.*

Sources M. Chamot, D. Farr, and M. Butlin, *The modern British paintings, drawings and sculpture*, 2 vols. (1964–5) [catalogue, Tate Gallery, London] • private information (1981) • *CGPLA Eng. & Wales* (1967) • *A painter's collection: an exhibition of paintings, drawings and sculpture from the collection of Edward le Bas, R.A.* (1963) [exhibition catalogue, Royal Academy of Arts, London]

Archives Tate collection, letters to Basil Creighton and Frances Creighton

Likenesses D. Grant, portrait, *c.*1947, priv. coll.

Wealth at death £286,554: probate, 16 June 1967, *CGPLA Eng. & Wales*

Le Blanc, Sir Simon (1748/9–1816), judge, was the second son of Thomas Le Blanc (1704–1765), of Charterhouse Square, London, and Ann Tully. Thomas Le Blanc, a wealthy merchant and a director of the South Sea Company, was descended from a Huguenot family of Rouen; his wife had a fortune of £20,000 at their marriage in 1739. Simon, who received £14,000 under his father's will in 1765, followed his brother Thomas (*b.* 1743) to Trinity Hall, Cambridge, where he was admitted pensioner on 1 January 1766; he was named scholar in that year and matriculated in Michaelmas term 1766. He was admitted to the Inner Temple in 1771 and called to the bar in February 1773. He graduated LLB from Cambridge in 1773 and was a fellow of Trinity Hall from 1779 to 1799.

Le Blanc joined the Norfolk circuit and by February 1787 was sufficiently eminent in the profession to be created serjeant-at-law; he was made king's serjeant on 4 March 1795 and was treasurer of Serjeants' Inn from 1798 to 1799. One of the most successful advocates of his generation, in the year 1790 he made 271 appearances in the court of common pleas; only one other barrister made more. His

Sir Simon Le Blanc (1748/9–1816), by Francis Wheatley

advice on cases was called upon by clients on many different issues; they included the inhabitants of Hinxton, Cambridgeshire, in 1792, whom he advised on right of common at enclosure; George Nugent-Temple-Grenville, first marquess of Buckingham, who retained him on the prosecution of deer-stealers in 1786; and many others, in Cambridgeshire and throughout the country. He was counsel for the University of Cambridge from 1791 to 1799. On 5 June 1799 he was made a justice of the court of king's bench, and knighted, taking his seat on the following day. Lord Campbell, who first saw him on the bench in June 1800, later described him as 'prim and precise' (Campbell, 4.108) in appearance and one of the best lawyers of his generation. In contrast Isaac Espinasse was less complimentary:

> In speaking, he was tame and unimpressive; his delivery was feeble, and totally destitute of that earnestness and seeming self-conviction of the truth of what he wished to impress upon the minds of others. No varied cadence ever relieved the ear—no quotation ever embellished his address to a jury. He was tamely correct, tedious, and unconvincing. (Espinasse, 319)

Espinasse added that Le Blanc was not popular with the bar and too full of his own importance to allow himself any familiarity.

Le Blanc's contributions to judgments were many, only some of which have been noted by historians, such as *Glazebrook* v. *Woodrow* (1799), on executory contracts; *Haycraft* v. *Creasy* (1801), on false representation of another's credit, in which he and the other puisnes overruled the lord chief justice, Lloyd Kenyon, first Baron Kenyon; and *R.* v. *Creevey* (1813), on libel by a member of parliament, in which his own direction at trial was overruled by Edward

Law, first Baron Ellenborough. He sat with other judges on a number of state trials, including that of James Hadfield, who fired on George III in 1800, but came to widest public notice in his conduct of other criminal cases. In June 1808 John Harriott Hart and Henry White, of the *Independent Whig*, were successfully prosecuted for libelling Le Blanc for his directions to the jury in the trials of captains Chapman (which he did conduct) and Bennett (which he did not) for murdering a young man and a boy through savage punishment. Chapman and Bennett had been acquitted; Hart and White were convicted, fined, and imprisoned for the libel on Le Blanc and another on the lord chief justice, Ellenborough.

Four years later Le Blanc was selected as one of the judges charged particularly with the suppression of Luddism. During the initial phase of machine-breaking in the midlands and the north some of the justices on assize circuit had directed or encouraged acquittals in spite of the scale of disturbances. John Bayley, a puisne justice of king's bench, did so at Nottingham in March 1812, at York in August 1812, and again, at Nottingham, in March 1815. George Wood, a baron of the exchequer, sat on a trial at Lancaster in August 1812 where thirty-eight were acquitted. The government was convinced that exemplary executions were necessary, and when special commissions were issued for assizes at Chester and Lancaster in May 1812, and at York in January 1813, care was taken to select judges of a different temper. Le Blanc sat with Sir Alexander Thomson at both Lancaster and York, at which twenty-five prisoners were executed in all. At York he tried the murderers of the woollen manufacturer William Horsfall, whose conviction was critical. The judges advised prosecuting counsel, James Alan Park, and Henry Hobhouse, the Treasury solicitor, that moving the executions of the three condemned men to Huddersfield would be unwise, as it would entail a respite, raising hopes of mercy. They were hanged at York two days after trial. Before the next convictions took place Le Blanc conferred with Park on the advantages of early hangings, as had been adopted at the Lancaster special commission. The judges also agreed to accept no applications for mercy but to leave the entire discretion with the secretary of state. Le Blanc and Thomson recommended mercy for only one of the seventeen sentenced to death.

In the 1780s, while a barrister, Le Blanc had chambers in Lincoln's Inn; on appointment to the bench he moved to Serjeants' Inn. His town house, where he died on 15 April 1816 in his sixty-eighth year, was in Bedford Square. He also had a country seat, Northaw House, near Barnet, Hertfordshire. He was buried under the altar of Northaw church. He made extensive bequests to nephews, his widowed sister, his sister-in-law, and their children. He had no children himself and never married.

DOUGLAS HAY

Sources Baker, *Serjeants*, 220, 460, 522 • John, Lord Campbell, *The lives of the chief justices of England*, 3rd edn, 4 vols. (1874) • ER • Foss, *Judges* • E. Foss, *Biographia juridica: a biographical dictionary of the judges of England … 1066–1870* (1870) • *GM*, 1st ser., 86/1 (1816), 871 • Holdsworth, *Eng. law* • J. Hutchinson, ed., *A catalogue of notable Middle Templars: with brief biographical notices* (1902) • D. Lemmings, *Professors of the law: barristers and English legal culture in the eighteenth century* (2000) • M. Lobban, *The common law and English jurisprudence, 1760–1850* (1991) • J. M. Neeson, *Commoners: common right, enclosure, and social change in England, 1700–1820* (1993) • W. P. Baildon, ed., *The records of the Honorable Society of Lincoln's Inn: the black books*, 4 (1902), 243 • Sainty, *Judges*, 38 • Sainty, *King's counsel*, 27 • *State trials* • M. Le Blanc, 'Notes on the descent of the family of Thomas Le Blanc of Cavenham, Suffolk', UCL, Huguenot Library • research file, Le Blanc, UCL, Huguenot Library • H. Wagner, 'Pedigrees and abstracts of Huguenot wills', UCL, Huguenot Library • [I. Espinasse], 'My contemporaries: from the notebooks of a retired barrister', *Fraser's Magazine*, 6 (1832), 316–19 • L. S. Sutherland, 'The City of London and the Devonshire–Pitt administration, 1756–7 (The Raleigh Lecture on History)', *PBA*, 46 (1960), 147–93, 190 • J. R. Tanner, ed., *The historical register of the University of Cambridge* (1917), 57 • will, PRO, PROB 11/1579, sig. 208 • Venn, *Alum. Cant.*, 2/4.128 • private information (2004) [S. Massil, Huguenot Library, London] • affidavit of William Richmond, 1800, PRO, KB 1/30, Hil 40 Geo III, pt 1 • affidavit of Thomas Bolton, 1803, PRO, KB 1/32/1,Ea 43 Geo III, pt 1

Archives PRO, corresp., HO 42/132

Likenesses J. Opie, oils, Trinity Hall, Cambridge • F. Wheatley, portrait; Sotheby's, 26 Nov 1975 [*see illus.*]

Wealth at death bequests of £30,000 in the funds, as well as real and other personal estate: will, PRO, PROB 11/1579, sig. 208

Le Blon [Le Blond], **Jacob Christofel** [Jakob Christoffel] (*bap.* **1667**, *d.* **1741**), miniature painter and colour-printmaker, was born at Frankfurt am Main, Germany, and baptized on 23 May 1667, the son of Christoff Le Blon (*bap.* 1639), bookseller, and Catharina Dorellin, the daughter of a confectioner. He was descended on his father's side from the engraving families of de Bry and Merian, but he appears to have been trained as a painter, claiming in the 1730s to have been a pupil of Carlo Maratta in Rome, where he signed and dated a miniature in 1697 (Kupferstichkabinett, Berlin). Johan van Gool, his early biographer, stated that he was brought from Rome as a miniature painter to Amsterdam in 1702 by the painter Bonaventura van Overbeek. Certainly he married Gerrarda Vloet (1679?–1716) there in February 1705, and in the same year was made, as a painter, a freeman of the city. The couple's first son, Theodorus, was born in 1706 but died in infancy. A second son, Christopherus, was baptized in September 1715.

In Amsterdam Le Blon began working on a theory of human proportions, and on the principles of light and shade, and colour mixing in painting, in consultation with the collector and amateur artist Lambert ten Kate and the painter and etcher Hendrick van Limborch. In 1707 he published *Generaale proportie voor de onderscheidene lengte der beelden van welbenesende menschelyke gestalte; ontwerpen tot ondersteuning van het oog*. Proportion was also to be a major preoccupation in his work on colour, and when, at The Hague about 1715, he described his principles to the Venetian amateur Antonio Conti, he emphasized that the Newtonian theory of colours had taught him 'the degrees of strength or weakness that must be given to colours in order to bring them into harmony' (Conti, 2. cxlviii). The book which was to explain his practice, *Coloritto, or, The harmony of colouring in painting: reduced to mechanical practice, under easy precepts, and infallible rules*, published in English and French in 1725, was still concerned entirely with painting.

But Le Blon was also exploiting his colour interests in the context of printmaking. He had printed etchings from at least 1710 and was developing the colour-mezzotint process for which he became famous, so that by 1711 the German traveller Zacharias Conrad von Uffenbach was able in Le Blon's workshop to examine examples of 'his special invention, to print engravings like miniature paintings' (Uffenbach, 3.534). The first of Le Blon's prints to be published in England, *The Napkin of St Veronica* (Singer, 10), after an oil by the artist now at Christ Church, Oxford, is still in this miniature style. It is likely that he seldom engraved his plates himself but was effectively a designer of colour separations. Uffenbach also stated that Le Blon was still mainly active as a miniature painter and was only just beginning to paint in oil.

Le Blon seems to have tried to patent his invention in The Hague, with no success, and in 1718 he moved via France to England, which he had already visited in 1710. Here he applied successfully for a royal letters patent for a method of colour printing in 'natural Coloris', with three plates in blue (the base plate), yellow, and red. Sets of colour separations showing these fundamental colours and some of their mixtures were in circulation by 1719; and, with the support of Lieutenant-Colonel John Guise, whom he may have met in France or the Netherlands, he soon set up the Picture Office in London for the large-scale production of colour prints. A catalogue of 1722 already listed some forty pieces. This manufactory had attracted some forty to fifty 'proprietors' by 1723; but Le Blon's business sense was limited and his imperfect method required much hand-finishing. He seems to have been removed as director of the works in 1722 and by 1725 the company was bankrupt.

But from about 1721 Le Blon had been exploring the possibility of adapting his system of colour proportions to the manufacture of tapestry, and in 1727 he secured a patent for the 'Art of weaving Tapestry on the loom' for fourteen years. He obtained permission to have Raphael's tapestry cartoons in the Royal Collection copied by Isaac Vogelsang (copies in the Ashmolean Museum, Oxford); weaving began by 1732 and a manufactory was established at Chelsea early the following year. It is clear from the detailed account by Cromwell Mortimer published in the *Philosophical Transactions of the Royal Society* in 1731 that Le Blon was obliged to make technical compromises in the interest of greater speed. For example, he introduced black and white in addition to his three 'primitive' colours; and, so far as is known, only a sample *Head of Christ* (from Raphael's *Miraculous Draught of Fishes*) was completed, and has survived in some sixteen examples, of which three are in the Victoria and Albert Museum in London, the Museum of London, and the Mormon Tabernacle in Salt Lake City, Utah. Weaving continued at Chelsea until the autumn of 1734, but by the following year Le Blon had transferred to Paris, where he was to remain until his death.

Le Blon set up a new printing office in Paris and secured a patent from Louis XV to print pictures for twenty years (from July 1739). He trained a number of assistants, notably Jacques-Fabien-Gautier Dagoty, whose family continued to produce colour mezzotints by a coarser version of Le Blon's process until the 1780s. With Catherine Poulle (*d.* 1741), whom he may have married, he had a daughter, Marguerite, born in 1736. Le Blon died on 15 May 1741 at his home at 16 rue Percée in the parish of St Séverin, Paris.

Le Blon's prints were largely of portraits and devotional subjects, but much of the eighteenth-century interest in his method of printmaking focused on its capacity to illustrate the human anatomy in full colour. Although only one of his own anatomical prints has survived—a dissection of the male genitals (Singer, 47)—many others are documented, and they form the largest proportion of the work of his followers. But his productions were also widely collected as exemplifying the theory of the three 'primary' colours, which became the basis of a good deal of colour science in the nineteenth century and is still (albeit with other sets of 'primaries') the fundamental principle of colour printing. In addition to his treatises *Generaale Proportie* and *Coloritto*, Le Blon published an English version of Lambert ten Kate's *Le beau idéal* (as *The Beau Ideal*) in London in 1732. Important collections of his prints are in the British Museum, London; the Kupferstichkabinett, Dresden; the Bibliothèque Nationale and the Bibliothèque de l'Arsenal, Paris; and the Yale Center for British Art, New Haven, Connecticut. Some of his oil paintings are in the Guise collection at Christ Church, Oxford. JOHN GAGE

Sources O. M. Lilien, *Jacob Christoph Le Blon, 1667–1741: inventor of three- and four-colour printing* (1985) • Vertue, *Note books*, vols. 3 and 6 • G. Wildenstein, 'Jakob Christoffel Le Blon, ou, Le secret de peindre en gravant', *Gazette des Beaux-Arts*, 6th ser., 56 (1960), 91–100 • J. Byam Shaw, *Paintings by old masters at Christ Church, Oxford* (1967) • H. W. Singer, 'Jakob Christoffel Le Blon', *Mitteilungen der Gesellschaft für vervielfältigende Kunst*, 1/2 (1901) • J. van Gool, *De nieuwe schouburg der Nederlantsche kunstschilders en schilderessen*, 1 (The Hague, 1750) • Z. C. von Uffenbach, *Merkwuerdige Reisen durch NiederSachsen, Holland und Engelland*, 3 (1754) • A. Conti, *Prose e poesie*, 2 (1756) • F. Rodari, ed., *Anatomie de la couleur: l'invention de l'estampe en couleurs* (Paris, 1996) [exhibition catalogue, Bibliothèque Nationale de France, Paris, 27 Feb – 5 May 1996, and Musée Olympique, Lausanne, 22 May – 1 Sept 1996] • Geburtenbuch, Stadtarchiv, Frankfurt am Main

Archives Archives Nationales, Paris, minutier central, actes des notaires de Paris, cote CXVII, 747; cote F–12–993, 1742, 7863 • Archives Nationales, Paris, cote E 1184A 2159, fol. 158; cote E 2166, fols. 122–3 • BL, Add. MS 4299, fols. 72–6; Add. MS 36126, fols. 175–7 • BL, Egmont MSS 47029, vol. CX • University of Amsterdam, Lambert ten Kate MSS

Wealth at death see inventory of property (without values), Archives Nationales, Paris, Archive des Notaires de Paris, Minutier Central, Cote LIII, 298, 15 May 1741

Le Blond [*née* Hawkins-Whitshed], **Elizabeth Alice Frances** (1860–1934), mountaineer and photographer, was the only child of Sir St Vincent Bentinck Hawkins-Whitshed, third baronet (1837–1871), of Killincarrick House, Greystones, co. Wicklow, and his wife, Alice (*d.* 1908), the youngest daughter of the Revd the Hon. John Gustavus Handcock. She was educated by governesses from the age of eight. Her father died in 1871, leaving her property in

Elizabeth Alice Frances Le Blond (1860–1934), by unknown photographer, 1910

Ireland, and she became a ward in chancery. She lived with her mother at Killincarrick and in London. By the end of her first London 'season' she was engaged to Colonel Frederick Gustavus *Burnaby (1842–1885), an adventurer who had travelled extensively in Russia and Turkey. They were married on 25 June 1879 at St Peter's Church, Cranley Gardens, London, and their only son was born in 1880.

As Mrs Burnaby she travelled 'on the borders of consumption' in 1881. After convalescence in Algiers, Hyères, and Menton, doctors sent her to Switzerland. In Chamonix she made several walks with friends and soon was inspired to climb to the Grands Mulets. Before descending from the hut, she put on her own boots for the first time in her life. Only several years later did she realize that she could do without a maid. In the summer of 1882 she returned and climbed Mont Blanc twice, as well as the Grandes Jorasses. Beginning in 1882–3, she made many ascents in winter with Eduard Cupelin, her guide, which she described in *The High Alps in Winter, or, Mountaineering in Search of Health* (1883), and *High Life and Towers of Silence* (1886). In this period her great-aunt Lady Bentinck wrote to her mother: 'Stop her climbing mountains! She is scandalizing all London and looks like a red Indian!' Photographs from this period show her climbing in a skirt that barely reached her knees. Le Blond later wrote in her memoir that 'I owe a supreme debt of gratitude to the mountains for knocking from me the shackles of conventionality' (Le Blond, 90).

During a maverick expedition to relieve General Charles Gordon at Khartoum, Fred Burnaby was killed at Abu Klea on 17 January 1885. In 1886 his widow married Dr John Frederic Main (1854–1892), professor of engineering at University College, Bristol, and the Royal College of Science, London. A complex marriage settlement of 1879 provided her husband with an income of £1000 a year from her lands in Ireland. After her marriage to Main, he became an investment banker and moved to Denver, Colorado, where he died on 10 May 1892. On 12 June 1900, in Kensington, she married (Francis Bernard) Aubrey Le Blond (*b.* 1869), of Aldeburgh, Suffolk, the eldest son of Francis Aubrey Le Blond, merchant. She lived apart from her husbands for long periods of time, for several years almost entirely in Switzerland, usually in St Moritz. She was active in winter sports such as tobogganing and ice-skating. After she became the first woman to pass the men's skating test, separate tests for men and women were abolished in St Moritz. She was among the first people to make bicycle tours through the Alps, and she raced early motor cars in hill-climbing competitions. She also founded the St Moritz Aid Fund to enable people to travel to St Moritz to convalesce.

As Mrs Main and Mrs Le Blond, she was often profiled in women's magazines and was the best-known woman mountain climber of her time. She published several books about the Alps and tales of mountaineering adventure. Since she climbed several times alone with other women, including a traverse of Piz Palü with Lady Evelyn McDonnell in 1900, she was among the earliest women to attempt 'manless' climbing. She stopped climbing in the Alps after the son of Joseph Imboden, her guide, was killed while climbing in 1895. She did, however, later climb with Imboden in Norway, which she described in *Climbing in the Land of the Midnight Sun* (1908). She also founded the Ladies' Alpine Club, first as a section of the Lyceum Club in 1907 and later as an independent organization in 1909. She served as the club's president during 1907–12 and 1932–4.

Next to mountaineering, her greatest interest was photography. She published *Hints on Snow Photography* in 1894, and was a medallist of the Royal Photographic Society. Her photographs illustrated her own books as well as many magazine articles and books in her areas of interest, such as Spanish cities, Italian gardens, and figure skating. She published genealogical and antiquarian books about her ancestors, including a two-volume work on Charlotte Sophie, Countess Bentinck, for which she carried out research in the Netherlands and Germany. In 1912 she toured China, Korea, and Japan with Aubrey Le Blond, during which he added to his collection of porcelains, which were later presented to the Victoria and Albert Museum. They returned from the Far East by the Trans-Siberian Railway and visited Russia in 1913.

After the outbreak of war in 1914, Le Blond volunteered at a hospital in Dieppe and remained there until the end of 1916, when she returned to England to take charge of the appeal department of the British ambulance committee. She had already raised funds with the Ladies' Alpine Club for a motor kitchen for the ambulance corps of the Vosges. For the British ambulance committee she raised £1200 each week through a variety of innovative fund-raising appeals. After the armistice she founded the British Empire Fund for the Restoration of Rheims Cathedral. The War Office also asked her to give lectures to troops in Britain and France, which she did with her own lantern slides on topics such as 'A day in the Alps' and 'Overseas France—Algeria, Tunisia, and Morocco'. She had been much impressed by Marshall Lyautey's pacification of Morocco. In 1920 she travelled to Morocco to meet Lyautey, whose *Lettres de Tonkin et de Madagascar* she translated into English in 1932. After she led the effort to erect a statue of Marshall Foch in London, Le Blond was made chevalier of the Légion d'honneur in 1933. Le Blond also founded the Forum, a club for women, and the Anglo-French Luncheon Club, which hosted French visitors in London. She made several visits to the United States after her son emigrated to California. Elizabeth Le Blond was recovering from a major operation at Mangalore, the home of her brother-in-law, Dr George Worthington, in Llandrindod Wells, Denbighshire, when she died on 27 July 1934. She was buried on 31 July at Brompton cemetery. PETER H. HANSEN

Sources E. A. Le Blond, *Day in, day out* [1928] • *The Times* (28 July 1934) • *Ladies' Alpine Club Yearbook* (1935) • E. L. S., 'In memoriam: Mrs Aubrey Le Blond', *Alpine Journal*, 46 (1934), 382–4 • *WWW* • M. Tindal, 'The champion lady mountaineer', *Pearson's Magazine*, 7 (Jan–June 1899), 354–64 • E. Whymper, 'Two lady climbers', *Girl's Own Paper* (15 Dec 1885), 164–7 • *Debrett's Peerage* • *Dod's Peerage* (1921) • M. Alexander, *The true blue: the life and adventures of Colonel Fred Burnaby, 1842–85* (1957) • Venn, *Alum. Cant.* • *CGPLA Eng. & Wales* (1934) • *DNB* • *The Times* (1 Aug 1934) • d. cert. • will, proved, Ipswich, 25 Oct 1934

Archives Alpine Club, London, Ladies' Alpine Club MSS

Likenesses photograph, *c.*1880, repro. in T. Wright, *The life of Colonel Fred Burnaby* (1908), 154 • photographs, 1898–9, repro. in Tindal, 'The champion lady mountaineer' • photographs, 1898–9, repro. in *Ladies' Alpine Club Yearbook* • photographs, 1898–9, repro. in *Alpine Journal*, 383 • photograph, 1910, Alpine Club, London [*see illus.*] • M. McLeod, oils, repro. in Le Blond, *Day in, day out*, frontispiece

Wealth at death £4410 14*s.* 6*d.*: resworn probate, 25 Oct 1934, *CGPLA Eng. & Wales*

Le Breton [*née* Aikin], **Anna Letitia** (1808–1885), writer, was born on 30 June 1808 at Broad Street, London, the first of five children of Charles Rochemont *Aikin (1775–1847), surgeon, and his wife, Anne (*d.* 1821), daughter of the Revd Gilbert *Wakefield (1756–1801), dissenting minister and defender of religious liberties, and his wife, Anne Watson. She was educated at home, in particular by her great-aunt, Anna Letitia *Barbauld (*née* Aikin) (1743–1825), poet and writer for children, and her aunt, Lucy *Aikin (1781–1864), also a poet and writer for children, as well as other members of the Aikin family. She married Philip Hemery Le Breton (1806–1884), barrister, in August 1833, and resided at Hampstead, London. Anna Letitia Le Breton's publications record the literary and political contributions of members of her family, particularly Anna Letitia Barbauld and Lucy Aikin. She co-edited Lucy Aikin's *Memoirs, Miscellanies, and Letters* (1864), edited her correspondence with Dr William Ellery Channing of Boston (1874), and wrote a *Memoir of Mrs Barbauld, Including Letters and Notices of her Family and Friends* (1874). Her final publication was *Memories of Seventy Years, by One of a Literary Family* (1883), edited by her daughter, Mary Emma Martin, novelist and writer for children. Predeceased by her husband, she died at her home, 6 Worsley Road, Hampstead, on 29 September 1885, and was buried at Hampstead cemetery. SUSAN J. LEVASSEUR

Sources A. L. Le Breton, *Memories of seventy years, by one of a literary family*, ed. M. E. Martin (1883) • B. Rodgers, *Georgian chronicle: Mrs Barbauld and her family* (1958) • *The Times* (1 Oct 1885) • A. L. Le Breton, ed., *Correspondence of William Ellery Channing DD and Lucy Aikin from 1826 to 1842* (1874) • A. L. Le Breton, *Memoir of Mrs Barbauld, including letters and notices of her family and friends* (1874) • *DNB* • d. cert. • *CGPLA Eng. & Wales* (1885)

Wealth at death £1323 18*s.* 7*d.*: probate, 26 Nov 1885, *CGPLA Eng. & Wales*

Le Breton, William Corbet (1815–1888), dean of Jersey, was the eldest son of William Le Breton (son of Dean François Le Breton) and Jane Hué, sister of Dean Corbet Hué; he was the nephew of Sir Thomas Le Breton senior, bailiff of Jersey. He was born at St Helier early in 1815, and was baptized in St Helier parish church on 17 March in that year. He was sent to Winchester College, where he fagged for Roundell Palmer, and entered Pembroke College, Oxford, in 1831 as a Morley scholar, graduating BA in 1835 with third-class honours in classics. After proceeding MA in 1837 he held a Jersey fellowship at Exeter College from 1837 until his marriage in 1842. He was ordained deacon in 1839 and priest in 1840, in the diocese of Oxford. In 1845 he became a curate of St Olave's in Southwark, and remained there until he was made dean of Jersey on 26 December 1849. His appointment occasioned some ill feeling among the clergy of Jersey, who petitioned that the office should be held by someone who had worked in the island. Le Breton held the deanship until his death, and was rector of St Saviour until 1875, when he transferred to the rectory of St Helier.

Le Breton was strikingly handsome, as was his wife, Emily Davis Martin, daughter of William Martin, whom he married at St Luke's Church, Chelsea, in 1842. They had a family of six sons and a daughter, Emilie Charlotte, who concentrated her parents' good looks in herself and became, as Lillie *Langtry, the most celebrated beauty of her time. Something of his daughter's reputation may have later coloured public opinion of Le Breton. In social life he attained a popularity which was perhaps excessive and rebounded against him. His private life was allegedly licentious, and became the subject of derogatory rumours which caused him to leave the island in 1880, when he consigned his clerical duties to the vice-dean, Philip Le Feuvre. He spent his remaining years in England, and died after a long illness, at his home, 161 Kennington Road, London, on 28 February 1888. He was buried in St Saviour's churchyard in Jersey. IAN MACHIN

Sources G. R. Balleine, *A biographical dictionary of Jersey*, [1] [1948], 366–7 • G. I. T. Machin, 'George Julian Harney in Jersey, 1855–63: a chartist "abroad"', *Annual Bulletin* [Société Jersiaise], 23/4 (1984), 478–95, esp. 483–4 • *The Times* (1 March 1888), 5 • *CGPLA Eng. & Wales* (1888)

Wealth at death £5: administration, 2 June 1888, *CGPLA Eng. & Wales*

Le Brun, John (*d.* 1865), missionary, was born in Switzerland but brought up in England, where he was educated by David Bogue at the missionary college at Gosport, Hampshire. He was ordained a Congregationalist minister in Jersey on 25 November 1813, and at about the same time was appointed missionary to Mauritius, which had been captured from the French in 1810. He set sail from England on 1 January 1814, with letters of recommendation from the directors of the London Missionary Society to Governor Robert Farquhar. According to his directors an important part of his mission was to prepare the way to the great island of Madagascar, and also to Bourbon.

Le Brun arrived at Port Louis, Mauritius, on 18 May 1814. In the following year the governor of the island spoke with satisfaction of his work to date, but Le Brun found it difficult to acclimatize to the new country: he was frequently in poor health, and his opposition to slavery meant that he and his congregation were placed under a police ban, making it hard to establish relations with non-whites.

In August 1818 Le Brun married Miss Mabille in Port Louis. They had two sons before her death on 9 July 1856, both of whom carried on Le Brun's missionary work after his death. From October 1832 until 4 March 1833 the family were in Cape Town, and then Le Brun returned to London on 22 May 1833.

In August 1833 the London Missionary Society, discouraged by government officials, abandoned its mission to Mauritius. But when the act for the abolition of slavery in all the British dominions was published in 1834, Le Brun chose to return independently to Mauritius, where he worked among emancipated slaves, mainly of Malagasy and Hovas origins. He built a large chapel in Port Louis, and established schools under the auspices of the Mico charity throughout the island. He also helped to settle Malagasy refugees escaping the persecution of Christians by Queen Ranavalona. In 1838 he sent one of his sons, Peter, to Tamatave to help more fugitives to leave Madagascar for the safety of Mauritius, where there was already a community of about 10,000 émigrés from that island, many of them having originally been imported either as slaves or as 'prize negroes' (Freeman and Johns, *Narrative of the Persecution of the Christians in Madagascar*, 276). Le Brun and his son did their best to convert as many as possible to Christianity, offering religious instruction in Port Louis and in Mokar (J. J. Freeman, *A Tour in South Africa*, 1851, 388). Le Brun was reappointed an agent of the London Missionary Society on 27 December 1841.

In 1851 Le Brun's son Peter again visited Madagascar, and after the death of Queen Ranavalona arranged at the court of King Radama II for government protection to be given to London missionaries entering the country. Le Brun died on 21 February 1865 at Port Louis.

S. P. Oliver, *rev.* Mary Heimann

Sources W. Ellis, *The martyr church: a narrative of the introduction, progress, and triumph of Christianity in Madagascar* (1870) • W. Ellis, *Three visits to Madagascar* (1858) • K. Jeffreys, *Widowed missionary's journal* (1827)

Likenesses H. T. Ryall, stipple (after J. Andrews), NPG

Lebuin [St Lebuin, Lebwin, Leofwine, Livinus] (*d. c.*775), missionary, went to the continent from an unknown part of England in the early 770s. He placed himself in the service of Gregory (*d. c.*775), abbot of St Martin's at Utrecht and administrator of that diocese. Gregory sent Lebuin as a missionary to the area of the River IJssel, a frontier region between the lands of the pagan Frisians and Saxons and the Frankish kingdom. He built the first church at Deventer, but it was soon destroyed by pagans. Lebuin died, supposedly on his feast day of 12 November, perhaps before Gregory, probably about 775, and certainly before 787; he was buried at Deventer. The church there was later rebuilt over his grave by Liudger, a native Frisian who had also been a pupil of Gregory of Utrecht and who was sent as a missionary to the region in 787 before becoming the first bishop of Münster.

The earliest, anonymous, life of Lebuin, the *Vita Lebuini antiqua*, identified in 1909, was written between 840 and 864 at the monastery of Werden, which Liudger had founded. It includes a famous report on the tribal assembly of the Saxons, at which Lebuin preached, holding a cross and gospel book, and warning prophetically that if the Saxons refused to convert they would be destroyed by a king who would be sent against them. The Saxons' attempts to kill him failed because Lebuin miraculously disappeared, and they allowed him to preach wherever he wished. The life was reworked by Hucbald of St Amand (*d.* 930). In later iconography Lebuin is represented as a priest in liturgical vestments, holding a book and a cruciform crozier to which a banner is attached.

Identity has been claimed for Lebuin with two other figures in the early medieval sources, one with much greater plausibility than the other. Lebuin's feast day, 12 November, is also that of *Livinus, the patron of St Lievens-Esse and St Lievens-Houtem (in modern Belgium). In the tenth century, Deventer, Esse, and Houtem were all in Hamaland, the ruler of which, Count Wichmann, was also *Burggraf* of Ghent, to where Livinus's supposed relics were translated, into the abbey church of St Bavo, in 1007. This, coupled with the shared date and the evident similarity of their names, makes it almost certain that Livinus is simply a doublet of Lebuin. The bishop Leofwine, one of seven Anglo-Saxon prelates on the continent who co-signed the admonitory letter that Boniface (*d.* 754) sent to Æthelbald, king of the Mercians, in 746 or 747, is much less likely to be identical with Lebuin. Apart from the chronological difficulty of casting the date of Lebuin's arrival on the continent back nearly thirty years, it is also the case that neither the nearest contemporary source for Lebuin, Altfrid's life of Liudger written in the second quarter of the ninth century, nor any other text calls him a bishop: he was only ever a priest.

Marios Costambeys

Sources C. H. Talbot, ed. and trans., *The Anglo-Saxon missionaries in Germany* (1954) • Hucbald of St Amand, 'Vita Lebuini antiqua',

[*Supplementa tomorum I–XV*], ed. A. Hofmeister, MGH Scriptores [folio], 30/2 (Stuttgart, 1926), 789–95 · W. Levison, *England and the continent in the eighth century* (1946) · Liudger, 'Vita Gregorii abbatis Traiectensis', [*Supplementa tomorum I–XII, pars III*], ed. O. Holder-Egger, MGH Scriptores [folio], 15/1 (Stuttgart, 1887), 66–79 · W. Diekamp, *Die Vitae Sancti Liudgeri* (Münster, 1881) · W. Kohl, ed., *Das Bistum Münster, 4/1: Das Domstift St. Paulus zu Münster* (Berlin, 1987)

Le Camus de Limare (*b.* 1736). *See under* Industrial spies (*act. c.*1700–*c.*1800).

Le Capelain, John (1812–1848), landscape and marine painter in watercolour, was born on 5 October 1812, the son of a Jersey printer and lithographer, Samuel Le Capelain (1788–1850), and his English wife, Elizabeth Anne Pinckney (1782–1851). He may have been born in London, as he can probably be identified with the John Le Capelain who was baptized on 1 November 1812 at the church of St Pancras. He received his artistic training from his father and lived for most of his life in the attic of his parents' large house in St Helier, where he worked with his father on lithographs until the latter retired from printmaking in 1834. Le Capelain also painted, mainly in watercolour but occasionally in oil. His watercolour of Mont Orgueil was lithographed and published in *Moss's Views of the Channel Islands* in 1829. From about 1832 Le Capelain lived and worked for a short time in England, where he exhibited in London, between 1833 and 1842, once at the Society of British Artists and once at the New Watercolour Society. In 1838 he was in France, painting coastal scenes; he was sketching in Scotland in 1841 and 1843.

Le Capelain's soft, atmospheric watercolours have always been particularly admired in his native island, where much of his work remains in the museum. After Queen Victoria's visit to Jersey on 2 and 3 September 1846, the States of Jersey commissioned an album of watercolours from him, bound in red morocco. It consists of a frontispiece, six views illustrating the royal visit, and nineteen landscapes showing the beauties of the island and the effects of different times of day and varying weather conditions. These were lithographed by Louis Haghe and published by the local printer Philip Falle, as *The Queen's Visit to Jersey* (1847). Delighted with this present, the queen commissioned from Le Capelain a series of views of the Isle of Wight. These were begun, but, before he could complete them, and despite treatment in France, Le Capelain died of galloping consumption at his home, 1 Hill Street, St Helier, on 17 October 1848; he was unmarried. He was buried in the new burial-ground, Green Street cemetery, St Helier, on 21 October. The obituary of the artist in *The Athenaeum* (28 October 1848, 1081) described him as 'a rival of the first artists of England as a painter of watercolours' and considered that Jersey had 'lost one of her most highly endowed sons' (*The Athenaeum*). A retrospective exhibition was held on the island in December 1848. Local enthusiasts wished to erect a monument to Le Capelain and acquire enough of his works to establish a national gallery in Jersey but, at that time of economic depression, financial support was not forthcoming. Two oils and sixteen watercolours were later acquired and hung in St Helier town hall. DELIA MILLAR

Sources J. Voak, *John Le Capelain, 1812–1848* (1988) [exhibition catalogue, Jersey Museums Service] · D. Millar, *The Victorian watercolours and drawings in the collection of her majesty the queen*, 1 (1995), 537–9 · *The Athenaeum* (28 Oct 1848), 1081 · *IGI*

Likenesses J. Le Capelain, self-portrait, miniature, repro. in Voak, *John Le Capelain*

Le Cène, Charles (*c.*1647–1703), religious controversialist, was born at Caen, Normandy, France. He studied successively at the protestant *académies* of Sedan (1667–9), Geneva (1669–70), and Saumur (1670–72). Following ordination at Caen on 14 September 1672, he became minister at the Reformed church at Honfleur. There he married and had at least one son, Michel Charles. Ten years later he left Normandy and became a probationary minister at the main Huguenot church at Charenton, near Paris. Denounced for Pelagian heresy, his beliefs were examined closely by the local consistory. Although Le Cène was befriended by one of the leading Charenton ministers, fellow Norman Pierre (later Peter) Allix, his position in what was already a divided church remained unresolved. Suspicions that he was an Arminian were heightened with the publication in Amsterdam of his *De l'état de l'homme après le péché et de sa prédestination* (1684). Like the controversial pastor Claude Payon, Le Cène argued that a man could save himself by means of his natural faculties and a careful reading of scripture. He expanded on his views on conversion, free will, and original sin in *Entretiens sur diverses matières de théologie* (1685), which he wrote jointly with Jean le Clerc.

After the revocation of the edict of Nantes in August 1685 Le Cène went first to the Netherlands and then to England, probably arriving in 1686. For a short period he joined the French conformist church established that year by Allix at Jewin Street, London (later at St Martin Orgar), but perhaps because his now overt Arminianism rendered exercise of his ministry difficult, before 1691 he returned to the Netherlands. Further evidence of the studies on which he had been engaged emerged in *Conversations sur diverses matières de religion* (Amsterdam, 1687), in which he advocated tolerance and liberty of conscience, and revealed a detailed knowledge of the work of William Chillingworth and other English theological writers. There survive ten volumes of manuscripts, totalling nearly 6000 densely written folios, mostly in Le Cène's hand: only a very small proportion are certainly his own compositions; the rest are copies and translations from many sources. The purpose of this was evident in his *Projet d'une nouvelle version françoise de la Bible* (Rotterdam, 1696). With a slight error, unfortunate in its context, he dedicated the work in fulsome terms to 'Matthieu Bocland, Honorable Membre du Parlement d'Angleterre': this must have been Maurice Buckland of Standlynch, Wiltshire, longstanding whig MP for Downton, perhaps introduced to him by Allix, now dean of Salisbury. Confident of the approbation of all Christians, Le Cène proposed a new translation of the Bible to eradicate the great number of errors in existing versions, to supersede pointless controversy over doctrine, and to revive piety; scripture brought into the clear light of day and purged of obscure literalism would be all that was necessary to promote holy living, the principal component of true theology. To illustrate his point he discussed some alleged mistakes, especially in the Geneva version, and in the process aired his own Socinian views. Jacques Gousset, who had heard and disliked his preaching in London, mounted an attack in *Considérations théologiques et critiques* (Amsterdam, 1698).

Le Cène may already have returned to London. In 1697 he informed the city authorities that he intended to 'teach and preach to a dissenting congregation' (Gwynn, 522) at the Embroiderers' Hall in Gutter Lane, but he was almost certainly thwarted following determined opposition from the French churches. His cause cannot have been helped by the publication by Hugh Ross of *An Essay for a New Translation of the Bible* (1701), in which Ross ironically, or perhaps appropriately, confessed that he had 'made bold with the Original' (sig. A2*v*); he also perpetrated further errors. Before Le Cène could bring the project to conclusion, he died in London in May 1703. His proposals were reissued in 1727 by his son Michel Charles, an Amsterdam bookseller who had also spent some time in England. Fourteen years later he issued a complete text, *La sainte Bible, nouvelle version françoise*, appending a life of his father, but it was not popular. Its use of bizarre forms of words and its replacement of 'tu' by 'vous' were disliked. In 1742 it was condemned by a synod of the Walloon church meeting at La Brille. VIVIENNE LARMINIE

Sources E. Haag and E. Haag, *La France protestante*, 10 vols. (Paris, 1846–59), vol. 6, pp. 457–60 · D. C. A. Agnew, *Protestant exiles from France, chiefly in the reign of Louis XIV, or, The Huguenot refugees and their descendants in Great Britain and Ireland*, 3rd edn, 2 (1886), 274 · E. G. Léonard, *A history of protestantism*, 2: *The Establishment*, ed. H. H. Rowley (1967), 393–4 · R. D. Gwynn, 'The distribution of Huguenot refugees in England, II: London and its environs', *Proceedings of the Huguenot Society*, 22 (1970–76), 509–68, esp. 522 · I. E. Gray, *Huguenot manuscripts: a descriptive account*, Huguenot Society quarto series, 54 (1983), 172–3 · *DNB* · J. P. Ferris, 'Bockland, Maurice', HoP, *Commons, 1660–90*

Archives French Hospital, La Providence, Rochester, Kent, MSS

Likenesses F. M. La Cave, line engraving, NPG

Leche, Cecilia la (*fl. c.*1350). *See under* Women medical practitioners in England (*act. c.*1200–*c.*1475).

Leche, Matilda la (*fl.* 1232). *See under* Women medical practitioners in England (*act. c.*1200–*c.*1475).

Le Chene, Marie-Thérèse (*b. c.*1887). *See under* Women agents on active service in France (*act.* 1942–1945).

Lechford, Thomas (*d.* in or after 1642), author and lawyer, was possibly a descendant of Henry Lechford (*d.* 1567) of Surrey, although his parents and place of birth are unknown. He was trained in law and was a member of Clement's Inn (one of the inns of chancery) but evidently was not admitted to the bar. The Massachusetts general court referred to him as 'an ordinary solicitor in England' (Massachusetts Colony Records, 2.206). His wife, Elizabeth, is briefly mentioned in his notebook, but there is no known record of their marriage, her family origins, or any child. Presumably they were married in England and she accompanied him on the voyage to Massachusetts.

Prior to his emigration Lechford attended the lectures of Hugh Peters at St Sepulchre, London, until 1629, when Peters was silenced by Archbishop Laud and fled to Rotterdam. Lechford spent some time in Ireland with Sir Thomas Wentworth. In the spring of 1637 he was a solicitor for the barrister William Prynne, who was convicted of libel when he publicly opposed Laud's church reforms and was sentenced to a brutal punishment in June. Lechford later wrote that he also 'suffered imprisonement, and a kind of banishment' for his role in Prynne's defence (*Plain Dealing*, xv–vi, 3). Both the Providence Island investors and the prince of Transylvania offered him 'a place of preferment', but he chose instead to emigrate to New England, where he landed on 27 June 1638 (Lechford, 'Notebook', 48).

Lechford's arrival in Boston came at the conclusion of the antinomian controversy surrounding Anne Hutchinson and her covenant of grace followers, and he soon found himself under scrutiny for opinions he expressed in a manuscript entitled 'Of prophecy' and several other writings. Indeed, Lechford had modified his earlier views and now argued in favour of episcopacy and apostolic succession, which entailed the establishment of bishoprics. Moreover, he questioned the prevailing New England belief that the Antichrist had already appeared on earth. In the rather naive hope that an open discussion would resolve his differences with the New England establishment he requested that Hugh Peters and several other ministers of his own choosing be appointed to an examining committee, 'who should soundly and maturely advise and consult of the matter' (Lechford, 'Notebook', 50). Presumably they did, but Lechford's opinions were none the less judged to be erroneous. He was consequently barred from membership in the church and from admission as a freeman of the colony.

On 8 June 1639 Lechford submitted a list of proposals to the general court for regulating judicial practice, which included the hiring of a public notary to record court actions and proceedings, a court secretary to write verdicts and writs, and the establishment of a fee structure in conformity with the inferior court of record in England. Lechford doubtless hoped that he would be appointed as notary or secretary in the general court of Massachusetts, but his dissenting religious opinions weighed against him. Alternatively, he relied upon occasional jobs as scrivener, conveyancer, and copyist. In 1639 he penned numerous copies of *The Abstract of the Lawes of New England*, as well as Robert Keayne's *Answeare before the Elders*. Writing to a friend in 1640, he complained of being 'kept from the Sacrament, and all places of preferment in the Commonwealth, and forced to get my living by writing petty things, which scarce finds me bread' (Lechford, 'Notebook', 287–8).

In summer 1639 Lechford was a lawyer for William and Elizabeth Cole in a property suit against Francis Doughty, but was disciplined by the court in September 'for going to the Jewry & pleading wth them out of Court' (Massachusetts Colony Records, 1.270). The following month he petitioned the court, acknowledging his 'delinquency inasmuch as he knew it was not to be done by the law of England' (Lechford, 'Notebook', 182–3).

Lechford's experience in New England had sharpened his criticism of the congregational way. In a 1640 letter copied into his notebook he declared that 'Christians cannot live happily without Bishops … nor Englishmen without a King' (Lechford, 'Notebook', 274). Thus, in October 1640 he was again admonished by the court 'not to meddle with controversies' (Massachusetts Colony Records, 1.273) in regard to religious 'tenets and disputations' (Lechford, 'Notebook', 440–1). Lechford meanwhile involved himself in the famous 'sow case' (1636–43), in which Richard Sherman and his wife brought suit against the wealthy merchant Robert Keayne for allegedly slaughtering the Shermans' pig. Initially siding with the Shermans and their advocate George Story, Lechford was persuaded of Keayne's innocence by the summer of 1641, and evidently advised the Shermans to withdraw their suit, which antagonized them and their supporters against him.

Lechford, who for the past year had been 'plucking up stakes' to return to England, sailed on 3 August 1641 on the same ship with Hugh Peters. Money for his passage may have been sent him by William Prynne (Lechford, 'Notebook', 275). Once again in London, he returned to Clement's Inn and the Church of England. In 1642 he published *Plaine Dealing, or, Newes from New England*. This was his public apology for his earlier dissent from the Church of England: 'I desire to purge myself of so great a scandall', he notes in the preface (p. 3). Indeed, it was his New England experience that compelled him to write this account of the congregational way, as fair warning against the rising tide of sectarian dissent in his native England. Lechford's legal training tempered his style, and he allowed descriptive detail to weigh as evidence for his case, relegating personal comments to the preface and marginal footnotes. Nevertheless, *Plaine Dealing* falls within the genre of heresiography, and his main purpose was to reveal the 'Anarchie and confusion' of Independency: 'for if all are Rulers, who shall be Ruled?' (pp. 5–6). Lechford had become convinced that an episcopal establishment, authorized by scripture, supported a coherent domestic and imperial rule; and, by way of example, he noted the inefficiency of the congregational churches in administering the conversion of indigenous peoples: 'all churches among them are equall, and so betweene many, nothing is done that way' (pp. 54–5). He died soon after the publication of his tract, but the details of his death are unknown. BARBARA RITTER DAILEY

Sources T. Lechford, 'Notebook kept by Thomas Lechford, esq., lawyer, in Boston, Massachusetts Bay, from June 27, 1638 to July 29, 1641', *Transactions and Collections of the American Antiquarian Society*, 7 (1885) • T. Lechford, *Plain dealing, or, Newes from New England*, ed. J. H. Trumbell (1867); repr. (1970) • *The Winthrop papers*, ed. W. C. Ford and others, 4 (1944), 85–7, 162 • 'Note to Lechford's *Plaine dealing*', *Collections of the Massachusetts Historical Society*, 3rd ser., 3 (1833), 397–405 • J. Winthrop, *The history of New England from 1630 to 1649*, ed. J. Savage, 2 vols. (1825–6); repr. (1972), vol. 1, pp. 45, 287, 289; vol. 2, pp. 6, 27, 36 • K. Kupperman, *Providence Island, 1630–1641* (1993), 255–6, 323 • N. B. Shurtleff, ed., *Records of the governor and company of the Massachusetts Bay in New England*, 5 vols. in 6 (1853–4), vol. 1, p. 270, 273, 310; vol. 2, p. 206 • P. F. Gura, *A glimpse of Sion's glory: puritan radicalism in New England, 1620–1660* (1984), 130–32
Archives American Antiquarian Society, Worcester, Massachusetts, MSS notebook

Lechmere [*alias* Stratford], **Edmund** (*c*.**1586–1640**), Roman Catholic priest, was the eldest son of Thomas Lechmere (*d*. 1605) and Anne Lechmere, of Fownhope, Herefordshire. He was educated at Brasenose College, Oxford, graduating BA in 1603. He became a Roman Catholic and crossed to the English College, Douai, obtaining degrees at the university there. In 1617 Matthew Kellison established all classes within the English College itself and Lechmere was appointed teacher of philosophy. Subsequently he studied at the Sorbonne in Paris under Gamache, and graduated BD there before returning to Douai, where he became vice-president to Kellison, and was ordained priest on 18 December 1622. He wrote a number of works of which *A Disputation of the Church wherein the Old Religion is Maintained* was published at Douai in 1629 and went through a number of editions. He also published *The Conference Mentioned by Doctour Featley … with some Notes* (1632) and *A Reflection of Certain Authors that are Pretended to Disown the Church's Infallibility* (1635). He was created DD at Rheims on 25 October 1633 and died at the English College, Douai, 'in the prime of his years', in September 1640.

THOMPSON COOPER, *rev.* G. BRADLEY

Sources G. Anstruther, *The seminary priests*, 2 (1975), 187 • E. H. Burton and T. L. Williams, eds., *The Douay College diaries, third, fourth and fifth, 1598–1654*, 1, Catholic RS, 10 (1911) • A. F. Allison and D. M. Rogers, eds., *A catalogue of Catholic books in English printed abroad or secretly in England, 1558–1640*, 1 (1956), 81 • Foster, *Alum. Oxon.* • P. Guilday, *The English Catholic refugees on the continent, 1558–1795* (1914)

Lechmere, Sir Nicholas (*bap*. **1613**, *d*. **1701**), judge and politician, was baptized in Hanley Castle, Worcestershire, on 4 October 1613, the eldest surviving son of Edmund Lechmere (1577–1650) and Margaret (*d*. 1635), daughter of Sir Nicholas Overbury of Bourton on the Hill, Gloucestershire. After an education at Gloucester School, Wadham College, Oxford (1631–4), and the Middle Temple he took up a career in the law, and was called to the bar on 4 June 1641. He married Penelope (*d*. 1690), daughter of Sir Edwin Sandys of Northbourne, Kent, on 12 November 1642; they had two sons. On the outbreak of civil war he was among those who formed an association of west midlands counties to support the army of Robert Devereux, earl of Essex. It is likely that after Worcestershire had fallen to the royalists Lechmere retreated to London, to his inn of court, but in September 1644 he was named to the embryonic Worcestershire county committee. As the county still lay under control of the king's supporters, Lechmere and his colleagues operated from Warwick Castle until April 1645, when the committee was able to set up at Evesham, newly fallen into parliamentarian hands. Lechmere was an energetic committee treasurer, introducing a very effective machinery of penal taxation against royalists. By March 1646 he was working as an agent of the committee for both kingdoms, and began to spend more time in London than in Worcestershire. When the royalist garrison at Worcester surrendered to parliament in July 1646 the county committee moved to the city, but Lechmere resigned as treasurer, and spent much time travelling between London and the county as the principal bearer of parliamentary instruction and opinion.

Lechmere's associates in London included political presbyterians and even crypto-royalists, and, at a time when provincial discontent against committees and the army ran high, these connections enabled him to secure the parliamentary seat of Bewdley without a contest on 4 July 1648. When the political tide turned against the conservatives later that year Lechmere deftly avoided becoming a victim of Pride's Purge, and instead became one of the first MPs to conform publicly to the republican government in February 1649. He was named to twenty committees of the Rump Parliament between January and June 1649, and remained busy as a committeeman in the house down to June 1651. Among the important executive committees to which he was appointed were the committee for the navy and customs, the committee for the army, and the committee for plundered ministers. In Worcestershire his standing was enhanced by his appointment as a JP and a commissioner for oyer and terminer. In this last capacity he rode the Oxford circuit for the first time in February 1649. His interests in the house were legal—he was a conservative lawyer, not a radical reforming one—and he specialized in introducing legislation to sell confiscated lands to replenish the empty coffers of the government. Religion was another area of legislative activity in which he was active—again, not as a radical reformer, but as a contributor to cautious expedients for maintaining a state-supported national ministry. His own religious outlook, documented in his surviving sermon notes, can best be described as orthodox puritan. Lechmere was present at the battle of Worcester on 3 September 1651, on the eve of which his house, Severn End, was occupied by Charles Stuart and Lechmere's former friend, now bitter enemy, Edward Massey.

After the expulsion of the Rump by Oliver Cromwell in April 1653, Lechmere found no place in the nominated assembly because his conservative approach to public affairs was seen as a check to the aspirations of godly radicals. When he was returned for Worcestershire to the first protectorate parliament in September 1654, his activities there were more focused on purely technical, legal matters, and he supported the 'Instrument of government' which governed the regime. In June 1655 he became attorney-general of the duchy of Lancaster, a profitable government office. On 15 July 1655 he was granted a licence to practise at the bar of all the Westminster courts, which gave him the privileges of the former order of king's counsel. He was a reliable organizer of the militia in Worcestershire against royalist-inspired insurgency in that year. In the second protectorate parliament Lechmere sat on a wide range of committees on economic issues, as well as on the technically legal committees pertinent to his high office. He helped solve problems of continuity in the legal system thrown up by 'The humble petition and advice', which he considered a 'Magna Charta' (*Diary of Thomas Burton*, 2.138), and took a hawkish line against the Quaker James Nayler and other notorious antinomians. Lechmere was a friend of Secretary John Thurloe, and walked in the funeral procession of Lord Protector Cromwell. He was foremost among those in Worcestershire loyal to Richard Cromwell, and with Thomas Foley spent £614 on ensuring that he was returned to the last Cromwellian parliament in 1659. He opposed the destructive tactics of the republicans in this assembly, but in March presaged his own shift of loyalty by praising the achievements of the Rump and declaring 'The humble petition and advice' to be a restoration of liberties encroached upon by Oliver Cromwell.

With the collapse of the protectorate Lechmere lost his legal office, but resumed his parliamentary career as a draftsman and committeeman. He broke his shoulder on a journey to the Monmouth assizes in August 1659, but was in Westminster in December to witness the last few months of the Rump. He stuck to his high opinion of this parliament; when Charles II was restored, however, he was able to draw on the help of a lawyer friend to obtain a pardon at the behest of Viscount Mordaunt. Lechmere escaped penalties at the Restoration beyond the loss of his local, central, and legal offices. Thereafter he kept busy in London as a senior member of the Middle Temple. He kept most of the land he had bought during the propitious times of the 1650s and rebuilt Severn End as a splendid mansion. He was whig and anti-Catholic in outlook, and suspected, as did many, that the great fire of 1666 was a popish outrage. At the revolution of 1688 his whig credentials and legal eminence recommended him to the government of William III, and 1689 was his belated *annus mirabilis*. He became in that year serjeant-at-law, second baron of the exchequer, and a knight, as well as deputy lieutenant of Worcestershire. In the 'bankers' case' of January 1692 his judgment was for the crown. He resigned from his judgeship on 29 June 1700, pleading extreme old age: he was by then eighty-seven. Lechmere died on 30 April 1701 at Hanley Castle, and was buried there on 2 May without a coffin. STEPHEN K. ROBERTS

Sources S. K. Roberts, 'Lechmere, Nicholas', HoP, *Commons, 1690–1715* [draft] • E. P. Shirley, *Hanley and the house of Lechmere* (1883) • *JHC*, 7–8 (1651–67) • *Diary of Thomas Burton*, ed. J. T. Rutt, 4 vols. (1828) • Lechmere's MS account of his life, priv. coll. [Church End, Hanley Castle, in the ownership of Sir Berwick Lechmere] • C. H. Hopwood, ed., *Middle Temple records*, 4 vols. (1904–5) • T. Nash, *Collections for the history of Worcestershire*, 2 vols. (1781–2); 2nd edn (1799) • *Diary of Henry Townshend of Elmley Lovett*, ed. J. W. Willis Bund, 4 pts in 2 vols., Worcestershire Historical Society (1915–20) • Foster, *Alum. Oxon.* • BL, Add. MS 39940–39942 • parish register, Hanley Castle, Worcestershire, 4 Oct 1613 [baptism] • parish register, Hanley Castle, Worcestershire, 2 May 1701 [burial] • PRO, PROB 11/460, fol. 297

Archives BL, sermon notes, MSS 39940–39942 • NRA, priv. coll., journal [copy] • Worcs. RO, legal papers

Likenesses V. Green, mezzotint, BM, NPG; repro. in Nash, *Collections* • portrait, repro. in Nash, *Collections*, 2 vols.; priv. coll.
Wealth at death very extensive landed interests: will, PRO, PROB 11/460, fol. 297

Lechmere, Nicholas, Baron Lechmere (1675–1727), politician and lawyer, was born at Hanley Castle, Worcestershire, on 5 August 1675, the second son of Edmund Lechmere (*bap.* 1614, *d.* 1703), barrister, of Hanley Castle, and his wife, Lucy, the daughter of Anthony Hungerford of Farleigh Castle, Somerset. He was admitted to the Middle Temple in 1693, was called to the bar in 1698, and over the next few years established himself successfully as a barrister. As counsel in several politically sensitive court cases he achieved early notoriety for his immoderate brand of whiggery and was taken under the wing of the leading junto whig, Lord Wharton, who helped to bring him into parliament for Appleby, Westmorland, in 1708. In the Commons he made an immediate impact as an able speaker, and in December 1709 was appointed to assist in the preparation of the articles of impeachment against the high-church tory divine Henry Sacheverell; he later took a leading part in the trial itself. At several key points during these proceedings, in February–March 1710, Lechmere powerfully argued the whig case against Sacheverell's preaching of 'absolute non-resistance', employing the radical Lockeian concept of an 'original contract' between government and subjects to demonstrate that the rationale behind Sacheverell's controversial sermons was a return to Roman Catholicism and the restoration of the exiled Stuarts to the crown after the queen's demise. Through Wharton's agency he transferred to the Cumberland borough of Cockermouth in the election later that year, and during the last four years of Queen Anne's reign he acted as one of the principal whig opponents of the tory ministry in the lower house. Hardly surprisingly, he was stripped of his status of QC in 1711, having taken silk in 1708. He persistently opposed the ministry's peace policy and warned against the dangers of an early sell-out to France and the possible consequences for the protestant succession. His aggressive and sometimes singular defence of dissenters' rights prompted one tory periodical to remark caustically that any new whig ministry could be expected to bring in a bill drafted by Lechmere 'for qualifying atheists, deists and socinians to serve their country in any employment' (Ellis, 195). As counsel in several government prosecutions against antiministerial propagandists, he deplored the practice 'of committing people without telling them of their crimes', which he likened to the Spanish inquisition. He was a willing accomplice in the composition of Richard Steele's explosive attack on the Oxford ministry, *The Crisis*, published in January 1714.

Stubborn, haughty, and opinionated, Lechmere was accomplished in confrontational politics, but to his whig colleagues he invariably seemed overbearing and awkward—characteristics which evidently stymied an otherwise promising career in the whig ministry after the accession of George I. Although he received immediate appointment as solicitor-general, his differences with Lord Chancellor Cowper forced his resignation in December 1715, and he soon afterwards broke with the government altogether over its draconian measures against the Jacobite rebels. Having aligned himself with Sunderland when the whig party split in 1717, he quickly emerged as Sunderland's chief spokesman in the Commons, and engaged in frequent clashes with Robert Walpole, the leader of the opposing whig faction. In June he was appointed chancellor of the duchy of Lancaster for life, and exchanged his parliamentary seat from Cockermouth to Tewkesbury, controlled by his elder brother. Appointment as attorney-general and as a privy councillor followed in 1718. In the following year he married Lady Elizabeth Howard (*d.* 1739), the daughter of Charles *Howard, third earl of Carlisle; the couple had no children. Soon after the whig reunion in April 1720 Lechmere was dismissed from his offices, having only just survived an investigation for alleged corruption. His subsequent attacks on Walpole over his handling of the South Sea crisis precluded him from the ministerial appointments of April 1721, although a barony was given him in September. He avoided open opposition to Walpole in the Lords until 1725, when he was disappointed in his hope of succeeding Macclesfield to the lord chancellorship. He died of 'apoplexy' at Campden House, Kensington, his London residence, on 18 June 1727, and was buried at Hanley Castle.

A. A. Hanham

Sources R. R. Sedgwick, 'Lechmere, Nicholas', HoP, *Commons* • *DNB* • *IGI* • F. H. Ellis, *Swift vs Mainwaring: The Examiner and The Medley* (1985)

Lecky, (William) Edward Hartpole (1838–1903), historian, was born on 26 March 1838 in Newtownpark, co. Dublin. He was the only son of John Hartpole Lecky (*d.* 1852) and his first wife, Mary Anne Tallents (*d.* 1839), who he married in 1837. The Leckys were of Scottish origin and settled in the north of Ireland in the early seventeenth century. Lecky's paternal grandfather married Maria Hartpole of Shrule Castle, near Carlow. Lecky's father was called to the bar, but did not practise. He lived comfortably off the revenues of his properties in Carlow and Queen's county. Lecky's mother was the daughter of W. E. Tallents of Newark, Nottinghamshire, who was the legal agent of the duke of Newcastle. After her early death at the age of twenty-two, Lecky's father married Isabella, daughter of Lieutenant-Colonel Eardley Wilmot of Queen's county, in 1841. A son and a daughter were the issue of this marriage. The second Mrs Lecky treated her stepson well; he was fourteen before he was told that Isabella was not his natural mother, but this did not lead to any change in relations between them. They remained good friends until her death in 1902.

Education From 1847 to 1852 the Leckys travelled widely through the British Isles. During this time Lecky began his schooling, first in Sussex, then at Kingstown, near Dublin, and later at the Royal School, Armagh. In September 1852 he went to Cheltenham College. His time at Cheltenham, which he never enjoyed, started badly. His father died, at the age of forty-six, within weeks of his arrival there.

(William) Edward Hartpole Lecky (1838–1903), by Julia Margaret Cameron, *c.*1868

Being unsporting and shy, he found himself often alone and any spare time he had he devoted to his hobbies of geology and poetry.

Lecky left Cheltenham in 1855 and prepared with a private tutor for the Dublin University matriculation. In the same year his stepmother married Thomas Henry Dalzell, eleventh earl of Carnwath (1797–1867), whose first wife had been the daughter of Henry Grattan. The family moved to Enniskerry, co. Wicklow.

Having obtained tenth place among forty candidates, Lecky entered Trinity College, Dublin, as a fellow commoner in February 1856. At Trinity he became more sociable and began to read widely. His chief companions were David Plunket, Edward Gibson (later lord chancellor of Ireland), and Gerald Fitzgibbon (later solicitor-general for Ireland and lord justice of appeal in Ireland). With these friends he attended 'the Hist', the Trinity College Historical Society, which had been founded by Edmund Burke, who was already one of Lecky's intellectual heroes. (Forty years later, when the centenary of Burke's death was commemorated at Trinity, Lecky proposed a toast to the memory of 'the greatest of all modern political philosophers'.)

Lecky took great pains with his speeches for 'the Hist'. He won its gold medal for oratory in 1859 and was on its committee in 1859–60. He engaged enthusiastically in the romantic rhetoric that was a staple of the society at this time, as it debated the great questions of the day: the nature of Irish and Italian nationality. In his commonplace book for 1859 he noted: 'The great evils of Ireland are mendicity and mendacity … The great desideratum in Ireland is a lay public opinion' (Lecky MSS, R.7.30). Such notes fed his speeches in 'the Hist', and those speeches formed the basis of his first published works on Irish and intellectual history.

Lecky selectively traced his early intellectual progress in an essay on 'Formative influences' in 1890. He acknowledged the particular importance of the writings of Richard Whately, archbishop of Dublin, and of Joseph Butler's *Analogy of Religion* (1736). To Whately and Butler, among others, he traced his inclination towards Christian rationalism. However, a college friend was to suggest that, at Trinity, Lecky read Shelley more than Whately and cared for the speeches of the Irish patriots Grattan and Curran above the sermons of Bishop Butler. Long before 1890, however, he was distancing himself from the romantic nationalism with which he had flirted in his youth.

Lecky graduated from Trinity College in 1859, content to take a pass degree. He then spent another year at Trinity and took a second-class divinity testimonium, before putting thoughts of a career in the church behind him.

Early writings There was some expectation that Lecky would become a Church of Ireland clergyman and take up a family living in Cork, but he wanted to be a man of letters. His first publications were *Friendship and other Poems* (1859), which he published under the pseudonym Hibernicus, and an essay on *The Religious Tendencies of the Age*, published anonymously in 1860. The poems were derivative, patriotic verses which owed more to the influence of Sir Walter Scott than to a love and understanding of Ireland, and they fell stillborn from the press (some reappeared in *Poems*, 1891). The essay was no more successful (it sold sixty-eight copies), but it was notable for its religious tolerance. In *Religious Tendencies* Lecky gave a sympathetic analysis of the various approaches to Christian worship adopted by the major churches in Britain. His capacity for putting forward the strongest arguments for each side in a debate was a quality for which he was to be praised throughout his career.

Lecky's first work of Irish history, *The Leaders of Public Opinion in Ireland* (1861), was no more successful than his poems or his theological essay. It sold thirty-four copies in 1861, but Lecky was to revise and republish it twice, and it became an important text in debates on the Irish question later in the century. The book traced the development of the idea of 'nationality with loyalty' in Ireland through essays on the political careers of Jonathan Swift, Henry Flood, Henry Grattan, and Daniel O'Connell. It also included a chapter on 'Clerical influences' (omitted in the revised editions), which argued that moral and political progress would only be possible in Ireland when the priest's influence in Irish politics had been curbed.

The book's patriotic purpose was to encourage a new secular national feeling, which would act as a check to sectarianism, and, earning the Irish the respect of England, lead to 'the coalescing of the sentiments of the two nations'. In 1861 Lecky retained some grandiose political ambitions of his own, dreaming of becoming a second Grattan. The 1871 edition of the work remained committed to the idea of the emergence of a new rational Irish patriotism, but was less confident about its imminent arrival. The changes Lecky made to the 1903 edition reflected the growth of his unionism and pessimism. He had refused to countenance Longman's publishing a cheap issue of *The Leaders* in 1886, fearing that it would be put to propagandist use by the Parnellites during the first home-rule crisis.

The intellectual histories Lecky travelled widely on the continent in the early 1860s. In the great libraries of Europe he read deeply into the history of the early middle ages and the development of the early church. His studies and his discovery of H. T. Buckle's *History of Civilization* (1857 and 1861), which he read and reread at this period, inspired him to continue with his literary career in spite of his initial disappointments. Buckle gave Lecky a sense of the grandeur of history and encouraged him to become a historian of ideas.

In 1863 Lecky proceeded MA at Dublin University and wrote an essay on 'The declining sense of the miraculous', which became the opening two chapters of his first successful book, *The History of the Rise and Influence of the Spirit of Rationalism in Europe* (1865). This philosophical history examined, with many diverting asides (a characteristic failing in Lecky), the decay of superstition in the face of reason. Rational Christianity, Lecky claimed, had ensured 'the moral development' of Europe: he argued that the Reformation let loose 'the germ of Rationalism' and he examined the progress of the idea up to 'the secularization of politics' after the French Revolution. Lecky was a liberal optimist in the 1860s. He wrote of a coming union of nations as 'the last and highest expression of the Christian ideal of the brotherhood of man'. The rights of nationalities, in the wake of Risorgimento fever, were described as the basis of political morality and he thought that the diffusion of the laws of political economy (already more subtle in Ireland than he knew) would eliminate war. He saw the dawning of a world of liberty, industry, and peace.

Rationalism, which was published fifteen times in Lecky's lifetime, raised him into the first rank of his literary contemporaries. It was an important contribution to history writing, which moved away from the great man theory to look at historical change as a result of impersonal and economic causes. There were some, however, who could not accept Lecky's complacency about the inevitable betterment of human character and society. George Eliot dismissed Lecky as a popularizer of the ideas of others and as an author who wrote for 'the general reader', who found in him an excuse for the 'utmost liberty of private haziness' (*Fortnightly Review*, 1, 1865, 43–55).

Lecky settled in London in October 1866 with chambers at 6 Albemarle Street and was elected to the Athenaeum in 1867. His next major work was his *History of European Morals from Augustus to Charlemagne* (1869), which expanded upon (and occasionally repeated) certain themes introduced in *Rationalism*. Indeed, it was a sort of prequel to *Rationalism*, examining the foundation of various moral codes and changes in standards of morality from the period of the later pagan empire to the re-establishment of the empire in the west. The book was criticized by the utilitarians, notably John Morley and James Fitzjames Stephen, for its attempt to unite a providential view of the progress of human affairs with a rational sensibility (*Fortnightly Review*, 5, May 1869, 29; J. F. Stephen, *Liberty, Equality, Fraternity*, 1873).

The message of *European Morals* was comforting for the mid-Victorians on at least two counts. Lecky implied that there could be a reconciliation of science and religion and counselled that old opinions did not need to be opposed but were made obsolete by the natural progress of civilization, perishing 'by indifference not by controversy'. Lecky thereby assured the mid-Victorians that there was no need for a loss of faith, in science or religion, nor for political revolution.

Marriage and *The History of England* On 14 June 1871 at the British embassy at The Hague, Lecky married Catharina Elisabeth Boldewina van Dedem, the eldest daughter of General Baron van Dedem (*d.* 1912) and his first wife, Baroness Sloet van Hagensdorp. Elisabeth was a lady-in-waiting to Queen Sophia of the Netherlands. With the queen's permission the wedding reception was held at the Dutch court. After a lengthy honeymoon in Europe, during which he corrected the proofs of the second edition of *The Leaders of Public Opinion in Ireland*, Lecky and his wife settled at 38 Onslow Gardens, London. Here they entertained many distinguished friends, including Carlyle, Leslie Stephen, Browning, Tennyson, Lord Derby, and Herbert Spencer. There was often an element of hero-worship and deference in Lecky's relations with such people. In 1873 Lecky was elected a member of the Literary Society and in 1874 of The Club, which had been founded by Dr Johnson.

From 1872 Lecky began collecting materials for his *History of England in the Eighteenth Century* (8 vols., 1878–90). This led him to do more archival work than was usual at this period, notably in Dublin, where he made those discoveries which gave the Irish portion of the history its particular and lasting value. Lecky determined that his *History of England* would relate not only the important political events of the life of the nation, but also introduce the reader to the moral, social, economic, and intellectual factors that shaped the country's progress. This, in part, he did, as well as illuminating numerous aspects of foreign and colonial policy.

Another purpose of the historical enterprise, however, was to refute the calumnies of J. A. Froude against the Irish. Lecky believed he had been set a personal challenge by Froude, who, in *The English in Ireland in the Eighteenth-Century* (1872–4), had written of the Irish as irredeemably degenerate. Froude's work, Lecky believed, could only open old wounds and further arouse sectarian passions in Ireland. In countering him, Lecky hoped to do 'some real service to history to the cause of truth and to the reputation of Ireland' (*Victorian Historian*, 122). To this end, he wrote a history of Ireland within his history of England. Irish matters took up over 40 per cent of the space in the first edition of *The History of England*, and a five-volume *History of Ireland in the Eighteenth Century* appeared separately within a twelve-volume cabinet edition of the work in 1892.

The History of England occupied Lecky for almost two decades. Volumes three and four, taking the story up to 1782, came out in 1882 and Lecky particularly impressed American critics by his impartiality in writing about the American War of Independence. In volumes five and six, which appeared in 1887 and which dealt with the development of French revolutionary ideas and their impact in Britain down to 1793, Lecky was able to show his appreciation of and debt to Edmund Burke. The last two volumes were published in 1890 and were almost entirely devoted to Irish politics from the emergence of the United Irishmen in the early 1790s to the signing of the Act of Union in 1801.

The History of England showed Lecky's prowess in narrative history, but it was read increasingly in the 1880s and afterwards as a manual for Irish politics. Gladstone was one of a number of late Victorian politicians who confessed to reading Lecky to enhance their understanding of the Irish question. Yet the situation was complicated by the fact that there seemed to be a tension between Lecky's history and his own politics. Lecky was seen as the defender of Irish nationality in his history and as a defender of the Anglo-Irish union in his politics. It was a commonplace to suggest that Lecky was the best man on both sides in the Irish question, and his various Irish writings have been appealed to by every side in the Irish conflict ever since.

Politics Lecky always saw himself as a Liberal, but he was wary of the party political manoeuvres of both Disraeli and Gladstone. The former he distrusted for what he regarded as 'an act of political dishonesty' which had no precedent in modern times: the overthrowing of the 1832 constitution by the passage of the 1867 Reform Act. The question of parliamentary reform, Lecky feared, was one upon which the Conservatives acted from 'a simple desire of place' (Lecky, *Memoir*, 52). Lecky was equally disgusted by what he believed to be Gladstone's attempt to buy the middle-class vote in the general election of 1874, with a promise of the abolition of income tax: the historian and the politician participated in a bad-tempered exchange over this issue in the *Nineteenth Century* in 1887. Two years later, in an introduction to a new edition of his *Democracy and Liberty*, Lecky offered one of the most critical contemporary assessments of Gladstone's work and character. He saw Gladstone as an honest man with a dishonest mind who, by skilful casuistry, could persuade himself that he was in the right, and then, his moral nature taking fire, act as if under a divine impulse.

Lecky had supported the disestablishment of the Church of Ireland in 1869 and, with reservations, the Irish Land Act of 1870, but he disapproved of almost all later concessions to the Irish nationalists and, upon Gladstone's adoption of home rule in 1886, he became a Liberal Unionist. Lecky wrote influentially against home rule in a number of letters to *The Times* in 1886 and in other journals (notably the *Nineteenth Century* in April 1886). A number of his letters were subsequently published as pamphlets by the Irish Loyal and Patriotic Union and the Irish Unionist Convention between 1886 and 1892. The main thrust of his argument in all these articles concentrated on his belief that an Irish democracy, motivated by a hatred of England, would never prove capable of governing Ireland as well as it could be governed from Westminster.

In October 1895 Lecky accepted an invitation to stand for parliament for Dublin University. He was proud to accept a seat that he saw as representing the property and intelligence of the Irish nation. He was elected by a majority of 746 in an unusually large poll of 2768 in a by-election in December 1895 (and he was unopposed in the general election of 1900). His first speech in the House of Commons in February 1896 was made on behalf of Irish prisoners condemned under the Treason Felony Act thirteen years earlier.

The debates in which Lecky engaged most prominently, in the relatively quiet years in which he was in parliament, were those on university education for Catholics in Ireland and the Irish land issue. On the university question, which had exercised parliament for many years, and which returned to its agenda in 1897, practical considerations forced Lecky to go against long-held principles. He had always been an advocate of non-denominational education and hoped that the tertiary education of Irish Catholics could be accommodated within Trinity College, Dublin. However, as Catholics were discouraged from attending Trinity by a church hierarchy that still perceived the college as a bastion of protestantism, Lecky supported a scheme for a Catholic university in Ireland. A denominational education was not likely to promote the highest intellectual standards, he believed, but it was better than no education at all.

On the land question, Lecky regarded himself as a representative of the besieged Irish landlords in parliament. Gladstone's Irish Land Act of 1881 and all his subsequent land legislation Lecky perceived as an invasion of the rights of property, motivated by a short-sighted and iniquitous desire to appease the Parnellites, the Fenians, and the Land League. He no longer differentiated between constitutional and violent Irish nationalism and saw all these forces as communistic in orientation. Indeed, the only Irish movement operating after 1886 about which Lecky was not dubious was Sir Horace Plunkett's co-operative movement. He called Plunkett 'the only constructive statesman in Ireland'. Returning the compliment, Plunkett dedicated *Ireland in the New Century* (1904) to the memory of Lecky, whom he described as his best guide in Irish public life.

The other political issue with which Lecky's name was widely associated in the 1890s was the old-age pensions question. As he explained in the press and in parliament, he remained, on this matter, an old-fashioned *laissez-faire* Liberal who believed that pensions would impair the industry of the working classes and encourage state socialism. He was the author of the minority report of the third royal commission on pensions in 1899.

Later works In 1896 Lecky published *Democracy and Liberty*, a long discursive treatise on contemporary politics in which the central question—the effect of democracy upon social and individual freedom—was obscured by many diversions. However, for all its faults in construction and some platitudinous sections, *Democracy and Liberty* did usefully explore such issues as the tyranny of the majority and the possibility of the democratic despot, and it included interesting reflections on proportional representation and referendums as means by which to limit the dangers of democracy. It also encompassed an early acknowledgement of the potential incompatibility of democracy and capitalism, pointing up the irony that the middle-class liberals, in rejecting economic democracy, thereby rejected the means to make political democracy significant. However, underpinning every chapter of *Democracy and Liberty* was Lecky's Burkean sense that the duty of parliament was primarily to represent the interests of property. This gave the book something of the quality of an elegy on the British constitution of 1832 to 1867, which Lecky described as the best the world had seen. This in turn revealed that Lecky, originally a prophet of progress, was, by the 1890s, crying out for the world to stand still.

In 1892, upon the death of E. A. Freeman, Lecky had declined the regius professorship of modern history at Oxford. He did not believe he had any great aptitude for lecturing or for academic duties and preferred to remain 'an isolated author'. His solitary position meant he was always something of an intellectual outsider, however, and he probably had more readers but less influence than many leading academics of his day.

Fourteen of Lecky's *Historical and Political Essays*, most of which dated from the early 1890s, were posthumously published by his wife in 1908. The most valuable essays were those on the nature of history. 'Thoughts on history' (based on a lecture on 'The art of writing history' delivered to the Royal Institution in 1868) and 'The political value of history' (an address delivered in 1892) reveal that Lecky saw history as a science and an art. The historian had to be artistic in his approach, but was obliged to ensure that truth always stood above poetry. He discussed the complexities of history and stood against reasoning by analogy, using the case of how different the demand for Irish home rule under a democratic constitution would be to a restoration of the 1782 constitution. Other interesting essays in the collection include 'The empire: its value and its growth', an inaugural address to the Imperial Institute which he delivered in November 1893, and 'Formative influences', the important biographical fragment which appeared in *Forum* in June 1890. There were also pieces, originally published in various British and American journals, on Irish history, the state of the Jews, and some biographical sketches, whose subjects included Carlyle, Peel, and Queen Victoria.

In autumn 1899 Lecky brought out *The Map of Life: Conduct and Character*, a volume of reflections, based on the notes of a lifetime, which achieved some popularity (2000 copies sold in the first week after publication). There was some implicit criticism of modern politics in this Victorian manual of good manners and right thinking, but it is generally more optimistic about the state of the nation than *Democracy and Liberty*.

Illness and death In the spring of 1901 an attack of influenza led to a weakening of Lecky's heart, from which he did not entirely recover. (Indeed, he had never been robust and there are abundant references to ill health in his commonplace books.) In the autumn of 1902 he took a cure at Nauheim, Germany, and in December he resigned his seat in parliament. In spring 1903 a third version of *Leaders of Public Opinion in Ireland* appeared, with numerous alterations. However, if Lecky intended it to become another unionist pamphlet, he was unsuccessful. Even when *Leaders* directly advanced the unionist case, it indirectly encouraged the Irish to take pride in nationalist leaders of the past. While Lecky emerged as a leading Irish unionist in the 1890s, he could do little to alter the fact that no other historian had contributed so much to the concept of the moral and constitutional invalidity of the Act of Union of 1801.

On 22 October 1903 Lecky died quietly in his study at 38 Onslow Gardens. His body was cremated at Golders Green crematorium on 26 October and his remains, after a service at St Patrick's Cathedral, Dublin, were buried in Mount Jerome cemetery, Dublin, on 28 October. His wife, Elisabeth, with whom he had no children, died on 23 May 1912 and was buried beside him. The Lecky chair of history at Trinity College, Dublin, was endowed by his widow, from the proceeds of her husband's property in Queen's county and Carlow. All his manuscripts she left to the library of Trinity College.

Assessment Honours conferred on Lecky included honorary LLD (Dublin, 1879; St Andrews, 1885; Glasgow, 1895), honorary DCL (Oxford, 1888), and honorary LittD (Cambridge, 1891). He was elected secretary for foreign correspondence to the Royal Academy in 1895. He was sworn of the privy council in 1897 and in 1902 he became one of forty-eight original members of the British Academy and one of the first twelve recipients of the Order of Merit and a full member of the Académie des Sciences Morales et Politiques of the Institut de France in 1902, having been a corresponding member since 1893. He was the president of the Royal Literary Fund in 1903. He kept a fine art collection, and was a particular admirer of Velázquez.

Lecky was by nature rather reclusive and in no way a man of the world. He sometimes appeared cold, but once his shyness was pierced, he could be a good, undemonstrative conversationalist. His voice was rather high-pitched and sometimes weak, and he betrayed some nervousness when speaking in parliament, but was a good after-dinner speaker when he did not attempt humour. He was tall and thin, with rather disjointed limbs, flapping hands, and a high forehead. Long, fair hair covered a dome-shaped head, in which the eyes were gentle, the nose long, and the down-turned lips full. The front of his face was clean-shaven, but he wore side-whiskers which met under his chin.

Lecky thought himself objective, but to a greater degree than many of his more obviously partisan contemporaries, he unconsciously applied Victorian moral standards to every age. He was a representative rather than a great Victorian, and he remains interesting as such. He stood at the crossroads in the evolution of history writing between the age of the gentleman scholar in the library and that of the professional scholar in the archives. Lecky was, however, notable on two counts: as a British historian of ideas and as the writer of Ireland's first '*philosophical* history' (he liked that Burkean phrase), for neither Young Ireland nor the Celtic revivalists produced a notable historian. His major narrative history was undertaken as a vindication of the Irish people, but he was a sharp critic of the careless or deliberately misleading application of arguments from Irish history to justify the patriotic cause. He was, therefore, both the first national historian of Ireland and the first 'revisionist' of the nationalist idealization of Ireland.

The biographical treatment Lecky has received has been scant. His widow produced a well-written *Memoir* in 1909, which is better than many such homages but which, in the nature of the enterprise, makes no effort to see Lecky in a wider intellectual context and conceals as much as it discloses. On the eve of the Second World War Lecky attracted interest, along with Henry Maine and J. F. Stephen, as one of the late Victorian critics of democracy (and as a prophet of the possibility of something like fascism growing out of democratic politics). Since 1945, while Irish historians have continued to refer to him as a founding father, there has been little attempt to gauge his importance as a historian of ideas. JOSEPH SPENCE

Sources D. McCartney, *W. E. H. Lecky: historian and politician, 1838–1903* (1993) · E. van D. Lecky, *A memoir of W. E. H. Lecky* (1909) · *DNB* · J. J. Auchmuty, *Lecky: a biographical and critical essay* (1945) · *A Victorian historian: private letters of W. E. H. Lecky, 1859–1878*, ed. H. M. Hyde (1947) · *The Times* (24 Oct 1903) · L. P. Curtis, introduction, in W. E. H. Lecky, *A history of Ireland in the eighteenth century* (1972) · B. E. Lippencott, *Victorian critics of democracy* (1938) · 'A college friend' [A. Booth], 'Early recollections of Mr Lecky', *National Review*, 43 (1904–5), 108–22 · E. Lawless, 'W. E. H. Lecky: a reminiscence', *Monthly Review*, 14 (Feb 1904), 41 · W. A. Phillips, *Lecky: a lecture in celebration of the centenary of Lecky's birth* (1939) · J. Morley, *Miscellanies*, 4th ser. (1909) · TCD, Lecky MSS · *CGPLA Eng. & Wales* (1903)

Archives Hunt. L., letters · TCD, corresp. and papers, incl. of his wife | ICL, letters to Thomas Huxley · NL Ire., Gavan Duffy MSS · NRA, priv. coll., letters to John Swinton · TCD, minute books of the College Historical Society · TCD, Hartpole MSS · TCD, corresp. with J. H. Bernard · TCD, letters to Knightley Chetwode · UCL, letters to Sir Edwin Chadwick · University of Pennsylvania, Philadelphia, Henry Charles Lea Library, Lecky–Lea corresp.

Likenesses J. M. Cameron, photograph, *c*.1868, NPG [*see illus.*] · M. Collier, pencil drawing, 1877, NPG · G. F. Watts, portrait, 1878, NPG · Elliott & Fry, carte-de-visite, *c*.1884, NPG; repro. in McCartney, *W. E. H. Lecky* · J. E. Boehm, bronze bust, 1890, NG Ire. · Russell & Sons, woodburytype photograph, *c*.1891, NPG · W. Rothenstein, lithograph, 1897, NPG · B. Stone, photograph, 1897, NPG · J. Lavery, oils, 1903, NG Ire. · Barraud, photograph, NPG; repro. in *Men and Women of the Day*, 3 (1890) · J. E. Boehm, bronze bust, TCD · J. E. Boehm, terracotta bust, NPG · G. John, bronze statue, TCD · W. Rothenstein, lithograph, BM · W. Rothenstein, lithograph, Bradford City Art Gallery · Spy [L. Ward], caricature, watercolour study, NPG; repro. in *VF* (27 May 1882) · G. J. Stodart, stipple (after H. T. Wells), NPG · H. T. Wells, drawing, Royal Collection · watercolour, NPG

Wealth at death £30,127 10*s*. 11*d*.: probate, 26 Nov 1903, *CGPLA Eng. & Wales*

Lecky, Squire Thornton Stratford (1838–1902), writer on navigation, born in co. Down, was the son of Holland Lecky of Bally Holland House, Bangor, co. Down, and Castle Lecky, co. Londonderry. He was sent to school at Gracehill, co. Antrim. At fourteen, without permission of his parents, he began his career at sea as midshipman on the *Alfred* (1291 tons), a sailing merchantman, bound for Calcutta. On his return home he apprenticed himself to James Beazley, a Liverpool shipowner, and, after serving his time on ships sailing to India, became in 1857 second mate of Beazley's *Star of the East*, a China clipper. He was subsequently second mate of an American ship, and then for two years first-class second master in the Indian navy, serving in the *Indus*, *Frere*, and *Napier* until the Indian fleet was disbanded. He then rejoined the merchant service and made voyages to North and South America. In 1864 he obtained his master's certificate, and was for some years second officer in the Inman Company's service. He was afterwards employed successively by Messrs Lamport Holt of Liverpool (for four and a half years) and by the Pacific Steam Navigation Company (for six years).

Lecky acquired a reputation for his nautical surveys of the Pacific and for detecting unmarked danger spots. In 1865 he detected off Rio de Janeiro Lecky Rock, a steep slightly submerged rock, surrounded by seven fathoms of water. Shortly afterwards he located a similar danger spot near Rat Island, and the Lecky Bank to the north-east of the mouth of the River Plate. In 1869 he published, as the result of a trip to Ceará in Brazil, a plan showing wide errors in earlier charts, as to both the shape of the land and the depth of the water. In 1874 plans of his were published by the Admiralty showing similar errors in charts of Port Tongoy, Chile. For many years his running surveys of the Strait of Magellan and a large part of Smyth's Channel (off Chile) and the water between Punta Arenas and Cape Pillar were the only trustworthy guides to navigation. His nautical surveying work, which was much appreciated by the Admiralty, covered the greater part of the coast of South America.

In 1876 Lecky sailed as a guest on Lord Brassey's yacht, the *Sunbeam*, but he left her at Buenos Aires, to sail for Calcutta as boatswain on the *City of Mecca*. In 1878 he became commodore captain of the British steamers of the American line from Liverpool to Philadelphia, a position which he enjoyed. He commanded the *British Prince* transport in the Egyptian campaign of 1882, and going to the front won the medal and the khedive's bronze star, and was commended by the Admiralty. He had previously received a commission as a Royal Naval Reserve officer, and retired with the rank of commander.

Squire Thornton Stratford Lecky (1838–1902), by unknown artist, *c*.1900

In his spare time Lecky wrote on navigation. He had taught himself mathematics and astronomy, and his direct style and avoidance, where possible, of technical language, made his books popular among seamen. His *Wrinkles in Practical Navigation* (1881) long remained the best work of its kind. In 1882 he published *The Danger Angle and Off-Shore Distance*, and in 1892 *Lecky's A, B, C and D Tables* for solving problems in navigation and nautical astronomy. He was an extra master, and passed the Board of Trade examination in steam machinery.

In 1884 Lecky was appointed marine superintendent of the Great Western Railway Company and successfully supervised their steamship services and docks, designing and overseeing the building of their ships. He also kept for eight years an automatic tide gauge, which demonstrated that the Admiralty tide tables for Pembroke Dock were in error. In 1898 Lecky's health failed and he retired on a pension, but the company retained him as consultant adviser. He was a younger brother of Trinity House, and an enthusiastic fellow of the Royal Astronomical and Geographical societies. He was for many years a member of the Mercantile Marine Association, and served on its council. Until within a few weeks of his death he was busy on a star atlas.

Lecky married twice, and a son from his first marriage and a son and daughter from his second survived him. He died at Orilla de Mar, Santa Catalina, Las Palmas, in the Canary Islands, on 23 November 1902, and was buried in the English cemetery there.

[ANON.], *rev.* ELIZABETH BAIGENT

Sources *The Times* (5 Dec 1902) · *Nautical Magazine*, 71 (1902), 759–64 · F. T. Bullen, 'A great merchant seaman', *Cornhill Magazine*, [3rd] ser., 14 (1903), 228–36 · private information (1912) · *CGPLA Eng. & Wales* (1903)

Archives CUL, letters to Lord Kelvin

Likenesses portrait, *c*.1900, NMM [*see illus.*] · photograph, repro. in S. T. S. Lecky, *Wrinkles in practical navigation* (1881)

Wealth at death £160 12*s*. 2*d*.: probate, 20 Jan 1903, *CGPLA Eng. & Wales*

Le Clerc, Jean (1657–1736), theologian and philosopher, was born on 29 March 1657 NS in Geneva, the second son of Étienne Le Clerc (1599–1676), professor at the *académie* in Geneva, and his second wife, Suzanne Gallatin, daughter of the counsellor Marin Gallatin. He received his education in Geneva at the Collège de Calvin from 1664 to 1672 and later at the *académie* until 1678. Upon leaving he had a good command of Latin, Greek, and Hebrew, skills which were to be very useful in his later career. Le Clerc did not take orders immediately, but became the private tutor of Gabriël, eldest son of Sarrasin de la Pierre, magistrate at Grenoble. He returned to Geneva with his pupil in 1680 and took the examinations for ordination as a minister. Despite objecting to its orthodoxy, he signed the *Consensus Helveticus*, a necessity if he were to preach in Switzerland. Later in 1680 he accompanied his pupil to Saumur. While the boy attended university, Le Clerc used his time there to improve his French and to take part in major theological debates over grace and predestination. Le Clerc's first book, published at Saumur in 1681, led to his being accused of Socinianism. In 1682 he visited London but failed to secure a suitable position—his appointment as curate in the French church at the Savoy ending in disagreement with the more orthodox members of the congregation—and settled in Amsterdam the following year. With the help of Philippus van Limborch, one of the most prominent spokesmen of the Arminians, he obtained a post at the Remonstrant seminary as professor of philosophy, Hebrew, and the humanities. On 11 February 1691 Le Clerc married Maria Leti (*d*. 1734), eldest daughter of the historian Gregorio Leti (1630–1701). Le Clerc frequently complained of the cost of living in the Dutch republic and tried to obtain a position in England with the help of his English friends, among whom were John Locke and Joseph Addison. As late as 1707 the latter tried, unsuccessfully, to have Le Clerc appointed librarian to Queen Anne. Richard Bentley is said to have opposed this appointment for personal reasons, but a more plausible explanation may be found in Le Clerc's unequivocal ideas on the separation of church and state, a sensitive issue in England.

Le Clerc was an all-round scholar who wrote, translated, and edited many theological, historical, and philosophical works as well as publishing editions of the classics and educational tracts. His *Logica* (1692) was dedicated to Locke and Robert Boyle. He is, however, probably known best for his scholarly journals in which he reviewed and announced many English works which he often obtained through the mediation of his English friends: *Bibliothèque Universelle et Historique* (1686–93), *Bibliothèque Choisie* (1703–13), and *Bibliothèque Ancienne et Moderne* (1714–27). His linguistic abilities ensured that the range of books discussed in his journals was wider than in many rival publications. Through his journals he played an important role in disseminating and popularizing in western Europe the scholarly and scientific ideas of English authors such as Locke and Newton. In 1705 (in *Bibliothèque Choisie*, 6.342–411) he published an *Eloge* on Locke, which was the foundation stone of Locke biography. He expressed his own often controversial ideas in a collection of essays entitled *Parrhasiana, ou, Pensées diverses sur des matières de critique, d'histoire, de morale et de politique* (2 vols., 1699–1701). After the death of his friend Philippus van Limborch in 1712 Le Clerc was appointed professor of ecclesiastical history at the Remonstrant seminary. He was never one to shun controversy and always advocated the employment of reason to arrive at the truth. According to Le Clerc it was a scholar's duty to reason and to publish his findings, regardless of the opinions of others. He considered the Bible an antique document which, although containing God's word, was not always to be believed literally. Exegesis and philology led him to publish a controversial French translation of the New Testament (1703), which resulted once again in accusations of propagating Socinianism.

In 1728 Le Clerc suffered a stroke but despite his illness was still paid his full salary of 1200 guilders a year by the seminary. In 1732 a second, major, stroke incapacitated him completely and his wife nursed him until her death on 4 November 1734. He was then cared for by the husband of a second cousin, Gabriel de Normandie, who arranged the sale of Le Clerc's books in 1735. Le Clerc died in Amsterdam on 8 January 1736 NS. An elegy on him was written by Jean Barbeyrac. MARJA SMOLENAARS

Sources A. Barnes, *Jean Le Clerc (1657–1736) et la République des Lettres* (Paris, 1938) · S. A. Golden, *Jean Le Clerc* (New York, 1972) · H. Bots and others, eds., *De 'Bibliothèque Universelle et Historique' (1686–1693): een periodiek als trefpunt van geletterd Europa* (Amsterdam, 1981) · A. N. M. Wijngaards, *De 'Bibliothèque Choisie' van Jean Le Clerc: een Amsterdams geleerdentijdschrift uit de jaren 1703 tot 1713* (Amsterdam and Maarssen, 1986)
Archives Bodl. Oxf., corresp. with J. Locke
Likenesses B. Picart, engraving, repro. in Wijngaards, *Bibliothèque Choisie*

Leclercq, Carlotta (1838–1893), actress, was born in London on 12 June 1838, one of the four daughters of Charles Clark (1797–1861), a pantomimist and ballet master, who performed under the name of Leclercq, and his wife, Margaret, *née* Burnet. She first appeared on stage in Bolton at the age of twenty months, as Cora's child in *Pizarro*, and as a child was Columbine in a pantomime at the Princess's. In 1853 she was Maddalina in J. Palgrave Simpson's *Marco Spada*; Charles Kean commented favourably on her performance as Marguerite in *Faust and Marguerite*. She went on to play Shakespearian roles, including Ariel in *The Tempest*, Nerissa in *The Merchant of Venice*, and Mrs Ford in *The Merry Wives of Windsor*. Her original parts included Diana in J. M. Morton's *Don't Judge by Appearances* (November 1855) and Mrs Savage in John Brougham's *Playing with Fire* (September 1861). For several years she played with Charles Albert Fechter at the Lyceum in such parts as Zillah in Brougham's *The Duke's Motto* (January 1863) and Lucy Ashton in Simpson's *The Master of Ravenswood* (December 1865), and at the Adelphi as Mercedes in *Monte Cristo* (October 1868). She went with Fechter to the USA in 1869, and returned to England in 1877. On 26 February 1877 she married John Nelson, an actor, following which her appearances were chiefly with him in the provinces. After his death, on 25 July 1879, she performed only rarely in London, but became noted as a theatrical teacher. She died at her home, 22 Edith Grove, Chelsea, on 9 August 1893.

Carlotta Leclercq (1838–1893), by Southwell Brothers [as Zillah in *The Duke's Motto* by John Brougham]

Her younger sister, **Rose Leclercq** (1843–1899), actress, was born at 14 Wilde Street, Liverpool on 2 February 1843, and on her sixth birthday played Ceres in *The Tempest* at Windsor Castle. On 8 October 1860 she appeared in Boucicault's *The Corsican Brothers* at the Princess's with Charles Fechter, and was the first Mrs Waverley in *Playing with Fire*. In October 1861 she played Desdemona to Fechter's Othello. In 1863 she was at Drury Lane, where she was the original Mary Vance in F. C. Burnand's *The Deal Boatman* and Astarte in Byron's *Manfred*. On 19 April 1864 she married Charles Perry Fuller, a dealer in horses, from whom she was divorced in 1871, having had a son, the actor Fuller Mellish (1865–1935). In 1868 she played Eliza in Boucicault's *After Dark* at the Princess's and Kate Jessop in his

Lost at Sea at the Adelphi; in 1875 she was the first Clara Ffolliott in *The Shaughraun* at Drury Lane. She continued to play both new and old roles for the next twenty years, including Olivia in *Twelfth Night* (Lyceum, July 1884) with Henry Irving and Ellen Terry, Marie Leczinska in W. G. Wills's *The Pompadour* (Haymarket, March 1888), and Lady Wargrave in Sydney Grundy's *The New Woman* (Comedy, September 1894). Her last original part was Mrs Beechinor in H. A. Jones's *The Manoeuvres of Jane* (Haymarket, October 1898). She played this character on 25 March 1899, and died a few days later, on 2 April 1899, from influenza and bronchial pneumonia at her home, 7 Stanley Mansions, Park Walk, Chelsea. She was buried at Kensal Green cemetery.

In her later days, Rose Leclercq had a matchless delivery, and was accounted the best, and almost the only, representative of the grand style in comedy.

JOSEPH KNIGHT, *rev.* J. GILLILAND

Sources *The life and reminiscences of E. L. Blanchard, with notes from the diary of Wm. Blanchard*, ed. C. W. Scott and C. Howard, 2 vols. (1891) · C. E. Pascoe, ed., *The dramatic list*, 2nd edn (1880) · 'Esther Sandraz', *The Theatre*, 4th ser., 14 (1889), 31–4 · 'The rake's will', *The Theatre*, 4th ser., 14 (1889), 100 · *The Era* (8 April 1899) · E. Reid and H. Compton, eds., *The dramatic peerage*, rev. edn [1892] · Boase, *Mod. Eng. biog.* · J. Hollingshead, *Gaiety chronicles* (1898) · C. Scott, *The drama of yesterday and today*, 2 vols. (1899) · J. Coleman, *Fifty years of an actor's life*, 2 vols. (1904) · A. T. C. Pratt, ed., *People of the period: being a collection of the biographies of upwards of six thousand living celebrities*, 2 vols. (1897) · *The Athenaeum* [various] · *The Times* [various] · d. cert. · d. cert. [Rose Leclercq] · b. cert. [Rose Leclercq] · J. Parker, ed., *Who's who in the theatre*, 6th edn (1930)

Archives Theatre Museum, London, letters

Likenesses W. W. Alais, line engraving (after photograph), NPG, Harvard TC · J. E. Baker, lithograph, Harvard TC · Southwell Bros., photograph, NPG [*see illus.*] · H. A. Thomas, lithograph, Harvard TC · portrait, repro. in Hollingshead, *Gaiety chronicles*, 265 · portrait, repro. in Scott, *The drama of yesterday and today*, vol. 2, p. 160 · portrait, repro. in Coleman, *Fifty years of an actor's life*, vol. 2, p. 618 · portrait, repro. in *The Theatre*, 14 (1889), 160 · portrait, repro. in *Era*, 13 · portraits, Harvard TC · two portraits (Rose Leclercq), Harvard TC

Wealth at death £1169 13*s*. 2*d*.—Rose Leclercq: administration, 8 May 1899, *CGPLA Eng. & Wales*

Leclercq, Henri Frédéric Laurent Ghislain (1869–1945). *See under* Farnborough scholars (*act.* 1896–1945).

Leclercq, Rose (1843–1899). *See under* Leclercq, Carlotta (1838–1893).

Leconfield. For this title name *see* Wyndham, John Edward Reginald, first Baron Egremont and sixth Baron Leconfield (1920–1972).

Le Courayer, Pierre-François (1681–1776), Roman Catholic priest and religious controversialist, was born on 17 November 1681 at Rouen, France, where his father, Pierre Le Courayer, was *conseiller rapporteur référendaire* of the *parlement* of Rouen's chancellery. He was educated at Vernon and at Paris, and in 1698 entered the congregation of Ste Geneviève in Paris. He became a canon regular in 1706, sub-librarian in 1711, and librarian in 1714, and by the age of forty had become renowned as a scholar. He supported the opposition to the anti-Jansenist papal bull *Unigenitus*

Pierre-François Le Courayer (1681–1776), by unknown artist, *c*.1727–40

and then began to study the subject of Anglican ordinations, corresponding with the archbishop of Canterbury, William Wake, and enjoying the friendship of the exiled Jacobite bishop Francis Atterbury. In 1723 his *Dissertation sur la validité des ordinations des anglois* was published, and an English translation appeared in 1725. The work pronounced that Anglican orders were unquestionably valid, and provoked hostile responses in France, above all from the Jesuits. The most important attacks were made by the Jesuit Jean Hardouin in 1724 and by the Dominican Michel Le Quien in the following year. Le Courayer replied to his critics in his *Défense de la dissertation* in 1726, but his thesis was condemned by a commission of French bishops, and faced with a possible trial for heresy he fled to England in January 1728.

In England Le Courayer was fêted. His friends already included Viscount Perceval, later first earl of Egmont, and the marquess of Blandford. Queen Caroline welcomed him at court, where he joined the eclectic clerical circle that she patronized. As John Milner, the Roman Catholic apologist, later—and rather bitterly—observed, Le Courayer 'was protected and almost idolized … by the [Anglican] clergy … and by some of the nobility who supported him in the most affluent and honorable manner' (Milner, 28). In 1727 the University of Oxford had conferred on him a DD by diploma; in an oration in the Sheldonian Theatre in 1733 he warmly expressed his gratitude to the university while denouncing the iniquity and malevolence of his adversaries. He was granted a Treasury pension initially of £100 per annum which was subsequently raised to £200. His *Dissertation* interested Charles Seager, a Puseyite, who produced an English edition in 1844.

Besides the *Dissertation* and its *Défense* Le Courayer produced, among other works, a translation into French of Paolo Sarpi's *Istoria del Concilio Tridentino* in 1736, another French translation, *Histoire de la Réformation, ou, Mémoires de Jean Sleidan* in 1767, and *A Declaration of my Last Sentiments on the Different Doctrines of Religion*, published posthumously in England in 1787. Caroline of Ansbach herself assisted in procuring subscriptions for the translation of Sarpi's work. Two volumes, containing thirty-four manuscript sermons in French, survive. The sermons discuss God's dealings with mankind and the duties of Christians, examining subjects such as faith, God's wisdom, patience, and justice, and the love and fear of God. However, they also contain pungent attacks on Romish practices or beliefs that Le Courayer regarded as superstitious or idolatrous and on claims by the papacy that he saw as unwarrantable pretensions.

Le Courayer never sought to leave the Roman Catholic church. But though he saw his opinions as unexceptionable, the Catholic hierarchy in England, as in France, thought differently. *The Grounds of the Old Religion* (1742), by Bishop Richard Challoner, was possibly a response to the *Dissertation*. Challoner wanted a 'retractation of … [Le Courayer's] errors, as public as his profession of them had been, and likewise his return to religious obedience' (Milner, 29). Since Le Courayer would not submit, when he attended mass in the Catholic chapels he was, by Challoner's orders, 'always publicly passed over by the officiating priest … at the altar rail' (ibid., 29).

Le Courayer gave a half-length portrait of himself to the University of Oxford in 1768. Now in the Bodleian Library, it shows a man in a white collar and alb, with a clean-shaven face, wavy brown hair, a pointed nose, and dark eyes; the countenance is thoughtful and gentle. Le Courayer was quiet and nervous by temperament; he gave charitably, lived frugally, and was a good conversationalist. In later life his eyesight deteriorated, and he eventually went blind. He was something of a valetudinarian, complaining of his poor digestion and afraid that he would not survive into old age.

None the less Le Courayer lived to the age of ninety-four, dying in London on 17 October 1776. In 1730 Archbishop Wake had written an assessment of the man. 'Father Courayer', he observed, was forced:

> to leave his own country, with his monastery and friends, and seek shelter with the necessaries of life among us here in England, whose cause he hath so learnedly and strenuously defended … Here he has lived an inoffensive life ever since, grateful to all honest men and scholars, and offensive only to those who could not bear the unanswerable truths established by him in his defence of our orders and consecrations … He is an excellent man, one of the best French writers that has appeared in the present age, and so honest that even that alone may suffice to render him justly esteemed by any fair and good man. (Sykes, 1.361–2)

Among Anglicans such a verdict seemed valid over forty years later. As a protagonist of the Church of England—and as he had wished—Le Courayer was buried in the cloister of Westminster Abbey. His grave is marked by a wall monument and by a floor slab. COLIN HAYDON

Sources J. Milner, 'A brief account of the life of the late R. Rev. Richard Challoner', in R. Challoner, *The grounds of the old religion*, 5th edn (1798) • monument and floor slab, Westminster Abbey cloister • G. V. Bennett, *The tory crisis in church and state: the career of Francis Atterbury, bishop of Rochester* (1975) • E. Préclin, *L'union des églises gallicane et anglicane: une tentative au temps de Louis XV. P.-F. Le Courayer (de 1681 à 1732) et Guillaume Wake* (1928) • N. Sykes, *William Wake, archbishop of Canterbury*, 2 vols. (1957) • S. Taylor, 'Queen Caroline and the Church of England', *Hanoverian Britain and empire: essays in memory of Philip Lawson*, ed. S. Taylor, R. Connors, and C. Jones (1998), 82–101 • Foster, *Alum. Oxon.* • Mrs R. Lane Poole, *Catalogue of portraits* (1920) [exhibition catalogue, reading room and gallery, Bodl. Oxf.]

Archives BL, corresp., Add. MS 35210 • Bodl. Oxf., theological MSS, MS Add. a 39 • Yale U., Farmington, Lewis Walpole Library, sermons

Likenesses portrait, *c*.1727–1740, NPG [*see illus.*] • pen and ink, and chalk drawing, Wellesley College, Massachusetts, Hope collection • portrait, Bodl. Oxf.

Le Couteur, John (1760–1835), army officer, was a member of an old Jersey family. He was born at Les Buttes in St John's parish in Jersey on 26 August 1760, the son of John Le Couteur (1718–1794), and Marie Bertault. He was educated at Guildford grammar school. In 1780 he obtained an ensigncy by purchase in the Old 95th foot, and in January 1781 he served with the 95th under Major Francis Peirson in the successful defence of Jersey against an invading French force. Immediately after this 'Battle of Jersey' he was promoted lieutenant in the Old 100th foot and went with it to India. He was present in a naval action in the Cape Verde Islands, and in some of the operations against Haidar Ali, and was appointed brigade-major to Colonel Thomas Humberston.

Le Couteur later served with General Mathews in Malabar, and was with him when he occupied Nagar (Bednur), while Tipu Sahib besieged him. After losing 500 men Mathews surrendered, and on 28 April 1783 the garrison marched out with the honours of war, the officers retaining their personal effects. Mathews was, however, accused by Tipu of having appropriated and divided the contents of the military chest; and he and nineteen officers were soon afterwards poisoned. Another party consisting of thirty-four subalterns, including Le Couteur, were sent as prisoners to Chitteldroog, where they were treated with great cruelty before being released at the peace in March 1784. Le Couteur wrote an account of the Malabar campaign in *Letters, Chiefly from India* (1790). He became captain-lieutenant in 1784, and captain in 1785, when the 100th was disbanded, and he was put on half pay.

Le Couteur returned to Jersey and became active in the politics and administration of the island; and in 1787 he became adjutant in a regiment of the Jersey militia. In 1792 he bought Belle Vue, St Aubin, Jersey, and the following year he married Marie (1774–1845), daughter of John (later Sir John) Dumaresq; they had two sons. In 1793 he was brought on full pay in the 11th foot, and was made brigade-major of the Jersey militia, which he vigorously reformed. From 1793 to 1795 he was in charge of the secret contacts, through Jersey, of the British government with French royalists, including Georges, Pichegru, and Laroche Jacquelin. In 1797 he became major in the 16th foot; however, he remained on the staff in Jersey until 1798, when he joined his regiment in Scotland, with the brevet rank of lieutenant-colonel. In 1799 he was appointed inspector of militia in Jersey, and in 1799–1800 he was assistant quartermaster-general in the island during the detention there of Russian troops from the Texel. He remained inspector of militia for twelve years. In 1808 he was gazetted colonel in the army, and in 1811 he was appointed a major-general on the staff in Ireland, and afterwards in Jamaica, where he commanded a brigade.

In 1813 Le Couteur was appointed lieutenant-governor of Curaçao and its dependent islands, whose inhabitants he found on the verge of starvation. Curaçao, off the coast of Venezuela, was a large trading centre, but the war with the United States in 1812 had prevented the arrival of corn from Britain, and orders in council prohibited the import of foreign grain. Le Couteur set aside the orders rather than expose the population to famine. When the island was restored to the Dutch after the peace in 1815, the legislative bodies, the native inhabitants, and Spanish refugees gratefully presented Le Couteur with addresses acknowledging his services to the colony. Le Couteur generously declined the duke of York's offer to put him down for a regiment, saying he did not feel entitled to the honour so long as a Peninsular officer remained unprovided for. Thereafter he lived at his Jersey home, Belle Vue. He became a lieutenant-general in 1821, and died at Belle Vue on 23 March 1835, aged seventy-four. He was buried at St Brelade's churchyard on 27 March.

Le Couteur's elder son, Colonel Sir John Le Couteur (1794–1875) of the 104th and 20th foot, was for a long time commander of the Jersey militia; he was also aide-de-camp to William IV and Victoria. He was an administrator and agricultural reformer in Jersey, and founded the Royal Jersey Agricultural and Horticultural Society. His scientific contributions to the study of wheat gained him the fellowship of the Royal Society in 1843, and he displayed 104 varieties of wheat at the Great Exhibition of 1851.

H. M. Chichester, *rev.* Ian Machin

Sources J. Stevens, *Victorian voices: an introduction to the papers of Sir John Le Couteur* (1969) • G. R. Balleine, *A biographical dictionary of Jersey*, [1] [1948], 378–82 • *United Service Journal*, 2 (1835), 379–82 • R. Mayne, *The battle of Jersey* (1981) • G. R. Balleine, *Balleine's history of Jersey*, ed. M. Syvret and J. Stevens, rev. edn (1981) • J. D. Kelleher, *The triumph of the country: the rural community in nineteenth-century Jersey* (1994)

Archives Jersey, Société Jersiaise

Lecoutz de Lévizac [Levizac], **Jean Pons Victor** (*c.*1750–1813), writer on the French language, was born at Albi in Languedoc of a noble family. He was educated for the church, became a priest when young, and obtained a canonry in the cathedral of Vabres, near St Affrique. In 1776 he received first prize for an idyll, 'Le bienfait rendu', from the Académie des Jeux Floraux. At the revolution he fled to the Netherlands, and from there to England. If, as seems probable, he was the Jean de Levizac who is mentioned by Plasse, he was at the time of his flight vicar-general of the diocese of St Omer.

For the rest of his life Levizac lived in London, taught French, and wrote numerous books on the French language. These included *L'art de parler et d'écrire correctement la langue Française* (1797, 1801), *Abrégé de la grammaire française* (1798), and a *French and English and English and French Dictionary* (1808, 1815). He also edited volumes of standard French authors. He died in London in 1813.

W. A. J. Archbold, *rev.* John D. Haigh

Sources J.-M. Quérard, *La France littéraire*, 5 (1833), 282 • J. Gorton, *A general biographical dictionary* (1841) • J. Watkins and F. Shoberl, *A biographical dictionary* (1816) • F.-X. Plesse, *Le clergé francais réfugié en Angleterre*, 2 vols. (1886), 2.439 • R. A. Davenport, *A dictionary of biography* (1831) • Watt, *Bibl. Brit.*

Le Davis, Edward (*fl.* 1671–1691), engraver and art dealer, was born in Wales and apprenticed as an engraver to David Loggan in London. George Vertue recorded information from a fellow engraver, John Sturt, that Loggan's wife:

> would have him [Davis] follow her in a livery & other servile offices, which he refus'd to do, & ran away to France, where he became acquainted with paintings & other parts of arts by which he gathered a good fortune at his return & became a great dealer in pictures. (Vertue, 2.29)

Davis's years in France can be followed from the plates he engraved there between 1671 and 1674 for the publisher François Chauveau. Nine large ones are recorded, as well as thirty small images of saints that have not been seen in modern times. They fall within the standard range of French production of the day, being religious plates after old masters or contemporaries.

Davis was back in London in 1675, when he engraved the frontispiece for S. Monteage's *Debtor and Creditor*. It was at this point that he added the French prefix 'Le' to his name, which he used in signing all his subsequent plates. He continued to make numerous engravings, almost invariably portraits, which have not yet been fully described. The matter is complicated by the number of unsigned plates that appear to have been produced by him. The finest of his plates was a full-length of Catherine of Braganza, made in 1682 as the frontispiece for the second volume of Moses Pitt's *English Atlas*.

Evidence about Le Davis's dealing activities can be found in various advertisements, notes by Vertue, and surviving auction catalogues. These are far from complete, but suggest that he was holding yearly auctions of mostly imported old master paintings at an auction house in St Albans Street in London. One sale held in 1691 comprised paintings from the collections of Cardinal Antonio Barberini (1607–1671) and Sir James Palmer (*d.* 1657).

The great connoisseur Pierre-Jean Mariette, writing in the eighteenth century, stated that Le Davis could have become a good engraver, for he cut the copper well. Given the high standards reigning in France, the implication that he never lived up to his abilities is reasonable; but in England Le Davis was the fourth leading engraver of his day, after Loggan, Robert White, and Peter Vandrebanc.

Antony Griffiths

Sources M. Préaud, *Bibliothèque Nationale inventaire du fonds français XVIIeme siècle*, 10 (1989), 12–19 • A. Griffiths and R. A. Gerard, *The print in Stuart Britain, 1603–1689* (1998), 208 [exhibition catalogue, BM, 8 May – 20 Sept 1998] • Vertue, *Note books*, 2.29, 192–3 •

Abécédario de P. J. Mariette, et autres notes inédites de cet amateur sur les arts et les artistes, ed. P. de Chennevières and A. de Montaiglon, 6 vols. (Paris, 1851–60), vol. 2, pp. 19, 67

Leddra, William (*d.* 1661), Quaker minister in America, was probably born in Cornwall, but apparently migrated early to Barbados. According to one authority, Leddra was a clothier before becoming an approved minister of the Society of Friends (Maule, 45). Nothing is known of his lineage or possible marriages or descendants. As a man committed to his faith, however, much is known, especially about his activities in New England during the years 1658–61. Indeed, Leddra has the unhappy distinction of serving that faith as its last New England martyr.

In March or April 1658 Leddra, accompanied by several other professing Friends from Barbados, arrived in Rhode Island. About mid-April Leddra and William Brend, a man of advanced years, embarked for Salem, Massachusetts. After a brief visit to Salem, where they were received warmly by the few Friends residing there, Leddra and Brend, feeling the call to press on to more dangerous territory, travelled to Boston, where they soon encountered considerable hostility. Jailed for five days without food, for which they had refused to work, these two suffered the humiliation of a public whipping. Brend, a particularly unco-operative prisoner, sustained even greater cruelty from his gaoler, so much so that he became comatose from repeated beatings. The townspeople, becoming sympathetic to Brend's condition of age and injury, gathered together the necessary prison fees for the release of both Brend and Leddra.

In Boston Leddra was joined by his fellow Quaker John Rous, who was returning to Boston even after being banished and told that if he came again he would be hanged. Both Leddra and Rous, who also came from Barbados and whose father was a lieutenant-colonel and a wealthy landowner there, requested that they be tried under the laws of England. Following denial of this reasonable and apparently legal request, each was whipped fifteen times; and while Leddra was cast out of the colony on pain of death should he return, Rous, like two other Quaker prisoners, suffered the loss of his right ear.

During the year 1659 Leddra spent some ten months in a prison in Plymouth, Massachusetts, before he again and deliberately braved the wrath promised him by the Boston magistrates. Having arrived in Boston in late 1660, he was imprisoned in a cell open to the natural elements, where a log was close-fastened to his leg by a heavy chain. Brought before the bar, bearing log and chain, he was condemned to be hanged from the gallows because he would not take off his hat, would not refrain from using 'thee' and 'thou'—two indications of Quaker identity—and particularly because he had returned to Boston.

Before his execution Leddra wrote two letters, the first about three months before his death and the second the day before. Both letters were often reprinted entire in America and England before the twentieth century; long passages from them were quoted during the twentieth. Each of these letters is appealing by virtue of its apparent homespun simplicity; for example, Leddra, the former clothier, is fond of using clothing as a metaphor, such as: God 'may have a garment ready to cover the nakedness of the weak' (Bishop, 384). Leddra demonstrates a lively imagination when he uses a 'Door of Life' conceit to close the longer of his two letters. After rejecting 'the lion of greedy desires', the faithful pass, so holds the minister, through 'the Door of Life' 'into the green and pleasant pastures of the folds', where they sate the righteous 'desires of their souls' (ibid., 384–5).

Such an elaboration suggests the artistry Leddra probably applied in the construction of his sermons. The second of his two letters, composed the day before his execution, contains no such elaboration. Here the prose reads as if it were written in haste under the stress of his impending judgment. Maxim piles on top of maxim: 'greater is He that is in you, than he that is in the world; for He will clothe you with humility' (Bishop, 387).

Following the earlier New England executions of such fellow Quakers as William Robinson, Marmaduke Stephenson, and Mary Dyer, William Leddra was taken to the gallows on Boston Common on 14 March 1661. A brother in the faith, Edward Wharton of Salem, 'caught his lifeless body as it fell from the scaffold' (Jones, 89n.). After stripping his body, the gaoler is recorded as having made the unlikely observation that Leddra 'was a comely man' (Sewel, 350; Bishop, 203), this remark evoking the biblical Jesus's execution. JOHN C. SHIELDS

Sources W. Sewel, *The history of the rise, increase and progress of the Christian people called Quakers* (1722) • G. Bishop, *New England judged* (1885) • J. Bowden, *The history of the Society of Friends in America*, 2 vols. (1850–54) • R. M. Jones, *The Quakers in the American colonies* (1911) • J. Whiting, ed., *A catalogue of Friends' books: written by many of the people called Quakers* (1708) • J. Besse, *A collection of the sufferings of the people called Quakers*, 2 vols. (1753) • D. Neal, *The history of new England: containing an impartial account of the civil and ecclesiastical affairs of the country, to the year … 1700*, 2 vols. (1720) • T. Maule, *New-England persecutors mauld with their own weapons* (1697) • W. Evans and T. Evans, eds., *The Friends' Library*, 14 vols. (1837–50), vol. 7, pp. 478–80 • E. C. Stedman and E. M. Hutchinson, eds., *A library of American literature*, 11 vols. (1889), vol. 1

Ledeboer, Judith Geertruid (1901–1990), architect and public servant, was born on 8 September 1901 at Almelo, in the Netherlands, the second of six children of Willem Ledeboer (1873–1943), a banker, and Harmina Engelbertha van Heek (1873–1959). The family moved to London soon after her birth, and she was educated at Wimbledon high school; Cheltenham Ladies' College; Bedford College, London; Newnham College, Cambridge (college scholar in history, 1921–4; MA, 1945); and Radcliffe College, Cambridge, Massachusetts (AM, economics, 1925). Though her interest in architecture was relatively late in developing she thought 'it was the job I was meant for' (Darley, 39). She trained at the Architectural Association, London (1926–31), and won the Henry Florence travelling studentship (1931). She was inspired by the success of the architect Elisabeth Scott, and worked as an assistant on Scott's Shakespeare Memorial Theatre, Stratford upon Avon.

Ledeboer practised architecture from 1934 in partnership with David Booth (1939–41 and 1946–62) and with John Pinckheard (1956–70). The firm of Booth, Ledeboer, and Pinckheard had offices in London and Oxford, designing mainly for clients in universities and the public sector. Commissions included the Institute of Archaeology and Classical Studies (1953–8), University of London; the Waynflete Building (1958–61), Magdalen College, Oxford; and housing for Lewisham and Newham borough councils in the 1950s and 1960s. Designed as part of the Festival of Britain (1951), Ledeboer's best-known project was the old people's home on the Lansbury estate, Poplar—a building type which she promoted in her writings and developed in a half-dozen other projects. Her Nuffield House (1951), Harlow, Essex, is a model of an architecturally interesting, low-cost local health centre; she was most closely concerned, however, with housing, and planned an entire neighbourhood unit at Hemel Hempstead new town (1950–55), which included houses, flats, and maisonettes, as well as shops.

Well-illustrated in the architectural press, Ledeboer's work was consciously not stylish, but thoughtfully designed, detailed for everyday use, and carefully considered in relation to its site and surroundings, which she often landscaped. Efficient and extremely able, she extended her practice to housing research, exhibition organization, and committee work devoted to providing social architecture. She succeeded Elizabeth Denby as organizer of the 'New homes for old' exhibitions (1934, 1936, 1938), which analysed the social and architectural problems associated with the slums; she proposed their clearance and replacement with modern, healthier accommodation, and added an assessment of rural housing (1938). At this time, as head of exhibitions at the Housing Centre Trust (HCT), a member of the committee, and later chairman (1951–63), she persuasively put the case for improved housing and social amenities through HCT lectures, exhibitions, publications (especially its *Housing Review*), and, most distinctively, through films.

Ledeboer became one of the most significant voices in post-war housing policy, helping to set housing standards that raised the quality of public-sector accommodation; at the Ministry of Health (1941–6) she was the first woman employed by the department then responsible for housing. She served as secretary to both the Dudley committee, which produced *Design of Dwellings* (1944), and the Burt committee (1942–6), which advised on construction methods—notably prefabrication. A member of the Building Research Board of the Department of Scientific and Industrial Research (1951–6), she sat on the influential Parker Morris committee (1961), whose space standards became mandatory in all public-sector housing (1967–81). At home in the corridors of power she believed in the efficacy of institutions and organizations and was an active member of the Royal Institute of British Architects (1932–76) and of the Institute of Landscape Architects (1942–77). An associate of Newnham College (1942–56), she was interested in education, especially girls' education, and designed kindergartens, adventure playgrounds, and a girls' school. She was appointed OBE in 1966.

Tall, and in her youth athletic, Ledeboer, who remained single, loved the countryside and designed two houses and gardens for herself in Surrey, where she enjoyed walking, raising livestock, and gardening. She died on Christmas eve 1990 at her home, Hilltop Farmhouse, Hambledon, near Godalming, where her ashes were scattered along a neighbouring track. LYNNE WALKER

Sources private information (2004) [Rita Brooking Clark, sister] · [A. B. White], ed., *Newnham College register*, 1: *1871–1923* (1964), 324 · associates' nomination papers, 1933; fellows' nomination papers, 1953, RIBA BAL · photographs and documents, RIBA BAL, Ledeboer MSS · G. Darley, 'Women in the public sector', *Women architects: their work*, ed. L. Walker (1984), 37–9 · *The Independent* (25 Jan 1991) · *Housing Review* (March–April 1991) · Schlesinger Library, Cambridge, Massachusetts, Radcliffe Archives · *Landscape Design Extra* (March 1991) · RIBA BAL, Photographs collection, MAL 91 · RIBA BAL, manuscripts and archives collection, SAG/88/4, DB/1-47 · articles and illustrations in the building press, including *Architect & Building News*, *Architectural Review*, *Housing Review*, *RIBA Journal*, *The Builder*, *Architects' Journal*, *Architectural Design* indexed by artist's name and building type in 'grey books', RIBA BAL · J. Fletcher Pott and L. B. Walker, interview, 1984 · membership lists, Institute of Landscape Architects, London · private information (2004) [M. Cleaver] · plan of Hughes Parry Hall, London, LMA, GLC/AR/BR/17/055326 · *RIBA Journal*, 69 (1962), 302–3 [obit. of David Booth] · *The Times* (1 Oct 1977) [obit. of John Pinckheard] · court minutes, 1952/3–1967/8, U. Lond., Senate House · MSS, Housing Centre Trust archive, London · Building Research Establishment Library, Elisabeth Denby papers · [E. Leopold], *Housing standards: a survey of new build local authority housing in London, 1981–1984* (1986) · private information (2004) [E. Leopold]

Archives LMA · priv. coll., papers · RIBA BAL, photographs collection · RIBA BAL, manuscript and archives collection | FILM BFI NFTVA

Likenesses photograph, *c*.1918, priv. coll.

Lederede, Richard de. *See* Ledred, Richard (*c*.1275–1360?).

Le Despencer. For this title name *see* Dashwood, Francis, eleventh Baron Le Despencer (1708–1781).

Le Despenser. For this title name *see* Wentworth, Thomas, second Baron Wentworth and *de jure* seventh Baron Le Despenser (1525–1584).

Lediard, Thomas (1685–1743), writer and surveyor, was probably born in Cirencester, Gloucestershire; details of his parents are unknown. He states that he was attached at different times to the staff of the first duke of Marlborough, and especially in 1707, on the occasion of the duke's visit to Charles XII of Sweden. Lediard does not appear to have been connected with the duke in any official capacity, and always travelled as a private gentleman at his own expense. He was probably at the time an attaché to the embassy at Hamburg, and was lent to the duke as a foreign secretary. He was afterwards for many years 'secretary to his majesty's envoy extraordinary in Hamburg', one of his duties being apparently to manage the opera there, in the pecuniary interests of his chief, Sir Cecil Wych. He also organized firework displays to celebrate royal birthdays between 1724 and 1729, and published descriptions of these in English and German. Nathan Bailey's *Dictionarium Britannicum*, to which Lediard contributed etymological information, further describes him as a 'professor of modern languages in lower Germany' on its title-page.

Lediard returned to England some time before 1730 and

settled in Smith Square, Westminster. Some time after this he was appointed justice of the peace for the liberty of Westminster, and was known as a 'useful and active magistrate'. During the next five years he worked on *The Naval History of England … from the Norman Conquest … to the Conclusion of* 1734, published in 1735. In February 1738 he wrote *A scheme, humbly offered to the honourable the commissioners for building a bridge at Westminster*, dedicated to Lord Sundon and Sir Charles Wager, the members of parliament for Westminster. About this time, possibly to some extent in consequence of this, he was appointed agent and surveyor of Westminster Bridge. It seems probable that he was the 'JP for Westminster' who was appointed in 1742 to succeed the recently deceased Nathaniel Blacherby as 'Treasurer for Westminster Bridge' (*GM*, 12.275, where, however, the name is printed 'John'), for on 13 July 1742 'the crown lands from Westminster Bridge to Charing Cross' were granted to him and Sir Joseph Ayloffe, bt, to hold 'in trust to the Commissioners appointed to build Westminster Bridge' (ibid., 12.385). On 9 December 1742 Lediard was elected a fellow of the Royal Society. In addition to his *Naval History*, he published other historical works, including a life of the duke of Marlborough (1736) and a continuation of Rapin de Thoyras's *History of England* (1737), covering the period from 1688 to 1714; he was also responsible for two English translations of works on ancient Germany and civil and historical architecture, as well as for editing *The German Spy* in which he describes his running of the Hamburg opera. Lediard was married to Helena (*d.* in or after 1744), about whom further details are unknown; the couple had five children. Early in 1743 Lediard resigned his appointment as surveyor of the bridge, and died shortly afterwards, in June 1743. He was succeeded in his office by his son Thomas, who was the author of *A Charge Delivered to the Grand Jury* (1754) and who died at Hamburg on 15 December 1759.

J. K. LAUGHTON, *rev.* ALEXANDER DU TOIT

Sources W. A. Lediard, *Genealogical information relating to the family of Lediard* (1957), 100 • *GM*, 1st ser., 12 (1742), 275, 385 • *GM*, 1st ser., 13 (1743), 337 • D. E. Baker, *Biographia dramatica, or, A companion to the playhouse*, rev. I. Reed, new edn, rev. S. Jones, 1 (1812), 447 • T. Lediard, *The German spy* (1738), 96–8 • *N&Q*, 3rd ser., 8 (1865), 351 • will of Thomas Lediard, PRO, PROB 20 • will of Elizabeth Lediard (sister), PRO, PROB 11/212, fols. 2r–3r

Archives BL, Birch, Sloane MSS

Likenesses C. Fritsch, line engraving, pubd 1726 (after J. S. Wahl), BM • line engraving, 1735, BM, NPG

Ledingham, Sir John Charles Grant (1875–1944), bacteriologist, was born on 19 May 1875 at Boyndie, Banffshire, the sixth child of the Revd James Ledingham, minister of Boyndie, and his wife, Isabella, daughter of the Revd James Gardiner, minister of Rathven. He was educated at Boyndie public school, Banff Academy, and the University of Aberdeen, where he distinguished himself in both classics and science. In 1895 he graduated MA with first-class honours in mathematics and natural philosophy. His ambition was to enter the Indian Civil Service, but he failed the examination.

Ledingham proceeded BSc in 1900 and DSc in 1910. He graduated MB ChB with honours in 1902, and with the Anderson travelling scholarship he went to Leipzig in the same year to study pathology under Marchand. After a year in the pathology department at Aberdeen University he went in 1904 to continue his bacteriological and immunological studies at the London Hospital. In 1905 Ledingham began his long association with the Lister Institute when he was appointed assistant bacteriologist in the serum department at Elstree. In 1906 he transferred to the main institute in London. He became chief bacteriologist in 1909, succeeding George Dean, and retained this post after he became director of the institute in January 1931. He married in 1913 Barbara, daughter of David Fowler, superintendent of the Banffshire Mental Hospital at Boyndie; they had one son and one daughter.

During the First World War Ledingham was for a time in charge of the bacteriological department of King George Hospital, Waterloo. He was then appointed a member of the medical advisory committee in the Mediterranean area in 1915, and in 1917 he became consulting bacteriologist to the forces in Mesopotamia. He was appointed CMG for his services in the following year.

In 1920 Ledingham took part in establishing the national collection of type cultures, acting as its secretary for the next ten years. Much of his time was spent on committee work, in particular for the Medical Research Council, the Local Government Board, the Ministry of Health, the London county council, the National Radium Commission, the British empire cancer campaign, and the bureau of hygiene. He was chairman of the tropical diseases committee of the Royal Society, and of the tropical committee of the Medical Research Council (1936). After the outbreak of the Second World War he served on several committees, one of which was concerned with the problem of war wounds.

In addition to his authorship of scientific papers, Ledingham contributed a number of reviews of subjects within his field. He was one of the team of contributors to the treatise on diphtheria published by the Medical Research Council in 1923. With Paul Fildes he was an associate editor of the council's *System of Bacteriology* (1929–31) to which he contributed the chapters on natural immunity, tularaemia, and production of active immunity; he also collaborated with William Ewart Gye in an introductory survey to the volume on viruses and virus diseases. He delivered the Harben lectures before the Royal Institute of Public Health in 1924 and the Herter lectures at Johns Hopkins University in 1934. He was a member of the Medical Research Council (1934–8) and president of the second International Congress of Microbiology in London in 1936.

Ledingham was elected FRS in 1921, FRCP (London) in 1924, and was knighted in 1937 for his contributions to science. In 1920 he was given the title of professor of bacteriology in the University of London and that of emeritus professor in 1942. After retiring from the Lister Institute in 1943 he continued his researches in the laboratories of the Imperial Cancer Research Fund at Mill Hill until he died at the Hendon Cottage Hospital, London, on 4 October 1944, after a short illness.

Ledingham's contributions to science show evidence of wide interests. They include studies in bacteriology, pathology, haematology, immunology, and research into viruses. Some 130 papers were published under his name or in collaboration with others between 1920 and 1943. His first important contribution, with Marchand, was a report of an obscure case of kala-azar. This proved the existence of the disease in China. He also produced studies on phagocytosis which appeared between 1908 and 1912. By the outbreak of war in 1914 he had made a comprehensive study of the role of the carrier in the spread of typhoid fever, and in 1912 he joined with J. A. Arkwright in writing the monograph, *The Carrier Problem in Infectious Diseases*. The pathogenesis of blood diseases was a field in which Ledingham had always been interested. He felt it had been dominated by morphological studies for too long. He was convinced of the need for experimental research into these obscure conditions. Several of his papers illustrate this belief.

During the last twenty years of his life Ledingham's chief interest was in the virus diseases. His work on the elementary bodies of vaccinia and fowl-pox supported the belief that the elementary body was the infecting agent. In 1923 he published his observations on the histology of the experimental lesions of tularaemia and of its serological diagnosis in humans. In 1935 he collaborated with Gye in research on the nature of the filterable tumour-exciting agent in fowl sarcoma.

Ledingham was keenly interested in the application of knowledge obtained in the laboratory to preventive medicine. He held strong views on the provision of clean and safe milk, and on the suppression of diphtheria by the active immunization of young children. Although shy in manner, laconic in speech, and sparing in praise, he encouraged his staff by his example and proved an able administrator. He derived his main interests outside work from his love of the countryside.

HUGH CLEGG, *rev.* TIM O'NEILL

Sources *The Lancet* (21 Oct 1944), 550–51 • *BMJ* (14 Oct 1944), 514–5 • Munk, *Roll* • *Journal of Pathology and Bacteriology*, 58 (1946) • S. P. Bedson, *Obits. FRS*, 5 (1945–8), 325–40

Likenesses A. Christie, portrait, 1921, RS • W. Stoneman, photograph, 1926, NPG • A. Christie, oils, Lister Institute, Elstree, Hertfordshire

Wealth at death £10,665 11*s*. 10*d*.: probate, 21 Nov 1944, *CGPLA Eng. & Wales*

Ledred [Lederede], **Richard** (*c*.1275–1360?), bishop of Ossory, may have come from Somerset, for in 1339 there was a certain Thomas of Ledrede 'of the county of Somerset', probably a kinsman, in his service. The suggestion that Ledred indicates Leatherhead in Surrey as his place of origin rests on supposition only. His date of birth is equally uncertain, but in 1356 the bishop was described as a centenarian, doubtless an exaggeration. Taking this observation with the date of his ordination as deacon, he was born probably about 1275.

Ledred entered the Franciscan order before being ordained deacon in 1297 by Robert Winchelsey, archbishop of Canterbury. For the next twenty years he disappears from sight. The Kilkenny annalist, Friar Clyn, observed that he had been at Avignon at the time of his appointment to the see of Ossory. The *Narrative of the Proceedings Against Dame Alice Kyteler*, composed almost certainly by Ledred himself, affirms that he was 'nurtured, educated and promoted' at the Holy See. He probably pursued his studies either at the *studium generale* of the Franciscan order at Avignon, or at the university founded there by Boniface VIII in 1303. The provision of 24 April 1317 appointing Ledred bishop of Ossory noted that his virtues included clean living and knowledge of letters, suggesting that he had come to the pope's attention because of his learning and zeal.

The Avignon connection is significant for two reasons. Ledred was the first bishop of Ossory to be provided under recent papal legislation. Unlike his elected predecessors, as often as not officials in the royal administration, Ledred put the interests of the church first. In his numerous conflicts with the king's ministers it was at Avignon that he sought and found refuge in periods of exile. More significantly, his presence in Avignon about the time of the suppression of the templars on charges of sorcery, heresy, and the worship of demons clearly made a deep impression on him. His appointment to the see of Ossory occurred only three years after the execution of Jacques de Molay, the grand master of the order of the Temple.

Ledred wasted no time in clarifying his priorities. Summoning a diocesan synod on 6 October 1317, he decreed that anyone suspecting the existence of heresy was to report to him within one month. Secular interference with church property, or defamation of churchmen, would result in immediate excommunication. Anyone presumptuous enough to do violence to the bishop or impede his jurisdiction would not receive a church burial but 'rather have his body cast upon a dunghill' (Gwynn, 57). By August 1320, to judge from a letter sent by the pope to the justiciar, no doubt based on complaints made by Ledred, there already existed serious conflicts between royal officials and the new bishop.

But it was Ledred's involvement in the trial of Alice Kyteler in 1324 on charges of sorcery and heresy that precipitated the most serious conflict in his tumultuous career. Alice was descended from a wealthy merchant family in Kilkenny, where the episcopal see was located. By virtue of her wealth and four marriages she had powerful political allies in both the palatinate of Kilkenny and the royal administration in Dublin. The occasion of the trial was the accusation by her stepchildren that they had been disinherited by Alice and her son, William Outlaw. It was alleged that she had acquired her wealth by disposing of three husbands by means of sorcery, and was in the process of dispatching the fourth in the same way. Given his predisposition to suspect heresy, which he associated with sorcery, Ledred transformed an essentially local dispute into a *cause célèbre*. He was bitterly opposed by the seneschal of the palatinate, Sir Arnold Poer, a relative of Alice's fourth husband, who imprisoned him in Kilkenny

Castle for seventeen days, and obstructed by the chancellor of Ireland, Roger Outlaw, another relative. Driven by his conviction that he had uncovered 'a diabolical nest' of heretics, Ledred in the end triumphed over his influential opponents, having appealed over their heads to the justiciar in a parliament assembled in Dublin in May 1324. His principal ploy, in this as in subsequent confrontations with authority, was to accuse his opponents of offering protection to heretics. Although Alice was forced to flee to England, he succeeded in having some of her alleged followers burnt at the stake, while others were flogged through the streets of Kilkenny.

Ledred pursued Sir Arnold Poer relentlessly, to the extent of making common cause with his enemies in a baronial war in 1327–8. The bishop had to clear himself of charges that he had encouraged men to violate the king's peace and foment attacks on Sir Arnold in parliament in 1328. Perhaps in response to these accusations he petitioned the king in the same year, accusing Sir Arnold of protecting heretics, treating the jurisdiction of the church and its sacraments with contempt, and ravaging clerical property. These serious charges were sufficient to coerce the Irish council into imprisoning Sir Arnold in Dublin Castle, where he died excommunicate in the following year without rite of burial.

Ledred's high-handed methods and liberal use of the charge of heresy were not calculated to win him friends in high places. Two powerful enemies, Roger Outlaw, the chancellor, accused of aiding heresy, and Alexander Bicknor, archbishop of Dublin, whom Ledred suspected of attempting to murder him, combined to discredit the bishop, with the result that he fled to Avignon in 1329, having failed to answer charges when summoned before the king's council. In spite of his restoration to royal favour in May 1331, and subsequent commands to the justiciar in 1339, Ledred was afraid to return to Ireland. Even after the death of Outlaw in 1341 Bicknor continued to obstruct him. Eventually, on 10 April 1347, Pope Clement VI exempted the diocese of Ossory from the metropolitan jurisdiction of the archbishop of Dublin, and commanded the archbishop of Cashel to investigate Ledred's claims that Bicknor was 'a notorious fosterer of heretics'.

But even Bicknor's death in 1349 did not bring peace. Ledred refused to allow a subsidy to be levied on the clergy of his diocese in 1351, so once again the temporalities of the see were resumed into the king's hand. Opposition to him continued to simmer. In 1356 John Thoresby, archbishop of York, wrote to the king expressing the desire of the clergy and people of Ireland to have Ledred removed because of his abuse of power and bouts of insanity brought on by extreme age.

Ledred's career was marked by an obsessive preoccupation with sorcery and heresy. There can be little doubt that, convinced he had uncovered a demonic conspiracy against Christian society, he introduced the demonic and heretical elements into the Kyteler inquiry. Thus an otherwise unremarkable case of sorcery marks a significant development of the witch stereotype in Europe, as Norman Cohn has rightly observed. His literary testament, apart from the *Narrative*, is exemplified by the episcopal register, the Red Book of Ossory, which contains some sixty lyrics, principally in Latin, written by the bishop for the vicars and clerks of the cathedral, so that 'their throats and mouths, consecrated to God, may not be polluted by songs which are lewd, secular, and associated with revelry' (Greene, iii–iv). The register also contains a two-page account of the exile of Thomas Becket, which suggests that Ledred saw himself cast in the role of a martyr in defence of the church. He died probably in 1360. His tomb, bearing the effigy of the only Franciscan bishop of Ossory, is located in St Canice's Cathedral, Kilkenny.

C. A. EMPEY

Sources F. de Ledrede, *A contemporary narrative of the proceedings against Dame Alice Kyteler*, ed. T. Wright, CS, 24 (1843) • *The annals of Ireland by Friar John Clyn and Thady Dowling: together with the annals of Ross*, ed. R. Butler, Irish Archaeological Society (1849) • G. O. Sayles, ed., *Documents on the affairs of Ireland before the king's council*, IMC (1979) • J. Raine, ed., *Historical papers and letters from the northern registers*, Rolls Series, 61 (1873) • N. Cohn, *Europe's inner demons*, rev. edn (1993) • A. Neary, 'The origins and character of the Kilkenny witchcraft case of 1324', *Proceedings of the Royal Irish Academy*, 83C (1983), 333–50 • A. Neary, 'Richard Ledrede: English Franciscan and bishop of Ossory, 1317–*c*.1360', *Journal of the Butler Society*, 2 (1984), 273–81 • R. L. Greene, ed., *The lyrics of the Red Book of Ossory* (1974) • The Red Book of Ossory, Representative Church Body Library, Dublin • A. Gwynn, ed., 'Provincial and diocesan decrees of the diocese of Dublin during the Anglo-Norman period', *Archivium Hibernicum*, 11 (1944), 31–117

Archives Representative Church Body Library, Dublin, Red Book of Ossory

Likenesses effigy, St Canice's Cathedral, Kilkenny

Le Druillenec, Harold Osmond (1911–1985), schoolmaster and concentration camp survivor, was born in the parish of St Ouen, Jersey, on 5 August 1911, the youngest of nine children of Vincent Le Druillenec, farm labourer, and his wife, Sainte-Françoise, *née* Sangan. His parents were originally from Brittany. Le Druillenec attended the local elementary school, Les Landes, from which he won a scholarship to Victoria College, Jersey, a public school. He completed his education at St Luke's College, Exeter, and commenced teaching in 1931 at New Street School, St Helier, Jersey. He was a popular and successful schoolmaster. He married Phyllis May Le Rossignol (*b*. 1909/10), daughter of Percy Alfred Le Rossignol, market gardener, of the parish of St Helier, Jersey, on 7 August 1937, and their only daughter, Mary, was born a year later.

The scarcity of food rations after the German occupation of Jersey in 1940 brought Le Druillenec into closer contact with his sister, Mrs Louisa Gould, who owned a small general shop in the remote parish of St Ouen and who was able to provide useful supplements to the meagre rations, in the form of local produce. This close contact was to bring disaster for them both. The German labour organization had brought into the island a large number of Russian prisoners to use as slave labour on the construction of fortifications. These unfortunate men lived in prison camps in various parts of the island and were seen by the civilian population to be badly treated and near starvation. One of these, Feodor Burrij, escaped from a working party at a quarry in St Ouen, and Mrs

Gould, who had recently received news that her elder son had been killed in action in 1941 while serving with the Royal Navy, took this young man into her home. While he was there, in hiding, Le Druillenec supplied him with a few necessities, such as socks, and helped him to learn English.

When Burrij had been concealed by Mrs Gould for about eighteen months, in May 1944, she was arrested by the occupying forces for retaining a radio receiver, against their orders. Burrij was spirited away to the home of another sister, Mrs Ivy Forster, but sufficient evidence was found to implicate all three, and each was sentenced by a court martial to three months' imprisonment, to be served in France. Mrs Forster was ill in the general hospital and, with the collusion of a medical intern, was found to be unfit to travel, but Mrs Gould and Le Druillenec were deported. St Malo was in ruins after allied bombardment, and while they were imprisoned in Rennes the gaol was hit by allied air raiders. Another member of their group managed to escape, but Mrs Gould and Le Druillenec were transported by separate trains, in cattle trucks, to Germany. The trains were delayed constantly by allied action, and at Belfort the brother and sister were able to shout a greeting as one train drew abreast of the other. This was their last meeting, as Mrs Gould was taken to Ravensbrück concentration camp, where she died in the gas chamber in 1945. Le Druillenec was taken to Neunegamme, a clearing centre for labour camps, and then, after a period making boathooks in Wilhelmshaven, was sent to Belsen, where he was found in the last stages of emaciation by the British liberating forces.

After prolonged hospital treatment, Le Druillenec recovered. He gave evidence at the Nuremburg war crimes trials and, in 1945, was given the honour of introducing the king's Christmas day broadcast. He said:

> At this very hour last year I, together with thousands of others, was standing on the parade ground of a German concentration camp; we had stood there for five hours at a temperature of twenty degrees below zero. When we entered that camp the German Commandant told us: 'You are entering a new world in which you will have no contact with the world outside. If you have wives and children forget them. You will never see them again!' For nearly all my comrades in that camp and for untold thousands who passed through the gates before us, those words were only too true. (private information)

Returning to Jersey after his recovery, Le Druillenec was appointed headmaster of St John's School, which combined, at that time, a village primary school with a collective secondary unit for the north-western parishes of the island. He filled this post until his retirement in 1971. In recognition of his wartime experiences, he was awarded the French médaille de la résistance, and in 1965 he was presented with a gold watch by the Russian government and invited to Moscow, with other Jerseymen who had helped escaped Russians, to meet the men whom they had helped. Upon his retirement he was a made OBE in recognition of his services to education. He returned to normal health after his release from imprisonment but the effect of his experiences remained. He died of heart failure at Overdale Hospital, St Helier, Jersey, on 10 February 1985. He was survived by his wife and daughter.

F. L. M. Corbet

Sources personal knowledge (2004) • private information (2004) • *Jersey Evening Post* (13 April 1995) • F. L. M. Corbet and others, *A biographical dictionary of Jersey*, [2] (1998) • b. cert. • m. cert. • d. cert.

Wealth at death residence and personalty to widow

Ledward, Gilbert (**1888–1960**), sculptor, was born on 23 January 1888 in Chelsea, the third child of the sculptor **Richard Arthur Ledward** (1857–1890) and his wife, Mary Jane Wood, descendant of a long line of Staffordshire master potters and figure makers. Richard Ledward was born at Burslem, Staffordshire, the son of Richard Perry Ledward, of the firm Pinder, Bowne & Co. of Burslem. He was employed as a modeller by that firm, and studied at the Burslem school of art; on obtaining a national scholarship he continued his studies at the national art school in South Kensington. There he obtained a gold medal for modelling from the life, and was appointed a master of modelling. He subsequently became modelling master at the Westminster and Blackheath schools of art. He exhibited at the Royal Academy from 1882 onwards, and his *A Young Mother* was favourably received. He made several good busts including one of W. E. Gladstone. Richard Ledward lived in Chelsea; he died there on 28 October 1890 and was buried at Perivale church, near Ealing. In 1883 he had married Mary Jane Wood, with whom he had four children, including Gilbert Ledward. Gilbert went to school at St Mark's College, Chelsea, leaving in 1901 when his widowed mother decided to take her five children to live in Germany. By 1905 Ledward was back in London starting full-time training as a sculptor at the Royal College of Art, where he studied under Edouard Lantéri. His fellow students included Charles Sargeant Jagger, Charles Wheeler, and William McMillan. They often worked directly from the nude, and their training prioritized modelling over carving. This generation was to occupy a transitory place between the late nineteenth-century New Sculptors and the twentieth-century modernists such as Henry Moore and Barbara Hepworth.

On 29 November 1910 Ledward went on to the Royal Academy Schools. In 1911 he married Margery Beatrix Cheesman (*d.* 1960); they had two daughters and one son. In 1913 he completed his first important commission, a stone *Calvary* at Bourton on the Water, Gloucestershire. In the same year he won the double honour of the academy travelling studentship and gold medal and the first Rome scholarship in sculpture. He travelled throughout Italy during the summer of 1914. Sketchbooks from this time, now held at the Royal Academy of Arts, indicate the works that appealed to and inspired him.

The outbreak of war brought Ledward's travels to an end, but 1917 found him back in Italy, on the front, serving as a lieutenant with the Royal Garrison Artillery. He was called home in April 1918 and seconded to the Ministry of Information as an official war artist. In this capacity he produced plaster reliefs for the Imperial War Museum which are typical of the dramatic compositions of soldiers in action surrounded by the accoutrements of battle that were developed in later memorial projects, notably at Harrogate in 1921 and Blackpool in 1923. Other war memorial commissions included Stockport, Abergavenny, Stonyhurst, and his best-known work, the guards division memorial in St James's Park, London (1926). For the Imperial War Graves Commission he sculpted two great lions for the *Memorial to the Missing*, Ploegsteert, Belgium. From 1927 to 1929 he was professor of sculpture at the Royal College of Art. From this point on his practice moved away from modelling monuments in bronze towards direct stone carving. Works exhibited at the Royal Academy at this time indicating this shift include *The Sunflower*, a life-size mother and child, in Glasgow Art Gallery and Museum; and *Monolith*, purchased for the Tate Gallery under the Chantrey bequest. In 1934 he founded the firm Sculptured Memorials and Headstones which advocated improvements in the design and carving of memorials and headstones in English churchyards and encouraged the use of local stones. Eric Gill and Sir Edwin Lutyens were among the firm's many distinguished supporters.

In 1932 Ledward was elected an associate of the Royal Academy and in 1937 became Royal Academician. Contemporaries regarded him as loyal to the aims and values of Burlington House and outspoken in his defence of academic traditions yet ready to praise the best in modern work. His adaptability made him a popular choice for a wide variety of post-war commissions. His many portrait busts include those of Bishop De Labilliere (1944), Rachel Gurney (1945), and Admiral Sir Martin Dunbar-Nasmith VC (1947). Other works that attracted considerable interest were his memorial to the Submarine Service, commandos, and airborne forces (1948) in the cloister of Westminster Abbey, the bronze figures of St Nicholas and St Christopher for the Hospital for Sick Children, Great Ormond Street (1952), the Sloane Square fountain (1953), and the great seal of the realm and the five-shilling piece for the coronation of Elizabeth II (1953). His last work, finished just before his death, was a great stone frieze, *Vision and Imagination*, above the entrance to Barclays Bank in Old Broad Street, London. Before starting this carving he toured Africa extensively, filling many sketchbooks with studies from which the final work derived.

In 1954–6 Ledward was president of the Royal Society of British Sculptors, and in 1956–7 a trustee of the Royal Academy. In 1956 he was appointed OBE.

Ledward's career developed alongside dramatic changes in the sculptor's profession. Trained in the conventions of the late nineteenth century he adhered to representational values grounded in realism that remained suited to public commemorative projects. His compositional strengths, particularly evident in his relief work, distinguish his First World War memorials from many of the more predictable solutions adopted by his contemporaries. An appreciation of the role of sculpture in public space, be it a city square or a country graveyard, rather than a gallery environment was at the heart of his practice. Never as unconventional as Gill or as radical as Jagger he represented the sculptural establishment with grace, appreciating that which was admirable in both the generations that preceded and succeeded him. An early bronze figure, *Awakening*, located in a garden on the Chelsea Embankment, very near to the house where he was born, is an unassuming yet enduring city landmark. Ledward died at 31 Queen's Gate, London, on 21 June 1960.

CATHERINE MORIARTY

Sources *DNB* · *Gilbert Ledward: drawing for sculpture: a centenary tribute* (1988) · P. Skipwith, 'Gilbert Ledward and the guards' division memorial', *Apollo*, 127 (1988), 22–6 · *CGPLA Eng. & Wales* (1960) · C. Moriarty, *The sculpture of Ledward Gilbert* (2003)

Archives Henry Moore Institute, Leeds, collection [of studies, photographs, press cuttings, and photocopy of typescript of his autobiography] · IWM · RA, sketchbooks | V&A, questionnaire completed for Kineton Parkes

Likenesses F. Marriott, drawing, priv. coll. · photographs, repro. in *Gilbert Ledward*

Wealth at death £41,617 12*s*. 2*d*.: probate, 21 Dec 1960, *CGPLA Eng. & Wales* · £814 14*s*. 7*d*.—Richard Arthur Ledward: administration, 23 Feb 1891, *CGPLA Eng. & Wales*

Ledward, Richard Arthur (1857–1890). *See under* Ledward, Gilbert (1888–1960).

Ledwich, Edward (1739–1823), antiquary, was born in Nicholas Street, Dublin, on 29 March 1739, the son of John Ledwich, a merchant. He was educated in the diocesan school, and then at Trinity College, Dublin, which he entered on 22 November 1755. He graduated BA in 1760 and LLB in 1763. He took holy orders, and was appointed vicar-general of Dromore, but, wishing to see the world, he obtained the chaplaincy of the 55th foot and spent time in America. Subsequently he was appointed to a curacy in the parishes of Coombe and Harnham, near Salisbury, Wiltshire, where he wrote a number of antiquarian works, including *Antiquitates Sarisburienses* (1771). In 1772 he exchanged his regimental chaplaincy for the living of Aghaboe, Queen's county, in 1772, and resided in Oldglas, Durrow, until his move to Dublin in 1790 or 1791. He was married but his wife's identity is unknown.

In 1778 Ledwich became involved in the Hibernian Antiquarian Society, which was set up by William Burton (later Burton-Conyngham), teller of the Irish exchequer, and Charles Vallancey, an officer of the engineers in Ireland. Ledwich's first publications on Irish antiquities appeared in Vallancey's journal, *Collectanea de Rebus Hibernicis*, in 1781, and included 'An essay on the study of Irish antiquities' and 'The history and antiquities of Irishtown and Kilkenny from original records and authentic documents'. These caused immediate controversy, because they challenged the dominant theories of Vallancey about Irish origins and early Irish society. While Vallancey maintained that the Phoenicians had colonized Ireland and ushered in a literate civilization long before the arrival of Christianity, Ledwich asserted a Scandinavian origin for the Irish, who, he alleged, had begun to experience the civilizing process only following the twelfth-century Anglo-Norman colonization, this process being far from complete. The disagreement quickly developed into a bitter feud and resulted in the breakup of the Hibernian Antiquarian Society in 1783. No longer allowed to write for

Vallancey's journal, Ledwich published further historical essays on religion in *Archaeologia* in 1785 and 1787. He also contributed essays on Irish music and the Irish harp to Joseph Cooper Walker's *Historical Memoirs of the Irish Bards* (1786).

Ledwich pursued all of these themes further in his influential *Antiquities of Ireland* (1790). This contained descriptions and none-too-accurate engravings of a number of Irish monuments, interspersed with short chapters which continued his dispute with Vallancey. It is noteworthy mainly for his rejection of the existence of St Patrick, who was accepted by all the churches as the foremost Christian missionary to Ireland. He admitted privately that he hoped to increase sales by this stunt. His scepticism, often seen as an Enlightenment trait and proclaimed by him as such, was always opportunistic and rarely consistent. He rejected Irish manuscripts as a historical source and yet used English translations of them regularly. He deplored what he saw as the romantic histories of Charles O'Conor and Charles Vallancey, and yet his own work is shot through with speculation and conjecture. For Ledwich antiquarianism was chiefly a political rather than a scholarly endeavour, another field on which contemporary issues, especially the Catholic question, were to be contested. His polemical writing was part of the conservative backlash against any further liberalization of the penal laws against Catholics and dissenters. Ledwich published an expanded edition of *Antiquities of Ireland* in 1804. He was a fellow of the Society of Antiquaries and a member of the Royal Irish Academy. He died at 19 York Street, Dublin, on 8 August 1823. CLARE O'HALLORAN

Sources E. Ledwich, letters to Joseph Cooper Walker, TCD, MS 1461, 1–7 • W. D. Love, 'The Hibernian Antiquarian Society', *Studies*, 51 (1962), 419–31 • *DNB* • J. Warburton, J. Whitelaw, and R. Walsh, *History of the city of Dublin*, 2 vols. (1818), 920 • D. MacCartney, 'The writing of history in Ireland, 1800–30', *Irish Historical Studies*, 10 (1956–7), 347–62 • Nichols, *Illustrations*, 7.816–56 [letters from Edward Ledwich to Thomas Percy and Richard Gough] • Burtchaell & Sadleir, *Alum. Dubl.*

Archives NL Ire., family corresp. and MSS | TCD, letters to Joseph Cooper Walker, MS 1461 (1–7)

Likenesses Shea, stipple (aged seventy-eight; after Cullen), NPG

Ledwich, Thomas Hawkesworth (*bap.* 1821, *d.* 1858), anatomist and surgeon, was the son of Edward Ledwich, an attorney who practised in Waterford, and his wife, Catharine Eleanor Hawkesworth. He was baptized on 11 October 1821 at St Mary's, Pembroke, where his family was living temporarily. His grandfather was Edward *Ledwich (1739–1823), the Irish antiquary. From early youth Thomas suffered from heart disease and asthma, and his health was always bad. He was educated at Waterford, and after having been apprenticed for some time to a medical practitioner there he studied medicine in Dublin. He became a fellow of the Royal College of Surgeons in Ireland in 1845, and immediately devoted himself to teaching and to anatomical research. In 1847 he became lecturer on anatomy at a private school of medicine in Dublin, then known as the Original School of Medicine, Peter Street, and he remained connected with the school until his death.

Ledwich was very popular and successful as a teacher, and was the most active and prominent man in his school. In lecturing he was remarkable for the clearness of his exposition and the vividness of his delivery. He wrote a number of minor contributions to surgical literature, of which the most noticeable were those in which he explained the views of the French school with reference to the drainage of wounds. He was also an industrious reviewer. He was a good pathologist, and he formed a valuable pathological museum. His great work, however, was a treatise entitled *The Anatomy of the Human Body*, which he wrote in conjunction with his brother Edward and published in 1852. This book did not contain any remarkable discoveries or new views, but it was a sound and trustworthy compendium of anatomy, and for many years it was a favourite textbook for students.

In July 1858 Ledwich's rapidly rising reputation was recognized by his appointment to the post of surgeon to the Meath Hospital, Dublin, in succession to Sir Philip Crampton. Not long before his death Ledwich married Isabella, daughter of Robert Murray of Dublin. On 29 September 1858 Ledwich died rather suddenly of pulmonary apoplexy at his home in York Street, Dublin, and was buried in the Mount Jerome cemetery. The Original School of Medicine changed its name to the Ledwich school of medicine in his honour shortly after he died. It retained the name until its amalgamation in 1887 with the school of the College of Surgeons.

CONOLLY NORMAN, *rev.* MICHAEL BEVAN

Sources C. A. Cameron, *History of the Royal College of Surgeons in Ireland* (1886) • [L. H. Ormsby], *Medical history of the Meath Hospital and County Dublin Infirmary* (1888) • *IGI*

Ledwidge, Francis Edward (1887–1917), poet, was born on 19 August 1887 at Janeville, Slane, co. Meath, Ireland, the eighth of the nine children of Patrick Ledwidge, an itinerant farm labourer (*d.* 1892), and his wife, Anne Lynch (1853/4–1926), a native of Slane. Of German origin, the name Ledwidge (also Ledwich, Ledwith) came to co. Meath with the Anglo-Normans. Patrick Ledwidge's premature death forced his wife and children out to work. Aged thirteen, Francis (Frank) Ledwidge left Slane national school to become a farmer's boy at 7*s.* a week. Strongly built, with a sensuous face and striking brown eyes, Ledwidge educated himself and wrote poetry—sometimes on gates or fence posts. The poems reflect his passion for the Boyne valley. He also worked as a shop assistant, 'yard boy', road mender, copper miner, supervisor of roads. In 1910 he began to publish poems in the *Drogheda Independent*. His writing and a temporary job as secretary to the County Labour Unions (1913–14) gave him hopes of permanent white-collar work. Ledwidge had been a trade union activist since 1906 (he was sacked from the copper mine for organizing a strike). His politics were nationalist as well as left-wing. With his brother Joseph he founded the Slane branch of the Irish Volunteers (1914), which, like the broader movement, split on the conflict of loyalties produced by the First World War. Ledwidge opposed John Redmond's call for home-rulers to enlist, yet joined the 5th battalion, Royal Inniskilling Fusiliers (24 October

1914). His mixed motives may have included disappointment in love.

Ledwidge's patron, Lord Dunsany, although an officer in the Inniskillings, opposed his enlistment. In 1912 Ledwidge had sent poems to Dunsany, a Meath landowner and man of letters, who gave him money, literary advice, and the run of his library. He promoted Ledwidge's poetry in Dublin and London, and Ledwidge became acquainted with W. B. Yeats and Katharine Tynan. *Songs of the Fields* (1915) successfully appealed to the English taste for rural poetry and to expectations created by the Irish revival. Dunsany's preface says: 'I have looked for a poet amongst the Irish peasants because … there was in daily use a diction worthy of poetry … an imagination capable of dealing with the great and simple things.' A postscript mentions Ledwidge's enlistment. Ledwidge served as lance-corporal at Gallipoli and in Serbia. He injured his back in the retreat to Salonika (December 1915). Following leave in Ireland (May 1916) he was court-martialled for extending his stay and for expressing sympathy with the Easter rising. In December 1916 the army posted him to the western front. On 31 July 1917 he was killed by a shell at the third battle of Ypres. He was buried in Artillery Wood cemetery, Boesinghe, Belgium.

Ledwidge's posthumous *Songs of Peace* (1917) includes poems written on war service and a well-known elegy for Thomas MacDonagh, a poet-leader of the Easter rising. Dunsany edited *Last Songs* (1918) and *Complete Poems* (1924). A revised *Complete Poems* appeared in 1974. Seamus Heaney's elegy for Ledwidge (*Field Work*, 1979) dubs him 'our dead enigma'. Ledwidge felt the irony of being called a British soldier while Ireland's political status was unacknowledged, but he was less conscious of aesthetic contradictions. Phrases like 'this bee-sucked bough of woodbine' ('June') owe more to Keats than to local observation and speech. Nor did war fundamentally disturb Ledwidge's romantic vision, and therefore his work has faded from view along with the double glamour of 'peasant poet' and 'soldier poet'. Yet occasional intensity, powered by a history that recalls John Clare and anticipates Patrick Kavanagh, keeps Ledwidge alive. *Francis Ledwidge: Complete Poems* was published in 1974, and an edition of his *Selected Poems* appeared in 1993, with a foreword by Seamus Heaney. E. LONGLEY

Sources A. Curtayne, *Francis Ledwidge: a life of the poet (1887–1917)* (1972) · *The complete poems of Francis Ledwidge*, ed. A. Curtayne (1974) · M. Amory, *Lord Dunsany* (1972) · d. certs. of Patrick Ledwidge and Anne Ledwidge, General Register Office, Dublin · Inniskilling Fusiliers Museum, Enniskillen

Archives Ledwidge Museum, Slane, Ireland, corresp., MS poems, memorabilia | NL Ire., Dunsany MSS

Likenesses photograph, 1915, Hult. Arch. · photographs, repro. in Curtayne, *Francis Ledwidge* · photogravure, NPG

Ledyard, John (1751–1789), traveller, was born at Groton in Connecticut, USA, the eldest of six children of John Ledyard, master of a merchantman in the West India trade, and Abigail, daughter of Robert Hempsted. On her husband's early death at sea in 1762 at the age of thirty-five, Abigail Ledyard was poorly provided for and so she found a home with her father in Long Island, but soon married again. As a result young John Ledyard was brought up at Hartford, Connecticut, by his paternal grandfather, and on the latter's death he came under the guardianship of Thomas Seymour, in whose law office he worked for a time. From 1772 to 1773 he studied at Dartmouth College in Hanover, New Hampshire, training as a missionary to the Indians. He aspired unsuccessfully to become a divinity student, but early in 1773 he joined, as a sailor, a ship bound from New London to Gibraltar. At Gibraltar he enlisted in a British regiment, but on his captain's representations he was sent back to his ship, in which he returned to New London in August 1774. He was now determined to travel, and to that end made his way to New York, from where he worked his passage to Plymouth in England, and then walked to London, where he arrived destitute. He had some wealthy relatives, collaterally descended, it would appear, from his great-grandfather, but when he called on them he was met with a request for some proof of his story, which he was unable to provide. He therefore enlisted in the marines, and possibly after presenting himself to Captain Cook joined the *Resolution* as a corporal and in her sailed from Plymouth on 12 July 1776 on Cook's third voyage. On Cook's return to Unalaska in October 1778 Ledyard was sent across the island where he located a Russian settlement, returning to the *Resolution* with three Russian seamen.

During the voyage Ledyard kept a journal, which, on the return of the ships to England, was, with all other journals, lodged with the Admiralty, to prevent the official history of the expedition being forestalled. For two years longer Ledyard continued to serve as a marine, but in 1782, being sent out to North America, he took an opportunity of deserting ship and returned to his family at Hartford where he took up residence with his uncle and former guardian. He was pressed to publish an account of Cook's third voyage, but as his journal was still at the Admiralty, he wrote an account from memory, filling it in with extracts from an anonymous account published in London in 1781, now attributed to John Rickman. Ledyard's book was published in Hartford as *A Journal of Captain Cook's Last Voyage to the Pacific Ocean* (1783), and though it cannot rank with accounts transcribed from strictly contemporary journals, it is of value as the story of events from the point of view of a corporal of marines.

After this Ledyard visited New York and Philadelphia in a vain attempt to obtain support for a scheme to open up trade to the north-west coast of America. He imagined that the furs of the sea otter would find a ready and extremely profitable market at Canton (Guangzhou). He made his way to Cadiz in 1784 and thence to Lorient and Paris, in the hope of obtaining support for such a scheme in Europe. In Paris he was received by Thomas Jefferson, and at one time had agreed on a scheme of co-operation with (John) Paul Jones, the naval adventurer, who was then in American service in France. When the negotiations with Jones broke down, Ledyard went to London where he was engaged to travel to the north-west coast of

America in a British ship, from where he proposed to walk across the continent to Virginia, but after sailing, the ship was recalled and the plan abandoned. He then decided to walk across Siberia in the hope of finding a ship to take him to Nootka. Jefferson approved this plan and sought a passport for Ledyard from the Empress Catherine, but this was refused. Nevertheless, with money advanced him by Sir James Hall and the support of Sir Joseph Banks, Ledyard reached Copenhagen on 1 January 1787 and Stockholm at the end of the month. Unable to cross the Gulf of Bothnia owing to the mildness of the season, Ledyard walked round the head of the gulf, a distance of about 1500 miles. It was in the depth of winter, he had no companion, and made no special provision either for lodging or feeding. He arrived at St Petersburg about seven weeks later, having travelled from January to March 1787, at an average rate of 200 miles a week.

After having waited in vain for some time at St Petersburg for a passport, as Catherine was absent, Ledyard was allowed to proceed, leaving the Russian capital on 1 June 1787. Dr William Brown, a Scottish physician, accompanied him as far as Barnaul, and thence he made his way, principally—if not entirely—on foot, to Yakutsk, visiting Lake Baikal on the way. At Yakutsk, which he reached on 18 September, he was detained by the governor, who insisted that the season was too advanced for him to travel; this was probably a mere pretext at the instigation, it has been supposed, of the Russian American Company, who were jealous of an outsider visiting their trading stations. While waiting at Yakutsk he met Joseph Billings, whom he had formerly known on board the *Resolution*, and returned with him to Irkutsk. Here he was arrested on 24 February 1788 by an order from St Petersburg, and sent back to Moscow, where he was questioned and then expelled from Russia after being warned not to repeat his attempt. He drew on Banks for a small sum and so returned to London after an absence of seventeen months, deeply disappointed at the frustration of his journey when success was so near. Banks received him with great kindness and introduced him to the politician Henry Beaufoy, who proposed that he should undertake a journey of exploration in Africa, on behalf of the African Association, the scheme being, in general terms, that he should make his way to Cairo and then cross Africa in the direction of the Niger, examining the towns and countries on its banks, returning to England by way of any of the European settlements on the west coast of the continent. This Ledyard readily undertook, and on reaching Cairo he sought to join a caravan to continue his journey. When its departure was delayed he was 'transported with anger', being seized soon after with a pain 'occasioned by bile'. This and his attempted cure led to his death three days later. He died on 10 January 1789, unmarried, in Cairo, where he was buried.

J. K. LAUGHTON, *rev.* ANDREW C. F. DAVID

Sources J. Sparks, *Travels and adventures of John Ledyard*, 2nd edn (1834) • S. W. Crompton, 'Ledyard, John', *ANB* • *John Ledyard's journey through Russia and Siberia, 1787–1788: the journal and selected letters*, ed. S. D. Watrous (1966) • M. Holmes, *Captain James Cook: a bibliographical excursion* (1952) • H. B. Carter, *Sir Joseph Banks, 1743–1820* (1988)

Archives Dartmouth College, Hanover, New Hampshire, corresp. and papers • New York Historical Society, letters and documents • priv. coll., papers | Harvard U., Jared Sparks collection, MS no. 112

Lee. *See also* Lea, Leigh.

Lee. For this title name *see* individual entries under Lee; *see also* Lockhart, Sir James, of Lee, Lord Lee (1588/1599–1674).

Lee, Alfred Theophilus (1829–1883), Church of England clergyman, born on 28 June 1829 at The Elms, Bedhampton, Havant, was the youngest son of Sir John Theophilus Lee GCH, of Lauriston Hall, Torquay, and his wife, Sophia, youngest daughter of Major Lawlor of Greenwich. After attending a school at Woolwich, he entered Christ's College, Cambridge, where he was elected a scholar in 1851 and gained the Porteous gold medal for his essay 'The slavery of sin' in May 1853. He graduated BA in 1853 and MA in 1856. In 1853 he married Euphemia, daughter of Marriott Dalway of Bellahill, near Carrickfergus, co. Antrim.

Lee took holy orders in 1853, becoming successively curate of Houghton-le-Spring, Durham (1853–5), senior curate and lecturer of Tetbury, Gloucestershire (1855–6), publishing in 1857 a history of Tetbury, chaplain to the marquess of Donegal (1857), and vicar of Elson, Hampshire (1857). From 1858 until 1872 he was rector of Ahogill, co. Antrim, and published an account of the parish church of St Colonanell, Ahogill. He was rural dean of Antrim (1860–72), surrogate of the diocese of Down and Connor (1860–65), and chaplain to the duke of Abercorn (1866–8). He was proctor for the diocese of Down and Connor in the Irish national synod in 1869, to the general convention in 1870, and to the general synod in 1871. He was also clerical assessor to the bishops' diocesan courts in 1870, and editor of the reports of the general convention and general synod of the Church of Ireland from 1860 to 1871. He was honorary secretary to the church institution for the province of Armagh from 1860 to 1870, and to the Society for Promoting the Gospel for the diocese of Connor from 1860 to 1871.

Lee was an energetic propagandist for the established Church of Ireland, publishing pamphlets, sermons, and articles in support of its position. His *Facts Respecting the Present State of the Church in Ireland* (1863) reached a fifth edition in 1868. Honorary doctorates were conferred on him by Trinity College, Dublin (1866), and Oxford University (1867). After Irish disestablishment was carried, he produced a commentary on the 1869 Irish Church Act. He returned to England in 1871 and was appointed secretary to the Church Defence Institution (1871–4) and the Tithe Redemption Trust, in which capacities he organized the defence of the established church's interests in England and Wales against the activities of nonconformist pressure groups. Lee died at his home, Lauriston House, Grange Road, Ealing, on 19 July 1883, leaving a widow and several children.

GORDON GOODWIN, *rev.* M. C. CURTHOYS

Sources *The Times* (21 July 1883), 10 · Crockford (1883) · Venn, *Alum. Cant.* · Boase, *Mod. Eng. biog.*
Archives LPL, corresp. with A. C. Tait and related papers
Likenesses portrait, repro. in *Church Portrait Journal*, 1 (1876), 25
Wealth at death £3996 14*s.* 5*d.*: probate, 13 Aug 1883, *CGPLA Eng. & Wales*

Lee, Ann (1736–1784), religious leader in England and America, was born in Manchester on 29 February 1736 to John Lees (or Lee), a poor blacksmith, and his wife (perhaps named Betty), a 'strictly religious, and very pious woman'. Lee was baptized in Manchester collegiate church on 1 June 1742. The family lived at Toad Lane and included Lee's five brothers and two sisters. Lee had no formal schooling and soon went to work cutting fabrics. Even as a child she is supposed to have had religious manifestations. According to her followers she claimed that the lusts of the flesh signalled the depravity of human nature, and she supposedly admonished her mother for sleeping with her father.

On 5 January 1762 Lee married Abraham Standerin (or possibly Stanley or Standley). The couple had a daughter, Elizabeth, who died on 7 October 1766. It appears that they had three other children who also died in infancy. Perhaps as early as 1758 Lee began to associate with the religious visionaries James and Jane Wardley in Bolton. Their religious society was known as Shakers (later the United Society of Believers in Christ's Second Appearing) because in meetings for worship they sang, danced, trembled, and screeched as the spirit moved them. The sect also assembled in homes to discuss theological beliefs and proclaimed theirs the only true religion. This society, which was probably influenced by the Quakers and the French Camisards, included other members of Lee's family, principally her father, her brother William, and a Betty Lees, possibly her mother.

When the Shakers became increasingly vocal and began to disturb Manchester's Church of England congregations, several members, including Lee, were apprehended and in some cases incarcerated. Tradition has it that she was locked up for two weeks in a cramped stone cell and would have starved but for the surreptitious visits of the future Shaker leader James Whittaker. Whittaker secretly fed Lee a concoction of wine and milk through the stem of a pipe inserted into a keyhole. Persecuted by mobs that stoned her and a brother that beat her, Lee deprived herself of food and sleep. She avoided her husband's affections, crying and groaning day and night, which made her husband glad to leave her bed. Lee was said to have perspired blood and confounded ministers with her capacity to speak seventy-two languages. She claimed to experience many spiritual insights, including visions that she would bring the gospel to America.

Whether because of sacred visions, government persecution, religious differences, or economic opportunities, Lee, her husband, and several other Shakers left for America in 1774. After a stormy crossing the group arrived in New York and dispersed to make a hard living. Later accounts of these years report that Lee worked as a washerwoman and that her husband worked for a blacksmith on what is now Pearl Street in Manhattan. The couple experienced severe financial problems when her husband sickened, forcing Lee to spend all of her time nursing him back to good health. But when he recovered, the couple's sexual differences would once again surface. According to Shaker testimonies he had 'lost all sense of the gospel, and began, in a very ungodly manner, to oppose [Lee's] faith, and finally refused to do anything more for her, unless she would live in the flesh with him, and bear children' (*Testimonies*, 1888, 8). Lee eventually left the city and her husband, possibly about 1776, and moved to upstate New York where some of the other Shakers had taken up farming at a place called Niskeyuna (now Watervliet).

The Shakers at Niskeyuna sought spiritual perfection in their ecstatic practices and believed that Christ had returned to their church. As early as 1778 people commented on their unusual religious exercises that continued to include dancing and whirling. But for the most part Lee and her group remained secluded until 19 May 1780, when New Light Baptist Joseph Meacham decided to visit the Shakers in supposed fulfilment of Lee's prophecies. His 'confession' initiated a period of mass conversions. The success and notoriety brought Lee new problems. In 1780 she was imprisoned for her opposition to military service during the American War of Independence. After her release she and several other leaders embarked on a missionary journey around New England that lasted over two years. The Shakers continued to convert many and also experienced renewed persecutions, especially in the town of Harvard, Massachusetts. In part due to Shaker charity, the sect attracted many poor people, and crowds often formed to scare the Shakers out of town. Mobs attacked and even stripped Lee to make sure she was not a witch or a British spy parading in women's clothing. The group returned to Niskeyuna in September 1783 and continued their religious work from there. When her brother William died in July 1784, Lee supposedly predicted her own forthcoming death. She died on 8 September 1784.

Lee was illiterate and left no written account of her experiences or beliefs. Later generations collected earlier anecdotes and gave Lee a religious designation that she had not claimed for herself. Nineteenth-century Shakers developed a mystical theology that viewed Lee as a female second appearance of Christ. In 1835 Shakers exhumed her body, examined her relics, and re-interred her at the Watervliet common burial-ground. Despite attempts to bulldoze the cemetery in the 1970s, it still stands, near a baseball stadium. Notwithstanding her many fasts, Lee appears to have been a large woman, who had brown hair and blue eyes. Her supporters claimed that she looked majestic to all, but to them she 'possessed a degree of dignified beauty and heavenly love transcending that of mortals' (*Testimonies*, 1888, 268).

CARLA GERONA

Sources *Testimonies of the life, character, revelations, and doctrines of Mother Ann Lee, and the elders with her*, 2nd edn (1888) [repr. New York, 1975] · *Testimonies of the life, character, revelations, and doctrines of Mother Ann Lee, and the elders with her* (1816) · S. J. Stein, *The Shaker experience in America: a history of the United Society of Believers* (1992) ·

C. Garrett, *Spirit possession and popular religion: from the Camisards to the Shakers* (1987) • S. Marini, *Radical sects of revolutionary New England* (1982) • J. M. Humez, '"Ye are my epistles": the construction of Ann Lee imagery in early Shaker sacred literature', *Journal of Feminist Studies in Religion*, 8/1 (1992), 83–103 • B. S. Youngs, *The testimony of Christ's second appearing* (1808) • R. Rathbone, *Reasons offered for leaving the Shakers* (1800)
Archives NYPL, Shaker Museum and Library, Old Chatham New York Shaker collections • Western Reserve Historical Society, Cleveland, Ohio, Shaker collections • Winterthur Museum, Delaware, Shaker collections
Likenesses Milleson, wood-engraving, repro. in Stein, *Shaker experience*

Lee, Arthur Hamilton, Viscount Lee of Fareham (1868–1947), politician and patron of the arts, was born on 8 November 1868 at the rectory, Bridport, Dorset, the youngest of the two sons and three daughters of the rector, the Revd Melville Lauriston Lee (1821–1870) and his wife, Emily Winter (*d.* 1918), daughter of Thomas Dicker, banker, of Lewes, Sussex. Lee had an unhappy childhood. His father died when he was two and his mother gave him into the care of a Miss Paterson, a strict disciplinarian with a 'curiously warped character'. He felt from then, he related later, simply 'superfluous and not wanted' (*Good Innings*, 9–11). At eleven he won a classical scholarship to Cheltenham College (where he became a life member of the college council in 1911 and was president from 1917 to 1939). He then entered the Royal Military Academy, Woolwich, and in 1888 joined the Royal Artillery. In 1889 he volunteered for service in China. While stationed there he undertook a lengthy mission secretly to gather information on the Russian fortifications at Vladivostok and received a number of official commendations. In 1891 he was promoted adjutant and posted to the Isle of Wight. In 1893 he was accepted for the post of teaching professor of military history, strategy, and tactics at the Royal Military College, in Kingston, Ontario, Canada. He remained there until 1898 when he was appointed British military attaché with the American army in Cuba during the Spanish-American War. He was made an honorary 'rough rider' and became a close friend of Theodore Roosevelt, with whom he maintained a 'constant and intimate' correspondence (*Good Innings*, 92). In 1899 Lee was appointed military attaché at the British embassy in Washington with the rank of lieutenant-colonel. On 23 December that year he married Ruth (*d.* 1966), daughter of John Godfrey Moore, one of the leading bankers in New York. They had no children. John Moore died shortly before the marriage took place and Ruth was left a substantial inheritance.

With no prospect of seeing active service in the Second South African War (1899–1902), Lee felt that he had little chance of further advancement within the army. Through contacts within the Conservative Party he investigated the possibility of a political career, and with the backing of the chief agent, Captain Middleton, he was chosen as the Conservative candidate for the Fareham division of Hampshire. He was elected in the general election of 1900. He quickly rose within the government, becoming civil lord of the Admiralty in October 1903. But in February 1905 he made in his constituency what the Liberal leader, Campbell-Bannerman, described as a 'most improper' speech (*Good Innings*, 89), in which he implied that Britain might strike first against Germany in an effort to destroy its naval fleet. This, at a time of growing suspicion between the two countries, 'virtually assured the Germans that their worst fears … were justified' (Steinberg, 198). Despite this incautious statement, he remained in the post until the resignation of the Balfour government at the end of 1905, and then was opposition spokesman on naval affairs until 1914.

In the House of Commons Lee demonstrated his independent political tendencies. In 1911 he opposed the measure introducing payment for MPs, arguing that it would lead to a corrupt parliament and would violate the principle of gratuitous public service. He was one of nine Unionist MPs who returned their salary cheques to the paymaster-general. In the following year he promoted the Criminal Law Amendment (White Slave Traffic) Bill as a private, non-party measure. He introduced it in an eloquent speech on the second reading and steered it through the committee and report with persistence and skill, in spite of considerable opposition, but with support from Reginald McKenna, the home secretary. Lee's political independence led the new Conservative leader, Bonar Law, to comment that 'The trouble with you is that your wife has too much money' (*Good Innings*, 76). This contributed to an estrangement between the two men.

During the initial stages of the First World War Lee served as a staff colonel and was appointed by Kitchener to serve in France as his personal commissioner to observe and report on the efficiency of the much criticized Army Medical Services. Having viewed the 'futile slaughter' on the front, Lee became increasingly frustrated with the conduct of the war by the Asquith government, and discounting the 'hopeless' Bonar Law, Lee sought out his former political opponent David Lloyd George as the one member of the government who, he considered, had 'sufficient courage and dynamic energy … to insist upon things being done' (*Good Innings*, 140). In October 1915 Lloyd George invited Lee to join him at the Ministry of Munitions as parliamentary military secretary and later, in his *War Memoirs*, expressed high praise of Lee's untiring industry, great resource, and practical capacity. In July 1916 he was appointed KCB for these services and on Lloyd George's transfer to the War Office Lee became his personal secretary. Lee was also useful to Lloyd George as a link with some of the younger tories; he was a member of the Unionist war committee in 1916 which acted as a focus of back-bench opposition to the Asquith coalition. When Lloyd George became prime minister later in 1916 Lee expected some reward, but was initially passed over in the allocation of offices and had to accept Lloyd George's explanation that Bonar Law's right of veto over Conservatives in the new coalition cabinet had stalled his career (*Good Innings*, 185).

In February 1917 Lloyd George, as prime minister, made Lee director-general of food production. Up to this time nothing had been done to increase the home production of food. Lloyd George in his first cabinet had included a minister of food control, whose function was to organize and regulate distribution. Two months later he took the first effective step to stimulate home production by the appointment of Lee as director-general, nominally under R. E. Prothero, president of the Board of Agriculture and Fisheries, but with direct instructions from himself to make a success of his important task. Lee conducted this new office with vigour and enthusiasm and Prothero recorded that 'his organizing gift amounted to genius', though subsequent research has suggested that the achievements of Lee's department were exaggerated (Bennett, 203–4). The Corn Production (Amendment) Bill which Lee promoted in 1918 to enable him to carry out a further extensive conversion of grass land to arable met with serious opposition as had the Corn Production Act in the previous year. It was severely amended in the Lords, as Conservative members of the war cabinet sought to curtail the powers of the food production department. Failing to agree with Prothero on this and other matters of policy Lee resigned at the end of July 1918. The end of hostilities was, however, approaching and Lee had made a big personal contribution to safeguarding the nation from acute food shortage. Without his energy and determination it would have been impossible to obtain the labour and machinery necessary for the large addition to the tillage area which he achieved. In January 1918 he had been appointed GBE and just before he resigned his work was recognized by his elevation (on 9 July 1918) to the peerage as Baron Lee of Fareham.

In August 1919 Lloyd George included Lee in his cabinet as president of the Board of Agriculture and Fisheries, and he was sworn of the privy council. He successfully carried the act which converted his board into a ministry, but his Agriculture Act of 1920, to amend and continue the Corn Production Act of 1917 and making permanent a guaranteed price for home-grown wheat and oats, was found to be unworkable and both acts were repealed in the following year.

In February 1921, when Lee was transferred to the Admiralty as first lord, the Washington conference on reduction and limitation of armaments was imminent. In the preliminary discussions on the defence committee, in the cabinet, and at the Imperial Conference, Lee, supported by the weighty authority of the first sea lord (Lord Beatty) and his assistant, Sir A. E. M. Chatfield, had an important part which he played with such success that he was selected to go to Washington as second British delegate with Balfour. His many American connections (Theodore Roosevelt's son was assistant secretary to the navy) made him a welcome guest and he acquired a great reputation as the exponent of British views, although, through the opposition of France and the failure of American support, he did not succeed in his attempt to secure the abolition of submarine warfare. The only result of this issue was the ineffective Root 'humanizing' resolution. The service which Lee rendered to Balfour and his country at this conference was rewarded with promotion to a viscountcy (on 28 November 1922). He had resigned office with Lloyd George's cabinet in that year and never again took part in politics.

After losing office Lee chaired three royal commissions: on the civil service in India (1923–4; he was appointed GCSI in 1925), London cross river traffic (1926), and police powers and procedure (1928), as well as the radium commission for four years. He was also chairman of the committee on police pay and pensions (1925). He was promoted GCB in 1929.

In 1917 the Chequers Estate Act was passed by which Lee and his wife presented to a trust, for the use of successive prime ministers for ever, the mansion and estate of over 1000 acres in Buckinghamshire which they had acquired in 1909 and entirely restored and equipped with appropriate furniture, works of art, and historical relics. In January 1921 the trust was brought into operation and Lord and Lady Lee finally left the house with its entire contents. They provided an endowment of £100,000 for its upkeep.

Lee had acquired a remarkable knowledge of painting and the fine arts generally before and during his years of furnishing Chequers, and he now began a second collection with zest and a rare flair for finding and acquiring masterpieces of all schools and dates, in which he revealed his real love and understanding of craftsmanship. He was active in the art sales of the 1920s, fuelled by the need of many gentry families to sell off their art collections during the post-war depression, and made many astute purchases. He bequeathed the whole to the Courtauld Institute of Art, the original conception of which was due to his imagination and energy. His idea originated in 1927, when he began to formulate a proposal for the establishment of an institute for the study of the history of art and for training museum experts linked to a university. In the following year his proposal was favourably received by the authorities of London University. In 1929 Lee gained financial backing from the industrialist and art patron, Samuel Courtauld, and from the art dealer, Joseph Duveen. Further negotiations with the University of London led to the announcement, in October 1930, of the creation of the Courtauld Institute of Art, under the management of a committee chaired by Lee. At Lee's suggestion William Constable was made the director of the institute, which opened in October 1932 offering degrees in the history of art, the first such degree course in Britain.

Again with Courtauld, Lee persuaded London University to accept the transfer from Hamburg of the famous Warburg Institute and library for the study of the humanities. He personally arranged for its removal and housing in London as a loan to himself until it was refounded in 1944. In 1940 he presented his extensive and valuable collection of early silver and other objects of art to Hart House, Toronto, in memory of his early associations with Canada. In 1924 he was appointed a trustee of the Wallace Collection and in 1926 of the National Gallery, being chairman in 1931–2. He was also for some time chairman of the Royal Fine Arts Commission. After leaving public life Lee's business dealings in the art world often involved 'rows and disputes less important, though no less vindictively pursued, than those which had punctuated his public career' (*Good Innings*, 5). Despite this, and the persistent image of Lee as the 'minor, pushing, politician who gave Chequers to the nation presumably in return for a peerage' (Gilbert, 303), it remains that Lee and his wife made a significant, and lasting, contribution to the nation's assets through their gifts. Lee died on 21 July 1947 at his Gloucestershire home, Old Quarries, Avening. There were no children of the marriage and the peerage therefore became extinct. V. W. BADDELEY, *rev.* MARC BRODIE

Sources T. H. Middleton, *Food production in war* (1923) • personal knowledge (1959) • private information (1959) • *The Times* (22 July 1947) • *A good innings: the private papers of Viscount Lee of Fareham*, ed. A. Clark (1974) • B. B. Gilbert, *David Lloyd George: a political life*, 2: *The organizer of victory, 1912–1916* (1992) • S. Courtauld, *The Times* (25 July 1947), 7 • J. Steinberg, 'The German background to Anglo-German relations, 1905–1914', *British foreign policy under Sir Edward Grey*, ed. F. H. Hinsley (1977) • S. Scott, 'The history of the Courtauld Institute of Art, part one: the founding fathers', *Courtauld Institute of Art News*, 8 (1999), 4–5 • N. B. Harte, *The University of London, 1836–1986: an illustrated history* (1986) • Burke, *Peerage* • R. Williams, *Defending the empire: the conservative party and British defence policy, 1899–1915* (1991) • G. R. Searle, *Corruption in British politics, 1895–1930* (1987) • K. O. Morgan, *Consensus and disunity: the Lloyd George coalition government, 1918–1922* (1979) • L. M. Bennett, *British food policy during the First World War* (1985)

Archives Courtauld Inst., papers | HLRO, corresp. with David Lloyd George • HLRO, corresp. with Andrew Bonar Law • HLRO, corresp. with J. St L. Strachey • NL Scot., corresp. with F. S. Oliver • Tate collection, corresp. with Lord Clark, and papers concerning his legacy • Wellcome L., reports to Lord Kitchener relating to army medical arrangements

Likenesses O. Edis, photographs, 1917, NPG • P. A. de Laszlo, oils, *c.*1921, Courtauld Inst. • J. Gunn, oils, *c.*1934, Cheltenham College • G. C. Beresford, photographs, NPG • photograph, repro. in Scott, 'History of the Courtauld'

Wealth at death £183,064 3*s.* 10*d.*: probate, 2 Jan 1948, *CGPLA Eng. & Wales*

Lee, Arthur Stanley Gould (1894–1975), air force officer, was born on 31 August 1894 in the King's Head inn, Emery Lane, Boston, Lincolnshire, the only son of Arthur Lee, a licensed victualler who later became a building contractor, and his wife, Clara Emily, *née* Gould. Nothing is known of his childhood or schooling. As with many young men of his generation, Lee's imagination was caught by the idea of flight, but there was no money to spare for flying lessons.

At the outbreak of war in 1914 Lee saw his chance to learn to fly and attempted to enlist in the Royal Flying Corps (RFC), but only qualified pilots (those who held a privately obtained Royal Aero Club brevet) were being considered. Lacking the technical qualifications necessary for training by the RFC as a mechanic, he joined the infantry, the 13th Sherwood Foresters, and was commissioned in February 1915. After two unsuccessful attempts to gain a transfer to the RFC, an opportunity arose when, in May 1916, as a result of the RFC's heavy losses, commanding officers were instructed not to obstruct volunteers. A further application led to secondment on temporary attachment to the RFC. Shortly afterwards Lee married, on 28 July 1916, Gwynneth, the daughter of Robert Lewis, a stationer; they had one daughter.

Arthur Stanley Gould Lee (1894–1975), by Walter Stoneman, 1945

After flying training, Lee was posted to France to serve with 46 squadron, arriving at the squadron on 22 May 1917. Based at La Gorgue, on the Ypres front, the squadron was equipped with the Sopwith Pup, a small, highly manoeuvrable single-seater fighter, but with the disadvantages of being slower than its German counterparts and having only one machine-gun—a Vickers, firing through the propeller arc—against the twin Spandaus carried by the German fighters. He flew with 46 squadron until 6 January 1918, when he was posted to home establishment. He had been promoted captain and flight commander on 21 November 1917, and had been shot down by ground fire three times during the battle of Cambrai. He had flown 118 patrols, been in combat fifty-six times, was credited with seven victories, and had flown 250 hours on active service. He was awarded a Military Cross for his work in France, and was gazetted on 4 February 1918. After the war he was posted to south-eastern area flying instructors' school. Passing out as a first-class instructor, he was then posted to 54 training squadron at Fairlop, Essex.

In October 1919 Lee was granted a short service commission in the Royal Air Force, and in March 1924, after several varied postings, was granted a permanent commission as a flight lieutenant in the general duties branch, RAF. His lectures to RAF recruits were published in 1923 as *The Spirit of Air Force Discipline*. On 4 November 1925 he was posted to Iraq to serve with no. 5 armoured car company, 'driving clapped out Rolls-Royce armoured cars' (Lee, *Fly Past*, 53). With eight RAF squadrons, these had been used to police the Turkish and Kurd insurgents, but the Turkish threat had been quashed before Lee's arrival, and only minor revolts were still breaking out in south-eastern Kurdistan. He was next posted to the staff of general headquarters in Baghdad. Promoted squadron leader in July 1927, he was posted back to England in August and entered the RAF Staff College at Andover, after which he was posted to 10 squadron, a night-bomber squadron flying Handley Page Hyderabads.

Lee's tour of duty with 10 squadron ended in February 1931, and he was posted to the Air Ministry. The growing threat of war in the mid-1930s led to the expansion of the RAF. Now a wing commander (July 1934), Lee was involved in the planning, working with civil servants until 1935, when he attended a course at the Imperial Defence College. In December 1935 he was posted to the command of the RAF station, Hornchurch, Essex, a key station in the air defence of London, but which was in some disarray, with low morale. By 1937, under Lee's leadership, the station was regarded as one of top status in every aspect—from defence operations and exercises to flying exhibitions and sport. An unwelcome posting back to Iraq followed, from which Lee was released by secondment to the Turkish air force as an instructor in October 1937. On 1 November 1938 he was promoted group captain. When war was declared in September 1939 he was still in Turkey, and only after delicate negotiations with the Turkish authorities was he able finally to leave the country, on 11 March 1941, posted as senior administration officer to headquarters, RAF Middle East, in Athens.

During the chaotic and mismanaged evacuation from Greece of the 58,000 men of the British army and RAF which began on 23 April 1941, Lee eventually took command of all the remaining RAF personnel in the Peloponnese once the other senior officers had left Greece by air. Over the next few days he succeeded in evacuating by sea and air more than a thousand men, in large and small groups, to the island of Kythera and hence to Crete, where Lee and his rearguard finally arrived on 30 April. Lee's party was the last official RAF contingent to leave Greece and Lee the last RAF officer; he departed from Crete for Cairo in a Sunderland flying boat. For his services he was awarded the royal order of George I of Greece (with swords).

From Cairo, Lee was posted to Middle East headquarters, RAF, where he served during the Iraq revolt of April 1941 and was responsible for sending reinforcements to the RAF cantonment at Dhuban. Posted back to England as senior air staff officer at 12 group, Fighter Command, in September 1941, he was mentioned in dispatches on 1 December 1942 for his service with 12 group. In 1944 he was posted to the Balkans as second in command of the armistice control commission in Romania and became friendly with King Michael and his family. As Romania became progressively under the rule of the Communist Party, Lee decided that little more could be done and asked to be transferred. In February 1945 he was given command of the British mission in Yugoslavia. Lee commanded the RAF mission and no. 37 military mission, with advanced headquarters in Belgrade, and was the link between Field Marshal Alexander and Marshal Tito, whom he saw at least once a week. On his official visits to the former partisan leader, Lee, who had been promoted air vice-marshal on 13 June 1945, found him initially friendly, but considered that he returned from a visit to Moscow, a 'different man' (Lee, *Fly Past*, 195), very pro-Soviet and critical of Britain and the USA. The position of the British and American missions became untenable; with Tito's agreement they decided to withdraw. Tito was nevertheless grateful for the help he had received from the British mission and the RAF during the war and sought to award decorations to some fifty people, of all ranks, in recognition of this, but the British government delayed granting permission for twenty-five years, until the breach with Yugoslavia was healed and Tito was finally allowed to confer his wartime awards. Lee was awarded Yugoslavia's highest war decoration, the partisan star with golden wreath.

Lee retired from the RAF in 1946 and took up a new career as a writer. He published four autobiographical works, all of high quality: *Special Duties* (1946), an account of his service in the Balkans, Turkey, and the Middle East; *No Parachute* (1968), his letters written in 1917; *Open Cockpit* (1969), on his First World War service in the RFC; and *Fly Past* (1974), reminiscences of his flying career. He also wrote an account of the royal house of Greece (1948), biographies of King Michael of Romania (1950), Helen, queen mother of Romania (1956), Robert Dudley, earl of Essex (1964), and Samuel Franklin Cody (1965), and, under the name Arthur Lee Gould, a novel, *An Airplane in the Arabian Nights* (1947).

Lee's first wife, Gwynneth, died in 1951, and on 15 January 1953 he married Winifrid Hilda (Fay) Atkinson, the widow of Squadron Leader M. R. Atkinson, who had been killed in air operations in 1942, and the daughter of Frederic William Molteni, an accountant. In 1972 Lee accepted the presidency of Cross and Cockade International, the society of First World War aero historians. He was a stockily built man of medium height, invariably cheerful and affable, and always ready to discuss aspects of the First World War in the air and his own experiences as a young fighter pilot in that war. He died on 21 May 1975 in King Edward VII's Hospital for Officers, Marylebone, London. ALEX REVELL

Sources A. S. G. Lee, *Fly past* (1974) • A. S. G. Lee, *Open cockpit* (1969) • A. S. G. Lee, *No parachute* (1968) • b. cert. • m. cert. • d. cert. • RAF Officers' Records, Gloucester • *WWW* • Kelly, *Handbk* (1958)
Archives Royal Air Force Museum, Hendon, MSS
Likenesses W. Stoneman, photograph, 1945, NPG [*see illus.*] • photographs
Wealth at death £9737: probate, 9 Sept 1975, *CGPLA Eng. & Wales*

Lee [*née* Spooner], **Catharine Anna** [Kate] (**1859–1904**), singer and folk-song collector, was born at Wellow House, Rufford, Nottinghamshire, on 9 March 1859, the third child and second daughter of Lucius Henry Spooner (*b.* 1817?) and his wife, Margaret Skottowe (*b.* 1829?), daughter of Richard Neville Parker of Waterview, co. Cork. The family's circumstances were modest middle-class, but there were legal and clerical connections, some grand, some eccentric. One of Kate Lee's aunts married A. C. Tait, who became archbishop of Canterbury. Among her cousins was Warden Spooner of New College, Oxford, famous for his Spoonerisms.

Lucius Spooner was a land agent and his family was peripatetic. By 1871 they had moved on from Nottinghamshire, and nothing is known of Catharine Spooner's childhood and education until she entered the Royal Academy of Music in London in January 1876. Her ambition was to study singing and to make a professional career; but her family had other ideas, and in December 1877 she married Arthur Morier Lee (1847–1909), a barrister from a Surrey family with interests in West Indies sugar. The marriage was conventionally happy and successful, and there were two children, born in 1879 and 1881.

Kate Lee still harboured musical ambitions and studied at the Royal College of Music, London, between 1887 and 1889. In 1892 her ambitions hardened into determination on hearing Wagner's operas, and she began a singing career, at first as an amateur, then as a professional from 1895. Lee called herself a contralto, but the critics perceived in her a 'big' mezzo-soprano voice comparable to that of Clara Butt. They attributed to her not only a voice of 'remarkable volume and purity' but also a 'rare power of artistic interpretation' (*The Times*, 16 Feb 1895). Her concert programmes reflected an increasing interest in traditional music: besides the standard repertory of Brahms and Schubert, Lee sang Hungarian songs arranged by the expatriate Francis Korbay, Irish material from the collections edited by Charles Stanford, and items from *English County Songs*, edited by Lucy Broadwood and J. A. Fuller Maitland. She joined the Irish Literary Society in 1895 and at about the same time began to collect English folk-songs. Most collectors of the 1890s were reluctant converts to field work and shrank from the social risks it entailed, but Kate Lee plunged in with the same boldness and determination as she had shown in making her concert career, helped by her interest in the fashionable pastime of cycling. On one occasion, learning of a Guy Fawkes celebration at which singing was likely, she dressed up as a waitress and helped to serve the meal, having smeared a little 'Yorkshire relish' on her cheeks for additional effect. She collected chiefly during holidays in Norfolk, but the high point of her collecting career was meeting the brothers James and Thomas Copper at Rottingdean, Sussex, in November 1898.

The initiative for the Folk Song Society's foundation came from the Irish Literary Society, in particular from A. P. Graves, its secretary; but it was Kate Lee who organized the preliminary meetings, intended to draw together other interested parties among the existing folk music collectors, the Folk Lore Society, and the musical establishment. The inaugural meeting was held on 16 May 1898, and Kate Lee became the society's first secretary. It was easier, however, to draw the interested parties together than to agree a policy, and in its early days the society was an uneasy mixture of people who saw it as a vehicle for scholarship and publication and those who wanted it to have a wider social role. The situation was complicated by the deep and irrational dislike felt for Lee by Lucy Broadwood, one of the leaders of the 'scholarly' party, who clearly believed that she would have been a better choice as secretary. The result of these divisions was that when Kate Lee became seriously ill from 1900–01 onwards, the Folk Song Society quickly became moribund.

Lee's illness was cancer: probably cancer of the cervix. By 1903–4 she knew that she was dying, and was at last persuaded to hand over the Folk Song Society's affairs to Lucy Broadwood, under whose direction it quickly recovered. The Lees spent most of their married life in Kensington, but during Kate Lee's illness they took a house at Stubbings, near Maidenhead, and Lee died there on 25 July 1904. She was buried in Stubbings churchyard three days later.

Kate Lee's life was spent struggling towards achievements whose benefits were felt by other people. By the example of a determined, enthusiastic, unconventional life she contributed towards the liberation of women. Through her folk-song collecting she helped to unlock England's rich store of traditional music, and when her name is mentioned today it is usually in connection with the Copper family. But her most important and lasting memorial was the folk music revival which effectively began in 1904, and for which the existence of the Folk Song Society was a necessary precondition. One can say of her, as of Sir Christopher Wren, that her monument is all around us. C. J. BEARMAN

Sources C. J. Bearman, 'Kate Lee and the foundation of the Folk Song Society', *Folk Music Journal*, 7 (1995–9), 627–43 • A. T. C. Pratt, ed., *People of the period: being a collection of the biographies of upwards of six thousand living celebrities*, 2 vols. (1897), 71 • L. E. Broadwood, diaries, Surrey HC • K. Lee, 'Some experiences of a folk song collector', *Journal of the Folk Song Society*, 1 (1899), 7–12 • A. P. Graves, *To return to all that: an autobiography* (1930), 265–7 • J. A. Fuller Maitland, *Journal of the Folk Song Society*, 2 (1905), 67 • *The Times* (16 Feb 1895) • entry register, 1883, 1887, Royal College of Music, London • entry register, 1876, Royal Academy of Music, London • *Southwark and Bermondsey Recorder and South London Gazette* (1 Feb 1902) [account of lecture by Kate Lee] • *CGPLA Eng. & Wales* (1904) • census returns, 1861, PRO, RG 9/2474 • private information (2004) [R. Strike] • college register, Balliol Oxf. • d. cert.

Likenesses photograph, repro. in Bearman, 'Kate Lee …'

Wealth at death £394 19*s.* 10*d.*: administration, 1 Oct 1904, *CGPLA Eng. & Wales*

Lee, Charles (1732–1782), revolutionary army officer in America, was born on 26 January 1732 in Chester, the youngest of seven children of Colonel John Lee (*d.* 1750), army officer, and his wife, Isabella Bunbury (*d.* 1766), niece of Sir Thomas Hanmer, Shakespearian scholar and speaker of the House of Commons. His father was comfortably well off, and his mother had inherited considerable wealth, so Lee was well provided for in his youth. Moreover, five of his six siblings died young, thus opening up greater opportunities for Lee and his surviving sister, Sidney Lee. When he was quite young, his father, whom he seems to have admired and perhaps loved, sent him to an academy in Switzerland to broaden his horizons and to learn foreign languages. He was eminently successful, mastering Greek and Latin, as well as four other European tongues, and acquiring habits of scholarship that he retained throughout his life. On 25 June 1746 he was enrolled in the King Edward VI Grammar School at Bury St Edmunds, where he studied for two years.

Early military career Even before his son entered grammar school Lee's father determined that he would become a professional soldier like himself. Hence, on 9 April 1746, Colonel Lee commissioned his son an ensign in his own regiment, the 55th foot, which was stationed in Ireland and soon to be renumbered the 44th. On 5 August 1750, two years after Lee had completed his education and joined his regiment, his father died. Acting as executor for his father's estate, he distributed legacies to his mother, his sister, and himself. By 1754 he and his mother were on extremely bad terms, probably because of a strain of capriciousness that ran in the Bunbury family, showing up in his mother, an uncle, a cousin, and himself. (In fact, Lee later admitted that he was of a temperamental disposition, given to fits of sulkiness and anger.) After that time, the only family member that held his affection was his sister, Sidney, a friendly, cultivated woman who like himself never married.

As Lee reached maturity he was a remarkable individual. He was tall and slender, with small feet and hands, a narrow, bony face, and a huge aquiline nose; his physiognomy was so arresting, even ugly, that his fellow officers nicknamed him Naso. But his scholarly bent, quick intelligence, fearlessness, and indomitable will, combined with his overweening ambition and vanity, marked him as a character that was anything but commonplace and caused observers to forget his physical characteristics. On 1 May 1751 he was commissioned a lieutenant in the 44th regiment and in 1755, at the outbreak of the Seven Years' War, went with his regiment to North America. He seems to have served in General Edward Braddock's campaign against Fort Duquesne in 1755, and was sent to Albany for garrison duty later in the year. Having become interested in the American Indians, he rhapsodized to his sister about their merits and lived with the daughter of White Thunder, a Seneca chieftain. With this woman, whom he described as 'a very great beauty' he had twins, a boy and a girl. Accepted into the Seneca tribe, he was named Ounewaterika, meaning 'boiling water, or one whose spirits are never asleep'. He was promoted captain in the 44th regiment on 11 June 1756, and a year later was with his regiment during the campaign against Louisbourg. In July 1758 he was severely wounded in an attack on Fort Ticonderoga. While recuperating in a hospital on Long Island, he argued with and pummelled an army doctor, who tried to kill him. In 1759, after recovering from his wound, he served with his regiment in the capture of Fort Niagara, and a year later was with Sir Jeffrey Amherst when Montreal fell to the British.

At the end of 1760 Lee returned to England, where he joined in political agitation for the retention of Canada when the war came to an end, and railed against the government. He was appointed major in the 103rd regiment on 10 August 1761. A year later, as part of a British expeditionary force, he accompanied his regiment to Portugal to fight invading Spaniards, with the temporary rank of lieutenant-colonel. On 5 October 1762 he led a brilliant raid against Spanish forces at Villa Velha, for which he was publicly thanked by his commander, Count Wilhelm La Lippe, and given a colonelcy in the Portuguese army. He returned to England in 1763 and in the next few years suffered a number of disappointments. Instead of receiving the preferment he expected, he was retired from the army as a major on half pay. In 1764 he bitterly criticized the performance of Amherst as commander-in-chief in America, and the earl of Bute's policies as prime minister, thus making it extremely unlikely that he would receive further promotion. He promoted a scheme to make his fortune by founding utopian military colonies on the frontier, but he actually lost money on the project. He joined the service of the Polish king, Stanislaus Augustus, in March 1765 as an aide-de-camp and in the following year accompanied the Polish ambassador on a trip to Turkey. After almost dying of exposure in the snowy Balkan mountains and surviving 'a dreadful earthquake' in Constantinople, he returned to England.

For the next two years Lee gambled on horses, criticized the government, and unsuccessfully sought promotion. In 1769 he rejoined King Stanislaus of Poland as a general and adjutant to fight against the Turks, but fell ill and had to leave the Polish service. He recuperated in Italy, where he fought a duel with a foreign officer, losing some fingers but killing his opponent. In 1771 he began a two-year tour through France and Switzerland, in search of a cure for the gout that had begun to afflict him and would do so for the rest of his life. Having returned to England he lived on a private income of at least £1000 per year. Although he was at last promoted lieutenant-colonel, his bitterness toward both king and parliament became more pronounced, and in late 1773 he determined to seek his fortune in America. On 10 November he arrived in New York, where he found the colonists agitating against tea duties and immediately took their side. He travelled through America in the next ten months, meeting prominent leaders and expressing zeal for their opposition to British 'tyranny'. In 1774 he wrote two pamphlets, one repudiating the tory ideas of the Episcopalian minister Myles Cooper, and another attempting to persuade colonists that their militiamen, fighting for freedom and virtue, could stand against the mighty British army.

War against the British By May 1775 Lee had decided irrevocably to cast in his lot with Americans in their fight against Britain. He declared that colonists would not, and should not, trust anyone who held no property among them, and purchased for £3000 an estate, which he named Prato Rio, in the Shenandoah valley, near the home of his friend Horatio Gates. On 17 June he was appointed second major-general in the continental army and five days later formally resigned his British commission, after being assured by congress that he would be compensated if he lost his property in England. His name, and the names of two other British officers supporting America's 'unnatural rebellion', was stricken from the British army's half-pay list on 3 August 1775. Early on 23 June he set out for Boston to take his place in a rebel army investing the city, in the company of General George Washington, newly appointed commander-in-chief, and other continental officers. He assumed command of the left wing of the army and in the next few months trained soldiers, erected fortifications, and urged Americans to declare independence. In December he assisted revolutionaries at Newport, Rhode Island, in preparing their defences, then moved on to New York city in early 1776 to do the same thing there.

When congress learned that General Richard Montgomery had been killed at Quebec on 31 December 1775, it resolved on 17 February 1776 to send Lee northward as his replacement. On 1 March, however, congress changed its mind, deciding instead to appoint Lee commander of the southern district. Having reached Williamsburg, Virginia, on 29 March, Lee remained there until 12 May, putting the defences of Virginia and North Carolina in order. He assumed command in Charles Town, South Carolina, on 4 June, organized the city's defences with the able assistance of Colonel William Moultrie, and repulsed a British attack on Fort Moultrie on the 28th. Returning to Washington's army at the peak of his fame in early October, he stopped at Philadelphia to request that congress reimburse him for his English property, which had recently been confiscated. Immediately that body voted to advance him the sum of $30,000. He rejoined Washington's army just as it was retreating from Manhattan. He assumed command of the left wing, helped impede the enemy's advance, and fought in the battle of White Plains on 28 October 1776. Two weeks later, on 10 November, he was left in command of a small army at White Plains when Washington marched southward with most of the Continentals to counter an enemy threat to New Jersey. Having already grown suspicious that Washington was mishandling his army, Lee was appalled in mid-November when forts Washington and Lee on the lower Hudson river fell to the British. Now convinced that Washington was incompetent, he began to vacillate in carrying out the commander-in-chief's orders. Throughout November and December, as Washington retreated across New Jersey toward the Delaware river, Lee received a number of letters urging him to follow on. By 12 December Lee finally had bestirred himself enough to reach Basking Ridge, New Jersey, with his contingent of soldiers. Having made his headquarters in a tavern 4 miles outside his lines, he wrote his friend Gates a letter in which he harshly condemned Washington for the loss of the forts. The following day he was captured by a detachment of British dragoons and taken to the headquarters of General William Howe in New York.

Fortunately for Lee, he had resigned his commission in the British army shortly after joining the Americans and so escaped being sent to England to stand trial as a deserter. Nevertheless, he remained a captive of Howe for the next sixteen months, urging congress to negotiate an end to the war with the British and scolding it for not doing enough to secure his release. As he reflected on events, he became convinced that the revolution was deleterious to both America and Britain. His rebel friends had not proven to be the liberty-loving, virtuous folks he had believed them to be in 1775, and he now was convinced they would lose the war. When congress refused to open peace talks, he furnished General Howe with information on how to defeat the Americans in the next campaign and threw himself open to suspicions that he had become a traitor. Having been exchanged for Major-General Richard Prescott on 5 April 1778, he returned to American service, still persuaded that the war was a mistake. On 9 April he informed congress that the continental army was inferior to the British in every way, and that it would be 'insanity' to meet the enemy in battle. Washington should remain on the defensive, harassing the British indirectly only when great opportunity presented itself.

Dishonour and dismissal Lee rejoined Washington's army at Valley Forge, Pennsylvania, as second in command on 21 May 1778 and immediately counselled the American generals to avoid battle at all costs. They agreed. But when the British army began to withdraw from Philadelphia towards New York on 8 June, Washington descried an opportunity to harass the enemy's retreat. On 24 June he ordered the marquis de Lafayette to hound the British rear and flanks with a force of 6000 men but to avoid a general engagement. When Lee learned of this operation he asserted his right as second in command to lead the detachment, even though he feared that he might find himself fighting redcoats in open battle. Washington acquiesced, and so on 28 June 1778 Lee lurched into the battle of Monmouth in an unhappy frame of mind. General Anthony Wayne began hostilities by attacking the British with his division, but was appalled when he discovered that Lee's forces were retreating in his rear. He also fell back, and the American retreat became a rout. At that point Washington arrived on the battlefield with the main army. Without allowing Lee to say a word in his own defence, the commander-in-chief angrily dismissed him from command and took charge of the battle. Soon Washington had restored order and fought the British to a standstill.

In a letter to Washington dated 1 July but written a day or two earlier, Lee vehemently demanded that his commander provide 'some reparation' for his public humiliation or that he be 'brought to a tryal'. The latter demand Washington was glad to comply with. On 30 June he charged Lee with misbehaviour before the enemy, making a shameful and disorderly retreat, and disrespect to the commander-in-chief. From 4 July to 12 August 1778 a court martial sat in Brunswick, New Jersey, to try the case. In the end the court found Lee guilty on all counts but imposed only a mild punishment of suspension from duty for one year. Lee remained with the army until September then removed to Philadelphia, where he wrote numerous letters to congress attempting to have his sentence reversed. On 3 December he published a 'Vindication' in the *Pennsylvania Packet*, abusing Washington so outrageously that congress two days later officially confirmed the court's sentence. Also because of his attacks on Washington he was compelled to fight a duel with Colonel John Laurens on 23 December in which he received a slight wound in the side. On 7 January 1779 he received a challenge from Wayne, who had taken issue with Lee's comments about Wayne's performance at Monmouth. Lee avoided this duel by publicly explaining that his comments were not meant to be critical of Wayne but were made only to defend himself at his trial.

Even as he strove against his many enemies in early 1779, Lee turned in his characteristically romantic fashion to writing 'crude reveries', one of which was a revision of his earlier scheme for planting military colonies in the west. Still campaigning for vindication, he arranged on 6 July to have his friend David Ramsay publish in the *Maryland Journal and Baltimore Advertiser* a series of 'queries' ardently defending Lee and harshly abusing Washington. Although much vexed by Lee's latest provocations, Washington refused to respond publicly, and so Lee abandoned his campaign against the commander-in-chief. His greater problem now was congress, for a movement was afoot in that body to dismiss him from the army because of his attacks on Washington. On 4 December James Forbes, delegate from Maryland, introduced just such a resolution, but it was handily defeated. When Lee heard of this action he fell into a white-hot rage, and wrote an insulting message to congress that guaranteed his dismissal but did not contain his resignation. On 10 January 1780 congress dismissed him from the army by the narrow vote of five states to four, with three divided and one not voting.

Having retired to Prato Rio in Virginia, Lee in June 1780 became estranged from Gates, who had come to doubt Lee's loyalty to the American cause. For the next two years he lived quietly, visiting extensively and breeding horses and dogs. In late September 1782, while visiting Philadelphia, he fell ill with a 'defluxion' of the lungs and died in a tavern on 2 October. According to some accounts, his death was mourned only by two faithful dogs, Minghini and Oswald, who remained by his bedside during his final agonies. Two days later, in a twist of irony that he might have appreciated, he was given a military funeral with all the pomp and ceremony that had been denied him in his final years. He was borne to the graveyard of Christ Church in Philadelphia and buried there, despite a provision in his will that he not be interred in or near any church.

Thus passed a remarkable person in American history. Eccentric in personality, whiggish in politics, more comfortable in opposition to causes than in support of them, he left a mixed legacy for the American cause that he so ardently embraced. At first he contributed mightily to mobilizing uncertain revolutionaries in both political and military matters, but as time went on it became clear that his genius in both areas had been overrated. Matters certainly were not helped by his 'distemper of … mind'. Hence it is debatable whether he was more an asset or a hindrance to the hard-pressed rebel cause.

Paul David Nelson

Sources *The Lee papers*, 4 vols. (1872–5) • J. R. Alden, *General Charles Lee: traitor or patriot?* (1951) • J. Sparks, *Lives of Charles Lee and Joseph Reed* (1846) • S. W. Patterson, *Knight errant of liberty: the triumph and tragedy of General Charles Lee* (1958) • J. Shy, 'Charles Lee: the soldier as radical', *George Washington's generals*, ed. G. A. Billias (1964), 22–53 • G. H. More, *'Mr Lee's plan — March 29, 1777', the treason of Charles Lee, major general, second in command in the American army of the Revolution* (1860) • W. S. Stryker and W. S. Myers, *The battle of Monmouth* (1927) • T. Thayer, *The making of a scapegoat: Washington and Lee at Monmouth* (1976) • T. J. Fleming, 'The "military crimes" of Charles Lee', *American Heritage*, 19 (1968), 12–15, 83–9

Archives NAM, account of capture of Ticonderoga and family papers • National Archives and Records Administration, Washington, DC, papers of the continental congress, no. 158 • Wayne State University Library, Detroit, corresp. and papers | L. Cong., George Washington MSS • priv. coll., letters to Lord Shelburne • PRO, Jefferey Amherst MSS, War Office 34/36 • U. Mich., Clements L., Clinton MSS

Likenesses G. R. Hall, engraving • G. R. Hall, stipple, NPG • R. P., line engraving, NPG; repro. in *History of American War*, 3 and 4 • Rushbrooke, oils, New York Historical Society • J. Trumbull, pencil sketch, Yale U. Art Gallery • line engraving, NPG

Lee [Lea], **Cromwell** (*d.* **1601**), compiler of an Italian dictionary, was younger son of Sir Anthony Lee (or Lea) of Burston and of Quarendon, Buckinghamshire, and his wife, the daughter of Sir Thomas *Wyatt. He was the brother of Sir Henry *Lee. Cromwell matriculated at St John's College, Oxford, probably in 1572, but took no degree, and afterwards spent some years travelling in Italy. Later in life he settled in Oxford, and there compiled an Italian–English dictionary, which he completed as far as the word *tralignato*. In 1575 he married Mary, daughter of Sir John Harcourt, and widow of Richard Taverner. Lee died in 1601 in the parish of St Cross Holywell, Oxford.

G. B. Dibblee, *rev.* Elizabeth Goldring

Sources Foster, *Alum. Oxon.* • Wood, *Ath. Oxon.*, new edn, 1.715 • D. Lysons and S. Lysons, *Magna Britannia: being a concise topographical account of the several counties of Great Britain*, new edn, 1 (1813)

Lee, Edward (**1481/2–1544**), archbishop of York, was a younger son of Richard Lee of Lee Magna in Kent, and grandson of Sir Richard Lee, lord mayor of London in 1461 and 1470. In later life Sir Thomas More, a friend of the family, affectionately recalled Lee's intellectual promise when a ten-year-old schoolboy.

Education and collaboration with Erasmus Admitted a demy of Magdalen College, Oxford, in 1495, and a fellow of the college in 1500, Lee graduated BA in 1501. The next year he migrated to Cambridge where he took his MA in 1502/3. After more than a decade of further study there he proceeded to the degree of BTh in 1515. He then moved to the continent and matriculated at Louvain on 25 August 1516. He also attended Bologna and gained his doctorate of theology from one of these two universities, incorporating as DTh at Oxford on 12 October 1531.

Lee financed his long academic career at least partially through church preferment. Ordained deacon in the diocese of London in 1504, he procured a prebend in Exeter Cathedral in 1509 which he retained until 1524, and in the same year *in commendam* the rectory of Freshwater in the Isle of Wight which he had vacated by 1513. In 1510, 1512, and 1513 he acquired prebends in the cathedrals of Salisbury, Lincoln, and Winchester respectively, the revenues of which he enjoyed until 1531.

At Louvain, where he had gone to further his knowledge of Hebrew and Greek, Lee for a time assisted Erasmus in the revision of his New Testament, but resented the fact that the older scholar did not give sufficient weight to his suggestions. Erasmus, for his part, always sensitive to any imputations of scholarly inaccuracy, turned violently against Lee when, after the publication of the second edition of the New Testament in 1519, he persisted in circulating his emendations. More did his utmost to mediate between the two men, begging Lee not to publish these emendations and to return to England, but undeterred later that year he brought out at Paris his *Annotationes Edouardi Lee in annotationes novi testamenti Disiderii Erasmi*. Having predictably drawn a vituperative reply from Erasmus, in 1520 he included these annotations in his book *Sunt in hoc volumine apologia Edouardi Loei contra quorundam calumnias*. The quarrel festered for years with Erasmus pursuing his vendetta in public and private and insinuating that Lee had been motivated by a desire for self-advancement. As late as 1526 Polydore Vergil tried to effect a reconciliation, but Lee sabotaged his efforts by demanding that Erasmus should be the first to apologize.

Foreign embassies While Lee's inflexibility greatly pained the English friends of Erasmus, his adherence to traditional Catholic orthodoxy in no way hindered his prospects in government service. He became a royal chaplain in 1520 and by 1523 the king's almoner, a stepping-stone to high promotion. In the autumn of 1520 he accompanied Henry VIII to his meeting with the emperor Charles V at the Field of Cloth of Gold, and some contemporaries subsequently believed Lee did the groundwork for Henry VIII's *Assertio septem sacramentorum* which appeared in July 1521. In the autumn of 1523 the king sent him on his first embassy to Nuremberg to confer the Order of the Garter upon the Archduke Ferdinand. His fellow delegate, Lord Morley, commented to Wolsey on Lee's wisdom and good management. Back in England Lee received the archdeaconry of Colchester which he resigned in 1531.

Having proved his competence in Germany, two years later Lee was selected by Wolsey to replace the resident English ambassador at the imperial court, Richard Sampson. In his passage through France in early December 1525 Lee characteristically warned the king and Wolsey about the prevalence of Lutheranism there and urged them to exclude from England all copies of Tyndale's translation of the New Testament. He reached Spain early in January 1526, less than a year after the Spaniards' defeat of the French at the battle of Pavia had transformed the balance of power in Europe. Thereafter for the next three and a half years he followed the imperial court around Spain. Charged with securing the release of the French king and the repayment of the English loan to the emperor, Lee complained in letter after letter about imperial procrastination. The eventual freeing of François I and his renunciation of undertakings he claimed he had made to the emperor under duress led to a new alliance between France, the pope, and the northern Italian states and a renewal of war in Italy. Late in 1526 Geronimo de' Ghinucci, the non-resident bishop of Worcester, who had previously represented Henry VIII at the Vatican, was dispatched to support Lee in Valladolid where they were joined by Thomas Cranmer for a few months at the beginning of 1527. Lee duly protested at the sack of Rome by Spanish troops in May 1527 and the ensuing imprisonment of the pope.

Fearing an all-dominant Spain, at this juncture Wolsey switched to working for a common front between England and France without fully informing his ambassadors of his change of direction, although Lee and Ghinucci had already become conscious of their declining influence at the imperial court, where from August 1527 rumours had begun spreading of Henry VIII's intention to repudiate his marriage to Katherine of Aragon, the emperor's aunt. Lee subsequently spent a considerable amount of time attempting to discredit a brief the Spaniards produced validating the marriage. In January 1528 he combined with the French ambassador in a declaration of war against Spain, which later in the year appeared in print at Antwerp as *Exhibita quodam, per E. Leum, oratorem Anglicum in consilio Caesareo ante belli indictionem*.

The emperor had been planning to go to Italy from late in 1528, and early in the next year Ghinucci was granted permission to leave for England. Without his guidance in legal matters Lee felt he could achieve little, and pressed for his own recall, sending Wolsey his last report from Spain on the emperor's desire for peace with France in August 1529.

On his return (which coincided with Wolsey's disgrace) Lee found his diplomatic expertise in more demand than ever, and after only a few weeks at court, in January 1530 he was included with Thomas Cranmer on a new embassy under the nominal command of Thomas Boleyn, recently created earl of Wiltshire, to try to persuade the pope and the emperor at Bologna to agree to the annulment of the king's marriage. Despite the failure of their mission Lee at last began to garner the rewards of his labours. In February 1530 he gained the chancellorship of Salisbury Cathedral together with the rectory of Odiham, later that month the prebend of Dunnington in York Minster, another prebend in St Stephen's Chapel in Westminster Abbey, and the archdeaconry of Surrey in July 1530, holding all these promotions until late in 1531.

Archbishop of York In July 1530 Lee signed the petition of the lords spiritual and temporal to Clement VII to grant the divorce and the following year composed a treatise against the dispensing power of the pope. Several times in 1531 Chapuys reported to Charles V on the deputations of leading laymen and churchmen sent by Henry VIII to Katherine of Aragon during which Lee among others remonstrated with the queen on her determination to have her marriage tried at Rome. In September 1531 he informed the emperor that in addition to advancing Stephen Gardiner to the bishopric of Winchester the king had given Lee the archbishopric of York, vacant since Wolsey's death in the previous November, to strengthen his cause in the House of Lords.

Consecrated on 10 December 1531, though still provided by the pope, Lee followed the other bishops in recognizing Henry VIII as the supreme head of the English church in 1532. In the autumn of that year he was nominated one of the regents to govern the country during the king's absence in France. Just before Christmas he made a brief visit to his diocese, but he had gone south by February when Chapuys related to the emperor that Lee and Gardiner were thought to harbour some scruples concerning Henry's marriage to Anne Boleyn, performed by Cranmer the previous month. Lee nevertheless participated in the festivities at Anne's coronation in June 1533, and was at Greenwich later in the month when Henry VIII made his appeal from the pope to a general council. In May 1534 the king again used Lee and Tunstall to try to persuade Katherine to repudiate her marriage and to advise her of the new act limiting the succession to the heirs of Henry VIII and Anne Boleyn.

Aware of the harm inflicted on the see of York through Wolsey's absence during the previous quarter of a century, Lee seems to have resolved from the start to be a very different archbishop from his predecessor, despite his constant occupation in secular business. First, and somewhat rashly, he attempted to assert his authority over the archdeaconry of Richmond, which had customarily enjoyed quasi-episcopal status, only for the archdeacon to complain vociferously to Cromwell over his interference. He achieved somewhat more success in protecting his patronage, on occasions contriving to fill a living in advance of an anticipated application from the king or Cromwell.

Perhaps with the intention of forestalling more drastic reform, in the summer of 1534 Lee began a series of visitations of religious houses in the vicinity of York until inhibited from proceeding further by the king at the end of September. His ensuing injunctions to the nuns of Clementhorpe, Nun Appleton, Sinningthwaite, and Esholt, the canons of Healaugh and Warter, and the monks of St Mary's in York itself all called for a stricter observance of the monastic rule.

Lee's insistence upon his rights also brought him into conflict with the towns of York and Beverley. After protests from York corporation the archbishop on Cromwell's prompting grudgingly dismantled his fishgarths in the River Ouse, but took an altogether harder line against his borough of Beverley where he disallowed the elections and temporarily arrogated to himself the power to nominate the twelve town governors.

Northern crisis With unco-operative northerners on the one hand and a suspicious monarch on the other, Lee was treading a very difficult path. In June 1535 he had to defend himself to the king against Sir Francis Bigod's accusations that he had failed to preach the royal supremacy with sufficient fervour. The same summer he dissuaded the Mount Grace Carthusians from following the example of the monks of the London Charterhouse, and claimed in October that northerners were obediently accepting the king as the supreme head of the church and the abolition of the primacy of Rome, only sticking at the rejection of the doctrine of purgatory. Despite these demonstrations of loyalty, he still considered it necessary in January 1536 to write to the king denying any connection with the spiritual confessor at Syon, Richard Reynolds, executed in the previous year, and disowning Bishop John Fisher who had been 'so stiff to die in these causes without good ground' (*LP Henry VIII*, vol. 10, no. 99). That winter and spring he went out of his way to co-operate with Cromwell's agents as first they visited the monasteries in his province and then, after the passing of the Act of Suppression, accepted the surrender of the houses with an income of less than £200 a year.

Throughout the early months of 1536 Lee worked hard to procure the information on livings in the province required by Cromwell to compile the *valor ecclesiasticus*, professing himself 'ready in this and all other things, as his conscience and learning will suffer, to follow the king's pleasure and commandment, so that our Lord be not offended, and the unity of the faith and the catholic church saved' (*LP Henry VIII*, vol. 8, no. 277).

The outbreak of the Pilgrimage of Grace in Beverley early in October 1536 made the archbishop's relationship with the central government even more precarious. Fearing retaliation from his aggrieved tenants Lee fled from Cawood to Pontefract where he became a prisoner of the rebels when Lord Darcy surrendered the castle on 20 October. He and the other gentlemen there then took the pilgrims' oath. Not without some justification Aske and his followers assumed that the archbishop sympathized with their aims for the restoration of the church's liberties, but Lee disappointed them by preaching a sermon advocating passive obedience in Pontefract Priory on 4 December. In January 1537, after Norfolk had brought the first insurrection to an end, Lee dared to question the wisdom of attempting to collect the clerical tenth while the north remained so volatile. During the second rising he stayed in his palace at Cawood and by so doing contributed to the quietness of the adjoining parts of the East Riding. To defend himself against allegations of treason in the aftermath of the uprising he drew up a very long exculpatory account of his involvement in the pilgrimage.

Conservative primate At this dangerous time Lee furnished yet further evidence of his religious conservatism. Appointed to a royal commission in February 1537 to devise a permanent religious settlement, together with the bishops of London, Lincoln, Bath, Chichester, and Norwich, he objected to the omission of four of the seven sacraments from the ten articles of 1536. Advised by Cromwell on ways to assuage the king's continuing displeasure, he preached several sermons in London in support of the royal supremacy in the summer of 1537, and on his return to his province worked closely with him to increase the number of loyal preachers in the north. The price Lee paid for his rehabilitation was the handover of even more of his patronage to Cromwell and his nominees. On the dissolution of the greater monasteries he successfully petitioned the king for the appointment as his suffragan of Robert Pursglove, the last prior of Guisborough, a man much in his own mould, and together they did their best to prevent the preaching of innovatory theological ideas in the diocese.

Still on occasions needed to give judgments affecting the king, in July 1540 Lee joined his fellow bishops in annulling the marriage of Henry VIII and Anne of Cleves. In the more conservative climate which prevailed after the passing of the Act of Six Articles and the fall of Cromwell he appeared somewhat less beleaguered, though as one who had sided with the rebels the archbishop still was faced with the indignity of having to seek his monarch's forgiveness on his knees, when Henry VIII visited York in the late summer of 1541.

A little earlier that year Lee surrendered to the crown the archdeaconry of Richmond which then formed part of the new see of Chester. Two years later he acquiesced in an exchange of lands with the crown under which the king gained the archiepiscopal manors of Beverley, Skidby, Bishops Burton, and Southwell in return for parcels of lands and impropriations previously belonging to the priories of Marton, Moxby, Newburgh, and Mount Grace of the same nominal value. Conscious to the end of his position as a servant of the state, only a few weeks before his death he was seeking advice about the maintenance of Scottish hostages billeted upon him by the government.

Lee died on 13 September 1544, aged sixty-two, and was buried in the south choir aisle of York Minster, at a spot marked by a brass which is no longer extant. In addition to his printed annotations to Erasmus's New Testament and speech made before the emperor in 1528, he also wrote a manuscript commentary on the Pentateuch and a tract against the dispensing power of the pope, and translated a collection of the lives of the saints. CLAIRE CROSS

Sources E. Lee, *Sunt in hoc volumine* (1520) • Borth. Inst., Abp. reg. 28 [Edward Lee] • 'Visitations in the diocese of York, holden by Archbishop Edward Lee (AD 1534–5)', *Yorkshire Archaeological Journal*, 16 (1900–02), 424–58 • *LP Henry VIII* • H. B. McCall, ed., *Yorkshire Star Chamber proceedings*, 2, Yorkshire Archaeological Society, 45 (1911) • J. S. Block, *Factional politics and the English Reformation, 1520–1540* (1993) • M. Bush, *The Pilgrimage of Grace: a study of the rebel armies of October 1536* (1996) • M. Bush and D. Bownes, *The defeat of the Pilgrimage of Grace* (1999) • C. Cross, 'The economic problems of the see of York: decline and recovery in the sixteenth century', *Land, church and people*, ed. J. Thirsk, British Agricultural History Society, 18, supplement (1970), 64–81 • A. G. Dickens, *Lollards and protestants in the diocese of York, 1509–1558* (1959) • M. H. Dodds and R. Dodds, *The Pilgrimage of Grace, 1536–1537, and the Exeter conspiracy, 1538*, 2 vols. (1915) • F. Drake, *Eboracum, or, The history and antiquities of the city of York* (1736) • Emden, *Oxf.*, 2.1122–3 • *GM*, 3rd ser., 15 (1863), 337 • *Fasti Angl., 1300–1541*, [Salisbury] • *Fasti Angl., 1066–1300*, [York] • J. K. McConica, *English humanists and Reformation politics under Henry VIII and Edward VI* (1965) • D. MacCulloch, *Thomas Cranmer: a life* (1996) • R. Marius, *Thomas More: a biography* (1984) • A. F. Pollard, *Wolsey* (1929) • G. Redworth, *In defence of the church catholic: the life of Stephen Gardiner* (1990) • J. J. Scarisbrick, *Henry VIII* (1968) • L. B. Smith, *Tudor prelates and politics, 1536–1558* (1953) • Venn, *Alum. Cant.*, 1/3

Archives BL, Cotton MSS, diplomatic letters to Henry VIII and Thomas Wolsey

Lee, Edwin (*d.* **1870**), writer on medical reform and spa physician, was born some time around the beginning of the nineteenth century. Nothing is known about his early years and information about his parents appears non-existent. He was articled under the Royal College of Surgeons, London, in 1822. He entered St George's Hospital as a medical student in 1824. He received the licence of the Society of Apothecaries in 1827 and the diploma of the Royal College of Surgeons in 1829. After qualifying he served as a house surgeon at St George's Hospital and then competed unsuccessfully for a similar position at the Birmingham General Hospital, losing the election by a single vote. From the early 1830s he spent long periods on the continent first at the Parisian hospitals, including the Hôtel Dieu, the Hôpital la Pitié, and the Hôpital Necker, where he studied under Civiale, inventor of the operation of lithotrity. This experience led in 1837 to his essay 'On the comparative advantages of lithotomy and lithotrity', which was awarded the Jacksonian prize by the Royal College of Surgeons, London. Later in the 1830s he attended medical schools and universities in Germany, including Munich and Berlin. While on the continent he became interested in two areas which were to dominate his career—spa treatment and medical reform.

Lee returned from the continent in the early 1840s and eschewed general practice to serve as a medical adviser to invalids in the resort town of Brighton. At the same time he increased the output of his medical writings. He did not, however, abandon his ambition of building a career in a London hospital, 'but … soon found, by personal experience, how little professional claims are estimated in competing for an hospital appointment' (Lee, *St George's*, 36). In late 1843 he failed in his attempt to gain an assistant surgeoncy at St George's Hospital during a notoriously ill-tempered contest. Lee's part in the proceedings was peripheral, but the experience shaped much of his later writings and activities, and arguably changed the direction of his career. At the next vacancy, in 1848, he declined to stand and published instead a pamphlet, *Hospital Elections and Medical Reform*, which he distributed 'liberally' to members of the profession, castigating the corrupt system of hospital elections. Later he was to describe St George's as 'that theatre of plots, and schemes' (Lee, *St George's*, 32).

By the 1840s Lee had already shown a general interest in medical reform in a series of works on medical organization on the continent, but his inability to obtain a hospital appointment, combined with other events, made of him an increasingly vocal campaigner against the medical establishment and for medical reform. He was particularly incensed by his failure to be made an honorary fellow of the Royal College of Surgeons following the introduction of a new charter in 1843. The charter had stipulated that a number of fellows would be created to act as an electorate for the college. Outrage, however, descended upon the heads of the college in 1844 when they created the new fellows. Not a few appeared to have been chosen arbitrarily. Lee himself was furious when, in his own words, he was 'unjustly excluded' (Lee, *Notes*, 24), and fired off angry letters to Sir James Graham, the home secretary, and Sir Benjamin Brodie, president of the college. Given Brodie's role as the powerful patriarch in the St George's elections, Lee took the matter as a personal slight.

Lee's interest in medical reform was such that he was invited to act as a witness to the 1848 select committee for medical registration and medical law amendment, where he was able to advance proposals previously put forward in *Remarks upon Medical Organisation and Reform* (1846). He advocated three faculties of medicine—in London, Edinburgh, and Dublin—each of which would control the examination process in its respective country. He continued writing about the state of the medical profession throughout the 1850s. Medical reform, however, provided just a few of the vast quantity of words spilled from his pen. His most extensive writings related to spas and other health resorts. His books on this subject often ran through three or four revised editions. Germany, Italy, and France were all covered in great depth, as were the British resorts of Bath, Brighton, Cheltenham, Leamington Spa, and many others. He also wrote about morality and ethics, stammering and squinting, and somnambulism, as well as producing critical tomes on hydropathy, homoeopathy, and animal magnetism, investigations into the nervous system, travel books with a vague medical bent, and works on the therapeutical uses of climate for treating diseases such as tuberculosis.

Lee's prolific writing was matched by his restless travelling. During the course of his career he lived in Cheltenham, London, and Brighton. He finally settled in Menton in the south of France, where he died on 3 or 4 June 1870. One of his obituarists stated that 'He was a kind of peripatetic Practitioner and spent the "season" in London or at some watering-place on the Continent' (*Medical Times and Gazette*, 679). Evidence for his nomadic life is found in various entries in the *London and Provincial Medical Directory* and later in the *Medical Directory*. Frequently his address was listed at London and Brighton, but sometimes his name was completely absent or recorded as 'travelling'. For example, in the mid to late 1850s he almost certainly served as a spa physician at Wiesbaden, his details given as such in the *London and Provincial Medical Directory* (1855). His place of death linked his preoccupations with the therapeutic value of climate and the mobility that had been required of him to survive as a practitioner without entering general practice. Behind him he left few traces, except his voluminous writings. His presence in censuses is at best elusive, and he is not to be found in the probate registers.

Lee's insistence on his ill-treatment, coupled with a burning sense of injustice, are persuasive, but his trials were, by no means, unique. The last thing he had wanted was to be nomadic: 'many persons would … look upon my removals as an indication of my being of an unsettled disposition'. Not so; he was forced into wandering by circumstance. Despite frugality—he had 'no expensive habits'—he met 'with but little encouragement or return' for his 'exertions'. He believed his situation was indicative of a wider professional malaise. 'What else but increasing deterioration of the profession is to be expected from the continuance of such a state of matters? Intrigue and jobbery, professional jealousies, and underhand practices, must continue to prevail' (Lee, *Additional Notes*, 39–40).

Lee's historical significance is to be found in three specific areas. First, while following in the footsteps of Sir James Clarke, author of *The Influence of Climate in the Prevention and Cure of Chronic Diseases* (1829), his well-received and widely quoted publications on continental spas and resorts were a precursor to the work of balneologists and climatologists such as Sir Hermann Weber. Second, by writing works such as *Bradshaw's Companion to the Continent* (1851), he was a travel writer who bridged the gap between the grand tour by carriage and the package tour by Thomas Cook. Finally, his very marginality within the medical profession, and his role as a 'reforming' practitioner attacking privilege and élitism, mark him as a representative of the thousands of practitioners whose ambitions were thwarted, but who continued the struggle to make a medical living outside general practice.

JAMES BRADLEY

Sources E. Lee, *St George's Hospital medical staff* (1859) • E. Lee, *Notes corroborative of the remarks in the 'St George's Hospital medical staff'* (1859) • E. Lee, *Additional notes corroborative of the remarks in the 'St George's Hospital medical staff'* (1860) • *The Lancet* (18 June 1870), 891–2 • *Medical Times and Gazette* (18 June 1870), 679 • E. Lee, *Remarks upon medical organisation and reform (foreign and English)* (1846) • *London and Provincial Medical Directory* (1847–71) • *Medical Directory of Great Britain and Ireland* (1845) • 'Select committee on medical registration and medical law amendment', *Parl. papers* (1847–8), 15.266–72, no. 210 [examination of Lee]

Lee, Elizabeth (1857/8–1920), biographer and translator, was born in Keppel Street, Russell Square, London, the daughter of Lazarus Lee (*b.* 1824/5), who dealt in ostrich feathers, and his wife, Jessie Davis (*b.* 1836/7). She was one of at least six children. Her family was Jewish, and had changed its name from Levi to Lee in mid-century. Her brother Solomon Lazarus also changed his forenames and as Sidney *Lee became second editor of the *Dictionary of National Biography*. Lazarus Lee was ambitious for his six children: Sidney was educated at the City of London School and Balliol College, Oxford, and Elizabeth at Queen's College, Harley Street, London, where she studied literature under its principal, the Revd Edward Hayes Plumptre. She travelled in France and Germany, studying languages and educational methods. She became a girls' secondary school English teacher, an editor, a translator of French and German literature and history, minor biographer, and compiler of school texts on literature, history, and art. She wrote articles for monthly magazines, notably *The Library*, and many articles for the *Dictionary of National Biography*. She was secretary of the English Association (1907–12), where she worked with Sir Arthur Acland, A. C. Bradley, and Frederic Boase. Her English Association leaflet *The Teaching of Literature in French and German Secondary Schools* (1907) was recognized by her appointment as officier d'Académie by the French ministry of public affairs.

Elizabeth Lee's career as a minor woman of letters was not unconnected to the circles in which her brother Sidney moved. Three factors in his life are crucial to understanding her work because of the opportunities they created: his interest in Shakespeare, his friends and associates and their publishing connections, and his involvement with the *Dictionary of National Biography*. At Oxford he had published two articles that attracted the attention of Frederick James Furnivall, the Shakespeare and early English texts scholar, who recommended him to Leslie Stephen when the *Dictionary of National Biography* project began. Another Shakespeare scholar and publisher, Arthur Henry Bullen, was at school and at Oxford with Lee. Elizabeth Lee's first published translation was *The English Novel in the Time of Shakespeare* (1890), from the work by Jean Jules Jusserand. Over the next thirty years she wrote, edited, translated, and contributed to another thirty books—most notably a biography, *Ouida* (1914), schools editions of the poetry of Thomas Gray, Oliver Goldsmith, and William Cowper, and selections from Thomas Carlyle and George Eliot. She translated Lucien Lévy-Bruhl's *Ethics and Moral Science* (1905), Petri Rosegger's *A Prisoner's Story of the Cross* (1905), and Georg Enge's *The Philosopher and the Foundling* (1906).

After Sidney Lee became editor of the *Dictionary of National Biography* Elizabeth contributed 110 articles: 67 to the first series (1885–1900), 14 in the supplements published in 1901, and 29 in the supplement for 1901–11. All but nine of her articles are on women. Of the 81 articles she wrote between 1892 and 1901, 79 are on women. She was not listed as a contributor until October 1892 (Sidney Lee had become sole editor in June 1891), though it is possible that she had been writing articles under her brother's name for some years before. It is noteworthy that Sidney had written twenty-two articles on women subjects in the twenty-seven volumes that appeared up to 1891, but only six in the thirty-six volumes that followed. It is conceivable that, at a time when female contributors were rare, Lee's new editorial authority simply gave him the opportunity to introduce Elizabeth as a contributor in her own right.

Elizabeth Lee was officially employed on the editorial staff of the *Dictionary of National Biography* as summarizer of volumes 31–5 in the *Index and Epitome* (1903). Her work is unremarkable, but it is noteworthy that she was given the job—the only female editor among nine men, many of whom had worked on the dictionary's staff in the past and had extensive editorial experience. She also helped to correct the proofs and to compile the index of the 1915 revision of Sidney Lee's *Life of William Shakespeare*.

Elizabeth Lee died, unmarried, on 10 July 1920 at home at 25 Holland Street, Kensington, and was cremated at Golders Green. Her death was a 'great sorrow' to Sidney Lee (*DNB*); they had worked closely together for thirty years, shared intellectual interests, and were very attached to each other. GILLIAN FENWICK

Sources *The Times* (13 July 1920) • 'Lee, Sir Sidney', *DNB* • G. Fenwick, *The contributors' index to the Dictionary of National Biography, 1885–1901* (1989) • G. Fenwick, *Leslie Stephen's life in letters* (1993) • G. Fenwick, *Women and the 'Dictionary of National Biography': a bibliography of DNB volumes 1885–1995 and 'Missing Persons'* (1994) • G. Fenwick, 'Sidney Lee', *Nineteenth-century British book-collectors and bibliographers*, ed. W. Baker and K. Womack, DLitB, 184 (1997), 244–51 • will • d. cert. • census returns, 1881

Archives John Murray, London, archives | Bodl. Oxf., Sidney Lee papers, letters

Wealth at death £2617 10s. 6d.: probate, 11 Sept 1920, *CGPLA Eng. & Wales*

Lee, Fitzroy Henry (1699–1750), naval officer, seventh son of Edward Henry Lee, second earl of the city of Lichfield (1663–1716), and Lady Charlotte Fitzroy (1664–1718), daughter of Charles II and Barbara, duchess of Cleveland, was born on 2 January 1699. His father, a staunch tory, had followed James II to Rochester after his departure from Whitehall in December 1688. Lee would later demonstrate a similar sympathy to the Jacobite cause. He entered the navy in 1717, and, after serving in the *Launceston* and *Guernsey*, passed his examination on 22 July 1720. In 1721 he was promoted lieutenant, and on 25 October 1728 he was appointed captain of the *Looe*.

Lee commanded the *Pearl* in 1731 and the *Falkland* in 1734; and from 1735 to 1738 he was governor of Newfoundland. Between 1738 and 1742 he commanded the *Pembroke* on the Mediterranean station, under Nicholas Haddock and Thomas Mathews. During the Jacobite rising of 1745 Lee was one of several British naval officers on whom the French called for assistance in planning an invasion. In the following year he went out as commodore and commander-in-chief on the Leeward Islands station, with a broad pennant in the *Suffolk*. In this capacity he made himself very unpopular among those under his command and merchants and residents in the West Indies. He was accused of incivility, drunkenness, and neglect of duty, and on 4 December 1746 Commodore Edward Legge was sent out to relieve him and try him by court martial. The complaints could not be substantiated, and Lee escaped trial. On his arrival in England, in October 1747, his promotion to rear-admiral, which had been suspended, was back-dated to 15 July. On 12 May 1748 he was advanced to vice-admiral of the white, but he had no further service, and died suddenly on 14 April 1750. 'Within a few hours of his death he had jocosely mentioned making his addresses to the relict of Sir Chaloner Ogle', who had died three days before him (*GM*, 188). He is described by Charnock as a 'free liver' (Charnock, 4.195), and was popularly spoken of as a man of debauched habits and foul tongue. It has been said that Fitzroy was the original of Tobias Smollett's Hawser Trunnion from *Peregrine Pickle* (1751). J. K. LAUGHTON, *rev.* PHILIP CARTER

Sources J. Charnock, ed., *Biographia navalis*, 4 (1796), 195 • *GM*, 1st ser., 20 (1750), 188 • J. Colin, *Louis XV et les Jacobites: le projet de débarquement en Angleterre de 1743–1744* (1901) • P. K. Monod, *Jacobitism and the English people, 1688–1788* (1989)

Archives BL, letter-books, Add. MSS 41738–41739 | Hunt. L., letters to Sir George Pocock

Likenesses portrait, *c.*1725, NMM

Lee, Francis (1661–1719), physician and millenarian, was born, probably at Cobham, Surrey, on 12 March 1661, the fourth son of Edward Lee and Frances Lee. He was related to the earl of Lichfield on his father's side and to the Percys of Northumbria on his mother's. He was orphaned at the age of four or five and placed in the care of a maternal aunt, Elizabeth Jenkins. Lee entered Merchant Taylors' School, London, on 11 September 1675. He matriculated at St John's College, Oxford, in 1679, proceeded BA on 9 May

1683 and MA on 19 March 1687, and was elected fellow of the college in January 1682. In 1691 he became chaplain to Ralph, Lord Stawell, of Somerton, Somerset, and tutor to his son, John Stawell; he was also tutor to Sir William Dawes, later archbishop of York. Lee's nonjuring principles led him to abandon the university, and from the summer of 1691 he travelled in Europe, visiting the Netherlands, Germany, and Italy. On 11 June 1692 he entered the University of Leiden, where he studied medicine. It was during this tour that Lee became involved with a number of pietists and followers of Jakob Boehme, including Johann Georg Gichtel and Pierre Poiret. He settled for two years in Venice, where he practised physic, before returning to England in 1694.

From this time Lee was closely associated with Jane *Lead, whose widowed daughter, Barbara Walton, he married in 1696 or 1697, in accordance with a divine revelation received by Lead. He subsequently lived in Lead's house in Hogsden Square, London. In 1697 he helped to found the Philadelphian Society, an ecumenical group of millenarians devoted to Boehme's ideas as interpreted by Lead. Members of the society believed that history was divided into seven ages, corresponding to the seven churches of Revelation; they themselves were inaugurating the sixth of these ages, in which the divisions of the church would be healed. Lee was co-editor, with his former schoolfellow Richard Roach, of the society's short-lived journal, the *Theosophical Transactions*.

Lee was under some pressure from his elder brother William and Henry Dodwell the elder to break with the Philadelphians. He defended his position vigorously in private correspondence and in *The State of the Philadelphian Society* (1697). The Philadelphians were criticized not only for their ecumenicalism, but also for their Boehmism, especially the role they accorded to the Virgin Sophia or Divine Wisdom in the godhead. While a forthright champion of the Philadelphians' ecumenicalism, Lee seemed less than candid in his defence of their heterodox teachings on divine gender. He distanced himself from his former associates after Lead's death had precipitated the society's collapse in 1704.

On 25 June 1708 Lee became a licentiate of the Royal College of Physicians. In 1709 he published *The History of Montanism* as the second part of a new edition of George Hickes's *The Spirit of Enthusiasm Exorcized*. This is generally regarded as a renunciation of his earlier Philadelphianism, but Lee never fully resolved the conflict in his personality between mystical enthusiasm and a more conventional high-church piety. It was also in 1709 that Lee began work on *An Epistolary Discourse, Concerning the Books of Esdras*, intended as an introduction to Simon Ockley's translation of the Esdraic Apocrypha. The work is permeated by Cabalism, as is Lee's 'Dissertations on the book of Genesis', published posthumously by his daughter in a selection of his writings, *Apoleipomena, or, Dissertations Theological, Mathematical, and Physical* (1752). This work also contains 'A short account of the author', which is curiously silent on Lee's Philadelphian associations.

In 1712 Lee lost the sight of his left eye, owing to a cataract. In 1719 he visited France, where he was in contact with the circle of Jeanne Guyon, one of the more controversial of the French quietists. Lee succumbed to fever while abroad, and died at Gravelines on 12 August 1719. He was buried in the precincts of the abbey at Gravelines, and subsequently reinterred within the walls of the building. He died intestate, and his estate was administered by his brother William in favour of his widow and his only child, Deborah Jemima.

Lee had a number of interests, and his writings include a short work of 1698, 'Proposals given to Peter the Great', suggesting various administrative and educational reforms. He was supposed to have inspired Robert Nelson in founding charity schools on the model of those he had seen in Halle, Germany. His principal concern was with religion, and especially with establishing an ecumenical spirit among the various churches. His personal piety was always one of high-church Anglicanism, even in his Philadelphian days, and there is no evidence to support the rumour that he converted to Roman Catholicism shortly before his death. B. J. GIBBONS

Sources F. Lee, *Apoleipomena, or, Dissertations theological, mathematical, and physical* (1752) • C. Walton, ed., *Notes and materials for an adequate biography of William Law* (1854) [incl. Lee's MSS] • DWL, Walton MSS, I.1.35; C-5-30; 24.109.7–9 • Munk, *Roll* • Wood, *Ath. Oxon.*

Archives LPL, letters | BL, letters to S. Ockley, Add. MS 15911 • DWL, Walton MSS

Lee, Sir Frank Godbould (1903–1971), civil servant and college head, was born at Colchester, Essex, on 26 August 1903, the eldest of three children and the only son of Joseph Godbould Lee and his wife, Florence Brown. Both parents were schoolteachers, and they soon moved to Brentwood. Frank, who attended Warley elementary school, won a scholarship to Brentwood School and from there in 1921 another to Downing College, Cambridge. He read English in part one of the tripos (1923) and history in part two (1924) and took a first class in both. He then passed into the Indian Civil Service, but, under parental pressure, returned to teach at Brentwood for a year. In 1926 he took the civil service examination again and entered the Colonial Office. He spent two years as district officer in Nyasaland and visited Cyprus and Bechuanaland. On 25 September 1937 he married Kathleen Mary, the daughter of Walter Harris, a chartered accountant in Hull, and spent the year 1938 at the Imperial Defence College.

In January 1940 Lee was transferred to the Treasury as a principal in the defence material division, dealing with the requirements of the service departments and the Ministry of Supply in all its aspects, including raw materials, oil, and the essential components. Here he made his mark, coping with the mass of work very largely on his own and becoming head of the division in 1943. In 1944 he went to Washington as deputy head of the Treasury delegation under R. H. Brand. There he became closely associated with Lord Keynes in negotiations over the end of lend-lease and the British loan agreement. He got on well

Sir Frank Godbould Lee (1903–1971), by Walter Stoneman, 1951

with Keynes and was able to deal with him on equal terms. A racy account by him of the lend-lease negotiations appears in chapter 19 of *Essays on John Maynard Keynes*, edited by Milo Keynes (1975).

In 1946 Lee returned to London as deputy secretary of the Ministry of Supply, dealing with the nationalization of the iron and steel industries. In 1948 he went back to Washington as a minister at the embassy, concerned with the distribution of Marshall aid. He returned to London in 1949 as permanent secretary of the Ministry of Food. In 1951 he became secretary to the Board of Trade, and in 1960 he returned to the Treasury as joint permanent secretary in charge of financial and economic policy. In 1962 he had a heart attack, and left the service. He was appointed CMG in 1946, KCB in 1950, and GCMG in 1959, and was sworn of the privy council in 1962.

Lee was an outstanding civil servant. Apart from an insatiable capacity for work, he was lucid and persuasive in argument, and had good personal relations with his staff, his colleagues in other departments, and his ministers, who were generally disposed to take his advice. His understanding of Americans and their ways was profound; in return Americans admired and liked him, as did his Commonwealth colleagues, and this was a great help in his negotiations. He drove himself too hard, welcoming responsibility, but tending to delegate too little to his staff. In his nine years at the Board of Trade he was an undoubted success, and this was perhaps the apogee of his official career. He also showed great promise in his brief spell at the Treasury, playing an influential part in the early days of incomes policy and, as a committed advocate of European integration, in the reappraisal of British policy towards Europe in 1960–62.

In 1962 Lee was elected master of Corpus Christi College, Cambridge, and threw himself into the life of the college and the university. He became chairman of the press syndicate, of the faculty board of engineering, and, as deputy to the vice-chancellor, of the university appointments board. He was also a member of the financial board of the university, and treasurer of the university rugby club. He was a governor of the Leys School, and vice-chairman of the board of Addenbrooke's Hospital, where he initiated a project for a sports and social centre for young doctors and nurses from the hospital which was completed after his death and named the Frank Lee Recreation Centre.

Outside Cambridge, Lee was a member of the council of the University of East Anglia, a governor of the London School of Economics, and a director of Bowaters. He was an honorary fellow of Downing College and received an honorary LLD from London University. He carried on all his varied activities with undiminished zest in spite of three further heart attacks and three strokes. He died in Cambridge on 18 April 1971.

Lee was a short, stocky man with a florid face, sharp pointed nose, and black, often crew-cut, hair. Energetic and forceful, he attacked the business in hand like a keen terrier attacking a large rat. He found enjoyment in work of all kinds and it was never a burden to him. He was full of humour, gregarious, and a lover of good food, good wine, and good company. He had a well-stocked and retentive mind and a fund of quotations and good stories. He was an avid reader of poetry, especially contemporary work. A good footballer in his youth, he played cricket whenever he could, and became a baseball fan. He wrote very little, and did not approve of public servants publishing their memoirs. But his Stamp memorial lecture of 1958, *The Board of Trade*, reveals much of his quality of mind and his approach to life. It was characteristic of him to decline a peerage, and to prefer appointment as a privy councillor. Before moving to Cambridge, the Lees lived a happy family and social life for twenty years at Much Hadham with their three daughters, all of whom followed their grandparents into the teaching profession.

SHERFIELD, *rev.* ALEC CAIRNCROSS

Sources *The Times* (29 April 1971) · personal knowledge (1986, 2004) · private information (1986, 2004)

Archives BLPES, corresp. with J. E. Meade · PRO, board of trade files, BT91

Likenesses W. Stoneman, photograph, 1951, NPG [*see illus.*]

Wealth at death £28,970: probate, 1 July 1971, *CGPLA Eng. & Wales*

Lee, Frederick, Baron Lee of Newton (1906–1984), trade unionist and politician, was born at 16 Ellison Street, Stockton Heath, Cheshire, on 3 August 1906, the son of Joseph William Lee, an iron moulder, and his wife, Margaret, *née* McKenna. The family moved subsequently to Salford where Lee was educated at Langworthy Road School. He served an engineering apprenticeship, but from 1930 to 1934 spent long periods unemployed. Subsequently he worked as a turner at the Metrovicks (Metropolitan Vickers) works in Trafford Park. Within this large plant he became chairman of the works committee and a member of the Manchester district committee of the Amalgamated Engineering Union (AEU). In 1944 and 1945 he was elected a delegate to the union's policy-making body, the national committee. On 23 April 1938 he married Amelia (Millie; *b.* 1914/15), daughter of William Shay, a crane driver. They had one daughter.

Although Lee's time on the factory floor and his trade union experiences remained central to his identity, from 1945 he became essentially a politician. His home had a strongly socialist culture, both his parents being members of the Independent Labour Party. Lee attended a socialist Sunday school in Pendleton and joined the West Salford Labour Party in 1922. He was active in national and local Labour Party campaigns from the early 1920s and sat on Salford city council from 1940 to 1945. He was elected as the AEU sponsored Labour MP for Manchester Hulme in the 1945 general election; following the abolition of this seat, he sat as MP for Newton from February 1950 until he retired from the House of Commons in February 1974.

Lee soon became recognized as one of the more talented trade union backbenchers in the 1945 parliament. He was the only trade union member among the fifteen signatories of the *Keep Left* pamphlet, a product of their critical discussions about government policy during the winter of 1947. He had no sympathy with the left-wing foreign policy concerns of most of the pamphlet's signatories, and his trade union ethic of solidarity meant that he had little toleration of ostentatious rebellion against the government. His enthusiasm for *Keep Left* focused on the sections on economic planning and public ownership. He also developed an early and enduring commitment to an incomes policy as a key element in socialist strategy. This attachment was informed by his experience at Metrovicks. In his view the complexities of localized bargaining could not generate rational and just solutions to problems of income distribution.

Lee subsequently became parliamentary private secretary to Sir Stafford Cripps, a relationship that he found particularly rewarding, and was a British delegate to the Council of Europe in 1949. Following the 1950 general election he entered the government as parliamentary secretary to the Ministry of Labour and National Service, working in turn with George Isaacs, Aneurin Bevan, and Alf Robens.

Lee felt that the ministerial resignations in April 1951 were unnecessary and he was one of the five parliamentary secretaries who sent a letter to Bevan in an unsuccessful attempt to persuade him not to resign. During the factional battles within the Labour Party that marked the early years in opposition, Lee played a reconciling role, seeking to limit the damage inflicted by ideological and personal antipathies. His most notable peace-making intervention came over the attempt to withdraw the whip from Bevan in March 1955. He voted for Bevan in the leadership election of December 1955, and his relationship with Hugh Gaitskell was never close. The Gaitskellites saw him simplistically as a left-winger and Gaitskell had a rather dismissive view of his ability. Nevertheless, from November 1959 he was elected annually to the parliamentary committee (shadow cabinet).

Following the decision of the 1960 Labour Party conference in favour of unilateralism Lee allied with Harold Wilson against what they characterized as Gaitskell's unnecessarily confrontational style. Wilson opposed Gaitskell for the leadership, and Lee contested the deputy leadership against George Brown and Jim Callaghan. In the second ballot Brown defeated him by 164 votes to 83. When Wilson was subsequently elected leader in February 1963, Lee was the only member of the parliamentary committee to vote for him.

Within the 1964 Labour cabinet Lee was appointed minister of power. This post posed two serious problems for him. Labour's 1964 manifesto included a commitment to renationalizing the steel industry, an indication for some within the government of socialist rectitude. Lee shared this sentiment, but the parliamentary situation—with a wafer-thin majority—was unfavourable. The Liberals opposed the policy and two Labour backbenchers, Desmond Donnelly and Woodrow Wyatt, were publicly hostile. The legislation was not passed until the parliamentary arithmetic had been transformed following the 1966 general election, and Lee had left the ministry. Inevitably the earlier frustrations had reduced his credibility.

The minister's second major challenge concerned the coal industry. Demand had been declining since 1957, and pit closures inevitably followed. The National Union of Mineworkers (NUM) anticipated that a Labour government would mean a different policy. Instead, closures on economic grounds accelerated. Lee presented delegates to the NUM conference in 1965 with the vision of a smaller, productive, mechanized, and high wage industry. But he insisted that loss-making collieries had to be closed. The NUM remained under the control of a loyalist right prepared to work with a Labour government; but in the longer term this experience of decline was one source of the radicalism that eventually transformed the politics of the union.

Lee became the last secretary of state for the colonies in April 1966, an appointment of limited duration given the pace of decolonization. In January 1967 he left the cabinet, but took on a responsibility much more in keeping with his talents. As chancellor of the duchy of Lancaster, he worked through the Department of Economic Affairs, liaising with workers and employers about the details of the government's prices and incomes policies. His enthusiasm for the project and his shop floor experience were strengths; but the political environment was discouraging. The 1966 economic crisis had meant that incomes policy became equated readily with a wage freeze and then wage restraint. Lee's belief that a constructive agenda was feasible encountered deepening union scepticism. Within his own union this was indicated by the election of another Metrovicks 'graduate', an opponent of statutory incomes policy, Hugh Scanlon, as AEU president in 1968. With the creation of the Department of Employment and Productivity in April 1968, responsibility for prices and incomes was transferred there. Lee's remaining responsibilities included the economic development of the northern region; he was also involved in the early committee discussions that produced the abortive white paper on trade union reform, *In Place of Strife*. He left the government in October 1969.

Following his retirement from the Commons, Lee accepted a life peerage in July 1974 as Baron Lee of Newton. He was an active member of the Lords; appropriately his last brief intervention in July 1983 was a defence of trade union democracy—and especially that of the engineers. He died at his home, 52 Ashton Road, Newton-le-Willows, St Helens, Lancashire, on 4 February 1984, and was buried at St Peter's Church, Newton-le-Willows. He was survived by his wife.

Fred Lee was stocky and genial, very conscious of his trade union roots and his regional identity. A thoughtful and hard-working parliamentarian, with a concern for party unity, his ministerial career from 1964 brought him more criticism than praise. Only in his work on incomes policy were his abilities and experience put to good use, but this occurred in a context which separated him from much trade union opinion. His political career was symptomatic of a planning and modernization agenda that had its roots in the experiences and debates of the 1930s and 1940s. The problems of implementation encountered by its advocates after 1964 arguably helped to engender radicalisms of both left and right. DAVID HOWELL

Sources I. Richter, *Political purpose in trade unions* (1973) • Lord Robens [A. Robens], *Ten year stint* (1972) • *The backbench diaries of Richard Crossman*, ed. J. Morgan (1981) • R. H. S. Crossman, *The diaries of a cabinet minister*, 3 vols. (1975–7), vols. 1–2 • *The Castle diaries, 1964–1976*, abridged edn (1990) • *The political diary of Hugh Dalton, 1918–1940, 1945–1960*, ed. B. Pimlott (1986) • J. Schneer, *Labour's conscience: the labour left, 1945–51* (1988) • b. cert. • m. cert. • d. cert. • personal knowledge (2004) • private information (2004) [Mrs Flint, daughter] • *WW*

Archives NRA, papers and press-cuttings • priv. coll., autobiography | FILM BFI NFTVA, party political footage

Wealth at death £73,308: probate, 9 May 1984, *CGPLA Eng. & Wales*

Lee, Frederick George (1832–1902), writer on theology, was born at School House, Thame, Oxfordshire, on 6 January 1832, the eldest son of Frederick Lee (*d.* 1842), sometime rector of Easington, Oxfordshire, and vicar of Stantonbury, Berkshire, and his wife, Mary, only daughter of George Ellys of Aylesbury. The Thame neighbourhood had been home to the Lee family from at least the sixteenth century. Lee's grandfather Thomas Tripp Lee had been vicar of Thame since 1795 and his father had returned there as curate. Both upheld the high-church tradition in the Church of England which descended from the Caroline divines of the seventeenth century through the nonjuring clergy of the eighteenth. This family influence, and his loyalty to the practices and doctrinal position of the church at Thame, dominated Lee's outlook and writings.

Lee was educated at Thame grammar school and matriculated at St Edmund Hall, Oxford, on 23 October 1851; after three years he failed to graduate. A contemporary commented that Lee's other interests distracted him from his studies. While still an undergraduate he contributed to various periodicals and published verses. In 1854 he won the Newdigate prize for a poem, *The Martyrs of Vienne and Lyons*, which went into several editions. He was admitted SCL (student of civil law) in the same year. The title Dr Lee by which he was widely known derived from an honorary DD conferred in 1879 by Washington and Lee University, Virginia. Lee entered Cuddesdon Theological College in 1854, and was ordained deacon in the same year to a title at Sunningwell, Berkshire, and priest in 1856. With his private means he did not need to depend on continuous ecclesiastical appointments, but was free to devote himself to causes of his choosing: they included the restoration of ritual to worship on aesthetic grounds, which paved the way to his interest in the reunion of the churches.

A photograph taken in middle life shows Lee as thickset and melancholy; it belies the mental energy that his considerable literary output must have required, but suggests, as does his verse, that his love for antiquity found him dissatisfied with the present. Uppermost was his longing for a return to an undivided Christendom. Still in his twenties, and while ministering for a short period at the Berkeley Chapel in John Street, Mayfair, he founded the short-lived *Union Newspaper*, which came to the notice of Ambrose Phillipps de Lisle, a prominent Roman Catholic. Together, in 1857, they established the Association for the Promotion of the Union of Christendom. Lee became secretary, and editor of the *Union Review*, a substantial periodical to which he was a frequent contributor. Both association and *Review* met with criticism. Lee became no stranger to opposition, which followed him to Scotland in 1860: when he was the incumbent of St John's, Aberdeen, his opinions divided the congregation. His supporters built for him a new large church, St Mary's, which the bishop of Aberdeen was unwilling to consecrate unless Lee acceded to terms regarding the use of unauthorized vestments, incense, and the positioning of lamps. Lee refused and in 1864 resigned. In 1867 he was presented to the living of All Saints', Lambeth, London, where he remained for thirty-two years. Virtually isolated from the main body of the Church of England, relegated to an unsalubrious backwater, he made it his own with elaborate ceremonial, processions of a hundred persons, persuasive preaching, and the use of his private money as relief for the poor.

Lee's writings were prolific and provide seventy-two separate entries in the catalogue of the British Library. They comprise devotional works, verse, novels, essays, sermons, and books on art and architecture, ceremonial, and the supernatural. He founded and contributed to many periodicals. His histories generally failed to be objective. Two works have been considered of value: the first is a translation from the Latin of the *Paraphrastica expositio articulorum confessionis Anglicanae* (1634) of Christopher Davenport (Franciscus a Sancta Clara) on the Thirty-Nine Articles, which Lee published with a commentary in

1865; the second is his *The Validity of the Holy Orders of the Church of England Maintained and Vindicated* (1870), which was well received. It has been suggested that Lee's researches made him question the validity of his orders, but as late as 1898 he wrote: 'to my defence of them, made 30 years ago … I unhesitatingly adhere' (Lee, 731).

In an enterprise of considerable eccentricity Lee in 1877 founded the Order of Corporate Reunion as a focal point for sympathizers of unity. He claimed that he and two fellow members had been consecrated bishops by prelates whose orders were held valid by three lines of succession in the churches of east and west. Lee, whose consecration was believed to have taken place near Venice, took the title 'bishop of Dorchester'. The consecration of Thomas Mossman, rector of East and West Torrington, Lincolnshire, as 'bishop of Selby' and of J. T. Seccombe, an Anglican layman, as 'bishop of Caerleon' were never satisfactorily explained. Secrecy, which has not been broken, bound members of the order, and though some 'ordinations' took place, it did not survive. Lee became disillusioned and recognized that he had made a mistake.

Lee married on 9 June 1859 Elvira Louisa, daughter of Joseph Duncan Ostrehan, vicar of Creech St Michael, Somerset; they had three sons and one daughter. His wife predeceased him in 1890, having joined the Roman Catholic church. Lee himself was received as a Roman Catholic on 11 December 1901, six weeks before his death, by Father Best of the London Oratory. He died, after a short illness, at his home at 22 Earl's Court Gardens, London, on 23 January 1902 and was buried in Brookwood cemetery, Surrey. MARGARET PAWLEY

Sources H. R. T. Brandreth, *Dr Lee of Lambeth* (1951) · M. Pawley, *Faith and family: the life and circle of Ambrose Phillipps de Lisle* (1993) · H. R. T. Brandreth, *Episcopi vagantes and the Anglican church* (1949) · P. F. Anson, *Bishops at large* (1964) · F. G. Lee, 'The O. C. R. and its work', *Nineteenth Century*, 44 (1898), 731–48 · J. H. Crehan, 'Black market in episcopal orders', *The Month*, 3rd ser., 2 (1970), 352–8 · *The Times* (25 Jan 1902) · m. cert.

Archives Bodl. Oxf., Oxfordshire and Buckinghamshire topographical notes and drawings · Bucks. RLSS, collection of Buckinghamshire prints · LPL, papers, mainly relating to Christian unity | Pusey Oxf., APUC, OCR MSS · Quenby Hall, Leicestershire, de Lisle archives · Stockerston Hall, Oakham, Rutland, de Lisle archives

Likenesses photographs, repro. in Brandreth, *Dr Lee of Lambeth*

Wealth at death £547 6*s*. 3*d*.: administration with will, 21 April 1902, *CGPLA Eng. & Wales*

Lee, Frederick Richard (1798–1879), landscape painter, was born on 10 June 1798 at Barnstaple, Devon, and baptized there on 15 July, the son of Thomas Lee and his wife, Mary. When young he joined the army, obtaining a commission in the 56th regiment and serving through a campaign in the Netherlands, but he left the army owing to weak health. Lee had practised painting as an amateur and now devoted himself to it as a profession. In 1818 he became a student at the Royal Academy. From 1822 until 1870 he exhibited on a regular basis in London; he exhibited 131 pictures at the British Institution, and from 1824 to 1870 171 pictures at the Royal Academy, exhibiting six pictures in the first exhibition held at Burlington House in 1869; he also exhibited twenty-four works at the Society of British Artists between 1825 and 1837. Lee is renowned for his sunlit, tranquil Devon landscapes, pastoral scenes with trees in full leaf and cattle standing in calm pools of water. John Ruskin described Lee's work as 'well intentioned, simple, free from affectation or imitation, and evidently painted with constant reference to nature' (*Art Journal*, 1908, 376). Apart from Devon, Lee painted landscapes throughout England, Scotland, and Wales. *Gathering Seaweed* (exh. RA, 1836; V&A) shows horses and figures between a still sea and sky, probably on the Lincolnshire coast. During the 1830s Lee painted views near Penshurst, Kent, for his patron, the collector William Wells of Redleaf, Kent, and an example, *Near Redleaf, Kent*, is at the Victoria and Albert Museum, London. Also at that museum is *Wooded Glen*, showing cattle standing in a stream; this painting is signed and dated 1860 by both Lee and his friend Thomas Sidney Cooper, the animal painter. From 1847 Lee and Cooper had a system of collaborating on paintings. Cooper states: 'We settled that he should paint the landscape part first, and send the picture up to me in an advanced state, the part where I was to introduce the cattle being only just covered over' (Cooper, 1.329).

Six oil paintings by Lee are in the Tate collection and in two of these Lee had the collaboration of Sir Edwin Landseer in painting figures and animals, and in another two works Cooper painted the cattle.

Lee owned Broadgate House at Pilton, near Barnstaple; he loved fishing, the sea, and yachting, and towards the end of his life he lived a great deal on board his yacht *Kingfisher*, in which he sailed around Europe, the Baltic, and as far as Africa and Australia. Understanding of the movement of the sea and waves breaking can be seen in pictures such as *The Breakwater at Plymouth* (exh. RA, 1856) and *Homeward Bound off Cape St Vincent* (exh. RA, 1863), depicting the contrast of sail and steamships. In 1864 Lee sailed to Italy and visited Garibaldi; his painting *General Garibaldi's Residence at Caprera—Looking across the Straits of Bonifacio towards Corsica* was exhibited at the Royal Academy the next year. Lee was elected an associate of the Royal Academy in 1834 and a Royal Academician in 1838; his diploma work held at the Royal Academy is *Morning in the Meadows* (1869). In 1870 Lee exhibited for the last time. He died on 5 June 1879 at Vliesch Bank Farm, Hermon Station, Malmsbury, Cape Colony, where some of his family were living. Lee was married, but of his wife nothing is known. He was a prolific painter primarily in oils but also in watercolour and his work can be seen in many collections; there are a good number of his oil paintings at the Royal Albert Memorial Museum and Art Gallery, Exeter.

L. H. CUST, *rev.* SARAH WIMBUSH

Sources G. Pycroft, *Art in Devonshire* (1883) · R. Parkinson, ed., *Catalogue of British oil paintings, 1820–1860* (1990) [catalogue of V&A] · C. A. Dars, ed., *Subject catalogue of paintings in public collections*, London, Tate Gallery old masters collection, vol. 2 (1990) · Graves, *Artists* · Graves, *RA exhibitors* · Wood, *Vic. painters*, 3rd edn · T. S. Cooper, *My life*, 2 vols. (1890) · *Art Journal*, new ser., 28 (1908), 376; 41 (1879), 184 · *North Devon Journal* (17 July 1879) · B. Ransom, 'Devon landscape artists: Frederick Richard Lee', *Devon Historian*, 49 (Oct 1994), 19–22 · photographs, Courtauld Inst., Witt Library · *CGPLA Eng. & Wales* (1879) · *IGI*

Likenesses J. Hollins, oils, 1850, priv. coll.; Bonhams 26 Oct 1989, lot 100 • H. Watkins, albumen print, 1855–9, NPG • J. & C. Watkins, two albumen cartes-de-visite, NPG
Wealth at death under £25,000: probate, 30 Sept 1879, *CGPLA Eng. & Wales*

Lee, Sir George (1700?–1758), ecclesiastical lawyer and politician, was the fifth son of Sir Thomas Lee, second baronet, and his wife, Alice, the daughter and coheir of Thomas Hopkins, a London merchant. Among his elder brothers was the judge William *Lee. On 21 March 1716 he was entered as a pensioner at Clare College, Cambridge, but he later moved to Christ Church, Oxford, where he matriculated on 4 April 1720 and took the degrees of BCL (1724) and DCL (1729). Having already entered the Middle Temple in 1719, on 23 October 1729 he was admitted as an advocate at Doctors' Commons, where he soon established a high reputation. The Lees were politically allied with the dukes of Bridgewater in Buckinghamshire, and Lee was returned to parliament as member for Brackley, Northamptonshire, on 25 January 1733, in the Bridgewater interest. He acted with the adherents of Prince Frederick, and his election as chairman of the committee of privileges and elections on 16 December 1741, when he defeated the ministerial nominee, Giles Earle, presaged Walpole's downfall. Through Lord Carteret's influence, and to the annoyance of the prince of Wales, he was appointed a lord of the Admiralty on 19 March 1742. As a result he was required to give up his parliamentary seat, as Bridgewater opposed his taking office. Lee later represented Devizes (1742–7), Liskeard (1747–54), and Launceston (1754–8). When Carteret lost his place as secretary of state, Lee refused the offers of his opponents and followed him into retirement.

On 5 June 1742 Lee married Judith (*c.*1710–1743), the second daughter of the Hanoverian tory MP Humphry Morice, of Werrington Park, near Launceston; the marriage was ended by Judith's death on 19 July 1743. There were no children.

Lee returned to the circle of Prince Frederick and by 1749 was, with the second earl of Egmont, one of the prince's closest advisers. It was intended that Lee should take a prominent part in forming an administration on Frederick's accession, and in some extant lists is named as chancellor of the exchequer. Immediately on the prince's death he joined the widow in burning all his private papers, and, in spite of the opposition of the Pelhams, was made treasurer of her household (1751). From 1751 until his death he held the offices of dean of arches and judge of the prerogative court of Canterbury, and he was duly knighted (12 February 1752) and, on the following day, was sworn of the privy council. Lee was offered the exchequer by Newcastle in 1755 as part of a scheme to bring Egmont, Lee, and their followers into the ministry and thus outflank Pitt, but Lee and his allies wanted first the freedom to vote against the Russian treaty, and this Newcastle could not allow. In 1757 he resigned his place of treasurer to the princess dowager in response to Lord Bute's rise into favour. Lee reluctantly agreed to be chancellor of the exchequer in a further attempt by Newcastle to include him in an anti-Pitt ministry, but the duke, almost at once and without 'the least notice' to those who had agreed to join him, abandoned his scheme.

Although he was an effective speaker, Lee's success in his profession disqualified him for the highest ministerial office. His legal judgments were held in high regard in the late eighteenth and nineteenth centuries, in particular an exposition of the nature and extent of the jurisdiction exercised by courts of law over ships and cargoes of neutral powers established within the territories of belligerent states, written in answer to a memorial from the king of Prussia, attributed to Lee and Lord Mansfield. Lee died suddenly at his house in St James's Square, London, on 18 December 1758 and was buried on 28 December in the family vault underneath the east end of Hartwell church, Buckinghamshire, alongside his wife.

W. P. Courtney, *rev.* Matthew Kilburn

Sources A. Newman, ed., 'Leicester House politics, 1750–60, from the papers of John, second earl of Egmont', *Camden miscellany, XXIII*, CS, 4th ser., 7 (1969), 85–228 • A. S. Foord, *His majesty's opposition, 1714–1830* (1964) • A. Edwards, *Frederick Louis, prince of Wales, 1707–1751* (1947) • W. H. Smyth, *Aedes Hartwellianae* (1851) • R. R. Sedgwick, 'Lee, George', HoP, *Commons*
Archives Bucks. RLSS, corresp. and papers • Hist. Soc. Penn., papers • HLRO, papers • Lincoln's Inn, London, commonplace book on ecclesiastical law • LPL, corresp. and legal papers • NMM, corresp. and notes on legal cases | CCC Cam., corresp. with Thomas Herring • Herts. ALS, letters to William Lee
Likenesses J. Faber junior, mezzotint (after J. Wills), BM, NPG

Lee, Sir (Albert) George (1879–1967), telecommunications engineer, was born at Conwy, Caernarvonshire, on 24 May 1879, the son of George Henry Payne Lee, a Post Office engineer, and his wife, Maria Agnes, *née* Bosmell. He grew up in Conwy, leaving there to attend the collegiate school, Llandudno. Little is known about his activities in the years after he left school until he joined the Post Office engineering department as an engineering assistant in London in November 1901, at a time when his father was engineer-in-charge of the Bangor section of the north Wales district of the Post Office. This was a period when the Post Office was integrating the diverse local services, which operated under the general oversight of the National Telephone Company, into a co-ordinated national whole. It was also a time when the application of scientific principles was beginning to produce important improvements and opportunities. On 25 May 1903 he married Susie Lydia Campbell (*d.* 1944), a widow, daughter of William Tanner, physician; they had one daughter.

Lee's innate drive and potential began to show itself in this fertile environment, for he made small but significant contributions to the redesign of experimental air-core loading coils on the new London–Birmingham telephone cable. Within five years he had graduated as BSc (London) after part-time study at Northampton Institute, Finsbury Technical College, and King's College, London.

By 1908 Lee had begun to contribute articles of increasing authority to technical journals and to establish his reputation as an expert on telephone transmission theory and practice. During the four years between 1908 and 1912 he experienced both 'field' management and command,

and achieved his father's rank of sectional engineer, at Bolton. Returning to the London headquarters in 1912, Lee was responsible for leading teams in the final stages of engineering integration of the national telecommunications systems into the overall Post Office network. On the outbreak of war in 1914 he was commissioned in the Royal Engineers signal service, becoming officer in charge of general headquarters signals area. Lee received the MC and continued his military service throughout the subsequent years of peace as lieutenant-colonel, Royal Corps of Signals (supplementary reserve).

When Lee returned to the Post Office his imagination was captured by the rapidly developing use of radio communications. Throughout the 1920s his interest was radiotelephony and -telegraphy for international communication. In 1921 he acted as British delegate to the inter-allied radio conference in Paris. In 1921–2 he visited Egypt and India to develop 'wireless' services with Britain. In 1923 he began work on transatlantic telephony in conjunction with the Atlantic Telephony and Telegraphy Company. This was at first experimental and included the building of Rugby radio station and, in 1926, the opening of a successful commercial service. From such beginnings developed, in the late 1920s and early 1930s, an empire-wide communications system of immense strategic and commercial significance.

In December 1931 George Lee was appointed engineer-in-chief, a post he held until his retirement from the Post Office in 1939. These were difficult years, with the aftermath of the depression, the rapidly changing international scene, and the threat of war.

When the Second World War broke out Lee became director of communications, research, and development at the Air Ministry, and in 1944 was appointed senior telecommunications officer in the Ministry of Supply. After the war he was a member of the Scientific Advisory Council of the Ministry of Supply and served as a member of the Royal Commission on Awards to Inventors from 1946 to 1955.

In 1929 Lee was vice-president of the Institute of Radio Engineers of America—the first Englishman to hold that honour. He was elected president of the Institution of Electrical Engineers for the year 1937–8. He was appointed OBE in 1927, and a knighthood was conferred upon him in January 1937. His first wife died in 1944 and on 1 February 1950 he married (Ivy) Laura Powell (*b. c.*1895), a widow, daughter of Edmund William Maidlow, builder.

Although he was an internationally recognized electrical engineer, a careful and meticulous administrator, and a man who cared about his fellow engineers, George Lee yet remained unknown as a person to his colleagues and staff. He was accepted and sought-after within the bounds of his official and professional activities but, to those who were even close colleagues, little was ever disclosed of the man, his deeper interests, his family, or his innermost thoughts. Memory and photographs evoke a short, neat, precise man looking out through small circular spectacles, the very confines of which seemed to exclude reference to any matter other than that in hand. Yet it is upon Lee's imaginative, specific judgements that the superstructure of much of today's global communications soundly rests. Lee died at his home, Chedworth, Cokes Lane, Chalfont St Giles, near Amersham, Buckinghamshire, on 26 August 1967. He was survived by his second wife.

J. H. H. MERRIMAN, *rev.*

Sources post office records, Post Office Archives, Freeling House, 23 Glasshill Street, London · *Electronics & Power, the Journal of the Institution of Electrical Engineers*, 13 (1967), 397 · *Post Office Electrical Engineers' Journal* · personal knowledge (1981) · private information (1981) · m. certs · d. cert. · probate

Likenesses photographs

Wealth at death £5217: probate, 31 Oct 1967, *CGPLA Eng. & Wales*

Lee, George Alexander (1802–1851), composer, was born in London, the son of a boxer, Harry Lee, who apparently kept the Anti-Gallican tavern in Shire Lane, Temple Bar. While a boy he is reported to have been in Lord Barrymore's service as a page, under the name 'Tiger', and is recorded as the first to bear that title. The talent he demonstrated for music and his pleasant voice enabled him to receive instruction in singing, and he began his career as a tenor and conductor at Dublin in 1822. He was engaged as a tenor at the Dublin Theatre in 1825. The following year he returned to London and appeared at the Haymarket Theatre, and in 1827 he was appointed conductor there. Shortly before this he had started a music shop in the Quadrant, Regent Street. Around the same time he also began writing music for the stage, notably for several plays at Covent Garden. His opera *The Sublime and the Beautiful* was produced there in 1828, and another, *The Nymph of the Grotto, or, A Daughter's Vow*, written in collaboration with Giovanni Liverati, was presented in 1829.

In 1829 he joined with the singer Melrose and John Kemble Chapman in managing the Tottenham Street Theatre for the purpose of producing English operas, but he was forced to secede from the management a year later following heavy penalties incurred by the lessees through certain infringements of the rights of the patent theatres. He then became co-lessee of Drury Lane with Captain Polhill, but retired after a single season. In 1831 he directed the Lenten oratorios at Drury Lane and Covent Garden, and in 1832 was appointed composer and music director to the Strand Theatre, where during 1834 he also took on managerial responsibilities. He ran a music shop in Frith Street between 1835 and 1836 and conducted and composed for the Olympic Theatre in 1845 and for Vauxhall in 1849. He was the pianist at the 'Poses plastiques' exhibition in Bow Street.

Lee's adaptations for the theatre included two of Auber's operas (*Fra Diavolo*, as *The Devil's Brother*, Drury Lane, 1831, and *Le lac des fées*, as *The Fairy Lake*, Strand Theatre, 1839). In all, his output for the stage included music for some twenty plays, burlettas, and melodramas. In addition, he composed a number of songs and ballads, of which the most popular were 'Away, away to the mountain's brow', 'Come where the aspens quiver', and 'The Macgregors' Gathering'. He also published two sets of eight songs, *Beauties of Byron* and *Loves of the Butterflies*, the words of the latter by Thomas Haynes Bayly, whose verses

Lee frequently set to music. His *Complete Course of Instructions for Singing* was published in 1872.

about 1840 Lee married the popular ballad singer Harriet *Waylett, *née* Cooke (1800–1851), whom he had known for about ten years and who had long been separated from her first husband, who died that year. Lee was devoted to her, and it is said that her death, on 29 April 1851, resulted in a shock from which he never recovered. In fact he died, in London, on 8 October of the same year.

R. F. Sharp, *rev.* David J. Golby

Sources A. Loewenberg, 'Lee, George Alexander', *New Grove*

Lee, George Augustus (1761–1826), cotton spinner and mill manager, was the only son of John *Lee (*d.* 1781), actor-manager, and his Portuguese-born actress wife. Lee's mother died early, and he was brought up by his sister Sophia. The children were well educated, and two of his five sisters, Sophia *Lee (*bap.* 1750, *d.* 1824) and Harriet *Lee (1757/8–1851), were to become authors. George 'became early imbued with a love of the sciences' (*Annual Biography and Obituary*, 11.245).

Lee's first recorded employment was in the 1780s as a clerk at the Northwich cotton mill of Peter Drinkwater, a Manchester merchant, who, in 1791, appointed him manager of a newly erected factory behind London Road, Manchester. A year later he left to become managing partner in the Chapel Street mill of the Salford Engine Twist Company owned by George and John Philips, Peter Atherton, and Charles Wood. Atherton and Wood left the company and by 1807 it had become known as Philips and Lee. Lee ran the business until his retirement, shortly before his death.

The Salford mill, among Manchester's largest, became a model enterprise: the mill was extended, using an original and fire-resistant cast-iron frame construction, albeit probably drawing on the earlier efforts of William Strutt and Samuel Bage; the application of the steam engine to cotton-spinning machinery was perfected; steam heating was introduced; gas lighting, reputedly the first for a cotton mill, replaced candles and oil around 1805; the machinery was constantly improved; and the workshops became a source of skill for the wider industry. Lee carefully co-ordinated production, experimented with cost analysis, and handled his workforce, whom he encouraged to organize a sick scheme, better than most. Even so, working hours were among the longest in Manchester. The Philipses' capital and Lee's astute management enabled the firm to negotiate the difficult years of the French and Napoleonic wars, and the firm's capital grew steadily. The mills became one of Manchester's sights and were visited by other industrialists, the scientific, and the curious, including William Edgeworth, an engineer who had worked for the Strutts, and the Swiss diarist J. C. Fischer.

Lee's abilities, the early patronage of Drinkwater and Philips, and his marriage in 1803 to Mary, daughter of the Revd John Ewart of Troqueer, drew him into the Manchester and midlands network of industrialists, engineers, scientists, liberals, and nonconformists. His five children were baptized in the exclusive Mosley Street Unitarian Chapel. His friends included the older and younger Soho partners and their workmen, particularly William Murdoch, on whose experiments with gas lighting he drew, and William Strutt (1756–1830). Among the mourners at his funeral in 1826 were the Ewarts, Manchester's cotton élite, and Benjamin Gott of Leeds. Lee's skills were held in high repute; he helped his friend William Henry in his experiments with coal gas, and was in all probability the G. Lee admitted to membership of the Manchester Literary and Philosophical Society in 1790. He was ever alive to fresh ideas, which he readily exchanged with friends, and visited factories in France, Prussia, and Switzerland. Lee had the greatest respect for the technical achievements of others; in 1811–12, he took a prominent part in efforts to obtain government recognition for Samuel Crompton, and he gave much information concerning the early cotton industry to the 1816 committee on the employment of children. Though 'capable of acts of the greatest disinterestedness' (*GM*, 281), he was not widely involved in public and charitable work.

Lee's wife, his son, and a daughter, predeceased him; for a time his sister Harriet was his housekeeper. Described in 1814 as 'one of the most outstanding Englishmen' (Henderson, 143) he died at his home, Singleton Brook, Cheetham Hill, near Manchester, on 5 August 1826 after 'a painful and lingering illness', and was buried five days later; he left his considerable estate to his surviving daughters. In 1829 Mary Ann (1805–1837), the eldest, married her cousin, William Ewart MP (1798–1869).

J. J. Mason

Sources A. E. Musson and E. Robinson, *Science and technology in the industrial revolution* (1969) · J. Tann, *The development of the factory* (1970) · W. H. Chaloner, 'Robert Owen, Peter Drinkwater, and the early factory system in Manchester, 1788–1800', *Bulletin of the John Rylands University Library*, 37 (1954–5), 78–102 · R. Owen, *The life of Robert Owen written by himself*, 1 (1857); repr. (1967) · A. Howe, *The cotton masters, 1830–1860* (1984) · W. A. Munford, *William Ewart M.P.* (1960) · W. O. Henderson, *J. C. Fischer and his diary of industrial England, 1814–1851* (1966) · J. C. Fischer, *Tagebücher* (1951) · *Manchester Guardian* (12 Aug 1826) · *Annual Biography and Obituary*, 9 (1825), 127–35 [obit. of Sophia Lee] · *Annual Biography and Obituary*, 11 (1827), 245–9 · *GM*, 1st ser., 96/2 (1826), 281–2 · G. W. Daniels, *The early English cotton industry, with some unpublished letters of Samuel Crompton* (1920) · W. Murdoch, 'An account of the application of the gas from coal to economical purposes', *PTRS*, 98 (1808), 124–32 · A. McCulloch and W. Buckley, 'Leaves from an old notebook', *Memoirs of the Literary and Philosophical Society of Manchester*, 74 (1929–30) · R. A. Smith, *A centenary of science in Manchester* (1883) · 'Select committee on the petition of Mr Samuel Crompton', *Parl. papers* (1812), 2.89, no. 126 · 'Select committee on the state of the children employed in the manufactories of the United Kingdom', *Parl. papers* (1816), 3.235, no. 397

Archives Birmingham Public Library, Birm. CA, letters to Boulton family

Wealth at death under £40,000: Lancs. RO, WCW George Augustus Lee of Salford, 5 Aug 1826

Lee, George Henry, third earl of Lichfield (1718–1772), politician, was born in London on 21 May 1718, eldest son of George Henry Lee, second earl of Lichfield (1690–1743), landowner, and his wife, Frances (1697/8–1769), daughter of Sir John Hales, fourth baronet, of Hackington, Kent,

George Henry Lee, third earl of Lichfield (1718–1772), by George Huddesford, 1777

and his first wife, Helen Mary Catherine Bealing; he had three younger brothers and six sisters. His mother was brought up as a Catholic by her father, who was styled second earl of Tenterden in the Jacobite peerage. Styled Viscount Quarendon until 1743, Lee was educated at Westminster School (1728–35), matriculated from St John's College, Oxford, in January 1736, and proceeded MA in 1738.

Promising and handsome, Quarendon was by-elected to parliament for Oxfordshire on 27 February 1740, and was re-elected in 1741. As a tory he spoke against the army establishments on 10 December 1740, but unlike his father did not vote for Robert Walpole's dismissal in February 1741. He was, however, a frequent critic of the government, and served as a member of the committee of inquiry into Walpole's administration. He was particularly hostile, as indicated by a long speech of 10 December 1742, to the influence of Hanover in British politics. After succeeding as earl, he denounced the subsidy to Hanoverian troops in his maiden Lords speech in December 1743. In Oxfordshire, where he had succeeded his father as lord lieutenant, he remained inclined to opposition and was active in the tory interest in the north of the county. He also succeeded to the lifelong sinecure of *custos brevium* in common pleas. He was created DCL at Oxford on 25 August 1743. He married, at the Queen Street Chapel in Bath, on 16 January 1745, Dinah (1718/19–1779), daughter and coheir of Sir Thomas Frankland, third baronet, of Thirkleby, Yorkshire, and his first wife, Dinah Topham. She was fourth in descent from Oliver Cromwell, as was he from Charles II. In 1747 he belonged to the tory junto seeking alliance with Frederick, prince of Wales, but was lampooned as a papist. He was a visitor to France before 1750.

In January 1759 Lichfield withdrew the day before a three-cornered contest for the chancellorship of Oxford University, to the advantage of another tory, Lord Westmorland, who defeated the whig candidate. Lichfield succeeded Westmorland as high steward of the university on 19 August 1760. On George III's accession he was one of the tories who returned to court, on being made a lord of the bedchamber on 9 December 1760. In 1762 he became captain of the band of gentlemen pensioners, and deputy ranger of Hampton Court Park, residing at the Stud Lodge, and was sworn of the privy council on 14 July. On 23 September that year, supported by Lord Bute, he succeeded Westmorland as chancellor of Oxford, by 321 votes to 168. An objection raised against him in 1759, on the grounds that he was a freeman of the city of Oxford, had since been nullified. The university created him DCL again, this time by diploma, on 27 September. He contrived to delay for five years an understanding that he would let a whig become high steward. Lichfield was not a strong chancellor, but he instituted the chancellor's prizes, and was commended for his ornamental conduct and costume in office: 'the graceful dignity, the political condescension, the *ne quid nimis* of the Chancellor were universally admired' (*GM*, 43.349). This restraint was absent from his drinking habits: Horace Walpole maintained that 'if he did not make the figure which his youth had promised, the Jacobites could not reproach him, as he had drowned his parts in the jovial promotion of their cause' (H. Walpole, *Memoirs of the Reign of George II*, ed. J. Brooke, 3 vols., 1985, 3.166–7). After 1760, however, Lichfield's attachment was to George III, and in 1766 he was giving dinners to members of the Commons courted by Lord Bute, and hostile to the Rockingham ministry. A fellow of the Society of Arts from 1767, he became its vice-president. He died on 19 September 1772, and was buried on 28 September at Spelsbury church, Oxfordshire, near his ancestral residence, Ditchley Park, the fine Palladian mansion built for his father. He bequeathed £7000 for the Lichfield clinical professorship, inaugurated in 1780, at Oxford, and was succeeded by his uncle Robert Lee (1706–1776), youngest son of the first earl. ROLAND THORNE

Sources GEC, *Peerage*, new edn, 7.646–7 • *Herald and Genealogist*, 3 (1866), esp. 483ff. • *Hist. U. Oxf.* 5: *18th-cent. Oxf.* • Cobbett, *Parl. hist.*, 11.951; 12.507, 979, 1027; 13.376 • E. Cruickshanks, 'Lee, George Henry', HoP, *Commons*, 1715–54 • *GM*, 1st ser., 42 (1772), 440 • *GM*, 1st ser., 43 (1773), 349 • *Report on the manuscripts of the earl of Denbigh, part V*, HMC, 68 (1911), 168, 178, 250, 256 • *Report on the manuscripts of the late Reginald Rawdon Hastings*, 4 vols., HMC, 78 (1928–47), vol. 3, p. 113 • Walpole, *Corr.* • *Manuscripts of the earl of Egmont: diary of Viscount Percival, afterwards first earl of Egmont*, 3 vols., HMC, 63 (1920–

23), vol. 3, p. 192 • E. Corbett, ed., *A history of Spelsbury* (1931), 194 • *DNB* • Foster, *Alum. Oxon.* • parish register, Spelsbury, Oxfordshire, 28 Sept 1772 [burial] • *Old Westminsters*, 2.563 • *Royal Kalendar* (1769), 20

Archives Oxon. RO, family and official corresp. and papers

Likenesses J. Wootton, group portrait, oils, 1744 (*Members of the Beaufort hunt*), Tate collection • G. Huddesford, portrait, oils, 1777, Bodl. Oxf. [*see illus.*] • engraving, BM • portrait, Radcliffe Infirmary, Oxford

Lee, Harriet (1757/8–1851), novelist and playwright, was the third of five surviving children of actors John *Lee (1725–1781) and Anna Sophia Lee (*b. c.*1725, *d.* in or after 1776). Their other children included Sophia Priscilla *Lee (*bap.* 1750, *d.* 1824), novelist and playwright, and George Augustus *Lee (1761–1826), textile manufacturer.

Harriet's parents both performed in theatres all over the British Isles. Her early life was extremely unsettled. In part because of John Lee's notoriously quarrelsome character, the family moved often between London and Bath until John died, when Harriet settled in Bath with her three sisters. Barely two months before her father died, she helped them open a girls' school there in December 1780, for which her elder sisters Charlotte (*b. c.*1748) and Sophia provided the expertise and the financing respectively.

'Mesdames Lees' quickly became 'a concern of magnitude' (Boaden, 1.211), and by 1786 moved to Belvidere House, 'a handsome, spacious, and airy mansion' (*Piozzi Letters*, 1.249 n. 7) atop a hill on Lansdown Road (now Belvedere Villas), whence it commanded a view of Sydney Gardens, far on the other side of the River Avon. These newly opened pleasure gardens featured frequent fireworks displays, and one former boarder describes how the girls would secretly watch through a high window after lights-out, until they heard the steps of Harriet Lee coming up the stairs to see what the commotion was about. At that sound they would give the alarm, trying to get back into their beds and appear to be sound asleep before she could reach the door.

No doubt encouraged by the example of her sister Sophia and by the financial stability of their school, Harriet published her first work, *The Errors of Innocence*, an epistolary novel in five volumes, in 1786. It was quickly followed by *The New Peerage, or, Our Eyes may Deceive Us* (1787), a comedy performed at Drury Lane on 10 November 1787. In that month Hester Thrale Piozzi first met Harriet. 'Miss Lees are charming women', she wrote on meeting them, 'and appear to deserve their very uncommon Success' (*Piozzi Letters*, 1.248). A year later Harriet had developed a particular friendship with Piozzi. She spent months at a time with the Piozzis as chaperone to Hester's ailing daughter Cecilia Thrale. In the summer of 1791 Piozzi encouraged a socially impossible match between Lee and Lorenzo Galeazzo Trotti (*b.* 1759), a member of a noble Milanese family who would have lost half his fortune had he married her. Harriet suffered a great deal from this frustrated attachment. It was years before she published again, but in 1797 she began bringing out new work at a furious rate. That year and the next saw the publication of her 'novel founded on facts', *Clara Lennox, or, The Distressed Widow* (2 vols., 1797), a three-act play, *The Mysterious Marriage, or, The Heirship of Roselva* (1798), and the first two volumes of her novella collection, *The Canterbury Tales* (5 vols., 1797–1805). Lee is best known for the latter work, and in particular for one Gothic novella, *Kruitzner*. It was often reprinted separately, and was later imitated by the poet Lord Byron (1788–1824) in his play *Werner, or, The Inheritance* (1822). Byron writes of *Kruitzner*, 'When I was young (about fourteen, I think), I first read this tale, which made a deep impression upon me, and may, indeed, be said to contain the germ of much that I have since written' (G. Gordon, Lord Byron, *Werner*, 1823, vii).

At the height of her literary success, in the summer of 1798, Lee was assiduously courted by philosopher and novelist William Godwin (1756–1836). She had considerable regard for him, but was put off by his superciliousness towards her in their intellectual disputes, and by his lack of respect for her religious faith in the teachings of the Church of England. She refused him, while desiring to maintain a friendship, but this seems to have lapsed.

Lee published one more novel a decade later, *Constantia de Valmont* (1799). By 1803 the Lee sisters could retire comfortably, closing their school after its twenty-third year. Lee's retirement was marred when her youngest sister, Anna (1760?–1805), hanged herself in their new home at Hatfield Place, South Lyncombe, near Bath. Lee suddenly stopped publishing new work after her sister's suicide. Harriet and Sophia left their house immediately afterwards, spending some time with their brother in Manchester, then living near Tintern Abbey before finally moving to Clifton, near Bristol, where the novelists Jane (1776–1850) and Anna Maria Porter (1780–1832) were their neighbours. Lee's only subsequent publication was her own dramatization of *Kruitzner*, which she had written before Byron published his. On the publication of his *Werner* in November 1822 she sent her five-act play *The Three Strangers* (1826) to Covent Garden. Although it was accepted immediately, Lee delayed its performance until 10 December 1825, possibly because of her sister Sophia's intervening illness and death.

After the death of Sophia, Lee stopped publishing altogether, although she lived and wrote for another quarter of a century. An album of her later poems and stories is preserved in the British Library (Add. MS 50197, fol. 31*v*); the verses it contains, many addressed to or written in memory of relatives and friends, are full of the sorrow of having survived all her loved ones. She died, unmarried, of heart failure at her home, 11 Vyvyan Terrace, Clifton, on 1 August 1851. April Alliston

Sources *The Piozzi letters: correspondence of Hester Lynch Piozzi, 1784–1821*, ed. E. A. Bloom and L. D. Bloom, 5 vols. (1989–99) • H. Lee and W. Godwin, letters, June–Aug 1798, Bodl. Oxf., MS Abinger c. 507/6 • *The memoirs of Susan Sibbald (1783–1812)*, ed. F. P. Hett (1926) • *DNB* • *GM*, 2nd ser., 36 (1851) • *Annual Register* (1851) • *Littell's Living Age*, 391 (8 Nov 1851) • A. Alliston, introduction, 'Chronology of events in the life of Sophia Lee', in *The recess, or, A tale of other times*, ed. A. Alliston (Lexington, KY, 2000) • K. A. Burnim, ed., 'The letters of Sarah and William Siddons to Hester Lynch Piozzi in the John

Rylands Library', *Bulletin of the John Rylands University Library*, 52 (1969–70), 46–95 • T. Fawcett, 'Leevites and others', *History of Bath Research Group Newsletter*, 23 (Jan 1994), 5–6 • Highfill, Burnim & Langhans, *BDA*, vol. 9 • will, PRO, PROB 11/2139, sig. 742 • J. Boaden, *Memoirs of Mrs Siddons*, 2nd edn, 1 (1831) • d. cert.

Archives BL, notebook, Add. MS 50197, fol. 31v | Bodl. Oxf., corresp. with William Godwin, MSS Abinger, b. 228/4, c. 507/6

Lee, Sir Henry (1533–1611), queen's champion, was born in Kent in March 1533, the eldest son of Sir Anthony Lee (*d.* 1550) of Quarrendon, Buckinghamshire, MP for the county in 1554, and Margaret, daughter of Sir Henry Wyatt of Allington Castle, Kent. The Lees of Quarrendon rose to prominence at the end of the Wars of the Roses, their fortunes established by Robert Lee, Sir Henry's grandfather. Henry could claim kinship to the earls of Essex and Leicester, to William Cecil, and even to Queen Elizabeth. He looked like his mother, who was painted by Holbein, and was educated by his uncle, Sir Thomas Wyatt, from whom he probably derived his tincture of letters. He may also have attended New College, Oxford.

Sir Henry Lee, in the phrase of his epitaph, served 'five succeeding princes, and kept himself right and steady in many dangerous shocks and utter turns of state' (Strong, 30), by being polite, politic, and well-connected. Entering Henry VIII's service at the tender age of fourteen, and succeeding his father only two years later, he had to grow up fast. He was knighted by the earl of Arundel on 2 October 1553. On 21 May 1554 he married Anne, daughter of the statesman William *Paget. This brought Lee immunity from being persecuted for his protestantism during Mary's reign, and Anne was to bear him three children; but it was not a happy marriage. Two sons, John and Henry, died young, and a daughter, Mary, after a scandalous elopement, followed them childless to the grave. Anne was of Catholic stock, Lee staunchly committed to the new reformed faith. His 'dearest deare', according to Aubrey, was not his wife but one who shared her name, Anne *Vavasour.

In 1559–1600 Lee accompanied Paget's son Henry on his continental tour. In 1563 he acquired London lodgings in the Strand. In 1568 he undertook a major journey to Antwerp, where he had his portrait painted by Anthonis Mor; to Augsburg, by way of Cologne and Speyer; and thence to Italy, where he visited Venice, Padua, Florence, and Rome. All the while he sent diplomatic dispatches to Leicester and, particularly, Cecil. He returned, in the phrase of William Scott, 'a well-formed traveller adorned with those flowers of knighthood, courtesy and valour' (E. K. Chambers, 37). Mor portrays him with a strong nose, a long jaw, and a mouth clamped grimly shut, avoiding the gaze of the spectator; but Lee could be engaging and kind. Not one but two men looked to him from their respective places of execution: Bishop Nicholas Ridley, in Queen Mary's reign, and the fourth duke of Norfolk, who had become embroiled in the Ridolfi plot against Elizabeth; Lee accepted from Ridley the tribute of a new groat and from Norfolk the embrace of a dying man and convicted criminal.

Sir Henry Lee (1533–1611), by Anthonis Mor, 1568

Lee prospered under Elizabeth, adored her, and was a chief architect of her myth. In 1571, the first year he is definitely recorded in the tilt-yard, he was appointed lieutenant of the royal manor of Woodstock. In 1573 the queen commended him for the part he played in the successful siege of Edinburgh, and in 1574 he was made master of the leash. The queen visited Woodstock in 1572 and 1574, and returned in 1575 for an unusually long stay. Lee's lavish reception for her on that occasion blended music, allegorical performance, and an oration from the vice-chancellor of Oxford University, Laurence Humphrey. The Fairy Queen hailed her English counterpart, who was also serenaded by an oak tree. In George Gascoigne's words, Elizabeth's royal head was, and no wonder, 'filled with conceites' (E. K. Chambers, 89). On 20 September the sequel to this inaugural entertainment was similarly successful, but the queen's happiness at Woodstock may have been slightly marred by unsatisfactory hunting.

In 1580 Lee became master of the armoury. It was in that capacity that he supervised the famous accession-day tilts, turning them into a large and spectacular public festival, the combat embroidered with speech-making and music and arranged in a flattering narrative. Contemporary jousting cheques record Lee's presence as queen's champion; and he directed and wrote much of the material. Occasionally his productions are touched with genius, as in the tribute to the dead Sir Philip Sidney, when lamentations were said over a riderless horse. Lee was hale and hearty, as John Aubrey records; excellent at tilting, as Sidney testifies; and he wore gorgeous armour:

his glistering mazor
A stately plume of orange mixed with azure

as Joshua Sylvester recalls (*Devine Weekes*, trans. Sylvester, 135).

On 17 November 1590 Lee resigned as queen's champion, the royal choir singing 'My golden locks, time hath to silver turned' on his behalf (R. Chambers, 590). This famous Elizabethan lyric, set to music by Dowland, may or may not be by Lee himself. In it and later poems he assumes a new identity as a religious hermit, substituting '*Vivat Eliza* for an *Ave Mari*' (Wilson, 38). But even after he had retired, his royal mistress required him to oversee the annual festival in her honour with which he was so closely associated. The celebrated Ditchley portrait of the queen (now in the National Portrait Gallery) has been called 'Lee's own picture of his life's heroine' (Strong, 154). Lee's devotion to Elizabeth culminated in 1592 with her visit to Ditchley, the manorial centre of his second territorial estate in Oxfordshire. In his lavish Spenserian entertainment, the queen rescued inconstant knights, chiefly Lee himself. Although he had retired, he told her, he had 'a verie courte in his own bosome, making presence of her in his soule, who was absent from his sight' (E. K. Chambers, 149).

Lee was also a businessman, with a particularly high profile in Oxfordshire. In the storm of 1570 he lost 3000 sheep, besides other horned cattle. The loan of £3000 which he received from the queen in 1576 became an embarrassment. He rebuilt Ditchley, and is said to have founded the grammar school at Aylesbury and given it a small endowment. In 1596 he made himself unpopular by enclosing many commons. His hopes of further preferment in the 1590s proved unfounded until he was made knight of the Garter in 1597, unusual for one not a peer. After the death of his beloved queen, he was there to honour the new monarch's arrival in London. In December 1603 James awarded Lee £200, which afterwards became an annuity. Aged seventy-one, Lee attended James's first tilt on 24 March 1604.

Although it is not known when the liaison began, Lee lived with Anne *Vavasour (*fl.* 1580–1621) in the 1590s after the death of his wife. This disreputable lady was mother to the earl of Oxford's illegitimate child. Lines ascribed to Ralegh are addressed to her. The story rather deflatingly goes that Lee's super-chivalrous entertainment of his queen in 1592 was partly intended to deflect her displeasure at this relationship. Queen Anne visited the Lee–Vavasour ménage in 1608 and in 1609 Lee went hunting with Prince Henry. He died, a rich man, in 1611, about 12 February. He was buried at Quarrendon.

EWAN FERNIE

Sources E. K. Chambers, *Sir Henry Lee: an Elizabethan portrait* (1936) • R. Strong, *The cult of Elizabeth* (1977) • *DNB* • J. Wilson, *Entertainments for Elizabeth I* (1980) • R. Chambers, ed., *The book of days: a miscellany of popular antiquities in connection with the calendar*, 2 (1863), 590 • E. Lodge, *Illustrations of British history, biography, and manners*, 3 vols. (1791) • *Brief lives, chiefly of contemporaries, set down by John Aubrey, between the years 1669 and 1696*, ed. A. Clark, 2 (1898), 30–31 • *Bartas his devine weekes and workes*, trans. J. Sylvester, 2 vols. (1605–6) • D. Lysons and S. Lysons, *Magna Britannia*, 1 (1806), 624

Archives BL, speeches, poems, etc., Add. MS 41499 | Oxon. RO, letters to Cecil [copies]

Likenesses A. Mor, oils, 1568, NPG [*see illus.*] • M. Gheeraerts, oils, 1590, Ditchley Park, Oxfordshire • M. Gheeraerts, oils, 1602, Armourers and Brasiers Company, London

Lee, Henry (*c.*1644–1713), philosopher and Church of England clergyman, was the son of William Lee, rector of Fletton, Huntingdonshire. Educated at Oundle School, he was admitted as a pensioner at Emmanuel College, Cambridge, on 4 July 1661, graduating BA (1665), MA (1668), and BD (1675). He was appointed a fellow by royal mandate in December 1667 and served as junior proctor in 1673–4. His degrees were incorporated at Oxford in 1669. Ordained deacon in Peterborough diocese on 20 September 1668 he was entered as a priest in the London diocese on 14 March 1674. Lee was rector of Titchmarsh in Northamptonshire from 1678, and of Brington, Huntingdonshire, from 1690 until his death.

Lee published one huge folio, *Anti-Scepticism, or, Notes upon each Chapter of Mr Lock's 'Essay Concerning Humane Understanding'* (1702), which he dedicated to the tory lord keeper, Sir Nathan Wright, who may have been his pupil at Emmanuel. Lee was a principal early critic of Locke, broadly similar in approach to John Norris, James Lowde, John Sergeant, Edward Stillingfleet, and G. W. Leibniz. His main charge was that Locke's epistemology led to scepticism, particularly in natural and revealed religion. Locke later came to be considered optimistic about the possibilities of human knowledge, but early critics thought that his attack on innate ideas undermined certainty. Lee read Locke as a pure sensationalist, or inductive empiricist, who derived knowledge only from sense experience, and he overlooked Locke's stress on ratiocination. 'If all knowledge comes by our senses or reflection … then there can be no certain knowledge of the truth of any general proposition whatever; because our senses can reach but to particulars' (Lee, 67). Lee defended innate ideas, but not naïvely as immediately known, since education and effort were necessary to develop our faculties. Some general principles were self-evidently true: while it might be held that it is some feature of the propositions themselves that makes them so, Lee thought them imprinted on our minds, or embedded in our natures, and that we have a natural disposition to receive them. Lee was irritated by Locke's new language of 'ideas' and was disturbed at his insistence that it is only our ideas that we know. He called Locke an idealist in the Platonic sense, and feared that Locke extinguished our confidence in the conformity of our ideas with external reality. Locke would not allow 'the real existence of any thing out of the mind itself' (ibid., sig. c2*r*). To guarantee a conformity between the mind's ideas and the external world Lee fell back on a Cartesian insistence that a good God would not allow our senses to be deceived. He was also disturbed by Locke's claim that much knowledge was probable rather than certain. Since testamentary knowledge was of this sort and biblical revelation was testamentary this threw doubt upon the scriptures. Further, Locke's apparent emphasis on custom, opinion, and education as sources of moral ideas rendered morality 'arbitrary [and] artificial', merely 'mutable sentiments'. Locke's citations of societies that accepted infanticide are 'instances given by the author to prove no law of nature'. In this Locke was 'exceeding Mr Hobbes in disservice to natural religion and morality' (ibid., sig. A1v, b2v, 19, 21). Lee was also alarmed at Locke's startling aside that matter might think, so that 'man may only be a species of machine' (ibid., 246). None the less he shared Locke's interest in the philosophical consequences of the new scientific atomism. For example, he pondered the problem of how motion was transferred when one body collided with another. He had read other work in this vein, such as Hobbes's *Seven Philosophical Problems*.

Locke's friends were dismissive of Lee's book. His bookseller told him, 'I hear from Cambridge that [it] hath no esteem there.' James Tyrrell told him, 'those few in Oxford that have read it, complain of the tediousness of it'; 'a book of controversy in a folio, larger than that he writes against is never like to gain many converts in an age when books of that kind are so little studied'. Part of the problem was that Lee was too judicious and too patiently expository. 'Oftentimes one cannot tell whether he writes for or against your opinion', and spends time explaining 'in his own way when indeed it was much clearer before' (*Correspondence of John Locke*, 7.654, 664, 684). However, Locke's enemy George Hickes, in *Spinoza Reviv'd* (1709), thought Lee's book had destroyed Locke:

> I am persuaded, had Mr Locke foreseen that such a book would have been written against his Essay, he would never have wrote that, and if he read it before he died, it must needs have been matter of grief, if not humiliation to him, to see his book, which all the atheists, and deists, and sceptics of the age cried up for a performance above whatever had been done by any philosopher, so perfectly demolished from part to part.

Lee was buried at Titchmarsh on 30 November 1713. He left two sons, Weyman (1681–1765), who went to King's College, Cambridge, and later became a barrister; and Henry, born about 1684, who attended Corpus Christi College, Oxford, and succeeded his father as rector in 1713. *Anti-Scepticism* was originally designed for their edification, and Lee included a preface to them, both then undergraduates. Henry junior, not Henry senior, was the author of an anti-deist book of 1730.

MARK GOLDIE

Sources H. Lee, *Anti-scepticism* (1702) • Venn, *Alum. Cant.* • Foster, *Alum. Oxon.* • *The correspondence of John Locke*, ed. E. S. de Beer, 7 (1982) • G. Hickes, preface, in W. Carroll, *Spinoza reviv'd* (1709) • J. W. Yolton, *John Locke and the way of ideas* (1968) • R. S. Woolhouse, *Locke* (1983)

Lee, Henry (1765–1836), actor and playwright, was born on 27 October 1765, apparently in Nottingham, where he was educated. His father died when he was young and his mother married a wealthy man named John Timm. However, she died soon after remarrying, and Henry did not benefit from his stepfather's money. He contributed poetical articles to Moore's Almanacks. He lived some time at Normanton, and soon after the age of twenty-one went to London and became an actor. Joining James Shatford's company at Newport Pagnell on 1 August 1787, he travelled with it, chiefly in the west of England. In January 1789 Lee was acting in Abingdon and from the summer of 1789 until 1791 he was in Brighton. In 1791 he left Brighton to become Shatford's partner in a theatre at Salisbury. In July 1793, in Salisbury, he married his first wife, the actress and singer Sarah Jane, daughter of the actor Simon Keys. She acted in London in the mid-1790s and died on 6 March 1797, childless. In 1793 Lee began managing a theatre in Dorchester and by 1799 he was managing the Taunton circuit, which included Barnstaple, Poole, and Guernsey. From 1796 until 1798 he seems to have been active in the Covent Garden scene.

Lee's farce *Throw Physick to the Dogs* was written about 1789 and after being performed in the country under the title *Jack of All Trades* was brought out at the Haymarket on 6 July 1798 (Genest, 7.387). It was acted twice, and then withdrawn and altered. The revised version was offered to George Colman the younger, but refused. Soon afterwards Lee charged Colman with borrowing the character of Caleb Quotem in *The Review, or, The Wags of Windsor*, a play of Colman's produced at the Haymarket on 1 September 1800. After Colman published his play Lee republished his farce under the title of *Caleb Quotem and his wife! or, Paint, poetry, and putty! An opera in three acts, to which is added a postscript, including the scene always play'd in 'The review, or, Wags of Windsor', but omitted in the edition lately published by G. Colman, with prefatory remarks* (1809).

In 1814 Lee married as his second wife a Miss Lloyd with whom he had a son and several daughters. He also wrote *Poetic Impressions, a Pocket-Book with Scraps* (1817); *Dash, a Tale in Verse* (1817); and *The Manager, a Melodramatic Tale in Verse* (1822). He continued to manage at Taunton for several years and from here published his two-volume *Memoirs of a Manager, or, Life's Stage with New Scenery* (1830). Lee, who described his life as irregular and eccentric, died in Long Acre, London, on 30 March 1836.

T. B. SAUNDERS, *rev.* REBECCA MILLS

Sources Highfill, Burnim & Langhans, *BDA*, 9.197–8 • *GM*, 2nd ser., 5 (1836), 546 • *The thespian dictionary, or, Dramatic biography of the eighteenth century* (1802) • Genest, *Eng. stage*, 7.387–91 • Watt, *Bibl. Brit.*, 2.593b • H. Lee and S. Arnold, *Songs, &c. in a new musical farce called 'Throw physick to the dogs'* (1798) • H. Lee, *Caleb Quotem and his wife! or, Paint, poetry, and putty!* (1809) • T. Gilliland, *The dramatic mirror, containing the history of the stage from the earliest period, to the present time*, 2 vols. (1808) • [J. Watkins and F. Shoberl], *A biographical dictionary of the living authors of Great Britain and Ireland* (1816) • D. E. Baker, *Biographia dramatica, or, A companion to the playhouse*, rev. I. Reed, new edn, rev. S. Jones, 1/2 (1812), 447

Lee, Henry (1826/7–1888), naturalist, succeeded John Keast Lord (1818–1872) as naturalist of the Brighton aquarium in 1872, and was for some time a director there. While at the aquarium he instituted important experiments on the migration of smelts, the habits of herring, and the nature of whitebait and crayfish. His *Aquarium Notes* (1875) for the use of visitors, was able and attractive. Lee was also author of *The Octopus* (1874), *The White Whale* (1878), *Sea Fables Explained* (1883), and *Sea Monsters Unmasked* (1883). The last two works were part of a series of handbooks issued in connection with the International Fisheries Exhibition in London in 1883. He also published *The Vegetable Lamb of Tartary: a Curious Fable of the Cotton Plant* (1887).

Lee was also an energetic collector of natural history specimens, and a skilful worker with the microscope. On

5 April 1866 he was made a fellow of the Linnean Society, and he was founder of the Croydon Microscopical and Natural History Club established on 6 April 1870. He was also a member of the Geological and Zoological societies of London. Following several years of ill health, he died at his home, Renton House, 343 Brixton Road, London, on 31 October 1888. His death certificate describes him as a hatter's furrier. He was married and was survived by at least one son, also called Henry Lee.

M. G. WATKINS, *rev.* YOLANDA FOOTE

Sources *Times and Field* (3 Nov 1888) • *Land and Water* (10 Nov 1888), 568 • Croydon Natural History and Scientific Society, *Croydon: the story of a hundred years* (1970–79) • private information (2004) • *CGPLA Eng. & Wales* (1888) • d. cert.

Archives Wellcome L., corresp.

Wealth at death £10,995 8*s.* 11*d.*: resworn administration, Nov 1889, *CGPLA Eng. & Wales* (1888)

Lee, Henry Augustus Dillon-, thirteenth Viscount Dillon (1777–1832), writer, eldest son of Charles Dillon-Lee, twelfth Viscount Dillon (*d.* 1813), KP, and his first wife, the Hon. Henrietta Maria Phipps (*d.* 1782), only daughter of Constantine, first Baron Mulgrave, was born in Brussels on 28 October 1777. He matriculated at Christ Church, Oxford, in 1795.

Trained as a soldier in the Surrey yeomanry and the Oxford militia, he became colonel in the Irish brigade on 1 October 1794, and was colonel of the duke of York's Irish regiment (101st foot) from August 1806 until its disbandment in 1817. In 1799 he was returned to parliament for the borough of Harwich. At the last general election of 1802 he was elected to one of the Mayo county seats and was re-elected in 1806, 1807, and 1812. He continued a member of the House of Commons until 9 November 1813, when he succeeded to his father's title. He spent most of his political career in opposition, and was an active proponent of Catholic relief.

Through his grandmother, Lady Charlotte Lee, daughter of the second of the extinct earls of Lichfield, Dillon inherited the estate of Ditchley Park, Oxfordshire, although latterly financial distress obliged him to live in Italy. In February 1807 he married Henrietta (1789–1862), daughter of Dominick and Margaret Browne and sister of the first Lord Oranmore. They had six sons and five daughters, among them Henrietta Maria *Stanley (1807–1895), political hostess and campaigner for women's education. He died, after much suffering, on 24 July 1832, at Lower Brook Street, Grosvenor Square, London.

Dillon is best-known for two pamphlets advocating Catholic emancipation, published in 1801 and 1805. He also wrote on military and political affairs, and published two novels, one of which was set in the seventeenth century.

ROBERT HARRISON, *rev.* MARIE-LOUISE LEGG

Sources *GM*, 1st ser., 102/2 (1832), 175 • Burke, *Peerage* • GEC, *Peerage* • HoP, *Commons*

Archives NL Ire. • Oxon. RO, Oxfordshire Archives

Lee, Holme. *See* Parr, Harriet (1828–1900).

Lee, James (1715–1795), nurseryman, was born in Selkirk, Scotland. He may have been a pupil at the grammar school in Selkirk, as he knew Latin. About 1732 he set out to walk to London, but when he reached Lichfield he caught smallpox. After he had recovered he completed his journey, and may have worked under Philip Miller at the Chelsea Physic Garden before he became gardener at Syon House, near Brentford, Middlesex. He later worked for the duke of Argyll at Whitton, Middlesex, an estate famous for its exotic plants.

About 1745 Lee and Lewis Kennedy (*d.* 1782) started the Vineyard nursery in Hammersmith, on the site of a former vineyard. Lee was a correspondent of Linnaeus, who named a genus, *Leea*, after him (a genus of tropical plants of the Vitaceae family); Lee's translation of Linnaeus's *Philosophia Botanica*, under the title of *Introduction to Botany* (1760, 10th edition 1810), was the first description of the sexual system of plants to appear in English. This work made Lee famous, bringing visitors from all over the world to the Vineyard nursery, including Pierre-Joseph Redoute, painter of the flowers at Malmaison. The nursery specialized in exotic plants, employing plant and seed collectors at the Cape of Good Hope and in the Americas. In 1771 Lee was one of a group of people who exchanged exotic plants with the Chelsea Physic Garden. In 1774 Kennedy and Lee issued a plant catalogue, and customers included Thomas Jefferson. The Vineyard nursery was the first supplier to sell the fuchsia commercially, in 1789, and it also introduced the *Buddleia globosa* from Peru. Lee published *Rules for Collecting and Preserving Seeds from Botany Bay* (*c.*1787), and in 1788 he raised the first seeds to be brought back from Botany Bay—the 'saw-leaved Banksia' was the first plant—and went on to specialize in plants from New Holland (Australia). The Vineyard was also said to have raised the first China rose, in 1787. Lee contributed to W. Aiton's *Hortus Kewensis* (1789), and the second edition (1810–1813) lists 135 plants first introduced into England, or first cultivated by the Vineyard nursery, during Lee's lifetime. The nursery survived until the 1890s. The exhibition hall at Olympia was built on the site.

Lee's wife, Martha, died in 1779. They had one son, Charles, who took over the nursery after Lee's death in partnership with Kennedy's son, and three daughters, including Ann Lee, a botanical artist. Lee died in Hammersmith, Middlesex, on 25 July 1795.

B. D. JACKSON, *rev.* ANNE PIMLOTT BAKER

Sources E. J. Willson, *James Lee and the Vineyard Nursery, Hammersmith* (1961) • M. Hadfield, *A history of British gardening*, 3rd edn (1979) • R. Webber, *The early horticulturists* (1968), ch. 7 • Desmond, *Botanists* • *Gardeners' Chronicle*, new ser., 16 (1881), 330–31 • M. Hadfield, R. Harling, and L. Highton, *British gardeners: a biographical dictionary* (1980)

Likenesses S. Freeman, stipple, BM, NPG; repro. in J. Lee, *An introduction to the science of botany*, 4th edn, rev. J. Lee (1810) • oils, repro. in J. Lee, *An introduction to the science of botany*, 4th edn, rev. J. Lee (1810)

Lee, James Prince (1804–1869), bishop of Manchester and headmaster, was born in London on 28 July 1804, the eldest son of Stephen Lee. His father came from a family of Levant merchants and had an interest in astronomy; elected FRS in 1789, he was assistant secretary and librarian of the Royal Society from 1810 until 1826, when he felt

James Prince Lee (1804–1869), by J. Lupton (after Sir John Watson-Gordon)

obliged to resign after criticizing the Greenwich observations of 1821, published under the supervision of John Pond, the astronomer royal. His mother was related to William Martin Leake, the classical topographer.

Entering St Paul's School, London, in 1813, Lee was captain of the school from 1822 to 1824, and gained the Campden and Perry exhibitions. He proceeded to Trinity College, Cambridge, as a sizar in 1824. Reckoned 'one of the most distinguished classical scholars ever known in the university', he became a scholar of Trinity and obtained the Craven scholarship in 1827. Ill health prevented him from entering for honours. After graduating BA in 1828, he was elected fellow of Trinity in October 1829 and gained a reputation as a successful private tutor. In 1830 he was ordained, proceeding MA in 1831. He relinquished his fellowship following his marriage on 25 December 1830 to Susannah, elder daughter of George Penrice of Elmridge, Worcestershire, with whom he had two daughters.

In 1830 Thomas Arnold appointed Lee fifth-form master at Rugby, where he remained until 1838, when he was appointed headmaster of King Edward's School, Birmingham, in succession to Francis Jeune. Housed in new buildings which were opened in 1838, the school, unlike Rugby, comprised primarily day-boys, and included all religious denominations. Lee was a remarkably successful teacher, placing the greatest emphasis on strict linguistic discipline. The first schoolmaster to use Joseph Butler's *Analogy of Religion* in the classroom, he was remembered for his inspiring teaching of the Greek New Testament. Among the pupils who came under his influence were Edward White Benson, the archbishop of Canterbury, and the Cambridge theologians, J. B. Lightfoot and B. F. Westcott. He also gained the favour of the prince consort, who visited the school during his headmastership. His reputation as a headmaster came to equal that of Thomas Arnold himself.

Lee's involvement in Birmingham civic institutions gained him the enmity of Thomas Gutteridge (*d.* 1880), a Birmingham surgeon and a disappointed candidate for an appointment at Birmingham General Hospital, of which Lee was a governor. In pamphlets addressed to Lord Calthorpe and the bishop of Worcester (1845–6), and at a public meeting, Gutteridge made allegations of corruption in the running of the hospital and the grammar school, specifically accusing Lee of drunkenness and of persecuting a subordinate. Lee, who was elected honorary canon of Worcester on 6 September 1847, took no action against the defamations until his nomination by Lord John Russell to the newly constituted see of Manchester (23 October 1847). A case before the queen's bench on 24 November 1847 led to an order restraining Gutteridge from further libels; he was subsequently found guilty at Warwick assizes of criminal libels on Lee (6 April 1848).

Lee's consecration took place at the Whitehall Chapel on 23 January 1848, and he was enthroned in the cathedral church, Manchester, on 11 February. A low-churchman, who attacked both 'papal aggression' in 1851 and ritualistic practices, Lee had Erastian tendencies (he approved of the Gorham judgment), which further alienated high-churchmen. His suppression of high-church innovations at Ringley Chapel, described in a pamphlet by Edward Fellows, assistant curate, was followed by an attack on the 'popish' fittings in the chancel of Broughton church, which drew a sharp reply from A. J. Beresford Hope (1851). Lee's charges (1851, 1855) showed a preference for evangelical styles of worship (Mark Smith, *Religion in Industrial Society*, 1994, 90). His headmasterly method of ruling his diocese, using rural deans to inform on his clergy, and his rather cold manner led to much opposition and distrust. His role in a dispute over the property of the dean and canons of Manchester Cathedral permanently harmed his relations with the chapter and he was rarely seen in the cathedral. The success of his episcopate lay in his organization of spiritual provision: he consecrated 110 new churches, created 163 new parishes and ecclesiastical districts, attached schools to new churches, and ordained some 500 clergy.

Lee was a member of the Manchester Literary and Philosophical Society and other learned societies, and was a prominent supporter of the establishment of the Manchester Free Library (1852). He collected a fine library, with an emphasis on art and British and foreign topography, though its particular strength lay in literature on the Greek Testament. His 'domineering manner' (Newsome, 127) has been suggested as the most likely explanation for the animus shown towards him by James Crossley, the Manchester antiquary, who relentlessly exposed errors in Lee's edition of Isaac Barrow's *Sermons and Fragments*

(1834), based on manuscripts in Cambridge. Some were shown to be spurious, though Lee's preface was more cautious as to their authenticity than his critics allowed. Crossley published a lampoon of Lee shortly after his death (see *N&Q*, 4th ser., 12, 1873, 145). Another local adversary, Samuel Crompton, a surgeon and secretary of the Manchester Medical Society, published allegations against Lee of maladministration in two local charities (1862).

Lee (or Prince Lee as he was sometimes known) 'was in frame rather spare, in stature scarcely above the middle height; his face was angular, his complexion pale' (*DNB*). Some of his faults of temper have been attributed to the pain he endured from inflammation of the eyes and neuralgia, for which he sought relief with heavy doses of laudanum. After suffering years of ill health, Lee died at his home, Mauldeth Hall, near Manchester, on 24 December 1869. He was buried at the neighbouring church of Heaton Mersey on the 31st. He bequeathed his library to Owens College, Manchester, but his will deliberately deprived his eldest daughter, Sophia Katherine, of any benefit from his estate as a mark of his disapproval of her marriage in 1854 to the Revd John Booker (*d.* 1895), curate of Prestwich and member of the Chetham Society. His younger daughter, Susannah Sarah, married in 1852 the Revd Charles Evans (*d.* 1904), headmaster of King Edward's, Birmingham, from 1862 to 1872. On her death in September 1875 Lee's widow, Susan, left £1000 to Owens College to provide two annual prizes for encouraging the study of the New Testament in Greek.

M. C. Curthoys

Sources D. Newsome, *Godliness and good learning* (1961), chap. 2 · E. W. Benson, *SALPISEI: a memorial sermon preached after the death of the Right Reverend J. P. Lee*, 2nd edn (1870) · Boase, *Mod. Eng. biog.* · Venn, *Alum. Cant.* · *DNB* · M. B. Hall, *All scientists now: the Royal Society in the nineteenth century* (1984)

Archives Chetham's Library, Manchester, papers · King Edward VI Grammar School, Birmingham, papers | Man. CL, Manchester Archives and Local Studies, corresp. with secretary of the Cathedral commission

Likenesses Duval & Co., carte-de-visite, NPG · J. Eastham, photograph, NPG · J. Lupton, mezzotint (after J. Watson-Gordon), NPG [*see illus.*] · M. Noble, bust, University of Manchester · D. J. Pound, stipple and line engraving (after photograph by A. Brothers), NPG; repro. in D. J. Pound, *Drawing room portrait gallery of eminent personages* (1859) · H. Robinson, stipple (after G. Richmond), NPG · portrait, King Edward's School, Birmingham · portrait, repro. in *ILN*, 12 (1848), 51 · portrait, repro. in *ILN*, 56 (1870), 55

Wealth at death under £40,000: probate, 26 Jan 1870, *CGPLA Eng. & Wales*

Lee, Jane (*d.* 1895). *See under* Lee, William (1815–1883).

Lee, Janet [Jennie], **Baroness Lee of Asheridge** (1904–1988), politician, was born on 3 November 1904 in Lochgelly, Fife, the third of four children (the older two of whom died in infancy) and only daughter of James Lee (*d.* 1951), miner and Independent Labour Party (ILP) activist, and his wife, Euphemia Greig (*d.* 1962), daughter of a commercial hotel-keeper; and granddaughter of Michael Lee, an Irish Catholic miner and Scottish labour leader. The Labour Party in Scotland was largely the ILP. Jennie's father was a friend of James Maxton, her grandfather a friend of Keir Hardie. The ILP, like the Communist Party,

Janet [Jennie] Lee, Baroness Lee of Asheridge (1904–1988), by Jorge Lewinski, 1968

fought to overthrow capitalism; unlike the Communist Party, it chose the parliamentary road. The ILP, with its ardent, militant, and uncompromising far-left politics, rooted in the class struggle fought daily in the Scottish coal fields, was woven into every fragment of the Lee family life.

Jennie, much loved by her parents, unusually was brought up as the son of the family, free of female domestic responsibilities, and free to join her father in his ILP work. (Her easily led younger brother, Tommy, was to emigrate to Australia where after serving in the navy he became dependent on heroin and on Jennie's handouts.) She was educated at Cowdenbeath secondary school, and then obtained local authority and Carnegie grants to train as a teacher at Edinburgh University (one of the few routes to a degree for a working-class girl) where she also studied law, gaining an ordinary MA, her teacher's certificate, and an LLB in 1926. Her first teaching post, at Glencraig School, in the bitter aftermath of the general strike, was unhappy but short-lived. Her upbringing, vividly described in her autobiography *Tomorrow is a New Day* (1939)—attending socialist Sunday school, collecting ILP subscriptions, joining great anti-war pacifist rallies, celebrating the 1917 Russian revolution, organizing politically correct lorry deliveries during the general strike—meant that she was always destined for a political life. She was 'swept into socialism long before the age of consent', said a friend, Benn Levy (Hollis, 10).

MP for North Lanark By the time Jennie left university, her vivid good looks and passionate evangelical style made her one of the finest platform orators on the Scottish Labour circuit. In July 1928 she was selected for North Lanark, a miners' seat, which she won for the ILP in a by-election in February 1929 (turning a tory majority of 2028 into a Labour majority of 6578), and held at the general election with a reduced majority of 4204 a few weeks later. She was an MP at the age of twenty-four, before she was old enough to vote. She was the youngest woman MP ever elected: gifted, passionate, and quite lovely. Men were besotted by her dark smoky beauty and her arrogant sexuality; women rather less so.

At Westminster Jennie was introduced by James Maxton, befriended by Ellen Wilkinson, mentored by Sir Charles Trevelyan, Labour minister for education; and educated in Hobsonian economics by her lover, Frank *Wise (1885–1933), MP for Leicester East, and in the folly of sectarian politics by Aneurin (Nye) *Bevan (1897–1960), MP for Ebbw Vale—all of them on the left. Jennie always reduced political issues to class issues, so she was dismissive of feminism, which she thought was a middle-class women's issue, and was reluctant to join the informal all-party group of women MPs led by Nancy Astor. As she told a woman friend (Mrs Suse Saemann), 'You are concerned with the problems of humanity; I am concerned with the needs and greeds of my class' (Hollis, 46).

Instead, as unemployment sharpened, Jennie savaged the policies of her minority Labour government (1929–31), led by Ramsay MacDonald and Philip Snowden, who, as the depression deepened, sought to balance budgets by cutting benefits to the unemployed. The Parliamentary Labour Party sat unhappily but loyally silent while its ILP members berated them for betraying their own class. The poor, said Jennie, were required to save the rich from ruin; they should be demolishing capitalism, not rebuilding it. Along with 230 Labour MPs who refused to join the coalition National Government, she lost her seat in the general election of 1931 (19,691 to 24,384 votes for the national candidate). When finally in July 1932 the ILP refused to bind themselves to official Labour Party discipline, and disaffiliated, Jennie went with them into the wilderness. Her Scottish roots, her ILP beliefs, and her sectarian instincts made her choose opposition. Nye Bevan tried to hold her in the Labour Party—'you Scottish dissenters' would be 'pure, but impotent … My Salvation Army lassie … I tell you, it is the Labour party or nothing' (Hollis, 64).

Campaigning out of parliament, the war, and MP for Cannock For Jennie, it proved to be nothing. She refought North Lanark for the ILP in the 1935 general election but, faced with an official Labour candidate, failed to regain her seat. For thirteen years she marked time, in politics but out of parliament, lecturing, broadcasting, dabbling in the law, campaigning for international revolutionary socialism, writing for the *New Leader*, helping Nye Bevan, Stafford Cripps, William Mellor, and the young Michael Foot to launch *Tribune* and the Unity campaign (which became the British expression of the Popular Front) in 1937 to fight fascism; until the Spanish Civil War and then the Second World War weaned her from the pacifism of the ILP and brought her back into mainstream Labour.

In 1940, summoned by Lord Beaverbrook ('You and I were against this bloody war. Now we have to win it for them'), Jennie toured barrage balloon factories ('aerial barbed wire') for his Ministry of Aircraft Production, urging people to keep working even as the bombs fell (Hollis, 93–4). When Hitler attacked the Soviet Union she quickly drafted a pamphlet, *Our Ally Russia* (1941), demanding greater support for the Russian war effort. Later in 1941 she criss-crossed the USA pressing it to enter the European war. 'Don't come back', said Nye, not entirely joking, 'until you have brought America into the War' (Hollis, 96). In June 1942 she finally resigned from the ILP. She defied the wartime electoral truce (which Nye described as 'political blackout') to stand against the official tory candidate as an independent in the Bristol Central by-election in February 1943, with the backing of Sir Richard Acland's Common Wealth Party and the support of the local vicar, Mervyn Stockwood, and against the bitter opposition of the party she had left, the ILP. She built her campaign around the Beveridge report, published in December 1942, and was expected to win. But on an electoral register depleted by bombing, evacuation, and conscription she lost by 5867 to 4308. In December 1944 she renounced splinter parties and all their works, rejoined the official Labour Party, and in the 1945 general election she won Cannock, a midlands mining seat, with a 19,634 majority, a seat she held through many boundary changes until 1970.

Jennie, Nye, and the Bevanites The early 1930s had been hard years for Jennie. She had not only lost her parliamentary life—she had also lost the love of her life, Frank Wise: a formidable and worldly man, twenty years older than Jennie, who died in his late forties from a brain haemorrhage in November 1933, leaving a widow and children as well as Jennie to mourn him. Nye Bevan, like Jennie from a mining background, had become a firm friend. (One evening, about to vote, Jennie had said, 'You know, Nye, we could be brother and sister.' He: 'Mmm—with a tendency to incest'; Hollis, 71.) Jennie, in the deepest depression after Frank's death, was consoled by Nye. He nagged her to marry him, which she did, on the rebound, on 24 October 1934. Together, they made a home at Lane End Cottage, Brimpton Common, in Berkshire; they then in 1944 moved to Cliveden Place in Chelsea, and finally to Asheridge Farm in Chesham, Buckinghamshire. Jennie's much-loved parents moved south to cook, keep house, and offer generous hospitality to their friends, both in the arts and in politics. In turn, their friends financially assisted them to live and travel first class. They developed warm and loyal friendships abroad, with Milovan Djilas in Yugoslavia, and with Jawaharlal Nehru and later Indira Gandhi in India. They had no children. 'A litter or none', said Nye, and Jennie chose none.

Nye was in love with Jennie; Jennie came to love and respect Nye, as during the war and much reviled he maintained a lonely courageous parliamentary opposition to Churchill's politics. The war made their marriage. Following the 1945 election Attlee made Nye minister for health and local government, where he built the National Health

Service, the greatest achievement of the Labour government. Although Jennie could expect office on her own behalf, she instead chose to sink her career into Nye's, at considerable personal cost, for she now believed he was Labour's next leader. 'He was doing what I wanted done, infinitely better than I could have done it' (Hollis, 197). Around them clustered the Bevanites (or Tribune group)—Richard Crossman, Barbara Castle, Michael Foot, Harold Wilson, Ian Mikardo, Tom Driberg—acting as a party within a party, seeking to keep Labour true to the socialist faith. In Nye's battles with Hugh Gaitskell during the 1950s, Jennie was seen as Nye's 'dark angel', his Lady Macbeth, always pulling him away from compromise and the centre and, true to her ILP roots, into confrontation, resignation—and opposition.

Jennie had sound physical health, although occasionally she suffered prolonged spells of depression; Nye was mentally immensely strong but his early years in the pits, together with his hard drinking, physically scarred him. His death from cancer on 6 July 1960 stunned the nation. Jennie was desolate, turned to drink, and withdrew from public life. Her glossy black hair turned silver; her health broke. She was lovingly cared for by her cousin Bettina Stafford, who moved from Scotland with her husband, Bill, and their small boy, Vincent, whom Jennie adopted as her surrogate son.

Minister for the arts, the Open University Jennie was rescued by Harold Wilson, who on Nye's and then (in January 1963) Gaitskell's premature deaths had become leader of the Labour Party. Following the 1964 general election he offered her a junior job. She refused health—a 'wreath for Nye'—so was given a loose responsibility for the arts, and was parked temporarily as a parliamentary secretary at the Ministry of Public Building and Works (1964–5), then moved to Anthony Crosland's Department of Education and Science, before becoming minister of state from 1967 to 1970. Her departmental colleagues and her senior civil servants despaired of her *grande dame* intransigent style; she in turn was deeply distrustful of the mandarins she thought were out to thwart her. She never learned to be a 'good' minister; but with the help of Arnold Goodman (whom she appointed to chair the Arts Council) she became the first and possibly the finest minister for the arts. All subsequent arts ministers were judged against her, and all failed.

Before Jennie, the arts were the 'high culture' of the élite—metropolitan, upper class, the leisure pursuit of the Oxbridge *cognoscenti* and the male connoisseur. Jennie insisted that the labour movement was entitled to 'bread and roses'. Her February 1965 white paper, *A Policy for the Arts, the First Steps*, stated that the arts could become accessible—diffused to the regions, to young people, to the trades unions, to the unemployed—without diluting their excellence. The best for the most. For Jennie it was simple; the arts were life-enhancing. They also represented sound politics and sound business. At a time of stringent government finance, she trebled the Arts Council grant from £3.2 million to £9.4 million in her six years; and while generously funding the great London flagship companies, of opera, theatre, ballet, orchestras, museums, and galleries, and sorting the new South Bank complex, she also supported artists outside London by building their audiences, purchasing their paintings, subsidizing their small poetry magazines, starting a National Film School, and housing the arts in dozens of new theatres and community arts centres across the land. She was much loved. When she went to the theatre, the audience rose to applaud her.

The other task Wilson entrusted to Jennie reflected his own enthusiasm for educational technology—to deliver a university of the air (or open university) offering distance learning to those who were immobile, tied by work, marriage, children, or disabilities to studying from home. She faced widespread opposition—from universities, old and new, who insisted (as with the arts) that open access was incompatible with academic excellence; from the adult education movement who argued that the greater educational need lay with remedial adult education; from the Labour left who wanted a working-class and not an open university (which might attract 'mere housewives'); from her cabinet colleagues who saw it as biting into their budgets; and from the tory right who thought it a costly irrelevance, which they would abolish if they won the next general election. But with Wilson's support, and Goodman's skills, she drove it through. A budget was agreed in July 1967. Walter Perry was appointed its vice-chancellor in May 1968, persuaded Margaret Thatcher in 1970 to back him, and accepted the first students for January 1971. By 1984 it was Britain's largest university, with 100,000 students. Wilson subsequently claimed that the Open University was the greatest achievement of his government.

On the way Jennie had collected admirers, and distinctions. She was sworn of the privy council in 1966, elected chairman of the Labour Party in 1967, awarded an honorary LLD from Cambridge in 1974, and became an honorary fellow of the Royal Academy in 1981. She republished Nye's *In Place of Fear* with an elegiac introduction of her own. She helped Michael Foot with his biography of Aneurin Bevan. However, she neglected her Cannock seat, which remained deeply suspicious of her work for the arts (too London, too toff). In the general election of 1970 her Labour majority of 11,000 became a Conservative majority of 1500. The swing against her was 11 per cent, double the national average and the highest in the country.

Wilson again rescued Jennie from depression and oblivion by appointing her to the Lords later in 1970, where she enjoyed a golden decade, fêted in the house and offering generous hospitality in her elegant Chelsea home, 67 Chester Row. In 1980 she completed her memoirs, *My Life with Nye*. From then on, she aged rapidly. Troubled by bad health—fractures, cataracts, ulcers, and breast cancer—she was increasingly confined to her home. She died of pneumonia at her home on 16 November 1988, her faithful cousin Bettina by her side. On 28 November her ashes joined Nye's, scattered on the Welsh hillside above Tredegar, Monmouthshire. PATRICIA HOLLIS

Sources P. Hollis, *Jennie Lee: a life* (1997) · J. Lee, *My life with Nye* (1980) · M. Foot, *Aneurin Bevan: a biography*, 2 vols. (1962–73) · J. Lee, MSS, Open University · J. Lee, *Tomorrow is a new day* (1939)
Archives Open University, Milton Keynes, MSS | FILM BBC WAC | SOUND BBC WAC
Likenesses J. Lewinski, photograph, 1968, NPG [*see illus.*] · photographs, Open University, Milton Keynes, Buckinghamshire · photographs, repro. in Hollis, *Jennie Lee*
Wealth at death £218,295: probate, 31 May 1989, *CGPLA Eng. & Wales*

Lee, Sir John (*d.* 1370), administrator, was the son of Geoffrey Lee, a knight of the shire and local official in Hertfordshire, and his wife, Denise. In 1316 his parents settled their lands in Albury, Hertfordshire, on John and his two brothers, Thomas and Robert. John at the time was probably very young, and his public career did not begin until the 1330s, when he was appointed to a few commissions of oyer and terminer. It was in the next two decades that his administrative career took off. At some point in this period Lee became steward of the household for Queen Isabella, a position he held until her death in 1358. Just before she died, Isabella prevailed upon her son, Edward III, to grant John an annuity of £40 when he took up knighthood. After Isabella's death, Lee moved over to Queen Philippa's household and became steward of her lands, service that earned him an additional 40 marks a year from the king for life. While still serving Philippa he also became steward of Edward's household in 1362, and he continued to hold the two posts simultaneously for several more years.

Despite his appointment to offices at the centre of government, Lee also acted on a number of local commissions in Hertfordshire and neighbouring counties. He was among those commissioned, for example, to enforce the Statute of Labourers in 1355, and was subsequently appointed to commissions of the peace, weights and measures, array, and oyer and terminer. His expertise as Isabella's and Philippa's steward was put to use on several commissions involving problems on the queens' estates. As steward of the king's household, he was commissioned in 1362 to investigate complaints made in parliament and elsewhere about oppressions committed by purveyors of the households of the king, queen, and royal children. On 10 October 1367 Edward named Lee as the keeper of the royal forests south of the Trent; unsurprisingly, he was out of court during much of his tenure as steward.

Lee's service to the crown brought ample rewards. Besides the annual fee he received from the crown, John also obtained a number of valuable wardships and marriages. He used his profits to purchase property near his family holdings in Albury and Clothall, Hertfordshire. In 1368, however, Lee was denounced in parliament for various misdeeds. William Latimer of Dorset accused him of having seized and dragged him to London, keeping him prisoner there until Latimer agreed to surrender his rights in a wardship and marriage. Lee then leased the lands back to Latimer, an arrangement that the latter was forced to recognize in the exchequer. Lee denied the charges, but the council did not accept his version of the story and found him guilty. He was also accused of cheating another man out of a wardship, saying that it pertained to the king. Others came forward to complain that Lee had misused his powers as steward to have individuals attached and brought before him, as though before the royal council, wherever he pleased and outside the places where pleas were ordinarily heard. On his authority as steward he forced men to answer in the Marshalsea court for acts committed outside the verge, and thus beyond the scope of his authority. Others he had seized and committed to prison in the Tower of London, without the king's authorization. He meddled in local courts by letting an approver go at large. Lee was thrown into the Tower until he paid a fine and ransom at the king's will.

The steward's jurisdiction had long aroused complaint, especially as the extent of the verge, the area 12 miles in radius from the king or guardian of the realm, tended to expand. The complaints against Lee, brought before the council by private petition, reflected these grievances, and foreshadowed a series of acrimonious attacks on the stewards and chamberlains in the 1370s. The growing unpopularity of the royal household at the end of the 1360s, coupled with the strains caused by the renewal of war in France, probably intensified anger over Lee's perceived use of the stewardship for personal profit and to harass his enemies.

Lee died on 22 January 1370, leaving a son and heir, Walter, who was then twenty-one years old. The identity of Walter's mother is unknown. SCOTT L. WAUGH

Sources F. Palgrave, ed., *The parliamentary writs and writs of military summons*, 2 vols. in 4 (1827–34) · *RotP*, vol. 2 · *Chancery records* · Rymer, *Foedera*, new edn · Tout, *Admin. hist.*, 3.234, 249, 259; 4.149, 161–2, 181 · *VCH Hertfordshire*, 3.79, 149, 223–4, 285, 310, 358, 477; 4.5, 7–8, 10, 67, 96, 461 · C. Given-Wilson, *The royal household and the king's affinity: service, politics and finance in England, 1360–1413* (1986), 48–50, 73 · *CIPM*, 13 no. 343

Lee, John (1725–1781), actor and theatre manager, first appeared as Condé in Nathaniel Lee's *The Massacre at Paris* at Goodman's Fields Theatre on 28 October 1745; of his earlier years nothing is known. He played the entire 1745–6 winter season with Hallam's company in roles that included Sir Charles in George Farquhar's *The Beaux' Stratagem*, Pedro in John Dryden's *The Spanish Fryar*, the ghost in *Hamlet*, Catesby in Nicholas Rowe's *Jane Shore*, and Southampton in John Banks's *The Unhappy Favourite*—leaving with a performance as Richard III on 3 March 1746. Thereafter he transferred to Drury Lane, where he made his début as Hotspur in *1 Henry IV* on 9 May 1746. However, he returned to Goodman's Fields on 11 November 1746, when, again playing Richard III, he began a season that saw him extend his repertory to take in the parts of Cassio in *Othello*, Hamlet, and the bastard in *King Lear*, as well as roles in Thomas Southerne's *Oroonoko*, Rowe's *The Fair Penitent*, *The Merry Wives of Windsor*, Thomas Otway's *Venice Preserv'd*, and James Thomson's *Tancred and Sigismunda*. In 1747 he joined the company at Richmond, where he first appeared as Ranger in Benjamin Hoadly's *The Suspicious Husband* on 3 October. Soon after, on 14 November 1747, he transferred to Garrick's new company at Drury Lane, playing with them for the first time as Edgar in *King Lear*. He continued with Garrick's company through the winter season of 1748–9, added a summer engagement at Richmond in 1749, and began again at Drury Lane on 19 September 1749. But on 5 October he deserted to Covent Garden and a salary of £10 per week. He made his début there for Rich on 23 October as Ranger—one of Garrick's favoured roles. He continued through the season in a series of increasingly high-profile parts, among them Essex in *The Unhappy Favourite*, Archer in *The Beaux' Stratagem*, Romeo, and Richard III. Lee began the next season at Covent Garden, but Garrick had sued him for breach of articles and he was forced to return to Drury Lane on 13 November 1750 and the modest role of Ross in *Macbeth*. There he stayed for two further winter seasons, with summer engagements at Richmond and Twickenham. During the summer of 1751 he was again at Richmond, this time with his wife, Anna Sophia (*d.* 3 Sept 1770), and they acted together in pairings that included Archer and Mrs Sullen in *The Beaux' Stratagem*, Romeo and Juliet, and Benedick and Beatrice. While his wife travelled to Dublin to join Thomas Sheridan's Smock Alley company, Lee was forced to continue with Garrick until mid-April 1752, when he too quit for Ireland. He performed at Smock Alley—as Romeo to his wife's Juliet on 20 May—only once, however, before he departed for Edinburgh and a new career as a manager.

Supported by Lord Elibank, Andrew Pringle, and other patrons, Lee assumed management of the Canongate Concert Hall, Edinburgh's only regularly producing theatre. His début season was under way by 16 July, when he performed Hamlet, and he continued with productions of *The Beggar's Opera*, *Romeo and Juliet*, Garrick's *Miss in her Teens*, and Richard Steele's *The Conscious Lovers*. Lee continued as an innovative manager for four years: overseeing a programme of renewal and improvement of the scenery and decorations, removing seats from the stage, and stopping visits behind the scenes during performances. He also initiated a series of summer tours by the Edinburgh company to Glasgow, Newcastle, and Edinburgh. James Dibdin acknowledged Lee's success in 'having been the first to raise the status and the *morale* of the theatre in Edinburgh' (Dibdin, 72).

Despite these exciting and challenging improvements, some sections of Edinburgh society opposed Lee's management and seem to have set upon an organized stratagem to wrest control of the theatre from him. The dispute was long, complex, and increasingly bitter, described by Lee himself in his pamphlet *Narrative of a remarkable breach of trust committed by a nobleman, five judges, and several advocates of the court of session in Scotland* (1772) and in Dibdin's *The Annals of the Edinburgh Stage* (1888). The result of action, counter-action, suit, and threat was that he was forced out of his position in favour of West Digges. On 23 February 1756 Lee's creditors seized the theatre even as he was performing on stage. The perfectly legal, but certainly rather distasteful, scheme saw Lee's wife and family turned out of their home and their furniture and property sold off, and the former manager himself put in gaol for two months. Even after his release the legal wranglings continued for some ten years.

Lee must have been relieved finally to leave Edinburgh and take up an engagement at Smock Alley, where he made his first appearance as Lear on 3 November 1756. However, controversy and legal argument followed him, and he was soon launched into a dispute with Sheridan over the terms of his engagement. Opposing sides of the dispute are described in Lee's pamphlet *Letters from Mr Lee to Mr Sheridan* and in the anonymous *Remarks on Mr Lee's Letters to Mr Sheridan* (both 1757). Lee limped on at Smock Alley until the end of the season before returning to Covent Garden for the first time in seven years. He began the winter season of 1757–8 on 11 November in one of his best roles, Richard III. Almost inevitably things fared badly. Although he was contracted to appear four times a week through the whole season, he in fact performed only four times in total: his opening engagement as Richard, then as Ranger on 18 November and 21 December, and finally as Bayes in the duke of Buckingham's *The Rehearsal*, on 24 January 1758. In *Mr Lee's Case Against J. Rich*, Lee accused the Covent Garden manager of breaking their signed contract and of refusing to meet with the actor and negotiate a settlement. Disgruntled and, he claimed, out of pocket, Lee left the capital for the Orchard Street Theatre in Bath, where he continued for three seasons. In August 1761 he also led a company to Winchester, and in 1760 and 1761 he again acted in Edinburgh.

Lee did not return to London until early 1762, when he made a handful of appearances at Drury Lane. However, in autumn of that year he again became a member of Garrick's regular company and continued there in a variety of roles—and in command of a salary of about £3 per week, a fee in the middle range of the pay list—in a more settled state until 1766. In 1762 and 1764 Lee had acted for the summer seasons in Manchester and briefly entered into management there in 1765. In the summer of 1766 he joined Spranger Barry's company to play Iago, Edmund, and Jaques in *As You Like It* in London. The following year he appeared in Edinburgh and even attempted to regain management there. He was more successful at Bath, where, in April 1768, he was appointed manager of the Bath Theatre Royal. He played the summer season with Foote's company at the Haymarket before taking up his post in Bath in the autumn, and remained there as manager until 1771. However, controversy plagued him throughout, with an obscure scheme to build a new theatre leading him once more to legal action. After leaving Bath he set upon a period of itinerant engagements—a series of concerts and readings at the Crown and Anchor tavern in the Strand in April 1772, a year or so in Ireland, and a return to Covent Garden on 11 October 1774 with a three-year contract. He left London at the end of the 1776–7 season and ended his career acting—and occasionally entering into management—in Bath and Bristol. Failing health forced his retirement, and his final role was as Macbeth at Bristol on 14 July 1780.

Although Lee was never a playwright proper, he did adapt old plays for contemporary production: his versions of *Romeo and Juliet*, *The Merchant of Venice*, *Macbeth*, and perhaps also *Much Ado about Nothing* for the Edinburgh house were described by the *Biographia dramatica* as 'literary murders' (Baker, 1.280). This brief but decidedly hostile account of Lee ascribed his litigiousness to an overrating of his own talent, arguing that 'It is remarkable, that he scarce ever was connected with any theatre that he did not quarrel with the manager or some person belonging to it' (ibid.). Lee died at Bath on either 19 or 20 February 1781, the cause, given in a letter held in the Enthoven Collection, being 'mortification of the bowels' (Highfill, Burnim & Langhans, *BDA*).

Lee and his wife may have had up to five daughters and one son: Sophia *Lee (*bap.* 1750, *d.* 1824) and Harriet *Lee (1757/8–1851) were both novelists and playwrights and also ran the Belvidere School in Bath; their sister Anna assisted them in this enterprise for the education of girls until, suffering from depression, she hanged herself on 23 October 1805. Lee's son, George Augustus *Lee (1761–1826), became a partner in the Manchester cotton-spinning firm Philips and Lee. ADRIENNE SCULLION

Sources Highfill, Burnim & Langhans, *BDA*, 9.201–9 • J. C. Dibdin, *The annals of the Edinburgh stage* (1888) • D. E. Baker, *Biographia dramatica, or, A companion to the playhouse*, rev. I. Reed, new edn, rev. S. Jones, 3 vols. in 4 (1812) • *The thespian dictionary, or, Dramatic biography of the eighteenth century* (1802) • Genest, *Eng. stage* • J. Lee, *Narrative of a remarkable breach of trust committed by a nobleman, five judges, and several advocates of the court of session in Scotland* (1772)
Likenesses engraving, repro. in *The Universal Museum*

Lee, John (1733–1793), barrister and politician, was born at Leeds on 6 March 1733, the youngest of the ten children of the cloth merchant Thomas Lee (1692–1736) and his wife, Mary, *née* Reveley (1691/2–1750). Although his early education remains obscure, he showed a commitment to the law and was admitted to Gray's Inn (1750) and to Lincoln's Inn (1754). He was called to the bar two years later and began to establish a formidable practice, principally on the northern circuit where he commanded high fees.

Lee's family had been associated with protestant dissent in Leeds and in particular supported the Unitarian Mill Hill chapel. Although his mother apparently wished him to become an Anglican clergyman, Lee himself was a committed Unitarian and a close friend of the Unitarian minister Joseph Priestley, his fellow Yorkshireman. It was probably through his nonconformity and its tinge of political radicalism that Lee was drawn, by the late 1760s, towards the parliamentary opposition. He came to the notice of Lord Rockingham, who used his influence in Yorkshire to secure Lee's appointment as recorder of Doncaster in 1769. Thereafter Lee acted as the legal adviser to Rockingham's party and began to acquire national prominence. In May 1769 he appeared before the Commons as counsel for the petitioners for the right of John Wilkes, elected for Middlesex, to take his seat. According to Burke, this performance 'established his reputation' (Copeland, 2.23) and it certainly placed him alongside the libertarian critics of George III and his ministers. In 1769, too, Lee married Mary (1734–1812), daughter of William Hutchinson of Staindrop, co. Durham, where Lee, despite his dismissal of landowning as 'the acquisition of dirty acres' (BL, Add. MS 34417, fol. 225), obtained a respectable house and estate. The couple had one child, Mary Tabitha (1777–1851).

Lee identified fully with the Rockinghamite hostility to the American war. He participated in the Yorkshire Association's campaigns for reform from 1779 to 1780, and was friendly with Christopher Wyvill. When Rockingham's friends took office in April 1782 Lee became solicitor-general, and Rockingham secured his election to the Commons for the small borough of Clitheroe. Thereafter Lee's political career followed the fortunes of his party. With Charles James Fox and Edmund Burke he resigned on Rockingham's death (1 July 1782) and was a warm supporter of the Fox–North coalition of 1783, which forced the second earl of Shelburne from office. Lee was again solicitor-general in April 1783, until he succeeded James Wallace as attorney-general the following November. He defended the India Bill of 1783 with a rashness and vituperation which incurred much criticism. After the removal of the coalition (December 1783) the *Morning Post* appraised the individual performances of the fallen ministers: 'Bill of fare for the Opposition: Lord North … Hung beef; Jack Lee … Hasty Pudding' (26 March 1784).

In opposition after 1783 Lee remained a supporter of Fox, but ill health limited his parliamentary attendance. He voted for parliamentary reform in 1785 and for repeal of the Test and Corporation Acts in 1789. He served as king's attorney and serjeant of the county palatine of Lancaster from 4 February 1782 until his death. Although not returned to parliament at the general election of 1790, he agreed later that year to serve as Lord Fitzwilliam's nominee for Higham Ferrers. He was the friend of several leading Unitarians, including Richard Price, and helped the Unitarian chapel of Theophilus Lindsey in London with legal advice and financial generosity. His friends included James Boswell and John Scott, the future Lord Chancellor Eldon, whose anecdote book records many instances of Lee's unaffected conviviality. But though an agreeable companion, Lee lacked polish. He belonged to the rough, fiercely competitive legal world of which Edward Thurlow was an exemplar, and N. W. Wraxall described him as 'a man of strong intellectual parts, though of very coarse manners' (*Historical and Posthumous Memoirs*, 2.370).

Lee died of cancer, combined with the effects of a riding accident, at his home, Malvern House, Staindrop, on 5 August 1793, and was buried in Staindrop parish church. His wife survived him. He offers an excellent example of the way in which the legal profession could provide the means for upward social mobility, and he remains a very rare case of a committed dissenter who held high office in the eighteenth century. G. M. DITCHFIELD

Sources G. M. Ditchfield, 'Some aspects of Unitarianism and radicalism, 1760–1810', PhD diss., U. Cam., 1968, ch. 4 • J. Brooke, 'Lee, John (?1733–93)', HoP, *Commons, 1754–90* [see also vol. 1] • HoP, *Commons, 1790–1820*, 4.401 • *The historical and the posthumous memoirs of Sir Nathaniel William Wraxall, 1772–1784*, ed. H. B. Wheatley, 5 vols. (1884), vol. 2, p. 370; vol. 3, pp. 58, 82, 86, 99, 112, 130, 182 • G. M. Ditchfield, 'Three unpublished letters of Joseph Priestley', *Enlightenment and Dissent*, 2 (1983), 101–6 • *Life and correspondence of Joseph Priestley*, ed. J. T. Rutt, 2 vols. (1831–2) • *The correspondence of James*

Boswell with David Garrick, Edmund Burke, and Edmond Malone, ed. G. M. Kahrl and others (1986), vol. 4 of *The Yale editions of the private papers of James Boswell*, research edn (1966–) • *Boswell: the applause of the jury, 1782–1785*, ed. I. S. Lustig and F. A. Pottle (1981), vol. 12 of *The Yale editions of the private papers of James Boswell*, trade edn (1950–89) • *Boswell: the English experiment, 1785–1789*, ed. I. S. Lustig and F. A. Pottle (1986), vol. 13 of *The Yale editions of the private papers of James Boswell*, trade edn (1950–89) • G. M. Ditchfield, 'Two unpublished letters of Theophilus Lindsey', *Transactions of the Unitarian Historical Society*, 20 (1991–4), 137–42 • R. G. Wilson, *Gentlemen merchants: the merchant community in Leeds, 1700–1830* (1971), 196, 236, 245 • *The correspondence of Edmund Burke*, ed. T. W. Copeland and others, 10 vols. (1958–78), vol. 2, p. 23; vol. 3, pp. 12–13; vol. 4, pp. 106–8, 419–20; vol. 5, pp. 77–9 • *Lord Eldon's anecdote book*, ed. A. L. J. Lincoln and R. L. McEwen (1960), 24–5, 60–61, 111–12, 127–8 • G. Thomas, earl of Albemarle [G. T. Keppel], *Memoirs of the marquis of Rockingham and his contemporaries*, 2 vols. (1852), vol. 2, pp. 106–32 • BL, Add. MS 34417, fol. 225 • *Morning Post* (26 March 1784) • will of John Lee, PRO, PROB 11/1239 • Durham RO, Lee MSS • J. Hunter, *Familiae minorum gentium*, ed. J. W. Clay, 1, Harleian Society, 37 (1894), 204–5 • *GM*, 1st ser., 63 (1793), 772–3

Archives Durham RO, corresp. and papers • U. Mich., Clements L., corresp. | BL, corresp. with Lord Auckland, Add. MSS 34412–34461 • JRL, corresp. of Theophilus Lindsey • Northants. RO, Fitzwilliam corresp. • Sheffield Central Library, Rockingham MSS, Wentworth Woodhouse MSS, X1603; X1604

Likenesses R. Stewart, mezzotint, pubd 1778, BM • J. Sayers, caricature, etching, pubd 1784 (after himself), NPG • J. Reynolds, oils, 1786, repro. in E. K. Waterhouse, *Reynolds* (1941) • C. H. Hodges, mezzotint, pubd 1788 (after J. Reynolds), BM, NPG • J. Nollekens, bust on monument, 1795, Staindrop church, co. Durham • S. W. Reynolds, mezzotint, pubd 1836 (after J. Reynolds), BM, NPG • J. Nollekens, bust, Wentworth Woodhouse, Yorkshire

Wealth at death over £10,000—probable value of estate at Staindrop, co. Durham, and personal estate incl. bequest of £4000 to daughter; residue to widow; legacies to servants: will, PRO, PROB 11/1239, fols. 340v–341r

Lee, John (*d.* 1804), wood-engraver, was possibly the son of the John Lee who published a series of *Twelve Prints of English Birds* in 1736. He lived in London, where he was active between about 1794 and 1804. He was a principal member of the London school of wood-engraving which was formed in response to the success of William Bewick's Newcastle-based revival of this medium, and his finest work has been compared to that of Bewick; indeed, in his *Treatise on Wood Engraving* (1839) John Jackson judged Lee to be the 'best of the London engravers' (Jackson, 627). Although it was designed for the cheap end of the market, his best work was a series of 'black-line cuts' to decorate the pages of *The Cheap Repository* (1794–8), a compilation of religious and moral tracts that was published by J. Marshall, in London, and S. Hazard, in Bath. All of his known work was produced for book illustration, and other examples appear in *A Wreath for the Brow of Youth*, a children's reading book dedicated to Princess Charlotte of Wales. Several of his architectural elevations, with the posthumous date of 1808, also appeared in John Britton's *The Architectural Antiquities of Great Britain* (1835). He operated from 68 Hatton Garden, the address which is inscribed alongside his signature, 'J. Lee Engraver on Wood', on some vignettes in the Bodleian Library in Oxford. Towards the end of his life he took on Henry White as an apprentice, but—as Lee died at Hatton Garden in March 1804—that student had to complete his training with Thomas Bewick. Lee was survived by his son James (*fl.* 1800–1875), who became one of the most prolific of the London wood-engravers; his work is often confused with that of his father. LUCY PELTZ

Sources Bénézit, *Dict.* • T. Clayton, *The English print, 1688–1802* (1997) • R. K. Engen, *Dictionary of Victorian wood engravers* (1985) • Farington, *Diary* • W. Chatto and J. Jackson, *A treatise on wood engraving* (1839) • J. Pye, *Patronage of British art: an historical sketch* (1845); facs. edn [1970]

Archives BL, Add. MS 4475, fol. 113

Lee, John (1779–1859), Church of Scotland minister and university principal, was born at Torwoodlee-Mains, in the parish of Stow, Edinburghshire, on 22 November 1779, the son of James Lee and his wife, Helen Patterson. He was educated at a school in Clovenfords, Selkirkshire, and went on to the University of Edinburgh in 1794, where he supported himself by teaching. He graduated MD in 1801. After serving for a short time in the army hospital service he commenced studying law, but finally, having previously been a member of the Associate Synod, decided to enter the Church of Scotland. In 1804 he was licensed to preach and became amanuensis, at Inveresk, to the Revd Alexander (Jupiter) Carlyle, who entrusted him with the manuscript of his autobiography on his death in 1805. Lee was ordained in 1807, and after acting for a few months as pastor of the Scotch Church, Hanover Street, London, was inducted as minister of Peebles. In 1812 he became professor of church history at St Mary's College, St Andrews, and was there chosen rector of the college. On 5 or 13 July 1813 he married Rose (*d.* 1833), the daughter of Thomas Masson or Mason, minister of Dunnichen. They had seven sons and four daughters.

In 1820 Lee became professor of moral philosophy in King's College, Aberdeen, but his lectures there were chiefly delivered by a deputy. In 1821 he resigned both professorships and accepted a call to the Canongate church, Edinburgh, when the degree of DD was given him by St Andrews University. In 1825 he was translated from the Canongate to Lady Yester's Church. He was made principal clerk of the general assembly in 1827 and was appointed a chaplain-in-ordinary to the king in 1830. In 1834 he became minister of the old church of St Giles, Edinburgh, and in 1840 he became dean of the Chapel Royal, Stirling.

Lee's successful career was somewhat impeded by his rivalry with Thomas Chalmers. The two men were personally antagonistic, an antagonism increased by the divergence of their views in church politics, as Lee was a committed moderate. They held opposite views in the disputes over poor law amendment and Catholic emancipation, and they were rivals for the Edinburgh chair in divinity in 1827. Lee's academic ambitions were once again thwarted by Chalmers in 1831: after lecturing regularly in divinity at Edinburgh University as a substitute for the infirm William Ritchie, Lee hoped to be appointed as successor to Hugh Meiklejohn, the professor of ecclesiastical history, when he died. Chalmers opposed the appointment on the grounds of plurality, although the income for the post was only £200 and it seemed unlikely that another candidate would be found to accept it. However, David Welsh, an unmarried cleric, was persuaded by Chalmers to accept the professorship. The next year Lee unsuccessfully contested the moderatorship with Chalmers. In 1835 Chalmers recommended the nomination of Lee for the moderatorship of 1836, but subsequently opposed him, after Lee had given evidence before a royal commission which was unfavourable to Chalmers's plans for church extension. Lee's evidence showed that, unlike Chalmers, he was well acquainted with the situation of the urban poor. He held a high view of the clerical profession, and was naturally out of sympathy with Chalmers's proposed laicization of the church ministry. An alternative candidate was elected to the moderatorship, and when, in 1837, Lee's supporters rallied round in an attempt to secure his election for that year, Chalmers renewed his opposition, and by various unscrupulous means discredited Lee and succeeded in smashing the whig evangelical wing of the church which he had come to represent. In order to escape Edinburgh, Lee accepted the appointment of principal of the United College of St Andrews, and in 1839 was appointed principal of St Andrews University. However, in 1841, when both men competed for the post of principal at the University of Edinburgh, Lee was elected. In that year, on 30 June, he married his second wife, Charlotte E. Wright (*d.* 1871). At the Disruption in 1843 Lee remained within the Church of Scotland, undertaking Chalmers's divinity classes and eventually succeeding him as professor of divinity. He held this appointment in conjunction with the principalship. In 1844 he was elected moderator of the assembly. As he was probably the most erudite cleric to remain in the Church of Scotland, it was a fitting recognition of his talents.

Lee wrote little during his busy career. His major works were *Lectures on the History of the Church of Scotland* (1860) and *The University of Edinburgh from 1583 to 1839* (1884). He was, however, a keen bibliophile, who collected a library of 20,000 volumes. In John Hill Burton's *The Book Hunter* (1862) he appeared as Archdeacon Meadows, a bibliomaniac who would buy several copies of a book which he owned already, and then, forgetting this, borrow a copy of the same book from a friend. But Lee's love of books was not a selfish one: in the 1820s he led a successful campaign to overturn the exclusive rights of the royal printers to print the Bible in Scotland, as their editions proved to be too expensive for the common man. He died on 2 May 1859 at the University of Edinburgh; his widow survived until March 1871. FERGUS MACDONALD

Sources *DNB* • B. W. Crombie and W. S. Douglas, *Modern Athenians: a series of original portraits of memorable citizens of Edinburgh* (1882), 135–7 • A. Grant, *The story of the University of Edinburgh during its first three hundred years*, 2 (1884), 271–4 • *Fasti Scot.* • *Proceedings of the Royal Society of Edinburgh*, 4 (1857–62), 212–17 • *The Scotsman* (7 May 1859), 4 • Lord Neaves, 'Memoir', *Inaugural addresses in the University of Edinburgh* (1861) • D. P. Thomson, *The lad from Torwoodlee* (1946) • *DSCHT* • S. J. Brown, *Thomas Chalmers and the godly commonwealth in Scotland* (1982)

Archives NL Scot., corresp. and papers • U. Edin. L., notebooks and papers | NA Scot., letters to Fox Maule • NL Scot., letters to Blackwoods • NL Scot., letters to Archibald Constable • U. Edin. L., letters to Archibald Constable • U. Edin. L., letters to David Laing • U. Edin., New Coll. L., letters to Thomas Chalmers • U. St Andr. L., corresp. with James David Forbes • U. St Andr. L., corresp. with lords Melville • U. St Andr. L., papers relating to University of St Andrews

Likenesses B. W. Crombie, caricature, coloured etching, 1847, NPG; repro. in B. W. Crombie, *Modern Athenians: a series of original portraits of memorable citizens of Edinburgh* (1882) • J. Archer, lithograph, BM • A. Edouart, silhouette, Scot. NPG • J. Watson-Gordon, two portraits, oils, U. Edin.

Wealth at death £3973 9*s*. 3½*d*.: inventory, 30 June 1859, NA Scot., SC 70/1/101/436

Lee [*formerly* Fiott], **John** (1783–1866), antiquary and astronomer, was born John Fiott on 28 April 1783, the eldest son of John Fiott, merchant of London, and his wife, Harriet, daughter of William Lee of Totteridge Park, Hertfordshire. The Fiotts originated from Dijon in the old kingdom of Burgundy; among his ancestors on his mother's side were Chief Justice Sir William Lee and the statesman John Hampden. He assumed the name of Lee by royal licence on 4 October 1815 under the terms of the will of his maternal uncle William Lee Antonie.

As John Fiott he was schooled at Mackworth in Derbyshire and admitted pensioner at St John's College, Cambridge, on 21 November 1801. He graduated BA as fifth wrangler in 1806 and was nominated Worts travelling bachelor in 1807. Having set his sights on northern Europe, he embarked for Göteborg, then under Danish rule, where, observing the importance of shipbuilding in those parts, he immediately bought copies of all the books on that subject for transmission to Cambridge. He reached the outskirts of Copenhagen on the eve of the British assault and witnessed the actual attack and the ensuing conflagration. Fiott was unimpressed by the Danes, whom he found a dour and colourless people. He visited the university towns of Lund and Uppsala, and Stockholm, before returning to Britain in February 1808. In April 1808 he was elected a fellow of St John's and the following May he went once more to Stockholm and Uppsala, a city which so pleased him that he stayed there until June 1809, in which year he proceeded to his MA.

Fiott next sampled naval life, by joining the Walcheren expedition in which his brother Lieutenant Fiott was involved, before returning to the university in September and remaining there until March 1810. He then joined HMS *Woolwich* on convoy to Gibraltar, from where he headed east, calling at Malta, Smyrna, and Constantinople. By January 1811 he was in Athens; after touring that neighbourhood he moved on to Hydra, Crete, Alexandria, and Cairo. After recovering from an attack of fever, he made for the Christian sites of Syria. At Aleppo he met the famous traveller John Lewis Burckhardt, who advised him on the purchase of manuscripts, coins, and medals, which afterwards formed part of the renowned library and museum at Hartwell House, Buckinghamshire. He indulged in a little tomb-robbing on Samos, uncovering vases and silver and gold ornaments before a letter arrived from the authorities ordering him to desist, which he did, although he regretted that a despotic government did not approve of what he saw as research. Tempted to excavate

John Lee (1783–1866), by Maull & Polyblank, 1855

again in the north of the island, he was once more sternly ordered to cease these unlicensed operations. A sojourn in Spain during the summer of 1813 preceded a visit in May 1814 to Elba, where he witnessed Napoleon's arrival before touring Italy. From there he returned to Britain in July 1815 via Germany and the Netherlands.

The death of his uncle in 1815 brought Lee not only his new name but also the valuable estates of Colworth in Bedfordshire, Totteridge Park, and others, and these were augmented in 1827, when he inherited from Sir George Lee, sixth baronet, the estate of Hartwell in Buckinghamshire, which had been in possession of the Lee family since 1617. Before that bequest arrived, however, he resumed his law studies and in due course took his LLD and was admitted in November 1816 to the College of Advocates, where he attended regularly for many years. After the courts of Doctors' Commons were abolished he was made a QC in 1864.

From this time Lee's life was divided between his profession, his duties as a landlord and country gentleman, and his scientific pursuits. He served as a JP from 1819, and as a high sheriff of Buckinghamshire in 1864. He married Cecelia Rutter on 25 October 1833, and after her death in 1854 he married Louisa Catherine Wilkinson; there were no children of either marriage. He took up the study of astronomy; he was a founder member of the Astronomical Society in 1824 and one of its most energetic fellows and a generous benefactor, serving as treasurer from 1831 (when it became the Royal Astronomical Society) to 1840 and as president in 1861–2. In 1831 he erected an observatory at Hartwell House to the design of his great friend Admiral William Henry Smyth, which he furnished with the best instruments available and where he employed, in turn, James Epps, Norman Robert Pogson, and James Glaisher as assistants. This devotion to astronomy led to an extensive correspondence with the leading astronomers of Europe, many of whom were among the friends who enjoyed his hospitality.

Lee was elected to the Royal Society and to the Society of Antiquaries; his antiquarian interests led him to accept the vice-presidency of the Buckinghamshire Architectural and Archaeological Society. In 1830 he assisted in the formation of the British Meteorological Society, holding office as treasurer and subsequently as president. He was the first president of the Numismatic Society in 1837, a founder member of the Royal Geographical Society in 1830, and member of the Society of Arts, the Geological Society, the British Archaeological Association, the Syro-Egyptian Society, the Asiatic Society of Bengal, and the Chronological Society, among others. He was a regular attender at meetings of the British Association for the Advancement of Science, and an indefatigable collector of rocks and fossils, which went into his museum together with the magnificent collection of cameos, gems, and coins garnered on his travels. Lee wrote little beyond a few papers in *Archaeologia* but paid for the publication of works compiled by Admiral Smyth, namely, the descriptive catalogue of his Roman brass medals (1834) and, more importantly, the *Aedes Hartwellianae* of 1851, with its *Addenda* of 1864, and *The Cycle of Celestial Objects* (1860), commonly known as *Speculum Hartwellianum*. The *Aedes* was subtitled 'Notices of the manor and mansion of Hartwell' and included a description of the observatory and its instruments, and observations made there by Epps and Smyth. Few books on travel and geography escaped Lee's notice; only light literature—poetry and belles-lettres—held no delights for him.

These scientific activities did not preclude a lively interest in the business and politics of everyday life. Lee, an uncompromising Liberal and an advocate of female suffrage, was an unsuccessful parliamentary candidate for Aylesbury (1835), Stafford (1847), and Buckinghamshire (1835, 1841, 1852, and 1863). Among his victorious opponents was Disraeli in 1852. According to his obituarist, Lee's final appearance on the hustings in 1863 distinguished him as 'perhaps the last man in England that sported in public a blue coat with brass buttons and yellow waistcoat' (*GM*, 592–3).

In his personal life Lee's habits and amusements were simple. He was a rigid teetotaller and a determined enemy of the use of tobacco in any form. He had strong religious views and was a staunch protestant. He was in favour of union between the Church of England and the protestant dissenters and stoutly opposed Tractarianism. Being prudent and economical, he was able to act with generosity towards other persons and institutions in need. His was the driving force behind the foundation in 1833 of the Buckinghamshire Infirmary, to which he gave 1000 guineas, and he continued to find time to visit and comfort the sick. His opinions, once framed, were inflexible, and only his practice of careful assessment before judgement saved him from the fault of obstinacy. His tendency to favour independent opinion over a majority view gave him the reputation of eccentricity where his views were founded on somewhat abstract codes of truth. Deaf to slander, he saw only the best side of people's characters, and he was credulous, even gullible, when confronted with knavery. In sum, he was seen as a just and upright magistrate, an obliging neighbour, a sincere and warm friend, and an admirable and loving husband. After a period of declining health, he died of jaundice at home at Hartwell House on 25 February 1866.

ANITA MCCONNELL

Sources *Memoir of John Lee* (1870?) • *Monthly Notices of the Royal Astronomical Society*, 27 (1866–7), 109–10 • *The Times* (1 March 1866), 11f [taken from *Pall Mall Gazette*] • *Proceedings of the Meteorological Society*, 3 (1866), 227–8 • W. H. Smyth, *Aedes Hartwellianae* (1851) • *GM*, 4th ser., 1 (1866), 592–3 • *Journal of the Royal Geographical Society*, 36 (1866), clxv • *Quarterly Journal of the Geological Society*, 23 (1867), xxxv • A. McConnell, 'Pen portraits of presidents: John Lee FRS', *Weather*, 52 (1996), 258–60 • d. cert. • *DNB* • *McCalmont's parliamentary poll book: British election results 1832–1918*, ed. J. Vincent and M. Stenton, 8th edn (1971)

Archives BL, letters, Add. MSS 47490–47493, 37185–37199 • Bodl. Oxf., corresp. • Bucks. RLSS, letters and papers • LPL, letters and papers • MHS Oxf., letters and papers • National Archives of Canada, Ottawa, letters relating to Canada • NL Aus., legal notebook • NMM, corresp. and papers relating to Franklin search expeditions • RAS, letters and papers • Royal Meteorological Society, Reading, letters • RS, letters • St John Cam., travel diary and corresp. • U. Oxf., Griffith Institute, notebooks | BL, letters to Charles Babbage, Add. MSS 37185–37199, *passim* • Bucks. RLSS, corresp. with Sir Henry Verney relating to a proposed Buckinghamshire county infirmary • CUL, letters to Joseph Bonomi • Herts. ALS, letters to his aunt Louisa Arrowsmith • Inst. EE, letters to Sir Francis Rolands • LPL, corresp. and papers relating to dissolution of Doctors' Commons • RAS, Hartwell MSS • RAS, letters to Royal Astronomical Society • RAS, letters to Richard Sheepshanks • St John's College, Oxford, St John's College muniments • Yale U., Beinecke L., letters to J. J. Pettigrew

Likenesses Maull & Polyblank, photograph, 1855, NPG [*see illus.*] • F. Croll, line engraving, NPG • R. Inwards, chalk drawing, RAS • T. H. Maguire, lithograph, BM, NPG; repro. in T. H. Maguire, *Portraits of honorary members of the Ipswich Museum* (1852) • lithograph, BM

Wealth at death under £7000: probate, 30 May 1866, *CGPLA Eng. & Wales*

Lee, John Edward (1808–1887), antiquary and geologist, was born at Newland, Kingston upon Hull, on 21 December 1808. His father having died when he was young, Lee was brought up by his uncles Avison and John Terry, owners of one of the most successful of Hull's Baltic merchants, and at sixteen entered their shipping office at Hull. An early interest in science was fostered by Hull's Literary and Philosophical Society, founded in 1822, and in its museum. For several years Lee travelled for the benefit of his health, visiting Norway and Sweden, and later Russia and other parts of the continent. During these years he learned French and German, and made sketches in the course of his travels.

On his return to Britain Lee joined the staff of J. J. Cordes & Co. (ironworks) at Monmouth. On 5 August 1846 he married Anne (1809–1885), daughter of Natham Graveley of Torquay; they lived at Caerleon Priory and raised two daughters and a son. In later years his wife's declining health led Lee to settle her at Villa Syracusa, Torquay, although he continued to spend most of his time at Caerleon.

In his leisure hours Lee turned to geology and the Roman archaeology of Caerleon. He was a founder of the Monmouth and Caerleon Antiquarian Society and a frequent contributor to its *Proceedings*. He aided the formation of Caerleon Museum, his chief work being *Isca Silurum, or, An Illustrated Catalogue of the Museum of Antiquities at Caerleon* (1862). He also published on Roman coins, translated and revised with the author Keller's *Lake Dwellings of Switzerland* (1866; enlarged edn, 2 vols., 1878), and made other European archaeological studies. He was a fellow of the Society of Antiquaries, subscribed to the British Association for the Advancement of Science, and was a member of the Devonshire Association and of the Torquay Natural History Society.

In connection with his geological interest Lee accumulated a vast collection of fossils, exchanging specimens and corresponding with other collectors in Europe and America. In 1859 he was elected fellow of the Geological Society of London. In 1868 he travelled to Italy with John Phillips to study Vesuvius, then active, and ten years later he accompanied Professor Roemer of Breslau to study the Devonian rocks of the Eifel district. Many of his sketches were reproduced in his *Notebook of an Amateur Geologist* (1881). Lee presented his fossils, comprising over 21,000 specimens in thirty-one cabinets, to the British Museum (Natural History) in 1885. He died at Villa Syracusa, Torquay, on 18 August 1887.

ANITA MCCONNELL

Sources J. E. Lee, *Notebook of an amateur geologist* (1881) • *Geological Magazine*, new ser., 3rd decade, 4 (1887), 526–8 • J. W. Judd, *Quarterly Journal of the Geological Society*, 44 (1888), 42–3 • *Report and Transactions of the Devonshire Association*, 20 (1888), 34–6 • private information (2004)

Archives Oxf. U. Mus. NH, letters to John Phillips

Wealth at death £159,488 3*s*. 7*d*.: resworn probate, Feb 1888, *CGPLA Eng. & Wales* (1887)

Lee, Joseph (1780–1859), enamel painter, was born on 16 January 1780, the son of John Lee of Islington, London, and his wife, Rachel, *née* Oldroyd. After an unsuccessful start in business, Lee turned to painting, in which he was probably self-taught, at about the age of thirty, when he studied the work of C. F. Zincke. He painted miniatures in enamel from the life, and also copied pictures in enamel, especially after works by B. van der Helst, George Romney, Jean Petitot, and Charles Boit. He was an occasional exhibitor at the Royal Academy from 1809 to 1853, and also exhibited with the Society of British Artists in Suffolk Street. With his wife, Ann (*d.* 1827), Lee had seven children, of whom Edwin Edmunds Lee and Walter Joseph Stooke Lee later became painters. In 1818 he was appointed enamel painter to Princess Charlotte of Wales, of whom he exhibited portraits in that year and in 1823 (the latter a copy of one by Dawe), and in 1832 a portrait of the duke of Sussex, after Phillips, having previously been appointed enamel painter to that prince. He also painted George IV after Sir Thomas Lawrence. Lee exhibited for the last time in 1853, and died at his home, 13 Victoria Place, Gravesend, Kent, on 26 December 1859, aged seventy-nine. Lee was apparently unsuccessful financially and in later years received an allowance from his nephew, Charles Lee, an architect. Daphne Foskett records that 'Lee, whose height was 5 ft. 8 in., used to carry an enamel of Napoleon I in his pocket as a show piece' (Foskett, 586). Enamel paintings by Lee are in the Victoria and Albert Museum, and the Wallace Collection, London. Another, of Prince Leopold of Saxe-Coburg-Saalfeld, signed in full on the reverse, is in the National Gallery of Ireland, Dublin.

L. H. CUST, *rev.* ANNETTE PEACH

Sources D. Foskett, *Miniatures: dictionary and guide* (1987) · *CGPLA Eng. & Wales* (1860)

Wealth at death under £200: administration with will, 10 March 1860, *CGPLA Eng. & Wales*

Lee, Laurence Edward Alan [Laurie] (1914–1997), writer, was born on 26 June 1914 at 2 Glenview Terrace, Slad Road, Uplands, Stroud, the third of the four children of Reginald Joseph Lee (1877–1947), civil servant, and his second wife, Annie Emily (1879–1950), daughter of John Light of Quedgeley, near Gloucester, and his wife, Emma. Reg Lee's first wife, Catherine Critchley, had died on 15 April 1910 giving birth to twins, who died six weeks later, leaving him with five children aged between two and nine. Annie Light answered his advertisement for a housekeeper, married him on 11 May 1911, and gave birth to Frances (1912–1916), Wilfred Jack Raymond (*b.* January 1913), Laurie, and Anthony Lisle (Tony; 1916–1957). Laurie's father, manager of the Co-op grocery store in Stroud, served in the Army Pay Corps at Greenwich during the First World War, then joined the civil service and remained in London for the rest of his life, leaving his wife to bring up her children and stepchildren alone. 'I, for one, scarcely missed him' his son later admitted (Lee, *Cider with Rosie*, 21).

Early years In June 1917 Annie Lee and the seven younger children moved from Stroud to the small village of Slad, a mile and a half away, where they rented a cheaper cottage 'with rooks in the chimney, frogs in the cellar, mushrooms on the ceiling, and all for three and sixpence a week'. 'My life began on the carrier's cart which brought me up from the long slow hills to the village', Lee wrote in the opening passages of his most famous book, the memoir of his childhood, *Cider with Rosie* (1959), '… then, I feel, was I born' (Lee, *Cider with Rosie*, 8). Between the ages of four and twelve he attended the village school, where he claimed he was 'a natural Infant, content to serve out my time' (ibid., 43). Nevertheless, he showed early talent, winning a medal for an essay on dabchicks in a national competition organized by the Royal Society for the Protection of Birds. By the time he was nine, his family discovered that he was already secretly writing 'very clever and amusing' stories which revealed 'a very strong imagination' (Gallagher, xx).

Life in the cottage was hand-to-mouth, cramped, and

Laurence Edward Alan Lee (1914–1997), by Ida Kar, late 1950s

chaotic, but Lee was 'perfectly content in this world of women'. His three 'generous, indulgent, warm-blooded, and dotty' half-sisters were 'the good fortune of our lives'. His mother, despite being 'deserted, debt-ridden, flurried, bewildered', possessed 'an indestructible gaiety' and was a lover 'of beauty & of books & of solitude' (Lee, *Cider with Rosie*, 55, 113; Grove, 1–2). She introduced Lee to poetry, encouraged him to draw and read, and paid 6*d*. an hour out of her husband's weekly remittance of £1 for him to have violin lessons from a peripatetic music teacher. A 'loving and dreamy' boy, according to his mother (Grove, 12), he suffered long bouts of debilitating illness throughout his childhood; frequent attacks of pneumonia and bronchitis left him with permanently weakened lungs, and after suffering concussion when he was knocked down by a bicycle he developed epilepsy.

In 1925 Lee transferred to the Central Boys' School, Stroud, where he developed 'a passion for out-of-school reading' which led to 'indiscriminate gorging' throughout his teens (Lee, *I Can't Stay Long*, 17). He graduated from reading thrillers and westerns at Woolworth's book store to Stroud Public Library, where he worked his way through the modern poets and discovered the prose works of Joyce, Huxley, and Lawrence (ibid., 16, 18). After leaving school two weeks before his sixteenth birthday he joined Messrs Randall and Payne, chartered accountants, of Stroud, as an office junior and took out a subscription from a travelling salesman for 'my own library at a shilling a week' (ibid., 19). When the vicar discovered him reading *Brave New World* (or *Sons and Lovers*; see Lee, *Cider with Rosie*, 206), confiscated, and burnt it, 'it was the end ... of my country childhood and of its carefree acquiescence' (Lee, *I Can't Stay Long*, 19).

Early in the summer of 1934 Lee resigned and, carrying only a small tent, his violin wrapped in a blanket, a change of clothes, a tin of treacle biscuits, and some cheese, he set out to walk to London. Taking a circuitous route so that he could see 'the real sea' (Lee, *As I Walked Out*, 229) for the first time, he busked his way along the south coast, sometimes earning as much in an hour as a farm labourer in a week. In London he took lodgings in Putney, worked as a builder's labourer during the day, and spent his evenings in Soho cafés opening 'the *Heraldo de Madrid*, which I couldn't read, and order[ing] Turkish coffee, which I couldn't drink'. He was also enjoying a string of romantic liaisons and 'scribbling poetry' (ibid., 248, 242). His poems had already appeared in the *Gloucester Citizen* and the *Birmingham Post*, but in October 1934 he won a poetry competition with 'Life', which was published in a national newspaper, the *Sunday Referee*.

Spain: 1935–1938 When his building job ended, Lee decided to go to Spain on what he said was little more than a whim (a former girlfriend having taught him one phrase in Spanish). In July 1935 he sailed to Vigo, then walked and made his way to the south coast, passing through Valladolid, Madrid, Toledo, Valdepeñas, Cordova, and Seville. He recognized characters from his own village in the peasants of Galicia and Andalucia; though they led 'hard and semi-starved lives', they welcomed him with almost medieval courtesy and hospitality. 'The violin was a passport of friendship wherever I went', he later reminisced: 'Here was I, a young boy, golden haired and beautiful, appearing from nowhere and bringing music which meant happiness ... I couldn't go wrong' (Grove, 57).

Lee spent the winter in Almunecar, a village 60 miles east of Malaga, working as a violinist and odd job man at the Hotel Mediterraneo. There he became the protégé of another temporary resident, Wilma Gregory (1886–1963), a 49-year-old Englishwoman with important left-wing and literary connections. 'I found him living as a vagrant, quite penniless & practically uneducated, with these really remarkable gifts for poetry, & art & music' (Grove, 69). In the preliminary skirmishes of the Spanish Civil War, Almunecar was accidentally bombarded by friendly fire, and when HMS *Blanche* arrived to evacuate British citizens on 1 August 1936 Lee returned to England with Gregory.

As I Walked out one Midsummer Morning (1969), Lee's book describing this period, made no reference to Gregory or the year he spent living with her as her 'nephew' (Grove, 75) at Padworth, near Reading, during which she supported him financially and enrolled him as a half-time student in the art department of the University of Reading. In September 1937 she took him to Montpellier, France, intending that he should study at the École des Beaux Arts, but Lee was anxious to return to Spain to join the International Brigades.

On 5 December 1937 Lee crossed the Pyrenees in a snowstorm and, with the assistance of republican sympathizers, re-entered Spain. There has been some confusion about exactly how long he stayed there and what part he played in the civil war, but he was actively involved and, with other veterans who had fought in the war, was granted Spanish citizenship in 1995. The debate centres on *A Moment of War* (1991), his memoir of this period, which describes his being three times arrested, imprisoned, and on the brink of being shot as a fascist spy, and graphically describes the disorganization, amateurism, and squalid living conditions endured by republican recruits.

According to records of the International Brigades and Lee's own passport, he was at Figueras on 11 December 1937, arrived at Albacete on 15 December and, on the following day, at the training centre at Tarazona. On 17 December, having already suffered two epileptic fits while in Spain, he was assigned to the cultural commission. His conduct was variously described as 'excellent' and 'exemplary', his politics as communist, and his character as 'responsible ... and trustworthy'. A report drawn up on 23 December concluded that he was 'a perfectly sincere comrade, who is very sympathetic to the Spanish government', but being 'generally speaking, physically weak, he will not be of any use at the front' (Grove, 93). A French visa was issued to him at Barcelona on 14 February 1938, and he left Spain on 19 February, with 'sale sin dinero' ('departed without money') stamped on his passport (Lee, *A Moment of War*, 536; Grove, 104).

Lee never claimed he had been recruited into active service or fought in the battle of Teruel (15 December 1937–20 February 1938): 'I trained as a soldier, but I was mainly used in the International Brigade headquarters in Madrid during the siege, making short-wave broadcasts to Britain and America' (Grove, 105). His violin, which he had taken with him to Spain and played on these radio broadcasts, again proved his saviour. Though his talents had been put to good use, this was not the role he had hoped to perform. He always regretted that he had been unable to do more and dedicated *A Moment of War* to 'the defeated'.

Lee's situation was further complicated by the fact that in August 1937, aged twenty-three, he had fallen passionately in love with the woman who was to be both his muse and his nemesis. Lorna Cecilia *Wishart, *née* Garman (1911–2000) [*see under* Wishart, Ernest Edward (1902–1987)], was twenty-six and married, with two young children. She was also, according to Lee, 'rich and demandingly beautiful, extravagantly generous with her emotions but fanatically jealous'; even his former girlfriends found her 'staggeringly beautiful and most unconventional' (Lee, *As I Walked Out*, 398; Grove, 83). They had become lovers almost immediately, and it was because of this 'entanglement' (Lee, *As I Walked Out*, 398), as well as his own altruistic motives, that Lee had decided to return to Spain.

Publication Wishart was waiting for Lee in London when he came back from Spain. They lived together until May 1939, when Wishart returned to her husband, who had undertaken to bring up her daughter by Lee, Jasmine (Yasmin) Margaret (*b.* 14 March 1939), as his own. Lee's epilepsy again prevented him being drafted for active service during the Second World War, but he worked as a sound technician for the General Post Office film unit (1939–40), then as a scriptwriter with the Crown Film Unit (1941–3) and the Ministry of Information publications division (1944–6). He also gained recognition as a poet: from 1941 his poems were published in *Horizon* and *Penguin New Writing* and broadcast, read by himself, on the BBC. In 1942 he was photographed looking like 'a rugged and Olympian roué' (Grove, 151) on Bognor beach by Bill Brandt for a series entitled 'Poets of democracy' in *Lilliput* magazine. His circle of literary friends now included Stephen Spender, Cyril Connolly, Cecil Day-Lewis, and John and Rosamond Lehmann, all of whom encouraged him to become a professional writer.

The day after his thirtieth birthday, Lee's first volume of poetry, *The Sun my Monument* (Hogarth Press, 1944), was published. It was dedicated to Wishart, but their affair was coming to an end as she had formed a relationship with Lucian Freud; however, Lee wore her signet ring until he died. He remained irresistible to women. He was extraordinarily good-looking—5 feet 10 inches tall, slim, with 'a golden blond, vulnerable, idealistic face'—and possessed great charm, 'the ultimate weapon, the supreme seduction … If you've got it, you need almost nothing else, neither money, looks, nor pedigree' (Grove, 29; Lee, *I Can't Stay Long*, 67). Children (and adults) were quickly won over by his sense of fun, his love of witty puns, and his ability to perform magic tricks, including fire-eating. Very few, even among his intimate friends, were aware of his constant struggle against illness and depression: 'I'm a melancholic man who likes to be thought merry' (Grove, 401).

Lee's output was prolific during these years: for the Ministry of Information he produced scripts for *Land at War* (1945), *Cyprus is an Island* (1945), and a propaganda film promoting the idea of national parks (1946); articles on his Slad childhood and his experiences in Spain for *Orion* and the BBC (1946–7); his first, highly acclaimed blank-verse play, *The Voyage of Magellan*, broadcast in 1946, and a second, *Peasants' Priest* (1947), performed at the Canterbury festival. He published a second volume of poetry, *The Bloom of Candles* (1947), but remarked that now 'Poems come out from time to time like rare and sickly orchids' (Grove, 224). He was to publish only one further volume of new poetry, *My Many-Coated Man* (1955), turning instead to journalism and, over the next three decades, writing evocative accounts of his travels in Europe, South America, India, and the East.

On 17 May 1950, aged thirty-five, Lee married eighteen-year-old Katherine (Kathy) Francesca Polge (*b.* 1931), niece of Lorna Wishart and, by marriage, of the poet Roy Campbell and the sculptor Jacob Epstein. He had met Kathy for the first time in Martigues when she was five and again in England at the end of the war. When they married Lee had just acquired his last salaried post, as chief caption-writer and creator of the eccentrics corner of the Lion and Unicorn pavilion for the Festival of Britain, for which he was appointed MBE in 1952. He and Kathy spent winter 1951–2 in Spain, a visit which resulted in *A Rose for Winter* (1955), but Lee could not shake off the ill health which dogged him. On his return to England he had a lung removed and thereafter referred to himself as 'Wun Lung Lee, the famous Chinese poet' (Grove, 267); while convalescing he wrote his first account of crossing the Pyrenees in 1937 for a BBC schools programme.

In 1957 the Hogarth Press offered Lee £500 'to give up all other work and get on with' *Cider with Rosie*, which had been commissioned ten years earlier (Grove, 289). The book was published to laudatory reviews in 1959, won the W. H. Smith award, and sold six million copies. Its success enabled Lee to buy Rose Cottage, Slad, 'in the heart of the village, six stumbling paces from the pub' (ibid., 339), though he never gave up his flat in Chelsea, which was the hub of his social life.

On 30 September 1963 Lee's daughter Jesse Frances (Jessy) was born; on the same day Laurie also became a grandfather when Yasmin, his daughter by Wishart, gave birth to Esther. He celebrated the birth of Jessy, 'the particular late wonder of my life' (Lee, *I Can't Stay Long*, 77), in a lyrical book, *The Firstborn* (1964), illustrated with his own photographs of mother and child.

As I Walked out one Midsummer Morning (1969), the second in Lee's autobiographical trilogy, was published ten years after *Cider with Rosie*. Disastrously for him, since his diaries were the basis of his work, his irreplaceable volumes for 1935–7 were stolen while he was in Spain with the BBC in 1969. Their loss made the writing of his last book, *A Moment of War*, more difficult. 'I was in despair', he wrote twenty years later. 'And the anxiety hasn't lessened. I feel myself imprisoned in the need to complete the trilogy' (Grove, 390). Ironically, the book was ultimately sharper and more moving because it was less reliant on detail.

Later years Music remained a solace throughout Lee's life; he was not only a skilled performer on violin and classical guitar, but also an extremely knowledgeable musicologist, with a particular love of classical music and jazz. He published anthologies of his journalism (*I Can't Stay Long*, 1975) and poetry (*Selected Poems*, 1983), and a tribute in prose to his wife and daughter, *Two Women* (1983), with his own remarkable photographs, but continued to work slowly and secretly on *A Moment of War*. 'In the last year I was only able to write a page a week, I couldn't dictate it; it was much too private and too painful … and in any case that is not my way of writing' (Grove, 479). By the time it was completed he was almost blind. *A Moment of War* was published to excellent reviews in 1991. A year later it was republished with *Cider with Rosie* and *As I Walked out one Midsummer Morning* as *Red Sky at Sunrise* and became a best-seller.

Lee himself had reached what he called the stage of 'immaculate degeneration' (Grove, 502) and was usually to be found in 'his' corner of the Chelsea Arts Club or The Woolpack at Slad. He died of bowel cancer at his home, Littlecourt, in Slad on 13 May 1997 and was buried on 20

May, as he requested, in the lower graveyard at Holy Trinity Church, Slad, 'between the pub and the church' (ibid., 510). His chosen epitaph was engraved on his tombstone: 'He lies in the valley he loved.' Lee was survived by his wife.

Though he preferred to think of himself as a poet, Lee's greatest contribution to English literature was his autobiographical trilogy. 'I belonged to that generation which saw, by chance, the end of a thousand years' life', he wrote of his Cotswold childhood (Lee, *Cider with Rosie*, 200). It was chance, too, that took him to Spain on the eve, and in the midst, of civil war. Writing in retrospect and with a poet's eye for lyrical description, he nevertheless avoided sentimentality, painting vivid and unforgettable pictures of a world which has since disappeared. Laurie himself said that *A Moment of War* was 'a book in which I tell a truth which is larger than my own particular experience'; in any case 'there is no pure truth, only the moody accounts of witnesses' (Grove, 493; Lee, *I Can't Stay Long*, 52). A well-publicized debate about the veracity of Lee's claims in *A Moment of War* ensued after his death. Much of the criticism was unjustified. Lee certainly did exaggerate the length of time he spent in Spain and probably embellished the accounts of his arrests on suspicion of being a spy. He was also incorrect on minor historical details, but he admitted this when *A Moment of War* was published. His diaries for the period were stolen and he therefore relied solely on his memory, necessarily fragmented and subjective, however vivid. Yet it is a no less authentic account of one man's particular experience.

Laurie Lee's books have been translated into half a dozen languages, adapted for radio and television, and been the subject of many documentaries. Despite the great public affection for him and his work, official recognition was limited. However, he was made a freeman of the City of London in 1982, and the people of Almunecar erected a monument in 1988 to the 'gran escritor' who had immortalized their town. JULIET BARKER

Sources L. Lee, *Red sky at sunrise* (1993) [incl. *Cider with Rosie*, 1–214, and *As I walked out one midsummer morning*, 215–406] • L. Lee, *A moment of war* in *Red sky at sunrise* (1993), 407–537 • L. Lee, *I can't stay long* (1975) • V. Grove, *Laurie Lee: the well-loved stranger* (1999) • J. Gallagher, ed., *Laurie Lee a many-coated man* (1998) • B. Hooper, *Cider with Laurie: Laurie Lee remembered* (1999) • H. Thomas, *The Spanish Civil War*, rev. 3rd edn (1990) • log book, 1914–47, Glos. RO, Slad primary school, MS S295/3 • admission register, 1903–68, Glos. RO, Slad county primary school, MS S295/5 • L. Lee, *The firstborn* (1964) • L. Lee, *Two women: a book of words and photographs* (1983) • private information (2004) [Katherine Polge, widow]

Archives Eton, letters • priv. coll. | FILM BFI NFTVA, *Muses with Milligan* • BFI NFTVA, *Cover to cover*, LWT, 6 Feb 1972 • BFI NFTVA, *About Britain*, HTV, 20 June 1979 • BFI NFTVA, *Verse, worse, and baby grand*, BBC Wales, 18 June 1979, 25 June 1979 • BFI NFTVA, *Mavis catches up with …*, Thames Television, 8 Nov 1989 • BFI NFTVA, *Great Westerners*, HTV, 21 Aug 1994

Likenesses portraits, 1934, repro. in Grove, *Laurie Lee*, nos. 14, 20, 24; priv. coll. • A. Devas, oils, *c*.1939, NPG • B. Brandt, photograph, 1942, Bill Brandt Archives Ltd; repro. in Grove, *Laurie Lee*, no. 22 • A. Devas, oils, *c*.1945, priv. coll. • I. Kar, bromide print, 1956–9, NPG [*see illus.*] • P. Wyeth, group portrait, 1960, Chelsea Arts Club, London • B. Warton, photograph, *c*.1960–1969, NPG • L. Bamber, bronze head, priv. coll.

Wealth at death £686,882: probate, 3 Sept 1997, *CGPLA Eng. & Wales*

Lee, Lennox Bertram (1864–1949), textile industrialist, was born on 7 November 1864 at 2 Camp Place, Camp Street, Broughton, Salford, the eldest son of the eight children of Sir Joseph Cocksey Lee (1832–1894), cotton spinner and merchant, and his wife, Henrietta Burleigh (*d.* 1922), daughter of James Hill, Independent minister at Clapham, London. He was educated at Thorpe Mandeville School and Eton College before serving in the Sherwood Foresters (1883–5), and travelling extensively in Africa. In 1889 Lee joined the Rossendale Printing Company, a family firm, which in 1899 he took into the Calico Printers' Association (CPA). This amalgamation brought together forty-six printing firms and thirteen merchants to form what was then the United Kingdom's largest company. Having rapidly acquired a reputation as one of the trade's leading practical men, Lee joined the CPA executive, and became its chairman in 1902. The CPA's initial performance proved disappointing, but under Lee's guidance the size of the board was reduced from an unwieldy eighty-four, nearly one-third of the original capacity was closed down, competition was limited by inter-firm agreements, and a research department was set up.

Following these successes, Lee was the undisputed choice as chairman of the board in 1908, a position he held until 1947, an unusual longevity within the corporate economy. By 1914 Lee had again reformed the CPA management and marketing structures, even if the company's main aim remained price stability through trade agreements and reduced capacity rather than the aggressive pursuit of growth. This conservative strategy allowed the CPA to share in the cotton industry's Edwardian summer, outwardly demonstrated by the opening of its new offices, the St James Building, Oxford Street, Manchester, in 1912, then the largest steel-framed building in Britain.

The First World War was a stark reminder to Lee that the textile industry faced threats from two directions: that of the home government, and that of foreign competition, principally from India and Japan. Lee was a thoroughly reluctant participant in government schemes to produce British dyes to replace German and Swiss ones, wholly disbelieving in the power of the official mind to intervene efficaciously in business concerns. On the other hand, he was prepared to serve on several committees, and to back the British Trade Corporation (1916–26) in its ill-fated schemes for commercial expansion. After the war, however, he became an insistent advocate of business as usual, leading efforts to repeal the Dyestuffs Act of 1920. More positively, Lee recognized the drastic need for his own firm, as for the cotton industry as a whole, to adjust in order to survive, as both the volume and the profitability of British trade slumped in the 1920s. But adaptation posed a dilemma which the CPA failed satisfactorily to resolve—namely was it to remain merely a congeries of family firms, effecting some economies of scale while maintaining its traditional role of printing goods on commission for 'merchant-convertors', or was it, as Lee wished, to become a large, centrally controlled and vertically integrated modern enterprise, producing, printing, and merchanting its own cloth? The company oscillated between these strategies, continuing the process of internal rationalization, but achieving only limited success in its attempt at vertical integration, specialist finishes, and direct-selling schemes.

With keen foresight, Lee also pioneered direct investment abroad, with printworks in China in 1928, in Egypt in 1934, and in India in 1936, followed by Java, Australia, and South Africa during the Second World War. Ironically, this strategy, which Lee had urged in the First World War, reached fruition only in the Second, while the excessive devolution of control abroad, favoured by the board, but not by Lee, squandered the CPA's opportunity to prosper as a truly multinational company. The CPA's defensive mentality was further confirmed in 1941, when following the major discovery of Terylene in its laboratories, it allowed ICI to develop this product under licence. The lucrative royalties from Terylene, however, gave Lee the satisfaction of restoring dividend payments (suspended since 1929) in 1947, the year in which he also resigned as chairman, having ensured the succession of his son, R. M. Lee (1902–1972). A tall, stately figure, whose goatee beard lent the mien of a Spanish grandee, Lee ultimately proved far more autocratic in manner than decisive in business strategy.

After the First World War, Lee continued to act as an important custodian and outspoken defender of Lancashire traditions and interests. In the 1920s he did so from within the Federation of British Industry, first as its Manchester chairman, and in 1929–30 as its president. In that role, and as a consistent free trader, he briefly held back the FBI's accelerating drift towards protection. He served on the influential Macmillan committee, urging in an addendum to the main report the need both for industrial rationalization and for close co-operation with trade unions, a reflection of his involvement in negotiations between employers and the TUC in the wake of the Mond–Turner talks. In the economic crisis of 1929–31 Lee resisted tariffs as likely to undermine, rather than encourage, the rationalization of industry, although throughout the 1930s he advocated an important role for government in backing up collective regulation by business.

With Manchester public life holding little attraction, Lee preferred to retreat to his Herefordshire estate at How Caple. He had lived there since 1901 with his wife, Edith Gertrude (*d.* 1964), daughter of Malcolm MacLellan of Glasgow, whom he married on 21 June 1892, and their three children. He played an active part in county society, reared pigs, and took a keen interest in the welfare of the Church of England and the architectural beauties of its buildings, especially as a benefactor of Hereford Cathedral. Lee died at home at How Caple Court on 14 December 1949 and was buried at How Caple. He had lived to see the jubilee of the CPA and oversee the publication of its history, itself a revealing chronicle of the frustrated vision and dynastic tenacity which had marked, and marred, his career. A. C. Howe

Sources A. C. Howe, 'Lee, Lennox Bertram', *DBB* • *Fifty years of calico printing: a jubilee history of the CPA* (1949) • S. Pitt, 'Strategic and structural change in the CPA, 1899–1973', PhD diss., London Business School, 1990 • P. L. Cook, *Effects of mergers: six studies* (1958) • *Herefordshire portraits past and present* (1908) • *Manchester Guardian* (16 Dec 1949) • *Manchester Evening News* (15 Dec 1949) • *Hereford Citizen* (16 Dec 1949) • *Hereford Times* (17 Dec 1949) • *Ross Gazette* (22 Dec 1949) • *The Times* (16 Dec 1949) • *CGPLA Eng. & Wales* (1950) • b. cert. • d. cert.

Archives Man. CL, Calico Printers' Association secretariat records • Tootals plc, Manchester, Calico Printers' Association board minutes | U. Warwick Mod. RC, CBI Predecessor Archive

Likenesses photograph, repro. in *Fifty years of calico printing*

Wealth at death £282,556 6*s*. 3*d*.: probate, 18 March 1950, *CGPLA Eng. & Wales*

Lee, Margaret Lucy (1871–1955), headmistress, was born at Hartley Wintney, Hampshire, on 14 July 1871, the elder of the two daughters of Revd Thomas William Lee (1833/4–1921) and his wife, Margaret Anne, daughter of Revd C. H. Lyon of Glen Ogil. Her father was headmaster of Hartford House, a preparatory school, but in 1875 became vicar of Leafield, near Witney, Oxfordshire. Lucy, as she was known at home, was taught to read by her mother, and by the age of six she had read much of *Paradise Lost*. She was then educated by governesses, from whom she gained a good knowledge of French and German. By the time she was twelve, the experience of taking a Sunday school class convinced her that teaching was her vocation. In 1888 she was sent to a fashionable girls' school in Warrington Crescent, London, where she formed a close relationship with one of the teachers, Miss Annie Sophia Batty (*d.* 1934). This developed into 'the most lasting intimate relationship of her life' (Lee, 11). She left Warrington Crescent in December 1889, determined to go to Oxford and then to return to assist Miss Batty in her teaching.

In 1890, overcoming her father's doubts about the value of higher education for women, Margaret Lee entered St Hugh's Hall, Oxford, a college particularly suitable for her, since it had been founded by Elizabeth Wordsworth specifically to cater for those (especially daughters of the clergy) who could not afford the fees at Lady Margaret Hall. She studied English literature under Professor A. S. Napier and philology under Professor Joseph Wright, gaining first-class honours in English in the Oxford University examination for women in 1892. This successful result appeased her father, who permitted her to remain at Oxford a further term, reading German and French and assisting Joseph Wright in preparing his grammatical works for the press. She also produced an edition, from a manuscript in the Bodleian Library, of *Narcissus: a Twelfe Night Merriment* (1893).

After teaching for two years with Miss Batty at Warrington Crescent, Miss Lee returned to Oxford in 1895 as vice-principal of St Hugh's, a post she held until 1896. In 1897 she became a lecturer in Middle English to the Association for Promoting the Education of Women in Oxford, which provided the bulk of teaching for women students. In 1898, at the invitation of Lilian Faithfull, she was appointed a part-time lecturer at King's College for Women, London, where her pupils included Edith Morley and Caroline Spurgeon. She resigned this in 1919. From 1915 until 1926 she also held a lectureship at University College, Reading. At Oxford, where she graduated MA by decree in October 1920 when degrees were opened to women, she was tutor in English to the Society of Oxford Students, comprising women students at Oxford living at home or lodging with families in the city, from 1913 to 1926. She never published original literary or philological work; teaching absorbed all her creative energies.

In addition to her work as a university lecturer, Margaret Lee founded with Miss Batty a private school at Oxford, originally intended for the daughters of dons. It grew rapidly and, after several moves, settled at 74 Banbury Road in 1918, when it became known as Wychwood School. The school (which was the subject of an article in *Queen* magazine, 3 September 1922) broke away from many of the conventions of contemporary girls' schools. A form of self-government was adopted, key decisions being made at weekly meetings of the school council, which included elected representatives of the pupils. Arts, crafts, and drama were encouraged. Former pupils at Wychwood recalled her Monday morning addresses to the school (which conveyed both practical sense and her enthusiasm for causes aimed at the betterment of mankind), her 'expressive bright blue eyes', and her taste for 'beflowered or beribboned' hats (Lee, 24–5). She was a vegetarian and teetotaller. Remaining as co-principal of Wychwood School until 1954, she was a notable example of those late Victorian college-educated women who set out to improve the tradition of girls' private school education. Margaret Lee died, unmarried, at her home, 77 Banbury Road, Oxford, on 26 December 1955.

DEBORAH QUARE

Sources *Memoir of Margaret Lucy Lee, largely based on her own diaries*, ed. M. M. Falk (1956) • *Wychwood School: its history and aims* • E. M. Snodgrass, J. E. Schuller, and M. L. Duffil, *A history of Wychwood School, 1897–1997* (1997) • St Hugh's Hall register, St Hugh's College, Oxford • M. L. Lee, 'A woman student at Oxford in the 1890s', *Oxford Magazine*, 4th week, Trinity term (1996), 11–12 • G. Avery, *The best type of girl: a history of girls' independent schools* (1991) • *CGPLA Eng. & Wales* (1956)
Archives Wychwood School, Oxford
Likenesses photographs, *c.*1895–1926, repro. in *Memoir of Margaret Lucy Lee*, ed. Falk, frontispiece, facing p. 13
Wealth at death £57,025 12*s.* 3*d.*: probate, 14 March 1956, *CGPLA Eng. & Wales*

Lee [*née* Aldridge]**, Mary** [*other married name* Mary Slingsby, Lady Slingsby] (*fl.* **1670–1685**), actress, performed initially with the Duke's Company and then, after its union with the King's Company in 1682, with the resulting United Company. Nothing is known about her family beyond her maiden name, Aldridge. Some time in 1670 she married John Lee, a minor actor with the Duke's Company, who died in the spring of 1680. Later that year she married—although the evidence is tentative—Sir Charles Slingsby, baronet (*d.* 1698). The marriage may have been informally contracted between the parties or clandestinely performed by a clergyman: one of those many marriages in Restoration London which were legally irregular but valid, if also often difficult to prove. Subsequently Mary Lee performed under the name of Lady Slingsby. It is uncertain how long—if at all—the couple lived together, given that Sir Charles sold his Kent estate and moved abroad, presumably to escape his creditors.

Mrs Lee's early roles capitalized on youthful sweetness: Eugenia in Edward Howard's *The Six Days Adventure* (1671), Leticia in Edward Revet's *The Town Shifts* (1671), Emilia in Joseph Arrowsmith's *The Reformation* (1673). However, in 1675 she appeared in a different type of role, that of a valiant woman, martial in demeanour and capable of violence, that also became a staple of her career. Amavanga in Settle's *The Conquest of China by the Tartars* assumes masculine dress to duel with the man she loves; Queen Deidamia in Thomas Otway's *Alcibiades* kills the king to secure her love for Alcibiades; Roxana in Samuel Pordage's *The Siege of Babylon* threatens male characters with a sword and then stabs herself. Perhaps most spectacular is the role of Tarpeia in the anonymous play *Romulus and Hersilia* (1683): Tarpeia, a Roman in love with an enemy Sabine, disguises herself as a soldier, endures wounds, challenges enemies, and ultimately, in good Roman fashion, falls on her sword to remove the dishonour she has caused to country and family; her father, weeping over the body of his daughter, says she was 'one of us; For tho she were a Virgin, she was martial' (*Romulus and Hersilia*, 1683, 51).

That statement summarizes nicely the roles Mrs Lee would play throughout her career: those of the virginal ingénue or the valiant woman, an odd juxtaposition. Her histrionic abilities must have been considerable: Elkanah Settle, known for bombastic language and excessive plots, wrote leading parts for her in five of his plays and in addition Mrs Lee played such demanding roles as Cleopatra in Sir Charles Sedley's *Antony and Cleopatra* (1677), Madam Fickle in Thomas D'Urfey's play of the same name, Bellamira in Nathaniel Lee's *Caesar Borgia* (1679), Regan in Nahum Tate's revision of *King Lear* (1681), and Marguerite in Lee's *The Princess of Cleve* (1681). She appears to have retired from the stage after 1685.

Contemporary writings make few references to Mrs Lee. Two lampoons mention her briefly: 'A Satyr on both Whigs and Tories' (July 1683) and the 'Satyr on players' (1684). The former mentions the royal roles for which Mrs Lee was known, and the latter, a scurrilous piece of writing, mocks her marriage to a baronet. The only other reference to her appears in the lord chamberlain's records. After she spoke the epilogue written by Aphra Behn for *Romulus and Hersilia* both women were ordered into custody 'to answer that affront for the same' caused by its reflections on the duke of Monmouth, although they appear to have been released quickly (Wilson, *All the King's Ladies*, 161). Mary Lee appears to have stopped acting after 1685 and nothing is known of her subsequently. A Dame Mary Slingsby, widow, was buried at St Pancras on 1 March 1694, but as Sir Charles died on 13 September 1698 it is uncertain whether this was Mrs Lee. The woman buried could be another Dame Mary (although the name of the most likely alternative, Sir Charles's mother, is unknown), but it is also possible that Mrs Lee and those around her did not know (or chose not to acknowledge) that the baronet was still alive in his financial exile.

DEBORAH PAYNE FISK

Sources Highfill, Burnim & Langhans, *BDA*, vol. 9 • W. Van Lennep and others, eds., *The London stage, 1660–1800*, pt 1: *1660–1700* (1965) • J. Downes, *Roscius Anglicanus*, ed. J. Milhous and R. D. Hume, new edn (1987) • E. Howe, *The first English actresses* (1992) • J. H. Wilson, *All the king's ladies: actresses of the Restoration* (1958) • J. H. Wilson, *Court satires of the Restoration* (1976) • J. H. Wilson, 'Theatre notes from the Newdigate newsletters', *Theatre Notebook*, 15 (1960–61), 79–84 • Genest, *Eng. stage* • GEC, *Baronetage*, 3.17

Lee, Matthew (1694–1755), physician and benefactor, was born in Northamptonshire, the son of William Lee. Between 1709 and 1713 he was educated at Westminster School, and then at Christ Church, Oxford, where he graduated BA (1717), MA (1720), MB (1722), and MD (1726). In addition to his medical studies at Oxford he also contributed to a book of poems on the death in 1715 of the eminent physician Dr John Radcliffe. Lee was married to Sarah Knapp, youngest daughter of John Knapp, although further details—other than that the marriage was childless—are unknown. After successfully practising medicine in Oxford, Lee moved to London in 1730. On 12 April of the following year he was appointed a candidate of the Royal College of Physicians and became a fellow on 3 April 1732. He was later appointed college censor (1734) and Harveian orator (1736), his oration being published in the same year. In 1739 he became physician to Frederick, prince of Wales, and was one of three doctors who attended the prince at his death in March 1751. Lee himself died on 26 September 1755 and was buried at the church of Little Linford in north Buckinghamshire. In his will he bequeathed funds to build an anatomy school at Christ Church, so realizing the plan first suggested by Lee's former associate, the physician John Freind. Work on a lecture theatre and dissection room began in 1766 and was completed at a cost of £1200. In addition, Lee left £140 p.a. for a university readership in anatomy (to which appointments are still made). Strict terms prevented the position being filled by ordained ministers and others whom it was feared would be prone to absenteeism. The first Lee's reader was John Parsons (1742–1785), appointed in 1767, at which date attendance at anatomy lectures became a compulsory part of Oxford's medical curriculum.

PHILIP CARTER

Sources *DNB* • C. Webster, 'The medical faculty and the physic garden', *Hist. U. Oxf.* 5: *18th-cent. Oxf.*, 683–723 • H. M. Sinclair and A. H. T. Robb-Smith, *A short history of anatomical teaching in Oxford* (1950) • Munk, *Roll* • H. Walpole, *Memoirs of King George II*, ed. J. Brooke, 3 vols. (1985)

Likenesses L. F. Roubiliac, marble bust, Christ Church Oxf.

Wealth at death donated £140 p.a. for readership in anatomy, University of Oxford, and £1200 for anatomy school

Lee, Nathaniel (1645x52–1692), playwright and poet, was born some time between the birth dates of his older brother Samuel and next younger brother, Daniel, in Hatfield (Hertfordshire), Middlesex, or Walthamstow (Essex), the second or third of ten or eleven children of Richard Lee DD (1612–1685), a prominent Anglican clergyman, and his wife, Elizabeth (*c.*1624–1714). Richard's father, William (*c.*1580–1646), was a merchant, landowner, and bailiff of Nantwich, Cheshire. Ordained an Anglican deacon in 1637, Richard Lee flourished as a presbyterian pluralist during the interregnum before conforming to the Church of England in 1662.

Early years and education No written records of Nathaniel Lee's childhood have been found, but it must have been intellectually and emotionally rich, judging from the family's level of education and the volumes in Dr Lee's extensive library. The eldest surviving son, Samuel (*b.* 1645)—an earlier Samuel seems to have died in infancy—was educated at Westminster School under Dryden's headmaster, Richard Busby, and three of the other boys, Daniel (*b.* 1653), Richard (1655–1725), and John (1663–1730), became Anglican priests. The youngest, Emmanuel (1667–1725), seems to have remained at Hatfield, a perennial debtor to his father and elder brothers. Little is known of the sisters, Anne (1658–1724)—buried as Anne Miller in Hatfield—and Mary (*b.* 1660), who married one Francis White and was buried in Hatfield as well. Dr Lee's private library, numbering over 1000 volumes at his death, comprised what were then standard works representing various religious viewpoints—Anglican, Cambridge Platonist, puritan, and Quaker—and a wide range of historical and philosophical subjects, many of which would later surface in Nathaniel's plays: providence and the infernal powers, ancient Rome, the Roman Catholic church, Renaissance France, contemporary psychology, political thought, and affairs of court and state.

Emerging from this busy, bookish family, Nathaniel Lee was nominated by his father's patron the earl of Salisbury for admission to Charterhouse School, originally founded for the poor but by Lee's time respected as a portal to university studies. After about seven years there (*c.*1658–65) he entered Trinity College, Cambridge, remaining as pensioner (1665), scholar (1668), BA (1669), and possibly fellow (1669–71). That Lee remained awhile as a fellow is suggested in a 1670 collection of verses mourning the death of his father's old patron, General George Monck, who had become duke of Albemarle. Lee's contribution is his first known poem, a clumsily written elegy 'On the Death of the Duke of Albemarle', which foreshadows his mature dramatic style only in its classical allusions and cosmic imagery. It is signed 'Nathaniel Lee, A.B. Trin,. Coll.', and perhaps it attracted the attention of George Villiers, second duke of Buckingham, before or during his visit to be installed as chancellor of Cambridge in summer 1671. One report says Buckingham admired the young poet, took him away to London, and then promptly lost interest in him (Spence, 1.280, item 677).

Early career in the theatre Certainly Lee was in London the next year, beginning a twenty-year career in the theatre world that gave him a few periods of heady success in return for poverty, increasing emotional distress, and insanity. In addition to literary abilities developed through his upbringing and formal education, he is said to have possessed a resonant voice and striking looks. Four of the six known portraits depict dark, shoulder-length hair (no wig), somewhat unkempt, framing a long, gaunt face with prominent nose, cheekbones, and chin; his dark eyes are fixed in an other-worldly gaze. Two of these renderings—the Garrick Club oil and the Watts engraving—emphasize the unfocused eyes and disorderly appearance, showing Lee in shirtsleeves with a nondescript article of clothing draped over one shoulder. The two likenesses about which the least information is known—oil paintings in the Dulwich Gallery and Clark Library—present a saner stare, more contrived pose, and more carefully arranged hair and costume. The Dulwich portrait romanticizes the costume with flowing hair pushed back and open-collared shirt beneath a high-necked waistcoat, possibly with a cape attached. In this depiction, Lee's hand rests on an unidentified bust, perhaps that of a Greek playwright or of Longinus (to emphasize the sublime imagination).

Whatever Lee's physical assets, his attempt to deploy them in an acting career—perhaps encouraged by his reputation for elocutionary skill—was cut short by stage fright, apparently after only two appearances on the boards: as Captain of the Watch in Nevil Payne's *Fatal Jealousie* (1672) and as Duncan in Sir William Davenant's version of *Macbeth* (1673). His fledgeling attempt at dramatic writing fared little better, for his *Nero* (1674) needed the protection of his powerful new patron, John Wilmot, earl of Rochester, against censorious critics. *Sophonisba* (1675), however, was a success and continued to be popular for more than a century, though Rochester, whose relationship with Lee had soured, damned the play as sentimental 'fustian' (Wilmot, 122). The loss of Rochester's esteem, coupled with the indifferent reception of *Gloriana* (1676), seems registered in Lee's complaint of 'blasted … hopes' and 'unjust fortune' (*Works*, 1.151).

But the connection with Rochester was replaced by what became a richly rewarding set of new relationships. Denouncing his 'Neronian Gambols' (*Works*, 1.219), Lee now entered his most productive and successful years by joining the circle of Rochester's greatest literary and social rival, the earl of Mulgrave, along with Mulgrave's more famous protégé, John Dryden. The bond with Dryden was sealed in Lee's poem 'To Mr. Dryden, on his Poem of Paradice', which commends the 'Monarch of Verse' for improving Milton in his opera *The State of Innocence* and urges Dryden to versify a comparison of Charles II with King David (ibid., 2.557–8). Returning the compliment in 'To Mr. Lee, on his *Alexander*' (1677), Dryden praises the younger author's passion and imagery (Dryden, 1.106–7). During the next five years, the literary output of this relationship grew substantially. Dryden contributed four prologues and four epilogues to plays by Lee; the two men collaborated on *Oedipus* (1678–9) and *The Duke of Guise* (1682); and Lee appended a complimentary poem to Dryden's great satire *Absalom and Achitophel* (1681).

These were Lee's peak years, both socially and professionally. In addition to Dryden and Mulgrave, his new friends also must have included Thomas Otway, his fellow actor and, later, fellow writer for the Duke's Company; Tom D'Urfey, contributor of an epilogue to the 1689 production of *The Massacre of Paris*; William Wycherley, who later wrote a compassionate, irreverent poem about Lee in Bethlem Hospital; and two younger Trinity College men, both disciples of Dryden: Richard Duke, who wrote the prologue to *Lucius Junius Brutus*, and Charles Saunders, author of *Tamerlane the Great* (1681). Lee was now dedicating his works to court luminaries such as the earls of Dorset and Pembroke, and Frances Stewart, the lovely duchess of Richmond, one of the king's favourite mistresses. He wrote a conventional panegyric on the wedding of the king's niece to William of Orange (*Works*, 2.553–6), and the royal family occasionally attended or commanded performances of his plays. The signs of high living were becoming visible in his growing paunch and red nose.

Theatrical success Meanwhile Lee enjoyed a series of stage successes, beginning with *The Rival Queens* (1677), still regarded as one of his best tragedies, and continuing with *Mithridates* (1678) and the first collaboration with Dryden, *Oedipus* (1678–9). The latter was produced at Dorset Garden in apparent breach of contract with the King's Company, and thereafter, until the merger of companies in 1682, all of Lee's plays were written for the Duke's players. This move may have contributed to the banning of *The Massacre of Paris* (possibly that same winter), for the current master of revels and court censor would have been Charles Killigrew, manager of the King's Company. When Lee's next play, *Caesar Borgia* (1679), also offended the censor, apparently with its violent anti-Catholicism (despite the subtler political message), he seems to have taken the hint. *Theodosius* (1680) avoids pointed allusions to the current regime, and its heroic anxieties and amorous dilemmas drew large audiences for a century. Emboldened by this new success, it seems, he resumed potent political commentary in *Lucius Junius Brutus* (1680), which became his last popular success before being banned after several performances, never to be revived in its original form.

Lee's reputation as a fashionable writer began to fade, despite repeated efforts to preserve it. In 1681, as if to emphasize his loyalty to the crown, he published a tribute 'To the unknown author of Absalom and Achitophel' hailing Dryden as 'a Milton' who 'the right Party chose' (*Works*, 2.559). The following year he penned a brief verse compliment 'To the author & translatour' of Richard Simon's *Histoire critique du Vieux Testament* and a fulsome ode to the duke of York, 'To the Duke on his Return' from exile (ibid., 2.560–61, 567). His second collaboration with Dryden, *The Duke of Guise* (1682), finally succeeded after a four-month prohibition for its political implications, but his last solo works, *The Princess of Cleve* (*c*.1683) and *Constantine* (1683), failed to attract much notice.

Looking back on this corpus of writing, it is possible to recognize Lee's distinctive style and major role in the development of English drama. His favourite topic, the mental pathology of political leadership, is typically developed through a dramatic form of lyricism. Without much analytical self-consciousness, his characters are emotionally driven into social or political patterns that are made perceptible to the audience, though usually not to the characters themselves, through a careful disposition of figurative content—imagery, spectacle, and allusions. In at least two respects, he led the other playwrights of his day: he anticipated Dryden in restoring blank verse to its favoured status in serious drama, and he started the transition from admirable heroes and happy endings, typical of serious plays of the 1660s, to the more pathetic, vulnerable characters and suicidal or homicidal conclusions that marked so many tragedies during the following two decades. Otherwise, he shared his contemporaries' penchant for adapting plots from history or romance in order to depict abuses of royal prerogative, and he contributed to all the important sub-genres of his day: villain tragedy, sentimentalized heroic play, high tragedy, and split-plot tragi-comedy.

Bethlem Hospital Less than a year after the production of *Constantine*, Lee became 'distracted' and on 11 November 1684 was admitted to 'Bedlam', the Bethlem Hospital for the insane. Friends gave financial support, and in 1685 his brother Daniel asked the board of greencloth, a branch of the royal household, to underwrite all expenses. The petition was granted, perhaps because the newly crowned James II recalled those flattering depictions in 'To the Duke on his Return', *The Duke of Guise* (as Henri of Navarre), and *Constantine* (as Dalmatius). From 1 January 1686 until Lee's release on 23 April 1688, his bills were paid by the court. The causes of his 'madness' can only be guessed at using the few extant reports by contemporaries. Anthony Wood points to an over-intense imagination (*Life and Times*, 3.112), Gerard Langbaine mentions alcoholism (Langbaine, 2.322–3), and Wycherley blames neglect, starvation, and a fiery temper (Wycherley, 3.233–7). Nor is much known about his behaviour and treatment while incarcerated. Sir George Etherege, in a letter from the continent, speaks of intermittent confinement (*Letters*, ed. Bracher, 135), and the anonymous author of 'Satyr Against the Poets' tells of painful fits, chains, and solitary confinement in the dark (though some of the wording comes from *Caesar Borgia*, V.i.262–8). Later commentators portray Lee with a shaved head submitting to the milk diet typically prescribed by Dr Edward Tyson, physician at Bethlem Hospital from 1684 to 1707.

Final years and reputation Somehow, Lee recovered sufficiently to be discharged in spring 1688. Taking lodgings in Duke Street (now Sardinia Street) close to the Theatre Royal, he drew a weekly pension of £10s. and tried to reconstitute his career. James II fled to France in December, and Lee greeted William and Mary with a competent, if unremarkable, panegyric to celebrate their coronation on 11 April 1689 (*Works*, 2.562–3). Later in the same year he again praised them in the prologue to a newly published version of *The Princess of Cleve*. In the dedication he asked his old patron, the earl of Dorset, who had become King William's lord chamberlain, to arrange a production of the once banned *Massacre of Paris*, which now seemed well aligned with the dominant political forces. The work was staged in November, the queen and maids of honour in attendance. But Lee never salvaged his former skill or health. According to anecdotists, the handsome, vigorous literary lion, with his congenial ways, abundant dark hair, and resonant voice had become a heavy-drinking caricature of his former self—red-faced, corpulent, and carbuncular. His last datable poem, 'On the Death of Mrs. Behn' (1689), conveys the pathos of his condition as he seems to long for another world 'where I shall never shed another Tear' (ibid., 2.564). In spring 1692 he was found dead in the streets. On 6 May he was interred in St Clement Danes, where today there is no sign of his grave.

Nor is there any sign of his manuscripts. Tom Brown once quipped that Lee composed a twenty-five act theatrical work while in Bethlem Hospital (Brown, pt 2, 130–31), and William Oldys wrote in 1730 that 'a Brother of this Nat Lees somewhere in or near the Isle of Ascholm in Lincolnshire … has a Trunk full of his Writing' (MS notes, c.28, g.1.). A similar remark to Edward Harley, earl of Oxford, suggests Oldys first heard of these manuscripts in early 1731, although they certainly do not appear in the Harleian collection (Oldys to earl of Oxford, 23 Feb 1731, *Portland MSS*, 6.36–7). The 'Brother' would have been the Reverend John Lee, rector of Bigby and Cadney, near the Isle of Axholme in Lincolnshire. John died in 1730, but his will does not refer to Nathaniel's papers. He leaves his entire estate to his wife, Sarah, who would most likely have left hers to John's married daughter Ann Langdon, or to some of her cousins, perhaps to Ann Lee Pitman Holmes.

Although Lee's plays never recovered their popularity on stage, every generation of critics since his death has felt compelled to assess his literary achievement. The dominant themes of this ongoing discussion have been his language (bombastic or sublime?), prosody (especially lyricism and the shift to blank verse), influence on genre (especially the move to affective tragedy), stage spectacle (mere sensationalism or carefully managed effects?), characterization (shallow contrivances or profound metaphors?), occultism, cynicism, and political stance. Intermittent surges of political and psychological criticism have made *Lucius Junius Brutus* and *The Rival Queens* his most frequently studied works, the former for its tortured analysis of republican ideology and legalism, the latter for its emotional power and psychological penetration.

J. M. Armistead

Sources *The works of Nathaniel Lee*, ed. T. B. Stroup and A. L. Cooke, 2 vols. (1954–5) • J. M. Armistead, *Four Restoration playwrights: a reference guide to Thomas Shadwell, Aphra Behn, Nathaniel Lee, and Thomas Otway* (1984), 167–259 • F. M. Link, *English drama, 1660–1800: a guide to information sources* (1976), 232–3 • J. M. Armistead, *Nathaniel Lee* (1979) • T. Brown, *Letters from the dead to the living*, pt 2 (1703), 130–31 • J. Dryden, 'To Mr. Lee, on his *Alexander*', *The works of John Dryden*, 1: *Poems, 1649–1680*, ed. E. N. Hooker and H. T. Swedenberg (1956), 106–7 • *Letters of Sir George Etherege*, ed. F. Bracher (1974), 135 • R. Ham, *Otway and Lee: biography from a baroque age* (1969) • G. Langbaine, *An account of the English dramatick poets* (1691); facs. edn with introduction by J. Loftis 2 vols. (Los Angeles, 1971), vol. 2, pp. 320–27 • *DNB* • *The manuscripts of Sir William Fitzherbert … and others*, HMC, 32 (1893), 273 • W. Oldys, manuscript notes to a copy of Langbaine's *Account*, BL, c.28.g.1 • *The manuscripts of his grace the duke of Portland*, 10 vols., HMC, 29 (1891–1931), vol. 6, pp. 36–7 • J. Wilmot, earl of Rochester, 'An allusion to Horace, the tenth satyr of the first book', *The complete poems of John Wilmot, earl of Rochester*, ed. D. M. Vieth (1968), 120–26 · 'Satyr against the poets', BL, Harleian MS 7317, fol. 64 · J. Spence, *Observations, anecdotes, and characters, of books and men*, ed. J. M. Osborn, new edn, 1 (1966), 280 · *The life and times of Anthony Wood*, ed. A. Clark, 3, OHS, 26 (1894), 112 · W. Wycherley, 'To Nath. Lee, in Bethlem', *The complete works of William Wycherley*, ed. M. Summers, 3 (1924), 233–7

Likenesses oils, *c.*1690, U. Cal., Los Angeles, William Andrews Clark Memorial Library · oils, *c.*1690, Garr. Club · W. Ridley, engraving, repro. in *The Monthly Mirror*, 13 (1802), following p. 75 · A. W. Warren, engraving, Harvard TC · J. Watts, mezzotint, BM, NPG, Harvard TC · oils, Dulwich Picture Gallery, London

Lee, (Richard) Nelson (1806–1872), pantomimist and theatrical entrepreneur, claimed that he was born on 8 January 1806 at Kew, Surrey, though this is unverified. He was the son of Lieutenant-Colonel Richard Lee, 63rd regiment of foot, who died in Martinique in 1811, and was probably brought up at Walworth, Surrey, with his elder brother James, with whom he attempted to set up a theatre in south London in 1822. During the 1820s he learned acting and juggling chiefly among the travelling fairs in and around London, and in 1827 was taken on by Robert Elliston as a utility player at the Surrey Theatre. He soon became a leading harlequin, and in 1831 wrote the pantomime for the Adelphi.

In 1836 Lee took over John Richardson's itinerant theatrical show in conjunction with his long-term business partner John Johnson, and in the same year briefly managed Sadler's Wells. In June 1838 he promoted and organized the Hyde Park fair to mark Queen Victoria's coronation, an occasion which was a success, made his fortune, and brought his name before the general public. In the same year he married Amelia Griffiths (1818–1870). They had eight children, the eldest being Nelson J. Lee (1842–1923), who was a writer of melodramas and acted as his father's amanuensis.

Lee's energy was prodigious, and until the 1850s he managed various minor London theatres, took Richardson's show round the fairs, and wrote several pantomimes each year. He lost much of his travelling show by fire (1845) and by riot (1850), and the fair he helped organize for the Great Exhibition in 1851 was a financial disaster. Lee was 'a hardy adventurer always courting success, encountering checks and often disaster but pursued an undaunted way' (Wilson, 53). In 1849 he took over the City of London Theatre, which, until it was sold for railway development in 1868, became the centre with which his name was most associated. His annual pantomimes were awaited with anticipation in east London. He wrote at least 230, in whole or in part, which were performed all over the country; his dramas, however, were less successful.

E. L. Blanchard and J. R. Planché may have achieved greater critical acclaim, but Nelson Lee (as he was universally known) was the most prolific and financially successful writer of pantomimes of his day. Thackeray wrote of him:

> I often think with gratitude of the famous Mr Nelson Lee—the author of I don't know how many hundreds of pantomimes—walking the summer wave at Margate or Brighton, revolving in his mind the idea of some new gorgeous spectacle of faëry, which the winter shall complete. (Seymour and Smith, 246)

Lee retired from the theatre in the mid-1860s and went on to mount regular entertainments at the Crystal Palace. He died at his home, 4 Nelson Cottages, Shrubland Road, Dalston, London, on 2 January 1872, perhaps the last of the fairground impresarios, who had regularly captivated the multitude by presenting a Shakespeare play in the open air in just fifteen minutes. He was buried in Abney Park cemetery, Stoke Newington, on 5 January.

Alan Ruston

Sources A. Ruston, 'Richard Nelson Lee and the Victorian pantomime', *Nineteenth Century Theatre Research*, 11/2 (1983), 106–11 · A. Ruston, 'Richard Nelson Lee and Nelson Lee Junior', *Nineteenth Century Theatre*, 13/1 and 2 (1990), 75–85 · A. E. Wilson, *East End entertainment* (1954), chap. 13 · *The Players*, 1/18 (28 April 1860), 137–8 · T. Frost, *Old showmen of old London fairs* (1874), 247, 254, 320, 346–55 · M. Williams, *Some London theatres past and present* (1883), 16, 52–3, 58–78, 82, 98, 101 · T. Horne, 'Nelson Lee', *The Era* (9 June 1906), 23–4 · *The Era* (7 Jan 1872), 9 · will, 1812, PRO, PROB 11/1538 [Col. R. Lee] · W. Seymour and J. Smith, *Happy Christmas* (1970), 246 · *Era Almanack and Annual* (1868), 23 · *The life and reminiscences of E. L. Blanchard, with notes from the diary of Wm. Blanchard*, ed. C. W. Scott and C. Howard, 2 vols. (1891), 408

Archives NYPL · Theatre Museum, London · U. Texas | PRO, petition HO/45/3291/72161

Likenesses carte-de-visite, Theatre Museum, London, Enthoven collection · photographs, Harvard TC · woodcut, repro. in *Illustrated Sporting News* (14 July 1866), 420 · woodcut, repro. in *The Players*, 137 · woodcuts, Harvard TC

Wealth at death under £9000: probate, 7 Feb 1872, *CGPLA Eng. & Wales*

Lee, Peter (1864–1935), trade unionist, was born on 20 July 1864 in a house in Duff Heap Row, Fivehouses, Trimdon Grange, in the Durham coalfield. His father, Thomas Lee, was also a miner but his mother, Hannah (*née* Simpson), was an educated woman, whose grandfather had been a schoolmaster and whose father had worked as a mill foreman in Lancashire. The Lee family moved frequently between Lancashire and Durham during Lee's early years, which may have accounted for a restlessness which seemed to be a part of the character of the young man. It certainly prevented regular attendance at school.

By the age of nine Lee was working as a piecer in a cotton mill and had a succession of jobs in the brickyards after this before going down the pit as a pony driver at Littletown colliery, Sherburn Hill, back in Durham. He was only ten. At thirteen he was putting, bringing the tubs back and forth from face to shaft, and by sixteen and a half had joined his father and older brother as a hewer of the coal. This hard and dangerous work was often reflected in the lifestyles of the men who did it, rough, drinking, gambling, and fighting men, whose social life centred on the pub. Even union meetings were held there when they were held at all. Lee built a reputation for hardness and had occasional confrontations with the police. His life remained nomadic as he moved around the northern coalfields looking for better places and better pay. He later calculated that he had worked in fifteen different pits between 1879 and 1886, some more than once.

In 1885 Lee thought to go to Australia, where silver had been discovered, but could not arrange an assisted passage. Instead, at the beginning of 1886 he went to the coal mines of Pennsylvania where an uncle was already working. He stayed about a year and also worked underground in Indiana and Kentucky. A mixture of homesickness and disillusionment propelled him back to Durham in 1887.

The experience, however, boosted Lee's confidence. He had occasionally acted as spokesman for the men in disputes with the management, and back in Durham at Wingate colliery he went to union meetings and was elected delegate to the council of the Durham Miners' Association (DMA). Neither his reading nor his writing were good, but in other respects he was a noticeable figure. In a world of small workmen he was 6 feet 1½ inches tall, with long black hair and grey eyes. He spoke clearly without an accent, probably through the influence of his mother who had read to her young family on winter evenings.

Lee also returned from America to marry Alice Thompson, a young dressmaker, whom he had known since they were children. She was religious and the marriage was celebrated at the Wesleyan church in Haswell on 29 February 1888. As Lee himself said much later, 'she took a great risk when she first threw in her lot with me. You should have seen me then—a man in the rough, with no education and a drunkard' (*The Times*). They lived with her parents for the first six weeks as Lee had been sacked, circumstances that emphasize the insecurity of working-class life. They had a son and three daughters.

Marriage brought some physical as well as temperamental stability, but after nearly four years as checkweighman at Wingate, Lee left his wife and young family in 1896 to work in the goldmines of South Africa. He returned after eighteen months, resuming work in the Durham pits and becoming checkweighman at Wheatley Hill in 1902. In many respects he was a changed man. He had improved his education during the nineties and his love of books later led to the conversion of one room in his home into a library. He gave up drinking and smoking and became a Methodist preacher. He was active in the union, though apart from two short spells on the executive it was 1919 before he was elected an agent of the miners. He soon became financial secretary of the DMA and in 1924 the executive and joint committee secretary. After the sudden death of W. P. Richardson he was appointed general secretary of the DMA in 1930, at the age of sixty-six. He was vice-president of the Miners' Federation of Great Britain and president the following year.

Lee came to trade union leadership late in life. In 1914, aged fifty, he was little known in the industrial and political world of Durham, but had already begun his work as a reformer in local government, notably in the fields of housing, roads, sanitation, and water supplies; and it was in those areas that he did most to improve the living standards of Durham people. He was chairman of Wheatley Hill parish council in 1903 and elected to Easington rural district council in 1907, later becoming chairman there too. His biographer noted the great attention to detail which buttressed his success. He kept a notebook for the parish council, the rural district council, and the Co-op, and one each for the young men's classes he taught, his public speaking, and preaching. In 1909 he was elected to the Durham county council, one of fewer than a dozen workers' representatives, and he was the obvious chairman when Labour won its first ever majority on a county council there in 1919. He sat continuously until 1932, serving two terms as chairman. In spite of the depressed state of the coal trade in inter-war Britain, Lee presided over improvements in the health of Durham people including falling infant mortality and death rates. Two most appropriate memorials to his work were the Burnhope Reservoir and the new town of Peterlee, which was named after him in 1954.

Lee died at his home, Bede Rest, in the city of Durham, on 16 June 1935 after a long illness. He was survived by his wife and children. He was buried in the cemetery at Wheatley Hill, which his own efforts had done much to provide. TONY MASON

Sources J. Lawson, *Peter Lee* (1936) • W. R. Garside, *The Durham miners, 1919–1960* (1971) • *DLB* • *The Times* (17 June 1935) • *Durham County Advertiser* (21 June 1935)

Lee [*née* Dashwood], **Rachel Fanny Antonina** (1773?–1829), alleged victim of abduction, was an illegitimate daughter of Francis Dashwood, eleventh Baron Le Despencer (1708–1781); her mother, who had been for eleven years Dashwood's companion, eventually became Mrs Barry. She was probably born in December 1773, but if De Quincey, who wrote of her and whose mother invited Mrs Lee to their house, is correct that she was twenty-two when he was seven her birth date would have been about 1770. She was educated in a French convent and endowed by her father with a fortune amounting to some £40,000. From 1789 to 1790 she lived in Kensington Square, London, with a Mrs Gordon whose sons, Loudon and Lockhart, she met when they came home for school holidays and who were to figure largely later in her life. While still under age she eloped to Scotland with Matthew Allen ('Handsome') Lee, whose main claim to fame was his good looks; they married on 9 March 1794 and separated on 4 January 1796.

Rachel went to live in Manchester, where she became acquainted with the De Quinceys through John Wesley's sister, who was a governess there. At that time she was described as having a classically beautiful face and figure, but being 'deplorably ignorant of English life and life universally' (De Quincey, 161). She played the organ well and was best known for her anti-Christian views, which she forcibly expressed in disputations with Christian clergymen. This led to continual quarrels with her friends and connections. In 1803 she was living in Bolton Row, Piccadilly, London, when she was carried off by the Gordon brothers, Lockhart by then a married clergyman and both Oxford graduates. The judgement as to whether she was abducted against her will depends on the assessment of the diametrically opposing evidence of Mrs Lee and the Gordons. When they arrived at Gloucester, Loudon Gordon came to her room in the hotel where they stayed for the night. Thither they were pursued at the instance of Mrs Lee's trustee, and Loudon Gordon, who was in debt, was arrested and sent for trial with his brother. Mrs Lee, under pressure from her husband, appeared as a witness at the trial which took place in Oxford on 6 March 1804 attended by a mob of 'gownsmen', who were harried by the police. Her evidence was to be that she was ignorant of English ways and had been led to believe that if she did not comply with the wishes of the brothers, Lockhart being armed with a pistol, she would have been harmed. Her demeanour in court, according to De Quincey, was far from that of the 'wild leopardess that had once worked her pleasure among the sheepfolds of Christianity' (De Quincey, 167). However, her examination was speedily stopped when she stated her disbelief in Christianity and could not take the oath. The Gordons were severely censured by the judge, but acquitted. The gownsmen sheltered Mrs Lee from the mob when she left the court. Loudon Gordon published an *Apology for the Conduct of the Gordons* in 1804 to show that, had the trial proceeded, it would have become clear that Mrs Lee had from the outset agreed with the 'elopement'. Lockhart Gordon's deserted wife died in the following May.

Mrs Lee was then sent by her friends to live with the family of a Gloucestershire clergyman whom, in her growing paranoia in matters of personal relations, she regarded as a persecutor. In 1807 she published *A Vindication of Mrs Lee's Conduct* and, with her intellect apparently unaffected by her personal obsessions, in 1808 she wrote, when living in Clarges Street, Piccadilly, under the pseudonym of Philopatria, an *Essay on Government*, the readership of which included Wordsworth.

Mrs Lee's husband committed suicide in that year and she returned to London, adopting the title of Baroness Le Despenser, to which she had no rightful claim, and continued to quarrel with her relatives and friends. Her *Memoirs of R. F. A.* appeared in 1812. She studied Hebrew, and published a translation entitled *The Hebrew epistle of Antonina Despenser entitled … a circular epistle to the Hebrews by H. V. Bolaffay* in 1821. About 1823 she wrote an *Investigation into the conduct of Lady Anne Dashwood and of Mr Delmar with respect to Antonina the Baroness Le Despenser* about her sister-in-law's alleged covetousness of her possessions. In 1825 *A Statement Including Charges Against Mr Henry Yorke* appeared. In 1828 she published *Remarks on a Will Said to have been that of Francis Dashwood Esq.* along with *A Statement Containing Charges Against Mr Thomas Marshall.* She died early in 1829.

RICHARD GARNETT, *rev.* J. GILLILAND

Sources L. H. Gordon, *Apology for the conduct of the Gordons* (1804) · T. De Quincey, *Autobiographic sketches*, 4 (1853) · *GM*, 1st ser., 74 (1804), 81, 485, 594 · *GM*, 1st ser., 99/1 (1829), 649 · R. F. A. Lee, *A vindication of Mrs Lee's conduct towards the Gordons* (1807) · [J. Watkins and F. Shoberl], *A biographical dictionary of the living authors of Great Britain and Ireland* (1816) · R. F. A. Lee, *Memoirs of R. F. A.* [*i.e. Rachel Fanny Antonina Lee*] (1812) · R. F. A. Lee, *Investigation into the conduct of Lady Anne Dashwood and of Mr Delmar with respect to Antonina the Baroness le Despenser* (1823?) · R. F. A. Lee, *Remarks on a will said to have been that of Francis Dashwood esq.* (1828) · R. F. A. Lee, *A statement containing charges against Mr Thomas Marshall* (1828) · R. F. A. Lee, *A statement including charges against Mr Henry Yorke* (1825)

Likenesses stipple, BM

Lee, Rawdon Briggs (1845–1908), dog breeder, born at Kendal, Westmorland, on 9 July 1845, was son of George Lee, Unitarian minister at Kendal, and proprietor and editor of the *Kendal Mercury.* His mother was Jane Agnes, daughter of Joseph Whitaker of Kendal, who was a friend of the painter Romney.

After education at the Friends' school, Kendal, Lee learned journalism under his father, whom he ultimately succeeded in the editorship of the *Mercury*, which he retained until 1883. But he gave much time to cricket and field sports, especially fishing and otter-hunting, and he became also an authority upon wrestling. In spite of defective eyesight he was one of the finest fly-fishers in England, with an unrivalled knowledge of angling in the Lake District.

Lee made his chief reputation, however, as a breeder of dogs. In 1869 he formed his first kennel, and his pack of Fellside terriers became well known to otter-hunters. But fox-terriers were his particular fancy. In 1871 he won the cup at the national show at Birmingham with a dog (Mac II) of this breed; and other prize-winners, such as Nimrod and Gripper, were exceptionally fine specimens. He was also successful with Dandie Dinmonts, pointers, collies, bull-terriers, Skye terriers, and Clumber spaniels. His English setter Richmond, after winning the highest honours at home, went to Australia to improve the breed. Lee acted as judge at dog shows held at Bath, Darlington, and Lancaster, but declined to adjudicate abroad. He finally retired from the show ring in 1892. A powerful advocate of field trials for sporting dogs, he did much to extend the movement which began in 1865.

Meanwhile, Lee, who had for several years written in *The Field* on angling and dog breeding, moved to London in 1883 and joined its staff, succeeding John Henry Walsh as kennel editor, and holding that post until June 1907. He also contributed occasionally to *Land and Water*, the *Fishing Gazette*, the *Stock-Keeper*, and other papers. He married in February 1907 Emily, daughter of Lieutenant Charles Dyer, and widow of Edward King, of Wavington, Bedfordshire. Injured in a carriage accident at Kendal, he suffered paralysis in spring 1907 while fishing and died in a nursing home at Putney on 29 February 1908. His body was cremated at Golders Green, and the ashes were afterwards buried in the family vault at Kendal.

Lee, who while living in London formed an excellent collection of books and pictures on sporting subjects, published the following works: *History and Description of the Fox-Terrier* (1889; 4th edn, enlarged, 1902); *History and Description of the Collie or Sheep Dog in his British Varieties*, illustrated by Arthur Wardle (1890); *History and Description of the Modern Dogs of Great Britain and Ireland: Non-Sporting Division*, illustrated by A. Wardle and R. H. Moore (1894; 3rd edn, 1915); *History and Description of the Terriers*, illustrated by the same artists (1894; 4th edn, 1915); *History and Description of the Modern Dogs of Great Britain and Ireland: Sporting Division*, illustrated by A. Wardle (2 vols., 1897; 4th edn, 1915). He also wrote, with Fred Gresham, the article on the dog in the *Encyclopaedia of Sport*, edited by the earl of Suffolk, H. Peek, and F. G. Aflalo (2 vols., 1897–8).

G. LE G. NORGATE, *rev.* JULIAN LOCK

Sources private information (1912) · *The Times* (2 March 1908) · *Westmorland Gazette* (7 March 1908) · *Kendal Mercury* (6 March 1908)

Lee, Sir Richard (1501/2–1575), military engineer and architect, was the eldest son of Richard Lee of Sopwell, Hertfordshire, and Elizabeth Hall of Ore, Sussex. His mother was a relative (possibly a niece) of Edmund Dudley, minister to Henry VII. It was perhaps through the Dudley connection that Lee gained a minor position within Henry VIII's household as a yeoman of the jewel house and (possibly in 1528) as a page of the king's cups with an annuity of £6. Keen to acquire patrons, he was known to Thomas Cromwell, earl of Essex, Sir Thomas Wriothesley, lord chancellor of England, Sir Ralph Sadler, Edward Seymour, earl of Hertford, and William Cecil, first Baron Burghley. His father and grandfather may have been masons and his own expertise as a building surveyor led to his employment by Cromwell to direct works at the latter's home at Hackney in 1535. Cromwell secured for him the post of surveyor at Calais, as well as defending him against detractors and helping him to secure various crown grants of land. His son Gregory stayed with Lee in France in 1539. Lee also received private commissions from Wriothesley at Titchfield, Hampshire.

Surveyor of Calais After his appointment on 8 August 1536 as surveyor of Calais, Lee did much, together with John Rogers, in the following eight years to maintain, expand, and modernize the military works there and in the pale. The post was an important one and well rewarded: a rent-free house in the borough, an annuity of £10, a salary of £20, a large staff including master masons, artificers, clerks, and—most importantly—draughtsmen, many of whose 'plats' (ranging from maps to detailed plans) survive among the Cotton Augustus manuscripts in the British Library, or in the collection of Sir William Cecil at Hatfield House. Lee's appointment was timely: previously the Tudor state had been parsimonious in its military building, but this changed dramatically in 1538–42. An unprecedented and high-profile meeting between Pope Paul III, Charles V, Francis I, and Cardinal Reginald Pole convinced the king and Cromwell that plans were being made for a Catholic crusade against England. It was apparent that the kingdom lay open to invasion unprotected by artillery fortifications. This gave rise to one of the largest construction programmes in Britain since the Romans. It was expensive and demanding: for Calais and its marches alone the building costs were £120,675 between September 1538 and January 1547.

When the works programme under Lee got under way it seemed that much of what was needed either did not exist (the wharf and harbour were derelict and had no crane) or was in a serious state of decay. Lack of building materials was acute (increasingly bricks could be procured locally, but dressed ashlar had to be transported from Kent) and workers were scarce. Over the next three years Lee directed not only extensive repairs, but also a massive rebuilding programme including the construction of new and formidable bulwarks. He was not yet thirty years old. In charge of a workforce of over 1000, he was never required to give a formal audit of expenditure and his work drew much praise. The duke of Norfolk commented to the French ambassador in London in 1541 that Calais was the strongest town in Christendom. In 1544 John Mason was similarly impressed and in 1557 the Venetian ambassador reported Calais to be an impregnable fortress. Most of this was Lee's work, from which he was relieved in December 1542. By then he had the reputation of being England's most accomplished military engineer.

In 1537 Lee had married Margaret, daughter of the Cornishman Sir Richard Grenville, marshal of Calais. Her parents and Grenville's uncle John Dudley, Lord Lisle, vigorously opposed the match. Cromwell assisted in reconciling Lee and Sir Richard, although Margaret's dowry was not agreed until 1550. The couple had two daughters, Anne and Maud (alias Mary). The latter married the son of another great Hertfordshire landowner, Sir Ralph Sadler.

Edward Seymour, who had been involved in the governmental debate over the works at Calais, was impressed by Lee and made sure that the young man accompanied him in April and May 1544 on his famous expedition to assault Edinburgh. For his part in this expedition Lee was rewarded with a knighthood on 11 May that year. He made a plan of both Leith and Edinburgh (although what survives in the Cotton Augustus manuscripts is a 'portrait' of the English army entering the city). Unable to take the castle or gain access to the upper town, however, the army looted. Craigmillar was assaulted and the palace of Holyroodhouse invaded. Lee was first to reach the abbey and made off with two of its notable artefacts: an eagle lectern (said to have been a gift from Pope Alexander VI) and a huge brazen font. He gave the lectern to his local church, St Stephen's in St Albans, and the font to the abbey church at St Albans.

Surveyor of the king's works On the sudden death of James Needham, surveyor of the king's works (1532–44), Lee was appointed to that post, an office which he held until 1 May 1547. In peacetime his duties would have centred on the royal palaces. But with the wars in France and Scotland, and more fortifications either planned or in construction, Lee had little time for domestic works. After his Scottish venture he went with the army to Boulogne, captured by Henry VIII in mid-September. There he gained great renown for beating off a French assault in October. He remained in France over the winter of 1544–5, overseeing the refortifications at both Calais and Boulogne. The need for this was urgent as Francis I had quickly set about constructing new fortifications around Boulogne in order to hem the English in. Noteworthy was a fort built on the other bank of the river, to a design by Antonio Melloni. At Fort d'Outreau, Lee and his colleague John Rogers encountered a revolutionary new approach to the art of fortification, but by 1546 English military engineers were 'quite abreast of the latest continental developments in the art of fortification' (Shelby, 144).

Berwick upon Tweed In September 1547 the protector, Somerset, gave Lee the task of designing a fortress at Eyemouth that would protect Berwick and a number of entrenched camps near by. Not yet fully master of this new structure, Lee built only one bastion, which meant that he had to insert two tunnels to allow gunners access to gunports to guard the face of the bastion. These seriously weakened the prime strength of this new form of defence: the massively thick earth walls. The mistake was not repeated; Dunglass (1548) and Berwick Citadel (1550–52) demonstrate his knowledge gained by experience.

When war broke out with France in 1557, Lee was again posted there and was in the duke of Savoy's army when St Quentin was captured. In January 1558, however, Calais was lost. Queen Mary's council immediately became fearful of the safety of England's northern Calais, Berwick upon Tweed. Lee was hastily recalled (his commission was dated 14 January 1558), provided with an enormous sum of money, and dispatched to the north with wide-ranging powers to raise a workforce, buy land and houses, and secure building supplies. He was on site by 17 March; his unprecedented salary of £1 a day gave rise to much comment and envy. Despite his experiences at Calais and Boulogne, Berwick posed considerable problems for Lee. Throughout 1558 he prepared plan after plan; all were subject to comment and revision by the queen's council. Questions as to the siting and extent of the new fortifications, what size to make the bastions, and to what design, the height and thickness of the curtain walls, whether or not to demolish the old castle, all preoccupied him. On the accession of Queen Elizabeth the council immediately decreed that the works should continue apace as 'if the late Quene had lyved' (*APC*, vii, 4). The overriding concern for Lee was how to meet the privy council's serious and justifiable apprehensions about the cost of the works while at the same time ensuring that Berwick could withstand a modern army equipped with artillery. For over a decade the programme was constrained by compromises and, unsurprisingly, the result was incomplete and flawed. Several experts interfered with Lee's work. In August 1559 Sir Ralph Sadler informed the council that so far the works did not sufficiently enhance the protection of the town. In January 1560 the duke of Norfolk pronounced them to be 'marvelous unapt' (*History of the King's Works*, 4.651). The new captain of the garrison, Sir James Croft, strongly deprecated Lee's intention to exclude the lower town from the walls. The crown then called in the military engineer Giovanni Portinari, who had been in service in England since the reign of Henry VIII; he worked at Berwick from 1560 to 1566 and found much to criticize in the size of Lee's bastions, the thickness of the curtain wall, and the failure to fortify all of the peninsula. Almost immediately he drew up counter-proposals, some of which disappeared mysteriously during his visit to Leith. Lee was seen to be the culprit. Most of Lee's schemes were ultimately adopted though at huge expense: at £128,648 this was by far the costliest building project of Queen Elizabeth's reign.

Although he spent much of his life on assignments, Lee continued to live in Hertfordshire, where he served as justice of the peace from 1543 to 1561 and from 1562 to 1575, and member of parliament in 1545. Between 1558 and 1566 he was not always at Berwick; in 1559 he was sent to survey the French fortresses in Scotland and later that year he was in Antwerp. In 1562 he was at Dieppe and Le Havre, and during his absences work advanced at Berwick under his competent deputy, Rowland Johnson. After his residence at Berwick during 1564–5 Lee undertook less work, although as late as 1573 (when he was over seventy years old) the earl of Essex requested that he might be sent to Ireland.

Land holdings and acquisitions Lee's positions allowed him a handsome income, which he invested in land. He also received other posts in recognition of his hard work. In March 1544, for example, he became, for a short time, receiver-general of the court of wards. His high profile and obvious enrichment laid him open, however, to allegations of peculation. The first serious accusation came after Cromwell's fall in 1540. The comptroller of Calais, Sir Edward Ryngeley, charged that Lee employed too many clerks, created sinecures for his friends, and wasted funds by hiring people for the calendar year when they could only work from March to October. Such accusations were often made against surveyors or officers of the crown who handled large sums of money, and Lee was able (with support) to withstand such attacks. He was pugnacious, resorting frequently to the law over his lands, and made enemies, in particular Sir Ralph Rowlett, a county rival. Lee was an assiduous investor and ploughed his rewards into property. Land near St Albans he bought from the crown in 1543 for £254, and during the year 1544–5 he paid out £3250 for more land in Hertfordshire. In addition to his purchases Lee was often granted lands as reward. In 1544 the manor of Hexton, Hertfordshire, was given to him, and his valiant service at Boulogne gained him a considerable share of the monastic lands at St Albans Abbey and Sopwell Priory. At Sopwell, where he had already purchased the buildings of the dissolved nunnery in 1538, he quickly demolished them, then refashioned the materials into his new home. As many others did, he benefited enormously from the Reformation: the rectory of Hexton (1547), the priory of Newent, Gloucestershire (1548), and the fee farm-rent of St Albans Abbey church (1533) all came to him. At the height of his powers Lee had consolidated his land into five manors and over 14,000 acres, at the centre of which was Sopwell Priory, increasingly known as 'Lee's place'. Most of these properties had been settled on his daughters, Mary and Anne, by the time he died at his manor house in Sopwell on 11 April 1575. He was buried on 25 April 1575 at St Peter's Church, St Albans.

Reputation Lee's career was a remarkable one; at the young age of thirty he emerged as 'the acknowledged English expert on military engineering' with 'a status and a reputation such as no man of his calling had enjoyed in the past' (*History of the King's Works*, 3.356). He was also a warrior and highly acquisitive. Lee affixed to the famous Holyrood font a brass plaque trumpeting his role in its history, but it was stolen during the civil war, when the borough was a parliamentary base. The lectern was removed in 1984 and returned to Edinburgh in 1999. But some of Lee's monuments have survived: his magnificent map of the Calais pale, Eyemouth fort, the artillery base at Dunglass, and the stupendous works at Berwick upon Tweed. An epitaph in the chancel of St Peter's Church, St Albans, celebrates his many accomplishments.

MARCUS MERRIMAN

Sources HoP, *Commons, 1509–58* • H. M. Colvin and others, eds., *The history of the king's works*, 3–4 (1975–82) • L. R. Shelby, *John Rogers: Tudor military engineer* (1967) • I. MacIvor, 'The fortifications of Berwick-upon-Tweed', *Antiquaries Journal*, 51 (1965), 65–96; *The fortifications of Berwick-upon-Tweed* (1967) [reprinted as] • M. H. Merriman, 'The forts of Eyemouth: anvils of union?', *SHR*, 67 (1988), 142–55 • D. Caldwell and G. Ewart, 'Excavations at Eyemouth, Berwickshire: a mid-sixteenth century *trace italienne* fort', *Post Medieval Archaeology*, 31 (1997), 61–119 • J. Harvey and A. Oswald, *English mediaeval architects: a biographical dictionary down to 1550*, 2nd edn (1984), 175–7

Lee, Richard (*c*.1774–1798?). *See under* London Corresponding Society (*act.* 1792–1799).

Lee, Richard Henry (1733–1794), revolutionary politician and planter in America, was born on 20 January 1733 in Westmoreland county, Virginia, the fourth of eight surviving children of Thomas *Lee (1690–1750) and Hannah (1701–1750), daughter of Philip Ludwell of Green Spring, Virginia, and his wife, Hannah. Lee's father, who amassed great wealth from plantations, land speculation, and lucrative appointments, and who served on the prestigious governor's council, exposed his son to the privileged society of the Virginia gentry. From an early age Lee also had regular contact with Great Britain and the Atlantic world. He was educated at Wakefield Academy in Yorkshire, several brothers and a sister lived in England and on the European mainland, and he later sent his own sons for training in Europe. On 3 December 1757 Lee married Anne Aylett (*d.* 1768), with whom he had four children. The summer following her death, in December 1768, Lee married Anne Gaskins Pinckard, with whom he had five children.

Unlike most landholding gentry of his era, Lee rented out the land and many of the slaves from his inherited estate. Lee established a residence, Chantilly, on property leased from his family's estate in Westmoreland county, where he had entered politics by gaining appointment as a justice of the peace, in 1757, and winning election to the colony's assembly, the house of burgesses, the following year. A celebrated orator, Lee attracted attention in the assembly by proposing a ban on the importation of slaves into Virginia. Lee argued that reliance on slave labour discouraged the immigration of skilled artisans, and prevented the improvements in agriculture and commerce that he observed in northern colonies. Lee challenged the established leadership in the house of burgesses by recommending a broader franchise, proposing debtor relief, and calling for the investigation of the powerful house speaker, John Robinson, who was later discovered to have made illegal loans to some of the colony's most prominent families.

Following reports of an impending American stamp tax imposed by the British parliament, Lee in November 1764

Richard Henry Lee (1733–1794), by Charles Willson Peale, *c*.1785

offered in the house of burgesses the original motion to submit formal protests to the king and parliament. As the date for the enforcement of the Stamp Act (passed in 1765) neared, Lee staged in Westmoreland county an elaborate procession, which included his own slaves in costume, and a mock hanging of the appointed collector of stamp duties in Virginia. In February 1766 he organized the Westmoreland Association, which pledged its signatories to resist any use of the excise stamps, and led the associators into a neighbouring county, where they demanded that a recalcitrant merchant forswear use of the stamps. Lee and others successfully called for closing Virginia's courts in order to prevent use of the stamps and to bring economic pressure on British merchants to lobby for repeal of the Stamp Act. Following parliament's repeal of the act in 1766, a Virginia newspaper revealed that in 1764 Lee had applied for appointment as the colony's collector of stamp duties. The embarrassment, however, did little to undermine his influence as one of Virginia's principal leaders in the resistance to imperial policy.

In May 1769, when Virginia's royal governor dissolved the house of burgesses in response to its resolutions opposing parliamentary duties on the colonies, Lee joined with George Washington and Patrick Henry to convene an extra-legal session to organize commercial resistance. As they considered the sort of non-importation agreement in effect in other colonies, Lee also urged the non-exportation of tobacco, which would have prevented the common form of payment Virginian planters made on debts owed to British merchants. The former burgesses were reluctant to take so radical a step, but they signed an agreement not to import a large selection of goods from Great Britain. In June 1770 Lee presented and won approval for a revised association in an attempt to secure more effective participation from merchants.

Lee's regular correspondence with two of his brothers, William, a tobacco merchant active in London politics, and Arthur, also resident in London, gave him a confidential source of intelligence about parliament and ministerial policy toward the colonies. Lee also established a correspondence with Samuel Adams, the popular leader of patriot opposition in Massachusetts. Their communication led to the formal establishment in 1773 of the correspondence committees that laid the basis for a united opposition to British policy.

As the imperial crisis worsened in the spring of 1774, Lee developed a plan to close the Virginia courts to all debt actions, drafted resolutions recommending a congress of deputies from all the colonies, and sponsored a resolution for a fast day, which provoked a dissolution of the house of burgesses and led to another non-importation association. Lee was among seven delegates chosen to represent Virginia at the continental congress in September 1774. There he offered the original motion for an intercolonial association to halt all imports of British goods and, after a year's delay, all exports to Great Britain. In the succeeding congress Lee continued at the forefront of organizing a united American resistance, and, with John Adams, moved toward independence by suggesting that states organize new governments. On 7 June 1776 congress approved Lee's resolution, declaring 'these United colonies are, and of right ought to be, free and independent States' (*Journals of the Continental Congress, 1774–1789*, 5, 1906). After assisting in the drafting of a constitution for Virginia in June, Lee returned to the congress in Philadelphia and signed the Declaration of Independence.

Lee served in congress until 1779 and again in 1784–5, when he was elected president of the congress, and in 1787, when he helped to draft the charter of government for the Northwest Territory. Lee also served in the Virginia house of delegates, 1777–8, and for most sessions from 1780 to 1785. During the war Lee became involved in the bitter controversy surrounding Silas Deane, a commissioner of congress who served in Europe with Lee's brother Arthur, and whose questionable private ventures led to his recall by congress.

Lee remained a skilful legislator, but much of his public service in the years following independence became consumed with attacks on the supposed loss of American civic virtue, and Lee's defensive posture often seemed at odds with his vision and originality as an organizer of colonial resistance. In the 1780s Lee became increasingly suspicious of the power of a national congress and anxious about the divisions he perceived between commercial improvement in the northern states and the stagnancy of what he called the 'Staple States'. He differed with old allies, such as Washington, who advocated granting congress the authority to raise revenue and regulate commerce. Lee retained an American continental perspective, however, and was convinced that the security of the new nation depended on the establishment of commercial ties with Europe. Lee declined a seat in the federal convention called to consider a new constitution in 1787, and, though he praised much about the resulting plan of government, he opposed ratification as long as the constitution lacked a bill of rights. It has been demonstrated that Lee was not, as long thought, the author of *Letters from the Federal Farmer*, published in opposition to ratification.

Lee served as one of Virginia's first senators in the federal congress that convened in the spring of 1789, and was elected the senate's president *pro tempore* on 18 April 1792. He retired from the senate on 8 October 1792 and resided at Chantilly until his death there, on 19 June 1794. He was buried at the Burnt House Field cemetery, Mount Pleasant, Virginia. BRUCE A. RAGSDALE

Sources P. Maier, 'A Virginian as revolutionary: Richard Henry Lee', *The old revolutionaries: political lives in the age of Samuel Adams* (1980), 164–200 • P. C. Nagel, *The Lees of Virginia: seven generations of an American family* (1990) • E. J. Lee, *Lee of Virginia, 1642–1892* (1895) • J. E. Selby, 'Lee, Richard Henry', *ANB* • *The letters of Richard Henry Lee*, ed. J. C. Ballagh, 2 vols. (1911–14) • *Memoir of the life of Richard Henry Lee and his correspondence*, ed. R. H. Lee, 2 vols. (Philadelphia, PA, 1825) • Lee corresp., Virginia Historical Society, Lee MSS • *Lee family papers* (1966) [microfilm] • G. S. Wood, 'The authorship of *The letters from the federal farmer*', *William and Mary Quarterly*, 31 (1974), 299–308

Archives University of Virginia, Charlottesville, family papers [microfilm] • Virginia Historical Society, Richmond, family papers, corresp.

Likenesses C. Willson Peale, oils, *c.*1785, Independence National Historical Park, Philadelphia, Pennsylvania [*see illus.*]

Lee, Robert (1793–1877), physician specializing in gynaecology and obstetrics, was born at Whitelaw in the parish of Melrose, Roxburghshire, the second son of John Lee, a major agriculturist. He was educated at Galashiels and entered Edinburgh University in 1806, aged thirteen and intended for the church, but then decided to devote himself to medicine. Lee graduated MD in June 1814, and also became a member of the Edinburgh College of Surgeons. He was physician's clerk at the Edinburgh Royal Infirmary to James Hamilton senior. During his Edinburgh period Lee was befriended by the abolitionists William Wilberforce and Zachary Macaulay, who introduced him to the physician and naval health reformer Sir Gilbert Blane. In 1817 Lee moved to London, where Blane arranged for him to attend on the son of a senior statesman who was afflicted with epilepsy. Lee spent the winter of 1821–2 studying medicine in Paris and dissecting with his friend William Cullen. After touring France and Italy as personal physician to an eminent family, Lee returned to England and became a licentiate of the Royal College of Physicians in March 1823 and a member of the Royal Medical and Chirurgical Society. He commenced practice in London as an obstetric physician.

Following a severe illness, perhaps brought on by constant attendance on cases of difficult labours in public institutions, Lee obtained an appointment with the East India Company, but then on the recommendation of Augustus Bozzi Granville he became physician to Prince

Robert Lee (1793–1877), by Frederick James Smyth, pubd 1851 (after John Jabez Edwin Mayall)

Vorontsov, governor-general of the Crimea and the Russian provinces on the Black Sea. Lee left England for Odessa in October 1824, and while there was responsible for introducing quinine for the treatment of fevers to the Crimea. He was presented to Tsar Alexander a few days before the tsar's sudden death from fever. Lee's account, *The Last Days of Alexander and the First Days of Nicholas*, which countered the impression that Alexander did not die a natural death, as well as outlining the social and political condition of Russia, was published in 1854 during the Crimean War by *The Athenaeum*. Lee returned to London with Prince Vorontsov in 1826, and again began to practise as an accoucheur.

In 1827 Lee was elected physician to the British Lying-in Hospital and began to lecture on midwifery, and in 1829 was appointed lecturer in midwifery at the Webb Street School with a salary of £150 per annum, and physician accoucheur to the Southwark Lying-in Institution. In 1830 he was elected fellow of the Royal Society on the recommendation of his benefactor Sir Gilbert Blane, and became secretary to the Royal Medical and Chirurgical Society, an office which he held until 1835. In 1832 he was elected physician accoucheur to the St Marylebone Parochial Infirmary and parish. In 1834 he obtained, through Lord Melbourne, the regius professorship of midwifery at the University of Glasgow, but his appointment aroused considerable local opposition and he resigned it after delivering his introductory address and returned to London. In 1835 he was appointed to the chair of midwifery and as lecturer in midwifery and the diseases of women at St George's Hospital, retaining the appointment until 1866.

Lee was a prolific researcher and author, and after settling in London in 1827 he studied and published on the anatomical structure and development of the nerves of the uterus and heart, the practice of midwifery, the pathology of diseases of the uterus, and on the treatment of diseases of women, hysteria, puerperal inflammation, tubal gestation and ovarian cysts, the treatment of sterility, the structure of the placenta, premature labour, and the use of the speculum. In a biographical sketch which appeared in March 1851 *The Lancet* listed thirty-one papers written by Lee, many of which had been published in the *Transactions of the Royal Medical and Chirurgical Society*, and others read before the Royal Society. Lee recorded an impressive number of case histories during his long practice, including all the significant occurrences of puerperal and uterine disease and difficult labours which came under his observation, utilizing his knowledge of shorthand, which he had acquired while a student in Edinburgh. Among his most important contributions to obstetrics are his *Clinical Midwifery* (1842), *Lectures on the Theory and Practice of Midwifery* (1844), and *Three Hundred Consultations in Midwifery* (1864). *Clinical Midwifery* contains 400 cases of difficult labour and was described as being of immense value for students and practitioners of midwifery. A second edition with 545 cases appeared in 1848.

Lee was admitted a fellow of the Royal College of Physicians in 1841, and in 1850 was appointed president of the Western Medical Society. He delivered the Lumleian lectures in 1856–7, the Croonian lectures in 1862, and was Harvarian orator at the college in October 1864, when he began his oration in Latin but, owing, one observer reported, to his poor grasp of the language, was forced to finish it in English. Lee was never awarded a medal by the Royal Society, and felt bitter at his lack of professional recognition. He had a fierce and well-publicized dispute lasting many years with Dr Snow Beck concerning the structure and formation of the nerves of the uterus. In 1845 the Royal Society's medal was awarded to Beck for his account. Lee vigorously opposed this, and the issue became a *cause célèbre* within the Royal Society and contributed to the resignations of the marquess of Northampton as president and Dr Peter Mark Roget as secretary in 1849.

Lee was an energetic and impetuous teacher and an outspoken man, with strong opinions, given to denounce those with whom he disagreed. He was a conservative in obstetrics, expressing concern about the safety of lying-in hospitals, suggesting that they be abolished, and strongly opposing caesarean section. Lee attracted large attendances at the Royal Medical and Chirurgical Society in 1850–51 to discuss papers on ovariotomy and the use of the speculum. In May 1850 he became one of the first to criticize surgical and instrumental interference in obstetrics, attacking the indiscriminate use of the speculum. Using data collected from St Marylebone Infirmary he demonstrated that cervical ulcerations were very rare and did not justify the use of the speculum. He ended his account with some horrific stories arising from misuse of the speculum, and protested against its repeated use on the grounds of propriety and morality, particularly among unmarried women. Lee vigorously opposed ovariotomy on the grounds of the difficulties in detecting the existence of disease and in assessing whether removal of the ovaries was practicable. In November 1850, at a meeting of the Royal Medical and Chirurgical Society, Lee analysed 162 operations for ovarian tumours carried out in Great Britain. A third of the cases were inoperable or there was no tumour present. Of 102 completed operations, 42 ended with the death of the patient. After Lee's denunciation ovariotomies were rarely undertaken in London until Thomas Spencer Wells revived the procedure in 1857. By 1862, when Lee renewed his attack on ovariotomies, which he claimed were being performed in the interest of greed rather than altruism, the tide had turned in favour of the operation. Lee also opposed the use of chloroform anaesthesia in childbirth, which he condemned as unnatural and potentially harmful, citing cases he had observed where chloroform had caused peritonitis or insanity; young and inexperienced mothers, Lee claimed, were 'decoyed to their destruction' by chloroform.

Lee worked indefatigably until 1875, when he retired from practice. He died suddenly at his home, 15 The Avenue, Surbiton Hill, Surrey, on 6 February 1877, and was buried at Kensal Green, London. He left a widow, Emily Auriol. Their son, Robert James Lee, was a physician, specializing in obstetrics and children's medicine; another son was a vicar. Robert Lee's extensive anatomical preparations were presented to the University of Cambridge. Lee was an indomitable worker and original researcher, anatomist, and physiologist, outlining a useful description of uterine innervation and pelvic contraction and its management, and was the first to examine the ovaries during menstruation. Lee's diary (written partly in shorthand) reflects his great anxiety about achieving a balance between his practice and research and publication. It also reveals Lee's jealousy of a number of his colleagues. Sir James Paget claimed that:

> Dr Lee was a strong instance of that fault which sometimes goes with honesty; he was so sure that his convictions were the results of hard and well-intentioned study; so sure that he sought the truth, and sought it in the right way, that he was wholly unable to believe that any one, with equal honesty, and almost equal industry, could arrive at conclusions different from his own. (*BMJ*, 10 March 1877, 306)

HILARY MARLAND

Sources 'Biographical sketch of Robert Lee', *The Lancet* (22 March 1851), 332–7 • Munk, *Roll* • diary of Robert Lee, 1793–1877, Wellcome L., MS 3218 • *BMJ* (17 Feb 1877), 217 • *BMJ* (10 Feb 1877), 177 • O. Moscucci, *The science of woman: gynaecology and gender in England, 1800–1929* (1990) • A. J. Youngson, *The scientific revolution in Victorian medicine* (1979) • A. Digby, *Making a medical living* (1994) • I. Loudon, *Death in childbirth: an international study of maternal care and maternal mortality, 1800–1950* (1992) • A. Dally, *Women under the knife* (1991) • D. E. Manuel, *Marshall Hall (1790–1857): science and medicine in early Victorian society* (1996) • J. Blomfield, *St George's, 1733–1933* (1933) • *DNB* • *CGPLA Eng. & Wales* (1877)

Archives Wellcome L., diary, correspondence and MSS, MS 3218, 5469 | NL Scot., letters to John Lee • RCP Lond., MSS

Likenesses F. J. Smyth, wood-engraving, pubd 1851 (after J. J. E. Mayall), Wellcome L. [*see illus.*] • bust, repro. in 'Biographical sketch of Robert Lee', 333

Wealth at death under £4000: administration with will, 28 Feb 1877, *CGPLA Eng. & Wales*

Lee, Robert (1804–1868), Church of Scotland minister, was born at Tweedmouth, Northumberland on 11 November 1804. He was the eldest of the three sons of George Lee, a shipbuilder, whose father had established the family in the trade; his mother was June, daughter of Robert Lambert. He was educated at Berwick upon Tweed grammar school, and worked for six years as a boat builder. In 1824 he was able to pursue his own ambitions, proceeding to the University of St Andrews where he distinguished himself in classics. An apocryphal tale records that he funded his entrance to the university by building a boat with his own hands to supplement his savings. While he was there, he maintained himself by more conventional means, spending his vacations as a tutor—on one occasion to the future novelist George John Whyte-Melville (1821–1878).

In 1833 Lee was elected minister of the Presbyterian chapel of ease at Arbroath, Forfarshire; in 1836 he was moved to the parish of Campsie, Stirlingshire. During this period, he contributed articles to the *Scottish Christian Herald*. On 21 June 1836 he married Isabella Carrick Buchanan; they had one son and four daughters. In 1840 he was an unsuccessful candidate for the chair of theology at Glasgow University; however, preferment soon came and on 29 August 1843 he was appointed minister of the church and parish of the Old Greyfriars, Edinburgh, where he remained until his death. In 1844 the University of St Andrews conferred on him the degree of DD, and in January 1847 he was installed as the first professor of biblical criticism in the University of Edinburgh, and dean of the Chapel Royal.

Lee was shaken by the threat of disestablishment following the Disruption of 1843 and disturbed by defections to the Episcopalian church. In his *Theses of Erastus Touching Excommunication* (1844) he defended church establishment vigorously enough to earn a lengthy review from W. E. Gladstone in the *Foreign and Colonial Quarterly Review*, in which the alarmed high-churchman accused Lee of whitewashing Erastus's heretical views. However, Lee looked to the reform of worship, rather than theological debate, to strengthen the established church. Uninfluenced by the contemporary enthusiasm in the Church of England and Church of Scotland for Catholic tradition, he was not involved in the foundation of the Church Service Society. He held that worship should consist of three elements—word, prayer, and praise—and seized the opportunity to amend 'unimpressive and ill-ordered worship' (Drummond and Bulloch, 193) when Old Greyfriars Church was burned down in January 1845. He introduced instrumental music, regular and consecutive readings from the Bible, ordered prayers, and the use of appropriate positions in response to the service. For the opening of the new church—ornamented with stained glass windows—on 14 June 1857, he composed and printed his own liturgy. Subsequently, Lee introduced an organ, the first to be used in a Church of Scotland service, to Old Greyfriars

Robert Lee (1804–1868), by James Edgar, 1853

in April 1864; in the same year he published *The Reform of the Church in Worship, Government and Doctrine: Part I, Worship*. Other works included *A Handbook of Devotion* (1845), *Prayers for Public Worship* (1857), and *The Clerical Profession, some of its Difficulties and Hindrances* (1866). Lee's innovations attracted a large and well-born congregation to a church which had declined under his predecessor, John Inglis (1763–1834), and his friends included influential and cultured laymen such as Sir John Archibald Murray, Lord Murray (1779–1859), and Alexander Russel (1814–1876) of *The Scotsman*.

Lee's liturgical innovations attracted criticism from conservative clergy, which was only exacerbated by his radical views on other church matters. In 1847 he opposed the sabbatarian movement's attempt to condemn the running of Sunday trains, arguing that the decision whether or not to travel on a sabbath should be left to the conscience of the individual. When the issue arose again in the 1863 general assembly, he stood firm with Norman McLeod and A. H. Charteris. Lee also supported radical educational reforms, advocating the acceptance of government grants for denominational education, opposing the university tests, and acting on the committee of the United Industrial School, a non-sectarian institution where religious and secular instruction were separated. His enthusiasm for freedom of worship and thought was further evidenced in his opposition to the Ecclesiastical Titles Bill of 1851, and his support for the private administration of baptism and communion. In 1864 he strongly favoured the abolition of patronage within the Church of Scotland, not as a means of facilitating a union with the Free Church, but as a measure which would give congregations some influence in the choice of a minister.

Lee's conservative critics did not refrain from action: on 23 February 1859, Lee was charged with unlawful innovations in worship before the presbytery of Edinburgh. The case came before the general assembly, which decided in his favour on 24 May, admitting his argument that all the changes in question—except the use of printed prayers—were authorized in the *Directory for the Publique Worship of God*. However, further proceedings followed in the Edinburgh presbytery in 1864, when the moderator of that year, William Robinson Pirie, succeeded in vesting control of worship in the presbyteries. Lee held his course, and, in March 1866, he was censured by the presbytery for celebrating the marriage of the Hon. Captain Arbuthnot and Mrs Ferguson Blair within his church, a ceremony not permitted in Presbyterian places of worship. The synod followed suit on 7 May. By way of a compromise, Lee offered to desist from reading prayers (rather than rendering them extemporarily), but this olive branch came too late to avert a summons before the general assembly. However, on 18 May 1867, four days after he had issued a final statement in *A Letter to the Members of the General Assembly*, as he was riding to the general assembly, he suffered a cerebral haemorrhage and was paralysed down his left side. He died at Torquay on 14 March 1868, and was buried in the Grange cemetery, Edinburgh, on 20 March. His widow was granted a civil-list pension of £100 a year on 17 November 1868. ROSEMARY MITCHELL

Sources R. H. Story, *The life and remains of Robert Lee DD*, 2 vols. (1870) · *Fasti Scot.* · R. Welford, *Men of mark 'twixt Tyne and Tweed*, 3 vols. (1895) · A. L. Drummond and J. Bulloch, *The church in Victorian Scotland, 1843–1874* (1975) · *DSCHT*

Archives U. Edin., New Coll. L., lectures and papers | NL Scot., letters to J. S. Blackie · NL Scot., corresp. with George Combe

Likenesses J. Edgar, oils, 1853, Scot. NPG [*see illus.*] · Hurst and Blackett, engraving, 1870 · portrait, repro. in Welford, *Men of mark* · portraits, repro. in Story, *The life and remains of Robert Lee DD* · sketch, repro. in Welford, *Men of mark*, 3.32

Wealth at death £6675 5s. 9d.: inventory, 11 Aug 1868, NA Scot., SC 70/1/140/131

Lee, Robert Warden (1868–1958), lawyer, was born at Hanmer, Flintshire, on 14 December 1868, the third son of the vicar, the Revd Matthew Henry Lee, later canon of St Asaph, and his wife, Louisa, daughter of Robert Warden. A scholar of Rossall School and of Balliol College, Oxford, he obtained a double first in classics (1889–91). He spent the years from 1891 to 1894 in the Ceylon civil service, where his experience as a magistrate and commissioner of requests awoke in him an interest in Roman-Dutch law, the common law of Ceylon.

Lee resigned for reasons of health and returned to England, where he was called to the bar by Gray's Inn in 1896, obtained the degree of BCL in 1898, practised before the privy council, mainly in appeals from Ceylon, and taught law both at Worcester College, Oxford, of which he became a fellow in 1903, and at London University, where he held the chair of Roman-Dutch law from 1906. In 1914 he went to Montreal as dean of the law faculty of McGill University. In the same year he married Amice Anna

Botham, daughter of Sir John Macdonell, the jurist. They had one daughter.

Oxford called Lee back as its first and only professor of Roman-Dutch law, and also as a fellow of All Souls, in 1921. He occupied the chair for thirty-six years, and only retired in 1956 at the age of eighty-seven after a serious operation. Most of his writing was done while he held the Oxford chair, but his most famous work, the *Introduction to Roman-Dutch Law*, of which five editions had appeared by 1953, came out in 1915. Admirably clear, attractive, and well proportioned, its concise and allusive language is designed, as he himself emphasized, to whet the appetite. Several generations of South African and Ceylon lawyers were brought up on it and as a laconic and ironical introductory work in the civil law tradition it can stand comparison with the *Institutes* of Gaius. Lee's two-volume work *Introduction to the Jurisprudence of Holland* (1926–36), including the work by Hugo Grotius and its English translation, is now of value chiefly for the translation and commentary. His *Elements of Roman Law* (1944), published in his seventies, was very successful with students.

Lee was a firm protagonist of codification and attached great importance to his part in producing the *Digest of English Civil Law* edited by Edward Jenks and two similar volumes on the law of South Africa (1950–54) which he edited in collaboration with A. M. Honoré, although they did not give the impetus he hoped to the movement for codification.

Lee was a fine teacher, whose pupils included at least six judges. All his pupils, distinguished or not, could implicitly rely on his painstaking care and loyal support of their interests. His loyalties were also engaged by All Souls College and by the inns of court, where he was for long reader in Roman and Roman-Dutch law to the Council of Legal Education. He received many honours, for he was, *inter alia*, a KC of the Quebec bar (1920), a fellow of the British Academy (1933), a bencher of Gray's Inn (1934), an honorary doctor of the universities of Lyons, the Witwatersrand, and Ceylon, president of the Society of Public Teachers of Law, and vice-president of the International Academy of Comparative Law.

Although Lee devoted a good part of his life to the study of Roman-Dutch law, he looked upon it with detachment. Himself a classical scholar who delighted in composing Latin verses—his *Series episcoporum Romanae ecclesiae* (1935) is an elegant example—he was impatient of the historical bent of some South African lawyers and was apt to say, with a twinkle, that the old authorities should be burned. This has not happened, but the modern legal systems of South Africa and Ceylon have now come to be regarded as distinct from the Roman-Dutch law of Renaissance Holland, and it has been said with some truth that this sturdy Victorian individualist was the last Roman-Dutch lawyer. Lee died at 11 Gray's Inn Square, London, on 6 January 1958. He was survived by his wife.

TONY HONORÉ, *rev.*

Sources H. G. Hanbury, 'Robert Warden Lee, 1868–1958', *PBA*, 44 (1958), 313–24 • F. H. Lawson, *American Journal of Comparative Law*, 7 (autumn 1958), 659–61 • *The Times* (7 Jan 1958) • personal knowledge (1971) • *CGPLA Eng. & Wales* (1958)

Likenesses W. Stoneman, photograph, 1938, NPG • K. Lloyd, pastel, priv. coll. • I. Plaente, charcoal drawing, priv. coll.

Wealth at death £24,208 15*s*. 5*d*.: probate, 31 March 1958, *CGPLA Eng. & Wales*

Lee, Rowland (*c*.1487–1543), administrator and bishop of Coventry and Lichfield, was the son of William Lee (*d*. 1511) of Morpeth, Northumberland, who was in 1509 receiver-general of Berwick-on-Tweed and other royal manors and lordships, and his wife, Isabel, daughter and heir of Sir Anthony Trollope of Thornley, co. Durham.

Lee and his family Rowland Lee was a tireless promoter of the interests of his family, especially those of his brother George. He secured for him livings in Essex and Yorkshire, and after he had become bishop of Coventry and Lichfield collated him to a prebend in Lichfield Cathedral (Bishopshull, 1537, exchanged for Wellington, 1538), then on 9 March 1541 advanced him to the office of treasurer of the cathedral with the prebend of Sawley. Lee also made his brother master of the hospital of St John the Baptist, Lichfield, on 23 March 1538 and dean of the collegiate church of St Chad, Shrewsbury, on 9 March 1541. Their sister Isabel also benefited from Rowland's patronage, when in 1528 he gave her a house attached to his Lichfield prebend of Curborough. She married Roger Fowler of Bromehill, Norfolk, who was killed fighting the Scots leaving four sons and three daughters. When she died, about 1538, Lee became the guardian of her children. He collated Brian and James Fowler to prebends in St John's, Chester, and Gnosall collegiate church, in James's case to fund his studies at Cambridge and the inns of court. By a settlement of 1540 he secured for Brian Fowler the lands of St Thomas's Priory, Stafford, granted to Lee himself the previous year. And for both James and Brian, as for their brothers, Rowland and William, and their sisters, Alice, Anne, and Jane, he obtained advantageous marriages into gentry families.

Education and early career Rowland Lee entered the University of Cambridge about 1503 to study civil law, aged about sixteen. He graduated in 1510 and proceeded DCnL in 1520. He also applied for incorporation at Oxford in 1524, whether successfully is unknown. Lee's qualifications pointed towards a career in the church and he was ordained subdeacon, deacon, and priest between 5 June and 18 December 1512. His studies were financed by a number of church livings. On 5 March 1509 he was given the rectory of Foston, Yorkshire, and when ordained he was recorded as already holding a prebend in Norton collegiate church in the diocese of Durham. By 1524 he also held the rectory of Washington in the same diocese. On 8 October 1520 Lee became an advocate and a member of Doctors' Commons. Shortly afterwards he acquired Banham rectory in Norfolk (26 October 1520), and Ashdon rectory, Essex (24 July 1522).

It was possibly at Doctors' Commons that Lee came to the attention of Geoffrey Blythe, bishop of Coventry and Lichfield. He presided over Blythe's consistory court at Lichfield Cathedral from 13 June 1525 until some time before 23 July 1527, and is also recorded on 4 June 1526 as Blythe's vicar-general, a position he retained until 6 November 1528. His tenure as Blythe's chancellor was brief but effective, for when he entered the diocese as its bishop in 1534 one of his company noted how he was 'so moche the better biloved for his gentle dealinge with theime in the tyme of his chauncellorshipp there' (SP 1/85, fol. 56). During this period Lee was made rector of Fenny Compton, Warwickshire (1 October 1526), and on the day of admission he displayed bulls from popes Leo X, Adrian VI, and Clement VII allowing him to hold benefices in plurality. The rectory was followed by the more prestigious prebend of Curborough in Lichfield Cathedral (7 April 1527). Lee's association with the diocese continued after he ceased to be chancellor, since he acted as the bishop's commissary in 1529. And while the see was vacant between 1531 and 1533 Lee helped ensure that the spiritualities of the diocese went to the crown.

Lee's restricted involvement with the diocese of Coventry and Lichfield after 1528 is explained by his increasing employment by Cardinal Thomas Wolsey. In April 1528 he collected revenue from Bromehill Priory, Norfolk, and in September he assisted Stephen Gardiner in the founding of Cardinal College, Ipswich, and the associated suppression of the religious houses of Felixstowe, Bromehill, and Rumburgh. In 1529 he acted as Wolsey's commissary-general in a visitation of the whole English church, and in this capacity suppressed Mountjoy Priory, Norfolk, visited the Ely Cathedral Priory, and took the fealty of the newly elected abbot of Shrewsbury. On 30 October 1528 he was recorded as an auditor in Wolsey's legatine court. Lee's work for Wolsey brought personal reward. On 8 September 1528 he became archdeacon of Cornwall, and as such sat in the convocation of Canterbury in November 1529. In February 1529 he claimed the prebend of Wetwang in York Minster, though without success, but in December 1531 he obtained the prebend of Sharrow in Ripon Minster, also in Yorkshire.

While he was in Wolsey's service Lee became friends with Thomas Cromwell. During 1530 Lee wrote to Cromwell at Wolsey's request asking for news of 'your good sped concernyng hys pardon' (SP 1/57, fol. 1). That he entered royal service after Wolsey's death was probably owing to Cromwell's rising fortunes at court. Confirmation of their friendship is provided by Lee's being presented by Cromwell to the vicarage of St Sepulchre, Newgate, London, on 19 August 1532 and by Cromwell's placing his son Gregory in Lee's care for periods in 1533 and 1534. Gregory's tutor, Henry Dowes, believed that Lee treated the boy as if he 'were his owne naturall sonne' (SP 1/85, fol. 56). Others recognized the closeness of the relationship between Lee and Cromwell. When Lancelot Collins, treasurer of York, heard that Lee was to become the bishop of Coventry and Lichfield, he told Cromwell, 'I rakune yow bechope thare yowre selffe' (SP 1/79, fol. 166).

Royal chaplain and master in chancery Between 1531 and 1534 Lee was actively engaged in royal business as one of the king's chaplains and a master in chancery. His earliest recorded labour for the crown came in February 1531 when he and John Oliver took the surrender of the priory of Christ Church, London. He subsequently directed a number of monastic elections. Lee also became increasingly involved in the business of Henry VIII's divorce from Katherine of Aragon. According to Nicholas Harpsfield it was Lee who reluctantly officiated at the secret marriage of Henry VIII and Anne Boleyn on 24 or 25 January 1533, but there is no further evidence for this. Lee is listed in Cromwell's remembrances of February 1533 with others who are believed to have met to discuss the Act of Restraint of Appeals to Rome. Two months later he recorded the need to 'attend apon my Lorde of Canterbury at Lambeth for the Kynges Mater' (SP 1/75, fol. 94), and was also involved in editing a collection of opinions on the royal divorce, which he urged to be shown to the king, 'in whos matre I shallnot be fownde oblivius' (ibid., fol. 178). These documents were probably prepared for presentation to the convocation of York, which was required to discuss the validity of the divorce. Sent north on 24 April to cajole or bully leading churchmen into supporting the crown Lee was opposed by Cuthbert Tunstall, bishop of Durham, but the northern convocation none the less supported the king's case, and Edward Leighton believed that this was due to the 'greate diligence, and laburs off maister Doctor Lee' (SP 1/76, fol. 61). Then on 10 December 1533 he appeared in Canterbury with Thomas Bedyll, to investigate the activities of Elizabeth Barton, the Nun of Kent, and her followers. Early in 1534 Lee and Bedyll, supported by the bishop of London, tried to persuade the nuns of Syon to acknowledge the validity of Henry VIII's marriage to Anne Boleyn.

Lee's loyalty and diligence on behalf of the crown was rewarded when he was elected bishop of Coventry and Lichfield on 10 January 1534, having been granted custody of the temporalities on the previous 18 December. Not everyone was pleased by Lee's elevation. On 1 November 1533 Stephen Vaughan, a merchant and royal agent based in Antwerp, had rebuked Cromwell for helping 'a molle and an eanemy to all godly lernyng into theoffyce of his dampnacon; a papiste, an idolator, and a flesshely preste unto a Busshopp of Chester' (SP 1/80, fols. 79–80). In fact Lee's religious views are not easy to define, as he made no outright declarations of faith, not even in his final will and testament. What mattered to Cromwell and the king was that Lee supported the royal supremacy by oath and deed.

While still bishop-elect Lee attended the southern convocation of late March 1534, signing its declaration that the pope had no more authority in England than any other foreign bishop. He is also named as attending the convocation of York, which made the same declaration on 1 June. During April 1534 he visited Bishop John Fisher of Rochester, incarcerated in the Tower of London for refusing the oath of succession. Lee was unable to persuade Fisher to conform, but he did warn that the old bishop was frail and would die unless mercy was shown, 'for the body can not bere the clothes on his bake' (BL, Cotton MS Cleopatra, E vi, fol. 160*v*).

Thomas Cranmer consecrated Lee as bishop of Coventry

and Lichfield at Croydon on 19 April 1534. He was one of the first bishops to take the oath recognizing the king as the supreme head of the Church in England. In early May he and Bedyll visited the monasteries of Sheen, Richmond, and Syon to try to persuade them to accept the royal supremacy. Then on 21 May they were at Huntingdon with Archbishop Edward Lee and Bishop Tunstall, in an unsuccessful attempt to persuade Katherine of Aragon to accept the divorce. On 28 May, Rowland Lee took an oath of fealty from a number of London Carthusians, and in mid-June, he and Bedyll attempted to persuade the Observant Friars of Richmond to take the oath of supremacy, but despaired that reason 'coulde not synk into their obstinatt heddes' (BL, Cotton MS Cleopatra, E iv, fols. 49–50*v*).

Lee and his diocese On 3 July 1534 Lee visited his diocese of Coventry and Lichfield as its bishop. By 10 August, however, he was at Shrewsbury as lord president of the council in the marches of Wales, and his preoccupation with the Welsh marches meant that the administration of the diocese was left to his officers, notably his chancellor, Dr David Pole, and his receiver-general, Richard Strete. Pole was a canon lawyer and advocate with great experience of diocesan administration, eventually becoming the bishop of Peterborough in 1557. On 10 February 1538 John Bird, bishop of Penreth (probably Pen-tyrch, near Llandaff) and later of Bangor, was appointed suffragan of the diocese. Meanwhile the consequences of the royal supremacy continued to affect Lee and his diocese. On 11 February 1535 he was required to display his support for the supremacy and to relinquish any papal bulls he owned, as well as those of his cathedrals, and on 7 June 1535 he received orders to preach against the power of the pope. He claimed that he was ready to go to his diocese to preach in person 'all though hertherto I was never in pulpitt' (SP 1/93, fol. 37). But despite Lee's initial enthusiasm it was his chaplain William Ducket who did the preaching.

Lee's name also appears on *The Institution of a Christian Man*, although he was not present at the vicegerental synod that produced the book. The king's growing involvement in ecclesiastical matters touched Lee and the diocese in more material ways. In April 1537 he discovered that Henry wanted Edward Seymour, Viscount Beauchamp, the future duke of Somerset, to have the bishop's London residence, known as Chester Place (it provided the site for Somerset House). Lee was compensated with the church of Hanbury, Staffordshire, in the following year. In 1538 the shrine of St Chads in Lichfield Cathedral was dismantled and the jewels and ornaments sent to Westminster, although Lee persuaded the king to allow the chapter to preserve the shrine itself, at least temporarily. In 1539 the monastic cathedral of Coventry was dissolved, despite Lee's objection that it was his 'principall see and hede churche' (BL, Cotton MS Cleopatra E iv, fol. 311). He also lost the large archdeaconry of Chester, when, on 4 August 1541, it became part of a new bishopric of Chester.

Lord president of the council in the marches of Wales Lee's primary concern, from 10 August 1534 until his death in January 1543, was Wales and the Welsh marches, where he replaced the ineffective John Voysey, bishop of Exeter, as lord president of the council in the marches of Wales. The council, which had judicial, administrative, and general surveillance duties over the principality, the semi-independent marcher lordships, the county palatine of Chester, and the English counties of Shropshire, Herefordshire, Worcestershire, and Gloucestershire, enjoyed considerable success in maintaining law and order under Lee's direction. Indeed, Lee's council was seen as an example to be followed by the council of the 1570s, when Dr David Lewis referred to Lee's presidency in terms of Joseph's wise rule over the Egyptians. William Gerard claimed in 1576 that Lee was an extreme punisher of offenders, and that fear brought the Welsh to obedience. One reason for this apparent success was the advancement of the council's authority through the statutes known as the pre-union legislation, which gave it the right to try felonies committed in the Welsh marches in the neighbouring English shires. Another important factor was Lee's willingness to travel round his jurisdiction—in the first year of his presidency he visited Shrewsbury, Chester, Newport in Shropshire, Bewdley, Presteigne, Wigmore, and Ludlow. He was adamant that his attendance in the marches was necessary, and thus often required his absence from parliament and convocation.

A popular tradition developed which branded Lee as a hanging judge—the Welsh chronicler Elis Gruffudd believed that the bishop had 5000 felons executed within the space of six years. Even the Lichfield chronicle claimed: *Iste Marchiam latrociniis purgavit* ('he purged the marches of brigands'; Wharton, 1.456). Even though these are obvious exaggerations they illustrate the power of Lee's reputation. Lee saw the theft of livestock as a major problem, and this is reflected in his favourite aphorisms, such as 'Wales is redacte to that state that oone thief taketh another, and oone cowe kepith an other' (SP 1/101, fol. 120), and the Shrewsbury chronicle's note of his claim that 'he wold macke the whyte sheepe keepe the blacke' (Leighton, 19). Lee's council eagerly punished notorious or persistent offenders like Lewis Gethyn and his associates, 'the most erraint & valyaint theves of all Wales', who were executed in August 1535 (SP 1/95, fol. 140), and its president was also determined to obtain justice for those felons who had escaped his jurisdiction. On 6 January 1535 Lee asked Cromwell to send him 'that greate rebellyon and outlawe' David Lloyd, and his accomplice Richard Hokulton, who had fled from Wales to Westminster (SP 1/101, fol. 20). And when he received the men, they were 'sent to ther triall according to Justice, which tomorowe they shall receyve (god pardon their sowles)' (ibid., fol. 122). He was also determined to punish members of the gentry involved in criminal activities, since the 'hanging of oone suche shulde cause fforty to take example to beware' (ibid., fol. 215). However, harshness was not the only characteristic of his regime, and Lee could show himself well aware of the factors that could lead people into crime. On

18 November 1535 he wrote that 'this skarsenes of grayne which riseth dayly here causeth no small roboryes in Wales' (SP 1/87, fol. 42). He was active in securing pardons for felons, especially if they had provided information on other malefactors, and this policy won approval and was advocated for Ireland in 1601.

Lee's preconceptions concerning Welsh and marcher society were intensified by his experience of law enforcement there, as he showed in 1536, when the government at Westminster proposed that the special privileges of the marcher lordships be abolished and a county administration, with justices of the peace, be constructed for the whole of Wales. Lee objected, claiming that 'there be very ffewe welshemen in Wales above Breknock that maye dispende ten pounde lande, and to saye truthe their discretion lesse then their landes' (SP 1/102, fol. 149). Yet despite Lee's comments on the people he governed there were exceptions to his general perceptions, since he clearly favoured some individual Welshmen. He petitioned for a John ap Rice to be taken into royal service, and greatly valued Sir Richard Herbert's support on the council in the marches. In any case, Lee's animadversions were not restricted to Welshmen, for when he wrote to Cromwell on 21 May 1538 his comments on Cheshire were as damning as those he sometimes uttered about Wales, asserting that 'I am sure more murders and manslaughters are done in Chesshire and the borders of the same within this yere, then in all Wales thiese ij yeres' (SP 1/132, fol. 153).

Rowland Lee died in January 1543, probably on the 25th, though the 24th, 27th, and 28th are also recorded. There is no evidence that he ever married. He was buried in St Chad's collegiate church, Shrewsbury, 'before the high aulter there under a toombe of marble stone' (Leighton, 19). The tomb was moved in 1720 to facilitate access to the altar. A man with a complex, even ambiguous, personality, Lee was perceived at his death as essentially an administrator with strongly conservative views on the governance of Wales. His conservatism also applied to his religion. Yet while he could be a harsh punisher of crime he could also show compassion and understanding to others, and although he showed little fervour for the new learning, in January 1539 he was reported to have wanted Coventry Cathedral to become a college of learned men for preaching. If the single-mindedness of his work for the council in the marches has masked his views on religious change, maybe that was because Lee himself preferred it that way. Perhaps he is best regarded as a conventional man of his time, as long as that judgement is applied not only to his training and career, but also to his relations with his associates and his family. It is his dealings with his kinsfolk that above all else add a human dimension to the personality of the hanging judge, a personality that still attracts both praise and criticism from commentators on Tudor Wales. MICHAEL A. JONES

Sources PRO, state papers, Henry VIII (SP 1) • BL, Cotton MSS • *LP Henry VIII*, vols. 1–18 • register of Archbishop Thomas Cranmer, LPL • [H. Wharton], ed., *Anglia sacra*, 2 vols. (1691); facs. edn (1969) [incl. Litchfield chronicle] • registers of Geoffrey Blythe and Rowland Lee, Lichfield joint RO, B/A/1/14, microfilm • M. A. Jones, '"An earthly beast, a mole and an enemy to all godly learning": the life and career of Rowland Lee, bishop of Coventry and Lichfield, and lord president of the council in the marches of Wales, *c*.1487–1543', MPhil diss., U. Wales, Cardiff, 1998 • treasurer of receipt, miscellaneous books, PRO, E 36 • inquisition post mortem, PRO, E 150/1047 • will, PRO, PROB 11/30 • chapter act book, 1521–75, Lichfield joint RO, D/3/2/1/4 • deeds of St Thomas's Priory, Stafford, Staffs. RO, D938 • *The institution of a Christian man* (1537) • R. Tresswell and A. Vincent, *The visitation of Shropshire, taken in the year 1623*, ed. G. Grazebrook and J. P. Rylands, 2 vols., Harleian Society, 28–9 (1889) • S. M. Leathes and others, eds., *Grace books*, 5 vols., Cambridge Antiquarian Society, Luard Memorial Series 1 (1897–1910) • W. A. Leighton, ed., *Early chronicles of Shrewsbury, 1372–1603* (1880) • J. Caley and J. Hunter, eds., *Valor ecclesiasticus temp. Henrici VIII*, 6 vols., RC (1810–34) • D. Lewis, 'The court of the president in the council of Wales and the marches from 1478 to 1575', *Y Cymmrodor*, 12 (1897), 1–64 [includes Elis Gruffudd's and Dr David Lewis's comments on Lee] • D. L. Thomas, 'Further notes on the court of the marches', *Y Cymmrodor*, 13 (1899), 97–163 [includes William Gerard's comments on Lee] • *Fasti Angl., 1300–1541*, [Coventry] • *Fasti Angl., 1300–1541*, [York] • *Fasti Angl., 1300–1541*, [Lincoln]

Archives Lichfield Joint RO, episcopal register | BL, Cotton MSS • PRO, state papers, letters and papers of the reign of Henry VIII, incl. letters to Thomas Cromwell, SP 1

Wealth at death Lee's grange valued at £208 5*s*. 2*d*. in 1543: Staffs. RO, deeds of St Thomas's Priory, D938/29

Lee, Samuel (1625?–1691), nonconformist minister and natural philosopher, was born in London, the only son of Samuel Lee (*d*. in or after 1669), a pious and prosperous haberdasher of Fish Street Hill. Anthony Wood recorded his birth date as 1625, but he may have been the Samuel Lee, son of Samuel, baptized at St Leonard Eastcheap on 29 August 1627. He was educated at St Paul's School, London, and in 1647 was admitted to Magdalen Hall, Oxford. On 14 April 1648 he was granted an MA by the parliamentary visitors, who on 3 October appointed him a fellow of Wadham College, where he immediately became bursar. Serving again as bursar in 1650 and 1654, Lee improved record keeping in the college, and remained there despite being recommended in January 1650 for a fellowship at All Souls. He was elected a junior proctor of the university for 1651, the visitors granting him a dispensation for the office as he was not yet of sufficient standing. In 1652 he was sub-warden of Wadham, and in 1653 dean. The following year the visitors, noting Lee's absence from the college, instructed him to return. He preached frequently in the Oxford area, but on 27 July 1655, at the urging of Oliver Cromwell, he reluctantly became rector of St Botolph without Bishopsgate, London. He did not resign his fellowship until 1657, and left his rectory some time before 30 August 1659, when he preached to the council of state, although he continued as a lecturer at nearby St Helen's. At an unknown date he married, perhaps Martha, the wife who survived him.

During his Oxford years Lee wrote *Orbis miraculum, or, The Temple of Solomon* (1659), dedicated to the warden and fellows of Wadham, a learned and amply illustrated description of the Jewish temple and its ornaments, priesthood, and ceremonies, interpreted typologically as foreshadowing Christianity. Edmund Calamy and Cotton Mather attributed to Lee *De excidio Antichristi*, a tract on Revelation otherwise unknown and not to be confused with a book of similar title by Edward Leigh. Anthony Wood's assertion that Lee also wrote *Chronicon Cestrense*, a work on Cheshire published as part of *The Vale-Royall of England* (1656), and the additions appended to the chronology of Christopher Helvicus's *Theatrum historicum* in the Oxford editions of 1651 and 1662, seems mistaken owing to the pro-episcopal and anti-Reformation sentiments expressed in the works.

Being without preferment at the Restoration, Lee was not, as Calamy supposed, ejected. For a time he retired to his property at Bignal, near Bicester, Oxfordshire. While at Wadham he had acquired an interest in the new science cultivated there under Wilkins; it was shared with his friend Charles Morton, and evident in his writings. He praised Francis Bacon and thought that old theories would be overthrown by experimentation; he was familiar with the scientific work of Descartes, Francis van Helmont, Robert Hooke, William Harvey, and Robert Boyle. This formed the backdrop to his being issued on 23 April 1666 with a licence to go to America, the Caribbean, or 'other western parts' (*Calamy rev.*, 321) to investigate natural rarities.

Wilkins's urgings to Lee to conform to the Church of England had less effect. He eventually returned to London, where he participated in the congregation of John Owen, whom he had known at Oxford, and preached to dissenting congregations. Although his associations were especially with learned Independents, whose congregational outlook he shared, it was as a presbyterian, living in Newington Green, Middlesex, that he was licensed in 1672 under the declaration of indulgence. He continued to publish works of edification. His *Contemplations on Mortality* (1669) had been dedicated to his father and intended to encourage him in old age. He contributed a discourse denying the infallibility of popes and councils to *The Morning Exercise Against Popery* (1675), and 'How to manage secret prayer' to Samuel Annesley's *Supplement to the Morning-Exercise at Criple-Gate* (1676). *Eleothriambos, or, The Triumph of Mercy* (1677) declared that God's mercies come when least expected, while *Ecclesia gemens* (1677) reflected on God's use of persecution to reprove his saints while anticipating God's justice against persecutors. Lee's sermon 'What means may be used towards the conversion of our carnal relations?', printed in *The Morning-Exercise at Cripple-Gate* (1677), offered advice on raising godly children. *Israel redux, or, The Restauration of Israel* (1677), introduced by Lee, printed for the first time two treatises by Giles Fletcher (1549–1611), ambassador to Russia, in which the Caspian Tartars were identified as descendants of the lost tribes of Israel. Lee avowed they would eventually return to their homeland, in accordance with biblical prophecy.

Following the death on 12 October 1677 of John Rowe, Lee published thirty of his sermons and replaced him as joint pastor with Theophilus Gale of the Independent congregation in Holborn, London. When Gale too died in February 1679, Lee became pastor of the congregational meeting in Newington Green. A timorous man, according to Calamy, with the accession of James II he feared the overthrow of protestantism. By 3 December 1685, when he made his will, he was living as a gentleman in Abbots Langley, Hertfordshire, with his wife, Martha, and four daughters under twenty-one, Rebecca, Anna, Lydia, and Elizabeth. On 24 June 1686 he sailed with his wife and daughters from Gravesend to New England, arriving in Boston on 22 August. He was well received, preached on notable occasions, and was lionized for his learning. Cotton Mather, who married as his third wife Lee's daughter Lydia (*d.* 1734), remarked that 'hardly a more universally learned person trod on the American strand' (C. Mather, *Magnalia Christi Americana*, 1852, 1.602) and drew extensively on Lee for his never published 'Biblia Americana'. Lee also played an important role in disseminating scientific knowledge to the new world; while in correspondence with the London botanist Nehemiah Grew he discoursed on American flora and fauna, and speculated that the Native Americans had derived from the Tartars and the Phoenicians. On 10 April 1687 he became pastor of the newly organized congregational church in Bristol, Rhode Island. That year he published two works in Boston, *The Joy of Faith*, which discussed the limits of reason, and *The Great Day of Judgement*, a sermon preached at Bristol assizes.

After the revolution of 1688 Lee decided to return to England. Ezra Stiles later recorded that Lee had been mortified by one daughter marrying a servant and another daughter someone who had deceived her about his fortune. He left Boston on 2 October 1691, but his ship was captured by a French privateer and taken to St Malo in Brittany. His wife and a daughter were sent to England, but Lee remained there as a prisoner, and sickened with fever. He died near the end of December and was buried in the heretics' burial-ground at St Malo. He left a considerable estate to his widow and daughters, and a library containing not only theological works and classical texts but also many books of medicine, physics, and chemistry. These scientific works remained in New England.

DEWEY D. WALLACE, JUN.

Sources *Calamy rev.*, 321 • Wood, *Ath. Oxon.*, new edn, 4.345–8 • R. B. Gardiner, ed., *The registers of Wadham College, Oxford*, 1 (1889), 172–3 • *DNB* • *The nonconformist's memorial … originally written by … Edmund Calamy*, ed. S. Palmer, [3rd edn], 1 (1802), 104–6 • G. L. Kittredge, ed., *Letters of Samuel Lee and Samuel Sewall relating to New England and the Indians* (1912) • 'Dr Stiles's account of the Reverend Samuel Lee', *Publications of the Massachusetts Historical Society* (1864–5), 219–20 • T. Hornberger, 'Samuel Lee (1625–1691), a clerical channel for the flow of new ideas to seventeenth-century New England', *Osiris*, 1 (1936), 341–55 • *The library of the late reverend and learned Mr. Samuel Lee* (1693) • *CSP col.*, 5.379, 485 • *CSP dom.*, 1655, 226, 254 • W. B. Sprague, *Annals of the American pulpit*, 1 (1859), 209–10 • *The diary of Samuel Sewall, 1674–1729: newly edited from the manuscript at the Massachusetts Historical Society*, ed. M. H. Thomas, 2 vols. (1973), vol. 1, pp. 120, 123, 127, 129, 131, 139, 177–8, 258, 279, 287 • will, PRO, PROB 11/409, sig. 70 • *IGI* [parish register of St Leonard, Eastcheap]

Wealth at death left property to wife and books to daughters; books were sold in New England: will, PRO, PROB 11/409, sig. 70

Lee, Samuel (1783–1852), orientalist, was born on 14 May 1783 at Longnor, a Shropshire village 8 miles south of

Shrewsbury, the youngest of eleven children, of poor parents. What is known of Lee's early life comes from a letter he wrote on 26 April 1813 to his benefactor, Jonathan Scott of Shrewsbury, who had been Persian secretary to Warren Hastings.

After receiving some elementary education at the village charity school at Longnor, Lee was apprenticed at the age of twelve to a Shrewsbury carpenter and joiner. He was fond of reading, and some Latin quotations which he saw in the houses he visited led him at seventeen to buy a *Ruddiman's Latin Grammar* at a bookstall and to learn it by heart. At first his wage was only 6*s*. per week, but he would buy a book, sell it, and buy another, and in this way he read all the standard Latin authors. In the same way, and encouraged by Scott, he managed to learn Greek and Hebrew, and before he was twenty-five had made progress in Chaldee, Syriac, Samaritan, Persian, and Hindustani.

Lee married at twenty-five, and discontinued his studies in order to increase his earnings from his trade, but the accidental loss of his tools in a burning house soon obliged him to seek a new, remunerative career, and, with the help of Archdeacon Corbett, he became teacher in Bowdler's foundation school, Shrewsbury. At the same time he gave private lessons in Persian and Hindustani. His talents were brought to the notice of the Church Missionary Society, and under its auspices he entered Queens' College, Cambridge, early in 1814, learning the mathematics required in two weeks. He graduated BA in 1818 and was soon afterwards ordained. He proceeded MA in 1819 (by special royal mandate), BD in 1827, and DD in 1833. He is said to have become, eventually, master of eighteen languages. In March 1819 he became professor of Arabic in the University of Cambridge, in 1823 chaplain of Cambridge gaol, and in 1825 rector of Bilton-with-Harrogate, Yorkshire. In 1831 he was appointed regius professor of Hebrew in the university, and retained the post until 1848. In 1831 he became a canon of Bristol Cathedral, and vicar of Banwell, Somerset, a living he held until June 1838, when he resigned it and became rector of Barley, Hertfordshire.

Lee's linguistic genius was shown in a prodigious scholarly output. He edited the New Testament in Syriac in 1816, and the Old Testament in Malay (1817–18) and in Syriac (1823). He also produced editions of the psalter and gospels in Arabic and Coptic, of Genesis and the New Testament in Persian, and of the New Testament in Hindustani. In addition to this, he superintended the publication of the prayer book in Hindustani, and wrote a history of the Abyssinian and Syrian churches. In 1821 he issued a *Sylloge librorum orientalium*, presenting various treatises on oriental literature, and a letter to J. Bellamy censuring his translation of the Bible. In 1823 he edited Sir William Jones's Persian grammar, and in 1827 issued a grammar of Hebrew (6th edn, 1844). 'Six sermons on the study of the Holy Scriptures' (1830) defended conservative orthodoxy against German rationalism and dealt with the interpretation of prophecy. In 1831 Lee wrote the Latin prolegomena to Bagster's polyglot Bible. In 1829 appeared *The Travels of Ibn Batuta*, translated from the Arabic (cf. *Blackwood's Magazine*, 49, 592). In 1833 a sermon entitled 'The duty of observing the Christian sabbath' maintained that our Sunday is the same day of the week as the original sabbath.

Lee was a dedicated pastor and preacher, with a buoyant temperament and a taste for vigorous, but amicable polemic. From an evangelical Anglican position he conducted a long controversy with Dr John Pye Smith on dissent, and contested Dr Pusey's views on the eucharist. In 1837 he published his translation of Job; in 1840 a lexicon, *Hebrew, Chaldee, and English*; in 1842 an edition, and in 1843 a translation, of the *Theophania* of Eusebius; in 1849 *An Inquiry into the Nature, Progress, and End of Prophecy*; and in 1851 an investigation of the visions in Daniel and St John.

Lee's first wife died when their children were still young, and in 1829 his only son died, aged seventeen, of consumption. A second wife died in 1837 at Banwell, Somerset, and on 9 September 1840, when his daughters were either married, or about to be so, he married his third wife, Anne Jenkins, daughter of the Revd Stiverd Jenkins of the old manor house at Locking, who survived him. Lee died on 16 December 1852 at the rectory at Barley, Hertfordshire, and was buried in a vault of the church.

THOMAS HAMILTON, *rev.* JOHN D. HAIGH

Sources A. M. Lee, *A scholar of a past generation: a brief memoir of Samuel Lee, D.D. … by his daughter* (1896) • *GM*, 2nd ser., 39 (1853), 203 • T. H. Horne, *An introduction to the critical study and knowledge of the Holy Scriptures*, 9th edn, 5 (1846) • Boase, *Mod. Eng. biog.* • Ward, *Men of the reign* • W. C. Taylor, *The national portrait gallery of illustrious and eminent personages, chiefly of the nineteenth century: with memoirs*, 4 vols. in 2 [1846–8] • *The Jewish Chronicle, 1841–1941: a century of newspaper history*, Jewish Chronicle (1949), 56 • d. cert. • *IGI*

Archives Shrops. RRC, letters to Jonathan Scott and others • Yale U., Beinecke L., letters to T. S. Pettigrew

Likenesses J. Thompson, stipple, pubd 1821 (after J. Gooch, 1821), NPG • W. T. Fry, stipple, 1846 (after R. Evans), BM, NPG; repro. in W. Jerdan, *National portrait gallery of illustrious and eminent personages*, 4 (1833) • attrib. R. Evans, oils, Trinity Cam.

Lee [*née* Wallis; *other married name* Bowdich]**, Sarah** (**1791–1856**), naturalist and author, was born on 10 September 1791 in Colchester, Essex, the third of four children and the only daughter of John Eglonton Wallis (*c*.1766–1833), grocer and linen-draper, and Sarah (*c*.1770–1839), daughter of Edward Snell (*c*.1744–1786) and his wife, Ann Wood (*c*.1750–1772). Her parents were nonconformists and owned considerable property. She learned to ride and fish, and enjoyed exploring the countryside.

Sarah Wallis's father went bankrupt in 1802, and later (probably in 1806 or 1807) moved the family to London. There Sarah met Thomas Edward *Bowdich (1791?–1824), whom she married on 9 January 1813. Soon afterwards the couple travelled more than 800 miles through Wales on horseback, studying foreign languages as they rode. In 1814 Thomas Bowdich secured a writership in the service of the Royal African Company; he was commissioned nearly a year later, and sailed to Cape Coast Castle in late 1815. Sarah Bowdich followed in 1816 with the couple's new-born daughter, Florence; along the way she caught a shark and helped to put down a mutiny. On her arrival in

September 1816 she found that her husband had temporarily gone back to England. While awaiting his return she made observations of the local culture and natural history, but she and her baby caught fever, from which Florence died. After her husband's return and successful inland expedition to the Asante, the Bowdichs sailed for England in February 1818. *En route* they stopped at Gabon, where they studied local flora and fauna. Sarah Bowdich's eighteen months in Africa established her as the first European woman ever to collect plants systematically in tropical west Africa.

In early 1819 the Bowdichs moved to Paris to study natural science in preparation for a second African expedition. Well received by the savants of the Institut de France, they became protégés of the eminent naturalist Georges Cuvier, who treated them like members of his family, allowing them the run of his collections and library. Sarah Bowdich, a regular at Cuvier's salons, was described as 'a sylph' and having a 'veritably angelic character'.

To support themselves the Bowdichs published several English translations of French texts between 1820 and 1822. Sarah Bowdich illustrated the books and prepared one volume, *Taxidermy* (1820), entirely on her own. By virtue of her zoological and botanical knowledge she was elected on 15 March 1820 an honorary member of the Wetterauische Gesellschaft für die Gesamte Naturkunde zu Hanau am Main, a membership she later publicized on the title-pages of her books. While in Paris the Bowdichs had three children, of whom two survived: Edward Hope Smith and Tedlie Hutchison. In midsummer 1822 the family left for Africa, stopping briefly at Lisbon and then spending fifteen months in Madeira, where they studied the island's natural history and where a daughter, Eugenia Keir, was born. Soon after arriving at Bathurst on the Gambia in November 1823 Thomas Bowdich caught fever; he died on 10 January 1824.

Penniless, stranded in Africa, and with three children to support, Sarah Bowdich set out to make a career of her art in natural history. Arriving back in London in mid-1824 she found that friends had taken up a collection for her support. By the next year she had prepared and published her husband's last manuscript, *Excursions in Madeira and Porto Santo*, adding three appendices of her own based on her experiences at Bathurst. Most significantly, however, her original descriptions of new species and genera of fish, birds, and plants, evaluated by Cuvier, established her as the first woman known to have discovered whole new genera of plants. Between 1824 and 1830 she often visited the Jardin des Plantes in Paris to consult with Cuvier. She also carried out errands for him and other leading scientists, among them the botanist Robert Brown and the Quaker physician Thomas Hodgkin, who had become her close friend in 1824.

The publisher Rudolph Ackermann persuaded Sarah Bowdich to write a story about Africa for his *Forget-me-Not* for 1826, an annual gift book to which she contributed until 1844. At about the same time, Lord de Tabley and William Pickering induced her to take up the project for which she is perhaps best remembered, *The Fresh Water Fishes of Great Britain*. The work, printed for fifty subscribers, appeared between 1828 and 1837. Each copy consisted of text and forty-eight individually hand-painted plates, appearing in twelve fascicules of four plates each. The book reflected Sarah Bowdich's exemplary command of both science and art; drawn from living specimens, the fidelity and lifelike quality of its illustrations were unique for their time. Now highly valued as a rare book, some of its observations were still of interest to scientists in the 1950s. While engaged in its production Sarah Bowdich contributed twelve articles to the *Magazine of Natural History*, wrote stories for the annual gift books, and reared her three children. Until late 1829 she continued to establish her career as Mrs Bowdich, only then revealing the secret that she had married Robert Lee, an assize clerk, on 29 July 1826.

Following Cuvier's death in 1832, Sarah Lee branched into biography with *Memoirs of Baron Cuvier* (1833), long the authoritative biography of Cuvier in English. In 1838–9 she interrupted her writing career to nurse her mother through her last illness. Having thereby suffered considerable loss of income, she then entered on her most prolific period of writing. Between 1840 and 1856 she published seventeen books and five short stories (both fiction and non-fiction), for both children and adults. Although well received her fiction was undistinguished, though her natural history ranked among the best informed and most popular. Her three most successful works were *Elements of Natural History* (1844), *Anecdotes of the Habits and Instinct of Animals* (1852), and *Anecdotes of the Habits of Birds, Reptiles and Fishes* (1853). The first of these, like *Taxidermy*, was on the privy council list of class books for national education; the last two were popular works for adults.

Sarah Lee also continued with her drawing, exhibiting at the 1843 summer exhibition of the Royal Academy of Art. It appears that she also occasionally painted plants and flowers for sale. In 1854 the government recognized her service as a popularizer of natural history by the award of a civil-list pension of £50. In all, she had published twenty-one books, twenty-two short stories, and twelve articles. From early 1856 she suffered increasingly poor health, and moved from London to her daughter Eugenia's house at George's Terrace, Erith, Kent, where she died of heart disease on 23 September 1856. She was probably buried in the churchyard of Old St Pancras Church, London. DONALD DEB. BEAVER

Sources Mrs. R. Lee [S. Lee], *Stories of strange lands* (1835) • *DNB* • private information (2004) [W. Klein] • T. E. Bowdich, *Mission from Cape Coast Castle to Ashantee*, 3rd edn (1966) • J. Bensusan-Butts, *Biographical dictionary of eighteenth century Colchester* [forthcoming] • Royal Literary Fund archives, files 465, 1414 • D. J. Mabberley, 'Edward and Sarah Bowdich's names of Macaronesian and African plants, with notes on those of Robert Brown', *Botanica Macaronesica*, 6 (1978), 53–66 • Mrs. R. Lee [S. Lee], *Taxidermy*, 6th edn (1843), preface • baptisms, Lion Walk Church, Colchester, 1785–1828, Essex RO • d. cert. • parish register (marriages), 29 July 1826, London, St Pancras • H. G. Adams, ed., *A cyclopaedia of female biography* (1857) • *The Field* (31 Dec 1887), 985 • *The Field* (14 Jan 1888), 53 • *GM*, 3rd ser., 1 (1856), 653–4 • *Literary Gazette* (11 Oct 1856), 784

Archives Duke U., medical library, papers relating to Africa · Musée de l'Histoire Naturelle, Paris, corresp. · RS | NHM, Robert Brown MSS

Lee, Sir Sidney (1859–1926), second editor of the *Dictionary of National Biography* and literary scholar, was born Solomon Lazarus Lee at 12 Keppel Street, Bloomsbury, London, on 5 December 1859, the elder son of Lazarus Lee, merchant, and his wife, Jessie Davis. He had a younger brother and four sisters, of whom the eldest of the family, Elizabeth *Lee, was a contributor to the *Dictionary of National Biography* and to its epitome, and a writer of textbooks and a translator from German. Although Jewish by upbringing Lee was not in adult life a practising member of his family's religion.

Lee was educated at the City of London School, then in Milk Street, Cheapside, under the headmastership of Dr Edwin Abbott, where (unusually for the time) there was a tradition of teaching English literature. In April 1871 Lee was awarded the Beaufoy prize for an essay on Shakespeare, starting early on a lifelong commitment to Shakespearian study. Among his school contemporaries were the Elizabethan scholar A. H. Bullen and the essayist (and later dean of Norwich) H. C. Beeching, both of whom remained his friends. Lee matriculated at Oxford as a commoner of Balliol College in October 1878. In November 1879 he was *proxime accessit* for the Brackenbury (history) scholarship, and was awarded a compensatory exhibition. He was placed in the third class of classical moderations in 1880, and in the second class of modern history finals in 1882, graduating BA in the same year. His college contemporaries acknowledged his erudition in one of the *Balliol Rhymes* (attributed to Beeching):

I am featly-tripping L-E
Learned in modern history,
My gown, the wonder of beholders
Hangs like a footnote from my shoulders.
(W. G. Hiscock, *Balliol Rhymes*, 1955, 13)

Two articles on Shakespearian themes written as an undergraduate, contributed to the *Gentleman's Magazine* in 1880, had attracted attention from established scholars, not least from F. J. Furnivall, whose encouragement of this undergraduate prodigy proved particularly valuable. He arranged a commission for Lee to edit Lord Berners's translation of *The Boke of Huon of Burdeux* for the Early English Text Society (the four volumes appeared between 1882 and 1887). Another editorial project at this time was the autobiography of Edward, Lord Herbert of Cherbury (1886; rev. edn, 1906). Lee had also during his time at Oxford provided some research assistance to Frederic Seebohm for his *The English Village Community* (1883).

The *Dictionary of National Biography* After graduating Lee took a temporary post with the earl of Portsmouth, tutoring his son the Hon. Oliver Wallop (later eighth earl), a Balliol undergraduate, at Eggesford, Devon, in autumn 1882. At that time Leslie Stephen had been asked by the publisher George Smith to plan 'A New Biographia Britannica', and was seeking a sub-editor whom he described as 'a man of knowledge, good at abstracting, looking up authorities and so forth, and an efficient whip

Sir Sidney Lee (1859–1926), by Frederick Hollyer

in regard both to printers and contributors' (Stephen to Edmund Gosse, 14 November 1882, U. Leeds, Brotherton L.). Furnivall urged Lee to apply, writing to Stephen, introducing his protégé in November 1882 as 'Sidney L. Lee of Balliol'. (Lee's application to Stephen is, like all his letters at the time, even to his mother, signed 'S. L. Lee', but he matriculated and graduated in his given names; his adoption of the name 'Sidney' instead of 'Solomon' was reputedly due to the advice of Benjamin Jowett, master of his college; Lee used 'Sidney Lee' *tout court* generally after about 1890.) Jowett wrote to Stephen commending 'a young man of excellent character and considerable abilities. He is very industrious and possesses a wide range of knowledge' (Bodl. Oxf., MS Eng. misc. d. 175). This magisterial commendation proved very accurate.

'He is free for any kind of work in your line, in Dec[emb]er', Furnivall wrote in a breezier style; 'You'd find him a good helper' (Bodl. Oxf., MS don. e. 121, fol. 80). Lee, who had been offered a newly established professorship of English at the University of Groningen, was appointed to the dictionary staff from March 1883 'to do literary and editorial work at Stephen's bidding', as he described it, at a salary of 'the preposterous sum of £300 per annum' (Firth, 'Sir Sidney Lee', 4). From the start editor and subeditor complemented each other nicely. Stephen later paid tribute to Lee's calmness and efficiency (in *Some Early Impressions*, reprinted in 1924), and his deputy's editorial skill made a decisive contribution to the immediate success and enduring reputation of the work. At the outset Stephen's own literary and editorial experience enabled him to commission authors and assign subjects, and Lee's taste for detail and appetite for checking and proof-reading ensured a high standard of editorial control. Stephen's special experience in eighteenth- and nineteenth-century literature was complemented by Lee's Elizabethan knowledge; Stephen made his main object the gathering and concise restatement of known information, but Lee was more willing to admit fresh material. Editor and deputy were at one in reducing verbosity and literary ornament (the 'no flowers, by request' principle, in Alfred Ainger's phrase), but Lee was allowed to find many opportunities to insert additional facts, provide copious bibliographical detail, and revise lists of authorities. Stephen was the first to concede that Lee

> had more aptitude for many parts of the work than I can boast of, for there were moments at which my gorge rose against the unappetizing, but I sorrowfully admit the desirable, masses of minute information which I had to insert. I improved a little under the antiquarian critics who cried for more concessions to Dryasdust, but Mr Lee had no such defect of sympathy to overcome. (L. Stephen, *Some Early Impressions*, 1924, 160)

Lee's 820 articles for the *Dictionary of National Biography*, which included a great many on minor subjects of all periods, ranged from lives of Elizabethan literary figures such as Roger Ascham to the much praised long account of Queen Victoria which rounded off both the era and the series. Even more important than his actual contributions, perhaps, was his businesslike determination that made such a success of the project. Lee had a special role in harrying delinquent contributors, and could on occasion be unduly sharp. He directed the enterprise with a punctuality that assured regular quarterly publication and kept the subscribers satisfied.

Stephen's industriousness was of a different temper, and he exhausted himself on the dictionary. The early volumes appeared on schedule with strong editorial involvement, efficiently handled in a way that led Stephen to feel he could take on other commitments, partly to provide him with relief from some of the more mechanical tasks that fell to the editor. Stephen's additional tasks included the inaugural Clark lectures in English literature at Trinity College, Cambridge, and he also felt bound, when his friend Henry Fawcett died in 1884, to write his biography. Prolonged overwork led to his collapse in autumn 1889. Mrs Stephen was alarmed and privately consulted Lee, who responded with tact and sympathy. The proprietor, George Smith, arranged for the editorship to be shared, so that volume 21 of the original edition was the first to bear both Stephen's and Lee's names. Furnivall, Lee's original sponsor, wrote again that 'It is a great honour … and has been won by your brain, work, and tact', adding 'Meantime, don't let Publishers tempt you to do other books. The Dict'll take all the steam you can put into it' (Bodl. Oxf., MS Eng. misc. d. 175). The senior editor's health did not improve greatly, and Lee was recognized as sole editor from volume 27 to volume 63. Stephen was able to contribute many further articles but was glad to be relieved of the burden of administrative control.

As the central editorial team expanded Lee drove it well but hard, working very long hours at evenings and weekends. With assistants like C. L. Kingsford, Thomas Seccombe, and later A. F. Pollard (from 1893) and E. I. Carlyle (from 1896), the office at 14 Waterloo Place became increasingly scholarly in composition. William Hunt wrote to Lee in 1911 that 'I and the others learnt a lot from our editors—sometimes by more or less painful experience, but the breaking in is over and the value of the lessons remains' (Bodl. Oxf., MS Eng. misc. d. 177, fol. 455). The assistants were enjoined to spend three hours at the British Museum each morning, and four hours at Waterloo Place each afternoon, without any tea break (which they much resented), and there was evening proof-reading work when necessary. By 1895 it had proved necessary to expand the dictionary's overall length from fifty to sixty volumes, not least as coverage in individual articles expanded through improvements in technique. Lee, with his own zeal for adding to knowledge, was able to persuade his proprietor that this was essential. 'You see', as Sir Charles Firth once put it simply, 'we all of us know so much more than we did when we began' (Pollard, 7).

Smith sponsored various periodic dinners for the contributors, which helped to emphasize collegiality among the central core of outside authors. The completion of the main work in June 1900 was a matter for public celebration, with civic banquets and regal compliments, all fully deserved. Stephen, elderly and increasingly deaf, found such ceremonies wearying, but Lee and Smith were suitably pleased. In May 1900 the prince of Wales attended a dinner party in their honour. A characteristic piece of dialogue was remembered: 'I hear you write about Shakespeare, Mr Lee.' 'Yes … ah … Yes. Yes, sir.' 'Stick to it, Mr Lee, stick to it. There's money in Shakespeare, Mr Lee' (D. Chapman-Huston, *The Lost Historian: a Memoir of Sir Sidney Low*, 1936, 213). The royal remark foreshadowed Lee's increasing involvement with matters Shakespearian.

As for the dictionary, there remained the problem of supplementation, to cover those (about 200 in all) who had been accidentally omitted from the main work, and the much larger constituency (about 800) who had died while the project was under way. By the time the supplement taking the dictionary up to 31 December 1900 was being planned Lee had both personally and through his editorship acquired an authority that enabled him to commission judiciously a series of authoritative articles on the recently dead. The obvious chronological terminus of the century had to be altered when Queen Victoria died on 22 January 1901. Smith, who himself died on 6 April 1901 (and in his will left Lee £500), had specially invited Lee to write the queen's life for the dictionary (and it also fell to him to write the entry for Smith, at his widow's particular behest).

'Private information; personal knowledge', the source list which concludes so many supplement entries for the following century, applied very well to Lee on Smith, where he had both the advantage of access to a private memoir and nearly two decades of work on one of the publisher's cherished projects. The same formula could in no way be applied to the queen-empress within a few months of her decease. Yet despite all the difficulties posed by prolonged reginal seclusion, defensive secretiveness on the part of courtiers, and the absence of personal documentation—especially for the latter part of the queen's life—Lee produced what for a virtual obituary notice is a highly satisfactory memoir. He could boast of having stated facts accurately, and to have respected both public interest and private feeling. The article, which runs to over 220 columns of the supplement, and has been calculated as containing 93,785 words, is structurally a sound piece of work, and in the circumstances was a truly remarkable feat. As A. F. Pollard remarked, 'Queen Victoria … ran to double the length of Shakespeare, though in her case bibliographical detail was as scanty as biographical was in Shakespeare's' (Pollard, 11). Revised to provide more detail and background commentary than the dictionary notice allowed it was published as a book in 1902 and a fourth edition came out in 1907. Although it did not adapt particularly well to book format it was the first serious attempt to present the queen's public and (so far as was then possible) her private life as a whole; fresh in tone though it was, its coverage was necessarily thinner for the second half of her life, where published sources were not available to any useful extent. The result, with some rather textbook-like appendices, was a good deal better than the other mere commemorations that appeared at the time. As the ancient historian J. B. Bury put it in a letter to Lee: 'I congratulate her late Majesty on having fallen so soon into the hands of a critical historian. She has hitherto been exploited by bookmakers and toadies' (Bodl. Oxf., MS Eng. misc. d. 175, fol. 351).

With the dictionary completed the task remained of producing the index and epitome, later known as the concise dictionary (*The Dictionary of National Biography: the Concise Dictionary*). This was published in spring 1903 and soon demonstrated its particular usefulness. It was followed in 1904 by a substantial volume of errata to the main work, presented as a bonus to dictionary subscribers. Necessarily detailed and indigestible this is something of a monument to Lee's meticulousness, which continued long afterwards; his own much annotated set of the original edition was bequeathed to the librarian and staff of the London Library (who deposited it with the project preparing the new edition, the *Oxford Dictionary of National Biography*). The conclusion of the main work, after which Lee was for several years able to turn back to his Shakespeare and Elizabethan studies, marks a point at which it is proper to turn to his work in that field of scholarship.

Shakespeare scholarship Lee's Shakespearian studies had, as mentioned above, begun early. His two *Gentleman's Magazine* articles published as an undergraduate had attracted the attention of established Shakespeare scholars such as J. O. Halliwell-Phillipps and F. J. Furnivall, and through the latter contributed to his appointment as Stephen's assistant on the *Dictionary of National Biography*. The first, 'The original of Shylock' (May 1880), suggested that the reputation of Queen Elizabeth's physician, Rodrigo Lopez, and the excitement provoked by his trial and execution in 1594, had led Shakespeare to a subtler, more complex depiction of a Jewish character than had been attempted by other playwrights. The second (October 1880) drew attention to the topical character of *Love's Labour's Lost*, the connections of characters' names to individuals in the circle of Henry of Navarre, and the play's other allusions to contemporary France. The first article formed the basis of a paper discussing Jewish life in Elizabethan England which Lee read to the New Shakspere Society on 10 February 1888 (*Transactions*, New Shakspere Society, 1887–92, 143). The topicality of Elizabethan drama was developed in two further papers read to the same society on 8 February 1884 and 22 October 1886 (ibid., 1880–86, 80; 1887–92, 1).

Despite his exacting work for the *Dictionary of National Biography*, Lee also maintained his Shakespearian work. His historical study *Stratford-on-Avon from Earliest Times to the Death of Shakespeare*, illustrated with pleasing sketches by Edward Hull, was published in 1885, and the following year he published an edition of the autobiography of Edward, Lord Herbert of Cherbury (1886; rev. edn, 1906). The Stratford history is a full and careful study in which the tradition of Shakespeare's poaching of Sir Thomas Lucy's deer is discussed with due scepticism; nevertheless Lee takes Justice Shallow to be a satirical portrait of Lucy. In an expanded 1890 edition Lee was no longer sceptical about the deer poaching story, and claimed that Shakespeare 'undoubtedly took a subtle revenge' on Lucy by satirizing him as Shallow in *The Merry Wives of Windsor*. Shifts from scepticism to certainty were to characterize much of Lee's literary scholarship.

In July 1897 volume 51 of the *Dictionary of National Biography* was published, containing Lee's first full biographical account of Shakespeare. In previous volumes of the dictionary, in articles on Mary Fitton (1889) and on Mary Herbert, countess of Pembroke, and her son William (both 1891), Lee had allied himself to the 'Pembrokian' party—that is, to the group of scholars who identified the 'Mr. W. H.', to whom *Shakespeare's Sonnets* (1609) were dedicated as their 'ONLIE BEGETTER', as William Herbert, third earl of Pembroke, and the so-called 'Dark Lady' of sonnets 127–52 as his mistress Mary Fitton. Rashly, he had claimed that 'Shakespeare's young friend was doubtless Pembroke himself'. However, by the time he wrote the entry on Shakespeare, Lee had become an equally convinced 'Southamptonite', identifying 'Mr. W. H.' with Henry Wriothesley, second earl of Southampton, to whom Shakespeare's narrative poems had been dedicated in 1593 and 1594. Lee's view of the *Sonnets* had undergone an even more radical transformation, or else he had reached the reluctant conclusion that it was not prudent for an ambitious man of letters to promulgate an image of England's national poet as emotionally devoted to a young nobleman. His abrupt withdrawal from any 'literal' meaning of sonnets 1–126 may have been a delayed response to the trial and imprisonment of Oscar Wilde. In April 1895 Wilde had cited Shakespeare in his own defence against Lord Queensberry's public description of him as a 'somdomite' [*sic*], explicitly equating his own relationship with Lord Alfred Douglas with the love celebrated in the *Sonnets*. By the time that Lee had committed himself in print to his third and final assessment of the *Sonnets*, that they were written entirely as 'literary exercises', Wilde was out of prison and living in France in terminal disgrace (see R. Ellmann, *Oscar Wilde*, 1987, 422 and *passim*).

The vehement prolixity with which Lee promoted his last, 'impersonal', reading of the *Sonnets* in many later writings may reflect continued discomfort on the matter. For the New York edition of the *Dictionary of National Biography*, published late in 1898, he made radical changes to the passage about the *Sonnets* in the Shakespeare entry. In the first, London, edition he had declared confidently that 'Shakespeare's relations with men and women of the court involved him at the outset in emotional conflicts, which form the subject-matter of his "Sonnets"'. The only purely 'artificial' ones, he claimed, are 153 and 154; 'In the rest of the "Sonnets", Shakespeare avows, although in phraseology that is often cryptic, the experiences of his own heart'. But in the New York edition he stated with equal assurance that the *Sonnets* 'seem to have been to a large extent undertaken as literary exercises. His ever-present dramatic instinct may be held to account for most of the illusion of personal confession which they call up in many minds'. Lee never publicly acknowledged that his own mind had been one of those in which, only a few months earlier, the *Sonnets* had appeared to be overwhelmingly 'personal', nor that he had been just as confident—twice—about the identity of the historical originals of Shakespeare's 'fair youth' and 'Dark Lady'. Much of his ensuing study of French and Italian Renaissance poetry, especially the sonnet, seems to have been informed by an almost desperate determination to discover models there for Shakespeare's 'purely literary' devotion to a young male patron.

Meanwhile Lee was also hard at work expanding his *Dictionary of National Biography* article on Shakespeare into the substantial, free-standing *Life of William Shakespeare* that was published in November 1898. This was received with great enthusiasm, going through four editions in two months. It was soon acknowledged as the standard life-and-works study of Shakespeare, full, sensible, and largely accurate in terms of the documents and scholarship then available. Two major twentieth-century scholars, E. K. Chambers and Samuel Schoenbaum, planned to write substantial biographies that would supersede Lee's, but neither in the event did so, each publishing only material towards such a biography rather than the book itself. In practice, Lee's *Life of William Shakespeare* dominated the field for the whole of the twentieth century.

Inevitably Lee's approach was circumscribed by the prudery of the time in which he was writing. For instance, he touches so obliquely on Anne Hathaway's pregnancy at the time of her marriage that an innocent young reader would not understand what was being alluded to, and might perhaps imagine merely that Anne had been seen in the company of young William so much that her social reputation required him to marry her. The orphaned Anne's guardians procured the marriage licence from the bishop of Worcester 'so that Shakespeare might have small opportunity of evading a step which his intimacy with his friends' daughter had rendered essential to her reputation' (Lee, *Shakespeare*, 1898, 22). Likewise his summary of John Manningham's anecdote about Shakespeare outwitting Richard Burbage in enjoying the sexual favours offered by a stage-struck citizen is so delicate that, as Schoenbaum observes, 'one might infer that the lady was entertaining her guests for tea' (ibid., 265; Schoenbaum, 336—see the full and hostile discussion of Lee as biographer of Shakespeare on pp. 367–82).

Nevertheless Lee was prepared to be candid on other matters, such as the tight hold Shakespeare held on money and property. In his chapter 'The practical affairs of life', which underwent numerous revisions, he calculated Shakespeare's annual income 'in the latter period of his life' at what Schoenbaum called the 'preposterously exaggerated' sum of £600, a figure that he revised upwards to £700 in the greatly expanded 1915 edition of the *Life*. Shakespeare's prestige and wealth appear to have improved in step with those of his biographer. Though Schoenbaum was to be scathing about Lee's dull style, 'essential mediocrity of mind' (Schoenbaum, 372), and occasional inaccuracies, his *Life* was hugely influential. For instance, it inspired James Joyce to a sequence of reflections on Shakespeare and his family. In the 'Scylla and Charybdis' section of *Ulysses*, Stephen Dedalus speculates on the date of *Hamlet*, asking 'What does Mr Sidney Lee, or Mr Simon Lazarus as some aver his name is, say of it?' (J. Joyce, *Ulysses: a critical and synoptic edition*, ed. H. W. Gabler, 1984, 1.416–17; see also D. Gifford, *Ulysses Annotated*, 1974, 20.220).

As Lee's employment on the *Dictionary of National Biography* drew to its close in 1900–01, his independent scholarship blossomed. He was Clark lecturer at Trinity College, Cambridge, in 1901–2, made a successful tour through the universities and colleges of the USA in 1903, and in October 1904 published the lectures he had delivered at the Lowell Institute, Boston, as *Great Englishmen of the Sixteenth Century*. His lecturing techniques, at first described as 'diffuse' (*DNB*), evidently improved in later years; and his literary expertise expanded to include careful bibliographical scrutiny of Shakespeare's texts, as well as a thorough investigation of European vernacular literature of the Renaissance. His Clarendon Press facsimile of Shakespeare's *Tragedies, Comedies and Histories*, based on the copy at Chatsworth, was published in 1902. It included an account of the methods by which publishers of the time procured their copy, as well as a discussion of the sources and value of the first folio's unique texts. His analysis of the volume's printing revealed many irregularities and signs of 'hasty and unconsidered arrangement and re-arrangement of the "copy"'. The Renaissance edition of the *Complete Works of William Shakespeare* was handsomely produced in forty volumes by John Murray in 1906–9, with a general introduction and annotation throughout by Lee. Each volume had a frontispiece by a contemporary artist and an individual preface by a contemporary writer. In the case of volume 38, *Sonnets*, the preface was not written by Lee—though he did write five of the other prefaces—but by the poet John Davidson, who found it impossible not to conclude that they 'contain a record essentially honest and sometimes terribly sincere'. The limited University Press edition published in New York in 1907–9 was identical except for being printed on even thicker paper.

Lee's two-volume collection *Elizabethan Sonnets* (1904) is valuable for its inclusion of some obscure sonnet sequences such as Giles Fletcher's *Licia* (1593), Barnabe Barnes's *Parthenophil and Parthenope* (1593), and Bartholomew Griffin's *Fidessa* (1596), but is marred by intrusive punctuation, with an explosion of exclamation marks. Much greater scholarly attention was devoted to edited facsimiles of important Shakespeare quartos for the Clarendon Press: *Hamlet* in 1902, and in 1905 handsomely produced limited editions of *Venus and Adonis*, *Lucrece*, *The Passionate Pilgrim*, *Shakespeare's Sonnets*, and *Pericles*. Each has a full and learned introduction incorporating a detailed account of its publication history and a descriptive census of copies, as well as a full survey of literary sources and analogues. In the case of *Venus and Adonis* this survey extends to poems and plays in Greek, Latin, Italian, French, and Spanish.

In the case of the *Sonnets*, however, Lee abandoned his normally cool, scholarly tone in his obsessive determination to prohibit the 'personal' reading which, only seven years earlier, had been his own: 'a purely literal interpretation of the impassioned protestations of affection for a "lovely boy", which course through the sonnets, casts a slur on the dignity of the poet's name which scarcely bears discussion' (W. Shakespeare, *Shakespeare's Sonnets … Facsimile of the First Edition 1609*, ed. S. Lee, 1905, 11). He also deviated from his habitual caution in bibliographical matters when recounting the career of Thomas Thorpe, publisher of the *Sonnets*, whom he was determined to downgrade to illegal procurer of the precious text: 'he held his own with difficulty for some thirty years in the lowest ranks of the London publishing trade'. According to Lee, Thorpe's publication of the *Sonnets* 'lacked authority, and was pursued throughout in that reckless spirit which infected publishing speculations of the day' (ibid., 29, 40.). (For a contrary view of Thorpe's career see K. Duncan-Jones, 'Was the 1609 *Shake-speares Sonnets* really unauthorized?', *Review of English Studies*, 34, 1983, 151–7). In a comparable, though less agitated, manner Lee was also determined to exonerate Shakespeare from any contact with George Wilkins in the composition of *Pericles*, seeing him working only with Wilkins's 'draft', not in direct association with Wilkins himself (W. Shakespeare, *Shakespeare's Pericles … 1609*, ed. S. Lee, 1905, 13–14).

Further edited facsimiles of Shakespeare quartos followed: *The Merchant of Venice*, *A Midsummer Night's Dream*, *King Lear*, and *The Merry Wives of Windsor*, all printed at Stratford upon Avon in 1908, and an edited facsimile of one source play, *The Chronicle History of King Leir* (1909). His source study was developed further in an article in the *Quarterly Review* (April 1909) on 'Ovid and Shakespeare's sonnets', and more substantially in a course of lectures sponsored by Oxford's Common University Fund in 1909 which formed the basis of his remarkably wide-ranging study, of continuing value, *The French Renaissance in England*.

Continued discomfort on the topic of the *Sonnets* is reflected in Lee's English Association lecture, *The Impersonal Aspect of Shakespeare's Art* (English Association Leaflet, 13, July 1909). Perhaps to the surprise of his audience he decided to consider plays alone: 'I omit the *Sonnets* of malice propense … Personally, I believe that the luxuriance of Shakespeare's dramatic instinct largely dominates that outburst of lyric melody which gives the *Sonnets* their life. That is my personal view'. However, as ever, he found it hard to let the topic go. He drew attention to the central problem, only to sideline it: 'the dominant topic of the *Sonnets*—an absorbing affection for a beautiful youth altogether transcending friendship—finds no place in the plays'. In a long footnote to the printed version he also paid awkward-sounding tribute to recent work on the *Sonnets* by H. C. Beeching, Sir Walter Raleigh, and A. C. Bradley, of whom the first named did view the *Sonnets* as autobiographical.

Other Shakespearian work included Lee's editorial and organizational role in the early stages of the preparation of the two volumes published as *Shakespeare's England*, edited by C. T. Onions (1916); a *Census of Extant Copies of the First Folio*, published as a companion volume to the 1902 facsimile of the Chatsworth copy; an account of fourteen further copies of the first folio (*The Library*, April 1906); *A Shakespeare Reference Library* (1910, 1925); and the *Catalogue of the Shakespeare exhibition held in the Bodleian Library at Oxford to commemorate the tercentenary of the death of Shakespeare* (1916). He also took an interest in contemporary performance: see, for example, the essay 'Shakespeare's King Henry the Fifth: an account and an estimate' (1900) associated with the production of the play at the Lyceum Theatre; and the book length study *Shakespeare and the Modern Stage, and other Essays* (1906).

Lee was always greatly interested in the New World. In four articles published in *Scribner's Magazine* during 1907 he explored the knowledge of America in Shakespeare's time and its influence in Spain and France as well as England. He also continued to expand the European context of Shakespeare's writings, with a British Academy lecture, 'Shakespeare and the Italian Renaissance' (1915), and a paper in the *Anglo-Italian Review*, 'Tasso in Shakespeare's England' (September 1918). In an inaugural address to the Modern Language Research Association (later the Modern Humanities Research Association) he stressed the peace-making influence of literature studied in an international context. This built on a lecture he had given in 1917, during one of the darkest periods of the First World War, 'Shakespeare and the Red Cross: an address delivered at the opening of the Shakespeare Exhibition at the Grafton Galleries on 19 January 1917' (published by the Chiswick Press, proceeds to the Red Cross). He claimed boldly that 'By rendering all the active aid we can to the British Red

Cross Society, and by demonstrating our appreciation of Shakespeare's mighty achievement, which conspicuously confirms our national credit, we are working for a single goal'.

Another side of Lee's literary work was his chairmanship of the executive committee of the Shakespeare Birthplace Trust from early in 1903 until his death. He played a key role in the development of Stratford as a literary shrine. Rather as his biographical work on Shakespeare provoked sharp assaults from Baconians and other anti-Stratfordians (see, for instance, George Stronach, *Mr Sidney Lee and the Baconians: a Critic Criticized*, 1904; Sir George Greenwood, *Sir Sidney Lee's New Edition of 'A Life of William Shakespeare': some Words of Caution*, 1916; John Denholm Parsons, *The great taboo in English literary circles: 5 questions addressed to the authority, Sir S. Lee*, 1919), his work for the trust immediately drew him into controversy. In a short illustrated book, *The Alleged Vandalism at Stratford-on-Avon* (1903), dedicated 'TO MY FRIENDS IN AMERICA', he responded to outspoken criticism of the trustees by the novelist and Stratford resident Marie Corelli ('The Body Snatchers', *King and Country*, April–June 1903). A benefaction by Andrew Carnegie enabled the trust to purchase four cottages in Henley Street, adjacent to the birthplace. However, what had most provoked Miss Corelli's wrath was a plan by the corporation to build a public library six doors further along Henley Street. Lee proved himself a pugnacious and loyal champion both of the trust and of the Flower family, 'which through three generations has devoted itself to the true interests of Stratford'. He also involved himself with the trust's acquisition of books: see, for instance, *Four quarto editions of plays by Shakespeare: the property of the trustees and guardians of Shakespeare's birthplace* (1908), and *England's Parnassus, 1900: a note by Sir Sidney Lee on the copy recently acquired by … Shakespeare's Birthplace* (July 1915). A decade later his own physical remains were interred in Stratford's cemetery.

Later career Although George Smith's widow had rewarded Lee with special bonuses for the lives of the late queen and of the founding publisher which he contributed to the first supplement to the *Dictionary of National Biography*, Lee had thereafter found his income decidedly inadequate once the dictionary was completed. Temporary jobs connected with the index and epitome and the errata were paid only as piecework, and he was involved with the 22-volume corrected reprint of 1908–9, which incorporated the accumulated amendments and became a standard text. The general impression that he was a member of the Smith, Elder staff stood in the way of his obtaining other suitable literary employment. Some paid literary work and lecturing (including the Clark lectures at Cambridge and a successful lecture tour in the United States in the following year) was available, and there was some civil service commission examining. Lee was, however, largely dependent on royalties from *Shakespeare* and *Queen Victoria*. In 1908 he failed to get the Goldsmiths' readership in English literature at Oxford. In Oxford in 1909 he did, however, give a course of lectures which were the origin of his *The French Renaissance in England* published the following year. Some relief soon came from further, though only temporary, full-time *Dictionary of National Biography* work.

George Smith had in a general way felt that it would be useful to continue the dictionary by periodic supplementations, fulfilling Lee's conception of the whole work as a 'living organism', but the commercial implications of this generous policy were not fully considered during his lifetime. Not until 1910 did Mrs Smith, to whom the dictionary had been bequeathed, commission Lee to undertake a decennial supplement, running from the queen's death to what was eventually agreed as the end of December 1911. Lee was engaged in this new task from October 1910 to the end of 1912. The old team of specialists, most of whom had a historical rather than a current interest in their subjects, had dispersed; indeed several were themselves ready for inclusion in the proposed new supplement. The Edwardian period was planned on a more generous scale than the previous volume of addenda had allowed; in the end there were three volumes, which ran to 2200 pages against the 1400 of the earlier supplement, which had moreover taken in omissions as well as additions. A new team therefore had to be assembled to handle this bulky proposition. The result necessarily has something more of the air of a very extended collection of obituary notices than the final register of a national pantheon.

There were indeed some objections to the supplement from those who felt, essentially, that it was all too recent and that balanced judgements were not yet possible on such recently dead personages. But the newly dead had been included throughout the main work, so far as alphabetization allowed, and it was only the decennial concentration that drew special attention to the reduced perspective. Lee, like Stephen before him, was adamant that the speed with which biographical materials tend to disappear meant that the danger lay not in undue haste, but in delay. The second supplement proved a valuable precursor of the later decennially extended series, though the later volumes were considerably scaled down.

Lee's own views on biography had been given a formal airing in his Leslie Stephen lecture, delivered in Cambridge in May 1911 and published that year as *Principles of Biography*. He had been much involved in raising funds to endow the lectureship, and so was a very appropriate choice of speaker. His theme was much broader than national biography, on which he had addressed the Royal Institution in 1896 (see *Cornhill Magazine*, March 1896). He considered biographers from Plutarch onwards, discussed Boswell and Lockhart, noted that 'discriminating brevity is a law of the right biographic method', but gave himself little space for the special branch of the subject, 'encyclopaedic or collective biography', to which he had devoted almost all his adult life. Here he emphasized 'the obligations of brevity and conciseness' which did not apply to individual or independent biography. 'The methods of national biography are Spartan methods heartlessly enforced by an editor's vigilance', he remarked, arguing that such disciplinary controls could be of much value to the 'independent biographer'. The principles that he tried to define in his lecture, without particular success, for 'the collective biographer's law-ridden factory' were at the time of his lecture in Cambridge being put to the test in the first decennial supplement.

Lee's articles in the supplement had included one on Leslie Stephen, but his major contribution was on King Edward VII, which ran to 128 columns. The notice of the late king was favourably received by press and public; they saw in it a refreshing frankness. As with Queen Victoria, Lee lacked 'personal knowledge', but he was now in a position to solicit much 'private information', even if some of it turned out to be unreliable. Within the royal household, however, and notably in Queen Alexandra's private secretary Sir Arthur Davidson, Lee's notice of King Edward aroused much hostility. References to the king's 'want of intellectual equipment', his having 'no broad political views', and his 'lack of originating political faculty' were seen to be inaccurate and insulting; the comment that their late master was 'unremitting in his attention to social pleasures' was reckoned unfair. Lee was heavily leant upon by several courtiers, who drew attention to Queen Alexandra's displeasure (based on reports she had read in Danish newspapers). They doggedly sought some form of published amendment. Any retraction would have compromised Lee and the supplement as a whole. He courteously refused to provide one, explaining that he had researched his article conscientiously. He had received and noted down much oral information, which came from many interviewees; they included A. J. Balfour, who swithered when challenged by courtiers. A new memoir, separately published and gently corrective in tone, and with access to confidential archives, was agreed upon, but this was negotiated at a time when Lee had taken up a new academic post. Little progress was made before summer 1914, after which the project was suspended for the duration of the war, not least because authoritative revelations about the conduct of Edwardian foreign policy could have had international repercussions. When the commission was revived the project had grown, access to royal archives was less problematic, perspectives had lengthened, and courtierly misgivings had been somewhat allayed. The scale of the proposed work was now very much larger than originally envisaged.

The two volumes of *King Edward VII: a Biography* (1925–7) ran to over 1500 pages of text, and proved to be a colossal effort for an ageing author in declining health and under mounting pressure from the court to complete his work. Lee managed to advance the task, with the assistance of secretaries and researchers. The result had an old-fashioned appearance, and certainly did not heed the strictures of Lytton Strachey, in his preface to *Eminent Victorians* (1918), on 'those two fat volumes, with which it is our custom to commemorate the dead'. Lee did, however, manage to include many quite deft touches in his portrayal of the king, such as a remark on the gourmand monarch that has become a classic of understatement: 'He had a splendid appetite at all times, and never toyed with his food' (S. Lee, *King Edward VII*, 2.408). Overall, however, the biography is diligently compiled rather than elegantly written, though its thorough documentation gives it some continuing value as a source. The first volume sold well—some 15,000 copies by the time of Lee's death; by then, however, he had completed no more than six chapters of its successor. His young assistant S. F. Markham, who had worked with him since summer 1923, was able to complete it swiftly and very competently from drafts and memoranda, also using manuscript sources newly available.

In 1917, the year after the death of George Smith's son-in-law Reginald Smith, its active partner, the firm of Smith, Elder & Co. was dissolved and the publishing business was transferred to John Murray's. Mrs George Smith and her family presented the *Dictionary of National Biography* to the University of Oxford, with the general intention that it should be kept up to date. Due gratitude was expressed, but the officials of the Clarendon Press, who knew Lee as (uncharacteristically) a procrastinator through his terminated editorship of the essays collected in the two tercentennial volumes of *Shakespeare's England* (commissioned in 1906, resigned by Lee in 1914 and published two years later), were wary of taking the former editor's prompt and over-insistent advice. Lee, who took a national interest standpoint that was far from being the press's main concern in 1917, wanted work to start immediately on preparing the next decennial volume. He sought an immediate commitment to continuing the dictionary. Here he faced an obstinate silence from the delegates (the press's managerial committee), and started to foment trouble. He lobbied hard: Ramsay MacDonald and Lord Curzon were among those to whom he wrote privately, and in public there were letters to *The Times*. Lee's interference was much resented, and he was given no voice in the continuance of the enterprise. The new volume was not agreed to until 1920, when the decision was confirmed to revert to greater selectivity rather than continue the profuse coverage of the Edwardian volume. By the time the first Oxford supplement, covering the years 1912–21, appeared in 1927, looking rather thin for a decade in which there had been many eligible wartime deaths to be considered, Lee himself was dead; he was, however, made the subject of a special prefatory memoir by his friend Sir Charles Firth.

Lee had for many years been an occasional lecturer and examiner in English literature in various London institutions. He eventually found himself a position that was the culmination of an energetic but intermittent teaching career, developed with missionary zeal in occasional lectures, university extension summer meetings, and Saturday evening classes at the Working Men's College, Mile End Road. At Toynbee Hall he arranged concerts and lectures, and was from 1890 president of the hall's Elizabethan Literary Society, attracting to its meetings many prominent Elizabethan scholars. In addition to specifically Shakespearian involvements he had been one of the founders of the English Association, chairing its first general meeting in 1907; he was its president in 1917.

In 1913 a professorship of English language and literature was established at the East End College, Mile End Road, and Lee was appointed to it. It was a strong appointment for the reconstituted college, but it matched Lee's own experience and interests, and he was very active in his professorship, both in teaching and administration, and on behalf of his students—latterly the many former servicemen in whom he took a special interest. His inaugural lecture, published as *The Place of English Literature in the Modern University* (1913), was much more ambitious than themes explored in his earlier public addresses. He appeared much more confident about his subject, and about university education as a whole, noting the recent election of an academic, Woodrow Wilson, as president of the United States. The value Lee now placed on the study of literature showed an almost missionary zeal for the subject: his concluding words were 'saving grace'. 'Reading', he urged his east London audience, 'is a wrestling with ideas greater than any we can create for ourselves'. Yet he did not view the most important function of literature as 'moral improvement' so much as its influence on 'the happiness of the student's life in all its future stages'. 'It has been said, a little extravagantly,' he continued, 'that reading can get the better of most physical sufferings, all indeed save the pangs of hunger.' But reading, and study, needed books, and he made a special plea for the development of the college library. He served as dean of the faculty of arts in the University of London from 1918 to 1922, but in 1924 resigned his chair to complete *Edward VII*. The east London college remained prominent in his affections. In his will he bequeathed to it £5000 for bursaries in English and a hundred books from his library; later, perhaps heeding the emphasis he had placed on the need for a strong library, the college bought the bulk of Lee's books on English literature—about 6000 volumes in all.

Lee was elected a fellow of the British Academy in 1910, and was knighted in 1911. He had been made an honorary DLitt at Oxford in 1907, at the installation of his Balliol contemporary Lord Curzon as chancellor of the university. The Victoria University of Manchester and Glasgow University also awarded him honorary doctorates. He was appointed a member of the royal commission on public records in 1910, and a trustee of the National Portrait Gallery from 1924. As well as his work, already mentioned, for the Shakespeare Birthplace trustees he served from 1907 as registrar of the Royal Literary Fund.

Lee was a phenomenally industrious worker, whose diligence restricted his social life. A lifelong bachelor, he had many friends who shared his scholarly interests; they included some of his principal *Dictionary of National Biography* contributors. He entertained them at his club (he was a member of the Athenaeum, by special election, from 1901) and at his home in south Kensington. His personal reputation was high in a profession that had evolved during his working life. George Saintsbury wrote of him in an obituary tribute: 'He is about the only man, I think, of the whole lot of us (including myself) from whom I have never heard an unkind speech about a fellow craftsman' (*The Times*, 6 March 1926). He was devoted to his sister Elizabeth, and her death on 10 July 1920 was a source of much sorrow. He had himself undergone a serious operation in 1921, and found that the labour of preparing *Edward VII* greatly taxed his strength. After he resigned his chair in 1924 to continue this burdensome task his health declined further during autumn 1925, and he died at his home, 108A Lexham Gardens, Kensington, on 3 March 1926. His body was cremated at Golders Green, and his ashes, by his own special request, were buried in the town cemetery at Stratford upon Avon.

ALAN BELL and KATHERINE DUNCAN-JONES

Sources *DNB*, xiii–xxvi • C. H. Firth, 'Sir Sidney Lee, 1859–1926', *PBA*, 15 (1929) • A. F. Pollard, *BIHR*, 4 (1926–7), 1–13 • G. Fenwick, *Contributors' index to DNB* (1989) • S. Schoenbaum, *Shakespeare's lives*, 2nd edn (1991), 506–26 • K. Duncan-Jones, ed., *Shakespeare's sonnets* (1998) • *CGPLA Eng. & Wales* (1926) • b. cert. • d. cert.

Archives BL, corresp. and papers relating to article on Edward VII, Add. MS 56087 • Bodl. Oxf., corresp. relating to *Dictionary of National Biography*, MSS Eng. misc. d. 175–181 • Bodl. Oxf., letters to his mother • Shakespeare Birthplace Trust RO, Stratford upon Avon, notes, corresp., and publishers' accounts | BL, letters to W. E. Gladstone and others • BL, corresp. with Macmillans, Add. MS 55044 • CUL, corresp. with the Royal Society of Literature • King's AC Cam., letters to Oscar Browning • Oxford University Press, archives • U. Edin. L., corresp. with James Halliwell-Phillipps • University College, Dublin, letters to D. J. O'Donoghue

Likenesses F. Dodd, black chalk drawing, 1920–1929?, NPG • W. Rothenstein, drawing, 1926, Goldsmiths College, London; repro. in S. Lee, *Elizabethan and other essays*, ed. F. S. Boas (1929), frontispiece • F. Hollyer, photograph, V&A [*see illus.*] • photograph, Hult. Arch.

Wealth at death £8910 10*s*. 7*d*.: London, 22 March 1926, Ledger 1926 (L–P), 55 • £6857 net personalty: *Evening News* (27 March 1926)

Lee, Sophia Priscilla (*bap.* **1750**, *d.* **1824**), novelist and playwright, was baptized on 13 May 1750 at St Paul's Church, Covent Garden, London, the second of five surviving children of the actors John *Lee (1725–1781) and Anna Sophia Lee (*b.* *c.*1725, *d.* in or after 1776). Their other children included Harriet *Lee (1757/8–1851), novelist and playwright, and George Augustus *Lee (1761–1826), textile manufacturer.

Lee's parents both performed in theatres all over the British Isles. Her early life was extremely unsettled. In part because of John Lee's notoriously quarrelsome character, the family moved often between London, Bath, Dublin, and Edinburgh. He was imprisoned for debt in the winter of 1756, leaving his evicted children destitute in Edinburgh, and again in 1772, when Sophia accompanied him in the king's bench. Lee describes herself as 'charged early in life with the care of a family' (Lee, 'Preface', *Chapter of Accidents*); it has since been assumed that she was the eldest daughter and lost her mother in childhood. She mentions an elder sister Charlotte (autograph letter, undated [1802?]), however, and their mother survived into Lee's twenties. She undoubtedly helped run the household because her mother performed and travelled often.

Lee planned her first play, *The Chapter of Accidents* (1780), while in debtors' prison with her father in 1772, and had written a novel before that. It was not until her father was on his deathbed, leaving his four daughters without prospect of any provision, however, that she overcame her reluctance to publish. Having submitted *The Chapter of Accidents* to Thomas Harris (*d.* 1820), manager of the Covent Garden Theatre and her father's employer at the time, she endured his contemptuous treatment and delays until the elder George Colman (1732–1794) produced it to acclaim at the Haymarket Theatre on 5 August 1780. A serio-comic play influenced by Diderot's *Le père de famille*, it was controversial in eliciting sympathy for a heroine who fails to maintain perfect virtue. It was performed over a hundred times in London and Bath by the early nineteenth century, was often reprinted, and was translated into French and German.

Lee earned enough from *The Chapter of Accidents* to finance a girls' school in Bath (where she and her three sisters had settled after her father's death), launched jointly with her sisters in December 1780. She continued to write. Although she first achieved fame as a playwright, her greatest work is *The Recess, or, A Tale of Other Times* (3 vols., 1783–5), a novel exploring the conflict between Elizabeth I and Mary queen of Scots told through the eyes of Mary's fictional daughters. It enjoyed immense popularity for many years and was translated into five languages. Its success established the taste for both Gothic and historical fiction, of which it is one of the earliest examples in English literature. Two years later Lee published a historical ballad about border warfare in the romantic spirit of *The Recess*: *A Hermit's Tale, Recorded by his own Hand and Found in his Cell* (1787). A tragedy, *Almeyda, Queen of Granada* (1796), was produced in London on 20 April 1796 with Lee's friend Sarah Siddons (1755–1831) in the title role. She contributed an introduction and two novellas, *The Young Lady's Tale: the Two Emilys* and *The Clergyman's Tale*, to her sister Harriet's *The Canterbury Tales* (5 vols., 1797–1805). At the height of this work's success, Sophia supported Harriet in her refusal of a marriage proposal urged by philosopher and novelist William Godwin (1756–1836).

By 1803 the Lee sisters could retire comfortably, closing their school after its twenty-third year. Lee was described by a pupil as 'very impressive in her manner, and very eloquent in her instruction. Her eye was brilliant and searching. She inspired her pupils with a respect that continued through life' (Boaden, 1.210). Another, 'much grieved at leaving the Misses Lee', describes Sophia at forty-seven as looking elderly, with grey hair and 'rather a stout figure … not at all good looking in her features', yet with 'perfect benevolence in the expression of her countenance' (*Memoirs of Susan Sibbald*, 35, 84). She appears at about this age in a portrait (*Monthly Mirror*, frontispiece) by her friend Sir Thomas Lawrence (1769–1830). Beloved by her pupils, Lee was admired in Bath society for her acerbic wit. Never married, in 1793 she adopted Elizabeth (Betty) Tickell (1781–1860), niece by marriage of Richard Brinsley Sheridan (1751–1816) and great-granddaughter of the poet Thomas Tickell (1685–1740).

Immediately after closing the school, Lee published her first written work, *The Life of a Lover* (6 vols., 1804), an epistolary novel thought to contain much personal history, and saw her comedy *The Assignation* produced at Drury Lane on 28 January 1807. Lee's retirement was marred when her youngest sister Anna (1760?–1805) hanged herself in their new home at Hatfield Place, South Lyncombe, near Bath. Whether discouraged by this blow or by the little success of her works published after retirement, or simply no longer financially motivated to struggle against the frustrations of the literary market place, Lee stopped publishing after the failure of *The Assignation*. She died at her home in Vyvyan Terrace in Clifton, near Bristol, on 13 March 1824, in the arms of Harriet. A practising member of the Church of England, she was buried on 18 March in St Andrew's churchyard, Clifton (destroyed in the Second World War). APRIL ALLISTON

Sources A. Alliston, introduction, 'Chronology of events in the life of Sophia Lee', in *The recess, or, A tale of other times*, ed. A. Alliston (Lexington, KY, 2000) • S. Lee, 'Preface', in S. Lee, *The chapter of accidents*, 1st edn (1780), ii–v • S. Lee, 'Preface', in S. Lee, *The life of a lover*, 1st edn, 6 vols. (1804), 1.v–xi • S. Lee, undated [1802?] autograph letter, *The two scribbling Mrs. P. P.'s: the intimate letters of Hester Piozzi and Penelope Pennington, 1788–1821*, ed. O. Knapp, rev. A. M. Broadley, extra-illustrated edn, 6 vols. (Misc. Bound Scripts, Firestone Library, Princeton University, Princeton, New Jersey, 1914), 3.160–61 • J. Lee, autograph letter, 29 Aug 1776, BL, Add. MS 29300, fol. 47 • *The memoirs of Susan Sibbald (1783–1812)*, ed. F. P. Hett (1926) • *The Piozzi letters: correspondence of Hester Lynch Piozzi, 1784–1821*, ed. E. A. Bloom and L. D. Bloom, 5 vols. (1989–99) • 'Biographical sketch of Miss Lee, with a portrait', *The monthly mirror, reflecting men and manners, with strictures on their epitome, the stage*, 2nd edn, 4 (July 1797), 6–11 • K. A. Burnim, ed., 'The letters of Sarah and William Siddons to Hester Lynch Piozzi in the John Rylands Library', *Bulletin of the John Rylands University Library*, 52 (1969–70), 46–95 • J. Boaden, *Memoirs of Mrs Siddons*, 2nd edn, 1 (1831) • T. Fawcett, 'Leevites and others', *History of Bath Research Group Newsletter*, 23 (Jan 1994), 5–6 • Highfill, Burnim & Langhans, *BDA*, vol. 9

Archives Bodl. Oxf., letters to William Godwin, Abinger deposit, c. 507/6

Likenesses W. Ridley, stipple (after T. Lawrence), BM, NPG; repro. in *Monthly Mirror* (1797)

Lee, Thomas (1551/2–1601), soldier, was the son of Benedict Lee (*d.* 1559), a Buckinghamshire landowner, and Margaret, daughter of Robert Packington of Worcestershire. He claimed kinship with the earls of Essex and was cousin to Sir Henry *Lee (*d.* 1611). He was English by birth and protestant in religion, yet his two wives were Old English recusants: Elizabeth Peppard, widow of John Eustace, whom he married in 1578, and Kinborough Valentine, whom he married in 1595. Lee's stormy military career, prolific writings, and colourful character illumine the Elizabethan experience in Ireland in all its complexity.

Early service in Ireland, before 1576 to 1589 Lee was in his early twenties when he first served in the 'enterprise of Ulster' under Walter, earl of Essex. In May 1580 he was before the English privy council, charged with highway robbery in Oxfordshire, and had to be bailed out of the town gaol. In the following year, he was back in Ireland as captain of a horse troop under Arthur, Lord Grey of Wilton, during the government's efforts to quell the rebellions of Gerald Fitzgerald, earl of Desmond, and of James Eustace, Viscount Baltinglass, and his brother Thomas, for

Thomas Lee (1551/2–1601), by Marcus Gheeraerts the younger, 1594

whose capture Lee took much credit. He earned the gratitude of the Dublin council for his 'forward' services. Archbishop Loftus reported that Lee had with his band of twenty-four horse 'done more good service than any one captain in this land' (PRO, SP 63/88/26). But his horse band ran amok in co. Tipperary, and Lee brought on his head the hostility of the most influential earl in Ireland, Elizabeth's cousin Thomas Butler, earl of Ormond. In February 1583 the government tried to discharge Lee's band, but he maintained that the horses and their equipment were his own property. Secretary Sir Geoffrey Fenton befriended Lee, recommending him for further service to Sir Francis Walsingham and hinting that he was not so much to blame as the earl of Ormond had alleged, adding that Lee 'is not without his portion of that common and secret envy which biteth most of us who serve here' (PRO, SP 63/100/52).

To consolidate his position in co. Kildare, Lee gained possession of the enfeoffed lands of Sir Walter Fitzgerald near Athy, south Kildare, and made the castle of Rebane his chief base. Trouble ensued with Sir Walter's heirs who put Lee briefly in Dublin Castle gaol; his early release in 1587 was secured for him by his influential cousin Sir Henry Lee. His horse company was disbanded; but far from being dispirited Lee travelled to court in 1589 to petition the queen and privy council, claiming that if he had twenty-five horse and fifty foot—half the usual number in horse and foot companies at this time—he would defend the borders of Kildare. The queen commended his economy but his critics in the Dublin council pointed out that Lee's activities would provoke rather than stop trouble since he was already involved in local factions. His loudest critic was Sir Nicholas White, Ormond's man at the council board. However, some months later Loftus admitted that Lee 'deserved what he asked for', that he had done better service than expected, and that he had 'so weeded those parts of that lewd sort of people as the inhabitants of their own report find greater quiet … than of many years they have had' (PRO, SP 63/109/56, 57).

In the winter of 1584/5 Lee was employed under Sir Henry Bagenal and Sir William Stanley in the repulsing of Sorley Boy MacDonnell's Scots in Antrim, suffering 'loss of horses to his great hindrance' (PRO, SP 63/115/39). In his own report to Walsingham he barely disguised his contempt for Bagenal. In the same letter he discoursed on his own position: 'I was amongst the rest as a common town dog at every hunter's call, appointed to attend his lordship [Sir John Perrot], but now turned off to get my food where I may' (Hill, 171, n. 157). Perrot employed him again in the autumn of 1585 in company with the O'Mores to pursue 'the notable traitor' Cahir Oge Kavanagh. Unfortunately their pursuit took them into Kilkenny, Ormond territory, where in a skirmish Lee captured the sheriff and killed several of his men; as he had Perrot's warrant for the operation he begged protection from the lord deputy. He also appealed to Walsingham for protection against Ormond. In October 1587 Lee's plot against Walter Reagh FitzGerald, chief of the bastard Geraldines of Leinster, was frustrated through the treachery of his own wife; this was the cause of Lee's separation from her. When in London in 1589 furthering his petition at court, Lee also had to answer the demands of his creditors at the council board, but took the opportunity to lodge complaints against Lord Deputy Perrot who ignored privy council letters ordering the payment of arrears for his services against Sorley Boy MacDonnell.

Servitor and soldier during the Nine Years' War, 1589–1599 Sir William Fitzwilliam, Perrot's successor, restored Lee's band of foot soldiers but occasioned new difficulties with Lee by refusing to pay his horsemen in sterling. His troubles multiplied in the 1590s; he brought charges against Sir Nicholas White alleging that his friends had burnt down one of Lee's houses. He was also in conflict with the St Michael family on account of his continued occupation of Castle Rebane. Sir Henry Lee continued his support, but Thomas additionally cultivated Robert, second earl of Essex, in whose eventual downfall Lee fatally shared. Meanwhile, in 1593 Fitzwilliam gave him command of a company in the forces sent to suppress Hugh Maguire's rebellion in co. Fermanagh. There he fought alongside his former friend Hugh O'Neill, earl of Tyrone, and Sir Henry Bagenal, both of whom commended Lee's bravery at the battle of the Erne fords at Beleek. He figures prominently in a pictorial map of the battle by John Thomas (BL, Cotton MS Aug. 1,ii,38). Lee's plan for the siege of Enniskillen Castle was at variance with Fitzwilliam's and that engagement ended in the slaughter of the defenders who had surrendered on terms. In March 1594, in a desperate effort to prevent the spread of the Ulster rising, Lee acted as an intermediary between O'Neill and the government's negotiators, Loftus, Gardiner, and Anthony St Leger.

In May 1594 Lee played for higher stakes in an important mission to the court to put forward O'Neill's grievances of two months earlier. In so doing he clearly took O'Neill's 'loyal' protestations at face value, and blamed the rebellion then brewing on the corrupt administration of Sir William Fitzwilliam, whose hatred of Lee was mutual. Fitzwilliam warned Burghley that Lee was 'indigent and desperate' and 'should be barred all access to her royal sacred person, sith her majesty may know otherwise all he can say' (*DNB*). Lee in turn portrayed Lord Deputy Fitzwilliam as the chief cause of the war in his *Informacion given to Queen Elizabeth against Sir William Fitzwilliams; his government in Ireland* (BL, Harley MS 35, fols. 258–65). (This unattributed manuscript has now been identified as Lee's work.) He demanded an independent inquiry into the ill-gotten gains of Fitzwilliam—some of them Lee's lands, given him after the Baltinglass rebellion. His criticisms were based on his own observations, experiences, and discussions with the Gaelic lords.

It is very likely that Lee's *Informacion Given to Queen Elizabeth* never reached her. Undaunted, he presented a longer treatise, *A Brief Declaration of the Government of Ireland*, which was also ignored; its importance was not recognized until printed by John Lodge in *Desiderata curiosa Hibernica* (1772). The tract gives a detailed account of Fitzwilliam's corruption, and sets out terms for a peaceful solution of the Ulster crisis.

In November 1595 Lee was again briefly imprisoned for wounding Dermot MacPhelim Reagh O'Byrne and killing his brother Kedagh on charges brought against him by Sir Henry Harrington. Sir William Russell, the new lord deputy, favoured Lee, entrusting him to fight against Hugh O'Donnell's Scottish mercenaries in O'Madden's country of north Connaught; his men fell on the Scots in their camp and utterly routed them. In the peace negotiations with O'Neill in 1596, however, Lee again played a mediator's part. He wrote to Burghley urging that 'the lieutenancy of the North' be given to O'Neill, and that Lee himself be sent to find out O'Neill's views and objectives. Lee would meet O'Neill in August 1597, but O'Neill was apparently not prepared to make a personal submission despite a declaration of safe conduct from the queen. Lee's mission was ineffectual; indeed his negotiating activities brought suspicion on his own head.

Before the year 1596 had ended Lee was back in his usual role of military captain. Russell continued to favour him; he reported that Lee had sent in the heads of seventeen traitors, and had him promoted to provost marshal of Connaught in April 1597, but Lee promptly sold the office to Dudley Norton. Perhaps his greatest military success in Ireland was the attack of his company on Fiach MacHugh O'Byrne in the Wicklow Mountains, after which Lee had the famous rebel's severed head sent to the court. His victory earned him not only the approbation of the queen but also the keepership of part of O'Byrne's lands and a commission from Russell to execute martial law throughout Leinster. But his enemies were busy and these now included Myler McGrath, archbishop of Cashel. No sooner was Russell replaced by Lord Burgh than Lee's O'Byrne lands were given to a Captain Clare and the command of the Wicklow garrisons to a Captain Montague, who accused Lee of treason with O'Neill; Lee spent twenty weeks imprisoned in Dublin Castle from February 1598. Later, in his 'The discoverye and recoverye of Ireland with the author's apologye' (BL, Add. MS 33743, fols. 1–188), Lee blamed his misfortune on the envy and malice of Thomas Jones, bishop of Meath, but it was Ormond and Sir Henry Harrington who brought twenty-nine charges of treason against him. They were based on hearsay, unsustainable written material, and unreliable witnesses, and Lee was released in July on bail of £1700 on condition that he stayed around Dublin.

In the aftermath of O'Neill's victory at the Yellow Ford and the overthrow of the Munster plantation in October 1598 Lee hatched a grandiose conspiracy to revenge himself on Ormond, who had taken the examinations against him. He incited Ormond's Gaelic tenantry to attack and defeat him, and hoped to reconcile O'Neill as lord president of Ulster, a post O'Neill had long coveted, according to Lee. Unwisely, Lee revealed his plan to Bishop Jones, whose colleagues on the council had him arrested. In his defence Lee could not produce sound proof that Ormond was in collusion with O'Neill.

Lee and Essex, 1599–1601 In April 1599, when Robert, earl of Essex, arrived in Ireland as lord lieutenant, Lee was released, but only on a public apology to Ormond on his knees before the assembled Dublin council. For Lee's services with Essex in Ireland we are reliant on his own words. However, his last attempt as a negotiator was a secret meeting at O'Neill's invitation, but with the connivance of Essex and his stepfather Sir Christopher Blount. According to Lee, O'Neill was then strident in his demands, confident of his allies, and dismissive of the enemy's military capacity. Moreover he wanted to bribe Lee to act as a double agent. Too late, Lee realized that he was being used by O'Neill; further allegations against him illustrate his continued contacts with O'Neill during the war.

Lee accompanied Essex on his flight from Ireland to the court at Nonsuch, on 24 September 1599, and was then put under house arrest, remaining under deep suspicion. Fresh allegations poured in against him from Ormond but these were countered by his cousin Sir Henry Lee, who even managed to get a privy council letter to Lord Mountjoy, Essex's successor in Ireland, to have his company of footmen restored. In prison Lee produced his third major writing, 'The discoverye and recoverye of Ireland with the author's apologye', dedicated to Sir Robert Cecil. It was never published, but judging by the number of extant copies it must have been widely read. His thesis, a strategy for the reconquest of Ireland, displays a detailed knowledge of military organization and operations there as well as an unusual concern for the common soldier. He gives full rein to his hatred of Ormond, claiming that he had never done the queen any good service, that it was only when she kept him in England that Ireland stayed quiet, and that Ormond would join the rebels if the Spanish landed. Lee then outlined conditions under which peace in Ireland could be gained: if present policy and tactics were to continue, the probable loss of Ireland to the crown was imminent. Indeed, if his previous advice had been taken the crisis need never have happened. Some of his practical suggestions for the recovery of Ireland were far-sighted, such as his advocacy of a free but protestant school in every shire, the removal of bishops from the administration, and the use of recusant incomes to pay for the hospital bills of sick and wounded soldiery. In the midst of a series of punishments for Jesuits he also suggested that no one should carry weapons on pain of death unless they spoke English and attended protestant services. The 'Apology' section of his treatise is virtually his autobiography, which of its nature is unfinished business.

In London, on 8 February 1601, Essex attempted a *coup d'état*, although Lee was not admitted to the circle of conspirators. However, on 12 February he made his final misjudgment in trying to persuade Sir Henry Neville and Sir Robert Crosse to join him in seizing the queen and forcing her to sign a release warrant for Essex. Lee was caught lurking outside the presence chamber and arrested. On 13 February he was examined, arraigned, tried, and found guilty of high treason at Newgate, and the following day he was hanged, drawn, and quartered at Tyburn, dying 'very Christianly'; his death hastened Essex's own execution. At his trial Lee admitted that 'it was ever my fault to be loose and lavish of my tongue', (he could have added, and with his pen equally violent and abusive) 'but that he cared not to live, his enemies were so many and so great' (*State trials*, 1.1403–10). In his defence he is also supposed to have added that he only meant 'to vex her [the queen] for half an hour, that she might live all the merrier all her life after' (*Salisbury MSS*, 12.575).

Lee is best known from his striking portrait by Gheeraerts in the Tate collection, painted in 1594 when he was aged forty-two, and by his writings. In some respects his military career in Ireland is typical of the younger sons of minor Elizabethan gentry, trying to carve out position and wealth. In other ways, however, Lee is not representative of the New English captains in Ireland in that he can be variously portrayed as a would-be mediator, yet ambiguous enough in his relations with O'Neill to be described as a double agent if not a conspirator. While a prisoner he was a prolific pamphleteer, exposing abuses and drawing up programmes for the conquest and government of Ireland. Although Lee was a minor actor on the Irish Elizabethan scene, his career gives insights into the major political leaders of the period. J. J. N. McGurk

Sources *CSP Ire., 1599–1600*, 417 · *CSP dom., 1598–1603* · [J. Lodge], ed., 'Lee's "A brief declaration of the government of Ireland"', *Desiderata curiosa Hibernica*, 1 (1772), 87–150 · Calendar of fiants, Elizabeth, nos. 3972, 4150, 4464, 5588, 5771, 6072, 6089, 6105, 6135 · J. S. Brewer and W. Bullen, eds., *Calendar of the Carew manuscripts*, 6 vols., PRO (1867–73), vol. 3, pp. 50, 180, 237, 243, 253, 332; vol. 4 · H. Morgan, 'Tom Lee: the posing peacemaker', *Representing Ireland: literature and the origins of conflict, 1534–1660*, ed. B. Bradshaw and others (1993), 132–65 · H. Morgan, *Tyrone's rebellion: the outbreak of the Nine Years' War in Tudor Ireland*, Royal Historical Society Studies in History, 67 (1993) · J. P. Myers, 'Early English colonial experiences in Ireland: Captain Thomas Lee and Sir John Davies', *Éire–Ireland*, 23/1 (1988), 8–21 · E. K. Chambers, *Sir Henry Lee: an Elizabethan portrait* (1936), chap. 7 · *Calendar of the manuscripts of the most hon. the marquis of Salisbury*, 24 vols., HMC, 9 (1883–1976), vol. 4, p. 206; vol. 8, p. 395; vol. 9, p. 414; vol. 10, pp. 85, 278, 300–01, 428; vols. 11–12 · P. E. J. Hammer, *The polarisation of Elizabethan politics: the political career of Robert Devereux, 2nd earl of Essex, 1585–1597* (1999) · *State trials*, 1.1403–10 · L. B. Smith, *Treason in Tudor England: politics and paranoia* (1986) · H. Morgan, 'Hugh O'Neill and the Nine Years' War in Tudor Ireland', *HJ*, 36 (1993), 21–37 · P. Croft, 'Libels, popular literacy and public opinion in early modern England', *Historical Research*, 68 (1995), 266–85 · G. Hill, *An historical account of the MacDonnells of Antrim* (1873) · BL, Add. MS 33743, fols. 1–188

Likenesses M. Gheeraerts the younger, oils, 1594, Tate collection [*see illus.*] · W. G. Strickland, portrait, repro. in *Royal Society of the Antiquaries of Ireland Journal*, 6th ser., 13 (1923)

Lee, Sir Thomas, first baronet (*bap.* **1635**, *d.* **1691**), politician, was baptized at Hartwell, Buckinghamshire, on 26 May 1635, the first son of Thomas Lee (*d.* 1643), of Hartwell, and his second wife, Elizabeth (*bap.* 1616, *d.* 1675), daughter of Sir George Croke, a judge of king's bench, of Waterstock, Oxfordshire. His mother married, as her second husband, Sir Richard *Ingoldsby (*bap.* 1617, *d.* 1685), Oliver Cromwell's cousin. On 31 March 1656 Lee married Anne (1630/31–1708), daughter of Sir John Davis (*d.* 1674), of Pangbourne, Berkshire. They had four sons, one of whom died young, and six daughters, one of whom predeceased her father. Lee achieved local office in January 1660 on the restoration of the Rump, and his interest at Aylesbury ensured the return of both himself and his stepfather for the convention of 1660. He was created a baronet on 16 August 1660.

Lee was re-elected to the Cavalier Parliament in 1661. In 1662 an act was passed to allow him to alter the terms of his marriage settlement. Although he seems to have opposed the attacks on Edward Hyde, first earl of Clarendon, lord chancellor, by the time of Clarendon's fall in 1667 Lee had become an effective critic of the government. In 1668 he sought to remove the oaths required by the Act of Uniformity, and in 1670 he was left off the Buckinghamshire bench over his opposition to the second Conventicles Bill in 1670. In 1673 his decision to second a motion for a supply of £1,200,000 brought forth accusations of bribery against him (which he saw fit to deny on his deathbed). He supported moves to comprehend within the Church of England all those willing to subscribe to the doctrinal articles of the Thirty-Nine Articles. By this date he was a confirmed Anglican, having passed on his ejected chaplain to his stepfather. Lee was also notable for his support for parliamentary privilege, particularly freedom of speech, and his rhetoric against a standing army.

In 1677–8 Anthony Ashley Cooper, first earl of Shaftesbury, considered Lee to be 'worthy', an assessment that Lee bore out when he continued to criticize the government. However, he was also cultivated by its spokesmen such as Sir Joseph Williamson. In 1678 he supported a bill to distinguish between popish recusants and other dissenters, to prevent the recusancy laws being used against protestants. Lee believed in the authenticity of the Popish Plot, which no doubt made him more suspicious of the court. He was returned for Aylesbury in the first Exclusion Parliament, playing a prominent role in ensuring that Edward Seymour was chosen speaker. However, he seems to have taken his chance for office, being named an Admiralty commissioner on 14 May 1679. In August 1679 Lee was re-elected for Aylesbury. Although he had voted for the Exclusion Bill, office blunted his effectiveness in the Commons and he was one of those whigs who resigned at the beginning of February 1680. In July 1680 Paul Barillon, the French ambassador, thought him one of the most considerable in the Commons and noted that he was a supporter of James Scott, duke of Monmouth, as preferred successor to Charles II. When parliament finally met in October 1680 Lee was regarded as favouring expedients over exclusion, although on 7 January 1681 he admitted the bill's necessity. Returned in February 1681 to the third Exclusion Parliament, he was elected on 25 March to the chair of the committee of election and privileges. His tenure lasted a mere three days before parliament was dissolved.

Lee retained local office during the tory reaction, but despite claiming a large majority he was defeated at Aylesbury at the 1685 election. James II's agents hoped that he would co-operate with the king's electoral strategy for repealing the tests because he had 'a good character as having always been against persecution, and an able man of parts and temper' (Duckett, 2.239), but he declined to commit himself and by the summer of 1688 he was urging the merits of intervention on William of Orange's agent, James Johnston. On 26 December he attended the meeting of members of Charles II's parliaments, and supported the move to have William take over the administration of the government. Lee switched to the county seat in the elections to the convention. On 4 February 1689 he expressed his concern in the convention Commons that the consideration of the Bill of Rights should consist of ancient rather than new rights. On 8 March 1689 he was named to the new Admiralty commission. He intervened to support the ministry on matters of supply while retaining a careful watch on the liberties of the subject, such as the impressment of seamen. Although expected to support the 'disabling' clause in the corporation bill he was too ill to attend on that day. He was returned for Aylesbury at the 1690 election. After the battle of Beachy Head on 30 June 1690, Lee was not averse to telling Queen Mary that he would not sign an order putting the command of the fleet in commission because the Admiralty commissioners had not recommended the officers so chosen.

By November 1690 Lee was too ill to attend the Admiralty board. He died of 'the dropsy' at his house in Chelsea on 19 February 1691, and was buried at Hartwell on 24 February. His autopsy revealed his 'vast bulk which was taken for a complication of distempers was nothing but fat' (Anne Pelham to Sir Edward Harley, 1 March 1691, BL, Add. MS 70121). He was succeeded in the baronetcy by his son Thomas; his second son was Sir William *Lee (1688–1754). His wife was buried at Hartwell on 23 September 1708.

STUART HANDLEY

Sources M. W. Helms and L. Naylor, 'Lee, Thomas I', HoP, *Commons, 1660–90* · 'Lee, Sir Thomas', HoP, *Commons, 1690–1715* [draft] · GEC, *Baronetage* · G. Lipscomb, *The history and antiquities of the county of Buckingham*, 1 (1831), 164 · A. Croke, *The genealogical history of the Croke family*, 2 vols. (1823), 1.604 · G. Duckett, *Penal laws and the Test Act*, 2 vols. (1882–3), 2.239 · M. Knights, *Politics and opinion in crisis, 1678–81* (1994) · *CSP dom.*, *1690–91*, 275 · Bodl. Oxf., Fleming newsletter 4, fol. 241 · *IGI* · D. R. Lacey, *Dissent and parliamentary politics in England, 1661–1689* (1969) · L. G. Schwoerer, *The declaration of rights, 1689* (1981) · J. Dalrymple, *Memoirs of Great Britain and Ireland*, new edn, 3 vols. (1790), 3.107–8 · N. Luttrell, *A brief historical relation of state affairs from September 1678 to April 1714*, 2 (1857), 179

Likenesses P. Lely, oils, Leicester Museum and Art Gallery

Lee, Thomas (1690–1750), planter and politician in America, was born on a Machodoc River plantation in Westmoreland county, Virginia, the fifth of the six surviving children of Richard Lee (1647–1715), planter and political leader, and his wife, Laetitia (1657–1706), daughter of Henry Corbin and his wife, Alice, also members of the Virginia tobacco élite. His parents were both born in Virginia of English ancestry.

Lee's family background decisively shaped his early life. Beginning about the age of ten, he received a grammar school education at the College of William and Mary in the colonial capital. Although as a younger son he inherited relatively little of the family fortune, kinship connections helped Lee to begin his adult career. In 1710, when his father resigned as naval officer for the South Potomac district, Thomas was appointed to replace him. This entitled him to a salary and a significant portion of the duties collected on various commodities shipped out of the district. A year later, family contacts in England helped him to gain appointment as the resident agent for the Northern Neck proprietary. Within the extensive area lying between the Potomac and Rappahannock rivers he was responsible for collecting the annual tax or quit-rent owed to the English proprietors. The position brought him not only substantial income but also a detailed knowledge of the unclaimed land still available within this portion of Virginia. Large land purchases advanced his personal fortune, and presumably facilitated his marriage in 1722 to Hannah Ludwell (1701–1750), a member of a prominent and wealthy family from the James River region. Ultimately the couple would have eleven children, including the revolutionary politician Richard Henry *Lee.

Lee's growing wealth also contributed to his political advancement. In 1720 he won a seat in the provincial assembly, but was removed when the incumbent's supporters demonstrated election irregularities. He returned to the assembly four years later and remained a member until 1733, when he was appointed to the governor's council, the upper house of the legislature. In 1749, when Governor William Gooch returned to England, Lee was the senior councillor, and he consequently became president of the council and acting governor of the colony. He held this position until his death in November 1750.

As a member of Virginia's élite, Lee received respect but also resentment from less powerful and prosperous colonists. In January 1729 fire destroyed his home at Machodoc, apparently the result of arson by convict servants, who stole a quantity of silver and other valuable property. Governor Gooch attributed the crime to anger at Lee's vigorous local law-enforcement. The loss encouraged Lee to begin construction of a more substantial house at Stratford, on the Potomac River. By the time of his death this plantation alone included 1800 acres of land and employed substantial numbers of African-American slaves and other workers. Lee's removal from Machodoc to Stratford seemingly encouraged further hostility toward him, because he retained his position on the Anglican vestry board of the Machodoc area and allegedly used his influence to pack the board with his relatives. These grievances, however, were formally expressed in a petition to the Virginia legislature only after Lee's death.

Throughout his life Lee remained involved in efforts to extend British control further into the North American interior. As agent for the Northern Neck proprietary, he came to recognize the value of western Virginia land and invested heavily in areas he considered as economically important. In 1744 he represented Virginia at the treaty of Lancaster, by which the Iroquois confederacy acknowledged British claims to much of the trans-Appalachian region. Five years later Lee helped to organize a group of investors from Virginia, Maryland, and England into the Ohio Company, which received from the crown a grant of 500,000 acres of western land and attempted to promote settlement. In sum, Thomas Lee's life reflected the roles of family connections, class frictions, and westward expansion in early Virginia and British America. He died on 14 November 1750 at Stratford, Westmoreland county, and was buried at Burnt House Field cemetery, also in Westmoreland. ALBERT H. TILLSON, JUN.

Sources J. A. Calhoun, 'Thomas Lee of Stratford, 1690–1750: founder of a Virginia dynasty', *Northern Neck of Virginia Historical Magazine*, 41 (1991), 4689–702 • P. C. Nagel, *The Lees of Virginia* (1990), 3–48 • E. Armes, *Stratford Hall: the great hall of the Lees* (1936) • J. A. Calhoun, 'A Virginia gentleman on the eve of the revolution: Philip Ludwell Lee of Stratford', *Northern Neck of Virginia Historical Magazine*, 46 (1996), 5360–78 • F. Harrison, *Landmarks of old Prince William: a study of origins in Northern Virginia* (1924) • B. J. Hendrick, *The Lees of Virginia: biography of a family* (1935), 24, 51–2, 64 • C. G. Lee, *Lee chronicle: studies of the early generations of the Lees of Virginia*, ed. D. M. Parker (1957), 64–6, 343–6 • W. M. E. Rachal, 'President Thomas Lee of Virginia', *Virginia Cavalcade*, 3 (summer 1953), 12–19 • J. W. Raimo, *Biographical directory of American colonial and revolutionary governors, 1607–1789* (1980)

Archives University of Virginia, Charlottesville, family papers

Likenesses attrib. Bridges?, portrait, 18th cent., priv. coll. • attrib. Bridges, portrait, 1700–99, repro. in G. Hood, *Charles Bridges and William Dering: two Virginian painters, 1735–1750* (1978), 89; priv. coll.

Wealth at death principally lands; debts (apparently substantial) omitted from will: Calhoun, 'Thomas Lee'

Lee, Vernon. *See* Paget, Violet (1856–1935).

Lee, William (*d.* **1614/15?**), inventor of the stocking frame; little is known of his life. Tradition placed his birth in Calverton in Nottinghamshire (Thoroton, 3.42), but others believed him to be a native of Sussex (*Lives*, ed. Walker, 2.32). The former is more likely; many Lees are recorded in Calverton parish registers, including a William, who died in 1607, leaving a gold ring to his eldest son, William, who may have been the inventor (Grass, 159–161). There was also an extensive hand-knitting industry in the east midlands, and the area was later dominant in the hosiery trade. Lee gained an MA degree, probably from Cambridge (Thoroton, 3.42), but possibly from Oxford (*Lives*, ed. Walker, 2.32). He has been claimed by Christ's College, Cambridge, who have a commemorative stained glass window to him, but he may also have been at St John's.

Lee invented the stocking frame about 1589, and brought it to London, where he seems to have worked to perfect it. There is no evidence, however, for the legends perpetuated by Henson and Grass that he demonstrated it before Queen Elizabeth, and failed to win her approval. The first definite reference to him in London is an indenture dated 6 June 1600, which claims that:

> William Lee hath by his long study and practice devised and invented a certain invention or artificiality being a very speedy manner of working and making in a loom or frame all manner of works usually wrought by knitting needles as stockings, waistcoats and such like. (partnership agreement, 1600)

In 1605, when seeking the freedom of the City of London, he had described himself as 'first inventor of an engine to make silk stockings' (proceedings of the court of aldermen, repertory 27, fol. 87). A further reference to him suggests that he was finding it difficult to establish his machine: he was admitted as a 'foreign brother' to the Weavers' Company in 1608, and undertook to pay £1 when he set up any loom for weaving, but there is no record of his having done so.

That so little is known about the inventor of a machine which gave employment to thousands has led to the creation of considerable legend. Tradition has it that he invented the machine after watching a woman knit, either his wife, who was trying to supplement the income he earned as a poor curate, or a lady who preferred her knitting to his courtship, and on whom he vowed revenge by depriving her of her occupation. There is no evidence at all that he was a clergyman, although the tradition was already established in the late seventeenth century, when he is depicted as such on the arms of the Worshipful Company of Framework Knitters, where a clergyman and a woman flank an early stocking frame. Some Victorian paintings, notably one by Alfred Elmore RA, exhibited in 1847, perpetuate this theme.

The knitting frame was a technically complex piece of machinery, which took many years to perfect. Nevertheless, it was the first real textile machine, albeit hand-powered, and therefore two centuries ahead of the mechanization of spinning and weaving. The context of its invention was a demand for better hosiery as a result of changes in male fashions. The transition from long robes to doublet and hose meant that the legs were on display. Knitted silk stockings, which moulded to the shape of the wearer's leg, were being worn on the continent in the early sixteenth century, and found their way into Britain where they were sold at a high price. Meanwhile, a considerable hand-knitting industry on a commercial scale had grown up in many regions of Britain, making stockings from wool and worsted. Lee, however, seems to have tried to develop his machine for the luxury market, making silk stockings, and therefore sought to have his machine accepted in London, the centre both of fashion and of the silk trade. In this he failed, as he is next heard of in France. On 16 February 1612, a contract was signed between William Lee, 'an English gentleman, at present a resident in this city of Rouen', and Pierre de Caux, a citizen of Rouen (Grass, 165–8). The contract makes it clear that they had established a company for manufacturing stockings of both silk and wool. Some machines had already been introduced into Rouen, and Lee was to supply others as well as to train French workers in their use. By 1614 there are references to Frenchmen working with Lee on silk stockings in Rouen but nothing more is heard of him.

The Framework Knitters' petition to Cromwell in 1657 indicates that various of Lee's workmen returned with their machines to Britain after his death. It is generally thought that William's brother, James Lee, had gone with him to France and returned after his brother's death. He entered into partnership with Aston, an apprentice of Lee's, and together they improved the original machine and began building numbers of them about 1620, probably in Nottingham. It would appear that William Lee's time in France was not long enough for the machine to succeed there, since Jean Hindret, an industrial spy, made a series of twenty-four technical drawings of the machines in Britain about 1656 and then began to construct them in France. Framework knitting was one of the last branches of the textile industry to be fully mechanized, both stockings and shawls being knitted on an improved version of Lee's frame on a domestic basis until the 1870s. It was the first textile machine, and a major invention, but its inventor remains a shadowy figure. All that is really known is that William Lee developed his frame for knitting silk stockings in the final decade of the reign of Queen Elizabeth, sought its acceptance in London, but then took it to France; he probably died in France in 1614 or 1615, before the knitting industry had become fully established there. MARILYN PALMER

Sources K. G. Ponting, 'In search of William Lee', *Knitting International*, 89 (Dec 1982), 79–83 • N. G. Harte, 'William Lee and the invention of the knitting frame', *Knitting International*, 96 (Feb 1989), 14–20 • E. W. Pasold, 'In search of William Lee', *Textile History*, 6 (1975), 7–17 • K. G. Ponting, 'In search of William Lee II', *Textile History*, 9 (1978), 174–5 • M. Grass and A. Grass, *Stockings for a queen: the life of William Lee, the Elizabethan inventor* (1967) • G. Henson, *History of the framework knitters* (1831); repr. with introduction by S. D. Chapman (1970) • W. Felkin, *A history of the machine-wrought hosiery and lace manufactures* (1867); repr. with introduction by S. D. Chapman (1967) • P. Lewis, 'William Lee's stocking frame: technical evolution and economic viability', *Textile History*, 17 (1986), 129–47 • J. Thirsk, 'The fantastical folly of fashion: the English stocking knitting industry, 1500–1700', *The rural economy of England* (1984), 235–57 • R. Thoroton, *The antiquities of Nottinghamshire*, rev. J. Throsby, 2nd edn, 3 vols. (1790–96), vol. 3 • *Letters written by eminent persons … and 'Lives of eminent men' by John Aubrey*, ed. J. Walker, 2 (1813) • Venn, *Alum. Cant.* • J. Stow and E. H. [E. Howes], *The abridgement or summarie of the English chronicle* (1607) • Weavers' Company freedom admission books, vol. 1, 1604–46, GL, fols. 47b, 48 • repertories of the court of aldermen, CLRO, REP 27, fol. 87

Archives Archives Départementales de la Seine-Maritime, Rouen, contract between William Lee and Pierre de Caux, and power of attorney naming William Lee • HMC, partnership agreement between William Lee and George Brooke

Likenesses portrait, 1660–99 • A. Elmore, portrait, exh. RA 1847 (with family) • F. Holl, engraving (after Elmore) • memorial window, Christ's College, Cambridge

Lee, Sir William (1688–1754), judge, was born at Hartwell, Buckinghamshire, on 2 August 1688, the second son of Sir Thomas Lee, second baronet (*c*.1661–1702), of Hartwell, MP for Aylesbury, and Alice, daughter of Thomas Hopkins of London, cutler. His grandfather was Sir Thomas *Lee, first baronet (*bap.* 1635, *d.* 1691), an important parliamentarian during the Restoration period.

As a younger son William Lee was expected to make his own way in the world; on 1 February 1704 he was admitted to the Middle Temple, and on 11 February he matriculated at Wadham College, Oxford, but did not take a degree. He was called to the bar on 22 June 1710, and is first noticed in the law reports as counsel in *R.* v. *Inhabitants of Ivinghoe*, which came before king's bench in Easter term 1717. This was a case of disputed settlement arising from a Buckinghamshire parish, and Lee demonstrated his familiarity with the relevant poor-law statutes and determined cases. No doubt like many junior counsel, he centred his early practice on arguing settlement cases before the county justices, with whom his family's local standing must have helped. He became recorder of Wycombe in 1718 and recorder of Buckingham in 1722, succeeding Alexander Denton, who had argued against him in *Ivinghoe*. His commonplace books show that he read widely among all kinds of learning, and he also must have had interest at court, because he was Latin secretary to the king between 1718 and 1730. At a date unknown he married Anne (*d.* 1729), daughter of John Goodwin of Bury St Edmunds, Suffolk. By 1725 he had made sufficient progress in his practice to forgo junior briefs, for he was made a king's counsel on 19 May, and in 1727 he was elected to parliament for Chipping Wycombe on his family's interest. He is not recorded as ever having spoken in the Commons, but supported the administration, and in 1728 was made attorney-general to Frederick, prince of Wales. In 1730 he appeared for the prosecution in *Castell* v. *Bambridge and Corbett*, an exceptional trial because it revived the archaic action of an appeal of murder and was brought following the acquittal of Thomas Bambridge, warden of the Fleet prison, who had been indicted for causing the death of Robert Castell, a prisoner for debt. The case arose out of the parliamentary inquiry into the prisons, which charged the prison officers with maladministration and extortion under duress, tending to murder in some cases, but the jury brought in a verdict of not guilty, despite Lee's efforts.

Having demonstrated his political reliability and legal competence, Lee was appointed a puisne justice of king's bench on 13 June 1730. His wife had died in 1729, and on 8 May 1733 he married Margaret, the daughter of Roger Drake and widow of Francis or James Melmoth, merchant, 'an agreeable young lady of £25,000 fortune' (Harris, 1.233). At the time he recorded the event in his notebook with the laconic entry 'I marryed to Mrs. M. M[elmoth], May 1733' (*Law Magazine*, new ser., 8, 1848, 70). Philip Yorke, first Baron Hardwicke, became chief justice in the same year, on the death of Robert Raymond, first Baron Raymond. The two men were already close, for Lee had assisted in the purchase of the Hardwicke estate in Gloucestershire. Their intimacy increased as colleagues, with the result that in February 1737, when Hardwicke became lord chancellor, he promised to nominate Lee to his old post. Lee duly became chief justice on 8 June 1737, and was knighted on the same day. He remained in that position for nearly seventeen years, and several contemporaries left glowing testimonials to his skill and impartiality on the bench. Later authorities have been less generous, noting particularly that he did little to advance doctrine when dealing with the increase in mercantile cases, preferring to leave difficult issues to the jury; but it was while Lee was chief justice that the court ruled that women who paid rates were entitled to vote in elections of parish officers, these being elections 'that did not concern the publick, or the care and inspection of the morals of the parishioners' (*Olive* v. *Ingram*, 1739). And in 1749, despite the attorney-general's opposition, he ruled that one Fitzgerald, who had been committed by a secretary of state on suspicion of high treason and held unlawfully for two years, should be discharged absolutely, no fact being alleged against him.

As chief justice of England, Lee presided at several of the trials for treason held before the special commission which sat at Southwark in the summer and autumn of 1746 to try the Jacobite rebels. Since the evidence for the defendants' participation in the rebellion was mostly incontrovertible, their counsel relied upon various justifications for their conduct, and Lee had to deal with some of these points. In *R.* v. *Townley* it was alleged that the defendant was entitled to be treated as a prisoner of war because he held a commission in the service of the Pretender, James Stuart, but Lee ruled that 'no man that is a liege subject of his majesty can justify taking up arms, and acting in the service of a prince that is actually in war against his majesty' (*State trials*, 18.345), and he reiterated this point in *R.* v. *Macdonald*, citing previous cases. Another prisoner, Alexander MacGrowther, claimed that he had been forced to join the rebellion by his lord, James Drummond, Jacobite third duke of Perth, on pain of burning his house and destroying his cattle and corn, but in his summing-up Lee observed that 'The only force that doth excuse, is a force upon the person, and present fear of death', citing a precedent established by Sir Matthew Hale (ibid., 18.393–4). But it was Lord Chief Justice Willes, not Lee, who presided on 29 October and ruled against the plea to the jurisdiction made by Alexander and James Kinloch on the ground of the Act of Union; Lee's ruling in *R.* v. *Wedderburn*, as to admitting evidence of overt acts not laid in the indictment, simply followed the court's determination in an earlier case.

At the end of the trials Lee was satisfied with the results, writing to his brother, 'the Rebells are likely to meet with a just Reward for their Sinns' (Lee MSS, box 9). In 1752 he tried William Owen, a bookseller, for seditious libel, Owen having published a pamphlet which criticized the proceedings of the House of Commons in its treatment of Alexander Murray, whom it had imprisoned for contempt. In his summing-up Lee gave it as his opinion that Owen was guilty in so far as he had sold the pamphlet, despite there being no evidence of seditious intent on his part. This was the orthodox interpretation in the law of libel at the time, but Murray's cause had attracted popular support, and the jury brought in a verdict of not guilty. He subsequently allowed the attorney-general's unsuccessful attempt to persuade them into a different verdict.

By 1752, after fifteen years as lord chief justice, Lee was tired and infirm. His wife died in May, and a few months later he was hinting a desire to retire with a peerage. His brother Sir George *Lee (1700?–1758), who was dean of the arches and judge of the prerogative court of Canterbury, had given political offence to the Pelhams, however, and Lee died in office on 8 April 1754, possibly at his town residence at Bloomsbury Square, London, after being struck with an apoplectic fit. He was then chancellor of the exchequer as well as chief justice, having been appointed as a formality on the death of Henry Pelham. At his own wish he was buried in the church at the family seat of Hartwell, on 17 April 1754, leaving all his estate including his residence at Totteridge, Hertfordshire, to William Lee, his son with his first wife. His surviving papers reveal a man of broad scholarly interests and great industry; he was also esteemed for his hospitality and had a 'General Character for Generosity and polite Literature' (William Lauder to Lee, 20 July 1750, Lee MSS, box 2), but there is little evidence of intellectual creativity or imagination. Despite his long service, it appears that he had little influence in judges' appointments, although he pressed the case for the regular payment of their salaries.

DAVID LEMMINGS

Sources *State trials* • E. Foss, *Biographia juridica: a biographical dictionary of the judges of England … 1066–1870* (1870) • *DNB* • Lee papers, Yale U., Beinecke L., Osborn collection • ER, vol. 93, 95 • diary of Dudley Ryder, 1752–4, Sandon Hall, Staffordshire, Harrowby MSS, 430, doc. 27, pts 2–4 • Holdsworth, *Eng. law*, vol. 12 • M. W. Helms and L. Naylor, 'Lee, Thomas I', HoP, *Commons, 1660–90* • John, Lord Campbell, *The lives of the chief justices of England*, 3rd edn, 4 vols.

(1874) • R. R. Sedgwick, 'Lee, William', HoP, *Commons, 1715–54* • 'Jotting book of a chief justice', *Law Magazine, or, Quarterly Review of Jurisprudence*, new ser., 7 (1847), 217–33, 8 (1848), 62–75 • G. Harris, *The life of Lord Chancellor Hardwicke: with selections from his correspondence, diaries, speeches, and judgments*, 3 vols. (1847) • will, PRO, PROB 11/808, fols. 48–9 • Sainty, *Judges* • Sainty, *King's counsel* • Foster, *Alum. Oxon.*

Archives Bucks. RLSS, papers • Yale U., Beinecke L., papers | BL, corresp. with Lord Hardwicke, Add. MSS 35584–35592, *passim*

Likenesses A. Ramsay, oils, 1746, Inner Temple, London • print, presented May 1789 • C. F. Barker, oils (after J. Vanderbank), NPG • J. Faber junior, mezzotint (after C. F. Barker, after J. Vanderbank), BM, NPG • G. Johnson, mezzotint, BM • monument, Hartwell church, Hertfordshire

Wealth at death estates at Totteridge in Hertfordshire, and in Suffolk and Derbyshire, totalling £967 p.a. in rent; also major investments in securities and stocks totalling £32,500

Lee, William (*fl.* **1768–1804**), slave, was probably born in the mid-eighteenth century in Virginia, the son of African slaves. He first appears in the historical record in 1768 when he was sold to George Washington by Mary Lee, a friend and neighbour of the Washingtons. William, who kept the surname Lee of his former master, became the personal body servant and butler of Washington, who referred to him mainly as Billy and Will.

About one-fifth of the population of the British North American colonies was of African descent, and not surprisingly many blacks, both free and slave, played important roles in the American War of Independence. The vast majority of active black participants sided with the British, usually taking up offers of freedom in exchange for service, but there were numerous instances of blacks serving in the American armed forces. Although free blacks were initially banned from service by congress, individual colonies (later states) continued established practices of recruiting them. Rhode Island, for example, raised an all-black battalion in 1776, which saw regular active service before being wiped out at Point Bridge on 14 May 1781. Although blacks had been in active service for some time, in March 1781 congress reversed its official position and promised freedom to all black enlistees who served for three years. Another category of service was the non-combat roles blacks performed for both sides. For most blacks it was a case of the familiar gruelling task of hard labour—digging ditches and building fortifications—but for others it was the equally familiar one of personal servant. It was in this latter capacity that William served.

Washington, like many American, British, and French officers, took his body servant with him on campaigns. In the case of slave-owning officers, this servant was usually a slave—William in Washington's case. Throughout the nine-year war, William tended to the personal needs of Washington and his guests. He was forever at Washington's side, enduring the hardships of the continental army as it struggled against the better trained and supplied British forces. He became a fixture of camp life. Washington's letters after the war to former comrades mention William, referring to him as 'your old acquaintance Will'. When painting Washington's portrait from memory while living in London in 1780, John Trumbull, a student of Benjamin West, included William in the background. When he requested items such as clothing on William's behalf, Washington mentioned him by name, which suggests that he was well known even to those outside the army (*Writings*, 8.11). When loyalists attempted to fabricate a series of letters from Washington in order to lessen the reputation of the general, they made their story more plausible by claiming the letters had been discovered with the capture of William. Often called the 'spurious letters', they were reprinted in London as *Letters from General Washington, to Several of his Friends in the Year 1776* (1777). When arranging for the preservation of his papers in 1797, Washington noted that 'Billy had never been one moment in the power of the enemy' as evidence of the letters' fabrication (*Writings*, 35.415). After the war William continued at Washington's side, serving as butler and messenger. In the Washington family portrait of 1796 William is the only person outside the family to be included. The appearance of slaves in family portraits at the time was not unusual, but the selection of William from the many slaves owned by Washington indicates William's continued importance and prominence in the Mount Vernon household.

At some point during or before the war, William married Margaret Thomas, a free black cook. The history of their relationship is unclear. Washington knew her, remarking that she was 'of my family' during the war and acknowledged her as William's wife, although he had hoped the relationship had ended when she stayed in Philadelphia and William returned to Mount Vernon. After she reached 'an infirm state' in 1784, however, William requested that she be brought to Mount Vernon. In a letter arranging her transportation, Washington remarked that he could not refuse the request 'as he has lived with me so long and followed my fortunes through the war with fidility' (*Writings*, 27.451).

By his later years William was an extremely large man, whose obesity Washington took as his own fault, claiming to have made so few demands on his personal servant. William was also incapacitated by a number of falls, the worst of which was during a postwar surveying mission. Charles Willson Peale remarked that 'by sliping on stones & being a heavy man the fall was severe' (*Selected Papers*, 2.696). He was so struck by the formerly robust William's state that he described the injuries in great detail in his diary, concluding 'How careful we ought to be to avoid similar accidents' (ibid.).

The depth of Washington's gratitude to William for his devoted service is most evident in the first president's will:

> And to my Mulatto man William (calling himself William Lee) I give immediate freedom; or if he should prefer it (on account of the accidents which have befallen him, and which have rendered him incapable of walking or of any active employment) to remain in the situation he now is, it shall be his option to do so: In either case however, I allow him an annuity of thirty dollars during his natural life, which shall be independent of the victuals and cloaths he has been accustomed to receive, if he prefers the first; and this I give him as a testimony of my sense of his attachment

to me, and for his faithful services during the Revolutionary War. (*Writings*, 37.277)

Whether or not William chose freedom is unclear. When Peale visited Mount Vernon in 1804, he 'inquired for the old Slave Servants of the General and was told they were all dead except William, his faithfull attendant through the war'. He found William making shoes, and although Peale mentioned the $30 annuity, he did not make reference to whether or not William had accepted freedom.

TROY O. BICKHAM

Sources S. Kaplan and E. N. Kaplan, *The black presence in the era of the American Revolution*, rev. edn (1989) • *The writings of George Washington from the original manuscript sources, 1745–1799*, ed. J. C. Fitzpatrick, 39 vols. (1931–44) • *Selected papers of Charles Willson Peale and his family*, ed. L. B. Miller (1988), vol. 2 • P. M. Voelz, *Slave and soldier: the military impact of blacks in the colonial Americas* (1993) • B. Quarles, *The negro in the American Revolution* (1961) • G. Mullin, *Flight and rebellion: slave resistance in eighteenth-century Virginia* (1972) • J. O. Horton and L. E. Horton, *In hope of liberty: culture, community and protest among northern free blacks, 1700–1860* (1997)

Likenesses J. Trumbull, portrait, oils, 1780 (of Washington at West Point), Metropolitan Museum of Art, New York • E. Savage, group portrait, oils, 1796 (the Washington family), Henry Francis du Pont Winterthur Museum

Wealth at death £30 p.a. annuity

Lee, William (1809–1865), watercolour painter, may have been the child baptized on 25 December 1809 at St Andrew's, Holborn, London, the son of Joseph and Hannah Lee. He was for many years a member and secretary of the Langham Sketching Club, All Souls Place, London. He was known as a painter in watercolours of English rustic figures and of scenes on the French coast. In 1845 he was elected an associate of the New Watercolour Society, becoming a full member in 1848. He was a regular contributor to their exhibitions, and he also exhibited three times at the Royal Academy between 1844 and 1854 and five times at the Society of British Artists between 1844 and 1855. Two of his paintings, *French Fisherwomen* (1855) and *Country Girl Standing beside a Fence with a Dish in her Hand* (1857), are in the Victoria and Albert Museum, London. He published *Classes of the Capital: a Sketchbook of London Life from Tinted Studies by W. Lee* (1841). Lee died at his home, 177 Euston Road, London, on 22 January 1865 after a long illness.

L. H. CUST, *rev.* ANNE PIMLOTT BAKER

Sources Mallalieu, *Watercolour artists*, vols. 1–2 • J. Johnson, ed., *Works exhibited at the Royal Society of British Artists, 1824–1893, and the New English Art Club, 1888–1917*, 2 vols. (1975) • Graves, *RA exhibitors* • Boase, *Mod. Eng. biog.* • *Art Journal*, 27 (1865), 139 • L. Lambourne and J. Hamilton, eds., *British watercolours in the Victoria and Albert Museum* (1980) • Bryan, *Painters* (1903–5) • private information (1892) [C. Cattermole] • *IGI*

Lee, William (1815–1883), Church of Ireland clergyman, was born on 3 November 1815 at Newport, co. Tipperary. He was the son of William Lee, curate of Newport, and afterwards rector of Mealiffe in the diocese of Cashel, and Jane, daughter of Richard White of Green Hall, co. Tipperary. In 1825 he was sent to the nearby endowed school of Clonmel, and on 20 October 1831 he entered Trinity College, Dublin, where he obtained the first (classical) scholarship in 1834. In August 1835 his father died, leaving a wife and five other children, but Lee nevertheless did well at university: at his degree examination in 1836 he obtained the first senior moderatorship in mathematics, and he won the Law mathematical prize in 1837 and the Madden fellowship premium in 1838. After graduating BA in 1837 he was elected a junior fellow in 1839 and proceeded MA in 1840.

In 1841 Lee was ordained in the Church of Ireland, and in 1844 he married Anne, daughter of William English of Farmley, Castleknock, co. Dublin. They had two sons and three daughters. In 1857 Lee was created DD and appointed professor of ecclesiastical history in the University of Dublin. In 1862 he became Archbishop King's lecturer in divinity, and also rector of the college living of Arboe in the diocese of Armagh. Archbishop Trench of Dublin made him his examining chaplain late in the year 1863 and in 1864 preferred him to the archdeaconry of Dublin and the rectory of St Peter's, Dublin. He played an influential role in the reconstruction of the Church of Ireland in the period immediately after disestablishment, becoming a prominent member of the house of convocation, and subsequently of the general convention. When it was proposed to give the laity a share in legislating on matters of doctrine and discipline, however, he entered a strong protest and ceased to attend. In February 1870 he was elected a member of the New Testament Revision Company. He was a prolific writer whose most important works include: *The Inspiration of Holy Scripture: its Nature and Proof*, (1854), *Three Introductory Lectures on Ecclesiastical History* (1858), and a *Commentary on the Revelation of St. John* (1882), in the Speaker's Commentary on the Bible. *The University Sermons of William Lee*, edited by G. Salmon and J. Dowden, were posthumously published (1886). Lee was a high-churchman and a learned theologian, of strong conservative convictions. His influence was great as a preacher and lecturer. He died of pneumonia at his home, 24/64 Merrion Square South, Dublin, on 11 May 1883 and was buried on 15 May at Mount Jerome cemetery, Dublin. A tablet was erected to his memory in St Peter's Church, Dublin. His daughter **Jane Lee** (*d.* 1895) studied Sanskrit and Lithuanian in Bonn, Germany, and was afterwards college administrator from 1889. She died on 6 November 1895 at her home in Elgin Avenue, Maida Vale, London.

GORDON GOODWIN, *rev.* DAVID HUDDLESTON

Sources J. B. Leslie, *Armagh clergy and parishes* (1911), 93–4 • *University sermons of William Lee*, ed. G. Solomon and J. Dowden (1886) • *The Athenaeum* (19 May 1883), 635–6 • H. Cotton, *Fasti ecclesiae Hibernicae*, 6 (1878), 58 • B. H. Blacker, *Brief sketches of the parishes of Booterstown and Donnybrook*, [new edn] (1874), 374–5 • [J. H. Todd], ed., *A catalogue of graduates who have proceeded to degrees in the University of Dublin, from the earliest recorded commencements to … December 16, 1868* (1869), 338 • Burtchaell & Sadleir, *Alum. Dubl.*, 2nd edn • R. B. McDowell, *The Church of Ireland, 1869–1969* (1975) • H. E. Patton, *Fifty years of disestablishment* (1922) • *CGPLA Ire.* (1883)

Archives TCD

Wealth at death £15,461 9*s.* 5*d.*: probate, 19 June 1883, *CGPLA Ire.* • £1488 18*s.* 6*d.*—Jane Lee: administration, 1896, *CGPLA Eng. & Wales*

Leech, David (1600x05–1657x64), Church of Scotland minister and poet, was probably a native of Montrose, Forfarshire, and the son of Andrew Leech (*d.* 1611), minister of

Maryton in the presbytery of Brechin, and his wife, Isabella Donaldson. David Leech's elder brother was John *Leech, the epigrammist. David presumably matriculated at King's College, Aberdeen, in 1620, where he graduated MA in 1624. He was appointed a regent of King's in 1628 and served as sub-principal from 1632 to 1638. The theses over whose public examination Leech presided were published first at Aberdeen in 1633, as *Positiones nonnullae philosophicae*, with regular printings of further theses: *Positiones nonnullae logicae et philosophicae* (1634, 1635, and 1636) and *Theses philosophicae* (1637). In April 1635 Leech gave a Latin funeral oration on the death of Bishop Patrick Forbes of Aberdeen, and it, with a Latin poem, was published in the collection of memorial pieces on the bishop's death. In 1637 he published an academic oration, *Philosophia Illachrymans*.

The next year Leech became the minister of Ellon, Aberdeenshire. He initially declined to take the national covenant, and fled to England. In 1639 he returned to Aberdeen. After his first 'penitentiall' sermon proved unsatisfactory, he regained the approval of the presbytery, following a second delivered on 21 September 1640 (Spalding, 1.199). In 1644 he had a vision of the sun at night, which was also witnessed by the beadle and other parishioners. His royalist tendencies surfaced later, for which the commission of the general assembly of the Church of Scotland cited him on 19 June 1646. At Aberdeen on 21 May 1647 the commission suspended him for these acts until the next general assembly. By 1643 Leech had married Elspeth Gordon. They had at least six children: Marie (*bap.* 4 Nov 1643), Andrew (*bap.* 9 Dec 1644), George (*bap.* 6 Feb 1648), David, Jean, and Elizabeth.

1648 marked momentous changes in Leech's life. On 25 February the kirk officially expressed a wish to have some versified additions to the psalter. The commission of the general assembly 'desired Mr Johne Adamson to revise Mr David Leitch's papers of poecie, and give his opinion to the commission thereof' (*General Assembly Commission Records*, 1.367; *Letters and Journals of Robert Baillie*, 3.554). On 5 April the commission informed the presbytery of Ellon that Leech was 'employed in paraphrasing the songs of the Old and New testaments' in Edinburgh (*General Assembly Commission Records*, 1.434). However, he abandoned the task to serve as the chaplain of one of the regiments of the engager army which invaded England. Escaping from the defeat of the army in Lancashire, he returned to Scotland, where he gained the parish of Kemnay and Craigern, in the Garioch, Aberdeenshire, on 15 January 1650. By late April 1651 he was chaplain of Colonel George Keith of Aden's foot (758 Aberdeenshire and Banffshire men) and Walter Forbes of Tolquhoun the younger's foot (659 Aberdeenshire men). He received £20 sterling for this service with the army, which included acting as a chaplain to Charles II. He accompanied the expedition to Worcester, where he became a prisoner of war on 3 September.

In 1653 Leech was created DD by Aberdeen University. On 16 May the presbytery of Edinburgh reported that he 'had a church on the roadway, not far from London' (*DNB*). He promised to return to Scotland by 1 November, but his parishioners wanted the benefice declared vacant. In October the kirk deprived him for deserting his parish and he never returned to Scotland. In 1657 he published in London a volume of Latin poetry, *Parerga Davidis Leochaei Scoto-Britanni*, intended as a first volume of his minor works; however, no other volume was ever published. He died sometime within the following seven years. On 23 June 1664 his unmarried daughters Jean and Elizabeth petitioned the privy council of Scotland for relief on the grounds that their deceased parents had been banished to England for their royalism. The council generously granted them £100 from the vacant benefices of the diocese of Aberdeen. Leech's contemporary Sir Thomas Urquhart described him as 'a most fluent poet in the Latin tongue, an exquisite philosopher and a profound theologian' ('Ekskybalauron', 124). EDWARD M. FURGOL

Sources *Fasti Scot.*, new edn • H. G. Aldis, *A list of books printed in Scotland before 1700* (1904) • *The letters and journals of Robert Baillie*, ed. D. Laing, 3 vols., Bannatyne Club, 73 (1841–2) • A. F. Mitchell and J. Christie, eds., *The records of the commissions of the general assemblies of the Church of Scotland*, 3 vols., Scottish History Society, 11, 25, 58 (1892–1909) • *Reg. PCS*, 3rd ser., vol. 1 • J. Spalding, *Memorialls of the trubles in Scotland and in England*, AD *1624 –* AD *1645*, ed. J. Stuart, 2 vols., Spalding Club, [21, 23] (1850–51) • *Presbytery of Aberdeen*, Spalding Club (1847–57) • J. Stuart, ed., *Selections from the records of the kirk session, presbytery, and synod of Aberdeen*, Spalding Club, 15 (1846) • 'Ekskybalauron, or, The discovery of a most exquisite jewel', *Tracts of the learned and celebrated antiquarian Sir Thomas Urquhart of Cromarty*, ed. [D. Herd] (1774) • W. Kennedy, *Annals of Aberdeen*, 2 vols. (1818) • P. J. Anderson, ed., *Officers and graduates of University and King's College, Aberdeen, MVD–MDCCCLX*, New Spalding Club, 11 (1893) • J. M. Laing, 'Some notes on the history of Kemnay', *Scottish Notes and Queries*, 2 (1888–9), 41 • NA Scot., PA. 16.2; PA. 163.24 • *DNB* • C. F. Skand, ed., *The funeral sermons, orations, epitaphs, and other pieces on the death of the Right Rev. Patrick Forbes, bishop of Aberdeen: from the original edition of 1635*, Spottiswoode Society (1845)

Leech, Humphrey [*alias* Henry Eccles] (**1571–1629**), Jesuit, was born at Drayton in Hales, Shropshire, of middle-ranking parents. Educated at Shrewsbury School, he matriculated from Brasenose College, Oxford, on 13 November 1590 but soon after was recalled home on the premature deaths of both parents. He then went on to Cambridge, where he graduated BA from Queens' College in 1593 and proceeded MA from Emmanuel College in 1596. Being incorporated MA at Oxford on 23 June 1602, he was appointed vicar of St Alkmund's Church, Shrewsbury, but not long after he returned to Oxford as chaplain or minor canon of Christ Church, where he gained a reputation as a preacher.

By reading widely in the fathers of the church, particularly St Vincent of Lérins, Leech appears to have adopted a more Catholic way of thinking. He delivered a sermon in Christ Church in 1607 on the text of Revelation 20: 12 considering the evangelical counsels of perfection—poverty, chastity, and obedience. His stance was criticized by those whom he considered the stricter Calvinists within the university. On 27 June 1608 he expanded his argument in a further sermon, distinguishing between the precepts of the Christian life 'and evangelical counsels performed by a small minority of men whose salvation is already certain', and denouncing Calvin as 'a blasphemous interpreter' (Dent, 236). He was summoned before a committee including the pro-vice-chancellor, Leonard Hutton, and subsequently before the vice-chancellor, John King, and suspended from preaching. His appeal to Archbishop Bancroft availed him nothing, and he withdrew to the continent.

Leech made the spiritual exercises at the Jesuit college of St Omer and was received into the Catholic church by John Floyd. He went on to publish his 'twelve motives, which perswaded me to embrace the Catholicke Religion', together with his offending sermon on the evangelical counsels, in a book entitled *A Triumph of Truth* in 1609. He was answered in the following year by two former Oxford colleagues of his, Sebastian Benefield, in *Doctrinae Christianae sex capita*, with an appendix refuting Leech's defence of the evangelical counsels, and Daniel Price, in *The Defence of Truth, Against a Book Falsely Called The Triumph of Truth*.

Proceeding to Rome on 19 March 1609, Leech entered the English College, assuming the name Henry Eccles. There he helped the rector Robert Persons in his reply to King James's 'late book of Premonition to all Christian Princes' with a book entitled *Dutifull and Respective Considerations* and attributed to 'a late minister & preacher in England', which was also published in 1609. Ordained priest on 21 April 1612, Leech remained at the English College, Rome, until 1618, when he was admitted into the Society of Jesus and sent to Liège. Subsequently, he was sent on the English mission to the Lancashire district, where he stayed with a Mr Massey at Puddington Hall, Hooton, Cheshire, until his death of consumption at Hooton on 18 July 1629. PETER MILWARD

Sources C. Dodd [H. Tootell], *The church history of England, from the year 1500, to the year 1688*, 2 (1739), 400–01 • Wood, *Ath. Oxon.*, new edn, 2.462–3 • Gillow, *Lit. biog. hist.*, 4.184–6 • H. Foley, ed., *Records of the English province of the Society of Jesus*, 1 (1877), 642–7; 2 (1875), 181–9; 6 (1880), 254 • P. Milward, *Religious controversies of the Jacobean age* (1978), 111, 167–8 • T. H. Clancy, *A literary history of the English Jesuits: a century of books, 1615–1714* (1996), 66–7 • Venn, *Alum. Cant.* • T. M. McCoog, *English and Welsh Jesuits, 1555–1650*, 2 vols., Catholic RS, 74–5 (1994–5) • C. M. Dent, *Protestant reformers in Elizabethan Oxford* (1983) • M. C. Questier, *Conversion, politics and religion in England, 1580–1625* (1996) • G. Anstruther, *The seminary priests*, 2 (1975), 188

Leech, John (*b.* **1566/7**), schoolmaster and author, was the son of John Leech, a member of a Cheshire family. He matriculated from Brasenose College, Oxford, on 29 November 1582, aged fifteen, became a fellow early in 1584 while still an undergraduate, graduated BA on 13 June 1586, and proceeded MA on 4 November 1589. It appears that he helped to organize the entertainments for Elizabeth I when she visited Oxford in 1592. With 'a natural propensity to classical learning', he 'took upon him to be a schoolmaster; and in truth such an one he was, that his equal could hardly be found in his time' (Wood, *Ath. Oxon.*, 352). It is not clear where he taught but his work was encouraged by Robert Johnson, archdeacon of Leicester and promoter of education in Rutland. Among his scholars in the 1590s was Sir John Digby, later first earl of Bristol.

Leech's *Certaine Grammar Questions*, published first about 1590 and reissued under this title or as *A Booke of Grammar Questions* several times up to 1651, was an early attempt—similar to that of John Stockwood—to supplement Lily's authorized grammar and provide (with explanations in English, not Latin) a plainer and more comprehensible text as the foundation of education. Nothing is known of Leech's personal life nor of the circumstances and date of his death. W. R. MEYER

Sources Wood, *Ath. Oxon.*, new edn, 2.352 • Foster, *Alum. Oxon.*, 1500–1714 [John Leche] • *Reg. Oxf.*, 2/1.230, 2/2.123, 2/3.135 • F. Watson, *The English grammar schools to 1660: their curriculum and practice* (1908), 267 • *ESTC*

Leech, John (*fl.* **1610–1624**), Latin poet, was born in Montrose, Forfarshire, the elder son of Andrew Leech (*d.* 1611), minister of Maryton; his brother, David *Leech, was also a poet. Some of John's books call him Leochaeus Celurcanus (Leech of Montrose). John Leech studied at Aberdeen from 1610, graduating MA in 1614.

Leech has been described as 'the most interesting of the Scottish Latinists after Buchanan'; but he lacked George Buchanan's 'rugged strength of character and capacity for hard work. Possessed of a facile style, he felt that the world ought to provide him an easy life in exchange for his graceful imitations of classical models' (Bradner, 163). The world proved largely unresponsive. He may have received some patronage from noblemen at James I's court, such as the earl of Pembroke; he may perhaps be the Mr Leech who was to consider places of settlement in Virginia on Pembroke's behalf in 1621. The overall picture is confused; he may have gained some royal approval, but was in gaol also for debt (Leask, 254). He probably produced the grammar book *Rudimenta grammaticae Latinae* (1624), ascribed to him by Ruddiman (Johnstone and Robertson, 218).

In one year, 1617, Leech produced an extraordinary selection of poetic *tours de force*, beginning with *Jani sperantis strena* ('A Hope-full January'), punningly addressed to Sir Thomas Hope. But *Jani maliferi strena* gives a more pessimistic picture, showing his disgust at the noisy mob. In *Lachrymae* he expresses exaggerated grief at King James's departure for England. For the first of May he is writing paradoxes about Nothing (one might compare Rochester and other authors on the topic) in *Nemo*, at sixteen pages the longest of these verse pamphlets, complete with an empty circle as illustration ('neminis effigies', a picture of no one, which the printer Thomas Finlayson is praised for drawing). His *Nemesis poetica* (also of 1617), dedicated to the poet and collector of poems Sir John Scot of Scotstarvet, offers ten pages of extravagantly rhetorical moaning in hexameters:

> O sortis crudele jugum! O non prospera fata
> Tantorum coeptis animorum! O ardua vitae
> Conditio!
> ('O hard yoke of fate! O fates unpropitious
> to noble designs! O hard condition of my life!')

Leech left Scotland on 1 October 1617 (according to his

epigram, book 3, p. 64, in *Musae priores*, 1620). On 19 November 1617 he wrote to Scot of Scotstarvet, saying that he was eager to be off from London. By 31 January 1618 he was in Paris. He studied law in Poitiers about 1618–19. Leech composed a poetic farewell to France on 1 May 1620, and by 16 June 1621 was writing again from London. Leech's many poetic friends included George Chalmers (Camerarius), who addressed *Sylvae Leochaeo suo sacrae* (Paris, 1620) to him.

Leech's major collection of verse, *Musae priores* (London, 1620), includes six books of love poetry (two to the girl Panthea; two of anacreontics; two of elegiacs). He is the first British author to make a large-scale attempt to master the short lines and loose morals associated with Anacreon: Herrick and Cowley followed in the vernacular. In the epigram Leech can be compared to his more famous contemporary, the Welshman John Owen: Owen, Walter Donaldson, and Buchanan appear in his poetry (as does George Villiers, then marquess of Buckingham, along with many Scottish magnates and other aristocratic figures). Leech can vie with the love poets of the neo-Latin tradition, such as Joannes Secundus, author of *Basia* ('Kisses') (1539). Leech is occasionally risqué, describing

> libellum
> castratum satis, et nimis pudicum.
> ('his little book castrated and too chaste'; Epigrams, book 4, *Musae priores*, 95)

He observes that Scots can take the occasional drink. Leech's love poetry has been criticized as conventional: 'the poems to Panthea are almost wholly mediocre' (Bradner, 165), perhaps influenced by his friend William Drummond. 'Panthea' may or may not have been real; she fails to convince Professor Bradner. These criticisms may be unfair in places; at any rate, they could be applied to much other Renaissance verse, in all languages. Leech says farewell to love poetry at the end of his elegies; like Milton, he is determined to attempt Latin epic (but never does). *Musae priores* also includes a wide selection of eclogues, including nautical and piscatory poems (like those of Sannazaro), showing an awareness of recent explorations.

Leech was an extremely prolific Latin poet; his chief rival among Scottish contemporaries was Arthur Johnston, whom in Leask's view he surpassed (Leask, 256), but whose later reputation outstripped his own. John Leyden translated his fine anacreontic 'Somnium' in the early nineteenth century; James Balfour had earlier put *Panthea* into Scots. Few others, apart from neo-Latin specialists and Aberdonian bibliographers, have taken notice. Leech was apparently short in stature, fond of fame, of smoking, and of gin (ibid.). The date of Leech's death is uncertain; if he survived into the 1660s, he may be the person whose bizarre end is described in *A strange and true relation of one Mr John Leech who lived in Huntingdonshire at a place called Ravely … carried twelve miles in the ayre by two furies* (1662).

D. K. Money

Sources L. Bradner, *Musae Anglicanae: a history of Anglo-Latin poetry, 1500–1925* (1940) • W. K. Leask, ed., *Musa Latina Aberdonensis*, 3: *Poetae minores*, New Spalding Club, 37 (1910) • J. F. K. Johnstone and A. W. Robertson, *Bibliographia Aberdonensis* (1929) • *STC, 1475–1640* • J. W. Binns, *Intellectual culture in Elizabethan and Jacobean England: the Latin writings of the age* (1990) • J. Leech, *Musae priores* (1620) • J. Leech, *Nemesis poetica* (1617) • J. Leech, *Nemo* (1617) • J. Leech, *Lachrymae* (1617) • P. J. Anderson, *Roll of alumni in arts of the University and King's College, Aberdeen* (1900)
Archives NL Scot., Advocates' Library

Leech, John (1817–1864), humorous artist and illustrator, was born at 28 Bennett Street, Stamford Street, London, on 29 August 1817 and baptized on 16 November at Christ Church, Southwark, London, the only son of John Leech, (*d. c.*1870), the assistant proprietor of the London Coffee House on Ludgate Hill, and his wife, Esther, *née* Amery. His father had been brought over from Ireland by his uncle, John Leech sen., of the London Coffee House, about 1813; he was a partner by 1819 and the sole proprietor of the establishment by 1823. The young John Leech was brought up therefore in an atmosphere of sociability, debate, and knowledge of the public prints, mixing with politicians, businessmen, and journalists in his father's public rooms.

Leech was adept with a pencil from an early age, and one of his sketches was shown to John Flaxman who commended it. He became a day boy at Charterhouse School, just north of St Paul's Cathedral, in January 1825 at the age of seven and a half. In September 1826 he became a boarder, joining a complement of about 600 boys in the historic school buildings. An outgoing, sporting boy, he did not shine academically and preferred fencing with Henry Angelo to study. He was well known for decorating his school books with drawings and became acquainted with a more senior boy, William Makepeace Thackeray, who remained a lifelong friend.

In 1833–4 Leech studied medicine at St Bartholomew's Hospital in London with a view to a medical career. He became friendly with fellow students such as Albert Smith, Percival Leigh, and Arthur à Beckett, whose literary careers were to be of great assistance to him, and he excelled in anatomical drawing under Dr Edward Stanley. After Bart's he was passed down through various doctors' practices but never succeeded in anything but his splendid caricatures and drawings. His medical career ended as suddenly as it had begun, in January 1834.

John Leech's father was a poor businessman and less worldly-wise than his uncle. The London Coffee House lost money and he decided to sell it and purchase another in Fleet Street. Within eight months this second business had failed and the elder Leech was in the court of bankruptcy. The effect of this collapse, a great disgrace in Victorian London, was to colour the remainder of the younger Leech's life and leave a great scar between father and son.

In the straitened circumstances of the Leech family, Leech's talents as a draughtsman changed from being a hobby to being a lifeline. He took up the popular medium of lithography and drew on stone a series of humorous street characters as 'Etchings and Sketchings by A. Pen, Esq' (1835). He admirably captured the mood of the moment by combining the caricature of types with the

John Leech (1817–1864), by Sir John Everett Millais, 1854

humour of sports, in a similar manner to Robert Seymour, his contemporary. It was in 1836 that he missed his first chance to be an illustrator of Dickens when he was shortlisted to take the place of the recently deceased Seymour on the highly popular *Pickwick Papers*.

In the same year Leech travelled to France and spent some weeks at Versailles studying with a French artist, one of the few illustrators of his generation to have done so. The result of his study was not only a reflection of the general reaction against scurrility in Britain but also a marked shift from the savage caricature of the Regency towards the new satire of the *comédie humaine* exemplified by Honoré Daumier and Paul Gavarni. This is at once apparent in the single-caricature lithographs issued by Spooner and Soffe in 1837–8, notably *Droll Doings* and *Funny Characters*, which are more domestic in subject. In the following two years Leech established himself as a fluent draughtsman and one who could as easily draw on stone as on steel. He had a great success in 1840 with his satire on the 'Mulready envelope' which had been developed by the newly created Post Office. In the same year he illustrated two books by Percival Leigh, *The Comic Latin Grammar* and *The Comic English Grammar*, with numerous wood-engraved illustrations, though his *tour de force* was the French-inspired *Children of the Mobility* (1841), a poignant skit on popular albums. In May 1842 he married Anne Viola (Annie) Eaton (*bap.* 1818, *d.* 1868) of Knutton, Staffordshire. They had a daughter, Ada, and a son, John George Warrington Leech. Mrs Leech was frequently the model for the popular 'Leech young ladies'.

By 1840 Leech was already 'second' illustrator to George Cruikshank in *Bentley's Miscellany*, but his great moment came in August 1841 when he became associated with the new magazine *Punch*. After a faltering start in the first and second volumes of the publication, he became a regular contributor from the end of 1842, often in harness with Percival Leigh. In July 1843 he began a series of 'Cartoons', full-page subjects satirizing the Westminster Hall murals. The name stuck and so Leech effectively gave to the English language the meaning of 'cartoon' as a large satirical print. For the next twenty years he produced hundreds of brilliant and incisive sporting and domestic illustrations for the weekly magazine. They were collected together as *Pictures of Life and Character* (1854–69) and reissued again in the 1880s. Leech created a dramatis personae of lovable characters who were instantly recognizable to the Victorian public: the sturdy British householder, the henpecked husband, the plain spinster, the intrepid sportsman Mr Briggs, the Brook Green volunteer, and the dandified and time-serving flunkey Jeames. The last was really the creation of the *Punch* contributor Thackeray in 1845, but Leech was to continue it for many years. His holidays were spent among his sporting friends hunting, shooting, and fishing in the shires, a rich quarry for his humour and sketches, often including landscape. He was always more at home in portraying the social scene than in setting down the 'big cut' or political cartoon, though he did some notable ones during the Crimean War, such as 'General Février Turned Traitor' (February 1855). He supplied numerous half-pages to the *Punch Almanacks* over the years, a task which he loathed, as he was a poor time-keeper and worked to the last minute. His frontispieces to the *Punch Pocket-Books* (1844–64), etched and coloured by hand, are among his most charming works.

Leech was also making a name as an illustrator of contemporary fiction, mostly by secondary writers, such as Douglas Jerrold's *Story of a Feather* (1846) and *A Man Made of Money* (1849), and Gilbert à Beckett's *Comic History of England* (1847) and *Rome* (1852). He brought his own drolleries to *Hood's Comic Annual* and the children's book *Jack the Giant Killer* (both 1843). He excelled in depicting precocious juveniles, as in his own *The Rising Generation* (1848).

Leech's greatest opportunity to work with a substantial author came with Charles Dickens's Christmas books (1843–8). His illustrations to *A Christmas Carol* (1843) remain the most enduring images of this classic, though his work for the later books was careless and less successful. He also acted in Dickens's amateur theatrical company. Perhaps his most important partnership came with his introduction by Thackeray to R. S. Surtees. Although Henry Alken and Phiz (H. K. Browne) had drawn for Surtees, Leech's caricatured but more modern approach was the perfect foil to Surtees's writing; *Mr Sponge's Sporting Tour* appeared in parts in 1852, followed by *Handley Cross* (1853) and three further novels by Surtees. Leech's Jorrocks and Soapy Sponge became part of the national consciousness. He worked extensively for *Once a Week*, *Punch*'s sister paper, and for the *Illustrated London News*. Two later successes were *A Little Tour in Ireland* (1859), in conjunction with his friend the Revd S. R. Hole, and *Puck on Pegasus* by C. Pennell (1861).

Leech was a tall, handsome man with fine features, a wave of brown hair, and blue eyes, all of which were best captured in John Everett Millais's portrait of 1854 (National Portrait Gallery, London). He dressed well and was a sociable figure among friends but shy of public acclaim. Like many *Punch* artists he yearned to be considered a serious painter. In the early 1860s he utilized a new patent for printing with rubber in order to enlarge some of his illustrations to painting size. These were then printed on canvas and coloured by the artist. He held two exhibitions of these 'sketches in oil' at the Egyptian Hall and the Auction Mart in London in 1862 and catalogues of all the exhibits were published. They were financial successes, greatly helped by Thackeray's favourable reviews.

Leech's lack of artistic training gave him a freedom of expression and a verve which was immediately popular with the public. Although his drawings lacked the precision of John Tenniel or the finesse of Millais, they had an immediacy which summed up the moment. For this reason he was extravagantly praised by Ruskin and suggested as an academician by Millais (royal commission on the Royal Academy, 1863, 185–6). Between 1845 and 1862 Leech had acquired increasingly bigger London houses, where he lived in some style. The expense drove him to take on more work and this taxed his physical strength. The onset of angina was not helped by the constant pecuniary demands from his indigent father and importunate sisters. He developed a sensitivity to street noise, particularly music (a frequent subject of his work). Affected by Thackeray's death in 1863, curative holidays failed to improve his health and he died at his home, 6 The Terrace, Kensington, London, on 29 October 1864 and was buried at Kensal Green cemetery, London, on 4 November. He was survived by his wife. SIMON HOUFE

Sources W. P. Frith, *John Leech: his life and work*, 2 vols. (1891) • F. G. Kitton, *John Leech, artist and humorist: a biographical sketch* (1883) • John Brown, 'John Leech', *North British Review*, 42 (1865), 213–44 • John Brown, *John Leech and other papers* (1872) • S. Houfe, *John Leech and the Victorian scene* (1984) • W. B. O. Field, *John Leech on my shelves* (1930) • G. Tidy, *A little about Leech* (1930) • S. K. Wilson, *Catalogue of an exhibition of works by John Leech* (1914) [exhibition catalogue, Grolier Club, New York] • J. Rose, *The drawings of John Leech* (1950) • M. Bryant and S. Heneage, eds., *Dictionary of British cartoonists and caricaturists, 1730–1980* (1994) • S. Houfe, *The dictionary of British book illustrators and caricaturists, 1800–1914* (1978) • H. Silver, 'The art-life of John Leech', *Magazine of Art*, 16 (1892–3), 115–20 • H. Silver, 'The home-life of John Leech', *Magazine of Art*, 16 (1892–3), 162–8 • G. L. P. B. Du Maurier, *Social pictorial satire* (1898) • *CGPLA Eng. & Wales* (1864) • parish records (baptism), Southwark, Christ Church, 16 Nov 1817 • records, 1825–6, Charterhouse School, London • *The Times* (31 Oct 1864)

Archives BL, Bentley MSS • Bodl. Oxf., Bradbury and Evans MSS, Eng. lett d 397 fols. 63–142 • Bodl. Oxf., MSS • Harvard U., Evans album • Punch Library, Silver diary • V&A, letters and notes to John Forster • V&A, correspondence • Hertfordshire, Dimsdale Collection

Likenesses J. E. Millais, pencil and watercolour, 1854, NPG [*see illus.*] • J. E. Boehm, plaster statuette, 1862, Dimsdale collection, Hertfordshire • Maclean, Nashvill, and Hass, carte-de-visite, 1862, NPG • J. Watkins and C. Watkins, carte-de-visite, 1862, NPG • J. E. Boehm, death mask, plaster bust, 1864, NPG • Butterworth & Heath, woodcut, BM • R. Doyle, double portrait, pen-and-ink caricature (with Tom Taylor), BM • M. Jackson, woodcut, BM, NPG • J. Leech, self-portrait, pencil and sanguine, Garr. Club • D. Todd, etching, NPG • woodcut, NPG; repro. in *Illustrated Review* (15 Nov 1872)

Wealth at death under £6000: probate, 29 Nov 1864, *CGPLA Eng. & Wales*

Leechman, William (1706–1785), Church of Scotland minister and university principal, was born at Dolphinton, Lanarkshire, the son of William Leechman, a farmer. First educated at the parish school he then attended the University of Edinburgh where he earned his MA on 16 April 1724. At Edinburgh he was greatly influenced by the professor of divinity, William Hamilton, later transmitting Hamilton's theological eirenicism to his own students in Glasgow. Following his graduation he was tutor to James Geddes, whose unfinished essay he later edited for posthumous publication by the Foulis brothers of Glasgow as *An Essay on the Composition and Manner of Writing of the Ancients, Particularly Plato* (1748). About 1727 he became tutor to William Mure of Caldwell and chaplain to his family. In the early 1730s, while accompanying the Mures to Glasgow, where they wintered, he was introduced to Francis Hutcheson, the new professor of moral philosophy, and began attending his lectures. Hutcheson soon became a mentor and dear friend to Leechman, closely monitoring his career until Leechman's appointment in Glasgow. In October 1731 the presbytery of Paisley licensed Leechman to preach, but it was not until 1736 that he was presented to the parish of Beith, near Caldwell, by Lady Eglington. He remained in Beith for seven years. During that time Hutcheson tried, without success, to persuade him to leave the 'pack of horse copers and smugglers of the rudest sort' (Francis Hutcheson to Thomas Drennan, Glasgow University Library, MS Gen. 1018.12) to whom he was preaching in order to serve a parish more suited to his education and taste in Hutcheson's native Belfast. In 1740 Leechman was elected moderator of the synod of Glasgow and Ayr, preaching before the synod on 7 April 1741 a sermon published by the Foulis brothers in September 1742 as *The Temper, Character, and Duty of a Minister of the Gospel*. It was reprinted many times and circulated widely during Leechman's lifetime.

In July 1743 Leechman married Bridget Balfour (*d.* 1792) of Pilrig, whose brother James Balfour later achieved recognition as a persistent critic of David Hume and as a lacklustre professor of moral philosophy at Edinburgh. Hume, a friend of the Mure family himself, had probably met him when Leechman was tutoring William Mure. On 2 May 1743 the Foulis brothers published another of Leechman's sermons, *The Nature, Reasonableness, and Advantages of Prayer*, which, like his earlier address, passed through several editions. Hume playfully commented to William Mure that he considered the sermon 'a very good one; tho' I am sorry to find the Author to be a rank Atheist' (*New Letters*, 11); he went on to provide stylistic criticisms for consideration for a second edition, suggesting that Leechman attend more to the sound of his words and achieve a smoother, more harmonious style.

When the Glasgow divinity chair became vacant in late

November 1743 Hutcheson was quick to promote Leechman for it, remarking that 'if he succeeds, it will put a new face upon Theology in Scotland' (Glasgow University Library, MS Gen. 1018.15). Other candidates for the position were their friend and fellow moderate minister William Craig of the Wynd Church, Glasgow, and the evangelical minister John MacLaurin of Ramshorn parish. Craig withdrew his candidacy for the chair early on, thus consolidating support for Leechman among the liberal minded university professors. In addition to Hutcheson, Leechman was supported by Alexander Dunlop (professor of Greek), Charles Morthland (oriental languages), Robert Simson (mathematics), Robert Hamilton (anatomy), and George Ross (humanity). The vote on 13 December left Leechman tied with MacLaurin, and the rector, George Bogle, used his deciding vote in Leechman's favour; he resigned from Beith on 3 January 1744. The presbytery of Glasgow refused to accept him as a member, however, charging that his sermon on prayer was heretical in advocating too little the merits of Christ. Leechman fended off the charges by appealing to the synod of Glasgow and Ayr, which hastily acquitted him and pressed the presbytery to admit him. For the next seventeen years he taught at Glasgow University, lecturing on the New Testament, divinity, Christian evidences, and homiletics. One evening a week was devoted to entertaining and conversation with his students at which he was said to have been far less adept than his wife, lecturing rather than listening to his pupils (*Autobiography*, ed. Burton, 93). He delighted, none the less, in his interactions with students. In his classroom lectures he followed the examples of both Hutcheson and William Hamilton in emphasizing practical religion, by refraining from metaphysical speculations, and remaining silent on issues he thought inappropriate to right religious faith and practice. Even when pressed by his students he never offered 'a dictatorial opinion, an infallible or decisive judgment' (Wodrow, 34). Instead, he endeavoured to impart the good taste and the eloquence which flows from a sincere and generous love of God.

When Hutcheson's successor, Thomas Craigie, fell ill in 1751 Leechman was one of those who filled in for him, lecturing on natural theology and on the first book of Hutcheson's *Compends*. During the illness of Principal Neil Campbell (1756–61) Leechman gradually acquired responsibility for most of the business of the university, serving as university chaplain and vice-principal. In 1759 he himself became ill, and was forced to give up teaching. He travelled to Bristol, drank the Clifton waters, and was restored to moderately good health. He returned to teaching until 1761 when, soon after Campbell's death, a royal commission made Leechman his successor. His years as principal were often stormy, with frequently contentious and irritable colleagues. Leechman's first goal was to reclaim some of the power and control over financial matters which had been lost during his predecessor's illness. This required challenging the role of the rector and vice-rector. Adam Smith, as vice-rector, ably met this challenge until his resignation in 1764. Finally, on 22 November 1770 the court of session resolved the conflict, granting Leechman financial control over the college. In addition to his responsibilities as principal he often preached at the college chapel and held open lectures on Sunday evenings.

Leechman was tall and gaunt with a grave demeanour, appearing to some as an ascetic reduced by prayer and fasting. He was admired for his elegance, his warm (but thoroughly moderate) piety, his modesty, fairness, and restraint. He was not a profound thinker, and published little more than several of his sermons. His biographical preface to Hutcheson's posthumous *System of Moral Philosophy* (1755) remains the standard biography of that philosopher. In 1753 he was a founding member of the Anderston Club, and he was later active in the Glasgow Literary Society. He received the degree of DD from Glasgow University in 1754 and was elected moderator of the general assembly of the Church of Scotland in 1757. In his latter years he took great pleasure in his small farm at Achinairn, near Glasgow. In the early 1780s he suffered two paralytic strokes and died in Glasgow on 3 December 1785. Four years later James Wodrow edited the two-volume *Sermons*, with his biographical account of Leechman.

THOMAS DAVIDSON KENNEDY

Sources J. Wodrow, 'Account of the author's life and of his lectures', in W. Leechman, *Sermons*, ed. J. Wodrow, 2 vols. (1789) • *Fasti Scot.* • T. D. Kennedy, 'William Leechman, pulpit eloquence and the Glasgow Enlightenment', *The Glasgow Enlightenment*, ed. A. Hook and R. B. Sher (1995), 56–72 • *Autobiography of the Rev. Dr. Alexander Carlyle … containing memorials of the men and events of his time*, ed. J. H. Burton (1860) • *New letters of David Hume*, ed. R. Klibansky and E. C. Mossner (1954) • J. Coutts, *A history of the University of Glasgow* (1909) • I. S. Ross, *The life of Adam Smith* (1995) • H. M. B. Reid, *The divinity professors in the University of Glasgow, 1640–1903* (1923) • J. H. Burton, *Life and correspondence of David Hume*, 2 vols. (1846) • priv. coll., Caldwell MSS • F. Hutcheson, letters, U. Glas. L., MS Gen. 1018 • U. Edin. L.

Archives U. Edin. L., lecture notes | NL Scot., letters to Mure family • Sheff. Arch., corresp. with Edmund Burke • U. Glas. L., F. Hutcheson, letters • U. Glas. L., letters to Joshua Sharpe relating to university finance

Likenesses J. Caldwall, line engraving, pubd 1789 (after W. Millar), BM, NPG

Leedes [*alias* Courtney], **Edward** (1599–1677), Jesuit, was a son of Sir Thomas Leedes KB and Mary, daughter and heir of Thomas Leedes of Northamilford, Yorkshire. He was born at Wappingthorne, the family seat in Sussex, on 27 September 1599, the younger of two brothers to join the Society of Jesus: Thomas (1594–1668) entered the noviciate in 1618. Both used Courtney as their alias. Sir Thomas Leedes, lord lieutenant of Sussex, was deemed a 'schismatic', that is, one who conformed to avoid financial and political ruin. At some unspecified date Sir Thomas was reconciled to the Roman church, put his affairs in order and went into voluntary exile in Louvain. Having studied humanities at the English College in St Omer, Edward matriculated at the English College in Rome on 9 October 1618 as a convictor, or boarder, under the name of Courtney. On 28/29 August 1621 he entered the Society of Jesus at the Jesuit noviciate in Rome. After he had completed his noviceship he taught grammar at Jesuit colleges in Sezza and Ancona. By 1627 he was back in Rome as a theologian at the Roman College. He was transferred to the English Jesuit college in Liège in 1629 where he was most likely ordained about 1630. He was professed of the four vows at Liège on 30 August 1634. Throughout the 1630s Jesuit catalogues list him at Liège as prefect of the church, professor of logic, professor of physics, and prefect of reading at table. The catalogues, however, do not record his sojourn in an English prison.

On a visit to London in the autumn of 1634 Courtney was arrested, charged with a denial of the oath of allegiance and supremacy, and committed to the Gatehouse prison. Earlier that year *A Patterne of Christian Loyaltie* (1634), published under the name of Sir William Howard but actually written by Thomas Preston OSB, argued that Catholics could, in good conscience, take the oath of allegiance. Courtney's strongly papalist Latin refutation, although it remained only in manuscript (since identified by David Lunn as MS Barb. 2384 in the Vatican Library), circulated widely enough to become a *cause célèbre* that involved the English court, secular and regular clergy, and Gregorio Panzani, official papal envoy to Queen Henrietta Maria. In a letter to Sir Francis Windebank on 23 April 1635 Courtney explained 'that the motives of my refusing the oathe were not treasonable intentions towards his Ma[tie.] or defect of allegiance, but most necessarye causes of Christian faith, apparently contayned in the Apostles' Creed and 10 Commandements' (Foley, 1.255–6). Throughout the controversy Courtney remained in prison until diplomacy and influence secured his release some time after the end of May in 1636. He then returned to Liège.

From 1641 until 1644 Courtney was the procurator of the English province in Brussels. In 1645 he moved to the English College in St Omer, where he served as rector from 1646 until 1649. He returned to England in late 1649 and worked in East Anglia and London, where he was socius to the provincial until 1652, when he was reassigned to Rome. Courtney was rector of the English College, Rome, from 1653 until 1656. After a year in London (1657) he was again procurator in Brussels and Antwerp (1658–9) before returning to England as provincial in 1660.

In Antwerp, Courtney met Charles II shortly before the restoration of the monarchy in 1660. As a result of the interview Courtney entertained high expectations for religious toleration. His hope was frustrated by political developments. Indeed, as provincial Courtney successfully blocked a move by some secular clergy to sacrifice the society in return for moderate toleration. Re-establishment of a strong financial base and recovery of religious fervour after the devastation of the civil war preoccupied Courtney's provincialate.

In June 1667 Courtney began his second term as rector of the English College, Rome. He remained in Rome until 1671 before returning to England. He ministered in Lincolnshire between 1672 and 1675. Because of ill health he was transferred to St Omer in 1676. He died there on 3 October 1677. Courtney's eulogist described him thus: 'he was equally distinguished for his prudence and virtue, which rendered him dear to God and man. The most close observer of his conduct could never discover any fault in him' (Foley, 1.263). Unfortunately his published works, funeral orations, martyrologies, and theological disputations, all written in exceptional Latin, lack the force and originality of his still unpublished manuscript on the oath of allegiance. THOMAS M. MCCOOG

Sources T. M. McCoog, ed., *Monumenta Angliae*, 1–2 (1992) • G. Holt, *St Omers and Bruges colleges, 1593–1773: a biographical dictionary*, Catholic RS, 69 (1979) • W. Kelly, ed., *Liber ruber venerabilis collegii Anglorum de urbe*, 1, Catholic RS, 37 (1940) • H. Foley, ed., *Records of the English province of the Society of Jesus*, 7 vols. in 8 (1875–83) • T. M. McCoog, *English and Welsh Jesuits, 1555–1650*, 2 vols., Catholic RS, 74–5 (1994–5) • A. F. Allison and D. M. Rogers, eds., *The contemporary printed literature of the English Counter-Reformation between 1558 and 1640*, 2 vols. (1989–94) • Gillow, *Lit. biog. hist.*, 4.186–8 • A. Kenny, ed., *The responsa scholarum of the English College, Rome*, 1, Catholic RS, 54 (1962) • C. M. Hibbard, *Charles I and the Popish Plot* (1983) • D. Lunn, *The English Benedictines, 1540–1688* (1980) • T. M. McCoog, 'The Society of Jesus in England, 1623–1688: an institutional study', PhD diss., University of Warwick, 1984

Archives Archivum Romanum Societatis Iesu, Rome • Stonyhurst College, Clitheroe • Vatican

Leedes, Edward (*c*.1627–1707), headmaster, was born at the rectory at Tittleshall, Norfolk, where his father, Samuel Leedes (*b. c*.1584, *d.* after 1632), was rector, as had been his grandfather, George. He was taught by one Briggs at the village school and proceeded to Christ's College, Cambridge, where he matriculated sizar on 5 June 1642. His tutor was Dr Ralph Widdrington, whose portrait Leedes kept in his chamber until he died. He graduated BA early in 1646 and MA in 1654.

By 1660 Leedes had become master of the grammar school at Newark-on-Trent, Nottinghamshire; some of his pupils went with him to King Edward VI School, Bury St Edmunds, on his appointment as headmaster there in 1663. In 1665 the school moved to new premises in Northgate Street; under Leedes it increased in numbers and distinction. His principal achievement was the creation of a splendid library which reflected the breadth of his scholarly interests, and for which he personally compiled a catalogue in 1673. He was a keen sportsman, keeping a pack of hounds which, by way of special reward, he would allow his pupils to follow. Although a supporter of James II's policy of religious toleration, he was disgusted when the king 'would stay no longer to defend himself and those that would have obeyed him, but left us all to the rabble and the Dutch' (Elliott, 70). Leedes published *English Examples* (1676), a selection of sentences for translation into Latin, which went to twelve more editions before the end of the century, joined by *New English Examples* (1685) and *More English Examples* (3rd edn, 1692). Among his other publications were *Methodus Graecam linguam docendi* (1690) and *Rudimenta Graecae linguae* (1693).

Leedes married Anne (*b.* 1646/7), daughter of Thomas Curtis, rector of Brandon, Suffolk. Their eldest son, Edward, was usher at Bury School from 1707 to 1712 and was himself a successful headmaster at Ipswich from 1717 to 1737. The second son, Samuel, and Leedes's brother John were both clergymen; Leedes himself seems unusually not to have taken orders. Anne Leedes died on 20 July 1707 aged sixty and was buried at Ingham, Suffolk. Her marble tablet there was already being cut by Drew the carver when Leedes made his will on 27 August that year. He left lands at Tittleshall and in several Suffolk villages, many portraits, and heirlooms to his sons, his eldest child, Anne, and his other daughters Elizabeth and Bridget. Singled out from what must have been a substantial private library was a Latin testament 'curiously bound in Turkey leather' which had belonged to his great-grandfather Robert Reymers; the Latin, Greek, and Hebrew books were shared between his sons, the English books among his daughters (PRO, PROB 11/499, fol. 110v). Leedes died on 19 November 1707 and was buried next to his wife in the chancel at Ingham. C. S. KNIGHTON

Sources BL, Add. MS 19166, 25–6 • Venn, *Alum. Cant.*, 1/1.68–9 • J. Peile, *Biographical register of Christ's College, 1505–1905, and of the earlier foundation, God's House, 1448–1505*, ed. [J. A. Venn], 1 (1910), 481 • R. W. Elliott, *The story of King Edward VI School, Bury St Edmunds* (1963), 64–74, 137–42 • I. E. Gray and W. E. Potter, *Ipswich School, 1400–1950* (1950), 68–71, 162 • PRO, PROB 11/499, fols. 109–11

Archives King Edward VI School, Bury St Edmunds | Bodl. Oxf., letters to Joshua Barnes

Likenesses oils, repro. in Elliott, *Story of King Edward VI School*, opposite p. 65

Wealth at death bequests of £1096; plus flock of sheep valued at £100; lands in several villages; also books, pictures, and valuables: will, PRO, PROB 11/499, fols. 109–11

Leeds. For this title name *see* Osborne, Thomas, first duke of Leeds (1632–1712); Osborne, Peregrine, second duke of Leeds (*bap.* 1659, *d.* 1729); Osborne, Francis, fifth duke of Leeds (1751–1799).

Leeds [Lydes]**, Edward** (*d.* **1590**), civilian and college head, was born at Benenden in Kent, the second son of William Leeds and Elizabeth Vinall. He graduated BA from Cambridge in 1542–3 (disproving the statement that he was a 'monk of Ely'), proceeded MA in 1546, and was created LLD in 1568. Leeds is listed on the rolls of Doctors' Commons as 'Edward Lydes'. He was made licentiate in civil law on 3 March 1560. Contrary to previous statements, he was never a practising advocate of Doctors' Commons. He did serve, however, as a master in chancery.

Leeds was appointed to various ecclesiastical posts including rector of Little Gransden, Cambridgeshire (from 20 June 1548 until 1563); Newton, Isle of Ely (1549–53); Elm, Isle of Ely-cum-Emneth, Norfolk (1552); Cottenham, Cambridgeshire (1560–81); and Croxton, Littleton, and Snailwell in Cambridgeshire (1571–80). He was also appointed prebendary of Ely (1559–84) and precentor of Lichfield and Canterbury in 1560–61, resigning the Lichfield post after only one year. He also served the chapelry of St Mary by the Sea in 1560. From 1550 to 1554 Leeds served the bishop of Ely, Thomas Goodrich, as chancellor, vicar-general, and commissary, acting on his behalf in visitations and other ecclesiastical causes. He was visitor at various times to the dioceses of Canterbury, Rochester, Peterborough, and Ely and was known to have destroyed altars and other vestiges of Roman Catholic practice during his tenure. Leeds also served as one of Bishop Goodrich's executors after his death in 1554. On 28 February 1559 he was appointed to the eighth stall in Ely Cathedral.

Under Elizabeth I, Leeds rose to prominence among the rulers and ministers of both church and government, an accomplishment that would directly benefit at least four Cambridge colleges during his lifetime. He became one of Matthew Parker's chaplains in 1559, and at the time of Parker's elevation to the archbishopric, Leeds's name appeared along with other civilians, appended to an opinion that was added to the *supplentes* clause of the letters patent affirming the validity of the confirmation and consecration. Also in 1559 William Cecil, then chancellor of the university, appointed him as an arbitrator, along with Parker and the vice-chancellor John Pory, to settle a dispute between the fellows of Queens' College and their president, Thomas Pecock. The dispute was over allegations of irregularities in the forms of admissions for students. Again, in 1568, Parker appointed him to settle another dispute at Corpus Christi College.

Leeds's work on these matters served him well, since there followed his appointment as master of Clare College in 1560, where he succeeded Thomas Bayly who retired and moved to Douai that same year. This appointment allowed Leeds to make a most significant contribution to Clare College in 1562, an endowment allowing for the maintenance of ten scholars. In that same year, Leeds was made master of the hospital of St John and Mary Magdalen in Ely. He successfully persuaded Elizabeth on 22 March to give him letters patent to convey the land and rents of the hospital to Philip Baker and Henry Harvey of Clare College. Harvey later became master of Trinity Hall, but not before presiding over several disputes that arose over enclosures of land, claimed to be part of the hospital of St John and Mary Magdalen. Parliament confirmed the letters patent in 27 Eliz. 32. The *Old Registry of Leases* directly credits Leeds and his influence in securing this grant:

> Wherein the College tasted of the good and free disposition of their good layde Queen Elizabeth and the special friendship of the Lord of Canterbury and his grace and singular favour of Sir William Cecell the secretary to the Queen's majesty and high Chancellor of the University of Cambridge. (Forbes, 76)

Leeds remained master of Clare until 1571 and gave 1000 marks for the building of Emmanuel College as well.

In 1570 Leeds purchased and rebuilt the manor house at Croxton, Cambridgeshire. He died on 17 February 1590 and was buried at Croxton church. A portrait of Leeds survived with descendants, but a more important likeness of him is found in a brass figure placed in the church at Croxton along with his epitaph. It is significant as one of the few examples of the dress worn by doctors of law and at court by king's counsel in the sixteenth century, showing that the dress was adopted from the ordinary walking dress of a late fifteenth-century nobleman.

JOHN F. JACKSON

Sources Clare College, Cambridge, Archives, Safe A, 3/65; A, 10/3; B, 5/2, i, ii, and iii; B, 5/58 • Cooper, *Ath. Cantab.*, 2.64 • *Correspondence of Matthew Parker*, ed. J. Bruce and T. T. Perowne, Parker Society, 42 (1853), 63–4 • J. Strype, *The life and acts of Matthew Parker* (1711), 55, 62, 72 • Venn, *Alum. Cant.* • [M. D. Forbes], ed., *Clare College, 1326–*

1926, 2 vols. (1928–30), vol. 1, pp. 76, 136–7, 198; vol. 2, p. 520 • N. Barwell, *Bindings in Cambridge libraries* (1929), 38–9 • R. Willis, *The architectural history of the University of Cambridge, and of the colleges of Cambridge and Eton*, ed. J. W. Clark, 2 (1886), 693 • J. R. Wardale, *Clare College* (1899), 52–4 • R. Eden, *Clare College and the founding of Clare Hall* (1998) • G. D. Squibb, *Doctors' Commons: a history of the College of Advocates and Doctors of Law* (1977), 79 • *CSP dom.*, 1547–90

Archives Clare College, Cambridge

Likenesses brass figure, Croxton church, Cambridgeshire

Leeds, Edward (*bap.* **1693**, *d.* **1758**), serjeant-at-law, was baptized at St Faith under St Paul, London, on 6 March 1693, the eldest son of Edward Leeds (1663x9–1729), citizen and mercer of London, and his wife, Elizabeth (*d.* 1718/19), daughter of Adam Woolley. He had two brothers and three sisters. His father was a prominent patron of dissenting ministers at Hackney and elsewhere.

On 2 May 1710 Leeds was admitted to the Inner Temple, and was called to the bar on 29 June 1718. In 1716 he was one of the founders of a club for dissenting bar students. Dudley Ryder wrote that Leeds 'has no very clear method, but has a great many good thoughts and actions' (*Diary of Dudley Ryder*, 224). While studying at the Inner Temple, Leeds's social position changed when his father inherited the family's country estate at Croxton in Cambridgeshire, adding to his property around the capital. On 6 October 1719 at All Hallows, London Wall, he married Ann (1701x3–1757), third daughter of Joseph Collett of Hertford Castle, formerly governor of Fort St George, India. Leeds became eminent as a case lawyer, and enjoyed a large chamber practice. In February 1742 he was summoned to take the coif as a serjeant-at-law, and in Trinity term 1748 was made a king's serjeant.

Leeds spent vacations at Croxton attending to county business; he advised on the composition of commissions of the peace in Cambridgeshire, and was an active turnpike trustee. William Cole described Leeds as 'a heavy dull Plodding Man, but [he] loved Antiquity' (Cole, fol. 67) and credited him with the collection of stone crosses placed around Croxton parish. He retired from practice in 1755, and died at Croxton on 5 December 1758. Leeds was survived by his two sons, Edward [*see below*] and Joseph (1730–1808), and two of his six daughters, Henrietta (1716–1765), second wife of John Howard the philanthropist, and Anne (1730/31–1759), who married on 31 May 1754 John Barnardiston, solicitor.

His elder son, **Edward Leeds** (1728–1803), lawyer and politician, was born on 30 November 1728, and was baptized on 20 December 1728 at St Clement Danes, Westminster. He entered the Inner Temple on 22 December 1743 and was called to the bar in 1752. According to Cole, Leeds was a 'most imptinent pracmatical Mortal' (Cole, fol. 67) and so bitter against the clergy that Cole had to remind him that his family had acquired their property entirely from the revenues of the church. He did not share his father's enthusiasm for practice, and instead sought to live as a country gentleman and pursue administrative office to augment his income. Following his father's death Leeds unsuccessfully lobbied his neighbour and political leader Philip Yorke, first earl of Hardwicke, and his son Philip, Viscount Royston, after 1764 second earl, for a succession of offices. He was eventually appointed sheriff of Cambridgeshire in 1768; the post had been offered by George Montagu, duke of Manchester, on behalf of his kinsman John, earl of Sandwich, the Yorkes' political rival in Cambridgeshire, but Leeds was careful to ask permission from Hardwicke before accepting. In 1771 he was offered a position at the office of hackney-coaches but rejected it—and £120 p.a.—as 'low and unpleasant enough' (Namier) and insufficiently salaried. On 21 January 1773, with Hardwicke's assistance, he was appointed a master in chancery, in exchange for the promise that he would appear occasionally at the bar.

Greatly to Leeds's disappointment his party persistently refused to nominate him MP for Cambridge, of which town he was sub-deputy recorder. He was a candidate for the deputy recordership, but was defeated by Charles Nalson Cole. At length, on 31 March 1784, he was elected MP for Reigate. Leeds was elected as a client of Hardwicke, but immediately chose to demonstrate his independence, voting against the government on the Westminster and Bedfordshire elections and not voting on the address. He assured Hardwicke that these had been individual matters of conscience, and in 1785 voted with Hardwicke and against Pitt on parliamentary reform, but his enthusiasm waned and he vacated the seat in May 1787.

Following the death of his brother-in-law John Howard in 1790 Leeds became one of Howard's executors. He used his position to limit the potentially wide legacies Howard had intended for the poor. He died, unmarried, in Charlotte Street, Bedford Square, London, on 22 March 1803, and was succeeded at Croxton by his brother, Joseph, a partner in the brewers Whitbread and Gifford; some of his personal property was inherited by his nephew Nathaniel Barnardiston. MATTHEW KILBURN

Sources L. B. Namier, 'Leeds, Edward', HoP, *Commons, 1754–90* • Cambs. AS, Leeds papers; Croxton estate papers • BL, Add. MS 35603, fol. 262; Add. MS 35606 fols. 309–10, 370–71; Add. MS 35679, fols. 129, 257, 259, 386, 411, 415, 421; Add. MS 35680, fols. 3, 4, 50, 71, 73–6, 105, 123, 136, 141, 164, 170, 184, 190, 220–21 • W. Cole, 'Practical antiquities of Cambridgeshire', 19, BL, Add. MS 5820, fol. 67 • *The diary of Dudley Ryder, 1715–1716*, ed. W. Matthews (1939) • Beds. & Luton ARS, Whitbread MSS [NRA 1123] • will, PRO, PROB 11/633, sig. 311 [Edward Leeds, father] • will, PRO, PROB 11/842, sig. 374 • H. W. Woolrych, *Lives of eminent serjeants-at-law of the English bar*, 2 vols. (1869) • *GM*, 1st ser., 38 (1768), 46 • *GM*, 1st ser., 73 (1803), 294, 379 • Musgrave's obituary, BL, Add. MS 5734, fol. 69 • *IGI*

Archives Lincoln's Inn, London, law reports • priv. coll., cash book and family history notes | Beds. & Luton ARS, Whitbread MSS • BL, Hardwicke MSS • Cambs. AS, Leeds MSS

Leeds, Edward (**1728–1803**). *See under* Leeds, Edward (*bap.* 1693, *d.* 1758).

Lee-Hamilton, Eugene Jacob. *See* Hamilton, Eugene Jacob Lee- (1845–1907).

Leeke, Sir Henry John (**1794–1870**), naval officer, was born at St John's, Isle of Wight. He was the son of Samuel Leeke, a deputy lieutenant of Hampshire who 'lost his life from the effects of over-exertion in the suppression of a riot' (O'Byrne, 643). Leeke entered the navy in 1803 under the patronage of his godfather, Lord Henry Paulet, on the

Royal William, guardship at Spithead. His service on her was probably nominal, and he did not go afloat until 1806, when he went out to the Mediterranean in the frigate *Iris*. He afterwards served in the *Royal Sovereign*, flagship of Vice-Admiral Edward Thornbrough, and in the *Terrible* under Paulet. As midshipman of the *Volontaire* he commanded a boat on the night of 31 October 1809, when four armed vessels and seven merchant ships were taken from under the batteries in the Bay of Rosas by the boats of the squadron. He was serving in the *Persian* when he was promoted lieutenant on 24 November 1810. She brought home a large number of prisoners, who attempted one night to capture the ship. Only Leeke and a quartermaster were on deck, but snatching up cutlasses, they stopped the rush of the Frenchmen, and kept them at bay until assistance arrived. He continued serving, chiefly in the Mediterranean, during the war, and was promoted to commander on 15 June 1814.

In 1818 Leeke married the second daughter of James Dashwood of Parkhurst, Surrey; they had at least two children—a son and a daughter. From 1819 to 1822 he commanded the sloop *Myrmidon* (20 guns) on the west coast of Africa. He imposed British order on indigenous coastal rulers, surveyed the coast, and suppressed the slave trade; he 'either liberated, or contributed to the release of 3,000 human beings' (O'Byrne, 644). At Bonny he compelled the king to agree to a treaty fixing the duty payable by British merchants on palm oil, which 'saved many thousands per annum to the importers of Liverpool' (ibid.). For assistance to a wrecked schooner he received a gold medal from the Portuguese government.

In 1824 Leeke was appointed to the yacht *Herald*, in which he took out the bishops of Barbados and Jamaica, and so had the opportunity of bringing home from the *Havana* a freight of upwards of $1 million in coinage. He was advanced to post rank on 27 May 1826. On 1 April 1835 he was knighted for his African services, and on 25 January 1836 was made KH.

From 1845 to 1848 Leeke was flag captain to Admiral Sir John West at Devonport, and in 1852 was appointed superintendent and commander-in-chief of the Indian navy. The duties were principally administrative; but when war with Persia began in November 1856 he commanded the squadron which convoyed the troops to the Persian Gulf, covered their landing, and on 10 November drove half the garrison out of Bushehr in a four-hour bombardment. In March 1857, after five years' service, he returned to England. He had been promoted to rear-admiral on 15 April 1854; on 1 October 1858 he was made a KCB. He became vice-admiral on 2 May 1860, and admiral on 11 January 1864. He died at his home, Uplands, near Fareham, Hampshire, on 26 February 1870.

J. K. Laughton, *rev.* Roger T. Stearn

Sources O'Byrne, *Naval biog. dict.* • *Annual Register* (1856), 255 • C. R. Low, *History of the Indian navy, 1613–1863*, 2 (1877), 240–382 • *The Times* (28 Feb 1870) • Boase, *Mod. Eng. biog.* • *Dod's Peerage* (1858) • J. B. Kelly, *Britain and the Persian Gulf, 1795–1880* (1968) • C. Lloyd, *The navy and the slave trade* (1949) • J. D. Hargreaves, *Prelude to the partition of west Africa* (1963) • *CGPLA Eng. & Wales* (1870)

Archives BL, letters to Sir Charles Napier, Add. MSS 40042 • BL OIOC, letters to Lord Elphinstone, MSS Eur. F87–9

Wealth at death under £10,000: probate, 22 April 1870, *CGPLA Eng. & Wales*

Leeke, Lawrence (*d.* 1357), prior of Norwich, is first recorded in 1315–16, probably shortly after becoming a Benedictine monk in Norwich Cathedral priory. Fifteen years later a payment of 25*s.* for him to go to Oxford almost certainly indicates that he had become a student there. In 1352 Bishop William Bateman quashed an election to the priorate of Norwich as irregular, and provided Leeke to the vacant office. In the following year he appointed Leeke to be his vicar-general in spirituals. Prior Leeke was likewise trusted by Bateman's successor, Thomas Percy, who appointed him one of his vicars-general in 1355 and again in 1356. He died in 1357. Leeke was the author of a eulogy of Bateman (who died in 1355), composed as the preface to a mortuary roll which was circulated to request prayers for the late bishop's soul. Written in high-flown Latin, it gives a generalized account of Bateman's life and career, and of his virtues as scholar, public servant, pastor, and Christian. Having apparently become detached from its accompanying roll, Leeke's memorial was in the sixteenth century in the possession of Bateman's foundation of Trinity Hall, Cambridge, where a transcript of it was made by the antiquary Robert Hare (Cambridge, Gonville and Caius College, MS 391/611). The original was later lost, but the early eighteenth-century antiquary Beaupré Bell made a copy of Hare's transcript and gave this to Trinity Hall, in whose library it is now MS 30. It is this version that was published in Francis Peck's *Desiderata curiosa* in 1735. Henry Summerson

Sources J. Greatrex, *Biographical register of the English cathedral priories of the province of Canterbury* (1997), 534 • Emden, *Oxf.*, 2.1125 • F. Peck, ed., *Desiderata curiosa*, 2 (1735), 1–4 • M. R. James, *A descriptive catalogue of the manuscripts in the library of Trinity Hall* (1907), 45 • M. R. James, *A descriptive catalogue of the manuscripts in the library of Gonville and Caius College*, 2 (1908), 453–4

Archives Gon. & Caius Cam., MS 391/611 • Trinity Hall, Cambridge, MS 30

Leemput, Remigius [Remy] **van** (**1607–1675**), painter and art collector, was of Flemish or possibly French origin and was baptized at Antwerp in December 1607. He was received into the guild of St Luke in Antwerp in 1628–9. By October 1635 he had settled in England and was living in Covent Garden, London. Van Leemput is listed in various contemporary inventories as Remee, Remy, and Old Remy. He was associated with the studio of Sir Anthony Van Dyck and established a reputation as a copyist. Series of small copies of Van Dyck's portraits, known as 'closet' pictures, were much in demand in the seventeenth century. They exist at Weston Park, Hampshire; Woburn Abbey, Bedfordshire (of the children of the fourth earl of Bedford); and in the Royal Collection. The latter two groups were both previously attributed to Theodore *Russell (*bap.* 1614, *d.* 1689), with whose works van Leemput's have been confused, but have subsequently been convincingly re-attributed to van Leemput (although several hands may have been at work in the Woburn series). A particularly fine example from the Woburn series, attributed to van Leemput, is the small portrait of Anne, Lady Digby, painted *c.*1641. The Royal Collection series, which includes copies after Sir Peter Lely and Samuel Cooper, as well as Van Dyck, was recorded in the reign of Queen Anne as by van Leemput and located in her bathing room. By the reign of George III they were associated with Russell but the traditional attribution to van Leemput is more convincing. Van Leemput was also paid £150 by Charles II for a life-size copy after Holbein's mural *Henry VII, Elizabeth of York, Henry VIII and Jane Seymour* (1537), originally commissioned by Henry VIII for Whitehall Palace. The Holbein wall painting was destroyed by the Whitehall fire of 1698 and van Leemput's copy of it and another one he executed (the latter now at Petworth House, Sussex) are the only records of the original full composition. Van Leemput also painted individual independent works such as the *Portrait of an Unknown Officer and Servants* at Lennoxlove, East Lothian.

As well as painting van Leemput was a collector and dealer, a leading figure in the London art world and he purchased a number of important works at the sale of Charles I's collections, including Van Dyck's famous *Charles I with M. de S Antoine* of 1633 (Royal Collection). Van Leemput attempted to sell the portrait in Antwerp but failed to find a buyer and the work was eventually reclaimed from him by the crown at the Restoration. The painting was widely copied and some of the smaller versions, such as that in the Museo del Prado, Madrid, have been attributed to van Leemput. A copy of one of Van Dyck's portraits of Queen Henrietta Maria, attributed to van Leemput, is in Dulwich Picture Gallery, London, described in the actor William Cartwright's original inventory as 'coped by oul Reme' (*Mr Cartwright's Pictures*, 34). His quirky, distinctive style is unmistakable in such works.

Van Leemput died in 1675 and was buried in St Paul's, Covent Garden, London, on 9 November, where his son Charles had been laid to rest on 19 September 1651. Another son, Giovanni Remigio, made a reputation for himself as a copyist in Italy and his daughter Mary also showed a talent for painting. She married Thomas Streeter, nephew of the serjeant-painter Robert Streeter. To his wife Anna Maria, van Leemput left all his estate including 'my house at Antwerpe upon the Meere and two small parcells of Land being near the said city of Antwerpe' (will). Van Leemput's considerable collection of works of art was sold at Somerset House on 14 May 1677.

L. H. Cust, *rev.* Ann Sumner

Sources H. Walpole, *Anecdotes of painting in England: with some account of the principal artists*, ed. R. N. Wornum, new edn, 3 vols. (1849), vol. 2, pp. 432–3 • Vertue, *Note books* • O. Millar, *The Tudor, Stuart and early Georgian pictures in the collection of her majesty the queen*, 2 vols. (1963), vol. 1, pp. 136–119 • M. Edmond, 'Limners and picturemakers', *Walpole Society*, 47 (1978–80), 60–242, esp. 187, 214 • *Mr Cartwright's pictures: a seventeenth century collection* [1987], no. 9 [exhibition catalogue, Dulwich Picture Gallery, London, 25 Nov 1987–28 Feb 1988] • A. Sumner, ed., *Death, passion and politics: Van Dyck's portraits of Venetia Stanley and George Digby* (1995), no. 16 [exhibition catalogue, Dulwich Picture Gallery, London] • will, PRO, PROB 11/349, sig. 118

Wealth at death money to wife; £200–£300 for her daughter; house at Antwerp 'upon the Meere'; also two parcels of land near Antwerp: will, PRO, PROB 11/349, sig. 118

Leeper, (Alexander Wigram) Allen (1887–1935), diplomatist, was born on 4 January 1887 in Melbourne, Australia, the elder of the two sons of Alexander Leeper (1848–1934), warden of Trinity College, Melbourne, and his first wife, Adeline Marian (1853–1893), the eldest daughter of Sir George Wigram Allen, politician and philanthropist. His younger brother, Reginald Wildig Allen *Leeper, was also a diplomatist. His father, a southern Irish protestant by descent, was fiercely loyal to the British empire. Leeper was educated at the Church of England grammar school, Melbourne, where he became head of school, and then at his father's college before proceeding in 1908 to Balliol College, Oxford. Having taken a first in Latin and Greek at Melbourne, he went on to take a first in Greats at Oxford in 1911. He found employment as an assistant in the Egyptian and Assyrian department of the British Museum in December 1912, which led to the publication of *Cuneiform Texts from Babylonian Tablets in the British Museum* (1920).

At the outbreak of war in 1914 Leeper attempted to enlist but was rejected as medically unfit, even for home defence. Determined to contribute to the war effort, he finally found war work in the propaganda department (Wellington House), moving from there to the intelligence bureau of the department of information. One of Leeper's colleagues was R. W. Seton-Watson, the proprietor of the journal *New Europe*. Leeper began to write for *New Europe* under the pseudonym Belisarius. He became particularly interested in Romanian issues, wrote a slim volume entitled *The Justice of Rumania's Cause* (1917), and was one of the founders of the Anglo-Roumanian Society, for which he acted as honorary secretary. He was also the author of several numbers of *The Times History of the War*.

In March 1918 most members of the intelligence bureau moved to the Foreign Office to form the nucleus of the new political intelligence department, which played a central role in British planning for the Paris peace conference. Leeper arrived in Paris in December 1918 and remained there, without a break, until 1920, working throughout for the Foreign Office section on Balkan affairs. He was appointed one of the British members of the Romanian and Yugoslav territorial claims commission and, because the senior British member, Sir Eyre Crowe, was occupied with other aspects of the peace conference, came to play an important role in drawing the frontiers of the new Europe. The communist seizure of power in Hungary caused great concern among the allies, and when, in April 1919, it was decided to send a special mission under Jan Smuts both to discuss regional issues with the new regime and possibly to open a line of communication to Lenin's government in Russia, Leeper was chosen to accompany him. In September 1919 he accompanied Sir

George Clerk on his special mission to Romania to secure the evacuation of its army from Hungary. His knowledge of south-eastern European issues was by this time sufficient for his name to be considered (alongside that of Arnold Toynbee) for the newly established Koraes chair in Greek studies at King's College, London.

After returning from the Paris peace conference Leeper was appointed a regular member of the Foreign Office, with the rank of second secretary, in March 1920. He became assistant private secretary to the foreign secretary, Lord Curzon, in December 1920, acquiring great influence with Curzon and being almost wholly responsible for initiating a more open relationship with the press. On 2 April 1921 he married Janet Christina Monteith Hamilton (*b*. 1898/9), daughter of Vereker Monteith Hamilton, artist, and niece of General Sir Ian Hamilton. They had one daughter. In February 1924 Leeper was promoted to first secretary and seconded to Australia to advise the prime minister, Stanley Bruce, on the reorganization of that country's department of external affairs. His report was described by J. R. Poynter as 'an important document in the history of Australian foreign policy' (Poynter, 'Leeper, Alexander', 56). On his return from Australia Leeper was appointed first secretary at the Vienna legation in December 1924. He used his spare time while posted there to begin a study, published posthumously, *A History of Medieval Austria* (1941). While in Vienna he witnessed the 'pan-European' congress and was the only Foreign Office official to take the idea seriously. He warned that Europe would ultimately form an economic bloc and that Britain would have to decide whether to be in or out.

In November 1928 Leeper returned to London as a member of the League of Nations and western department and in August 1933 became its head upon his promotion to counsellor. His main work now came to concern arms control, and he was intimately involved in the Geneva disarmament conference. He worked closely with his chief, and old friend, Sir Robert Vansittart, sharing to some degree his world-view. Leeper in particular worked on the British proposal for the prohibition of aerial bombardment on the territory or shipping of another state, attempting to find a solution that maintained Britain's ability to deploy air power in the policing of its empire while giving it some measure of protection from aerial attack. A strong supporter of the League of Nations as a vehicle for improving international relations, he was prompted to adjust his views by the rise to power of the Nazis in Germany.

A gifted linguist, Leeper could read fifteen languages with ease and converse in seven or eight. Together with his brother, he was an exponent of Britain pursuing cultural diplomacy. His principal recreational interests were reading, travel, and Shakespeare's plays. Religiously devout, he moved from the Anglican evangelical environment of his youth to Anglo-Catholicism. A deeply humane and modest person, he could, when necessary, forcefully argue a case to a senior figure with an unflinching courage. He was appointed CBE (1920) and CMG (1935). He died at 5 Collingham Gardens, Earls Court, London, on 24 January 1935, following the rupture of his gall-bladder. He was survived by his wife and daughter. ERIK GOLDSTEIN

Sources papers, CAC Cam. • H. Nicolson, 'Allen Leeper', *Nineteenth Century and After*, 118 (1935), 473–83 • PRO, foreign office MSS • H. Seton-Watson and C. Seton-Watson, *The making of a new Europe: R. W. Seton-Watson and the last years of Austria-Hungary* (1981) • J. Headlam-Morley, *A memoir of the Paris peace conference, 1919*, ed. A. Headlam-Morley, R. Bryant, and A. Cienciala (1972) • R. Clogg, *Politics and the academy: Arnold Toynbee and the Koraes chair* (1986) • J. R. Poynter, 'Leeper, Alexander (1848–1934)', *AusDB*, vol. 10 • J. R. Poynter, *Doubts and certainties: a life of Alexander Leeper* (Melbourne, 1997) • m. cert. • d. cert. • *WWW, 1929–40* • *FO List*

Archives CAC Cam., corresp. and diaries | PRO, foreign office MSS, FO 371 • UCL, school of Eastern European and Slavonic studies, R. W. Seton-Watson MSS | FILM IWM FVA, home footage • IWM FVA, news footage

Wealth at death £311 9*s*. 3*d*.: probate, 7 March 1935, *CGPLA Eng. & Wales*

Leeper, Sir Reginald Wildig Allen [Rex] (1888–1968), diplomatist, was born on 25 March 1888 at Toxteth Park, Glebe, Sydney, New South Wales, the second son and youngest of the four children of Alexander Leeper (1848–1934), classical scholar, and his first wife, Adeline Marian (1853–1893), daughter of Sir George Wigram Allen, solicitor and politician. His elder brother, (Alexander Wigram) Allen *Leeper, was also a diplomatist. Leeper (who was known throughout his life as Rex) was educated at Melbourne grammar school (where he was head of school, in 1905) and Trinity College, Melbourne. He excelled as a student of the classics at both institutions, also displaying at university a talent for modern languages, which was recognized by the award of scholarships for Italian and Japanese. He graduated in 1909. Later that year, he entered New College, Oxford. In 1911 he obtained his second BA, with a second-class degree in modern history.

The idea of a life and career outside Australia had taken root while Leeper was at Oxford. He was rejected for a British Museum post, and after an unsuccessful interlude with a British trading company in India, he joined the department of information's intelligence bureau in 1916, having been invalided out of the southern Indian mounted territorial force the previous year. On 30 December 1916 he married his first cousin, (Margaret) Primrose Dundas Allen (1890–1987), daughter of George Boyce Allen, of Oxford. They had two daughters, Elizabeth (*b*. 1918), and Ann (*b*. 1922). Leeper entered the Foreign Office as a temporary clerk in March 1918, serving briefly in the political intelligence department, and was appointed CBE in 1920 for his work in connection with the Paris peace conference. He was promoted second secretary in September 1920, and joined the Foreign Office's northern department. One of his earliest duties was to negotiate the exchange of Maxim Litvinov for Robert Bruce Lockhart, the British consul in Moscow, who had been detained by the Soviet authorities. He went on to serve in Warsaw (1923–4), where he was promoted first secretary in February 1924, Riga (1924–5), Constantinople (1925–7), and Warsaw again (1927–9), returning to the Foreign Office in March 1929; he had acted as chargé d'affaires in each of his postings. He was promoted counsellor in August 1933, and appointed CMG in 1936.

Two subjects dominated Leeper's professional life during the 1930s: the threat of fascism in Europe, and improving the usefulness of propaganda in peace and war. Anthony Eden remembered him as 'an early prophet of the Nazi menace' (Eden, 203). At considerable risk to his career, he used his position as a Foreign Office official to support the activities of politicians opposed to the policy of appeasement, such as Winston Churchill. As one of 'Van's boys'—the coterie of younger officials favoured by the permanent under-secretary in the Foreign Office, Sir Robert Vansittart—he transformed British approaches to propaganda when head of the Foreign Office news department from 1935. His pioneering work provided a sound foundation for Britain's propaganda efforts during the Second World War. He was also the driving force behind the establishment in 1934 of the British Council, the country's first national 'cultural propaganda' body.

From August 1940 Leeper acted as an assistant under-secretary in the Foreign Office. He revived, and served as director of, its political intelligence department between 1938 and 1943. From 1940 to 1941 he headed SO 1, the first (propaganda) division of the Special Operations Executive, and from 1941 to 1943 was director of the country headquarters of the political warfare executive. He worked at Woburn Abbey, Bedfordshire, from November 1940. The battles within Britain's wartime security establishment and Leeper's uneasy relationship with his ministerial chief, Hugh Dalton, eventually disillusioned and exhausted him, and he was relieved to be appointed ambassador to the Greek government in March 1943.

Based in Cairo until October 1944, and then in Athens, Leeper's main task was to restore British influence in Greece by ensuring the return of the king of the Hellenes to a democratic state, and by neutralizing any threats to national stability, principally that posed by the communists. He succeeded, due in large measure to his diplomatic and political skills, and to the firm support of the prime minister, Winston Churchill, whose romantic love of Greece was expressed in a barrage of telegrams to Leeper. These enjoined him, for example, to display those 'qualities of imperturbability and command which are associated with the British Diplomatic Service' (PRO, FO954/11B, no. 131, 07/04/44). Leeper obliged, reporting on one occasion that, despite privation and danger, the embassy's occupants were 'in excellent heart but getting terribly short of whisky' (PRO, FO954/11B, no. 475, 05/12/44). The communist insurgency was eventually defeated, with the help of British troops, and in March 1946 elections confirmed the ascendancy of the monarchists. Two months later Leeper was appointed ambassador to Argentina. There he was involved closely in the complex negotiations that led to the signing of the Anglo-Argentine trade treaty, or Andes agreement, in February 1948. He retired from diplomacy the following December. He was promoted GBE on retirement, having been promoted KCMG in 1945.

In retirement Leeper accepted directorships of several companies, including De Beers Consolidated Mines Ltd and the Mexican Light and Power Co. He also served as vice-president of the British Council from 1948. He died of cerebrovascular arteriosclerosis and cancer of the prostate at his London home, 9 Cornwall Gardens, Kensington, on 2 February 1968. He was survived by his wife and two daughters. A memorial service was held at St Paul's, Knightsbridge, on 12 February.

Leeper, who inspired great loyalty from his subordinates, possessed the organizing and negotiating abilities of the ablest civil servant. He even looked the part, one contemporary describing him as 'tall and spare, with the thoughtful, concentrated face of some old-time papal secretary' (Delmer, 62). He could be 'political', going beyond his brief in the pre-war Foreign Office and in Greece, although the seriousness of both situations demanded unorthodox methods, and he was proven justified in each instance. There may have been something of the politician *manqué* about him; if so, his gifts were put to good use, as founder of the British Council, an anti-appeaser and wartime propagandist, and in Greece and Argentina.

DEREK DRINKWATER

Sources R. Cockett, *Twilight of truth: Chamberlain, appeasement and the manipulation of the press* (1989) • J. Poynter, *Doubts and certainties: a life of Alexander Leeper* (1997) • P. M. Taylor, *The projection of Britain: British overseas publicity and propaganda, 1919–1939* (1981) • P. Papastratis, *British policy towards Greece during the Second World War, 1941–1944* (1984) • R. Leeper, *When Greek meets Greek* (1950) • F. Donaldson, *The British Council: the first fifty years* (1984) • *FO List* (1949) • *Liber Melburniensis* (1965) • *The Second World War diary of Hugh Dalton, 1940–1945*, ed. B. Pimlott (1986) • *The Times* (5 Feb 1968) • N. Rose, *Vansittart: study of a diplomat* (1978) • PRO, FO954/11B • H. Macmillan, *The blast of war, 1939–1945* (1967) [vol. 2 of autobiography] • *The diaries of Sir Robert Bruce Lockhart*, ed. K. Young, 2 vols. (1973–80) • *The diplomatic diaries of Oliver Harvey, 1937–1940*, ed. J. Harvey (1970) • M. Balfour, *Propaganda in war, 1939–1945: organisations, policies and publics in Britain and Germany* (1979) • S. Delmer, *Black boomerang* (1962) • Lord Gladwyn, *Memoirs* (1972) • A. Eden, *Facing the dictators* (1962) • H. Macmillan, *War diaries: politics and war in the Mediterranean, January 1943 – May 1945* (1984) • J. R. Poynter, 'Leeper, Alexander (1848–1934)', *AusDB*, vol. 10 • B. Pimlott, *Hugh Dalton* (1985) • N. Cowper and R. Teale, 'Allen, Sir George Wigram (1824–1885)', *AusDB*, vol. 3 • *The diaries of Sir Alexander Cadogan, 1938–1945*, ed. D. Dilks (1971) • A. Roberts, *'The holy fox': a biography of Lord Halifax* (1991) • T. Barman, *Diplomatic correspondent* (1968) • J. A. Page, *Perón: a biography* (1983) • M. R. D. Foot, *SOE: an outline history of the Special Operations Executive, 1940–46* (1984) • O. Lancaster, *Classical landscape with figures* (1947) • J. Lees-Milne, *Harold Nicolson: a biography, 1930–1968* (1981) • C. M. Woodhouse, *The story of modern Greece* (1968) • New College register (1909–11) • *WWW, 1961–70* • *Who's who in Australia* (1965) • Burke, *Peerage* • d. cert.

Archives Balliol Oxf. • CAC Cam. • State Library of Victoria, Melbourne, La Trobe manuscript collection, letters and MSS, MS 11129 | BL, corresp. with P. V. Emrys-Evans, Add. MS 58236 • CAC Cam., corresp. with his brother A. W. A. Leeper | FILM BFI NFTVA, news footage

Likenesses W. Stoneman, photograph, 1948, NPG • photograph, repro. in *The Times* • photograph, repro. in Donaldson, *British Council*, facing p. 18

Wealth at death £105,468: probate, 4 April 1968, *CGPLA Eng. & Wales*

Lees, Andrew John (1949–1994/5), conservationist and environmental campaigner, was born on 8 June 1949 at

Sandown Nursing Home, 14 Sandown Road, Great Yarmouth, Norfolk, the eldest among the four boys of Edward Andrew Lees (*b.* 1923), hotelier and Great Yarmouth borough councillor, and his wife, Beryl, *née* Whiteley (1927–1993). Andrew Lees was a son of Norfolk with a passion for its big skies, low-lying landscape, and traditional village culture. Most of all he loved its myriad of rivers and streams, dykes, marshes, and fens, and its rich diversity of wildlife.

In 1967 (after education at St George's School, Harpenden) Lees enrolled at the University of Wales in Cardiff to study zoology, botany, and philosophy. After graduating with honours in 1971 he worked as a field scientist with the Nature Conservancy Council (NCC). The NCC had a statutory responsibility to protect the best of Britain's natural environment by designating certain areas as 'sites of special scientific interest' (SSSIs). Lees's uncompromising commitment to nature conservation first emerged in 1978 when surveying Crymlyn bog in Wales. Having determined that this unique habitat was a potential candidate for special protection he organized the local community and the media to stop it being turned into a rubbish tip. In 1981, working with Friends of the Earth (FOE), he obtained leave for judicial review of NCC's failure to notify part of the bog as a SSSI. The NCC backed down and the site was given SSSI protection. This was Lees's first environmental campaign success. His adherence to scientific discipline and knowledge of environmental laws, combined with his ability to attract media attention and generate local support, provided the winning formula that defined his future environmental campaign strategies.

Disillusioned with the NCC, Lees left Wales in late 1981 and returned to his native Norfolk. The broads were under serious threat from proposals to build deep drainage and barrier systems that would turn the wetlands into vast prairies of cereal production. In 1982 Lees helped to set up Broadlands Friends of the Earth and was appointed as its chairman. He lobbied the media, exposed the environmental contradictions in the government's agricultural policies, and succeeded in galvanizing local and national opinion against the drainage scheme. In 1986, after much campaigning, large tracts of marshlands were designated an environmentally sensitive area (ESA). Two years later, under intense public pressure, the government passed the Norfolk and Suffolk Broads Act. The broads were protected: a success due in large measure to Lees's tenacious campaigning and commitment.

In 1985 Lees was appointed FOE national campaign officer for the countryside and pesticides, and in 1986 as water pollution and toxics campaigner. Pollution in any form was unacceptable to him: agricultural pesticides, sewage discharges, leachate from landfill sites, and traffic pollution. Any activity that threatened human health or the environment would be challenged. He continued to apply his winning campaign formula with vigour and determination. He organized the 'dirty dozen' campaign to expose a group of highly toxic chemicals, many of which were later banned. He pioneered the use of judicial review of government legislation. He used formal complaints procedures to ensure proper implementation by the British government of European Community environmental laws, becoming a well-known figure to officials in Brussels. He was extremely wary of the government's plans in 1987 to privatize the water industry, which he felt would undermine water quality in the United Kingdom. He exposed the poorly regulated and weak standards of sewage treatment and showed that concentrations of pesticides in many drinking water supplies breached legal standards. The Water Resources Act, which was implemented in 1991, included much higher environmental standards and tighter regulatory controls for the protection of water quality than had previously been expected. This was one of Lees's greatest achievements.

Lees's environmental concerns extended beyond the UK. In 1988 he and a fellow FOE campaigner, Charles Secrett, went to Nigeria and exposed the illegal dumping of 8000 tons of mainly Italian toxic waste at Koko on the Niger delta. Lees was incensed that a so-called developed country could show such scant regard for the health and well-being of local people in a developing country. Not content simply to expose those responsible, he continued to track the waste on the *Karin B* cargo ship. With nowhere for the ship to go the *Karin B* saga became an international scandal and a major embarrassment to the European Union, which later introduced new regulations restricting the shipment of hazardous waste to developing countries.

In 1990 Lees became FOE's national campaigns director. His enthusiastic and combative campaigning style never abated. He would work day and night to get results, and he expected the same level of commitment from his colleagues. He was demanding and motivating in equal measure. His single-minded and often uncompromising approach would sometimes infuriate his colleagues. But he was also empowering and supportive, always encouraging others to realize their aspirations, hopes, and dreams.

Lees's intense love of life and nature extended beyond environmental campaigning. He had a lively interest in philosophy, politics, and art that shaped his own unconventional perspective on life. But it was his partner from 1984, Christine Orengo (*b.* 1955), a theoretical biologist, who provided balance in his often over-stressed life. They were a devoted couple. She described him as a wonderful listener, the most caring and loving of partners, completely supportive, and a great strength in times of crisis.

In 1994 Lees turned his attention to Madagascar, the world's fourth largest island and home to some of the most remarkable flora and fauna on earth. QIT, a mining company owned by Rio Tinto Zinc, was proposing to mine parts of the island for titanium dioxide. The mining operation threatened to produce 2 billion tons of titanium dioxide over forty years, and destroy huge swathes of unique littoral forest and sand dunes, along with the livelihood of thousands of local farmers and fishermen. This was a *cause célèbre* of international proportions. Lees went to Madagascar with a photographer, Paul Hellyer, just before Christmas 1994, with the intention of making a film documentary to support his campaign. Sadly, he never completed the project. On new year's eve, despite suffering from chronic diarrhoea, he decided to go into Petriky Forest alone to shoot one last piece of film. Hours later, when he failed to rendezvous with his taxi, there was panic. Eventually his body was found in a small clearing in Petriky Forest on 7 January. There was no indication of foul play. His camera equipment was intact. The autopsy later indicated that he had died of heat exhaustion. He was buried in Norfolk.

Lees was a scientist with principles: a professional campaigner who won international acclaim and respect for his work on the environment. His abrupt and tragic death sent shock waves around the world. Tributes poured in from friends and adversaries alike. The media variously described him as 'a secular saint', 'a man of deep principles', and 'an environmental campaigner of a kind we will not see again', the man who 'effected more positive environmental change than any Secretary of State in the government'. A former European commissioner, Lord Clinton-Davis, commented on Lees's remarkable ability to influence an audience by his unassailable evidence and penetrating logic. Following his death the Andrew Lees Memorial Trust Fund was set up to help the people of Madagascar, and the Libanona Ecology Centre was dedicated to his memory. Perhaps the most poignant of memorials erected in his honour is the one at Pant-y-sais fen, the northern limb of the Crymlyn bog, where Lees's remarkable campaigning career began. The memorial carries a quotation from him: 'At some point I had to stand up and be counted. Who speaks for the butterflies?'

JOHN BARWISE

Sources *The Independent* (9 Jan 1995) · *The Guardian* (9 Jan 1995) · *The Times* (13 Jan 1995) · *The Guardian* (14 Jan 1995) · www.broads-authority.gov.uk, 14 Jan 2002 · www.nwjones.demon.uk/foe2/kilcrym.htm, 20 Jan 2002 · personal knowledge (2004) · private information (2004) [Edward Lees, Christine Orengo, Tony Long, Mary Taylor, Charles Secrett] · b. cert. · *CGPLA Eng. & Wales* (1996) · www.andrewleestrust.org.uk, 18 Jan 2002

Likenesses D. Mansell, photograph, 1984, Hult. Arch. · photograph, repro. in *The Independent*

Wealth at death under £125,000: administration, 20 March 1996, *CGPLA Eng. & Wales*

Lees, Charles (1800–1880), painter, was born on 11 July 1800 in Cupar, Fife, the son of Charles Lees, a linen manufacturer, and his wife, Catherine Tarbane. He studied art in Edinburgh where he received tuition from Sir Henry Raeburn. Lees first exhibited at the Institution for the Encouragement of the Fine Arts in Scotland; a small full-length portrait was shown in 1824 and *Portrait of a Gentleman* in 1825. Lees was elected an associate of the Scottish Academy in March 1829 and admitted as an academician that same year. He exhibited there throughout his life, his early works being predominately portraits. On 22 June 1832 he married Agnes Loudon of Dairsie, Fife. It is not known when he remarried, but his death certificate records that he was the widower of Elizabeth Christie. He had four sons: Archibald, Charles, Robert, and Henry. A portrait of a medical officer of the Royal Navy shown at the Royal Scottish Academy in 1861 was probably a portrait of Charles, who served as a Royal Navy surgeon.

In 1832 Lees exhibited *The Cameronian Sunday Evening* at the Society of British Artists in London but the picture did not sell and he exhibited the same painting at the Scottish Academy the following year. Lees went to Rome in 1832, where he hoped to remain for a year or two. On his return to Edinburgh in 1835, he exhibited *Church of San Carlo al Corso, Roma* at the Scottish Academy. He lived in Edinburgh for the rest of his life, exhibiting infrequently at the Royal Academy in London between 1841 and 1857.

Lees painted a number of members of the Royal Scottish Academy, including the Revd David R. Arnott, chaplain to the academy (1861–77), and the painter J. E. Lauder. Both these portraits were painted on panel, while that of another academician, David Scott, was painted on zinc. They were painted very precisely using small, neat brushstrokes, and while they do not have flair his portraits are of some merit. Lees had a lifelong interest in the Royal Scottish Academy, serving as treasurer from 1868 to 1880. His diploma work, *Summer Moon—Bait Gatherers* (1858), is a glorious subject but is sadly deficient in depth and feeling. However, his sporting pictures, produced mainly in the 1850s and 1860s, are more celebrated.

Lees's sporting paintings included both portraits and scenes of golfers and curlers that recorded actual competitions. The golfer Sandy Pirrie and golf ball manufacturer Allan Robertson both sat to Lees (both Scot. NPG). *The Golfers at St Andrews* (1847; priv. coll.) includes portraits of Sir David Baird and Sir Ralph Anstruther, and their competitors Major Playfair and John Campbell of Saddell (engraving in Scot. NPG). *A Grand Match Played over St Andrews Links* contains numerous portraits (1865); previously hung in the Royal and Ancient clubhouse, St Andrews, it was engraved by Charles E. Wagstaffe in 1850. Lees's *Grand match of the Royal Caledonian Curling Club Linlithgow between the north and south of the Forth* (1853; priv. coll.) was exhibited posthumously at the Royal Scottish Academy in 1880; it had earlier been engraved by John Le Conte of Edinburgh and published by W. Forrester of Edinburgh in 1858 (BM). The engravings indicate the contemporary public interest in sporting images and where Lees's reputation now lies. He died at his home, 19 Scotland Street, Edinburgh, on 28 February 1880 after suffering a stroke.

L. H. CUST, *rev.* LUCY DIXON

Sources *Art Journal*, 42 (1880), 172 · R. Billcliffe, ed., *The Royal Glasgow Institute of the Fine Arts, 1861–1989: a dictionary of exhibitors at the annual exhibitions*, 4 vols. (1990–92), vol. 3 · Bryan, *Painters* · Graves, *RA exhibitors* · A. Graves, *A century of loan exhibitions, 1813–1912*, 2 (1908) · Graves, *Brit. Inst.* · J. Halsby and P. Harris, *The dictionary of Scottish painters, 1600–1960* (1990) · P. J. M. McEwan, *Dictionary of Scottish art and architecture* (1994) · W. D. McKay and F. Rinder, *The Royal Scottish Academy, 1826–1916* (1917) · H. Smailes, *The concise catalogue of the Scottish National Portrait Gallery* (1990) · A. M. Stewart and C. de Courcy, *Royal Hibernian Academy of Arts: index of exhibitors and their works, 1826–1979*, 3 vols. (1985–7) · B. Stewart and M. Cutten, *The dictionary of portrait painters in Britain up to 1920* (1997) · M. A. Wingfield, *A dictionary of sporting artists, 1650–1990* (1992) · bap. reg. Scot. [Robert Lees, son] · d. cert. · Edinburgh and Leith directories, City of Edinburgh Library · *IGI*

Archives Royal Scot. Acad., letters and paintings

Likenesses photographs, Royal Scot. Acad.
Wealth at death £1479 14s. 6d.: confirmation, 8 Sept 1880, *CCI*

Lees, Derwent [*formerly* Desmond] (**1884–1931**), painter, was born on 14 November 1884 in Clarence, Tasmania, the ninth child of William Lees, bank manager, and his wife, Gertrude Knox, both of whom were born in England. Originally named Desmond, Derwent Lees took his first name from the river on which Clarence is situated. He was educated at Melbourne grammar school and is said to have gone on to Melbourne University, but there is no formal record of his attendance there; he studied art in London (following a brief stay in Paris) at the Slade School of Fine Art, University College (1905–7), under Frederick Brown and Henry Tonks; a fellow student was J. D. Innes, with whom he developed a close friendship. Lees went several times with Innes to France, painting in Caudebec (Normandy), Bozouls (the Auvergne), and Collioure (Roussillon). Having won many prizes at the Slade for his brilliant draughtsmanship, Tonks appointed him to teach there, which he did from 1907 to 1918. (The Slade School has nineteen of his drawings in its collection.) He travelled widely in Europe, visiting Poland, Russia, Belgium, Germany, Italy, and Spain; however, repeated visits to France, to Ffestiniog in north Wales, and to Dorset with Innes and Augustus John were of the greatest importance to his art. Between 1911 and 1916 he was an exhibiting member of the Friday Club which had been founded in 1905 by Vanessa Bell. He exhibited in London at the Alpine Club Gallery, Brook Street Gallery, Goupil Galleries, and Redfern Gallery, at the Walker Art Gallery in Liverpool, and at the New English Art Club, of which he became a member in 1911. Three of his pictures were included in the celebrated Armory show in New York in 1913 (the American collector John Quinn owned eight of his paintings) and his first one-man show was at the Chenil Galleries in London in 1914. On 21 July 1913 he married his model, Edith Gilbert (Lyndra) Price (*b.* 1890/91), daughter of John Frederick Price.

Lees's work is close in style to that of Innes and John (the latter of whom he depicted in the nude with his mistress Dorelia, as Adam and Eve), being freely painted, often in intense colours, flat in pattern, and evoking wild landscape and mountainous country, often including lyrically romantic female figures; *The Blue Pool, Dorset* (1911) and *Lyndra by the Pool* (1914), both in Manchester City Galleries, are very characteristic. A photograph of the Slade picnic in 1912 shows Lees in the company of, among others, Dora Carrington, C. R. W. Nevinson, Mark Gertler, David Bomberg, and Stanley Spencer; he was of average height, wore his hair combed back, had an oval face with a heavy mouth, and in the photo has a brooding expression. He wears a suit with a collar and tie, which was evidently his custom; he appears similarly dressed in a painting by Innes, *Moonlight and Lamplight* (*c.*1908, priv. coll.), showing him seated in an interior. Lees was lame, having suffered a serious accident falling from a horse before he left Australia; his head was injured and his right foot was amputated. He wore a prosthetic wooden foot which did not, however, interfere with an active life; indeed, he is said to have climbed up the outside of the Chenil Galleries on one occasion and then to have had a fight with the owner, Jack Knewstub, who lived at the top. In 1918 he began to experience severe mental disorder and was unable to work during the last thirteen years of his life, which were passed in an asylum. He died at 1 West Park Road, Epsom, Surrey, on 28 March 1931. The Tate collection owns four of his works, including *Métairie des abeilles* (1912), and his paintings are also in the collections of many other British and Australian museums. Alan Windsor

Sources H. Lew, *In search of Derwent Lees* (1996) · *The Times* (30 March 1931) · m. cert. · d. cert.
Likenesses J. D. Innes, oils, *c.*1908, priv. coll. · group photograph, 1912, repro. in G. Gerzina, *Carrington: a life of Dora Carrington* (1990) · D. Lees, self-portrait, etching, *c.*1917, NPG

Lees, Edwin (**1800–1887**), botanist, was born at Worcester on 12 May 1800, the son of Thomas Lees (1772–1809), a woollen draper in that city, and Elizabeth (*b.* 1777), the eldest daughter of James Terrill, a Birmingham baker and confectioner. Following his father's early death his mother remarried in 1814 and probably thanks to her prosperous Birmingham relations Lees was educated at a boarding-school there, though the wide knowledge of botany and literature (especially poetry) he subsequently displayed was largely self-acquired. He was apprenticed in his early teens to a master printer. About 1828 he married Sarah, a native of Tewkesbury about whom little is known, and set up as a printer and bookseller in Worcester High Street. That same year he published, under the pseudonym Ambrose Florence, a guide to the city and cathedral with a list of local plants appended, and a few months later started a quarterly, the *Worcestershire Miscellany*, intended as a vehicle for local history, which survived for only five issues. Scarcely longer lived was another product of that initial burst of enthusiasm, the Worcester Literary and Scientific Institute, of which he acted as joint secretary.

Lees's long career as an author effectively opened in 1834 with the publication of *Illustrations of the Natural History of Worcestershire*, which, though attributed to Dr Charles Hastings, was substantially his work. Election to fellowship of the Linnean Society in 1835 was followed soon after by the sale of his shop, removal to the neighbourhood of Tewkesbury and the start of nearly thirty years as a freelance writer. *The Botanical Looker-Out* (1842) and *The Botany of the Malvern Hills* (1843) were the first fruits of his release from the ties of a business, the former the product of a series of walking tours in Wales and south-west England. The early 1840s also marked the beginning of more than two decades of study of blackberries, an intriguingly complex group of plants just then attracting the attention of field botanists. In 1844 the Botanical Society of London devoted seven successive meetings to an exposition by him of the forms of blackberries that he had succeeded in discriminating, mainly in the west midlands, several of which he was subsequently to describe. By comparison his other botanical work was lightweight and journalistic, some of it marred by a modish Romanticism carried to excess.

Lees's most important legacy locally came from his gifts as an organizer. Though otherwise of retiring habits, he was genial and kindly with a flair for informal instruction. In 1847, at the instance of Professor James Buckman, he founded the Worcestershire Naturalists' Club, on the model of similar bodies then springing up across the country in which the emphasis was on field meetings. Elected the first president, he was ever to remain its most active member. Almost at the start he proposed that the club compile a much-needed flora of the county, an objective realized twenty years later in *The Botany of Worcestershire*. It was apparently at his suggestion too that the Woolhope Naturalists' Field Club initiated in 1868 the annual fungus forays in Herefordshire for which it became nationally famous.

Lees was always anxious to share his profound interest in the local countryside and repeatedly spoke up against the wanton destruction of wildlife, including heedless collecting, at a period when such views were unfashionable. As early as 1828 he predicted the eventual creation of nature reserves. After his first wife died he returned to Worcester and about 1880 married a widow, Jane Bridges, a farmer's daughter of St John's and Broughton Hackett. Lees died in Worcester, at his house at Green Hill Summit, off London Road, on 21 October 1887; he was buried at Pendock, near Ledbury, on 28 October. His wife survived him.

B. D. JACKSON, *rev.* D. E. ALLEN

Sources M. M. Jones, *The lookers-out of Worcestershire* (1980) · *Berrow's Worcester Journal* (29 Oct 1887) · W. Mathews, *Journal of Botany, British and Foreign*, 25 (1887), 384 · J. Amphlett and C. Rea, *The botany of Worcestershire* (1909), xxi–xxv · 'The lady who did not eat sixpennyworth', *Transactions of the Worcestershire Naturalists' Field Club*, 1/new ser. (1983), 247–9 · *Transactions of the Woolhope Naturalists' Field Club*, 34 (1952–4), 242–3 · M. Lawley, *The bygone botanists of Herefordshire* (1996) · *CGPLA Eng. & Wales* (1887)

Archives U. Birm. L., corresp. · Victoria Institute, Worcester, letters · Woolhope Naturalists' Field Club, Hereford, notebook | NHM, corresp. with C. E. Broome

Likenesses S. Cole, oils, 1869 · photograph, Woolhope Naturalists' Field Club, Hereford; repro. in Lawley, *Bygone botanists of Herefordshire*

Wealth at death £2370 10*s*. 10*d*.: probate, 1 Dec 1887, *CGPLA Eng. & Wales*

Lees [*married name* Craven], **Florence Sarah** (1840–1922), nurse, was born in Blandford, Dorset, on 31 March 1840, the only daughter of Henry Lees, physician, and his wife, Sarah Matilda Phythian. Henry Lees deserted his family and Florence was brought up by a half-brother, an Oxford don, who sent her to school in London. In 1864 the family moved to St Leonards, where Florence helped her mother in visiting the sick. In 1866 she went to the Nightingale school at St Thomas's Hospital, London, as an observer for four months, as her mother would not allow her to be a probationer. During the following year she visited Germany and studied at the Kaiserswerth institute under Pastor Fliedner, subsequently visiting and studying in hospitals in Europe.

At the outbreak of the Franco-Prussian War Florence Lees volunteered for military nursing, and the crown princess of Germany, Queen Victoria's eldest daughter, put her in charge of a hospital at Marange, and later at Homburg. For her services she was awarded the cross of the German order of merit. After the war she studied in the United States and was impressed by the ideas of Palmer Howard, who maintained that nurses should be educated in the manner of medical students and pay for their training. Florence Lees argued, with some justification, that the current nurse training, even at St Thomas's, was deficient and did not give a systematic, planned education and that it failed to attract educated ladies looking for a worthwhile career. This was anathema to Florence Nightingale, who pointed out that 'the object was to encourage ladies to work'. Nightingale was also fearful of producing what she called 'medical women'. She maintained that 'the less knowledge of medicine that the matron has the better (1) because it does not improve her sanitary practice (2) because it would make her miserable and intolerable to doctors' (Cope, 121). The nurse must not only nurse, she must promote sanitary science, a subject in which she thought doctors were deficient. Later she did modify her views on medical lectures though she was always ambivalent as to whether the nurse should be the doctor's assistant or an autonomous practitioner. However, she was at one with Florence Lees in arguing against William Rathbone and the Liverpool concept of district nurses as welfare workers supervised by a ladies voluntary committee, insisting that the district nurse must have a higher training and be accountable to a superintendent who was herself a highly trained nurse.

In 1874 Florence Lees was asked to make a survey of the hospitals and nursing practices in London to see if a scheme such as hers would be viable. This she did almost single-handed, leaving a useful picture of the nursing situation in London at that time. As a result, with the help of the order of St John, the Metropolitan and National Nursing Association was founded to provide trained nursing for London with its headquarters in Bloomsbury and Miss Lees as the superintendent. After much controversy she converted the committee to the idea of a district nursing service as a corps of trained, educated women under the superintendence of a highly trained nurse. For this reason Florence Lees can be considered the founder of modern district nursing.

On 16 September 1879 Florence Lees married the Revd Dacre Henry Craven (*d.* 1922), son of Major Charles Cooley Craven, an army physician. It was a happy marriage: Dacre Craven supported her work and became the secretary to the home in Bloomsbury Square. They had two sons, the empress of Germany being a godparent to the elder, who committed suicide in 1928; the younger was killed in 1917. In 1887 Florence Craven, backed by the empress, and together with Florence Nightingale and William Rathbone, persuaded Queen Victoria to devote most of the women's jubilee offering to establish a national district nursing service. Using the Metropolitan and National Nursing Association as a model thus was established Queen Victoria's Jubilee Institute for Nurses (later the Queen's Nursing Institute): the queen's nurses. Mrs Craven served on the council and advised on training and in

1889 published *Guide to District Nurses and Home Nursing*, which became the vade-mecum for district nurses for many years. She was awarded the jubilee medal and the cross of St John of Jerusalem and remained, together with her husband, closely associated with district nursing until they retired to Essex in 1918.

Florence Craven died on 19 October 1922 at her home, 3 East Terrace, Walton on the Naze, Essex, two months after her husband, saying that she could not live without him. She was buried at Walton on the Naze, where there is a fine brass memorial to the Craven family in the parish church. MONICA E. BALY

Sources b. cert. • letter, from Mrs Edwin Bedford to Lady Stocks, Wellcome L., Queen's Nursing Institute archives • LMA, Cadbury letters, HI/ST/NTS/Y 161 • F. Lees's survey, printed booklet, June 1875, LMA, HI/ST/NC.C15 • M. Baly, *Florence Nightingale and the nursing legacy* (1997) • M. Stocks, *A hundred years of district nursing* (1960) • M. Baly, *A history of the Queen's Nursing Institute* (1987) • M. Baly, 'Profiles of pioneers: Florence Lees', *History of Nursing Journal*, 3/1 (1990), 85 • private information (1993) • m. cert. • d. cert. • Z. Cope, *Florence Nightingale and the doctors* (1958)

Archives Wellcome L., Queen's Nursing Institute *Guide to district nurses* (1889) [copies] | Wellcome L., Queen's Nursing Institute archives, lectures given by Mrs Dacre Craven to nurses and the public [copies]

Likenesses photographs, *c.*1880–1889

Wealth at death £2603 1*s.* 8*d.*: probate, 1923, *CGPLA Eng. & Wales*

Lees, Frederic Richard (1815–1897), temperance advocate, was born on 15 March 1815 at Meanwood, near Leeds, the only child of Joseph Lees (*c.*1795–1845), who conducted a school there, and his first wife, Anne (1796–1815), the daughter of Ephraim Sanderson of Aberford, also a schoolmaster. Joseph Lees remarried in 1816 and had nine children with his second wife, Isabella Bickerdyke. Prominent in local radical circles, he served as secretary of the Leeds Political Union in 1832. He sent his eldest son to Mr Compton's school in Bury (1825–8), and then articled him to a solicitor named Wailes in Leeds (1828–36).

Lees made his living as a temperance writer, editor, and speaker. One of the pioneers of teetotalism in the north of England, he took a pledge against drinking any kind of alcohol in 1835. Two years later he became joint secretary of the British Association for the Promotion of Temperance. From 1840 to 1844 he edited and published the *British Temperance Advocate and Journal*, and from 1844 to 1850 edited the *Truth Seeker*. In 1854 the new United Kingdom Alliance appointed him as a travelling secretary. Two years later Lees won the prize that the alliance offered for the best statement of the case for prohibition, published as the *Alliance prize essay, or, An argument, legal and historical, for the legislative prohibition of the liquor traffic*.

Despite frequent ill health Lees wrote incessantly. His principal books and shorter publications were reprinted as *The Selected Works* (8 vols., 1884–7) and *The True Thinker* (6 vols., 1891–7). Lees emphasized secular and scientific arguments against alcoholic drink. To enhance his position as the philosopher of temperance, he styled himself Doctor after 1842, when he received an honorary degree from a minor German university.

Intense and inflexible, Lees often courted controversy. As a young man he offended the orthodox by challenging the inerrancy of the Bible and in the 1840s flirted with pantheism. Ironically, he died a member of the Church of England. He irritated traditionalists by his demand, as early as the 1840s, that non-intoxicating grape juice be used in the eucharistic sacrament. With Dawson Burns he published *The Temperance Bible Commentary* (1868) to establish that the Bible never sanctioned fermented wine. Lees was forced to resign his alliance office in 1858 after he had accused the English-born American temperance reformer John Gough of being a secret drinker, and Gough sued him for libel. Radical in his political views, Lees upset many reformers when his independent candidacy at Leeds helped bring about the defeat of the incumbent Liberal MP, Edward Baines, in 1874. Lees headed a minority faction of the Good Templar fraternal temperance organization in the British Isles during a worldwide schism. He had joined the templars in 1869 while on a lecture tour in the United States, a year after Joseph Malins organized the first English lodge. Lees denounced the secession that Malins instigated in 1876. Malins claimed to be fighting for the right of black people in the American south to join the templar society, but Lees, an old abolitionist, regarded the real motive as a grab for power. Lees and Malins became adversaries in an expensive, acrimonious, and protracted law suit.

Lees enjoyed a happy family life. In 1838 he married Mercy Joanna Jowett (*d.* 1870), the daughter of a Leeds printer; they had two children, Frederic Arnold (1847–1921), a physician, surgeon, and botanist, and Mary Eleanor, who later married Freeman Whatmoor. On 25 September 1878 he married Mrs Sarah Barnesley, *née* Brooks, of Manchester, who died in 1889 at the age of fifty-eight. He lived most of his adult life at Meanwood, near Leeds, but he died at 1 Park Road, Halifax, on 29 May 1897. He was buried at Meanwood on 1 June. His son, Frederic Arnold Lees, contributed an introduction to the biography written by (George) Frederic William Lees (*b.* 1872), perhaps his son or a son of one of F. R. Lees's half-brothers. DAVID M. FAHEY

Sources G. F. W. Lees, *Dr Frederic Richard Lees, FSA Edin., a biography with an introductory appreciation and bibliography by Frederic Arnold Lees, LRCP* (1904) • D. M. Fahey, 'Lees, Frederick Richard (1815–97)', in J. O. Baylen and N. J. Gossman, *Biographical dictionary of modern British radicals*, 3 (1988), 518–23 • D. M. Fahey, *Temperance and racism: John Bull, Johnny Reb and the Good Templars* (1996) • L. L. Shiman, *Crusade against drink in Victorian England* (1988) • B. Harrison, *Drink and the Victorians: the temperance question in England, 1815–1872* (1971) • N. Longmate, *The waterdrinkers* (1968) • P. T. Winskill, *Temperance standard bearers of the nineteenth century: a biographical and statistical temperance dictionary*, 2 (1898) • J. Newton, *Alliance News* (March 1915), 44–6

Likenesses E. Fithian, pencil sketch, 1892, repro. in Lees, *Dr Frederic Richard Lees*

Wealth at death £4717 1*s.* 2*d.*: probate, 15 Dec 1897, *CGPLA Eng. & Wales*

Lees, George Martin (1898–1955), geologist, was born at Dundalk, co. Louth, Ireland, on 16 April 1898, the third child of George Murray Lees, civil engineer, of Edinburgh, and his wife, Mary Martin. From St Andrew's College, Dublin, he went to the Royal Military Academy at Woolwich.

Commissioned at seventeen in the Royal Artillery, he served in France but soon transferred to the Royal Flying Corps, in which he won the MC. After a tour of duty as flying instructor in Egypt he went to Mesopotamia for further active service, winning the DFC in air operations. He took part in the capture of Kirkuk from the Turks, making a forced landing behind the Turkish lines in what became the Kirkuk oilfield, regaining the British lines on foot by following geological outcrops seen from the air.

After the war Lees joined the civil administration in Iraq (1919–21), serving as assistant political officer in the mountainous Halabja district close to the Persian frontier. At the time of the insurrection he had an exciting escape, but later returned to Kurdistan. He resigned from the Iraq administration in April 1921 and began to study geology, in which he had become interested in Kurdistan. After a few months at the Royal School of Mines he joined the Anglo-Persian Oil Company (later the British Petroleum Company Ltd) in June 1921, as assistant geologist, without formal academic qualifications. The wisdom of this appointment was soon revealed by the excellence of his geological work and his appointment in 1930 as chief geologist of his company at the early age of thirty-two, a post he held with distinction until 1953.

In 1922–5 Lees was in the Middle East on geological surveys. In the winter of 1924–5 he accompanied an eminent Hungarian geologist, Hugo de Böckh, on a geological reconnaissance of south-west Persia, an experience which played an important part in his further geological education. In 1925–6 he made, with K. Washington Gray, a geological reconnaissance of Oman. During subsequent study leave at the University of Vienna (1926–8) he attended lectures by F. E. Suess and L. Kober, both eminent geologists with worldwide interests, and was awarded a PhD for a thesis on his Oman work, subsequently published by the Geological Society of London. In following years Lees examined oil prospects and oil company geological methods in many countries, including the United States, Canada, Egypt, Germany, and Australia. Under his geological direction his company in the Middle East discovered more oil for fewer wells drilled than the world had yet seen. Over 100,000 square miles of mountainous Persia were also geologically surveyed at appropriate scales. In 1933 he initiated a new programme of oil search in England and Scotland which resulted in the discovery of the east midland oilfields in 1939: these explorations added much new information to British geology, discovering the Yorkshire potash deposits as a by-product. During the war of 1939–45 Lees was seconded for a period to the petroleum division of the Ministry of Fuel and Power and also carried out a special mission for the prime minister in the Far East. Other successful explorations which he helped to initiate and which came to fruition in post-war years were those in Nigeria, Libya, and Abu Dhabi (Trucial Coast).

In 1943 Lees was awarded the Bigsby medal of the Geological Society of London 'for his important geological work in Persia and Oman, and for his share in the discovery of oil in England'. In 1948 he was elected FRS. During subsequent years he was appointed a member of the Geological Survey Board and served on the councils of the Geological Society and Royal Society and on other committees. For the two years of 1951 and 1952 he was president of the Geological Society, becoming the first geologist practising his profession in industry to achieve this distinction. His two presidential addresses, on 'Foreland folding' and 'The evolution of a shrinking earth', aroused considerable interest. In 1954 he was awarded the Sidney Powers memorial medal of the American Association of Petroleum Geologists, their highest distinction, never previously given to a non-American, for service to Middle East geology. Lees's publications, mostly on the Middle East, number about forty.

Lees had all the characteristics of a leader—outstanding personality, quickness of apprehension, capacity for constructive thinking, abundant common sense, skill in exposition, good humour, and reasonableness; in discussion he was a catalyst and a listener rather than a talker. His geological career coincided with the discovery and development on scientific lines of the world's largest oilfields, to which his contribution was unique.

In 1931 Lees married Hilda Frances, writer and musicologist, daughter of Francis Baugh Andrews, architect and antiquary; they had one son. Lees died at St Mary's Hospital, Paddington, London, on 25 January 1955, after two years' illness following a life of vigour and good health.

N. L. FALCON, *rev.* ROBERT BROWN

Sources R. W. Ferrier, *The history of the British Petroleum Company*, 1: *The developing years, 1901–1932* (1982) • J. H. Bamberg, *The history of the British Petroleum Company*, 2: *The Anglo-Iranian years, 1928–1954* (1994) • W. J. Arkell, *Memoirs FRS*, 1 (1955), 163–73 • private information (1971) • *CGPLA Eng. & Wales* (1955) • BP Archive, University of Warwick

Archives U. Cam., Centre of South Asian Studies, corresp. and papers relating to Iraq and Kurdistan • University of Warwick, BP Archive

Likenesses Sayer, photograph, GS Lond.

Wealth at death £30,721 19*s*. 11*d*.: probate, 2 April 1955, *CGPLA Eng. & Wales*

Lees, Sir Harcourt, second baronet (1776–1852), political pamphleteer, was born on 29 November 1776, the eldest son of Sir John Lees, baronet (1739–1811), and his wife, Mary, the eldest daughter of Robert Cathcart of Glandusk, Ayrshire. His father saw service in Germany under the marquess of Granby, and was private secretary to Lord Townshend during his administration of Ireland, where he was secretary to the Post Office from 1784. He was created a baronet in 1804. Lees was educated at Rathmines School, co. Dublin, at Trinity College, Dublin, and at Trinity College, Cambridge, where he graduated BA in 1799 and proceeded MA in 1802. He took holy orders, and was preferred to the rectory and vicarage of Killaney, co. Down, was collated to the prebend of Fennor in the church of Cashel in 1800, and to that of Tullycorbet in the church of Clogher in 1801; he resigned both stalls in July 1806. He succeeded his father as second baronet in 1811, and in or before October 1812 he married Sophia (*d*. 1874), daughter of Colonel Thomas Lyster of Grange, co. Roscommon. They had four sons and four daughters; their fourth son was William Nassau *Lees.

Lees was a prolific pamphleteer and lobbyist in the protestant interest. He warned of Jesuit-inspired conspiracies to massacre protestants and advocated firm repression, coupled with proposals for state payment of the Roman Catholic clergy so as to neutralize their political influence. His protestantism was of a conservative and political kind and he was strongly critical of the growing evangelical influence in Ireland. His writing was characterized by extreme animation of style and, in 1825, after he called on protestants to arm themselves against Roman Catholics, the Irish administration considered prosecuting him. His publications tended towards discursive titles, such as *Theological extracts; selected from a late letter written by a popish prelate to his grace the archbishop of Dublin, with observations on the same, and a well-merited and equally well-applied literary flagellation of the titular shoulders of this mild and humble minister of the gospel; with a complete exposure of his friend the pope and the entire body of holy impostors* (n.d.; 1822?). Short titles of other typical works include *The Antidote, or, 'Nouvelles à la main'* (1820), *Letter to Mr. Wilberforce … [on] the Whigs* (1820), *An Address to the King's Friends* (1820), and *Most Important: Trial of Sir Harcourt Lees* (1823). Lees died at his home, Blackrock House, near Dublin, on 7 March 1852.

J. M. RIGG, *rev.* JOHN WOLFFE

Sources *GM*, 1st ser., 54 (1784), 558 • *GM*, 1st ser., 74 (1804), 590 • *GM*, 1st ser., 81/2 (1811), 292 • *GM*, 1st ser., 82/2 (1812), 492 • *GM*, 2nd ser., 37 (1852), 518 • Liverpool MSS, BL • H. Cotton, *Fasti ecclesiae Hibernicae*, 1 (1845), 132–3 • H. Cotton, *Fasti ecclesiae Hibernicae*, 3 (1849), 103 • *The Times* (10 March 1852) • Venn, *Alum. Cant.* • E. Lodge, *Peerage, baronetage, knightage and companionage of the British empire*, 81st edn, 3 vols. (1912) • *BL cat.* • Burke, *Peerage*

Archives BL, corresp. with second earl of Liverpool, Add. MSS 38291–38295, *passim* • Lpool RO, letters to E. G. Stanley • PRO NIre., corresp. with first marquess of Anglesey • W. Sussex RO, letters to fifth duke of Richmond

Likenesses H. Meyer, stipple, pubd 1824 (after oil portrait by T. C. Thompson), BM, NPG • stipple (after T. C. Thompson?), NG Ire.

Lees, William Nassau (1825–1889), army officer and orientalist, was born on 26 February 1825, the fourth son of Sir Harcourt *Lees, second baronet (1776–1852), political pamphleteer, and his wife, Sophia, daughter of Colonel Lyster of Grange, co. Roscommon, Ireland. He was educated at Nut Grove and at Trinity College, Dublin, but took no degree. He was appointed to a Bengal cadetship in 1846, and was posted to the 42nd Bengal native infantry as ensign in March 1846. He was promoted lieutenant in 1853 and by 1885 he reached the rank of major-general. He was for some years principal of the Calcutta madrasa, where he was professor of law, logic, literature, and mathematics. He was also secretary to Fort William College, Persian translator to the government, and government examiner in Arabic, Persian, and Urdu for all branches of the service. As well as being for some years part proprietor of the *Times of India* newspaper, he was a constant contributor to the daily press on all Indian topics. He appears to have left India in the mid 1850s and settled in London.

In 1857 the University of Dublin conferred on Lees the honorary degree of LLD, and he also received a doctorate of philosophy from Berlin. He became a member of the Royal Asiatic Society of Great Britain and Ireland in 1872. A staunch Conservative in politics, he twice sought to enter parliament, but without success. He died of cirrhosis of the liver at his home, 64 Grosvenor Street, Grosvenor Square, London, on 9 March 1889, aged sixty-four.

Lees was a distinguished oriental scholar. In 1853, when still an ensign, he brought out an edition of Abu Isma'il Basri's *The Footooh al-Sham: being an Account of the Moslim Conquests in Syria*, and edited or co-edited various other works (see *Centenary Review of the Bengal Asiatic Society*, 1885). The Arabic work for which he is more remembered by eastern scholars is his *Commentary of Az-Zamakhshari*, an exegesis of the Koran. In Persian scholarship, his *Nafahatu 'l-Uns* of Jami, and *Biographical Sketch of the Mystic Philosopher and Poet Jámí* (1859), as well as his *Vis u Rámin*, which has been described as a poetical version of an original Pahlavi romance, are worthy of attention. Lees co-edited and supervised the publication of many editions of Persian and Arabic books, including Morley's edition of the *Tarikh-i-Baihaki*, and Ahmad Khan's edition (1868) of the *Tarikh-i-Firuz Shahi* by Ziyya al-Din Barani, an interesting account of which is in volume 3 of C. P. H. Rieu's *Catalogue of Persian Manuscripts in the British Museum* (4 vols., 1879–95), as well as the *Tabakat i-Nasiri* (1863) by Minhaju al-Din al-Jurjani.

Lees also contributed extensively to the *Journal of the Royal Asiatic Society of Great Britain and Ireland* and to the *Journal of the Asiatic Society of Bengal*. He published several handbooks on oriental languages for the use of candidates for the East India Company, as well as books on such widely different topics as the laws on the sale of land in India and *The Drain of Silver to the East, and the Currency of India* (1864).

H. M. CHICHESTER, *rev.* PARVIN LOLOI

Sources J. Foster, *The peerage, baronetage, and knightage of the British empire for 1880*, [2 pts] [1880] • *East-India Register and Directory* (1803–44) • *East-India Register and Army List* (1845–60) • *Journal of the Royal Asiatic Society of Great Britain and Ireland*, new ser., 21 (1889), 463–6 • *The Athenaeum* (16 March 1889), 345 • Boase, *Mod. Eng. biog.* • J. S. Crone, *A concise dictionary of Irish biography*, rev. edn (1937) • Allibone, *Dict.* • C. E. Buckland, *Dictionary of Indian biography* (1906) • d. cert.

Wealth at death £10,523 18s. 4d.: resworn probate, March 1890, *CGPLA Eng. & Wales* (1889)

Leese, Sir Oliver William Hargreaves, third baronet (1894–1978), army officer, was born in London on 27 October 1894; he was the eldest in the family of three sons and one daughter of Sir William Hargreaves Leese, second baronet (1868–1937), of Send Holme, Send, Surrey, and senior partner of Freshfields, solicitors, and his wife, Violet Mary (*d.* 1947), daughter of Albert George Sandeman, of Presdales, Hertfordshire. Educated at Ludgrove School and at Eton College, where he excelled at cricket and football, Leese was commissioned into the Coldstream Guards in August 1914. During the First World War he was wounded three times (the third nearly fatally in October 1916), was appointed DSO (1916), and was twice mentioned in dispatches.

From 1920 to 1922 Leese was adjutant of the 3rd battalion, Coldstream Guards. He then (1922–5) became adjutant of the Officers' Training Corps at Eton. He studied at the Staff College, Camberley, in 1927–8 and in 1933 he married Margaret Alice (*d.* 1964), daughter of Cuthbert Leicester-Warren, of Tabley House, Knutsford, country gentleman; they had no children. After occupying various posts he became general staff officer, grade 2, at the War Office in 1935, and in the following year took command of the 1st battalion, Coldstream Guards. He succeeded his father as baronet in 1937. In 1938 he went to India as chief instructor at the Staff College, Quetta.

In 1940 Leese was recalled home, and held five posts, including that of deputy chief of the general staff of the British expeditionary force (BEF) until the evacuation of France. He helped prepare the outline plan for the Dunkirk evacuation. He was promoted major-general in 1941. He then formed the guards armoured division, training it with great thoroughness and enthusiasm. In September 1942, with the rank of temporary lieutenant-general, he was sent for by General B. L. Montgomery to command 30th corps, Eighth Army, before the battle of El Alamein, his task being to break through the German minefields so that the armour could fan out. With Australian, New Zealand, South African, and Indian divisions under his command Leese made a vital contribution to victory, causing Montgomery to inform Sir Alan Brooke that 'the best soldier out here is Oliver Leese—first class' (Hamilton, 2.46). The relationship between Montgomery and Leese is important. Montgomery regarded him as a great friend and Leese considered his superior the finest general in the field since the duke of Marlborough. Leese was a perfect foil to Montgomery, being intensely loyal though not a yes-man, and thoroughly disliking publicity.

After a refit Leese's corps led the advance to Tripoli and Mareth. In March 1943 Sir H. R. L. C. Alexander asked Montgomery to release Leese so that he could command the First Army. Montgomery refused, though he could have spared him ten days later, after the battle of Mareth, and this might have made a great difference to Leese's career. As it was, Alexander then took control himself. In July 1943, with Canadian troops under his command, Leese landed in Sicily and penetrated along the eastern side of the island. He then took 30th corps back to England.

At the end of December 1943 Leese was appointed to succeed Montgomery as general officer commanding Eighth Army before Monty could return and prevent his departure, as General Sir Frank Simpson put it. In March 1944, the American Fifth Army having failed to capture Cassino, Alexander ordered Leese to take the Eighth Army across the Apennines, a task he completed in utter secrecy, in order to capture the monastery position. Partly thanks to the Polish corps (led by General Anders), which respected Leese more than any other British commander, the battle was won in May. When on reaching the 'Gothic line' the Eighth Army was held up, Leese again moved with complete surprise eastwards to the Adriatic, and breached its defences.

In October 1944 Leese became commander-in-chief, allied land forces, south-east Asia, with his headquarters in Calcutta. He was directed to establish the Fourteenth Army under General W. J. Slim in central Burma by the end of 1945 but, partly due to his drive, Burma was recaptured by June. There then occurred a setback in Leese's military career. He started planning the invasion of Singapore for September 1945. Slim was tired and requested three months' leave in England. As Leese required a commander in India, with combined operations experience, to plan the landings, he suggested to Lord Louis Mountbatten, supreme allied commander, south-east Asia, that Slim should command the Twelfth Army in Burma to mop up, and a new invasion commander be appointed. Mountbatten instructed Leese to sound out Slim, who agreed at first, and then retracted, preferring retirement and implying that Leese had sacked him. Mountbatten then dismissed Leese for exceeding instructions. Leese never disclosed his version but in his diaries Alanbrooke wrote that after reprimanding Leese, who took it in manly fashion, never blaming anyone else, he still had a 'feeling that, although he may have been at fault, he had a raw deal at the hands of Mountbatten' (Fraser, 498). Leese next became general officer commanding-in-chief, eastern command. He retired from the army in 1946.

Leese then turned to horticulture, becoming expert on mushrooms, cacti, and bonsai trees. He wrote three books on cacti, accumulated a collection at Worfield Gardens, Shropshire, and travelled extensively collecting specimens, being known affectionately as Cactus Pete. He won many gold medals at the Chelsea flower show and was often found by his stand producing, from memory, Latin names of exhibits (just as he had given lectures on military strategy without notes). He was elected to the Royal Horticultural Society floral committee.

As national president of the British Legion (1962–70) Leese changed its image, increasing a declining membership by 50,000, and always contacting local branches on his travels abroad. While president of the combined cadet force association (1950–71) he encouraged close relations between the services and schools with cadet units. He ran the El Alamein reunion, and was chairman of the Old Etonian Association, a director of Securicor, lieutenant of the Tower of London, and colonel of the Shropshire yeomanry. Cricket was a great love of his, as was fly fishing. President of Warwickshire County Cricket Club (1959–75) and of the Shropshire County Cricket Club, he was prominent in their administration. He was elected president of MCC (1965–6) and accompanied their tour of Australia.

A tall, strong man, informal, unorthodox in dress, with the manner (which masked an astute mind) of a Wodehouse character, Leese possessed a sense of humour and schoolboy fun but was sometimes impatient and intolerant and had an explosive, petulant temper. His refusal to get immersed in paperwork (though he never took an important decision without the most detailed examination) gave him more time to see his troops, waving to those he passed, as they did to him, or appearing unexpectedly on a gun site. He regarded as important the distribution of 'comforts' to them. He surrounded himself with predominantly young officers whom he sent on important missions with complete confidence, having instilled in them his determination 'to achieve'. He offered warm hospitality in his Eighth Army mess, among whose visitors were George VI (who knighted Leese in the field at Arezzo), Winston Churchill, and J. C. Smuts. A prolific letter writer (once sending at least 150 postcards from Australia), he kept up with a variety of friends. His will-power was such that he overcame a leg amputation when he was seventy-nine. His determination 'never to look back' was an important part of his character.

Leese was appointed CBE (1940), CB (1942), and KCB (1943). In 1944 he was awarded the Virtuti Militari, the highest Polish military honour. He also won the Croix de Guerre and was a commander of the Légion d'honneur and of the American Legion of Merit. Leese died on 22 January 1978 at his home, Dolwen, Cefn-coch, Llanrhaeadr, Montgomeryshire. He was succeeded in the baronetcy by his brother, Alexander William (1909–1982). In 1982 the baronetcy became extinct.

I. M. CALVOCORESSI, *rev.*

Sources B. L. Montgomery, *The memoirs of field-marshal the Viscount Montgomery of Alamein* (1958) · N. Hamilton, *Monty*, [3 vols.] (1981–6) · D. Fraser, *Alanbrook* (1982) · personal knowledge (1986) · private information (1986) · *WWW* · *The Times* (23 Jan 1978) · *CGPLA Eng. & Wales* (1978) · Burke, *Peerage* (1980) · R. Ryder, *Oliver Leese* (1987)

Archives IWM, MSS | CAC Cam., letters to G. N. M. Bland · King's Lond., Liddell Hart C., letters to Sir Charles Grant | FILM BFI NFTVA, 'General Leese takes over command of Eighth Army', Gaumont British News, 15 Jan 1944 · BFI NFTVA, 'Eighth Army commander looks round', British News, 20 March 1944 · BFI NFTVA, news footage · IWM FVA, 'Leese being knighted by George VI', War Pictorial News, 28 Aug 1944, WPN 173 · IWM FVA, 'General Sir Oliver arriving in Olumbo to take up his new appointment as head of 11th Army group', British Movietone News, 30 Nov 1944, NMV 808-2 · IWM FVA, actuality footage · IWM FVA, documentary footage · IWM FVA, news footage | SOUND IWM SA, oral history interview

Wealth at death £112,661: probate, 30 March 1978, *CGPLA Eng. & Wales*

Leese, Sir William Hargreaves, second baronet (1868–1937), lawyer, was born at Send Holme, Send, near Guildford, Surrey, on 24 August 1868, the eldest son of Sir Joseph Francis Leese, first baronet (1845–1914), cotton spinner and later recorder of Manchester (1893–1914) and MP for Accrington (1892–1910), and his wife, Mary Constance Hargreaves (*d.* 1928). He was educated at Winchester College and at Trinity College, Cambridge (1887–90), where he developed a keen interest in cricket and acting, which he retained for the rest of his life. His own desire was for a military career but instead he followed his father's wishes and became a barrister of the Inner Temple. He was called to the bar in 1893, the year in which he married Violet Mary Sandeman (*d.* 1947), daughter of Albert George Sandeman (1833–1923), head of the Sandeman drinks business (1868–1923), a director of the Bank of England (1868–1918), and its governor (1895–7). There were three sons and a daughter of the marriage.

In his early years at the bar, Leese forged his own link with the Bank of England through its solicitors, Freshfields, who instructed him as junior to Sir Charles Mathews in a number of prosecutions for forgery. A closer connection was offered to Leese when Freshfields invited him to join them as a partner, an invitation he accepted. He was disbarred, admitted a solicitor, and became a partner in Freshfields in 1906.

From the beginning Leese worked, as intended, on Bank of England matters which had been, since 1819, always conducted by a member of the Freshfield family. Dr Edwin Freshfield, who had recruited him, was senior partner of the firm and was at this time in his seventies. Neither his son, Edwin Hanson Freshfield, nor his nephew James William Freshfield, though both partners in the firm, had shown the interest in or dedication to the practice of law of the family's three previous generations. Following the death of Dr Freshfield in 1918 and the retirement from practice of his son in 1921, Leese became the senior partner of the firm. He succeeded his father as second baronet in 1914.

Under Sir William's leadership the firm was modernized. The telephone was brought out of the basement, a lift was installed, and considerable refurbishment of the offices at 31 Old Jewry (which the firm had occupied since 1898) was carried out. Sir William's own room, with its handsome mahogany desk, thick carpet, and walls hung with choice watercolours, was apparently much admired in the City—such tasteful luxury being at that time unusual in the offices of City solicitors. He had style; Sir Godfey Morley of Allen and Ovary recalled (in 1978) a visit to Freshfields in the 1930s when he was an articled clerk: 'It was a hot summer's day and Sir William was sitting without his jacket (unusual in those days) wearing a most beautiful silk shirt' (Morley, 9).

From 1914 to 1930 Sir William bore sole responsibility for the Bank of England's legal work. This included acting for the trustees of the loans developed to ease the payment of German reparations, and for the Securities Management Trust which held the bank's interest in the merged firms of Armstrong, Whitworth & Co. and Vickers Ltd. In the 1930s, as the bank's involvement in industrial organization became greater and Sir William also became involved in the international loans made to Austria and Hungary under the auspices of the League of Nations, other Freshfield partners were appointed to take on parts of the bank's work. In 1935 Leslie Peppiatt was recruited from the British American Tobacco Company to understudy Sir William's work for the bank.

Despite such a busy professional life—and Sir William was an active member of the Council of the Law Society—for many years he found time to give free legal advice at Cambridge House in the East End and to take an interest in the Boy Scout movement. He was widely respected in the City and beyond, not least for his ability to find solutions to difficult problems with common sense, tact, and friendliness.

Sir William's sporting interests encompassed golf, horse-racing, and dry-fly-fishing as well as cricket. His enthusiasm for the stage never faltered and he continued to participate in the dramatic productions of the Old Stagers and the Windsor Strollers. He died suddenly of heart failure on 17 January 1937 while on holiday at the Victoria Hotel, Sidmouth, Devon. He was succeeded as third baronet by his eldest son, Oliver William Hargreaves *Leese. JUDY SLINN

Sources J. Slinn, 'Leese, Sir William Hargreaves', *DBB* • J. A. Slinn, *A history of Freshfields* (1984) • *The Times* (22 Jan 1937) • *WWW* • G. Morley, *Allen and Ovary* (1978) • Venn, *Alum. Cant.* • Burke, *Peerage* • *CGPLA Eng. & Wales* (1937) • b. cert. • d. cert.
Likenesses portrait, repro. in Slinn, *History of Freshfields*
Wealth at death £53,951 7s. 8d.: probate, 15 March 1937, *CGPLA Eng. & Wales*

Leeson, Henrietta Amelia (1751–1826). *See under* Lewis, William Thomas (1746?–1812).

Leeson [*née* Plunkett], **Margaret** (1727–1797), courtesan and writer, was born at Killough, co. Westmeath. The daughter of Matthew Plunkett, a Catholic landowner with estates at Corbetstown and Killough, and his wife, the former Miss A. O'Reilly, she was the third youngest of eight surviving siblings. Her early life was pleasant and she received 'the best education the county could afford' (*Memoirs*, 5). Then her mother and eldest brother died of fever and her father became a chronic invalid. The estate was made over to her brother Christopher Plunkett. He was a bully and Margaret was frequently beaten; on one occasion her riding habit had to be cut from her swollen limbs. Eventually she escaped his tyranny and went to live with a married sister in Dublin. While there she was seduced by a Mr Dardis, gave birth to a daughter, and was disowned by her family. She attempted to get by on her own, selling what little clothing and jewellery she had to make ends meet. On the verge of starvation she met Thomas Caulfeild, a wine merchant and a cousin of the earl of Charlemont; she became his mistress. He treated her kindly and they had a son together. Then Caulfeild, at the insistence of his family, married a suitable heiress but settled annuities on his mistress and their child. Margaret's annuity was conditional on good behaviour; it was stopped when she began to keep company with other courtesans. When their son died the second annuity lapsed.

Margaret's next lover, an Englishman named Leeson, whose surname she used as her professional name, seems to have intended to marry her but was too jealous for his own good. As it happened Margaret preferred the company, though not the purse, of John Lawless, a distant connection of the countess of Clonmel. Leeson employed the sculptor John Van Nost as a private detective. Van Nost's reports described late-night parties, junkets, and secret assignations with Lawless. Naturally she was cut adrift without a penny. Lawless stood by her. They moved into a small house on Wood Street, Dublin, where they lived together for four years. During that time they had three children, none of whom survived. Increasingly there were jealous rows and eventually he left without warning to take up employment with the New York banking house of Smith and Ramage.

Margaret's next liaison was with a foundation scholar in Trinity College, one Thomas Lambert. It is the first of her affairs that can be roughly dated, having occurred between his graduation in 1767 and the termination of his scholarship in 1770. After Lambert, Margaret changed professional tack and moved away from keeping, where the woman was supposedly the property of a single lover, and into joint ventures with other prostitutes. She attended the notorious meeting of Dublin prostitutes held in October 1776 (*Freeman's Journal*, 17 Oct 1776). By the late 1770s she was running a house in Drogheda Street in partnership with her friend Sally Hayes.

In November 1779 the Drogheda Street house was wrecked by the Pinking-dindies, a gang of street rowdies under the leadership of the balloonist Richard Crosbie. Margaret successfully prosecuted Crosbie and then sold up to move to London. After a glittering season she returned to Dublin and established herself in a new brothel in Wood Street. There her clients included prominent Dublin merchants, almost all of the lord lieutenant's aides-de-camp, quantities of noblemen, including Joseph Leeson, the first earl of Milltown, and David La Touche, first governor of the Bank of Ireland. By 1783 the Wood Street premises had begun to suffer from subsidence so Mrs Leeson commissioned the building of a new establishment at Pitt Street. Her clients there included politicians, noblemen, actors, journalists, and lawyers. The most spectacular of these was Charles Manners, duke of Rutland and lord lieutenant of Ireland. On his first visit, late in the spring of 1784, he arrived in the state coach with a full complement of outriders. Margaret subsequently refused admission to the earl of Westmorland, Rutland's successor in office, because of his persistent cruelty to his wife.

By 1791 or 1792 Margaret began to plan her retirement. She went through a form of marriage to Barry Yelverton junior, only to be bought off by his father, Yelverton senior, then chief baron of the exchequer in Ireland. Late in 1792 or early in 1793 she sold Pitt Street and moved to Blackrock but swiftly ran through her savings to end up in a sponging-house run by one of her former clients. In desperation she decided to cash in her last saleable asset—the story of her life.

The first two volumes of her *Memoirs* were published in 1795 and sold at a profit of £500. She spent this money in a matter of months but had finished work on a third volume by the late summer or early autumn of 1796. Shortly afterwards, returning on foot from a visit to Drumcondra, she was set upon by thieves and raped. Infected with some form of venereal disease she reacted badly to the available treatment and died on 22 March 1797 in poor lodgings in Temple Bar. Three days later she was buried in St James's churchyard. The third volume of her *Memoirs* was posthumously published. MARY C. LYONS

Sources *The memoirs of Mrs. Leeson, madam*, ed. M. C. Lyons (1995) • *Dublin Evening Post* (1779–97) • *Public Register, or, Freeman's Journal* (1763–97) • Burtchaell & Sadleir, *Alum. Dubl.*, 2nd edn • J. Watson and others, *Gentleman's and Citizen's Almanack*, various edns (1750–) • *Wilson's Dublin directory*, various edns (1753–) • *Abstracts from the companion to the grave* (1778) • *An heroic epistle from Kitty Cut-a-Dash to*

Oroonoko, 2nd edn (1778) • *Dublin: a satirical essay in five books. By a young author* (1788)
Likenesses J. Watson, engraving, *c.*1780–1787 (after W. Hoare), NL Ire.
Wealth at death died a pauper: *Memoirs of Mrs. Leeson*, ed. Lyons, 227–52

Leeson, Spencer Stottesbery Gwatkin (1892–1956), headmaster and bishop of Peterborough, was born in Twickenham, Middlesex, on 9 October 1892, the son of John Rudd Leeson (*c.*1850–1927), a surgeon who had worked with Joseph Lister, who later became first mayor of the new borough of Twickenham, and a freethinker whose independent views contrasted strongly with the piety of his wife, Caroline (*c.*1855–1930/31), daughter of Frederick Gwatkin, solicitor, of Lincoln's Inn. Both parents had been married before (Leeson had eight half-brothers and -sisters) and both influenced him deeply. He grew up with a respect for middle-class integrity and a sympathy for the man in the street which gave him a sureness of touch later to prove one of his most considerable assets.

In 1905 Leeson went from the Dragon School, Oxford, as a scholar to Winchester College, where, although not a notable figure, he was deeply affected by the life which he later described in *College, 1901–1911* (1955). Never reckoning himself an arbiter of taste, he was peculiarly impressionable; the buildings of Winchester, with their atmosphere of intellectual activity, were an inspiration, as at Chartres later. He was similarly affected at both Winchester and Oxford by music, in which again, with no pretence of catholic or critical appreciation, he allowed himself to be 'overwhelmed'. Already there was to be observed the religious inspiration which derived from his mother.

In 1911 Leeson went up to Oxford with a New College scholarship and in 1913 secured a first in classical honour moderations, on the strength of which he was awarded a 'war degree' in 1916. His contemporaries remembered him as a man who seemed to have the 'gift of universal friendliness' (*Spencer Leeson, a Memoir*, 21). His characteristic greeting had a zest and wholehearted attention which won him devoted followers. He developed an eloquence which, interrupted by a slight stammer that did not embarrass him, was used to great effect. He would apologize for speaking from notes and for not producing a paper. The notes were three words on half an envelope, but the address would have a masterly coherence as well as a striking extempore quality which made him on occasion one of the most effective speakers of his day. The interests of Lionel Curtis and L. S. Amery in imperial questions attracted him, as did Christian socialism preached by Scott Holland and John Carter at Pusey House.

In August 1914 Leeson enlisted and was commissioned. He went to Flanders in March 1915 but was soon invalided home as a result of a severe bout of influenza affecting his heart. In September he joined naval intelligence, in which he worked until the war ended. His marriage in 1918 to Mary Cecil (1895–1967), daughter of Dr Montagu Lomax, gave him not only an unusually happy family life (they had one son and three daughters), but also a 'business manager'. Able administrator though he was, he could never be bothered with his own affairs and left them to his wife.

Spencer Stottesbery Gwatkin Leeson (1892–1956), by Elliott & Fry, 1949

In 1919 Leeson joined the Board of Education, where he found a cause on which he could lavish that passionate interest in social conditions which he had developed at Oxford. Colleagues were impressed as well as amused by his seriousness about education—a seriousness at which he could always laugh himself. In his five years at the board he came under influences which affected him permanently, in particular that of Sir Amherst Selby-Bigge, whom he served as private secretary. In 1922 he was called to the bar by the Inner Temple.

When Leeson was offered a post at Winchester College in 1924 it was clear that the choice could hardly have been better both for the school and for Leeson himself. He had an enthusiasm and abandon which, with his ability, made him the ideal teacher for clever boys. In later years when he expected similar success in teaching, despite an exceptionally heavy programme of outside engagements, he was to some extent disappointed. But at Winchester and in his early years at Merchant Taylors' School, London, he was one of the most successful teachers of his generation. He went to Merchant Taylors' as headmaster in 1927. The school had become somewhat out of date in spite of his predecessor's scholarly distinction, but particularly as a social problem the post appealed to Leeson. He understood the background of boys and governors. His personal energies were poured out in teaching, in the inspiring of his staff, and in securing the confidence of governors and parents. When he urged the governors to move the school from the grim and restricted buildings in Charterhouse Square he received much support: the case for and against had been debated for many years. The final choice of Sandy Lodge, a spacious site on the outskirts of north-west London, was a brilliant one; and the challenge of planning and bringing into life what was virtually a new school gave a new outlet for his energies.

His task achieved, Leeson succeeded A. T. P. Williams at Winchester, where he remained for eleven years (1935–46). There, with his growing sense of Christian mission, he expected almost too much: when Wykehamists proved that they would also be boys, they were falling short of his sacred ideal for them. Some of them, indeed, indignantly questioned his sincerity. They were wrong to do so. Unrealistic he may have been, and too ready to believe the best of people, but it was a weakness which enabled him to inspire. In practical terms the onset of war and all its distracting problems prevented him from doing more than consolidate the reforms of his predecessor. Nevertheless it was a remarkable headmastership, and the younger members of his staff, in particular those who left Winchester, as Leeson had done, to look after great day schools, owed him a special debt.

Some of Leeson's most important work was done as chairman of the Headmasters' Conference (1939–45, an exceptionally long tenure); Winchester colleagues who criticized him for absenteeism had little notion of what he was doing for other schools. His influence in the conference from the first was exercised to try to make school religion a reality. War may have made his task easier. He certainly inspired the conference with his own conception of the teacher's vocation, and persuaded it of the importance of religion as the mainspring of education in every school; he also emphasized the importance of opening the doors to children from less privileged families. The latter belief he was able to further through his influence on the 1944 Fleming report. His hand can also be detected in the provisions for religious observance in schools made by the 1944 Education Act.

In 1939, after years of uncertainty, Leeson was ordained deacon and, in 1940, priest. Religion had finally come to displace even education as his main concern. By 1946 it was natural for him to step aside serenely and become rector of St Mary's Church in the docks area of Southampton, characteristically seeking a job in what he called 'the Church's front line'. His gift for getting on with parishioners and for making his small staff feel that they were doing great service, his interest in Sunday schools and in the reconstruction of the bombed church, and his contact with the civic authorities and the university all contributed to his success. As at Winchester he was increasingly claimed by national causes; he would have thought it wrong ever to refuse the chairmanship of an educational body. In 1949 he was consecrated bishop of Peterborough. There the same themes were repeated: devotion to every educational cause; determination to know every parish priest in his diocese; readiness to undertake any job of preaching or speaking in which he reckoned he could do God's work. During the last fifteen years of his life he drove himself too hard for there to be enough time for thought. His speeches and sermons were in consequence less effective, although he could still rise to a great occasion. But his complete devotion to his clergy won their deep affection, beset as many of them were by dwindling rural congregations and meagre stipends. A breakdown in 1952 should have proved a warning; by 1955 it was apparent that the appalling accumulation of tasks eagerly accepted could not be sustained. He died in St Thomas's Hospital, London, on 27 January 1956 and was buried on 31 January at Headbourne Worthy, Hampshire. His early death disappointed many who saw in him a potential archbishop, and indeed his gifts might well have found fuller expression in that role than in his headmasterships, however distinguished.

Leeson published a number of books, the most ambitious being his Bampton lectures, published as *Christian Education* in 1947. These surveyed the history of Christian education and sketched his own optimistic policy for the church in relation to the Education Act of 1944. His writings were by no means so important as his life and the spoken word of his early addresses, which made him for years a dominating figure in English education.

Leeson's portrait was painted by Oswald Birley for Merchant Taylors' more sympathetically than it was by Rodrigo Moynihan, who in his portrait for Winchester gave the misleading impression of a scheming prelate. Nobody disliked more heartily the trappings of power. But it is in photographs (such as those reproduced in *Spencer Leeson, a Memoir*, 1958) that the characteristic looks of puzzled seriousness or unaffected delight may be seen.

W. F. Oakeshott, *rev.* R. D. H. Custance

Sources S. Leeson, *Spencer Leeson, shepherd, teacher, friend: a memoir by some of his friends, etc.* (1958) • personal knowledge (1971) • private information (1971) • private information (2004) • S. S. G. Leeson, *College, 1901–1911* (1955) • F. W. M. Draper, *Four centuries of Merchant Taylors' School, 1561–1961* (1962) • headmaster's reports, 1935–46, Winchester College Archives • J. P. Sabben-Clare, *Winchester College* (1981); 2nd edn (1989) • *The Times* (28 Jan 1956)

Archives NL Wales, Lewis MSS, letters to Sir J. H. Lewis • Winchester College Archives

Likenesses O. Birley, oils, 1935, Merchant Taylors' School, Northwood • R. Moynihan, oils, 1948, Winchester College, Hampshire • Elliott & Fry, photograph, 1949, NPG [*see illus.*] • photographs, repro. in Leeson, *Spencer Leeson*

Wealth at death £15,178 8s. 10*d*.: probate, save and except settled land, 9 March 1956, *CGPLA Eng. & Wales*

Leete, William (*c*.1613–1683), colonial governor, was born in Keyston, Huntingdonshire, the son of John Leete and Anna Shute. His maternal grandfather, Robert Shute, was a judge of the king's court, and may have influenced William's decision to practise law. As registrar for the bishop of Ely's court at Cambridge, Leete became deeply affected by the persecution of nonconformists, which led him to adopt puritan beliefs.

Leete married Anne Payne (*d.* 1668), daughter of the Revd John Payne of Southoe, on 1 August 1636. In 1639 they emigrated to New England with the Revd Henry Whitfield. Leete signed Whitfield's group's shipboard plantation covenant on 1 June 1639, and after arrival at Quinnipiac (later New Haven) he helped to establish a new plantation at Menunkatucke, later called Guilford. Leete was an original proprietor of Guilford, and a pillar of its church. He served as the plantation's clerk for twenty-two years (1639–62) and was chief magistrate there from 1651 to 1664.

Leete signed Guilford's acceptance of New Haven colony's articles of confederation on 27 October 1643, after the formation of the defensive alliance of the United Colonies of New England made union of the plantations around New Haven a practical necessity. From that date Leete was a deputy from Guilford to the colony's general court until 1649. He was the commissioner from New Haven to the United Colonies from 1655 to 1664, and served as the colony's deputy governor from 1658 to 1661. He became acting governor upon the death of Francis Newman on 18 November 1660, and was subsequently elected governor every year until the colony was absorbed into Connecticut in 1665.

Events following the Restoration tested Leete's courage and political skill. By engaging in stalling tactics, casuistry, and overt resistance that to a degree he later regretted, he successfully resisted the efforts of royalist agents to capture the regicides William Goffe and Edward Whalley, who were sheltered within New Haven colony from 1661 to 1664. Concern that a royal backlash might focus on the colony's lack of a charter probably led Leete to suggest to the Connecticut governor, John Winthrop the younger, that Winthrop seek a royal charter incorporating both New Haven and Connecticut as independent entities within a single colony. Under the terms of the charter Winthrop secured in 1662, however, New Haven's lands were simply absorbed into Connecticut. Upon notification of this, Leete helped to launch a spirited and sustained resistance to Connecticut's attempted annexation.

Tension between the two colonies continued until the arrival in April 1664 of royal commissioners charged with examining conditions in New England, capturing the regicides, and subduing the Dutch in New Amsterdam. The potential jeopardy they posed to both colonies helped to produce a quick resolution of the dispute. After the commissioners made clear that New Haven's lands would be subsumed within royalist New York or puritan Connecticut, Leete grudgingly helped to effect New Haven's submission to the latter. The colony was officially absorbed into Connecticut on 5 January 1665.

To help soften the blow of annexation, Connecticut elected Leete to the position of assistant from 1665 to 1669. His elevation in that year to deputy governor, a post he held continuously for the next seven years, was, however, certainly a recognition of his ability as a leader. Leete became governor of Connecticut upon the death of John Winthrop the younger on 5 April 1676, in the midst of the violent uncertainties of the devastating Anglo-Amerindian conflict known as King Philip's War. He was elected governor on 11 May 1676 and held the post continuously until his own death in Hartford, Connecticut, on 16 April 1683.

Leete's first wife, Anne, mother of their nine children, died on 1 September 1668. On 7 April 1670 he married Sarah, the widow of Henry Rutherford. She died on 10 February 1674. Leete's third wife, Mary, the widow of the New Haven governor Francis Newman and of the Revd Nicholas Street, survived him by only eight months, dying on 13 December 1683. William Leete was buried before 18 April 1683 in the ancient burial-ground in Hartford.

WALTER W. WOODWARD

Sources E. L. Leete, *The family of William Leete, one of the first settlers of Guilford, Conn., and governor of New Haven and Connecticut colonies* (1884), 9 • C. Mather, *Magnalia Christi Americana*, 7 bks in 1 vol. (1702), 29–30 • R. D. Smith, *The history of Guilford, Connecticut* (1877) • C. M. Andrews, *The rise and fall of the New Haven colony* (1936) • I. M. Calder, *The New Haven colony* (1934) • B. C. Steiner, *Governor William Leete and the absorption of New Haven colony by Connecticut* (1891) • L. Aiken Welles, *The regicides in Connecticut* (1935), 6–14 • W. Leete, 'Correspondence', *Collections of the Massachusetts Historical Society*, 4th ser., 7 (1865), 538–86 • *Letters of Jack Davenport, puritan divine*, ed. I. M. Calder (1934) • J. Leete, *The family of Leete* (1906) • C. J. Hoadley, ed., *Records of the colony and plantation of New Haven*, 2 vols. (1858) • D. Pulsifer, ed., *Acts of the commissioners of the united colonies of New England* (1859), vols. 9–10 of *Records of the colony of New Plymouth in New England*, ed. N. B. Shurtleff and D. Pulsifer (1855–61) • J. H. Trumbull and C. J. Hoadly, eds., *The public records of the colony of Connecticut*, 15 vols. (1850–90), vols. 1–2

Archives Mass. Hist. Soc.

Leeves, William (1748–1828), composer, was born on 11 June 1748, the son of Henry Leeves of Kensington. He entered the 1st regiment of foot guards as an ensign on 8 June 1764, was promoted lieutenant on 23 February 1772, and retired in February 1776. In 1779 he took holy orders, and by the patronage of Mr and Mrs Pulteney was appointed rector of Wrington, Somerset, where Hannah More was among his parishioners. He remained there for the rest of his life. On 4 May 1786 he married Anne, youngest daughter of Samuel Wathen MD; they had at least three sons and a daughter. A good musician and a competent cellist, in 1772 Leeves wrote music to the song 'Auld Robin Gray' by Lady Anne Barnard. Lady Anne had originally written her words in order to supersede the coarse lyrics associated with the tune 'The Bridegroom Greets', but Leeves's music rapidly superseded it. Leeves's authorship of the music was not made public until 1812, when he acknowledged it in the dedication to his *Six Sacred Airs*. Leeves also wrote a good deal of poetry, some of which was published. He died at Wrington on 25 May 1828.

AUGUSTUS HUGHES-HUGHES, *rev.* K. D. REYNOLDS

Sources A. M. Moon, *In memoriam: the Rev. W. Leeves* (privately printed, [Brighton], 1873) • *GM*, 1st ser., 98/2 (1828), 91 • Grove, *Dict. mus.* (1927) • *Army List* (1765) • F. W. Hamilton, *The origin and history of the first or grenadier guards*, 3 vols. (1874)

Likenesses engraving, 1773, repro. in Moon, *In memoriam*

Le Fanu, Alicia (1753–1817). *See under* Le Fanu, Philip (1735–1795).

Le Fanu, Alicia (*b.* 1791, *d.* in or after 1844). *See under* Le Fanu, Philip (1735–1795).

Le Fanu, Sir Michael (1913–1970), naval officer, was born in Lindfield, Sussex, on 2 August 1913, the son of Commander Hugh Barrington Le Fanu RN and his wife, Georgiana Harriott Kingscote. He came of an Irish Huguenot family and was educated at Bedford School and the Royal Naval College, Dartmouth. After the usual junior officer's training at sea and ashore, he spent three years in destroyers before specializing in gunnery in 1938. After qualifying he was appointed to the staff of the commander-in-chief, Mediterranean, until in October 1939 he left to become gunnery officer of the cruiser *Aurora*. There his character and personality developed to a remarkable degree and he was mentioned in dispatches for his competence and bravery during the Norwegian campaign; he was awarded the DSC for his services in a very successful night action against a heavily escorted Italian convoy in November 1941.

In June 1942 Le Fanu joined the staff of the commander-in-chief, Home Fleet, as gunnery assistant and was most successful in training numerous new and refitted ships. From March 1944 until the end of the year when he was promoted commander he served as gunnery officer of the new battleship *Howe* which joined the Far East Fleet and operated with distinction in the Indian Ocean and the Pacific. As a commander he was appointed liaison officer to the American 3rd and 5th fleets, a post which he held until the end of the war with Japan. He distinguished himself by his clear thinking, his ability to mix well, and by his humour. With a United States captain he was responsible for the arrangements for the surrender of Japan aboard the battleship *Missouri* on 2 September 1945. Le Fanu was awarded the Legion of Merit in recognition of his services to the American navy.

It had become clear that Le Fanu was an officer of altogether exceptional ability. He had been granted two years' seniority during the war which enabled him to be promoted commander at the early age of thirty-one; and after the war his appointments were planned to give him the necessary experience for the highest rank.

A spell ashore as experimental commander at the Portsmouth gunnery school was followed by sea service as executive officer of the cruiser *Superb*, where Le Fanu again showed his gifts of leadership and his ability to get the most out of officers and men. Promoted captain in 1949, he went as naval assistant to the controller, gaining useful experience of Whitehall. Then followed, in 1951, his first command: of the 3rd training squadron at Londonderry, where the main activities were anti-submarine, a task which was new to him. In 1952–3 he was employed on special duties in the Admiralty under the chief scientist in order to investigate the many problems of atomic warfare. There followed a year at the Imperial Defence College before taking command in 1954 of HMS *Ganges*, the boys' training establishment at Harwich. He moved next to the aircraft-carrier *Eagle* (1957–8), an important command in which he was a great success and quickly gained the respect and confidence of naval aviators. On promotion to rear-admiral in 1958 Le Fanu was a well-qualified officer with experience in almost every sphere of naval activity.

Le Fanu's first appointment as admiral was in the newly created post of director-general, weapons (1958–60), where he found many difficult problems connected with the development of new equipment. His next post was as second in command of the Far East station (1960–61), where he gained golden opinions by the flexibility of his thinking and by his mental and physical endurance. In the important appointment of controller of the navy (1961–5), with a seat on the Board of Admiralty, he followed through a radical reorganization of the material departments. He was promoted vice-admiral in 1961 and full admiral in 1965.

In that year Le Fanu was appointed to the command of the three services in the Middle East with his headquarters at Aden where conditions were most difficult both in the city and in the hinterland. He was able to develop a very high morale at a time of withdrawal and disillusion and the evacuation was conducted with skill and precision.

It had long been clear that Le Fanu would become first sea lord, a post to which he was duly appointed in 1968. It was a time of reductions in the fleet when the decision to phase out the aircraft-carriers had already been taken. But by great personal efforts at home and abroad, and by skilled advocacy and intelligent administration in Whitehall, he retained the confidence of the service and maintained its morale. In October 1970 he should have taken over the post of chief of the defence staff—the highest position in any service—but illness intervened. He retired at the age of fifty-six with the rank of admiral of the fleet and died in London on 28 November 1970. He was appointed CB (1960), KCB (1963), and GCB (1968).

In 1943 Le Fanu married Prudence Grace, daughter of Admiral Sir Vaughan Morgan; they had two sons and one daughter. It was a happy marriage and his wife took a full share in all social activities—wheeled by Le Fanu or carried up gangways, for she had been disabled by polio when she was a girl. She died in 1980.

Le Fanu was perhaps the most unusual officer of his generation in the navy. He was an exceptional leader and administrator and he had the knack of getting his point of view across to politicians. Moreover, he was well read and well informed on many subjects, not exclusively naval; besides being witty he had a useful talent for pithy verse. While he could be very firm when necessary he gained most of his aims by sympathy and kindness. Nothing was ever too much trouble and he displayed a deep sense of gratitude to friends. When he had the opportunity he gave much of his time to boys' clubs; for he had the common touch and knew no barriers of rank, or age, or class.

Peter Gretton, *rev.*

Sources *The Times* (30 Nov 1970) • personal knowledge (1981) • private information (1981) • *WWW* • *CGPLA Eng. & Wales* (1971)
Archives FILM IWM FVA, actuality footage • IWM FVA, news footage
Wealth at death £40,843: probate, 10 May 1971, *CGPLA Eng. & Wales*

Le Fanu, Peter (1749–1825). *See under* Le Fanu, Philip (1735–1795).

Le Fanu, Philip (1735–1795), translator, was born on 13 March 1735 and baptized in St Peter's Church, Dublin, the eldest of nine children of William Le Fanu (1708–1797) and Henriette Roboteau (1709–1789). His family, which appears first in the mid-sixteenth century in Vire, a town to the south-west of Caen, fled from France following the revocation of the edict of Nantes and came to Ireland in the 1730s following a period in London. His father, William, was baptized in Caen in 1708 while his mother was from Puygibaud, near Saintes. She was a member of an old protestant family and her marriage settlement brought William a fortune of £800. They were married on 28 May 1734 in St Peter's Church, Dublin, according to the rites of the Church of Ireland, to which many Huguenots conformed, and continued to live in the city where William prospered as a merchant and banker acquiring extensive property in King's county, co. Westmeath, and Dublin.

At the age of twelve Philip Le Fanu was sent to the school of the Yorkshire Quaker Abraham Shackleton in Ballitore, co. Kildare, from where he proceeded to Trinity College, Dublin, in 1750. He was elected to a scholarship in 1753, and graduated BA in 1755 and MA in 1758.

Le Fanu was ordained into the Church of Ireland and was licensed as a curate in the parish of St Luke, Dublin, in January 1759. In May of the following year he was presented to the rectory of Clonegal in co. Wexford, and to this was added the vicarage of Carbery, co. Kildare, in 1767, but this latter preferment was of little value as there was no glebe or house and he does not appear to have lived there.

On 23 April 1768 in St Peter's Church, Dublin, Le Fanu married Rebecca (*d.* 1809), daughter of Edward Newton of Umrigar, co. Wexford, and widow of Benjamin Brownrigg; they do not appear to have had any children. Le Fanu subsequently lived at Umrigar, and while there resumed his studies in Trinity College, acquiring the degrees of BD and DD in 1776. His learning was evidenced by two publications: a translation entitled *Letters of Certain Jews to Monsieur Voltaire* (1777) and *An Abridgement of the History of the Council of Constance* (1780) which was reprinted with an appendix in 1787.

Le Fanu died in Grafton Street, Dublin, in January 1795 and was buried on 17 January in the chancel vault of St Peter's Church, Dublin, where his widow was interred on 28 April 1809.

Philip's brother **Peter Le Fanu** (1749–1825) was born on 12 September 1749 and was educated at Dr Buck's school and later Trinity College, Dublin, from which he proceeded BA in 1769. Ordained into the Church of Ireland, he became a fashionable preacher. Peter Le Fanu was successively curate of the Dublin parishes of St Michan and St Luke before his appointment as prebendary of Tassagard in St Patrick's Cathedral, Dublin, in 1795. In 1798 he was appointed rector of Dunlavin, co. Wicklow, but returned to Dublin in 1810 to be perpetual curate of St Bride's and the chaplain of the Rotunda Hospital. He married Frances Knowles, granddaughter of Thomas Sheridan and aunt of the dramatist Sheridan Knowles. His principal dramatic work was 'Smock Alley Secret', an occasional prelude, which was performed at the Smock Alley Theatre, Dublin, in 1778, but was never published. Peter Le Fanu died at his home, 9 Camden Row, Dublin, in 1825.

Philip's sister-in-law **Alicia Le Fanu** [*née* Sheridan] (1753–1817) was born in January 1753, the eldest daughter of Thomas *Sheridan (1719?–1788), actor and orthoepist, and Frances Anne *Sheridan, *née* Chamberlaine (1724–1766), novelist and playwright. Alicia was educated briefly with her brother Richard Brinsley *Sheridan at Samuel Whyte's school in Grafton Street, Dublin, then with her sister at home in London. On 11 October 1781 Alicia married Philip's brother Joseph. She took part in Dublin literary society, especially in private theatricals, and wrote a patriotic comedy, *Sons of Erin*, which received only one performance at the Lyceum Theatre in London on 13 April 1812. Alicia Le Fanu died in Dublin on 4 September 1817 and was buried in St Peter's churchyard on 6 September.

Her niece **Alicia Le Fanu** (*b.* 1791, *d.* in or after 1844), novelist and poet, was the daughter of another of Philip's brothers, Henry Le Fanu (1747–1821), a captain in the 56th infantry who served through the siege of Gibraltar, and Anne Elizabeth Craford, *née* Sheridan (*bap.* 1756, *d.* 1837), younger daughter of Thomas. Henry Le Fanu had a precarious financial existence, being dependent on an uncertain allowance from his brother-in-law Richard Brinsley Sheridan, and died on 9 August 1821 in Northampton. Alicia's first book was *The Flowers, or, The Sylphid Queen* in 1809. Her poems were generally verse fables with moral messages while her historical romances, such as *Strathallan* (1812) and *Henry IV of France* (1826), both in four volumes, are melodramatic and long-winded, though they contain some pointed satire and a few memorable comedic lines. In 1824 she published *Memoirs of the Life and Writings of Mrs Frances Sheridan*, an account of her grandmother, which depended heavily on unsubstantiated family tradition. It is not clear when she died, although she is known to have died in Dublin, but she was alive in 1844 when Caroline Norton managed to secure £150 for her from the Royal Bounty Fund.

THOMAS SECCOMBE, *rev.* RAYMOND REFAUSSÉ

Sources T. P. LeFanu, *Memoir of the Le Fanu family* (privately printed, Manchester, 1924) • J. B. Leslie, *Ferns clergy and parishes* (1936) • Burtchaell & Sadleir, *Alum. Dubl.*, 2nd edn • parish register, Dublin, St Peter, Representative Church Body Library, Dublin, P45 • *BL cat.* • J. B. Leslie, unpublished biographical succession list of the clergy of the diocese of Dublin, Representative Church Body Library, Dublin, MS 61/2/4/2 • J. B. Leslie, unpublished biographical succession list of the clergy of the diocese of Kildare, Representative Church Body Library, Dublin, MS 61/2/7 • *IGI*

Le Fanu, (Joseph Thomas) Sheridan (1814–1873), novelist and newspaper proprietor, was born in Lower Dominick Street, Dublin, on 24 August 1814, the second child and elder son of Thomas Philip Le Fanu (1784–1845), then a curate in the parish of Saint Mary, later chaplain to the Royal Hibernian Military School, and his wife, Emma Lucretia, *née* Dobbin (*d.* 1861), daughter of Dr William Dobbin, Church of Ireland clergyman. The Le Fanus were a conventional middle-class Irish protestant family, of Huguenot origin. The novelist's paternal grandmother was a sister of Richard Brinsley Sheridan, playwright and radical whig MP. A further element of political dissent entered the family through his mother, Emma Dobbin, whose father attended Robert Emmet at the scaffold. The privileged location of Le Fanu's birthplace in the Phoenix Park provided security for the boy's early childhood. In 1826 the family moved to Abington in co. Limerick; T. P. Le Fanu had been an absentee rector of Abington parish for several years, and now became additionally dean of Emly.

(Joseph Thomas) Sheridan Le Fanu (1814–1873), by unknown artist, 1842

Limerick in the late 1820s was an uncomfortable place in which to meditate on family legacies: the agrarian violence which culminated in a 'tithe war' across Ireland had its origins in the county.

Sheridan Le Fanu was educated privately in Abington glebe house during the disturbances, before entering Trinity College, Dublin, in 1832. In addition he studied law at the King's Inns and 'ate his dinners' in the London inns as required by Tudor statute. He graduated BA in 1836, and was called to the Irish bar. His subsequent legal practice was negligible, though he held a sinecure as court tipstaff for some years.

In the College Historical Society (founded 1770) and the *Dublin University Magazine* (founded 1832), Le Fanu discovered two very different platforms for his views. The 'Hist.' was a general debating forum which graduates still pursuing legal qualifications frequented. As treasurer in 1837 Le Fanu found it necessary sometimes to borrow money for his own expenses, an early sign of the financial anxieties which dogged his adult life. The dominant figure in student politics was Thomas Osborne Davis, whose romantic nationalism impressed Le Fanu without convincing him. The *Dublin University Magazine* on the other hand, had been established by young men distressed by the whig electoral victory of 1831 and the inevitability of a reform act. Among the early editors, Isaac Butt was closest to Le Fanu: both were sons of the glebe, lawyers by profession, and novelists by aspiration.

Contributions to the *Dublin University Magazine* appeared anonymously, yet Le Fanu went to the trouble of inventing a narrative persona—Father Francis Purcell, a Catholic priest—for the series of stories he published during Butt's editorship. A rather later tale, 'Spalatro' (1843), published during the editorship of Charles Lever, mixed anti-Catholicism with domestic anxiety about the death of his own sister Catherine in 1841 and also perhaps about her sexual well-being; the locations are happily remote, in Italy. These narrative acrobatics find their counterpart in Le Fanu's politics. In summer 1840 the Irish Metropolitan Conservative Society (IMCS) had explored in a private debate the advantages possibly to be gained from a repeal of the union between Great Britain and Ireland. Isaac Butt played a central role in the discussions. Disillusion with Westminster persuaded (at least temporarily) these young Irish tories that an exclusively Irish arena of political contestation might offer a better prospect of frustrating the Catholic nationality of Daniel O'Connell. It was never more than a pipe dream, but the onset of famine in 1845 quickly exposed the weakness of the social constituency for which the IMCS spoke. Le Fanu's active participation in mid-August 1840 puts him among those members who at least contemplated such a drastic shift of policy with regard to Britain.

On 18 December 1843, with Isaac Butt as one of the witnesses, Le Fanu married Susanna Bennett (*c.*1823–1858), third youngest child of George Bennett QC (1777–1856). The couple had four children, two of whom made very minor artistic careers—the eldest, Eleanor Frances (1845–1903), as the novelist Russell Gray, and the youngest, George Brinsley Le Fanu (*b.* 1854), as a book illustrator. The marriage was beset with difficulties from the outset, as Le Fanu conducted an odd flirtatious correspondence with his wife's sister Elizabeth.

Le Fanu's first published novel, *The Cock and Anchor* (1845), was set during the Irish viceroyalty of Thomas, earl of Wharton (1648–1715), and deftly exploited Jonathan Swift's excoriating satire of the whig grandee. His second, less accomplished novel, *The Fortunes of Colonel Torlogh O'Brien* (1847), had probably been written earlier. Both apply Walter Scott's model of historical fiction to explore Irish mid-nineteenth-century anxieties, including sexual ones.

The second phase of Le Fanu's writing career reflected the convergence of his newspaper proprietorship and his emotional and creative needs. By September 1840 he had acquired an interest in two Dublin papers, *The Statesman* and *The Warder*. The first of these proved more trouble than it was worth, and he was probably relieved when it failed in 1846, for he had ceased to write leading articles twelve months earlier. *The Warder* was made of sterner stuff, less 'low' in tone and less prone to confuse the ecclesiastical with the parliamentary side of toryism; Le Fanu retained his position in it until 1870. Nevertheless a libel action in 1845, arising from a letter *The Warder* had published on the topic of factory conditions, was not the last of his troubles. In 1849 *The Warder* was obliged to editorialize in his defence, even to the point of admitting that the office of tipstaff was worth no more than £10 p.a.

Le Fanu's distinctive literary merits as a writer emerge in *Ghost Stories and Tales of Mystery* (1851), in which his exceedingly marginal association with some of the revolutionaries of 1848 is transformed into a theme of innate and ineradicable guilt. In 1852 Le Fanu sought the tory nomination for the constituency of Carlow, but without success. By then his public image was that of fictionalist rather than political tyro, even though his work remained hermetically anonymous.

Susanna Le Fanu gradually succumbed to medical and religious distress. Her death on 16 April 1858 left the widower with a young family and little income; only his ageing mother appeared to provide solace. Her death three years later led quickly into a period of Le Fanu's most prolific writing, commencing with the novel *The House by the Church-Yard* (serialized in the *Dublin University Magazine* from October 1861; published in three volumes in 1863).

The humiliations arising from *The Warder* did not deter Le Fanu from seeking a larger stake in Dublin journalism, first attempting to buy the local *Daily Express*, and then succeeding as co-editor of the *Dublin Evening Mail*. The need to secure a personal income would appear to have outweighed any consideration of real political influence. In buying the journal which published his first attempts at fiction, Le Fanu displayed greater enterprise. He acquired the *Dublin University Magazine* in July 1861, three months after his mother's death. In its columns he serialized much of his own best fiction: *The House by the Church-Yard* (1861–3), *Wylder's Hand* (1863–4), *Maud Ruthyn and Uncle Silas* (1864), followed by six other novels of lesser quality. From the editorial chair, he dictated no striking policy, even taking the Fenian rising of 1867 in his leisurely stride. He was generous to obscure contributors, notably Patrick Kennedy, and published a disproportionate amount of fiction by women, including his daughter Eleanor and his niece Rhoda Broughton.

From this base Le Fanu was able to place his fiction with London book publishers (notably Richard Bentley) and to gain admission to metropolitan journals such as *All the Year Round* and *Temple Bar*. In the 1860s his work negotiated between English settings (often Derbyshire and thereabouts) and what be might termed undeclared Irish provenances. His best novel, *Uncle Silas*, was set on the Derbyshire borders, though its origins lay in a short story of the 1830s set in Ireland. Its use of a female narrator was extended in later work such as 'Carmilla' (serialized in the *Dark Blue*, December 1871 to March 1872), a masterpiece of construction and subversive sexual characterization. He was also an enquirer into ill-mapped spiritual zones, using his knowledge of Swedenborgianism in *Uncle Silas* and some of the stories of *In a Glass Darkly* (1872).

Sheridan Le Fanu disposed of the *Dublin University Magazine* in March 1870. He did not follow his erstwhile friend Isaac Butt into the home rule movement. Having become a virtual recluse, he died on 7 February 1873 in the house at 18 Merrion Square, Dublin, later occupied by An Comhairle Ealaíon (the Irish Arts Council): it had been his father-in-law's home and in it Susanna Bennett, his wife, had died almost fifteen years earlier. He was buried on 11 February in Mount Jerome cemetery, Dublin. Their elder son, Philip (1847–1879), squandered what remained of a decent inheritance. Even the pictures and books which the novelist had preserved during his lean years were dispersed beyond trace.

W. B. Yeats acknowledged a debt to *In a Glass Darkly* in the early versions of his play about Jonathan Swift, *The Words upon the Window-Pane* (1934), which had accommodated a character named Le Fanu. James Joyce more openly acknowledged *The House by the Church-Yard* as a quarry for materials used in *Finnegans Wake* (1939). Elizabeth Bowen wrote an influential introduction to *Uncle Silas* (Cresset Press, 1947); her own post-Second World War fiction, beginning with *The Demon Lover and other Stories* (1945) owes not a little to Le Fanu's disturbing blend of the occult and the banal. His transgressions across the boundaries of gender, genre, and nation have assisted a revival of interest in the late twentieth and early twenty-first centuries.

W. J. McCormack

Sources TCD, Le Fanu MSS · U. Leeds, Brotherton L., Brotherton papers · PRO NIre., Dufferin and Ava MSS · W. R. Le Fanu, *Seventy years of Irish life* (1893) · T. P. Le Fanu, *Memoir of the Le Fanu family* (1924) · W. J. McCormack, *Sheridan Le Fanu and Victorian Ireland* (1980) · *Wellesley index*, vol. 4 (1987)

Archives King's AC Cam., corresp., literary MSS, and papers · NL Ire., account book for *Dublin University Magazine* | BL, letters to Royal Literary Fund, loan 96 · PRO NIre., letters to Helen Selina Sheridan, Lady Dufferin · U. Leeds, Brotherton L., letters to Bessie Pigott Bennett

Likenesses watercolour drawing, 1842, NPG [*see illus.*]

Wealth at death under £600—in England: administration with will, 28 March 1873, *CGPLA Ire.*

Le Fayre, Mark (*d.* 1417/18), merchant, is of uncertain origins, but his unusual names, and his interest in Freefolk, Hampshire, point to a connection with the baronial Husee family, possibly as an illegitimate son. Sir Mark Husee, heir to the lord of Freefolk, died in 1346, and the surname Le Fayre may signify the vair (ermine) of the Husee arms. Husee contacts, including the earls of Arundel, perhaps helped him make his way.

Le Fayre, who entered the Winchester merchant guild in 1366 or 1367, came to dominate that city's long-distance commerce in a way that no single merchant had done in earlier and more prosperous times. He dealt in woollen cloth, for the making and finishing of which Winchester became a notable centre in his time, and imported large quantities of Gascon wine through Southampton. Between 1383 and 1408 he regularly sold wine in Winchester. He also shipped wine from Southampton to London, and by 1400 was supplying it to the king. Between 1371/2 and 1404/5 he exported cloth through Southampton. His sales of cloth in Winchester were on a smaller scale. In 1408 he was the only merchant not a Londoner to sell cloth to the royal household, and in 1414 claimed to be owed nearly £448 for cloth and wine supplied to Henry IV. He also imported woad, iron, oil, wax, and salt, and supplied woad and potash to the Winchester dyeing trade. On occasion he shipped wool to Calais and exported corn to Bordeaux. An entrepreneur in the cloth industry, he put out work to weavers and supervised a dyehouse. He had debtors, including clergy and knights, in London and at least five counties.

Le Fayre rose high in Winchester and was often active in the capital on its behalf. His first known civic position was as a bagman (collector of revenues) in 1377, and in 1378–9 he was the senior bailiff. He represented Winchester in seven of the nine parliaments between 1385 and 1395, and in six between 1399 and 1417. First elected as mayor for 1398–9, he held the office four more times (1402–3, 1408–9, 1411–12, 1413–14). Constable of the Winchester staple in 1390–91, he was aulnager for Hampshire between 1408 and 1415, and had a royal commission to seize Flemish ships in 1415.

Le Fayre's earliest known property holdings were for commercial use, and included shops in Winchester High Street where cloth was sold, a shop with the same speciality in St Giles's Fair outside Winchester, a stone cellar on a prime site for wine dealing in Southampton, and a wine tavern in Winchester, all acquired well before 1400. His spacious Winchester residence occupied a secluded site, but was in Parchment Street, close to High Street and the cloth-working district. He was probably living there by 1381, but only as tenant of the Inkepenne family, wool merchants before 1350 whose wealth probably exceeded Le Fayre's. His occupancy of the house where they had lived was a sign of success. About 1400, when he would have been well over fifty, his career became more sedentary, a change marked by tenure of the mayoralty, a shift in investment from trade to rents, and probably a more direct engagement in cloth production. He built several houses, a sound investment since, despite the contraction of the city, rents for good-quality buildings rose until about 1410. In that year he purchased tenements which he rebuilt as an inn, a prominent place of resort in High Street. At the same time he organized the repair of an inn belonging to the city, promising to lend money for the enterprise should it be needed. In 1412 the net annual value of his lands in Winchester, Southampton, Romsey, Freefolk, and Wiltshire (probably Salisbury) was given as £46. The estate reflects his interest in towns associated with the cloth trade, and is notable for its lack of rural holdings, apart from his country seat at Freefolk acquired in 1403. In 1417 his Winchester holdings alone brought in about £34, one of the most valuable rent rolls in the city.

By 1386 Le Fayre had married his first wife, Joan. Later he made provision for properties to descend to his daughter Catherine and her heirs. By 1398 Catherine had married John Newman, a Salisbury merchant who died in 1402. Later that year she married Henry Somer (*d.* 1450), a rising and highly regarded crown servant. Le Fayre stood surety for Somer more than once, and with him acquired property in London. The two men probably began their alliance before 1400, possibly in connection with the Southampton wine trade and through the influence of Somer's patron, Archbishop Thomas Arundel (*d.* 1414). Joan died in 1410, and in the following year Le Fayre married Agnes Langestoke. At that time he settled Freefolk on Somer and Catherine, and arranged for his Winchester freeholds to be settled on himself, Agnes, and his heirs. Somer gained control of the Winchester property early in 1417, and just over year later, Le Fayre having died around the end of 1417, bought out Agnes's claim. A fortune created by a Winchester merchant thus came to contribute a regular, if declining, income to an influential official based in London. The city of Winchester later acquired the freeholds and commemorated Le Fayre and Joan as benefactors.

DEREK KEENE

Sources D. Keene and A. R. Rumble, *Survey of medieval Winchester*, 2 vols., Winchester Studies, 2 (1985) [Somer le Fayre] • HoP, *Commons, 1386–1421* [le Faire, Hussey, Somer] • GEC, *Peerage* • *VCH Hampshire and the Isle of Wight*, 4.282 • *VCH Wiltshire*, 6.85n. • J. C. C. Smith, ed., *Index of wills proved in the prerogative court of Canterbury, 1383–1588*, 2 (1885), 386 • L. F. Salzmann, *English industries of the middle ages* (1913), 158 • J. M. Kaye, ed., *The cartulary of God's House, Southampton*, 2, Southampton RS, 20 (1976), 248, 336

Archives Hants. RO, Winchester city archives • Southampton Borough Records, deeds | BL, Stowe MS 846

Wealth at death approx. £46 p.a.—lands

Lefebvre, Rolland [*known as* Lefebvre de Venise] (*c.***1608–1677**), painter, was born in Anjou, possibly in Bagneux, near Saumur. Nothing is known of his parents. He painted allegorical and historical subjects, miniatures, and portraits. He studied for many years in Italy, and for a long time lived in Venice. He may have been in England in 1633, but he was in Italy in 1636, when he was admitted to the Accademia di San Luca in Rome. He returned to his native France later in life, and presented his work to the Académie Royale de Peinture et de Sculpture in Paris on 30 December 1662. On 6 January 1663 the Académie Royale decided to accept him on the basis of his reputation, merit, and experience in Italy, rather than wait until he had produced his formal reception piece, on the condition that he paint a portrait of Jean-Baptiste Colbert or possibly Charles le Brun. It is unclear whether he ever completed this work. Instead, on 4 January 1665, he submitted a tableau, *Truth Presenting herself to the Academy*. The Académie Royale confirmed his reception, not as a history painter of the highest prestige but as a portrait painter. He was dissatisfied with this and wrote a letter that was read at a meeting of the Académie Royale on 14 March 1665 asking for the return of his painting and the moneys he had paid, which the academicians granted; he was excluded from the academy the same day. He was received into the Académie de St Luc in Paris on 24 May 1665. Lefebvre moved to England about 1676. He died in Bear Street, near Leicester Fields, London in 1677, and was buried in St Martin-in-the-Fields.

Bainbrigg Buckeridge wrote that Lefebvre was 'better at designing, as appears by his works, than at Painting. He had a particular excellence in staining marble, which he did several times for Prince Rupert' (Buckeridge, 373). This last statement, though repeated, has not been confirmed by other sources. Vertue says some of his paintings were 'very obscene' (Vertue, *Note books*, 2.94). His portrait of Jean-Michel de Cigala (1668) is known from an engraving by Étienne Picart, and that of Hilaire Clément (1667) from an engraving by Jean-Louis Roullet (1689). A miniature of Oliver Cromwell at the Mappin Art Gallery, Sheffield, is thought to be his work. He is often confused with Claude Lefebvre, a well-known painter in Paris at the same time, who did not go to England, and Valentin Lefebvre, who lived for many years in Venice, where he engraved works of Titian, Paolo Veronese, and others.

L. H. CUST, *rev.* ARIANNE BURNETTE

Sources M. A. de Montaiglon, *Procès-verbaux de l'Académie Royale de Peinture et de Sculpture, 1648–1792*, 1 (1875) • [B. Buckeridge], 'An essay towards an English school of painting', in R. de Piles, *The art of painting, with the lives and characters of above 300 of the most eminent painters*, 3rd edn (1754), 354–439 • G. Duplessis, *Catalogue de la collection des portraits français et étrangers conservée au Département des Estampes de la Bibliothèque Nationale* (Paris, 1897) • Vertue, *Note books*, vol. 2 • Thieme & Becker, *Allgemeines Lexikon* • P. de Chennevières and A. de Montaiglon, *Abecedario de P. J. Mariette et autres notes inédites de cet amateur sur les arts et les artistes* (1854–6) • *Histoire de l'Académie de Saint-Luc* (1915) • E. K. Waterhouse, *The dictionary of British 16th and 17th century painters* (1988) • H. Walpole, *Anecdotes of painting in England: with some account of the principal artists*, ed. R. N. Wornum, new edn, 2 (1849); repr. (1862) • Bénézit, *Dict.*, 4th edn, vol. 8 • J. Turner, ed., *The dictionary of art*, 34 vols. (1996) • L. R. Schidlof, *The miniature in Europe in the 16th, 17th, 18th, and 19th centuries*, 1 (1964) • *DNB*
Archives Courtauld Inst., Witt Library

Lefevre, Charles Shaw-, Viscount Eversley (1794–1888), speaker of the House of Commons, was born on 22 February 1794 in Bedford Square, London. He was the eldest son of Charles Shaw, a barrister, of a Yorkshire family, and MP for Reading from 1802 to 1820, and his wife, Helena, only daughter of John Lefevre, a member of a Huguenot family long settled at Heckfield Place, Hartfordbridge, Hampshire; on their marriage the family name became Shaw-Lefevre. Sir John Shaw-*Lefevre was Charles's younger brother.

Shaw-Lefevre was educated at Winchester College, and Trinity College, Cambridge, where he graduated BA in 1815, and MA in 1819; he was called to the bar at Lincoln's Inn in 1819, but practised very little. 'Only fit to be a gamekeeper' was his mother's verdict on her son, an excellent shot. On 24 June 1817 he married Emma Laura (*d.* 1857), daughter of Samuel *Whitbread, and his wife, Elizabeth (daughter of the first Earl Grey). They had three sons, none living beyond the age of six, and three daughters. His relations with his wife later deteriorated, only her death preventing a formal separation.

Shaw-Lefevre at once took to politics, and in 1820 was active in his brother-in-law Samuel Whitbread's contest for Middlesex, but from his father's death in 1823 he lived mainly at Heckfield Place in Hampshire, interesting himself in county business and the yeomanry. In 1830 he entered parliament for Lord Radnor's pocket borough of Downton in Wiltshire, and in 1831, after a severe contest, was returned for Hampshire. The county was divided into two constituencies by the act of 1832, and from then until his elevation to the peerage, he sat for the northern division. He was a steady supporter of the whig government, but though he moved the address in 1834, he spoke rarely.

Charles Shaw-Lefevre, Viscount Eversley (1794–1888), by Sir Hubert von Herkomer, 1882

For some years he was chairman of a committee on petitions for private bills, and in 1835 was chairman of a committee on agricultural distress. He was chairman of the select committee on procedure in 1838, and carried his report almost unanimously. By attending closely to the work of these committees and to the forms of the house, and by his natural fair-mindedness and good temper, he gained a reputation which led to his selection in 1839, in spite of Spring-Rice's claims to be the government candidate, to succeed Abercromby in the speaker's chair. He was the only candidate certain of radical support, and was thus the choice of the party rather than of its leaders. He was elected in a full house on 27 May by 317 votes to 299 for Henry Goulburn. He was re-elected in 1841, in spite of Peel's possession of a majority which could easily have ousted him, and again in 1847 and 1852, on each occasion unanimously. He proved himself a speaker of distinction. He set himself to reform procedure, and during the stormy debates on Irish questions in O'Connell's time, and afterwards on free trade, maintained order firmly and impartially. He was very dignified, strong, and tactful, and the business of the house benefited greatly by his election. Asked how he selected members to speak, he replied: 'Well, I have been shooting rabbits all my life, and have learnt to mark the right one' (*The Times*, 29 Dec 1888). A volume of his decisions was published by Robert Bourke in 1857, and to Shaw-Lefevre is due the removal of many unsuitable forms now forgotten. In the same year, having served longer than any speaker except Onslow, he decided to retire, and withdrew on 11 March.

Shaw-Lefevre was raised to the peerage on 11 April as Viscount Eversley of Heckfield, and received a pension. He was nominated a church estates commissioner, which office he resigned in 1859 on becoming an ecclesiastical commissioner, and was a trustee of the British Museum. He declined the governor-generalship of Canada in 1861 and in 1867 chaired the Parliamentary Boundary Commission consequent on the Reform Bill of that year. He was president of the Royal Agricultural Society in 1863, and of the Statistical Society from 1877 to 1879. Though often present, he rarely spoke in the House of Lords; he was high steward of Winchester, governor and lord lieutenant of the Isle of Wight, colonel of the Hampshire yeomanry, and until July 1879 was chairman of quarter sessions. He was made a GCB in 1885. He took a keen interest in shooting and in agriculture, and, looked after by his unmarried daughter, Emma Laura, was active almost until his death. He died on 28 December 1888 at his house, Heckfield Place, in Hampshire, but was buried beside his wife at Kensal Green cemetery, London, on 2 January 1889.

J. A. Hamilton, *rev.* H. C. G. Matthew

Sources F. M. G. Wilson, *A strong supporting cast: the Shaw Lefevres, 1789–1936* (1993) • GEC, *Peerage* • J. A. Manning, *The lives of the speakers of the House of Commons* (1850) • *The Times* (29 Dec 1888)

Archives Hants. RO, corresp., notebooks, and papers | BL, letters to W. E. Gladstone, Add. MSS 44374–44491 • BL, corresp. with Sir Robert Peel, Add. MSS 40428–40602 • BLPES, corresp. with Sir Joshua Jebb • Hants. RO, letters to William Wickham and Sophia Emma Wickham • NL Scot., corresp. with Lord Rutherford • NRA, priv. coll., letters to S. H. Walpole • PRO, corresp. with Lord John Russell, PRO 30/22 • UCL, corresp. with Sir Edwin Chadwick • Wellcome L., letters to John Hodgkin

Likenesses H. von Herkomer, portrait, 1882, priv. coll. [*see illus.*] • carte-de-visite, 1892, NPG • Caldesi, Blandford & Co., carte-de-visite, NPG • J. Doyle, pen-and-ink sketch, BM • G. Hayter, group portrait, oils (*The House of Commons, 1833*), NPG • W. Holl, stipple (after G. Richmond), NPG, BM • J. Partridge, group portrait, oils (*The fine arts commissioners, 1846*), NPG • R. T., wood-engraving, BM; repro. in *ILN* (1889) • M. A. Shee, oils, Palace of Westminster, London • etching (after F. Sargent), NPG

Wealth at death £167,894 8*s*. 6*d*.: probate, 17 April 1889, *CGPLA Eng. & Wales*

Lefevre, George John Shaw-, Baron Eversley (1831–1928), politician, was born in Battersea, Surrey, on 12 June 1831, the only surviving son of Sir John George Shaw-*Lefevre (1797–1879), clerk to the parliaments, and his wife, Rachel Emily (1801–1885), daughter of Ichabod Wright, of Mapperley Hall, Nottinghamshire. His father's elder brother was Charles Shaw-*Lefevre, Viscount Eversley, speaker of the House of Commons, while his mother's brother was Ichabod Charles *Wright (1795–1871), the translator of Dante. Shaw-Lefevre also had six sisters, including Rachel Emily (1829–1889), who married Arthur Charles Hamilton *Gordon, first Baron Stanmore, and Madeleine Septimia Shaw-*Lefevre, first principal of Somerville College, Oxford. He was brought up in a whig-Liberal atmosphere of dedicated public service, administration, and politics at a time when the distinctions between a political and governmental career were not as sharp as they later became.

Early parliamentary career Lefevre was educated at Eton College before going up to Trinity College, Cambridge, in

George John Shaw-Lefevre, Baron Eversley (1831–1928), by unknown photographer

1849, graduating in 1853. He was called to the bar by the Inner Temple in 1854 and practised briefly. During this period, he also travelled widely in North America, the eastern Mediterranean, and north Africa. On 24 March 1874 Lefevre married Constance Emily Moreton (*d.* 1929), only daughter of Henry John Moreton, later third earl of Ducie. She remains a shadowy figure, a retiring woman, committed to local good works and for many years an invalid. Marriage gave Lefevre financial independence but not great wealth, and he was later to receive a political pension. There were no children.

Lefevre contested Winchester unsuccessfully in 1859, before being elected as member for Reading in 1863, which he represented until 1885. In foreign affairs he broadly supported Palmerston's policy, although, as a firm supporter of the union in the American Civil War, he was suspicious of Britain's neutral stand. Later he was an important supporter of international arbitration over the question of the Alabama payment. At home Lefevre was a radical and in favour of an extended franchise, the abolition of church rates, and disestablishment of the Church of Ireland. He was a committed Gladstonian on issues of trade and state expenditure, remaining so throughout his life. He had a voracious appetite for public affairs, quickly mastering a subject, and using his expertise persistently and often effectively. To those less committed he could appear a bore, with Lord Richard Grosvenor describing him as having 'not one grain of human sympathy in his composition' (Grosvenor to Gladstone, 3 May 1882, Gladstone MS, BL, Add. MS 44315, fol. 73).

Lefevre's earliest official duties in 1863 were as the legal member on the royal commission on fisheries, whose report led to the removal of all restrictions on the industry under the Sea Fisheries Act of 1868.

In parliament Lefevre soon came into contact with a diverse group of radicals, most of whom had been influenced by the writings and person of John Stuart Mill, including John Morley, Frederic Harrison, and Lord Edmond Fitzmaurice, each of whom was as long-lived as Lefevre himself. Lefevre's efforts in two fields in the mid-1860s proved to be of long-term significance. The first concerned the preservation of and public access to the commons and royal forests around London. As a result of a particular concern about Wimbledon Common, Lefevre became a member of a Commons select committee investigating the issue, which called for the public's rights to be safeguarded. This led in July 1865 to the founding of the Commons Preservation Society, the first pressure group committed to preserving open spaces and extending public rights of access to land in Britain. Lefevre quickly became its chairman, a position he held almost continuously for the rest of his life. The society brought together an eclectic group of upper-class radical and academic figures, including Mill, T. H. Huxley, Thomas Hughes, James Bryce, Sir Charles Dilke, Henry Fawcett, and Octavia Hill, a social mix that was to characterize much of the environmental and conservation movement for the next century. The society, through a combination of parliamentary action, litigation, and public campaigning, progressively secured the preservation of royal forests and metropolitan and rural commons for public benefit. Lefevre wrote the history of those battles in *Commons, Forests and Footpaths* (1894, revised edn 1910). In many ways this achievement proved to be Lefevre's most lasting memorial.

The second also involved property rights. In April 1868, along with Mill and Russell Gurney, Lefevre introduced a bill to entitle married women to own and manage their own property on the same principles as if they were single. Lefevre chaired the more important of two select committees on the subject, before a new bill was introduced and passed in 1870 as the Married Women's Property Act, 1870. Although a much diluted and amended version of the original bill, it was an important first step in the advance of all women to equal property rights. Lefevre continued to work for its legislative improvement.

Into office Lefevre quickly secured office, first as a civil lord of the Admiralty in Russell's government (April–June 1866), which gave him a lifelong interest in naval affairs, and in December 1868 as secretary of the Board of Trade under the light rein of John Bright in Gladstone's first government. He was responsible for legislation in 1870 requiring life insurance companies to publish accounts, and a General Tramways Act which gave the opportunity in the longer term for local authorities to take private tramways into public control. He was disappointed not to receive advancement on Bright's retirement early in 1871 but was somewhat mollified by becoming secretary to the Admiralty under G. J. Goschen, a post he held until the dissolution of parliament in early 1874, fielding all questions relating to naval estimates, shipping, and safety at sea.

During Disraeli's government (1874–80) Lefevre continued as an active radical member, extending his own expertise in relation to the laws of landed property. He supported reform of the laws of primogeniture and entail, cheaper and easier conveyancing, amendment to the game laws, the extension of public rights over commons, and the creation of peasant proprietors in Ireland. He presented all of these issues in a historic context in which he contrasted the immobilism of the English law to the dynamic changes that had taken place in Europe and North America. He believed that the wider ownership of property was synonymous with social progress and political stability. He chaired the select committee on the purchase clauses of the 1870 Irish Land Act (1878), and his writings on these subjects were published together as *English and Irish Land Questions: Collected Essays* (1881). He was the first English politician to propose peasant proprietorship as a major strand in any comprehensive settlement of the land question in Ireland. He was president of the Royal Historical Society from 1877 to 1878.

In April 1880 Lefevre returned to the Admiralty before being appointed first commissioner of works (November 1880 – November 1884) and sworn of the privy council. In this largely executive office with a low political profile, he excelled, rapidly mastering detail and presenting arguments relating to public buildings, metropolitan planning, and the functioning of the palace of Westminster with clarity and confidence. His two tenures of this office (to which he returned with a seat in the cabinet in 1892 in Gladstone's fourth government) had a significant impact on the metropolitan landscape. Hyde Park Corner was re-ordered, the Constitution Arch repositioned, and the unpopular Wellington equestrian statue removed, alterations were initiated to Westminster Hall and the Tower of London, and an extension to the National Gallery approved, along with the completion of the new law courts in the Strand. The royal parks were made more open to the public, and finally in 1894 a site on Millbank was agreed with Sir Henry Tate for a new gallery of modern British painting. Lefevre's most significant legislative work was the passing of the Ancient Monuments Protection Act in 1883, an alternative to the earlier unsuccessful attempts led by Sir John Lubbock to establish public powers to preserve ancient structures. Lefevre failed however in his persistent attempts to remove the memorials in Westminster Abbey to a new cloister, and in his desire to secure approval for a set of buildings to house the Admiralty and the War Office overlooking Whitehall and the Mall.

Gladstone also sought to use Lefevre's expertise in other spheres, most notably on English and Irish land reform. Lefevre often annoyed his political master by enthusing in public about peasant proprietorship at a time when Gladstone was keen to secure agreement for his tenurial reforms. Despite this, his name was widely canvassed as a possible successor to W. E. Forster in late 1881 as Irish chief secretary, although it was not in fact until October 1884 that he was offered the post in succession to his radical colleague, Sir George Trevelyan. By this time, he had become a firm opponent of continued coercion for Ireland and felt his appointment would be inconsistent with serving with Lord Spencer as his senior colleague in Dublin. He was later to regret his refusal, as he saw Morley emerge as Gladstone's favourite disciple in Irish affairs. A month later, in November 1884, he accepted the office of postmaster-general with a seat in the cabinet, which he held until the fall of the government in June 1885. He added the sixpenny telegram to the range of services provided.

During these months Lefevre was involved along with his radical colleagues, Joseph Chamberlain, Sir Charles Dilke, Sir George Trevelyan, and John Morley, in their attempt to fashion an alternative Irish policy to that being proposed by Lord Spencer. This was centred on the establishment of a devolved central board in Dublin for domestic affairs, alongside a closer working relationship with the Irish nationalist members led by Charles Stewart Parnell. This proved unacceptable to the cabinet and, when Spencer proposed renewed coercion, Lefevre along with Chamberlain and Dilke threatened Gladstone with resignation. Later Lefevre proposed a possible compromise of bringing in any coercion by proclamation, an idea not fully discussed at the time of the government's defeat and resignation on its budget on 8 June.

Electoral defeat and subsequent career In the general election of November 1885, Lefevre was defeated at Reading. It was a critical moment to be out of parliament, and he played little part in the political crisis surrounding Gladstone's introduction of a Home Rule Bill. His frustration was underscored by his bizarre suggestion to Gladstone that he might become a 'working' lord lieutenant of Ireland. He was returned to the Commons on 21 April 1886 as member for Central Bradford in succession to W. E. Forster, a seat he held until again defeated in 1895. He remained a strong supporter of Gladstone's home-rule policy, and vigorously and provocatively attacked the coercive policy adopted by A. J. Balfour against the Plan of Campaign. In particular he identified with the tenants evicted from the Massareene, Clanricarde, and Vandeleur estates, writing and speaking in their defence, and making highly publicized visits to Ireland, at times courting arrest. He firmly believed that the government should be seeking arbitration in these disputes, and continued to urge their reinstatement after the return of the Liberals to office in 1892, a stance which did not improve his relations with John Morley as chief secretary.

As first commissioner for works (1892–4) once more and president of the Local Government Board (1894–5), Lefevre was responsible for the London (Equalization of Rates) Act of 1894, and personally incorporated the maintenance of footpaths as a public duty on local authorities for the first time. He remained one of Gladstone's most loyal lieutenants, and in particular sided with him in the dispute over the increases in naval expenditure in 1894 which provoked Gladstone's final retirement. He played little part in the subsequent struggle for the Liberal leadership, and devoted a considerable amount of energy from 1894 to 1896 as chairman of the royal commission into the depression of agriculture, which failed to produce an agreed report or recommendations.

Lefevre's defeat at the general election was a bitter blow, which he saw as the direct result of local political scheming led by Sir Alfred Illingworth, hostile to his conciliatory stance towards organized labour. Never a man to remain idle, Lefevre was elected in February 1897 to the newly formed London county council as a Progressive member for the Haggerston division of Shoreditch, using his previous ministerial experience to promote metropolitan improvement and slum clearance. The possibility of a return to the Commons continued to be canvassed until 1903, especially during the Second South African War to which he was passionately opposed. But deafness made this increasingly unlikely. Having resettled in 1896 at Abbotsworthy House in the village of Kings Worthy, near Winchester, he retired in 1901.

Thereafter Lefevre confined himself to a vigorous political activity through his pen, despite being given a public forum through his elevation to the House of Lords as Baron Eversley of Old Ford by Campbell-Bannerman early in 1906. A passionate Gladstonian, he challenged the arguments of the tariff reformers in Cobden Club publications, he deplored the growth in expenditure on armaments (especially those of Winston Churchill at the Admiralty), he applauded John Burns's ministerial resignation on the outbreak of the First World War, and thought a British continental engagement fundamentally mistaken. At the same time, he continued to do battle for free public access to common land and historical monuments, as well as rekindling his much earlier opposition to any form of proportional representation as a result of the Speaker's Conference in 1917. During his eighties he also wrote three long works on *Gladstone and Ireland* (1912), *The Partitions of Poland* (1915), and *The Turkish Empire: its Growth and Decay* (1917), the last of which, prompted by the Dardanelles campaign, represented a return to interests stimulated by a visit to the theatre of the Crimean War sixty years before.

A handsome man, Lefevre remained mentally active until the last few weeks of his life. He died at his home, Abbotsworthy House, Kings Worthy, near Winchester, on 19 April 1928, and was buried at Kings Worthy four days later. He was survived by his wife, who died on 27 February 1929. On his death the barony became extinct. Hightown Common, near Ringwood, on the edge of the New Forest, was later purchased by the Commons Preservation Society as a memorial to him, the ownership being vested in the National Trust.

Lefevre was not a clubbable politician; ambitious, hardworking, self-promoting, argumentative, and stubborn, he had no personal following and his ministerial advance was cut back by his personality and the political transformations of the years 1885–6. His career demonstrates how long was the Gladstonian shadow cast over English radicalism with its concern for free trade, cheap government, non-interventionist foreign and colonial policy, and the statutory extension of individual liberties. Lefevre's principles and personality proved to be the grit that contributed significantly to the causes of conservation, public access, peasant proprietorship in Ireland, and the advancement of women. He had no known religious opinions. ALLEN WARREN

Sources F. M. G. Willson, *A strong supporting cast: the Shaw Lefevres, 1789–1936* (1993) [appx 2 (351–5) incl. most complete list of Shaw Lefevre's writings] • GEC, *Peerage* • Lord Eversley [G. Shaw-Lefevre], *Commons, forests, and footpaths: the story of the battle during the last forty-five years for public rights over the commons, forests, and footpaths of England and Wales*, rev. edn (1910) • Haddo House, Aberdeenshire, Haddo House MSS • L. Holcombe, *Wives and property: reform of married women's property law in nineteenth-century England* (1983) • T. W. Heyck, *The dimensions of British radicalism: the case of Ireland, 1874–95* (1974) • Gladstone, *Diaries*
Archives Haddo House, Aberdeenshire, Haddo MSS • NRA, priv. coll., corresp. and papers | BL, corresp. with Sir Charles Dilke, W. E. Gladstone, Lord Gladstone, Sir Robert Peel, Add. MSS 43887–43922, 44153, 46050–46082, 41227 • Bodl. Oxf., corresp. with Sir William Harcourt • Bodl. Oxf., letters to F. W. Hirst • Hants. RO, letters to Sophia Emma Wickham • HLRO, letters to David Lloyd George • NL Scot., corresp., mainly with Lord Rosebery • U. Birm. L., corresp. with Joseph Chamberlain
Likenesses photograph, NPG [*see illus.*]
Wealth at death £17,291 13*s*. 1*d*.: probate, 11 June 1928, *CGPLA Eng. & Wales*

Lefevre, Sir George William (**1798–1846**), physician and traveller, was born at Berkhamsted, Hertfordshire. He is known to have had two brothers, but nothing more is known of his family background. After apprenticeship to a medical practitioner in Shropshire, he studied medicine at Edinburgh University, and at Guy's and St Thomas's hospitals in London, and he graduated MD at Aberdeen on 4 August 1819. He was threatened with pulmonary disease, and on the advice of Dr Pelham Warren decided to go abroad. After failing to obtain an Indian appointment, he went to Pau with a patient, who died there of phthisis. Lefevre then returned to England. He was admitted a licentiate of the Royal College of Physicians on 1 April 1822, but having failed in his candidature as physician to a dispensary he decided to go abroad again, and, through the influence of the surgeon Benjamin Travers, became physician to a Polish nobleman, with whom he travelled for nine years—five in France and the rest in Austria, Poland, and Russia. His position gave him the opportunity of observing the domestic life of the Polish nobility, in many of whose castles he stayed.

Lefevre finally left his employer at Odessa and went to St Petersburg, where he engaged in private practice and became physician to the British embassy and to the English hunt. In 1831 he was put in charge of a district during the cholera epidemic, and published, in London, *Observations on the Nature and Treatment of the Cholera morbus now Prevailing Epidemically in St Petersburg*. His experience led him to oppose the indiscriminate use of the purgative calomel (mercury chloride) and opium in the treatment of the disease, to favour the use of other purgatives, and to avoid astringents. His alleged remedies were later shown to be positively harmful, though possibly not more so than those he opposed. However, his methods of observation were advanced in that he recognized the value of clinical thermometry. In 1832 he came to England for a short time, but he returned to Russia and was soon knighted by patent for his services to the embassy. In 1836–7 he published in the *British and Foreign Medical Review* descriptions of the history and state of medicine in Russia which provided a valuable insight into a relatively obscure subject.

Lefevre then settled in London, in 1842, and on 30 September was admitted a fellow of the Royal College of Physicians. In 1843 he published anonymously *The Life of a Travelling Physician* (3 vols.), describing his travels on the continent, his residence in Poland and Russia, and the social life in Poland and in the English factory at St Petersburg. This book was followed by the pamphlet *Advantages of Thermal Comfort* (1843), on the temperature of rooms, clothing, and bedmaking, suggested by his Russian experience of the effects of a severe climate on health and on sick persons. In 1844 he published *An Apology for the Nerves*, which was of importance mainly for identifying his authorship of his first work, and, by drawing attention to the state of his own nerves, for foreshadowing the mode of his death.

Lefevre's already unstable frame of mind was further unsettled by the mental illness of his wife, the death of his children, and the loss, while he was abroad, of many friendships. He lived with a friend, Mr Myers, at Lower Brook Street, Grosvenor Square, after his return to London, and then with another friend, Dr Nathaniel Grant, in Thayer Street, Manchester Square, London. Both knew of his periodic depressions, which led ultimately to his death: Lefevre died on 12 February 1846 at Grant's house, when he killed himself by swallowing prussic acid. A verdict of 'temporary insanity' was recorded by the coroner. Lefevre was buried at Kensal Green cemetery, Middlesex. He was survived by his wife. ELIZABETH BAIGENT

Sources Munk, *Roll* • *GM*, 2nd ser., 25 (1846), 537 • W. F. Chambers, *Address to the Royal Medical and Chirurgical Society of London 2/3/1846* • N. H. Schuster, 'English doctors in Russia in the early nineteenth century', *Proceedings of the Royal Society of Medicine*, 61 (1968), 185–90 • *Provincial Medical Directory* (1847), 178–9 • *DNB*
Wealth at death under £6000—personal property in England: *London and Provincial Medical Directory*, 1 (1847)

Lefevre, Sir John George Shaw- (**1797–1879**), civil servant, was born at 11 Bedford Square, London, on 24 January 1797, the second of four sons of Charles Shaw (1758–1823), and his wife, Helena (1767–1834), daughter and heiress of John Lefevre of Heckfield Place, Hampshire. Charles Shaw, who assumed the additional name of Lefevre on his marriage into that Huguenot family, sat as an MP from 1792 to 1820. John was educated at Dr Faithfull's school at Warfield, and then at Eton College, before entering in 1814 Trinity College, Cambridge, where he was a close friend of Denis Le Marchant. He graduated BA as senior wrangler and first Smith's prizeman in 1818, proceeding MA in 1821, having been elected a fellow of Trinity in 1819. He went out of residence, travelling in France and Italy, where he studied Italian and modern Greek and established the foundations of his later facility in languages. He entered at the Inner Temple in 1822, and was called to the bar in 1825. He married in 1824 Rachel Emily (1801–1885), daughter of Ichabod Wright, a Nottingham banker, with whom he had a family of two sons and six daughters.

On settling in London during the 1820s Shaw-Lefevre moved in intellectual whiggish circles. Through his father he gained election as FRS in 1820, and in the following year he was elected one of the founder members of the Political Economy Club, remaining a member until 1831. From 1828 until 1846 he was a member of the Society for the Diffusion of Useful Knowledge, promoted by Lord Brougham. At the same time he developed a successful legal practice as a conveyancer, handling from 1826 the land dealings of the earls Spencer. The Spencer connection led to his appointment by Lord Grey's government in November 1831 to redraw county constituency boundaries in readiness for the Reform Act of 1832. His success in carrying out this sensitive assignment raised his political prospects and, standing as a whig, he was elected for Petersfield in December 1832, but early in 1833 he was unseated on petition. In April 1833, on Althorp's recommendation, Lord Stanley appointed him under-secretary for the colonies, where he had particular responsibility for distributing the £20 million compensation to slave owners in the West Indies provided for under the Emancipation Act. Althorp's influence led to his appointment in August 1834, together with Frankland Lewis and George Nicholls, as one of three commissioners responsible for implementing the Poor Law Amendment Act. This involved both a heavy administrative burden and much public obloquy.

Shaw-Lefevre found the strain of the poor-law commission overwhelming and was happy to transfer, in June 1841, to the vacant joint secretaryship of the Board of Trade, responsible mainly for the legal business falling on the department and especially the regulation of joint-stock companies. He represented the Board of Trade on the council of government schools of design, and became embroiled in the heated arguments as to how best government might encourage industrial design. He retained political ambitions, and in July 1847 was brought forward by a committee chaired by Sir Edward Ryan, and including Babbage, Brougham, and Macaulay, to stand as a reforming candidate for the Cambridge University parliamentary seat. He finished at the foot of the poll. In June 1848 he was able to leave the busy departmental work at the Board of Trade when Lord John Russell appointed him to the more leisurely position of deputy clerk to the parliaments (where his brother, Charles Shaw-*Lefevre, later Viscount Eversley, was speaker), and succeeded Sir George Henry Rose in 1855 as clerk of the parliaments. He held the clerkship until his retirement in March 1875. During his period of office he prepared an analysis of the standing orders of the House of Lords, achieved a more orderly publication of statutes, and helped the work of the Historical Manuscripts Commission.

Shaw-Lefevre's services were in constant demand for various commissions, inquiries, and other public work. He was an unsalaried charity commissioner (1835–7) and a member of the colonization commission for South Australia (1835–40), chaired by Robert Torrens. After that commission was revoked he became an unpaid colonial land and emigration commissioner (1841–6). In 1836 he was appointed one of the original thirty-eight members of the senate of the University of London, which received its charter as an examining and degree-awarding body in that year, serving as vice-chancellor from 1842. His mathematical training qualified him for membership of the commission appointed in 1838 to consider replacements for the official standards of weights and measures destroyed by fire in the houses of parliament. In 1842 he served on a Treasury committee to investigate frauds connected with the issue of exchequer bills. He was an unpaid member of the British Museum commission (1847–50) and the ecclesiastical commission (from 1847). In 1847 he was called upon to settle the row between the Royal Scottish Academy, the Edinburgh Royal Institute, and the Board of Manufactures regarding support for art and the training of artists in Scotland. His recommendations to the Treasury led to the scheme for a national gallery in Scotland. He also reported to the Treasury on the Scottish Fishery Board (1848) and reviewed the unpopular annuity tax, levied to pay the stipends of the Scottish clergy (1849).

Serving as an unsalaried member of the episcopal and capitular revenues commission (1849–50), Shaw-Lefevre was made an unpaid member of the church estates commission, created to oversee the management of the Church of England's property. On both commissions he was the whig government's nominee charged with protecting the interests of lay tenants of the church's lands. Later in 1850 he was appointed to investigate the affairs of the New Zealand Company. He was one of the five members of Macaulay's committee of 1853 which drew up the famous scheme for open competitive recruitment to the civil service of the East India Company, and he served on the inns of court commission (1854–5) which investigated legal education. In 1855 he was appointed one of the civil service commissioners, charged with organizing the examinations for posts in the home civil service which replaced the old patronage system. All these were unpaid, and he was extremely scrupulous about not taking on additional remunerative employments when receiving an official salary; the traditional stipend of £20 and a butt of ale for undertaking the auditorship of Trinity College was the only emolument he had received in addition to his income as poor law commissioner. He looked instead for honorary recognition, which was slow in coming. He was appointed CB in April 1848 and knighted (KCB) on Palmerston's recommendation in January 1857, but only after he had felt obliged to distribute a printed memorandum of his official services.

In 1858 Shaw-Lefevre gave up his position as church estates commissioner, and early in 1862 poor health caused him to stand down from the civil service commission and the vice-chancellorship of London University. His final unsalaried services were as a member of the digest of laws (1867–70) and standards of weights and measures (1867–8) commissions, and as one of the commissioners responsible for redrafting the statutes of the ancient public schools (1868) following the report of the Clarendon commission. In 1871 he presided over the education section of the Social Science Association congress at Dublin.

Oxford University conferred the degree of honorary DCL upon him in 1858. He continued to learn languages late in life, taking up Russian when he was sixty-five. In 1873 he translated and published *The Burgomaster's Family* from the Dutch. Shaw-Lefevre died at Cliftonville, Margate, Kent, on 20 August 1879.

Shaw-Lefevre was one of the generation of administrators who, following the passage of parliamentary reform in 1832, carried through the whig programme of renovating British institutions. He was assiduous and conscientious, with a remarkable capacity for assimilating knowledge. His official life was largely behind the scenes, and contemporaries noted that he never overcame the timidity which deterred him from positions exposing him to public criticism (Willson, 226). He belonged to a dynasty active in public life: among his children were George John Shaw-*Lefevre, Baron Eversley, and Madeleine Septimia Shaw-*Lefevre. His second daughter, Rachel Emily, married Arthur Hamilton Gordon, Baron Stanmore.

M. C. CURTHOYS

Sources F. M. G. Willson, *A strong supporting cast: the Shaw Lefevres, 1789–1936* (1993) • *DNB* • Boase, *Mod. Eng. biog.* • Venn, *Alum. Cant.* • S. E. Finer, *The life and times of Sir Edwin Chadwick* (1952) • G. F. A. Best, *Temporal pillars: Queen Anne's bounty, the ecclesiastical commissioners, and the Church of England* (1964) • J. M. Collinge, *Officials of royal commissions of enquiry, 1815–70* (1984)

Archives HLRO, corresp. and papers | BL, corresp. with W. E. Gladstone, Add. MSS 44358–44724, *passim* • BL, corresp. with Sir Arthur Hamilton-Gordon, Add. MS 49224 • HLRO, letters to Thomas Greene • LUL, letters to Lord Overstone • NA Scot., corresp. with Lord Dalhousie • PRO, letters to Lord Granville, PRO 30/29 • W. Sussex RO, letters to duke of Richmond • Wellcome L., corresp. with the Hodgkin family

Likenesses J. Watson-Gordon, oils, 1847, Scot. NPG • Ape [C. Pellegrini], watercolour drawing, NPG; repro. in *VF* (1871) • portrait, repro. in *The Graphic*, 11 (1875), 291–2 • portrait, repro. in *ILN*, 2 (1843), 93

Wealth at death under £12,000: probate, 26 Sept 1879, *CGPLA Eng. & Wales*

Lefevre, Madeleine Septimia Shaw- (1835–1914), college head, was born on 6 May 1835, the seventh child and fourth daughter of Sir John George Shaw-*Lefevre (1797–1879), civil servant, and his wife, Rachel Emily Wright (1801–1885). George John Shaw-*Lefevre, Baron Eversley, was an elder brother. She was educated at home in the succession of London residences taken by her father in his official career. During 1866–7 she visited her sister Rachel and brother-in-law, Arthur Charles Hamilton *Gordon, in New Brunswick and Trinidad, where the latter was colonial governor.

Though she must have learned much from the conversation of her family, Madeleine Shaw-Lefevre, who, like three of her sisters, remained unmarried, was drawn late into public work. Her involvement in social work probably came about through her friendship with Lady Ducie (her brother's mother-in-law), a founder member of the Workhouse Visiting Society and connected with the National Association for the Promotion of Social Science. By 1877 Madeleine was on the committee of the Metropolitan Association for Befriending Young Servants, founded by Mrs Nassau Senior, and was an active 'visitor' on behalf of the association.

Madeleine Shaw-Lefevre's social work brought her to the attention of the committee of the council of Somerville Hall, Oxford, who, early in 1879, were seeking a warden for the newly founded undenominational hall for women students. Choice of a head for the institution was difficult because undefined: there was in 1879 no body of women distinguished by academic qualifications or by professional public service. Madeleine Shaw-Lefevre was not in the original shortlist, but was approached by John Percival, president of Trinity College and chairman of the council, and was elected on 3 May 1879. In her brief period of committee work she had acquired a reputation for hard work, wisdom, and tact, while her family's Liberal political connections further recommended her to the Somerville council. Her father, as vice-chancellor of London University, had privately favoured the earliest moves to open London degrees to women, and her brother, who promoted reform of the law relating to married women's property, was an energetic fund-raiser for Somerville. She had the additional qualification of having been, since 1885, a trustee at Bedford College for Women in London.

Miss Shaw-Lefevre was a reluctant candidate. She loved family life and dreaded the solitariness of her new position. She accepted it for one year only, and that on condition that she need not stay in Oxford during vacations. She was paid £100, with free board and lodging. Somerville Hall was housed in Walton Manor, a simple house, less grand than the homes of some of its students, set in three rough acres of paddock off the Woodstock Road. Living conditions must have seemed austere to the warden. Her duties were not onerous. There were twelve students in 1879, and the numbers did not rise above forty-three in her time. In 1885 the West Buildings (still little changed) were opened. West Buildings were run by a deputy warden, with their own drawing-room and dining-room. Students from House and West would pay calls on one another, leaving cards as their mothers had taught them.

Miss Shaw-Lefevre's function was to make a women's hall of residence acceptable in an ancient university city where women had been treated with little respect outside a family setting. She sought the advice of Anne Jemima Clough, and modelled arrangements at Somerville on those of Newnham Hall, Cambridge (rather than those of Girton, which sought to copy the men's colleges). In collaboration with her deputy at Somerville, Clara Pater, she was responsible for what Charlotte Green, a member of the council, described as 'the wise establishment of precedents in the conduct of life in a women's college' (Green, 165). She successfully ensured that opponents of women at Oxford were given no opportunity to attack the new institution. She believed that the Hall should resemble a house party. A few of the first students were well-to-do, in a period when wealth displayed itself in dress, especially in millinery. Others were young and socially inexperienced. She steered them between dowdiness and ostentation. Yet her rule was not felt to be oppressive. Her father had friends in Oxford and she was a valued guest at dinner parties. Distinguished men as well as women visited the warden, giving at least one student the impression that 'Oxford passed in freely' to them. Ruskin, at first hostile to the idea of women students, came to tea, saw the girls playing tennis on the rough lawn, and presented his complete works and a case of cut sapphires, later set in a jewelled necklace to be worn as the principal's chain of office.

During Miss Shaw-Lefevre's principalship women began (1884) to be admitted to university examinations. Teaching was arranged by the Association for the Education of Women, under Mrs Bertha Johnson; the first woman tutor was appointed at Somerville in 1882. Somerville had no chapel. From the beginning it had asserted its religious independence. Miss Shaw-Lefevre was a traditional but not an enthusiastic Anglican. She read prayers daily in the dining-hall but never talked about religion. She was for her time widely travelled, taking leave of absence during 1885–6 to visit the Hamilton-Gordons in Ceylon.

Madeleine Shaw-Lefevre's dignified grace survives in the portrait hanging over the principal's chair in Somerville College. She carried her head beautifully. Ordinarily she had an aristocratic casualness in dress, but could appear when the occasion called for it as a very great lady. Elizabeth Wordsworth described her as 'the very antipodes of the clumsy, masculine blue-stocking who was the favourite bugbear of the opponents of women's education' (Wordsworth, 5). At fifty-four, in the last year of her principalship, she seemed to one student, the Indian feminist Cornelia Sorabji, 'a very old lady' (Willson, 307). She presided over the first decade of Somerville. Traditions acceptable to Oxford were formed. In her time eighty-two Somervillians went out into the world, thirteen of them with firsts. In 1889 she went back to live quietly with her unmarried sisters, remaining on the council of the college until her death at her home, Greenhill Farm, Farnham, Surrey, on 19 September 1914. She was buried, with others of her family, at Ascot. ENID HUWS JONES

Sources E. W. [E. Wordsworth], 'Miss M. Shaw Lefevre', *Oxford Magazine* (16 Oct 1914), 5–6 • T. H. Green, 'Miss M. Shaw Lefevre', *Times Educational Supplement* (6 Oct 1914), 165 • F. M. G. Willson, *A strong supporting cast: the Shaw Lefevres, 1789–1936* (1993) • P. Adams, *Somerville for women: an Oxford college, 1879–1993* (1996) • V. Farnell, *A Somervillian looks back* (1948) • *Somerville College register, 1879–1971* [1972] • Somerville College, Oxford • *CGPLA Eng. & Wales* (1914)
Archives Somerville College, Oxford
Likenesses R. Jacomb-Hood, oils, Somerville College, Oxford
Wealth at death £12,957 7*s.* 6*d.*: probate, 10 Nov 1914, *CGPLA Eng. & Wales*

Le Févre, Nicaise [Nicasius, Nicolas] (*c.*1610–1669), chemist, was born in Sedan, France, the son of Claude Le Févre (*c.*1569–*c.*1630), a protestant apothecary born in Rouen who settled in Sedan about 1597, and Françoise de Beaufort, daughter of a local family of apothecaries and physicians. Le Févre was educated at the protestant academy of Sedan, then apprenticed to his father in 1625. His father died before his apprenticeship was completed and he was taken under the tutelage of Abraham Duhan, doctor of medicine and professor of philosophy at the academy. Le Févre practised as an apothecary in Sedan until 1646 when he moved to Paris where Samuel Cottereau Du Clos, protestant and physician to the king, became his patron. He began to offer lectures in pharmaceutical chemistry, some of which were attended by English émigrés. John Evelyn (1620–1706) attended a course of his lectures in February 1647. In 1652 Le Févre obtained the privilege of a royal apothecary and was appointed demonstrator of chemistry at the Jardin du Roi by Antoine Vallot (1584–1671), first physician to Louis XIV.

At the Restoration, Le Févre was called to London as professor of chemistry to Charles II on 15 November 1660 and was appointed apothecary-in-ordinary to the royal household on 31 December of that year. Charles entrusted him with the management of the laboratory at St James's Palace which Le Févre furnished with supplies from France. He became a fellow of the Royal Society on 4 December 1661 and his election as an original fellow was confirmed on 20 May 1663.

Le Févre was an able practical chemist and a lucid, learned, and accurate author. His principal published work was *Traicté de la chymie* (2 vols., 1660). An English translation by 'P. D. C., Esq.', one of the gentlemen of the privy chamber, was published in London in 1664 and again in 1670. German and Latin versions also appeared. He claimed that this book was the result of thirty years' work, but his ideas were nearly all derived from others, chiefly Basil Valentine, Paracelsus, van Helmont, and Glauber. The treatise was important for transmitting German chemistry into French and English circles. It stands at a pivotal point in the history of chemistry and Le Févre's importance lies in the fact that much of his work was later assimilated into the popular chemical textbook of Nicolas Lemery (1675). Lenglet-Dufresnoy published an edition of Le Févre's *Traicté* considerably augmented by Dumoustier (5 vols., 1751).

Le Févre divided chemistry into three branches, philosophical, medical or iatrochemical, and pharmaceutical. Predominantly practical, his work was intended largely for the apothecary and his interest in pharmaceutical chemistry is revealed in the careful attention to detail which he shows in his *Discours sur le grand cordial de Sir Walter Rawleigh*, published in 1664. Le Févre died in the parish of St Martin-in-the-Fields, London, in the spring of 1669; on 21 April of that year his estate was administered to by his widow, Philibert. N. G. COLEY

Sources P. Dorveaux, 'L'Apothicaire Le Febvre Nicaise dit Nicolas', *Proceedings of the third international congress of the history of medicine* (1922), 207–12 • O. Hannaway, 'Le Febvre, Nicaise', *DSB* • J. P. Contant, *L'enseignement de la chimie au Jardin Royal des Plantes de Paris* (1952), 88–90 • J. Read, *Humour and humanism in chemistry* (1947), 101–14 • J. R. Partington, *A history of chemistry*, 3 (1962), 17–24 • H. Metzger, *Les doctrines chimiques en France du début du XVIIe à la fin du XVIIIe siècle*, 1 (1923); repr. (1969), 62–82
Likenesses Edelinck, sculpture, repro. in Read, *Humour and humanism in chemistry*, 102 • engraving, repro. in E. Evans, *Catalogue of a collection of engraved portraits*, 2 (1853), 150

Lefort, Cecily Margot (1900–1945). *See under* Women agents on active service in France (*act.* 1942–1945).

Lefroy, George Alfred (1854–1919), bishop of Calcutta, was born on 11 August 1854 at Aghaderg, co. Down, Ireland, the fourth son of the Very Revd Jeffrey Lefroy (*d.* 1885), dean of Dromore, and his wife, Helena, *née* Trench (1820–1908). There were nine children in the family, three girls and six boys. Lefroy was educated at Marlborough School (1865–74), and in 1874 entered Trinity College, Cambridge, where he also taught at the Jesus Lane Sunday school. At Cambridge he fell under the influence of the regius professor of divinity, B. F. Westcott, and Professor J. B. Lightfoot. These two members of the so-called 'Cambridge triumvirate' urged undergraduates to undertake a special mission to educated Hindus and Muslims in India on the model of the classical Alexandrian school, where Clement and Origen had used Greek thought to reinterpret Christianity to educated Romans. In 1877 Lefroy joined five other men to inaugurate a celibate high-church brotherhood, the Cambridge Mission to Delhi, affiliated with the Society for the Propagation of the Gospel (SPG). Lefroy took a first-class degree in the theological tripos in 1878, was ordained priest in 1879, and arrived in Delhi before the end of the year. He became head of the Cambridge brotherhood in 1881, and head of the SPG mission in Delhi (which included St Stephen's Community, an Anglican sisterhood), in 1891.

Committed to an élitist model of clerical influence, Lefroy assumed pastoral responsibility in Delhi for a small Indian Christian community of poor leatherworkers whose piety he found suspect, and he reduced their numbers through the exercise of ecclesiastical discipline. Accomplished in Urdu, he conducted public disputations with learned Muslims which drew large crowds to Delhi's mosques but brought few converts to Christianity. His greatest long-term influence came through establishing prestigious Christian institutions, especially St Stephen's College and St Stephen's Hospital for Women.

Lefroy's conflict between missionary ideals and imperial power deepened after his consecration in 1899 as bishop of Lahore, with episcopal responsibility for the Punjab's extensive military chaplaincies. Despite his association with the government, Lefroy became a favourite with the nationalist press for his statements expressing a generous attitude toward the new national movement. In the face of stubborn opposition he promoted Indian clergymen to positions of diocesan authority and encouraged an interracial, semi-monastic order—the Brotherhood of the Imitation of Christ—centred on the Christian *sadhu* Sundar Singh. But these initiatives were overshadowed by Lefroy's public statements deploring the effects of Hinduism and Islam on the Indian moral character and by his opposition to the appointment of the first Indian head of St Stephen's College, S. K. Rudra. By the time of his consecration as bishop of Calcutta and metropolitan of India in 1913, it was clear to him that the Cambridge Mission's hopes of an Indian–Christian synthesis of East and West had not been fulfilled.

Lefroy enjoyed sports and vigorous walks but after 1911 suffered from painful arthritis and recurrent malaria. His illnesses caused him to resign his bishopric, on Christmas day 1918. He died in Calcutta on 1 January 1919 and was buried in Calcutta Cathedral. JEFFREY COX

George Alfred Lefroy (1854–1919), by Bourne & Shepherd

Sources H. H. Montgomery, *The life and letters of George Alfred Lefroy* (1920) · J. Cox, 'A bishop in search of a church: George Alfred Lefroy', *After the Victorians: private conscience and public duty in modern Britain*, ed. S. Pedersen and P. Mandler (1994), 55–76 · *The Times* (7 Jan 1919) · D. O'Connor, *Gospel, raj and swaraj: the missionary years of C. F. Andrews, 1904–14* (1990) · H. P. K. Skipton, *George Alfred Lefroy, bishop of Calcutta* (1919)

Archives Bodl. RH, Society for the Propagation of the Gospel archives · CUL, corresp. with Lord Hardinge · LPL, corresp. with Edwin James Palmer, etc.

Likenesses Bourne & Shepherd, photograph, NPG [*see illus.*] · photograph, repro. in Pedersen and Mandler, eds., *After the Victorians*, 54

Wealth at death £6621: *The Times* (30 Jan 1919), 11

Lefroy, Harold Maxwell (1877–1925), entomologist, was born on 20 January 1877 at Itchel House, Crondall, Hampshire, the fourth son of Charles James Maxwell Lefroy, landed proprietor, and his wife, Elizabeth Catherine McClintock. He was educated at Marlborough College and King's College, Cambridge, where he matriculated at Michaelmas 1895. Pursuing his boyhood interest in insects he achieved a first class in the natural sciences tripos, part one, and took his BA in 1898. After less than a year as assistant master of Seaford College, Sussex, Lefroy became the entomologist for the newly created department of agriculture in the West Indies, arriving at Barbados on 24 December 1899. In lectures to sugar planters, in pamphlets, and in articles for the *West Indian Bulletin*, he produced detailed accounts of the insect pests of sugar cane, and of thrips that attacked cacao trees. Lefroy's colonial experiences quickly convinced him of the centrality of the applied entomologist and his insecticides as 'tools of empire'.

In April 1903 Lefroy arrived in Calcutta to take up an appointment as entomologist to the government of India. He began his career in India working under E. P. Stebbing at the Indian Museum, but soon became connected with the Imperial Agricultural Research Institute at Pusa. The following year he married Kathleen Hamilton O'Meara, daughter of William O'Meara of British Guiana. During the nine years that he spent in India, Lefroy 'revolutionized all previous methods of studying the insect pests of agricultural crops' (Stebbing). In addition to serving on the managing committee of the Bombay Natural History Society, and producing numerous entomological pamphlets and articles, he wrote two major texts. His first, *Indian Insect Pests*, appeared in 1906. With the assistance of F. M. Howlett, he followed this three years later with *Indian Insect Life*.

In 1912 Lefroy accepted a position as professor of entomology at the Imperial College of Science and Technology in South Kensington; he arrived in England in January 1913. Already a fellow of the Entomological Society (1900) and the Zoological Society (1902), he quickly became an active participant in London's scientific circles. But he openly declared himself an applied scientist. Identifying himself as the representative of colonial economic entomologists he asserted that the naming of insects was best left to metropolitan museum staff who were accustomed to working with dead specimens. He later reiterated this position in his definitive textbook, *Manual of Entomology* (1923). Between 1911 and 1914 the British Museum (Natural History) engaged him to deal with economic entomological enquiries, and upon the creation of the Imperial Bureau of Entomology in 1912 he joined the committee of management as the representative for India. In 1913 he became honorary curator of the insect house at the zoological gardens. At about the same time he was asked to deal with an infestation of death watch beetles in the roof timbers of Westminster Hall. Contemporaries consistently remembered Lefroy as a man of boundless energy. One manifestation of this was his driving technique. A friend recalled:

> He was an ardent and dangerous motorist. It was an experience to be driven by him in a car whose battered wings gave little confidence, as fast as the car could go, through London traffic, in company with a biscuit-box of noxious living insects, a few glass bottles of poisons, and a cylinder of some lethal gas. (*The Times*, 15 Oct 1925)

On 17 April 1914, this motoring passion resulted in a near fatal accident.

Although rejected for service in the First World War Lefroy instructed sanitary officials, doctors, and army officers on the dangers of insects as vectors of disease. In the same capacity he served as temporary lieutenant-colonel in the Mesopotamian field force in 1916. And at the behest of the British Wheat Commission he and R. A. Lowe travelled to Australia to vanquish a large infestation of weevils in stored wheat in early 1918. An original member of the Association of Economic Biologists (established in 1904), Lefroy served as honorary secretary in 1914 and as honorary editor of the association's journal, the *Annals of Applied Biology*, from 1914 to 1916. His involvement with the association was indicative of his desire for professional recognition. Aware of his roles as both scientist and publicist Lefroy freely used Royal Institution lectures, newspapers, popular magazines, wireless broadcasts, and even cinematograph films to promote his subject. Lefroy's decision to become chair of the panel of applied biology at the College of Pestology was undoubtedly motivated by the same professional and entrepreneurial aspirations.

In the end Lefroy succumbed to the thing that he saw as his greatest tool in the struggle for professional recognition—insecticides. On Saturday 10 October 1925 he was overcome by a gas insecticide of his own invention while working at his laboratory at Imperial College. He rallied for several hours before exposing himself to a final fatal dose. Presciently he admitted, 'The little beggars have got the best of me this time' (*The Times*, 17 Oct 1925). Later that day Lefroy was found unconscious on the floor of his laboratory; he never regained consciousness. He was rushed to St George's Hospital, where he died at 6.25 p.m. on 14 October 1925. At an inquest held two days later it was revealed that Lefroy was a victim of 'very chronic toxaemia which had been carrying on for a period of six or seven years' (ibid.). Mourned by his wife and only son, Cecil, Harold Maxwell Lefroy was buried at Kensal Green cemetery, London, on 17 October 1925. J. F. M. Clark

Sources *The Entomologist*, 58 (1925), 279–80 · *Entomologist's Monthly Magazine*, 61 (1925) · *Journal of the Bombay Natural History Society*, 30 (1925) · *Nature*, 116 (1925), 651–2 · *The Times* (15 Oct 1925) · *WWW*, 1941–50 · H. A. Ballou, 'Entomology in the West Indies', *West Indian Bulletin*, 11 (1911), 282–317 · J. F. M. Clark, 'Science, secularization, and social change: the metamorphosis of entomology in nineteenth-century England', DPhil diss., U. Oxf., 1994 · W. B. Bierley, 'The Association of Applied Biologists and the *Annals of Applied Biology*: a retrospect (1904–1938)', *Annals of Applied Biology*, 26 (1939), 178–95 · 'Professor Lefroy's death: inquest verdict', *The Times* (17 Oct 1925) · Venn, *Alum. Cant.*, 2/4 · N. D. Riley, *The department of entomology of the British Museum (Natural History), 1904–1964: a brief historical sketch* (1964) · P. L. G. Bateman, 'The imperial entomologist', *Antenna*, 2 (Jan 1978), 5 · E. P. Stebbing, 'The late Professor Lefroy', *The Times* (19 Oct 1925) · 'Report of the committee for 1912–13', *Parl. papers* (1914), 57.375, Cd 7050–22 [entomological research] · 'War on the weevil: how Australian crops were saved', *The Times* (27 Oct 1919) · b. cert. · d. cert.

Wealth at death £1268 11*s*. 9*d*.: probate, 8 Dec 1925, *CGPLA Eng. & Wales*

Lefroy, Sir John Henry (1817–1890), army officer and meteorologist, born at Ashe, near Whitchurch, Hampshire, on 28 January 1817, was son of John Henry George Lefroy (*d.* 1823), rector of Ashe, and his wife, Sophia, youngest daughter of Revd Charles Cottrell, rector of Hadley, Middlesex. Lefroy was grandson of Antony Lefroy of Leghorn, the catalogue of whose collection of coins and antiquities was printed in 1763. After his father's death in 1823, his mother moved with her family of six sons and

Sir John Henry Lefroy (1817–1890), by Alessandro Ossani, 1879

five daughters to Itchel Manor, near Farnham, Hampshire, which had been left to her husband a few years before his death.

Education and early military career Lefroy was sent to private schools at Alton and at Richmond. In 1828 two of his brothers accidentally discovered an important hoard of Merovingian and English gold coins and ornaments on Crondall Heath, and he thus acquired a taste for antiquarian research. In January 1831 he passed into the Royal Military Academy, Woolwich, and on 19 December 1834 was commissioned second lieutenant, Royal Artillery, and stationed at Woolwich. A strong evangelical throughout his adult life, he joined, with eight or nine young officers, in a weekly meeting in one another's rooms for Bible reading and prayer, and, with the sanction of the commandant and chaplain, these young men opened an evening Sunday school for soldiers' children. He served at Woolwich three years, varied by detachment duty at Purfleet and the Tower of London, and was on duty with his battery at London Bridge at Victoria's coronation. On 10 January 1837 he was promoted lieutenant and in August was sent to Chatham, where he used the Royal Engineers' school of instruction, making a special study of practical astronomy.

In 1838 Lefroy, with Lieutenant Eardley Wilmot, proposed the formation of an institution to provide Royal Artillery officers with opportunities of professional instruction. The scheme was first suggested to Lefroy by a study of the manuscript records of a regimental society which had been started in 1771 and came to an untimely end. Colonel Cockburn, head of the Royal Laboratory at Woolwich arsenal, submitted the proposal to the authorities, and when the Royal Artillery Institution was founded was the first president of the committee of management, and Lefroy the secretary.

Taking magnetic observations The government assented to a British Association recommendation to establish magnetical observatories in various colonies for simultaneous observation with foreign stations, and agreed to send a naval expedition to take simultaneous observations in high southern latitudes. Lefroy and Eardley Wilmot were in April 1839 selected, on the recommendation of Major Edward Sabine, then engaged in a magnetic survey of the British islands, to go to St Helena and the Cape of Good Hope respectively to take magnetic observations. After instruction during the summer in magnetic work at Dublin from the leading expert in magnetism, Professor Humphrey Lloyd, who became Lefroy's lifelong friend, the two lieutenants embarked in HMS *Terror* for St Helena on 25 September. At Madeira they took barometers to the top of the Pica Ruivo, measured its altitude, and descended with plants for the expedition's naturalists. The results of these measurements are given in the *Narrative of the Voyage of the Antarctic Expedition*. The voyage was long, as the survey work required the expedition to take a devious course by the Canaries, Cape Verde Islands, St Paul's, Trinidad, and Martin Vas, off the Brazilian coast, and Lefroy did not arrive in St James's Bay at St Helena until 31 January 1840. He remained at St Helena until 1842, making magnetic observations, and during his stay assisted at the disinterment of the remains of Bonaparte for removal to France.

In July 1842 Lefroy was transferred to the observatory at Toronto. In 1843 he made the remarkable journey which, undertaken for magnetic research, established his reputation as a geographer. In April 1843 he left Toronto with Corporal William Henry, Royal Artillery, and travelled to Lachine, and from there to Hudson's Bay, partly by canoe and partly on snow-shoes. The principal object of the expedition was to discover the geomagnetic characteristics of British North America and to attempt to locate the magnetic north pole. During the journey Lefroy made two lengthy halts, the first at Fort Chipewyan, at the west end of Lake Athabasca, where magnetic and meteorological observations were made every hour of the twenty-four from 16 October 1843 to 29 February 1844, months of Arctic darkness; the second at Fort Simpson on the McKenzie River, where similar observations were made continuously during April and May 1844. Magnetic observations were also made every two minutes for hours together during periods of magnetic disturbance when the temperature in the observatories could not be kept above 0 °F. During this survey Lefroy traversed about 5475 miles, and made observations at 314 stations *en route*.

The magnetic results of this expedition were communicated to the Royal Society by Sabine (with whom Lefroy had various disagreements), and long remained the chief authority for the determination of the approximate position of the forces of magnetic intensity in North America.

Lefroy's continuous and painstaking method of observation was recognized as the ideal standard for work of the kind, and his work was much praised by later experts. Lefroy's magnetic and meteorological observations were published by the government.

During Lefroy's expedition in North America many observations were taken of the aurora borealis, which formed the subject of two papers, one published in the *Philosophical Magazine* and the other in *Silliman's Journal*. In November 1844 Lefroy resumed work at Toronto, where he lived for the next nine years. On 30 November 1845 he was promoted captain. In June 1848 he was elected FRS. In 1849 he founded the Canadian Institute at Toronto, and was its vice-president (1851–2) then president (1852–3). He cultivated the friendship of American men of science, including Agassiz and Henry.

In 1853 the Toronto observatory was transferred to the colonial government, and Lefroy returned to England. He joined his battery at Woolwich, and went with it to the camp of instruction at Chobham. The Royal Artillery Institution had somewhat declined after he ceased to be secretary in 1839, but in 1849 the evidence given by Captain Eardley Wilmot before a committee of the House of Commons had aroused public interest in it, and a grant of public money had been made for the erection of a suitable building. Lefroy was again appointed secretary, the laboratory being fitted up under his direction, and on 1 February 1854 the new building was opened.

In view of the coming war, and the need of a good portable textbook, Lefroy compiled in 1854 the useful *Hand book of Field Artillery for the Use of Officers*, which was published by the institution, and 300 copies were sent to the Crimea in July 1854. It was used by the War Office until 1884 as a textbook for artillery officers.

Scientific adviser to the army In 1854 Lefroy became secretary of the Patriotic Fund, which brought him into contact with the duke of Newcastle, war minister, who in December made him his confidential adviser in artillery matters. He was made 'scientific adviser on subjects of artillery and inventions', and to meet questions of pay and military precedence was made a senior clerk in the War Office. His duties consisted principally in examining and reporting on military inventions, to which was added the 'foreign legions' and correspondence connected with them. At that time the professional advisers of the master-general of the ordnance on artillery matters were the select committee, composed of nine artillery officers whose average length of service was forty-nine years, and the youngest of whom was sixty-four. Lefroy managed to get this committee abolished and a new one, of younger men, appointed, with power to obtain the best possible outside scientific opinion. Lefroy remained in the same post at the War Office under Lord Panmure, and was one of the first to recognize the importance of rifled ordnance. On his recommendation a battery of 15-pounder rifled shell guns was ordered from Herr Bashley Brittan in 1855, but the order was cancelled at the end of the war. Lefroy was promoted lieutenant-colonel on 24 September 1855.

In October 1855 Lefroy was sent by Lord Panmure, at two days' notice, to Constantinople, to confer with Brigadier-General Storks on the condition of the hospital staff in the East and on the accommodation of the sick at Scutari. He made the acquaintance of Florence Nightingale, whom he much admired and with whom he enjoyed a lifelong friendship. Panmure's confidence in her was partly due to Lefroy's reports. Lefroy supported her work, and corresponded with her on military hospitals and nurses from 1856 to 1868. He also, after the war, helped her establish reading-rooms for soldiers. While at Constantinople he tried to obtain for the Rotunda artillery museum, Woolwich, one of the huge bronze guns from the fort on the Asiatic side of the Dardanelles, but it was only after eleven years of effort that his wish was accomplished.

In 1856 a reorganization of the system of military education was undertaken by Lord Panmure, secretary of state for war. Lefroy prepared a detailed scheme, and some of his proposals, including for competition and grading, were adopted at the new Staff College at Camberley, though other of his proposals, including that the Staff College be at London, were rejected. Panmure wanted Lefroy to implement the latter's comprehensive scheme as the first director-general of military education, but this ran counter to royal and military politics. So in February 1857 Lefroy was appointed only inspector-general of army schools. Regimental education was placed under his direction, and he organized a large staff of trained schoolmasters. In September 1858 he drew up a paper on the importance of establishing a school of gunnery, and it is to his foresighted initiative that the school at Shoeburyness was due. He was promoted brevet colonel on 24 September 1858.

Lefroy was a member of the royal commission on the defence of the United Kingdom appointed in August 1859. Its recommendations resulted in the defence loan, and the controversial fortifications known as 'Palmerston's follies'. The same year, in view of possible hostilities, he was sent with Lieutenant-Colonel Owen, Royal Engineers, by Lord Derby to report on the fortresses of Gibraltar, Malta, and Corfu. On the abolition of the office of inspector-general of army schools in 1860 Lefroy became secretary of the ordnance select committee, and in 1864 president of that committee, with the rank of brigadier-general. He became a regimental colonel on 9 February 1865. From December 1868 to March 1870 he was director-general of ordnance, with the temporary rank of major-general. He carried through the formation of a class for artillery officers who wished to prepare themselves for special appointments, and to the 'advanced class'—later the Artillery College—the regiment owed much. He was a member of the 1868 royal commission on military education, but resigned before completion of the inquiry. While Lefroy was director-general of ordnance the controversial 'control department' was introduced—under Sir John Pakington (secretary of state for war 1867–8) and his successor Cardwell—into the administration of the army. Lefroy recognized the necessity for a better organization of the supply departments of the army, but keenly opposed the attempt to secure it by converting the accountants and commissariat of the army into its controllers. He was unable, however, to secure the rejection of the new scheme, and early in 1870, finding his position untenable, he resigned his appointment, and on 1 April retired from the army with the honorary rank of major-general. In the previous month he had been made a CB. For ten years he had held most important posts in connection with artillery at a time when ordnance and ammunition developed immensely, and his scientific attainments and untiring energy were of great value at a critical period of change. His last service at the War Office was as member of a committee presided over by Sir Frederick Chapman in 1870 to consider the proposed submarine mining defence of certain harbours of the kingdom.

Later career From April 1871 to May 1877 Lefroy was governor and commander-in-chief of Bermuda. He brought together original documents on the early history of the colony, and published them in two bulky volumes, with maps, charts, and views. He collected the indigenous flora, introduced new cereals and vegetables, and brought a skilled gardener at his own expense from England to superintend their cultivation. He also resumed meteorological and magnetic observations. Everything concerning the welfare of his government, civil and military, social, literary, and scientific, interested him, and the island's inhabitants found in him a firm friend. While at Bermuda he strongly recommended on moral and economical grounds a reduction of the length of imprisonment courts martial were empowered to award. On his return home in 1877 he contacted Sir Henry Thring, then drafting the amended Mutiny Act, and a more lenient code resulted.

Lefroy was made a KCMG in 1877, and from October 1880 to December 1881 was briefly governor of Tasmania, where he was active and popular. While there he communicated to its Royal Society a paper, 'On the magnetic variation at Hobart', which gave the result of his observations with the 4 inch azimuth compass made in 1881 and discussed secular change of the magnetic variation on the southern coast of Australia.

Lefroy returned to England in 1882, and made his last contribution to magnetic science by the publication in 1883 of the diary of his Canadian magnetic survey. In this résumé of the principal work of his life the lines of equal value of magnetic intensity on his maps differ considerably from Sabine's in the *Philosophical Transactions* in 1846 and 1872. This resulted from different methods: Sabine attempting the best mean results of a great continent, but Lefroy the exact results for a portion of that continent.

Lefroy was twice married: first, on 16 April 1846, to Emily Merry, the daughter of Sir John Beverley *Robinson, bt, chief justice of Upper Canada; they had two sons and two daughters, and Emily died in 1859. Secondly, on 12 May 1860, he married Charlotte Anna, eldest daughter of Colonel T. Dundas of Fingask and widow of Colonel Armine Mountain; she survived her husband.

Lefroy was tall, with sharply cut features, very slim, alert in movement, genial, cheerful, and chivalrous. His exertions for the welfare of soldiers and their families continued throughout his military career. His good works were unpretending and unobtrusive. He was honorary secretary and later a commissioner of the Patriotic Fund, an active member of the committee of the Royal School for Daughters of Officers of the Army, and for some years chairman of its house committee.

As a labour of love Lefroy devoted his evenings for many months in 1863–4 to arranging, classifying, and cataloguing the collection in the Rotunda artillery museum at Woolwich. He was for two years a member of the Royal Society's Kew committee. He became FGS in 1853, and was LLD (1884) of McGill College, a fellow of the Society of Antiquaries, and member of other learned societies and of the Royal Colonial Institute. In 1880 he was president of the geographical section of the British Association at Swansea, and again in 1884 at Montreal, and delivered the presidential addresses. On his return he suffered from heart weakness and bronchitis, and his last years were marred by frequent illness. In 1885 and 1886 he was a member of the general committee of the Universities Mission to Central Africa, and in 1887 and 1888 was a vice-president. His many and varied publications, from 1841 to 1888, included articles and books on meteorology, botany, terrestrial magnetism, artillery, military history, numismatics, and the Bermudas.

Lefroy resided in London for several years after his retirement from public life; but failing health led him to Cornwall, where he died at Lewarne, near Liskeard, on 11 April 1890. He was buried near his birthplace at Crondall in Hampshire. R. H. Vetch, *rev.* Roger T. Stearn

Sources *Proceedings* [Royal Geographical Society], new ser., 12 (1890) • *Proceedings of the Society of Antiquaries of London*, 2nd ser., 13 (1890) • *Minutes of the Proceedings of the Royal Artillery Institution*, 18 (1890) • B. Bond, *The Victorian army and the Staff College, 1854–1914* (1972) • E. T. Cook, *The life of Florence Nightingale*, 2 vols. (1913) • R. Biddulph, *Lord Cardwell at the war office: a history of his administration, 1868–1874* (1904) • E. M. Spiers, *The late Victorian army, 1868–1902* (1992) • Boase, *Mod. Eng. biog.* • C. M. Whitfield and R. A. Jarrell, 'Lefroy, Sir John Henry', *DCB*, vol. 11 • *AusDB* • Kelly, *Handbk* • Burke, *Peerage*

Archives NA Canada, family corresp. • priv. coll. • Royal Artillery Institution, Woolwich, London, papers • Yale U., Sterling Memorial Library, journals | BL, corresp. with Florence Nightingale, Add. MS 43397 • CUL, letters to Sir George Stokes • Inst. EE, corresp. with Sir Francis Ronalds • PRO, letters to Sir Edward Sabine, BJ3 • Tyne and Wear Archives Service, Newcastle upon Tyne, letters to Sir Andrew Noble • Tyne and Wear Archives Service, Newcastle upon Tyne, letters to Lord Rendel

Likenesses portrait, 1853, repro. in Bond, *The Victorian army and the Staff College*, facing p. 126 • portrait, 1853, repro. in *The Graphic* (26 April 1890), 533 • A. Ossani, portrait, 1879, priv. coll. [*see illus.*]

Wealth at death £10,618 12*s*. 7*d*.: resworn probate, May 1891, *CGPLA Eng. & Wales* (1890)

Lefroy, Thomas Langlois (1776–1869), judge and politician, was born on 8 January 1776, the eldest son of Anthony Lefroy of Newton Perry, co. Limerick, and Anne Gardiner. He entered Trinity College, Dublin, in 1790, and after a distinguished university career graduated BA in 1795. He was instrumental in the re-establishment in 1794 of the College Historical Society. He entered Lincoln's Inn, London, in 1793, and King's Inns, Dublin, in 1794, and he was called to the Irish bar in 1797. He visited Bath and was known to

Jane Austen. Lefroy married in 1799 Mary, only daughter and heir of Jeffrey Paul of Silver Spring, co. Wexford. They had four sons (a number were also called to the bar) and three daughters.

Lefroy commenced practice at the bar in 1800 and went the Munster circuit. His abilities in chancery work enabled him to give up going on circuit after some years. He published *Observations on Proceedings by Elegit* (1802) and was joint editor with John Schoales of *Reports on Cases in the Irish Court of Chancery under Lord Redesdale, from 1802 to 1806*. He was called to the inner bar in 1816, became third serjeant in 1818, a bencher of King's Inns in 1819, second serjeant in 1820, and first serjeant in 1822. He declined offers of judicial appointments three times, in 1820, 1821, and 1822. It was one of the functions of the first serjeant to act as a temporary commissioner of assize when one of the judges was unable to travel on circuit, and Lefroy resigned his position as first serjeant in 1830 when he considered an official suggestion (that he might apply to be exempted from this duty) to be an infringement of the judicial functions of the position and an interference with the administration of justice.

Lefroy lived in Dublin at 18 Leeson Street, and at Newcourt, near Bray, co. Wicklow. He acquired an estate at Carrigglass, co. Longford, and built a substantial manor house between 1838 and 1848 to the design of Daniel Robertson. He was an evangelical churchman and a strong Conservative, at a time when religious issues, such as Catholic emancipation and the non-payment of tithes, were at the centre of political debate in Ireland. He was a strong opponent of Daniel O'Connell.

Lefroy stood unsuccessfully for parliament in the Dublin University constituency in 1827, but he succeeded in being elected in 1830 and thereafter held his seat at each election up to (and including) 1841. He made no great figure in the House of Commons, though he spoke often. His support of Peel was rewarded, not over-generously, by a relatively junior judicial appointment in 1841, as a puisne judge (baron) of the court of exchequer. He held that position until 1852, when Derby, in the first of his three ministries, appointed him to be chief justice of the queen's bench in Ireland, in succession to Francis Blackburne.

Lefroy was a diligent, competent, and conscientious judge, but he is best remembered for the fact of his promotion to such a senior position at the age of seventy-six and his continuation in office to the age of ninety. The Conservatives, under Derby, were in office for only brief intervals in the 1850s and 1860s, and although Lefroy's advanced age necessarily created an expectation that he might die at any time or be compelled by ill health or failing powers to retire, he was not prepared to retire voluntarily until the choice of his successor was in the hands of the tories. In 1856 a debate was initiated in the House of Commons on the alleged incapacity due to age of a number of the Irish judges, including Lefroy. In May 1866 questions were asked in both the House of Lords and the House of Commons about the capacity of Lefroy to discharge his judicial functions, following a macabre incident in the previous year when, owing to poor light in a court house, he had been assisted in reading and pronouncing a sentence of death. He held his position until July that year, when Lord Derby replaced Lord John Russell as prime minister and Lefroy could safely resign. He died at Newcourt on 4 May 1869, and was buried at Mount Jerome cemetery, Dublin. DAIRE HOGAN

Sources T. Lefroy, *Memoir of Chief Justice Lefroy* (1871) • D. Hogan, '"Vacancies for their friends": judicial appointments in Ireland, 1866–1867', *Brehons, serjeants, and attorneys: studies in the history of the Irish legal profession*, ed. D. Hogan and W. N. Osborough (1990), 211–29 • F. E. Ball, *The judges in Ireland, 1221–1921*, 2 vols. (1926) • *CGPLA Eng. & Wales* (1869)

Archives Carrigglas Manor, co. Longford | NL Ire., Farnham MSS

Likenesses C. Moore, marble bust, 1839, TCD • S. C. Smith the elder, oils?, 1852–5, Carrigglas, co. Longford, Ireland • S. C. Smith the younger, oils, *c.*1872, King's Inns, Dublin • G. Hayter, group portrait, oils (*The House of Commons, 1833*), NPG • H. Robinson, stipple and line engraving (after G. Hayter), BM, NPG • mezzotint, BM, NPG

Wealth at death under £30,000: probate, 2 Aug 1869, *CGPLA Ire.*

Lefroy, William (1836–1909), dean of Norwich, was born on 6 November 1836 in Dublin, the eldest of the four children of Isaac and Isabella Lefroy. He had two brothers and one sister. The family's background was humble, and after education at the St Michael-le-Pole Latin school in Dublin, Lefroy began work for the *Irish Times*, first in the printers' office and then as a journalist. This gave him a lifelong affection for, and rapport with, the press. During his spare time he read for holy orders and studied for the BA degree at Trinity College, graduating in 1863. He was awarded the divinity testimonium in 1864, MA and BD in 1867, and DD in 1889.

In 1864 Lefroy was ordained deacon and appointed curate of Christ Church, Cork. The eloquence of his preaching soon attracted attention, and in 1866, the year after his ordination to the priesthood, he was invited to become incumbent of St Andrew's, Renshaw Street, Liverpool. At this time St Andrew's was a proprietary chapel controlled by the Gladstone family, with a large congregation drawn by the preaching of the previous incumbent, R. W. Forrest. Lefroy rose to this daunting challenge, filling the chapel's 1800 seats through a combination of pulpit oratory and conscientious pastoral care. A small, wiry, excitable man of boundless energy, deep affections, and great personal charm, Lefroy exerted considerable influence not only over his own congregation but also over the merchant princes of Liverpool. This enabled him to raise funds to build new churches in Bootle and Everton, and made him a valuable supporter of the scheme for a Liverpool bishopric. As a member of the Liverpool school board from 1876 Lefroy's energetic defence of voluntary schools earned him the epithet 'the War-horse' from his colleagues. Lefroy was married twice. No information is available about his first marriage. He married secondly, on 11 February 1878 at Malta, Mary Ann, daughter of Charles MacIver of Calderstone, Liverpool, with whom he had two daughters. The younger daughter, Mary Ann, married Sir Percy Bates, bt.

In theology Lefroy was a staunch evangelical and an outspoken protestant. He gave the Donnellan lectures at Trinity College, Dublin, in 1887–8, taking as his subject 'The Christian ministry: its origin, constitution, nature, and work', and offering a sustained critique of the views of the broad-churchman Edwin Hatch and the Anglo-Catholic Charles Gore. With the consecration of his fellow evangelical J. C. Ryle as first bishop of Liverpool in 1880, Lefroy was appointed to an honorary canonry. Further preferment followed as he became rural dean of Liverpool South (1884) and later archdeacon of Warrington (1887). Lefroy was appointed dean of Norwich in June 1889 on the retirement of E. M. Goulburn. His twenty years as dean were marked by a thorough restoration of the fabric of the cathedral, the installation of a new organ, and the inauguration of Sunday evening services in the nave designed to appeal to the unchurched inhabitants of the city. Lefroy worked to make Norwich Cathedral a centre for worship and evangelism, and he achieved considerable success. His reforming schemes extended beyond Norwich, to convocation and to the church congress, and his ideas on clergy sustentation, put forward in 1895, did much to shape the Queen Victoria Clergy Fund of 1897. He was an active freemason, and was chaplain to the grand lodge of England in 1899–1900.

Lefroy made a visit to the Alps every year from 1867 to 1909, taking a summer chaplaincy for the Colonial and Continental Church Society. The English churches at Zermatt, Riffel Alp, the Rhône glacier, and Adelboden owed much to his enthusiasm. He was taken ill at the Riffel Alp Hotel at Zermatt in early August 1909 and died there on 11 August. The funeral took place two days later at Holy Trinity, Riffel Alp, and Lefroy was buried beside the church.

MARTIN WELLINGS

Sources H. Leeds, *Life of Dean Lefroy* (1909) · *DNB* · *The Record* (13 Aug 1909) · *The Record* (20 Aug 1909) · *The Times* (12 Aug 1909) · *WWW, 1897–1915* · C. Dunkley, ed., *Official report of the church congress* (1907), 129–36 · B. Baring Gould, *In memoriam: the Very Rev. William Lefroy* [1909]

Archives Norfolk RO, corresp. relating to chapter and estate business

Likenesses Bassano, photographs, 1894, NPG · Blackden, portrait, Norwich Cathedral · wood-engraving (after photograph by Russell & Sons), NPG; repro. in *ILN* (22 June 1889)

Wealth at death £11,184 1s. 10d.: probate, 28 Sept 1909, *CGPLA Eng. & Wales*

Leftwich, William (1770–1843), confectioner and ice merchant, was born in Aldford, near Chester, in 1770, the son of William Leftwich (1743/4–1809) and his wife, Martha Barns (1732/3–1818). He was descended from an old family of local landowners, the Leftwich family of Leftwich Hall, Cheshire.

Leftwich moved to London and set himself up as a wholesale confectioner, with outlets in Fleet Street and Kingston upon Thames. He became increasingly frustrated by his inability to preserve food, especially dairy products, during hot summer months. In the early nineteenth century ice was used for this purpose only in a most limited way, on a few country estates and in the area around Barking, where it was collected from the marshes most winters. Leftwich seems to have been among the first to realize that the widespread use of ice for preserving food would be both highly beneficial and immensely profitable. Accordingly, he chartered a vessel to go from Great Yarmouth to Norway early in 1822, returning in May of that year with a cargo of 300 tons of ice. Confirmation that importing ice was not then regular practice comes from the uncertainty of customs officers in London as to what import duties to levy; they delayed so long in coming to a conclusion that Leftwich feared his cargo might melt. When it was eventually landed and sold at auction there was widespread interest in this novelty, as well as sufficient demand from fishmongers and pastry-cooks for Leftwich apparently to realize a considerable profit.

In this action Leftwich was well ahead of his time, as Norwegian ice later became widely used for refrigeration. In particular, the advent of the railways ensured that fresh fish, meat, and dairy produce could be speedily transported to urban centres. Previously most food had become unfit for human consumption after forty-eight hours: henceforth the use of ice extended its 'shelf life', and undoubtedly contributed to contemporary improvements in diet and food hygiene.

It was probably similar concerns which led to Leftwich's interest in adequate water supplies. In 1825 he used an artesian tube to sink what was then the largest well known in the country, 80 feet deep and 30 feet wide. Other wells followed, and Leftwich seems to have prospered. He died on 17 November 1843, at his home at 43 Cumberland Market, Regent's Park, London. He was buried in Kensal Green cemetery. Almost nothing is known of his family life, but there were fourteen people with the name Leftwich buried in three graves in Kensal Green cemetery between 1841 and 1904, seven of them, including William, in the same grave between 1841 and 1851. His son Thomas registered his death.

D. E. MATHEW, *rev.*

Sources 'Great Yarmouth and the ice trade', *Norfolk Weekly Standard* (11 Dec 1908) · T. Ashbourne, 'The ice trade', *Yarmouth Archaeology* (1989) · E. David, *Harvest of the cold months* (1994) · d. cert. · memorial, Aldford churchyard

Le Gallienne, Richard Thomas (1866–1947), poet and essayist, was born in West Derby, Liverpool, on 20 January 1866. He was the eldest son of John (originally Jean) Gallienne (1843–1929), who became manager of the Birkenhead Brewery, and his wife, Jane (*c.*1839–1910), daughter of Richard Smith of Baxenden, Lancashire, the overlooker in a cotton mill. In keeping with the Celticism of the 1890s, in which he was a leading figure, Le Gallienne's ancestry was from Ireland, Scotland, and the Channel Islands. He restored 'Le' to his surname in the early 1880s. Le Gallienne grew up to share with his mother an interest in literature, especially poetry. In 1875 he entered Liverpool College, where he pursued a distinguished career, being elected McNeill scholar in 1877. In 1881 his father apprenticed him to a firm of chartered accountants. While there he became a book collector and cultivated Liverpool literary society; one of his new friends, the Scottish printer John Robb, produced Le Gallienne's first book, *My Ladies Sonnets*, in 1887. In this period there were two major events

Richard Thomas Le Gallienne (1866–1947), by W. & D. Downey, pubd 1894

which influenced his career: Oscar Wilde's lecture at the Claughton Music Hall, Birkenhead, in December 1883, and the attention and encouragement of Oliver Wendell Holmes three years later.

In the autumn of 1887 Le Gallienne and his friend the actor Jimmy Welch approached the actor–manager Wilson Barrett outside the Royal Court Theatre, Liverpool. Welch obtained a role in a London production and Le Gallienne made an important contact. Within a few months he began to review books for *The Academy*, and made the acquaintance of John Lane. Following his failure in his final accountancy exams in December 1888 Le Gallienne left for London in earnest, serving for a time as Wilson Barrett's private secretary and biographer, and meeting such literary figures as Swinburne, Meredith, and Wilde. Although Le Gallienne had to return to Liverpool in October 1889, owing to the asthma from which he was a persistent sufferer, he was back in London in the spring of 1891. In June he became book critic for *The Star*, where he inherited the pseudonym 'Logroller', a title well suited to his reviewing practice. Shortly afterwards, on 22 January 1891, he married Mildred, daughter of Alfred Lee, the manager of a Liverpool carting firm. Her early death in 1894 was a sore blow: they had one daughter, Hesper Joyce. The emotional legacy of Le Gallienne's love for his first wife can be found in his subsequent fiction: she was, for example, the inspiration for the character of Angel in *Young Lives* (1899). With W. B. Yeats, Ernest Rhys, Lionel Johnson, and others, Le Gallienne was one of the original members of the Rhymers' Club, meeting in the Cheshire Cheese, off the Strand, but in 1892, he broke with the Rhymers in order to criticize decadence.

In 1889 the first work published by Elkin Mathews's and John Lane's Bodley Head was a collection of Le Gallienne's verse, *Volumes in Folio*. In 1892 he became the firm's reader, and was able to recommend such writers as Francis Thompson, John Davidson, Laurence Binyon, Lionel Johnson, and Kenneth Grahame; he also helped in the publication of the *Yellow Book*, to which he also contributed.

Pushing himself and his often whimsical and plangent writings ceaselessly, Le Gallienne achieved real literary success with the publication of *The Quest of the Golden Girl* (American edition, 1896; English edition, 1897), a quintessentially nineties dream of erotic idealism. On 12 February 1897, at Marylebone Town Hall, London, he married Julie, daughter of Peter Norregard, of Copenhagen, a railway director: she was a journalist. They had one daughter, Eva, who became an actress, but Le Gallienne's infidelity and alcoholism broke up the marriage in 1903, after which he emigrated to the United States. Le Gallienne's status was in any case in decline, following the end of the *fin-de-siècle* movement, the atmosphere of which he recalled in the nostalgic short-story collection *Painted Shadows* (1904) and in the popular study *The Romantic '90s* (1926). In America his productivity continued, but not his fame. Following his divorce he married Irma, formerly wife of the American sculptor Roland Hinton Perry, on 27 October 1911, in Darien, Connecticut. Their daughter Gwen achieved a reputation as a portrait painter. In 1930 Le Gallienne moved to France, where he wrote the regular Paris column for the *New York Sun*. Some of these essays were republished in *From a Paris Garret* (New York, 1936; London, 1943) and *From a Paris Scrapbook* (New York, 1938), the latter sharing the 18,000 franc prize from the French government for the best book of the year written about France by a foreigner. After the fall of France in 1940 the Le Galliennes took refuge in Monte Carlo, where they suffered privations as a result of Richard's refusal to broadcast for the German authorities. In 1945 the couple returned to Menton, where Richard died at the Villa Beatrice, rue Albert, on 15 September 1947, following a collapse and asthma attack. He was buried on 17 September in the cemetery above the town, not far from the grave of Aubrey Beardsley, his collaborator on the *Yellow Book*. Le Gallienne's contemporary reputation depended on his character, appearance ('like Botticelli's Head of Lorenzo', William Rothenstein said; Hyde, xxi), and almost ninety books. Today his limpid poetry barely earns a place even in period anthologies, though his prose work captures the air of nineties affectation and nostalgia in a manner still worthy of attention.

MURRAY G. H. PITTOCK

Sources R. Whittington-Egan and G. Smerdon, *The quest of the golden boy: the life and letters of Richard Le Gallienne* (1960) • R. Whittington-Egan, 'The quest of the golden girl', *The 1890s: an encyclopedia of British literature, art, and culture*, ed. G. A. Cevasco

(1993), 491–2 • M. G. H. Pittock, 'The quest of the gilt-edged girl', *The 1890s: an encyclopedia of British literature, art, and culture*, ed. G. A. Cevasco (1993), 490–91 • M. G. H. Pittock, *Spectrum of decadence* (1993) • K. Beckson, *London in the 1890s* (1992) • H. M. Hyde, introduction, in R. Le Gallienne, *The romantic '90s*, new edn (1951) • J. G. Nelson, *The early nineties: a view from the Bodley Head* (1971) • personal knowledge (1951) [*DNB*; H. Montgomery Hyde]

Archives Bodl. Oxf., papers • Howard University, Washington, DC, papers • Lpool RO, corresp. and papers • New York University, Fales Library, corresp. • Ransom HRC, papers • University of San Francisco, corresp. and literary papers | Harvard U., Houghton L., letters to Grant Richards • Ransom HRC, corresp. with John Lane • Richmond Local Studies Library, London, corresp. with Douglas Sladen • U. Leeds, Brotherton L., letters to Edmund Gosse • U. Lpool, letters to John Fraser and papers • U. Reading, letters to Charles Elkin Matthews

Likenesses W. & D. Downey, photograph, pubd 1894, NPG [*see illus.*] • M. Beerbohm, caricature, drawing, 1900, UCLA, Clark Memorial Library • M. Beerbohm, pen and Indian ink drawing, V&A

Wealth at death £4600 12*s*. 7*d*.—in England: probate, 13 March 1948, *CGPLA Eng. & Wales*

Legat, Francis (1755–1809). *See under* Boydell, John, engravers (*act*. 1760–1804).

Legat, Hugh (*fl. c*.1399–1427), scholar and prior of Redbourn, a native of Hertfordshire according to John Bale, was probably a member of the family that held a manor at Abbots Walden in that county, belonging to the Benedictine monks of St Albans, and assisted the monastery in at least one important crisis, although his vernacular work, as Grisdale notes, has been transmitted in a dialect of the west midlands. He entered the abbey of St Albans in the last years of the fourteenth century and studied at Oxford, probably at Gloucester College where the monks of St Albans maintained a strong presence. He remained there for at least a part of the abbacy (1401–20) of William Heyworth, for his commentary on *Architrenius*, dedicated to Heyworth, was written there. It seems he completed a first degree, for in the list of electors of Abbot John Whethamstede in 1420 he is described as 'Bachelor in Theology'.

Legat is distinguished for his literary interests. At Oxford and later at St Albans he joined a group of scholars, both monks and seculars, at work on Latin literature and rediscovering classical rhetoric. Probably his earliest work was an elementary commentary, in nine books, on the *Architrenius*, a satirical poem written at the close of the twelfth century by Jean de Hauville, which, he explains in his prologue, Legat wrote as a diversion from his other studies. Legat's commentary, mutilated at beginning and end, is extant in a fifteenth-century hand in Bodl. Oxf., MS Digby 64. John Bale quoted Legat's preface from a more perfect copy. A Latin letter, written as a rhetorical exercise, is ascribed to him in a fifteenth-century collection (BL, Harley MS 5397, fols. 130*r*–131*v*). This too is likely to be an Oxford composition. These interests he continued on his return to St Albans, acquiring early copies of rhetorical and grammatical texts for the abbey library. Bale also attributes to him a commentary on the *Philosophiae consolatio* of Boethius and *Epistolae ad diversos*, for which he gives incipits from a copy seen at Norwich. These are not known to have survived. Later in his career Legat was active as a preacher both for his own house and for the general chapter of the English Benedictines. In 1420 he was named among preachers for the meeting of the general chapter. Only one sermon, in English, survives which can certainly be attributed to him, in Worcester Cathedral Library, MS F.10, fols. 8*r*–31*v*. It reflects his interest in secular literature as well as a concern for pastoral care.

By 1420, when he attended the election of John Whethamstede, Legat had become prior of the cell of Redbourn, close to St Albans. In 1427, he was assigned by Abbot Whethamstede to the northernmost cell of the abbey at Tynemouth. Nothing further is known of him.

James Tait, *rev*. James G. Clark

Sources Emden, *Oxf.*, 2.1125–6 • Bale, *Cat.*, 518–19 • Bale, *Index*, 171, 215 • H. E. Salter, W. A. Pantin, and H. G. Richardson, eds., *Formularies which bear on the history of Oxford*, 2 vols., OHS, new ser., 4–5 (1942), 435–6 • D. M. Grisdale, ed., *Three Middle English sermons from the Worcester chapter manuscript F.10* (1939) • W. A. Pantin, ed., *Documents illustrating the activities of … the English black monks, 1215–1540*, 3 vols., CS, 3rd ser., 45, 47, 54 (1931–7) • Bodl. Oxf., MS Digby 64 • BL, Harley MS 5397, fols. 130*r*–131*v* • *Gesta abbatum monasterii Sancti Albani, a Thoma Walsingham*, ed. H. T. Riley, 3 vols., pt 4 of *Chronica monasterii S. Albani*, Rolls Series, 28 (1867–9)

Archives BL, Harley MS 5397, fols. 130*r*–131*v* • Bodl. Oxf., MS Digby 64 • Worcester Cathedral, MS F.10, fols. 8*r*–31*v*

Legate, Bartholomew (*d*. 1612), radical separatist and convicted heretic, was the son of William Legate, a substantial householder of Hornchurch, Essex. The extended Legate clan was among the most ancient and successful families of the royal liberty of Havering. By the mid-sixteenth century members of the family, including Bartholomew's father, frequently occupied local offices, while others appear to have been participating in the cloth trade with the Low Countries. Although nothing is known of Bartholomew's formal education, Thomas Fuller later claimed that as an adult he possessed a 'confident carriage, fluent tongue', and was 'excellently skilled in Scripture' (Fuller, 61). During Legate's formative years Hornchurch was a hotbed of radical puritanism, owing in part to the presence of the nonconformist firebrand and schoolmaster John Leech, who regularly preached and catechized out of his household, and who was on one occasion accused of Anabaptism by the archdeacon of Essex. By 1587 it was alleged that Leech's house had become a haven for people claiming that the Church of England 'had neither churches, sacraments, neither good government' (McIntosh, 208). A year later Bartholomew Legate, now described as a gentleman, was presented at the assizes for not attending church; by the end of that year he owed £80 in recusancy fines, the authorities apparently making no discrimination at this point between Catholics and separatists. Two years later a man named Thomas Legate, possibly Bartholomew's brother, was indicted together with John Leech on the charge that Legate had refused to have his child baptized.

It would appear that during these years Legate and his brothers, Thomas and Walter, were together moving towards ever more radical ecclesiological and theological positions. Having rejected the Church of England, they now began to call into question the legitimacy not merely of that institution but also of some of the fundamental doctrinal verities that had been transmitted through the centuries by the Catholic church—most importantly, the doctrines of infant baptism and the Trinity, both of which they now condemned as corrupt vestiges of popish tyranny. It is possible that the brothers may have been exposed to Dutch Anabaptist ideas, for during these years Bartholomew was engaged in the international cloth trade; in the 1590s he petitioned the Cecils for a licence to export kerseys. Regardless of how they arrived at their opinions, by 1600 Henoch Clapham, himself a veteran of the Anglo-Dutch separatist milieu, complained of them as 'our English Arrians', who 'denie all Baptisme and Ordination, till new Apostles be sent to execute those parts to the Gentiles, and *Elias* the Thisbite do come for that end' (Clapham, *Antidoton*, 33). Clapham later elaborated on this description, providing a full-blown caricature of the 'Legatine-Arian' in his *Errour on the Right Hand* (1608), a polemical attack on radical puritan folly. Here Clapham attributed to the 'Legatine-Arians' the belief that

> The Church being to be latent and invisible for many yeares, so that her place was no more to be found; it must accordingly follow, that there could be no more a visible Church, till some notable men were stirred up of God, to raise it again out of the dust. (Clapham, *Errour*, 29)

Christ, meanwhile, was taken to be 'a meere Man, as was Peter, Paule, or I: Once whereas we have the Spirit in measure, and were borne in sinne; he hath the Spirit beyond measure, and was borne free from sinne.' Their reasoning on this point was as follows: 'it being meere Man that sinned, it must be meere Man that must satisfie Gods justice' (ibid., 43–4, 45). In other words, they seem to have argued that if Christ were truly God, the traditional view of a substitutionary atonement would collapse; only if Christ were a perfect, sinless man could the traditional view be maintained without contradiction. Having arrived at these eccentric positions, the brothers appear to have begun to proselytize with a prophetic zeal; as one observer put it, 'these *Legats* had a conceit, that their name did (as it were) foreshew and entitle them, to be the new Apostles, that must doe this new worke' (Jessop, 76–7). It is impossible to determine how widely their ideas spread, but they clearly attracted at least some followers: the puritan minister Thomas Gataker later reported that he had engaged in a theological discussion with one such unnamed admirer, whom Gataker described only as 'a Gentleman-like man' (Gataker, 38–9).

During this period the brothers appear to have been living for at least part of the time in London itself. Predictably, they soon found themselves in trouble with the authorities. In 1612 the French ambassador alleged that Bartholomew had been in prison since 1600. Fuller claimed, however, that for much of this period of incarceration in Newgate, he was given permission to 'go abroad'. Walter allegedly drowned in the Old Foord River about 1603, while Thomas at some point joined Bartholomew in Newgate and was said to have died there about 1607. Bartholomew, meanwhile, was repeatedly brought before the bishop of London's consistory, where he obstinately maintained his opinions, predictably denying the legitimacy of the English church and publicly threatening to sue the court for false imprisonment. By this time, the would-be prophet had come to the attention of James I, who reportedly summoned Bartholomew before him on several occasions. Ever enamoured of theological disputation, the king allegedly tried to steer the heretic away from his positions on the divinity of Christ, only to be frustrated in his attempts at theological subtlety.

In early 1612, on the heels of James's very public dispute with the alleged Socinian Vorstius, and after the appearance of Edward Wightman, a second accused anti-Trinitarian heretic, the king appears to have determined to make an example of Legate. On 11 January Archbishop George Abbot wrote to Lord Chancellor Ellesmere notifying him of the king's desire to prosecute Wightman and Legate, and requesting a judgment from the judges on the proper procedure for cases of heresy. This question settled, Legate was convented on 21 February before the consistory of St Paul's, presided over by Bishop John King and strengthened by bishops Richard Neile, Lancelot Andrewes, and John Buckeridge. Here he was charged with, and ultimately convicted of, thirteen points of anti-Trinitarian error. Legate was handed over to the secular power by *significavit* (ecclesiastical writ) dated 3 March, and on 11 March James commanded Ellesmere to make out a writ *de haeretico comburendo* under the great seal for the execution of Legate. Legate stubbornly refused all overtures for his recantation, and on 18 March he was accordingly burned in Smithfield amid a huge throng of onlookers. While there is little evidence that his ideas exerted more than a fleeting influence on the religious life of his day, Legate's career stands as a testimony to the power of radical puritanism to produce novel, and sometimes frankly heterodox, ideas and theological formulations. DAVID R. COMO

Sources H. Clapham, *Antidoton, or, A soveraigne remedie against schisme and heresie* (1600) • H. Clapham, *Errour on the right hand* (1608) • E. Jessop, *A discovery of the errors of the English Anabaptists* (1623) • T. Fuller, *The church-history of Britain*, 11 pts in 1 (1655) • M. McIntosh, *A community transformed: the manor and the liberty of Havering, 1500–1620* (1991) • T. Gataker, *An answer to George Walkers vindication* (1642) • *Diary of Walter Yonge*, ed. G. Roberts, CS, 41 (1848) • J. P. Collier, ed., *The Egerton papers*, CS, 12 (1840) • *Calendar of the manuscripts of the most hon. the marquis of Salisbury*, 14, HMC, 9 (1923), 86 • PRO, ASS 35/30/2; French transcripts, PRO, 31/1, fol. 93*r*

Legate, John (*c*.**1562–1620/21**), printer, was probably born into a family of Hornchurch, Essex. After serving an apprenticeship with Christopher Barker, the queen's printer, he was freed by the Stationers' Company on 11 April 1586. With English printing at the time almost wholly concentrated in London, he might have expected to follow his career there. Instead, although having no obvious connection with either town or university, he perhaps saw in the position of university printer at Cambridge, made vacant by the death of Thomas Thomas in 1588, an opportunity to escape from the London trade: later, his mother-in-law claimed to have encouraged him in this.

Following Thomas's death, Legate married Thomas's stepdaughter Alice Sheres at Great St Mary's, Cambridge, on 6 February 1589, and was appointed university printer on 2 November 1589. After a legal dispute over the value of Thomas's estate (he claimed, with some justification, that the printing type was too worn to be of use) he settled with his wife in Thomas's former house. However, the ensuing dispute with his mother-in-law, conducted in the vice-chancellor's court, provides a vivid picture of the fractious household. Between 1590 and 1609 he also rented a shop at the west end of Great St Mary's Church.

From here, Legate developed the pattern of publishing established by Thomas, and in 1591 completed the first Bible to be printed at Cambridge, closely copied in its design from equivalent London editions. He confronted the Stationers' Company (who resented such a challenge to their former monopoly) with his cheap editions of classical authors, though his reputation was probably widest for printing many of the works of the highly popular theologians William Perkins and Andrew Willet, both ardent protestants. In 1600 he introduced the device that was to become familiar on Cambridge books, bearing the motto *Hinc lucem et pocula sacra* ('Whence issue light and the sacred draughts of wisdom'). Though trained in London, Legate retained an independent, even buccaneering, attitude to the conventions of the book trade: cultivating connections with Edinburgh after 1603, risking the displeasure of Justus Lipsius whose work Legate printed without permission, and willing to put his name to work that he had not printed. In 1599 he shared in a piracy of Sidney's *Arcadia*.

Legate remained at Cambridge until 1609 or 1610, his departure for London perhaps being connected with the death of his mother-in-law at Cambridge in January 1610. At Cambridge, his business was assumed by his former apprentice Cantrell Legge, whose imprints overlap with those of Legate from 1607. Once re-established in London (for a time at least in Trinity Lane, in the City), he worked closely with the bookseller Simon Waterson. Though no longer at Cambridge, he continued to call himself printer to the university until his death at some date between 1 December 1620, when he signed his will, and 2 January 1621, when he was noted as 'lately Deceased' by the Stationers' Company (Arber, *Regs. Stationers*, 4.45). Legate and his wife had twelve children, of whom John [*see below*], their eldest son, succeeded to his father's business.

John Legate (*bap.* 1600, *d.* 1658), printer, was the eighth child and eldest son of John Legate and his wife, Alice. He was born in Cambridge and baptized at Great St Mary's on 8 June 1600. He was freed by patrimony in the Stationers' Company on 6 September 1619, and married Agatha (*bap.* 1602, *d.* 1660), the daughter of Robert Barker, the king's printer, for whom Legate acted briefly as deputy at Newcastle upon Tyne in 1639. In 1650, after a period of decline in his London business, he was appointed university printer at Cambridge, though he made of this little more than a commercial convenience, and to the irritation of the university authorities did not choose to work there: on 10 October 1655 he was dismissed. In London he served twice as warden of the Stationers' Company between 1651 and 1653. His address was in Little Wood Street, where he died, 'distempered in his senses', on 4 November 1658. The administration of his estate was granted to Agatha on 16 November. DAVID MCKITTERICK

Sources D. McKitterick, *A history of Cambridge University Press*, 1 (1992) • *STC, 1475–1640* • Arber, *Regs. Stationers* • *VCH Essex* • court books, Stationers' Company, London • CUL, department of manuscripts and university archives • parish register, Cambridge, Great St Mary, Cambs. AS, 8 June 1600 [baptism: son, John] • *DNB* • apprenticeship registers, Stationers' Company, London • G. E. B. Eyre, ed., *A transcript of the registers of the Worshipful Company of Stationers from 1640 to 1708*, 3 vols. (1913–14), vol. 2, pp. 284–5 • will, GL, MS 9171/245, fols. 5*v*–6*v* • administration of estate of John Legate the younger, PRO, PROB 6/34, fol. 294*r*

Legate, John (*bap.* **1600**, *d.* **1658**). *See under* Legate, John (*c.*1562–1620/21).

Le Geyt, Philippe (*bap.* **1635**, *d.* **1716**), jurist, was born in the vingtaine of Mont à l'Abbé in the parish of St Helier, Jersey, and was baptized in St Helier parish church on 26 April 1635. He was the eldest son of Philippe Le Geyt (*bap.* 1602, *d.* 1669) and his wife, Jeanne Seale (*bap.* 1604, *d.* 1680). Le Geyt's royalist father was in Elizabeth Castle when it surrendered to the parliamentarians in 1651, and during his time there his house was pillaged by the parliamentarians; subsequently, in order to escape confiscation of his property, he compounded by paying two years' income. He had been greffier from 1642 until 1651 and he then became a jurat. He was put out of that office in 1651 and reinstated to it in 1660, from which time he served until his death. Philippe Le Geyt, the son, was educated at the protestant Academy of Saumur, and he later studied law at Caen and at Paris. He is first heard of in Jersey in 1660 when he was appointed greffier. Ten years later he was appointed jurat in succession to his father.

In 1671 Le Geyt was one of a delegation of three from Jersey to represent the states before the privy council. The council had sent some orders in 1668 intended to improve the administration of justice in the island, but the royal court of Jersey had given them a trial and found them unworkable. They were consequently withdrawn by the council, but then reintroduced with only minor alterations by an order in council of 19 May 1671. The court found the revised version no more workable than the original one. At the states meeting of 27 July 1671 a committee was appointed to examine them and to determine whether they infringed in any respect the privileges of the island. Le Geyt was on this committee, which reported back to the states, who then appointed the delegation of three to go to London to make representation about the orders and to request the sending of a commission to prepare a code of laws for the island. After nearly fifteen months' wait in London they returned having accomplished nothing.

In 1676 Le Geyt succeeded Jean Poingdestre as lieutenant-bailiff. He served in that office first under Bailiff Sir Edward de Carteret and second under Bailiff Philippe de Carteret. When the latter died Le Geyt acted as judge-delegate. He almost certainly played a large part in drawing up an abstract of the privileges of Jersey, a work that was subsequently suppressed. It was published in the twentieth century together with his work entitled 'Loix et coutumes de l'Isle de Jersey': together these two works are often called the *Code Le Geyt*. When, in 1694, a new bailiff, Edward de Carteret, was appointed, Le Geyt asked to be relieved of his work as lieutenant-bailiff. He remained, however, a jurat until 1711, when he obtained discharge from that office by an order in council on account of his infirmity. It was after resigning from the post of lieutenant-bailiff that he found the time to write, and almost all of his works are from this period, except the 'Procédé des commissaires Pyne and Napper', which was finished in 1692 and concerns the royal commission of 1591.

Le Geyt was highly regarded by his contemporaries as an able and upright judge. He is also said to have been a man of deep piety who, particularly towards the end of his life, after his retirement from public office, spent much time in prayer and meditation. In 1686 he presented a silver baptismal dish to the parish church of St Helier. It is on account of his extensive legal writings that Le Geyt is chiefly remembered. These writings in French show a profound knowledge of Roman law, of the old Norman coutumiers, and of the precedents of the royal court of Jersey. In places his Calvinist piety also shows clearly. His legal writings are still widely used today on those matters in which the Norman customary law has not been superseded by more recent statute legislation. Le Geyt's writings were not printed until the nineteenth century, after François Jeune, then dean of Jersey, bought the manuscripts at auction and offered them to the states of Jersey, who printed them in four volumes. Le Geyt never married. He lived the last years of his life in the household of his nephew, the only son of his only brother, John. He died on 31 January 1716, having caught a cold on his way home from church, and he was buried on 3 February in St Helier parish church. HELEN M. E. EVANS

Sources R. P. Marett, 'Notice sur la vie et les écrits de Mons. Le Geyt', *Les manuscrits de Philippe Le Geyt, ecuyer, lieutenant-bailli de l'île de Jersey sur la constitution, les lois et les usages de cette île*, 1 (1846), ii–xl • Sorsoleil, *Éloge de Monsieur Le Geyt de l'île de Jersey* (1716) • nineteenth-century transcript of the registers of baptisms, marriages, and burials in the parishes of Jersey, St Helier, and St Brelade, Jersey Law Society, States Building, Royal Square, St Helier, Jersey • J. A. Messervy, 'Liste des jurés-justiciers de la cour royale de Jersey, 1274–1665', *Annual Bulletin* [Société Jersiaise], 4 (1897–1901), 213–36 • J. A. Messervy, 'Liste des jurés-justiciers de la cour royale de Jersey [pt 2]', *Annual Bulletin* [Société Jersiaise], 4 (1897–1901), 275–93 • J. A. Messervy, 'Liste des baillis, lieut.-baillis et juges-délégués de l'île de Jersey', *Annual Bulletin* [Société Jersiaise], 4 (1897–1901), 92–116 • J. A. Messervy, 'Greffiers de la cour royale de Jersey', *Annual Bulletin* [Société Jersiaise], 8 (1915–18), 206–17
Archives Jersey Library, Halkett Place, St Helier, Jersey, Falle Collection, five notebooks bearing the title 'Œuvres de Monsieur Le Geyt'
Likenesses drawing, Jersey Museums Service; repro. in A. Glendinning, *Did your ancestors sign the Jersey oath of association roll of 1696?* (1995), 32 • lithograph, Jersey Museums Service • portrait, Royal Court Room, Jersey

Legg, John Wickham (1843–1921), physician and liturgical scholar, was born at Alverstoke, Hampshire, on 28 December 1843, the third son of George Legg, a printer and bookseller, of Alverstoke, and his wife, Ellen Austin. Samuel Wilberforce was vicar of Alverstoke from 1840 until his appointment as bishop of Oxford in 1845, and the church revival which he began in this parish probably influenced the young Wickham Legg. After education at Winchester College, he entered University College, London, in order to study medicine, and became a pupil of Sir William Jenner. He won the gold medal of his year, and having qualified MRCS in 1866 became, on Jenner's recommendation, personal physician to Prince Leopold, afterwards duke of Albany, with whose family he maintained a lifelong friendship. After resigning this post in 1867 he spent a year studying in Berlin before taking up an appointment as curator of the museum of pathology at University College in 1868. In the same year he took his MD degree at London and became MRCP; he was elected FRCP in 1876. In 1870 he was appointed casualty physician at St Bartholomew's Hospital, and in 1878 was elected assistant physician; he was also lecturer in pathology in the medical school from 1879. In addition, he had a growing consulting practice and made considerable contributions to medical literature, of which his treatise, *Haemophilia* (1872), is probably the best known.

In 1887, after two attacks of rheumatic fever, Wickham Legg decided to abandon medicine; he resigned his appointments, gave away his medical books, and retired from practice in order to pursue his interest in the study of liturgy. As early as 1875 he had been elected a fellow of the Society of Antiquaries, and he now had the leisure to bring to his liturgical studies the accurate scientific method and eagerness for research which had made his reputation as a physician. In this new field of learning he soon obtained a considerable reputation, his first major contribution to liturgical scholarship being his edition (1888) of the *Quignon Breviary* of 1535. He was one of the founder members, in 1890, of the Henry Bradshaw Society for the publication of rare liturgical texts. For that society he edited the *Westminster Missal* (3 vols., 1891–7), the *Second Recension of the Quignon Breviary* (2 vols., 1908, 1912), and seven other volumes, and he was chairman of the council from 1895 until 1915. His researches in the libraries of western Europe bore fruit in essays printed in the publication of various learned societies; collections of a number of his essays were published as *Ecclesiological Essays* (1905) and *Essays Liturgical and Historical* (1917). He also edited the Sarum missal from three early manuscripts for the Clarendon Press in 1916. His *English Church Life from the Restoration to the Tractarian Movement* (1914), which showed that from 1660 to 1833 traditional church doctrines and practices had prevailed more commonly than was supposed, was an intelligent attempt to redress the jaundiced view of eighteenth-century Anglicanism usually adopted by contemporary Tractarian historians. In 1913 the University of Oxford conferred on him the honorary degree of DLitt in recognition of his liturgical scholarship.

In ecclesiastical as in medical matters Wickham Legg's

mind was strongly conservative. Emphasizing the importance of church tradition, he became increasingly hostile both to liberal theology and to Anglo-Catholic experiments. He would relate humorously how in 1886 he had been described as 'one of a conspiracy to restore the ceremonial of fifty years ago', and he preferred traditional high Anglican ceremonial, reverently performed, to ritualist innovations. He held that his contemporaries lacked both the knowledge and the taste to revise the prayer book successfully, and opposed the revision in some learned and hard-hitting pamphlets. In 1910 he was elected a member of the house of laymen of the province of Canterbury, where he maintained the position of a strong high-churchman in the Tractarian tradition.

In appearance Wickham Legg was of medium height, portly, with a handsome face and fine head. In 1917 his sight became impaired, and at the end of his life he was almost blind. He possessed a rare charm of manner, and was an entertaining raconteur as well as host to a large circle of friends. He was acquainted with many foreign savants, including the future Pope Pius XI who, as prefect of the Ambrosian Library, was Legg's guest at Oxford at the commemoration of Roger Bacon in 1914.

Wickham Legg married in 1872 Eliza Jane, daughter of Richard Houghton, of Sandheys, Great Crosby, near Liverpool. Their son, Leopold George Wickham Legg, was an editor of the *Dictionary of National Biography*. On his wife's death in 1908 Wickham Legg moved to Oxford, where he resided until his death at his home, 82 Woodstock Road, on 28 October 1921. He was buried at Saltwood, Kent.

S. L. Ollard, *rev.* G. Martin Murphy

Sources A. E. Garrod, *St Bartholomew's Hospital Reports*, 55 (1922), 1–6 • A. Ward and C. Johnson, 'J. W. Legg, 1843–1921: a contribution towards the rediscovery of British liturgical scholarship', *Ephemerides Liturgicae*, 97 (1983), 70–84 • A. Ward and C. Johnson, 'A forgotten liturgical scholar: John Wickham Legg', *Notitiae* [Vatican City, Congregatio pro Sacramentis et Cultu Divino], 21 (1985), 115–21 • A. Ward and C. Johnson, 'Diary of an Anglican liturgist in Rome in 1906', *Notitiae* [Vatican City, Congregatio pro Sacramentis et Cultu Divino], 22 (1985), 563–5 • private information (1927) • personal knowledge (1927) • *WWW, 1916–28*

Archives Bodl. Oxf., corresp. and papers | Church of England Record Centre, London, letters to A. M. Davis and F. C. Eeles • St George's Chapel, Windsor, letters to Canon J. N. Dalton

Likenesses portrait, repro. in Garrod, *St Bartholomew's Hospital Reports*

Wealth at death £10,652 4*s*. 10*d*.: probate, 4 Jan 1922, *CGPLA Eng. & Wales*

Legge [*née* Finch], **Augusta, countess of Dartmouth (1822–1900)**, philanthropist, was born on 18 February 1822, eldest of the two sons and two daughters of Heneage Finch, fifth earl of Aylesford (1786–1859), and his wife, *née* Lady Augusta Greville (*d*. 1845). She grew up at the family home at Packington in Warwickshire, and was educated by a governess of strong religious principles. She early became a devoted churchwoman, to the consternation of her family: 'I was not confirmed till I was nineteen', she later recalled, 'and my mother very much wished me to go to a ball the night before, and I was thought strange for not going' (How, 204). On 9 June 1846 at St James's, Westminster, she married a childhood friend, William Walter Legge, Viscount Lewisham (1823–1891), who in 1853 succeeded his father as fifth earl of Dartmouth. It was a happy marriage, although one of her daughters was to comment that 'When I first remember her she was always ill. She had a very large family though only five of us [two sons and three daughters] grew up' (How, 212).

The family lived at Sandwell, near Birmingham, until 1853, when they took over the main Dartmouth family residence, Patshull Hall, near Wolverhampton. Unwilling to see Sandwell let to tenants, Lady Dartmouth persuaded her husband to use the house for a charitable purpose of benefit to the people of the Black Country. After a false start as a school for training girls for domestic service, the institution eventually settled down as a school for girls 'who, more or less gently born, were in needy circumstances' (How, 209). The first head of the school was Laetitia Frances Selwyn, sister of the bishop of Lichfield, and it remained open until the death of Lord Dartmouth in 1891. Lady Dartmouth was also active at a local level in the Girls' Friendly Society, in the Ladies' Home Mission Association, the Mothers' Union, and the Church of England Waifs and Strays Society. She also formed clothing clubs and lending libraries for her tenants and poor neighbours, and supplied the largest of the local villages with the services of a parish nurse.

After her husband's death in 1891, Lady Dartmouth retired to Woodsome Hall, another of the family houses, near Huddersfield. She had previously spent time in the area, and was known to the local independent loomworkers, whom she had assisted by selling their linsey when they were under great pressure of competition from factories. Now based in the newly formed diocese of Wakefield, she was instrumental in the formation of the Mothers' Union there, of which she served as diocesan president. Moreover, in 1892 she established the All Saints' Home for orphaned baby boys, under the auspices of the Church of England Waifs and Strays Society, in the neighbouring parish of Almondbury. She supervised this home personally, keeping the accounts and managing its affairs; she had a highly regarded capacity for business, and a motherly relationship with the boys.

Brought up in the country, Lady Dartmouth was an active agriculturalist. She took charge of the poultry yards at Patshull, and originated (by cross-breeding) the Andalusian bantam. She was particularly proud of the fact that she supplied all the birds for her elder son's twenty-first birthday celebrations. Until late in life she was to be found walking her grounds accompanied by her terriers, occasionally indulging in a surreptitious rat hunt. Lady Dartmouth died from a fall at Woodsome Hall on 1 December 1900, and was buried three days later at Patshull.

K. D. Reynolds

Sources F. D. How, *Noble women of our time* (1901) • GEC, *Peerage* • *The Times* (3 Dec 1900) • *The Times* (4 Dec 1900) • *The Times* (6 Dec 1900) • *Our Waifs and Strays*, 7/201 (Jan 1901), 4

Archives Staffs. RO, family papers

Likenesses Whitelock Bros., photograph, repro. in How, *Noble women of our time*

Wealth at death £7031 9*s*. 2*d*.: probate, 5 Feb 1901, *CGPLA Eng. & Wales*

Legge, Edward (*c.*1710–1747), naval officer, was the fifth son of William *Legge, first earl of Dartmouth (1672–1750), and Lady Anne Finch (*d.* 1751), daughter of Heneage Finch, first earl of Aylesford. He entered the Royal Navy as a volunteer on the *Royal Oak* in July 1726, one of the fleet under Sir Charles Wager bound for the relief of Gibraltar. He afterwards served in the *Poole*, the *Kinsale*, the *Salisbury*, and the *Namur*, before passing his lieutenant's examination in July 1732. He was promoted lieutenant of the *Deptford* (50 guns) in March 1734 and became third lieutenant on the *Somerset* (80 guns) in the following August. On 26 July 1738 he was appointed captain of the *Lively* (20 guns). By the end of the year the *Lively* was decommissioned, but during the first half of 1739 the prospect of war with Spain increased and in July, Legge became captain of the *Pearl* (40 guns).

In January 1740 the *Pearl* was assigned to the secret expedition to the Pacific under the command of Commodore George Anson. During the spring and early summer the expedition prepared at Spithead. On 30 June, Legge was moved to the *Severn* (50 guns), which was also part of Anson's force. The expedition sailed for the South Seas on 18 September 1740. By the time the force reached Cape Horn the vessels were in a sickly condition, and the *Severn* appears to have been suffering extremely from disease. On 10 April 1741, during the terrible storms that marked their passage around Cape Horn, the *Severn* and the *Pearl* lost sight of the rest of the squadron. After seven days, with desperately weak crews, Legge and the captain of the *Pearl*, George Murray, decided to submit to the dictates of the winds, and ceased trying to rejoin Anson. The two ships arrived at Rio de Janeiro on 6 June 1741. After recouping as best they could, they departed on 19 December 1741 for Barbados. Legge finally left for England on 11 March 1742, and arrived at Portsmouth on 15 April. Later accusations of Legge's desertion were not supported by Anson, as a result of which he did not suffer professionally as a consequence of this abortive voyage.

On 6 June 1743 Legge became captain of the *Hampshire* (50 guns) and on 6 October he was moved to the *Medway* (60 guns), in which he held command from 11 November until 21 March 1744. In April 1744 he commanded the *Strafford* (60 guns), which in September was attached to Vice-Admiral Thomas Davers's squadron bound for Jamaica. They arrived at Port Royal on 11 March 1745. At some point in his career Legge appears to have made a study of military engineering as he cited his expertise in this science as grounds for succeeding Commodore Charles Knowles in the command of the Leeward Islands station. Although his request was ignored at the time, it may have set down an important claim for the future.

By the mid-1740s Legge was well placed for promotion, his elder brother Heneage *Legge being counsel to the Admiralty from February 1744 and another brother, Henry *Legge, an Admiralty commissioner from April 1745. On his return from the West Indies he was given command of a new ship, the *Windsor* (60 guns), being built at Woolwich. However, Legge spent much of the late summer of 1746 as a member of Admiral Thomas Mathew's court martial at Deptford. During this time his claims for a good command were given periodic attention in correspondence between the duke of Bedford, first lord of the Admiralty, and other members of the Admiralty commission. The trial ended on 22 October and two days later Legge was rewarded with command of the Leeward Islands station. Before his departure he was given additional orders to suspend his predecessor, Commodore Fitzoy Henry Lee, pending a court martial.

Legge sailed on 4 January 1747 and after a very difficult passage reached Barbados on 13 April. He arrived at English Harbour, Antigua, on 28 April and suspended Lee. The cause of Lee's suspension was an address to George II by the assembly of Antigua, complaining of Lee's failure to protect trade. The prosecution had to be brought by the assembly but, to Legge's growing frustration, it dragged preparations on for months. Finally, when the court martial sat on 24 July 1747 the construction of the case was declared illegal and Lee was sent to England with the homeward bound trade. During this time Legge became thoroughly disillusioned with the islanders and irritated with the ministry in London for sending instructions to him in response to pressure from their agents. In his letter to the Admiralty on 5 August 1747 he despaired as 'it seems to me to require an artful Casuist rather than an able or faithful Servant' to command on the station (Legge, to Thomas Corbett, 5 Aug 1747, PRO, ADM 1/305, fol. 422). Other grievances raised included the islanders' collusion with the French and Dutch, their disregard for the other islands and their misrepresentations to London. Copies of his correspondence were sent home to illustrate and justify his behaviour.

Legge died in the Leewards on 19 September 1747. This was unreported in England, and he was elected MP for Portsmouth, being declared on 15 December 1747. News of his death arrived four days later. RICHARD HARDING

Sources *DNB* · captains' letters 'L', 1731–50, PRO, ADM 1/2039–43 · commanders-in-chief: Leeward Islands, 1745–7, PRO, ADM 1/305 · *Correspondence of John, fourth duke of Bedford*, ed. J. Russell, 3 vols. (1842–6) · BL, Anson papers, Add. MS 15956 · captain's log—*Severn*, PRO, ADM 51/888 · captain's log—*Medway*, PRO, ADM 51/613 · J. Charnock, ed., *Biographia navalis*, 4 (1796), 380–82 · R. Walter and B. Robbins, *A voyage round the world in the years MDCCXL, I, II, III, IV*, ed. G. Williams (1974) · will, PRO, PROB 11/760, sig. 55 · PRO, ADM 6/424

Archives PRO, ADM 1/2039–2043; 1/305; 51/888; 51/613

Legge, George, first Baron Dartmouth (*c.*1647–1691), naval officer, was the eldest son of Colonel William *Legge (1607/8–1670) and his wife, Elizabeth, *née* Washington (*d.* 1688). He was educated at Westminster School and at King's College, Cambridge. In 1666 he served as a volunteer in the fleet during the Four Days' Battle, probably with his cousin Edward Spragge, although in that year he also witnessed powers of attorney granted by John Kempthorne, an alternative candidate as Legge's first naval patron. He became captain of the *Pembroke* on 4 April 1667. The duke of York's subsequent remark that Legge 'was, he knows not how, made a captain after he had been but one voyage at sea' (Pepys, *Diary*, 9.39–40) was partly prompted by the fact that after barely a month in the command,

George Legge, first Baron Dartmouth (*c*.1647–1691), after John Riley, *c*.1685–90

Legge lost the *Pembroke* in collision with the *Fairfax* in Torbay on 11 May 1667, and in later years Legge himself regretted his lack of early training. About November 1667 Legge married Barbara (*d*. 1718), daughter of Sir Henry Archbold of Abbots Bromley. Their only son of eight children, William *Legge, was born in 1672.

By 1668 York's opinion of him had improved sufficiently for Legge to become one of the duke's grooms of the bedchamber, and in October 1669 he became captain of a company in the Tower of London. In 1670 he became lieutenant-governor of Portsmouth in succession to his father. Legge became captain of the *Fairfax* on 13 January 1672, took part in Sir Robert Holmes's attack on the Dutch Smyrna convoy in March, and on 28 May fought at the battle of Solebay. He left the *Fairfax* on 18 July 1672, taking command of the *York* briefly before returning ashore in August. For the 1673 campaign, he commanded the *Royal Katherine*, fighting in the second battle of the Schooneveld (4 June) and at the Texel (11 August), where he defended Prince Rupert's shattered flagship *Royal Prince* for three hours. Legge was heavily involved in the faction-fighting within the officer corps in 1673, a consequence of the failure to secure a decisive victory, and sought to moderate the more extreme criticisms of Prince Rupert's appointments and tactics made by some of the duke of York's other clients.

Life ashore The period of the Third Anglo-Dutch War also saw Legge gain a succession of important positions on land. In 1672 he became lieutenant-general of the ordnance, in 1673 master of the horse to the duke of York and governor of Portsmouth, and in February 1673 he was elected MP for Ludgershall, becoming identified as a staunch supporter of the court. In May 1678 he was appointed general of artillery with the English army in Flanders, although the intended French war never broke out. During the exclusion crisis, Legge spoke on a number of occasions in parliament (to which he was elected for Portsmouth twice in 1679 and again in 1681) in support of himself and the duke of York, thereby scandalizing the earl of Shaftesbury and whig opinion. 'I am the duke of York's servant, and I will serve him affectionately, but … I will live and die a Protestant, and am as loyal as my family has always been', he stated on 12 May 1679, while on 11 November 1680 he cried 'if my master the duke be popish, God's curse be on him that was the cause of it' (A. Grey, *Debates of the House of Commons*, 10 vols., 1769, 263, 454–5). He again spoke against exclusion at Oxford on 26 March 1681, shortly after his appointment as master of the ordnance. While the duke was in exile in Brussels and Edinburgh, Legge was one of his chief correspondents, informing him of political developments in London. His high-profile support of the duke led to growing pressure for him to surrender one of his major posts, the mastership of the ordnance and the governorship of Portsmouth. York felt that the loss of one of the posts would be a direct attack on him:

> I am glad you have Portsmouth still, and wish his majesty had but a few more like your self, that considered his service as you do, and venture as frankly as you do … if they have you part with Portsmouth, there is no remedy. (*Dartmouth MSS*, 1.65, 72)

In the event, Legge was forced to 'part with Portsmouth', but he was quickly compensated, becoming a privy councillor on 3 March 1682 and being elevated as Baron Dartmouth on 2 December of the same year. Between these events, on 6 May he survived the wreck of the *Gloucester* on the Lemon and Oar Sands off Cromer. The ship was carrying York back to Scotland to settle his affairs there, and Legge, with sword drawn, held back a crowd which might have overturned the longboat to ensure that the duke could get away in it. Legge himself was saved by the *Katherine* yacht. He served as master of Trinity House from 1683 to 1685, then as an elder brother until his death.

In 1683 Charles II and his ministers decided to evacuate and demolish Tangier, an English colony since 1661, as a cost-cutting exercise. Dartmouth was involved in the discussions from an early stage, thwarting the duchess of Portsmouth's suggestion that the colony should be sold to France. He was appointed admiral on 2 August 1683, flying his flag in the *Captain*, and with additional commissions and instructions to act as general of land forces and governor of Tangier. Samuel Pepys, who had been counted one of Dartmouth's enemies as recently as 1679, joined the expedition as his secretary, and the fleet sailed from Spithead on 19 August, arriving at Tangier on 14 September. Dartmouth's time at Tangier was taken up with a succession of problematic tasks: the physical demolition of the town and the great breakwater or mole, the settling of compensation claims by the inhabitants, and the need to convince the *alcaïd* of Alcazar that the English forces were strong enough to resist a Moorish attack (a feat accomplished partly by bluff, when seamen were dressed as soldiers at Dartmouth's first meeting with the *alcaïd* on 28 September). Moreover, Dartmouth was all too aware that his many factional opponents at court would use his absence to denigrate him, and criticism of the length and expense of his stay did indeed increase. Pepys's diary of the period, published under the title *Tangier Papers*, gives a revealing insight into Dartmouth's problems and personality at this time. He was determined to remedy what he perceived as the abuses in the navy, encouraged by the Admiralty commission of 1679–84 and his rival Arthur Herbert (the previous admiral in the Mediterranean), and attempted to introduce new rules governing officers' seniority. He swung between on the one hand the optimistic beliefs that the duke of York's return to the Admiralty would remedy all, and that the king would support him against his enemies at home, and on the other a melancholic pessimism:

> The king would do him right in it … adding that he must and would do the thing though it cost him his life and the laying of his bones here, so that the work might be well done (2 Oct 1683) … the king and the duke of York were very good at giving orders and encouragement to their servants in office to be strict in keeping of good order, but were never yet found stable enough to support their officers in the performance of their orders when they had done (7 March 1684) … talking with him of the present differences between him and Herbert, upon which he talks very melancholy and as one that is weary of the service and would rather retire than have any more to do with it (if he could … pay his debts, which he says do not exceed £10,000 and that his estate is and will be really £4,000 a year). (*Tangier Papers*, 35, 221, 245)

Dartmouth abandoned Tangier on 6 February 1684, firing the last mine himself, and his fleet arrived back in Plymouth Sound on 31 March. He was received warmly by the king at Windsor on 11 April. The reception, far better than Dartmouth himself had expected, was partly because his former enemies the earl of Sunderland and the duchess of Portsmouth now sought his friendship as part of their plan to outmanoeuvre the marquess of Halifax. In May and June, Dartmouth attempted to use his seemingly strong position to launch a new faction, opposed to France and popery, but his erstwhile ally Sunderland rapidly thwarted him, and Dartmouth was in ill health for some time.

Service under James II On James II's accession, Dartmouth became master of the horse, constable of the Tower of London, and colonel of the Royal Fusiliers, and was in regular attendance on the king during his reign—accompanying him, for example, to the midlands in the late summer of 1687. He was one of the witnesses to the birth of the prince of Wales in June 1688, and was generally regarded as one of the king's leading Anglican advisers. Throughout this period contemporaries noted the ongoing factional struggle between, on the one hand, himself and his close friend the Catholic Sir Roger Strickland, and, on the other, Arthur Herbert and his friend John Churchill. On 24 September 1688 Dartmouth was appointed to command the fleet which had been mobilized to defend against an expected invasion from the Netherlands, and joined his flagship on 3 October. He superseded Strickland, who remained his vice-admiral, and prepared to confront Herbert, appointed by William III to command the invasion fleet. The personal animosity between Dartmouth and Herbert had even led to an offer by the former in September to meet his enemy at Ostend 'at what time and with what arms' he chose (BL, Egerton MS 2621, fols. 9–10). The fleet moved to the Gunfleet anchorage off Harwich in mid-October. While it lay at anchor, Dartmouth struggled to suppress Williamite sentiment in the fleet: many of his officers owed their early promotion to Herbert, or else had close links with the conspiracy in the army headed by John Churchill. He was well aware of 'caballing' among his captains and especially of the activities of Lord Berkeley of Stratton, whom he moved into the next ship to his to keep a closer watch on him, and of the duke of Grafton, who was involved in a shadowy and abortive scheme to kidnap and supplant Dartmouth. At councils of war on 26 and 28 October the captains of the fleet decided not to cross to the Dutch coast. An attempt to sail on the 30th was thwarted by the wind, and when the Dutch left Hellevoetsluis on 1 November, the stiff north-easterly that favoured them kept Dartmouth's fleet at the Gunfleet. He finally got out on 3 November, too late to prevent William's landing at Torbay, and another council of war, on 5 November off Beachy Head, resolved not to attack what was believed to be a much larger Dutch fleet. Dartmouth returned to the Downs, attempted to sail west again on 16 November, but was driven by storms into Spithead.

Dartmouth's failure to intercept the invasion fleet seems to have caused him genuine agony, although he did not see what else he could have done: 'I take myself for the most unfortunate man living … I am not conscious to myself of any wrong step I have made unless it be too much assurance of my own success' (Dartmouth to James, 5 and 7 November 1688, *Dartmouth MSS*, 3.264, 266). James II, whose often contradictory orders and advice had done little to ease Dartmouth's task, publicly exonerated him of any blame, but privately came to suspect that his admiral had been implicated in the conspiracy. In turn, Dartmouth's attitude to the king changed during November and December. On 28 November he wrote to James imploring him to summon a free parliament, and opposed the king's plan to send the prince of Wales to France from Portsmouth, arguing that such an act would make him guilty of treason and would inevitably lead to war with France. One of his captains, Matthew Aylmer, smuggled a letter (dated 29 November) from William of Orange into his toilet, where he found it on 12 December. The letter proposed that Dartmouth join his fleet to Herbert's. Knowing that James had already made one attempt to leave the country, Dartmouth responded positively, effectively surrendering the fleet to William's control on

13 December. However, it is impossible to reconstruct completely his motives and correspondence in this period: two pages of his letter-book, covering the crucial period from 7 to 10 December, were cut out by his wife (NMM, Dar/16, pp. 44–7). His subsequent letters reveal apparently genuine grief at the king's departure and concern for his own future, despite William's reassurances. Dartmouth remained in command of the fleet until 10 January 1689, when William ordered him to come to his presence. He was stripped of his other offices in the revolution, but took the oath of allegiance to William and Mary on 2 March 1689. Early in 1691 he was accused by Viscount Preston of sending intelligence to the Jacobites about the fleet and Portsmouth, and of being the putative commander of a Jacobite fleet. For some months, the ministry debated whether or not there was sufficient evidence against him, but on 12 July he was arrested at his country house, Holt. On 14 July he was examined by a panel of ministers headed by his old schoolfriend the earl of Nottingham. Dartmouth vigorously denied Preston's accusations, although he had to admit meeting Preston briefly during his last visit to London. He was committed to the Tower at the end of July, and died there of apoplexy on 25 October 1691. He was buried with his father at Holy Trinity Minories, London.

Dartmouth's command of the fleet that failed to prevent William of Orange's invasion, and thereby the 'glorious revolution', has guaranteed his place in history, if only as one of history's losers. In the 1850s Macaulay's attempt to portray him after that revolution as an out-and-out Jacobite spurred his descendants to publish many of his papers in an attempt to vindicate him, and subsequent publication of primary sources, especially of Pepys's *Tangier Papers*, has enabled still more rounded assessment of Dartmouth to be made. Although he undoubtedly handled the Tangier expedition competently, the personality traits that he revealed at that time, and in his subsequent short-lived political career, indicate how unsuited he was to command in 1688, when strength of character and decisiveness were required. Dartmouth was comparatively inexperienced at sea, having spent twenty-three months there in the preceding twenty-two years, and certainly wholly inexperienced in command of a fleet at war; he was naturally indecisive, alternated between self-doubt and exaggerated self-belief, and was unable to impose himself on a divided, factious fleet. Ultimately, James II's early doubts about the competence of the young Captain Legge proved prophetic. J. D. Davies

Sources *The manuscripts of the earl of Dartmouth*, 3 vols., HMC, 20 (1887–96), vols. 1, 3 • NMM, Dartmouth MSS • Staffs. RO, Dartmouth papers, D(W) 1778 • F. Devon, *A vindication of the Right Honourable the first Lord Dartmouth from the charge of conspiracy or high treason, brought against him in the year 1691, and revived by Macaulay in his 'History of England'*, 1855 (1856) • J. D. Davies, 'James II, William of Orange, and the admirals', *By force or by default? The revolution of 1688–1689*, ed. E. Cruickshanks (1989), 82–108 • J. D. Davies, *Gentlemen and tarpaulins: the officers and men of the Restoration navy* (1991) • *Seventh report*, HMC, 6 (1879) • *Report on the manuscripts of the marquis of Downshire*, 6 vols. in 7, HMC, 75 (1924–95), vol. 1 • E. B. Powley, *The English navy in the revolution of 1688* (1928) • *The Tangier papers of Samuel Pepys*, ed. E. Chappell, Navy RS, 73 (1935) • R. C. Anderson, ed., *Journals and narratives of the Third Dutch War*, Navy RS, 86 (1946) • *Report on the manuscripts of Allan George Finch*, 5 vols., HMC, 71 (1913–2003), vol. 3 • correspondence of James II with Dartmouth, 1679–89, BL, Add. MS 18447 • P. M. Cowburn, 'Christopher Gunman and the wreck of the *Gloucester*', *Mariner's Mirror*, 42 (1956), 113–26, 219–29 • Pepys, *Diary* • HoP, *Commons*, 1660–90, 2.724–6 • P. Le Fevre, 'Another false misrepresentation', *Mariner's Mirror*, 69 (1983), 299–300 • BL, Egerton MS 928, fol. 12 [powers of attorney granted by John Kempthorne, 1666] • *Memoirs of Thomas, earl of Ailesbury*, ed. W. E. Buckley, 2 vols., Roxburghe Club, 122 (1890) • BL, Egerton MS 2621, fols. 9–10 • GEC, *Peerage*

Archives Cumbria AS, Carlisle, reports • NMM, journals, letter-books, and papers • Staffs. RO, corresp. and papers | BL, MS 18447

Likenesses oils, NMM • portrait (after oils by J. Riley, *c*.1685–1690), NPG [*see illus.*]

Legge, George, third earl of Dartmouth (1755–1810), politician, was born on 3 October 1755 and was baptized at Lewisham, Kent, on 26 October, son of William *Legge, second earl of Dartmouth (1731–1801), politician, and Frances Catherine Nicoll (1732/3–1805), only daughter and heir of Sir Charles Gunter Nicoll. Styled Viscount Lewisham, he was educated at Harrow School (1770–71) and at Christ Church, Oxford, where he matriculated on 22 October 1771 and graduated BA in 1775 and DCL in 1778. After making a grand tour to France and Italy, he entered the House of Commons as MP for the Admiralty seat of Plymouth on 5 June 1778. He made his maiden speech on 17 March 1779 against the bill for the relief of protestant dissenters and he gave loyal support to the North administration in which his father served. At the general election in 1780 he chose not to stand again for Plymouth and was elected unopposed for the county of Stafford. His father attempted to procure a place in government for him but, after many false hopes, he was appointed lord of the bedchamber in the prince of Wales's household in 1782. On 24 September 1782 Lewisham married Lady Frances Finch (1761–1838), the second daughter of Heneage Finch, third earl of Aylesford, and Charlotte Seymour, daughter of the sixth duke of Somerset. They had a large family of nine daughters and five sons.

Lewisham followed Dartmouth's lead in continuing to support North in the Fox–North coalition and in 1783 he was appointed lord warden of the stannaries. After the dismissal of Fox and North from office he faced a contest at the 1784 general election against a wealthy Pittite rival, Lord Gower, who enjoyed the principal interest in the county. Not surprisingly, Lewisham looked for another seat but he was defeated at Tregony and Fowey. His enforced retirement from Westminster politics lasted until Pitt's resignation from office; on 19 May 1801 he was appointed president of the India board, having been sworn of the privy council on 17 March. Lewisham was summoned to the Lords as Baron Dartmouth on 15 June 1801 but he never sat as such, succeeding his father as third earl of Dartmouth on 15 July 1801. Relinquishing his office on the India board, he became lord steward of the household on 15 August 1802 and lord chamberlain on 14 May 1804. He also enjoyed office as a trustee of the British

Museum (1802–10) and as colonel of the Birmingham regiment of volunteers. He was appointed knight of the Garter in 1805. Dartmouth died, aged fifty-five, at Dawlish, Devon, on 10 November 1810, and was buried on 24 November in his family vault in Holy Trinity Minories, Haydon Square, London. He was succeeded by his eldest son, William Legge (1784–1853), as fourth earl.

J. M. Rigg, *rev.* S. J. Skedd

Sources GEC, *Peerage* • J. Brooke, 'Legge, George, Viscount Lewisham', HoP, *Commons* • Foster, *Alum. Oxon.* • *GM*, 1st ser., 80 (1810), 500 • *DNB*
Archives Staffs. RO, corresp. and papers • Staffs. RO, journal attributed to him • Staffs. RO, receipt book and diary | Birm. CA, letters to Boulton family • BL OIOC, letters to David Scott, MS Eur. F 18 • Linn. Soc., letters to Sir James Smith
Likenesses J. Zoffany, oils, 1772–8 (*The tribuna of the Uffizi*), Royal Collection • W. Evans, stipple, pubd 1808 (after W. Lane), BM, NPG • W. Daniell, etching, pubd 1809 (after G. Dance), BM, NPG • C. Heath junior, line engraving (after T. Phillips), BM, NPG • J. Spilsbury, mezzotint (as a boy; after J. Reynolds), BM

Legge, Heneage (1704–1759), judge, was born in March 1704, the second son in the family of six sons (two of whom died in infancy) and two daughters of William *Legge, first earl of Dartmouth (1672–1750), and his wife Lady Anne Finch (*d.* 1751), third daughter of Heneage *Finch, first earl of Aylesford. Legge was the great-grandson of Heneage Finch, first earl of Nottingham, who was lord chancellor from 1674 to 1682. He was admitted to the Inner Temple in 1723, and called to the bar in 1728. On 12 December 1734 he was appointed high steward of Lichfield, and in February 1740 he was appointed king's counsel and elected a bencher of the Inner Temple. He married Catherine (*d.* 1759), daughter of Jonathan Fogg, merchant, of London, in 1740. They had one son and two daughters. In 1744 he was appointed counsel to the Admiralty and auditor of the Royal Naval Hospital, Greenwich.

In June 1747 Legge was appointed fourth baron of the exchequer, replacing Sir James Reynolds, and a serjeant-at-law. His compassionate conduct of the trial of Mary Blandy, charged with poisoning her father, at the Oxford assizes in March 1752 was remarked on at the time, although she was convicted, and hanged for murder. He opposed the Habeas Corpus Extension Bill of 1758. Legge died on 30 August 1759.

J. M. Rigg, *rev.* Anne Pimlott Baker

Sources Baker, *Serjeants*, 523 • Foss, *Judges*, vol. 8 • W. Musgrave, *Obituary prior to 1800*, ed. G. J. Armytage, 1, Harleian Society, 44 (1899) • *GM*, 1st ser., 29 (1759), 442 • H. Walpole, *Memoirs of King George II*, ed. J. Brooke, 3 vols. (1985) • T. Harwood, *The history and antiquities of the church and city of Lichfield* (1806)
Archives Bodl. Oxf., corresp. and papers • Bucks. RLSS, notebook of legal precedents and papers • Staffs. RO, papers

Legge, Henry Bilson (1708–1764), politician, was born Henry Legge on 29 March 1708, the fifth of the eight children of William *Legge, first earl of Dartmouth (1672–1750), politician, and his wife, Lady Anne Finch (*d.* 1751), the daughter of Heneage *Finch, first earl of Aylesford, and his wife, Elizabeth Banks. His father was a Hanoverian tory who held several high offices under Queen Anne, the most important being secretary of state for the southern department (1710–13). Of Legge's surviving brothers, Heneage *Legge (1704–1759), a lawyer, was appointed to the exchequer bench. Edward *Legge (*c.*1710–1747) was a captain in George Anson's expeditionary squadron in 1740–41 and, as a commodore, was in command of a squadron when he died of a fever at Barbados. His eldest brother, George Legge, Viscount Lewisham (1705–1732), left a son, William *Legge, second earl of Dartmouth, to whom Legge became political mentor. Of Legge's two sisters, Anne died in 1740 aged about twenty, and Barbara (1701–1765) married Sir Walter Wagstaffe Bagot, fifth baronet.

Legge may have accompanied his elder brothers to Mr Ellis's school at Colney Hatch, Middlesex, and reportedly was attending Westminster School, London, in 1724 together with his friend John Eardley Wilmot. Legge was short and slightly built, with dark hair, brown eyes, and regular features. He was cheerful and optimistic in nature, and his lively sense of humour helped him make friends easily. He was entered at Christ Church, Oxford, on 29 March 1726, where his parents intended he would prepare for a career in the Anglican church. On 10 February 1728, however, he signed on as an ordinary seaman in the convoy for the Newfoundland fishing fleet, which allowed him to visit Mediterranean ports on the return route. Serving under Captain Lord Vere Beauclerk, he made the voyage a second time and advanced to midshipman, but left his ship and presumably the navy in September 1731. How he employed his time during the next two years is unknown.

In 1733 Edward Walpole introduced Legge to his father, Sir Robert Walpole, whom Dartmouth said showed him 'extreem goodness' and 'uncommon generosity' (Lord Dartmouth to Sir Robert Walpole, 25 Aug 1733, CUL, Houghton MS 2028). Walpole, as chancellor of the exchequer, appointed Legge as his secretary in February 1736, and, when he was unable to make him junior secretary to the Treasury in 1739, obtained for him in October the office of chief secretary to the lord lieutenant for Ireland, William Cavendish, third duke of Devonshire. Legge continued, however, to work in London because there was no vacancy for him in the Irish parliament. Walpole arranged his election to the House of Commons on 27 November 1740 for the pocket borough of East Looe, Cornwall, and on 9 May 1741, for the pocket borough of Orford, Suffolk. The post of Treasury secretary finally opened for him on 30 April 1741. Horace Walpole wrote that his father was fond of Legge 'to the greatest degree of partiality' (Walpole, 1.126), which may be why Legge dared, at the end of 1741, either to offer or to attempt to marry Sir Robert's daughter Maria. The only account of this affair says that Sir Robert banished Legge from his sight, but the author, Horace Walpole, was in Italy at the time. Walpole still thought well enough of Legge to secure him a half interest in a customs sinecure just before he resigned in 1742 and to include him in a family gathering in 1743.

When Legge was dismissed from the Treasury in the purge of Walpole's associates, he still had friends and relatives of all political persuasions, and so was able to secure help from an opposition whig, John Russell, fourth duke of Bedford, in obtaining on 16 July 1742 the office of surveyor-general of woods and forests north and south of the Trent. His earlier posts had brought him in contact with all the important politicians in Walpole's circle. Now he was further from the centre of government but had leisure to pursue his favourite sport, shooting, which supplanted cricket. On 20 April 1745 he was appointed to the Admiralty board, which already included five of his friends: Bedford as first lord, Beauclerk, Anson, George Grenville, and John Montagu, fourth earl of Sandwich. He was the only civilian on the board with either naval or governmental experience. He wrote many of the board letters to the frequently absent Bedford and served on Commons committees on naval affairs. Henry Pelham thought enough of his abilities to designate him to read the Commons' reply to the king's address on 17 October 1745 and to bring him to the Treasury board on 27 June 1746, the natural progression of office for rising young politicians. Legge continued to work on naval affairs in the Commons, and he read the reply to the king's address again in 1746. An intestinal infection drove him to Bath in May 1747 and kept him ill for a further three months. The death of his brother Edward in September was a further blow.

In the following year, 1748, the luxury of having a wide circle of political friends proved to be damaging to Legge's career. Critics of the administration's handling of the War of the Austrian Succession, and even Pelham himself, were demanding that Frederick II of Prussia be asked to pressurize France to come to terms. Any mission to Berlin was doomed to fail because George II distrusted his nephew and because Frederick wanted to supplant Austria as Britain's chief ally. After persuading George II, Thomas Pelham-Holles, duke of Newcastle, secretary of state for the southern department, on 19 January 1748 proposed Legge to be envoy because of 'his capacity and integrity' and his 'intimacy and friendship' with Sandwich, who was the delegate to the upcoming peace congress (the duke of Newcastle to the earl of Sandwich, 19 Jan 1748, BL, Add. MS 32811, fol. 87). William Pitt, who had urged a Prussian alliance, praised Legge's appointment. Legge's departure was delayed by the resignation of the northern secretary, Philip Stanhope, fourth earl of Chesterfield, on 6 February 1748. Legge supported as his successor first Sandwich, then, when the earl proved unacceptable, Bedford. Newcastle took this opportunity to obtain George II's consent for his transfer to the northern department because he wanted to accompany the king to Hanover. Sandwich, then at The Hague, soon received false reports that Legge had supported Henry Fox against himself and immediately set about undermining Newcastle's opinion of Legge. Further delays, including a stop at Hanover, prevented Legge from meeting Frederick before the preliminary peace treaty was signed on 30 April. He received no new instructions from Newcastle on how he should proceed, and became entangled in Frederick's plan to displace Austria by offering George II his support on an imperial electoral issue. All the blame fell on Legge when negotiations inevitably soured. After reading the abuse that Newcastle and George II heaped on Legge, Pelham defended him as 'more able and as willing to serve those that serve him as any one I have been acquainted with, in that way, for a great while' (Coxe, 1.447).

Legge spent the rest of the year dealing with reparations claims for captured Prussian ships. He returned to London in February 1749 and, thanks to Pelham, was consoled with an appointment as treasurer of the navy in March. Thereafter he turned his attention to private affairs, in 1749 purchasing properties in north-east Hampshire to make up a small estate and in 1750 buying the lease of the office of ranger of the royal forests of Alice Holt and Woolmer, Hampshire, where he could pursue freely his sport of shooting. After his marriage at Hinton Ampner on 11 September 1750 to Mary Stawell (1726–1780), the only daughter and heir of Edward Stawell, fourth Baron Stawell (*c*.1685–1755), and Mary Stukeley (*d.* 1740), the couple resided at the Great Lodge of Holt Forest, an easy ride from London. This was perhaps the happiest time of Legge's life, when he said that he had:

> drawn so many Bills upon fortune which she has answer'd at sight that I begin to fancy that I have an Open Credit upon Her for every thing I wish. Even that great Disaster which was the capital one of my life & the greatest check upon my Career has in the event prov'd the most fortunate circumstance, for it has enabled me to marry a much prettier girl … of a Temper & Understanding that make me completely happy. (Henry Legge to Benjamin Keene, 16 July 1751, English MS 668, 1)

The Legges' only child, Henry, was born on 22 February 1757.

The balanced political arrangement constructed by Pelham fell apart at his death on 6 March 1754. His successor at the Treasury, Newcastle, 'with a view to please all our friends', asked Legge to become chancellor of the exchequer (the duke of Newcastle to William Pitt, 2 April 1754, BL, Add. MS 32735, fol. 10). Legge himself 'did all that was possible to avoid it, consistent with honour & character & the obligations I owe to those who found me Nobody & have made my Fortune' and said: 'all I have now to do is to look out for the first favourable opportunity of making my retreat' (Henry Legge to John Eardley Wilmot, 26 March 1754, Wilmot MSS). This option seemed to open when an inheritance from a first cousin of his father, Leonard Bilson of Mapledurham, which was worth about £1200 a year, reverted to Legge only days after he accepted office, on condition that he took the additional surname of Bilson. Legge secured as his official residence the house in Downing Street formerly occupied by Walpole, which is now no. 10. He was not made leader of the Commons and was rarely consulted on financial matters by Newcastle, who soon suspected him of joining Pitt and Fox in plotting against him. Legge's inability to reply quickly in debate certainly made it difficult for him to oppose these two, whom he felt should be given higher office. After Legge on 23 July 1755 omitted to sign a warrant for a subsidy payment because he disapproved of subsidies, Pitt seized on the issue to pressurize Newcastle, who had them both turned out of office on 20 November.

When the furore over the loss of Minorca led to Newcastle's resignation on 26 October 1756, Legge, saying 'I cannot escape without shamefully running away', resumed the office of chancellor under William Cavendish, fourth duke of Devonshire, at the Treasury, with Pitt as southern secretary (Henry Legge to the first earl of Guilford, 9 Nov 1756, Bodl. Oxf., MS North d. 7, fol. 67). With Pitt frequently ill, defence of policy fell to Grenville and to Legge, who could gain no support from financiers for his methods of raising money. George II, who had always resented these ministers who had been forced on him, dismissed Pitt on 6 April 1757, whereupon Legge resigned.

Tortuous negotiations involving Newcastle and John Stuart, third earl of Bute, produced in June an administration with Pitt, Newcastle, and Legge back in their former offices. Legge had wanted to head the Admiralty board but was rejected by the king. This more inclusive ministry proved successful, guiding Britain to victory in the Seven Years' War. Allowed to work more closely with Newcastle, Legge suggested new means of raising the enormous sums needed to pay for the war and effectively defended the budget in the Commons. His formal speeches were always well prepared, so that even Horace Walpole praised them as clear and concise. When the customs place provided by Walpole reverted to Legge in 1758, he considered giving up his seat and requesting a peerage because he felt that Pitt no longer respected him, but was prevailed on by Newcastle to remain. When the place reverted again in 1759, he vacated his seat for Orford and extracted the promise of a peerage for his wife before agreeing to remain in office. Hearing he was free, some whigs in Hampshire asked him in October to stand for the county. For the past three years he had enjoyed some favour at the court of the prince of Wales, and therefore was shocked to find himself opposed in Hampshire by a candidate supported by the prince and his adviser Bute. This misunderstanding destroyed Legge's relations with that court and led eventually to his dismissal from office. Newcastle, who preferred to retain Legge as the chancellor least objectionable to him, put his own and the ministry's electoral influence behind Legge. Newcastle also persuaded George II to make Mary Legge Baroness Stawell on 21 May 1760. Keen to settle old scores after his accession, George III dismissed Legge from office on 16 March 1761. He was, nevertheless, re-elected for Hampshire on 8 April and, after Newcastle resigned the following year, joined the whig opposition.

Legge maintained his interest in finance by preparing and giving to Newcastle analyses of the debt and revenue in November 1761 and February 1762 and by speaking on financial affairs in the Commons. When the question arose of his ever taking the office of chancellor again, however, Legge told Newcastle that he had no desire for 'the high office of first Clerk of the Treasury in the House of Commons' and that 'I can be very happy out of all office whatsoever as long as I maintain the good opinion of the respectable part of Mankind, & that I will do my best to endeavour to carry to the grave with me' (Henry Legge to the duke of Newcastle, 17 Sept 1763, BL, Add. MS 32951, fol. 67). Having suffered bouts of vomiting and diarrhoea for the past five months, Legge went to Bath in December 1763 to recover his health. Despite remissions that raised false hopes, he gradually wasted away, adding jaundice to his symptoms, all typical of liver failure. He left London for Tunbridge Wells in late July and died there on 23 August 1764. Newcastle learned from the executors that Legge had left little or no money, and an estate which, together with his wife's estate, was worth about £6000 a year. Legge was buried with the Stawells at Hinton Ampner, Hampshire, on 5 September. His papers are not extant, and his character and actions have in the past been judged unfavourably primarily on the basis of statements, now known to be biased, in Horace Walpole's writings. Legge's letters reveal a man no better or worse than other younger sons who made their fortune through holding office under the crown, but one with a better sense of humour and less vindictiveness than his contemporaries.

P. J. KULISHECK

Sources P. J. Kulisheck, '"The favourite child of the whigs": the life and career of Henry Bilson Legge, 1708–1764', PhD diss., University of Minnesota, 1996 • BL, Newcastle MSS • J. C. D. Clark, *The dynamics of change: the crisis of the 1750s and English party systems* (1982) • R. Middleton, *The bells of victory: the Pitt–Newcastle ministry and the conduct of the Seven Years' War, 1757–1762* (1985) • E. J. S. Fraser, 'The Pitt–Newcastle coalition and the conduct of the Seven Years' War, 1757–1760', DPhil diss., U. Oxf., 1976 • CUL, Cholmondeley (Houghton) correspondence • JRL, Legge MSS, English MS 668 • Wilmot papers, Yale U., Beinecke L., Osborn collection • Bodl. Oxf., North MSS • W. Coxe, *Memoirs of the administration of the Right Honourable Henry Pelham*, 2 vols. (1829) • H. Walpole, *Memoirs of King George II*, ed. J. Brooke, 3 vols. (1985) • R. Lodge, 'The mission of Henry Legge to Berlin, 1748', *TRHS*, 4th ser., 14 (1931), 1–38 • parish register (baptism), 18 April 1708, Westminster, St Margaret's • *DNB* • J. E. Wilmot, *Memoirs of the life of the Right Honourable Sir John Eardley Wilmot*, 2nd edn (1811) • parish register, Hinton Ampner, 5 Sept 1764 [burial]

Archives Hants. RO • JRL, English MS 668 | BL, Newcastle MSS • BL, letters to Lord Anson, Add. MSS 15946, 15956 • BL, correspondence with Lord Holland, Add. MS 51388 • Chatsworth, Devonshire MSS • Lewis Walpole Library, Farmington, Connecticut, Sir Charles Hanbury Williams MSS • priv. coll., letters to James Oswald • U. Nott., Hallward Library, Pelham MSS in Newcastle (Clumber) MSS • Woburn, Bedford MSS

Likenesses S. Slaughter?, double portrait, oils, *c*.1737 (with Sir Robert Walpole), Gov. Art Coll. • W. Hoare, oils, *c*.1754, Gov. Art Coll. • R. Houston, mezzotint (after W. Hoare), BM, NPG • Johnson, mezzotint (after W. Hoare), NPG • mezzotint (after W. Hoare), BM, NPG

Wealth at death £6000 p.a., with wife's estate: Newcastle to Ashburnham, 4 Sept 1764, BL, Add. MS 32962, fol. 17

Legge, James (1815–1897), Sinologist and missionary, was born on 20 December 1815 in Huntly, Aberdeenshire, the youngest of the four sons of Ebenezer Legge (1770–1848), a successful drapery merchant, and his first wife, Elizabeth (*née* Cruickshank; *d.* 1817). Born into in a 'middling class' household in a 'little grey town' in the lowlands of Scotland, Legge was reared in a rigorously evangelical culture that stressed zealous 'Sabbatarian' devotion, missionary concerns, and educational self-improvement. Legge himself recalled this religious heritage in his unfinished autobiography, 'Notes of my life' (*c*.1896), noting both his boyish pleasure in finding a missionary book in his house containing some strange Chinese characters and his father's high regard for education and a missionary vocation.

From the more liberal perspective of his later life he admitted that there was sometimes 'an error on the side of strictness' in the religious practices at that time.

Legge's early education at the Huntly parish school and the Aberdeen grammar school stressed the translation of Latin and Greek; particularly influential were Latin versions of the Psalms, the Westminster shorter catechism, and the writings of George Buchanan (1506–1582) about Scottish history. Later he distinguished himself academically at King's College, Aberdeen, graduating with an MA and highest honours as the Huttonian prizeman of 1835. During his college years he cultivated his unusual linguistic facility for Latin and Greek and developed an interest in the Scottish common-sense philosophers. After graduation Legge taught Latin and mathematics at a secondary school in Blackburn, Lancashire. Caught up in a crisis of religious conscience as he went out into the world and haunted by a vision of the mother he never knew, he relates that it was only now that he was able to make a personal decision to enter the Congregational ministry and become a 'truer and more consistent servant of Christ'. In September 1837 he entered Highbury College in Middlesex where he began his studies for a master of divinity degree. Drawn to the foreign missions since his childhood, before long he made a commitment to the London Missionary Society and embarked upon the study of Chinese in London with the returned missionary Samuel Kidd.

In 1839 Legge was ordained at Trevor Chapel, London, and married Mary Isabella Morison (1817–1852). He set out that same year on a sailing ship with his new wife for the Anglo-Chinese College in Malacca, an institution for the education of Chinese and Malayan youth established in 1818 by the pioneering protestant missionary Robert Morrison (1782–1834). He intensified his efforts to master the Chinese written language and various spoken dialects; although fluent in Cantonese, he never felt fully comfortable in Mandarin. With one of his advanced students, Ho Tsun-sheen, he produced a two-volume translation of a popular Chinese novel. Here also he continued with his regular custom of early morning study, a habit that he would maintain until his death. By 1841 Legge had taken over as the principal of the college and, with the impetuous confidence of youth and religion, was actively seeking ways to extend his educational and religious mission into China itself.

With the opening of China to the West in 1842 as a result of the First Anglo-Chinese War, the London Missionary Society moved its base of operations to several treaty ports along the coast. Legge was put in charge of the society's mission house in the new colony of Hong Kong. In 1848 a theological seminary was established there, of which he also took charge. Except for various furloughs home and brief travels within mainland China, he spent almost a third of his long life (from 1843 to 1873) in this notoriously brash and dynamically polyglot British commercial outpost. Never much of a mass converter, Legge was generally more successful as a transcultural educator of the Chinese and of his fellow missionaries and countrymen. An accomplished missionary-scholar, a conscientious pastor (at the Nonconformist Union Chapel), a rare transgressor of cultural and racial boundaries (especially in his professional and personal associations with influential Chinese such as Ho Tsun-sheen, Hong Rengan, and Wang Tao), and a whiggishly liberal, judicious citizen of the colony, he participated in most of the significant theological, social, and political issues of the period. The rancorous 'term question', which concerned the best way to translate the biblical 'God' into Chinese and the gradual emergence of more liberal missionary methods were among the religious questions which exercised him. Social concerns of his included the creation of a new system of non-sectarian general education for the Chinese of the colony. He was also interested by political questions: for example, he criticized government policies concerning opium, gambling, and the Taiping uprising. His greatest and most lasting contribution to transcultural understanding was his massive translation *Chinese Classics* (first edn, 7 vols., 1861–72; second edn, 5 vols., partially 'revised', 1893–5). This bravely conceived and meticulously executed work was the greatest single achievement of Western Sinological scholarship during the nineteenth century and, though dated in style, remained the standard English version of these texts even in the late twentieth century.

In 1859, after the sudden death of his first wife in Hong Kong, Legge had married Hannah Mary Willetts, *née* Johnstone (1822–1881). He returned home to Scotland in 1873 to rejoin his wife and children. He had two sons and two daughters with Hannah Mary, and a stepdaughter; his two living daughters with Mary Isabella were grown and married. His younger son, Thomas Morison *Legge (1863–1932), became a medical inspector of factories. On his return he formally retired from missionary work to devote himself to his Chinese scholarship. At this point in his lifelong intellectual pilgrimage Legge had moved away from an antagonistic condemnation of heathen religions to a more sympathetic, academic, and 'comparativist' appreciation of the greatness of Confucius and ancient Chinese civilization recorded in texts that were now found to have both secular and sacred authority. These developments were crystallized by his acceptance of a fellowship at Corpus Christi College and his appointment in October 1876 to the newly endowed chair of Chinese at Oxford University, the first nonconformist to achieve a professorship.

A robust and big man, Legge's bright red hair and unruly side locks had started to turn to a silvery sheen as he entered his sixth decade and a new career, but as described by some Oxford acquaintances he always seemed to possess the hearty good health, simple humour, earnest dignity, and indefatigable industry of a Scot from the country. At Oxford he continued and extended his translations of the Chinese classics by his participation in Max Müller's Sacred Books of the East (50 vols., 1879–1910), a monumental project that defined both academic 'orientalism' and the new discipline known as the 'comparative science of religions'. Legge's translations of the Chinese texts in the series make up volumes 3, 16, 27, and 28 on Confucianism and volumes 39 and 40 on the new category of Taoism. Besides the Sacred Books volumes and numerous articles, reviews, and lectures during this period, Legge published an influential 'comparative' study, *The Religions of China* (1880), as well as lengthy annotated translations of Buddhist texts (1886), the Nestorian monument (1888), and ancient Chinese poetry (1895). This period from 1876 to his death may be designated the 'Leggian epoch' in the emergence of Sinology as a professional academic discipline (with its characteristic emphasis on a unique 'classical' and 'Confucian' China) awkwardly associated with the larger discursive domain of oriental and comparative scholarship.

Legge should also be remembered for playing a noteworthy role in the liberalization of Oxford University. He was actively involved in the promotion of a new multicultural curriculum and examination system, in the religious and intellectual emergence of nonconformity at Oxford, and in the establishment of women's education at Somerville College. Having suffered a stroke after completing his Friday class on elementary Chinese composition, he slipped into a coma and three days later, on 29 November 1897, died at his home, 3 Keble Terrace, Oxford. He was buried at Wolvercote cemetery, Oxford, on 3 December. As was said about the death of Confucius, the old professor's teaching was done and it was as if he had silently 'passed behind a cloud'. Legge's passage from an early evangelical missionary career to the new, more secular, academic 'sciences' of Sinology and comparative religions epitomizes some of the most significant religious and intellectual changes during the Victorian era and belies his image as a hopelessly apologetic and outdated missionary-translator. N. J. GIRARDOT

Sources J. Legge, 'Notes of my life', *c.*1896, Bodl. Oxf. [typed copy] • J. Legge, 'Notes of my life', *c.*1896, SOAS, Archives of the Council for World Mission (incorporating the London Missionary Society) [orig. handwritten MS] • H. E. Legge, *James Legge, missionary and scholar* (1905) • L. Ride, 'Biographical note', *The Chinese classics* (1960), 1.1–25 • N. J. Girardot, *The Victorian translation of China: James Legge's oriental pilgrimage* (2002) • Lau Tze-yui, 'James Legge (1815–1897) and Chinese culture: a missiological study in scholarship, translation and evangelization', PhD diss., U. Edin., 1994 • Wong Man Kong, 'A pioneer at the crossroads of East and West: James Legge', MPhil diss., Chinese University of Hong Kong, 1993 • L. F. Pfister, 'James Legge', *An encyclopedia of translation*, ed. Chan Sin-wai and D. E. Pollard (1995), 401–22 • L. F. Pfister, 'Some dimensions in the works of James Legge (1815–1897)', *Sino-Western Cultural Relations Journal*, 12 (1990), 29–50 • L. F. Pfister, 'Some dimensions in the works of James Legge (1815–1897)', *Sino-Western Cultural Relations Journal*, 13 (1991), 33–48 • L. F. Pfister, 'Clues to the life and academic achievements of one of the most famous nineteenth-century European Sinologists—James Legge (AD 1815–1897)', *Journal of the Hong Kong Branch of the Royal Asiatic Society*, 30 (1990), 180–218 • N. J. Girardot, 'The course of Sinological discourse: James Legge and the nineteenth century invention of Taoism', *Proceedings of the 33rd International Congress of Asian and North Africa Studies*, 4 (1992), 1–7 • N. J. Girardot, '"Finding the way": James Legge and the Victorian invention of Taoism', *Religion*, 29 (1999), 107–21 • N. J. Girardot, 'Ritual combat during the Babylonian era of Sinology', *The Oracle*, 2 (1999), 8–24 • T. H. Barrett, *Singular listlessness: a short history of Chinese books and British scholars* (1989)

Archives Bodl. Oxf., journals and papers • Emory University, Atlanta, Georgia, Pitts Theological Library • NYPL • SOAS, corresp., papers, and sermons | Bodl. Oxf., Max Müller MSS • College of William and Mary, Williamsburg, Virginia, Earl Gregg Swem Library, Robert Nelson MSS • Hong Kong Government Gazette • Oxford University Press, archive • Hong Kong Colonial Office records

Likenesses J. E. Christie, portrait, CCC Oxf. • J. Cochran, steel engraving (after H. Room), NPG • G. Richmond, portrait, repro. in Legge, *James Legge, missionary and scholar* • H. Room, portrait (with three Chinese students), Council for World Missions, London; repro. in Legge, *James Legge, missionary and scholar* • photographs, engravings, Bodl. Oxf., Legge papers • photographs, engravings, London Missionary Society Archive, Legge papers • photographs, engravings, SOAS, Council for World Missions archive, Legge papers

Wealth at death £5539 13*s.* 9*d.*: probate, 6 Aug 1898, *CGPLA Eng. & Wales*

Legge, Thomas (*c.*1535–1607), playwright and college head, was born in Norwich, son of Stephen Legge and his wife, Margaret, daughter of William Larke. His home was in Cambridge from 1552 until his death in 1607: first as pensioner at Corpus Christi College (1552–5), then as scholar and fellow of Trinity College (1555–68), fellow and tutor of Jesus College (1568–73), and finally as master of Gonville and Caius from 1573 until 1607. He proceeded BA in 1556–7, MA in 1560, and LLD in 1575. He was chosen by John Caius in 1573 to be his successor as master of Gonville and Caius. They were alike in being laymen tolerant in matters of religion and in their place of birth; but Legge was much the more genial of the two men and had gathered a flock of pupils at Jesus, many of whom migrated with him to Caius in 1573. There he fostered a community of fellows, some of them of advanced protestant views, some the opposite; he allowed students from Catholic or recusant backgrounds to join the college. At least six became Jesuits, one a Benedictine monk, ten—including the martyr John Fingley—became secular Roman Catholic priests. But a majority of the fellows were of protestant, some, at least, of puritan tendency; and it is abundantly clear that Legge was a man who sincerely believed in religious toleration. Most of the fellows did not; and in 1582 he and some of his colleagues were delated to the chancellor of the university, Lord Burghley, on eighty-eight charges varying from tolerance of recusants to maladministration. Lord Burghley does not seem to have taken the charges very seriously, and the storm presently abated; by 1587 all the insurgents had left the college, many of them to country livings. Legge's later career was more peaceful; and in 1587–8 and again in 1592–3 he was vice-chancellor of the university—presiding, ironically, in 1587 over the opening ceremonies at Emmanuel College, the home of moderate puritans.

A part of Legge's difficulties with his protestant colleagues lay in his fondness for music and drama; and he was himself a notable dramatist. His Latin *Richardus tertius*, in the Senecan mode, was performed in St John's College hall in 1579. His *Solymitana clades*, 'The destruction of Jerusalem', has been recently rediscovered; both have been edited by Dana M. Sutton. *Richardus tertius* is the earliest known Elizabethan history play, and there 'seem to be no grounds for excluding the possibility that Shakespeare had read *Richardus Tertius*' (Legge, 1.xxi).

Beside his work for the college, Legge had another career, as a civil (Roman) and canon lawyer. His legal learning was considerable, and the Gonville and Caius College Library still contains a remarkable collection especially of late medieval and sixteenth-century legal treatises bequeathed by Legge. A commonplace book also survives, which confirms that he was more interested in the practical than the theoretical aspects of Roman law, following the Italian civilians whose works chiefly interested him. Like many civilians, Legge practised in the church courts: first as commissary of the university from 1579, then as commissary of the diocese of Ely—his colleague as vicar-general was his friend Richard Swale, whom he had appointed president of Caius and shared with him the accusations of the insurgent fellows. From 1590 they were admitted as advocates in Doctors' Commons, the centre of practice in church courts and admiralty courts; and Legge was also made a master in chancery. Their practice as canon lawyers makes it abundantly clear that Legge and Swale were not crypto-recusants, as some supposed—but helps to explain their reputation, since civil and canon lawyers were often exposed to the charge.

Legge died in Cambridge on 12 July 1607, and in 1619, on the initiative of his friend John Gostlin, physician and master of Caius (1619–26), a monument was erected to him in the college chapel, where he had probably been buried: at its foot is a heart between two hands, symbol of the devoted friendship of Gostlin and Legge, a fitting reminder of a genial, kindly, and tolerant man in an age of intolerance. C. N. L. Brooke

Sources P. Stein, 'Thomas Legge, a sixteenth-century English civilian and his books', *The character and influence of the Roman civil law: historical essays* (1988), 197–208 • C. N. L. Brooke, *A history of Gonville and Caius College* (1985); repr. with corrections (1996), 79–93 • J. Venn and others, eds., *Biographical history of Gonville and Caius College*, 1: *1349–1713* (1897), 73 • J. Venn and others, eds., *Biographical history of Gonville and Caius College*, 3: *Biographies of the successive masters* (1901), 64–9, 280, 283 • T. Legge, *The complete plays*, ed. D. M. Sutton, 2 vols. (1992–3) • G. B. Churchill, *Richard III up to Shakespeare* (1900); repr. (1976), 265–395 • J. Caius, *The annals of Gonville and Caius College*, ed. J. Venn (1904), 185–215 • J. Venn, *Early collegiate life* (1913), 80–103, 146–50 • J. Heywood and T. Wright, eds., *Cambridge University transactions during the puritan controversies of the 16th and 17th centuries*, 1 (1854), 314–41 • C. Brooke, 'In commemoration of Blessed John Fingley, 26 November 1986', *The Caian* (1987–8), 110–14 • exit book, 1592–1618, Gon. & Caius Cam. • BL, Lansdowne MS 33, fols. 91–128

Likenesses effigy on monument, 1607, Gon. & Caius Cam. • oils, Gon. & Caius Cam.

Wealth at death readily recoverable debts to him, £565 5*s.* 0*d.*; debts doubtful, £213 5*s.* 0*d.*; debts desperate, £838 8*s.* 4*d*; also landed property; modest personal effects; scarlet gown value £3: CUL, vice-chancellor's court, inventory of Legge, 10 Dec 1607

Legge, Sir Thomas Morison (1863–1932), factory inspector, was born on 6 January 1863 in Hong Kong, the younger son of Reverend James *Legge (1815–1897), missionary and Chinese scholar, and his second wife, Hannah Mary Willetts, *née* Johnstone (1822–1881). He was educated at Dollar Academy, Clackmannanshire, at the City of London School, and at Magdalen College School, Oxford, to which he transferred when his father became the first professor of Chinese at Oxford University in 1876. In youth he suffered prolonged ill health following an attack of typhoid fever. Legge entered Oxford University as a non-collegiate student in 1882, migrating to Trinity College in 1884, where he graduated with second-class honours in the natural sciences (physiology) in 1886. He received his medical training at St Bartholomew's Hospital, London, qualifying MB BCh in 1890. He gained his DPH (Cantab.) in 1893, and MD (Oxon.) in 1894. Legge then studied public health on the continent, investigating sanitary arrangements in several cities and publishing his findings in *Public Health in European Capitals* (1896). The favourable reception accorded this work helped secure his appointment as secretary to the royal commission on tuberculosis (1896–8). Following publication of the commission's report he worked briefly under Arthur Newsholme who was then medical officer of health for Brighton. In 1898, at a time of mounting public concern about occupational ill health, he was appointed the first medical inspector of factories. His initial salary was £600 p.a.

Legge's appointment to the factory inspectorate formed part of a shift in policy on industrial regulation, one aspect of which was the introduction of specialist inspectors. Before assuming his duties Legge had no particular knowledge of industrial disease, but he tackled his duties with great energy and soon became a leading expert in the field. His early work on lead poisoning established a reputation which grew to encompass most industrial diseases. A chief inspector of factories, D. R. Wilson, described him as 'not only the pioneer, but the greatest living authority on occupational disease'. Legge's professional achievement was to promote awareness of industrial health within the Home Office, to advance medical understanding of a number of occupational diseases, and to help raise health standards in the workplace.

In 1902, at the annual meeting of the British Medical Association, Legge was honorary secretary of the section of industrial hygiene and diseases of occupation. Three years later he was vice-president of the same section. In the same year, 1905, he was Milroy lecturer at the Royal College of Physicians, taking as his subject industrial anthrax. Legge sat on official committees on compensation for industrial diseases (1906–13) and anthrax (1913–18). He travelled widely on official business and lectured frequently on industrial medicine at venues including Manchester University (1920–32), King's College, London (1920–24), and University College, London (1922–9). In 1919 he undertook a lecture tour of North America. He was appointed CBE in 1918 and given a knighthood in 1925; in 1923 he was the Royal College of Physicians' Bissett-Hawkins medallist.

Shy to the point of appearing rude, Legge possessed firm convictions and a strong social conscience. His official career ended on a point of principle. In 1921 he represented the British government on the advisory hygiene commission of the International Labour Office at Geneva, helping to draft an international convention to ban the use of lead paint inside buildings. When the time came to implement its terms the British government issued regulations which fell far short of the agreement it had signed five years earlier. Legge resigned his post in protest on 29 November 1926, explaining his decision in a letter to *The Times* (1 December 1926). At the time of his retirement his salary was £1200 p.a. From 1930 Legge was medical adviser to the social insurance section of the Trades Union Congress.

Legge wrote *Thirty Years' Experience of Industrial Maladies* (1929); his *Industrial Maladies* (ed. S. A. Henry, 1934) was published posthumously. He co-authored *Cattle Tuberculosis* (1898) with Harold Sessions, and *Lead Poisoning and Lead Absorption* (1912) with Sir Kenneth Goadby. His *Industrial Poisoning from Fumes, Gases and Poisons* (1913) was a translation of a work by J. Rambousek. Legge contributed many papers to edited books and journals. Between 1919 and 1932 he was honorary consulting editor of the *Journal of Industrial Hygiene*.

In youth Legge was an accomplished swimmer and skater. In adulthood his main recreational interest was stained glass, a subject on which he was an authority. An enthusiast for the arts in general, he was a keen watercolourist, especially of industrial subjects.

Legge married Norah Elizabeth Mack of West Grinstead, Sussex, in 1904. They had two sons and one daughter. He died suddenly at his home, Wintergreen, in Warlingham, Surrey, on 7 May 1932. He was buried at All Saints' parish church, Warlingham. P. W. J. Bartrip

Sources *The Lancet* (14 May 1932), 1069–70 · *BMJ* (4 Dec 1926), 1066 · *BMJ* (14 May 1932), 913–14 · T. M. Legge, preface, *Industrial maladies*, ed. S. A. Henry (1934), viii–xiii · *Journal of Industrial Hygiene*, 14 (1932), 235–6 · R. Murray, 'Sir Thomas Morison Legge: a disciple of Charles Turner Thackrah', *Journal of the Society of Occupational Medicine*, 35 (1985), 23–8 · *The Times* (9 May 1932) · *The Times* (12 May 1932) · *The Times* (16 May 1932) · *Dollar Magazine*, 24 (1925), 113–16 · *Industrial Medicine and Surgery*, 23 (1954), 427–8 · *Medical News*, 9 (25 Oct 1963)

Archives priv. coll., papers

Wealth at death £1223 7*s*. 11*d*.: probate, 30 June 1932, *CGPLA Eng. & Wales*

Legge, (Harry) Walter (1906–1979), impresario and record producer, was born in Keith Grove, Ravenscourt Park, London, on 1 June 1906, the son (there was to be a younger sister) of Harry Legge (*b*. 1871) and his wife, Florence (*b*. 1871). His father was a successful tailor, and Legge was educated until the age of sixteen at Latymer High School, in Hammersmith, where he excelled at languages. As a young man, Legge collected records as a hobby, and, encouraged by his father, he also regularly attended Royal Albert Hall Sunday concerts. In these circumstances, he was soon able to teach himself to read music and German, though he never received any formal training as a musician. He acquired 'a fine ear, understanding of style and unusual linguistic prowess' (*New Grove*, 611).

Legge was expected to follow his father's trade but, determined to pursue a career in classical music, he secured a job in 1927 with the HMV record shop in London's Oxford Street, part of the Gramophone Company. This lasted only a few months because he criticized the company's policy. Undeterred, he obtained further employment with the company, this time as writer of sleeve notes and articles for *The Voice*, HMV's monthly magazine for retailers, which he also edited. In this capacity he began attending recording sessions and quickly impressed HMV's musical director Fred Gaisberg with his musical knowledge and discernment. In 1931, when the classical business slumped in the great depression, Legge conceived the ingenious idea of Society Editions whereby a minimum number of subscribers guaranteed in advance to buy certain proposed recordings. The first project was a collection of Hugo Wolf songs and its success led to subsequent recordings of works by Bach, Beethoven, Sibelius, Delius, Mozart, and others. Legge soon started to take an active role in the recording studio, first in the production of Society Editions and later also for the HMV recording programme of local British artists like Myra Hess, Benno Moisiewitsch, and Walter Goehr.

(Harry) Walter Legge (1906–1979), by unknown photographer

In 1934 Legge met Sir Thomas Beecham for the first time. Beecham quickly became impressed with him and insisted that Legge supervise all his recording sessions: a demand to which Fred Gaisberg readily agreed since Beecham was one of the few artists with whom Gaisberg did not get on well. Beecham also made Legge assistant artistic director of his opera company at Covent Garden, giving Legge freedom to engage all the singers and conductors. Always critically appreciative of the talents of performers, Legge provided Beecham with a dazzling array of fine singers and conductors until the outbreak of war in 1939 put an end to opera at Covent Garden. Throughout the 1930s Legge remained active as a musical journalist. He first wrote for *The Gramophone* magazine in 1928, and in 1932 became music critic for the *Manchester Guardian*, covering such disparate events as the 1933 season at Bayreuth (with Adolf Hitler in the audience) and the Russian ballet's visits to London. He later wrote for the *Times Saturday Review* and for the American journal *High Fidelity*.

During the Second World War, Legge's poor eyesight

prevented him doing war service but he worked for Entertainments National Services Association (ENSA), organizing classical concerts for the armed forces and war workers. The Gramophone Company had by this time become EMI, and Legge also continued to supervise classical recordings. When hostilities ceased, Legge joined EMI's revived international artistes department as manager of the Columbia label and, together with David Bicknell, who was manager of the HMV label, immediately began to restore EMI's artiste roster, placing under exclusive contract Herbert von Karajan, Wilhelm Furtwängler, Dinu Lipatti, Walter Gieseking, Elisabeth Schwarzkopf, and many others. In 1941 Legge married the singer Florence Annie (Nancy) *Evans; they had one child, Helga Maria. The marriage was dissolved in 1948, and in 1953 Legge married his second wife, the soprano Elisabeth Schwarzkopf (*b.* 9 Dec 1915); there were no children from this marriage.

Outside the record business, Walter Legge also had a galvanizing impact on the performance of music in Britain. According to *New Grove*, he 'always worked to raise standards of musical execution and interpretative artistry' (611). With this intent in 1945 he brought the Philharmonia String Quartet into being, and was its musical director. Legge also founded his own orchestra, the Philharmonia. Although he later remarked that he established it merely as a hobby, Legge undoubtedly felt the need for a virtuoso British symphony orchestra with which he could make recordings and thus set new, superior standards of musical performance. Beecham conducted its first public performance, a programme of Mozart, at Kingsway Hall on 27 October 1945. Karajan became its principal conductor, and guest conductors included Wilhelm Furtwängler, Arturo Toscanini, Guido Cantelli, Carlo Maria Giulini, and many others. When Karajan left to succeed Furtwängler as principal conductor of the Berlin Philharmonic Orchestra, Legge appointed Otto Klemperer to take his place with the Philharmonia. Not content, in 1957 Legge created the Philharmonia chorus, in order to perform Beethoven's ninth symphony (with Klemperer as conductor). The chorus too 'was immediately recognised as a choir without peer' (*New Grove*, 611). The Philharmonia and its chorus together were 'an elite whose virtuosity transformed British concert life' (ibid.).

The period from 1945 to 1964 was a golden age for both Legge and EMI, when Legge's talents as both record producer and impresario reached their peak. Throughout these years he continued to place under contract to EMI the greatest artistes in the world, enriching London's musical life with his Philharmonia concerts and making a vast number of outstanding recordings that set standards unlikely ever to be surpassed. However, by June 1963 Legge felt that his freedom to make recordings was severely restricted by EMI's newly formed international classical repertoire committee, whose function was to control all the company's classical recording activities. He therefore tendered his resignation on notice of one year, but in March 1964, after a disagreement with Otto Klemperer over the recording of Mozart's *Die Zauberflöte*, Legge departed and made no further recordings for EMI except those involving his wife, Elisabeth Schwarzkopf. He remained active in musical life on the continent, however, organizing concerts and producing recordings for other firms.

Legge died at Cap Ferrat, France, on 22 March 1979. One of his wife's recordings that he had produced closed his memorial service at St James's, Piccadilly. Although Legge was a generous and delightful host and an irresistible conversationalist, he was also ruthless in the pursuit of his own ends, though these were invariably connected with the art of music and his contribution to it. The pianist Gerald Moore once aptly described Legge as 'a Diaghilev where music is concerned'. As a record producer and musical impresario Legge was undoubtedly without equal, and 'his activities have immensely benefited musical performance and appreciation all over the world' (*New Grove*, 612). PETER MARTLAND

Sources M. Tobin, 'Walter Legge: the early years', *International Classical Record Collector Magazine*, 2 (Sept 1995), 7–19 · E. Schwarzkopf, *On and off the record* (1982) · staff file, EMI Music Archive, Hayes, Middlesex · W. Mann, 'Legge, Walter', *New Grove* · *Daily Telegraph* (27 March 1979)
Archives EMI Music Archive, Hayes, Middlesex | SOUND BBC Broadcasting House
Likenesses photographs, 1957–65, Hult. Arch. · photographs, EMI Music Archive, Hayes, Middlesex [*see illus.*]

Legge, William (1607/8–1670), royalist army officer, was the eldest son of Edward Legge (*d.* 1616), vice-president of Munster, and his wife, Mary, daughter of Percy Walsh of Moyvalley, co. Kildare. The family of Legge had been long established in London, and had occupied several offices in the City; but Edward, as the son of a second son, had had to make his own way, which he did through naval exploits and settlement in Ireland. William was the eldest of six sons; two died in childhood, and the others pursued military or naval careers. His godfather was Henry Danvers, earl of Danby, president of Munster. It was reported later that Danby was instrumental in bringing him out of Ireland and assisting in the search for office, after the death of his father.

Early career As his younger brothers were to do, Legge embarked on a military career. The details of his service on the continent are lacking, but it was later claimed by his son that he joined the Dutch and Swedish forces in the Thirty Years' War. He certainly returned to England in the deepening political crisis of 1638, and was appointed inspector of the defences of Newcastle and Hull. His experience and natural ability were recognized when he was made master of the armoury and lieutenant of the ordnance for the first bishops' war. From his store at Hull, and with a small staff, he supplied arms and munitions to the forces in the north from September 1638 to the end of the second bishops' war in September 1640. He was required to travel constantly from Hull to the Tower of London, headquarters of the ordnance office, and his own house on Tower Hill; during 1641 he carried messages from the army camped in Yorkshire to the royal court. When some officer-courtiers fell under suspicion in the

William Legge (1607/8–1670), by Jacob Huysmans, *c.*1670

Long Parliament for plotting to assist the king by direct action, he was examined on oath in the Commons in October. He said that he had brought a petition from the army to London, but had burnt it. Only his powerful friends in the Lords saved him from imprisonment in December, and there was alarm in parliament when he returned to Hull the following month with the king's commission.

Legge's attempt to get the townsmen to admit the earl of Newcastle in January 1642 failed. He was still there when the king moved his court to York in April 1642, and Hull became the focus of the political struggle for the arms of the kingdom. He moved to Newcastle, where the earl was preparing forces to secure the town. In June he was condemned as a delinquent by parliament.

Legge found time, in the midst of this political crisis, to marry (on 2 March 1642) Elizabeth (*c.*1616–1688), the eldest daughter of Sir William Washington of Sulgrave Manor, Northamptonshire, and sister of another future royalist officer, Colonel Henry Washington. They had several children; their eldest son, George *Legge, who was to succeed his father as lieutenant-general of the ordnance, was created first Baron Dartmouth in 1682. William's younger brother Robert also held a prominent military—and politically sensitive—post at this crucial juncture, as deputy to Lord Goring, governor of Portsmouth.

First civil war Legge was among the first to join the king at Nottingham in August, when the latter was preparing to raise the royal standard. It was there that he met the newly arrived Prince Rupert. Together they improvised a petard from an apothecary's mortar, for a projected attack on Coventry. A few days later, at Southam, Warwickshire, mistaking the enemy's quarters for his own, he became one of the first prisoners of war in the unfolding conflict. He was sent to London and lodged in the Gatehouse prison. He escaped in October and was next recorded as captain of the Royal Life Guard of foot at Oxford in January 1643.

But it was as a cavalry officer, and technical expert, patronized by Rupert, now general of horse, that Legge rapidly rose to prominence. By April 1643 he was major of the prince's cavalry regiment, and he was with him in all the actions of the mounted arm that year. He was at the capture of Cirencester; the attack on the besiegers at Lichfield Close, where he was briefly taken and immediately rescued; and the abortive relief of Reading. Taking part in Rupert's celebrated Chalgrove raid on 18 June 1643, he again found himself for a moment captive before John Hampden's hastily assembled force was dispersed (and Hampden mortally wounded). He was present at the siege of Gloucester in August–September 1643. At the battle of Newbury later that month his conduct drew praise from the king himself, who offered him a knighthood. He declined it.

When parliament took over the national machinery for arms production, storage, and distribution, centred on the Tower of London, the king had to recreate his own munitions industry in his new capital of Oxford. Legge had an important part to play as the royalist master of the armoury. He sat on an early council of war when arms supply matters were being discussed in December 1642. Late in 1643 he commandeered the mill at Wolvercote, 3 miles north of the city, for the making of swords. A forge was set up, for the same purpose, at Gloucester Hall, empty of students. Considerable sums were assigned to him from the limited revenues available to the king. He lodged, when at Oxford, in early 1644, in one of the largest houses in St Aldate's parish, near the royal court at Christ Church.

Legge continued close to Rupert during the campaigning of 1644. He was at the relief of Newark in March, and was left in charge of Chester by the prince on his journey north to assist Newcastle at York. Rupert commended Legge to the authorities of the city as his 'Sergeant-Major and General of my Ordnance' and a 'person every way qualified for so great and important a trust' (Warburton, 2.425–6). He did not remain long in that post, but it is uncertain whether he was with the prince at Marston Moor.

In the winter months that followed Legge was quartered with his troops at Faringdon in Berkshire, but, with the death in action of the previous governor of Oxford, Sir Henry Gage, on 11 January 1645, he was appointed to succeed him. Rupert, now commander-in-chief of the king's forces, was instrumental in the choice. Honours followed; he was elected a freeman and alderman of the city (18 March), made a groom of the bedchamber (12 April), and created DCL by the university (16 April). Rupert further commissioned him, on 7 May 1645, to take charge of the ring of strongholds protecting Oxford. He seems to have been generally popular with the city, court, and army, a remarkable feat in the increasingly divided counsels of the king. He was often spoken of as 'honest Will' Legge.

Rupert wrote frequently to him, and the thirteen holograph, partly enciphered, letters which survive from the period March–July 1645 provide a telling commentary on royalist strategy and politics in a key period. His intimacy with Rupert aroused jealousy, however, with the factions hostile to the prince.

With the comprehensive royalist defeat at Naseby on 14 June 1645 the smouldering resentments in the high command broke into open warfare. It was to Legge that Rupert confided his bitter feelings about Lord Digby, the royal secretary; while, for his part, the secretary thought it worth while to convince Legge of his innocence. When Rupert surrendered Bristol in September, Digby persuaded the king that the prince and his associates had committed treason, and that other garrisons would soon be betrayed. Rupert was dismissed, and ordered from the kingdom; Legge, in common with others of the prince's appointees, was removed as governor of Oxford, and placed under arrest on 14 September 1645.

But the failure of Digby to produce any evidence of treachery—'more particular proofs'—and a period of reflection by the king, led to Legge's partial reinstatement. Thereafter he worked tirelessly, when Charles returned to Oxford, to effect a reconciliation between sovereign and prince. Rupert was allowed to remain in the royal headquarters. At the fall of the city to Fairfax on 22 June 1646 Legge was listed among the prince's followers, given a pass, and allowed the benefit of the surrender terms. In due course he compounded for his estate, and was fined at a tenth, £40. This modest sum may have been an indication of his comparative poverty (or successful concealment of lands, perhaps in Ireland), his political acceptability as a go-between in the 1647 negotiations with Charles, or the generosity of the Oxford articles.

Imprisonment and obscurity Little is known of Legge's whereabouts until he joined the king in captivity at Holmby House in July 1647. With John Ashburnham and Sir John Berkeley he engineered the king's flight to Carisbrooke Castle in the Isle of Wight on 11 November, but escaped the censure this move attracted. 'Legg had had so general a reputation of integrity and fidelity to his master', wrote Clarendon, 'that he never fell under the least imputation or reproach with any man.'

> He was a very punctual and steady observer of the orders he received, but no contriver of them; and though he had in truth a better judgment and understanding than either of the other two, his modesty and diffidence of himself never suffered him to contrive bold counsels (Clarendon, *Hist. rebellion*, 4.266)

When Legge was ordered by parliament to be restrained, his friendship with the governor, Robert Hammond, delayed but did not prevent his imprisonment. This was, however, brief for by January 1648 he had obtained some limited freedom, and made his way to join other royalists in the Channel Islands. He returned to the mainland to take part in the activities of Kent plotters during the second civil war, and was reported secretly conferring with others, including his brother-in-law, Colonel Henry Washington, at Gravesend in April 1649.

Legge's Irish connections, and longstanding friendship with the king's representative there, the marquess of Ormond, persuaded the new king, Charles II, to send him with a ship of Rupert's fleet to Kinsale in summer 1649. It was captured in July, however, and he was imprisoned in Exeter gaol, where he remained for over three years. A family tradition, repeated in Collins's *Peerage*, that he went to Scotland with the king, appears to be without foundation. In March 1653 he was granted a pass to go abroad, but there is no record of his activities during the royalists' exile. In 1659 he was named by the king one of five commissioners to treat with potential supporters in England, and was actively involved in plots to restore the king. The failure of these led to his imprisonment in the Tower from July to 30 September 1659.

The Restoration At the Restoration, Charles II offered to create Legge an earl, 'which he modestly declined, having a numerous family with a small fortune, but told the king he hoped his sons might live to deserve his majesty's favour' (*Collins Peerage*, 4.113). He recovered his old posts of master of the armouries and groom of the bedchamber, and was made lieutenant-general of the ordnance. He was MP for Southampton in the Cavalier Parliament from 1661 until his death. He aided the return of Rupert to England, and travelled to Ireland for a time, where his estates were restored and augmented. As head of the ordnance office at the Tower he occupied a large house in the Minories, the liberty close to the Tower, where many of the arms makers and their workshops were located. He received an income of £2000 p.a. in fees as general, including poundage of 6*d*. in the pound, a similar amount as treasurer, and profits arising from the lease of royal forests in Hampshire. His wife had a pension of £500 p.a. Under his guidance the department acquired a reputation for good management and financial probity, a contrast to the pre-civil-war office. Unlike the Navy Board it remained creditworthy, in spite of the big expansion of its activities and costs in the Second Anglo-Dutch War.

Legge died in the Minories on 13 October 1670, aged sixty-two, and was buried in the north chancel vault of Holy Trinity Church there. Prince Rupert and five dukes, it was said, attended the funeral. He left a sizeable estate, including lands in Ireland and valuable leases, and £4000. In 1673 a memorandum of his services to the crown was drawn up by his eldest son, no doubt to assist his own bid for the generalship, which he achieved in 1679.

IAN ROY

Sources Dartmouth papers, William Salt Library, Stafford [formerly held by the family at Patshull House, near Wolverhampton, and reported on by the HMC, vols. 2, 11 (appx 5), 15 (appx 1); see also stray item printed in I Roy, ed., *Royalist ordnance papers*, 2 vols., Oxfordshire RS, 43, 49 (1964–75), 227–9] • E. Warburton, *Memoirs of Prince Rupert and the cavaliers*, 3 vols. (1849) • *CSP dom.*, *1637–40*; *1649–53*; *1659–62*; *1666–7* • *Collins peerage of England: genealogical, biographical and historical*, ed. E. Brydges, 9 vols. (1812) • *DNB* • I. Roy, ed., *The royalist ordnance papers, 1642–1646*, 2 vols., Oxfordshire RS, 43, 49 (1964–75), 25, 28, 179, 427–9, 466 • M. Toynbee and P. Young, *Strangers in Oxford: a side light on the first civil war, 1642–1646* (1973), 195–6 • 'Memoirs of Sir John Berkeley', *Select tracts relating to the civil wars in England*, ed. F. Maseres, 1 (1815), 353–94 • Clarendon, *Hist. rebellion* •

P. R. Newman, *Royalist officers in England and Wales, 1642–1660: a biographical dictionary* (1981) • P. Watson, 'Legge, William', HoP, *Commons, 1660–90* • H. C. Tomlinson, *Guns and government: the ordnance office under the later Stuarts* (1979) • E. M. Tomlinson, *A history of the Minories, London* (1907) • J. Le Neve, *Monumenta Anglicana*, 5 vols. (1717–19), vol. 2, p. 144

Archives Staffs. RO, MSS • Yale U., Beinecke L., corresp.

Likenesses W. Dobson, bust, *c*.1645, NPG • by or after J. Huysmans, oils, *c*.1670, NPG; repro. in *Historical portraits, 1628–1714*, 198 • J. Huysmans, portrait, *c*.1670, priv. coll. [*see illus.*] • P. Lely?, repro. in Tomlinson, *A history of the Minories, London* • oils (after a type by J. Huysmans, *c*.1670), NPG

Wealth at death possibly over £5000, including estate, at time of death: Tomlinson, *Guns and government*

Legge, William, first earl of Dartmouth (1672–1750), politician, the only son of the eight children of George *Legge, first Baron Dartmouth (*c*.1647–1691), and his wife, Barbara (1649/50–1718), the daughter and coheir of Sir Henry Archbold of Abbots Bromley, Staffordshire, was born on 14 October 1672. He was educated at Westminster School, and while there witnessed Bishop Sprat read the declaration of liberty of conscience in the abbey (20 April 1688). He then went to King's College, Cambridge, where he graduated MA in 1689. He succeeded his father as second Baron Dartmouth on 25 October 1691, but, rather than embarking on a career in politics, just before his twenty-first birthday he was granted leave to travel abroad. He spent the next two years undertaking an extensive grand tour, which included waiting on Princess Sophia in Hanover, a visit to Vienna, and a sojourn in Rome. Following his return he took his seat in the Lords on 22 November 1695.

Politically, Dartmouth was a moderate, although on religious matters he exhibited a distrust of clerical power in matters of state. His loyalty to the revolution regime was absolute, and he was 'one of the first that signed the voluntary Association' (Burnet, 5.11) in the spring of 1696. Nevertheless, on most political matters he was a tory. On 23 December 1696 he signed the protest against Fenwick's bill of attainder. His decision to do so was a seminal event in his early career for 'the violent, unrelenting ill-usage' (Dartmouth MSS, D1778/Iii/1) which he met with after Fenwick's trial justified him in his opposition to 'anything that was for his majesty's [William III] advantage or personal satisfaction' (ibid.). As yet, however, he had other priorities: as early as 1696 his mother had remarked upon his need to 'find a good wife' (ibid.), and on 18 July 1700 he married Lady Anne Finch (*d*. 1751), the third daughter of Heneage Finch, first earl of Aylesford. This proved a fruitful match, yielding six sons (two of whom died in infancy) and two daughters.

Following the death of King William, Dartmouth told Queen Anne that on her accession day 'Twas all joy without the least alloy' (Burnet, 5.11). The queen evidently believed him, and he became something of a favourite whom she was able to protect in office throughout her reign. On 19 June 1702 he was appointed a commissioner of the Board of Trade, and four days later was admitted a member of the privy council. He declined being sent to Hanover on a mission to the electress of Hanover, on the ground that 'he was very sensible that whoever was employed between her majesty and her successor would soon burn his fingers' (ibid., 5.13), and in 1704 refused the appointment of ambassador to Venice. During the middle years of Anne's reign John Macky described him:

> He sets up for a critick in conversation, makes jests, and loves to laugh at them; takes a great deal of pains in his office, and is in a fair way of rising at court; is a short, thick man of fair complexion. (*Memoirs of the Secret Services*, 89)

Rise at court he did, despite some disgruntlement among the whigs, who objected to his occasional votes with the tories. His survival at the Board of Trade owed something to his low profile; indeed, he did not attend a single meeting of the board in 1708. However, when the queen was finally persuaded to turn to the tories, and needed a candidate to indicate that a change of ministry was imminent, it was on her initiative that Dartmouth was chosen on 15 June 1710 to replace Sunderland as secretary of state for the southern department. On 2 November 1710 he was also made joint keeper of the signet for Scotland with James, duke of Queensberry. Swift's *Examiner* for 1 February 1711 praised him as:

> a man of letters full of good sense, good nature, and honour; of strict virtue and regularity in his life, but labours under one great defect—that he treats his clerks with more civility and good manners than others in his station have done the queen. (Swift, 3.436)

On 5 September 1711 Dartmouth was created Viscount Lewisham and earl of Dartmouth, and later that month signed the preliminary articles of peace with France. In December he expressed his disapproval to the queen of the intended creation of the twelve peers, fearing 'it would have a very ill effect in the House of Lords, and no good one in the kingdom' (Burnet, 6.94–5). Consistently, he had opposed the grant of an English peerage to the duke of Hamilton on constitutional grounds. Prince Eugene, on his visit to England in 1712, found him 'very pliable, a great stickler for the tory party, but not much bred to business, of a tolerable sense, and easily led' (GEC, *Peerage*, 4.88). No doubt Dartmouth fared badly when compared with his fellow secretary Bolingbroke, and certainly he could not compete with his colleague's skill in the conduct of the peace negotiations. Thus on 16 August 1713 he was allowed to resign the secretaryship in order to become lord privy seal. He remained loyal to Lord Oxford in his struggle with Bolingbroke, so retained his office and was present on the queen's deathbed when she appointed the duke of Shrewsbury as lord treasurer; he acted as one of the lords justices until the arrival of George I in England, when he was relieved of his office.

Dartmouth then retired into Staffordshire and thereafter played only a peripheral role in national politics. He remained a firm supporter of the Hanoverian succession, and 'never in his whole life held any sort of correspondence with the pretender or his followers' (*Dartmouth MSS*, 1.329). He opposed the impeachment of Lord Oxford in 1717–18 and remained committed to the tories until in 1739 he helped to ease his son Henry into office by transferring his proxy to a government supporter. Perhaps his most enduring monument was the annotated copy of Burnet he left in his library, which provided a tory refutation of the period's most whiggish historian. Dartmouth died at Blackheath on 15 December 1750, aged seventy-eight, and was buried in Trinity Church in the Minories on the 21 December. His wife died on 30 November 1751, and was buried in the Dartmouth vault of Trinity Church in the Minories on 7 December following. Three of his sons (Heneage *Legge, Henry *Legge, and Edward *Legge) became important politicians in their own right, but he was succeeded as second earl by his grandson William *Legge, the son of his eldest son, George.

Dartmouth's town house was situated in Queen Square (now known as Queen Anne's Gate), Westminster. The adjoining Dartmouth and Lewisham streets were named after him. However, he spent more time at Dartmouth House, Blackheath, and Sandwell in Staffordshire.

STUART HANDLEY

Sources *Bishop Burnet's History* • *DNB* • Staffs. RO, Dartmouth papers, D1778/V; D/1778/Iii • *The manuscripts of the earl of Dartmouth*, 3 vols., HMC, 20 (1887–96), vol. 1, pp. 293–330; vol. 3, pp. 147–65 • *Memoirs of the secret services of John Macky*, ed. A. R. (1733), 89 • will, PRO, PROB 11/785, sig. 7 [proved in 1751] • N. Luttrell, *A brief historical relation of state affairs from September 1678 to April 1714*, 6 vols. (1857) • *The prose works of Jonathan Swift*, 3: *The Examiner and other pieces written in 1710–11*, ed. H. Davis (1941) • G. S. Holmes, *British politics in the age of Anne* (1967), 19, 205, 389, 427 • I. K. Steele, *Politics of colonial policy: the board of trade in colonial administration, 1696–1720* (1968), 112–14, 174–5 • C. Jones, 'The impeachment of the earl of Oxford and the whig schism of 1717: four new lists', *BIHR*, 55 (1982), 66–87, esp. 81 • GEC, *Peerage*

Archives BL, diplomatic corresp., Add. MSS 22205–22207 • Staffs. RO, accounts, commonplace book, papers, and official papers | BL, corresp. with Lord Lexington, Add. MSS 46543–46545 • BL, corresp. with duke of Newcastle and others, Add. MSS 32727–33069, *passim* • BL, corresp. with Lord Strafford, Add. MS 22211 • CKS, corresp. with James Stanhope • NA Scot., corresp. with Lord Levan

Likenesses J. Fitfer, line engraving, NPG • portrait, repro. in *Bishop Burnet's history*, 9

Legge, William, second earl of Dartmouth (1731–1801), politician, was born on 20 June 1731 in Marylebone, Middlesex, the second and only surviving son of George Legge, Viscount Lewisham (1704?–1732), politician, and his wife, Elizabeth (1707–1745), the daughter and heir of Sir Arthur Kaye, third baronet, of Woodsome, Yorkshire. Under the Stuarts the family had been tories. Legge's grandfather William *Legge, first earl of Dartmouth, willing to accept a Hanoverian succession, secured his advancement in the peerage in 1711 but withdrew from politics after the death of Queen Anne. George Legge's death from smallpox on 29 August 1732 led the young William to inherit the title on 15 December 1750. Not yet twenty, he would never experience politics in the House of Commons.

Legge's mother remarried in 1736; her husband was the widowed Francis North, Lord North and Grey, later first earl of Guilford. At the age of five, Legge thus acquired a stepbrother one year his junior: Frederick *North, the future prime minister. This established a lifelong connection. The loss of his mother on 21 April 1745 was mitigated by his inclusion within the North family. Educated at Westminster School, he matriculated at Trinity College, Oxford, on 14 January 1749 and was consequently still *in statu pupillare* when, the following year, he became the second earl.

William Legge, second earl of Dartmouth (1731–1801), by Thomas Gainsborough, 1769

Frederick North had also attended Trinity College. The stepbrothers were companions for a grand tour of Europe that occupied three years from 1751. This, if not an intellectual awakening—the University of Leipzig was declared to be much inferior to Oxford—did not provide an introduction to continental vice. For Dartmouth, Italy proved an especially rich source of works of art. A leisurely progress introduced them to a number of courts and brought a meeting in 1752 in Hanover with the duke of Newcastle who, always alert to political recruiting, took note of Dartmouth's potential utility.

Soon after his return to England, Dartmouth married, on 11 January 1755, Frances Catherine (1732/3–1805), the only daughter and heir of Sir Charles Gunter Nicholl and his wife, Elizabeth Blundell, later duchess of Ancaster. A long and happy marriage escaped financial difficulties with the provision of a dowry of over £100,000. This may have made possible the acquisition of a London house at 1 St James's Square, occupied by Dartmouth from 1755 until his death. He had inherited from his grandfather two other properties, a mansion on the south side of Blackheath in Kent and a residence at Sandwell, near West Bromwich, which he favoured, extended considerably, and where, in all circumstances, he spent each summer. A further property, the bequest of his mother, less regularly visited, was Woodsome Hall, near Huddersfield.

Dartmouth's family of eight sons and a daughter, all of whom lived to adulthood and would include a bishop and an admiral, as well as his heir, George *Legge, who succeeded him as third earl of Dartmouth, did not create financial difficulties. At his death the family estate was said to be worth £14,000 a year and had been carefully maintained: at Sandwell he had paid particular attention to the needs of midlands merchants and manufacturers.

Powerful religious conviction united Dartmouth and his wife. This was present from the earliest days of their marriage: by 1757 they were firmly committed to evangelical beliefs. In the years that followed, Dartmouth, displaying virtually no interest in political questions, became linked to the Wesleys, Whitfield, William Romaine, and the countess of Huntingdon. This made his entry into politics, when he joined the Rockingham ministry in 1765, occasion general surprise, not least to himself. He had accepted, after characteristic demurrals and consultations, an offer of the presidency of the Board of Trade, while claiming 'to have never entertained a serious thought of taking a part in administration' (Langford, 39). North's refusal to join him meant that all the duke of Newcastle's skills had been needed to persuade him to accept office on 19 July 1765.

Totally lacking in political experience, Dartmouth was compelled to come rapidly to terms with an office placed by circumstances at the centre of policy making. The ministry had to deal with the problem of colonial protests against the Stamp Act. Much of the relevant information was received by the Board of Trade. Dartmouth's attitude, unchanged during the next ten years, was formed with relative ease: first, in the event of a conflict of powers, parliament possessed undeniable and permanent supremacy over the colonies; second, with proper handling, such a situation could be averted or resolved. Benevolent gestures could accompany an unchallengeable principle. Accordingly, to ensure the repeal of the Stamp Act—of which Dartmouth had disapproved—it was necessary to pass a Declaratory Act to persuade a suspicious parliament that its supremacy would unquestionably be sustained. This met with his full support. Nevertheless, within a year the ministry had collapsed. When Pitt formed its successor, Dartmouth was asked to continue at the Board of Trade, but he refused when his request for promotion to secretary of state was rejected, and he left office on 16 August 1766.

A lengthy withdrawal from politics followed. The policies of Hillsborough, his successor at the Board of Trade and, after 1768, the American secretary of state, did not win Dartmouth's support, even though links with Rockingham grew steadily weaker. North's political advancement—he became chancellor of the exchequer in September 1767—in no way threatened their personal relations. In that year Dartmouth gave less consideration to the problems of the Townshend duties than to the pressing need, in the opinion of her followers, for him to assume the countess of Huntingdon's role, should she succumb to illness. The regular meetings at Dartmouth's house were called for prayers, not politics. Although in January 1771 North was to offer him a cabinet post, Dartmouth, now out of touch with Rockingham, would, not for the first or last time, decline.

Dartmouth's religious commitment gained wide recognition. He secured the ordination of the former slaver John Newton and his installation as curate at Olney, where he also provided support for the poet William Cowper. He offered the living of West Bromwich to William Romaine, Lady Huntingdon's chaplain, and, on his refusal, appointed in turn the evangelicals Edward Stillingfleet and William Jesse. With the aid of Sir John Ramsden, he secured the appointment of Henry Venn of Clapham, whom he hailed as a 'faithful labourer', as vicar of Huddersfield.

More distant missions also claimed his attention. In 1766 he met Samson Occum, the first Native American pupil of Eleazar Wheelock's charity school in Connecticut, who had been sent to raise funds for the school. Evangelical support was extensive, if marked by debate between Wheelock and the English trustees, of whom Dartmouth was one. Wheelock was determined to move the school further north into New Hampshire and obtain a charter of incorporation for a college open to others and with American trustees. This did not find favour with the English board. To win their support it was proposed that it be called Dartmouth College. This with a site at Hanover in New Hampshire was announced in July 1770. Dartmouth had played no significant part in the creation of an institution 'named without his permission and incorporated against his known wishes' (Bargar, 14) but through this means an enduring recognition was his unanticipated reward.

In the summer of 1772 North, prime minister since January 1770, established political relations with Dartmouth: a protracted cabinet dispute, turning on land grants in the Ohio valley, led to Hillsborough's resignation and, as rivals sought to succeed him, an apparent weakening of North's leadership. This was averted when North persuaded Dartmouth to accept the office, so bringing into the cabinet a trusted and benevolent ally. Benjamin Franklin, asked some months before who might be more acceptable than Hillsborough to the colonists, had replied: 'there is Lord Dartmouth: we liked him very well when he was head of the Board formerly and probably should like him again' (Benjamin Franklin to William Franklin, 19 Aug 1772, *The Papers of Benjamin Franklin*, ed. L. W. Labaree and others, 1975, 19.258). Gratitude for his part in the repeal of the Stamp Act had been demonstrated by North American gifts to Lady Dartmouth for her menagerie at Sandwell.

Initially, only as firm a radical as Sam Adams could remark that 'I wish I could hear something more of Lord D to qualify him for his high office, than merely that he is a *good* man' (Adams to Arthur Lee, 9 April 1773, R. H. Lee, *Life of Arthur Lee*, 1829, 2.199). Certainly the new secretary proved altogether more accessible than Hillsborough: his predecessor would not, as Dartmouth did in June 1773, have opened a private correspondence with Thomas Cushing, the speaker of the Massachusetts assembly. But an undeniable desire to find ways of resolving differences did not lead to effective policies.

The three major problems inherited from Hillsborough—the resolution of the *Gaspée* incident, the patrol ship burned by Rhode Islanders; the extent and form of western expansion; and the provision of constitutional government for Quebec—were still unresolved when at the end of January 1774 news of the Boston Tea Party reached ministers.

Dartmouth's reaction confirmed his political principles. Parliamentary supremacy remained beyond question: the colonists could not fail to pay duty on tea, let alone destroy it. If, as proved the case, the executive authority did not prevail, legislation must be introduced. Dartmouth agreed with North on the necessity of such a step, even though he hoped that an admission of unjustifiable actions would restore good relations between the imperial government and the colonists.

However, until this came about, redress had to be sought through parliamentary measures: between 19 February and 2 June 1774 four statutes to establish order came into being. These closed the port of Boston, amended the Massachusetts charter, regulated the administration of justice, and provided military quarters in North America. Dartmouth did not find their acceptance difficult, only expressing hopes for a cautious enforcement. He had made no noticeable contribution to their passage, though on 2 May he introduced the bill which would become, on 22 June, the Quebec Act, a measure that opponents declared to be a further, fifth step towards imperial elimination of colonial liberties.

This reassertion of parliamentary supremacy in matters of imperial regulation still did not force Dartmouth to believe that colonial interests needed to conflict with those of the mother country. Coercive legislation was necessary and regrettable but could be transient. If compensation was offered for the destruction of property, the tea duty might be repealed; with imperial authority restored the port of Boston could reopen; a military presence was justifiable but no more than a reaction to events.

These hopes were soon seen to be misplaced. The Coercive Acts had not reduced Massachusetts to order but, on the contrary, had stimulated opposition. Even so, Dartmouth still hoped to negotiate a solution. Intermediaries, including Franklin, were found, and a proposal put forward in December 1774 that commissioners should meet colonial delegates 'to discuss and settle all claims, and Parliament to confirm, if approved what they should agree upon' (Donoghue, 215). George III was not impressed and, although Dartmouth persisted in urging acceptance on the cabinet, only North proved in the least sympathetic. Dartmouth made it clear that, if negotiations failed, he was prepared to subdue colonial resistance. By February 1775 that seemed necessary and Dartmouth's role steadily diminished. North assumed responsibility for a last effort to combine potential concessions and imperial control.

When, in April 1775, fighting at Lexington and Concord turned a political into an armed conflict, Dartmouth lost the capacity to conduct American affairs. Continuing to favour conciliation he was unable to accept, even had he grasped the urgency of the situation, any colonial approaches. As usual, the summer of 1775 was passed at Sandwell.

In November 1775 the duke of Grafton resigned as lord privy seal. This provided Dartmouth with an opportunity to escape from an office that, now American policy was based on the suppression of rebellion, he could not occupy. North did not wish to lose him from the cabinet but had offered his position to Lord George Germain. After extended negotiations, Dartmouth became lord privy seal on 10 November 1775 and remained a member of the cabinet.

Dartmouth's political significance had effectively ended. Although he remained in government until 1782, his role was largely nominal and his presence spasmodic: North would have proposed him as lord lieutenant of Ireland in October 1776 but for the well-founded belief that the offer would have been declined. His stepbrother's fall from office in March 1782 brought a final end to a career that owed almost nothing to personal ambition. The office of lord steward of the household, which he occupied from April to December 1783 during the Fox–North coalition, possessed no political significance. In July 1786 North, as chancellor of Oxford University, bestowed a last appointment. He urged acceptance of the office of high steward, 'though it is accompanied by no emolument, and I believe by no function whatever' (Valentine, 2.440). The honour was accurately described.

Dartmouth died in Blackheath on 15 July 1801 and was buried in Holy Trinity Minories on 3 August. By the time of his death he had been almost entirely forgotten. His part in the politics of the American War of Independence, never clear-cut, had passed from view; his religious activities no longer commanded attention. As his sympathies for the colonists had been constrained by an unswerving belief in parliamentary supremacy, so his attachment to evangelical religion was bounded by a fixed attachment to the Church of England. His public and personal actions, however directed by conscience, did not challenge accepted institutions, either in church or state.

In office Dartmouth has been judged 'conscientious and not ungifted' (Langford, 39). His under-secretaries, John Pownall and William Knox, might have found it difficult to agree—Knox considered him unsuited by character for political life, a verdict confirmed by Dartmouth's preference to occupy himself with the affairs of Sandwell rather than of Whitehall. If the judgement that he was 'a lethargic office holder' (Basye, 181) is too severe, his capacity to influence policy in the years before the outbreak of the American War of Independence was small.

Dartmouth's distinctive quality and the one which secured general recognition was personal virtue. On that account George III held him in high esteem and Lord North continued to solicit a support which, after November 1775, became largely passive. As he had entered government, so he left it—on personal grounds. Of his resignation as lord privy seal the king wrote: 'I have esteemed him ever since I have thoroughly known him in another light than any of his companions in Ministry' (Valentine, 2.321). It was a generous and representative note on which to bid him political farewell. PETER MARSHALL

Sources *The manuscripts of the earl of Dartmouth*, 3 vols., HMC, 20 (1887–96) · *The manuscripts of Rye and Hereford corporations*, HMC, 31 (1892) · B. D. Bargar, *Lord Dartmouth and the American revolution* (1965) · P. D. G. Thomas, *Tea party to independence* (1991) · B. Donoghue, *British politics and the American revolution: the path to war, 1773–75* (1964) · P. Langford, *The first Rockingham administration, 1765–1766* (1973) · *VCH Staffordshire*, 3.44–91 · L. J. Bellot, *William Knox* (1977) · A. Valentine, *Lord North*, 2 vols. (1967) · *DNB* · GEC, *Peerage* · R. S. Lea, 'Legge, George', HoP, *Commons* · *GM*, 1st ser., 71 (1801), 768 · A. H. Basye, *The lords commissioners of trade and plantations, commonly known as the board of trade, 1748–1782* (New Haven, CT, 1925)

Archives Boston University, Mugar Memorial Library, letter-book · NA Canada [microfilm at Staffs. RO] · Staffs. RO, corresp. and MSS | Birm. CL, letters to Matthew Boulton · BL, corresp. with General Amherst and General Haldimand, Add. MSS 21695, 21697 · BL, letters to second Lord Hardwicke, Add. MSS 35611–35620 · BL, Newcastle MSS · BL, 'Present state of the British colonies in America', returns made to Dartmouth as secretary of state · Bodl. Oxf., North MSS, trustee and estate papers · NA Canada, corresp. and papers relating to British North American colonies · PRO, official papers as colonial secretary, 30/2 · U. Mich., Clements L., Gage MSS · U. Mich., Clements L., Knox MSS

Likenesses J. Reynolds, oils, *c*.1757–1759 (in peer's robes), Thomas Coram Foundation, London · T. Gainsborough, portrait, 1769, priv. coll. [*see illus.*] · W. Evans, stipple (after T. Gainsborough), BM, NPG · T. Gainsborough, portrait, repro. in B. Bailyn, *The ordeal of Thomas Hutchinson* (1974) · C. Warren, line engraving, BM, NPG; repro. in *The Senator* (1792) · line engraving, BM, NPG; repro. in *London Magazine* (1780) · portrait (after N. Hone, 1777) · portrait (after J. Reynolds?), Dartmouth College, Hanover, New Hampshire

Wealth at death £14,000—value of family estate

Leggett, Sir Frederick William (1884–1983), civil servant, was born at 54 Paul Street, West Ham, Essex, on 23 December 1884, the son of Frederick John Leggett, a police constable, and his wife, Frances Mary, the daughter of William Murphy of Huntingdon. He was educated at the City of London and Strand schools and King's College, London, before entering the Board of Trade as an executive officer in 1904. On 22 March 1913 he married Edith Guinevere, (1887/8–1949), the daughter of Henry Kitson of Woodford, with whom he had one son and three daughters.

Leggett became successively the private secretary to the parliamentary secretary of the Board of Trade in 1915 and of the newly established Ministry of Labour in 1917. He spent the remainder of his career within the ministry, rising to deputy secretary from 1942 to 1945, when he retired. He was appointed CB in 1933 and knighted in 1941 (KBE 1951).

Leggett made his reputation in industrial relations, and in recognition of his prowess Ernest Bevin, on becoming minister of labour and national service in 1940, bestowed on him the title of chief industrial commissioner. This title had been in abeyance since the enforced resignation of Sir George Askwith in 1919 and was particularly apposite because, as an outspoken and somewhat awkward personality, Leggett shared many of Askwith's characteristics—although he never took them to such extremes. As a conciliator, Leggett's success depended on three principal factors. The first was his encyclopaedic knowledge of industrial practices and personalities. The second was his ability to win the trust of both sides and, in Bevin's words, 'fondle' a dispute so that agreement was forthcoming on how to settle not just the current but also any future dispute (Bullock, 120). The third was what has euphemistically been called his superhuman ability 'to defy all needs of nature', so that negotiations came to a sudden, successful conclusion as the other parties started to suffer acute physical discomfort or sheer exhaustion (private information, St J. Wilson). These skills particularly came into their own in the 1930s and resolved major disputes in the cotton industry in 1932 and the London theatre in 1935. The former led to the Cotton Manufacturing Industry (Temporary Provisions) Act of 1934, which exceptionally gave legal force to any voluntary agreement reached by the new conciliation board. The latter similarly led to the creation of the London Theatre Council, which among other things introduced standard contracts for actors.

Leggett was controversial because underpinning his negotiation of such agreements was a commitment to an extreme form of the voluntaryism which characterized the industrial relations policy of the ministry and successive governments from the 1920s to the early 1960s. He fervently believed that 'the preservation of order in a democracy depends on a personal sense of responsibility' and that any lasting settlement had accordingly to be built up from below by the parties directly concerned. Any outside intervention—be it by government, international bodies (such as the International Labour Organization, on which he was the government representative from 1932 to 1944), or national organizations such as the TUC—jeopardized lasting success by introducing extraneous issues and by enabling the warring parties to evade their mutual responsibilities. Even strikes or lock-outs were preferable if they eventually forced the two sides to acknowledge economic 'reality' (Leggett, 674). This commitment led Leggett even to oppose the government's role as a model employer and initiatives designed to improve work practices such as trade boards, with their responsibility of introducing minimum wages to specific industries. Indeed to one prospective member of such a board, who protested he was 'strongly laissez-faire so he might himself be out of sympathy with what he was doing', he replied that his beliefs were 'a strong reason for offering him an appointment' (BLPES, Beveridge papers, IIb 31–2). This opposition to state intervention equally covered initiatives in economic and welfare policy.

Leggett's commitment to industrial autonomy was appreciated by many employers and trade unionists, and especially by Bevin, whom he came to know well on a government industrial mission to the USA in 1926 and at the International Labour Organization. He therefore warmly welcomed Bevin's appointment as minister. The two, however, quickly fell out. As minister, Bevin wanted to influence wage settlements and Leggett continued fiercely to defend the independence of conciliators and arbitrators. Bevin also wanted to modernize industrial conditions by introducing a 'new code of conduct, inspection, enforcement and welfare' (Lowe, 241). This was naturally inimical to Leggett, and a major battle ensued over the controversial Catering Wages Act of 1943. Leggett's knighthood was a recognition of the fact that he was not to be made permanent secretary. Such a promotion would, regardless of policy differences, have been inappropriate anyway because he was not a born administrator. Despite producing trenchant minutes on major issues, he preferred not to confide his thoughts to paper and, as has been diplomatically expressed, he could be as exasperating as a colleague as he was delightful as a friend (Emmerson, 34). His handling of an awkward file was notorious because it would not return for several months, if at all.

Leggett, a tall lean man with only one eye and a disarming sense of humour, enjoyed a long and active retirement. He was a member of the British reparations mission to Moscow in 1945 and the Anglo-American committee into Palestine in 1946. He sat on many industrial inquiries, including that into the London docks disputes in 1950–51 (as chairman), and was the industrial relations adviser for the Anglo-Iranian Oil Company from 1947 to 1960. He was vice-president of the Royal College of Nursing from 1948 until his death. Following the death in 1949 of his first wife he married on 7 August 1957 Beatrice Melville Sheppard, a widow and the daughter of Joseph Roe. Leggett, who in retirement lived at Angmering-on-Sea, Sussex, died in HRH Princess Christian's Hospital, Windsor, on 28 June 1983. His wife survived him. RODNEY LOWE

Sources *The Times* (30 June 1983) • F. W. Leggett, 'The settlement of labour disputes in Great Britain', *Meeting of minds*, ed. E. Jackson (New York, 1952) • E. Wigham, *Strikes and the government, 1893–1974* (1976) • R. Lowe, *Adjusting to democracy* (1986) • R. Crossman, *Palestine mission* (1946) • A. Bullock, *The life and times of Ernest Bevin*, 2 (1967) • H. Emmerson, 'Masters and servants', unpublished autobiography • BLPES, Beveridge MSS, IIb 31–2 • PRO, Ministry of Labour papers, LAB 2, LAB 10 • private information (2004) • C. J. Wrigley, ed., *A history of British industrial relations*, 2–3 (1987–96) • b. cert. • m. cert. [Edith Guinevere Kitson] • m. cert. [Beatrice Melville Sheppard] • d. cert. • Kelly, *Handbk* (1947) • *WWW*

Archives PRO, ministry of labour papers, LAB 2, LAB 10

Wealth at death £98,094: probate, 6 Sept 1983, *CGPLA Eng. & Wales*

Leggett, Trevor Pryce (1914–2000), judo master, was born on 22 August 1914 at 39 The Avenue, Brondesbury, London, the third son of Lewis Ernest Leggett (1885/6–1943) and his wife, Isabel Mabel, *née* Pryce (1885/6–1965). His father, a child prodigy pianist, was a professional violinist and for some years led the orchestra at Covent Garden under Sir Thomas Beecham; his mother was a registered nurse and later a housewife. The parents' marriage was dissolved on 11 January 1939.

Educated at Mill Hill School, north London, Leggett's earliest ambition was to be a concert pianist and, when still at school, he earned extra pocket money by playing the organ at a local church. His father, while sending him to the finest piano teachers, discouraged him from becoming a professional pianist. Instead Leggett attended King's College, London University, and graduated at the age of twenty in 1934 with an LLB. He was totally obsessed with music, and his health suffered through lack of exercise. To remedy this, at the age of sixteen in 1930 he joined the Budokwai, founded in 1918 by Gunji Koizumi (1885–1965), where he started judo. Earlier, when he was fourteen, he had already started meditation, a practice he continued for the rest of his life. These two disciplines, judo training under Koizumi and Yukio Tani (1881–1950) and meditation under the guidance of Dr Hari Prasad Shastri (1882–1956), whom he met in 1938, had a deep and lasting effect on his life. He had a profound respect for Dr Shastri and regarded him as his mentor in matters spiritual, dedicating all his books of that nature to him. Shastri, a teacher of adhyatma yoga (the yoga of self knowledge), revered all the great meditation traditions, and Leggett followed his example, disdaining any narrow-minded approach to spiritual topics.

Leggett's judo career took him to Japan in 1939; later he was to reach the highest grade (sixth dan) then ever attained by a non-Japanese. At the same time he studied the Japanese language, both spoken and written, and also continued his meditation practices by studying Zen Buddhism. It was some time in 1940 that he joined the British embassy and when war broke out he was interned along with the other diplomats. Following repatriation, he arrived home in October 1942. Having joined the Ministry of Information he was sent on a Japanese language refresher course at the School of Oriental and African Studies where he had private sessions with the eminent orientalist Arthur Waley. In 1943 he was posted to the Far Eastern Bureau in India; it later merged with the South East Asia Command, where he held the rank of major in its psychological warfare division.

Leggett joined the British Broadcasting Corporation in 1946, rising to be head of the Japanese section, a position he held until early retirement in October 1969 at the age of fifty-five. Judo was not neglected; he returned to the Budokwai, where he took over the training of the advanced students, raising many to international standard and arranging for some to study in Japan in the 1950s, with others following later. Leggett closely followed the tenets of Dr Jigoro Kano (1860–1938), founder of the system of ju-jitsu he called judo, who regarded it as a training for life, of developing a mature character with the ultimate aim of moral rectitude.

At a height of 6 feet 3 inches, Leggett was of imposing presence. Slightly stooped in the manner of many tall men, he was beset by illnesses for most of his life. For instance, in 1946 he was lucky to survive a severe stroke, which left him with defective vision. His first book *A First Zen Reader*, was published in 1960, followed by over thirty others, some being translations from ancient Japanese treatises on Zen, others on yoga, judo, golf (his handicap was six), chivalry, and shogi (Japanese chess in which he reached professional standard). A translation from Sanskrit of a newly discovered commentary by the great Indian philosopher Sankara (*c.*AD 700) occupied him for about seventeen years. Other works were in Japanese, along with hundreds of articles. For some works, such as

The Old Zen Master (2000), he drew on both his own experiences and stories from Christianity, Judaism, Islam, Hinduism, and Buddhism, as well as Japanese and other sources such as judo, using parables in a masterly fashion. He lectured widely, regularly at the Buddhism Society (which recorded many of his talks on tape) and to theosophical groups. In 1984 he was awarded the order of the Sacred Treasure by the emperor of Japan for his contribution to Anglo-Japanese relationships.

On 2 August 2000, nearly blind, Leggett died in St Mary's Hospital, Praed Street, London, from a stroke and septicaemia. He had never married. He was cremated on 11 August 2000 at Mortlake crematorium, Richmond, and his ashes were later scattered on the River Thames by the Royal Botanical Gardens, Kew. RICHARD BOWEN

Sources priv. coll., Leggett collection • R. Bowen, *A history of British judo* [forthcoming] • R. Bowen, 'Trevor Leggett', *Britain and Japan: biographical portraits*, ed. H. Cortazzi, 4 (2002) • *The Times* (16 Aug 2000) • *Daily Telegraph* (11 Aug 2000) • www.kanosociety.org/trevor_leggett.htm, 20 Feb 2002 • www.leggett.co.uk

Archives Trevor Leggett Adhyatma Yoga Trust | priv. coll. | SOUND Buddhist Society, 58 Eccleston Square, London

Likenesses B. Hardy, three photographs, 1949, Hult. Arch. • photographs, repro. in www.kanosociety.org/trevor_leggett.htm

Wealth at death £270,649—gross; £267,693—net: probate, 18 Jan 2001, *CGPLA Eng. & Wales*

Legh, Alexander (*c*.1435–1504?), administrator and diplomat, came from Caragill, Aston Moor, in Cumberland. Educated at Eton College (1445–50) and King's College, Cambridge (from January 1451), he graduated MA in 1457–8. Appointed warden of Freckenham chantry, Kent, in February 1462, and then rector of Fen Ditton, Cambridgeshire, in May 1468 (an appointment that he resigned in April 1473), Legh entered royal service as canon of St George's Chapel, Windsor Castle, in November 1469.

In September 1470 Alexander Carlile, serjeant of the minstrels, and Legh, king's chaplain, warned Edward IV of the defection of John Neville, Marquess Montagu, to Henry VI, so enabling Edward to escape to Flanders. When Edward regained the throne in 1471 Legh was rewarded with numerous ecclesiastical benefices, including prebends of York, Exeter, Rochester, Ripon, and St Stephen's, Westminster, the mastership of Sherburn Hospital, Durham, and the rectory of Spofforth, Yorkshire. Royal almoner by *c*.1474, he was a member of the king's council by 1477–8.

During the 1470s Legh often acted as a diplomat—something for which his training in canon law at Cambridge would have been a useful preparation, as it was for other men who served as ambassadors. He carried Edward IV's ratification of the treaty of Utrecht with the Hanse to Bruges in July 1474, and he was particularly active as an envoy to Scotland between 1475 and 1480. Praised by James III for his 'grete prudence, lawte and diligence', this 'traist clerk and counsaloure' (PRO, E 39/102/28) conveyed private messages between James and Edward IV, paid the instalments of Princess Cecily's dowry to the Scots each February from 1475 to 1479, in St Giles's Church, Edinburgh, and helped to resolve naval and border grievances. Legh's embassy of March–April 1475 helped preserve Anglo-Scottish peace in the period leading up to Edward's expedition to France. James III used Legh to propose additional Anglo-Scottish marriage alliances between his brother the duke of Albany and Margaret of Burgundy, and between George, duke of Clarence, and his own sister Margaret, while in 1480 Edward IV sent Legh to Edinburgh with an ultimatum calculated to undermine the existing Anglo-Scottish accord.

After the ensuing war, on 24 August 1482 Legh became controller of the newly recaptured Berwick, receiving £283 to repair the town and castle. Chamberlain, customer, and supervisor of works at Berwick for Richard III, in December 1483 he was also appointed one of the surveyors of the walls and bridge at Newcastle upon Tyne. He was present in Nottingham Castle in September 1484, at a reception for Scottish envoys, and helped to negotiate an Anglo-Scottish truce.

Under Henry VII, however, perhaps due to ill health, perhaps to his Yorkist links, Legh slipped into relative obscurity, though he retained many clerical positions. He had suffered an 'infirmite' in early 1477 (delaying his journey to Scotland from February to April), his health deteriorated *c*.1491, and an apparent stroke in 1499 led to the appointment of a coadjutator at Sherburn and also at Houghton-le-Spring, where he had become rector in 1490. Apparently resident in Durham during a dispute with Sir Robert Plumpton over the tithes due to Spofforth rectory (*c*.1490–1494), Legh was chancellor of the bishop of Durham (1490–91), and assisted in border negotiations with the Scots in May 1491. He was awarded annuities amounting to £81 6*s*. 8*d*. from three of his benefices and was still alive on 11 December 1503, but probably died soon afterwards. DAVID DUNLOP

Sources Emden, *Cam.* • Cooper, *Ath. Cantab.*, 1.520 • [J. T. Fowler], ed., *Acts of the chapter of the collegiate church of SS. Peter and Wilfrid, Ripon, AD 1452 to AD 1506*, SurtS, 64 (1875) • [J. T. Fowler], ed., *Memorials of the church of SS Peter and Wilfrid, Ripon*, 2, SurtS, 78 (1886), 189 • M. P. Howden, ed., *The register of Richard Fox, lord bishop of Durham, 1494–1501*, SurtS, 147 (1932) • *CPR, 1467–1509* • *CClR, 1468–509* • *CDS*, vol. 4 • PRO, exchequer Scots documents, E 39 • D. Dunlop, 'The "redresses and reparacons of attemptates": Alexander Legh's instructions from Edward IV, March–April 1475', *Historical Research*, 63 (1990), 340–53 [a critical edition of BL, Cotton MS Vespasian C.xvi, fols. 121–6] • *RotS*, vol. 2 • Rymer, *Foedera*, 3rd edn, vol. 5 • R. Horrox, ed., *BL Harleian MS 433* (1979–83), vols. 1, 2, 4 • C. L. Scofield, *The life and reign of Edward the Fourth*, 2 (1923) • T. Stapleton, ed., *Plumpton correspondence*, CS, 4 (1839), 52, 105–6

Archives BL, Cotton MS Vespasian C.xvi, fols. 121–6 • PRO, E 39/96/21; E 39/102/23; E 39/102/25; E 39/55; E 39/56; E 39/102/28; E 39/60; E 39/102/29, 30, 31

Wealth at death annual pensions of £8, 20 marks, and £60 from Monkton, Spofforth, and Houghton-le-Spring, respectively: Howden, ed., *Register of Richard Fox*, 144–8; Fowler, ed., *Acts of chapter*, 298–9

Legh [Leigh], **Gerard** (*d.* 1563), heraldic writer, was the son of Henry Legh, draper, of Fleet Street, London, and his first wife, Isabel Cailis or Callis. Born in London, he was educated at the expense of Robert Wroth of Durants in Enfield, Middlesex, and Richard Goodrich was also a benefactor; both men were distinguished lawyers. Although

Legh is said by Wood, and later by Thomas Moule, to have studied at Oxford, this may well be incorrect. It appears that he was apprenticed to his father and joined the Drapers' Company. This association was strained when Legh apparently took the part of the government rather than the city in some political question. Subsequently he became a member of the Inner Temple. He travelled in France, and was planning a journey to Venice the year before his death. He died of plague on 13 October 1563, and was buried on the 15th at St Dunstan-in-the-West, where a wall monument was erected to his memory. He left a widow, Alice, and four daughters. His will conventionally disposes of his goods in three equal parts, for his wife, for his daughters, and for other bequests, including 20s. left to 'Vaer and the crew of myrthe … to be usedd as they shall thynke goodd, soe yt be in potatyon and locutyon' (*Accedens*, 1863, 16). There were also legacies that hint at important connections: a book to Sir William Cecil and a clock to Sir Edward Saunders, chief baron of the exchequer. He also left money to the poor of St Dunstan's parish.

Legh's only published work was *The Accedens of Armory* (London, 1562; reprinted 1568, 1576, 1591, 1597, and 1612, the last supposedly 'newly corrected and augmented', though the work was in fact ineptly done). The prefatory address is by Richard Argall of the Inner Temple, who was himself remembered in Legh's will, and Legh's epistle preceding it is addressed 'To the honorable assemble of gentlemen in the Innes of Court and Chauncery' (Legh). The book is mainly a dialogue between 'Gerarde the Herehaught and Legh the Caligat Knight' (ibid.). The *Accedens* has been dismissed as 'a medley of irrelevant learning', and it is true that Legh was more interested in symbolism than was required for a simple description of blazon. Thus Woodcock and Robinson understandably find his suggestions for considering the physiognomy of the grantee of a coat of arms among the 'wilder advice' given by early modern heraldists. Yet Dennys, who also finds some of Legh 'complex', argues that such colour symbolism was clearly in the tradition of medieval heraldry. His book's popularity suggests that Legh's discussions of heraldic symbolism, as well as his linking of chivalry to virtue and heraldry to fable, was admirably suited to Tudor England. Certainly it seems to have been particularly well adapted to the class-conscious claims of the gentry, whose obsession with pedigrees and coats of arms were almost as much a reaction to social mobility as an anachronistic longing for chivalry. It may also have appealed to readers among those same 'upstarts' who, despite the discouragement of their social superiors, found armoury a useful adjunct to their claims to gentle status.

Legh's learning is evident if idiosyncratic; he cites not only classical authors but also Chaucer and other medieval authorities, even giving a usually overlooked version of the Lear story. The book's plate of the fictitious panther herald (fol. 228) is thought to represent Legh himself, and the book has numerous illustrations of coats of arms, including full achievements for several contemporaries. The original manuscript of the *Accedens* is now in the College of Arms. J. F. R. DAY

Sources G. Legh, *The accedens of armory* (1582) • T. Moule, *Bibliotheca heraldica Magnae Britanniae* (privately printed, London, 1822) • *DNB* • T. Woodcock and J. M. Robinson, *The Oxford guide to heraldry* (1990) • R. Dennys, *The heraldic imagination* (1975) • A. R. Wagner, *The records and collections of the College of Arms* (1952) • Wood, *Ath. Oxon.*, new edn, 1.428 • '*The accedens of armory* by Gerard Legh, 1562', *Herald and Genealogist*, 1 (1863), 42–68, 97–118, 268–72 • F. Heal and C. Holmes, *The gentry in England and Wales, 1500–1700* (1994)

Legh, Peter (1669–1744). *See under* Legh, Richard (1634–1687).

Legh, Richard (1634–1687), politician, was born on 7 May 1634, the second but first surviving son of Thomas Legh DD (1593/4–1639), and his wife, Lettice (1610–1648), daughter of Sir George Calverley, of Lea, Cheshire. Legh's father was the rector of Walton on the Hill and Sefton in Lancashire until his death on 27 May 1639. The death of his cousin Peter Legh on 2 February 1642, following a duel, left his childless uncle Francis heir to Lyme. When Francis died on 2 February 1643 Legh inherited the Lyme estates. Legh was educated at Winwick grammar school, where the presbyterian rector, Charles Herle, was a trustee of his uncle Francis's will. On 18 June 1649 Legh was admitted to St John's College, Cambridge, and on 23 May 1653 he entered Gray's Inn.

Almost as soon as Legh came of age he was embroiled in county politics. The elections to the second protectorate parliament in 1656 saw Legh elected for Cheshire as part of a slate of gentry candidates agreed to by the new major-general, Tobias Bridge, because it kept the republican John Bradshaw out of the Commons. He was returned again for Cheshire in 1659. He was imprisoned in York in May 1659, and hence he avoided involvement in Sir George Booth's royalist uprising.

In the elections for the Convention of 1660 Legh supported the return of Booth for Cheshire and came in himself for the borough of Newton in Lancashire, where his family owned the dominant interest, Legh having strengthened it with the purchase of the barony of Newton for £3500 in 1660. He was licensed on 31 December 1660 to marry Elizabeth (1642–1728), daughter of Sir Thomas Chicheley of Wimpole, Cambridgeshire. The marriage took place on 1 January 1661. They had six sons and seven daughters, one son and two daughters dying young. Legh's estate was calculated at £4500 p.a. when he was considered for the new order of knights of the Royal Oak, but an account book for 1662–3 suggests a rental of £2678 per annum. He was an inactive member of parliament, although generally a court loyalist, whom Anthony Ashley Cooper, first earl of Shaftesbury, labelled 'doubly vile' in 1677–8. He retired from parliament in 1679, but returned members of his extended family to the Exclusion parliaments. Legh was active in local affairs in the wake of the Rye House plot and Monmouth's rebellion. Following the accession of James II he returned his son, Peter [*see below*], to parliament in 1685. Legh died at Lyme on 31 August 1687, and was buried on 6 September at

Winwick. An inventory of the contents of the house at Lyme and its farm and stables totalled £4179 14*s.* 4*d.* His widow was buried at Winwick on 4 June 1728.

Peter Legh (1669–1744), politician and nonjuror, was born on 22 August 1669, the fourth child and the first son of Richard Legh and Elizabeth Chicheley. He was educated privately at home, but as a child he was entered at Gray's Inn, on 2 February 1673. Legh survived an attack of smallpox in autumn 1683. His father ensured Legh's election to parliament for Newton in 1685, his maternal uncle, Sir John Chicheley, acting as chaperon for his first appearance in the chamber. His youth was remarked upon, and a motion made for the expulsion of minors, but no action was taken possibly because the earl of Plymouth's son, Thomas Windsor, looked even younger.

Legh was licensed on 21 December 1686 to marry Frances (1670–1728), daughter of Piers Legh (*d.* 1671) of Bruche, Poulton, Lancashire, and his second wife, Abigail, and the heir of her half-brother, also Piers Legh, who had died in 1685. They had one son, who died in 1725, although Legh assumed responsibility for the upbringing of his own younger siblings. Legh was able to plead his youth in October 1687 when declining to serve as a deputy lieutenant under the Roman Catholic lord lieutenant, Caryll Molyneaux, third Viscount Molyneaux. Legh remained passive at the revolution in 1688, declining to support the adherents of the prince of Orange. He never stood for parliament again, and he refused the oaths to William and Mary. This political stance brought with it problems, such as the threat of double taxation and the possibility that the government would treat him as disloyal. In March 1694 he lost his place in the Lancashire commission of the peace. On 17 July 1694 Legh was arrested for treason in what was known as the Lancashire plot, following allegations by an informer, John Lunt. He was kept prisoner in Chester Castle until the end of August before being transferred to London, questioned by the secretary of state, Charles Talbot, duke of Shrewsbury, and sent to the Tower. He was then sent back to Chester where his trial collapsed for lack of evidence, Lunt and his accomplices having been discredited and no witnesses appearing against him on 24 October 1694. After this escape Legh made a deal with the only challenger to his electoral dominance at Newton, Thomas Brotherton, who had assisted his defence at his trial, and after that Legh was able to return without challenge two MPs for the remainder of his life.

Legh kept a low political profile but he was again incarcerated in Chester following the discovery of the assassination plot in 1696. Following the accession of Queen Anne, Legh returned to the commission of the peace, and in 1708 there was a concerted effort to persuade him to take the oaths, Sir William Dawes, bishop of Chester, holding several meetings with Legh. Legh was present at the decisive vote at the meeting of the group of Jacobite sympathizers known as the Cheshire Club which decided not to join the northern English part of the Jacobite rising of 1715, following which the members ordered their portraits to be painted to commemorate the wisdom of their decision. However, with several brothers implicated in the rebellion Legh found himself taken into custody again in September 1715, and in 1722 he felt it prudent to seek out the protection of Simon, first Viscount Harcourt.

Legh's wife died on 17 February 1728, and was buried at Winwick. In the absence of children Legh settled his estates on his nephews, the children of his deceased brother Thomas. Legh died in January 1744, being buried on 16 January at Winwick. STUART HANDLEY

Sources E. Legh, Baroness Newton, *Lyme letters, 1660–1760* (1925) · E. Legh, Baroness Newton, *The house of Lyme from its foundation to the end of the eighteenth century* (1917) · I. Cassidy, 'Legh, Peter', HoP, *Commons, 1660–90* · E. Baines and W. R. Whatton, *The history of the county palatine and duchy of Lancaster*, new edn, ed. J. Croston and others, 4 (1891), 388–9 · I. Cassidy and M. W. Helms, 'Legh, Richard', HoP, *Commons, 1660–90* · W. Beaumont, *A history of the house of Lyme* (1876), 143–84 · J. S. Morrill, *Cheshire, 1630–1660: county government and society during the English revolution* (1974), 287–95 · P. J. Pinckney, 'The Cheshire election of 1656', *Bulletin of the John Rylands Library*, 49 (1966–7), 387–426 · *The diary of Henry Prescott, LLB, deputy registrar of Chester diocese*, ed. J. Addy and others, 3 vols., Lancashire and Cheshire RS, 127, 132–3 (1987–97), vol. 2, pp. 127, 132–3 · *The manuscripts of Lord Kenyon*, HMC, 35 (1894) · JRL, Legh of Lyme MSS · L. K. J. Glassey, *Politics and the appointment of the justices of the peace, 1675–1720* (1979) · J. Wilford, *Memorials and characters together with the lives of divers eminent and worthy persons* (1741), 122–6 · Foster, *Alum. Oxon.* · J. L. Chester and J. Foster, eds., *London marriage licences, 1521–1869* (1887), 831

Archives JRL, papers | NRA, priv. coll., letters to his wife

Likenesses P. Lely, portrait, 1660, repro. in Legh, *House of Lyme*, 218–19 · Cooper, miniature, *c.*1670, repro. in Legh, *House of Lyme*, 266–7 · G. Kneller, portrait, 1702 (Peter Legh), repro. in Legh, *The house of Lyme*, 356–7

Wealth at death see inventory, incl. house, farm, stables, £4179 14*s.* 4*d.*; account book for 1662–3 suggests £2678 p.a.

Legh, Sir Thomas (*d.* **1545**), diplomat and ecclesiastical administrator, appears to have originated from Cumberland; little is known of his family background other than that his father, John, and brother William farmed near Calder. The family probably were a cadet branch of the Leghs of Issal. He married Joan Cotton (*d.* 1556/7), who after his death married Sir Thomas Chaloner; Legh's only child, Katherine, married James Blount, sixth Lord Mountjoy, in 1558. His cousin Rowland Lee became bishop of Coventry and Lichfield. Thomas was educated at Cambridge, perhaps at St Nicholas's Hostel or St Michael's Hostel, and proceeded BCL in 1527 and DCL in 1531. He was perhaps originally destined for the priesthood, as a Thomas Legh is noted as resigning the canonry of St Sepulchre's Chapel, York, in April 1531. He was admitted to the College of Advocates in the court of arches on 7 October 1531.

In the period December 1532 to March 1533 Legh was appointed by King Henry VIII as ambassador to Denmark; Chapuys considered him to be a 'doctor of low quality for this mission' (*LP Henry VIII*, vol. 6, no. 19). Legh cited Katherine of Aragon to appear at Dunstable for Cranmer's inquiry into the validity of her marriage to Henry, and was present at the pronouncement at Lambeth on 28 May 1533. Recommended by his cousin Rowland Lee to Thomas Cromwell, during the rest of 1533 he was involved in monastic business including the election of a new abbot of Rievaulx. That autumn 'young Dr Legh' was again to be sent to Denmark, but by October the mission had been cancelled. Instead, in February 1534, Legh was sent as an ambassador to Lübeck to establish the extent of common religious ground and a basis for an alliance. He visited Hamburg and negotiated with representatives of Bremen before returning home in June; he maintained involvement in the affairs of Denmark and Hamburg during early 1535.

In June 1535 Legh was interrogating a servant of Bishop John Fisher, before the latter's trial. At this time Richard Layton wrote to Cromwell requesting that both Legh and himself should be given commissions for visiting monastic houses in the north, as both had friends a dozen miles from every religious house there. It was, however, probably in the midlands that Legh began his role as commissioner in the royal visitation of 1535–6; he is first identified as a monastic visitor, accompanied by his registrar John ap Rice, at Worcester Priory. During August and September Legh visited religious houses in the Worcester, Salisbury, Bath and Wells, and Winchester dioceses. At this stage Legh's abrasive personality can be identified in his complaint that Layton was not implementing the tight injunctions specified for each religious house. Even when later given discretion over some aspects of the injunctions by Cromwell, Legh decided to 'release none' and included among his reasons 'it might advantage Cromwell to gratify them' (*LP Henry VIII*, vol. 9, no. 265). It is evident that Legh assisted in the organization of the visitation. His letter with ap Rice to Cromwell from Winteney on 24 September 1535 reveals that they had devised the restrictions on the bishops' diocesan powers that were in place during the visitation.

At the end of September 1535 Legh began his tour of the London, Ely, parts of Lincoln, and Norwich dioceses. In October he was strongly criticized by Cromwell for his behaviour during the visitation. In letters to Cromwell, ap Rice accused Legh of being 'too insolent and pompatique' in his dealings with the religious and he 'handleth the fathers where he cometh very roughly', he adopted a 'satrapike countenance', his fees were excessive, and 'he hath twelve men waiting on him in a livery' (*LP Henry VIII*, vol. 9, no. 622). Legh stridently, but not convincingly, denied these accusations, ending his own letter to Cromwell 'Veritas Liberabit' (*LP Henry VIII*, vol. 9, no. 621). In December he joined Layton for the visitation of York province, the last major section of the royal visitation. In the period up to the end of February 1536 they investigated over 120 religious houses and secular colleges. Their 'comperta' from this visitation are the basic information used to produce the famous document, the 'Compendium compertorum' (PRO, SP 1/102, fols. 91–110), which has been unfairly represented by many historians as evidence for the falseness of the commissioners.

The Pilgrimage of Grace, in late 1536, sought 'condyne punishment for their extortions in their tyme of visitation', reflecting the brusque treatment the religious had received from Legh and Layton (Fletcher and MacCulloch, 136). The northern risings of 1536–7 evidence the widespread hatred for Legh: in the Lincolnshire rebellion his cook was hanged; and in January the commons arrested his servant at Muncaster, Cumberland, and the 'country rose' (*LP Henry VIII*, vol. 11, no. 714). Legh is apparently noted in the last verse of the Sawley ballad where the pilgrims seek 'God thym amend' (PRO, SP 1/108, fol. 217*r*). He examined prisoners involved in the rebellion, including Robert Aske. Aske, in his last extant letter, wrote to 'good Mr Doctor' asking him to send some money and clothes (*LP Henry VIII*, vol. 12/1, no. 1175 (3)).

In March 1537, Legh's attempts (eventually successful) to obtain the mastership of Burton Lazer drew the response from the duke of Norfolk 'what a pity it were that such a vicious man should have the governance of that honest house' (*LP Henry VIII*, vol. 12/1, no. 629). In August, Legh had a commission to visit the archdeaconries of Coventry, Stafford, Derby, and part of Cheshire. In January 1538, on Cromwell's instructions, he implemented the 'voluntary' surrender of Muchelney Abbey, Somerset, at which he is noted as a 'Master of Chancery'. He then travelled north, accepting the surrender of Holm Coltram Abbey in March before visiting the York province. In May he oversaw the surrender of Woburn Abbey and examined the abbot on his papal sympathies. Between 1538 and 1540 Legh assisted at over sixty-nine monastic dissolutions, accelerating their surrender and arranging pensions for the redundant religious—the last he attended was on 26 January 1540 at Wenlock. In 1539 he had been present at the defacing of St Cuthbert's shrine, finding the saint 'lying whole' and uncorrupted.

Legh profited handsomely from being a visitor, acquiring advowsons, leases, and rewards from religious houses. However, his biggest gains occurred after the monastic suppressions. He obtained the lease of house, site, and lands at Calder, St Bees, Croxton (for a short time), St Oswald's, Guisborough, and Halliwell, among others. In 1542 he was described as one of the 'commissioners in the borders' and was responsible for transporting £2000 to the treasurer of the borders, less £40 to cover his own costs. On 11 May 1544, after the burning of Leith, he was knighted by the earl of Hertford, who commended Legh to the king.

Legh played a key part in protecting Archbishop Cranmer in the prebendaries' plot of 1543. Foxe states that the king sent to York for Dr Legh, giving him a ring to emphasize his role as the monarch's representative. Legh instituted surprise raids 'all in one moment' on enemies of Cranmer, obtaining incriminating evidence and saving the archbishop from being confirmed as 'the greatest heretic in Kent' (Nichols, *Narrative*, 252–3). In May 1545 he took the surrender of Christ Church Cathedral and King Henry VIII College at Oxford. He had been returned as MP for Wilton in January, and may have been an MP on earlier occasions. He fell so ill in 1545 that by August the earl of Hertford mistakenly reported him dead. His actual death occurred on 25 November 1545 and he was buried at St Leonard, Shoreditch. The greater part of Legh's estates were willed to his brother William's eldest son, also called Thomas. The supervisors of his will included 'my especial good lord' the archbishop of Canterbury and Sir Richard Rich, chancellor of the court of augmentations.

There survives a description and sketch of a monumental brass plate on Legh's tomb, part of which read:

> Great was his wisdom, and greater was his wit
> His usage comely, with no sad change dismayed.
> (Ellis, 53–4)

In contrast, correspondence reveals Legh as a man difficult to handle, who regularly caused irritation to Thomas Cromwell. It is evident, however, that Legh's brusque character helped make him effective and valuable in completing commissions for Cromwell and the king.

ANTHONY N. SHAW

Sources PRO, SP 1/70–208 • *LP Henry VIII*, vols. 5–21, *addenda* • HoP, *Commons*, 1509–58, 2.513–15 • R. P. Littledale, 'Some notes on the Patricksons of Ennerdale', *Transactions of the Cumberland and Westmorland Antiquarian and Archaeological Society*, new ser., 25 (1924–5), 128–243, esp. 131 • *The diary of Henry Machyn, citizen and merchant-taylor of London, from AD 1550 to AD 1563*, ed. J. G. Nichols, CS, 42 (1848), 123, 404 • will, PRO, PROB 11/30, fols. 348v–350r • Cooper, *Ath. Cantab.*, 1.87 • [C. Coote], *Sketches of the lives and characters of eminent English civilians, with an historical introduction relative to the College of Advocates* (1804), 29 • A. Fletcher and D. MacCulloch, *Tudor rebellions*, 4th edn (1997), 136 • [J. T. Fowler], ed., *Rites of Durham*, SurtS, 107 (1903), 102–3 • J. G. Nichols, ed., *Narratives of the days of the Reformation*, CS, old ser., 77 (1859), 252–3 • H. Ellis, *The history and antiquities of the parish of St Leonard, Shoreditch, and liberty of Norton Folgate* (1798), 53–4 • BL, Harley MS 6063, fol. 15

Archives BL, Cotton MS Cleopatra E.iv • BL, Cotton MS Titus B.i • BL, Harley MS 6148, 604 • PRO, SP 1

Likenesses effigy on a brass plate, repro. in Ellis, *History and antiquity of the parish of St Leonard's*

Wealth at death house and lands at Hageston, Middlesex; lease of Haliwell Priory and lands; lease of St Bees, Cumberland; lease of manor, house, and lands at Calder, Cumberland; property at Cambridge; house at St Oswald's Priory, Yorkshire; various advowsons: will, PRO, PROB 11/30, fols. 348v–350r

Legh, Thomas Wodehouse, second Baron Newton (1857–1942), politician, was born at Hillington, King's Lynn, Norfolk, on 18 March 1857, the eldest of the three sons and two daughters of William John Legh, first Baron Newton (1828–1898), and his wife, Emily Jane (*d.* 1901), daughter of the Ven. Charles Nourse Wodehouse, archdeacon of Norwich. The Legh family had held substantial property in the Cheshire area since the time of Agincourt, including the great country house, Lyme Park, at Disley, near Stockport. Legh attended Eton College from 1870 to 1874 where, in his own words, 'he did as little work as possible' to pass (Newton, 6). His parents withdrew him from the school and sent him travelling on an extended trip through Europe with a private tutor. In 1876 he entered Christ Church, Oxford, graduating in 1879 with a fourth class in modern history. The same year, largely through the influence of his mother's relatives lords Kimberley and Currie, he was accepted into the Foreign Office.

On 24 July 1880 Legh married Evelyn Caroline (*d.* 1931), daughter of a Cheshire landowner, William Bromley-Davenport. They had three daughters and two sons. In 1881 he was appointed as an attaché in Paris, where he served until 1886, and where his life was 'extremely pleasant and there had been just enough work to keep me from idleness' (Newton, 35). In August 1886 he successfully stood as Conservative candidate at the by-election for the Newton division of South-West Lancashire, vacated when the sitting MP, R. A. Cross, was created a peer. As an MP he 'served obscurely' (Southern, 834) until he succeeded to the peerage on the death of his father in December 1898.

On entering the House of Lords Newton quickly came to the conclusion that reform of the house was desperately required, largely, in his view, as a means of strengthening it as a bulwark against what he saw as the inevitable advance of socialism. He was also spurred on in his belief by his perception of the capacities of many of his fellow Conservative peers. They included 'pig-headed imbeciles … so grossly ignorant that they went into the wrong lobby' he wrote in his diary, and the rejection of the Education Bill of 1906 was 'a ridiculous exhibition of [a] majority consisting of ignoramuses' (Southern, 835). He introduced into the Lords in 1907 an (unsuccessful) bill proposing changes to the composition of the house, to make it consist of hereditary peers and life peers appointed by the government of the day.

Newton was also unsuccessful with a number of other measures he proposed in the Lords, including the removal of conscientious objection to vaccination, amendments to the betting laws, and the introduction of smoke abatement regulations and the twenty-four-hour clock. He helped found the National Service League after the demands of the Second South African War had seemed to show the existing system of voluntary enlistment to be inadequate for Britain's military needs.

But, as Southern suggests, 'Newton's principal interest for the historian … lies in his role in securing the Parliament Act of 1911' (Southern, 835). This act, designed to remove from the upper house the power of absolute veto over bills, was re-introduced by the Liberal government after it had fought the second 1910 election on the issue in December. Official Conservative policy was to abstain from the vote on the bill, because it was realized that if the bill was lost the Liberal prime minister, Asquith, would advise the king to create enough new peers to swamp the house. But a number of Conservatives—the 'diehards'—were determined to vote against the bill. The Conservative leadership needed some of their followers in the House of Lords to support the bill, but were politically unable to promote this publicly as the resentment created could have resulted in a larger vote against. Newton, with a prominence resulting from his long history of advocating Lords reform, was chosen as their 'stooge' (Southern, 837) in this plan. At Lord Lansdowne's request, Newton independently contacted a large number of Conservative peers, seeking their support for the bill. His diary entries indicate that he was successful in convincing twenty-six to side with the government. The final margin, on 10 August 1911, in favour of the bill was seventeen. Newton himself abstained, later commenting on the courage of those Conservatives who voted for the bill and suffered the opprobrium of others within the party, but, disappointed in the lack of leadership shown by the Conservative front bench, he decided his reputation would ultimately not 'be utilised to save their face' (Southern, 839).

In 1915 Newton was appointed paymaster-general in the Asquith coalition government, and was sworn of the privy council. From March 1916 until August 1919 he was an assistant under-secretary at the Foreign Office, with his responsibilities including negotiations regarding prisoners of war. He was very successful at this task, organizing numerous exchanges which resulted in the release of thousands of British prisoners by the Germans and the Turks. This work brought him, he said, 'for the first and the last time the sweets of popularity' (*The Times*, 23 March 1942, 6).

In 1919 Newton achieved a significant victory in parliament on the issue of the rights of former 'enemy aliens' in Britain. Under the terms of a new Aliens Restriction Bill, those who fell into this category (even without having been interned during the war) would have to prove why they should not be deported from the country. Newton, despite admitting his belief that Britain 'had been far too lax in the past in admitting swarms of undesirable aliens, who had given a great deal of trouble and had engaged in seditious activities' (Newton, 277), fought this provision in the Lords and sought to place the onus of proof in these cases back onto the government. After the bill had been sent back twice to the House of Commons, Newton's amendment was accepted, and he saw his victory as:

> a historic event. The occasions on which the Lords had defeated the Commons were few … It was a moral issue … the action of the House of Lords did more to enhance its position than anything which had occurred for a long time.

He regarded this episode as 'the most creditable incident' in his parliamentary career (Newton, 279).

Newton wrote two biographies, of Lord Lyons (1913) and of Lord Lansdowne (1929). He was widely travelled and spoke fluent French and German. With a quiet and modest manner, he was respected in parliamentary committees as a hard and conscientious worker, a reputation far different from the one he had gained in his school and university days. He was, with little recognition being given, a significant figure in the parliamentary struggles of his time. In private life, despite his wealth he lived unostentatiously and his habits were frugal. He died at his home at 75 Eaton Square, London, on 21 March 1942, and after cremation his ashes were interred at St Mary's Church, Disley, on 26 March. MARC BRODIE

Sources *The Times* (23 March 1942) • D. Southern, 'Lord Newton, the conservative peers and the Parliament Act of 1911', *EngHR*, 96 (1981), 834–40 • Lord Newton [T. W. Legh], *Retrospection* (1941) • J. Turner, *British politics and the Great War: coalition and conflict, 1915–1918* (1992) • *The letters of Arthur Balfour and Lady Elcho, 1885–1917*, ed. J. Ridley and C. Percy (1992) • Burke, *Peerage* • *The Eton register*, 4 (privately printed, Eton, 1907) • *CGPLA Eng. & Wales* (1943)

Archives NRA, priv. coll., diaries | Bodl. Oxf., corresp. with Sir H. Rumbold • CUL, corresp. with Lord Hardinge and minutes • HLRO, corresp. with John St Loe Strachey • U. Leeds, Brotherton L., letters to E. Gosse

Likenesses A. T. Nowell, oils, *c.*1908, Lyme Park, Cheshire • Spy [L. Ward], caricature, NPG; repro. in *VF* (14 Oct 1908) • W. Stoneman, photographs, NPG • photograph, repro. in *The Times*, 6

Wealth at death £85,408 1*s.* 9*d.*: probate, save and except settled land, 24 Aug 1942, *CGPLA Eng. & Wales* • £191,401 12*s.* 1*d.*: further grant, limited to settled land, 11 May 1943, *CGPLA Eng. & Wales*

Le Grand, Antoine (1627/8–1699), Franciscan friar and philosopher, was born in the neighbourhood of Douai, in the Spanish Netherlands. Nothing is known of his life until he entered the English province of the Franciscan Recollects at St Bonaventure's, Douai, in 1647; he took his vows in 1648. Ordained priest in 1653, he was appointed a lector in philosophy in 1655. In the following year he was appointed to preach and hear confessions, and was sent to teach philosophy in London, where it seems that his courses were followed by sons of the Roman Catholic gentry. How long this school of philosophy continued is not known, but Le Grand produced a series of writings on philosophy whose influence and circulation went far beyond his own circle.

Le Grand early wrote two works in French. The first, *Le sage des stoïques, ou, L'homme sans passions, selon les sentiments de Sénèque* (The Hague, 1662), denounced any concession to one's feelings and was dedicated, inappropriately perhaps, to King Charles II. The second was *L'épicure spirituel, ou, L'empire de la volupté sur les vertus* (Douai, 1669), in which Le Grand retracted some of his earlier criticisms of Epicurus, interpreting him in a way which brought him close to Stoicism. But it is as an ardent Cartesian that Le Grand was best known and most influential. Known as the Abbreviator, he summarized Descartes's philosophy in a series of books which were designed for the use of students. In 1671 he published in London *Philosophia veterum e mente Renati Descartes, more scholastico breviter digesta* and the next year, encouraged by its favourable reception, particularly at Cambridge, expanded it into *Institutio philosophiae secundum principia Renati Descartes, nova methodo adornata et explicata, ad usum juventutis academicae* (1672), printed by J. Martyn, printer to the Royal Society. This was followed by further works in which he set out observations of natural phenomena accounted for in accordance with Cartesian principles, and defended the Cartesian theory that animals are mere machines. These three works were later translated into English under the auspices of Richard Blome and published as *An Entire Body of Philosophy According to the Principles of the Famous Renate Descartes* (1694), but Le Grand was not entirely happy with this translation, writing that so much had been added, omitted, and changed by the editor that he did not know whether he ought to acknowledge it as his own.

Le Grand also defended Descartes in several controversies. He defended the Cartesian doubt, the distinction of mind and body, and the argument from the idea of God to his real existence against the criticism of Samuel Parker in *Apologia pro Renato Descartes, contra Samuelem Parkerum* (1679), and in his last years became involved in an acrimonious controversy with the Roman Catholic priest John Sergeant, who had attacked the whole 'way of ideas' as seen in Descartes, Malebranche, and Locke in his *Method to Science* (1696) and *Solid Philosophy Asserted* (1697). Le Grand replied with *Dissertatio de ratione cognoscendi, et appendix de mutatione formali* (1698). Sergeant returned to the attack, but Le Grand died before he could reply again.

Within the Franciscan order Le Grand held a succession of offices. The English province held chapters every three years, with occasional intermediate chapters, and these chapters were responsible for appointing friars to positions within the province, normally for three-year periods. In 1671 Le Grand was appointed guardian of London, with responsibility for friars working in that area. In 1674, relinquishing that position, he was elected a definitor, adviser to the minister provincial. He alternated between these two posts from 1671 until 1690. In 1691, as the minister provincial was too ill to preside, Le Grand was unanimously chosen by the definitors to chair the intermediate chapter. In 1695 he acted as secretary of the chapter, chairman of the definitors' meeting, and guardian of Oxford. He was living at this time at Tusmore in Oxfordshire as chaplain to Mr Henry Fermor and tutor to his sons. In 1698 Le Grand was elected minister provincial and next year carried out a visitation of English Franciscan houses on the continent. A feature of his time as provincial was the requirement that lectors in philosophy at Douai should spend six months teaching their students mathematics at the conclusion of their philosophy course. After returning from Bruges to London, Le Grand died there of apoplexy on 26 July 1699, aged seventy-one.

Le Grand, whose books were recommended for study at Oxford and Cambridge, was an important link in the transmission of Cartesian ideas and their popularization in England. He is also interesting as showing that a Roman Catholic priest could occupy an influential position in English intellectual life even at a time when persecution was by no means over. His life and work link the two worlds of Catholic recusancy and the new philosophy of the later seventeenth century. RICHARD ACWORTH

Sources minutes of chapter meetings of the English Province of the Order of Friars Minor (Recollect), St Antony's Friary, Forest Gate, London, Archives of the English Province OFM • A. Le Grand, preface, *Institutio philosophiae secundum principia Renati Descartes* (1672) • A. Le Grand, *Dissertatio de ratione cognoscendi* (1698), preface • 'The necrology of the English Franciscans', *The English Franciscan nuns, 1619–1621, and the friars minor of the same province, 1618–1761*, ed. R. Trappes-Lomax, Catholic RS, 24 (1922) • D. Garber and M. Ayers, eds., *The Cambridge history of seventeenth-century philosophy*, 2 vols. (1998) • C. Dodd [H. Tootell], *The church history of England, from the year 1500, to the year 1688*, 3 (1742) • *Biographia universalis*, suppl. 71 (Paris, 1842) [incl. complete bibliography of Le Grand's writings] • *DNB* • A. Pyle, ed., *The dictionary of seventeenth-century British philosophers* (2001) • J. Gascoigne, *Cambridge in the age of the Enlightenment* (1989), 55 • *Hist. U. Oxf.* 4: *17th-cent. Oxf.*, 410 • J. McLoughlin, 'Antony Le Grand', *The Franciscan* (Nov 1955), 4–5

Archives St Antony's Friary, Forest Gate, London, Archives of the English Province of the Order of Friars Minor, MS minutes of chapter meetings of the English Province of the Order of Friars Minor (Recollect)

Likenesses W. Faithorne, line engraving, NPG

Legrew, James (1803–1857), sculptor, was born in 1803 at Caterham, Surrey, and baptized there on 2 November that year, the son of the rector, James Legrew (1769–1856), and his wife, Elizabeth Harrison. He was descended from Huguenot refugees. Legrew quickly became proficient in ancient and modern languages, and showed considerable promise as a child in animal modelling. He went on to study sculpture under Sir Francis Chantrey (*c*.1821–1830) and in 1822 he received the silver palette from the Society of Arts. He also enrolled in April 1822 as a student at the Royal Academy Schools where he gained the silver medal in 1824 and in 1829 won the gold medal for *Cassandra Dragged from the Altar of Minerva* which he exhibited at the Royal Academy in 1830. Over the next twenty-seven years he was a frequent exhibitor, contributing to the academy some thirty pieces, including royal and ecclesiastical portrait commissions, alongside two works at the British Institution and five at the Suffolk Street Gallery of the Society of British Artists.

Legrew travelled extensively in Italy in the early 1840s, working for some time in Rome before returning to London where he resided first in Ebury Street, Pimlico, and then at St Alban's Road, Kensington. In 1844 he sent to the Westminster Hall competition two of his most famous works, *The Last Prayer of Ajax* and *Milton Dictating to his Daughters*. In the same period Legrew also executed some monumental work in London, Ely, and Sussex churches and cathedrals. Known for his by turns heroic and pathetic neo-classical figures drawn from the Bible and classical mythology, Legrew's work included *Cupid* (1839; Birmingham Art Society), and groups including *Samson Breaking his Bonds* (1843; formerly at Crystal Palace) and *The Murder of the Innocents* which he sent to the Great Exhibition. He was also a writer on sculpture; he wrote a short life of Flaxman, and *A Few Remarks on the Sculpture of the Nations Referred to in the Old Testament* (1845). After the death of his father in 1856 Legrew became depressed and he committed suicide at his Kensington home on 15 September 1857. He was unmarried. During his lifetime Legrew's work was felt to be 'finely proportioned' but 'too smooth' and the poses of his figures 'liable to question' (*Literary Gazette*, cited in Gunnis, 237–8). By the 1950s, however, Rupert Gunnis argued that his work had never received the encouragement it deserved.

L. H. CUST, *rev.* JASON EDWARDS

Sources Redgrave, *Artists* • Allibone, *Dict.* • M. H. Grant, *A dictionary of British sculptors from the XIIIth century to the XXth century* (1953) • R. Gunnis, *Dictionary of British sculptors, 1660–1851* (1953); new edn (1968) • Boase, *Mod. Eng. biog.* • Graves, *Artists* • *The exhibition of the Royal Academy* (1826–57) [exhibition catalogues] • *IGI* • S. C. Hutchison, 'The Royal Academy Schools, 1768–1830', *Walpole Society*, 38 (1960–62), 123–91, esp. 174

Le Grice, Charles Valentine (1773–1858), writer, was born on 14 February 1773 in Bury St Edmunds, the eldest of eight children of Revd Charles Le Grice (1741–1792), incumbent of St James, Bury, and his wife, Sophia Anne Day (*d.* 1830). Valentine, named after his birth date, was admitted to Christ's Hospital, London, in 1781. There Val, as he was known, distinguished himself as a Grecian, or one of the select students who would be expected to go on to university, and was a friendly rival of his fellow Grecian Coleridge. In his Elia essay, 'Christ's Hospital five and thirty years ago', Charles Lamb, another bluecoat boy and friend, recollects the 'wit-combats' between Le Grice and Coleridge and in 'Grace before meat' remembers Le Grice's waggishness. In 1792 Le Grice entered Trinity College, Cambridge, where he continued his friendship with Coleridge who was at Jesus College. Before taking his BA in

1796 Le Grice was elected a scholar at Trinity and won a silver cup for declamation.

In the year he graduated Le Grice left for Cornwall to tutor William John Godolphin Nicholls of Trereife in Madron parish, near Penzance. Nicholls was the only son of Mary Ustick Nicholls (*d.* 1821), the wealthy widow of John William Nicholls. Widow and tutor were married on 16 May 1799, and shortly thereafter Le Grice was ordained. He became perpetual curate of St Mary's, Penzance, in 1806 and remained in that position until 1831. In 1805 he earned his Cambridge MA. On the death of his stepson in 1815, Le Grice inherited Trereife and its lands. In 1821 his wife died. Fond of travel, Le Grice also enjoyed his life in Cornwall as squire and parson. As a clergyman he occasionally felt the call to enter into controversy. In 1814, for instance, he preached against the 'danger' of Methodist revivalism, and in 1824 he published a challenge to the consistency of belief of a prominent Unitarian.

Among Le Grice's more ambitious secular publications were *The Tineum* (1794), a miscellany of prose and verse, some of it written at Christ's Hospital; *Analysis of Paley's Principles* (1796), designed for students preparing for examination; and his translation from the Greek of Longus's *Daphnis and Chloe* (1803). All were of sufficient interest to be listed in the 1816 *Biographical Dictionary of Living Authors*, along with his Cambridge prize declamation and some of his sermons. Several sonnets—'On Charles Lamb Leading his Sister to the Asylum', 'In Reminiscence of the Poet Coleridge', 'On my First and Only Visit to the Poet Wordsworth'—recall literary friends and acquaintances. 'The Genius of Chatterton', another sonnet, reflects Le Grice's considerable interest in Chatterton, on whose sister he once called. He contributed to the *Critical Review*, his reviews characterized, in Oscar Wellens's words, by 'uncompromising critical severity'. His many pieces in the *Gentleman's Magazine* include his 1834 'College reminiscences of Mr Coleridge', memorable for its description of Coleridge holding forth in his rooms to 'conversation-loving friends'.

Le Grice's friends and associates sometimes judged him severely. Coleridge in 1794, Lamb in 1796, Wordsworth and Robert Southey in 1807, all expressed contempt for Le Grice in letters to third parties. The remarks of Coleridge and Lamb are petty; those of Wordsworth and Southey contain more serious charges, that Le Grice, writing for the *Critical Review*, was giving vent to hatred of Coleridge by venomously attacking Coleridge and his friends. According to Wordsworth, Le Grice was a 'most malignant Spirit'; to Southey, Le Grice's mind was 'perverted & mischievous'. But Wellens, who finds no evidence that Le Grice hated Coleridge, argues that Wordsworth and Southey misunderstood Le Grice whose severe criticisms were rather an attempt to uphold traditional neoclassical standards against the new Romantic poetry. In later life, at any rate, Le Grice met on cordial terms with all four: with Coleridge in 1833 at Highgate and Trinity; with Lamb, also in 1833, in Edmonton; with Southey at Trereife in 1836; and with Wordsworth at Rydal Mount in 1841.

A rich man, Le Grice lived out his days in Cornwall. In March 1858 he wrote 'some account of myself', with particulars about his son Day Perry Le Grice and his grandson: 'I have a son in fine health nearly sixty years of age, and a grandson who is now at Oriel College, where his father was before him' (Hazlitt, 24). Le Grice refers to his own good health, notes his years as clergyman in Penzance, and speaks of his service and that of his son as magistrates. Nine months later Le Grice died at Trereife on Christmas eve 1858. After a funeral procession led by his tenants, he was buried in Madron.

W. P. Courtney, *rev.* John H. Schwarz

Sources E. Blunden, 'Coleridge's fellow Grecian', *Eibungaku Kenkyū* (1956), 47–81 · *The letters of Charles and Mary Lamb*, ed. E. W. Marrs, 3 vols. (1975–8), vol. 1, pp. xxxi–xxxii, 9–10 · O. Wellens, 'C. V. L.: Wordsworth's 'most malignant Spirit' …', *Elizabethan and modern studies: presented to professor Willem Schrickx on the occasion of his retirement*, ed. J. P. Vander Motten (Ghent, 1985), 309–15 · R. Madden, 'The old familiar faces', *C. Lamb Bulletin*, new ser., 6 (April 1974), 113–21 · H. Penneck, 'The Rev. C. Val. Le Grice', *GM*, 3rd ser., 4 (1858), 322–4 · W. C. Hazlitt, *The Lambs: their lives, their friends, and their correspondence* (1897), 23–4 · *DNB* · [J. Watkins and F. Shoberl], *A biographical dictionary of the living authors of Great Britain and Ireland* (1816) · S. T. Coleridge, letter of 11 Dec 1794, *Collected letters of Samuel Taylor Coleridge*, ed. E. L. Griggs, 1 (1956), 135 · letter, 12 July 1807, *The letters of William and Dorothy Wordsworth*, ed. E. de Selincourt, 2nd edn, 1: *The early years, 1787–1805*, rev. C. L. Shaver (1967), 134–5

Archives Cornwall RO, travel journals

Wealth at death £1500: administration with will, 14 Feb 1859, *CGPLA Eng. & Wales* · £7218 10s.: administration with will, 28 July 1885, *CGPLA Eng. & Wales*

Legros, Alphonse (1837–1911), artist, was born on 8 May 1837 in rue La Verrerie, Dijon, France, the third of four children of Lucien-Auguste Legros, a notary's clerk born in Toulon in 1807, and his wife, Anne-Victoire Barrié, originally from La Rochelle. A good part of his childhood was spent with cousins in the small village of Véronnes-les-Petites, some 20 miles north-east of Dijon. The roots of Legros's profound attachment to rural life are to be traced among the variegated landscape of low hills, enlivened by little rivers and patches of woodland, which proved an especially fertile source of imagery during the second half of his career.

Training and early success Legros's formal education was neglected; able to read, but writing only with difficulty, he was apprenticed at the age of eleven to 'maître' Nicolardot, a house painter and artist of popular images. He may also have attended the local École des Beaux-Arts, but only briefly. In 1851 the family moved to Lyons, where Legros found employment under J.-B. Beuchot, but at the end of the year they were in Paris. Legros painted scenery at the Opéra under Charles Cambon (1802–1875) but also undertook a more rigorous artistic training at the École Impériale de Dessin, Paris, where he came under the influence of the singular and revolutionary method of Horace Lecoq de Boisbaudran (1802–1897), reliant on the training of the artist's visual memory. Fellow pupils included Henri de Fantin-Latour (1836–1904), Jules Dalou (1838–1902), Auguste Rodin (1840–1917), and Jean-Charles Cazin (1841–1901). In February 1855 Legros gained admission to the École des Beaux-Arts. He made little headway there, and stopped attending in 1857 when he first had a work accepted at the Salon, *Portrait du père de l'artiste* (Musée de Tours). Through Fantin, Legros met the American J. A. M. Whistler and the three dubbed themselves the Société des Trois, linked by their sympathies for Courbet's realism, but also, in the case of Legros and Whistler, by a serious commitment to etching. The medium appeared popular, spontaneous, and personal, free of the pretensions of much salon art. After a brief trip to Spain, which probably took place in 1860, Legros developed the theme of the church interior, already a favourite of his, into one of his early masterpieces in the medium, *A Spanish Choir*; an impression was acquired by the South Kensington Museum that same year. In 1861 the publisher Cadart issued Legros's *Esquisses à l'eau-forte*, a portfolio of twenty-four subjects, which the artist dedicated to the poet Baudelaire. Legros played a leading role in the creation of the Société des Aquafortistes, which issued its first portfolio in 1862 and was much praised by Baudelaire in his article 'L'eau-forte est à la mode'; he became a friend during these years, although Legros's spine-tingling etchings made in 1860 to illustrate a new edition of the poet's translations of Poe were never published.

Whistler first took Legros to London in 1861 and his brother-in-law Francis Seymour Haden acquired Legros's 1859 Salon success *L'angélus*. *L'ex-voto* (Musée des Beaux-Arts, Dijon), exhibited in 1861, was admired but considered too dependent on Courbet. Legros's most ambitious works of these years, *La visite au village* and *La fête du grand-père* (both lost), also owed much to Courbet's aggrandizement of popular customs, and pursued a similar theme of the tensions between town and country. Incorporating figure studies made in the open air, they sought to bring the landscape painter's control of natural light to figure subjects usually made in the studio, a preoccupation of many of this generation, which resulted in Monet's *Déjeuner sur l'herbe* and *Femmes au jardin* (Musée d'Orsay, Paris) a few years later. Legros's stylistic predilection for Holbein and Dürer further accentuated the 'primitive' in his work, a feature that aligned him with the avant-garde, but made him a less likely candidate for the official commissions he thought his due. By 1863 Legros was desperate for some recognition of his gifts; the débâcle of the Salon des Réfusés, when Whistler and Manet, the other young painter he most admired, were the object of public scorn, encouraged him to abandon, temporarily at least, any hope of success in France and move to London.

Legros in London In London, Legros was welcomed by an advanced set of independent painters including Rossetti and Watts; crucially, he found many buyers, chiefly among the émigré Greek community centred around the consul Constantine Ionides. He made an impression at artistic gatherings by his energetic renditions of French operetta, an expression of the young man's lively temperament which in later years was submerged in melancholy. Legros rapidly established a presence in London and exhibited at the Royal Academy in 1864, at the Dudley Gallery, and at Gambart's French Gallery. Rossetti went on to effect introductions to many of his own patrons including James Leathart, for whom Legros painted a subject from *Hamlet*, and William Graham, who commissioned *Cupid and Psyche* (1867; Tate collection). These varied demands encouraged the painter to experiment still further and in 1868 the Royal Academy exhibited *Hans Holbein Showing some of his Pictures to Henry VIII*, a lost work which at once catered to the English taste for costume pictures and took an incident from the life of a favourite artist as a metaphor for his own condition as a foreigner seeking approval from a new audience. On 28 November 1864, at St John the Evangelist, Brixton, Legros married Frances Rosetta Hodgson, a young woman he had met in his lodging house and who had been able to converse with him in French; she was just sixteen, and pregnant with their first child. Quite apart from his aversion to writing, Legros never learned more than the most basic English and his wife became the artist's lifelong secretary and interpreter. This role was subsequently shared with their eldest son, Lucien, born in 1865. The marriage eventually produced nine children; three died in infancy, and none married. In his later teaching at the Slade School of Fine Art, Legros relied on a succession of able 'massiers', senior students, to interpret whatever meaning could not be conveyed by expletive or gesture.

By 1867 Legros was almost reluctant to show his work in Paris. His *Lapidation de Saint Étienne* gained a second-class medal at the Salon that year, but the pull of England remained stronger, despite the entreaties of the critic Duranty, who claimed Legros as a rival to Manet as leader of the younger generation. With the publication of his *Fifty Impressions of Ten Etchings* in 1869, Legros sought to extend appreciation of his printmaking and present a riposte to Whistler; the breach of their friendship in 1867 was never repaired. Legros's gifts as a teacher first emerged clearly in his tuition of George Howard, later ninth earl of Carlisle and a major patron, who funded the painter's extended journey to Italy in 1871–2. Links with French artists were again renewed in 1870–71, when many took refuge in London from the Prussian advance and the commune. Monet looked up Legros and ten years later sought his help over an exhibition of the impressionist group in London (which came to nothing). At the insistence of Degas, Legros sent a group of etchings to the second impressionist show in Paris in 1876.

Official recognition Notwithstanding the patronage of Prince Leopold, fourth son of Queen Victoria (*Death and the Woodcutter*, 1875; National Gallery of Ontario, Ottawa), and the leading Liberal MP Charles Dilke, who commissioned a portrait of the republican Gambetta (Musée d'Orsay, Paris), Legros was still deep in debt. Financial stability came for the first time in 1876 when he was appointed professor at the Slade School of Fine Art, University College, London. The departing professor, Edward Poynter, with Watts and Burne-Jones all strongly supported the Frenchman against the preferred English candidate, the little-known W. H. Fisk. Legros's teaching was conventional, but his insistence on the quality of line was decisive for a generation of English artists including H. S. Tuke, Charles

Furse, and William Strang; it laid the foundation for the 'Slade tradition' of fine draughtsmanship of which Augustus John became the leading exponent early in the new century. Etching and, later, sculpture were also introduced to the syllabus. The 'demonstration heads' Legros painted in under two hours revealed the showman in him, displaying the verve he captured effortlessly with the etching needle or burin, but so often lost in his large canvases. These proved so successful that he went on two tours in 1879–80, painting before invited audiences of art students and local worthies in Sunderland, Manchester, Aberdeen, and Liverpool, where the products of these performances can still be found.

Legros was naturalized a British citizen on 13 October 1880. This was also the year of the foundation of the Society of Painter-Etchers, with Haden as president and Legros one of six founder members. The first exhibition, held in 1881, did not manifest any great influence of Legros, and much of the work was by amateurs. It did, however, include the earliest plates by Rodin, who had been instructed in drypoint by Legros during a visit to London which renewed a friendship that had lapsed over twenty years previously. The visit of Rodin to London also prompted a new departure for Legros, an interest in sculpture. The modern revival of the cast portrait medal, indebted to the early Renaissance models of Pisanello, was due to Legros; he also made several figures including the bronze *Torse de femme* (Fitzwilliam Museum, Cambridge; only one plaster, for the life-size *La femme du marin*, survives in the Fitzwilliam Museum), and, late in life, two bronze fountains for the sixth duke of Portland at Welbeck Abbey. Rodin later called on Legros and their classmate the painter Jean-Charles Cazin to visit Calais in 1884, in an attempt to gain favour for his maquette of *The Burghers of Calais*. With or without Legros's help, the commission was confirmed the following year.

Later years Legros left the Slade in 1893. 'Vingt ans perdus' he is said to have remarked. His final years were certainly more productive, with dozens of etchings and a series of exquisite portrait heads in metal point, although he painted little. Legros also began to exhibit regularly in Paris again, and in 1898 held a large one-man show at L'Art Nouveau. The macabre streak of the earlier Poe illustrations continued through the six plates of *Death and the Woodcutter* (*c.*1875–1906) and the long series of *The Triumph of Death* (*c.*1892–1900), yet another homage to Holbein; this work is sometimes characterized as overly pessimistic but Legros emerges as possibly a truer symbolist than he ever was a realist, his *fin-de-siècle* fatalism at last finding an audience. He won the admiration of a younger generation of high-minded artists, including Charles Holroyd, with whom he visited Italy in 1896, and Charles Shannon. He also worked to promote an undervalued classicist of the previous generation, the sculptor Alfred Stevens. In 1885 the print historian Henri Béraldi had produced an updated version of a catalogue of Legros's prints which comprised 258 items; by 1900, when Legros was honoured with a large retrospective at the Musée du Luxembourg, Paris, this number had increased to 572. The largest collection of his prints is in the Bliss collection in Boston Public Library. Legros's health now began to decline; he lived for part of the year at Brasted Chart in Kent and often spent winters abroad; in 1904 he sold the house on Brook Green, Hammersmith, where he had lived since 1874 and moved to Watford. He died at Melbury, Clarendon Road, Watford, on 8 December 1911. It was in the Hammersmith cemetery that he had chosen to be buried, alongside the three children he had already laid to rest there (the family grave was subsequently overlaid). His death was marked by the largest-ever retrospective yet mounted by the Tate Gallery, versions of which were later shown in Birmingham, Manchester, Nottingham, and York.

TIMOTHY WILCOX

Sources T. Wilcox, *Alphonse Legros, 1837–1911*, trans. M. Guillaume (1987) [exhibition catalogue, Musée des Beaux-Arts, Dijon, 12 Dec 1987 – 15 Feb 1988] • M. Geiger, 'Alphonse Legros (1837–1911): peintre, graveur, sculpteur', thesis, École du Louvre, 1953 • L. Legros, biography of Alphonse Legros, U. Glas. L., special collections department • J. Bailly-Herzberg, *L'eau-forte de peintre au XIXe siècle: La Société des Aquafortistes, 1862–1867*, 2 vols. (1972) • M. Crouzet, *Un méconnu du réalisme: Duranty (1835–1880)* (1964) • C. Ricketts and C. Dodgson, *A catalogue of paintings, drawings, etchings and lithographs by Professor Alphonse Legros (1837–1911) from the collection of Frank E. Bliss* (privately printed, London, 1922) • P. Attwood, 'The medals of Alphonse Legros', *The Medal*, 5 (1984), 7–23 • C. P. Weisberg, *The realist tradition: French painting and drawing, 1830–1900* (1981) • A. Seltzer, 'Alphonse Legros: the development of an archaic visual vocabulary in nineteenth-century art', PhD diss. State University of New York at Birmingham, 1980 • *CGPLA Eng. & Wales* (1911) • W. Rothenstein, *Men and memories: recollections of William Rothenstein*, 2 vols. (1931–2) • A. S. Hartrick, *A painter's pilgrimage through forty years* (1939) • Archives Nationales, Paris

Archives priv. coll., family papers • U. Glas., Centre for Whistler Studies | Bibliothèque d'Art et d'Archéologie, Paris, Clément-Janin papers • Boston PL, Bliss collection • U. Glas. L., Harold Wright MSS • V&A, Ionides collection

Likenesses H. de Fantin-Latour, oils, *c.*1858, Tannenbaum collection, Toronto • A. Legros, self-portrait, etching, 1858, Boston PL • A. Legros, self-portrait, etching, 1858, BM • A. Legros, self-portrait, pen and ink, 1858, FM Cam. • J. A. M. Whistler, oils, 1860–64, National Gallery of Art, Washington, DC • F. Braquemonde, etching, 1861, Bibliothèque Nationale, Paris • L. Carroll, photograph, *c.*1863, U. Texas, Gernsheim collection • H. de Fantin-Latour, 1865 (in Hommage à Delacroix), Musée d'Orsay, Paris • J. Dalou, terracotta bust, *c.*1875, Musée de Dijon • G. F. Watts, etching, *c.*1879, NPG • J. B. Clark, etching, 1880, NPG • A. Legros, self-portrait, etching, 1880, BM • R. Lehmann, crayon drawing, 1880, Musée d'Orsay, Paris • R. Lehmann, drawing, 1880, BM • A. Rodin, bronze bust, *c.*1882, Man. City Gall. • A. Besnard, ink and gouache drawing, 1883, Musée d'Orsay, Paris • A. Legros, self-portraits, etchings and lithographs, *c.*1885–*c.*1906, BM • M. Zambaco, terracotta head, *c.*1886 • W. Rothenstein, lithograph, *c.*1900, BM, NPG • C. Shannon, oils, *c.*1900, NPG • A. Legros, self-portrait, silverpoint, 1903, Uffizi, Florence • A. Legros, self-portrait, bronze medal, 1907, BM • G. C. Beresford, photographs, NPG • F. Braquemonde, etching, BM, NPG • C. J. Durham, etching, NPG • C. Holroyd, etchings, BM, NPG • C. Holroyd, oils, Tate collection • E. R. Hughes, etching, NPG • A. Legros, self-portrait, etching, Bradford City Art Gallery • A. Legros, self-portrait, etching, Carlisle Art Gallery • A. Legros, self-portrait, etching, Hugh Lane Municipal Gallery of Modern Art, Dublin • A. Legros, self-portrait, pencil drawing, Uffizi, Florence • F. Regamey, etching, NPG • C. H. Shannon, lithograph, BM, NPG •

W. Strang, etching, NPG • photograph, repro. in *Bliss collection catalogue* (1922) • photograph, Tate collection • photograph, UCL
Wealth at death £438 16*s*. 6*d*.: probate, 20 Dec 1911, *CGPLA Eng. & Wales*

Le Grys, Sir Robert (*bap.* 1571?, *d.* 1635), translator, may have been a son or other close relative of Richard Grice, a captain in Ireland under Elizabeth and a deputy vice-admiral of Munster in the first decade of the seventeenth century. Alternatively, he may have been a son of Charles Le Grys, gentleman, of Billingford, Norfolk (*fl.* 1548). Nothing is known of his mother. Le Grys states in the preface to his translation of *Velleius Paterculus his Romane Historie* (1632) that he 'never was a grammar schoole boy', but he may have matriculated at Emmanuel College, Cambridge, in 1585. If so, he was baptized on 12 June 1571.

In 1603 Le Grys was a groom of the privy chamber, in which position he remained for several years. By 1618 he bore the title of captain, and throughout the 1620s he served in the king's forces in Ireland and Wales. He was knighted on 16 August 1628, almost certainly as a reward for military service. He evidently had connections to the admiralty, for in 1633 he was made captain for life of the castle of St Mawes, Cornwall, a lucrative post paying more than £50 per year. On 22 May 1630 he married Mary Trefusis of Lezant, Cornwall, a member of an armigerous family with ties to the admiralty. This may not have been his first marriage; no records of children survive.

During the 1620s and 1630s Le Grys was involved in a great deal more than military service. In February 1628 he had succeeded in inventing 'a medium for the preservation of sheep from the rot' that was expected to earn £1000 per year (*CSP dom.*, *1627–8*, 551). In 1633 he offered to Charles I his services as tutor to the prince of Wales, proposing to 'render Latin his linguam vernaculam … so that if Sir Robert lived till the Prince were seven years old, the nimblest Latinist should find him his match'. He promised to teach him French, Italian, and Spanish as well, and to 'feed his mind' with histories, in which he had 'not yet met with any one that has read more than himself, nor whose memory has more faithfully kept what has been committed to it' (*CSP dom.*, *1633–4*, 375). Le Grys says that he began his translation of John Barclay's 1621 Latin *Argenis* (1628), his most important work, at the direct command of Charles I. Put into English twice before Le Grys's translation, Barclay's historical romance cum political treatise allegorized events at the French court of Henri IV and also at the court of James I, where Barclay had been a groom of the bedchamber at the same time Le Grys was a groom of the privy chamber. Charles may have commissioned the translation because *Argenis* gives strong support to the ascendancy of the monarch over parliament; at the same time Thomas May's translations of the embedded verse, made for an earlier English translation and included at the suggestion of Le Grys's printer, emphasize the work's denunciation of tyranny. In 1632 Le Grys published his translation of *Velleius Paterculus his Romane Historie, in 2 Bookes*. He dedicated this work to Sir Thomas Jermyn, governor of Jersey and member of the privy council. Le Grys may also have been the author of the no longer extant 'Nothing Impossible to Love: a Tragi Comedy by Sr. Robert Le Greece', entered in the Stationers' register on 29 June 1660. There is no earlier record of the play, but nor is there any record of a later Sir Robert Le Grys.

Le Grys's last years were spent in controversy. His commission as captain of St Mawes Castle, although lucrative, introduced him to a tense and fractious military community. Sir Francis Vivian, whose grandfather had been created first captain of the castle under Henry VIII and in whose family the captainship had remained since, had been removed from the post of captain after being convicted in the Star Chamber in 1632 of stealing his soldiers' wages. Le Grys arrived at St Mawes in July 1633, and was apparently in residence for about nine months. He quickly came into conflict with Captain Hannibal Bonithon, who had been lieutenant of the castle under the absentee Vivian and seems to have been hoping for the post of captain himself. Le Grys made the mistake of dismissing Bonithon, and within a few months Bonithon had preferred charges against him to Edward Nicholas, secretary of the admiralty, accusing him of letting the castle decay substantially under his watch. Le Grys appeared before the admiralty to defend himself in April 1634, but the court ordered Bonithon to be reinstalled as lieutenant and appointed a committee to survey the castle that included a John Trefusis, probably a relative of Le Grys's wife, and that issued a bill for repairs in August 1634. It is unclear whether Le Grys was formally removed from his post; he died in London on 2 February 1635, of unknown causes, and the captainship was next granted to Thomas Howard, earl of Arundel and Surrey, on 23 March 1635. Le Grys's estate at the time of death is unknown.

Amelia Z. Sandy

Sources *CSP dom.*, *1627–8*; *1633–4* • S. P. Oliver, *Pendennis and St Mawes* (1875) • J. L. Vivian and H. H. Drake, eds., *The visitation of the county of Cornwall in the year 1620*, Harleian Society, 9 (1874) • *CSP Ire.*, *1509–1603* • Venn, *Alum. Cant.*, 1/1 • W. A. Shaw, *The knights of England*, 2 vols. (1906) • D. Gilbert, *The parochial history of Cornwall: founded on the manuscript histories of Mr Hals and Mr Tonkin*, 4 vols. (1838) • C. H. Cooper and T. Cooper, 'Sir Robert Le Grys', *N&Q*, 3rd ser., 3 (1863), 504–5 • G. C. Boase, *Collectanea Cornubiensia: a collection of biographical and topographical notes relating to the county of Cornwall* (1890) • R. Le Grys, 'Preface', *Velleius Paterculus his Romane historie* (1632)

Leguat, François (1638–1735), traveller and author, was probably born in October 1638 at St Jean-sur-Veyle, in the province of Bresse, France, the son of Huguenot parents. He was possibly a descendant of Pierre le Guat, seigneur de la Fougère and secretary to the duke of Savoy from 1511 to 1534.

In order to avoid persecution for his faith following Louis XIV's revocation of the edict of Nantes in 1685, Leguat left France for Holland, where he arrived on 6 August 1689. There he volunteered to take part in the scheme of Henri, Marquis Du Quesne, to establish a Huguenot colony on the island of Bourbon in the Indian Ocean. Leguat was one of ten adventurers who sailed on 10 July 1690 from Amsterdam to Texel aboard the frigate *Hirondelle*. On 4 September the ship departed Texel, arriving at the Cape of Good Hope on 16 January 1691. Leguat's presence at the Cape is proved by his extant letter of complaint concerning the captain of the ship. Sailing from the Cape, bad weather forced them to seek harbour at the uninhabited island of Rodrigues, which was reached on 30 April 1691. There, in what he later described as an Edenic tropical island idyll, the group attempted to settle. He made a survey of the island, describing the solitaire, a flightless bird similar to the dodo and also now extinct, and the presence of dugongs, a species of aquatic mammal. However, tensions eventually arose among the settlers, apparently caused by the absence of female company, and they made a hazardous crossing to Mauritius, where they arrived on 29 May 1693.

At Mauritius later that year Leguat and his comrades fell foul of the Dutch governor, Rudolphe Deodati, who at first imprisoned them on the small Île aux Vacoas, off Port South-East. On 26 September 1696, along with two surviving comrades, he was shipped on to Batavia, Java, where they arrived on 15 December. It was not until 23 April 1697 that their freedom was eventually granted. They departed from Batavia on 28 November 1697, Leguat engaging as a soldier on a vessel bound via the Cape to Flushing, Holland. There they arrived on 28 June the following year.

In early 1707 Leguat left Holland for England, where he was naturalized in 1709. In 1716 he was recorded as living in the parish of St Giles-in-the-Fields, Middlesex, and on 17 February of that year he married Catherine Uchard. It has also been claimed that while in London he became acquainted with Sir Hans Sloane and the botanist Baron A. von Haller. He died at the remarkable age of ninety-six in early September 1735. His will, dated 19 July 1716, was registered on 5 September 1735. The bulk of his possessions in England and France he left to his wife.

An account of his travels was published simultaneously in London and Amsterdam in late 1707 (although the imprint gives 1708) as *Voyage et avantures de François Leguat, et de ses compagnons, en deux isles desertes des Indes Orientales. Avec la rélation des choses les plus remarquables qu'ils ont observées dans l'Isle Maurice, à Batavia, au Cap de Bonne-Esperance, dans l'Isle de Ste. Helene, et en d'autres endroits de leur route*, in two volumes. Editions in English and Dutch followed in 1708, that in English being titled *A New Voyage to the East Indies by François Leguat and his Companions*. The book was a great success, and was reprinted frequently in English, French, Dutch, and German. A meticulously edited edition of the English translation was issued by the Hakluyt Society in 1891.

Soon after it was published it became clear that at least the preface to Leguat's book had been contributed by another French protestant refugee in England, François Maximilien Misson, and doubts arose during the eighteenth century as to authenticity of the work. Perhaps the most persuasive argument for its fictitious nature was provided in the early twentieth century by the scholar Geoffroy Atkinson, who, following a minute analysis of the text, concluded that Misson was the author of the whole work and that Leguat was a purely fictional character. Such was the influence of Atkinson that the book was subsequently frequently consigned to the literary genre of the imaginary voyage, characterized by such works as Defoe's *Robinson Crusoe* (1719). Others, such as Van Eeghen, took the middle ground in concluding that the work was 'a story of personal experience, embroidered by an ingenious editor or collaborator' (Van Eeghen, 410). Perhaps Van Eeghen's most important contribution was in providing evidence for the existence of Leguat in London between 1709 and his death in 1735. In the most exhaustive recent analysis of the controversy Alfred North-Coombes has demonstrated (1991), perhaps conclusively, the essential veracity of Leguat's remarkable narrative.

Andrew Grout

Sources A. North-Coombes, *The vindication of François Leguat*, rev. 2nd edn (1991) • G. Atkinson, *The extraordinary voyage in French literature from 1700 to 1720* (1922) • I. H. Van Eeghen, 'The voyages and adventures of François Leguat', *Proceedings of the Huguenot Society*, 18 (1947–52), 396–417 • M. Ducasse, 'Le voyage de François Leguat dans l'océan Indien (1690–1698)', *Revue Historiques des Armées*, pt 1 (1996), 12–20 • P. B. Grove, *The imaginary voyage in prose fiction* (1961) • R. H. Grove, *Green imperialism: colonial expansion, tropical island Edens, and the origins of environmentalism, 1600–1860* (1995) • PRO, PROB 11/673, fol. 79 • H. du Quesne, *Un projet de république à l'île d'Eden, l'île Bourbon en 1689 … Réimpression d'un ouvrage disparu publié en 1689 …* (1887) • *The voyage of François Leguat of Bresse to Rodriguez, Mauritius, Java, and the Cape of Good Hope*, ed. S. P. Oliver, 2 vols., Hakluyt Society, 82–3 (1891)

Lehmann [*married name* Bedford], **Elizabeth Nina Mary Frederica** [Liza] **(1862–1918)**, composer and singer, was born on 11 July 1862 at 139 Westbourne Terrace, London, the daughter of the painter Rudolf *Lehmann (1819–1905) and his wife, the composer Amelia Lehmann ('A. L.'), *née* Chambers (1820–1903). Always known as Liza, she spent the first five years of her life in Italy before her parents returned to England and settled in London. Apart from a year spent at a day school she was privately educated, and her first music teacher was her mother. She also studied singing with Alberto Randegger and Jenny Lind and composition with Niels Ravnkilde and Wilhelm Freudenberg. Encouraged by both her parents to embark on a career as a professional musician, Lehmann made her formal début as a lyric soprano at a Monday Popular Concert in London in 1885 at the age of twenty-three. Over the next nine years she was in great demand as a concert singer, and she performed at both private and public venues throughout Britain. Her repertory included both her own songs, which started appearing in print in 1888, and various seventeenth- and eighteenth-century English songs which she discovered in the British Museum.

On 10 October 1894 Lehmann married the amateur composer Herbert Bedford, son of John Thomas Bedford, and retired from the public stage. She turned instead to composition, and in 1896 she wrote her best-known work, the song cycle *In a Persian Garden*, for four voices and piano. Lehmann saw this as her 'first serious composition' (Lehmann, 70), and one critic described it as 'one of the most impressive works ever penned by a female composer' (*MT*, 38, 1897, 20). A setting of a selection of verses from ʿUmar Khayyam's *Rubaiyat* in the translation by Edward FitzGerald, *In a Persian Garden* captured the *fin-de-siècle* fascination with the Orient and philosophy of living for the moment.

Elizabeth Nina Mary Frederica Lehmann (1862–1918), by Flora Lion, 1915

It is still sometimes performed today, and at the end of the twentieth century was widely heard throughout Britain and the United States.

The song cycle was not commonly used by British composers in the late nineteenth century, and Lehmann can be credited with establishing the genre in Britain. Further cycles included the intense and moving *In Memoriam* (1899), for baritone or mezzo-soprano and piano, to sections from Tennyson's poem of the same name. The births of her two sons, Rudolf (*b.* 1897) and Leslie (*b.* 1900), inspired several works either written for children or reflecting childhood. Among these were the much-loved cycles *The Daisy-Chain* (1900), for four voices and piano, to poems by Robert Louis Stevenson and others, and its sequel *More Daisies* (1902). Humour also became an important element of Lehmann's work, as in the cycles *Nonsense Songs*, incorporating 'The Songs that Came out Wrong from Alice in Wonderland (Lewis Carroll)' (1908), for four voices and piano, and *Four Cautionary Tales and a Moral* (1909), to poems by Hilaire Belloc, for two voices and piano. Always well crafted and using compelling melodies, such light-hearted works were in great demand from both the public and Lehmann's publishers. In addition they provided a vital source of income when Bedford fell into financial difficulties. Lehmann found it harder to gain a hearing for what she described as her 'more ambitious work' (Lehmann, 117) and, as her more popular music became widely known, faced growing disapproval from critics previously enthusiastic.

In 1904 Lehmann was the first woman to be commissioned to compose the music for a musical comedy. *Sergeant Brue*, with a libretto by Owen Hall and lyrics by J. Hickory Wood, was an undoubted success, playing in London for 290 performances between 1904 and 1905. Other stage works were the light opera *The Vicar of Wakefield* (1906), to a libretto by Laurence Housman after Oliver Goldsmith, and an operatic version of the morality play *Everyman* (1915).

While cultivating an acceptably ladylike image as devoted mother and wife (clearly reflected in her published memoirs *The Life of Liza Lehmann*, which appeared posthumously in 1919), Lehmann always remained fiercely professional. Towards the end of her life she toured the United States, took up a post at the Guildhall School of Music, and served as the first president of the Society of Women Musicians (established in 1911). In 1916 she was devastated by the death of her beloved son Rudolph during military training and could not continue with many of these activities. She died at her home at Hatch End, Pinner, on 19 September 1918.

Sophie Fuller

Sources L. Lehmann, *The life of Liza Lehmann* (1919) · S. Fuller, 'Women composers during the British musical renaissance, 1880–1918', PhD diss., U. Lond., 1998 · E. Evans, 'Modern British composers: Liza Lehmann', *Musical Standard*, 20 (17 Oct 1903), 242 · A. Lawrence, 'Women and musical composition: a chat with Miss Liza Lehmann (Mrs Herbert Bedford)', *Young Woman*, 8 (1899–1900), 414–16 · 'Mr and Mrs Herbert Bedford (Liza Lehmann)', *Strand Musical Magazine*, 3 (1896), 158–9 · 'To the young musician who would compose: an interview with Mme Liza Lehmann', *Musical Standard*, 33 (1903), 373–5 · *MT*, 38 (1897), 20 · m. cert. · S. Bedford, *Liza Lehmann*, Collins Classics English Song Series, vol. 4 (CD no. 15082) [sleeve notes] · *The Times* (21 Sept 1918)

Archives priv. coll., MSS | Richmond Local Studies Library, London, corresp. with Douglas Sladen

Likenesses F. Lion, lithograph, 1915, NPG [*see illus.*] · portrait, repro. in *Strand Musical Magazine*, 158 · portrait, repro. in J. A. Sadie and R. Samuel, eds., *New Grove dictionary of women composers* (1994), 276

Lehmann, Hermann (1910–1985), biochemist and human geneticist, was born on 8 July 1910 in Halle, Saxony, Germany, the youngest of the four children of Paul Lehmann (*d. c.*1927), publisher, and his first wife, Bella, *née* Apelt (*d. c.*1913). His parents were both German. His eldest sister, Bertha, left Germany in the mid-1930s for New York, where she worked as a trained nurse. His second sister, Ruth, had left Germany earlier for Jerusalem as the wife of Ernst Wertheimer, a professor at Hadassah University. His third sister died aged eighteen. He also had a half-brother, from his father's second marriage, who settled in England and pursued a business career.

Lehmann received his early education at a state school in Halle. In 1923, following the collapse of his father's business, Lehmann's family moved to Dresden, and until 1928 he attended the Gymnasium zum Heiligen Kreuz. Wishing to pursue a career in medicine, in the summer of 1928 he enrolled on the medical course in the University of Freiburg im Breisgau. Later, he moved to the medical school at Frankfurt, where his family had settled after the death of his father, and passed the pre-clinical examination in July 1930. After a short spell of laboratory training in Berlin he went to Heidelberg to complete his clinical training. His work towards an MD degree was carried out in Heidelberg, but because of Nazi policies affecting Jews, it was presented in Basel in 1934. Lehmann subsequently returned to Heidelberg to work as an unpaid assistant in the laboratory of Otto Meyerhoff at the Kaiser Wilhelm Institute, where he developed his love of biochemistry, carried out his early research, and published his first scientific papers.

In 1936 Lehmann moved to Cambridge (having already worked there briefly with Frederick Gowland Hopkins), where he obtained a PhD in 1938 with a thesis entitled 'Aspects of carbohydrate metabolism in the absence of molecular oxygen', which was awarded the Darwin prize at Christ's College. After a short period of internment as a 'friendly alien' at the beginning of the Second World War, Lehmann married Benigna Norman-Butler, a music teacher and accompanist, in 1942. They had four children: Susanna, a musician and translator; Ruth, also a part-time musician; Paul, an associate professor of microbiology in the medical school at Toledo, Ohio; and David, who died aged eighteen as the result of an accident. In 1943 Lehmann became an officer in the Royal Army Medical Corps. It was during his service in India and, later, Uganda, as a colonial medical research fellow, that he developed his lifelong research interest in inherited blood diseases, particularly those of haemoglobin. After returning to England in 1949 he became consultant pathologist at Pembert Hospital, Kent, before being appointed to St Bartholomew's Hospital, London, as senior lecturer in chemical pathology in 1951. In 1963 he moved to Addenbrooke's Hospital in Cambridge and was appointed honorary director of the Medical Research Council's Abnormal Haemoglobin Research Unit, and in 1967 he became the first professor of clinical biochemistry at Cambridge University—a position he held until 1977, when he became emeritus professor.

While in Uganda, Lehmann had become interested in sickle-cell anaemia. Stimulated by Linus Pauling's work in the USA showing that this disease was an inherited disorder of haemoglobin, he began a systematic search for abnormal human haemoglobins in many different populations throughout the world. As the techniques of protein chemistry became more sophisticated Lehmann was able to characterize many of these variants at the molecular level. This work provided important information about the origins of human races and how inherited abnormalities of a protein such as haemoglobin can give rise to a variety of different diseases. He also made early observations on the inheritance and causes of the thalassaemias, the commonest inherited disease of humans, also, like sickle-cell anaemia, caused by defective haemoglobin production. This work culminated in 'Molecular pathology of human haemoglobin' (*Nature*, 219, 1968, 402–9), a brilliant paper written in collaboration with M. F. Perutz, in which the authors were able to relate the many different inherited abnormalities of human haemoglobin to its structure and function, both in health and disease.

Lehmann also made important contributions in other fields, including the study of myoglobin, the population genetics of blood groups, inherited disorders of human enzymes, and the characterization of the haemoglobin of many different species. But he was, more than anybody, responsible for cataloguing the enormous wealth of human genetic variation reflected in the human haemoglobin variants and hence for providing important insights into human population genetics, evolution, and the clinical diversity of disorders that result from inherited diseases.

Because of his international research interests Lehmann was well known in laboratories the world over, and he published widely with collaborators from many different countries. His laboratory in Cambridge was a training ground for young haematologists and human geneticists from many countries. He was extremely kind to young people and had broad cultural interests and an unquenchable curiosity and enthusiasm for his field. In 1977 he travelled together with D. J. Weatherall throughout China to search for haemoglobin diseases. During this trip he had a major confrontation with officials because he wished to enter Mongolia to obtain blood samples to search for a particular abnormal haemoglobin. Although almost seventy, in poor health, and with the full might of bureaucracy against him, he won the day and was able to find his beloved haemoglobin variant in the Mongolian races.

Lehmann was widely honoured for his work and was elected FRS, in 1972, and to many other fellowships and honorary degrees. He became CBE in 1980. He died in Cambridge after a short cardiac illness on 13 July 1985, and was buried there. He was survived by his wife.

D. J. WEATHERALL

Sources RS · J. V. Dacie, *Memoirs FRS*, 34 (1988), 405–49 · R. G. Huntsman, 'Professor Hermann Lehmann: a personal tribute', *Acta Haematologica*, 78 (1987), 71–3 · D. J. Weatherall, 'Hermann Lehmann', *BMJ* (27 July 1985), 288–9 · M. M. Wintrobe, *Hematology, the blossoming of a science* (1985), 358–9 · *WWW* · personal knowledge (2004)

Archives RS | Bodl. Oxf., Society for Protection of Science and Learning file · Girton Cam., corresp. with D. M. M. Needham | SOUND IWM SA, tape

Likenesses G. Argent, photograph, 1980, repro. in Dacie, *Memoirs FRS*

Wealth at death £99,025: probate, 11 Dec 1985, *CGPLA Eng. & Wales*

Lehmann, (Rudolph) John Frederick (1907–1987), publisher and author, was born on 2 June 1907 at Bourne End, Buckinghamshire, the fourth and youngest child and only son of Rudolph Chambers *Lehmann, oarsman, contributor to *Punch*, and Liberal MP, and his wife, Alice Marie, daughter of an American, Harrison Davis, and descended on her mother's side from Sir John Wentworth, an eighteenth-century governor of New Hampshire. In the house and garden of Fieldhead, where he was brought up with his sisters, Rosamond *Lehmann, Beatrix, and Helen, the profession of letters was powerful as both living presence and lively inheritance. His paternal grandmother belonged to the notable Scottish publishing family Chambers (whence his father's second name), and a great-uncle of his father was W. H. Wills, assistant editor with Charles Dickens of *Household Words*.

Lehmann went as a king's scholar to Eton, where he edited *College Days*. Among his contemporaries were Eric Blair (George Orwell), Henry Yorke (Henry Green), and Cyril Connolly. He read history and modern languages at

Trinity College, Cambridge, where he obtained a second class (division one) in both part one of the history tripos (1928) and part two of the modern and medieval languages tripos (1930). There his close friendship with Julian Bell, nephew of Virginia Woolf, plunged him so irresistibly into the Bloomsbury circle that by 1931 he was working as factotum at the Hogarth Press, which also published *A Garden Revisited* (1931), his first volume of poems. His verse, praised for metrical skill, elegiac tone, and clarity of diction, followed at rare intervals, ending with the *Collected Poems* of 1963, a self-critically thin volume.

As Nazism took grip in Germany, Lehmann left publishing to live as a poet in Vienna, a city he monitored as Christopher Isherwood did Berlin. The first of his three volumes of autobiography, *The Whispering Gallery* (1955), reflects the hardening of his anti-fascist view of that 'pink' decade, while with heartache he faced the dilemma that was to dog him insolubly: whether to be impresario or artist. In 1935 he founded the twice-yearly (often irregular) hard-bound *New Writing*, which abruptly lost its left-wing élitism when in 1940 it burgeoned, as the paperback *Penguin New Writing*, into part of the war effort. This magazine was his masterpiece. Four or six issues a year during the Second World War all sold out their 75,000 or more copies within days. A morale booster of high potency, a documentary record of war by the men fighting it, packed full of poets and story-writers who were his own discoveries, this was the voice of cultural survival.

In 1938 Lehmann had bought Virginia Woolf's share of the Hogarth Press, but when his partnership—vigorously described in *Thrown to the Woolfs* (1978)—ended in 1946, he launched his own firm, John Lehmann Ltd. His good-looking books—225 titles by 1954, when his supportive printers withdrew—reintroduced British readers to the wider world at a crucial post-war point. Saul Bellow, George Seferis, and Gore Vidal ornamented his list, as did the no less influential Elizabeth David. His services to European letters earned him the Légion d'honneur (1958), the Greek order of George I (1954), and an honorary DLitt at Birmingham (1980). He was appointed FRSL (1951) and CBE (1964).

Lehmann's subsidy from the *Daily Mirror* in 1954 to found the *London Magazine* and maintain the aesthetics of humanism was soon dropped. The magazine tottered on too conservatively for the current *Zeitgeist* until Alan Ross took it over in 1961. For the remainder of his life Lehmann took visiting professorships in America and engaged in literary journalism and reminiscence of reflective quality, especially in his popular studies *Lewis Carroll* (1972), *Virginia Woolf* (1975), and *Rupert Brooke* (1980). In his books, of which there were many, his writing was always courtly and finished, expressive only between the lines, except in the homosexually libidinous novel *In the Purely Pagan Sense* (1976), which he predicted would lose him his friends. It did not.

Lehmann was a tall, broad, and formidable figure, whose guttural voice and avuncular presence filled a room, with eyes, as William Plomer put it, 'like forget-me-nots within a skull'. His gardens (and gardening) he loved. At his frequent parties at his Egerton Crescent home in London, where he had the generosity to confront young writers with their elder peers, his rooms were ablaze with massed flowers from the country. For much of his life he shared homes in London and near Crawley, Sussex, with the dancer Alexis Rassine.

Lehmann died after a long illness, in which hip operations had interrupted his mobility, in a nursing home at 29 Devonshire Street, Westminster, on 7 April 1987.

DAVID HUGHES, *rev.*

Sources *Daily Telegraph* (9 April 1987) • *The Independent* (10 April 1987) • A. T. Tolley, ed., *John Lehmann, a tribute* (1987) • J. Lehmann, *In my own time* (1969) • *CGPLA Eng. & Wales* (1987) • personal knowledge (1996)

Archives Eton, letters • Princeton University Library, papers • Ransom HRC, corresp. and papers • U. Cal., Berkeley, Bancroft Library, corresp. and papers | King's AC Cam., letters to G. H. W. Rylands • U. Reading L., corresp. with Ewald Osers • U. Sussex Library, corresp. with Leonard Woolf • UCL, letters to Alex Comfort

Likenesses photograph, Hult. Arch.

Wealth at death £244,753: probate, 28 Oct 1987, *CGPLA Eng. & Wales*

Lehmann, Rosamond Nina (1901–1990), novelist, was born on 3 February 1901 in Bourne End, Buckinghamshire, the second child and second daughter in the family of three daughters and one son of Rudolph Chambers *Lehmann, journalist, Liberal MP, and oarsman, and his wife, Alice Marie, *née* Davis. The Lehmanns were an affluent and gifted family. Rosamond Lehmann's great-grandfather was Robert Chambers (1802–1871), who co-founded the publishing company Chambers; and her great-uncle was the artist Rudolf Lehmann. Of the four Lehmann children, three grew up to distinguish themselves in the arts—Lehmann herself; her younger sister Beatrix, who became an actress; and John *Lehmann, the poet, editor, and publisher. 'I was bound to write,' Lehmann recalled in old age. 'I never considered anything else as a possibility.'

Lehmann was educated at the family home, Fieldhead, until she won a scholarship to read English at Girton College, Cambridge, in 1919. At Cambridge she contributed occasional pieces to *Granta*, the magazine founded by her father, and met (Walter) Leslie *Runciman, from 1949 second Viscount Runciman of Doxford (1900–1989), son of the nonconformist shipping magnate and Liberal elder statesman Walter *Runciman, first Viscount Runciman of Doxford. After graduating with second classes in English (1921) and modern and medieval languages (1922), she and Runciman married in December 1923 and moved to Newcastle. The marriage was brief and unsatisfactory, and it had already broken down when Lehmann's controversial first novel, *Dusty Answer*, was published in 1927. This was both a critical and a popular success, its sales enhanced by the author's reputation as a society beauty. Her second novel was, in contrast, poorly received by the critics, who were disconcerted by the glum northern setting and two unhappy marriages described in *A Note in Music* (1930). Lehmann's own marriage had been dissolved in 1928 and in the same year she had married the colourful Wogan *Philipps (1902–1993), who in 1962 became the second Baron Milford, artist and communist son of Laurence Richard

Rosamond Nina Lehmann (1901–1990), by Howard Coster, 1944

Philipps, first Baron Milford, businessman. A son, Hugo, was born in 1929, and a daughter, Sarah (Sally), in 1934.

Between 1932 and 1953 Lehmann wrote the four novels by which she will be remembered: *Invitation to the Waltz* (1932), *The Weather in the Streets* (1936), *The Ballad and the Source* (1944), and *The Echoing Grove* (1953). The books are autobiographical in tone, with certain themes and preoccupations occurring throughout, notably the heroine's experience of compelling but destructive sexuality, and the conflict between intelligence and passion. Modern criticism now stresses Lehmann's role in asserting the centrality of female experience, whereas she was once stigmatized as a writer of 'women's novels'. She has been commended not only for her treatment of particular issues such as homosexuality and abortion, but also for her technical skill, which became fully apparent in her handling of the non-linear chronological and narrative complexities of *The Echoing Grove*.

Between 1930 and 1939 Lehmann lived at Ipsden House, Oxfordshire, where she entertained a wide circle of acquaintances, including Leonard and Virginia Woolf, Lytton Strachey, Dora Carrington, W. H. Auden, Christopher Isherwood, and Stephen Spender. By 1939 her second marriage had also failed and in 1941 she began a relationship with the married poet Cecil Day-*Lewis (1904–1972), with whom she lived for several years. Her own marriage was dissolved in 1944, but when Day-Lewis was eventually divorced in 1951 he married Jill Balcon. The effect of his desertion was traumatic, although the tragic turning-point of Lehmann's life occurred in 1958 when her daughter, who had recently married the writer P. J. Kavanagh, contracted poliomyelitis in Jakarta and died, aged twenty-four. Lehmann wrote nothing of literary significance for many years afterwards and devoted herself instead to spiritualism. Her impressionistic autobiography, *The Swan in the Evening* (1967), reiterates her belief in Sally's continuing life, and in her last, confusing, novel, *A Sea-Grape Tree* (1976), the spirit of Sibyl Jardine, monstrous protagonist of *The Ballad and the Source*, converses telepathically with the heroine. Other publications include translations of Jacques Lemarchand and Jean Cocteau; a play, *No More Music* (1939); *The Gipsy's Baby, and other Stories* (1946), and several spiritualist works.

The reprinting of Lehmann's books by Virago Press in the 1980s brought her a new and appreciative audience. In 1982 she was created CBE and a fellow of the Royal Society of Literature. In 1986 she was made an honorary fellow of Girton College. She was also president of the English Centre of International PEN; a member of the council of the Society of Authors, and vice-president of the College of Psychic Studies.

Rosamond Lehmann was tall and beautiful, with almond-shaped eyes, a firm mouth, and a warm, impulsive manner. She died on 12 March 1990 at her London home, 30 Clareville Grove. JUDITH PRIESTMAN, *rev.*

Sources *The Times* (14 March 1990) · *The Independent* (14 March 1990) · *The Independent* (24 March 1990) · J. Lehmann, *The whispering gallery* (1955) · S. Day-Lewis, *C. Day-Lewis: an English literary life* (1980) · R. Lehmann, *Rosamond Lehmann's album* (1985) · J. Simons, *Rosamond Lehmann* (1992) · M. Laski, 'Woman in love', *London Review of Books* (1–20 April 1983) · *The Times* (9 Feb 1984)

Archives King's AC Cam., papers | CUL, letters to Siegfried Sassoon · Harvard University, near Florence, Italy, Center for Italian Renaissance Studies, letters to Bernard Berenson · King's AC Cam., letters to John Hayward · King's AC Cam., letters and postcards to G. H. W. Rylands · Tate collection, corresp. with Lord Clark · U. Durham L., letters to William Plomer · U. Reading L., letters to Herberth Herlitschka and Marlys Herlitschka

Likenesses H. Coster, photograph, 1944, NPG [*see illus.*]

Wealth at death £196,629: probate, 1991 · £22,000: probate, 1991

Lehmann, (Wilhelm Augustus) Rudolf (1819–1905), portrait and genre painter, was born on 19 August 1819 in Ottensen, near Hamburg, Germany, the fourth of seven children of Leo Lehmann (1782–1852), a miniature painter, and his wife, Friederike Dellevie (1792–1884). Following a lacklustre education at the Johanneum in Hamburg, Lehmann journeyed to Paris in March 1835 to join his eldest brother, Henri, a talented pupil of Ingres. Rudolf remained in Paris for two years, studying at a private academy and at the Louvre before enrolling in the École des Beaux-Arts. Through an aunt who lived in Paris he became acquainted with the city's cultural élite.

In 1837 Lehmann journeyed to Munich, where he studied with the Nazarene painters Peter von Cornelius and William von Kaulbach. In autumn 1839 he joined his brother Henri in Rome, earning a meagre living by painting copies after Raphael, Jacopo da Pontormo, and other

Italian masters. The success of his first original painting, *Chiaruccia* (a girl in Abruzzi costume walking through a cornfield), sent to the Paris Salon in 1842, encouraged Lehmann to concentrate on scenes of Italian peasant life. He received a third-class medal for his picture of a Capri grape-gatherer, exhibited at the Salon in 1843, and second-class medals for pictures shown in 1845 and 1848. He received numerous commissions for such paintings, many of which were engraved. Lehmann also had a thriving portrait practice and occasionally painted historical subjects. His ambitious painting *Sixtus V Blessing the Pontine Marshes* was purchased at the Salon in 1846 by the French government for the museum at Lille. Lehmann continued to exhibit at the Salon until 1859.

In 1849–50 Lehmann returned to Hamburg for eighteen months. Before returning to Rome he visited London for the first time, and exhibited his first paintings at the Royal Academy in 1851. Ten years later, following a lengthy courtship, he married Amelia Chambers (1820–1903), the sister of his brother Frederick's wife and daughter of the Scottish writer and publisher Robert Chambers. She was highly esteemed as a singer, music teacher, and arranger of songs. They had four daughters, of whom the eldest, Elizabeth *Lehmann (1862–1918) became one of England's foremost female composers. The family lived in Rome, where Lehmann's studio attracted an illustrious crowd of international visitors. Edward, prince of Wales, bought several of the artist's paintings and commissioned *La lavandaja di terracina* (1864), a characteristic depiction of a lovely Italian peasant, exhibited at the Royal Academy in 1866 and at the International Exhibition in 1875.

In 1866 Lehmann settled in London with his family and was naturalized as a British citizen. He and his wife led a glittering social life, hosting musical soirées attended by luminaries in literature, science, and the arts. Many of the same people sat to Lehmann for their portraits. His paintings of the novelist Wilkie Collins, the metallurgist and electrician Sir William Siemens, and the poet Robert Browning (a great friend whom Lehmann painted on several occasions) are in the National Portrait Gallery, London. From the 1840s, Lehmann made pencil sketches of eminent contemporaries, each of them signed by the sitter (BM). Eighty of them were reproduced in *Men and Women of the Century; being a Collection of Portraits and Sketches by Mr. Rudolf Lehmann* (1896). Lehmann's impressive social connections and cosmopolitan travels dominate his autobiography, *An Artist's Reminiscences* (1894), which he divided into two sections: 'Places I Have Seen' and 'People I Have Met'. He was created a knight of the order of the Falcon by the grand duke of Saxe-Weimar, but received no official professional honours in England during his long and productive career. Lehmann exhibited his last painting at the Royal Academy in 1904, six months before his death on 27 October 1905 at his home, Bournemede, Bushey, Hertfordshire. His cremated remains were buried at Highgate cemetery, Middlesex.

ROBYN ASLESON

Sources R. Lehmann, *An artist's reminiscences* (1894) • J. Dafforne, 'The works of Rudolf Lehmann', *Art Journal*, 26 (1874), 169–72 • J. Lehmann, *Ancestors and friends* (1962) • *The Times* (28 Oct 1905), 6 • catalogues of the Paris Salons, 1842–59 • Graves, *RA exhibitors* • H. C. Marillier, ed., *Men and women of the century: being a collection of portraits and sketches by Mr. Rudolf Lehmann* (1896) • Thieme & Becker, *Allgemeines Lexikon*, vol. 22 • *Magazine of Art*, 20 (1896–7), 264–6 • *Men and women of the time* (1899) • *The Athenaeum* (4 Nov 1905) • *WWW*, 1916–28

Archives Princeton University, New Jersey, family MSS, C0746

Likenesses H. Lehmann, pencil, 1847, repro. in Lehmann, *Ancestors and friends* • photograph, 1868, L. Cong. • photograph, *c.*1885, repro. in J. Maas, *Victorian art world in photographs* (1984) • photograph, *c.*1894, repro. in Lehmann, *An artist's reminiscences* • H. von Herkomer, oils • R. Lehmann, self-portrait, oils, Uffizi Gallery, Florence • R. Lehmann, self-portrait, oils, Kunsthalle, Hamburg

Wealth at death £34,866 17*s.* 6*d.*: resworn probate, 21 Dec 1905, *CGPLA Eng. & Wales*

Lehmann, Rudolph Chambers (1856–1929), journalist and oarsman, was born in Ecclesall, Sheffield, on 3 January 1856, the eldest in the family of three sons and one daughter of Frederick Lehmann, businessman, and his wife Nina, daughter of Robert *Chambers (1802–1871), the Edinburgh publisher. The artist Rudolf Lehmann (1819–1905) was his great-uncle. He was educated at Highgate School and Trinity College, Cambridge, taking a second class in the classical tripos (1878). He was president of the union (1876), a noted boxer, captain of first Trinity boat club, and twice rowed in the university trial eights. On coming down he was called to the bar in 1880 (Inner Temple) but soon abandoned legal practice. An ample private income allowed him time to indulge his tastes for writing, politics, and rowing.

At Cambridge, Lehmann had founded *Granta*, which he continued to edit for some years after leaving university. Much of his prose and verse, light-hearted in nature but containing some good pieces on rowing, appeared in *Punch*, of whose table he was a member for thirty years from 1890. Less happy were his efforts during the late 1890s to revive *The Speaker* as an organ for radical ideas, and his editorship of the ailing *Daily News* from 1901 to 1902. He did not find the day-to-day life of a professional journalist congenial.

A public-spirited man, Lehmann was high sheriff of Buckinghamshire during 1901–2 and he was long active in the affairs of the National Liberal Federation. He unsuccessfully contested parliamentary seats in Cheltenham in 1885, Central Hull in 1886, and Cambridge town in 1892 before being elected in 1906 for the Harborough division of Leicestershire. He had opposed the Second South African War, and South African issues were one of his major concerns as an MP. He retained his seat in January 1910 but declined to stand again the following December. Deteriorating health and financial worries, following careless judgements by his stockbroker in 1907, contributed to this decision. His name was on the list of H. H. Asquith, had the prime minister been forced to create new Liberal peers in 1911.

Sport, more especially rowing, was his constant pleasure. An inspiring coach, he was in considerable demand by both Oxford and Cambridge for their boat race crews throughout the 1890s. He captained Leander in 1894 and 1895 and was elected a steward of Henley royal regatta in

1898. Secretary of the Amateur Rowing Association from 1893 to 1901, he tried unsuccessfully to widen its narrow definition of an amateur. He coached abroad on a number of occasions, always refusing any kind of payment, even for his expenses, and his three visits to Harvard between 1896 and 1898 were rewarded by an honorary degree. Nevertheless he was suspicious of international competition, especially the Olympic movement, fearing it would turn what was intended to be pleasure into too serious a business.

Talented but without driving ambition, Lehmann was during his last years handicapped by Parkinson's disease. But his gift of friendship remained, reinforced by his marriage in 1898 to Alice Marie, daughter of Harrison Davis, of old New England puritan stock. Of their four children (one son and three daughters), three subsequently distinguished themselves—Beatrix as an actress, (Rudolph) John *Lehmann (1907–1987) as a man of letters, and Rosamond Nina *Lehmann (1901–1990) as a novelist. Lehmann died on 22 January 1929 at Fieldhead, the house he had built at Bourne End, Buckinghamshire.

ERIC HALLADAY, *rev.*

Sources J. Lehmann, *The whispering gallery* (1955) • J. Lehmann, *Ancestors and friends* (1962) • *CGPLA Eng. & Wales* (1929)
Archives NRA, letters and papers | King's AC Cam., letters to Oscar Browning • NL Aus., letters to Alfred Deakin
Wealth at death £59,358 8*s*. 0*d*.: probate, 6 April 1929, *CGPLA Eng. & Wales*

Le Hunte, Sir George Ruthven (1852–1925), colonial governor, was born on 20 August 1852 at Artramont, co. Wexford, Ireland, the son of George Le Hunte, high sheriff of the county, and his wife, Mary, the daughter of Edward *Pennefather, chief justice of Ireland. He was educated at Eton College from 1866 to 1868 and matriculated from Trinity College, Cambridge, in 1870. He took a second-class degree in law and history in 1873 and graduated MA in 1880. Intending to practise law, he was admitted to the Inner Temple in November 1874, although he was not called to the bar until he was on leave from the colonial service in 1881.

In 1875 Le Hunte became private secretary to Sir Arthur Hamilton-Gordon (a younger son of George Hamilton-Gordon, fourth earl of Aberdeen), who was leaving his governorship of Mauritius to become the first governor of Fiji after its cession to the crown by the high chiefs. In Fiji, Le Hunte served as magistrate both in the colony and in the Western Pacific high commission. He proved an able officer in Gordon's administration, which was noted for its preservation of the Fijian system of rank, and for its protection of indigenous society in the face of European planters and the immigrant Indian labour force that had been imported to work the land. Land ownership was largely the preserve of the Fijians. On 14 February 1884, while on leave from Fiji, Le Hunte married Caroline Rachel Clowes, the daughter of John Clowes of Burton Court, Eardisland, Herefordshire, with whom he had a son and a daughter. His son predeceased him.

Le Hunte's work was well thought of by Gordon. After Gordon had left the colony to become governor of New Zealand, he supported Le Hunte's appointment as president of Dominica in the Caribbean in 1887. In 1894 Le Hunte was promoted to become colonial secretary of the colony of Barbados, where he encountered opposition between a government seeking to protect indigenous interests and an economically vital settler community. Three years later he was transferred as colonial secretary to Gordon's former colony of Mauritius in the Indian Ocean, where the problems of colonial government were similar, except that the settler community was French from its earlier colonial history. In 1898 his work was recognized by his appointment as CMG.

In the following year Le Hunte's former Fijian colleague Sir William MacGregor left his governorship of British New Guinea, and Le Hunte was appointed to succeed him in a difficult post. The territory was administered under a cumbersome arrangement of Colonial Office and three Australian colonies which provided £15,000 per annum, a grant which was soon to expire. Le Hunte faced a colony which was rugged, hazardous, and largely unexplored. It was undeveloped, with limited resources in men and money. He had no taste for the arduous exploratory journeys of his predecessor, but introduced some needed reorganization of central administration. More than half his term was spent lobbying for funds in Australia, whose new federal commonwealth was to take over British New Guinea. Le Hunte was essentially a 'headquarters' man, and his major field expedition was a punitive one, against a Papuan group which had killed and eaten two missionaries, in April 1901. Following criticism of his action, a second visit was made in 1902 to attempt reconciliation.

In 1903, after several years in a difficult and demanding post, Le Hunte was appointed governor of the state of South Australia within the Australian federation, and advanced to KCMG. His talents were well suited to this largely ceremonial office, which Sir John Anderson of the Colonial Office had described to the Australian prime minister, Sir Edmund Barton, as 'presiding over mothers' meetings and paying two thousand a year for the privilege' (Barton MSS). Le Hunte had no private income and, although he had been successful enough to be reappointed, he preferred to accept the post of governor and commander-in-chief of Trinidad and Tobago in December 1908, another post earlier occupied by Sir Arthur Gordon.

In his new, and last, governorship, Le Hunte was faced with the familiar problems of a plural society in a tropical colony: a resident planter community, which could exert strong pressures on the government, an immigrant Indian labour force under indenture, and an indigenous population whose rights and welfare needed protection. He was able to negotiate these reefs without major disasters. In 1912 he was created GCMG, and three years later he retired from the colonial service to Sandridge, Crowborough in Sussex. From 1917 he served on the London Appeal Tribunal which dealt with cases of conscientious objection to military service in the war.

Le Hunte was a tall man (6 feet 2 inches), of distinguished features (with a walrus moustache), a humane

Christian gentleman who had been an Anglican lay reader in Fiji. Although he offered frequent advice on policy and personnel to the Australian government after he had left New Guinea for South Australia, and, as a beneficiary of Sir Arthur Gordon's 'Fijian nursery', believed in patronage, he was not a keen judge of character; he could not accept the adverse judgement of a royal commission on his own protégé, Captain F. R. Barton, formerly of the West India regiment, whose appointment he had urged as administrator of British New Guinea in 1904. But he was a 'safe pair of hands' as the governor of small, potentially difficult colonies. On 29 January 1925 he died of cancer at Sandridge, Crowborough, Sussex, and was buried at Crowborough. F. J. West

Sources PRO, CO [Fiji, Dominica, Barbados, Mauritius, British New Guinea, South Australia, Trinidad and Tobago] • Commonwealth Archives, Australia [British New Guinea] • State Archives, South Australia • NL Aus., Atlee Hunt MSS • NL Aus., Alfred Deakin MSS • NL Aus., Barton MSS • m. cert. • d. cert. • G. R. Le Hunte, *Six letters from the Western Pacific* • D. Langmore, 'Le Hunte, G. R.', *AusDB*, vol. 10 • *WWW* • *The Eton register*, 3 (privately printed, Eton, 1906)
Archives Commonwealth Archives, Canberra • NL Aus., Deakin MSS • NL Aus., Atlee Hunt MSS • PRO, CO corresp. • State Library of South Australia, Adelaide, Mortlock Library of South Australiana, South Australia Archives
Likenesses photograph, Government House, Adelaide, South Australia

Lehzen, (Johanna Clara) Louise, Baroness Lehzen in the Hanoverian nobility (1784–1870), royal governess, was born on 3 October 1784 in Hanover, among the younger of the seven daughters and two sons of Joachim Friedrich Lehzen, a Lutheran pastor, and his wife, Melusine Palm, daughter of a clergyman. Joachim Lehzen had known the disgraced Queen Caroline Matilda of Denmark during her exile in Celle. After serving in the von Marenholtz family, in December 1819 Louise Lehzen came to England to become the governess of Princess Feodore, daughter from her first marriage of the duchess of Kent; earlier in the same year the duchess had given birth to another daughter, who would become Queen Victoria.

In 1824 Lehzen was appointed governess to Victoria, as well as to her half-sister, remaining as lady in attendance and Victoria's constant companion after her education was placed in other hands. From 1830 she held no official position at court, hampered by her lowly social origins, despite the Hanoverian barony which was conferred on her by George IV in 1827. More important was the intense dislike of Sir John Conroy, comptroller of the household of the duchess of Kent. Seeking to establish himself as Victoria's chief counsellor, against the day of her accession, he viewed the baroness as a rival and sought to have her removed from the household. But she was firmly entrenched in Victoria's affections, and, moreover, was regarded by George IV and William IV as a bulwark against the ambitions of Conroy; she retained her position. In Victoria's eyes she was 'the *most affectionate, devoted, attached*, and *disinterested* friend I have' (*Girlhood*, ed. Esher, 1.138).

After Victoria's accession, Lehzen remained her constant attendant; the duchess of Kent had little access

(Johanna Clara) Louise Lehzen, Baroness Lehzen in the Hanoverian nobility (1784–1870), by Princess Victoria, 1833

to her daughter, but Lehzen occupied an adjoining bedroom with a connecting door, withdrawing during political audiences and returning immediately afterwards. She also enjoyed considerable control over the queen's expenditure: her signature was required to authorize the payment of all tradesmen's bills. Her influence was criticized, especially by those hostile to German influence at court, as was her penchant for gossip, characteristics which made her a ready scapegoat in the Lady Flora Hastings scandal. More importantly, fear of losing Lehzen was one of the causes of Victoria's intransigence during the 'bedchamber' crisis of 1839.

The arrival of Prince Albert in 1840 ended Victoria's dependence on Lehzen. Albert, determined that his wife should rely on him alone, came early into conflict with her attachment to the baroness. By 1842, he was describing her as 'A crazy, stupid intriguer, obsessed with the lust of power, who regards herself as a demi-God, and anyone who refuses to recognise her as such is a criminal' (Hudson, 184), and actively sought to wean Victoria from her dependence on her former governess. In September 1842 Lehzen was persuaded to retire, with an annual pension of £8000. She returned to Germany, settling in Bückeburg with her sister (who died three months later). She remained there with her mementos of the queen, whom she saw briefly in 1862, and died there, unmarried, on 9 September 1870. She was buried in the Jetenburger cemetery at Bückeburg, where Victoria erected a memorial to her.

Lacking the sophistication to survive in a royal court, and apparently without personal ambition, Lehzen had none the less been a formative influence of Victoria's character. As an educator, she had not imparted a great deal of information to the young princess, but provided a clear set of moral imperatives and encouraged in them the strength of will which had enabled her to foil the plans of Conroy. Perhaps remembering the unfortunate Queen Caroline Matilda, she wrote that she could 'pardon *wickedness* in a Queen, but not *weakness*' (Hudson, 19).

K. D. REYNOLDS

Sources *DNB* • *The girlhood of Queen Victoria: a selection from her majesty's diaries between the years 1832 and 1840*, ed. Viscount Esher [R. B. Brett], 2 vols. (1912) • S. Weintraub, *Victoria: biography of a queen* (1987) • E. Longford, *Victoria RI* (1964) • K. Hudson, *A royal conflict* (1994) • *The letters of Queen Victoria*, ed. A. C. Benson, Lord Esher [R. B. Brett], and G. E. Buckle, 9 vols. (1907–32) • D. D. Aldridge, *Scandinavica*, 31 (1992), 94–6 [review article]
Archives Herts. ALS, corresp. with Lord Conyngham • Herts. ALS, corresp. with Lord Lytton
Likenesses Queen Victoria, drawing, 1833, Royal Collection [*see illus.*] • Koepke, miniature, Royal Collection

Leicester. For this title name *see* Beaumont, Robert de, count of Meulan and first earl of Leicester (*d.* 1118); Robert, second earl of Leicester (1104–1168); Breteuil, Robert de, third earl of Leicester (*c.*1130–1190); Breteuil, Robert de, fourth earl of Leicester (*d.* 1204); Grandmesnil, Petronilla de, countess of Leicester (*d.* 1212); Amice, countess of Rochefort and *suo jure* countess of Leicester (*d.* 1215) [*see under* Breteuil, Robert de, fourth earl of Leicester (*d.* 1204)]; Montfort, Simon de, eighth earl of Leicester (*c.*1208–1265); Briouze, Loretta de, countess of Leicester (*d.* in or after 1266); Eleanor, countess of Pembroke and Leicester (1215?–1275); Montfort, Amaury de, styled eleventh earl of Leicester (1242/3–*c.*1300); Edmund, first earl of Lancaster and first earl of Leicester (1245–1296); Thomas of Lancaster, second earl of Lancaster, second earl of Leicester, and earl of Lincoln (*c.*1278–1322); Henry of Lancaster, third earl of Lancaster and third earl of Leicester (*c.*1280–1345); Lacy, Alice, *suo jure* countess of Lincoln, and countess of Lancaster and Leicester (1281–1348) [*see under* Thomas of Lancaster, second earl of Lancaster, second earl of Leicester, and earl of Lincoln (*c.*1278–1322)]; Dudley, Robert, earl of Leicester (1532/3–1588); Dudley, Lettice, countess of Essex and countess of Leicester (*b.* after 1540, *d.* 1634); Sidney, Barbara, countess of Leicester (*c.*1559–1621); Sidney, Robert, first earl of Leicester (1563–1626); Sidney, Robert, second earl of Leicester (1595–1677); Sidney, Philip, third earl of Leicester (1619–1698); Coke, Thomas William, first earl of Leicester of Holkham (1754–1842); Coke, Thomas William, second earl of Leicester of Holkham (1822–1909).

Leicester, John Fleming, first Baron de Tabley (1762–1827), art patron, was born at Tabley House, Nether Tabley, near Knutsford, Cheshire, on 4 April 1762, the eldest surviving son of Sir Peter Leicester, fourth baronet (1732–1770), and his wife, Catherine (*d.* 1786), coheir of Sir William Fleming, bt, of Rydal, Westmorland. His father was the son of Sir John Byrne, third baronet, of Timogue, Ireland, and his wife, Merial, the only child of Sir Francis Leicester, third baronet; he took by act of parliament his

John Fleming Leicester, first Baron de Tabley (1762–1827), by James Northcote, *c.*1803

mother's name of Leicester in 1744, and came into possession of the Leicester estates in Cheshire. An art patron himself, he erected Tabley House in 1760–68 to the design of John Carr, near the old hall. Sir Peter Leicester died on 12 February 1770, and was succeeded by his son John, who was educated at home and at Trinity College, Cambridge (1781–4), and was instructed in drawing by Robert Marris, Thomas Vivares, and Paul Sandby. From June 1784 to July 1786 Leicester toured Switzerland and Italy, where he met Sir Richard Colt Hoare with whom he sketched and visited the galleries in Rome; from about 1801 they shared a holiday villa on Lake Bala. Many of Leicester's sketches, chiefly landscapes, together with some loosely finished pictures in oil, are still at Tabley House. He was not amused when J. M. W. Turner, who painted a pair of views of Tabley in 1808, sent him a bill for giving him lessons. Leicester also executed a set of lithographic prints from his own drawings of landscapes, birds, fishes, and other wildlife.

Leicester became 'the greatest patron of the national school of painting that our island ever possessed' (*GM*, 273). He was buying British paintings by 1789 and his penchant for works from British artists was further encouraged from 1818 by William Paulet Carey (1759–1839), an Irish artist turned propagandist for modern British art, who was fine arts editor of the *Literary Gazette*; the editor of this magazine, William Jerdan, became another supporter. From about 1800 Leicester commissioned fancy pictures of his mistress, Emily St Clare, but she was pensioned off with an allowance of £700 p.a. and her portraits hidden when, on 9 November 1810, he married a granddaughter of the architect Sir William Chambers, Georgiana Maria Cottin (1794–1859); portraits of Lady Leicester by Lawrence and William Owen are still at Tabley. The couple had two sons.

Leicester's patronage of British art was highly public-spirited: in 1805 he acquired the lease of 24 Hill Street, Mayfair, and immediately converted part into a gallery, to which (from April 1818) the public was admitted most years during the season. By 1808 he had converted three rooms at Tabley into another picture gallery. In 1810 he was treasurer of the short-lived Calcographic Society, established to help engravers. In 1823 he gave two pictures to the Royal Irish Institution (of which he was an honorary member, as too of the Royal Cork Society of Arts), to encourage the creation of a national gallery in Dublin. In March 1823 his offer to sell his collection to the nation to create a 'National Gallery for British Art' was refused by the prime minister. And in 1825 he sought the support of others in the foundation of the Manchester Institution. In the 1820s he broadened the scope of his collection to include history paintings and sculpture, although the core of it remained landscapes and fancy subjects; notable omissions were works by David Wilkie and Constable.

Leicester was also interested in music and in natural history, especially birds and fishes. Shortly before his death he planned with William Jerdan an elaborate 'British Ichthyology'. He was also noted as an excellent pistol shot. In politics he was a moderate whig, joining Brooks's Club in 1790. He was MP for Yarmouth, Isle of Wight, from 1791 to 1796, for Heytesbury, Wiltshire, from 1796 to 1802, and for Stockbridge, Hampshire, in 1807. In 1799 he opposed Irish union, and he consistently supported the prince regent, an intimate friend. He was lieutenant-colonel of the Cheshire militia (1784–96), and from 1797 colonel of the regiment eventually called the King's regiment of Cheshire yeoman cavalry, which he raised and helped to finance. The regiment received the thanks of the prince regent and government for helping to disperse the blanketeers in Lancashire in 1817 and the meeting at Manchester known as the Peterloo massacre on 16 August 1819. He was created Baron de Tabley (a wag suggested the alternative title of 'De Tableaux') on 16 July 1826, a promotion which he had eagerly awaited since 1811. He died at Tabley House on 18 June 1827, after being taken seriously ill the previous December, and was buried at Great Budworth, Cheshire. His widow subsequently married his nephew, the Revd Frederick Leicester.

Leicester's annual income of £12,000 was derived from Cheshire land and salt mines at Northwich (admired by Sir Richard Colt Hoare); his artistic and military expenditure, however, left him insolvent. An executor, his first cousin once removed, Thomas Lister Parker, also a collector, who had had to sell his own Lancashire house some years before, ordered the immediate auction of the pictures at Hill Street, which realized £7466; in 1828 the salt mines too were auctioned. Tabley and the pictures there, except for some sold in 1912 and 1927, descended in Leicester's family until 1975, when they became the property of the University of Manchester. The main rooms of the house were later opened to the public. Leicester's grandson John Byrne Leicester *Warren, third Baron de Tabley (1835–1895), was a poet.

ALBERT NICHOLSON, *rev.* SELBY WHITTINGHAM

Sources D. Hall, 'The Tabley House papers', *Walpole Society*, 38 (1960–62), 59–122 • W. Carey, *Some memoirs of the patronage and progress of the fine arts in England and Ireland* (1826) • P. Cannon-Brookes, *Paintings from Tabley* (1989) • HoP, *Commons, 1790–1820* • S. Whittingham, 'A most liberal patron: Sir John Fleming Leicester, bart., 1st Baron de Tabley, 1762–1827', *Turner Studies*, 6/2 (1986), 24–36 • *GM*, 1st ser., 97/2 (1827), 273–4 • *Literary Gazette* (23 June 1827), 397 • G. Ormerod, *The history of the county palatine and city of Chester*, 2nd edn, ed. T. Helsby, 1 (1882), 610, 626 • Farington, *Diary* • C. Hussey, 'Tabley Old Hall, Cheshire [pts 1–3]', *Country Life*, 54 (1923), 50–58, 84–90, 114–20 • W. McKay and W. Roberts, *John Hoppner, R.A.*, 2 vols. (1909–14) • J. Wilson, 'Hoppner's "Tambourine girl" identified', *Burlington Magazine*, 130 (1988), 763–7 • M. Butlin, 'A hitherto unnoticed sale from the collection of Sir John Leicester', *Turner Studies*, 11/1 (1991), 30–31 • F. Leary, *The earl of Chester's yeomanry cavalry, 1797–1897* (1898) • GEC, *Peerage*

Archives Ches. & Chester ALSS, corresp.

Likenesses J. Reynolds, J. Northcote, and J. Simpson, oils, 1790–1826, Tabley House, Cheshire • J. Northcote, oils, *c.*1803, Tabley House, Cheshire [*see illus.*] • J. Northcote, oils, *c.*1803, Browsholme Hall, Lancashire • J. Ward, oils, 1824, Tabley House, Cheshire • G. Jones, oils, 1825, Tabley House, Cheshire • H. Meyer, stipple, BM, NPG • S. W. Reynolds, mezzotint (after J. Reynolds and J. Northcote), BM, NPG

Wealth at death insolvent • £12,000 p.a., mainly from land and salt mines in Cheshire: Farington, *Diary*

Leicester, Richard of. *See* Wetheringsett, Richard of (*fl. c.*1200–*c.*1230).

Leicester, Robert (*c.*1266–1327x34), Franciscan chronologist and theologian, originally came from Leicester and was a novice of the Franciscan convent there. About 1294 he was made lector of the Franciscan convent at Hereford through the patronage of Richard Swinfield, bishop of Hereford (*d.* 1317). By 1300, when he was unsuccessfully presented for licence to hear confessions in the diocese of Lincoln, Leicester was sub-lector of the Northampton convent. Subsequently he became forty-eighth master of the Oxford Franciscans, probably in 1321–2, and soon after that he was lecturing at the order's convent in Avignon. The date of his residence in Avignon can be determined as before 1325 by inference from his treatise *Super egenum et pauperem Christum*, in which he presented a defence of the Spiritual Franciscan position on poverty (which maintained that Christ and the apostles had owned no property). Leicester is unlikely to have written such a treatise after the papal bull *Cum inter nonullos* of 1325, in which the extreme Spiritual views were declared heretical, since there is no record of proceedings being initiated against him by the papacy. John XXII (*r.* 1316–34) does not mention Leicester as one of those English Franciscans to be arrested in 1329–30 for dissenting from the bull. The prologue to the treatise, however, was written in response to the bull and added later. The treatise afterwards belonged to Thomas Duffield, chancellor of Lincoln Cathedral, who presented it to his cathedral library in 1422. It exists in one manuscript, CUL, Add. MS 3571, fols. 246*r*–257*v*. Leicester was back in Oxford by 1325, when he was associated with

Nicholas Tyngewick as a *magister extraneus* at Balliol College, with responsibility for determining whether the college statutes permitted members to attend lectures in faculties other than arts. The *magistri* ordained that it was not permissible.

In his youth Leicester wrote works on Jewish chronology, contained in Bodl. Oxf., MS Digby 212. These comprise *De compoto Hebreorum aptato ad Kalendarium* (1294), *Compotus Hebreorum purus*, and *Commentariolus super tabulas in tractatu primo supra recensito descriptas*, sometimes known as *De ratione temporum* (1295). These works may have been written at the request of Bishop Swinfield, who asked Leicester for instruction in the computation of calendars. Leicester's treatises show an appreciation of the merits of the Jewish calendar, but on the grounds that it supplied a rational and comprehensive biblical chronology rather than on purely scientific grounds. His work in this field relied somewhat on Roger Bacon (*d.* 1294), and also on a Jewish writer he calls 'Rabada filius Hahaha' (probably Rabbi Abraham bar Hiyya). He died between 1327 and 1334, probably at Bury St Edmunds, rather than, as Bale thought, Lichfield. Bale gives 1348 (implausibly) as the date of his death.

Robert Leicester is to be distinguished from the Robert of Leicester (*fl.* *c.*1250–*c.*1280) who was a doctor of theology in Paris, and whose *Distinctiones* is preserved in Cambridge, Pembroke College, MS 87. Emden considered it probable that the author of the early works on computation was a different figure altogether from the Robert Leicester presented for licence to hear confessions in 1300, and indeed from the author of the treatise on poverty. The Robert unsuccessfully applying to hear confessions may have been a different man, but there seems little reason why the same Franciscan should not have written in youth on mathematics and in maturity on theology. ANDREW JOTISCHKY

Sources C. Walmsley, 'Two long lost works of William Woodford and Robert of Leicester', *Archivum Franciscanum Historicum*, 46 (1953), 458–70 · CUL, Add. MS 3571 · A. G. Little, *The Grey friars in Oxford*, OHS, 20 (1892) · Emden, *Oxf.* · J. D. North, 'Astronomy and mathematics', *Hist. U. Oxf.* 2: *Late med. Oxf.*, 103–74

Archives CUL, Add. MS 3571, fols. 246r–257v | Bodl. Oxf., MS Digby 212

Leichhardt, (Friedrich Wilhelm) Ludwig (1813–1848?), natural scientist and explorer in Australia, was born on 23 October 1813 at Trebatsch, near Beeskow, then in Saxony but after 1845 in the mark of Brandenburg, Prussia, the fourth son and sixth of the eight children of Christian Hieronymus Matthias Leichhardt, farmer and minor official, and his wife, Charlotte Sophie, *née* Strählow. Leichhardt grew up in very modest circumstances: he was educated at Trebatsch, and at schools in nearby Zaue and Cottbus, before attending the universities of Berlin (1831 and 1834–6) and Göttingen (1833) where he began his study of the natural sciences. He left university without a degree, his poverty preventing him from paying the necessary fees. In 1837 Leichhardt joined William Nicholson, a fellow student at Berlin, who lived in Clifton, Bristol. From this date until 1841 the two studied medicine and natural science at the Royal College of Surgeons, the British Museum, and the Jardin des Plantes, and in the field in England and on the continent. Nicholson supported Leichhardt throughout this period, and in 1841 equipped him to travel to Australia to study the as yet undocumented natural history of the new land.

Leichhardt arrived in Sydney in 1842 and spent his time studying and lecturing on the natural history of the region but his hopes of an official position in a museum or the botanical garden came to nothing. He left the town to explore the Hunter River valley (1842–3) and the area between Newcastle, on the Hunter, and the Moreton Bay district, near Brisbane (1843–4), returning to Sydney to publish and lecture on his geological and natural historical discoveries. Frustrated by the lack of official support for exploration, Leichhardt, who had by this time won a considerable reputation, organized a private, rather ramshackle, party which between 1844 and 1845 traversed nearly 3000 miles between Jimbone in the Darling downs, about 150 miles west of Brisbane, and Port Essington, on the north coast of Arnhem Land, by way of the Gulf of Carpentaria. Leichhardt returned to Sydney in 1846 as the leader of the longest Australian exploration to date and was accorded a rapturous welcome, a government reward, money from an admiring public, and honours from the geographical societies of London and Paris (1847). His *Journal of an Overland Expedition in Australia* (1847) was a work of science, not a popular traveller's tale. The object of exploration was the testing of scientific hypotheses, not adventure.

Leichhardt planned a second journey into the interior, financed by the rewards from the first. In 1846 his party set out from the Darling downs again, but was forced by rain and fever to return the following year. In March 1848 a fresh party set out from the Condamine River, there flowing north-west, hoping to travel inland, skirting the northern edge of the desert. Last seen on 3 April at Cogoon, still in the Darling downs, the party disappeared without trace.

The lost party received something of the same treatment as Franklin's and Scott's. In the 1850s and 1860s expeditions were sent to find Leichhardt's men, although, unlike Franklin's and Scott's parties, the fate of Leichhardt's was never established. Like Franklin and Scott, Leichhardt was initially hailed as a gallant hero, and accorded the 'Strahlenkrone des Märtyrers'—'the glorious crown of the martyr'—(Ratzel, 213) who perished in the cause of science and extending European influence. Later, criticism of Leichhardt's leadership, like that of Franklin and particularly of Scott, was voiced, notably by Chisholm. As with the polar explorers, Leichhardt's reputation was cultivated after his death by his family, in his case by the publication of his private letters in 1881, and has continued to inspire both popular and scholarly biographies. Leichhardt was the inspiration for the character Voss in Patrick White's novel of the same name.

Leichhardt was unquestionably single-minded and determined, and his scientific works, published in England, Germany, and Australia, and his unpublished papers bear witness to his success as a scientist who could formulate imaginative hypotheses and test them rigorously against empirical data. ELIZABETH BAIGENT

Sources *AusDB* • W. Cooper and G. McLaren, 'Friedrich Wilhelm Ludwig Leichhardt, 1813–?1848', *Geographers: biobibliographical studies*, 17, ed. G. J. Martin (1996), 52–67 • L. Leichhardt, *An explorer at rest*, ed. E. M. Webster (1986) • A. H. Chisholm, *Strange new world* (1955) • F. Ratzel, 'Leichhardt, Ludwig', *Allgemeine deutsche Biographie*, ed. R. von Liliencron and others, 18 (Leipzig, 1883), 210–14 • C. Roderick, *Leichhardt the dauntless explorer* (1988) • D. Sprod, *Proud intrepid heart* (1989) • E. Connell, *The mystery of Ludwig Leichhardt* (1980) • L. Leichhardt, *The letters of F. W. Ludwig Leichhardt*, ed. M. Aurousseau, 3 vols., Hakluyt Society, 133–5 (1968) • H. Haufe, *Entdeckungsreisen in Australien; Ludwig Leichhardt, ein deutsches Forscherschicksal* (1972) • L. Leichhardt, *Dr L. Leichhardts Briefe an seine Angehörigen*, ed. E. Neumayer and O. Leichhardt (1881)
Archives Mitchell L., NSW • State Library of New South Wales, Sydney, Dixson Library | Mitchell L., NSW, J. Gilbert MSS
Likenesses Schmalfuss, portrait, 1855, Heimat Museum, Beeskow, Germany • E. Wolf, portrait, 1938 (after Schmalfuss) • C. Rodius, drawing • lithograph (after drawing by C. Rodius), Mitchell L., NSW

Leifchild, Henry Stormonth (1823–1884), sculptor, born in Moorgate, London, was the fourth son of William Gerard Leifchild of Moorgate and The Elms, Wanstead, Essex, and nephew of John Leifchild DD. He married Marion, daughter of Henry Clarke of King Street, Covent Garden, London; they had no children. He studied from 1844 at the Royal Academy Schools, and from 1848 to 1851 in Rome. He first exhibited at the Royal Academy in 1844, sending *The Mother of Moses Leaving him on the Banks of the Nile*. At the Great Exhibition of 1851 he exhibited his statue, *Rispah Watching over the Dead Bodies of her Sons*, and that, like his later groups *Bacchus Awakening Ariadne*, *The Torchbearers*, *Minerva Repressing the Wrath of Achilles*, *Lot's Wife*, and *Wrecked*, besides various busts, attracted favourable attention. He was the successful competitor for the guards' memorial at Chelsea Hospital in London. Seven models in plaster of his most important works were presented by his widow and family to the Castle Museum in Nottingham, all but one of which were destroyed by a curator before 1929. He is today best-known for the Robertson mausoleum (*c*.1867) in Warriston cemetery, Edinburgh. A heroic seated figure of *Erinna*, dated 1860, is at the Royal Holloway and Bedford New College, Egham, Surrey. Leifchild resided most of his life in Stanhope Street, Regent's Park, London, and died on 11 November 1884 at 15 Kirkstall Road, Streatham Hill, London. He was multitalented, excelling not only in his profession but also as a draughtsman, carver, and musician.

L. H. CUST, *rev.* CHRISTOPHER WHITEHEAD

Sources R. Gunnis, *Dictionary of British sculptors, 1660–1851* (1953), 238 • B. Read, *Victorian sculpture* (1982), 187–8 • Graves, *RA exhibitors* • M. H. Grant, *A dictionary of British sculptors from the XIIIth century to the XXth century* (1953), 147 • *The Athenaeum* (29 Nov 1884), 701 • private information (1892)

Leifchild, John (1780–1862), Congregational minister and writer, was born on 15 February 1780 at Barnet, Hertfordshire, the elder son and fourth in the family of two sons and three daughters of John Leifchild, cooper, a Methodist, and his wife, a Miss Bockman, daughter of an artist whose paintings hung at Hampton Court Palace. As a child Leifchild heard John Wesley preach in Barnet, and this made a deep impression on him. He was educated at Barnet grammar school from 1789, leaving at the age of eleven or twelve to work for his father, and from 1797 he worked for a cooper in St Albans. In 1799 or 1800 he moved to London, still working as a cooper, and attended the Wesleyan chapel in Great Queen Street. His first wife died in childbirth in 1804. About 1803 he joined the Workhouse Community at City Road Chapel, spending his Sundays preaching in workhouses. By now he was moving away from Wesleyan views, and in 1804 he was invited to study at the Independent Hoxton Academy.

In 1808 Leifchild became minister of the Independent chapel in Hornton Street, Kensington. On 4 June 1811 he married Elizabeth Stormonth (*d.* 1855), eldest daughter of John Farquhar, a surgeon in India, who had changed his name on inheriting an entailed estate near Forfar in Scotland. They had one son. After Elizabeth's death Leifchild published a memoir of her life, *The Minister's Help-Meet* (1856). From 1824 to 1830 he was minister of Bridge Street Chapel, Bristol, and he filled it with a congregation of 900. From 1831 to 1854 he was minister at Craven Chapel, Bayswater, London, where his congregation grew to 2000. He became a famous preacher, and although he retired in 1854 he continued to preach, at Queen's Square Chapel, Brighton, until 1856. He was one of those involved in the formation of the Evangelical Alliance in 1846, the aim of which was to bring evangelical Christians together for combined action.

Leifchild was a prolific writer throughout his life, and his many publications included *A Help to the Private and Domestic Reading of the Holy Scriptures* (1829), *The Plain Christian Guarded Against some Popular Errors Respecting the Scriptures* (1841), *Original Hymns* (1842), *Christian Union, or, Suggestions for Promoting Brotherly Love among the Various Denominations of Evangelical Protestants* (1844), and *The Christian Emigrant, containing Observations on Different Countries, with Essays, Discourses, Meditations, and Prayers* (1849). With George Redford he edited *The Evangelist*, a monthly magazine, from May 1837 to June 1839. Leifchild died on 29 June 1862 at his home, 4 Fitzroy Terrace, Gloucester Road, Regent's Park, London, and was buried in Abney Park cemetery. ANNE PIMLOTT BAKER

Sources J. R. Leifchild, *John Leifchild* (1863) • R. Tudur Jones, *Congregationalism in England, 1662–1962* (1962) • *Congregational Year Book* (1863), 235–9 • J. B. Brown, *John Leifchild: a sketch of his character and ministry* (1862) • J. Graham, *The victor crowned: thoughts on the life of J. Leifchild* (1862)
Archives DWL, corresp. and papers
Likenesses J. Linnell, mezzotint, pubd 1836, NPG • Baugniet, engraving, 1854, repro. in Leifchild, *John Leifchild*, frontispiece • W. Dickes, stipple, 1854 (after C. Baugniet), NPG • T. Blood, stipple (after J. R. Wildman), BM, NPG; repro. in *Evangelical Magazine* (1825) • R. Woodman, stipple, BM; repro. in *Congregational Magazine* (1825)
Wealth at death under £4000: probate, 17 July 1862, *CGPLA Eng. & Wales*

Leigh. *See also* Lea, Lee.

Leigh, Alexander (*c.*1683–1772), local government officer and industrial promoter, was born at Millgate, Wigan, but little else is known about his origins. During his lifetime his home town of Wigan was transformed from an archaic borough dominated by craft companies and disputes over burghal rights, office holding, and parliamentary elections, to the archetype of Dickens's Coketown. As a prominent agent of the change, Leigh founded a large fortune and a notable lineage.

From about 1710 to 1760 Leigh dominated the borough administration of Wigan: he held many of the key offices, serving as mayor (1727, 1737, and 1759), bencher (1726, 1741, 1760–62, and 1765), town clerk (1733–6), town attorney (1743–53), and town justice (1760). During these fifty years he also managed the parliamentary electorate of Wigan in association with Robert Holt, Holt's son Edward, and his own son Robert. First to benefit from the often violent chicanery of 'their high and mightinesses Leigh and Holt' (NL Scot., Crawford MS 47/2) was James Barry, earl of Barrymore, who was MP for Wigan (1715–47), and also its mayor (1725 and 1734). Although Leigh initially acted against the interest of Sir Roger Bradshaigh, third baronet (1675–1747), who also represented Wigan in parliament (1695–1747) and served as mayor, he and the Holts subsequently became close associates of the Bradshaighs. In an acrimonious dispute in 1759–60 Leigh set up, as senior alderman, an alternative borough administration, of which he made himself mayor. By 1761 he had lost control of Wigan, and 'Corporation feuds … moderated into peace; for the Electors, doubtless, have discovered that beating out of brains did not contribute to the honesty or worth of the elected' (Walker, 34).

Leigh married his first wife, Elizabeth, before 1709, and they had seven children between 1709 and 1718. Four died in infancy, and a fifth at the age of twenty-one. Their son Robert (1713–1741) also practised as an attorney and was active in Wigan politics until his early death. In addition Leigh had an illegitimate son (who died in 1725) with Mary Tootell. On 22 July 1728 Leigh married Dorothy (*b.* 1705), daughter of Robert Holt; they had seven children between 1729 and 1737.

As the agent or trustee of many local landowners and steward of seventeen manor courts, Leigh was experienced in proving and exchanging manorial titles, and therefore common and mineral rights. Oversight of the local affairs of the Bradshaighs, who spent most of their time at court in London, gave Leigh considerable expertise in estate and colliery management. In 1737 and 1738 he kept Bradshaigh minutely informed about a fire in his Haigh colliery (yet without mentioning that six colliers were killed in the disaster). He bought Hindley Hall estate from the Hindley family, and in 1721 he obtained an act to enclose Hindley commons; this was steered through parliament by Bradshaigh and Barrymore, against strong local opposition. By about 1750 Leigh also had land in Manchester (developed as Cannon Street), Wigan (including Whitely Hall), Orrell, and Ince. Leigh's estates contained rich coal deposits as did land acquired next to his own in Orrell on the marriages in 1762 and 1760 of his sons Holt (1731–1785) and Edward (*b.* 1733) to two wealthy sisters of a neighbouring family. By 1770 the Leigh family owned 4 million tons of high-grade coal in Orrell; and reserves in Hindley, Ince, and Aspull, though not as well located relative to waterways until after Alexander's death, were even bigger.

Mining developed rapidly after the River Douglas was made navigable from Wigan to the Ribble estuary. Contractors appointed in 1720 did not do the work, and the parliamentary commissioners for the project (including Barrymore) appointed Alexander Leigh and Alexander Radcliffe of Ormskirk to complete it in 1731. Leigh took over five-sixths of the enterprise and Robert Holt one-sixth in 1737. Although the commissioners declared the navigation finished in 1742 within the stipulated eleven years, the first receipts were earned in 1744, and the business did not move into consistent profit until 1753. At this point Leigh announced that annual dividends would be paid, and he sold two shares of one thirty-sixth each. The total cost of the waterway was over £23,000; however, receipts from tolls on coal shipments grew nearly ninefold between 1748 and 1754, and annual profits between 1753 and 1755 averaged nearly £200 and were climbing steeply. Leigh operated collieries on the river, traded coal to the Ribble estuary and the Lancashire coast, and made money from rents on coal yards, way-leaves, and coal royalties. Threats to impose sea-borne coal duties on boats crossing estuarine and coastal waters were fought off in parliament by Barrymore and Bradshaigh.

A few weeks before his death, Leigh sold his twenty-nine of the thirty-six navigation shares for £14,500 to the proprietors of the Leeds and Liverpool Canal, who thereby gained control of waterway access to the Wigan coalfield. Holt Leigh had already sold the two shares he had received from Edward Holt to the canal company for £2000 in 1768, days after a cancelled agreement for the transfer of all of his father's shares to him in return for settling debts of only £6335. The Orrell and Wigan estates were not bequeathed in Alexander's will, and must have been transferred before his death to Holt Leigh.

Alexander Leigh's powers were perhaps failing as he moved into his late eighties, though he granted mortgages in the last year of his life and the will drawn up within weeks of his death was signed with the usual bold flourishes in a firm hand. Judged on his behaviour in Wigan affairs, Leigh was domineering and cantankerous. In his later years it seems that he continued to be unscrupulous: in his quarrels with and threats against Sir Roger Bradshaigh and Edward Holt, in the chancery suit he began in 1755 against the other beneficiaries of Robert Holt's will of 1740, in the sour tone of his bequest to his wife, in his contractual dealings with his son Holt, and in his sale agreement with the Leeds and Liverpool Canal Company (it excluded the land necessary to run the navigation, which was obtained by returning a share). When he died at his lifelong home in Millgate, Wigan, in 1772, the only surviving members of his family were his widowed granddaughter of his first marriage, Cicely Harvey, to whom he bequeathed £3000, his sons Holt and

Edward from his second marriage, and his second wife. He was buried at All Saints, Wigan, on 27 November 1772. Holt Leigh was Alexander's elder surviving son and principal heir; like his father he was an attorney and had considerable business acumen, and he amassed more land and coal rights (including the marriage portion and paternal inheritance of his only surviving brother, Edward). He also rebuilt Whitely Hall as Leigh Place in the five years after his father's death. Despite the 'folly and profligacy' of his unmarried 'mature years' (*VCH Lancaster*, 4.120), Holt Leigh's son and heir, Sir Robert Holt Leigh, first baronet, of Hindley Hall (1763–1843) was MP for Wigan between 1802 and 1820. He left an income of over £14,000 a year for life to a distant kinsman, Thomas Pemberton, who took the name Pemberton Leigh in 1842.

JOHN LANGTON

Sources calendar of the Wigan Corporation Archives, Wigan Archives Service, Leigh, Borough Court Leet Rolls [vol. 2, 1692–1834 (n.d.)] • M. Cox, 'Sir Roger Bradshaigh, 3rd baronet, and the electoral management of Wigan, 1695–1747', *Bulletin of the John Rylands University Library*, 37 (1954–5), 120–64 • D. Anderson, *The Orrell coalfield, Lancashire, 1740–1850* (1975) • J. Langton, *Geographical change and industrial revolution: coalmining in south west Lancashire, 1590–1799* (1979) • C. Hadfield and G. Biddle, *The canals of north west England*, 1 (1970) • *VCH Lancashire*, vol. 4 • A. Walker, *Remarks made on a tour from London to the lakes of Windermere and Cumberland in the summer of 1791* (1792) • R. Bradshaigh, correspondence with G. Winstanley, 12 Oct 1946, NL Scot., Crawford MS 47/2 • HoP, *Commons* • will, proved, Chester, 1 Dec 1772, Lancs. RO

Archives NL Scot., Crawford MSS • Wigan Archives Service, Leigh, Leigh-Pemberton MSS • Wigan Archives Service, Leigh, canal letter-book | Gredington Hall, Shropshire, Kenyon MSS • Lancs. RO, Clifton MSS • Wigan Archives Service, Leigh, Walmsley MSS

Wealth at death see will, proved 1 Dec 1772, Lancs. RO

Leigh, Anthony (*d.* 1692), actor, was 'of a good Family, and born in *Northamptonshire*' (Betterton, 32). Nothing more is known of his origins. He probably arrived in London in 1671; in December, the lord chamberlain arrested him and several other actors for performing without a licence. During this same period, Leigh married one Elinor, probably the actress Elinor Dixon, who first performed in Howard's *The Women's Conquest*, about September 1670. She acted subsequently under the name of Elinor Leigh or Mrs Leigh until 1707. Their parish church, St Bride's, Fleet Street, London, records the baptism of eight children: Marmaduke (*bap.* 15 March 1676), Eleanor (*bap.* 26 April 1678), Francis (*bap.* 28 July 1680), Eleanor (*bap.* 10 Sept 1681), Anthony (*bap.* 3 July 1684), Charlot (*bap.* 23 Sept 1686), John (*bap.* 22 July 1688), and Anne (*bap.* 22 July 1691). Another son, Michael, is not mentioned in the parish registers. Best known of these children is Francis, who became an actor in the eighteenth century.

Leigh's arrest late in 1671 may have impressed upon him the necessity of joining a patent company. The following year he appeared for the first time with the Duke's Company, performing the role of the fop Pacheco in Joseph Arrowsmith's *The Reformation*. The prompter John Downes claims that Leigh joined the Duke's Company in 1673 and it is likely he performed the part of Alexas in Samuel Pordage's *Herod and Mariamne* later that year. Leigh

Anthony Leigh (*d.* 1692), by Sir Godfrey Kneller, 1689 [as Father Dominic in *The Spanish Fryar* by John Dryden]

appears not to have become a staple of the company until the 1676 season but continued acting with it until its union with the King's Company in 1682; like many other theatre personnel he was absorbed into the newly formed United Company, where he found a home until his death in 1692.

Leigh is best known for his comic roles. John Downes says he was especially 'Eminent in this part of Sir *William* [in Thomas Shadwell's *The Squire of Alsatia* (1688)], & *Scapin* [in Thomas Otway's *The Cheats of Scapin* (1676)]. Old *Fumble* [in Thomas Durfey's *A Fond Husband* (1677)]. Sir *Jolly Jumble* [in Otway's *The Souldiers Fortune* (1680)]. *Mercury* [in *Amphitrion* (1690)]. Sir *Formal* [in Shadwell's *The Virtuoso* (1676)], *Spanish* Fryar [(1680)], *Pandarus* in *Troilus and Cressida* [(1679)]' (Downes, 86). Leigh's comic skills made him a favourite speaker of prologues and epilogues; indeed, several include comic business between him and James Nokes, the other brilliant comedian of the Restoration stage. In the prologue to D'Urfey's *The Virtuous Wife* (1679) the great Restoration actress, Elizabeth Barry, pouts that

Underhil, *Jevan Currier*, *Tony Lee*,
Nokes, all have better Characters than me
(*Works of Aphra Behn*, 2.200)

Barry threatens to 'throw up her Parts' until dramatists

write her better roles, but, soothed by Nokes and Leigh, ultimately decides against losing her 'share' in the company.

Performance records indicate that Leigh also possessed extraordinary range as an actor. For instance, he appeared in such sombre roles as the senator, Aelius, in Thomas Shadwell's redaction of *The History of Timon of Athens* (1678) and Antonio, 'A fine Speaker in the Senate', in Thomas Otway's *Venice Preserv'd* (1682). He was capable of impersonating a young blade like Frugal, one of 'Three wild Fellows of the Town, that Ramble to Sea, and desert their Wives' in D'Urfey's *A Commonwealth of Women* (1685). He even donned skirts for the role of Lady Addleplot, 'A Lusty flaunting imperious Lady, a highflown Stickler against the Government, and always railing at it, in talking of Politicks', in D'Urfey's *Love for Money* (1691). So convincing were Leigh's powers of impersonation that the earl of Ailesbury was convinced the actor modelled his performance on Lady Fenwick: '… the famous comic, Mr Lee, in woman's clothes represented her to the life, and so exactly had her features and complexion that one could hardly have distinguished one from the other' (Van Lennep, 1.393).

Despite this versatility Leigh mainly performed one of several comic types. Often he enacted pimps, such as Pandarus and Sir Jolly Jumble; Security, 'A Bawd and Usurer', in Nahum Tate's *Cuckolds-Haven* (1685); and Petro, the 'Suppos'd Pimp to the two Curtezans' in Aphra Behn's *The Feign'd Curtezans* (1679). Lustful prelates, such as Ascanio Sforza, a 'Buffoon Cardinal' in Nathaniel Lee's *Caesar Borgia* (1679), the Abbé in Thomas Southerne's *Sir Anthony Love* (1690), and the bishop of Hereford in *King Edward the Third* (1690), were another speciality. He also represented blustering military men, such as Rogero in Thomas Southerne's *The Disappointment* (1684) or Major Oldfox in William Wycherley's *The Plain Dealer* (1682–3 revival). The description of Major-General Blunt in Shadwell's *The Volunteers* (1692) sketches the type: 'An old Cavalier Officer, somewhat rough in Speech, but very brave and honest, and of good Understanding, and a good Patriot'. Several times Leigh was cast in farces derived from *commedia dell'arte*, suggesting that he could perform not only psychologically quirky characters, but also broad roles requiring physical dexterity. He appeared as Trappolin in Tate's *A Duke and No Duke* (1684), Harlequin in William Mountfort's *The Life and Death of Doctor Faustus, Made into a Farce* (1685–6?), and Scaramouch in Aphra Behn's *The Emperor of the Moon* (1687).

Most of all Leigh was known for playing peevish or foolish old men. D'Urfey, Behn, and Shadwell seemed especially keen to take advantage of his genius in this regard, writing several memorable roles for him. D'Urfey first created this comic type in Old Fumble, a role Leigh played in *A Fond Husband* (1677). In a similar vein were the parts of Sir Lubbery Widgeon in *The Virtuous Wife* (1679); Sir Oliver Oldcut, 'Chairman to the Committee of Sequestrations, a busie Factious fellow', in *The Royalist* (1682); and Justice Grub, 'An old Peevish Country Justice, an hater of the Town, and its Fashions', in *A Fool's Preferment* (1688). Behn wrote for Leigh the titular role of Sir Patient Fancy, 'An old Rich Alderman, and one that fancies himself always Sick' (1678); Sir Anthony Meriwill, 'An old Tory Knight of Devonshire', in *The City Heiress* (1682); and Sir Feeble Fainwou'd, 'An old Alderman to be married to Leticia', in *The Lucky Chance* (1686). Shadwell's creation, Sir William Belfond, perhaps best exemplifies the comic type:

> A Gentleman of above 3000£ *per annum*, who in his Youth had been a Spark of the Town; but married and retired into the Country, where he turned to the other extreme, rigid, morose, most sordidly covetous, clownish, obstinate, positive, and froward.

Such was Leigh's comic genius that contemporary references to him abound. Behn mentions him several times in prologues and epilogues, as well as in the preface to *The Lucky Chance*. Other dramatists, such as John Crowne, Nicholas Brady, and D'Urfey also allude to him. Crowne claimed in the preface to *City Politiques* (1683) to have taught him the part of Bartoline, down to the lisp. Frequently Leigh's name is coupled with the comic actor James Nokes, as the epilogue to Behn's play *The False Count* (1681?) typifies:

> If to make People laugh the business be,
> You Sparks better Comedians are than we;
> You every day out fool ev'n *Nokes* and *Lee*.
> They're forc'd to stop and their own Farces quit,
> T'admire the Merry-*Andrews* of the Pit.
> (*Works of Aphra Behn*, 2.341)

The fullest and most flattering description of Leigh comes from Colley Cibber's *Apology*. At one point Cibber goes so far as to credit the actor with single-handedly resuscitating otherwise moribund dramatic characters: 'Characters that would make the Reader yawn, in the Closet, have by the Strength of his Action, been lifted into the lowdest Laughter, on the Stage' (Cibber, 86). Cibber is especially good at contrasting the respective comic techniques of Nokes and Leigh. If Nokes was the more 'natural' comedian, Leigh nevertheless showed more versatility:

> *Leigh* was of the mercurial kind, and though not so strict an Observer of Nature, yet never so wanton in his Performance, as to be wholly out of her sight. In Humour, he lov'd to take a full Career, but was careful enough to stop short, when just upon the Precipice: He had great Variety, in his manner, and was famous in very different Characters. (Cibber, 86)

Cibber also mentions that Leigh 'was much admir'd by King *Charles*, who us'd to distinguish him, when spoke of, by the Title of *his Actor*' (ibid., 89). He also reports that James II was 'highly displeas'd' at Leigh's shenanigans during a performance of Sir Robert Howard's play *The Committee* in Oxford. Evidently the comedian alluded none too flatteringly to the conversion of Obadiah Walker, head of University College, to Roman Catholicism during the reign of James II.

Anthony Leigh and his wife were good friends of the Shadwells; they both witnessed Shadwell's will and testified to its authenticity. Leigh died shortly after the playwright, either on 21 or 22 December 1692; according to Cibber, Leigh contracted a fever after hearing of the death of William Mountfort, the playwright and actor who was ambushed and killed by Captain Hill and several other men. Leigh was buried in his parish church, St Bride's, Fleet Street, London, on 25 December 1692. Several images of him have come down from the Restoration. In 1689 the earl of Dorset commissioned a portrait of him by the great portrait painter, Godfrey Kneller, which has been in the National Portrait Gallery since 1900. There is a copy, perhaps by Ranelagh Barret, in the Garrick Club, and a number of engravings based on one or both of these paintings circulated during the eighteenth century.

Deborah Payne Fisk

Sources Highfill, Burnim & Langhans, *BDA*, vol. 9 • W. Van Lennep and others, eds., *The London stage, 1660–1800*, pt 1: *1660–1700* (1965) • C. Cibber, *An apology for the life of Colley Cibber*, new edn, ed. B. R. S. Fone (1968) • P. Danchin, ed., *The prologues and epilogues of the Restoration, 1660–1700*, 7 vols. (1981–8), vols. 3–6 • J. Downes, *Roscius Anglicanus*, ed. J. Milhous and R. D. Hume, new edn (1987) • *The works of Aphra Behn*, ed. J. Todd, 7 vols. (1992–6) • J. H. Wilson, *Court satires of the Restoration* (1976) • [P. A. Motteux], *The Gentleman's Journal* (Dec 1692) • PRO, LC 5/14, 19 [reversed] • T. Betterton, [W. Oldys and others], *The history of the English stage* (1741) • parish register, St Bride's, Fleet Street, London, 25 Dec 1692 [burial]

Likenesses G. Kneller, oils, 1689, NPG [*see illus.*] • R. Barret?, portrait (after G. Kneller), Garr. Club • J. Smith, mezzotint (after G. Kneller), BM

Leigh, Augustus Austen (1840–1905), college head, born at Wargrave, Berkshire, on 17 July 1840, was the sixth son of James Edward Austen (from 1836 Austen Leigh), who when he died in 1874 was vicar of Bray (Berkshire), and Emma (*d.* 1876), daughter of Charles Smith (1756–1814), MP, of Suttons in Essex.

Austen Leigh entered Eton College as a colleger in 1852; in 1858–9 he played cricket for the school. In 1859 he entered King's College, Cambridge, as a scholar on the foundation; he gained a Browne medal for Latin ode, and a members' prize for Latin essay in 1862, graduated as fourth classic in 1863, and proceeded MA in 1866. In 1862 he became fellow of his college, where two of his brothers, Edward Compton Austen Leigh (1839–1916) and William Austen Leigh (*d.* 1921), also held fellowships. He was ordained deacon by the bishop of Lincoln (visitor of the college) in 1865, but his experience as curate of Henley-on-Thames, 1865–7, convinced him that he was unsuited for parochial work and he never proceeded to priest's orders.

In 1867 Austen Leigh returned to King's College, where he spent the rest of his life. He was tutor (1868–81), dean (1871–3, 1882–5), and vice-provost (1877–89), and was then, on the death of Richard Okes, elected provost (9 February 1889), gaining a large majority over the other candidate, Henry Sidgwick. Shortly after his election he married, on 9 July 1889, Florence Emma (*b.* 1856/7), eldest daughter of George Benjamin Austen Lefroy. They had no children. Austen Leigh's work was that of an administrator, and his leading characteristics were fair-mindedness, courtesy, and unsparing industry. Although an essentially conservative figure, who set great store by college chapel and who regretted the ending of religious tests, he effected far-reaching changes in his college. As a result of a long series of reforms, which took shape in two successive bodies of statutes, ratified in 1861 and 1882 respectively, the college ceased to be a close corporation of Eton collegers. In the furthering of these reforms and in guiding their progress, lay the principal achievement of Austen Leigh's life. To him was largely due the establishment of a tutorial system, which turned the college into an effective centre of teaching. He also promoted closer relations between dons and undergraduates. As provost, he set about uniting the college, which had suffered from a division between the Etonian 'best set' and the outsiders recently admitted, and went on to preside with striking success over a period of remarkable intellectual growth.

In 1876–80 and again in 1886–90 he was a member of the council of the senate of Cambridge University, and was vice-chancellor, 1893–5. From 1883 to his death he was president of the Cambridge University Musical Society and from 1886 president of the university cricket club. He was an active member of the governing bodies of Eton and Winchester colleges, from 1889 and 1890 respectively. His only published work was a *History of King's College* (1899). On 28 January 1905 he died suddenly in his home, the provost's lodge in King's College, of angina pectoris, and was buried at Grantchester. His wife survived him.

M. C. Curthoys

Sources W. Austen-Leigh, ed., *Augustus Austen Leigh, … a record of college reform* (1906) • C. N. L. Brooke, *A history of the University of Cambridge*, 4: *1870–1990*, ed. C. N. L. Brooke and others (1993) • S. Rothblatt, *The revolution of the dons: Cambridge and society in Victorian England* (1968) • L. P. Wilkinson, *A century of King's* (1980) • Venn, *Alum. Cant.* • *CGPLA Eng. & Wales* (1905) • m. cert. • d. cert.

Archives CKS, corresp. relating to King's College • Hants. RO, extracts from diaries and reminiscences | CUL, letters to Lord Acton • King's AC Cam., letters, mainly to Henry Bradshaw • King's AC Cam., letters to Oscar Browning

Likenesses J. Collier, oils, 1897, King's Cam.

Wealth at death £9027 1*s.* 8*d.*: probate, 9 March 1905, *CGPLA Eng. & Wales*

Leigh, Chandos, **first Baron Leigh** (1791–1850), poet and literary patron, was born in London on 27 June 1791, the only child of James Henry Leigh (1765–1823) MP, of Adlestrop, Gloucestershire, and Julia Judith Twisleton (*d.* 1843), daughter of Thomas Fiennes, thirteenth Baron Saye and Sele. At Harrow School (1799–1808/9) Chandos Leigh was awed by Byron's pugilistic ferocity and formed a warm and lasting friendship with the master, Samuel Parr. In 1810 he matriculated at Christ Church, Oxford, where he attended several terms. After making the grand tour with his tutor Philip Shuttleworth (afterwards bishop of Chichester), Leigh entered London social life and published his first volumes of poems and essays. He formed theatrical acquaintanceships with General Richard Fitzpatrick, Richard Brinsley Sheridan, and Edmund Kean, and Holland House acquaintanceships with Lord Byron, Sir John Cam Hobhouse, and Sir James Mackintosh. On 7 June 1819 he married Margarette (*d.* 1866), eldest daughter of the Revd William Shippen Willes; they had ten children. The Leighs of Adlestrop and the Leighs of Stoneleigh Abbey were alike descendants of Sir Thomas Leigh, lord mayor of London in 1558. In 1813 Stoneleigh Abbey estate was inherited by James Henry Leigh, from whom in 1823 it devolved to Chandos Leigh, with property in several counties worth an estimated £90,000 per annum. In May 1839 Chandos Leigh was created Lord Leigh of Stoneleigh, the fifth Baron Leigh having died without issue in 1786.

After his marriage Leigh lived in the country and received little notice from his famous literary contemporaries. He was a distant cousin of Jane Austen and Sir Egerton Brydges; with Mary Shelley he gave private financial assistance to (James Henry) Leigh Hunt (named after Chandos Leigh's father); the vicar of Stoneleigh was appointed tutor to the Shelleys' son Percy. Leigh Hunt left a glowing character in his autobiography, comparing his patron to Henry Fielding's Squire Allworthy. Chandos Leigh was a trustee of Rugby School and contributed to various literary causes. Poetry was his chief vanity; he published over two dozen volumes, mostly in small or private editions. Written over four decades, his lyrics, epigrams, epistles, and descriptive effusions record a lifetime's reflections in the decorous manner popularized by the literary annuals. Most of the volumes reprint a core selection of favourite poems; early verse is collected in *Juvenile Poems, and other Pieces* (1817) and middle-period verse in *Poems, now First Collected* (1839). The early verse is mildly libertine, the later mildly pious. The principal work is a sequence of verse epistles addressed 'to a friend in town' arguing liberal positions on the aesthetic and economic questions of the day. Byron was ever the point of departure: he mentions Leigh as a potential purchaser of Newstead, and Byron's portrait by Thomas Phillips hung over the mantle in the library at Stoneleigh Abbey. Chandos Leigh thought and lived as a more civilized Byron might have done; the scarcely concealed character Leigh gives of Byron in 'Dives loquitur: in imitation of a great poet' is telling criticism of a man he obviously admired.

Chandos Leigh championed free trade and liberal policies not always popular at home in Warwickshire. He certainly had enemies. In 1844 his title was challenged by other descendants of Sir Thomas Leigh and over thirty rioters forcibly entered Stoneleigh Abbey in search of evidence. Four years later an inquest was held into the spectacular charge that in 1814 Leigh had assisted his mother in stealthily removing a monument and coffin plates from the family vault—supposedly buried, along with the bodies of several witnesses, under a bridge abutment on the estate. The bridge was left intact and the charges dismissed as fabulous, but not before a parade of witnesses had testified to poisonings, mysterious disappearances, and irregular doings among the family retainers. In 1850 Leigh suffered a partial paralysis and went to Europe in an attempt to recover his health. He died at Bonn on 27 September 1850. He was buried on 8 October in the chancel of Stoneleigh church, where a marble monument was erected to his memory. His eldest son, William Henry Leigh, succeeded as second baron.

David Hill Radcliffe

Sources *DNB* • 'Leigh family', *GM*, 1st ser., 93/2 (1823), 585–6 • *GM*, 2nd ser., 34 (1850), 656–8 • 'Extraordinary investigation', *The Times* (9 May 1848) • 'Death of Lord Leigh', *The Times* (3 Oct 1850) • L. Hunt, *The autobiography of Leigh Hunt, with reminiscences of friends and contemporaries*, 3 vols. (1850) • C. Griffin, *Stoneleigh Abbey, thirty four years ago, containing a short history of the claims to the peerage and estates, and a catalogue of the confessed and suspected crimes* (1848) • 'Stoneleigh Abbey', *An historical and descriptive guide to Warwick Castle, Kenilworth Castle, Guy's Cliff, Stoneleigh Abbey, the Beauchamp Chapel, Charlecote Hall, Stratford, Coombe Abbey, and other places of interest in the neighbourhood* (1854) • *The letters of Mary Wollstonecraft Shelley*, ed. B. T. Bennett, 2 (1983) • *Byron's letters and journals*, ed. L. A. Marchand, 4 (1975) • *Jane Austen's letters*, ed. D. Le Faye, 3rd edn (1995) • A. Blainey, *Immortal boy: a portrait of Leigh Hunt* (1985) • W. Derry, *Dr Parr: a portrait of the whig Dr Johnson* (1966) • Foster, *Alum. Oxon.* • M. G. Dauglish and P. K. Stephenson, eds., *The Harrow School register, 1800–1911*, 3rd edn (1911) • Burke, *Peerage* (1956)

Archives BL, letters to his family, RP4390 [copies] • Shakespeare Birthplace Trust RO, Stratford upon Avon, letters and papers • Yale U., Beinecke L., letters to members of his family [photocopies in BL, RP 4890] | BL, corresp. with Samuel Butler, Add. MS 34589, fols. 114, 119 • BL, letters to Leigh Hunt, Add. MSS 38109, 38110, 38523 • Bodl. Oxf., corresp. with Sir Thomas Phillipps • Bucks. RLSS, letters to Thomas Tyringham Bernard • Shakespeare Birthplace Trust RO, Stratford upon Avon, legal documents concerning Lord Leigh

Likenesses G. Hayter, oils, Stoneleigh Abbey, Warwickshire • marble monument, Stoneleigh church, Warwickshire • stipple, BM

Wealth at death 'estates in four counties, estimated at £90,000 a year': Griffin, *Stoneleigh Abbey*, iii; will, Shakespeare Birthplace Trust RO, Stratford upon Avon

Leigh, Charles (*bap.* **1572**, *d.* **1605**), merchant and sea captain, was baptized on 12 March 1572 at Addington, Surrey, the seventh of eight children of John Leigh (*d.* 1576) and his wife, Joan (*d.* 1593), daughter and heir of Sir John Oliph of East Wickham, Kent. Little is known about his early life or marriage. He had a son Oliph, baptized on 16 June 1597, and a daughter named Milcah living in 1612. He made his career as a merchant and sea captain; the earliest reference to his activities can be found in the records of the high court of admiralty for 1596. Charles Leigh and William Resould are identified as merchants of London associated with Sir Francis Carew and Captain Nicholas Sawnders in the voyage of the *Expedition of London*, which had carried the *Blue Lyon* of Emden into Plymouth as a prize. Carew was the nephew of Leigh's grandfather Nicholas Leigh; as a favourite of both the queen and Lord Burghley, it may well have been Carew who brought Charles to the notice of the court. By the later 1590s both Burghley and his son Robert Cecil seem to have regarded Leigh as a dependable servant in maritime enterprises.

In 1597 Leigh, together with Abraham and Stephen van Harwick, Dutch merchants resident in London, undertook a voyage to the Gulf of St Lawrence intended to monopolize the walrus fishery by establishing a colony on Ramea (the Magdalen Islands). The venture had Burghley's encouragement, and the latter's decision to people the colony with the Brownist congregation of Pastor Francis Johnson may explain how Leigh was drawn into it. It is not likely that Leigh was a separatist himself, even though George Johnson acclaimed him as 'a brother in the faith with us' (Johnson, 111). Leigh's cousin, a London merchant named Boys, was incarcerated for his association with Francis Johnson and died in prison. The latter married his widow, Thomasin Boys, in 1594. Charles

Leigh, 'who called the Pastors wife cosen' (ibid., 106), would have been the logical commander to convey the first English 'pilgrims' to the New World.

Leigh set sail from Falmouth on 28 April 1597 as captain of the *Hopewell*, accompanied by the *Chancewell* with Stephen van Harwick as captain. Francis and George Johnson and two others went as the advance party for the Brownists. The ships reached the Grand Banks by 18 May, entering Conception Bay two days later. They then coasted southward round Cape Race, losing each other in fog off Placentia Bay on 5 June. Leigh continued westward, noting the bird colonies and walrus on Bird Rocks and catching cod, which bit 'almost as fast as we could hale them into the ship' (Hakluyt, 8.167). When he rounded the south-western tip of the Magdalens and entered Pleasant Bay on 18 June, Leigh found Breton and Basque ships already ensconced in Halabolina and Grand Entry harbours, mustering between them about 200 men. Some 300 Mi'kmaqs were also encamped there fishing. Leigh suspected one of the Basque ships to be Spanish and confiscated its arms, provoking near mutiny from his crew when he refused to let them seize the vessel as prize. The Bretons, Basques, and Mi'kmaqs joined forces on 20 June to drive Leigh out of the bay. Leigh's crew refused to reconnoitre alternative sites in the gulf. Turning back eastward the *Hopewell* was signalled by the crew of the *Chancewell*, which had run aground near St Anne's Bay on Cape Breton and been looted by the Basques. Leigh took the survivors aboard and decided to return the Brownists to England. During July he tried to recoup his losses from the Basques. Encountering a Breton ship in the pay of the Catholic league off Belle Île, he took command of her and set sail for England with the four Brownists as passengers, leaving the *Hopewell* to make for the Azores in search of further prizes. Leigh reached England on 5 September 1597. He wrote up an account of his voyage, subsequently published in Richard Hakluyt's *Principal Navigations* (1600), and submitted a proposal to the privy council to garrison the southern harbours of the Magdalens.

There is no evidence whether Leigh returned to the Gulf of St Lawrence. In September 1601 Cecil and Lord Admiral Charles Howard commissioned him to take the *Marigold*, owned by his brother Oliph [*see below*] and the queen's *Lion's Whelp*, to the Mediterranean for 'reprisal of pirates and Spaniards' (PRO, SP 98/2, fol. 93). The vessels took a Hamburg prize, but Leigh's share of the booty was sequestered in Algiers. In 1603, with the knowledge of Cecil and Howard, Leigh set forth the *Lioness* to the 'South Seas' commanded by his partner Richard Gifford. Gifford left the ship off the coast of Spain, hearing that privateering had been discontinued by the accession of James I. The *Lioness* was captured by the Spaniards and Leigh was still trying to make good his losses from Gifford in 1604.

Gifford's aborted voyage was probably connected to Charles Leigh's preparations to settle the first English colony in Guiana. Leigh had gone out to reconnoitre that coast in 1602 after returning from Algiers. Cecil and Howard supported the project to give the English a foothold in South America, but it was financed largely by Leigh's brother Oliph and other family connections. Leigh set sail in the *Olive Plant* on 28 March 1604. He carried out forty-six men and boys and a Guiana native named William who had been living in England. After making landfall in the mouth of the Amazon, Leigh brought his vessel into the River Wiapoco (Oyapock) on 22 May. The natives near the river mouth were used to trading with the English and Dutch and 'very willing to have him and his people abide' (Purchas, 16.310). Leigh hoped they would assist him in searching for rich civilizations or goldmines in the interior. His plans were frustrated by his men, who preferred privateering in the Caribbean and refused to clear land for settlement upriver. He was forced to settle in the native villages near the river mouth to get his company to remain. In early July, Leigh sent the *Olive Plant* back to England, carrying four native hostages and letters to Oliph Leigh, other family, James I, the privy council, and Howard. By September he and his men were sick with fever and increasingly suspicious of their native hosts, although the latter continued to support the idle colonists. When the *Olive Plant* returned to the Wiapoco in January 1605 with men and supplies, some of the settlers 'had not in three monethes time beene a stones cast from their houses' (ibid., 16.339). Leigh decided to return to England but died of fever on 20 March 1605, shortly before the ship sailed, and was buried secretly ashore. A second supply vessel failed to reach the remaining colonists, who were brought home by visiting Dutch and French traders during 1605 and 1606.

Charles Leigh's eldest brother, **Sir Oliph Leigh** (1559–1612), was born at Addington on 24 November 1559. He married Jane, daughter of Sir Thomas Browne of Betchworth, Surrey, on 4 June 1577. They had one son, Francis, baptized at Addington on 6 September 1590. Oliph Leigh inherited the manor of Addington, together with property in Newdigate, Ockley, and Wotton in Surrey, on the death of his grandfather Nicholas Leigh on 30 July 1581. He subsequently acquired the manors of East Wickham and Foxgrove in Kent through his mother. He was knighted by Elizabeth I some time after 1586, in which year he was still listed as having the rank of esquire when he contributed £10 to the free school at Guildford. After the accession of James I he informed the privy council that the tenant of the manor of Addington had an ancient right, recorded in Domesday, to make a dish of 'herout or pigernout' in the king's kitchen on the day of his coronation. The privy council chose not to avail itself of this service, assigning his request to the category of 'claims unexamined' on 26 July 1603 (PRO, SP 14/2, no. 76). During the next two years he was much occupied in organizing his brother's unsuccessful attempt to colonize the Wiapoco. He was the owner of the *Olive Plant* which carried Charles Leigh and the settlers out in March 1604. He bore the chief responsibility for the rapid first supply of men and provisions, paying particular attention to his brother's request for hatchets, beads, and knives for trade with the natives. His second ship, the *Oliph Blossome*, sent out with a further sixty-seven colonists in April 1605, missed the Guiana coast and deposited its passengers on St Lucia, where most succumbed to the assaults of hostile Caribs or starvation. Although his Guiana investments brought him very little profit, Oliph seems to have prospered in the early years of James I's reign. He held the office of keeper of the Great Park at Eltham, which he surrendered for £1200 in 1609. He was granted the office of keeper of the New Park at Horne in Kent for life in 1607. He died on 14 March 1612: as requested in his will, his son erected a monument 'in the chauncell of the parish church of Addington, wherein shall be sett downe the ages, tyme of death, matches, and yssues of my grandfather, my father, and myselfe'. The handsome alabaster and black marble memorial still survives. Sir Oliph's widow was also buried at Addington on 28 June 1631. JOYCE LORIMER

Sources R. Hakluyt, *The principal navigations, voyages, traffiques and discoveries of the English nation*, 8, Hakluyt Society, extra ser., 8 (1904), 166–82 • S. Purchas, *Hakluytus posthumus, or, Purchas his pilgrimes*, 4 (1625); repr. Hakluyt Society, extra ser., 16 (1906), 309–51 • G. Johnson, *A discourse of some troubles and excommunications in the banished English church at Amsterdam* (1603) • J. Nicholl, *An houre glasse of Indian newes* (1607) • PRO, HCA13/38, no. 33; HCA24/64, nos. 41, 75; HCA24/65, no. 74; HCA24/71, nos. 62, 161 • PRO, SP 12/285, no. 42; SP 98/2, fol. 93; SP 14/2, no. 76; SP 14/35, no. 49; SP 14/45, 21 May 1609; SP 14/58, 14 Nov 1610 • PRO, E 190/12/3, fol. 22 • PRO, C 142/328 n. 162 • K. R. Andrews, 'Caribbean rivalry and the Anglo-Spanish peace', *History*, new ser., 59 (1974), 1–17 • D. B. Quinn, 'England and the St Lawrence, 1577–1602', *Merchants and scholars*, ed. J. Parker (1965), 117–43 • D. B. Quinn, 'The first pilgrims', *William and Mary Quarterly*, 23 (1966), 359–90 • K. R. Andrews, 'Sir Robert Cecil and Mediterranean plunder', *EngHR*, 87 (1972), 513–32 • G. Leveson-Gower, 'Notices of the family of Leigh of Addington', *Surrey Archaeological Collections*, 7 (1880), 77–123 • will, PRO, PROB 11/119, sig. 24 [Sir Oliph Leigh] • *VCH Surrey*, 4 • parish register, Addington, Surrey [Charles Leigh: birth, parents' data, religion; Oliph Leigh: parents' data, spouse's death, death] • A. F. Kinney, *Titled Elizabethans: a directory of Elizabethan state and church officers* (1973)

Leigh, Charles (1662–1701?), physician and naturalist, was born at Singleton Grange, Lancashire, the son of William Leigh of Singleton in the Fylde, and great-grandson of William Leigh BD, rector of Standish. He became a commoner of Brasenose College, Oxford, on 7 July 1679, matriculated on 18 July 1679, aged seventeen, and graduated BA on 24 May 1683. Wood records that Leigh left Oxford in debt and went to Jesus College, Cambridge, where he graduated MD in 1690. For a time Leigh practised in London but at a later date he lived at Manchester, and had an extensive practice throughout Lancashire. On 13 May 1685 he was elected FRS and promised that he would 'to the Utmost of my Capacity give you an account of the Naturall Curiosities here' (Hunter, 115).

Some of Leigh's papers read before the Royal Society are printed in *Philosophical Transactions*. He also published the following separate works: *Phthisologia Lancastriensis, cui accessit tentamen philosophicum de mineralibus aquis in eodem comitatu observatis* (1694, reprinted Geneva, 1736), *Exercitationes quinque, de aquis mineralibus; thermis calidis; morbis acutis; morbis intermittentib.; hydrope* (1697), and *The natural history of Lancashire, Cheshire, and the Peak in Derbyshire; with an account of the British, Phoenic, Armenian, Gr. and Rom. antiquities found in those parts* (1700). He wrote three pamphlets in 1698 in reply to R. Bolton's *Heat of the Blood* and one in reply to John Colebatch on curing the bite of a viper. According to T. D. Whitaker, Leigh's 'vanity and petulance' were 'at least equal to his want of literature'. His *Natural History* is little more than a translation of his earlier Latin treatises.

Leigh married Dorothy, daughter of Edward Shuttleworth of Larbrick, Lancashire, with whom he received a moiety of the manor of Larbrick, afterwards surrendered in payment of a debt owed by Leigh to Sergeant Bretland. Leigh left no children. His widow died before 1717, and Leigh himself is said to have died in 1701 but there is some doubt on this point, as evidenced by Thomas Hearne, writing on 30 October 1705: 'I am told Dr Leigh, who writ the *Natural History of Lancashire*, has divers things fit for the press, but that he will not let them see the light because his *History* has not taken well' (MS diary, iv. 222). The plant *Leighia* cass. commemorates Leigh's name.

C. W. SUTTON, *rev.* MICHAEL BEVAN

Sources Venn, *Alum. Cant.* • M. Hunter, *The Royal Society and its fellows, 1660–1700: the morphology of an early scientific institution* (1982) • Desmond, *Botanists*, rev. edn • Wood, *Ath. Oxon.* • J. P. Earwaker, ed., *Local gleanings relating to Lancashire and Cheshire*, 2 vols. (1875–8), 68 • J. E. Bailey, Cheetham Library, MS bundle 7 • H. Fishwick, *The history of the parish of Kirkham in the county of Lancaster*, Chetham Society, 92 (1874), 183, 189 • G. Ormerod, *The history of the county palatine and city of Chester*, 2nd edn, ed. T. Helsby, 1 (1882), xxxiii • J. P. Malcolm, *Lives of topographers and antiquaries who have written concerning the antiquities of England* (1815) • T. D. Whitaker, *An history of the original parish of Whalley*, 3rd edn (1818)

Likenesses P. Rothwell, line engraving (after W. Faithorne, 1812), Wellcome L. • J. Savage, line engraving (after W. Faithorne), BM, Wellcome L.; repro. in C. Leigh, *The natural history of Lancashire, Cheshire, and the Peak in Derbyshire* (1700)

Leigh [*née* Kempe], **Dorothy** (*d.* in or before **1616**), writer, was the daughter of William Kempe of Finchingfield, Essex, according to a contemporary 'heraldic book' (BL, Harley MS 6071). Further details of her parentage are unknown. She married Ralph Leigh (*d.* *c.*1616), a gentleman of Cheshire who served under the earl of Essex at Cadiz. They had three sons, George, John, and William; the last became rector at Groton in Suffolk and is mentioned in letters by John Winthrop between 1626 and 1630 (for example, Winthrop, 1.347). An alternative hypothesis (Morant, 2.363) makes her the daughter of Robert Kempe and his wife, Elizabeth, daughter of Clement Higham of Barrow-Hall in Suffolk, and sister of William Kempe (1555–1628). It is unlikely, however, that the woman who died in 1616, the mother of young children, had a brother aged sixty-one at the time, and Morant makes no mention of her work.

The Mothers Blessing was published in 1616, subtitled, 'The Godly Counsaile of a Gentlewoman, not long since deceased, left behind her for her Children'. Twenty-three editions of this work were published, of which sixteen are extant, the latest dated 1674. Leigh utilizes the 'mother's advice book', a popular genre which could legitimize a woman's writing at a time when it was readily seen as an 'unchaste' act. She justifies her writing through the idea of leaving advice to her young sons, as a mother's love 'is hardly contained within the bounds of reason', and structures the text around this idea, most chapters being entitled 'the [nth] cause of writing is …'. Mother's advice books are typically prefaced with an epistle from the male printer recording the author's death and innocence of publication. Leigh's death is recorded in the book's title, but she markets the book herself in dedicating it to Princess Elizabeth, the queen of Bohemia. Her projected readership, moreover, expands from her sons to a wider, and female, one: once Leigh has defined the third cause of writing as 'to move women to be careful of their children', this larger female audience hovers behind subsequent chapters.

Leigh claims for herself a strong moral position by writing on religious themes, identifying herself clearly as a protestant who condemns the 'vain prayers' of Catholics, and exhorting women to be chaste: the woman who is 'unclean' is 'worse than a beast'. She also expresses more radical views, however, in particular on women's rights in marriage and on rape and its significance for women. In instructing her sons on their 'choice of wives' she argues for women's emotional rights in marriage and their equality with their husbands. Leigh advocates female learning and validates this not only through its religious focus, but also as a defence against male threat. A woman's reading thus becomes a defence against listening to wicked male persuasion. Engaging with the long-standing debate over rape, she argues, contentiously, that rape does not undermine a woman's chastity. The feelings of shame experienced by women after rape, she contends, signify their innocence, exemplified particularly in those who commit suicide. The great number of editions of Leigh's work testifies to the popularity of her writing.

JOCELYN CATTY

Sources D. Leigh, *The mothers blessing* (1616) · 'An heraldic book', BL, Harley MS 6071 · P. Morant, *The history and antiquities of the county of Essex*, 2 (1768) · *N&Q*, 4th ser., 2 (10 Oct 1868) · J. Winthrop, *The history of New England from 1630 to 1649*, ed. J. Savage, 1 (1825) · B. Travitsky, ed., *The paradise of women: writings by Englishwomen of the Renaissance* (1981) · J. L. Klein, *Daughters, wives, and widows* (1992) · *STC, 1475–1640* · *ESTC*

Leigh, Edward (1603–1671), writer, was born at Shawell, Leicestershire, on 24 March 1603, the second but eldest surviving son of Henry Leigh (1587–1630), gentleman, of Rushall Hall, Staffordshire, and his first wife, Anne (*d.* 1611), daughter of Anthony Lisle of Wootton in the Isle of Wight. Thanks to his father's generosity, as he later explained, he had a 'liberal education', attending Walsall grammar school, where he was taught by Mr Loe, before undergoing 'a double apprenticeship' (Leigh, 'Epistle Dedicatory', *Select and Choyse Observations*), first at Magdalen Hall, Oxford, where he matriculated on 24 October 1617, graduated BA in 1620, and proceeded MA in 1623, and then at the Middle Temple, which he entered on 30 October 1624. When his legal education was interrupted by London's great plague of 1625 he travelled for six months in France, 'with great improvement to himself and his studies' (Leigh, *Three Diatribes*, 5–6). On 10 February 1629 he married, at Walsall, Elizabeth Talbot (*d.* 1707) from Shropshire. Their younger son was the poet Richard *Leigh.

Leigh's upbringing was notable for its fervent puritanism, which owed much to his stepmother, Ruth Scudamore, and to his university tutor, William Pemble. By the late 1630s Leigh and his wife were members of the godly circle based at Banbury in Oxfordshire. Here he became an acolyte of the puritan minister, William Whateley, who baptized Leigh's daughter Anne on 15 May 1638. On Whateley's request, Leigh jointly published, with Henry Scudder, the minister's manuscript work on the book of Genesis as *Prototypes* in 1640, a year after Whateley's death. Biblical exegesis was also the leitmotif of most of Leigh's own publications, for as he declared in the 'Epistle Dedicatory' to his *Treatise of the Divine Promises* (1633), his chief motive in writing, 'next unto the promoting of God's glory was the benefit of Christians'. Undoubtedly his most notable work was his *Critica sacra*, a philological study of the Hebrew and Greek words of the Old and New testaments, initially published in two separate editions in 1639 and 1642. This lexicon became a standard work of reference, winning the plaudits of scholars like William Gouge and Thomas Fuller, earning him the respect of James Ussher, and being translated into several foreign languages. However, pagan subjects also featured in Leigh's literary output, as shown by his *Selected and Choice Observations Concerning the Twelve Caesars* (1635).

By the autumn of 1640 Leigh had returned to Staffordshire, where most of his estates lay. He was appointed a JP of the county on 12 August 1641, but because of his parliamentarian sympathies, as evinced by his support in late March 1642 for a Staffordshire petition in favour of the Militia Bill, he was removed by royal command the following August. Parliament subsequently restored him to the bench, and he eventually became *custos rotulorum*. Leigh was active early in the civil war, first raising a troop of horse for the parliamentary cause, with which he served at Lichfield Cathedral close in April 1643. He subsequently joined the parliamentary forces in Stafford, where he officered an infantry regiment. He had also garrisoned his family seat at Rushall, Staffordshire, but on 28 March 1643 his formidable young wife was forced to surrender it to the king's troops after a brief siege. Leigh was also an active member of the Staffordshire parliamentary committee, supporting the peace party faction led by the earl of Denbigh. On 30 September 1644 he presented a pro-Denbigh petition from Staffordshire to the House of Commons which, together with a speech he made on that occasion, was published at his own expense as *A Speech of Colonell E. Leigh* (1644).

In October 1645 Leigh stood as a parliamentary candidate in a by-election at Stafford and won by a single vote. Leigh's victory greatly perturbed his political opponents such as Sir William Brereton, who thought Leigh had been 'all along possessed of a rotten faction', while conceding that he was 'a religious gent' and thus capable of being brought to 'a right understanding' (*Letter Books*, 2.216–18). As a recruiter MP, Leigh proved very much to the fore in the ecclesiastical arena: for example, he was appointed a member of the committee of plundered ministers on 15 May 1646, a visitor for the regulation of Oxford University on 10 February 1647, and, at some unspecified date, chairman of the select committee investigating unlicensed preaching. He was nominated to the Westminster assembly of divines, in which he served as a teller, but although he subscribed to the solemn league and covenant on 28 January 1646 and was branded 'a dangerous prisbyterian' (Kidson, 36) by royalists, his preferred form of church government was a primitive episcopacy along the lines advocated by his friend Archbishop Ussher.

Leigh's parliamentary career came to an abrupt halt during Pride's Purge on 5 December 1648, when he was not only forcibly excluded from the Commons by the New Model Army, but also kept a prisoner for at least five weeks in the King's Head tavern in the Strand. For the next decade he held aloof from active engagement in politics, disapproving of regicide and of Cromwell's broad-church policies in particular. However, he continued to publish, and some of his works bore on contemporary debates, as did Christopher Cartwright's *The Magistrates Authority in Matters of Religion* (1647), to which he had written a preface. His religious tomes included *A Treatise of Divinity* (1646), *The Saints Encouragement in Evil Times* (1648), *Annotations upon All the New Testament* (1650), and *A Treatise of Religion and Learning* (1656), and he edited Lancelot Andrewes's *A Learned Discourse of Ceremonies Retained and Used in the Christian Churches* (1653). As a Middle Templer he retained an interest in the English legal system, publishing in 1652 *A Philological Commentary, or, An Illustration of the most Obvious and Usefull Words in the Law*, and in 1658 a book on the court of chancery, while an interest in topography led to his *England Described* (1659).

With the fall of the protectorate Leigh returned briefly to public life as one of the members of the restored Rump Parliament. He fully endorsed the Restoration, which he marked with a historical study, *Choyce Observations of all the Kings of England from the Saxons to the Death of King Charles the First* (1661), but in time he became increasingly disillusioned with Charles II's government and found refuge in 'a way of retirement' (*Choyce Observations*, 218–19). None the less he published in 1671 *Three Diatribes or Discourses* on foreign travel, money, and the measurement of distance. He died on 2 June that year at Rushall Hall, and was interred in the chancel of Rushall church four days later. In his will he made bequests to his immediate family, household servants, tenantry, neighbours, and several ejected ministers in Staffordshire, enjoining them all 'to make Religion their great business' (PRO, PROB 11/358, fol. 129).

Leigh was described by Amon Wilbee in his *Prima pars de comparatis comparandis* (1647) as 'a man of fiery disposition' (pp. 19, 26, 39) and by another contemporary as 'a cunning man' (Kidson, 36). Two engraved portraits of Leigh at the ages of forty-eight and of sixty suggest that he had a rather thickset appearance, with large eyes, prominent nose, and moustache and goatee beard. While not an original thinker, he impressed contemporary writers not only for the 'industry' of his literary output, but also for its sheer range, prompting one 'judicious divine' to remark, 'Sir you labour to make us idle' (Leigh, *A System or Body of Divinity*, preface). JOHN SUTTON

Sources Wood, *Ath. Oxon.*, new edn, 3.926–31 • S. Shaw, *The history and antiquities of Staffordshire*, 2 (1801), 65, 69 • J. C. Wedgwood, 'Staffordshire parliamentary history [2]', *Collections for a history of Staffordshire*, William Salt Archaeological Society, 3rd ser. (1920–22), 78–82 • F. W. Willmore, *Records of Rushall* (1892), 47–9, 80–81, 83 • R. M. Kidson, 'Active parliamentarians during the civil wars', *Collections for a history of Staffordshire*, Staffordshire RS, 4th ser., 2 (1958), 43–70 • D. H. Pennington and I. A. Roots, eds., *The committee at Stafford, 1643–1645*, Staffordshire RS, 4th ser., 1 (1957) • C. H. Firth and R. S. Rait, eds., *Acts and ordinances of the interregnum, 1642–1660*, 3 vols. (1911) • *JHC*, 4–6 (1644–51) • S. W. Carruthers, *The everyday work of the Westminster assembly* (1943), 192 • PRO, PROB 11/358, fol. 129 • *The letter books of Sir William Brereton*, ed. R. N. Dore, 2, Lancashire and Cheshire RS, 128 (1990), 216–18 • E. Leigh, 'Epistle dedicatory', *Select and choyse observations containing all the Roman emperors* (1657) • E. Leigh, *Three diatribes or discourses* (1671) • E. Leigh, 'Preface', *A system or body of divinity* (1654) • H. A. C. Sturgess, ed., *Register of admissions to the Honourable Society of the Middle Temple, from the fifteenth century to the year 1944*, 1 (1949), 114 • N. W. Tildesley, ed., *Rushall and Pelsall parish registers* (1985)

Likenesses T. Cross, line engraving, 1650, BM, NPG; repro. in E. Leigh, *Critica sacra*, 3rd edn (1650), frontispiece • J. Chantry, line engraving, 1662, BM, NPG; repro. in E. Leigh, *Critica sacra*, 4th edn (1662), frontispiece

Wealth at death £800 p.a. *c*.1662: Kidson, 'Active parliamentarians', p. 36

Leigh, Egerton (1815–1876), antiquary and politician, was born on 17 March 1815 at Broadwell Manor House, Gloucestershire, the only son of Egerton Leigh (1779–1865) of West Hall, High Leigh, Cheshire, and his wife, Wilhelmina Sarah (*d*. 1849), daughter of George Stratton of Tew Park, Oxfordshire. The Leigh or Legh family had been settled in Cheshire for more than five centuries and was one of the leading families of the county.

Leigh was educated at Eton College and then followed a military career. On 12 April 1833 he became a cornet in the 2nd dragoon guards (Queen's Bays), being promoted to lieutenant on 19 June 1835 and to captain on 18 December 1840. In 1843 he retired from the regular army and joined the 1st Cheshire militia, which he left with the rank of honorary colonel in 1870.

On 20 September 1842 at St George's, Hanover Square, London, Leigh married Lydia Rachel, the second daughter and coheir of John Smith Wright of Bulcote Lodge, Nottinghamshire. They had five sons and one daughter.

In 1872 Leigh was high sheriff of Cheshire, and the next year he entered parliamentary politics. He was a staunch Conservative and was president of several party organizations in mid-Cheshire. At a by-election in March 1873 he was elected as one of the members of parliament for the mid-Cheshire division. At the general election of 1874, when the Conservatives were returned to power, he was returned unopposed, together with the Hon. Wilbraham Egerton. He remained an MP until his death in 1876. Leigh made little impact on national politics and his views were straightforward and conventional: he advocated maintenance of the union of church and state, a combination of secular and religious education, and economy in the public expenditure.

Leigh was an archetypal country gentleman, of handsome appearance and a quiet and courteous manner. He was a very popular figure in his native county, belonged to most of the county societies, and was an active magistrate. Apart from his military and political interests, he was a keen antiquary, with a wide knowledge of his county's history. His special interests were archaeology, local ballads and folklore, and Cheshire dialect. He published several works, the most important of which were *Ballads and Legends of Cheshire* (1867) and *A Glossary of Words used in the Dialect of Cheshire* (1877). The latter, published posthumously, was largely based on the collections of Roger Wilbraham. Leigh's main aim in compiling his glossary was to catalogue as many Cheshire words as he could before they disappeared from use. In his introduction to the glossary, he cites 'emigration, railways and the blending of shires' as the main threats to his county's dialect.

Leigh died on 1 July 1876 at Cox's Hotel, 55 Jermyn Street, London, and was buried in Rostherne churchyard, Cheshire. SIMON HARRISON

Sources *Chester Chronicle* (8 July 1876) · *Chester Courant* (5 July 1876) · Boase, *Mod. Eng. biog.* · G. Ormerod, *The history of the county palatine and city of Chester*, 2nd edn, ed. T. Helsby, 1 (1882)
Likenesses engraving, repro. in E. Leigh, *A glossary of words used in the dialect of Cheshire* (1877) · wood-engraving, NPG; repro. in *ILN* (15 July 1876)
Wealth at death £30,000: probate, 18 Aug 1876, *CGPLA Eng. & Wales*

Leigh, Evan (1810–1876), manufacturer of textile machinery, was born on 21 December 1810 at Ashton under Lyne, Lancashire, the son of Peter Leigh, a cotton spinner of Ashton under Lyne, and his wife, Mary. He travelled on the continent for two years and, in 1828, he became the manager of his father's mill. On 26 September 1831 he married Anne, daughter of James Allen of Macclesfield; they raised three sons and five daughters.

An early sign of Leigh's inventive capacity was his coupling of hand mules in 1832, an innovation which reduced the cost of mule spinning by 40 per cent. In 1849 he patented the twin-screw propeller, which was adopted in the 1860s for both merchant and naval vessels. In 1850 he retired from cotton spinning in order to begin the manufacture of textile machinery. He established the Junction Works in Manchester in 1856, and there invented the loose-boss top roller, which came into universal use on the drawing-frame. He originated in 1856 the self-stripping flat carding engine. In 1861 he patented a pontoon ferry for the purpose of transporting trains across the channel; he improved his plans in 1867 and published in 1870 a pamphlet entitled *A Plan for Conveying Railway Trains across the Straits of Dover.*

Leigh suffered five years of illness after a visit to Egypt in 1862. In 1869 he retired from the Junction Works in order to practise as a consulting engineer. To this end he established in 1869 the firm of E. A. Leigh & Co. in Boston, Massachusetts, as importers of the machinery which he shipped from Liverpool. In order to make information

Evan Leigh (1810–1876), by John Smith

about the latest machinery more widely available, especially in the USA, he published the illustrated work *The Science of Modern Cotton Spinning* (2 vols., 1871), which embodied the results of forty-five years of practical experience, and which was reprinted three times within six years. Leigh took out twenty-four patents and defended the patent system against its critics. He was a member of several societies and professional bodies, among them the Society of Arts, the Inventors' Institute, the Institution of Naval Architects, the Institution of Mechanical Engineers, the Institution of Civil Engineers, and the Manchester Scientific and Mechanical Society, of which he served as president in 1875–6. He was the author of many papers and pamphlets on mechanical subjects.

Leigh died at his home, Clarence House, Clarence Street, Chorlton-on-Medlock, near Manchester, on 2 February 1876, and was buried at Harpurhey cemetery, near Manchester, on the 8th. He was survived by his wife. His eldest surviving daughter, Mrs Ada M. Lewis, was founder of the British and American Mission Home in Paris, which was opened in March 1876, and of which she was for a long time lady president. D. A. FARNIE

Sources A. Hildebrandt, 'A memoir of the late Evan Leigh', *Proceedings of the Manchester Scientific and Mechanical Society*, 10 (1876), 3–8 [with portrait] · *PICE*, 44 (1875–6), 229–31 · *Institution of Mechanical Engineers: Proceedings* (1877), 19–20 · *Manchester Weekly Times* (5 Feb 1876), 7v · Boase, *Mod. Eng. biog.* · *CGPLA Eng. & Wales* (1876)
Archives Harvard U., Baker Library, Dun and Bradstreet ledgers (for Boston Massachusetts) for firm of E. A. Leigh and Co.
Likenesses J. Smith, stipple, NPG [*see illus.*] · portrait, Sci. Mus., pictorial collection · portrait, repro. in Hildebrandt, 'A memoir of the late Evan Leigh'

Wealth at death under £7000: probate, 9 March 1876, *CGPLA Eng. & Wales*

Leigh, Sir Ferdinando (*c*.1585–1654), royalist army officer, was the only son of Thomas Leigh (*d*. 1594) of Middleton, West Riding of Yorkshire, and his wife, Elizabeth Stanley, possibly a member of a cadet branch of the Lancashire Stanleys, earls of Derby, and a maid of honour to Elizabeth I about 1595. Leigh was twice a widower before he was thirty, having been married first to Margery, daughter of William Cartwright, and subsequently to Mary (*d*. *c*.1615), daughter of Thomas Pilkington. About 1617 he married Elizabeth, daughter of Robert Tyrwhit of Cameringham, Lincolnshire, with whom he had two sons who died young, and two daughters. His fourth wife was Anne, daughter of Edmund Clough, with whom he had two sons and two daughters. After his father's death he inherited considerable estates in Middleton near Leeds (which included a coal mine), and at Rothwell and Haigh. In April 1617 he was knighted at York. Probably through his mother's family connections he was appointed governor of the Isle of Man for the earl of Derby in 1622, a post which he held until 1624. He was a gentleman of the king's privy chamber and contributed £100 to the royalist cause when Charles I assembled the Yorkshire gentry at York. Leigh was not appointed to the commission of array in 1642, but during the first civil war he served as a colonel of horse in his regiment, the active command of which was apparently undertaken by his son-in-law, Sir John Kaye. In February 1644 Leigh was recovering from wounds or illness at York. He was at Skipton Castle when the garrison surrendered to parliamentarian forces in December 1645 and faced the sequestration of his estates in Middleton in March the following year. In 1650 he was threatened by the committee for advance of money with the forced sale of his property. He died at Pontefract on 19 January 1654, and was buried there in the ruined Low Church.

E. T. BRADLEY, *rev*. J. R. DICKINSON

Sources R. V. Taylor, ed., *The biographia Leodiensis, or, Biographical sketches of the worthies of Leeds* (1865), 90–91 • R. Thoresby, *Ducatus Leodiensis, or, The topography of … Leedes*, ed. T. D. Whitaker, 2nd edn (1816), 222 • P. R. Newman, *Royalist officers in England and Wales, 1642–1660: a biographical dictionary* (1981), 228 • J. W. Clay, ed., *Yorkshire royalist composition papers*, 3, Yorkshire Archaeological Society, 20 (1896), 100–01 • J. W. Clay, 'The gentry of Yorkshire at the time of the civil war', *Yorkshire Archaeological Journal*, 23 (1914–15), 349–94, esp. 366 • W. A. Shaw, *The knights of England*, 2 (1906), 162 • J. Foster, ed., *The visitation of Yorkshire made in the years 1584/5 … to which is added the subsequent visitation made in 1612* (privately printed, London, 1875), 45 • 'Liber Scaccarii', 1622, Manx Museum Library, Douglas, Isle of Man, 53 • book of allowance, Castle Rushen, 1624, ingates and outgates, 1620–29, Manx Museum Library, Douglas, Isle of Man • J. R. Dickinson, *The lordship of Man under the Stanleys: government and economy in the Isle of Man, 1580–1704*, ed. P. H. W. Booth, Chetham Society, 3rd ser., 41 (1996), 355 • *A catalogue of the inquisitions post mortem for the county of York for the reigns of James I and Charles I*, Yorkshire Archaeological and Topographical Association, record ser., 1 (1885) [with *A catalogue of the Yorkshire wills at Somerset House, for the years 1649 to 1660*, ed. F. Collins] • M. A. E. Green, ed., *Calendar of the proceedings of the committee for advance of money, 1642–1656*, 2, PRO (1888), 924

Archives CKS, letters to Lady Foulis and papers

Wealth at death see Collins, ed. *Catalogue*

Leigh, Francis, first earl of Chichester (*d*. 1653), politician and courtier, was the son and heir of Sir Francis Leigh (*d*. 1625), and Mary, daughter of Thomas *Egerton, Viscount Brackley, and great-grandson of Sir Thomas Leigh (or Lee) of Stoneleigh; he was born at his father's seat at Newnham Regis, Warwickshire. His father was made KB at the coronation of James I on 25 July 1603, sat in the parliaments of 1601, 1604, and 1621 respectively, and was a member of the Derby House Society of Antiquaries, together with Sir Henry Spelman, Sir Robert Cotton, and William Camden. He was an intimate friend of the latter, who left him by his will £4 for a memorial ring. Some pieces by Leigh are preserved in Thomas Hearne's *A Collection of Curious Discourses Written by Eminent Antiquaries*. Francis Leigh entered the University of Oxford in 1613, and was admitted at Lincoln's Inn two years later. He was knighted, either in 1613 or in 1618, and was created a baronet by James I on 24 December 1618. On 31 July 1617 he married the widow Susan Banning, daughter of Richard Northam, but she died soon after; they had no children. After her death he married, in 1617 or 1618, Audrey (*d*. 1652), widow of Sir Francis Anderson and eldest daughter of John Boteler, Baron Boteler of Brantfield. The couple had two daughters.

Leigh's second marriage to the niece of the royal favourite George Villiers, duke of Buckingham, explains his meteoric rise at court. He was elected MP for Warwickshire in a by-election after the elevation of Sir Fulke Greville to a peerage in 1621, and for Warwick in 1625. He was raised to the peerage as Baron Dunsmore by letters patent dated 31 July 1628. A close ally of Fulke Greville, Lord Brooke, Dunsmore was an opposition peer in 1640. In the Short Parliament he opposed the motion that supply should precede redress of grievances. He actively campaigned for the summoning of a second parliament later that year. However, the militancy, religious radicalism, and popularity of the crown's opponents in Warwickshire helped restore Dunsmore's sense of loyalty, which was further encouraged by the king himself. He was made captain of the band of gentlemen pensioners and sworn privy councillor in 1641, much to the dislike of the House of Commons, and on 15 March the following year he signed a protest with five other lords against the militia ordinance. On the outbreak of civil war he subscribed money to levy forty horse 'to assist his Majesty in defence of his Royal person, the two houses of Parliament, and the Protestant religion' (Peacock, 9). Executing the Warwickshire commission of array, men under Dunsmore's command were early exponents of the royalist excess in the harassment of the godly which parliamentarian propagandists exploited so well. Consequently Dunsmore attracted no little hatred among the saints in arms. In August 1642 his park at Newnham was despoiled of its venison by the parliamentarian soldiers quartered under his old associate Lord Brooke at Coventry.

On 3 July 1644 the king fortified Dunsmore's loyalty by creating him earl of Chichester. In May 1645 he was on the commission appointed to govern Oxford during the king's absence. He was, however, more of a courtier than a soldier, and was several times employed as commissioner on the part of the crown, notably to meet the Scottish commissioners at Ripon in the autumn of 1640 and those of the parliament at Uxbridge in 1645. Clarendon had no high opinion of Chichester's qualities as a statesman, describing him as of a froward and violent disposition, deficient in judgement and temper, whose 'greatest reputation was, that the earl of Southampton married his daughter, who was a beautiful and a worthy lady' (Clarendon, *Hist. rebellion*, 2.533). David Lloyd, on the other hand, writes of him as 'a stout, honest man in his council', with 'a shrewd way of expressing and naming' his views (Lloyd, 653).

Chichester appeared several times before the committee for the advance of money, being assessed in November 1645 to pay the sum of £3000; he was given a year in which to make payment. In October 1646 parliament annulled his and many other honours, granted since 20 May 1642, when the great seal had passed from parliamentary control with the flight of Lord Keeper Littleton to the king at York. On 26 January 1647, Chichester having paid £1000 and given security for £1847 more, his sequestration was suspended. However, in 1650 his fine was assessed at £3594 by the committee for compounding. He died at his home, Apps Court, Surrey, on 21 December 1653, and was buried in the chancel of Newnham church. His two daughters survived him; Elizabeth, second wife of Thomas Wriothesley, fourth earl of Southampton, and Mary, wife of George Villiers, fourth Viscount Grandison, whose granddaughter married Robert Pitt, and was mother of the first earl of Chatham. The earldom devolved, according to a special limitation, upon Leigh's son-in-law the earl of Southampton; the barony of Dunsmore, together with the baronetcy, became extinct.

Thomas Seccombe, *rev.* Sean Kelsey

Sources Foster, *Alum. Oxon.* • GEC, *Baronetage*, 1.118 • GEC, *Peerage*, 3.193–4 • A. Hughes, *Politics, society and civil war in Warwickshire, 1620–1660* (1987) • W. A. Shaw, *The knights of England*, 2 (1906) • E. Peacock, ed., *The army lists of the roundheads and cavaliers*, 2nd edn (1874) • D. Lloyd, *Memoires of the lives … of those … personages that suffered … for the protestant religion* (1668) • will, PRO, PROB 11/240, fols. 401–2 • *CSP dom.*, 1641–3, 347

Wealth at death disposed of extensive real estate in Warwickshire and elsewhere, on which gifts and bequests valued at £10,000 were devised: will, PRO, PROB 11/240, fols. 401–2 • est. pre-war income of £3000 p.a.: Hughes, *Politics*, 26

Leigh, Henry Sambrooke (1837–1883), writer and playwright, was born in London on 29 March 1837, the son of James Mathews *Leigh (1808–1860), painter and author, and his wife, Elizabeth, *née* Ashley. Leigh began to write poetry from an early age. Collections of his lyrics include: *Carols of Cockayne* (1869), *Gillott and Goosequill* (1871), *A Town Garland: a Collection of Lyrics* (1878), and *Strains from the Strand* (1882). As their titles indicate, he drew on London life in his poetry, and one contemporary critic described him as 'a veritable Londoner' (*ILN*, 648).

Leigh also translated many French comic operas, including *Le roi carotte* (3 June 1872) and *Voyage dans la lune* (15 April 1876). His first dramatic effort, however, had been a collaboration with Charles Millward in a musical spectacle for the Theatre Royal, Birmingham. Between 1871 and 1883 his works appeared on various London stages, and included *Bridge of Sighs*, staged at St James's Hall on 18 November 1872, and *Cinderella*, an opera performed on 2 May 1884 (although the words were published two years earlier).

Leigh was a Spanish, Portuguese, and French scholar. In addition to his translations, he edited *Jeux d'Esprit Written and Spoken by French and English Wits and Humorists* (1877). He was a brilliant and witty conversationalist, and a humorous singer. Leigh died in his rooms in Lowther's Private Hotel, 35 Strand, London, on 16 June 1883, and was buried in Brompton cemetery on 22 June.

G. C. Boase, *rev.* Megan A. Stephan

Sources *ILN* (30 June 1883), 648–50 • W. D. Adams, *Dictionary of English literature*, 2nd edn [1878], 342 • Boase, *Mod. Eng. biog.*, 2.375 • Allibone, *Dict.* • *IGI* • d. cert.

Likenesses R. Taylor, wood-engraving, 20 June 1883 (after a sketch from memory by W. Mackay), NPG; repro. in *ILN* • W. Mackay, drawing, repro. in *ILN* (10 June 1883), 648

Leigh, James Mathews (1808–1860), art teacher and painter, was the son of James Mathews (*bap.* 1775), a well known bookseller in the Strand, London, and his wife, Elizabeth. He was the nephew of the comic actor Charles Mathews (1776–1835). He studied painting under William Etty RA, with the intention of becoming a history painter. He first exhibited at the Royal Academy in 1828, when he showed two portraits and a religious painting, *The Good Samaritan*. He exhibited there again in 1830 and 1832, before leaving for the continent, where he studied the works of the old masters and gained a familiarity with European art academies. On 4 October 1834 he married Elizabeth Ashley at St Martin-in-the-Fields, Westminster. At this time he also began to write, and following his *The Rhenish Album* (1836), subtitled 'the Journal of a Travelling Artist, etc.', in 1838 he published privately a historical play in five acts entitled *Cromwell*. After a second visit to Europe, Leigh resumed his career as a painter, and continued to exhibit sacred subjects and portraits at the Royal Academy from 1839 to 1849. As well as at the Royal Academy, Leigh exhibited at the British Institution (from 1827 to 1845), and with the Society of British Artists in Suffolk Street (from 1825 to 1844). Among works shown there was a portrait of the celebrated art teacher Henry Sass (1827). He also showed several works at the Liverpool Academy between 1841 and 1845, including, in 1841, a picture intriguingly titled *The First Whiff of Chartism*. The same year, encouraged by the painter John Rogers Herbert, Leigh opened a painting school in London at 79 Newman Street, to the north of Oxford Street. This school was soon to rival the celebrated institution already inaugurated by Henry Sass. Leigh's school, which was run along the liberal lines of a French atelier, was available to male and female fee-paying students, who were able to study anatomy, antique sculpture, and the living model, as well as attending weekly sketching meetings. Among those who passed through Leigh's school were William Makepeace Thackeray, Dante Gabriel Rossetti, and William Holman Hunt.

Leigh was described by a pupil as 'a strongly built man, with good broad forehead, a piercing eye, square jaw, and thin lips, with a look of great firmness and determination' (Marks, 1.22–3). He habitually smoked a long pipe and dressed eccentrically in a black velvet cap and cassock. An accomplished linguist and scholar, Leigh was also renowned among his students for his kindness, his lively conversation, and his sharp wit, for which reason he was known as Dagger Leigh. Criticizing Hunt's remarkable attention to detail, he remarked presciently, 'If Holman Hunt had to paint Everton toffee he would go to Everton to paint it' (Storey, 90). Towards the end of his life Leigh suffered from cancer of the tongue, caused by years of incessant pipe smoking. He died at his home, 79 Newman Street, London, on 20 April 1860 and was buried in Highgate cemetery. After his death Leigh was succeeded as principal by Thomas J. Heatherley (1826–1914), whose name the art school still bears today. Leigh's son, Henry Sambrook *Leigh (1837–1883), is separately noticed.

MARTIN POSTLE

Sources Redgrave, *Artists* • Graves, *Artists* • *Royal academy catalogues* (1828–49) • G. A. Storey, *Sketches from memory* (1890) • H. S. Marks, *Pen and pencil sketches*, 2 vols. (1894) • M. Postle and W. Vaughan, *The artist's model from Etty to Spencer* (1999) • *IGI*

Leigh, Jared (1724–1769), painter of landscapes and seascapes, was descended from the Leighs of West Hall, High Leigh, Cheshire. A letter from Trinity College, Oxford, dated to 1757–8 and thanking him for his donation of a picture, *Dead Christ*, which he presented to the University Museum, is addressed to Jared Leigh, jun., esq., indicating that his father was of the same name (*N&Q*, 148). He became a proctor in Doctors' Commons, and with his wife, Elizabeth (1729/30–1807), had several children, one of whom, Clara Maria *Pope (*bap.* 1767, *d.* 1838) married firstly the painter Francis Wheatley RA. He exhibited twenty-three pictures with the Free Society of Artists from 1761 to 1767, including classical scenes, sea views, and landscapes including views of Africa and the Mediterranean, suggesting that he pursued some travel. Leigh died prematurely in London on 1 May 1769 and was buried there at St Andrew by the Wardrobe.

W. A. J. ARCHBOLD, *rev.* KATE RETFORD

Sources Redgrave, *Artists* • *N&Q*, 5th ser., 8 (1877), 148 • Graves, *Artists* • A. Wilson, *A dictionary of British marine painters* (1967), 51 • Graves, *Soc. Artists* • E. Edwards, *Anecdotes of painters* (1808); facs. edn (1970), 28 • M. H. Grant, *A dictionary of British landscape painters, from the 16th century to the early 20th century* (1952), 116 • J. Gandon and T. J. Mulvany, eds., *The life of James Gandon* (1846), 213 • Bryan, *Painters* (1903–5) • *IGI*

Leigh, John (*c.*1689–1726?), actor and playwright, was possibly born in Ireland (according to William Chetwood's *A General History of the Stage*). A George Leigh was acting in Dublin about 1673 and may have been John's father. John Genest also considers the possibility that he was son 'to the famous Anthony Leigh' (Genest, 2.647) [*see* Leigh, Anthony (*d.* 1692)] and was a deserter from the Drury Lane company. Nevertheless, both Genest and Chetwood favour the Irish connection, and this seems the more likely, given that Rich recruited a number of the players, probably including Leigh, for his new theatre from Dublin's Smock Alley theatre company. John Leigh played Captain Plume in George Farquhar's *The Recruiting Officer*, given as the opening performance of the new Lincoln's Inn Fields playhouse (18 December 1714). Chetwood quotes some lines written on the back of one of the bills: ''Tis right to raise Recruits, for faith, they're wanted; For not one acting Soldier's here 'tis granted' (Chetwood, 179). Presumably the anonymous writer found John Leigh as undistinguished a soldier as the others in the company. In fact, there was a second Leigh at Lincoln's Inn Fields, Francis, from whom John was distinguished by the sobriquet Handsome Leigh. Indeed, Chetwood commenting on this says that John Leigh's good figure was 'the chief advantage in the Parts he perform'd' (Chetwood, 178). Francis Leigh also played at Drury Lane, whereas John Leigh spent almost all his remaining career at Lincoln's Inn Fields. E. L. Avery's *The London Stage* does not always distinguish between the two, but John did maintain a strong position in the company until the advent of Lacy Ryan and Thomas Walker, although his less frequent appearances in the mid-1720s may possibly have been due to illness.

Whatever his merits as an actor, John Leigh was a regular member of the Lincoln's Inn Fields company until 1726, playing a range of important roles. Among the roles he took in the first season, apart from that of Captain Plume, were Bellman in William Congreve's *The Old Bachelor*, Dick in John Vanbrugh's *The Confederacy*, Essex in *The Unhappy Favourite* by John Banks, Valentine in *Love for Love* by Congreve, Carlos in *Love Makes a Man* by Colley Cibber, and the Governor in Thomas Southerne's *Oroonoko*. He reprised the role of Plume on a number of occasions, as well as the parts of Carlos and Valentine; he probably also played the latter two at William Pinkethman's theatre where he is known to have appeared in summer 1718. Highfill, Burnim, and Langhans list a large number of roles that Leigh took at Lincoln's Inn Fields; many are solid supporting roles, but he also played a range of leading roles, among them Banquo and Macduff in *Macbeth* and Bolingbroke in *Richard II*. Although a staunch member of the Lincoln's Inn Fields company, John Leigh, like many of his contemporaries (and, as Highfill, Burnim, and Langhans wryly comment in *BDA*, 'every performer named Leigh or Lee'), also acted at the summer fairs, in his case Southwark fair, where he both appeared at and managed the 'John Leigh-Hall Great Theatrical Booth'.

Leigh is also credited with two plays, both of which were staged at Lincoln's Inn Fields. The first, *The Pretenders* (first performed 26 November 1719, and published as *Kensington Gardens* in 1720), is described by Genest as 'a moderate C[omedy]' (Genest, 3.31). Leigh played the role of Lord George Bellmour. The play only managed a short run, playing for six days, or, as Chetwood puts it, 'walked consumptively six Nights, and then expir'd' (Chetwood, 179). It appears to acknowledge the contribution of William Greville, seventh Baron Brooke, to Lincoln's Inn Fields, calling him 'the first subscriber towards the support of our theatre' (Genest, 3.32). Despite the relative lack of success of *Kensington Gardens*, Leigh made a second attempt with *Hob's Wedding*, acted (for the first time on 11 January 1720) in a double bill with the three-act *The Half-Pay Officers*, by Charles Molloy. Leigh's play is in effect a sequel to Thomas Doggett's *The Country Wake* and is, at least in part, composed of scenes not included in that play. Again, the run was short, but it provided an opportunity for two benefit performances. It seems that Leigh made one further attempt at play writing; he is recorded as having paid a Mr Miars 10 guineas in 1724 for 'his damage in buying and printing the Farce of the Shephard written and sold Mr. Walker and Mr. Leigh but never acted' (Highfill, Burnim & Langhans, *BDA*, 9.234). If this was ever published, there is no remaining record of it.

Leigh seems to have made his last appearance at Lincoln's Inn Fields on 14 April 1726 as Phorbas in *Oedipus*, by John Dryden and Nathaniel Lee, and most sources take this to be the year of his death. ROLAND METCALF

Sources Genest, *Eng. stage* • W. R. Chetwood, *A general history of the stage, from its origin in Greece to the present time* (1749) • E. L. Avery, ed., *The London stage, 1660–1800*, pt 2: 1700–1729 (1960) • Highfill, Burnim & Langhans, *BDA*

Leigh, John (1812–1888), medical officer of health, was born on 8 June 1812, reputedly at Foxdenton Hall, Chadderton, near Oldham, but possibly in Liverpool, the son of Thomas Leigh (*c*.1778–1847), druggist and tea dealer of Ashton under Lyne, and his wife, Hannah (*b*. *c*.1778), daughter of Hugh Shaw of Saddleworth. He later claimed affinity with the Leighs of West Hall, High Leigh, Cheshire, and the earls of Bridgewater (Ormerod, 1.456–7), but Stancliffe doubts the validity of this claim (Stancliffe, 277), and Egerton Leigh of High Leigh refers to him only as 'my talented young friend Mr John Leigh' without attributing kinship (E. Leigh, x). He was educated at the Moravian school at Fairfield and apprenticed in 1827 to William Dyson, surgeon, of Ashbourne. In 1831 Leigh went to Manchester for further training at the infirmary and associated medical schools, and he subsequently lectured in two schools in chemistry and forensic medicine. From 1834 to 1837, holding the licence of the Society of Apothecaries of London, Leigh was physicians' clerk (resident medical officer) at the Manchester Infirmary. Following additional surgical training at Guy's Hospital, London, he proceeded to membership of the Royal College of Surgeons in 1837.

Thereafter Leigh practised from 26 St John Street, Deansgate, Manchester, and became registrar of births and deaths of the Deansgate sub-district, analyst to Manchester gasworks, and consultant to chemical manufacturers. A fellow of the Chemical Society, while experimenting with coal-tar he resolved the basic chemistry of aniline dyes, which he reported to the British Association for the Advancement of Science in 1842 and in subsequent papers. However, he failed to patent his discoveries, and others profited commercially from them. He published various papers on public health, that with Ner Gardiner, the superintendent registrar, being the definitive description of Manchester's 1849 cholera outbreak. In 1844 he lectured to the Manchester Royal Institution on the sanitary condition of Manchester, and the next year he published a pamphlet praising Alderman Alexander Kay for his long-standing interest in the condition of the inhabitants of Manchester.

In 1868, after intense pressure from the Manchester and Salford Sanitary Association for the appointment of a medical man to spearhead a reversal of the city's notoriously poor status in public health, Leigh was appointed Manchester's first medical officer of health by a majority vote of the council, at a salary of £500 per annum, while retaining his private practice. He made strenuous efforts, detailed in his annual reports, to improve the health of the population. He worked to overcome the prevalent infectious diseases, including smallpox and typhus, through district inspections, the notification of infectious disease, disinfestation of clothing and houses, and the provision of baths, wash-houses, open spaces, parks, and hospital beds; and he campaigned for the total abolition of cellar dwellings. Leigh's report of 1868 to the corporation suggesting the need for more isolation hospitals led to the opening in 1871 of a new fever hospital at Monsall to the north of the city.

Leigh also urged the council not to pursue wholesale clearance of slum housing, but to upgrade 'back to back' houses by opening the wall between each pair, so as to create 'through-houses'. When he took office, the majority of dwellings in the centre of Manchester were in courts, with privy-middens and cesspools for excreta, classically described earlier by James Kay and Friedrich Engels. Leigh introduced a general pail-closet system with cinder sifters to replace the middens. He did not favour water systems, partly because of distrust about the sustainability of Manchester's water supply, but also because his pail system yielded saleable manure, potentially benefiting the council. By the end of the century Leigh's system had failed because Manchester's householders did not maintain the closets adequately, and evidence emerged that council workers secretly discharged raw sewage in volume into the River Medlock. At Leigh's death, though the health of Manchester residents had improved substantially, it still remained the worst of the large cities of the country.

Leigh had many interests. He assisted E. W. Binney in pioneering geological surveys in and around Manchester. During one, at Newtown, near Collyhurst, they discovered a number of fossil shells not previously described. One was named in Leigh's honour *Rissoa leighi*. Leigh also published several poetic works, including *Lays and Legends of Cheshire* (1880), and was president of the Spenser Society and poet laureate of John Shaw's Club. His large library contained a fine reference collection of English plants, and many rare books, including a celebrated collection of Bewick's works, reflecting an ornithological interest. He was a founder of the local Rosicrucians: twelve gentlemen who dined monthly and made antiquarian field visits. John Harland, another founder, recorded each meeting in his newspaper, the *Manchester Guardian*. At the inaugural meeting at Leigh's home, Leigh himself presented a paper on a bronze statue of Jupiter Stator, excavated at Campfield, Manchester.

Leigh married, on 29 August 1840, Marianne (*c*.1809–

1847), daughter of Robert Goodwin of Ashbourne, Derbyshire, and they had a daughter, Marianne, and a son, Francis; on 11 October 1848 he married Elizabeth (*c*.1820–1891), daughter of William Collier of Weaste, Salford, with whom he had two daughters, Gertrude and Beatrice, and three sons, Arthur, Piers Henry, and Egerton. On becoming medical officer of health, Leigh moved to a new home, Sandiway, in the emerging Manchester suburb of Whalley Range. In 1879 he erected a large mansion in the Tudor style, in Hale Barns, Cheshire, which he called the Manor House, moving again to become one of Hale Barns's first commuters. He died there, from cardiac disease, on 11 November 1888, still in office. His will gave a life interest in his estate to his widow, and the residue to his three daughters, seemingly excluding his three surviving sons. Leigh was buried on 15 November 1888 in the nearby churchyard at Timperley. W. P. POVEY

Sources 'Mr John Leigh, M.R.C.S., medical officer of health for Manchester', *Health Journal*, 5/50 (July 1887) • court of examiners' examination, candidates' declaration and recognition of lecturers' books, and register of licentiates, Society of Apothecaries, London • annual reports, medical officer of health, 1868–88, Manchester • G. Ormerod, *The history of the county palatine and city of Chester*, 2nd edn, ed. T. Helsby, 1 (1882) • F. S. Stancliffe, *John Shaw's 1738–1938* (1938) • J. Leigh and N. Gardiner, *History of the cholera in Manchester in 1849* (1850) • J. V. Pickstone, *Medicine and industrial society: a history of hospital development in Manchester and its region, 1752–1946* (1985) • census returns for Deansgate, Manchester, 1841, 1851; for Withington, Hulme, 1861, 1871, 1881; for Altrincham, 1881 • J. Leigh, will, 24 July 1885, proved at Chester, 12 Feb 1889, Ches. & Chester ALSS, 91/ 40, 172–6 [microfilm] • E. L. [E. Leigh], *Ballads and legends of Cheshire* (1867) • E. W. Binney, 'Sketch of the geology of Manchester and its vicinity', *Transactions of the Manchester Geological Society*, 1 (1841), 35–66 • Society of the Rosy Cross (Rosicrucians), rules and minutes 1852–9, Chetham's Library, Manchester, Mun. Ab.18 • *Manchester Guardian* (12 Nov 1888) • *Manchester Courier* (12 Nov 1888) • *Manchester City News* (17 Nov 1888) • *BMJ* (17 Nov 1888), 1138 • *The Lancet* (17 Nov 1888) • J. Niven, *Observations on the history of public health effort in Manchester* (1923) • examination book 181, 1837, RCS Eng. • d. cert. • *IGI* • *Manchester City News* (15 Dec 1888) • parish register, Middleton, Lancashire, St Leonard's Church, 8 Nov 1815 [baptism]

Archives JRL, scientific papers; literary works • Man. CL, MOH annual reports; scientific papers; literary works • Manchester Museum, Geological Collection, fossils • RCS Eng., scientific papers • Sale Library, Trafford, literary works incl. autographed copies • Wellcome L., scientific papers

Likenesses photograph, *c*.1887, repro. in 'Mr John Leigh, M.R.C.S.'

Wealth at death £2763 16*s*. 7*d*.: resworn probate, March 1890, *CGPLA Eng. & Wales* (1889)

Leigh [*née* Brown], **Mary** [Marie] (*b*. **1885**, *d*. in or after **1965**), militant suffragette, was born in Manchester and was a schoolteacher until her marriage to a builder named Leigh. More details of her family have proved impossible to trace, because of the ubiquity of her name. From 1906 until 1913 Mary Leigh was a member of the most militant of the women's suffrage organizations, the Women's Social and Political Union (WSPU). Mary Leigh was herself one of the first to engage in the acts of violent and escalating militancy which marked the later phases of the WSPU's campaigns, for which she was to be imprisoned on more than nine occasions.

On 30 June 1908, following Prime Minister Asquith's refusal to meet a WSPU delegation, Mary Leigh and Edith New smashed the windows of 10 Downing Street. They were arrested and sentenced to two months' imprisonment. When they were released on 23 August, they were greeted by a brass band and accorded a ceremonial welcome breakfast attended by Emmeline and Christabel Pankhurst. Mary Leigh immediately resumed her campaigning, acting as drum-major of the WSPU drum and fife band, which often accompanied their processions and demonstrations. Then on 17 September 1909 Mary Leigh conducted a rooftop protest at Bingley Hall, Birmingham, where Asquith was addressing a meeting from which all women had been excluded. Using an axe, she and Charlotte Marsh tore slates from the roof and threw them at the police below, causing some injuries, and at Asquith's car. For this Leigh was sentenced to three months' hard labour for assault, and one month for damage to property. On arriving at Winson Green gaol in Birmingham, she broke the window in her cell in protest, demanding to be treated as a political offender. She embarked on a hunger strike (a tactic which had previously secured the release of suffragettes on grounds of ill health), and became one of the first suffragettes to be forcibly fed. Her graphic account of the horrors of forcible feeding was published while she was still in prison. The WSPU was incensed, and initiated legal proceedings against the home secretary, prison governor, and prison doctor on Mary Leigh's behalf, opening a defence fund in her name. The case was brought to trial in December 1909, and the jury found for the defence, upholding the defence's claim that forcible feeding had been necessary to preserve life and that minimum force had been used.

During 1910 Mary Leigh was involved in by-election work in Wales, and on 18 November ('black Friday') was among the many women injured in violent scuffles with the police near the houses of parliament following the dropping of the Conciliation Bill. On 21 November 1911 she was again arrested, following the organized window-breaking campaign which accompanied another deputation to the House of Commons, and was sentenced to two months' hard labour for assaulting a policeman (she claimed it was in self-defence). On 18 July 1912 she was in Dublin, where she threw a hatchet into Asquith's carriage; later that evening she and Gladys Evans went to the Theatre Royal, Dublin, where Asquith had recently seen a performance, and set fire to the curtains, threw a burning chair into the orchestra pit, and set off several small bombs. Mary Leigh conducted her own defence at her trial on 6 August, and her speech was reported as the focal point of the proceedings. She was convicted, and sentenced to five years' penal servitude. The sentence was condemned by the WSPU, and tributes to Mary Leigh's courage filled the pages of its newspaper, *Votes for Women*; Christabel Pankhurst, however, later denied that Leigh and Evans's actions had been specifically sanctioned in advance by the organization. Mary Leigh undertook a hunger strike of six weeks, which left her in an emaciated condition, and she was released on licence. (The case was eventually dropped after prolonged litigation about the terms of the licence.)

Following the events in Dublin, Mary Leigh became disillusioned with the WSPU, which she felt had not responded adequately to her lengthy prison sentence. Consequently she involved herself increasingly with Sylvia Pankhurst's breakaway suffrage organization, the East London Federation of Suffragettes (ELF). In October 1913 she was badly injured during scuffles with the police at an ELF meeting at Bow Baths. She continued to work with the ELF long after the WSPU's campaign ceased in 1914. During the war years she applied for war service, but was rejected because of her criminal record. Reverting to her maiden name, Brown, she gained a place on an RAC course to train as an ambulance driver. Little is known of Mary Leigh's life after this time. She apparently took part in the first Aldermaston march (1958), and as a committed socialist regularly attended the May day processions in Hyde Park. She was a founder of the Emily Wilding Davison lodge, a memorial to her suffrage comrade who died after throwing herself under the hooves of the king's horse at the 1913 Epsom Derby. Every year Mary Leigh made the pilgrimage to Morpeth, Northumberland, to tend Davison's grave. In later years she continued to recall with pride her days in the WSPU, and stood by her actions as a suffragette. Mary Leigh gave two interviews in 1965; nothing is known of her after this. MICHELLE MYALL

Sources M. Myall, 'No surrender: the militancy of Mary Leigh, a working-class suffragette', *The women's suffrage movement: new feminist perspectives*, ed. M. Joannou and J. Purvis (1998), 173–88 • A. Morley and L. Stanley, *The life and death of Emily Wilding Davison* (1988) • M. Leigh, *Fed by force: how the government treats political opponents in prison* (Oct 1909?) • D. Mitchell, interview with Mary Leigh, 1965, Museum of London, David Mitchell collection • A. Rosen, *Rise up, women! The militant campaign of the Women's Social and Political Union, 1903–1914* (1974) • D. Atkinson, *The suffragettes in pictures* (1996)

Archives Women's Library, London, Mary Leigh and Helen Brown MSS | Museum of London, David Mitchell collection

Likenesses Brooke, photograph, 1927, Hult. Arch. • photographs, Museum of London, Suffragette Fellowship Collection; repro. in Atkinson, *Suffragettes in pictures*

Leigh, (Elizabeth) Medora (1814–1849), alleged daughter of Lord Byron, was born on 15 April 1814 at Six Mile Bottom, near Cambridge, acknowledged as the fourth of the seven children of Colonel George Leigh (1770/71–1850) and his wife, the Hon. Augusta Mary, *née* Byron (1784–1851). She was named Medora after the heroine of the romance *The Corsair*, begun by George Gordon, Lord *Byron (1788–1824) in December 1813 at the height of his relationship with Augusta Leigh, his half-sister. The allegation that Medora was the child of their incestuous union is not proven, but an 'incestuous' motif marked Medora's life. In 1829 she became pregnant by a cousin, Henry Trevanion (1805?–1855?), the husband of her eldest sister, Georgiana, and the couple eloped to France in 1831 using the alias Aubin. There was one surviving child of the liaison, Marie (1834–1873), later Sister Saint Hilaire. Medora's relationship with Trevanion had broken down by 1838. She was now dependent on sporadic and inadequate financial assistance from her hard-pressed mother. In 1840 she became the resistant object of Lady Byron's controlling financial magnanimity, and the recipient of Lady Byron's account of her incestuous conception. Her memoir of her life, down to 1843, was written at this time to justify her position (it was published by Charles Mackay from the MS in 1869). In 1844 she recovered some freedom of action by a loan of £500 on a deed of appointment for £3000 (on the reversionary interest of Byron's marriage settlement). On 23 August 1848 she married Jean-Louis Taillefer (1810?–1877), a retired French soldier of the hussars with whom she had one son, Elie (1846–1900). She died of smallpox on 28 August 1849 at Lapeyre in Aveyron, southern France, where she is buried. MALCOLM KELSALL

Sources *Medora Leigh: a history and autobiography*, ed. C. Mackay (1869) • R. de V. de Régie, *Le secret de Byron* (1927) • F.-J. Temple, *Le tombeau de Medora* (1988) • C. Turney, *Byron's daughter: a biography of Elizabeth Medora Leigh* (1972) • *The life and letters of Anne Isabella, Lady Noel Byron*, ed. E. C. Mayne (1929) • D. L. Moore, *Ada, countess of Lovelace* (1977) • J. S. Chapman, *Byron and the honourable Augusta Leigh* (1975) • M. Rees, 'Medora's grave', *Byron Journal*, 10 (1982), 104 • M. Elwin, *Lord Byron's family: Annabella, Ada and Augusta, 1816–1824* (1975) • M. Elwin, *Lord Byron's wife* (1962) • H. B. Stowe, *Lady Byron vindicated* (1870) • R. Milbanke, *Astarte, a fragment of truth concerning George Gordon Byron*, new edn (1921)

Archives Bodl. Oxf., Lovelace MSS • Bodl. Oxf., family MSS

Likenesses daguerreotype (aged about twenty-eight), repro. in Moore, *Ada, countess of Lovelace*; priv. coll. • engraving, Morgan L.; repro. in Turney, *Byron's daughter* • portrait (possibly Medora Leigh), Newstead Abbey Collections, Nottingham; repro. in Turney, *Byron's daughter*

Wealth at death £3000—deed of appointment: will, Temple, *Le tombeau de Medora*, 105

Leigh, Sir Oliph (1559–1612). *See under* Leigh, Charles (*bap.* 1572, *d.* 1605).

Leigh, Percival (1813–1889), satirist, son of Leonard Leigh of St Cross, Winchester, was born at Haddington, Scotland, on 3 November 1813. He was educated for the medical profession at St Bartholomew's Hospital, London, where he became good friends with the illustrator John Leech, as well as Albert Smith and Gilbert À Beckett. But although he became LSA in 1834 and MRCS in 1835, he and Leech found their real calling in comic literature, and they banded together in 1840 to produce three books: *The Comic Latin Grammar*, *The Comic English Grammar*, and *The Fiddle-Faddle Fashion Book*. This last was an exceedingly popular *jeu d'esprit*, containing colour illustrations of some fifty men in the most ridiculous assortment of male and female attire. A fourth work, *Portraits of Children of the Mobility*, appeared in 1841, and was so popular that the pair were immediately recruited to *Punch* on its formation a few months later.

At *Punch* Leigh rubbed elbows—quite literally, at its dinners—with William Makepeace Thackeray, Henry Mayhew, and Thomas Hood, and he was the first to carve his initials into the *Punch* table. He published *Jack the Giant Killer* in 1843, and, a good amateur actor, was a member, with Dickens, Leech, and Douglas William Jerrold, of the company which performed Ben Jonson's *Every Man in his Humour* on 21 September 1845 at Miss Kelly's Theatre, Dean Street, Soho (later the Royalty), in which Leigh took the role of Oliver Cob. As a result of these plaudits he was named deputy editor of *Punch* under Mark Lemon, but was prevented from becoming Lemon's successor by Shirley Brooks.

Leigh's best work—though the only one not illustrated by Leech—appeared in 1849, *Yᵉ manners and customs of yᵉ Englyshe: drawn from yᵉ quick by Richard Doyle, to which be added some extracts from Mr. Pips hys Diary*. Originally appearing serially in *Punch*, it owes much to Doyle's illustrations. But Leigh's application of ancient phraseology to modern affairs, such as a shareholders' meeting, made a decided hit. It is a clever, sarcastic chronicle of prevailing fashions and opinions, and its enlarged edition of 1876 was still in print in 1949. As with nearly all his works, the humour hinges on the schoolroom. Thus he was known jocularly among his friends as the Professor, and the best likeness of him is a caricature by Leech in their last book, *Paul Prendergast, or, The Comic Schoolmaster* (1859)—as an absent-minded professor, twirling his cane and pulling out his hair.

In 1850 Leigh lived at 10 Bedford Street, Bloomsbury, London, but before 1860 he had moved to Oak Cottage, 221 Hammersmith Road, Hammersmith, where he died on 24 October 1889. He was the last survivor of the early writers for *Punch*, though his weekly contributions had ceased to appear in the magazine for some fifteen years. His wife, Letitia, *née* Morrison, predeceased him.

W. A. J. Archbold, *rev.* Katharine Chubbuck

Sources W. P. Frith, *John Leech: his life and work*, 1 (1891) • R. G. G. Price, *A history of Punch* (1957), 33, 68, 100–07, 129, 136 • *Still crazy after all these years: Punch at 150* (1991) • J. Forster, *The life of Charles Dickens*, new edn, ed. A. J. Hoppé, 1 (1966), 375–7 • G. Everitt, *English caricaturists and graphic humourists of the nineteenth century* (1886), 282 • *The Athenaeum* (2 Nov 1889), 600 • 'Percival Leigh, 1813–89', *The new Cambridge bibliography of English literature*, [2nd edn], 3, ed. G. Watson (1969), 1390 • *CGPLA Eng. & Wales* (1890)

Likenesses photograph, *c*.1880–1889 (with Sir Francis Burnard), repro. in *Punch at 150* • J. Leech, caricature, repro. in P. Prendergast [P. Leigh], *Paul Prendergast, or, The comic schoolmaster* (1859)

Wealth at death £10,817 18*s*.: probate, 4 Jan 1890, *CGPLA Eng. & Wales*

Leigh [*alias* Layton, Metcalfe], **Philip** (1650/51–1717), Jesuit, was born in February 1650 or 1651 in Lancashire, the youngest of four sons (possibly there were more children) of Alexander Leigh (*d*. in or before 1676) and Anne, *née* Taylor, of Orrell, Wigan. An elder brother, John, also became a Jesuit. Educated at the English College at St Omer from 1667 (or earlier) until 1671, he departed in the latter year to the English College, Rome, where he was ordained priest on 13 April 1675. He was a good scholar and defended the theses of theology in a public disputation at the college in Rome. In 1678 he left Rome, and he joined the Jesuits in that year. He was soon appointed to Gateshead in the Durham district where he worked as a missionary for more than twenty years during which he was for some years the local Jesuit superior. From the time of his coming to England he usually went by the names of Layton or Metcalfe. In the reign of James II he had a spacious chapel in Gateshead and opened a classical or grammar school which did not survive the revolution of 1688. When Bishop Leyburn, the vicar apostolic, came to Newcastle and Gateshead in 1687 he confirmed more than 300 persons. In January 1688 Leigh preached a sermon 'on the day of thanksgiving' before the mayor of Newcastle, Sir William Creagh, which was subsequently printed by Henry Hills, the king's printer. It was described early in the nineteenth century by Dr Weedall, president of Oscott, where the library possessed a copy: 'it displays learning, piety and moderation' (*Catholic Miscellany*, 1826, 334). After two years in London Leigh moved to Wales about 1710, and became chaplain to the earl of Powis at Powis Castle. From about 1713 he served on the mission at Holywell, where he was superior of the Jesuits in north Wales. During these years he is believed to have edited *The Life and Miracles of St Wenefride, Virgin, Martyr and Abbess, Patroness of Wales* (1712), originally translated by the Jesuit priest John Falconer and printed by the press of the English College at St Omer in 1635. Leigh died at Holywell on 31 or possibly 1 January 1717, and was probably buried there.

Geoffrey Holt

Sources H. Foley, ed., *Records of the English province of the Society of Jesus*, 5 (1879), 661; 7 (1882–3), 449 • G. Holt, *The English Jesuits, 1650–1829: a biographical dictionary*, Catholic RS, 70 (1984), 147 • G. Holt, *St Omers and Bruges colleges, 1593–1773: a biographical dictionary*, Catholic RS, 69 (1979), 162 • J. Gillow and J. S. Hansom, eds., 'A list of convicted recusants in the reign of Charles II', *Miscellanea, V*, Catholic RS, 6 (1909), 75–326 • J. R. Baterden, ed., 'The Catholic registers of the secular mission in Newcastle-upon-Tyne', *Miscellanea, XVI*, Catholic RS, 35 (1936), 198–324, esp. 199, 201 • W. Kelly, ed., *Liber ruber venerabilis collegii Anglorum de urbe*, 2, Catholic RS, 40 (1943), 83–4 • A. Kenny, ed., *The responsa scholarum of the English College, Rome*, 2, Catholic RS, 55 (1963), 613 • A. de Backer and others, *Bibliothèque de la Compagnie de Jésus*, new edn, 4, ed. C. Sommervogel (Brussels, 1893), 1600 • [J. Leyburn], *Bishop Leyburn's confirmation register of 1687*, ed. J. A. Hilton, A. J. Mitchinson, B. Murray, and P. Wells (1997), 62–7 • G. Oliver, *Collections towards illustrating the biography of the Scotch, English and Irish members, SJ* (1838), 118 • F. Blom and others, *English Catholic books, 1701–1800: a bibliography* (1996) • Archives of the British Province of the Society of Jesus, London • Westm. DA

Leigh, Ralph Alexander (1915–1987), French scholar, was born in Poplar, Tower Hamlets, London, on 6 January 1915, the son of a journeyman tailor. His mother died tragically when he was nine. He won a scholarship to Raines' Foundation School for Boys and then won Drapers' Company and London county council scholarships in 1933 to study French at Queen Mary College, London University, graduating BA with first-class honours in 1936. A Clothworkers' Company scholarship enabled him to continue his studies at the University of Paris from 1937 to 1939. During the Second World War he served with the Royal Army Service Corps, reaching the rank of major in 1944; he was posted to Berlin during 1945–6. On 6 July 1945 he married, at Hackney register office, the pianist Edith Kern (1914–1972), whom he had met at the Sorbonne in 1938; she was the daughter of Theodore Kern, a schoolmaster. They had a son and a daughter.

In 1946 Leigh was appointed lecturer in French at the University of Edinburgh. The basis of his remarkable book collection, now in Cambridge University Library, was laid in that city. In 1952 he moved to Cambridge as a university lecturer in French; he became university reader in 1969 and held a personal professorship of

French from 1973 until his retirement in 1982. He was also in 1952 elected a fellow of Trinity College, where he was praelector for many years and a remarkable teacher. He was elected FBA in 1969 and was appointed CBE in 1977 and chevalier of the Légion d'honneur in 1979 (he was to have been made officier in 1988). He held honorary doctorates at the universities of Neuchâtel, Geneva, and Edinburgh, and was due in 1988 to be honoured at Oxford.

Leigh was the sole editor of one of the great scholarly achievements of the twentieth century, the *Correspondance complète de Jean-Jacques Rousseau* (53 vols., 1965–98). His choice of Rousseau for so much intent and inventive attention was made early, and was neither light nor accidental. While a student, he had discovered, with an irritation that never left him, the shortcomings in erudition and intellect of the previous edition. The brilliant outsider (born in Geneva, not France) whose arguments for justice and freedom were sharpened by a sense of exclusion and laced by derision, whose work had been misinterpreted and even deformed, who was hypersensitive and persecuted, evoked resonances in the young scholar of the 1930s, himself born into a poor East End Jewish family.

Leigh's work goes far beyond what is usually expected in an edition of the letters even of a great thinker and complex personality such as Rousseau. It contains far more letters than were recorded in previous collections and editions. It is based not on a printed tradition but on collation of the actual manuscript where it still exists. It gives variants and different versions of letters systematically and not sporadically. These versions are particularly important in the case of Rousseau because they illuminate cruxes in Rousseau's thought or in the course of his reaction to events in his life (for instance, the letter on Providence to Voltaire, 18 August 1765, where the complex changes traced may shed crucial light on Rousseau's evolving anti-materialism). Leigh identified and tracked down the lives of several thousand persons mentioned in the letters; where relevant he printed the letter to which Rousseau replied or the reply it evoked. Even more strikingly, he continued the collection beyond the date of his subject's death, so that the vexed question of Rousseau's influence on the French Revolution receives illumination from the papers. In the last volumes of his edition, Leigh published letters of reaction to Rousseau's death, but also accounts from the press, from memoirs, and from ephemera, which amount to a vast canvas of Rousseau's posthumous presence in France. It has become apparent after Leigh's own death that the edition has laid down a new set of measures and expectations about what such an enterprise, so conducted, can contribute to a community's knowledge; in this case, the community reaching out well beyond a group of the learned and scholars of the period that it might first seem to have addressed. The edition has become a standard work of reference for material beyond Rousseau, and has been placed on the open shelves of the Bibliothèque Nationale de France. This makes of it an emblem of its message: the intellectual, and not merely scholarly, importance of the detail of the field from which the great work arises.

Tall, short-sighted, and gangling, Leigh was an eloquent and witty debater whose urbanity would turn to passion and fury in the face of suffering and injustice. He loved music and wrote poetry, and his formidable intelligence engaged in whatever his eyes sparkling behind his glasses turned to consider. His enjoyment of the Johnson Club, as of the peculiarities of life within a Cambridge college (where he lived after the death of his wife in 1972), and of social and academic success was real enough. But these never outweighed the delight in scholarship, the keener if it were sharp and polemical, or the utter respect for intellectual achievement that he lived by. Having earlier suffered a heart attack, he died in the Addenbrooke's Hospital, Cambridge, on 22 December 1987 and was buried in Trumpington cemetery. MARIAN HOBSON

Sources *The Times* (23 Dec 1987) • *The Independent* (4 Jan 1988) • R. Wokler, *PBA*, 84 (1994), 369–91 • private information (2004) [John Leigh, son; Martha Leigh, daughter; Rose Mendel] • holograph CVs, copies of material for grant applications • m. cert. • d. cert. • Queen Mary College, London, archives • S. Harvey, M. Hobson, D. J. Kelley, and S. S. B. Taylor, eds., *Reappraisals of Rousseau: studies in honour of R. A. Leigh* (1980) • M. Hobson, J. T. A. Leigh, and R. Wokler, eds., *Rousseau and the eighteenth century: essays in memory of R. A. Leigh* (1992)
Archives CUL, notes for scholarly work
Likenesses photograph, Trinity Cam., archives • photograph, repro. in Wokler, *PBA*, facing p. 369
Wealth at death £333,745: probate, further grant, 5 July 1988, *CGPLA Eng. & Wales*

Leigh, Richard (1649/50–1728), poet, was the younger son of Edward *Leigh (1603–1671), of Rushall, Staffordshire, writer and MP, and Elizabeth Talbot (*d.* 1707). He entered Queen's College, Oxford, on 23 March 1666 aged sixteen and proceeded BA on 19 June 1669. Wood writes that he left Oxford for London, and became an actor in the duke of York's or the King's Company. There were other actors named Leigh in the period (Anthony and John Leigh), but no records survive of a Richard Leigh in either company, and, given Leigh's subsequent career, Wood may have been mistaken.

While still a young man, Leigh wrote a prose tract attacking Dryden, entitled *The Censure of the Rota on Mr. Dryden's Conquest of Granada*, an attack which irked Dryden, who subsequently referred to Leigh as 'the Fastidious Brisk of Oxford'. Leigh also wrote *The transproser rehearsed, or, The fifth act of Mr. Baye's play: being a postscript to the animadversions* [by Marvell] *on the preface to Bishop Bramhall's 'Vindication' showing what grounds there are of fears and jealousies of popery* (1673) for 'the assigns of Hugo Grotius and Jacob van Harmine, on the North Side of Lac Lemane'. Lowndes describes this as scurrilous and indecent. More recently, Smith calls it 'the most successful effort to rail at Marvell in his own manner, visualizing him as a "Coffee House *virtuoso*"' (Marvell, xiii). It is wrongly ascribed by Andrew Marvell to Dr Samuel Parker. Leigh also published *Poems upon Several Occasions and to Several Persons* (1675).

In his will dated 22 March 1726, Leigh described himself as a doctor of physick of Wolverhampton, and directed that his body should be buried near his father's, in the chancel of St Michael's Church, Rushall. The will was proved on 12 September 1728.

T. B. SAUNDERS, *rev.* JOANNA MOODY

Sources Watt, *Bibl. Brit.*, 2.597 • W. T. Lowndes, *The bibliographer's manual of English literature*, ed. H. G. Bohn, [new edn], 3 (1864), 1336 • F. W. Bateson, *The Cambridge bibliography of English literature*, 2 (1940), 283 • A. Marvell, *The rehearsal transpros'd*, ed. D. I. B. Smith (1971), xiii • Wood, *Ath. Oxon.*, new edn, 4.533 • Foster, *Alum. Oxon.* • H. MacDonald, introduction, in R. Leigh, *Poems, 1675* (1947), v–xvi

Leigh, Richard Arthur Austen- (1872–1961), printer and historian, was born on 17 May 1872 at Calder Lodge, Maidenhead, Berkshire, the fifth of six children of Cholmeley Austen-Leigh (1829–1899), printer, and his wife, Melesina Mary, *née* Chenevix (*d.* 1918), daughter of Richard Chenevix, archbishop of Dublin. Both his parents were English and of Huguenot descent.

The traditions into which Richard Austen-Leigh was born, and to which he willingly adhered, shaped his life and filled his leisure. Many of his family had been Etonians and he followed his elder brother Edward Chenevix Austen-Leigh to Eton College. From Eton he went up to King's College, Cambridge, as a scholar, at a time when his uncle Augustus Austen-Leigh (1840–1905) was provost and vice-chancellor of the university. He was awarded a first class in the classical tripos (1894). Having acted at Eton, he continued to do so at Cambridge, where he was president of the Cambridge Amateur Dramatic Club in 1894; he excelled in female parts and was particularly acclaimed as Mrs Malaprop in Sheridan's *The Rivals*.

Like an uncle before him, Austen-Leigh became a clerk in the House of Commons (1897–1900), but after the death of his father he resigned and joined his brothers as a director in the family printing firm of Ballantine & Co. His younger brother, Charles Raymond, died in 1901 at the age of twenty-seven, leaving the elder brothers to manage Ballantine's, later Ballantine, Spottiswoode. Under their direction, the firm expanded and prospered. On joining Ballantine's, Austen-Leigh was admitted to the livery of the Stationers' Company, and from the end of the First World War was active in the company's affairs. On 28 July 1906 he married (Vera Estelle Stephanie Maria de las) Mercedes Trench (1884/5–1927).

Austen-Leigh's family's history and those of his old school and college fascinated him. In the years before the Second World War, when a large printing house could still fit in small-scale jobs, Spottiswoode's was printer to the Eton Press and King's, and privately printed Austen-Leigh's own books. *Bygone Eton: an Illustrated Guide to the Buildings of Eton College* (1906) and *Bygone Kings: being a collection of views of the buildings at Kings College, Cambridge, with descriptive notes* (1907) are examples of Spottiswoode's fine book design and production. Through such works as *Eton under Barnard, 1754–65* (1904), *Etoniana*, a journal of research into the history of Eton, which he edited from 1920, and to which he contributed many articles, and *The Eton College Register, 1698–1770* (1921 and 1927), a unique source of biographical information on Old Etonians, he came to be regarded as the unofficial historian of the school. His interest in Cambridge printing extended to the university press and he recommended the very able John Lewis as Cambridge University printer, which led to a collaboration with Stanley Morison as typographic designer, transforming the standard of Cambridge printing in the inter-war years. He also published a number of guides to the history and architecture of King's.

Jane Austen's Life and Letters (1913), written jointly with his uncle William Austen-Leigh, drew on letters and papers in the family's possession together with those published by Lord Brabourn, and was the definitive biography for its day. An interest in his Huguenot roots led to publication of several papers in the journal of the Huguenot Society (of which he was president, 1934–7), which his firm printed. A tall, imposing figure, with a ready wit, and a skilful negotiator, Austen-Leigh was active in trade organizations. He was the Livery Committee's first chairman (1920–27) and persuaded the court to permit a checklist to be made of the company's historic archives which literary scholars and bibliographers had used since the late eighteenth century. It was published by the Bibliographical Society in 1926. He was president of the Federation of Master Printers in 1922, chairman of the Joint Industrial Council of the Printing Trade (1927–8), and founding chairman of the International Bureau of Federations of Master Printers (1933–49). From 1934 to 1936 he was president of the Bibliographical Society. At the beginning of the Second World War he organized the move of the federation's offices from Berlin to Paris and was subsequently made a chevalier of the order of Leopold (Belgium) and commandeur de mérite commercial (France). Austen-Leigh was also chairman of the committee of management of the National Benevolent Institute (1936–45), president of the festival of the Printers' Pension Corporation (1941), and editor of the Master Printers' *Annual* (1920–61). In the meantime, he continued his work on his family history. *The Pedigree of Austen*, a genealogy, was privately printed in 1940 and *Austen Papers, 1704–1856*, a volume of family letters, was published in 1942. Although neither measures up to modern scholarly methods, they make available material which might otherwise never have been known. His first wife having died in 1927, in 1941 he married Margaret Thruston (*d.* 1986).

Austen-Leigh became a trustee of the Jane Austen Memorial Trust in 1949 when Chawton was bought as a study centre. In 1954–5, at the age of eighty-two, he was master of the Stationers' Company. Richard Austen-Leigh died on 18 October 1961 at his home, Isel Hall, Cockermouth, Cumberland. The material he had amassed for a revised and enlarged edition of the *Life and Letters* was incorporated in the posthumously published *Jane Austen: a Family Record* (1989).

ROBIN MYERS

Sources *WWW, 1961–70* • Venn, *Alum. Cant.* • admissions register, King's Cam. • Cambridge class lists • G. W. Cole, *Index to bibliographical papers published by the Bibliographical Society and the Library Association, London, 1877–1932* (1933) • R. A. Austen-Leigh, *Pedigree of Austen*, ed. D. Gilson, rev. edn (1995) • The beadle's book, Apprentice memorandum book, Court books, Archive of the Stationers' Company, London • *Eton College Chronicle* (7 Dec 1961) • *The Times* (20 Oct 1961) • *International Bulletin for the Printing and Allied Trades* (Oct

1961) • *Master Printers' Annual* (1962) • *Eton Chronicle* (7 Dec 1961) • *Annual Report of the Council* [King's College, Cambridge] (1962), 20–21 • *Proceedings of the Huguenot Society*, 20 (1958–64), 372–3 • m. cert. [Vera Mercedes Trench] • d. cert.

Archives Hants. RO, corresp. and MSS • priv. coll., diaries | Eton, letters to the provost • Jane Austen House, Chawton, letters to R. W. Chapman and T. E. Carpenter • King's AC Cam., letters to Oscar Browning

Likenesses group photograph, 1931 (with members of the Council of Administration of the International Bureau of Printers), repro. in *International Bulletin for the Printing and Allied Trades* • photograph, Stationers' Company, London, album of photographs of masters of the company • photograph, repro. in *International Bulletin for the Printing and Allied Trades*

Leigh, Samuel (*b.* 1645/6, *d.* in or after 1686), translator and poet, was the son of Samuel Leigh, of Boston, Lincolnshire. He entered Merton College, Oxford, in Michaelmas term 1660 as a commoner, and matriculated on 12 December 1661 aged fifteen. In the same year his metrical translation of the Psalms, *Samuelis Primitiae, or, An Essay towards a Metrical Version of the Whole Book of Psalms*, was published, with a dedication to Leigh's 'father-in-law' Charles Pott: not his father-in-law in the modern sense, but rather his stepfather. According to Wood, the amateurishness of Leigh's translation is due to the extenuating circumstances of 'youth and sickness' (Wood, *Ath. Oxon.*, new edn, 4.478).

Leigh's pedestrian style notwithstanding, the volume is recommended to the reader with fulsome praise by the well-known presbyterians Thomas Manton and Gabriel Sanger. Holland attributes their plaudits to Leigh's financial prospects and his family's presbyterian links rather than sincere appreciation of his talents. Of the latter there is no further proof: *Samuelis Primitiae* was the only work Leigh ever published.

It seems that Leigh left university without completing his degree and may have been the Samuel Leigh who entered Lincoln's Inn as a student on 23 April 1663. Apparently he spent the rest of his life living off his patrimony and was still alive in 1686.

ARTEMIS GAUSE-STAMBOULOPOULOU

Sources Foster, *Alum. Oxon.*, 1500–1714, 3.899 • W. P. Baildon, ed., *The records of the Honorable Society of Lincoln's Inn: admissions*, 1 (1896), 289 • J. Holland, *The psalmists of Britain*, 2 vols. (1843), 2.54–5 • Wood, *Ath. Oxon.*, new edn, 4.478 • *DNB*

Likenesses W. Faithorne, line engraving (aged fifteen), BM, NPG; repro. in S. Leigh, *Samuelis Primitiae* (1661) • pen-and-ink drawing, NPG

Leigh, Sir Thomas (*d.* 1571), mayor of London, was the son of Roger Leigh of Wellington in Shropshire. He was apprenticed to Thomas Seymer, a member of the Mercers' Company, and was made free in 1526. From 1528 until 1540 Leigh rented a tenement in Basinghall from the Mercers, at the rate of 26*s.* 8*d.* He was one of those for whom membership of the Mercers was a gateway to the profitable overseas trading monopoly of the Merchant Adventurers; the two organizations were closely associated in this period. References in official papers to a Thomas Leigh, who was acting as a merchant of the staple at Antwerp by February 1528, and who in the following year was in a position to advance substantial credit to the government's

Sir Thomas Leigh (*d.* 1571), by unknown artist

representative in that city, are likely to be to the future lord mayor. It is not known for how long Leigh continued his activities as an overseas trader, but as late as January 1559 he was referred to as 'merchant of staple'.

It is clear that Leigh became a wealthy man. He was admitted to the Mercers' Company livery in 1535, and in 1546 was living in a great mansion in the Old Jewry. More London properties accumulated in his possession. In 1549 he rented the parsonage of St Mary Colechurch from the Mercers, at a rent of £7 p.a. In 1550, in exchange for the lease of a parsonage, the company granted to him the fee simple of the sextons' and priests' chambers on the north side of St Thomas of Acon, together with a payment of £27. During the reign of Edward VI, Leigh also acquired property outside London, notably in Warwickshire, at Stoneleigh and elsewhere, and in Gloucestershire, at Adlestrop and Maugersbury. His considerable wealth was poorly reflected in subsidy assessments for £400 in 1549 and for £300 in 1559 and 1564; it undoubtedly strengthened Leigh's advance towards political influence in the city. His path was also smoothed by marriage, before 13 March 1536, to Alice Coverdale, daughter of John Barker of Shropshire and niece and principal heir of the mercer and alderman Sir Rowland Hill, who was lord mayor of the city in 1549–50.

Leigh became a warden of the Mercers' Company in 1543 and master in 1553, serving in each capacity twice. In 1550 he was elected to the common council of the city as a representative of Coleman Street ward. On 27 October 1552 Leigh became alderman for Castle Baynard ward, on the nomination of Alderman Sir George Barne, then lord mayor, and others. It was agreed to grant him a two-year respite from the position of sheriff; but in 1555 he was duly nominated for and accepted that unpopular duty. From 15 September 1556 he sat as alderman for Broad Street ward, attending court sessions in Christ's Hospital. From 15 March 1558 until the year of his death he represented Coleman Street ward. During this period of almost twenty years' continuous service as an alderman, he attended about half the sessions.

The accession of Elizabeth in 1558 coincided with his term as lord mayor and was important to the safety of the transition. But the emotions of the London protestant crowds were not confined to their attendance at the famous royal progress through the city. It seems that members of the congregation of Bow church engaged in the 'pulling down of the images and the sacrament and defacing the vestments and books'. Their action was approved by many, and no complaint was made. But the incident came to the ears of the privy council, which wrote to Leigh protesting at this 'outrageous disorder'. He was sharply reminded of:

> an exhortation made by the Queen's majesty unto him on Candlemas day last past, and straitly commanded to use the best means he could to bolt out the doers hereof, and to cause them to be apprehended and committed to ward. (*APC*, 7.77)

Nevertheless, Leigh's loyalty to the new monarch and her government and religion was recognized: he was knighted before 15 January 1559.

By the onset of his last years Leigh had amassed an enormous fortune: among the cancelled bonds ordered to be paid by the privy council in 1571 were debts to him of more than £7000. He died on 17 November 1571 and was buried in the Mercers' chapel. His will, dated 20 December 1570 and proved on 14 December 1571, confirms that he had already settled the main bulk of his landed property on his children at the time of their marriages. His moveable property was to be divided into equal parts: one to be settled on his wife, one to be divided equally—with no respect for gender or seniority—on his four sons and five daughters, and one to be granted to the relief of the poor of London, Southwark, and elsewhere. To the Mercers he left a heavy silver-gilt hanap or lidded cup, hallmarked 1499–1500, known as the 'Leigh cup'. Sir Thomas seems to have regarded his wife, Alice, with great affection, charging his children to 'behave yourselves like good, honest gentle, obedient children towards your mother … not forgetting the motherly love she had unto you in bringing you up out of your cradle to this present day'. Alice herself founded an almshouse at Stoneleigh in 1579. She long outlived her husband, dying at what must have been a very great age in 1604.

In William Jaggard's *A View of all the Right Honourable the Lord Mayors* there are woodcuts of five mercers who reached that position, including Thomas Leigh. Jaggard's habit of reusing his woodcuts invites caution as to how truly Sir Thomas is represented. There is no doubt, however, of the substance of the dynasty that the merchant founded, notably in Warwickshire. His eldest son, Rowland (aged twenty-six in 1568), ancestor of the lords Leigh, established his seat at Longborough, Gloucestershire. The ancestry of William Pitt can be traced, via Francis Leigh, earl of Chichester, to the third son, Sir William Leigh. Lord Melbourne was descended from Thomas Leigh's daughter Winifred. STEPHEN WRIGHT

Sources R. Benbow, *Table of London citizens involved in city government, 1558–1603* (1992) • R. Benbow, *Notes to the index of London citizens* (1992) • A. B. Beaven, ed., *The aldermen of the City of London, temp. Henry III–[1912]*, 2 vols. (1908–13) • will, PRO, PROB 11/53, sig. 48 • J. Strype, *Annals of the Reformation and establishment of religion … during Queen Elizabeth's happy reign*, new edn, 2 (1824), 71 • *APC*, 1558–75 • *VCH Gloucestershire*, vol. 6 • *LP Henry VIII*, vol. 4 • I. Doolittle, *The Mercers' Company* (1990) • J. Johnson, *Tudor Gloucester* (1985) • *DNB* • HoP, *Commons, 1558–1603*

Likenesses line engraving, BM, NPG • oils, priv. coll. [*see illus.*] • woodcut, repro. in W. Jaggard and T. Pauyer, *A view of all the right honourable the lord mayors of this honorable citty of London* (1601)

Wealth at death amassed an enormous fortune: will, PRO, PROB 11/53, sig. 48

Leigh, Thomas, first Baron Leigh (1594/5–1672), landowner and local politician, was the eldest son of Sir John Leigh (*d.* 1608) of Stoneleigh and Ursula, daughter of Sir Christopher *Hoddesdon of Leighton Buzzard, Bedfordshire, and great-grandson of Sir Thomas *Leigh (*d.* 1571). He was educated at Magdalen College, Oxford, matriculating on 4 November 1608. Two years later, on 11 November 1610, at the age of fifteen, he married Mary, the daughter and coheir of Sir Thomas Egerton, eldest son of the lord chancellor, also Sir Thomas *Egerton. This early marriage was almost certainly linked to the death of his father in 1608 and the need to settle his future during the lifetime of his grandfather Sir Thomas Leigh of Stoneleigh, first baronet. The couple's eldest daughter was born in 1614 and during a long marriage they had five sons and six daughters.

On 1 February 1626 Leigh succeeded his grandfather as second baronet, inheriting an estate that encompassed Stoneleigh, Warwickshire, Hamstall Ridware, Staffordshire, and Leighton Buzzard, Bedfordshire. He was admitted to the Warwickshire bench in April 1626, but excused himself from service as a commissioner for the forced loan. He represented Warwickshire in the parliament of 1628–9 and with his cousin Sir Francis Leigh (created Baron Dunsmore in 1628) was a leading figure in the county during the 1630s. His income at this time was at least £2500 per annum. He served as sheriff in 1636–7, when he was reported as saying of the ship money levy that 'he did not mean to trouble himself in the business farther than he must needs' (Hughes, 107). During the year of his shrievalty he was visited at Stoneleigh by the antiquary William Dugdale, to whom he lent the Stoneleigh ledger book and later other records.

Like many leading gentlemen who had manifested reservations over the forced loan and ship money, Leigh's opposition to the king's policies did not extend to rebellion. At the outbreak of the civil war he supported the king, being one of the eleven out of twenty-one resident justices in the county to attend the king's musters in 1642.

In August 1642 Charles I stayed at Stoneleigh for three days while his army bombarded Coventry. When making his composition with parliament Leigh was to claim that he went with the king on his departure from Stoneleigh, but was neither himself in arms nor assisted with men or money. However, on 1 July 1643 he was created Baron Leigh of Stoneleigh 'in testimony of his stedfast loyalty' to the king (W. Dugdale, *Antiquities of Warwickshire*, 1656, 173) and is one of the few gentlemen to whose service in the civil war the royalist William Dugdale made reference in his *Antiquities of Warwickshire*. In October 1644 he was taken prisoner by Sir Thomas Middleton, being sent to London on parole, but was rescued by his own party. He subsequently paid £4895 in composition to parliament for his estate. His youngest son, Ferdinand, died in 1655 while a student at Lincoln's Inn and his funeral sermon was preached by the royalist cleric Bruno Ryves and published the following year. Leigh himself subscribed to a ceremonial form of religion, to which he gave expression in the preamble to his will.

Leigh's joy at the restoration of the monarchy was overshadowed in April 1662 by the death of his eldest son, Thomas, who sat in parliament for Staffordshire. Drawing up his will a decade later, he left £4000 to be divided between his three granddaughters by Thomas, provided they married with the consent of his eldest surviving son, Charles, who was established at Leighton Buzzard. The bulk of his considerable estate he left to his 21-year-old grandson Thomas, the son of Thomas by his second wife, Jane, daughter of Patrick Fitzmaurice, Lord Kerry. He died on 22 February 1672 and was buried two days later at Stoneleigh alongside his wife, who had predeceased him in 1669. JAN BROADWAY

Sources GEC, *Peerage*, new edn • A. Hughes, *Politics, society and civil war in Warwickshire, 1620–1660* (1987) • J. Gresley, *The Cistercian abbey of Stoneley-in-Arden* (1854) • will, PRO, PROB 11/388, fol. 50 • J. Burke and J. B. Burke, *A genealogical and heraldic history of the extinct and dormant baronetcies of England, Ireland and Scotland*, 2nd edn (1841); repr. (1844), 307 • Foster, *Alum. Oxon.*, 1500–1714, 3.899 • B. Ryves, *A sermon preached at Lincolns-Inne, July 15th 1655* (1656)

Archives Coventry Archives, corresp., mainly with mayor and justices of Coventry | Shakespeare Birthplace Trust RO, Stratford upon Avon, Stoneleigh MSS

Likenesses oils (after H. Stone), Lamport Hall, Northamptonshire

Wealth at death considerable; left £4000 to granddaughters; settlement of £1000 to eldest son concerning land in Warwickshire; also further land in Bedfordshire, out of which he was to pay brother £1500; bulk of estate to grandson: will, PRO, PROB 11/388, fol. 50 • £2500 p.a.; income in 1630s: Hughes, *Politics & society*

Leigh, Thomas Pemberton, **Baron Kingsdown** (1793–1867), lawyer, was born in London on 11 February 1793, the eldest son of Robert Pemberton (*d.* 1804), chancery barrister, and his wife, Margaret, eldest daughter and coheir of Edward Leigh of Bispham Hall, Lancashire. His father, a member of a family settled near Warrington in Lancashire, and a descendant of Sir Francis Pemberton, chief justice of the common pleas, died in 1804. Though he had earned a good income, he had been unable to save money, and his widow was left poorly off, considering the size of his family—three sons and two daughters. Accordingly Thomas Pemberton, who had been for four years at Dr Horne's school at Chiswick to be prepared for Westminster and Oxford, was obliged to give up all hope of a university career, and, leaving Dr Horne's school at the age of sixteen, went into the office of a solicitor, Mr Farrer, for twelve months, and then became a pupil in the chambers of his uncle, Edward Cooke, a barrister in good chancery practice. He had been a studious and diligent boy, left school a fair scholar, and was throughout his life fond of classical studies. He earned £100 to £150 a year before being called to the bar by drawing equity pleadings, according to the practice of the day, for solicitors. He was called to the bar at Lincoln's Inn in 1816. His youth had been, as he called it, 'gloomy and joyless', but he had read diligently, and success came rapidly. He made the hitherto unprecedented sum of £600 in his first year. Though he joined the northern circuit and occasionally appeared before parliamentary committees on election petitions, his practice was almost exclusively in equity. Before he was thirty his income was £3000 a year. In 1829 he became a king's counsel, and divided with Bickersteth the practice of the rolls court, which, when Bickersteth became Lord Langdale, he entirely dominated. In April 1831 he entered parliament for Rye as a staunch Conservative, after an election at which great violence was displayed; he spoke with great effect against the Reform Bill, and afterwards published his speech. He lost the seat in 1832, began and abandoned a candidature for Taunton, and was elected in January 1835 for Ripon, a seat which he retained as long as he remained in parliament. He declined in December 1835 Sir Robert Peel's offer of the solicitor-generalship in his first administration, as well as Lord Lyndhurst's offer of a puisne judgeship. With characteristic diffidence he distrusted his judicial fitness, and preferred to remain undisputed leader of the chancery bar. Until 1838 he spoke little in the Commons, when he joined with Sugden, his colleague in the representation of Ripon, in resisting the privilege claim of the House of Commons in the case of *Stockdale* v. *Hansard*, his best-known speech, supported by his pamphlet-letter to Lord Langdale (1837). He afterwards took a large share in the arrangements made for settling the matter by act of parliament. In 1841 the vice-chancellorship was offered him and refused, but he accepted from Sir Robert Peel in 1841 the post of attorney-general for the duchy of Cornwall.

In January 1843 Pemberton came into a life income of upwards of £14,000 a year on the death of Sir Robert Holt Leigh, a distant relative and large Lancashire landowner, whose admiration he had won by successfully conducting a case for him in 1831. He then assumed the name of Leigh in addition to his father's surname, Pemberton, and took a step unusual among lawyers by deciding to retire in mid-career to his country seat, Torry Hill, near Sittingbourne, Kent, and to the country sports he loved. Sir Robert Peel made him thereon chancellor of the duchy of Cornwall and a privy councillor, and it was arranged that when he left the bar he should become one of the members of the judicial committee of the privy council. He resigned his seat for Ripon in the spring of 1843, and his practice at the bar at the end of that year.

In February 1844 Pemberton Leigh began attendances at the judicial committee of the privy council, which continued for twenty years. He also devoted considerable time to the affairs of the duchy of Cornwall, and thus became a close friend and admirer of Prince Albert. During his tenure of the chancellorship he succeeded in rehabilitating the finances of the duchy, and in accumulating a considerable fund during the minority of the prince of Wales. Honours were repeatedly offered to him and refused. It was expected that he would have been lord chancellor in 1849. Four successive governments, beginning with Lord John Russell's in 1853, offered him a peerage. Lord Derby pressed the lord chancellorship on him in vain, though it is said that he promised to take it if the interests of the Conservative Party, of which he remained a staunch supporter, imperatively demanded it.

Pemberton Leigh also spent much time on the judicial committee, which had been reorganized in 1833 but had not yet settled to its new role. He was an important influence in shaping that role. He was especially influential in imperial cases, becoming an authority on Indian land tenure on which subject he delivered many important judgments, as he also did on allied subjects such as succession rights and mortgages (Simpson, 411). Following the decision in *Bremer* v. *Freeman* (1857), he promoted what became known as Lord Kingsdown's Act, which dealt with the wills of British subjects living abroad. He was a member of the committee when it pronounced on the Gorham case and the *Essays and Reviews* case, 'revealing himself to be against persecution and proscription within the Church of England' (ibid.). In 1854 Lord Aberdeen requested him to take especial charge of appeals in prize cases, and he uniformly interpreted the law of blockade, capture, and prize with a liberal bent towards freedom of trade. When created Baron Kingsdown in 1858 by the Conservative government he also became a member of the appellate tribunal of the House of Lords, and, though he never really approved of it as the ultimate court of appeal, was a much needed source of judicial strength there. In his later years indolence and distaste for judicial activity somewhat grew on him, and at length, after a lingering illness, he died at Torry Hill on 7 October 1867. He was unmarried, and his title became extinct. He was buried at Frinsted church, near Sittingbourne.

Kingsdown was much admired by his legal colleagues for his fastidious and elegantly drafted judgments. He was known as a pious member of the Church of England. His reputation survives in his speech in *Ramsden* v. *Dryson* (1866) on the concept which became known as proprietary estoppel, his dissenting judgment still being of relevance. J. A. HAMILTON, *rev.* H. C. G. MATTHEW

Sources T. P. Leigh, *Lord Kingsdown's recollections of his life at the bar and in parliament*, ed. E. L. Pemberton (1868) • 'Lord Kingsdown's recollections', *EdinR*, 129 (1869), 40–68 • *The Times* (8 Oct 1867) • *GM*, 4th ser., 4 (1867), 674 • A. W. B. Simpson, ed., *Biographical dictionary of the common law* (1984) • GEC, *Peerage*

Likenesses W. Walker, mezzotint, pubd 1846, BM, NPG • W. Holl, stipple (after G. Richmond), BM, NPG

Wealth at death under £100,000: probate, 29 Oct 1867, *CGPLA Eng. & Wales*

Leigh, Valentine (*d.* **1563**), merchant and writer, was the son of Robert Leigh and his wife, Leillman, both of whom he predeceased. Nothing more is known of his early life. He later became a prosperous London mercer, and resided on Lodde Lane in the St Lawrence Jewry parish. He and his wife, Katheryn, had at least three children: Robert (the eldest), Richard, and Agnes, all of whom survived him, as did a brother, Nicholas. Leigh was of strong protestant leanings, as is reflected in *Deathes Generall Proclamation, or, Five Preceptes of Vertuous and Honest Lyfe*, published in 1561. His more significant work, *The Most Profitable and Commendable Science of Surveying*, was published in 1577 (twice), 1578, 1588, 1592, and 1596. This treatise was a popular, practical guide, largely for self-surveyors, and is mentioned in John Norden's standard work, *The Surveiors Dialogue* (1610).

A third work has been attributed to Leigh, *The Pleasaunt Playne and Pythye Pathewaye Leadynge to a Vertuous and Honest Lyfe*, which possibly dates from 1552. It takes the form of a dialogue in verse between a young man (the author, V.L.) and an old man, whom the author asks for advice. The old man asks him his age and name, and he replies that he is under twenty-one, and called Nitnelave—an anagram of Valentine (*Pleasaunt Patheway*e, sig. A2r). On the strength of this, *ESTC* attributes the text to Leigh, but it has also been attributed to Urban Lynyng.

When Leigh died he owned two houses (next to each other), a lute, several bibles, and other books. He also employed at least two servants, whom he provided for in his will dated March 1563. It was proved in December that year. BEN LOWE

Sources V. Leigh, *Deathes generall proclamation, or, Five preceptes of vertuous and honest lyfe* (1561) • commissary court of London, GL, MS 9171/15, fol. 178 [1563] • Tanner, *Bibl. Brit.-Hib.* • A. McRae, *God speed the plough: the representation of agrarian England, 1500–1660* (1996) • M. Fitch, ed., *Index to testamentary records in the commissary court of London, 1489–1570*, 2, British RS, 86 (1974) • G. Huelin, *Think and thank God: the Mercers Company and its contribution to the church and religious life since the Reformation* (1994) • *ESTC*

Wealth at death two houses; various lands and tenements; several parchment bibles and other books; a lute; miscellaneous household goods and plate; about £20 in gifts to friends and family: will, proved, Dec 1563

Leigh, Vera Eugenie (**1903–1944**). *See under* Women agents on active service in France (*act.* 1942–1945).

Leigh, Vivien [*real name* Vivian Mary Hartley; *married name* Vivian Mary Olivier, Lady Olivier] (**1913–1967**), actress, was born in Darjeeling, India, on 5 November 1913, the only surviving child of Ernest Richard Hartley and his wife, Gertrude Robinson Yackje. She spent the first six years of her childhood in India, where her father was a junior partner in a firm of exchange brokers in Calcutta. Her mother, who was of French-Irish descent, carefully superintended her small daughter's upbringing, and the books and music that early appeared in the nursery had a warm welcome. In 1920 the Hartleys returned to England and placed their daughter in the Convent of the Sacred

Vivien Leigh (1913–1967), by Laszlo Willinger, 1940

Heart in Roehampton, where Maureen O'Sullivan was a fellow boarder. Even as a child Vivian Hartley was a leader in style, and her beautifully chosen clothes were not a little coveted. Although bored by conventional school lessons, she lost no opportunity in absorbing what interested her, and her letters home urged many extra lessons in ballet, piano, and violin. Visits to the theatre fed the child's dramatic instinct, and she took part each term in school productions, making her début as Mustardseed in *A Midsummer Night's Dream*.

When Vivian Hartley was thirteen her parents extended her education by taking her on a European tour. This tour, which included study in schools and convents in France, Italy, and Bavaria, gave her fluency in three languages and a liberal experience of great value. She made the utmost use of her five years abroad, visiting the great art galleries, attending opera, concerts, and the theatre, while her natural taste for beauty and quality was nourished by the international fashion designers. When she returned to England at eighteen, she was abundantly prepared to conquer the theatre world. Her clear green-blue eyes, chestnut hair, and delicate features were enhanced by a flawless complexion, and she walked with an assured grace.

Scarcely had she enrolled as a student at the Royal Academy of Dramatic Art when she announced her engagement to a young barrister, Herbert Leigh Holman. The fashionable wedding that followed in December 1932 at St James's, Spanish Place, George Street, London, and the establishment of a new pattern of living engrossed her until after the birth of her daughter in October 1933. Characteristically, this was recorded in her diary—'Had a baby—a girl'. Gradually, however, her ambition to become an actress again grew restless, and in August 1934 she interrupted a family yachting cruise to return home, just in case she should be called for a small part in a film. Her reward came in one line in the film *Things are Looking Up*, with Cicely Courtneidge. More small parts now began to come her way, and she decided upon the stage name Vivien Leigh.

Less than a year after her entry into films Vivien Leigh was given the stage opportunity that she needed when casting had been held up for a young actress to play a leading part in *The Mask of Virtue* by Carl Sternheim. Since the first requirement was exceptional beauty, Vivien Leigh conquered everyone concerned at the first interview. The play, produced at the Ambassadors Theatre in 1935, was not a success, but the young actress was acclaimed 'a star of unusual promise'. It was very much to her credit that the adulation she received did not turn her head, but like the good professional that she wished to be she took the exposure of her inexperience intelligently and began to learn her craft. Within twenty-four hours of her successful press reviews Vivien Leigh had signed a five-year contract with Alexander Korda, but she had to wait another year before Korda was ready to cast her in *Fire over England* (1937). The occasion, when it came, was fateful, bringing her into a professional relationship with Laurence Kerr *Olivier (1907–1989). They were soon very much in love. She was already an admirer of his acting, and the four months they spent working daily together on the film were deeply influential in her subsequent development. Aware of her limitations, and working constantly to overcome them, Vivien Leigh eagerly accepted the challenge to play Ophelia to Olivier's Hamlet when the Old Vic production was invited to appear in Elsinore, Denmark, in June 1937. Under expert tuition, her voice—which had been light and small—gained in strength, and her willingness to learn so won her director's admiration that she was cast for Titania in the Old Vic production of *A Midsummer Night's Dream* at Christmas 1937.

With the offer to play Scarlett O'Hara in the film *Gone with the Wind* (1939) Vivien Leigh saw her first chance to break the image of a Dresden china shepherdess—a comparison that she despised. Although she had no sympathy for Scarlett, the actress could recognize 'a marvellous part' when she saw one, and she seized and exploited every facet of her heroine, who gave her both an Oscar award and international status as a film star.

Following the dissolution of their previous marriages, Vivien Leigh and Laurence Olivier were married in California on 30 August 1940. They made the film *Lady Hamilton* (1941), then returned to England—Olivier to service in the Royal Navy, and Vivien Leigh to establish a wartime home for them both. She was eager to return to the theatre, making her appearance in *The Doctor's Dilemma* by Bernard Shaw at the Haymarket in 1942. This was followed a year later by a three-month tour of north Africa in which she appeared in a concert party with Beatrice Lillie for the armed services. In a letter home she confesses to 'one of the most exciting and often the most moving experiences I have ever had'.

Vivien Leigh had been an actress for almost ten years before her capacity to carry the action of a play was tested. In Thornton Wilder's *The Skin of our Teeth* (Phoenix, 1945) as Sabina she showed a new authority in her work, and evidence that she could now stand unsupported. In 1947 her husband was knighted. In a demanding ten-month tour of Australia and New Zealand with Olivier with the Old Vic Company in 1948 she had abundant classical opportunities to prepare her for the tragic role of Antigone, in which she made a great impression when they returned to London in 1949. Critics, who had been cautious over her early successes, observed that 'this is a new Miss Leigh altogether', and they complimented her on her extended vocal range and 'fanatical force of character'. The actress was now seen in full maturity; when she appeared as Blanche in Tennessee Williams's *A Streetcar Named Desire* at the Aldwych in October of the same year she received a storming ovation for a performance of uncommon subtlety, and she filled the theatre for eight months. Another Oscar award was given to her for her film performance in the same role.

Although Vivien Leigh appreciated her film successes, it was more important to her to succeed as her husband's equal in the theatre. Her great joy was to act with Olivier, and in spite of her fears that she was not yet ready for the demanding variety of Cleopatra, she accepted the challenge to appear, under the joint management of herself and her husband, in two plays on alternate nights, *Caesar and Cleopatra* by Shaw and *Antony and Cleopatra* by Shakespeare, at the St James's in 1951. Under her husband's direction, she gave a performance that satisfied both scholars and the general public. The Oliviers' first season together at Stratford upon Avon in 1955 culminated in a powerfully effective production of Shakespeare's *Titus Andronicus* by Peter Brook. In May 1957 this production was selected to represent the Memorial Theatre Company on a prestige tour of European capitals for the British Council. On such occasions Vivien Leigh appeared in her natural element—a distinguished guest, a gracious hostess, and totally professional. Colleagues paid warm tribute to the unvarying quality of her performances, which remained constant throughout a gruelling social programme. Her tact and consideration for the press were tireless and individual. However, she repeatedly began to suffer from manic phases in which she lost physical control of herself and abused her husband verbally in public. Olivier finally decided that he could no longer tolerate the situation. In 1957 Vivien Leigh and Laurence Olivier appeared together for the last time, at the Stoll Theatre in *Titus Andronicus*. It was during this run that Vivien Leigh interrupted a debate in the House of Lords to protest—without avail—against the projected demolition of the St James's Theatre.

The last decade of Vivien Leigh's life, although marked by the same high level of performance in plays by Jean Giraudoux and Noël Coward, among others, had lost its radiance. Her marriage to Olivier was dissolved in December 1960; they had no children. She continued to act, making a new reputation for herself in the musical *Tovarich* in New York in 1963, but her delicate constitution could not sustain a career single-handed; the fire of a shared grand passion for the theatre had gone out. Her career had been interrupted from time to time by nervous collapse when she had driven herself too hard and by the tuberculosis that caused her death on 8 July 1967 at 54 Eaton Square, London, during preparations for her appearance in Edward Albee's *A Delicate Balance*. That night the exterior lights of London's West End theatres were darkened for an hour. She was cremated at Golders Green.

Vivien Leigh received the knight's cross of the Légion d'honneur in 1957. FREDA GAYE, *rev.*

Sources A. Edwards, *Vivien Leigh: a biography* (1977) · F. Gaye, ed., *Who's who in the theatre*, 14th edn (1967) · F. Barker, *The Oliviers* (1953) · A. Dent, *Vivien Leigh: a bouquet* (1969) · G. Robyns, *Light of a star* (1968) · *The Observer* (16 Feb 1949) · *The Observer* (16 Oct 1949) · *The Times* (10 July 1967) · private information (1981) · *CGPLA Eng. & Wales* (1967)

Archives King's AC Cam., letters to G. H. W. Rylands

Likenesses B. Park, bromide print, 1935, NPG · Madame Yevonde, modern colour dye, 1936, NPG · L. Willinger, bromide print, 1940, NPG [*see illus.*] · Y. Karsh, bromide print, 1954, NPG · D. Edward, oils (as Henriette in *The mask of virtue*), priv. coll. · A. John, oils, priv. coll. · A. K. Lawrence, oils (as Blanche in *A streetcar named Desire*), Theatre Museum, London · photographs, Hult. Arch.

Wealth at death £252,681: probate, 29 Nov 1967, *CGPLA Eng. & Wales*

Leigh, Walter (**1905–1942**), composer, was born on 22 June 1905 at 62 Alexandra Road, Wimbledon, London, the son of Ernest Leigh, a life assurance accountant, and his wife, Charlotte Emmeline Lindemann. His mother, a German concert pianist, was his first teacher, and from the age of eight he had piano lessons from the organist Harold Darke. He was educated at University College School, Hampstead, and read English at Christ's College, Cambridge, graduating with a BA (third class) in 1925. From 1927 to 1929 he studied composition with Paul Hindemith at the Hochschule für Musik in Berlin, and while still in Germany he wrote *Three Pieces for Amateur Orchestra* (1929), which were published in Zürich and performed at the 1929 Baden-Baden festival. These were the first of several works written specially for amateurs, under the influence of Hindemith, who believed in giving amateurs new music that they could play.

Leigh decided against a teaching career in the hope of being able to make a living as a composer, and was appointed musical director of the Festival Theatre in Cambridge from 1931 to 1932 after the success of *Aladdin, or, Love will Find the Way Out*; this pantomime—the first of the famous 'Baddeleigh' entertainments devised by Walter Leigh and V. C. Clinton-Baddeley—was first performed at the Festival Theatre before transferring to the Lyric, Hammersmith, at Christmas 1931. Leigh's post as musical director involved providing the incidental music for a different play each week, and after a year he moved to London to work as a freelance composer. He again collaborated with Clinton-Baddeley in two comic operas: *The Pride of the Regiment* (1932), performed first in Cambridge and then at St Martin's Theatre, London, and *Jolly Roger* (1933), which ran for six months at the Savoy Theatre and the Lyceum in London. On 5 August 1933 he married Frances Marion Folliott, daughter of F. G. Blandford of Cambridge; they had two sons and one daughter.

At the same time Leigh was writing chamber music, and his *Sonatina* (1930) for viola and piano had its first performance in 1932 at the International Society for Contemporary Music festival in Vienna. His piano music included *Music for Three Pianos* (1932), a virtuoso piece commissioned by the piano manufacturers Messrs Challen. He first worked for the BBC in 1932, and in 1935 he was commissioned to write a 'Jubilee overture' (later renamed the *Agincourt Overture*) for George V's silver jubilee. His trio for flute, oboe, and piano (1935), and some of his light orchestral music, including the *Interlude for Theatre Orchestra* (1932), were regularly broadcast.

Leigh became involved in experimental work for several documentary films, in the early days of sound films, including the title music for *6.30 Collection* (1932) for the Empire Marketing Board, the first documentary film made entirely with authentic sound. For this he orchestrated and conducted the sounds produced by typewriters, sandpaper, an empty beer bottle, and the studio bell, as well as more conventional instruments including cymbals, a triangle, and a trumpet. When the General Post Office film unit, headed by John Grierson (1898–1972), was set up, Leigh wrote the music for Alberto Cavalcanti's comedy *Pett and Pott* (1933). Grierson then asked him to write the music for *Song of Ceylon* (1934), made for the Ceylon Tea Board, and he was put in charge of all the sound: this film won the prix du gouvernement Belge at the Brussels film festival in 1935. When Associated Realist Film Producers was formed in 1936 to make documentary films for industry, Leigh became a consultant.

Leigh had written the incidental music for several stage productions, including the experimental piece *Genesis 2* (1934), which had three performances at the Fortune Theatre, and *Public Saviour No. 1* (1935) at the Piccadilly Theatre, and in 1936 he was commissioned by the Greek Play Society at Cambridge University to write the incidental music for Aristophanes' *The Frogs*, a production which transferred to the Chiswick Empire. This was followed by *Victoria Regina*, a very popular series of scenes about the life of Queen Victoria by Laurence Housman for which Leigh arranged the music and which opened at the Lyric Theatre in June 1937, the summer of George VI's coronation. Leigh turned to revue in the late 1930s, writing the music for several of the revues put on by Herbert Farjeon, including *Nine Sharp* at the Little Theatre in 1938 and *In Town Again* at the Criterion in 1940.

Influenced by Hindemith's belief that all music should be of use, and should be well written whatever its purpose, Leigh was always a serious and meticulous composer, whether writing light music for the theatre or experimenting with the avant-garde as in his film music. His best-known work was the *Concertino* (1936) for harpsichord and string orchestra. His last works were *Eclogue* (1940) for piano, and music for the revues *Diversion* (October 1940) and *Diversion No. 2* (January 1941). Leigh joined a tank regiment, the 4th Queen's Own hussars, at the start of the Second World War, and was killed in action on 12 June 1942 near Tobruk, Libya. He was survived by his wife.

ANNE PIMLOTT BAKER

Sources R. Wimbush, 'The younger English composers, 2: Walter Leigh', *Monthly Musical Record*, 68 (June 1938), 138–42 · *New Grove*, 2nd edn · E. Sussex, *The rise and fall of British documentary* (1975) · BBC WAC · J. P. Wearing, *The London stage, 1890–1959* (1976–93) · *MT*, 83 (1942), 255 · *Christ's College Magazine*, 48 (1942), 18 · b. cert. · *CGPLA Eng. & Wales* (1943)

Archives BL, music collections, music MSS, and papers, Add. MSS 65105–65134, 69418–69419

Likenesses Sasha, double portrait, photograph, 1933 (with Marion Blandford), Hult. Arch.

Wealth at death £584 1s. 9d.: administration, 'limited', 26 Feb 1943, *CGPLA Eng. & Wales*

Leigh, William (1550–1639), Church of England clergyman, was born at Westhoughton, Lancashire. He was one of several young men from the north-west to attend Brasenose College, Oxford, which he entered in 1571. Elected a fellow on 24 November 1573, he graduated BA the following month and MA on 29 May 1578. Probably soon after, Leigh took up pastoral duties in Lancashire. In 1582 Preston became the first of five centres to inaugurate yearly synods, set up with episcopal authority, in order to propagate the gospel. Leigh acted as one of the moderators of the exercise at the town and was appointed a justice of the peace, but he did not confine his activities to Lancashire. On 24 July 1584 he applied for a university licence to preach at Paul's Cross in London, and in that year became vice-principal of Brasenose.

Leigh resigned his Brasenose fellowship on 24 November 1587, having in 1586 been presented by William Chaderton, bishop of Chester, to the rectory of Standish, near Wigan. A conscientious and godly minister, Leigh was one of several zealous preachers, including Richard Midgley of Rochdale and Oliver Carter of Manchester, who in October 1590 wrote to John Piers, archbishop of York, during his visitation of the diocese. Affirming that they used only the Book of Common Prayer in services, the group drew attention to the 'gross idolatry and heathenish prophanations' common in the area, and to the malice of popish opponents. If Leigh needed a powerful patron, he found one in Henry Stanley, fourth earl of Derby, who was also generous to some of his co-signatories. The earl was a zealous protestant commended by the government for his energy in dealing with recusancy, and Leigh is known to have preached at least eleven times before him between 1587 and 1590.

Leigh's sermon at the funeral of Katherine Brettagh, on 3 June 1601, published as *Death's Advantage Little Repasted*, is an expression of his puritan piety, tempered in the hostile environment of Lancashire, with its 'paucity of professors' and 'barrenness of faith'. Here, as he lamented in a later sermon, even the godly seemed destined to fight a good but unavailing fight: 'our souls are sad, our zeal is cold, our spirits are dumpish, our faith is frail, we have no courage for the truth' (Leigh, *First Step*, 24, 26). Shortly after the accession of James I, however, there were more rewarding tasks. Leigh preached before the new king and was appointed a tutor to Prince Henry, and in June 1608 he was made master of Ewelme Hospital, Oxfordshire. Leigh strongly identified with the patriotic protestant cause, marking the first anniversary of Guy Fawkes's plot with the publication of *Great Britain's Great Deliverance from the Great Danger of Popish Powder*. During an earlier sermon, he had rejoiced at the defeat of Spain: 'the Lord had no sooner blown upon all their pomp and pride, but their spirits were daunted, their armies were discomforted, the great Armada was scattered, beaten and broken'. By 1612, when this sermon was published, many were looking back nostalgically to days of remembered national and religious militancy. If Leigh shared the mood, it was not reflected in his remarks on King James, under whose rule 'the flowers flourish and the kingdoms are united, religion prospereth and superstition withereth' (W. Leigh, *Queene Elizabeth, Paraleld in her Princely Vertues*, [1612], 96, sig. A5).

Neither superstition nor popery was quite a spent force, however. In August 1612, Leigh was involved in the trials at Lancaster assizes of nineteen people charged with having caused deaths and injuries by diabolical means. Evidently still a JP, he took a statement from a fourteen-year-old girl, Grace Sowerbuts of Samlesbury, who claimed to have been bewitched. Ten of the accused were convicted of witchcraft, and it was probably Leigh who preached the sermon delivered before their execution. Meanwhile Leigh continued his pastoral duties. He contributed towards the restoration of Standish church, and in 1616 donated an oak pulpit. From the following year, as Nicholas Assheton recorded in his diary, he regularly preached before auditories of Lancashire gentlemen.

Leigh married Mary Wrightington of Wrightington, Lancashire, who died before him, and they had three sons and three daughters. He did not win high honours in the church, but certainly prospered. In his will, dated 28 October 1638, he was able to leave £20 to the poor of Wigan, Westhoughton, and Standish, and in 1633 he had set up a trust fund to the value of £12 p.a. in favour of the free school at Standish. But these were just a small part of his wealth, which included Singleton Grange, in the Fylde, and which, at his death, amounted to more than £1100, including £258 in ready money. Leigh was the great-grandfather of the Lancashire antiquary Charles Leigh. He died at Standish on 26 November 1639, at the age of eighty-nine, and was buried two days later in the chancel of the parish church, where an inscribed brass serves as his memorial. STEPHEN WRIGHT

Sources will, 28 Oct 1638, Lancs. RO, WCW William Leigh • R. C. Richardson, *Puritanism in north-west England: a regional study of the diocese of Chester to 1642* (1972) • W. Ffarington, *The Derby household books*, ed. F. R. Raines, Chetham Society, 31 (1853) • F. R. Raines, ed., 'A visitation of the diocese of Chester, by John, archbishop of York', *Chetham miscellanies*, 5, Chetham Society, 96 (1875) • W. Dugdale, *The visitation of the county palatine of Lancaster, made in the year 1664–5*, ed. F. R. Raines, 2, Chetham Society, 85 (1872) • B. Coward, *The Stanleys, lords Stanley and earls of Derby, 1385–1672: the origins, wealth and power of a landowning family*, Chetham Society, 3rd ser., 30 (1983) • C. M. Dent, *Protestant reformers in Elizabethan Oxford* (1983) • G. T. O. Bridgeman, *The history of the church and manor of Wigan, in the county of Lancaster*, 4 vols., Chetham Society, new ser., 15–18 (1888–90) • C. A. Leigh, *Natural history of Lancashire, Cheshire, and the Peak in Derbyshire* (1700) • F. Gastrell and F. R. Raines, eds., *Notitia Cestriensis, or, Historical notices of the diocese of Chester*, 2/3, Chetham Society, 22 (1850) • Foster, *Alum. Oxon.* • [C. B. Heberden], ed., *Brasenose College register, 1509–1909*, 2 vols., OHS, 55 (1909) • Wood, *Ath. Oxon.*, new edn, 2.642 • E. Peel and P. Southern, eds., *The trials of the Lancashire witches* (1985) • *The journal of Nicholas Assheton*, ed. F. R. Raines, Chetham Society, 14 (1848) • M. Tonge, 'The Lancashire witches', *Transactions of the Historic Society of Lancashire and Cheshire*, 83 (1931) • J. Swain, 'The Lancashire witch trials of 1612 and 1634 and the economics of witchcraft', *Northern History*, 30 (1994), 64–85

Wealth at death £1135: will, 28 Oct 1638; Ffarington, *Derby household books*, 117–19

Leighton, Alexander (*c*.1570–1649), religious controversialist, was probably born at Guildy, Monikie, near Dundee, the son of Duncan Leighton or Lichtoun; his mother is unknown. He was related to the Leightons of Usan and Ulyshaven, near Montrose, who held many important local offices. In 1587 he graduated MA at St Andrews. He was apparently ordained before 1603, although no record of this has been found, since he was employed as a lecturer in various churches in Newcastle upon Tyne from then until 1612. By 1611 he had married a widow surnamed Mears or Means, with whom he had four children: Robert *Leighton (*bap.* 1612, *d.* 1684), later archbishop of Glasgow; Elisha, later Sir Ellis *Leighton (*d.* 1685), royalist colonel and Restoration intriguer; James; and Elizabeth. He applied at least once for a living, but in vain, later claiming that his failure to gain preferment was 'for keeping a good conscience' (A. Leighton, 57). In 1617 he changed career and enrolled at the University of Leiden as a medical student. He found lodgings with Thomas Brewer, who funded the Pilgrim Press and probably gave Leighton useful publishing contacts. Brewer's other lodgers included John Bastwick, another medical student, with whom Leighton became friends. Leighton submitted a thesis on hypochondriacal melancholy and graduated MD from Leiden in 1619, returning to London in the same year.

Leighton applied to the College of Physicians for a licentiateship but was refused on the grounds that he had been a minister and thus could not be licensed as a physician. He then practised without a licence. He was also involved in other illegal activities—private prayer meetings (conventicles) and collective fasts. He had joined the Blackfriars church founded by Henry Jacob, and his first three publications were all printed by the press of the Ancient (separatist) church of Amsterdam which was run by Sabine Staresmore, a member of Jacob's church who regularly visited the Netherlands. Leighton apparently became known outside London as well, visiting Boston and Leicester for theological debates.

Leighton's first wife died before 1625, when Caleb was born, his first child with his second wife, Isobel (*c*.1600–1653). She was the daughter of Sir William Musgrave of Cumberland. They were also to have a daughter, Sapphira. In 1624 Leighton published *Speculum belli sacri, or, The Looking Glass of the Holy War*. Written in the currently popular

Alexander Leighton (*c.*1570–1649), by Wenceslaus Hollar, *c.*1641

style of a military treatise, it urged the abolition of episcopacy and military action in support of the protestant cause in Europe. Leighton strongly opposed Prince Charles's marriage to a Catholic: 'be not unequally yoked … with that lincie-woolsie match' (*Speculum belli sacri*, 194–5). However, he gave little indication of what form of church government he favoured. His *A Friendly Triall of the Treatise of Faith of Mr Ezekiel Culverwell* appeared in the same year, its essential message being that only the elect were saved. Leighton's house was searched by the Stationers' Company, and his family briefly imprisoned, but Leighton appealed to the king, who 'ordered that neither Prelates, nor others, should trouble me further' (A. Leighton, 68). Temporarily at least more cautious, Leighton's next work, *A Shorte Treatise Against Stage Players*, appeared anonymously in 1625.

In early 1628, reflecting the high expectations of many awaiting the new session of parliament, Leighton organized a petition for the abolition of episcopacy, obtaining 500 signatures. He then went to the Netherlands, apparently originally intending to publish the petition itself. Instead he composed *An Appeale to the Parliament, or, Sions Plea Against the Prelacy*, which urged king and parliament to abolish the English episcopate and seize its wealth, before assuming the leadership of the protestant cause in Europe. The assassination of Buckingham had been a sign from God, 'who … removed the greatest *nayl*, in all their tent and will you not follow home?' (*Sions Plea*, 176). While preparing his book Leighton was offered the post of minister to the English church at Utrecht, and he was ordained in March 1629. He had sent copies of *Sions Plea* to every MP, unaware that Charles had dissolved parliament. In May Isobel Leighton was about to join him when news came that he had been dismissed following disagreements over the observance of ceremonies. Dr Bastwick, her husband's university friend, housed the family until Leighton returned in July. Bastwick also found Leighton a medical post in Colchester, but he stayed there only briefly. Back in London, he returned to Jacob's church and to unlicensed medicine.

On 17 February 1630, as Leighton left church, he was arrested, 'clapt in irons', and thrown into 'a nasty doghole full of rats and mice' in Newgate (A. Leighton, 3). His house was searched: the pursuivants held a pistol to little Caleb's head to persuade Isobel to co-operate. Because of the prison conditions, Leighton became seriously ill: he claimed that 'all his hair and skin came off' (ibid., 89). His wife represented him at his trial for sedition in Star Chamber in June, although Leighton submitted an answer to the attorney-general's charges, adamantly refusing to reveal the names of the signatories to his petition. He was sentenced to pay £10,000, be degraded from holy orders, be pilloried and whipped at Westminster, have one of his ears cut off, one side of his nose slit, and his face branded with SS (for sower of sedition), to be then carried back to prison and after a few days to have the whole punishment repeated at Cheapside, and then to be imprisoned for life. On 4 November (the delay being due to an outbreak of plague in London) Leighton was brought before the high commission court to be degraded from holy orders. He declined its jurisdiction and refused to take off his hat, foreshadowing in this as in other ways the radicals of the next generation.

On the night before his punishment was due Leighton escaped from prison by changing clothes with a visitor. A description of him was circulated, asking recipients to look for 'a man of low stature, with a fair complexion, yellowish beard, and a high forehead' (BL, C.59.i.3). Leighton's followers were disappointed by this attempt to evade martyrdom, but he was quickly recaptured: on 26 November he was pilloried in a snowstorm for two hours. His left ear was nailed to the pillory before being cut off, and he received thirty-six lashes before being branded. Unsurprisingly, he was 'in a fever' on 5 December (Birch, 69). The second part of the sentence seems to have been remitted.

Leighton was sent to the Fleet prison. By 1635 he was earning enough as a doctor to his fellow prisoners to afford a private chamber. In 1637 Isobel took William Prynne (on trial for sedition, like Leighton) a beaver hat as a gift. This gesture may have reminded the authorities of Leighton's existence. In February 1638 he was moved into the common prison. When he was released by parliamentary order in 1641, he could 'neither see, hear, nor walke' (A. Leighton, 3). In prison Leighton wrote two poems which, surely uniquely, describe the feelings of a victim of the Laudian episcopate:

Beegoard in bloud of cruell p[relates] scourge
Dismemberd ears, eares, stigmatized, to urge
Me to despaire to earths and heavens grace,
That to the sun I nere might showe my face.
A dismale, savage spectacle I rise
An act unparrallelled to eternize.
I am not superstitiouse: yet I feare
The auctors of my tragedie will weare
My marks upon their cauterized browes
Allthwgh my bloud in bowles they now carouse.
(Condick, 'Self-revelation', 202)

This prophecy of reprisal was to prove particularly true in Leighton's own case when in December 1642 parliament appointed him keeper of Lambeth Palace, which had been commandeered as a military prison. He was permitted to charge 2*s.* to ordinary prisoners, 4*s.* to esquires and knights, and 5 marks to persons of higher degree. One of his royalist prisoners, Sir Roger Twysden, wrote bitterly of Leighton's acquisitiveness: 'he loved money, would not abate one peny though he were very ritch … upon my denyal of rent I was threatened with harder usage' (Larking, 175). As with all Laudian victims, parliament promised Leighton large sums which never materialized, but Lambeth provided ample compensation.

The fortunate survival of his library (in Dunblane Cathedral Library) demonstrates that Leighton was a man of learning and wide interests: his writings show familiarity with Latin, Greek, Hebrew, and French. The Leighton family remained united and affectionate despite many differences in its political and religious views. This must surely be partly due to Leighton himself, a man who, despite his fiery prose style, seems to have been personally charming. Bastwick wrote of him, 'he always joined in any festivity; his jests and drolleries quite won my heart' (Bastwick, 69–70); and the royalist Twysden commented, 'I parted with great kindness from Dr Leighton, the man beeing no ill-dispositioned person' (Larking, 175).

Despite his sufferings Leighton seems to have had an iron constitution, visiting Scotland several times after his release. In 1648 he was probably the author of *To All the Honest, Wise, and Grave-Citizens of London*, which urged Londoners to resist the army and distrust generals whose families were not city-dwellers. In June 1649 his son Robert applied for leave of absence owing to his father's sickness, and Leighton died soon after, probably in London; his son was back in his parish by early September. Leighton's will divided his books between his sons, divinity books going to Robert, physic books to Elisha, and humanities books to Caleb. FRANCES CONDICK

Sources A. Leighton, *An epitome, or, Briefe discoverie … of the … great troubles that Dr Leighton suffered in his body, estate and family* (1646) · *JHC*, 2 (1640–42) [9 Nov, 13 Nov, 28 Nov, 1 Dec, 30 Dec 1640; 9 April, 21 April, 11 June, 23 June 1641; 9 Nov, 17 Dec, 23 Dec, 27 Dec 1642] · *JHC*, 3 (1642–4) [1 Jan 1643] · J. Bastwick, *Flagellum pontificis et episcoporum Latialium* (1635) · L. B. Larking, ed., 'Sir Roger Twysden's journal [pt 4]', *Archaeologia Cantiana*, 4 (1861), 131–202, esp. 175 · G. du Rieu, ed., *Album studiosorum academiae Lugduno Batavae, MDLXXV–MDCCCLXXV: accedunt nomina curatorum et professorum per eadem secula* (The Hague, 1875), 61 · S. Foster, *Notes from the Caroline underground: Alexander Leighton, the puritan triumvirate, and the Laudian reaction to nonconformity* (1978) · C. F. Leighton, *Memorials of the Leightons of Ulishaven* (1931) · F. M. Condick, 'The self-revelation of a puritan: Dr Alexander Leighton in the 1620s', *BIHR*, 55 (1982), 196–203 · J. Brand, *The history and antiquities of the town and county of the town of Newcastle upon Tyne*, 1 (1789), 321, 375, 412 · [T. Birch and R. F. Williams], eds., *The court and times of Charles the First*, 1 (1848), 61–9 · G. Davidson, 'Robert Leighton, his family and his library', *Transactions of the Society of the Friends of Dunblane Cathedral* (1959), 44–9 · F. M. Condick, 'The life and works of Dr John Bastwick, 1595–1654', PhD diss., U. Lond., 1983 · D. Plooij, *The Pilgrim Fathers from a Dutch point of view* (1932) · J. Bruce, preface to S. R. Gardiner, ed., 'Speech of Sir Robert Heath, attorney-general, in the case of Alexander Leighton', *Camden miscellany, VII*, CS, new ser., 14 (1875), iii–xiii · E. A. Knox, *Robert Leighton, archbishop of Glasgow* (1930) · D. Butler, *The life and letters of Robert Leighton* (1903) · PRO, PROB 11/211, fol. 54

Archives BL, answer to the charges against him in star chamber, Sloane MS 41 · BL, poems and other writings, Sloane MS 346 (a medieval manuscript), fols. 10–22 · Inner Temple, London, answer to the charges against him in star chamber, Misc. MS 19, fols. 41–5 · PRO, petition to Charles I, SP 16/408/168 · PRO, letters to Isobel Leighton, SP 16/103/39; SP 16/138/10, 23, 90; SP 16/142/114 | University of Stirling / Dunblane Cathedral, Leighton Library

Likenesses W. Hollar, etching, *c.*1641, BM, NPG [*see illus.*]

Wealth at death £1700 bequests; plus extensive library: PRO, PROB 11/211, fol. 54

Leighton, Alexander (1800–1874), writer and literary editor, was born in Dundee, the son of Alexander Leighton, corn merchant, and his wife, Janet Green. He is said to have distinguished himself at Dundee grammar school and to have become a lawyer's clerk after studying medicine at Edinburgh University, but he took no MD degree.

In 1836–7 Leighton became editor and principal contributor to the series Wilson's Historical, Traditionary, and Imaginative Tales of the Borders, and of Scotland, which had begun to appear from the pen of John Mackay Wilson in 1835. The first six-volume series of Tales, completed in 1840, was an enormous popular success, capitalizing on the taste for traditional or traditional-looking Scottish stories created by Sir Walter Scott. It was followed by further, much augmented, editions in 1857–9 and 1863–9 in which the text was revised, and new tales added, by Leighton.

A smaller collection for which Leighton was solely responsible, the *Curious Storied Traditions of Scottish Life* (1860), went into a second series and further editions in the space of two years. This marks the beginning of an association with the Edinburgh publisher William Nimmo. Nimmo published most of Leighton's later writings, which continued to appear into his late sixties. These included further stories, traditional and contemporary; a novel, *Shellburn* (1865); and lives of Scott and Byron for Nimmo editions of those authors (both 1861). A jobbing writer, he was nevertheless not a mere hack: his odd and scarcely commercial volume *The Principal Songs of Robert Burns Translated into Mediæval Latin Verse* (1862), for example, was praised by Carlyle.

Leighton lived quietly, even reclusively, in Edinburgh through his decades of popular success. He died at his home, 10 George Street, on 24 December 1874, his stooping figure, bright eye, and pale face—said to resemble portraits of John Locke—having already vanished from Edinburgh literary circles a few years previously when a progressive paralysis set in. He was survived by his wife, Ann, *née* Barrowman. STUART GILLESPIE

Sources *The Scotsman* (26 Dec 1874) • Boase, *Mod. Eng. biog.* • J. M. Wilson, *Wilson's Tales of the Borders … with biographical notices of the contributors, by James Tait* (1881) • *DNB* • d. cert. • *Nomina eorum, qui gradum medicinae doctoris in academia Jacobi sexti Scotorum regis, quae Edinburgi est, adepti sunt, ab anno 1705 ad annum 1845*, University of Edinburgh (1846)

Wealth at death £92 13*s*. 8*d*.: confirmation, 30 June 1875, NA Scot., 70/1/171, 513–7

Leighton, Charles Blair (1823–1855), artist and printer, was born on 6 March 1823, the son of Stephen Leighton and Helen Blair. From the age of fourteen he was apprenticed to a silver-engraver but after serving his seven-year training he opted for a change of career. He had always devoted his spare time to drawing and was evidently gifted as he was accepted as a student at the Royal Academy. From his early twenties, in 1843, until the year before his death he practised as an artist and sent more than twenty paintings to the Royal Academy exhibitions, and several others to the British Institution in 1853 and 1855 from his home in Red Lion Square, Holborn, London. Given his commitment to the human figure and his time spent studying anatomy, his greatest strength was in figure painting and consequently most of the subjects he executed were either portraits or history paintings of literary and biblical subjects, such as *Moses Raising the Brazen Serpent* (1843) or *The Assassination of Richard III* (1843). Charles Blair Leighton enjoyed modest success as an artist but the most outstanding artist in the family was Edmund Blair Leighton (1853–1922), his son with his wife, Caroline Boosey, daughter of the music publisher Thomas Boosey. Elected to the Institute of Painters in Oil Colours in 1887, he too was a regular exhibitor at the Royal Academy, where he exhibited genre and figure paintings almost annually between 1878 and 1904.

Charles Leighton and his younger brother **George Cargill Leighton** (1826–1895) were most prominent as publishers of colour prints, trading as the Leighton Brothers. George Leighton was born in 1826, and was indentured to the wood-engraver George Baxter (1804–1867) when he was only ten years old. This apprenticeship was to prove especially influential to the young Leighton's career. Not only did Baxter specialize in colour book illustrations but he was a pioneer of colour woodblock print technology. In 1835 he patented a new technique for oil colour printing where the key design was transferred from a single intaglio print and the colour developed by individual woodblocks, inked with an oil colour. As this resulted in highly nuanced 'prints of subtle colouring and minute detail' (Engen, *Wood Engravers*, 25) Baxter christened this technique 'picture-printing'.

In 1843, after finishing his seven-year indenture, George Leighton joined several other of Baxter's pupils to establish a colour printing company named Gregory, Collins, and Reynolds. They were one of a number of firms to employ Baxter's patented technique under licence. In 1849, after the three partners went their separate ways, George went into partnership with his brother Charles and the firm continued under the name Leighton Brothers, at 19 Lamb's Conduit Street. It was also in this year that Baxter's patent expired. When he filed for its renewal, his former pupil Leighton contested this, stating that he had a right to employ the same technique and that using it under licence was diminishing his livelihood. Even if his motives were entirely self-interested, the fact that Leighton fought this case in court single-handedly and without any legal aid is an indication of his confidence and resolve. He was, however, unsuccessful in his petition and Baxter won the case. Consequently Leighton was no longer able to employ Baxter's methods of printing intaglio plates with woodblocks and, according to Ruari McLean, having to do without this facility 'probably helped to ensure his commercial success' (McLean, 191). In contrast, Leighton Brothers specialized in colour printing from numerous separate colour plates whose careful registration they ensured. Such was the quality of their results that in 1851 they exhibited at the Great Exhibition; they also won a commission to produce colour plates for the *Art Journal*. Moving to premises at 4 Red Lion Square in 1852, over the following years they produced subtle and splendidly coloured plates for a number of volumes where the colour was essential to the success of the book. For example, in 1853, they illustrated *The Poultry Book*, a serious work on the breeding of poultry with 'vivid portraits' (ibid., 192) of these birds. They also produced the plates for various other art and illustrated books including George Barnard's *Landscape Painting* (1854) and Harriet Martineau's *The English Lakes* (1858).

Following Charles Blair Leighton's death on 6 February 1855 at Kingsland, Middlesex, George became a regular printer of colour plates for the *Illustrated London News*. This was a fortunate move as only two years later Leighton became its publisher until the year before his retirement, in 1884. Of consistently high quality, his coloured plates of flowers, birds, and domestic animals along with the intricate and brightly coloured covers were undoubtedly integral to the success of the *Illustrated London News*.

From Stanhope House, a factory in Drury Lane, George Leighton continued to produce art-quality illustrations for a variety of publications including *Gems of English Art* (1869). Later in his career he was also associated with a number of attractively illustrated children's books. Indeed, in 1885, when he sold up the business to the lithographers Vincent Brooks, Day & Son, he passed over the colour woodblocks for Warren and Routledge's Toy Book series to the wood-engraver Edmund Evans.

George Cargill Leighton died at his home, Fairlight, Shepherd's Hill, in Highgate, Middlesex, on 8 May 1895. Although he was married it is not known if he was survived by any children. LUCY PELTZ

Sources R. K. Engen, *Dictionary of Victorian engravers, print publishers and their works* (1979) • R. K. Engen, *Dictionary of Victorian wood engravers* (1985) • D. Bank and A. Esposito, eds., *British biographical*

archive, 2nd series (1991) [microfiche] • S. Houfe, *The dictionary of 19th century British book illustrators and caricaturists*, rev. edn (1996) • G. W. Friend, *Index of painters and engravers … declared at the office of the Printseller's Association, London* (1894) • Graves, *RA exhibitors*, 5.168 • R. McLean, *Victorian book design and colour printing*, rev. edn (1972) • d. cert. [George Cargill Leighton]

Wealth at death £6016 9s. 2d.—George Cargill Leighton: probate, 6 June 1895, *CGPLA Eng. & Wales*

Leighton, Clara Ellaline Hope [Clare] (**1898–1989**), engraver, was born on 12 April 1898 at 40 Abbey Road, St John's Wood, London, the second of the three children of Robert Leighton (1858–1934), a writer and journalist, and his wife, Marie (1865/6–1941), a writer of romantic fiction who was the daughter of Captain James Connor.

Clare Leighton, whose education was largely private, began painting as a child under the guidance of her father and his brother Jack, a professional artist. After the family's move to Keymer, Sussex, in 1915, she attended classes at Brighton College of Art, and between 1922 and 1923 studied painting under Sir Henry Tonks at the Slade School of Fine Art, and wood-engraving under Noel Rooke at the Central School of Arts and Crafts, London. Attracted by the medium's wide range of effects, she thereafter practised mainly as a wood-engraver, supporting herself by teaching art in schools until she could earn a living as an illustrator. Her first subjects were farmers and bargees at Bishop's Stortford, Hertfordshire, the market town to which the Leightons moved in the early 1920s, and working-class people remained a preferred theme after she left home for Bloomsbury, London, around 1923—the year in which her work was first seen at the annual exhibition of the Society of Wood Engravers.

In 1924 Leighton showed her prints to the radical journalist Henry Noel *Brailsford (1873–1958), who published examples in the *New Leader* in April of that year. Further engravings appeared in the *London Mercury* and *The Forum* between 1925 and 1926. Leighton's technique was refined in sketches of landscapes and peasants made on trips to France, Italy, and the Balkans between 1923 and 1927, and she returned from America in 1925 with enough illustrating contracts to occupy her for several years. Independent prints (always signed 'Clare Leighton') and illustrations for Thornton Wilder (in *Bridge of San Luis Rey*, 1929) and Thomas Hardy, an author for whom she felt a special affinity (in *The Return of the Native*, 1929), earned her a reputation on both sides of the Atlantic, and by 1930, the year in which she gained first prize at the International Engravers Exhibition at the Art Institute of Chicago, she was an associate member of both the Society of Wood Engravers and the Royal Society of Painter-Etchers. A selection of her work, *Woodcuts*, introduced by Hilaire Belloc, was published in 1930.

In 1927 Clare Leighton moved to accommodation near Brailsford's Hampstead flat. Brailsford, separated from his alcoholic wife, was twenty-five years her senior, but Leighton shared the left-wing politics of his circle and found intellectual stimulus and fulfilment in the relationship. Her oil portrait of Mohandas Gandhi (1931) marks one of the points at which their paths crossed. At their joint home, Four Hedges, near Monks Risborough, Buckinghamshire, to which they moved in 1931, Leighton engraved her *Lumber Camp* series (1931), the well-known *Bread Line, New York* (an example of social realism, 1932), and several single engravings for American print clubs. But the major projects from the 1930s are three books she wrote as well as illustrated: *The Farmer's Year* (1933), a sombre vision of life on the land at a time of agricultural depression; the phenomenally successful *Four Hedges* (1935), a personal chronicle of a year in her Chiltern garden; and *Country Matters* (1937), a nostalgic celebration of English rural life on the eve of the Second World War.

Clara Ellaline Hope Leighton (1898–1989), by Powys Evans

In 1939 Leighton left Brailsford to begin a new life in the United States, where she became a citizen in 1945. She travelled widely in her adopted country, observing the American way of life at first hand, and finally settled at Chapel Hill, North Carolina, in 1943. In the English edition of her *Southern Harvest* (1943) she declared that 'the true character of a people is to be found in its workers' (p. 6), an idea also explored in engravings for *North Carolina Folklore* (1952–64), a survey published by Duke University, Durham, North Carolina, where she was visiting lecturer from 1943 to 1945. The many commissions postdating her 1951 move to Woodbury, Connecticut, include engravings for *The Book of Psalms* (1952); *Where Land Meets Sea* (1954), a tribute to the Cape Cod tideline she loved; and an illustrated edition of the works of Henry David Thoreau (1961). In her later years she turned from wood-engraving, which makes exacting demands on the eyes, to stained-glass (notably in the transept windows for St Paul's Cathedral, Worcester, installed 1962) and mosaic (*Christ Rising from the*

Earth, for the chapel of the Holy Family of Nazareth Community, Monroe, Connecticut, 1966–7). In 1988, on account of failing health, Leighton moved into a nursing home. She died, unmarried, on 4 November 1989, and her ashes were buried at Waterbury cemetery, Connecticut.

Convinced that wood-engraving was an art for the masses rather than for an élite, Clare Leighton worked independently of the private presses. Her popular success was founded on a disciplined technique, powerful compositions, and a gravity of content and sincerity of feeling that derives from artists such as Samuel Palmer. 'No one in our time', wrote Eric Gill in Gollancz's publicity leaflet for *The Farmer's Year*, 'has succeeded better in presenting the nobility of massiveness and breadth of life of the earth on a scale so grand.' The artist herself, who possessed a gift for friendship with people of all races and classes, was influential as a teacher, lecturer, and author of two respected texts: *Wood-Engravings and Woodcuts* (1932) and *Wood-Engravings of the 1930s* (1936). COLIN CAMPBELL

Sources P. Jaffé, *The wood engravings of Clare Leighton* (1992) • D. Leighton, 'Chronology of Clare Leighton', in A. Stevens and D. Leighton, *Clare Leighton: wood-engravings and drawings* (1992), 6–11 [exhibition catalogue, AM Oxf.] • W. D. Fletcher, 'Clare Leighton: the artist and her work', *Clare Leighton, an exhibition: American sheaves, English seed corn* (Boston, 1977), 1–5 [exhibition catalogue, Boston Public Library] • private information (2004) • C. Leighton, *Tempestuous petticoat* (1948)

Archives priv. coll., notes for an autobiography

Likenesses P. Evans, drawing, NPG [*see illus.*] • C. Jenkins, photographs, repro. in C. Leighton, *Wood-engravings and woodcuts* (1932) • C. Leighton, self-portrait, pencil drawings, repro. in C. Leighton, *Sometime-never* (1939) • photograph, repro. in Fletcher, 'Clare Leighton'

Leighton, Sir Elisha [Ellis] (*d.* **1685**), royalist courtier and government official, was the third son of the Scottish physician and presbyterian divine Alexander *Leighton (*c.*1570–1649), and younger brother of Robert *Leighton (*bap.* 1612, *d.* 1684), bishop of Dunblane and archbishop of Glasgow. His mother was a widow surnamed Mears or Means whom his father had married by 1611. Though baptized Elisha, he was known throughout his adult life as Ellis, a gesture symbolic, if not symptomatic, of his rejection of his Calvinist upbringing.

While his violently anti-episcopalian father had suffered imprisonment and mutilation for attacks on Archbishop Laud, Ellis Leighton served in the royalist army in the civil war, rising to the rank of colonel. He was arrested at Kingston, Surrey, in August 1647 on an information that he had been commissioned to raise troops 'to engage the kingdom in a new war' (Rushworth, 7.779), and briefly imprisoned in Windsor Castle. After the execution of the king he went abroad, to return in the autumn of 1649 with a commission from the duke of Lorraine to raise a regiment. He was again arrested, examined before the council of state, and warned as to his conduct; he was evidently released, for in December 1650 Charles II appointed him to act in Scotland, under the third earl of Lothian, as his secretary for English affairs. At this time Leighton could still be described as 'a perfect Presbyterian' (Warner, 1.208). After the king's defeat he escaped to Rotterdam in the company of the duke of Buckingham, whose close friend and political associate he had become. Besides being considered 'a very vicious man', he was also presumed to be an 'atheist' (ibid., 1.289). Buckingham sent him to London in 1652 with a sealed letter for Oliver Cromwell. It was reported at the royalist court that he had been well received by Cromwell, with whom he had enjoyed two hours' private conversation, but the proceedings of the council of state tell a different story: the letter was returned to Leighton without comment and he was required to leave the country. At his return to Antwerp he seems to have suffered a serious mental breakdown, from which he emerged a Catholic convert, at least in name; Bishop Burnet, for one, was highly sceptical of his grasp of Catholic doctrine. Doubts were also expressed, in various quarters, about his real political loyalties.

Ever the opportunist, Leighton broke with Buckingham in 1656 and entered the employment of the duke of York, in which capacity he was knighted at Brussels in April 1659. He was at this time acting as a go-between for the royalists and their contacts in England, which again brought some suspicion of double-dealing. Given his doubtful history and mercurial character he cannot seriously have expected a great reward at the Restoration, but his quick wit made him welcome at court, and he was always ready to exploit his various connections and friendships. Through the influence of the duke of York he became secretary of the Royal African Company. He was granted a share in the secretaryship of the prize office in 1664, and the following year was appointed as one of the king's counsel in the Admiralty court. This latter preferment required a doctorate of laws, which Cambridge University conferred on him at the king's request, then admission as a civilian, and finally entrance into the Middle Temple (in 1667), where he was called 'of grace' in 1670. Since 1667 he had been one of the counsel to the Navy Board. According to Pepys, he did not shine in his new profession: 'for a speech of forty words' he was 'the wittiest man that ever he knew in his life, but longer, he is nothing; his judgment being nothing at all, but his wit most absolute' (Pepys, 5.300). Leighton also involved himself in the fledgeling Royal Society, of which he was elected a fellow in 1663, but was unable to maintain interest and was excluded in 1678 for failing to meet his subscriptions. His only 'scientific' achievement was the invention of a patented device, described by John Evelyn as 'iron axle-trees' (Evelyn, 3.516), to facilitate the motion of carts or carriages.

Leighton had long since made his peace with Buckingham after their earlier estrangement and in 1670, on Buckingham's recommendation, was sent by the king to France, under cover of promoting his axle-trees, to broach at the French court the question of a possible alliance—an exploit of which he boasted much in later life. Soon afterwards he went to Ireland as chief secretary to the new lord lieutenant, John, Lord Berkeley. The post offered obvious financial opportunities, which Leighton seized: he secured grants for himself, devised and published an official gazette, which brought profits to his office, and shamelessly solicited bribes. Unusually for a chief secretary, he also practised at the Irish bar. He was equally determined to maximize the political potential of his position. His correspondence with the secretary of state, Lord Arlington, reeked of flattery and careerism: 'you have raised so many men in the world', he wrote, 'that I am anxious to be under your protection' (*CSP Ire., 1669–70* and *addenda*, 269–70). As a Catholic chief secretary in a distinctly pro-Catholic administration he was also well placed to advance the objectives of the duke of York's faction, and those of his old patron Buckingham, through his close association with Colonel Richard Talbot, who himself aspired to the leadership of the Catholic interest in Ireland. But Leighton was not really happy in Dublin: the climate disagreed with him, and his health suffered. More important, his political schemes faltered. His avowed Catholicism made him a lightning conductor for criticism of Berkeley's viceroyalty in its supposed over-indulgence of Catholics, and he was personally blamed for the most flagrant examples of authoritarian government—not always unfairly, as can be seen in the case of Dublin corporation, whose remodelling, according to Berkeley's 'new rules', was undertaken under Leighton's supervision. He was briefly recorder under the reconstructed corporation, and made a notorious speech to the aldermen, subsequently printed, that offered a high-flying interpretation of royal authority: in his opinion borough corporators were 'creatures of the monarchy' who 'ought to have no politic maxims of their own' and should subject themselves as far as possible to 'the will and personal power of the prince' (Gilbert and Weldrick, 5.558–62). As the cabal administration disintegrated, he also suffered the intrigues of Irish and English factions seeking to undermine his standing with the lord lieutenant, perhaps as a preliminary to the modification of government policy in Ireland. However, he seems to have retained the trust both of Berkeley and of Buckingham.

Recalled from Ireland with the lord lieutenant in 1672, Leighton accompanied Berkeley as an unofficial secretary on his embassy to Paris in 1675. This episode precipitated his ruin, for he assumed the part of agent for those English merchants whose ships had been taken by French privateers. Once again he could not resist the opportunity to extort bribes, but this time the merchants complained to the privy council and Leighton could no longer rely on his powerful friends. He was committed to the Tower to await prosecution and in the meantime was stripped of an Irish pension he had acquired as chief secretary. Somehow he contrived to escape, and after hiding for a time (in disguise) at Falmouth took ship for France in November 1676. He returned to England in 1677 to surrender himself into custody, but must have escaped again, or skipped bail, for he was rearrested at Dover in October 1678 (not only for his past crimes, but also, it was said, because his name had cropped up in Titus Oates's evidence about the Popish Plot) and conveyed to Newgate. His health was failing, however, and he was probably released on compassionate grounds. In August 1682 he was once more in Paris and contemplating a return to England, this time for good. He seems to have been provided with lodgings in Whitehall, from which he launched fruitless appeals for the restoration of his Irish pension. He died in the parish of St Andrew, Holborn, on 9 January 1685, leaving a daughter, Mary, as his sole heir, and was buried at Horsted Keynes, Sussex; nothing is known of Mary's mother. Burnet's verdict on him, though naturally hostile, recognized his talents as well as his weaknesses:

> though he loved to talk of great sublimities in religion, yet he was a very immoral man … lewd, false and ambitious. He was a papist of a form of his own: but he had changed his religion to raise himself at court … He maintained an outward decency, and had more learning, and better notions, than men of quality, who enter into orders in the church, generally have. Yet he was a very vicious man. (*Bishop Burnet's History*, 1.246–7)

D. W. HAYTON

Sources *Le Neve's Pedigrees of the knights*, ed. G. W. Marshall, Harleian Society, 8 (1873) • *DNB* • *The Nicholas papers*, ed. G. F. Warner, 1, CS, new ser., 40 (1886) • *Bishop Burnet's History* • *CSP dom.*, *1648–84* • *CSP Ire.*, *1669–70* • M. Hunter, *The Royal Society and its fellows, 1660–1700: the morphology of an early scientific institution* (1982) • *Seventh report*, HMC, 6 (1879), 268, 373, 471, 494 • Pepys, *Diary*, 5.300 • J. T. Gilbert, R. M. Gilbert, and J. F. Weldrick, eds., *Calendar of the ancient records of Dublin*, 18 vols. (1889–1922) • J. Rushworth, *Historical collections*, new edn, 7 (1721), 779, 792 • *Calendar of the manuscripts of the marquess of Ormonde*, new ser., 8 vols., HMC, 36 (1902–20), vol. 4, p. 464 • W. A. Shaw, *The knights of England*, 2 (1906), 225 • Venn, *Alum. Cant.*, 1/3.72 • Evelyn, *Diary*, 3.516 • H. A. C. Sturgess, ed., *Register of admissions to the Honourable Society of the Middle Temple, from the fifteenth century to the year 1944*, 1 (1949), 174

Leighton, Frederic, Baron Leighton (1830–1896), painter, was born on 3 December 1830, the son of Dr Frederic Septimus Leighton (*d.* 1892), a physician living at 13 Brunswick Terrace, Scarborough, and his wife, Augusta Susan (*d.* 1865).

Family background, childhood, and education Leighton had two surviving siblings, both sisters: Alexandra, who was older than he, and Augusta, who was younger. His paternal grandfather, Sir James Leighton, was also a doctor, and had served for a period as physician to the court of the tsars at St Petersburg (a career which had provided money-making opportunities that, it was said, provided the basis of the Leighton family's financial independence). Sir James died in 1832, and at about the same time his son and daughter-in-law and their young family moved from Yorkshire to London, where they lived at 22 Argyle Street, off the Gray's Inn Road. Leighton's father continued in medical practice, and in 1838 was appointed lecturer in forensic medicine at the Middlesex Hospital. In the later 1830s the family lived at 7 Upper Gower Street, Bloomsbury.

Although Leighton was enrolled at University College School when aged about eight, and intermittently attended lessons there, the course of his education was disrupted by the frequent European travels that his family undertook. In 1839 a visit to Paris seems to have been Leighton's first sight of the continent. In the following year, probably as a consequence of a severe attack of rheumatic fever suffered by Leighton's mother, after which it was felt that she needed to be taken away from London, they visited Rome, where Leighton was given

Frederic Leighton, Baron Leighton (1830–1896), by George Frederic Watts, 1871

drawing lessons. They were back in London during the following winter, but in 1841 they travelled through Germany and Switzerland back to Italy, on this occasion remaining for a period in Florence. Again Leighton was given art lessons, and by this time he had begun to draw of his own accord. In the latter part of 1842 the family returned to Germany, passing the winter of 1842–3 in Berlin (where Leighton studied at the Academy of Art); then in 1843 they moved first to Munich and then to Frankfurt am Main (where he studied at Stellwag's academy in the Hochstrasse). In 1845 the family transferred from Frankfurt to Florence, where Leighton enrolled at the Accademia di Belle Arti. Leighton was a precocious linguist, and rapidly became fluent in French, German, and Italian.

In 1846 Leighton's father bought a large house on the Bockenheimerlandstrasse in Frankfurt, which was the family's principal home until 1853. In October 1846 Leighton enrolled as a student at the Städelsches Kunstinstitut in Frankfurt, the director of which was the Nazarene painter Philip Veit. The following year he progressed to the life class, as well as studying under the landscape painter Jacob Becker. In 1848 political upheavals in Germany drove the Leighton family out of Frankfurt, first to Brussels (where Leighton made contact with various Belgian artists, including Anton Wiertz and Louis Gallait), and then on to Paris. In Paris in 1849 he attended the atelier of Alexandre Dupuis as well as copying in the Louvre. In 1850 the family felt it safe to return to Frankfurt. Thus Leighton re-enrolled at the Städelsches Kunstinstitut, where in that year Edward von Steinle—who became a friend and artistic mentor to Leighton—was appointed director. In 1850 Leighton exhibited his first large-scale and ambitious painting, *Cimabue Finding Giotto in the Fields of Florence* (Baroda Museum and Picture Gallery, India).

Formative years in Italy and France In summer 1851 Leighton visited London, to see the Great Exhibition and to visit his grandmother Lady Leighton, who lived in Bath. During this stay he seems to have intended to make contact with his contemporaries among English painters, meeting Alfred Elmore, William Powell Frith, and E. M. Ward. He may have had some knowledge of the Pre-Raphaelite Brotherhood, formed in 1848, but appears to have had no contact with any of its members. Later in 1851 he returned to Frankfurt to begin work on the painting upon which his early reputation would be based, *Cimabue's Madonna* (Royal Collection; on loan to National Gallery, London).

In August of the following year Leighton set out from Frankfurt for Rome, travelling part of the way with his master Steinle, and passing through the Austrian Tyrol, Verona, Venice, and Florence. Soon after his arrival in November 1852 he took a studio in the via della Purificazione. Rome in the early 1850s was still regarded as a city to which young artists would want to travel—and Leighton seems to have enjoyed the convivial and stimulating social life that it offered. Among the artists he met there were the German Nazarene painters Peter Cornelius and Johann Friedrich Overbeck, while somewhat later he embarked on close and lifelong friendships with the Staffordshire-born painter George Heming Mason—then living in the city and painting Campagna landscape subjects—and the Italian patriot and landscape painter Giovanni Costa. In February 1853 he met and made friends with Adelaide Sartoris, a retired singer who had once been famous for her soprano roles, notably in the operas of Vincenzo Bellini. She recognized Leighton's talent as an artist and introduced him to a fashionable circle of connoisseurs and patrons, in Italy and later also in England.

In 1854, after a visit to Germany and then to England (where his father had settled in Bath, having bought a house in The Circus), Leighton returned to Rome and took a studio in the via Felice. There he worked in earnest on *Cimabue's Madonna* and another large painting, to be entitled *The Reconciliation of the Montagues and Capulets* (Agnes Scott College, Decatur, Georgia). These two works—which seemed to represent alternative courses for the forward development of his art—were both finished in the early months of 1855, and were dispatched by Leighton to, respectively, the Royal Academy in London and the Universal Exhibition in Paris. *The Reconciliation* was a dark-toned and lugubrious painting, which remained unsold until it was sent as part of a travelling exhibition of British art to the United States in 1857–8. *Cimabue's Madonna Carried in Procession through the Streets of Florence* (to give the painting its full title), the subject of which was inspired by Vasari, shows a procession of figures leading through the streets of Florence as the *Ruccelai Madonna* was carried to the church of Santa Maria Novella. The composition is brightly lit and carefully constructed, and depends upon a formula of symmetrical flanking elements (made up of massed groups of figures) and a central lacuna occupied by Cimabue and Giotto themselves. The painting was enthusiastically received at the academy exhibition of 1855, with rapturous accounts of it in newspapers and periodicals, and much excitement attaching to its purchase, on the recommendation of Prince Albert, by Queen Victoria. Among the few who expressed themselves less than delighted by it were John Ruskin and the Pre-Raphaelite Dante Gabriel Rossetti.

In the autumn of 1855 Leighton transferred from Rome to Paris, taking a studio in the rue Pigalle. Once again, he threw himself into artistic social life, meeting painters of an older generation, including the great Ingres, as well as many of Ingres's followers among mid-century Romantic French artists. He also knew the landscape painters Gabriel-Alexandre Decamps and Constant Troyon, and admired the works of Charles Daubigny, J.-B.-C. Corot, and J.-F. Millet. In Paris, Leighton assimilated the principles of 'l'art pour l'art', which, although having originated in German aesthetic theory of the early nineteenth century, had been more recently promulgated by Théophile Gautier and Charles Baudelaire. These held that art was a self-fulfilling philosophy that was too important to serve merely as a means of didactic information or form of literary illustration. Leighton was a vital figure in the transfer of such ideas into a progressive sphere of English painting after his eventual move to London in 1859.

In 1856 Leighton began an intense and romantically tinged friendship with an Englishman named Henry Greville, carried on between London and Paris. Other new friends from the late 1850s were Henry and Augusta Hoare, of the banking family. Also living in Paris in these years were a number of English or English-speaking artists, such as those described by George du Maurier in the novel *Trilby* (1894), notably the American James Whistler. Leighton seems, however, to have kept apart from the bohemian antics of this circle. In London he was a member of the Hogarth Club, founded in 1858, which allowed him to make contact with a progressive circle of painters that was forming in those years and which included Rossetti and Edward Burne-Jones among other quondam Pre-Raphaelites. Among his fellow Hogarth Club members were forward-minded patrons such as James Stewart Hodgson—who in due course assembled a remarkable collection of works by Leighton.

Between October 1858 and the summer of 1859 Leighton returned to Rome, where he stayed at the Albergo del Sole and used his old studio. In November 1858 he embarked on the series of paintings of Nanna Risi, the model and mistress of the German artist Anselm Feuerbach. These remarkable works, of which *A Roman Lady* (*La Nanna*) (Philadelphia Museum of Art) and *Pavonia* (priv. coll.) are examples, seem to be meditations on female sexual allure explored by one who was largely indifferent to that mechanism. Two of the series were shown in 1859 at the Royal Academy, where reviewers were struck by their erotically charged, and even menacing, character. F. G. Stephens of *The Athenaeum* lauded the 'proud look … worthy of a Lucrezia Borgia' (*The Athenaeum*, 7 May 1859, 618). The prince of Wales had seen these *La Nanna* paintings in Leighton's studio in Rome, and succeeded in purchasing one of them—*Nanna* (*Pavonia*) (Royal Collection)—although it had in fact already been promised to another client.

Also during winter 1858–9 Leighton made painting expeditions into the Campagna, and then in the early summer of 1859 he spent a period of five weeks on the island of Capri. There he drew his famous and much admired silverpoint *Study of a Lemon Tree* (priv. coll.) and made delicious landscape oil sketches done before the motif and without revision, so as to capture fleeting meteorological effects or times of day. This visit to Capri seems to have been a deliberate withdrawal from the hectic life that he had come to lead as an increasingly well-known figure in the art worlds of Paris, Rome, and London. There he made the decision that the long period of restless alternation between these different cities should end, and so in the summer of 1859 he arrived in London and took a studio at 2 Orme Square. Although Leighton remained a frequent traveller for the rest of his life, from this time forward London was his professional base and his home.

The 1860s Leighton's reputation as a rising talent of the English art world was by no means clearly established at the time that he settled in London. The glittering success of *Cimabue's Madonna*, of 1855, must have seemed a distant memory—and had in any case been compromised by the abject failure of the painting that had appeared the year after, *The Triumph of Music* (unlocated, probably destroyed). The two exhibited *La Nanna* pictures of 1859 were seen as his best works since 1855, but in the same year his *Samson and Delilah* was refused at the British Institution. During the first half of the 1860s Leighton was still seen as an outsider, particularly at the Royal Academy. In 1861 his works were badly hung there, although well received critically. In the following two years he seems to have gone to lengths to demonstrate the range and serious-minded character of his art, with subjects from the Old and New Testaments—*The Star of Bethlehem* (priv. coll.) and *Jezebel and Ahab* (Scarborough borough council)—appearing in 1862 and 1863. About this time Leighton had volunteered to paint a fresco mural of *The Wise and Foolish Virgins* for St Michael's Church in Lyndhurst, Hampshire—an important work that occupied him intermittently for several years. It represented his second large-scale composition and utilized again the device of symmetrical flanking elements on either side of a pivotal central figure. A further opportunity to treat religious subjects occurred when he was commissioned to make nine illustrations of Old Testament subjects for Joseph Cundall (later taken over by the Dalziel brothers and eventually incorporated into the *Dalziel Bible Gallery*). Leighton was not inclined personally towards religious faith, describing himself to Steinle in a letter of this period as 'really a profane fellow' (Barrington, 2.91).

Leighton's most remarkable paintings of the 1860s were of the so-called aesthetic type, without ostensible subject and ambiguous in the identification of the figures in anthropological, social, or even, on occasions, gender terms. This amounted to a rejection of the conventions of British art, which held that paintings should lend themselves to easy interpretation of narrative subjects, in favour of ideas about the function and purpose of art that had circulated on the continent. Thus the insular and unsophisticated English art establishment saw Leighton as an unwelcome and insidious intruder. Possibly the most alarming among the works of this type that he sent to the academy was that entitled *Lieder ohne Worte* (Tate collection), of 1861. The contrived composition and artificial nature of the physiognomic and figurative types was witnessed by a remark that Leighton made to his father: '*Before* I began to paint "Lieder ohne Worte" … I intended to make it *realistic*, but from the first moment I began I felt the mistake, and made it professedly and pointedly the reverse' (Barrington, 2.62).

Leighton was prominent among the group of progressive artists who led the classical impulse in English painting in the middle years of the decade. Works by him such as *Mother and Child (Cherries)* (Blackburn Museum and Art Gallery) derive from meditations on the way the rhythmic patterns or folds of drapery reveal the underlying form of a figure. Leighton's second great processional painting, and the work that marked his arrival as a classical artist, *The Syracusan Bride* (priv. coll.), was the sensation of the 1866 Royal Academy exhibition. A mass of figures are placed across the width of the composition as in a sculpted bas-relief and in poses which derive from the artist's study of ancient sculpture. The subject of the painting comes from the second *Idyll* of Theocritus. However, the theme of the painting is treated without narrative drama and fulfils the expectation of aesthetic philosophy that no form of art should be dependent for its interpretation on another. Later Leighton looked back on his shift towards classical subjects and the representation of historical or genre subjects in antique settings as having happened gradually over a period of years, or so he explained to Joseph Comyns Carr in 1873:

> By degrees my growing love of form made me intolerant of the restraints and exigencies of costume and led me more and more, and finally, to a class of subjects, or more accurately to a state of conditions in which supreme scope is left to pure artistic qualities … These conditions classic subjects afford. (J. Comyns Carr, *Coasting Bohemia*, 1914, 114)

Leighton first put his name up for election as an associate of the Royal Academy in 1861. It was not until 1864, however, that following the success of two of his academy exhibits that year—*Golden Hours* (priv. coll.) and *Dante in Exile* (priv. coll.)—he was elected. And then he waited a further four years to become a member. There was a faction within the Royal Academy that resented his precocity and remained suspicious of his continental training. Leighton's connections with fellow artists in the early years that he lived in London were as much with the group that were to lead the then nascent aesthetic movement as with the artistic establishment.

The Royal Academy exhibition of 1869 was both the first to be staged in the new galleries at Burlington House and the first in which Leighton, as a full member of the academy, had the opportunity to influence the complexion of the display, as in that year he served on the hanging committee. Paintings of classical and mythological subjects by older artists such as George Frederic Watts and Edward Armitage were shown in conjunction with works by younger painters. These were either the followers or associates of Rossetti, such as John Roddam Spencer Stanhope, Frederick Sandys, and Simeon Solomon, or a group of painters who accepted Leighton as their leader, such as William Blake Richmond, represented by *A Procession in Honour of Bacchus at the Time of the Vintage* (priv. coll.), and Edward John Poynter, who showed a religious subject, *The Return of the Prodigal Son* (Forbes Magazine Collection, New York). Leighton seems to have intervened personally to admit Albert Moore's *A Venus* (York City Art Gallery) and Sandys's *Medea* (Birmingham City Art Gallery), a fearsome and sexually charged image which had been the centre of a furore when refused at the 1868 Royal Academy exhibition. Among Leighton's particular friends whose works were included in the exhibition of 1869, perhaps in some degree as a result of his influence, were George Heming Mason (represented by *Girls Dancing*; Bradfield College, Berkshire) and Giovanni Costa (who showed two works—*Porto d'Anzio* and *Near Leghorn*; both untraced).

Leighton's own classical subjects at the Royal Academy exhibition of 1869 included *Daedalus and Icarus* (priv. coll.) and *Electra at the Tomb of Agamemnon* (Ferens Art Gallery, Hull). In addition, his diploma piece, *Saint Jerome* (RA), was on display. The prominence of Leighton's own paintings and the works by his artistic confederates at the exhibition indicates that he was by then established on the professional trajectory that led to his election as president of the Royal Academy (in 1878) and his eventual arrival as the most respected and influential figurehead in the London art world.

Classical subjects After a period of ill health in 1870 Leighton returned to the Royal Academy in 1871 with three extraordinary paintings, which seemed to offer alternative treatments of classical subjects. The largest and most imposing of these, *Hercules Wrestling with Death for the Body of Alcestis* (Wadsworth Atheneum, Hartford, Connecticut), continues along a path of theatrical presentation of a mythological legend, depending as it does on Euripedes' play *Alcestis*. *Cleobolus Instructing his Daughter Cleoboline* (priv. coll.) represents a more intimate and domestic type of reconstruction of the ancient world. By contrast, *Greek Girls Picking Pebbles by the Sea* (priv. coll.) is the culmination of Leighton's move towards a type of subjectless classicism. Here, instead of taking a mythological theme, the artist has simply arranged four elegant female figures across the width of the composition. No attempt has been made to combine these elements into a logical scheme of perspective; indeed, their disparate scales and apparent disrelation each to the next contribute to the spectator's sense of the unreality of the scene. *Greek Girls Picking Pebbles* is a challenging and extremely modern painting of the English aesthetic movement, and one that derives from the same instinct towards classical abstraction and the sensuous manipulation of mood through colour that Albert Moore and James Whistler, among London-based artists, were also exploring. At the same time it was a most learned and considered painting, which reflected the artist's long meditation on historic schools of painting. The left-hand figure is a quotation from Guido Reni's *Atalanta and Hippomenes*, which Leighton had seen in the Prado Museum in Madrid.

Among Leighton's oil paintings of the 1870s and 1880s were various works which returned to the processional type that he had first attempted with *Cimabue's Madonna* in the 1850s. *The Daphnephoria* (Lady Lever Art Gallery, Port Sunlight) was commissioned by Leighton's friend James Stewart Hodgson, and was hung in his country house on the North Downs in Surrey. The work, first exhibited at the Royal Academy in 1876, takes its subject from Proclus's *Chrestomathia*, but represents a subject that was dreamed of by the Theban general Polemates rather than a principal event or main action from that text. Therefore, although the painting may be described as classical in a formal sense—with its frieze-like distribution of nude or draped figures, and carefully manipulated symmetries built around a central figure carrying a lyre—it subscribes to the precepts of aestheticism in its concern with the transmission of a trance-like mood and its indifference to the documentation of an event from ancient literature.

Leighton's last and perhaps best-known processional composition, *Captive Andromache* (Manchester City Art Gallery), painted in 1886–8, likewise raises questions about strict classical authenticity. The subject of the painting is inspired by the passage in the *Iliad* where Hector, the Trojan leader, imagines what the fate of his wife, Andromache, might be were he to be killed in battle. Thus the event represented is only obliquely suggested to the imagination of the reader rather than occurring as a central episode of the ancient text. In the painting we see Andromache dressed in the black robes of a widow and taken into captivity by Pyrrhus, son of Achilles. She is obliged to stand with other women to collect water from a cistern, and among the crowd are some who seem to be aware that she was once the wife of a great warrior. Her tragedy is conveyed in compositional terms, because here once again Leighton has resorted to placing the key figure of the piece within a central lacuna which both identifies and isolates her from the surrounding groupings.

Landscape From the late 1850s onwards Leighton painted landscape subjects in the course of his travels away from London, usually adopting a horizontal format on a small scale. Once or twice in his early career he attempted to rework these views in the studio to provide paintings which might be sent to exhibitions. He discovered, however, that the truthfulness of effect was lost in the process, and that the large-scale paintings became wooden and lifeless. Leighton painted landscape sketches for his own satisfaction, and as a means of reflecting on the forms of nature. The resulting works were very little known, as he only occasionally allowed them to be seen outside his own studio, and yet they remain among his most beautiful and individual works.

In three trips to the Mediterranean and the Orient in successive years in the late 1860s Leighton brought his landscape painting to a level of the utmost simplicity and refinement. In 1866 he travelled in the south of Spain, from which trip came *Mountains Near Ronda—Puerta de los Vientos* (Tate collection), in which he shows the structure of a distant range of mountains against a sky that seems to burn with heat. In the following year, 1867, Leighton made a long tour through Constantinople and western Turkey, returning via the islands of Rhodes and Lindos and staying for periods in Athens and Venice. He was spellbound by the sheer brilliance of light in the southern landscape, and looked for ways of reproducing the effect. Two Aegean subjects, *Isle of Chios* (Manchester City Art Gallery) and *Bay Scene, Isle of Rhodes* (priv. coll.), represent alternative treatments of the sunlit sea, looking towards and away from the light. In none of these views does Leighton introduce any of the devices whereby more conventional landscape painters suggest distance to the eye; he relies instead on what was known as aerial perspective, the precise manipulation of degrees and intensities of tone to give paintings a naturalistic quality.

In 1868 Leighton made a voyage down the Nile as far as Philae. He travelled alone, but the viceroy Isma'il Pasha, to whom Leighton had a letter of introduction from the prince of Wales, provided a steamer and retinue of staff. The purpose of the trip, which lasted about six weeks, was to see the archaeological remains, and Leighton kept a journal that describes each place visited. His greatest pleasure (as well as what he described on one occasion as 'a sort of discipline') was to sketch the riparian landscape and monuments in oil. An extraordinary sequence of at least thirty oil sketches derives from the journey. It was in the course of these three expeditions of the 1860s that Leighton pioneered and perfected his characteristic landscape style, and they mark the period when he was most prolific as a landscape painter. In 1873 he visited Damascus, painting there among other works a view of the house of his friend Richard Burton, but as he grew older he seems to have found it more difficult to summon the detachment needed to concentrate on landscape painting.

Portraiture Leighton was well aware of the demands that were made upon his contemporaries who allowed their professional practices to become portrait manufactories. As president of the Royal Academy from 1878, he knew very well that there was an oversupply of portraits to the summer exhibitions in London—both because people in society wanted to see the paintings of themselves and of their families exhibited in public displays, and because the artists themselves were eager to show off their latest works in the hope of receiving further and even more munificent commissions.

Leighton felt himself to be above this trade; nor was he impressed by or in need of the vast financial rewards that artists such as John Everett Millais reaped from it. Only on very rare occasions did he allow himself to paint what might be described as a society portrait, although his painting in 1878 of the Countess Brownlow (Belton House, Lincolnshire) might be regarded as representative of that type. Leighton was at heart a shy man who hesitated to intrude into the personalities of people whom he did not know well. The best of his portraits were therefore of men and women of whom he was fond and with whom he felt at ease. Among his female sitters, most were rather younger than he and, it seems, were individuals of marked temperament. For example, the portrait that he painted of Mrs James Guthrie in 1864–5 (Yale U. CBA) speaks of a relationship of affection and mutual respect between painter and sitter. Of the men he painted, two are pre-eminent (and, significantly, both were close friends of the artist). Leighton's portrait of the explorer–adventurer and translator of the *Kama Sutra*, Richard Burton, is in the National Portrait Gallery in London, while that of the Italian patriot and painter Giovanni Costa is in a private collection in Australia.

Leighton also painted a series of delightful portraits of the children of his friends—starting with the painting of about 1860 of May Sartoris, the daughter of his old friend Adelaide (now in the Kimbell Art Museum, Fort Worth, Texas). From the mid-1870s comes his portrait of the same sitter as a young woman, shortly after her marriage, now in the collection of Leighton House in London. As a group, this series speaks of Leighton's affection both for the parents of these various sitters and for their offspring, whether represented as children or in the early years of their adult lives, but whom he had known in each case since their infancy.

Working method Leighton was in a sense an aberrant figure in the context of English Victorian art, having been trained in, and subscribing to, an academic method of work. His practice was to make multiple chalk studies from the nude and the draped figure, so as to ensure an assured treatment of the figurative elements within a composition. At the same time he would refine the arrangement of the elements of the painting in small sketches, into which the shapes of the posed figures would be placed. Finally, he would work up the compositions in swiftly treated oil sketches, so as to have clear in his mind the overall impression of colour and tone that the finished painting would give. By this elaborate technique, which in certain instances took a number of years to run its complete cycle, Leighton organized the compositions of his large and complex paintings.

Other projects and activities From the early 1860s, when Leighton had painted the mural *The Wise and Foolish Virgins* for St Michael's, Lyndhurst, he had sought opportunities to paint works for public display. A decade later he undertook to paint schemes of decoration to occupy two lunettes for the south court of the South Kensington Museum, *The Arts of Industry as Applied to War* (on which he worked from 1872 to 1879) and *The Arts of Industry as Applied to Peace* (1873–85). From the start, Leighton encountered difficulties with the pretend fresco medium, and the project seems to have become a chore. Despite his belief that an artist had responsibilities to work for the widest possible audience and to provide ornament for public buildings, works of this type from his hand were chilly and impersonal affairs. What would have been the most prominent of Leighton's works on public display, had the project come to completion, was for the dome spandrels of St Paul's Cathedral, London. A design for one of these, showing the subject from the resurrection, *'And the Sea gave up the Dead which were in it'*, was shown at the Royal Academy in 1882, and was later worked up as an independent composition (now in the Tate collection). On one further occasion, in the mid-1890s, he undertook a mural subject—entitled *Phoenicians Bartering with Ancient Britons*—for the royal exchange building in the City of London.

Although the total number of his works as a sculptor was quite small, Leighton was none the less one of the most distinguished producers of bronze castings and clay models of figurative subjects of his generation, and a powerful influence on younger sculptors such as Hamo Thornycroft and Alfred Gilbert. His career as a sculptor commenced in the mid-1870s, and the first work that he exhibited—*Athlete Wrestling with a Python* (Tate collection)—made a sensation at the 1877 Royal Academy exhibition and was bought by the trustees of the Chantrey bequest. Later works of sculpture by Leighton were *The Sluggard*, the figure of a nude athlete stretching himself after sleep, and a subject entitled *Needless Alarms*, which shows a child frightened by a frog. Both these latter subjects appeared at the Royal Academy in 1886, and each was issued as a statuette in multiple editions.

In addition, Leighton made designs for a medallion to celebrate Queen Victoria's golden jubilee in 1887, showing a figure representing the British empire enthroned with her right hand holding the sword of justice, and in her left a symbol of victory. Around the figure are shown emblems of agriculture and industry, as well as a personification of commerce. Mention should also be made of the tomb that Leighton designed to contain the body of Elizabeth Barrett Browning, who died in Florence in 1861; this still stands in the protestant cemetery in Florence.

Role in artistic life It seems that Leighton had always aimed to gain a position of influence within the Royal Academy, and that he believed that the academy was the ideal institution to foster and safeguard the professional interests of artists. The fact that he himself had to wait so long to become a full member of the academy seems not to have made him less enthralled by the institution, and this is notwithstanding the fact that most distinguished painters among Leighton's contemporaries—for example, Ford Madox Brown, William Holman Hunt, Dante Gabriel Rossetti, and Edward Burne-Jones—despised the academy as an old-fashioned and merely self-serving professional cartel.

The Grosvenor Gallery was intended by its founder and proprietor Sir Coutts Lindsay as a deliberate rival to the academy, and a place to which painters of whom he approved, whether or not they were previously academy exhibitors, would prefer to send their works. Yet when it was set up in 1877 Leighton was aggrieved. He promptly set about the task of persuading artists to maintain loyalty to the academy, and to follow his example of sending only lesser works to the Grosvenor exhibitions in New Bond Street. Leighton even attempted to draw into the academy fold painters whose fame resulted from the acclaim that attached to the early Grosvenor shows—notably Burne-Jones—offering associate status of the academy without the need to stand for election. Against his better judgement, Burne-Jones was persuaded to accept this offer—and even showed a work at the summer exhibition of 1886, *The Depths of the Sea* (priv. coll.)—before seeing sense and resigning.

Leighton was active within the academy from the very start. In 1869 he was elected a visitor to the Royal Academy Schools, and in due course he instituted reforms in the running of the schools. He helped organize the academy winter exhibitions, the first of which took place in 1870. Although he had not been on friendly terms with Sir Francis Grant, the fox-hunting and portrait-painting president of the Royal Academy who died in October 1878, none the less Leighton's prominence within the institution made him Grant's natural successor. He was elected on 13 November 1878, and was knighted. His academy addresses were presented biennially from 1879, treating themes such as the relationship between art, morality, and religion, and national schools of art; they were undeniably dull in presentation and in content. Leighton's self-portrait of 1880, commissioned for the Collezione degli Autoritratti at the Uffizi Gallery in Florence, in which the artist shows himself wearing academic robes and standing before a cast of the Elgin marbles, such as was displayed in his own studio, and revealing the gold medal of the president of the Royal Academy at his breast, conveys the self-image that the artist sought for himself.

In the wider sphere of the arts, Leighton was again an indefatigable campaigner. In 1873 he gained W. E. Gladstone's support in the campaign to persuade the British Museum to buy the Castellani collection of antique sculptures; in 1882 he encouraged the trustees of the National Gallery to buy paintings from the Hamilton Palace sale; and in 1884 he advocated the purchase of various works, including the Van Dyck equestrian portrait of Charles I from Blenheim Palace. He served as a trustee of the Chantrey bequest, and used his influence to secure paintings under the terms of the endowment which were relatively progressive, including John Singer Sargent's *Carnation, Lily, Lily, Rose* (Tate collection). He was involved in the programme to complete Alfred Stevens's memorial to the duke of Wellington in St Paul's Cathedral, and he also joined William Morris and John Ruskin in their campaign to protect the west front of St Mark's Basilica in Venice from reconstruction. He served on the selection juries of a succession of international exhibitions, notably those held in Paris in 1878 and 1889, and that in Berlin in 1891.

Leighton was immensely businesslike in the conduct of his professional affairs. He made a handsome living from his art, although his income was much less than that earned by painters such as Millais who had allowed themselves to be overtaken by the demand for portraits. His outgoings must in large part have been connected with the fine house he built for himself, and the paintings and works of art that he accumulated to display in it. Leighton first commissioned the architect George Aitchison to build a modest villa, Leighton House, in the Kensington side street Holland Park Road in 1864, and moved there in the autumn of 1866. Gradually a community of fellow artists assembled around Leighton, with George Frederic Watts and Valentine Cameron Prinsep becoming his immediate neighbours. In 1877 Leighton asked Aitchison to create an Arab hall as an extension to the house, which was loosely modelled on the Norman-Arabic palace La Zisa in Palermo and which survives as one of London's most beguiling artistic interiors.

Leighton House provides much evidence of Leighton's way of life in London, with its spacious reception rooms and magnificent and richly furnished studio, all of which lent itself to entertaining, and particularly to musical parties. Society at the highest level attended these receptions, and the house was used as a command centre for the conduct of the art life of the nation. It is said that Leighton had wished that the house should be passed down as the official residence of successive presidents of the Royal Academy, but this intention was not expressed in his last testament.

Leighton's late career Leighton was clearly absorbed by the idea of the transitions between life and death and death and rebirth, themes which occur in a series of metaphysical paintings of biblical and mythological subjects from the mid-1860s onwards. *Ariadne Abandoned by Theseus: Ariadne Watches for his Return: Artemis Releases her by Death* (Salarjung Museum, Hyderabad) and *Hercules Wrestling with Death for the Body of Alcestis* (Wadsworth Atheneum, Hartford) represent two essays on the theme of death, while a later mythological subject, *The Return of Persephone* (Leeds City Art Gallery), shows the release of Persephone from her annual period of imprisonment in Hades as a supernatural rebirth, her body symbolically raised as if by the osmotic power of spring. *Clytie* (priv. coll.), Leighton's last painting, shows a figure who is dying because human will is defeated, and who is controlled by forces beyond our comprehension. Religious subjects such as *Elisha Raising the Son of the Shunamite* (Leighton House) and *Elijah in the Wilderness* (Walker Art Gallery, Liverpool) similarly show the moment when life returns by the power of divine intervention.

By the time when *'And the Sea gave up the Dead which were in it'* was painted, Leighton had abandoned the Hellenism of his middle period in favour of a style that was darker and more ominous (although always highly crafted). The new solemnity of his art from the late 1880s onwards owed much to his study of the work of Michelangelo, for whom he felt 'a profound reverence [and] who satisfies those modern sides of our nature that the Greeks leave untouched' (Jones and others, 194).

The artist's final masterpiece—*Flaming June* (Museo de Arte de Ponce, Puerto Rico)—is itself a meditation on the cycles of existence, between sleep and waking, through the seasons of the year, and from life into death, and is the last of Leighton's abstract evocations of mood in the form of a single female figure. Without narrative reference or association, the painting takes its theme from the rippling patterns of flame-coloured draperies worn by the sleeping woman and the sense of heat and airlessness of midday in a southern climate. The woman represented draws her legs up as she lies sideways on a bench, while her head rests in sleep on her left arm and against a marble parapet. Above and beyond this low wall is a view over a wide expanse of sea, which reflects the burning brightness of the sun, and a distant horizon of mountains. The sky is a pinkish-ochre colour, which lends an oppressive and enervating tone to the scene, and yet the quality of light cast over the sleeping figure is soft and subtly coloured, filtered by the awning that is glimpsed at the upper edge of the composition.

From the early 1880s onwards, through to the end of Leighton's career, one particular model appears most frequently in his work. Her adopted name was Dorothy Dene, and so close was the friendship between her and Leighton that there were rumours of a love affair. Born Ada Alice Pullen, she came from an impoverished family in New Cross, and was one of several daughters, each of whom was notably beautiful in a way that was suggestive of classical art and literature; Edith and Lena Pullen were Dorothy's sisters, and each also modelled to Leighton. Dorothy Dene had ambitions as an actress, and was encouraged and assisted in these by Leighton himself in the 1880s. Her performance on stage was apparently disappointing, but it has been suggested that Leighton's attempts to model and promote a working-class girl from south London as a classical tragedienne—unsuccessful though they may have been, and observed with fascination mixed with scorn by contemporaries in the world of theatre and the arts—were the inspiration for George Bernard Shaw's *Pygmalion* (first performed 1913).

Final years Leighton's mother died in 1865, while his father lived on until 1892. The artist's own health began to break down in 1894, when he suffered an attack of angina. He was recommended to rest, and in the following year, after the selection of the Royal Academy summer exhibition was complete, he set out for north Africa, where it was hoped he might recuperate. In June, back in London, he offered his resignation as president of the academy. Later in the year he travelled to Ireland, and then in the autumn made a long tour of Italian cities, including Venice, Naples, Rome, Florence, and Siena. In the new year honours list for 1896 he was raised to the peerage as Baron Leighton of Stretton, becoming the first artist ever to be so treated—an honour that reflected Lord Salisbury's desire to broaden membership of the House of Lords and may also have reflected Leighton's long friendship with the prince of Wales, as well as his prominence and dedication to the cause of the arts in British public life.

On 25 January 1896 Leighton died at his home, Leighton House. With him at his house were his sisters, Alexandra and Augusta, as well as two close friends, the painter Valentine Cameron Prinsep and Samuel Pepys Cockerell. Dorothy Dene was brought to his bedside shortly before the moment of death, and his last recorded words were 'My love to the Academy' (Barrington, 2.334). His body lay in state in the octagon room at the Royal Academy, and then on 3 February his funeral and burial took place at St Paul's Cathedral. He was represented, according to custom, by one work at the summer exhibition of 1896—the unfinished painting *Clytie*. A sale of the contents of the artist's studio was held in July 1896, and an exhibition for sale of his drawings was mounted at the Fine Art Society in December. In 1897 a large memorial exhibition of Leighton's work was shown at the Royal Academy.

Critical fortunes Leighton's works were by no means universally admired in his lifetime. He had many critical failures, and even the paintings upon which his contemporary reputation rested—notably the great series of processional paintings, *Cimabue's Madonna*, *The Syracusan Bride*, *The Daphnephoria*, and *Captive Andromache*, that punctuate his career at approximately eleven-year intervals—were not without their detractors. As a young man he had been made to wait embarrassingly long to be accepted into the ranks of the Royal Academy, not being elected a full member until 1868 (whereas Millais, Leighton's near contemporary, was an associate in 1853 and a member in 1863). Then, it seems that even before his career was ended, by his death at the age of sixty-five, a faction had emerged that was offended by the polished choreography of Leighton's figurative machines, or so his biographer Edgcumbe Staley indicated in 1906 when he wrote: 'in 1889 the fashion of running Leighton down had become all but universal—only the very *élite* of the art world remained true' (Staley, 138). Even friends and followers such as George Frederic Watts and William Blake Richmond were prepared to comment disparagingly on the artificiality and lack of spontaneity of Leighton's art, while, among artists who represented an opposite camp, Edward Burne-Jones described the president's work as 'theatrical', castigating compositions in which the 'emotions are developed in just the same way as emotions are on the stage' (*Burne-Jones Talking*, 124).

From the large and imposing paintings of edifying subjects that Leighton frequently sent to the summer exhibitions at the Royal Academy, to the more informal figurative subjects of men and women, usually studied from models found in the course of his long sojourns in the countries of southern Europe each summer and autumn, the artist was admired by his contemporaries for his virtuosity in the handling of paint and the manipulation of colour rather than for the intellectual content of his art.

Christopher Newall

Sources E. Rhys, *Sir Frederic Leighton, bart., P.R.A.: an illustrated chronicle* (1895) • A. Corkran, *Frederic Leighton* (1904) • Mrs R. Barrington, *Life, letters & work of Frederic Leighton*, 2 vols. (1906) • E. Staley, *Lord Leighton of Stretton, PRA* (1906) • A. L. Baldry, *Leighton* (1908) • L. Ormond and R. Ormond, *Lord Leighton* (1975) • R. Dorment, G. Hedberg, L. Ormond, R. Ormond, and A. Staley, *Victorian High Renaissance* (1978) [exhibition catalogue, Man. City Gall. and other locations, 1978–9] • *Burne-Jones talking: his conversations, 1895–1898*, ed. M. Lago (1981) • C. Newall, *The art of Lord Leighton* (1990) • S. Jones and others, eds., *Frederic Leighton, 1830–1896* (1996) [incl. a full bibliography; exhibition catalogue, RA, 15 Feb – 21 April 1996] · T. Barringer and E. Prettejohn, eds., *Frederic Leighton: antiquity, Renaissance, modernity* (New Haven, 1999) · *CGPLA Eng. & Wales* (1896)

Archives Hunt. L., letters · Kensington Central Library, London, corresp. · Leighton House Museum, London, corresp. and papers · RA, corresp., diary, sketchbooks · UCL, corresp. relating to the duke of Wellington's memorial | Baylor University, Waco, Texas, Armstrong Browning Library, letters to Robert Browning · BL, letters to Lady Dilke, Add. MS 43907 · BL, letters to W. E. Gladstone, Add. MSS 44411–44789 · BL, letters to Sir Austen Layard, Add. MSS 38992–39099 · Bodl. Oxf., letters to John Callcott Horsley and family · Bodl. Oxf., letters to F. G. Stephens · Castle Howard, North Yorkshire, letters to ninth earl of Carlisle · FM Cam., letters, mainly to Sidney Colvin · JRL, letters, mainly to Manchester City Art Gallery · JRL, letters to Fairfax Murray · JRL, letters to Marion Spielmann · Kensington Central Library, London, letters, incl. some to George Mason · NL Wales, letters to Johnes family · Northumbd RO, Newcastle upon Tyne, letters to Sir Matthew Ridley · RA, letters to A. H. Church · Watts Gallery, Compton, Surrey, letters to G. F. Watts

Likenesses F. Leighton, self-portrait, drawing, *c*.1848–1850, NPG · H. Hasselhorst, pencil drawing, *c*.1850, Städelsches Kunstinstitut, Frankfurt · A. Hendschel, etching, *c*.1850–1852 (students at the Städelsches Kuntinstitut), Städelsches Kuntinstitut, Frankfurt · F. Leighton, self-portrait, 1852, repro. in S. Jones and others, *Frederic Leighton, 1830–1896* (1996), no. 1 [exhibition catalogue, Royal Academy of Arts, London] · F. Leighton, self-portrait, oils, 1852, Städelsches Kunstinstitut, Frankfurt · F. Leighton, self-portrait, pencil caricatures, 1852, RA · E. von Steinle, pencil and chalk drawing, *c*.1852, BM · E. von Steinle, two chalk and wash drawings, 1852 (with Count Enrico Gamba), Staatliche Museen zu Berlin, Sammlung der Zeichnungen · E. von Steinle, pencil caricatures, 1852, RA · C. Silvy, photograph, 1860–65, V&A · D. Wynfield, photograph, 1864, repro. in Ormond and Ormond, *Lord Leighton*, pl. 67 · D. W. Wynfield, print, *c*.1864, NPG · H. N. O'Neil, group portrait, oils, 1869 (*Forty-three members in the billiard room of the Garrick Club*), Garr. Club · G. F. Watts, portrait, 1871, repro. in Ormond and Ormond, *Lord Leighton*, pl. 93 · G. F. Watts, portrait, 1871; Sothebys, 8 June 199, lot 24 [*see illus.*] · J. Tissot, caricature, chromolithograph, 1872, NPG; repro. in K. Matyjaszkiewicz, *James Tissot, 1836–1902* (1984), no. 52 [exhibition catalogue, Barbican Art Gallery, London]; for *VF* (12 June 1872) · F. Dupuis, oils, 1880, Leighton House, London · A. Legos, etching, *c*.1880, BM · F. Leighton, self-portrait, 1880, repro. in S. Jones and others, *Frederic Leighton, 1830–1896* (1996), no. 84 [exhibition catalogue, Royal Academy of Arts, London] · F. Leighton, self-portrait, oils, 1880, Uffizi Gallery, Florence · G. F. Watts, oils, exh. RA 1881, RA · G. F. Watts, two related oil paintings, 1881, NPG; related watercolour, Leighton House, London · F. Leighton, self-portrait, oils, 1882, Aberdeen Art Gallery, MacDonald collection · S. P. Hall, pencil drawing, 1889 (with Clifford Lloyd), NPG · R. Lehmann, drawing, 1889, BM · F. Pegram, drawing, 1889, V&A · R. Robinson, photograph, 1890, repro. in S. Jones and others, *Frederic Leighton, 1830–1896* (1996), p. 20 [exhibition catalogue, Royal Academy of Arts, London] · G. F. Watts, portrait, 1890, repro. in Ormond and Ormond, *Lord Leighton*, pl. 143 · T. Brock, bronze cast, *c*.1892, RA; repro. in S. Jones and others, *Frederic Leighton, 1830–1896* (1996), p. 19 [exhibition catalogue, Royal Academy of Arts, London] · R. Carter, miniature, 1895–6, NPG · T. Brock, recumbent bronze effigy, *c*.1901, St Paul's Cathedral, London · S. Boyes, stone statue, 1909, V&A, South Front · M. Beerbohm, double portrait (*A man from Hymetus*; with D. G. Rossetti), repro. in M. Beerbohm, *Rossetti and his circle*, new edn (1987) · H. J. Brooks, group portrait, oils (*Private view of the Old Masters Exhibition, Royal Academy, 1888*), NPG · J. Brown, stipple (after H. T. Wells, 1881), BM · R. Cleaver, group portrait, pen and ink (*Hanging committee, Royal Academy, 1892*), NPG · Elliott & Fry, carte-de-visite, NPG · Elliott & Fry, photograph, NPG · H. Furniss, pen-and-ink sketch, NPG · G. Grenville Manton, group portrait, watercolour (*Conversazione at the Royal Academy, 1891*), NPG · Kingsbury & Notcutt, photograph, NPG · Lock & Whitfield, woodburytype photograph, NPG; repro. in W. Downey and D. Downey, *Cabinet portrait gallery* (1890), vol. 1 · London Stereoscopic Co., two cartes-de-visite, NPG · R. W. Robinson, photograph, NPG; repro. in *Members and associates of the Royal Academy of Arts* (1891) · E. L. Sambourne, woodcut (with Sir Robert Peel), NPG; repro. in *Punch* (10 May 1884) · Walery, photograph, NPG · J. & C. Watkins, carte-de-visite, NPG · woodcut, NPG; repro. in *Hornet* (9 Jan 1878) · chromolithograph (after watercolour by S. P. Hall), NPG; repro. in *Society* (5 May 1883) · prints (after photographs), NPG · stone medallion on decorative frieze, Stroud School of Science and Art

Wealth at death £168,836 14*s*. 5*d*.: resworn probate, Jan 1897, *CGPLA Eng. & Wales* (1896)

Leighton, George Cargill (1826–1895). *See under* Leighton, Charles Blair (1823–1855).

Leighton, Henry. *See* Lichton, Henry (1369x79–1440).

Leighton, Henry (*d.* 1669), language teacher, was a Scot educated mainly in France. While serving in the royal army at Oxford he intruded himself by stealth at dusk on 1 November 1642 into a mass creation of masters of art commanded by Charles I. After the king's defeat he settled at Oxford, becoming one of several instructors in the French language who made a living on the fringe of academic life.

Leighton is chiefly remembered for privately publishing at Oxford in 1659, by his own account to please his friends, a French grammar in Latin, *Linguae Gallicae addiscendae regulae*, dedicated to Henry O'Brien, only son of the earl of Thomond and one of his pupils. Leighton described the work as a 'divertissement' to fill time not occupied with more serious studies. He offered grammatical rules and guidance on pronunciation, as well as a list of irregular verbs. The fact that a finer and enlarged second edition appeared in 1662, this time at the printer's expense, suggests a demand for the work.

Wood says Leighton was of doubtful character and that 'in some respects he debauched young men' (Wood, *Ath. Oxon.: Fasti*, 2.30). It appears that he never married. He died from a fall on the stairs at St John's College, Oxford, where he had a room allowed him, on 28 January 1669. He was buried the next day at St Giles's Church. Two witnesses testified that he had expressly indicated all his possessions, valued at £32 3*s*. 10*d*., should go to his friend Harry Hunton of Great Tew, Oxfordshire. While his books were worth only £1 10*s*. 0*d*., the old soldier died possessed of two swords, a swordstick, a crossbow, a prospective glass, and a considerable quantity of unscholarly clothing, with some gold and silver ornaments.

GORDON GOODWIN, *rev.* A. J. HEGARTY

Sources Wood, *Ath. Oxon.: Fasti* (1820), 29–30 · K. Lambley, *The teaching and cultivation of the French language in England during Tudor and Stuart times* (1920), 203–4 · H. Leighton, *Linguae Gallicae addiscendae regulae* (1659); 2nd edn (1662) · F. Madan, *Oxford literature, 1651–1680* (1931), vol. 3 of *Oxford books: a bibliography of printed works* (1895–1931); repr. (1964) · chancellor's court wills, Oxf. UA, Leighton fol. 32*r* · chancellor's court inventories, Oxf. UA, Leighton fol. 82*r*

Wealth at death £32 3*s*. 10*d*.: inventory, Oxf. UA, Leighton fol. 82*r*

Leighton, John [*pseud.* Luke Limner] (**1822–1912**), artist and book cover designer, was born on 15 September 1822, the first of seven children of John Leighton (1800–1883), bookbinder and publisher, and his wife, Sarah (1799–1877), daughter of the artist James Baynes (1766–1837). His father was in business with his uncle James, as J. and J. Leighton, bookbinders. Leighton studied as an artist in the studios of Henry Howard RA and Thomas Seddon. He wrote and illustrated a number of works under the pseudonym of Luke Limner. Possessed of exceptional ability, with wide-ranging interests, he also produced book cover designs.

The Great Exhibition of the Works of Industry of All Nations in 1851 offered Leighton a significant opportunity: he executed a number of bookbinding designs for J. and J. Leighton, as Luke Limner, his design for the binding of a William IV royal Bible being reproduced in the official catalogue of the exhibition. He also designed the commemoration shield of the Great Exhibition, which was executed in electrotype by the company of Elkington and subsequently used as ornamentation to blotting books. Leighton was awarded a prize medal for his designs by the jury of fine arts. In the 1850s and the 1860s he continued to be active in the organization of international exhibitions.

In 1852 and 1853 David Bogue published Leighton's *Suggestions in Design … for the Use of Artists and Art Workmen* (which appeared under the name Luke Limner). Leighton's mastery of line in relation to the design of all ages is readily apparent in this work which provided a source of inspiration for Leighton's designs, for both cloth and paper covers, and also for book illustrations. Examples of Leighton's monogram, a crossed capital 'J' and 'L', are on every plate. In his later work Leighton's monogram is a single capital 'L'. Both monograms were used regularly to sign his book illustrations and cover designs.

Leighton created over 400 cover designs in the 1850s and 1860s, some of which were for serial publications, though the majority of his work was for monographs. For *The Keepsake* his cover design was first used in 1849. It was repeated each year until 1857. He made different upper cover vignettes for each year of the *Court Album* from 1850 to 1855. He carried out much work for two publishers in these years: for Griffith and Farran he made over forty designs; for Routledge he created over eighty. The series Routledge's British Poets provides an early example of the reuse of vignette design by Leighton for many of the individual volumes published in the 1850s.

Leighton's densely ornamented design for R. H. Barham's *Ingoldsby Legends* was reused six times in the 1860s and 1870s. For another equally popular title, *Robinson Crusoe*, Leighton made four different designs for three publishers between 1859 and 1864. Longmans provided Leighton with opportunities to make more complex designs, as well as textual illustrations. The cover design for James Doyle's *A Chronicle of England* (1864) is one example. Longmans also published Jacob Cats's *Moral Emblems, with Aphorisms, Adages and Proverbs of All Ages and Nations* (1860), edited and translated by Richard Pigot, with illustrations and a cover design by Leighton. Editor and illustrator collaborated again on *The Life of Man, Symbolized by the Months of the Year* (1866), which contained passages selected from ancient and modern authors. Longmans published several editions of the hymnbook *Lyra Germanica: the Christian Life* (1855); the 1868 edition has illustrations and a lavish cover design by Leighton.

John Leighton [Luke Limner] (**1822–1912**), by Herbert Watkins, late 1850s

Between 1879 and 1895 Leighton executed a number of designs for the Glasgow publisher William Mackenzie, whose practice it was to issue the same text either in parts within paper covers, or in bound volumes with cloth covers. For seven titles, Leighton created designs for both the paper and the cloth covers. Leighton collaborated with his brother Henry, who engraved the designs for the paper covers for three publications: J. Taylor's *The Family History of England* (6 vols., 1870–73), H. M. Hozier's *The Russo-Turkish War* (1879), and *The National Burns*, edited by G. Gilfillan (2 vols., 1879–80). In his last published work Leighton proposed improvement to *Tubular Transit for London* (1902). Leighton worked for nearly seventy publishers, between 1845 and 1902.

Distinguishable by his sheer proficiency as well as by his artistic talent, Leighton's work as a book illustrator also showed him capable of providing a rich vein of comic art in the 1840s and 1850s. He also created more studied work in the 1850s and 1860s, often within the prevailing fashion for gothic design and motifs. He designed covers for a wide range of subject material, including religion, engineering, history, natural history, and particularly imaginative literature. His commissions from a few publishers spanned many years. His cover and spine designs are frequently a marvel of intricate line within a confined space. Above all, Leighton provided designs that the publishers wanted, often incorporating deft touches of humour with a flourish.

Leighton died, unmarried, at his home, 32 Pinner Road, Harrow on the Hill, Middlesex, on 15 September 1912, his ninetieth birthday, and was buried on 21 September 1912 in the family tomb, situated in the graveyard of the church of St Mary, Harrow. The mosaic on the south side of the tomb shows a red lion rampant within a shield. The words 'Light On' (a pun on Leighton) are underneath the lion. EDMUND M. B. KING

Sources S. Pantazzi, 'John Leighton, 1822–1912', *The Connoisseur*, 152 (1963), 262–73 · G. Dry, 'John Leighton and bookbinding design in England, 1845 to 1880', PhD diss., University of Munich, 1984–5 · D. Ball, *Victorian publisher's bindings* (1985) · L. Limner [J. Leighton], *Suggestions in design* (1852–3) · R. McLean, *Victorian publishers' book-bindings* (1974) · R. McLean, *Victorian book design and colour printing* (1963) · *CGPLA Eng. & Wales* (1912) · tombstone, St Mary's Church, Harrow on the Hill, Middlesex · *The Times* (18 Sept 1912) · *The Times* (23 Sept 1912)

Archives Bodl. Oxf., John Johnson MSS

Likenesses H. Watkins, print, 1856–9, NPG [*see illus.*] · J. Leighton, self-portrait, photograph, *c.*1870, HR HRC · J. Leighton, self-portrait, photograph, repro. in J. Leighton, *Tubular transit for London* (1902) · J. Leighton, self-portrait, photograph, repro. in J. Leighton, *On Japanese art* (1863)

Wealth at death £830 2*s.* 4*d.*: probate, 8 Oct 1912, *CGPLA Eng. & Wales*

Leighton, Kenneth (1929–1988), composer, was born on 2 October 1929 at Wakefield in the West Riding of Yorkshire, the younger son and second of two children of Thomas Leighton (*d.* 1979), a nurse, and his wife, Florence Dixon (*d.* 1973). His exceptional musical ability showed itself early. Kenneth, fair with auburn hair, sang in the choir of Wakefield Cathedral and played the piano for morning assembly at Holy Trinity Boys' School. At the Queen Elizabeth Grammar School after 1940 he began to compose in earnest. Vaughan Williams and Walton were his models.

Leighton left Wakefield in 1947 with a Hastings scholarship to read classics at Queen's College, Oxford, where he switched to music in his fourth year, studying with Bernard Rose. Important early works such as *Veris gratia* (1950) were first performed by the Newbury String Orchestra under Gerald Finzi. Then in 1951 he won the Mendelssohn scholarship, which enabled him to spend a year in Rome as a pupil of Goffredo Petrassi. He studied the music of Bartók, Dallapiccola, Berg, and above all Hindemith, whose influence proved lasting. In Italy too he met Lydia Vignapiano, the secretary whom he married in 1953. Their children, Angela and Robert, were born in 1954 and 1958.

On his return to England in 1952 Leighton worked at the Royal Marines School of Music, Deal. He moved to the University of Leeds in 1953 and the University of Edinburgh in 1955. As a lecturer he specialized in composition, counterpoint, and the music of the sixteenth and twentieth centuries. His own works started to receive critical acclaim. *Fantasia contrappuntistica*, winner of the Busoni prize in 1956, combined two abiding interests: virtuoso pianism and intricate neo-baroque forms. Leighton was himself a brilliant pianist, outstanding in the neo-classical repertory. He also revered J. S. Bach, making it his custom to play the forty-eight preludes and fugues complete each new year's eve.

The cello concerto premièred at the Cheltenham Festival in 1956 and the cantata *The Light Invisible* (1958) helped make Leighton's name. His instrumental music at this time was largely atonal, but his serialism was never dogmatic and he characteristically tempered it with considerable lyricism. By 1960, when Oxford awarded him a doctorate, his musical idiom had reached maturity: while very chromatic, it possessed an underlying tonality, which grew more pronounced over subsequent decades. Listeners were often struck by the contrast between wistful elegiac passages and bursts of nervous rhythmic energy.

Leighton began in the 1960s on his significant body of music for organ. The demanding *Prelude, Scherzo, and Passacaglia* (1963) and the short *Paean* (1966) both became established pieces in the repertory, and an organ concerto (1970) was generally applauded. He simultaneously emerged as an eminent composer of sacred works, ranging from large-scale cathedral music through an unaccompanied setting of the Latin mass (1964) to very singable diatonic hymns and services for small church choirs. 'Lully, lulla', an arrangement of the Coventry carol, is perhaps his best-known composition. Plainsong elements found their way into some of his chamber music.

A serious-minded man, well read in philosophy, Leighton responded emotionally to Christian texts and subjects while still wrestling with the problems of belief. He valued music as a coming together of the spiritual, intellectual, and physical. Composition for him was instinctive and personal, a means of sincere self-expression; yet he felt a duty to serve an exterior purpose. Therefore he was happy to undertake diverse commissions for churches, schools, and individuals. Performers associated with him include pianist Peter Wallfisch, organist Dennis Townhill, and tenor Neil Mackie.

Though receptive to fresh influences, Leighton looked askance at radical experimentalism. Indeed, the state of contemporary music sometimes depressed him, and his warm praise for Messiaen rather underlined his reticence about some other composers. He ignored transient fashions and the coterie which propagated them. While the critics were writing off symphonic music, he produced piano concertos and a symphony which won the Trieste prize in 1965.

In 1968 Leighton went back to Oxford as university lecturer and fellow of Worcester College in succession to Edmund Rubbra, but only two years later Edinburgh recalled him as Reid professor of music (in which post he remained until his death). Leighton, a down-to-earth, beer drinking, pipe smoking Yorkshireman, was devoted to Scotland, its history, literature, and landscape. Never one for small talk or parties, he liked to walk the hills with his dogs and inspect archaeological sites. Friends and colleagues appreciated his dry self-deprecating humour, and students respected his kindness as well as his intellect. The professor, bespectacled and latterly bearded, wore his favourite old tweed jacket and woollen tie on almost all occasions. In teaching he emphasized craftsmanship and communication and resisted excessive compartmentalization: the study of music should not become separated from practical music-making. Among his pupils were James MacMillan and Nigel Osborne.

During vacations Leighton composed at the piano for a few hours each morning in the music room of his home: 9 Bright's Crescent, Edinburgh. From the symphony no. 2 (1974) onwards, many discerned a gradual mellowing of his style, and this less stringent, more visionary voice may be heard in the opulent symphony no. 3 (1984) and *Earth, Sweet Earth* (1986). The opera *Columba*, with libretto by Edwin Morgan, was performed in 1981 and 1986.

Divorced in 1980, Leighton married his second wife in Edinburgh on 14 March 1981. Josephine Ann Prescott (*b.* 1936), an American microbiologist, had four children from a previous marriage. The Royal College of Music elected him a fellow in 1982. He died at 38 McLaren Road, Edinburgh (where he had recently moved), from cancer of the oesophagus on 24 August 1988. His remains were cremated in Edinburgh and his ashes were interred in Glen Sannox cemetery on the Isle of Arran.

Kenneth Leighton left a large output: ninety-six opus numbers, plus sixty other works. By the close of the century the vast majority had been published and nearly half released on compact disc. Much of his finely crafted music shows a certain romanticism. Anthems and services by Leighton are sung in churches across the world.

JASON TOMES

Sources *New Grove*, 2nd edn • private information (2004) [Josephine Ann Leighton, widow] • 'Roger Fulton talks to Kenneth Leighton', *New Edinburgh Review*, 5 (Feb 1970), 25–7 • H. Truscott, 'Two traditionalists: Kenneth Leighton and John McCabe', *British music now*, ed. L. Foreman (1975), 145–54 • A. Thomson, 'Kenneth Leighton (1929–1988): a personal memoir', *Organists' Review*, 75 (1989), 165 • F. Routh, 'Composer-pianist of musical impetus', *The Guardian* (31 Aug 1988) • J. V. Cockshoot, 'The music of Kenneth Leighton', *MT*, 98 (1957), 193–6 • P. Moger, 'Kenneth Leighton's organ music', *MT*, 126 (1985), 553–5 • D. Webster, *Musical Opinion*, 111 (1988), 328 • 'Kenneth Leighton', *MT*, 129 (1988), 620 • *The Times* (27 Aug 1988)
Wealth at death £74,292.67: confirmation, 23 Jan 1989, *CCI*

Leighton, Margaret (1922–1976), actress, was born on 26 February 1922 at Barnt Green, Worcestershire, the elder of two daughters in a family of three children of Augustus George Leighton, businessman in the cotton trade, and his wife, Doris Isabel Evans. She was educated at the Church of England College, Edgbaston, Birmingham, and began work as an assistant deputy stage manager at Barry Jackson's Birmingham Repertory Theatre, making her first appearance on stage in 1938, aged sixteen, as a cockney girl in *Laugh With Me*.

For the next few years Leighton played innumerable parts with Basil Langton's Travelling Repertory Theatre, rejoining Barry Jackson in December 1942. Leighton was

Margaret Leighton (1922–1976), by Dorothy Wilding, *c.*1952

something of a protégée of Jackson and his 'adjutant', the South African-born director H. K. Ayliff. Her contemporary Paul Scofield commented that 'hers was a formidable combination of talent and beauty … she assimilated from H. K. a kind of female version of his towering qualities and his authority' (O'Connor, 147).

In 1944 Laurence Olivier, Ralph Richardson, and John Burrell came to see her perform and asked her to join their newly formed Old Vic company. For £17 a week she made her London début as the Troll King's Daughter in Ibsen's *Peer Gynt*. She remained with this historic company for three years, playing other parts including Yelena in Chekhov's *Uncle Vanya*, Regan to Olivier's Lear, Roxane to Richardson's Cyrano, and the Queen to Alec Guinness's Richard II.

On 16 August 1947 Leighton married Max Reinhardt (1915–2002), the publisher, living in some style in Albany, Piccadilly, and in a country house near Guildford. A year later she entered films, appearing as Flora MacDonald in *Bonnie Prince Charlie* for Alexander Korda's London films, and as the daughter in *The Winslow Boy* by Terence Rattigan with Robert Donat. Under contract to Korda, she was in great demand on both stage and screen, although she never perhaps achieved the success in films that might have been expected. She was divorced from Reinhardt in 1955.

In the theatre Leighton continued to thrive, playing a 'deeply touching' Celia in T. S. Eliot's *The Cocktail Party* (1950), and Masha in an all-star *Three Sisters* by Chekhov (1951) which reunited her with Ralph Richardson. They appeared together at Stratford upon Avon the following year as the Macbeths and as Prospero and Ariel. It was thought that Richardson had fallen in love with her during the Old Vic season, but Leighton was also playing a delightful Rosalind (although Kenneth Tynan found her 'rather like a popular head girl') opposite Laurence *Harvey (1928–1973), and was falling in love herself. Born Hirsch Moses Skikne in Lithuania, Harvey was making a name for himself in films. They married, on a ship moored off Gibraltar, in 1957; passionate and tempestuous, they were very much the celebrity couple, playing their private lives in public.

Leighton was enjoying huge and glamorous success in theatres on both sides of the Atlantic. At the Haymarket in 1953 she played Orinthia in G. B. Shaw's *The Apple Cart*, starring with Noël Coward. They also made some sparkling recordings together of his plays and poetry, and he considered her to be a peerless interpreter of his work. In 1954 she began a long run (nearly four years in London and New York) as Anne Shankland and Sybil Railton-Bell in the double bill of Terence Rattigan's *Separate Tables*, co-starring with Eric Portman and winning a Tony award as best actress. In *Variations on a Theme* (1958) Rattigan provided her with a role whose inspiration lay in Leighton's marriage to Harvey. The play was not a success.

Leighton was a radiant Beatrice to Sir John Gielgud's Benedick in New York (1959), and then scored another US triumph as Hannah Jelkes in Tennessee Williams's *The Night of the Iguana* (1962), playing with Bette Davis and winning a second Tony award. Her marriage to Harvey now over, she at last found happiness and stability with the actor Michael *Wilding (1912–1979), the son of Henry Wilding and his wife, Ethel Thompson. They were married in 1964; it was Wilding's fourth marriage—his second wife had been Elizabeth Taylor with whom he had two sons.

Apart from an acclaimed Cleopatra at Chichester in 1969, for which she was the Variety Club's best actress, Leighton's later stage performances did not really match the achievements of earlier years. She had continued to work extensively in both film and television. On film she appeared in John Ford's *Seven Women* (1966) and was querulous and dotty in *The Madwoman of Chaillot* (1969) and chilling as the mother in *The Go-Between* (1970), for which she was Oscar nominated and won the British equivalent. Leighton had made her first appearance on television in 1955 in *A Month in the Country* by Turgenev; later appearances included *Gaslight* (1960), *The Vortex* (1968), and Gertrude to the Hamlet of Richard Chamberlain—television's Dr Kildare—in 1970, for which she won an Emmy.

Leighton made her last appearance on stage in 1975, in an adaptation of Ivy Compton-Burnett's *A Family and a Fortune* with her friend Alec Guinness, acting her role in a wheelchair. She had in fact been ill for some years with multiple sclerosis, the crippling effects of which she bore with great bravery. Always a wildly social figure (Coward and Rattigan both adored her, she adorned their arms at many a function, and Rattigan's house in Brighton included a permanent bedroom for Leighton), she lived with Wilding in a cottage near Chichester known locally as Vodka Villa. Tall, sometimes painfully thin, with sorrowful blue eyes, she had beauty, grace, intelligence, wit, and 'cheerful vulgarity' (Stephens, 122). The writer Enid Bagnold spoke of her as 'an extraordinary and shining woman, made of moonshine and talent and deep self-distrust, astonished at success' (*The Times*, 14 Jan 1976). Appointed CBE in 1974, she died on 13 January 1976 in Chichester. ALEX JENNINGS

Sources I. Herbert, ed., *Who's who in the theatre*, concise 16th edn (1978) · E. Katz, *The international film encyclopedia* (1980) · *The Times* (14 Jan 1976) · microfiche, BFI · M. D. Candee, ed., *Current Biography Yearbook* (1957) · D. Hickey and G. Smith, *The prince, being the public and private life of Larushka Mischa Skikne, a Jewish Lithuanian vagabond player, otherwise known as Laurence Harvey* (1975) · G. O'Connor, *Ralph Richardson: an actor's life* (1982) · G. Wansell, *Terence Rattigan* (1995) · R. Stephens, *Knight errant: memoirs of a vagabond actor* (1995) · S. Morley, *The great stage stars: distinguished theatrical careers of the past and present* (1986) · private information (2004) · m. cert. [Max Reinhardt] · D. Quinlan, *The illustrated directory of film stars* (1981)

Archives FILM BFI NFTVA, *Those British faces*, Channel 4, 13 June 1993 · BFI NFTVA, home footage · BFI NFTVA, performance footage | SOUND BL NSA, performance recordings

Likenesses photographs, 1950–76, Hult. Arch. · D. Wilding, photograph, c.1952, NPG [*see illus.*] · A. Wysard, airbrush drawing (as Flora MacDonald), NPG; repro. in *Strand Magazine*, 116 (1948), 699

Leighton, Robert (*bap.* 1612, *d.* 1684), archbishop of Glasgow, was baptized on 1 October 1612 at St Nicholas's, Newcastle upon Tyne, probably the second son of Alexander *Leighton (c.1570–1649), then lecturer in the town, and his first wife (*d.* before 1625), whose previous husband was called Means or Mears; Elisha *Leighton (*d.* 1685) was his brother. In 1617 his father went to Leiden to study medicine; following his graduation in 1619 he practised as a physician in London, where he attended the separatist church at Blackfriars. In 1627 Robert was sent to the University of Edinburgh. His patron was Sir James Stewart of Goodtrees, who had to use his influence in Leighton's favour after he was excluded for contributing to a student satire on the provost. Leighton expressed great regret to his father for this misdemeanour, and otherwise won a good reputation with his teachers. He graduated MA on 28 May 1631.

Early career Leighton then spent several years travelling in Europe, in France and at Douai in the Spanish Netherlands, where he had relations among the Roman Catholic clergy. He perfected his Latin, Greek, and Hebrew, learned to speak French like a native, and read widely in theology. He came into contact with the European reaction to formalism in the church, later expressed in Jansenism, pietism, and quietism, and akin to the views expressed in Scotland by the 'Aberdeen doctors', who also regarded the polity of the church as less important than personal piety.

Following his return to Scotland, Leighton was licensed by the presbytery of Edinburgh, in July 1641. On 16 December he was ordained by the presbytery of Dalkeith and inducted to the parish of Newbattle, whose patron was the earl of Lothian, a covenanter. Leighton had been present at the Glasgow assembly in 1638 and in 1643 he signed the solemn league and covenant. However, he hated controversies 'not excepting those with Papists', and there

Robert Leighton (*bap.* 1612, *d.* 1684), by Robert White

was already a tension between this attempt to avoid involvement in public affairs and the pressures exerted by contemporary conflicts in the church. In 1648 parliament resolved in favour of the engagement but the church opposed this. Leighton attracted mild censure for not reading the declaration against it in person and for failing to attend the general assembly when the issue was being debated. When obliged to rebuke the engagers in his own congregation, he exhorted them to repent of their immoralities 'without meddling with the quarrel on the grounds of that war'.

Leighton's personality as minister of Newbattle was reserved and private, lacking vanity or aggression. He engaged in fasting and his only pleasure was taking rides. His English accent and politeness created some barriers in his pastoral work among the nine hundred communicants of the parish. He communicated more effectively from the pulpit, arguing for longer texts and shorter sermons and exhibiting a preaching style which was regarded as unusual owing to his preference for a 'discourse on some common head', 'rather than expounding and dividing a text, raising doctrines and uses', as Robert Baillie put it. Leighton's style was more natural and less methodical than was fashionable and this can be seen in his posthumously printed work. He argued for simpler catechisms and himself wrote one for children, published in 1693. An essay entitled 'The rule of conscience' is an attack on presbyterian rebelliousness, based on a clear use of the term 'conscience' as an attribute of the individual's relationship to God in opposition to those bent on 'extending its legislative power' until they were 'sufficiently warranted to do what they please … above the reach of all checks from any power on earth'. Leighton's Erastianism derived from his latitudinarian approach to church government, itself a sign of his placing of personal faith above church organization.

London and Edinburgh, 1649–1660 Leighton visited London annually and in 1649 was granted leave to spend several months there during his father's final illness. In 1652 the synod of Lothian sent him there to negotiate the release of Scottish ministers captured at Alyth and Worcester. While in England, Leighton decided to resign his charge both for health reasons and because he was finding it difficult to follow the party line of the church. The presbytery refused to accept his resignation and asked Lord Lothian to urge him to remain. Meanwhile, the town council of Edinburgh had elected him to the principalship of the University of Edinburgh. Leighton accepted this post from Oliver Cromwell, though the ministers of Edinburgh were against it, and started his duties on 3 February 1653.

Leighton was principal and also professor of divinity. He preached before the university on Sunday morning and in a rota with the other professors on Sunday afternoon. His weekly sermon to the students was open to the townspeople. Gilbert Burnet believed he had the highest reputation of any man in Scotland and described his preaching at this time: 'His thought was lively, out of the way and surprising, yet just and genuine,' and commented on the 'grace and gravity of his pronunciation'. Leighton continued to eschew ecclesiastical controversy, though with difficulty. He went frequently to London and met Cromwell's courtiers. On the other hand he was appointed a member of the general assembly of 1653, which was dispersed by Cromwell's officers. He gave covenants to the students in line with official church policy, while encouraging them to avoid 'that itch for polemical and controversial theology which is so prevalent and infectious'. He also expressed the wish for a grammar school in every parish supported by a simple Latin grammar for children.

Bishop of Dunblane The tensions within Leighton's position came to a head on the restoration of episcopacy in 1661. He was sympathetic to a combination of presbyterian and episcopal systems. However, when offered a bishopric, either through his brother's influence at court or through his own journeys there as agent for Lord Lothian, Leighton was most reluctant to accept. He was consecrated along with James Sharp on 15 December 1661 at Westminster Abbey in London and, like Sharp, agreed to be reordained as a political necessity rather than to prove a point of principle. Pressure from Charles II himself played a part in Leighton's acceptance of a bishopric. So too, apparently, did the desire to use his position to create a peaceful church settlement. For the rest of his life he was involved in the uncomfortable working out of some form of accommodation between his own personal priorities and the political powers to whom he had committed himself, along with the fragmentation, realignments, and conflict within the church.

This discomfort was evident from 1661. Leighton insisted on the smallest of the Scottish dioceses, Dunblane. He abandoned Sharp's party on the return to Scotland and travelled from Morpeth alone. He did not like the inaugural banquet. He was not involved in the consecration of new bishops at Holyrood in May 1662, nor did he become involved in the political role of the episcopacy either in parliament or in the lords of the articles, though he did attend the former in 1662 to defend ministers unwilling to take the oath of allegiance by arguing for their right to define their own sense of it. His independent line led to his omission from the church commissioners in 1663.

Synods and presbyteries, once restored, now derived their authority from the bishops. Leighton alarmed his fellow bishops by inviting his own synod to meet him a month early and by asserting that its members should have free voting rights. However, he insisted on conformity and won it from all but one of his ministers and the great majority of the people under his charge, as his diocese was not so sympathetic to the covenanting movement as others in the south and west. The register of the synod of Dunblane shows Leighton encouraging in the clergy reverence in public worship, the use of longer texts and a plain and useful style in sermons, the restoration of daily service in church, use of the Lord's prayer, creed, and *Gloria patri*, and the regular visitation and catechizing of their flocks. Above all he repeated his belief in the primacy of holiness in heart and life.

In 1665 Leighton went to London to offer his resignation to Charles II, complaining that government policy was 'so violent that he could not concur in the planting to the Christian religion itself in such a manner, much less a form of government'. After his resignation was turned down, he worked up his ideas on church government into a 'scheme of accommodation' which argued that moderate episcopacy was compatible with the solemn league and covenant and that episcopacy governing the church in conjunction with synods and presbyteries was different from the episcopacy against which the covenant had been drawn up. He suggested that no minister need promise canonical obedience to the bishop or approve of episcopacy in principle, and that bishops could act merely as chief presbyter at ordinations and permanent moderators of the church. In 1667 the new government of Alexander Stuart, earl of Moray, and John Hay, earl of Tweeddale, organized a conference with members of the privy council, to which Leighton brought six of his ministers and these ideas. A change of policy did not occur until 1669, when the government of John Maitland, earl of Lauderdale, passed the first indulgence and revived the idea of accommodation when it became apparent that dissent was becoming more extreme.

Archbishop of Glasgow Alexander Burnet, archbishop of Glasgow, had been deprived for opposing indulgence, under an act of 1669 which declared the external government of the church to be an inherent right of the crown. His post was offered to Leighton, who refused it twice, after which Tweeddale argued that he was undermining the policy of indulgence. When Charles II wrote to Leighton personally, then summoned him to London and ordered him directly, he finally accepted the archbishopric on condition that he could put into practice his scheme of accommodation. Leighton tried to do this in various ways in 1670. The synod of Glasgow set up a committee to hear complaints against ministers, but it was ineffective. Six 'evangelists' were sent round the western parishes to argue his case; despite large turnouts, this had little lasting influence. Meetings with dissenters also proved inconclusive, despite pressure behind the scenes by Tweeddale through the duchess of Hamilton. There was a suggestion that the accommodation might win support if it were enacted into law, but the mutual distrust of government and dissenters was too great and a final reply from dissenting ministers in 1671 proved unsatisfactory.

Leighton agreed to continue in his role despite having 'done my utmost to repair the temple of the Lord', and was installed as archbishop of Glasgow in October 1671. He continued to have difficulty in filling twenty-five vacant parishes and argued for the appointment of indulged ministers to the vacancies. But he was now less in tune with Lauderdale's policy, which paid more attention to Sharp than to Leighton and had hardened towards those resisting the second indulgence of September 1672. The established clergy were also becoming impatient with the attempts to reach agreement with dissenters, and the government was becoming alarmed at the increase in conventicles. Leighton appears to have been sympathetic to the suggestion of Gilbert Burnet that a national synod should be called with a view to abandoning episcopacy if disorder could not be contained. He reported to Lauderdale that he felt that containment of dissent was now the only policy; he regarded persecution as 'scaling heaven with ladders fetched out of hell'. In April 1673 Leighton went to London once again to resign his see, but Charles II persuaded him to remain in office for a year from August 1673. On visiting the king in June 1674 he was told to stay until the end of the year, after which his resignation from the archbishopric was finally accepted.

Retirement Leighton lived briefly at the University of Edinburgh but then moved to Broadhurst in Horsted Keynes, Sussex, the home of his sister, Saphira Lightmaker. Charles II wrote to him again in 1679 after the murder of Sharp and the rising which led to the battles of Drumclog and Bothwell Bridge, asking him to return to Scotland to lead a policy of clemency and act as a negotiator 'for persuading all he could of both opinions to as much mutual correspondence and concord as could be'. Leighton's own description of such negotiations previously had been 'a drunken scuffle in the dark'. He did not undertake this commission. In Sussex he continued to study and to preach and pray in local churches. In 1684 he went to London to meet the earl of Perth, the Scottish chancellor, who had desired his spiritual advice. Leighton met Bishop Burnet and told him that despite appearances he was 'very near his end'. Two days later, on 25 June 1684, he died of pleurisy, in Burnet's presence, at The Bell inn, Warwick Lane, London. He was buried in the chancel of the church at Horsted Keynes, where his brother Elisha was laid seven months later.

Leighton's historiographical reputation has been consistent with regard to his spiritual and theological influence but varied with regard to his ecclesiastical career. His personal unworldliness was widely attested. He shrank from ostentation, retaining contempt for riches and honours and even his own reputation. On accepting the bishopric he had said that 'one benefit will arise from it. I shall break that little idol of estimation my friends have for me, and which I have so long been sick of.' He was abstemious, fasted frequently, and maintained long periods of private devotion. He gave away what he could spare and employed others as the agents of his charity so that he might avoid the credit. He founded two bursaries in philosophy at Glasgow University and confirmed one at Edinburgh, and made permanent provision for the poor and elderly in Dunblane, Edinburgh, Glasgow, and Sussex. He left his library of fifteen hundred volumes, many with his own marginalia, to the diocese of Dunblane along with an endowment of £100 for their housing and upkeep. His will of 17 February 1683 gave the executors, his sister Saphira and her son Edward Lightmaker, complete discretion to bestow the rest of his estate on charitable causes he had recommended to them.

Leighton printed nothing in his lifetime and gave instructions that his manuscripts should not be published. His sister was persuaded to contravene this and Henry Fall edited the publication of Leighton's sermons, commentaries, lectures, and addresses between 1692 and 1708, while apologizing if his 'Stile is not after the Mode and dress of those times'. Burnet found his 'language was too fine, too much laboured and too full of figures and sentences' but it proved popular in print. His works were widely reprinted in whole or part in the nineteenth century, much being made of his respect for Thomas à Kempis and his own emphasis on the imitation of Christ through the virtues of humility, meekness, and charity. The *Dictionary of National Biography* refers to him as a saint as a matter of course.

Leighton's political reputation in the twentieth century has reflected the position of the authors writing about him. Buchan saw him as an English liberal with Platonist leanings; Cowan condemned his 'remarkable capacity for personal survival and self-advancement'; and Cameron commented on contemporaries' doubts about his 'holy wobbling'. Buckroyd believed that, though he has been portrayed as the man who could have saved the Scottish church at the Restoration, 'his total indifference to matters which had rent the church asunder rendered him unacceptable to either side'. Leighton was an anomalous figure in the seventeenth-century Scottish church because of his English and continental connections and his latitudinarian views. He never resolved the conundrum between his belief that the form of church government mattered less than personal piety and his sense of obligation to work towards its settlement.

HUGH OUSTON

Sources E. A. Knox, *Robert Leighton* (1930) · J. Buchroyd, *Church and state in Scotland, 1660–81* (1980) · *DSCHT* · J. H. S. Burleigh, *A church history of Scotland* (1960) · D. Reid, ed., *The party-coloured mind* (1985) · J. M. Allen, *Only my books* (1985) · D. Laing, ed., *The Bannatyne miscellany*, 3, Bannatyne Club, 19b (1855) · W. R. Rogier, *Bishops and presbytery* (1958) · P. Butler, ed., *Archbishop Leighton's practice of the presence of God* (1910) · I. B. Cowan, *The Scottish covenanters, 1660–1688* (1976) · *Bishop Burnet's History* · *IGI* [parish register of St Nicholas, Newcastle upon Tyne] · will, PRO, PROB 11/377, sig. 103 · *DNB* · J. Buckroyd, *The life of James Sharp, archbishop of St Andrews, 1618–1679* (1987)

Archives Dunblane Cathedral Museum, legal papers and letters · NL Scot., letters and papers · U. Glas. L., sermons preached at Newbattle | BL, letters to duke of Lauderdale, Add. MSS 23128–23137

Likenesses R. White, line engraving, BM, NPG [*see illus.*] · oils, U. Edin.

Wealth at death approx. £1500; plus library of 1500 volumes: will, *Bannatyne miscellany*, vol. 3; will, PRO, PROB 11/377, sig. 103

Leighton, Robert (1822–1869), poet, was born in Murraygate, Dundee, on 20 February 1822, the eighth of the fourteen children of David L. Leighton (*d.* 1828) and his wife, Janet, *née* Gloag (*d.* 1835). In 1834 his mother married a farmer named Fleming, of East Friarton, Fife, and on her death a year later he settled with his brother William, a shipowner, in Dundee. He attended Dundee Academy until 1837, when he entered William's business.

In 1842–3 Leighton went round the world as a supercargo in one of his brother's ships, visiting Sydney and returning by Valparaiso. He then entered the service of the London and North Western Railway at Preston. In 1850 he married Elizabeth Jane Campbell, daughter of a retired Scottish schoolmaster living in Liverpool, the 'Eliza' of his dramatic and reflective poems. They had nine children. By this time he had contributed a number of poems and songs to pamphlet publications including the popular lyric 'Jenny Marshall's Candy, O'. Between 1854 and 1858 he managed the Ayr branch of a firm of Liverpool seed merchants and published *Rimes and Poems* (1855) under the pseudonym Robin. In 1858 he visited his brother William, who had settled in America. He subsequently travelled for the Liverpool firm in the agricultural districts of England, Scotland, and Ireland, and brought out various editions of his poems.

In March 1867 Leighton met with an accident near Youghal, and became an invalid. During his illness he transcribed and prepared further works of poetry. His *Scotch Words and the Bapteesement o' the Bairn* (1869) was reprinted a number of times. He died, as a result of his accident, at Liverpool on 10 May 1869, and Emerson, writing to Leighton's brother William in 1871, paid a high compliment to Leighton's 'purity and manliness of thought, and the deep moral tone which dictated every verse'. Two collections were published posthumously: *Reuben* (1875) and *Records* (1880).

T. W. BAYNE, *rev.* SARAH COUPER

Sources J. G. Wilson, ed., *The poets and poetry of Scotland*, 2 (1877), 432–3 · Boase, *Mod. Eng. biog.*, 2.378 · C. Rogers, *The modern Scottish minstrel, or, The songs of Scotland of the past half-century*, 6 (1857), 163 · R. Inglis, *The dramatic writers of Scotland* (1868), 63 · private information (1892) [Leighton's son, R. Leighton] · R. Leighton, *Scotch words* (1869) [incl. biography] · *Christian Leader* (20 Aug 1885)

Archives NRA, corresp. with Jeffrey Inglis • University of Dundee Library, corresp. with Jeffrey Inglis [copies]

Leighton, Stanley (1837–1901), politician and antiquary, was the second son of Sir Baldwin Leighton (1805–1871), of Loton Park, Shropshire, seventh baronet, an authority on economic policy, and his wife, Mary, daughter and eventual heir of Thomas Netherton Parker of Sweeney Hall, Oswestry, the author of several pamphlets on rural economy. He was born at Loton on 13 October 1837 and educated at Harrow School and at Balliol College, Oxford, where he took a third in law and history in 1858. In 1861 he was called to the bar from the Inner Temple, but ceased practising on succeeding in 1871 to his mother's property at Sweeney Hall, where he devoted himself to local affairs.

At the general election in 1874 he was defeated by ninety-nine votes, standing as a Conservative for Bewdley. In 1876, he stood for North Shropshire at a by-election; local tories preferred to put forward their own candidate, but Leighton won by thirty-seven votes with Liberal support. Even so, his principles were uncompromisingly Conservative, and, though preserving a considerable independence of judgement, he quickly won the confidence of those who originally opposed him, and continued to represent North Shropshire and (after the division of the county in 1885) the Oswestry division until his death. His style of speaking was not well suited to the House of Commons, and his influence there was mainly due to his recognized position as a convinced supporter of the established church. He was a devoted churchman, and took a leading part in the establishment of the Clergy Pensions Institution. In the house of laymen he represented the diocese of Lichfield. He also took a prominent part in all public matters in north Shropshire, and commanded the Oswestry volunteer corps from 1871 to 1880.

Leighton visited India in 1867–8 and the West Indies in 1890, but his chief interest outside public life was antiquarianism. He became FSA in 1880, was a vice-president of the Shropshire Archaeological Society from its foundation, and published papers in its *Transactions*. He was president of the Cambrian Archaeological Association in 1893, and in 1897 he founded the Shropshire Parish Register Society. He was an accomplished amateur artist, and made large collections for an illustrated history of the fine ancient houses of Shropshire. One volume, *Shropshire Houses Past and Present* (1901), consisting of drawings and descriptions of fifty houses, was in the press at the time of his death; it contained only a fraction of his collection of materials.

Deeply interested in religious education, Leighton helped to reorganize the school for Welsh children of both sexes which had existed in London under the auspices of the Society of Antient Britons since 1715. The Elementary Education Act of 1870 rendered superfluous its original purpose, and mainly through Leighton's initiative it was converted in 1882 into a school for the secondary education of girls of Welsh parentage at Ashford in Middlesex.

In 1873 Leighton married Jessie Marie, daughter and coheir of Henry Bertie Watkin Williams Wynn, of Nantmeichiad, Montgomeryshire. They had a son and a daughter. Leighton died unexpectedly at 70 Chester Square, London, on 4 May 1901 and was buried at Oswestry.

F. G. Kenyon, *rev.* H. C. G. Matthew

Sources *Oswestry Advertiser* (8 May 1901) • W. P. W. Phillimore, *Diocese of Hereford*, 4: *Stanton Lacy*, Shropshire Parish Registers, (privately printed, London, [1902])
Archives BL OIOC, journal of Indian tour • LPL, corresp. and papers relating to tithes • Oswestry Branch Library, Oswestry, papers • RGS, travel notes on West Indies • Shrops. RRC, sketches
Likenesses J. E. Millais, oils, *c*.1896; priv. coll., 1912 • wood-engraving (after photograph by Maull & Fox), NPG; repro. in *ILN* (5 Oct 1895)
Wealth at death £28,524 7*s*. 6*d*.: probate, 31 July 1901, *CGPLA Eng. & Wales*

Leighton, Thomas of (*fl.* 1293–1294), blacksmith, took his name from Leighton Buzzard in Bedfordshire. The earliest medieval blacksmith whose works, name, and contract survive, Thomas may have learnt his outstanding skills at nearby Dunstable Priory, which, in 1283, produced one of the first mechanical clocks in England. This was work for a skilled blacksmith. The wording (*fecimus horologium*) suggests the clock was made by a member of the community, one who may, moreover, have been connected with the decorative ironwork on the church door at Eaton Bray. The dies used for the stamped foliage here differ in detail from those used by Thomas, but the general arrangement of scrolls is comparable. In 1293 or 1294 Thomas was commissioned to make the ironwork around the tomb of Queen Eleanor (*d.* 1290) at Westminster Abbey and to deliver it from Leighton, for £12 with £1 extra, the latter presumably for carriage and installation. The grille is made of protective iron bars covered with naturalistic foliage scrolls. A very similar design was once at St Denis, Paris, and this is likely to have provided the model. The foliage is formed by die-stamped impressions: identical dies are used on the west and vestry door hinges at Leighton Buzzard and similar ones are found at Turvey church nearby. Leighton Buzzard church was being completed in 1288 and was probably consecrated shortly afterwards by Oliver Sutton (*d.* 1299), bishop of Lincoln. The Turvey scrolls are less assured than those at Leighton Buzzard and are likely to be earlier, *c*.1270–80. Sutton frequently stayed near Leighton Buzzard and in 1290 officiated at Queen Eleanor's funeral. He may have suggested Thomas for the commission, in the absence of a qualified royal smith. Thomas had no direct influence on other smiths—essentially he was the most accomplished exponent of the stamped technique which fell out of fashion in the fourteenth century. He is not mentioned in the 1297 tax assessment for Leighton Buzzard which could mean he was dead by then.

Jane Geddes

Sources [B. Botfield and T. H. Turner?], eds., *Manners and household expenses of England in the thirteenth and fifteenth centuries, illustrated by original records*, Roxburghe Club, 57 (1841), 131, 135, 138 • J. Geddes, 'English decorative ironwork, 1100–1350', PhD diss., U. Lond., 1978, 144–52 • M. Viollet le Duc, *Dictionnaire raisonné de l'architecture*, 6 (1866), 61 • *Richard of Wallingford: an edition of his writings*, ed. and trans. J. D. North, 3 vols. (1976), vol. 2, p. 363 [Lat. orig., with parallel

Eng. trans.] • J. S. Gardner, *Ironwork*, rev. W. W. Watts, 4th edn, 1 (1927), 83–4; repr. (1978)

Leighton, Sir Thomas (*c.*1530–1610), soldier, was a son of John Leighton of Wattlesborough, Shropshire (*d.* 1532), esquire of the body to Henry VIII and MP for Shropshire, and his wife, Joyce, daughter of Edward Sutton, second Baron Dudley. Like Ambrose Dudley, earl of Warwick, and Robert Dudley, earl of Leicester, Thomas Leighton was a great-great-grandson of John Sutton, first Baron Dudley. His career was strongly influenced by family connections, which placed him at the core of the Dudley clientele. It may be inferred that he was a conspirator against the crown in Mary's reign and implicated in the plot of 1555–6 led by his first cousin Henry Dudley. In 1559 Elizabeth I named Leighton, along with known plotters exiled in France, as 'serviceable' and welcome to return to England. In summer 1560 Leighton served as captain of 200 foot soldiers during the Scottish campaign (PRO, SP 70/59/3). He may earlier have fought for Henri II in the war with England (1557–9): in 1563, when seeking to lead a force of 100 lances, he noted 'that is the kynd of servis I have been broght up in and do most love, besides I knowe as well as most men the manner of the servis of the Frenche with all the contry' (ibid.).

Leighton's French language skills, which were to shape his career, probably originated in this period. In October 1562 he served with distinction at Rouen, commanding the English forces sent to aid the Huguenots. At the capture of Rouen he was wounded and taken prisoner, avoiding the galleys or worse by the intercession of Henri, comte de Damville. He was exchanged, only to be named as one of the English hostages upon Warwick's withdrawal from Le Havre in 1563. A recommendation from the Dudleys resulted in a captaincy for Leighton in Henry Sidney's colonizing enterprise in Ireland (1565–7); he also became a member of the corporation for the settlement of Munster. Connections at court brought more substantial returns. Leighton had been named by William Cecil in his list of Leicester's particular friends, which can now be dated to spring 1565, and he was created a gentleman of the privy chamber in 1568. In May of that year Elizabeth sent him to Mary, queen of Scots, and the earl of Moray to encourage a composition between their parties.

Leighton served near Pontefract in suppressing the northern uprising of 1569. He was appointed governor of Guernsey on 14 April 1570 and took up residence, over the years advancing works at Castle Cornet (where he employed the engineer Paul Ivy) and encouraging the island's developing presbyterian polity. The natives persistently challenged many aspects of his government, particularly in the decade 1579–89; generally Leighton enjoyed the privy council's support in these disputes. He also continued in favour in diplomatic affairs, and was employed on an embassy in 1574 seeking to reconcile Charles IX with Alençon. In 1577 he visited the Low Countries to encourage peace between the states and Don John of Austria.

In 1578 Leighton married Elizabeth, daughter of Sir Francis Knollys, a gentlewoman of the privy chamber and first cousin once removed of the queen. His wife's sister Lettice, countess of Essex, married Leicester in the same year. Leighton was knighted in May 1579. The scurrilous *Leicester's Commonwealth* (1584) inevitably characterized him as one of the earl's 'most obliged dependents' (Peck, 105). In 1585 the queen granted him the manor and park of Feckenham, Worcestershire. He was sent to represent the Huguenot cause before Henri III in June 1588. Diplomatic responsibilities did not diminish military obligations, and later that summer Leighton was a commissioner organizing defences and a senior officer of the royal camp at Tilbury. He was made deputy in Normandy to the earl of Essex in 1591. Trusted by the queen to supervise her favourite's military ardour, and prey to gout, Leighton found himself in exasperating circumstances.

Leighton's governorship did not bring unmixed relief. He and Guernsey's royal court once more were in dispute before the privy council in 1597. Again Leighton emerged with honour. He may well have felt some satisfaction in providing a refuge for the eminent puritan Thomas Cartwright, whom he employed as chaplain at Castle Cornet (1595–1601). He devoted other energies to preserving game on the island of Herm; sadly in 1597 this retreat saw the drowning, with his tutor Isaac Daubeney, of Walter St John, son of Leighton's daughter Elizabeth, the wife of John St John. Leighton's other child, Thomas, married Mary, daughter of Edward, eleventh Baron Zouche. Lord Zouche acted in 1600–01 as Leighton's lieutenant in Guernsey. Thomas junior also served as lieutenant, being sworn in on 10 September 1604. The latter died in Guernsey and was buried in St Peter Port church on 25 September 1617.

Leighton joined the council in the marches of Wales in 1601. In the same year he was appointed to the quorum on the commission of the peace of Worcestershire. He represented the shire in the parliament of 1601 where, appropriately given his puritan convictions, he was appointed to committees for bills for penal reform and against blasphemous swearing. The ill-fated bill for prohibiting the transport and sale abroad of iron ordnance touched Leighton's own patent. The stout defence of the royal prerogative made before the Commons by his father-in-law, Sir Francis Knollys, and the bill's failure, cannot have been unwelcome.

Leighton's waning status under James I was symptomized by concessions made to Guernsey's authorities in 1607–8. Less significance may have attached to his military office at the former frontier, and his puritanism may also have lost him favour. He was elderly, and his onetime patron long beyond secular influence. Leighton died in Guernsey and was buried in the parish church of St Peter Port on 1 February 1610. The record of this referred, in French, to his government of the island as 'fortunate'. An early modern interlineation has altered the meaning to 'most unfortunate'. Traditionally Leighton was recalled in Guernsey with just such rancour, notwithstanding his distinction and his contributions to the island's military security and religious independence. In England he is barely remembered at all. D. M. OGIER

Sources HoP, *Commons, 1558–1603*, 2.458–60 · A. J. Eagleston, 'Guernsey under Sir Thomas Leighton, 1570–1610', *Report and Transactions* [Société Guernesiaise], 13/1 (1937), 72–108 · PRO, SP 70/59/3 · Hatfield House, MS 155, art. 28 · Priaulx Library, Guernsey, St Pierre Port burial register; 'Papier ou livre des colloques des églises de Guernezey' · 'Jugements', Royal Court Guernsey, vol. 2 · R. Tresswell and A. Vincent, *The visitation of Shropshire, taken in the year 1623*, ed. G. Grazebrook and J. P. Rylands, 2 vols., Harleian Society, 28–9 (1889) · Shrops. RRC, MS 1060/463 [John Leighton] · D. C. Peck, ed., *Leicester's commonwealth: the copy of a letter written by a master of art of Cambridge (1584) and related documents* (1985) · F. B. Tupper, *History of Guernsey* (1876) · S. Smiles, *Industrial biography* (1863) · G. Adlard, *The Sutton-Dudleys of England* (1863) · private information (2004) [Simon Adams]

Archives PRO, accounts, pipe office, rolls 249, 3551, 3554, 3555, 3560–3563, 3572, 3573 · PRO, declaration of accounts, audit office, bundle 2513, rolls 539B, 540–544 | BL, advice for privy council, Add. MS 48152 · BL, payment, Add. MS 48162 · BL, reput in the cause of complaint of inhabitants of Guernsey against him, Add. 11405 · BL, request for payment for ammunition, Add. MS 22724 · BL, letters to Lord Zouche, Egerton 2812, *passim*

Leighton, Sir William (*c.*1565–1622), poet and composer, of Plash Hall, Plaish, Shropshire, was the elder of two sons of William Leighton (*d.* 1607), chief justice of the Welsh marches, and Isabella, daughter of Thomas Onslowe. Besides his probable attendance at Shrewsbury School (from *c.*1578) little is known of Leighton's early life in Shropshire; by the time he had become established as a gentleman pensioner at court he was married to Winifred (*d.* 1616), daughter of Simon Harcourt, of Ellenhall, Staffordshire. This marriage produced a son and two daughters.

In 1603 Leighton published his first book in London, *Vertue Triumphant, or, A Lively Description of the Foure Vertues Cardinall*. 'Dedicated to the Kings Majestie', this book probably appeared in the first half of that year (though after the death of Queen Elizabeth in March) as it probably precipitated his knighthood, which was conferred at Whitehall on 23 July, two days before the coronation of James I. In this adulatory poem to the new king Leighton describes his admiration for the recently deceased Queen Elizabeth:

> Elizaes losse made wet the driest eies,
> And spred sad sorow through our state and land

but explains how his grief is tempered by his joy at the arrival of her successor:

> But present blisse shone from the glorious skies
> For mightie love strecht forth his holy hand.

After 221 stanzas in this vein, the knighthood can hardly have come as a surprise.

Leighton did not remain in the king's favour for long, however, perhaps in part because of his controversial support for the young Robert Dudley, which in 1605 cost Leighton a hefty fine. Luck continued to fail him, as did his precarious finances, and he was soon sued for debt by Sir William Harmon, and outlawed in 1608, which led to his imprisonment in 1610.

Leighton was probably still in prison in 1613, when he published *Tears or Lamentations of a Sorrowful Soul*—a collection of hymns, prayers, and lamentations expressing his humility and contrition for his sins, and begging salvation and help from God, while simultaneously berating Him for abandoning Leighton in his time of need. It is clear from the prefatory material that this must have been Leighton's first published work since *Vertue Triumphant*. There are prefatory notes and verses by the diplomat Arthur Hopton, John Lepton, and the divine John Layfield, among numerous others keen to show solidarity for their friend in his continuing misfortune.

In his prefatory 'Declaration … to the religious and devoute' Leighton promises shortly to add to this collection 'sweete Musicall Ayres and Tunable Accents, whereof some of the plainest sort are mine owne Ayres and the rest are done by expert and famous learned men in that science and facultie'. And within a year (still perhaps from his imprisonment) he had managed to persuade a number of distinguished musicians and composers (including William Byrd) to contribute work to a new volume, which was published in 1614. Of the fifty-five songs in this collection, comprising the work of twenty-one different composers, the first part consists of eighteen 'consort songs', settings of Leighton's poems for voices with treble viol and lute accompaniment (the first eight settings are by Leighton himself); the second and third parts of the collection are made up of partsongs for voices unaccompanied.

Leighton died—probably intestate—in 1622, and was buried in London on 31 July at St Bride's, Fleet Street.

Daniel Hahn

Sources BL, Add. MS 24489 · BL, Harley MS 1396 · BL, Harley MS 1241 · *DNB* · BL, Cotton MS, Claudius C.III · *New Grove*

Leighton, William (1841–1869), poet, was born at Dundee on 3 February 1841, the son of David Leighton, a master baker, and his wife, Elizabeth, *née* Inglis. He was the nephew of Robert Leighton (1822–1869), poet. When he was in his seventh year the family settled in Liverpool, where he received a good education and became a clerk for a Spanish merchant.

From 1864 until his death Leighton worked for a firm engaged in the Brazil trade. He was rapidly promoted to the position of managing and confidential clerk. He devoted every spare moment to either reading or writing. Leighton began writing verses at an early age and during his last five years he was an active member of literary and debating societies, and contributed poems to *The Compass*, a local literary paper, and to the *Liverpool Mercury*. William Makepeace Thackeray accepted for the *Cornhill Magazine* his 'Leaf of Woodruff', but Leighton meanwhile, impatient of editorial delay, had already published it in *The Compass*. He gradually mastered a smooth and easy style, and his lyrical poetry often evinces a thoughtful piety. Poems such as 'Eighteen Hundred and Sixty-Two', 'The Seasons', 'Baby Died Today', and 'Rose' display very considerable versatility and promise.

Leighton died of typhoid fever in Liverpool on 22 April 1869, and was buried in Anfield cemetery, Liverpool. There is a window to his memory in St Ann's Church, Brookfield, Highgate Rise, London. His complete poems were edited posthumously in 1890.

T. W. Bayne, *rev.* S. R. J. Baudry

Sources *The poems of William Leighton* (1890), biographical preface • W. Norrie, *Dundee celebrities of the nineteenth century* (1873) • Boase, *Mod. Eng. biog.* • private information (1892) [Robert Leighton]
Likenesses A. Swan, photograph, repro. in Leighton, *Poems*

Leighton, William Allport (1805–1889), botanist, was born on 17 May 1805 at the Talbot Hotel, Shrewsbury, the only son of William Leighton, keeper of the Talbot Hotel, and his wife, Lucy Maria, daughter of John Allport of Prescot, near Baschurch, Shropshire. He was educated at Mr Case's school on Claremont Hill, Shrewsbury, and at Wolverhampton grammar school. He attended the former with Charles Darwin, who was subsequently credited with rousing in Leighton an interest in plants. In 1822 Leighton was articled to a solicitor in Shrewsbury, and in 1827 married Catherine, youngest daughter of David *Parkes, a Shrewsbury antiquary. The couple had at least two sons. He later married a Mrs Sarah Gibson with whom he had a son; she survived him.

On the death of his father Leighton inherited a competency, and abandoned the study of the law in favour of the church. He matriculated at St John's College, Cambridge, and graduated BA in 1833. On his return to his native town he deferred ordination in order to draw up a county flora. In 1841 he published his *Flora of Shropshire*, complete with his own etchings. In 1843 he was ordained deacon and priest. He was priest at Lichfield until 1846, when he became curate of St Giles, Shrewsbury. In 1848 he resigned his cure to dedicate himself to botany.

Soon after the completion of his *Flora*, Leighton turned his attention to lichens, a field in which he was much helped by William Barrer, the leading British lichenologist of the day. In 1851 the Ray Society published his *Angiocarpous Lichens Elucidated by their Sporidia*. Between 1837 and 1879 he published over fifty papers or books on lichens, his major contribution being *Lichen Flora of Great Britain* in 1871. He was a keen follower of the well-known Finnish lichenologist William Nylandel, and made use of spore characters in his descriptions of lichens. He was elected FLS in 1865.

In the early 1880s Leighton found the strain on his eyesight too great to allow him to pursue his studies and he gave his collection to the national herbarium at Kew (whence it was later transferred to the Natural History Museum). He died at his home, 2 Luciefelde, Shrewsbury, on 25 February 1889. He is commemorated by the lichen genera *Leightonia trevis* and *Leightoniella henssen*.

B. D. Jackson, *rev.* D. J. Galloway

Sources D. L. Hawksworth and M. R. D. Seaward, *Lichenology in the British Isles, 1568–1975* (1977) • F. A. Stafleu and R. S. Cowan, *Taxonomic literature: a selective guide*, 2nd edn, 2, Regnum Vegetabile, 98 (1979) • *The autobiography of Charles Darwin, 1809–1882*, ed. N. Barlow (1958) • d. cert.
Archives NHM, herbarium and type specimens • RBG Kew, letters • Shrops. RRC, papers on lichens, botanical notes, and extracts
Likenesses photograph, repro. in Hawksworth and Seaward, *Lichenology in the British Isles*
Wealth at death £6822 0s. 1d.: probate, 30 March 1889, *CGPLA Eng. & Wales*

Leiningen, Ernest Leopold Victor Charles Auguste Joseph Emich. *See* Ernest (1830–1904).

Leinster. For this title name *see* Cholmondeley, Robert, earl of Leinster (1584–1659); Schomberg, Meinhard, duke of Leinster and third duke of Schomberg (1641–1719); Kielmansegg, Sophia Charlotte von, *suo jure* countess of Darlington and *suo jure* countess of Leinster (1675–1725); Fitzgerald, James, first duke of Leinster (1722–1773); Fitzgerald, Emilia Mary, duchess of Leinster (1731–1814); Fitzgerald, William Robert, second duke of Leinster (1749–1804).

Leinster, saints of (*act. c.*550–*c.*800), were holy men whose cults are located in south-eastern Ireland. 'Leinster' here stands as the early medieval counterpart to the modern counties of Carlow, Dublin, Kildare, Kilkenny, Laois, Wexford, and Wicklow. Although all or most of counties Meath, Westmeath, Longford, Offaly, and Louth were at times considered part of Leinster, their saints are covered separately in this work [*see* Meath, saints of].

Cóemgen [Kevin] (*fl.* 7th cent.), whose feast day is 3 June, is recorded as the founder of Glenn-da-locha (Glendalough, co. Wicklow). His death is recorded in the annals of Ulster under the year 618, but the entry is an addition made by Cathal Mac Maghnusa, for whom these annals were written in the late fifteenth century. It is recorded again at 622 'according to others'. In the *Chronicum Scotorum* and the annals of Tigernach he is said to have been the biblical age of 120 years at this death. There is, therefore, no certainty of the date of his death. In the ninth-century Stowe missal he is counted among the priests, but because of his ascetic reputation, he was twinned with Paul the Hermit. The uncertain pedigrees of the saint trace his ancestry to the Dál Messin Corb, an early Leinster dynastic group that held sway in the fifth and sixth centuries.

The earliest biographical material for Cóemgen probably dates from some two centuries after the saint's lifetime. There are two extant lives in Latin and three in Irish, dating in their present form to between the twelfth and the seventeenth or eighteenth centuries. The latest in date is like a pilgrim's guide to Glendalough. The earliest life upon which some of this extant material was based may date to approximately 800. Cóemgen is credited with the foundation of a number of churches in the counties of Wicklow, Dublin, and Kildare. His biographers bring him into contact with twenty ecclesiastical figures and in his genealogy his mother and sisters are the mothers of other saints. Much of this information arose as a means of expressing the relationship between his principal church of Glendalough and churches dependent upon it or in alliance with it. In 790 Cóemgen's relics were taken on circuit along with those of Mochua of Clondalkin (a dependent church). Glendalough became the seat of a diocese, its most famous abbot being St Laurence O'Toole (Lorcán Ua Tuathail).

Máedóc [Aidan] (*fl.* 7th cent.), whose feast day is 31 January, was the founder of the church of Ferns (co. Wexford) and patron of Drumlane (co. Cavan) and Rossinver (co. Leitrim). His name, Mo-Áed-óc, means 'my little Áed'; he is also known as Aidan. According to tradition, he was born on the island crannóg of Inis Brechmaige in Templeport Lake (co. Cavan). His father, Sétna, was of the Uí Moccu Uais (a branch of the Airgialla). His mother, Eithne, was of the Uí Amalgaid (Tirawley, co. Mayo). After an education in Wales with St David he returned to Leinster where he established his principal foundation of Ferns. His death is recorded in the annals of Ulster as an addition to the year 625 by their fifteenth-century compiler Cathal Mac Maghnusa. *Chronicum Scotorum* and the annals of Tigernach have it noted at 625 and again at 656 and 659. The later date may refer to a similarly named saint, Áed (feast day 11 April), whose church was Cluain Mór Máedóc (Clonmore, co. Carlow). The latter was a member of the Uí Dúnlainge dynasty of north Leinster, from the valley of the River Tolka. It can be shown that there was a deliberate conflation of the two lives of these saints for political purposes in the eleventh century. From the late tenth century, the main segment of the Uí Chennselaig dynasty based at Ferns was opposed by a rival branch based at Clonmore. In 1040 Diarmait mac Máel na mBó, the Uí Chennselaig king who was soon to become ruler of the whole province, plundered Clonmore as part of a ruthless elimination of his rivals. It is likely that the life of Máedóc was rewritten at the time of Conchobar Ua Laidhgneáin, abbot of Ferns and St Mullins (or Tech Moling: Timolin, co. Kildare), who died in 1062, in order to suppress the cult of Áed. By introducing Brandub, a king of Leinster who supposedly died in 605, it also served to enhance the prestige of Brandub's descendant, Diarmait mac Máel na mBó. The same circumstances probably gave rise to the association of Máedóc with Mo Ling, founder of St Mullins.

By the twelfth century, the centre of Máedóc's cult had shifted from Leinster to Drumlane (co. Cavan, in the diocese of Kilmore). The lives of Máedóc deriving from this area are written in Irish and provide important evidence for the relationship between the church and lay society in the Uí Ruairc territory of Bréifne. In the fifteenth century the centre of Máedóc's cult moved again, for political reasons, to Rossinver in what is now co. Leitrim.

Finten [Fintan, Munnu] (*fl.* 7th cent.), whose feast day is 21 October, was the founder of Tech Munnu (Taghmon, co. Wexford). His four extant lives, all depending on a common original, say that his father, Tailchán, was of the Cenél Conaill (a branch called the Cenél mBóguine, south co. Donegal) and his mother, Fedelm, of the Uí Maine, a people on the River Shannon in the midlands, part of which was absorbed by the Uí Néill. The historically most important part of the biographical information on Finten shows few anachronisms and reflects political relationships in the mid-eighth century among the Fothairt, the Síl Máeluidir, the Síl Cormaic, and the monastery of Taghmon.

An alternative origin for the saint is given by Adomnán, who reports in his life of Columba that one of his informants was a disciple of Finten. Adomnán says that Finten was the son of Tailchán, of the people of 'moccu Moie'. He says that Finten was devoted to studies of divine wisdom and wished to go to Iona on pilgrimage. While he was discussing the matter with a priest of his own people, Colum Crag, monks arrived announcing the death of Columba a few days earlier, on Sunday 9 June 597. Finten sailed to Iona and asked Columba's successor Baithéne if he could be admitted as a monk. Baithéne replied that Columba had prophetically revealed to him that Finten was destined to found his own monastery. He was sent back to construct his own religious house in south Leinster.

Much of Finten's hagiography is garbled, but appears to present him as an arch conservative in Irish religious practice. A letter from Cummian to Abbot Ségéne of Iona written *c.*633 describes how a 'whited wall' (Latin 'paries dealbatus') arose and argued for the old method of Easter dating, after it was thought that agreement had been reached on a new method at a synod held in 629 or 630 at Mag Léna, near Durrow. The 'whited wall' seems to represent Finten: he appears in the same guise in a record of a synod at Mag nAilbe (on the River Barrow), where he was opposed by Mo Laisse of Leighlin.

Fintan [Fintán moccu Echdach] (*d.* 603?) was the founder and patron saint of Clonenagh (Cluain Ednech or Ednig), situated in the territory of the Loígsi (partially represented by the modern co. Laois). Although Fintan's eighth-century life gave his father a different name (Cremthann, Crumthann) from the one in the genealogies (Gabríne or Gabrén), all were agreed that, by paternal descent, he was of the Fothairt, a scattered people, principally of Leinster, to which Brigit was also believed to belong. The family background of his mother, Findnait, is unknown. Fintan belonged to the same generation of monastic founders as Columba of Iona and Cainnech of Aghaboe. His short life has as one of its principal concerns the situating of the saint in relation to these other monastic leaders of his generation. Thus, in his infancy, Columba of Iona is said by the life to have prophesied his greatness. This may be a reaction, in part, to the close friendship, attested in Adomnán's life of Columba, between the founder of Iona and another saint of the Loígsi, Bishop Colmán moccu Loígse, connected with a church a few miles to the east of Clonenagh. St Cainnech of Aghaboe (only about 8 miles to the south-west of Clonenagh, but in the neighbouring kingdom of Osraige) is likewise shown as an ally; yet he also appears as the leader of a delegation seeking to persuade Fintan to relax the severity of his monastic rule.

The terms in which the manner of life at Clonenagh is described suggest that the arguments advanced by Cainnech may have resembled those put forward by Gildas a generation earlier against the more extreme ascetics of his day. Similarly, the description of the mode of life at Clonenagh, although very brief, resembles that given by Rhigyfarch in his life of St David, probably using an earlier source: of the two marks of extreme asceticism in Rhigyfarch's account—renunciation of any use of the plough in agriculture and renunciation of any drink apart from water—the first recurs in the life of Fintan. Fintan's separation from the world is portrayed in the life as virtually complete, and it is clear that this is the rhetorical stance of the hagiographer, though it may also have been the aspiration of the saint. Born in the desert, Fintan was almost immediately handed over to a priest to be fostered and educated; when he founded his monastery, the life makes no mention of any royal participation; kings are mentioned only once—wicked kings who plundered the home of the dead father of one of his monks. The only appearance of the ordinary laity, once Fintan has been born, is as perpetrators of homicide, as the subjects of miracles, or as possible candidates for the monastic life. Fintan's feast day is given in the martyrologies of Tallaght and Óengus as 17 February; this may explain why his obit is given as the first entry under 603 in the annals of Ulster; but alternatively, since the source of the early annals was Iona, this may reflect the high esteem in which he was held by the Columban community.

A somewhat later figure was **Máel Ruain** (*d.* 792), founder and patron saint of Tallaght, co. Dublin, who was the central figure in what historians have described as the monastic reform movement known as the Céli Dé, 'Clients of God'. His feast day, 7 July, is given in the martyrology of Tallaght, completed *c.*830 and reflecting the interest of his circle in earlier saints, both Irish and non-Irish. The versified counterpart, known as the martyrology of Óengus the Culdee (*Félire Óengusso Céli Dé*), is of the same period. Possible supporting evidence that Máel Ruain was indeed the founder of Tallaght (called Máel Ruain's Tallaght, Tamlachtae Máele Ruain, after him) is given by a note in the martyrology of Tallaght for 10 August, 'Máel Ruain came to Tallaght with his relics of the holy martyrs and virgins' (ed. Best and Lawlor, 62). The word *tamlachtae* means a burial-ground but in the eighth century this was not necessarily yet attached to a church. Tallaght is not attested before Máel Ruain; the note may thus refer to a foundation rather than merely to the arrival of relics.

The evidence for Máel Ruain may be divided into ninth-century texts written by his disciples and their allies, and other texts of much less certain date such as 'The Unity of Máel Ruain', a list of his monastic associates preserved in a twelfth-century manuscript. The most important ninth-century text is that called by modern scholars 'The monastery of Tallaght'. This is a collection of the sayings and practices of Máel Ruain and others, such as Máel Díthruib, 'Devotee of a Desert', anchorite of Terryglass, who died in 841. Some of its material also occurs in another collection of such sayings called 'The rule of the Céli Dé'. The relationship between the collections has not yet been fully elucidated, but it is clear that they owe much to the model offered by collections of the teachings of the monks of the Egyptian desert, notably a text well-known in Ireland, the *Conferences* of John Cassian. Historians have seen Máel Ruain as the principal leader of a movement aiming at an ascetic revival within Irish monasticism in opposition to current laxity. They have also seen him and his allies as the originators of the 'culdees' or Céli Dé, who by the twelfth century were widespread in Scotland as well as in Ireland. It remains uncertain how far this picture will stand up to critical examination. It has also been claimed that the Céli Dé were instrumental in promoting vernacular religious literature, and it has been suggested that this Irish revival of the late eighth and early ninth centuries may owe something to monastic reform under Charlemagne. CHARLES DOHERTY

Sources *Ann. Ulster* • W. Stokes, ed., 'The annals of Tigernach [8 pts]', *Revue Celtique*, 16 (1895), 374–419; 17 (1896), 6–33, 119–263, 337–420; 18 (1897), 9–59, 150–97, 267–303, 374–91; pubd sep. (1993) • W. M. Hennessy, ed. and trans., *Chronicum Scotorum: a chronicle of Irish affairs*, Rolls Series, 46 (1866) • *AFM* • S. Mac Airt, ed. and trans., *The annals of Inisfallen* (1951) • D. Murphy, ed., *The annals of Clonmacnoise*, trans. C. Mageoghagan (1896); facs. edn (1993) • J. F. Kenney, *The sources for the early history of Ireland* (1929) • C. Plummer, *Miscellanea hagiographica Hibernica*, Subsidia Hagiographica, 15 (Brussels, 1925) [Société des Bollandistes] • M. Lapidge and R. Sharpe, *A bibliography of Celtic-Latin literature, 400–1200* (1985) • R. Sharpe, *Medieval Irish saints' lives: an introduction to Vitae sanctorum Hiberniae* (1991) • C. Plummer, ed., *Vitae sanctorum Hiberniae*, 2 vols. (1910) • C. Plummer, ed. and trans., *Bethada náem nÉrenn / Lives of Irish saints*, 2 vols. (1922) • W. W. Heist, ed., *Vitae sanctorum Hiberniae*, Subsidia Hagiographica, 28 (Brussels, 1965) [Société des Bollandistes] • W. Stokes, ed., *Lives of saints from the Book of Lismore* (1890) • P. Ó Riain, ed., *Corpus genealogiarum sanctorum Hiberniae* (Dublin, 1985), section 713 [*Lucht Óentad Máele Ruain*] • A. S. Mac Shamhráin, *Church and polity in pre-Norman Ireland: the case of Glendalough* (Maynooth, 1996) • A. S. Mac Shamhráin, 'The "unity" of Cóemgen and Ciaráin: a covenant between Glendalough and Clonmacnoise in the tenth to eleventh centuries', *Wicklow: history and society*, ed. K. Hannigan and W. Nolan (Dublin, 1994), 139–50 • A. S. Mac Shamhráin, 'Prosopographica Glindelachensis: the monastic church of Glendalough and its community sixth to thirteenth centuries', *Journal of the Royal Society of Antiquaries of Ireland*, 119 (1989), 79–97 • C. Doherty, 'The Irish hagiographer: resources, aims, results', *The writer as witness* [Cork 1985], ed. T. Dunne (1987), 10–22 • *Adomnán's Life of Columba*, ed. and trans. A. O. Anderson and M. O. Anderson, rev. edn, rev. M. O. Anderson, OMT (1991) • M. Walsh and D. Ó Cróinín, eds., *Cummian's letter De controversia paschali together with a related Irish computistical tract De ratione conputandi* (Toronto, 1988) • M. A. O'Brien, ed., *Corpus genealogiarum Hiberniae* (Dublin, 1962) • *Félire Óengusso Céli Dé / The martyrology of Oengus the Culdee*, ed. and trans. W. Stokes, HBS, 29 (1905) • R. I. Best and H. J. Lawlor, eds., *The martyrology of Tallaght*, HBS, 68 (1931) • E. J. Gwynn, ed., 'The rule of the Céli Dé', *Hermathena*, 44 (1927), 65–87, 97–103 • E. J. Gwynn and W. J. Purton, eds. and trans., 'The monastery of Tallaght', *Proceedings of the Royal Irish Academy*, 29 C (1911), no. 5, 115–79 • K. Hughes, *The church in early Irish society* (Dublin, 1966) • P. O'Dwyer, *Céli Dé: spiritual reform in Ireland, 750–900* (1981) • W. Reeves, *The Culdees of the British Isles as they appear in history, with an appendix of evidences* (Dublin, 1864); repr. (1994)

Leintwardine, Thomas (*c.*1363–1423), theologian and churchman, was a native of Herefordshire, but his life was substantially that of a fellow, sojourner, and eventually provost of Oriel College, Oxford, and a theologian lecturing in the schools. He was master of arts and scholar in theology in 1387, and bachelor of theology in 1394, and was ordained acolyte on 18 February 1391 and deacon on 8 June 1392. That he comes to notice primarily in connection with disputed elections to the provostship of Oriel, as a supporter of the successful candidate Master John Middleton in 1386–7, of the unsuccessful candidate Master John Paxton in 1402, and as an eventually vindicated candidate himself in 1417–19, probably gives a false impression of his activities: he was busy in the college as dean in 1394 and as an agent for the acquisition of college property in 1394 and 1396. He may have been the compiler of the register of college muniments made about 1397, which was certainly made by a fellow present at a college meeting in 1389. He seems to have lost his fellowship, under protest, as a consequence of his promotion to the chancellorship of St Paul's on 18 June 1401, but evidently continued to live in college, where he appears in the treasurer's accounts for 1409–15, and as a defender of authority against the turbulence of some of the fellows in 1411. In 1417, on the death of the provost Master William Corfe, at the Council of Constance, he was elected by one party of the fellows to succeed; another party elected the logician Master Richard Garsdale, but after a lawsuit lasting until 1419 Leintwardine was confirmed. He evidently resigned in 1421; he retired to St Paul's, and died in 1423.

As chancellor of St Paul's, Leintwardine played some part in the life of the church. Although an associate of the one-time heretic Master Nicholas Hereford, with whom he pledged a book in a university loan chest after the latter was reconciled with the authorities, he showed no evident sign of sympathy with the Lollard party in Oxford or the country at large; but he acted for Archbishop Henry Chichele (*d.* 1443) in negotiations with the university over the latter's scheme for the promotion of graduates in 1417, and was present at the trial of Master William Taylor for heresy in the chapter house of St Paul's in February 1423. He left to Oriel his copy of Aquinas's commentary on the *Sentences* of Peter Lombard (now Oxford, Oriel College, MS 8); his copy of Peter the Chanter on the gospels is now Oxford, Merton College, MS 212. His commentary on the epistles of St Paul was evidently valued by Abbot John Whethamstede of St Albans (*d.* 1465), who had a copy of it made, but is not now extant. Leintwardine is an early instance of the churchman who remained for the majority of his working life a teaching fellow of an Oxford college, a prototype of the Oxford don of later centuries.

Thomas Leintwardine is not to be confused, as by Tanner, with Richard Leintwardyne, a chaplain of William Courtenay, archbishop of Canterbury (*d.* 1396), who was presented to the living of Aldington, Kent, on 1 December 1390, and to Chartham, Kent, on 26 July 1392, and who was appointed archdeacon of Cornwall on 5 April 1395.

JEREMY CATTO

Sources Januensis, 'Catholicon', Hereford Cathedral Library, MS O.vii.8 · Peter the Chanter, gospel commentary, Merton Oxf., MS 212 · T. Aquinas, *Sentences* commentary, Oriel College, Oxford, MS 8 · treasurer's accounts, Oriel College, Oxford, vol. 1 (1409–15) · register of William Courtenay (Canterbury), LPL, fols. 63*v*–65*r* · register of Thomas Arundel (Canterbury), LPL, fols. 107*r*, 198*r*, 425*v* · register of Philip Repingdon, Lincs. Arch., episcopal register xiv, fols. 415*v*–416*v* · C. L. Shadwell and H. E. Salter, *Oriel College records*, OHS, 85 (1926) · Tanner, *Bibl. Brit.-Hib.*, 475 · D. Wilkins, ed., *Concilia Magnae Britanniae et Hiberniae*, 3 (1737), 381 · Emden, *Oxf.*, 2.1131–2

Leiper, Robert Thomson (1881–1969), helminthologist, was born on 17 April 1881 in Witch Road, Kilmarnock, Scotland, the eldest of three children of John Leiper (*d.* 1895), tailor, and his wife, Jessie Aird. He was educated at the board school, Coters End, and at Warwick School, after his family moved south, and he spent a year at Mason

Robert Thomson Leiper (1881–1969), by unknown photographer, 1938

College, Birmingham, before entering Glasgow University's medical school. Although he graduated MB, ChB, in 1904, helminthology was and remained his major interest; he published over 130 articles in that field. This interest was stimulated by a visit to Millport marine station with his cousin, J. F. Gemmill FRS, while still at school in England and by becoming an honorary librarian at the station during his years as a medical student.

After graduation Leiper won a Carnegie research scholarship in biology, which enabled him to examine the Platyhelminthes collected during the Scottish Antarctic expedition of 1902. In January 1905 Patrick Manson appointed him the first lecturer in helminthology at the London School of Tropical Medicine, then situated at the Royal Albert docks in Greenwich. But with such limited experience in the field, he spent the next two years in a process of self-education and research, and did not begin his teaching duties at the London school until 1907. These duties involved teaching helminthology to medical graduates reading for the diploma in tropical medicine.

In those two years Leiper travelled to the Gold Coast to study the Guinea worm, *Dracunculus medinensis*, a nematode worm which causes large and highly unpleasant skin ulcers. He was able to discover the elusive male worm, and, more importantly, showed that infection was acquired by ingesting the fresh-water crustacean *Cyclops*, containing the larval stages of the worm. In 1906–7 he spent eighteen months in Cairo working under the internationally acclaimed German parasitologist Arthur Looss. While there he first learned about the human blood-fluke *Schistosoma*, the cause of schistosomiasis or bilharzia, endemic to the Nile valley and delta; it was the disease with which Leiper's name became inextricably linked. Leiper married Ceinwen Saron (*d.* 1966), a dentist, daughter of William Jones, builder, and his wife, Mary Davies, in 1908; they had one son and two daughters.

In March 1914 Leiper and Surgeon-Lieutenant E. L. Atkinson (1881–1929) arrived in Shanghai to ascertain, if possible, the life cycle of the oriental blood-fluke, *Schistosoma japonicum*, which, unlike the Egyptian fluke, was parasitic also in other animals and therefore susceptible to experimental investigation. Leiper had been sent by the advisory committee of the Tropical Disease Research Fund, and Atkinson's inclusion in the team indicated that the disease had become a concern to British military authorities. Looss, in Egypt, had provided evidence which suggested that the schistosome worm, unlike other known flukes, was transmitted directly from person to person without a snail intermediate host and thus had a life cycle similar to that of hookworm. Although the Chinese expedition was a failure, Leiper visited Japan where he learnt from Japanese workers that the life cycle of *S. japonicum* did indeed involve a snail intermediate host and that humans became infected when forked-tailed larvae (cercariae) from these snails bored through the skin to enter the blood vessels. But with the outbreak of war and still worried about the situation in Egypt, the War Office sent Leiper there as consultant parasitologist, with the honorary rank of lieutenant-colonel, Royal Army Medical Corps. He was required to investigate the disease in order to suggest preventive measures for the British garrison stationed there.

While attached to the British army Leiper showed in a series of papers published in the *Journal of the Royal Army Medical Corps* that the life cycle of the Egyptian schistosomes involved passage through snail intermediate hosts, and he offered advice on how to avoid contact with the cercariae liberated from these snails. He was then discharged from the army, having satisfied his military commitments, but later in 1915 returned to Egypt, where he concluded his work by showing that there were two human schistosome species in Egypt, *S. haematobium* and *S. mansoni*, each with a different life cycle. The former utilized the snail *Bulinus contortus* as its intermediate host, the latter *Planorbis* (*biomphalaria*) *boissyi*. Until Leiper's work, much controversy had surrounded the question of whether there were one or two human schistosomes in Egypt. As a result of this work Leiper was promoted to be professor of helminthology, in 1919, at the London school. In 1924 he became director of the department of parasitology.

Although this work in Egypt represented the highlight of Leiper's scientific researches, there were others of significance. In 1912, for example, he discovered that tabanid flies transmitted the larvae of the nematode *Loa loa* in west Africa. His work was not restricted to the tropics nor to human parasites. He investigated 'grouse disease' in Scotland and in the early 1920s received grants from the Ministry of Agriculture to investigate the parasites of farm animals.

For the rest of his working life Leiper devoted much of his time to the collection and presentation of helminthological literature. In 1923, for example, he founded the *Journal of Helminthology*, and in 1929, as a result of the Imperial Agricultural Research Conference, eight bureaux were formed to collect and disseminate scientific information on agriculture. One of them, the Imperial Bureau of Agricultural Parasitology (later the Commonwealth Bureau of Helminthology), was housed in the Institute of Agricultural Parasitology at Winches Farm, St Albans, which Leiper had acquired in 1925 as a field station for his work on the parasites of sheep and goats and on the nematodes of plants. The filing and indexing of material by the bureau led, in 1932, to the publication of *Helminthological Abstracts*, an annual resumé of parasitological literature. Leiper was also intimately involved in the Rockefeller Foundation's decision during the 1920s to fund in part the building of the London School of Hygiene and Tropical Medicine, which was then opened at its new site on Gower Street. He retired from the London school in 1945, but remained as director of the Commonwealth Bureau until 1958.

An enormously energetic, determined, wiry, and canny Scot, Leiper was a difficult man with whom to work, but he nevertheless inspired loyalty in many of his staff and students. He enjoyed controversies—probably because of his ability to outsmart most people—and was not afraid of making enemies; indeed he seemed to believe that people worked better when social frictions existed.

Leiper was elected FRS in 1923 and FRCP in 1936, was appointed CMG in 1941, and received the LLD degree from Glasgow University in 1955. His expertise in parasitology and tropical medicine led to service on many committees of such bodies as the Royal Society of Medicine, the Royal Society of Tropical Medicine and Hygiene, the British Medical Association, the Colonial Office, and the Agricultural Research Council. He also received the Mary Kingsley medal of the Liverpool School of Tropical Medicine and the Bernhard Nocht medal from the Tropeninstitut, in Hamburg. He also took an interest in local affairs and served on local government bodies in St Albans. Leiper died at his home, Homestead Down, Green Lane, Wheathampstead, St Albans, on 21 May 1969. JOHN FARLEY

Sources 'Festschrift for R. Leiper', *Journal of Helminthology*, 35, supp. (1961) • S. Willmott, 'Robert Thomson Leiper, 1881–1969', *International Journal of Parasitology*, 11 (1981), 423–4 • J. Farley, *Bilharzia: a history of imperial tropical medicine* (1991) • P. C. C. Garnham, *Memoirs FRS*, 16 (1970), 385–404 • *DNB*

Archives London School of Hygiene and Tropical Medicine

Likenesses photograph, 1938, Wellcome L. [*see illus.*] • J. Adam, photograph, repro. in Garnham, *Memoirs FRS*

Wealth at death £46,656: probate, 27 Oct 1969, *CGPLA Eng. & Wales*

Leir (*supp. fl. c.*820 BC). *See under* Monmouth, Geoffrey of (*d.* 1154/5).

Leishman, James Blair (1902–1963), English scholar and translator, was born on 8 May 1902 at Craigard, Thursby, Cumberland, the eldest son of Matthew Shaw Leishman, a tea merchant, and his wife, Sarah, *née* Crossfield. He attended Earnseal School, Arnside, Westmorland, and, from the age of fourteen, Rydal Mount, Colwyn Bay. In 1922 he went to St John's College, Oxford, where, having taught himself Greek, he obtained second-class honours in *literae humaniores* in 1925. In 1927 he took a first in English and in 1929 he was awarded a BLitt for a study of the early seventeenth-century Parnassus plays. He was appointed assistant lecturer at University College, Southampton, in 1928.

In 1946 Leishman left Southampton to take up a university lectureship at Oxford, being made senior lecturer in 1948. He was lecturer in English at St John's College from 1948 to 1960, when he was elected a senior research fellow. In 1963, shortly before his death, he was elected a fellow of the British Academy.

Leishman published regularly, concentrating mainly on the poetry of the early seventeenth century with works such as *The Metaphysical Poets* (1934), *The Monarch of Wit* (1951) on John Donne, and *Themes and Variations in Shakespeare's Sonnets* (1961). Both this last, and his study of Andrew Marvell, which appeared after his death, are informed by his wide reading of classical and European literature. His books and articles were well received in their day. *The Year's Work in English Studies* (42.124) described *Themes and Variations* as 'the most penetrating study for years'; some, especially his books on Donne and Marvell, are still valued by students as good introductions to their subjects.

However, it is as a translator of German poetry, especially of Rainer Maria Rilke, that Leishman will be remembered. He started to teach himself German at Oxford and, initially at the request of a friend who wanted to read Rilke in English, translated a number of poems which were published by the Hogarth Press in 1934. They proved successful, and he continued to bring out further volumes throughout his life. Leishman also translated a selection by another German poet, Friedrich Hölderlin (1944), and in 1956 he produced a volume with translations of thirty odes of Horace in the metres of the original, accompanied by an introduction explaining the differences between Latin and English versification.

For some, Leishman remains *the* translator of Rilke. It is largely thanks to him that almost the whole corpus of Rilke's poetry is available to the English speaker, and he did much to bring about the recognition of Rilke as one of the key voices of the twentieth century. This was a monumental achievement, especially when one remembers both the innate difficulty of Rilke's poetry and the fact that the work was carried out alongside regular publications in his main field. One volume, the *Duino Elegies* (1939), was done in collaboration with the poet Stephen Spender, and, although in some respects it is now outdated, it still sets a standard by which others are judged.

Though never a fully-fledged Germanist, Leishman came to be regarded as an authority on the interpretation of Rilke, even by German scholars. His translations are informed by the meticulous scholarship that characterized his editorial work together with an appreciation of both the technical aspects of versification and subtler details of poetic style such as rhythm, register, and sound quality. Leishman wrote: 'What have I attempted to do? To reproduce the essential. And what is not essential in a successful Rilke poem? Virtually nothing' (trans. from Leishman, 'Betrachtungen', 137). Where this approach is successful, the results can be remarkable, but it has been criticized for the attempt to import German constructions and metres into English. In his study of Rilke translations, Roy Woods wonders, 'If Rilke's rhythm is the tension that results from overlaying an artificial metrical pattern on natural rhythms of speech, how can copying the metrical structure reproduce the same tensions in a language like English?' (Woods, 18).

Leishman was himself aware of some of these objections, appealing to the authority of Rilke himself, who told a translator not to pay attention to those who criticized her translations as 'un-Italian', and commenting, 'There is a lot of "un-ness" in Rilke's poetry, and to fail to reproduce at least some of it would distort the original' (Introduction to *Selected Works*, 23). Many translators have in recent years taken different approaches to Rilke, but that they can do so is in many ways due to Leishman's pioneering work. The best summary of his achievement is perhaps that by William Gass who, after listing what he sees as the faults of Leishman's translations, concludes they are 'the faults of a friend, for J. B. Leishman, more than anyone else, has given us our poet, Rilke, in English' (Gass, 77).

Literature was Leishman's life and, though he was a somewhat dull lecturer, his tutorials were fuelled by his enthusiasm for his subject, and were inspiring; as for his regular Thursday evening at-homes, they were long remembered by students. He never married and, though not a recluse, he was not particularly gregarious by Oxford standards; but he had his regular evening in the common room, with 'his ritual pipe, his Tory snorts at the Welfare State and his appearance as of a genial and benevolent witch' (*Oxford Magazine*). Ever since his schooldays, when illness left him with a weakened chest, he had been a keen walker and, in a routine that not even college meetings were allowed to disrupt—perhaps one reason why he had to wait so long for his fellowship—his afternoons were devoted to excursions on foot or bicycle. In the heavy brown tweed knickerbocker suit he invariably wore, Leishman was a distinctive figure around Oxford, especially when riding out to stay with friends for the weekend, his heavy bicycle loaded down like the White Knight's horse. His summer vacations were generally spent in the mountains of Germany or Switzerland. While returning from a walk near Zeneggen, Valais, Switzerland, on 14 August 1963, he slipped and fell to his death.

MICHAEL MITCHELL

Sources *The Times* (17 Aug 1963) • J. Butt, 'James Blair Leishman, 1902–1963', *PBA*, 49 (1963), 459–65 • J. B. Leishman, 'Betrachtungen eines englischen Rilke-Übersetzers', *Gestalt und Gedanke*, 8 (1963),

137–55 • R. M. Rilke, *Selected works*, ed. and trans. J. B. Leishman, 2: *Poetry* (1960) • W. Gass, *Reading Rilke: reflections on the problems of translation* (2000) • R. Woods, *Through a glass darkly: poetry of R. M. Rilke and its English translations* (1996) • *The Year's Work in English Studies*, 42 (1961) • b. cert. • B. A. W. and J. D. M., 'J. B. Leishman', *Oxford Magazine* (14 Nov 1963), 75 • A. Sillery and V. Sillery, *St John's College biographical register, 1919–1975* (1978)
Archives LUL, translations of Rilke's poetry
Likenesses photograph, repro. in Butt, 'James Blair Leishman'
Wealth at death £34,194 1*s*. 8*d*.: probate, 28 Nov 1963, *CGPLA Eng. & Wales*

Leishman, Thomas (1825–1904), Church of Scotland minister and liturgical scholar, born at his father's manse on 7 May 1825, was the eldest son, in a family of thirteen children, of Matthew Leishman DD (1794–1874), minister of Govan, who was leader of the middle party at the time of the Disruption in 1843. His mother was Jane Elizabeth Boog (*d.* 1874). A brother, William, was professor of midwifery in the University of Glasgow from 1868 to 1894. Ancestors on both sides had distinguished clerical careers, and family tradition claims collateral connection with Principal William Leechman (Leishman; 1706–1785) of Glasgow University. After education at Govan, Leishman attended Glasgow high school and, in 1838, Glasgow University; graduating MA in 1843, he became a distinguished classical scholar and a confirmed bibliophile. After attending the Divinity Hall, he was licensed as a probationer by the presbytery of Glasgow on 7 February 1847, and became assistant at Greenock. From 1852 to 1855 he served the parish of Collace, near Perth, and from 1855 until 1895 that of Linton, Teviotdale, in the presbytery of Kelso. Leishman, while effectively ministering to a rural district, soon became a leader in presbytery and synod. Enthusiastic for the revival of the original order of reformed worship in Scotland, which he thought had deteriorated through borrowings from English dissent, he was among the first to join the Church Service Society, formed in 1865. In 1866 he became a member of its editorial committee, where he worked chiefly in collaboration with George Washington Sprott. In 1868 Sprott and Leishman published an annotated edition of the Book of Common Order, commonly called 'Knox's liturgy', and the *Directory for the Public Worship of God Agreed upon by the Assembly of Divines at Westminster*, which became a standard authority. Leishman later brought out a second edition of the *Westminster Directory* in 1901 as part of the series of Scottish liturgies issued by the Church Service Society.

Leishman graduated DD from Glasgow University with a thesis published as *A Critical Account of the Various Theories of the Sacrament of Baptism* (1871). In 1875 he published a plea for the observance by the Church of Scotland of the five great Christian festivals, entitled: *May the Kirk Keep Pasche and Yule?* 'Why not,' he answered, in the words of Knox, 'where superstition is removed.' Owing to ill health, the winter of 1876–7 was spent in Spain and in Egypt, and Leishman added to earlier studies in the continental reformed liturgies an investigation of the Mozarabic and Coptic service books. A keen defender of the validity of Presbyterian ordination, he joined Sprott and others in a formal protest against the admission by the general assembly of 1882 of two congregational ministers to the status of ordained ministers. In 1892 Leishman helped William Milligan to found the Scottish Church Society to defend 'Catholic Doctrine as set forth in the Ancient Creeds and embodied in the Standards of the Church of Scotland'. He took an active part in the work of this society, contributing papers to its conferences, and twice (1894–5, 1901–2) acting as its president. To a work in five volumes, *The Church of Scotland Past and Present*, edited by R. H. Story (1890), he contributed a valuable section, 'The ritual of the Church of Scotland', which has remained a standard reference. Leishman defined his ecclesiastical position in *The Moulding of the Scottish Reformation* (Lee lecture for 1897); *The Church of Scotland as She Was, and as She Is* (John Macleod memorial lecture for 1903); in an address entitled 'The vocation of the church' at the Church of Scotland congress in 1899; and in lectures on pastoral theology which were delivered by appointment of the general assembly at the four Scottish universities in 1895–7. He was moderator of the general assembly of 1898 at which he welcomed Frederick Temple, the first archbishop of Canterbury to visit the supreme court of the Church of Scotland.

Leishman married, on 25 March 1857, his cousin, Christina Balmanno Fleming (1831/2–1868); they had five sons and two daughters. Leishman's third son, James Fleming, was ordained to succeed him at Linton on 7 March 1895, and Leishman then moved to Edinburgh. There he died at his home, 4 Douglas Crescent, on 13 July 1904; he was buried at Linton on 16 July. At Hoselaw, in a remote corner of the parish where Leishman used to conduct cottage services, a chapel was erected by public subscription to his memory in 1906.

Leishman, whose manners were full of gentle dignity, was described by A. K. H. Boyd as 'the ideal country parson, learned, devout, peace-loving, pretty close to the first meridian of clergyman and gentleman' (Boyd, 670).

James Cooper, *rev.* D. M. Murray

Sources J. F. Leishman, *Linton leaves* (1937) • G. W. Sprott, *The character and work of the late Very Revd Thomas Leishman* (1904) • *Fasti Scot.* • A. K. H. Boyd, 'The new liturgics of the Scottish kirk', *Blackwood*, 148 (1890), 659–75 • *Glasgow Herald* (14 July 1904) • *Life and Work* (Nov 1904) • D. M. Murray, 'The Scottish Church Society, 1892–1914: the high church movement in the Church of Scotland', PhD diss., U. Cam., 1975
Archives U. Glas. L., Church Service Society papers
Likenesses photograph, 1898, Assembly Hall of the Church of Scotland, Edinburgh
Wealth at death £11,474 6*s*. 8*d*.: confirmation, 10 Aug 1904, *CCI*

Leishman, Sir William Boog (1865–1926), bacteriologist and pathologist, was born in Glasgow on 6 November 1865, the fourth of six children and youngest of the three sons of William Leishman (1833–1894), regius professor of midwifery in the University of Glasgow, and his wife, Augusta Selina, eldest daughter of George Drevar, of Rosehill, Blackrock, co. Dublin. The divine, Thomas Leishman, was his uncle. Leishman attended Westminster School and studied medicine at the University of Glasgow, where he graduated MB CM in 1886. He entered the Army Medical Service in 1887, passing fifth into the Army Medical

School at Netley in Hampshire. After three years' home service he was posted to India, where he spent the next seven years (excluding a year's sick leave in 1892–3). He saw active duty during the Waziristan campaign of 1894–5 and was awarded the medal and clasp.

In 1899 Leishman was promoted to the rank of major in the Royal Army Medical Corps and posted back to Netley, in charge of the medical wards. He spent his spare time working in the laboratory of the professor of pathology, Almroth Wright, and of his assistant professor Major David Semple. He was rewarded for this initiative when he succeeded as assistant professor of pathology in 1900. This appointment gave Leishman his first real opportunities for original research, and he combined an existing interest in microscopy with the expansive view of pathology presented to him by Wright. He enjoyed three major achievements in the following three years, and this period established his reputation in the fields of military public health, and microbiology.

In 1900 Leishman identified the causative parasite of kala-azar or Dum-dum fever. However, this work was not published until 1903, when Lieutenant-Colonel Charles Donovan of the Indian Medical Service confirmed the discovery, and Ronald Ross coined the term Leishmaniasis to cover all conditions associated with this and closely allied parasites. In 1901 Leishman modified Romanovsky's stain, rendering the diagnosis of malaria much easier, especially in the tropics, where facilities were often limited. Wright's interest in infection and immunity and his development of practical techniques attracted Leishman's attention, and in 1902 Leishman developed a method for quantitatively estimating the phagocytic power of the blood. In the same year Leishman married Maud Elizabeth, eldest daughter of Lieutenant-Colonel Edward Gunter, of the East Lancashire regiment; they had four children: one son and three daughters.

In 1903 the Army Medical School was transferred from Netley to Millbank, London, and Leishman was appointed professor of pathology, a post he held until 1913. In this ten-year period he continued to work on kala-azar and developed the practical use of anti-typhoid vaccine under the auspices of the anti-typhoid committee. A large quantity of the vaccine was held at the Royal Army Medical College, and within two weeks of the outbreak of war in August 1914, 170,000 doses were issued to the troops. It has been estimated that without the use of this vaccine in the First World War there would have been about 551,000 cases of typhoid, with more than 77,000 deaths; in the event there were 21,139 cases and 1191 deaths. Before the outbreak of war Leishman had begun to investigate pathogenic spirochaetes, and with the cessation of hostilities found the time to conclude his work on the life cycle of the *Spirochaeta duttoni*, the cause of relapsing fever, which is conveyed by the tick *Ornithodoros moubata*. In 1920 he presented the results of this research in the Horace Dobell lecture before the Royal College of Physicians.

When Leishman's professorship terminated at the end of January 1914, he became the War Office's expert on tropical diseases on the army medical advisory board; he also continued his own research work in the laboratories at the Royal Army Medical College for a time. In October 1914 he joined the British expeditionary force as adviser in pathology, and organized the pathological laboratories in France and Flanders. He chaired War Office committees on 'trench fever' and 'trench nephritis', new conditions in military medicine, consequent on stationary warfare. In April 1918 he returned to England, to duty at the War Office, and he was gazetted major-general in October that year. In June 1919 he became the first director of pathology at the War Office. In July 1923, he was appointed medical director-general of the army medical services, with the rank of lieutenant-general. He showed good administrative skills and had already proved himself a very successful teacher and promoter of research.

Leishman was knighted in 1909, and created CB in 1915, KCB (military) in 1924, and KCMG in 1918. He was made honorary physician to King George V in 1912, and a commander (1915) and grand officer (1925) of the Légion d'honneur; he received the Distinguished Service Medal of the United States of America and was three times mentioned in dispatches. He was elected a fellow of the Royal Society in 1910 and served on its council and on many committees. He was elected a fellow of the Royal College of Physicians in 1914, and to his great delight in 1925 he was made a member of the Athenaeum, in recognition of his distinction in public service and science. He was an original member of the Medical Research Committee (later Council) from 1913 to 1923 and was re-elected in 1926. He was president of the Society of Tropical Medicine and Hygiene in 1911–12, and of the section of comparative medicine of the Royal Society of Medicine in 1926, and he chaired the foot-and-mouth research committee at the Ministry of Agriculture in 1924. Glasgow and McGill universities each conferred on him an honorary LLD degree. He gave the Harben lecture (1910) on anti-typhoid inoculation, and the Linacre lecture (1925) at St John's College, Cambridge, on health in the tropics.

Leishman was an accomplished landscape artist and musician. He was also a keen sportsman and sailed a small yacht during his years at Netley. Contemporaries described him as universally liked and respected both within and beyond the military service. He died in London after a short illness, on 2 June 1926, at Queen Alexandra's Military Hospital, Millbank, and was buried in Highgate cemetery three days later; his wife survived him. In recognition of his association with military medicine, memorial tablets were placed in the chapel of the hospital and in the pathological laboratory of the Royal Army Medical College, Millbank.

H. D. ROLLESTON, *rev.* HELEN J. POWER

Sources *Journal of Pathology and Bacteriology*, 29 (1926), 515–28 • *The Times* (3 June 1926) • private information (1937) • personal knowledge (1937) • *The Lancet* (12 June 1926), 1171–3 • *BMJ* (12 June 1926), 1013–16 • *CGPLA Eng. & Wales* (1926)

Archives Wellcome L., notebook as professor of pathology, and drawings, papers, and photomicrographs relating to various fevers, etc.

Likenesses J. Hassall, oils, *c.*1926, Royal Army Medical Corps, Camberley, Surrey • Bassano Ltd, photograph, Wellcome L. • Lafayette Ltd, photograph, Wellcome L. • photograph, repro. in *Journal of Pathology and Bacteriology* • photograph (with Hyacinthe Vincent), Wellcome L. • photographs, Royal Army Medical Corps, Camberley, Surrey • portrait, repro. in *BMJ* • portrait, repro. in *The Lancet*

Wealth at death £7898 3*s*. 10*d*.: probate, 13 Sept 1926, *CGPLA Eng. & Wales*

Leisler, Jacob (*bap.* **1640**, *d.* **1691**), merchant and rebel leader in America, was baptized on 31 March 1640 in Frankfurt am Main, Germany, the first of eight children of the Revd Jacob Victorian Leisler (1606–1653), and his wife, Susanne Adelheid, *née* Wissenbach (1612–1694). His father, a noted Calvinist minister, studied divinity at the University of Geneva before accepting the pulpit of the French Reformed church in Frankfurt am Main. Leisler grew up in a pious, French- and German-speaking household, and later learned Greek, Latin, English, and Dutch. On the death of his father in 1653 his mother settled in Hanau, and Leisler enrolled in a military academy, learning tactics, drill procedures, geography, and law. In 1658–9 the family moved to Amsterdam, where Leisler worked verifying Dutch–English translations for Cornelius Melyn, a shareholder in the Dutch West India Company and landholder in New Netherland. Melyn probably influenced Leisler's decision to go to the company's North American colony. On 27 April 1660 Leisler, recently commissioned as a West India Company military officer, embarked aboard the *Gilded Otter* to seek his fortune in the New World.

Leisler quickly established himself in the fur and tobacco trades with contacts in Boston, London, Leiden, and Amsterdam. He joined New Amsterdam's Dutch Reformed church on 24 October 1661, and served three two-year terms as a deacon. On 18 March 1663 he wed the widow Elsie Van der Veen, *née* Tymens (*c.*1635–*c.*1708), who had four children from her previous marriage. She and Leisler had two sons and five daughters. His wife's stepfather, Govert Lookermans, was one of New Amsterdam's leading merchants. Following the English conquest which secured the colony for James, duke of York, in 1664, Leisler expanded his trade interests and erected a grand house in the city. He invested in real estate, and in 1674 was assessed for taxes as the seventh wealthiest merchant in the city.

Prior to 1689 Leisler played a modest role in public life and did not seek the patronage of English governors Edmund Andros and Thomas Dongan, who governed New York, as the city was renamed, from 1674 to 1689. Resenting Andros's interference in the Dutch Reformed church, in 1676 Leisler protested against the governor's appointment of a non-orthodox minister to the congregation at Albany. Dongan tried to draw Leisler into the governing circle, commissioning him to the court of Admiralty in 1682 and as a captain in the militia in 1684, but as a committed Calvinist Leisler was wary of the Catholic governor and worried about the legality of his appointments. The duke of York's decision to subsume New York within the dominion of New England upon his succession to the throne as James II in 1685, and the arrival of Huguenot refugees following the revocation of the edict of Nantes in 1685 by Louis XIV, increased Leisler's fears of a Catholic conspiracy against the protestant cause at home and abroad.

In April 1689 news of the revolution of 1688 and the fall of the dominion of New England reached New York, raising fears of a possible French attack in favour of James II. When the lieutenant-governor, Francis Nicholson, and his merchant supporters failed to make adequate provision for the city's defences or to declare for William and Mary, Leisler assumed command of a revolt by the city's militia. Suspecting a Catholic, pro-Stuart conspiracy, he secured the city for William and Mary and protestantism. The arrival of New York's replacement royal governor, Thomas Sloughter, was delayed until March 1691. In the interim Leisler governed the colony with a committee of safety, supported by city tradesmen and farmers, and sections of the merchant community. Merchants who had worked closely with Andros and Dongan opposed Leisler and misrepresented his activities to the London authorities. Early in 1690 Leisler struck down provincial trade regulations and levied taxes to garner support and funds for a campaign against the French in Canada, provoking protests from merchants and the leaders of provincial towns. On 1 May he convened the first intercolonial convention ever held in North America, drawing delegates from Massachusetts, Connecticut, and Plymouth to plan the campaign. When the attack went badly he resorted to coercive measures to bolster provincial support for his flagging administration. Following Sloughter's arrival he surrendered the city and, with his lieutenant and son-in-law Jacob Milbourne, was hastily tried for treason and hanged on 16 May 1691. They were first buried near the gallows but were reburied on 20 September 1698 in the grounds of the Dutch church in New York. Contests between Leisler's supporters, who considered him a martyr for protestantism and the city's liberty, and his opponents, who considered Leisler a tax evader and megalomaniac, reverberated in New York politics for the ensuing twenty years. SIMON MIDDLETON

Sources D. W. Voorhees, 'The "fervent Zeale" of Jacob Leisler', *William and Mary Quarterly*, 51 (July 1994), 447–72 • D. W. Voorhees, '"In behalf of the true Protestant religion": the Glorious Revolution in New York', PhD diss., New York University, 1988 • J. K. Reich, *Leisler's rebellion: a study of democracy in New York, 1664–1720* (Chicago, 1953) • D. Merwick, *Possessing Albany, 1630–1710: the Dutch and English experience* (New York, 1990) • C. H. McCormick, *Leisler's rebellion* (New York, 1989) • T. J. Archdeacon, *New York City, 1664–1710: conquest and change* (Ithaca, NY, 1976) • E. B. O'Callaghan, *Documentary history of the state of New York*, 4 vols. (Albany, 1848–51), 2.1–438 • E. B. O'Callaghan, B. Fernow, and J. R. Brodhead, eds., *Documents relative to the colonial history of New York*, 15 vols. (1853–85), vols. 2–5 • 'Documents relating to the administration of Jacob Leisler', *Collections of the New York Historical Society*, 1 (1868), 239–426 • D. J. Maika, 'Commerce and community: Manhattan merchants in the seventeenth century', PhD diss., New York University, 1995 • private information (2004) [D. W. Voorhees, ed., Jacob Leisler papers project, New York University] • J. O. Evjen, *Scandinavian immigrants in New York, 1630–1674* (1974)

Archives New York University

Wealth at death land in Manhattan, Long Island, and 6100 acres in Westchester county; in 1680s acquired control of wife's step-father's estate valued at 332,000 guilders; also owned and had shares in at least nine ships; attainder meant everything was confiscated

Leitch, Charlotte Cecilia Pitcairn [Cecil] (**1891–1977**), golfer, was born on 13 April 1891 at Monimail, Silloth, Cumberland, the sixth of the seven children and fourth of the five daughters of Dr John Leitch (1849–1896), medical practitioner and botanist, formerly of Monimail, Fife, and his wife, Catherine Edith (1858–1937), second daughter of the Revd Francis Redford. She was educated at home and at Carlisle Girls' High School.

Completely self-taught on the windswept links of Silloth-on-Solway, all the sisters were championship golfers, Cecil, Edith (Guedalla), and May (Millar) being English internationals.

Cecil Leitch herself made a dramatic début as a seventeen-year-old in the 1908 British ladies' championship at St Andrews when, although she lost in the semi-final, her decisive and powerful game was immediately hailed as setting a new standard for women's golf. A strong but graceful figure, already with a commanding presence, employing an unorthodox flat swing and palm grip to produce shots of exceptional length and accuracy, she was soon established among the leaders. Her first appearance for England, however, was not until 1910 when the residential qualification was specially reduced from twenty to eighteen years. In the same year, receiving half a stroke over seventy-two holes, she defeated the leading amateur, Harold Hilton, in the first challenge match to test the disparity between men and women players, a result as much publicized on the suffragette platform as in golfing circles. In 1912 she won the French championship, and by 1914, when at Hunstanton she took her first British Open as well as the French and English titles, she was recognized as the foremost woman player of the day and one of the game's greatest personalities.

After the war Cecil Leitch retained all her championships, winning the British on its resumption in 1920 at Newcastle, co. Down, and in 1921 at Turnberry. Her dominance was undisputed until a shock defeat by Joyce Wethered (later Lady Heathcoat Amory) in the 1920 English final. Thereafter, apart from a year when an arm injury kept Cecil Leitch out of action, their duels were front-page news, arousing an enthusiasm unmatched by any successor. The historic final of the 1925 British Open at Troon before a crowd of thousands, when she succumbed to Joyce Wethered at the thirty-seventh hole, was regarded by Cecil Leitch as her greatest match. She regained the title at her final attempt in 1926 at Harlech, thus winning it in each of the four home countries, and retired from competition in 1928. Her record included victory in the French championship five times, the English twice, and the Canadian once. The margin of 17 up and 15 to play by which she won the Canadian final has not been equalled in any major championship. She represented England in thirty-three matches, losing only three, and was an honorary member of twenty-five clubs and five associations. In 1967 she was elected to the American Golf Hall of Fame.

Before journalism was ruled as violating the amateur status Cecil Leitch contributed regular articles to newspapers and magazines on all aspects of the game, and published three books, *Golf for Girls* (1911), *Golf* (1922), and *Golf Simplified* (1924). She served for some years on the council of the Ladies' Golf Union, with a term as chair, until disagreement with its new form of constitution in 1928 caused her resignation. By that time she was living in the south of England, and turned her energies to business, firstly to the antiques world and later as a working director of the Cinema House group, which was concerned

Charlotte Cecilia Pitcairn [Cecil] **Leitch** (**1891–1977**), by unknown photographer, 1914

largely with introducing the first foreign films to Britain. At the same time she allied herself with the ideals of the infant National Playing Fields Association, on whose executive and finance committees she was to serve devotedly for nearly fifty years. Always an excellent speaker, she made numerous appeals and also organized fund-raising tournaments, receiving the president's certificate for her services in 1963 (she became a vice-president in 1967). Her equally long spell with the Kent County Playing Fields Association saw the introduction there of the popular Five Club competitions which she had first devised in 1947 for the Veteran Ladies' Golf Association. She was also on the executive of the Central Council of Physical Recreation and the publicity council of the YWCA. She was an active member of the Embroiderers' Guild. The Women Golfers' Museum was her proudest achievement; on the founding committee in 1938 and subsequently chair until her death, she was responsible for building up a remarkable collection of memorabilia and books. She established it as the only museum of its kind accessible to the public.

Conscientious and thorough with a keen mind and firm opinions but not lacking in humour, Cecil Leitch was often critical but never unfair, and her generosity and concern for others were sincere. Equally ready to support the veterans or to counsel young players, she fiercely defended amateurism in golf. In 1976 she revisited Silloth as lady president to present the British amateur trophy. She was on the platform the following year at the European professional ladies' final. A month later, on 16 September 1977, she died at her home, 20 Chatsworth Court, Pembroke Road, London. Her remains were cremated at Golders Green on 20 September, and a memorial service was held on 17 March 1978 at St James's Church, Piccadilly. She was unmarried. M. S. Millar

Sources *DNB* • D. Steel and P. Ryde, eds., *The Shell international encyclopaedia of golf* (1975) • E. Wilson, *A gallery of women golfers* (1961) • D. Caird, 'Miss Cecil Leitch looks back', *Fairway and Hazard* (April 1969), 42–4 • *The Times* (17 Sept 1977) • *The Guardian* (20 Sept 1977) • *Sunday Telegraph* (6 Nov 1977) • *Golf Illustrated* (29 Sept 1977) • C. Leitch, autobiographical memoirs • personal knowledge (2004) • private information (2004) • Presbyterian church records, Silloth, Cumberland

Archives British Golf Museum, St Andrews, trophies and artefacts • Museum of Scotland, Edinburgh, books, photographs, and papers • Women Golfers' Museum, collection | FILM BFI NFTVA, news footage

Likenesses photograph, 1914, Hult. Arch. [*see illus.*] • Sports and General Press Agency, photograph, 1926, priv. coll. • photographs, Royal Mid-Surrey Golf Club, Richmond, Surrey • photographs, Royal St David's Golf Club, Harlech, Merioneth

Wealth at death £77,342: probate, 19 Dec 1977, *CGPLA Eng. & Wales*

Leitch, Isabella (1890–1980), nutritional physiologist, was born on 13 February 1890 at Lambreck Cottage, Grantown-on-Spey, Moray, in Scotland. She was the third of six daughters (a son was stillborn) of John Leitch (*d.* 1907) and his wife, Isabella McLennan. At the time of her birth her father was a postmaster. He resigned when expected to deliver telegrams on the sabbath, and later worked as a marine engineer. Isabella Leitch was educated at Peterhead Academy and at Aberdeen University, where in 1911 she graduated MA with honours in mathematics and natural philosophy, and in 1914 BSc in zoology. Latin, political economy, moral philosophy, plant and animal physiology, and embryology were among the extra courses she took.

In 1914 Leitch began her research career working in Professor A. Krogh's zoophysiology laboratory in Copenhagen; she was supported by the Carnegie Trust, first as a scholar and then as a fellow. Her work on Mendelian characteristics in beans, metabolism of peas, and haemoglobin in invertebrates earned her a DSc from Aberdeen University in 1919.

After returning to Scotland in 1919 Leitch was unable to find employment in a laboratory so, using her extensive knowledge of languages (eventually she was proficient in eleven), she worked as a translator. In 1923 she was appointed temporary librarian in the Reid Library at the Rowett Research Institute, Aberdeen, where further temporary jobs followed—first as an assistant in the physiology department, working mainly on iodine, and then as personal assistant to the director, Dr John Boyd Orr. In this role, as when librarian, she collated information from the literature and drafted research reports. Boyd Orr was passionate in his aim to make nutritional research a matter of international political debate. A. M. Thomson stated that it would be hard to exaggerate the influence that Isabella Leitch had on what was known at the Rowett as 'the gospel according to Sir John' (Thomson, 'Problems and politics', 317).

In 1929 Leitch returned to the Reid Library where the Bureau of Animal Nutrition had just been established as the first of a number of imperial (from 1949, Commonwealth) bureaux. Originally the bureau simply received reports on the nutritional studies in progress at centres within the British empire, and sent research digests back to them. In 1931 the bureau issued the first volume of *Nutrition Abstracts and Reviews*, no longer a mere compilation of reports but a journal that aimed to abstract all literature bearing on nutrition. Isabella Leitch is generally recognized as having been the major force behind the bureau and its publications for the next twenty-nine years. Her official position was variously designated as assistant to the editor, editor, deputy director (1940–45), and director (1945–60), but to those privileged to work with her she *was* the bureau (Thomson, *British Journal of Nutrition*, 2). After her 'retirement' she worked as an abstractor for a further eighteen years.

Leitch's publication list, spanning more than fifty years, goes far beyond her output as an editor: it comprises research papers, reviews (for example, on calcium requirements in humans), and technical reports, including one on the feeding of camels and another, with W. Z. Billewicz, on nutritional information coded for machine retrieval using punched cards. In 1964 she and F. W. Hytten published a monograph, *The Physiology of Human Pregnancy*, and in 1976, aged eighty-six, she was joint author with A. W. Boyne and G. F. Garton of *Composition of British Feedingstuffs*.

As a nutritional expert Isabella Leitch attended meetings of the League of Nations and, after the Second World War, worked with several of the groups set up by the United Nations Organization, in particular with the Food and Agriculture Organization, being, *inter alia*, a member of its standing committee on nutrition; she also served on the UNESCO co-ordinating committee on abstracts and indexing of the medical and biological sciences. Other bodies with which she was involved included the Medical Research Council and the Agricultural Research Council. A founder member of the Nutrition Society, she was elected to honorary membership in 1979. She served on the editorial board of the *British Journal of Nutrition* (1947–9) and as an editor (for the Scottish group meetings) of the *Proceedings of the Nutrition Society* (1944–7).

Leitch's somewhat frail appearance, which she attributed to childhood malnutrition, belied her strength of character. Of powerful intellect and always forceful in discussion, Isabella Leitch did not suffer fools gladly but she relished arguments with worthy opponents. She was fiercely proud of being a Scot and supported women's suffrage. Once, when one of Emmeline Pankhurst's daughters, whom she resembled, was speaking in London, Isabella Leitch stood by, ready to lure the police away if necessary. She enjoyed good conversation, reading (especially Georgette Heyer's novels), her roses, classical music, and her family, to whom she was very generous; she had no interest in money for herself.

In 1949 Leitch was appointed OBE in the list of birthday honours; the true significance of her work was further highlighted in 1965 when the University of Aberdeen conferred on her the honorary degree of doctor of laws, in recognition of her work for humanity. Appropriately, a building at the Rowett was named after her. She left Aberdeen in 1978 to join her daughter, first in the United States, and then in Australia. She died in hospital on 21 July 1980, from obstruction of the bowel, in Warwick, Queensland, where she was buried in the Eden Gardens cemetery three days later. ANN SILVER

Sources A. M. Thomson, *British Journal of Nutrition*, 45 (1981), 1–4 • A. M. Thomson, 'Problems and politics in nutritional surveillance', *Proceedings of the Nutrition Society*, 37 (1978), 317–32 • J. Boyd Orr, 'History of the Rowett Institute 1913–1945', *Progress in nutrition and allied sciences*, ed. D. P. Cuthbertson (1963), 1–15 • *Nutrition Abstracts and Reviews*, 1 (1931) • Carnegie Trust for the Universities of Scotland, 'Minutes of the fifty-eighth meeting of the executive committee', 1919 • *Aberdeen University Review*, 41 (1965–6), 118–19 • private information (2004) • *WWW*

Likenesses photographs, priv. coll.

Wealth at death approx. A$25,000: private information

Leitch, Richard Principal (*c*.1827–1882). *See under* Leitch, William Leighton (1804–1883).

Leitch, William Leighton (1804–1883), landscape painter and drawing-master, was born in Glasgow on 2 November 1804, the son of Richard Leitch, who had been in the navy and army and retired in 1815, and Elisabeth Hardie. Educated in Glasgow, Leitch worked in a lawyer's office and a weaver's shop, and then as a house painter, but spent his evenings drawing with Daniel Macnee. On 20 June 1824 he

William Leighton Leitch (1804–1883), by David Octavius Hill and Robert Adamson

married Susanna Smellie (*d*. 1868); this happy union produced five sons and two daughters. Despite his lack of formal training, from August 1824 he painted scenery at the Theatre Royal, Queen Street, Glasgow. When the theatre collapsed he moved to Ayrshire, where he spent two years painting snuff-box lids before moving to work as a scene-painter in London, where he lived until his death. Befriended by David Roberts, Leitch worked at the Prince of Wales's Theatre in Tottenham Street, and then (from 1832) at the Pavilion Theatre. Much impressed by the paintings of Clarkson Stanfield, whose style he emulated, he exhibited two drawings at the Society of British Artists in 1832. A stockbroker, Mr Anderden, saw his work and commissioned him to illustrate a book he was writing and recommended that he take lessons in watercolour from Copley Fielding. Anderden paid for him to travel to the continent from the autumn of 1833, and he looked after his family during his four-year absence.

Leitch travelled to the Netherlands, down the Rhine, and through Switzerland to Italy. He studied in Venice but ran out of money and began to give landscape painting lessons to English families. He travelled via Ferrara, Bologna, and Florence, and arrived in Rome by late 1834; here he earned his living by teaching aristocratic patrons, and he met John Gibson, Bertel Thorwaldsen, and Horace Vernet. After visiting Naples and Sicily in 1835–6 and then returning to Rome, he travelled back to London in 1837. Later he described this journey as 'the most interesting part of all my artistic life' (MacGeorge, 57), and he returned home with innumerable studies in oils and watercolour from nature and from old masters.

In Rome, Leitch had met Lord Richard Cavendish who—in addition to arranging for the artist to give watercolour lessons to the earl of Radnor's children—showed his work to the earl of Carlisle and his daughter, the duchess of Sutherland, mistress of the robes to Queen Victoria. She in turn showed his pictures to the queen and Prince Albert, who commissioned two paintings from the artist. Leitch quickly acquired a circle of aristocratic pupils, including the duchess of Buccleuch, the duchess of Manchester, the countess of Rosebery, Lady Shaftesbury, and Louisa, Lady Ashburton. Another pupil, Charlotte, Viscountess Canning, lady of the bedchamber, arranged for Leitch to teach the queen to paint landscapes in watercolour and her lessons with him continued until 1865—she described him as 'a very good simple man', whom she recommended as a teacher whenever she could (Queen Victoria's journal, 30 Sept 1846, Royal Archives, Windsor Castle). J. A. M. Whistler was less complimentary, reacting to a mention of the artist's name with 'Leitch? Leitch? Didn't he teach the Queen—or did she teach him?' Leitch also taught the royal children and later the princess of Wales, who was his last and, by the 1870s, his only pupil; from 1864 he was given an annuity by the queen. Nearly 200 of his watercolours and drawings remain in the Royal Collection.

Leitch suffered all his life from an acute form of migraine or asthma, which became worse with age. In 1854 his health was so bad that he travelled to Rome with Sir Coutts Lindsay, one of his pupils, who found the painter a 'charming companion … [and] an excellent guide': he commented that he had 'never met anyone who could impart knowledge so clearly, or who had so definite a system of art instruction' (MacGeorge, 109). Leitch exhibited five oil paintings and five watercolours at the Royal Academy between 1841 and 1861, but later he painted only watercolours. Of these, he exhibited 220 at the British Institution, the Suffolk Street gallery of the Society of British Artists, and the New Watercolour Society. For twenty years, until his death on 25 April 1883 at his home, 124 Alexandra Road, St John's Wood, London, he was vice-president of the New Watercolour Society; the society held a loan exhibition of his paintings in that year. After his death his remaining works (which bear a studio stamp) were sold at Christies from 13 to 17 March 1884 and on 17 April 1884.

William Leighton Leitch's eldest son was **Richard Principal Leitch** (*c.*1827–1882), landscape painter. 'An excellent water-colour painter and a good draughtsman on wood' (MacGeorge, 112), he exhibited between 1844 and 1860 at the Royal Academy as R. Leitch Junior, at first from his father's address. His *View on the River Limpopo with a Herd of Hippopotami* (reproduced in the *Illustrated London News* of 5 January 1856) was among scenes painted for Gordon Cumming's South African Entertainment at 232 Piccadilly, London, in 1856. He also signed an engraving based on one of Charles Wirgman's watercolour sketches of China in the *Illustrated London News* (1857–8). In September 1857 he was in Normandy painting watercolours for Queen Victoria. Thereafter, especially when his father was ill, he painted extensively for the queen and gave lessons to her children; the styles of father and son are often confused. William Leitch stated that both Richard and a younger son, William, were 'most graciously set a-going' by the queen (letter of 28 Nov 1882; private information). Richard Leitch published drawing manuals in the 1870s and early 1880s and worked as an illustrator for journals such as *The Quiver* and *Good Words*. His wife died a few months before him in 1882, leaving two children.

DELIA MILLAR

Sources A. MacGeorge, *William Leighton Leitch, landscape painter: a memoir* (1884) · Mallalieu, *Watercolour artists* · D. Millar, *The Victorian watercolours and drawings in the collection of her majesty the queen*, 2 (1995) · d. cert. · *CGPLA Eng. & Wales* (1883) · private information (2004) · *DNB* · birth and bap. reg. Scot. · m. reg. Scot.

Archives Royal Arch.

Likenesses E. F. Bridell-Fox, chalk drawing, 1861, Scot. NPG · Elliott & Fry, carte-de-visite, NPG · D. O. Hill and R. Adamson, photograph, Scot. NPG [*see illus.*] · D. Macnee, pen-and-ink sketch, repro. in MacGeorge, *William Leighton Leitch* · Maull and Polyblank, carte-de-visite, NPG · carte-de-visite, repro. in D. Millar, *Queen Victoria's life in the Scottish highlands* (1985), pl. 85 · woodcuts, BM

Wealth at death £20,254 6*s*. 2*d*.: resworn probate, June 1884, *CGPLA Eng. & Wales* (1883)

Leith, Sir James (1763–1816), army officer, of an old Scottish family, was the third son of John Leith (*d.* 1763), of Leith Hall, Kennethmont, Aberdeenshire, and his wife, Harriot, daughter and heir of Alexander Steuart of Auchluncart. James was born at Leith Hall on 8 August 1763. He was educated by a private tutor, and afterwards at Marischal College, Aberdeen, and at the military school at Lille. In 1780 he was appointed second lieutenant in the 21st fusiliers, and after promotion into the 81st, or Aberdeenshire Highlanders, obtained his company in 1782. This regiment was disbanded in Edinburgh in 1783. In 1784 Leith was posted to the 50th foot at Gibraltar, and served as aide-de-camp, first to General Sir Robert Boyd, and afterwards to generals Charles O'Hara and David Dundas (1735–1820), in the operations at Toulon in 1793. He received a brevet majority, and on 25 October 1794 was commissioned as colonel, to raise the Aberdeen fencibles, which were embodied in July 1795 as the Princess of Wales's or Aberdeenshire Highland regiment of fencible infantry. Leith commanded the regiment in 1798 in Ireland, and until it was disbanded there in April 1803. In the same year he was appointed colonel of the 13th battalion of the army of reserve, and in 1804 brigadier-general.

After serving on the staff in Ireland, Leith joined Sir John Moore's army, and as major-general commanded a brigade in the Hon. John Hope's division during the Corunna retreat, where he distinguished himself by heading a charge of the 59th in the action at Lugo on 9 January 1809. He took part in the battle of Corunna, and commanded a brigade in the Walcheren expedition. In the summer of 1810 he joined the Peninsular army, and was at first posted to a brigade in Sir Rowland Hill's division, with charge of the division, so as to leave Hill's hands free.

Leith commanded a body of British and Portuguese, which became the 5th division of the army, in the lines of Torres Vedras and at Busaco. (His account of this action is in the Wellington *Supplementary Despatches*, 6.635–9.)

A recurrence of Walcheren fever necessitated Leith's return home on sick leave; but he rejoined the army after the fall of Ciudad Rodrigo in January 1812, and commanded the 5th division at the last siege of Badajoz. On the night of the assault on the town, Leith's division was ordered to make a feint on the Pardaleras, to be followed, if practicable, by a real attack on the San Vincente bastion. This was gallantly carried by escalade by Major-General George Townshend Walker's brigade, supported by Leith with some other troops of the division. Leith was severely wounded at the head of his division in the desperate fighting with the French centre about Arapiles, at the battle of Salamanca, on 22 July 1812. He was sent home, and in 1813 he was made KB for distinguished conduct at Corunna, Busaco, Badajoz, and Salamanca, where, in personally leading a successful charge, 'he and the whole of his personal staff were severely wounded'. He also received 'honourable augmentations' to his family arms in consideration of his services at Badajoz and Salamanca.

In 1813 Leith became a lieutenant-general, a rank he had held locally in Spain and Portugal since 1811. He rejoined the Peninsular army on 31 August 1813, two days before the final assault on San Sebastian, where he was again disabled while directing the movements of his division. Leith, who was temporarily replaced by Major-General Andrew Hay, remained with the army, on the sick list, for a couple of months, and then went home again. In 1814 he was appointed commander of the forces in the West Indies, and governor of the Leeward Islands. Wellington wrote cordially congratulating Leith on obtaining 'one of the most lucrative positions in the service', but suggesting that he should calculate his expenditure on 'the lowest scale suitable to the situation he occupies' (*Dispatches of the Duke of Wellington*, 7.213). Leith arrived at Barbados on 15 June 1814. He implemented the restoration of the French West Indian islands to the Bourbons; but on the news of Bonaparte's return from Elba, most re-hoisted the tricolour. So an expedition was sent from Barbados in June 1815 under Leith, to secure the islands for Louis XVIII. Martinique and Marie-Galante were reoccupied without trouble, but at Guadeloupe there was sharp fighting before the place surrendered on 8 August 1815, a month after the general peace. For his services then, the British government presented Leith with a sword valued at 2000 guineas; he also received the grand cordon of military merit from Louis XVIII. Leith was made a GCB on 2 January 1815, and for his Peninsular services had the Portuguese grand cross of the Tower and Sword, and the gold cross and clasp for Corunna, Busaco, Badajoz, Salamanca, and San Sebastian. He died of yellow fever at Pilgrim, Barbados, after six days' illness, on 16 October 1816, and was buried the next day. His nephew Sir Andrew Leith Hay was his heir.

H. M. CHICHESTER, *rev.* ROGER T. STEARN

Sources Chambers, *Scots.* (1835) • Burke, *Gen. GB* • *LondG* • *GM*, 1st ser., 86/2 (1816) • W. F. P. Napier, *History of the war in the Peninsula and in the south of France*, new edn, 6 vols. (1886) • *The dispatches of … the duke of Wellington … from 1799 to 1818*, ed. J. Gurwood, new edn, 4–7 (1837–8) • *Supplementary despatches (correspondence) and memoranda of Field Marshal Arthur, duke of Wellington*, ed. A. R. Wellesley, second duke of Wellington, 15 vols. (1858–72), vols. 6, 13 • A. L. Hay, *A narrative of the Peninsular War*, 2nd edn, 2 vols. (1834)

Archives JRL, corresp. and papers • NA Scot., corresp. and papers | BL, letters to Lord Spencer • BL, corresp. with Sir James Willoughby Gordon, Add. MS 49486 • PRO NIre., corresp. with Lord Castlereagh

Likenesses B. Burrell, pencil, chalk, and watercolour drawing, Scot. NPG • C. Picart, stipple (after J. Wright), BM, NPG

Leith, Theodore Forbes (1746–1819), physician, was born in Aberdeenshire, the second son of John Forbes Leith (*d.* 1781) and Jean Morrison (*d.* 1767), eldest daughter of Theodore Morrison of Bogny. He studied medicine at the University of Edinburgh, where he graduated MD on 12 September 1768. His thesis was read on 31 August 1768, and was published by the university press. It was on the delirium of fever, and was dedicated to his tutors, William Cullen and John Gregory. He married Marie d'Arboine in 1776; they had three sons and three daughters. He married, second, in 1789, Lucy, eldest daughter of Andrew Crunkshorn, of Rochester, and they had a son and a daughter. He practised at Greenwich, Kent, and was elected FRS in 1781, and licentiate of the Royal College of Physicians on 26 June 1786. On the death of his elder brother in 1806 he inherited Whitehaugh, Aberdeenshire, where he subsequently moved. He died there from lockjaw, after breaking his collarbone, on 6 September 1819.

NORMAN MOORE, *rev.* CLAIRE L. NUTT

Sources Munk, *Roll* • T. Thomson, *History of the Royal Society from its institution to the end of the eighteenth century* (1812) • T. F. Leith, 'Tentamen Pathalogicum inaugurale de delirio febrili', 1768, U. Edin. L. • Burke, *Gen. GB*

Leitner [*formerly* Sapier], **Gottlieb Wilhelm** (1840–1899), educationist and orientalist, was born at Pest, Hungary, on 15 September 1840. His name at birth, which was registered with the Jewish community of Pest, was Gottlieb Sapier. He was the only son (there was a younger daughter) of Leopold Sapier, a woollen merchant of Pest, and his second wife, Maria Herzberg. (The father also had four children by a first marriage: most other members of his family spelt their surname Saphir.) Leopold Sapier was the elder brother of Moritz Gottlieb Saphir (1795–1858), a renowned German-language satirist and editor. He was also the elder brother of Israel Saphir, a merchant of Budapest, whose son Adolph Saphir (1831–1891) converted to protestantism, moved to Britain, and became a well-known Presbyterian minister and theologian in London. In 1845 Leopold Sapier died and, possibly for reasons connected with the failure of the 1848 revolution in Hungary, his widow moved with her two children to Constantinople. There she married Dr Johann Moritz Leitner (1800–1861), a Hungarian-born physician who had converted from Judaism to protestantism and was serving as a medical missionary to the Jews of the Ottoman empire, chiefly in Palestine, under the auspices of the London Society for Promoting Christianity Amongst the Jews. Dr Leitner adopted his wife's two children, and Gottlieb Wilhelm

Leitner (as he was henceforth known) always referred to him, inaccurately, as his real father. In 1861, in his petition for British naturalization, Leitner stated that he was an Anglican. Although he invariably shrouded his early life in considerable mystery, it was widely known in the Anglo-Jewish community that he was of Jewish origin. His obituary notice appeared in the *Jewish Chronicle* newspaper as did entries on his life in several Jewish biographical dictionaries.

It was as a youth in Constantinople that Leitner's gift for languages became evident; his abilities were so remarkable that *The Times* in its obituary (25 March 1899) stated that 'as a linguist he probably had no living rival in the area of his knowledge'. He had learned fifteen languages by the time he left school and apparently knew fifty at the time of his death. For several years he also studied Islamic learning in Constantinople schools. At the age of fifteen he was appointed first-class interpreter to the British commissariat at Constantinople with, extraordinarily, the rank of honorary colonel. He was a student for seven months at the Malta protestant college and, about 1858, moved to London. He became a student at King's College, London, receiving a certificate in divinity in April 1859. In the same year he became a lecturer in Arabic, Turkish, and modern Greek at King's College and two years later, at the age of only twenty-one, was there appointed professor of Arabic with Mohammedan law. Soon afterwards he received an MA and a PhD from the University of Freiburg. In May 1862 he was naturalized as a British subject. He was admitted a student at the Middle Temple in November 1869 and was called to the bar in November 1875, but did not practise.

In 1864 Leitner was appointed to the post of principal of the Government College at Lahore, and spent the next fifteen years in India. His achievements in that country in the fields of both education and scholarly research were very considerable. He helped to raise £32,000 to transform the Government College into the Oriental University of the Punjab. He attempted, with considerable success, to convince the local government and religious leaders, both Hindu and Muslim, to support Western science and the type of Western learning taught at the new university. He founded a number of schools, literary societies, and free public libraries on the English model, and published journals in English, Urdu, and Arabic. The best-known of these, founded in Lahore as *Indian Public Opinion*, changed its name to the *Civil and Military Gazette*. It had the distinction of employing Rudyard Kipling as an assistant editor, and Kipling published many of his earliest verses and stories in this periodical. In 1865–6 Leitner, accompanied only by one English companion (who died in the Himalayas), conducted a series of important ethnographical expeditions to the previously almost unexplored mountain regions of Kashmir, an area he termed 'Dardistan', recording and attempting to classify the hitherto unknown languages of the area, tongues of great linguistic obscurity. In 1866 he barely escaped alive from an attack by warring Kashmiris. He later published a number of works on his explorations, notably *Results of a Tour in Dardistan* (1877), *The Languages and Races of Dardistan* (1889), and *Dardistan in 1866, 1886, and 1893* (1893). Widely acknowledged in Britain as one of the greatest experts on India's languages and cultures, Leitner in 1876 first suggested the famous Hindustani title of Queen Victoria as empress of India, kaisar-i-Hind, which became the accepted translation throughout India.

Leitner had always been notable as one of the few Europeans who mixed freely with the native Indians, treating them as social and intellectual equals. In 1879 he left India to pursue research at Heidelberg University and in 1881 returned to England, where he attempted to found a centre for the study in Europe of the culture and history of India and the Islamic world. In 1882 he wrote a *History of Indigenous Education in Punjab* which dealt with controversial subjects such as women's education. In the following year he succeeded in purchasing the vacant building of the Royal Dramatic College in Woking, Surrey, and established the Oriental Institute. This body, which by the 1890s was accredited for the purposes of granting degrees recognized by the University of Lahore, trained Asians living in Europe for the learned professions and taught Asiatic languages to Europeans wishing to travel in the East. It also contained an Oriental Museum and a notable art collection. Perhaps its most significant feature was the fact that it contained the first mosque to be founded in Great Britain, the well-known Shah Jahan Mosque at Woking, opened late in 1889 with a bequest from Shah Jahan, the begum of Bhopal, and designed in a charming oriental style by W. I. Chambers. Leitner was a tireless advocate of the fair treatment of Islam by the West, in 1889 producing a pamphlet entitled *Muhammadanism* which attempted to refute the baseless attacks made upon that faith by Englishmen and other Westerners. Leitner's genuine sympathy for the cultures of Asia marked him out as an early advocate of what is now termed 'multiculturalism', many decades ahead of its time. Lacking sound funding, the Oriental Institute regrettably did not survive Leitner's early death, closing in 1899. The Woking mosque was closed between 1899 and 1912, when it reopened on a permanent basis.

Leitner received many honours during his lifetime. He was made a knight of the order of the Iron Cross of Austria, and an honorary member of the Hungarian Academy of Sciences, of the French École des Langues Orientales, and of the German Hochstift. He was awarded an honorary doctorate of laws by the University of Heidelberg, and was generally known as 'Dr Leitner'. He also won a diploma for the promotion of education at the 1873 Universal Exhibition in Vienna, and was an honorary member of many learned societies throughout Europe. He had a number of devoted followers, among them J. H. Stocqueler, editor of *The Orientalist*, who published a biography of him in 1872. Leitner was a man of some means (he probably inherited money from his Hungarian relatives) and, from the 1880s, served as a director of the Delhi and London Bank. In appearance, he was a short, dark-haired man with very prominent bushy sideburns. While some regarded him as headstrong, wilful, and conceited, few questioned his energy or intellectual competence.

In October 1869 Leitner married, in Frankfurt am Main, Olympia Caroline, daughter of Heinrich Schwaab, a merchant who acted as the German and American consul at Broussa, near Constantinople. They had one son, Henry, who became an electrical engineer. In 1873 Leitner's sister Elisabeth married Charles Frederick Amery, an official of the Indian forestry commission. Their eldest son, Leopold Charles Maurice (formerly Moritz) Stennett *Amery (1873–1955), became a prominent Conservative politician and cabinet minister, serving from 1940 to 1945, appropriately in view of his uncle's career, as secretary of state for India.

In 1898 Leitner fell ill and, early in 1899, travelled to Bonn to take the waters at the Godesburg spa. There he contracted pneumonia, and he died at Bonn on 22 March 1899; his wife survived him. W. D. RUBINSTEIN

Sources L. S. Amery, *My political life*, 1: *England before the storm* (1953) • J. Keay, *Eccentric travellers* (1982) • J. Keay, *The Gilgit game* (1993) • J. R. Whiteman and S. E. Whiteman, *Victorian Woking* (1970) • *A history of Woking* [supplied by Surrey RO] • *The Times* (25 March 1899) • *Jewish Chronicle* (31 March 1899) • marriage licence and sister's divorce proceedings [which show the orig. surname to be 'Saphir'] • b. cert. • private information (2004) [Judith Brody, John Keay] • *Surrey Advertiser* (1 April 1899) • A. Crosby, *A history of Woking* (1982), 114–16 • *Woking History Journal*, 1 (1989), 25–7 • *ILN* (1 Nov 1884) • W. D. Rubinstein, 'The secret of Leopold Amery', *History Today*, 49/2 (1999), 17–23 • W. D. Rubinstein, 'The secret of Leopold Amery', *Historical Research*, 73 (2000), 175–96 • family tree of the Hungarian Saphir family [researched for Professor Rubinstein by Family Tree–Csaladfa, Budapest, 1999] • H. A. C. Sturgess, ed., *Register of admissions to the Honourable Society of the Middle Temple, from the fifteenth century to the year 1944*, 2 (1949)

Archives Bodl. Oxf., corresp. with Lord Kimberley • CAC Cam., L. S. Amery MSS

Likenesses bust, repro. in *The mosque centenary* (*c*.1989); formerly at Oriental Institute, Woking • engraving, repro. in Keay, *Eccentric travellers*, 192 • photograph, repro. in Keay, *The Gilgit game*, 26

Wealth at death £17,941 2*s*. 6*d*.: administration, 2 June 1899, *CGPLA Eng. & Wales*

Lejeune [*married name* Thompson], **Caroline Alice (1897–1973)**, film critic, was born on 27 March 1897 at Didsbury, Manchester, the youngest in the family of five daughters and three sons of Adam Edward Lejeune (*d*. 1898/9) and his wife, Jane Louisa, daughter of Alexander MacLaren, a nonconformist minister. Adam Lejeune belonged to a Huguenot family who had settled in Germany; as a young man he had moved from Frankfurt to Britain to learn the cotton trade. Caroline never knew her father, who died in Switzerland before she was two years old; but presumably he left his widow comfortably well off, for the children were brought up without anxiety in a large house with servants and a nanny.

Caroline Lejeune was educated at Withington Girls' School, Manchester. But there were more potent influences, for C. P. Scott, editor of the *Manchester Guardian*, was a close friend of her mother and a regular visitor to the Lejeune household; he was to be the patron and supporter of the career of the youngest child. She was expected to go to Oxford and she passed responsions, then the entrance examination to the university. But she took a dislike to the place and, electing instead to work from home, after taking a secretarial course and working as a secretary, she enrolled in the English school of Manchester University; she left with a first-class degree (1921). She was already writing for the *Manchester Guardian* while she was still a student. Those were the days of the Beecham Opera Company at Manchester and D'Oyly Carte seasons; delightedly she became a reviewer. But she was sensitive also to the younger arts of the period and at the age of twenty-four she took a decision—she would be a film critic.

It was a bold and courageous step. In 1921 there were no regular film critics in England, and certainly no women film critics; the cinema was not yet taken seriously. A suggestion came from C. P. Scott: such work, he said, would have to be done from London. A graduate scholarship from Manchester University paved the way. Lejeune would read at the British Museum, write a thesis, and obtain a PhD. With her mother, a significant force in her career who would settle near her wherever she went, she moved south. By the beginning of 1922 she had a film column of her own in the *Manchester Guardian*, signed C.A.L. Three years later she married (Edward) Roffe Thompson (*d*. 1973), a journalist and later editor of *John Bull*. He was the son of Edward Thompson, a musician. However, she never changed her professional name and it was as C. A. Lejeune that she was to be known. Presently the couple settled, with her mother living close by, in Pinner. In 1928 a son, their only child, was born; and in the same year Caroline Lejeune moved, with the blessing of C. P. Scott, from the *Manchester Guardian* to *The Observer*. She wrote for the paper for over thirty years, making its film criticism well known.

A pioneer, Lejeune was already writing about television before the Second World War; but it is on her recognition of the achievements of cinema that her distinction rests. She came to the post at a crucial time. The screen was still silent when she began; the years of invention and development and experiment were to come. She was there to see the coming of sound and the victory of colour. She was not herself a friend of revolution; on the contrary she was a non-political writer. But she never shrank from the new or the unfamiliar. She was among the few who welcomed the advent of the 'talkies'; she saw Eisenstein's *Battleship Potemkin* in Berlin long before it reached Britain and was quick to hail the startling film with enthusiasm. She also saw the cinema from the other side of the screen. At Pinner she lived within reach of the Pinewood and Denham studios, which were being built between the wars. Her house was hospitable to the great figures of the British cinema; Alexander Korda, Alfred Hitchcock, and Michael Balcon were her friends. In her way she was an educator; she noted the absurdities of a popular medium and she recorded wittily but without malice. Her clear, lively, literate style persuaded a whole generation to look with attention at the creative genius of the screen.

After her retirement in 1960 Lejeune never went to the cinema. She received an honorary DLitt from Durham University in 1961. In the same year she completed a novel, *Three Score and Ten*, which had been left unfinished by Angela Thirkell; her autobiography, *Thank You for Having Me*, appeared in 1964. There had been an early study, *Cinema* (1931), and a lively collection of her reviews, *Chestnuts in her Lap* (1947). She was a home-keeping figure; she never went to Hollywood, never attended the continental festivals so much frequented by later critics. Her final years were spent in the quiet of her home and the garden which she loved. She died on 31 March 1973 at her home, Lane End, Hillside Road, Pinner. Her husband and her son, Anthony Lejeune, survived her, the former for only six months. DILYS POWELL, *rev.*

Sources C. A. Lejeune, *Thank you for having me* (1964) · personal knowledge (1986) · A. Crawford and others, eds., *The Europa biographical dictionary of British women* (1983) · d. cert.
Likenesses C. Beaton, photograph, 1942, NPG
Wealth at death £20,304: probate, 16 May 1973, *CGPLA Eng. & Wales*

Le Jeune, Henry (1819–1904), history and genre painter, was born in London on 12 December 1819, the son of Anthony Le Jeune, a professional musician of Flemish origin. Le Jeune hailed from a musical family, his grandfather and brothers also being musicians. His sister developed an interest in photography, working in Italy. At a young age, Le Jeune expressed a desire to be an artist, and his family encouraged him to study the collections in the British Museum. In 1834 he was admitted to the Royal Academy Schools; there, after obtaining four silver medals in succession, he exhibited his first work in 1840, *Joseph Interpreting the Dream of Pharaoh's Chief Butler*. In 1841 he earned the gold medal for his *Samson Bursting his Bonds*, exhibited at the British Institution in 1842. He married Dorothy Lewis Lewis (*fl.* 1820–1900), daughter of James Dalton Lewis, a lieutenant in the Royal Navy, on 21 June 1844, and together they had five sons and three daughters.

Le Jeune worked in both oil and watercolour. He exhibited eighty-four pictures at the Royal Academy between 1840 and 1894, and twenty-one at the British Institution between 1842 and 1863. Early in his career Le Jeune painted biblical themes, such as the *Liberation of the Slaves* (1847), purchased by Prince Albert and now in the Royal Collection at Osborne House, as well as literary themes often drawn from Shakespeare (*Prospero and Miranda*, 1844) or Spenser (*Una and the Lion*, 1842). In the 1850s, however, he began to devote himself to genre scenes, especially depictions of children, and it is for these works that Le Jeune gained his greatest measure of fame. In 1858 the *Art Journal* commented that, 'whatever merits his other pictures possess, his real strength lies in his representations of those "small folk"' (p. 267). Subjects such as *Early Sorrow* from 1869 (Royal Holloway College) and *Children with Toy Boat* (Manchester City Galleries) from 1865 characterize these works, which were praised for their 'truth, beauty, and natural expression' (ibid.).

While Le Jeune continued to exhibit works at the Royal Academy and the Society (later Royal Society) of British Artists, he was appointed headmaster of the morning class at the Government School of Design at Somerset House. He held this post until 1848, when he was appointed curator of the painting school of the Royal Academy,

Henry Le Jeune (1819–1904), by Maull & Polyblank

an office that allowed him to teach painting. Le Jeune held this post until 1863. That year he was elected an associate of the Royal Academy, and although he never achieved the rank of academician, in 1886 he was named an honorary retired associate.

Le Jeune remained in London his entire life, retiring to Hampstead about 1864. He died at his home, 155 Goldhurst Terrace, Hampstead, on 5 October 1904, and was buried at Kensal Green cemetery. MORNA O'NEILL

Sources J. D. Champlin and C. C. Perkins, eds., *Cyclopedia of painters and paintings*, 4 vols. (1888) · 'British artists, their style and character: no. XXXVIII, Henry Le Jeune', *Art Journal*, 20 (1858), 265–7 · *WW* (1905) · Graves, *Brit. Inst.* · J. Chapel, *Victorian taste: the complete catalogue of paintings at the Royal Holloway College* (1982) · O. Millar, *The queen's pictures* (1977) · C. E. Clement and L. Hutton, *Artists of the nineteenth century and their works: a handbook containing two thousand and fifty biographical sketches*, rev. edn, 2 vols. in 1 (Boston, MA, 1884) · Bryan, *Painters* (1876) · Wood, *Vic. painters*, 3rd edn · A. G. Temple, *Art of painting in the queen's reign* (1897) · *Men of the time* (1872) · *Concise catalogue of British paintings*, Man. City Gall., 2 vols. (1976–8) · J. Johnson, ed., *Works exhibited at the Royal Society of British Artists, 1824–1893, and the New English Art Club, 1888–1917*, 2 vols. (1975) · m. cert. · *CGPLA Eng. & Wales* (1904)
Likenesses Elliott & Fry, photograph, NPG · Lock & Whitfield, carte-de-visite, NPG · Maull & Polyblank, carte-de-visite, NPG [*see illus.*] · wood-engraving, NPG; repro. in *ILN* (27 July 1863)
Wealth at death £1383 18*s*. 9*d*.: probate, 24 Oct 1904, *CGPLA Eng. & Wales*

Le Keux family (*per.* 1800–1885), engravers, came to prominence with **John Le Keux** (1783–1846), engraver, who was born in Sun Street, Bishopsgate, London, on 4 June 1783, and baptized, at St Botolph without Bishopsgate, in September, the son of Anne, *née* Dyer, and Peter Le Keux, a wholesale pewter manufacturer who came from a large and flourishing Huguenot family. While apprenticed to his father John Le Keux began experiments in engraving on the quart pots of London publicans and, in 1800, turned his attention to copperplate. Some of his drawings were praised by James Basire II (1769–1822), the engraver to whom his younger brother Henry [*see below*] was already apprenticed, and he was consequently transferred to Basire by his father for the remaining four years of his apprenticeship. Under Basire he acquired that peculiar skill in architectural engraving which characterized his work, developing a very fine yet free style in the linear manner. John Le Keux married Sara Sophia, daughter of John Lingard, on 27 September 1809, at St Mary's, Lambeth; their son John Henry Le Keux [*see below*] inherited his father's skill in engraving.

The publications of John Britton generated much of John Le Keux's best work from the outset of his career, and it in turn contributed very largely to the success of those volumes. He produced several of the plates for *Architectural Antiquities of Great Britain* (1807–26), 400 plates for *Cathedral Antiquities of Great Britain* (1814–35), and an even greater number, after various artists, for *A Dictionary of the Architecture and Archaeology of the Middle Ages* (1836–9). Of equal importance was his contribution to publications illustrated by A. C. Pugin, including *Specimens of Gothic Architecture* (1821–3) and *Examples of Gothic Architecture* (1831–6), both written by E. J. Willson. With his brother Henry he engraved Pugin's illustrations to *Engraved Specimens of the Architectural Antiquities of Normandy*, edited by Britton (1828). Other architectural subjects included engravings after J. P. Neale for *Abbey Church of St Peter, Westminster* (1818–23), with a text by E. W. Brayley, and for *Views of the most Interesting Collegiate and Parochial Churches in Great Britain*, the first volume of which was co-written by John Le Keux and J. P. Neale (1824–5). His engravings after Frederick Mackenzie for James Ingram's *Memorials of Oxford* (1837) sparked his own publication *Memorials of Cambridge*, with plates after Mackenzie and J. A. Bell, and a text by Thomas Wright and the Revd Harry Longueville Jones (1841–2); some of these plates were subsequently used for C. H. Cooper's *Memorials of Cambridge* (1860–66). Of the *Memorials of Oxford* 'an early reviewer noted approvingly that the publication of views of Oxford's "halls of learning imposes a check upon future innovators"' (*Hist. U. Oxf.* 6: *19th-cent. Oxf.*, xvii).

Le Keux also engraved two plates after J. M. W. Turner: *Rome from the Farnese Gardens* for James Hakewill's *A Picturesque Tour of Italy* (1818–20) and *St Agatha's Abbey, Easby*, for T. D. Whitaker's *An History of Richmondshire* (1823).

John Le Keux died on 2 April 1846, and was buried at Bunhill Fields cemetery, London. The poet and humorist Thomas Hood was apprenticed to John Le Keux and his brother Henry. Lionel Cust mentioned that John Le Keux 'may be considered, perhaps, the best engraver of his day in the somewhat mechanical style then in vogue' (*DNB*). Le Keux often worked for up to sixteen hours a day. Nineteenth-century commentators had noted the important contribution his atmospheric architectural engravings made to the revival of Gothic architecture in Britain. These have remained popular and are often reproduced. It is for his fine engravings of Gothic and Gothic revival architecture that John Le Keux is chiefly remembered.

Henry Le Keux (1787–1868), engraver, was born on 13 June 1787, and baptized at St Dunstan's, Stepney, the younger brother of John Le Keux. As apprentice to the younger James Basire, Henry Le Keux worked on the *Oxford Almanack* and on plates for the Society of Antiquaries. Then, about 1808, he established himself as an architectural engraver by contributing to such of Britton's publications as *The Beauties of England and Wales* (1801–18). Associated with his brother John in some of his architectural work, he contributed to *Cathedral Antiquities of Great Britain*, and produced the famed plate *The Interior of Henry VII's Chapel* for J. P. Neale's *Westminster Abbey*. He also collaborated with Edward Blore, engraving several fine plates for his *Monumental Remains* (1826), of which publication he was part proprietor.

Henry Le Keux was equally known as an engraver of illustrations to literary works. His work after J. M. W. Turner includes seven plates for Sir Walter Scott's *Provincial Antiquities* (1826) and two for Scott's *Poetical Works* (1834), two rare steel plates for Samuel Rogers's *Italy* (1830), and *St Herbert's Island* for Rogers's *Poems* (1834), the last of which he considered his finest achievement. His engravings after John Martin appeared in various of the fashionable annuals, including *Forget-me-Not* (1829) and *The Keepsake* (1832).

As a mature engraver Henry Le Keux returned to work on the *Oxford Almanack*, advising on the change to steel engraving and then engraving five issues (1832–9). In 1838 he was consulted by the Bank of England, together with Henry Corbould and William Wyon, regarding a new design of banknote. He then retired from engraving and moved to Bocking in Essex, where he worked for Samuel Courtauld & Co., crape manufacturers, until a short time before his death. As a member of the Associated Society of Engravers he engraved some paintings by Canaletto and Claude in the National Gallery, his last work being after the latter's *Embarkation of St Ursula* (1846). He died, apparently unmarried, after a short illness on 11 October 1868, and was buried at Halstead, Essex. While he did not attain quite the same degree of proficiency as his brother, Henry Le Keux engraved the whole of his plates himself, without the assistance of pupils.

John Henry Le Keux (1812–1896), engraver and illustrator, was born in Argyll Street, Euston Road, London, on 23 March 1812, the son of John and Sara Le Keux. He studied under James Basire III (1796–1869) before assisting his father and adopting his style. His first independent plate was engraved in 1832, after Samuel Prout's *City and Bridge of Prague*, for the annual *Continental*.

J. H. Le Keux made his name as an architectural engraver

during the 1830s on such publications as George Godwin's *A Short Account of the Temple Church, London* (1837), illustrated by R. W. Billings, and *The Travellers' Club House* (1839), illustrated by J. Hewitt. However, his most significant achievements in the medium were produced two decades later, when he began to work with John Ruskin on the author's illustrations to *The Stones of Venice* (1851–3) and *Modern Painters* (1856–60). Ruskin became friendly with Le Keux and paid him to teach line-engraving to George Allen, his assistant and publisher; in 1890 Allen received Le Keux's engraving tools. During the same period he also engraved plates for C. H. Hartshorne's *Illustrations of Alnwick, Prudhoe, and Warkworth* (1857), after T. O. S. Jewitt's illustrations, and J. H. Parker's *Mediaeval Architecture of Chester* (1858). At the close of the decade the Norwegian government employed him to execute thirty-one large plates of Trondheim Cathedral, after illustrations by F. W. Schiertz and H. E. Schirmer; they were published in 1859 with an accompanying text by Peter Andreas Munch. A talented draughtsman, J. H. Le Keux exhibited architectural drawings at the Royal Academy (1853–65) and engraved plates after his own designs for the *Oxford Almanack* (1855–70). He also wrote several papers on medieval armour and ornamental metalwork, which appeared in the *Journal of the Archaeological Institute* and the proceedings of other antiquarian societies.

On 23 June 1841 J. H. Le Keux patented an improvement in line-engraving whereby two steel or copper plates were employed, one carrying the subject, the other a 'ground'. Colour could be used, and two or more plates employed. It is uncertain why he never made use of this commercially, though it has been variously suggested that it was too expensive or time-consuming, and that it would interfere with high-quality engraving.

On 16 April 1863 Le Keux married Frances Andrews, and a year later he moved to Durham. There he acted as manager to a firm of publishers and booksellers with which his wife was connected. He continued to produce engravings and paint in watercolours for his own amusement into his seventies. He died at his home, 26 Old Elvet, Durham, on 4 February 1896, and was buried in St Nicholas's Church in that city. DAVID WOOTTON

Sources B. Hunnisett, *An illustrated dictionary of British steel engravers*, new edn (1989), 59–60 · Boase, *Mod. Eng. biog.* · *DNB* · *GM*, 2nd ser., 25 (1846), 224 · *GM*, 280 (1896), 647 · Redgrave, *Artists* · *The Athenaeum* (15 Feb 1896), 224 · C. Knight, ed., *Biography*, 3 (1856) · J. F. Waller, ed., *The imperial dictionary of universal biography*, 3 vols. (1857–63) · Ward, *Men of the reign*, vol. 2, p. 535 · H. M. Petter, *The Oxford almanacks* (1974) · *Hist. U. Oxf.* 6: *19th-cent. Oxf.* · *CGPLA Eng. & Wales* (1868) · *CGPLA Eng. & Wales* (1896) · S. Houfe, *The dictionary of 19th century British book illustrators and caricaturists*, rev. edn (1996)
Archives BL, corresp. [John Le Keux, John Henry Le Keux, Henry Le Keux] · V&A NAL, corresp. [John Le Keux, Henry Le Keux, John Henry Le Keux] · Yale U., Beinecke L., corresp. [John Le Keux, Henry Le Keux]
Likenesses Hills & Saunders, carte-de-visite (John Henry Le Keux), NPG
Wealth at death under £1000—Henry Le Keux: probate, 31 Oct 1868, *CGPLA Eng. & Wales* · £179 4s. 1d.—J. H. Le Keux: probate, 6 Aug 1896, *CGPLA Eng. & Wales*

Le Keux, Henry (1787–1868). *See under* Le Keux family (*per.* 1800–1885).

Le Keux, John (1783–1846). *See under* Le Keux family (*per.* 1800–1885).

Le Keux, John Henry (1812–1896). *See under* Le Keux family (*per.* 1800–1885).

Lekeux, Peter (1648–1723), master weaver, was born in Canterbury, Kent, the third son of John Lekeux, weaver, and Antoine Le Quien. The Lekeux were a well-established family of weavers, who had first gone to Canterbury as Huguenot refugees in the late sixteenth century. Peter served his apprenticeship in Canterbury, then moved to London, being admitted to the Weavers' Company in 1675. He married Marie (*d.* 1723), the daughter of Pierre Marescaux (Peter Marescoe), on 7 August 1681. As Marescaux was one of the leading master weavers in the rapidly expanding London silk industry, and a man of some wealth, it was an influential alliance for Lekeux's career, and on Marescaux's death in 1710 he inherited considerable property and one third of his estate.

Peter Lekeux was the first of three master weavers of the same name to play a leading role in the Weavers' Company, making the Lekeux family among the most important in the English silk industry for nearly 100 years. In 1692 he was a founder member of the Royal Lustring Company, a joint-stock company set up to weave lustrings, glazed silks whose production and trade was previously a French monopoly. Its success was such that in 1695 legislation was proposed seeking to break the monopoly the company had rapidly established, Lekeux petitioning the House of Lords against the bill. He was active, too, on behalf of the Weavers' Company, helping to formulate its policy and standing as its spokesman in giving parliamentary evidence. A man of wide experience both of the London industry and overseas trade, he was as confident in presenting a detailed memorandum to the House of Lords on trade with Italy and Portugal as he was in explaining to the commissioners for trades and plantations what kinds of textiles were made in the different regions of England. His evidence was particularly significant during the anti-calico campaign of 1719–20, an episode of vigorous lobbying by members of the silk and woollen industries which helped to secure legislation prohibiting the sale, use, and wear of printed calico.

Peter Lekeux bore the title of colonel, indicating his rank between 1710 and 1722 in the Tower Hamlets regiment of the London trained bands (in which he had served as captain from 1691 to 1697, and major from 1697 to 1708). He also served as a justice of the peace, commissioner of sewers, and commissioner for land tax in the county of Middlesex. At his death in Stepney, Middlesex, in 1723 he was able to leave substantial property to his sons and grandsons, but none appears to have entered the silk trade.

Peter Lekeux (*bap.* 1684, *d.* 1743), one of the executors of Lekeux's will, was his nephew; he was baptized on 17 February 1684 at the French church, Threadneedle Street,

London, the son of his elder brother John (*b.* 1647) and Susannah Didier (*d.* 1719). He had been apprenticed as a silk weaver in 1703 at the late age of nineteen, made free in January 1712, and later the same year went on to the livery of the Weavers' Company. This was the start of a long association which saw him become an upper warden of the company in 1728 and be elected to the court of assistants, the governing body, in 1734. His activity on company business included fighting legislation against the wearing of materials containing precious metal, the last attempt at sumptuary legislation in England, shortly before his death in London on 20 June 1743. He bore the rank of captain in the London trained bands. Peter Lekeux had married Sarah Bloodworth on 29 July 1712 and of their four children he left a sum to his son Peter 'in consideration of the care and management of his father's business' (will, fol. 78).

Peter Lekeux (1716–1768) had been apprenticed to his father in February 1730. He was not made free until 1745, perhaps because he had been working exclusively for his father, but joined the livery of the Weavers' Company immediately, and rose in its ranks to reach the highest office, upper bailiff, in July 1764. Also a distinguished master weaver in the London silk industry, living and working throughout his life in or close to Spitalfields, he left all his property at his death in London on 9 December 1768 to his wife, probably called Mary, naming no children or partners to continue his business. CLARE BROWNE

Sources P. K. Thornton and N. Rothstein, 'The importance of the Huguenots in the London silk industry', *Proceedings of the Huguenot Society*, 20 (1958–64), 60–94 • N. Rothstein, *Silk designs of the eighteenth century: in the collection of the Victoria and Albert Museum, London, with a complete catalogue* (1990) • N. Rothstein, 'The calico campaign of 1719–1721', *East London Papers*, 7 (1964), 3–21 • D. C. A. Agnew, *Protestant exiles from France in the reign of Louis XIV, or, The Huguenot refugees and their descendants in Great Britain and Ireland*, 2nd edn, 1 (1871) • will, PRO, PROB 11/590, fol. 78

Wealth at death £1440 goods and bequests; also substantial property in London: will, PRO, PROB 11/590, fol. 78

Lekeux, Peter (*bap.* **1684**, *d.* **1743**). *See under* Lekeux, Peter (1648–1723).

Lekeux, Peter (**1716–1768**). *See under* Lekeux, Peter (1648–1723).

Lekpreuik [Lekprevick]**, Robert** (*fl.* **1561–1581**), printer, worked primarily in Edinburgh. A Robert Lekpreuik was banished for life on 8 August 1532 for 'unspecified offences', but Lekpreuik's known career in the book trade began in 1561 with his printing of the Scots confession (Durkan, 'Heresy', 364). Throughout the 1560s and early 1570s his press was by far the most productive in Scotland, surpassing the incumbent printer John Scot, and being aided by support from the general assembly, beginning with a £200 loan for printing the Psalms (which appeared in 1564). Lekpreuik proved his usefulness to the kirk by producing *The Forme of Prayers* (1562), a protestant service book based on Genevan practice, along with three polemics against Quintin Kennedy in 1563, one by John Knox. In the following year he attained financial security, as well as roman type fonts, through a contract with Alexander Clerk. Further material for the kirk followed, notably an edition of the service book which included the metrical Psalms and Calvin's catechism (1564); John Carswell's translation of this work into Gaelic, the *Foirm na nurrnuidheadh* (1567), the first Scottish Gaelic publication; and the *Ordour and Doctrine of the Generall Faste* (1566). In 1565 Lekpreuik was authorized to print parliamentary records, and to this governmental work he added other commissions, including an epithalamion on the wedding of Mary and Darnley (1565).

With the outbreak of civil war Lekpreuik sided with the 'king's men', and by 14 January 1568 he was designated 'our soverane lordis imprentar', being given exclusive rights to print all official material for twenty years, with a £200 fine for violators (Livingstone and others, 6.28). On 14 April Lekpreuik was given similar rights to the Geneva Bible, though he never completed an edition. Support from the kirk continued with a £50 pension in 1570, and Lekpreuik continued to print other commissions, including Henryson's translation of Aesop (1570), Blind Harry's *Wallace* (1570), and Barbour's *Bruce* (1571), all funded by Henry Charteris.

Lekpreuik was cautioned by the Edinburgh council on 2 June 1570 for printing books (probably items by Robert Sempill) without its licence, and by 14 April 1571 he was forced to flee his premises at Netherbow in the city when Maitland of Lethington, suspecting him of planning to print George Buchanan's satire 'Chamaeleon', sent men from the castle to apprehend him. Lekpreuik spent a few months in Stirling, then moved to St Andrews, all the while printing material in favour of the infant James VI, including Buchanan's *Admonition* (1571) and *[D]Etectioun of … Marie Quene of Scottis* (1572). In April 1572 Lekpreuik was cautioned by the regent, Morton, to cease printing uncensored material.

By January 1574 Lekpreuik was back in Edinburgh, where he printed John Davidson's controversial *Dialog … Betuix a Clerk and ane Courteour*. This led quickly to his prosecution under a 1552 act concerning printers, and he was imprisoned in Edinburgh for between four and seven years. In 1577 he was left £20 by the printer and bookseller Thomas Bassendyne, who died that year and had for some time previously been providing Lekpreuik with an annual pension of 10 merks, and in 1580 he brought a process against the English printer Robert Wodehouse. Lekpreuik produced several works in 1581, including a lament for Morton and a catechism by Patrick Adamson, for whom he had printed earlier in St Andrews. A work by John Colville dated 1582 may have come from Lekpreuik's press, but otherwise he printed nothing further. A deceased Robert Lekpreuik is mentioned in a reversion from 1581, but this was probably not the printer.

Lekpreuik was not only a printer, but also a bookbinder and bookseller, operating as the latter from his home in the Netherbow; where he learned these skills is unknown. As Lekpreuik accepted a few 'commissions from court Catholics' in the mid-1560s, his press was not guided strictly by protestant convictions, but his attachment to the reformed kirk is clear from his overall work, particularly Davidson's 1574 poem, which he must have known would put him at risk (Mann, 151). A printer with a wide range of commissions, Lekpreuik was important above all to the formative kirk.

T. F. Henderson, *rev.* Martin Holt Dotterweich

Sources H. G. Aldis, *A list of books printed in Scotland before 1700*, rev. edn (1970) [updated currently at the NL Scot. (www.nls.uk/catalogues/resources/scotbooks/intro.html)] · M. Livingstone, D. Hay Fleming, and others, eds., *Registrum secreti sigilli regum Scotorum / The register of the privy seal of Scotland*, 6 (1963), 28, 53, 186, 388 · C. T. McInnes, ed., *Accounts of the treasurer of Scotland*, 12 (1970), 312, 380 · R. Dickson and J. P. Edmond, *Annals of Scottish printing* (1890), 198–272 · A. Mann, *The Scottish book trade, 1500–1720* (2000) · J. Durkan, 'Contract between Clerk and Lekpreuik for printing the Book of Common Order, 1564', *The Bibliothek*, 11 (1983), 129–35 · T. Thomson, ed., *Acts and proceedings of the general assemblies of the Kirk of Scotland*, 3 pts, Bannatyne Club, 81 (1839–45), 1.164 · W. Scott and D. Laing, eds., *The Bannatyne miscellany*, 3 vols., Bannatyne Club, 19–19b (1827–55), vol. 2, pp. 202–3 · *APS*, *1424–1567*, 488–9; *1567–92*, 249 · J. Durkan, 'Heresy in Scotland: the second phase', *Records of the Scottish Church History Society*, 24 (1990–92), 342–3

Leland, John, the elder. *See* Leylond, John (*d.* 1428).

Leland, John (*c.*1503–1552), poet and antiquary, was born in London on 13 September in an unspecified year. Most of the surviving information about his early life, including the day of his birth, comes from his own poetry. Slightly older than his friend William Paget, the future royal secretary, he must have been born shortly before 1505–6. He had an elder brother, also called John, who became a physician, and they were orphaned when the antiquary was a young boy. Presumably they were related to Sir William Leyland of Morleys Hall, near Leigh in Lancashire, whose estate Leland described in one of his peregrinations and to whom he wrote an unpublished encomium. After his parents' deaths Leland was adopted by one Thomas Myles, who sent him to St Paul's School where, according to his own account, he studied under the headmaster William Lily and made the acquaintance of many of the figures who would become his later patrons: Paget, Antony Denny, Thomas Wriothesley, and Edward North.

Cambridge and Paris From St Paul's, Leland went to Cambridge where he was a member of Christ's College—'ut qui Grantae, in Collegio Christi nomini sacro, bonis artibus operam dederim' ('I was one who took pains with the liberal arts at Cambridge, in the college dedicated to Christ's name'; *De scriptoribus*, 84)—by approximately 1519. He was admitted BA in 1522. Soon afterwards he was a prisoner of the king's bench. According to his petition to Thomas Wolsey he was arrested after having reported the treasonous activities of an unnamed knight who was in contact with Richard de la Pole in France. (Most scholars have dated this petition to 1529, but this is impossible since Pole died in 1525.) After Cambridge, Leland entered the Lambeth household of Thomas Howard, second duke of Norfolk, and acted as tutor to the latter's ill-fated sixth son, Thomas, later to die in the Tower under sentence of death. He went to Oxford after the death of the duke in 1524 and according to Anthony Wood was associated with All Souls College. (Wood's source for this information was the 'sure tradition' passed from Leland's friend Thomas Caius of All Souls to Thomas Allen of Gloucester Hall.) In the dedicatory letter to Henry VIII prefacing his *Cygnea cantio* Leland stated that it was the king who sent him to Oxford. He quickly became dissatisfied with the conservative attitude to education at Oxford, however, and later complained to Paget that 'Sors vel ad obstreperos me duxit iniqua sophistas' ('An unfavourable fortune led me to noisy sophists'; Carley, 'John Leland in Paris', 30, 32). A verse encomium to Thomas Lupset, in which he requested to be made a member of his household, probably dates from approximately this period. In spite of his dissatisfaction he must still have been in Oxford in 1526, when he congratulated his friend Edward Wotton on the latter's return from Italy.

From Oxford, Leland set out for the continent with the stated intention of studying in France and Italy, but there is no evidence that he ever got as far as Italy. In 1528 the treasurer of the chamber's accounts record a quarterly payment of £25s. for 'Sir John Leylonde's exhibition' (*LP Henry VIII*, 5.305). Basing himself in Paris he presumably lived a kind of 'freelance' student life with the English–German nation, perfecting, as he would later relate, his skill at poetry. He cultivated the great continental scholars, singling out for his admiration Guillaume Budé, Jacques Lefèvre d'Etaples, Paolo Emilio, and Jean Ruel. He also wrote flattering verses to Janus Lascaris. Particularly influential on him was François du Bois, professor of rhetoric and principal of the Collège de Tournai. From Bois Leland seems first to have developed his passion for the Latin poet Ausonius, who would become the inspiration for his own river poem, and for the study of ancient texts. Bois, for example, introduced him to a manuscript of the late twelfth-century poet Joseph of Exeter, the corpus of whose works he would spend many years attempting to track down. This antiquarian bias, which shaped his future work, is described in his verse epistles, and he observed to his friend Robert Severs at Cambridge that he was making it his task to dig out from obscurity manuscripts of the ancients.

While in France, Leland kept up contact with his English friends and benefactors, sending, for example, verses to Lord Mountjoy to accompany a 'small gift', quite possibly a book. His friend Richard Hyrde, who had been one of the masters in More's household, came to visit him in Paris before going to Italy as physician to Stephen Gardiner and Edward Foxe in 1528. There is some evidence that Wolsey was Leland's chief advocate during these years. Leland addressed at least one encomium to Wolsey and John Bale lists a lost *Panegyricon ad cardinalem* among Leland's works. By his own account, moreover, it was Wolsey who collated him to the rectorship of Laverstoke, Hampshire, although it is not clear when precisely this occurred.

Leland must have been back in England before 10 November 1529 when he resigned the Laverstoke living. He was made a royal chaplain and on 17 June 1530 rector of Pepeling in the marches of Calais, where there is no evidence he ever set foot, and on 12 July 1536 he was granted a licence of non-residence for the living. After Wolsey's fall

Leland no doubt began cultivating Cromwell as a potential patron. On 12 July 1533 he was granted a papal dispensation to hold up to four benefices, the income from which was not to exceed 1000 ducats, provided that he take subdeacon's orders within two years and priest's orders within seven. Earlier that year, with Nicholas Udall, who had lent him money while he was a poor student in Oxford, he prepared verses for the pageants celebrating the royal entry of Anne Boleyn into London, 'whereof some were set up, and some other were spoken and pronounced' (*LP Henry VIII*, 6.564); these were probably commissioned by the duke of Norfolk and Cromwell. What is possibly the presentation copy (BL, Royal MS 18 A. lxiv) was retained in Henry's collection and was published by John Nichols in the first volume of *The Progresses and Public Processions of Queen Elizabeth* (London, 1788), pages i–xx. In 1533–4 Leland composed liminary verses for Udall's *Floures for Latine Spekynge: Selected and Gathered out of Terence* (STC 23899). In 1534 'Layland, priest', described as one of the royal chaplains, gave the king two books of stories at the new year and received in turn a gilt vessel with a cover. In 1535 he was made a prebendary of Wilton Abbey, Wiltshire, with the livings of North Newnton and West Knoyle, near Mere, attached.

Collecting and cataloguing books According to his later 'new year's gift' to Henry, published in 1549 as *The Laboryouse Journey*, in 1533 Leland received some sort of commission from the king, of which no record survives, 'to peruse and dylygentlye to searche all the lybraryes of monasteryes and collegies of thys your noble realme' (*Itinerary*, ed. Toulmin Smith, 1.xxxvii). Elsewhere in his writings he refers to a 'diploma' which he carried with him as he travelled from establishment to establishment. The surviving book-lists in his so-called *Collectanea* were almost all completed before the dissolutions of the houses that he visited, although he did on occasion return to religious establishments after their fall. During this phase of his activities, when he was normally on good terms with the religious, he rarely removed books from their ecclesiastical homes and his primary motivation in examining libraries was to compile lists of works by British authors and 'de viris illustribus' in general. His first extended journey took place *c.*1533 when he made a tour of the west country. In 1534 he was at York, where with Sir George Lawson he defaced a *tabula* containing a reference to the pope's authority in England. Citing a now lost document among the 'Papers of State', Anthony Wood claims that Leland wrote to Cromwell on 16 July 1536, only a matter of months after the passage of the bill for the suppression of all religious houses with an annual income of less than £200, requesting assistance in preserving books that were fast being dispersed: 'whereas now the Germanes perceiving our desidiousness and negligence, do send dayly young Scholars hither, that spoileth them, and cutteth them out of Libraries, returning home and putting them abroad as Monuments of their own Country' (Wood, *Ath. Oxon.*, 1.67).

By the mid-1530s Leland had made the acquaintance of John Bale and in 1536 Bale wrote a letter to him, praising his antiquarian efforts and offering to be of assistance in any way he could. He also dedicated his unpublished history of the Carmelite order in England, *Anglorum Heliades*, to Leland. In 1537 Leland wrote to Cromwell requesting Bale's release from prison where the latter had been confined on account of his preaching. Much later, in a revised version of *Kynge Johan*, Bale held him up as a witness for the British cause against the papists, Verity pleading with the (by then) mad Leland to awake from his 'slumbre' to 'wytnesse a trewthe for thyne owne contrayes sake' (Bale, 84).

Leland's precise role in the re-formation of the royal library in the 1530s and 1540s is difficult to unravel. Based on his use of the term 'antiquarius', generations of scholars assumed that he had some sort of official position as 'king's antiquary'. This is not the case, and Leland seems to have appropriated the term in analogy with continental humanist practices. Nor is there any indication in household accounts, admittedly incomplete, that he received any payment as librarian. He was not, as has been widely maintained, the author of a list of books treating history and divinity drawn up from a visitation of Lincolnshire houses *c.*1530. In his *Antiphilarchia* Leland did, however, relate that Henry had the libraries in three palaces—Greenwich, Hampton Court, and Westminster—refitted for the reception of monastic books. According to the 'new year's gift', moreover, Leland conserved books in goodly number for the Royal Collection as well as for himself. Yet, although he made select lists of books from about 140 foundations, less than a dozen of the hundreds of monastic books in the Royal Collection can be shown to have arrived there through his agency. Possibly he was responsible for the rescue of a number of the others, but no record remains; perhaps many of the items he acquired were later deaccessioned.

Travelling in England There is some evidence that Leland kept on searching out books after the fall of the monasteries and his copy of a letter authorizing him to use any books in the 'late' monastery at Bury St Edmunds that might 'forder hym yn setting forth such matiers as he writith for the King's Majeste' still survives (*Itinerary*, ed. Toulmin Smith, 2.148). By about 1539, nevertheless, his chief concerns had shifted to topography and local history. Inflamed by a patriotic desire to see the places he had read about in ancient histories and chronicles, he spent by his own account some six years in travelling throughout Henry's dominions, so that:

> there is almost neyther cape nor baye, haven, creke or pere, ryver or confluence of ryvers, breches, washes, lakes, meres, fenny waters, mountaynes, valleys, mores, hethes, forestes, woodes, cyties, burges, castels, pryncypall manor places, monasteryes and colleges, but I have seane them and noted in so doynge a whole worlde of thynges verye memorable. (*Laboryouse Journey*, ed. J. Bale, 1549, sig. D.iiiiv)

The precise chronology of Leland's journeys, of which there seem to have been about five, is impossible to determine and only once did he give a date for his setting out: on 5 May 1542 he began an extensive tour of the west country. An earlier journey began in Wales and brought him to

Shropshire, up to Chester and across to Yorkshire, down to the east midlands, Worksop and Bedford, and home again. Other trips included the west midlands, Yorkshire again, and places further north. The accounts of more than one trip have been lost. His notebooks suggest his procedure: sometimes he made maps and measured distances, he asked information from local inhabitants, and he also examined books and charters. He compared sources and noted when there were disparities or when information seemed to be unreliable. During the travels themselves he took rough notes, which he later amplified; normally he kept both rough and fair copies. Although he never managed to produce the many works he envisaged, his undertaking was an extraordinarily ambitious one and marks the beginning of English topographical studies.

Last years On 31 March 1542 Leland was presented to the rectory of Great Haseley, near Thame in Oxfordshire. He was made a canon and prebendary of King Henry VIII College, Oxford, on 26 March 1543 and was one of the signatories of its surrender in 1545. (When an inquisition post mortem was taken in 1551 he still occupied the rectories of Pepeling and Great Haseley, and the prebends of North Newnton (called in this document East Knowle) and West Knoyle in the dissolved abbey of Wilton, and had an annuity of £26 13*s.* 4*d.* from the dissolved King Henry VIII College.) According to the 1541 subsidy roll, in which he was assessed for £100 and required to pay £2 10*s.*, he was living in Cornhill ward. He was later discharged on the grounds that he was liable to the clerical tenth and the clerical subsidy. (His brother, John Leland, who was listed in the parish of St Michael-le-Querne, was assessed at £50.) On 13 August 1546 his house in the site of the former Charterhouse was alienated to one Joan Wilkinson. Presumably the undated letter he wrote to his friend Mr Bane in Louvain, requesting the services of a toward young man, learned in Latin and Greek, relates to this final phase of his activities. A number of his short encomia can also be dated to the 1540s; no doubt he was trying to consolidate his position and drum up increased financial patronage. In an undated poem to Thomas Cranmer he described the mass of wonderful material he had brought together at his house which would never see the light of day without the archbishop's generous support; possibly it was this poem that led to ecclesiastical appointments of 1542 and 1543, or possibly it was written later. Some time in 1546, no doubt after the treaty of Campe or Ardres of 8 June 1546, Leland was sent by Henry to obtain trees, grafts, and seeds in France, including 100 pear and apple trees from Rouen.

In 1549 John Bale published his annotated edition of the 'new year's gift' as *The Laboryouse Journey & Serche … for Englandes Antiquitees* (STC 15445), in which he testified that Leland had suddenly fallen mad some three years previously. Elsewhere in his commentary on the tract he dates Leland's collapse at 1547, the year of Henry's death. In 1551 Leland's elder brother, residing in the parish of St Michael-le-Querne and described as his heir, was granted custody of his person and his property. Various theories of the cause of his madness were propounded: his friends alleged grief over spiteful treatment by enemies; others suggested realization of his inability to produce the grandiose works he had promised, or divine retribution for heresy. Bale, who knew him well, states that he was vainglorious, and John Caius alleges that although learned he was a boaster. Later generations saw Leland's madness as a symbol of the fate of the scholar, a warning against overapplication to abstruse studies. In a recent professional diagnosis it has been suggested that Leland suffered from manic-depressive illness which may well have been aggravated by Henry's death, as well as from a 'magpie complex', that is an obsession with collecting, from which insanity provided the only escape. He died on 18 April 1552 and was buried in his brother's parish church. John Stow mentioned a monument, but this was destroyed in the great fire of 1666. His brother, described as a citizen of London and minstrel, died early in 1558. Although married, the elder John was also childless.

Engravings of at least two likenesses survive, although the originals have disappeared. The better known is that of Charles Grignion (1717–1810), taken from a bust at All Souls now lost, which shows a clean-shaven individual attired in the Roman manner. The original was almost certainly the work of Louis François Roubiliac. In 1824 Thomas Charles Wageman published an engraving deriving from a portrait dated to 1546 and misattributed to Hans Holbein. By this time Leland was bearded and considerably heavier. An etching of what appears to be a different portrait was published in *European Magazine*, 10 (1786), page 161; it was then in the possession of the heirs of Rowe Mores of Low Layton, Essex.

Poetry During his lifetime Leland published relatively few works, most of which were Latin poems. The first of these was his *Naeniae in mortem T. Viati, equitis incomparabilis*, published by Reyner Wolfe (in whose house later tradition had him residing at the time of his death) in 1542 (STC 15446). It was dedicated to Henry Howard, earl of Surrey, described by Leland as Wyatt's literary heir. This elegy, written a matter of weeks after Wyatt's death on 11 October 1542, is based on classical models and contains references to nymphs, the phoenix, and the contest of the gods over the apotheosis of the dead poet. Three years later he wrote another lamentation, this one commemorating Sir Henry Dudley, eldest son and heir of John Dudley, Viscount Lisle and later duke of Northumberland, who died at Boulogne. Entitled *Naenia in mortem splendidissimi equitis Henrici Duddelegi*, it was published by John Mayler (STC 15445.5). Leland's *Genethliacon illustrissimi Eaduerdi principis Cambriae*, completed in 1543 and published by Reyner Wolfe (STC 15443), was a revised version of a poem begun at the time of Prince Edward's birth in 1537. The poem, rich in topographical allusions, is remarkable for the description of Elizabeth's accomplishments—Leland met the queen at Ampthill when he was invited by John Cheke to see the young prince. The presentation copy, printed on vellum, survives as Clare College, Cambridge, MS O 6 26. There are three poems celebrating Henry's victories in France. The first, *Fatum Bononiae Morinorum*, was published by Wolfe in 1544 (STC 15442.5). This was followed by *Bononia Gallo-mastix in laudem felicissimi victoris Henrici VIII* in 1545, published by Mayler (STC 15441.7). Both of these celebrate the siege and capture of Boulogne in 1544. The *Laudatio pacis*, published by Wolfe in August 1546 (STC 15442), was written almost immediately after the treaty of Campe or Ardres was concluded.

Leland describes his most ambitious poem, the *Cygnea cantio*, published by Wolfe in 1545 (STC 15444), as his own swansong to the poetic arts. The poem relates a journey down the Thames from Oxford to Greenwich, and provides detailed topographical and historical information in the long accompanying commentary in prose. Some 250 of Leland's miscellaneous shorter poems were edited by Thomas Newton and published in 1589 (STC 15447). No autograph manuscript of these poems survives, but John Stow made a copy shortly after Leland's death, now MS Tanner 464.iv in the Bodleian Library, Oxford. This manuscript, which was consulted by Newton but which was not his copy text, contains twenty-eight poems not printed by Newton and fuller versions of others. The earliest poems may date to Leland's time at Cambridge, but others seem to have been written shortly before his descent into madness. Some appear to be literary exercises, some were meant to accompany gifts, often books, and many were addressed to patrons, potential as well as those whose attention he had already secured. Some, such as the verses to John Barret and the tributes to Chaucer, were extracts from the three books of epigrams written, as he stated elsewhere, in his youth. With the exception of the verses to Anne Boleyn and the *Fatum Bononiae Morinorum*, all the published poems were reprinted by Thomas Hearne in his editions of Leland's works.

Antiquarian writings During his lifetime Leland published only one work in prose, his *Assertio inclytissimi Arturii regis Britanniae* (also by Wolfe; STC 15440); a translation was published by Richard Robinson in 1582 (STC 15441). The presentation copy to Henry VIII on vellum, now C.20.b.3 in the department of printed books of the British Library, contains a correction in Leland's own hand. Growing out of his *Codrus, sive, Laus et defensio Gallofridi Arturii contra Polydorum Vergilium* (which was later published in abbreviated form in the accounts *De viris illustribus*), the *Assertio* attempted to establish the validity of Arthur's historical existence through a comprehensive analysis of ancient texts, place names, ancient artefacts, and landscape features. Another lengthy prose work, the *Antiphilarchia*, was cast as a dialogue between a reformer and a Romanist over the *Tu es Petrus* text. Completed after Henry assumed the kingship of Ireland in 1541, it has never been printed, but what was no doubt the presentation copy survives in Cambridge University Library as MS Ee.5.14.

By 1545 Leland had a clear idea of the works he wished to produce and he provided detailed lists in the *Cygnea cantio* and in his 'new year's gift'. He planned a dictionary of British writers, *De viris illustribus*. This work, published under the title of *Commentarii de scriptoribus Britannicis* by Anthony Hall in 1709, was divided into four books and contained almost 600 entries arranged in chronological order. Although he had still been revising it as late as 1545, it was nearing completion when he became insane. Leland also envisaged a 'table', presumably some sort of map of Britain, to be engraved in silver or brass. This was to be accompanied by a descriptive text or *Liber de topographia Britanniae primae*, giving ancient names of places and peoples. Next was to come a work to be entitled *De antiquitate Britannica* or *Civilis historia*, which would be arranged shire by shire and would include as well adjacent islands. Following this there was to be a study of noble families in three books, *De nobilitate Britannica*. In the 'new year's gift' Leland emphasized that the data for these latter three projects was in hand and no doubt he was referring to the materials that were later published by Thomas Hearne as *The Itinerary of John Leland the Antiquary* (Oxford, 1710–12; etc.) and *Joannis Lelandi antiquarii de rebus Britannicis collectanea* (Oxford, 1715; etc.). Three further works were mentioned in the *Cygnea cantio* and all three figure in Bale's commentary to the 'new year's gift'. The first was a *Vita Sigeberti regis*, portions of which no doubt survive in the fifty-seventh chapter of *De scriptoribus*. Materials pertaining to the other two, *De academiis Britannicis* and *De pontificibus Britanniae*, are scattered throughout Leland's notes, but it seems unlikely that the plans were very far advanced.

In his *Index Britanniae scriptorum* Bale lists other works by Leland, many with incipits, which he himself had seen. *Antiquitates Britannie* is the title Bale gave to an unpublished notebook, now in the British Library (Cotton MS Julius C.vi, fols. 1–89), made up of extracts relating to Britain taken primarily from classical authors. Others, such as the *Descriptiones Anglie* and *Dictionarium Britannicolatinum*, are titles that Bale applied to extracts from Leland's notebooks. The lost *De titulo regis ad Scotiam*, which Bale saw in the royal library and in the library of Thomas Caius, must have been based on the short text printed in *Collectanea* (3.2–10). A copy of the *Panegyricon ad cardinalem* was at Westminster Palace in 1542 and no doubt the encomium to Anne of Cleves also found its way into the Royal Collection. In a section of the itineraries dealing with Kent (*Itinerary*, ed. Toulmin Smith, 4.57) Leland made a note 'Let this be the firste chapitre of the booke'; the book to which he refers must be the *Itinerarium Cantie* dedicated to Henry, which Bale saw in Caius's library.

Literary afterlife According to tradition Leland's papers were assigned to his friend Sir John Cheke by Edward VI and there is some evidence to support this. In the letter he wrote to Matthew Parker in 1560 Bale describes seeing a copy of Sicardus of Cremona's now lost lives of the popes in Leland's study when Cheke had charge of it. According to John Foxe's *Acts and Monuments* Bale borrowed a copy of Leland's *De catalogo virorum illustrium* from Cheke when Bale and Foxe were dwelling together in the house of the duchess of Richmond (that is, in 1548). When Cheke left England in 1554 there appear to have been dispersals, and damage also occurred at an early stage. Cheke himself presented four volumes to Humphrey Purefoy, whose son Thomas gave them to a cousin, William Burton, the historian of Leicestershire, in 1612. Some papers passed to William, Lord Paget, and others to William Cecil, Lord Burghley, who was married to Cheke's sister. It is possible that the sale of Leland's library on 18 May 1556, from which John Dee obtained medieval manuscripts, was a result of Cheke's arrest in Brussels almost immediately beforehand. Ultimately most of Leland's own surviving papers got to Burton, who in 1632 and later gave to the Bodleian Library the *Collectanea* and *De scriptoribus* (now Bodl. Oxf., MSS top. gen. c.1–4) and seven of the eight volumes of the *Itineraries* (now Bodl. Oxf., MSS top. gen. e.8–14). The eighth, made up of stray leaves from the other volumes, which he had lent to a friend and could not recover, was given by Charles King of Christ Church about 1677 (Bodl. Oxf., MS top. gen. e.15). Apart from the *Antiquitates Britannie* acquired by Cotton there are stray fragments in other collections. Leland's papers were widely circulated after Leland's death and Stow's transcripts included three books of the itineraries which later went missing. John Bagford believed Stow possessed a volume on the antiquities of London, now lost, which he incorporated into his own *Survey*, but this seems unlikely. Other missing material may have included an itinerary of East Anglia and accounts of some Warwickshire towns.

These vicissitudes notwithstanding, from the time of Bale onwards scholars voiced concern that Leland's papers should be preserved. In her early twentieth-century edition of the *Itinerary* (1.xix) Lucy Toulmin Smith observes that 'The blessing of John Bale must have rested upon Thomas Hearne', who brought the *Itinerary* and the *Collectanea* into print. But even before Hearne's heroic enterprise the notes circulated, and copies in varying degrees of completeness were made by prominent scholars, to exert an immense influence. Few historians and antiquaries did not use Leland's work, and many acknowledged their debt, starting with Bale. In the following generation Leland's followers included both William Harrison and William Camden, ranging like him across the whole country, and local historians like William Lambarde, in his ground-breaking survey of Kent, and John Stow, who used Leland's notes for his great *Survey of London* of 1598. In the following century not only did scholars of the eminence of Dugdale, and the less methodical John Aubrey, use Leland's work, but so too did the pioneering natural historian Robert Plot. For Anthony Wood, not always generous with praise, Leland was 'that singular light and ornament of Great Britain' (Wood, *Ath. Oxon.*, 1.197). In the eighteenth century, too, Leland's writings were influential; they were fundamental, for instance, to the *Bibliotheca Britannico-Hibernica* (1748) of Thomas Tanner, who originally intended to do no more than reproduce Leland's *De scriptoribus*. By more recent generations Leland's notes are valued particularly for the unique insight they provide into Tudor England, and for their witness to the final phase of English monasticism. They continue to be regularly cited in local histories, in scholarly editions of medieval British authors, and in such bio-bibliographical works as the *Oxford Dictionary of National Biography* itself. JAMES P. CARLEY

Sources *The itinerary of John Leland the antiquary*, ed. T. Hearne, 3rd edn, 9 vols. (1768–9) • *Joannis Lelandi antiquarii de rebus Britannicis collectanea*, ed. T. Hearne, 6 vols. (1715); [3rd edn] (1774) • *Commentarii de scriptoribus Britannicis, auctore Joanne Lelando*, ed. A. Hall, 2 vols. (1709) • *The itinerary of John Leland in or about the years 1535–1543*, ed. L. Toulmin Smith, 5 vols. (1906–10); repr. with introduction by T. Kendrick (1964) • *John Leland's itinerary: travels in Tudor England*, ed. J. Chandler (1993) • [W. Huddesford], ed., *The lives of those eminent antiquaries, John Leland, Thomas Hearne, and Anthony à Wood*, 1 (1772) • E. Burton, *The life of John Leland* (1896) • Emden, *Oxf.*, 4.350–51 • T. C. Skeat, 'Two "lost" works by John Leland', *EngHR*, 65 (1950), 505–8 • L. Bradner, 'Some unpublished poems by John Leland', *Proceedings of the Modern Language Association of America*, 71 (1956), 827–36 • J. W. Binns, *Intellectual culture in Elizabethan and Jacobean England: the Latin writings of the age* (1990), 18–26 • J. P. Carley, 'John Leland in Paris: the evidence of his poetry', *Studies in Philology*, 83 (1986), 1–50 • J. P. Carley, 'The manuscript remains of John Leland: "The king's antiquary"', *Text*, 2 (1985), 111–20 • J. P. Carley, 'John Leland and the contents of the English pre-dissolution libraries: Lincolnshire', *Transactions of the Cambridge Bibliographical Society*, 9 (1989), 330–57 • T. D. Kendrick, *British antiquity* (1950), 45–64 • A. Momigliano, 'Ancient history and the antiquarian', *Journal of the Warburg and Courtauld Institutes*, 13 (1950), 285–315 • Wood, *Ath. Oxon.*, new edn, 1.67, 197–204 • M. McKisack, *Medieval history in the Tudor age* (1971) • D. C. Douglas, *English scholars, 1660–1730*, 2nd edn (1951) • S. A. E. Mendyk, *Speculum Britanniae: regional study, antiquarianism and science in Britain to 1700* (1989) • J. Bale, *Kynge Johan: a play in two parts*, ed. J. P. Collier, CS, 2 (1838) • R. G. Lang, ed., *Two Tudor subsidy assessment rolls for the city of London, 1541 and 1581*, London RS, 29 (1993)

Archives NRA, historical and topographical MSS | BL, Cotton MS Julius C.vi • BL, Royal MS 18A. lxiv • Bodl. Oxf., MS Tanner 464, 4 • Bodl. Oxf., MSS top. gen. c.1–4, e.8–15 • CUL, MS Ee. 5.14

Likenesses T. C. Wageman, engraving, pubd 1824 (after portrait, 1546) • C. Grignion, engraving (after lost bust, probably by L. F. Roubiliac), All Souls Oxf. • etching, repro. in *European Magazine*, 10 (1786), 161

Leland, John (1691–1766), Presbyterian minister and theological writer, was born at Wigan, the second of three sons of devout parents, on 18 October 1691. He contracted smallpox at five and lost his mental powers for almost twelve months. A year or two later his father was bankrupted by standing surety for some friends, but found a business opening in Dublin, to which the family moved. After regular schooling Leland and a close friend, Thomas Maquay (1694–1729), who became minister at Plunket Street, Dublin, in 1717, went through their 'Course of Philosophy' together under 'a celebrated Teacher at that Time' before undertaking theological studies under the direction of local Presbyterian ministers (Weld, preface). If they attended an organized programme in philosophy this perhaps points to James McAlpin's academy at Killyleagh, the only philosophy school for Irish dissenters 'celebrated' at that period. Leland was ordained co-pastor to Nathanael Weld (1660–1730) at New Row, Dublin, on 16 December 1716 and moved to the congregation's elegant new Georgian building in Eustace Street in 1728. After Maquay's death Leland took responsibility for helping to raise his children. He married Maquay's widow, Ann, in 1731, but further children of their own died in infancy. Unlike Maquay, whose congregation contained 'some very hot Northerns' (Leland to Thomas Steward, 20 April

1725) and enforced subscription to the Westminster confession, Leland avoided association with the synod of Ulster and, with the exception of two pamphlets (*The Case Fairly Stated* and *A Defence of The Case Fairly Stated*, Dublin, 1754) on the crown's rights in financial matters, he also stayed out of political controversy. He was created MA of Glasgow University in 1734 and DD of King's College, Aberdeen, in 1739.

A diligent pastor, Leland was also the foremost theological writer among eighteenth-century Irish dissenters. After two early pieces against the papacy (a sermon on the anniversary of the Gunpowder Plot in 1728 and an account of a debate with Francis Lehy, 'a popish priest', in 1730) his published work was devoted largely to defences of the Christian religion, conceived in non-sectarian terms. It was undertaken in two phases: the first, a critical exposition of the arguments and strategies of deistic writers, is presented in a series of works beginning with tracts against Matthew Tindal (1734), Thomas Morgan (1739), and Henry Dodwell the younger (1744); it culminates in *A View of the Principal Deistical Writers that have Appeared in England in the Last and Present Century* (1754), in the form of letters ostensibly for Thomas Wilson, rector of St Stephen Walbrook. The second phase, proceeding from a historical account of ancient pagan religion until the coming of Christ, is designed to show that even among civilized nations a supernatural revelation is needed; this is presented in *The Advantage and Necessity of the Christian Revelation Shewn from the State of Religion in the Ancient Heathen World* (1764), a work that cost Leland more labour than any other. His mature works were completed in the face of mounting incapacity. From May 1753 until his death he depended on pastoral assistants to help him conduct his Sunday ministrations.

By a 'deistical writer' Leland means one whose aim is to impugn the necessity, authenticity, or excellence of the Christian revelation, or who claims the adequacy of mere reason to discover the principles of true religion, or the sufficiency of natural religion to secure eternal happiness. He sought to counteract what he considered to be a diminution of zeal for the study of scripture and divine worship; a decline of personal morality and an increase in public vice and corruption; and a dangerous indifference towards the inevitability of divine retribution in this world and the next. Although he supposed those whom he judged to be 'deistical' to be united in their purpose to discredit Christianity he found no consensus of doctrine among them: each went about his task in his own way. Since not all of them were explicitly anti-Christian his first duty was that of an 'unmasker'—that is, the removing of 'different disguises and appearances' that concealed their real intent. Objections by some respected Christians to his inclusion of Shaftesbury among the deistic writers caused him to review his presentation. In a supplement to the second edition of *A View* (1756) he commends Shaftesbury for insisting on the purity of ethical motivation but blames him for tracing Christianity's motivation solely to the fear of retribution. Since that is not the case and since, Leland suspected, Shaftesbury knew better, his portrayal of Christian morality as a morality of fear must be a wilful misrepresentation. The fact that deistic authors reduce Christianity to caricature in order to discredit it is taken as evidence that the case for Christianity is more formidable than they like to admit. Other writers treated by Leland as deistic are Charles Blount, Thomas Chubb, Anthony Collins, Herbert of Cherbury, Thomas Hobbes, John Toland, Thomas Woolston, and the author of *The Resurrection of Jesus Considered* (Peter Annet). A second volume of *A View*, dated 1755, devotes four chapters to Hume, which were later extended to eight, and twelve to continuing an earlier campaign against Bolingbroke. Leland tries hard to place Hume's critique of religious thinking within the context of the overall philosophy of his *Enquiry Concerning Human Understanding* but cannot reconcile Hume's allegiance to causal reasoning with his nescience as to the nature of the causal connection—an illuminating instance of the commentator's projecting onto his subject the 'contradictions' that he expects of an infidel work. In discussing Hume's critique of miracle reports Leland is indebted to William Adams.

One of Leland's main arguments against the deists is their lack of agreement about the principles of natural religion. If as rational beings they cannot agree on these principles and put them into practice we may not expect that mankind in general will do so, and we must conclude that there is need of revelation. *The Advantage and Necessity of the Christian Revelation* applies the same argument to the failure of pagan antiquity, in spite of its civilization and learning, to realize a state of true religion. Leland is careful not to assert the incapacity of human reason to discover the principles of natural religion—the existence and nature of God, the moral duty of mankind, and retribution in a life to come—but contends that these principles were first delivered to mankind in an original revelation. The advantage of Christianity over natural religion is twofold: it offers both a remedy to mankind's failure to adhere perfectly to the moral law, and a more perfect account of the principles of natural religion than had been hitherto known. On the co-operation of reason and revelation he cites Selden, Grotius, Pufendorf, Cudworth, and Locke. Although disagreeing in general with the account of the origin of religion in Hume's *Natural History* he approves Hume's comment that mankind in earliest times could not have come to knowledge of the being and attributes of God by merely natural enquiry.

Leland composed many sermons and himself prepared the four-volume selection that was published posthumously in 1768–9. These *Discourses on Various Subjects* present a version of Christianity suitable to an enlightened age. They represent Christianity as a moral religion consisting of divinely ordained duties that can be refounded on rational grounds. In a pair of sermons on 1 Corinthians 10: 31 (vol. 1, nos. 20–21) he accepts the standard formula among protestants for the end of man—to glorify God—but interprets it morally. The glory of God is equated with divine perfection, which cannot be added to or diminished by human action. Since, however, God is the best of beings we must live in a way consistent with his perfections, exemplifying those that can be cast as moral duties and delighting in and adoring the rest. Since this is the proper end of man human happiness is its consequence. This moral religion, which is equivalent to the religion of nature, is set within the history of redemption, which is marked by the Creation and Fall, the Mosaic and Christian revelations, and the end of the world, when, as in the case of the Deluge, God will intervene and change the course of nature.

Leland's theology was orthodox enough and broad enough to appeal both to mainstream and to more radical dissenters; many leading Anglicans subscribed for his *Discourses* and editions of *A View* continued to appear until the mid-nineteenth century, with two American editions. Leland died in Dublin, of a lung infection, on 16 January 1766, and was survived by his wife.

VICTOR NUOVO and M. A. STEWART

Sources I. Weld, *A sermon … on occasion of the much lamented death of the reverend and learned John Leland DD* (1766) • I. Weld, preface, in J. Leland, *Discourses on various subjects*, 4 vols. (1768–9), vol. 1 • MS correspondence of Thomas Steward, Magee University College Library, Londonderry, MS 46, items 14, 69 • register of diplomas, U. Glas., Archives and Business Records Centre, MS 21320, p. 29 • P. J. Anderson, ed., *Officers and graduates of University and King's College, Aberdeen, MVD–MDCCCLX*, New Spalding Club, 11 (1893) • T. Witherow, *Historical and literary memorials of presbyterianism in Ireland, 1623–1731* (1879), chap. 45 • Eustace Street meeting-house, vestry minutes, Unitarian Church Library, Dublin • V. Nuovo, 'Leland, John', *Dictionary of eighteenth-century British philosophers*, ed. J. W. Yolton and others (1999), 544–8 • I. Rivers, *Reason, grace, and sentiment: a study of the language of religion and ethics in England, 1660–1780*, 2 (2000) • L. Stephen, *History of English thought in the eighteenth century*, 3rd edn, 2 vols. (1902) • M. Wall, *Catholic Ireland in the eighteenth century* (1989), 54

Likenesses Hall, engraving, 18th cent. (after unknown artist), repro. in J. Leland, *The advantage and necessity of the Christian revelation*, frontispiece • J. Brooks, mezzotint (after A. Lee), BM • portrait; formerly in possession of Revd Dr Thomas Wilson, rector of St Stephen Walbrook, London

Leland, Thomas (1722–1785), historian and Church of Ireland clergyman, was born in Dublin, and after education at Thomas Sheridan's school there he entered Trinity College, Dublin, as a pensioner in 1737. He graduated BA (1742) and MA (1745), and was elected a fellow in 1746. In 1754, with his childhood friend John Stokes, he published *The Philippic Orations of Demosthenes*, a text and Latin translation with notes. He was one of the men of letters who visited the earl of Charlemont at Marino, co. Dublin, and was on intimate terms with the earl's family. Charlemont persuaded him to publish an English translation, *The Orations of Demosthenes Against Philip*, which appeared in parts from 1754 to 1761 and in a complete edition in 1770, and was frequently reissued. In 1758 he published *The History of Philip, King of Macedon* and in 1764 *A Dissertation on the Principles of Human Eloquence*.

During this time Leland continued his academic career at Trinity, taking the degrees of BD in 1752 and DD in 1757. In 1761 he was appointed professor of history at the college, and in 1762 professor of oratory. A second edition of the *Dissertation* appeared in 1765, with strictures on William Warburton's *Doctrine on Grace*. This gave rise to a controversy about the style of the New Testament in which Bishop Hurd was Leland's chief opponent. In 1768, Leland became chaplain to Lord Townshend, lord lieutenant of Ireland. Townshend's influence secured for him the posts of vicar of Bray, co. Wicklow, and prebendary of Rathmichael in St Patrick's Cathedral in the same year. It was at Bray that he began his *History of Ireland from the invasion of Henry II, with a preliminary discourse on the ancient state of that kingdom*, which was published in 1773. This work, which covers Irish history from the twelfth century to the capitulation of Limerick in 1691, has never been highly regarded. The schoolmaster Richard Shackleton was induced by an anonymous correspondent, who pretended to be Leland, to write his opinion of the book to the author, and this led to a real correspondence on the history. In 1766 Leland bought the Irish manuscript chronicle later printed as the *Annals of Loch Cé* at a sale of the books of John Fergus, and gave it to Trinity College Library. On 29 September 1773 he became vicar of St Anne's, Dublin. In the following year Charlemont supported his unsuccessful candidature for the provostship of Trinity College. When in Dublin he lived at 18 Clare Street. Two of his sermons on days of appointed fast (13 December 1776 and 10 February 1779) were published separately, and a collected volume, *Sermons on Various Subjects*, appeared posthumously in 1788 in Dublin. He gave up his fellowship for the college living of Ardstraw in Londonderry in 1781, and divided his time between the rectory there and Dublin for the rest of his life. He died in Dublin in August 1785. Leland had a son called John, who was admitted to Lincoln's Inn in 1776 and called to the Irish bar in 1780. However, there is no record of Leland's wife's name, and it is not even certain that he was ever married.

NORMAN MOORE, *rev.* ALEXANDER DU TOIT

Sources 'Some account of the life and writings of the author', J. Leland, *Sermons on various subjects*, 1 (1788), xxix–lvii • A. J. Webb, *A compendium of Irish biography* (1878), 289–90 • Burtchaell & Sadleir, *Alum. Dubl.* • *The manuscripts and correspondence of James, first earl of Charlemont*, 1, HMC, 28 (1891), 195, 206, 278, 282, 286, 294, 320, 324, 383, 390 • *The manuscripts and correspondence of James, first earl of Charlemont*, 2, HMC, 28 (1894) • *Anthologica Hibernica*, 1 (Jan–June 1793), 165–8 • W. M. Hennessy, ed. and trans., *The annals of Loch Cé: a chronicle of Irish affairs from AD 1014 to AD 1590*, 1, Rolls Series, 54 (1871), vii • W. P. Baildon, ed., *The records of the Honorable Society of Lincoln's Inn: admissions*, 1 (1896), 485 • W. Harrison, *Memorable Dublin houses* (1890), 59 • E. Kilmurray, *Dictionary of British portraiture*, 2 (1979), 132

Archives Northants. RO, corresp. with Edmund Burke • Royal Irish Acad., Charlemont MSS and corresp. • Sheff. Arch., corresp. with Edmund Burke

Likenesses J. Reynolds, oils, *c.*1776, Staatsgalerie, Stuttgart • J. Dean, mezzotints, 1777 (after J. Reynolds), NG Ire. • attrib. T. Hickey, oils, NG Ire.

Lely, Sir Peter (1618–1680), portrait painter and art collector, was born on 14 September 1618 in Soest, Westphalia. His father, Johan van der Faes, an infantry captain of a Dutch regiment serving the elector of Brandenburg, was originally from The Hague, where the van der Faes family owned a number of fashionable properties. The

Sir Peter Lely (1618–1680), self-portrait, *c.*1660

pseudonym Lely appears to have originated from the carved decoration of a lily on one such property, In de Lelye, on the western side of the Noordinde. His mother, Abigail van Vliet, was from a wealthy and respectable Utrecht family.

Early work and career In October–November 1637 a Pieter Lely is listed in the minutes of the Guild of St Luke in Haarlem as a pupil of the artist Frans Pieter de Grebber. It is not known how long he remained with de Grebber in Haarlem—where, according to Houbraken, he gained a reputation as an excellent portrait painter—or when exactly he arrived in England, but it is now generally accepted that he was in London by about 1643. As a talented and ambitious young artist it is possible that he arrived in England with the specific intention of succeeding Van Dyck, who had died two years previously, as the king's painter. According to Vertue, Lely spent his first few years in England working for the successful portrait painter and picture dealer George Geldorp, pursuing what an early commentator, Bainbrigg Buckeridge, called 'the Natural Bent of his Genius, in Landtskips and Painted with small Figures, as likewise Historical Compositions' (Buckeridge, 445). Paintings such as the *Amorous Couple in a Landscape* (Valenciennes Museum) and *Diana and Nymphs Bathing* (Musée des Beaux-Arts, Nantes) clearly show the influence of fellow Dutch artists such as Jacob van Loo, Abraham van Cuylenberg, and Cornelius van Poelenburg.

An early self-portrait is incorporated into one of the largest of this type of painting, *The Concert*, from the late 1640s (Courtauld Inst.), which represents a group of musicians in an arcadian setting seated beside two courtly ladies with a third, semi-naked young woman, viewed from behind. Although long assumed to be a portrait of *Sir Peter and his Family*, it is now accepted as an allegory of Music, Love, and Beauty, with Lely the figure playing the bass violin. In keeping with a style and type of painting characteristic at this point in Lely's career, it also shows, in the seated portraits of beautiful courtly women, an early awareness of Van Dyck's work and, through that, of sixteenth-century Venetian painting, while at the same time foreshadowing Lely's own later female portraits.

According to Buckeridge, Lely soon found 'the practice of *Face-Painting* more encourag'd here' and therefore 'turn'd his study that way, wherein, in a short time, he succeeded so well that he surpass'd all his Contemporaries in Europe' (Buckeridge, 445). In contrast to his later portraits of sophisticated Restoration courtiers and renowned beauties, the portraits of the 1640s and 1650s show a quieter, more reflective quality, often incorporating the arcadian and musical themes of his earlier work. Examples are a series of five portraits of musicians (three in a private collection; two in the Tate collection), *The Music Lesson* (priv. coll.), signed and dated 1654, and a number of portraits of children dressed in arcadian costume, such as *The Little Girl in Green* (priv. coll.), *Henry Sidney, Earl of Romney* (priv. coll.), or *Jocelyn Percy in an Arcadian Vest* (Petworth House, Sussex).

Major commissions The Percy, Herbert, and Sidney families, together with the Capels, Dormers, and Dysarts, were among Lely's most important patrons during the civil war and Commonwealth years. For the Capel family, whose second son, Henry, became a close friend, Lely produced a number of half-length and double portraits which Vertue, visiting the Capel house, Cassiobury Park, in 1731, described as 'the best and highest perfection that ever I saw painted by Sr. P. Lelly' (Vertue, *Note books*, 4.17). For Elizabeth Murray, countess of Dysart, who remained a lifelong supporter, he painted several portraits, including a memorable three-quarter length with her black pageboy (Ham House, Surrey), which is clearly dependent on Van Dyck's *Princess Henrietta of Lorraine* (Iveagh Bequest, Kenwood House, London), one of the many Van Dycks formerly in Charles I's collection. An even more important patron and contact was Algernon Percy, tenth earl of Northumberland. Through Northumberland's impressive art collection Lely would have had access to some of the most highly esteemed works by artists such as Titian, Mantegna, Correggio, Rubens, and Van Dyck, which, in the case of the last-named, were to have a profound influence on his own development as an artist. In 1647, the same year Lely was made a freeman of the Painter-Stainers' Company in London, he painted a group portrait of the children of Charles I—James, duke of York, Princess Elizabeth, and Henry, duke of Gloucester—then in Northumberland's care (Petworth House). Although the work is much grander in scale and less intuitive than Van Dyck's earlier royal groups (one of which Lely was shortly and briefly to own), the influence of Van Dyck's work is immediately apparent. In the following year Lely produced a double portrait of Charles I, by then in captivity, with his second son, James, duke of York (Syon House). The image is in retrospect a poignant and muted one and must have strengthened Lely's artistic position, especially the link with Van Dyck, inspiring Lely's friend the poet Richard Lovelace to write his well-known poem, published separately in his collection of poems entitled *Lucasta* in 1649, 'To my worthy friend Mr. Peter Lely: on that excellent picture of his majesty, and the duke of York, drawne by him at Hampton-Court'. It is unclear exactly who commissioned these works, but recent research (Wood) suggests that Northumberland commissioned the double portrait *Charles I with James, Duke of York* while the group portrait of the royal children was painted for Charles I.

During these years Lely seems to have played a strategic game, working for important former court patrons in London, possibly maintaining links with exiled royalists at The Hague, where he had family property, and developing contacts with influential parliamentary and Commonwealth figures. In 1653, together with Geldorp and Sir Balthasar Gerbier, he petitioned parliament, unsuccessfully as it transpired, for the commission to decorate Whitehall Palace with a series of paintings celebrating parliament's civil war victories and inset with portraits of its generals and commanders. For 'the great Room, formerly called the Banqueting House' they proposed a large group portrait commemorating 'the whole Assemblie' of parliament; for the opposite wall a group portrait of members of the council of state (BL, Stowe MS 184, fol. 283). The following year Lely painted Oliver Cromwell (Birmingham City Museums and Art Gallery), versions of which are in the Pitti Palace, Florence, and the National Gallery of Ireland, Dublin, although the face probably derived from a Samuel Cooper miniature rather than a fresh *ad vivum* sitting with the Protector. By 1658 Lely was described by the historian William Sanderson as one of the seven 'English Modern Masters' of note in portrait painting (Sanderson, 5). Two years later, on 20 June 1660, he had established sufficient reputation and influential supporters to be sworn in to the post of Charles II's principal painter, although he was not formally appointed by the king's letter of privy seal until 25 February 1662. The first instalment of his annual pension of £200 'during pleasure as formerly to Sr A. Vandyke' was made in October 1661 (Gibson, 116). He was granted naturalization by parliament on 16 May 1662 and exempted from paying local taxes on his house (ibid.).

Royal portraiture Unlike Van Dyck, who held a virtual monopoly of royal portraiture during Charles I's reign, Lely was the most prominent and successful of a number of Restoration artists who painted Charles II. Recent research has suggested he had only three sessions of sittings with the king, resulting in three *ad vivum* head studies. Notable examples of his portraits of Charles (although only partly by Lely) include a full length in garter robes (Royal Collection), a three-quarter length, standing, in armour (Royal Collection), and a rather informal, seated full length in garter robes (Suffolk county council, Euston Hall, Suffolk). Numerous copies of these and other portraits were produced; in Lely's studio at his death there were seventeen copies of portraits of Charles II. Interestingly the king seems to have owned no finished portrait of himself by Lely. Although he painted Queen Catherine of Braganza on a number of occasions—for example, in a three-quarter length portrait, seated, with hands folded in her lap, dressed in cream satin (Royal Collection)—her preferred artist was not in fact Lely but the Catholic Flemish artist Jacob Huysmans. Lely's more important royal patrons were the king's brother, James, duke of York, and his first wife, Anne Hyde. His first portraits of them were the magnificent pendants (Scot. NPG) to commemorate their wedding in 1660, commissioned by Anne's father, the chancellor, Edward Hyde, first earl of Clarendon. Along with the equally grand double portrait of Anne's brother, Lord Cornbury, and his wife, they hung in richly carved frames in Clarendon's picture gallery, in Worcester House, Strand, defiant challenges to Clarendon's collection of Van Dycks. Lely may have met the Hyde family, in exile in the Netherlands, when he made a brief return visit to The Hague in 1656 to attend to family business. Direct commissions from the duchess began several years later in the early 1660s when, over a four- to five-year period, she commissioned him to paint a group of three-quarter length portraits, known as *The Windsor Beauties* (Royal Collection), of the most beautiful women at her own and the queen's court. Independent portraits of Anne herself were also commissioned during this period—for example, a full length in a white satin dress, seated on a chair of state, which Pepys saw in Lely's studio on 18 June 1662, and, a few years later, a seated full length, holding a tress of hair in her right hand, and a three-quarter length of this same type (all in the Royal Collection). For the duke of York, Lely produced *The Flaggmen*, a series of thirteen three-quarter length portraits of flag officers who had served under him during the battle of Lowestoft in June 1665, although in contrast to *The Windsor Beauties*, which with one exception are autograph Lelys, all but the heads of *The Flaggmen* are studio works. Another important and prominent patron, especially during the 1660s, was the king's chief mistress, Barbara Villiers, countess of Castlemaine and duchess of Cleveland, who seems to have been something of an inspiration to Lely (see below). His role portraits of her as Minerva, the Virgin Mary, Mary Magdalen, and her namesake St Barbara represent some of his most dramatic female portraits and helped establish her reputation as temporarily the most beautiful, rapacious, and powerful woman at court.

Lely's studio Pepys recorded in a diary entry for 18 July 1666 that Lely was so busy that his next free appointment for a sitting was in six days' time, between seven and eight in the morning. To help meet the increasing demand for his work from court circles, Lely ran a large and well-organized studio. As early as 1648 he had employed—briefly—Robert Hooke, the future architect. Four years later he applied to the Painter–Stainers' Company for permission to take on an apprentice, and as he became busier and more successful he employed greater numbers of assistants. Among those who worked in his studio were

Joseph Buckshorn, Jan van der Eyden, Bartholomew Fleshier, Thomas Hawker, Frederick Sonnius, and Henry Tilson. Some who went on to enjoy individual success were employed for relatively short periods, for example, the French artist Nicholas Largillière and the English artist John Greenhill, while others, such as John Baptist Gaspars, who painted postures and draperies for Lely, was so closely linked with Lely that contemporaries referred to him as 'Lely's Baptist'. Another artist whose close association with Lely obscures his own independent practice as a landscape painter was the artist and collector Prosper Henry Lankrink, who painted some of Lely's landscape backgrounds and flower and ornamental details.

Although Lely was highly secretive about his method of working, only rarely allowing assistants or close friends such as the fellow artist Mary Beale to watch him paint, he seems to have followed methods similar to those used by Van Dyck. Sitters were booked in at hourly intervals, usually as was traditional from 9 a.m. to 4 p.m., although, as Pepys noted, it could be earlier if Lely was exceptionally busy. A quick chalk sketch would be the basis of the composition, with sitters able to choose postures or poses from a large selection of numbered examples in the studio. The easel would be placed at an angle to catch the light, with Lely standing some 6 feet from the sitter, the light falling over his left shoulder. Over a terracotta-coloured underpainting the outline of the sitter's hair would be indicated, although only the area of the face itself would be carefully worked up; the study for the duke of York's head (NPG) gives an excellent idea of this technique. Lely then took a hog bristle 'pencil' or brush and laid in the flesh colour for the hands before painting the drapery in a middle tint. No further sittings would be required and the painting was passed to an assistant for completion, with studies of hands or drapery available for further guidance. If necessary, lay figures, listed in Lely's posthumous studio sale, could be draped with some of the many pieces of fabric and cloth kept specifically as props. Before leaving the studio the portrait would be passed back to Lely for final finishing. Increased pressure of work meant that in many cases only the head would have been painted by Lely, understandably provoking criticism from some sitters. A great many works were copied in the studio by assistants, mostly to supply the demand for images of royal patrons and court beauties. To help facilitate such copying, Lely seems to have used a particular copying device which involved a piece of white or black muslin being placed over the picture to be copied, which was then screwed onto the copying frame. The image was traced onto the muslin with chalk and the image transferred by placing the muslin over a fresh piece of canvas and patting the tracing with a clean handkerchief. According to a letter Lady Chaworth wrote to her brother Lord Roos in October 1674, Lely required two weeks for a copy to be made, in this case of her sister-in-law's portrait, which was to be sent to a friend.

The pigments for the colours so characteristic of many of Lely's portraits—saffron, apricot, cinnamon, and russet—together with the less usual range of cooler pinks and blues, were mostly ground in the studio by an assistant, John Young, although some paints would be bought from professional colourmen. Lely preferred lean rather than rich oily pigments, but as he became busier his paint, particularly in his draperies, became thinner and broader. This seems to have been caused by a change in technique from the mid-1660s, whereby he exchanged his earlier double layer of preparatory ground for a single layer which could be applied more quickly to the canvas. Shortly after this, again to cope with increasing demands on his time, the earlier variety of poses and postures became more limited and repetitive.

Lely as a collector Pressure of work was also the reason, according to Buckeridge, for Lely's decision to form his impressive collection of old master and contemporary paintings, sculpture, prints, and drawings, as he was too busy to travel to Italy and study the work of other artists at first hand.

> In his younger Days, he [Lely] was very desirous to finish the Course of his studies in *Italy*, but being hinder'd from going thither by the great Business he was perpetually involv'd in, he resolv'd to make himself amends, by getting the best *Drawings*, *Prints* and *Paintings* of the most celebrated *Italian* hands. (Buckeridge, 445)

Although there was a well-established tradition on the continent of artists forming collections, Lely was really the first artist to do so in England. Exactly when he began to collect is not known, although his early association with George Geldorp, a recognized dealer and buyer at the Commonwealth sales of Charles I's collection, must surely be significant. Like Geldorp, Lely was himself a buyer at these sales, purchasing eight paintings—'A Picture of the Kinge, the Duke of York and the Princess Royall' and 'A Picture of Cupid and Psiche', both by Van Dyck, 'A Picture of an old Man with a shell in his hand', 'A Picture made by Carecelly', 'A Picture of Tirburgh', 'A Picture of an Hermit', 'A Picture of Fettey', and 'A Landscape of Bredenburgh'; four sculptures—'A Statue of Helen', 'A Centaur in Brass', 'Foure Heads in Marble', and 'The Trionke of a body in Marble'; and a picture frame, which were all later returned in 1661 to the committee for the restoration of the royal collection (House of Lords, main papers relating to the king's goods, May 1660 to 11 June 1660, no. 86). At his death Lely owned no fewer than 575 paintings, although over half (about 320) were works either by himself or his studio. Of the rest the largest proportion were by Dutch and Flemish and then north Italian artists, with a few paintings by French and Spanish artists. It was a very wide-ranging collection, with portraits, landscapes, and religious paintings predominating, and smaller numbers of mythological, still-life, and *vanitas* subjects. Many artists were represented by a single painting, though there were several examples by others, such as Van Dyck, Rubens, Antonio Mor, Veronese, Tintoretto, and Jacopo Bassano. In the case of Van Dyck, Lely owned twenty-two portraits, twelve of which were of women, including *Lady Elizabeth Thimbelby and Dorothy, Viscountess Andover* (National Gallery, London). In addition he owned two religious paintings, a *Crucifix* and a *Blessed Virgin and*

Saviour, plus a number of copies after Van Dyck. His collection of drawings and prints was perhaps even more impressive; Lely proudly considered it to be 'the best in Europe' (Beale, MS Rawl. 8.572). It totalled some 10,000 items, all identifiable from the 'PL' stamp applied posthumously by one of his executors, the lawyer Roger North. It was particularly strong in sixteenth-century Italian drawings, especially the work of Raphael and Parmigianino, although Dutch, Flemish, and some English artists were also represented. His print collection was of a particularly high quality, with large numbers of rare examples and early states by Marc Antonio Raimondi and Van Dyck. Little is known about how the collection was formed, though many items were probably acquired through dealers such as the Dutch-born Gerrit von Uylenburgh, who worked briefly in Lely's studio and who, according to the colourman Charles Beale, had valued the collection at approximately £10,000. Others could have been bought by Lely directly from London-based artists, given to him as gifts, or acquired through relatives of deceased collectors. In the case of his many Van Dycks, he may have bought some from Van Dyck's widow, though more probably he benefited from the sequestration of royalist estates. Such a collection gave Lely a high status and a reputation as a connoisseur and an arbiter of taste, adding style to his extravagant way of life and without doubt contributing to the substantial debts outstanding at his death. Moreover, the dispersal of the collection through three highly publicized and well-organized sales in 1682, 1688, and 1694 was of fundamental importance to the development of the auction as a professional venue for buying and selling works of art.

Buckeridge believed Lely's own 'wonderful *Style* in Painting … his correct Draft, and beautiful Colouring … and the pleasing Variety of his Postures' were the result of 'daily conversing with the Works of these great Men' (Buckeridge, 445). Van Dyck's influence is certainly apparent in many of Lely's female portraits, especially in their range of poses, attributes, and settings, the use of fabric and gestures to convey movement and poise, and their mixture of contemporary and romanticized dress. His Parmigianino drawings were similarly influential, giving to many of Lely's full-length female portraits an earlier Renaissance aesthetic of beauty and grace, and, like many other works in the collection, would have provided a potential pattern book of ideas, compositions, and poses. Given Lely's belief that 'Painting is nothing more than Draught' (Talley, 316), his drawing collection, like his own preparatory studies, would have had clear pedagogic value for his studio assistants.

Later years From 1650 until his death in 1680 Lely lived in a house in the north-east corner of the still-fashionable piazza in Covent Garden. With a frontage of only 29 feet, the house must have been quite narrow, with a number of small wainscoted rooms, including a dining-room, a parlour, a room behind the parlour, a room over the parlour, a bedchamber, and a closet, as listed in his executors' account book. The workroom or studio and the great room were presumably the more public rooms of the house. Sitters would wait and be received in the great room, where many of the largest and most important works from Lely's collection must have been displayed, although Pepys on one of his frequent visits to Lely's studio could clearly see other fine pictures in other rooms in the house. On one visit he enviously recorded the lavish lifestyle Lely clearly enjoyed, noting how well his table was laid for his supper. At the time of his death Lely kept four servants and a housekeeper, Mrs Fane. He also had a house at Kew and properties at Greetwell and Willingham in Lincolnshire and in The Hague. He never married, but with his common-law wife, Ursula, who died shortly after giving birth to a son in 1674, Lely had two surviving children—a son and heir, John Lely, whose schooling was a heavy financial responsibility for Lely's executors, and a daughter, Anne, who only a few months before his death returned home to live with him. Perhaps unaccustomed to having his comfortable routine disturbed, and with genuine fatherly concern that she 'might see something of ye world', Lely asked a friend, Dr Nicholas Denton, to introduce her to people of her own age (Verney and Verney, 2.238). John Lely later married the wealthy daughter of Sir John Knatchbull, while Anne married a Peter Frowd of Gray's Inn in December 1693 and died soon afterwards in childbirth.

Pepys may have found Lely 'a mighty proud man … and full of state' after a visit to the studio on 25 March 1667 (Pepys, 8.129), but to close friends such as Charles and Mary Beale, Hugh May (whose long friendship with Lely was celebrated in their famous double portrait of *c.*1675; Audley End, Essex), Roger, Dudley, Francis, and Montagu North, or the printseller Richard Tompson, he must have been a relaxed and entertaining companion, enjoying an evening with Robert Hooke drinking his 'rare but heady wine' (*The Diary of Robert Hooke, 1672–1680*, ed. H. W. Robinson, 1935, 209), or discussing art with the Norths while looking over his collection. According to Vertue, Charles II took 'grate Pleasure in his Conversation, which he found to be as agreeable as his Pencil' (Vertue, *Note books*, 2.148). He could be generous with friends, as in the encouragement he gave Mary Beale, allowing her the rare honour of watching him work, and supportive of younger artists, as in the endorsement he gave to the work of George Freeman, a painter and tapestry designer. But his supposed discomfiture at the talent of his assistant Greenhill and the threat posed by the rivalry of Verelst, which saw him temporarily remove himself to his house at Kew, or his alleged refusal to attend upon the fire judges in the City to paint their portraits (the commission eventually went to John Michael Wright), suggest an arrogance and hauteur conveyed in a number of his self-portraits, for example, the three-quarter length holding a small figurine (NPG) or the beautiful pastel (FM Cam., formerly with the Lely family), where he represents himself as an elegant courtier and fitting heir to Van Dyck. He was clearly confident, well read (his library contained works by Torquato Tasso and Edmund Spenser), and a fine connoisseur, but, according to Roger North, a poor businessman. In a period noted for its scepticism he seemed surprised about his success, agreeing with a friend that he knew he was no great painter, but 'I am the best you have' (Richardson, 228).

For his entire Restoration career Lely dominated court portraiture. Other artists' work was often judged in the context of his or Van Dyck's, with many contemporaries regarding Lely as the latter's natural successor, especially from the way Lely presented himself in his self-portraits, the lavish lifestyle he adopted, and the way he ran his studio. Both artists may have been acclaimed primarily for their portraits, but they were also highly regarded as painters of other genres. Lely had to wait longer for his knighthood, which was granted shortly before his death, and, unlike Van Dyck, had to contend with occasional competition, but overall his position was equally prized. He did have his detractors, such as those ladies of the Bagot family who chose to have their portraits painted by J. M. Wright in 1676, whom they felt was more 'moderate' in comparison to Lely, and he was frequently charged with making his paintings, especially of women, too alike. As one contemporary wrote, 'all his Pictures had an Air one of another, all the Eyes were Sleepy alike. So that Mr Walker Ye Painter swore Lilly's Pictures was all Brothers & Sisters' (BM, Add. MS 22950, fol. 41). While many of his portraits are arguably more individualized than this view maintains, the issue of likeness is central to an understanding of Lely's construction of female beauty. Unlike some Renaissance theorists who advocated an ideal of beauty composed from the best features of the most beautiful women, Lely had an ideal based on a specific facial type, allegedly the heavy brows and hooded, almond shaped eyes of Barbara Villiers. As Lely himself was supposed to have remarked, 'it was beyond the compass of art to give this lady her due, as to her sweetness and exquisite beauty' (*Reliquiae Hearnianae*, ed. P. Bliss, 1869, 2.57–8). With his male sitters, Lely was accused of making them appear blacker and more morose than they actually were. Lady Chaworth again wrote to her brother to say she had 'made the copier correct' this particular fault 'of Mr Lilie's' (BM, Add. MS 22950, fol. 41). To the poet John Dryden, writing after Lely's death, 'he drew many graceful pictures, but few of them were like. And this happened to him, because he always studied himself more than those who sate to him' (Dryden, *Works*, 3.5–6).

Death and reputation Lely died suddenly in his studio in his house in Covent Garden on 30 November 1680, from some sort of seizure, having been visited there that morning by his friend and physician, Dr William Stokeham. He left debts and legacies totalling about £9000, which explains why his executors were forced to sell his famous collection. He had made his will on 4 February 1679 after being urged to do so by another close friend, the lord keeper, Francis North. Although he had been naturalized, his foreign birth meant that his estate would have reverted to the crown, rather than gone to his children, had he died intestate. The will confirms an indenture, made the previous day, of a settlement on his son, John, of his manor of Willingham, as well as the life interest of the farm rents on that estate, and a life-term lease of the manor and rectory at Greetwell, held from the church at Lincoln. His executors were Roger North, Hugh May, and Dr Stokeham, who were instructed to provide for Lely's two surviving children and be responsible for their schooling and eventual marriage. Also mentioned is a codicil, where Lely would leave specific legacies to particular friends and servants, although it seems no such codicil was ever made. The main beneficiary was Lely's son and heir, John; Lely's daughter, Anne, was to receive £3000; his sister Katherina Maria Werk, the widow of a Gelderland burgomeister, £2000. Each of the executors was to receive £100 as a 'kind Remembrance of their Friendship and in Recompense of their care and Trouble'. A further £100 was to go to the poor of the parish of St Paul's, Covent Garden, where Lely was buried (with thirteen official mourners attending his funeral), £50 to the rebuilding of St Paul's, and £100 for a monument to himself. This was commissioned from the sculptor Grinling Gibbons and based on one of Lely's self-portraits (the exact one is not known); on 5 March 1684 the executors' account book records a payment of 1*s*. 6*d*. to a porter 'to carry Sr Peters picture to Mr Gibbons' (BL, Add. MS 16174, fol. 61*v*); the monument was destroyed by fire in 1795.

Lely's artistic legacy lived on long after his death. The many copies after his work, and prints made after his portraits by printmakers such as Isaac Beckett and Alexander Browne, ensured his continuing influence on younger portrait painters such as Willem Wissing, who took over some of Lely's clientele after his death, as well as later generations of artists such as Sir Joshua Reynolds. Some nineteenth-century commentators such as William Hazlitt were very critical of his work, especially his female portraits, describing *The Windsor Beauties* as 'a set of kept-mistresses, painted, tawdry, showing off their theatrical or meretricious airs and graces, without one real touch of real elegance or refinement, or one spark of sentiment to touch the heart' (*The Complete Works of William Hazlitt*, ed. P. P. Howe, 1934, 10.38). By the early twentieth century C. H. Collins-Baker's *Lely & the Stuart Portrait Painters* (2 vols., 1912) helped reinstate Lely's position and technical competence. A later monograph by R. B. Beckett (1953) and the magisterial work of Sir Oliver Millar, especially his National Portrait Gallery exhibition catalogue of 1978, refocused scholarly attention on an artist who had become an unfashionable and rather maligned figure of English art history. After an interval of over twenty years, the exhibition 'Painted Ladies' at the National Portrait Gallery in 2001 and its accompanying publication, although focusing only on Lely's female portraits, those images Oliver Millar refers to as 'the most familiar and vulnerable aspect of Lely's achievement' (Millar, *Tudor, Stuart and Early Georgian Pictures*, [1/2].125), have provided a new generation of viewers with the opportunity to evaluate the abilities of one of the most technically gifted and artistically sophisticated English portrait painters.

DIANA DETHLOFF

Sources A. Houbraken, *De groote schouburgh* (Amsterdam, 1719), vol. 2 • [B. Buckeridge], 'An essay towards an English school of painters', in R. de Piles, *The art of painting, and the lives of the painters* (1706), 398–480 · Vertue, *Note books* · F. Verney and M. Verney, *The Verney memoirs during the seventeenth century* (1925) · 'Booke of orders and constitutions', London Painter-Stainers' Company · W. Sanderson, *Grafice, or, The use of pen and pensil* (1658) · K. Talley, *Portrait painting in England: studies in the technical literature before 1700* (1987) · J. Wood, 'Van Dyck and the earl of Northumberland: taste and collecting in Stuart England', *Van Dyck 350*, ed. S. Barnes and A. K. Wheelock jun., Studies in the History of Art, 46 (Washington, 1994), 281–324 · *The poems of Richard Lovelace*, ed. C. H. Wilkinson (1930) · 'Original book of accompts of the Hon. Roger North, Dr William Stokeham and Hugh May, executors of Sir Peter Lely, during the years 1679–1692', BL, Add. MS 16174 · 'Proposal to the parliament of Sir Balthazar Gerbier, knt., Peter Lely and George Geldorp concerning the representing in oil, pictures of all the memorable achievements since the parliament's first sitting, c. 1651', BL, Miscellaneous Historical Papers, Stowe MS 184, fol. 283 · *The manuscripts of his grace the duke of Rutland*, 4 vols., HMC, 24 (1888–1905), vol. 2 · Pepys, *Diary* · O. Millar, *Sir Peter Lely* (1978) [exhibition catalogue, NPG] · K. Gibson, '"Best belov'd of kings": the iconography of Charles II', 3 vols., PhD diss., U. Lond., 1997 · D. Dethloff, 'The executors' account book and the dispersal of Sir Peter Lely's collection', *Journal of the History of Collections*, 8 (1996), 15–51 · C. Beale, notebook, 1677, Bodl. Oxf., MS Rawl. 8°572 · main papers relating to the king's goods, May 1660 to 11 June 1660, no. 86, House of Lords · O. Millar, 'Abraham van der Doort's catalogue of the collection of Charles I', *Walpole Society*, 37 (1958–60) · J. Richardson, *Essay on the theory of painting* (1717) · memorandum books of Ozias Humphry, RA, BM, Add. MS 22950, fol. 4 · will, PRO, PROB 11/365, fols. 45v–47 · O. Millar, *The Tudor, Stuart and early Georgian pictures in the collection of her majesty the queen*, 2 vols. (1963)

Archives Wilts. & Swindon RO, inventory of his collection of paintings | BL, executor account book, Add. MS 16174 · V&A, sale catalogue of his collection of paintings

Likenesses P. Lely, self-portrait, oils, *c.*1660, NPG [*see illus.*] · P. Lely, self-portrait, oils, *c.*1665–1670, Uffizi, Florence · P. Lely, self-portrait, oils, *c.*1675 (with H. May), Audley End House, Essex · I. Beckett, mezzotint (after P. Lely), BM, NPG · A. de Jode, line engraving (after P. Lely), BM, NPG

Le Maçon, Robert [Robert La Fontaine] (**1534/5–1611**), Reformed minister and diplomat, was born at Illiers, near Chartres, in the Orléanais, France; his parents' names are unknown. In 1557 he was one of the founding ministers of the important Reformed church in Orléans, which became the capital of the Huguenot movement during the first war of religion in France in 1562. There he also probably met and married, about 1557, his first wife, Anne (*d.* 1605), who, according to the 1593 census of aliens in London, originally came from that city.

La Fontaine (as he was usually known, being sieur de la Fontaine) fled to England at the time of the St Bartholomew's day massacre in 1572, and in October 1574 was appointed minister of the French and Walloon refugee church in London. Throughout his long pastorate he worked diligently to establish and maintain Calvinist orthodoxy among this congregation. In 1578 he revised the church's written 'discipline', the first revision since the church had been re-established under Elizabeth I in 1560. He also composed a Calvinist catechism for the members of his own flock, translated into English and published in 1580 as *A catechisme and playne instruction for children which prepare themselves to communicate in the holy supper*, and published in French in 1602 as *Catechisme et instruction familière pour les enfans qui se preparent à communiquer à la saincte cène*.

La Fontaine also maintained a correspondence with protestant leaders throughout Europe, such as Theodore Beza in Geneva and Philippe Du Plessis-Mornay in France. In 1578 he helped Du Plessis compose his protestant manifesto, *Traité de l'eglise*. During Henry IV's wars against the Catholic League and Spain in the 1590s, Du Plessis arranged to have La Fontaine appointed the French king's unofficial representative in England. La Fontaine was most heavily involved in the complex political and military negotiations between Henry IV and Elizabeth I during their mutual war against Spain from 1595 to 1598. He was in direct communication with both monarchs, and maintained a wide correspondence with influential royal councillors, such as Villeroy in France and Burghley and Robert Cecil in England, and with nobles such as the duc de Bouillon and the earl of Essex. He was one of the few French negotiators who took part in drawing up the treaty of Greenwich in 1596, chosen because, as the chief French negotiator, De Sancy, wrote to him, 'we did not think that we could employ anyone more trustworthy than you, nor one who would be more acceptable to them [the English negotiators]' (Kermaingant, 46–7). By this time La Fontaine was sixty-one (preface to *Les funerailles de Sodome*, 2nd edn, 1610), and after Henry's peace with Spain in 1598 he withdrew himself from active diplomacy, but throughout the following years he continued to maintain contact with Du Plessis and remained an important link between the Huguenots in France and the English church and government. In 1601, at the French Reformed church's national synod at Gergeau, he even presented a proposal to unite the English and French churches, with little success.

The previous year La Fontaine had published the first edition of a series of sermons on the story of Lot, *Les funerailles de Sodome et de ses filles*. In August 1605 his wife, Anne, died, and six months later, on 25 February 1606, he married, as his second wife, Maturine Doute (or Doubts; *d.* 1621), also a native of Orléans. By the end of his life, La Fontaine had spent almost exactly half of his years in France and half in England. He died in 1611, and was buried in his parish of St Anne Blackfriars, London, on 6 November, his death even attracting the notice of John Chamberlain (*The Chamberlain Letters*, ed. E. M. Thomson, 1966, 319) and Isaac Casaubon. His widow died on 15 February 1621. His family maintained a foot in both countries. His son, Louis, a king's councillor who had assisted his father in his diplomatic activities, maintained the family name in France, as the sieur de la Fontaine et d'Ancreville. Meanwhile his three daughters—Anne, Rachel, and Sara—all married male members of the Harderet family, another prominent refugee family, and remained in England.

CHARLES G. D. LITTLETON

Sources F. de Schickler, *Les églises du réfuge en Angleterre*, 3 vols. (Paris, 1892) · C. Littleton, 'The French church of London in European protestantism: the role of Robert le Maçon, dit de la Fontaine, minister, 1574–1611', *Proceedings of the Huguenot Society*, 26 (1994–7), 45–57 · MSS 3–4, consistory minutes, 1578–1615, French Protestant Church of London, Soho Square · A. M. Oakley, ed., *Actes du consistoire de l'église française de Threadneedle Street, Londres*, 2,

Huguenot Society of London, 48 (1969) · J. H. Hessels, ed., *Ecclesiae Londino-Batavae archivum*, 3 vols. (1887–97) · P. Auguis, ed., *Mémoires et correspondance de Philippe du Plessis-Mornay*, 12 vols. (1824–5) · P. Laffleur de Kermaingant, *L'ambassade de France en Angleterre sous Henri IV: la mission de Jean de Thumery* (1886) · J. Berger de Xivrey, ed., *Recueil des lettres missives de Henri IV*, 9 vols. (1843–75) · T. Birch, *Memoirs of the reign of Queen Elizabeth*, 2 vols. (1754) · J. Quick, *Synodicon in Gallia reformata*, 2 vols. (1692) · I. Scouloudi, *Returns of strangers in the metropolis, 1593, 1627, 1635, 1639: a study of an active minority*, Huguenot Society of London, 57 (1985) · *The registers of the French church, Threadneedle Street, London*, 1, ed. W. J. C. Moens, Huguenot Society of London, 9 (1896) · parish register, St Ann Blackfriars, GL, MS 4510/1 [marriage, 25 Feb 1606; burial, 6 Nov 1611]

Archives BL, Cotton MSS, Caligula E vii, ix · BL, Cotton MSS, Galba E vi, ix · BL, Lansdowne MSS 43–55, 102–106 · LPL, papers of Anthony Bacon, MSS 654, 657 · PRO, State Papers Foreign, Elizabeth I

Wealth at death approx. £900 bequests — £150 to repay loan from consistory; £600 to widow; £15 to poor of churches; £53 to relations and servants; £150 library to the consistory of French church; plus £12 household contents; basin, ewer, and silver cup to eldest son; residue divided equally among children: will, PRO, PROB 11/118, sig. 103

Leman, Anna Margharetta (1704?–1743). *See under* Brett, Anne, countess of Macclesfield (1667/8–1753).

Leman, Sir John (1544–1632), merchant and mayor of London, was born at Saxlingham, Norfolk, a younger son of John Leman of Beccles in Suffolk and the neighbouring Norfolk village of Gillingham, and his wife, Mary, the daughter of John Alston of Pevenham in Bedfordshire. Nothing is known of his education before he became a merchant. Apart from his remarkable longevity and the fact that, unusually for a civic dignitary, he never married, Leman is noteworthy for his generous philanthropic benefactions and provides an apt illustration of the tendency for the principal economic interests of many London aldermen to be in domestic wholesale rather than overseas trade. Settled in London but with continuing close connections with Suffolk, a county which, during his lifetime, was acquiring increasing importance as a source of metropolitan butter and cheese supplies, Leman was well placed to profit from this trade. Another wholesaling interest was the trade in pepper received as dividend from his investment in East India Company joint stocks.

Leman was prominent in civic activities, becoming prime warden of the London Fishmongers' Company in 1605, in which year he was elected alderman for Portsoken ward, transferring to Langbourne ward in 1616 and to Cornhill in the following year. He served as a sheriff of London in 1606–7 and as lord mayor in 1616–17. He was knighted by James I on 9 March 1617. His mayoralty saw a more than usually magnificent mayoral pageant, *Chrysanaleia, the Golden Fishing, or, Honour of Fishmongers*, with text by the official city poet, Anthony Munday. Drawings of the devices here presented are still preserved in Fishmongers' Hall. As lord mayor, Leman acquired a reputation for hospitality, sumptuously entertaining several privy councillors and lords at his house near Billingsgate on Easter Monday 1617, while earlier, in February, he had extended lavish hospitality to the French ambassador and

Sir John Leman (1544–1632), by unknown artist, 1616

his train, even though, as John Chamberlain reported, the lord mayor 'poore man had been at death's doore these sixe or seven weekes' (*Letters of John Chamberlain*, 2.55). However, he survived and lived on for a further fifteen years.

A major problem of Leman's mayoralty was the provision of a loan of £100,000 demanded from the city by James I early in 1617. Although the initial efforts of the lord mayor and his civic colleagues were warmly praised by the king, the government's tone soon changed to sharp criticism of their delays which were imputed 'either to backwardnes and ill affeccion … or to the negligent and indiscreate carriage of the same' (Overall, 4.75). In the end only £96,466 of the required £100,000 was forthcoming. Only a handful of the contributors to the loan received satisfaction when repayment fell due after one year and indeed many still remained unsatisfied when Leman died in London on 9 March 1632. He was buried on 3 May in the now demolished church of St Michael, Crooked Lane, where a splendid funerary monument testified in Latin to his manifold virtues.

Among the beneficiaries of Leman's will, dated 8 July 1631, was Christ's Hospital, of which he had been president since 1618, and which gained lands in Whitechapel valued at £2000. There were smaller legacies (£150 in all) to St Bartholomew's Hospital and Bridewell, and provision for the poor of several parishes and for sea coal for the needy inhabitants of the almshouses of his livery company. Spiritual needs were not neglected, notably a legacy of £1000 to be invested to provide an annual payment of £10 to the preachers at Paul's Cross and a stipend of £40 for a Thursday lecturer 'of honest and good life and conversation' for the church of St Mary-at-Hill. Nor did Leman forget his East Anglian origins. In addition to his purchase of the manor of Warboys in Huntingdonshire from Sir Oliver Cromwell, he had in 1605 bought the manor of Brampton, a few miles south of Beccles. His most notable East Anglian benefaction was the school in Beccles which still bears his name and which was to be built together with a house for the master on a messuage bequeathed by Leman. The school was to serve forty-eight local pupils (all but four of them from Beccles) and to be endowed with lands in nearby districts to the value of at least £800 out of the income from which the resident master and usher were to be supported. The curriculum was to differ from those of grammar schools in that it was to be confined to the three Rs and religious catechizing. The school still flourishes today, though with a wider curriculum.

Robert Ashton

Sources A. B. Beaven, ed., *The aldermen of the City of London, temp. Henry III–[1912]*, 2 vols. (1908–13) • G. E. Cokayne, *Some account of the lord mayors and sheriffs of the city of London during the first quarter of the seventeenth century, 1601–1625* (1897) • W. K. Jordan, *The charities of London, 1480–1660: the aspirations and achievements of the urban society* (1960) • E. A. Goodwyn, *A century of a Suffolk town: Beccles, 1760–1860* [1968] • *Analytical index, to the series of records known as Remembrancia, preserved among the archives of the City of London*, Corporation of London, ed. [W. H. Overall and H. C. Overall] (1878) • *CSP col.*, vols. 4–6 • *The letters of John Chamberlain*, ed. N. E. McClure, 2 (1939) • R. Ashton, *The crown and the money market, 1603–1640* (1960) • R. Ashton, *The city and the court, 1603–1643* (1979) • R. R. Sharpe, *London and the kingdom*, 2 (1894) • Tai Liu, *Puritan London: a study of religion and society in the City parishes* (1986), 157 • P. S. Seaver, *The puritan lectureships: the politics of religious dissent, 1560–1662* (1970), 345 • A. I. Suckling, *The history and antiquities of the county of Suffolk*, 2 vols. (1846–8) • private information (2004) [Joanna Gooderham]

Likenesses oils, 1616, Royal Collection [*see illus.*] • oils, second version, Christ's Hospital, Horsham

Leman, Thomas (1751–1826), antiquary, was born at Kirstead, Norfolk, on 29 March 1751, the only son of John Leman (1705–1777), Church of England clergyman, of Wenhaston Hall, Suffolk, and Anne Reynolds (*d.* 1796), daughter of Clement Reynolds of Cambridge. After attending a school at Uggeshall, Suffolk, he entered Emmanuel College, Cambridge, as a pensioner on 15 September 1770, became a fellow-commoner, and took his BA in 1775. He was elected a fellow of Clare College, took holy orders, proceeded MA in 1778, and was readmitted to Emmanuel on 9 November 1783 as a Dixie bye-fellow. Here he formed a lasting relationship with William Bennet, later bishop of Cloyne. Bennet conferred on him the chancellorship of Cloyne in May 1796, which Leman treated as a sinecure and was compelled to resign in 1802 on account of his non-residence. With Bennet, he visited every Roman and British road station in Great Britain. He corresponded extensively with other antiquaries, mainly about British prehistory and the Roman period, and in 1788 was elected FSA.

Leman's reputation as a scholar greatly impressed contemporaries, and contributions were sought by, or sometimes offered by him to, writers of county histories. He wrote short chapters or supplied materials for the histories of Leicestershire, Hertfordshire, Essex, and co. Durham which appeared in his lifetime. He supplied maps of British tribes and of Roman roads and campaigns for J. N. Brewer's *Introduction to the Beauties of England and Wales* (1818) and for Sir Richard Colt Hoare's edition of *The Itinerary of Archbishop Baldwin through Wales* (1806). Of particular significance was his involvement in the planning and execution of *The History of Ancient Wiltshire*, published by Sir Richard Colt Hoare between 1810 and 1821.

Most of Leman's work was conducted within the dogmatic and bookish framework of classical literary studies typical of his time, which on occasion led to friction with those such as William Cunnington, who were producing new evidence about the prehistoric past using purely archaeological methods. But he did point the way forward in certain areas: he was among those who began to appreciate that the prehistoric past could be divided into three ages—of stone, bronze, and iron—and that British prehistory could be interpreted in terms of a series of invasions by different peoples. He appreciated the need for accurate records, so that material little understood in his day might benefit future generations better able to make use of it. Some of his advice on practical matters, such as excavation procedure and the correct appreciation of etymological evidence, was sound. His own fieldwork was devoted to tracing the Roman roads of Britain, and his surviving notes are valuable to modern researchers. In common with most of his contemporaries, however, he accepted as genuine the forged *Itinerary* of Richard of Cirencester, and the edition of this work which appeared with critical notes in 1809 owed much to him.

Leman had no benefice and lived the life of an independent gentleman of means at Bath. He was a founder and original trustee of the Bath Institution. He was married twice, first on 4 January 1796 to Frances Champion (*d.* 1818), daughter and heir of William Nind, barrister, and the widow of Colonel Alexander Champion of Bath. Following her death on 15 January 1818, he married in January 1819 Frances Hodges, daughter of Sir Robert Deane, baronet, and widow of Colonel John Hodges.

Leman died at his house in the Royal Crescent, Bath, on 17 March 1826, and was buried at Walcot, near Bath. He was survived by his second wife. An elaborate cenotaph of his own design, with the armorial bearings of his family and its connections, was erected to his memory in Wenhaston church.

Gordon Goodwin, *rev.* A. E. Brown

Sources Nichols, *Illustrations*, 6.435–54 • G. Monkland, *The literature and literati of Bath: an essay* (1854) • R. W. Bagshawe and T. W. Bagshawe, 'An early antiquary and his friends', *Bedfordshire Magazine*, 9 (1963–5), 57–60 • R. H. Cunnington, *From antiquary to archaeologist: a biography of William Cunnington*, ed. J. Dyer (1975) • K. Woodbridge, *Landscape and antiquity: aspects of English culture at Stourhead, 1718 to 1838* (1970) • Venn, *Alum. Cant.* • H. I. Longden, *Northamptonshire and Rutland clergy from 1500*, ed. P. I. King and others, 16 vols. in 6, Northamptonshire RS (1938–52), vol. 7, p. 235 • *GM*, 1st ser., 96/2 (1826), 373–4

Archives BL, letters, Add. MSS 38288, 35652, 35746, 35752, 35527 • Bodl. Oxf., notes and genealogical papers • Glos. RO, genealogical notes • Luton Museum and Art Gallery, topographical and genealogical notes, notes on Roman roads • Suffolk RO, Ipswich, historical notes and papers relating to parish of Wenhaston | Devizes Museum, Wiltshire, Wiltshire Archaeological and Natural

History Society, notes on Ridgeway and Roman roads, corresp. with William Cunnington and Sir Richard Colt Hoare

Le Marchand, David (1674–1726), ivory carver, was born on 12 October 1674 in Dieppe, the son of Guillaume le Marchand, a painter and possibly also a carver of ivory, and his wife, Madeleine Levasseur, who married in 1658. After the revocation of the edict of Nantes in 1685 Le Marchand, a Huguenot, emigrated (presumably with his parents) to Edinburgh, for in 1696 he was permitted to open a shop there, on condition that he trained local apprentices in his unusual craft. His earliest signed medallion dates from that year, and portraiture became his speciality, although he also carved a few mythological and religious statuettes. By 1705 (and possibly as early as *c.*1700, after the death, in 1699, of Jean Cavalier, ivory medallist to William III and Queen Mary) he had moved to London, where he became naturalized in 1709 and where he spent the rest of his career.

Le Marchand's patrons included royalty—James II, Queen Anne, and George I; nobility—the earls of Leven and of Cromarty, the dukes of Perth and of Marlborough; and whig politicians and intellectuals—such as John Flamsteed, astronomer royal; Samuel Pepys; Sir Christopher Wren; Sir Thomas Guy, founder of the hospital; and William Stukeley, the pioneer archaeologist. He also made portraits of Huguenot artists, such as Michael Garnault, and City of London businessmen, including Sir John Houblon and the Rapers. His known *œuvre*—nearly all signed and some dated—stands at some eighty pieces. Of these ten are in the British Museum and fifteen in the Victoria and Albert Museum, London, while many remain in private hands, often with descendants of their subjects. The largest collection of his work is in a private collection in Toronto, Canada.

Le Marchand's early style was influenced by those of other carvers in Dieppe, such as Jean Mancel, and of his gifted predecessor in London, Jean Cavalier. His earliest portraits, in profile and in low relief, were on an oval plaque, or 'medallion'. Le Marchand also aspired to more ambitious kinds of portraiture, and carved a substantial, masterly bust-in-the-round of John Locke (untraced), perhaps as early as 1697. Other busts on varying scales followed: Anne Churchill, countess of Sunderland (1699 or later; V&A); an anonymous lady, formerly identified as Anne Nellthorpe (1704; priv. coll.); John Vesey, archbishop of Tuam (1702; priv. coll.); Francis Sambrooke (1704; priv. coll.); John, first Baron Somers (1706; Wimpole Hall, Cambridgeshire); Sir Isaac Newton, in two or three versions (1714; National Gallery of Victoria, Melbourne; 1718; BM); and George I (1716; V&A). Le Marchand's busts and plaques of Locke and Newton were much imitated contributions to the iconography of these famous sitters and were probably referred to by marble sculptors such as Rysbrack and Roubiliac when called upon later in the eighteenth century to carve images of such 'British worthies'.

As Le Marchand's self-confidence and technique improved he began to use thicker plaques of ivory, so that the head and shoulders project boldly off the flat background. He probably made preliminary models from the life in wax, for its ductile nature is reflected in the way he then carved the drapery in deeply channelled, sinuous folds. A calligraphic rendering of the curls of the fashionable periwigs and incisively chiselled facial features, as well as precise details of costume, even down to buttons and buttonholes, complete portraits with brilliant characterization redolent of the spirit of the reigns of Queen Anne and George I. They are among the most impressive portraits ever to have been carved in ivory.

Le Marchand's statuettes and narrative plaques are far fewer in number than those of the average continental European ivory carver, partly because of the protestant objection to much Christian imagery, but they are as fine as the portraits. Most intricate is his rendering on a miniature scale of a marble group, *Saturn Abducting Cybele*, while a *Crucified Christ* demonstrates his competence in rendering anatomy and suggesting emotion (both are in the Victoria and Albert Museum, London).

Le Marchand died, probably a pauper, in the French Hospital, Bath Street, Finsbury, London, on 17 March 1726. In the following June the archaeologist William Stukeley noted with regret the death of 'the famous cutter in ivory Monsr. Marchand, who cut my profile' (*Family Memoirs of the Rev. William Stukeley*); his diary also records Stukeley's sitting to Le Marchand for his portrait on 11 July 1722.

CHARLES AVERY

Sources T. Hodgkinson, 'An ingenious man for carving in ivory', *Victoria and Albert Museum Bulletin*, 1/2 (April 1965), 29–32 • S. R. Houfe, 'A whig artist in ivory: David Le Marchand (1674–1726)', *Antique Collector* (April 1971), 66 • J. Kerslake, 'Sculptor and patron? Two portraits by Highmore', *Apollo*, 95 (1972), 25–9 • R. Foah, 'David Le Marchand's Madonna and child', *Muse: Annual of the Museum of Art and Archaeology, University of Missouri–Columbia*, 7 (1974), 38–43 • C. Avery, 'David Le Marchand: Huguenot ivory carver (1674–1726)', *Proceedings of the Huguenot Society*, 24 (1983–8), 113–18, pl. 17–20 • C. Avery, 'Missing, presumed lost: some ivory portraits by David Le Marchand', *Country Life* (6 June 1985), 1562–4 • T. Murdoch, *The quiet conquest: the Huguenots, 1685 to 1985* (1985), 208–12, nos. 303–10 [exhibition catalogue, Museum of London, 1985] • C. Theuerkauff, ed., *Elfenbein: Sammlung Reiner Winkler*, 2 vols. (Munich, 1984–94), vol. 1, pp. 89–92, nos. 46–7; vol. 2, pp. 58–9, no. 20; 160. • C. Avery, *David le Marchand, 1674–1726: 'An ingenious man for carving in ivory'* (1996) • M. Baker, 'Exhibition reviews: Edinburgh, London and Leeds, David le Marchand', *Burlington Magazine*, 88 (1996), 838–9 • records of the burgh of Edinburgh, 1689–1701, Edinburgh City Archives • C. Avery, 'Le Marchand, David', *The dictionary of art* (1996), vol. 19, p. 130 • C. Avery, 'Precursor of eighteenth-century English portrait sculpture: David le Marchand', *British Art Journal*, 1/1 (1999), 27–34 • *Publications of the Huguenot Society*, 'Quarto Series', 17 (1923), 85; 18 (1924), 22; 29 (1926), 90 • *The family memoirs of the Rev. William Stukeley*, ed. W. C. Lukis, 1, SurtS, 73 (1882), 131 • Journal des commissaires of the French hospital 'La Providence', *Publications of the Huguenot Society*, 'Quarto series', 52, 53 [under Le Marchant, David] • Vertue, *Note books*, 2.47, 69–70; 3.13, 17, 50, 61; 4.166

Likenesses J. Highmore, oils, *c.*1723, NPG • D. Le Marchand, self-portrait, ivory; Christies, 1969

Le Marchant, Sir Denis, first baronet (1795–1874), politician, second and eldest surviving son of Major-General John Gaspard *Le Marchant (1766–1812) and his wife, Mary (*d.* 1811), eldest daughter of John Carey, was born at Newcastle upon Tyne on 3 July 1795. The death of his father at Salamanca meant that he was brought up by his maternal aunt and her husband, Peter Mourant, of Candic, Guernsey. He was educated at Eton College, where his name occurs in the school lists for 1805 and 1808, and at Trinity College, Cambridge, but seems to have taken no degree, and was called to the bar at Lincoln's Inn in 1823. In 1828 he published the *Proceedings of the House of Lords in the Gardner Peerage Claim*, in which case he had appeared for the petitioner. Upon the recommendation of William Brougham, a friend of Le Marchant's from Cambridge, Henry Brougham, on becoming lord chancellor in 1830, appointed him his principal secretary. During the debates on the Reform Bill he attended nightly in the House of Commons, and greatly distinguished himself by the reports which he prepared for the use of ministers. He was appointed clerk of the crown in chancery in 1834, and in that year edited a highly successful pamphlet, *The Reform Ministry and the Reform Parliament*, to which his intimate friend Lord Althorp, and also Lord Stanley, Lord Palmerston, and Sir James Graham were contributors; it ran through nine editions. From 1836 to 1841 he was secretary to the Board of Trade, and during the last few months was also a whip. Melbourne created him a baronet in August 1841. Le Marchant was bottom of the poll at Harwich in 1841, won Worcester in 1846, but retired the next year. In the Russell administration of 1847 he was under-secretary for the Home department, and in 1848 returned to the secretaryship of the Board of Trade. In 1850 he was appointed chief clerk to the House of Commons, which office he held until he retired with the thanks of the house in 1871.

On 9 January 1835 Le Marchant married Sarah Eliza (*d.* 1894), fourth daughter of Charles Smith of Sutton, Essex, with whom he had two sons and two daughters. He published privately in 1841 a memoir of his father; edited in 1845 Walpole's *Memoirs of the Reign of George III*, with notes; and, at the request of Frederick, Earl Spencer, wrote the *Memoirs of John, Viscount Althorp*, which, being left incomplete at his death, was completed and published, in 1876, by his son, Sir Henry Denis Le Marchant. He died on 30 October 1874 at his home, 21 Belgrave Place, London.

J. A. HAMILTON, *rev.* H. C. G. MATTHEW

Sources *The Times* (4 Nov 1874) • Boase, *Mod. Eng. biog.* • *The Greville memoirs, 1814–1860*, ed. L. Strachey and R. Fulford, 8 vols. (1938)
Archives HLRO, corresp. and papers • NRA, priv. coll., corresp. and papers | BL, corresp. with Lord Holland, Add. MS 51591 • Borth. Inst., letters to Sir Charles Wood • ING Barings, London, corresp. with Baring family • PRO, corresp. with Lord John Russell, PRO 30/22 • U. Durham L., corresp. with third Earl Grey • W. Sussex RO, letters to duke of Richmond • Woburn Abbey, letters to duke of Bedford
Likenesses J. Phillips, group portrait, oils (*The House of Commons, 1860*), Palace of Westminster, London • wood-engraving (after photograph by Kilburn), NPG; repro. in *ILN* (1851) • wood-engraving, NPG; repro. in *ILN* (1874)
Wealth at death under £9000: probate, 5 Feb 1875, *CGPLA Eng. & Wales*

Le Marchant, John Gaspard (1766–1812), army officer, born on 9 February 1766 at his maternal grandfather's house near Amiens, in Picardy, France, was the eldest son of John Le Marchant (a retired officer of the 7th Queen's Own light dragoons who was from a distinguished and ancient Guernsey family) and his wife, Marie Hirzel, daughter of Count Hirzel de Gratien, *maréchal de camp* of the Swiss guards in the service of France. In Paris the infant was christened John (after his father) and Gaspard (after Admiral Gaspard de Coligny, a Hirzel ancestor) by the Revd Buck, chaplain to the British ambassador. Le Marchant was sent to a boarding-school, Morgan's, in Bath, where he successfully challenged a persistent bully, met Sidney Smith, the future admiral, and was dubbed a dunce by the headmaster, Dr Morgan. After having been brought home, he became studious and, with the help of the family butler, an American loyalist and a man of some education, made up for past neglect by acquiring habits of application that lasted through life. However, he continued to possess a turbulent temper.

John Gaspard Le Marchant (1766–1812), by Philip Jean, 1787

On 25 September 1781 Le Marchant was appointed ensign in the Wiltshire militia and almost at once called out the colonel for allegedly insulting him. The colonel had the wisdom to smooth matters over, and another duel Le Marchant planned at York was stopped by the peace officers. He was appointed ensign in the 1st foot on 18 February 1783, and on the eve of embarking with his regiment for Gibraltar (February 1784) was enticed to a gaming house in Dublin by a superior officer, who won £250 from him. The loss practically meant the sacrifice of his commission, but the regimental paymaster came to his rescue after Le Marchant gave a promise, which he religiously kept, never to touch cards again. He spent three years in garrison at Gibraltar, unable to enjoy a full social life through need to repay the loan and occupying his spare moments in sketching and painting watercolours of scenery in Spain and on the coast of distant Morocco.

Stricken with yellow fever, Le Marchant survived dosing with Jesuit bark, purging, bleeding, and blistering, and returned to Guernsey on sick-leave, where he courted Mary (Polly) Carey (*d*. 1811), eldest of the fourteen children of John Carey, a law officer (jurat) of Guernsey. Neither family approved of an immediate marriage and Le Marchant returned to Gibraltar. On 30 May 1787 he moved to the 6th dragoons as a cornet, in June 1789 commanding George III's escort from Dorchester to Weymouth, where he attracted the king's attention and through his influence advanced to lieutenant in the 2nd dragoon guards on 18 November 1789. Meanwhile, he had married Mary, on 29 October 1789. During the campaign in Flanders (1793–4) he commanded a troop of the 2nd dragoon guards, having been promoted captain on 31 December 1791. On the eve of his first action he confessed in a letter to his wife: 'The forms of religion I do not respect, but the principle I rever [*sic*], and as devoutly as any man I seek the protection of the Supreme' (Thoumine, 14). Towards the end of 1793 he was attached to Lieutenant-General William Harcourt's staff and for a time, as senior officer present, commanded the 2nd dragoon guards in the field. Early in the new year his father died; and on 11 March 1794 he purchased a majority at regulation price in the 16th Queen's light dragoons, continuing to serve in Flanders until September.

Le Marchant was appalled at the poor performance of the British cavalry in Flanders. During 1796 he designed a lighter, curved sabre which was used experimentally in his regiment and later adopted by others, and for this initiative Lord Cornwallis, master-general of the ordnance, and Mr Osborne, the celebrated sword-cutler from Birmingham, both presented him with swords. He also devised a more effective system of cavalry sword-exercise, which was incorporated in a new drill book and which he demonstrated to regular and reserve units throughout the country.

Through the patronage of the duke of York, on 6 April 1797 Le Marchant was appointed lieutenant-colonel without purchase in Hompesch's hussars, moving rapidly to the 29th light dragoons on 29 May and finally to the 7th Queen's Own light dragoons on 1 June, where he insisted on rigorous training, mastery of tactics, and personal commitment by officers. In Flanders he had witnessed the professional ineptitude of staff officers and, in 1798, he began drafting a scheme for a national military college. The duke of York, the commander-in-chief, on being sounded out, observed: 'I can hardly recommend you to sacrifice your time and talents to a project which seems so very unlikely to succeed' (Le Marchant, 65). Nevertheless, Le Marchant refined his ideas in 'An outline of a plan for a regular course of military instruction' for infantry and cavalry officers, envisaging one department dealing with staff duties, the second for cadets seeking their first commission, and a third to provide an educational grounding for entrants to the second department. In addition, a 'legion' of 200 potential non-commissioned officers would train alongside cadets of the second department. In March 1799 he recorded a more favourable response from the duke of York, and on 4 May an embryo first (senior) department, the staff training college, opened in High Wycombe, Buckinghamshire, with Le Marchant as commandant. In December the duke of York chaired a committee which approved the first two departments, rejected the third and the legion, and awarded Le Marchant £500 to cover 'the unavoidable expenses to which he has been exposed during the long period in which he has been engaged in this undertaking' (ibid., 99). A royal warrant, issued on 24 June 1801, formally established the Royal Military College with General Sir William Harcourt (who had been his commander in Flanders) as governor, and Le Marchant himself as lieutenant-governor and superintendent-general at an annual salary of £300. On 17 May 1802 the second (junior) department was opened at Marlow, Buckinghamshire, with Lieutenant-Colonel James Butler appointed its superintendent, and later its commandant. Le Marchant remained at High Wycombe as lieutenant-governor, with oversight of both departments, each of which had its own commandant. However, he found Butler resentful of his perceived interference, and, disappointingly, Harcourt proved an unhelpful absentee. He strove hard at High Wycombe to overcome the antipathy of students to academic subjects; but he was, in practice, powerless to improve standards at Marlow. Plans to build a new college for co-location of the two departments at Sandhurst Park on Bagshot Heath in Surrey made little headway, and Le Marchant's further proposal for organization of an army general staff gained scant support. To Colonel William Stewart he expressed despair at the intransigent, narrow-minded prejudice he faced. Stewart acknowledged his 'cruel difficulties' but urged him to 'persevere, and this country must be grateful at last' (Thoumine, 105). In January 1807 he had to defend himself before a board of general officers against accusations of calumny by Harcourt, after he had once more complained to the governor of inefficiency at Marlow. The following year he was refused permission to train the Portuguese army and was thus condemned to 'the old humdrum routine [which] I am heartily tired of' (ibid., 127).

Le Marchant had gone on half pay as a lieutenant-colonel in 1803, had been promoted colonel on 30 October 1805, and in 1808 was re-designated 'lieutenant-governor and inspector-general of instructions [*sic*]' at the Royal Military College, with a total annual income of £1898. In addition, he had a colonel's pay and the proceeds of private rents in Guernsey. He was promoted major-general on 4 June 1811 and shortly afterwards visited Sandhurst to see the progress of work on the college. Within a week he received notification 'that your situation at the College is incompatible with your rank in the Army' (Thoumine, 140). Le Marchant protested to the duke of York that he had devoted twelve years to developing an organization which had trained more than 200 staff- and 1500 regimental officers. He said that he would, nevertheless, 'cheerfully' resume an active career, but 'respectfully' drew attention to the annual loss of £500, which would adversely affect his large family, especially in view of additional need to support a major-general's 'establishment' abroad. 'Great pecuniary difficulties' were inevitable; and he further remarked to his brother-in-law, Colonel Tom Carey, that 'all I want is bread' (ibid., 142–3).

To no avail. On 25 July 1811 Le Marchant returned to the active list as lieutenant-colonel in the 6th dragoon guards, and on 10 August he sailed from Portsmouth to command the heavy brigade in the Peninsula. Within days of arriving in Lisbon he learned that Mary had died after giving birth to their tenth child. He was present at the capture of Ciudad Rodrigo, on 20 January 1812, and at Llerena on 19 April 1812 when he scattered two French regiments of cavalry with three squadrons of the 5th dragoon guards. At the battle of Salamanca on 22 July, Le Marchant's brigade was posted at the right centre of the allies. Ordered to 'charge at all hazards' (Thoumine, 191) in support of Lieutenant-General Sir Edward Pakenham's flank attack, shortly after 5 p.m. Le Marchant rode his 1000-strong brigade decisively forward to complete the rout of the French left, personally cutting down six of the enemy. Then, leading a detachment of the 4th light dragoons in a minor skirmish after the main action, he fell, mortally wounded. In Pakenham's words, he 'died sabre in hand giving the most princely example' (Longford, 354). Two days later he was buried in an olive grove near the village of Los Arapiles, close to Salamanca. Parliament voted an annual pension of £1000 to his family and £1500 for a memorial to him in St Paul's Cathedral, London.

Of Le Marchant's surviving children (four sons and five daughters, another having died in infancy), Carey Le Marchant, lieutenant and captain in the 1st (Grenadier) guards, was killed in action in 1814; Denis *Le Marchant (1795–1874) was made a baronet and became a government minister; John Gaspard *Le Marchant (1803–1874), also knighted, became a colonial governor; and Thomas Le Marchant (1812–1873) retired as a major. Le Marchant, who because of his Guernsey background retained a noticeable French accent, was slim, nearly 6 feet tall, and was an excellent horseman. He produced many watercolours and sketches, played the flute, read widely, and was devoted to his wife, with whom he conducted a regular and lengthy correspondence while apart. In politics he was a moderate whig, and was once approached to enter parliament. When at High Wycombe he supported a school for poor children at his own cost, at a time when opinions respecting popular education were much divided. A careful administrator and energetic reformer, Le Marchant rarely slept more than five hours a night. His restless, innovative spirit frequently offended more lethargic superiors, and the impetuosity displayed in youth never fully left him. He wrote numerous military papers, but his main publications were *Cavalry Sword Exercise* (1796), *Elucidation of Certain Points in HM Regulations for Cavalry* (1797–8), and *Instructions for the Movement and Discipline of the Provisional Cavalry* (1797–8). JOHN SWEETMAN

Sources *Army List* • D. Le Marchant, *Memoirs of the late Major-General Le Marchant* (1841) • R. H. Thoumine, *Scientific soldier: a life of General Le Marchant, 1766–1812* (1968) • E. Longford [E. H. Pakenham, countess of Longford], *Wellington*, 1: *The years of the sword* (1969) • A. F. Mockler-Ferryman, *Annals of Sandhurst* (1900) • Burke, *Peerage* (1887) • *DNB* • R. Cannon, ed., *Historical record of the second, or queen's regiment of dragoon guards* (1837)

Archives Guille-Allès Library, Guernsey • priv. coll. • Royal Artillery Institution, Woolwich, London, corresp.

Likenesses P. Jean, miniature, 1787, priv. coll. [*see illus.*] • J. D. Harding, drawing, repro. in Thoumine, *Scientific soldier*, facing p. 149 • J. Smith, medallion on monument, St Paul's Cathedral, London • engraving (after J. D. Harding), repro. in Le Marchant, *Memoirs of the late Major-General Le Marchant* • oils, Staff College, Camberley, Surrey • portraits, Royal Military Academy, Sandhurst • sketches, Royal Military Academy, Sandhurst

Le Marchant, Sir John Gaspard (1803–1874), army officer and colonial administrator, the third son of the ten children of Major-General John Gaspard *Le Marchant (1766–1812) and his wife, Mary, *née* Carey (*d.* 1811), was born in England. On 26 October 1820 he was appointed ensign in the 10th foot. In 1821 he purchased a commission as lieutenant in the 57th foot, and in 1825 a commission as captain, first in the 57th, and then in the new 98th foot, in which regiment he served as major in the Cape in 1832. In 1835 he exchanged to an unattached majority, and was appointed adjutant-general, with the rank of brigadier-general, in the British Auxiliary Legion in Spain, where he served in the First Carlist War under generals Sir De Lacy Evans and Sir Charles Chichester. He was in action at Bilbao in September 1835 and was present at the heights of Arleban in Alava (16–18 January 1836), the raising of the siege of San Sebastian and the storming of the Carlist lines (5 May 1836), the passage of the Urumea, the taking of Passages, the general action at Alza in October 1836, and the general actions at Ernani on 10, 13, 15, and 16 March 1837. The queen of Spain created him knight bachelor in 1838 and permitted him to wear the Spanish decorations of San Fernando and Charles III.

On 28 May 1839 Le Marchant married Margaret Anne Taylor, the third daughter of Revd Robert Taylor of Clifton Campville, Staffordshire, and the granddaughter of Revd John Watkins of Clifton Hall; they had several children. Also in 1839 he purchased the lieutenant-colonelcy of the 99th foot, returning from Mauritius, and in 1845 he was transferred to the 85th light infantry, returning from the West Indies. In both of these regiments he instilled severe discipline and introduced elaborate financial arrangements. A dedicated soldier, Le Marchant left the 85th regiment in 1846 to take up an appointment to a civil post in Newfoundland on the understanding that this would advance his military career. He duly became colonel in 1851, major-general in 1858, and lieutenant-general in 1864, but he did not serve in the Crimean War. He acted as lieutenant-governor of Newfoundland from February 1847 to June 1852; lieutenant-governor of Nova Scotia from June 1852 to December 1857; governor of Malta from 1859 to 1864 (when he held the local rank of lieutenant-general); and commander-in-chief at Madras from 1865 to 1868. He was made GCMG in 1860 and KCB in 1865, and became a lieutenant-general and colonel of the 11th (Devonshire) regiment. Le Marchant died of liver disease at his home, 80 St George's Square, London, on 6 February 1874. His interests, apart from soldiering and administration, included riding and farming.

H. M. CHICHESTER, *rev.* LYNN MILNE

Sources *ILN* (14 Feb 1874), 163 • P. B. Waite, 'Le Marchant, Sir John Gaspard', *DCB*, vol. 10 • *Colonial Office List* (1873) • *CGPLA Eng. & Wales* (1874) • d. cert.

Archives BL, corresp. relating to Crimea, Egerton MS 2972 • priv. coll. | Bodl. Oxf., corresp. with Sir John Crampton • National Archives of Malta, corresp. with Odo Russell • U. Durham L., corresp. with third Earl Grey • U. Nott. L., dispatches to duke of Newcastle

Wealth at death £14,000 0*s.* 0*d.*: administration with will, 13 April 1874, *CGPLA Eng. & Wales*

Lemare, Edwin Henry (1865–1934), organist and composer, was born on 9 September 1865 in Ventnor, Isle of Wight, the son of Edwin Lemare, music teacher and organist, and his wife, Margaret, *née* Wicker. He spent his boyhood on the island and was a chorister and organ pupil, under his father's direction, at Holy Trinity Church, Ventnor. Then, in 1876, he won a John Goss scholarship to the Royal Academy of Music, where he studied for six years under George and Walter Macfarren and the organists Charles Steggall and Edmund Hart Turpin. In 1882 he was made organist at St John's Church, Finsbury Park, London. He first established a reputation as a concert organist at the International Inventions Exhibition at South Kensington in 1885; there he played works by Louis Lefébure-Wély, Alexandre Guilmant, Bach, and other composers twice daily for a total of over 100 recitals to demonstrate the new tubular-pneumatic action of the one-manual Brindley and Foster organ. This further led to his employment by competing organ-builders.

In 1886 Lemare began recitals twice a week at the Park Hall, Cardiff, and in the same year he was appointed organist at the parish church and the Albert Hall, Sheffield. In 1892 he returned to London, as organist of Holy Trinity, Sloane Street, and on 1 June he married Marian Broomhead Colton Fox (*b.* 1863/4), daughter of Barnard Platts Broomhead Colton Fox, solicitor. He also became an organ professor and examiner for the Associated Board of the Royal Academy of Music and the Royal College of Music. In 1897 he followed his vicar to St Margaret's, Westminster, where a new Walker instrument was installed.

Lemare's performances in the concert hall were by now leading to his being compared with virtuosi such as the pianists Ignacy Jan Paderewski and Leopold Godowsky. His reputation was heightened by his own organ compositions, among which he enjoyed particular success with *Andantino in D♭* (1892), which was also arranged for small orchestra by Gustav Holst. In 1900–01 he made his first tour of the USA and Canada, sponsored by the organ manufacturer John Austin. The tour encompassed over 100 recitals and led to Lemare's becoming one of the Austin Organ Company's most ardent champions. His marriage meanwhile having failed, on 7 January 1902 he married Elsie Frances (*b.* 1876/7), daughter of David Reith, honorary canon of Rochester Cathedral. He seemingly also married again after he settled in the USA when he became organist of the Carnegie Institute in Pittsburgh from 1902 to 1905.

As time went on Lemare's recitals triumphed to the extent that he became the highest-paid organist in the world. Altogether tours took him across the Atlantic several dozen times and across the Pacific four times, his appearances in Melbourne and Sydney being noteworthy events. In 1908 he inaugurated the huge Hope-Jones pipe organ at Ocean Grove, New Jersey, and in 1915 he performed a series of 121 concerts on the Austin organ at the Panama-Pacific Exposition. When that instrument was relocated to San Francisco's Civic Auditorium in 1917, he became municipal organist there. He remained until 1921, when he took a similar post at City Hall in Portland, Maine, and later he was in Chattanooga, Tennessee, where in 1927 he designed an especially impressive Austin organ.

Lemare's virtuoso organ compositions embraced some 200 opus numbers. They included two symphonies, published in 1899 and 1906, a sonata, a toccata and fugue, and various services of thanksgiving. He also made transcriptions of a wide range of compositions, ranging from Handel's 'Largo' and Schubert's *Serenade* to Tchaikovsky's *Romeo and Juliet* overture and Elgar's *Pomp and Circumstance* march no. 1, via Suppé's *Poet and Peasant* overture and some Neapolitan songs. His transcriptions and performances of Wagner compositions were of especial note, originating a style of registering and organ-scoring that did much to develop organ tone qualities. He made some 120 player rolls for the Aeolian and Welte companies.

In 1925 Lemare's *Andantino in D♭* achieved renewed popularity when adapted by Ben Black and Neil Moret into the song 'Moonlight and Roses'. However, even these royalties could not prevent him from declining into poverty when his health, fame, and technique began to fade. He died in Hollywood on 24 September 1934. In 1956 a volume of his memoirs, augmented by reminiscences by his wife and friends, was published in Los Angeles as *Organs I have Met*.

ANDREW LAMB

Sources P. Hale and W. Osborne, 'Lemare, Edwin (Henry)', *New Grove*, 2nd edn • b. cert. • m. certs. [M. B. C. Fox; E. F. Reith] • www.orgel.com/music/lemare-e.html, 16 Sept 2001 • *CGPLA Eng. & Wales* (1935)

Likenesses portrait, repro. in www.orgel.com/music/lemare-e.html, 13 Sept 2002

Wealth at death £90—in England: administration with will (limited), 29 Jan 1935, *CGPLA Eng. & Wales*

Lemare, Iris Margaret Elsie (1902–1997), conductor and concert organizer, was born on 27 September 1902 at 43 Emperor's Gate, Kensington, London, the daughter of Edwin Henry *Lemare (1865–1934), organist, and his wife, Elsie Reith (*b.* 1876/7). After studying at Bedales School in Hampshire she continued her education at the Jacques Dalcroze School of Eurhythmics in Geneva. In 1925 she entered the Royal College of Music, London, where she studied the organ under George Thalben-Ball and won the Dove prize. At the college she was permitted by the principal, Sir Hugh Allen, to attend the conducting class run by Malcolm Sargent, though it is said that Sargent tended to ignore her presence since she was the only female student. She received greater encouragement from Adrian Boult and from fellow students such as Howard Ferguson, Imogen Holst, Constant Lambert, Michael Tippett, and George Weldon, all of whom participated in the musical activities of the college orchestras and appreciated her talents as a conductor.

In 1931, in association with the composer Elisabeth Lutyens and the violinist Anne Macnaghten, Lemare founded the Macnaghten–Lemare concerts, the purpose of which was 'to present contemporary music of differing trends in which British music predominates'. From 1934 to 1937 these were known as the Lemare concerts. Beginning in the form of three chamber music concerts, performances were initially held at the Ballet Club Theatre, after which the venue transferred to the Mercury Theatre in Notting Hill Gate. Between 1931 and 1935, compositions by some twenty-seven composers were performed, including works by Benjamin Britten, Gerald Finzi, Patrick Hadley, Gordon Jacob, Elisabeth Lutyens, Elizabeth Maconchy, Alan Rawsthorne, and Grace Williams. Every effort was made to reduce expenses: composers having works performed were each expected to sell a minimum of ten tickets. A notable part in stimulating the interest of public and critics alike in the concerts was played by Vaughan Williams, who provided both professional support and financial assistance. It was through the Macnaghten–Lemare concerts that Britten's music received its first performance: the *Sinfonietta*, op. 1, was given in 1933, followed by his choral work *A Boy was Born*. Britten also performed in the concerts as a viola player. Tippett's first string quartet was given its first performance in 1935. In 1950 the concerts were revived as the Macnaghten concerts.

A notable event in Iris Lemare's life was her invitation from Adrian Boult to conduct the BBC Symphony Orchestra in 1936 and 1937; she was the first woman ever to do so. She was also the conductor of the Oxford Chamber Orchestra and the Carlyle Singers. From 1935 to 1939 she gave annual performances of opera at Pollards, a large country house in Essex owned by the Howard family, Handel's *Xerxes* being among the works selected. During the Second World War she established her own orchestra, which performed with soloists including Geza Anda, Peter Donohoe, Joan Hammond, and Benno Moiseivitch. From 1970 to 1984 she was conductor of the Durham County Opera and Opera Nova, performing operas by Britten, Maconchy, and Menotti among others, together with the première of McCabe's *The Play of Mother Courage*. Her last years were spent in lecturing, adjudicating, and examining, primarily in the northern counties. A person of winning charm, she pursued a wide range of interests, including climbing, swimming, skiing, campanology, and ornithology. She died, unmarried, at her home, 10 St Nicholas Croft, Askham Bryan, York, on 23 April 1997, and was cremated. Iris Lemare is remembered not only as the first professional British woman conductor, but also as a tireless supporter of the music of British composers.

G. R. Seaman

Sources *The Times* (8 May 1997) • *The Independent* (13 May 1997) • *Daily Telegraph* (15 May 1997) • b. cert. • d. cert.
Archives U. Warwick Mod. RC, Crossman–Lemare MSS
Likenesses photograph, repro. in *The Times*
Wealth at death £728,146: probate, 22 Sept 1997, *CGPLA Eng. & Wales*

Le Marquand, Cyril (1902–1980), Jersey senator and businessman, was born in St Lawrence, Jersey, on 6 March 1902, the only son of Joshua Le Marquand and his wife, Lilian Mabel, *née* Le Feuvre. His father and uncle were joint owners of the flourishing local corn chandlery and seed and animal fodder merchants Le Marquand Brothers. He attended Victoria College, Jersey, from 1916 to 1919, and then joined the family business.

In the 1930s Le Marquand took a keen interest in economics and politics, both local and national. He attained prominence in the island by leading the opposition to spraying the potato crop with arsenate of lead against the threat of Colorado beetle, and addressed a mass gathering of farmers on the subject in the Royal Square, St Helier. On 18 August 1927 he married May Irene Le Gros. There were twin daughters of the marriage, Elaine and Denise.

At the outbreak of war, in 1939, Le Marquand and his family went to England, where he was appointed assistant director of animal foodstuffs for the Ministry of Food, working in Wales, where he joined the Home Guard. A number of prominent Channel Islanders in exile formed a discussion group to produce a blueprint for political and social reform in the islands when they should be liberated, and drew up an influential document entitled *Nos îles*. Le Marquand was one of this group. On his return to Jersey in 1945, he became a founder member of the Jersey Progressive Party and stood unsuccessfully in the election for deputies that year. He gave evidence to the privy council committee on states reform in 1946, and when a reformed states assembly was elected in 1948 he and his cousin and business partner, John Le Marquand, were among a dozen members of the Progressive Party elected to the new house. As Jersey politicians were unpaid they continued to take an active part in the family business. He served on the committee of essential commodities, which organized food rationing, later becoming its president, and was a moving spirit in the formulation of the compulsory contributory social security scheme. This scheme, which revolutionized island life by the provision of sickness benefit, old age pensions, and free hospital services, caused great social division and was strenuously opposed by the farming community upon whose custom Le Marquand Brothers relied. Nevertheless Le Marquand topped the island-wide poll for senators in 1957.

Le Marquand served on several important states committees, but it was as president of the finance committee (later finance and economics committee), the Jersey equivalent of chancellor of the exchequer, that he really made his mark. The states of Jersey had entered into an agreement with the Westminster government, in 1927, that all necessary steps would be taken to stem the flow of wealth from the United Kingdom to the island for the avoidance of tax. In 1946 United Kingdom citizens began to invest in cheap mortgages on Jersey properties as a loophole in this agreement, and Le Marquand introduced and persuaded the states of Jersey to adopt the borrowing control (Jersey) law, 1947, to block it.

The application of the British government to join the European Common Market seemed likely to provoke a constitutional crisis for the islands, and Le Marquand was elected vice-president of the constitution and Common Market committee in 1967. The committee, of which Senator Ralph Vibert, an experienced local advocate, was president, and which was reinforced by the bailiff (Sir Robert Le Masurier), the law officers, the greffier (clerk) of the states, and two eminent English international lawyers, was involved in protracted high-level discussions over a period of five years. It was seen that under article 227(4) of the treaty of Rome, Jersey as a 'European territory for whose external relations the United Kingdom was responsible' might well lose its right to self-government and independent taxation. In the event, special terms were agreed whereby Jersey would retain its fiscal autonomy and constitutional rights but would extend its right to free trade with the United Kingdom to embrace the European Community. This famous victory led to subsequent economic growth and contributed largely to the prosperity of the island.

Le Marquand died on 27 February 1980 in St Helier, while still active in politics and business. He was survived by his wife and daughters. His contribution to the establishment of the Jersey finance industry was recognized by Williams and Glyns Bank, which established a Senator Cyril Le Marquand scholarship to assist students reading banking, business, and economics in higher educational institutions in the United Kingdom, and by the states of Jersey, which named its new and imposing Treasury and income tax offices in St Helier, Cyril Le Marquand House.

F. L. M. Corbet

Sources *Jersey Evening Post* (6 Nov 1978) · *Jersey Evening Post* (28 Feb 1980) · *Jersey Evening Post* (7 Oct 1980) · *Jersey Evening Post* (31 Aug 1982) · F. L. M. Corbet and others, *A biographical dictionary of Jersey*, [2] (1998) · personal knowledge (2004) · private information (2004)

Lemass, Seán Francis [*formerly* John Francis] (1899–1971), taoiseach, was born John Francis Lemass in Ballybrack, co. Dublin, on 15 July 1899, the second of the seven children of John Timothy Lemass, a Dublin hatter, and his wife, Frances Phelan, of Kilkenny. A scholarship student at the Christian Brothers' O'Connell Schools in Dublin, he abandoned his formal education before he was sixteen to join the Irish Volunteers. He fought in the General Post Office during the 1916 rising, and was briefly imprisoned before being released because of his youth. He re-entered education by taking a commercial course at Rosse's College, but he soon abandoned this in favour of his work as an officer in the volunteers; his work at his father's shop in Capel Street provided him with a modest income and a cover for these activities, which included an important intelligence function. He was arrested by British forces in December

Seán Francis Lemass (1899–1971), by unknown photographer, 1942

1920 and interned at Ballykinlar in co. Down until December 1921, when he was released as part of a general amnesty.

Early life and political career The outbreak of the civil war that followed the signing of the treaty found Lemass on the anti-government side: he was a senior member of the republican garrison in the Four Courts, Dublin, from where he was captured, but escaped. Recaptured in December 1922, he was interned by the free state government in the Curragh from December 1922 until the end of the conflict in October 1923. At the end of the civil war he began to play an increasingly important part in the political activities of the Sinn Féin movement. With Eamon de Valera, whose loyal lieutenant he was for four decades, he steered that organization along a narrow path towards full participation in constitutional politics, a path signposted by his own election to the Dáil for Dublin South City in November 1924 at a time when Sinn Féin was still following an abstentionist policy. In 1926, with de Valera, he was involved in the exodus from Sinn Féin that led to the establishment of Fianna Fáil, and he became its joint honorary secretary in November of that year. In the following year, with abstentionism abandoned, he joined his leader and other Fianna Fáil deputies in the Dáil, where he became party spokesman on industry and commerce. His early career in politics and in the party was marked by two central preoccupations: economics and organization.

Self-taught—his years as an internee had been put to good use—he was influenced by the protectionist policies of Arthur Griffith, but was also, from as early as 1929, when he wrote an important policy document for the party, conscious of the economic challenges of free trade. His organizational skills were legendary: he envisaged his party as a two-way information system, providing local intelligence to policy makers as well as forming the backbone of a command system controlled from the centre.

On 24 August 1924 Lemass married Kathleen Hughes (*c.*1901–1985), daughter of a middle manager in a Dublin department store. Their daughter Maureen, who later married Charles Haughey, Lemass's successor but one as taoiseach, was born in 1925; their other children were Peggy (*b.* 1927), Noel (*b.* 1929), and Sheila (*b.* 1934). Noel followed his father into politics but with less prominence: he was a junior government minister in 1969–73 and died in 1976.

Into government Lemass became the youngest member of de Valera's first cabinet when appointed to the department of industry and commerce on 9 March 1932: he was a member of every Fianna Fáil cabinet thereafter, serving as a minister and as taoiseach for a total of twenty-eight years before he retired in 1966. With the exception of a brief period during the war, he occupied the same ministerial post to which he was first appointed: under his tenure the department became synonymous with industrialization. Although his own policies were outwardly indistinguishable from the protectionism of colleagues during this early period, they had a somewhat different long-term objective: traditional Fianna Fáil policy envisaged an almost entirely self-sufficient Ireland, whereas Lemass rapidly came to see the protective network of tariffs and quotas behind which they were trying to construct a native industrial base primarily as scaffolding which could and should eventually be dismantled. Although protection—and substantial investment in public works and housing—helped to boost output and improve living standards, and successive acts governing the control of manufacturers brought industrial production increasingly under native control, his growing disenchantment with the lacklustre contribution of many Irish entrepreneurs led him to continue to promote the state's role. The nationalization of transport services during the Second World War was a case in point, as was his involvement in the development of the Irish national airline, Aer Lingus, at the end of the war. Turf production and tourism were two further activities whose development took place largely as a result of his initiatives.

Another aspect of Lemass's policy framework had profound electoral consequences, helping to cement the traditional Fianna Fáil electoral base of small farmers and urban workers. This was his development of close links with the trade union movement, which stood the party in good stead for many years. The same policy produced a series of generally progressive pieces of industrial legislation, notably the Conditions of Employment Act (1936). Lemass's radical ideas on agricultural reorganization were, however, largely rebuffed by cabinet colleagues fearful of their electoral consequences.

Lemass saw the end of the war as a major opportunity for new plans and programmes, and effectively oversaw the introduction of economic planning in 1945–7. His appointment as tanaiste (deputy prime minister) in 1945 was already a sign of de Valera's confidence in him. A period of intense electoral volatility between 1948 and 1957, however, had two profound effects. One was to encourage de Valera to retain the leadership of his party until a very advanced age (and thus effectively to deny Lemass the succession for a time); the other was to segregate Ireland from the period of intense economic growth which accompanied the rebuilding of post-war Europe. Lemass sat out part of his time in opposition as managing director of the *Irish Press*; his organizational and managerial skills, by now well honed, were exercised in this enterprise to considerable effect. By 1957, at the beginning of a second lengthy period of uninterrupted Fianna Fáil rule, emigration was haemorrhaging the country's productive base, and disenchantment and disillusion were rife. At this point, partly at the prompting of key public servants—notably T. K. Whitaker, then secretary of the department of finance—Lemass set about revivifying the economy by introducing new emphases on export-led growth and inward investment: when he was elected as taoiseach on 23 June 1959, he was finally in a position to implement his blueprint for growth.

As taoiseach Lemass was, however, still beset by internal and external problems. Internally, Irish industrial production was still sluggish: entrepreneurs had become too much accustomed to protection, and some civil servants feared the consequences of dismantling tariffs. Externally, Ireland's dependence on the UK market depressed prices of agricultural exports. He also had to deal with the recrudescence of IRA violence between 1956 and 1962. He moved rapidly on all fronts. The Industrial Development Authority, whose establishment by a predecessor government he had opportunistically opposed at the time, became a major source of inward investment; he created and extended a whole series of relationships with employers and trade unions which led to the introduction of national wage-rounds and the creation of a range of committees designed to enhance industrial productivity; he pushed Ireland's candidacy as a member of the Common Market; and in 1965 he responded to an invitation from the Northern Ireland prime minister, Terence O'Neill, to visit Belfast, which inaugurated a new and hopeful era in cross-border political and economic relationships. Less publicly, but equally significantly, he oversaw a series of key judicial appointments, notably to the Supreme Court, whose members he expected to be more interventionist in defining and extending social rights; and he established, also in 1965, an all-party advisory committee on the constitution introduced by de Valera in 1937, partly with an eye to possible developments in Northern Ireland, but also partly with an eye to the need for change in social policy areas such as divorce, which the constitution explicitly prohibited.

Lemass's approach to Northern Ireland policy, although not clearly perceived at the time, marked a significant break from that of his predecessor as leader of Fianna Fáil. Whereas de Valera had always insisted on the right of the Irish people as a whole to self-determination, thus minimizing the rights of the Unionists in Northern Ireland (apart from conceding their right to maintain a subordinate parliament), Lemass emphasized the need for reconciliation, and so laid the foundation for a policy which, without ever explicitly accepting a Unionist veto, began to recognize the importance of Unionist consent to any proposed new constitutional arrangements. In other areas, too, his style diverged markedly from de Valera's: although outwardly a practising Catholic, he had reserves of scepticism absent from his predecessor's make-up; and he conspicuously did not share (except at election times) de Valera's passionate devotion to the Irish language or his belief that it could be revived as the country's principal means of communication. He was also much more openly internationalist, seeing Ireland's contribution as a member of the United Nations forces in the Congo as a sign of more effective involvement in the international community. In foreign policy he was—not least because of his admiration for American industrial practices and policies—pro-America in general, although he supported efforts by his foreign minister, Frank Aiken, to engineer a debate on the admission of China to the United Nations and to devise a treaty aimed at preventing the proliferation of nuclear weapons.

Lemass's thoroughly modern and decisive approach caught the temper of the times. As emigration began to fall, industrial output began to grow, and inward investment began to increase, the air of optimism was palpable. As the 1960s proceeded, however, the rejection of Britain's and Ireland's bid to join the Common Market put a substantial brake on industrial progress; agricultural prices, deprived of the potential boon of the common agricultural policy, remained depressed; and a combination of inflationary wage settlements and industrial unrest began to remove some of the lustre from his earlier achievements. Throughout the latter part of this period his health had been deteriorating: he was a heavy pipe-smoker, and his lungs were seriously affected. His resignation as taoiseach on 10 November 1966, prompted by ill health, was none the less relatively sudden.

Lemass was the recipient of a number of honours, most notably the grand cross of the order of St Gregory the Great (a papal decoration) in 1948, just after losing office at a general election, an honorary doctorate in economics from the National University of Ireland in 1954, and an honorary LLD degree from the University of Dublin in 1965. His private life was utterly unostentatious, enlivened only by a gambling streak which drew occasionally adverse political comment: playing poker, betting on horses, and, in later years, the occasional round of golf were his only distractions from a highly organized working life. Between his retirement as taoiseach in 1966 and his withdrawal from active politics at the election of 1969, he worked in a relaxed way as a government backbencher, his only official involvement being as a member of the all-party committee on the constitution, which he himself had founded and which issued its report in 1967. He acquired a number of relatively modest directorships on his retirement, largely in order to ensure continuing financial support for his wife, Kathleen. He died in the Mater Hospital, Dublin, on 11 May 1971 of pyopneumothorax, and was buried on 14 May at Dean's Grange cemetery. JOHN HORGAN

Sources J. Horgan, *Seán Lemass: the enigmatic patriot* (1995) · V. Browne, *The Magill book of Irish politics* (1981) · J. Lee, *Ireland, 1912–1985* (1989) · B. Farell, *Chairman or chief?* (1971) · *DNB* · personal knowledge (2004) · private information (2004) · b. cert. · d. cert.
Archives TCD, corresp. with Thomas Bodkin | FILM BFI NFTVA, 'Sean Francis', 13 May 1971
Likenesses photograph, 1942, Hult. Arch. [*see illus.*] · S. O'Sullivan, oils, *c*.1960, priv. coll. · photographs, Hult. Arch.
Wealth at death Ir£43,586: probate

Le Masurier, Sir Robert Hugh (1913–1996), bailiff of Jersey, was born on 29 December 1913 in St Helier, Jersey, the son of William Smythe Le Masurier (1875–1950) and his wife, Mabel Harriet, *née* Briard. His father was a well-known local solicitor and keen yachtsman who later distinguished himself, as commodore of the St Helier Yacht Club, by organizing the flotilla of small boats which evacuated British soldiers from St Malo in 1940. Robert attended Victoria College, the local public school, where he won a scholarship to Pembroke College, Oxford, from which he graduated with second-class degrees in jurisprudence in 1935 and in civil law in 1936. He then joined the Jersey legal practice Le Masurier, Giffard, and Poch, of which his father was a partner, and was called to the bar in the royal court, Jersey, in 1938.

Like his father, Le Masurier was a keen sailor, and on the outbreak of the Second World War he joined the Royal Naval Volunteer Reserve. He was commissioned as a sub-lieutenant in 1939, rose to the rank of lieutenant-commander by 1944, served in minesweepers, and won the Distinguished Service Cross for gallantry in 1942. One of his wartime exploits was of personal significance to him as it involved an attempt to gather intelligence from his native island, under German occupation. As part of a naval intelligence division plan, he approached the island in command of a motor torpedo boat, intending to make a secret landing. The quiet engine failed and the sound of the normal engines alerted the occupying troops, who played searchlights on the craft, so the attempt had to be abandoned. During the war Le Masurier met Helen Sophia Sheringham (*d*. 1999), daughter of Hubert Valentine Sheringham, while she was serving in the Women's Royal Naval Service. They married in 1941. There were two daughters and one son of the marriage.

Le Masurier returned to Jersey upon demobilization and resumed his place in the family firm; his fine legal brain won him the respect of his colleagues. Then, in 1955, he accepted the crown appointment of solicitor-general, and in 1958 was promoted to attorney-general of the royal court of Jersey. The bailiff, Sir Alexander Coutanche, was by then planning to retire. Knowing that his deputy, C. S.

Sir Robert Hugh Le Masurier (1913–1996), by unknown photographer

Harrison, was in failing health, he pressed for Le Masurier to be made a lieutenant-bailiff, and upon the succession of Harrison as bailiff in 1961 Le Masurier became his deputy. The death of Harrison, after only six months in office, brought Le Masurier to the highest office in the government of Jersey in April 1962. In this dual role he was an immediate success, impressing the royal court with his wise and well-reasoned judgments and presiding over the states of Jersey forcefully and impartially.

The twelve years during which Le Masurier was bailiff of Jersey saw much development in the European Economic Community and tremendous growth in the Jersey finance industry. Le Masurier succeeded in maintaining the dignity and independence of the Jersey constitution and of the high office of bailiff to which he had been appointed. He was knighted in 1966. After retirement, in 1974, he continued his public service by chairing the Jersey Rent Control Tribunal and an inquiry into the structure of the honorary police service in 1979.

In private life Sir Bob, as he was familiarly known, was a devoted family man. He continued to be a keen yachtsman and enjoyed woodwork, at which he was very proficient. He was a fluent speaker of Jersey Norman French, a supporter of L'Assembliée d'Jèrriais (the local language society), and a member of the Société Jersiaise and of the National Trust for Jersey. He was a humble person, who enjoyed easy social relations with people from all walks of life, and a lifelong supporter of the parish church of St Helier. He died at Oaklands Manor, Jersey, on 30 July 1996, and after a funeral service at St Helier's parish church, attended by members of the royal court, states of Jersey, and a large number of friends and admirers, his remains were cremated and the ashes scattered, according to his wishes, on Les Minquiers reef of rocks. He was survived by his wife and children. F. L. M. Corbet

Sources personal knowledge (2004) · private information (2004) [family] · *WWW* · *Who's who in the Channel Islands* (1967–87) · *The memoirs of Lord Coutanche*, ed. H. R. S. Pocock (1975) · *The Times* (9 Aug 1996) · *Jersey Evening Post* (31 July 1996) · *Jersey Evening Post* (6–7 Aug 1996) · Burke, *Peerage* · F. L. M. C. [F. L. M. Corbet], 'Le Masurier, Sir Robert Hugh', in F. L. M. Corbet and others, *A biographical dictionary of Jersey*, [2] (1998), 241–3

Likenesses photograph, repro. in F. L. M. Corbet and others, *Biographical dictionary of Jersey*, facing p.183 · photograph, News International Syndication, London [*see illus.*]

Lemberg [Limberg, Limburg], **Tideman** (*c*.1310–1386), merchant and banker, came of a family which had migrated to the Westphalian town of Dortmund, in north-west Germany, during the thirteenth century, and there joined the influential guild of shoemakers and tanners. Nothing is known of his youth and apprenticeship, but there is evidence for his taking an active part in the trade with England from 1339—not surprisingly, since Hanseatic merchants from Dortmund had been playing an important part in the English wool trade from about 1275. Between 1340 and 1350 Lemberg was one of Edward III's leading bankers. In order to finance his wars in France the king badly needed larger sums of money than could be raised from the crown's regular income, through direct taxation or by additional wool subsidies granted by parliament, while his former Florentine bankers, the Bardi and Peruzzi, had collapsed in 1340 and so were no longer at his disposal. During the 1340s, at first along with his Westphalian compatriots Johann vom Walde, Johann Klepping, and others, and afterwards in company with English merchants like Walter Chiriton and Gilbert Wendlinburgh, Lemberg negotiated five substantial loans, for a total of more than £100,000, on the king's behalf. It is difficult to analyse the structure of these transactions in detail, because new loans might be agreed before the earlier ones had been repaid; methods of repayment might be altered while a loan was still outstanding, and it is seldom possible to tell which payments were made for which loans. Repayments of the king's debts were made from customs on exported wool; the lenders might be given licences to export specified quantities of wool, wool-fells, and hides, or granted customs reductions or even exemptions, or customs revenues might be in part transferred to the king's creditors, or placed in pawn to them. These transactions were so organized that the loans were made on the continent, where the king needed the money, while repayments were made in England, so that the German merchants then had at their disposal the money they needed for buying wool. And at the same time dangerous and costly shipments of money could be avoided.

Lemberg won Edward III's particular favour in 1343, when he made two loans, of nearly 50,000 florins (£8850), to redeem the royal crowns and other jewels which in 1339 had been given in pledge to Archbishop Baldwin of Trier and certain citizens of Cologne respectively. The king's German creditors, headed by Lemberg, consequently came to be temporarily possessed both of the entire customs revenue from wool shipped out of all the English ports from Bristol to Newcastle, and of one part of the revenues of the cocket seals. The extent of their profits cannot be calculated exactly, but they were clearly substantial. Lemberg's commercial activities, too, benefited considerably from the confidence that Edward III placed in him, which in 1347 gave him the opportunity to secure for all Hanseatic merchants a limited exemption from customs duties.

After that year Lemberg no longer confined his activities to trading in wool. In 1347 he farmed the coinage dues from all the Cornish tin mines (at 40*s*. per hundredweight), and secured for three years the entire revenue from the stannaries of Devon and Cornwall. At this time Lemberg, who already owned a house in London, seems to have intended to settle permanently in England, and may even have aimed at becoming a country gentleman, since in 1348 he purchased estates in several counties. But when the final settlement of the large sums due to him was being organized at the exchequer in the spring of 1352, numerous irregularities came to light. It became increasingly difficult for Lemberg to prove the legitimacy either of his demands or of the payments he had already received. He was accused of embezzlement, of illegal dealings in royal bonds, and of dishonest use of tin scales, and several actions were brought against him. In 1352 his tin supplies were confiscated in compensation for irregular receipts from the customs, and he was even temporarily arrested. Lemberg was able to negotiate a settlement with the king and with his English creditors, but he was obliged to leave England. He sold his estates to the sons of William de la Pole (*d*. 1366) and moved to Cologne.

In 1359, however, Lemberg returned to England. He farmed the lead and copper mines at Alston Moor, Cumberland, and acquired the right to exploit them as he pleased, having negotiated an agreement with the crown under which the latter took 15 per cent of the profits. A debt of 5000 marks at the exchequer was pardoned by the king, to whom Lemberg once more became a lender, this time of 1000 marks. In return he and his partners received customs reductions at Boston. However in 1363 he finally left England. At first he moved to his native town of Dortmund, but strained relations with its leading families made it impossible for him to remain there, and so in 1367 he once more settled in Cologne, where he was active in the wine trade and as a financier. He gave generous support to the Carthusian monastery of St Barbara, and in his will remembered other religious houses and collegiate churches in Cologne, among them the Augustinian friary, where he was laid to rest following his death in Cologne on 29 July 1386. V. HENN

Sources *Chancery records* • K. Kunze, ed., *Hanseakten aus England, 1275–1412* (1891) • *Dortmunder Kaufleute in England im 13. und 14. Jahrhundert: ein Quellennachweis*, ed. G. Luntowski (1970) • L. von Winterfeld, *Tidemann Lemberg: ein Dortmunder Kaufmannsleben aus dem 14. Jahrhundert* (1927) • A. Beardwood, *Alien merchants in England, 1300–1377* (1931) • I. M. Peters, *Hansekaufleute als Gläubiger der Englischen Krone, 1294–1350* (1978)

Lemens, Balthasar van (**1637–1704**), painter, was born in Antwerp. His 'early genius [having] soon distinguishd it self', he went to England not long after the restoration of Charles II in 1660. Vertue records that 'Mr. Le Mense learnt under Decretz' (Vertue, *Note books*, 1.127); presumably this was Emanuel de Critz. Vertue also noted that van Lemens was 'expecting to meet with suitable encouragement' (ibid., 2.136). This does not appear to have been forthcoming, however. Early commentators hint at misfortunes 'in the latter part of his life, wherein he was often in trouble' (Buckeridge, 405), which made it necessary for him to undertake work for other people, drawing and making sketches to assist both painters and engravers; chief among these was Paul van Somer, the mezzotint engraver. Bainbrigg Buckeridge, writing *c*.1706, thought van Lemens's drawings and sketches 'excellent, and by some thought much better than many of his finished pieces' (ibid.), while Vertue judged 'his Invention' as 'very fruitfull being as serviceable in his drawings for others as to himself' and his sketches 'free & masterly' and 'of a good manner of Design' (Vertue, *Note books*, 2.136–7).

Van Lemens had some success in painting small history pieces, allegories, and landscapes. Buckeridge describes these as 'very pleasing and well coloured. His manner was free, and often very graceful' (Buckeridge, 404). His works, known through mezzotint engravings by John Smith, include *St George*, several cupids, and *Venus and Adonis*; his *Acteon Changed into a Stag by Diana* was engraved by Nicolas de Larmessin the younger. For his patron, the amateur architect William Emmett, he painted portraits of Emmett and his wife, a ceiling painting of the nine muses (after 1698; destroyed) for their house in Bromley, Kent, and religious subjects. According to Vertue, van Lemens had a brother who practised in Brussels and who painted his portrait. He died in London in 1704, of 'a Diabetis in the 66 year of his Age … & was buried in the Chappell Church yard Westminster' (Vertue, *Note books*, 2.137).

L. H. CUST, *rev*. ARIANNE BURNETTE

Sources [B. Buckeridge], 'An essay towards an English school of painting', in R. de Piles, *The art of painting, with the lives and characters of above 300 of the most eminent painters*, 3rd edn (1754), 354–439 • Vertue, *Note books*, vols. 1–2 • F. W. H. Hollstein, *Dutch and Flemish etchings, engravings and woodcuts ca. 1450–1700*, 10 (1954) • E. Croft-Murray, *Decorative painting in England, 1537–1837*, 1 (1962) • H. Walpole, *Anecdotes of painting in England: with some account of the principal artists*, ed. R. N. Wornum, new edn, 2 (1849); repr. (1862) • Thieme & Becker, *Allgemeines Lexikon*, vol. 23 • E. K. Waterhouse, *The dictionary of British 16th and 17th century painters* (1988) • R. H. Wilenski, *Flemish painters, 1430–1830*, 1 (1960) • *DNB*

Likenesses S. van Lemens, portrait

Le Mesurier, Havilland (**1758–1806**), merchant and commissary officer, was born on 8 May 1758 in Guernsey, the youngest of the five sons of John Le Mesurier (1717–1793), hereditary governor of Alderney, and his wife, Martha (*d*. 1764), the daughter of Peter Dobrée of Guernsey and his wife, Martha. He briefly attended Winchester School (1770–71) before joining his father and eldest brother, Peter, in a merchant house which made large profits from privateering in the American War of Independence. On 27 June 1782 he married Elizabeth Dobrée, the daughter of Isaac Dobrée and Martha de Beauvoir of Guernsey, and in the same year he joined a large commercial undertaking in Le Havre. On his return from the continent he established himself among the prospering community of Channel Island merchants in London.

The commercial crisis associated with events in Europe and the outbreak of war with France in 1793 reduced Le Mesurier's fortunes to a nadir and, needing employment, he accepted a commissariat commission in the army sent to assist the Dutch. Service in the commissariat was not generally esteemed, but Le Mesurier's integrity and abilities were such that he was rapidly promoted deputy commissary-general. As such, he won commendation from generals Walmoden and Dundas for trying to instil efficiency into the chaotic and ill-led system of supply during the terrible winter retreat of 1794–5. After his return to England he entered a lucrative partnership with his brother Paul as merchants and privateer-owners based in Austin Friars in the City of London.

From his painfully gained appreciation of the vital role of supply in warfare, Le Mesurier set out the model of a commissariat service in two important and detailed manuals, *A System for the British Commissariat on Foreign Service* (1796) and *The British Commissary* (1798). His stipulations, in particular, on the financial aspects of supply, and on the prompt and full payment of contractors and peasants, proved invaluable to Wellington and other British commanders.

In the spring of 1797, with invasion threatening, Le Mesurier was appointed commissary-general of the southern district of England. Apart from technical preparations to resist a French landing, he believed that, if the enemy arrived, the civilian population should know precisely what it must do, and the consequences of not doing it, and in his *Thoughts on a French Invasion* (1798) he explained in popular and patriotic terms the government's plan of resistance. When Brook Watson, Le Mesurier's incompetent superior in the continental campaign, was appointed over his head as commissary-general of all England, Le Mesurier took offence and resigned in June 1800 after a heated disputation.

In 1801 Addington's administration replaced Pitt's and Le Mesurier was appointed commissary-general to the army then preparing to return from Egypt following the peace of Amiens. His vigour and efficiency were again in evidence and, as the peace started to break down, he saw further service in Malta and Naples. However, when Watson retired at the end of 1805, Pitt was back in office and Le Mesurier was passed over for the promotion that he might have expected. His response was to publish *Two Letters to the Commissioners of Army Accounts* (1806), exposing abuses in the commissariat. Before he could enter into further controversy on the issue, Le Mesurier died at his house, 3 Austin Friars, Great George Street, Westminster, on 5 March 1806, leaving one daughter and four sons. In a will made in 1801, he named his wife and brother Thomas as his executors, though he substituted his eldest son, Havilland, for Elizabeth following her death in 1804.

W. R. MEYER

Sources *GM*, 1st ser., 76 (1806), 290–91 • E. F. Carey, 'Peter Le Mesurier, governor of Alderney, 1793–1803', *Report and Transactions* [Société Guernesiaise], 10 (1926–9), 56 • will, PRO, PROB 11/1440, fols. 141*v*–142*v* • T. F. Kirby, *Winchester scholars: a list of the wardens, fellows, and scholars of … Winchester College* (1888), 265 • J. P. Warren, 'Extracts from the diary of Elisha Dobrée', *Report and Transactions* [Société Guernesiaise], 10 (1926–9), 520 • R. Glover, *Peninsular preparation: the reform of the British army, 1795–1809* (1963), appx A • W. R. Meyer, 'Paul Le Mesurier, lord mayor of London', *Report and Transactions* [Société Guernesiaise], 21 (1981–5), 701–14

Archives BL, MSS, letters to Baron de Löw, Lieutenant-General Don, George Rose and earl of Liverpool; memorial to the treasury • Devon RO, corresp. with first Viscount Sidmouth

Wealth at death see will, PRO, PROB 11/1440, fols. 141*v*–142*v*

Le Mesurier, Havilland (1783–1813), army officer, son of Havilland *Le Mesurier (1758–1806), commissary-general of the army, and his wife, Eliza or Elizabeth, *née* Dobrée (*d.* 1804), was originally intended for a partnership in his father's business. He was educated at a school at Salisbury, and afterwards at Westminster School, and early in 1800 was sent to Berlin to learn German. There he acquired military tastes, and in January 1801 became an ensign in the Royal Staff Corps. He was promoted lieutenant in one of the limited-service companies added to the 20th foot, but the company was reduced at the peace of Amiens, and Le Mesurier, who had been with his father in Egypt and Italy, was appointed lieutenant, 83rd foot. In August 1803 he entered the senior department of the Royal Military College, Marlow, and was sent to reside at Kiel in Holstein to improve his German. On 25 August 1804 he was promoted captain, 21st foot, and, after passing well at Marlow, was employed on the quartermaster-general's staff in Kent and Sussex. He was a deputy assistant quartermaster-general under Sir John Moore in Sweden, and at Corunna.

On returning to the Peninsula in April 1809, Le Mesurier was appointed by Marshal Beresford a supernumerary lieutenant-colonel in the 14th (Algarves) Portuguese infantry. The regiment was at Chaves, in a wretched state, the officers old and inefficient, and from 200 to 400 of the men constantly sick. Provisions were scarce and very high-priced, and not another British officer was within 50 miles of the place. Le Mesurier succeeded to the command, won the confidence of the officers and men, and brought the regiment into good order. He was appointed Portuguese military secretary to Wellington in April 1811, and was present at the battle of Fuentes d'Oñoro (5 May 1811), but soon resigned his post and returned to his regiment.

On 3 October 1811 Le Mesurier became a brevet lieutenant-colonel in the British service, and was appointed commandant of the frontier fortress of Almeida, where he showed much skill and activity in bringing the defences and the garrison into a state of efficiency. On government land, and on the government account, he raised corn enough for the maintenance of Almeida within range of its guns, and with the fatigue labour of the garrison he raised enough potatoes to supply 2500 men for three months. When Wellington prepared for his final advance, Le Mesurier was appointed to command the 12th Portuguese infantry. He was shot through the back of the head, leading his regiment in the battle of the Pyrenees, on 28 July, and died on 31 July 1813, at the age of thirty. Le Mesurier, though not robust, and suffering much from fever and ague during the Peninsular campaign, was very active. He translated one or two French military works, and was entrusted by Marshal Beresford with compiling the Portuguese army regulations, which were nearly completed at the time of his death.

H. M. CHICHESTER, *rev.* ROGER T. STEARN

Sources *GM*, 1st ser., 83/2 (1813), 499, 685 · *GM*, 1st ser., 84/1 (1814), 90–94 · *Army List* · A. J. Guy, ed., *The road to Waterloo: the British army and the struggle against revolutionary and Napoleonic France, 1793–1815* (1990) · R. Muir, *Britain and the defeat of Napoleon, 1807–1815* (1996)
Archives Devon RO, corresp. with first Viscount Sidmouth

Le Mesurier, John (1781–1843), army officer and governor of Alderney, was the eldest son of Governor Peter Le Mesurier (*d.* 1803) and grandson of Governor John Le Mesurier (*d.* 1793). Alderman Le Mesurier and Commissary Havilland *Le Mesurier were his uncles. He was appointed ensign in 1794 in the 132nd highlanders, from which short-lived corps he was promoted into the 89th regiment, and became captain-lieutenant in 1796. He served with a flank battalion commanded by Colonel Stewart in the Irish rising of 1798, and later with his regiment in 1799–1800 at the occupation of Messina in Sicily after the blockade and capture of Malta under General Thomas Graham, Lord Lynedoch. He served in the campaign in Egypt in 1801, including the battles before Alexandria, the defence of Rosetta, and the surrender of Cairo. After the fall of Alexandria the 89th embarked on Lord Keith's fleet on a secret expedition, the supposed destination of which was Brazil; on reaching Malta peace was found to have been declared, and the regiment returned to Ireland.

After attaining his majority in the 89th in 1802 Le Mesurier retired on half pay. The government of Alderney, to which he succeeded on his father's death in 1803, was originally granted to an ancestor, Sir Edmund *Andros, by Charles II, and was renewed to Le Mesurier's grandfather, John, by George III, for ninety-nine years, in 1763. Le Mesurier married in 1804 Martha, daughter of Alderman Peter Pochard of London, a native of Guernsey, and they had one son, who took holy orders. Le Mesurier, who, while on the half-pay list, attained the rank of major-general, resigned the post of governor at the end of 1824. He was the last holder of the post. He died at his home, Bradfield Place, near Reading, on 21 May 1843, aged sixty-two.

H. M. CHICHESTER, *rev.* JAMES FALKNER

Sources *Army List* · *GM*, 2nd ser., 19 (1843), 105, 204
Likenesses G. Engleheart, miniature, 1803, priv. coll.; Sothebys, 26 Nov 1931

Le Mesurier, John [*real name* John Elton Halliley] (1912–1983), actor, was born in Bedford on 5 April 1912, the only son and younger child of John Halliley, a well-known and long-established family solicitor, and his wife, Mary Le Mesurier. He spent his early years at Bury St Edmunds before being sent away to school, first to Grenham House at Birchington in Kent and then to Sherborne School in Dorset. While at school (which he thoroughly disliked) he managed to visit a great many West End plays and in particular and perhaps significantly the farces presented at the Aldwych Theatre by Tom Walls and Ralph Lynn. On leaving school he was already determined to be an actor but, being diffident at expressing such an ambition to his family, he allowed himself to become an articled clerk to a firm of Bury St Edmunds solicitors, Greene and Greene. He then drifted into the theatre through the Fay Compton Studio of Dramatic Art. He adopted his mother's maiden name as his stage name.

Le Mesurier gained considerable experience in the theatre of the 1930s. His first job was at the Palladium Theatre, Edinburgh, at a salary of £3 10*s.* per week. Then followed a season at Oldham and various touring shows until 1940 when he joined the Royal Armoured Corps. He was sent to India and enjoyed what he was to describe as a 'comfortable war with captaincy thrust upon me'. He was demobilized in 1946 and began the many roles which seemed to make few demands on his acting talents—barristers, doctors, vicars, naval commanders, family solicitors, courtiers, air force officers—which he played to such perfection. He became an indispensable figure in the gallery of second-rank players which were the glory of the British film industry in its more prolific days.

It became almost impossible to sit through any home-grown comedy without expecting to encounter at some time that inimitable brand of bewildered persistence under fire which Le Mesurier made so very much his own. The character he cumulatively created will be remembered when others more famous are forgotten, not just for the skill of his playing but because he somehow embodied a curiously British reaction to the madness of the modern world—endlessly perplexed as he was by the dizzying and incoherent pattern of events, but doing his courteous best to ensure that resentment never showed. Like Woody Allen he rarely smiled. His characteristic expressions were the twitch and the lopsided grin, the raised eyebrow, the grimace, and the world-weary sigh that passed over his face.

Le Mesurier first attracted critical attention as a supporting player in popular British comedies like *Private's Progress* (1955)—he was the psychiatrist with a tic—and *I'm All Right Jack* (1959)—as a time-and-motion expert. During this period too he frequently appeared on television with his close friend Tony Hancock and he had a leading part in the Hancock film *The Punch and Judy Man* (1962), giving a beautifully judged and extremely sad performance as a sand artist. Later films included *Carlton-Brown of the F.O.* (1958), *We Joined the Navy* (1962), *The Wrong Arm of the Law* (1962), *Mouse on the Moon* (1963), *The Pink Panther* (1963), *The Liquidator* (1965), *The Wrong Box* (1966), and *Casino Royale* (1967).

In 1966, on television, Le Mesurier was in the comedy series *George and the Dragon* with Sidney James and Peggy Mount, but it is for his portrayal of Sergeant Wilson in the Home Guard television series *Dad's Army* (from 1968) that he is most remembered. This he wonderfully sustained over a period of nine years. The stroke of genius was the casting of Arthur Lowe as Captain Mainwaring, the bank manager, and Le Mesurier as Sergeant Wilson, his clerk, rather than the other way around. This made the series a much more acute commentary on class in the Second

World War, with a lower-middle-class Mainwaring lording it over his upper-middle-class public school subordinate, to whom he constantly felt, and was made to feel, inferior.

Le Mesurier married three times. In 1939 he married the actress June Melville, daughter of Frederick Melville, dramatic author and theatre manager. There were no children and after the war this marriage was dissolved. In 1949 he married the comedian Hattie *Jacques (1922–1980), daughter of Robin Rochester Jacques, who had been a test pilot in the Royal Flying Corps. They had two sons, Robin and Kim. This marriage was dissolved in 1965 and in 1966 he married Joan Malin, former wife of Mark Eden and daughter of Frederick Daniel Long, manager of a Ramsgate funfair.

Though mainly in demand as a comedy actor, Le Mesurier could be equally effective in straight parts. One of his best was in Dennis Potter's television play *Traitor* in 1971. He played a character based on the spy Kim Philby and turned in a memorable performance of a drunken stammering wreck of a man, holding court to Western journalists in a Moscow flat. It gained him the best television actor award from the Society of Film and Television Arts, and demonstrated how much more he could have achieved if he had chosen to be other than what he called a 'jobbing actor'. His other straight work for television included the lead part in David Mercer's play *Flint* and Marley's Ghost in *A Christmas Carol*. He was last seen in an adaptation of the novel of Piers Paul Read, *A Married Man* (1983).

Tony Hancock, of whose unofficial repertory company he was long a member, loved Le Mesurier's air of gloom and always called him Eeyore. Behind this apparent gloom, however, the inner Le Mesurier was the very opposite; ringing up to propose a meal or a party or a night out, the sepulchral voice would first murmur 'Playtime?' He loved jazz clubs and was a talented jazz pianist himself. He liked late-night restaurants at midnight and was the one who would drive the others home if they had celebrated too extravagantly. He died on 15 November 1983 at Ramsgate Hospital. His whimsical sense of humour and baleful view of life were typified by his death announcement in *The Times*: 'John Le Mesurier wishes it to be known that he conked out on November 15th. He sadly misses family and friends.' DEREK NIMMO, *rev.*

Sources J. Le Mesurier, *A jobbing actor* (1984) · *The Times* (16 Nov 1983) · personal knowledge (1990) · private information (1990) · J. Le Mesurier, *Dear John* (2001)

Archives FILM BFI NFTVA, 'The unforgettable John Le Mesurier', ITV1, 9 Sept 2001 · BFI NFTVA, performance footage | SOUND BL NSA, performance recordings

Le Mesurier, Paul (1755–1805), merchant and politician, was born on 23 February 1755 in Guernsey, the third of the five sons of John Le Mesurier (1717–1793), hereditary governor of Alderney, and his wife, Martha, daughter of Peter Dobrée of Guernsey and his wife, Martha. Le Mesurier's commercial career began in the City of London, where, 'from a little office over a gateway in Cloak Lane, he lived many years with very little success' (*City Biography*, 43), trading with his native island.

From 1776, however, he was in partnership at Walbrook with Noah Le Cras, the two enjoying great success as prize agents in the American War of Independence. Also in 1776, on 10 October, he married Mary Roberdeau, niece of Mrs Le Cras and daughter of Isaac Roberdeau, a substantial Spitalfields silk manufacturer, of Huguenot descent.

Le Mesurier's work as a propagandist in the campaign against Charles Fox's India Bill was rewarded by his election in April 1784 as an East India director, his election as MP for Southwark at a by-election in June 1784, and his unopposed return as alderman of Dowgate ward in the following October. His Foxite opponent in the large Southwark division was defeated by only eleven votes, 'at a most enormous expense' and after 'one of the hardest elections upon the Reports' (obituary, *GM*, 85). In the Commons he was vigorous and generally loyal to Pitt. He spoke for the corporation of London's policies of parliamentary and electoral reform and as an East India director defended Warren Hastings.

During his year as City sheriff (1786/7) Le Mesurier calmed and relieved the distress in Newgate caused by the delayed sailing of the first convict fleet to Australia and frustrated an attempt by Lord George Gordon to make mischief in the gaol. His attempt to revive the laws against forestalling and regrating in the London markets failed. As lord mayor of London (1793/4), at the start of the war against France, he used a mixture of firmness and expediency effectively to deal with riots directed against the 'crimping' of men into the army and with unruly protests about assessments under the new Militia Act. He was returned as MP for Southwark in 1790 but stood down at the general election of 1796. In 1789, 1794, 1799, and 1804 he was re-elected as an East India director. A leading force in the Honourable Artillery Company, he was the volunteer unit's colonel from 1794 until his death. He was noted as a philanthropist, serving on the governing bodies of the Eastern Dispensary, the Asylum for Female Orphans, and the London Huguenot Hospital.

Suave and urbane, though not physically handsome, Le Mesurier was markedly respectable, balanced, and efficient. His marriage produced five children, the younger of his two sons, Thomas, being archdeacon of Malta for thirty-four years. From about 1803 he suffered increasingly from 'a lethargic affection' (obituary, *GM*, 85) and he died at his house in Upper Homerton, near Hackney, on 9 December 1805. He was buried on the 19th at Christ Church, Spitalfields. Essentially a middle-man in both politics and trade, his general enlightenment and flexibility stopped at the ideas of the French Revolution, to which he was an inveterate opponent. The *City Biography* (43) described him as having 'almost as much wit as Alderman Curtis, but none of his conviviality'. W. R. MEYER

Sources W. R. Meyer, 'Paul Le Mesurier, lord mayor of London', *Report and Transactions* [Société Guernesiaise], 21 (1981–5), 701–14 · *GM*, 1st ser., 76 (1806), 84–6 · 'A short statement of the riots which took place this month so far as respects the City of London', *GM*, 1st ser., 64 (1794), 721–3 · J. Stevenson, 'The London "Crimp" riots of

1764', *International Review of Social History*, 16 (1971), 40–58 • Cobbett, *Parl. hist.*, 26.1167–72 • 'Guildhall intelligence', *Daily Universal Register* (27 Jan 1787), 4 [debate contributions of Sheriff Le Mesurier as an alderman of the Court of Common Council] • *Daily Universal Register* (7 June 1787), 3 [see report of *The King* v. *Lord G. Gordon* (re Newgate)] • *The Times* (21 Aug 1794), 2c [speech of lord mayor on balloting of London householders under the new Militia Act] • *The Times* (20 Dec 1805), 4a [report of funeral] • HoP, *Commons* • *City biography: containing anecdotes and memoirs of … the aldermen and other conspicuous personages of the corporation and City of London*, 2nd edn (1800), 43 • PRO, PROB 10/3731 • will, PRO, PROB 11/1435, sig. 849

Archives Guernsey Museum, St Peter Port, armorial china | NA Scot., memorial to H. Dundas for a new company to settle Bulam

Likenesses C. Tomkins, portraits, repro. in *The British volunteer* (1799)

Wealth at death under £25,000: PRO, PROB 10/3731

Le Moine, Abraham (*d.* 1757), theological writer, born in France, was one of the Huguenot refugees to England. He married Ann Saubère on 7 February 1721 at St James's, Duke's Place, London. They had at least two children, Abraham (*b.* 10 Feb 1724) and Joseph, both of whom entered Merchant Taylors' School, London, in 1735. The former graduated BA from St Catharine's College, Cambridge, in 1744.

From 1723 to 1743 Le Moine was chaplain to the French Hospital in London. His translations into French (1728–9) of Bishop Edmund Gibson's *Pastoral Letters* were read in the American colonies as well as in France, and he likewise translated Gibson's *Letters Against Libertines* (1732) and several works by Bishop Thomas Sherlock. He also wrote, in French, a *Dissertation* (1735) on the writings of Thomas Woolston. In 1729 he became chaplain to the duke of Portland, who in 1738 presented him to the rectory of Everley, Wiltshire; his handwriting appears in the parish register until 11 July 1756. His principal work, the *Treatise on Miracles* (1747), was a 'solid and full answer' (Allibone, *Dict.*, 1.1083) to Thomas Chubb, and was extracted in the *Gentleman's Magazine* in 1749 (19.161–3). He also wrote works directed against Conyers Middleton and Bolingbroke.

As doctor of divinity Le Moine, or possibly his son, was collated prebendary of Salisbury on 22 December 1753, though there is no record of either receiving this degree. Le Moine died in January 1757 and was buried at St James's, Paddington, on 13 January, but his tombstone has disappeared. J. G. ALGER, *rev.* ADAM JACOB LEVIN

Sources D. C. A. Agnew, *Protestant exiles from France, chiefly in the reign of Louis XIV, or, The Huguenot refugees and their descendants in Great Britain and Ireland*, 3rd edn, 2 vols. (1886) • D. Lysons, *The environs of London*, 3 (1795), 338 • R. C. Hoare, *The history of modern Wiltshire*, 4 (1822), 12 • *GM*, 1st ser., 88/2 (1818), 116 • Venn, *Alum. Cant.* • *IGI* • N. Sykes, *Edmund Gibson, bishop of London, 1669–1748: a study in politics & religion in the eighteenth century* (1926), 254 • Allibone, *Dict.* • M. J. P. Picot, *Mémoires pour servir à l'histoire écclésiastique*, 2nd edn, 4 vols. (1815–16), 4.291 • *Fasti Angl.* (Hardy), 2.672

Lemoine, Henry (1756–1812), author and bookseller, was born on 14 January 1756 in Spitalfields, London, and baptized in the French Huguenot church of La Patente in Brown's Lane, Spitalfields, on 1 February 1756. He was the only son of Henry Lemoine, a French protestant refugee, and Anne I. Cenette, a native of Guernsey. His early education took place at a local free school supported by contributions from French Calvinists.

In 1770, aged fourteen, Lemoine was apprenticed to a local stationer and rag merchant. To his employer's annoyance, Lemoine immersed himself in books, a passion that would last throughout his life. Finding a position more suited to his interests, about 1773 he started in the employ of one Chatterton, a bookseller and baker. Although Lemoine was apprenticed in the latter occupation, he now began contributing material to London periodicals. By the mid-1770s he had found work in London as a French teacher at a Vauxhall boarding-school by posing as a monolingual Frenchman. He was discharged when caught speaking fluent English to the school's maids.

Lemoine's future was now looking bleak, but his prospects improved when, coming of age in 1777, he inherited some property in Jersey from his aunt Ann Le Moine, who had died in 1766. With these funds he established a bookstall in the Little Minories, Aldgate, from which he also sold quack remedies, especially Dr Thomas Marryat's 'bug-water'. By 1780 Lemoine had moved his business west to Bishopsgate, and, as a result of his continued contribution to the periodical press, had become a familiar face in the circles of London's minor *literati*. He was often to be seen dining at George Lackington's house in Chiswell Street, and became a close acquaintance of David Levi, a noted Jewish apologist. On 8 January 1786 he married Anne Swires at St Luke's (Old Street, Finsbury) in London.

During the 1780s Lemoine's literary endeavours had proceeded apace. In 1786 he offered to the public four volumes of *The Kentish Curate, or, The History of Lamuel Lyttleton*, a mildly salacious work, complete with the usual false pretensions to moral probity. About this time he also produced an edition of Cleland's *Fanny Hill*, although no copies of this seem to be extant. By 1788 his wealth was such that, on 8 October, he was able to become a freeman of the Leathersellers' Company by redemption.

The early 1790s saw further success for Lemoine. He published a version of Blair's *The Grave* ('altered into rhime from the blank verse') in 1790, and launched a number of short-lived, entertaining periodicals: the *Conjuror's Magazine*, later renamed the *Astrologer's Magazine* (started 1792), and the *Wonderful Magazine and Marvellous Chronicle* (started 1793). The year 1794, however, marked a downturn in Lemoine's fortunes. Now engaged in the copperplate printing business, he had imprudently given credit to two booksellers, both of whom defaulted. Lemoine's subsequent debt led to imprisonment, and to separation from his wife. To add to his woes, in the following year he was forced to give up his bookstall, and took to the streets as an itinerant bookseller or chapman. In modern terminology he was a book-runner, collecting books from diverse sources, and then selling them to trade. As always, he supplemented his now meagre income through hack writing.

However, Lemoine did produce work of substance during this period, including the brief 'Present state of printing and bookselling in America' (first printed in the *Gentleman's Magazine*, 1796). In the following year he produced *Typographical Antiquities*, a history of the process and art of printing, and the work for which he is chiefly remembered. Also in 1797, he wrote *The Art of Speaking, upon an Entire New Plan*.

In addition to hack writing and book-running, Lemoine occupied his later years with work on Adam Clarke's bibliographical dictionary, and the opening in 1807 of a small bookstall in Parliament Square. During the period 1810–12 he displayed his expertise on the subject of Judaism in the pages of the *Gentleman's Magazine*. In the last year of his life he started the *Eccentric Magazine*, but his hand-to-mouth existence had undermined his health, and he did not live to see the first issue. Henry Lemoine died in St Bartholomew's Hospital, London, on 30 April 1812.

DAVID GOLDTHORPE

Sources W. Granger and others, *The new wonderful museum, and extraordinary magazine*, 5 (1807), 2218–40 · *GM*, 1st ser., 82/1 (1812), 493 · *GM*, 1st ser., 82/2 (1812), 673 · G. Smeeton, *Biographia curiosa, or, Memoirs of remarkable characters in the reign of George the Third* (1822), 50–51 · D. C. McMurtrie, 'Introduction', in H. Lemoine, *Present state of printing and bookselling in America* (1929) · H. Wilson, *Wonderful characters*, 1 (1821), 73–8 · *Fly leaves* (J. Miller, 1855), 50–53 · C. H. Timperley, *Encyclopaedia of literary and typographical anecdote*, 2nd edn (1842), 106, 110, 847–8 · Nichols, *Lit. anecdotes*, 2.279; 3.692, 727–8; 9.517, 551 · Watt, *Bibl. Brit.*, 2.674 · *IGI* · *DNB*

Likenesses engraved plate, repro. in Smeeton, *Biographia curiosa*, 51 · etching, BM, NPG; repro. in *Wonderful Magazine* (1806)

Lemon, Denis Edward (1945–1994), newspaper proprietor and restaurateur, was born on 11 August 1945 at Berryfield House, Bradford-on-Avon, Wiltshire, the eldest child and only son of Albert Edward Lemon, an executive officer with the Assistance Board, and his partner, Jane Kenyon, formerly Unsworth (1912–1988), a clerical officer with the Inland Revenue. While he was still a child the family relocated to Herne Bay and subsequently to Whitstable, Kent, and from 1956 to 1960 he was a student at the Simon Langton Grammar School for Boys in Canterbury, Kent. Early aware of his burgeoning homosexuality, Lemon decanted himself to London within a handful of years of his leaving school. Initially he studied and worked in accountancy, but he soon found himself more congenial employment in a record shop in south London. Music was a lifelong passion and he was as enthused by grand opera as he was by rock and roll, by divas as diverse as Maria Callas, Ethel Merman, and Dusty Springfield, by American show tunes or free-form jazz.

Towards the end of the 1960s (following the passing into law in 1967 of the Sexual Offences Act, which partially decriminalized homosexual acts between males over the age of twenty-one which took place in private), Britain's gay life was both expanding and becoming more visible. Lemon's exploration of and participation in the capital's gay life drew him steadily towards sexual politics and the evolving Gay Liberation Front, a facsimile of the American original (though with considerably less clout), which began meeting at the London School of Economics

Denis Edward Lemon (1945–1994), by unknown photographer, 1977

in 1970. By this time a gay press of sorts existed, heavily reliant upon showbusiness features, short stories, and pin-up photographs. The idea of a community newspaper (informed, informative, and politically aware) was first mooted in 1971. In 'The love that dared to speak its name' Lemon wrote:

> Founded … by Andrew Lumsden and myself, the paper was first published in June 1972. Andrew came from a professional journalistic background; mine was a 'fading hippy' one. I had more than a few friends in what was quaintly called the 'underground press' and presumed to have learned enough from them to give me the enthusiasm and impertinence to consider such a publishing venture not only viable but necessary. (Lemon)

The first issue of *Gay News* was run by a short-lived collective; by August 1972 Lemon had become sole editor and he remained in that position until he sold the newspaper almost ten years later. The paper did not long survive his departure.

Although he was an occasional contributor to *Gay News* and subsequently a regular contributor (writing on crime fiction) to *Gay Times*, Denis Lemon was not a journalist, and his vital contribution to gay publishing was as a far-sighted administrator and entrepreneur who was hard-nosed enough to get a gay newspaper up and running and keep it going in the face of hostility. The newspaper was to become highly respected and eventually boasted a wide range of distinguished contributors. It was, however, his publication in June 1976 of James Kirkup's poem 'The Love that Dares to Speak its Name' which propelled Denis Lemon into the dock at the Old Bailey and to international celebrity as the first man to be convicted on a charge of blasphemous libel in more than fifty years. He published Kirkup's poem because he thought 'the message and intention of the poem was to celebrate the absolute universality of God's love', although he admitted it was 'probably not a great work of literature' (Lemon). Not everyone viewed the poem in the same light as Lemon and an outraged reader dispatched a copy to Mary Whitehouse, the campaigner against pornography, who instigated a prosecution for blasphemous libel. Judge Alan King-Hamilton disallowed expert testimony on the literary, sociological, or theological qualities of the poem, and Denis Lemon and Gay News Ltd were found guilty—Lemon being fined £500 and sentenced to nine months' imprisonment, suspended for eighteen months, and subsequently quashed by the Court of Appeal.

Lemon sold *Gay News* in 1982 and eventually moved to Exeter (he became a restaurateur at the Exeter Arts Centre) in an attempt to regain the anonymity he had lost. He became increasingly reclusive and devoutly Christian in the years leading to his death at Exmouth from an AIDS-related illness on 21 July 1994. He was buried on 28 July at Alphington parish church, Alphington, Exeter, Devon. He was survived by his long-time partner, Nick Purshouse.

PETER BURTON

Sources P. Burton, *Parallel lives* (1985) · P. Burton, 'Remembering Denis', *Amongst the aliens* (1990) · G. Hanscombe and A. Lumsden, *Title fight* (1983) · D. Lemon, 'The love that dared to speak its name', *Gay Times* (July 1992) · *The Times* (23 July 1994) · *The Independent* (23 July 1994) · *The Guardian* (22 July 1994) · b. cert. · personal knowledge (2004) · private information (2004)

Likenesses photograph, 1977, Hult. Arch. [*see illus.*] · photograph, repro. in *The Times* · photograph, repro. in *The Independent*

Lemon, Sir Ernest John Hutchings (1884–1954), engineer and railway administrator, was born on 10 December 1884 at Okeford Fitzpaine in Dorset, the son of Edward Lemon, agricultural labourer and craftsman, and his wife, Martha Mary Lemon, *née* Rose. He was educated in the local primary school and sang in the choir, where he attracted the notice of the rector, who soon recognized his promise. One of the rector's daughters married the younger brother of Arthur Pillans Laurie, principal of Heriot-Watt College, Edinburgh (1900–28), who befriended Lemon and arranged for his apprenticeship to the North British Locomotive Company at their Hyde Park works in Glasgow. During his apprenticeship he also attended Glasgow Technical College. Lemon often spoke of his gratitude to Laurie for his start in life. In 1905 he worked for a time in the drawing-office of Brown Brothers & Co. in Edinburgh and attended Heriot-Watt College to obtain his professional status as a mechanical engineer. Later he worked for two years in the running department of the Highland Railway, and in 1907 joined Hurst, Nelson & Co., where he was employed in negotiating payments by the railways for damage in transit to privately owned wagons. The Midland Railway was impressed by his efficiency and in 1911 appointed him chief wagon inspector. On 15 October 1912 Lemon married Amy (*b*. 1886/7), daughter of Thomas Clayton, farmer; they had two sons. He was later transferred to the Derby carriage and wagon works where his flair for large-scale production found its opportunity and in 1917 he became works superintendent. During the war he was responsible for building ambulance trains and in 1918 he was appointed OBE in recognition of his work in this field.

When the railways were amalgamated into four large companies in 1923 Lemon became divisional superintendent with responsibility for the London, Midland, and Scottish Railway (LMS) carriage and wagon works at Derby, Earlestown in Lancashire, and Newton Heath, Manchester, where he soon installed mechanized construction of rolling-stock. In 1927 he became carriage and wagon superintendent to the LMS and in 1930 he went with the railway's vice-president and a group of railway engineers to the United States to study the working of American railroads. On his return he was appointed chairman of a committee, called the 'lightning committee' because of its quick report, which foreshadowed many of the changes introduced into the LMS during the thirties under Lemon's vigorous, modernizing leadership. In 1931 he became chief mechanical engineer and in the following year traffic and commercial vice-president. This new position gave Lemon's fertile imagination full scope and the railway quickly reaped the benefits of his technical and organizational ability and his progressive attitude. He reorganized the motive power depots to make more efficient use of locomotives, permitting a reduction in the locomotive fleet and in its associated workforce. At the same time he accelerated LMS passenger train services and improved freight services through the modernization and mechanization of goods facilities which he oversaw. Lemon took a special interest in the recruitment and training of personnel, improving apprenticeship schemes, and increasing graduate recruitment. The foundation of the School of Transport at Derby and the introduction of training films for railway staff were also due to his initiative. In all this Lemon owed much to the backing and encouragement of Lord Stamp, chairman of the LMS, and his wise judgements of Lemon's many schemes. It was a most happy combination of two minds, poles apart in outlook and experience, but with mutual trust and confidence.

As the result of the reputation Lemon had made as a planner of production, in 1938 he went to the Air Ministry as director-general of aircraft production, with a seat on the Air Council. He was closely associated with Sir Wilfrid Freeman who soon assimilated the secrets of Lemon's planning techniques. The Air Ministry had only a small production section, which Lemon quickly enlarged, adding some half-dozen directorates to organize the work. He also reorientated the central planning section, which gained great importance in the complex tasks ahead of it, as Lemon had foreseen. In all this he had Freeman's wholehearted support, and the organization remained unaltered after its transfer to the Ministry of Aircraft Production. Lemon also succeeded in persuading the aircraft industry to adopt the procedure of subcontracting the manufacture of component parts, and his wide contacts with the engineering industry contributed to the rapid increase in production. His vision, drive, and creative resourcefulness provided the transformation vital for the unprecedented expansion of aircraft supply during the critical early war years.

In 1940 Lemon returned to the LMS, and in 1941 he was knighted in recognition of his great contribution to the Royal Air Force. Stamp's death later in the year was a great blow to him and he was never quite the same man afterwards. He resigned from the LMS in 1943, after a short spell of secondment to the Ministry of Production, and was then appointed chairman of a commission to consider the post-war reconstruction and planning of the railways. In 1948 he chaired a committee set up by the Ministry of Supply to consider the standardization of engineering products, and for a time he served as a member of the committee on the organization of the British Standards Institution.

Lemon had a fertile, imaginative brain, always seeking to find fresh and more efficient ways of doing things. He also had the gift of inspiring his colleagues with his own drive and sense of urgency. Under his leadership the LMS was perhaps the most consistently forward-looking and innovative of the big four railway companies. He was a pioneer of mechanized production and one of the early presidents of the Institution of Production Engineers. He died at Woodcote Grove, Chalk Lane, Epsom, on 15 December 1954. HAROLD HARTLEY, *rev.* RALPH HARRINGTON

Sources *The Times* (17 Dec 1954) • *The Times* (23 Dec 1954) • *The Engineer* (24 Dec 1954) • *Engineering* (31 Dec 1954) • J. Marshall, *A biographical dictionary of railway engineers* (1978) • O. S. Nock, *LMS steam* (1971) • d. cert. • *CGPLA Eng. & Wales* (1955)

Wealth at death £14,266 10*s*. 3*d*.: probate, 25 March 1955, *CGPLA Eng. & Wales*

Lemon, George William (1726–1797), schoolmaster and writer, was born in Middlesex, of unknown parents. He was admitted sizar of Queens' College, Cambridge, on 8 March 1744 and graduated BA in 1748. Ordained priest at Ely on 18 March 1753, he was presented to the vicarage of East Walton, near King's Lynn, and to the nearby rectory of Gaytonthorpe, in 1755. He lived at East Walton until 1767, and on 31 May 1760 married Elizabeth Young (1735–1804), of that parish.

In January 1768 Lemon accepted an ushership at Bury St Edmunds grammar school and on 23 December 1769 he was elected high master of Norwich grammar school, in succession to the Revd Edward Symonds. The school's fortunes were declining when Lemon took up his new post, on Lady day 1770, and he could not reverse the trend. The situation became so desperate that a group of parents complained about his poor management and the lack of discipline in the school, and he was ordered to attend court on 7 December 1777 to hear the charges against him. He resigned on 5 January 1778 but continued in post until Michaelmas, when the new high master, Samuel Parr, was elected. Lemon's failings as a schoolmaster almost certainly prompted the publication of new school ordinances in May 1778. Four daughters of Lemon and his wife were baptized at St Luke's in Norwich, and a son had been baptized on 6 October 1769 at St James's in Bury St Edmunds.

Lemon returned to East Walton, where he remained until his death, a quiet country clergyman and an industrious scholar. In 1774 he had published a new Greek grammar in which he 'endeavoured … to remove those Obstructions, which have lain in the way of my young Pupils, and smooth those rugged paths, in which the former Grammars have bewildered and perplexed them' (G. W. Lemon, *Graecae grammaticae rudimenta, ordine Nova, ac faciliori ratione, tradita*, 1774, iii–iv). He intended to replace the Eton grammar, then in use in Norwich School, with his own grammar and a larger companion volume, which never materialized. Likewise he failed to complete a new English translation of Virgil's *Aeneid* and published only specimens of his work, in 1773. His principal publication, *English Etymology, or, A Derivative Dictionary of the English Language*, was printed by subscription in 1783. Praised in the *Critical Review* at the time, it is an eccentric and useless exposition of his theory that most English words were derived from a Greek radix, notwithstanding the dialects that they may have passed through. A close friend of Edward Spelman (*d.* 1767), Lemon completed his history of the Wars of the Roses and published it in 1792. Lemon died on 4 October 1797 at East Walton, where he was buried. His wife died in 1804, and a tablet commemorating them both is in the church. O. W. TANCOCK, *rev.* S. J. SKEDD

Sources Venn, *Alum. Cant.* • *GM*, 1st ser., 67 (1797), 982–3 • *IGI* • J. Johnstone, 'Memoirs', in *The works of Samuel Parr*, 8 vols. (1828), 1.161 • H. G. Bohn, *Bibliotheca Parriana* (1827), 698 • H. W. Saunders, *A history of the Norwich grammar school* (1932), 312–15 • *Critical Review* (March–April 1784) • memorial inscription, East Walton church, Norfolk

Lemon, Margaret (*b. c.*1614), artist's model, was English by birth, but the variant spelling of her name, Lemans, suggests that she may have had Flemish ancestry; the approximate date of birth is based on her apparent age in Van Dyck's earliest paintings of her. Apart from the period *c.*1629–1645, when she was living in London, little is known of her life. Probably still in her teens, she appears to have been a courtesan when Van Dyck made her his mistress, during his second stay in England (1632–41). She presided over his houses in Blackfriars and Eltham, where he entertained both Charles I and members of the nobility who were his patrons, although there is no evidence that she actually met the king. The Czech engraver Wenceslaus Hollar, who was not liked by Van Dyck, famously described Margaret as a woman of explosive temperament, who once in a fit of jealous rage attempted to end her lover's painting career by biting off his thumb (Urzidil, 47). Van Dyck himself remarked on her financial extravagance (Cust, 136) and there were rumours that she had entertained his friend Endymion Porter at Van Dyck's house in Blackfriars while he was on the continent. Yet her beauty, vivacity, and musical ability seem to have offset the more combustible aspects of her nature. She played the viola da gamba, and Van Dyck painted her at the instrument on at least two occasions.

Van Dyck's early portraits of Margaret show a flirtatious

Margaret Lemon (*b. c.*1614), by Sir Anthony Van Dyck

young woman with a brilliant complexion, dark brown hair, and brown eyes. His fascination with her is attested to by the number of times he chose to paint her. The Van Dyck paintings for which she modelled are many and varied and include mythological subjects, such as *Cupid and Psyche* (Royal Collection) and a lost portrait of Margaret as Flora, which survives in a preparatory sketch (priv. coll.), as well as religious works, including two *Lamentations* (Alte Pinakothek, Munich; Royal Museum of Arts, Antwerp), for which Margaret served as model for the Virgin Mary. Her impact on Van Dyck's art can be measured both by the length of time she acted as his model and by the number of paintings for which she is known to have posed. Twelve of these paintings, either originals or contemporary copies, survive, including five portraits. No other seventeenth-century woman without substantive ties to the aristocracy was painted as often.

Margaret had presumably left Van Dyck's household before his marriage to Mary Ruthven in 1639. She continued to live in London and posed, both during Van Dyck's lifetime and afterwards, for other aspiring artists, mostly from London's Netherlandish community. Her position as both his model and his mistress seems to have made her an object of artistic interest for these painters, who used her as a model, probably in the hope that both her looks and her reputation would attract public notice to their work. They included Cornelis Jansen van Ceulen, Adriaen Hanneman, and Peter Lely (for whom Margaret modelled, notably, for *The Concert*; Courtauld Inst.). Among the most important portraits of her by this group of artists is the earliest known miniature by Samuel Cooper (*c.*1635–1641), which shows her dressed as a young cavalier. Cooper's last known miniature (1671; priv. coll.) may also be a portrait of Margaret. Of Van Dyck's lost painting of her as Flora no fewer than three seventeenth-century engravings and two contemporary copies, all by different artists, are known, indicating that her impact on the group of painters who succeeded Van Dyck was significant. The place and date of her death are not known.

Susan E. James

Sources S. E. James, 'Margaret Lemon: model, mistress, muse', *Jaarboek van het Koninklijk Museum voor Schone Kunsten Antwerpen* (1999) • S. E. James, 'The model as catalyst: Nicholas Lanier and Margaret Lemon', *Jaarboek van het Koninklijk Museum voor Schone Kunsten Antwerpen* (1999) • Vertue, *Note books*, vols. 1–2 • H. Walpole, *Anecdotes of painting in England: with some account of the principal artists*, ed. R. N. Wornum, new edn, 1 (1849); repr. (1862) • BL, Egerton MS 1636, fol. 102 • J. Urzidil, *Hollar: a Czech émigré in England* (1942) • L. Cust, *Anthony Van Dyck: an historical study of his life and works* (1905) • file on 'Van Dyck's *Andromeda chained to a rock*', Los Angeles County Museum of Art • M. M. Damm, 'Van Dyck's mythological paintings', PhD diss., U. Mich., 1966 • C. Brown and others, *Van Dyck, 1599–1641* (1999) [exhibition catalogue, Koninklijk Museum voor Schone Kunsten, Antwerp, 15 May – 15 Aug 1999, and RA, 11 Sept – 10 Dec 1999]

Likenesses A. Van Dyck, oils, 1629, Baltimore Museum of Art, Maryland, Jacob Epstein collection • A. Van Dyck, oils, 1629, Galleria di Palazzo Bianco, Genoa • A. Van Dyck, oils, 1629, Pommersfelden, Graf von Schonborn collection • school of A. Van Dyck, oils, *c.*1633–1634, Alte Pinakothek, Munich • A. Van Dyck, oils, 1634–6, Alte Pinakothek, Munich • A. Van Dyck, oils, *c.*1634–1636 • S. Cooper, miniature, watercolour on vellum, *c.*1635–1641, Institut Neerlandais, Paris, Fondation Custodia, Collection F. Lugt • A. Hanneman?, oils, *c.*1636 (after A. Van Dyck), Newnham Hall, Northamptonshire • C. J. van Ceulen, oils, 1637; Christies, 1916 • A. Van Dyck, oils, *c.*1638–1639, Hampton Court Palace, London • engraving, *c.*1641–1646 (after A. Van Dyck), Tokyo collection • oils, *c.*1641–1646 (after A. Van Dyck), Longleat House, Wiltshire • W. Hollar, engraving, 1646 (after A. Van Dyck), BM • A. Hanneman, oils, 1652 (after A. Van Dyck); Christies, 1978 • S. Cooper, miniature?, watercolour on vellum, 1671, priv. coll. • P. Lely, oils, Courtauld Inst., Lee Collection • P. Lely, oils; Sothebys, 9 Dec 1981 • A. Lommelin, engraving (after A. Van Dyck), repro. in M. Mauquoy-Henrickx, *L'iconographie d'Antoine van Dyck* (1956) • J. Morin, engraving (after A. Van Dyck), repro. in A. P. F. Robert-Dumesnil, *Le peintre-graveur*, 2 (1836) • A. Van Dyck, oils, Royal Collection [*see illus.*] • A. Van Dyck, oils, Blenheim Palace, Oxfordshire • A. Van Dyck, oils, Royal Museum of Arts, Antwerp • A. Van Dyck, pen and Indian ink wash on paper, Institut Neerlandais, Paris, Fondation Custodia, Collection F. Lugt • A. Van Dyck?, oils, Los Angeles County Museum of Art

Lemon [*née* Smith], **Margaretta Louisa** (1860–1953), bird protectionist, was born at Hythe, Kent, on 22 November 1860, the daughter of Captain William Elisha Smith and his wife, Louisa Barclay. Nothing is known of her early years; as an adult she became involved in animal welfare, acting as one of the main proponents of the Royal Society for the Protection of Birds (RSPB) for more than fifty years. Her inspiration was the account in Eliza Brightwen's *Wild Nature Won by Kindness* (1890) of the slaughter of breeding egrets to obtain feathers for the plumage trade. The feathers were used to trim the hats of ladies; during church services Margaretta Smith would note which women were wearing feathers and send them a polite note to make them aware of the horrors inflicted in order to provide their fashion accessories. In 1889 she joined a near-neighbour in Croydon, Mrs Eliza Phillips (1823–1916), in organizing Fur, Fin and Feather afternoons at 11 Morland Road, Croydon; simultaneously a group calling itself the Society for the Protection of Birds was founded in Manchester by Emily Williamson.

When the two groups merged at a meeting at the RSPCA's Jermyn Street headquarters in London in 1891, it seems that the Manchester group provided the name and the London group the energy. A barrister, Frank Edward Lemon (*c.*1859–1935), drew up the constitution of the merged organization. On 25 May 1892 Etta Smith married Lemon. Since no reference can be found to the couple having met through their mutual concern with bird protection, it might be assumed that they knew one another before Miss Smith became involved, and that she recommended Frank Lemon as a legal adviser.

Margaretta Lemon became the first honorary secretary of the society in 1893 and served in this capacity until 1904, when the society was incorporated by royal charter. Frank then took her place, while she became honorary secretary of the society's publications and watchers committee, as well as preparing all the agendas, writing minutes, and handling general correspondence. For the next thirty-one years the couple worked in tandem as the driving force behind the society, during a period when its achievements included the passage of the Importation of Plumage (Prohibition) Act, 1922; the establishment of the society's first nature reserve; some sharply focused educational activities, such as the public school essay competition and Bird and Tree weeks; and improvements in the protection of birds legislation. However, towards the end of the Lemons' reign at the RSPB there were signs of the innovators becoming staid and resisting new ideas.

Descriptions of the Lemons show two very different personalities. The existing oil portraits and photographs confirm these differences: it is easy to see in Frank's features his

> genial, kindly manner, unfailing tact and good temper, and ready humour, no less than his knowledge of men and things, and his tolerant and equitable judgment, particularly in times when difficulties had to be confronted or differences of opinion blended into harmony. (*Bird Notes*, 16, 1935, 6)

His wife's portrait and photographs, on the other hand, show a direct gaze and a determined mouth. The address by the Revd J. B. Phillips at her memorial service in 1953 creates the image of a formidable woman:

> I have known her only eight and a half years, but I have rarely met anyone of quicker intelligence or with a more ready wit or a livelier sense of humour. She had tremendous courage; she had great tenacity of purpose and she had a directness of approach which those who did not know her might sometimes think brusque. But behind all that was an immense love of her fellow men—and of all her fellow creatures, for we do not forget her championship of wild birds. (*Bird Notes*, 25, 1953, 293)

Mrs Lemon's obituarist in *Bird Notes* was Miss M. G. Davies, a member of the staff of the RSPB, who confirmed the fierceness of her former employer: 'To office staff she was something of a dragon at times, but no one in trouble ever appealed for her help in vain, when all the forces at her command were called into play' (*Bird Notes*). Her formidable qualities showed themselves in the early 1930s when some of the younger council members of the RSPB felt that the old guard should be changed. It was proposed and accepted that when the professional secretary of the society (Linda Gardiner) retired in 1935 she should be replaced by a man. This proposal—apparently based on the presumption that a male secretary would give the society greater *gravitas* and acceptability—was resented by the two female assistant secretaries (one of whom, Phyllis Barclay-Smith, was involved in international conservation and was well regarded as an ornithologist). Angered by exclusion from candidacy for the position on the grounds of gender, they confronted Mrs Lemon, in her capacity as acting honorary secretary following Frank's death, in April 1935, demanding to be regarded as of equal standing with the new secretary, although accepting that he would be *primus inter pares*. Whether such a novel proposition might ever have been accepted is doubtful, but the assistant secretaries ensured its failure by stating that, if their requests were not met, they would regretfully be forced to resign. Mrs Lemon swiftly accepted their resignations. In her anger she omitted their names in her brief note about their resignation in the society's magazine.

The issue of the direction in which the society was going was covered in an editorial in *The Field* in February 1936, and at the society's annual meeting in March questions were asked about the society's gambling in real estate, its inaction over cage birds, excessive administrative expenses, the advanced age of the women involved with the society, and the dismissal of officers at a moment's notice. Clearly Mrs Lemon was the target of these questions, which resulted in the society's council setting up a six-man committee under Julian Huxley, then secretary of the Zoological Society. Some of their proposals were adopted, but the one aimed at preventing a self-perpetuating governing body met stiff opposition. It was another twenty-four years before council accepted that its members should be elected for a fixed term, after which they would be ineligible for re-election within a year; Mrs Lemon had been dead six years by then.

Margaretta Lemon was not an ornithologist, and never had any pretensions to be one, despite having been elected to membership of the British Ornithologists' Union. Indeed, she seemed to mistrust ornithologists: during the first decades of the RSPB's existence she felt that they were indifferent or even hostile to its effort, a hostility that she attributed to the fact that one of the principal objects of the society was to curb the activities of egg collectors and skin hunters.

Bird protection was not Mrs Lemon's only good cause: she was also involved with the Royal Earlswood Institution and the Crescent House Convalescent Home, Brighton. During the First World War she was Voluntary Aid Detachment commandant at the Redhill Clinic, a function that she performed well enough to be made an MBE in the 1920 new year's honours. She died on 8 July 1953 at Annandale, Warwick Road, Redhill, and was buried at Reigate. NICHOLAS HAMMOND

Sources T. Samstag, *For love of birds: the story of the Royal Society for the Protection of Birds, 1889–1988* (1988) · N. Hammond, 'Conservation and sister organisations: Royal Society for the Protection of Birds', *Enjoying ornithology*, ed. R. Hickling (1983), 158–64 · *Bird Notes*, 25 (1953), 293 · *Bird Notes*, 16 (1935), 6 · b. cert. · m. cert. · d. cert.
Archives Royal Society for the Protection of Birds Library
Likenesses oils, 1935?, Royal Society for the Protection of Birds, The Lodge, Sandy, Bedfordshire · photographs, Royal Society for the Protection of Birds, The Lodge, Sandy, Bedfordshire
Wealth at death £13,770 5*s*. 5*d*.: probate, 19 Oct 1953, *CGPLA Eng. & Wales*

Lemon, Mark (1809–1870), magazine editor and playwright, the only child of Martin Lemon (*d*. 1817) and Alice Collis, was born on 30 November 1809 in Oxford Street, London. Both parents had rural roots. Martin Lemon could trace his descent from Cornish yeomen, while his wife came from prosperous Northamptonshire stock. At the age of eight Mark lost his father and was sent to live with his paternal grandparents at Church House Farm, Hendon, Middlesex. His mother, meanwhile, began a new career as a milliner in Oxford Street. Mark became a boarder at Cheam School for a while and came under the influence of its headmaster, James Wilding. Some of his school experiences were woven into his second novel, *Loved at Last* (1864). The death of Lemon's grandfather in 1820 was the possible reason for the end of Mark's spell at Cheam. Three years later his grandmother died, and at the age of fourteen he was sent to Boston, Lincolnshire, to learn the hops business under the guidance of his uncle, Thomas Collis.

Early career and the foundation of *Punch* By 1836 Lemon had returned to London and in March of that year was living in Soho. A year later he was working in a Kentish Town brewery run by the brother of his mother's second husband. From 1834 to 1837 his light verse and sketches under the pen-name Tom Moody appeared in the *New Sporting Magazine*. From September 1837 he also contributed to *Bentley's Miscellany* while Charles Dickens was the editor. Lemon saw his first play, a farce entitled *The P. L., or, 30, Strand*, produced at the Strand Theatre on 25 April 1836. This was followed in July by his first melodrama, *Arnold of Winkelreid*, which was staged at the Surrey Theatre. A meeting with the actor and composer Frank Romer led to their collaboration on *Rob of the Fen* (an adaptation of the German *Des Falkners Braut*), which appeared at the English Opera House in July 1838. Lemon was introduced to one of Romer's sisters, Helen (Nelly) Romer (*c*.1817–1890), whom he eventually married on 28 September 1839, and with whom he had three sons and seven daughters. However, with the closure of the brewery early in the following year Lemon was left without a regular income, though he was soon found a new post as landlord of the Shakespeare's Head in Wych Street, off Drury Lane, London. Although popular with his 'guests', as he preferred to call his clientele of mainly poets, playwrights, artists, and journalists, Lemon proved to be an incompetent businessman, and by the close of 1840 had been sacked.

In early June 1841 fellow playwright Henry Mayhew introduced Lemon to Joseph Last, a printer, who had already introduced Mayhew to the engraver Ebenezer

Mark Lemon (1809–1870), by Horatio Nelson King

Landells. The latter wished to finance the launch of a new comic journal modelled on Philipon's Paris *Charivari*. This was a bold initiative, given that *Figaro in London*, the comic newspaper with which the nascent *Punch* was most commonly compared, had folded two years earlier. Its closure was symbolic of a decline in the fortunes of satirical journalism which was due partly to a period of relative political calm, partly to the death of its most obvious target, George IV, and partly also to the growth of Chartist newspapers, which provided an alternative voice for radicalism. Lemon was none the less attracted by the idea, and over the next few weeks became involved in discussions. Eventually a definite plan emerged. Initially Lemon was to share the editorial responsibilities with Mayhew and the Irish dramatist Stirling Coyne. Last was to be the printer, Landells the engraver, and the publisher was to be William Bryant. Several writers were approached for contributions, including Douglas Jerrold, Gilbert à Beckett, and Percival Leigh. Among the artists were to be Archibald Henning, Birket Foster, and John Leech. The title *Punch* was chosen after some debate, and Lemon set about preparing a prospectus, which was duly circulated throughout the capital. Lemon saw the new comic weekly, which was due to make its début on 17 July 1841, as 'a refuge for destitute wit' and an 'asylum for the thousands of orphan jokes … the millions of perishing puns, which are now wandering about without so much as a shelf to rest upon' (Adrian, 30–31). However, he also promised features on politics, fashion, police, reviews, fine arts, music and drama, and sport. The first number of *Punch* appeared on the date set and the leading article by Lemon expanded on the prospectus. The new paper would provide 'pleasing instruction' as well as harmless amusement, and would be conducted in a liberal, humanitarian spirit. Despite the investment of money and talent in it, *Punch* did not take off as expected, and had Lemon not ploughed back a fee of £30 received for his playlet *The Silver Thimble* the third issue would not have appeared. The proceeds from a farce by Lemon, *Punch*, also helped to keep the paper going. As a *Punch* contributor in this period Lemon was kept busy with his serial 'The Heir of Applebite', which ran from August to November 1841.

Editor of *Punch* With the acquisition of *Punch* by Bradbury and Evans in December 1842 Lemon became sole editor, possibly in recognition of his financial help. An embittered Henry Mayhew never adjusted himself to a new subservient role under Lemon, and in 1847 he accused his former friend of welshing on an agreement to share the proceeds from certain plays on which they had collaborated. Under the inspired leadership of Lemon, who possessed a genuine gift for getting the best out of his contributors, *Punch* prospered. In 1842 William Makepeace Thackeray was recruited to the team; Horace Mayhew arrived a year later, and in 1844 Tom Taylor made his début. John Leech, who began his first *Punch* cartoon in 1842, and Richard Doyle were the two outstanding artists taken on by Lemon in the first decade. Apart from 'The Heir of Applebite' Lemon's own contributions to *Punch* tended to be short fillers, though he also wrote 'Songs for the Sentimental' and similar verse effusions, many of which had a keen social emphasis. Lemon's humanitarianism encouraged social and political satirists, most notably the brilliant Jerrold, to submit their best material to *Punch*, though the magazine's strong radical flavour was tempered somewhat by the more conservative contributions of men like Thackeray, Tom Taylor, and John Leech. It was Lemon who accepted 'The Song of the Shirt', a fierce indictment of the harsh working conditions of seamstresses by Thomas Hood, for the 1843 Christmas number, against the advice of his staff. As a result the circulation of *Punch* was tripled overnight. Yet behind the magazine's social conscience lurked a genuine philistinism, particularly towards the visual arts, and a narrow jingoism. Lemon oversaw a protracted campaign against Prince Albert, who was ridiculed for collecting pre-Renaissance Italian art, for patronizing the German portraitist Winterhalter, and for dabbling, alongside his wife, in etching. The Art Union and the Schools of Design were also satirized, as was the emerging Pre-Raphaelite Brotherhood, which *Punch* depicted as an unnatural 'foreign' departure from the English tradition in genre painting.

Lemon's uncanny instinct for discovering fresh talent led *Punch* towards even greater prosperity in its second and third decades. Doyle's resignation in 1850 (in protest at the magazine's anti-Catholic campaign) opened the door for John Tenniel, a draughtsman with even greater gifts, and in the following year Lemon recruited the equally gifted Charles Keene. The humorist Shirley Brooks was poached by Lemon from *Punch*'s rival the *Man in the Moon* at about the same time, and eventually became deputy editor. Henry Silver, whose intimate diary recorded the proceedings at the weekly *Punch* dinners (another Lemon innovation), arrived in 1857. The artist George du Maurier became a regular in 1864, just after the writer F. C. Burnand was taken onto the staff by Lemon. With the death of Jerrold in 1857 *Punch* lost its only genuinely radical voice, though by this time the magazine's earlier anti-establishment tone had been replaced by one that reflected the views and aspirations of its largely professional middle-class readership. *Punch*'s respectability was acknowledged by Lemon himself when he admitted that his magazine kept 'to the gentlemanly view of things' (Adrian, 58). As editor of Britain's leading comic weekly he received £1500 annually, the highest salary ever paid for such a position up to that time. Courted as a celebrity, he was admitted to the Garrick Club and attended Reform Club dinners presided over by the chef Alexis Soyer. Nevertheless, despite his success he did not jettison his liberalism, and at *Punch* dinners was often the sole voice of humanitarianism in discussions over social policy.

Lemon's circle Lemon's friends outside *Punch* included Herbert Ingram, whom he had first met while living in Boston as a boy. He acted as Ingram's chief adviser during the launching of the *Illustrated London News* in May 1842, and thereafter was responsible for each Christmas supplement of the magazine until Ingram's death in 1860. He was Ingram's right-hand man during his successful Liberal campaign for the Boston constituency in 1856, during which he was joined by several of his *Punch* colleagues. In the following year Ingram turned the editorial work of his recently acquired *London Journal* over to Lemon, but a decision to reprint the Waverley novels in its pages proved disastrous and Lemon resigned. Lemon was also first editor of *The Field*, which Bradbury and Evans launched in January 1853. In this part-time post he renewed his association with Robert Surtees, who became his principal hunting correspondent and general adviser, but his own contributions consisted largely of surplus material from *Punch* and the *Illustrated London News*. He was replaced as editor by J. H. Walsh at the close of 1857.

Lemon's friendship with Charles Dickens was a close and long-lasting one. Although he contributed to *Bentley's Miscellany* while Dickens was editor, it is unlikely that the two men met until after the first issue of *Punch* appeared. In April 1843 Lemon was formally invited to dinner by Dickens and their friendship grew. Lemon and *Punch* stalwart Gilbert à Beckett adapted Dickens's *Chimes* for the Adelphi in February 1844. *The Haunted Man* followed in 1848. Lemon and Jerrold probably acted as Dickens's sub-editors during the latter's short stint in charge of the *Daily News* in January 1846. A shared passion for amateur theatricals cemented their friendship. Lemon appeared as Brainworm and Dickens as Bobadil in Jonson's *Every Man in his Humour*, which played at the Royalty and at the St James Theatre in the autumn of 1845. The production was transferred to Manchester and Liverpool in the summer of 1847, and in the following year the play was revived in London, alternating with *The Merry Wives of Windsor*, in which Lemon appeared as Falstaff alongside Dickens. During the more lengthy provincial tour that followed Lemon and Dickens supplemented their Shakespearian repertoire with roles in various farces. In a campaign to raise funds for the Guild of Literature and Art, Lemon and Dickens appeared again in Jonson's play at Lytton's Knebworth in November 1850, and in the following May, after a performance in Lytton's *Not So Bad As We Seem*, Lemon joined Dickens in *Mr Nightingale's Diary*, a piece that they had co-written. Further provincial tours followed late in 1851 and in 1852. Lemon also took part in productions at Dickens's small private theatre in Tavistock House, notably in Wilkie Collins's melodramas *The Lighthouse* (1855) and *The Frozen Deep* (1857). Lemon and his family had become frequent visitors to Dickens's home since the latter had moved to Tavistock House in November 1851, though the new neighbours were already fellow members of a weekly walking club, had taken nocturnal strolls around London together, and had been on excursions, such as a tour of Salisbury Plain in 1848. In the following year Dickens submitted his one and only contribution to *Punch* (an attack on the suburban water supply), but Lemon deemed it unsuitable.

Other writings; later life The end of Lemon's long friendship with Dickens came in 1858 when Lemon neglected to publish in *Punch* his friend's proclamation outlining the reasons for a separation from his wife, Catherine, who had been advised by Lemon. The two men were eventually reconciled in 1867. The break with Dickens coincided with Lemon's move from London to Crawley, Sussex, in May 1858. At the spacious Vine Cottage he entertained his *Punch* colleagues, including Shirley Brooks, who replaced Dickens in Lemon's affections, and John Tenniel, who modelled his illustrations of Alice in Lewis Caroll's *Alice in Wonderland* on Lemon's daughter Kate. Lemon also involved himself in parish affairs. He used his influence to bring street lighting to Crawley, helped promote cultural events, resurrected stage-coach travel, and raised money for a new fire engine. At the one-roomed Malthouse, a mile from his home, Lemon wrote prodigiously until his death. He continued to write plays, including the anti-suffragist *Women's Suffrage, or, Petticoat Parliament* (1867), but the bulk of his output in this period was fiction, and in particular novels. His first book, *The Enchanted Doll*, a collection of fairy tales, had appeared in 1849, and had been followed by four collections of contributions to periodicals, *Prose and Verse* (1852), *The Heir of Applebite* and *Our Lodgers* (1856), and *Betty Morrison's Pocket Book* (1856). At Crawley Lemon prepared a collection of Christmas pieces from the *Illustrated London News*, *A Christmas Hamper* (1860), which was followed by two novelty items, *The Jest Book* (1864), a compendium of mainly old jokes, and *The New Table Book* (1867). He also continued to write for children. *The Legends of Number Nip* (1864) is a rendering of Johann Karl Musaeus's *Rübezahl* with illustrations by *Punch* artist Charles Keene. *Tinykin's Transformations* (1869) is a fairy tale set in Saxon times. Lemon wrote his first novel in Crawley; *Wait for the End* (1863) is a moralistic tale centring on the lives of two brothers and their progeny. This was followed by *Loved at Last* (1864) and the more highly regarded *Falkner Lyle* (1866), both of which had strong romantic themes. *Leyton Hall* (1867) was a novella set at the time of Charles I. In the same year appeared a full-length novel, *Golden Fetters*, which had a contemporary setting. Lemon's final unpublished novel, *The Taffeta Petticoat*, was completed shortly before his death and drew on years of accumulated knowledge of the theatre, of metropolitan life, and the era of coaching. All Lemon's fiction suffers from unwanted authorial intrusions into the narrative and much of it is marred by a patronizing attitude towards women, extreme prudishness, and a saccharine sentimentality, though his powers of observation and humour are a saving grace.

Early in 1862 Lemon delivered a highly successful series of illustrated lectures on the history of London, using as sources such authorities as Stow, Camden, Pepys, and Evelyn. In spring this entertainment toured the provinces, and in 1867 the material was published as *Up and Down the London Streets*. In 1863 he toured with an adaptation of his own drama *Hearts are Trumps*. With his heavily bowdlerized interpretation of Shakespeare's Falstaff from *Henry IV*, Lemon realized a personal ambition to rescue the reputation of a favourite character. On opening in London in October 1868 his Falstaff performances were well received, but provincial tours in the following year resulted in heavy financial losses and were a strain on his declining health. Lemon died at Vine Cottage, Crawley, on 23 May 1870 after a series of short illnesses, and was buried at Ifield church on 27 May. R. M. HEALEY

Sources A. A. Adrian, *Mark Lemon: first editor of 'Punch'* (1966) · R. G. G. Price, *A history of Punch* (1957) · M. H. Spielmann, *The history of 'Punch'* (1895) · R. M. Healey, '*Punch* and the arts, 1841–51', MA diss., U. Birm., 1976 · *The letters of Charles Dickens*, ed. M. House, G. Storey, and others, 3–8 (1974–95) · E. Johnson, *Charles Dickens: his tragedy and triumph*, abridged edn (1977) · J. Hatton, *With a show in the north: reminiscences of Mark Lemon* (1871) · N. Cross, *The common writer: life in nineteenth-century Grub Street* (1985) · L. W. Fisher, *Lemon, Dickens, and 'Mr Nightingale's diary': a Victorian farce* (1988) · R. D. Altick, *'Punch': the lively youth of a British institution, 1841–1851* (1997) · *Sussex Agricultural Express* (31 May 1870)

Archives Harvard U., MSS · Haverford College Library, Pennsylvania, MSS · Hist. Soc. Penn., MSS · Hunt. L., letters · New York University, Fales Collection · NL Scot., MSS · NYPL, Berg Collection · priv. coll. · U. Edin. L., MSS · U. Texas, MSS · University of Victoria, British Columbia, MSS · London, Punch Office MSS | BL, correspondence with Macmillans, Add. MS 55041 · Cleveland, Ohio, Adrian MSS

Likenesses photograph, *c*.1860, repro. in Adrian, *Mark Lemon*, facing p. 106 · death mask, 1870, repro. in Adrian, *Mark Lemon*, 204 · A. E. Downing, etching, NPG · R. Doyle, pen-and-ink caricature, BM · H. Furniss, NPG · H. N. King, photograph, NPG [*see illus.*] · Sem [G. Goursat], watercolour caricature, NPG · Swain, woodcuts, BM · cartes-de-visite, NPG · wood-engraving (after photograph by H. J. Whitlock), NPG; repro. in *ILN* (4 June 1870) · woodcut (after photograph by London Stereoscopic Co.), NPG; repro. in *Illustrated Review* (15 Feb 1872)

Wealth at death under £800: probate, 14 Jan 1871, *CGPLA Eng. & Wales*

Lemon, Robert (1779–1835), archivist, born in London, was the son of Robert Lemon, chief clerk of the record office in the Tower of London. After education at Norwich grammar school under his uncle George William Lemon and assisting his father at the tower for about eighteen months, he was appointed clerk in the state paper office on 24 June 1795. In 1798 he helped to compile the appendix to the *Report on Internal Defence*, which chiefly relates to the preparations made against the threatened invasion of 1588. Lemon worked with his father in preparing the calendars of the charter rolls and inquisitions ad quod damnum, and of the inquisitions post mortem. In February 1801 he became second clerk. The keeper, John Bruce (1745–1826), was also historiographer to the East India Company, and compiled the *Annals* of the company (1810) with Lemon's assistance. Lemon became deputy keeper of the state paper office on 23 January 1818, and began to arrange categories of records including royal letters, Irish and Scottish correspondence, royalist composition papers, and Gunpowder Plot papers.

In the course of his work Lemon discovered the manuscript of Milton's treatise *De doctrina Christiana*. Thereupon, on the advice of Sir Robert Peel, then home secretary, a commission for publishing records of historical value was issued on 10 June 1825, and renewed on 14 September 1830. Lemon was appointed secretary. By his exertions the documents belonging to the reign of Henry VIII were arranged for publication. In 1833 the state papers were removed from Scotland Yard and Great George Street to a repository built for them in St James's Park, in which Lemon had private apartments assigned to him. He was married and with his wife, Sarah (1772–1826), he had a son, Robert *Lemon, who was also an archivist, and a daughter. Elected FSA in May 1824, he contributed to the *Archaeologia* (21.148–57) the warrant of indemnity to Lord Treasurer Middlesex for the jewels sent to Charles, prince of Wales, in Spain. Among those who benefited by Lemon's knowledge was Sir Walter Scott, as the postscript appended in November 1829 to the cabinet edition of *Rob Roy* testifies. Lemon illustrated his copy of Scott's novel with transcripts of historical documents. He died on 29 July 1835, and was buried in Kennington churchyard, London. GORDON GOODWIN, *rev.* G. H. MARTIN

Sources *GM*, 2nd ser., 4 (1835), 326–8 · *The Greville memoirs*, ed. H. Reeve, 4th edn, 3 (1875), 44 · *GM*, 1st ser., 96/2 (1826), 283 [death of Sarah Lemon]
Archives U. Edin. L., corresp. and papers relating to state paper office | BL, letters to W. R. Hamilton and others [index of MSS vi (1985)]
Likenesses M. Gauci, lithograph, BM, NPG

Lemon, Robert (1800–1867), archivist, possibly born in London, was the son of Robert *Lemon (1779–1835), archivist, and his wife, Sarah (1772–1826). He was employed under his father in the state paper office, where he compiled the indexes to *Valor ecclesiasticus temp. Hen. VIII* (*Report of Record Commission*, 1836, appx, 770), and discovered in 1826 an original portrait of Milton. In November 1835 he was appointed senior clerk. Lemon suggested that calendars of the state papers should be compiled and published, and he first interpreted the cipher which had previously rendered large masses of those papers unintelligible. The first two volumes of the *Domestic Series*, 1547–90, were published under his editorship in 1856 and 1865. He was married, and had a large family. He died at his home, 10 Ovington Square, Brompton, London, on 3 January 1867.

Lemon was elected FSA on 3 March 1836. His single contribution to the *Archaeologia* (vol. 37) consists of a commentary appended to a letter addressed to John Stanhope in 1588, giving particulars of the Spanish Armada. He also contributed to the Society of Antiquaries' *Proceedings*. In 1846 he rearranged the society's library, and compiled catalogues of its valuable collections of broadsides and proclamations. His *Catalogue* of the broadsides, with an introduction by John Bruce FSA, was published by the society in 1866. GORDON GOODWIN, *rev.* G. H. MARTIN

Sources *Proceedings of the Society of Antiquaries of London*, 2nd ser., 3 (1864–7), 481–2 · *The Athenaeum* (24 Jan 1857), 107–8 · *GM*, 1st ser., 96/2 (1826), 61, 283 · *GM*, 2nd ser., 4 (1835), 545 · [R. Lemon], 'Lemon's calendar of state papers', *GM*, 3rd ser., 2 (1857), 446–51 · *GM*, 4th ser., 3 (1867), 261 · *CGPLA Eng. & Wales* (1867)
Archives S. Antiquaries, Lond., papers relating to Society of Antiquaries Catalogue of Proclamations | BL, letters to Sir Robert Peel and others · Bodl. Oxf., corresp. with Sir Thomas Phillipps
Wealth at death under £16,000: probate, 26 Jan 1867, *CGPLA Eng. & Wales*

Lempriere, Charles (1818–1901), politician and speculator, born at Exeter on 21 September 1818, was second son of John *Lemprière (*c.*1765–1824), compiler of the *Classical Dictionary*, and his second wife, Elizabeth, daughter of John Deane of Salisbury. He entered Merchant Taylors' School in February 1825 and matriculated at St John's College, Oxford, in 1837, his school entitling him to the fellowship which he held from 1837 until his death. He took a third in *literae humaniores* and a third in mathematics in 1841, a BCL in 1842, and DCL in 1847.

Lempriere was called to the bar from the Inner Temple on 22 January 1844, and for a time did work for Alexander James Edmund Cockburn, who always remained his friend. On joining the western circuit he made good progress, but soon became involved in risky financial ventures, the consequences of which involved him in difficulties lasting almost until his death. In pursuance of these schemes he travelled for some time in Egypt and the Near East. Meanwhile he interested himself in politics on the Conservative side. He had been one of the earlier members of the Conservative Club (1841) and from 1850 was an active tory agent. He was one of a group of drunken tories who threatened to throw W. E. Gladstone out of the window at the Carlton Club in London in 1852. He acted as a controversial but unsuccessful tory agent for the Oxford University seat, his tactics in 1853 (when he slipped in a last-minute candidate against Gladstone at a by-election) and in 1859 leading to his denunciation in pamphlets. In 1861 Lempriere was dispatched by Sir Moses Montefiore on a private mission to Mexico, then in the midst of civil and financial disturbance, to defend, as far as was possible, threatened British interests. *Notes in Mexico in 1861 and 1862* (1862) recorded his impressions. On that journey he also visited the United States; *The American Crisis Considered* (1861) vigorously supported the Confederacy.

In 1865 Lempriere was back in England and again active in elections. In June 1866 he contested Winchester at a by-election so as to force a contest, but he polled only forty-six votes. In 1867 Lord Derby rewarded his services by the colonial secretaryship of the Bahamas. Political feeling at that time ran high in the islands, and it was not long before Lempriere's strong tory opinions brought him into difficulties. He was accused of interfering in elections, and had to resign. Scenes of great disorder followed; Lempriere's house was robbed and his papers destroyed. Rather than return to Britain, he went to the United States, where he had previously made the acquaintance of Horace Greeley, who now employed him as a writer for *The Tribune*. After Greeley's death in 1872 Lempriere entered on the oddest stage of his exotic career. He organized a colony of young Englishmen at Buckhorn in West Virginia, on the lines of that afterwards attempted at Rugby, Tennessee, by Thomas Hughes, who is reputed to have suggested the idea to Lempriere. The 'colony' failed, the colonists were half starved, and in 1879 Lempriere was back in England and again engaged in financial projects. In the pursuit of these he travelled in most countries of Europe. His last undertaking was in connection with the valuation of the great Partagas tobacco estates in Cuba, in which he was employed by a syndicate (1887–9). From that time onwards he remained mostly in England, occasionally residing for some months at a time in Belgium and Luxembourg, where he had many friends. His debts continued to constrain him and it was said that he maintained his fellowship at St John's College so as to avoid prosecution. He died unmarried at 205 North End Road, London, on 30 October 1901. His executor was Hannah Houlton, spinster. A. T. S. GOODRICK, *rev.* H. C. G. MATTHEW

Sources J. B. Payne, *Monograph of the house of Lempriere* (1862) · W. R. Ward, *Victorian Oxford* (1965) · personal knowledge (1912) · *Hist. U. Oxf.* 6: *19th-cent. Oxf.* · *CGPLA Eng. & Wales* (1901)
Likenesses oils, St John's College, Oxford · oils, Seigneurie of Rozet, Jersey, Channel Islands
Wealth at death £180: probate, 21 Nov 1901, *CGPLA Eng. & Wales*

Lemprière, John (*c*.1765–1824), classical scholar, was born in Jersey, the son of Charles Lemprière, solicitor-general of Jersey, and his wife, Elizabeth, daughter of James Corbet. He was educated at Winchester College and at Pembroke College, Oxford, where he graduated BA in 1790, MA in 1792, BD in 1801, and DD in 1803. In 1788 he interrupted his studies to act as an assistant master at Reading School, where the headmaster was Richard Valpy, also a Jersey man and graduate of Pembroke. Lemprière appears to have been ordained in 1789, since he preached at St Helier's church, Jersey, in that year.

While at Reading, Lemprière published his *Bibliotheca classica, or, A classical dictionary containing a full account of all the proper names mentioned in antient authors* (1788). An enlarged edition appeared in 1797. The work went through numerous editions. It was translated into Latin in Holland in 1794, and was registered as the property of an American citizen in 1825. In this form it passed through seven editions in eight years under the editorship of Professor Charles Anthon, who expanded it greatly. This version was adopted by the English classical scholar E. H. Barker who expanded it further. F. D. Lemprière, the nephew of the compiler, produced another still larger version. Anthon, Barker, and F. D. Lemprière added material of their own, but reprinted most of the original articles verbatim. A revised edition of the original dictionary appeared in 1949 and had been reprinted six times by 1984.

In 1791 Lemprière was master of the grammar school at Bolton, Lancashire. From 1792 until 1809 he was headmaster of Abingdon School. He also served as curate of Radley and reader at St Nicholas's Church, Abingdon. About 1792 he married Miss Willince of Abingdon. On 18 December 1813 he married, secondly, Elizabeth, daughter of John Deane of Salisbury; Charles *Lempriere, politician, was a son from this marriage. Lemprière was neither an effective headmaster nor a conscientious priest. During his time at Abingdon most of the teaching was done by an usher, and numbers in the school fell sharply, so it became difficult to find candidates for the school's numerous closed scholarships to Pembroke College, Oxford. With the connivance of the high-master of St Paul's and John Smith (*d*. 1809), master of Pembroke (who was an old Pauline), Lemprière offered to secure a Pembroke scholarship for any boy who was sent to him on payment of the boarding fee and 20 guineas. In a few years at least eight boys who had been educated at St Paul's were put down in the Pembroke registers as having been at Abingdon. In 1809 a new master, George William Hall, came into office at Pembroke and Lemprière resigned from Abingdon. His failure to hold sufficient regular services at St Nicholas's led to a complaint to the bishop of Salisbury in 1796, and in 1799 the vestry refused to pay his stipend. He closed the church and it remained unused until 1800, when he was appointed vicar of St Helen's, Abingdon, and the usher took his place at St Nicholas's.

While at Abingdon, Lemprière published the first volume of an English translation of Herodotus with notes, but did not complete the work. He also published a *Universal Biography … of Eminent Persons in All Ages and Countries* (1808). The articles are brief, and no authorities are cited. In 1809 he became master of Exeter grammar school with a salary of £40 a year and a house, and held the post until about 1823, when he retired in consequence of a dispute with the trustees of the school. In 1811 he was presented to the rectory of Meeth, Devon. This living, together with that of Newton Petrock, to which he was appointed in 1823, he held until his death, which took place from a fit of apoplexy on 1 February 1824, in Southampton Street, Strand, London.

Lemprière's dictionary is a remarkable achievement for

an undergraduate of twenty-three. It has remained popular because it is so readable; the factual information it contains is more accurately recorded elsewhere, but his concise accounts (particularly those of mythological characters), with their elegant phrasing and ironic wit, often recall the tone of his older contemporary, Edward Gibbon. The work was widely used by writers in the nineteenth century, although its influence on Keats (who possessed two copies) is now disputed. As in Johnson's dictionary, the personality of the lexicographer speaks through many of his entries, and Lempriére's own opinions are sometimes extravagantly expressed, as when he states that 'Aristophanes is the greatest comic dramatist in world literature; by his side Molière seems dull and Shakespeare clownish'. A novel entitled *Lempriére's Dictionary*, by Lawrence Norfolk, was published in 1991.

RICHARD SMAIL

Sources *GM*, 1st ser., 94/1 (1824), 283 · *GM*, 1st ser., 59 (1789), 834, 1031, 1067 · *GM*, 1st ser., 61 (1791), 740 · F. A. Wright, *Lemprière's classical dictionary* (1984) · Allibone, *Dict.* · Foster, *Alum. Oxon.* · W. Plees, *An account of the island of Jersey* (1817) · N. Carlisle, *A concise description of the endowed grammar schools in England and Wales*, 2 vols. (1818)
Likenesses oils, St John Cam. · oils, Pembroke Cam.

Lemprière, Michel [Michael] (**1606–1671**), magistrate and local politician, was the eldest of the four children of Hugh Lemprière (1562–1624), seigneur of Diélament, and at various times lieutenant-bailiff and judge-delegate of Jersey, and his second wife, Jeanne (*d.* 1647), daughter of Jean Hérault, greffier, and his wife, Allès Le Geyt. Hugh Lemprière's eldest son, Philippe, son of his first wife, Sara (1573–*c.*1599), daughter of Helier Dumaresq and Françoise Hamptonne, inherited the fief of Diélament, and Michel settled, as the younger sons of the family were accustomed to do, at a large house in the vingtaine of Maufant in the parish of St Saviour. He is often referred to as the seigneur of Maufant, though strictly speaking there was no such fief and therefore no such title. The chronicler Jean Chevalier comments on this appellation, saying that it arose from Michel Lemprière's living in the largest house of the vingtaine of that name.

Lemprière was elected a jurat of the royal court of Jersey in January 1637 and at once occupied a leading place in the opposition to the bailiff of the island, Sir Philip De Carteret. The part that he played has led to his being styled the Hampden of Jersey (Payne, 236), though the comparison is not particularly apt. An important factor in the early progress of the parliamentary party in Jersey was the widespread feeling in the island against the dominant De Carteret family, and in particular Sir Philip De Carteret, who had been unwisely allowed by Charles I to combine with the post of bailiff those of lieutenant-governor and farmer of the revenues. The attitude taken up by Lemprière and his friends, among whom was David Bandinel, was condemned by William Prynne, whom De Carteret had befriended while he was in prison on the island from 1637 to 1640. In 1642, with four other jurats and three clergymen, Lemprière prepared a petition to parliament containing twenty-two articles of accusation against Sir Philip de Carteret, who was at the time in London. This produced no immediate effect, but the feeling against De Carteret steadily grew. In February 1643 Lemprière was appointed by the parliamentary committee for the defence of the kingdom as a special commissioner, together with François De Carteret, who refused to act, Benjamin Bisson, Abraham Hérault, and Henry Dumaresq, to suspend De Carteret, and in the meantime to take over the government from his hands. At a meeting of the states summoned in the following month, upon De Carteret's producing the royal commission appointing him bailiff, Lemprière, who alone of his party was present, forthwith displayed his commission from the parliament. De Carteret promptly ordered his officers to turn him out of the assembly as a traitor. But Lemprière with undaunted courage insisted that De Carteret should submit to the parliament's order for his apprehension. The unpopular bailiff had to retire for refuge to Elizabeth Castle, and Lemprière was one of the signatories of the letter initially rejecting De Carteret's appeal for permission to see his family, though at the last moment the request was granted. Sir Philip died on 23 August 1643. Three days later the parliamentary commissioner, Major Lydcot, arrived, and named Lemprière bailiff of the island. The latter at once took the oath of bailiff, and administered that of lieutenant-governor to Lydcot. For the next three months the island was under Lemprière's rule, but during that period he did not enjoy the unanimous support of the population and was unable to restrain even his own officers from going over to the royalist party. No progress was made against the castles, which were still in royalist hands. On the arrival of Sir George De Carteret in the island with a royal commission Lemprière at once fled with the remnant of his followers to London, embarking by stealth on 21 November 1643.

A royal warrant dated 1643 was issued for the arrest of the parliamentary leaders, Lemprière's name standing first on the list. His property was sequestrated, and in 1645 he was tried in his absence, found guilty of high treason and hanged in effigy. During his eight years' exile in London he wrote with his fellow exiles and former jurats Abraham Hérault and Henry Dumaresq the narrative entitled 'Pseudo-mastix: the lyar's whipp' (first printed in 1888) in response to Prynne's defence of Sir Philip De Carteret in *The Lyar Confounded* (1645). After Sir George De Carteret's capitulation to Sir James Haines on 15 December 1651, Lemprière at once returned and resumed his office as parliamentary bailiff. During this second tenure of office he acted with wisdom and patriotism, as well as with conspicuous moderation. He zealously endeavoured to secure for Jersey the goodwill of the parliament, and confirmation of its ancient privileges. In February 1652 he sent a full account of the civil government of Jersey to the speaker of the House of Commons, by his friend Colonel Stockall, strongly deprecating any change in the constitution. In February 1654 Cromwell issued an order to Lemprière, superseding the old method of election of jurats and nominating some Jerseymen, including two Lemprières, to that office. However, some of these were variously unable or unwilling to serve and Lemprière could not hold a full court, for which the presence of seven of the twelve was necessary. He was also given the control of the militia, in which 'malignants' were replaced by his own adherents. In his capacity of commissioner for compounding with delinquents he is generally allowed to have been lenient and as a judge fair and able. Lemprière seems to have stood high in the esteem of the protector, though the latter lent a cold ear to his proposal for excluding the clergy from the island's state assembly.

Lemprière married Sara (1630–1690), daughter of François De Carteret, seigneur of La Hague, jurat and judge-delegate, and his wife, Judith Le Febvre, at St Peter's parish church, Jersey, on 31 March 1657. His two sons and three daughters, the youngest of whom died in early childhood, were baptized as infants at St Helier parish church in the years 1665–1670. The statement (Balleine, 119, 142) that both he and his brother Nicholas had become Anabaptists by 1643 is mistaken in the case of Michel, though Nicholas did apparently become an Anabaptist, whether then or later, for his daughter Sara was baptized at St Helier in July 1678, aged twenty-four.

On the Restoration Lemprière's estates were granted to a royalist, John Nicolls; but this grant was afterwards declared to be void because Lemprière, 'late pretended bailiff of Jersey … though guilty of great offences, is restored to his estates' (*CSP dom.*, *1660*, 442). The exact date of his death is not known, but he was buried in St Helier parish church on 14 February 1671.

THOMAS SECCOMBE, *rev.* HELEN M. E. EVANS

Sources transcript of the registers of baptisms, marriages, and burials in the parishes of Jersey, Jersey Law Society, St Helier, Jersey, Channel Islands Family History Society • *Journal de Jean Chevalier*, ed. J. A. Messervy, 9 parts (1906–14) • 'Notice sur les Lempriére, seigneurs de Diélament', *Annual Bulletin* [Société Jersiaise], 8 (1915–18), 258–90 • G. R. Balleine, *Balleine's history of Jersey*, ed. M. Syvret and J. Stevens (1981) • S. E. Hoskins, *Charles the Second in the Channel Islands*, 2 vols. (1854) • J. A. Messervy, 'Liste des baillis, lieut.-baillis et juges-délégués de l'île de Jersey', *Annual Bulletin* [Société Jersiaise], 4 (1897–1901), 92–116 • J. B. Payne, *Armorial of Jersey*, 2 vols. (1859–65) • *CSP dom.*, *1660*, 442 • M. Lempriére, H. Dumaresq, and A. Hérault, 'Pseudo-mastix: the lyar's whipp', *Annual Bulletin* [Société Jersiaise], 2 (1885–9), 309–55

Lempriére, William (*b.* before **1789**, *d.* **1834**), military physician and writer, was the third son of Thomas Lempriére of Jersey. He entered the Army Medical Service when young and by 1789 was attached to the garrison of Gibraltar. In September 1789 Sidi Mahommed, emperor of Morocco, asked the commandant at Gibraltar to send an English doctor to attend his son, Mawlay Absolom, who was suffering from a cataract. Lempriére accepted the commission, and left Gibraltar on 14 September 1789; on 28 October he reached Taroudannt, where he attended the prince with great success. His only rewards, however, were 'a gold watch, an indifferent horse, and a few hard dollars'. He was then summoned to attend some women of the sultan's harem, and, having reached them on 4 December 1789, was detained in Morocco a long time against his will and was not allowed to leave until 12 February 1790, again with miserable remuneration.

After his return from Morocco Lempriére published an account of his travels in *A Tour from Gibraltar to … Morocco* (1791). The work aroused most interest for its description of the sultan's harem. A number of its minor inaccuracies were addressed in a *Corrective Supplement to Wm. Lempriére's Tour* (1794), by Francisco Sanchez.

Lempriére was next appointed surgeon to the 20th or Jamaica regiment of light dragoons, about 1790. He spent five years in Jamaica, and on his return to England published *Practical Observations on the Diseases of the Army in Jamaica* (1799). Lempriére left the army with the rank of deputy inspector-general of hospitals, and lived for many years in the Isle of Wight; there he published *A report on the medicinal effects of an aluminous chalybeate water, lately discovered at Sandrocks, in the Isle of Wight* (1812), and lectured at the Isle of Wight Philosophical Society. Lempriére died at Bath on 24 July 1834.

G. P. MORIARTY, *rev.* ELIZABETH BAIGENT

Sources J. B. Payne, 'Monograph of the house of Lempriére', *GM*, 2nd ser., 2 (1834), 333 • *Army List* • Allibone, *Dict.*

Lendy, Auguste Frederic (**1826–1889**), army officer and military tutor, was born in France, became a captain of the French army staff, and came to England as military tutor to the Orléans princes. According to Evelyn Wood, his pupil in 1861, Lendy was a handsome man from a royalist family from near Perpignan in the south of France, he had served in Algeria, and he left the army after the establishment of the 1848 republic. In 1853 he published in London *The Principles of War*, an 'elementary treatise' for 'young military students', dedicated to Colonel J. M'Douall, commanding the 2nd Life Guards, 'for his kind patronage'.

About the time of the Crimean War (1853–6) Lendy set up his private Practical Military College of Sunbury (of which he was director) at Sunbury House, Sunbury-on-Thames, Middlesex, for a long time one of the most successful of the much abused army 'crammers', which prepared candidates for Woolwich, Sandhurst, and Staff College entrance. He was considered 'the Doyen of private military teachers' (*Broad Arrow*, 479). Ian Hamilton, Lendy's pupil in 1870, wrote in his memoirs that Lendy was a much better teacher than the masters at Wellington, and 'keen on the success of *all* his pupils'. Hamilton described Lendy as having 'longish hair; long side-whiskers of the sort called Dundreary; loud check trousers and legs held wide apart … eyes that looked at you as a corkscrew looks at a bottle' (Hamilton, 174–5). According to Evelyn Wood, Lendy was very quick-minded and had an exceptional memory for dates. After becoming naturalized in November 1861, Lendy was for twenty years an officer in the 4th Royal Middlesex militia: ensign (1859), lieutenant (November 1862), captain (May 1866), retiring with the honorary rank of major on 1 February 1879. He was married to Sophia, *née* Bulley or Bolley, and they had children (see below).

Lendy's special interest was fortification, especially of the elaborate schools of Vauban and Cormontaigne. He claimed in 1861 that 'three-fourths of the English Staff have read Fortification with me' (*Treatise on Fortification*, vi). He published two textbooks on it: *Elements of Fortification* (1857) was a short 'elementary treatise' intended to give general knowledge to young officers; *Treatise on Fortification, or, Lectures Delivered to Officers Reading for the Staff* (1862) was a substantial work of 538 pages, considered the best textbook on its subject in English. He also published works on military surveying, military history, and other military subjects.

A fellow of the Linnean Society (1861), Lendy was an active horticulturist, a distinguished amateur orchid-grower (whose collection included rare plants featured in the gardening press), and a successful exhibitor at upper Thames valley flower shows. In 1888 he was on the floral committee of the Royal Horticultural Society. He died at his home, Riverside Lodge, Sunbury-on-Thames, on 10 October 1889, in his sixty-fourth year. His funeral was at Brookwood cemetery, near Woking, on 15 October.

A. F. Lendy's son **Charles Frederick Lendy** (1863–1894), army officer, was born at Sunbury-on-Thames, Middlesex, on 7 January 1863, and educated in France and Germany, at Harrow School (1877–8), and at the Royal Military Academy, Woolwich. He was commissioned lieutenant in the Royal Artillery on 16 February 1883, was promoted captain on 15 March 1892, and served in Britain, Gibraltar, and Bermuda.

From May 1890 Lendy was on secondment to the British South Africa Company in Mashonaland and took a vigorous part in the violent and controversial imposition of company rule. He served first at Charter. In March 1892 he commanded a punitive force of police and volunteers, with a 7-pounder gun, sent by L. S. Jameson from Fort Salisbury against a sub-chief, Gomwe (Ngomo), who had allegedly robbed a white trader. When Gomwe refused to surrender Lendy bombarded his kraal, killing him and twenty-two others. Lendy reported: 'a very wholesome lesson has been given to all the Chiefs in the district' (Mason, 158). Rhodes and the settlers approved, but in Britain Lord Knutsford, the colonial secretary, stated that Lendy had acted 'with recklessness and undue harshness' (Blake, 101), and Henry Labouchere and others criticized Lendy and his 'Ngomo atrocities' (Keppel-Jones, 244). Colonial Office officials considered him provocative, 'such a fire-eater' (ibid.), and that the company should get rid of him. Lobengula later said of him, 'he has no holes in his ears, and cannot or will not hear' (Keppel-Jones, 250). In March 1893 Lendy was appointed resident magistrate at Fort Victoria, near the *de facto* boundary between company-occupied Mashonaland and the Ndebele (Matabele) kingdom. In July 1893 he prepared defences at Fort Victoria, and led a small force against Ndebele warriors who were raiding nearby Shona kraals. He claimed the Ndebele fired first, but historians have considered that his force attacked first and that his report was mendacious, containing 'so many lies' (Keppel-Jones, 243). He was again criticized in Britain, by Labouchere's *Truth* among others. For the Matabele campaign (1893–4) Lendy raised but declined command of the Victoria column (commanded instead by Allan Wilson). He served in the campaign, commanding the artillery. In November and December 1893 he was in the force under Major Patrick William Forbes sent from Bulawayo to pursue the fleeing Lobengula. Relations were bad between Forbes and Lendy and his friend Commandant Pieter Johannes Raaff, and after the destruction of the Shangani patrol Lendy and Raaff accused Forbes and gave evidence against him at the court of inquiry at Bulawayo. Lendy died at Bulawayo, Mashonaland, on 14 January 1894, reportedly from inflammation of the bowel 'in consequence of a strain brought about while pursuing his hobby of "Putting the shot"' (Ransford, 263).

C. F. Lendy's younger brother, **Edward Augustus William Lendy** (1868–1893), army officer, was born on 13 February 1868 at Sunbury-on-Thames and educated at Haileybury College (1881–3) and the Royal Military College, Sandhurst (1886–7). He was gazetted second lieutenant, West India regiment, on 21 December 1887, and promoted lieutenant on 31 July 1889. He served in Sierra Leone and in February 1890 was awarded the DSO for his part in the 1889 operations against slave traders at Foulah Town in the Sierra Leone hinterland. In 1892 he was appointed, with the local rank of captain, inspector-general of the paramilitary Sierra Leone frontier police. Contrary to the policy of James Christopher Ernest Parkes, the Creole head of the department of native affairs, Lendy wanted his men to free any domestic slave they believed was going to be sold. After more slaves were freed the Colonial Office decided for Parkes and the 'frontiers' were restricted to seizing only slaves in transit. Lendy resented civilian criticism of his police. He was eager for active service and from 1891 pressed for punitive expeditions. He and Colonel Alfred Burdon Ellis of the 2nd battalion, West India regiment, urged an expedition to expel the Sofas who were raiding the hinterland. Officials opposed it but the Colonial Office ordered the Sofa expedition. The British force, commanded by Ellis, mostly men of the West India regiment, with a frontier police detachment under Lendy—who wanted to return to army service and had arranged with the War Office to defer his transfer—started out in December 1893. In the early morning of 23 December, encamped at Waima in eastern Sierra Leone near the French frontier, they were attacked by a French force which mistook them for Sofas (the 'Waima incident'). Lendy's police were mostly undisciplined recruits, and they ran into huts and started firing indiscriminately. According to contemporary accounts Lendy, trying to restore order, in the confusion was accidentally shot and killed by his own men. He was buried at Waima the next day and his fellow officers erected a memorial cross to him. After his brother's death, Sunbury residents erected a fountain as a memorial to the two brothers.

ROGER T. STEARN

Sources *Broad Arrow* (19 Oct 1889) · *Gardeners' Magazine* (19 Oct 1889) · *Gardeners' Chronicle*, 3rd ser., 6 (1889), 450 · A. F. Lendy, *The principles of war* (1853) · A. F. Lendy, *Elements of fortification* (1857) · A. F. Lendy, *Treatise on fortification, or, Lectures delivered to officers reading for the staff* (1862) · I. Hamilton, *When I was a boy* (1939) · E. Wood, *From midshipman to field marshal*, 2 vols. (1906) · J. Smyth, *Sandhurst: the history of the Royal Military Academy, Woolwich, the Royal Military College, Sandhurst, and the Royal Military Academy, Sandhurst, 1741–1961* (1961) · B. Bond, *The Victorian army and the Staff College, 1854–1914*

(1972) • E. M. Spiers, *The late Victorian army, 1868–1902* (1992) • J. Roach, *Public examinations in England, 1850–1900* (1971) • C. Duffy, *Fire and stone: the science of fortress warfare, 1660–1860* (1996) • *Parl. papers* (1867–8), vol. 60 • Boase, *Mod. Eng. biog.* • *CGPLA Eng. & Wales* (1889) • J. H. Stogdon, ed., *The Harrow School register, 1845–1937*, 1 (1937) • *Army List* (1885–93) • *Hart's Army List* (1885–93) • F. C. Morgan, ed., *List of officers of the royal regiment of artillery from June 1862 to June 1914*, 2 (1914) • A. Keppel-Jones, *Rhodes and Rhodesia: the white conquest of Zimbabwe, 1884–1902* (1983) • S. Glass, *The Matabele war* (1968) • P. Mason, *The birth of a dilemma: the conquest and settlement of Rhodesia* (1958) • R. Blake, *A history of Rhodesia* (1977) • O. Ransford, *The rulers of Rhodesia: from earliest times to the referendum* (1968) • L. H. Gann, *A history of Southern Rhodesia: early days to 1934* (1965) • J. O'Reilly, *Pursuit of the king: an evaluation of the Shangani patrol* (1970) • W. D. Gale, *One man's vision: the story of Rhodesia* (1935) • *Encyclopaedia Rhodesia* (1973) • L. S. Milford, ed., *Haileybury register, 1862–1891* (1891) • *Annual Register* (1893) • M. C. F. Easmon, 'A note on the Waima incident', *Sierra Leone Studies*, new ser., 18 (Jan 1966), 59–61 • C. Fyfe, *A history of Sierra Leone* (1962) • C. Fyfe, *Sierra Leone inheritance* (1964) • C. G. Hancock, 'Notes on the Waima incident', *Sierra Leone Studies*, 19 (Nov 1933), 168–71 • B. Dyde, *The empty sleeve: the story of the West India regiments of the British army* (1997) • b. certs. [Charles Frederick Lendy; Edward Augustus William Lendy]

Wealth at death £1743 13*s*. 10*d*.: resworn probate, June 1890, *CGPLA Eng. & Wales* • £554 19*s*. 10*d*.—Edward Augustus William Lendy: administration, 4 Oct 1894, *CGPLA Eng. & Wales*

Lendy, Charles Frederick (1863–1894). *See under* Lendy, Auguste Frederic (1826–1889).

Lendy, Edward Augustus William (1868–1893). *See under* Lendy, Auguste Frederic (1826–1889).

Le Neve, Cornelius. *See* Neve, Cornelius de (*b*. before 1594, *d*. 1678).

Le Neve [Neve], **Jeffrey** (1579–1653), astrologer and medical practitioner, was born on 15 April 1579, the son of John Le Neve, and became a merchant and alderman of Great Yarmouth. He was also in the king's customs service as a 'quarter waiter', and in November 1626 he was nominated deputy water bailiff of Dover.

In 1620 Le Neve served as bailiff of Great Yarmouth, and in 1626 he excited a great commotion in the corporation by proposing to substitute a mayor for the two bailiffs who had hitherto governed the town. He was requested to resign his alderman's place but obtained a letter from the king ordering his restitution. The corporation refused to comply, and after a long controversy the privy council resolved to 'be no more troubled in the business' (*CSP dom.*). On 4 April 1628 Le Neve, with three others, was commissioned to put in execution the statute of 33 Hen. VIII for encouraging the use of archery, receiving a fee of 1*s*. on every branch cut for a bow. The abuses allegedly committed by Le Neve and his colleagues formed the subject of several petitions to the king and their commission was revoked by proclamation on 23 August 1631. Thinking to avenge himself for the loss of this lucrative position Le Neve unsuccessfully petitioned on 30 March 1630 for licence to export 600 lasts of herrings for twenty-one years at £50 a year.

After these rebuffs Le Neve decided to make a career in medicine, in which he already had some expertise. He crossed to the Netherlands where he matriculated in the medical faculty at Leiden on 15 June 1632 and at Franeker five days later; five days after that he was awarded an MD at Franeker. On his return he established himself in London as a medical practitioner and astrologer.

Contemporaries differed as to Le Neve's proficiency. William Lilly said he had only 'some small smattering in Astrology' (Lilly, 26), whereas John Gadbury, who admired his politics, called him 'one of the best Astrologers that lived in his time' (Gadbury, 179). Le Neve's main work was *Vindicta astrologiae judiciariae, or, The Vindication of Judiciarie Astrologie*, a collection of five hundred horary figures and judgements calculated between 1636 and 1641. Most of the cases concern lost or stolen goods, missing spouses, runaway servants and children, courtship, and strayed animals; the circumstantial details make it a valuable social document. Le Neve had designed it for the press but Lilly, to whom he showed the manuscript, dismissed it as full of errors and it remained unpublished. It survives as MS Ashmole 418 in the Bodleian Library. Dr Thomas Clayton, regius professor of medicine and first master of Pembroke College, Oxford, helped Le Neve draft the prefatory epistle, along with Richard Dukeson, rector of St Clement Danes, Le Neve's parish church. A Latin translation, by Miles Beveridge of Pembroke College, is now MS Ashmole 400. In his epistle Le Neve spoke of his forty-four years' experience in astrology, which he had learned from his uncle Geoffrey le Neve (*c*.1525–1613). This Geoffrey, or Jeffrey, was doubtless the compiler of the series of annual almanacs for Great Yarmouth published from 1604, in which he described himself variously as physician, student in mathematics, and gentleman. After his death the series continued under the same name, probably now compiled by his nephew, the subject of this article, before being taken over by a John Neve, gentleman, for the years 1626–61. Le Neve was married and had children but nothing is known of his wife, who died in his lifetime.

A supporter of the royalists during the civil war, Le Neve lost some of his property, and took refuge with the king at Oxford. Lilly, who described Le Neve as 'a very grave Person, laborious and honest, of tall Stature and comly Feature', noted that he died suddenly, 'almost in the very Street', on 2 September 1653, near Tower Hill (Lilly, 26). Letters of administration were granted to his son Robert, who had assisted his medical practice and later worked with Dr John Southwell before being licensed in 1662 by the College of Physicians of London. Robert also took over the family almanac, which was published under his name from 1662 to 1672. In 1643 Le Neve's daughter had married the astrologer John Mallet (1615–46). Le Neve's astrological papers passed into the hands of Elias Ashmole.

Bernard Capp

Sources W. Lilly, *Mr William Lilly's history of his life and times: from the year 1602, to 1681*, 2nd edn (1715); repr. with introduction by K. M. Briggs (1974) • G. Le Neve, 'Vindicta astrologiae judiciariae', Bodl. Oxf., MS Ashmole 418 • B. S. Capp, *Astrology and the popular press: English almanacs, 1500–1800* (1979) • *The visitation of London, anno Domini 1633, 1634, and 1635, made by Sir Henry St George*, 2, ed. J. J. Howard, Harleian Society, 17 (1883) • *CSP dom.*, 1625–33 • R. W. Innes Smith, *English-speaking students of medicine at the University of Leyden* (1932) • J. Gadbury, *Collectio geniturarum, or, A collection of nativities* (1662) • *The obituary of Richard Smyth … being a catalogue of all such persons as he*

knew in their life, ed. H. Ellis, CS, 44 (1849) · C. J. Palmer, *The perlustration of Great Yarmouth*, 3 vols. (1872–5), vols. 1–2
Archives Bodl. Oxf., MSS Ashmole

Le Neve, John (*b.* 1679, *d.* in or before 1741), antiquary, was born on 27 December 1679 in Great Russell Street, Bloomsbury, London, the only son of John Le Neve (1649–1693), a landed gentleman with property in Essex, Herefordshire, and Northamptonshire, and his second wife, Amy (*d.* 1687), daughter of John Bent of London and his wife, Anne. Brought up after his parents' death by two guardians, his relatives Peter Le Neve and John Boughton, he went to Eton College as a day pupil in 1692 and then in 1694 to Trinity College, Cambridge; he matriculated in 1696 but left that year without a degree. In January 1699 he married his cousin and Boughton's sister Frances, who was the daughter of Thomas Boughton of Kings Cliffe, Northamptonshire, and Elizabeth Le Neve, sister of Le Neve's father. Le Neve and Frances had three sons and five daughters.

Encouraged by Peter Le Neve, whose antiquarian notes were at his disposal, Le Neve's first work, *Memoirs, British and foreign, of the lives and families of the most illustrious persons who died in the years 1711 and 1712*, was published in two volumes in 1712–14. His greatest work, *Fasti ecclesiae Anglicanae*, which appeared in 1716, contained 11,051 entries on England's major ecclesiastical dignitaries down to the year 1715. This was a colossal undertaking that drew both on Le Neve's own research and the collections of others, including that of the antiquarian dean of Peterborough, White Kennett, whose encouragement and support Le Neve was keen to acknowledge. It was Kennett who had dissuaded him from his original intention simply to revise Francis Godwin's *De praesulibus Angliae* (1616) and to expand the scope of the work, but while Browne Willis was to call Kennett 'the real compiler of that useful work' (Hardy, xvi), this would be unfair to Le Neve. Indeed, Le Neve's importance lies in that as well as using the collections of other scholars and clerics—among them Sir Robert Cotton, Matthew Hutton, Roger Dodsworth, Thomas Tanner, and William Fleetwood—he directly consulted primary sources such as the bishops' registers in various dioceses to compile his *Fasti*. Although initially poorly received and with only forty-five original subscribers (twenty-seven of whom were bishops), 750 copies of the work were printed and its value was soon recognized, as shown by the number of copies possessed and annotated by notable men of the eighteenth century, such as Browne Willis (who planned to publish his own additions to the volume), Thomas Tanner, Richard Rawlinson, William Cole, and Richard Gough. Its continued importance has been ensured by the publication of revised editions by Sir Thomas Duffus Hardy in 1854, and by J. M. Horn and others from 1967 onwards.

Le Neve's other major publication was *Monumenta Anglicana, being inscriptions on the monuments of several eminent persons deceased in or since the year 1700, to the end of 1715* (1717), supposedly 'a specimen of a much larger work', which drew on Peter Le Neve's manuscripts and information from the masons who carved the actual monuments recorded. Supplements to this work covering the periods 1650–79 and 1680–99 were published in 1718, and in 1719 a fourth volume appeared for the period 1600–49. Le Neve intended to take the work back to 1400 but, although he carried out research for this, no volume covering this part of the project was printed, and Le Neve instead had to satisfy himself with a fifth volume containing those monuments dating between 1650 and 1718 'collected since the publication of the former volumes'.

Le Neve's last published work was *The lives and characters … of all the protestant bishops of the Church of England since the Reformation* (1720) but, like all his publications, this was not a financial success and in the event only two parts, listing the archbishops of Canterbury and York, were printed. Facing severe difficulties as a result, and despite selling the manor of White Roothing in Essex, which he had inherited from his father, to Robert Sumner in 1717, Le Neve was ordained a priest in the Church of England, probably largely to provide him with a livelihood. Under the patronage of William Fleetwood, bishop of Ely, to whom *Fasti* had been dedicated, he was presented to the living of Thornton-le-Moor, Lincolnshire, in January 1722. Even this did not save him from his creditors and in December that year he was imprisoned in Lincoln gaol for insolvency. The date and place of his death are unknown, but it was not until 23 May 1741 that a new rector was appointed to Thornton-le-Moor, 'vacant by the death of John le Neve, the last incumbent' (*DNB*).

Nicholas Doggett

Sources T. D. Hardy, introduction, *Fasti Angl.* (Hardy), xiii–xx · J. M. Horn, introduction, *Fasti Angl., 1300–1541* · J. L. Chester and J. Foster, eds., *London marriage licences, 1521–1869* (1887) · BL, Harley MSS 3605–3616 · *GM*, 1st ser., 11 (1741), 278 · *DNB*
Archives BL, antiquarian collections, Harley MSS 3605–3625, 5317, 5321, 6098, 6127, 6404–6418 · CUL, biographical collections

Le Neve, Peter (1661–1729), herald and antiquary, was born on 21 January 1661 in London, and baptized at St Michael, Cornhill, on the following day. He was the second of the eight children (and the elder of the two who survived, both sons) of Francis Neve (1620–1681), citizen and upholsterer of London, and his wife, Avis (*d.* 1679), daughter of Peter Wright of London, merchant. An armorial that he compiled as a boy displays an early interest in heraldry perhaps derived from his father's occupation as an upholsterer, work which then involved heraldic funerals. He was educated at Merchant Taylors' School, London (1673–6), and admitted pensioner, aged sixteen, at Trinity College, Cambridge, on 10 April 1677, but did not take a degree. He was admitted to the Middle Temple on 30 May 1679 but was not called to the bar. On 27 January 1683 he married, at St Katharine by the Tower, Prudence (*d.* 1724), daughter of John Hughes, alias Herbert, a merchant in Bristol. By this time he had altered his surname to Le Neve, as had his distant kinsman Sir William Le Neve (1592–1661), Clarenceux king of arms. Le Neve and his wife had twin daughters who died in infancy.

On 15 December 1684 Le Neve was appointed a deputy chamberlain of the exchequer, and accounts for the year ending 29 September 1692 record an annual payment of

£60 for this office. He was appointed Rouge Croix pursuivant by patent dated 17 January 1690. On 13 August 1690 he answered a complaint of his fellow deputy chamberlain John Lowe about his failure to arrive in the office before eleven or twelve in the morning. Le Neve's answer, that his habitation at the College of Arms, near St Paul's, prevented his attendance at nine o'clock, was accepted. In 1692 he entered a pedigree at the heralds' visitation of London. In 1698 his brother, Oliver Le Neve (1662–1711), killed Sir Henry Hobart in a duel and had to leave the country. In his absence Le Neve managed his estate at Great Witchingham, in Norfolk, and arranged for his safe return in 1700.

In 1703 Le Neve purchased the manuscript collections of the deceased Sir Thomas St George, Garter king of arms, and in the following year bought the place of Richmond herald from its holder, Henry Dethick. Having suffered from a fistula in 1694–5 he was again ill between 1703 and 1706. None the less he was appointed Richmond herald by patent dated 5 April 1704, two days before the death of Norroy king of arms, whom he succeeded by patent dated 25 May 1704. In December 1705 deputy chamberlains Le Neve and Lowe delivered an account of the exchequer records in the Treasury, which was subsequently published. The report in a letter of 22 March 1706 from John Millicent to Oliver Le Neve that Le Neve had been turned out of his 'Receivership' seems to be inaccurate, since in 1708 he described himself as senior deputy chamberlain and on 8 March 1712, while still a deputy chamberlain, he petitioned unsuccessfully to succeed Charles Cole as chamberlain. By the date of his will, 5 May 1729, he described himself as 'late one of the Under Chamberlains of the Court of Receipts in the Exchequer'.

In December 1707 Le Neve was one of the original members of an antiquarian society that met at the Young Devil tavern in Fleet Street for less than a year. In 1711 he succeeded to his brother's estate at Great Witchingham, worth some £2000 p.a. He traced the ultimate male heir of the settlor, a London blacksmith named John Neve, and purchased his interest for £10. A large part of his antiquarian collections relates to Norfolk and Suffolk; his most valuable acquisition was the Paston letters, which he bought from William Paston, second earl of Yarmouth. A fellow of the Royal Society from 1712, he was elected president of a refounded antiquarian society, which first met in July 1717 in the Mitre tavern, Fleet Street, and which continued as the Society of Antiquaries; he retained the presidency until 1724. Like a number of other early fellows of the society he was a freemason, and in religion a unitarian, although he was regarded as an atheist by Stephen Martin Leake, his successor as Norroy. He had a reputation for miserliness, yet according to Leake, he would 'give more for a Book than it was worth, grudging no expence of that sort' (Coll. Arms, MS SML 65/18–20). Leake, who knew Le Neve only in his last five years, took a sceptical view of his scholarship:

> he had collected a good Library, and knew a great deal of Antiquity & Heraldry, but with little Judgment Expressed himself very ungracefully in speaking, and worse in Writing, being altogether a dry Antiquary, and though he made large Collections, from his niggardly disposition they were upon such scraps of paper that it will [be] difficult for any person to make a proper use of them. (ibid.)

Politically a whig, Le Neve, with other heralds, opposed the appointment of the tory John Anstis as Garter, even after Anstis obtained a reversionary patent from Queen Anne in 1714. Anstis was in prison as a suspected Jacobite when Garter died in 1715 but his claims to the position were set aside until 1718. During the vacancy Le Neve officiated at the Garter investiture, in Hanover in December 1716, of the grandson and brother of George I, Frederick Lewis, later prince of Wales, and Ernest Augustus, later duke of York. Following the death of his wife, Prudence, who was buried at Great Witchingham on 18 August 1724, Le Neve married on 26 July 1727 at Sparham, Norfolk, Frances (*d.* 1751), the daughter of Robert Beeston, a miller of Witchingham and one of Le Neve's tenants. During his first marriage he kept as his mistress Mrs Carnegie, also known as Durham Dolly. Le Neve died at Great Witchingham on 24 September 1729 and was buried in the parish church there on 1 October. He attempted to bequeath his estate to the three daughters of his brother, Oliver. Before he had purchased the remainder John Norris, the barrister who drew up the settlement, had traced the remainderman and purchased his interest for £30. Norris's descendants successfully secured the estate against Le Neve's nieces following prolonged litigation.

By his will Le Neve left his heraldic and genealogical collections to be disposed of as directed in any signed memorandum found with his papers. An unsigned paper in his hand left them to the College of Arms, but this was not considered to give the college an enforceable title. A sale of Le Neve's books and manuscripts was held over twelve days from 22 February 1731, during which period over 2000 printed books and 1252 manuscript lots were sold; the latter included 584 heraldic manuscripts from Sir Thomas St George's collection, 72 pedigree rolls, 22 portfolios of pedigrees, and 28 boxes of charters. Le Neve's executor Thomas *Martin (1697–1771) married his widow, Frances, in January 1732 and thereby obtained the remainder of Le Neve's manuscript collection, including the celebrated Paston letters.

In his will Le Neve directed that his collections relating to Norfolk and Suffolk should be deposited in Norwich Cathedral or in some other public building in Norwich 'for the use of curious persons'. These collections formed the basis of the five-volume *History of Norfolk* (1739–75), which was largely written by Francis Blomefield. Most of these manuscripts are deposited in the Norfolk and Suffolk county record offices; Le Neve's manuscript three-volume 'Pedigrees of baronets' and a charter collection are in the College of Arms. His manuscript 'Pedigrees of the knights' (BL, Harley MS 5801) was edited by G. W. Marshall and published by the Harleian Society in 1873. Le Neve's phenomenal industry is reflected in the fact that his collections are to be found in many manuscript repositories.

The Great Witchingham parish register contains 'An epitaph on Peter Nevis Norroy who lived and dyed an Infidell'. It reads:

Here underneath this gracious stone
Lies Peter Neve, that faithful one;
His life and death declar'd the man
Deny it neighbours if ye can!

THOMAS WOODCOCK

Sources W. H. Godfrey, A. Wagner, and H. Stanford London, *The College of Arms, Queen Victoria Street* (1963), 114–15 • A. Wagner, *Heralds of England: a history of the office and College of Arms* (1967), 346–7 • M. Noble, *A history of the College of Arms* (1804), 383–5 • F. Rye, ed., *Calendar of correspondence of family of Oliver Le Neve* (1895) • J. Evans, *A history of the Society of Antiquaries* (1956) • A. R. Wagner, *The records and collections of the College of Arms* (1952), 35*n*, 36, 38, 44 • heralds' visitation of London, 1692, Coll. Arms, K9 61–2 • P. J. Willetts, *Catalogue of manuscripts in the Society of Antiquaries of London* (2000) • *DNB* • A. W. Hughes Clarke and R. H. D'Elboux, *The registers of St Katharine by the Tower 1666–1686, marriages part III* (1947), 71 • Venn, *Alum. Cant.* • A. Tanner, 'The best laid plans: Peter Le Neve and his misappropriated manuscripts', *Genealogists' Magazine*, 27 (2002), 208–13

Archives Beds. & Luton ARS, notes relating to the De Grey family, Barons Lucas • BL, collections for a history of Norfolk, Add. MSS 8839–8843 • BL, diary and commonplace book, Add. MS 61903 • BL, Dunwich collections, notes, Add. MSS 34653, 35819–35821 • BL, printed works with his MS notes and additions [copies] • Bodl. Oxf., collections relating to foreign countries • Bodl. Oxf., Norfolk collections • Bodl. Oxf., notes and copies from MSS • Bodl. Oxf., pedigrees • Coll. Arms, baronets' pedigrees and MSS • Coll. Arms, collections of deeds and charters • CUL, commonplace book • Devon RO, genealogical notes • Folger, diary • Herts. ALS, MS of visitations of Hertfordshire with later notes and additions • Lyon Office Library, Edinburgh, abstracts of inquisitions in various hands with his annotations • Norfolk RO, antiquarian and family corresp. • Norfolk RO, collections relating to Newton Flotman • Norfolk RO, Essex pedigrees and index of Norfolk manors • Norfolk RO, notes, collections, and papers • Norfolk RO, notes and papers relating to Norfolk • Norfolk RO, papers on Knyvett and related families • Norfolk RO, pedigree of the Tylney family • PRO, corresp. and papers as deputy chamberlain to exchequer, SP 46/139 • S. Antiquaries, Lond., heraldic and genealogical collections • Suffolk RO, Bury St Edmunds, books of petitions, grants of arms • Suffolk RO, Ipswich, collections for a history of Norfolk and Suffolk with MS additions by T. Martin • Suffolk RO, Ipswich, volume of extracts from cartularies, monastic registers, and other documents relating to medieval Suffolk • U. Hull, Brynmor Jones L., pedigree of the Thoresby family | BL, autograph and antiquarian collections, Harley MSS • Essex RO, Chelmsford, letters to W. Holman • Norfolk RO, corresp. with his brother, Oliver • Wakefield Reference and Information Library, Norfolk collections

Likenesses J. Ogborne, line engraving, pubd 1773 (after G. Vertue, 1731), BM, NPG • oils, Coll. Arms

Wealth at death life interest only in the Great Witchingham estate; left £100 p.a. to his widow, Frances: will, PRO, PROB 11/627–34

Le Neve, Sir William (*bap.* **1592**, *d.* **1661**), herald and genealogist, was baptized William Neve at Aslacton, Norfolk, on 1 July 1592, the eldest son of William Neve (*d.* 1609), eldest son of Laurence Neve of Aslacton and of his wife, Anne, daughter of John Aldham of Shimpling. He assumed the name of Le Neve, and in 1627 he received from Sir William Seagar, Garter king of arms, confirmation of the antiquity of his lineage, and of the right to bear the following arms and crest: 'Arms: Argent on a cross sable five fleurs de lys of the field. Crest out of a crown ducal or a silver lily stalked leaved and seeded gold. No supporters.' The preamble, dated 5 May 1627, reported

> that William Leneve, esq., York herald, is lineally descended from the ancient family of Leneve who bear their arms as above depicted and in the reign of Edward III and of former kings were owners of a seignory then named Lenenbes … in Tivetishall in the county of Norfolk. (Le Neve-Foster, 2)

Le Neve seems to have cultivated an early and continuing interest in heraldry and antiquities. In 1618 his ordering of escutcheons for the funeral of a Robert Wolmer, of Flixton, Suffolk, had trenched on the prerogatives of the office of arms, but the authorities were disposed to indulgence. Later he acquired much of the library of Sir William Dethick, and was in possession of many original medieval rolls of arms, of which in 1638 some were reproduced in facsimile by the painter William Sedgwick. Le Neve had already been appointed Mowbray herald-extraordinary by a patent of 24 June 1624, the ceremony having taken place at Arundel House five days later. On 25 November 1625 he became herald of York; James Balfour, later Lyon king of arms, reported in 1628 that his duties were 'only for matters of ceremony and antiquity, as coronations, funerals, marriages, christenings, tilts, tourneys and triumphs' (Wagner, 232). On 3 January 1634 he was advanced to the office of Norroy king of arms and on 23 April he was knighted at Whitehall. On 22 June 1635 he became Clarenceux king of arms. Such a position carried the right and the responsibility to carry out visitations, and in 1634, the year before his promotion, no fewer than thirteen counties had been visited. But the new Clarenceux was prevented by Sir John Borough, Garter king of arms, from carrying out such duties, until the coming of civil war made them impossible.

In October 1642, after the king set up his headquarters at Oxford, most of the officers of arms joined him, and their number seems to have included Le Neve. He was certainly present at the battle of Edgehill. Here he was sent by the king with a proclamation demanding that the parliamentarian forces lay down their arms, which was snatched from him. Blindfolded and brought before the earl of Essex, he complained bitterly of 'the indignity and injury done to his office, contrary to the law of nations, which standers by laughed at' (Clarendon, *Hist. rebellion*, 2.355–6).

In 1646 Le Neve was replaced as Clarenceux, Arthur Squibb being granted the post by a parliamentary ordinance of 21 October. For the next years nothing is known of his movements, but in 1658 he was adjudged to be insane. Soon after the Restoration, and despite protests directed to Clarendon, Sir Edward Walker, newly appointed Garter king of arms, was authorized on 20 July 1660 to execute Le Neve's office during his illness. Such a solution did not survive the bitter rivalry between Walker and Edward Bysshe. In March 1661 a fresh investigation confirmed his incapacity and soon afterwards Bysshe was appointed Clarenceux. He died, unmarried, at Hoxton on 15 August

1661 and was buried at St Benet Paul's Wharf. Some writings attributed to him may be found among the Ashmole manuscripts in the Bodleian Library, Oxford.

STEPHEN WRIGHT

Sources A. Wagner, *Heralds of England: a history of the office and College of Arms* (1967) • M. Noble, *A history of the College of Arms* (1804) • A. W. Hughes Clarke and A. Campling, eds., *The visitation of Norfolk … 1664, made by Sir Edward Bysshe*, 2 vols., Harleian Society, 85–6 (1933–4) • P. Le Neve-Foster, *The Le Neves of Norfolk: a family history* (privately printed, Sudbury, 1969) • W. Rye, *Norfolk families*, 2 vols. in 5 pts (1911–15) [1911–1913 edn incl. 1915 Index nominum] • G. D. Squibb, *The high court of chivalry* (1959) • Clarendon, *Hist. rebellion* • *Calendar of the Clarendon state papers preserved in the Bodleian Library*, 5: *1660–1726*, ed. F. J. Routledge (1970), 42 • *DNB* • private information (2004) [T. Woodcock] • W. H. Godfrey, A. Wagner, and H. Stanford London, *The College of Arms, Queen Victoria Street* (1963)

Archives BL, sale of his library, Add. Ch 71076 • Coll. Arms, heraldic collections • S. Antiquaries, Lond., papers relating to grants of arms, etc. | Bodl. Oxf., MSS Ashmole • Norfolk RO, copy made by him of the Norfolk visitation made by John Raven

Leney, William Satchwell (1769–1831), engraver, was born in London on 16 January 1769, the son of Alexander and Susannah Leney, and articled to Peltro William Tomkins. He practised in line and stipple, and was employed on John Boydell's great edition of Shakespeare, for which he executed five plates after Fuseli, Downman, W. Miller, J. Graham, and Boydell. He won a gold medal for his *Descent from the Cross* after Rubens. Much of his earlier printed work, however, consisted of portrait illustrations for Bell's *British Theatre*: for example, *Mrs Siddons as Isabella* (1792) and *Mr Wilson as Sir Francis Wronghead (The Provoked Husband)*, both after De Wilde.

About 1806 Leney left England with his wife, Sarah, *née* White, with whom he eventually had nine children. He settled in Greenwich Street, New York, where he engraved some small portraits of George Washington, John Adams, Captain Lawrence of the *Chesapeake*, Robert Fulton, and other notable Americans.

In 1812 Leney entered into partnership with William Rollinson, a banknote engraver, in a portrait engraving firm in New York. He later moved to Longue Point, near Montreal, in 1820, where he engraved the first banknotes for the Bank of Montreal and a series of large views around Quebec and Montreal. On retiring from business he took a farm on the St Lawrence River. He died at Longue Point on 26 November 1831.

F. M. O'DONOGHUE, *rev.* ELEANOR TOLLFREE

Sources M. B. H., 'Leney, William Satchwell', *DAB* • Redgrave, *Artists*, 268 • W. S. Baker, *American engravers and their works* (1875) • W. S. Baker, *Engraved portraits of Washington, commemorative of his death* (1899) • *Engraved Brit. ports.*, 4.644

Leng, John (1665–1727), Latin scholar and bishop of Norwich, was born at Thornton-le-Dale, near Pickering, Yorkshire. He received his early education at St Paul's School, London, and obtained an exhibition at St Catharine's College, Cambridge, where he was admitted a sizar on 26 March 1683, graduating BA (1686), MA (1690), BD (1698), and DD (1716). He was elected a fellow of the college on 13 September 1688, and subsequently became a very efficient tutor. He obtained great distinction as a Latin scholar. In 1695 he published an edition of Aristophanes' *Plutus* and *Clouds* with a Latin translation, and in 1701 he edited the magnificent Cambridge edition of Terence, adding a dissertation on the metres of the author. He also published a revised edition of Sir Roger L'Estrange's translation of Cicero's *De officiis*. In 1701 he preached the sermon at the consecration of the new chapel at St Catharine's College by Simon Patrick, bishop of Ely. In 1708 he was presented by his old pupil, Sir Nicholas Carew, to the rectory of Beddington, Surrey, which he held *in commendam* to his death. In 1717 and 1718 he delivered the Boyle lectures, which were published to acclaim in the following year, his subject being 'The natural obligations to believe the principles of religion and divine revelation'. In addition Leng published fourteen single sermons preached on public occasions, including one before the Society for the Reformation of Manners at Bow church on 29 December 1718. He became chaplain-in-ordinary to George I, and in 1723 was appointed bishop of Norwich. He was consecrated at Lambeth by Archbishop Wake on 3 November of the same year. During his short episcopate Leng gained a good reputation as 'a man of modesty and diligence', than whom 'no one could be further from pride, or show more true humility in his station'; William Whiston calls him 'a good and learned man' (*Life*, 547). Leng was twice married. His first marriage produced no children; his second was to Elizabeth, daughter of a 'Mr Hawes of Sussex', with whom he had two daughters, Elizabeth and Susanna. Three years after being appointed bishop, Leng died on 26 October 1727 in London of smallpox. He was buried in St Margaret's, Westminster, where a mural tablet was erected to his memory in the south aisle of the chancel.

EDMUND VENABLES, *rev.* PHILIP CARTER

Sources Venn, *Alum. Cant.* • F. Blomefield and C. Parkin, *An essay towards a topographical history of the county of Norfolk*, [2nd edn], 11 vols. (1805–10), vol. 3 • C. J. Abbey, *The English church and its bishops, 1700–1800*, 2 vols. (1887) • PRO, PROB 11/618, fols. 423v–424r • *The life of Mr William Whiston written by himself*, 2nd edn (1753)

Archives BL, ordination book, Add. MSS 41500–41501

Leng, Sir John (1828–1906), newspaper proprietor and politician, was born on 10 April 1828 at Hull, the son of Adam Leng of Hull and his wife, Mary, daughter of Christopher Luccock, land surveyor, of Malton, Yorkshire; he was the younger brother of Sir William Christopher *Leng (1825–1902). At Hull grammar school Leng showed a precocious interest in journalism, co-editing a magazine with his fellow pupil Charles Cooper, later editor of *The Scotsman*. Leng's first appointment after his education was as assistant master at a private school, but he soon abandoned this for journalism. Letters sent for publication to the *Hull Advertiser* attracted the attention of its editor, who encouraged Leng to learn shorthand before taking him on as a reporter and sub-editor's assistant in 1847. Leng remained a newspaperman for the rest of his life.

Leng quickly gained the all-round expertise required of a journalist on a provincial newspaper. The sub-editor, 'being lazy and too fond of drink, no sooner found that his assistant was capable of doing his work than he gave him the greater part of it' (*Newspaper Press Directory*, 11). Leng soon replaced him, combining sub-editing with the duties of chief reporter and drama and music critic. By 1851, when twenty-three, he was thus well qualified to take on the editorship of the *Dundee Advertiser*, a bi-weekly, established in 1801, which had seen better times. He transformed it into one of Scotland's leading daily papers.

Leng's business acumen was quickly recognized by the proprietors of the *Advertiser*, who made him a partner in 1852; thereafter the paper was issued under the imprint of John Leng & Co. Having inherited cramped premises in Argyll Close and a single press which could print only 350 copies per hour, Leng introduced significant changes in production. In 1859 the *Advertiser* moved to a new building in Bank Street and three new triple-reel presses were eventually installed, each able to print up to 20,000 copies per hour. Leng pioneered illustration in daily newspapers, utilizing first the relatively primitive pantographic method and later zincography. He was quick to adopt new ways of news gathering, opening in 1870 a London office in direct telegraphic communication with Dundee. Almost half a century later the *Advertiser* continued to run a column proudly headed 'News of the world: flashed from Fleet Street over our private wire'.

From the late 1850s Leng began to expand and diversify his newspaper business. The *People's Journal*, published weekly from 1858, was especially successful, building up a circulation of 250,000 for its ten local editions. It aimed 'not to write *down* but to write *up* to the good sense of the working classes' and, from its earliest editions, gave generous space to the literary efforts of its readers (Donaldson, 11, 30–31). Though the *Daily Advertiser*, a halfpenny paper started in 1859, was soon abandoned, Leng issued the *Dundee Advertiser* as a daily from 1861. An illustrated magazine, the *People's Friend*, incorporating abridged versions of contemporary novels, was published from 1869, allowing more scope for the improving, literary journalism which Leng was anxious to encourage. As early as 1863 he had commissioned the popular Scottish novelist, David Pae, author of *The Factory Girl*, to write exclusively for the *Advertiser*. Leng & Co. published an evening newspaper in Dundee, the *Evening Telegraph*, from 1877. He was chairman, after 1893, of the Donside Paper Mills which supplied newsprint to the presses in Dundee.

Leng's editorial line reflected his staunchly Liberal politics. When one of the Dundee seats fell vacant in 1889 he was invited to stand by the local party and was returned unopposed. He retained his seat against Conservative opposition in 1892, 1895, and 1900, retiring in 1905. An advanced radical and advocate of devolution, or 'home rule all round', Leng was prominent in support of Gladstone's second Home Rule Bill in 1892–3. He also advocated temperance reform, taxation of land value, and registration reform. An energetic pamphleteer, he campaigned vigorously for improvements in the postal service, for employers' liability, and for reductions in the working hours endured by railwaymen; he also took a special interest in the welfare of Crimean War veterans. Leng was knighted at Rosebery's suggestion in 1893, matching the title conferred six years earlier on his brother, who owned a Conservative newspaper in Sheffield. In the same year he became deputy lieutenant for Dundee. He was honoured again in 1902, a year after his retirement as editor of the *Advertiser*, when he was made an honorary burgess. St Andrews conferred an honorary doctorate two years later. His recreations included yachting.

Leng's prodigious energy found further outlet in extensive travel. Visits to the United States in 1876, India and Ceylon in 1896, the eastern Mediterranean in 1897, Egypt and Sicily in 1902, and the United States and Canada in 1905 were each recorded in published volumes. To the end of his life he sustained a youthful enthusiasm for new ideas and experiences; 'his belief in progress remained firm to the last' (*Dundee Advertiser*, 13 Dec 1906). In 1906 at the Newspaper Society Leng opposed the committee of imperial defence's proposal that, in emergency or war, only official news should be published, warning it would mean 'a state press directed and controlled by not improbably incompetent and injudicious underlings of government departments … altogether alien to my ideas of what an enlightened and influential press should be' (Morris, 151). However, the society agreed to co-operate, so Leng protested in 'An open letter to the press of the United Kingdom' in his *Dundee Advertiser* (20 July 1906).

Leng married twice: first, in 1851, to Emily, elder daughter of Alderman Cook of Beverley, Yorkshire, who died in 1894, leaving two sons and four daughters; and second, in 1897, to Mary, daughter of William Low of Kirriemuir, who survived him. Leng's health had been failing for some time, and he died at Delmonte, near Monterey, California, during a visit on 12 December 1906. His body was cremated and the ashes brought back and interred at Vicarsford cemetery, near Newport, Fife. DILWYN PORTER

Sources *DNB* • *Dundee Advertiser* (12 Dec 1906) • *Dundee Advertiser* (13 Dec 1906) • *The newspaper press directory* (1907), 11 • *Advertising* (July 1901), 532–8 • W. Donaldson, *Popular literature in Victorian Scotland* (1986) • *The Newspaper Owner* (15 Dec 1906) • *WWW, 1897–1915* • *WWBMP*, vol. 2 • A. J. A. Morris, *The scaremongers: the advocacy of war and rearmament, 1896–1914* (1984)

Archives Dundee Central Library, papers | NL Scot., corresp. mainly with Lord Rosebery

Likenesses J. Archer, portrait, 1889 • B. Stone, photographs, 1898–9, NPG • W. Q. Orchardson, oils, exh. RA 1902, Dundee City Art Gallery

Wealth at death £76,624 3*s*. 1*d*.: confirmation, 9 Feb 1907, *CCI*

Leng, Sir William Christopher (1825–1902), journalist and newspaper proprietor, was born at Hull on 25 January 1825, the elder son of Adam Leng, a Hull businessman, and his wife, Mary, daughter of Christopher Luccock, architect, of Malton. Sir John *Leng (1828–1906) was a younger brother. After education at a private school, where he showed a taste for literature, Leng was apprenticed in 1839 to a wholesale chemist in Hull, for whom he later worked as a commercial traveller before setting up his own business in 1847.

Meanwhile in anonymous contributions to the *Hull Free Press*, including sketches of notable citizens (published as a book in 1852), Leng campaigned vigorously for practical measures of reform such as slum clearance and improved safety on cargo vessels. He is credited with first suggesting to Samuel Plimsoll (1824–1898) the crusade which led to the introduction of the Plimsoll line, as a safeguard against overloading, following the Merchant Shipping Act of 1876. Alienated by the self-interested opposition of prominent Hull Liberals to slum clearance, Leng abandoned his original party affiliation and declared himself a Conservative, a relatively painless transition in the era of Disraelian 'tory democracy'. Brought up as a Wesleyan Methodist, he joined the evangelical wing of the Church of England.

In spite of Leng's and his brother John's divergent political opinions, Leng was a regular contributor of articles on municipal and national affairs to the *Dundee Advertiser*, which his brother edited from 1851. In 1859 he gave up his chemist's business in Hull and lived in Dundee until 1864, writing for the *Advertiser*. During the American Civil War he was prominent among Scottish journalists in supporting the cause of the north.

In 1864 Leng joined Frederick Clifford (1828–1904) in the purchase of the *Sheffield Daily Telegraph*. He became its managing editor, and lived in Sheffield for the rest of his life. As publishers, Leng & Co. invested boldly, purchasing extensive new premises at Aldine Court in 1872 and installing linotype machinery, at that time something of a novelty. The paper, which was almost moribund when Leng took over, quickly became a great Conservative power in the north of England. Its influence was sufficient to thwart Joseph Chamberlain's parliamentary ambitions when he stood at Sheffield in 1874. As J. L. Garvin later noted, the *Telegraph* at that time and under Leng's direction had become 'the cleverest Conservative organ in the country' (Koss, 1.219).

Leng was fearless in advocacy of what he deemed the public interest. In 1867, at some personal risk, he denounced the intimidation of non-union labour by Sheffield trade unionists under the leadership of William Broadhead (1815–1879), inducing the government to appoint a royal commission of inquiry which fully substantiated his allegations. He was the original of Mr Holdfast in Charles Reade's *Put Yourself in his Place* (1870), a novel based on Broadhead's career. In recognition of his services Leng was presented in April 1868 with his portrait by H. F. Crighton and a purse of 600 guineas, subscribed by men of all political opinions.

In the last quarter of the nineteenth century Leng's Sheffield-based newspaper publishing business continued to expand; a *Weekly Telegraph*, a *Sunday Telegraph*, and, most important, the *Evening Telegraph and Star* were added to his stable. He remained active as a journalist, reporting descriptively for the *Daily Telegraph* on his travels in Europe, and was active, too, in local politics, where he served as vice-chairman and chairman of the Sheffield Conservative and Constitutional Association. Leng was rewarded with a jubilee knighthood, awarded on the recommendation of Lord Salisbury in 1887. Salisbury had a high regard for the *Sheffield Daily Telegraph*, that 'clever organ of Jingoism' (Koss, 1.295).

In 1860 Leng married Anne (1833/4–1893), daughter of David Stark of Ruthven, Forfarshire, and widow of Harry Cook of Sandhurst, Australia; her sister was first wife of his brother John. His two sons, C. D. Leng and W. St Quentin Leng, became partners in the *Sheffield Telegraph*. Leng died on 20 February 1902 at his home, Oaklands, Collegiate Crescent, Sheffield, and was buried in Ecclesall churchyard. A. H. Millar, *rev.* Dilwyn Porter

Sources K. G. March, 'The life and career of Sir William Leng: a study of the ideas and influence of a prominent Victorian journalist', MA diss., Sheffield University, 1966 • *In memoriam, Sir William Leng, kt* (1902) • *Sheffield Daily Telegraph* (20 Feb 1902) • *Dundee Advertiser* (20 Feb 1902) • W. Shepherdson, *Reminiscences in the career of a newspaper: starting a 'daily' in the provinces* (1876) • S. E. Koss, *The rise and fall of the political press in Britain*, 1 (1981)

Likenesses H. F. Crighton, oils, 1868; Sheffield town hall, 1912 • Spy [L. Ward], caricature, chromolithograph, repro. in *VF* (8 March 1890)

Wealth at death £163,897 5*s.* 6*d.* (in UK): probate, 17 April 1902, *CGPLA Eng. & Wales*

Lenihan, Maurice (1811–1895), journalist and local historian, was born on 8 February 1811 at Waterford, son of James Lenihan, a woollens merchant. He was one of a family of fifteen. His mother came from Carrick-on-Suir. He first attended a dame-school and went on to St John's College, Waterford, but from twelve to twenty he was at Carlow College, where he was a pupil of Dr Daniel William Cahill, and was a skilful violin player. On the completion of his education he began his career as a journalist, with the *Tipperary Free Press* in Clonmel, of which his cousin, John Hackett, was proprietor. He next worked for the *Waterford Chronicle*, and here his articles in favour of the agitation against tithes made his reputation. He was a close friend of Daniel O'Connell, and between 1832 and 1844 helped to organize his larger meetings, and reported the speeches of O'Connell and Richard Lalor Sheil. In 1841, when the *Limerick Reporter* was established, he was appointed editor, but early in 1843 left it to join the staff of the *Cork Examiner*, the proprietor of which was John Francis Maguire. During his short residence in Cork Lenihan made the acquaintance of Father Theobald Mathew, who induced him to take the temperance pledge and became his lifelong friend. Before the end of the year he was asked by O'Connell and Bishop Power of Killaloe to edit a paper in Nenagh, co. Tipperary, supporting the repeal movement; and O'Connell, in a meeting at Limerick, announced the establishment of the *Tipperary Vindicator* under Lenihan's editorship. In this paper Lenihan exposed a police plot known as the Shinrone conspiracy, and obtained the dismissal of the detective, Parker, who was its leader, and of eleven policemen who had assisted him. In 1849 he bought up the *Limerick Reporter* and incorporated it with the *Tipperary Vindicator*. Lenihan's newspaper followed a line of moderate nationalism. Although he was a friend of Thomas Francis Meagher, and visited him in prison, Lenihan correctly forecast that Young Ireland would end in 'smoke or worse'.

Lenihan became interested in the history of Limerick, and from time to time wrote articles for his paper dealing with the sieges. He knew both George Petrie and Eugene

O'Curry, and with their encouragement, and at the suggestion of Archbishop Leahy of Cashel, in 1866 he published *Limerick: its History and Antiquities*. This history superseded the earlier works by Ferrar and Fitzgerald and John James Macgregor. Two of his primary sources, the papers of the Revd James White and the Limerick manuscripts of John D'Alton, he had in his own possession; and he was one of the first who had access to the manuscript works of Dr Thomas Arthur, the friend of Sir James Ware. He also consulted the chartulary of Edmund Sexton, and obtained valuable matter from the Carew MSS through Lord Gort, and the papers in the possession of the Hon. John Vereker. A list of nearly 150 sources for the work is given in the preface. Good maps, copious appendices, and an index add to its value.

Lenihan, besides contributing to periodicals, had collected materials for histories of Tipperary and Clare, but they were never utilised. Between 1866 and 1868 he published a series of articles in his paper, 'Reminiscences of a journalist'. He took an active part in municipal affairs, was mayor of Limerick in 1884, and was named a justice of the peace by his friend Lord O'Hagan. He was a member of the Society for the Cultivation of the Irish Language, and in 1863 was elected a member of the Royal Irish Academy. He died on 25 December 1895 at 17 Catherine Street, Limerick. His son, James Lenihan, succeeded him as editor and proprietor of his paper.

G. Le G. Norgate, *rev.* Marie-Louise Legg

Sources *Limerick and Tipperary Vindicator* (31 Dec 1895) • *The Times* (26 Dec 1895)
Archives NL Ire.

Lennard, Francis, fourteenth Baron Dacre (1619–1662), politician, was born at Chevening, Kent, on 11 May 1619 and baptized at Paulerspury in Northamptonshire on 20 January 1620, the eldest son of Richard, thirteenth Baron Dacre (1596–1630), and his first wife, Elizabeth, daughter of Sir Arthur Throckmorton. Dacre succeeded his father at the age of only eleven, and was brought up by Sir Francis Barnham. After a brief spell at Merton College, Oxford, where he matriculated in 1634, Dacre travelled to the continent in 1635, and may have remained there for the rest of the decade. He returned to England before the summoning of the Long Parliament, however, during the early stages of which he sided with the small group of peers who were most active in supporting the reforming measures adopted by the House of Commons. He appears to have been a witness against Thomas Wentworth, earl of Strafford, and in the early weeks of 1642 joined those future parliamentarian peers who protested against the Lords' decision to oppose the Commons' resolution to put the kingdom in a 'posture of defence'. These peers also voted for root and branch reform of the church, and sought to settle the militia under parliament's control. As a result of his stance Dacre was nominated lord lieutenant of Herefordshire in 1642, but although he was one of the small band of peers who remained in London rather than join the king at Oxford, his zeal for the parliamentarian cause may have subsided thereafter. The frequent calls for him to attend the Lords were usually met with excuses that he could not travel to Westminster because of illness and the poor quality of Sussex roads. He clearly spent much of his time at his seat, Herstmonceux Castle, Sussex, where he was able to indulge his passion for the relatively novel pastime of yachting.

During the second half of the 1640s, however, Dacre's parliamentary activity increased, as he worked with the political presbyterians at Westminster, one of the most important of whom was his uncle, Sir Philip Stapilton. During much of 1647 the presbyterians were particularly powerful on the committee for Irish affairs at Derby House, and Dacre was one of six presbyterian peers appointed to that body. His most important work was as one of the commissioners sent to negotiate with the army at Saffron Walden in April 1647 with a view to arranging both the disbandment of troops and the transfer of regiments to Ireland. This presbyterian policy caused much resentment among the army, and marked Dacre out as a leading conservative peer. Similarly, he was subsequently among the ten peers who voted against the bill for the establishment of the high court of justice to try Charles I in 1649. As a result he was regarded as a malignant by many radical members of the Rump, and he was soon removed from local office for refusing to take the engagement.

Dacre may have travelled to the continent again in 1650, although he returned to England in time to secure election as one of the knights of the shire for Sussex in Cromwell's parliament of 1654. He was one of only two peers to sit in the Commons after having previously sat in the House of Lords, although he took little part in the proceedings of the parliament, and he was probably no supporter of the protectorate regime. Cromwell's allies were evidently relieved when Dacre decided to travel abroad once again, in late 1655, since they feared that he might be appointed *custos rotulorum* of Sussex. Thereafter Dacre played no further part in parliament during the 1650s and resurfaced only after the Restoration, when he was one of the most prominent grandees from Sussex who welcomed the return of Charles II.

For much of Dacre's life he was embroiled in a series of protracted legal battles over various parts of his estate, particularly his attempt to secure control of ancestral lands in the north of England. This battle, which was not settled until the 1650s, was made more complex by the rival claim of the Howard family, earls of Arundel, as well as by the occupation of the estates by the Scottish army in the 1640s. The years of litigation were eventually brought to an end by means of arbitration, and the agreement, while dividing the lands, was probably to the advantage of Dacre. The latter's financial position had been hampered by the years as a royal ward, during which time his guardian had been obliged to pay £5000 to the crown each year, as well as 4000 marks for composition of his marriage. The effect of this and other disputes on Dacre was dramatic, and he reputedly died with debts of £18,000 and an estate worth only £8500. Creditors claimed that his estate brought him £6000 per annum, although this appears unlikely.

Dacre married, in 1641, Elizabeth (1625–1686), daughter of Paul, first Viscount Bayning, and Anne, dowager Viscountess Dorchester. The marriage resulted in three sons and three daughters, but appears to have been far from harmonious. Although promised a portion of £20,000, Dacre's executors would later claim that he received less than half of this amount. When he drew up his will in 1655 he made no mention of his wife, and when Dacre left England in the same year William Goffe wrote that he did so 'on some discontent betwixt him and his lady' (Thurloe, *State papers*, 4.190). Their dispute outlived Dacre by means of a legal battle between Dacre's widow, their children, and his executors. Dacre himself died at his lodgings in St Martin's Lane, Westminster, on 12 May 1662, and he was buried at Chevening in Kent. His son was created earl of Sussex and married the natural daughter of Charles II, whom he himself had served as a gentleman of the bedchamber. J. T. PEACEY

Sources HoP, *Commons, 1690–1715* [draft] · GEC, *Peerage* · T. Barrett-Lennard, *An account of the families of Lennard and Barrett* (1908) · Essex RO, Chelmsford, Barrett-Lennard MSS, D/DL · will, PRO, PROB 11/308, fol. 59 · CKS, Stanhope papers, U 1590 · *Sixth report*, HMC, 5 (1877–8) · *CSP dom.*, *1638–50* · A. Fletcher, *A county community in peace and war: Sussex, 1600–1660* (1975) · *JHL*, 4–10 (1628–48) · A. Woolrych, *Soldiers and statesmen: the general council of the army and its debates, 1647–1648* (1987) · Thurloe, *State papers*
Archives Essex RO, Chelmsford, estate and other papers | CKS, Stanhope MSS, U 1590
Likenesses P. Lely, double portrait, oils, *c.*1650 (with his wife), Eydon Hall, Northamptonshire · P. Lely, oils, Horsford Manor; copy, AM Oxf.
Wealth at death £7933—personal estate: inventory, PRO, PROB 4/9634; will, PRO, PROB 11/308, fol. 59

Lennard, Sampson (*d.* **1633**), antiquary, was described in the *Dictionary of National Biography* as the son of William Lennard of Chevening, Kent, and his wife, Anne, daughter of John Perkins of Richmond, Surrey, but he was probably their grandson, his parents being Sampson Lennard (*b.* *c.*1533) and his wife, Eleanor Cresswell (*b.* *c.*1535) of Odiham, Hampshire. Nothing is known of Lennard's education, but as a young man he served with the army of the Netherlands in the 1580s. By 1605 he was married (his wife's name is not known) and living in Westminster, attempting to attract patronage and to earn a living through translation. In 1606 he dedicated a translation from the Italian of Buoni's *Problems of Beauty* to his kinsman Sampson Lennard, the husband of Margaret Fiennes, Baroness Dacre, and a translation from the French of Charron's *Of Wisdom Three Bookes* to Henry, prince of Wales. *Of Wisdom* ran to four editions in his lifetime. In 1609 he published a moderately protestant composition of his own, entitled *An exhortatory instruction to a speedy resolution of repentance and contempt of the vanities of this transitory life*. Such moderation may have failed to attract sufficient patronage, for in 1612 he dedicated a translation of Du Plessis-Mornay's *History of the Papacie* to the prince of Wales, expressing the hope that he might 'live to march over the Alpes, and to trayle a pike before the walls of Rome' behind the prince's standard.

It is unknown through whose auspices Lennard obtained the position of Rose Rouge pursuivant in the College of Arms in 1613. In 1616 he was promoted Bluemantle. He is credited with the compilation of the oldest extant catalogue of the college's library. In 1619 he undertook the visitation of Warwickshire and Leicestershire with Augustine Vincent and of Cornwall, Devon, Wiltshire, Dorset, and Somerset with Henry St George between 1620 and 1623. In the factional dispute within the College of Arms he supported Camden against Brooke and contributed triumphant congratulatory verses to Vincent's *Discouverie of Errours* (1622). In 1624 he dedicated a translation of Perrin's *Luther's Forerunners* to William, earl of Pembroke, invoking the memory of his service with Sir Philip Sidney at Zutphen.

It is not known whether Lennard succeeded in attracting further patronage, but his installation of his wife and daughters at Derby House against the rules of the college suggests his means were limited. He died in August 1633 and was buried on 17 August at St Benet Paul's Wharf, Upper Thames Street, London. He left three daughters, his wife having predeceased him in 1621.

JAN BROADWAY

Sources W. H. Godfrey, A. Wagner, and H. Stanford London, *The College of Arms, Queen Victoria Street* (1963), 196–7 · A. Wagner, *Heralds of England: a history of the office and College of Arms* (1967), 227–8, 231 · J. Perrin, *Luther's forerunners*, trans. S. Lennard (1624), dedication · P. Du Plessis-Mornay, *The history of iniquitie: that is to say, the history of the Papacie*, trans. S. Lennard (1612), dedication · will, PRO, PROB 11/166, sig. 73 · P. Charron, *Of wisdome three bookes*, trans. S. Lennard (1606), dedication · W. A. Littledale, ed., *The registers of St Bene't and St Peter, Paul's Wharf, London*, 4 vols., Harleian Society, register section, 38–41 (1909–12)
Archives BL, 1619 visitation of Leicestershire, Stowe 623 [copy] · BL, 1620 visitation of Devon and Cornwall, Add. MS 34101 [copy] · BL, heraldic collections, Harley MSS 1178, 1452 · Coll. Arms, library catalogue
Likenesses R. Vaughan, line engraving, pubd 1658, BM
Wealth at death left silver, furniture, clothes, books: will, PRO, PROB 11/166, sig. 73

Lennie, William (**1779–1852**), grammarian and educational benefactor, established himself in 1802 as a teacher of English at Edinburgh, where he remained until his death. He became known for his *Principles of English Grammar* (1816), to which he added a key (1816). The work proved very popular and was steadily revised and reprinted through the nineteenth century; a ninety-third edition appeared in 1894. Despite its manifest popularity with generations of schoolmasters it exhibits the characteristic weaknesses of traditional school grammars—subservience to Latin and insulation from contemporary language scholarship.

Lennie died at 23 St Andrew's Square, Edinburgh, on 20 July 1852. In his will he made a number of notable educational bequests. To a school at Craigend, Perthshire, he left an endowment of £10 per annum. To the town council of Edinburgh he bequeathed the lands of Auchenreoch, Dumfriesshire, for founding in Edinburgh University four bursaries of £12 each, to be called the Lennie bursaries. They were to be given for literary education only, and the bursars were enjoined to repay the amounts received by them as soon as they were able; those who did so were to have the nomination of their successors. The residue of the rents was to be equally divided between Trinity Hospital and James Gillespie's Hospital, Edinburgh, and after the lapse of certain annuities a further sum of £200 p.a. was to be added to the fund.

GORDON GOODWIN, *rev.* JOHN D. HAIGH

Sources *GM*, 2nd ser., 38 (1852), 319 • Boase, *Mod. Eng. biog.*, 2.388 • *BL cat.*, 189.187–8

Lennon, John (1768–1846), merchant navy officer, was born on 12 November 1768 at Downpatrick, co. Down, Ireland. Nothing is known of his family, education, or early life, though he may have served as a midshipman in the navy during the Anglo-American War. In December 1796, while commanding the schooner *Favorite* of Martinique, carrying a letter of marque, he was severely wounded, and his ship was taken, after a fierce engagement, by a heavily armed French privateer. Lennon was held as a French prisoner and later, for four months at Havana, as a prisoner of the Spanish. On 28 August 1798, while commanding the *General Keppel*, also of Martinique, he was capsized in a squall on passage from Philadelphia. After suffering great hardships Lennon and some of his crew were rescued by a passing schooner.

Lennon performed various daring feats in the West Indies in 1806–9; but his most remarkable exploits were in the *Hibernia*, a Cowes-built barque which he commissioned, pierced for twenty guns—eighteen carronades and two long 9-pounders—though when fully laden with cargo she carried more guns than hands to work them. She was launched on 10 February 1810 and sailed on her first voyage, for Martinique, on 14 March. Lennon traded in her for some years from the West Indian island of St Thomas. In 1812, on the outbreak of war with the United States, orders were issued that no vessels should leave the island without convoy, because of American privateers. In September 1812 the *Hibernia* and three other merchant ships, whose aggregate cargoes were valued at half a million sterling, had long been waiting. Governor Maclean agreed to their sailing without convoy, on condition that Lennon hoisted his pennant as commodore. Sailing on 13 September, Lennon was soon chased by the *Rossie*, an American privateer of superior force under Commodore Barney. In a running fight on 19 and 20 September Lennon repulsed the American but was harassed continually by him until he brought his vessels safe into the English Channel on 18 October 1812.

Fifteen months later, while returning to St Thomas, Lennon was attacked, on 11 January 1814, off the island of Saba, by the schooner *Comet* of Baltimore, an American privateer of sixteen guns and 136 men under Captain Boyl. In 1813 Lennon had landed all his guns except for four carronades and the two long guns, but he beat off the *Comet* after a nine-hour fight, in which twelve out of his crew of twenty-two were killed or wounded. Arriving at St Thomas on 12 January 1814, Lennon received the heartfelt congratulations of the inhabitants. The masters of merchant ships there subscribed 50 guineas for a commemorative sword, a subscription of £550 was raised for the crew, and an inscribed silver salver, costing £105, was bought for Lennon. Two lawsuits followed with the underwriters of the *Hibernia's* cargo (insured for £40,000), who refused to pay any part of the repair costs. As a result Lennon and his owners were liable for £8000 damages, not half of which would have been incurred if Lennon had surrendered.

Lennon was married: his wife's name was Mary and they had two daughters. He died in retirement at his home, 6 Windsor Terrace, Plymouth, on 27 August 1846. A shot in the back, received in 1796 and still lodged in his diaphragm, had moved to his lungs, causing a bronchial infection which killed him.

Lennon's career illustrates the successes and hazards of that mixture of legitimate trade and commerce raiding often practised in the West Indies. Between 1812 and 1814 the threat to British commerce from United States privateers proved increasingly serious, and the rewards made to captains who evaded or outfought them reflected the relief felt by the maritime community. In 1841, when Lennon's reminiscences were published (as *Chivalry of the Merchant Marine* by D. Burn), attempts were made to secure a knighthood for his services. These were unsuccessful, but formed part of a campaign to promote and encourage the merchant navy.

H. M. CHICHESTER, *rev.* P. K. CRIMMIN

Sources D. Burn, *Chivalry of the merchant marine* (1841) • d. cert. • will, PRO, PROB 11/1988 • E. P. Brenton, *The naval history of Great Britain, from the year 1783 to 1822*, 5 vols. (1823–5) • *Naval and Military Gazettes* (24 July 1841) • *Naval and Military Gazettes* (7 Aug 1841) • *Naval and Military Gazettes* (21 Aug 1841) • *Naval and Military Gazettes* (18 Sept 1841)

Wealth at death left £2000 to wife; £10 to a servant; remainder of real and personal estate to be sold, invested in funds from which widow and two daughters to receive annual income: will, PRO, PROB 11/1988

Lennon, John Ono (1940–1980), musician, composer, and political activist, was born John Winston Lennon at Oxford Street Maternity Hospital, Liverpool, on 9 October 1940, the only child of Julia Stanley (1914–1958), a cinema usherette, and Alfred (Freddy) Lennon (1912–1976), a merchant seaman. Three half-sisters were born to his mother subsequently, including Julia, who later wrote a book about her relationship with John. Alfred Lennon's family came from a working-class Irish background while Julia Stanley's was more lower-middle class; both, however, were described by their acquaintances as 'fun-loving' (Julia, indeed, seems to have been regarded by her four sisters as somewhat irresponsible), and there was musical talent on both sides of John's family. Alfred was often away at sea, and the marriage was rocky; he left for good in 1942. Julia's precarious circumstances and dubious liaisons led to a family decision that John would be better brought up by her sister Mary (Aunt Mimi to John) in the respectable suburb of Woolton, where Mary's husband George Smith ran a dairying business. John was the son that Mimi never had, and she brought him up with passionate affection but also with strictness and an eye to middle-class standards. The ambivalent attitudes to social class apparent in the adult Lennon—millionaire and

John Ono Lennon (1940–1980), by Annie Leibovitz, 1970

'working-class hero', to quote the title of one of his own songs—may have had their seeds in tensions generated by the relationship between his natural and adoptive families.

From child to Beatle John's feelings for his mother remained warm, and he saw a lot of her: she was entertaining and became a rock 'n' roll fan; she taught him his first guitar chords. But, having lost his father, and then the man who became a substitute—George Smith died in 1955—John suffered an even more traumatic blow when Julia was killed in a road accident in 1958, right outside Mimi's home. Again, it is difficult not to link to these childhood experiences Lennon's later resentments and neuroses concerning absent mothers and fathers, not to mention a pervasive sense of alienation and pain in much of Lennon's music, and a defensive abrasiveness in his behaviour.

As a young child Lennon was bright and bookish, inquisitive about religion (he later described seeing visions), and fond of listening to the radio (*The Goon Show* was a particular favourite). But he found little to interest him at Dovedale primary school, with the partial exception of art lessons, and, on moving in 1952 to Quarry Bank high school, this lack of application—'he was a bohemian, even as a boy', said Mimi later (Coleman, 129)—was coupled with a determined campaign of rebellion against what he took to be petty discipline and a tedious curriculum. His school performance sank steadily, and only his interest in art survived: his 'Daily howl' exercise book, containing satirical verses and cruel caricatures of teachers and others, became notorious, and foreshadowed the style and content of his later published works of humorous poetry and prose, *In his Own Write* (1964) and *Spaniard in the Works* (1965). Disastrous results in the general certificate of education examinations meant that only one educational route remained open: art college.

The British art schools at this time offered opportunities for a new sort of rebel: the grammar school drop-out. At Liverpool College of Art (1957–60) Lennon's progress continued talented but wayward. He went out of his way to antagonize staff. He dressed and performed the part of 'arty teddy boy', spent more time drinking and womanizing than in class, and positioned himself as an aggressive, charismatic loner. And then there was music. While still at Quarry Bank, Lennon had been bowled over by rock 'n' roll and, never lacking in ambition—'When I was about twelve … I used to think I must be a genius but nobody's noticed' (Wenner, 64)—had decided he wanted to be 'bigger than Elvis' (ibid., 70). He had formed a skiffle group—the Quarry Men—and by 1957 this was playing at local gigs. In July of that year, in a celebrated encounter, Paul McCartney heard and was impressed by the band, and by Lennon, at a Woolton fête. During Lennon's time as an art student, the group went through several names: Johnny and the Moondogs, the Silver Beetles, and finally the Beatles. There were also several changes of personnel: McCartney had joined in 1957, lead guitarist George Harrison in early 1958, and Lennon's fellow art student and best friend Stuart Sutcliffe was also in the group at this stage. After several attempts to find the right drummer, Pete Best joined in 1960. The group's local reputation grew as Lennon pushed its repertoire away from skiffle and towards rock 'n' roll, and he and McCartney began writing songs together. At last John Lennon had found a focus for his talents.

After a short Scottish tour in 1960, the Beatles were booked into a residency—the first of several—at a Reeperbahn club in Hamburg. Here Lennon worked on his macho, all-action performance style, the band learned to play lengthy sets and entertain often aggressive audiences, and they were introduced both to pep pills (the first of many stimulants) and to the local pseudo-existentialist beatnik scene by the artists Klaus Voormann and Astrid Kirchherr; it was the latter who designed the striking 'mop-top' hair-style that became the group's visual trademark in their early years. Armed with a new image and a new professionalism, the Beatles took Merseyside, especially the Cavern Club, by storm during 1961; *Mersey Beat*, a new Liverpool music paper, featured Lennon's writings; and a local record shop owner, Brian Epstein, became their manager. After several attempts to secure a record contract, Epstein succeeded with the EMI label Parlophone, and the Beatles' first national release, a Lennon–McCartney original called 'Love me do', entered the singles chart in October 1962. By this time Ringo Starr had replaced Pete Best as drummer, and Stuart Sutcliffe had died, shockingly, of a brain haemorrhage in Hamburg in April—another emotional trauma for Lennon.

Of the four Beatles singles released in Britain in 1963, three reached number one, to be followed by two more in 1964. In April 1964, immediately after their first American tour, the Beatles had five singles occupying the top five positions in the US *Billboard* singles chart. Two albums in each year—*Please Please Me* and *With the Beatles* followed by *A Hard Day's Night* and *Beatles for Sale*—all reached number one in Britain, and featured a mixture of cover versions and Lennon–McCartney original compositions. From January 1963 appearances on television (including the *Ed Sullivan Show* in the USA) became commonplace, and the feature film *A Hard Day's Night*, a comic pseudo-documentary of the Beatles' frantic lifestyle directed by Richard Lester, was a great success in 1964. The characteristics of 'Beatlemania'—screaming audiences, obsessive (especially female) fans, sieges of hotel rooms—emerged in 1963 and reached a level of hysteria in 1964 on both sides of the Atlantic. The first signs of official recognition also appeared, with an appearance in the royal variety show in November 1963 (Lennon famously inviting those in the expensive seats to 'rattle their jewellery' rather than clap), a civic reception in Liverpool in 1964, and, also in 1964, a Foyle's literary luncheon to honour the success of Lennon's *In his Own Write*. The Northern Songs publishing company, which ensured a constant flow of royalty income to Lennon and McCartney, was formed in February 1963. By mid-1964 Lennon was a millionaire, and had set up home in a Surrey mansion with his wife, Cynthia, *née* Powell, whom he had met as a student at the College of Art and married on 23 August 1962, together with their son, Julian (*b.* 1964); Julian himself later enjoyed a career as a pop singer–songwriter.

Although it was difficult at this point to isolate Lennon's musical contribution, the qualities defining the Beatles' quickly consolidating style and, within that, Lennon's and McCartney's compositional territory, were clear enough. The core influence came from the rock 'n' roll classics, but they drew from a broader range too, including professional New York songwriters such as Goffin and King, African-American vocal groups, Tin Pan Alley standards, and country singers like the Everly Brothers; and they grafted onto these foundations a quite specific lyricism—a bit 'folky', often modal, with an innocence and brashness extending as they matured into a bitter-sweet quality. With help from the producer George Martin, they were at the forefront in developing new studio effects. In a wider context, the Beatles' image—irreverent, witty, unapologetically provincial and streetwise—set much of the tone for the emergent pop culture centred on 'swinging London'. Both inside and outside the group, Lennon was regarded as the leader and chief image-maker, and his ability to put down pomposity with acerbic one-liners became notorious. But already, though he loved the fame and wealth, he was feeling the strain of media pressure and of constant public exposure. Later, he spoke bitterly about the 'fuckin' humiliation' of enforced politeness; of being presented with cripples to bless (so it seemed); of being made to perform like 'circus animals', and of the martyrdom inseparable from being an artist (Wenner, 11, 16, 20). His attempt to escape the transformation of John Lennon into 'John Beatle' in the service of the 'Beatles myth' dominated the later years of his career.

The Beatles: from peak to breakup By 1965 Lennon (along with the other Beatles) was a leading media personality, constantly seen at exclusive London clubs, restaurants, and theatres. The Beatles were also a British success story to be boasted of by politicians (particularly by the prime minister Harold Wilson), and they were controversially awarded MBEs in June of that year. Touring and performing were becoming increasingly wearing: at a concert in Shea Stadium, New York, in August (preserved on a BBC film), hardly a note of music could be heard above the screams of the 56,000 fans in the audience. Perhaps in response to such public pressures, Lennon at home in Weybridge was rather reclusive, and also sybaritic—overeating, over-drinking, and over-spending on luxury consumer items. This was, he later recalled, his 'fat Elvis period' (Coleman, 363). A different response was his typically blunt remark, in a London *Evening Standard* interview in March 1966, that the Beatles 'were more popular than Jesus now'; although 'Jesus was all right', he argued, 'Christianity … will vanish and shrink' (Thomson and Gutman, 72). The statement attracted no attention in Britain, but when it was reprinted in the USA in July it led to a storm of protest, especially across the 'Bible belt', with radio bans and bonfires of Beatles records. At the start of their third American tour in August, Brian Epstein forced Lennon to apologize. The Beatles' concert on 29 August in San Francisco was their last live performance anywhere.

During 1964–5 Lennon got to know the American singer–songwriter Bob Dylan. Dylan allegedly introduced Lennon to the pleasures of marijuana, which became his drug of choice until it was largely superseded by LSD in 1965–6. (In 1968 he was convicted on a marijuana possession charge, a fact which, some years later, the US authorities used as part of their attempt to deny him residential status.) By 1966 Lennon was taking prodigious quantities of LSD, a habit interrupted temporarily in 1967–8 when chemical routes to expanded spiritual awareness were replaced by an infatuation with transcendental meditation, as taught by a rather dubious Indian guru, Maharishi Mahesh Yogi. A trip to India in February–April 1968 for a meditation course ended with, in Lennon's eyes, their guru's fraudulence being exposed (his disillusion being expressed in his 1968 song about the Maharishi, 'Sexy Sadie'), and his LSD consumption resumed, coupled now with heroin and cocaine.

Lennon's music during this period was undoubtedly affected by drugs, particularly LSD, which opened a way into hidden areas of his psyche but which also, he later claimed, temporarily destroyed his ego with false claims to spiritual insight: 'it was only another mirror' (Wenner, 78). The mysterious and often disturbing atmospheres created in such songs as 'Tomorrow never knows', 'She said she said' (both 1966), and 'Strawberry Fields forever' (1967), the tinkly hallucinatory quality of 'Lucy in the sky with diamonds' (1967), and the terrifying collage ('I'd love to turn you on') that ends 'A day in the life' (1967) all suggest links with what is known of LSD-driven hallucinogenic experiences. But Lennon's (and the Beatles') music was changing in other ways in this period too. Lennon in particular was impressed by the way that Bob Dylan was using rock sounds as the setting for more complex, personal, and poetic (sometimes surreal) lyrics than had been usual in pop songs, and many of his own compositions ('Nowhere man', 'Help', 'I'm a loser', 'Norwegian wood') became more 'inward'—and indeed autobiographical. Both he and McCartney were developing wider artistic interests—in electronic music such as that of Stockhausen, in contemporary art, and in avant-garde 'happenings'—and the engagement with India, however superficial, represented a growing awareness of musical cultures beyond western pop. Fast-improving studio technology, together with George Martin's increasing input into the Beatles' record production, resulted in several Lennon tracks (the surreal 'I am the walrus' and the experimental pieces that went under the title 'Revolution', both recorded in 1968) which could not be performed live; it was this factor, alongside revulsion at the effects of Beatlemania, that led to the decision to move from live performance into the studio, a transition foreseen as early as 1963 by the ever restless Lennon: life is a 'fast run', he once said (Coleman, 352). These experimental tendencies can be detected in the albums of 1965 (*Help!*—more successful than the film of the same name to which it formed the soundtrack—and *Rubber Soul*), and the accompanying singles, but they reached a peak on *Revolver* (1966) and *Sergeant Pepper's Lonely Hearts Club Band* (1967). The latter, with its pop art collage sleeve by Peter Blake, its studio wizardry, and its status as an early 'concept album', was undoubtedly one of the most influential musical products of the 1960s. The enthusiastic reception given to the Beatles' development by such classical music critics as William Mann of *The Times* was later dismissed as over-intellectual 'bullshit' by Lennon (Wenner, 72), but it marked the importance of their contribution to what can be seen now as a decisive cultural shift.

Sergeant Pepper was a key emblem in the so-called 'summer of love' of 1967, by which time, Lennon, like the other Beatles, had adopted the shoulder-length hair, exotic clothing, and love-and-peace discourse typical of the counter-cultural hippies. Shortly after the album was released, the Beatles, surrounded by hosts of other pop luminaries, recorded a new Lennon composition, 'All you need is love', live on a worldwide television satellite link-up, *Our World*, with an estimated audience of 44 million. His politics were as yet ill-defined. On his 'Revolution' tracks, produced while the huge anti-Vietnam War demonstrations and other startling 'events' of 1968 were raging, he is ambivalent about the need for violent revolution, but 'All you need is love' can be regarded as the start of a commitment to a peace politics which he never abandoned.

Lennon's work for peace, and his broader political thinking, were given added focus and momentum through his meeting and subsequent liaison with the performance artist Yoko Ono (*b.* 1933). Born into a wealthy Japanese business family, Ono had been brought up partly in Tokyo, where after the Second World War both Zen Buddhism and a transplanted Dadaism were fashionable, and partly in the USA, where, in the 1950s and 1960s, she became active in the avant-garde New York scene—particularly in the mixed-media 'happenings' associated with such artists as John Cage and the Fluxus group. Lennon met Ono on 9 November 1966 at an exhibition of her work at the Indica gallery in London. He was intrigued by its Dadaist absurdity: one exhibit invited the observer to climb a stepladder and look through a magnifying glass which, when peered through, revealed in tiny letters the word 'yes'. Their relationship, at first apparently intellectual, developed through 1967, and by May 1968 the two were lovers. Ono was ever-present during the recording sessions for the double album released in 1968 (*The Beatles*, otherwise known as 'the white album' after its pure white sleeve), even contributing to some of Lennon's songs, and they were now living together openly. To Lennon, Ono represented the weird but alluring world of 'art', as well as becoming, arguably, Paul McCartney's rival for his intellectual affections, and a mother-substitute standing in both for the absent Mimi and for his dead mother (in later years, he often referred to Ono as 'mother'). Her avant-garde repertoire also provided models for peace happenings: in June 1968 she and Lennon travelled to Coventry to plant two acorns 'for peace' in the grounds of the cathedral, the first of many such 'events'. They married on 20 March 1969, Lennon having been divorced by his first wife, Cynthia, on 8 November 1968, while Ono was divorced from her first husband, Anthony Cox, on 2 February 1969.

The advent of Yoko Ono, who was much resented by the other Beatles, crystallized in Lennon a dissatisfaction with Beatle-ism and a desire to go his own way which had been developing in him for some time. On 27 August 1967, at the beginning of the excursion into transcendental meditation, Brian Epstein died suddenly of an accidental drug overdose. 'I knew that we were in trouble then … I thought, "We've fuckin' had it"', said Lennon later (Wenner, 52), and indeed the two disruptions taken together clearly signalled the beginning of the end for the Beatles. With Lennon distracted—by meditation, drugs, and Ono—McCartney took over the effective leadership, with mixed results. Apple Corps, an idealistic hippy-capitalist company including a record label, set up by the Beatles in 1968 to support and market new cultural projects, proved a financial disaster, and efforts to retrieve the situation, which set Lennon against McCartney, exacerbated strains that were in any case already growing. Early in 1969 Lennon announced to his fellow Beatles that he was breaking the group up. Some collaborative work continued—the final album, *Let It Be*, was not released until May 1970, and the legal dissolution, in a High Court action, did not come until March 1971—but the end was now unavoidable. The Beatles' late-period music—mainly the albums *The Beatles* (1968), *Abbey Road* (1969), and *Let It Be*

(1970), together with soundtracks for the television film *Magical Mystery Tour* (1967) and the animated film *Yellow Submarine* (1968)—included some fine songs, but their production was much more individualistic, Lennon's efforts pointing towards distinctive modes of his post-Beatles career: some heavy and anguished, some flippant, others meditatively, even sentimentally, lyrical.

Lennon, Ono, and politics During the same period, Lennon had begun working with Ono. Two albums of avant-garde tape music were issued, *Unfinished Music No. 1: Two Virgins* (November 1968, recorded in May 1968 during their first night together) and *Unfinished Music No. 2: Life with the Lions* (May 1969), the first including a controversial image of the pair naked on its sleeve. The Plastic Ono Band, a scratch group set up to perform Lennon's and Ono's repertory, began to appear in concerts—most dramatically in Toronto in September 1969, an event documented on the album *Live Peace in Toronto* (1969)—and put out the Lennon singles 'The Ballad of John and Yoko', 'Give peace a chance', 'Cold turkey' (all 1969), 'Instant karma!' (1970), 'Power to the people' and 'Happy Xmas! War is over' (both 1971). Screenings of avant-garde films made by Lennon and Ono also took place. More important than all of this, at least to them, were the 'happenings for peace'. Their 'honeymoon' in March 1969 was devoted to a 'bed-in for peace' lasting seven days in the Amsterdam Hilton Hotel; during this they gave hundreds of interviews publicizing their peace message. Several other bed-ins and 'bag-ins' followed (in the latter, Lennon and Ono 'appeared' in a large bag), together with poster campaigns (for Christmas 1969, their posters, in eleven cities worldwide, read 'War is over! If you want it') and other demonstrations. On 25 November 1969 Lennon returned his MBE 'in protest against Britain's involvement in the Nigeria–Biafra thing, against our support of America in Vietnam, and against "Cold turkey" slipping down the charts' (Coleman, 524). In many of the songs accompanying the peace campaign, Lennon cultivated a new anthemic simplicity, in which he explicitly aimed to provide chants suitable for collective singing: for example, 'All we are saying is give peace a chance'. Many listeners found his new music crude compared with his Beatles work, and they often ascribed the shift to Ono's influence, but the peace campaign achieved enormous publicity, and its agitprop style was probably indebted not only to Ono's skill at politicizing conceptual art ('con-art', as she herself described it) but also to contemporary political demos and especially the activities of the French situationists. It is true, though, that Lennon was completely immersed in his relationship with his new partner at this time and on 22 April 1969 he formally changed his middle name from Winston to Ono.

Lennon was still not without psychological troubles, however: the Apple financial crisis, the messy break-up of the Beatles, the sale of Northern Songs (a public company since 1965) in September 1969, separation from his son, Julian, and the pressure of living twenty-four hours a day with Ono, much of it in public, were among the causes, but the problems also lay deeper in Lennon's psyche. Once again, an answer (or so it seemed) appeared, this time in a book entitled *The Primal Scream* by the American psychotherapist Arthur Janov. Janov offered a somewhat vulgar Freudian method of rediscovering the primal self: stripping away accumulated ego-defences, acknowledging childhood traumas, and screaming away the pain. This therapy came as a revelation to Lennon who, with Ono, spent four months in mid-1970 undergoing a course of treatment at Janov's institute in California. For Lennon, the pain related first and foremost to his abandonment by, and loss of, his mother, but it may be that the therapy also facilitated a final rejection of one 'Lennon'—that which had enabled the Beatles myth—and the discovery, or construction, of another. As Lennon commented, 'it's just like Primal is like another mirror' (Wenner, 21). At any rate, the effects of 'primal' are clear in two events that occurred late in 1970: the issue of the first solo Lennon album (*John Lennon/Plastic Ono Band*) and the large-scale interview with *Rolling Stone* magazine published in January 1971, in which Lennon discussed the album, his past, and his future. Taken together these two statements mark a watershed, the definitive end of Lennon the Beatle (and perhaps of the sixties as a cultural entity) and the start of the second half of his career.

The music is sparse and elemental—melodically, harmonically, texturally—the content avowedly autobiographical ('I'm in me own head. I can't be in anybody else's'; Wenner, 52). The moods are personal, confessional, often anguished ('Mother', 'Working class hero', 'My mummy's dead'), the vocal style ranging between stoicism and scream. In 'God' Lennon dispatches past myths: 'I don't believe in magic … I don't believe in Jesus … I don't believe in Elvis … I don't believe in Zimmerman [Bob Dylan] … I don't believe in Beatles / I just believe in me / Yoko and me / And that's reality.' In his *Rolling Stone* interview he links the change in content to both a historical shift ('the dream is over … we gotta … get down to so-called reality') and to an aesthetic turn towards simplicity, manifested in one-take recording, as compared to that 'dead Beatles sound or dead recording sound'), and the virtues of rock 'n' roll: 'The thing about rock 'n' roll … is that it's real … You recognise something in it which is true, like all true art … If it's real, it's simple usually, and if it's simple, it's true' (Wenner, 31, 21, 100–101). In a conjunction that was of course not new but nevertheless was unusual within vernacular culture, 'advanced' political and social ideas were melded with an artistic theory of popular realism.

Life and death in New York In September 1971, as if marking this shift geographically, the Lennons moved to New York, at first to the bohemian Greenwich Village, later to an up-market apartment in the Dakota Building close to Central Park. Lennon spent the rest of his life in New York, although not until July 1976 was his application for permanent residence approved after a protracted and bitter dispute with the US authorities. The paranoia in government circles which led to the attempt to deport Lennon on grounds of his political radicalism, together with the dirty tricks used to discredit him, were later documented in Jon Wiener's book *Come Together: John Lennon in his Time* (1985).

And his views *were* now radical. In 1969 he used to describe himself as a 'Christian communist' but by the time of an interview with the socialist magazine *Red Dwarf* in March 1971 he seemed to be toying with revolutionary Maoism. He supported militant Irish republicanism, African-American radicals such as Angela Davis and George Jackson, and the White Panther John Sinclair. He was also fast learning feminism from Yoko Ono. In his early New York days, he wrote songs addressing all these issues ('Woman is the nigger of the world', 'Sunday bloody Sunday', and others) and associated with the new left veterans Jerry Rubin and Abbie Hoffman. Lennon's personal life remained turbulent too. He constantly sniped at the more conservative McCartney (as in the song 'How do you sleep?'), and his relationship with Ono was often rocky, especially when he was drinking heavily. In October 1973 Ono insisted on a separation. Lennon's 'lost weekend', as he later called it, lasted for some fifteen months, and was spent mostly in Los Angeles, much of it in the company of his friend the broadcasting personality Elliot Mintz, and in the pursuit of drunken antisocial behaviour. Lennon kept in contact with Ono, however; indeed, Ono had arranged for her secretary, May Pang, to accompany Lennon, and almost certainly a sexual relationship between the two developed. Gradually Lennon pulled out of his riotous lifestyle; his single 'Whatever gets you thru the night' (October 1974), recorded with Elton John, became his first post-Beatles number one hit in the US, and on 28 November 1974 he made a surprise concert appearance with Elton John in New York (Ono, unknown to him, being in the audience). Lennon returned to the Dakota, and to Ono, in January 1975.

Musically, Lennon's recorded output between 1972 and 1975 is largely disappointing. After the masterly album *Imagine* (1971), a follow-up to *Plastic Ono Band* but, as Lennon put it, with added honey coating, his American period produced *Some Time in New York City* (1972), a politically audacious but artistically dubious product of his theory at the time that pop records should be as transient and sloganized as newspapers; two albums of originals, *Mind Games* (1973) and *Walls and Bridges* (1974), which are at best uneven; and an album of rock 'n' roll covers, *Rock 'n' Roll*, recorded initially with the producer Phil Spector at the very beginning of the 'lost weekend' in notoriously chaotic sessions, but not issued until February 1975.

For some time after this it appeared that there might be no further recordings from John Lennon. Ono became pregnant and, after several previous miscarriages, gave birth to a son, Sean, on 9 October 1975. Lennon's recording contract with EMI expired in February 1976 and he did not renew it. He became a house-husband and devoted himself to bringing up Sean, leaving management of the Lennon–Ono business to his wife. She proved as efficient at her side of this arrangement as he was typically obsessive, even faddish, in his domestic duties. Lennon mellowed dramatically, and his musical tastes broadened, as the image of a recluse, lost to pop music, took hold. But by 1980 he was talking about creative work again, and in August he and Ono recorded a new album, released in November by Geffen Records as *Double Fantasy* (other tracks from the same sessions appeared in 1984 on *Milk and Honey*). Some found this music overly sentimental, even mawkish, although some tracks—'Beautiful boy', addressed to Sean, 'Woman', addressed to Yoko, and '(Just like) Starting over', the (number one) single—stood out. In any case, the records both shrank and mushroomed in significance when on 8 December 1980 John Lennon was shot at the entrance to the Dakota Building by Mark Chapman; he died shortly afterwards in Roosevelt Hospital, and was cremated at Hartsdale crematorium, New York, on 10 December. The response to his death—vigils everywhere, messages of sympathy pouring in, and continuous broadcasts of Lennon's music—was such as to suggest that a major world figure had died. Chapman, changing his plea from not guilty to guilty, was sentenced to life imprisonment; Fenton Bresler's book *The Murder of John Lennon* (1989) argues that he may have been the tool of a CIA conspiracy, but no conclusive evidence has emerged that he was anything other than a psychopathic fantasist in search of celebrity and consumed by hatred of the famous. Victim at the last, ironically, of a pathology which he had both indulged and excoriated, Lennon left an estate estimated to be worth around $150 million, half going to Ono and half to a charitable trust.

Posthumous events and overall achievement In a strange way, an important new phase in John Lennon's life was now beginning, as he became perhaps culturally the most pervasive dead rock star (outshining even Elvis Presley). Reissues and re-packages of his (and of the Beatles') recordings continued to pour out. A good deal of previously unreleased material also appeared. It ranged from *Live at the BBC* (1994), a collection of Beatles radio broadcasts from 1962 to 1965, to two albums of early 1970s Lennon tracks, *Live in New York City* and *Menlove Avenue* (both 1986). It included, most dramatically, a new Lennon single, 'Free as a bird'/'Real love' (1995), put together from a home-made Lennon tape and instrumental overdubs added in 1994 by the other Beatles. The glossiest package was the late-1990s *Beatles Anthology*, with television, video, book, and CD components, the latter including many outtakes of famous tracks. At the same time Lennon songs were covered by many other performers, and some—including Paul McCartney, Queen, Pink Floyd, Paul Simon, and Elton John—composed and recorded tribute songs to him. The British Performing Right Society established a scholarship in his name in 1982, and he was inducted into the Rock 'n' Roll Hall of Fame in 1994. His musical influence burst into particular prominence during the 1990s Britpop phenomenon, and was especially evident in the work of the band Oasis.

There were also several exhibitions of Lennon's drawings, re-showings of films he made with Ono, and publication of a new collection of his writings: *Skywriting by Word of Mouth* (1986). Out of many radio, television, and film documentaries, the films *Imagine: John Lennon* (1988), made by Ono, *Backbeat* (1994), telling the story of the Beatles in Hamburg, the BBC radio series *In my Life: John Lennon Remembered* (1990), and *The Lost Lennon Tapes*, broadcast by the US radio company Westwood One weekly for four years, from 1988, stood out. Two major interviews with Lennon in his last year were disseminated, the first by the BBC (*The Lennon Tapes*, 1981), the second by *Playboy* magazine (*The Playboy Interviews*, 1982). Biographies included Ray Coleman's celebratory *Lennon: the Definitive Biography* (1984, rev. 1995) and Albert Goldman's muckraking *The Lives of John Lennon* (1988), and there were memoirs of varying degrees of interest from, among others, Cynthia Lennon, May Pang, Lennon's half-sister Julia Baird, and his father, Freddy (in a book published by his widow). Lennon manuscripts (of drawings, writings, song lyrics, etc.) and memorabilia became highly prized: one of his Rolls-Royces, for example, sold for $2.2 million in 1985, while an amateur tape of him singing with the Quarrymen in 1957 fetched £78,500 at Sothebys in 1994.

Lennon was also commemorated in public events and locations. The city of Liverpool honoured him in several ways, most strikingly by renaming its airport the John Lennon Airport in 2002. A John Lennon Museum opened in Tokyo in 2000. Of many streets and parks named after him, the most famous is the 3½-acre garden in New York's Central Park opened in 1984 and named Strawberry Fields. Often these events and memorials were connected to Lennon's work for peace. In 1990 a ceremony in the United Nations building in New York included the playing of a tape of Lennon speaking on the subject, and was broadcast around the world. In times of war—the Gulf War in 1991, and the World Trade Center attack in 2001, for instance—Lennon's peace songs invariably emerged on the airwaves, often accompanied, as in those two cases, by attempts at censorship. At the same time, commercial exploitation of his fame, often furthered by Yoko Ono herself, continued unabated and was seen by many as incongruous. It included the licensing of his song 'Instant karma!' to a television commercial for Nike trainers in 1992, and the exhibiting in 1993 of Ono's bronze replicas of the bloodstained spectacles and bullet-riddled shirt Lennon was wearing on the night of his murder (available for $25,000 and $35,000 respectively).

But Lennon himself, hungry for fame and at the same time torn apart by it, would have relished the irony inherent in his iconic yet contested public status. Critics of his 'canonization' have pointed to his often ugly personal behaviour, and have argued that his taste for self-publicity and his aggressive espousal of a constantly changing sequence of belief systems, each one apparently definitive, reveal both hypocrisy and artistic and political faddism. This seems too harsh. To an almost unprecedented degree, he lived his adult life in public and in highly mediated forms. In popular existentialism, situationism, and new left theories made up of equal parts Herbert Marcuse and Herman Hesse, he found ways of understanding his own fierce commitment to 'reality'—to a life and art produced 'authentically', 'in the moment'. The peculiarities of his psycho-biography (especially his childhood traumas) and social location (sensitive grammar school layabout, stranded between cultures and classes) meant that the results took highly personal and contradictory forms, and, when these were placed within the pressures of the public context, the rudeness, violence, social gaffes, and constant switches of direction were a predictable consequence. Lennon's search for the 'real me' was worked out through a sequence of 'performed identities', a narrative that was traced not only musically but also on the surface of his own body, through a bewildering succession of visual personae. In the process, he also revealed the fault lines of society to itself, on the broadest level through his crucial roles in both the would-be universalistic mood of the 1960s—youth counter-culture to the fore—and in the more fragmented, wary, cynical feel of the 1970s; and through his dauntless, if at times naïve, embodiment of the shift from one to the other.

The intermeshing of public and private explains how, to Lennon, life, art, and politics could come to seem hardly distinguishable. In this he was at once a creature of the mass media's star-making machinery and a child of Dada, Fluxus, and sixties narcissism. On this level, his political songs—'commercials for peace' (Howlett and Lewisohn, 86–7), or for revolution or justice—contain the quintessential Lennon. In a further irony, however, it is Lennon the musician—the sound of Lennon rather than his life—that will probably survive most strongly. He was a considerable rhythm guitarist—not outstanding technically but an energizing band presence, a 'cinéma vérité guitarist', as he put it (Wenner, 48)—and a charismatic stage performer. He possessed one of the most memorable rock voices, instantly recognizable and hence apt for his 'first-person music' (ibid., 29), and capable of great expressive variety; and yet, characteristically, he distrusted it, always begging producers to treat it, distort it, and turn it into (presumably) a vocal persona. As a songwriter and composer, he had a gift for striking lyric and melodic phrases—usually concise, self-contained, and somehow static—coupled with an original aural imagination, resulting in songs which, at their most memorable, function as epiphanies, summoning up particular worlds of feeling or consciousness. The materials of 'Help!', 'I'm a loser', 'She said she said', 'Strawberry Fields forever', 'A day in the life', 'I am the walrus', 'Come together', 'Working class hero', 'Imagine', 'Across the universe', and many more may be rooted in the everyday—Lennon's working method was to immerse himself in the vernacular flux of memory, emotion, events, and cultural detritus and, once inspiration struck, the transfer into artistic ideas seems to have been fast—but the songs transform these into precisely imagined visions with their own aesthetic substance. To describe this body of work as pop music of unusually high quality is accurate (and essential if Lennon's insistence on the virtues of simplicity is to be respected) but it does not adequately highlight the scope of an achievement which, more persuasively than that of any other musician of his generation, pointed towards both the concrete creative possibilities in rock music and their potential political resonance.

RICHARD MIDDLETON

Sources R. Coleman, *Lennon: the definitive biography* (1995) · J. Wenner, ed., *Lennon remembers: the Rolling Stone interviews* (1973) ·

K. Howlett and M. Lewisohn, eds., *In my life: John Lennon remembered* (1990) • A. Peebles, ed., *The Lennon tapes: John Lennon and Yoko Ono in conversation with Andy Peebles* (1981) • D. Sheff, *The Playboy interviews with John Lennon and Yoko Ono* (1982) • E. Thomson and D. Gutman, eds., *The Lennon companion: twenty-five years of comment* (1987) • *The Beatles anthology* (2000) • M. Braun, *Love me do: the Beatles' progress* (1964) • H. Davies, *The Beatles* (1968) • P. Norman, *Shout! The true story of the Beatles* (1981) • A. Goldman, *The lives of John Lennon* (1988) • I. MacDonald, *Revolution in the head: the Beatles' records and the sixties* (1994) • G. Giuliano and B. Giuliano, *Lost Lennon interviews* (1996) • J. Wiener, *Come together: John Lennon in his time* (1985)

Archives priv. coll., Lennon estate | FILM BFI NFTVA, 'John Lennon story', 1982 • BFI NFTVA, 'Lennon', 5 May 1990 • BFI NFTVA, 'Imagine: John Lennon', BBC2, 1 Jan 1996 • BFI NFTVA, documentary footage • BFI NFTVA, performance footage | SOUND BL NSA, documentary recordings • BL NSA, performance recordings

Likenesses L. McCartney, two platinum prints, 1967–8, NPG • A. Leibovitz, bromide print, 1970, NPG [*see illus.*] • I. Macmillan, photograph, 1971, priv. coll. • A. Leibovitz, colour print, 1980, NPG • photographs, Hult. Arch. • portrait, repro. in B. Gruen, *Listen to these pictures: photographs of John Lennon* (1985) • portrait, repro. in D. Hoffmann, *John Lennon* (1985) • portrait, repro. in P. Norman, *Days in the life: John Lennon remembered* (1990) • portrait, repro. in A. Solt and S. Egan, *Imagine John Lennon* (1988)

Wealth at death £2,522,317: probate, 20 Feb 1981, *CGPLA Eng. & Wales*

Lennox. For this title name *see* individual entries under Lennox; *see also* Stewart, John, tenth earl of Lennox (1424x9–1495); Stewart, Matthew, eleventh earl of Lennox (*d.* 1513); Stewart, John, twelfth earl of Lennox (*d.* 1526); Douglas, Lady Margaret, countess of Lennox (1515–1578); Stewart, Matthew, thirteenth earl of Lennox (1516–1571); Stewart, Robert, earl of Lennox and earl of March (1522/3–1586); Stuart, Frances, duchess of Lennox and Richmond (1578–1639); Stewart, Esmé, first duke of Lennox (*c.*1542–1583); Stuart, Ludovick, second duke of Lennox and duke of Richmond (1574–1624); Stuart, Esmé, third duke of Lennox (1579?–1624); Stuart, James, fourth duke of Lennox and first duke of Richmond (1612–1655); Villiers, Mary, duchess of Lennox and Richmond (1622–1685); Stuart, Charles, sixth duke of Lennox and third duke of Richmond (1639–1672); Stuart, Frances Teresa, duchess of Lennox and Richmond (1647–1702).

Lennox family (*per. c.*1300–1425), nobility, was established in the twelfth century in the region from which it was named, in the south-western highlands of Scotland, but became of national importance only at the end of the thirteenth century, with **Malcolm Lennox**, fifth earl of Lennox (*d.* 1333). Having probably succeeded his father and namesake in the early 1290s, the younger Malcolm became a committed supporter of Robert Bruce in his attempt to revive an independent Scottish kingship in the early months of 1306. He attended Robert's enthronement on 25 March and shared fully in the misfortunes of the new king's allies in the years immediately following. The earldom of Lennox was forfeited to Edward I, who assigned it to his principal supporter in the Firth of Clyde, Sir John Menteith. The defeat of Robert's forces at the battles of Methven and Dalry in summer 1306 reduced Malcolm to the status of a fugitive; John Barbour's *Bruce* preserves a tale of his narrow escape when the Scottish king and his men were being pursued by sea in the Firth of Clyde. However, the earl's fortunes recovered as a result of Robert I's increasingly successful military and political campaigns from 1307 onwards. Lennox was with Robert on campaigns in the west during 1308, and appended his seal to the letter sent by the nobles of Scotland to the king of France in the first parliament of the reign in March 1309. He was similarly one of the signatories of a more famous diplomatic communication, the so-called 'declaration of Arbroath' sent by the Scottish nobility to Pope John XXII in 1320.

Although never one of the major beneficiaries of Robert I's patronage, Malcolm Lennox received a number of important grants from him, including that of the hereditary sheriffdom of Clackmannan in 1309 and above all the sheriffdom and castle of Dumbarton, the principal stronghold in the area of his earldom, in 1321. After Robert's death in 1329 Malcolm apparently remained loyal to his infant son, David II. On 19 July 1333 pro-Bruce forces attempting to relieve an English siege of Berwick were badly defeated at the battle of Halidon Hill. English chroniclers record the earl of Lennox among the Scottish casualties.

Malcolm Lennox was succeeded by **Donald Lennox**, sixth earl of Lennox (*d.* 1361x4), the son of his marriage to a woman named Margaret, said to have been a sister or daughter of an earl of Mar. Donald issued a number of charters dealing with lands and offices within the Lennox, but played little part in the wider affairs of the kingdom. In September 1357 he was one of the Scottish magnates who agreed to the ransom arrangements for David II, captured by the English at the battle of Nevilles Cross in 1346 (in which Donald himself took no part). Otherwise little is known of his activities. He seems to have died between 2 May 1361 and 20 November 1364. The identity of his wife is unknown. He had no surviving sons and was succeeded as *suo jure* countess by his daughter **Margaret Lennox** (*d.* in or before 1392) and her husband, **Walter Faslane** (*d.* in or before 1392), who is referred to as earl of Lennox in an indenture of 20 November 1364, but who thereafter used the courtesy title 'lord' of Lennox. Margaret's marriage to Walter was probably concluded in the 1340s and may well have been designed to keep the earldom in the comital family, since he was a descendant of Alwin, second earl of Lennox (*d. c.*1214x17), and as such the head of a major cadet branch of the Lennox kindred. From about the time of his marriage, Walter may have been treated as Donald's *de facto* heir, explaining why he witnessed many of the earl's charters and received grants of important offices within the earldom.

As 'lord' of Lennox Walter Faslane attended the coronation of Robert II on 26 March 1371 but was not particularly prominent in the governance of the kingdom thereafter. Towards the end of his life his hold on the earldom may have been challenged by his son **Duncan Lennox**, eighth earl of Lennox (*d.* 1425). In 1385 Walter and Margaret resigned the earldom in favour of Duncan, who received a great seal charter confirming the arrangement and began to use the title earl of Lennox. The resignation may not have been entirely voluntary, or some aspects of the new arrangement may have displeased Walter and Margaret, for in August 1388 they repeated their resignation of the earldom in Duncan's favour, but this time reserving their 'liferent' rights in the Lennox. Duncan may have achieved an uncontested supremacy in the Lennox only after the deaths of his parents, in both cases before 17 February 1392.

Duncan's career as eighth earl was dominated by his increasingly close links to the family of Robert Stewart, duke of Albany. By the early 1390s he had no legitimate male heirs (though he had four illegitimate sons), but did have three legitimate daughters, probably born of his marriage to Helen Campbell, daughter of the Campbell lord of Lochawe, for which he obtained papal approval in 1373. On 17 February 1392 Duncan entered into a contract for the marriage of his eldest daughter, Isabel, to Robert Stewart's eldest son, Murdoch. By the terms of the contract Isabel and Murdoch and their successors were recognized as heirs to the earldom should Duncan fail to produce any legitimate male heirs before his death. On 8 November 1392 Robert III gave his consent to the entailing of Lennox in favour of Murdoch Stewart and his heirs. The entailing arrangement (which ruled out the possibility of the earldom being partitioned between Duncan's daughters) tied Lennox to one of the most powerful figures in the kingdom, for Albany was first guardian of the kingdom for the incapacitated Robert III from 1402 until the latter's death in 1406, and then, as a result of the capture of the heir to the throne, Prince James, by the English in the same year, governor of Scotland. When the duke died in 1420, Duncan's son-in-law Murdoch succeeded his father as both duke of Albany and governor.

Earl Duncan's close connection to the Albany Stewart family eventually proved his undoing, as he was caught up in the bitter political dispute between the Albanys and King James I after the latter was released from English captivity in 1424. At the forefront of resistance to James was Duncan's grandson Walter Stewart, who had built a personal following in the earldom of Lennox and had been opposed to the entire idea of negotiating James's release. Walter, whose increasingly rebellious courses did much to undermine his father's position, was arrested on the king's orders in May 1424, and before January 1425 James had also detained Earl Duncan and imprisoned him in Edinburgh Castle. In March 1425 Duncan's daughter Isabel and his son-in-law Murdoch were also taken into custody, and it became clear that the duke and his kinsmen were to face trial in a parliament called for May 1425. The king's actions provoked a rebellion in the Lennox led by another of Duncan's grandsons, James Stewart, who attacked the royal burgh and castle of Dumbarton on 3 May, although with limited success. On 25 May Duncan, Duke Murdoch, and Murdoch's son Alexander were tried in parliament at Stirling, convicted, and summarily executed; Walter Stewart had suffered the same fate on the previous day. Earl Duncan was reputed to be over eighty years of age at the time of his execution. According to a later chronicler all four men were buried in the Dominican friary in Stirling.

Earl Duncan's daughter Isabel recovered control of the earldom of Lennox after James I's death in 1437. She died about 1458, without legitimate heirs, and the comital title was eventually claimed by the descendants of Duncan's second daughter, Elizabeth, and her husband, John Stewart of Darnley. Their grandson, another John Stewart, was acknowledged as earl in 1488. S. I. Boardman

Sources J. Dennistoun, ed., *Cartularium comitatus de Levenax*, Maitland Club, 24 (1833) • W. Fraser, *The Lennox*, 2 vols. (1874) • G. W. S. Barrow and others, eds., *Regesta regum Scottorum*, 5–6, ed. A. A. M. Duncan and B. Webster (1982–8) • *CDS*, vols. 1–4 • W. Bower, *Scotichronicon*, ed. D. E. R. Watt and others, new edn, 9 vols. (1987–98), vols. 7–8 • *APS*, 1124–1567 • C. Innes, ed., *Registrum episcopatus Glasguensis*, 2 vols., Maitland Club, 61 (1843) • C. Innes and P. Chalmers, eds., *Liber s. Thome de Aberbrothoc*, 2 vols., Bannatyne Club, 86 (1848–56) • GEC, *Peerage*, 7.585–96 • *Scots peerage*, 5.324–43 • S. I. Boardman, *The early Stewart kings: Robert II and Robert III, 1371–1406* (1996) • M. Brown, *James I* (1994)

Lennox, Lady (Georgiana) Caroline. *See* Fox, (Georgiana) Caroline, *suo jure* Baroness Holland of Holland (1723–1774).

Lennox, Charles, first duke of Richmond, first duke of Lennox, and duke of Aubigny in the French nobility (1672–1723), landowner, natural son of *Charles II (1630–1685) and Louise Renée de Penancoët de *Kéroualle, duchess of Portsmouth (1649–1734), was born in London on 29 July 1672. On 9 August 1675 he was created baron of Settrington, Yorkshire, earl of March, and duke of Richmond, Yorkshire, in the peerage of England, and on 9 September 1675 Baron Methuen of Tarbolton, earl of Darnley, and duke of Lennox in the peerage of Scotland. The two dukedoms had reverted to Charles II as nearest male heir of Charles Stuart, duke of Richmond and Lennox (1640–1672), who had died without issue. Louis XIV also gave him the dignity of duke of Aubigny in remainder to his mother.

Early in January 1693 Richmond married Anne Belasyse (*d.* 1722), widow of Henry, second Baron Belasyse of Worlaby, and daughter of Francis, Lord Brudenell. They had three children: Charles *Lennox, second duke of Richmond (1701–1750), Louise (1694–1717), who married James, third earl of Berkeley, and Anne (1703–1722), wife of William Anne Keppel, second earl of Albemarle. In August 1675 Richmond was granted Richmond Castle in Yorkshire. On 18 April 1681 he was installed KG and on 12 July of that year he was named governor of Dumbarton Castle. On 22 January 1682 he was appointed master of the horse, on the removal of the duke of Monmouth, the duties of the office being exercised during his minority by three commissioners. He and his mother paid a visit to France in March 1682. About April 1683 he became high steward of the city of York. The duchess of Portsmouth was uneasy about her son's prospects, and she procured letters patent naturalizing him in France, which were registered on 22 January 1685. But Charles II was sufficiently generous, and

Charles Lennox, first duke of Richmond, first duke of Lennox, and duke of Aubigny in the French nobility (1672–1723), by Sir Godfrey Kneller, *c*.1703–10

in addition to an annuity of £2000 charged on the lands of Lord Grey, he gave him a royalty on the coal dues, which Richmond's descendant in 1799 exchanged for an annuity of £19,000 from the consolidated fund. When Charles was dying he recommended Richmond to his brother. James II, however, hated the duchess of Portsmouth, and removed the duke from the mastership of the horse on 6 February 1685 on the alleged ground that the office could not be exercised by deputy. James was more concerned for the youth's spiritual prospects and made his mother promise to rear him as a Roman Catholic.

For the rest of his career Richmond changed his allegiance and religion to suit his circumstances. First, together with the duchess of Portsmouth, he went to France about August 1685 and remained there for a year. He was duly presented to Louis XIV and was well received. He formally professed the Roman Catholic faith in the presence of the French king in the chapel at Fontainebleau after mass on 21 October 1685. His mother's pension was now raised to 20,000 livres and she wished it to be settled on her son. At the revolution of 1688 Richmond again came to Paris; but his character was now better understood and on 1 January 1689 he found it necessary to protest his loyalty to James to the French king, who politely replied that he knew him too well to suspect anything. He tried a military career. He wished to go on the Irish expedition but was told that he was too young and too little. He served, however, in August 1689 as a volunteer at the attack on Valcours in the army of the marshal d'Humieres, and the next year, while making the campaign as aide-de-camp to the duke of Orléans, was laid up at Neustadt with what was thought to be an attack of smallpox. In September 1690 Louis gave him a company in the Royal regiment of horse. He was not, however, satisfied with his position and in February 1692 he secretly left the court and proceeded, by way of Switzerland and Germany, to England. In writing to De Barbezieux he said that he was going where he would have higher rank and a more plentiful revenue. Narcissus Luttrell mentions a report that he had stolen his mother's jewels. The family pension from Louis was reduced on his departure to 12,000 livres, and continued to his mother, who thought her son out of his senses.

In England Richmond found it convenient to change both his politics and his religion, and on Whitsunday 15 May 1692 was received again into the Church of England. He made his peace with William III, on 14 November 1693 he took his seat in the House of Lords, and he served as aide-de-camp in the Flanders wars throughout the reign. In 1696 he was suspected of some complicity in the Jacobite schemes. He purchased a country estate at Goodwood in Sussex in 1697. He naturally took a leading part in the opposition to the resumption bill in April 1700. In 1702, by the death of Frances, dowager duchess of Richmond, third wife of Charles Stuart, duke of Richmond, he came into possession of the Lennox estates, in which she had enjoyed a life interest under the grant to Richmond in 1680. Richmond promptly sold the estates to a purchaser who resold them to the duke of Montrose. At the coronation of Anne he bore the sceptre and the dove, but he ceased to be a whig before the close of the reign. He visited Paris in May 1713, and while there again in July 1714 was mysteriously wounded near the Pont Neuf. He probably became a whig once more at the Hanoverian accession, as he was made lord of the bedchamber to George I on 16 October 1714 and privy councillor of Ireland on 5 August 1715.

In 1684 John Evelyn described him as 'a very pretty boy' (Evelyn, *Diary*, 24 Oct 1684). John Macky thought him 'good-natured to a fault, very well bred, and hath many valuable things in him, is an enemy to business very credulous, well shaped black complection much like King Charles II' (*Memoirs of the Secret Services*, 48), and in 1723 Thomas Hearne considered him 'a man of very little understanding, and though the son of so great a King as Charles II was a man that was struck in with everything that was Whiggish and opposite to true monarchical principles' (*Reliquiae*, 2.162). His final years saw a sorry decline into drunkenness and the duc d'Aumont informed the duchess of Portsmouth that 'bad companions often spoil the best intentions' (Goodwood MS 6). He made his will on 24 May 1723 and died at Goodwood on 27 May 1723. After a funeral on 3 June, he was buried in Henry VII's chapel, Westminster Abbey, on 7 June 1723. His body was removed to Chichester Cathedral on 16 August 1750 and re-interred in the family vault in the lady chapel. The eighth duke of Richmond said of his ancestor that 'although at one time and another he filled various more or less important public offices, yet his unfortunate propensity for being everything by turns and nothing long effectually militated against any chance of his name being emblazoned upon the scroll of fame' (Lennox, 1.xv).

TIMOTHY J. MCCANN

Sources *DNB* · W. Sussex RO, Goodwood MSS · F. W. Steer, 'The funeral account of the first duke of Richmond and Lennox', *Sussex Archaeological Collections*, 98 (1960), 156–64 · Earl of March [C. H. G. Lennox], *A duke and his friends: the life and letters of the second duke of Richmond*, 2 vols. (1911) · B. Bevan, *Charles the Second's French mistress: a biography of Louise de Keroualle, duchess of Portsmouth, 1649–1734* (1972) · H. Forneron, *Louise de Kérouälle, duchess of Portsmouth, 1649–1734*, ed. and trans. Mrs G. M. Crawford (1887) · J. Delpech, *The life and times of the duchess of Portsmouth*, trans. A. Lindsay (1953) · J. Kent, *Records and reminiscences of Goodwood and the dukes of Richmond* (1896) · *Memoirs of the secret services of John Macky*, ed. A. R. (1733) · *Reliquiae Hearnianae: the remains of Thomas Hearne*, ed. P. Bliss, 2nd edn, 3 vols. (1869)

Archives W. Sussex RO, Goodwood papers

Likenesses W. Wissing, oils, *c.*1681, Goodwood House, West Sussex · G. Kneller, oils, *c.*1703–1710, NPG [*see illus.*] · J. Faber junior, mezzotint, 1731 (after G. Kneller), BM, NPG · attrib. H. Gascar, oils (as a boy), Goodwood House, West Sussex · attrib. T. Hudson, oils (as a boy), Goodwood House, West Sussex · attrib. G. Kneller, oils (as a child), Goodwood House, West Sussex · attrib. G. Kneller, oils (as a young man), Goodwood House, West Sussex · G. Kneller, oils (in youth), Goodwood House, West Sussex · P. Lely, oils (as a child), Goodwood House, West Sussex · W. Wissing, mezzotint (after R. Dunkarton), BM, NPG

Lennox, Charles, second duke of Richmond, second duke of Lennox, and duke of Aubigny in the French nobility (1701–1750), politician and sportsman, was born at Goodwood, near Chichester, on 18 May 1701, the only son of Charles *Lennox, first duke of Richmond, Lennox, and Aubigny (1672–1723), and his wife, Anne (*d.* 1722), the widow of Henry, second Baron Belasyse of Worlaby, and the daughter of Francis, Lord Brudenell. He was the grandson of *Charles II by Louise de Kérouälle, duchess of Portsmouth. He married, at The Hague, on 4 December 1719, Sarah (1706–1751), the eldest daughter and coheir of William Cadogan, first Earl Cadogan, apparently to settle a gambling debt between their parents, and almost immediately left on the grand tour. Accompanied by Tom Hill, his tutor and lifelong friend, he visited the Netherlands, France, Austria, and Italy, and returned to England in 1722. In his absence he was elected MP for Chichester and Newport in March 1722, and sat for Chichester. On his return he entered the army and was made captain in the Royal Regiment of Horse Guards. He was also reunited with his wife, and enjoyed an unusually happy marriage; the couple had twelve children, including Charles *Lennox, third duke of Richmond, George *Lennox, Lady Caroline Lennox [*see* Fox, Caroline, Baroness Holland of Holland (1723–1774)], who later married Henry Fox, Lady Emily Lennox [*see* Fitzgerald, Emilia Mary], who married the first duke of Leinster, Lady Louisa Lennox [*see* Conolly, Lady Louisa Augusta], who married the Irish politician Thomas Conolly, and Lady Sarah Lennox [*see* Napier, Lady Sarah], later wife of the Hon. George Napier.

On 27 May 1723 Lennox succeeded his father as the second duke and inherited Goodwood. Although he never

Charles Lennox, second duke of Richmond, second duke of Lennox, and duke of Aubigny in the French nobility (1701–1750), by Jean Baptiste van Loo

rebuilt the house he commissioned detailed plans from Alessandro Galilei and Colen Campbell, and added a front designed by Matthew Brettingham. He enlarged the estate by purchasing neighbouring manors, populated his park with buildings such as the Shell House, and established a well-known menagerie. He rebuilt Richmond House in Whitehall, based on plans commissioned from Lord Burlington, and encouraged Canaletto to paint the views from the front and rear of the house. In November 1734, on the death of his grandmother, he succeeded to the dukedom of Aubigny, and spent three months in France in 1735 claiming his inheritance. It became his custom to visit Aubigny each autumn, and he often combined these visits with journeys to The Hague to stay with his cousins the Bentincks or his wife's family, the Cadogans. In addition to these titles he was created KB on 27 May 1725 and KG on 16 June 1726.

In adult life Richmond divided his time between a military and a political career. On 8 April 1724 he was appointed aide-de-camp to George I, a position confirmed by George II on his accession. He rose to the rank of brigadier-general (2 July 1739) and lieutenant-general (6 June 1745). He attended George II to the scene of the war in 1743, when he acted as the duke of Newcastle's agent, and was present at Dettingen, while in 1745 he led the government forces in pursuit of the Pretender and assisted at the reduction of Carlisle. He was appointed colonel of the Royal Regiment of Horse Guards on 13 February 1750.

The accession of George II also saw Richmond appointed lord high constable of England, in which capacity he served at the king's coronation (11 October 1727). In the following week he was made a lord of the bedchamber. On 7 January 1735 he was appointed as master of the horse, and two days later he was sworn a member of the privy council. First as a supporter of Robert Walpole's government, and later as a personal friend of the Pelhams, he was a staunch defender of the whig party and the Hanoverian succession. He was a loyal and disinterested servant to the first two Georges, and was 'thoroughly zealous for both the Government and the Administration'. He described himself as 'bred up from a child in Whig principles' (BL, Add. MS 32700, fol. 264), and told Newcastle: 'I never can, nor never will vote against my principles' (BL, Add. MS 32707, fol. 155). He was trusted as an intermediary in the king's quarrel with Frederick, prince of Wales, in 1737–8, and was chosen as one of the lords justices of the realm during George II's absences in Hanover in 1740, 1745, 1748, and 1750. At the conclusion of the War of the Austrian Succession in 1748 he was asked to undertake a special embassy to Paris. In 1749 he gave the well known firework display for the duke of Modena as a codicil to the peace at which the king and the court were present.

Richmond was also a figure of importance in local politics. He was mayor of Chichester in 1735, dominated the city council throughout his life, and succeeded the duke of Somerset as high steward of the city in 1749. He controlled one of the two parliamentary seats in Chichester, on condition that the inhabitants were free to choose the other. He intervened unsuccessfully at New Shoreham in 1734 and Arundel in 1747, but between them he and Newcastle ensured that Sussex returned two government supporters unopposed throughout his life. Other positions included his appointment as grand master of the freemasons of the grand lodge of England in 1724, and as elder brother of Trinity House in 1737 and master from 1741 to 1745. After a long contest with the earl of Pembroke, who earlier had been his rival for the mastership of the horse, he was elected a governor of the Charterhouse in 1739.

With regard to his intellectual pursuits, Richmond was a devotee of opera, and in 1725 was elected a governor of the Royal Academy of Music. Owen MacSwiney, who toured Italy for scores and singers for the academy, reported to Richmond, who also received the dedication of the libretto of the academy's production of Ariosti's *Artasere* in 1724. He was one of the first patrons of Canaletto, and his dining-room at Goodwood was framed with the paintings of allegorical tombs of famous Englishmen commissioned by MacSwiney from contemporary Bolognese and Venetian artists. Richmond's scholarly interest also led him to the study of medicine, science, and antiquity. In 1728 he was awarded a doctorate in law at the University of Cambridge, and in June of that year he was elected a fellow of the Royal College of Physicians. In 1741 he was president of the London Hospital, and he was one of those responsible for the hospital's move to Whitechapel Mount. He was elected a fellow of the Royal Society in 1724, and in September 1728 he was invited to attend a meeting of the Académie Royale des Sciences in Paris. These were not simply honours paid to his rank and station. Richmond patronized early inoculators in Sussex, he collected information on local earthquakes in 1734 and the Chichester smallpox epidemic in 1739, and he observed and reported on Abraham Trembley's experiments on hydra in 1743. He was elected a fellow of the Society of Antiquaries in 1736, and in March 1750 became president.

Richmond's greatest enthusiasm, however, was reserved for sport. In 1730, having commissioned a design from Burlington, he built a hunting lodge at Charlton. In the following year he became master and sole proprietor of the Charlton hounds, and, from that moment, the Charlton hunt became the most important meeting in the country, and remained so until the duke's death in 1750. He was perhaps the most famous patron of cricket in the first half of the eighteenth century. He pioneered organized cricket in Sussex by challenging Sir William Gage to matches in 1725 and 1727. In the latter year, when arranging two cricket matches with Mr Broderick of Peper Harow in Sussex, he drew up the first formal rules of the game. For the next twenty years the duke's team played regular matches in London, Surrey, and Kent, and he acted as sponsor to the famous team which represented Slindon.

Richmond died of cancer of the bladder on 8 August 1750 at his house in Godalming and was buried in Chichester Cathedral. He was survived by his wife, who died on 25 August the following year. Horace Walpole described Richmond as 'vastly lamented' (Walpole, 2.223), and, although Queen Caroline described him as 'so half-witted so bizarre and so grandseigneur, and so mulish, that he is as troublesome from meaning well and comprehending so ill, as if he meant as ill as he comprehends' (J. Hervey, *Some Materials towards Memoirs of the Reign of King George II*, ed. R. Sedgwick, 3 vols., 1931, 3.82), he was always spoken of with affection and respect by his contemporaries. Lord Hervey wrote in his diary that 'there never lived a man of more amiable composition; he was friendly, benevolent, generous, honourable, and thoroughly noble in his way of acting, talking and thinking' (ibid., 3.12), and in a letter to Stephen Fox that 'the Duke of Richmond was cheerful and entertaining which he always is' (*Hervey and his Friends*, 207). For Henry Fielding, who helped Richmond in his campaign against the Sussex smugglers, the duke was 'one of the worthiest of magistrates, as well as the best of men', and wished that 'his life for the good of mankind had been prolonged' (Fielding, *An Enquiry into the Causes of the Late Increase of Robbers*, 1751, 69).

TIMOTHY J. MCCANN

Sources Earl of March [C. H. G. Lennox], *A duke and his friends: the life and letters of the second duke of Richmond*, 2 vols. (1911) • *The correspondence of the dukes of Richmond and Newcastle, 1724–1750*, ed. T. J. McCann, Sussex RS, 73 (1984) • J. Marshall, *The duke who was cricket* (1961) • S. Rees, *The Charlton hunt: a history* (1997) • L. P. Curtis, *Chichester towers* (1966) • S. Tillyard, *Aristocrats: Caroline, Emily, Louisa and Sarah Lennox, 1740–1832* (1994) • M. M. Reese, *Goodwood's oak: the life and times of the third duke of Richmond* (1987) • T. P. Connor, 'Architecture and planting at Goodwood, 1723–1750', *Sussex Archaeological Collections*, 117 (1979), 155–93 • T. J. McCann, '"Much troubled with very rude company": The second duke of Richmond's menagerie at Goodwood', *Sussex Archaeological Collections*, 132 (1994), 143–9 • T. J. McCann, 'Cricket and the Sussex county by-election of 1741', *Sussex Archaeological Collections*, 114 (1976), 121–6 • *Lord Hervey and his friends, 1726–38*, ed. earl of Ilchester [G. S. Holland Fox-Strangways] (1950) • J. Hayes, 'Parliament Street and Canaletto's views of Whitehall', *Burlington Magazine*, 100 (1958), 341–9 • E. Gibson, 'Owen Swiney and the Italian opera in London', *MT*, 125 (1984), 82–6 • G. Knox, '"The tombs of famous Englishmen" as described in the *Letters of Owen Macswiney to the duke of Richmond*', *Arte Veneta*, 37 (1983), 228–35 • Walpole, *Corr.* • GEC, *Peerage* • W. Sussex RO, Goodwood MSS • BL, Holland House MSS • BL, correspondence with Lord Newcastle, Add. MSS 32700, 32707

Archives W. Sussex RO, Goodwood MSS | BL, Newcastle MSS • BL, Holland House MSS • BL, letters to P. Collinson, Add. MSS 28726–28727 • BL, letters to Lord Hardwicke, Add. MSS 35586–35601 • BL, correspondence with Lord Newcastle, Add. MSS 32688–32818, 33066 • BL, Sloane MSS, letters to Hans Sloane • Devon RO, Seymour MSS, letters to duke of Somerset

Likenesses M. Dahl?, oils (in youth), Goodwood • J. Faber, mezzotint (after J. B. van Loo), BM, NPG • J. Faber, mezzotint (after J. Vanderbank), BM, NPG • G. Kneller?, double portrait, oils (with his wife), Goodwood • G. Kneller?, oils (in youth), Goodwood • J. B. van Loo, portrait; Sothebys, 13 Nov 1996, lot 39 [*see illus.*] • J. B. van Loo, portrait, oils, Goodwood • W. Smith, oils, Goodwood • Zoffany, oils, Goodwood • portrait, Deene Park

Lennox, Charles, third duke of Richmond, third duke of Lennox, and duke of Aubigny in the French nobility (1735–1806), politician, the son and heir of Charles *Lennox, second duke of Richmond, Lennox, and Aubigny (1701–1750), politician, and his wife, Sarah (1706–1751), the daughter of William Cadogan, first Earl Cadogan, was born on 22 February 1735 in Arlington Street, Westminster, London.

Education and early career Descended from Charles II and his mistress Louise de Kéroualle, Lennox was styled earl of March until succeeding his father in 1750. He entered Westminster School in 1746. Much of his education, however, came under the tutelage of Abraham Trembley, a biologist who became famous for proving that the marine polyp was a form of animal life rather than a plant. Basing themselves in Geneva, Trembley and his pupil travelled extensively on the continent, making the acquaintance of Montesquieu, Fontenelle, and Frederick the Great among others. Several months were spent at the University of Leiden, where the duke took a degree in 1753.

While on the continent Richmond was attracted to a military career. His brother-in-law and guardian, Henry Fox, was secretary at war and well placed to assist. Commissioned an ensign in the 2nd foot guards in 1751, Richmond was made a captain in the 20th foot (1753) and lieutenant-colonel in the 33rd foot (1756), with which he served in the Netherlands and Germany. In 1758 he was made colonel of the 72nd foot. In that year he took part in

Charles Lennox, third duke of Richmond, third duke of Lennox, and duke of Aubigny in the French nobility (1735–1806), by George Romney, 1775–7

the raid on Cherbourg and the following year was at Minden, where he served as aide-de-camp to Prince Frederick of Brunswick. Although he left active service in 1760, he retained a lifelong interest in military affairs and later served for thirteen years as master-general of the ordnance. He was periodically promoted through the general officer ranks, becoming a field marshal in 1792, and he took a keen interest in the Sussex militia after becoming lord lieutenant of the county in 1763.

As a young man Richmond developed a wide range of interests which he pursued throughout his life. He was especially fond of art. A founder member of the Society of Arts in 1754, the duke created a sculpture gallery at his house in Whitehall in 1758 that was open to 'any painter, carver, sculptor or other artist and youth over twelve years of age, to whom the study of statuary might be useful' (Reese, 58); it was ultimately taken over by the Incorporated Society of Artists in 1770. He was also a patron of George Stubbs and George Romney. He was elected a fellow of the Royal Society in 1756. Early on he embarked on a long-term project of expanding and developing his estates around his country seat of Goodwood in Sussex. Here he indulged enthusiasms for scientific agriculture, building, fox-hunting (spending £7000 on a heated kennel for his dogs), and horse-racing. Building the famous racecourse at Goodwood was the last major project of his life.

Richmond married, on 1 April 1757, Lady Mary Bruce (1740–1796), the daughter and coheir of Charles Bruce, third earl of Ailesbury and fourth earl of Elgin, and his third wife, Lady Caroline Campbell. Horace Walpole described the marriage as 'the perfectest match in the world; youth, beauty, riches, alliances, and all the blood of all the kings from Robert Bruce to Charles II' (Reese, 65). Though childless, the union was happy, if not characterized by perfect fidelity: the duke provided in his will for three illegitimate daughters by his housekeeper.

Richmond and the Rockingham whigs Richmond returned to England and became more involved in politics in 1760. His prospects for a successful career must have seemed promising at the dawn of George III's reign. He enjoyed an income of about £19,000 p.a., most of it coming from a tax of 1*s*. per chaldron on all coal shipped from Newcastle (a grant originally made by Charles II to his grandfather, the first duke), connections with many powerful families, and an appointment as a lord of the bedchamber in November 1760. Moreover, his younger sister, Lady Sarah Lennox, was temporarily the object of the new king's affections. Things went awry, however, as Richmond promptly offended the king by resigning the bedchamber after only a month when his brother, Lord George Lennox, was passed over for a place as one of the king's aides-de-camp. The king's dislike of Richmond would persist over the next two decades.

Although he was counted a follower of his brother-in-law Henry Fox, Richmond stood on the fringe of politics until the formation of the first Rockingham administration in the late summer of 1765. Through the auspices of his uncle the third earl of Albemarle, and the duke of Cumberland, he was named ambassador to France and later made a privy councillor. He had hoped for something better and accepted the position reluctantly, but he acquitted himself well before returning to England in the spring of 1766 to support the administration's repeal of the Stamp Act. Although he had taken his seat in the upper house in 1756, the controversy over repeal marked his first important participation in parliamentary debates; after hearing him speak Edmund Burke predicted: 'I think he will become a considerable man' (*Correspondence*, 1.244). Following the resignation of the duke of Grafton as one of the secretaries of state in April, Richmond was eventually named his successor after more veteran politicians declined to serve. The accession of one so inexperienced was seen by some as a sign of the ministry's weakness, and Richmond held the position for only seven weeks before it fell. Offended by the earl of Chatham's offer of another embassy, he went into opposition and gradually developed close political relationships with Rockingham and Burke. He provided Chatham with a rude welcome to the Lords on the latter's second appearance in the house on 10 December 1766; the two exchanged angry words when Richmond accused Chatham of behaving with insolence. Other peers intervened lest the altercation get out of hand, and both men apologized to the house. Richmond proceeded to establish himself as a frequent and able speaker, thereafter opposing the Chatham and Grafton administrations on almost every topic that came before parliament.

Richmond, however, never quite penetrated the inner circle of the Rockingham party's leadership. For one thing, his beloved seat at Goodwood placed him at a considerable distance from the rest of the party's leaders, most of whom were based in the north and adjoining areas of the midlands. Richmond also lacked a large following in the Commons, as his electoral influence was limited to nearby Chichester. Nevertheless he became one of the most visible of opposition figures. During 1771 he took over the leadership of the parliamentary party when Rockingham was forced by his wife's ill health to remain at Bath. He did a creditable job, keeping the party's forces together, maintaining an uneasy alliance with Chatham and his followers (now in opposition), and organizing the main opposition attack on the North ministry's handling of the crisis with Spain over the Falkland Islands.

The opposition made little dent in North's majorities, and Richmond was periodically despondent at the ineffectiveness of opposition efforts. His restless nature inclined him to action, however. In 1773 he took the lead in resisting the North ministry's plans to reform the East India Company. Richmond fought a two-front battle, rallying opposition to the ministry's proposals in the company's court of proprietors and then leading a rather ragged effort in the House of Lords to prevent passage of the ministry's legislation. He failed on both counts. Equally unsuccessful were his efforts to secure passage of dissenters relief bills in 1772 and 1773, a cause consistent with his belief in religious toleration.

By 1774 the worsening relations between Great Britain and the American colonies had come to dominate politics. Richmond played a leading role in his party's unsuccessful efforts to oppose the legislation that brought the crisis to a head in 1774 and 1775. His opposition on American questions was comprehensive and originally reflected the Rockinghamite view that, while parliament possessed legislative supremacy over the colonies (as stated in the Declaratory Act of 1766 that Richmond had supported), it should not use its power to force the colonists to submit to parliamentary taxation. He resisted the North administration at every step, speaking frequently in the upper house and offering a variety of resolutions and protests. Like many of his fellow whigs, he believed that curtailment of American liberty would herald oppression at home. Once hostilities began he continued his opposition, and he was relentless in criticizing the ministry's management of the war effort. He was one of the first of the Rockingham party to take the view that the Declaratory Act needed to be repealed as a barrier to a settlement, and he was an early convert to the idea of American independence. His pertinacity made him one of the most visible members of the opposition and one of those most resented by North's supporters. In 1780 Charles Jenkinson, tiring of parliament's having to deal with a steady stream of motions from the duke, termed him a 'plagueing fellow' and remarked: 'If there were two dukes of Richmond in this country, I would not live in it' (Olson, 9n). After France entered the war, references were made in the ministerialist press to Richmond's French ancestry (he had officially registered his French dukedom in 1776). When in 1780 the

Morning Post characterized him as a traitor, Richmond responded by successfully bringing an action for libel against the paper's editor, Henry Bate. His attacks on ministers and others involved in the war effort were often couched in personal terms and did little to win him friends. In 1779 his reproach of Lord Chancellor Thurlow's modest origins brought the famous retort that Richmond's own presence in the Lords was the result of 'the accident of an accident' (Reese, 151); in 1781 his criticism of Lord Rawdon's role in the execution of the South Carolina militia leader Isaac Hayne almost led to a duel before Richmond issued an embarrassing retraction.

Richmond sought co-operation with other members of the opposition, cultivating for several years a friendship with the earl of Shelburne, a leading Chathamite. At other times his efforts served only to dramatize the differences between the Rockingham and Chathamite wings of the opposition. After France entered the war in 1778, Richmond and his party colleagues argued that the American colonies should be given up so that the war effort could be concentrated against France. Chatham clung to the hope that somehow the war could be ended with the empire intact if more loosely structured. It was, in fact, amid an impassioned reply to Richmond's motion to withdraw British forces from North America that Chatham dramatically collapsed on the floor of the House of Lords on 7 April 1778 in what proved to be his last speech.

Richmond and parliamentary reform It is as an advocate for parliamentary reform that Richmond is most remembered. He showed a fondness for radical causes early in his political career: in 1765 he visited John Wilkes during the latter's exile in Paris, and he later supported Wilkes's attempts to have his outlawry overturned and his election for Middlesex validated, alienating his Fox in-laws in the process. By the later 1770s the leaders of the opposition detected a sense of crisis in the country, and a constant theme of their rhetoric was that the American war was a catastrophe brought on by an incompetent ministry kept in power by a corrupt system of government. Various schemes for reform emerged. Many of Richmond's party colleagues placed their hope in a campaign for economical reform that would reduce the patronage available to the ministry, while others were attracted to the association movement led by Christopher Wyvill, which advocated, among other things, the reform of parliament by an enlarged membership from county constituencies in the House of Commons. Richmond, though supporting the efforts of such reformers (and serving on the Westminster committee that was part of Wyvill's movement), went further in his prescription for reform. He came to believe that reform, to be lasting, must be broadly based and focused on parliament. Attracted to the pamphlet literature circulating out of doors, he was particularly taken with John Cartwright's *The Legislative Rights of the Commonalty Vindicated, or, Take your Choice!*, first published in 1776, which advocated manhood suffrage for all over eighteen, annual parliaments, more equal representation, and vote by ballot. The two became friends, and in 1780 Richmond joined Cartwright and other advocates of reform in the Society for Constitutional Information. He drew up a bill providing for manhood suffrage, equal election districts, and annual parliaments—Richmond differed from Cartwright in feeling that voting should be public—and on 2 June 1780 he asked leave to introduce his bill into the House of Lords. His timing was exceptionally unfortunate—the Gordon riots began that day and the capital was in disorder. Leave was refused, and the riots created an atmosphere that was hardly conducive to reform. Richmond remained committed to the cause, however, and in 1783 for the first time published his plan for parliamentary reform in a pamphlet, *Letter to Colonel Sharman*, ostensibly in response to questions from the Irish Volunteers. His advocacy of such measures alienated him from many of his Rockinghamite colleagues, especially Burke, who had declined Richmond's request for copies of his own anti-reform speeches so that the duke's presentation of his bill could be made more effective. Richmond's ideas placed him among the more extreme reformers of the day, and his pamphlet was used as an argument for parliamentary reform for many years to come; it was reprinted in 1792, 1795, 1797, 1817, 1824, and 1859. He himself later changed his views in response to the French Revolution, and by 1795 he was condemning agitation for parliamentary reform: 'nothing less is meant by it than to overturn the Constitution' (Reese, 220).

Richmond and the crisis of 1782–1784 From 1782 Richmond's reform activity was increasingly overshadowed by the political crisis that marked the end of the American war. As the North ministry's position became untenable following the British surrender at Yorktown, members of the opposition were brought into office by a reluctant George III. Rather than yield to a 'party' administration composed largely of Rockingham and his followers, the king successfully insisted on one that included other elements of the opposition, notably Shelburne (with whom Richmond had become close) and the remnants of Chatham's followers. The involvement of Richmond in the arrangements was a point insisted upon by Rockingham, and the king moderated his personal dislike of the duke (who for his part apologized for his long absence from court) and approved his appointment as master-general of the Ordnance with a seat in the cabinet. He was also made a knight of the Garter (17 April 1782). Richmond found a new focus for his energy at the Ordnance and immediately began to develop plans for an overhaul of its operations. Formed in March 1782, the second Rockingham administration lasted but three months before being terminated by the marquess's death. The king then turned to Shelburne, whereupon most of the Rockingham whigs, led by Charles James Fox, Richmond's nephew, and the duke of Portland, resigned. Richmond may have hoped to become Rockingham's successor, and his friendship with Shelburne had cooled somewhat after the latter had preferred the earl of Pembroke to Lord George Lennox for the military governorship of Portsmouth. However, Richmond stuck with Shelburne, and retained his position in the new cabinet. His effort to prevent resignations by other members of the Rockingham administration was largely unsuccessful and resented by his nephew. Richmond's situation grew increasingly uncomfortable, however, as he chafed at Shelburne's failure to keep the cabinet informed of progress in the peace negotiations then going on in Paris. As details became known, Richmond became more alienated. He felt that the proposed cessions of territory to the United States were too large, and he was shocked at Shelburne's apparent willingness to cede Gibraltar to Spain. In January 1783 he ceased attending cabinet meetings, though he kept the Ordnance, where his enthusiasm for reform continued unabated. When the treaties came before the Lords the following month, Richmond told the house he 'freely owned he did not like the terms of the treaties', but that 'he should not vote on the question' (Cobbett, *Parl. hist.*, 23.385). The peace preliminaries narrowly passed the Lords but were defeated in the Commons by the emerging coalition of the followers of Fox and North, leading to Shelburne's resignation. Richmond was not on good terms with his nephew and was horrified by his union with North. With the greatest reluctance the king accepted a coalition ministry nominally headed by the duke of Portland. Richmond declined Portland's offer of retaining the Ordnance or becoming secretary at war, stating that he could never serve with North and his followers. He thereafter bent his efforts towards overturning the coalition. The occasion came with the coalition's India Bill. After the king let it be known that he would consider any peer who voted for the bill as his enemy, Richmond met with William Pitt the younger and lords Temple, Gower, and Thurlow to plan its defeat in the Lords. He subsequently took a major role in the key debate of 15 December 1783 that decided the bill's fate, skilfully turning the language of Rockingham's protest of 1773 against North's Regulating Act against those of the marquess's former followers who now supported the coalition. In the aftermath of the coalition's dismissal Richmond and others rallied around Pitt, and Richmond eventually agreed to join his administration by returning to the Ordnance. He advised against an immediate dissolution of parliament and provided valuable moral support to Pitt as he waged an uphill but ultimately successful battle in the Commons to secure the minimum legislation necessary to keep the government going.

Richmond and Pitt Richmond was initially one of the more influential members of Pitt's cabinet. After the defeat of Pitt's relatively modest parliamentary reform proposal in 1785, Richmond increasingly devoted his energies to reforming the Ordnance. Here he had already succeeded in substituting salaries for fees in paying departmental office-holders. He worked to make the Ordnance more efficient by reforming its finances. He began a topographical survey of the south coast that ultimately became the Ordnance Survey and organized the forerunner of the Royal Horse Artillery. He also fostered several improvements in small arms. Less successful was his plan for erecting major new fortifications to protect the dockyards at Plymouth and Portsmouth, another interest he shared with John Cartwright. His proposal to spend £400,000 over eight years created controversy and caused parliament to appoint a committee of professional military and naval officers to evaluate the plan. Reports that he sought to influence the committee weakened the impact of its favourable report. Despite Pitt's active support in the Commons, in 1786 the lower house defeated the scheme by the casting vote of the speaker. The defeat was a major blow to Richmond's political prestige and helped to sustain the public image of him, satirized in *The Rolliad*, as lavish in the expenditure of public money but miserly with his own. Richmond actually spent his own money freely, and despite attempts at economy left £180,000 in debts at his death.

Richmond gradually became less active in the cabinet and more distanced from the prime minister. He resented the elevation in 1790 of Pitt's cousin William Grenville to the peerage so that he could take the ministerial lead in the House of Lords. By the time war with revolutionary France began in 1793 he was often on bad terms with other members of the cabinet, especially Henry Dundas. He made a further enemy in the king's second son, the duke of York. York had fought a duel in 1789 with Charles Lennox, Richmond's nephew and heir, and in 1794 he blamed Richmond's management of the Ordnance for his failure to take Dunkirk. Moreover, Richmond's earlier advocacy of parliamentary reform came back to embarrass the ministry at a time when it was attempting to stifle political radicalism. In 1794 two members of the London Corresponding Society for Parliamentary and Social Reform on trial for treason, Thomas Hardy and John Horne Tooke, mounted a successful defence by citing Richmond's 1783 pamphlet as the basis of their platform and summoned Richmond and Pitt as witnesses. By January 1795 Richmond had become a liability, and Pitt replaced him with Marquess Cornwallis. The last member of Pitt's original cabinet to leave office, Richmond blamed his removal on the duke of York.

Richmond never held political office again, though he retained his position on the staff and was made colonel of the Royal Regiment of Horse Guards. He did make periodic forays into politics, eventually associating himself with the prince of Wales. In 1798 he tried to intercede with the government on behalf of another nephew, the Irish rebel Lord Edward Fitzgerald. He remained keenly interested in military matters. He opposed Pitt's Additional Force Bill and effectively frustrated its implementation in Sussex. His last intervention in parliamentary politics came in support of Lord King's motion to establish a committee on defence in 1804. He died on 29 December 1806 and was buried in Chichester Cathedral.

Political character and significance Through a career marked by much frustration, Richmond was one of the most visible and erratic political figures of his generation. He was undoubtedly possessed of intelligence, oratorical ability, humanitarian impulses, and persistence, but his abilities were often dissipated among changing enthusiasms or obsession with details. William Grenville noted that his mind, though 'ingenious and acute … and in diligence and perseverance rarely equalled', was offset by other tendencies: 'In office, he laboured too much at detached objects and minute details, harassing to his inferiors and perplexing to himself' (Jupp, 45). Nathaniel Wraxall remarked that 'he was ever active detecting and exposing abuses, real or imaginary' (*Historical and Posthumous Memoirs*, 2.60). Richmond once admitted to Burke: 'I pass in the world for very obstinate, wrong-headed, and tenacious of my opinions' (Olson, 12), to which list his contemporaries might have added tactlessness. He made for a difficult colleague. Rockingham was the only close political associate with whom he did not eventually fall out, and even that relationship would likely have been put at risk had the marquess lived long enough for their differences over parliamentary reform to come to a head. Richmond also had a remarkable ability to inspire dislike. In the world of high politics this was likely a result of his habit of making personal and public attacks. His final falling out with Shelburne (by then marquess of Lansdowne) in 1787 was typical, taking the form of a public wrangle in the House of Lords, diverting consideration from Pitt's commercial treaty with France, over whether Shelburne had approved of Richmond's fortification plan in 1783. When rumours of a duel proved to be false, Sir Gilbert Elliot remarked: 'The general wish I think was that one should be shot and the other hanged for it' (*Life and Letters*, 1.135). His personal unpopularity with members of the lower house was thought by many to have been responsible for the defeat of his fortification scheme in 1786. Despite his reputation as a reformer, Richmond never achieved popularity with the wider public. In particular his income from the coal duties (which he sold to the government in 1800 for £728,333) was often resented as burdensome to the poor. His abandonment of the cause of reform in the 1790s left him open to the charge of apostasy. Yet, despite its disappointments and contradictions, his career was not without impact. He was for almost two decades the most visible and forceful opposition presence in the House of Lords, enlivening debates and raising questions that helped to define the politics of the day. In office, specific reforms at the Ordnance proved fruitful and lasting, and his proposal for parliamentary reform became a permanent part of the radical tradition.

WILLIAM C. LOWE

Sources A. Olson, *The radical duke* (1961) • M. M. Reese, *Goodwood's oak* (1987) • J. Cannon, *Parliamentary reform, 1640–1832* (1972) • J. Cannon, *The Fox–North coalition: crisis of the constitution, 1782–4* (1969) • *The correspondence of Edmund Burke*, ed. T. W. Copeland and others, 10 vols. (1958–78) • I. R. Christie, *Wilkes, Wyvill and reform: the parliamentary reform movement in British politics, 1760–1785* (1962) • J. Ehrman, *The younger Pitt*, 3 vols. (1969–96) • *The correspondence of King George the Third from 1760 to December 1783*, ed. J. Fortescue, 6 vols. (1927–8) • Cobbett, *Parl. hist.*, 23.385 • H. V. Bowen, *Revenue and return* (1991) • L. G. Mitchell, *Charles James Fox and the disintegration of the whig party, 1782–1794* (1971) • *The life and correspondence of Major Cartwright*, ed. F. D. Cartwright, 2 vols. (1826) • G. Thomas, earl of Albemarle [G. T. Keppel], *Memoirs of the marquis of Rockingham and his contemporaries*, 2 vols. (1852) • *The historical and the posthumous memoirs of Sir Nathaniel William Wraxall, 1772–1784*, ed. H. B. Wheatley, 5 vols. (1884) • *Life and letters of Sir Gilbert Elliot, first earl of Minto, from 1751 to 1806*, ed. countess of Minto [E. E. E. Elliot-Murray-Kynynmound], 3 vols. (1874) • GEC, *Peerage* • P. Jupp, *Lord Grenville, 1759–1834* (1985)

Archives BL, corresp., Loan MS 57 • W. Sussex RO, corresp. and papers | Birm. CA, letters to Matthew Boulton • BL, letters to J. Caryll, Add. MSS 28233–28235 • BL, letters to James Adair, Add. MSS 50829–50830, 53800–53815 • BL, letters to P. Collinson, Add. MS 28727 • BL, corresp. with Lord Grenville, Add. MS 58937 • BL, corresp. with Lord Holland, Add. MSS 51424, 51802 • BL, corresp. with duke of Leeds, Egerton MS 3498 • BL, corresp. with duke of Newcastle, earls of Chichester, Add. MSS 32723–33112, *passim* • Bodl. Oxf., corresp. with Sarah Napier • CKS, letters to William Pitt • Glos. RO, corresp. with Granville Sharp • NRA, priv. coll., letters to Lord Selborne • PRO, letters to William Pitt, PRO 30/8 • Sheff. Arch., corresp. with Edmund Burke • Sheff. Arch., letters to Lord Rockingham • U. Nott. L., letters to duke of Portland

Likenesses oils, *c.*1740 (as a child), Goodwood House, West Sussex • J. Reynolds, oils, exh. RA 1758, Goodwood House, West Sussex • G. Stubbs, group portrait, oils, *c.*1762, Goodwood House, West Sussex • G. Romney, oils, 1775–7, NPG [*see illus.*] • J. Sayers, etching, pubd 1782 (after himself), NPG • W. Evans, stipple, pubd 1808 (after G. Romney), BM, NPG • attrib. P. Batoni, oils, Goodwood House, West Sussex • J. S. Copley, group portrait, oils (*The collapse of the earl of Chatham in the House of Lords, 7 July 1778*), Tate collection; on loan to NPG • C. Mengs, oils, Goodwood House, West Sussex • G. Romney, oils, Goodwood House, West Sussex • G. Stubbs, group portrait, Goodwood House, West Sussex

Wealth at death estimated own income at £28,550, March 1799, incl. £18,355 from coal duties; sold coal duties to government for £728,333, 1800; debts. *c.*£180,000 at death: Reese, *Goodwood's oak*, 233–6

Lennox, Charles, fourth duke of Richmond and fourth duke of Lennox (1764–1819), army officer, born in Scotland (reportedly in a barn when his mother was on a fishing party) on 9 September 1764, was the eldest son of Lieutenant-General Lord George Henry *Lennox (1737–1805) and his wife, Louisa, eldest daughter of William Henry Kerr, fourth marquess of Lothian. He was educated privately by Mr Kempson.

Lennox, who was secretary to his uncle, the master-general of the ordnance, from 1784 to 1795, entered the army in 1785. While captain in the Coldstream Guards in 1789, after the duke of York complained about the king's having appointed Lennox to a company in the duke's regiment without consulting him, he challenged the duke to a duel which occurred on 26 May on Wimbledon Common, Lennox's bullet grazing the duke's curl, and the duke firing in the air. The duke declared that he had no animosity against Lennox, and had merely come out to give him satisfaction. The officers of the guards having passed a resolution that Lennox had 'behaved with courage, but from the peculiarity of the circumstances not with judgment', Lennox subsequently exchanged with Lord Strathnairn his captaincy in the guards for the command (lieutenant-colonel) of the 35th foot, then stationed in Edinburgh.

On 3 July, before joining the 35th, he fought a duel in a field near Uxbridge Road, London, with Theophilus Swift, who had published a pamphlet criticizing his character. Swift was wounded, but not fatally. When Lennox joined the 35th in Edinburgh, the castle was illuminated in his honour. He was also presented with the freedom of the city, and elected an honorary member of the corporation of goldsmiths. He made himself popular with the 35th by playing cricket with the soldiers, then an unusual thing for an officer to do. He married on 9 September 1789 Lady Charlotte Gordon (1768–1842), eldest daughter of Alexander *Gordon, fourth duke of Gordon, and they had seven sons, including the writer William Pitt *Lennox, and seven daughters. She was described as 'excessively proud, and disdainful of persons of inferior rank' (GEC, *Peerage*, 10, 1945, 844) and allegedly ruined her husband by gambling.

Lennox served with the 35th in the Leeward islands. At St Dominica in 1794 the regiment was afflicted with yellow fever, 40 officers and 600 rank and file succumbing. In 1795 Lennox obtained the rank of colonel, and was appointed aide-de-camp to the king, and in 1798 he became major-general. In 1800 he was made colonel-commandant, and in 1803 was promoted colonel of the 35th. He became lieutenant-general in 1805, and general in 1814. In 1790, through the influence of his uncle, the duke of Richmond, he became MP for Sussex, in succession to his father, as a supporter of Pitt, and he continued to represent the county until he succeeded to the dukedom of Richmond and Lennox on the death of his uncle, on 29 December 1806. On 1 April 1807 he was sworn of the privy council, and, after three others had refused, was appointed lord lieutenant of Ireland, Colonel Arthur Wellesley (afterwards duke of Wellington) being chief secretary. He spent much, maintaining quasi-regal state, and, although favouring protestants and against Roman Catholic emancipation, was reportedly popular. In 1811–12 he attempted to prevent the establishment of an elected Catholic assembly. KG in March 1812, he was lord lieutenant until 1813. He then resided with his family in Brussels. He held the posts of governor of Hull, 1813–14, and Plymouth, 1814 until his death. On 15 June, the night before Quatre Bras, the duke and duchess gave, at their rented house in the rue de la Blanchisserie, their ball, 'the most famous ball in history' (Longford, 416). Richmond was present at the battle of Waterloo, unofficially with Wellington's suite, though Wellington had tried to send him home: 'Duke, you have no business here' (Longford, 451).

Lennox 'was a great lover and patron of athletic sports, indeed for a foot race, few men [were|] able to compete with him' (A. Haygarth, *Scores and Biographies*, 1862, 1.63). He came of a family who had contributed a great deal to the growth of cricket in the eighteenth century and he himself played the game for some twenty-two seasons. He was 'a good and successful batsman and an excellent wicket-keeper' (ibid.). He was president of the Hambledon Club and one of the founders of the Marylebone Cricket Club (1787) which superseded the White Conduit Club, of which he was also a member. He retained his enthusiasm for cricket all his life, arranging a match at Brussels just before the battle of Waterloo and supporting the game in Canada during his time as governor-general.

The Richmonds continued to live in Brussels until 1818 when Richmond was appointed governor-in-chief of British North America. He reached Quebec in July 1818. The house of assembly was dominated by Louis-Joseph Papineau's party, and they and Richmond disagreed over financing of government. In 1819 Richmond, determined to maintain the royal prerogative, prorogued the assembly. In the summer of 1819 he went on an extensive tour of Upper and Lower Canada. He died in agony in a barn a few miles from Richmond, Upper Canada, of hydrophobia, on 20 August 1819. The disease probably resulted from a bite on the hand by a newly purchased young pet fox at William Henry (Sorel, Quebec). He was buried on 4 September in the cathedral of the Holy Trinity, Quebec. He was succeeded as duke by his eldest son, Charles Gordon-*Lennox (1791–1860). His third daughter, Georgiana, born in 1795, married on 7 June 1824 William, twentieth Baron de Ros, and died on 16 December 1891.

T. F. HENDERSON, *rev.* ROGER T. STEARN

Sources GEC, *Peerage* • *GM*, 1st ser., 59 (1789) • *GM*, 1st ser., 89/2 (1819) • HoP, *Commons* • J. Paterson, *Kay's Edinburgh portraits: a series of anecdotal biographies chiefly of Scotchmen*, ed. J. Maidment, 2 vols. (1885) • *Short review of the recent affair of honor between the duke of York and Lieutenant Colonel Lenox* (1789) • T. Swift, *Letter to the king* (1789) • E. Longford [E. H. Pakenham, countess of Longford], *Wellington*, 1: *The years of the sword* (1969) • A. J. Guy, ed., *The road to Waterloo: the British army and the struggle against revolutionary and Napoleonic France, 1793–1815* (1990) • G. F. G. Stanley, 'Lennox, Charles', *DCB*, vol. 5 • T. W. Moody and others, eds., *A new history of Ireland*, 5: *Ireland under the Union, 1801–1870* (1989)

Archives NL Ire., correspondence relating to Ireland • Queens University Archives, Kingston, Canada, MSS relating to Canada • W. Sussex RO | BL, correspondence with Lord Liverpool, Add. MSS 38242–56, 38320–28, 38568, *passim* • BL, letters to Sir Robert Peel, Add. MSS 40185–86 • E. Sussex RO, correspondence with Lord Gage • NA Scot., correspondence with Lord Melville

Likenesses G. Shepheard, watercolour drawing, *c*.1795, Lord's, London, MCC collection; *see illus. in* Hambledon cricket club (*act. c*.1750–*c*.1796) • J. Hoppner?, oils, 1809, Goodwood, West Sussex • J. Kay, etching, BM, NPG • J. Nollekens, bust (probably fourth duke), Goodwood, West Sussex • attrib. S. J. Rochard?, miniature, NPG • G. Romney, oils (in youth), Beaverbrook Art Gallery, Fredericton, New Brunswick, Canada • W. Theed jun., bust, Royal Military Academy, Sandhurst • oils, Goodwood, West Sussex • sketch (in youth), Goodwood, West Sussex

Lennox, Charles Gordon-, fifth duke of Richmond and fifth duke of Lennox (1791–1860), landowner and politician, was born Charles Lennox on 3 August 1791, the eldest of the seven sons and seven daughters of Charles *Lennox, fourth duke of Richmond (1764–1819), and his wife, Charlotte (1768–1842), daughter of Alexander *Gordon, fourth duke of Gordon. He was educated at Westminster School, and in 1810 he joined the 13th dragoons. Lord March—by which courtesy title he was known until he succeeded to the dukedom in 1819—served briefly as aide-de-camp to his father, at that time lord lieutenant of Ireland, and then went to the Peninsula where he served as aide-de-camp and assistant military secretary to the duke of Wellington from July 1810 to July 1814 and was seriously wounded at the battle of Orthes in February 1813. He was at Waterloo, as aide-de-camp to the prince of Orange, subsequently rejoining Wellington's staff. In 1816 he retired from the army on half pay, as a lieutenant-colonel. He received the silver war medal with clasps: years later, in 1847, largely as a result of his persistence in raising the matter in the Lords, the Peninsular War medal was at last

Charles Gordon-Lennox, fifth duke of Richmond and fifth duke of Lennox (1791–1860), by James Andrews (after John Andrews, 1841)

awarded to all the veterans, who gratefully presented him with a handsome piece of plate in 1851.

Lord March was MP for the family seat of Chichester from October 1812 until his succession to the dukedom on the death of his father, then governor-in-chief of British North America, in November 1819. With his war service on the one hand and his marriage on the other he did not have much time for the House of Commons. On 10 April 1817 he married Caroline (1796–1874), eldest daughter of Henry William *Paget, first marquess of Anglesey, and his first wife, Caroline Villiers. They had five sons and five daughters, the eldest, Charles Henry Gordon-*Lennox, born in February 1818. After the end of the war Richmond concentrated on racehorses, family life, and farming on the family estate. With the help of his close friend Lord George Bentinck he developed the annual race meeting at Goodwood, which had been started in 1801 by his great-uncle the third duke, into one of the outstanding social and sporting events in the racing calendar. Invitations to the great house parties at Goodwood were much prized. The duke was also a racehorse owner, and his horses won the Oaks in 1827 and 1845. He became a steward of the Jockey Club in 1831. A considerate landlord and keen aristocratic farmer, he helped in the improvement of the breed of Southdown sheep, and was a popular choice as vice-president of the Smithfield Club in 1832, and as president of the Royal Agricultural Society from 1845 until his death. 'The Duke of Richmond appears nowhere to such advantage as in his own house', Lord Stanley noted in 1851,

> Surrounded by a tenantry among whom he is deservedly popular, engaged in the personal superintendence of his large property, or in local business, which he understands well, extending an abundant hospitality, not to a few fashionable friends, but to all in the rank of gentleman with whom he has anything to do—enjoying life, and helping others to enjoy it—he is far more in his element than when addressing the Lords, or ranting at a provincial meeting. (*Disraeli, Derby and the Conservative Party*, 62)

It was, however, through addressing the Lords that he became one of the leading public representatives of the agricultural interest.

In the Lords in the later 1820s Richmond spoke about corn and wool, the latter in such astonishing fiscal and statistical detail that Bentinck was credited with ghosting his speech (*Hansard* 3, 19, 5 May 1828, 345). Greville commented waspishly that

> he happens to have his wits, such as they are, about him, and has been quick and neat in one or two little speeches … [he did very well on the wool question]. Besides, his fortune consists in great measure of wool, he lives in the country, is well versed in rural affairs and the business of quarter sessions, has a certain calibre of understanding, is prejudiced, narrow-minded, illiterate, and ignorant, good-looking, good-humoured, and unaffected, tedious, prolix, unassuming, and a duke. There would not have been so much to say about him if an idea had not existed in the minds of some people of making him Prime Minister and successor to the Duke of Wellington. (*Greville Memoirs*, 1.204–5)

This was in 1829, and over Catholic emancipation he emerged as an ultra-tory, sharply critical of his old commander, Wellington, and persuaded that parliament needed to be made more representative of 'weighty' opinion to prevent any repetition of such scandalous measures. He did not have much of a following among the tories, but Earl Grey offered him a place in the reform ministry (November 1830) all the same. He accepted the offer of the Ordnance department, but the army chiefs were so indignant at the idea of a half-pay lieutenant-colonel being in command that the offer had to be withdrawn; he regarded the alternative suggestion of becoming master of the horse as insulting, and in the end ingloriously settled for being postmaster-general. He promptly went down into Sussex, it being the time of the Swing riots, and 'had a battle with a mob of 200 labourers, whom he beat with fifty of his own farmers and tenants, harangued them, and sent them away in good humour' (*Greville Memoirs*, 2.70). He was a combative supporter of the reform bills, at times savaging his former tory friends, and in November 1831 startled the cabinet by suddenly suggesting 'extending the right of representation to Colonies, whose members, without appearing so, would be, he said, a sure counteraction to the force of popular clamour and temporary excitement in the House of Commons' (A. D. Kriegel, ed., *The Holland House Diaries*, 1977, 86). This exhausted his vein of radical conservatism, and in May 1834 he resigned, along with Graham, Ripon, and Stanley, on conventional Anglican objections to the appropriation clause in the Irish Church Bill, and he moved, after a spell on the cross-benches, back into the Conservative camp.

In January 1842, strangely in view of his later stand on

the corn laws, Peel offered him a cabinet position as lord privy seal, to replace the duke of Buckingham who had resigned over the proposal to alter the sliding-scale duties. This was declined. Increasingly alarmed by the activities of the Anti-Corn Law League, which launched its rural campaign in 1843, uncertain of the strength of the government's attachment to the corn laws, and unsettled by the independence of the tenant farmers in mobilizing in self-defence under the leadership of Robert Baker of Writtle, Essex, Richmond took the lead in January 1844 in the formation of an agricultural protection society, with himself as president, Buckingham as vice-president, and the support of forty or fifty landlords, the tenant farmers of Baker's association, and similar bodies in several other counties. The society quickly became known as the Anti-League, but although it attracted considerable support in the country Richmond's call to the membership to be 'up and doing' in December 1845 did not have any noticeable effect on events, although it did something to prevent any general repudiation of the tenantry's attachment to their landlords. Richmond himself was vehement in his opposition to repeal and spoke repeatedly in the Lords against the Corn Importation Bill, most notably in the second reading debate when he claimed that repeal 'will shake the very foundations of the Throne, will cripple the Church, endanger our institutions, and convert our hitherto happy and contented people from a state of comparative comfort into one of misery and wretchedness' (*Hansard* 3, 86, 25 May 1846, 1109). He supported the protectionist party of Derby and Disraeli, and was offered, but refused, office in Derby's 1852 ministry; but after 1846 he was not politically active.

On the death of his uncle, the fifth, and last, duke of Gordon, in 1836 he inherited Gordon Castle in Banffshire and vast Scottish estates, and took the additional surname of Gordon; he coveted the Gordon dukedom as well, but its revival, for his son, had to wait until 1876. As well as being lord lieutenant and vice-admiral of Sussex, and high steward of Chichester, he was hereditary constable of Inverness Castle and chancellor of Marischal College, Aberdeen. He died on 21 October 1860 at the family mansion, 51 Portland Place, London, of dropsy, and was buried in the family vault in Chichester Cathedral on 30 October. His second daughter, Augusta Katherine (1827–1904), married in 1851 Field Marshal the Prince William Augustus Edward of Saxe-Weimar. His second son, Lord Fitzroy George Gordon-Lennox, was lost at sea in the steamer *President* in 1841.

Richmond's third son, **Lord Henry Charles George Gordon-Lennox** (1821–1886), politician and speculator, was born at Goodwood on 2 November 1821. After attending Westminster School and Christ Church, Oxford, where he graduated BA in 1843, he was précis writer to the foreign secretary, Lord Aberdeen. He was brought into the Commons as member for Chichester in 1846 by his father, who made the sitting member, his brother Lord Arthur Lennox (1806–1864), the clerk of the ordnance, resign the seat so that a protectionist demonstration could be made. Lord Henry was a lord of the Treasury in 1852 and again in 1858–9, secretary to the Admiralty in 1866–8, and first commissioner of public works in 1874–6, and continued to sit for Chichester until 1885. His resignation from office in July 1876 because of unsavoury publicity about the Lisbon Tramways Company, of which he was a director, was held at the time to have been an act of over-scrupulous propriety, since he was thought to have entirely clean hands. The fifteenth earl of Derby, who had been a close friend of Lord Henry in his youth, recorded a rather different opinion after Henry's death on 29 August 1886. 'He was by far the cleverest of the family', Derby noted,

> and had to a certain extent educated himself, which except the Duke none of the rest have done. He accomplished a fair parliamentary success, and held several minor offices. With his position, and being as he was ambitious, it seemed as if he ought to have gone higher: and perhaps he would, but for an unlucky speculation, which caused him to be mixed up in sundry not very creditable affairs, and in the end caused his retirement from office … I do not believe he ever did, or connived at, anything dishonest: but no man could be associated with Albert Grant and come away with perfectly clean hands. In addition to this, his manner was affected, and his temper irritable: so that he was never popular in the society of his own class: but he lived much among actors, speculators, and small hangers-on to newspapers: and in this Bohemian world he was much appreciated. He was always in money difficulties from which marriage with a rich widow [on 25 Jan 1883, to Amelia Susannah, widow of John White of Arddarroch, Dumbarton] did not extricate him: for his debts were once at least paid by his family: and latterly he went through the bankruptcy court. (*Later Derby Diaries*, 73–4)

F. M. L. Thompson

Sources *DNB* • *Hansard 2* (1828), 19.345 • *Hansard 3* (1846), vol. 86; (1828), 86.1109 • *Disraeli, Derby and the conservative party: journals and memoirs of Edward Henry, Lord Stanley, 1849–1869*, ed. J. R. Vincent (1978) • *The diaries of E. H. Stanley, 15th earl of Derby, 1869–1878*, CS, 5th series, 4 (1994) • *The later Derby diaries … selected passages*, ed. J. Vincent (privately printed, Bristol, 1981) • *The Greville memoirs*, ed. H. Reeve, new edn, 8 vols. (1888) • *The Greville diary*, ed. P. W. Wilson, 2 vols. (1927) • *VCH Sussex*, vol. 2 • *A portion of the journal kept by Thomas Raikes esq. from 1831 to 1847: comprising reminiscences of social and political life in London and Paris during that period*, 4 vols. (1856–8) • T. L. Crosby, *English farmers and the politics of protection, 1815–1852* (1977) • *The Times* (22 Oct 1860), 7 • Boase, *Mod. Eng. biog.* • *CGPLA Eng. & Wales* (1860) • Burke, *Peerage*

Archives W. Sussex RO, corresp. and papers | BL, corresp. with Lord Holland, Add. MS 51802 • BL, letters to Sir Robert Peel, Add. MSS 40232–40525, *passim* • BL, corresp. with Lord Ripon, Add. MSS 40863, 40880 • BLPES, corresp. with Sir Joshua Jebb • Lpool RO, letters to fourteenth earl of Derby • PRO NIre., corresp. with marquess of Anglesey • U. Durham L., letters to second Earl Grey

Likenesses S. Lane, oils, exh. RA 1842, Goodwood House, West Sussex • H. Weekes, bust, 1845, Goodwood House, West Sussex • H. Weekes, bust, 1845, Goodwood House, West Sussex • J. Andrews, engraving (after J. Andrews, 1841), NPG [*see illus.*] • G. Hayter, group portrait, oils (*The trial of Queen Caroline, 1820*), NPG • G. Hayter, group portrait, oils (*The House of Commons, 1833*), NPG • T. Heaphy, watercolour drawing, NPG • W. Salter, group portrait, oil study (*Waterloo banquet at Apsley House*), NPG; version, Goodwood House, West Sussex • W. Salter, group portrait, oils (*Waterloo banquet at Apsley House*), Wellington Museum, London • attrib. F. Wilkin, oils, Goodwood House, West Sussex • group portrait, Goodwood House, West Sussex • oils (in old age), Goodwood House, West Sussex

Wealth at death under £120,000: probate, 17 Dec 1860, *CGPLA Eng. & Wales*

Lennox, Charles Henry Gordon-, sixth duke of Richmond, sixth duke of Lennox, and first duke of Gordon (1818–1903), landowner and politician, was born on 27 February 1818 at Richmond House, Whitehall, the eldest of the five sons and three daughters of Charles Gordon-*Lennox, fifth duke of Richmond (1791–1860), and his wife, Caroline (1796–1874), eldest daughter of Henry William *Paget, first marquess of Anglesey. Known as the earl of March from his grandfather's death in August 1819 until his succession to the dukedom, he was educated at Westminster School and Christ Church, Oxford. After graduating BA in 1839 he went straight into the Horse Guards, from which he retired, as captain, in 1844. Meanwhile, at the 1841 general election, he was elected as Conservative MP for West Sussex, where the Richmond influence was considerable, and held the seat until his father's death in October 1860. In 1842 he became aide-de-camp to the duke of Wellington, and on 28 November 1843 he married Frances Harriett, the eldest daughter of Wellington's private secretary, Algernon Frederick *Greville, who was also Bath king of arms and a kinsman of the fourth earl of Warwick. They had four sons and two daughters, their last child, Walter Charles, being born in 1865.

MP and agriculturalist For a while the earl of March continued his military career, as aide-de-camp (1852–4) to Lord Hill, Wellington's successor as commander-in-chief, but he devoted much of his time to establishing a reputation in the House of Commons as an authority on agriculture. Joining the Royal Agricultural Society in 1838, within six months of its formation, and serving as a member of its council from 1852 to 1857, he took a serious interest in farming matters, and laid the foundations for his agricultural popularity as duke. He became well known for the improvements made to the Goodwood flock of Southdown sheep and the Gordon herd of shorthorns, and was a knowledgeable president of the Smithfield Club (1866 and 1875), the Shorthorn Society (1889), and the Royal Agricultural Society (1868 and 1883). As the heir to a famous protectionist father he inevitably belonged to the protectionist wing of the tory party in the 1840s, and hence had little chance of holding office, apart from a few months as president of the poor-law board in Lord Derby's second administration in 1859.

Conservative leader in the Lords He entertained ambitions somewhat beyond his abilities, but as a tory duke after 1860, with parliamentary experience, an exemplary attendance record, and unquestioning loyalty to his leaders, Richmond had a secure political future. When Cranborne, Carnarvon, and General Peel resigned from Derby's third administration in March 1867 he joined the 'leap in the dark' cabinet as president of the Board of Trade, unhesitatingly accepting the astonishing about-turn on the franchise issue. After Derby's death in 1869 the party chose as its leader in the Lords not Salisbury (as Cranborne had become) who had yet to work his passage back into the party's favour, nor Cairns, able lawyer and recent lord chancellor but rather an Irish upstart, but a traditional duke endowed with good sense 'and not the slightest inclination to epigram' (*The Times*, 28 Sept 1903, 5), or, as one historian has put it, 'an amiable but ineffective nonentity' (Blake, 516). The duke was a reasonably moderate leader of the opposition in the Lords, trying, ineffectually, to water down the great Gladstonian measures on the Irish church, Irish land, and education; and on the Ballot Bill, where he moved a futile and absurd amendment making secret voting optional, so far forgetting himself as to assert that Lord Granville 'has not a tittle of foundation for the language he has used' in calling Richmond a despot ordering his bands of tory lords to vote this way and that, an outburst which prompted the reading of the standing order 'for avoidance of offensive speeches … that all personal, sharp, or taxing speeches be forborn' (*Hansard* 3, 211, 17 June 1872, 1841).

When Disraeli formed his government in February 1874 Richmond continued as leader in the Lords and became president of the council, although he would have preferred the War Office which, understandably, went to the far more able Gathorne-Hardy. As lord president Richmond presided over the education department,

> a man of little calibre with no particular interest in education, an aristocratic amateur of the old type, whose main concern seems to have been to get the business of the session over and depart to the Scottish moors with that other hammer of the grouse, Lord Cairns. (Smith, 244)

Fortunately the vice-president of council, Lord Sandon (later third earl of Harrowby), in charge of education in the Commons, understood the subject thoroughly and knew precisely what he wanted to do, within the 1870 structure, to protect the educational interests of the church against any further nonconformist inroads. Richmond from time to time showed his resentment of Sandon and of his successor as vice-president, Lord George Hamilton, in outbursts typical of a weak character faced with more able and independent subordinates, but competently steered through the Lords the government's chief education measure, the 1876 Education Bill, which aimed at helping the voluntary schools bolster their pupil numbers through a modified form of compulsory education. In August 1876 he ceased to be leader in the Lords on Disraeli's transformation into Lord Beaconsfield. His control of the house faltered in 1877 when he was forced to withdraw his burials bill after an amendment allowing nonconformist services in Anglican churchyards was carried against him.

Cabinet minister Richmond spoke on all matters of government business, often, as with merchant shipping regulations, with little knowledge or conviction. His real interest was to act as virtual minister of agriculture, a non-existent position given a slight cloak of plausibility by the fact that in virtue of his presidency of the privy council the veterinary department came within his departmental responsibilities, along with education. He steered the 1875 Agricultural Holdings Bill through the Lords, contriving without embarrassment to commend both the fairness of giving tenant farmers compensation for the unexhausted value of improvements they had made to their farms and the fairness of allowing landlords to contract out of any obligation to grant such compensation. Because of its permissive nature this act was almost completely ineffective, but it was a small achievement to get 'tenant right' for English and Welsh farmers into law, something first put before parliament in 1848 by Philip Pusey, and Richmond himself was to be partly responsible for giving the concept some teeth in the 1883 Agricultural Holdings Act.

Richmond's main agricultural performance as a cabinet minister was on cattle disease, a serious outbreak in 1877 prompting him to strengthen the regulations introduced after the great cattle plague of 1866. His Contagious Diseases (Animals) Bill was intended, so he argued, not to ensure that infected beef did not enter the food chain but to ensure that infected (foreign) cattle did not come into contact with healthy British beasts, by introducing compulsory slaughter of all foreign cattle at their port of entry. He imagined that this was self-evidently a desirable policy and was taken aback by the public outcry that it was a protectionist measure in disguise which would force up the price of meat, benefiting British farmers and hurting consumers. It is a measure of his political innocence, and obstinacy, that he went ahead with the bill, although in December 1877 Derby and Cross, in a cabinet discussion of the plan 'for giving effectual protection against cattle-plague … warned our colleagues of the formidable opposition they would have to face, & of the danger of setting town against country' (Stanley, 461). Ploughing ahead with more determination to please the agricultural interest than regard for either political or common sense, he claimed in the second reading debate on the bill in March 1878 that far from being a measure of protection it would, miraculously, render Britain independent of foreign cattle supplies, increase the supply of meat and reduce its price for all classes (*Hansard* 3, 238, 1878, 748). In June and July 1878, while the Congress of Berlin was sitting, cabinet meetings were much occupied with cattle disease, and finally induced Richmond to make a string of concessions which had the effect of permitting imports of live cattle, without compulsory slaughter on arrival, from countries which were certified by the privy council to be free from disease. Sweden, Norway, Denmark, Spain, and Portugal were those initially named as exempt from the operation of the bill, and an exasperated Lord Sandon commented in his cabinet journal: 'Why did not the Duke of Richmond and our farming friends come to see this sooner, so as not to expose us to the odium in the Towns of interfering with the meat supply?' (Howard and Gordon, 37).

There were good grounds for the letter which Derby recorded he received from Salisbury in December 1874:

> Letter from Salisbury, who has got in his mind the notion that there is in some quarters a project for making the D of Richmond the next premier, when Disraeli's health compels him to resign, an event which Salisbury evidently considers as not far distant. He protests against this, says it must not be allowed, that the Duke is unfit for the post, that his appointment would justify the title of the 'stupid party' as applied to us, and that in the event of a vacancy I must assert my claim to the position … I answer … agreeing as to the unfitness of the Duke. (Stanley, 184)

The notion that Richmond was a suitably dignified and passably experienced territorial grandee to lead the tories had been around in 1868 when the previous Lord Derby retired, and was still present, at least in Richmond's own mind, in 1881 when, after Beaconsfield's death, he told an understandably startled Gathorne-Hardy that only the duchess's poor health had prevented him becoming the leader. 'I was rather surprised', Hardy noted,

> to find that in resigning the leader's crown he gave indications he would fain have kept it, and he revealed the real reason for renouncing it. He told me that he had said to Salisbury, 'If Lady S were the Duchess of Richmond you never would have been leader.' (*Diary of Gathorne Hardy*, 476)

Later career; 'the farmers' friend' By 1881 Richmond's political career was in fact almost over. His service as 'the farmers' friend' (a title publicly given him at the York meeting of the Royal Agricultural Society in 1883 in an address by the prince of Wales) continued after the fall of the Beaconsfield government, in his chairmanship of the royal commission on the depressed state of the agricultural interest, which had been appointed in 1879 and made its final report in 1882. Known at the time—and to historians since—as the Richmond commission, it is his principal claim to fame, although his personal contribution to its proceedings and recommendations was not conspicuous. One recommendation was to remove the permissive element from the 1875 Agricultural Holdings Act, which he had insisted was essential to the preservation of private property, and to make compensation to tenants an obligation on landlords, which was done in the 1883 act. A more congenial recommendation was for the establishment of an agriculture ministry, which was eventually set up in 1889. None of the recommendations did much for the farmers, but the evidence collected by the commission has proved useful for historians.

In 1884 Richmond played a part in settling the crisis provoked by the tory peers in rejecting the Franchise Bill and insisting on a simultaneous Redistribution Bill. Victoria held him in high regard, summoned him to Balmoral, and urged him to persuade the more obdurate peers to accept a compromise, which he achieved to her satisfaction. She wrote to him in November remarking on the 'favourable turn affairs are at last taking, and which she feels has been greatly owing to the firm and patriotic tone the Duke, and also Lord Cairns, has held' (*Letters of Queen Victoria*, 2nd ser., 3.578). The association with Cairns was basic to his political views, and enduring. Derby had noted how, throughout the Near Eastern crisis of 1877–8, Richmond had consistently echoed the views of Cairns, typically noting, of a cabinet meeting on 27 December 1877, that 'Cairns took a specially active part, Richmond backing up all he said with a persistent fidelity which was almost comic' (Stanley, 471). Richmond's final cabinet appearance was as the first ever secretary of state for Scotland in the 1885–6 Salisbury cabinet.

Richmond's Scottish credentials were impeccably authentic and aristocratic. His father had inherited the bulk of the Gordon estates in Banff and Aberdeen when the last duke of Gordon died in 1836, and Richmond became very fond of Gordon Castle and the Scottish estates. He usually spent three or four months every year at Gordon Castle for the fishing in the Spey, and at Glenfiddich Lodge for the grouse shooting (often with Cairns); and he treated the property as rather more than just a sporting estate, gaining a reputation for benevolence among his tenantry and building a harbour at Port Gordon to stimulate the local economy. In 1861 he became chancellor of the University of Aberdeen. It was in this context of lordly Scottishness that in 1874 Victoria proposed the revival of the dukedom of Gordon, as a consolation prize for Richmond on ceasing to be leader in the Lords, writing to Disraeli that the revival 'would be a right and proper thing, as well as very popular in Scotland. It is not right', she continued,

> that when these great possessions pass into English hands they should be treated as a secondary possession, and in some cases, like lord Aveland, who has Drummond Castle, or who will have it when his mother dies, probably be treated like a shooting place. By conferring this great title on the D of Richmond it will at once do away with this, and have the very best effect. (*Letters of Queen Victoria*, 2nd ser., 2.355)

The new title was conferred in January 1876.

Nevertheless, Richmond always treated Goodwood as his primary possession, and spent most of the year there and in Belgrave Square. Although he was elected to the Jockey Club in 1838 he did not inherit his father's passion for racing, and confined his efforts to keeping up the glitter of the annual Goodwood meeting as a great social gathering. He always had a large house party for race week, with kings and queens, emperors and empresses, frequently among his guests. An admirer of tradition, he revived the old Charlton hunt at Goodwood, which had once been as fashionable as Melton Mowbray, and the hunt servants in canary livery kept the course at the races; because of the cost the hounds were disposed of some years before his death, the canary liveries surviving. In the same spirit he clung to the use of the tall hat, even at Goodwood, but by 1899 he and Lord Howe were the sole members of the house party to wear one. Lord lieutenant of Banff from 1879, in Sussex he was outranked by the duke of Norfolk and had to be content with becoming chairman of the new West Sussex county council after 1888. The real world also caught up with him in another way, when in 1893 his grandson and the future eighth duke, Charles Henry, married Hilda, eldest daughter of Henry Brassey, the third son of the great railway contractor Thomas *Brassey.

Richmond's wife died in 1887 after many years of poor health, and his elder, unmarried, daughter Caroline became his companion and acted as hostess for him in his later years. Richmond died at Gordon Castle on 27 September 1903, having enjoyed a good summer there since July, and was buried in the family vault in Chichester Cathedral on 3 October. F. M. L. THOMPSON

Sources *DNB* • *The Times* (28 Sept 1903), 5 • *The diaries of E. H. Stanley, 15th earl of Derby, 1869–1878*, CS, 5th series, 4 (1994) • *The letters of Queen Victoria*, ed. G. E. Buckle, 3 vols., 2nd ser. (1926–8), vols. 2–3 • *Hansard 3* (1872), 211.1841; (1878), 238.748 • C. Howard and P. Gordon, eds., 'The cabinet journal of Dudley Ryder, Viscount Sandon', *BIHR*, special suppl., 10 (1974) [whole issue] • *The diary of Gathorne Hardy, later Lord Cranbrook, 1866–1892: political selections*, ed. N. E. Johnson (1981) • R. Blake, *Disraeli* (1966) • P. Smith, *Disraelian Conservatism and social reform* (1967)

Archives W. Sussex RO, corresp. and papers | BL, corresp. with Lord Carnarvon, Add. MS 60768 • BL, corresp. with Lord Cross, Add. MS 51267 • Bodl. Oxf., corresp. with Benjamin Disraeli • Herts. ALS, letters to Lord Lytton • PRO, letters to Lord Cairns, PRO 30/51 • Suffolk RO, Ipswich, letters to Lord Cranbrook

Likenesses W. Webb, oils, 1825, Goodwood House, West Sussex • J. Brown, stipple, pubd 1861 (after photograph by Maull & Polyblank), NPG • F. Grant, oils, *c*.1876, Goodwood House, West Sussex • G. Reid, oils, *c*.1885, Goodwood House, West Sussex • H. Gales, group portrait, watercolour (*The Derby cabinet of 1867*), NPG • Lock & Whitfield, woodburytype photograph, NPG; repro. in T. Cooper, *Men of mark: a gallery of contemporary portraits* (1882) • Russell & Sons, cabinet photograph, NPG • Russell & Sons, photograph, NPG; repro. in *Our conservative and unionist statesmen*, 1 (1897) • Southwell Bros., cartes-de-visite, NPG • G. J. Stodart, stipple and line print (after photograph by W. N. Malby), NPG • A. Thompson, caricature, chromolithograph, repro. in *VF* (26 March 1870) • prints, NPG

Wealth at death £353,573 9*s*. 6*d*.: probate, 6 Feb 1904, *CGPLA Eng. & Wales*

Lennox [*née* Ramsay], **(Barbara) Charlotte (1730/31?–1804)**, novelist and writer, was born in Gibraltar, the youngest of the five children of Captain James Ramsay (*c*.1677–1742) of Dalhousie, Edinburghshire, Scotland, and Catherine (*d*. 1765), sister of the Revd William Tisdall of Carrickfergus, co. Antrim, Ireland. She was probably baptized Barbara, the name entered on her marriage certificate, or perhaps Barbara Charlotte. Her early life is obscure, partly because she herself chose to fictionalize it: 'Nothing is more public than her writings,' observed Bishop Warburton, 'nothing more concealed than her person' ('Memoirs', 33). The facts must be sought in her semi-autobiographical novel, *The Life of Harriot Stuart, Written by Herself* (1750), the records of her father's military career, and the anonymous 'Memoirs of Mrs. Lenox' (1783). Other accounts are little more than uncritical paraphrases of *Harriot Stuart*, of no independent biographical value; the 'Memoirs' also paraphrase the novel but add much specific detail.

Charlotte's father was promoted captain of an independent company of foot of New York in 1738 and stationed in Albany until his death on 10 March 1742. His widow and children remained in New York for a few years, until Charlotte accepted a position as companion to Mary Luckyn, the widow of Sir William Luckyn, bt, of Messing Hall, Essex. On her arrival in England, however, the fifteen-year-old Charlotte apparently discovered that Lady Luckyn had become deranged after the death in 1746 of a son, the Revd Charles Luckyn, and the position was no longer open. Charlotte spent a short, evidently unhappy term as companion to Lady Isabella Finch, in the hope of a place at court, and dedicated her first publication, the unremarkable *Poems on Several Occasions* (1747), to her. She then ruined these prospects by an imprudent marriage to Alexander Lennox, 'an indigent and shiftless Scot' (Isles,

18.326), at the marriage factory of St George's Chapel, Mayfair, on 6 October 1747.

Marriage and early success At the time of the marriage, Lennox's husband was reportedly working for the printer William Strahan, but he does not appear in Strahan's meticulous list of his apprentices, and he was already unemployed in 1752. Croker identifies him as the lieutenant of the Surrey militia who claimed the earldom of Lennox in 1768 as 'lineal heir-male' of Alexander, brother of Duncan, eighth earl (*d.* 1425). The identification is supported to some extent by his wife's belief that he was a relative of the Murrays of Broughton (Isles, 19.185), who was descended from Donald, Earl Duncan's illegitimate son, while his 'Birth misfortunes' (as Lennox tactfully referred to them in a letter written probably to Samuel Johnson; Chicago Historical Society) may explain why his petition was rejected by the House of Lords. Apart from this lieutenancy, the only position he is known to have held was as deputy waiter in the customs (1773–82), thanks to the generosity of the duke of Newcastle. It is said that the duke granted it in lieu of a pension for Charlotte, at her request.

After her marriage, Lennox briefly tried her hand as an actress, but without success. Horace Walpole, who saw her at Richmond in 1748, described her performance as 'deplorable' in a letter to George Montagu (3 September 1748; Walpole, *Corr.*, 9.74), but she enjoyed a benefit as Almeria in *The Mourning Bride* at the Haymarket on 22 February 1750. Her first novel, *Harriot Stuart*, attracted Samuel Johnson's admiration; he celebrated its publication in December 1750 with an all-night party, with a laurel wreath and 'a magnificent hot apple pie' decorated with bay leaves (Hawkins, 121–2). Comparing her to Frances Burney, Elizabeth Carter, and Hannah More, he exclaimed, 'Three such women are not to be found. I know not where I could find a fourth, except Mrs. Lennox, who is superior to them all' (*Applause of the Jury*, 212). He remained her friend to the end of his life, writing prefaces, dedications, subscription proposals, and other minor contributions for her publications, and introducing 'our Charlotte' to the London literary scene (*The Letters of Samuel Johnson*, ed. R. W. Chapman, 1952, no. 36).

Lennox was fortunate in her male friends: Joseph Baretti taught her Italian, Thomas Birch translated one of her odes into Latin, and the earl of Cork and Orrery promoted her novels with Andrew Millar (Lennox's chief publisher and employer) and, together with Johnson and others, assisted her with her translation of *The Greek Theatre of Father Brumoy* (1760). David Garrick produced her *Old City Manners* (1775), an adaptation of *Eastward Ho* by Jonson, Chapman, and Marston, which ran for seven nights, and Samuel Richardson suggested improvements to her second and best-known novel, *The Female Quixote, or, The Adventures of Arabella* (1752), while Henry Fielding warmly praised it in his *Covent Garden Journal*. Though posterity has often unjustly attributed her literary distinction to the contributions of these illustrious male friends, there can be no doubt that their support was invaluable to a struggling woman writer.

Women found Lennox less winning, even those who admired her novels: 'nobody likes her', Mrs Thrale opined (*Fanny Burney's Diary*, 75), while Lady Mary Wortley Montagu 'was roused into great surprise and indignation' by Lennox's satiric portrait of Lady Isabella Finch as 'Lady Cecilia' in *Harriot Stuart* (letter to Lady Bute, 1 March 1752; *Complete Letters*). The poet Elizabeth Carter condemned her poetry, declaring: 'It is intolerably provoking to see people who really appear to have a genius, apply it to such idle unprofitable purposes' (Small, 9). The writer Laetitia Matilda Hawkins scorned her housekeeping, and 'several Ladies … were astonished to see a gentlewoman's hands in such horrid order' (Isles, 19.416). 'How each in her mistaken task delights!', sneered an anonymous squib; 'L[ennox] works Muslin and Macaulay writes' (ibid., 19.432). Johnson, visiting Mary (Burney) Brookes and the painter Catherine Reid, 'heard of you [Lennox] at both houses, yet, what much surprised me I heard no evil' (ibid., 19.46–7). He had clearly heard plenty on other occasions. The only woman who seems to have risen above this storm of 'feminine disapprobation' was the actress Mary Ann Yates (Small, 10, 228). Possibly Johnson and Richardson's female acquaintance begrudged Lennox so much famous male attention, but certainly she seems to have done little to placate them with her prickly demeanour and the ease with which she was offended.

Lennox was unable to repeat the success of her first two novels, in part because demand unaccountably slumped in the 1750s. Her experience parallels the comparative failures of Fielding's *Amelia* (1751) and Richardson's *Sir Charles Grandison* (1753–4). Nevertheless, her *Female Quixote* became a classic, reprinted in the series of Harrison (1783), Cooke (1799), and Barbauld (1810), and translated into German (1754), French (1773 and 1801), and Spanish (1808)—title-pages of her later publications regularly style her 'the Author of The Female Quixote'. The novel deserves the critical and commercial success it secured for Lennox. It recounts the adventures and misadventures of Arabella, the Quixote of the title, who like Cervantes' Don Quixote confused chivalric romances with reality. At a time when novels were eagerly read by the public yet treated with suspicion by arbiters of literary taste, Lennox uses her character to demonstrate the mistakes that can be made by treating life as if it were a romance penned by Madame de Scudéry or Madame de Lafayette. What complicates Lennox's satire of romances is the fact that while her heroine lives in this fantasy world she enjoys the upper hand in the battle of the sexes, and a variety of startled men find themselves ill-equipped to deal with the eccentric heroine. Though Arabella is ultimately awoken from her dream of romance—by an elderly clergyman, appropriately enough—Lennox has demonstrated just why the romance was so appealing to women living in a thoroughly patriarchal society.

Literary toil and domestic problems A later novel, *Henrietta* (1758), was a modest success, reprinted in Harrison's series and twice translated into French, but it was a *succès d'estime* and Lennox indignantly complained that the booksellers reaped most of the benefit from her 'slavery'

(Small, 28). *Harriot and Sophia* (serialized, 1760–61, and reprinted as *Sophia*) and *Euphemia* (1790) suffered an even cooler reception. To support herself and her husband, Lennox turned to translating, in which her production was more profitable, though not to her. She seems, however, to have preferred it, finding it a less demanding task than writing novels. Her translation *Memoirs of Maximilian de Bethune, Duke of Sully* (1755) sold steadily: there were fifteen editions to 1856, including a Scottish 'piracy' (1773); after the case of *Donaldson* v. *Becket* (1774) abolished the London book trade's claim to perpetual literary property, the work was shared out to the trade, and James Dodsley was obliged to decline Lennox's offer of a revised and corrected version. It was all too incomprehensible, she declared, erroneously supposing that *Donaldson* v. *Becket* had revived her original title.

Lennox's *Shakespeare Illustrated* (1753–4) was a pioneering attempt to identify and translate his sources, 'with critical remarks'. Unfortunately, her neo-classical bias tended to overstate the critical importance of the original plots (the 'soul' of drama, for Aristotle) and understate the value of their poetic, psychological, and dramatic elaboration, and her strictures followed on the heels of William Lauder's scandalous indictment of Milton for plagiarism (1747–50). Nevertheless, Lennox's work is a milestone in the historical interpretation of vernacular literature, precedented only by Zachary Grey's edition of *Hudibras* (1744). It remained for Johnson, who playfully suggested that she try her hand at Milton 'when Shakespeare is demolish'd' (Isles, 19.38–9), to adjust the balance, by affirming the transcendent value of 'nature', 'truth', and 'the mirror of life' in his edition of Shakespeare of 1765. Some, like Garrick, found her criticisms of the bard intolerable: 'In the Whole, I imagin'd that you had betray'd a greater desire of Exposing his Errors than of *illustrating* his Beauties' (ibid., 19.41).

The Lennoxes never stayed in any one lodging for long, except for an extended residency in Somerset House, London (1768–73), by favour of Henrietta, duchess of Newcastle. Their two surviving children, Harriot Holles (1765–1782/4) (the duchess's goddaughter) and George Lewis (*b.* 1771), were so belated that it is possible that Charlotte suffered earlier miscarriages. Another son is said to have died in infancy, which may explain her unspecified, severe 'distress' in 1759 ('Memoirs', 36; Small, 27). According to Johnson, her husband treated Charlotte 'very harshly', and the unhappy couple may have lived separately at various times.

After 1760 Lennox's literary production dwindled, possibly as a result of her greater financial security and the demands of raising children. Dislodged from Somerset House in 1773, she proposed an illustrated edition of *The Female Quixote*, only to exasperate her subscribers by expanding her project into three volumes of a collected *Works* (1775). This, and a proposal for a revised edition of *Shakespeare Illustrated* (1793), came to nothing.

Lennox's portrait was sketched by Sir Joshua Reynolds about 1775, but survives only in engraved copies by H. R. Cook and F. Bartolozzi. Neither engraving quite matches contemporary descriptions of her features, which were plain and 'much pitted with the small-pox' (Séjourné, 142). Yet they accurately reflect her own self-image as she elaborated it to her friends and the Literary Fund, the source of all subsequent biographies until 1966. There her father figures grandly as lieutenant-governor of New York, Lady Luckyn is her mother's aristocratic sister, and Charlotte's (that is, Harriot Stuart's) patrons discard her from envy of her poetic talent and beauty.

Lennox had become an exalted, wooden, female worthy, a 'Living Muse', canonized in a painting by Richard Samuel (1779) alongside Catharine Macaulay, Hannah More, Elizabeth Montague, Elizabeth Griffith, and others—a rather lower position on Parnassus than Johnson would have chosen, but remote and above all unrewarded. The Lennoxes separated permanently in 1793. George Lewis, a literary prodigy, was apparently led to 'the brink of utter ruin' by his 'most unnatural father' in 1793 (Small, 59)—the result of which was his emigration to America. Lennox spent the rest of her life in solitary penury, supported by the Literary Fund and the kindness of George Rose and William Beloe. She died on 4 January 1804 at Dean's Yard, Westminster, and was buried in Broad Court cemetery, Westminster, in an unmarked grave.

Posthumous reputation In the nineteenth century Lennox's memory was kept green by her Johnsonian associations and by the American scenes she introduced into *Harriot Stuart* and *Euphemia*, which earned her the title of 'the first American novelist'. More recently, feminist studies have put right these inequities, with critics such as Janet Todd and Jane Spencer giving Lennox the attention she deserves in their studies of eighteenth-century women writers. *The Female Quixote* retains its freshness and humour 250 years after its publication, and internet searches reveal a continued interest in the works of Charlotte Lennox. Her reputation as a virago has been vindicated by her literary abilities. Her life had been regularly embittered by her savage resentment of real or imaginary slights, which only frequent quarrels with her friends relieved—with what justification one can only conjecture today. Johnson's condescension to the clucking fury of his 'Dearest Partlet' (Isles, 19.420) was probably compounded of a real sense of her worth, a long history of mutual affection, impatience with her shrewish punctilio, and (unavoidably) a conviction of the superiority of 'male reason' over 'female emotion'. If the outlet for her literary talents was limited, however, there was no ready remedy: it was no doubt easier for Johnson to sustain a sense of his own worth in bondage to the booksellers than for Lennox; it is also true that he was massively her superior in education and abilities, and that his marriage never ruined his opportunities. One can hardly blame Lennox for escaping from these grim realities into genealogical fantasy and the surrogate pleasures of beautiful, fierce, and talented *alter egos*, unsuccessfully menaced by male importunity. Still, as a person, she is perhaps most human when she boasts her hand at making gooseberry tarts and apple dumplings (Small, 50). Not that the kitchen was her proper sphere, but, a true Quixote, she was at her best humorously braving her shabby reputation for traditional womanly skills, instead of helplessly ranting against such spiteful slander. HUGH AMORY

Sources 'Memoirs of Mrs Lenox, the celebrated author of *The female Quixotte*, and other works', *Edinburgh Weekly Magazine*, 18 (1783), 33–6 · D. Isles, 'The Lennox collection', *Harvard Library Bulletin*, 18 (1970), 317–44 · D. Isles, 'The Lennox collection', *Harvard Library Bulletin*, 19 (1971), 36–60, 165–86, 416–35 · M. R. Small, *Charlotte Ramsay Lennox, an eighteenth-century lady of letters* (New Haven, Conn., 1935) [incl. bibliography and iconography] · P. Séjourné, *The mystery of Charlotte Lennox, first novelist of colonial America* (Aix-en-Provence, 1967) · J. Boswell, *The life of Johnson*, new edn, ed. J. W. Croker, 5 vols. (1831) · C. Lennox, *The life of Harriot Stuart, written by herself*, ed. S. K. Howard (Madison, Wisc., 1995) · *Fanny Burney's diary*, ed. J. Wain (1961) · J. Hawkins, *The life of Samuel Johnson, LL.D*, ed. B. H. Davis (New York, 1961) · W. Robertson, *Proceedings relating to the peerage of Scotland, from January 16 1707 to April 29 1788* (1790), 335–6 · D. Warrand, ed., *Hertfordshire families* (1907), 171ff. · *Boswell: the applause of the jury, 1782–1785*, ed. I. S. Lustig and F. A. Pottle (New York, 1981) · William Strahan archive, list of apprentices, BL, Add. MS 48803A, fol. 103 · J. Todd, ed., *Dictionary of British women writers* (1989) · J. Spencer, *The rise of the woman novelist from Aphra Behn to Jane Austen* (1987) · *The complete letters of Lady Mary Wortley Montagu*, ed. R. Halsband, 3 vols. (1965–7) · Highfill, Burnim & Langhans, *BDA* · Charlotte Lennox to [Samuel Johnson?], 3 Feb 1752, Chicago Historical Society, MS na Br, 1752, Feb. 3, Len.

Archives Harvard U., Houghton L., collection

Likenesses R. Samuel, group portrait, oils, exh. 1779 (*The nine living muses of Great Britain*), NPG; repro. in Wordsworth and Hebron, eds., *Romantic women writers*, 25 · F. Bartolozzi, stipple (after J. Reynolds), BM, NPG; repro. in S. Harding, *Shakespeare illustrated* (1793) · H. R. Cook, engraving (after J. Reynolds), repro. in *Lady's Monthly Magazine* (June 1813) · Page, engraving (after R. Samuel)

Lennox, Donald, sixth earl of Lennox (*d.* 1361x4). *See under* Lennox family (*per. c.*1300–1425).

Lennox, Duncan, eighth earl of Lennox (*d.* 1425). *See under* Lennox family (*per. c.*1300–1425).

Lennox, Emilia Mary. *See* Fitzgerald, Emilia Mary, duchess of Leinster (1731–1814).

Lennox, Lord George Henry (1737–1805), army officer and politician, the eighth child but second surviving son of Charles *Lennox, second duke of Richmond (1701–1750), courtier, and his wife, Sarah Cadogan (1706–1751), was born at Richmond House, Whitehall, London, on 29 November 1737. He was educated at Westminster School and travelled abroad on the grand tour, with his brother Charles *Lennox, the third duke of Richmond (1735–1806), under the tutelage of Abraham Trembley. For a time he studied at the University of Leiden and undertook scientific studies under Jean Allamand. On 25 December 1759 he married Louisa Kerr, the daughter of William Henry *Kerr, Lord Ancram and later fourth marquess of Lothian, and his wife, Lady Caroline D'Arcy. They had one son, Charles *Lennox (1764–1819), who, on the death of his uncle in 1806, succeeded as fourth duke of Richmond, and three daughters.

Lennox had a long military career, and George III held a high opinion of him as a soldier. Having been commissioned ensign in the 2nd foot guards on 15 February 1754 he was appointed aide-de-camp to the duke of Cumberland, campaigned in Germany in 1757, and took part in the

Lord George Henry Lennox (1737–1805), by George Romney, 1779

expedition to Cherbourg on the French coast in 1758. On 8 May 1758 he was appointed lieutenant-colonel of the 33rd foot, in succession to his elder brother. In 1760 and 1761 he served in Germany, and on 20 February 1762 was made aide-de-camp to the king with the rank of colonel. On 29 December 1762 he obtained the command of the 25th foot, which he held until his death; in 1763 he was brigadier to the forces in Portugal. In 1769 he went, with his regiment, to Minorca, where he quarrelled with the governor, General Mostyn, about the quality of the wine served to the men and was court-martialled for disrespect to a superior officer. When Lennox was ordered to make a written apology, his brother Richmond advised him to resign his regiment, but the order was remitted to an oral apology. Mostyn afterwards tried to prosecute the wine merchant, Fabrigas, but lost the case in 1773 and was forced to pay £10,000 in damages to Fabrigas. Lennox became major-general on 15 May 1772, lieutenant-general on 29 August 1777, and constable of the Tower of London in 1783; he was sworn of the privy council on 9 February 1784 and was promoted full general on 12 October 1793. He was afterwards made governor of Plymouth.

As a politician, Lennox prospered under the protection of his brother. He was elected MP for the family borough of Chichester in 1761 and was mayor of the city in 1763 and 1772. In 1765 he accompanied the duke on his embassy to France and was left chargé d'affaires in the latter's absence, but he declined the offer of an embassy to Russia in 1767. From 1767 to 1790 he served as one of the knights of the shire for Sussex, and on his retirement was succeeded in his seat by his son, Charles Lennox. Having followed his brother in supporting the administrations of

Bute and Grenville before going over to the Rockinghams in 1765, Lennox voted consistently with the opposition between 1774 and 1782.

In 1764 Richmond purchased the manor of West Stoke and conveyed it to Lord George, who made it his family seat. He died there on 22 March 1805 and was buried in Chichester Cathedral on 29 March. Lennox was described by his sister Lady Sarah Bunbury as 'formal from vanity, and likes or dislikes from pique and prejudice' (*Correspondence of Emily, Duchess of Leinster*, 2.131).

W. A. J. Archbold, *rev.* Timothy J. McCann

Sources S. Tillyard, *Aristocrats: Caroline, Emily, Louisa and Sarah Lennox, 1740–1832* (1994) • M. M. Reese, *Goodwood's oak: the life and times of the third duke of Richmond* (1987) • *Correspondence of Emily, duchess of Leinster* (1731–1814), ed. B. Fitzgerald, 3 vols., IMC (1949–57) • A. G. Olson, *The radical duke* (1962) • J. Brooke, 'Lennox, Lord George Henry', HoP, *Commons*, 1754–90 • P. Sumner, 'The 25th foot in Minorca, 1771', *Journal of the Society for Army Historical Research*, 19 (1940), 19–33 • J. R. Baker, *Abraham Trembley: scientist and philosopher, 1710–1784* (1952) • H. K. James, 'Some Sussex bookplates of the eighteenth century', *Sussex Notes and Queries*, 6 (1937), 163–8 • *The correspondence of King George the Third from 1760 to December 1783*, ed. J. Fortescue, 6 vols. (1927–8) • H. Walpole, *Memoirs of the reign of King George the Third*, ed. G. F. R. Barker, 4 vols. (1894) • *Memoirs of Sir James Campbell of Ardkinglas, written by himself*, 2 vols. (1832), 1.176–81 • GEC, *Peerage* • *Report on the manuscripts of Earl Bathurst, preserved at Cirencester Park*, HMC, 76 (1923) • *GM*, 1st ser., 75 (1805), 294, 580

Archives BL, Bathurst MSS • Hunt. L., letters to Sir George Yonge • NAM, Townshend MSS, letters to George Townshend • NL Scot., letters to Lord Charles Hay • W. Sussex RO, Goodwood MSS

Likenesses P. Batoni, oils, 1752–3, Goodwood, West Sussex • G. Romney, portrait, 1779; Leger Galleries, London, 1986 [*see illus.*] • G. Chiesa, portrait, NAM • G. Romney, portrait, Goodwood, West Sussex • G. Stubbs, group portrait, oils (with his brother the third duke of Richmond and General Jones), Goodwood, West Sussex

Lennox, Lord Henry Charles George Gordon- (1821–1886). *See under* Lennox, Charles Gordon-, fifth duke of Richmond and fifth duke of Lennox (1791–1860).

Lennox, Lady Louisa Augusta. *See* Conolly, Lady Louisa Augusta (1743–1821).

Lennox, Malcolm, fifth earl of Lennox (*d.* 1333). *See under* Lennox family (*per. c.*1300–1425).

Lennox, Margaret, *suo jure* **countess of Lennox** (*d.* in or before 1392). *See under* Lennox family (*per. c.*1300–1425).

Lennox, Lady Sarah. *See* Napier, Lady Sarah (1745–1826).

Lennox, Sir Wilbraham Oates (1830–1897), army officer, fourth son of Lord John George Lennox (1793–1873), second son of Charles, fourth duke of Richmond, was born on 4 May 1830 at Molecomb House, Goodwood, Sussex. His mother was Louisa Frederica (*d.* 12 Jan 1865), daughter of Captain the Hon. John Rodney MP, third son of Admiral Lord Rodney. He was educated privately and at the Royal Military Academy, Woolwich, being commissioned second-lieutenant, Royal Engineers, on 27 June 1848. His further commissions were: lieutenant (7 February 1854), second-captain (25 November 1857), brevet major (24 March 1858), brevet lieutenant-colonel (26 April 1859), first-captain (1 April 1863), brevet colonel (26 April 1867), regimental major (5 July 1872), lieutenant-colonel (10 December 1873), major-general (13 August 1881), lieutenant-general (12 February 1888), and general (28 June 1893).

Lennox, after the usual course at Chatham and a few months at Portsmouth, embarked on 20 November 1850 for Ceylon, where he shot elephants and other big game. In August 1854 he went direct from Ceylon to the Crimea, where he arrived on 30 September; he was employed under Major Frederick Chapman in the trenches of the left attack on Sevastopol, and had also charge of the engineer park of the left attack. He was present at the battle of Inkerman on 5 November, having come off the sick list for the purpose. His conduct on 20 November won him the Victoria Cross (awarded 24 February 1857) for his bravery in establishing a lodgement in Tryon's rifle pits and helping to repulse enemy attacks; he was the first engineer officer to win the VC. On 9 December he was appointed adjutant to the Royal Engineers of the left attack. He acted as aide-de-camp to Chapman with Eyre's brigade at the attack of the Redan on 18 June, and was present at the fall of Sevastopol, after which he was adjutant of all the royal engineer force in the Crimea until the army was broken up. He arrived home on 5 August 1856. He was mentioned in dispatches and awarded the Mejidiye (fifth class).

Lennox was adjutant of the Royal Engineers at Aldershot until he again left England on 25 April 1857 as senior subaltern of the 23rd company, Royal Engineers, to take part in the Second Opium War. At Singapore the force was diverted to India, against the mutiny, and Lennox reached Calcutta on 10 August. On the march to Cawnpore he took part on 2 November in the action at Khajwa under Colonel Powell. The captain of his company was then severely wounded, and Colonel Goodwyn, Bengal Engineers, having fallen sick on 14 November, Lennox became temporarily chief engineer on the staff of Sir Colin Campbell. As such he served at the second relief of Lucknow. He submitted a plan of attack which Campbell adopted. He took a conspicuous part in the operations, and the relief was accomplished on 17 November. He continued to act as chief engineer in the operations against the Gwalior contingent, and in the battle of Cawnpore on 6 December. He commanded a detachment of engineers at the action of Kali Nadi under Campbell on 2 January 1858, and at the occupation of Fatehgarh. He was assistant to the commanding royal engineer, Colonel Henry Drury Harness, in the final siege of Lucknow from 2 to 21 March.

After the fall of Lucknow Lennox commanded the engineers of the column under Brigadier-General Robert Walpole for the subjugation of Rohilkhand, and was active in various engagements between April and November. On 30 November he left Lucknow as commanding royal engineer of the column under Brigadier-General Eveleigh to settle the country to the north-east, and was present at the capture of Umria on 2 December. He commanded the 23rd company Royal Engineers at the action on 26 December under Lord Clyde at Barjadua or Chandu in the Trans-Gogra campaign, at the capture of Fort Majadua on the 27th, and at the action at Banki on the Rapti on 31 December. Lennox was mentioned in dispatches, and rewarded with a brevet majority and a brevet lieutenant-colonelcy.

Lennox left India in March 1859, and on his arrival home was appointed to the Brighton subdivision of the south-eastern military district. From 14 June 1862 until 31 October 1865 he was deputy assistant quartermaster-general at Aldershot. On 30 March 1867 he was made a CB, military division, for his war services. From November 1866 he was for five years instructor in field fortification at the School of Military Engineering, Chatham, where his energy and experience were of great value. He originated a series of confidential professional papers to keep engineer officers up to date with matters which could not be published, and a series of translations of important foreign works on military engineering. He also started the Royal Engineers' Charitable Fund, which has been of great benefit to the widows and children of soldiers of his corps. In 1868 he visited Koblenz and reported on the experimental siege operations. In 1869 he was on a committee on spade drill for infantry, and accompanied Lieutenant-General Sir William Coddrington to the Prussian army manoeuvres. In summer 1870 he visited Belgium to study the Antwerp fortifications. From November 1870 to March 1871 he was attached officially to the German armies in France during the Franco-Prussian War, and was at the sieges of Paris, Mézières, and Belfort.

On 13 November 1871 Lennox was appointed assistant superintendent of military discipline at Chatham, and was on a committee on pontoon drill in December. In 1872 he again attended the military manoeuvres in Prussia. In December 1873 he went to Portsmouth as second in command of the Royal Engineers, and remained there until his appointment on 24 October 1876 as military attaché at Constantinople. He visited Montenegro in connection with the armistice on the frontier, and arrived in Constantinople in December. During the Russo-Turkish War, from April to December he accompanied the Turkish armies in Bulgaria.

In March 1878 Lennox went to the Curragh, Ireland, as commanding royal engineer until his promotion to major-general in August 1881. From 2 August 1884 he commanded the garrison of Alexandria, and during the Gordon relief expedition (1884–5) organized the landing and dispatch to the front of the troops, the Nile boats, and all the stores of the expedition. From Egypt he was transferred on 1 April 1887 to the command of the troops in Ceylon, but his promotion to lieutenant-general vacated the appointment in the following year, and he returned home via Australia and America. He was made KCB on 30 May 1891. He was director-general of military education at the War Office from 22 January 1893 until his retirement from the active list on 8 May 1895. He patented a light, portable table for camp use, and invented Tug-of-War and Pallas Word-Game. His energy, resolution, and decisiveness apparently fitted him for high command, and his kindness and Christian character endeared him to many.

Lennox married, first, at Denbigh, on 16 July 1861, Mary Harriett (*d.* 22 July 1863), daughter of Robert Harrison of Plas Clough, Denbighshire; they had a son, Gerald Wilbraham Stuart (1862–1937), lieutenant in the Black Watch. He married secondly, in London, on 12 June 1867, Susan Hay (*d.* 6 April 1912), youngest daughter of Admiral Sir John Gordon Sinclair of Stevenson, eighth baronet, and they had three sons.

Lennox contributed to the *Professional Papers of the Royal Engineers* and compiled *The Engineers' Organisation in the Prussian Army for Operations in the Field, 1870–1* (1878). He was writing a memoir of Sir Henry Harness's Indian career when he died at 49 Lupus Street, Pimlico, London, on 7 February 1897. He was buried in the family vault at Brighton cemetery on 15 February.

R. H. VETCH, *rev.* ROGER T. STEARN

Sources *The Times* (8 Feb 1897) · *Royal Engineers Journal*, 28 (April–May 1898) · A. W. Kinglake, *The invasion of the Crimea*, [new edn], 9 vols. (1877–88) · *Official journal of the engineers' operations at the siege of Sebastopol*, 1 and 2 (1859) · J. W. Kaye, *A history of the Sepoy War in India, 1857–1858*, 9th edn, 3 vols. (1880) · G. B. Malleson, *History of the Indian mutiny, 1857–1858: commencing from the close of the second volume of Sir John Kaye's History of the Sepoy War*, 3 vols. (1878–80) · J. G. Medley, *A year's campaigning in India: from March 1857 to March 1858* (1858) · E. T. Thackeray, *Two Indian campaigns in 1857–1858* (1896) · L. Shadwell, *The life of Colin Campbell*, 2 vols. (1881) · C. Hibbert, *The great mutiny, India, 1857* (1978) · *In relief of Gordon: Lord Wolseley's campaign journal of the Khartoum relief expedition, 1884–1885*, ed. A. Preston (1967) · A. D. Lambert, *The Crimean War: British grand strategy, 1853–56* (1990) · Burke, *Peerage* · Kelly, *Handbk* · E. W. C. Sandes, *The military engineer in India*, 1 (1933) · Boase, *Mod. Eng. biog.* · *WWW*

Archives BL, corresp. with Sir Austen Layard, Add. MSS 39013–39017, 39130, 39144–39146

Likenesses C. Silvy, carte-de-visite, 1861, NPG · portrait, repro. in T. E. Toomey, *Heroes of the Victoria cross* (1895), 55 · wood-engraving (after photograph by Russell & Sons), NPG; repro. in *ILN* (20 Feb 1897)

Wealth at death £4094 8*s.* 4*d.*: probate, 10 May 1897, *CGPLA Eng. & Wales*

Lennox, Lord William Pitt (1799–1881), army officer and writer, was the fourth son of Charles *Lennox, fourth duke of Richmond (1764–1819), and his wife, Lady Charlotte Gordon (1768–1842), eldest daughter of Alexander *Gordon, fourth duke of Gordon. He was the godson of William Pitt, who left him an engraved sword in 1806, and a cousin of Charles James Fox. He was born on 20 September 1799 at Winstead Abbey, Yorkshire, and baptized in the private chapel there, allegedly from the bowl of a favourite retriever named Tip, which became William's nickname. Lennox himself reported that his early education was neither systematic nor strict and that he was better with a pony than with books. He attended Westminster School under Dr Cary from 1808 to 1813, where flogging was rife, and he was fag to the future earl of Mar among others. This period he described in his book *Percy Hamilton* (1851). His holidays were spent in Phoenix Park, Dublin, where his father was lord lieutenant, and where Lennox developed a passion for amateur dramatics. In 1813 Lennox was gazetted a cornet in the Royal Horse Guards (Blues) through the patronage of Arthur Wellesley, later duke of Wellington, whom he had met in 1808. Later that year he and a friend escaped at night from school to go to the theatre and spend the night in a hotel.

They were betrayed, and the headmaster, instead of expelling him on the spot, sent him to spend an extra school year with a tutor.

On 8 August 1814 Lord William accompanied Wellington as an unpaid attaché to his embassy in Paris, and was there during the peace negotiations. In 1815 he was attached to General Sir Peregrine Maitland's staff, and was present at his mother's famous eve of Waterloo ball in Brussels. An accident when riding a Cossack horse in a race on 15 April 1815 precluded him from taking an active part in the battle of Waterloo, but he was able later to give a lively description of the scene, which he observed. He then rejoined his regiment in England. On 18 June 1818 he departed for Canada in HMS *Iphigenia* as an extra aide-de-camp to his father, who had been appointed governor-in-chief of British North America. Back in London, he was summoned at the last minute to be a page to Lord Hill at the coronation of George IV on 19 July 1821. He was promoted captain on 28 March 1822.

Lord William's life as described in his several volumes of autobiographical writings consisted mainly of social engagements, particularly at the theatre. He married the singer Mary Ann *Paton on 7 May 1824 and they had one daughter who died young. The marriage was dissolved by the Scottish court of session in 1831 and by act of parliament in 1834. Disraeli used Lord William as a model for Lord Prima Donna in his novel *Vivian Grey* (1827). In 1831 Lord William was elected as MP for King's Lynn, in which capacity he served for four years. He spoke on the Reform Bill and on regulating child labour, and supported the whig government on fees paid on vessels in quarantine and on the Anatomy Bill. He was, however, more interested in sport, particularly horse racing, and social life, and turned his attention to writing. In addition to his personal recollections and several undistinguished novels, he contributed to the *Sporting Review*, *Diadem*, the *Book of Beauty*, *Once a Week*, the *Illustrated London News*, *Land & Water*, and the *Court Journal*. He was described by the *Saturday Review* as 'a pleasant, amusing good-natured gossip'. *Memoirs of Madame Malibran* by Lady Merlin (1840) was based on a manuscript by Lennox. His autobiographical works, including *The Story of my Life* (3 vols., 1857), *Fifty Years' Biographical Reminiscences* (2 vols., 1863), and *Celebrities I Have Known* (4 vols., 1876–7), provide a rich fund of anecdotal material. He got married again, in 1854, to Ellen Smith, who died in 1859, and they had one son, William, who died unmarried in 1907. On 17 November 1863 he married his third wife, Maria Jane Molyneux (*d.* 1916), who later wrote a novel, *Castle Heather* (1888). By this time in his life he was not a rich man and supplemented his income by lecturing, in 1865 answering an advertisement for a lecturer at the Clapham Athenaeum. His subjects included physical education, reminiscences of Wellington, and reminiscences of Theodore Hook, 'His Hoaxes and Jokes'. He continued writing, and his last publication was *Plays, Players, and Playhouses at Home and Abroad* (1881). He died at his home, 34 Hans Place, London, on 18 February 1881 and was buried in Brompton cemetery on 25 February.

G. C. BOASE, *rev.* J. GILLILAND

Sources W. P. Lennox, *Fifty years' biographical reminiscences*, 2 vols. (1863) • W. P. Lennox, *My recollections from 1806–1873*, 2 vols. (1874) • [W. P. Lennox], *Three years with the duke of Wellington, or, Wellington in private life … by an ex-aide-de-camp* (1853) • W. P. Lennox, *The story of my life* (1857) • Burke, *Peerage* • W. D. Adams, *Dictionary of English literature*, rev. edn [1879–80] • Allibone, *Dict.* • Boase, *Mod. Eng. biog.* • *The Times* (19 Feb 1881) • *The Times* (22 Feb 1881) • *ILN* (26 Feb 1881) • *Saturday Review*, 16 (1863), 327–8

Archives BL, letters to Royal Literary Fund, loan 96 • Wellcome L., letters to Henry Lee

Likenesses H. Meyer, stipple and aquatint engraving, 1824 (after F. P. Stephanoff), BM • F. P. Stephanoff, watercolour drawing, V&A

Wealth at death under £10,000: resworn probate, Feb 1882, *CGPLA Eng. & Wales*

Leno, Dan [*real name* George Wild Galvin] (**1860–1904**), comedian, was born on 20 December 1860 at 6 Eve Place, London—not on the site of St Pancras Station, as often recounted, but just to the north. He was one of several children of John Galvin and his wife, Louisa, *née* Dutton, 'The Singing and Acting Duettists', known as Mr and Mrs Johnny Wild. No record of their activities has been found and their address in a poor part of London suggests that audiences did not rate them highly. George learned to entertain as an infant and in 1864 joined his parents on stage at the Cosmotheca Music-Hall, Paddington, under the billing 'Infant Wonder, Contortionist, and Posturer'. By 1866 his father was dead, reputedly through drink, and Mrs Galvin had married William Grant, a bibulous comedian of Irish extraction with the stage name of Leno. The family settled in Liverpool, where George and his older brother Jack formed a clog-dancing double act known as 'The Great Little Lenos'. Jack left to learn a trade and George probably made his first solo appearance aged nine at the Britannia Music-Hall, Glasgow, as the 'Quintessence of Irish Comedians' (meaning performer of comic songs; patter was introduced into music-hall later by Leno himself). His 'Irishness' dated from a visit to Ireland in 1869, and was reinforced by the stage name Dan Patrick. The family appeared in Dublin at the same time as Charles Dickens, who was giving readings. The story goes that, after watching the boy perform, Dickens said to him: 'Well done, little man. You'll make headway' (Brandreth, 12).

The young Leno received little schooling; touring the northern music-halls took all his time. By 1880 his clog dancing had become so good that he won the world championship at Leeds, though he still formed part of 'The Comic Trio (Mr & Mrs Leno and Dan Patrick) In Their Really Funny Entertainments, Songs and Dances'. By the time he appeared in the sketch 'Doctor Cut-'em-up' at the Grand Varieties, Sheffield, he had finally become Dan Leno and was a celebrity in the provinces. On 15 December 1884 he married the eighteen-year-old Sarah Reynolds, known as Lydia, a singer from Sunderland who was already pregnant; two years later he left the family troupe to make his first London appearance since childhood.

Leno opened at the Foresters' Music-Hall, Mile End, at £5 a week. Though billed as 'The Great Irish Comic Vocalist and Clog Champion', he slowly phased out his dancing in favour of character studies such as 'Going to Buy Milk for the Twins' and 'When Rafferty Raffled his Watch'. His fame spread and he was soon being billed as 'All the Rage' and 'The Talk of London'. During his years in variety he had begun to modernize solo comedy. Confining song to the start and finish of his act, he developed a style of patter in which life's adversities were made hilarious by mixing the humdrum with the surreal. Rather than being addressed directly, his audiences were like eavesdroppers on his attempts to explain some predicament to an acquaintance of limited understanding. This person 'could not grasp the situation until it had been put to him from every possible—and impossible—point of view' (Wood, xii). Leno's material and technique were captured in recordings made not long before he died. The sound quality is poor, but as an evocation of the nonpareil of music-hall they are priceless. He did not tell jokes, but presented the commonplace in fantastic guise. His shopwalkers, grocer's assistants, beefeaters, huntsmen, racegoers, firemen, fathers, henpecked husbands, and garrulous wives were the most ordinary of mortals turned into comic archetypes. 'All that trite and unlovely material, how new and beautiful it became through Dan Leno's genius' (Beerbohm, 349), wrote Max Beerbohm. Leno's comedy does not translate well to the page. So much depended on the look of comic wistfulness which audiences found irresistible:

> That face so tragic, with all the tragedy that is written on the face of a baby monkey, yet ever liable to relax its mouth into a sudden wide grin and to screw up its eyes to vanishing point over some little triumph wrested from Fate.
> (ibid., 350)

A Kinora reel showing him opening a bottle of champagne is too brief to reveal his range of expression, and the other films he made are lost, but the records give a flavour of his 'pleading, coaxing, arguing voice, hoarse with its eagerness, yet mellow with sheer kindliness and sweetness of character' (Wood, 222). Contemporaries observed a touch of Irish in his accent, though the records hint at his youth in the north of England.

As well as topping the bill in music-hall Leno appeared in burlesque and musical comedy, and from 1888 to 1903 starred in the Drury Lane pantomime every Christmas, generally as dame. His stage partner Herbert Campbell was as large and stolid as Leno was small and restless. They would use the script as a basis for invention and work gradually towards a finished performance. Rehearsals could seem so unpromising that spectators doubted the scene would be funny at all; they were rarely at their best until some nights after opening, causing Bernard Shaw to write of one appearance: 'I hope I never again have to endure anything more dismally futile' (Brandreth, 45). Even Beerbohm conceded that Leno did not do himself justice until he had 'collaborated with the public' (Beerbohm, 350), but he was exceptional in giving each of his dames a personality of her own, from extravagant queen to artless gossip. He and Campbell were so popular that in *Sleeping Beauty* they caused laughter even when the audience could not see them, simply by arriving on stage in closed palanquins, exchanging the lines 'Have you anything to do this afternoon, my dear?'—'No, I have nothing on', and being carried off again.

At his peak Leno earned £250 a week. He and Lydia bought substantial houses, first in Akerman Road, Brixton, then in Atkins Road, Clapham, employing a coachman and living in some style. Of their six children, three—Ernest, Sidney, and May—were to follow their father on to the stage, Sidney as Dan Leno junior. Away from home Leno was susceptible to any hard-luck story and gave away large sums of money. He co-founded the Grand Order of Water Rats, was president of the Music Hall Benevolent Fund, and supported his mother and stepfather, tolerating Grant's claim that he was 'the most famous man on earth—and I trained him!' (Wood, 99). The hyberbole scarcely varied when Leno went to America in 1897, billed as 'The Funniest Man On Earth'. He had only qualified success: one paper reported that the house roared its approval; another complained that his English humour was out-of-date. The following year he became the hero of *Dan Leno's Comic Journal*, the first real person to be so immortalized. *Dan Leno: hys Booke* (1899) was probably ghosted for him by T. C. Elder, who successfully hit off his style. In 1901 he performed his 'Huntsman' sketch for Edward VII at Sandringham: 'My friend said to me, when you come to a ditch, take it. So I took it. Well, I say I took it, I took about a pint-and-a-half.' The monarch was sufficiently amused to present him with a breast-pin. He became known as 'the king's jester' and at forty-one seemed set for ever-greater success, but heavy drinking and erratic behaviour had begun to affect his work. He was obsessed with the idea of playing Richard III, buttonholing the actor–manager Sir Herbert Beerbohm Tree with his proposals. Angry outbursts off-stage were the background to fluffed lines and inaudibility in performance. Treatment in a mental home proved fruitless, and Leno died at home, aged forty-three, on 31 October 1904. 'So little and frail a lantern could not long harbour so big a flame', wrote Beerbohm (Beerbohm, 349); other accounts referred to brain fag and exhaustion. In fact the cause of death was too shocking to be made public. It was certified as 'general paralysis of the insane', a euphemism for tertiary syphilis. Unaware of the truth, the thousands who eight days later watched Leno's cortège on its way to Lambeth cemetery, Tooting, mourned a man who had made them laugh. His legacy is such that Peter Ackroyd built a novel, *Dan Leno and the Limehouse Golem* (1994), around him, and the comedy of *ITMA*, the Goons, Frankie Howerd, and *Monty Python* owes something to his example. Charlie Chaplin called him the greatest comedian since Grimaldi; many consider that time has not overturned his judgement. JAMES HOGG

Sources J. H. Wood, *Dan Leno* (1905) • G. Brandreth, *The funniest man on earth: the story of Dan Leno* (1977) • M. Beerbohm, *Around theatres*, new edn (1953) • T. C. Elder, *Dan Leno: hys booke*, ed. J. Duncan (1968) • *DNB* • private information (2004) [B. Anthony] • B. Anthony, 'Leno, Dan', *Who's who in Victorian cinema*, ed. S. Herbert and L. McKernan (1996) • J. Fisher, *Funny way to be a hero* (1976) • C. MacInnes, *Sweet Saturday night*, [new edn] (1969) • H. Scott, *The early doors: origins of the music hall* (1946) • H. G. Hibbert, *Fifty years of a*

Londoner's life (1916) • C. Collier, *Harlequinade* (1929) • B. Anthony, 'A Kinora discovery', *Sight and Sound*, 59 (1989–90) • P. Ackroyd, *Dan Leno and the Limehouse golem* (1994) • b. cert. • m. cert. • d. cert.
Archives Theatre Museum, London | Jerwood Library of the Performing Arts, London, Mander and Mitchenson theatre collection, photographs, programmes, bills, and cuttings | FILM BFI NFTVA, performance footage • Fox Talbot Museum, Lacock, Wiltshire, home footage | SOUND BL NSA, performance recordings
Likenesses S. C. Cavin, bust, 1895, Theatre Royal, Drury Lane, London • rotary photograph, 1903, NPG • D. Leno, self-portrait, pen-and-ink sketch, NPG • postcard photograph, NPG
Wealth at death £10,994 16s. 7d.: administration, 9 Dec 1904, *CGPLA Eng. & Wales*

Le Noir [*née* Smart]**, Elizabeth Anne** (*bap.* **1754**, *d.* **1841**), poet and novelist, was baptized on 21 November 1754 at Canonbury House, Islington, the second daughter of Christopher *Smart (1722–1771), poet. Her mother, Anna Maria Carnan (1732–1809), with whom Smart had eloped, was the stepdaughter of the publisher John Newbery, who had married Mary Hounshill Carnan, widow of William Carnan, publisher of the *Reading Mercury*. In London Christopher Smart wrote for Newbery, who placed the young family in lodgings in Canonbury House where Elizabeth Smart was born and spent her first seven years, familiar with another inmate, Oliver Goldsmith, and with Samuel Johnson, to whom she (not a 'Miss Hunter') addressed a question about his strange gestures (Boswell, *Life*, 183 n. 2, 512–13). After one visit to her father in the madhouse about 1758 Elizabeth Smart may never have seen him again. Roman Catholics like their mother, she and her sister Marianne spent three years from about 1763 to 1766 in a Boulogne convent. In 1762 Newbery had turned the management of her father's *Reading Mercury* over to Anna Maria Smart, and on his death in 1767 he left the business to her and her brother John, who, when he died in 1785, left his half of the business to his two nieces. In 1793 Marianne Smart married a former apprentice to the business, Thomas Cowslade, who succeeded to the management of the paper in which he was followed by three of their sons. Anna Maria Smart made her daughter unhappy by discouraging her literary efforts (which Newbery encouraged) and, Elizabeth later wrote, 'I was born under a cloud where discouragement on the part of others and diffidence on my own have always left me' (Sharp MS 28, 13 July 1831). But for fifty years she produced an annual 'Newsman's address' or 'Ode' for the initial paper of the year. On their mother's death in 1809 the sisters inherited the remaining half-share of the paper.

After 1789 Elizabeth Smart joined with the rest of the Catholic community in assisting the great number of French refugees in Reading, and in 1795 she married the Chevalier Jean Baptiste Le Noir de la Brosse, who was dependent on a £60 pension. There seems little reason to confound the chevalier with the émigré Pierre Valery Le Noir, who taught French language, literature, and pronunciation and published a great variety of poetry, orations, and textbooks. This man died in 1833 and Elizabeth Le Noir's husband was apparently still living when she died in 1841. The pair had no children, but Le Noir adopted her niece and god-daughter Eleanora Cowslade (*b.* 1792), with whom she opened a boarding-school.

Elizabeth Le Noir did not publish until she was fifty, when, under financial pressure and perhaps to advertise her school, she issued her 'first child', *Village Anecdotes, or, The Journal of a Year, from Sophia to Edward, with Original Poems*, in 1804. George Dyer learned of the manuscript and arranged publication. That year verses from the work, 'On Seeing a Ship Sail', and a warm review of the book announcing much delight with 'many very beautiful pieces of poetry' appeared, remarking that the author was said to have 'possessed much of the poetical spirit of her father' (*GM*, 1st ser., 74, 1804, 661–2). A second revised edition in three volumes with additional characters and poems was published by subscription in 1807 and dedicated to her father's friend Charles Burney DMus, and there was a third edition in 1821. In 1808 appeared *Clara de Montfier, a Moral Tale, with Original Poems*, dedicated through the offices of Burney to Lady Charlotte Greville. This work too was popular enough to be issued in a second edition in 1819 as *The Maid of La Vendée … with Critical Remarks by Dr. Burney and the Rev. Christopher Hunter. Conversations, Interspersed with Poems, for the Amusement and Instruction of Youth* in three volumes appeared in 1812. In 1823 her lines 'To W—H—, with a Pen Knife' were published, accompanied by praise of her work which noted that Burney had pronounced *The Maid of La Vendée* the best work of the kind he had ever read, and that her two-volume *Conversations* was 'best of all', 'skilfully blending instruction with amusement' (*GM*, 1st ser., 93/1, 1823, 582–3). Le Noir's best-known work, her *Miscellaneous Poems* in two volumes, dedicated to Viscountess Sidmouth, was printed in Reading in 1825–6, but never advertised in London. Le Noir also claimed a work, *Meditations on the Gospel from the French*, a translation in four volumes, but noted it to be 'little known, but much approved'. In 1830 Le Noir and her niece moved their academy to Caversham Priory, near Reading. She died at Caversham Priory on 6 May 1841, aged eighty-six.

Discouragement and diffidence impeded Elizabeth Le Noir's writing career, and her works, approved in her day, are now difficult to find, but Mary Russell Mitford admired them and wrote that her 'books when taken up one does not care to put down again' (M. R. Mitford, *Recollections of a Literary Life*, 1852, 3.101). She left at her death an unpublished comedy, an incomplete collection of her newsman's odes, and many less ambitious works, and wrote:

> my pen has been my solace through sickness and sorrow; it has been my introduction to valuable and steady friends, & therefore I must not complain of it, if it has brought me little of fame & less of profit. (Sharp MS 28, 22 Aug 1831)

Betty Rizzo

Sources E. Le Noir, letters to Cuthbert Sharp, 13 July 1831, 30 July 1831, 22 Aug 1831, Durham Cath. CL, Sharp MS 28, 217–45 • E. Le Noir, letter to E. H. Barker, 21 March 1825, Bodl. Oxf., MS Bodley 1006, fols. 245–6 • E. Le Noir, letter to E. H. Barker, [n.d.], Bodl. Oxf., MS Montagu d.14, fols. 122–3 • 'The Catholic registers of Reading', *Catholic Record Society Miscellanea*, 32 (1780–1840), 117–91 • A. Sherbo, *Christopher Smart, scholar of the university* (1967) • *GM*, 1st ser., 74

(1804), 661–2, 668 • *GM*, 1st ser., 93/1 (1823), 582–3 • *GM*, 2nd ser., 15 (1841), 667 • registers, Islington, St Mary's
Archives Bodl. Oxf., letters to E. H. Barker • Durham Cath. CL, letters to Cuthbert Sharp

Lens [Laus] **family** (*per. c.*1650–1779), artists, was probably settled in England by **Bernard** [i] **Lens** (1630/31–1707/8), who was described by George Vertue as a 'Dutch Preacher' (Vertue, *Note books*, 5.5) ('4 or 5 books written in English by him … scriptural matters'), and as a 'painter' who died in England 'Feb 5. 1707/8. Aged 77. lyes buried in St. Brides London' (ibid., 5.62).

Michel Huber (1727–1804) noted that **Bernard** [ii] **Lens** (1659/60–1725) was 'fils de Bernard Lens, habile peintre en émail' ('son of Bernard Lens, skilled painter in enamel'; Huber, 9.90). Vertue noted that Bernard [ii] Lens was a 'mezsotintor scraper' (Vertue, *Note books*, 5.62) (there are collections of his mezzotints in the British Museum and the Yale Center for British Art, New Haven, Connecticut) and that he also 'drew for engravers principally Mr Sturt [John Sturt, 1658–1730] … for plates books &c.' (ibid., 4.184). In 1697, with Sturt, he set up a drawing-school, one of the first in England, near the Hand and Pen, in St Paul's Churchyard, London, which continued until at least after 1710. In 1705 Lens was appointed drawing-master at Christ's Hospital, a charity school where drawing was taught as a vocational subject, for example, in mapping or navigation. Vertue noted that he 'dy'd 28 April 1725. aged 66—buried at St Brides—fleet Street' (ibid., 5.62), leaving several sons. John Lens (1683/4–*c.*1716), a drawing-master from 1703 at 'Major' John Ayres's school at the Hand and Pen, near St Paul's School, was portrayed by his brother Bernard [iii] Lens in a miniature inscribed 'John Laus, aet 24 Gunner. B. Laus aetat.26 fecit. March ye 24, 1708' (ex Sothebys, 25 May 1964). A younger son of Bernard [ii] Lens, Edward (*c.*1685–1749), succeeded his father as drawing-master at Christ's Hospital; on his death his son, John (*b.* 1725), applied unsuccessfully for the post, which was awarded to Alexander Cozens.

The most successful of Lens's sons was **Bernard** [iii] **Lens** (1682–1740). An inscription on his self-portrait in miniature (NPG) records his date of birth: 'Bernard Lens/ Pictor … Born may:ye.29:1682'. In 1698 he was formally apprenticed to 'Sturt' (presumably his father's partner, John Sturt) of the Goldsmiths' Company, of which he himself chose to be made free only in 1729, the year in which his son Peter Paul Lens (*b.* 1714/15, *d.* in or after 1754) was apprenticed under him. On 30 November 1706, in Gray's Inn Chapel, Bernard [iii] Lens had married Katherine Woods (*b. c.*1681). They are known to have had at least three sons. Vertue noted that one of these, presumably the eldest, also called Bernard, was 'no Artist—but was promoted to some little office in the Exchequer' (Vertue, *Note books*, 5.63), apparently with the help of Horace Walpole. The work of Peter Paul and the third son, Andrew Benjamin Lens, is noticed below.

The work of Bernard [ii] Lens and his artist sons Bernard [iii] Lens and Edward Lens often overlapped, although Bernard [iii] Lens was the only miniature painter. It is often not clear which member of the family was responsible for any given piece of work. One example is a drawing manual, *A New and Compleat Drawing Book* (1750), which has traditionally been wholly attributed to the younger Bernard Lens, and yet the frontispiece describes 'Mr Lens' as 'Drawing Master to Christ's Hospital', a position in fact held by his father and brother Edward. The text and figural plates are adapted from other drawing manuals by, for example, Gérard de Lairesse and Charles-Alfonse Dufresnoy, and many of the engraved coastal and fortress scenes are after drawings by other members of the Lens family. As Bernard [iii] Lens also had at least two sons who became artists, the attribution of drawings by members of the Lens family is complex. Some drawings are signed by individual members of the family, but they so often copied each others' drawings that attribution of the often unsigned topographical pen and ink wash drawings must be uncertain. (Examples are in the British Museum and the Yale Center for British Art.) The variety of topographical work undertaken by Bernard [iii] Lens and his sons is reflected in the sale held at his death: 'His Catalog. of limnings drawings sold—22[d] June 1740/1 … Views of Bath … Wokeyhole—Bridgnorth Shropshire … Richmond … Portsmouth … Windsor … Eaton. Glastonbury Glocestershire shropshire—Rochester … Greenwich. London Hampton Court &c. London &c. different Exercise of the Granadiars, colourd' (Vertue, *Note books* 3.100; the last work is now in the V&A).

It can be equally unclear to which Lens a contemporary writer might be referring. In 1707 a letter written to Robert Harley, father of Edward Harley (later second earl of Oxford, a miniature collector and patron of both Vertue and Bernard [iii] Lens), stated:

> You was pleasd to desire me to speak to a person that could teach your son, Mr Edwd, to draw. I have sent for Mr Lens, a very able and the best master we have in London—a sober, diligent man, and very carefull. His rate for teaching is a guinea entrance, and half-a-crown a time (for an hour's staying). (Goulding, 41)

This letter could refer to Bernard [ii] or Bernard [iii] Lens, for by this date the latter was twenty-five, and throughout his career he worked as a fashionable drawing-master. Notable students included Horace Walpole, who in his own copy of Vertue's notes annotated a reference to him: 'was my master, H. W.' (Vertue, *Note books*, 5.62), and Lady Helena Percival (a landscape by her is in the British Museum). In addition to drawing, Bernard [iii] Lens taught miniature painting: among his pupils were Princess Mary, the daughter of George II and Queen Caroline (Mary's miniature of her sister Louisa is in the Royal Collection), and Catherine da Costa (miniatures by her of her family are held by the Jewish Museum, London).

In his notes Vertue usually referred to Bernard [iii] Lens as a 'limner'. This was the traditional term for a painter in watercolour, although during Lens's lifetime it gave way to the term 'painter in miniature' or 'miniature painter'. Vertue says that Lens was mistakenly designated 'enameller' on his appointment to the service of George I and George II, and explained that the mistake originated in the lord chamberlain's records: 'Mr Lens limner. Is calld his Majestyes Enameller. In the books of the chamberlains Office. & his warrant. Which was causd by Mr. Boit Enameller when he procurd the place, he got the stile to be alter'd from Limner to Enameller' (Vertue, *Note books*, 3.50). Lens was officially registered 'Painter in Enamell in Ordinary' on 16 January 1720. In his own, presumably later, inscription on a self-portrait (priv. coll.) he significantly replaced the incorrect designation 'enameller' with the Italian for limning, *miniatura*: 'Bernard Lens Pictore ad vivum. Aged : 37 : Fecit Oct ye : 18 : 1718. Painter in Minatura [*sic*] in Ordinary to his Majesty King George' (Goulding, cat. no. 148). Vertue added that 'Mr Lens has no Sallery' (Vertue, *Note books*, 3.50).

Bernard [iii] Lens's earliest-known dated miniature, *Portrait of Dr Harris* (1707; Yale U. CBA) is important for being the earliest dated miniature painted in Britain on ivory rather than the traditional vellum support. Lens pioneered the use of ivory in Britain, but it was Rosalba Carriera, a Venetian artist, who probably first used ivory in place of vellum as a support. Her self-portrait on ivory was accepted as her diploma piece for the Academy of St Luke in 1704. *Dr Harris*, painted only three years later, when Lens was twenty-five, is sufficiently competent not to be a first attempt at limning. It is not known whether Lens received tuition in traditional limning on vellum, but at this date limning was an established amateur pastime and he would not necessarily have been taught by a professional limner. Carriera never visited England, and there is no evidence that Lens travelled abroad. He probably heard of the use of ivory or saw examples of miniatures painted on ivory in the homes of clients and pupils who had travelled to Italy on the grand tour. He seems not to have understood Carriera's methods of working on the difficult ivory surface. He worked more cautiously, first using touches of graphite to sketch the sitter. Like Carriera he abandoned the seventeenth-century technique of laying in a ground, called a carnation, in the face, leaving the ivory as the ground. But he mixed his pigments with more gum, thus easing the adhesion between ivory and paint, and he worked the features in both stipple and hatching. The effect is harder, tighter, and less free than Carriera's work. Like Carriera he painted the background in solid colour, but unlike her he did not break it up and soften it with stipples, but occasionally added a few dry hatches. Both his technique and less assured draughtsmanship contributed to the stiffer appearance of his miniatures. None the less, it is evident that Lens was responsible for encouraging the use of ivory in Britain, not just through the example of his miniatures, but also through teaching.

Bernard [iii] Lens also made limned copies of old master paintings on vellum, continuing a respected tradition begun by Peter Oliver, who had made copies for Charles I of paintings in the king's collection. Vertue noted that one of Lens's pupils, Catherine da Costa, 'copy'd pictures that mr lens her instructor had coppyd … mostly all the remarkable pictures of fame in england painted by rubens Vandyke & other masters' (Vertue, *Note books*, 3.115). Large copies, such as *Landscape with Bathers* (V&A), after Vandervart, would have been expensive, and it is likely that they were commissioned by a collector rather than produced speculatively. There is a bill from Edward Harley for work commissioned from Bernard [iii] Lens: '1719. A large half length of Mathew Prior, Esqr., on a large skin of Vellum … after a French Pictor' (Goulding, 41) (priv. coll.). In contrast, it was possibly a speculative venture to paint a series of copies on vellum, with sixteenth-century style solid blue backgrounds, of kings and queens of England and including the lord protector, Oliver Cromwell (six examples are in the V&A). These are roughly painted and seem to have been produced rapidly, with some examples contributed by Andrew Benjamin Lens, the son of Bernard [iii] Lens. These miniatures probably appealed to collectors who wanted more expensive and 'authentic' versions of the popular engraved 'heads' published by, for example, Vertue. The most frequently encountered historical 'head' by Bernard [iii] Lens, also known in versions by his pupil Catherine da Costa, is that of a so-called Mary Queen of Scots (a version by da Costa is in Ham House, Surrey). Lens also copied Samuel Cooper's famous miniature of Oliver Cromwell; one example on vellum dated 1717 is in the Royal Collection, another on ivory dated 1723 is at Welbeck Abbey. Both are signed and inscribed with a note that they were taken from the original Cooper belonging to Thomas Frankland.

Bernard [iii] Lens collected historical miniatures, especially those by Samuel Cooper; Vertue noted that Lens 'has two or three heads, the womans faces only finisht, the finest I ever saw of Cooper' (Vertue, *Note books*, 1.108). He also advised collectors on the care of their collections. Notably he worked for Edward Harley, second earl of Oxford (whose collection of miniatures is housed today at Welbeck Abbey, Nottinghamshire). The simple stained black pear-wood frames he produced to house pieces from the earl's collection are still known today as 'Lens frames'.

Bernard [iii] Lens's knowledge of limnings made in the sixteenth and seventeenth centuries is reflected in some of his *ad vivum* miniatures; for example, his portraits of the family of Richard Whitmore MP (two of which are in the V&A, the remainder illustrated in Christies' sale catalogue of 2 November 1971), have a flat blue background in imitation of the Elizabethan miniatures which he encountered in numerous collections. His portraits of contemporaries include miniatures of Mohawk and Mahican members of a group which made a historic visit to Queen Anne in London in 1710 (British Museum).

Lens's work on the traditional vellum support, where the vellum is laid onto card backed with gesso, shows his knowledge of seventeenth-century professional limning techniques, as in, for example, a self-portrait (NPG). However, it seems that he did not have a particular motivation in his choice of support, nor did he follow any apparent strategy or consistency with regard to the impact of that choice. Thus historical copies which could more appropriately be on vellum are on ivory, while some contemporary portraits are on vellum rather than the more modern ivory. During Lens's early career there were few other professional limners in London. Peter Cross (*c*.1645–1724) was still practising in 1707 (his *Katherine Tufton* (V&A) is dated 1707), the year that Lens painted his first known dated miniature. Vertue noted: 'Mr Zurick [Johann Zurich, *c*.1685–1735] … of Dresden … comeing to England about 1714 or 15 his generall employment was limning', but added that Zurich (whose work cannot be identified today) could not rise to equal those artists already 'established in reputation and merit, as mr Bernard lens. Mr. Rechter. [Christian Richter, 1682–1732, a Swedish limner] Mr Zinke enamaller' (Vertue, *Note books*, 3.76–7). Zurich was apparently the only painter of miniatures at this early date, apart from Lens, who painted on ivory, which Vertue noted later in 1735 was 'A manner much used of late years amongst the limners' (ibid.).

Lens became a member of the Rose and Crown club, along with Zincke, Vertue, and William Hogarth. A painting of the *Virtuosi of London*, begun by John Smibert in 1724 but now known only from a marginal sketch in Vertue's *Note Books*, includes Lens, although he evidently was not present at the group sittings, being represented by a painting on an easel: 'in the large painting/piece of the Virtuosi of London … Lens on the Easel a profil' (Vertue, *Note books*, 3.24). Of the eighty-five members of the Rose and Crown club, half, including Lens, attended the academy in Queen Anne Street founded by Sir Godfrey Kneller in 1711. Kneller's influence may be seen in a few of Lens's compositions: his miniature of a child called Jane Codd (V&A) borrows the somewhat awkward pose used by Kneller in his portrait of *Mrs Voss and Child* (engraved by I. Smith), and his miniature of George I (V&A) is copied from a print after a portrait by Kneller; the miniature is inscribed on the reverse with an exact transcription of the lettering on the print.

Vertue noted that Bernard [iii] Lens died:

> Decemb. 1740—Christmas Eve … at his house near Hyde park Hospital—after his long Illness, being sweld (dropsical) by very slow and continud degres carryd him off. By a dropsy. he was buried at Kensington church. (born Oct. 18, 1681 [*sic*]. Ob 24 Decembr. 1740—aeta : 59—2 month—) leaving two sons professors of the Art of Painting limning—&c. (Vertue, *Note books*, 3.100)

One of these sons was **Andrew Benjamin Lens** (*c*.1713–*c*.1779), miniature painter and drawing-master. His year of birth is inferred from a portrait of him by his father dated 1723 in which he appears to be about ten years old (V&A). He exhibited at the Society of Artists and the Free Society of Artists from 1764 until 1779. The other son was **Peter Paul Lens** (*b*. 1714/15, *d*. in or after 1754). His year of birth is inferred from a miniature of him aged fifteen and dated 1729. No works are known by P. P. Lens after about 1750, but the address given in an advert for a 'Lens, miniature painter' in the *Public Advertiser* (1 December 1754) implies that he was still active in 1754. P. P. Lens became notorious as a member between 1737 and 1738 of a 'hell-fire' club in Ireland called The Blasters, possibly in Dublin, which he visited about 1737. Vertue confused the identity and reputations of the two sons, but clearly meant P. P. Lens when he referred to 'Young Lens, calld the *reprobate*' (Vertue, *Note books*, 3.88). He later described him as 'An Ingenious Youth. Whose vile, athestical conversations and behaviour, publickly practised (for some such wicked blasphemous affair in Ireland. He was forc'd to fly away)' (ibid., 3.106). Other artists with the name of Lens are also known. A John Lens advertised three times in the *Daily Advertiser* during 1752–3 and offered his services in the issue of 14 September 1752 as teacher of drawing and miniature painting, while in the issue of 2 October 1753 he described himself as a 'miniature painter' and was promoting 'a new drawing book'. It is possible that this is the same John Lens (1703–1779) whose death was recorded in the *Gentleman's Magazine* (49, 1779, 566). He was a miniature painter who was engaged to teach drawing at the Revd d'Latournelle's academy in Norwich. He also taught watercolours and painting on silk until 1763, when he began to advertise as a land-steward. The *Public Advertiser* (7 August 1765) carried an advertisement by a Thomas Lens for 'Miniature Painting'. The relationship of these men to the Lens family of artists has not been established.

KATHERINE COOMBS

Sources Vertue, *Note books* · R. W. Goulding, 'The Welbeck Abbey miniatures', *Walpole Society*, 4 (1914–15) [whole issue] · J. Kerslake, *National Portrait Gallery: early Georgian portraits*, 2 vols. (1977) · M. Huber and C. G. Martini, *Manuel des curieux et des amateurs de l'art*, 9 (Zürich, 1808) · B. S. Long, *British miniaturists* (1929) · lord chamberlain's appointment books, 1714–33, PRO, LC 3/63–4 · K. M. Sloan, 'The teaching of non-professional artists in eighteenth-century England', 2 vols., PhD diss., U. Lond., 1986, esp. chap. 2, appx c · E. Croft-Murray, 'Catalogue of British drawings in the British Museum', vol. 2, BM, department of prints and drawings · J. Murdoch and others, *The English miniature* (1981) · A. Crookshank and the Knight of Glin [D. Fitzgerald], *The watercolours of Ireland: works on paper in pencil, pastel and paint, c.1600–1914* (1994)

Likenesses B. Lens, self-portrait, miniature, 1708, Ickworth House, Suffolk · B. Lens, self-portrait, miniature, 1721, NPG · B. Lens, miniature, 1723 (Andrew Benjamin Lens as a child), V&A · B. Lens, self-portrait, miniature, 1724, AM Oxf. · L. P. Biotard, line engraving, pubd 1750–51 (after B. Lens), BM; repro. in *Drawing Book* (1750–51)

Lens, Andrew Benjamin (*c*.1713–*c*.1779). *See under* Lens family (*per. c*.1650–1779).

Lens, Bernard (1630/31–1707/8). *See under* Lens family (*per. c*.1650–1779).

Lens, Bernard (1659/60–1725). *See under* Lens family (*per. c*.1650–1779).

Lens, Bernard (1682–1740). *See under* Lens family (*per. c*.1650–1779).

Lens, John (1756–1825), serjeant-at-law, was born on 2 January 1756 in Norwich, son of John Lens, a well-known land agent in the city. He was educated first at a school in Norwich, and then by the Revd John Peele. In 1775 he matriculated at St John's College, Cambridge; he graduated BA in 1779, when he was fourth wrangler and chancellor's medallist, and MA in 1782. After leaving Cambridge Lens entered Lincoln's Inn, where he was called to the bar on 16 June 1781. He at first joined the Norfolk circuit, but soon transferred himself to the western circuit, which he led for many years. On 12 June 1799 Lens became a serjeant-at-law, taking the motto *Libertas sub rege pio*; he became king's serjeant on 19 April 1806 and in 1819 king's prime, or ancient serjeant, in succession to Samuel Shepherd. Lens was named a lay fellow of Downing College, Cambridge, in its charter in 1800, was treasurer of Serjeants' Inn from 1806 to 1823, and succeeded Spencer Perceval in 1807 as counsel to the University of Cambridge. In 1816 Lens appeared for the defendant in *Wyatt* v. *Gore* (a libel action by the surveyor-general of crown lands in Canada against the governor of Upper Canada), and for the plaintiff in *Lord Rivers* v. *King* (the Cranborne Chase boundaries case). On 1 October 1818 he married Mrs Nares, widow of John Nares, son of Sir George Nares, a judge of the common pleas; they had at least one child.

A friend and adherent of Charles James Fox, Lens was a whig by conviction, and might, had he chosen, have represented the University of Cambridge in parliament. But he was as indifferent to honours as he was completely disinterested; in December 1813, on the appointment of Sir Robert Dallas to the bench of the common pleas, he declined the solicitor-generalship, although it was pressed upon him by the prime minister at the request of the prince regent, who was his friend. In 1817 Lens retired from his circuit at the height of his powers in order to make way for younger men, but he continued to practise in London, acting also as commissioner of assize on the home circuit in 1818 in place of Lord Ellenborough. He refused the chief justiceship of Chester, and Lord Ellenborough strongly recommended him as his own successor in the office of lord chief justice.

Lens became seriously ill in 1823 and, after an operation, gave up all professional activity. He died at Ryde, in the Isle of Wight, on 6 August 1825, and was buried in the family vault in Huntingdonshire. His wife had predeceased him on 15 June 1820. Lens was an elegant scholar and a perfect gentleman, a sound lawyer and an eloquent pleader; and, in spite of the fact that he was an 'aquatic' (a water drinker), a popular and respected leader of the western circuit, 'a truly amiable, venerable and learned Gentleman' (*The Times*, 18 July 1818).

J. A. Hamilton, *rev.* David Pugsley

Sources H. W. Woolrych, *Lives of eminent serjeants-at-law of the English bar*, 2 vols. (1869) • Amicus Curiae [J. P. Collier], *Criticisms on the bar* (1819), 123–34 • *GM*, 1st ser., 95/2 (1825), 373–4 • Mrs Hardcastle, *Life of Lord Campbell*, 1 (1881), 313, 330–31 • John, Lord Campbell, *The lives of the chief justices of England*, 3 (1857), 225–6, 289 • Venn, *Alum. Cant.* • Baker, *Serjeants* • Sainty, *King's counsel*, 33–7 • *The Times* (18 July 1818) • *The Times* (11 Aug 1825) • *The Times* (16 Aug 1825)

Likenesses C. Penny, stipple, pubd 1825, NPG • F. C. Lewis, stipple (after E. Coffin), BM, NPG

Lens, Peter Paul (*b.* 1714/15, *d.* in or after 1754). *See under* Lens family (*per. c.*1650–1779).

Lenshina, Alice Mulenga (1920–1978), visionary and founder of the Lumpa church in Northern Rhodesia, was born in 1920 in the Chinsali district of the northern province of Northern Rhodesia. Her given name was Mulenga. Alice was her baptismal name, and Lenshina, a Bemba form of the Latin word *regina*, was a name which she chose for herself. She was the daughter, by a junior wife, of Lubusha Kasaka. He was the son of a chief, a member of the extensive royal family of the Bemba people, and became a district messenger, a minor functionary in the colonial administration. Chinsali district, though remote, was an area of political and religious importance. It was the scene of strong competition between two Christian missions, the protestant United Free Church of Scotland (later Church of Scotland) based at Lubwa from 1905, and the Roman Catholic Missionaries of Africa—the White Fathers—mission based at Ilondola from 1934. Among the early missionaries at Lubwa was the Revd David Kaunda, whose son Kenneth became the first president of Zambia in 1964. The first vice-president, Simon Kapwepwe, also came from Chinsali district and, together with Kenneth Kaunda, had his primary education at Lubwa Mission.

In September 1953 Lenshina became seriously ill with cerebral malaria at Kasomo village, about 5 miles from Chinsali. She fell into a deep coma and was not expected to recover:

> But after a few days she slowly regained consciousness and to everybody's surprise claimed to have met the saviour Jesus Christ, who had sent her back to earth with a special message and a new commitment. As a sign of her vocation she began to compose beautiful hymns according to traditional modalities. (H. Hinfelaar, *Bemba Women and Religious Change*, 1994, 73)

She was subsequently baptized at Lubwa Mission. Her near-death experience and baptism initiated a revival movement which was welcomed by the young Scottish missionary at Lubwa, the Revd Fergus MacPherson, and by the church elders. She maintained for a while a close relationship with MacPherson and named a daughter, Catherine, after his child who had died at Lubwa.

Within two or three years, however, the revival movement within the Church of Scotland mission church had, with its strident call for repentance, taken on some of the characteristics of a witchcraft eradication movement, and had grown into an independent church. The Lumpa (meaning superior) church began to compete aggressively with both the protestant and Catholic mission churches in the area and was seen by the colonial government as a political threat. The church was led by the *badikoni*—deacons—and built its own churches. Its leaders included leading members of Lubwa families, including the Kaundas, Kapwepwes, and Makasas. Kenneth Kaunda's elder brother, Robert, was a leading member, and helped in the composition and writing down of Lenshina's hymns. Lenshina's husband, Petros Chintankwa (*d.* 1972), also played a leading part in the organization. At its peak in the late 1950s the church may have had as many as 150,000 adherents in five districts of the northern and eastern provinces.

The Lumpa church was seen at first as close to the African National Congress, but a split in the nationalist movement in 1958 and the formation of the more militant United National Independence Party (UNIP), led by Kenneth Kaunda, led to competition for adherents between the new party and the new church. Increasing friction between church members and UNIP supporters, especially from the later months of 1962, led Lumpa leaders to order their followers to move out of villages, where they lived alongside UNIP supporters, and to establish separate villages. About 30,000 supporters, both Bemba and Tumbuka speakers, segregated themselves in thirty or forty villages—some of them stockaded. The conflict reached a peak in the months before independence—July to October 1964. During that time about 1000 people were killed in clashes between UNIP members and Lenshina's followers, and between the security forces and the latter. According to official figures, almost 500 of the deaths were caused by security force action. About 15,000 of Lenshina's followers became refugees in the Congo. Some have remained there ever since. The so-called Lumpa revolt, and its violent suppression, cast a shadow over the decolonization process and the last months of colonial rule—a time when Kenneth Kaunda was prime minister and head of government, but the governor, Sir Evelyn Hone, retained responsibility for law and order.

It was generally recognized that Alice Lenshina had herself played little or no part in the political activities of the movement which was founded in her name. In her last interviews she regretted the political direction which the movement had taken and blamed this on the deacons. She regretted that this had weakened the religious impact of her message—which Hinfelaar sees as having much to do with the sanctity of marriage, and the uplifting of commoners and of women.

Alice Lenshina was never brought to trial, but was detained with her husband in the Mumbwa district in August 1964. In March 1965 she was placed in restriction in the Kalabo district near the border with Angola. She escaped with her husband in October 1967, was gaoled for six months, and was again restricted in the Mkushi district. In May 1970 she was placed in detention. In the early 1970s her large temple church at Kasomo was destroyed by the government. She was finally released from detention in December 1975, but was placed under house arrest in New Chilenje compound, Lusaka. Her husband died on 6 October 1972. She died on 7 December 1978 at New Chilenje, Lusaka, and was buried at Kasomo village.

HUGH MACMILLAN

Sources H. F. Hinfelaar, *Bemba-speaking women of Zambia in a century of religious change* (1994) • J. Hudson, *A time to mourn: a personal account of the 1964 Lumpa Church in Zambia* (Lusaka, 1999) • F. Macpherson, *Kenneth Kaunda of Zambia: the times and the man* (Lusaka, 1974) • J. J. Grotpeter, B. V. Siegel, and J. R. Pletcher, *Historical dictionary of Zambia*, 2nd edn (1998)

Likenesses photograph, repro. in Hudson, *A time to mourn*, 15 and cover

Lenthall, Sir John (1624/5–1681), politician and lawyer, was the only surviving son of William *Lenthall, created Lord Lenthall under the protectorate (1591–1662), of Burford Priory, Oxfordshire, lawyer and speaker of the House of Commons, and Elizabeth (*d.* 1662), daughter of Ambrose Evans of Loddington, Northamptonshire. On 12 September 1640 he matriculated, aged fifteen, from Corpus Christi College, Oxford. Following his father in the law, he was admitted in the same year to Lincoln's Inn, and was called to the bar in 1647. Elected MP for Gloucester in 1645, he survived Pride's purge of parliament in December 1648 and continued to sit in the Rump Parliament until 1653. During this period he served as a commissioner for the army, as JP for Berkshire and Oxfordshire, and as a member of the assessment committees for Gloucester. He was a commissioner for the trial of King Charles I but did not sit.

Between 1643 and 1654 Lenthall was one of the six clerks in chancery, petitioning in July 1655 to obtain the office for life after it was transferred to another. He defended his right to the post by the laws of God, Magna Carta, and parliament, and called on Protector Oliver Cromwell to compensate his subjects 'as other kings have done and as I fear not but you will do … with the miracle and greatness of your wisdom and justice' (*CSP dom.*, *1655*, 230). Although the petition was unsuccessful Lenthall was valued enough by the protector to be knighted in March 1658, and in January 1659 was reported to be a 'fit person to be trusted with the command of Windsor Castle', where he was made governor and commanded a regiment of foot (*JHC*, 7.814). During the 1650s he married Mary (*d.* after 1667), daughter of Sir William Ashcombe of Alvescot, Oxfordshire.

Although Anthony Wood described Lenthall as the 'grand braggadocio and liar of the age' (Wood, *Ath. Oxon.*, 3.608), Edmund Ludlow believed him to be 'a better oratour than his father' (Ludlow, 172). He is chiefly admired for his stance in the Commons during the debate over the Indemnity Bill of 1660, which demanded that the perpetrators of regicide be called to justice. On 12 May Lenthall rose and proclaimed, 'he that first drew his sword against the king committed as high an offence as he that cut off the king's head'; this was the only attempt to recognize that it was not merely those who signed Charles I's death warrant who were guilty of involvement in his death (*JHC*, 8.24). Lucy Hutchinson wrote in her memoir that Lenthall spoke 'with so much courage and honour as was not matched at that time in England' (Hutchinson, 279). The presbyterians in the house were angered by the speech, calling Lenthall to the bar; he was severely reprimanded by the speaker, who announced that 'there is much of poison in the words, and that they were spoken out of design to set this house on fire', and sent him briefly to the Tower of London (*JHC*, 8.24).

Lenthall left the Commons on 23 May 1660 after it was found that Sir George Stonhouse had 'a greater number of voices' for Abingdon after a double return (*JHC*, 8.24). In November he was arrested for hiring a man to take an impression of the great seal of England, but later released on £3000 bail. During 1661 he reportedly frequented Nonsuch House, a coffee house in Covent Garden, where prominent republicans such as John Wildman and Henry Neville met and were suspected of plotting to restore the Long Parliament with the help of disbanded army officers. Lenthall landed himself in further trouble when, after marrying as his second wife Mary (*d.* in or before 1678), widow of Sir James Stonhouse and daughter of John Blewett, he was found guilty of cheating his stepchildren out of their estate portions, and a bill was introduced to compensate them.

Lenthall seems to have settled down with his third wife, Katherine (*d.* 1692), daughter of the cavalier Eusebius Andrews. Perhaps under the influence of the Andrews family he became reconciled to the monarchy, and in 1678 was knighted by Charles II, who dined with Lenthall at his Burford Priory home before meeting with his parliament in Oxford. That he was knighted by both protector and king is perhaps symbolic of Lenthall's political beliefs, in his ability to separate the office from the body of the king, thereby allowing him to accept more than one form of government. He died on 9 November 1681 and was buried at the church in Besselsleigh, Berkshire.

SARAH CLAYTON

Sources M. W. Helms and B. Jaggar, 'Lenthall, John', HoP, *Commons, 1660–90*, 2.733 • *JHC*, 4 (1644–6) • *JHC*, 7–8 (1651–67) • L. Hutchinson, *Memoirs of the life of Colonel Hutchinson*, ed. N. H. Keeble (2000) • Wood, *Ath. Oxon.*, new edn, vol. 3 • *CSP dom.*, *1655–6*, *1661–2* • Foster, *Alum. Oxon.* • E. Ludlow, *A voyce from the watch tower*, ed. A. B. Worden, CS, 4th ser., 21 (1978) • R. L. Greaves, *Deliver us from evil: the radical underground in Britain, 1660–1663* (1986) • *N&Q*, vols. 5, 12 • *DNB* • D. Underdown, *Pride's Purge: politics in the puritan revolution* (1971)

Archives Hunt. L., letters to Temple family

Likenesses S. Harding?, watercolour drawing, NPG

Lenthall, William, **appointed Lord Lenthall under the protectorate** (**1591–1662**), lawyer and speaker of the House of Commons, was born in June 1591 at Henley-on-Thames, Oxfordshire, the second son of William Lenthall (*d.* 1596) and Frances Southwell.

William Lenthall, appointed Lord Lenthall under the protectorate (**1591–1662**), by unknown artist, after 1643

Family background and early career The main branch of the Lenthalls was settled at Latchford, Oxfordshire, but had moved there from Hertfordshire several generations before William's birth. His father, William, who also was a second son, lived at Wilcote, near Charlbury. His mother, Frances, of Horsham St Faith, Norfolk, was the sister of a Jesuit poet, Robert Southwell, and Lenthall's family only became protestant after William senior died in 1596. After attending Thame School, Lenthall matriculated at St Alban Hall, Oxford, on 23 January 1607, but left without taking his degree. He was more successful at Lincoln's Inn, to which he was admitted in 1609: he was called to the bar on 14 October 1616. From 1633, as a bencher, he was a senior figure in the government of his inn, and was its Lent reader in 1638. Naturally for one who was becoming prominent in legal circles, Lenthall built up a successful legal practice. By 1640, on his own evidence, his income from advocacy was £2500 a year. From 1621 he was recorder of Woodstock, and secured this office probably through the intervention of Lawrence Tanfield, a relative of Lenthall by his marriage to Elizabeth (*d.* 1662), daughter of Ambrose Evans of Loddington in Northamptonshire. Further public office came to Lenthall in the 1630s. He was appointed to the Oxfordshire bench of magistrates on 9 July 1631, and added Gloucester to his recorderships in 1638. He was granted a lease of two Berkshire hundreds in 1636, which made him technically an office-holder under the crown. In 1634 he bought Burford manor and rectory, once the home of Lucius Cary, Viscount Falkland, for £7000, adding this property to Bessels Leigh manor in Berkshire, south-west of Oxford, which he had acquired in 1630.

Lenthall's parliamentary career began in 1624, when he sat for New Woodstock in Oxfordshire. Apart from his being nominated to seven committees in this assembly, he spoke in defence of John Lambe, chancellor of the diocese of Peterborough. Lambe, a zealous prosecutor of puritans, was facing charges of extortion. Lenthall reported from a committee that considered the offences of Dr Cradock, chancellor of Durham, to be more serious.

Lenthall sought a seat in at least one of the first three parliaments of Charles I, and intimated to the corporation of Woodstock his frustration at being passed over: 'you know what a disgrace it was to me the last time, the not choosing me amongst you' (Berks. RO, D/EL1/o.5/12). He was very keen to get into the parliament of April 1640, and Woodstock duly obliged. He was prominent in this assembly, offering judicious observations on procedure, and was evidently alive to the possibility that the indignation of MPs discussing the ship-money verdicts might make 'a party betwixt the king and the kingdom' (*Diary of Sir Thomas Aston*, 107). On 23 April, 2 May, and 4 May Lenthall was called to chair grand committees of the house, on which occasions the speaker handed over control of debate to him. Ship money, parliamentary grievances, and the king's message on supply were the momentous topics for debate subject to Lenthall's chairing, and it was doubtless his performance on these occasions that recommended him to members as speaker of the second parliament of 1640.

The Long Parliament In that parliament Lenthall sat again for Woodstock. When it assembled on 4 November the king discovered that his preferred candidate for the chair, Sir Thomas Gardiner, had failed to be returned to the house. He identified Lenthall as speaker after scrutinizing the list of lawyers who had been returned: Lenthall's main qualification to Charles was that he had 'no ill reputation for his affection to the government both of Church and State' (Clarendon, *Hist. rebellion*, 221). The secretary of state, the elder Sir Henry Vane, proposed Lenthall, and on the following day the king indicated his approval. Lenthall's speech in response began with customary expressions of unworthiness, but then outlined a view of the role of parliaments in general and the one in session in particular. He saw its potential as an opportunity to repulse 'invaders of the church and commonwealth' and thus free the king 'from the interpretation of misdoing' (*Mr Speaker his Speech to his Majestie*, 3–4). Coupled with his articulation of requests for freedom of arrest, liberty of speech, and access to the king on matters of importance, Lenthall's was a bold, if brief, opening statement.

The Lenthall that emerges from the journal of Sir Simonds D'Ewes, no particular friend of his, was in the opening months of the Long Parliament very much in control of proceedings in the house. On 5 December he moved that bills should be read for the first time in the mornings only, and between November 1640 and the following March pledged £1500 security for sums raised for the armies in the north. Lenthall certainly encountered difficulties. On 9 January 1641 Sir Henry Mildmay blamed him for letting too many speak during a debate, and on 9 March he was accused of partiality in a squabble between members. On 2 November 1641 D'Ewes recorded two errors by the speaker. When black rod left after requiring the Commons' presence at the House of Lords, Lenthall asked MPs whether he should be called back for an answer, and he was later made to look foolish by D'Ewes over a point of precedence. But he could bite back. On the day of this latter accusation he reproved the house for moving from one subject to another, and as early as 26 November 1640 established that catching the speaker's eye would establish precedence in a debate.

Part of Lenthall's role as speaker was to act as the voice of the Commons in formal dealings with the king, and he delivered speeches, most of which were published, on the occasion of presenting bills for royal assent. On 13 May 1641 he spoke on the theme of 'no peace to the king, no prosperity to the people' (Nalson, 243). As the gulf widened between king and parliament during the months after the execution of Thomas Wentworth, earl of Strafford, the speaker's speeches must have sounded increasingly hollow. When the sudden sound of cracking woodwork was mistaken by MPs for an armed attack on the house on 19 May, Lenthall was the first to spot their embarrassing error. On 22 June 1641 his speech in the Lords on the occasion of granting limited supply in the bill for tonnage and poundage was based on the conceit of weighing the royal prerogative in the scales against the property of the subject. On 3 July he delivered another speech which attempted assurances of normal relations between king and parliament. That he genuinely saw his function as providing stability in a worsening political crisis is suggested by the level of his official hospitality: he entertained a wide range of MPs and public figures at his house at Charing Cross during the first two years of the parliament. He was awarded £6000 by the king towards these expenses, and Lenthall complained many years later that over half of this was never paid.

On 9 September 1641 the House of Commons adjourned until 20 October, placing its business during the recess in the hands of a committee which included many critics of the king but not Lenthall, who was granted leave to go to the country. When the house reassembled, Lenthall began to find the long sittings physically exhausting, and was to do so over many years to come. He pleaded on 19 November that 'he could not hold out to sit daily seven or eight hours' (*Journal*, ed. Coates, 172–3). On 2 December he described in a speech to the king the work of that parliament as 'without intermission, scarce of a day, nay an hour in that day, to the hazard of life and fortune' (Nalson, 2.707), but by then he was desperate to be relieved of the speakership, pleading the prospect of financial ruin if he continued.

On 4 January 1642 the king attempted to arrest five members of the Commons and one of the Lords, and entered the House of Commons in search of them. Lenthall's response, on his knees before his sovereign and under massive psychological pressure, was to defend his office:

> May it please your majesty, I have neither eyes to see nor tongue to speak in this place but as this house is pleased to direct me whose servant I am here; and humbly beg your majesty's pardon that I cannot give any other answer than this is to what your majesty is pleased to demand of me. (Rushworth, 4.478)

Whether precisely these words were spoken is open to doubt, but in essence this, rather than the flowery and conciliatory speech foisted on him and published by parliament for propaganda purposes, was what was said. Lenthall's defence of his office was further proof of his capabilities, which were materially acknowledged by the House of Commons in its award of £6000 to him on 9 April. A month after the attempt on the members, Lenthall delivered the last of his speeches to the king, stuffed with biblical allusions on the theme of reconciliation, and inviting Charles I to rid himself of false counsellors.

The speaker during the civil war Lenthall is said to have read the same prayer every morning he took the chair in the Long Parliament, and presided as the Commons moved into the uncharted waters of executive authority. His competence during the period of nearly two years between the parliament's first sitting and the outbreak of civil war had been demonstrated in a number of clarifications of Commons procedure. A penalty was to be imposed on a member who persisted in speaking when another had the floor; the duration of parliamentary privilege before and after sittings was established; and while one piece of business occupied the house, a motion on another could not be made. In divisions, those who voted for standing orders of the house stayed in, while those seeking a change left the chamber. In the workings of committees, no vote affecting the property of a subject was to be taken without the prior knowledge of the house; no vote at a committee and not reported by the house could be made a rule for a court of justice. When at the naming of a committee, any man rose to speak, the clerk was to stop writing, and when witnesses came to the chamber, the bar should be down if the house was sitting, up if in grand committee. All these rules and orders were established under Lenthall's speakership during 1640 and 1641. Some may well only have confirmed existing practice, but that they were codified as rules suggests a self-consciousness in the Commons in this period that Lenthall must have helped foster.

During Lenthall's speakership parliament gained access to the printing press for the first time. Both houses were involved in printing orders, declarations, acts, ordinances, and sermons, but the Commons took the lion's share of this parliamentary output, which began as an estimated 8 per cent of publications as a whole in 1641, and had reached 23 per cent by 1645. After the outbreak of civil war, however, more important than either the development of procedure in the house or its expanding programme of publishing was the evolution of the committee system of Lords and Commons into an effective, if byzantine, executive machine for running those parts of the country under parliamentary control. Here Lenthall's influence as speaker was limited, and he played no significant role in the drafting of legislation on crucial topics such as penal taxation of royalists, nor in the creation of the structure of committees. His role remained as the spokesperson of the Commons, which made him at once uniquely visible—as recipient and author of letters on parliamentary business—and (for his biographer), peculiarly elusive. There are occasional glimpses of his personal views. On 21 November 1642, he argued forcefully that the Commons should send peace proposals to the king, countering suggestions that this might offend parliament's supporters: no peace could be made without propositions. There seems no evidence to suggest that Lenthall was ever in sympathy with the diehard protestants who sought 'root and branch' ecclesiastical reform.

It is clear that even before 1640 Lenthall's personal finances were a preoccupation of his. Having cited them as a reason for wishing to resign the chair, he saw them become even more unstable as a result of civil war. His estates were in the Oxford area, which made them liable to confiscation by the royalists, and he later claimed they brought him no income during five years. On the other hand, further grants of high office came to him. On 8 November 1643 he became master of the rolls in succession to Sir Julius Caesar, according to Anthony Wood, a hostile commentator, through the 'continual importunities of his covetous and snotty wife' (Wood, *Ath. Oxon.*, 3.603). He had been proposed for the office by the Commons nearly a year previously. It was in normal times worth perhaps £3000, but the disruption to normal legal process caused by the civil war devalued its financial potential, as did the abolition of the court of wards and the ending of episcopal appointments with their attendant fees. Lenthall reckoned that £2000 a year was lost to him through these missing opportunities. When he became a commissioner of the great seal in October 1646, amid confused votes in the House of Lords and the House of Commons, he was alleged to have gained a further £1500; the chancellorship of the duchy of Lancaster, which came to him in 1647, brought another £1000. There can have been comparatively few citizens outside the mercantile élite who could have lost as much in a burglary as he did on 2 June 1649. In the early hours of that morning a labourer broke into Lenthall's London house and stole £1900 in 'numbered moneys' (Jeaffreson, 3.189). The burglar was later apprehended, tried, and sentenced to hang; the case was still active in December 1651, when an accomplice was arrested. Radical republicans noted Lenthall's instinct to insist on enforcing his own interests in property disputes. In 1658 Richard Salwey, an associate of the younger Sir Henry Vane, complained of Lenthall's oppressive conduct towards smaller men in Wychwood Forest, Oxfordshire. Allegations that the speakership alone brought him £7730 a year prompted him in 1660 to publish a detailed account of his offices, which argued that his public service was given at the cost of much income that he might normally have expected. Even so, it is hard not to sympathize with the view that material reward mattered to him more than a little, even if the judgement that 'he minded mostly the heaping up of riches' (Wood, *Ath. Oxon.*, 3.606) was born of sheer prejudice.

In the summer of 1647 Lenthall again stuck out for the privileges of parliament when his office came under pressure, this time from the London crowd that included apprentices and disbanded soldiers. On 31 July, amid scenes of disorder in Westminster occasioned by a reaction against the growing power of the parliamentary armies, especially the New Model, and the oppressions of local committees, Lenthall published a personal statement. Votes in the Commons had been forced, making them void in his judgement, and he feared further violence. It was time to withdraw, he asserted, when 'they shall jostle, pull and hale the Speaker all the way he went down to his coach, and force him to avoid their violence to betake himself to the next coach he could get into for refuge' (*A Declaration of William Lenthall Esquire*, 6). He was therefore taking himself to the army, and would return only when free to resume his office. Fifty-seven other MPs felt the same way, and it was not until 6 August that he returned, after having attended a review of the army at Hounslow Heath. From this point Lenthall was a sympathizer with the Independents, and with other MPs who had fled to the army signed an engagement with them, but there is little evidence that this association extended to the wider political projects of his protectors. On 15 November he conveyed assurances of the Commons to Sir Thomas Fairfax that they had tried to address the army's concerns over arrears of pay and continuing free quarter; he assured the lord general of the Commons' continuing sympathy with the soldiers, arising from MPs' regard for them, 'and the value they put on their past services' (*A Full Relation*, 3).

Royalist newspapers during 1648 portrayed Lenthall as the tool of the Independents, engaged in various ploys to manipulate the house in their interests. His own deathbed assertion that he went along with the Independents only because they swore to restore the king to his rights, while he knew the presbyterians never would, seems hollow, and was little more than a commentary on the eclipse of the latter group in 1662. At the end of July 1648 he 'startled the saints' vote drivers' (*Mercurius Pragmaticus*, 18, 26 July – 1 Aug 1648) by using his casting vote when the house was tied 57 to 57 in favour of continuing negotiations with the king, an indication that the Independent leaders could not rely on him in all circumstances. In the following month Lenthall was caught out when he unsuccessfully attempted from the speaker's chair to identify the anonymous author whose revelations in *Mercurius Pragmaticus* were proving damaging, and was left 'in his dumps, and the whole house in a laughter' (*Mercurius Pragmaticus*, 21, 15–22 Aug 1648). He was silent at Pride's purge of the house on 6 December 1648, and so was probably advised of it in advance: indeed, he warned MPs on 4 December that voting for the treaty of Newport with the king would mean their own destruction. Certainly he was consulted on several occasions by Independent leaders during the crisis of December, and had to send to Fairfax to allow a number of MPs into the house to progress normal business. On 18 December the commissioners of the great seal met Oliver Cromwell and Colonel Richard Deane at Lenthall's accommodation at the Rolls Chapel, and planned further consultations, presumably on the plans to try the king. But there is nothing to suggest that Lenthall played any active part in the events which led to the regicide. His attitude towards it was never put to the test formally, as he was not asked to take the dissent from the vote to continue treating with the king.

Speaker during the Commonwealth Once the republic had been proclaimed Lenthall found himself, by virtue of his office as speaker, the leading citizen of England. The king's arms were removed from above his chair in the Commons chamber, and Lenthall was honoured by the City of London in June 1649 and was the first to take the engagement of loyalty to the Commonwealth when it was distributed for mass subscription in October. He was no longer speaker of the House of Commons, but of a unicameral parliament; a warship was named after his office. None of this meant a substantial change of role, however; there is no evidence that he became more important as a politician in his own right. He remained cautious and conservative in his approach to public affairs. In August 1649 he used his casting vote to block the establishment of a presbyterian church structure in England, in defiance of informed advocacy by leading republican politicians such as William Purefoy. This was not because Lenthall was holding out for a more radical solution, but because what had been proposed was a change to the manifestly unsatisfactory *status quo*. As master of the rolls he was involved in discussions on the reform of chancery, but it was left to later governments to make substantive change in this area of the law. After the battle of Worcester on 3 September 1651 Lenthall rode through London in the same coach as Lord General Oliver Cromwell, in a show of solidarity between parliament and the military, but this was not a hint of Lenthall adopting a new radical outlook. When discussions on constitutional change took place at the speaker's house that autumn, between leading soldiers and politicians, there is nothing to suggest that he held views that were distinct from the preference for a limited monarchy voiced by the other leading lawyers present. On the other hand, the allegations by the informer Thomas Coke that Lenthall was involved in a presbyterian–royalist conspiracy to undermine the republic are of interest only as a further indication that he moved in conservative, not radical, political circles.

On 20 April 1653 Lenthall was at the centre of what is known to posterity as his second set-piece performance as speaker, when the Rump Parliament was forcibly dissolved by Oliver Cromwell and other leading army officers. As on 4 January 1642 his office was challenged by a show of force, and again he rose to the occasion, assuring Major-General Thomas Harrison that he would not come down from the chair unless forced. Harrison's own account, stating that he politely gave the speaker his hand, and that he came quietly down and left the chamber, seems convincing: Lenthall must have realized the futility of resistance. Unsurprisingly, he had come to symbolize the shortcomings of the Rump, and found no place in the nominated assembly that sat between July and December 1653. Indeed, as soon as the Rump was expelled, the council of state which then held supreme authority commenced proceedings against Lenthall's brother Sir John Lenthall, who was widely regarded as a corrupt and oppressive manager of the upper bench prison. Nevertheless, William Lenthall was never *persona non grata* to the successive regimes of Oliver Cromwell, and he retained his office as master of the rolls throughout. He welcomed the inauguration of the protectorate in December 1653 as a rescue from 'the brink in my judgment of confusion and desolation'. He looked forward to the safeguarding of property and the return to 'our ancient and true ways of God's worship', further confirmation of his thoroughly conservative and unquestioning cast of mind (Spalding, 166).

Speaker and Cromwellian office-holder In elections to the first protectorate parliament, which opened on 4 September 1654, Lenthall was returned for Oxfordshire and Gloucestershire, preferring to sit for the former constituency. He was brought again to the chair as speaker, in what must have appeared to critics of the Rump as an assertion of continuity. After the dissolution of the assembly in January 1655 he was prepared to court the disapproval of

Lord Protector Cromwell on legal issues. Chancery reform was again being promoted, on this occasion by an ordinance of the council of state, with Cromwell's backing. As master of the rolls, the principal judge of that court, Lenthall held out for a time against the legislation, indeed in May 1655 protesting 'that he would be hanged at the rolls gate before he would execute it' (*Diary of Bulstrode Whitelocke*, 409). Bulstrode Whitelocke and Sir Thomas Widdrington resigned as commissioners of the great seal over the issue but to their disgust Lenthall then conformed: 'his profit, and fear to offend, overswayed all other considerations' (Whitelocke, *Memorials*, 4.202).

When the second protectorate parliament was summoned Lenthall retained his Oxfordshire seat. He was not elected to the chair, but was a prominent participant in the proceedings, offering observations on procedure and comments on the range of business before the house. On 30 December 1656, in a speech on the constitution, he spoke in favour of parliament's claim to have inherited the legislative rights of abolished component parts of the ancient constitution, and argued that it had the right to judge any matter, even if there was no statute in support. He took a hawkish line on the Quaker James Nayler—'I never heard of such a horrid sin as this, in all my life' (*The Diary of Thomas Burton*, ed. J. T. Rutt, 4 vols., 1824, 1.66–7)—and declared himself content with the quality of local magistrates. He acted as a spokesman for adventurers in Ireland, promoting the interests there of Gloucester corporation, where he was still recorder. Public faith creditors were another group that benefited from Lenthall's advocacy in this parliament. He was among the 'kinglings' who pressed the crown upon a reluctant Cromwell; after Bulstrode Whitelocke resigned from the committee when this component of the *Humble Petition and Advice* was rejected, Lenthall was left as a senior figure in the committee that went forward to conclude the new constitutional arrangements. His earlier critical stance on changes to legal procedure now behind him, his speeches in parliament were supportive of the protector. He was duly rewarded with a seat in the new second chamber, which he took up on 10 December 1657, not without some agitation on his part for a place. Edmund Ludlow recounted a story that Lenthall declared the value of the place to be that it bestowed the title of peers on his posterity.

Lenthall's support for a Cromwellian monarchy and his elevation to the 'other house' as Lord Lenthall fuelled allegations of self-serving corruption on his part that were never far away from published comment on him. In Lenthall's pomp as speaker of the Rump, it was not only Thomas Coke's allegations of his alleged conspiring that circulated. As early as July 1649 a tract originating in the army was published in London claiming to reveal details of his royalist associations and cover-ups. By 1658 it was personal financial gain, rather than sympathy with the cause of monarchy, that was alleged to be Lenthall's motive in public life. That he became rich through public office is beyond question, as is his regard for wealth and status. Much of the criticism came from victims of injustice or unredressed grievances, however, and Lenthall's high office provided them with a target for eye-catching revelations that could be lurid and impossible to authenticate, as in the case of John Bernard, who in 1657 alleged that Lenthall and his faction attempted to 'drive on the pope's and Jesuits' interest' against the protector (Bernard, 7).

Collapse of the republic and the restoration of monarchy On 6 May 1659 Lenthall was visited at the house of the master of the rolls, first by leading army officers and then by a group of sixteen Rumpers. In the light of the collapse of Richard Cromwell's protectorate, they designed the restoration of the Rump, and called on Lenthall to play a part in the recall, and to resume as speaker. It was clear that this was a most unwelcome invitation, and Lenthall pleaded ill health and old age, adding that he was now unsure whether the execution of Charles I had in fact terminated the existence of the Long Parliament. Observers thought he was reluctant to lose his Cromwellian peerage. His further plea that he was in spiritual preparation for communion cut no ice with his visitors, and when the republican leaders bypassed him to summon MPs he was forced to put himself at their head to resume the sitting of the Rump the following day. Despite his reluctance to accept the office, Lenthall now wielded greater theoretical power than in his first period as speaker of the Commonwealth: he was head of the armed forces, and on 14 May became keeper of the great seal. Ominously, royalists began to speak favourably of him. Divisions between parliament and the army under John Lambert deepened, however, and on 7 October Lenthall was obliged to urge the City to remain faithful to the civil authority. On the 13th parliament was blockaded by soldiers, and Lenthall was forced into dialogue with some of them from his coach, which had to turn back from Westminster. To his remonstrance that he was their general, he was told that his claim would have had more substance if he fought with them against the royalist Sir George Booth at Winnington Bridge. It was reported that Lambert personally dismissed Lenthall to his face as a fool.

In the final months before the restoration of Charles II Lenthall began to manoeuvre away from the republicans. On 25 November 1659 he was thought to be in touch with General George Monck. On 23 December another meeting took place at the speaker's house, at which Lenthall was among a group who put themselves at the head of a group of soldiers disaffected from Charles Fleetwood. The following day a rendezvous of soldiers at Lincoln's Inn Fields gave their loyalty to the speaker, regretting the interruption to parliament and calling Lenthall, who was much gratified to be able to take control of the Tower in a torchlight procession, 'father of their country' (*Mercurius Politicus*, 22–9 Dec 1659). On the 26th the Rump resumed its sitting once more. The next day Lenthall wrote to Whitelocke a letter to encourage him to attend in order to bolster parliament's authority, but within weeks he was absenting himself because of gout, suspected to be a tactical illness to avoid having to take the republican inspired oath of abjuration against the royal family. He was away from the house for ten days. By 4 February 1660

Lenthall was co-operating fully with Monck in London, and received him in state as speaker, Monck standing behind the chair. It was now clear that Lenthall had broken completely with the republicans. He refused to co-operate with their scheme to hold elections to fill places in parliament, and persisted in defying them to send him to the Tower, or elect another speaker. His stand, with Monck's army behind, made possible on 21 February the admission of the MPs secluded at Pride's Purge. On 14 March he was rewarded with the office of chamberlain of Chester. If he was the author of advice to the future king, dated 28 March, whose author claimed to have given both Charles I and his eldest son much unheeded advice in the last crisis to beset the monarchy, it was an astonishingly brazen act of presumption and an early repudiation of his former republican colleagues. By early April there were those among Charles's advisers who were arguing that Lenthall should be forgiven his past.

When elections were held for the convention Monck lobbied to have Lenthall elected for Oxford University, and a petition on his behalf was read in convocation on 7 April, but to no avail. Lenthall sent £3000 to Charles II at Breda, with a request that he might retain the mastership of the rolls, but received the cold response that it had been allocated elsewhere. Lenthall headed the list of those excepted from the Act of Indemnity but who were not to be tried for life, and was denounced particularly by William Prynne, but his money and collaboration with Monck ensured that he was simply barred from public office for life. His appearance on 12 October at the trial of the regicide Thomas Scot, to swear that Scot had spoken in parliament in favour of executing the king, was viewed by republicans and even some monarchists as disgusting, in the light of his famous defence of parliamentary privilege in 1642. He retired to Burford, and made a deathbed confession of his involvement in the events of January 1649: 'I confess with Saul, I held their clothes whilst they murdered him, but herein I was not so criminal as Saul was, for God, thou knowest, I never consented to his death' (Wood, *Ath. Oxon.*, 3.608). He requested that the sentence (in Latin) 'I am a worm' should be his only epitaph, and died on 3 September 1662 at Burford; his wife had died the previous April. He was buried at Burford church two days later, and left property mainly in that area. His only son, John *Lenthall, survived him.

Assessment The allegations of personal weakness that were levelled against Lenthall by his critics do not bear close scrutiny. The view of Edward Hyde, earl of Clarendon, that it was his personal inadequacy that failed to keep in check the more unruly, extreme critics of the monarchy was an attempt to discredit the body that eventually brought Charles I to trial. Lenthall's conduct in the early years of the Long Parliament suggests a speaker who had every intention of maintaining his office, and of contributing to the procedures of the house. His dignified defiance of Charles I in January 1642 was in itself a guarantee of his special place in the pantheon of speakers, and this was not the only occasion on which he took a stance and held it. He lacked the politician's instinct for riding events, however, and had no political vision. Had it not been for his rescue by the army in 1647 from the mob, he would probably not have thrown in his lot with the Independents for so long; in many respects, he was the kind of conservative who would have been a victim of the army in 1648. Nor did he evince any of the godly enthusiasm that marked the republicans. Tradition was important to his religious outlook; royalists sneered at his religion (or lack of it) in 1659. The allegations of avarice and underhand behaviour that persisted through his career in high office are encountered too frequently to be ignored. His personal character seemed significantly less noble than the offices of state on acquiring which he had so evidently set his heart. STEPHEN K. ROBERTS

Sources Berks. RO, D/EL1/0.5/12 • *The journal of Sir Simonds D'Ewes from the first recess of the Long Parliament to the withdrawal of King Charles from London*, ed. W. H. Coates (1942) • *The journal of Sir Simonds D'Ewes from the beginning of the Long Parliament to the opening of the trial of the earl of Strafford*, ed. W. Notestein (1923) • H. Elsyng, *Memorials of the method and manner of proceedings in parliament* (1670) • *The Short Parliament (1640) diary of Sir Thomas Aston*, ed. J. D. Maltby, CS, 4th ser., 35 (1988) • B. Whitelocke, *Memorials of English affairs*, new edn, 4 vols. (1853) • Wood, *Ath. Oxon.*, new edn, vol. 3 • W. Lenthall, *A declaration of William Lenthall esquire* (1647) [Thomason tract E 400(32)] • *Calendar of the Clarendon state papers preserved in the Bodleian Library*, ed. O. Ogle and others, 5 vols. (1869–1970) • 'A narrative of the late parliament (so-called)' (1657), *Harleian miscellany*, ed. W. Oldys and others, 10 vols. (1808–13), vol. 6, p. 503 • 'A second narrative of the late parliament (so called)', *The Harleian miscellany*, ed. W. Oldys and T. Park, 10 vols. (1808–13), vol. 3, pp. 470–89 • R. Spalding, *Contemporaries of Bulstrode Whitelocke, 1605–1675* (1990) • *The diary of Bulstrode Whitelocke, 1605–1675*, ed. R. Spalding, British Academy, Records of Social and Economic History, new ser., 13 (1990) • *The memoirs of Edmund Ludlow*, ed. C. H. Firth, 2 vols. (1894) • Clarendon, *Hist. rebellion* • J. G. Nichols and J. Bruce, eds., *Wills from Doctors' Commons*, CS, old ser., 83 (1863) • *Mercurius Pragmaticus* (1648–9) • *A full relation of the proceedings of the rendezvous of that brigade of the army that was held in Corkbush field in Hartford parish* (1647) [Thomason tract E 414(13)] • S. Kelsey, *Inventing a republic* (1997) • Thurloe, *State papers*, vol. 7 • W. H. Turner, ed., *The visitations of the county of Oxford … 1566 … 1574 … and in 1634*, Harleian Society, 5 (1871) • J. Nalson, *An impartial collection of the great affairs of state*, 2 vols. (1683) • Birm. CA, 602993/128; 603503/193 • *JHC*, 2–7 (1640–59) • *Ten articles already proved upon oath against an evil member now in the parliament* (1649) [Thomason tract 669.f.14(52)] • W. Lenthall, *Mr Speaker his speech to his Majestie* (1640) [Thomason tract E 774(4)] • W. Lenthall, *Mr Speaker's letter* (1641/2) • W. Lenthall, *Mr Speaker's speech before the king* (1641) • W. Lenthall, *Mr Speaker's speech in the Lords* (1641) • *A true relation of the unparaleld breach of parliament* (1641/2) [Thomason tract E 181(31)] • Diary of Walter Yonge, BL, Add. MS 18777 • *The king's majestie's demand* (1642) • J. Bernard, *Truth's triumph over treacherous dealing* (1657) • S. Lambert, *Printing for parliament*, List and Index Special Ser., 20 (1984) • *The diaries and papers of Sir Edward Dering, second baronet, 1644 to 1684*, ed. M. F. Bond (1976) • G. E. Aylmer, *The state's servants: the civil service of the English republic, 1649–1660* (1973) • E. S. Cope and W. H. Coates, eds., *Proceedings of the Short Parliament of 1640*, CS, 4th ser., 19 (1977) • J. Rushworth, *Historical collections*, new edn, 8 vols. (1721–2) • *An account of the gains of the late speaker Lenthall* (1660) • *A more exact and necessary catalogue of pensioners in the Long Parliament* (1660) • Foster, *Alum. Oxon.* • *State trials*, vol. 5 • parish register, Burford, 5 Sept 1662, Oxon. RO [burial] • Foss, *Judges*, vol. 5 • *A copie of a letter sent by Mr Speaker, to all the corporations in England* (1642) [Thomason tract E 133(2)] • W. Lenthall, *The speech of Master Speaker* (1642) [Thomason tract E 199(36)] • B. Worden, *The Rump Parliament, 1648–1653* (1974) • D. Underdown, *Pride's Purge: politics in the puritan revolution* (1971) • R. Bell, ed., *Memorials of the civil war … forming the concluding volumes* *of the Fairfax correspondence*, 2 vols. (1849) • A. Davidson, 'Lenthall, William', HoP, *Commons, 1604–29* [draft] • *DNB* • J. C. Jeaffreson, ed., *Middlesex county records*, 3 (1888)

Archives Bodl. Oxf., corresp. | Berks. RO, corresp. • BL, corresp., Add. MS 64867

Likenesses oils, after 1643, NPG [*see illus.*] • S. Cooper, miniature, 1652, NPG • H. Paert?, Palace of Westminster, London • Van Weesop, group portrait (with his family), Speaker's House, Palace of Westminster, London

Wealth at death bequests of £1000; lands around Burford: Nichols and Bruce, eds., *Wills from Doctors' Commons*, 111–18

Lenton, Francis (*fl.* 1629–1653), poet, was probably born in Northamptonshire. A Lenton family owned lands in Northamptonshire, Buckinghamshire, Nottinghamshire, and Lincolnshire. Lenton certainly has some connections to the county, as he wrote a marriage hymn honouring Margarite Banister of Passenham (part of the prefatory material to Henry Lawes's *Ayres and Dialogues* of 1653). Furthermore, his biographer Lota Snider Willis asserts that he was related to the Lentons of Aldwincle (Willis, 8–9). A Simon Lenton of Aldwincle was granted land in Rockingham Forest, an area important to the Montagu family with whom Francis Lenton had some contact (an undated quarto MS collection of gratulatory verses and carols addressed to Edward Montagu, Baron Montagu of Boughton, is now part of the collection of the duke of Buccleuch in Dalkeith House, Dalkeith, Scotland).

The dedication to Lenton's first published work, *The Young Gallants Whirligigg* (1629), claims that 'I once belonged to the Innes of court'. However, his name does not appear in the register of admissions. Despite the uncertainty of his status, he does seem to have been part of the poetic coteries centred upon the inns of court during the 1620s and 1630s. The *Whirligigg* is a moralistic account of the trials of a country student when he is exposed to the temptations of London. The text is a standard cautionary tale which attacks the immorality of the corrupt city. A model student through school and Oxford, the protagonist, once in the city, swiftly goes off the rails:

His parents him supply to buy him bookes
As hee pretends: but stead of Cokes Reports,
Hee's fencing, dauncing, or other sports.

The hero 'learns the postures of the cap and knee' and runs the gamut of courtly activities: he falls in love and writes bad poetry; dances masques in the inns of court; goes to the theatre; is spendthrift and debauched; gambles, drinks, falls into debt, and is undone (and imprisoned); mourns his woes and turns to God. The epilogue bids those 'blyth yong Rufflers' who will mock the work to:

glory in what you may,
Till lusty youth is vanished away.

Lenton's second work, *Characterismi, or, Lentons Leasures* (1631), presents satirical portraits and caricatures of various city types from 'Gallant Courtier' to 'Whore', 'Gamester', 'Common Drunkard', and 'Innes a Court Gentleman'. This volume was relatively popular, and went through three editions during the 1630s.

Lenton became attached in some nominal capacity to the court of Henrietta Maria, and throughout the 1630s composed various works and masques which espoused her version of Catholicism. The title-pages of these works identify him variously as the 'Queenes Poet' and 'Gent, one of Her Majesties Poets'. This was an honorary role that had been previously filled by Sir William Davenant. In 1634 Lenton became involved in the controversy surrounding William Prynne's *Histriomastix* (1633). A member of the inns of court, Prynne had insulted the queen by, among many other things, including the entry 'women actors, notorious whores' in his index. In response to this perceived insolence, James Shirley wrote a masque of reconciliation which attempted to distance the student body from the extremism of Prynne's tract. Lenton's work *The Innes of Court Anagrammatist, or, The Masquers Masque in Anagrammes* (1634) anagrammatizes the names of the leader and sixteen students who danced this masque, and so further allies the inns of court with the cult of the queen. Lenton dedicates the work 'To the Foure Honourable Societies, and famous Nurseries of Law, the Innes of Court', addressing them as:

The creame o'th kingdome, either in your wealth,
Wit, learning, valour, or iust lawes lov'd health
Who, by your worthy breedings, births, and blood,
Are chose for Guarders of your countries good.

Jove and Juno command the inns to undertake:

a most renowned taske,
Onely present them a most renowned Maske.

This masque, Shirley's *Triumph of Peace*, heals domestic rancour and celebrates the neoplatonic harmony of the royal union.

In 1638 Lenton published the approbative *Great Britains Beauties, or, The Female Glory*. This celebrated the women of the court in a succession of anagrams and acrostics that were physically 'Presented at White-Hall on Shrove Tuesday at Night, by the Queenes Majestie and her Ladies'. These works reflected the Catholicism of the queen and celebrated the cult of Mary. The verses in praise of the queen and her ladies in *Great Britains Beauties* deployed a particularly religious tone. As Erica Veevers has observed, the imagery and 'language of Marian devotion applied to the Queen by Lenton, and specifically related to this masque, could hardly be more explicit' (Veevers, 147). The subtitle of this work may be an allusion to Anthony Stafford's book about the Virgin Mary, *The Femall Glory* (1634).

Many of Lenton's poems and anagrams were circulated via manuscript to a select coterie. Some of the anagrams making up *Great Britains Beauties* were collected in a manuscript presented to the earl of Dorset that is now preserved as Beinecke Library, Yale University, MS b.205. This collection illustrates the idealized neoplatonism and chastity of Henrietta Maria's court, and is entitled 'The virgin knott of honor, or, Vesta's anagramatist exprest in anagrams and explications upon the names of sacred Junoes handmaydes the six lovely nimphs of Hisperides by titles ye mayds of honor'. The author is 'Fra: Lenton gent & scholler in the court of arcadia'. More important still are two works that Lenton scribally published in manuscript form during the late 1630s and early 1640s: 'Queene Esters Haliluiahs and Hamans Madrigalls

Expressed and Illustrated in a Sacred Poeme' (1637) and 'The Muses Oblation' (1641). 'The Muses Oblation' celebrated in anagrams, acrostics, and an 'Encomiastick Gratulation' the honours newly conferred by Charles upon Sir James Stonehouse in 1641. The piece was written to seek patronage from Stonehouse. There is a copy in the Houghton Library, Harvard University, MS Eng. 178, and another described by Hazlitt (Hazlitt, *Collections*, 1.140).

Lenton's choice of Esther as a subject is interesting, given that the story is particularly used by Catholics. It was employed by such writers as Nicholas de Caussin to show how beauty and chaste love could be used in God's service. Such ideas were very influential at court during the 1630s. The poem on Esther appears at Huntington Library, MS HM 120, and is dedicated to Sir Anthony and Lady Cage; there are later copies in the British Library (Add. MS 34805, a 1638 version dedicated to Thomas Coteel) and the Houghton Library, Harvard University (MS Eng. 178.2, a 1649 version). Two other copies are described by Hazlitt (Hazlitt, *Collections*, 1.255). The Harvard copy is particularly interesting, given Lenton's early career, for the dedication to 'His Excellence the Illustrious valiant and most Religious Prince: Thomas Lord Fairefax Captain Generall of All the Forces for the Parliament etc And to his vertuous Consort'. This is signed 'Your Excellencyes most reall and devoted Honouror: Francis Lenton'. This manuscript, and the dedicatory poem 'To the Honorable, Valiant, and Ingenious Colonel Richard Lovelace, on his Exquisite Poems' which appears in *Lucasta* (1649), confirm that Lenton was alive past 1642, the date which was once assumed to be the year of his death.

JEROME DE GROOT

Sources L. S. Willis, *Francis Lenton, queen's poet* (1931) • E. Veevers, *Images of love and religion: Queen Henrietta Maria and court entertainments* (1989) • K. Sharpe, *The personal rule of Charles I* (1992) • M. Butler, 'Entertaining the palatine prince: plays on foreign affairs, 1635–37', *Renaissance historicism: selections from English literary renaissance*, ed. A. F. Kinney and D. S. Collins (1987), 265–93 • A. Shell, *Catholicism, controversy and the English literary imagination* (1999) • W. H. Rylands, ed., *The visitation of the county of Buckingham made in 1634*, Harleian Society, 58 (1909)

Archives Harvard U. • Hunt. L. • Yale U. | BL, Add. MS 34805

Lenton, John (*bap.* **1657**?, *d.* **1719**), violinist and composer, was perhaps the John Linton, son of Nicholas and Joan, baptized at St Andrew's, Holborn, on 4 March 1657. He was sworn as violinist at the English court on 2 August 1681 and served among the private musick until his death. His presence is noted among the musicians at the coronations of James II and of William III and Mary II and in various routine journeys to Windsor and Newmarket. He was one of the violinists attending William III into the Netherlands in 1691. Lenton was sworn as an extraordinary gentleman of the Chapel Royal on 10 November 1685, but he never progressed to an ordinary post. However, he was made groom of the vestry in 1708 and records show him in full attendance when the chapel was at Windsor each summer thereafter. Somehow he combined his chapel duties with an active life as composer both at court and also for the London theatres. Unfortunately much of his surviving music is lacking one or more parts, but it shows considerable skill and inventiveness. For the court there are suites celebrating William III's return to London (November 1697?) and the new year 1699 (or 1700) and he wrote at least twelve suites for plays produced between 1682 and 1705, mostly for Betterton's company at Lincoln's Inn Fields.

Among Lenton's published works are *A Consort of Music of Three Parts* (1692), in which he was joined by his court colleague Thomas Tollett, and *A Three Part Consort of New Musick* (1697), whose popularity led to three editions. Of particular importance is his *The Gentleman's Diversion* (1693), again unfortunately incomplete, apparently the second earliest extant violin tutor after *Apollo's Banquet* (1678). On publication it was available from Lenton's 'House over against the Green Ball in Brownlow-street near Drury Lane'. The music (all duets) is by Lenton and fourteen of his contemporaries, mostly from court. He was also active as an editor, 'carefully' correcting *Wit and Mirth, or, Pills to Purge Melancholy*, volume 4 (1706), and *The Dancing-Master*, volume 2 (1710), was also 'corrected by J. Lenton' according to the *Post Boy* of 8 April that year. He died before 13 May 1719, when James William replaced him in the private musick; his widow, Anne, was granted administration of his estate on 21 May, when he was described as of the parish of St James, Westminster. His place of burial is unknown. Manuscripts of his compositions can be found in the British Library, the Fitzwilliam Museum in Cambridge, Yale School of Music, New York Public Library, and the Nanki Library, Tokyo.

ANDREW ASHBEE

Sources A. Ashbee and D. Lasocki, eds., *A biographical dictionary of English court musicians, 1485–1714*, 2 vols. (1998) • A. Ashbee, ed., *Records of English court music*, 9 vols. (1986–96), vols. 6–8 • A. Ashbee and J. Harley, eds., *The cheque books of the Chapel Royal*, 2 vols. (2000) • M. Boyd and J. Rayson, 'The gentleman's diversion: John Lenton and the first violin tutor', *Early Music*, 10 (1982), 329–32 • C. L. Day and E. B. Murrie, *English song-books, 1651–1702: a bibliography with a first-line index of songs* (1940) • M. Tilmouth, 'A calendar of references to music in newspapers published in London and the provinces (1660–1719)', *Royal Musical Association Research Chronicle*, 1 (1961) • C. A. Price, *Music in the Restoration theatre* (1979) • P. Holman, *Four and twenty fiddlers: the violin at the English court, 1540–1690*, new edn (1993) • C. Sharpe, 'An annotated bibliography of early English violin tutors published 1658–1731 including reissues and subsequent editions of single works', *A handbook for studies in 18th-century English music*, 10 (1999), 1–50

Archives BL, letters, Sloane 4065

Leo, Alan [*formerly* William Frederick Allen] (**1860–1917**), astrologer, was born William Frederick Allen at 6.10 a.m. on 7 August 1860 in Great College Street, Westminster, the only son of a Scottish ex-soldier, who disappeared when Allen was about nine, and a member of the Plymouth Brethren sect. Circumstances of poverty impelled him into working from the age of sixteen at a variety of jobs, including chemist's assistant, grocer, sewing machine salesman, and engineering shop manager. Meanwhile, however, he had learned about astrology from an astrological herbalist in Nottingham at the age of eighteen; four years later, he discovered the idea of reincarnation

Alan Leo (1860–1917), by unknown photographer, c.1895

and karma, and by twenty-eight he was deep into the study of natal astrology.

In 1888 Allen settled at 12 Lugard Road in Peckham, and about that time he changed his name to Alan Leo, to reflect the preponderance of planets in that sign in his horoscope. His 'exoteric' job was now that of chief salesman for a confectionary firm, but his 'esoteric' life was dominated by the stars. On 21 November 1889, together with another astrologer, F. W. Lacey or Aphorel, Leo began his first monthly periodical, the *Astrologer's Magazine*.

That summer another young astrologer, Walter Richard Old (known as Sepharial), had introduced Leo to the members of a lodge of the Theosophical Society that had been formed by Madame Blavatsky herself two years earlier. Meetings took place at her 'lamasery' at 17 Lansdowne Road, Holland Park. In May 1890 Leo formally joined the society, of which he remained a lifelong adherent. He also became a member of several lodges of freemasonry.

By late 1891 Leo was the sole proprietor of his periodical, and combined his work as a commercial traveller with extensive lecturing around the country. In February 1893, through a theosophical contact in Southampton, he met—and two years later, on 23 September 1895, married—Ada Elizabeth Murray Phillips (1858–1931), soon better known as Bessie Leo. Theirs was a celibate but happy union. (For reasons of spiritual purity, Leo was also a committed teetotaller, non-smoker, and vegetarian.)

By 1895 Leo had sent out over 4000 free horoscopes to new subscribers, but was barely breaking even. He also felt discouraged by the reluctance of his fellow astrologers (especially those led by A. J. Pearce) to convert to his theosophical orientation. This started Leo on his long search for an approach that was at once more practical and more metaphysical. The first issue (August 1895) of a new periodical, *Modern Astrology*, announced this programme: 'The time has come to modernise the ancient system of Astrology' ('Introduction', 1). Leo followed this up by founding an astrological society on 14 January 1896—the first of several.

In 1898 the Leos bought 9 Lyncroft Gardens, West Hampstead, and Alan Leo wound up his other commercial activities. *Modern Astrology* was starting to cover its expenses, but Leo was desperate for a way to attract new subscribers without the burden of sending out endless free horoscopes. The solution he hit upon was twofold: first, to offer the public a 'test' horoscope for 1s.—this resulted, according to Leo, in 20,000 being sent out in the first three years—and second, a system of facsimiles whereby a person's horoscope would be calculated, then carbon-copied sheets of interpretation for each planetary position stapled together and sent off. Thus was born the production line which, suitably computerized, is still the way modern astrological business is conducted. By 1903 Leo employed nine people, and in 1909 he took offices at 42–3 and 50 Imperial Buildings, Ludgate Circus.

With indefatigable energy Leo also produced seven books in a series entitled Astrology for All, and fourteen pocket manuals. All pursued the programme of a popular occult astrology, but the last, *Esoteric Astrology*—a bewildering pot-pourri of auras, etheric bodies, and 'higher' planetary rulerships—revealed its limits.

By now Leo had inspired a considerable number of more unscrupulous astral 'professors', working the West End and attracting considerable critical comment in the press. He was thus the obvious target for a charge under the Vagrancy Act of 1824 (5 Geo. IV c. 83), which forbade the activities of 'every Person pretending or professing to tell Fortunes', and on 29 April 1914 Leo was summoned to appear at Mansion House on 6 May to answer that charge. Among the witnesses attending on Leo's behalf was Annie Besant, and the trial was widely reported. The case was dismissed, however, when it emerged that the horoscopic reading for Inspector Hugh McLean had been sent out when Leo was away in India. The lord mayor, presiding, refused Leo's costs.

Leo was now more determined than ever to replace the planetary 'influences' of what he regarded as 'the fatalistic school of materialistic Astrology' (A. Leo, *The Astrologer and his Work*, 25) with psychological 'tendencies', in keeping with his slogan, 'Character is Destiny' (*Modern Astrology*, 25, 1914, 299). However, this ambition encountered another obstacle, as Leo admitted, in the widespread public desire not for self-knowledge but precisely for prediction of the future. About this time, the Leos purchased Dollis Lodge, Dollis Avenue, in Finchley. On 13 July 1914 they invited seventeen others to the founding meeting of yet another new body, namely the Astrological Lodge of the Theosophical Society. Unlike the others, this one still exists, and virtually all contemporary astrological organizations in Britain are its offshoots.

However, another blow was about to fall. On 2 July 1917 Leo was again served with a summons on the charge of fortune-telling (though not, this time, of taking money for it). The trial was again held at Mansion House, on 9 and 16 July, and despite a more sympathetic hearing from Mr Alderman Moore, Leo was found guilty, and fined £5 with £25 costs. (The sentence could have been three months' hard labour.) Leo's downfall was the fact that despite his protestations of principles, tendencies, and free will, his horoscope for Inspector Nicholls had included the remark that 'at this time a death in your family circle is likely to cause you sorrow'.

Such an outcome cruelly exposed Leo's failure to free astrology from the taint of fortune-telling. Rather than appeal against the decision, Leo decided he must recast his entire system and cut out any prediction whatsoever. Typically, he started this work when supposedly on holiday with Bessie in Bude, Cornwall, in the summer of 1917, but on 30 August he died suddenly of a brain haemorrhage at 10 Burn View, Bude.

Despite astrology's enduring stigma, Leo succeeded in realizing much of his ambition. His marriage of popular astrology with esoteric occultism, and of mass marketing with individual soul-searching, resulted in a kind of middle-class magic that is not so much an aberration as an expression of late modernity. Increasingly translated into psychological terms, it is still a fixture of contemporary culture. PATRICK CURRY

Sources P. Curry, *A confusion of prophets: Victorian and Edwardian astrology* (1992) • B. Leo and others, *The life and work of Alan Leo, theosophist-astrologer-mason* (1919) • A. Leo, *The astrologer and his work* (1911) • *Modern Astrology*, 28/12 (Dec 1917) • *Occult Review*, 26 (1917), 343–9 • 'Alan Leo', *Old Moore's Monthly Messenger*, 7/3 (Dec 1913), 50–52 • *The Co-Mason*, 9 (1917), 139–40 • A. Leo, 'The observatory', *Modern Astrology*, 14/6 (Dec 1903), 183–91 • A. Leo, 'The status of the astrologer', *Modern Astrology*, 25/7–8 (July–Aug 1914), 289–393 • *Modern Astrology*, 28/9 (Sept 1917), 257–87 • *Modern Astrology*, 28/10 (Oct 1917), 296–302, 303–6
Likenesses photograph, *c.*1895, BL [*see illus.*] • photograph, repro. in *Modern Astrology*, 17 (1906) • photograph, repro. in A. Leo, *The art of synthesis*, 3rd edn (1912), frontispiece
Wealth at death £1959 9*s.* 2*d.*: probate, 10 Dec 1917, *CGPLA Eng. & Wales*

Leoba [St Leoba, Lioba, Leofgyth] (*d.* **782**), abbess of Tauberbischofsheim, was the leading female contributor to her kinsman *Boniface's mission to pagan Germany. Her full name was Leofgyth. Leoba was the only child of elderly parents, Dynne and Æbbe, and entered the monastery of Wimborne as an oblate in the time of Abbess Tetta. She was educated there by Eadburh (*fl.* 716–746), who knew Boniface and was in correspondence with him. Four lines of verse composed by Leoba in the style of Aldhelm have been preserved in a letter she sent to Boniface in the period after 732 when Boniface began attracting religious from England to work with him. Leoba reminds him of his kinship with her mother and friendship with her father. Subsequently Boniface invited her to join him in Germany, but her move there cannot be dated securely. A passage in her life by Rudolf of Fulda has been interpreted as linking her arrival to the time of the dispatch of Boniface's follower Sturm to Rome in 748, but it is not certain that Rudolf intended such chronological precision, and a letter from Boniface to Leoba and other Anglo-Saxon women known to have worked in Germany provides some support for the idea that she had settled in Germany before 748. Boniface founded a nunnery at Tauberbischofsheim, near Würzburg, for Leoba, but according to Rudolf she had a wider authority over all the nuns working with Boniface, comparable to that which Sturm exercised over the monks. Before his departure to Saxony and martyrdom in 754, Boniface reinforced Leoba's position, symbolized by his gift to her of his cowl, and instructed her to continue the work she had begun under his direction.

Leoba's kinship with Boniface must have been of key importance for the authority she continued to enjoy after 754, but that should not detract from her own innate abilities as a spiritual leader. Tauberbischofsheim became a major training centre for Anglo-Saxon religious women working in Germany and several of Leoba's nuns became abbesses themselves, including Thecla, a kinswoman, who became abbess of Kitzingen and of Ochsenfurt, and another West Saxon, Walburg, who succeeded her brother Winnebald as head of the monastery of Heidenheim. According to her biographer, Leoba was an inspirational monastic leader and renowned for her learning in the scriptures, the fathers, and ecclesiastical law. Tauberbischofsheim also had an important role to play in the evangelization of its locality and as abbess Leoba had a difficult and sometimes dangerous position; her hagiography is notable for miraculous events which show her in an active role. One incident reported by Rudolf concerns a false accusation that one of the nuns was the mother of a dead baby found in a millpond, which caused considerable ill feeling against the nunnery. Leoba organized an impressive round of church services and processions and caused the real culprit to confess. On another occasion local panic about a severe storm obliged Leoba to validate the power of God by confronting the storm directly.

Leoba's influence went beyond her immediate locality and the work of the men and women she trained. She was also influential at the courts of Pippin III and his son Charlemagne, and was particularly close to Charlemagne's wife, Hildegard, though, according to Rudolf, Leoba 'detested the life at court like poison' (Rudolf of Fulda, 'Vita Leobae', 129). She was also apparently consulted by bishops on spiritual matters and on ecclesiastical discipline. After Boniface's death Leoba visited Fulda regularly to pray at his tomb and to speak with the monks; as Rudolf stresses, she was an exception to the rules which otherwise prevented women from entering the male preserve. In her old age, having been abbess for twenty-eight years, Leoba gave up her abbacy and retired with a few nuns to Schornsheim, near Mainz, a royal estate which, according to a surviving charter, was made available to her by the gift of Charlemagne.

Leoba died at Schornsheim on 28 September 782 attended by her Anglo-Saxon chaplain Torhthat, who seems to have been a member of the community at Tauberbischofsheim for many years. Her death is recorded in the necrology of Fulda. Boniface had requested that she be buried in his own tomb, but although she was buried at Fulda it was not considered appropriate to reopen Boniface's grave and she was at first buried near him in the crypt of the main church. Abbot Eigil subsequently translated her remains to the west porch and a number of miracles are reported at her tomb from this time, including the healing of a Spaniard who came to

Fulda after a fruitless tour of the shrines of Italy and France and was cured through the joint intervention of Boniface and Leoba. Following an extensive programme of rebuilding at Fulda during the abbacy of Hrabanus Maurus (822 to 841 or 842), Leoba's remains were translated again in 836 or 838 and placed in a reliquary behind an altar, dedicated to Mary and the female virgins of Christ, in the crypt of a new church on the nearby hill of Petersburg, where her remains can still be visited. It may have been in preparation for this translation that Hrabanus commissioned Rudolf, a monk of Fulda, to compose his life of St Leoba, which was completed before the body was transferred. The work is dedicated to a nun called Hadamout and drew upon the recorded remembrances of female disciples of Leoba, including her kinswoman Thecla, who may also have been formerly a nun at Wimborne; they evidently recalled her with affection and respect. BARBARA YORKE

Sources [Rudolf of Fulda], 'Vita Leobae abbatissae Biscofesheimensis auctore Rudolfo Fuldensi', [*Supplementa tomorum I–XII, pars III*], ed. G. Waitz, MGH Scriptores [folio], 15/1 (Stuttgart, 1887), 118–31 · M. Tangl, ed., *Die Briefe des heiligen Bonifatius und Lullus*, MGH Epistolae Selectae, 1 (Berlin, 1916), nos. 29, 96, 67 · 'Rudolfi miracula sanctorum in Fuldenses ecclesias translatorum', [*Supplementa tomorum I–XII, pars III*], ed. G. Waitz, MGH Scriptores [folio], 15/1 (Stuttgart, 1887), 328–41 · C. H. Talbot, ed. and trans., *The Anglo-Saxon missionaries in Germany* (1954) · T. Reuter, ed., *The greatest Englishman: essays on St Boniface and the church at Crediton* (1980) · S. Hollis, *Anglo-Saxon women and the church* (1992), 271–300 · P. H. Coulstock, *The collegiate church of Wimborne Minster* (1993) · J. Schwarz, ed., *1150 Jahre Petersberg* (1986) · B. Yorke, 'The Bonifacian mission and female religious in Wessex', *Early Medieval Europe*, 7 (1998), 145–72 · Y. Hen, '*Milites Christi utriusque sexus*, gender and the politics of conversion in the circle of Boniface', *Revue Bénédictine*, 109 (1999), 7–31

Leofric, earl of Mercia (*d.* 1057), magnate, was the son of Leofwine, son of Ælfwine. Leofwine was created ealdorman by Æthelred II in 994. He retained his rank after the Danish conquest (*AS chart.*, S 1384), though his eldest son, Northmann, was murdered at Christmas 1017, on Cnut's orders. His sphere of office is uncertain: under Æthelred he had held Worcestershire and Gloucestershire, but these shires, with that of Hereford, were given to Danes early in Cnut's reign. It is possible that Leofwine became ealdorman of Mercia in succession to Eadric Streona (*d.* 1017). His son Eadwine (killed at the battle of Rhyd-y-groes in 1039) may have been Earl Ranig's deputy in Herefordshire (S 1462), and Leofric, who attests charters as *minister* from 1019 to 1026, was perhaps sheriff in Worcestershire under Earl Hakon (S 991). Leofwine probably died soon after his last attestation in 1023.

Leofwine was given land in Warwickshire in 998 (*AS chart.*, S 892), but the family may have come from the east, rather than the west, midlands. In the religious houses of west Mercia they have a reputation as spoliators. Æthelred II gave Leofwine land at Mathon, Herefordshire (S 932), which probably belonged to Pershore Abbey and bestowed on Northmann an estate at Hampton, Worcestershire, later claimed by Evesham (S 873); Leofwine, Eadwine, Leofric, and a fourth son, Godwine, are accused of seizing lands belonging to the church of Worcester. In contrast, the religious establishments of the east midlands remember them kindly. It may have been Northmann who gave Twywell, Northamptonshire, to Thorney Abbey (S 931), and Leofwine was commemorated as a benefactor at Peterborough, a house ruled between 1052 and 1066 by his great-nephew, Abbot Leofric. Earl Leofric's son *Ælfgar (*d.* 1062?) was a benefactor of Crowland. In the Confessor's reign, Sexi of Woodwalton, Huntingdonshire, a benefactor of Ramsey, claimed kinship with Earl Leofric; and descendants of the family may have survived in the east midlands even after 1066.

Leofric married *Godgifu (*d.* 1067?), probably at some time before 1010, and he first attests as earl in 1032, though he may have been promoted in the late 1020s. John of Worcester, indeed, has Leofric succeed to the earldom of his brother Northmann, but there is no evidence that Northmann ever held the rank of earl. Whatever the extent of his father's power, Leofric himself was certainly earl of Mercia, a post which he held through the reigns of four kings. In 1035 he supported Harold I (*d.* 1040), Cnut's son with Ælfgifu of Northampton, against Harthacnut (*d.* 1042), who was backed by his mother, Emma, and Earl Godwine. Leofric's championship of Harold may stem from the marriage, probably in the late 1020s, of his son Ælfgar with Ælfgifu, arguably a kinswoman of Harold's mother. In Harthacnut's reign, Leofric participated in the harrying of Worcester in 1041, in punishment for the murder of two housecarls sent to collect the geld of 1040; but it was Earl Godwine whom Harthacnut sent to dig up the body of Harold I and throw it into the Thames marshes.

In the Confessor's reign, Leofric was among those who in 1043 advised the king to deprive his mother, Emma, of her treasure, and rode with him to Winchester to implement this decision. There seems to have been considerable rivalry between the Mercian earls and the family of Earl Godwine. In 1047 and 1048 Leofric counselled against sending ships to aid Godwine's nephew, Swein Estrithson, against his Norwegian rivals for the kingdom of Denmark; he also supported the king against Godwine in 1051, but advised him against an outright attack on the earl. When Godwine and his family fled, it was Leofric's son Ælfgar who received Harold Godwineson's earldom in East Anglia; and when the family forced the king to reinstate them in 1052, Leofric allowed Osbern Pentecost, whose castle in Herefordshire had been a cause of dissension, to escape through Mercia to Scotland. Ælfgar regained East Anglia in 1053, when Harold became earl of Wessex, though he was exiled (temporarily) in 1055. In the following year Gruffudd ap Llywelyn, Ælfgar's erstwhile ally, killed the warlike bishop of Hereford, Leofgar (formerly Earl Harold's chaplain), on 16 June, and it was Leofric who assisted Harold and Ealdred, bishop of Worcester, to make peace; the bishops of Worcester, on whose lands the Mercian earls were encroaching, had close connections with Godwine's family. This is Leofric's last recorded appearance and he died the following year.

Lands in Warwickshire and Shropshire are still entered in Leofric's name in Domesday Book. They are probably his personal estates, for John of Worcester says that he endowed Coventry Abbey out of his own patrimony and that of Godgifu, and Coventry's manor at Southam had certainly been held by Leofwine (*AS chart.*, S 892). Coventry was established in or before 1043 as a family monastery and mausoleum and is the only house actually founded by Leofric and Godgifu. Both Coventry's pre-conquest abbots were connected with Leofric: Leofwine (*c*.1043–1053) was the son of Wulfwine of Selly Oak, who by 1066 was commended to Leofric's grandson *Eadwine [*see under* Ælfgar] and may originally have been the man of Leofric himself; and when Leofwine became bishop of Lichfield in 1053, Coventry passed into the control of the earl's nephew, Leofric of Peterborough, who died in 1066. In 1071 Leofwine resigned his see and returned to Coventry, apparently as abbot.

John of Worcester praises Leofric's generosity, not only to Coventry but also to Much Wenlock in Shropshire, Leominster, Herefordshire, the churches of St John and St Werburgh at Chester, Stow St Mary in Lincolnshire, Worcester itself, and Evesham; Domesday Book adds his gift of Austrey, Warwickshire, to Burton Abbey, Derbyshire, and the Evesham chronicle records his building and endowment of the church of Holy Trinity. John's praise is somewhat surprising, since the monks of Worcester remembered Leofric, his father, brothers, and grandsons, and several of the men commended to him, as despoilers of church land. His only known grant to Worcester, of lands at Wolverley and Blackwell (*AS chart.*, S 1232), is no more than the return of two of the six estates taken from the church by his father; the others remained in the hands of Leofric and his adherents. Myton, Warwickshire, which Cnut gave to Abingdon Abbey, was also held in 1066 by Leofric's descendants (S 967).

Leofric's piety, though genuine, seems to have been of the conventional kind, which did not preclude the use of ecclesiastical land for the enrichment of his family. His relations with Burton illustrate the point. The abbey may have received Austrey, but six other estates given by its founder were held by Leofric's family in 1066 and the house itself was, like Coventry, in the hands of his nephew Leofric of Peterborough. Burton was founded by the north Mercian nobleman Wulfric Spot (*d.* 1002x04) but his family fell from power soon after his death; his brother Ælfhelm was murdered on King Æthelred's orders in 1006 and Morcar, husband of his niece Ealdgyth, met the same fate in 1015. Much of the land held by Wulfric and his kin is later found in the hands of Leofric's family, who probably took over the patronage of his abbey. The families may have been connected by marriage, for Ælfgifu, wife to Leofric's son Ælfgar, is probably Wulfric Spot's godchild, Morcar and Ealdgyth's daughter; it may not be coincidental that these names were given to two of her children with Ælfgar.

The same connection with Wulfric Spot might underlie Leofric's relations with Evesham. Its abbot from 1014 to 1044 was Ælfweard, also bishop of London from 1035. He was allegedly a kinsman of Cnut, but is perhaps more likely to have been related to Cnut's English wife, Ælfgifu of Northampton (*fl.* 1006–1036), daughter of Wulfric Spot's brother Ælfhelm. Æfic, Ælfweard's prior (*d.* 1037/1038), became confessor to Leofric and his wife, Godgifu, and it was he who persuaded Leofric to restore the lands at Hampton, Worcestershire, given by Æthelred II to Northmann.

Ecclesiastical benefactions were also a means to acquire influence through patronage. Leofric's gifts to Leominster may be a response to Cnut's removal of Herefordshire from Mercian control in his father's time. Leominster's support would be a powerful asset, for the estates of the church were extensive enough to put north Herefordshire beyond the control of any ordinary secular authority. After Earl Ranig's death, Leofric's rival here was Swein Godwineson, who attempted to obtain Leominster's land by marrying its abbess, an escapade which brought about his own exile and the house's dissolution. In this instance Leofric's benefactions came to nothing, but he was more successful elsewhere. Stow St Mary, Lincolnshire, had been founded by the Eadnoth who was bishop of Dorchester from 1034 to 1049 and whose successor Wulfwig (1053–67) solicited Leofric's aid to establish and endow a college of priests. Leofric's involvement with Stow extended his influence outside his earldom, into a shire where his family had become prominent by 1066; in the same way, his gifts to the two Chester churches reflect (and perhaps prefigure) the wealth and influence in the shire enjoyed by his grandson Eadwine. By 1066, when Eadwine and Morcar were earls of Mercia and of Northumbria respectively, the family's estates were worth nearly £2500, and were scattered over seventeen shires, with the greatest concentrations of land lying in Shropshire, Staffordshire, Cheshire, and Yorkshire.

Leofric died in 1057, on either 31 August or 30 September, at his manor of King's Bromley, Staffordshire, and was buried at Coventry. John of Worcester's words may stand as his epitaph: 'the wisdom of this earl during his lifetime was of great advantage to the kings and all the people of the English' (John of Worcester, *Chron.*, s.a. 1057).

ANN WILLIAMS

Sources *ASC*, s.a. 1039, 1055, 1056 [text C]; s.a. 1043, 1051, 1055, 1057 [text D]; s.a. 1006, 1015, 1017, 1035, 1051, 1057, 1066 [text E] • John of Worcester, *Chron.* • *Hemingi chartularium ecclesiæ Wigorniensis*, ed. T. Hearne, 2 vols. (1723) • F. E. Harmer, ed., *Anglo-Saxon writs* (1952) • Ordericus Vitalis, *Eccl. hist.*, 2 • F. Barlow, *Edward the Confessor* (1970) • P. H. Sawyer, ed., *Charters of Burton Abbey*, Anglo-Saxon Charters, 2 (1979) • R. Fleming, *Kings & Lords in conquest England* (1991) • S. Keynes, *An atlas of attestations in Anglo-Saxon charters, c.670–1066* (privately printed, Cambridge, 1993) • S. Keynes, 'Cnut's earls', *The reign of Cnut*, ed. A. R. Rumble (1994), 43–88 • P. A. Clarke, *The English nobility under Edward the Confessor* (1994) • J. Hunt, 'Piety, prestige or politics? The house of Leofric and the foundation and patronage of Coventry Abbey', *Coventry's first cathedral: the cathedral and priory of St Mary* [Coventry 1993], ed. G. Demidowicz (1994), 97–117 • A. Williams, *The English and the Norman conquest* (1995) • A. Farley, ed., *Domesday Book*, 2 vols. (1783), 1.238*v*, 239, 243*v*, 252*v*, 259*v* • W. D. Macray, ed., *Chronicon abbatiae de Evesham, ad annum 1418*, Rolls Series, 29 (1863) • S. Keynes, *The diplomas of Æthelred II, 'the Unready', 978–1016* (1980) • D. Knowles, C. N. L. Brooke, and V. C. M. London, eds., *The heads of religious houses, England and Wales*, 1: *940–1216* (1972) • *The letters of Lanfranc, archbishop of Canterbury*, ed. and trans. H. Clover and M. Gibson, OMT (1979) • C. R. Hart, *The early charters of eastern England* (1966) • A. Williams, '"Cockles amongst the wheat": Danes and English in the western midlands in the first half of the eleventh century', *Midland History*, 11 (1986), 1–22 • A. Williams, 'An introduction to the Worcestershire Domesday', *The Worcestershire Domesday*, ed. A. Williams and R. W. H. Erskine (1988), 1–31, esp. 20–28 • A. Williams, 'A vice-comital family in pre-conquest Warwickshire', *Anglo-Norman Studies*, 11 (1988), 279–95 • J. Hunt, 'Land tenure and lordship in tenth- and eleventh-century Staffordshire', *Staffordshire Studies*, 4 (1991–2), 9–13 • D. Roffe, 'The *Historia Croylandensis*: a plea for reassessment', *EngHR*, 110 (1995), 93–108 • W. D. Macray, ed., *Chronicon abbatiae Rameseiensis a saec. x usque ad an. circiter 1200*, Rolls Series, 83 (1886) • *The chronicle of Hugh Candidus, a monk of Peterborough*, ed. W. T. Mellows (1949) • F. Barlow, ed. and trans., *The life of King Edward who rests at Westminster* (1962) • *The Vita Wulfstani of William of Malmesbury*, ed. R. R. Darlington, CS, 3rd ser., 40 (1928) • *AS chart.*, S 891–2, 906, 931–2, 991, 1384, 1423, 1459–60, 1462, 1478, 1536 • D. Hill, *An atlas of Anglo-Saxon England* (1981), map 182

Leofric (*d.* **1072**), bishop of Exeter, a priest with an impeccable Old-English name, nevertheless came probably from Cornwall. John of Worcester calls him *Brytonicus* (British). In the lost Plympton cartulary it was recorded that his brother and steward, Ordmaer, administered his Cornish estate, Tregear in Roseland, and that Ordmaer's son and grandson, Osbert and John Sor, inherited an interest. This family was still holding the manor of Tolverne in Roseland of the bishop of Exeter in the thirteenth century. Leofric, for reasons unknown, was brought up and educated in Lotharingia, possibly in the cathedral church of St Stephen's, Toul (Meurthe-et-Moselle). There he would have received a good grounding in the literary and devotional culture produced by the Carolingian renaissance. He also became an admirer of St Chrodegang's rule for canons. When King Æthelred's son Edward (later called the Confessor), who likewise had spent much time in exile, returned in 1041 to join his half-brother, King Harthacnut, and to succeed him in 1042, Leofric accompanied him as his chaplain. The background to their relationship is unknown; but the ties were close, for Leofric remained a member of the Chapel Royal until, when Bishop Lyfing died in 1046, he was rewarded with two of that bishop's dioceses, Devon and Cornwall. Nevertheless, although clearly remaining on good terms with the king and queen, he seems thereafter to have avoided royal service and so passed unscathed through the several crises of the reign. Instead, he devoted himself to the reform of his large 'province'.

With royal and papal permission, Leofric quickly effected a radical reorganization, replacing his two sees, St Germans and Crediton, with one in the Benedictine monastery within the walled borough of Exeter, and, moreover, substituting canons for the existing community. By 1050 the basic changes had been made, and, according to documents produced at Exeter to protect the revolution, the king and queen escorted the bishop to his enthronement in his new cathedral. The ministering clergy were given the rule of St Chrodegang; Leofric's own copy, in Old English and Latin, of a version of the eighth-century rule in the form promulgated for the Carolingian empire by the Council of Aachen in 817 is extant. It envisaged the bishop and his clergy forming a small and close community, living together in a quasi-monastic fashion, but undertaking some external pastoral duties. There is, however, hardly any evidence for the actual conditions at Exeter before 1133. A history of the see produced before Leofric died claims that he was an active visitor and preacher in his diocese, an instructor of the clergy, and a builder of churches. But, aided by probably only a small group of canons, one of whom would have been the single archdeacon, the scope of his government would have been limited.

Documents produced in Leofric's church, although probably exaggerating the poverty he inherited, indicate the main areas in which he enriched it. He was content with the vast hoard of relics, mostly King Æthelstan's gift, and the existing monastic buildings, and concentrated on increasing its estates and furnishings, including the library. Inventories of all its possessions were drawn up shortly before his death. He had recovered some lost properties and contributed his own. In the league table of pre-twelfth-century manuscripts, the Exeter scriptorium comes fourth, after Canterbury, Salisbury, and Worcester. Leofric inherited the famous Exeter book of Old-English poetry, which has been dated *c*.950–970, and acquired many volumes, some from Canterbury (for example, the Leofric missal). Consequently the Exeter scriptorium was a prime exponent of Anglo-Caroline minuscule, style IV, associated with the Canterbury scribe Eadwig Basan. Among Exeter's losses were its archives, damaged by fire before 1019; and inevitably these were replaced by fabrications. A surprising feature of Exeter charters of the period is, however, the poor Latinity and general ineptitude.

Unharmed by the Norman conquest, Leofric died on 10 February 1072 and was buried in the crypt of his cathedral church at Exeter. When Bishop William Warelwast rebuilt it, he translated Leofric's remains; but the site has never been found. In 1568 a tomb was created for Leofric against the east wall of the south tower. FRANK BARLOW

Sources *ASC*, s.a. 1044, 1046, 1047 [texts E, C, D] • John of Worcester, *Chron.* • *Willelmi Malmesbiriensis monachi de gestis pontificum Anglorum libri quinque*, ed. N. E. S. A. Hamilton, Rolls Series, 52 (1870) • A. S. Napier, ed., *The enlarged rule of Chrodegang*, EETS, 150 (1916) • R. W. Chambers, M. Förster, and R. Flower, eds., *The Exeter book of Old English poetry* (1933) • F. E. Warren, ed., *The Leofric missal* (1883) • F. Barlow, ed., *Exeter, 1046–1184*, English Episcopal Acta, 11 (1995) • F. Barlow, *The English church, 1000–1066: a history of the later Anglo-Saxon church*, 2nd edn (1979) • F. Barlow and others, *Leofric of Exeter: essays in commemoration of the foundation of Exeter cathedral in AD 1072* (1972) • D. W. Blake, 'Bishop Leofric', *Report and Transactions of the Devonshire Association*, 106 (1974), 47–57 • P. Chaplais, 'The authenticity of the royal Anglo-Saxon diplomas of Exeter', *Essays in medieval diplomacy and administration* (1981), 1–34 • P. W. Conner, *Anglo-Saxon Exeter: a tenth-century cultural history* (1993)

Leofric (*fl.* **1070–1071**). *See under* Hereward (*fl.* 1070–1071).

Leofwine, earl (*d.* **1066**), magnate, was a younger son of Earl *Godwine (*d.* 1053) and his wife, *Gytha [*see under* Godwine]. He attested royal charters between 1043 and 1054 as *minister* or *nobilis*, usually with his elder brothers *Harold II (before 1045) and *Tostig (*c*.1029–1066). This might suggest that he was the fourth brother (*Swein, the eldest, who died in 1052, was earl from 1043); but he may have been younger than *Gyrth, who seems to have been promoted to an earldom before him. Leofwine attested as earl from 1059, but there are no charters between 1055 and that date, and it is usually presumed that he received part of the earldom of Ralph, earl of Hereford, on the latter's death in 1057. His command included Hertfordshire, Middlesex, and probably Buckinghamshire, but the evidence linking him with Kent, Surrey, and Staffordshire is unreliable. Leofwine is associated with his brother Harold (as Gyrth is with Tostig), fleeing with him to Ireland in 1051, when the rest of the family went to Bruges, and Harold's presence looms large in the shires of Leofwine's earldom; it was he, not Leofwine, who held the great comital manor of Hitchin, Hertfordshire, and the brothers shared the lordship of eighteen burgesses at Hertford itself. The same pattern can be seen in Buckinghamshire, and even in Middlesex Harold as well as Leofwine was one of the major tenants. Leofwine's lands outside his earldom, amounting to about 75 hides (or the equivalent) in Kent, Sussex, Surrey, Somerset, and Devon, are relatively modest and perhaps represent his inheritance from his father; this must be the case with his five estates in Devon, which are clearly comital in origin. Leofwine led the forces of his earldom to the battle of Hastings on 14 October 1066 and was killed with his brothers Harold and Gyrth; the Bayeux tapestry shows him wielding his axe before falling to the Norman cavalry. ANN WILLIAMS

Sources *ASC*, 1051–2, 1066 [text E] • D. M. Wilson, ed., *The Bayeux tapestry* (1985) • F. E. Harmer, ed., *Anglo-Saxon writs* (1952) • F. Barlow, *Edward the Confessor* (1970) • P. A. Clarke, *The English nobility under Edward the Confessor* (1994) • A. Williams, 'The king's nephew: the family, career, and connections of Ralph, earl of Hereford', *Studies in medieval history presented to R. Allen Brown*, ed. C. Harper-Bill, C. J. Holdsworth, and J. L. Nelson (1989), 327–43 • S. Keynes, *An atlas of attestations in Anglo-Saxon charters, c.670–1066* (privately printed, Cambridge, 1993) • R. Abels, 'An introduction to the Hertfordshire Domesday', *The Hertfordshire Domesday*, ed. A. Williams and G. H. Martin (1991) • A. Farley, ed., *Domesday Book*, 2 vols. (1783), 1.10v, 134

Likenesses Bayeux tapestry, repro. in Wilson, ed., *The Bayeux tapestry*, pl. 68

Leominster. For this title name *see* Fermor, William, Baron Leominster (1648–1711).

Leon, Beatrice Augusta de (1900–1991). *See under* Leon, Jack de (1902–1956).

Leon, Delia de (1901–1993). *See under* Leon, Jack de (1902–1956).

Leon, Henry Cecil [*pseud.* Henry Cecil] (1902–1976), writer and judge, was born on 19 September 1902 at the rectory, Norwood Green, Middlesex, the youngest of the three sons (there were no daughters) of Joseph Abraham Leon, analytical chemist, and his wife, Esther Phoebe Defries. He was educated at St Paul's School, of which he was a foundation scholar. His eldest brother, destined for the law, was killed in action in the First World War. Leon joined Gray's Inn, where he had a book-lined flat up many flights of wooden stairs, and was admitted as an exhibitioner to King's College, Cambridge. He obtained second classes in classics (part one) in 1921 and law (part two) in 1923. Called to the bar in 1923, he acquired a considerable practice by exercising the four qualities he was later to cite as necessary for success in his engaging book of advice, *Brief to Counsel* (1958): speed of understanding, patience in listening, integrity, and the capacity for hard work.

As early as 1930, together with his surviving brother, Leon was able to present his parents, whose means had always been modest, with their first car and with someone to drive it: an early example of a notorious generosity. Success also enabled him, on 9 August 1935, to marry Lettice Mabel (1904/5–1950), daughter of Henry David Apperly, of Chalfont St Peter, whom he later characterized in his discursively anecdotal autobiography *Just within the Law* (1975) as 'the most skilful dentist for whom I have ever opened my mouth' (p. 112). In 1939, from a sense of duty, he joined the Army Officers' Emergency Reserve; he was called to the 1/5 battalion of the Queen's Royal regiment, in which he gained the MC (1942) at the battle of Alamein for, in the words of his commanding officer, 'sheer refusal to be intimidated by every kind of enemy projectile' while taking weapons through a minefield gap. It is typical of his fundamental modesty that the award goes unmentioned in his autobiography.

Leon had not long resumed his bar career when his wife was stricken by cancer. He at once applied for a county court judgeship in order to spend as much time as possible with her in the country. She died in 1950, and Leon was to express in his autobiography his gratitude 'for the happiness which she gave me during the short fourteen years of our marriage' (p. 131). On 29 December 1954 he married Barbara Jeanne Ovenden (*b.* 1911/12), daughter of Thomas Blackmore, farmer, of Weston-super-Mare. It was a marriage, he later said, as happy as his first. Neither marriage resulted in children, but he was extremely proud of his stepson, Barbara's son, and his three 'step-grandchildren'.

To restore his income (county court judges then received only £2000 p.a.) Leon began writing, under the name Henry Cecil. First came a collection of stories, *Full Circle* (1948), based on diverting tales told to his fellow soldiers on board ship, and then a succession of twenty-four novels, of which *Brothers in Law* (1955), made into a play then a film, brought him most success. They are written much as their author talked, amusingly, with ingenuity and shrewd illustrative anecdote but ballasted with common sense and an uncompromising belief in goodness. Yet they are never 'goody-goody': his sense of mischief, noted of himself in an article, 'I haven't changed since I was eight', is too pervasive for that.

Leon served as a county court judge at Brentford and Uxbridge, Middlesex, from 1949 to 1953 and at Willesden, London, from 1953 to 1967, a term marked by compassion and reform. He instituted an unofficial welfare officer system to help litigants after trial; thanks largely to his instigation, debtors faced with prison were obligatorily informed of their rights, and such imprisonment was at once cut by half. His conduct on the bench, he said of himself, was marked by frequent intervention, occasionally from his sense of mischief, at other times from his passion for properly conducted justice. This latter prevented his admitting in undefended divorce cases less than strict proof, and eventually at his request the lord chancellor relieved him of divorce work.

Leon's latter days, bow-tied as ever, were much enjoyed. Some six months before his death, giving the Saintsbury oration—he was a most clubbable person—he quoted with high approval Charles Lamb on retirement: 'I walk about, not to and from'. But he also served—as chairman of the British Copyright Council (from 1973) and of the Society of Authors and in lecturing and talking to students and others. Henry Cecil Leon died of a heart attack on 21 May 1976 at the Royal Sussex County Hospital in Brighton. Although he is best-known for his light novels set in the world of the law, and the handful of these which were adapted in other media, he also had a legal career which, but for a personal tragedy, might have taken him high. His half-dozen books on legal matters demonstrate the shrewdness of judgement and the same sense of fun which marks out his fiction. The aim that he offered to a correspondent who, he feared, would be soured by a legal reverse was to lead a 'happy, sensible and useful life'. That was the life that he himself enjoyed.

H. R. F. Keating, *rev.*

Sources H. C. Leon, *Just within the law* (1975) • personal knowledge (1986) • private information (1986) [Barbara Leon, widow] • b. cert. • m. certs. • d. cert.

Archives BBC WAC, corresp. with BBC

Wealth at death £6282: probate, 18 Aug 1976, *CGPLA Eng. & Wales*

Leon, Jack de (1902–1956), theatre manager and impresario, was born on 12 August 1902 at Colon, Panama, the second of eight children of Michael de Leon (1868–1914), merchant, and his wife, May Miriam Maduro (1881–1964). His love of drama developed from when he operated a puppet theatre as a child. In 1911 the family moved to London where he was educated at University College School, Hampstead. After brief forays into the import trade and publishing, he was articled to the legal practice of Indermaur and Brown in London in 1923. On 30 August 1921, at the St John's Wood synagogue, he married Beatrice Lewisohn [*see below*], an actress and founder of a drama school.

In 1924, encouraged by Beatie's mother and with financial help from his elder sister, Delia [*see below*], de Leon leased the Prince's Hall, Kew Bridge, Brentford, Middlesex, which had formerly served as a dance hall, a skating rink, and a cinema. It opened as the Q Theatre on 26 December 1924 with *The Young Person in Pink*, a comedy by Gertrude Jennings, and with Milton Rosmer as the production manager. Beatie was in the cast, making her professional début. Although their first production had already achieved success in London's West End, the de Leons' intention was to specialize in wholly new plays in the hope that after a week-long trial at the Q, they would be taken up by West End managers. The policy proved sufficiently successful for the theatre critic James Agate to write: 'Clever Mr Jack de Leon that what you think today … the West End managers often think tomorrow' (*Sunday Times*, 25 July 1926, 6). By now de Leon had surrendered his solicitor's articles. His own first play, *The Man at Six*, written under the name of Noel Doon and in collaboration with Steve Donohue, was produced at the Q on 16 January 1928.

Criticism of the contractual arrangements with new writers and a series of practical problems led the de Leons to relinquish management of the Q in March 1929. Their association was renewed two years later when Beatie reopened the theatre for a season of plays performed by students from her drama school.

Although he remained closely involved with the Q, de Leon's own future was expanding as a playwright and impresario associated increasingly with productions, including revues, in the West End and on provincial tour, and writing a number of film scripts. He also became an expert in stage lighting; his light cues were included in the publication of his version of Goethe's *Faust* which he produced at the Q in April 1948. *The Man at Six* was produced at the Queen's Theatre at Easter 1929. For a few months in 1929 he leased the newly built Duchess Theatre. In April 1930 *The Silent Witness*, written again by de Leon and Donohue, opened at the Comedy Theatre. De Leon was involved with the production of Noel Scott's *Traffic* at the Lyceum Theatre in July 1930 and with *Rocklitz* by Marjorie Bowen at the Duke of York's Theatre in February 1931.

Gradually the Q became re-established on a fully professional basis, but now with Beatie in overall charge, and reverted to including in its programme new plays, many of which transferred to the West End. Among these in 1933 was de Leon's most ambitious and untypical play, *Francis Thompson*, based on the life of the poet. It was said to have 'several scenes which catch at one's throat' but to 'emphasise too much the prostitute element' (*The Stage*, 9 March 1933, 12).

In the next twenty years the Q was a training ground for actors, producers, stage managers, and technicians. Among those whose careers began or were nurtured there were Richard Attenborough, Dirk Bogarde, Phyllis Calvert, Joan Collins, Joan Hickson, Vivien Leigh, Margaret Lockwood, James Mason, and Michael Wilding, and the director Peter Brook. Between 1938 and 1940 the de Leons ran the Embassy Theatre, Swiss Cottage, London, alongside the Q. In 1943 and 1944 de Leon put on summer seasons at the Savoy Theatre, Kettering.

De Leon's role as impresario created such West End successes as *See How They Run* at the Comedy Theatre in 1945, *The Giaconda Smile* at the New Theatre in 1948, *To Dorothy a Son* at the Savoy Theatre in 1950, and *And So to Bed* at the New Theatre in 1951. His last West End production was *The Count of Clerambard* at the Garrick Theatre in 1955. Competition from television and, more immediately, a leaking roof and insufficient financial support from the Arts Council and the local authority, led to the closure of the Q on 19 February 1956. De Leon died from a heart attack on 21 September 1956 at his mother's home, 254 Kew Road, Kew, Surrey, and was cremated at Golders Green on 23 September.

De Leon was tall and elegant with a shock of black, later grey, wavy hair. He always dressed in dark suits or a black jacket, waistcoat, and striped trousers. 'He was a barrister manqué … [with] that sort of investigative mind, a natural feel for the dramatic and an arresting voice' (Barrow, 67).

His wife and co-founder of the Q Theatre, **Beatrice Augusta** [Beatie] **de Leon** [*née* Lewisohn] (1900–1991), was born on 22 November 1900 at 26 Darnley Road, Hackney, London, the ninth child of Bernhard Lewisohn (1850–1906), boot manufacturer, and his wife, Lydia Moses (1865–1939). As a child she was taught by her widowed mother to recite and was often taken to the local theatre in Dalston and to the Royal Opera House, Covent Garden, London. She was educated in London at Lady Hollis's School, Skinners' School, and Northfield high school. At thirteen she left to learn shorthand and typing and she worked until 1916 in clerical positions before she followed an older brother, Victor, to train at Herbert Beerbohm Tree's Academy of Dramatic Art (later the Royal Academy of Dramatic Art). With Delia de Leon she founded the London Academy of Dramatic Art in 1923.

Beatie de Leon acted occasionally at the Q but suffered from chronic stage fright and was far happier training others or in management. After the closure of the Q and de Leon's death she and the couple's only child, Jean, ran the De Leon Drama School in association with Richmond Adult College for some thirty years. She retired in 1984. Subsequently she became an 'angel', investing in West End shows including the musical *Oliver*. She was warm-hearted and had immense courage and drive. Dirk Bogarde compared her to a bright-eyed wren or robin, 'eager, alert, determined … [and] amazingly unsentimental' (Barrow, xv). She died of cancer on 16 February 1991 at the home she shared with her sister-in-law Delia, King's Lodge, Kew Green, Kew, Surrey, and was cremated at Golders Green on 19 February.

Jack de Leon's sister **Delia de Leon** (1901–1993), actress, was born at Colon, Panama, on 10 February 1901. In 1909 she was sent to Jamaica to be educated at a school run by English women. She moved to London with her family in 1911. She had two ambitions: 'to be an actress and … to come to an understanding of God' (Barrow, 78). She appeared in a number of productions at the Q between 1925 and 1935, initially under the name of Delia Delvina, and was in *The Children of the Moon* when it transferred from the Q to the Royalty Theatre, London, in October 1926. She became a disciple of the Indian avatar, Meher Baba (1894–1969), in the 1930s. She was both generous and impractical. Pete Townsend wrote of the 'passion, constancy, meticulousness, and enormous anxiety' which combined in an 'endearing eccentricity' (de Leon, xiv). She never married. Her autobiography, *The Ocean of Love*, was published in 1991. She died on 21 January 1993 at Abbeyfield, 4 Ennerdale Road, Kew, and was cremated at Mortlake on 31 January.

C. M. P. Taylor

Sources K. Barrow, *On Q: Jack and Beatie de Leon at the Q theatre* (1992) • D. Bogarde, *A postillion struck by lightning*, pbk (1988) • D. de Leon, *Ocean of love* (1991) • *The Times* (22 Sept 1956) • *The Independent* (19 Feb 1991) • *The Independent* (5 March 1993) • *Sunday Times* (25 July 1926) • *The Stage* (9 March 1933) • *The Stage* (22 Sept 1956) • *The Stage* (7 March 1991) • m. cert. [Jack de Leon] • d. cert. [Jack de Leon] • b. cert. [Beatrice de Leon] • d. cert. [Beatrice de Leon] • d. cert. [Delia de Leon] • private information (2004) [Mrs Jean de Leon Mason, daughter]

Likenesses photographs, priv. coll.

Wealth at death £4035 7*s.* 4*d.*: administration, 20 Nov 1956, *CGPLA Éire* • £8193—Beatrice de Leon: probate, 8 April 1991, *CGPLA Eng. & Wales* • under £125,000—Delia de Leon: probate, 10 May 1993, *CGPLA Eng. & Wales*

Leonard, Daniel (1740–1829), lawyer and politician in America and public official in Bermuda, was born in Norton, Massachusetts, on 29 May 1740, the only son of Colonel Ephraim Leonard and his wife, Judith Perkins. His father's militia office qualified Daniel to rank third in the Harvard College graduating class of 1760 and to a captaincy in the first class of Harvard fencibles, a student military body created during the Seven Years' War. He read law with Samuel White of Taunton, Massachusetts, and his classmates elected him valedictorian. His commencement oration dealt in Latin with the origins of English liberty in the Magna Carta. In 1766 he received an AM degree from Yale College. After four years of living with his parents and practising law in Norton, he was appointed justice of the peace for Bristol county. On 2 April 1767 he married Sarah White, who died a year later. In 1770 he married Sarah (*d.* 1806), daughter of Captain John Himock, a Boston merchant, whose estate in 1769 enabled Daniel and Sarah to build a mansion on the Taunton, Massachusetts, town green. They had three children.

A high-living and successful lawyer, in 1769 Leonard became king's attorney for Bristol county and was elected to the Massachusetts house of representatives. He protested against the removal of the legislature from Boston to Cambridge in 1769 by demanding the recall of Governor Francis Bernard and demanding that Lieutenant-Governor Thomas Hutchinson return the court to Boston. As a member of the Taunton committee of correspondence in 1773, he joined in calling for the removal of Governor Hutchinson and Chief Justice Peter Oliver. Offended by the Boston Tea Party, he voted on 14 February 1774 against a resolution for Oliver's removal. The rumour network buzzed with speculation that he enjoyed riding to court in a chariot and wearing a gold chain around the brim of his hat. 'Discerning ones soon perceived', John Adams later recalled, 'that wealth and power must have charms to a heart that delighted in so much finery and indulged in such unusual expense'. Hutchinson, Adams wrote, 'courted Leonard with the ardor of a lover, reasoned with him, flattered him, overawed him, frightened him, invited him to come frequently to his house' (Shipton, 642). On 29 May 1774 Leonard signed a complimentary address to the departing Hutchinson and on 15 August joined other Massachusetts lawyers in welcoming the military governor, Thomas Gage. He was appointed to the newly created mandamus (royally appointed) council under the terms of the Massachusetts Government Act in 1774 (one of the four notorious Coercive Acts passed by parliament to punish Massachusetts for the Tea Party) but his Taunton neighbours, carrying clubs, demanded his resignation from the council. Leonard and the other mandamus councillors sought protection of British troops in Boston.

There between 12 December 1774 and 3 April 1775 Leonard published seventeen essays in the *Massachusetts Gazette*, under the pseudonym Massachusettensis, each answered by John Adams, writing as Novanglus. Adams incorrectly assumed that Massachusettensis was his old friend and tireless newspaper polemicist Jonathan Sewall. Adams's confusion was significant because Leonard himself developed into an amazingly astute adversary. The debate between 'Massachusettsman' and 'New Englandman' was a subtle, wide-ranging discussion in which both writers forced the other to plumb the depths of their respective ideological positions. Leonard's was one of the first accounts of the pre-revolutionary controversy to examine the complex interaction of struggles between patriots and loyalists in each colony, on one level, and the merging of these conflicts at the continental level. Mindful of the British origins of American colonial liberty, Adams countered Leonard's depiction of a British empire designed to foster political liberty with a theory of empire as a league of self-governing entities.

The Massachusettensis letters are Leonard's major claim to a place of prominence among the leading loyalists in revolutionary America. Leonard matched Adams's ability to write at several levels. Both writers didactically offered historical guidance, legalistically applied colonial or British law, imaginatively constructed rival models of imperial constitutionalism, and adroitly pushed the hot buttons of Massachusetts partisanship. Leonard did so through appeals to 'fear, anger, honor, pride, virtue, and communal and imperial loyality' (Mason, xi). Rising to each other's bait, Adams and Leonard knew how to go for the jugular. Leonard wrote:

> Our patriots have been so intent on building up American rights that they have overlooked the rights of Great Britain and our own interest. Instead of proving that we were entitled to privileges that our fathers knew our situation would not admit us to enjoy, they have been arguing away our most essential rights

—among them British protection and participation in a future empire which might have increasing benefits to distribute to mother country and colonies alike (Mason, 36–7). In a telling critique of the first continental congress in his letter 'Massachusettensis, no. 16', he detected the functional shift in the nature of the congress that had occurred between the final days of the first congress in late October 1774 and in plans for a second congress to assemble in May 1775, as the congress evolved from a constituent assembly into a revolutionary tribunal presuming to possess 'the collected wisdom of the continent'. That accumulated 'wisdom', Leonard wrote with withering scorn, consisted of 'every particle of disaffection, petulence, ingratitude, and disloyalty that for ten years past have been scattered through the continent' (Mason, 94). Stripped of vituperative intent, those four abusive terms were also an accurate and astute depiction of the structure of American patriot ideology.

While seeking refuge from the patriots in the Boston garrison town in 1775, Leonard served as solicitor-general to the customs commissioners and volunteered for military action in the assault on Bunker Hill. When the British evacuated Boston in March 1776 the Leonard family joined in the exodus, settling briefly in Halifax, Nova Scotia, where he once more served as legal counsel to the customs commissioners. By August 1776 he had made his way to London where he became an active member of the loyalist exile community. In 1780 he was appointed chief justice of New Ireland, an abortive colony to be established between New England and Nova Scotia which never materialized. Instead Leonard accepted the post of attorney-general in Bermuda, and in 1781 became chief justice and a member of the council there. He visited the United States in 1806 and 1808, the latter visit to arrange for guardianship of his son, Charles, who had become mentally deranged. He retired to London in 1815 where he prospered as a barrister at the Inner Temple and presided over gatherings of loyalist exiles who came together periodically to eat 'an American Sunday dinner' of 'salt fish, beefstake, and apply pie' (Shipton, 647). After seeing a figure on his roof whom he took to be a burglar and preparing to defend himself, Leonard died on 27 June 1829 of an accidentally self-inflicted gunshot wound.

ROBERT M. CALHOON

Sources C. K. Shipton, *Sibley's Harvard graduates: biographical sketches of those who attended Harvard College*, 14 (1968) • R. Calhoon, *The loyalists in revolutionary America, 1760–1781* (1972) • B. Mason, ed., *The American colonial crisis: the Daniel Leonard–John Adams letters to the press, 1774–1775* (1972)

Wealth at death $14,000: Shipton, *Sibley's Harvard graduates*, vol. 14, p. 647

Leoni, Giacomo [James] (*c.*1686–1746), architect, a Venetian first heard of at Düsseldorf in 1708, arrived in Britain early in the second decade of the eighteenth century. He claimed to have been 'Architect to his most serene Highness the Elector Palatine' (G. Leoni, *The Architecture of A. Palladio*, 1716–20, title-page); although this remains unproven, his residence at Düsseldorf is known from an inscription on a short manuscript treatise. His arrival in Britain was announced with his edition of translations (1715–19) of Palladio's *Quattro libri dell'architettura* (1570). In this work Leoni replaced the original woodcuts with copperplate-engravings produced by distinguished craftsmen in London and in Amsterdam where the printshop of Bernard Picart was the base for distribution of the book, which carried a French text, through Europe. The English translation was the work of Nicholas Dubois (*c.*1665–1735), and was based on a French edition of 1650 rather than on the 'Italian Original' mentioned on the title-page. While a complete English translation of Palladio was a key text in the growing interest in that architect, it was soon noted that Leoni's plates took liberties with Palladio's buildings. Although he claimed to have seen Palladian buildings for himself, as early as 1719 the young Lord Burlington noticed errors in his depiction of a cornice in Vicenza, and the elevation of the Villa Valmarana was substantially redesigned. A considerable subscription list accumulated during the course of the publication of the work; either Leoni or, more probably, Dubois ensured that half the artisan subscribers were members of building trades.

Leoni approached the practice of architecture by grounding himself in architectural theory. The manual written in Düsseldorf had concerned the orders according to the precepts of Palladio; for his first English patron, Henry Grey, duke of Kent, he wrote 'Compendious Directions for Builders'. This may have been presented as early as 1713, by which time Leoni was involved in the greater labour of preparing the edition of Palladio. This theoretical preparation yielded practical fruit in a commission from the duke of Kent to modernize his house at Wrest in Bedfordshire, but although Leoni's designs were sent abroad to receive the comments of distinguished foreign architects such as Fillipo Juvarra, nothing came of them. Another early patron was James, Earl Stanhope, first lord of the Treasury, for whom he designed a triumphal arch for George I intended for Hyde Park, but this too came to nothing. Leoni's first recorded building appears to have been Queensberry House, 7 Burlington Gardens, for John Bligh, Lord Clifton, in 1721, which was built on Lord Burlington's Westminster estate. This early and prominent participation in the development of the estate suggests that, briefly, Palladio's editor may have enjoyed a measure of collaboration with Lord Burlington; at this time the earl was building up his collection of the drawings of Inigo Jones, and Colen Campbell, whose own designs had considerable impact on Leoni, was working for Burlington.

Over the next thirty years Leoni was involved in the construction of over a dozen substantial country houses, including a small group in the north-west of England, and at least six London houses; two church monuments are also known to be by him. This activity brought him little prosperity, and in 1734 one patron, Lord Fitzwalter of Moulsham, Essex, provided £25 to him, 'being in distress' (Edwards, 53). Nor does a substantial body of work survive on which an assessment of his work can be based: Moulsham (1728) was demolished in 1816, Bodecton Park, Sussex (1738), in 1826, Lathom, Lancashire (*c*.1740), in 1929. Two of his greatest schemes, for Carshalton, Surrey (1723–7), and Thorndon, Essex (1733–1742), were never completed. The narrow record of his extant works can be widened slightly by engraved designs of projects which he published in 1729. The country houses adhere to a slightly austere Palladian formula: many of the fronts are tall and only barely articulated, though the survival of either Carshalton or Thorndon might have modified this severe impression. Leoni's most extensive surviving work is Lyme Park, Cheshire (*c*.1725–35), where he ingeniously adapted the formalities of his Palladianism to the complexities of an earlier house. The galleries are carried on an arcade round the interior court, masking the irregularity of the space, while the projecting Ionic portico on the south front was one of his grandest statements. Little evidence of his interest in the villa form survives but a small group of town houses, including Queensberry House, shows that he took part in the fashionable development of the city of Westminster.

Publication continued to provide Leoni with the possibility of additional income, but his interests were erudite and ambitious. From as early as 1719 he was intending to publish a translation of Alberti's *De re aedificatoria* and the first volume appeared in 1726. Again the translation was not his (it was by John Ozell); his main contribution was the preparation of drawings for the engravers. In the third volume, published by 1730, he included *Some Designs for Buildings both Publick and Private*, a collection of engravings of eight of his designs, three of which had been executed, including Carshalton and Queensberry House. Towards the end of his life he was preparing to publish a 'Treatise of Architecture and ye Art of Building Publick and Private Edifices … Containing Several Noblemen's Houses & Country Seats' of his own design, but this was cut short by his death. Leoni died on 8 June 1746 after a month's illness, during which his benefactor Lord Fitzwalter had sent him £8 8*s*. 'par charité' (Edwards, 64). He was buried in St Pancras old churchyard, Middlesex, and left a wife, Mary, and two sons, one of whom was probably a clerk to Matthew Brettingham. T. P. CONNOR

Sources Colvin, *Archs.* • R. Hewlings, 'James Leoni, *c*.1686–1746: an Anglicized Venetian', *The architectural outsiders*, ed. R. Brown (1985), 21–44 • E. Harris and N. Savage, *British architectural books and writers, 1556–1785* (1990) • T. P. Hudson, 'Moor Park, Leoni and Thornhill', *Burlington Magazine*, 113 (1971), 657–61 • T. Friedman, 'Lord Harrold in Italy, 1715–16: four frustrated commissions to Leoni, Juvarra, Chiari and Soldani', *Burlington Magazine*, 130 (1988), 836–45, esp. 837–40 • J. Cornforth, 'Lyme Park, Cheshire [pts 1–2]', *Country Life*, 156 (1974), 1724–7, 1998–2001 • A. C. Edwards, ed., *The account books of Benjamin Mildmay, Earl Fitzwalter* (1977)

Archives Beds. & Luton ARS, Lucas MSS • Cliveden, Buckinghamshire, Cliveden album • JRL, Legh of Lyme MSS

Leonowens [*née* Edwards], **Anna Harriette** (1831–1915), educator and travel writer, was born in Ahmadnagar, India, on 6 November 1831, the younger daughter of Thomas Edwards (*c*.1803–1831), formerly a cabinet maker of St George the Martyr parish, London, then a sergeant in the sappers and miners, and his wife, Mary Anne (1815/16–1873), who was possibly the illegitimate Eurasian daughter of William Vawdrey Glasscott (*d*. 1821), lieutenant in the Bombay army. Anna's father died before her birth, leaving the family penniless. On 9 January 1832 her mother married Patrick Donohoe, a corporal in the engineers, soon seconded to the public works department where he served successively as sergeant overseer (in Deesa), assistant supervisor (in Aden) and deputy commissary (in Poona).

It is likely that Anna first met the Irish-born Thomas Lean Owens (*bap*. 1823, *d*. 1859), in the mid-1840s, when he was paymaster sergeant with the 28th regiment at Deesa. Her parents opposed the connection which was temporarily broken when Donohoe was transferred to Aden in 1847, taking his by then large family with him. There they encountered the resident chaplain, the Revd George Percy *Badger, and his wife, Maria, a missionary schoolmistress. When the Badgers embarked on an extended tour of Egypt and Palestine, probably in 1849, Anna accompanied

Anna Harriette Leonowens (1831–1915), by Napoleon Sarony, *c.*1870

them. Her intellectual curiosity was stimulated by Badger, a noted orientalist and keen observer of colonial imperialism in the Middle East. It was he who introduced Anna to the study of languages (she eventually mastered eight), encouraged her interest in Eastern culture and religion, and sharpened her skills of observation and analysis.

Upon her return to India, Anna married 'Leon' Owens on Christmas day 1849, in Poona; he was then a clerk in the commissary general's office at Bombay, but by May 1852, when their first child, Selina, died, he was employed by R. Frith & Co., Bombay mess agents. At about this time Anna broke completely with her family, and the couple, their surname now conflated to Leonowens, went to Perth, Western Australia. There they had a second child, who died after only a few months; a third child, Avis, was born in 1854, and a fourth, Louis, in 1856. Anna, then known as Harriet, advertised a Young Ladies' School, at Perth in 1854. In February 1857 the family sailed from Perth to Singapore and went thence to Prince of Wales Island (later Penang) where Thomas ran a hotel. He died of apoplexy in Penang on 8 May 1859 and was buried in Northam Road cemetery.

Left impoverished with children to support, his widow opened a school in Singapore. Then in 1862 she took an appointment arranged by the Borneo Company to teach the wives and children of Rama IV of Siam, popularly known as King Mongkut. The king fathered some thirty-nine sons and forty-three daughters, procreation being a royal duty which he took seriously. The children and their mothers, along with several thousand other women and retainers (most of whom were given to the king by those seeking royal favour), lived in seclusion in Nang Harm, a walled city within the royal palace. Mongkut, an enlightened modernizer who had fostered contacts with both Americans and Europeans, wanted his children to receive a Western education, but the missionary wives whom he engaged initially had as their main object the conversion of their pupils to Christianity. Leonowens, the first Western woman to live in the palace, was contracted to 'do [her] best endeavour for knowledge of English language, science and literature and not for conversion to Christianity' (King Mongkut, letter of 26 Feb 1862, in A. Leonowens, *Governess at the Siamese Court*, 1954 edn, vii).

Taking Louis with her (but sending Avis to a London boarding-school), Leonowens served Mongkut for nearly six years, first as teacher and latterly as one of his foreign language secretaries. In her first role she is best remembered for tutoring the future King Chulalongkorn, and for intervening on behalf of the women of Nang Harm, whom she saw as enslaved and oppressed; in her second she was important to Mongkut's strategy of opening Siam to Western influence, while at the same time frustrating the territorial ambitions of France, America, and Britain. Her decidedly ambiguous position at court fed palace intrigue and fostered animosity from the Anglo-French diplomatic community. In consequence she mixed mainly with American missionaries, assimilating their professional antipathy to the heathen and polygamous king, and this later coloured her published accounts of life in Siam. Overwork, poor pay, unrelenting stress, and recurring tropical illnesses led her to secure a furlough and sail for England in July 1867. In his farewell speech Mongkut remarked: 'You ought to know you are [a] difficult woman and more difficult than generality' (King Mongkut, in A. Leonowens, *Governess at the Siamese Court*, 1954 edn, xv). Nevertheless, they seem to have respected and even perhaps liked each other.

After a brief sojourn in England and Ireland, where Louis was installed in a boarding-school, Leonowens sailed with Avis for New York in November 1867, in search of the bracing climate which her health was thought to need, and in anticipation of renewed contact with various American friends. Efforts to renegotiate her post at the Siamese court were unsuccessful, and Mongkut's death on 1 October 1868 terminated any ideas of return. Contact with the royal family, however, continued over many years, facilitated by correspondence, occasional meetings (including a memorable one with Chulalongkorn in London, in August 1897), and the considerable business success of Louis Leonowens in Siam, under Chulalongkorn's patronage, beginning in the 1880s.

Leonowens decided to remain in the United States where, again needing to support herself and her family, she opened a school on Staten Island; more significantly, she began to write about her life in Siam. An article in the *Atlantic Monthly* in 1869 was the prelude to two books, *The English Governess at the Siamese Court* (1870; English edn as *Governess at the Siamese Court*, 1870) and *The Romance of the*

Harem (1873; English edn as *The Romance of Siamese Harem Life*, 1873). Both, but especially the second, are a mixture of biography and snippets of history and myth, frequently misrepresented. Almost immediately Leonowens was accused of having invented salacious and barbaric incidents of life in Siam, in order to titillate her audience and thus increase sales. Her books and the lecture engagements to which they gave rise did, however, bring her an income (always precarious) and an entrée into the literary circles of New York and Boston, where her many friends included James T. Fields, Henry Wadsworth Longfellow, Sarah Orne Jewett, and Harriet Beecher Stowe.

Her daughter's marriage in 1878 to Thomas Fyshe, a Scottish banker, greatly improved Leonowens's financial situation. She subsequently made her home with them in Halifax, Nova Scotia, but continued to work, notably as a writer for the *Youth's Companion*, an American periodical as whose correspondent she visited Russia in 1881. Her *Life and Travels in India* (1884), a competent travel work with little biography, was less successful than the earlier books, and her final study, *Our Asiatic Cousins* (1889), was barely noticed. Leonowens is best remembered in Halifax for her leadership in art education initiatives, social activism, and women's suffrage. From the late 1880s she spent two extended periods in Germany, supervising the education of her grandchildren; after 1901 she lived with the Fyshe family in Montreal, Canada, where she was active in arts and crafts advocacy and hospital charity work. Blinded by a stroke in 1912 and confused by age, she lingered until 19 January 1915, when her death went largely unnoticed. She was buried two days later in Mount Royal cemetery, Montreal.

Leonowens would probably have been entirely forgotten had Margaret Landon not published a romanticized biography, *Anna and the King of Siam* (1944), with a shorter version, *Anna and the King* (1952), on which were based a theatrical musical and films, *Anna and the King of Siam* (1946), *The King and I* (stage, 1951; screen 1956), and *Anna and the King* (Twentieth Century Fox, 1999). The stage and screen versions present an even more fanciful picture of Siam than did Leonowens's books, but are less offensive (although still patronizing) about Mongkut, who is depicted as endearing but childlike. These productions in turn led to several accounts in English by Thai and Western scholars on the true nature of the king and his reign. These did little, however, to alter the Hollywood image and have themselves been criticized for their condoning of slavery and general repression of women and children. Direct attacks on Leonowens also failed to subvert her influence. A. B. Griswold, in *King Mongkut of Siam* (1961), undermined her claim to historical accuracy and questioned her emotional stability; Ian Grimble called her 'a mischief-maker, a squalid little girl … one of those awful little English governesses, a sex-starved widow' (*New York Times*, 8 Aug 1970, p. 25); while W. S. Bristowe, in *Louis and the King of Siam*, revealed how far she had invented the story of her ancestry and early life. New research has strengthened the argument for mixed ancestry and various family secrets, but has refuted much of Bristowe's genealogical research, his claim that Leonowens was raised in squalor and deprivation, and his insinuation that she travelled unchaperoned and alone with the unmarried Revd Badger. Despite, or perhaps because of, their shortcomings, her life and writings captured the imagination of the Western public, although the strident and unflattering portrayal of one of their greatest kings has continued to offend the Thai people. As one of the first westerners to write about Siam, and as one in unique contact with the king at a critical juncture in the country's history, Leonowens is remembered for having created an enduring if inaccurate image of Siam in the eyes of the West. ELIZABETH BAIGENT and LOIS K. YORKE

Sources Avis Fyshe MS, Wheaton College, Wheaton, Illinois, Kenneth and Margaret Landon Southeast Asia collection · M. Landon, *Anna and the king of Siam* (New York, 1944) · W. S. Bristowe, *Louis and the king of Siam* (1976) · L. S. Dow, *Anna Leonowens: a life beyond 'The king and I'* (Lawrencetown Beach, Nova Scotia, 1991) · Bombay ecclesiastical records, BL OIOC · Bombay marriages, BL OIOC · parish register, St Mary's Church of Ireland, Enniscorthy, co. Wexford, NA Ire. [baptism, husband] · PRO, records of HM 28th regiment, War Office 12 · Nova Scotia Archives and Records Management, Halifax, Nova Scotia, Phyllis R. Blakeley fonds · *Bombay Calendar and General Directory* [and variant titles] (1844–51) · *Bombay Almanac and Book of Direction* (1850–57) · Bengal ecclesiastical records, BL OIOC · Bombay army muster rolls and casualty returns, BL OIOC · A. B. Griswold, *King Mongkut of Siam* (New York, 1961) · L. K. Yorke, 'Edwards, Anna Harriette (Leonowens)', *DCB*, vol. 14 · J. Corfield, 'Anna Leonowens and the Australian connection', *Ancestor*, 24/4 (1998), 6–7 · Bombay baptisms, BL OIOC · Bombay burials, BL OIOC · Bombay military consultations, BL OIOC · Bombay wills, BL OIOC · Nova Scotia Archives and Records Management, Halifax, Nova Scotia, Local Council of Women (Halifax) fonds · Nova Scotia Archives and Records Management, Halifax, Nova Scotia, Nova Scotia College of Art and Design fonds · Hunt. L., Annie Adams Fields papers, James T. Fields collection · *East-India Register and Directory* (1822) · *Montreal Gazette* (20 Jan 1915) · *New York Times* (8 Aug 1970) · L. K. Yorke, *Anna Leonowens, 1831–1915: the life and times of a 'difficult woman'* [forthcoming]

Archives Hunt. L., James T. Fields collection, letters to Annie Adams Fields · Wheaton College, Illinois, Kenneth and Margaret Landon Southeast Asia collection | FILM 'Anna Leonowens: getting to know you', BBC, 1999 · 'Anna and the king: the true story', Foxstar Productions (1999) · Foxstar Productions, 'Anna and the king: the real story of Anna Leonowens', 1999 · *Women adventurers*, History Television, 2001

Likenesses N. Sarony, photograph, *c.*1870, Wheaton College, Illinois, Kenneth and Margaret Landon Collection [*see illus.*] · W. Notman & Son (Montreal), photographs, 1903–11, McCord Museum, Montreal, Quebec, Notman photographic archives · R. Harris, oils, 1905–6, Confederation Centre Art Gallery and Museum, Charlottetown, Prince Edward Island

Leopold, Prince, first duke of Albany (1853–1884), fourth and youngest son of Queen *Victoria and Prince *Albert, was born Leopold George Duncan Albert at Buckingham Palace on 7 April 1853. The birth was the first at which Victoria was assisted by the use of chloroform. He was early diagnosed as a haemophiliac, and suffered from epilepsy; the illness conditioned his entire life. Victoria was obsessively protective of him, and grew more so after Albert's death. He shared Albert's scholarly tastes from an early age; his principal tutor was Robert Hawthorn Collins, afterwards comptroller of his household, with whom he went into residence at Oxford in 1872, matriculating at

Prince Leopold, first duke of Albany (1853–1884), by W. & D. Downey, 1872

Christ Church. He lived at Wykeham House, St Giles', and attended (in the academic dress of a gentleman commoner) the lectures of the professors of history, poetry, music, fine art, and political economy, and studied science at the museum and modern languages at the Taylor Institution. He was very attached to Oxford, where he was relieved of the constant anxiety of his mother, who referred to the city as 'very odious'.

In 1876 Leopold left the university with the honorary degree of DCL, and established himself at Boyton House, Wiltshire. His attempts to assert his independence, despite his frequent illness, upset, alarmed, and, increasingly, infuriated the queen, who regarded his refusal to accompany her to Balmoral in 1878 as little short of treason. He compounded the offence by going to Paris without mishap, and the queen submitted to his travelling in France, Germany, Switzerland, and Italy; in 1880 he made a tour in Canada and the United States. In 1878 he was elected president of the Royal Society of Literature, and in 1879 vice-president of the Society of Arts. He was an effective public speaker, and took a lively interest in questions of education, favouring university extension and technical education, in public speeches. He supported the Royal Institution in Aid of the Deaf and Dumb, and advocated the establishment of a national conservatoire of music under the influence of his friendship with Arthur Sullivan. Frustrated by the limitations imposed on him by his health and position, Leopold threatened to stand for parliament as an 'extreme radical'; instead he consulted Disraeli, who persuaded the queen to use him as a confidential secretary (incidentally enabling them to circumvent her official secretary, Sir Henry Ponsonby, whose Liberal sympathies were at odds with those of the queen). He was given the keys to the government dispatch boxes, a privilege to which the prince of Wales was not admitted.

In 1881 Leopold was created duke of Albany, earl of Clarence, and Baron Arklow. Victoria's general opposition to her children marrying was heightened in his case, but by 1881 he was actively seeking a wife. Frances Maynard (later Lady Warwick) was suggested, but she married his equerry, Lord Brooke. In the autumn of 1881 he met Princess Helen of Waldeck-Pyrmont (1861–1922), and, having informed her fully about Leopold's health, Victoria gave her consent to the 'risk and experiment' of the marriage, which took place in St George's Chapel, Windsor, on 27 April 1882. The queen gave them Claremont in Surrey as a wedding present. To the queen's surprise, they produced a daughter the following February (*Alice, later countess of Athlone). Leopold's wife was expecting a second child (*Charles Edward, later duke of Saxe-Coburg and Gotha, born on 19 July 1884) when he was sent to Cannes to escape the harsh weather early in 1884. While there, he slipped on a staircase, bringing on an epileptic fit and brain haemorrhage, from which he died at the Villa Nevada on 28 March 1884. His remains were interred in St George's Chapel, Windsor, on 6 April.

Leopold had resented the restrictions placed on him by his illness and his over-protective mother, and, rather than succumbing to invalidism, sought to be useful: in 1883 he applied to go to Canada as governor-general, following the term of his brother-in-law, the marquess of Lorne. In this, as in so much, he was thwarted by his mother's intervention. Commenting on the death of a haemophilic nephew, he wrote, 'it is perhaps better that this dear child has been spared all the trials and possible miseries of a life of ill-health like mine' (Van der Kiste, 78).

J. M. Rigg, *rev.* K. D. Reynolds

Sources J. R. Ware, *Life and speeches of Prince Leopold* (1884) · *Darling child: private correspondence of Queen Victoria and the crown princess of Prussia, 1871–1878*, ed. R. Fulford (1976) · *Beloved mama: private correspondence of Queen Victoria and the German crown princess, 1878–1885*, ed. R. Fulford (1981) · J. Van der Kiste, *Queen Victoria's children* (1986) · S. Weintraub, *Victoria: biography of a queen* (1987)

Archives Bodl. Oxf., autograph collection · Royal Arch., corresp., incl. that of duchess of Albany | BL, corresp. with W. E. Gladstone, loan 73 · BL, letters to Lady Knightley, Add. MS 46360 · Bodl. Oxf., corresp. with Doyle Family · Bodl. Oxf., letters to Friedrich Max Müller

Likenesses W. & D. Downey, photograph, 1872, Royal Arch. [*see illus.*]

Leopold I (1790–1865), king of the Belgians, was born on 16 December 1790 in Coburg, the eighth child and third son of Prince Francis Ferdinand of Saxe-Coburg-Saalfeld (1750–1806), heir to the German duchy of Coburg, and Augusta Caroline Sophia of Reuss-Ebersdorff (1757–1831). His baptismal names were Leopold George Chrétien Frederick. Charles Theodore Hoflender, head of ecclesiastical

Leopold I (1790–1865), by Franz Xaver Winterhalter, 1840

administration for Coburg and first professor at the Collegium Casimirianum, oversaw his education. He was confirmed in the Lutheran church on 12 September 1805, and left Coburg in the winter of 1805–6, Napoleonic troops having overrun it.

Leopold then joined the Russian army; Tsar Alexander's brother Grand Duke Konstantin was his sister Anna's husband. The treaty of Tilsit (1807) returned the duchy of Coburg to Leopold's eldest brother, Ernest, and the two brothers travelled to Paris to meet Napoleon, who asked Leopold to act as his aide-de-camp. Leopold refused, returned instead to the Russian army, and fought at the battles of Lutzen, Bautzen, Kulm, and Leipzig. He was appointed to the military order of St George of Russia and accompanied the tsar on his triumphal march through Paris following Napoleon's defeat.

Marriage to Princess Charlotte It was as part of the tsar's retinue that Leopold travelled to London in 1814, where he met Princess *Charlotte (1796–1817), daughter of the prince regent and heir presumptive to the British throne; their first encounter was accidental, on the back stairs of Pulteney's Hotel. At the time arrangements were being made for Charlotte's engagement to the prince of Orange, but she, known for her beauty and cultivated, independent spirit, alighted on Leopold—who in contrast to Orange was tall, handsome, and soldierly—as a more suitable husband. Tellingly in view of his later role in shaping modern European constitutional monarchy, she regarded his freedom from party ties in Britain an important recommendation. Leopold remained in London after the Russian delegation had departed, and moved from a flat above a grocer's shop on Marylebone High Street (reflecting the family's low income) to a residence of the Count Beroldingen in nearby Stratford Place. Their courtship letters were in French, though according to Lord Lauderdale, Leopold had 'a mania for England and English manners' (Sturt, 216). He was warmly received at the end-of-season ball at Carlton House, and the match was encouraged by, among others, the dukes of Kent and York, although with the regent (who, taking his cue from a favourite expression of Leopold's, nicknamed him le Marquis Peu à Peu) his relations were cool, and remained so (Hibbert, 93).

Napoleon's escape from Elba and return to power saw Leopold return to the Russian army at the head of a cavalry division. After the French emperor's final defeat at Waterloo (Leopold's division arrived too late for the battle) Leopold undertook negotiations on behalf of his brother for the enlargement of the duchy of Coburg. Pleading these diplomatic commitments, he resisted entreaties to return to England from the prince regent and an increasingly frustrated Princess Charlotte. He finally crossed the channel in February 1816, and the couple were married on 2 May at Carlton House by the archbishop of Canterbury. The marriage settlement gave Leopold the rank of army general, English citizenship, and a generous annual stipend of £50,000. Charlotte, whose original preference for Leopold had been pragmatic (she had told her confidante Mercer Elphinstone on 8 November 1814 that she was 'not in the least in the world in love with him'), now hailed him as 'the perfection of a lover' (*Letters of the Princess Charlotte*, 180, 242). Once feisty, she now submitted to his dislike at seeing ladies in the saddle and ceased to ride; Leopold for his part grew a moustache to please her. They settled at Claremont House, Esher, Surrey, but enjoyed life together for barely eighteen months, as Charlotte died on 6 November 1817, following the traumatic birth of a stillborn son. Baron Stockmar, Leopold's private secretary, later recorded that his master 'never recovered the feeling of happiness which had blessed his short married life' (*Memoirs of Baron Stockmar*, ed. F. M. Muller, 1872, 1.67).

Leopold remained in England for the next fourteen years. He was accorded the title of royal prince and the military rank of field marshal, and lived on at Claremont on his vast pension, giving rise to murmurs of discontent in parliament: particular objection was felt to his profiting, as a state pensioner, from the produce of his Surrey estate. He angered George IV by paying a private visit to Queen Caroline at the height of the divorce proceedings against her in 1821. (During her exile in Italy Leopold made no contact, giving rise to accusations of crowd-pleasing opportunism.) Thereafter he left England for a time to visit his own mother, and to travel to Florence, Naples, and Vienna.

By this time Leopold had acquired another connection

within the British royal family. After Charlotte's death the sons of George III had bestirred themselves to ensure the survival of the dynasty; Edward, duke of Kent, had married Leopold's sister Victoria of Saxe-Coburg-Saalfeld, and a daughter—Alexandrina Victoria—was born on 24 May 1819. After Kent's death in February 1820 Leopold granted his sister a pension of £3000 (which he could certainly afford) and encouraged her to remain in England in spite of the attitude taken towards her by her royal brothers-in-law, which ranged from indifferent to hostile. He provided funds too for the education of his niece, who later recalled her visits to Claremont as the 'brightest epoch of my otherwise rather melancholy childhood' (*Letters of Queen Victoria*, 1.14). A slight distancing factor was his sister's disapproval of his private life; he had installed his mistress, the German actress Kristina Bauer, in a house overlooking Regent's Park, and continued to have numerous affairs even after his second marriage.

First king of the Belgians Leopold had little to do in the United Kingdom; having been married to the heir presumptive to the throne he was effectively a king without a country. The first opportunity for him to rectify this omission came in February 1830, when he was put forward by France, Britain, and Russia for the throne of the newly established kingdom of Greece; finding that little popular support existed for him on the ground, he prudently declined the offer. His refusal was later recalled with gratitude by Victoria; Richard Barham, the pseudonymous Ingoldsby, took a less charitable—and widely held—view of his decision:

> Some say in hope to rule for his niece
> He hath refused to be king over Greece.
> (Weintraub, 64)

In October 1830, however, the revolt of the former Habsburg territories in the Netherlands against Dutch rule, and the establishment of a provisional government in Brussels, provided Leopold with another opening. The London conference on the future of Belgium, as the new kingdom became known, was held in the following month and involved France, Britain, Prussia, Austria, and Russia. Apart from setting the boundaries of the new state the five powers' main concern was to select a suitable constitutional monarch. The initial favourite was the duke of Nemours, son of the French king, Louis Philippe, but the prospect of expanded French influence sparked objections, and Leopold emerged as a compromise candidate. His selection was confirmed by the vote of a Belgian national congress on 4 June, and—with expressions of regret at leaving his adopted home of England—he accepted the invitation. (He forwent some, but not all, of his pension and maintained establishments in England for which he had little use; this became the subject of press criticism, to which he reacted with uncomprehending irritation.) Dressed in the uniform of a lieutenant-general of the Belgian army, he was inaugurated as the first king of the Belgians on 21 July 1831.

Before Leopold had finished his inaugural tour of the country the Dutch had amassed 50,000 troops along the border. The Belgian army, ill-trained and half the size, was no match—in spite of Leopold's own engagement with Dutch forces near Louvain—but the invading army retreated at the threat of French intervention. The new state survived, albeit on terms less favourable than Leopold would have liked (he even threatened abdication). Belgian independence and neutrality was finally guaranteed by the treaty of London in 1839. In the meantime Leopold had strengthened his position with the country's Roman Catholic hierarchy by marrying on 9 August 1832 Louise Marie d'Orléans (1812–1850), the eldest daughter of Louis Philippe, the king of the French, on 9 August 1832. According to Charlotte Brontë the Brussels court to which he brought her was as gloomy as a conventicle. Their children were raised as Catholics; the eldest surviving son, Leopold Louis Philippe Marie Victor (1835–1909), was married to the Habsburg archduchess Marie-Henriette—an example of the dynastic empire-building for which the Coburgs won repute. Leopold also brokered the marriage between his nephew Prince Ferdinand of Saxe-Coburg-Kohary and Queen Maria of Portugal in 1836, and married another nephew and a niece into the house of Bourbon. His daughter Marie Charlotte (1840–1927)—known by her second name in honour of Leopold's first wife, reputedly at the suggestion of his second—married another Habsburg, Archduke Ferdinand Maximilian of Austria. He later became emperor of Mexico—with consequences fatal for himself and catastrophic for the mental health of his widow.

Mentor and matchmaker to Queen Victoria With his niece Victoria, Leopold maintained a steady correspondence from her childhood onwards. Their letters ranged from personal matters to court intrigue and national and international politics. They give an unparalleled insight into the mind of the young princess and her development of a sense of her destiny and constitutional role. Leopold's position in her life in the years leading up to 1837—something between a father figure and an *éminence grise*—was exemplified in a letter of 19 November 1834, in which Victoria thanked him for sending her an extract about Queen Anne 'to show what a Queen ought not to be', and requested 'that you will send me what a Queen ought to be' (*Letters of Queen Victoria*, 1.50). In June 1837, with the health of William IV clearly rendering Victoria's succession imminent, Leopold advised her to keep the Melbourne ministry in office, that she would 'do wisely' by showing herself 'attached to the English Protestant Church as it exists in the State' (ibid., 94), and—above all—to train those around her to offer their opinion only when she asked for it. When she ascended the throne he prudently declined her invitation to visit Britain for fear of giving the appearance of interference, but made the trip in September 1839 and on numerous occasions thereafter.

Leopold's most lasting contribution to the history of the British empire—and his most triumphant piece of matchmaking—was his energetic promotion of the union of Victoria and his nephew Prince Albert of Saxe-Coburg-Saalfeld. This had been a pet project of his even before he arranged Albert's first visit to England, in May 1836, in the teeth of opposition from William IV. Victoria, however, would not be hurried into marriage; having found another confidante in Lord Melbourne she chafed at her uncle's overbearing influence and early became wise to his attempts to embroil her in Belgian affairs and his own international politicking. Leopold was shocked at the change in her tone towards him but bided his time and continued, through the agency of Stockmar, to groom Albert for the role of royal consort that he himself had been denied. His patience was rewarded and, though his relationship with Victoria inevitably altered, their correspondence continued unbroken until he died. In reply to his condolences on the death of Albert in 1861, she addressed him as 'Dearest, kindest, father' (Weintraub, 304). Afterwards, with his accustomed wiliness, he urged her to end her seclusion by invoking the popularity and high profile of the prince of Wales.

Constitutional monarch As king of the Belgians Leopold was active in promoting commerce and industry, and gave sanction in 1834 to the first railway on the European continent. He left domestic policy largely to his ministers; the lessons in constitutional monarchy absorbed during his time in England may have helped to ensure his survival of the revolutions of 1848 that toppled, among others, his father-in-law. He concerned himself more directly with foreign affairs; his diplomatic abilities were widely regarded and he was regularly called to act as an arbiter in international disputes.

Leopold made his last trip to England in April 1865 and, having been in declining health for a decade, returned to Belgium suffering from bronchitis. He died on 10 December 1865 at Laeken, Brussels. After lying in state at the Palais Royal dressed in the full uniform of a Belgian general, he was given a state funeral on 16 December. He was buried at Laeken, alongside his second wife, the wishes of his subjects having taken preference over his own desire to be buried at Windsor alongside Princess Charlotte. His eldest son succeeded him as Leopold II, whose rule in the Congo made his name a byword for colonial exploitation.

JANET L. POLASKY

Sources L. Lichtervelde, *Léopold I et la formation de la Belgique contemporaine* (1929) • T. Juste, *Leopold I: roi des Belges*, 2 vols. (1868) • A. Notebaert, 'Leopold I', *België en zijn koningen* (1990), 7.27 • C. Bronne, *Léopold I: roi des Belges* (1943) • J. Carlier, *La correspondence de la reine Victoria avec le roi Léopold I* (1908) • *Leopold Ier et son règne* (1965) [exh. cat.] • E. Corti and C. Buffin, *Léopold I: oracle politique de l'Europe* (1927) • G. Kirschen, *Léopold avant Léopold I* (1988) • A. Simon, *Léopold I* (1963) • H. Pirenne, *Histoire de Belgique*, 7 (1932) • C. Bronne, 'La reine Victoria et l'oncle Leopold', *Synthèses, Revue Européenne*, 97 (1954), 308–23 • E. Cammaerts, *The keystone of Europe* (1939) • *Letters of the Princess Charlotte*, ed. A. Aspinall (1949) • S. Weintraub, *Victoria: biography of a queen* (1987) • *The letters of King George IV, 1812–1830*, ed. A. Aspinall, 3 vols. (1938) • A. T. Holme, *Prinny's daughter: a life of Princess Charlotte of Wales* (1976) • D. M. Sturt, *Daughter of England: a new study of Princess Charlotte of Wales and her family* (1951) • *The letters of Queen Victoria*, ed. A. C. Benson and Lord Esher [R. B. Brett], 3 vols., 1st ser. (1907) • 'Belgium', *Encyclopaedia Britannica*, 9th edn (1875–89) • E. Longford, *Victoria RI* (1964) • C. Hibbert, *George IV* (1973)

Archives BL, corresp. • Ministry of Foreign Affairs, Brussels • Royal Arch. • Royal Palace, Brussels | Lpool RO, letters to fourteenth earl of Derby • U. Durham L., corresp. with second Earl Grey • U. Southampton L., letters to Lord Palmerston

Likenesses E. Quenedey, engraving, 1808, Royal Collections of Belgium • F. X. Winterhalter, portrait, 1840, Musée National du Château de Versailles, France [*see illus.*] • A. Dutrieux, statue, 1849, Royal Palace, Brussels • L. Ghémar, lithograph, 1856, Royal Palace, Brussels, Archives • L. De Winne, oils, Royal Palace, Brussels • W. T. Fry, engraving (Leopold and Charlotte), Royal Library of Belgium, Brussels • Nadar, photograph, Archives photographiques, Paris • F. X. Winterhalter, oils, Royal Palace, Brussels • bust in pastel, Royal Palace, Brussels

Le Patourel, (Herbert) Wallace (1916–1979), army officer, was born on 20 June 1916 at Kyrton, Fosse André, St Peter Port, Guernsey, the younger of two sons of Herbert Augustus Le Patourel (1874–1934), advocate, and from 1929 to 1934 procureur (attorney-general), and his wife, Mary Elizabeth (Minnie), *née* Daw (1873–1956), daughter of John Henry and Mary Daw, tenant farmers from Devon. His elder brother, John Herbert Le Patourel (1909–1981), was an eminent medievalist.

Le Patourel (known as Wally in Guernsey and Pat in his regiment) was educated at Elizabeth College, Guernsey, and always wanted to be a soldier. During his last year at school his father died, and he was persuaded that it was his duty to stay in the island and look after his mother. So in 1934 he became a bank clerk and satisfied his military aspirations in 1936 by joining the Royal Guernsey militia as a second lieutenant. His mother settled into widowhood and Le Patourel received a legacy of £500. This enabled him to prepare for the army entrance examination. In 1937 he transferred to the Hampshire regiment (supplementary reserve of officers) and in 1938 was granted a regular commission in the regiment.

Within a year the Hampshires went to France. In 1940 Le Patourel was evacuated from Dunkirk and was mentioned in dispatches. Two years in the UK followed but in November 1942 the 2nd battalion of the Hampshires sailed for Tunisia. Almost at once they were involved in the battle for the Tebourba Gap. On the fourth day of a fierce battle, 3 December 1942, Z company, commanded by Le Patourel, came under heavy fire from high ground. A brave attempt by an already depleted platoon from Z company failed to win it back. Then Le Patourel requested permission to make one last effort to dislodge the Germans. The citation for his award read:

> This officer then personally led four volunteers under very heavy fire to the top in a last attempt to dislodge the enemy machine guns. Major Le Patourel rallied his men and engaged the enemy, silencing several machine gun posts. Finally when the remainder of his party were killed or wounded, he went forward alone with a pistol and some grenades to attack the enemy machine guns at close quarters. From this action he did not return.

He was believed to be dead, and his Victoria Cross was awarded 'posthumously'. In fact he had been badly wounded and was taken prisoner, sent to hospital in Italy, and, as a seriously wounded prisoner, was repatriated in September 1943. Happily he recovered his health and was able to rejoin the service. In 1944 he landed in Normandy on D-day plus four as a senior staff officer, brigade major with the 53rd (Welsh) infantry division, serving with them until the end of the war in Europe.

(Herbert) Wallace Le Patourel (1916–1979), by Elliott & Fry, 1961

Le Patourel's subsequent career was varied and distinguished. From 1945 to 1947 he instructed in India at the Quetta Staff College. In 1948 he was appointed instructor at Warminster School of Infantry. On 26 October 1949 he married Babette Theresa Beattie (*b.* 1925) of Guernsey in the Town Church, where his father had been churchwarden; they had two daughters. The following year Le Patourel trained as a parachutist and was appointed second in command of the 2nd battalion of the Parachute regiment, serving in the Middle East. In 1953 there followed a staff appointment as a deputy assistant adjutant-general at the War Office. In 1954, now a lieutenant-colonel, he commanded the 14th battalion of the Parachute regiment and the 5th battalion of the Royal Hampshire regiment (TA) at Southampton. From 1957 to 1959 he was in Washington, DC, as general staff officer to the British joint services mission. In 1959, promoted to brigadier, he moved to Ghana as deputy commander of its army. While there he had a heart attack but was able to serve for two more years as deputy commander of 43 (Wessex) division district. In 1962 he retired.

Le Patourel's first three years as a civilian were spent as manager of the Fowey–Bodinnick ferry in Cornwall. Then in 1966 he joined Showerings Vine Products as executive assistant to the directors. In 1969 Showerings took over Harveys, the Bristol wine merchants, and Le Patourel became for the rest of his life a director of Harveys. During his Bristol years he lived in the county of Somerset and was appointed deputy lieutenant in 1974. He planned to spend his retirement raising Jacob's sheep and bought a farm in Chewton Mendip, but he died there of heart failure two years before his sixty-fifth birthday, on 4 September 1979, and this dream was never fulfilled. He was buried at Chewton Mendip on 11 September.

Le Patourel's regimental obituary described him as a kind and conscientious officer who never spared himself and got the best out of those he commanded. He met adversity calmly. He had energy, endearing charm, and a lively sense of humour. Despite his great achievements he remained a modest man. The citation for his VC concluded: 'Major Le Patourel's most gallant conduct and self sacrifice, his brilliant leadership and tenacious devotion to duty … were beyond praise.' He was survived by his wife and daughters. R. E. IRVINE

Sources *WWW* · L. J. Marr, *Guernsey people* (1984), 125–7 · *Royal Hampshire Regiment Journal*, 68 (1979), 176–8 · H. S. Daniel, *Regimental history: the royal Hampshire regiment*, 3: *1918–1954* (1955) · B. Perrett, *The Hampshire tigers* (1997)

Archives Royal Hampshire Regiment Museum, Winchester, medals and uniform | SOUND talk for the BBC, 1943/1944

Likenesses Elliott & Fry, photograph, 1961, NPG [*see illus.*] · T. Cuneo, oils, 1980, Royal Hampshire Regiment Museum, Winchester · photograph, Royal Hampshire Regiment Museum, Winchester

Wealth at death £77,974: probate, 5 Dec 1979, *CGPLA Eng. & Wales*

Lepell, Mary. *See* Hervey, Mary, Lady Hervey of Ickworth (1699/1700–1768).

L'Epine, Francesca Margherita de (*d.* **1746**), singer, was reputedly Tuscan, possibly French, but her origins and parentage are not known for certain; her mother and sister (possibly the singer Maria Gallia) at some stage lived in London. The belief that L'Epine was the 'Italian lady' who appeared at York Buildings, London, in 1693 is unfounded; her first known stage appearance was in two Venetian opera seasons, at the Teatro San Giovanni Grisostomo in 1698/9 and the Teatro Sant' Angelo in 1699/1700. The earliest evidence of her presence in London is a May 1703 receipt (now lost)—signed Françoise Marguerite—for 20 guineas 'for one day's singing in the play call'd the Fickle Shepherdess' (Moore, plate facing p. 335); she may have arrived with musicians from Rome and Venice who performed at York Buildings on 3 November 1702. Although L'Epine's name does not appear in any advertisements until 29 May 1703, her early fame is attested in two 1703 play prologues, for Joseph Trapp's *The Tragedy of King Saul* and Richard Wilkinson's *Vice Reclaim'd*. The latter bears witness not only to her talent and to the already strong hostility between spoken and sung theatre, but also to her connection with the composer Jakob Greber (*d.* 1731):

> Singing and Dancing is the only Grace
> And Shakespear's well wrought Scenes will have no Place,
> With Fam'd L'Epine, and great Greber's Base.

L'Epine's appearances at the Lincoln's Inn Fields Theatre, and at Tunbridge Wells in August 1703, featured Greber's music. Nicholas Rowe and others called her 'Greber's PEGG' (Rowe, 7), but she also established a relationship with Daniel *Finch, second earl of Nottingham (1647–1730), accepting an invitation to his estate after singing at

Tunbridge Wells, and benefiting from a financial subscription conducted by him that autumn. Many contemporaries assumed that their connection was a romantic one. Although she sang Greber's compositions during her first season at Drury Lane Theatre, beginning on 29 January 1704, she left England for the summer, and apparently did not take up Greber's music again on her return.

Unlike many other foreign singers, L'Epine endeavoured to learn English: her Saturday night entr'acte performances for Drury Lane featured songs by Henry Purcell, as did her occasional appearances in concert venues and at court. Her popularity apparently inspired jealousy: in February 1704 Catherine Tofts, another singing star at Drury Lane, published a letter disclaiming responsibility for the misbehaviour of her servant, who had thrown oranges at L'Epine during a performance (*Daily Courant*). L'Epine and Tofts were both important in the foundation of Italian opera in London, working first for John Rich at Drury Lane and then, following their mounting dissatisfaction with Rich and the lord chamberlain's ensuing separation of spoken and sung theatre in 1708, at John Vanbrugh's Queen's Theatre, Haymarket.

L'Epine does not seem to have had roles in the first few Italian operas in London. Perhaps her looks were the reason; Burney explains that

> she was so swarthy and ill-favoured, that her husband used to call her Hecate, a name to which she answered with as much good humour as if he had called her Helen. But with such a total absence of personal charms, our galleries would have made her songs very short, had they not been executed in such a manner as to silence theatrical snakes, and command applause. (Burney, *Hist. mus.*, 2.670–71)

L'Epine's looks may also have benefited her, however, as she was thought suitable for male as well as female roles. For over a decade from 1706, when she replaced Tofts in the title role in *Camilla* (music by Bononcini, arranged by Haym), L'Epine was a linchpin of London's operatic stage, appearing for example as female lead in J. C. Pepusch's pasticcio *Thomyris* (1707), Francesco Conti's *Clotilda* (1709), Giovanni Bononcini's *Almahide* (1710), and *Calypso and Telemachus* (1712) by John Hughes and John Galliard, and as male lead in Colley Cibber's and Pepusch's *Venus and Adonis* (1715), Cibber's *Myrtillo and Laura* (1715), and *Apollo and Daphne* by John Hughes (1716). She took part in Handel's earliest operas for London, taking over Goffredo in *Rinaldo* in 1712 and creating the demanding roles of Eurilla and Agilea in *Il pastor fido* (1712) and *Teseo* (1713) respectively. Donald Burrows suggests she may have created Galatea in Handel's *Acis and Galatea* (1718) (Burrows, 96). L'Epine also substituted for others at short notice: in at least five operas she played more than one role, and she made a brief comeback from retirement in 1720 to substitute for an ailing singer, playing three roles in three different operas in one week.

Although John Downes's 1708 speculation that she had 'got by the Stage and Gentry, above 10000 Guineas' (Downes, 97) is undoubtedly an exaggeration, L'Epine was highly valued: for the Queen's Theatre's 1708 season her salary was £400—equal to Tofts, and just below the starring castrato Valentini (£430). In 1712/13 L'Epine was still awarded a salary of £400 (though paid only £105), but this was £100 to £200 below several new Italian stars. Similarly, for two concerts given for the duchess of Shrewsbury in Kensington in 1712 and 1713 she received £20, half the wage of newer singers.

L'Epine retired from the stage in May 1719, possibly to marry Johann Christoph *Pepusch (1666/7–1752); though the date of their marriage is unknown, their only child, John, was baptized on 9 January 1724. The couple were associated from at least 1714, however, with L'Epine following Pepusch from the Queen's Theatre to Lincoln's Inn Fields (1714) and then to Drury Lane (1716). They lived and took pupils for some time at Boswell Court, Carey Street; by 1730 they had moved to Fetter Lane, and in 1737 they moved to the Charterhouse when Pepusch became organist there. L'Epine died in London on 8 August 1746 and was interred in the Charterhouse burying-ground on 12 August. SUZANNE ASPDEN

Sources D. F. Cook, 'Françoise Marguérite de L'Epine: the Italian lady?', *Theatre Notebook*, 35 (1981), 58–73, 104–13 · W. Van Lennep and others, eds., *The London stage, 1660–1800*, 5 pts in 11 vols. (1960–68) · Highfill, Burnim & Langhans, *BDA*, 4.292–6 · J. Milhous and R. D. Hume, eds., *Vice Chamberlain Coke's theatrical papers, 1706–1715* (1982) · Burney, *Hist. mus.*, new edn · J. Downes, *Roscius Anglicanus*, ed. J. Milhous and R. D. Hume, new edn (1987) · E. L. Moore, 'Some notes on the life of Françoise Marguérite de L'Épine', *Music and Letters*, 28 (1947), 341–6 · *Daily Courant* (8 Feb 1704) · *London Evening-Post* (12–14 Aug 1746) · N. Rowe, *Poems on several occasions* (1714) · J. Hawkins, *A general history of the science and practice of music*, 5 vols. (1776); new edn, 3 vols. (1875) [repr. 1875–83] · L. Lindgren, 'Venice, Vivaldi, Vico and opera in London, 1705–1717: Venetian ingredients in English pasticci', *Nuovi studi Vivaldiani: edizione e cronologia critica delle opera*, ed. A. Fanna and G. Morelli (1988), 633–66 · J. Milhous and R. D. Hume, 'Opera salaries in eighteenth-century London', *Journal of the American Musicological Society*, 46 (1993), 26–83 · D. Burrows, *Handel* (1994) · R. Wilkinson, *Vice reclaim'd* (1703) · [J. Trapp], *The tragedy of King Saul* (1703)

Likenesses attrib. M. Ricci, portrait, 1708–1709? (*A rehearsal of an opera*)

Le Piper [Lepipre], **Francis** (*d.* **1695**), artist, the son of Noel Le Piper, belonged to an important Flemish family which had settled in England and owned property at Canterbury. His father made a large fortune as a merchant, and gave Le Piper a liberal education, but he showed a talent for art, and devoted himself to drawing. Having substantial private means, he drew for his amusement, selecting humorous or comic subjects. According to the memoir by Buckeridge, from whom all modern knowledge of Le Piper derives, his memory was so good that he could draw exact likenesses of anyone whom he had merely passed in the street. He was very corpulent, fond of the bottle and good living, and a jovial companion: some of his best drawings were made on the walls of taverns in London, such as the Mitre in Stocks Market and the Bell in Westminster. Le Piper travelled much on the continent, where he closely studied the works of the great painters, and he once extended his travels as far as Cairo in Egypt. He drew landscapes and humorous compositions and caricatures, and frequently etched subjects on silver plates for his friends, who used them as lids to their tobacco boxes. Late in life he took to modelling in wax, and executed bas-reliefs in this manner with some success. Having run through much of the fortune inherited from his father, Le Piper at one time worked for the mezzotint engraver Isaac Beckett. But after his mother's death he inherited further property and reverted to his earlier lifestyle. A fever was the result, and through medical inexperience it proved fatal; Le Piper died, unmarried, in Aldermanbury, and was buried in St Mary Magdalen, Bermondsey, on 23 July 1695.

Le Piper's only surviving paintings are from a set of twelve small sketches of scenes from *Hudibras*, of which four are in the Tate collection and three in Rye Art Gallery. Of the many drawings by him that Buckeridge mentioned, only four are now known, all in the British Museum. He also designed several of the heads for Paul Rycart's *History of the Turks* (1687), which were engraved by William Elder. His brother Peter Le Piper, a merchant in London, owned most of his brother's drawings; he married Sarah, the daughter of Sir Gabriel Roberts, with whom he had a large family.

L. H. CUST, *rev.* ANTONY GRIFFITHS

Sources [B. Buckeridge], 'An essay towards an English school of painters', in R. de Piles, *The art of painting, with the lives and characters of above 300 of the most eminent painters*, 2nd edn (1744), 354–430 • E. Croft-Murray and P. H. Hulton, eds., *Catalogue of British drawings*, 1 (1960), 424–5 • *The Tate Gallery: report of the trustees, 1963–4* (1964), 30–31 • priv. coll. [1892], Frere family MSS
Likenesses E. Luttrell, mezzotint (after portrait), BM

Le Quesne, Charles (1811–1856), historian, was born in Jersey, the eldest son of Nicholas Le Quesne, a jurat (magistrate) of the royal court. From early youth he showed a strong predilection for the study of political economy, and his first publication comprised a series of articles on commercial questions relating to the Channel Islands. He had previously contributed these to the *Guernsey and Jersey Magazine* between 1836 and 1838, and the collection was edited by Jonathan Duncan (1799–1865). In 1848 Le Quesne published a remarkable essay, *Ireland and the Channel Islands, or, A Remedy for Ireland*. He attributed the discontent in Ireland mainly to the system of land tenure, and suggested the application to Ireland of the land system of the Channel Islands, which divided the land among many small proprietors. His *Constitutional History of Jersey* appeared in 1856 and became a standard work, from which quotation was frequently made in lawsuits relating to the Channel Islands which were heard before the privy council. The *History* was written in English, and printed many valuable documents for the first time. Some of its contents were borrowed from Edward Durell's edition of Philip Falle's *History of Jersey* (1837). Le Quesne's *History* is cited in more modern works such as G. R. Balleine's *History of Jersey* (rev. edn, 1981).

Le Quesne was elected a jurat of the royal court of Jersey on 2 July 1850; he was an officer in the island artillery, and was president of the Jersey chamber of commerce. He was also an active and liberal member of the states of Jersey. Although attached to the constitution of the island, he was a staunch supporter of useful and progressive reform, for which there was considerable demand in the 1850s and later. He was married to Kate, daughter of Colonel English RE. Le Quesne died at St Helier on 18 August 1856, and was buried at Green Street cemetery, Jersey, on the 22nd.

E. T. NICOLLE, *rev.* IAN MACHIN

Sources G. I. T. Machin, 'George Julian Harney in Jersey, 1855–63: a chartist "abroad"', *Annual Bulletin* [Société Jersiaise], 23/4 (1984), 478–95 • Boase, *Mod. Eng. biog.* • J. B. Payne, *Armorial of Jersey*, 2 (1865)

Le Queux, William Tufnell (1864–1927), author and self-publicist, was born on 2 July 1864 at 5 Mina Terrace, Southwark, London, the eldest son of a Frenchman, William Le Queux (or Lequeux; *c.*1823–1890), draper's assistant, and his English wife, Henrietta Marie (*b.* 1837), daughter of Thomas Henson, clock and watch maker. The 1871 census reported an apparently impecunious household, with one illiterate general servant girl and two lodgers. Le Queux's own accounts of his life are unreliable, and little is known definitely. He claimed to have been educated privately in London and at Pegli, near Genoa, to have studied art in Paris until 1884, and to have travelled and worked on the continent. He also claimed to have been a journalist in Paris, and to have been encouraged by Zola to write novels. In the 1880s he did work as a journalist in England on various local papers and on *The Globe*, but he left it in 1893 and devoted himself principally to writing fiction, though still contributing intermittently to newspapers.

Le Queux's first novel was *Guilty Bonds* (1890), a melodrama about Russian nihilists. He was a prolific writer who, in addition to short stories and articles, averaged over five novels a year, a total of more than two hundred. He wrote, rapidly and carelessly, melodramatic thrillers of crime and love, with enticing titles such as *A Secret Sin*, *The Indiscretions of a Lady's Maid*, *Sins of the City*, and *Wiles of the Wicked*. He was proudly 'cosmopolitan', and many of his novels were set in continental and other exotic locations, with a knowingness of hotels and casinos, and a smattering of French and Italian phrases. His hero was usually a well-born, wealthy clubman: travelled, worldly, and somewhat cynical. His heroine was young, beautiful, well dressed, and usually mysterious and under the influence of the villain. His villains were wicked, often foreign, and ingenious. Their crimes included murder by bizarre methods: explosive bon-bons, a cobra in bed, and—in *The Death Doctor* (1912), his most repulsive fiction—tetanus in soap and rabies in ointment, and attempted murder by an electrified statue. He became one of the most popular novelists, whose extensive and varied readership reportedly included Queen Alexandra and A. J. Balfour, and did include the young Dennis Wheatley and Graham Greene. Indicative of his popularity, in 1898 he was among the highest paid fiction writers at 12 guineas per thousand words, the same rate as Thomas Hardy and H. G. Wells.

Most influential and controversial of Le Queux's fiction were his tales of invasion and of espionage. G. T. Chesney's *The Battle of Dorking* (1871) had established the popular genre of future-war fiction, and in 1893 Alfred Harmsworth commissioned from the little-known Le

William Tufnell Le Queux (1864–1927), by Frederic G. Hodsoll [standing, with his publisher]

Queux a serial, 'The Poisoned Bullet', which was published in *Answers*, and then in book form as *The Great War in England in 1897* (1894). A tale of surprise French invasion, it warned of British vulnerability and military unpreparedness. In the period of defence anxiety following the Second South African War, Le Queux joined the National Service League. From about 1905 he was a self-proclaimed patriot and a Germanophobe defence publicist, one of those condemned by their opponents as 'scaremongers'. He was active in Roger Pocock's Legion of Frontiersmen. In 1906 Le Queux, advised by Lord Roberts and H. W. Wilson, wrote for Lord Northcliffe's *Daily Mail*—the largest-circulation daily paper—a sensational serial of German invasion, 'The invasion of 1910', later published in book form. It warned of British vulnerability and German atrocities, and urged the introduction of compulsory military training as demanded by Lord Roberts and the National Service League. Much publicized, denounced, and satirized, it became Le Queux's best-known work.

From the 1890s Le Queux wrote fiction warning of French, Russian, and later German spies in Britain. In 1909 his sensational serial 'Spies of the Kaiser' appeared in D. C. Thompson's *Weekly News*, then was expanded into the book *Spies of the Kaiser: Plotting the Downfall of England*. This aroused much concern, and readers wrote to Le Queux reporting alleged spies. He passed the letters to Lieutenant-Colonel J. E. Edmonds of MO5 who used them, with other evidence, some from Le Queux, to convince the committee of imperial defence of the necessity of a secret service, leading to the establishment of the Secret Service Bureau (later MI5 and MI6).

An avid self-publicist, Le Queux wrote his way from obscurity to wealth and celebrity. The profits from his thrillers bought the image and lifestyle to which he aspired: the cosmopolitan clubman, man of the world, and man of mystery. Boyishly enthusiastic, opportunist, snobbish, name-dropping, sociable yet secretive, delighting in being mysterious, he was apparently a sort of Walter Mitty. He presented himself as a hero involved in dangerous adventures, and listed 'revolver practice' in his *Who's Who* entry. He claimed an expert knowledge of crime and criminology. He claimed he was an expert on spying and that he was involved in espionage and counter-espionage for Britain, and he gave public lectures warning of foreign spies. His appearance, however, was not that of his fictional heroes. He was portly, genial, and wore pince-nez. The *Morning Post* obituarist wrote that he was 'an amiable and placid little man, who looked as if he caught the 9.15 from Ealing to the City every morning'. He became for a time the Birmingham consul of the republic of San Marino and wore his gorgeous uniform for publicity photographs; he gained and proudly wore continental orders.

Le Queux travelled widely. His anonymous Balkan reportage, *An Observer in the Near East* (1907), was anti-Austrian and pro-Serbian. He repeatedly changed residence, sometimes living in Italy. On 23 November 1887 he married Florence Alice, 25 years old, daughter of Alfred Thomas Dowsett, artist (deceased). In January 1901 she died after fracturing her skull by falling down steps at their Lambeth home: the inquest ruled accidental death. On 22 February 1902 he married at Kensington register office an Italian, Luisa Gemma (declared age 27 years), daughter of Ferdinando Cioni. *Cassell's Magazine*, presumably echoing Le Queux, described her as 'a member of one of the oldest Florentine families' (*Cassell's Magazine*, Dec 1904, 693). They had no children, and by 1910 they had separated.

Le Queux was involved in various business ventures, including allegedly selling army boots to the Bulgarian government and film making. In 1913 he did not pay his wife money due under the deed of separation and she took bankruptcy proceedings against him. In October he told the assistant official receiver he had lost money on unsuccessful attempts to operate a casino in Corfu and to sell war stores to Serbia, and that until 1910 his annual income had been £5000 and his annual expenditure £3000. He was declared bankrupt and had to resign his consulate. His losses suggest his fantasizing may have spilled over into his business ventures, and he may have been gullible and deceived.

Like other 'scaremongers' Le Queux flourished during the First World War. He was an amateur spy hunter, lectured extensively on espionage and the German threat, wrote for Horatio Bottomley's *John Bull*, demanded the internment of enemy aliens, and denounced the German 'invisible hand' in Britain. He wrote sensational anti-German fiction presented as fact, including *German Spies in England* (1915) and *Love Intrigues of the Kaiser's Sons* (1918), and in a similar mode wrote *Rasputin the Rascal Monk* (1917) and *The Minister of Evil* (1917).

After 1918 Le Queux continued to write thrillers. *Rasputinism in London* (1919), for example, was about a Clapham curate—a Keble man and 'satanic scoundrel'—who established a Rasputinist cult among rich women drug takers based in the Cromwell Road. Le Queux continued his amateur wireless experiments, with more publicity than originality. In 1923 he published his unreliable, largely fictitious memoirs, *Things I Know about Kings, Celebrities and Crooks*. Apparently resenting lack of official recognition in Britain, from 1923 he spent much time in Switzerland, skiing and writing tourist publicity. After several weeks' illness, he died from heart failure on 13 October 1927 at the Links Hotel, Knocke, Belgium, and was cremated at Golders Green, London, on 19 October.

Before and during the war, although criticized, Le Queux had been influential, but by 1927, according to the *Morning Post* obituarist, 'with the cultured reader he passed as a modern variant of Baron Münchausen'. Le Queux's own version of his life was essentially repeated in N. St B. Sladen's *The Real Le Queux* (1938), in derivative reference works, and belatedly in *Missing Persons* (1993). However, from the 1970s into the 1990s historians researching Le Queux, 'spy fever', 'scaremongers', and the secret service revealed further information, which formed the basis of a more accurate, if less flattering, portrayal.

ROGER T. STEARN

Sources R. T. Stearn, 'The mysterious Mr Le Queux', *Soldiers of the Queen*, 70 (1992) • D. A. T. Stafford, 'Conspiracy and xenophobia: the popular spy novels of William Le Queux, 1893–1914', *Europa* [Montreal], 4/2 (1981) • W. Le Queux, *Things I know about kings, celebrities and crooks* (1923) • N. St B. Sladen, *The real Le Queux* (1938) • *The Times* (14 Oct 1927) • *Morning Post* (14 Oct 1927) • *Daily Mail* (14 Oct 1927) • *Daily Express* (14 Oct 1927) • *Manchester Guardian* (14 Oct 1927) • *The Times* (1 Nov 1913) • *Morning Post* (1 Nov 1913) • *WWW* • I. F. Clarke, *Voices prophesying war, 1763–1984*, new edn (1970) • A. J. A. Morris, *The scaremongers: the advocacy of war and rearmament, 1896–1914* (1984) • C. Andrew, *Secret service: the making of the British intelligence community* (1987) • N. Hiley, 'Decoding German spies: British spy fiction, 1908–18', *Intelligence and National Security*, 5/4 (1990), 55–79 • D. French, 'Spy fever in Britain, 1900–1915', *HJ*, 21 (1978), 355–70 • B. Porter, *Plots and paranoia* (1989) • *Le Queux: Magazine of the Society of William Tufnell Le Queux*, 4 (Feb 1997) • m. cert. [Luisa Gemma Cioni]

Archives Local Studies Library, Richmond, London, corresp. with Douglas Sladen • NAM, Roberts MSS

Likenesses F. G. Hodsoll, double portrait, photograph (with his publisher), NPG [*see illus.*] • photographs, repro. in Le Queux, *Things I know about kings* • photographs, repro. in Sladen, *The real Le Queux*

Lerner, Meyer (1857–1930), rabbi, was born in Czestochowa, Poland, on 10 March 1857, the son of Mordechai Lerner, a leather merchant. At the age of nine he was sent to the *yeshivah* (Talmudic college) of Biala. Between the ages of thirteen and sixteen he studied in Eisenstadt, near Vienna, under Rabbi Salomon Kutner, to whom he had been recommended by his uncle Rabbi Abraham Jener, the *av bet din* (senior judge of the Jewish ecclesiastical court) of Cracow. Rabbi Kutner in turn recommended the promising student to Rabbi Ezriel Hildesheimer of the Adas Yisroel Synagogue in Berlin, who had been his predecessor at Eisenstadt and was one of the foremost exponents of neo-Orthodoxy in Europe. While remaining strictly Orthodox, Hildesheimer and his school were imbued with the scholarly spirit of the German *Wissenschaft des Judentums* that set a high value on a secular as well as a religious education. Hildesheimer became Lerner's patron, paying for private instruction in Greek and Latin and transferring him to the Orthodox rabbinical seminary that he had founded in Berlin. At the Hildesheimer Seminar, Lerner continued his studies under Rabbi David Zvi Hoffmann, and his *semicha* (rabbinical ordination) was conferred by Hildesheimer himself.

At twenty-one Lerner matriculated at Berlin University, where he studied philosophy and oriental languages. His treatise *Bereshit Rabba* (Midrashic commentary on the book of Genesis) was awarded a prize in 1879, and three years later he gained his doctorate at the University of Leipzig. In 1886 Lerner married Henriette, a daughter of Rabbi Hirsch Plato of Cologne and a granddaughter of the outstanding exponent of German neo-Orthodoxy Rabbi Samson Raphael Hirsch.

Lerner was appointed rabbi of Wintzenheim, near Colmar in Alsace, in 1884 and remained there for six years. In January 1890 he was one of four shortlisted candidates for chief minister of the London Federation of Synagogues, a post especially created and underwritten by Samuel Montagu, banker and Liberal MP for Whitechapel. Montagu had founded the federation in 1887 as an umbrella body for the multitude of independent synagogues and prayer circles (*hevrot*) that had grown up among Jewish immigrants in the East End of London. A semi-public preaching competition was held at the Jewish Workingmen's Club, Great Alie Street, east London, from which Lerner emerged as the winner by thirty votes to six. Lerner took up residence at 46 Great Prescott Street, Aldgate, and concerned himself with the religious needs of his Yiddish-speaking neighbours. He founded the Sabbath Observance Society to assist Jews to keep the Jewish sabbath (from sunset on Friday to nightfall on Saturday), notwithstanding the considerable economic pressures dictating otherwise. In the autumn of 1892, together with Montagu, Lerner successfully intervened to save 100 Jewish tailors from losing their jobs in a non-Jewish firm because they refused to work on the Jewish festival of *Succot* (Tabernacles). Part of his job was to preach against the 'Jewish Socialists, Atheists and Nihilists' who were regarded by the Anglo-Jewish establishment as a deleterious influence on East End Jewry.

Lerner was taken aback at the poor standard of Jewish education in England. In 1890–92 he carried out a thorough investigation into the state of Hebrew education. His report found both the traditional system of religious study in the *heder* (private schoolroom) and the education on offer in state board schools, and even in the Jews' Free School, to be wanting. He proposed sweeping reform of the system and advocated the use of English as the language of instruction rather than Yiddish. Lerner's initiatives met with a disappointing response but sowed the seeds for the later formation of the Jewish Religious Education Board.

The chief minister of the federation came into conflict with Chief Rabbi Hermann Adler to whom he was supposed to defer. Under pressure from 'progressive' elements, Adler was willing to introduce some English and certain modifications into the liturgy of congregations within the establishment United Synagogue. In May 1894 Lerner quit Britain to become rabbi of Altona and Schleswig-Holstein, a position he retained until 1926.

Lerner was a rabbinic scholar of considerable stature, a fact that was little appreciated in England. He published in Hebrew and German. His writings included studies of commentaries on the Torah and the Mishnah as well as rabbinical responsa on contemporary issues in Jewish law, for instance the Jewish prohibition of cremation. His most important work was his two-volume *Torat haMishnah* (1915, 1928), which dealt with the origin of the oral tradition in Jewish law.

Sympathetic to Zionism, Lerner took an active interest in the Hovevei Tsion 'Lovers of Zion' societies in London. In 1905 he set up the Moriah society that sought 'to restore the ancient ruins, and the national and religious culture of the Jews'. However, he found himself at odds with both the secular majority and the *mizrakhi* religious wing of the Zionist movement. In 1930 Moriah merged with the non-Zionist strictly Orthodox political party Agudat Yisrael.

Rabbi Lerner died in Altona, Germany, in early July 1930. His death received only a brief mention in the London *Jewish Chronicle*. SHARMAN KADISH

Sources *Jewish Chronicle* (11 July 1930) • *Jewish Encyclopedia* (1904) • C. Roth, ed., *Encyclopaedia Judaica*, 16 vols. (Jerusalem, 1971–2) • J. Jung, *Champions of orthodoxy* (1974) • S. Wininger, ed., *Grosse jüdische National-Biographie*, 4 (1930), 33–4 • G. Alderman, *The Federation of Synagogues* (1987), 28–32

Archives U. Southampton, unpublished biography, MS 116/131

Likenesses photograph (as a young man), repro. in Jung, *Champions of orthodoxy* • photograph (as an old man), repro. in C. Roth, ed., *Encyclopedia Judaica*, 16 vols. (1971–2)

Lerpinière, Daniel (1745–1785). *See under* Boydell, John, engravers (*act.* 1760–1804).

Le Sage, Sir John Merry (1837–1926), journalist and newspaper editor, was born at Clifton on 23 April 1837, the only son of John Sage of Clifton and his wife, Elizabeth Godfrey; he adopted the name Le Sage in middle life. Educated at Bristol, Sage became a reporter on the *Torquay Directory* and the *Western Morning News* at Plymouth before obtaining an appointment in London on the *Daily Telegraph*. His connection with that paper, begun in 1863, remained unbroken until his retirement sixty years later.

Le Sage's principal journalistic success as a special correspondent consisted of getting through to London, hours ahead of his rivals, an account of the entry of the German army into Paris in January 1871; he remained in Paris throughout the commune. He attended the coronations at St Petersburg of Alexander III (1881) and Nicholas II (1894), was in Egypt in 1882 at the time of Sir Garnet Wolseley's expedition against Arabi Pasha, and was received in audience by Pope Leo XIII and by Sultan Abdul Hamid. He did not, however, achieve marked distinction as a writer at the *Daily Telegraph*.

Le Sage's talents were better displayed in an executive capacity. He enjoyed the confidence in turn of Joseph Moses Levy, the original proprietor of the *Daily Telegraph*, and that of his son, Edward Levy-Lawson, first Baron Burnham. The latter was in full direction and control of the paper for more than thirty years before he was raised to the peerage in 1903, and Le Sage was his trusted right-hand man. Later, when the Hon. Harry Levy-Lawson, afterwards second Baron Burnham, took charge, Le Sage served the son as loyally as he had served the father and the grandfather. For almost forty years Le Sage was managing editor, and, in his contacts with the staff in the daily conduct of the paper, the autocrat of Peterborough Court. He strongly maintained the traditions by which the *Daily Telegraph* had established its special position, which Edmund Yates once described as 'the organ of the knife-board of the omnibus'. Le Sage regarded the middle class as the backbone of the country, and had little sympathy with democratic reform and reformers: 'To let well alone' was one of his working principles. News interested him more deeply than politics, and the minutiae of any political controversy bored him. He liked it presented, as he said, 'in six lines'. Le Sage made up his mind quickly—a sovereign editorial virtue. As a judge of men he reposed great faith in what he called his 'journalistic instinct', which worked 'in flashes'. The criticism of outsiders he met with imperturbability: it was a fixed article of his creed that enemies of the *Daily Telegraph* always came to a bad end, sooner or later.

Le Sage's gifts were better suited to the last two decades of the nineteenth century than to the first two of the twentieth: the rapid rise of the 'new journalism' in the late nineteenth century took him by surprise, and the *Daily Telegraph* suffered accordingly. He responded to the challenge, but his age and inability to delegate hampered him. The anxieties and responsibilities of the First World War, however, gave him new vigour: nothing but illness or holidays kept him, even when past his eightieth year, from his usual office routine. For many years he had rooms in Clement's Inn, and, punctual to the minute, twice a day, he trod the Fleet Street pavement—an erect, imposing, and well-groomed figure. Outside Fleet Street Le Sage was hardly known. He cultivated few social and no political relationships, he never wrote a letter except under compulsion, and he never made speeches. He was a lieutenant of the City of London, but the only public recognition he received was the knighthood bestowed on him in 1918 in recognition of his long services to journalism, and more especially of the *Daily Telegraph's* steady support of the national policy during the First World War.

In his younger days Le Sage travelled widely: in later life he enjoyed the gossip of the Garrick Club, and was a keen cricket enthusiast. He married three times; nothing is known of his first marriage. He married second, on 16 December 1868, Clara Ellen (*d.* 1873), daughter of Charles Henderson Scott, legal reporter, with whom he had one son and one daughter, and, third, in 1874, Elizabeth Lord (*d.* 1933), daughter of John Burton Martin, of London, with whom he had two sons. Le Sage retired from the *Daily Telegraph* in June 1923, and died on 1 January 1926 at his home, 25 Ranelagh Avenue, Hurlingham, Barnes.

J. B. FIRTH, *rev.* JOSEPH COOHILL

Sources *Daily Telegraph* (2 Jan 1926) • personal knowledge (1937) • D. Griffiths, ed., *The encyclopedia of the British press, 1422–1992* (1992)
Archives CUL, corresp. with Lord Hardinge
Likenesses Owl, caricature, mechanical reproduction, NPG; repro. in *VF* (20 Aug 1913)
Wealth at death £17,166 7*s.* 7*d.*: probate, 22 Feb 1926, *CGPLA Eng. & Wales*

Lescallier, Daniel, Baron Lescallier in the French nobility (*fl.* **1789–1790**). *See under* Industrial spies (*act. c.*1700–*c.*1800).

Lescher, Mary Adela [*name in religion* Mary of St Wilfrid] (**1846–1927**), college head, was born at Hampstead, Middlesex, the third of the five children of Joseph Sidney Lescher (1803–1892/3), a partner of the wholesale druggists Evans, Lescher, and Evans and a second-generation member of a family from Alsace, France, who were zealous Roman Catholics. His wife, Sarah Harwood (*d.* 1856), Mary's mother, was the daughter of a West India merchant in Bristol and a member of a staunch Baptist family, but she converted to Catholicism two years after her marriage. The oldest brother, Wilfrid (1847–1916), entered the Dominican order in 1864. Mary's only sister died at the age of five.

Mary, known as Adela in the family, was educated by governesses at home and in France, where the family had gone for health reasons, until her mother's death in 1856, after which she was sent to the Benedictine school at Winchester, Hampshire (later at East Bergholt in Suffolk), where she had an aunt in the order, and for a short time at the Dominican school at Stone. She left boarding-school in 1864 and continued her studies in languages, music, and literature at home under her brother's former tutor.

Mary had two older cousins, Frances Lescher (Sister Mary of St Philip), who was the principal of Notre Dame Teacher Training College at Mount Pleasant, Liverpool, and Annie Lescher (Sister Mary of St Michael), who was also a sister in the Institute of Notre Dame. In May 1869 she entered the mother house of the Notre Dame order, dedicated 'to teach the poor in the most neglected places', at Namur, Belgium, and took the name Sister Mary of St Wilfrid. She returned to England in September 1871 as a professed sister to teach in the Notre Dame boarding-school at Clapham, London. After a bout of rheumatic fever she convalesced at Mount Pleasant and was then appointed to the college staff there to lecture in botany, English, and music. In 1886 she became mistress of the boarders, instructed the senior girls, and taught psychology. In 1892 she was appointed superior of Everton Valley convent, Liverpool, which ran a convent day school, several elementary schools, and a pupil-teacher centre where boarders were prepared for entry into the Mount Pleasant Training College.

In April 1893 Archbishop Eyre of Glasgow invited the Sisters of Notre Dame to establish a Roman Catholic teacher training college in Scotland which would relieve female students from the need of travelling to Liverpool or London for training. A site was chosen at Dowanhill, in the west end of Glasgow, near the university, which had just opened its classes to women. The college was officially established in December 1893 with Sister Mary of St Wilfrid as its first principal, assisted by four sisters. The first female Roman Catholic teachers to receive their training in Scotland began their course of study in January 1895. Sister Mary of St Wilfrid took an active part in the training of the students and through her singleness of purpose made the venture a success.

A major achievement of Notre Dame College was the development of practical science teaching and the revolutionizing of biology teaching. A 'practising school', which was to include both a secondary school and the first Montessori school in Glasgow, was opened next to the college in 1897 and new schools were opened in Dumbarton (together with a convent) in 1908 and Milngavie in 1912. A staunch member of the Educational Institute of Scotland, Sister Mary of St Wilfrid encouraged all her students to join. As sister superior she was manager of the Notre Dame schools until May 1919, when Notre Dame Training College was transferred to the national scheme and came under the control of the national committee for the training of teachers. She retired as sister superior in 1919. She had been instrumental in founding a Notre Dame association for former students and the Glasgow University Catholic Women's Association. She also set up a branch of the Scottish Needlework Guild to make garments for the poor and vestments for missions, and, after a stay in a nursing home in 1904, had set up the Association of Catholic Nurses of the Sick. Sister Mary of St Wilfrid died at Notre Dame Convent, Dowanhill, Glasgow, on 7 May 1927, and was buried on 11 May at Dalbeth cemetery.

LESLEY M. RICHMOND

Sources Notre Dame College magazines (1909–26) • D. Gillies, *A pioneer of Catholic teacher-training in Scotland: Sister Mary of St Wilfrid* (privately printed, Quidenham, 1978) • T. A. FitzPatrick, *No mean service: Scottish Catholic teacher education, 1895–1995* (1995)
Archives Sisters of Notre Dame Archive, Speke Road, Woolton, Liverpool • St Andrew's College, Bearsden, Glasgow
Likenesses photograph, St Andrew's College • photograph, repro. in Gillies, *A pioneer of Catholic teacher training in Scotland*

Lesieur, Sir Stephen (*d.* **1630x38**), diplomat, was born in Geneva and first arrived in England about 1575; nothing is known of his parentage and childhood. By 1581 he was a servant of Sir Philip Sidney, travelling between England, the Low Countries, and the Rhineland, delivering letters and supplying information about central European politics, the war between Spain and the Dutch provinces, and possible plots brewing against Queen Elizabeth. For roughly four years he laboured to secure the release of the English envoy Daniel Rogers from Spanish forces, nearly falling prey to kidnappers in May 1584. When Rogers was finally freed in September he blamed Lesieur for at least two and a half years' delay spent wooing women at the court of the duke of Cleves and in Antwerp. Lesieur flatly denied the charges. In 1585 he worked as an envoy between the English forces and the rebel Dutch estates, especially in Brabant. After the Spanish took Antwerp, Lesieur tried to return to England but was taken captive while crossing the channel and imprisoned at Dunkirk by November 1585. Negotiations for his release did not succeed until May 1587, in part because of the death of his patron, Sir Philip Sidney, in 1586.

Lesieur returned to England in summer 1588. Having obtained a licence five days earlier as of St Benet's parish, London, on 26 December 1592 at St Martin-in-the-Fields he married Mary, widow of Francis Littleton. Edward 'Leysure' was baptized and buried at the same church in 1596; Stephen 'Leysure' was baptized there in 1597. In the late 1590s Lesieur served on English diplomatic missions to the Holy Roman empire regarding trade disputes with the Hanseatic League. In 1602–3 he went on an embassy to Denmark, and when Queen Elizabeth died, his absence, he claimed, prevented him from receiving due recompense for his services. During the reign of James I Lesieur continued his work for the crown, drafting and translating diplomatic correspondence and receiving in return the proceeds from various forfeitures, recusancy fines, foreclosures, and outstanding debts, some of which he had to collect. On 25 March 1608 he received a knighthood and was then dispatched on an embassy to Florence in 1608–9 which failed, apparently due to his threatening the grand duke. During his next embassy, to Prague in 1610–11, he was caught in the crossfire between Emperor Rudolf and his brother and rival, Matthias, and was nearly stoned by an enraged mob. Lesieur returned to Germany in 1612 during the Jülich–Cleves crisis, with a commission to assist protestant princes through a peaceful mediation among the rival parties. Matthias, now emperor, did not welcome this interference and declared Lesieur unacceptable due to allegations of diplomatic misconduct. Though he parried the charges he incurred further disfavour by donating 7000 florins to the building of a Calvinist church and was recalled in 1614. He tried unsuccessfully to become ambassador to the Netherlands in 1615 and a clerk of the court of wards in 1618.

In 1627, citing forty years of service in fifteen embassies, Lesieur asked King Charles I to honour and increase his annual pension of £50 granted by King James. In 1630 the exchequer paid Lesieur £25. His will, dated in the probate copy 12 February 1605 (that is, 1606), but from internal evidence probably drawn up in 1626 or 1636, revealed him to be living in Chiswick. After bequests of £5 to the poor of the parish, and a bed to a former servant, the residue of the estate went to 'my beloved brother in lawe' Sir Edward Wardour (knighted in 1618). The date of Lesieur's death is unknown. Wardour, as executor, proved the will on 2 October 1638. B. C. PURSELL

Sources *CSP dom.*, *1581–90*; *1601–18*; *1627–31* • *CSP for.*, *1581–8*; *1597–1602* • *CSP Venice*, *1610–15* • E. A. Beller, 'The negotiations of Sir Stephen le Sieur, 1584–1613', *EngHR*, 40 (1925), 22–33 • J. L. Chester and G. J. Armytage, eds., *Allegations for marriage licences issued by the bishop of London*, 2 vols., Harleian Society, 25–6 (1887) • T. Mason, ed., *A register of baptisms, marriages, and burials in the parish of St Martin in the Fields … from 1550 to 1619*, Harleian Society, register section, 25 (1898), 26, 27, 78, 141 • PRO, PROB 11/178, fol. 165*r* • W. B. Patterson, *King James VI and I and the reunion of Christendom* (1997), 156, 294–5 • W. A. Shaw, *The knights of England*, 2 (1906), 144
Archives PRO, SP 80/2

Lesley, Alexander (1693–1758), Jesuit, was born at Pitcaple Castle, Garioch, Aberdeenshire, on 7 November 1693, the third son of Alexander Lesley (or Leslie), ninth baron of Pitcaple (*b.* 1656, *d.* in or after 1710), landowner, and his second wife, Henrietta Irvine of Drum (*b.* after 1643, *d.* in or after 1710). He entered the Scots College at Douai on 24 October 1708, where he completed a course in humanities. His studies were continued at the Collegio Romano, in Rome, and he entered the Society of Jesus as a novice on 12 November 1713. He taught literature at Sora and Ancona, passed through a theological course at the Collegio Romano, and then lectured on the Greek language there. He was appointed teacher of philosophy at the Illyrian College of Loreto, but in 1728 was sent to the Scottish mission, and worked in Aberdeenshire. Owing to the suspicion of Jesuits in Scotland, Lesley travelled in secret, concealing his identity and even attending a meeting of Presbyterian elders. While he was in Scotland he took the four vows and became a full member of the society.

In 1734 Lesley returned to Italy and taught at Ancona and Tivoli. He went to England in 1738 at the request of Lord Petre, who wanted the services of an ecclesiastic who was also an antiquarian. Lesley was associated with the English province of the society, and in 1741 was a missioner in the 'College of the Holy Apostles', which had been founded by Lord Petre's family in 1633 and which comprised Essex, Suffolk, Norfolk, and Cambridgeshire. Returning to Rome in 1744 he was prefect of studies in the Scots College until 1746, and professor of moral theology for two years in the English College (1746–8). In 1749 he was associated with the Jesuit scholar Emanuel de Azevedo in preparing the *Thesaurus liturgicus*, and he is considered by some authorities to have played a major part in contributing to those works which made Azevedo famous.

Lesley fixed his residence in the Collegio Romano, where he died on 27 March 1758, having published only a fragment of the projected thesaurus. This was the *Missale mixtum secundum regulam beati Isidori dictum mozarabes* with a preface, notes, and appendix, published in Rome in 1755. It was a reprint of the Mozarabic missal printed at Toledo in 1500 by order of Cardinal Ximenes. Lesley's preface and 145 pages of notes were regarded by contemporary scholars as important contributions to knowledge of the Mozarabic rite and its variations. Lesley is said to have left several works in manuscript, mostly in Latin, on historical and antiquarian subjects, including numismatism and the Roman army, but these do not appear to be extant. His English writings included a refutation of Middleton's *Pagan and Modern Rome Compared* and several abridgements of works on English and Scottish history, which were acquired by his friend Father Thorpe at his death.

ALEXANDER DU TOIT

Sources Labouderie, 'Lesley, Alexandre', *Biographie universelle ancienne et moderne*, ed. L. G. Michaud and E. E. Desplaces, new edn

(Paris, 1843–65), vol. 24 · Colonel Leslie [C. J. Leslie], *Historical records of the family of Leslie, from 1067 to 1868–9*, 3 (1869) · H. Foley, ed., *Records of the English province of the Society of Jesus*, 5 (1879); 7 (1882–3) · J. F. S. Gordon, *Ecclesiastical chronicle for Scotland*, 4 vols. (1867), vol. 4 · G. Oliver, *Collections towards illustrating the biographies of the Scotch, English and Irish members of the Society of Jesus*, 2nd edn (1845) · P. J. Anderson, ed., *Records of the Scots colleges at Douai, Rome, Madrid, Valladolid and Ratisbon*, New Spalding Club, 30 (1906) · A. de Backer and others, *Bibliothèque de la Compagnie de Jésus*, new edn, 4, ed. C. Sommervogel (Brussels, 1893) · D. Wimberley, *A short account of the family of Irvine of Drum* (1893) · R. D. Caballero, ed., *Bibliothecae scriptorum Societatis Jesu supplementa*, 2 vols. in 1 (Rome, 1814–16)

Lesley [Leslie], **John** (1527–1596), bishop of Ross, historian, and conspirator, was born on 29 September 1527, the eldest illegitimate son of Gavin Lesley, parson of Kingussie, Inverness-shire, a descendant of the Lesleys of Balquhain. His mother was apparently a Ruthin, daughter of the laird of Gormack, but her forename remains unknown.

Education and early career in Scotland Lesley was destined for an ecclesiastical career and on 19 July 1538, while still a scholar in the province of Moray, he was granted a dispensation to allow him to become a priest. An able boy, he graduated MA from King's College, Aberdeen, and on 15 June 1546 was ordained acolyte in the cathedral church there. At nineteen he was inducted to a canonry, and about three years after that, in 1549, he went to France to continue his studies. After reading theology, Greek, and Hebrew in Paris, he moved to Poitiers where he studied canon and civil law for four years. He also spent some time in Toulouse before returning to Paris. Following a further year there he gained his doctorate in civil and canon law.

Appointed a canonist in King's College, Aberdeen, in 1553, Lesley was back in Scotland by the following April, but it was not until April 1558 that he finally took major orders and became official of the diocese of Aberdeen. Settling down to a career in Scotland, he was on 2 July 1559 made parson, canon, and prebendary of Oyne. By January 1561 he had made his mark sufficiently to be summoned to Edinburgh, along with learned colleagues from Aberdeen, to dispute with John Knox and other leading reformers on the subject of the mass. According to Knox, Lesley said little, though Lesley himself claimed that he and the others argued their case vigorously. He also recalled later that he and the rest of the Aberdeen deputation were kept in Edinburgh to hear the reformers preach and indeed were held prisoner until they gave sureties that they would appear for trial if summoned.

When François II of France, husband of Mary, queen of Scots, died in 1560, Lesley was sent by the earl of Huntly and other prominent Roman Catholics in the north of Scotland to visit the young queen and invite her to return home. He was to say that if she landed at Aberdeen more than 20,000 Catholics would rally to her cause. He was admitted to her presence at Vitry, Champagne, on 15 April 1561, and although Mary refused to contemplate the plan he suggested she invited him to remain in her entourage. After her return that August, Lesley's career advanced rapidly under her patronage. In 1562 he became professor of canon law in King's College, Aberdeen, and on 19 January

John Lesley (1527–1596), by unknown artist

1565 he was made an ordinary judge in the court of session. That same year he was given a place on the privy council, taking his seat for the first time on 18 October 1565. In February 1566 he acquired the abbacy of Lindores, Fife, and less than two months afterwards the queen presented him to the bishopric of Ross, vacant since the recent death of its incumbent, Henry Sinclair.

Lesley was by now Mary's chief adviser on ecclesiastical affairs. He was with her in Holyroodhouse the night that David Riccio was murdered in her presence, and after her escape from the palace she turned to him for advice. When she was pregnant with the future James VI she entrusted Lesley with the will she had made and the inventory of her priceless jewels, and according to George Buchanan's highly suspect account it was Lesley who later suggested that Bothwell should abduct the queen. Lesley denied this, claiming that Mary had subsequently told him of her great distress at having married her third husband, knowing that the bishop had always disapproved of the relationship. Lesley's support for Mary was unwavering during the final months of her reign and, although he retired to his bishopric after he and her other supporters failed to have her released from Lochleven, he set out to join her at Hamilton as soon as she sent him word of her escape.

England By the time Lesley arrived, Mary had already been defeated at Langside and had fled to England, but it was not long before she sent for him and gave him a commission to be one of her representatives at the official inquiry at York to investigate both her complaints that her subjects had wrongfully deposed her, and the earl of Moray's counter-claims that she had been an accomplice in the murder of her second husband, Lord Darnley. Lesley disapproved of the York inquiry, for he realized that Mary's weakened position would be made much worse by any confrontation with Moray. However, he seconded 'briefly and pithily' (Donaldson, 114) the opening speech made on her behalf by Lord Herries and believed that he had found a means of delivering her when he and William Maitland of Lethington devised a plan for her to marry Thomas Howard, fourth duke of Norfolk. As a protestant the duke would presumably be acceptable to Elizabeth I as a restraining influence on Mary.

Lesley also cultivated his acquaintance with Guerau de Spes, the ambassador to England of Philip II of Spain, and in the winter of 1568–9 wrote *A defence of the honour of the right high, mightye and noble Princess Marie, queene of Scotland*, which he published in London in 1569. This treatise defended Mary against charges of complicity in Darnley's murder and asserted her right, as great-granddaughter of Henry VII, to be recognized as heir presumptive to the throne of England. By the time Lesley's book appeared the inquiry at York had moved to Westminster and its inconclusive findings made public on 10 January 1569.

The following month Lesley joined Mary at Tutbury Castle, but soon afterwards he and Lord Boyd, another of her commissioners, were arrested and held prisoner at Burton upon Trent. Deprived of the revenues of his bishopric Lesley persuaded Elizabeth I to intervene with the regent Moray on his behalf, but no money was forthcoming and the bishop had to rely on financial assistance from Spain, arranged by Mary. Lesley was released in April 1569, and he continued to hope for the successful outcome of the Norfolk marriage plan until in October Elizabeth found out about it and sent Norfolk to the Tower. Interrogated by the English privy council, Lesley gave a detailed account of all the discussions in which he had been involved, but assured his questioners that nothing of significance had passed between Mary and Norfolk since the previous June. Further trouble ensued in November when Moray insisted that Lesley had been implicated in the rising of the Roman Catholic earls of Northumberland and Westmorland in the north of England and the bishop was once more arrested. This time he was kept in the town house of the bishop of London and questioned at Hampton Court by the privy council. He strenuously denied any involvement, and in May 1570 was set free.

Lesley's principal aim throughout was to negotiate Mary's restoration to the throne of Scotland, and by the time official discussions for her return collapsed in May 1571 he was embroiled in the Ridolfi plot, reviving the plan for marrying the queen to Norfolk, who had been released from the Tower. This conspiracy came to light when Ridolfi's messenger, Charles Baillie, was captured at Dover carrying cipher letters. By bribing a jailer Lesley managed to gain possession of the incriminating documents, and he ordered his secretary to forge innocuous replacements which he hoped to substitute for the originals. Baillie, however, under threat of torture confessed everything and Norfolk's role in the plot was revealed. Ignoring Lesley's claims to be too ill to leave his bed, four members of the privy council entered his house and questioned him. He lied about the identity of the people mentioned in the cipher letters and was moved to the house of the bishop of Ely, in Holborn in central London, while investigations continued. Finally, Norfolk admitted that he had been corresponding with Mary, queen of Scots, and was sent back to the Tower.

After further questioning by Lord Burghley, three other privy councillors, and the solicitor- and attorney-general, Lesley was also sent to the Tower for refusing to make a full confession. Ever the realist he promptly decided that 'Folly was it to conceal the truth any more, seeing the matter was discovered' (Lockie, 110). Two days after his incarceration, with assurances from Burghley that his evidence would not be used against anyone else, he embarked upon a series of confessions during which he gave elaborate details of the entire conspiracy. As a result Norfolk was executed. In the course of his revelations Lesley apparently admitted Mary's complicity in the murder of Darnley and was even alleged to have charged her with having poisoned François II and plotted to murder Bothwell. 'A flayed priest, a fearful priest', Mary said tersely when she heard (*CSP Scot.*, 1571–4, 81) but she herself knew what it was to act under duress. She had signed her abdication to save her own life after her friends assured her that a document extracted by force had no legality, and Lesley's confessions in the Tower did not end her reliance on him, though her trust in him must have been shaken.

Lesley remained in prison for eighteen months after Norfolk's execution, writing pious meditations for Mary. The king's party in Scotland tried to have him extradited, but the French king intervened on his behalf and Elizabeth finally allowed him to move to less oppressive imprisonment in the castle of the bishop of Winchester, at Farnham. Lesley then composed a learned and obsequious Latin oration which he sent to Elizabeth, pleading for his liberty and promising that if he were released his behaviour would be 'honest and quiet' and that he would thereafter live 'as a private man and follow my study and contemplation … without meddling in affairs of estate' (Murdin, 54–7; Lockie, 111). Always flattered by a compliment to her knowledge of the classics, Elizabeth agreed to his release. On 16 November 1573 the privy council told him that he was free to go, on condition that he left the country. He was, indeed, no longer any threat, for his confession had damaged him with English Catholics, and Mary's last stronghold in Scotland, Edinburgh Castle, had finally fallen to the king's party.

France Scotland was now governed by the protestant James Douglas, fourth earl of Morton, and much as Lesley would have liked to return north it was not safe for him to do so. He urged Burghley to intervene on his behalf, and was told that if he stayed quietly on the continent for a year or two, Elizabeth would try to persuade Morton to pardon him and restore him to his living. Recognizing that this was his best chance for the future, Lesley crossed to France in January 1574 and made his way to Paris, where he assured the English ambassador that he was now a new man. A month later he published the obsequious oration to Elizabeth, with an even more obsequious introductory letter.

Having spent the spring and summer of 1574 trying to ingratiate himself at the French court, Lesley hurried to Lyons after the death of Charles IX to greet the new French king, Henri III, on behalf of Mary, queen of Scots. In his speech of welcome he thanked the French for securing his own release and urged Henry to intercede on behalf of Mary. Aware that his remarks would swiftly be reported in London, he sent Burghley a hasty message explaining that he had merely gone to Lyons to deliver a letter from Mary, had thought it only diplomatic to make a little speech there, but had now returned to Paris and his accustomed life of study and contemplation. In reality, an ascetic existence was hardly to his taste. Contemporaries commented on his fondness for good food and fine wine; he had left three illegitimate daughters behind in Scotland; and James Beaton, archbishop of Glasgow, Queen Mary's ambassador in Paris, heartily disliked him for his garrulous indiscretions.

Italy Despite his failings Lesley had considerable diplomatic skills and in 1575, a jubilee year in the Catholic church, Mary agreed to his request that she should send him as her ambassador to Pope Gregory XIII. The bishop travelled to Rome with a retinue which included his friend Ninian Winzet, formerly schoolmaster of Linlithgow and for a time the confessor of Queen Mary. During his stay in Italy, Lesley busied himself writing a Latin history of Scotland designed to impress the pope with Scottish constancy to the Roman Catholic church. This was eventually published in Rome in 1578.

His own country was never far from Lesley's mind, and his interest was caught when he heard talk of Scottish abbeys and monasteries in Germany. These *Schottenklöster* had originally been founded for Irish monks who called themselves *Scoti*, and the term later caused considerable confusion as to their identity. In 1514 a rival had succeeded in having the Irish abbot of Regensburg ejected on the doubtful grounds that he was not a Scot. There may have been a genuine misunderstanding, for there were many Scottish traders in Regensburg and it is possible that they believed that the abbey really was the preserve of the Scots. A new Scottish abbot was duly appointed and he in turn inserted Scots into other houses in the Regensburg congregation. For a time, the *Schottenklöster* flourished, but by the middle of the century the number of monks had dwindled and those few who did remain were mostly German.

Lesley decided to take up the cause. Determined to effect a Roman Catholic revival in Scotland, not least because he wished to regain his position of power and influence there, he decided that the German houses could provide livings for exiled Scottish ecclesiastics who could then train missionaries for Scotland. He urged the pope to appoint Ninian Winzet as abbot of Regensburg, which Gregory XIII did on 13 June 1577. Everything depended on a change in the political situation in Scotland and there is good reason to suppose that Lesley had a hand in the plot of his fellow exile Thomas Stucley to send a force to Liverpool with the intention of releasing Queen Mary from her current imprisonment at Sheffield. Spanish aid was required and as usual the Spanish procrastinated, with the result that Stucley's plans to sail to England were never carried out.

There were, however, interesting developments in both Scotland and England. On 12 March 1578 Morton was forced to resign the regency and the eleven-year-old James VI was seized by Lesley's great friend John Stewart, fourth earl of Atholl, and Colin Campbell, sixth earl of Argyll. At about the same time Mary heard mistaken reports that Elizabeth was dying of tuberculosis. Already elated by the news of Morton's fall, Mary allowed herself to believe that she would soon be ruling both Scotland and England. Even if Elizabeth died, of course, there remained the problem of James VI. Mary had always refused to recognize her son as king, for she held that the crown was rightfully hers, and indeed she and Lesley had often discussed having James kidnapped and taken to France, to be brought up as a Roman Catholic by her Guise relatives. Deluded by false assurances that her son was now devoted to her, Mary had come to believe that he and her nobles would do whatever she wished. Lesley laboured under no such misapprehension, and in order to persuade the pope to approve plans for Mary's restoration he devised a proposal for joint sovereignty, whereby Mary and James would rule together. This compromise was accepted by Gregory XIII.

Germany With such exciting developments the time had obviously come for Lesley to return home. He was still set on pushing forward his scheme for the German monasteries and with Mary wanting to enlist the support of the emperor he decided to travel back to Scotland by way of Germany. Gregory XIII optimistically made him administrator of the church of Moray and sent briefs to the Scottish nobility, commending Lesley to them and urging them to renounce heresy. Armed with letters from both the pope and Mary, Lesley finally set out some time before 10 August 1578. He travelled through northern Italy into Austria, and received a warm welcome from Archduke Ferdinand before riding on to Bavaria to speak to its duke. Towards the end of September he was in Prague, telling the emperor that Mary, queen of Scots, was being held prisoner because of her religion, outlining her just claim to the English throne, and describing hopes for her restoration. He carefully avoided any mention of her alleged complicity in the murder of Darnley. Having secured promises of assistance from the emperor and a gift of 500 florins, he continued his travels through Germany and was just about to cross into Lorraine to visit the Guises when he was captured by Prince Georg Johann, count of Lützelstein, a protestant nobleman who had mistaken him for the papal legate, the archbishop of Rossano. His papers were temporarily seized and he was held for about a month.

As soon as he was free Lesley made his way to Paris. The English ambassador refused to see him and so he wrote a long letter to Burghley, claiming that he had spent the past three years quietly composing his *History* before negotiating the return of the Scottish monasteries. Making no allusion to his activities on behalf of Queen Mary, he hoped that Burghley had not forgotten his promise to ask Elizabeth I to intervene on his behalf with the Scottish authorities. Burghley made no reply, for a catalogue of the bishop's papers had been sent from Lorraine to Sir Francis Walsingham, and Lesley's clandestine activities were exposed.

The final years Forced to stay on in Paris, Lesley received discouraging news. His friend Atholl had long since lost his influence over James VI and he died on 24 April 1579. Lesley then became involved in the dispatch to Scotland of the king's kinsman Esmé Stewart, urging him before he went to try to convert James to Catholicism. He continued to correspond with Stewart as he rose high in the young king's favour, and in the spring of 1580 Lesley was rumoured to be in Dieppe, waiting to cross to Scotland. However, he remained in France, where he was appointed suffragan and vicar-general to the archbishop of Rouen. Still trying to win favour with Elizabeth I he revealed to her ambassador in July 1580 the articles of a papal league recently concluded against England. He may have been partly inspired by fears for the safety of Queen Mary, for if England were invaded by Roman Catholic forces her captors might well have killed her. The archbishop of Glasgow took a less charitable view and suspected that Lesley was already in Elizabeth's pay.

Lesley never did return to Scotland. In June 1587, after Mary's execution, he was comprised in an act of pacification by the Scottish parliament, but that would have required him to give a confession of faith. On 29 May 1589 an act was passed putting into force previous legislation against Lesley and others, regardless of recent remissions, but another act was passed on 23 June 1591 declaring that the tacks and dispositions made by him from the bishopric of Ross since his restitution and the act of 1587 were in fact valid.

During the French civil war Lesley encouraged the citizens of Rouen to hold out against a besieging force, in the summer of 1591, and he was rewarded by Pope Clement VIII on 16 December 1592 with translation to the bishopric of Coutances in Normandy. Unable to take up his appointment because of the unsettled state of the country, he is said to have retired to a monastery of Augustinian canons at Guirtenburg (or Gertrudenberg) near Brussels, where he died on 31 May 1596, and where he was buried. However, no reliable record has been found of such a monastery, and Lesley's place of death and burial is consequently uncertain.

For many John Lesley's name was synonymous with serpentine scheming, but there is no denying that he was a highly skilled negotiator, an accomplished lawyer, and a diligent historian. His *Defence of the Honour of … Marie, Queene of Scotland* was reprinted many times and he was one of the editors of the first edition, in 1566, of the parliamentary records of Scotland. His intimate knowledge of the archives, and of both Scottish and English chronicles, was obviously advantageous when he decided to compose his continuation of Boece's *Scotorum historia* (1527), even if it did cause him some intractable problems in trying to reconcile his various sources (Boece had concluded in 1437). Lesley's vernacular *History of Scotland* (presented to Queen Mary in 1570) begins with a study of James II, provides the first full-scale account of the reign of James III, and contains a description of the rule of James V that is much more detailed than, for instance, that given by John Knox. Lesley's desire to uphold the monarchy made him somewhat too uncritical of both James IV and James V, but, despite both a certain lack of objectivity and a number of errors copied from previous writers, his *History* remains a classic work containing many valuable observations.

Like any leading figure caught up in the religious controversies of the sixteenth century, Lesley has received widely differing assessments of his career from subsequent historians. For Froude he was 'a man of infinite faithfulness, courage and adroit capability' (Froude, 9.282). To the historian of the Scottish monasteries in Germany his achievement in having Scottish abbots appointed to the houses at Regensburg and Erfurt was 'an outstanding diplomatic success' (Dilworth, 23), yet David Mathew could characterize him as 'that loquacious and indolent gourmet' (Mathew, 115). In fact whatever his perceived deficiencies there is no doubting that John Lesley showed an extraordinary tenacity in pursuit of his many schemes to restore Queen Mary to her throne, the Roman Catholic faith to Scotland, and himself to his former position of power.

ROSALIND K. MARSHALL

Sources D. M. Lockie, 'The political career of the bishop of Ross, 1568–80: the background to a contemporary life of Mary Stuart', *University of Birmingham Historical Journal*, 4/2 (1954), 98–145 · J. Anderson, *Collections relating to the history of Mary, queen of Scotland* (1727–8), vol. 1, p. 1; vol. 3, p. 6 · M. Dilworth, *The Scots in Franconia* (1974), 23–7, 30, 33–4, 157–8, 213–14, 243 · J. Lesley, *The history of Scotland*, ed. T. Thomson, Bannatyne Club, 38 (1830) · N. Williams, *Thomas Howard, fourth duke of Norfolk* (1964); repr. as *A Tudor tragedy: Thomas Howard, fourth duke of Norfolk* (1989), 135–44, 149, 152–4 · J. Leslie, *The historie of Scotland*, ed. E. G. Cody and W. Murison, trans. J. Dalrymple, 2 vols. in 4 pts, STS, 5, 14, 19, 34 (1888–95) [1596 trans. of *De origine moribus, et rebus gestis Scotorum libri decem* (Rome, 1578)] · *A collection of state papers … left by William Cecill, Lord Burghley*, ed. W. Murdin, 2 (1759), 52 · A. Fraser, *Mary, queen of Scots* (1969) · G. Donaldson, *The first trial of Mary, queen of Scots* (1969), 35, 109, 114, 120, 140, 173, 193, 196, 204, 205 · J. B. A. T. Teulet, ed., *Papiers d'état, pièces et documents inédits ou peu connus relatifs à l'histoire de l'Écosse au XVIème siècle*, 3 vols., Bannatyne Club, 107 (Paris, 1852–60), vol. 3, pp. 62, 187, 209, 219, 222 · J. Dowden, *The bishops of Scotland … prior to the Reformation*, ed. J. M. Thomson (1912) · W. Forbes-Leith, ed., *Narratives of Scottish Catholics under Mary Stuart and James VI* (1885), 135–8 · [J. Lesley], *Mary, queen of Scots and the prince her son*, ed. R. McLure (1913) · A. Shephard, *Gender and authority in sixteenth-century England* (1994), 3–33 · *CSP Spain*, *1568–79*, 75, 85, 90, 97 · *CSP Rome*, *1558–71*, 215–30, 320–22; *1572–8*, 40, 356–7, 407, 423–4, 446, 465–6, 478–9, 485 · J. A. Froude, *History of England*, 12 vols. (1856–70), vol. 9, pp. 282 · C. McGladdery, *James II* (1990), 137–8 · N. Macdougall, *James III: a political study* (1982), 282–3 · N. Macdougall, *James IV* (1989); repr. (1997), 301 · J. Cameron, *James V: the personal rule, 1528–1542*, ed. N. Macdougall (1998), 346 · D. Mathew, *The Celtic peoples and Renaissance Europe* (1933)

Archives BL, Cotton MSS, corresp.

Likenesses G. Jamesone, oils, 17th cent., Marischal College, Aberdeen • Barlow, engraving (after G. Jamesone), Scot. NPG • eleventh earl of Buchan, pencil drawing, Scot. NPG • P. van Gunst, engraving (after A. van der Werff), Scot. NPG; repro. in I. de Larrey, *Histoire d'Angleterre, d'Ecosse, et d'Irlande*, 4 vols. (Rotterdam, 1697–1713) • oils, Scot. NPG • portrait, Marischal College, Aberdeen [*see illus.*]

Lesley, William Aloysius. *See* Leslie, William Aloysius (1641–1704).

Leslie. *See also* Lesley.

Leslie, Agnes, countess of Morton (*d.* in or after **1606**), noblewoman, was a daughter of George *Leslie, fourth earl of Rothes (*d.* 1558), and his third wife, Agnes Somerville (*d.* 1543), daughter of Sir John Somerville of Cambusnethan. She was married, by contract dated 19 August 1545 (revised 1554) when she and her future husband were still children, to William *Douglas (*c.*1540–1606), eldest son of Sir Robert Douglas of Lochleven who was killed at the battle of Pinkie in 1547. In order to make the contract binding her father paid Agnes's tocher (dowry) of £1000 Scots immediately while the laird of Lochleven promised to infeft Agnes in the liferent of the barony of Fossoway in Perthshire, worth £100 Scots a year. The couple's actual marriage may date from about 1555 when William, then about fifteen years of age, was served heir to his father. Agnes's family was early associated with the Anglophile-protestant party in Scotland. Her eldest brother, Norman, master of Rothes, and her uncle John Leslie of Parkhill were among the assassins of Cardinal David Beaton in 1546. Agnes and her husband entertained Mary, queen of Scots, at their island castle of Lochleven, Kinross-shire, in 1563. On Queen Mary's deposition in July 1567 she was warded by the Lords in Lochleven Castle where she remained until her escape eleven months later. The first few months of the queen's detention, when she was in a state of nervous and physical collapse and suffered a miscarriage, probably forged personal contacts with the Lochleven women, especially with Agnes Leslie and her mother-in-law, Lady Margaret Erskine, who lived in the household. Agnes, who was pregnant during Mary's stay with the family, is said to have slept in the queen's room.

After being suspected of involvement in the so-called Ruthven raid (1582) William Douglas went into exile in France between 1584 and 1586, and from there he wrote letters to his wife which reveal not only his own movements abroad but also the extent to which he relied on Agnes's management of their affairs at home. In 1585 he asked her for money, 'if it were but ane hundred crownis, for I am neir ane end of the silver that I had already' (Thomson, Macdonald, and Innes, 1). While the laird was abroad the chamberlains wrote to Agnes on estate and other business, including the important matter of allocating the arable land among the tenants, which on one occasion the chamberlain on the family's Roxburghshire lands urged her to 'haste over' and supervise (NA Scot., GD150/3440/6). Even when her husband was at home Agnes was personally involved in the running of their widespread lands. She was present with him when the tenants' rents were received and estate accounts audited at the family's more convenient residence of The Newhouse (on the site of Kinross House gardens) on the shores of Lochleven. She travelled to their barony of Auchterhouse in Angus (Forfarshire), sometimes by sea, where she 'held house in mucking time', supervising agricultural and building operations—'to freight of my Lady and deals, 16*s.* 8*d.*', a clerk noted on one occasion—and loaned her own horse for the harrowing (NA Scot., GD150/2727). In 1591 she wrote to her husband about the difficulty of obtaining a decent price from the tenants for the grain rents which she was trying to sell back to them; 'they will offer but four merks for meal and bere [barley] for all the prigging [haggling] that John Douglas and I can make' (Thomson, Macdonald, and Innes, 1.176–7). She purchased wine in Dundee and arranged for its shipment by ferry to Fife. Household supplies, food, and clothes were purchased from Dundee and Edinburgh merchants and tailors, and the constant supply of medicinal comfits and herbs demanded by her husband's ill health from Sarah Kerwood, an Edinburgh 'sweetmeat wyfe'.

Agnes and her husband spent time each year in Edinburgh where they rented lodgings from an Edinburgh merchant, David Somer. In 1588 she became countess of Morton when William Douglas succeeded to that earldom on the death of Archibald Douglas, who had been earl of both Angus and Morton. She and her husband enjoyed a married life of over fifty years, having been married young. They had five sons, all of whom predeceased their parents: Robert (the eldest); James, commendator of Melrose; Sir Archibald of Kellour; Francis; and Sir George of Kirkness. They also had seven daughters, known as 'the seven pearls of Lochleven': Margaret, married to Sir John Wemyss of Wester Wemyss; Christian, who married first Laurence, master of Oliphant, and second Alexander, first earl of Home; Mary, who married as his second wife Walter, Lord Ogilvy of Deskford; Euphemia, who married as his second wife Thomas Lyon of Baldukie, master of Glamis; Agnes, married to Archibald, seventh earl of Argyll; Elizabeth, who married as his third wife Francis, ninth earl of Erroll; and Jean, who died unmarried in 1606. Agnes survived her husband, who died in 1606, and she is last recorded in that year; the date of her death is not known. MARGARET H. B. SANDERSON

Sources NA Scot., Morton muniments, GD 150 • T. Thomson, A. Macdonald, and C. Innes, eds., *Registrum honoris de Morton*, 2 vols., Bannatyne Club, 94 (1853) • *Scots peerage*, 1.198; 6.371–4; 7.281–92 • M. H. B. Sanderson, *Mary Stewart's people: life in Mary Stewart's Scotland* (1987)

Archives NA Scot., Morton muniments

Leslie, Alexander, first earl of Leven (*c.*1580–1661), army officer, was the illegitimate son of George Leslie, captain of Blair Castle in Atholl. By one account he was born in Balvenie, by another in the Abbot's House at Coupar Angus. The only mention of his mother in his own lifetime states that she was 'a wench in Rannoch' (*Scots peerage*, 5.373). Family historians assert that George Leslie subsequently married Alexander's mother, thus legitimizing him, but this is incompatible with references to his bastardy in his later life. The estimate of his birth date is based on his being said to have been over eighty at the time of his death. In a letter Leslie referred to Sir Robert Campbell of Glenorchy as his 'foster-brother' (NA Scot., GD112/39/68/14), suggesting that he spent part of his childhood in Argyllshire. He received little formal education, and the tale that he could neither read or write receives some support from the fact that there appear to be no papers surviving in his own hand, and his signatures to documents are in clumsy and childish letters.

Swedish service Leslie chose to make a career as a soldier, and fought in the English forces supporting the Dutch in the Netherlands under Sir Horace Vere in 1605–7 before transferring to the Swedish service as an ensign in 1608. 'When he was in but a Mean Condition' (Macfarlane, 2.43) he married Agnes Renton (*d.* 1651), daughter of the laird of Billie in Berwickshire, and by 1638 his second son was old enough to be a colonel in the Swedish service.

By 1626 Leslie himself had reached the rank of colonel, and was serving as governor of Pillau. He was knighted by Gustavus Adolphus on 23 September 1627, at the ceremony in which Gustavus was himself invested as a knight of the Garter by representatives of Charles I. In July 1628 Leslie was appointed governor of Stralsund by Gustavus, in what was to prove the first move towards Swedish involvement in the Thirty Years' War in Germany. The imperialist general Wallenstein had advanced to the Baltic coast of Germany, and only the Hanseatic port of Stralsund remained in protestant hands. Early in July a contingent of Scots mercenaries in the Danish service had reinforced the garrison, and Gustavus had then agreed to take over from the Danes responsibility for helping the city authorities resist attack. Thus without intervening directly in the war Sweden could preserve one port in friendly hands for use as an entry-point to Germany. Leslie commanded a force of Scots dispatched by Gustavus which landed soon afterwards, on 7 July, and a few days later the imperial army began to withdraw. Wallenstein had evidently decided to abandon the siege before Leslie's arrival, but the way in which the Swedes publicized their relief of the city as a great protestant victory brought glory to Leslie, aided by ecstatic (if incoherent) praises of his valour by his countryman Robert Monro, who was serving in the Danish–Scots force in Stralsund.

As governor of Stralsund Leslie worked to strengthen the fortifications, while the Swedish garrison built from about 3000 men at the end of 1628 to 5700 by June 1630. At times he was despondent: he feared his troops would desert, they were weakened by illness, and he himself was badly paid and 'my services are counted for naught … Let a man be appointed here who has a better political head than I have' (Fischer, *Sweden*, 92). However, between March and June 1630 he succeeded in occupying the island of Rügen, ensuring that an imperialist withdrawal was not followed by Danish occupation, and when Gustavus landed in Germany with a Swedish army in July 1630 Leslie marched with him as one of his commanders. At the first major Swedish success, the storming of Greifenhagen on 25 December, the artillery barrage was supported by fire from a fleet of riverboats led by Leslie.

In April 1631 Gustavus named Leslie along with the marquess of Hamilton as commanders of a force which the latter had undertaken to raise in Britain to serve under Gustavus. Leslie was also instructed to negotiate with north German cities to win their support for Hamilton's venture, and to try to levy extra regiments. He also visited Britain to help Hamilton with recruitment there, and when about 6000 men landed at the mouth of the Oder in August, Leslie led them to Stettin and then up the Oder towards Frankfurt. Many of Hamilton's men soon died of disease and hunger, but Leslie was in command of a detached part of the force which occupied Frankfurt, Crossen, and Gubin. In November Gustavus ordered him to Mecklenburg, to serve as major-general under Field Marshal Ake Tott. He took part in the recapture of Magdeburg in January 1632, but he was shot in the left foot while commanding Tott's army at the siege of Boxtelude, an injury that left him with a limp for life. He was carried to Hamburg to recover, and from there sent 9000 rixdaler, the rewards of a successful campaign, home to Scotland. Leslie took part in the victory at Lutzen on 7 November 1632 in which Gustavus was killed, and in the years that followed he continued to serve in the Swedish campaigns in Germany. Brandenburg surrendered to him in March 1634, but defeat at Nördlingen in September forced the Swedes to abandon all their conquests in southern Germany, and the peace of Prague early in 1635 temporarily brought fighting to an end.

Leslie briefly returned to Scotland and invested the wealth he had acquired in land, taking the name of his estate of Balgonie in Fife as his territorial designation. Returning to Germany he was given command as field marshal of the Swedish army in Westphalia early in 1636. He relieved Osnabrück and Hanau, but in 1637 the Swedish armies were pushed back, and Leslie retired to Stettin before going to Stockholm in September for discussions with the Swedish chancellor, Alex Oxenstierna.

From Sweden to Scotland Since the marquess of Hamilton had returned from his German venture to Britain in 1632 Leslie had kept in touch with him, treating him as his patron and stressing that though he was serving the Swedish crown he saw this as service to Charles I, since one of the war's objectives was to restore Charles's nephew, the elector palatine, to the estates he had lost to the imperialists in the early stages of the Thirty Years' War. In May 1636 Leslie ventured to write to Charles himself stressing that doing some acceptable service to the king or his relatives 'I should accompt my cheifest earthlie happiness' (Fraser, 2.85). Early in 1638 he visited England, met the king, and again indicated his willingness to serve him: if Charles raised an army, he would be happy to lead it to restore the elector. He also received the king's permission to remove his household to the continent (23 March). By this time, however, Charles's attention was being diverted by events in Scotland, where opponents of his innovations in religion and other policies had seized power, signing the national covenant in February 1638. Leslie's intention of moving his family to Germany suggests that his first reaction to these events was that he should distance himself from them, and he may well have regarded the growing conflict between the covenanters and the king as an unfortunate provincial quarrel among protestants that would distract attention from the central conflict between protestants and Catholics in Europe.

If so, a visit to Scotland changed his viewpoint dramatically, and he adopted the covenanters' perspective, in which their revolt was seen as a part of the great European religious struggle. Charles I, whom Leslie had previously looked to for support for the protestant cause, was seen as moving towards Catholicism, and thus posing a threat to protestantism in Britain which must be resisted. The cause for which Leslie had long fought in Germany now demanded that he serve in Scotland. He was doubtless influenced by ties of kinship as well as of ideology. In spite of his illegitimacy he identified strongly with the Leslie kin, and its head was the earl of Rothes, who in 1636 had married one of Leslie's daughters. Rothes was the outstanding noble leader of the covenanters at this stage, and it seems likely, there already being talk of civil war, that Leslie was urged to make himself available to command the covenanters' army if necessary.

In June 1638 Leslie wrote to the Swedish national council, enclosing a copy of the national covenant. Though he was returning to Sweden, he asked to be allowed to leave that country's service quickly, as he wished to return to Scotland promptly, fearing that an English naval blockade would be imposed which would prevent this. Serving the covenant, he revealed, he regarded as a matter of defending religion and national liberty. The Swedes decided that, in view of his loyal service, and because he was moved by 'patriotic loyalty alone' (Murdoch, 49) he should be allowed to go. In fact Swedish foreign policy was moving towards support for the covenanters, and indeed Leslie may have known in advance that his request to retire would be favourably received. Granting Leslie a pension of 800 rixdaler might be a deserved reward for past service, but the added gift of two cannons and 2000 muskets shows which side in the British conflict the Swedes were on.

Outwardly, it was said that Leslie was retiring through ill health, his career over, but few can have believed this—except John Spalding, who reported that Leslie, 'ane gentleman off bass birth, who had servit long and fortunatly in the Germane warris', having acquired wealth in great abundance, had returned 'to sattill him self besyde his chief, the Erll of Rothass' in Fife, and that only then was he seduced by Rothes into joining the covenanters (Spalding, 1.130).

Rumours that Leslie would return to Scotland to serve against the king were widespread enough by the summer of 1638 for it to be believed (as Leslie had feared) that English naval vessels which were stopping Scottish merchant ships were not, as they claimed, looking for arms but for Leslie. When he left Sweden, he did so 'in a small bark' (*Letters … Baillie*, 1.111) to avoid attention, arriving in Scotland towards the end of the year.

The first bishops' war At first Leslie acted as military adviser to the covenanters without holding any formal position among them. That he had been one of the lieutenants of the great Gustavus Adolphus gave him an authority which was an important boost to the covenanters' morale as they prepared to resist their own king and the greatly superior resources of England and Ireland potentially at his disposal. Moreover, in Leslie they had a military leader of great experience in one of the most admired armies in Europe, who also could advise of the procurement of arms, and had contacts with many of his fellow Scottish officers serving on the continent. Many were to be encouraged by him to return to their homeland and serve under him.

From the first the willingness of the noble-dominated committees that controlled the rebel regime to follow Leslie's advice was remarkable, and he showed skill and tact in combining the diverse elements at his disposal into an effective army. He needed to make full use of veterans returning from Europe, with up-to-date professional experience, to train and lead, but he had to do this without alienating a Scottish society dominated by landlords who assumed that it was their right and duty to recruit men in the localities and lead them. Leslie blended these two potentially conflicting elements in a masterly fashion. His army was organized on modern lines, in regular regiments with fixed hierarchies of officers, but they were raised by nobles and lairds, and most were commanded by such men as colonels. Below the rank of colonel, however, experienced professional officers were intermixed with enthusiastic landed amateurs. A modern army was produced without compromising social structure.

In the action that began the first bishops' war, the seizing of Edinburgh Castle on 21 March 1639, Leslie led a group of nobles and others to the castle gate to talk with the king's garrison about surrendering. Nothing was agreed, and as Leslie and his companions withdrew they left a petard (bomb) at the gate. Once it was blown in, parties of men ready with axes and ladders stormed in and took the castle. Immediately thereafter a force of several thousand men was dispatched to Aberdeen to subdue the royalist marquess of Huntly. The ambitious young earl of Montrose led the force, but Leslie was sent with him, and remained in Aberdeen until Huntly had submitted. Then, having dealt with internal threats, he marched most of his men south so that he could concentrate on preparing an army on the border to resist invasion from England. At a 'convention' of covenanters at Edinburgh on 9 May he was issued with a commission as general of all Scottish forces, with wide powers to raise men, appoint officers, and do everything necessary to organize an army, and to undertake operations necessary 'for the defence of the covenant, for religion, croune, and countrie'. He was to be answerable to civil and ecclesiastical law, and to the 'counsall of estait' (which soon became known as the committee of estates), but he could punish anyone of 'whatsoever ranke, qualitie, or degrie, who shall not do his dewty' without anyone questioning the punishment, 'aither of his kin, friends or acquaintances' (Terry, 43–4). The covenanters were well aware of the dangers of rivalry and feuding undermining their efforts, and had deliberately chosen to give military power to a man who could prevent such problems arising because he stood outside the tensions that might cause them. Though he was a Leslie, he was of obscure and illegitimate birth, without social rank to clash with the claims of others, and having spent the majority of his life abroad, he was associated with no faction.

There was no thought in 1639 of entering England, and Leslie's strategy was simply to build up an army sufficient to deter attack. Numbers were vital, and the need to hasten men to the army as quickly as possible forced the normally rather taciturn Leslie into eloquence, in a stream of letters to individuals and general summonses. In May he stressed the need for speed in the military build-up. The safety of the whole country depended on border defence. In such circumstances only enemies of cause and country would hold back. 'Remember that your chartour chists are lying at the Borders', he urged landowners, meaning that their titles to their lands would not be safe if the king triumphed. Lesser men were urged that none should stay at home 'when strangers are hired for 3s. a day to make us all slaves' (*Letters … Baillie*, 2.438–9).

By the beginning of June the rival armies faced each other over the Tweed. After a few minor English incursions over the river Leslie concentrated his men at Duns, ready for a major engagement. If there was to be fighting it was up to the king to make the first move and, faced with the obvious determination and readiness of the Scots, and the failure of his efforts to provide an overwhelmingly strong army, Charles agreed to listen to approaches from the covenanters for a peace. The treaty of Berwick, fine words that settled nothing in the long term, was quickly agreed, and on 20 June Leslie disbanded his army. The almost bloodless first bishops' war was over.

Political stalemate continued, but the treaty was a major humiliation for Charles I. Faced with Leslie's army, he had not dared to risk fighting. The covenanters, though disappointed there had not been a more decisive outcome, were thrilled—even astonished—by the success of their defiance. Much of the credit went to Leslie, as is indicated by Robert Baillie's outburst of praise for his skill:

> We were feared that emulation among our Nobles might have done harme, when they should be mett in the fields; bot such was the wisdome and authoritie of that old, little, crooked souldier, that all, with an incredible submission, from the beginning to the end, gave over themselves to be guided by him, as if he had been Great Solyman. Certainlie the obedience of our nobles to that man's advyces was as great as their forbears wont to be to their King's commands: yet that was man's understanding of our Scott's humours, that gave out, not onlie to the nobles, bot to verie mean gentlemen, his directions in a verie homelie and simple forme, as if they had been bot the advyces of their neighbour and companion; for, as he rightlie observed, a difference would be used in commanding sojours of fortune, and of sojours voluntars, of whiche kind most part of our camp did stand. (*Letters … Baillie*, 1.213–14)

The second bishops' war As part of the Berwick settlement Charles demanded that Leslie's commission be withdrawn. The Scots refused, but Leslie solved the problem by resigning voluntarily. He was then approached on the king's behalf to command a force of ten or twelve thousand Scots to be sent to Germany to help the elector palatine. The offer was tempting, for the cause was one which Leslie cherished, but it was obvious that the scheme was a ruse intended to deprive the covenanters of their eminent general and many of their best troops. Leslie said he would only consider the plan if the king got agreement from the Scottish parliament to pay the troops. This, given the covenanters' domination of Scotland, was clearly impossible, and the plan was abandoned.

The year 1640 saw preparations for a new war. Both sides were clear that decisive action was necessary: the conflict evaded in 1639 had to be concluded. In November 1639 Leslie had indicated that he was willing to serve as general again, but there was controversy over the terms of his commission. It was proposed that a committee should be named to work with him in commanding the army, but he indicated that he regarded this as an unacceptable limitation on his powers. Therefore, on 17 April 1640 he was given a commission which gave him much the same powers as in 1639, though a subcommittee was named which was to accompany him.

As the build-up on the border neared completion in July, Leslie joined the army at Duns. The English forces facing him were in no state to take offensive action, and Leslie confidently crossed the Tweed into England on 20 August. His strategic objectives were clear, and were easily accomplished. Marching south without encountering opposition he reached the Tyne at Newburn. English forces trying to block his passage fled after a short encounter on 28 August, freeing Leslie to attack Newcastle in the rear, where its defences were weakest. An attack was rendered unnecessary when the English garrison withdrew without a fight, and on 30 August Leslie was able to occupy the town. The strategic advantage in holding Newcastle was far greater than a map might suggest. Not only was it one of the richest towns in England, but coalfields in the locality provided London's fuel supply. By cutting that off the Scots had struck at the heart of England, putting increasing political pressure on the king as winter approached.

Leslie's reputation was now at its peak. Under him Scottish organization, unity, high morale, and clear objectives had triumphed over English muddle, disorganization, and uncertainty. However, he remained alert. There was a danger that now strategic advantage had been gained the Scots would relax, and Leslie was aware that in the bargaining for a settlement that would follow the covenanters must maintain the strength of their army if the best results were to be obtained. On 28 October Charles was forced by the continuing readiness of the Scots for action to agree by the treaty of Ripon not only that the Scottish army would remain in England until the outlines of a peace settlement were agreed, but that it should be paid by England.

Nearly a year later Leslie was still at the head of his army when Charles I came north to reach a final settlement with the covenanters. On 13 August 1641, when he reached Newcastle, the whole Scottish army was drawn up before the king, after which he dined with Leslie before proceeding to Edinburgh. The army now withdrew from England and was disbanded at Leith on 27 August, while Charles and Leslie drove through Edinburgh together in a coach, with crowds cheering this bizarre pairing of rebel general and defeated king. Leslie is said to have been effusive in swearing never to fight against the king again, and indeed, now that religion was secure, offering to serve him against those who unjustly attacked his power. Like other leading covenanters he was well rewarded for past rebellion by a king hoping to buy future loyalty. On 23 September 1641 he was created earl of Leven. However, he quickly discovered that there was a sting in the tail. His second-in-command, Lord Almond, had been promoted to earl of Callendar, and his patent was dated a week before Leven's, and thus he would have precedence over his commander. Leven was furious when he discovered this, taking it to be a deliberate insult. Charles wrote a few months later assuring him that it had been a mistake, and he would see Leven got the precedence he sought. This was never confirmed, but with the country under the control of the covenanters his precedence was accepted in his lifetime, only to be lost by his successor in 1661.

A settlement with the king having been confirmed, Leven resigned his post as general. Parliament promised him a gift of 100,000 merks (about £5500 sterling). The governorship of Edinburgh Castle and a seat on the privy council of Scotland completed the rewards for his services.

Ireland However, the next stage in Britain's snowballing civil wars soon called Leslie back to command. The Irish Catholic rising of October 1641 was seen as threatening not only Scottish and English settlers in Ulster but the security of protestant Britain as a whole, and an agreement was made whereby Scotland would send an army of 10,000 men to Ulster, to be paid by the English parliament. Leven was now over sixty, but his fame made it almost inevitable that he be given command of this army—to encourage its men, satisfy the English, and scare the Irish. His commission as general was dated 7 May 1642 but the army was effectively commanded in its first months by Major-General Robert Monro. Only when it had reached its full strength did Leven cross to Ulster, landing on 4 August 1642. He soon found himself frustrated, both by the enemy and by his own men. The Irish, as he discovered in leading two expeditions against them, melted away as soon as he advanced but regrouped afterwards. The enemy 'will not be caught but at his advantage' (NA Scot., GD406/1/1787). In the pattern that was to dominate warfare in Ireland in the years that followed, all he could do was devastate the countryside in the hope of defeating the enemy by famine. As for his own men, he found the officers bitter at lack of pay and supply, and (as war between king and parliament loomed in England) uncertain in their loyalties. The mercenary principle that loyalty was due only to effective paymasters was widespread. Faced with disrespect from officers and an inability to pursue an effective strategy, Leven withdrew to Scotland in October, and never again visited the army that until 1648 he nominally commanded. James Turner, a hostile witness, summed up Leven's stay in Ireland by quoting the remark 'That the Earle of Levens actions made not such a noyse in the world as these of Generall Lesley' (Turner, 25). Age, and the satisfaction of ambition by fame and a noble title, left him little motivation for becoming bogged down in an unwinnable provincial campaign.

The English civil war Leven's performance in Ireland had been unimpressive, but his return to Scotland late in 1642 may have reflected more than disappointment. While he had been in Ireland the English civil war had begun, and Scotland's future depended on who was victorious. Many covenanters saw that to sit on the sidelines if the king looked like being victorious would be a recipe for disaster, as he would then use his power to destroy them. It may well be, therefore, that Leven was summoned back to Scotland because his military advice was needed. As, in the course of 1643, the king's armies gained the upper hand in England, the likelihood of the Scots agreeing to parliament's pleas for military aid increased. Long before a treaty was negotiated, the English parliament made it clear that it looked to Leven to lead an army to its rescue, writing to him on 19 July that his service would be rewarded in accordance with 'the high Esteem they have of the worth and abilities of your Excellency' (Terry, 175–6). By August the Scots had begun preparations to raise an army, and on the 26th the convention of estates commissioned Leven as lord general. 'It is true, he had past manie promises to the King, that he would no more fight in his contrare; bot, as he declares, it was with the express and necessar condition, that Religion and Countrey's rights were not in hazard' (*Letters … Baillie*, 2.100). These causes were now indeed in hazard, and on 19 January 1644 the first units of his new army of over 20,000 men crossed the Tweed.

From the first the achievements of Leven's army were disappointing to both his Scots and English masters. Easy success in the bishops' wars led to expectations that he would achieve quick and decisive victory. As in 1640 Leven's first objective was Newcastle, whose royalist garrison was starving London of coal, but though he again crossed the Tyne the town was now resolutely defended, the garrison being reinforced by the marquess of Newcastle's royalist army just before the Scots arrived. Initial attempts at an assault were driven back and a formal siege began. Just holding Newcastle's army in the north, preventing it from moving south to help the king's other armies, brought considerable military advantage to parliament, but it was not the spectacular success that had been expected. Leven's political masters, realizing that Newcastle would not fall quickly, ordered him to march south to join parliamentary armies threatening York. They helped in the achievement of a major victory at Marston Moor on 2 July, when the allied armies destroyed the army that Prince Rupert had brought to attempt the relief of the city, but the victory was marred for Leven by the fact that, though his army played a major part in the outcome of the battle, he himself was forced by initial royalist successes to flee the battlefield. Admittedly he was not alone: with Lord Fairfax and the earl of Manchester he made up a trio of generals embarrassed by having fled from a field of victory—though the malicious Turner gleefully insisted that Leven fled furthest, not drawing bridle for 24 miles (Turner, 38). Perhaps his wounded pride received some consolation from his chaplain's slick interpretation of events: 'God would not have a generall in the army, he himself was Generall,', so he had made Leven and the others flee (R. Douglas, 'Diary', *Historical Fragments, Relative to Scottish Affairs, from 1635 to 1664*, ed. J. Maidment, 1833, 64).

Marston Moor was one of the decisive battles of the war, but political tensions led to controversy over whether the English or the Scots had contributed most to victory. York surrendered on 16 July, Leven marched his men back to continue the siege of Newcastle, and the town was at last stormed on 19 October. However, in the year that followed, Leven's task was complicated by conflicting loyalties. While he had been sent to England to secure victory for parliament, which paid (or, rather, increasingly failed to pay) his men, his and his army's loyalties were primarily to Scotland, and from September 1644 to August 1645 the covenanting regime was shaken, and ultimately almost destroyed, by the remarkable victories of the royalist marquess of Montrose. Resources were diverted from Leven to face this threat, and he and his men in fighting the war in England tended to be distracted by looking over their shoulders, anticipating that they might have to march home to save the regime. Leven was thus reluctant during 1645 to obey the demands of parliament that he advance south, fearing this might let English royalist forces, and even the king himself, slip into Scotland to join Montrose. In May he moved into Westmorland after intelligence reports suggested that 'the King was bending his course with a flying Army' (Terry, 354) towards Scotland. Only after the threat had passed in June did he march south, and on 30 July he laid siege to Hereford. However, upon the king again moving northwards he sent all his cavalry back to Nottingham, and on news of Montrose's victory at Kilsyth on 15 August it hastened back to Scotland to restore the covenanting regime. Leven, starved of supplies, threatened by royalist forces, and lacking cavalry, decided it would be prudent to withdraw the rest of his army, and raised the siege of Hereford on 30 August. The English alleged he had lacked zeal in attempting to take the town, and resented an army that it had hired giving priority to Scotland's interests. Leven, on the other hand, resented the neglect of his army by both Scots and English, and was angered that commissions granted to commanders leading forces in Scotland against Montrose ignored his position as lord general of all Scottish forces. Therefore, in September, after the covenanters' victory at Philiphaugh had forced Montrose to flee to the highlands, Leven announced that he intended 'to lay doun my charge, being now become unable to performe such duty as I wold for the publique' (Terry, 379). Age, military problems, and the political complications of the English civil war had decided him that the time for retirement had come.

The threat of resignation, however, temporarily turned complaints of his lack of success into expressions of appreciation. Even now he was seen as a military leader whose lack of involvement in political intrigue made him invaluable as a commander, and to dispense with the lieutenant of the great Gustavus would be bad for morale. Guarantees of his supremacy as lord general came from Scotland, the promise of a jewel worth £500 sterling and thanks for services rendered from London. Mollified, Leven agreed to continue in command, and he was besieging Newark-on-Trent in May 1645 when the defeated Charles I fled to the Scots army rather than fall into the hands of his English enemies. Under Leven's supervision Charles remained a prisoner in Newcastle until January 1647, when the Scots, despairing of reaching a peace agreement with him, handed him over to the English and withdrew their army to Scotland.

Final years Even now Leven retained office as lord general, and the Scottish parliament promised him a jewel worth 10,000 merks (about £550 sterling) and an annual salary of the same amount. When, in 1648, the engagers (an alliance of moderate covenanters and royalists) raised an army to invade England, consideration was given to retaining him in command, in spite of his infirmity and his dislike of the engagement, but in the end 'with threats and promises they moved old Lesley to lay downe his place' (*Letters … Baillie*, 3.45) on 11 May. Leven's own account was that he had refused the command in spite of 'all importunities and profferred incouragements' (Fraser, 1.432). None the less, it was decreed that, though he would not lead the army in England, he would become lord general of any additional forces that needed to be raised in Scotland.

After the engagers were defeated in England by Cromwell, however, the forces that mustered in Scotland under Leven's nominal command, far from supporting the engagers, replaced the collapsing regime with the 'kirk party' rule of the stricter covenanters. Leven presided at a banquet in Edinburgh Castle for Oliver Cromwell, who had come north to ensure that a settlement was made satisfactory to him, while the kirk party rewarded Leven on 4 January 1649 by restoring his full status as lord general.

By mid-1650, however, Scotland had swung round to support for Charles II, who had been brought to Scotland from exile in the Netherlands, and English invasion threatened. In parliament on 22 June Leven announced that he was laying down office 'for his age and other reasons', but parliament again insisted that he remain in office 'for his happey carriage in his former conducte of ther armies', pointing out that he had a very able deputy in Lieutenant-General David Leslie, and promising that no more would be asked of him than 'his grate age might comport with' (J. Balfour, *Historical Works*, 4 vols., 1824,

4.54–5). Thus Leven's responsibility for the initially effective defence against Cromwell's invasion, and for the disastrous defeat at Dunbar on 3 September (at which he was present), was more nominal than real, though he accepted liability for the defeat. Parliament exonerated him, yet again (in March 1651) refusing his attempts to resign. When Charles II undertook his despairing invasion of England, Leven remained behind with the committee of estates to try to organize defence, though the report that he refused to raise men 'unlesse he were Commander-in-Cheife' (C. H. Firth, ed., *Scotland and the Commonwealth*, 1895, 6) indicates that his touchiness about his rights as general remained. He was with the remnants of the committee at Alyth in Forfarshire when it was captured by the English on 28 August, and was sent to the Tower of London. Respect for his achievements, aided by the efforts of an English son-in-law, soon bought him freedom. He was allowed to stay with Ralph Delavall of Seaton Delavall in Northumberland, and was able to visit London in 1654 in order to try to regain possession of his Scottish estates, and (doubtless helped by a letter from Queen Kristina to Cromwell pleading for him) he was then allowed to return to Scotland, reaching his home at Balgonie on 25 May. His wife had died in June 1651 on the estate that he had bought at Inchmartine (and vaingloriously renamed Inchleslie) in 1650, but she had been buried at Markinch, the parish in which Balgonie lay, and Leven spent most of his remaining years there. However, he did not entirely give up involvement in military affairs. In 1655, after royalist risings in the highlands had been defeated, the English were eager to dispose of former rebels by having them enlist for foreign service. Leven was reported to have contracted to supply men for Sweden, earning a stinging letter of rebuke from the again exiled Charles II: 'I looke upon all designes of that kind as most prejudiciall to my service, and mischievious to the kingdome' (C. H. Firth, ed., *Scotland and the Protectorate*, 1899, 297). But in February 1656 Lord Cranstoun, another of Leven's sons-in-law, was licensed to levy 1000 men for Sweden. The regiment was sent to Poland, but in 1657 many of its men deserted, some taking service with Charles II. Before Lord Cranstoun sailed, Leven had assigned him his right to his Swedish pension: if Cranstoun could get his arrears paid, the money was to be divided equally between the two men. Cranstoun later corresponded with Leven from Sweden about raising another 2000 men for Swedish service, but nothing came of this. Leven survived the restoration of monarchy, and took his seat in parliament in January 1661—and lost his coveted precedency over the earl of Callendar. But before his covenanting career brought any further indignities on him, he died at Balgonie on 4 April 1661, and was buried five days later at Markinch.

The Scottish Lion of the North Leven's biographer C. S. Terry found him an exasperating subject. 'He is consistently placid, almost depressingly prosaic', 'He has left little, save deeds, to unlock the recesses of his character. In his despatches he is above everything precise, curt, prosaic. He spends few words on principles or motives' (Terry, viii, 3). Partly no doubt this is because illiteracy or semi-literacy meant that he left no truly personal letters, but he does seem to have been a man who rose to eminence through solidity rather than brilliance. He was trustworthy, assiduous, a good organizer, excellent at working with others. Association with Gustavus Adolphus brought him a glamour that his own character could not have earned. When he returned to Scotland in 1638, he carried the mantle of the Lion of the North to shield their cause.

Leven's greatest achievements came in 1639–40. In 1639 he inspired confidence in the Scots, that in the awesome step of defying their king they not only had God on their side but a real chance of military success. The following year defence gave way to a sharp, decisive offensive that ended the war in a few days, with little bloodshed, and little opportunity for English sympathy for Scottish grievances to turn into patriotic reaction against invasion. Even allowing for the incompetence of the forces he faced, the achievement of 1640 is impressive.

In England in 1644–7 Leven's achievements were again notable. Scottish intervention was, arguably, the turning-point of the war. But Leven's reputation had outrun what was possible in practical terms, and his dilemma over whether his primary task was to protect Scotland or to serve the English parliament led at times to indecision and over-caution. Fettered by such complications he proved competent rather than inspiring. For his subsequent reputation it would probably have been better if he had succeeded in retiring in 1645, while memories of Marston Moor were still strong, rather than let himself become the aged figurehead who presided over military disaster in 1650–51.

Leven made his career, and a fortune, as a professional soldier. James Turner (perhaps with a touch of jealousy) accused him of avarice, and undoubtedly he fought for wealth as well as glory and causes he believed in. He enjoyed his eminence and his rank as an earl. A surprising touch of whimsy shows in his choice of a nominal payment for his lands to his feudal superior the king—a feather (referring to helmet plumes) 'to denote his calling as a soldier' (*Historical Notices*, 1.167) to be paid annually. His desire to have his deeds remembered was indicated in his will (1656), which specified that his family was to keep a jewel that Gustavus Adolphus had given as a perpetual 'memoriall of the King of Swedines respectes to me' (Fraser, 3.175). This was evidently a gold medal Gustavus had had struck after the relief of Stralsund, presenting a copy to Leven, and it is still in the possession of his descendants. The early glories of the covenanting wars might have been sullied by subsequent disasters, but the glory of having fought under the greatest protestant military hero of the age remained untarnished. DAVID STEVENSON

Sources *DNB* • *Scots peerage* • GEC, *Peerage* • *APS* • C. S. Terry, *The life and campaigns of Alexander Leslie, first earl of Leven* (1899) • W. Fraser, ed., *The Melvilles, earls of Melville, and the Leslies, earls of Leven*, 3 vols. (1890) • *The letters and journals of Robert Baillie*, ed. D. Laing, 3 vols., Bannatyne Club, 73 (1841–2) • T. A. Fischer, *The Scots in Germany* (1902) • T. A. Fischer [E. L. Fischer], *The Scots in Sweden* (1907) • M. Roberts, *Gustavus Adolphus*, 2 vols. (1953–8) • S. R. Gardiner, *History of England from the accession of James I to the outbreak of the civil war*,

10 vols. (1883–4) • J. Turner, *Memoirs of his own life and times, 1632–1670*, ed. T. Thomson, Bannatyne Club, 28 (1829) • W. Macfarlane, *Genealogical collections concerning families in Scotland*, ed. J. T. Clark, 2 vols., Scottish History Society, 33–4 (1900) • E. M. Furgol, *A regimental history of the covenanting armies, 1639–1651* (1990) • Colonel Leslie [C. J. Leslie], *Historical records of the family of Leslie, from 1067 to 1868–9*, 3 vols. (1869) • Breadalbane muniments, NA Scot., GD 112 • Hamilton muniments, NA Scot., GD 406 • Leven and Melville muniments, NA Scot., GD 26 • J. Spalding, *Memorialls of the trubles in Scotland and in England, AD 1624 – AD 1645*, ed. J. Stuart, 2 vols., Spalding Club, [21, 23] (1850–51) • S. Murdoch and A. Grosjean, 'Scotland, Scandinavia and Northern Europe, 1580–1707', www.abdn.ac.uk/ssne/ • S. Murdoch, 'The house of Stuart and the Scottish professional soldier, 1618–1640: a conflict of nationalities and identities', *War: identities in conflict, 1300–2000*, ed. B. Taithie and T. Thornton (1998) • A. Grosjean, 'General Alexander Leslie, the Scottish covenanters and the Rikstrad debates, 1638–1640', *Shaping identities: ships, guns and bibles in the North Sea and the Baltic states*, ed. A. Macinnes, T. Riis, and F. Pederson (2000), 115–38 • *Historical notices of Scotish affairs, selected from the manuscripts of Sir John Lauder of Fountainhall*, ed. D. Laing, 2 vols., Bannatyne Club, 87 (1848) • A. Grosjean, 'Scotland: Sweden's closest ally?', *Scotland and the Thirty Years' War, 1618–1648*, ed. S. Murdoch (2001), 143–69

Archives NA Scot., corresp. and papers • NA Scot., muniments | NA Scot., letters to the Campbells of Glenorchy

Likenesses attrib. G. Jamesone, portrait, Scot. NPG • M. Vandergucht, line engraving, BM, NPG; repro. in E. Ward, *The history of the grand rebellion … digested into verse*, 3 vols. (1713) • line engraving, BM • line print, BM; repro. in J. Ricraft, *A survey of England's champions* (1647) • oils, Scot. NPG • oils, priv. coll.; repro. in Terry, *Life and campaigns*

Leslie, Alexander (*fl.* **1796–1798**), radical bookseller and publisher, was born in Jedburgh, moving to Edinburgh some time before 1796. Before becoming Bookseller to the Rabble, as he liked to describe himself, he was apprenticed in Edinburgh, possibly to one Andrew Leslie, shoemaker. Leslie was to claim in 1796 that he had 'uniformly adhered to … the glorious cause' and that it was 'persecution' which had forced him to give up his apprenticeship (BL, Add. MS 27815, Francis Place MSS, fols. 74–5), a story which, given the prevalence of such acts of persecution of radicals in the 1790s, has a strong air of credibility about it. On 29 December 1797, having set up as a 'patriotic bookseller' in Nicolson Street, Edinburgh, he married Janet Young, daughter of Patrick Gow, a Glasgow weaver.

An extant catalogue of Leslie's, taken from his shop in early 1798, shows that he stocked and distributed a wide range of radical pamphlets, songbooks, and poems. These included Jacobin classics such as Joel Barlow's *Advice to the Privileged Orders in the Several States of Europe*; Thomas Paine's major political works of the 1790s, including both parts of *The Rights of Man*; and several translations of major works of the European Enlightenment, such as Voltaire's *Dictionnaire philosophique* and Beccaria's *Dei delitti e delle pene* (*On Crimes and Punishments*). He also stocked a broad array of more populist radical works, many of which were published by the London radical bookseller Daniel Isaac Eaton. These included, for example, Eaton's famous serial publication *Politics for the People* and James Parkinson's *Pearls Cast before Swine, by Edmund Burke, Scraped together by Old Hubert* (1793) and *Revolutions without Bloodshed, or, Reformation Preferable to Revolt* (1794).

Leslie played a crucial role in the dissemination of radical propaganda and tracts in Scotland between 1796 and 1798, and outside Scotland. He dealt closely with a number of important radical printers and booksellers from London, notably Eaton, but also John Smith, J. S. Jordan, John Bone, and Thomas Evans, all members of the London Corresponding Society (LCS). He also appears to have had links with Thomas Spence, the bookseller and radical land reformer. At several times during this period, he dispatched large orders of pamphlets to Eaton, Smith, Jordan, Bone, and Evans, as well as to John Ashley, at this stage secretary of the LCS. In 1796 he had written to the society offering his services as a confidential correspondent, claiming to have contacts in the west, north-east of Scotland, and in the borders. He also spoke of the eagerness for radical publications in Scotland at that time. Extracts from his daybook for 1796–7 indicate that he did business with a network of radical booksellers and printers which included Edinburgh, Leith, Glasgow, Paisley, Kelso, Hamilton, Hawick, Jedburgh, Dunbar, and Newcastle, south of the border. His customers also included leading radicals from several parts of Scotland, for example, James Craigendallie and Robert Sands from Perth.

As well as selling and distributing radical works printed and published in London, Leslie was joint publisher of several pamphlets with London's radical printing fraternity, further emphasizing the closeness of the connections between them. For example, John Martin's *A letter to the Hon Thomas Erskine, with a postscript to the Right Hon Lord Kenyon, upon their conduct at the trial of Thomas Williams* (1797) was published with John Smith, John Bone and Thomas Evans, and T. G. Ballard. He also published several pamphlets on his own account, including Edinburgh editions of Paine's *Agrarian Justice* and *A Letter to George Washington*, a translation of Helvétius's *Catechism*, as well as a number of radical poems.

The exact nature of Leslie's politics is hidden from full view. Radicals in these years were acutely conscious of the prudence of secrecy, given official and judicial hostility; the language they used in correspondence was deliberately elliptical. Nevertheless, as a republican and deist, Leslie was on the extremist fringe of Scottish radical opinion in this period. In one letter to a fellow radical, a weaver from Kilsyth, he referred to 'these cursed Brigands or Ruffians, for they are a race of Monsters that ought to be exterminate the Earth, Kings & Priests have in all ages been a Curse to Mankind in Making Ruinous & Bloody War' (NA Scot., JC 26/293). It seems highly likely that Leslie was also a member of the United Scotsmen, a shadowy body linked to a wider insurrectionary conspiracy embracing Ireland and England. In August 1797 a fellow radical wrote to him from Linlithgow: 'I think the Soceity [*sic*] in London is doing well. I hope they will give Arastockrats a Sweet very Soone' (ibid.). He was a frequent visitor to Glasgow—on one trip he had got married—visiting radical groups in various places *en route*. Among the pamphlets seized from his shop were two in the name of the British Union Society, a breakaway group of impatient extremists from the LCS, formed in August 1797. In 1796 he sent an order of books to Colonel Despard, who was to lead an abortive and failed insurrectionary conspiracy in 1801–2.

Given Leslie's prominence in Scottish radical circles, and the nature of the literature he was circulating, it is unsurprising, therefore, that he was apprehended in November 1797 as part of a wider executive crackdown against radicals in the aftermath of the militia riots and against a background of deteriorating political and military conditions in Ireland. He was charged with distributing seditious and blasphemous writings, namely Paine's *Rights of Man* and the *Age of Reason*. Admitted to bail of 600 merks (£33 6*s*. 8*d*.) on 2 April 1798, he was called to appear at the high court on three occasions. On the final call, on 28 May, when Leslie failed again to appear, Lord Eskgrove handed down a sentence of fugitation and outlawry against him. He forfeited his bond of caution, and all his moveable goods were escheated to the crown.

Leslie's importance to the history of Scottish radicalism in the 1790s is considerable. His brief career as a bookseller illuminates not only networks of radical communication in Britain in the years that followed the first major wave of government repression, but also some of the ideological influences shaping Scottish radical opinion in a period when, following the suppression of the British convention, it fades from clear view. Bob Harris

Sources justiciary MSS, NA Scot., JC 26/293 · *ESTC* · BL, Francis Place MSS, Add. MS 27815 · H. W. Meikle, *Scotland and the French Revolution* (1912) · F. J. Grant, ed., *Register of marriages of the city of Edinburgh, 1751–1800*, Scottish RS, 53 (1922)

Archives BL, Place MSS, Add. MS 27815 · NA Scot., records of high court of justiciary

Leslie, Andrew, fifth earl of Rothes (*c*.**1530–1611**), magnate, was the eldest legitimate son of George *Leslie, fourth earl of Rothes (*d*. 1558), and his wife, Agnes (*d*. 1543), daughter of Sir John Somerville of Cambusnethan, Lanarkshire. Andrew married three times: first, in 1548, he married Grizel (*d*. 1573), daughter of Sir James *Hamilton of Finnart, with whom he had six children including James, master of Rothes, who predeceased him; in 1573 he married Jean (*d*. 1591), daughter of Patrick *Ruthven, third Lord Ruthven, with whom he had two children; and in 1592 he married Janet, daughter of David Durie of that ilk, with whom he had four. He succeeded to the earldom on the death of his father in 1558. However, his claim was hotly disputed by his illegitimate half-brothers Norman and William, and the dispute was resolved only in 1566, when Queen Mary reaffirmed Andrew Leslie's title on condition that he granted lands in the Carse of Gowrie to William. Norman *Leslie had been a leader in the conspiracy to murder Cardinal David Beaton in 1546, and the fourth earl had at times been assured to England, making it less than surprising that the fifth earl should have become an active supporter of religious reform. In 1559 Rothes joined the lords of the congregation, and took part in their manoeuvres against the regent, Mary of Guise, and her French allies in Perthshire and Fife. In 1560 he was one of the signatories of the treaty of Berwick which guaranteed the English assistance that ensured success for him and his fellow reformers. He also attended the assemblies which ended papal authority in Scotland and which replaced it with a new confession and the first Book of Discipline.

Appointed a privy councillor in 1561, Rothes was largely inconspicuous during the early part of Mary's reign, at least until she married Darnley on 29 July 1565. Disapproval of that union on religious grounds and ties of kinship through marriage to the Hamiltons were probably the main considerations which then stirred him into action, so that in August 1565 he joined Moray and others in the short rebellion known as the chaseabout raid. In March 1566, when he was due to stand trial for his part in the rising, Rothes was one of those who struck a deal with Darnley, undertaking to support the latter's claim to the crown matrimonial in return for the charges against him being dropped. After the murder of Riccio on 9 March it was the queen herself who granted remissions to Rothes and the others, as she skilfully created divisions among her opponents. Rothes had certainly been implicated in the murder, but he now detached himself from Moray and the other ringleaders, and by 1568, like a number of noblemen and lairds from Fife with good protestant credentials, he had pledged his support to Mary despite her Catholicism.

This move may well have been connected with the feud in which Rothes was then engaged with Patrick, Lord Lindsay, one of the queen's bitterest opponents. Lindsay strongly disputed Rothes's claim to inherit his father's position as sheriff of Fife, and this contentious issue remained a source of friction until Lindsay finally gave up the struggle in 1575. Whatever his motives, Rothes fought on the queen's side at Langside and was active on her behalf thereafter, notably in his attempts to seek French assistance for the beleaguered garrison in Edinburgh Castle. In March 1570 the earl of Sussex reported that Rothes had come back from France with promises of aid. Rothes maintained his allegiance to Mary until August 1571, when like many of her supporters he recognized the futility of persisting in the struggle against the 'king's men'.

The early stages of Morton's regency saw Rothes being called upon to use his negotiating skills, when in April 1573 he was asked to mediate between the government and the castilians besieged in Edinburgh Castle. But Kirkcaldy of Grange, their leader, replied by presenting a series of unrealistic demands which would have to be met before the garrison would surrender. There were contemporary rumours that Rothes had encouraged Grange to hold out in the hope that help would materialize from France, possibly arising from the fact that his old enemy Lord Lindsay was now provost of Edinburgh, as well as from his own reported travels abroad. However, a statement by the privy council in April 1573 strongly denied this allegation.

For most of the remaining years of Morton's regency Rothes was inconspicuous, though in August 1574 he served as a member of a judicial expedition which visited north-east Scotland. In October 1575 he was on sufficiently good terms with the regent to entertain him at Ballanbreich, his castle in Fife, during one of Morton's journeys between his two main residences of Dalkeith and Aberdour. Rothes did not support Morton during the crisis of March 1578, being appointed to replace Lord Glamis as one of the commissioners to whom the regent handed over the custody of Edinburgh Castle, but neither was he particularly active against him. But his services were obviously valued, for in July he became a member of the privy council formed after Morton's recovery of power. However, apart from sitting on the jury at his trial in June 1581, Rothes made no other contribution of note to the second phase of Morton's administration and indeed he was rarely prominent in national affairs thereafter. Notwithstanding, he was one of the noblemen appointed by James VI to remain with him at St Andrews after he escaped from the Ruthven raiders in June 1583, and in the following year he was present with the king and the earl of Arran when they were besieged in Stirling Castle by Angus and the Hamiltons. His brief spell as lieutenant and justiciar of the south-eastern counties in 1584 was presumably a reward for his loyalty to Arran's administration. In 1588 he was one of the officials appointed to enforce anti-Catholic legislation, and in 1593 he was a member of the commission which tried the pro-Spanish 'northern earls'.

Rothes can hardly be regarded as a key figure under either Mary or James. Relatively prominent in his earlier years, he later sank into near anonymity, possibly because he was preoccupied with family matters and the administration of his extensive earldom. As early as 1577 it was said of him that he was 'given to quietness, and comes seldom to Court. He was once thought to be of great enterprize, but now deals little' (*CSP Scot.*, 1574–81, 254). He died in Fife in 1611 and was succeeded by his grandson John *Leslie, sixth earl of Rothes. G. R. HEWITT

Sources *CSP Scot.*, 1569–83 • *Scots peerage*, 7.292–7 • *Reg. PCS*, 1st ser., vols. 2–4 • D. Calderwood, *The history of the Kirk of Scotland*, ed. T. Thomson and D. Laing, 8 vols., Wodrow Society, 7 (1842–9), vol. 3 • *CSP for.*, 1558–89 • *John Knox's History of the Reformation in Scotland*, ed. W. C. Dickinson, 2 vols. (1949) • Lord Herries [John Maxwell], *Historical memoirs of the reign of Mary queen of Scots*, ed. R. Pitcairn, Abbotsford Club, 6 (1836) • D. Moysie, *Memoirs of the affairs of Scotland, 1577–1603*, ed. J. Dennistoun, Bannatyne Club, 39 (1830) • *DNB* • G. Donaldson, *Scotland: James V–James VII* (1965) • G. Hewitt, *Scotland under Morton* (1982) • GEC, *Peerage*, new edn, 11.195–7 • G. Donaldson, *All the queen's men* (1983)

Leslie, Andrew (1818–1894), shipbuilder, was born on 1 September 1818 at Garth, Dunrossness, in the Shetland Islands, the only son and younger of the two children of Andrew Leslie (*d.* 1829), a crofter, and his wife, Christina, *née* Allison. When he was six weeks old his parents were evicted, and his father moved the family to Aberdeen, working as a cartman and on coastal ships out of Aberdeen. After his father's death the family moved back to the Shetland Islands. At the age of thirteen Leslie began work as a rivet catcher before starting an apprenticeship as a boilermaker at the iron works of John Vernon & Co. in Aberdeen. He also studied technical drawing at evening classes with Charles Mitchell, who later established an iron shipyard on the Tyne. He was promoted to foreman, but left in the early 1840s to set up his own business in Aberdeen as a boilermaker and blacksmith.

In 1853 Leslie moved to Tyneside, leased 9 acres at Hebburn in open country east of Hebburn Quay on the south bank of the Tyne, and founded an iron shipyard and boiler works. After a brief partnership with John Coutts, a Scot who at Walker in 1840 had established the Tyne's first iron shipyard, which had since failed, Leslie became sole owner of the Hebburn yard. Because of the shortage of local labour, he recruited most of his skilled craftsmen from Aberdeen, to the extent that Hebburn became known as 'little Aberdeen'. He launched his first ship, the steamship *Clarendon*, in 1854, but progress was slow after this, at a time when most ships were still being built in wood, and the yard had an annual average output of 2000 tons during the first decade. From the beginning many of Leslie's ships were for overseas customers: twelve of his first twenty ships were for Russian owners, beginning with the 1000 ton *Mogoustschi* for the Russian Steam Navigation and Trading Company for its new service from London to Odessa. He built more than sixty ships in all for Russian companies, and his first steel-framed vessel, the *Grand Duchess Olga*, launched in 1880, was built for the Russian S. E. Navigation Company. His principal English customer was Holts, the Liverpool shipping line, from 1861.

By 1863 Leslie had built fifty-three ships, and his business was valued at £90,000. Needing more capital for the business, he entered into negotiations with Thomas Coote, a local businessman, who in 1863 bought a partnership for his son, Arthur, who had served his apprenticeship at Denny & Co., the Dumbarton shipyard. Arthur Coote later married Leslie's adopted daughter. The company became known for its paddle steamers, beginning with the *Enterprise* in 1864. It built many cross-channel paddle steamers, including the twin-hulled *Calais-Douvres*, launched in 1877. Between 1863 and 1875 output grew to more than 10,000 tons a year, and in the period 1876 to 1885, despite the depression of the mid-1880s, average output was 16,000 tons, with a peak in 1881 of 23,500 tons. By 1885, 260 ships had been built at the Hebburn yard, and there was employment for more than 2000 men. Although Leslie had no sympathy for the trade union movement, giving evidence to the royal commission on trade unions (1867–9), he managed to retain the loyalty of his workmen, many of whom stayed with the firm all their lives.

From 1860 there was increasingly close co-operation between Andrew Leslie & Co. and the marine engineering firm R. and W. Hawthorn, with Hawthorns supplying thirty-one sets of machinery for ships built in Leslie's yard between 1860 and 1870. Following Leslie's retirement in 1885 the two firms amalgamated to become R. and W. Hawthorn, Leslie & Co. Ltd.

From 1859 until 1880 Leslie lived in Wallsend House, Wallsend, across the river from the yard, and played an important part in local affairs. He was a member of the first Wallsend school board, and its first vice-chairman, and he was one of those who worked to establish a local board of health, which was set up in 1867: he was elected to the board in 1869 and served until 1878. He served as a

Tyne improvement commissioner for thirteen years, and was a JP for Northumberland and Durham. He also did much to develop Hebburn. He built more than four hundred houses for his workmen, with gas lighting supplied from the gas-producing plant in his shipyard. He was the chairman of the meeting that established the Hebburn Co-operative Society in 1866, and contributed to the cost of building a school and a workmen's institute. Leslie was a presbyterian and donated £900 in 1873 for the building of St Andrew's Presbyterian Church in Hebburn, close to the shipyard, for his Scottish workmen and their families. He was a member of the Institution of Mechanical Engineers from 1858, and of the Institution of Naval Architects from 1882.

Leslie was married to Margaret, *née* Jordan (*c.*1829–*c.*1888); they had one adopted daughter. Leslie died on 27 January 1894 at his home, Coxlodge Hall, Gosforth, Newcastle upon Tyne, and was buried on 1 February at Rosebank cemetery, Edinburgh. ANNE PIMLOTT BAKER

Sources J. F. Clarke, *Power on land and sea: … a history of R. & W. Hawthorn Leslie & Co. Ltd* (1979) • J. F. Clarke, *Building ships on the north east coast*, 1: *c.1640–1914* (1997) • D. Dougan, *The history of north east shipbuilding* (1968) • J. F. Clarke, 'Leslie, Andrew', *DBB* • *The Times* (31 Jan 1894) • *Newcastle Daily Chronicle* (29 Jan 1894) • *Newcastle Daily Leader* (29 Jan 1894) • *Jarrow Express* (2 Feb 1894) • *Shields Gazette* (29 Jan 1894) • *Newcastle Weekly Chronicle* (2 Feb 1894) • census returns, 1881 • W. Richardson, *History of the parish of Wallsend and Willington* (1923) • memorial tablet, St Andrew's Church, Hebburn, co. Durham

Archives Durham RO, Leslie company records

Likenesses photograph, repro. in Clarke, 'Leslie, Andrew'

Wealth at death £161,275: Clarke, 'Leslie, Andrew'

Leslie, Sir Bradford (1831–1926), civil engineer and author, was born on 18 August 1831 in London, the second son and second of the three children of Charles Robert *Leslie (1794–1859), painter and Royal Academician, and his wife, Harriet Stone (1799–1879). After receiving a classical education at Mercers' School, London, Leslie, at the age of sixteen, was apprenticed for five years to Isambard Kingdom Brunel, who waived his usual fee of £1000 in return for one or two paintings by Charles Leslie. Bradford Leslie was an apt pupil and rapidly became a good engineer—a process facilitated, he believed, by his previous drudgery at Greek and Latin. In 1851 while still apprenticed to Brunel, Leslie was sent as an assistant engineer to the construction of the bridge over the Wye at Chepstow. Work on further Brunel projects followed: the Dock branch of the Gloucester and Dean Forest Railway; resident engineer at the famous bridge over the Tamar at Saltash where he had charge of the sinking—using compressed air—of the large caisson for the central pier; construction for the Victoria Railways in Australia including the Stoney Creek and Saltwater River bridges; superintendence of the heavy forgings for Brunel's *Great Eastern* steamship, and assistance at its launch in January 1858. Leslie married, on 21 January 1855, Mary Jane Eliza (*d.* 1886), daughter of William Honey, a civil engineer of Plymouth; they had four daughters and a son.

In 1858 Leslie began his long association with India. He

Sir Bradford Leslie (1831–1926), by George Dunlop Leslie, 1888

became a resident engineer of the Eastern Bengal Railway (EBR), to which Brunel was the consulting engineer, in charge of building certain large bridges and viaducts, notably those over the Kumar and Ichamati Rivers where he used compressed air caissons to sink the wells for the piers. He sometimes worked in the caissons, demonstrating the willingness to participate in the dangers of the work he was supervising that he exhibited throughout his professional life.

Leslie returned to Britain in 1862 and was appointed principal engineer for the construction of the Ogwr Valley Railway in south Wales and, that task completed, re-entered the service of the EBR in October 1865. As the EBR's chief resident engineer (1865–71) for the construction of the Goalundo extension in the northern Gangetic delta, Leslie was responsible for the bridge across the formidable Gorai River, the largest deltaic branch of the Ganges. This difficult piece of engineering was facilitated by Leslie's invention of an ingenious boring device to sink caissons nearly one hundred feet into the shifting river bed to found securely the piers on which the bridge rested. The Goalundo extension opened in January 1871 and Leslie returned to England. In April 1872 he was chosen from a list of ten applicants, among whom were some well-known engineers, to be the consulting engineer (1872–4) for the Oudh and Rohilkhund Railway (O&RR). October 1872 saw Leslie back in India to examine the operations of the O&RR and, on special commission, to report on measures to be taken to protect the large bridges on the Delhi line of the Sind, Punjab, and Delhi

Railway in the aftermath of their partial failures in the previous high water season.

Leslie also became involved in the construction of a floating road and pedestrian bridge across the Hooghly between Calcutta and Howrah where the river was deep, rapid, subject to large tidal fluctuations, exposed to cyclones, and carried considerable ocean and river traffic. Leslie, out of personal interest, had considered the problems presented by such a crossing while he was the EBR's chief resident engineer and had decided that a floating bridge was the best solution, a design and partial model for which he prepared and which he showed to the viceroy of India, Lord Mayo, when the latter opened the Gorai Bridge in early 1871. Thus, when the decision to bridge the Hooghly was made, Lord Mayo favoured a floating structure despite the objections of many experts. A floating bridge, 1530 feet long and 60 feet wide, was begun in January 1873 and completed in October 1874. Coincidently, completion of the construction of the bridge came under the supervision of Leslie who became municipal engineer of Calcutta in 1874. During Leslie's short stint as municipal engineer (1874–6) he completed water supply and drainage works begun by his predecessor. However, in July 1876 he returned to railway work as the agent (1876–87) of the large East Indian Railway (EIR) and also, 1876–82, the chief engineer. As agent he had administrative charge of a railway system that extended over 1518 miles by 1887.

While agent, Leslie introduced a number of innovations, notably the replacement of wooden wagons by iron ones of larger capacity, cast-iron sleepers, and the employment of Indians as drivers of goods trains. He also became involved in the plans to bring the EIR directly into Calcutta via a bridge crossing the Hooghly at Naihati. Although his design for the bridge was not accepted he did supervise its construction, an engineering task he retained after pressure of work led him to relinquish the position of chief engineer in 1882. This, the Jubilee Bridge, was begun in 1882 and opened in 1887; it was a substantial structure for which Leslie was created KCIE on 15 February 1887. During his time as the EIR's agent Leslie also became a fellow of the University of Calcutta and a member of its governing senate. He subsequently received an LLD from the same university.

Leslie returned to England in April 1887, his health undermined by repeated attacks of malaria and the emotional toll of seeing his wife, three of his four daughters, and his son-in-law die within the space of three years. On the way home with his two orphan granddaughters their ship was wrecked off Corsica. While carrying the younger grandchild to safety Leslie slipped and badly injured a knee, leaving him with a noticeable limp for the rest of his life, notwithstanding which, and a thigh broken in his eighty-fourth year when he was knocked down in London by a bicycle, he remained remarkably healthy, vigorous, and sociable until close to his death.

Soon after his return to England Leslie began to practise as a consulting engineer. He remained active professionally until 1925. In 1889 he acted as a British juror at the Paris Exhibition and was made an *Officier de l'instruction publique* by the French government. He became chairman and engineering adviser to the Southern Punjab Railway in 1895 and presided over the Company's board meetings until October 1925. He briefly visited India in 1899 to promote his ideas for a larger floating bridge across the Hooghly to replace the one completed in 1874. However, his ideas were not then nor later received with favour and when, in 1921, a fixed, cantilever design for a new bridge was accepted he criticized it vigorously.

Leslie became a full member of the Institution of Civil Engineers in 1872 and served on its council from 1889 to 1895. To the institution he thrice made detailed presentations on the bridges in India with which he had been most closely connected. It is upon those bridges—the Gorai, the Hooghly floating bridge, and the Hooghly Jubilee Bridge—that Leslie's place among the important civil engineers of the later nineteenth century particularly rests. For his presentations and the accomplishment behind them the institution honoured him with a Telford medal and premium (1872), a Watt medal and a Telford premium (1878), and a Stephenson medal and a third Telford premium (1888). Leslie wrote several articles on engineering subjects including a pamphlet (1880) proposing a railway tunnel across the English Channel: a buoyant steel cylinder 16 feet in diameter anchored 40 feet beneath low tide levels through which trains would speed in a thirty-minute passage. He remained an active writer, as well as sending letters to *The Times* on a variety of subjects, until his final year. He died at his home, 171 Maida Vale, London, on 21 March 1926 and was buried at Falmouth three days later. He was survived by one daughter and a son, Lieutenant-Colonel Sir Bradford Leslie (1867–1936). IAN J. KERR

Sources *The Times* (22–4 March 1926) • *PICE*, 224 (1926–7), 377–9 • *The Engineer* (26 March 1926) • B. Leslie, 'Account of the bridge over the Gorai River, on the Goalundo extension of the Eastern Bengal Railway', *PICE*, 34 (1871–2), 1–23 • B. Leslie, 'The Hooghly floating bridge', *PICE*, 53 (1877–8), 2–14 • B. Leslie, 'The erection of the "Jubilee" Bridge carrying the East Indian Railway across the River Hooghly at Hooghly', *PICE*, 92 (1887–8), 73–96 • B. Leslie, *Channel railway* (1880) • B. Leslie, *A new chapter in the history of permanent way* (1924) • G. Huddleston, *History of the East Indian railway* (1906) • agreements of staff, East Bengal railway, 1862–9, BL OIOC, L/AG/46/10/35 • minutes of board of directors of the Oude and Rohilkhund railway, 10 April 1872, BL OIOC, L/AG/46/16 • *DNB* • *Calcutta University Calendar, 1887* (1886) • m. cert. • d. cert.

Archives BL OIOC

Likenesses G. D. Leslie, portrait, 1888, priv. coll. [*see illus.*] • photograph (in later years), repro. in *The Engineer*

Wealth at death £19,889 9*s*. 4*d*.: probate, 27 April 1926, *CGPLA Eng. & Wales*

Leslie, Charles (1650–1722), nonjuring Church of Ireland clergyman, was born in Ireland, probably in Dublin, on 17 July 1650, the sixth son of John *Leslie (1571–1671), bishop successively of Orkney (1628–33), Raphoe (1633–61), and Clogher in Ireland (1661–71), and Katherine Cunningham (1620–1694), daughter of Alexander Cunningham, dean of Raphoe. He married Jane Griffith, the daughter of the dean of Ross, Richard Griffith, soon after his ordination in

Charles Leslie (1650–1722), attrib. George White

1681. They had two sons, Robert (*d.* 1744) and Henry, and a daughter (sources do not provide her name).

Early years and education Named for the martyred king, Charles I, Leslie began his education at age ten at Enniskillen grammar school in co. Fermanagh. He was then admitted as a commoner to Trinity College, Dublin, on 4 August 1664, graduating BA and, in 1673, MA. On the death of his father in 1671 he went to London to study ecclesiastical and civil law at the Temple. He practised law until 1680, when he chose to pursue a career in the church, being ordained deacon in 1680 and to the priesthood in 1681. Returning to his family's estate at Glaslough, Ireland, he served his brother John, the dean of Dromore, as assistant curate at Donagh in co. Monaghan. As most of his parish was Roman Catholic or Presbyterian he had few duties, leaving him time for study and for service as justice of the peace for Monaghan. Leslie was appointed chancellor of the cathedral of Connor on 13 July 1686 through the influence of Henry Hyde, second earl of Clarendon, who called Leslie a 'man of good parts, admirable learning, an excellent preacher, and of an incomparable duty' (Singer, 1.405).

Leslie became well known for his zealous opposition to Roman Catholicism. Though a strong royalist, he nevertheless strongly opposed James II's attempts to place Roman Catholics in political and judicial offices in Ireland, including the candidate for high sheriff of Monaghan in 1687. He opposed James's claim to have the dispensing power to suspend the Test Act, arguing that the appointment of Catholics was illegal under English law. He also debated with Roman Catholic representatives of the titular bishop of Clogher, the Catholic Patrick Tyrell, at Monaghan and then at Tynan in co. Armagh. The monarch's activist Catholicism severely tested Leslie's allegiance to the Stuarts. Though he denied the incident, whig opponents such as Gilbert Burnet and William King accused him of fomenting a riot in Ireland by calling for James's removal from the throne. According to Burnet, Leslie's speech so stirred up the crowd that several people died in the riot, yet after the revolution of 1688 Leslie switched sides and 'became the violentest Jacobite in the nation'. The source for the charge was King, the Archbishop of Dublin, with whom Leslie exchanged a series of pamphlets concerning James's alleged persecution of protestants in Ireland (*Burnet's History*, 6.34). Leslie's involvement in these events remains uncertain and they stand at odds with his later allegiance, at great cost to himself, to the Stuarts.

Jacobite and nonjuror years Leslie's fortunes changed with the revolution of 1688. He was then residing on the Isle of Wight for health reasons, but soon afterwards the Leslies moved to London, where his connections with the Hyde family, especially the second earl, led to his appointment as chaplain to the Hyde household at Cornbury, Oxfordshire. In the autumn of 1689 he preached at the parish church of Charlbury and at the nonjuror oratory at Ely House, London, where on 30 January 1690, at Clarendon's request, he delivered a sermon to commemorate the martyrdom of Charles I. Leslie refused to take the required oath of allegiance to William and Mary on 2 February 1690, leading to the loss of his clerical and judicial offices in Ireland. He became a member of the nonjuror community in London and used his talents to support nonjuror, Jacobite, and tory causes, becoming friends with leading nonjurors including George Hickes, Robert Nelson, Francis Cherry, and Henry Dodwell. Cherry's home at Shottesbrooke was a leading nonjuror centre and occasionally served Leslie as a hiding place when arrest warrants were issued because of his political activities. Dodwell, like Leslie, was a graduate of Trinity College, Dublin. As the Church of Ireland had suffered significantly under James II, it produced few nonjurors and Jacobites, but Leslie and Dodwell proved to be among the most gifted and influential early nonjuror writers and important representatives of the tradition of the Caroline divines in the Church of Ireland.

Although he had yet to publish before the revolution, Leslie quickly became a prominent and politically active nonjuror writer. Burnet charged that his violent Jacobitism led to his engagement in 'many plots, and in writing many books against the revolution and the present government' (*Burnet's History*, 6.34). Leslie's publishing career began with his anonymous response to William King's defence of the revolution, *The State of the Protestants of Ireland under the Late King James' Government* (1691). King, at the time dean of St Patrick's, Dublin and writing anonymously, declared that the revolution was a necessary response to James's persecution of Irish protestants. Leslie's *An Answer to a Book, Entitled the State of the Protestants of Ireland* (1692), written from Glaslough, accused King of disowning the principles of passive obedience and non-resistance he had once preached by placing the power of government in the hands of the people and countenancing rebellion, thereby destroying all prospects for peace in human society. Attached was the first account of the massacre at Glencoe, Scotland, in 1692, which charged William III with complicity in the incident. He expanded this account in *Gallienus redivivus, or, Murthere will out &c.: being a true account of the de-witting of Glencoe, Gaffney, &c.* (1695). These accusations led the government to issue a warrant and he was arrested on board a ship bound for the Netherlands in September 1694; he escaped, however, and continued his polemical campaign against William III and the whigs. During the 1690s Leslie served as a primary conduit of information between the nonjuring community in England and the Stuart court, making several trips to St Germain, and may have obtained permission from James II for the consecration of George Hickes and Thomas Wagstaffe as nonjuror bishops.

After Anne succeeded William III in 1702, Leslie took part in the tory renaissance of the early years of her reign. He found literary success, possibly with the help of influential members of the government, by advocating the revival of tory and high-church positions. Besides numerous books and pamphlets supporting the tory cause he published a biweekly newspaper known as *The Rehearsal* from 1704 to 1709. Though he remained more Jacobite than tory, he found a receptive audience among tories, who appreciated his strong rebuttal to whig positions on issues such as occasional conformity, episcopacy, and divine-right monarchy. His *Rehearsal* served as a leading voice for legislative attempts to ban the practice of occasional conformity, which allowed dissenters to qualify for public office by taking the sacrament in the Church of England. Leslie and other tories believed that if the practice continued it could eventually threaten the viability of both the established church and the monarchy. In *The Rehearsal* he also reminded his readers that it was whigs and dissenters who had destroyed episcopacy and monarchy during the civil war. Leslie also may have found it useful to support Anne in the hope that the Pretender, James III (James Francis Edward Stuart), might be restored to the throne at Anne's death.

By 1710 Leslie had become disillusioned with the tory party, which had come under the leadership of proponents of the Hanoverian succession. Tories also grew uncomfortable with him for chiding their inconsistency in backing the revolution and then returning to the principles of non-resistance and passive obedience once their positions in government were safe. Disgruntled by Leslie's charges, Henry Sacheverell considered publishing a response, though, as Thomas Hearne noted, Leslie had defended tory and high-church positions in his *Rehearsal* 'much better than they can or durst do themselves', for Leslie spoke 'with boldness, & discover'd some truths which their complyance would not permit them to do' (*Remarks*, 3.36). Despite his service to the tory party, it had become concerned about being associated with his fanaticism, especially after Burnet criticized Leslie by name during the Sacheverell trial for his positions on dissenters and occasional conformity; the government closed down his paper in March 1709, and he was forced to plead a royal pardon.

Though the tories shunned him Leslie continued to defend divine-right monarchy and episcopacy, responding to Burnet's attacks with *The Good Old Cause, or, Lying in Truth* (1710), which caused sufficient concern to the government that it ordered his arrest in July 1710. His failure to appear for questioning by 8 August led to his being declared an outlaw. In poor health, the Leslies hid for six months at Francis Cherry's home at White Waltham. In 1711 Leslie fled to the continent and the safety of the Jacobite court, arriving at St Germain on 17 April.

Leslie not only provided journalistic support for tory and Jacobite causes but by 1711 had also become an active Jacobite agent. In April 1711, in a letter entitled 'Memorial of Sieur Lamb', he reported to the Stuart court that Scotland was ripe for invasion and that 'the princess of Denmark' (Queen Anne) was 'favourably inclined towards the King her brother; and that she would choose rather to have him for her successor, than the prince of Hanover' (Macpherson, 2.211–12). He claimed that the only objection given against the Pretender concerned his religion, 'but that is not imputed to him as a fault, but as his misfortune and ours'. Though James should not show that he 'is capable of dissembling his religion', on his return to England he should not bring more priests than he personally needed. Additionally, James should allow his protestant followers at St Germain to gather freely for worship and on his landing have a minister of the Church of England 'of approved character' preach to the people. Militarily Leslie advised James to bring with him Irish troops, which would be agreeable to the highlanders, and bring the duke of Berwick, who could quell any disputes among the Scottish nobility about command of the army (ibid., 2.214–16).

Leslie and his wife had travelled to the Stuart court at St Germain at the personal invitation of James III. Leslie's wife ceased to be mentioned after 1712, so it is likely that she died then after years of illness and living in hiding. Leslie remained part of that court from 1711 to 1719, serving as the protestant chaplain, first at St Germain and Bar le Duc in France and then, after the failure of the revolt of 1715, in Italy. He offered Anglican services in a private chapel for Anglican members of the exiled court in both France and Italy. The Pretender may have attended services on occasion and may have allowed Leslie to engage him in theological conversation, but these opportunities diminished over time. Though hopeful that the Pretender would convert to the Church of England, Leslie resisted attempts by Viscount Bolingbroke and others actively to attempt his conversion. Bolingbroke charged that Leslie had been used by the Pretender who 'not only refused to hear himself, but that he sheltered the ignorance of his priests, or the badness of his cause, or both behind his authority, and absolutely forbid all discourse concerning religion' (H. Saint John, Viscount Bolingbroke, *The Works of Lord Bolingbroke*, ed. D. Mallet, 5 vols., 1754, 1.170). Leslie's nineteenth-century biographer denied this charge, stating that he would never have confided in Bolingbroke, as his 'notorious indifference to religion would have been sufficient to prevent any confidential communications between Leslie and him on the subject' (R. Leslie, *Life*, 491).

Leslie continued using his polemical skills in support of the Pretender's cause, writing several pieces, including *A letter from Mr. Leslie to a member of parliament in London in support of the Stuart claim to the throne* (1714), which was written to persuade parliament to overturn the Act of Settlement of 1701 and consider the Chevalier's claim. Leslie described the Pretender as a handsome, wise, cheerful, unbigoted man, who had promised to secure the future of the Church of England by waiving his right of episcopal nomination. His defence of the Chevalier led one anonymous writer to charge James of harbouring the nation's greatest traitors, with Leslie being 'the most notorious of all of 'em; which is of itself sufficient to warrant driving him about like a scape-goat, and put a price on his head' (*Remarks on Lesley's Two Letters from Bar le Duc*, 1715, 4).

Though Leslie remained loyal to the Pretender, the difficulty of holding protestant services in Italy led him to return to Paris in June 1717. In 1719, suffering from gout and in generally poor health, he sought help from friends in England to return home to Ireland. With the help of Roger Kenyon he published a two folio-volume edition of his theological works. By 1721 he had raised £750 in subscriptions, with more than 500 members of the Lords and Commons as subscribers. Lord Sunderland finally gave the needed permission for Leslie to return, with the stipulation that he cease his political activities; in the autumn of 1721 he went back to the family estate at Glaslough for the first time since 1691. He died at his home on 13 April 1722 and was buried in the Glaslough churchyard.

Political writings Leslie's published works included dozens of political and religious tracts and books, with a strong connection between his political and theological writings. Rooting his thought in the patriarchalism of Robert Filmer, he offered an antidote to the contractualism of John Locke and his followers, including Benjamin Hoadly and Daniel Defoe. As Filmer's most prominent interpreter, Leslie insisted that God ordained a hierarchical political structure for all aspects of society, whether civil, religious, or familial. Fathers reigned supreme in the home, bishops in the church, and the monarch in national government. The revolution of 1688 which brought the eviction of James II and the ascendancy of William and Mary was, therefore, a humanly designed abrogation of this divinely ordered society. Sacred and civil governments, in Leslie's perspective, stood in two parallel lines, and though remaining distinct and separate they should protect and support each other. If one took liberties regarding the church then it seemed logical that one would take seditious attitudes toward the state (*The Rehearsal*, 1 Oct 1707).

In defence of the church's independence from state control Leslie wrote *The Case of the Regale, and the Pontificate Stated* (1700), which H. J. Laski called the 'ablest of his many able performances' (*Political Thought in England*, 1920, 104). There he argued against the deprival of the nonjuring bishops, insisting that the government must allow bishops freely to exercise their episcopal duties and that only convocation could deprive bishops of their spiritual offices and jurisdiction. Though the deprival of the nonjuror bishops was an illegal act of aggression against the church, the schism did not begin until bishops were consecrated in place of those deprived, for 'not till then, were there bishops and anti-bishops, and opposite altars set up' (Leslie, *Regale*, 74–5).

Leslie's most prominent political work was his journal, *The Rehearsal*. In opposition to whig interests in church and state, represented by John Tutchin's *Observator* and Daniel Defoe's *Review*, the paper supported tory causes including a ban on occasional conformity. Response to Leslie's journalistic positions reflected party lines. Gilbert Burnet wrote that Leslie rejected any form of resistance to government, 'deriving government wholly from God, denying all right in the people, either to confer or coerce it' (*Burnet's History*, 6.34–5). Thomas Hearne, however, commented that the 'rehearsals are full of excellent reasoning as well as wit, and very well contrived for the security of our constitution and good principles, and the church, and the personal reputation of the clergy attacked by slanders of the wicked party' (*Remarks*, 2.152).

In *The Finishing Stroke: being a Vindication of the Patriarchal Scheme of Government*, published just prior to his flight to the continent in 1711, Leslie argued that ecclesiastical, civil, and military governments all had their origins in Adam. These three governments in time coalesced into two forms, spiritual and temporal, with bishops ruling over the spiritual realm and the king possessing both civil and military authority. Since civil government began with Adam, who had no human superior, no independent state of nature ever existed, and therefore there was not a time without a civil government for the people to establish (Leslie, *Finishing Stroke*, 14–15).

In his tract *Cassandra* (1704), Leslie affirmed royal absolutism and denied that the people had a right of resistance, even if the government unjustly invaded their property. Taking up arms and deposing the monarch was a usurpation of governmental power and dissolved the divinely ordained constitution, by which God ruled the world (*Cassandra*, 5). Similarly, in *The Best Answer Ever was Made* (1709) he defended non-resistance in response to Benjamin Hoadly. Leslie turned to St Paul to prove that even if a magistrate was 'guilty of male-administration', this did not mean that he should 'forfeit his office, or ought to be resisted', for resistance to 'authority lead to damnation, since it was *resistance to an ordinance* of God' (Leslie, *Best Answer*, 6).

Leslie believed that political whiggism and religious dissent were linked. In the *Wolf-Stript of his Shepherd's Clothing* (1704) he blamed religious dissent for the rebellion of 1641, the Rye House plot, and Monmouth's rebellion. He spoke of republicans and whigs as 'Jack Presbyter's lay elders', for 'rebellion is his lay face, as schism is his ecclesiastical'. Political rebellion and schism were the same thing, with only the object of resistance being different, since all dissenters would agree that they had a common enemy in 'the church and the crown' (Leslie, *Works*, 1832, 6.445). He implicated moderate or latitudinarian churchmen in whig fanaticism in *The New Association of those called Moderate-Church-Man* (1702), in which he charged latitudinarian whigs with seeking to pull down the church by allowing dissenters into the church through comprehension.

Theological writings. Leslie's theological works were largely apologetic in nature, offering defences of theological orthodoxy against deism, Judaism, latitudinarianism, Socinianism, and the Quakers. John Hunt described his theology as 'orthodox Episcopalian, adhering rigidly to Church dogmas and holding Episcopacy necessary to the essence of a church' (*Religious Thought in England*, 1871, 2.83). The best known of his apologetical works was the *Short Method with the Deists* (1694), which was written as a letter, probably for Henry Hyde's sister, Frances Kneightly, who stayed with the Leslies during a period of attraction to deism. There he sought to defend trinitarian orthodoxy and the centrality of the doctrine of satisfaction, which he called 'the foundation of the Christian Religion' (Leslie, *Works*, 1832, 6.64). The book became a classic theological response to deism and continued to be reprinted well into the nineteenth century. As in most of Leslie's works, theological positions had political consequences; therefore, he insisted that deism led inevitably to contractualism. Blurring the distinctions between deists and Socinians, he criticized both for rejecting the doctrine of satisfaction. He sought to prove the historicity of the biblical miracles through their conformity to four rules of evidence, which placed great trust in the reliability of scripture and the testimony of liturgical rites, such as the eucharist (Leslie, *Works*, 1721, 1.11). In addition, explaining miracles based on secondary causes led to the rejection of scripture, for if it was 'false in part, we cannot trust to it either in whole or in part' (ibid., 1.15). He wrote similarly against the Jews in *A Short Method with the Jews*, arguing that their rebellion against God's laws had led to their experiencing God's wrath through the ages. Therefore, whig adherents of Locke's contractualism should understand that disobedience to God's order for society would lead to judgment. These two works, along with *The Truth of Christianity Demonstrated* (1711) later appeared in William Jones's *The Scholar Armed Against the Errors of the Times* (2 vols., 1800), which described the *Short Method with the Deists* as containing 'an unanswerable proof of Christianity from the evidences of its facts' (vol. 1, preface).

Leslie's belief that Socinianism posed a pernicious threat to the stability of the Church of England led him to attack John Tillotson and Gilbert Burnet, who, he believed, displayed Socinian tendencies. In *The Charge of Socinianism Against Mr. Tillotson Considered* (1695) he charged the new archbishop of Canterbury with exhibiting antitrinitarian views, denying that Christ's death served as satisfaction for sin, and rejecting the doctrines of hell and eternal punishment, all of which meant that humanity did not need the atoning work of Christ on the cross (p. 9). Though Tillotson might deny his Socinianism, Leslie charged that Socinians were adept at 'altering the meaning of words, so that no words can almost bind them' (p. 3). Therefore, Tillotson's embrace of Socinianism had reduced Christianity to little more than a moral prop to ordered government. This pamphlet led to a decade-long outburst against the alleged Socinianism in the church. Other anti-Socinian works included *A Letter to a Friend* (1694) and *Second Letter to a Friend* (1694), and *The Socinian Controversy Discussed in Six Dialogues* (1708).

While in hiding during the early 1690s Leslie and his family lodged with a Quaker family, whom he allegedly converted. This encounter led to the publication of nine books in response to the Quaker faith. Finding their theology and disregard for the sacraments troubling, he charged them in the *Snake in the Grass* (1697) with being agents of Satan and the largest and most dangerous example of enthusiasm in Britain. This enthusiasm was 'more dangerous than atheism' because atheism attracted only the 'unthinking and debauch'd, while Enthusiasm steals away many devout and well-meaning persons' (Leslie, *Works*, 1721, 2.3–4). Like the latitudinarians, Quakers exhibited a Socinian Christology and denied the doctrine of satisfaction (ibid., 2.77). Believing his polemical efforts were successful, he claimed in *The Present State of Quakerism in England* (1701) that many Quakers were renouncing their faith and seeking baptism in the Church of England, while many others remained Quakers but rejected the Socinian doctrines or had begun to 'colour and gloss their words to make them bear a Christian sense' (ibid., 2.642–3). As evidence for this change he pointed out that in responding to his works the Quakers George Whitehead and Joseph Wyeth had put a Christian meaning on Quaker doctrines. This might deceive outsiders but it would have raised concerns among true Quakers. His other anti-Quaker works included *A Discourse Proving the Divine Institution of Water Baptism* (1697), *Satan Disrobed from his Disguise of Light* (1698), and *A Defence of a Book Entitled, the Snake in the Grass* (1700).

Having argued against Roman Catholicism before the revolution, Leslie added two tracts, *The Case Stated between the Church of Rome and the Church of England* and *The True Notion of the Catholic Church, in Answer to the Bishop of Meaux's Letter to Mr. Nelson*, in defence of the Church of England. In *The Case Stated* he denied Rome's claim to be the mother church, suggesting that Jerusalem was the mother church and that scripture was silent concerning the supremacy of Peter or whether Peter was the bishop of Rome. Then in *The True Notion* he declared that God appointed neither a universal monarch nor a universal bishop; any arguments for a universal bishop being the source of peace and unity might equally be made for a universal monarch. In another work, which was more political in nature, *Discourse Against Marriages with those of Different Communions* (1702), Leslie blamed the troubles of Charles I and his successors in large part on Catholic marriages.

When the usages controversy erupted among the nonjurors, a controversy that irreparably divided the small nonjuring community over the necessity of certain eucharistic practices, Leslie was in exile on the continent. Though he did not play an active role in the controversy he contributed two tracts for the nonusages party, arguing against the expediency of restoring the four usages that included the invocation of the spirit, the oblation, prayers for the dead, and adding water to the wine. In *A letter from Mr. Leslie to his friends against alterations or additions to the liturgy of the Church of England* (1718) and *A Letter from the Rev. Mr. Charles Leslie Concerning the New Separation to Mr. B—* (1719), Leslie argued that though the usages might be primitive they were not essential. Therefore, it was not expedient to insist on adherence to the usages and divide the already small nonjuror community. Finally, one had to ask if the Church of England had been in schism since the Reformation because it lacked these liturgical elements.

Leslie's apologies for the true English church took a more scholarly turn in *A Dissertation Concerning the Use and Authority of Ecclesiastical History*, where he tried to demonstrate the usefulness of history as moral example. Ecclesiastical history was the most beneficial to humanity, for while secular history might make one a statesman or politician, ecclesiastical history 'will make us wise unto salvation' (Leslie, *Works*, 1832, 1.411–12). On an apologetical level he called for a study of the primitive fathers as an antidote to both Roman Catholicism and nonconformity. He believed that history proved the church of the apostles was neither papist nor presbyterian, but strongly episcopal. He also castigated the universities for neglecting the study of the primitive church and focusing on the modern systems of divinity, especially those that were German and Dutch.

Leslie's influence Reviled by many, as evidenced by Mark Noble's comment that 'Leslie had much learning, but more faction; some wit but more scurrility' (*A Biographical History of England*, 3 vols., 1806, 1.140), others found much help in Leslie's writings. The respect given him can be seen in Samuel Johnson's remark that he was 'a reasoner, and a reasoner who was not to be reasoned against' (Boswell, *Life*, 4.286). Leslie's works continued to be republished throughout the eighteenth century, finding a new audience at the end of the century in the Hutchinsonians, including George Horne, Charles Daubney and William Jones. The Hutchinsonians found his defence of divine-right monarchy and defence of the episcopacy as the essence of the church extremely helpful as the regime of George III faced the challenges of the American and French revolutions. William Jones, in his *Life of Bishop Horne*, wrote that 'these two volumes [Leslie's *Theological Works*] may be considered as a library in themselves to any young student of the Church of England' (Allibone, *Dict.*, 1.1085). Though Leslie never swerved from his loyalty to the Stuarts, the Hutchinsonians made use of his works, including a 1750 reprint of *The Rehearsal*, to defend the Hanoverian regime. As Jonathan Clark notes, Leslie's 'increasing currency in the later eighteenth century seems to have evoked no awareness of his political disaffection to an earlier Hanoverian' (Clark, 219–20). During the nineteenth century his works continued to find an audience, with his *Short Method with the Deists* becoming a classic apologetic against deism. Tractarians also found Leslie's defences of episcopacy and orthodox Christology attractive and several of his works were published in the Tracts for the Times.

By the end of the century Leslie's biographer bemoaned Leslie's 'undeserved and unfortunate neglect during the nineteenth century', which he blamed on the demise of the political viability of Jacobitism and a decline in theological learning among the clergy (R. Leslie, *Life*, 1–2). Despite this neglect, Thomas Macaulay affirmed that Leslie's abilities were such that had he not remained steadfast in his Jacobitism, he would have 'obtained high preferment in the Church of England'. Macaulay, however, placed greater value on his qualifications as a constitutional scholar than as a theologian, suggesting that Leslie had been 'studying English history and law, while most of the other chiefs of the schism had been poring over the Acts of Chalcedon, or seeking for wisdom in the Targum of Onkelos' (*History of England from the Accession of James II*, 5 vols., 1856, 4.360). Leslie Stephen, likewise, commented that Leslie was 'no despicable master of the art of expressing pithy arguments in vigorous English' (*English Thought in the Eighteenth Century*, 2 vols., 1927, 1.195).

Some modern scholars have dismissed Leslie and the Jacobite cause as having little realistic hope of success. This is seen in Bruce Lenman's comment that 'it may be doubted whether his political activities ever had much relationship to reality, let alone any chance of changing it' (*The Jacobite Risings in Britain, 1689–1746*, 1980, 113). There is, however, a growing recognition of Leslie's importance to conservative political and religious movements during the eighteenth century. J. A. W. Gunn points out that eighteenth-century tories and high-churchmen looked to Leslie for help in challenging whig pretensions, as he subjected 'co-ordinate power to the cruelest inquisition, arraigning it before the prayer-book and the statute-book. This, rather than his fruitless loyalty to the Stuarts has been recognized as the focus of his political thought' (*Beyond Liberty and Property*, 1983, 164). Similarly, J. C. D. Clark describes Leslie not only as 'one of the most able intellects in the Stuart cause', but also as 'a vigilant and trenchant opponent of doctrinal error in the church' (Clark, 282). ROBERT D. CORNWALL

Sources R. Leslie, *Life and writings of Charles Leslie, M.A.* (1885) • C. Leslie, *The theological works of the Reverend Charles Leslie*, 2 vols. (1721) • C. Leslie, *The theological works of the Reverend Charles Leslie*, 7 vols. (1832) • W. Frank, 'Charles Leslie and theological politics in post revolutionary England', PhD diss., McMaster University, 1983 • W. Frank, '"The excellent rehearser": Charles Leslie and the tory party, 1688–1714', *Biography in the eighteenth century*, ed. J. Browning (1987), 43–68 • J. H. Overton, *The nonjurors: their lives, principles, and writings* (1902) • D. Jellett, 'The journalistic career of Charles Leslie, 1688–1711', MA diss., Auburn University, 1981 • Colonel Leslie [C. J. Leslie], *Historical records of the family of Leslie, from 1067 to 1868–9*, 3 vols. (1869) • A. Kippis and others, eds., *Biographia Britannica, or, The lives of the most eminent persons who have flourished in*

Great Britain and Ireland, 2nd edn, 5 (1793), 2917–2920 • *Bishop Burnet's History of his own time*, another edn, 6 vols. (Edinburgh, 1753) • J. McGuire, 'The Church of Ireland and the "Glorious Revolution" of 1688', *Studies in Irish history presented to R. Dudley Edwards*, ed. A. Cosgrove and D. McCartney (1979), 137–49 • *Remarks and collections of Thomas Hearne*, ed. C. E. Doble and others, 3, OHS, 13 (1889) • *The correspondence of Henry Hyde, earl of Clarendon, and of his brother Laurence Hyde, earl of Rochester*, ed. S. W. Singer, 2 vols. (1828) • W. Scott, ed., *A collection of scarce and valuable tracts … Lord Somers*, 2nd edn, 13 vols. (1809–15) • Burtchaell & Sadleir, *Alum. Dubl.* • Allibone, *Dict.* • J. Macpherson, ed., *Original papers: containing the secret history of Great Britain*, 2 vols. (1775) • R. Ryan, *Biographia Hibernica*, 2 vols. (1821) • A. Boyer, *The history of Queen Anne* (1735) • A. Chalmers, ed., *The general biographical dictionary*, new edn, 32 vols. (1812–17) • J. C. D. Clark, *English society, 1688–1832: ideology, social structure and political practice during the ancien régime* (1985) • *DNB*

Likenesses F. Chereau, line engraving (after A. S. Belle), BM, NPG • Vertue, engraving, repro. in Leslie, *Theological works of the Reverend Charles Leslie* • attrib. G. White, mezzotint (after portrait), BM, NPG [*see illus.*] • engraving, repro. in Leslie, *Life and writings of Charles Leslie* • mezzotint, BM, NPG

Leslie, Charles [*nicknamed* Mussel-Mou'd Charlie] (**1676/7–1782**), ballad singer and songwriter, was reputed a natural son of Leslie of Pitcaple, which lies in the Garioch in Aberdeenshire. He was what contemporaries called a 'flying stationer', making his living by composing and arranging songs, often on political subjects, which he then had printed as pamphlets or chapbooks; these he performed and sold throughout his territory, which seems to have covered most of the east coast of Scotland between Fraserburgh and Edinburgh, but centring on the city of Aberdeen and its hinterland. He was a kenspeckle figure: rakishly thin and red-headed, with long lugubrious features and a small severely pursed mouth, which resembled a mussel—hence his nickname.

Leslie was a sort of strolling journalist, whose visits were eagerly anticipated because he always carried the latest news; he was also well versed in folklore and genealogy, and 'When he knew of any to be hang'd at Edinburgh, he was sure to be there that day for their last speech and dying words' (Olson and Morris, 318).

Details survive of only one of Leslie's publications, *Three excellent new songs: 1. A new song, called The Jacobite's lamentation: 2. The true Briton's thought: 3. John Armstrong's last goodnight* (1746), although there is probably a good deal which has not survived. In politics he was staunchly Jacobite, as indeed were many of his auditors, since the north-east was the heartland of Jacobitism in the lowlands of Scotland. Notwithstanding this,

> The Magistrates of Abdn, [Aberdeen] were very illnaturd to him they often put him into Jail for singing, and asked him what for he did it, why says Charlie for a bit of bread, why says the Provost, cannot you sing other songs than that rebellious ones, ay says Charlie but they winna buy them (Olson and Morris, 319)

Leslie had been 'out' in the rising of 1715 and during that of 1745 he was rounded up by the whiggish magistrates of Aberdeen and incarcerated with other prominent local Jacobites. Following the defeat of the government forces under the laird of MacLeod at the battle of Inverurie (23 December 1745), however, the guardhouse was emptied to accommodate whig prisoners, and according to one source, Leslie had the satisfaction of watching the provost, James Morison, being compelled to toast the health of the chevalier at the cross of Aberdeen while bellowing out his new song, 'MacLeod's Defeat at Inverury', in his characteristic 'deep hollow roar' (Kinloch, iii–viii):

> … godless Whigs, wi' their intrigues,
> Together did convene, man,
> At Inverury, on the riggs,
> On Thursday afternoon, man.
> Macleod came down frae Inverness …
> Came cross the Murray Firth, man,
> But ye shall know before ye go,
> The Gordons marred their mirth, man …

Charles Leslie died in the autumn of 1782 at the age of 105, and was buried at Old Rayne in the county of Aberdeen.

William Donaldson

Sources '"Biographia Lesleyana" or life of Charles Lesley, the Aberdeen ballad-singer', *The ballad book*, ed. G. R. Kinloch (1827), iii–viii • P. Buchan, ed., *An interesting and faithful narrative of the wanderings of Prince Charles Stuart and Miss Flora MacDonald, after the battle of Culloden … and several Jacobite poems and songs* (1839) • I. A. Olson and J. Morris, 'Mussel-Mou'd Charlie's (Charles Leslie) 1745 song: "McLeod's defeat at Inverury"', *Aberdeen University Review*, 58 (1999–2000) • M. E. Brown, 'The street laureate of Aberdeen: Charles Leslie, alias Mussel Mou'd Charlie, 1677–1782', *Narrative folksong: new directions*, ed. C. L. Edwards and K. E. B. Manley (1985), 362–78 • W. Donaldson, *The Jacobite song* (1988) • W. Walker, *The bards of Bon-Accord, 1375–1860* (1887) • J. Hogg, *Jacobite relics of Scotland* (1819–21) • *Aberdeen Journal notes and queries*, 2 (1909), 28 • *Scottish Notes and Queries*, 3rd ser., 4 (1926), 157

Likenesses J. Wales, oils, Fyvie Castle, Aberdeenshire • engraving, repro. in Buchan, *An interesting and faithful narrative*

Leslie, Charles Robert (**1794–1859**), literary genre painter and author, was born in Clerkenwell, London, on 19 October 1794, the eldest son of Robert Charles Leslie (*d.* 1804), a prosperous Philadelphia clockmaker, and his wife, Lydia Baker (1766/7–1824). Leaving a business partner behind, his father had moved to England in 1793 with his wife and their three daughters, in order to improve his business connections.

Early years After their return to the Philadelphia area in 1799, young Leslie showed such an interest in drawing that when his father sent him to a nearby school in New Jersey he specified that he should be allowed to draw. At about ten Leslie attended the University of Pennsylvania, through the kindness of some professors, to complete his education but, as he told William Dunlap, he was 'more attentive to drawing' than to any of his studies (Dunlap, 241). After his father's death his mother took in boarders and his older sister Eliza gave drawing lessons, but they were too poor to pay for Leslie's education as an artist, so in 1808 he became an apprentice at fourteen, bound for seven years to Messrs Bradford and Inskeep, Philadelphia publishers. Nearly three years later Samuel T. Bradford, a senior partner who had become fond of young Leslie, saw some theatrical sketches he had done, including a watercolour of the visiting English actor George Frederick Cooke as Richard III (1811) and, recognizing talent, offered to help raise a subscription for him to study painting for two years in London. As it happened, Bradford was a director of the Pennsylvania Academy of the Fine Arts.

Through his efforts the academy not only hung five of Leslie's watercolour drawings in their annual exhibition of 1811 but also accepted him as a pupil and contributed $100 towards his education abroad. The art critic, John Neal, noted in 1823 that Leslie 'was considered a marvel and a prodigy' who needed only to be sent to London to become 'a finished miracle' (Dickson, 16). Bradford even published engravings after some of Leslie's theatrical illustrations in his firm's monthly publication *Mirror of Taste*, with a description of the artist as an untaught 'genius'. When sufficient money was raised Leslie took his first lessons in oil painting, which had been offered as a gift from the portraitist Thomas Sully, before leaving for England.

Move to England On 3 December 1811 Leslie arrived in Liverpool and continued to London with a letter of introduction from Sully to Benjamin West, the American-born president of the Royal Academy. The ageing West and his former student Washington Allston soon became Leslie's favourite teachers, although Leslie also enrolled, for further training, as a student at the academy on 23 March 1813. With these mentors, and sharing lodgings with their student Samuel F. B. Morse, Leslie found himself under the influence of compatriots who were highly dedicated history painters. Allston, the most charismatic of them all, became particularly influential and his manner can be seen in some of Leslie's early work, such as in the distinctive illumination of flesh in both his early portrait *Nathaniel West* (1812; Salem Marine Society, Massachusetts), and his experimental history painting, *Timon of Athens* (1812; Athenaeum, Philadelphia). Leslie, however, was in an eclectic phase. In 1813 he exhibited *Personification of Murder* (1813; priv. coll.) at the Royal Academy. Showing an assassin gripping a sword as he steals from a cave at midnight, this image from *Macbeth* reverts to a couple of his early Philadelphia drawings of actors in its element of caricature. Both *Murder* and *Timon*, like so much of Leslie's work, evince a lifelong love of English literature and the stage. They also reflect, in their anatomical drawing, the careful studies Leslie had made from the academy's antique casts, the Townley marbles in the British Museum, and the Elgin marbles in a temporary building near Burlington House.

Major works The first large picture that Leslie attempted was *The Witch of Endor Raising the Ghost of Samuel before Saul* (1814), which he painted for exhibition under West's guidance. While its appearance is unknown, it is clear from its size (80 x 98 inches) and subject that at this time Leslie was considering a career as a history painter. His next major work, *The Murder of Rutland by Lord Clifford* (1815; Pennsylvania Academy of the Fine Arts, Philadelphia), from Shakespeare's *Henry VI*, reveals that his sensitivity to colour and paint texture was steadily increasing and his sources of inspiration were becoming more varied. The close-up, melodramatic presentation of *Rutland*, for instance, recalls scenes by artists such as James Northcote from John Boydell's Shakspeare Gallery of a generation earlier.

Leslie painted half-length portraits to support himself and to exhibit, as a means of enhancing his reputation, he painted some theatrical characters and history subjects, but he had not yet found his own particular métier. Several factors finally caused him to change direction. One was the near meteoric rise in reputation of the English genre painter David Wilkie. Leslie must have been made especially aware of Wilkie when he travelled to Paris in 1817 with Wilkie's friend, the painter William Collins, and Allston. He was asked about the newly famous Wilkie, as he reported, in Paris. Then there were the recent exhibitions at the British Institution on Hogarth (1814) and Dutch and Flemish painting (1815). Finally Allston's friend

Charles Robert Leslie (1794–1859), by John Partridge, 1836

Washington Irving helped to re-direct Leslie toward light-hearted genre scenes, akin to his Philadelphia work, by employing him in 1817 to illustrate two of his comical works: *History of New York* by Knickerbocker and *The Sketch Book*.

Encouraged by these precedents, Leslie made a first major trial in a different speciality by exhibiting *Sir Roger de Coverley Going to Church* (1819; priv. coll.), generally in the style of Wilkie, at the Royal Academy in 1819. The immediate success of this portrayal of eighteenth-century country manners, taken from Joseph Addison's serial in *The Spectator*, determined the future course of Leslie's career. Apart from this picture, some of his finest early literary genre scenes include *Sancho Panza in the Apartment of the Duchess* (1824; Petworth House, Sussex), *Slender, with the Assistance of Shallow, Courting Anne Page* (1824–5; Yale U. CBA), and *Uncle Toby and the Widow Wadman* (1832; V&A). He composed his pictures and determined facial expressions as if he were interpreting and directing a play, with real people as actors. Although he painted quickly, he took time over researching his historical subjects so as to be as authentic as possible in such details as costume and background. By deserting history painting for the sake of smaller, literary subjects often based on humorous or sentimental passages from well-known texts, Leslie appealed not only to the increasingly middle-class purchasing public, but also to the changing taste of some of his fellow artists. In 1821 he was elected an associate at the Royal Academy, and in 1826 Royal Academician.

According to a small, bust-length *Self-Portrait* (*c*.1820; priv. coll.), Leslie as a young man had a pleasing appearance with thick dark hair and arched eyebrows. With his background of genteel poverty he was a perceptive, principled, and relatively cautious person. His early biographer Tom Taylor thought that he valued 'good taste and moderation as much in art as in manners' (*Recollections*, xv). With other artists he never pushed himself forward, but rather took the part of loyal friend and genial companion. His particular friends, whom he regarded with great affection, included Allston, Morse, John Constable, Washington Irving, and Gilbert Stuart Newton. With Irving and Newton he shared a whimsical sense of humour. At an auction, for instance, a country dealer sitting next to Leslie exclaimed at the high price paid for one of Leslie's pictures and turned, unknowingly, to the artist for agreement. Leslie appeared shocked. 'Monstrous, is it not?', he replied, and later recounted the incident to his friends with amusement (ibid., xxxi). The growing depth of his English friendships helped to postpone his return to the United States. The Pennsylvania Academy of the Fine Arts, appreciating Leslie as potentially another West, always remained supportive from afar, repeatedly exhibiting his work and even holding an exhibition centred on *The Murder of Rutland* in 1816, but between 1819 and 1820 as Dunlap reported, Leslie finally decided to spend his life in London. Some time before 1824 he met the Londoner Harriet Honor Stone (1799–1879), whom he married on 11 April 1825, in the parish of St Marylebone, Middlesex, and with whom over approximately the next ten years he had six children.

Portraits In addition to his genre pictures Leslie continued to paint portraits, including some family groups. Among his finest are early works done with great facility, which in a Romantic vein emphasize through posture and glance the inner life of the sitter. They include *Louisa Johnson Adams* (1816; Department of State, Washington, DC), *Washington Allston* (*c*.1816; National Academy of Design, New York), and *John Howard Payne* (*c*.1820; Museum of Fine Arts, Boston). The bust-length portrait of Allston, perhaps his best—with its sketchy, unfinished clothing and sparkling, sidelong glance—, has the effect of having been achieved effortlessly, and yet the portrait is striking in its immediacy. There is this same sense of a thinking presence in Leslie's most famous portrait, that of Sir Walter Scott (1824; Museum of Fine Arts, Boston), painted from life, on commission, during Leslie's visit that year to Scotland.

Leslie's decision to remain in England, with the exception of short trips, was unexpectedly tested in 1833. Without his knowledge, his only brother, Tom, obtained for him the post of teacher of drawing at the Military Academy of West Point in upstate New York. After much hesitation and consulting with friends, including his loyal patron the third earl of Egremont, Leslie agreed to go. He arrived at West Point via Philadelphia, with his wife and children early in November, and, after five unhappy winter months in which his wife fell ill and a promised studio was never built, he finally left in mid-April 1834 for England with his family.

Broadening his *œuvre* Although Leslie became relatively formulaic with his literary subjects, he did occasionally branch out with other kinds of multi-figure compositions, for example, his historical subject picture *Lady Jane Grey Prevailed upon to Accept the Crown* (1827; priv. coll.) and his contemporary genre scenes, such as *Londoners Gypsying* (1820; Geffrye Museum, London), *Fairlop Fair* (1841; priv. coll.), and *The Shell* (*c*.1848; priv. coll.). Yet he did not have a chance to develop his reputation differently until 1838 when, through the influence of his patrons Henry Richard Fox, third Baron Holland and Lady Holland, he was admitted to Westminster Abbey to witness Queen Victoria's coronation. Afterwards he began a picture of the event, which the queen subsequently commissioned. The moment chosen was calculated to please by referring to her virtue. As he worked on his large picture, *Queen Victoria Receiving the Sacrament after the Coronation* (1838–43; Royal Collection), Leslie took the opportunity of portraying the queen and many of the nobility included in the picture from life sittings. He exhibited the painting at the Royal Academy and the queen rewarded him with a second commission for a picture of the christening of the princess royal (1841; Royal Collection). Leslie also broadened his *œuvre* with various small landscapes. These digressions would be less interesting if his son, the artist Robert C. Leslie, had not reported that his father late in life regretted that he had been limited in the subject matter of his paintings: he wished he had painted more from contemporary life. Leslie had been repeatedly commissioned to churn out reprises of his popular literary subjects or variations on them, some of which were reproduced by engravers on both sides of the Atlantic and disseminated as prints. Apart from Egremont and Holland, who collected his work, his patrons also included members of the middle class such as Richard Newsham (1798–1883) of Preston, Lancashire, and Daniel Roberts (1798–*c*.1880) of London, for whom his literary subjects held a strong appeal. The judgement of Taylor that his best pictures, in terms of subtlety of colouring, are his early ones, from about 1819 to 1838, has never been challenged.

Leslie is unusual among artists who attempted similar historicized literary scenes in that he was, according to Strong, 'a major pioneer of accuracy in costume' (Strong, 62). One contemporary reported that Leslie's costuming, taken from old prints and pictures, at least had 'the air of truth' (ibid., 62). Whether contemporary genre scenes or historical reconstructions from literature, his paintings aspire, as Taylor noted, to 'the function of pleasing and refining' (*Recollections*, lxxii); they are inspired by the concept of painting as poetry and are concerned, as Dunlap rightly noted, with 'select', rather than everyday life (Dunlap, 2.248). Decoratively composed and naturalistic, they are always 'easy, elegant and impressive' (ibid.).

Authorship His long association with literary men, as well as artists, compelled Leslie, after Constable's death, to collect materials and attempt the first biography of his friend. His *Memoirs of the Life of John Constable* (1843; 2nd edn 1845) is an invaluable biographical resource. He followed this with his *Handbook for Young Painters* (1854), based on his lectures as professor of painting at the Royal Academy (1847–52). In these Leslie endorsed the views of Sir Joshua Reynolds given in his lectures at the Royal Academy and set out in his *Discourses*. At the end of his life Leslie set aside his unfinished *Autobiographical Recollections* to concentrate on his fourth book, a biography of Reynolds. In poor health, Leslie worked on this until a month before his death, at his home, 2 Abercorn Place, St John's Wood, London, on 5 May 1859. He was buried in Kensal Green cemetery, London. *The Life and Times of Sir Joshua Reynolds* was completed by Taylor and published in 1865.

DORINDA EVANS

Sources *Autobiographical recollections of the late Charles Robert Leslie, R.A.*, ed. T. Taylor (1860); repr. with introduction by R. Hamlyn (1978) · W. Dunlap, *History of the rise and progress of the arts of design in the United States* (New York, 1834); repr. (1969), 2.238–50 · R. C. Leslie, 'With Charles Robert Leslie, R.A.', *Temple Bar*, 107 (March 1896), 353–69 · E. B. Green, 'Charles Robert Leslie', PhD diss., George Washington University, 1973 · D. Evans, *Benjamin West and his American students* (1980) · G. Jackson-Stops, 'Some sources for the paintings of C. R. Leslie', *Antiques*, 135 (Jan 1989), 310–21 · R. Strong, *And when did you last see your father? The Victorian painter and British history* (1978) · D. S. Macleod, *Art and the Victorian middle class: money and the making of cultural identity* (1996) · *CGPLA Eng. & Wales* (1859) · H. E. Dickson, 'Selections from the writings of John Neal (1793–1876)', *Pennsylvania State Bulletin*, 37 (1943), 16 · J. Dafforne, *Leslie and Maclise: the British school of painting, specimens of the works of our most famous artists with biographical and descriptive notices* [n.d., 1870?] · J. Dafforne, *Pictures by Charles Robert Leslie, R.A. with descriptions and a biographical sketch of the painter* (1872)

Archives priv. coll., family papers · Tate collection, corresp. and papers | Harvard U., Houghton L., MSS · Hist. Soc. Penn., Dreer collection · NL Scot., corresp. with Archibald Constable · V&A NAL, letters to John Forster

Likenesses C. R. Leslie, self-portrait, oils, 1814, NPG · C. R. Leslie, self-portrait, oils, *c*.1815, Historic Hudson Valley, Tarrytown, New York · C. R. Leslie, self-portrait, oils, *c*.1820, priv. coll. · J. Partridge, oils, 1836, NPG [*see illus.*] · C. H. Lear, chalk drawing, 1846, NPG · C. W. Cope, pencil sketch, *c*.1862, NPG · A. B. Wyon, bronze medallion, exh. RA 1872, NPG · C. R. Leslie, self-portrait, oils, Tate collection · Mayall, albumen carte-de-visite, NPG

Wealth at death under £8000: resworn probate, Jan 1862, *CGPLA Eng. & Wales* (1859)

Leslie, David, first Lord Newark (1601–1682), army officer, was the fifth son of Patrick Leslie, Lord Lindores, of Pitcairly, Fife, commendator of Lindores, and his wife, Lady Jean Stewart, second daughter of Robert, first earl of Orkney.

Early military career, 1630–1640 David Leslie started his military career as a captain in Alexander Leslie's foot in the Swedish army about 1630. In 1631 he was a captain in John Ruthwen's foot in the same service. There is a record of a Captain David Leslie who appears in Russian service under Alexander Leslie of Auchintoul in 1632. He bore testimonials from Charles I which honoured him as a commander in wars of France, Germany, Sweden, and the Low Countries. Gustav II Adolf sent Auchintoul and about 100 Scottish officers to aid the Russian army with the idea of tying down the Poles and securing the Swedish eastern flank when they entered Germany. David Leslie rejoined the Swedish army in 1634 as a colonel of cavalry. In August 1640 he petitioned to leave Swedish service after being wounded in battle. The Swedish Riksråd (royal council) records show that he and Colonel James Lumsden asked to return to Scotland at the same time. On 10 August both these officers were rewarded with a separation deal which included 200 muskets and 200 suits of armour each, and for Leslie a pension of 1000 riksdaler and gold chain. Leslie's and Lumsden's action and gift indicate a desire to join the covenanters in the bishops' wars. Leslie did not actually leave Sweden until November 1640, when he left for Scotland via Hamburg and so missed any combative part in the war.

The first civil war On 28 July 1643 the Scottish convention of estates contracted Leslie for three years' military service for £18,000 Scots. On 24 November 1643 he was appointed major-general in the Scottish army under Alexander Leslie, first earl of Leven, which crossed the Tweed on 19 January 1644, also holding the rank of a colonel of horse. The part played by Leslie in the battle of Marston Moor on 2 July was vital to the success of the anti-royalist coalition. Robert Baillie, the Scots presbyterian minister, asserted that Leslie 'in all places that day was his [Cromwell's] leader' (*Letters and Journals of Robert Baillie*, 2.204, 209, 218). He commanded three regiments of 900 Scots horse (his own, Balcarres's, and Kirkcudbright's) in the third line of the allied left-wing cavalry commanded by Cromwell. As his line advanced, they swept away the royalist musketeers supporting the first line of Lord Byron's horse, then routed some of Prince Rupert's and Byron's

David Leslie, first Lord Newark (1601–1682), by or after George Jamesone

retiring infantry. According to his fellow officer Colonel William Stewart of the Galloway foot, then 'he charged the enemies horse (wth whom L. Generall Cromwell was engaged) upon the flankes and in a very short space the enemies whole cavalry was routed' (*Full Relation of the Victory Obtained*, 1644, 5). After that success Cromwell and Leslie checked the pursuit of their horse, allowing the shattered royalist right wing to flee back to York. They formed their men up on the east side of the battlefield, then charged and routed the cavalry under George, Lord Goring. Following an attack on the main body of royalist foot, 'Generall Major Lesley charged the Earl of Newcastle's brigade of Whitecoats and cut them wholly off … and after them charged a brigade of Greencoats, whereof they cut off great numbers and put the rest to flight' (ibid., 9). After the surrender of York, Leslie was sent forward in advance to join the earl of Callendar in the siege of Newcastle, but on the arrival of Leven he was dispatched to the north-western shores, and defeated the forces of Musgrave and Fletcher in Westmorland, capturing Thirlwall Castle. He then laid siege to Carlisle, which surrendered on 28 June 1645.

Meanwhile, on 28 February 1645 the Scottish estates promoted him to lieutenant-general of horse. During that month he had led three Scottish cavalry regiments and 2000 foot in Cheshire in support of Sir William Brereton's parliamentarian forces. While employed in the midland shires in dogging the movements of the king in July–August 1645, preventing him from advancing northwards to effect a junction with Montrose in Scotland, he was suddenly summoned to Scotland by the committee of estates that he might, if possible, retrieve the disaster of Kilsyth on 15 August and check the career of the victorious Montrose. At the head of 4000 horse, on 6 September he entered Scotland by Berwick, where he had an interview with the fugitive committee of estates. His original design was to intercept Montrose at the Forth, but learning at Prestonpans that he was still in the south of Scotland, he resolved to attack him there. By a rapid march southward he surprised Montrose in the early morning of 13 September while the low grounds of Philiphaugh, on which Montrose had encamped, were enveloped in mist, and almost annihilated his forces, Montrose himself, with a few horse, escaping to the highlands. The glory of the victory was sullied by the massacre of the camp-followers, including a large number of Irish women. This apparently was done in retribution for excesses committed by Montrose and in line with British policy of executing Irish troops captured outside Ireland. After his victory Leslie advanced northwards to the Lothians, and thence convoyed the committee of estates to Glasgow, where his services were rewarded with a gift of 50,000 merks and a chain of gold or jewel, worth £7200 Scots. He then proceeded to Forfarshire, and for a time made Forfar his headquarters; but when it was discovered that Montrose was no longer dangerous, he returned to England and rejoined the Scottish army under Leven at Newark-on-Trent.

The rise of the covenanter regime Leslie became field commander after Leven's withdrawal to Scotland. In late December 1646 or early January 1647 the French ambassador, Bellieure, tried unsuccessfully to bribe Leslie to support Charles I. After the surrender of the king to the English in January 1647, the Scottish army returned home. It was reduced to 7200 foot and horse and, under the command of Leslie with the rank of lieutenant-general, was sent to the north of Scotland to extinguish the embers of insurrection there. After capturing the castles of the Gordons, and executing forty-two Irish prisoners, then chasing Huntly and his followers to their highland fastnesses, Leslie passed into Argyll, whence he drove the Macdonalds and their Irish allies out of Scotland. The 300-man garrison of Dunaverty Castle, which had made a strenuous resistance, were massacred without mercy after their surrender. On Mull he had an additional fourteen Irish soldiers killed.

In 1648 Leslie was offered the command of the horse in the army of the engagers for the rescue of the king; but, like the earl of Leven, he declined to serve on account of the disapproval of the kirk authorities. In September, after the defeat of the engagers at Winwick-Warrington, near Preston, Leslie took command of the whigmore rebellion against the engager regime. The successor kirk party regime appointed him lieutenant-general of the army, in practice the chief command given Leven's physical indisposition. The radical covenanters' alignment with the English parliament ended on 5 February 1649, when the Scots declared Charles II king. In March–May 1649 Leslie suppressed royalist risings against the kirk party, while a letter of September 1649 from Leven indicates that Leslie had kept the Swedes informed of British affairs. That month royalists seized the Orkneys and he established garrisons in northern Scotland to check them. In April 1650 Montrose landed in Caithness to effect the restoration of Charles II without acceptance of the covenants, and Leslie was dispatched against him from Forfarshire with a large force. As usual, his movements were characterized by great expedition, but to no avail since Colonel Archibald Strachan of the northern forces totally routed Montrose's forces at Carbisdale while Leslie was still far to the south. Montrose escaped, but through Neil Macleod of Assynt he was delivered up to Leslie, who conducted him in an ignominious manner to Edinburgh, where he suffered execution.

Commander of the covenanter army When Charles II agreed to mount the throne of Scotland as a covenanted king, Leslie continued as commander of an army that grew from just over 5000 men to 23,000 foot and horse. To deal with the emergency the English council of state recalled Cromwell from Ireland to conduct an invading force into Scotland. Leslie, on the enemy's approach, made no attempt to hold the south of Scotland, but devastated the open country between Berwick and Edinburgh. Outside Edinburgh he awaited Cromwell's arrival behind a line of defence selected and fortified with such skill that it was practically impregnable. Finding it equally impossible to cut off his supplies or entice him from his lines of defence, Cromwell was ultimately compelled from lack of provisions to withdraw to Dunbar. Keeping the high grounds to the west, Leslie closely attended his retreat, and while pushing forward a detachment to seize the pass of Cockburnspath, and thus to cut off his escape to England, drew up the main body of his forces on the slopes of the Lammermuirs. Cromwell was undoubtedly outmanoeuvred. He himself practically acknowledged that his case was desperate. It has been generally supposed that, had Leslie been left to his uncontrolled judgement, he would have maintained his attitude of masterly inactivity. For this the chief direct evidence is the statement of Burnet that Leslie told the committee of estates that by 'lying there all was sure, but that by engaging with gallant and desperate men all might be lost' (*Bishop Burnets's History of his Own Time*, 1839, 36). Leslie also declined to accept responsibility for the defeat on the ground that he 'had not the absolute command' due to interference from the committee of estates 'contrare to his mind' (Thurloe, *State papers*, 1.69; *Letters and Journals of Robert Baillie*, 3.111). He nevertheless attributed his defeat simply to the failure of his men, after moving down from the hills, to stand to their arms during the night, and of the officers to stay by their troops and regiments. He also affirms that, had they followed his counsel, Cromwell would have been defeated as completely as Montrose was at Philiphaugh. In any case, he was anticipated by Cromwell, who at the break of day on 3 September gave the order to advance before the Scots under Leslie were drawn up in line. Thus, though the more disciplined troops made at first a desperate resistance, the case of the Scots was from the beginning hopeless, and, to use the words of Cromwell, they soon 'became as stubble' to his horsemen. No fewer than 3000 were slain almost where they stood, and over 10,000 taken prisoner.

Leslie escaped and reached Edinburgh by nine o'clock; but no attempt was made to hold it, and the committee of estates ordered a rendezvous of the army under his command to be held at Stirling. From Stirling Leslie marched to Perth, and thence by Dundee to Aberdeen, in order to make final arrangements with the northern loyalists, who had risen against the kirk party on behalf of the king. On 24 October a letter was sent him by Middleton, the general of the loyalists, desiring a union against the common foe, and on the 26th a band was subscribed by Huntly, Atholl, and other lords acknowledging the solemn league and covenant. On the 29th an act of indemnity was therefore proclaimed at Perth, and on 4 November the loyalists laid down their arms and accepted the act by a treaty with Leslie at Strathbogie. This was followed by the coronation of the king at Scone on 1 January. Leslie had already, on 23 December, been exonerated 'of all imputation anent the miscarriage at Dunbar', and on his return from the north he took up a position at Torwood, between Stirling and Falkirk, to prevent the passage of Cromwell northward. It was so well chosen, and so well defended by entrenchments, that when Cromwell, whose operations had been delayed by illness, arrived before it in June, he regarded an attack on it as hopeless.

Throughout the winter and spring of 1651 the committee of estates and army staff became filled with engagers and royalists and Leslie's status declined. On 17 July 1651 the English succeeded in forcing a passage into Fife, and on 2 August occupied Perth, thus threatening both to cut off Leslie's supplies and to take him in the rear. The country to the south of Leslie had necessarily, however, been left open, and the Scots therefore resolved to pass into England and march on London. The manoeuvre might have been successful had the royalists in England shown more alacrity in utilizing their opportunity, had the Scots seized a point near the Welsh royalist recruiting grounds, or had Cromwell shown less promptitude in dealing with the crisis. The endeavour to introduce Charles to the English as a covenanted king was, moreover, in itself a hopeless error. It caused dissension even among his Scottish supporters, and it scared away the English royalists from his banner. That in such circumstances Cromwell would triumph was a foregone conclusion, and Leslie seems to have foreseen that defeat was inevitable. Clarendon states that Leslie told the king that he was 'melancholy indeed, for he well knew that the army, how well soever it looked, would not fight' (Clarendon, *Hist. rebellion*, 3.540). Clarendon attributes the detention of the Scots army at Worcester to the fatigue caused by the long march, but probably it rather indicated the presence of doubt and despair in the counsels of the leaders as exemplified in Leslie's quarrelling with the more royalist, conservative lieutenant-general John Middleton. Insufficient energy was shown in strengthening its defences against Cromwell's arrival. 'There was', says Clarendon,

> no good understanding between the officers of the army. David Leslie appeared dispirited and confounded, gave and

> revoked his orders, and sometimes contradicted them. He did not love Middleton, and was very jealous that all the officers loved him so well. (ibid., 3.550)

It would appear that when all was practically lost, the king desired to make a charge with the horse, and then probably it was that David Leslie was seen riding 'up and down as one amazed or seeking to fly' (*CSP dom.*, *1651*, 437). Leslie does not seem to have shown greater alacrity in flight than Middleton. They made their escape together with a considerable body of horse, the number, according to Clarendon, reaching 4000. They appear to have lost considerable numbers from panic on their journey, but, had it not been for dissensions and recriminations, might have reached Scotland in safety. In Yorkshire, however, Leslie and Middleton separated themselves, either accidentally or designedly, from their discontented followers, and were taken prisoner with 1000–1200 horse by Colonel John Birch at Blackstone Edge on 9 September. On 24 October Leslie was committed to the Tower. By Cromwell's Act of Grace he was fined £11,000, subsequently reduced to one-third of that sum. Latterly he obtained some relaxation of his imprisonment, but he was not granted his liberty until 1660.

Restoration and last years After the Restoration Leslie was, on 3 August 1661, in recognition of his services to the royal cause, created Lord Newark by patent to him and heirs male of his body. A pension of £500 per annum was also bestowed on him. He consistently attended the Scottish parliament between 1662 and 1681. On 10 June 1667 the king sent him a letter assuring him of his continued confidence in his loyalty. From 1667 to 1681 Newark commanded one of the two Fife militia horse troops. In 1681 as a sign of his religious and political loyalties, as now held, he signed the declaration against the covenants and opposing the king in arms.

Newark and his wife, Jane (*d.* 1713), daughter of Sir John Yorke, had three sons: David, who succeeded him, Charles, who died young, and James, who became a colonel; and five daughters, Helen, who died young, Elizabeth, married to Sir Archibald Kennedy of Culzean, Mary, married first to James Kinloch of Gilmerton and secondly to Sir Alexander Ogilvy of Forglen, Margaret, married to Colonel James Campbell, fourth son of Archibald, ninth earl of Argyll, Anne, who died young, and Jane, who died young. Newark died of an apoplexy at his home, Newark Castle, St Monance, Fife, in February 1682, and was buried at St Monance.

T. F. Henderson, *rev.* Edward M. Furgol

Sources *APS* • *The letters and journals of Robert Baillie*, ed. D. Laing, 3 vols. (1841–2) • J. Turner, *Memoirs of his own life and times, 1632–1670*, ed. T. Thomson, Bannatyne Club, 28 (1829) • *The historical works of Sir James Balfour*, ed. J. Haig, 4 vols. (1824–5) • *CSP dom.*, *1639–49* • [W. Thompson], *Montrosse totally routed at Tividale in Scotland by Lieutenant-General Lesley* (1645) • *General Leslie's speech in the parliament of Scotland* (1647) • *A victory obtained by Lieutenant-General David Lesley in the north of Scotland* (1650) • *Reg. PCS*, 3rd ser. • *Report on manuscripts in various collections*, 8 vols., HMC, 55 (1901–14), vol. 5 • *The memoirs of Henry Guthry, late bishop*, ed. G. Crawford, 2nd edn (1748) • Clarendon, *Hist. rebellion* • P. Newman, *The battle of Marston Moor* (1981) • *The letter books of Sir William Brereton*, ed. R. N. Dore, 2 vols., Lancashire and Cheshire RS, 123, 128 (1984–90) • military muster rolls, Krigsarkivet, Stockholm, 1630/36, 1631/22, 24 • D. Fedosov, *The Caledonian connection* (1996) • N. A. Kullberg, S. Bergh, and P. Sondén, eds., *Svenska riksrådets protokoll*, 18 vols. (Stockholm, 1878–1959), vol. 8, p. 184 • *Rikskansleren Axel Oxenstiernas skrifter och brefvexling*, 1/9 (Stockholm, 1946), 514–15 • GEC, *Peerage*

Archives NA Scot., letters to laird of Glenorchy

Likenesses eleventh earl of Buchan, pencil and chalk drawing, 1795, Scot. NPG • C. Tiebout, stipple, pubd 1795 (after G. Jamesone), BM, NPG; repro. in J. Pinkerton, *The Scottish gallery* (1799) • by or after G. Jamesone, oils, Scot. NPG [*see illus.*] • Vandergucht, engraving (after Van Dyck), repro. in Clarendon, *Hist. rebellion*

Wealth at death owned part of St Monans, Fife, and had a home there

Leslie [*née* Oppenheim], **Doris** [*other married name* Doris Fergusson Hannay, Lady Fergusson Hannay] (**1891–1982**), novelist, was born at 66 Westbourne Grove, London, on 9 March 1891 of Jewish descent. Her parents were Samuel Oppenheim, a tobacconist, and his wife, Sarah Elkan. Doris was evasive about her early life. She said she was educated privately in London and Brussels, and then after she showed a gift for drawing her father sent her to a school of art in London. It is certain that at fifteen she decided to become an actress against her father's wishes, and won a scholarship to the drama section of the Guildhall School of Music. Her stage début was as Viola in *Twelfth Night* at the Old Vic. She also appeared with the Birmingham repertory theatre. While still in her teens she married John Leslie, another actor. He died shortly after the marriage; she kept his name for the rest of her life. Her second marriage was to R. Vincent Cookes, but she did not publicly acknowledge this marriage for 'religious reasons' (Ashley).

After her first husband's death Doris Leslie lost interest in acting and resumed her art studies, this time in Florence. She kept regular diaries while in Italy and realized that writing was her vocation. On her return to England she wrote her first novel, *The Starling* (1927), set in Florence. Its success committed her to writing, although she later dismissed her four subsequent novels, *Fools in Mortar* (1928), *The Echoing Green* (1929), *Terminus* (1931), and *Puppets' Parade* (1931), as trivial. But *Full Flavour* (1934), a fictional account of the long life of a woman who makes a success of her father's business, in the then popular dynasty chronicle genre, established her reputation. It was quickly translated into five languages and adapted for the stage. It was dedicated to her mother, who did not live to see it published. In 1936 Doris Leslie published *Fair Company*, another 'leisurely' tale, this time spanning four generations of an English family from the Regency up to the 1930s.

Some of the many characters in *Full Flavour* and *Fair Company* reappear in the crowded pages of the Victorian-to-First World War chronicle of *Concord in Jeopardy* (1938), but Leslie's loose style and uninspired plotting were beginning to make readers unhappy with just well crafted historical backgrounds. Moreover she unsuccessfully attempted to psychologize Concord and make him a symbol. *Another Cynthia: the adventures of Cynthia Lady Ffulkes (1780–1850) reconstructed from her hitherto unpublished memoirs* (1939), a tale of a Moll Flanders figure who snares titled lovers, was more 'lively'. This was a word often used by critics to describe Leslie's work, although the diary format she used in fact renders action as more reported than experienced. On 21 November 1936 she married Walter Fergusson Leisrinck Hannay (1904–1961), a London physician who was knighted in 1951. There were no children of the marriage.

During the Second World War Leslie was slightly wounded while serving in civil defence as an air raid warden. The battle of Britain featured in *House in the Dust* (1942), in which a bombed house triggers the memories of her central character, Jennifer. However, the twentieth-century anachronisms, in what was largely a tale of Victorian childhood, irritated the critics. Also in the 1940s came a series of 'fictional biographies', first of Chopin in *Polonaise* (1943), and then of Lady Arabella Stuart in *A Wreath for Arabella* (1948). These were not scholarly works of biography but vivid and colourful portraits designed to entertain. She also produced novels such as *Folly's End* (1944) and *The Peverills* (1946). In the 1950s Leslie published *The Great Corinthian* (1952), an entertaining biography of the prince regent, and novels which included *Peridot flight: a novel reconstructed from the memoirs of Peridot, Lady Mulvarnie, 1872–1955* (1956). Hutchinson reprinted *Another Cynthia*, *Folly's End*, and *The Peverills* in 1956 as *Tales of Grace and Favour*.

After Sir Walter's death in 1961 Doris Leslie converted to Roman Catholicism, moved to Devon, and began to breed and show English bulldogs. She became a real celebrity when BBC television broadcast her *Peridot* series. Over her lifetime she wrote more than sixteen popular novels and seventeen biographies, and while they were not critically esteemed, particularly as historical fiction came under fire in the 1960s, her books were widely enjoyed in Britain and America. Her biographies, which later included works on François Villon (1962), Elizabeth Chudleigh (1974), and Richard the Lionheart (1977), were often as finely wrought as her best historical novels.

Doris Leslie was a striking woman with very dark eyes and black bobbed hair. Unable to type, she wrote all her books in longhand and had her hand insured for a large amount of money. She had settled near East Grinstead, Sussex, when she died of renal failure on 31 May 1982 at the Royal Sussex County Hospital, Brighton.

LEONARD R. N. ASHLEY

Sources L. R. N. Ashley, 'Doris Leslie', *British novelists between the wars*, ed. G. M. Johnson, DLitB, 191 (1998), 214–17 • S. J. Kunitz and H. Haycraft, eds., *Twentieth century authors: a biographical dictionary of modern literature* (1942) • S. J. Kunitz and V. Colby, eds., *Twentieth-century authors: a biographical dictionary of modern literature, first supplement* (1955) • L. Henderson, ed., *Twentieth-century romance and historical writers*, 2nd edn (1990) • b. cert. • m. cert. [Walter Fergusson Leisrinck Hannay] • d. cert.

Leslie, Frank [*formerly* Henry Carter] (**1821–1880**), engraver and publisher, was born at Ipswich on 29 March 1821, the son of Joseph Leslie Carter, a prosperous glove manufacturer, and his wife, Mary Elliston. His boyhood was spent learning glove making in his father's factory, and at the age of seventeen he was sent to London to work in the drapery business of an uncle. In 1841 or 1842, aged twenty, he married Sarah Ann Welham, with whom he had three sons. Both at Ipswich and in London Carter indulged a passion for drawing, sketching, and engraving, particularly on wood. To conceal this from his father, who intended for him a career in trade, he took to signing his woodcuts Frank Leslie. It was under this name that he found employment in 1842 in the engraving department of the *Illustrated London News*. He was soon put in charge of that department, and there he learned the techniques of pictorial printing.

Carter was 'a pushing, lively fellow, with a head full of projects' (Mott, 378). Perceiving a greater demand for his skills in America he emigrated to New York with his family in 1848 and opened for business in a shop on Broadway as F. Leslie, engraver (he changed his name to Frank Leslie by law in 1857). He soon won an important commission illustrating for the impresario P. T. Barnum. Leslie next went to Boston, to prepare woodcuts for Frederick Gleason's new illustrated weekly, but returned to New York in 1852. Once he had accumulated sufficient capital he began publishing on his own account, launching *Frank Leslie's Ladies Gazette of Fashion* as a New York periodical in January 1854. Later that year he purchased, cheaply, the *New York Journal of Romance*, an illustrated story paper; under his skilful management it turned a healthy profit. The success of these two ventures made possible his great ambition: the publication of *Frank Leslie's Illustrated Newspaper*, which first appeared on 14 December 1855.

Frank Leslie's Illustrated contained 'the seeds not only of Leslie's success but of modern picture-text magazines and news weeklies' (Tebbel and Zuckerman, 18). It was a weekly magazine offering for 10 cents sixteen pages of news, sport, arts reviews, and later, fashion. Central to its success were the quality of its large illustrations and the speed with which they appeared: pictures in the *Illustrated* generally followed events within about two weeks, a quickness not matched by any competitor until after the civil war. Leslie achieved this by the simple but effective innovation of dividing the woodblock into thirty-two squares that could be engraved simultaneously and then screwed together, cutting the time for the production of a double-page illustration from a fortnight to a single day. Though at first the *Illustrated* struggled, by its third year it had over 100,000 readers. The arrival of *Harper's Weekly* in 1857 represented direct competition, which Leslie countered by cutting the price of the *Illustrated* to 6 cents. Circulation rose to 164,000 before the civil war and reached a peak of around 200,000. It survived as a title (latterly *Leslie's Weekly*) until 1922.

Less dignified in tone than *Harper's*, the *Illustrated* unashamedly liked sensation and, while it gave good coverage to events such as Commodore Perry's historic visit to Japan, 'its artists seemed to do their best work with murders, prizefights, and disasters' (Mott, 378). But it was also a serious investigative journal, and in 1858 its picture power exposed the political and administrative corruption that had rendered New York's milk supply a health hazard. Images of dying and diseased cows fired public interest in the 'swill milk' business and led to an official committee of inquiry. Leslie, however, did not carry the same clarity of moral conviction towards the civil war, and the *Illustrated*, which was anti-abolitionist and had a significant southern readership, pursued neutrality in the early days before backing the Union in mid-1861.

Edited from 1861 by the archaeologist Ephraim George Squier, the *Illustrated* was Leslie's flagship publication, but his list expanded to include weekly and monthly story papers, joke papers, news-sheets, pictorials, and a German-language weekly, *Die Illustrierte Zeitung* (1857). He also diversified into book publication, the civil war providing rich opportunities for this; the *Pictorial History of the War of 1861* (1861–2) was followed by several other works in a similar vein. The 1870s marked the zenith of the Frank Leslie publishing house, based in an impressive five-storey building at 537 Pearl Street. Leslie amassed a considerable fortune, with which he liberally entertained his numerous friends at a magnificent residence in Saratoga. After the breakdown of his marriage in the late 1850s he separated from his wife in 1860 and became enamoured of Miriam Florence Squier, *née* Follin, formerly Peacock (1836–1914), wife of the editor of the *Illustrated* and herself the editor of two Leslie periodicals, the *Chimney Corner* and *Lady's Journal*. Having obtained his own divorce in 1872 Leslie helped to secure hers in 1873, and they were married later that year. In her publishing acumen and social vivacity the red-headed Miriam Leslie was more than a match for her new husband, her third, and in time her legend outgrew his. The tone of their social life was evident in the luxurious railroad journey that they made from New York to California, with a small entourage of writers and artists, in 1877. It resulted in Miriam Leslie's book *California: a Pleasant Trip from Gotham to the Golden Gate* (1877).

This journey also symbolized Frank Leslie's fascination with the growth of the railroads in America. He saw early on the publishing potential that this offered and launched several series of cheap books intended to capitalize on it. The major series was the Home Library of Standard Works by the Most Celebrated Authors, begun in 1877. Books that might normally cost as much as $2 were made available by the Home Library for 10 or 20 cents at station kiosks, newsstands, and even on the trains themselves. Between 1876 and 1877, when railroad expansion was at its height, Leslie tripled his book production, 'catering to the developing mass market for cheap reprints to read aboard trains' (Stern, *Mass Entertainment*, 186).

When the Leslie publishing machine was at its fullest stretch it ran into trouble, the victim of the general business depression of 1877 but also of a loss of focus on Leslie's part. He made one of his heaviest trade losses on the lavishly illustrated *Historical Register of the United States Centennial Exposition, 1876* (1877). Facing imminent ruin he made an assignment of his property for the benefit of creditors in September 1877, although by the time of his death he had reduced his debts to only $100,000. He died of throat cancer at his home on Fifth Avenue, New York, on 10 January 1880. In the last days of his life he put the publishing house that he had built into the hands of his wife, Miriam, who proved adept at running it. She soon cleared the remaining debt, changed her name to Frank Leslie, and retired from the business in 1900 a wealthy woman.

Leslie represented a new breed of editor in American journalism, a personality in his own right, and an innovator in the techniques of mass publishing and marketing. At his peak, in the 1850s, he was 'a striking figure': 'Short and broad but handsome, his heavy black beard thrusting out below a pair of penetrating eyes, he virtually radiated energy' (Tebbel and Zuckerman, 20). He had built his success on the simple precept 'Never shoot over the heads of the people' and, perhaps because of this, he had limited national influence: in the end he did far more to amuse and entertain than to inform and instruct.

MARK POTTLE

Sources *DNB* • G. Everett, 'Leslie, Frank', *ANB* • M. B. Stern, *Publishers for mass entertainment in nineteenth-century America* (1980) • F. L. Mott, *American journalism: a history of newspapers in the United States through 250 years, 1690–1940* (1941); repr. (1947) • J. Tebbel and M. E. Zuckerman, *The magazine in America, 1714–1990* (1991) • M. B. Stern, *Imprints on history: book publishers and the American frontiers* (1956)

Leslie, Fred [*real name* Frederick George Hobson] (**1855–1892**), actor and singer, was born at 56 Artillery Place, Woolwich, London, on 1 April 1855, the youngest son of Charles Hobson, a prosperous military outfitter, and Sarah Hobson, *née* Pye. After schooling in Woolwich, Lewisham, and Pas-de-Calais he worked in commerce and performed in amateur theatricals under several different names. In 1878 the flat-faced but darkly handsome young man made his professional début, as 'Mr Lewis', at the Royalty Theatre, under the management of Kate Santley. Since Miss Santley's main diet was *opéra bouffe*, his second role there (under the name 'Mr Leslie') was a singing one, the aged Agamemnon in *La belle Hélène*. His useful baritone voice proved ideally suited to the various musical-comic roles in the French *opéras comiques* which were the rage of the time, and thereafter, although he mixed younger roles with the older character ones which he fancied his speciality, he played very largely in musical shows. He appeared in several such pieces with Selina Dolaro at the Folly, took a leading (young) part in *La petite mademoiselle* at the Alhambra, and then, confirmed at the age of twenty-three as a top musical-theatre comedian, followed this success with a run of lead musical-comic roles in London and New York. Leslie married his childhood girlfriend Louisa (Louie) Agate on 20 December 1879; they had three children, the eldest of whom, Leslie, went on the stage in the 1900s (as Fred Leslie) for a successful career as a light comedy supporting and, later, leading man in musical comedy.

On his return to London, Leslie created a fine low-comedy part in the successful new musical *Les manteaux noirs*, and then in 1882 introduced what would be the most memorable part of his career, the title role in a comic opera, *Rip Van Winkle*, written especially to his measure by the librettist and the composer of the moment, H. B.

Farnie and Robert Planquette. Leslie scored a veritable triumph as Rip, but a quarrel over wages led him to quit the part after a year's run and to return to America, where he played a season with the country's top comic opera company, run by John McCaull. The outstanding singing-comedy role of Ollendorf in a revival of *The Beggar Student* provided him with another fine vehicle in which to return to Britain, but thereafter interesting roles rather lacked, and Leslie's career faltered momentarily. He was reduced to appearing in an amateurish piece called *Fay o' Fire* (alongside a young beginner called Marie Tempest) when the opportunity came which would lead him on to the second half of his double-peaked career. He was offered the part of the thief-taker Jonathan Wild in a full-length 'new burlesque' version of the Jack Sheppard story to be produced at the Gaiety in 1885, with that theatre's adored 'principal boy', Nellie Farren, as Jack. *Little Jack Sheppard* was a huge success, Leslie and Farren were huge successes in it, and thereafter Leslie worked only for the Gaiety manager, George Edwardes. Through the next seven years, and just five shows (*Monte Cristo Jr*, *Frankenstein*, *Ruy Blas and the Blasé Roué*, *Miss Esmeralda* (revival), and *Cinder-Ellen up-too-Late*), he and Farren went unchallenged as the British theatre's outstanding and outstandingly popular pair of musical-theatre stars, and as the centre people and virtual *raison d'être* of the six-year blaze of the new burlesque tradition. They played their shows at the Gaiety, around the provinces, in America, and in Australia (1888–9), until Nellie Farren was forced from the stage by illness in 1892. The new burlesque tradition was itself tottering by this stage, but Leslie (who had had a hand in the writing of three of the shows, plus another allowing his fellow comedian Arthur Roberts to play in *Guy Fawkes Jr*) and Edwardes were planning one further piece of the kind when Leslie was overcome by 'enteric fever', and died at his lodgings at 8 Tavistock Chambers, Hart Street, on 7 December 1892, at the age of thirty-seven. He was buried in Charlton cemetery, Greenwich.

Fred and Nellie thus never had a period of theatrical decline, and this fact undoubtedly helped them to remain in theatrical annals as one of the most brilliant and adored musical-comic partnerships of all time, a partnership which perhaps unfairly clouded the memory of the first part of the career of a player whom Clement Scott called 'one of the great lyric and comic artists of my time'. KURT GÄNZL

Sources W. T. Vincent, *Recollections of Fred Leslie*, 2 vols. (1894) • K. Gänzl, *The British musical theatre*, 2 vols. (1986) • K. Gänzl, *The encyclopedia of the musical theatre*, 2 vols. (1994) • *The Era* • *Who's who in the theatre* • b. cert. • d. cert.

Likenesses St James Photographic Co., woodburytype photograph, NPG; repro. in *The Theatre* (1884) • cartoons, Harvard TC • photograph, repro. in Vincent, *Recollections of Fred Leslie* • photograph, repro. in Gänzl, *The encyclopedia of the musical theatre* • photograph (as Rip van Winkle), British Musical Theatre Collection • photograph (with Farren), British Musical Theatre Collection • woodcuts, caricatures, Harvard TC

Wealth at death £16,545 4*s*. 2*d*.: probate, 3 Feb 1893, *CGPLA Eng. & Wales*

Leslie, George, first earl of Rothes (*c*.1417?–1489/90), magnate, was the only son of Norman Leslie of Fythkill in Fife, who died about February 1440, and Christian, daughter of Sir John Seton of Seton. He inherited a considerable collection of lands, mainly on the east coast: Leslie in the Garioch; Rothienorman, Fowlis Mowat, and Cushnie in the adjoining earldom of Mar; Rothes in Moray; Fythkill and Tacis in Fife; and Cairny in Perthshire. Consequently he was among the first Scottish nobles elevated to the new rank of lord of parliament in the minority of James II, becoming first Lord Leslie of Leven probably in 1445—a creation, if not a date, confirmed by two extant charters issued by him with this style in 1448. He further increased his status through important marriage alliances and by providing local support to the adult James II in the king's dealings in north-east Scotland.

On 5 November 1457 Leslie served on the Aberdeen assize of error which found against the claim of Thomas, Lord Erskine (of whom Leslie held lands), to the earldom of Mar, so confirming it as a crown possession. Leslie was rewarded by James II on 20 or 21 March 1458 with the earldom of Rothes (based on his castle barony in Morayshire), the barony of Ballinbreich in Fife, confirmation of all his other lands, and the erection of Leslie-Green into a burgh of barony. James II clearly intended Rothes to be a royalist counterweight in north-east Scotland to the earls of Orkney, Crawford, and Huntly. But the remainder of Rothes's career seems to have been low-key and troubled. In May 1459 his annulment of his second marriage on the grounds of relationship within the fourth degree was disputed by William Sinclair, third earl of Orkney (*d.* 1480), whose son and daughter were by then married to Rothes's children from this marriage. Arbitration by the chapter of St Andrews Cathedral allowed the annulment, granted on 22 May 1459, and legitimation of the offspring. The latter was presumably Sinclair's concern, along with some £500 Scots which by 'certain contracts' of marriage Rothes had been bound to pay Sinclair in 1459. (Sinclair's successor would litigate against the second earl of Rothes for this in 1498–9.) That on 15 October 1464 the privy council declared Rothes not guilty of forging the signet of the late James II on a royal acquittance of debt of 200 merks may also point to financial problems.

Rothes attended parliament often between 1467 and 1481 and on 8 February 1476 received the barony of Balmain in Kincardineshire after the forfeiture of John MacDonald, earl of Ross and lord of the Isles. But he was never a regular royal charter witness and seems to have withdrawn from national affairs into neutrality just before the first of the civil wars of James III's reign, in 1482. At some stage, though, there was an apparent rift within the Leslie family (perhaps dating back to Rothes's marriage annulment in 1459): on 10 February 1487 James III ordered Rothes—who suffered 'personal apprehension' by the sheriff of Aberdeen—on pain of immediate ward in Dumbarton Castle to provide for his grandson and heir, George, master of Rothes [*see below*], who was to continue in the king's retinue.

The earl's subsequent fortunes are uncertain, but he

died between 31 August 1489 and 24 May 1490 and was probably buried in Leslie churchyard, Fife. He and his first wife, Margaret, daughter of John Lundin of that ilk, whom he married *c.*1435, had a daughter, Margaret. About 1440 he married Christian, widow of Alexander Leslie, earl of Ross, and daughter of Walter Haliburton of Dirleton and Isabel Stewart (daughter of Robert Stewart, duke of Albany). They had three children: Andrew, who died before January 1478, having married Elizabeth, daughter of William Sinclair of Orkney; Elizabeth, who married William Hay, third earl of Erroll, another north-east magnate; and Christian, who married William Sinclair, later Lord Sinclair. Rothes's third wife was Elizabeth Campbell.

George Leslie, second earl of Rothes (*d.* 1513), second surviving son of the first earl of Rothes's only son, Andrew, was infefted on 25 May 1490 in his grandfather's lands, with the addition of Balmullo in Fife. But his career was racked by legal actions over feudal casualties and criminal activity, and he was pursued by the crown and several individuals (including his wife, the bishop of Moray, and the earl of Orkney and Caithness). Probably as a result of his support for James III in 1487–8, Rothes was pursued before the lords of council on 22 October 1490 for arrears of non-entry (payment due to the crown by a tenant-in-chief when lands are first acquired) for Ballinbreich, for which he was to pay over £800 Scots and more in kind to Patrick Hepburn, earl of Bothwell (*d.* 1508), then guardian of James IV; three days later he was pursued by his grandfather's widow for two years' wrongful occupation of Ballinbreich, which she claimed to own. Rothes failed to compear, and his lands were seized and distrained to yield the sum required. Significantly, about this time Rothes's father-in-law, Archibald Douglas, fifth earl of Angus (*d.* 1514), was gradually being displaced from his political and territorial offices.

Rothes, though, was as much a crook as a victim. On 23 April 1498 he was fined £100 Scots for non-compearence at Cupar justiciar's court to answer for the murder of one George Leslie, or Dunlop, and he subsequently became a fugitive, failing to compear in court to face the charges four times between 1500 and 1509. On each occasion he was fined £1000 Scots, declared an outlaw, and had his goods forfeited to the king. This was despite crown attempts to rehabilitate Rothes: on 2 March 1506 James IV granted to William Leslie, brother and heir of George, the right to counsel the earl not to waste 'so noble and famous a house', so disinheriting his rightful heir. But Rothes's intractability left him open to royal fiscal opportunism. In March 1508 Rothes lost his Fife lands for alienating some of them without royal licence and was fined £2210 Scots for eighty-five years' non-entry to Balmain (which the first earl had been given only in 1476, unaware of the previous tenant's debts). The king granted out many of Rothes's other lands and collected their feudal revenues anew, until the Leslies recovered them after the battle of Flodden.

The second earl of Rothes died between 24 February and 31 March 1513. Some time between 1484 and 1488 he married Jane or Janet (*d.* before 10 July 1494), fifth daughter of the fifth earl of Angus. They had no children, and Rothes was succeeded by his brother William.

Michael A. Penman

Sources J. M. Thomson and others, eds., *Registrum magni sigilli regum Scotorum / The register of the great seal of Scotland*, 11 vols. (1882–1914), vol. 2 · Colonel Leslie [C. J. Leslie], *Historical records of the family of Leslie, from 1067 to 1868–9*, 3 vols. (1869) · G. Burnett and others, eds., *The exchequer rolls of Scotland*, 6–12 (1883–9) · T. Dickson, ed., *Compota thesaurariorum regum Scotorum / Accounts of the lord high treasurer of Scotland*, 1 (1877) · J. B. Paul, ed., *Compota thesaurariorum regum Scotorum / Accounts of the lord high treasurer of Scotland*, 2–4 (1900–02) · [T. Thomson] and others, eds., *The acts of the lords of council in civil causes, 1478–1503*, 3 vols. (1839–1993) · [T. Thomson], ed., *The acts of the lords auditors of causes and complaints*, AD *1466–*AD *1494*, RC, 40 (1839) · *APS*, *1424–1567* · *Scots peerage* · N. Macdougall, *James III: a political study* (1982) · N. Macdougall, *James IV* (1989) · *Fourth report*, HMC, 3 (1874) · *Johannis de Fordun Chronica gentis Scotorum / John of Fordun's Chronicle of the Scottish nation*, ed. W. F. Skene, trans. F. J. H. Skene, 2 vols. (1871–2) · GEC, *Peerage*
Archives NA Scot., muniments, GD 204

Leslie, George, second earl of Rothes (*d.* **1513**). *See under* Leslie, George, first earl of Rothes (*c.*1417?–1489/90).

Leslie, George, fourth earl of Rothes (*d.* **1558**), nobleman, was the eldest of the four children of William Leslie, third earl of Rothes (*d.* 1513), and Janet (*fl. c.*1490–*c.*1520), daughter of Sir Michael Balfour of Montquhannie. Earl William was killed at the battle of Flodden (9 September 1513) within a few months of the death of his elder brother, George *Leslie, the second earl [*see under* Leslie, George, first earl of Rothes (*c.*1417?–1489/90)], and before he had taken full legal possession of the estates, so the fourth earl was served heir to both.

While still a young man, Rothes formed a liaison with Lady Margaret Crichton (*b.* before 1496, *d.* in or after 1545), daughter of William, third Lord Crichton, and Lady Margaret Stewart, second sister of James III. She was the widow of, first, William Todrick and, second, George Halkerston, both burgesses of Edinburgh. In a charter of 1 April 1517 her relationship with Rothes is defined as 'eius sponsa affidate per verba de futuro cum carnali copula inde secuta'—that is, his wife by plighting of troth followed by physical consummation (*Registrum magni sigilli*, 3.148). There is no surviving record of a formal ceremony, however, and on 27 December 1520 the marriage was declared by the rector of Flisk to have been invalid from the beginning, on account of consanguinity. Nevertheless, the children of the union were to be considered legitimate because the couple had lived together in ignorance of the impediment. Those children were Norman *Leslie, master of Rothes (*d.* 1554), William of Cairney, Robert of Ardersier and Findrassie (*d.* 1588), Janet (*d.* 1591), and Helen (*d.* 1594). Shortly before 20 July 1525 Rothes married Elizabeth Gray, daughter of Andrew, second Lord Gray, and widow of John Lyon, fourth Lord Glamis, and of Alexander Gordon, third earl of Huntly, but they had no children, and she was dead before 4 October 1527. Before 29

January 1530 Rothes had remarried; his third wife was Agnes (*d.* 1543), daughter of Sir John Somerville of Cambusnethan and widow of John, second Lord Fleming. Their children were Andrew *Leslie, later fifth earl of Rothes, Peter, parson of Rothes, James, ancestor of the Leslies of Ballybay in Ireland, Euphemia (*d.* 1588), Agnes *Leslie, Beatrix, and Elizabeth. It is possible that Rothes married Margaret Crichton after the death of Agnes Somerville, since a charter of 31 May 1542 refers to the former as countess of Rothes, but two charters of 21 October 1542 do not accord her this title. By 10 April 1543 he was married to Isobel Lundy (*d.* in or before 1550), daughter of Lundy of Lundy and widow of David Lindsay, eighth earl of Crawford (*d.* 1542), but they had no children. Rothes seems to have had four illegitimate children: Walter Leslie of Cowcairnie, Robert Leslie, who was legitimated in October 1557, Christine, who was legitimated in November 1553 and whose mother was Christian Wood, Lady Balcaskie, and Katherine, the daughter of Helen Forsyth.

During the minority of James V, Rothes had co-operated with the regime of the sixth earl of Angus, James's hated stepfather, but was nevertheless accepted into the service of the adult king. On 1 June 1529 he was appointed hereditary sheriff of Fife and the office was confirmed in 1540. On 16 November 1532 he was made an extraordinary lord of session, and in 1533 he was entrusted with the detention of the archbishop of St Andrews, who was suspected of dealings with the king of England. Rothes was one of the nobles who travelled to France with James V in September 1536, but he returned to Scotland in October with Lord Erskine to take possession in the king's name of Dunbar Castle, the former property of John Stuart, duke of Albany, who had died in May that year. In August 1537 John Lyon of Knockany was executed for treasonably concealing a conspiracy by Janet Douglas, Lady Glamis, to kill the king, and also of plotting to poison the earl of Rothes: Rothes had been in dispute with the Lyons (the lords Glamis) for some years over the wardship of the earldom of Erroll.

At the battle of Solway Moss (24 November 1542), John Leslie of Parkhill and Cleish, one of Rothes's younger brothers, was captured and became assured to the king of England. Rothes himself was also initially pro-English and in July 1543 served the governor, the earl of Arran, who was then negotiating with Henry VIII, at the siege of Linlithgow; but in September Arran was reconciled with Cardinal Beaton, the leader of opposition to England, and Rothes was captured and warded in Craignethan Castle in November. In December 1543 Rothes was readmitted to the council, and during the 'rough wooing'—the campaigns of devastation by which King Henry attempted to break Scottish resistance in 1544–5—he was active in defending Scotland, especially the Fife coast, from English attacks. On 29 May 1546 Cardinal Beaton was murdered at St Andrews by a gang of Fife lairds who included Norman Leslie, master of Rothes, and John Leslie of Cleish; both were convicted of treason and forfeited. Rothes' brother James, and his sons William and Robert, were also subsequently associated with the killers of Beaton, so it is hardly surprising that Rothes himself was suspected of being an accessory to the murder. On 28 June he appeared before the council to protest his innocence but by September he had fled to Denmark. By the spring of 1547 the Scottish government agreed to give Rothes a formal trial to clear his name. He returned home and on 15 July was acquitted of all charges at an assize held near Yarrow Water, where he was serving with the army. The official record states that Rothes had lately returned from a trip to Hungary, but this is clearly an error for Denmark. After the battle of Pinkie (10 September 1547) both Arran and Rothes considered coming to terms with England, but when French help arrived in the summer of 1548 Rothes renewed his activity in the defence of the realm and assented to the treaty of Haddington, made with France on 7 July.

Once the war with England was concluded, Rothes was sent back to Denmark as ambassador; there, between April and June 1550, he successfully persuaded King Christian III to defer pursuit of his claims to the islands of Orkney and Shetland until Mary, queen of Scots, was an adult. In the parliament of 14 December 1557 Rothes was one of the lords appointed to act as Scottish ambassadors to witness the marriage of Mary to the dauphin in Paris. He narrowly escaped being drowned on the voyage, but carried out his duties and seems to have impressed the French, one of whom described him as a 'puissant seigneur pour le pays' (*CSP Scot.*, 1547–63, 1.207). However, this was to be his last public duty, for he and several of his colleagues were taken violently ill on the way home. There were rumours of a French plot to poison the ambassadors but accidental food poisoning is perhaps a more likely explanation. Rothes died at Dieppe, probably on 28 November 1558. ANDREA THOMAS

Sources *LP Henry VIII*, vols. 7–21 • J. M. Thomson and others, eds., *Registrum magni sigilli regum Scotorum / The register of the great seal of Scotland*, 11 vols. (1882–1914), vol. 3 • *Scots peerage* • T. L. Christensen, *The earl of Rothes in Denmark* (1983) • Colonel Leslie [C. J. Leslie], *Historical records of the family of Leslie, from 1067 to 1868–9*, 3 vols. (1869) • R. K. Hannay, ed., *Acts of the lords of council in public affairs, 1501–1554* (1932) • *Fourth report*, HMC, 3 (1874) • J. B. Paul, ed., *Compota thesaurariorum regum Scotorum / Accounts of the lord high treasurer of Scotland*, 5–10 (1903–13) • M. Livingstone, D. Hay Fleming, and others, eds., *Registrum secreti sigilli regum Scotorum / The register of the privy seal of Scotland*, 8 vols. (1908–82), vol. 1, 1488–1529; vol. 4, 1548–56 • *CSP Scot., 1547–63* • J. Cameron, *James V: the personal rule, 1528–1542*, ed. N. Macdougall (1998) • G. Burnett and others, eds., *The exchequer rolls of Scotland*, 14–19 (1893–8) • R. Pitcairn, ed., *Ancient criminal trials in Scotland*, 7 pts in 3, Bannatyne Club, 42 (1833) • *APS, 1424–1567*

Leslie, George [*name in religion* Archangel] (*d.* **1637**?), Capuchin friar and missionary, son of James Leslie of Peterstone, Aberdeen, and Jane Wood, was born into a protestant family. Having become a Catholic he entered the Scots College in Rome in 1608 but left to become a Capuchin friar, taking Archangel as his name in religion. He claimed in April 1618 to have worn the Capuchin habit for eleven years. In November 1617 he wrote from Bologna to the cardinal-protector of Scotland, Maffeo Barberini, whom he would have known in Rome, saying that his studies for

George Leslie (*d.* 1637?), by unknown engraver

the priesthood were now completed and asking for faculties to hear the confessions of the many Scottish, English, and Irish banished for their religion and living near him. Further letters to Barberini described the difficulties he faced in his work with these exiles. Writing from Pisa in July 1618 he asked for favour to be shown to his cousin Thomas Dempster, and from Bologna in October 1619 recommended another relative, George Conn.

Four years later, in August 1623, Leslie wrote from London telling Barberini (now Pope Urban VIII) that he was with the Spanish ambassador but would soon go to stay with the Catholic Lord Herries in south-west Scotland. Before long, however, he was in the north-east of the country and had written a polemical tract, 'Where was your church before Luther?', which is only known from a reply published in 1624 by Andrew Logie, minister of Rayne, Aberdeenshire, entitled *Raine from the Clouds upon a Choicke Angel*. In March 1626 the Congregatio de Propaganda Fide in Rome considered Leslie's report about Catholics in Scotland attending heretical sermons. It was a period of vigilant action against missionary priests; a list of these in the north-east included Leslie (whom the privy council singled out as a Capuchin), and among their resetters (shelterers) was his brother William. In December 1628 the privy council ordered the arrest of Capuchin Leslie, while another brother, Francis, was accused of resetting priests, making libellous writings and pasquils, and hearing mass said by Capuchin Leslie.

By January 1630 Leslie was in Paris and there he wrote to his relative Colonel William Sempill, explaining why he had left Scotland: first because the French Capuchin given charge of all the order's missions had decided that only French friars should serve in them; and second to answer charges made against him to *propaganda fide*. He also listed the many conversions he had made; they included his own family and persons of rank in diverse parts of Scotland. In April 1631 Leslie was completely exonerated. The prefect of the Capuchin mission in England had testified in his favour and various Scottish Catholics had praised his exemplary life and his efforts to confute and convert heretics, saying that he had done more good than other religious priests and pleading for his return to Scotland. This was passed on to the Capuchin general superior but Leslie was instead appointed guardian of the friary at Monte Giorgio in the marches of Ancona, where he remained until 1634.

In July 1633 Leslie's offer to return to Scotland had been considered by *propaganda fide* and in December faculties were given for his apostolate and for exemption when necessary from Capuchin observance. Little is known about his activities in Scotland. In 1635 he had to take refuge with the Capuchins in Dublin but in November of that year he reported to Rome about the dire straits of Scottish Catholics. He died, most probably in 1637, in his mother's house 'against the mill of Obein [Aboyne]' (Hay, 214) on Deeside and was buried in Glen Tanar churchyard.

Though there are many references to Leslie's polemical writings it is difficult to judge in the absence of surviving printed copies how much was actually published. Leslie was a dedicated missionary and a shrewd observer but hardly a celebrity, yet it has been said that more has been published about him than about any other Scot except Queen Mary Stuart. A biography entitled *Il cappuccino scozzese*, by Giovanni Battista Rinuccini, archbishop of Fermo, was published at Macerata in 1644. It was based on conversations when Leslie was at Monte Giorgio, near Fermo. Although the work reads like a medieval romance Rinuccini was a shrewd ecclesiastic and in the later 1640s was papal envoy to Ireland; he gathered what he could from other sources and declared that he had been unable to discover any information about Leslie's second missionary period. The book was an instant success, being published again and again in Italian, then in French, then in most of the languages of Catholic western Europe. The French edition of 1660, twenty-three years after Leslie's death, contained substantial additions, including a wholly fanciful account of his second missionary effort. Further editions in various languages added fabulous episodes. Jesuit students at Metz in 1657 produced a play of Leslie's life in seventy-six scenes and in 1673 an Italian stage version was published. However, no English version was published and in fact Scots Catholics deplored the publication. In the later nineteenth century publications in English appeared, ranging from the legendary version for the edification of the faithful to blunt accusations of mendacity. T. G. Law concluded that Leslie was a lying braggart, a view that hardly fits the person revealed in Leslie's letters. A more nuanced approach is now usual. The crucial factual inaccuracy in what Rinuccini says he learned from Leslie was the latter's birth to noble parents at Monymusk in Aberdeenshire, which belonged to the titled Forbes family. Two sons of that family had, however, been Capuchins, each taking the name of Archangel. It seems likely that Rinuccini, however it came about, had attributed to Archangel Leslie a conflation of the stories of the Forbes brothers and indeed of other friars too.

MARK DILWORTH

Sources F. Callaey, *Essai critique sur la vie du P. Archange Leslie* (Paris and Couvin, 1914) · Colonel Leslie [C. J. Leslie], *Historical records of the family of Leslie, from 1067 to 1868–9*, 3 (1869), 408–9, 415–35 · A. Dean, 'George Archangel Leslie, *il cappucino scozzese*', *Innes Review*, 49 (1998), 66–76 · C. J. Gossip, 'From Monymusk to Metz: Archangel Leslie on the European stage', *Aberdeen University Review*, 46 (1975–6), 137–50 · F. X. Martin, 'A thwarted project: the Capuchin mission to England and Scotland in the seventeenth century, 1608–1660', *Miscellanea Melchor de Pobladura*, ed. I. Villapadierna, 2 (Rome, 1964), 211–41 · T. G. Law, 'The legend of Archangel Leslie', *Collected essays and reviews of Thomas Graves Law, LL.D*, ed. P. H. Brown (1904), 332–64 · T. G. Law, 'Archangel Leslie of Scotland: a sequel', *Collected essays and reviews of Thomas Graves Law LL.D*, ed. P. H. Brown (1904), 365–76 · T. G. Law, 'The bibliography of the lives of two Scottish Capuchins', *Edinburgh Bibliographical Society I*, Session (1890–91), 1–12 · C. Giblin, 'The "Acta" of propaganda archives and the Scottish mission, 1623–1670', *Innes Review*, 5 (1954), 39–76 · [W. A. Leslie], *Laurus Leslæana explicata* (Graz, 1692) · A. Bellesheim, *History of the Catholic Church in Scotland*, ed. and trans. D. O. H. Blair, 4 (1890), 75–81 · M. V. Hay, *The Blairs papers (1603–1660)* (1929), 213–14
Archives PRO, letters, PRO 31/9/128, fols. 159–75 · Vatican, letters, Barb. Lat. 8618, fols. 123 ff.
Likenesses engraving, NPG [*see illus.*]
Wealth at death practically nothing: Hay *Blairs papers*, 214

Leslie, Sir Harald Robert, Lord Birsay (1905–1982), judge, was born on 8 May 1905 at South Shields, co. Durham, the only son of Robert Leslie, master mariner, and his wife, Margaret Mowat Cochrane. His parents were both natives of Stromness, Orkney, and although he spent most of his life in southern Scotland, Leslie considered himself an Orcadian. His father died of a heart condition while serving in the merchant navy during the First World War, and Leslie professed that his only ambition had been to go to sea, but he was dissuaded from doing so by his widowed mother. His early childhood was spent in the borders, where he attended Berwickshire high school, Duns. He later moved to Glasgow and was educated at Glasgow high school and at Glasgow University, where he took MA (1927) and LLB (1930) degrees. He became a solicitor in 1930 and practised in Glasgow, but he found the life uncongenial and studied briefly for the ministry of the Church of Scotland. In 1937 he was called to the Scottish bar. He had been active in the Officers' Training Corps, and in 1939 he volunteered for active service. When his posting was delayed he briefly served as a stoker on a small steamer running military supplies around Scapa Flow. He was later commissioned into the Royal Scots and served throughout the war. He was mentioned in dispatches and appointed a military MBE; in 1945 he transferred to the reserve with the rank of lieutenant-colonel. In the same year he returned to practice at the bar, and on 27 December married Robina Margaret Marwick, the daughter of James George Marwick, a provost of Stromness. She had served as a doctor with the British forces in Germany and was among the first allied medical personnel to enter Belsen concentration camp. They set up home in Edinburgh and adopted a son and a daughter.

Between 1947 and 1951 Leslie served as an advocate depute under the Labour administration, acting as a prosecutor in the High Court of Justiciary. Despite having few connections in the law, his promotion was rapid and he took silk in 1949. At the bar his outstanding talent was as a jury pleader at a time when civil jury trials in actions for damages for personal injuries took up much of the business of the Court of Session. He was at his best when representing the pursuer, and was frequently successful. Later he defended the mass murderer Peter Manuel until his client, who was subsequently found guilty and hanged, dismissed him and took over his own defence. Although Leslie was not considered to be in the front rank as a lawyer, his powerful presence, coupled with his oratorical gifts and a stalwart independence, placed him among the most prominent advocates of the day. He was able to deploy to great advantage a rich bass voice which he enhanced with a pleasingly modified Orkney intonation.

While Leslie was admired by many of his brother advocates, in the narrow world of Parliament House the admiration was not universal. His determinedly homely delivery, his readiness to appeal to the emotions of juries (and even of judges), and his lack of enthusiasm for minute legal analysis did not endear him to elements of the legal establishment, and in particular to Lord Clyde, the lord president, whom he warmly disliked, and with whom he had several bitter courtroom confrontations. Nevertheless, in 1956 he was made sheriff of Roxburgh, Berwick, and Selkirk, when such appointments were seen as the route to elevation to the Supreme Court bench.

In 1959 Leslie stood for election as dean of the Faculty of Advocates (the leader of the Scottish bar), and in the first ballot his popularity enabled him to defeat the powerful establishment candidate I. H. Shearer QC. He was ultimately defeated by the compromise candidate, W. I. R. Fraser QC (later Lord Fraser of Tullybelton, lord of appeal). In 1961 he was translated to the (part-time) sheriffdom of Caithness, Sutherland, Orkney, and Zetland, an appointment which gave him considerable personal satisfaction. In 1965 he was appointed chairman of the Scottish land court, with the rank and tenure of a judge of the Court of Session, and took the title Lord Birsay from a village in Orkney. The land court had been set up in 1912 to adjudicate on disputes between crofting tenants and their landlords following upon the granting of security of tenure in the wake of the suffering caused by the highland clearances. Later it assumed a wider jurisdiction under the Agricultural Holdings Acts. While the court's headquarters were in Edinburgh, its jurisdiction was peripatetic and Leslie regularly sat in remote parts of Scotland, often in village halls and other even less formal surroundings.

His genuine interest in the people and their culture, his approachability and his pragmatism fitted him well for this work and his public popularity and reputation increased.

It was in the wider field of public affairs that Leslie made his greatest mark on Scottish life. In the general election of 1950 he stood as Labour candidate in the Orkney and Shetland constituency, but was defeated by Jo Grimond, who subsequently held the seat for many years for the Liberals. Leslie appeared incapable of refusing any request for help or service in the charitable or public sphere, and accepted a vast range of appointments. Among them were the chairmanships of the Scottish Advisory Council on the Treatment of Offenders, the Committee on General Medical Services in the Highlands and Islands, the National Savings Committee for Scotland, and the Scottish Advisory Committee on the Travelling People. He was also a vice-president of the Boys' Brigade, trustee of the Scottish Architectural Heritage Trust, and president of the Scottish national dictionary. In that capacity he led an appeal for a concise Scots dictionary which, when it was ultimately published after his death, was dedicated to his memory. He was an elder of the Church of Scotland for nearly fifty years and sat on many committees of the general assembly. The culmination of his life of public service was his appointment as lord high commissioner to the general assembly of the Church of Scotland in 1965 and 1966.

Leslie was in constant demand as a speaker and rarely declined an invitation. He would travel considerable distances at his own expense to address modest local gatherings as readily as he would undertake important after-dinner speeches. His reputation preceded him and his audiences were readily captivated by his homely eloquence, although even his admirers conceded that the content sometimes took second place to the charm of his delivery. Throughout his public life his natural warmth and generosity won him much affection across a wide range of Scottish society. He was appointed CBE in 1963. In 1966 he received LLD degrees from Glasgow and Strathclyde universities and in the same year was made an honorary fellow of the Educational Institute of Scotland in recognition of his services to education. In 1973 he was made a knight of the Order of the Thistle. He died of a coronary thrombosis on 27 November 1982 at his home, 27 Queensferry Road, Edinburgh. His wife survived him.

PHILIP

Sources personal knowledge (2004) • private information (2004) • d. cert. • records of Faculty of Advocates, Edinburgh • *WWW*

Archives Orkney Archives, Kirkwall, corresp. with E. Marwick

Leslie, Henry (1580–1661), Church of Ireland bishop of Down and Connor, was born at Leslie, Fife, Scotland, the third son of James Leslie and the grandson of George *Leslie, fourth earl of Rothes (*d.* 1558), and his third wife, Agnes Somerville.

Education and early career Leslie was educated at the University of St Andrews from where he graduated doctor of divinity. In 1614 he went to Ireland. He was ordained priest in 1617. In 1619 his kinsman Robert Echlin, bishop of Down and Connor, collated him to the prebendary of Connor and the rectory of Muckamore. When Leslie preached at the triennial visitation of the archdiocese he came to the attention of the archbishop of Armagh, Christopher Hampton. Subsequently, Leslie was appointed to the vicarage of St Peter's, Drogheda in 1620. He also became one of the archbishop's chaplains. In 1622 he was appointed to the rectories of Kilcluny and Beaulieu, and in 1624 he became rector of Clonoe and Arboe. Each of these livings was held *in commendam*. Early in the 1620s he married Jane Swinton, with whom he had three sons and two daughters. Of his sons, Robert was successively bishop of Dromore, of Raphoe, and of Clogher, and James and William were captains in the royalist forces in the civil war.

In 1622 Leslie preached before the royal commissioners at Drogheda. This sermon was published the following year, entitled *A Treatise Tending to Unitie*: it was the first publication by one of the most prolific authors of early to mid-seventeenth-century Ireland. In this sermon he considered the reasons for the lack of conformity in religion in Ireland and proposed a means to achieve conformity. To overcome the obduracy of Irish Catholics to the reformed religion, Leslie urged the commissioners to compel the Irish to church. On 9 July 1625 Leslie preached before Charles I at Windsor. This sermon was also published and its theme was once again Irish Catholics' obstinacy in relation to the Church of Ireland. Some time later that year Leslie was made a royal chaplain, as he was so titled in his next publication, *A Warning for Israel* (1625). This was based upon a sermon given in Christ Church, Dublin, on 30 October 1625. In this sermon he made an analogy between the Samaritans and the Jews, and the Irish and the English. As the Jews did not trust the Samaritans so too were the English to be wary of the Irish. The consequence of ignoring this warning would be detrimental for the nation, and so he exhorted his congregation and readers to turn from sin in order to avoid God's wrath. In 1627 Leslie once again preached before the king at Woking, the text of the sermon being published that year.

Dean of Down That same year the king donated the deanery of Down to Leslie. Almost immediately Leslie set about trying to rectify the alienations that encumbered this living. In 1628 he obtained a licence to proceed in the courts of justice against those who held alienated church lands that belonged to him by right of his deanery. A commission was also established to discover concealed rectories that could be used to augment the deanery. In 1629 the commission, consisting of Sir John Denham and Sir William Jones, made a report that concurred with Leslie's claims that the deans of Down had received no benefit of the land granted in a 1609 charter that re-erected the dean and chapter of Downpatrick. In 1631 king's letters were issued ordering the lord justices to augment the deanery of Down with the rectories of Beally, Tierreloghe, and Balliculter. The net effect of this was to increase the value of the deanery of Down from £40 in 1615 to £90 in 1633. Leslie's litigious nature is also evident when he was appointed to the treasurership of St Patrick's, Dublin, in 1628. The same year Ambrose Aungier was appointed by a different patron to the same living. The case went to England, and it was not until 1632 that Leslie took possession of the dignity.

Leslie was concerned with the Presbyterian revivals in east Ulster. In 1631 he wrote to John Maxwell, a minister in Edinburgh, about nonconformists in his diocese, and described, in disparaging tones, the fits that the Presbyterians experienced in their congregational meetings. He claimed that this situation had arisen because the bishop was weak, and proposed to oppose the nonconformists if he was supported in this endeavour. These attitudes, of upholding and prosecuting the church's rights, endeared Leslie to the emerging Laudian party of the early 1630s. So when Lord Deputy Wentworth called a convocation in 1634, Dean Leslie was seen as a loyal representative and was appointed prolocutor in the lower house. In this position he was directed to prohibit any discussion regarding the adoption of the new canons of the church. Furthermore, he came to the attention of the lord deputy's chaplain, John Bramhall, who recommended him as a capable clergyman to William Laud.

Bishop of Down and Connor In 1635 Leslie was rewarded with the bishopric of Down and Connor and was consecrated at St Peter's, Drogheda, on 4 October 1635 by Archbishop James Ussher. The only living that he was allowed to retain *in commendam* with the bishopric was the prebend of Mullaghbrack in the diocese of Armagh. The following year he was made a member of the court of high commission. However, he appears to have been one of the least active members of the court. By this stage Leslie was preoccupied with the problem of nonconformity in his diocese, and the court of high commission was not the primary instrument used to deal with this problem. Instead, nonconformity was dealt with at the local level. At his primary visitation Leslie preached to his clergy to subscribe to the newly established canons of the Church of Ireland. Five of the clergymen present refused and, though Leslie attempted to persuade them to conform, their refusal eventually led him to suspend them. Leslie and a nonconformist wrote conflicting accounts of this confrontation. Leslie's account, published as a *Treatise on the Authority of the Church* (1637), attempted to play down the role of John Bramhall in the proceedings. He accompanied this defence of the hierarchy and the church's right to correct disobedience with a discourse on kneeling and the importance of ceremonies. By 1637 he was able to report that he was having some success in bringing his people to conformity and was able to present lists to Wentworth of communicants that kneeled.

These achievements were to be short-lived, as the developments in Scotland that gave rise to the solemn league and covenant were to have grave implications for the diocese of Down and Connor. On 26 September 1638 Leslie gave a sermon at Lisburn that was later published as *A Full Confutation of the Covenant* (1639). In this sermon he equated Presbyterianism with rebellion and appealed to the loyalty of his congregation and readers to eschew nonconformist ideas. Leslie was one of the leading Scots in Ireland who signed the petition that gave rise to the black oath. He also kept the lord deputy informed of the activities of covenanters in his diocese. In September 1638 he informed Wentworth that those he had previously brought to conformity had revolted. Furthermore, Scottish traders and merchants defied the local authorities in seeking support for the covenant. Wentworth directed Leslie to inquire into the names of the covenanters and those who had revolted from their conformity. In his reply Leslie singled out the churchwardens as the guiltiest because they refused to present their fellow laymen. In an earlier sermon he had identified them as the ringleaders of separation. To counteract this problem the bishop sought and received a warrant from the lord deputy to arrest and imprison on bail those who refused to appear before him or his officers or who refused to perform all lawful decrees, sentences, and orders. This incident was to form the ninth article of Strafford's impeachment.

Although Leslie was very much preoccupied with the problem of nonconformity he did attempt to institute reforms in his own diocese. He managed to improve the revenues of the see from £300 to £1000 per annum by 1641. Legal difficulties meant that this had taken over four years to effect. Leslie also proposed to rebuild the cathedral of Downpatrick, which had been in disrepair for well over a century. In 1638 he wrote for aid to Laud, who in turn wrote to Wentworth. To undertake this work it was proposed that an act of state be passed for the diocese to make a general contribution. Leslie also suggested to Wentworth (earl of Strafford from 1640) that a commission be established to re-tax livings in his diocese. This would increase the royal revenue from his diocese by a quarter. Nevertheless these developments were to be short-lived, as the attempts to reconstruct the church foundered with the impeachment of Strafford and Bramhall and collapsed with the outbreak of the 1641 rising. Although a petition was presented in parliament against Leslie in 1641, his real troubles began when he was informed in October of that year that Dungannon, Charlemont, and Newry had fallen to the rebels.

Royalist As a result of the rebellion Leslie left his home at Lisburn. In 1643 he deposed that he had lost £8000 in total. He eventually found his way to Oxford, where he preached before the king and the parliament. Two of his discourses were printed: *A Sermon Preached 9 February 1643 in St Mary's Oxford before the House of Commons* which focused on the need for repentance in troubled times, and *The Blessing of Judah Explained and Applied to the Present Time*, in praise of Charles I. Leslie returned to Ireland some time before 1645, and in 1646 he signed a petition to the lord lieutenant, the duke of Ormond, from the clergy of the Church of Ireland for the free exercise of religion according to the liturgy and canons of the church and for the provision of an adequate maintenance until they were restored to their benefices. The following year the city of Dublin was surrendered to the parliamentary forces, and subsequently the Book of Common Prayer was prohibited. Leslie appears to have followed Ormond to England, and, after the execution of the king, he followed Charles II to the Netherlands. In June 1649 he preached before the king at Breda on the subject of the martyrdom of King Charles. This sermon was later published and reprinted a further three times. Here he expounded on 1 Corinthians 28 and compared the execution of Charles I to the crucifixion of Christ. Despite the numerous similarities identified by Leslie, he postulated that Charles had suffered a worse fate, deeming his execution more illegal and crueller that Christ's crucifixion.

Leslie returned to Ireland in the early 1650s and was one of only four members of the episcopal bench that remained in Ireland during the Commonwealth period. In 1653 he received a government pension of £120. In 1659 he preached before Colonel Hill's family on the subject of praying. This sermon formed the basis of Leslie's final publication, *A Discourse of Praying with the Spirit and with the Understanding* (1660), prefaced by a letter by his friend Jeremy Taylor. This work displays Leslie's continued antipathy to Presbyterianism and in particular his disdain for Presbyterians' style of extempore prayer. He concluded with a defence of set forms of prayer, particularly those found in the Book of Common Prayer. Following the Restoration, Leslie was translated to the bishopric of Meath by letters patent on 19 January 1661. However, he did not live long enough to effect the re-establishment of the church in that diocese, as he died in Dublin on 7 April 1661. He was buried at Christ Church, Dublin, on 10 April 1661; Dr Thomas Price, bishop of Kildare, preached the funeral sermon. From his son James the Leslie family of Ballybay, co. Monaghan, were descended. CIARAN DIAMOND

Sources J. B. Leslie, *Clergy of Connor* (1993) · J. B. Leslie, *Armagh clergy and parishes* (1911) · J. B. Leslie and H. B. Swanzy, *Biographical succession lists of the diocese of Down* (1936) · *The whole works of Sir J. Ware*, rev. W. Harris (1739) · H. Cotton, *Fasti ecclesiae Hibernicae*, 3 (1849) · G. Radcliffe, *The earl of Strafforde's letters and dispatches, with an essay towards his life*, ed. W. Knowler, 2 vols. (1739) · Colonel Leslie [C. J. Leslie], *Historical records of the family of Leslie, from 1067 to 1868–9*, 3 vols. (1869) · R. Mant, *History of the Church of Ireland*, 2 vols. (1840), vol. 1 · J. D. McCafferty, 'John Bramhall and the reconstruction of the Church of Ireland, 1633–1641', PhD diss., U. Cam., 1996 · E. P. Shirley, *History of the county of Monaghan* (1879) · R. Lascelles, ed., *Liber munerum publicorum Hiberniae … or, The establishments of Ireland*, 2 vols. [1824–30] · *Report of the Laing manuscripts*, 1, HMC, 72 (1914) · *Report on the manuscripts of the late Reginald Rawdon Hastings*, 4 vols., HMC, 78 (1928–47), vol. 4 · J. Rushworth, *Tryal of Strafford* (1680) · *CSP Ire., 1625–47* · A. Ford, *The protestant Reformation in Ireland, 1590–1641* (1987) · J. T. Gilbert, ed., *A contemporary history of affairs in Ireland from 1641 to 1652*, 3 vols. (1879–80) · T. Carte, *An history of the life of James, duke of Ormonde*, 3 vols. (1735–6) · J. H. Murnane, *At the ford of the birches: the history of Ballybay, its people and vicinity* (1999) · St J. D. Seymour, *The puritans in Ireland, 1647–1661* (1921) · 'The life of Henry Leslie', NL Ire., MS 10241 · depositions, Down, 1641, TCD, MS 837

Archives PRO, papers, SP 63 · PRO NIre., family MSS, D/3406/D · Sheffield Central Library, Strafford manuscripts, vol. 20

Likenesses portrait; formerly in the possession of the Leslie family at Ballybay, 1892, now lost?

Leslie, Henry David (1822–1896), composer and conductor, was born in London on 18 June 1822, the fourth of nine children (five sons and four daughters), and the first son to survive infancy, of John Leslie, a fashionable tailor and keen amateur viola player, and his wife, Mary Taylor. He was educated at the Palace School, Enfield, before unenthusiastically joining the family firm. A lugubrious looking, bespectacled, and later whiskery young man, he began musical studies in his mid-teens, studying the cello with Charles Lucas. He later played the cello at the Sacred Harmonic Society concerts.

In 1840 Leslie published his op. 1, a Te Deum and Jubilate in D. In 1848 his symphony in F was performed by the prestigious Amateur Musical Society under Michael Balfe. His anthem 'Let God arise' was first performed at the Norwich festival of 1849: Charles Lucas called it 'the best antiphonal work since the days of Handel', and *The Times* found in it 'gifts that are accorded to few'. The next decade saw a dramatic overture, *The Templar*, the oratorios *Immanuel* (1854) and *Judith* (1858), and some chamber music. The *Birmingham Gazette* hailed *Judith* as a 'great work', but the second part of *Immanuel* contains probably the finest music Leslie wrote. About the same time came two cantatas, *Holyrood* (1861) and *Daughter of the Isles* (1862), and two works given at Covent Garden: the operetta *Romance, or, Bold Dick Turpin* (1860) and the romantic opera *Ida, or, The Guardian Storks* (1865). The only major late work was a programmatic second symphony, *Chivalry*, first performed in 1881 at the Crystal Palace. He edited *Cassell's Choral Music* (1867) and other collections of early partsongs.

In 1857 Leslie married one of his pupils, Mary Betsy, the daughter of William Henry Perry, a physician, and moved to her family home, Bryn Tanat, Llansanffraid, near Oswestry on the Welsh border. They had four sons and one daughter. The second son, William, became a master of the Musicians' Company, and the third, Charles, played cricket for Middlesex and England.

In 1847 Leslie became honorary secretary of the newly founded Amateur Musical Society, and from 1855 its conductor. He had also taken charge of a madrigal society which performed in the Hanover Square Rooms and which from May 1856 was known as Henry Leslie's Choir. A basic group of about thirty singers swelled on some orchestral occasions to 240, and over three decades gave several London concerts each year, prepared with a care for detail unique in Britain at the time, though its effects were later attacked as too calculated, even 'effeminate', and many regretted the drift from a pure partsong repertory to grandiose 'mixed concerts' with popular soloists. Leslie wrote a hundred or so partsongs for the choir, including 'O memory', 'The pilgrims', and 'Annabelle Lee', which became best-sellers.

By the late 1870s Leslie (and many critics) felt that some of his singers were 'becoming a little ropy' and that he himself was tired and stale. A final triumph came at the Paris Exhibition of 1878, where he and Arthur Sullivan organized the British musical element, and Leslie's choir won first prize in the international choral competition. Two years later, after a command performance at Windsor Castle, he disbanded it, and although it was revived at public request under Albert Randegger, with Leslie as president and later conductor (1885–7), and attracted such stars as Charles Santley, it was finally disbanded in 1887.

In 1864 Leslie realized a long-held ambition in setting up a National College of Music, in Piccadilly, to rival the continental conservatories. Although Sullivan, Julius Benedict, and other prominent musicians were among the professors, it collapsed after only two years. A second attempt (in 1878) led to the foundation of the Royal College of Music in 1883. Leslie was always interested in the training of village choirs, and in retirement he launched the Oswestry Festival of Village Choirs, which absorbed him for some years until underfunding brought it to an end. He died on 5 February 1896 at Boreatton Park, Baschurch, Shropshire, after several years of ill health, and was buried in Llanyblodwel churchyard. He was survived by his wife. JOHN HOLMSTROM, *rev.* ANNE PIMLOTT BAKER

Sources *New Grove* • Boase, *Mod. Eng. biog.*, vol. 3 • *The Times* (7 Feb 1896) • *ILN* (15 Feb 1896) • *The Times* (15 Feb 1850) • *Magazine of Music* (Sept 1890) • *Musical World* (25 March 1848) • *Musical World* (24 May 1850) • *Musical World* (2 March 1854) • *Musical World* (26 June 1858) • *Musical World* (31 July 1858) • *Musical World* (4 Feb 1860) • *Musical World* (9 Feb 1861) • *Musical World* (11 July 1863) • *Musical World* (2 Jan 1864) • *Musical World* (18 Nov 1865) • *Musical World* (16 Feb 1867) • *Musical Gazette* (31 May 1856) • *MT*, 19 (1878), 427 • *MT*, 21 (1880), 399 • *Musical Standard* (24 Dec 1881) • *Oswestry Advertiser* (5 Nov 1879) • *CGPLA Eng. & Wales* (1896)

Likenesses T. G. Cooper, pen-and-ink drawing, *c.*1868–1872, NPG • J. B. Folkard, oils, 1878, Royal College of Music, London • portrait, repro. in *ILN*, 198

Wealth at death £452 5*s.*: probate, 3 June 1896, *CGPLA Eng. & Wales*

Leslie, John. *See* Lesley, John (1527–1596).

Leslie, John, of Parkhill (*d.* 1585). *See under* Castilians in St Andrews (*act.* 1546–1547).

Leslie, John (1571–1671), Church of Ireland bishop of Clogher, was born at Crichie, Aberdeenshire, on 14 October 1571, the eldest son of George Leslie and his wife, Marjorie. He was educated at the University of Aberdeen and on the continent, principally in France, where he is said to have spent over twenty years. While abroad he acquired a reputation as a linguist and is reputed to have spoken Spanish, Italian, French, and Latin fluently, earning from the Spanish the title 'Solus Lesleius Latini Loquitur'. During this period he was ordained and became chaplain to various English noblemen. At some point he spent time in Oxford, and may have been the 'Dr John Lesley' recorded as studying in the 'public library' in 1618 (Wood, *Ath. Oxon.*, 4.846). In 1621 he was made a domestic chaplain to the king. Three years later he received the degree of DD from Cambridge by royal mandate and obtained the living of Hartlebury, Gloucester. In 1625 he exchanged this living for the rectory of St Faith, London, and the same year he was appointed rector of St Martin Vintry.

Leslie may have served as chaplain to the duke of Buckingham, whom he is said to have accompanied on the expedition to the Île de Ré and at the siege of La Rochelle. It was probably through Buckingham's influence that in 1628 Leslie was appointed to the bishopric of the Isles. Appointed in 1631 to the Scottish privy council, Leslie used this body to attempt to impose conformity in his diocese. In 1631 he called the chief men of the diocese to subscribe to the articles of Perth and proceeded against those who did not conform, actions which drew the ire of some fellow Scottish clergy, who attacked him because they believed he had Arminian leanings.

Leslie's association with Caroline religious policy became more apparent after he was translated in June 1633 to the bishopric of Raphoe in Ireland. With the aid of Sir Thomas Wentworth and the arbitration of John Bramhall, bishop of Derry, Leslie was able to increase the annual income of his see from £600 to £1000. This was achieved through legal suits and by obtaining the surrender of old leases from his tenants and the regranting of new leases with increased rents and fines for terms of about sixty years.

Larger revenues enabled Leslie to construct an episcopal palace. The foundation-stone was laid on 17 May 1636 and he took up residence on 14 December 1637; the total cost of the work was £3500. Then in his sixties, on 6 June 1638 Leslie married Katherine (1620–1694), daughter of Alexander Cunningham, dean of Raphoe. They had at least eight children, of whom only two survived to adulthood: John Leslie, later dean of Down, and Charles *Leslie (1650–1722).

With assistance from Wentworth and the archbishop of Canterbury, William Laud, Leslie prosecuted covenanters in his diocese. In 1638 he disciplined Abraham Pont and his wife who, at a conventicle in the diocese of Raphoe, preached against the jurisdiction of bishops and urged the congregation to take the covenant. Leslie was also a signatory to the petition that gave rise to the infamous 'black oath'. His castle was to become a refuge for the British and for protestants in north Donegal when the uprising of 1641 broke out. Leslie also raised, maintained, and commanded a company of foot soldiers to defend the castle and took part in a number of expeditions for which he earned the epithet 'the Fighting Bishop'. He is said to have transported arms to Londonderry through hazardous conditions. He also relieved Sir Ralph Gore and his company, who were besieged in Magherabeg, even though other forces were available to come to their assistance. This tenacity was also displayed in the fact that the castle was one of the last strongholds to surrender to the Commonwealth forces in 1651.

Leslie was one of the few members of the episcopal bench to remain in Ireland during the interregnum. He also appears to have acquiesced somewhat with the Commonwealth regime. In 1653 he received a pension of £100 from the state; this was increased two years later to £120 and subsequently to £160, in consideration of the money expended by Leslie on repairing the castle at Raphoe. In 1654 he received £10 for preaching in the precinct of Derry. He also held a yearly lease of former episcopal land in the parishes of Raphoe and Tarboyne from the Commonwealth regime. However, Leslie appears to have retained episcopalian sympathies: in 1658 it was hinted that he helped to hinder presbyterians in Raphoe from exercising their discipline, and it was said that he used the Anglican liturgy in private with his family.

Leslie's royalist sympathies were displayed at the Restoration when, it was said, he rode from Chester to London in just under twenty-four hours in order to pay his respects to Charles II. In August 1660 he petitioned the crown for the deanery of Raphoe, to be held *in commendam* with his bishopric, which, by then, was of an insufficient value to support his family. This request was granted in February 1661 but that autumn, on his translation to the bishopric of Clogher, he resigned both livings. In his petition to the crown Leslie also requested relief for the expenses incurred in building his castle and defending it during the uprising. The result of this was a king's letter in 1660 for a grant of 4000 acres in the barony of Kilmacrenan, co. Donegal, or elsewhere. In December that year Leslie petitioned the king once again: that he was much in debt and that the grant of 4000 acres was not yet perfected. In response the king directed Leslie to submit his claim to the next parliament. When parliament met in summer 1661, the bishop was awarded £2000 sterling, which he probably used when he purchased Ballyglasslough, also known as Glaslough, co. Monaghan. A patent of 1665 made these lands into one entire manor and confirmed it to Leslie.

Subsequently, the family seat at Glaslough became known as Castle Leslie. Here, after a number of false rumours about his death, Leslie died on 8 September 1671. At the time of his death he was reputed to be one of the oldest bishops in Christendom, being just over a month short of his 100th birthday. He was buried in St Saviour's, Glaslough, which he had constructed at his own cost, and a monument was erected there commemorating the chief events of his life. His castle was attacked in 1690 and among the books that were destroyed were a number of Leslie's own writings; these included unpublished works on memory and on meditation. Leslie's widow died on 28 January 1694. CIARAN DIAMOND

Sources J. B. Leslie, *Clogher clergy and parishes* (1929) • J. B. Leslie, *Raphoe clergy and parishes* (1940) • *The whole works of Sir James Ware concerning Ireland*, ed. and trans. W. Harris, 1 (1739) • H. Cotton, *Fasti ecclesiae Hibernicae*, 3 (1849) • Wood, *Ath. Oxon.*, 4.845–8 • Venn, *Alum. Cant.* • *Journal of the House of Commons [of Ireland]*, 2nd edn, 1–2 (1763) • R. Newcourt, *Repertorium ecclesiasticum parochiale Londinense*, 1 (1708) • 'Memorials at Glaslough, co. Monaghan', *Journal of the Association for the Preservation of the Memorials of the Dead, Ireland*, 7 (1907) • E. P. Shirley, *History of the county of Monaghan* (1879) • *The works of the most reverend father in God, William Laud*, 6, ed. J. Bliss (1857) • G. Radcliffe, *The earl of Strafforde's letters and dispatches, with an essay towards his life*, ed. W. Knowler, 2 vols. (1739) • *Reg. PCS*, 2nd ser., vols. 4–5 • *CSP Ire.*, 1634–70 • *CSP dom.*, 1671 • T. Sweeney, *Ireland and the printed word: a short descriptive catalogue of early books … relating to Ireland, printed, 1475–1700* (Dublin, 1997) • D. G. Mullan, *Episcopacy in Scotland* (1986) • *DNB* • R. C. Simington, *The civil survey of counties Donegal, Londonderry and Tyrone*, 3 (1937)

Archives PRO NIre., letters to Francis Guthrie

Leslie, John, sixth earl of Rothes (*c.*1600–1641), politician, was the only son of James Leslie, master of Rothes (*d.* 1607), Fife, and his second wife, Catherine, daughter of Patrick Drummond, Lord Drummond. His father died in March 1607 and his education began under the direction of his mother; following her resignation in December 1608, it was continued by James Drummond, earl of Perth.

John Leslie, sixth earl of Rothes (*c.*1600–1641), attrib. Samuel Cooper, *c.*1635–40

Leslie succeeded to the peerage on the death of his grandfather Andrew *Leslie, *de facto* fifth earl of Rothes, in 1611. He was served heir to his elder half-brother James (who had died unmarried in 1604) in 1613, and to his great-grandfather George *Leslie, fourth earl of Rothes, in 1621. The young earl married Lady Anne (*d.* 1640), daughter of John *Erskine, earl of Mar, by contracts dated 10, 21, and 28 December 1614. They had a son and two daughters, Mary and Margaret. Rothes was appointed justice of the peace for Elgin and Forres, and Nairn, in 1616, and was sheriff-principal of Fife in 1619. As befitting the family's high status among the nobility of the realm, Rothes bore the sword of state at the parliaments of 1617 and 1621, and attended the privy council in 1620.

In matters of religion, Rothes appears as an ardent opponent of the crown's attempts to force episcopacy upon the Scottish church. He was one of the few members of the nobility to vote against the five articles of Perth at the parliament of 1621, along with John Elphinstone, Lord Balmerino, John Campbell, Lord Loudoun, John Hay, Lord Yester, and John Ross, Lord Ross. Indeed, Rothes recorded in 1625 that one of the most controversial policies of James VI's reign had been 'the imposing of certain novations upon the kirk' (*Correspondence of Sir Robert Kerr*, 1.36). It is likely that the foremost influence on Rothes in the latter regard emanated from his wife, Anne Erskine. She was, like her sister Catherine, one of the earl of Mar's troublesome presbyterian daughters, and a fervent 'conventicling matron' (Wells, 123). If the couple had hoped for a change of religious heart with the accession of a new king, then their hopes were soon dashed. Charles I's attempts to enforce kneeling at communion, in accordance with the five articles, had revived deep concerns over the direction of religious policy in Scotland by 1628. As a consequence, Rothes's name lay at the head of a petition (penned in 1630), which called on the king to restore the 'simple forme of Divine Worship … free of pomp and ceremonies, with peace and puritie of doctrine' that Scotland had previously enjoyed (Scot, 327). By the latter date, opposition to the crown's religious policy was growing, and Rothes's signature was accompanied by that of Balmerino, Loudoun, Yester, and Ross, as well as that of Colin Mackenzie, earl of Seaforth, John Kennedy, earl of Cassillis, and John Melville, Lord Melville.

Nevertheless, it would be wrong to view Rothes's opposition to the crown purely from the standpoint of religious scruple. For the earl and his co-petitioners of 1630, the refusal of 'libertie to pastours and ther congregatiouns' to practise religion according to their presbyterian principles mirrored a similar state of affairs in the civil estate. In 1625 Rothes had complained of 'the impairing of the libertys of the Nobility both in Counsell and Parliament' under James VI (*Correspondence of Sir Robert Kerr*, 1.37–8), a comment that reflected his concern regarding the absolutist tendencies of the crown. Charles's act of revocation of the same year, about which the nobility of Scotland were not consulted, did little to alleviate such fears. Under the proposed legislation, all church property in the hands of laymen reverted to the crown. Rothes had a personal interest in the proposed act, since his brother Patrick had been commendator of Lindores Abbey in Fife, a title and income inherited by the earl on his brother's death. In 1626 the earl was sent to London, with other commissioners, to petition against the revocation. At first the king 'stormed at the petition as of too high a strain from petitioners and subjects' (Balfour, 2.153), a royal stance which was precisely the cause of Rothes's complaint. Ultimately, however, a compromise was reached as a result of the consultation which the earl so desired. The settlement included, in the case of Rothes, a mitigation of duties due to the crown from a tobacco monopoly and the retention of a tack of the feu duties from the abbacy of Lindores.

It was the apparent willingness of Rothes to act in his own (particularly financial) interest which allowed his detractors to claim that he was 'unrestrained … by any scruples of religion, which he only put on when the part he was to act required it, and then no man could appear more conscientiously transported' (*DNB*). Yet such a verdict is unduly hard on Rothes, who—despite his determination to maintain his privileged status and lifestyle—regarded the curtailment of religious and civil liberties as symptoms of the same disease. Thus the earl remained resolutely opposed to royal absolutism. On the visit of Charles to Scotland in 1633 Rothes denounced as unwarrantable the act of parliament that conjoined an acknowledgement of the royal prerogative with that of the king's authority to determine the apparel of the judges, magistrates, and the clergy. At parliament Balmerino, Loudoun, and John Lindsay, Lord Lindsay, joined Rothes in his opposition to the bill. In particular, the quartet viewed the clause 'anent his majesties royal prerogative and [the] apparel of kirkmen' as a further encroachment on the ecclesiastical independence of the kirk (Anderson, *Scot. nat.*, 375), and presented a petition to that effect. The king, however, refused to have the bill divided. Thereafter, a majority of the votes declared in its favour, and an attempt by Rothes to challenge the correctness of the numbers was overruled by a furious Charles. At the closing of parliament on 20 June 1633 the king treated Rothes with the 'utmost coldness' (ibid.), and in a display of royal petulance denied him the right to bear the sceptre during the closing ceremony. On the pretext of failing to settle his accounts with the exchequer, Rothes was 'put to the horn' in December of the latter year. To further demonstrate his anger, Charles revoked plans for the creation of the earldoms of Loudoun and Lindsay, while Balmerino (held to be the author of the petition) was indicted on a charge of treason in 1634. The king was soon to relent, raising Loudoun and Lindsay to the peerage and pardoning Balmerino, but the affair confirmed Rothes's suspicions regarding the intentions of the king towards the government and religion of Scotland.

It is unsurprising, therefore, that Rothes, Balmerino, Loudoun, and Lindsay became the 'pryme foor noblemen' of the covenanting revolution (Johnston of Wariston, *Diary*, 282). The four men had, at some time prior to 1637, drawn up a secret band 'to overthrow the bishops' (Spalding, 1.76). Rothes personally headed the opposition to the proposed introduction of the prayer book into the services of the kirk in July of that year, and—aided and abetted by Archibald Johnston of Wariston, then an obscure Edinburgh lawyer—was the chief organizer of the movement against episcopacy. He addressed a circular letter to the noblemen and gentlemen who had hitherto held aloof, urging them to take a firm stand on behalf of the liberties of the kirk. Along with Loudoun and Balmerino, Rothes ordered the revision of the new version of the covenant drawn up by Wariston and Alexander Henderson, minister of Leuchars. Wariston and Rothes worked closely together on the details of the progress of the revolution, and produced *A short relation of proceedings concerning the affairs of Scotland from August 1637 to July 1638*, a pamphlet which was largely the work of Wariston, but to which Rothes appended his name. Rothes was one of a deputation appointed to meet the king's commissioner to the assembly, the marquess of Hamilton, on his arrival in Scotland, and gave him warning of the attitude of the covenanters towards the king's proposals. At the general assembly of Glasgow in 1638, Rothes is said to have 'spoken more than all the ministers, except the moderator', Johnston of Wariston (*DNB*), and when the commissioner attempted to dissolve the gathering he presented a protest, successfully preventing the action. Thereafter, the assembly presided over the removal of bishops from the kirk, the abolition of the court of high commission, and the repudiation of all the crown's former religious innovations.

In the face of such defiance, Hamilton threatened that Charles would march north to Scotland in person with 40,000 men. The threat prompted Rothes to seek the support of his kinsman Alexander Leslie (later earl of Leven), in preparation for armed resistance. While Leslie drilled Rothes's dependants and followers in Fife, the earl advised the purchase of arms and accoutrements in the Netherlands, and the recall of the experienced Scottish officers serving in foreign countries. In March 1639 Rothes and other nobles, with 1000 musketeers, brought the royal ensigns of the kingdom (the crown, sword, and sceptre) to the castle of Edinburgh. In response, the king issued a proclamation excepting nineteen leaders of the covenanters, including Rothes, from pardon. Nevertheless, Rothes and his supporters gave notice that they would continue to adhere to the assembly of Glasgow, and were summoned to confer with Charles at Berwick. As the principal spokesman of the opposition, the earl's uncompromising attitude in privy conference led the king to denounce him angrily as an equivocator and liar.

In recognition of his role as one of the undisputed heads of the revolutionary government of Scotland, Rothes was appointed a lord of the articles at the parliament held in Edinburgh in September 1639, and a member of the committee of estates in July 1640. Having failed to negotiate a settlement with his old adversary, Charles was soon forced to summon the Short Parliament in order to raise supplies for an invasion of Scotland. Yet the House of Commons proved as refractory as their Scottish counterparts, who, to make matters worse, anticipated Charles by invading England. On 27 August 1640 Rothes, in command of a regiment, and as one of the committee of the estates, accompanied Leslie's army across the Tweed. The occupation of Newcastle by Rothes sealed the fate of Charles's Scottish policy and the earl was one of the commissioners sent to London in November to conclude the negotiations for a treaty.

In the midst of the troubles, personal tragedy struck the household of Rothes. Anne, countess of Rothes, was smitten by a 'hectic fever' and died on 2 May 1640. She 'was interred in the new aisle of Leslie church, on 25 May', at which date, according to her presbyterian principles, the burial took place 'without any funeral ceremony' (Balfour, 2.427). In November 1640 Rothes departed for London to conclude the peace treaty, and remained at court in England. He was said to have found 'the gaiety of the English court … congenial' (*DNB*), and his 'popular talents and persuasive eloquence' soon won Charles's respect (J. Leslie, earl of Rothes, ii). His contemporaries support this assessment of his character: the diarist Robert Baillie thought him a 'good courteour … who is like to first with both king and queen' (*Letters and Journals of Robert Baillie*, 1.354); and Clarendon noted that he was 'pleasant in conversation, [but] very free and amorous' (*DNB*). His financial situation, on the other hand, was by this time precarious. Rothes's will valued his various properties and their contents in excess of £40,000 Scots, but at the time of his death he possessed little ready money, the contents of his purse amounting to £104. The troubles had apparently caused him to neglect the collection of rents from his tenants, some of whom had not paid 'fermes and dewties' for four or five years. In addition, his 'pay as colonell' was eighteen months in arrears, and the consequent debt amounted to some £4000. In all, Rothes was owed over £12,000 by his various debtors, with no indication as to when—if ever—he could recover the outstanding amounts.

Understandably, Rothes sought to relieve his position by pursuing royal patronage. He hoped to obtain an office in the royal household, and, through the king's mediation, to gain the hand of the countess of Devonshire, who possessed an income of about £4000 a year. He had also negotiated a pension of £10,000 from Charles, who hoped in return to employ Rothes as an unofficial emissary in Scottish affairs. The covenanting government, however, regarded such payment as little short of bribes, and had forbidden its commissioners from accepting monetary 'benefits'. In an attempt to justify his actions, Rothes wrote that he was not 'lyabl to the Letter wryten to us not to accept benefits, which can only be meant within the kingdom [of Scotland]; yet, I desyr never to be in a condition [of which] my Comerads shall not aprov' (*Letters and Journals of Robert Baillie*, 1.226). The note was addressed to Johnston of Wariston, who was one of the earl's closest confidants, and asked for his opinion to be given 'frely'. Unfortunately, Wariston's reply has not survived, but events—in the form of Rothes's death—conspired to end the matter. In August 1641, the earl was to have accompanied Charles into Scotland, in a further attempt to achieve a final settlement. For his part, the king expected 'by [Rothes's] help and interest to have gained such a party in Scotland as would have been more tender of his honour than they after expressed themselves' (*DNB*). Before either man could embark on that mission, however, 'my Lord Rothes, one of the Scottish Comissioners, departed this world [at Richmond, Surrey, on 23 August] having beine sicke a great while of a burning fever' (BL, Sloane MS 1467, fol. 139). His body was transported to the country of his birth, and Rothes was laid to rest at his parish kirk of Leslie, Fife, on 21 November 1641. According to Sir Thomas Hope, the king's advocate, the earl's death was 'muche lamentit' in Scotland (Hope, 152). It was a mark of the respect in which the king came to hold Rothes, that he bestowed the pension Rothes had sought upon his only son, John *Leslie, seventh earl and first duke of Rothes (*c.*1630–1681), 'to begin at Martinmas 1641' (Colonel Leslie, 108).

There is little doubt that the resistance of the Scots to crown policy was greatly strengthened by the ability, eloquence, and resolution of Rothes. His opposition (and that of other 'pryme' noblemen such as Balmerino, Loudoun, and Lindsay) was not the result of any single overriding principle, but was caused by a number of factors. These included his wife's fervent presbyterianism, the perceived religious radicalism of the crown, royal absolutism, and crushing financial insecurity, all of which represented a threat to the nobility of Scotland. The confluence of these factors in the 1630s converted Rothes's natural conservatism into revolutionary energy. That energy had dissipated on the rack of the covenanting government by 1641, and the earl reverted to type. He was not the first (nor would he be the last) member of the nobility to view royal patronage as his saviour. Ultimately, Rothes could not conceive of political society without a king.

VAUGHAN T. WELLS

Sources D. Calderwood, *The history of the Kirk of Scotland*, ed. T. Thomson and D. Laing, 8 vols., Wodrow Society, 7 (1842–9) • Edinburgh testaments, NA Scot., CC8/8/61, fols. 2r–3r • *Scots peerage* • GEC, *Peerage* • *Correspondence of Sir Robert Kerr, first earl of Ancram, and his son William, third earl of Lothian*, ed. D. Laing, 2 vols.,

Roxburghe Club, 100 (1875), vol. 1 • W. Scot, *An apologeticall narration of the state and government of the kirk of Scotland* (1846) • J. Spalding, *Memorialls of the trubles in Scotland and in England, AD 1624 – AD 1645*, ed. J. Stuart, 2 vols., Spalding Club, [21, 23] (1850–51) • *The historical works of Sir James Balfour*, ed. J. Haig, 4 vols. (1824–5) • *Diary of Sir Archibald Johnston of Wariston*, ed. G. M. Paul and others, 3 vols., Scottish History Society, 61, 2nd ser., 18, 3rd. ser., 34 (1911–40) • 'Fragment of the diary of Sir Archibald Johnston, Lord Wariston, 1639', ed. G. M. Paul, *Wariston's diary and other papers*, Scottish History Society, 26 (1896), 1–98 • *The letters and journals of Robert Baillie*, ed. D. Laing, 3 vols. (1841–2) • *A diary of the public correspondence of Sir Thomas Hope of Craighall*, ed. T. Thompson (1843) • J. Leslie, earl of Rothes, *A short relation of proceedings concerning the affairs of Scotland from August 1637 to July 1638* (1830) • Colonel Leslie [C. J. Leslie], *Historical records of the family of Leslie, from 1067 to 1868–9*, 3 vols. (1869) • *Bishop Burnet's History of his own time*, new edn (1850) • Anderson, *Scot. nat.* • V. T. Wells, 'The origins of covenanting thought and resistance', 1997 • BL, Sloane MS 1467 • *DNB* • *Fasti Scot.*, new edn, vol. 4 • *Leslie House*, Church of Scotland [n.d.]

Likenesses attrib. S. Cooper, miniature, *c.*1635–1640, priv. coll. [*see illus.*] • portrait, repro. in Leslie, *Short relation*

Wealth at death £55,283 Scots: Edinburgh testaments, March 1643

Leslie, John, duke of Rothes (*c.*1630–1681), politician and nobleman, was the only son of John *Leslie, sixth earl of Rothes (*c.*1600–1641), and his wife, Lady Anne Erskine (*d.* 1640), daughter of John *Erskine, earl of Mar (*c.*1562–1634). Following his father's death on 23 August 1641 he succeeded to the earldom at the age of about eleven. He was placed into the care of his tutors, Alexander Leslie, earl of Leven and Archibald Campbell, marquess of Argyll. On account of the covenanting wars his education was much neglected. 'He had', says Burnet, 'no advantage of education, no sort of literature, nor had he travelled abroad; all in him was mere nature' (*Burnet's History*, 186). In recognition of his father's services to Charles I, on 23 September 1641 a grant was made to him of £10,000 Scots yearly for life. He married when still under age, by contract dated 1 January and 4 February 1648, Lady Anne Lindsay (*d.* in or after 1689), daughter of John *Lindsay, earl of Crawford-Lindsay (1596–1678), with whom he had two daughters.

Rothes was one of the first noblemen to wait on Charles II on his arrival from Breda in 1650, and on 20 December of that year he was appointed colonel of one of the Fife regiments of horse. He carried the sword of state at the coronation of the king at Scone. In command of his regiment he accompanied the Scots army into England and was taken prisoner at the battle of Worcester on 3 September 1651. Having been committed to the Tower of London, he was at first granted liberty to visit Scotland under heavy security in December 1652. Similar permission was granted in 1653 and 1654. Owing to the influence of Elizabeth Murray, countess of Dysart, he obtained leave to visit Scotland again in January 1657. However, in January 1658 Oliver Cromwell committed him to Edinburgh Castle after a quarrel broke out between him and Viscount Howard. The supposed cause of the disagreement was Rothes's pursuit of the viscount's wife. While he was imprisoned his estates were sequestered. He was released in December 1658 by General George Monck, paying on 2 February 1659

John Leslie, duke of Rothes (*c.*1630–1681), by Sir Peter Lely, *c.*1662–5

a fine of £4000 Scots imposed on him under the Act of Pardon and Grace.

Rothes travelled to visit the king at Breda in 1660 and accompanied him on his triumphant return to England. His fidelity was rewarded at the Restoration with the grant of £1000 sterling yearly for life in place of his former pension granted by Charles I. When the new government was formed in Scotland Rothes was appointed president of the privy council. He was a key member of the recalled committee of estates, which met from August to December 1660. He courted the burghs in late 1660 in order to secure their support at the ensuing meeting of the Scottish parliament, and with the approval of the secretary of state, the earl of Lauderdale, he was involved in manipulating those elections. On 1 June 1661 he was named a lord of session and a commissioner of the exchequer. In 1662 he went to London to justify the proceedings of the earl of Middleton in the billeting affair and to press for the immediate establishment of episcopacy, and when the synod of Fife was engaged the same year in preparing for an act establishing their government, in the king's name, he dissolved the synod and commanded the ministers to retire, under pain of treason. On the fall of Middleton in 1663 Rothes was appointed to the post of lord high commissioner, overseeing the proceedings of the parliament that met on 18 June. In the same year he succeeded his father-in-law as lord high treasurer and was appointed captain of the troop of lifeguards and general of the forces in Scotland. Following the death of the earl of Glencairn in 1664, on the recommendation of

Archbishop James Sharp, he was chosen as the keeper of the privy seal until another successor was named.

Rothes now held the three highest offices in the kingdom. In November 1665 he made a tour of the west in order to enforce a series of measures aimed at eliminating religious dissent. He caused considerable scandal by taking with him his mistress, Lady Anne Gordon, sister of the duke of Gordon. He angered Lauderdale by voting against his instructions regarding taxation in the Convention of Estates in 1665. As lord high treasurer he controlled the public purse, but widespread corruption flourished under his rule. His policy of using military force to crush religious nonconformity made his administration highly unpopular, and he was largely made a scapegoat for the outbreak of the Pentland rising in 1666. His personal conduct in office had long been the subject of much criticism. 'He delivered himself', said Gilbert Burnet, 'without either restraint or decency to all the pleasures of wine and women. He had but one maxim, to which he adhered firmly, that he was to do everything, and deny himself in nothing, that might maintain his greatness, or gratify his appetites' (*Burnet's History*, 187). Through the intervention of Lauderdale, Rothes was dismissed from power in April 1667. Because of his personal friendship with Charles II he was stripped of all his offices 'by degrees' since 'the doing so all at once would have looked much more to the disadvantage of the person' (*Lauderdale Papers*, 2.71). Despite protesting that his inability to read Latin and his inexperience in legal matters made him an unsuitable candidate he was induced to take on the vacant position of chancellor in October. It was widely known that his apparent promotion was nothing more than a design to remove him from a position of authority.

Throughout the following decade Rothes remained a prominent public figure, frequently in attendance at sessions of parliament. As his only rival, he was instrumental in the fall of the earl of Tweeddale in 1671. Through the intervention of the duke of York he was, on 29 May 1680, created duke of Rothes, marquess of Ballenbreich, earl of Leslie, viscount of Lugton, Lord Auchmutie and Caskiebery. The title was limited to the heirs male of his body. He had not long to enjoy the accession of rank, as he died of jaundice at Holyroodhouse on 27 July 1681. He was buried at night with great splendour on 23 August in the cathedral of St Giles, Edinburgh. Subsequently his body was removed to Leslie, Fife. His dukedom became extinct, but Rothes's elder daughter, Lady Margaret (*d.* 1700), who had in 1674 married Charles Hamilton, fifth earl of Haddington, succeeded as countess of Rothes.

GILLIAN H. MACINTOSH

Sources *Scots peerage* • *Bishop Burnet's History of my own time*, new edn, ed. O. Airy, 2 vols. (1897–1900); H. C. Foxcroft, *A supplement to Burnet's History of my own time* (1902) • *The letters and journals of Robert Baillie*, ed. D. Laing, 3 (1842) • G. Mackenzie, *Memoirs of the affairs of Scotland* (1821) • Anderson, *Scot. nat.*, vol. 3 • NL Scot., Lauderdale MS 3424 • *The Lauderdale papers*, ed. O. Airy, 2, CS, new ser., 36 (1885) • GEC, *Peerage*

Archives NRA, priv. coll., political corresp. | BL, letters to Lauderdale, Charles II, etc., Add. MSS 23113–23138, 23242–23248, 28747 • Buckminster Park, Grantham, corresp. with duke of Lauderdale • NA Scot., corresp. with Sir William Bruce • NA Scot., Yule collection, scroll warrant book of the earl of Rothes, GD 90/2/260

Likenesses P. Lely, portrait, *c.*1662–1665, priv. coll. [*see illus.*] • L. Schuneman, oils, 1667, Scot. NPG • C. Picart, stipple (after P. Lely), BM, NPG; repro. in E. Lodge, *Portraits of illustrious personages of Great Britain*, 4 vols. (1823–34)

Leslie, John, ninth earl of Rothes (1679–1722), politician, was the eldest son of Charles Hamilton, fifth earl of Haddington (*c.*1650–1685), and Lady Margaret Leslie (*d.* 1700), elder daughter of John Leslie, seventh earl and first and only duke of Rothes. He was born in August 1679 and baptized on the 21st of that month at Tyninghame, Haddingtonshire. His formative years were spent at Leslie, where his parents lived after the death of Margaret's father in 1681. On her death, on 20 August 1700, John succeeded her as ninth earl of Rothes, the dukedom having become extinct on the death of Margaret's father. (As the eighth holder of the earldom was a countess, John Leslie is sometimes called the eighth earl.) On 29 April 1697 Leslie married Lady Jean Hay (*d.* 1731), daughter of John *Hay, second marquess of Tweeddale, and they had eight sons and four daughters.

In parliament Rothes was, according to the court spy John Macky, 'a warm assertor of the liberties of the people and in great esteem, also of vigilant application for the service of his country' (*Memoirs of the Secret Services*, 229). He supported the revolution settlement, but was accused by the Jacobites of being a turncoat for, they claimed, after having expressed great regard for the house of Stuart 'alass! he had neither enough of sense nor honesty to resist the first temptation' (Lockhart, 1.94–5). He was one of the three commissioners chosen by the duke of Hamilton's party to petition Queen Anne in February 1704 regarding the loyalty of her Scottish subjects and to request that Scottish troops should not be paid with English money. On 17 October 1704 he was appointed lord privy seal, with an annual salary of £1000, but held the office for only one year.

Rothes zealously assisted the creation of the union of 1707 and was chosen as one of the sixteen representative peers of Scotland, a position he held until his death. On the accession of George I, in 1714, he was appointed vice-admiral of Scotland and in the following year, lord high commissioner for his majesty to the general assembly of the Church of Scotland, which he held until 1721.

Rothes was very active on the government side during the Jacobite rising of 1715. Soon after its outbreak he attempted with 500 men to occupy Perth in advance of the rebels, but was forestalled by them on 18 September 1715. When, on 26 September 1715, a party of Jacobites tried to proclaim James Stuart, the Pretender, at Kinross he led a detachment of the Scots Greys who scattered the rebels, captured Sir Thomas Bruce of Kinross, and, on 28 September, took him to Stirling. In retaliation Jacobites raided Leslie House, searched the house for arms, and then, having broken open the church doors, dug up the coffins from the family burial place and desecrated them. Undaunted,

John Leslie, ninth earl of Rothes (1679–1722), attrib. John Scougall

on 17 October, Rothes with 300 volunteers, and Lord Torphichen with 200 horsemen, marched on Seton House, then garrisoned by the Jacobites, but found them too strongly entrenched and withdrew after an exchange of fire. At the battle of Sheriffmuir (13 November 1715), he commanded a body of sixty gentlemen volunteers, and is said to have behaved with great gallantry. He also raised the Fifeshire militia, and when Rob Roy garrisoned Falkland and made the palace his headquarters for raiding the neighbourhood, Rothes attacked the palace on 2 January 1716 but was repulsed with loss by the rebels who had been forewarned. Rothes turned his own house into a royal garrison, and with a few troops and Swiss soldiers kept the highlanders in check. In acknowledgement of Rothes's service the king made him governor of Stirling Castle in 1716, an appointment which he retained until his death. In the same year, through Lord Townshend, secretary of state, he received a commission as chamberlain of Fife and Strathearn, with an annual salary of £320. Other positions held by him were lord lieutenant of the counties of Fife, Kinross, and Aberdeen, and heritable sheriff of Fife.

George Lockhart, a Jacobite and therefore a somewhat biased witness, said of Rothes that he

> had not, that I know of, one good property to recommend him, being false to a great degree, a contemmer of honour and engagements, extreamly ambitious, ridiculous, vain, and conceited (tho' of very ordinary parts and accomplishments), extravagantly proud, and scandalously mercenary (Lockhart, 1.94)

This judgement is almost certainly unfair. Rothes might well have been vain, conceited, and ambitious, but he showed considerable courage and gallantry on the battlefield and was steadfast in his loyalty to the government. A more fitting epitaph was provided by his deputy at Stirling Castle, Colonel Blackader, who, after witnessing Rothes's death, wrote 'I never saw any man die more as a Christian hero, with so much natural fortitude, and such lively faith. He was pleasant in his life, and pleasant in his death' (Crichton, 526). He died on 9 May 1722 at Leslie House; his eldest son, John *Leslie, succeeded him as tenth earl of Rothes. His wife survived him by nine years, dying on 4 September 1731. ANDREW M. LANG

Sources *DNB* • W. Fraser, *Memorials of the earls of Haddington*, 2 vols. (1889) • G. Lockhart, *The Lockhart papers: containing memoirs and commentaries upon the affairs of Scotland from 1702 to 1715*, 2 vols. (1817) • *Scots peerage* • Burke, *Peerage* • GEC, *Peerage*, new edn • A. Crichton, *The life and diary of Lieut. Col. J. Blackader of the Cameron regiment* (1824) • *Memoirs of the secret services of John Macky*, ed. A. R. (1733) • P. Rae, *The history of the late rebellion* (1718) • G. H. Rose, *A selection from the papers of the earls of Marchmont*, 3 vols. (1831) • J. Redington, ed., *Calendar of Treasury papers*, 6 vols., PRO (1868–89) • J. Redington and R. A. Roberts, eds., *Calendar of home office papers of the reign of George III*, 4 vols., PRO (1878–99) • W. Fraser, *The earls of Cromartie, their kindred, country and correspondence*, 2 vols. (1897) • *The manuscripts of the Marquess Townshend*, HMC, 19 (1887)

Archives NA Scot., letters to Cornelius Kennedy • NA Scot., letters to duke of Montrose

Likenesses attrib. J. Scougall, portrait; Christies, 10 April 1992 [*see illus.*] • oils, Scot. NPG

Leslie, John, tenth earl of Rothes (1698?–1767), army officer, was the eldest son of John *Leslie, ninth earl (1679–1722), and Jean (*d.* 1731), second daughter of John Hay, second marquess of Tweeddale. His first commission was as captain in General Wynn's regiment of dragoons (the 9th), raised in 1715 following the Jacobite rising. He transferred to the 3rd foot guards (the Scots guards) as captain and lieutenant-colonel on 17 July 1717. On 21 January 1721 he was made lieutenant-colonel of the 21st regiment of foot (Royal Scots Fusiliers). He succeeded as earl of Rothes on the death of his father in May 1722, and retained his father's post as governor of the castle of Stirling, where he was captain of the independent company garrisoned there. He was also chamberlain of Fife and Strathearn between 1722 and 1727. In 1723 he was chosen as a representative peer for Scotland, and was re-elected in 1727, 1747, 1754, and 1761. Under the Heritable Jurisdictions Act of 1747, he disposed of the hereditary sheriffdom of Fife, which had long been held by the Rothes family, to the government, receiving in compensation the sum of £6268 16*s*., though he claimed £10,000.

Having continued in the army, Rothes was appointed on 25 May 1732 to the command of the 25th regiment of foot (later the King's Own Scottish Borderers). He was promoted to the rank of brigadier-general on 2 July 1739. On 25 May 1741 he married Hannah (*d.* 1761), second daughter of Matthew Howard of Thorpe, Norfolk. On 1 January 1743 he was made major-general and acted in this rank at the battle of Dettingen. He received a commission as colonel of the 2nd troop of Horse Grenadier Guards on 25 April 1745, and took part in the battle of Rocoux in October of the following year, gallantly heading the charge of the first line of cavalry. He was appointed lord lieutenant of

Fife in 1746. He was promoted to the rank of lieutenant-general on 5 August 1747. In 1750 (16 January) he was appointed colonel of the 2nd regiment of dragoons, and in April following took command of the 3rd regiment of foot guards. In 1751 he joined the military staff in Ireland where he spent the remainder of his military career.

On 3 March 1753 Rothes was created a knight of the Order of the Thistle. In 1754 he was made governor of Duncannon Fort, in 1756 he became an Irish privy councillor, and in 1758 was put in command of all the forces in Ireland. On 8 June 1763 he was granted the freedom of Edinburgh. Following the death of his first wife in Dublin in 1761 he married second, on 27 June 1763, Mary (1743–1820), daughter of Gresham Lloyd. Her mother, Mary, married second, Thomas Hamilton, seventh earl of Haddington, in 1750. Rothes was made a full general on 19 March 1765. He died on 10 December 1767 at Leslie House, Leslie, Aberdeenshire, which during his time was destroyed by fire and rebuilt. He was buried at Leslie on 17 December. He had children from his first marriage only, two sons and two daughters, of whom the eldest son, John, succeeded him as eleventh earl, and the eldest daughter, Jane Elizabeth, subsequently became the twelfth holder of the title. The countess of Rothes married Bennet *Langton, the Greek scholar and friend of Dr Johnson. She died at Exeter, aged seventy-seven, on 14 January 1820.

HENRY PATON, *rev.* JONATHAN SPAIN

Sources C. Dalton, *George the First's army, 1714–1727*, 2 vols. (1910–12) · GEC, *Peerage*, new edn · Burke, *Peerage* (1999)

Archives BL, corresp. with duke of Newcastle, Add. MSS 32693–32915, *passim* · NL Scot., corresp., mainly with the fourth marquess of Tweeddale · U. Nott. L., papers; memorial; letters to Henry Pelham

Likenesses J. Macardell, mezzotint (after J. Reynolds), BM, NPG, NG Ire.

Leslie, Sir John (1766–1832), mathematician and natural philosopher, was born on 17 April 1766 at Largo, Fife, Scotland, the youngest child of Robert Leslie (*d.* 1804), a joiner and cabinet-maker, and his wife Anne Carstairs of Largo. Though he attended three local schools for only about a year he learned mathematics at home from his father and elder brother, Alexander, and was encouraged to study by Spence Oliphant, minister of Largo.

University and early career, 1779–1805 In 1779 Leslie entered the local University of St Andrews where he pursued mathematics under Nicholas Vilant. Next year Leslie's precociousness attracted the attention of Thomas Hay, eighth earl of Kinnoul, chancellor of the university, who paid the cost of his education with the intention that he should enter the church. While an undergraduate he became friendly with John Playfair and the wealthy Ferguson brothers, Robert and Ronald, of Raith, near Kirkcaldy, Fife. In 1785 Leslie proceeded to the University of Edinburgh where he was formally registered as a divinity student but devoted his efforts to mathematics, natural philosophy, chemistry, moral philosophy, and anatomy, attending the classes of Playfair, John Robison, Joseph Black, Dugald Stewart, and Alexander Monro secundus

Sir John Leslie (1766–1832), by John Henning, *c.*1805

respectively. On Kinnoul's death in 1787 Leslie unobtrusively relinquished a clerical career for which he had little enthusiasm. In 1787–8, his last session at Edinburgh, he was befriended by Adam Smith who employed him to teach his nearest relative, David Douglas. Leslie also took other private pupils and wrote his first paper, which was communicated in 1788 by Playfair to the Royal Society of Edinburgh; the society published it in 1790. Through Playfair he met James Hutton, the geologist.

Early in 1788 Leslie began to tutor a fellow student, Thomas Randolph, of Virginia. Supported by recommendations from Playfair and Robison, Leslie went to Virginia in November 1788 to be private tutor to Thomas and his brother William. By summer 1789 this American venture had failed: Thomas became difficult and his mother's death led to the breakup of the family. Back in Scotland Leslie sought posts unsuccessfully for six months. Armed with letters of recommendation from Smith he went to London hoping to become a lecturer on natural philosophy but he lacked the necessary grander instruments and was not prepared to demonstrate trifling experiments. He also hoped to become a private mathematics tutor to a grandson of the third earl of Bute but was rejected on the insulting ground that he was a Scot. At this time Leslie was also let down by Nevil Maskelyne, the astronomer royal, who offered to make Leslie his assistant, an invitation withdrawn when the existing assistant unexpectedly recovered his health. Leslie was so desperate that he approached the ninth earl of Kinnoul, nephew of his former patron, and considered unwillingly a career in the Church of Scotland.

In 1790 Leslie's fortunes improved. Through William Thomson, a Scot who had moved to London to become a miscellaneous writer, Leslie wrote the notes for a new edition of the Bible which Thomson published. For Strahan and Cadell he translated Buffon's *Histoire des oiseaux* (9 vols., 1793), a task occupying two years from April 1790. This literary hack work enabled Leslie to begin acquiring that financial security which he thought was the foundation of intellectual independence. From April 1790 until the end of 1792 he was private tutor at Etruria, Staffordshire, to Thomas Wedgwood, a fellow student at Edinburgh. For this he was paid £150 per annum and enjoyed the use of Wedgwood's apparatus and library.

When Wedgwood's poor health ended the arrangement, Leslie returned to Largo, his base until 1805. Again unemployed he contemplated and sometimes pursued visionary schemes but his salvation once again was literary hack work, this time as a writer from summer 1794 for the *Monthly Review* edited by Ralph Griffiths to whom Leslie had been recommended by Wedgwood and Alexander Chisholme, a chemical assistant at the Wedgwood works. Leslie wrote for the *Monthly Review* until 1808, his most frequent contributions dating from 1795 and 1796. In these years Leslie was an unsuccessful candidate for the chairs of natural philosophy at the universities of St Andrews and Glasgow respectively. He failed at the former because he was then an extreme whig and an atheist who deplored the Erastianism of many of the Scottish clergy. His failure at St Andrews confirmed his opposition to the so-called moderate faction in the Church of Scotland and to clerical juntas and bigotry in general. In 1797 Leslie was relieved of financial worries by Thomas Wedgwood who settled an annuity of £150 on him for life. He used his independence well: by 1804 he had published six papers and his *Experimental Enquiries into the Nature and Properties of Heat* (1804), which brought him the Rumford medal of the Royal Society of London in 1805. Drawing on the ideas of Hutton and Boscovich, Leslie proposed that heat was a material compound and not a form of motion. His contemporaries, especially Count Rumford, who regarded Leslie as a plagiarist, ignored his theories; but they took cognizance of his instrumental innovations, such as a heat source which became known as Leslie's cube and a sensitive heat detector which he called the differential thermometer, and they recognized that he had established several basic laws of heat radiation.

Atheist mathematician, 1805–1819 In autumn 1803 Leslie was yet again pressed financially as a result of inflation and a rash investment. Once more he undertook literary drudgery. Yet again he looked to an academic post but late in 1804 failed a second time to secure the chair of natural philosophy at St Andrews and early in 1805 competed, on Playfair's advice, for the Edinburgh chair of natural philosophy to which Playfair was elected, leaving his mathematics post vacant. Leslie's fifth attempt to gain a Scottish university chair was successful: in March 1805 he was elected professor of mathematics at Edinburgh, but amid great controversy. Before his election the Edinburgh moderates had insinuated that Leslie was an atheist. They adduced note xvi of his *Heat* in which he had written favourably about the doctrine of the sceptical David Hume that causation was nothing more than an observed constant and invariable sequence of events. When they brought forward their own candidate, Thomas MacKnight, an Edinburgh clergyman, Stewart and Playfair protested against the uniting of clerical and academic posts and objected to the intended clerical domination of the University of Edinburgh on the pattern of St Andrews. After Leslie's election the Edinburgh moderates, determined to oust Leslie, took the affair to the general assembly of the Church of Scotland, its highest forum, which decided in May 1805 by the narrow majority of 96 to 84 that the affair be dropped and Leslie be left undeposed from his mathematics chair. In a highly acrimonious controversy, Stewart, Playfair, and Leslie settled old personal scores, but the affair had political and ecclesiastical impacts. It was one of the first successes of nineteenth-century Scottish whiggery. It also confirmed the rise in the Church of Scotland of the evangelicals who defeated their traditional moderate opponents by taking the risk of supporting Leslie, a suspected atheist, and embracing the views on causation held by the atheist Hume.

As professor of mathematics Leslie strove to render his classes more respectable and more profitable. Though he lacked the clear exposition and elocution of Playfair his audience in the 1810s never dropped below 100 and reached a maximum of 180. As a textbook writer he published at intervals parts of what he at first intended to be a complete course of mathematics. His best known text, *Elements of Geometry, Geometrical Analysis, and Plane Trigonometry* (1809), which was speedily translated into French and German, reached a fourth edition in 1820. Characteristically Leslie presented mathematics, with its requirement of patient and accurate reasoning, as a vital part of liberal education. Though he was capable of using continental analysis and algebra in his research publications and on occasion taught them in an advanced class, in his general teaching he followed Playfair in presenting Greek geometry and trigonometry as by far the most important types of mathematics: continental analysis and algebra, with their mechanical facility, use of negative and complex numbers, and unrigorous short cuts, were in contrast philosophically suspect and pedagogically inadequate. Leslie also maintained his interest in heat and instruments, sometimes working at the home of the Ferguson brothers and devising in 1810 a machine for making ice, the principle of which had been published in 1777 by Nairne. Leslie contributed fifteen articles on mathematics and physical science to the *Supplement to the Fourth, Fifth, and Sixth Editions of the Encyclopaedia Britannica* (1824) edited by his friend Macvey Napier, whom he helped greatly. From 1809 Leslie supplemented the lucid writings of Playfair in the *Edinburgh Review* with seven contributions on the history of science and travel in his characteristically ornate, almost affected, style.

Natural philosopher, 1819–1832 Leslie enjoyed continental travel in his vacations. On his return from Holland in summer 1819 he heard of Playfair's death. Having deputized for Playfair, who was abroad in 1816–17, Leslie was the natural choice for the Edinburgh natural philosophy chair which was more suited to his talents and widely regarded as senior to that of mathematics. He was elected professor of natural philosophy in autumn 1819, having fought off a short-lived challenge from the Revd Thomas Chalmers, the candidate of the evangelicals, led by Andrew Mitchell Thomson and including David Brewster, who objected to Leslie's notorious atheism. The fixed annual salary of Leslie's new chair was £52 compared with that of £148 for mathematics so he was more dependent for emolument on class fees. Though Leslie lacked Playfair's elegance, taste, and judgement he greatly surpassed his predecessor in two ways. His course, occupying 120 hours, was much wider in scope. It was lavishly illustrated by about a thousand experiments using new apparatus which by 1826 had cost £1600 of which Leslie provided £900. In one respect, however, Leslie was constrained by the open access to the university classes: many of his students, totalling about 150 per annum, were mathematically ignorant. In 1823 Leslie proposed to solve this problem by giving an additional class in special physics but the university senate banned it because of alleged interference with other subjects such as mathematics. At the elementary level he was temporarily successful. In 1826–7 he followed his rival, T. C. Hope, the professor of chemistry, in giving popular lectures before a mixed audience, an unseemly venture which was not repeated.

Always paying attention to his own fortunes, both intellectual and financial, in 1822 Leslie employed as counsel three leading whig lawyers, Francis Jeffrey, Henry Cockburn, and James Wellwood Moncreiff, in a legal action against *Blackwood's Edinburgh Magazine* for libels accusing him of dishonesty, plagiarism, impiety, and dishonouring scripture. He won damages of £100 on two of the four counts. Keen to promote his visibility Leslie wanted to display his best experiments to the royal suite when George IV paid his celebrated visit to Edinburgh in 1822 and to furnish the monarch with 6–8lbs of ice every day. Past his best as a researcher, Leslie continued writing. In 1823 he published chiefly for the use of his class *Elements of Natural Philosophy*, the first of three intended volumes; but, as with his mathematics series, the plan was not completed. His crowning benefaction to the *Encyclopaedia Britannica* (7th edn, vol. 1) was his *Dissertation … exhibiting a general view of the progress of mathematical and physical science, chiefly during the eighteenth century* which brought him £200 and continued Playfair's unfinished account published in 1816.

Suspicious of learned societies as incorporated juntas, Leslie was never a fellow of the Royal Society of London which had rejected an early paper of his; elected a fellow of the Royal Society of Edinburgh in 1807 he took no part in its affairs; but he did prize his election in 1820 as a corresponding member of the Institute of France. Though subsequently distinguished pupils attended Leslie's lectures, his idiosyncrasies precluded any of them from becoming a disciple.

In later life Leslie was not prepossessing in his appearance. Lampooned in a student magazine as Edinburgh's Falstaff, he was short and fat with a florid face, his front teeth projected, and he tottered when walking. A strong and active man, he ate big meals at the end of which he was capable of devouring 2 pounds of almonds and raisins. He dressed slovenly but, in an attempt to appear engaging, the affluent and vain but grubby bachelor dyed his hair purple. His great intellectual powers were combined with a love of financial reward which even his friends thought unseemly. He could be disparaging about his fellow savants and his honesty in scientific matters was questioned by Rumford, Brewster, and Thomas Young. In his private life, however, he was a warm friend, a reliable relative, free from that affectation so characteristic of his literary style, and above all placable.

Early in 1832 Leslie was created a knight of the Royal Guelphic Order on the recommendation of Henry Brougham, the whig lord chancellor. Later that year Leslie caught a severe cold while superintending some improvements on the estate at Coates, near Cupar, Fife, which he had bought in the 1820s. Contemptuous of medicine he neglected his ailment and suffered erysipelas in one of his legs. On 31 October he imprudently worked in his grounds, soon became very ill, and died from erysipelas on 3 November 1832 at Coates. A loyal Fifer to the end, he was buried at Largo on 9 November 1832.

Jack Morrell

Sources M. Napier, 'Memoir of Leslie', in J. Leslie, *Treatises on various subjects of natural and chemical philosophy* (1838), 3–46 • Leslie letters, U. Edin. L. • letters, NL Scot., Leslie MSS • Chambers, *Scots.* (1855) • J. B. Morrell, 'The Leslie affair: careers, kirk, and politics in Edinburgh in 1805', *SHR*, 54 (1975), 63–82 • J. B. Morrell, 'Science and Scottish university reform: Edinburgh in 1826', *British Journal for the History of Science*, 6 (1972–3), 39–56 • R. G. Olson, 'Count Rumford, Sir John Leslie, and the study of the nature and propagation of heat at the beginning of the nineteenth century', *Annals of Science*, 26 (1970), 273–304 • R. G. Olson, 'Scottish philosophy and mathematics: 1750–1830', *Journal of the History of Ideas*, 32 (1971), 29–44 • *Wellesley index* • W. Bennet, *Report of the trial by jury, Professor John Leslie against William Blackwood, for libel in Blackwood's Edinburgh Magazine* (1822) • J. Kay, *A series of original portraits and caricature etchings … with biographical sketches and illustrative anecdotes*, ed. [H. Paton and others], 2 vols. in 4 (1837–8) • *The Scotsman* (7 Nov 1832) • *Edinburgh Evening Courant* (8 Nov 1932) • b. cert. • W. P. Anderson, *Silences that speak* (1931) • private information (2004)

Archives NRA Scotland, priv. coll., corresp. and notebooks • NRA, priv. coll., family corresp. and papers • U. Edin. L., notebooks and papers | BL, letters to Macvey Napier, Add. MSS 34611–34615 • BM, Banks MSS • Keele University Library, Wedgwood MSS • Lincs. Arch., corresp. with J. S. Langton • NL Scot., corresp. with Sir Joseph Banks • NL Scot., corresp. with Archibald Constable • U. Edin. L., letters to James Brown • U. St Andr. L., corresp. with James David Forbes

Likenesses J. Henning, chalk drawing, *c.*1805, Scot. NPG [*see illus.*] • W. Wastle, etching, pubd 1819, BM, NPG; repro. in J. G. Lockhart, *Peter's letters to his kinsfolk* (1819) • H. Cook, stipple, pubd 1833 (after A. Chisholm), BM, NPG • J. Caw, oils (after portrait by D. Wilkie), U. Edin. • F. Chantrey, pencil drawing, NPG • J. Rhind, marble bust (after S. Joseph), Scot. NPG • portrait, repro. in Kay, *A series of original portraits*, no. 152

Wealth at death under £10,000: Chambers, *Scots.*

Leslie, Sir John Randolph [Shane], **third baronet** (**1885–1971**), author, was born on 24 September 1885 at Stratford House, 11 Granville Place, in London, the eldest of the four sons of Sir John Leslie, second baronet (1857–1944), and his wife, Léonie Blanche (1857–1943), pianist, youngest

Sir John Randolph Leslie, third baronet (1885–1971), by Howard Coster, *c.*1954

daughter of Leonard Jerome of New York, and sister of Lady Randolph Churchill. His boyhood was spent in Ireland. He was educated at Ludgrove School, London, and then at Eton College, which he left in order to learn French at the Sorbonne. He returned to take up a place at King's College, Cambridge, where he obtained a second class in part one of the classical tripos in 1907. At Cambridge he became a Roman Catholic and an Irish nationalist, persuasions which deeply affronted the Anglo-Irish protestant ascendancy into which he had been born. He began to use the Irish form of his name—Shane.

Having changed his religion and renounced the Irish estates entailed on him, in the winter of 1907 Leslie travelled to Russia and stayed with Lev Tolstoy at Yasnaya Polyana. Leslie was in awe of Tolstoy and as a tribute to him he 'became a confirmed vegetarian and promised to learn to plough' (Leslie, *Long Shadows*, 116). After leaving Cambridge, Leslie studied scholastic philosophy at Louvain University, became attached to the Brethren of the Divine Compassion and other clergy houses in the East End of London, and 'dallied on the threshold of a monastery until the college boat club begged me to return to Cambridge and row in the May boat' (ibid.). During this period his first cousin Winston Churchill, who was in favour of home rule, showed interest in Leslie's political views and introduced him to John Redmond, leader of the Irish nationalists in the House of Commons. Inspired by Redmond, Shane agreed to stand for Londonderry as a nationalist in the 1910 election. He narrowly lost the seat and set off to raise interest in the Gaelic movement in America where he worked with Bourke Cockran the Irish orator, who was a friend of Churchill's. Both Cockran and Leslie were seeking to lessen the dislike of the American Irish for England. While in America, Leslie met and married in June 1912 Marjorie (1881–1951), writer and youngest daughter of Henry Clay Ide, judge of the Vermont supreme court and governor-general of the Philippines, and sister of Anne, Mrs Bourke Cockran. They had a daughter and two sons. As well as working politically Leslie began to produce books of verse. In the First World War his brother Norman, a captain in the rifle brigade, was killed (Leslie recovered his brother's body from the battlefield near Armentières) and Leslie, attached to a British ambulance corps, was on his way to the Dardanelles when he became ill and was placed in a military hospital in Malta. Here he wrote his first major book, *The End of a Chapter*, which described the civilization he now saw perishing. Published in 1916, it made his name and anticipated in its fluency, nostalgia, and candour the character and style of his later work.

During 1916 and 1917 Leslie worked in Washington with the British ambassador, Sir Cecil Arthur Spring-Rice, who was trying to soften Irish American hostility to Britain and convince the United States of the urgency of declaring war against Germany. Leslie published a magazine entitled *Ireland* and strove with Spring-Rice to establish understanding between Westminster and Washington. Perhaps the bravest thing that Leslie ever did—certainly the most perspicacious—was to implore the British politicians not to execute the leaders of the 1916 Easter rising in Dublin. His arguments went unheeded: sixteen Irish leaders were shot. In 1918 Shane Leslie's political career suffered when Sinn Féin wiped out the nationalist party. But after the war Leslie took an unofficial role in the exchanges for the Irish treaty in 1921, and to the end of his life was passionate about the future of a united Ireland.

From 1916 to 1926 Leslie worked as editor of the *Dublin Review* and during the 1920s and 1930s he wrote *Henry Edward Manning: his Life and Labours* (1921), *Mark Sykes: his Life and Letters* (1923), a biography of his friend and cousin, *The Skull of Swift* (1928), and *Studies in Sublime Failure* (1932). His biography of Mrs Fitzherbert (1939), mistress of George IV, was in a sense a family history: the Leslies claimed descent from the daughter of the affair. And from his pen also came three novels: *Doomsland* (1923), about his Ulster boyhood; *The Oppidan* (1922), a discerning book about Eton College; and *The Cantab* (1926), describing the adventures of a Cambridge undergraduate. The first edition of the autobiographical novel, which was deemed sexually explicit, caused Leslie's tenure at the *Dublin Review* to be ended, and was banned by Rome. He also wrote in verse *Jutland, a Fragment of Epic* (1930) and, being a classical scholar, he produced *The Greek Anthology* (1929). His *American Wonderland* (1936) and the autobiographical *The Film of Memory* (1938) appeared shortly before the Second World War. From 1940 to 1945 Leslie served in the Home Guard at the London headquarters of General Sir Hubert Gough. There on his camp-bed he wrote *The Irish Tangle for*

English Readers (1946) about the increasing bitterness engendered around his Monaghan home. He succeeded to the baronetcy in 1944. His last book, *Long Shadows*, published in 1966 when he was over eighty, presented a final memoir. Small books of verse were interspersed throughout his other work and many anthologies include his poems. For the *Dictionary of National Biography* he wrote the notices of W. P. Ward, Mark Sykes, Michael Logue, and Alfred Noyes. He was an associate of the Irish Academy and had an honorary LLD from Notre Dame University.

Leslie, a striking man particularly in old age, had fine conversational powers and wit. To the end of his days he could galvanize the most erudite audience with his lectures or entrance with reminiscence. The well-turned phrases of his writings were outmatched by the speed of his repartee. Keenly interested in reforestation, he led a campaign for more general planting and was well known in the organization Men of the Trees. After the death of his first wife he married Iris Carola (*d.* 1993), daughter of Charles Miskin Laing, in 1958. Leslie died at 14 New Church Road, Hove, on 14 August 1971. His elder son, John Norman Ide (*b.* 1916), succeeded to the baronetcy.

ANITA LESLIE, *rev.* CLARE L. TAYLOR

Sources S. Leslie, *Long shadows* (1966) • S. Leslie, *The film of memory* (1938) • *WWW* • b. cert. • d. cert.

Archives CAC Cam., papers relating to biography of Admiral Beatty • Eton, letters to his family • Georgetown University, Washington, DC, MSS • NL Ire., MSS, MIC/1606, T/3827 • NRA, priv. coll., corresp. and MSS • NRA, priv. coll., letters • TCD, papers relating to biography of J. P. Mahaffy • University of Notre Dame, Indiana, MSS | CUL, letters to Francis Meynell • Eton, letters to Marjorie Madan • King's Cam., letters to librarian • NRA, priv. coll., letters to Norman Moore • St Patrick's College, Maynooth, letters to Canon Lyons • TCD, corresp. with John Dillon • W. Sussex RO, letters to Wilfrid Scawen Blunt

Likenesses H. Coster, photograph, *c.*1954, NPG [*see illus.*] • F. Whiting, portrait, 1956, repro. in Leslie, *Long shadows* • J. Eves, portrait, Castle Leslie • J. Lavery, oils, Hugh Lane Municipal Gallery of Modern Art, Dublin • C. Sheridan, bust, Castle Leslie • F. White, portrait, Monaghan Museum • photograph, University of Notre Dame, Indiana, archives

Wealth at death £11,590: probate, 22 Oct 1971, *CGPLA Eng. & Wales*

Leslie [*married name* Burr], **May Sybil (1887–1937)**, chemist, was born on 14 August 1887 at Cloverfield, Woodlesford, Yorkshire, the daughter of Frederick Leslie, coalminer (and later bookseller), and his wife, Elizabeth Dickinson. She was educated at Leeds high school and on graduation in 1905 was awarded a West Riding county scholarship to study at the University of Leeds. She graduated with a first-class BSc degree in 1908 and the following year was awarded an MSc for research under H. M. Dawson. Her investigation, on the rate of reaction of iodine and acetone, has since become a classic in the field of chemical reaction kinetics.

In 1909 Leslie was awarded an 1851 Exhibition scholarship which she used to travel to Paris to work with Marie Curie on the extraction of new elements from the products of the radioactive decay of thorium. She spent two years at the Curie Institute, then returned to England to work for the year 1911–12 at Manchester University with another famous pioneer researcher in radioactivity, Ernest Rutherford. There she continued her work with thorium and extended her studies to the element actinium. In 1912–14 she taught at the Municipal High School for Girls in West Hartlepool, while commencing a study on ionization in non-aqueous solvents with Dawson at Leeds. In 1914, at a time when women rarely obtained academic positions other than at women's colleges, Leslie was appointed assistant lecturer and demonstrator of chemistry at the University College in Bangor, Wales.

In 1915, Leslie accepted a position as research chemist at the government explosives factory at Litherland near Liverpool. During the First World War, many male scientists had been called up for service in the armed forces and there was a desperate need for qualified research chemists to supervise the production of chemicals needed for the war effort. Her particular research elucidated the chemical reactions involved in the formation of nitric acid (a component for the synthesis of explosives) and as a result she was able to identify the optimum industrial conditions for the process. Increasing the efficiency of this process was so essential to maximizing explosives production that, after the war, she was awarded a DSc degree by the University of Leeds in recognition of her contribution. In 1916, she was promoted to chemist in charge of laboratory at Litherland. The following year, the Litherland factory closed and she was transferred with the same rank to the government factory in Penrhyndeudraeth, north Wales.

In 1920, Leslie was appointed to the University of Leeds as demonstrator in the department of chemistry, rising through the ranks to a position as lecturer in the department of physical chemistry in 1928. She was an active researcher, and she also wrote *The Alkaline Earth Metals* (1925) and co-authored *Beryllium and its Congeners* (1926), two titles in J. Newton Friend's comprehensive series, A Textbook of Inorganic Chemistry. Both books were published under her married name, M. S. Burr.

Leslie married Alfred Hamilton Burr (1885–1933) a lecturer in chemistry at the Royal Technical College, Salford, on 29 September 1923. She resigned her position at Leeds in 1929 and moved with Burr to Scotland in 1931 when he was appointed head of the chemistry department at Coatbridge Technical College. Following Burr's death in 1933, she moved back to Leeds where her first project was the completion of her deceased husband's research on wool dyes. She also resumed research work with Dawson. Later, she was a sub-warden at Weetwood Hall, a women's residence, from 1935 to 1937. She was elected associate of the Institute of Chemistry in 1918 and fellow of the Chemical Society in 1920. She died of lung cancer at Mahlstan, Bardsey, near Leeds, on 3 July 1937, her early death possibly being the result of exposure to high levels of radiation during her time at the Curie Institute. She was cremated at Lawnswood crematorium on 6 July 1937.

MARELENE F. RAYNER-CANHAM

Sources G. Rayner-Canham and M. Rayner-Canham, 'A chemist of some repute', *Chemistry in Britain*, 29 (1993), 206–8 • H. M. Dawson, *JCS* (1938), 151–2 • b. cert. • m. cert. • d. cert. • *Yorkshire Post* (6 July 1937)
Archives U. Leeds, Edward Boyle Library, MSS and papers • U. Leeds, A. Smithells collection, letters
Likenesses photograph, U. Leeds, university archives
Wealth at death £8765 15*s*. 5*d*.: confirmation, 2 Oct 1937, *CCI*

Leslie, Norman, master of Rothes (*d*. 1554), landowner and soldier, was the eldest son of George *Leslie, fourth earl of Rothes (*d*. 1558), and Margaret Crichton, natural daughter of William, third Lord Crichton and Princess Margaret, daughter of King James II. Norman, who was regarded as an accomplished young man, was for a time a yeoman of the chamber to James V, and is referred to as the king's familiar servant. He was a considerable landowner, jointly with his father and independently, with lands in Fife, Moray, Forfarshire, Perthshire, and Aberdeenshire, including land belonging to the nunnery of Elcho, whose property had long been at the disposal of his family. In 1541 his father resigned to him the family's hereditary office of sheriff of Fife. He himself frequently wadset (mortgaged) land to others for loans of money. Other sources of income and influence included purchases from the crown of the rights of ward and marriage in lands of which the heir was under age, and the escheats of individuals who had been forfeited for various crimes. He obtained a remission (pardon) for his absence from the musters of the royal army in 1543 and 1544.

It may have been a land dispute that first soured Leslie's relations with Cardinal David Beaton, with whom he had at one time been on friendly terms. In 1543, for example, it was at the cardinal's instigation that the lands of Wemyss, Fife, which the king had granted to the Leslies on the forfeiture of Sir James Colville, were restored to their former owners. There were other sources of growing antipathy between Leslie and the cardinal. Norman fought at Solway Moss in November 1542, was taken prisoner, and with other Scots was released on promising to assist Henry VIII's plans for a union of England and Scotland, plans which were furthered by the Anglo-Scottish marriage treaty of the summer of 1543. The aims of the Anglophile party to which Leslie belonged ran counter to the cardinal's Francophile policies. Leslie's family also identified with the growing number of laity who favoured reform of the church, some aspects of which echoed Henry VIII's attack on the church's property and authority. Transactions in the Rothes family papers sometimes reveal their association with others in the Anglophile-reformist party, including the Melvilles of Raith, Kirkcaldys of Grange, Lindsays of the Byres, Mr Henry Balnaves the lawyer, and the priest Norman Gourlay who was put to death for heresy in 1534. Norman Leslie's name appears in a list of those who in 1544 were pardoned for, among other offences, 'disputing the holy scriptures and reading forbidden books' (*Register of the Privy Seal*, 1543–8, no. 820).

In April 1544 Henry VIII was informed that the master of Rothes and others were prepared to take the cardinal's life on assurance of the English king's protection after the deed was done. Nothing came of their offer at this time. In fact there seems to have been a brief attempt at reconciliation between Leslie and the cardinal, for on 24 April 1544 they signed a bond of manrent (mutual support). In July 1544, along with Lord Gray, Leslie lent military support to the cardinal's attempt to force the appointment of John Charteris of Kinfauns as provost of Perth, but the failure of the coup is said to have disillusioned Leslie as to the advantages of alliance with the cardinal. Leslie fought in the Scots army which repulsed an English force at Ancrum Moor on 27 February 1545, where he led a contingent of spearmen from Fife. His relations with the cardinal deteriorated, culminating, it is said, in a violent personal quarrel. By then he was probably a leader of the conspiracy that rapidly took shape against Beaton's life with the knowledge of the English authorities.

The execution of George Wishart for heresy at St Andrews on 1 March 1546 brought to a head the plans of the group of frustrated Anglophiles and religious dissidents whom Leslie led. In the early hours of Saturday 29 May they succeeded in entering St Andrews Castle, turned out the guards and household servants, and murdered Beaton in his private apartments. If the assassins knew of an alleged plot by Beaton to encompass the downfall of a number of his Fife opponents, regarding which papers were said to have been found in the castle after his death, they may have acted to forestall his attack. Norman Leslie did not himself strike a blow at the cardinal but his familiarity with the household may have facilitated the evacuation of the castle before the deed. Contemporary accounts describe him as leader of the assassins and as captain of those men, known as *castilians, who proceeded to hold St Andrews Castle against the governor's somewhat half-hearted siege. So confident was he that he occasionally led a sortie into the town, setting fire to the local friaries and on one occasion bullying the clergy of St Salvator's collegiate church into granting a charter of their lands to an ally of his own.

Leslie was denounced rebel on 30 July 1547. Because of his own and his father's part in the plot against Beaton the family's property was forfeited to the crown, but had been recovered by the earl of Rothes by the time of his death on 16 September 1558, whereupon Norman's younger brother Andrew *Leslie succeeded as fifth earl of Rothes. On the fall of St Andrews Castle in August 1547 Norman was taken prisoner to France with other castilians. They were detained in Cherbourg Castle, where Leslie was among those who resisted the order to attend mass, but on 6 October 1547 they were transferred to Mont St Michel, whence they later escaped. Leslie is said to have briefly visited Scotland, but fear of arrest took him to Denmark, thence to England where the accession of Mary Tudor in 1553 caused him to return to France, where he took service in the army of King Henri II during his wars with the emperor Charles V. He showed considerable bravery at the siege of Renti in August 1554, and at one point attacked a superior force of imperial cavalry at the head of thirty Scots horsemen. He was fatally wounded, and in spite of the attention of the French king's own surgeons died of his wounds on the 29th. Many regretted his death, and also that by the outcome of his vendetta against the cardinal 'he lost himself and the expectation which was generally held of his worth' (*History of the Church*, 1.188).

Leslie married Isobel, or Elizabeth (*d.* in or after 1568), daughter of John *Lindsay, fifth Lord Lindsay of the Byres, in 1541. They had no children. She was confirmed in possession of her conjunct-fee lands despite her husband's forfeiture. Leslie had two natural sons, Robert and John, legitimated on 25 February 1554.

MARGARET H. B. SANDERSON

Sources *Scots peerage*, 7.279–92 · J. M. Thomson and others, eds., *Registrum magni sigilli regum Scotorum / The register of the great seal of Scotland*, 11 vols. (1882–1914), vol. 3 · *Memoirs of his own life by Sir James Melville of Halhill*, ed. T. Thomson, Bannatyne Club, 18 (1827), 25–6 · J. Spottiswood, *The history of the Church of Scotland*, ed. M. Napier and M. Russell, 3 vols., Bannatyne Club, 93 (1850), vol. 1, pp. 163, 177–8, 188 · *John Knox's History of the Reformation in Scotland*, ed. W. C. Dickinson, 1 (1949), 52–63, 75–8 · Rothes muniments, NA Scot., GD 204 · M. Livingstone, D. Hay Fleming, and others, eds., *Registrum secreti sigilli regum Scotorum / The register of the privy seal of Scotland*, 1 (1908) · J. B. Paul, ed., *Compota thesaurariorum regum Scotorum / Accounts of the lord high treasurer of Scotland*, 6–7 (1905–7) · acts of the lords of council and session, NA Scot., CS6, xxviii · register of acts and decreets, NA Scot., CS7, xxviii · J. H. Burton and D. Masson, eds., *The register of the privy council of Scotland*, 1st ser., 14 vols. (1877–98) · *LP Henry VIII*, vols. 19/1, 21/1 · T. Thomson, ed., *A diurnal of remarkable occurrents that have passed within the country of Scotland*, Bannatyne Club, 43 (1833) · G. Chalmers, *Caledonia, or, An account, historical and topographic, of north Britain*, 3 vols. (1807–24), 2 · E. Dupont, 'Les prisonniers écossais du Mont Saint Michel (en Normandie) au XVIe siècle', *SHR*, 3 (1905–6), 506–7

Archives NA Scot., Rothes muniments, GD 204

Leslie, Robert, of Inverpeffer (*d.* 1536). *See under* College of justice, procurators of the (*act.* 1532).

Leslie, Thomas Edward Cliffe (1826–1882), economist, second son of Edward Leslie (1792–1865), prebendary and treasurer of Dromore and rector of Annahilt, co. Down, a descendant of Charles Leslie, the nonjuror, was born in the county of Wexford on 21 June 1826. His mother was Margaret, daughter of the Revd Thomas E. Higginson of Lisburn. He was at first educated by his father, and afterwards at King William's College in the Isle of Man, and then from 1842 at Trinity College, Dublin, where he took a classical scholarship in 1845, and graduated BA with a senior moderatorship and gold medal in ethics and logic in 1847.

Leslie's original intention seems to have been to pursue a legal career; he was admitted to the Irish bar in 1850 and proceeded to the degree of LLB in 1851—also at Trinity College, Dublin, which later recognized his distinction by conferring an honorary LLD upon him in 1878. He had entered Lincoln's Inn in 1848 and was for two years a pupil in a conveyancer's chambers. Although he was called to the bar at Lincoln's Inn in Easter term 1857, he never practised. Before this his interests had come to lie more in the philosophy of law than in the practice of it and even in 1851 had broadened to include economic studies. Consequently Leslie gained appointment to the chair of jurisprudence and political economy in Queen's College, Belfast, in 1853. As his professorial duties permitted him to reside for most of each year in London he continued his legal studies there, and attended the lectures of Sir Henry Sumner Maine. From Maine, Leslie learned the value of the historical and comparative method in jurisprudence, and he inferred the need for a similar approach in political economy. He also studied the philosophy of Auguste Comte, but although he accepted Comte's view of political economy as a department of the science of society he never became a Comtist, unlike his friend and contemporary John Kells Ingram.

As Ingram himself wrote, 'Leslie's work may be distributed under two heads, that of applied political economy, and that of discussion on the philosophical method of the science' (Ingram, *Encyclopaedia Britannica*, 478). It is upon his work under the latter head that Leslie's enduring reputation as an economist rests, but it was to applied political economy that he initially turned his attention. His first publication, *On the Self-Dependence of the Working Classes under the Law of Competition*, read to the Dublin Statistical Society in April 1851, showed him already critical in some respects of the classical theory of wages, but not employing the method which in later years he adopted from Maine. In his only published lecture at Queen's College, Belfast, he turned to a different topic, *The Military Systems of Europe Economically Considered* (1856), a subject which he followed up in several later articles, becoming one of a very few economists of the later Victorian era who dealt seriously with the economic implications of growing militarism. One of his articles on this subject, in *Macmillan's Magazine* (September 1860), attracted the notice and later secured him the friendship of J. S. Mill. In 1864–5 he took part in the controversy on the effects of gold discoveries on prices, stressing that the rise in prices observed in many countries was due not only to increased gold supplies but also to the widening of markets by improved communications and the consequent equalization of price levels within, as well as between, countries.

Between 1865 and 1870 Leslie also made significant contributions to the debate then taking place on the economic condition of Ireland. He took an unfavourable view of emigration, pointing out that the rise in money wages in Ireland since 1850 was not due, as many argued, to a reduced supply of labour so much as to increased world prices. He was also critical of the consolidation of small into large farms, urging the creation of peasant proprietorship, which would allow and encourage profitable cultivation of small-holdings. Leslie's advocacy of small-scale farming was based on firsthand knowledge of the tenure and cultivation of land in various countries in Europe. Two autumn holidays, in 1868 and 1869, passed with Léonce de Lavergne at his country seat, Peyrusse in La Creuse, and some tours in Belgium, Westphalia, and other parts of the continent, furnished Leslie with materials which formed the basis of a volume of essays entitled *Land Systems and Industrial Economy of Ireland, England, and Continental Countries*. On its publication in 1870 it was highly praised by Mill in a review article in the *Fortnightly*.

It was not until 1868 that Leslie began to publish his ideas on the philosophical method of political economy, criticizing the dominance of deduction from limited premises in classical economic analysis and following the lead of F. D. Longe and W. T. Thornton in attacking the wages-fund doctrine. In 1870 he published an article on 'The political economy of Adam Smith', pointing out that it combined the deductive and inductive methods and contending 'that we have two systems of political economy claiming descent from him': one, the Ricardian 'reasoning entirely from hypothetical laws'; the other, 'of which Malthus in the generation after Adam Smith, and Mr Mill in our own, may be taken as representative', combining deduction with induction, as Smith himself had done. In subsequent essays he continued to attack the Ricardian approach and in 1876 published in *Hermathena* his fullest statement 'On the philosophical method of political economy', urging that it 'must be historical, and must trace the connection between the economical and the other phases of national history'.

Leslie's critique of Ricardian analysis gained the attention of such economists as W. S. Jevons and Alfred Marshall, who saw the future of their discipline as requiring the use of other methods besides the historical, but he himself never succeeded in producing a systematic economic treatise using the methods he advocated. In consequence his contemporaries saw his work as fragmentary and tended to underestimate the value of the many papers he had published. They attributed his failure to publish an authoritative treatise partly to a preponderance in him of the critical over the constructive faculty, partly to the loss, while travelling in France in 1872, of the manuscript of a work which he was preparing on the economic and legal history of England, and partly to chronic ill health, the result of kidney disease. Early in 1882 it seemed that this might compel him to resign his chair, and friends and colleagues organized a memorial to Gladstone requesting a civil-list pension for him; but before the matter could be decided Leslie died, unmarried, at his lodgings, 48 Botanic Avenue, Belfast, on 27 January 1882.

R. D. Collison Black

Sources 'Political and economical heterodoxy: Cliffe Leslie', *Westminster Review*, 120 (1883), 470–500 • J. K. Ingram, 'Leslie, Thomas Ed. Cliffe', *Encyclopaedia Britannica*, 9th edn (1875–89), vol. 14, pp. 477–8 • J. S. Mill, 'Leslie on the land question', *Essays on economics and society*, ed. J. M. Robson (1967), vol. 5 of *The collected works of John Stuart Mill*, ed. J. M. Robson and others (1963–91), 669–85 • *The later letters of John Stuart Mill, 1849–1873*, ed. F. E. Mineka and D. N. Lindley, 4 vols. (1972), vols. 14–17 of *The collected works of John Stuart Mill*, ed. J. M. Robson and others (1963–91), vol. 1 • 'Professor T. E. Cliffe Leslie', *Hibernia* (1 March 1882), 38–9 • G. M. Koot, 'T. E. Cliffe Leslie, Irish social reform, and the origins of the English historical school', *History of Political Economy*, 7 (1975), 312–36 • G. M. Koot, *English historical economics, 1870–1926* (1987) • G. C. G. Moore, 'T. E. Cliffe Leslie and the English *Methodenstreit*', *Journal of the History of Economic Thought*, 17 (1995), 57–77 • T. W. Moody and J. C. Beckett, *Queen's, Belfast, 1845–1949: the history of a university*, 2 vols. (1959) • J. Lipkes, *Politics, religion and classical political economy in Britain* (1999) • Burtchaell & Sadleir, *Alum. Dubl.* • Colonel Leslie [C. J. Leslie], *Historical records of the family of Leslie, from 1067 to 1868–9*, 3 (1869), 328–9 • *Annual Register* (1882), 113 • *The Athenaeum* (4 Feb 1882), 158 • *Belfast News-Letter* (28 Jan 1882) • *The Times* (28 Jan 1882) • *The Times* (30 Jan 1882) • W. S. Jevons, *The Economist* (4 Feb 1882) • Boase, *Mod. Eng. biog.* • entrance books, TCD • register of deaths, 28 Jan 1882

Archives NA Ire., registered papers, letters, and testimonials relating to academic appointments • NL Ire., letters to J. E. Cairnes • PRO NIre., letters to John Kells Ingram

Likenesses photograph, Queen's University, Belfast

Wealth at death £405 3*s*. 7*d*.: probate, 3 April 1882, *CGPLA Ire.*

Leslie, Sir Walter, lord of Ross (*d.* 1382), soldier and royal retainer, was a younger son of Sir Andrew Leslie, lord of Leslie (*d.* 1320x24), and Mary Abernethy (*d.* in or before 1355), daughter and heir of Sir Alexander Abernethy of that ilk. He had two elder brothers, Andrew and Norman, and two younger half-brothers, Alexander and William Lindsay, from his mother's marriage to her second husband, Sir David Lindsay of Crawford. Walter seems to have started his career as an esquire in the household of his kinsman Thomas Stewart, earl of Angus, but by the end of the 1350s, having been knighted between 23 October 1357 and 24 October 1358, he had joined his brother Norman in the service of David II. Like many of David II's favoured retainers, Walter and Norman Leslie were active crusaders, obtaining numerous safe conducts for expeditions to the Holy Land and the Baltic crusades. Walter's exploits were commemorated in the Saracen's head crest adorning his coat of arms in the late fourteenth-century 'Armorial de Gelres' and may well have provided the inspiration for a now lost vernacular work, 'The Tail of Syr Valtir the Bald Leslye'. In 1363–5 Walter and Norman, possibly at the instigation of David II, seem to have been involved in the crusade organized by Pierre I of Cyprus which ended in the sack of Alexandria (where Norman Leslie may have been killed).

On Walter Leslie's return to Scotland he was the beneficiary of considerable royal favour. Before 13 September 1366 David II forced through the marriage of his favourite to Euphemia *Ross [*see under* Ross family], daughter and heir of William, earl of Ross, despite the earl's opposition to the match. Then in February 1370 he granted the royal thanages of Kincardine, Aberluthnott, Fettercairn, and Aberchirder to Walter and Euphemia and their heirs. In October of the same year, moreover, the king intimidated Ross into a formal entailing of his earldom in favour of Walter and Euphemia. Overall, David II apparently viewed Leslie as a dependable and forceful agent for the interests and authority of the crown in the north of the kingdom. The death of his royal patron in February 1371, and the fact that David's successor, Robert II, was the brother-in-law of the earl of Ross, brought about a decline in Leslie's political influence. A fairly regular witness to David's later charters, he no longer witnessed royal charters after 1371. Despite this, King Robert allowed him to retain all the crown lands granted to him in the 1360s and failed to take any action over a complaint delivered to him in June 1371 by the earl of Ross, detailing King David's unfair treatment of the earl and his brother and the resultant resignation of land and title in favour of Leslie.

After Ross's death on 9 February 1372 Leslie adopted the courtesy title lord of Ross as the husband of the earl's daughter and heir, although his influence within the earldom may well have been limited by the opposition of local lords and kindreds, particularly the male line descended from the earl's brother Hugh. In addition, the earldom of Ross was one of the areas made subject to the authority of Robert II's son Alexander Stewart, lord of Badenoch, when he was appointed the king's lieutenant in the north in October 1372. Leslie seems to have continued his career as a crusader and mercenary after 1372 and obtained a succession of English safe conducts for travel overseas. He died at Perth on 27 February 1382; his widow, Euphemia, married Alexander Stewart, but this liaison ended in a politically inspired divorce in 1392.

Leslie and his wife had at least two children, Alexander and Mary. Alexander Leslie became earl of Ross and married Isabel Stewart, daughter of Robert Stewart, duke of Albany, brother of Robert III. Alexander died on 8 May 1402, leaving a daughter and heir, Euphemia, who in 1415 resigned her rights in the earldom in favour of Albany's son John Stewart. Euphemia Leslie seems to have died unmarried and childless after her resignation. Mary Leslie married Donald, lord of the Isles, and after her brother's death Donald of the Isles claimed the earldom of Ross in right of his wife. The son of Donald and Mary, Alexander, eventually had his claim to Ross recognized by the crown, and the earldom remained with the lords of the Isles until it was forfeited to James III in 1478. S. I. BOARDMAN

Sources W. Bower, *Scotichronicon*, ed. D. E. R. Watt and others, new edn, 9 vols. (1987–98), vol. 7 • J. M. Thomson and others, eds., *Registrum magni sigilli regum Scotorum / The register of the great seal of Scotland*, 2nd edn, 1, ed. T. Thomson (1912) • R. J. Adam, ed., *The calendar of Fearn: text and additions, 1471–1667*, Scottish History Society, 5th ser., 4 (1991) • *CEPR letters*, vols. 2, 4 • R. Wedderburn, *The complaynt of Scotland*, ed. A. M. Stewart, STS, 4th ser., 11 (1979) • *RotS*, vol. 1 • W. H. Bliss, ed., *Calendar of entries in the papal registers relating to Great Britain and Ireland: petitions to the pope* (1896) • A. MacQuarrie, *Scotland and the crusades* (1985) • A. H. Dunbar, 'Facsimiles of the Scottish coats of arms emblazoned in the "Armorial de Gelre"', *Proceedings of the Society of Antiquaries of Scotland*, 25 (1890–91), 9–19 • G. Burnett and others, eds., *The exchequer rolls of Scotland*, 1 (1878) • S. I. Boardman, *The early Stewart kings: Robert II and Robert III, 1371–1406* (1996)

Leslie, Walter, Count Leslie in the nobility of the Holy Roman empire (1606–1667), army officer and diplomat, was born in Aberdeenshire, the second son of John Leslie of Balquhain (*d.* 1622), and his third wife, Jean Erskine, daughter of Sir Alexander Erskine of Gogar. By 1624 he had escaped the financial troubles of the family and was fighting in the service of the United Provinces. In 1628 he was at Stralsund on the Baltic, and by 1630 he was serving on the side of the Spanish Habsburgs in the War of the Mantuan Succession (1628–31). By 1631 Leslie had moved northwards again, to help the imperialists' attempt to repel the Swedes under Gustavus Adolphus. On 8 August 1632 he fought at Freistadt, having joined the multinational regiment of Count Adam Trčka, but was captured with a fellow Scot, John Gordon. As prisoners they received the admiration and compliments of the Swedes for their prowess.

The entrepreneurial Leslie quickly acquired prestige in the imperial army following his release. Later in 1632 he was given command of 1000 dragoons at the garrison at Eger (Cheb) in Bohemia, where Gordon commanded Count Adam's Nen-Trčka regiment. Leslie was based there until 1634. Meanwhile his Calvinist background did not prevent him from securing promotion to second-in-command of the regiment. By 1633 he had established contacts that were to lead to his involvement in the plot to dismiss, 'dead or alive', the obscurely motivated imperialist general Albrecht von Wallenstein and his last allies, who included Trčka. On 18 February 1634 Ferdinand II authorized the execution of the plot, the general having made a disastrous attempt from his winter quarters at Pilsen (Plzeň) to persuade his subordinates to maintain their loyalty. Wallenstein was thus forced to make a journey via Eger, arriving there in the afternoon of 25 February, on his way towards a presumed escape to Saxony.

It was Gordon and Leslie, along with the Irishman Walter Butler, another regimental commander, who were instrumental in deciding the final course of events. All appear to have been trusted by Wallenstein to the last since Leslie had been sent to meet him the day before, in the general's apparent belief that the Scot could still be counted on. On the morning of the fateful day, the loyal Count Ilow had tried to win Leslie, Gordon, and Butler over from their unquestioning allegiance to the emperor.

Wallenstein had apparently been feeling ill and had retired to his bedroom in the former burgomaster's house, while his four remaining advisers, including Ilow, accepted an invitation from Leslie and Gordon to a feast at the nearby castle. While all joined to make toasts to the absent *generalissimo*, the drawbridge was closed and a signal came from Leslie for a group of Scottish and Irish dragoons to enter. They slew all four as the others watched, proclaiming 'Vivat Ferdinandus, vivat domus Austria!'. An Irishman, Deveroux, then went with a small group to Wallenstein's residence, found him defenceless in his bed-clothes, and killed him. It remains uncertain whether the gruesome legend that the general's corpse was then conveyed through the streets of the town in a manure-cart to be dumped with the other bodies is entirely accurate.

Nevertheless the events demonstrated to surprised contemporaries the hitherto unknown influence of Leslie within the imperial army. After arriving in Vienna on 6 March he was awarded the post of imperial chamberlain and on 16 April the command of two regiments. Earning ever more favour, he soon converted to Roman Catholicism. However, his subsequent military career was sporadic and frequently disastrous, and absenteeism led to his being deprived of his last regiment by 1642. His main prize at Eger in fact proved to be the award of Trčka's grand estate, at Neustadt (Novemberé Mesto-nad-Metují), a prize which far outweighed the significance of his involvement. Through baroque-inspired renovations there and particularly following his acquisition of the title count (*Reichsgraf*) on 26 June 1637, he expressed his noble claims by various means in order to increase his prestige at court.

Leslie's post-1636 friendships with ambassadors from the British Isles, Basil, Lord Feilding, Sir Thomas Roe, Thomas Howard, earl of Arundel, and Sir Heneage Finch, were to lead to co-operation, both in bringing about the release of Prince Rupert of the palatinate from prison in 1638, and in attempts to restore the privileges of the palatinate to Charles Louis, the elder son of the exiled royal family, during negotiations at Regensburg in 1636 and again in 1640–2. In 1642, as his reward for these services, Leslie requested an appointment for his elder brother William Leslie (*d.* 1671) to the privy chamber of Charles I. His power in imperial affairs further increased after marriage to Anna Franziska Dietrichstein, daughter of Maximilian, prince of Dietrichstein, which occurred in 1647. He later also gained possession of Wallenstein's palace in Prague, but it was his acquisition of the castle of Oberpettau (Ptuj) in Styria from the Jesuits at auction in Zagreb in 1656 which signalled his new role in the south-eastern Habsburg lands.

Leslie was sent to negotiate loans in Italy, a trip which included a meeting with Pope Innocent X in Rome on 21 April 1645. By 5 January 1650 he had become warden of the Slavonian marches and on 23 August he was appointed field marshal and general on the so-called 'Croatian–Slavonian military frontier'. In 1657, already an adviser to the imperial privy council, he was appointed vice-president of the war council. Five years later he sent back money to another brother in Scotland, Alexander Leslie (*d.* 1677), and in his will of 27 May 1663 he not only left money for him and two other brothers still in Aberdeenshire, but arranged to have his Styrian and Bohemian estates fall to his nephew, Alexander's son James. Hence James Leslie and another nephew accompanied him, following his award of the order of the Golden Fleece on 6 May 1665, on his last, lavish embassy, to Constantinople. He died on 3 March 1667 and was buried in the Scottish Benedictine abbey in Vienna. DAVID WORTHINGTON

Sources H. Hallwich, 'Leslie, Walther, Graf von', *Allgemeine deutsche Biographie*, ed. R. von Liliencron and others, 18 (Leipzig, 1883), 437–44 • Colonel Leslie [C. J. Leslie], *Historical records of the family of Leslie, from 1067 to 1868–9*, 3 (1869), 241–72 • *DNB* • P. Brouček, 'Leslie, Walter, Graf von', *Neue deutsche Biographie*, ed. Otto, Graf zu Stolberg-Wernigerode (Berlin, 1953–) • PRO, state papers: Germany, SP 81, vol. 51, fol. 203 • M. Toegel and others, eds., *Der schwedische Krieg und Wallensteins Ende: Quellen zur Geschichte der Kriegsereignisse der Jahre 1630–1635* (Prague, 1977), 450 • B. Badura and others, eds., *Der grosse Kampf um die Vormacht in Europa: die Rolle Schwedens und Frankreichs* (Prague, 1978), 227, 434 • E. Schmidhofer, 'Das irische, schottische und englische Element im kaiserlichen Heer', PhD diss., University of Vienna, 1971 • P. Taverner, *Caesaria legatio quam … comes de Leslie* (1672) • W. Crowne, *A true relation … emperor of Germanie* (1637) • R. B. Mowat, 'The mission of Sir Thomas Roe to Vienna, 1641–42', *EngHR*, 25 (1910), 264–75 • *Report on the manuscripts of the earl of Denbigh, part V*, HMC, 68 (1911), vi, 21, 56 [1634–39] • A. Svoboda, *Prague* (1968), 181

Archives Státní Oblastni Archiv, Zámrsk, Czech Republic, family archive • U. Aberdeen, family papers | Österreichisches Staatsarchiv, Vienna, Kriegsarchiv, 'Hofkriegsrat-Protokolle, 1626–67' / 'Feldakten' • BL, Arundell MSS and others • PRO, state papers: Germany, 1636–67 • Steiermarkisches Landesarchiv, Graz, Austria, 'Handschriften'

Likenesses L. Kilian, line engraving, 1637, BM, NPG • L. Venetiis, oils, 1664?–1666, Pokrajinski Muzej, Ptuj • oils, *c.*1666, Royal Collection • J. Hofreuther, oils, 1736, Cheb Museum Collection • portrait, repro. in Taverner, *Caesaria legatio*

Wealth at death wealthy: will, Leslie, *Historical records*, 531–4

Leslie, William (*d.* 1654), university principal, was the only son of Alexander Leslie (*d.* after 1603), minister of Rothes, Fife, and his second wife, Jane Harvie (*d.* 1639). He had three half-brothers and three half-sisters from his father's first marriage. He was educated at King's College, Aberdeen, becoming grammarian or humanist there in 1603. He then progressed to regent in 1617 and sub-principal in 1623. He received his doctorate after 1627, and on 5 November 1632 he was admitted principal. He was thus a key player in the struggle between the supporters of the old and new foundations of the college, eventually emerging as a leader of the new foundation faction following the death in 1635 of Patrick Forbes, bishop of Aberdeen. His position on the rival foundations under the chancellorship of Bishop Forbes is unclear, and he had been promoted under Forbes and contributed two Latin elegies to the volume commemorating his death. It was because of his championship of the new foundation that the royal visitation procured by supporters of the old foundation in April 1638 found him 'to have been defective and guilty in his office', although also of 'good literature, life and conversation' (*Fasti Aberdonenses*, ed. C. Innes, Spalding Club, 26, 1854, 288).

A more serious threat to Leslie's position came from the supporters of the national covenant promulgated in February 1638. The rigid approach favoured by the covenanters went against the predominant trend of thinking in Aberdeen, which favoured toleration of inessential details of religious practice in order to promote protestant unity against the threat from Catholicism. To the covenanters this smacked of encouraging popery, and a delegation was sent to Aberdeen in July 1638 to persuade the college to submit to the covenant. The response from Aberdeen was a printed set of fourteen *Demands* to be put to covenanting ministers, which Leslie signed, the authors becoming known as the Aberdeen doctors. The tract quickly became known outside Scotland, for on his return to Scotland the king's commissioner, the marquess of Hamilton, thanked the doctors for their role in challenging the legitimacy of the covenant, and forwarded a letter from Charles I, which indicated that the king was 'satisfied' with their efforts. The *Demands* provoked a reply and a veritable pamphlet war ensued. However, neither Leslie nor any of his colleagues felt able to attend the Glasgow general assembly of November 1638, although one member from Aberdeen did sit, as he was sent by Leslie and others to undermine old foundation supporters.

Partly as a result of Leslie's manoeuvring over the new foundation, the Glasgow assembly ordered a visitation of Aberdeen for April 1639. When the marquess of Montrose arrived with an army to back it up, Leslie took ship for Berwick. On 11 April 1639 he was duly deposed as principal for failure to attend the visitation. Leslie returned to Aberdeen in August 1639 and sent a supplication to the general assembly asking to be restored to office and offering to accept the recent reforms of the church. Meanwhile, he kept a low profile, although he again took up residence in the college. His deposition as principal was confirmed by the general assembly which met in Aberdeen in July 1640, although even then he remained living in college.

In 1642 Leslie went to reside with the marquess of Huntly. He then lived with his kinsman Alexander Douglas of Spynie, the son of the bishop of Moray. He died at Spynie of cancer in 1654. He was unmarried. To Sir Thomas Urquhart he was 'one of the most profound and universal scholars of his time' (*Fasti Scot.*, 7.365), although his lack of publication was put down to modesty and what James Gordon called 'his retired monastic way of living, being naturally melancholian' (Stevenson, 118).

James Cooper, *rev.* Stuart Handley

Sources *Fasti Scot.*, new edn, 7.365; 6.348 • D. Stevenson, *King's College, Aberdeen, 1560–1641: from protestant Reformation to covenanting revolution* (1990) • D. Macmillan, *The Aberdeen doctors* (1909) • J. Spalding, *The history of the troubles and memorable transactions in Scotland and England, from 1624 to 1645*, ed. J. Skene, 2 vols., Bannatyne Club, 25 (1828–9) • R. S. Rait, *The universities of Aberdeen: a history* (1895) • D. Littlejohn, ed., *Records of the sheriff court of Aberdeenshire*, 3 vols. (1904–7), 3.484 • P. J. Anderson, ed., *Officers and graduates of University and King's College, Aberdeen, MVD–MDCCCLX*, New Spalding Club, 11 (1893) • J. D. Ogilvie, 'The Aberdeen doctors and the national covenant', *Papers of the Edinburgh Bibliographical Society*, 11 (1912–20), 73–86 • J. Gordon, *History of Scots affairs from 1637–1641*, ed. J. Robertson and G. Grub, 3, Spalding Club, 5 (1841), 231–2 • G. D. Henderson, *The burning bush: studies in Scottish church history* (1957), 75–93

Leslie, William (1621/2–1707), Roman Catholic priest and missioner, was born between October 1621 and April 1622, the son of Alexander Leslie of Conrack, Moray, and his wife, Agnes Gordon of Cormellat. He entered the Scots College, Douai, in September 1636. In October 1640 he went to the Scots College, Rome, was ordained priest on 15 June 1647 after seven years' study, and in September 1647 proceeded to Paris to prepare for mission work in Scotland. In the winter of 1649 to 1650, however, six Scottish secular priests meeting in Paris, having decided to petition Rome to give them a superior and financial support, agreed that Will Leslie should remain in Rome as their agent.

Leslie's single-minded and lifelong aim was to establish a body of secular priests, with one of them as bishop, controlling the Roman Catholic church in Scotland. Most mission work in Scotland was being done by Jesuits; the rectors of all Scots colleges except that in Paris were Jesuits, and students of the Scots College, Rome, became Jesuits rather than secular priests. Although the Roman Congregatio de Propaganda Fide existed to oversee all missionary work, Jesuits were not responsible to it but directly to the pope. Leslie worked tirelessly to increase *propaganda*'s influence and in autumn 1661 was appointed its archivist.

Leslie's influence was increasingly powerful, not only with *propaganda* but also with other church dignitaries and even with popes—of whom he served under eight—and after 1688 with the Jacobite court in exile. Everything affecting the Scottish mission became his concern. He kept a close watch on the Scots College in Rome, sending complaints, memos, and petitions about its rectors and their administration, particularly to *propaganda*, and was in constant touch with the Paris college, which acted as a staging post and sent students to Rome. Though he declined to assist the missionary plans of the Scottish Benedictines in Germany, he welcomed their assistance to the mission superior in Scotland.

Leslie's life's work was successful. In 1694 Rome appointed a vicar apostolic, Thomas Nicolson, to whom the Jesuit missioners submitted in 1701. When Leslie died on 23 April 1707, having been enfeebled from the 1690s by kidney stones, the Scottish clergy comprised two bishops, Nicolson and a coadjutor, and a majority of secular priests. Leslie's countless lengthy letters (which gained him the sobriquet the Homilist) were long-winded, moralizing, but also outspoken. His consistent opposition, and indeed antipathy, to the Jesuits is plain to see, though his alleged plotting to have their missionary practices in China condemned is at least not proven.

Mark Dilworth

Sources W. J. Anderson, ed., 'Abbé Paul MacPherson's history of the Scots College, Rome', *Innes Review*, 12 (1961), 3–172 • J. F. S. Gordon, ed., *The Catholic church in Scotland* (1874) • B. M. Halloran, *The Scots College, Paris, 1603–1792* (1997) • M. Dilworth, *The Scots in Franconia* (1974) • M. V. Hay, *Failure in the Far East: why and how the breach between the western world and China first began* (1956) • P. J. Anderson, ed., *Records of the Scots colleges at Douai, Rome, Madrid, Valladolid and Ratisbon*, New Spalding Club, 30 (1906) • Colonel Leslie [C. J. Leslie], *Historical records of the family of Leslie, from 1067 to 1868–9*, 3 (1869), 372–3

Archives BL, Blairs letters, letters to Scots College, Paris

Leslie, William (1657–1727), Roman Catholic prince-bishop of Laibach, was the second son of William Leslie, laird of Warthill, and his wife, Anne, daughter of James Elphinstone of Glack; she was reportedly the grand-niece of the famous bishop of Aberdeen, William Elphinstone. He went to King's College in Aberdeen at the age of eleven, with an elder brother, and for a short time thereafter became schoolmaster in the parish of Chapel of Garioch before venturing south to Padua, northern Italy. Here he appears to have quickly become a Roman Catholic, in 1675 transferring to the Scots College at Rome and on 5 April 1681 becoming a member of the priesthood. However, he returned to Padua and to the seminary of Cardinal Barbarigo in the same year, since the Scottish mission was, at that time, unable to afford the maintenance of any more priests. His attempts to return to Scotland in 1683, presumably for missionary work, were thwarted due to problems in obtaining the required money *en route* in France.

In 1684 Leslie was called to Styria to visit his relative Count James Leslie (1635–1694). He appears to have settled into a more sedentary life in Graz, before embarking on a course of studies in philosophy, theology, and church law in Vienna and Rome. From here he proceeded to take up several ecclesiastical positions in Austria and Hungary as well as that of archdeacon in Cilli, where he remained despite being offered a seemingly more attractive post at Trieste in 1710. His correspondence in the 1680s demonstrates a detailed knowledge of military events on the nearby Habsburg–Ottoman frontier in Bosnia and Croatia. A second plan to return to Scotland in 1686, to settle unspecified family affairs on behalf of Count James, was unsuccessful. In 1698 he returned to Padua to take up a post at the university there, as professor of theology. Subsequently, as a member of the privy council of Emperor Joseph I, he also travelled on diplomatic missions to many European courts; the acclaim for these led to his appointment on 6 April 1716 as bishop of Waitzen.

Two years later, on 5 January 1718, following the unexpected death of the prince-bishop F. K. von Kaunitz at the Carniolan see of Laibach, Leslie was nominated as his successor. He appears to have kept a detailed and regular record of his visitations there and apparently arranged regular church assemblies. He also maintained contacts with his Aberdeenshire family, including a letter dated 25 February 1718 to his elder brother, Alexander, at Warthill, in which he expressed his obvious joy at his latest appointment: 'It has pleased his Majesty to transport me out of Hungary, which is a country not much civilised or cultivated as yet for conversation, nor secure from foreign or intestine wars' (Leslie, 3.303–4). He stated his delight at having been given a 'much more honourable preferment' (ibid.) in Laibach, a post which also included the title of prince of the Holy Roman empire.

On 1 July 1725 Leslie sent home, besides a copy of his diploma from Padua, a portrait of himself, the whereabouts of which is now unknown. However, the accompanying letter offered the following advice for future correspondence from Scotland, which he refers to as 'the Land of Cakes': 'You may direct to me in this manner—"To the Bishop of Laybach, Metropolitan of Carniola, betwixt Vienna and Venice, Privy Councillor to his Imperial Majesty"' (Leslie, 3.304). Leslie died in Laibach on 4 April 1727, leaving money to his relatives in Styria, alongside a generous annual pension to be paid to an old colleague in Rome and Padua, Robert Strachan. In addition to this a large sum of his fortune went to the support of both the Scots College and the Scottish mission based in Rome. He was buried in Laibach Cathedral on the banks of the Ljubljanica River. DAVID WORTHINGTON

Sources F. Dolinar, 'Wilhelm, Graf von Leslie', *Die Bischöfe des Heiligen Römischen Reiches: 1648 bis 1803*, ed. E. Gatz (1990), 268–9 • Colonel Leslie [C. J. Leslie], *Historical records of the family of Leslie, from 1067 to 1868–9*, 1, 3 (1869) • W. Leslie, letters to Mr H. Hughes, 1686–8, BL, Add. MS 41842 • J. F. S. Gordon, ed., *The Catholic church in Scotland* (1869), 514–636 • *DNB*

Archives BL, letters to H. Hughes, Add. MS 41842 • Nadškofijski Archiv, Ljubljana, Slovenia

Wealth at death 1000 Roman crowns to the Scottish mission and 1000 florins to the Scots College in Rome; also pension of 50 Roman crowns p.a. to be paid to Mr Robert Strachan: Gordon, ed., *The Catholic church in Scotland*, 576

Leslie, William Aloysius (1641–1704), Jesuit, was born in Aberdeenshire, the fourth of five sons of Alexander Leslie of Balquhain, Count Leslie (*c*.1597–1677), and his wife, Jean Elphinstone, daughter of James Elphinstone of Glask. The only known feature of Leslie's appearance is a hare-lip. He was enrolled in the Scots College, Rome, on 6 January 1657 and, after resigning a canonry of the cathedral church of Wratislaw, entered the Society of Jesus at Rome at the age of twenty-five, being then a doctor of divinity. For some time he taught philosophy at Perugia, and on 30 March 1674 he was appointed superior of the Scots College at Rome, which he governed for nine years. On his petition, in conjunction with his cousin William Leslie, agent at Rome for the Scottish clergy, the festival of St Margaret, which previously had been celebrated in Scotland only, was inserted in the Roman breviary and missal. He also published *Vita di S. Margherita, regina di Scozia, racolta da diversi autori* at Rome in 1675. Despite this co-operation to promote the cult of the Scottish patroness, there were many disputes between agent and rector, the most serious arising from the latter's designs to persuade students to seek dispensation from their mission oath in order to join the Jesuits. The strenuous efforts of the agent put an end to that practice. In 1683 Father William Aloysius Leslie left Rome for the Scottish mission, where he became Jesuit superior. In 1687 a rumour that he might be appointed bishop caused consternation among the secular clergy. By 1690 he was superior of the Jesuit house in Graz, where he managed to procure the freedom of Catholic priests and laymen who had been captured in the British revolution by getting his brother, Count James Leslie, to intercede with Emperor Leopold on their behalf. In Graz he published *Laurus Leslaeana*, a history of the Leslie family. From 1692 until 1695 he was superior of the Scots College in Rome for the second time. During the last nine years of his life Leslie served the mission in Scotland, once again as Jesuit superior. In this capacity, on 7 February 1701, he signed a declaration of Jesuit acceptance of the authority of Bishop Thomas Nicolson who had been appointed vicar apostolic for Scotland in 1694. William Aloysius Leslie died in Scotland, probably in Aberdeenshire, on 26 March 1704. THOMPSON COOPER, *rev.* BRIAN M. HALLORAN

Sources W. A. Leslie, *Laurus Leslaeana* (1692), para. 66 • Colonel Leslie [C. J. Leslie], *Historical records of the family of Leslie, from 1067 to 1868–9*, 3 (1869), 111, 117 • H. Foley, ed., *Records of the English province of the Society of Jesus*, 7 (1882–3), 454 • W. J. Anderson, ed., 'Abbé Paul MacPherson's history of the Scots College, Rome', *Innes Review*, 12 (1961), 3–172, esp. 39–55, 57–89, 167 • M. V. Hay, *Failure in the Far East: why and how the breach between the western world and China first began* (1956), 29, 32, 36, 61–4, 66–7, 70, 83–4., 123 • P. J. Anderson, ed., *Records of the Scots colleges at Douai, Rome, Madrid, Valladolid and Ratisbon*, New Spalding Club, 30 (1906), 42 • G. Oliver, *Collections towards illustrating the biography of the Scotch, English and Irish members, SJ* (1838), 13 • P. F. Anson, *Underground Catholicism in Scotland* (1970), 86 • J. F. S. Gordon, *Ecclesiastical chronicle for Scotland*, 4 vols. (1875), vol. 4, pp. 196–8 • *Catholic Miscellany*, 9 (1828), 38

Archives BL, Blairs letters, corresp. • Scottish Catholic Archives, Edinburgh, corresp.

Lesly [Leslie], **George** (*d.* **1701**), Church of England clergyman, was Scottish by birth: in seeking the patronage of the earl of Westmorland in the preface to one of his works, Lesly described his effort as 'the frozen conception of one born in a cold Climate' (Lesly, *Divine Dialogues*, sig. A2r). He was associated with Aberdeen, and has been accounted as an author associated with the town in the standard bibliographical work on the writers of Aberdeen. He almost certainly attended the university there. The title-page of Lesly's last publication described him as

MA (Lesly, *Israel's Troubles and Triumph*, title-page), and there was a 'Georgius Lesly, Aberdonensis, A. M.' recorded among the alumni of Aberdeen University in the lists for the years 1666–70 (Anderson, 29).

After finishing at university Lesly travelled south into England. He was installed as the rector of Wittering in Northamptonshire on 17 December 1668, where he remained for almost twenty years. Lesly resigned this position to become the minister at Olney in Buckinghamshire on 11 November 1687.

Lesly's first work, *Joseph Reviv'd* (1676), was a paraphrase in verse of the last twelve chapters of the book of Genesis, and *Israel's Troubles and Triumph* (1699) was a similar poetic treatment of Exodus. In *Divine Dialogues* (1678) Lesly undertook a commentary on biblical stories, such as the destruction of Sodom and Gomorrah, and Abraham's sacrifice of Isaac. This work also contained a reprint of *Joseph Reviv'd*, and *Divine Dialogues* itself was reprinted in 1684. In 1678 Lesly published five of his sermons collected under the title *The Universal Medicine*, which also reached a second edition in 1684. Another sermon, delivered in conjunction with a fast ordered by William and Mary in 1689, developed the themes of the need to pray for deliverance in times of trouble and the assurance of God's covenant to answer those prayers. In this sermon Lesly commented on the threats of war by the French, promoted by the papacy, 'to fright and terrifie the Worshippers of the true God, (the Protestants of these Kingdoms) out of their God, their Religion, Lives and Liberties', and he suggested how all feared this intimidation unless they 'be profest papists, or mistaken Loyalists' (Lesly, *A Sermon Preached March 12, 1689*, 1690, 4, 18).

A manuscript note on the British Library copy of *Israel's Troubles* states that Lesly was buried at Olney on 17 March 1701. WARREN JOHNSTON

Sources J. F. Kellas Johnstone and A. W. Robertson, *Bibliographia Aberdonensis*, ed. W. D. Simpson, Third Spalding Club, 2 (1930), 450, 487–8, 526, 586 • P. J. Anderson, ed., *Roll of alumni in arts of the University and King's College of Aberdeen, 1596–1860* (1900), 29 • H. I. Longden, *Northamptonshire and Rutland clergy from 1500*, ed. P. I. King and others, 16 vols. in 6, Northamptonshire RS (1938–52), vol. 8, p. 241 • G. Lesly, *Divine dialogues: viz. Dives's doom, Sodom's flames, Abraham's faith*, 2nd edn, 2 (1684) • G. Lesly, *Israel's troubles and triumph* (1699)

Le Squyer, Scipio (1579–1659), record keeper and antiquary, was the eldest son of Edmund Le Squyer (*d.* 1620) (third son of George Squyer), later rector of King's Nympton, Devon, and his wife, Martha, second daughter of Mark Slader of Bath. He left home for London in 1597, and was a student at an inn of chancery, New Inn, for four years from 1599. In 1603 he became marshal of his fellow Devonian John Doddridge (later Sir John and justice of king's bench). Before 1620 Le Squyer married Frances, third daughter of Sir Hugh Brawne; they had at least two sons and two daughters.

While retaining his marshal's position until Doddridge's death in 1628, in 1620 Le Squyer entered crown service as one of the two deputy chamberlains in the receipt of the exchequer. He apparently continued as a deputy chamberlain until 1655, when, with essentially unchanged duties, he was appointed one of the two chamberlains of the exchequer and keeper of its records. The officers gained some of their fees from those wishing to consult Domesday Book and other records in their custody; it was a matter at their discretion whether to index or calendar the records. Le Squyer was as active in this side of his work as had been his predecessor and friend, Arthur Agarde, and about twenty volumes of his abstracts and calendars survive (JRL). In 1627 he was granted an extra £10 p.a. for his 'extraordinary service and charges in sorting, ordering and digesting' the contents of the Westminster treasuries. In April 1643 he was acting escheator of Devon and Cornwall.

Le Squyer also had a disinterested fascination with the records of the middle ages, especially those of the west country. He was a friend of such antiquaries as Sir Robert Cotton (with whom he swapped medieval manuscripts and from whose collection he copied extracts), Sir Simonds D'Ewes, and Sir William Dugdale, who thanked him as 'a gentleman of great knowledge in Antiquities and a special furtherer of this worke' (*The Antiquities of Warwickshire*, 1730, 913).

A more general indication of Le Squyer's interests is given by the catalogue of his library, which he drew up in 1632 when he had just moved house to Long Acre, Covent Garden. Quite apart from over 200 manuscripts, many heraldic or about Devon and some medieval, he owned nearly 500 printed books, including about 130 each of 'theological' and 'historical' works, over seventy works of 'Poesy' and over forty of 'Morality'. He had made his own translations of one of the 'Psalms and Prayers' of Cardinal John Fisher (although his theological books show a puritan tendency) and of 'The life and death of Edward II', and he had part of the original manuscript of the *Advancement of Learning* by Francis Bacon.

By 1656, Le Squyer had married his second wife, Elizabeth. He died in September 1659 and was buried in Westminster Abbey; in his will he had requested that he should be buried near to Agarde's monument there. Elizabeth Le Squyer survived her husband. NIGEL RAMSAY, *rev.*

Sources F. Taylor, 'An early seventeenth century calendar of records preserved in Westminster Palace treasury', *Bulletin of the John Rylands University Library*, 23 (1939), 228–341 • F. Taylor, 'The books and manuscripts of Scipio le Squyer, deputy chamberlain of the exchequer, 1620–1659', *Bulletin of the John Rylands University Library*, 25 (1941), 137–64 • J. J. Alexander, 'Escheators of Devon & Cornwall (1450–1643)', *Devon and Cornwall Notes and Queries*, 16 (1930–31), 202–8 • J. L. Chester, ed., *The marriage, baptismal, and burial registers of the collegiate church or abbey of St Peter, Westminster*, Harleian Society, 10 (1876), 151 • C. Worthy, *Devonshire wills: a collection of annotated testamentary abstracts* (1896), 106

Archives JRL, books and MSS • S. Antiquaries, Lond., notes from Domesday Book

Lesse, Nicholas (*fl.* 1548–1550), translator, is identified simply as 'Londoner' on the title-page of two of his publications. The eighteenth-century *Bibliotheca Britannico-Hibernica* by Thomas Tanner further identifies Lesse as 'civis et mercator', which seems reasonable, but there is no clear evidence of his admission to the freedom of the city. As a minor participant in the mid-century debates over the place of justification and predestination in English protestant theology, Lesse translated a work by Philip Melancthon, as *The Justification of Man by Faith Only* (1548). He also translated other works, published as: *The Minde and Judgement of Maister F. Lambert of Avenna, of the Wyll of Man* (1548); *The Censure and Judgement of the Famous Clark Erasmus of Roterodam* (1550); *A Worke of the Predestination of Saints Wrytten by the Famous Doctor S. Augustine* (1550); and *The Twelfe Steppes of Abuses* (1550), which was attributed to St Augustine or St Cyprian and printed by the noted protestant publisher John Day. Additionally Tanner attributes to Lesse a translation of a work by Martin Luther, as *Commentaries on Two Epistles of St Peter*, as well as translations of Polydore Vergil's *De inventoribus rerum* and Aepinus's *Psalms*; but if Lesse did produce these works no copy or contemporary reference survives.

Lesse's one original work, *An Apologie of the Worde of God*, was appended to his translation of Melancthon. He dedicated his 1548 works to the king and denounced the errors of the two groups—identified as Jews and papists—that reject God's free gift of Christ's grace. As well as considering justification by faith, his writings also dealt with the ramifications of a Reformed ecclesiology that promoted the doctrine of the visible and invisible church. In the 1550 dedication of his *A Worke of the Predestination of Saints* to Anne, duchess of Somerset, Lesse identified the major target of his efforts as not the Catholic world, but the emerging and vocal tradition of protestants who adopted some measure of human freedom or choice in salvation. Known as 'freewill protestants', their theological position was declared to be a threat to orthodoxy by more Calvinist reformers such as Lesse. According to Lesse, these misguided freewill protestants seemed reformed in appearance, but 'ther mischeif is cloked with a double face of holiness ten tymes more religious to seem to than were the superstitious and arrogant papists' (Lesse, *A Worke of the Predestination of Saints*, sig. A. III). Nothing more is heard from him after 1550. GARY G. GIBBS

Sources Tanner, *Bibl. Brit.-Hib.* · P. Melancthon, *The justification of man by faith only*, trans. N. Lesse (1548) · N. Lesse, *An apologie or defence of the worde of God* (1548) · St Augustine, *A worke of the predestination of saints*, trans. N. Lesse (1550)

Lessingham, Jane [*née* Jane Hemet; *married name* Jane Stott] (**1738/9–1783**), actress, was born in 1738 or 1739 if the age at death inscribed on her tombstone was correct. Nothing is known about her parents, although a brother served as a witness at her marriage in 1753. Very little is known about her personal life before coming to the stage. As Jane Hemet, spinster, she was married to John Stott, naval commander, at St Paul's, Covent Garden, in 1753. In their divorce proceedings in 1765, recorded in *Trials for Adultery* (1780), witnesses attested to the fact that Mrs Stott had given birth to a daughter during the three years her husband was away at sea. John Taylor in his *Records of my Life* (1832) recalled that she lived with the poet Samuel *Derrick (1724–1769) as his wife and that Derrick was responsible for bringing her to the stage. If so, it seems probable that their relationship began in the years when her husband was at sea, as they coincide with her initial appearance on the stage as Desdemona in *Othello* in 1756. She did not appear again until February 1762, when she played the title role in Nicholas Rowe's *Jane Shore*. She evidently took the name Lessingham as her stage alias and used it first in March 1762, when she played Sylvia in *The Recruiting Officer* by George Farquhar. Taylor also noted Lessingham's ability as a comic actress, but further described her as an extraordinary character who frequented coffee houses in men's clothing.

Lessingham remained at Covent Garden until 1763, but subsequently worked at Smock Alley Theatre in Dublin and at Drury Lane in London, as well as at provincial theatres in Bath, Bristol, and Richmond. She returned in 1767 to Covent Garden, where she remained for the duration of her career. There was always some suspicion that she maintained her position at Covent Garden because of her long-standing relationship with the theatre manager Thomas *Harris (*d.* 1820). David Garrick thought her not worth the £4 a week she demanded in 1767 and refused to re-employ her at Drury Lane. As Harris's mistress she was a focal point in the managerial disputes at Covent Garden in 1768; she was named several times in the pamphlets, arguing for her right to a private dressing-room and to particular roles, specifically that of Imogene in *Cymbeline*. The critic Francis Gentleman did not think she was worth all the fuss, and in *The Theatres* (1772) described her as a 'tasteless milksop'. William Hawkins was more complimentary in his *Miscellanies in Prose and Verse* (1775), commenting that she was agreeable in comedy but dismal in tragedy. Such criticism is borne out by the roles she favoured: Clackit in *The Guardian* by Garrick, Madame Florival in *The Deuce is in him* by George Colman the elder, Nerissa in *The Merchant of Venice*, and Lady Anne in *Richard III*. Harris himself was quick to defend her and in *The Ring: an Epistle, Addressed to Mrs. L—M* (1768), amid protestations of her beauty and virtue, argued that she was as strong a performer as Elizabeth Barry and Mary Ann Yates.

Jane Lessingham also won a reputation for her writing: there were rumours that she herself wrote *The Ring*, and she advertised two publications that either never appeared or were published in such small numbers as not to have survived. *Expostulations with George Colman* was advertised as forthcoming in December 1767, and a pamphlet entitled *The Hampstead Contest* was mentioned in a legal dispute over some property in 1775. The *Town and Country Magazine* noted in May 1777 that she 'still amuses herself and the world, with her pen in the public papers'.

Jane Lessingham's last appearance on the stage was in November 1782 as Jacintha in Benjamin Hoadly's *The Suspicious Husband*. Her salary of £7 a week in the last five seasons of her career places her below the premier performers Mary Ann Yates and Frances Abington in prestige and talent, but well above the poorer actresses, who were paid less than £1 a week. She died on 13 March 1783, and was buried four days later in Hampstead churchyard. Her will, written in the December before her death, left her estate to Thomas Harris in trust for the use of her sons Thomas, Charles, and Edwin. A fourth son, William Frederick, was also named, but there was no mention of the daughter she bore while she was married to John Stott. The will was signed 'Jane Hemet' and was proved by Thomas Harris in 1784. The original stone on her grave, bearing her maiden name, was replaced in 1802 by her son William Frederick with a stone inscribed 'Mrs. Jane Lessingham of the Theatre Royal, Covent Garden', and noting her age as being forty-four. K. A. CROUCH

Sources Highfill, Burnim & Langhans, *BDA* • *Trials for adultery, or, The history of divorces: being select trials at Doctors' Commons … from the year 1760*, 7 vols. (1779–80) [rebound in alphabetical order of cases] • [T. Harris], *The ring: an epistle, addressed to Mrs. L—M* (1768) • *Conduct of the four managers of Covent Garden Theatre, freely and impartially examined, both with regard to their present disputes, and their past management* (1768) • J. Taylor, *Records of my life*, 1 (1832), 5–9 • *The letters of David Garrick*, ed. D. M. Little and G. M. Kahrl, 2 (1963), 565, 582 • *Town and Country Magazine*, 9 (1777) • F. Gentleman, *The theatres: a poetical dissection* (1772), 77 • W. Hawkins, *Miscellanies in prose and verse, containing candid and impartial observations on the principal performers belonging to the two Theatres-Royal, from January 1773 to May 1775* (1775) • tombstone, churchyard, Hampstead

Likenesses C. Grignion, engraving, pubd 1775 (as Ophelia in *Hamlet*; after drawing by J. Roberts), repro. in J. Bell, ed., *Bell's edition of Shakespeare's plays* (1775) • Walker, engraving, pubd 1776 (as Mrs Sullen with William T. Lewis as Archer in *The stratagem*; after Barralet), repro. in *The new English theatre*, 12 vols. (1776–7) • Thornthwaite, engraving, pubd 1777 (as Oriana in *The inconstant*; after J. Roberts), repro. in J. Bell, *Bell's British theatre* (1777) • engraving, pubd 1777 (with portrait of Justice Addington), repro. in *Town and Country Magazine* • Terry, engraving, pubd 1779 (as Flora in *She would and she would not*) • J. Zoffany, group portrait, oils (*The Merchant of Venice*, trial scene; as Nerissa with Charles Macklin as Shylock), Tate collection • engraving (as Sylvia in *The recruiting officer*)

Lessore, (Elaine) Thérèse (**1884–1945**). *See under* Sickert, Walter Richard (1860–1942).

Lessore de Saint-Foix [*née* Brook], **Helen** [*known as* Helen Lessore] (**1907–1994**), painter and gallery director, was born on 31 October 1907 in Highbury, London, the elder of two daughters of Abraham Brook (*c*.1876–1944), a furrier, and Edith Berliner (1881–1935), who were both Jewish. She owed her gift for art to her mother (English-born, in a Frankfurt family of Spanish descent). From her father (more recently arrived from Lithuania) she inherited a readiness to uproot herself, but a lack of business sense.

Helen Brook was a quiet, serious girl, determined to become a painter (so she claimed) 'from the age of three' (private information). Winning first prize in a newspaper competition entered while still at Highbury Hill high school took her, in 1924, to the Slade School of Fine Art. Here, Henry Tonks taught 'truth to nature': a rigorous adherence to observed reality; while the art historian Tancred Borenius lectured on the 'great tradition' in European painting, and the underlying principles of old master composition. She continued to win first prizes, but had to wait (as she put it) 'until Rex Whistler' (one year her senior) 'was gone' (private information).

Helen Lessore de Saint-Foix [Helen Lessore] (**1907–1994**), by Michael Ward, 1987 [at her eightieth birthday exhibition, in front of her painting *Symposium II*]

When she left the Slade in 1928, Helen Brook tried illustrating Goethe's *Wilhelm Meister*, but failed to find a publisher. She applied (also without success) to Bertrand Russell for a teaching post at Beacon Hill School; so she mastered shorthand and typing, and, in 1931, became secretary to Frederick Lessore de Saint-Foix (1879–1951) at the Beaux Arts Gallery, Bruton Place, London. On 24 November 1934 they married.

Her husband, twenty-eight years Lessore's senior, was a sculptor (the gallery, originally a coach-house and stable, had been his studio); he belonged to a distinguished family of artists, which included his grandfather Emile Lessore (the Wedgwood ceramics painter), his sister (Elaine) Thérèse *Lessore [*see under* Sickert, Walter Richard], and his brothers-in-law Alfred Powell (of the arts and crafts movement) and Walter *Sickert, who was the gallery's leading exhibitor. Soon Sickert's influence—broader brushstrokes and bolder colours—became apparent on the careful drawing and subdued palette Lessore owed to her Slade training; but painting had to take second place to gallery work, and then to motherhood. Two sons were born, in 1937 and 1939.

Fat years were followed by lean. After the war, separation from her husband led Lessore to a spell teaching at Langford Grove (under its redoubtable head mistress Elizabeth Curtis) followed by a partial reconciliation. For her painting, the modernism of the school of Paris proved an example less easily digested than Sickert's, and she later destroyed many of her experiments of the 1940s.

In November 1951 Frederick Lessore died, and Helen Lessore took over the gallery, by then in decline. Lacking the resources to chase established favourites, she sought out the young and unfashionable. The dictates of necessity corresponded, in this case, with the inclinations of instinct. Her first successes came with four young realists who went on to triumph at the 1956 Venice Biennale: the critic David Sylvester labelled them 'the Kitchen Sink School'; more importantly, he brought her Francis Bacon, who showed with her (in 1953) and remained a friend thereafter. Before the war she had considered Sickert the foremost painter in England (her first published article, in 1932, had been an appreciation of his late work). Now she wrote several pieces about Bacon, whom she admired equally, and felt held a corresponding position in the post-war world.

During these years Lessore nurtured the talents of a dozen young painters who later won recognition, and rescued an equal number of their elders from neglect. Showing these artists brought credit—in 1958 she was appointed OBE—but precious little profit, and in 1965 the gallery was forced to close. In tribute to her Andrew Forge wrote: 'Self-sacrificing, jealous, reckless, she was in some respects an ideal dealer. In others, she was a failure. In the end the gallery went under flags flying' (Forge, 6). For the remainder of the decade she struggled to earn a living as a portrait painter. In 1970–72 a group of friends came to her help, providing a fund for her support.

Twenty years of tranquillity remained. The paintings of Lessore's late maturity capture a harmonious vision of family and friends in idyllic settings based on the house and garden in Camberwell to which she had moved. Here she wrote *A Partial Testament*, published in 1986, a meditation on the artists of her time in whom she felt the 'great tradition' of Western painting had been preserved and extended. To some—Bacon, Frank Auerbach, Leon Kossoff, Michael Andrews, and Craigie Aitchison—she had given exhibitions; of others—Giacometti, Balthus, and Lucian Freud—she had shown only occasional examples.

Many of them reappear portrayed in Lessore's largest and most ambitious painting, *The Symposium* (Tate collection), a composition distantly echoing Leonardo's *Last Supper*, but remoulded to represent a world of the intellect reminiscent of Raphael's *School of Athens*. (Bacon, Freud, Auerbach, Kossoff, and Andrews were indeed, by then, known as the school of London.) In 1984 the Tate dedicated a major exhibition, 'The hard-won image', to Lessore, allotting this work a central role in a survey of contemporary British figurative painting. The Fine Art Society marked her eightieth year (1987) with a retrospective show. Shortly before this, she had become a senior Royal Academician. She had survived long enough to enjoy the legend beginning to form around her. Richard Morphet (Tate keeper of modern British painting), to whom this later recognition was partly due, characterized her in these terms: 'Her appearance was of a grave beauty … her presence had a certain severity that was allied to her stringency of judgement, but these traits went hand in hand with a lively curiosity and notable warmth' (Morphet). Helen Lessore died on 6 May 1994 and was buried in St John's churchyard, Hampstead. HENRY LESSORE

Sources private information (2004) · personal knowledge (2004) · R. Morphet, *The Independent* (9 May 1994) · A. Forge, *Helen Lessore and the Beaux Arts Gallery* (1968) [exhibition catalogue, Marlborough Gallery, London]
Archives FILM BBC programmes | SOUND BBC programmes
Likenesses M. Ward, photograph, 1987, NPG [*see illus.*] · A. Snowdon, photograph, repro. in *The Independent*

Lester, Frederick Parkinson (1795–1858), army officer in the East India Company, third son of John Lester, merchant, of Racquet Court, Fleet Street, and his wife, Elizabeth Parkinson, born on 3 February 1795, was educated at Mr Jephson's academy at Camberwell and at Addiscombe College (1810–11). He qualified for a commission on 22 April 1811. His commissions, all in the Bombay artillery, were: second-lieutenant (25 October 1811), lieutenant (3 September 1815), captain (1 September 1818), major (14 May 1836), lieutenant-colonel (9 August 1840), brevet colonel (15 March 1851), and major-general (28 November 1854). Of his forty-five years of service thirty-seven were in India, chiefly as acting commissary of ordnance, commissary of stores, and secretary to (and afterwards ordinary member of) the military board. A system of double-entry bookkeeping introduced by him was, in 1834, ordered to be generally adopted in the Ordnance department. As an ordinary member of the military board he was 'specially thanked for his zealous and efficient services' by the governor of Bombay in April 1847. Lester was deeply religious, and his leaving a mess breakfast table at which Sir John Keane was present, in protest against the profane conversation, placed him temporarily under an official cloud.

In April 1857 Lester was appointed to command the southern division of the Bombay army, with headquarters at Belgaum, and assumed command there on 12 May 1857. His actions during the months of May to September 1857 were believed by Sir George Le Grand Jacob 'in all probability to have prevented an explosion at Belgaum' (Jacob, 218). He repaired the fort, moved the powder and ammunition inside the fort, deported suspected sepoys, and moved guns, gun carriages, and horses into the fort. In addition he organized night-time patrols (chiefly of civilian volunteers) and moved the depot of HM 64th regiment, with 400 European women and children, into the fort. He vetoed the proposal of the commanding officer of the 29th Bombay native infantry, backed by the political agent, Mr Seton-Karr, to disarm the regiment as potential mutineers on the ground of the inadequacy of any European force for the task, and the possibility of a failure which would end in disaster. On the arrival of British troops (10 August 1857) he supervised the court-martial, execution, and other punishment of rebels. One of these courts-martial consisted entirely of Indian non-commissioned officers, a testament to Lester's wise leadership. The measures were among the precautions which prevented the insurrection spreading to western India, and Lester was hardly given the credit due to him for them.

Lester married first, in 1828, at St Thomas's Church, Bombay, Helen Elizabeth Honner, and they had two children who died in infancy. Second, in 1840, he married at Mahabaleshwar, Charlotte Pratt, daughter of the Revd Charles Fyvie; they had five children. Lester was found dead in his bed of heart disease at 7 a.m. on 3 July 1858, at Belgaum. H. M. CHICHESTER, *rev.* JAMES FALKNER

Sources BL OIOC · *East-India Register and Directory* (1832) · *East-India Register and Directory* (1840) · *East-India Register and Army List* (1856) · P. Cadell, *History of the Bombay army* (1938) · G. L. G. Jacob, *Western India* (1871) · *GM*, 3rd ser., 5 (1858), 243

Lester, Mary. *See* Farr, Florence Beatrice (1860–1917).

Lester, Muriel (1883–1968), peace campaigner and writer, was born on 9 December 1883 at Gainsborough Lodge, Leytonstone, Essex, the third daughter of Henry Edward Lester (1834–1927) and Rachel Mary, *née* Goodwin (1853–1918). Henry Lester was a wealthy businessman; he also served as president of the Essex Baptist Union, as an overseer, a magistrate, and chairman of West Ham school board. It was from her father that Muriel acquired the two main driving forces of her life—her religion and her strong social conscience; from her mother she inherited a love of nature, books, music, travel, and a certain 'style' which Muriel never lost, even in her 'voluntary poverty'.

Educated at a progressive day school, Wanstead College, Lester then attended St Leonard's School in St Andrews. A chance outing to London's East End in 1902 first opened her eyes to the existence of dire poverty. She determined to renounce her own wealth and to work and live with the poor. In 1914, with the help of her sister, Doris, she opened Kingsley Hall, in Bow, to serve local people as a combined community centre and church. They also erected there the first purpose-built children's nursery. Muriel Lester served as a Poplar borough alderman, 1922–5, and opened a second Kingsley Hall, in Dagenham, in 1930.

Encouraged by her reading of Tolstoy, Muriel took a pacifist stance in 1914 and joined the newly formed Christian pacifist organization, the Fellowship of Reconciliation. From tentative beginnings in Hyde Park she grew in stature as a public speaker. She also discovered another advocate of non-violence—Mohandas K. Gandhi—and travelled to India to meet him in 1926: this was to be the first of many such trips and the start of a warm friendship. In 1931, attending the round-table conference in London, Gandhi stayed with her at Kingsley Hall, Bow.

In 1934 Muriel Lester began her work as travelling secretary for the International Fellowship of Reconciliation. Over the next twenty-five years she courageously carried a message of Christian non-violence into the very heart of conflict situations all over the world—in India, the Far East, the USA, Central and South America, Europe, the Soviet Union, Africa, and even communist China. Muriel campaigned against war, and the trade in arms and drugs; she challenged social, racial, and religious prejudice; championed the poor, the starving, conscientious objectors, and prisoners of war; and urged women to fulfil their potential as peacemakers and clergy.

Muriel Lester had a large following in the USA and threatened to become something of a *cause célèbre* there in 1941. She had been on a speaking tour of the country at the outbreak of the war but after a trip to South America found the British authorities blocking her re-entry. She was held in a detention camp in Trinidad, forcibly repatriated, imprisoned briefly in Holloway gaol and had her passport confiscated. It was testimony to her outstanding ability to preach the pacifist cause that the British government could not afford to let her return to the USA just as Roosevelt was attempting to woo Americans into joining the allied war effort.

Muriel Lester was equally at home whether cleaning out latrines in an ashram or taking tea in the White House. She mixed easily with the humble but impressed many influential figures—Clement Attlee, George Lansbury, Lord Lytton, Lord Halifax, Gandhi, Nehru, Kenyatta, Mandela, H. G. Wells, Eleanor Roosevelt, Madame Chiang Kaishek, Sybil Thorndike, and Vera Brittain. With a ready sense of humour, she had a gift for making people feel good. Yet she was not always a 'comfortable' person to know. There was an implicit challenge in her faith and lifestyle, which invariably became explicit when she spoke.

Muriel Lester was an exponent of practical Christianity, but her writings also reveal a deep spirituality. In addition to copious *Travel Letters*, she wrote numerous articles and had over twenty works published, including two autobiographical accounts, *It Occurred to Me* (1939) and *It So Happened* (1947). During a trip to Japan she was once dubbed Mother of World Peace; more formal recognition of her work came in 1964 when Muriel was awarded the freedom of the borough of Poplar. She died on 11 February 1968 at her home, Kingsley Cottage, 47 Baldwin's Hill, Loughton, Essex. A thanksgiving service for her life was held at Kingsley Hall, Bow, on 4 April; her body was donated to science. JILL WALLIS

Sources J. Wallis, *Mother of world peace: the life of Muriel Lester* (1993) · *CGPLA Eng. & Wales* (1968)

Archives Bancroft Road Library, Tower Hamlets, London, local history collection, papers · Fellowship of Reconciliation, Nyack, New York, papers · Kingsley Hall, Dagenham, Essex, corresp., drafts, diaries, notebooks, unpublished articles | Swarthmore College, Swarthmore, Pennsylvania, peace collection | SOUND BL NSA, documentary recordings

Likenesses photograph, Kingsley Hall, Dagenham, Essex, Muriel Lester archives · photographs, Swarthmore College, Swarthmore, Pennsylvania, peace collection · photographs, Tower Hamlets Local History Library and Archives, London · photographs, Fellowship of Reconciliation MSS, Nyack, New York

Wealth at death £958: probate, 6 May 1968, *CGPLA Eng. & Wales*

Lester, Sean [*formerly* John Ernest] (1888–1959), journalist and international civil servant, was born John Ernest Lester on 27 September 1888 at Woodburn, Carrickfergus, Antrim, Ireland, the son of Robert John Lester, the owner of a Belfast grocers, and Henriette Mary Ritchie. He was educated at the Methodist college, Belfast. In 1905 he began a career in journalism with the Unionist paper the *North Down Herald*, but he soon also joined the Irish nationalist cultural association, the Gaelic League. Lester believed that nationalism was not just for Catholics and joined the Irish Republican Brotherhood in 1908 and Sinn Féin in 1909. From the early 1900s he styled himself Sean Lester, Sean being the Irish form of John, in line with his belief in the Irish cultural movement. He was now chief reporter for the Unionist *Dublin Evening Mail* and the *Dublin Daily Express*. He was not involved in the 1916 Easter rising, but his nationalist affiliations led him to change papers and he held the post of news editor of the Dublin-based *Freeman's Journal* from 1916 to 1922. In 1920 he married Elizabeth Ruth Tyrrell, the daughter of Alderman J. Tyrrell of Belfast and the younger sister of Air Vice-Marshall Sir William Tyrrell. They had three daughters, Ann, Dorothy, and Patsy.

Following the establishment of the Irish Free State in 1922, Lester joined the publicity department of the young state's department of external affairs, rising to become director of publicity from 1925 to 1929. In the latter year he was made Ireland's permanent representative of the League of Nations at Geneva. He was given a wide latitude in formulating Irish league policy by Dublin. He played a central role in Ireland's election to the League of Nations council in 1930. Until 1933 he represented Ireland at many council sessions and at numerous international conferences. This active role led Lester to become the chairman of the league committees that were attempting to broker solutions to territorial disputes between Peru and Colombia and between Bolivia and Paraguay. Lester was also closely involved with the league's attempts to bring to a peaceful end the Japanese invasion of the Chinese province of Manchuria.

His work on the council led Lester into the career of an international civil servant. He was seconded to the service of the League of Nations in the autumn of 1933 and took up the office of high commissioner in the league-controlled free city of Danzig in January 1934. He saw his duty as trying to negotiate a compromise between the German and Polish populations of the city and to protect it against the ravages of Nazism. After the Nazis secured control of the city's assembly and began to persecute its non-German inhabitants, Lester protested and faced a harsh campaign of Nazi intimidation. He resigned and returned to Geneva in 1937.

At the League of Nations, now greatly reduced in power, Lester took up the vacant post of deputy secretary-general (the previous occupant having been Jean Monnet). He was involved mainly in administrative tasks until the outbreak of war in September 1939. He then came into conflict with the pro-axis secretary-general of the league, the Frenchman Joseph Avenol. The two men clashed over the future of the league, with Avenol wanting to hand it over to the axis powers, whom he expected to win the war. Lester became acting secretary-general in September 1940, on Avenol's resignation, and held the post until 1946. He and his skeleton staff had the thankless task of keeping the league in operation through to the post-war era. Lester regarded these years as the hardest in his life; the impact of the strain of work and separation from his family, until 1945, was immense. In April 1946 he presided over the final assembly of the league, dissolving it on 31 July 1947. He was retrospectively made secretary-general from 1940 to 1947.

There was no role for Lester in the new United Nations, as he was tainted both by league service and as a citizen of a former neutral state. He retired to the small village of Recess in co. Galway, Ireland, to fish and garden. There were rumours in 1945 that he might be a candidate for the presidency of Éire, but this did not materialize. He was made an honorary LLD of Dublin University in 1947, and received an equivalent honour from the National University of Ireland in 1948. In 1945 he received the Woodrow Wilson Foundation award for his distinguished service in maintaining the league throughout the war. In the same year he took over the post of president of the permanent Norwegian-Swiss conciliation commission. In 1956 he was appointed a member of the Irish national group that nominated candidates to fill vacancies in the membership of the International Court of Justice.

Lester was a courageous international civil servant who strove for the ideals of international co-operation. The failure of the League of Nations and the inward looking nature of much mid-twentieth century Irish historiography meant that it was only in the latter part of the century, with the beginning of detailed research into Irish foreign policy and a renewal of interest in international organizations after the end of the cold war, that Lester re-emerged from virtual historical anonymity. He died at the Calvary Hospital, Galway, on 13 June 1959.

MICHAEL J. KENNEDY

Sources M. Kennedy, *Ireland and the League of Nations, 1919–1946* (1996) · S. Barcroft, 'The international civil servant: the League of Nations career of Sean Lester', PhD diss., TCD, 1972 · NA Ire., Department of Foreign Affairs archives · *The Times* (15 June 1959) · *DNB* · *CGPLA Eng. & Wales* (1960)

Archives NA Ire., Department of Foreign Affairs archives · Palais des Nations, Geneva, Switzerland, League of Nations archives · priv. coll., personal diary | Department of Foreign Affairs, Iveagh House, Stephens Green, Dublin, Ireland, Francis Cremins MSS

Likenesses J. Sleator, oils, League of Nations Library, Geneva

Wealth at death £13,101 13*s*. 9*d*. in England: probate, 11 April 1960, *CGPLA Eng. & Wales*

Lestock, Richard (*b*. in or before **1679**, *d*. **1746**), naval officer, was the second son of Richard Lestock (*d*. 1713), captain in the navy and magistrate for Middlesex. Lestock senior was one of the commanders of merchant ships who were invited by the Admiralty on 26 December 1690 to volunteer for naval service, and was speedily appointed captain of the *Cambridge* on 6 January 1691, taking post from that day. His son Richard may have been born on 22 February 1679 though it is more probable that he was born some years earlier. In April 1701 Lestock was appointed third lieutenant in his father's ship, the *Cambridge*; he subsequently served as lieutenant in the *Solebay*, *Exeter*, and *Barfleur* (flagship of Sir Cloudesley Shovell during the battle of Malaga). In 1705 Shovell promoted him master and commander of the fireship *Vulture*, in which capacity he was active ashore in the relief of Barcelona and capture of Alicante. Lestock took post in the *Fowey* (32 guns) on 29 April 1706. He helped destroy a 64-gun French warship near Almeria (December 1706) before being ordered to join Sir George Byng for the attempt on Toulon (1707). The *Fowey* was present at the capture of Minorca (1708). On 14 April 1709 during her passage from Alicante to Lisbon, however, the *Fowey* fell in with two enemy 40-gun frigates and was captured after a running fight of several hours. Lestock was shortly afterwards exchanged, and on his return to England was tried by court martial for the loss of his ship and fully acquitted on 31 August 1709. From 1710 to 1712 he commanded the *Weymouth* in the West Indies. After she was paid off he went on half pay until 1717 when he commanded the *Panther* (50 guns) in the Baltic. The fleet commander, Byng, put him in charge of a seven-ship squadron to cruise off Göteborg and in the Skagerrak against Swedish privateers, and Lestock acquitted himself well. He was second captain of Byng's flagship, the *Barfleur*, during the battle off Cape Passaro in 1718.

Since Lestock had apparently impressed the most highly placed and influential admiral of the 1720s, it is puzzling that he remained on half pay for almost a decade. Probably at this time he married Sarah, of Chigwell Row in Essex. An infant named Richard Lestock, baptized at Chigwell on 14 July 1723, may have been their son, but presumably died young; there was also a daughter, Elizabeth, who survived her father. In addition James Peers, who was promoted captain of the *Kingston* at Jamaica by Lestock on 26 August 1732, was then spoken of as Lestock's son-in-law; however he may have been his stepson according to the language of the time, and hence the son from a previous marriage of the widow Sarah Peers. Lestock was appointed to command the *Princess Amelia* in 1728. The next year saw him in the *Royal Oak*, which went to the Mediterranean under Sir Charles Wager in 1731. On 21 February 1732 he was moved into the *Kingston*, to go to the West Indies as commander-in-chief at Jamaica. On 6 April he received his instructions and an order to wear a red broad pennant, but contrary winds delayed his departure until 29 April. Just three weeks later, however, Sir Chaloner Ogle was appointed commander-in-chief at Jamaica and on 15 June a letter written by the lords themselves ordered Lestock to strike his flag and return to England. No reason was assigned; but Lestock, writing from Port Royal on 21 November, reporting the arrangements he had made for his passage, added:

> My affair being without precedent I cannot say much, but such a fate as I have met with is far worse than death, many particulars of which I doubt not will be heard from me when I shall be able to present myself to my lords of the admiralty. (PRO, ADM 1)

Why he was suddenly superseded in this way remains a mystery, but it may be connected with his being passed over for flag-rank in 1733 and 1734, when five captains of lesser seniority were promoted.

Nevertheless Lestock continued in active service throughout the decade. On 22 February 1734 he was appointed captain of the *Somerset*, which was stationed as guardship in the Medway, and he continued in her until April 1738, when he was shifted to the *Grafton* at the Nore. As senior officer he was zealous and occasionally overly zealous in arresting vessels that had no right to wear an official pendant. In August 1739 he became captain of the *Boyne*, one of the ships which in the following year went to the West Indies with Sir Chaloner Ogle.

Soon after Lestock's arrival in the West Indies Vice-Admiral Edward Vernon authorized him to fly a broad pennant as commodore and third in command of the fleet. Lestock was regularly summoned to Vernon's naval councils of war; in the operations against Cartagena he actually commanded in the attack on Fort San Luis on 23 March 1741, when the *Boyne* was severely damaged. That summer Lestock, in the *Princess Carolina*, with many other large ships which were ordered home, convoyed the trade to England. Shortly after his arrival he was appointed to the *Neptune* to command a large reinforcement going to the Mediterranean.

Lestock's sailing was, however, delayed for several weeks, and he did not join Vice-Admiral Nicholas Haddock until the end of January 1742, and then with the ships so shattered by bad weather, and the crews so disabled by sickness, many having died, that the long-expected reinforcement was of no immediate use. On 13 March 1742 Lestock was promoted rear-admiral. When, a couple of months later, Haddock was compelled by ill health to return to England, Lestock became acting commander-in-chief in the Mediterranean. He both hoped and expected to be appointed to the command from England, and to have his original seniority restored. The news that Vice-Admiral Thomas *Mathews was on his way out to supersede him was a bitter disappointment. Mathews, in accepting the command, had stipulated that Lestock should be recalled and Lestock soon asked to be appointed to the West Indies command. The two men had had ample experience of each other when Mathews was commissioner at Chatham and Lestock was in charge of the local guardships. Upon arrival Mathews openly criticized Lestock's performance, and countermanded his appointments. For eighteen months, however, the two were seldom together. Mathews, much occupied by his diplomatic duties, looked to Lestock for help in administering the fleet, and from time to time wrote home complaining of the burden which Lestock's bad health threw on him. The government at home had sufficient reason to replace and re-assign Lestock, who was, on 29 November 1743, promoted vice-admiral of the white, but he remained second-in-command to Mathews.

Lestock's name will always be connected with the battle of Toulon (11 February 1744). By adhering to a restrictive interpretation of the fighting instructions and declining to take any initiatives he contributed to a monumental naval failure. The trouble began on the evening of 10 February when he halted his rear division before it attained its proper position in line abreast. During the night a local current caused it to drift even farther away so that by daybreak at least 5 miles separated it from the rest of the fleet. Lestock promptly made sail, but could not close the gap and missed the battle. Mathews had signalled repeatedly all morning for him to make more sail, twice sending a lieutenant in a boat. Lestock said he was doing all he could (this became a disputed point) and observed that some of his ships were foul and slow. Yet not all were slow, and he did not order the faster ones forward independently, nor when Mathews hoisted the signal to engage did he seize an opportunity to engage a group of four lagging Spanish ships. Lestock was a man who readily nursed resentments, and the possibility that a soured spirit explains his backwardness cannot be dismissed. His argument, however, was that, as the signal for the line was still flying, he was bound primarily to keep the line, and to engage only when he could do so in the line. Regarding the preceding night, he claimed that he was required by the rules to 'bring to' the moment the flagship gave the signal regardless of the signal for a line abreast (a dubious interpretation). Dissatisfied with these explanations, Mathews suspended him and sent him home, but did not charge him.

Lestock immediately threw blame on various captains not in his division and especially on Mathews, whom he charged publicly. Nevertheless, opinion high and low ran strongly against him, nor did he fare well in the pamphlet war that ensued. But during a parliamentary enquiry which Lestock's political friends managed to obtain, Mathews was vanquished. This investigation into the battle by the House of Commons occupied many days in March–April 1745 and was capped with anti-Mathews speeches by Henry Fox and George Grenville. Lestock had been his own best witness. The MPs were impressed by his coolness, overt exactitude, and lofty comments on the importance of discipline (i.e., fighting in good order). Mathews's conduct of the battle was viewed as the antithesis, an image that matched the admiral's heated and disorganized efforts at explanation (he sat as an MP during the proceedings). A pro-Mathews pamphleteer ridiculed Lestock's pedantic insistence on rules by referring to him as 'Mr. Discipline' (*Ad—l M—ws's Conduct*, 20–23), but Lestock won the debate within parliament.

Meanwhile factional politics were moving in Lestock's favour, and the authorities regarded Mathews's popularity 'out of doors' with grave suspicion. The Admiralty board contrived to avoid having a court martial composed of officers favouring Mathews and eagerly anticipated Lestock's acquittal. In early May 1746 Henry Bilson Legge informed his chief, the first lord, that Lestock's defence would be, he believed, 'very short, as the whole seems entirely unnecessary' (*Correspondence of John, Fourth Duke of Bedford*, 1.90). There is every sign that the exoneration of Lestock was arranged. The court, in fact, carried it to an extreme, for in every way conceivable the members found no possible fault in Lestock's conduct. Subsequently, the same court cashiered Mathews.

The public was not convinced. As a naval historian writing in 1758 observed, the 'nation could not be persuaded that the vice-admiral ought to be exculpated for not fighting' and the admiral cashiered for fighting (*The Naval History of Great Britain*, 4 vols., 1758, 4.270). The Admiralty chose not to release the evidence of either of these courts martial, and uncertainty about pivotal facts and circumstances persisted for a long time. Thus Robert Beatson was able to conclude that Lestock 'shewed a zeal and attention which gives a very advantageous idea of his capacity as a seaman and an officer' (Beatson, 1.220), while the verdict in John Campbell's *Lives of the British Admirals* was that he 'ought to have been shot'. No one has analysed the battle more closely than Admiral Sir Herbert Richmond, who was struck by 'the extraordinary partiality' shown to Lestock in his trial. Scrutinizing the evidence, he also found that a crucial portion of the master's log of Lestock's flagship had been obliterated and that other logs of rear-division ships had been altered (Richmond, 2.268–71).

There are clues that Lestock had a scientific bent and that he gave serious thought to fighting instructions and signals (Vernon was a mentor in this). Yet his conduct on the day of battle, his arguments in defence of that conduct, and the court martial's acceptance of those arguments had a dreadful result: official endorsement was given to an idealized, rigid interpretation of the line-of-battle signal that was ill-suited to the Royal Navy's circumstances and purposes in eighteenth-century sea warfare.

Two days after his acquittal (3 June 1746) Lestock was promoted admiral of the blue and notwithstanding his fragile health given command of a large squadron. The original orders called for an attack on Quebec, but circumstances made that impossible and a descent upon the French coast was substituted. Lestock and the military commander, General James St Clair, chose Lorient, but protested that they could not plan properly. Nevertheless, the force was landed efficiently and, despite mistakes by the engineers, nearly succeeded in taking the city. The public saw nothing but failure, but from beginning to end Lestock performed his part helpfully and expertly.

Lestock hoped to be appointed naval commander of a spring expedition to North America when suddenly his health gave way and he died of a stomach ailment on 13 December 1746, possibly in London or Portsmouth. His wife had predeceased him on 12 September 1744. In her will no child is mentioned except Elizabeth, who proved the will on 9 January 1747. This daughter married James Peacock, a purser in the navy. Lestock seems to have been on bad terms with his family. In his will, dated 17 July 1746, he left all his property to William Monke of London, an apothecary, with the exception of £200 to 'my honoured friend Henry Fox, now secretary-at-war', to buy a memento. Daniel A. Baugh

Sources H. W. Richmond, *The navy in the war of 1739–48*, 3 vols. (1920) • B. Tunstall, *Naval warfare in the age of sail: the evolution of fighting tactics, 1650–1815*, ed. N. Tracy (1990) • Cobbett, *Parl. hist.*, 13.1250–83 • P. A. Luff, 'Mathews v. Lestock: parliament, politics and the navy in mid-eighteenth-century England', *Parliamentary History*, 10 (1991), 45–62 • [R. Lestock], *A narrative of the proceedings of his majesty's fleet in the Mediterranean, by a sea-officer* (1744) • *Vice-Adm—l L—st—k's account of the late engagement near Toulon, … as presented by him the 12th of March 1744–5* (1745) • *Vice-Adml Lestock's recapitulation, As spoke by him at the bar of the Honble House of Commons, on Tuesday, the 9th of April, 1745* (1745) • *Ad—l M---ws's conduct in the late engagement vindicated* (1745) • *GM*, 1st ser., 16 (1746), 189 • R. Beatson, *Naval and military memoirs of Great Britain*, 2nd edn, 6 vols. (1804) • *The Byng papers: selected from the letters and papers of Admiral Sir George Byng, first Viscount Torrington, and of his son, Admiral the Hon. John Byng*, ed. B. Tunstall, 3 vols., Navy RS, 67–8, 70 (1930–32) • J. H. Owen, *War at sea under Queen Anne, 1702–1708* (1938) • T. Lediard, *The naval history of England*, 2 vols. (1735) • R. Harding, *Amphibious warfare in the eighteenth century: the British expedition to the West Indies, 1740–1742*, Royal Historical Society Studies in History, 62 (1991) • *Correspondence of John, fourth duke of Bedford*, ed. J. Russell, 3 vols. (1842–6) • J. Campbell, *Lives of the British admirals*, 8 vols. (1812) • *N&Q*, 6th ser., 6 (1882), 287 • PRO, ADM 1 • D. Lysons, *The environs of London*, 4 (1796), 126 • private information (2004) [Richard Harding]

Archives BL, papers relating to his conduct off Toulon, Add. MS 29512 • PRO, ADM 1; ADM 3

Likenesses J. Wollaston, oils, *c.*1740, NMM; repro. in Tunstall, *Naval warfare in the age of sail*, 83 • J. Faber junior, mezzotint, 1746 (after J. Wollaston), BM, NPG

Lestor, Joan, Baroness Lestor of Eccles (1927–1998), politician, was born on 13 November 1927 in Vancouver, British Columbia, Canada, the daughter of Charles Lestor, journalist, actor, and political activist, and his wife, Esther, a textile worker who had been a shop steward in the Garment Workers' Union in east London. At the time of her birth her father was working for the union bulletin of the International Workers of the World (the 'Wobblies'). The family moved to the UK when she was five, and her father became a leading member of the Socialist Party of Great Britain.

Lestor attended Blaenafon Secondary School, Monmouthshire, and William Morris Secondary School, Walthamstow, before training as a teacher at Goldsmiths' College, London (where she was awarded a diploma in sociology). Her experience in the education system of meeting people with different views made her challenge the Marxism of her family, and at twenty-four she found an ideological home in the Labour Party. She became a primary school teacher in Walthamstow, and on 5 January 1952 married John McGregor (*b.* 1927/8), book salesman, son of John McGregor, railway driver. There were no children of the marriage, which was dissolved shortly afterwards.

In 1958 Lestor began ten years of service on Wandsworth council, where she began her life work of developing pre-school facilities for children, in the provision of which Britain lagged behind other developed countries. In 1962 she was elected to the London county council and the executive committee of the London Labour Party. Meanwhile she had left primary school teaching in order to run her own day nursery school in south London. In 1964 she fought her first parliamentary election, for West Lewisham, almost taking the constituency from the Conservatives. In the following year she was adopted as Labour candidate for Eton and Slough, which she won in 1966, holding the seat until Labour's disastrous election defeat of 1983.

As a frequent speaker at the party conference and a representative of the young, progressive side of the party, Lestor was a natural choice for office, and in October 1969 Harold Wilson appointed her under-secretary at the Department of Education and Science, where she remained until the government's defeat in June 1970. After Labour's return in February 1974 she was made under-secretary at the Foreign Office, with responsibility for Africa, a position that she held for fifteen months with praise from career diplomats for her 'enthusiasm, interest and easy informality' on foreign visits (*Castle Diaries*, 403), but in June 1975 she was removed from the post; the decision shocked her senior colleague Barbara Castle, who thought that she had been 'a breath of fresh air in that airless institution' (ibid., 416). It was widely suspected (including by Lestor herself) that foreign secretary James Callaghan had lobbied for her removal because she did not fit in with his conservative view of world affairs, a claim that he denied. She was moved back to education, a post from which she resigned in February 1976 over cuts in the education budget, remarking in her resignation letter that 'investment in education is as important as investment in industry' (*The Guardian*).

Joan Lestor, Baroness Lestor of Eccles (1927–1998), by Godfrey Argent, 1970

Her dramatic presence and authentic left-wing conscience made Lestor a 'darling of the party' and a national executive committee (NEC) member from 1967 to 1982 (chairman, 1977–8). Like others of similar views her fortunes were linked with those of the crown prince of the left, Tony Benn. She was part of Benn's 'alternative cabinet' of advisers until the end of the 1970s, but abstained in the deputy leadership contest of 1981, which was the litmus test of commitment for party activists. The result was the loss of her NEC seat; she regained it in 1987, serving on the committee thereafter for another ten years. In Slough her concern for racial equality helped to establish a firm Labour base among Asian voters. She was a vice-president of the anti-apartheid movement, at one time an editor of the anti-fascist magazine *Searchlight*, and consistently campaigned against racism.

In her four years out of parliament from 1983 Lestor worked for the World Development Movement, and was able to carry forward her campaign for the rights of children when she was sponsored by several trade unions to set up a unit to look at child abuse, including sexual abuse, a subject that was not receiving the official attention that it merited. She was also ahead of her time in her focus on teenage pregnancy and poor nutritional standards in young children. She returned to the House of Commons in 1987, as MP for Eccles, and was a shadow spokesman on such issues as children, young offenders, the family, and overseas aid. She retired from the shadow cabinet in 1996 because of ill health. Her last contribution, in 1997, was in a debate on child poverty. She left the Commons at the 1997 general election and was ennobled as Baroness Lestor of Eccles later in that year.

Lestor's red hair and strapping physique meant that her physical presence as much as her forthright views impressed themselves upon her listeners. Following the dissolution of her marriage to John McGregor she did not marry again, but adopted two children, David in 1967 and Susan in 1969, thus pioneering the adoption of children by single women. She cited 'playing with children' when asked to name a hobby (*WWW*). She died at the Trinity Hospice, Clapham, London, on 27 March 1998, of motor neurone disease. She was survived by her two adopted children. JAD ADAMS

Sources *The House Magazine* (10 May 1993) • *The Guardian* (28 March 1998) • *The Times* (30 March 1998) • *The Independent* (30 March 1998) • *The Castle diaries, 1974–1976* (1980) • T. Benn, *Against the tide: diaries, 1973–1976* (1989) • J. Adams, *Tony Benn: a biography* (1992) • *WWW* • m. cert. • d. cert.

Archives U. Lond., Institute of Education, corresp. with World Education Fellowship

Likenesses G. Argent, photograph, 1970, NPG [*see illus.*] • photograph, 1980, Hult. Arch. • photograph, *c.*1980–1989, repro. in *The Independent* (28 March 1998) • photograph, 1991, repro. in *Daily Telegraph* (28 March 1998) • G. Herringshaw, photograph, repro. in *The Guardian* • photograph, repro. in *The Times* (28 March 1998)

Wealth at death £301,772—gross; £296,660—net: probate, 10 Dec 1998, *CGPLA Eng. & Wales*

Le Strange, Guy (1854–1933), orientalist, was born on 24 July 1854 at Hunstanton, Norfolk, the youngest of the three sons of Henry L'Estrange Styleman *Le Strange (1815–1862) of Hunstanton Hall, church decorative painter, and his wife, Jamesina Joyce Ellen (*d.* 1892), youngest daughter of John Stewart MP, of Belladrum, Inverness-shire. He was educated at Clifton College and the Royal Agricultural College, Cirencester, and later spent long periods abroad, at first with his mother in Paris. After his marriage in 1887 to Wanda Irene, eldest daughter of William Cornwallis *Cartwright MP, of Aynho Park, Northamptonshire, he lived in Florence. There were no children of this marriage.

While he was in Paris Le Strange's interest in oriental studies was awakened by his contact with Julius Mohl, professor of Persian at the Collège de France, and husband of the society hostess Mary Mohl. Julius Mohl persuaded him in spite of extremely bad sight to learn Persian. At the same time he also studied Arabic. In 1877 he travelled to Persia, where he remained until 1880, the first-fruits of the visit being an edition (with W. H. D. Haggard, 1882) of the *Vazir of Lankuran*, a Persian comedy, enlivened by some witty and racy notes. The title-page, which calls the work 'a text-book of colloquial Persian for the use of travellers', shows Le Strange's preoccupation with the practical side of oriental scholarship; and it was always characteristic of him to be concerned more with subject matter than with philology. It was not until many years later, in 1915, that he again published a Persian text, the *Nuzhat al-Qulub*. In the meantime he worked at the historical geography of the Middle Eastern Muslim lands, and it is in this field that he made his chief contribution to oriental scholarship. He began in 1884, while staying at Haifa with his brother-in-law Laurence Oliphant, with a translation of Muqaddasi's *Description of Syria, Including Palestine* (1886), which was followed by *Palestine under the Moslems* (1890), *Baghdad under the Abbasid Caliphate* (1900), and *The Lands of the Eastern Caliphate* (1905). In 1890 he published a three-volume edition and translation of *The Correspondence of Princess Lieven and Earl Grey*.

After his wife's death in 1907 Le Strange settled in Cambridge, becoming a member of Pembroke College, of which his friend E. G. Browne was a fellow. With Browne and others he became active in the affairs of the memorial fund to E. J. W. Gibb, the publications of which include several works edited or translated by him—a remarkable achievement for a man with such poor sight. In 1912 he became almost totally blind, yet refused to be overcome by his difficulties. Not only did he continue his oriental work but he took up the study of Spanish, and translated several books from Spanish. He died at the Evelyn Nursing Home, Trumpington Road, Cambridge, on 24 December 1933. R. LEVY, *rev.* PARVIN LOLOI

Sources *The Times* (27 Dec 1933) • R. A. Nicholson, 'Guy Le Strange', *Journal of the Royal Asiatic Society of Great Britain and Ireland* (1934), 430–32 • personal knowledge (1949) • *Cox's county who's who series: Norfolk, Suffolk, and Cambridgeshire* (1912) • *CGPLA Eng. & Wales* (1934)

Archives FM Cam., corresp. with C. M. Doughty

Wealth at death £13,024 15*s.* 1*d.*: probate, 9 Feb 1934, *CGPLA Eng. & Wales*

L'Estrange, Sir Hamon (1583–1654), politician, was the third but eldest surviving son of Sir Nicholas L'Estrange (*d.* 1592) and his wife, Mary, daughter of Robert Bell of Beaupré Hall, Outwell, Norfolk. Of ancient Norfolk lineage, the L'Estrange family of Hunstanton can be traced back to the eleventh century. The family fortune was made by L'Estrange's great-great-grandfather, Thomas, who was an esquire of the body to Henry VIII and accompanied him to the Field of Cloth of Gold in 1520. L'Estrange inherited Hunstanton as a minor in 1592, and in 1601 was at Queens' College, Cambridge. His guardian, Sir John Peyton, arranged his marriage the next year, on 8 June, to Alice Stubbe (*d.* 1656), the daughter of Richard Stubbe (Peyton's lawyer) and his wife, Anne, the widow of L'Estrange's great-uncle, Sir John L'Estrange. Peyton received £1000 from Stubbe for his part in the transaction. L'Estrange was still of nonage so, while he was released from his wardship, it was necessary for his estates to be held in trust—a role undertaken by two leading members of the Norfolk gentry, Sir Henry Hobart and Thomas Oxburgh.

As a senior gentry figure in the county L'Estrange played a prominent role in its affairs throughout his life. He was pricked as sheriff in 1608 and through the patronage of Hobart he was appointed a deputy lieutenant in 1625. He also served twice as knight of the shire for Norfolk (1614 and 1621) and in 1625 he exploited his local prominence to gain a seat at Castle Rising. His role in the 1614 election bears close scrutiny as not only did he ally himself with Sir Henry Bedingfield, a prominent Catholic, but he and Bedingfield in collaboration with his cousin, Sir James Calthorpe, the sheriff, adjourned the election at the last moment from Norwich to Swaffham. This effectively foiled the plans of Sir Henry Rich to gain a seat. Rich waited in Norwich with a group of freeholders and the backing of Thomas, earl of Suffolk, but could not reach Swaffham in time to influence the election.

L'Estrange played little role in the 1614 parliament, waiting until the last day to make his maiden speech in the house when he called for the Commons to vote on whether to send a reply to James's letter dissolving the parliament. He travelled to the 1621 parliament in the company of his wife and they took rooms with a Mr Haywood in Westminster at £1 10*s*. per week. Through L'Estrange's meticulous accounts it is clear that this was the only time that Alice L'Estrange visited London and while her husband attended the house she bought a variety of goods for the family and Hunstanton Hall. During the parliament L'Estrange called stridently for the punishment of Sir Giles Mompesson, the notorious monopolist: 'Mompesson said he was justice *par excellentium*. I may say *per pestilentiam*, for he hath plagued the country' (Notestein, Relf, and Simpson, 2.168) and he later moved that he be expelled from the Commons. He also introduced a bill concerning salt marshes, which, if enacted, would have granted title to landowners to hold and use land down to the low water mark. The bill proceeded no further than the first reading stage, probably because it overturned the well-established common-law maxim that the dividing line between county and admiralty jurisdiction was the edge of the water. In 1625 L'Estrange attended the London sitting of parliament but along with many of his fellow MPs he absented himself from the Oxford sitting.

L'Estrange continued to play a prominent role in Norfolk affairs during the 1630s. A cultured and articulate man, he avidly purchased books to add to his library and maintained an interest in music and hawking. However, the civil war shattered his peaceful existence and along with his sons, Sir Nicholas *L'Estrange (*bap.* 1604, *d.* 1655), Hamon *L'Estrange (1605–1660), and Roger *L'Estrange (1616–1704), he supported the king. He was disarmed in December 1642 and when King's Lynn declared for Charles I in August 1643 he was named as governor of the town. Besieged by the earl of Manchester, King's Lynn was forced to surrender on 16 September. Despite heavy financial losses L'Estrange managed to escape immediate sequestration of his estates by the terms of surrender, but he could not hide for ever and Hunstanton was eventually sequestered in 1649. Although in his last years he was badly affected by gout, he patronized the foremost English viol composer, John Jenkins, and brought him to reside with the family at Hunstanton Hall. L'Estrange died there on 31 May 1654 and was buried in Hunstanton church where his gravestone reads:

in Heaven at home, o blessed change!
Who while I was on earth, was Strange!
(Blomefield, 10.326)

CHRIS R. KYLE

Sources F. Blomefield and C. Parkin, *An essay towards a topographical history of the county of Norfolk*, [2nd edn], 11 vols. (1805–10), vol. 10 • Norfolk RO, L'Estrange papers • C. Oestman, *Lordship and community: the L'Estrange family and the village of Hunstanton Norfolk* (1994) • R. W. Ketton-Cremer, *Norfolk in the civil war: a portrait of a society in conflict* (1969) • HoP, *Commons* [draft] • W. Notestein, F. H. Relf, and H. Simpson, eds., *Commons debates, 1621*, 7 vols. (1935) • *IGI* • *JHC*, 1 (1547–1628) • M. J. Prichard and D. E. C. Yale, eds., *Hale and Fleetwood on admiralty jurisdiction*, SeldS, 108 (1993) • A. Ashbee, *Harmonious musick of John Jenkins* (1992) • M. A. E. Green, ed., *Calendar of the proceedings of the committee for compounding … 1643–1660*, 4, PRO (1892), 2690–91 • W. A. Shaw, *The knights of England*, 2 vols. (1906) • Venn, *Alum. Cant.* • W. Harvey, *The visitation of Norfolk in the year 1563*, ed. G. H. Dashwood and others, 2 vols. (1878–95)

Archives Norfolk RO, papers

Wealth at death approx. £3000 p.a.: Norfolk RO, L'Estrange MSS, P10

L'Estrange, Hamon (1605–1660), theologian and historian, second son of Sir Hamon *L'Estrange (1583–1654) of Hunstanton, Norfolk, and his wife, Alice, *née* Stubbe or Stubbs (1585–1656), was baptized at Sedgeford, Norfolk, on 9 or 29 August 1605. His family had been seated at Hunstanton on the north Norfolk coast since the twelfth century. He was admitted to Gray's Inn on 12 August 1617 at the age of eleven, but educated at Eton College. He became a fellow-commoner of Christ's College, Cambridge, in 1623, taking lessons in music at a regular monthly expense of 6*s*. 8*d*. He enrolled at Lincoln's Inn on 16 June 1626, but was not called to the bar. His life was passed instead, he says, 'in the vales of rural recess' (*DNB*), presumably in Norfolk, and devoted to theological study. His earliest work was *God's Sabbath*, a work of straightforward sabbatarian polemic, published in 1641, which attempted to prove the divinity and immutability of the sabbath as a religious institution. Dedicated to the Long Parliament, and to his father, supposedly it helped subsequently to inform the sabbatarianism of the Westminster assembly.

On the outbreak of the civil wars L'Estrange threw in his lot with the king. He was sent for as a delinquent for affronting the parliamentary committee for the county of Norfolk. L'Estrange and his brother Roger were involved, with their father, in the attempted delivery of King's Lynn to the royalist forces, and he is also stated to have been at a little later period a colonel in the royal army. He displayed in the event a more yielding disposition than his father or brother. Writing to the earl of Manchester on 31 August 1644, he craved the assistance of the earl, 'having referred himself to a strict soliloquy and reconciled his opinion to the sense of the parliament' (*DNB*).

As the sense of parliament changed, so, evidently, did the fortunes of Hamon L'Estrange. In 1649 his estate was sequestered. He appealed to the barons of the exchequer, and complained of the violation of his rights under the articles for the surrender of Lynn to the earl of Manchester. In March 1651 his fine was set at £105, which he had paid by 17 September following, obtaining discharge for his estate accordingly. However, neither he nor his father appear to have resumed full control of their estate by the time the compounding commissioners ordered that their property remain under sequestration until further order in June 1652.

In 1651 L'Estrange took part in the controversy surrounding the discussions between Charles I and the marquess of Worcester several years earlier on the differences between protestantism and Catholicism. L'Estrange styled himself a 'votary' of the reformed church in the face of those who would categorize as popishly affected both himself and men like him, and took the opportunity to dismiss the claims of the Catholic church to be the sole judge of the meaning of scripture in controversies. In the dedicatory epistle, addressed to Lady Anne L'Estrange of Hunstanton, he proclaimed himself one of those champions of protestantism:

> who dare tell Rome to her teeth, that that thing which she calls her Religion is but meer Policy, not founded upon Christ or his Apostles, but new modell'd in most, and those the weightiest Points, within these last five hundred years.

He also took up the defence of the English liturgy against Smectymnuus, his thoughts on which were annexed to the *Answer to the Marques of Worcester*.

In 1655 L'Estrange published *The Reign of Charles I*, a history of the reign to May 1641. Fuller described it as 'an handsome history likely to prove as acceptable to posterity as it hath done to the present age' (*DNB*). This has been claimed as one of the earliest attempts at impartiality in accounting for the tensions which led to the civil war in England. Certainly L'Estrange himself believed that he was setting the record straight by offering 'a modest vindication of this King in some particulars, not reflecting upon the fatall proceedings against him' (preface). Clearly this was not how Peter Heylyn saw it. His own excoriating *Observations* on the history of the reign of King Charles (1656) criticized L'Estrange's history for its hasty composition, and consequent omissions, misunderstandings, and errors. Heylyn dismissed its style as so lofty that 'no English reader can climb over', as well as its 'pre-ingagements in a party' (dedicatory epistle). This rebuke drew from L'Estrange a defence in an enlarged and revised edition published the same year. Returning fire, Heylyn now described L'Estrange as 'stiffly principled in the Puritan tenets, a semi-presbiterian at the least in the form of church government, a nonconformist in matter of ceremony, and a rigid sabbatarian in point of doctrine' (*DNB*). The charge inspired L'Estrange to write the work which has become his most lasting legacy, one of the earliest historical studies of Anglican liturgy, *The Alliance of Divine Offices*, in which he asserted his affections for the established liturgy and the proscribed Book of Common Prayer. He rejected all the main objections of the liturgy's Catholic and puritan detractors, his lengthy title claiming to show 'the conformity it beareth with the Primitive Practice, and giving a fair prospect into the Usages of the Ancient Church'. L'Estrange concluded that 'our Liturgy in the most, and those the most noble parts (those of sacred extraction excepted) were extant in the usage of the Primitive Church long before the Popish Masse was ever dreamt of' (preface), and that it was wrong to insist that common prayer worship was an illegal doctrine solely of man's devising. These arguments well exemplify the 'low' Anglicanism so objectionable to those neo-Laudians like Heylyn who led the assault on comprehension and a broad-based church settlement at the Restoration.

L'Estrange died on 7 August 1660, and was buried at Pakenham, Suffolk. He was married twice, first, by a licence dated 24 July 1634, to Dorothy Laverick, daughter and heir of Edmund of Upwell, Norfolk, and second to Judith Bagnall of London, who survived him. He had five sons and five daughters. His eldest son, also Hamon, the executor of his estate, married three times and left a large family. He died on 4 May 1717, aged eighty, and was buried at Holm by the Sea. His father's works have been occasionally assigned to him in error. Second and third editions of L'Estrange's *Alliance of Divine Offices* appeared in 1690 and 1699.

W. A. SHAW, *rev.* SEAN KELSEY

Sources *DNB* • M. A. E. Green, ed., *Calendar of the proceedings of the committee for compounding … 1643–1660*, 5 vols., PRO (1889–92) • G. Fisher, 'The Le Stranges of Hunstanton Hall', *East Anglian Magazine*, 6 (1946–7), 666–8 • P. V. Marshall, 'Hamon L'Estrange and the rise of historical liturgiology in seventeenth-century England', ThD diss., General Theological Seminary, 1982 • *Calendar of the Clarendon state papers preserved in the Bodleian Library*, ed. O. Ogle and others, 5 vols. (1869–1970) • Fuller, *Worthies* • F. Blomefield and C. Parkin, *An essay towards a topographical history of the county of Norfolk*, [2nd edn], 11 vols. (1805–10), vol. 10 • Venn, *Alum. Cant.* • J. Foster, *The register of admissions to Gray's Inn, 1521–1889, together with the register of marriages in Gray's Inn chapel, 1695–1754* (privately printed, London, 1889), 7 • *Lincoln's Inn admissions register*, 1 (1896), 200 • will, PRO, PROB 11/301, fols. 313*v*–314*r*

Wealth at death He settled £80 p.a. on his wife for as long as she remained a widow, put down £500 for portions for two of his daughters, and another £700 for a third. He also bequeathed the £1000 of his wife's portion to cover these commitments. He devised a legacy of £100 for his son William at the conclusion of his apprenticeship: PRO, PROB 11/301, fols. 313*v*–314*r*

L'Estrange, Hamon (*bap.* **1674**, *d.* **1767**), legal and religious writer, was baptized at Pakenham, Suffolk, on 9 April 1674, the son of Hamon L'Estrange of Pakenham, and his second wife, Barbara, daughter of Edward Bullock of Faulkbourn, Essex; his grandfather was Hamon *L'Estrange (1605–1660), theologian and historian. He became fellow-commoner of Christ's College, Cambridge, in 1692 and a justice of the peace in 1702. He married Christian Isabella Harvey of Cockfield, Surrey, and they had three daughters. He died at Bury St Edmunds, where he was then living, on 11 August 1767, survived by two of his children; he was buried at Holm.

In 1720 L'Estrange published *The Justices' Law*, which consisted of an abstract of all the acts relating to the powers of justices of the peace. Most of his later publications, however, dealt with theological or moral topics. *Some Important Duties and Doctrines of Religion Prov'd from the Sacred Scriptures*, which also outlined his views on deism, appeared in 1739. A book entitled *Essays on the Being of a God, his Governing and Preserving Providence* (1753) was followed in the same year by another work devoted to the delights of conjugal life. In 1762 he wrote *A Legacy to the World*, which was an attempt to promote practical Christianity; the second edition of this work also contained a pamphlet entitled 'Justification by faith alone' by John Berridge (1767).

J. M. RIGG, *rev.* NORMA LANDAU

Sources G. A. Carthew, *The hundred of Launditch and deanery of Brisley, in the county of Norfolk*, 2 (1877), 447–8 • Venn, *Alum. Cant.* • F. Blomefield and C. Parkin, *An essay towards a topographical history of the county of Norfolk*, 5 vols. (1739–75) • *IGI*

Le Strange, Henry L'Estrange Styleman (1815–1862), decorative painter, was born on 25 January 1815 in Hunstanton, Norfolk, the only son of Henry Styleman of Snettisham and Hunstanton, and his wife, Emilia, daughter of Benjamin Preedy. He was the great-grandson of Armine, daughter of Sir Nicholas L'Estrange, third baronet. (The baronetcy had become extinct in 1760.) He was educated at Eton College, and, after leaving Christ Church, Oxford, with a BA in 1837, he travelled in Portugal, Spain, and Egypt. On 23 July 1839 he assumed the name of Le Strange by royal licence; two days later he married Jamesina Joyce Ellen Stewart (*d.* 1892), daughter of John Stewart of Belladrum, Inverness-shire. Also in 1839 he was declared coheir of the barony of Camoys by the House of Lords, and in 1841 coheir to that of Hastings. In 1847 he made an unsuccessful attempt to enter parliament for West Norfolk.

Le Strange was an art lover, and he painted himself. In 1847 Sir George Gilbert Scott began extensive restorations at Ely Cathedral, which included a new ceiling in the west tower, and Le Strange prepared a design for its decoration in 1853. This was accepted in 1854, and he completed it in 1855. In 1856 he was invited by the dean and chapter to submit a design for the decoration of Scott's wooden ceiling, recently added to the roof of the nave; he began painting the roof in 1858. In 1860 he was invited to work with the architect William Butterfield on the decoration of St Alban the Martyr, Holborn, London, and spent two years making the designs. In February 1862 he was appointed a member of the royal commission which was to examine the state of fresco painting in England.

Le Strange died suddenly of heart disease at 7A Portland Place, London, on 27 July 1862. His wife, three sons, including Guy *Le Strange, and three daughters survived him. He was buried at Hunstanton. He had only completed six of the twelve bays of the roof in Ely Cathedral, and his friend Thomas Gambier Parry completed the remaining bays in 1864 as a memorial to him. His designs for St Alban the Martyr were painted by his cousin, Frederick Preedy. There is a stained-glass window by Preedy in St Mary's, Hunstanton, commemorating Le Strange, who helped in the restoration of the church.

L. H. CUST, *rev.* ANNE PIMLOTT BAKER

Sources J. Burke and J. B. Burke, *A genealogical and heraldic history of the extinct and dormant baronetcies of England, Ireland and Scotland*, 2nd edn (1841); repr. (1844) • Burke, *Gen. GB* (1914) • private information (1892) [H. Le Strange] • *IGI* • Foster, *Alum. Oxon.* • *Cambridgeshire*, Pevsner (1954), 288–9, pl. 7 • P. Moore, *Three restorations of Ely Cathedral* (1973) • *North-west and south Norfolk*, Pevsner (1962), 211–13 • *CGPLA Eng. & Wales* (1862)

Wealth at death under £20,000: probate, 5 Nov 1862, *CGPLA Eng. & Wales*

Lestrange [Le Strange], **John (III)** (*c.*1194–1269), marcher lord, was the son of John (II) Lestrange (*d.* January 1223), grandson of John (I) Lestrange (*d.* before 1178), and great-grandson of Roald ('Rivallonus Extraneus') (*d.* before 1158) who was a tenant in Norfolk of the founder of the Fitzalan dynasty, Alan fitz Flaald, before 1122. Roald's description was from 1166 Anglicized as Lestrange or Lestraunge (the form 'Strange' comes much later); in its first English context it presumably differentiated the family from fitz Flaald and other Bretons, and from Normans also. Anjou has been suggested as their land of origin. The numeration *tertius*, *quartus*, and so on began with John (III).

In Norfolk John (II) acquired Hunstanton through his mother, whose father had held it of Roger (I) Bigod in 1086; in the twelfth century, service to the Angevins and to the Fitzalans brought John (II) and his three brothers scattered but considerable grants in Shropshire, and particularly a block of manors, including Ness and Osbaston (not all of them annexed to England until 1536), near the Fitzalans' *caput* at Oswestry, being 'the most advanced outpost from the Shropshire side in that part of the debatable land' disputed with the Welsh. The Lestranges succeeded Richard de Belmeis and Pain fitz John as part of the twelfth-century answer to problems posed by the proximity of the Welsh of Powys, but in contrast to the families of Belmeis and fitz John the Lestranges lasted for several generations.

John (II) acquired Knockin (pronounced Nuckin) in Osbaston from the sisters and coheirs of his cousin Ralf (*c.*1198). In imitation of grander families the Lestranges developed on that unpromising site a castle, a small church, and a village. (A modern aerial photograph exists; M. Watson and C. Musson, *Shropshire from the Air*, 1993, 71.) A market and fair were later added; it was possibly Guy (*d.* 1179), brother of John (II), who commissioned from the Herefordshire school of sculptors some elaborate carvings in the church at Alveley, near Bridgnorth, which were discovered in the twentieth century in a nearby inn. But the attribution to Guy fails if, as seems possible, the carvings came not from Alveley church but from Romsley chapel two miles away (Mercer, chap. 2).

John (I) Lestrange was appointed sheriff of Shropshire for a second term after the inquest of 1170, and held Shrewsbury and Bridgnorth castles for the king in 1173–4; John (II) showed the same consistent loyalty. He and his son, John (III), were alike sheriffs of both Shropshire and Staffordshire. The latter served in 1214 under King John in Poitou, and between 1233 and 1240 was successively appointed by Henry III constable of the castles of Montgomery, Shrewsbury, Bridgnorth, and Chester. He spent a long life in defending the Welsh border as a marcher lord, and during the rebellion of Simon de Montfort supported the crown. One of his two daughters, Hawise, married Gruffudd ap Gwenwynwyn, prince of Powys Fadog; from them descended the Charltons, lords of Powys. John (III) Lestrange died in 1269.

John (III) and his wife, Lucia, daughter of Robert of Tregoz, had four sons: John (IV), Hamo, Roger, and Robert. Roger Lestrange of Ellesmere, Shropshire, was a knight of the royal household, and a lieutenant of Edward I in the Welsh wars of 1277, 1282–3, 1287, and 1294; in the first two wars Roger at various times held important castles such as Dinas Brân, Builth (a new stronghold), and Montgomery; in the second war it was he who reported to Edward the death of Llywelyn and of the flower of his people and was then the first to move against the Welsh castle of Bere; later he raised troops.

Despite Roger's services, no Lestrange received any territorial reward in Wales itself after the English success of 1282–3; Roger himself received an individual summons to parliament in 1295 and in five generations the family had thus risen from the status of successor of a Domesday mesne tenant to baronial dignity. Roger's title died with him in 1311. Roger's brother Robert was father of Fulk Lestrange of Blackmere (near Whitchurch, Shropshire), who—freed from the demands of Welsh wars—served against the Scots, and was appointed seneschal of Aquitaine in 1322, dying two years later. His barony of Lestrange of Blackmere (1309) passed with an heiress to the Talbot family in 1383 and later fell into abeyance.

John (III)'s eldest son, John (IV), himself a Montfortian, was drowned early in 1276; his son John (V) (*d.* 1309) was in royal service and was summoned to parliament from 1299 onwards as John Lestrange of Knockin; he is deemed to have become Lord Strange. Five generations of his descendants held the title, which an heiress took to the earls of Derby. They held the barony of Strange with the earldom of Derby until the former went into abeyance in 1595; this abeyance was terminated in 1921. Another barony of Strange was created in error (in 1628) for the seventh earl of Derby, and has become merged with the dukedom of Atholl. The fourteenth- and fifteenth-century Lestranges married well, but into English families; however, Owain Glyn Dŵr himself was the great-grandson of John (V) Lestrange.

The family achieved three baronies but no earldom; it was Hamo Lestrange of Ellesmere, the only son of John (III) not so far treated, who in a short life became the only Lestrange to achieve a royal marriage. He joined the Lord Edward at an important moment in 1263, followed the future king on his crusade, and in Cyprus in 1272 married a widowed queen. This was Isabella of Ibelin, Lady of Beirut, widow of Hugh II, king of Cyprus and Jerusalem, and a descendant of those vidames of Chartres who outshone most medieval families in their rise from insignificance to riches and titular eminence. In comparison with the splendours of the palace at Beirut the castle at Knockin must have seemed unutterably provincial; Hamo himself behaved in Outremer with the pragmatism necessary on the Welsh border, committing Beirut to the custody of the Mameluke sultan Baibars whose successor was to terminate the failing western hold on the coast of Syria. Hamo's death was known in England by late April 1273, and there appear to have been no children from the most exotic of the Lestrange marriages. J. F. A. Mason

Sources GEC, *Peerage* · H. Le Strange, *Le Strange Records* (1916) · R. W. Eyton, *Antiquities of Shropshire*, 12 vols. (1854–60), vol. 10 · *VCH Shropshire*, 3.1–32 · R. R. Davies, *Conquest, coexistence, and change: Wales, 1063–1415*, History of Wales, 2 (1987) · E. Mercer, *English architecture: the Shropshire experience* [forthcoming]

L'Estrange, John (1836–1877), antiquary, was born at Norwich on 18 January 1836 and given the surname of his natural father, a plumber and glazier, whose first name was not stated on John's marriage certificate. Nothing is known of his mother unless she is identified by an entry in the 1851 census for Heigham, the Norwich hamlet where L'Estrange and his family passed the whole of their lives. One Francis L. Estrange, shop assistant, aged forty, was living with Harriet Courtnell, a seamstress of thirty-two. No son is admitted, but it is a small step from L. Estrange to L'Estrange. From the age of twenty-one John was employed in the Norwich stamp office, and eventually became the senior clerk under the distributor of stamps. A Roman Catholic, he married Mary (*b.* 1835/6), the eldest daughter of Henry Maris, a saddler of Bacton, Norfolk, and his wife, Mary, an assistant to a milliner, at Norwich on 4 June 1858.

L'Estrange, who had been enthused for and instructed in local history by the Revd F. C. Husenbeth of Costessey, Norfolk, devoted his entire leisure to the subject. He transcribed the court books of the city, the records of the Guild of St George, early churchwardens' accounts, and lists of the freemen of Norwich, King's Lynn, and Yarmouth. From wills in Norwich registry he made extensive extracts to throw light on the building history of the city churches and life in the late medieval parishes. What little he published is still valued by East Anglian historians. When Samuel Tymms died in 1869 the *East Anglian Notes and Queries* he had edited for publication in monthly parts from 1864 ceased abruptly, and L'Estrange produced twenty-four parts of a worthy successor, the *Eastern Counties Collectanea*, in 1872–3. Judging from the rarity of the work, its editor was not able to recruit sufficient subscribers to avoid financial loss. He wrote several articles for Walter Rye's *Norfolk Antiquarian Miscellany* and for *Norfolk Archaeology*, some of which appeared after his death. His finest achievement was his *Church Bells of Norfolk* (1874), for few counties have such a complete and detailed campanology. He drew on churchwardens' accounts for payments made to bell-founders, and recorded pre-Reformation inscriptions including those defaced by iconoclasts in the 1640s, not only in Norfolk but also in Suffolk. His preface shows that, despite his humble situation, he earned the respect and fruitful co-operation of antiquaries and scholars all over England.

The demands of a large family and the expense of his historical pursuits kept L'Estrange poor. Eventually he felt driven to forge the signature of his superior, Francis Gostling Foster, the distributor of stamps, in order to embezzle money and steal stamps worth over £3000. Charged at Norwich police court in July 1877, he was committed for trial at the next county assizes. On 4 August he pleaded guilty to fraud and theft, and it was argued in his defence that he was of unblemished character, universally respected in Norfolk and Suffolk, and completely devastated by the realization of what he had done. Sir James FitzJames Stephen, sentencing him to seven years' penal servitude, stated that an educated man could not be dealt with less severely than an ignorant one. Within three weeks of L'Estrange beginning his sentence at Millbank prison, Walter Rye set about the task of helping Mary L'Estrange, left with six children aged between five and seventeen, and utterly destitute. He solicited subscriptions to a fund for the family, and arranged nearly 10,000 pages of antiquarian notes into nineteen lots, printed a catalogue to show them at their best, and offered the collection to the Norfolk and Norwich Antiquarian Society for £100. The Revd C. R. Manning turned the offer down, so Rye took written bids, accepting the best after alerting under-bidders. He paid handsome sums for fifteen lots himself, promising them to Norwich Library at his own death, but before the fate of the collection was settled L'Estrange died in Millbank on 13 October 1877. Newspaper reports state that he died 'of a fistula', and the death certificate has the even less plausible 'natural acute atrophy of liver from mental emotion and grief', but G. W. Marshall, who knew him well, states with more credibility that he committed suicide. He was buried in Norwich cemetery on 19 October. His widow immediately moved the family from Pear Cottage, Union Street, to open a small grocer's shop in William Street, still in Heigham, and took boarders and a lodger, but three of the children died without reaching adulthood. Rye edited the most important manuscripts he had acquired for posthumous publication, giving their compiler full credit. It took thirty-five years for three of L'Estrange's calendars of freemen to appear in print: Norwich (1317–1603) in 1888 (found to be incomplete), Yarmouth (1429–1800) in 1910, and King's Lynn (1292–1836) in 1913. J. M. Blatchly

Sources W. Rye, *Norfolk families*, 2 vols. in 5 pts (1911–13) · C. Mackie, *Norfolk annals: a chronological record of remarkable events in the nineteenth century*, 2: 1851–1900 (1901), 278 · *DNB* · note by G. W. Marshall in his copy of J. L'Estrange, *Eastern Counties Collectanea* (1872–3) · W. Rye, *An index to Norfolk topography* (1881), xvii–xxii · *Norwich Mercury* (7 July 1877) · *Norwich Mercury* (8 Aug 1877) · *Norwich Mercury* (17 Oct 1877) · census returns, 1851, 1861, 1871, 1881 · m. cert. · Norwich directories · d. cert. · Norwich cemetery records
Archives Norfolk RO, Bolingbroke MSS · Norfolk RO, Bulwer MSS · Norfolk RO, Colman MSS · Norfolk RO, corresp. with Walter Rye, collected notes on Norfolk history

Lestrange, Sir Nicholas (1515–1580). *See under* Lestrange, Sir Thomas (*c.*1490–1545).

L'Estrange, Sir Nicholas, first baronet (*bap.* 1604, *d.* 1655), collector of anecdotes, was baptized on 27 March 1604 at Hunstanton, Norfolk; he was the third but eldest surviving son of Sir Hamon *L'Estrange (1583–1654), MP, and his wife, Alice (*d.* 1656), daughter of Richard Stubbe (*d.* 1619), lawyer and MP of Sedgeford, Norfolk, and his wife, Anne. L'Estrange was privately educated at Hunstanton before attending Trinity College, Cambridge, in 1622, and two years later Lincoln's Inn. In 1629 his father purchased a baronetcy for him, at the cost of £300 plus £100 in charges. On 26 August the following year L'Estrange married Anne (1612–1663), daughter of Sir Edward Lewkenor of Denham, Suffolk. They had eight sons and three daughters.

L'Estrange was an avid observer of seventeenth-century life and he compiled a manuscript volume of anecdotes, 'Merry Passages and Jests' (BL, Harley MS 6395). In total he collected over 600, though many of them were so coarse that when the collection was published in the nineteenth century only 141 were deemed suitable to be printed. Although the author of the volume is unnamed, L'Estrange can be identified as such since many of the anecdotes noted as being from the author's own knowledge are marked S. N. L. (that is, S[ir] N[icholas] L'[Estrange]). He also travelled throughout the county visiting friends and relatives, to whom he attributed many of the anecdotes found in the volume. Both his brothers, Hamon *L'Estrange and Sir Roger *L'Estrange, are given as authorities, his father is named over thirty times and his mother in excess of forty. The remainder of the attributions reveal his connections with other Norfolk gentry, including Sir William Spring, Sir Francis Russell, Clement Spelman, Sir Robert Bell, Sir Drue Drury, Sir John Hobart, and Sir Miles Hobart. The collection reveals that L'Estrange played an active role as a senior member of the Norfolk gentry and was often present at the assizes and parliamentary elections at Norwich as well as taking part in hunts and hawking sessions. Furthermore the anecdotes present an unparalleled view of provincial life at the time and of the interaction between members of the gentry, as well as of the gossip of the taverns and quarter sessions. The slur on the penmanship of Sir Drue Drury and how it could affect the pleading of benefit of clergy provides a good example: 'Sir Drue Drury being an ill scribe, having writt a thing very ill, Sir Robert Bell check't him thus: "Fie, Drue, pr'ythe write so that a man may be saved by the reading on't however"' (Thoms, 1).

During the 1640s L'Estrange shared the royalist views of his father and two brothers though he does not appear to have played an active role in the civil wars. His account of the Norfolk elections to the Long Parliament of the 1640s and the candidacy of the noted puritan Tobias Frere reveal his sympathies:

> Tobias Fryar, a pretended zealote, but true ringleader and head of all factious and schismaticall spiritts in the country, puft up with the pride and strength of his party, would needs be stand to be K[nigh]t (or rather K[nave]) of the shire for Norff[olk] but fell most shamefully short and lost it, with many squibs and disgraces: only, for his comfort, a True Disciple of his sayd, 'However, I am sure Mr Fryar stood for Christ Jesus, for none but reprobates and prophane wretches went against him.' (Thoms, xxvii)

L'Estrange was not removed as a colonel of militia foot in Norfolk until October 1642, after he had declined to attend a meeting of militia commanders in Norwich assembled by the authority of a parliamentary ordinance. He politely claimed that his lack of horses would inhibit him from attending this or any other meeting. Following this, the Norfolk parliamentary commanders ordered that his house should be searched and any arms removed. However, unlike his father and brothers, he avoided the sequestration of his estates. He died on 24 July 1655 at Hunstanton, where he was buried. Chris R. Kyle

Sources W. J. Thoms, ed., *Anecdotes and traditions, illustrative of early English history and literature*, CS, 5 (1839) • R. W. Ketton-Cremer, *Norfolk in the civil war: a portrait of a society in conflict* (1969) • GEC, *Baronetage* • F. Blomefield and C. Parkin, *An essay towards a topographical history of the county of Norfolk*, [2nd edn], 11 vols. (1805–10), vol. 10 • C. Holmes, *The eastern association in the English civil war* (1974) • HoP, *Commons* [draft] • parish register, Hunstanton, 27 March 1604, Norfolk RO [baptism] • *CSP dom.*, *1625–60* • Bodl. Oxf., MS Tanner 69, fols. 200–01 • *The manuscripts of the duke of Leeds*, HMC, 22 (1888)

Archives BL, Harley MS 6395 | BL, letters to J. Perceval, Add. MSS 46955–46956

Likenesses oils, Hunstanton Hall, Norfolk

Lestrange [Strange], **Sir Roger** (*d*. 1311), soldier and administrator, was active and apparently of age by 1265. He benefited from the grant of rebel lands in that and the following year and in 1267 he received his first royal commission, to inquire into the trespasses committed against the king by the men of the rebellious earl of Derby in southern Lancashire. In May 1270 he was appointed sheriff of Yorkshire, an office he continued to hold until October 1274. Although he had interests in many counties, Lestrange was especially active in Cheshire, Shropshire, and Staffordshire, and his prominence in the Welsh marches led to his being much involved in Edward I's conquest of Wales. In 1276 he was sent on a special mission to the marches, and he fought against the Welsh in 1277, when he was empowered to receive the submissions of individual Welshmen, and was given the custody of Oswestry Castle, which he held until 1279. He played a particularly important part in the campaign of 1282, when he commanded a section of Edward's army; his force was credited by a Peterborough chronicler with the defeat and death of Prince Llywelyn near Builth (of which he became bailiff) in November that year. Lestrange wrote to the king to report his success—'Llywelyn ap Gruffudd is dead, his army defeated, and all the flower of his army dead' (Edwards, 84–5). He also led the campaign against the Welsh rebellion of Rhys ap Mareddud in 1287, and was sent to Wales by the king on another special mission in 1294. He served on the continent in 1295 and 1297.

At the parliament at Acton Burnell on 21 October 1283 Lestrange was appointed chief justice of the forest south of the Trent. He held the office until 12 February 1297, and the forest seems to have occupied much of his attention during that period. He held some forest eyres, and some of his forest eyre rolls have survived. In 1291–2, however, he served as a royal envoy on a mission to the papal court, and he was summoned by name to several parliaments and royal councils. Throughout his career he received many marks of favour from King Edward, whom he served for many years as a household knight, but seems to have remained in debt to him. In 1306, in consideration of his long service and great expenses in his service, the king granted that Lestrange's executors should not be impeded by reason of his debts to the king from having sufficient of his goods to bury him and provide for his obsequies in a fitting manner. In the last years of his life, after giving up the forest justiceship, he was apparently largely inactive, and is recorded in 1298, 1302, and 1310 as being in poor health, though in 1301 he was involved in assessing the king's wastes in his forests north of the Trent and he also sealed the barons' letter to the pope.

Lestrange died on 31 July 1311. His first wife was Maud, former wife of Roger (II) de Mowbray. She had died by 1275, when he received her lands in dower, at a rent of 200 marks, during the minority of the heir, which lasted until late 1278; his second wife, named Eleanor, was dead by 1280; a third wife, also Maud or Matilda, is mentioned in 1307. Also in 1275 he received a life grant of Ellesmere hundred and castle in Shropshire, and some manors there, which he had received as a gift from his brother Hamo and had surrendered to the king; it remained his principal lordship. Lands in Buckinghamshire and Bedfordshire, including the site of Bedford Castle, part of his third of the barony of Beauchamp of Bedford, which he held by the courtesy of England in right of his first wife, descended to her heir John (I) Mowbray.

David Crook

Sources C. Moor, ed., *Knights of Edward I*, 4, Harleian Society, 83 (1931), 299–301 • *Chancery records* • *CIPM*, 5, no. 351 • J. G. Edwards, *Calendar of ancient correspondence concerning Wales* (1935), 84–5, 124–5 • L. B. Smith, 'The death of Llywelyn ap Gruffydd: the narratives reconsidered', *Welsh History Review / Cylchgrawn Hanes Cymru*, 11 (1982–3), 200–13 • F. Palgrave, ed., *The parliamentary writs and writs of military summons*, 1 (1827), 849–50 • A. Hughes, *List of sheriffs for England and Wales: from the earliest times to AD 1831*, PRO (1898), 161

Archives PRO, E 32; SC 1/19 nos. 8, 9; SC 1/23, nos. 174–177

Wealth at death held a few estates: *CIPM*, 5, no. 351

L'Estrange, Sir Roger (1616–1704), author and press censor, was born on 17 December 1616 at Hunstanton Hall, Norfolk, the third son of Sir Hamon *L'Estrange (1583–1654), author and MP, and his wife, Alice Stubbe (1585–1656), daughter of Richard Stubbe of nearby Sedgeford. His elder brothers were Sir Nicholas *L'Estrange, first baronet (*bap*. 1604, *d*. 1655), who succeeded to the family estate, and Hamon *L'Estrange (1605–1660), theological writer and historian. After three years at Sedgeford School, a year at Westminster School, and two years at Eton College, Roger was admitted on 6 November 1634 to Sidney Sussex College, Cambridge. On 6 February 1637, without having taken a degree, he entered Gray's Inn.

Military service and exile In the spring of 1639 L'Estrange accompanied Sir Hamon northward to take part in the unpopular first bishops' war against the Scots. In the early stages of the civil war he fought on the royalist side at Newark and at Edgehill. On 13 August 1643 he took part with Sir Hamon in the seizure of King's Lynn, which was held until 19 September when terms were agreed for a withdrawal. On 28 November 1644 he was issued with a royal warrant authorizing him to regain the town through bribery. Betrayed by an accomplice and apprehended unheroically in an alehouse in his slippers, L'Estrange was tried by court martial at London and on 28 December was sentenced to death for spying. Although the prosecution had been initiated by parliament, the legality of the sentence was questioned both by the Lords and by Prince Rupert, who argued in a letter to his military opponent, Essex, that L'Estrange was entitled to 'fair quarter'

Sir Roger L'Estrange (1616–1704), attrib. John Michael Wright, *c.*1680

(Kitchin, 17–18). Reprieved after much difficulty, he languished in Newgate, inaugurating his career as a published writer with a series of appeals for release issued between 1644 and 1646. Early in 1648 he was suffered to abscond and was soon involved as an agitator in the abortive Kentish uprising that began on 21 May. Here he proved a firebrand in speeches, warrants, and letters, but was of little help in the military campaign, which was easily won by Fairfax. Distrusted now by his own side, he fled to Holland, defending his conduct in *L'Estrange his Vindication to Kent* (1649), which earned him the patronage of Hyde. A vivid recollection in *The Observator*, 1/213, of 'Michael Angelo's great piece of the Day of Judgement' makes it possible that L'Estrange travelled as far as Rome. He speaks in *Discovery upon Discovery* of having passed 'a matter of eight months' in the house of the warrior cardinal Friedrich, Landgraf von Hesse-Darmstadt, a notable convert from protestantism, but does not specify its location (R. L'Estrange, *Discovery upon Discovery*, 1680, 9). He found solace in exile from Seneca's *Epistulae morales*, which he valued 'next to the Gospel itself' as 'the most sovereign remedy against the miseries of human nature' and which he later translated (R. L'Estrange, *Seneca's 'Morals'*, 1678, xii).

Return to England and pre-Restoration pamphleteering In August 1653 L'Estrange took advantage of Cromwell's policy of accommodation to return to England. He was clearly seen as a catch, since Cromwell intervened personally to nullify the previous sentence of death. By an order of 31 October he was freed from attendance on the council of state, subject to his providing £2000 bail to appear if called and undertaking 'to do nothing prejudicial to the commonwealth' (*CSP dom.*, 1653–4, 225). On 31 May 1654 his father died at Hunstanton. Despite being a younger son, L'Estrange received an inheritance sufficient for him to live 'like a gentleman' in London (*The Observator*, 1/290). Here he extended his musical and literary friendships and was the dedicatee in 1655 of Thomas Fuller's political fable *Ornitho-Logie, or, The Speech of Birds*. An incident of this period gave rise to the derisive nickname Noll's Fiddler. Visiting Whitehall, L'Estrange came across a viol consort in the apartment of Cromwell's master of music, John Hingeston, and was offered a part. During the playing Cromwell came through the door, listened for a while, then left. Viol (not violin) playing was a tradition in his family, Sir Nicholas being a notable collector and editor of viol music in manuscript. Dame Alice's account book records that in 1636 Thomas Brewer was paid £2 for 'teaching of Roger on the voyall' (Norfolk RO, L'Estrange accounts, 7). It is likely that the brothers also had music lessons from John Jenkins, a dependant of the family. Variants on the 'fiddler' jibe were far from the only ones directed at L'Estrange. Bunyan in *The Holy War* called him Mr Filth; to Ralph Wallis he was Old Crack-Fart and the Devil's Bloodhound; to the whigs he was to be Towzer, Hodge, Don Rugero, or simply Roger. In the dialogues of *The Observator* he calls himself Nobs.

Cromwell's death in 1658 brought L'Estrange back to political journalism. During the confused months preceding the Restoration he was one of a group of royalist pamphleteers advocating the dismissal of the Rump Parliament and the calling of a free parliament. It was now that he found his true vocation as a knight of the pen rather than the sword, and he laid the foundation for his long career as a propagandist, censor, pamphleteer, and editor in the Stuart interest. His *No Blind Guides* (20 April 1660), written in reply to Milton's *Brief Notes upon a Late Sermon*, crowned the insult of its title with the motto 'If the blind lead the blind, both shall fall into the ditch'. Still distrusted by many of his own party, he defended his conduct during these busy months in *L'Estrange his Apology: with a Short View of some Late and Remarkable Transactions* (June 1660), a kind of collected works incorporating the texts of nineteen (in some copies twenty-one) of his already published pamphlets. These were the writings that prompted his boast that he 'ventured hanging for His Majesty's service, in those times, as fair and as often perhaps, as any man in the three kingdoms' (*The Observator*, 2/80).

Regulator of the press With the Restoration accomplished, L'Estrange established himself as a spokesman for the most vindictive party of the old royalists. *A Caveat to the Cavaliers* (July or August 1661) and *A Modest Plea both for the Caveat and the Author of It* (28 August 1661) were responses to James Howell's attempt in *A Cordial for the Cavaliers* (1661) to defend the king against the charge of indifference to the sufferings of uncompensated loyal officers. However, as long as the government's policy remained one of oblivion and indemnity, L'Estrange's views were an embarrassment to it. An established pattern of vigorous self-justification was continued in *To the Right Honourable,*

Edward, Earl of Clarendon ... the Humble Apology of Roger L'Estrange (3 December 1661). His *Interest Mistaken, or, The Holy Cheat* (1662 for 1661), directed at the presbyterians, showed him once again to be ahead of his party. In *The Relapsed Apostate* (14 November 1661) and *State-Divinity* (4 December 1661) he crossed swords, not for the last time, with Richard Baxter, and in the closely argued *Toleration Discussed* (1663) with Edmund Calamy. *A Memento, Directed to All those that Truly Reverence the Memory of King Charles the Martyr* (11 April 1662) was again dedicated to Clarendon. The preface to this speaks of his having spent six years in gaol for the royal cause, which is two more than is currently recorded. Both his principles and his intemperate manner of declaring them were now thoroughly familiar. The presbyterian Edward Bagshawe, awaiting an attack on his *Animadversions*, wittily published a *Second Part ... with an Answer to All that L'Estrange Intends to Write* (1662). Once Clarendon turned decisively against the presbyterians, L'Estrange's extremism was vindicated and he became an acknowledged mouthpiece of the administration. Throughout this period of intense pamphleteering L'Estrange had also acted as an informer on illegal anti-government printing and bookselling. The task was not an easy one: in 1664 Richard Atkyns estimated that there were 'at least 600 booksellers that keep shops in and about London and two or three thousand free of the Company of Stationers' (R. Atkyns, *The Original and Growth of Printing*, 1664, 16). On 24 February 1662 L'Estrange's initiative was regularized by an appointment as an unpaid surveyor of the imprimery under Secretary of State Nicholas. He argued the necessity of the office in his *Truth and Loyalty Vindicated* (7 June 1662), and was to exercise it with intermissions until 1688.

At this time action against printers and publishers of seditious material was taken either under the Treason Act of 1660 or under powers of the crown that were acknowledged in common law, although not formulated in a statute. The licensing of books was conducted by Sir John Berkenhead under an order in council of 29 October 1660. The Act of Uniformity, which received royal assent on 19 May 1662, demanded a more refined mechanism of control. This was given by the Licensing Act, whose full title was 'An act for preventing the frequent abuses in printing seditious, treasonable and unlicensed books and pamphlets, and for regulating of printing and printing presses'. The act specifically forbade the printing of any matter 'contrary to ... the doctrine or discipline of the Church of England' and, among other measures, re-established a system of compulsory pre-publication licensing, modelled on that of the Star Chamber ordinance of 1637. Section 15 of the act legitimized the practice of entering and searching premises merely suspected of containing seditious books, only the houses of peers being exempt. These intrusions were performed under a general warrant issued to one of the secretaries of state—the legal basis for L'Estrange's subsequent activity as surveyor. Following the ejectments of the following August, the threat of the act was used to deter nonconforming clergy from re-establishing their ministry in the medium of print.

L'Estrange's nominal surveyorship was given official status by letters patent of 15 August 1663, which conflated the role of surveyor with that of licenser. They also gave him a sole privilege of 'writing, printing and publishing all narratives or relations not exceeding two sheets of paper and all advertisements, mercuries, diurnals and books of public intelligence' together with other forms of ephemeral printing (Siebert, 292–3). As a licenser, supplanting Sir John Berkenhead, he was responsible for all books apart from those on law, heraldry, divinity, physic, and philosophy, which went before other authorities, and those printed at the universities. His imprimatur appears on a great number of books from the first period (ending in May 1679) during which the act was in force, although other books, known to have been licensed, omit it. The post brought no official salary but offered obvious opportunities for self-enrichment. A document of 3 June 1676 alleges a subvention of £50 a year from the playhouses 'besides presents', £500 a year for quacks' bills and books, and a fee of a shilling a sheet for both new books and reprints (Kitchin, 200–02). However, the post was far from a sinecure, as Henry Oldenburg found when he occupied it from February to April 1675. The licenser's responsibilities included the rewriting of exceptionable passages. William Lilly complained that his almanacs had been 'macerated, obliterated, sliced and quartered' by 'old Crackfart' (B. Capp, *English Almanacs, 1500–1800*, 1979, 48–9). However, it was as surveyor, operating from an office above the bookseller Henry Brome's shop in Ivy Lane, London, that L'Estrange now achieved notoriety. His ambitions for the post are given in his *Considerations and Proposals in Order to the Regulation of the Press* (3 June 1663). Self-regulation by the Stationers' Company, as he never failed to argue, could not be hoped for when many of its leading members were themselves opposed to the Anglican settlement and nearly all were profiteers in one way or another from the sale of forbidden books at enormous mark-ups. In a letter to the earl of Arlington of 17 October 1664 L'Estrange spoke of having outlaid £500 of his own money in the first year on 'entertaining spies and instruments' for the supervision of the press (Kitchin, 152–3). His most pressing task was to control the circulation of Fifth Monarchist prophecies and of the last speeches of executed regicides. Livewell Chapman, Francis Smith, Giles and Elizabeth Calvert, Simon Dover, and Thomas Brewster were charged with involvement in one Fifth Monarchist series that appeared during 1661. Dover, Brewster, John Twyn, and Nathan Brooks were arrested in connection with publications timed to coincide with the rising of 12 October 1664. Twyn, whom L'Estrange had apprehended in the act of printing a tract, was executed for treason. The others named endured long periods in gaol, with Brewster and Dover dying while prisoners and Calvert dying not long after his release. Ralph Wallis, the cobbler of Gloucester, who in 1664 was the quarry of one of L'Estrange's most troublesome pursuits, was able to jest his way out of prison with a promise to 'scribble as much against the fanatics' (*CSP dom.*, *1664–5*, 156–7). But it was usually L'Estrange who had the last laugh as when, in his translation of Quevedo's *Visions*, he placed Chapman in hell. Summarizing these busy years, L'Estrange later claimed to have 'suppressed above 600 sorts of seditious pamphlets' (*CSP dom.*, *1670*, 502).

The clause in L'Estrange's letters patent concerning 'diurnals and books of public intelligence' gave him control of *The Intelligencer*, an official weekly news-book, previously conducted by Berkenhead and Henry Muddiman. L'Estrange transformed the weekly into a shorter bi-weekly by adding the *Newes*, which after a brief period of independence was numbered consecutively with *The Intelligencer*. L'Estrange proved a poor news journalist, preferring to recast the publication as an anti-dissenter political organ. Even in that capacity P. W. Thomas judges that he lacked Berkenhead's 'polished way of insinuating biased views', regarding him as 'brutal and heavy handed' (P. W. Thomas, *Sir John Berkenhead: a Royalist Career in Politics and Polemics, 1617–1679*, 1969, 225–6). He ingratiated himself with Pepys in an attempt to secure naval news and was used in return when Pepys wished to gain favourable publicity for the earl of Sandwich. L'Estrange continued publication in London during the great plague (perhaps involuntarily, since he mentions having the plague in his own house), when the administration moved to Oxford. On 29 January 1666 his lagging enterprise was abolished in favour of the *London Gazette*, which had begun publication as the *Oxford Gazette* on 16 November 1665. His departure from the news field was sweetened by royal pensions of £200 and £100 respectively, although both were difficult to collect and the first lapsed in 1674.

The great fire of 1666 devastated the book trade, which was then clustered around St Paul's Cathedral with much of its stock actually stored in vaults under the building. Printers and booksellers now set up in a variety of new locations in which it was difficult to supervise them. There was also a greater incentive for them to produce forbidden books in the hope of quick returns. In 1668 three supposedly loyal booksellers were elected by royal command to the governing body of the Stationers' Company, which now became more active in exercising its independent powers of arrest and seizure, but mainly at the expense of popish books, which L'Estrange had generally tolerated, while dissenting books remained freely procurable. Moreover, the company's confiscations were often, in his own later words, 'only the removing them from one warehouse to another' (*CSP dom.*, *July–September 1683*, 341). On 19 May 1670 he wrote to Arlington asserting that the press had become 'as foul and licentious as ever'. He appended two proposed by-laws dealing with seditious publications, which he wished to have inserted into the Stationers' Company's charter, and he declared himself prepared to launch a new campaign of suppression as soon as he was afforded 'credit and supply'. But he also warned that 'the people concerned have grown more peremptory, and become better instructed in the niceties of the case, and the failures of the act for printing' (*CSP dom.*, *1670*, 227–8). Confirming the last claim, an attempt by one of his agents on 6 July to arrest a compositor in John Streater's shop was met with a denial of the validity of the secretary's warrant which then erupted into a riot during which the prisoner escaped. The proposed by-laws were the subject of a *quo warranto* of 19 August 1670 that was withdrawn when the company agreed to make voluntary changes to the charter; but these were not the stringent conditions desired by L'Estrange. In any case they only affected the company's own members, whereas much suspect bookselling was handled by non-members, such as haberdashers operating under bishops' licences. On 24 September he reported to Joseph Williamson on an interview with the king about proposals to discipline the company and to place booksellers who were not members under its control. These administrative measures, like many others he planned, were never enacted; however, in the following January he was awarded a monopoly of all blank papers printed on one side only (such as legal documents and receipts), for which he received a fixed amount per ream.

The matter of the new by-laws was to occupy L'Estrange for more than a decade, only being resolved as part of the general remodelling of charters in the closing years of the reign. Meanwhile he had to deal with difficulties in his relationship with his superiors and the parliament. In September 1674 the replacement of Arlington as secretary of state by his deputy Williamson led to the loss of the larger of L'Estrange's pensions and appears to have seen him suspended from his functions for a time. However, L'Estrange's powers were always greater than those he was formally allowed. He could do damage simply as an informer, as many documents in the state papers show; moreover, he seems never to have thrown away a potentially incriminating document or publication. No doubt it was this wealth of private information that brought about his reconciliation with Williamson, who normally preferred to have no rivals in his control of intelligence.

The expiry of the Licensing Act on 27 May 1679 (Knights, 156—the legal date is often mistaken) deprived L'Estrange of both his offices, though his name appears as a licenser on a few books published subsequently. It also left him financially embarrassed. His opponents had long alleged that his considerable income had been squandered on gambling and women. Now a wife, Anne, daughter of Sir Thomas Doleman, whig clerk of the council, and a young family added to his outlays. In *A Short Answer to a Whole Litter of Libels* (1680), he concedes that he 'ran away with her … And that, without a portion too' (p. 2). Between 1678 and 1686 the St Giles-in-the-Fields register records the birth of six children to the couple: Hamon, Ann, Nicholas, Margery, Roger, and John. Hamon died on 7 February 1684, prompting a touching tribute in *The Observator*, 2/15. Only Roger (1685–1705) and Margery, who embarrassed her father by becoming a Roman Catholic, are known to have survived him.

Anti-whig journalism By 1679, with the press completely out of control, there was a renewed demand for L'Estrange's other craft of political editorialist and pamphleteer. Having produced little of note during the 1670s apart from *A Discourse of Fishery* (1674), written for Williamson, he replied to Andrew Marvell's *An Account of the Growth of Popery* (1677) with *An Account of the Growth of Knavery* (1678), in which he compared the current agitations with those of 1641. During the Popish Plot turmoil, he put himself forward in a series of pamphlets as the voice of reason and scepticism. Cautiously at first, and then with increasing boldness, he began to question the fabrications of Titus Oates and William Bedloe. His *The History of the Plot*, which appeared late in 1679, was not openly disbelieving but drew attention to inconsistencies and contradictions in the existing narratives. This line of attack was continued in *The Free-Born Subject* (1679), *A Further Discovery of the Plot*, *Discovery upon Discovery*, and *L'Estrange's Narrative of the Plot*, and less formally in the two parts of his dialogue *Cit and Bumpkin* (all 1680). His comic gifts were also in evidence in 'The Committee', an allegorical caricature of the sects published with a verse 'Explanation' (1680). In April 1680 he was made a justice of the peace for Middlesex and he received a secret services grant of £100.

In responding to his attacks the whigs made L'Estrange the target of a huge body of satire in prose, verse, and caricature. He figured prominently in the pope-burning processions organized by the Green Ribbon Club: in that of 17 November 1680 he was playing a violin side-by-side with the 'popish midwife', Elizabeth Cellier. On Gunpowder Treason day, 1682, rioters seized furniture from his house in Holborn to make a bonfire, stopping people for money to buy drink with which to toast 'the destruction of Towzer and the Pope' (T. Harris, *London Crowds in the Reign of Charles II: Propaganda and Politics from the Restoration until the Exclusion Crisis*, 1987, 187). Whig propaganda asserted univocally that he was a crypto-Catholic and thus a secret sympathizer with the Popish Plot. L'Estrange's attempts in *L'Estrange No Papist* (1681) and elsewhere to free himself from this accusation were oddly muted and did little to convince either his opponents or many on his own side. However, he continued a favourite with the Anglican clergy, whose cause he defended against the dissenters and with whom he socialized in Sam's Coffee House. In October 1680 he was accused by Miles Prance of having attended mass at the queen's chapel and by Oates of having suborned Simpson Tonge to swear that evidence for the Popish Plot presented in 1679 by Oates and Tonge's father, Israel, had been a fabrication. L'Estrange defended himself successfully before the privy council on 6 October, when 'His Majesty's speaking well of Mr L'Estrange, he was acquitted' (Luttrell, 1.57), and again on 13 October. However, when Oates and Prance then took their charges to the Lords' committee for examinations and an order was issued for him to be attached L'Estrange found it prudent to abscond. He travelled first to Edinburgh, where he was protected by the duke of York, whose side he had taken in *The Case Put, Concerning the Succession* (1679), and then to The Hague where on 1 February 1681 he asserted his orthodoxy in a letter to Thomas Ken. He was removed from the commission of the peace in December 1680.

L'Estrange's return to England in February 1681, following the last session of the second Exclusion Parliament, was perfectly timed for both himself and his party. On 28 March 1681 Charles secured the constitutional initiative against the whigs by unexpectedly dismissing the new parliament assembled at Oxford. Within a few days one of L'Estrange's most effective pamphlets, part one of *The Dissenters' Sayings*, was on sale and on 13 April 1681 he issued the first number of *The Observator* which, appearing at an average of three times a week over the next six years, was to prove the most powerful organ of tory propaganda. The paper is composed throughout as a dialogue between two speakers, A (later Tory, Observator and, briefly, Courantier) and Q (later Whig, then Trimmer). It is normally Q's role to be slapped down, but he is always allowed to make some telling points and the best of the papers convey an enlivening sense of a vigorous mind in dialogue with itself. Deploring its influence, Burnet noted that the 'greater part of the clergy … being now both sharpened and furnished by these papers, delivered themselves up to much heat and indiscretion' (*Bishop Burnet's History*, ed. Burnet and Burnet, 1.461). Its success, as well as advancing L'Estrange's influence, allowed him to restore his finances through gifts and testimonials. Never one to forget old scores, L'Estrange returned to the case of young Tonge in *The Shammer Shammed* (February 1682). This was also a means of extending his pursuit of Prance and Oates, his accusers of 1680. On Easter Sunday (16 April) 1682 Prance and L'Estrange both took the sacrament at St Giles in order, respectively, to assert and deny the queen's chapel story. As an agitator L'Estrange assisted with the management of the City election of 18 May 1682, at which the return of a tory mayor, Sir John Moore, and two tory sheriffs ended whig control of the Middlesex juries. Moore was the addressee of his *A Word Concerning Libels and Libellers* (1681). That the court party, and especially its Yorkist faction, survived the whig assault and was able from 1681 to go strongly on the offensive owed much to L'Estrange's courage and persistence. In November 1682 tribute was paid to him as Sheva in lines 1025–36 of *The Second Part of Absalom and Achitophel*, which had probably been written by the previous May. Opposition versifiers had their turn in *Strange's Case Strangely Altered* (1680), in which he is illustrated as Towzer the dog with a broom—his publisher Henry Brome—fixed to his tail, 'The Protestant Satire' (c.July 1684), and 'A Heroic Scene' (1686) (Lord, 2.367–73, 3.511–40, 4.80–94). In this last skit, which parodies the style of the heroic play, Old Hodge and Johnny the sincere (Dryden) try unsuccessfully to persuade Oliver's Porter, an inmate of Bedlam, to convert to Rome. The most effective of the many prose attacks was *The Observator Proved a Trimmer* (December 1684): L'Estrange devoted over a month of *Observators* to answering it. Throughout the 1680s he remained the tory lightning rod for whig polemics; however, with the opposing voices falling silent owing to persecution or exile, he soon found himself beyond much danger of being answered. Robert Stephens, a messenger of the press who had converted to the whig side, agitated unsuccessfully during 1683 to have *The Observator* suppressed with other newspapers. A lord mayor's warrant to this effect issued in October did no more than irritate L'Estrange, who regarded himself as protected by his 1663 patent.

In March 1683 it was reported that L'Estrange was 'very indisposed with fits' (Luttrell, 1.252)—he was to have a second attack in April 1692. A newsletter cited in *The Observator*, 1/304, claims that he 'fell down dead … at Sam's Coffee-House'. There is also a curious reference of 1681 to 'lunatic paroxysms' (J. P., *Mr L'Estrange Refuted*, 9). The exposure of the Rye House plot in June and the ensuing trials found him fully engaged. In July 1683 he published *Considerations upon a Printed Sheet*, defending Lord Russell's execution. The state papers for the year show him repeatedly supplying information on the movements of suspected persons. The consolidation of court control over the City brought about a long-pursued triumph over the Stationers, who were issued with a new, restrictive charter on 23 March 1684. Throughout this period of tory triumph, *The Observator* continued its hounding of Oates and Prance. In February 1684 L'Estrange had been given custody of a collection of the elder Tonge's papers and subsequently took depositions and enlisted witnesses for Oates's trial before Jeffreys, which took place in June 1685. The information so collected is summarized in *A Brief History of the Times* (1687). Prance was tried in May–June 1686; he confessed his perjury and, like Oates, he was pilloried and whipped.

By the time of these trials L'Estrange was serving a new king. In March 1685 he was forced by James on the unwilling electors of Winchester as their candidate for parliament and on 30 April he was knighted. One of the earliest acts of the parliament that met on 19 May 1685 was to reinstate the Licensing Act and with it L'Estrange's positions as licenser and surveyor, which had been extinguished in 1679. It was an *Observator* of this period that prompted Macaulay's stricture that 'from the malice of L'Estrange the grave was no hiding place, and the house of mourning no sanctuary' (T. B. Macaulay, *The History of England from the Accession of James II*, 5 vols., 1861–5, 1.393). In June 1686, L'Estrange was sent to Scotland to promote the repeal of the Test Acts by the Scottish parliament, keeping *The Observator* going with groups of papers on general political topics.

L'Estrange's zeal in the royal cause revived questions about his religion. While he may have profited from the seizure of Catholic books, he was free of any vindictiveness against Catholics as such, remembering only that they had been loyal supporters of the crown during the civil wars and had cared for him during his years of exile. In *A Brief History of the Times* he is careful to exculpate them from responsibility for the death of Sir Edmund Berry Godfrey, which he maintained to have been suicide. Under James he was a firm advocate of passive obedience and the dispensing power; however, he never took the further step of conversion, and the closing down of *The Observator* with the issue of 9 March 1687 would seem to indicate that there were limits to how far he could assent to the Romanizing programme. His other difficulty was that at crucial times under both Charles and James his position had been compromised by royal desire to appease the dissenters as a means of achieving toleration for Catholics. In 1687 he made it clear that he would accept toleration as an obedient subject, but was opposed to it as a member of the established church. Other sources, admittedly hostile, paint him as a sceptic and a mocker. The whigs remained convinced that he had converted to Rome in the 1650s and had worked throughout his career as an undercover agent of the Holy See. Yet a man who was so definite in all his opinions should be allowed to be so about his religion, which he always insisted was that of the Church of England.

Final years With the revolution of 1688, L'Estrange's government service ended abruptly and he was removed for the second time from the commission of the peace. On 16 December 1688 he was imprisoned in Newgate for 'writing and dispersing treasonable papers against the government' (*Kenyon MSS*, 211). He was excluded from the Act of Indemnity in 1690 and was rounded up as a known Jacobite in 1691 and 1696 on the occasion of the Ashton and Fenwick conspiracies, but without anything being charged against him apart from refusal, in the second case, to take the oaths. Advanced years prevented him from being regarded very seriously. Queen Mary is said to have made an anagram on his name, usually quoted as 'Lye Strange Roger'; however, William was an appreciative reader of L'Estrange's *Aesop*. On 7 April 1694 Anne L'Estrange died, having damaged both their fortunes through compulsive gambling. L'Estrange's last years were plagued by poverty and declining health. On 3 September 1700, while at work for the booksellers on his complete translation of the works of Josephus, he wrote to John Caryll 'I have neither eyes nor fingers for many words' (BL, Add. MS 28237, 4*r*). He died on 11 December 1704, in St Giles-in-the-Fields parish, aged eighty-seven, and was buried in the church.

Personality and writings Violent in his political battles and often brutal in enforcing his will on his enemies, L'Estrange in private life was agreeable company and a *bon vivant*. Even his dealings with errant stationers seem often to have taken place in taverns. Pepys described him in 1664 as 'a man of fine conversation I think; but I am sure, most courtly and full of compliment' (Pepys, 4.348). To Evelyn, who knew him well, he was 'a person of excellent parts, abating some affectations' (Evelyn, *Diary*, 4.439). Nine of his witticisms are recorded in his brother Sir Nicholas's *Merry Passages and Jests*. Opponents were prone to characterize him as a rake, addicted to women and gambling, and more recent writers never fail to cite John Dunton's remark that he 'would wink at unlicensed books, if the printer's wife would but—' (Dunton, 349). He confronts this accusation in *The Observator*, 1/290, but so evasively that one suspects that there must have been some truth to it.

L'Estrange's skill as a viol player has already been mentioned. Four compositions by him for the instrument are preserved in the manuscript additions to a Bodleian Library copy of the 1659 edition of Christopher Simpson's *The*

Division Viol, originally owned by John Covell, master of Christ's College, Cambridge. In his licenser's preface to the second edition of Simpson's work, L'Estrange refers to the author as 'my Familiar Friend' and the subject as 'my singular entertainment, and delight' (A3*v*). The improvisatory skill of division playing was the basis for L'Estrange's friendship with Simpson's most famous pupil, Sir Robert Bolles, who in 1672 bequeathed L'Estrange a silver posset cup. A shared culture of domestic viol playing reinforced a political link with other royalist families such as those of North, Derham, and Pettus. However, he was also a patron of the new musical styles introduced into England by the violin virtuosi Thomas Balthazar and Nicola Matteis, and he was a supporter of Thomas Britton's early experiments at giving regular public concerts. Matthew Locke's treatise on thorough-bass, *Melothesia* (1673), and John Bannister's *New Airs and Dialogues* (1678) were both dedicated to him. Locke speaks of him as a long-term patron.

L'Estrange was an enormously prolific writer. Wing's *Short-Title Catalogue* assigns 130 titles to him, and others no doubt remain undiscovered. His visibility as an author was accentuated by the fact that many of his works ran through several editions: in particular, a number of the post-Restoration tracts were reprinted at the time of the Exclusion Bill crisis. His early career was aided by the efforts of his regular publisher, Henry Brome, and Brome's wife, Joanna. With his office directly above Brome's bookshop in Ivy Lane it was an easy matter for him to revise and augment even during the production of a particular edition, making the bibliography of his pamphlets a matter of great complexity. While he did not create the profession of political journalist, he was the most important link between the controversialists of the civil war period and the newspapermen of Queen Anne's reign. His vigorous, colloquial prose and mastery of dialogue form were greatly admired. Sutherland describes L'Estrange's idiom as

> that of the tavern and the market-place mixed with the fashionable slang of the day, appealing not only to gentlemen and scholars but to men of affairs, to shopkeepers and artisans. (J. R. Sutherland, *English Literature of the Late Seventeenth Century*, 1969, 355)

His name, several times included in the titles of his works, was undoubtedly a selling point, and one which the countless attacks and replies confirmed in its drawing power.

In addition to his work as a pamphleteer L'Estrange produced translations of Francisco Quevedo y Villegas's satirical *Sueños* (1667), Giovanni Bona's *Manuductio ad coelum* (as *A Guide to Eternity*, 1672), the younger Seneca's *Epistulae morales* (1678), Cicero's *De officiis* (1680), twenty-two of Erasmus's *Colloquia* (1680 and 1689), Cervantes' *Novellas exemplares* (as *The Spanish Decameron*, 1687), Aesop's *Fables* (in two parts, 1691 and 1699), the third book of Tacitus's *Histories* (1694, as part of a group translation), and the works of Josephus (1709), as well as some lighter pieces from Spanish and an eirenic *Apology for the French Protestants* (1681). He also contributed suggestions to Laurence Eachard's collaborative translations of Terence and to three plays by Plautus (1694). The very popular Seneca translation, published as *Seneca's 'Morals' by Way of Abstract*, presents the source at about a third of its original length and substantially rearranged. L'Estrange's Preface explains that he had 'reduced all his scattered ethics to their proper heads, without any additions … more than of absolute necessity for the tacking of them together'. Dunton thought that it and the version of *De officiis* would 'live as long as the world' (Dunton, 349). The *Aesop*, on the other hand, was actually an assemblage of fables and facetiae from a variety of sources, ancient and modern, the second volume being wholly unAesopian. The trenchant reflections added to the individual fables possess a strong political animus and were to draw severe criticism from the later whig fabulist Samuel Croxall; but all L'Estrange's translations have some degree of political colouring. *Five Love-Letters from a Nun to a Cavalier* (1678), a translation of the pseudonymous *Lettres Portugaises*, is of interest for the development of epistolary fiction in Behn and later writers. L'Estrange's method of translation was closer to that of the Augustan 'imitation' than what Dryden called 'metaphrase': its aim is always to bring the author into a racy English present. In the works of Josephus he was reliant on a French translation and in the edition of Tacitus on Sir Henry Savile's earlier English one. His frequent verbal liberties and colloquial style offended purists and it became fashionable for a time to decry the translations as unfaithful to the tone and dignity of their originals. Thomas Gordon in 1728 found them full of 'technical terms, of phrases picked up in the street from apprentices and porters' and stigmatized his sentences as 'lively nothings, which can never be translated (the only way to try language) and will hardly bear repetition' (T. Gordon, *The Works of Tacitus*, 2 vols., 1728–31, 1.30). It is true that L'Estrange will often use a vivid but vague colloquial phrase to avoid giving a clear answer to a compromising question. But generally there is much to relish in what he called his 'honest Dunstable English' (*The Observator*, 3/69).

In considering L'Estrange's contribution to the growth of journalism and the profession of journalist it can never be ignored that he was always the voice of a party and for most of the time on its payroll, and that he never for a moment accepted the desirability of a free press. While there were times in his career when he became too extreme for his masters, he never gave them any excuse to doubt his fidelity. At an early age his views were set in a mould that was never broken of loyalty to the crown and implacable hostility to puritanism in all its manifestations. He was to remain the civil war warrior all his life. His opponents, whether of the Stationers' Company or of the sects, were enemies in a conflict for which no armistice had ever been declared and which might still be pursued to the death. When pressed to justify repression, he would cite Bacon's 'Of seditions' or argue, as in the very first *Observator*, that failure to enforce religious uniformity had already cost 'the life of a prince, the blood of two or three hundred thousand of his subjects, and a twenty-years-rebellion'. Such a mindset was to earn L'Estrange the hearty dislike not only of whigs of all periods but also of liberal tories: even Kitchin, his most knowledgeable and sympathetic biographer, makes no attempt to defend his moral character. And yet it is difficult not to respect his courage and tenacity, especially when displayed against opponents as ruthless as Oates and Shaftesbury. His hatred of hypocrisy and ingratitude was genuine and lifelong. HAROLD LOVE

Sources G. Kitchin, *Sir Roger L'Estrange: a contribution to the history of the press in the seventeenth century* (1913) • F. S. Siebert, *Freedom of the press in England, 1476–1776* (1952) • N. H. Keeble, *The literary culture of nonconformity in later seventeenth-century England* (1987) • J. G. Muddiman, *The king's journalist, 1659–1689: studies in the reign of Charles II* (1923) • S. Parks, ed., *Freedom of the press: Sir Roger L'Estrange's tracts and others, 1660–1681* (1974) • A. Ashbee, *The harmonious music of John Jenkins* (1992) • G. de F. Lord and others, eds., *Poems on affairs of state: Augustan satirical verse, 1660–1714*, 7 vols. (1963–75) • M. Knights, *Politics and opinion in crisis, 1678–1681* (1994) • H. Weber, *Paper bullets: print and kingship under Charles II* (1996) • R. L'Estrange, *The Observator*, 1/289 (13 Feb 1683) [replies to accusations] • R. L'Estrange, *The Observator*, 1/290 (14 Feb 1683) [replies to accusations] • *The loyal Observator, or, Historical memoirs of the life and actions of Roger the Fiddler* (1683) • *Bishop Burnet's History of his own time*, ed. G. Burnet and T. Burnet, 2 vols. (1724–34) • Pepys, *Diary* • J. Dunton, *The life and errors of John Dunton … written by himself* (1705) • N. Luttrell, *A brief historical relation of state affairs from September 1678 to April 1714*, 6 vols. (1857) • *The manuscripts of Lord Kenyon*, HMC, 35 (1894) • Hunstanton register, Norfolk RO • register, Sidney Sussex College, Cambridge

Archives BL, letters to J. Caryll, Add. MSS 28237, 28618 • BL, letters to secretary of state, Add. MSS 41803–41805 • Norfolk RO, L'Estrange MSS

Likenesses attrib. J. M. Wright, oils, *c*.1680, NPG [*see illus.*] • R. White, line engraving, 1684 (after G. Kneller), BM, NPG; repro. in R. Lestrange, *Fables of Aesop and other eminent mythologists* (1692)

Sir Thomas Lestrange (*c*.1490–1545), by Hans Holbein the younger, 1536

Lestrange [Le Strange], **Sir Thomas** (*c*.1490–1545), landowner and administrator, was the eldest son of Robert Lestrange, esquire (*d*. 1511), and Anne Lestrange, heir to Sir Thomas Lestrange of Walton, Warwickshire. Upon the death of his father in 1511, when he was in his early twenties, he inherited scattered estates in west Norfolk centred on Hunstanton, a number of leasehold properties in central and south Norfolk, and two highly profitable Suffolk manors at Thorpe Morieux and Felsham. In 1501 he had married Anne, daughter of Sir Nicholas Vaux, later first Baron Vaux of Harrowden, Northamptonshire, and Elizabeth, who was the daughter and heir of Henry, Baron Fitzhugh, and the widow of Sir William Parr. The lives of husband and wife are exceptionally well documented thanks to the survival of a substantial Lestrange archive, now deposited in the Norfolk Record Office, Norwich. As well as recording the fortunes of the family estates over some six centuries, it contains family settlements and letters which illuminate the alliances, influence-brokering, and other public activities of generations of Lestranges. Above all, a splendid series of household accounts provides unusually detailed information about the daily lives of the family.

In his early adult life Thomas Lestrange was a member of Henry VIII's inner circle of courtiers, attending the king as squire of the body at the Field of Cloth of Gold in 1520 and accompanying him to Calais in 1529; he was knighted at Whitehall in the latter year. When Hans Holbein the younger made his first visit to the English court in 1526–8 he made a chalk drawing of Lestrange, which was later elaborated into a portrait in oils depicting him in his maturity. After the mid-1530s Sir Thomas took little part in court affairs; the last summonses to attend which he received were in 1533, to the marriage of King Henry and Anne Boleyn and to the new queen's coronation, where he acted as a servitor at the queen's board during the state banquet, and in 1536 'to the dethe of the Queen', apparently to witness Anne's execution. For the remainder of his life Sir Thomas Lestrange fulfilled a variety of official duties in Norfolk; he was sheriff of the county in 1530, sat on the commission for the peace, and acted as a royal commissioner for the *valor ecclesiasticus* and inquiries preceding the dissolution of the monasteries within his part of Norfolk: Coxford (1534), Westacre (1538), Great Massingham (1538), and Walsingham (1538). These activities do not appear to have posed any religious difficulties for him. In 1527 the weekly lists of 'strangers', guests at Hunstanton Hall, included the priors of Coxford, Walsingham, and the Austin friary of King's Lynn, and the abbot of Ramsay. These social connections bore fruit in Sir Thomas's acquisition of leases and purchases of lands from monastic superiors before their houses were dissolved. There was a transitory awkwardness when in December 1537 he was appointed commissioner with Richard Leighton to produce an inventory of goods missing from Westacre Priory and to sequester the remainder, as he had himself bought from Coxford Abbey 'an aulter of ymages of alabaster' for 10*s*. through the good offices of Richard Southwell. His own religious opinions may have been shifting towards protestantism as on 28 June 1538 the household accounts record the purchase of 'a Byble' for 12*s*. As a magistrate Sir Thomas was called in May 1537 to inquire into the so-called Walsingham conspiracy, a locally organized protest at the anticipated closure of the priory with an accompanying loss of employment. Lady Lestrange, who oversaw the household accounts, noted sombrely 'paid at Norwich Walsingham and Lynn when you rode to the execution of the traytors' (Norfolk RO, LC P3). As a client of Thomas Howard, third duke of Norfolk, Sir Thomas was summoned with fifty men to attend the duke in Lincolnshire to confront the rising there in 1536. His connection with the duke was a long-standing one. Visits, letters, and gifts of game were regularly exchanged, and in 1539 Sir Thomas was called upon, unsuccessfully in the event, to mediate in the dispute over the election of knights of the shire for Norfolk between the duke's nephew Edward Knyvett and Sir Thomas's young kinsman Richard Southwell.

During the 1530s and 1540s Lestrange's personal wealth was steadily increasing. Judicious sales of outlying land and the purchases of islands of monastic land within the estate served to consolidate Lestrange holdings. The profits of fold-course sheep farming were augmented by the raising of fat cattle on the richer pastures of the holding in central Norfolk in and around Godwick. At the same time a venture in coastal shipping between Heacham and Newcastle upon Tyne was expanded. These public and mercantile activities took place against the background of prosperous family life at Hunstanton Hall. Lady Anne supervised the many activities of household and estate. The extended family of her own children, their spouses, and subsequent grandchildren lived on such terms of equal provision that the generations cannot be clearly distinguished. The household was clothed and fed in the main from local resources, though supplies of wine were bought through Sir Thomas's butlership of King's Lynn and better quality cloth and silks obtained from Norwich. A substantial yearly purchase of spices was made from Stourbridge fair at Cambridge. The household expenses also include payments to 'the Minstrells of Lynn' (1536/7), 'the Singing Children of Beston', 'the King's Players' (1537), and 'the Duke of Suffolk's Trumpettes' (1538) (Norfolk RO, LC P3).

Hospitality accounted for a regular part of the domestic expenditure. This too was directed by Lady Anne, whose family from Northamptonshire and Cambridgeshire, Vaux and Tresham cousins, were frequent guests whose visits were regularly returned. Sir Thomas's circle extended beyond branches of his own kin to influential citizens of Norwich, such as Alexander Steward, mayor of the city, to fellow magistrates, and to officers in the duke of Norfolk's household at Kenninghall. There were constant visits from neighbours, and also from gentry from further afield such as John Robsart and Lady Boleyn. They appear in the guise of personal friends rather than as representatives of any particular political or religious alignment within the county. Not surprisingly, Sir Thomas himself was in demand among the county gentry as a convivial companion who enjoyed dicing and playing at cards, though with only moderate success; his most frequent personal expenses were for hawking, shooting, and hunting with hounds. These activities seem not to have been curtailed by increasing ill health from 1538. Payments for physicians and medicaments during recurrent attacks of 'colique and the stone' (Norfolk RO, LC P4), which he suffered on visits to neighbouring friends as well as at home, became increasingly frequent. Visits from the surgeon as well as from different physicians from Norwich, Dereham, and Stamford, urine examinations, and the administration of large quantities of drugs including 'white poppy seed' accounted for a substantial sum in the household accounts. His death, possibly from kidney failure, took place at Hunstanton Hall on 16 January 1545. So unexpected was it that his will remained in draft form only, with no executors named. His burial in the chapel on the north side of the chancel of Hunstanton parish church took place on the following day.

Sir Nicholas Lestrange (1515–1580), the eldest son of Sir Thomas Lestrange and Anne Vaux, was born at Hunstanton Hall in 1515. Educated in Norfolk and at the inns of court, he spent the greater part of his adult life away from the family estates, either in London on his father's legal affairs or in the employment of the third and fourth dukes of Norfolk, and also, briefly, as a client of Lord Protector Somerset. In 1526 he married Ellen, daughter of Sir William Fitzwilliam of Milton, Northamptonshire, who appears to have spent her whole married life, in company with their five children, with her husband's family at Hunstanton Hall. Nicholas Lestrange was appointed to the commission of the peace for Norfolk in 1538. During the next decade he enhanced his standing at court, in 1547 becoming steward for life of the lands of the widowed duchess of Richmond, and in 1552 being proposed to Princess Elizabeth as her officer. Notwithstanding his close connection with the third duke of Norfolk, in 1547 he sat upon the jury empanelled at Norwich to inquire into the alleged treason of Henry Howard, earl of Surrey. During the temporary eclipse of the Howards he saw service under Somerset on the Scottish campaign and was knighted by him at Roxburgh in September 1547. In the following year he was sheriff for Norfolk and Suffolk and was obliged to return hastily from London to take part in the suppression of the several risings in East Anglia which together constituted Ket's rebellion. Malicious rumours circulating in Norfolk that he had been slow to act against insurgents from the south-west of the county as they marched to join Ket at Norwich, waiting instead until the arrival of the main relieving force under the earl of Warwick, may be explained by the fact that his brother and son were being held as hostages in the rebel camp at Downham.

In 1553 Lestrange conspicuously failed to support Princess Mary, but soon became once more a prominent officer at Kenninghall. With the support of the fourth duke of Norfolk he became MP for King's Lynn in 1555, and in 1557, after Cambridge had declined to accept him at Norfolk's recommendation, for the newly enfranchised borough of Castle Rising. He represented Castle Rising again in 1558, 1559, 1563, and 1571. In 1555 he supported Sir Anthony Kingston in opposing an anti-protestant bill, but this can hardly be regarded as evidence for his devotional allegiance, since he seems to have been no more than conventionally observant in his religious practice. Apart from this episode Lestrange appears to have been almost entirely inactive in parliament. By contrast, he was deeply involved in Howard affairs. In 1569 he acted as trustee for the lands of Philip, earl of Arundel, and accompanied Norfolk on his Scottish expedition, acting as confidential messenger to the privy council. As the duke's amanuensis he wrote a brusque rejoinder to a letter from John Foxe, the duke's former tutor, who as early as 1566 warned against a marriage with Mary, queen of Scots. He was fortunate to escape relatively undamaged from the duke's fall, suffering no worse than a series of privy council examinations during a year's imprisonment. Thereafter he prudently avoided public notice, though he was still attentive to his Arundel trusteeship until the earl reached his majority in 1578.

Sir Nicholas had inherited a flourishing estate. After the death of his first wife about 1546 he married in January 1547 Katherine, *née* Hide (*d.* 1589), widow of Nicholas Mynne of Barsham, a Norfolk neighbour and old hawking companion. A pair of portraits by the monogrammist H. W. possibly commemorates their marriage. His mother moved from Hunstanton Hall to Godwick; without her supervision the estate and household accounts become much less detailed and after 1548 change their form. In 1549 Sir Nicholas was involved in an expensive lawsuit over the marriage of his eldest son, Hamon, to Elizabeth Hastings, a cousin who had been brought up at Hunstanton Hall but who was the ward of Sir Anthony Brown KG. Sir Nicholas had to find 1000 marks in compensation money which was raised by a £500 mortgage on the estate. In 1571, in his retirement after the execution of the duke of Norfolk, Sir Nicholas sold the manor of Hunstanton to Hamon. His movements thereafter are obscure but his wife seems to have lived in King's Lynn where Sir Nicholas had owned property since the 1550s. Nevertheless the Hunstanton parish register records his burial in the church there on 19 February 1580, in accordance with the wish expressed in his will that he should be interred 'withowte pompe or pryde of sumptuows or costlye Funeralles' (Norfolk RO LC AE4). JOY ROWE

Sources Norfolk RO, Lestrange collection, A5T; C4; C53/6; Q34; A38; B4; AE3, 4–5; A42; P1–4; NG2 • chancery, inquisitions post mortem series II, PRO, C 142/27/19; C 142/71/72; C 142/196/20 • *LP Henry VIII*, vols. 4–21 • BL, Harley MS 416, fols. 154, 186–7 • HoP, *Commons, 1509–58*, 2.522–3 • B. M. Harris, *English aristocratic women* (2002) • N. M. Fuidge, 'Lestrange (Strange), Sir Nicholas', HoP, *Commons, 1558–1603*, 2.462–3 • *Calendar of the manuscripts of the most hon. the marquis of Salisbury*, 1, HMC, 9 (1883), 189, 196, 214, 517, 533, 548 • parish register, Hunstanton, Norfolk RO [burial, also Nicholas Lestrange and Katherine Lestrange] • C. Oestmann, *Lordship and community: the Lestrange family and the village of Hunstanton* (1994), 14–15, 146 • T. H. Swales, 'Opposition to the suppression of the Norfolk monasteries: expressions of discontent before the Walsingham conspiracy', *Norfolk Archaeology*, 33 (1962–5), 254–65 • D. MacCulloch, 'Kett's rebellion in context', *Past and Present*, 84 (1979), 36–59 • K. T. Parker, *Holbein's drawings at Windsor Castle* (1945), 48, pl. 43 • R. Strong, *Holbein: the complete paintings* (1980), 72, pl. 103 • R. Strong, *Hans Eworth* [1965], 21, pls. 41, 42 [exhibition catalogue, City of Leicester Museums and Art Gallery and NPG, 10 Nov 1965 – 9 Jan 1966] • G. Anstruther, *Vaux of Harrowden: a recusant family*, 2nd edn (1953), 8 • F. Blomefield and C. Parkin, *An essay towards a topographical history of the county of Norfolk*, [2nd edn], 11 vols. (1805–10), vol. 10, p. 318 • J. L. Chester and G. J. Armytage, eds., *Allegations for marriage licences issued from the faculty office of the archbishop of Canterbury at London, 1543 to 1869*, Harleian Society, 24 (1886), 9

Archives Norfolk RO, collections, estate papers, household accounts, personal papers | BL, Harley MS 416, fol. 186 • Norfolk RO, Hunstanton parish register I [microfilm]

Likenesses H. Holbein the younger, chalk drawing, 1526–8, Royal Collection • H. Holbein the younger, oils, 1536, Kimball Art Museum, Fort Worth [*see illus.*] • H. Holbein the younger, oils, 1536, repro. in Oestmann, *Lordship and community*, frontispiece; priv. coll.

Wealth at death £600—total receipts: PRO, C 142/71/72 • £180—lands: *Lordship*, 133, Norfolk RO, LC P1–4

Le Sueur, Hubert (*c.*1580–1658x68), sculptor, was born in Paris, the third son of Pierre le Sueur (*d.* 1616), a master armourer, and his wife, Lucrèce le Long (*d.* 1620). He had several relatives who worked metal as founders and goldsmiths, but it remains uncertain where he learned to cast monumental sculpture. In 1634 Henry Peacham claimed that it was under Giambologna (1529–1608), and hence in Florence. This is certainly possible, for there are spans of several years between documents attesting Le Sueur's presence in Paris (1596, 1602, 1604) and 1609, the year of his marriage to Noémie Le Blanc (*d.* 1620), when, fully trained, he took on an apprentice, but there is no corroboratory evidence. However, Peacham's remark may have been intended to support Le Sueur's artistic pretensions, quoting a prestigious name with whom the sculptor wished to be associated. In fact, Le Sueur could perfectly well have been trained under skilled bronze founders active in Paris such as Barthélémy Prieur or Pierre Biard. Indeed, despite their technical excellence, the coarseness of modelling in his major bronzes in England, when compared with—for example—those by Francesco Fanelli, a rival hired latterly by Charles I—let alone those by Giambologna and Antonio Susini—belies a training in Italy.

In 1610 Le Sueur moved to the hôtel of the duc de Nevers, on the site of the hôtel de Nesles, where in 1541 Cellini had established a bronze foundry which was kept going after his departure by his goldsmithing pupils and may still have been functional. In the same year, when Le Sueur had his son Henri baptized, he chose as godparents (instead of the grandparents, as was normal for a first child) Henri de Loménie, a private secretary to Henry IV, and his sister Catherine, which implies that he was socially ambitious. In 1612 he received a prestigious commission for a statue in bronze of the constable of Montmorency to go on a pre-existing bronze horse at Chantilly, the first such statue to be erected in France (its head survives in the Louvre). Its success probably resulted in his official appointment under Louis XIII as *sculpteur ordinaire du roi* in January 1614.

Meanwhile, the demise in 1611 of Prieur perhaps encouraged Le Sueur to turn to the production of statuettes, including one of the young Louis XIII on horseback, signed by the artist, and a larger very similar bronze of the same subject, together with one of Henri IV (all V&A). The latter rears over a fallen enemy, a separate figure that has only recently come to light and been reunited. In these years Le Sueur may also have cast a portrait bust of the court painter Martin Freminet, who died in 1619 (Louvre). In 1617 Le Sueur was contracted to cast four large angels and various other components for the high altar in the church of the Grands Augustins, Paris (dem. 1674). In 1622 he carved a monument to Guillaume du Vair, keeper of the seals (crypt of the abbey of St Denis), and four big commissions ensued for grand tombs with praying figures (*priants*) in the traditional French mode.

By 1620 Le Sueur had lost both parents and his wife, Noémie, and by 1623 a sister too. In 1624 he married Marie Le Senne, and may therefore have been ready for a move. An opportunity arose in mid-1625 with an invitation to accompany to England Charles I's new bride, Henrietta Maria. Louis XIII relinquished to his sister and new brother-in-law the least proficient and least well-paid of the royal bronze founders. Le Sueur wound up his affairs in Paris, and by 1626 was recorded as a foreign 'picture drawer' living near Drury Lane. The following year he received £20 for modelling twelve statues for the catafalque of James I in Westminster Abbey, designed by Inigo Jones. Though ephemeral, these no doubt prepared the sculptor for producing the statuary in bronze required for two great tombs next commissioned from him: the first, in 1628, was for the second duke and duchess of Lennox and Richmond, and the second for the fourth duke of Buckingham (assassinated 1628) and for his duchess (*d.* 1634) (both King Henry VII's chapel, Westminster Abbey). These are, by English standards, impressive and were partly inspired by Pietro Torrigiano's royal tombs with bronze effigies and ornaments of a century earlier. Le Sueur's two pairs of effigies are clad in ornamental armour (recalling the traditional products of his family) or delightfully embroidered and bejewelled dresses, but are stiff and lifeless. Even the allegorical figures of mourners around them are ill-modelled and inexpressive. The only ambitious figure, on the earlier tomb, was one of Fame—supposedly flying in mid-air and trumpeting—which is a competent but uninspired copy of one by Pierre Biard for a tomb in France (1597; Louvre). Both were ultimately derived from 'flying' figures of Mercury by Giambologna.

In 1628 and 1629 Hubert and/or his wife were witnesses at various baptisms in the French church, Threadneedle Street (whose records are vital for his private life), while in December an equestrian portrait of Charles I was commissioned by Sir Richard Weston, then lord treasurer, and later earl of Portland. By mid-January 1630 Le Sueur visited Mortlake Park, Roehampton, to decide on the location in Weston's garden of this statue, described as 'Carolus Magnus' (with the flattering double entendre of the emperor Charlemagne). The statue was to cost £600 and be ready in eighteen months. Le Sueur was enjoined to 'take the advice of the King's riders of great horses for the shape and action both of the horse and his Majesty's figure on the same' (*CSP dom.*, *16 Jan 1630*, 167, 54). Charles I subsequently owned a bronze statuette which may have embodied the first fruits of Le Sueur's studies in the royal stables (Ickworth, Suffolk). The monumental statue is signed and dated 1633. In 1644 parliament ordered the statue to be taken from Roehampton to Covent Garden to be sold. There it was lost sight of, probably in the crypt of St Paul's, Covent Garden, until it was discovered in 1655 and sold for scrap metal to 'John Rivet, a brazier … with strict orders to break it in pieces' (G. Vertue, *Anecdotes of Painting in England*, 3 vols., 1862, 2.394). Rivet pretended to have melted it down and offered for sale items that he claimed to have fashioned from its metal. Actually he had secreted the statue in his yard and produced it after the Restoration, whereupon it was claimed by Weston's son, Jerome, whose widow eventually sold it to Charles II in 1675 for £1600. It was erected at Charing Cross on a high pedestal designed by Christopher Wren or Grinling Gibbons and carved by Joshua Marshall.

In January 1631 the crown began to pay £100 annual rent on a house for the sculptor; by the end of May he had been to Rome and back, to make moulds of certain ancient statues of which the king wanted copies to be cast in bronze for his gardens at St James's Palace. Some are now in the East Terrace Garden at Windsor Castle and in the gardens at Hampton Court. Over the following months there were several payments for bronze statues whose subjects were not always specified, some of which may have been casts from these moulds, while others may have been portrait statues of the king and queen.

Le Sueur's first bust of Charles I and his only one in marble is fully signed and dated 1631 (V&A): the waxed tips of its moustache have weathered away, leaving traces on the cheeks. Its strict frontality and the absence of any implicit movement were very old-fashioned and pedestrian by this date, indicating either Le Sueur's indifference or his incapacity. Recalling far earlier French busts of Charles I's father-in-law, Henri IV, it became the normal 'icon' of the monarch and was widely reproduced in bronze with minor variations of apparel and regalia. Most notable of these is the version showing the king in a helmet with a dragon for its crest, as St George, an image that Charles I particularly favoured (Stourhead, Wiltshire). This was in the Royal Collection, so Le Sueur made greater use of his imagination than usual. The other bronze busts were distributed to significant locations either by the king or his courtiers, including Duke Humfrey's Library in the Bodleian Library, Oxford; St Paul's Church, Hammersmith; and the Market Cross, Chichester. The same iconic head was used by the economical sculptor for his equestrian statue, as well as for several full-length statues of the king on his own (formerly Royal Exchange and St Paul's, Covent Garden, London) wearing armour or paired with one of his queen—equally immobile (Canterbury quadrangle, St John's College, Oxford; also, formerly, Queen Street, London)—or of his father, James I (Winchester Cathedral; also, formerly, on the roofline of the façade of old St Paul's Cathedral, London). All the statues in London fell victim to the iconoclastic zealotry of the Commonwealth in the early 1650s.

It was for Queen Henrietta Maria that Le Sueur executed his most important secular commissions, the bronze figures for two fountains in the grounds of her palace, Somerset House, on the banks of the Thames. The smaller fountain was crowned with a statue of Mercury, for which the king paid £100 in 1639 and—though not further described—this is likely to have been a full-size copy (or even a cast) of Giambologna's celebrated composition, of which a cast had been sent from Florence to Henri IV in France in 1598.

Also copied from Giambologna (albeit perhaps from engravings rather than the original fountain of Neptune in Bologna, which he probably had not seen) was Le Sueur's fountain of Arethusa. The crowning figure, called 'Arethusa' in the earliest description (1659), has sometimes been called Diana, though it sports none of her usual attributes. John Evelyn's attribution of the fountain in 1662 to Le Sueur's Italian rival Fanelli caused further confusion until recently, when close examination showed that its style and bland modelling were instead those of the French bronze founder. The statue is posed as gracefully as Le Sueur knew how in a classical *contrapposto* and with elegantly spread fingers to emphasize her fastidious femininity. Eight subsidiary statues, four boys supporting dolphins with open mouths and four nubile sirens expressing water from their breasts through nozzles, are closely derived from the prototypes by Giambologna. This concept may well have been suggested to the unimaginative but ambitious sculptor by the king or the queen, both of whom were familiar with the work of the older master and also wished to introduce sophisticated Italianate fountains to their country. Despite the overtly pagan and sensuous subject matter—which did offend some of the puritans who beheld it—Oliver Cromwell recognized that it was a prestigious example of classical taste and decreed that it should be removed to Hampton Court. Later still, in 1712, it was removed and the components were mounted incongruously on a high limestone pedestal which destroyed its original pyramidal design (Bushy Park, Middlesex).

Meanwhile, Le Sueur created other tombs for titled patrons, two in Westminster Abbey (Lord and Lady Cottington, 1634; Sir Thomas Richardson, 1635) and one in St Peter's, Wolverhampton (Sir Richard Leveson, 1633). His portrait busts include likenesses of Lord Herbert of Cherbury (1631); Sir Peter Le Maire (1631; St Margaret's Lothbury, London); Robert Bertie, first earl of Lindsey (Yale U. CBA); and Archbishop Laud (1635; St John's College, Oxford). All manifest the same woodenness as his royal portraits, which was to be made embarrassingly apparent by comparison with the busts in marble of the king by François Dieussart and Bernini, which reached England in 1637. Worse was to befall Le Sueur: in 1635 the king granted a pension to an immigrant from Genoa, Francesco Fanelli, who was an expert at casting bronze thinly (and thus economically) and was also a gifted modeller. The last payments from the crown to Le Sueur date from 1637 and 1638, the former being for 'divers brass heads, statues and images' (*CSP dom.*, *1637*, 197, 28), and the latter for the pair of bronze statues of Charles I and James I for Winchester Cathedral, as well as a bust of James I (Banqueting House, Whitehall). Le Sueur was last recorded in London as a witness to a Huguenot baptism on 31 January 1641; by 1643 Peter Besnier had been appointed sculptor to the king and Le Sueur appeared in a legal document in his native Paris. His discomfiture was—fortunately for him—concealed by the general flight of artists from London upon the outbreak of the civil war.

In France Le Sueur had to face competition not only from his well-established contemporary Francesco Bordoni (the son-in-law of Pietro Francavilla), but also from younger sculptors with Italian training, Simon Guillain and Jacques Sarrazin, who were well versed in the new baroque style. Accordingly he fell back on his expertise as a foundryman, in June 1643 casting four copies of a bust by Jean Warin of Cardinal Richelieu, and in 1648 copies of some classical originals in France for the gardens of different courtiers. His daughter Marguérite married well in 1650 and again in 1657, enabling her father and mother to end their days in comfort in a house near St Germain-des-Prés, which they sold in 1658, the last date when Le Sueur was recorded as living; by 1668 his wife was widowed.

An oval medallion initialled W (probably for Claude Warin) and dated 1635 shows Le Sueur balding, smartly clad, and wearing a floppy ruff and a gold chain. The profile is encircled by an inscription emphasizing that he was 'sculptor to two Kings' (i.e. of France and Great Britain). On the reverse some bees hover round new branches sprouting from a blasted tree stump in an open landscape lit by a radiant sun, inscribed 'sudore parta' ('brought forth by the sweat of the brow'; BM). This is a word play on the sculptor's surname, for in French 'sueur' means sweat. CHARLES AVERY

Sources C. Avery, 'Hubert le Sueur: the unworthy Praxiteles of King Charles I', *Walpole Society*, 48 (1980–82), 135–209, pls. 31–62 [repr. in C. Avery, *Studies in European sculpture*, 2 (1988), 145–235] • C. Avery, 'Hubert le Sueur's portraits of King Charles I in bronze at Stourhead, Ickworth and elsewhere', *National Trust Studies*, 1 (1979), 128–47 [repr. in C. Avery, *Studies in European sculpture*, 1 (1981), 189–204] • D. Howarth, 'Charles I, sculpture and sculptors', *The late king's goods*, ed. A. MacGregor (1989), 73–113 • P. Evelyn, 'Hubert le Sueur's equestrian bronzes at the Victoria and Albert Museum', *Burlington Magazine*, 137 (1995), 85–92 • G. Bresc-Bautier, 'L'activité parisienne d'Hubert le Sueur sculpteur du roi (connu de 1596 à 1658)', *Bulletin de la Société de l'Histoire de l'Art Français* (1985), 35–54 • C. Avery, 'Le Sueur, Hubert', *The dictionary of art*, ed. J. Turner (1996) • G. Fisher and J. Newman, 'A fountain design by Inigo Jones', *Burlington Magazine*, 127 (1985), 531–2 • J. Harris, 'The Diana fountain at Hampton Court', *Burlington Magazine*, 111 (1969), 444 • M. Whinney, *Sculpture in Britain, 1530 to 1830*, rev. J. Physick, 2nd edn (1988), 86–90 • *CSP dom.*, *1630–40* • D. G. Denoon, 'The statue of King

Charles I at Charing Cross', *Transactions of the London and Middlesex Archaeological Society*, new ser., 6 (1933), 460–85
Archives Archives Nationales, Paris, Minutier Central
Likenesses C. Warin, bronze medallion, 1635, BM; repro. in M. Jones, *A catalogue of the French medals in the British Museum*, 2: 1600–1672 (1988), no. 299

Le Sueur, Pierre (1811–1853), politician in Jersey, was born in November 1811 in a house in Broad Street (La Grande Rue), St Helier, Jersey, the youngest son of François Le Sueur, a blacksmith on the island. He was educated at Le Gros's school, St Helier, and in 1827, aged fifteen, became a clerk in a lawyers' office (Le Gallais and Hugh Godfray) which was the headquarters of the Laurel (Conservative) Party. In 1835 he went to study law in Paris under Beaufils, and on his return to Jersey his employers in the law firm obtained his nomination as one of the six advocates (barristers) in the island. He was sworn in on 10 December 1836 and (after further study in Paris) began to practise in the following October. He surprised his patrons by declining to join the Laurel ranks, becoming instead an ardent supporter of the Rose (Liberal) Party, of which he soon became leader. His name as an advocate was made largely through his dogged and ultimately successful defence from 1837 to 1841 of the Revd Edward Durell, rector of St Saviour's, Jersey, who was accused of sodomy. Le Sueur's legal services were much in demand, and the call for them was usually well justified by his skill in finding loopholes for clients who seemed to have little hope. His opponent in the Royal Court (as in the States, the island parliament) was frequently François Godfray, a leading member of the Laurel Party. Le Sueur's cool and quietly persuasive method of arguing was in marked contrast to Godfray's tempestuous oratory.

In 1839 Le Sueur was elected constable (chief administrative official) of St Helier parish. He held this post until his death, being re-elected four times and having a seat in the States by virtue of his office. It was in this capacity that Le Sueur performed his most memorable work, showing himself one of the most effective constables in Jersey's history. The rapidly growing town of St Helier, and the island as a whole, benefited in many ways from his reforming zeal. At a time when public health reform, especially by providing effective sewerage systems, was being pressed on the British mainland by Edwin Chadwick, Le Sueur inaugurated in 1845 and carried through (against complaints from ratepayers about the cost) the construction of a complete network of underground sewers in St Helier. He also commenced a fire brigade, had some of the streets widened, and insisted that slum landlords improve their properties. Public appreciation of his many-sided efforts was eventually his. In 1848 he was presented with a handsome gift of plate, vases, and silverware bought by 1200 subscribers at a cost of £330, a very substantial sum for the time.

Despite his commitment to popular welfare, Le Sueur had to uphold the law when confronted with popular disturbance, and in 1847 he intervened effectively to prevent the theft of flour from the St Helier town mills by a large crowd. Complaints about the high price of bread, caused partly by protectionist policies, led hundreds of workers to march on the town mills and drive away waggons loaded with flour. But Le Sueur was on the scene and managed to stop this process, compelling the return of the flour to the mills. Subsequent rioting was quelled by the local militia. On the day after this incident he opened a fund to relieve distress caused by the dearth. Two years later he had to make special arrangements to deal with the spread of cholera from France. In regard to constitutional reform Le Sueur favoured moderate change, but he was a loyal 'nationalist' who defended the States against current attempts to reduce its powers and to institute the direct authority of the Westminster parliament over Jersey.

Le Sueur died suddenly on 16 January 1853, aged only forty-one. He was buried in Green Street cemetery, St Helier, and an obelisk erected to his memory by public subscription still stands in Broad Street, opposite the house where he was born. In 1873 the States voted to commission from W. M. Hay portraits of both Le Sueur and François Godfray, and these hang in the Royal Court.

Ian Machin

Sources G. R. Balleine, *A biographical dictionary of Jersey*, [1] [1948], 451–4 · J. D. Kelleher, *The triumph of the country: the rural community in nineteenth-century Jersey* (1994) · G. R. Balleine, *History of Jersey*, rev. M. Syvret and J. Stevens (1981) · J. Stevens, *Victorian voices: an introduction to the papers of Sir John Le Couteur* (1969)
Likenesses W. M. Hay, oils, 1873, Royal Court, St Helier, Jersey, Channel Islands

Letchworth, Thomas (1738–1784), Quaker minister, was born on 5 October 1738 at or near Woodbridge, in Suffolk, the fifth child of Robert Letchworth (*c.*1694–1782), a Quaker leather stay maker, and his wife, Elizabeth (*c.*1704–1784), daughter of John Squirrell of Ipswich. During his childhood, his parents moved to Norwich, where, at seven years of age, he preached from a tombstone. The family moved to London about 1755; Letchworth completed his schooling at Joseph Dancer's school at Hertford, after which he served an apprenticeship with J. Brecknock, an Anglican shopkeeper in Epping. Soon afterwards he embarked in trade, as a tallow chandler, from a shop in Crispin Street, Spitalfields, London, where he continued to live until at least 1765. On 21 March 1759 he married Sarah (1742–1828), daughter of Thomas and Sarah Burge of London, at Savoy meeting-house in the Strand; Sarah was a woman of considerable property. They had three sons, two of whom died in infancy. Having moved to Ampthill in Bedfordshire, after a short period Letchworth returned to London and lived at Wandsworth Common. Not a natural businessman, he gave up his shop and moved into publishing and bookselling, editing the short-lived *Monthly Ledger, or, Literary Repositor* from 1773 to 1775; in the latter year he published the first edition in England of the journal of John Woolman, the American Quaker.

Letchworth was recognized as a minister in Devonshire House meeting, London, while still a young man. He was an earnest and eloquent preacher, remembered as 'an intelligent, well-informed, and liberal-minded Christian'

(Matthews, 4), whose abiding interests were 'the mysterious operations of the human mind [and] the passions which actuate it' (*Twelve Discourses*, preface). He appears not to have travelled widely in the ministry but he was well known in London. His power as a preacher attracted many to his local meeting at the Park Meeting-House, Southwark. Twelve of his discourses, taken down in shorthand, were published posthumously in 1787. Opinions of Letchworth within the Quaker community were divided. To his admirers he was cultured, fluent, and 'entirely devoid of sectarian bigotry' (Frost, 174). The plainer elements of the Quaker establishment cooled towards him, probably because of his liberal views, but he continued to have the friendship of the wealthier, more worldly members of the society, who latterly supported him financially.

A spare figure, who had been consumptive when young, Letchworth fell ill early in 1784 and moved to Walworth to be nearer to medical friends in London. He died at the home of his friend Joseph Rand at Newbury in Berkshire on 7 November 1784, and was buried (at his own request) in the Quaker burial-ground at Reading on 14 November. He was survived by his wife, who died on 7 October 1828.

ANGUS J. L. WINCHESTER

Sources W. Matthews, *The life and character of Thomas Letchworth* (1786) • *The records and recollections of James Jenkins*, ed. J. W. Frost (1984), 156–7, 174–7 • *Twelve discourses delivered chiefly at the meeting house … in the park, Southwark, by the late Thomas Letchworth* (1787) • digest registers of births, marriages, and burials, RS Friends, Lond. [Suffolk, London and Middlesex, Berkshire and Oxfordshire quarterly meetings] • 'Dictionary of Quaker biography', RS Friends, Lond. [card index] • *DNB* • *Annual Monitor* (1830), 26
Likenesses oils, *c*.1770, Museum of Fine Arts, Boston

Le Texier, Anthony A. (*c*.1737–1814), monologuist and theatre manager, was born about 1737 in Lyons, France, of good, though not noble, family. Little is known of his early life, but by 1770 he was a cashier in the office of the ferme générale at Lyons. Having a strong inclination towards the theatre, he participated in amateur theatricals wherever he could, one particular triumph being in Jean-Jacques Rousseau's *Pygmalion* in June 1770. Since his social status prevented him from becoming a professional actor, he began to hold play-readings in which he would perform all the parts himself.

By 1774 Le Texier's readings had become popular and, abandoning his secure position with the ferme générale, he went to Paris. After only two recitals there he was a sensation. However, the extraordinary amount of adulation he received turned his head, and he became insufferably arrogant. When reciting in front of Louis XV, who, exhausted after a day's hunting, fell asleep during his performance, Le Texier is said to have woken the king by slamming a book in front of him. Once he had lost royal support—the king considered his performances 'too noisy' (Highfill, Burnim & Langhans, *BDA*)—official questions started being asked about his having left his post at Lyons without permission, and he was accused of peculation. He fled Paris, spent a few months acting comedies before Voltaire at Ferney, and, via the Austrian Netherlands and Weimar, finally reached England in September 1775.

In London Le Texier became acquainted with David Garrick, who thought his talents 'very extraordinary' (Hedgepath, 273). Their initial correspondence shows a relationship of mutual respect and admiration, but when Le Texier tried to exploit the friendship by urging Garrick to intercede with the French ministry Garrick refused. Not long after, possibly because of Le Texier's arrogant behaviour, he withdrew his patronage.

Apart from liaising with Garrick, Le Texier was a frequent guest of Henry and Hester Thrale, of Horace Walpole at Strawberry Hill, and of many others. He also recited in front of George III and participated in amateur theatricals at various country houses. In 1777, for example, he took the title role in Rousseau's *Pygmalion* and played the violin for George Mason-Villiers, Viscount Villiers, and his guests at Bolney Court, Henley-on-Thames, Buckinghamshire. In that same year he began bringing out by subscription the *Journal Étranger de Littérature, des Spectacles et de Politique*. This magazine was especially valuable for its theatrical criticism, but for unknown reasons it was discontinued after a year.

Le Texier was particularly associated with the house of William Craven, sixth Baron Craven, and his wife, Elizabeth (formerly Lady Elizabeth Berkeley), at Newbury in Berkshire. Lady Craven was the energizing force behind various amateur theatricals, for which she employed Le Texier's assistance. At a charity performance directed by Lady Craven at Newbury Town Hall on 11 and 12 May 1778, Le Texier played the Dutch Gardener in her translation of *Le somnambule*, by Antoine de Ferrol, comte de Pont-de-Veyle. This was an opéra comique in which Le Texier probably also sang.

From 1778 to 1779 Le Texier was acting manager of a small but good company of singers and dancers in a King's Theatre season which included the first performances of the famous castrato Pacchierotti. He returned for the following season, but resigned or was discharged on or after 27 December 1779.

From around 1780 Le Texier resumed giving solo readings at his house in Lisle Street. For English audiences his one-man shows had the added allure of being in French. Sylas Neville, describing an evening at Le Texier's in his diary, mentions that 'his pronunciation is extremely pure & correct, which makes it an excellent amusement for those who wish to improve themselves in the French language' (Highfill, Burnim & Langhans, *BDA*). Another way in which Le Texier helped promote French culture was his publication, between 1785 and 1787, of forty plays by various French playwrights.

Between 1792 and 1798 Le Texier was engaged as gentleman-in-ordinary to the household of the margrave and margravine of Ansbach (formerly Lady Craven) at Brandenburg House. A sort of private theatrical manager, he wrote, acted, directed, and had a decisive part in arranging visual and musical effects. His wife, the Drury Lane dancer Mary Ross, whom he had married by 1793, and his daughter also took part in the presentations he organized.

For the season of 1795–6 Le Texier had been recalled as acting manager at the King's Theatre. On 25 May 1797 he planned and conducted a celebration of the wedding of George III's daughter Princess Charlotte, princess royal, to Prince Friedrich of Württemberg at Ranelagh. On that occasion he was also responsible for a magnificent display of fireworks. Together with Joseph Rossi, an opera dancer, Le Texier had been involved in organizing pyrotechnics since at least 1791.

The *True Briton* of 10 April 1797 named Le Texier as a bankrupt, but given his many connections this probably did not prevent him from continuing his theatrical activities. However, the remainder of his life was spent in comparative obscurity, and the circumstances of his death in 1814 are unknown. MIRIAM G. MURTIN

Sources Highfill, Burnim & Langhans, *BDA* • S. Rosenfeld, *Temples of Thespis: some private theatres and theatricals in England and Wales, 1700–1820* (1978) • F. Hedgepath, *Garrick's French friends* (1912) • A. A. Le Texier, *Ideas on the opera offered to the subscriber, creditors and amateurs of that theatre by Mr. Le Texier, translated from the French* (1791) • *True Briton* (10 April 1797)

Lethaby, William Richard (1857–1931), educationist and architect, was born at Grosvenor Street, Barnstaple, on 18 January 1857, the only son and youngest of two children of Richard Pyle Lethaby (*d.* *c.*1904), of Barnstaple, and his wife, Mary Rowe Crago (*d.* 1870). His father was a lay preacher of the local Bible Christian chapel, and Lethaby grew up in a strictly religious, working-class household. It was also a politically radical one, shaping the visions of a free and fair society that impelled his architectural life.

Early life Lethaby's father was a skilled carver and gilder. The boy, known in the family as Willem, showed an early aptitude for making and inventing, rigging ships, erecting peepshows, and forming shapes out of a geometric toy called Tangram. The busy seaport routines of Barnstaple entranced him: 'ship-shape' was the phrase he later applied to prime examples of functional design. Lethaby resisted his early formal schooling, first at an institution run by a Plymouth Brother, then at the local grammar school, finding that 'Arithmetic and grammar and what they call history were horrid bores and mostly gibberish to me' (W. R. Lethaby, *Home and Country Arts*, 1923, 131). He was a child who learned best by doing. Education through experience was to be the basis of his work as a teacher of design.

Once he had enrolled at the Barnstaple Literary and Scientific Institute, taking part-time night classes in drawing, Lethaby's special abilities emerged. He now won the first of many art and architectural prizes awarded to him over the next decade. He came under the beneficent if erratic influence of a local architect, poet, and artist, Alexander Lauder, to whom he was articled at the age of fourteen. Lauder had a generous approach to building crafts, insisting that all his labourers should have an understanding of one another's craft 'so that each might feel that he

William Richard Lethaby (1857–1931), by unknown photographer

was building a house and not just practising carpentry, bricklaying or plumbing' (*RIBA Journal*, 64, 1957, 218). Lethaby's holistic attitude to architecture was being formed at an early stage.

In 1878 the highly motivated but still excruciatingly shy young Lethaby left Barnstaple. First he joined the office of Richard Waite at Duffield in Derbyshire, a practice specializing in agricultural building. He then worked briefly with T. H. Baker in Leicester. After winning the Royal Institute of British Architects (RIBA) Soane medal for 1878–9 for a Renaissance-style 'building to accommodate four learned societies', he set out to prove himself in London. His friend and contemporary C. R. Ashbee, in an unpublished memoir (King's College Library, Cambridge), was later to identify the Dick Whittington strain in Lethaby. His high promise was recognized by Norman Shaw, the most successful Victorian country house architect, who appointed Lethaby his chief assistant in succession to Ernest Newton. From relative obscurity Lethaby now found himself, aged only twenty-one, in charge of one of the most sophisticated London architectural practices of its day, where his colleagues included Edward Prior, Mervyn Macartney, Arthur Keen, and Gerald Horsley. His assiduous brilliance made him invaluable. An acquaintance once referred to Lethaby as Shaw's pupil. 'No', Shaw replied, 'on the contrary it is I who am Lethaby's pupil' (Weir).

During his decade in Shaw's office, from 1879 to 1889, Lethaby worked on such now famous buildings as New

Scotland Yard, London, and Cragside, Northumberland. The immense elaborately carved marble fireplace he designed for Cragside is a perhaps surprising early work from the critic who would later eschew useless decoration. But Lethaby embodied numerous artistic contradictions. Strongly influenced by Ruskin, Lethaby was travelling widely in Britain and abroad, especially in northern France, where Gothic church architecture was a revelation to him. His intense appreciation of the buildings of the past and his urge to relate past experience to the present made Lethaby the most important theoretician of design and architecture in the first quarter of the twentieth century.

Architectural practice In 1889 Lethaby set up his own practice in Bloomsbury. He completed only six buildings in his lifetime. Four of these were country houses: Avon Tyrrell, near Christchurch, on the edge of the New Forest (1893); The Hurst at Four Oaks, near Birmingham (1893); Melsetter House at Hoy in the Orkneys (1898); and High Coxlease at Lyndhurst, Hampshire (1900–01). Having by now been drawn into the arts and crafts circles of William Morris and Philip Webb, whose biography he would eventually write, Lethaby departed from the more conventional architectural approach of Shaw's office. At Melsetter House, in particular, he achieved a highly original combination of the rational and the romantic. May Morris, on a visit, recognized Melsetter, in its Orkney island setting, with its steeply pitched roofs and white roughcast walls, as a building out of one of her father's prose romances, 'a sort of fairy palace on the edge of great northern seas' (*RIBA Journal*, 39, 1932, 303). Lethaby's only urban building, the Eagle Insurance office in Colmore Row, Birmingham (1899–1900), is a tall, austere stone structure surmounted by a highly characteristic cornice featuring a large eagle flying through symbolic suns and clouds.

Lethaby's vision of architecture as 'building touched with emotion' (Lethaby, *Ernest Gimson*, 2) reached its apotheosis in his last commission. The small-scale village church at Brockhampton in Herefordshire (1901–2) is built of local red sandstone. The roof is suspended on massive jointed stone arches. The interior has a simple strength and spiritual grandeur that anticipate Le Corbusier's La Chapelle at Ronchamp. The roof is a high concrete vault covered by traditional local thatch. Brockhampton has frequently been cited as one of the greatest monuments of the arts and crafts movement (Davey, 64). It was built by direct labour, in the manner recommended by Lethaby's mentor Philip Webb. But the strain of acting as his own master builder brought the abnormally sensitive Lethaby to the verge of nervous collapse.

Arts and crafts education As a young man, Lethaby had experienced the exhilaration of the beginnings of the arts and crafts movement. He had been a privileged attender at the legendary suppers at Gatti's in the Strand, when Morris addressed his young disciples on the socialist future. Lethaby became convinced of the redemptive role of handicraft in achieving a newly democratic social order: 'beauty can only be brought back to common life by our doing common work in an interesting way' (Lethaby, *Form in Civilisation*, 162). He was one of the moving spirits in the foundation of the Art Workers' Guild in 1884 and the Arts and Crafts Exhibition Society four years later. With his friends Ernest Gimson, Sidney Barnsley, and other young architect-craftsmen he set up Kenton & Co., a small idealistic furniture making company obviously inspired by William Morris's own firm. There is a rare example of Lethaby's furniture in the Victoria and Albert Museum, London.

From the middle 1890s Lethaby's considerable energies were concentrated on disseminating Morris's ideas to a new generation, expanding upon Morris's view of the importance of manual skills. Lethaby insisted 'A work of art is first of all a well-made thing' (Lethaby, *Form in Civilisation*, 221). In 1894 he was appointed art inspector to the newly established London county council's technical education board. When the board set up its own specialist training school, the Central School of Arts and Crafts, in 1896, Lethaby was appointed joint director with the sculptor George Frampton. Since Frampton was rarely present, Lethaby had freedom in evolving the curriculum and appointing his own staff.

Lethaby put a new emphasis on workshop training and recruited as teachers distinguished craft practitioners. May Morris gave classes in embroidery; Douglas Cockerell taught bookbinding; Alexander Fisher led a revival of the lost art of enamelling. The most influential teacher was Edward Johnston, whose classes in writing and illuminating, attended by Eric Gill and Noel Rooke, resuscitated the book arts in Britain. Lethaby was himself an inspirational presence, described by a student as patrolling the school 'like a white moustached rabbit, with a quick, dark eye' (Backemeyer and Gronberg, 19). The Central School, as it developed first in Regent Street and then in its purpose-designed new premises in Southampton Row, affected the whole direction of twentieth-century European design education. The German design expert Hermann Muthesius described it as 'the best organised contemporary art school' (N. Pevsner, *Academies of Art Past and Present*, 1940, 265). The Bauhaus, when it opened in 1918 in Weimar, was set up on similar lines.

In 1900 Lethaby was appointed professor of the school of ornament and design at the Royal College of Art, where he attempted, with partial success, to introduce a study of the practical needs of production into a syllabus up to then dominated by the copying of drawings and plaster casts. He occupied these two key London educational posts concurrently until his resignation from the Central School in 1911.

Design theory Lethaby was a reformer whose beliefs in the moral significance of art were expressed in the surge of books, articles, and lectures that continued for five decades, amounting to the most impressive body of sustained design polemic since John Ruskin. His first substantial piece of writing, *Architecture, Mysticism and Myth* (1891), defined and encouraged the spiritual instincts which ran in counterpoint to the simple life principles of the arts and crafts. Lethaby's wide-ranging study of artistic symbolism went into several editions, being republished as *Architecture, Nature and Magic* in 1956. His deep understanding of the arcane and exotic was shown in *The Church of Sancta Sophia, Constantinople* (1894), written with H. Swainson. This detailed analysis was the result of a visit made in 1893, when Lethaby disguised himself in women's clothes to enter the building, then barred to English men. Lethaby's championing of the Byzantine was responsible for a new eastern tendency in British architecture, notably the Roman Catholic cathedral in Westminster by John Bentley. Lethaby's knowledge of the buildings of England was unrivalled in his period. He had joined William Morris's Society for the Protection of Ancient Buildings as a young man and had become the conservation lobby's most influential propagandist by the turn of the century.

In 1906 the child of the Bible Christian chapel was appointed surveyor to the fabric of Westminster Abbey, a post Lethaby sustained until 1927. He compared his role to that of 'the family butler' (*TLS*, 17 April 1933), introducing a new policy of mending and cleaning which led to the discovery of many hidden treasures including medieval carvings and wall paintings. Lethaby's *Westminster Abbey and the King's Craftsmen: a Study of Medieval Building* (1906) was followed by *Westminster Abbey Re-Examined* (1925). His concerns for the future of great cities, particularly his beloved London, produced some of the most cogent of his writings. He resisted any schemes to 'grandify' London. For Lethaby, intimacy was of the essence. He suggested (in a lecture to the Arts and Crafts Exhibition Society in 1896) that 'we should begin on the humblest scale by sweeping streets better, washing and whitewashing the houses, and taking care that such railings and lamp-posts as are required are good lamp-posts and railings, the work of the best artists available'.

From his own close involvement in the techniques of handmaking Lethaby arrived at an acceptance of the potential of the machine. His practical background made him appreciative of new materials and constructional techniques. His collaborative competition entry for the new Liverpool Cathedral (1902; not built) is structurally original, exploiting mass concrete. From around 1910 Lethaby was urging the use of scientific method in designing to create a democratic 'efficiency style'. In defining his machine aesthetic he regarded a good industrial product as a work of art 'in a secondary order—shapely, smooth, strong, well fitting, useful; in fact, like a machine itself' (Lethaby, *Form in Civilisation*, 36).

Lethaby's artistic humanism reached its widest circulation with the publication of *Form in Civilisation: Collected Papers on Art and Labour* (1922). This shows him as the pioneer of rationality, the crucial link between the arts and crafts movement and the Design and Industries' Association, which he helped to found in 1915. From his brilliantly concise, impassioned writings emerged the concept 'form follows function', which dominated European modernist design.

Personal life and reputation Lethaby was a small, neat man with a genius for aphorisms: 'Modernism conceived as a style is only archaeology'; 'Art can only be done before people know about it'; 'The superior man is willing to accept inferior things' (*TLS*, 17 April 1953). His English radical conservative vision of design embraced 'simple well-off house-keeping in the country, with tea in the garden; Boy-scouting and tennis in flannels' (Lethaby, *Form in Civilisation*, 209). His moral qualms and his dilatory manner made him an unpopular committee member. He rode his bicycle as if he and the machine were one. He overcame his emotional reticence to marry, late in life and after a long courtship, Edith Rutgers Crosby (1850–1927), in 1901. She was six years his elder, the intellectual daughter of a Berlin clergyman. She cheerfully undertook such domestic duties as transcribing his writings for the printer and translating documents of the Deutscher Werkbund for the Design and Industries' Association, while regretting his dislike of organized religion. They had no children and she predeceased him. When Lethaby died in London on 17 July 1931 he was buried with her in the churchyard at Hartley Wintney near their country home in Hampshire. The tombstone is inscribed 'Love and Labour are all'.

By the time of his death Lethaby had become an isolated figure. Depressed by what he saw as widespread dilution of the modernist principles he had espoused, he refused the award of the RIBA gold medal in 1924. It was only with the growth of design history studies, from the 1970s, that W. R. Lethaby, with his advocacy of the unassuming, unadorned, and practical, began to be seen as the formative influence on British twentieth-century design.

FIONA MACCARTHY

Sources G. Rubens, *William Richard Lethaby: his life and work, 1857–1931* (1986) • S. Backemeyer and T. Gronberg, eds., *W. R. Lethaby, 1857–1931: architecture, design and education* (1984) • T. Garnham, *Melsetter House* (1993) • P. Davey, 'The guide: the search for earthly paradise', *Arts and crafts architecture* (1980), 56–67 • W. R. Lethaby, *Form in civilisation: collected papers on art and labour* (1922) • W. R. Lethaby, *Philip Webb and his work* (1935) • W. R. Lethaby, 'Ernest Gimson's London days', in W. R. Lethaby, A. H. Powell, and F. L. Griggs, *Ernest Gimson: his life and work* (1924), 1–10 • R. W. S. Weir, *William Richard Lethaby* (1938) • *CGPLA Eng. & Wales* (1931)

Archives Central St Martin's College of Art and Design, London, archive • Royal College of Art, London, archive • Society for the Protection of Ancient Buildings, London, minutes and papers | Art Workers' Guild, London, minutes and papers • BL, corresp. with Sir Sydney Cockerell, Add. MSS 52730–52732 • NAAD, London, records of Arts and Crafts Exhibition Society • NAAD, London, records of Design and Industries' Association • Norfolk RO, report on ancient bishop's throne of Norwich Cathedral • RIBA BAL, corresp. with William Begley • RIBA BAL, letters to Lord Manners and notes relating to Acton Tyrell • RIBA BAL, corresp. with H. H. Peach • RIBA BAL, papers relating to Philip Webb and his work, incl. MS and typescript drafts • RIBA BAL, letters to Stephen Wheatley • V&A, letters to Sir Sydney Cockerell

Likenesses W. Rothenstein, drawing, *c.*1921 • G. Bayes, bronze bust, *c.*1923, Art Workers' Guild, London • G. Bayes, bronze plaque, *c.*1924, RIBA • photograph, RIBA BAL, photographic collection [*see illus.*]

Wealth at death £16,057 9*s.* 3*d.*: probate, 24 Aug 1931, *CGPLA Eng. & Wales*

Lethame, John (*d. c.*1549). *See under* College of justice, procurators of the (*act.* 1532).

Lethbridge, Joseph Watts (1817–1885), minister of the Countess of Huntingdon's Connexion and Congregational minister, was born at Plymouth on 20 January 1817. He entered Cheshunt College in 1842, and in 1846 the Countess of Huntingdon's Connexion, in which he served at Kidderminster, at Rochdale, and then at Melbourne, Derbyshire (1850–55). He joined the Congregationalists, and was placed in charge of their church at Byfield, Northamptonshire. In 1862 he moved to Leicester, and from there in 1868 to Wellingborough where he retired in 1883, and where he died on 27 July 1885. He published a number of minor works, including *Woman the Glory of Man* (1856), and *The Idyls of Solomon: the Hebrew Marriage Week Arranged in Dialogue* (1878). J. M. Rigg, *rev.* Timothy C. F. Stunt

Sources *Congregational Year Book* (1892) • Boase, *Mod. Eng. biog.*

Lethbridge, Walter Stephens (1772–1831), miniature painter, was born on 13 October 1772 in Charleton, Devon, the only child of William Lethbridge, farmer, and his wife, Mary Stephens. He was educated at a school in Kingsbridge, Devon, and then apprenticed to a house painter named Drew before acting as assistant to a travelling artist in England and Scotland for several years. He returned to Devon to marry Elizabeth, *née* Mudge (*d.* 1826) on 4 July 1797 in Kingsbridge, and in 1798 they moved to London where some sources say Lethbridge enrolled as a student at the Royal Academy Schools.

Having taken lodgings at an establishment in Covent Garden run by a theatrical agent, Lethbridge soon developed a large clientele among the leading figures of the stage. He moved to a studio in the Strand about 1802, where he worked for almost thirty years, broadening his patronage to include leading society figures and members of the aristocracy, such as William Chambers (Abbot Hall Art Gallery, Kendal), Dr John Wolcot (alias Peter Pindar), and Samuel Horsley, bishop of St Asaph (National Portrait Gallery, London). His likenesses of the earl and countess of Huntingdon and Henry Nugent Bell were engraved for Bell's *Huntingdon Peerage* (1821). Lethbridge exhibited at the Royal Academy and the Society of British Artists between 1801 and 1829, only retiring to Plymouth in 1830 after having made an unpopular second marriage following the death of his first wife. His second wife, whom he had married on 19 March 1827 at St Martin-in-the-Fields, London, and who outlived him, was also called Elizabeth Mudge. A relative of his late wife, she had lived with the Lethbridges for several years as a domestic servant. He died in Plymouth of a stroke in May 1831 and was buried in Stonehouse churchyard, Plymouth. V. Remington

Sources W. Mannin, 'Memoir of the life of Walter Stephens Lethbridge', NPG, Heinz Archive and Library, MS 1863 • D. Foskett, *Miniatures: dictionary and guide* (1987), 343, 589 • B. S. Long, *British miniaturists* (1929), 271 • L. R. Schidlof, *The miniature in Europe in the 16th, 17th, 18th, and 19th centuries*, 1 (1964), 497 • Graves, *RA exhibitors* • B. Stewart and M. Cutten, *The dictionary of portrait painters in Britain up to 1920* (1997) • G. C. Williamson, *Catalogue of a collection of miniatures belonging to the Lord Hothfield* (1916), 79–80 • R. Walker, *The eighteenth and early nineteenth century miniatures in the collection of her majesty the queen* (1992), 352 • *IGI* • parish registers, Charleton, Devon, 1560–1861

Likenesses W. S. Lethbridge, self-portrait, watercolour on ivory, exh. RA 1818 (with his wife); Christie's, 13 May 1997

Letheby, Henry (1816–1876), analytical chemist and public health official, was born in Plymouth. He began his study of chemistry at the Cornwall Polytechnic Society in Falmouth. In 1837 he enrolled in Aldersgate Street medical school, where he was a class prizewinner and subsequently assistant of Jonathan Pereira (1804–1853), professor of chemistry at the London Hospital and of materia medica at the Pharmaceutical Society. Letheby became a licentiate of the Society of Apothecaries in 1837, and graduated MB from London University (1842) and MA and PhD from an unknown German university in 1858 (he was probably a non-resident student). Letheby's early research interests were in comparative anatomy and in the late 1840s and early 1850s he published papers on the leech, on electric fishes, and on human pathological anatomy.

After succeeding Pereira in the London Hospital chair of chemistry and toxicology in 1846, Letheby began to follow his mentor's interests in practical and forensic chemistry, particularly gas and water analysis and toxicology. By 1848 he was sufficiently prominent to receive *The Lancet's* endorsement for the prestigious appointment of City of London medical officer of health, but came fourth behind John Simon. On Simon's appointment in 1855 as medical officer to the General Board of Health, Letheby was elected as the City's medical officer; he was already serving as its gas examiner. By this time he had become active in the crusade against the adulteration of foods and drugs and, in a controversy with Arthur Hassall, claimed credit for much of the scientific work that led to the first anti-adulteration act (1855).

Letheby served as medical officer (and after 1855 as public analyst) for nineteen years during a period of depopulation as the City became a financial centre. While he was successful in building a department that improved housing, prosecuted vendors of adulterated foods, and led to significantly lowered mortality, Letheby never acquired the popularity of his more colourful predecessor, Simon. It was complained that Letheby treated his City posts as part-time work and also that he was a paid partisan of the London water companies, then under scrutiny for providing inadequate supplies of poor quality water. In 1861 Letheby had begun a series of monthly water analyses, underwritten by the companies, which tended to give an optimistic view of the quality of the water supply; in 1867 he was almost the only expert to exonerate water from causing cholera in east London.

Because of failing health, Letheby resigned his City posts in February 1874. He was a member of the Chemical and Linnean societies, and a founding member of the Society of Metropolitan Medical Officers, whose president he was in 1874. His most lasting work is chronicled in his annual reports on the health of the City of London. He was also author of *Food, its Varieties, Chemical Composition, etc.* (1870), first given as the Cantor lectures to the Royal Society of Arts, and translated into French in 1869. He was also

Henry Letheby (1816–1876), by W. & D. Downey

an innovator in photometric approaches to gas analysis and the colorimetric analysis of water. Letheby died on 28 March 1876 at his home, 17 Sussex Place, Regent's Park, London, and was buried in Highgate cemetery on 30 March. He was survived by his wife, Elizabeth.

CHRISTOPHER HAMLIN

Sources *Medical Press and Circular* (5 April 1876), 290–91 · *JCS*, [29] (1876), 618 · R. Lambert, *Sir John Simon, 1816–1904, and English social administration* (1963) · C. Hamlin, *A science of impurity: water analysis in nineteenth century Britain* (1990) · E. W. Stieb and G. Sonnedecker, *Drug adulteration: detection and control in nineteenth-century Britain* (1966) · *Chemical News* (7 April 1876), 146 · *ILN* (15 April 1876), 373–4 · *The Analyst*, 1 (1876), 15 · *BMJ* (8 April 1876), 451 · *The Lancet* (13 Oct 1855), 348, 351

Archives Guildhall RO, reports and records as City of London medical officer of health

Likenesses W. & D. Downey, photograph, NPG [*see illus.*] · engravings (after photographs), repro. in *The Graphic*, 13 (1876), 381 · wood-engraving (after a photograph by Barraud and Jerrard), NPG; repro. in *ILN*, 373 · woodcut, NPG

Wealth at death £25,000: probate, 5 May 1876, *CGPLA Eng. & Wales*

Letherland, Joseph (1699–1764), physician, was born at Stratford upon Avon, Warwickshire. He entered the University of Leiden on 30 September 1722, and graduated MD on 5 July 1724 with an inaugural dissertation, 'Veterum medicorum sententiae de phrenitide curanda', which was published in the same year. He was made a doctor of medicine of Cambridge by royal mandate on 9 April 1736, and thus qualified for the fellowship of the Royal College of Physicians. He was admitted there as a candidate on 30 September 1736, and as a fellow on 30 September 1737, and subsequently held the office of censor and other college posts. He was elected physician to St Thomas's Hospital on 7 July 1736, and resigned in 1759. In 1761 Letherland was appointed physician to Queen Charlotte on the recommendation of William Heberden (1710–1801), who had declined the honour.

Letherland always practised in London, but never became well known to the public, though he was highly regarded by his colleagues for his knowledge and professional achievements. His classical learning was shown in a reply to Conyers Middleton's dissertation on the servile nature of Roman physicians, in which he vindicated the position of the Roman doctors: *Notae breves in dissertationem de medicorum apud Romanos conditione a C. Middleton editam* (1726). This was his only individual publication, but he is known to have contributed to John Fothergill's *Account of the Sore Throat Attended with Ulcers* (1748). The historical section, which identified the disease as that described by Spanish physicians in the sixteenth and seventeenth centuries, is accepted to be his work. Indeed, he has the credit of being the first to draw attention to this disease (diphtheria) in 1739, though he modestly never asserted his claim to priority.

Letherland died in London on 31 March 1764, and was buried in the church of St Mary Aldermanbury, where a memorial to him was placed.

J. F. PAYNE, *rev.* CLAIRE L. NUTT

Sources Munk, *Roll* · E. Peacock, *Index to English speaking students who have graduated at Leyden University* (1883) · St Thomas's Hospital, London · S. C. Lawrence, *Charitable knowledge: hospital pupils and practitioners in eighteenth-century London* (1996)

Lethieullier, Sir John (1632/3–1719), merchant and local politician, was the eldest of the three sons of Jane Delafort of London and Jan le Thieullier (1591–1679), a French protestant from Valenciennes who was brought to England in 1605 and established himself first in Ilford, Essex, and later in Lewisham, Kent. John was to become one of the most distinguished and successful members of his large and prosperous family, and he occupies a significant place in that second generation of Huguenot families which, like his friends the Houblons, distinguished themselves in late seventeenth-century London trade and contributed notably to the 'financial revolution' of the 1690s and beyond. Under the auspices of the Barber–Surgeons' Company, of which he became master in 1676, he was apprenticed to alderman Sir John Frederick (1601–1685), an eminent merchant who became lord mayor of London in 1661, and in 1658 he married Anne Hooker (*d.* 1702/3), the eldest daughter of a future lord mayor. Her plump, pretty looks were much admired by Samuel Pepys (a fellow parishioner of St Olave's, Hart Street) who also paid tribute to her husband as 'a pretty, civil, understanding merchant'. Through his powerful connections Lethieullier was well placed to succeed in City government, and he also established himself quickly in London's overseas trade.

Lethieullier specialized initially in the export of English textiles to southern Europe and the Levant, buying extensively from East Anglian and west of England manufacturers and superintending the dyeing and finishing in partnership with his brother-in-law, Charles Marescoe, but his interests became increasingly diversified. In 1669, for example, he was importing sugar from Portugal and iron from the Netherlands while exporting lead and tin to Venice and Rotterdam. He became a member (and later director) of the Levant Company and by 1673 was also a director of the East India Company. At the same time he was involved with the Hamburg trade in English textiles and German linens carried on by the declining company of Merchant Adventurers, of which he became governor, and with the new Royal African Company of 1671, in which he served as a director after 1681.

Having served Tower ward as a common councilman from 1672 to 1675 and performed a term as a sheriff in 1674–5, during which he was knighted, Lethieullier was chosen as alderman for Cripplegate ward but quickly secured his discharge without bearing the usual fine. Nevertheless, through his father-in-law and in his own right, he was an influential figure in City affairs, and he was able to intervene successfully to save his sister Leonora's second husband, Jacob David, from the full financial penalties of his frauds. The career of his brother Sir Christopher (1639–1690) closely matched his own, since the latter traded within the Levant Company (of which he became a director), served as a sheriff in 1688–9 (when he was knighted), and held his place as an alderman for Coleman Street ward before and after the revolution of 1688. His other brother, William (1646–1728), also prospered as a merchant and served the City as a common councilman.

Lethieullier acquired several properties outside London, which proved their value in the years of the plague and fire. He retained his father's ties in Essex with a house at Low Leyton, and he followed him to Greenwich, where about 1680 he built a substantial mansion called Lewisham House. He also purchased Sutton Place at Sutton-at-Hone in Kent, while in London he acquired, among other properties, Buckingham House in College Street, the former mansion of the second duke, George Villiers.

Lethieullier did not retain close ties with the French protestant community from which he stemmed, but in 1681 he was appointed as trustee for a fund set up to support French refugees in linen manufacture at Ipswich. He also served his Hart Street parish as a trustee of its charities, and when he died, in his eighty-sixth year, at Lewisham House on 4 January 1719, was buried at St Alfege, Greenwich, where his churchyard monument, erected by a grandson, also records his two sons, John and William, and his three daughters, Anne, Letitia, and Leonora. In a very lengthy will of 6 May 1709, with several codicils, he distributed his real property between his sons and gave £10,200 to his unmarried daughters, Letitia and Leonora, as well as £1000 in addition to his marriage settlement for Anne, now Lady Dodwell. He also left sums of £100 for the French church in Threadneedle Street, and for Christ's Hospital and St Thomas's Hospital. H. G. Roseveare

Sources L. B. Ellis, 'The Lethieullier family', *Proceedings of the Huguenot Society*, 19/2 (1953–4), 60–67 • J. R. Woodhead, *The rulers of London, 1660–1689* (1965), 107–8 • S. Young, *The annals of the Barber-Surgeons of London: compiled from their records and other sources* (1890), 556–7 • *Markets and merchants of the late seventeenth century: the Marescoe–David letters, 1668–1680*, ed. H. Roseveare, British Academy, Records of Social and Economic History, new ser., 12 (1987); repr. (1991) • will, PRO, PROB 11/567, sig. 12

Archives GL, repertories of the court of aldermen • PRO, Chancery Masters' Exhibits, C.114/63–78

Wealth at death approx. £100,000: will, PRO, PROB 11/567, sig. 12

Lethieullier, Smart (1701–1760), antiquary, the second son of John Lethieullier (*d.* 1737), businessman and financier, of Aldersbrook Manor House, Little Ilford, Essex, and his wife, Elizabeth Smart, daughter of Sir Joseph Smart of Havering, was born at Aldersbrook Manor House on 3 November 1701. The family, originally of Brabant, had come to London to escape persecution, in 1605. Its fortunes rose with the enterprising career of Smart's grandfather Sir John *Lethieullier (1632/3–1719), in Pepys's words 'a pretty, civil, understanding merchant'. He was sheriff of London in 1674–5 and completed the transition from successful trade to landownership and social recognition when, in 1693, he bought the Aldersbrook estate: it became the principal seat of the family. After Eton College, Smart entered Trinity College, Oxford, in February 1720 and graduated MA in July 1723. On 5 February 1726 this 'polite gentleman' (Nichols, 5.3) married Margaret Sloper (*d.* 1753), daughter of William Sloper, of Woodhay in Berkshire. About this time he was painted by George Knapton, a fellow member of the Society of Dilettanti, in the soft, pastel-like colours favoured by that artist. The sitter is wearing a fine silver waistcoat which may have been part of his wedding outfit and holding a half-unfurled sketch of a contemporary building, in the Palladian style. It may be his own plan for alterations to one of the Lethieullier properties. With an ample fortune, scholarly tastes, and some skill as a draughtsman, he proceeded to make a life's work of the study and collecting of antiquities. With it went the arduous but fashionable and stimulating necessity of travelling in France, Italy, Germany, and all parts of Britain.

After Lethieullier inherited Aldersbrook on his father's death (1 January 1737) he set about improving the grounds in the contemporary taste and built a hermitage for his collections. His collection was large, but it was discriminating, the work of a true antiquarian, and an invaluable resource for scholars. It made a material contribution to the more accurate view of the past characteristic of the Enlightenment. He corresponded and wrote articles tirelessly on subjects ranging from the Ambesbury banks to the Bayeux tapestry. Some were published posthumously in *Archaeologia*. A few, such as that on the shrine of St Hugh in Lincoln Cathedral (*Archaeologia*, 1, 1770), have stood the test of time. He wrote about Roman objects found at Leyton, Essex, for Gough's edition of *Camden's Britannia* (1789). In Rome Lethieullier had dealings with the antiquary Ficoroni; at home he was in contact with such scholars as Richard Pococke and Dr Ducarel, author of *Anglo-Norman Antiquities, &c* (1767). The celebrated art collector Dr Meade was another acquaintance. Lethieullier's folios included one of finely painted drawings of ancient marbles, and others of Saxon and later objects, many of which came into the possession of Horace Walpole. Fossils, so significant in later scientific advance, were another interest: his two large cabinets were described by his friend Peter Collinson as 'a great collection, which excells most others' (*GM*, 443). Lethieullier made an illustrated manuscript catalogue of the rarer specimens. He became a fellow of the Royal Society, a member of the pioneering Spalding Society (elected 1733), and fellow of the Society of Antiquaries (elected 1725).

The Lethieulliers had no children. Margaret died on 19 June 1753, Smart on 27 August 1760 at Aldersbrook; he was buried, probably three days later, in Little Ilford church, as is recorded on the monument in the family mausoleum (which he may have designed himself) on the north side of the nave. Aldersbrook, the manor of Birch Hall at Theydon Bois, and other estates were inherited by his niece Mary, the daughter of his younger brother Charles Lethieullier (1718–1759), fellow of All Souls College, Oxford. Another relation was Smart's cousin the Egyptologist Colonel William Lethieullier, who bequeathed mummies to the British Museum. Between 1756 and 1760 his son Pitt and Smart Lethieullier further endowed the museum with manuscripts, coffins, fragments of statues, bronzes, and manuscripts.

In 1760 Lethieullier's library was sold at auction. His remaining collection found its way into various hands. A few years after his death Aldersbrook was bought by Sir James Long, who pulled down the manor house and the hermitage and built a farmhouse. Today the park is the City of London cemetery. GEOFFREY TREASURE

Sources L. B. Ellis, 'The Lethieullier family', *Proceedings of the Huguenot Society*, 19/2 (1953–4), 60–67 • C. H. I. Chown, 'The Lethieullier family of Aldersbrook House', *Essex Review*, 35 (1926), 203–20 • P. Morant, *The history and antiquities of the county of Essex*, 1 (1768); repr. with introduction by G. H. Martin (1978), 27–8 • E. Walford, *Greater London*, 1 (1883) • S. Lethieullier, 'letters', *Archaeologia*, 1 (1770), 26–9, 56–9, 73–9 • 'Mr Lethieullier's observations on sepuchral monuments', *Archaeologia*, 2 (1773), 291–300 • L. Cust and S. Colvin, eds., *History of the Society of Dilettanti* (1898), 261–9 • Nichols, *Lit. anecdotes*, 5.368–72 • *GM*, 1st ser., 30 (1760), 394, 443 • T. Murdoch, ed., *The quiet conquest: the Huguenots, 1685–1985* (1985), 154 [exhibition catalogue, Museum of London, 15 May – 31 Oct 1985] • *IGI* • Foster, *Alum. Oxon.* • R. A. Austen-Leigh, ed., *The Eton College register, 1698–1752* (1927) • monumental inscription, Little Ilford church, Essex

Archives BL, drawings, Add. MSS 27348–27350 • priv. coll., correspondence • priv. coll. | BL, letters to Dean Lyttelton, Stowe MS 752 • BL, correspondence with E. M. Da Costa, Add. MS 28539 • NA Scot., letters to Sir John Clerk

Likenesses G. Knapton, oils, *c*.1725, Breamore House, Hampshire

Wealth at death great: estates; house; collections

Lethlobar mac Loingsig (*d.* 873), king of Ulster, was the son of Loingsech mac Tommaltaig. Although his father had not held the kingship either of Dál nAraidi or of Ulster, his grandfather, Tommaltach mac Inrechtaig (*d.* 790), had held both. At this period there were two dynasties among the Dál nAraidi; the one to which Lethlobar belonged was centred in Mag Line (around the town of Antrim), while another branch, centred in Eilne between the Bann and the Bush (around the town of Coleraine), was known as 'Dál nAraidi of the North'. The other major kingdoms of the province of Ulster (east of the River Bann) were Dál Fiatach and Uí Echach Cobo, respectively in the eastern and western parts of what is now Down. Uí Echach Cobo were aligned both genealogically and politically with Dál nAraidi, making a loose but potentially powerful block along the east side of the River Bann.

Little is known of Lethlobar apart from his appearance in king-lists of Dál nAraidi and Ulster and in the twelfth-century poem *Clann Ollaman Uaisle Emna* ('The nobles of Emain are the children of Ollam'). He is directly noticed in the annals in only two entries. The first occurred in 828, only three years after the death of his predecessor as king of Dál nAraidi, when Lethlobar defeated a viking army; the second was his non-violent death, as a very old man, in 873. At the beginning of his reign, at least, there were also kings of the Dál nAraidi of the North: while the annals of Ulster, s.a. 828, entitle Lethlobar 'king of Dál nAraidi', they call Cináed mac Echdach, in his obit in 832, 'king of the Dál nAraidi of the North', and they give the same title to Flannacán mac Echdach (possibly Cináed's brother) in his obit in 849.

Lethlobar's reign fell within a period of major viking activity, and Cenél nÉogain were also putting pressure on the northern Dál nAraidi; the crucial question, therefore, is whether this relative silence in the annals indicates relative peace or is merely a consequence of the location of the annalist in the midlands rather than in the north. Probably the silence indicates a degree of success. A distinction can be drawn between the earlier and later parts of Lethlobar's reign as king of Dál nAraidi. His victory in 828 did not prevent serious developments in the 830s: one of the principal churches of the province, Connor, was sacked in 832; a crannog at Lough Bricrenn (Loughbrickland, Down) in the kingdom of Uí Echach Cobo was taken in 833; and viking pressure in the north-east came to a head with the establishment of a camp on Lough Neagh in 839, from which 'they plundered the peoples and churches of the north of Ireland' (*Ann. Ulster*, s.a. 839). They remained there until early in 841, but in that year new camps were established at Linn Duachaill (by Annagassan on the coast of co. Louth) and Dublin; the main scope of viking attacks then shifted southwards to the midlands. For the next generation, the main sufferers in north-eastern Ireland were the Dál nAraidi of the North and Dál Fiatach, both coastal kingdoms exposed to attack from the Hebrides and the Isle of Man.

In 866, by which time Lethlobar was overking of the province of Ulster but was also growing old, the king of Cenél nÉogain, Áed Findliath mac Néill, now also king of Tara, 'plundered all the naval camps of the Foreigners, that is the coastland of the North, both Cenél nÉogain and Dál nAraidi' (*Ann. Ulster*, s.a. 866). The coastland of Dál nAraidi must signify Dál nAraidi of the North rather than Lethlobar's inland kingdom of Mag Line. A final, more local, sign of Lethlobar's success is that his son, Macc Étig, grandson, and great-grandson were all both kings of Dál nAraidi and overkings of the province of Ulster; his daughter, Barrdub, married his predecessor as king of the province, Matudán mac Áeda of Dál Fiatach.

BENJAMIN T. HUDSON

Sources *Ann. Ulster* • F. J. Byrne, 'Clann Ollaman Uaisle Emna', *Studia Hibernica*, 4 (1964), 54–94 • M. C. Dobbs, ed. and trans., 'The Ban-shenchus [3 pts]', *Revue Celtique*, 47 (1930), 283–339; 48 (1931), 163–234; 49 (1932), 437–89 • M. A. O'Brien, ed., *Corpus genealogiarum Hiberniae* (Dublin, 1962) • B. T. Hudson, *Prophecy of Berchán* (1996) • T. W. Moody and others, eds., *A new history of Ireland*, 9: *Maps, genealogies, lists* (1984)

Lethlobor. *See* Lethlobar mac Loingsig (*d.* 873).

Lett, Sir Hugh, baronet (1876–1964), surgeon, was born at Waddingham, Kirton, Lincolnshire, on 17 April 1876, the son of Richard Alfred Lett, who had graduated in Dublin in 1869 and subsequently went into general practice in Lincolnshire, and his wife, Bithiah, daughter of William Appleford. Hugh Lett was the eldest of eight children, one of whom, Phyllis, became famed as a contralto, and another, Eva, principal of Ripon Diocesan Training College. Lett was educated at Marlborough College; in later years he became a governor and president of the Marlburian Club. From preclinical studies at Leeds he entered the London Hospital in 1896. He was a dedicated student, qualified MB, BCh (Victoria) at Leeds in 1899, took the conjoint diploma of the royal colleges in 1901, and passed the FRCS in 1902. In his earlier years he was active in the students' union as president of the cricket and fencing clubs. After qualification he held most of the resident appointments at the London Hospital: in 1902 he became surgical registrar, in 1905 assistant surgeon, and in 1915 full surgeon. In 1906 Lett married Helen (*d.* 1963), daughter of the famous surgeon Sir George Buckstone Browne; they had three daughters.

From 1909 to 1912 Lett served as a lecturer in anatomy and clinical and operative surgery. His writing, while not frequent, covered many subjects. In 1905 he published a study of ninety-nine cases of advanced breast cancer treated by removal of the ovaries, one of the earliest studies of hormonal manipulation in this disease. Although a general surgeon, his main interest was in urology and for many years he was in charge of the hospital's urological department. He was an excellent teacher and always showed great courtesy to his patients and the nurses, but in the operating theatre he had a tendency to irritability which seemed out of character.

Lett served throughout the First World War, first as a surgeon at the Anglo-American Hospital at Wimereux (1914–15), then the Belgian field hospital at Furnes (1915), and subsequently in Egypt. He was promoted to major in the Royal Army Medical Corps. For his services he was appointed CBE in 1920. Between the two world wars Lett began to find operating sessions wearisome. Fortunately he had great abilities as an administrator, which he became free to use for the benefit of his colleagues and the country by retiring at a comparatively early age from active surgical practice in December 1934. He became consulting surgeon, an honorary appointment, to the London Hospital. His association with the Royal College of Surgeons of England was long, close, and extremely valuable. He served as examiner from 1923 to 1925. He was a Hunterian trustee from 1942 to 1962, and chairman from 1955 to 1959. In 1936 he delivered the Bradshaw lecture, 'Early diagnosis of renal tuberculosis', and in 1942 the Thomas Vicary lecture, 'Anatomy at the Barber Surgeons' Hall'. On the council from 1927 to 1943 he was president for three years from 1938, a period of considerable difficulty because of the anxieties of the war. He took a personal interest to safeguard the valuable possessions of the college. He travelled to Aberystwyth in the summer of 1939 and arranged the removal of the most valuable paintings, books, and other treasures to the National Library of Wales. During 1940 he secured a generous grant from the Rockefeller Foundation to evacuate the library to the west country. Lett was later associated with the rebuilding of the Hunterian Museum which had been destroyed in an air raid. Lett was created a baronet in 1941, and in 1947 was appointed KCVO in recognition of his work for the King Edward's Hospital Fund, of which he had been an honorary secretary since 1941. He was the first chairman of the Staff College for Ward Sisters established by the fund.

During the Second World War Lett was chairman of the committee for the allocation of medical manpower. In 1946–8 he was president of the British Medical Association at a time when the National Health Service was coming into being and he gave the presidential address, 'Medicine in the post-war world'. He was also president of the sections of surgery and urology of the Royal Society of Medicine (1932–3) and of the Hunterian Society (1917), and an honorary fellow of both. In 1911 he became a liveryman of the Worshipful Society of Apothecaries and a freeman of the City of London, and played an active part in the society's activities. He joined the court in 1931 and was master in 1937–8. He was also a masonic grand officer. He received an honorary DCL from Durham and an honorary ScD from Cambridge.

Lett was a tall, thin man of serious demeanour, kindly and affable, and without any affectation. He was meticulous in all his professional dealings, and was an admirable committee chairman with a wealth of experience and common sense. He was interested in music and himself became an accomplished cellist. In his latter years his eyesight failed. He died at his home, Water's Edge, The Beach, Walmer, Kent, on 19 July 1964.

HAROLD ELLIS

Sources R. H. O. B. Robinson and W. R. Le Fanu, *Lives of the fellows of the Royal College of Surgeons of England, 1952–1964* (1970) • Z. Cope, *BMJ* (25 July 1964), 251 • *The Times* (20 July 1964), 12 • *CGPLA Eng. & Wales* (1964) • *WWW*

Likenesses J. Gunn, oils, RCS Eng. • J. Gunn, oils, Society of Apothecaries, London • photograph, RCS Eng.
Wealth at death £102,875: probate, 28 Oct 1964, *CGPLA Eng. & Wales*

Lettice, John (1737–1832), Church of England clergyman, was born on 27 December 1737 at Bozeat, Northamptonshire, son of the Revd John Lettice and his wife, Mary, daughter of Richard Newcome, rector of Wymington. His father was rector of Strixton and vicar of Bozeat, but died when he was fourteen, and left him to the guardianship of a maternal uncle. He was educated at Oakham School, under Mr Powell, and admitted in 1756 to Sidney Sussex College, Cambridge, where he matriculated on 20 July, and graduated BA in 1761, MA in 1764, STB in 1771, and STP in 1797.

Lettice became a fellow of his college, and in 1764 obtained the Seatonian prize with a poem entitled *The Conversion of St Paul*, which was published in 1765, and was reissued in the *Musae Seatonianae* in 1772. It was reprinted in 1787 and 1808. Lettice married, first, a daughter of John Newling, an alderman of Cambridge; she died in January 1788. Second, on 25 May 1788, he married a daughter of Dr Hinckley of the parish of St Mary Aldermanbury, City of London.

In March 1765 Lettice spent an evening with Dr Johnson, who was visiting Cambridge. In 1768 he accompanied Sir Robert Gunning as chaplain and secretary to the British embassy at Copenhagen, was present at the palace revolution in 1772, and subsequently visited other parts of the continent. He was a staunch opponent of reform of the University of Cambridge, accusing its supporters of misrepresentation in a sermon in 1788.

A skilled linguist, Lettice mastered Danish and a number of other European languages. In addition to sermons, he published a variety of other works: *Letters on a Tour through Various Parts of Scotland in 1792* was followed in 1803 by a plan for evacuating the coastal population if an invasion was threatened. *A Village Catechist* appeared in the same year, and in 1812 he produced *Fables for the Fireside*. He also wrote a work about clerical eloquence. In collaboration with Thomas Martyn, he translated Ottavio Antonio Bayardi's book *Antichità di Ercolano* into English as *The Antiquities of Herculaneum* in 1773, and 'The immortality of the soul', a poem, from the Latin of Isaac Hawkins Browne.

In 1785 Lettice was presented by his college to the tiny living of Peasmarsh, Sussex; in 1799 he was tutor to the Beckford family, and on 21 February 1804 was nominated by Bishop Buckner to the prebend of Sleaford in the diocese of Chichester, both of which preferments he held until his death on 18 October 1832 at the vicarage, Peasmarsh. Lettice was a strong preacher, being chosen by both Bishop Ashburnham and Bishop Buckner as preacher at visitations in 1787 and 1788. In his later years he was chaplain to the duke of Hamilton. He was greatly respected by his parishioners, who erected a monument to his memory. W. A. SHAW, *rev.* WILLIAM GIBSON

Sources Venn, *Alum. Cant.*, 2/4 • J. Lettice, *Sermon preached at the primary visitation of the bishop of Chichester* (1798) • Nichols, *Lit. anecdotes* • *GM*, 1st ser., 59 (1789), 466 • *GM*, 1st ser., 102/2 (1832), 477–9
Archives Bodl. Oxf., corresp., mainly with William Beckford • CUL, corresp. with James Plumptre
Wealth at death approx. £50 p.a. income as vicar of Peasmarsh

Lettou, John (*fl.* 1475–1483), bookbinder and printer, may have come from the eastern Baltic, since his name, Lettou, was the Middle English form for Lithuania. But by this date such a name no longer guaranteed a person's immediate origins. Seventeen books printed between 1475 and 1480 are attributed to the workshop of the 'Indulgence Binder' now identified as Lettou. The identification depends upon the use of waste strips cut from an indulgence of 1480 used in the binding of a Bible, printed by Gotz in 1480, which now belongs to Jesus College, Cambridge. Since this waste would have been found only in the workshop of the printer, and the indulgence was printed by Lettou, he must have been both the printer and the binder.

Two copies of this indulgence issued by John Kendale were printed in a type identified as Lettou's. They are identical with one printed by Caxton earlier that year. Also in 1480 Lettou printed one further indulgence, together with the *Questiones* of Antonius Andreae (possibly a reprint of the Vicenza edition of 1477) and *Expositiones super psalterium* by Thomas of Wales. The two books were printed by Lettou in London for a William Wilcock. The type in these works was that used by a printer in Rome, John Bulle, in 1478–9. Lettou printed no other books on his own, perhaps because Wilcock withdrew financial support. Six books, presumably from 1482–3 though they are undated, were printed in London near All Saints' Church by Lettou in partnership with William Maclyn: Littleton's *Tenores novelli*, the *Abbreviamentum statutorum*, three yearbooks from Henry VI's reign, and a *Dialogus* without printers' names. The type for these books is inferior to that in Lettou's own books. Nothing further is known of Lettou's life; it is assumed he died about 1483. N. F. BLAKE

Sources E. G. Duff, *The printers, stationers, and bookbinders of Westminster and London from 1476 to 1535* (1906) • H. R. Plomer, *Wynkyn de Worde and his contemporaries from the death of Caxton to 1535* (1925) • E. G. Duff, *Early printed books* (1863) • G. Pollard, 'The names of some English fifteenth-century binders', *The Library*, 5th ser., 25 (1970), 193–218 • E. G. Duff, 'Early chancery proceedings concerning members of the book trade', *The Library*, new ser., 8 (1907), 408–20 • H. Bradshaw, 'Notice of a fragment of the "Fifteen Oes" and other prayers printed at Westminster by W. Caxton about 1490–91: preserved in the library of the Baptist College, Bristol', *Collected papers of Henry Bradshaw*, ed. F. Jenkinson (1889), 341–9

Letts, John (*bap.* 1772, *d.* 1851), stationer and diary publisher, was baptized on 21 June 1772 at St Peter's Church, Cornhill, London, the third of the three children of John Letts and his wife, Anne, *née* Beaman, who were both also baptized and married in the parish.

After serving an apprenticeship as a bookbinder, Letts set up business as a stationer in the City of London in 1796. His premises were in the Royal Exchange, and his clientele included merchants and traders in the City. One of the chief requirements of the latter, apart from the regular recording of financial transactions, was a need to know about the movements of ships to and from the Port of London. This they obtained from a diary in which prominence was given to the working week, with a cash ruling through the diary section and tide tables in the opening pages.

Letts sensed that there could be a market for more general diaries of this type, but ones that were future-dated, so that the diary owner could plan ahead and not simply record the events of the day. His first such diary was issued in 1812 as a deliberately commercial product. Unlike existing diaries, it simply printed the dates of a six-day working week, Monday to Saturday, with no information other than the public holidays as they fell. The publication was branded by a printed label on the front cover 'Diary. 1812. Sold by John Letts Stationer. Royal Exchange'. There was soon a public demand for more informative contents, and by the early 1820s Letts was publishing a range of diaries in different sizes and formats, incorporating in their pages governmental, legal, commercial, and astronomical information, as what was essentially a combination of a detailed almanac and a day-to-day dated notebook.

On 4 February 1800 Letts married Mary Spicer, in Saffron Walden, Essex. They had two sons, John and Thomas *Letts, who were also baptized at St Peter's, Cornhill. Mary died on 6 October 1815, aged forty-two, and was buried at St Stephen's, Coleman Street. On 16 November 1816, at St Michael's, Bishop's Stortford, Hertfordshire, Letts married his second wife, Frances Debenham (1788–1848), then aged twenty-eight. John and Frances had twin sons and two daughters.

The commercial publication of Letts's diary proved to be a success, and the booklet was well received by the merchants and shipping personnel whose patronage Letts sought. However, although Letts realized that a more general publication might well appeal to a wider market, his initial commercial activity was modest, and two factors rather militated against any immediate expansion. The first was that his output was restricted to local consumers in particular lines of business. The second was that he was not a natural businessman, and pursued his chosen trade more with a sense of stolid optimism than with a genuine entrepreneurial flair. The diaries were in a sense simply an extension of his basic skills as a bookbinder. It might also be added that the 1830s were not overall a favourable time for commercial development. It was thus left to his son, Thomas, who took over the firm in the 1830s, to move the business significantly forward, and to diversify it into maps and stationery products and to find an overseas response to these, especially in the English-speaking world of the burgeoning British empire.

By the time Thomas took over, Honest Jack Letts, as he had come to be known, was living in retirement with his wife at Broxbourne, Hertfordshire. It was there that Frances predeceased him, dying of dysentery on 30 April 1848, aged fifty-nine. John survived her for less than three years, dying of dropsy on 25 March 1851. Although both wife and husband ended their days in Broxbourne, they were each buried at St Olave's, Hart Street, London, where John's eldest son was rector. The Revd John Letts officiated at his mother's funeral, but not his father's.

The family firm later came to bear the name not of its founder, John Letts, but of Charles Letts, Thomas's son, who broke with the company in 1881 to set up independently. John Letts's own firm went into liquidation in 1885.

ADRIAN ROOM

Sources private information (2004) · F. Vivian, ed., *Letts keep a diary: an exhibition of the history of diary keeping in Great Britain from 16th–20th century in commemoration of 175 years of diary publishing by Letts* (1987) [exhibition catalogue, Mall Galleries, London, 28 Sept – 25 Oct 1987] · W. H. Beable, 'Charles Letts's diaries', *Romance of great businesses*, 2 (1926), 211–20 · parish records (baptism), 21 June 1772, St Peter's, Cornhill, London · parish records (marriage), 4 Feb 1800, Saffron Walden · parish record (marriage), 16 Nov 1816, St Michael's, Bishop's Stortford · parish records (burial), 29 March 1851, St Olave's, Hart Street, London · parish records (burial), 1848, St Olave's, Hart Street, London [Frances Letts]

Likenesses oils, *c.*1820, priv. coll.

Wealth at death left £100 to elder son: will

Letts, Thomas (1803–1873), stationer, was born at Stockwell, London, the son of John *Letts (*bap.* 1772, *d.* 1851), bookbinder, and his wife, Mary Spicer (*d.* 1815). Thomas was educated at Dr Crosby's school at Greenwich, and then apprenticed to his father. John Letts had left the bookbinding trade to set up as a printer and stationer at 95 Old Royal Exchange. He experimented with ruled and dated books for day-by-day transactions and in 1816 began to publish 'Letts's diary or bills owed book and almanack', the first commercially produced diary of its kind. The venture was successful and when Thomas took over the business on John's retirement in 1835 the firm was printing twenty-eight varieties of such diaries, ranging from foolscap folio, at one day per page, to small pocket diaries.

Letts also issued interest tables, medical diaries, office calendars, parliamentary registers and guides, ledgers, logbooks, clerical diaries, and washing books. The sale gradually increased to several hundred thousands annually, and Letts erected large factories at New Cross. He acquired a property at Chale, Isle of Wight, and in 1864, on the occasion of the Shakespeare tercentenary, he erected a small Doric temple in the neighbouring woods as a memorial to the poet.

Letts married twice: first, on 21 January 1837, Harriet Cory, with whom he had three sons and a daughter; after her death he married, on 26 February 1842, Emma Horwood Barry, with whom he had seven children. He died at his home, 23 Granville Park, Lewisham, London, on 9 August 1873, and was buried at Norwood cemetery. He was survived by his second wife.

Thackeray, in his Roundabout papers, no. 18, first published in the *Cornhill Magazine* for January 1862, made 'Letts's diary' the text of a new year sermon. He declared his preference for 'one of your No. 12 diaries, three shillings cloth boards; silk limp, gilt edges, three and six; French morocco, tuck ditto, four and six'.

The diary side of the stationery business grew so vast

that Letts, confronted with the need to raise working capital, converted in 1870 to a limited liability company, Letts, Son & Co., the son being Charles John Letts (*b*. 1839). Unfortunately the hoped for profitability failed to materialize, the shareholders grew increasingly dissatisfied, and Charles resigned in 1881 to set up Charles Letts & Co. Letts, Son & Co. went into liquidation in 1885, and the copyrights were purchased by Cassell Sons & Co., later sold to Hazell, Watson, and Viney Ltd. Charles Letts subsequently began anew from a modest base and his family business prospered throughout the twentieth century.

ANITA MCCONNELL

Sources Charles Letts & Co., *The romance of the business of a diary publisher* (1949) · A. A. Letts, 'Letts, Charles John', *DBB* · *CGPLA Eng. & Wales* (1873)
Archives NL Wales, travel journals
Likenesses photograph, repro. in Charles Letts & Co., *The romance of the business of a diary publisher*, 5
Wealth at death under £800: probate, 24 Dec 1873, *CGPLA Eng. & Wales*

Lettsom, John Coakley (1744–1815), physician and philanthropist, was born on 22 November 1744 at Little Vandyke, one of the Virgin Islands, West Indies, the son of Edward Lettsom, plantation owner, and his wife, Mary *née* Coakley. The Lettsoms were a Quaker family, originally from Cheshire.

Early life and education When six years old, Lettsom was sent to England for his education. In due course he came under the notice of Samuel Fothergill of Warrington, also a Quaker and the younger brother of the celebrated physician John Fothergill. After a year learning a trade in Liverpool, Lettsom was apprenticed in April 1761 to Abraham Sutcliff, a surgeon and apothecary at Settle, Yorkshire. Through Sutcliff he acquired a good knowledge of Latin, while plant gathering on the moors laid the foundations for his later botanical interests. After five years' apprenticeship he went to London, where John Fothergill arranged for him to serve as a surgeon's dresser at St Thomas's Hospital and introduced him to medical practice. He also attended the lectures of George Fordyce.

After his father's death Lettsom returned to the West Indies, in October 1767, to take possession of a plantation his father had bequeathed to him. He there performed a characteristically generous gesture: 'The moment I came of age', he recalled in 1791, 'I found my chief property was in slaves, and without considering of future support, I gave them freedom, and began the world without fortune, without a friend, without person, and without address' (Pettigrew, 2.36). Lettsom then went into practice in the Caribbean, rapidly amassed some £2000, and with this he returned to London and embarked upon a medical career. In October 1768 he entered the University of Edinburgh, where he studied under William Cullen and Francis Home; and after visiting several universities on the continent he graduated MD at Leiden on 20 June 1769, writing his dissertation (*Dissertatio inauguralis medica: sistens observationes ad vires Theae pertinentes*) on the pathological effects of tea drinking. In 1770 he became licentiate of the College of Physicians and FSA; in 1773 he was elected FRS.

John Coakley Lettsom (1744–1815), by T. R. Poole, 1809

Medical practice and family life Setting up in practice in London from a house in Basinghall Street, Lettsom proved highly successful, partly thanks to indefatigable activity. In 1782 he noted that 'sometimes for the space of a week, I cannot command twenty minutes' leisure in my own house' (Pettigrew, 1.21). A year later he reported that 'since 1769 when I first settled in London I have not taken one half day's relaxation' (ibid., 1.27). By 1791 he observed that 'during the last nineteen years not one holiday have I taken' (ibid., 2.53).

Lettsom acquired many prominent patients, including Lord Shelburne and Thomas Erskine. His busy practice made him wealthy. By the age of forty he had acquired the capital's top practice, with an income of £3600, in 1784, and £4500 two years later; from 1786 to 1800, when he was fifty-six, his earnings amounted to as much as £12,000 annually. His marriage on 31 July 1770 to Anne Miers also gained him a considerable fortune. The couple had a large family. One son, Samuel Fothergill Lettsom, and two daughters, married respectively to Dr Philip Elliott and Mr John Elliot of Pimlico, survived him. The latter was the father of Sir Henry Miers Elliot. Several children died before him, including his eldest son, John Miers Lettsom (1771–1799), a physician of promise and father of William Nanson *Lettsom.

Lettsom was a highly sociable man; he entertained extensively at his house, Grove Hill, Camberwell, he was received by George III, and he kept up an extensive correspondence with (among others) George Washington, Benjamin Rush, Benjamin Franklin, Erasmus Darwin, and Albrecht von Haller. Although a lifelong Quaker, he was not of the stern variety—indeed he was something of a ladies' man. Despite Quaker pacifism, he became physician to the Camberwell volunteer infantry in September 1803, declaring, 'may I fall by the sword rather than live to see this free country the domain of a Corsican murderer and usurper!' (Pettigrew, 2.129–30). He was widely regarded as a social climber, being caricatured in the *Westminster Magazine* in 1782 in the guise of 'Dr. Wriggle' in 'Dr. Wriggle, or, The art of rising in physic'.

A prolific author Lettsom was an ardent believer in the benefits of useful knowledge, medical advice, and moral exhortation, and a tireless writer on such topics; he produced books and pamphlets against drunkenness, for example, and on the evils of tea drinking. In *The natural history of the tea tree with observations on its medical qualities, and effects of tea-drinking* (1772) he argued that the habit made society enervated and effeminate. He championed a multitude of improving projects, among them soup kitchens; characteristically, he could not resist writing a pamphlet giving recipes for different kinds of soups. Passionate about education, in 1795 he wrote a work on the management of boarding-schools, with advice on games, diet, attire, and cleanliness. Lettsom also found time to direct his attention to beehives, believing that they could become 'appendages both of ornament and utility to the gardens about the metropolis' (*Hints for Promoting a Bee Society*, 1796). Within 20 miles of London, he judged, no fewer than 50,000 beehives might be maintained, bringing in a guinea per hive per annum.

By 1802 Lettsom had collected his improving essays into *Hints Designed to Promote Beneficence, Temperance, and Medical Science*. These three volumes contained essays on such varied subjects as poverty, discharged prisoners, prostitution, infectious fevers, a Samaritan society, crimes and punishments, wills and testaments, lying-in charities, deaf mute people, village societies, blind people, a society for promoting useful literature, hints to masters and mistresses, religious persecution, humane parties, Sunday schools, the Philanthropic Society, dispensaries, hydrophobia, sea-bathing infirmaries, and a substitute for wheat bread; in this last Lettsom advocated the use of Indian corn and offered characteristically detailed instructions for making thrifty porridge. Lettsom's literary activity was the more remarkable, because most of his works as well as his private letters were written in his carriage while driving about to see his patients.

Philanthropic and professional activities Lettsom rendered genuinely important public services as a philanthropist, taking part in the foundation of several valuable institutions. In 1770 he united with others in founding the General Dispensary in Aldersgate Street, the first of its kind in London, and in 1773 he became one of its physicians, publishing a pamphlet setting out its aims. The dispensary gave free out-patient treatment to the poor through its resident apothecary, and inaugurated a tradition of domiciliary visiting by the medical staff. In 1774 Lettsom brought out *Medical Memoirs of the General Dispensary*, containing records of cases treated there. He also assisted William Hawes and others in founding the Royal Humane Society in 1774, to resuscitate the drowned, and he was the driving force behind the establishment of the Royal Sea-bathing Infirmary at Margate in 1791, designed mainly to permit tuberculous patients to convalesce.

Lettsom's name is, however, chiefly connected with the Medical Society of London. Floating the idea in his *Hints on the Establishment of a Medical Society of London* (1773), he became one of the society's founders in 1773. He supported it by the gift of a freehold house in Bolt Court, Fleet Street, and of a considerable library, and also by the foundation of a gold medal (called the Fothergillian, after his patron), to be given annually for a medical essay. His own name was commemorated in the Lettsomian lectures given in the society. The aim of the society was to promote research as well as conviviality, and papers were regularly delivered. The society proved especially popular with those excluded for religious reasons from the inner circles of the Royal College of Physicians. In 1812 Lettsom became president of the newly founded Philosophical Society of London, and he contributed several lectures to it.

Though piqued at his exclusion, as a Quaker, from the fellowship of the College of Physicians, Lettsom was a zealous upholder of the dignity of his own profession. To that end in 1776 he waged a newspaper war against the German quack uroscopist Theodor Myersbach, though being answered in *The impostor detected, or, The physician the greater cheat: being a candid enquiry concerning the practice of Dr. Mayersbach; commonly known by the title of the German Doctor … being a full refutation of the sophistical arguments and invidious reflections of Dr. Lettsom and others* (1776). Continuing his onslaught, in 1804 he persuaded the editor of the *Medical and Physical Journal* to print each month an anonymous letter attacking a quack. He directed the first of these against William Brodum, proprietor of a 'nervous cordial', declaring his medicines had killed thousands and making other disparaging remarks about Brodum's character. Brodum promptly sued, and the case was settled out of court with Lettsom paying costs.

Lettsom had been a supporter of smallpox inoculation from early in his career, and he aided in the foundation of the Society for General Inoculation; his belief in the feasibility and desirability of mass inoculation, expressed in *A letter to Sir Robert Barker, knt., F. R. S. and George Stacpoole, esq.; upon general inoculation* (1778), brought him into controversy with Thomas, Baron Dimsdale. Lettsom expressed his views in *An answer to Baron Dimsdale's review of Dr. Lettsom's observations on the baron's remarks respecting a letter upon general inoculation* (1779). When vaccination was introduced, after initial hesitation he quickly became an ardent advocate in print and person of the new practice, and he warmly supported Edward Jenner's claims to public recognition. He also took an active part in promoting the erection of a memorial to John Howard.

Alongside botany, fossils, and natural history, another subject in which Lettsom interested himself was scientific agriculture. He was involved in the introduction of the mangel-wurzel, first brought to notice by Sir Richard Jebb in 1786. Lettsom translated a pamphlet on the subject (*An Account of the Mangel-wurzel, or Root of Scarcity*, from the French of the Abbé de Commerell, 1787); he grew the seed himself and imported a large quantity, which he distributed to farmers and others in Britain as well as in Europe, America, and the West Indies.

Later years and death Lettsom was a truly benevolent man, sometimes charged by his friends with indiscriminate charity: 'Who will thank us for dying rich!', he commented in 1786 (Pettigrew, 1.118). Nevertheless, his munificence, aggravated by his lavish expenditure, brought pecuniary difficulties. Towards the close of his life, straitened circumstances compelled him to part with his suburban house, Grove Hill, Camberwell, which he had built in 1779 and where he had laid out a fortune on a museum, library, and botanical garden. Shortly before his death a large West Indian fortune was bequeathed to him and his grandson by the widow of his son, Pickering Lettsom.

After forty-five years' incessant occupation in his profession, Lettsom died at his house, Sambrook Court, Basinghall Street, London, on 1 November 1815; he was buried in the Quaker burial-ground, Coleman Street, Bunhill Row.

J. F. Payne, *rev.* Roy Porter

Sources J. J. Abraham, *Lettsom, his life, times, friends and descendants* (1933) • *Memoirs of the life and writings of the late John Coakley Lettsom*, ed. T. J. Pettigrew, 3 vols. (1817) • R. Porter, '"I think ye both quacks": the controversy between Dr Theodor Myersbach and Dr John Coakley Lettsom', *Medical fringe and medical orthodoxy, 1750–1850*, ed. W. F. Bynum and R. Porter (1987), 56–78 • E. Rose, 'John Coakley Lettsom and English medicine in the Georgian period', *Transactions of the College of Physicians of Philadelphia*, vol. 32, pp. 57–59 • S. Thomson, *John Coakley Lettsom and the foundation of the Medical Society: being the presidential address delivered before the Medical Society of London on October 8th, 1917* (1918) • J. C. Trent, 'John Coakley Lettsom', *Bulletin of the History of Medicine*, 22 (1948), 528–42 • *GM*, 1st ser., 85/2 (1815), 469–73 • *European Magazine and London Review*, 3 (1783), 440–41 • 'Character of Dr John Coakley Lettsom', *European Magazine and London Review*, 10 (1786), 395–6 • *European Magazine and London Review*, 68 (1815), 393–8 • *Westminster Magazine* (1782)

Archives Medical Society of London • Royal Medical and Chirurgical Society of London • Wellcome L., autobiography and notes • Wellcome L., corresp. • Wellcome L., lecture notes and MS collection | Yale U., Beinecke L., corresp. with James Boswell

Likenesses T. Holloway, line engraving, 1787, Wellcome L. • T. Holloway, line engraving, 1792, Wellcome L. • W. Ridley, stipple, 1800 (after S. Medley), Wellcome L. • silhouette, aquatint, 1801, Wellcome L. • stipple, 1804 (after S. Medley), Wellcome L. • T. R. Poole, wax medallion, 1809, RCP Lond. [*see illus.*] • W. Skelton, engraving, 1817, Wellcome L. • W. Holl, stipple (after S. Medley), Wellcome L. • T. Holloway, line engraving, BM, NPG; repro. in *European Magazine* (1787) • S. Medley, oils, Medical Society, London • W. Skelton, line engraving, BM, NPG; repro. in Pettigrew, *Memoirs*

Wealth at death under £7000: Abraham, *Lettsom*

Lettsom, William Nanson (1796–1865), textual scholar and translator, was born in London on 4 February 1796, the only son of John Miers Lettsom MD (1771–1799) and his wife, Rachel Nanson. He was the eldest grandson of John Coakley *Lettsom (1744–1815), physician, naturalist, and author. Lettsom was educated at Eton College and was admitted to Trinity College, Cambridge, as pensioner, on 24 September 1813. He was admitted to Lincoln's Inn on 2 May 1815. He graduated BA in 1818 and MA in 1822. While at Trinity College he won prizes for poems and epigrams in Latin. Financially independent, he was able to indulge his interest in literature.

In addition to the Latin poems written while at Cambridge, Lettsom translated the *Nibelungenlied* with the title of *The Fall of the Nibelungens; otherwise the Book of Kriemhild* in 1850. The translation is in couplets, to which he appended a prefatory note on the title itself. He added a number of endnotes on the text, some running to one or two pages. A revised edition was published in 1901 with a 'Special introduction' by William H. Carpenter, professor of Germanic philology in Columbia University. An anonymous *Song of Flogawaya*, a parody on Longfellow's *Song of Hiawatha*, published in 1856, is Lettsom's. His chief claim to fame, if only of a limited kind, however, is linked with the names of William Sidney Walker and Alexander Dyce. Walker, who entered Trinity College, Cambridge, on 16 February 1814, was Lettsom's contemporary and friend, both having been at Eton at about the same time. Walker became a fellow of the college in 1820 and died in 1846, leaving a mass of manuscript notes on the text and versification of Shakespeare's works. Lettsom edited many of these as *Shakespeare's versification and its apparent irregularities explained by examples from early and late English writers* in 1854, with subsequent editions in 1857 and 1859. He also published *A critical examination of the text of Shakespeare with remarks on his language and that of his contemporaries together with notes on his plays and poems* (3 vols., 1860), the editions all bearing Walker's name.

The 1860 *Critical examination* has a 'Preliminary notice' (pp. vii–x), having to do with John Payne Collier's annotated copy of the Shakespeare second folio, and a long 'Preface' (pp. xi–lviii), both by Lettsom. The preface is an apologia for Lettsom's labours as an editor, not 'accustomed to the critical study of our old authors' (p. xii), and an explanation of his methods. There are remarks on the Shakespeare editions of Alexander Pope, Sir Thomas Hanmer, and William Warburton, focusing on their treatment of Shakespeare's text. Later editors, Edward Capell and Samuel Johnson especially, come in for extended comment, and, in short, the preface is a brief history of the various treatments of Shakespeare's text, with many examples of editorial absurdities. The chief value of Lettsom's 1860 edition lies in the wealth of illustrative quotations and parallels adduced by Walker. Lettsom's notes, signed 'Ed.', include readings from the Shakespeare quartos and folios, emendations from a number of editors, and an occasional conjectural emendation of his own.

There is a complimentary reference in Lettsom's preface to the 1860 work to Alexander Dyce (p. xxvi), and in his conclusion Lettsom acknowledges 'the kindness of Mr. Dyce in advising me on several points on which I had occasion to consult him' (p. lvii). Dyce, for his part, in the preface to his edition of Shakespeare (6 vols., 1857), acknowledged Lettsom's assistance, including access to Walker's unpublished papers on Shakespeare. In the second edition of his Shakespeare edition (1866) he wrote:

> Though the frequent occurrence of Mr. W. N. Lettsom's name is a sufficient proof that I am greatly indebted to him, it by no means shows the full extent of my obligations, for on every one of the plays he has favoured me with not unimportant suggestions, of which I have silently availed myself. (1.xxiii)

Both men resided in London, Dyce at Oxford Terrace and Lettsom at 43 Westbourne Park, Paddington, where he died of 'a disease of a cancerous nature' on 3 September 1865 (*GM*, 790–91). Dyce was at his side when Lettsom died. ARTHUR SHERBO

Sources Venn, *Alum. Cant.* • *GM*, 3rd ser., 19 (1865), 790–91 • W. S. Walker, *A critical examination of the text of Shakespeare*, ed. W. N. Lettsom, 3 vols. (1860) • *The works of William Shakespeare*, another edn, rev. A. Dyce, 6 vols. (1857) • *CGPLA Eng. & Wales* (1865)

Wealth at death under £30,000: probate, 18 Sept 1865, *CGPLA Eng. & Wales*

Leuchars, Patrick (*d.* in or after **1383**), administrator and bishop of Brechin, probably came of a Fife family. He would have entered the Augustinian priory of St Andrews before taking the parsonage of Tyninghame, whose patronage belonged to the bishop of St Andrews, in 1344. He had exchanged it for or also had Tannadice when he was elected to the see of Brechin after 3 May 1351. This election, possibly engineered by Queen Joan at a time when David II's return from captivity in England was possible, was quashed by the pope, who provided Leuchars on 17 November 1351; he was consecrated within a month, presumably at Avignon. After the king's brief visit to Scotland in 1351–2, Leuchars is found as chancellor in March and December 1353. Although he had lost office by 12 February 1354, he was present at a council on 1 April 1354, held to discuss the king's ransom. Royal authority crumbled under the ineffectual regency of Robert Stewart in 1354–7, but the impending return of the king saw a chancellor, Leuchars, appointed by 26 September 1357. He continued to hold office during the subsequent years of heavy taxation and political wrangling and, while it is uncertain what his duties were in chancery, the two acts of revocation of title increased the business of that office significantly. He sat regularly at the exchequer until January 1369, and was twice an ambassador to England in 1360–62. The king made Edinburgh a *de facto* capital, but travel was still required and may have become increasingly difficult for Leuchars. He is last found as chancellor on 4 March 1370; his successor occurs a month later.

Leuchars was the last member of a religious order to hold the office of chancellor. Clearly a strong supporter of David II during his years of captivity, he lost office during the regency of Robert Stewart and was rewarded by David II's support after 1357. He was not prominent under Robert II, but was present at the parliament of 1373. Ten years later, early in June 1383, he resigned his see at Avignon on account of age, receiving a pension of 100 merks from its revenues. The date of his death is unknown, and he may not have returned to Scotland. A. A. M. DUNCAN

Sources G. W. S. Barrow and others, eds., *Regesta regum Scottorum*, 6, ed. B. Webster (1982) • A. A. M. Duncan, 'The regnal year of David II', *SHR*, 68 (1989), 105–19 • G. Burnett and others, eds., *The exchequer rolls of Scotland*, 2 (1878) • J. Dowden, *The bishops of Scotland … prior to the Reformation*, ed. J. M. Thomson (1912), 182–3

Leuthere (*d.* **675/6**), bishop of Winchester, was a Frank who was the nephew of *Agilbert (*d.* 679x90), sometime bishop of the West Saxons and later bishop of Paris. Leuthere originated from the Soissons area in Francia, and since his name is a form of Clothar, a name borne by three Frankish kings, it is likely that he was related to the Merovingian royal family. His name is also basically the same as that of the contemporary king of Kent, Hlothhere (*d.* 685), which suggests that Leuthere had family links with the Kentish royal house. Here one is reminded that his uncle, Agilbert, likewise had the Frankish form of a Kentish royal name, Æthelberht.

According to Bede (*Hist. eccl.* 3.7), in 670 Cenwalh, king of the West Saxons, wished to recall Agilbert to become once more a bishop in his kingdom, but Agilbert declined the offer because he was now bishop of Paris. In his stead he sent his nephew Leuthere, who was already a priest. Leuthere was consecrated bishop by Theodore of Canterbury in 670 and he held the see of Winchester from 670 to 675 or 676. As bishop he attended the Council of Hertford in 672. In 675 he appeared in a charter granting land at Malmesbury for the foundation of a monastery there. The beneficiary of this grant was Aldhelm, later bishop of Sherborne, whom Leuthere may have ordained priest. Leuthere's successor Hædde witnessed the Malmesbury charter as abbot, but later in the same year Hædde appears in another charter as bishop, alongside Leuthere. This may suggest that at least briefly Leuthere ruled Winchester jointly with his successor. In both charters the style of Leuthere's witness reveals use of a so-called Frankish 'humility formula', an observation which supports the argument that it was Frankish, rather than Italian, models which formed the basis of early charter writing in England. The second charter of 675 granted land at Bath for the foundation of a monastery. It is Leuthere's last appearance in the record and he died in that year or the next.

Interestingly, Bertha, the abbess of the new double monastery at Bath, bore the same name as Æthelberht of Kent's Frankish queen, a name similar to that of Bertila who began her career at the double monastery of Jouarre with which Leuthere had strong family connections. The little that is known about Leuthere therefore strengthens the impression that there was a powerful Frankish influence upon the early development of the church in southern England, and that at the centre of that influence lay the family of Leuthere. PAUL FOURACRE

Sources Bede, *Hist. eccl.*, 3.7 • *AS chart.*, S 1245, 51 • P. Sims-Williams, 'Continental influence at Bath monastery in the seventh century', *Anglo-Saxon England*, 4 (1975), 1–10 • H. P. R. Finberg, *The early charters of the west midlands* (1961) • P. Wormald, *Bede and the conversion of England: the charter evidence* (1984?)

Leven. For this title name *see* Leslie, Alexander, first earl of Leven (*c.*1580–1661); Melville, David, third earl of Leven and second earl of Melville (1660–1728).

Levens [Levins], **Peter** (*fl.* **1552–1587**), lexicographer, is said to have been born 'at or near Eske in Yorkshire', possibly Eske in Holderness as a family of that name lived there (Wood, *Ath. Oxon.*, 237). He probably was, like a number of others at this period, both a lexicographer and a medical practitioner, as well as a teacher. His life is obscure apart from a few details of his education and his publications. He went to Oxford in 1552, and was admitted BA on 6 July 1556. On 14 January 1557 he was elected as a Yorkshire pensioner-fellow of Magdalen College, and supplicated for the MA degree in February 1560, but no date of admission is recorded. He left his fellowship the same year. He then taught at a grammar school for some time and practised medicine; Wood described him as an 'eminent physician'.

Levens's *Manipulus vocabulorum*, 'the most original lexicographical venture in 16th-century England', was published in 1570 (Stein, *English Dictionary*, 226). Only three copies are now known to exist. The many northern wordforms in the dictionary accord with the claim about his origins. The work is relatively modest in size, and was clearly meant as a cheap alternative to the impressive but costly folio dictionary by Richard Huloet, a point which Levens labours in the dedication. It is also intended by its author for beginners, as the work is in English, not Latin.

The *Manipulus vocabulorum* broke new ground in English lexicography in several important respects. It is a reverse or rhyming English–Latin dictionary, alphabetized by the last syllable of the word, the first such work attempted in English. Levens incorporates a number of comments on English spelling, pronunciation, and morphology. He also indicates the stress in certain polysyllabic words, marking strong stress with an accent. These features are explained at some length in his preface. There are also systematic comments on the derivation of English endings from Latin or Greek, and explanations of word formation are provided. He also treats grammar more extensively than did his predecessors.

Levens accounts for homonymy and polysemy by creating multiple headwords, as in the two entries for 'A pricke', six for 'yong', two for 'to sticke' and so on, the last of these indicating his awareness of phrasal verbs. He also marked certain words as obsolete or obscure, another feature which adds historical linguistic value to his work.

Some years later Levens published *A Right Profitable Book for All Diseases, called the Path Way to Health* (1587), a modest but successful medical remedy book, which was republished a number of times, being reissued in 1587, 1596, 1608, and 1632. No details of his death, circumstances, or his family have been established. R. W. McConchie

Sources *DNB* · Wood, *Ath. Oxon.*, 1st edn, 1.237 · G. Stein, *The English dictionary before Cawdrey* (1985) · G. Stein, 'Peter Levins: a sixteenth-century English word-formationalist', *Neuere Forschungen zur Wortbildung und Historiographie der Linguistik: Festgabe für Herbert E. Brekle zum 50. Geburtstag*, ed. B. Asbach-Schnitker and J. Rogenhofer (1987), 287–302 · *STC, 1475–1640* · J. Kerling, *Chaucer in early English dictionaries: the old-word tradition in English lexicography down to 1721 and Speght's Chaucer Glossaries* (1979) · J. Kerling, 'English old-word glossaries, 1553–1594', *Neophilologus*, 63 (1979), 136–47 · De W. T. Starnes, *Renaissance dictionaries: English–Latin and Latin–English* (1954) · P. Levens, *Manipulus vocabulorum: a rhyming dictionary of the English language*, ed. H. B. Wheatley (1867)

Likenesses I. Chantrey, line engraving, NPG; repro. in P. Levens, *The path way to health*, new edn (1664)

Lever, Sir Ashton (1729–1788), natural history collector, eldest son of Sir (James) Darcy Lever (*d.* 1742), knight, and his wife, Dorothy (*d.* 1777), daughter of the Revd William Ashton, was born on 5 March 1729 at the family seat, Alkrington Hall, near Manchester. He was educated at the Manchester grammar school and attended Corpus Christi College, Oxford, as a gentleman commoner, matriculating on 1 April 1748 but not taking a degree. He was a keen hunter and kept very fine horses and dogs.

For some years after completing his education Lever lived with his widowed mother in Manchester and collected live birds. He subsequently moved to Alkrington Hall. His aviary was considered the best in the kingdom, enhanced with many species imported through London. About 1760 he turned his attention to shells and fossils, prompted initially by the purchase of a hogshead of shells at Dunkirk. His birds were freed or given to friends in order to concentrate on his new passion. A few years later he resumed collecting birds, this time stuffed, having determined after visiting the display at Spring Gardens that he would excel it.

As Lever's collection gained in reputation increasing numbers of people visited it and he was forced, instead of welcoming them as acquaintances of his friends, to designate one day each week for admission of the public. In an effort to control numbers further he excluded those who arrived on foot. The popularity of the display eventually prompted him to transfer it to London, despite the objections of his wife, Frances Bayley (1746–1802), whom he had married on 23 December 1764.

In 1773 Lever was elected fellow of the Royal Society and at about the same time the museum, or Holophusikon as Lever styled it, was installed in Leicester House, Leicester Square, London. The collection sprawled through sixteen rooms and encompassed not only shells and minerals, but stuffed animals from around the globe, weapons, and artefacts from the south Pacific, many of which were associated with the Cook expeditions. While the museum boasted an 'Antique Room', this part of the collection was confined primarily to medals and casts, their value entirely dwarfed by his natural history and ethnographic material. He encouraged donations and circulated information about preserving specimens. Lever advertised aggressively and claimed patronage from many distinguished admirers. The entrance fee varied from 5*s*. 3*d*. to a half-crown, and an annual ticket could be bought for 2 guineas.

Lever's museum became well known and in 1778 he was knighted. He intended for the collection to be considered in scholarly terms and it was indeed lauded as curious and instructive by fellow collectors and naturalists. Some of his specimens were cited in Latham's *Synopsis of the Birds* (1781–5) and the collection partially described and illustrated in Shaw's *Museum Leveriani* (1792).

By 1783 it was clear that, whatever its importance to natural history, the Holophusikon was not a financial success and Lever was obliged to dispose of the collection in order to pay off debts. Unable to find a buyer despite his (and others') conviction that it should belong to the nation, Lever obtained parliamentary permission to award the collection as first prize in a lottery. However, of the 36,000 tickets printed, only 8000 were sold, realizing for Lever far less than the £53,000 purportedly spent in assembling the museum.

The lottery was drawn in March 1786 and won by an

estates agent, James Parkinson (1730–1813), who took possession. He moved it to a purpose-built rotunda on the Surrey side of Blackfriars Bridge in 1787 but was also unable to profit from the display. The collection was sold by auction in 1806, an event which lasted sixty-five days. The catalogue was written by the naturalist and collector Edward Donovan.

An eccentric man, Lever squandered a fortune on the collection which was to have been his legacy. With its alienation and dispersal, he lost not only his passion but all tangible evidence of his claim to a place in the annals of natural history. After disposing of his museum, Lever returned to Alkrington where he resumed the life of a country gentleman. Less than two years later, while serving as a magistrate in Manchester, Lever suffered an apoplectic fit and died at Alkrington Hall the following day, 31 January 1788. P. E. KELL

Sources 'An account of Sir Ashton Lever', *European Magazine and London Review*, 6 (1784), 83–5 • A. Chalmers, ed., *The general biographical dictionary*, new edn, 20 (1815), 219 • G. Shaw, *Musei Leveriani explicatio* (1792) • T. Taylor and R. Owen, *Leicester Square: its associations and its worthies* (1874) • 'A description of the Holophusicon, or, Sir Ashton Lever's museum', *European Magazine and London Review*, 1 (1782), 17–21 • 'Curiosities', *GM*, 1st ser., 53 (1783), 219–21 • W. J. Fitzpatrick, *The life of Charles Lever*, new edn [1884], 2 • *European Magazine and London Review*, 13 (1788), 143 • E. Axon, 'The Bayley family of Manchester and Hope', *Transactions of the Lancashire and Cheshire Antiquarian Society*, 7 (1889), 193–228 • W. J. Smith, 'Sir Ashton Lever', *Transactions of the Lancashire and Cheshire Antiquarian Society*, 72 (1962), 61–9 • J. C. H. King, 'New evidence for the contents of the Leverian Museum', *Journal of the History of Collections*, 8 (1996), 167–86 • election certificate, RS

Archives FM Cam., letters and packet of papers relating to Leverian Museum

Likenesses W. Nutter, stipple, pubd 1787 (after S. Shelley), BM, NPG • W. Holl, stipple, pubd 1835 (after S. Shelley), NPG • W. Angus, line engraving, BM; repro. in *European Magazine*, 6 (1784), 83 • J. Flaxman, Wedgwood medallion, Brooklyn Museum, New York

Lever, Charles James (1806–1872), novelist, was born on 31 August 1806 at 35 Amiens Street, Dublin, the second son of James Lever (*d.* 1833), and his wife, Julia, *née* Candler (*d.* 1833). Lever's father, a successful building contractor, had gone to Ireland from Lancashire in 1787, and his mother was of an Anglo-Irish family from Kilkenny. John, Lever's only sibling, was born in 1796 and spent his working years as a Church of Ireland clergyman.

Early life and education As a child, Lever attended various private schools in Dublin; in October of 1822 he entered Trinity College, Dublin, as a pensioner. Never a very diligent student, Lever nevertheless graduated in the autumn of 1827 with a BA degree, and the friendships and associations he formed at Trinity among the sons of Ireland's protestant middle class would prove most enduring. In 1828 Lever travelled to Germany and enrolled at Heidelberg University, after short stays in the Netherlands and Austria. Lever found Germany greatly to his liking and frequently returned in later years.

Some time before 1830 Lever visited Canada, either as a doctor or as a tourist (the date is disputed by his biographers, as is his status on board ship), and his various adventures with the local populations, both settler and native, surfaced in print in *Harry Lorrequer* (1839) and elsewhere. Lever maintained in later years that he had spent some time living with an Indian tribe in the Tuscarora district of Canada (Stevenson, 17); eventually tiring of the life but being told the tribe would not allow him to leave, he escaped with the aid of an Indian named Tahata. When the two finally reached Quebec, a merchant friend of Lever's father arranged for his passage back to Ireland. Amazingly, Lever managed to bring back a canoe as a souvenir, which he is said to have used to navigate Dublin's canals.

Charles James Lever (1806–1872), by John Jabez Edwin Mayall

Medical career and first writings Back home, Lever took up his medical studies again as a resident student at Stevens' Hospital, attending lectures at the medico-chirurgical school in Park Street and Sir Patrick Dunn's Hospital. Despite failing his medical exams, Lever obtained the degree of bachelor of medicine from Trinity College in 1831. By the summer of 1832 a cholera epidemic had broken out and Lever was employed by the Clare board of health as doctor to the district of Kilrush and Kilkee. By all accounts he was a popular and successful physician, but he was profoundly affected by the poverty and disease of the area and even years later he was to write that 'to recall some of the incidents was an effort of great pain' (Stevenson, 39). As the epidemic abated, the offer of a dispensary at Portstewart, on the north shore of co. Londonderry, appealed to him at a time when money was scarce and his prospects in Dublin looked grim.

About September 1832 (no accurate document exists to authenticate the date) Lever married Kate Baker (*d.* 1870), daughter of W. M. Baker, master of the Royal Hibernian

Marine School, and they installed themselves in Portstewart. In January of 1833 Lever's mother died and was buried in St Thomas's Church, Dublin. Lever's father died two months later in Tullamore, King's county, where he had gone in his grief after his wife's death to live with his son John. Lever then found himself heir to a half-interest in £500 p.a. and a house full of furniture, but with no family in Dublin and no base of operations there, his attachment to the city was broken. Despite some success, Lever soon realized that Portstewart would fail to supply enough work to keep his growing family happy (daughter Julia was born in 1833) and his gambling debts paid. Writing seemed to offer an easy way to make money. Lever's introduction to literature had really begun in his student days with various short pieces for Irish journals such as *Saunders*, the *Cork Quarterly Magazine*, the *Dublin Literary Gazette*, and the *Irish National Magazine*, but it was not until the birth of the *Dublin University Magazine* in 1833 that he found a home for his particular brand of Irish tale. Following in the steps of William Hamilton Maxwell's comic Irish sketches in *Wild Sports of the West of Ireland* (1832) and his military *Stories of Waterloo* (1834), Lever submitted one instalment of what was later to become *The Confessions of Harry Lorrequer* to the *Dublin University Magazine*. The serial was accepted and ran from February 1837; the book was issued in volume form in 1839 with illustrations by Phiz. Although the series did not appear under Lever's name, the identity of the author was soon discovered and Lever found himself much sought after. So began a lifetime of writing quickly, to order, with all of the concomitant difficulties surrounding serial publication at that time.

By May of 1837 Lever had left Ireland for Brussels in search of a more lucrative medical practice; he found it among the expatriate families there who were as charmed by his newly found fame as an author as they were by his skill as a doctor. In July 1837 the Levers' son Charles was born, followed in August 1839 by their daughter Kate. The success of *Harry Lorrequer* was soon followed by *Charles O'Malley: the Irish Dragoon*, also in the *Dublin University Magazine* in 1840, and published by Curry in 1841, and *Our Mess* (vol. 1, *Jack Hinton, the Guardsman*; vols. 2 and 3, *Tom Burke of 'Ours'* in 1843–4. These early works owe perhaps more to the eighteenth-century style of comic sketch than to nineteenth-century realism. Lever admired Maria Edgeworth as much as Walter Scott, and his novels continued to have a regional focus, an Irish voice, and a historical dimension associated with the Anglo-Irish middle-class view of Ireland's place in the empire. Despite a series of more lucrative offers throughout his career from English publishers such as Bentley, Lever always felt a sense of loyalty to Ireland and its beleaguered publishing industry, which had never recovered from the restrictions placed on it by the Act of Union in 1800. In 1841 Lever was invited to become editor of the *Dublin University Magazine*—an offer he accepted over Bentley's one of the editorship of his *Miscellany*, saying simply that to edit Bentley's journal would entail living in London.

Editorial duties and mid-century fiction In 1842 Lever gave medicine up for ever and moved to the sort of house his characters would have felt at home in, a Jacobean mansion called Bridgehouse, at Templeogue, 4 miles south-west of Dublin. The house became a mecca for those interested in fine hospitality and witty conversation. The young Thackeray visited Lever there, looking for material for his *Irish Sketch Book* (1843), later dedicated to Lever. An anonymous obituary in the *Dublin University Magazine* highlights Lever's expansive personality:

> We well remember those pleasant *noctes*,—the beaming face of our host, every muscle trembling with humour, the light of his merry eye, the smile that expanded his mouth, and showed his fine white teeth, the musical ringing laugh that stirred every heart, the finely-modulated voice uttering some witty *mot*, telling some droll incident, or some strange adventure. Indeed, Lever was one of the best *causeurs* and *raconteurs* to be met with, and managed conversation with singular tact; never seeking to monopolise the talk, but, by the felicity of some remark thrown in at the right moment, insensibly attracting the attention of all, till he was master of the situation, and then went off in one of his characteristic sallies. How many of his witty sayings and racy anecdotes are still in the memory of his friends! ('Charles Lever', *Dublin University Magazine*, July 1872, 106)

The life of an editor, though, was not all that Lever had imagined. He found the unrelenting drudgery uncongenial, and nationalist feeling in Ireland militated against his brand of self-parody. He was savagely attacked by William Carleton in *The Nation* in October 1843 for 'disgusting and debasing caricatures' of Irishmen (Stevenson, 141) and denounced by devout Catholics for his depiction of jolly priests. His defence in the *Dublin University Magazine* of Thackeray's ironic portrayal of Ireland further incensed an increasingly politicized readership. Despite these criticisms, circulation of the magazine under his editorship rose to 4000 copies per month, the highest figure it ever attained. Lever was often guilty of indiscretion in his editorials and of making the influential the butt of practical jokes, but he had hoped, perhaps innocently, to translate his fame as a writer into some sort of governmental post on the continent that would allow him to live and write easily.

By February of 1845, having given up both his editor's chair and trying to win favour with the government, Lever had moved his family back to Brussels. He would never live in Ireland again. His few years in Dublin produced numerous short pieces for the *Dublin University Magazine*, as well as serials and works issued in volume form: *Arthur O'Leary: his Wanderings and Ponderings in many Lands* (1844), *Nuts and Nutcrackers* (1845), *Tales of the trains, being some chapters of railroad romance, by Tilbury Tramp, queen's messenger* (1845) (both collections of short pieces from the magazine), *The O'Donoghue: a Tale of Ireland Fifty Years Ago* (1845), and *St Patrick's Eve* (1845). Further wanderings in Germany and Italy led the family to settle eventually in Florence in 1847, Lever supporting their wanderings through further contributions to the *Dublin University Magazine*, the sale of the family home in Dublin, royalties, and more novels. *The Knight of Gwynne: a Tale of the Time of the Union* (1847) is one of Lever's best books, the work of mature imagination, dealing sensitively with the political wrangling and self-interest surrounding the passing of the Act of Union in 1800. Travel formed the basis for new plots: *Roland Cashel* (1850), a rather dark satire of Dublin middle-class life, *Confessions of Con Cregan, the Irish Gil Blas* (1850), and *Diary and Notes of Horace Templeton Esq., Late Secretary of Legation at ---* (1848), which concerns the ramblings of a civil servant come to Italy to die.

By February of 1850 Lever had started writing the opening chapters of two books concurrently, a practice engaged in occasionally before this time but now become the rule: *Maurice Tiernay, the Soldier of Fortune*, which ran in the *Dublin University Magazine* from April 1850 to December 1851 (volume form, 1855), and *The Daltons, or, Three Roads in Life* (1852). The efforts were patchy; friends urged Lever to take more time to write, lest his work become repetitive. Lever's reply reveals how close he felt to desperation: 'But how am I to live meanwhile? While I am training for the match I'll die of hunger' (Downey, 1.312–13). A daughter, Sydney, had been born in 1849; Lever had lost money when the Irish publishing firm of Curry was bankrupted; insurance premiums were due; his son Charles was proving difficult to place in a suitable profession; and the sort of life that he desired on the continent was always expensive. Looking to Dublin again for encouragement and recognition, Lever published *Sir Jasper Carew, his Life and Experiences* in 1855, *The Dodd Family Abroad* (1854), whose adventures sound much like the Lever family's own, and *The Martins of Cro' Martin* (1856).

Civil service and later literary work Lever had never given up hope of securing some kind of employment in the civil service, and the late 1850s brought a renewal of rumours of posts to be offered once a Conservative government gained power. Late in 1858 he was appointed vice-consul at La Spezia at a salary somewhat less than £300 per annum: 'as I like the place, and there is nothing—actually nothing—to do, I have thought it best to accept it' (Stevenson, 236). In fact the post suited Lever admirably. It provided a small measure of financial security, and allowed him to get on with the business of writing. Several novels followed from Italy in quick succession: *The Fortunes of Glencore* (1857), *Davenport Dunn: a Man of our Day* (1859), *Gerald Fitzgerald, 'the Chevalier'* (1859), and *One of them* (1861).

Lever's relations with Dickens had been amiable for some time; October 1859 saw the two negotiating for a new serial for *All The Year Round*, and *A Day's Ride: a Life's Romance* began its monthly appearance in August of 1860. Despite Dickens's best editorial efforts, the story was a failure. Lever was writing *One of them* at the same time as *A Day's Ride*, and seems to have felt that the serial project was of less importance than the volume for Chapman and Hall. Dickens wrote to Lever with bad news on 6 October 1860:

> Whether it is too detached and discursive in its interest for the audience and the form of publication, I cannot say positively; but it does not *take hold*. The consequence is, that the circulation becomes affected, and that the subscribers complain. (Dickens to Lever, 6 Oct 1860, *Letters of Charles Dickens*, 9.321)

As a result, Dickens decided to run *Great Expectations* alongside the remaining parts of Lever's novel, and Lever suffered the humiliation of having his story relegated to the magazine's back pages.

The early years of the next decade were marred by the ill health of Lever's wife, and the mounting debts and dissolution of his son, who suffered an internal haemorrhage and died in 1863 at the age of twenty-six. The furious production of Lever's early years as a writer began to slow, and his work took on a more studied appearance. In February of 1864 he began a series of anonymous occasional pieces for *Blackwood's Magazine*. Topical and amusing, the essays were edited by John Blackwood whenever Lever's enthusiasms threatened to border on the slanderous. The arrangement lasted until May 1872, Blackwood publishing selections under the title *Cornelius O'Dowd upon Men and Women and other Things in General* in several volumes (1864, 1865). Lever's frequent outrage at the vagaries of Italian and English politics would often be worked off by writing another 'O'Dowd'. Other novels of the period include *Barrington* (1863), *Luttrell of Arran* (1865), *Tony Butler* (1865), *A Rent in a Cloud* (1865), and *Sir Brook Fossbrooke* (1866). Ill health and flagging spirits dogged Lever during the latter half of the decade. In February of 1867 he took up the consulship at Trieste, a location that proved insalubrious. In a letter to John Blackwood, Lever laments, 'Trieste means no books, no writing, no O'D., no leave nor go of any kind, but moral death, and damnation too' (Stevenson, 275). Serials for *St Paul's* and the *Cornhill Magazine* became *The Bramleighs of Bishop's Folly* (1868), *Paul Goslett's Confessions in Love, Law, and the Civil Service* (1868), and *That Boy of Norcott's* (1869).

Final years Lever was devastated by the death of his wife Kate in April of 1870, and despite being in poor health himself, decided to make one last journey to London and Ireland to gather material for what was to be his final novel, *Lord Kilgobbin: a Tale of Ireland in our Own Time* (1872). The trip confirmed his status in the literary world; constant engagements precluded seeing anything much of the country, though they proved gratifying to his ego. In the spring of 1871 Lever was awarded an honorary degree of LLD from Trinity College, news of which reached him back in Trieste. John Blackwood and his family visited Lever at the Villa Gasteïger in May 1872 where they found him rather weak but in good spirits. On 1 June 1872, however, Lever died of heart failure. He was buried on 3 June in the British cemetery at Trieste. His reputation has suffered much since his death. He is chiefly remembered for his first two novels, whose comic depictions of stage Irishmen and women angered writers like Yeats and Lady Gregory. But this is to ignore, as Yeats did, his later work: considered, often deeply critical both of English attitudes toward Ireland and of the prevailing Irish Ascendancy view of the people. The fault lies partly with nineteenth-century publishing practices—forcing authors to write too quickly, and too much—and partly with an audience that was ultimately unwilling to see beyond stereotypes.

E. S. Tilley

Sources L. Stevenson, *Dr Quicksilver: the life of Charles Lever* (1939) • E. Downey, *Charles Lever: his life in his letters*, 2 vols. (1906) • W. J. Fitzpatrick, *The life of Charles Lever*, new edn [1884] • T. Bareham, ed., *Charles Lever: new evaluations*, Ulster Editions and Monographs, 3 (1991) • M. Sadleir, *Dublin University Magazine: its history, contents and bibliography* (1938), vol. 5, no. 4 of *The Bibliographical Society of Ireland papers* • R. McHugh, 'Charles Lever', *Studies*, 27 (1939), 247–60 • A. N. Jeffares, 'Lever's *Lord Kilgobbin*', *Essays and Studies by Members of the English Association*, new ser., 28 (1975), 45–57 • W. J. McCormack, *Ascendancy and tradition in Anglo-Irish literary history from 1789 to 1939* (1985) • B. Sloan, *The pioneers of Anglo-Irish fiction: 1800–1850* (1986) • J. S. Crone, *A concise dictionary of Irish biography* (1928) • [J. H. Slingerland], 'The *Dublin University Magazine*, 1833–1877, and the *University Magazine*, 1878–1880', *Wellesley index*, 4.193–213 • S. Haddelsey, *Charles Lever: the lost Victorian* (2000)

Archives Hunt. L., corresp. and notebooks • Morgan L., notebook • NL Ire., 'Downey List', MS 10061(4) • Princeton University Library, New Jersey, corresp. and literary MS • Ransom HRC, papers • Royal Irish Acad., journals • U. Cal., Los Angeles, corresp. | BL, letters to Royal Literary Fund, Loan MS 96 • Herts. ALS, letters to earl of Lytton • NL Scot., corresp. with Blackwoods

Likenesses S. Louer, portrait, 1842?, repro. in Downey, *Charles Lever*, vol. 1 • S. Pearce, chalk drawing, 1849, NG Ire. • Dalziel, woodcut, BM • J. J. E. Mayall, photograph, NPG [*see illus.*] • H. T. Ryall, stipple (after S. Louer), NPG • R. Taylor, woodcut (after a photograph by C. Watkins), NPG; repro. in *The Illustrated Review* (1 July 1871) • photograph, repro. in Downey, *Charles Lever*, vol. 2 • wood-engraving (after a photograph by C. Watkins), NPG; repro. in *ILN* (15 June 1872)

Wealth at death under £4000: probate, 16 Oct 1872, *CGPLA Eng. & Wales*

Lever, Christopher (*fl.* **1598–1627**), religious writer and poet, was possibly a kinsman of the brothers Thomas Lever (1521–1577) and Ralph *Lever (*c.*1530–1585), successively masters of Sherburn Hospital, co. Durham, in whose firm protestant tradition he stood. Probably a king's scholar at Durham School in 1588, he matriculated as a sizar from Christ's College, Cambridge, about 1593 and graduated BA early in 1598. Thereafter, although he claimed eminent patrons, his career is obscure.

In 1607 Lever published *Queene Elizabeths Teares* and *A Crucifixe, or, A Meditation upon Repentence and the Holy Passion*. The former, dedicated to Robert Cecil, earl of Salisbury, and containing commendatory verses by I. C., R. K., and Robert Parker, celebrated in verse Elizabeth's 'resolute' resistance to her persecution by Bishop Stephen Gardiner during the reign of Mary. The latter was dedicated to his 'singular good Lord and Patron' Richard Bancroft, archbishop of Canterbury, in recognition of 'the many testimonies I have of your Lordships gratious respecting me' (A3). The following year Bancroft was again the dedicatee of Lever's patriotic anti-Catholic *Heaven and Earth, Religion and Policy* (1608), in which he stressed the obligations of the clergy to live up to their high calling and the superior claims of religion over politics and of bishops in the counselling of kings. Two years later saw the first of several editions of *The Holy Pilgrime*, an exposition of the central doctrines of protestantism, designed to 'direct the simple'. 'Yet unprofest in any particular place of charge, eyther in Church or State' (A3*v*), the author dedicated the work to Adam (later Sir Adam) Newton, tutor of Prince Henry and dean of Durham, to Thomas Murray, tutor of Prince Charles and master of Sherburn Hospital, and to the prebendaries of Durham Cathedral.

One Christopher Lever was vicar of Heighington, co. Durham, from 1613 until his death in 1623; he was buried there on 27 November. However, despite the plausible coincidence of place, this seems not to have been the author. Lever's *The Historie of the Defendors of the Catholike Faith* appeared in 1627 with a dedication by the author to Charles I. From a similar perspective to that of his earlier works it surveyed the record of English monarchs from Henry VIII to James I and passed judgement on their religious achievements. On the one hand Henry was guilty of 'remisse and cold proceeding in the worke of Reformation' (chapter 6) and Mary, who was compared to Catherine de' Medici, of a catalogue of shortcomings, including the restoration of monasteries and idolatry, the persecution of Elizabeth, and marriage to Philip of Spain. She was absolved in the matter of the death of Lady Jane Grey, unavoidable in difficult circumstances; rebellion was always unjustified. On the other hand were Edward, like King Josiah, James, defending the true faith both in Scotland and England, and 'this Phoenix Queene Elizabeth … without Comparison' (334), who had laboured for protestantism at home and abroad. The final chapter, 'Of the diversity of religion', dismissed as false papist objections that the credibility of protestantism was undermined by its diversity: 'for the corne may bee good, which lyeth mingled with Chaffe, and so must the church of God lie until the day of Judgement' (369). Nothing further is known of Lever. VIVIENNE LARMINIE

Sources Venn, *Alum. Cant.* • *STC*, *1475–1640*

Lever, Darcy (**1760?–1839**), writer on seamanship, probably born in 1760, was the eldest son of the Revd John Lever of Buxton, Derbyshire, and Mary, daughter of Isaac Shaw of Altrincham. He was a nephew of the collector and antiquary Sir Ashton Lever. In January 1770 he was entered in the Manchester School. He afterwards went out to India, where his life is described as 'a somewhat eventful one'. His activities must have been profitable, as he returned to England at a comparatively early age, apparently enjoying a comfortable income. In 1808 Lever published at Leeds *The young sea officer's sheet anchor, or, A key to the leading of rigging and to practical seamanship*. In 1819 a second edition was published in London and Philadelphia. This lively work, illustrated by himself, was designed for the education of the practical seaman. Original in concept, it met with immediate success, and for the next forty years continued in steady use as a standard textbook for young officers of the Royal Navy and the merchant marine. The introduction states that the work was planned many years before and was then finished 'for the advantage of a young gentleman whose inclinations led him to the choice of a sea-faring life'. Lever afterwards settled in Pontefract, and towards the end of his life divided his time between Alkrington Hall, near Manchester, the original seat of his family, and Edinburgh, where he died on 22 January 1839. He married Elizabeth, only child of the Revd William Murgatroyd: they had eight children. A note in

Mariner's Mirror (87, 2001, 76–7), 'Darcy Lever as inspiration for Jane Austen's "Mr Darcy"', describes recent discoveries about Lever's career on the stage.

J. K. LAUGHTON, *rev.* JOHN H. HARLAND

Sources J. F. Smith, ed., *The admission register of the Manchester School, with some notices of the more distinguished scholars*, 1, Chetham Society, 69 (1866), 155 • J. F. Smith, ed., *The admission register of the Manchester School, with some notes of the more distinguished scholars*, 2, Chetham Society, 73 (1868), 280 • E. Baines and W. R. Whatton, *The history of the county palatine and duchy of Lancaster*, new edn, ed. J. Croston and others, 2 (1889), 352–3 [family tree of Lever, of Alkrington and Kersall] • E. Hargrave, *Early Leeds volunteers* (1919)

Lever, Sir (Samuel) Hardman, baronet (1869–1947), accountant, was born on 18 April 1869 at 21 Bedford Place, Bootle, Lancashire, the younger of the two sons of Samuel Lever, a cotton dealer, and his wife, Elizabeth, *née* Cain. Only the forename Samuel appears on his birth certificate. His father had married at an early age and died when aged only twenty-one. The younger Samuel was educated at the Merchant Taylors' School, Great Crosby, and was then articled to T. T. Rogers of Liverpool; he achieved a certificate of merit in the final examinations of the Institute of Chartered Accountants in England and Wales in 1890. Soon afterwards he left Liverpool for New York and joined the accountancy firm of Barrow, Wade, Guthrie & Co. Some years later he became a partner, and also set up an office in London under the name of Lever, Anyon, and Spence. In 1900 he married Mary Edythe, the daughter of Matthew Hamilton Gault of Montreal. There were no children of the marriage.

In 1915 the minister of munitions, Lloyd George, then engaged on a large programme of national factory construction, was much exercised about production costs and the control, in general, of profits arising from munitions contracts. He was advised to seek the services of the best obtainable expert in cost accountancy, a science then more developed in the United States than in Britain. Lever was recommended and travelled from New York at very short notice in August 1915. Officially he became assistant financial secretary to the Ministry of Munitions with a wide range of duties, but he was forced to concentrate more and more on the institution of costing systems in the national factories. His brief was to ensure that efficient costing techniques and controls were applied internally and that cost-effective agreements should take the place of competitive contracts for the supply of munitions. Many companies which had previously been unaware of the advantages of costing methods had, therefore, to install costing systems, and began at last to appreciate their value.

When, at the end of 1916, Lloyd George became prime minister, his appointments included several personalities with little or no parliamentary experience and no particular interest in politics. Lever's appointment as financial secretary to the Treasury was a questionable one, for his ambitions did not lie in that direction, and his past experience did not demonstrably fit him for an office which demands at once a knowledge of national finance and of parliamentary procedure. He was never, in fact, called upon to carry out the normal duties of his post, for within two months of his appointment he was transferred to another sphere of activity for which he was eminently fitted.

The British government had virtually exhausted all the dollar resources it could command to cover the large commitments into which it had entered for American supplies. In the course of January 1917 it became clear that someone enjoying the confidence of the government must go to New York to be in intimate contact with J. P. Morgan & Co., who acted as agents for the government in placing orders and finding funds to pay for them. Lever, who was made a KCB in February that year, was the obvious choice since he had lived for many years in New York, and was in touch with and had the confidence of America's industrial and financial leaders. He arrived in America in February 1917, and became the official Treasury representative after the United States entered the First World War in April. He was also in close touch with the Canadian government on all financial relations with Great Britain. He did not return to England until the war was over, when he received a baronetcy (1920). He was also a chevalier of the Légion d'honneur and a commander of the order of the Crown of Italy.

After the war Lever became a director of several leading industrial companies and was also called upon from time to time for further public services. He was Treasury representative at the Ministry of Transport from 1919 to 1921, a member of the Weir committee on electricity, which recommended the construction of the national grid, and served as chairman of a committee set up in 1927 to inquire into the inland telegraph service. As the threat of war with Germany loomed, Lever in 1938 headed an air mission to Canada, which led to the construction in that country and the United States of aircraft which proved invaluable during the Second World War, and six months later he undertook a similar mission to Australia and New Zealand.

Lever, never thought of as anything but Sammie among his wide circle of friends on both sides of the Atlantic, was essentially a sturdy figure. Once described in New York as 'a Britisher who made American noises' (*DNB*), he was, apart from the noises, essentially British and liberal minded. He took a love of cricket with him to the United States, and even managed in his youth to play it there. In later life he was a keen golfer and an ardent angler.

A prominent cost accountant, who played a significant role in war-time Anglo-American financial relations, Lever died on 1 July 1947 at his home, Northlands, Abbey Hill Road, Winchester. He was survived by his wife, and the baronetcy became extinct.

JOHN RICHARD EDWARDS

Sources S. Marriner, 'The ministry of munitions, 1915–19, and government accounting procedures', *Accounting and Business Research*, 10 (1980), 130–42 • E. Jones, *Accountancy and the British economy, 1840–1980: the evolution of Ernst & Whinney* (1981) • 'Institute of Chartered Accountants in England and Wales', *The Accountant* (17 Jan 1891), 51 • K. Burk, ed., *War and the state: the transformation of British government, 1914–1919* (1982) • *CGPLA Eng. & Wales* (1947) • d. cert. • private information (2004) • b. cert.

Archives PRO, official papers, T186
Wealth at death £202,997 10*s.* 6*d.*: probate, 26 Aug 1947, *CGPLA Eng. & Wales*

Lever, (Norman) Harold, Baron Lever of Manchester (1914–1995), politician and businessman, was born in Cheetham, Manchester, on 15 January 1914, in a family of four sons and one daughter of Bernard Lever, textile merchant, and his wife, Bertha. Both parents were Orthodox Jews; their parents had emigrated from Lithuania at the end of the nineteenth century. An elder brother, Leslie, was a Labour councillor, lord mayor of Manchester, MP for the Ardwich division of Manchester, and life peer. Lever was educated at Manchester grammar school and Manchester University, where he read law; he was called to the bar (Middle Temple) in 1935. After practising on the north-western circuit from 1935 to 1939, he served with the RAF regiment from 1939 to 1945. He was MP for the Exchange division of Manchester from 1945 to 1950, and for the Cheetham division (later renamed Manchester Central) from 1950 to 1979. In 1939 he married Ethel Sebrinski, a medical student, daughter of Mendel Samuel, and former wife of Harris Sebrinski; the marriage was dissolved shortly afterwards. In 1945 he married Betty Featherman (known as Billie), daughter of Myer Woolfe, and former wife of Monty Featherman; she died in 1948, shortly after the birth of their one daughter. In 1962, after a long affair with the bridge player Erika (Rixi) *Markus (1910–1992), he married, third, Diane Zilkha, daughter of Saleh Bashi, a wealthy Lebanese banker, with whom he had three further daughters.

Lever was an extraordinary combination of kindness, wit, and commercial acumen. He was a bridge player of international standing. But his interest in partisan politics diminished with age. It was thus that, during Labour's years in opposition after 1951, he was not the most assiduous of members. He once sent a postcard to his chief whip (whom he had not notified of his absence), reading: 'Weather wonderful. Wish you were here.' His most notable achievement during these years was his sponsorship, as a private member, of the Defamation Act of 1952, which, *inter alia*, removed from authors the risk of unintentional defamation of real persons with the same name as fictional characters. When Labour returned to office in October 1964, Lever paid the price for his previous neglect of the House of Commons. Wilson omitted him from his government. This, however, gave him the opportunity to display his financial and legal expertise in criticism of James Callaghan's 1965 Finance Bill, which introduced both a corporation tax and a capital gains tax. Lever's performance eclipsed the official opposition. He was undisturbed by the humiliation he inflicted on his own government. This remarkable exhibition of wit, eloquence, and mastery persuaded Wilson to bring Lever into the government. After a probationary period as a chairman of commons standing committees, during which his wit relieved many a tedious session, Lever was recruited to the government in 1967 as joint parliamentary under-secretary of state at the Department of Economic Affairs and then as financial secretary to the Treasury, from 1967 to 1969. He joined the cabinet in 1969 as paymaster-general and deputy to Tony Benn at the Ministry of Technology. When Labour was defeated at the 1970 general election, he became chairman of the public accounts committee, a post he held until 1973.

Although sometimes criticized on the left because of his reputation for great wealth and his right-wing views on policy, Lever was nevertheless highly popular in the Parliamentary Labour Party, and achieved regular election to the shadow cabinet while Labour was in opposition between 1970 and 1974. As a strong 'European' he resigned with Roy Jenkins in 1972, when Labour proposed a referendum on membership of the EEC. However, he stood successfully for re-election at the beginning of the subsequent session. He would have achieved high office in the Labour cabinet formed after the February 1974 general election, had he not suffered a stroke in December 1972. He was out of politics for a year and, while he suffered no diminution in intellect, Wilson considered that his health forbade appointment to a major government department. Instead he joined the cabinet as economic adviser to the prime minister with the portfolio of chancellor of the duchy of Lancaster. He served until the defeat of the Callaghan government in May 1979.

The expansionary policies followed by the Heath government in its last two years of office exacerbated the inflationary problems it inherited, as well as moving the balance of payments into substantial deficit. A further deterioration in the balance of payments followed when, in the autumn of 1973, the Organization of Petroleum Exporting Countries (OPEC) quadrupled oil prices. At the outset of the 1974 Labour government, this critical conjuncture served to maximize Lever's influence. He was concerned to counteract the deflationary consequences of the oil price increase, which was threatening higher unemployment. With the majority of Keynesian economists, he pressed for reflation, to be funded by borrowing. He sometimes appeared to exert greater influence on economic policy than Denis Healey, the chancellor of the exchequer, especially as his recommendations were politically convenient for a government facing re-election later in 1974. Lever also devised politically advantageous interventions in the market place when, for example, he persuaded the building societies, in 1974, to eschew an increase in interest rates in return for a temporary loan from the government and, in 1975, managed the rescue with public money of the car manufacturer Chrysler UK, which its parent company, the American Chrysler Corporation, had declared an intention to liquidate. Thereby Lever achieved popularity even on the left of the Parliamentary Labour Party, which saw in him an enabler of their social policies despite the surrounding economic crisis. Lever's influence lessened as the economic crisis worsened and as Healey became more confident in the discharge of his responsibilities, to the extent of announcing his rejection of Keynesianism in 1975. When the UK was forced to seek assistance from the International Monetary Fund in the autumn of 1976, Healey and Lever found themselves on opposite sides of the argument, but Prime

Minister Callaghan, after long debate in cabinet, threw his weight on Healey's side and against Lever's optimistic view that International Monetary Fund conditionality could be escaped.

Lever was made a life peer in 1979. When the Social Democratic Party was formed in 1982, largely owing to differences within the Labour Party on Europe, Lever explained that he could not join because he had received his peerage from Callaghan. But he was understanding of the motives leading to the defection of others with whom he had previously been associated politically. In retirement he suffered increasing ill health as a result of a series of strokes. He died in London on 6 August 1995. He was survived by his third wife, and his four daughters.

EDMUND DELL

Sources H. Wilson, *Final term: the labour government, 1974–1976* (1979) • E. Dell, *A hard pounding: politics and economic crisis, 1974–76* (1991) • D. Healey, *The time of my life* (1989) • House of Commons, official report, vols. 702–3, 712–16 • *The Castle diaries, 1974–1976* (1980) • T. Benn, *Office without power: diaries, 1968–72* (1988) • T. Benn, *Conflicts of interest: diaries, 1977–1980*, ed. R. Winstone (1990) • T. Benn, *Against the tide: diaries, 1973–1976* (1989) • J. Callaghan, *Time and chance* (1987) • B. Pimlott, *Harold Wilson* (1992); repr. (1993) • P. Ziegler, *Harold Wilson: the authorized life* (1993) • *The Times* (7 Aug 1995) • *The Independent* (7 Aug 1995) • *WWW*

Likenesses photograph, repro. in *The Times* • photograph, repro. in *The Independent*

Lever, Ralph (*c*.1530–1585), Church of England clergyman, was the fifth son of John Lever of Little Lever, Lancashire, and his wife, Elenor Heyton, and the younger brother of Thomas *Lever. Educated at Eton, he progressed to St John's College, Cambridge, where he graduated BA in early 1548 and proceeded MA in 1551, dates which suggest that he was born about 1530. In 1549 he was a fellow of the college. On the accession of Queen Mary he went to the continent, a move doubtless connected with his partisanship for Lady Jane Grey in July 1553. His precise destination is unknown and it has been assumed that he remained 'a wandering scholar' (Garrett, 218). By 1559 he was back in England, becoming a senior fellow of St John's. He was incorporated at Oxford in 1560 and awarded his DTh at that university in 1578. When he married is unknown, but he and his wife, Margaret, had ten children.

During the early 1560s Lever appears to have become tutor to the family of Walter Devereux, first earl of Essex, and in 1563 he published a book on chess, *The most Noble, Ancient and Learned Play called the Philosopher's Game*, describing it on the title-page as invented 'for the honest recreation of students, and other sober persons, in passing the tediousness of time to the release of their labours and exercise of their wits'. Another book, *The Art of Reason*, 'teaching a perfect way to argue and dispute', was dedicated to Essex in 1573. Lever's fascination with logical processes, which he approached in a somewhat pedantic manner, had a significant bearing on his career. By the mid-1560s he had secured the patronage of James Pilkington, bishop of Durham, who made him his chaplain and in 1565 promoted him to the rectory of Washington; in 1566 to the archdeaconry of Northumberland; and in 1567 to a prebend in Durham Cathedral. However, it was not long before the relationship came under strain. During the episcopal visitation of 1572 Lever clashed with Pilkington's chancellor Robert Swift over the content of the visitation articles. Called before the consistory for disobedience, Lever resigned in order to avoid deprivation.

Lever resigned the rectory of Washington in 1576 in favour of his brother John, but the legal complexities implicit in the move initiated a dispute with one Anthony Garforth who also claimed the living. In 1575 he became rector of Stanhope, but resigned in 1577 in order to take up the mastership of Sherburn Hospital, vacant because of the death of his brother Thomas. At Sherburn he continued the reforms implemented by his predecessor, eventually procuring an act of parliament in 1585 'so that not the master and a few have the commodities, but the living wholly bestowed on the poor' (Marcombe, 291). Under this act the number of brethren was increased from sixteen to thirty; leasing policy was regulated; and it was ruled that the master should be a preacher with no other cure.

But although Lever's determination bore fruit at Sherburn, he had a much less positive impact on the Durham chapter. Despite the fact that he shared similar religious views to Dean William Whittingham and the puritan 'inner ring' of prebendaries, he was never a fully fledged member of the group and his profit from the 'lotteries' of chapter leases in 1572 and 1575 was small. Partly because of this he became opposed to Whittingham and made a series of complaints against his government, culminating in a petition to the queen to undertake a royal visitation in 1578. The new bishop of Durham, Richard Barnes, who was to assist in this task, made Lever his chaplain. However, when the commission met Lever became disillusioned because virtually all of its deliberations centred on the question of Whittingham's ordination, rather than on his alleged corruption. Consequently he fell out with Barnes and ultimately with the new vice-dean, Robert Bellamy. Writing to Burghley in September 1582, he complained, 'There was never a preacher so misused by a bishop as your orator hath been by the Bishop of Durham' (Marcombe, 265).

The appointment of Tobias Matthew as dean in 1583 began to calm an embarrassing situation. Thereafter Lever appears to have devoted his energies to a scheme to reform the chapter and other perceived abuses within the Church of England. On 12 January 1585 he submitted a document to the queen 'touching the canon law, the English papists, and the ecclesiastical officers of this realm' (Durham University Library, York book, fol. 36). With regard to the cathedral he suggested a thorough revision of the statutes, 'defective in sundry points touching religion and government', and an end to all 'back reckoning' about the difficulties of the 1570s (Marcombe, 245). The chapter, however, was hostile to his plans and he died in March 1585 before the new scheme could be properly considered. He was buried in Durham Cathedral, where his widow, who subsequently married Thomas Walker of Whitwell, requested interment in 1616.

Lever was a man of high principles who believed he spoke with the authority of God. He was blunt, fearless, and persistent, Robert Bellamy characterizing him as 'a man born to argue' (Marcombe, 267). Sir Michael Hickes believed he was 'distempered' and in 1583 Lever wrote to Burghley explaining how he was prone to uncontrollable fits of sobbing which rendered him helpless at times. According to Whittingham's biographer he finally 'fell mad … being at last followed by the boys and children with wonderment' (Green, 36). Lever may well have been suffering from a manic depressive illness, and contemporaries believed that the disruptions at Durham, caused largely by his persistence, were having a damaging effect both on the diocese and on the church in general.

DAVID MARCOMBE

Sources D. Marcombe, 'The dean and chapter of Durham, 1558–1603', PhD diss., U. Durham, 1973 • Venn, *Alum. Cant.*, 1/3.78 • C. H. Garrett, *The Marian exiles: a study in the origins of Elizabethan puritanism* (1938) • *The registers of Cuthbert Tunstall … and James Pilkington*, ed. G. Hinde, SurtS, 161 (1952) • York book, U. Durham L., archives and special collections, MSS DRv/2; DR III/3, fol. 36 • J. Strype, *Annals of the Reformation and establishment of religion … during Queen Elizabeth's happy reign*, new edn, 1/1 (1824) • BL, Lansdowne MS 36 • *APC*, 1577–82 • state papers, domestic series, Elizabeth I, PRO, SP/12, 149; 176; 162; 219 • G. Allen, ed., *Collectanea ad statum civilem et ecclesiasticum comitatus Dunelmensis* (1763–99) • Durham Cath. CL, Sharpe MS 51 (Randall MS) • H. C. Porter, *Reformation and reaction in Tudor Cambridge* (1958) • Foster, *Alum. Oxon.*, 1500–1714, 3.903 • G. J. Armytage, ed., *The baptismal, marriage, and burial registers of the cathedral church … at Durham, 1609–1896*, Harleian Society, register section, 23 (1897) • W. H. Longstaffe and J. Booth, eds., *Halmota prioratus Dunelmensis*, SurtS, 82 (1889) • high commission act book 9, Borth. Inst. • exchequer, king's remembrancer, deposition, PRO, E 134/23 & 24 Eliz. Mich. 12 • A. M. E. Green, ed., 'Life of Mr William Whittingham, dean of Durham', *Camden miscellany, VI*, CS, 104 (1871)

Lever [Leaver], **Thomas** (1521–1577), Church of England clergyman and writer, was born at Little Lever in Lancashire, the second of seven sons of John Lever and his wife, Elenor, daughter of the merchant Richard Heyton. Little is known of his early life. Like three of his brothers, Ralph *Lever, Richard, and John, Thomas was educated at St John's College, Cambridge, where he graduated BA in 1541–2, became a fellow in 1543 after being turned down a year earlier, proceeded MA in 1545, and in 1548 became senior fellow (3 July) and college preacher (23 September). At Cambridge Lever became friends with Roger Ascham, and quickly became the leader of the more advanced evangelical party that forced the resignation of the Lutheran master of St John's, John Taylor. In late 1548 Lever and Roger Hutchinson took part in a dispute with leading Catholics over the mass. Lever preached at St Paul's in London on 2 February 1550, and also a Lenten sermon before Edward VI on 16 March, while in April he tried unsuccessfully to persuade Joan Bocher to recant her Anabaptist heresies. Nicholas Ridley, bishop of London, ordained (or re-ordained) him deacon on 24 June and priest on 10 August. Lever preached at Paul's Cross on 14 December. These sermons of 1550, each of which had gone through at least three published editions by the end of 1551, castigated the rich for their exploitation of the poor commons, the church for its hypocrisy and sloth, and the government for its corruption and neglect of primary and university education, and established Lever as one of the most dynamic of the reforming preachers. He was active in this capacity in his native Lancashire, and the re-establishment of Sedbergh grammar school in Yorkshire in April 1551 may perhaps be credited to Lever, as a consequence of his decrying its spoliation during his Lenten sermon, when he exclaimed 'For Gods sake, you that be in aucthoritie, loke upon it' (Lever, *Sermons*, 81). Two editions of Lever's *A Meditacion upon the Lordes Prayer* were also published in 1551. In May, Lever served as chaplain to the marquess of Northampton during the latter's embassy to France.

Lever became master of St John's by royal mandate on 10 December 1551. The following year he graduated BTh and was commissioned to investigate a dispute over the mastership of Clare College. He preached one last time at court while the king lay ill during Lent 1553, prompting John Knox to write of this sermon that Lever 'planelie spak the desolation of the common weill, and the plagues which suld follow schortlie' (J. Knox, *A Godly Letter Sent to the Faythfull in London, Newcastle, Barwyk, etc.*, 1553). After the king's death Lever supported the claim of Lady Jane Grey, and on 15 July 1553 he supped with the duke of Northumberland, who had gone to Cambridge to proclaim her queen. But with the failure of Jane's cause and Mary Tudor secure on the throne, on 28 September, Lever gave up his mastership at the same time that twenty-four other fellows of St John's resigned their positions. Soon afterwards he fled to Strasbourg with a group of students from Oxford and Cambridge, arriving there on 24 February 1554. Lever, along with Cuthbert Hugh of Magdalen College, Oxford, reached Zürich on 10 March, where he had gone ahead to arrange accommodation for the students. While making these arrangements Lever became acquainted with Heinrich Bullinger, who facilitated his travels through Lentzburg, Bern, and Lausanne on his way to Geneva, where he arrived on 7 April. In Geneva, Lever attended a number of John Calvin's lectures and sermons.

Apart from at least one trip back to Zürich in October 1554, Lever appears to have remained in Geneva until 17 January 1555, and to have kept in frequent correspondence with Bullinger, and with the English students who had arrived in Zürich on 5 April 1554. Lever was in Frankfurt by 12 February 1555, where he entered into a controversy with John Knox over which prayer book to use. Both he and Knox opposed using the Genevan book of order without the approval of all the exile communities, but they also refused to use the current English prayer book. Lever's attempt to introduce his own service was rejected by the congregation, and set off a bitter rivalry with Knox, who along with William Whittingham sought Calvin's assistance. At this point Lever may have gone to Strasbourg to encourage Richard Cox to come to Frankfurt. Knox soon claimed that due to 'the subtle undermining of Mr. Lever … the whole Church was broken', especially after he brought in John Jewel, 'who had been at the Masse in England', to preach (Knox, 'Narrative', *Works*, 4.42–3). Cox arrived in Frankfurt on 13 March, Knox was banished on the 26th, and on 5 April Lever signed the letter Cox sent to Calvin explaining recent events and the prayer book revisions. By 13 October, Lever was back in Geneva, and in December was invited to replace Miles Coverdale as pastor at Wesel. He passed through Strasbourg (4 January 1556) before reaching Wesel, where he remained until the spring of 1557, when the congregation asked him to leave. He and a small group of supporters looked for a new home, and were probably in Bern by May, planning to visit English exiles in Basel. Bern officials finally permitted them to settle at Aarau, by 11 August 1557. Over the next eighteen months Lever lived at the home of Hans Dür, with his brother, and preached in the town church.

In November 1558 Elizabeth I succeeded to the English throne, and Lever received a licence to leave Aarau on 11 January 1559. On 16 January he was still there, when his small congregation agreed to participate in a Genevan initiative against ceremonies. Soon afterwards he was back in England, but immediately came into disfavour with the new queen for questioning her assumption of the title of supreme head of the church; he may, however, have helped to persuade her to settle for the title of supreme governor. During his continental exile Lever wrote and published in Geneva *A Treatise of the Right Way from Danger of Synne* (1556), which appeared in a second edition in 1571. In April 1559 Lever married a widow (her identity is unknown) who already had three children, and they had a son, Sampson, and a daughter who was born in July 1560. About June 1559 he was appointed minister of St John's, Bablake, Coventry, and archdeacon of Coventry about the same time. In a letter to Sir Francis Knollys and Sir William Cecil, dated 17 September 1560, Lever urged a complete investigation into the recent death of Amy Robsart, Lord Robert Dudley's wife, making it clear that he was troubled by the impact that rumours were having locally, and indicating that others in Coventry were similarly concerned. On 28 January 1563 he was made master of Sherburn Hospital, Durham. As a member of the convocation of 1562 he subscribed to the Thirty-Nine Articles while still hoping for a more reformed church. On 21 February 1564 he was made a prebendary of Durham Cathedral by the bishop, James Pilkington, an old friend from days at St John's College and in exile. During the vestiarian controversy Lever objected to wearing the surplice, and wrote to Cecil and Leicester on 23 February 1566 opposing the persecution of those who, out of conscience, shared his beliefs. In 1567 Lever wrote the preface to the Marian martyr John Bradford's *Godly Meditations uppon the Ten Commaundementes*, and appended to it his own *A Meditation on the Tenth Commandment*. On 9 November that year his radical reforming tendencies and rhetoric led Pilkington to relieve him of his prebend, but he retained his other benefices in Sherburn and Coventry. Lever preached the sermon at the funeral of his fellow radical William Turner, dean of Wells, in July 1568.

Lever's preaching and activities were closely monitored after the northern uprising of 1569–70. He and three other evangelical ministers were cited before ecclesiastical commissioners at Lambeth in 1571 for breaches in church discipline. Best known for his fiery and uncompromising preaching, Lever's three sermons of 1550 were first published collectively in 1572, and his *Treatise of the Right Way from Danger of Synne* appeared in a new edition in 1575. In the 1570s he circulated a series of notes for the 'reformacion of the mynistrye and mynisters', hoping to raise standards by insisting that ordained clergy should have an actual living or cure, to be held on condition of their preaching and administering the sacraments. Based on continental reformed models, his proposals would have given local congregations a greater role in the selection of ministers (especially to livings whose patrons were non-resident), and provided for the suspension of clergymen who failed to perform their duties or proved morally suspect and impenitent. That was relatively uncontroversial, though it cannot be shown that anything came of his proposals, but on 18 June 1577 Lever had another major confrontation with the government, when Thomas Bentham, bishop of Lichfield and Coventry, wrote to him in the queen's name directing him to stop the prophesyings he had been encouraging in his archdeaconry. Lever had continued to preach in a black gown in London churches, and it was during a journey from London to Sherburn in early July 1577 that he died on the road at Ware. He was buried in the chancel of the chapel of Sherburn Hospital, under a blue marble stone carved with a cross, a bible, a chalice, and an epitaph recalling the most influential years of his life: 'Thomas Leaver Preacher to King Edward the Sixte. He died in July 1577.' His brother, Ralph *Lever, succeeded him as master of the hospital on 16 July.

Ben Lowe

Sources T. Lever, *Sermons, 1550* (1870) • Cooper, *Ath. Cantab.*, vol. 1 • C. H. Garrett, *The Marian exiles: a study in the origins of Elizabethan puritanism* (1938) • V. W. Leaver, *Thomas and Ralph Lever: protestant reformers during the Edwardian Reformation in sixteenth century England* (1986) • *DNB* • M. A. Simpson, 'Of the troubles begun at Frankfurt, A.D.1554', *Reformation and revolution*, ed. D. Shaw (1967), 17–33 • *The works of John Knox*, ed. D. Laing, 6 vols., Bannatyne Club, 112 (1846–64), vol. 4 • H. Robinson, ed. and trans., *Original letters relative to the English Reformation*, 1 vol. in 2, Parker Society, [26] (1846–7) • T. Baker, *History of the college of St John the Evangelist, Cambridge*, ed. J. E. B. Mayor, 2 vols. (1869) • E. Miller, *Portrait of a college: a history of the College of Saint John the Evangelist, Cambridge* (1961) • T. Lever, 'A preface showing the true understanding of God's word', in *The writings of John Bradford*, ed. A. Townsend, Parker Society, 31 (1848), 565–8 • T. Lever, 'Meditation on the tenth commandment', *The writings of John Bradford*, ed. A. Townsend, Parker Society, 31 (1848), 569–71 • T. Lever, *A meditacion upon the Lordes prayer* (1551) • T. Lever, *A treatise of the right way from danger of synne … nowe newly augmented* (1571) • R. O'Day, *The English clergy: the emergence and consolidation of a profession, 1558–1642* (1979) • C. Haigh, *Reformation and resistance in Tudor Lancashire* (1975)

Lever, William Hesketh, first Viscount Leverhulme (1851–1925), soap manufacturer and philanthropist, was born on 19 September 1851, at 16 Wood Street, Bolton, seventh child and elder son of James Lever (1809–1897), wholesale and retail grocer, and his wife, Eliza, daughter of William Hesketh, cotton mill manager, of Manchester.

William Hesketh Lever, first Viscount Leverhulme (1851–1925), by William Strang, 1918

He had eight sisters and a brother. He was educated privately in Bolton, and at Bolton Church Institute (1864–7). On his sixteenth birthday he was given a copy of Samuel Smiles's *Self-Help*, which provided his secular credo. He was a lifelong Congregationalist, who applied many of that sect's ideals in his business life, though he developed an interest in Christian Science. He was put to work in the family grocery in 1867, and admitted to a junior partnership worth £800 a year in 1872.

In 1874 Lever married Elizabeth Ellen (*d*. 1913), daughter of Crompton Hulme, linen draper, a neighbour in Wood Street. They had been friends since childhood; she was a kindly, resilient woman, to whom he remained devoted. Their only surviving child, William, was born fourteen years after their marriage, in 1888; he inherited his father's titles, and published a biography of him in 1927.

The soap business Although Lever was a grocer by trade, his instincts were those of a marketing man. He studied not only the habits of his father's customers, who were chiefly poor Lancashire housewives, but also American techniques of brand naming, advertising, and sales promotion, for he admired the successful provision of household necessities and minor luxuries at a moderate price to a new mass of American consumers. An additional grocery branch was opened at Wigan, organizational reforms were made, large premises were built, and new commitments were undertaken, including a line of soap tablets marketed from 1874 as Lever's Pure Honey Soap. The elder Lever, with the conservatism of age, was anxious at these measures, but their success disarmed opposition.

In 1884 Lever decided to trade on his own account in a soap made largely from vegetable oils rather than the customary tallow. His brother, James Darcy Lever (1854–1910), agreed to join him in the firm of Lever Brothers. Their father hesitated to support the scheme, though he eventually provided some capital. William Lever had no technical knowledge, and did not invent the soap, but recognized its potential popularity with housewives. His great strokes were to give his soap the registered brand name of Sunlight, and to provide packaging that made it easily recognizable and served as a guarantee of quality. Other great brand names associated with him were Lux soap powder and Vim household cleaner, which he registered in 1894. His vigorous advertising and promotion created a demand which no retailer dared ignore. Competitors resented but emulated his methods. Initially Sunlight soap was supplied by other manufacturers for sale by Lever Brothers, but in 1885 the firm bought a soapworks at Warrington and thereafter made its own soap.

The need for a large factory soon became pressing, and in 1887 Lever bought 52 acres, later extended to 500 acres, conveniently situated on the Mersey, near Bebington in Cheshire. He conceived the idea of a colony of industry to be called Port Sunlight, where his workpeople should live near his works. There were picturesque houses and gardens, together with many social and sporting amenities. Manufacture began there in January 1889. Though ruling his model community as a benevolent despot, he introduced a co-partnership scheme in 1909.

Lever travelled extensively, spreading his business overseas, opening branches or agencies in the colonies, United States, and European countries. In addition he undertook five world tours between 1892 and 1923–4, always travelling with a large and pompous retinue. His early travel articles were published in a book entitled *Following the Flag* (1893).

Some of Lever's foreign ventures made slow progress, but generally the profitable development of his affairs was continuous. In 1890 Lever Brothers was made a limited company, and in 1894 it was floated to the public with a capital of £1.5 million, divided equally into preference and ordinary shares. No ordinary shares were offered publicly, and Lever, who became chairman, gradually acquired all of these. He initiated a policy of amalgamation with other soap makers, either by purchase or interchange of shares, which resulted in a wide control over the soap-making trade. In 1906 he proposed a new and greater amalgamation of soap companies, which was denounced by the *Daily Mail* and other newspapers controlled by Lord Northcliffe, who anticipated a loss of advertising revenue. During the autumn of 1906 they directed at Lever many startling accusations, including fraudulent trading and sweated labour. The Sunlight business was damaged by these attacks, and other soap firms were alarmed into abandoning the proposed amalgamation. Lever was the first witness in a libel action brought by his company in 1907, and testified so forcefully that the defendants immediately offered a settlement. Lever Brothers received a total of £141,000 from Northcliffe's newspapers—at that date the highest libel payment ever made—and Lever used these sums to endow Liverpool University with a school of tropical medicine (of which he was chairman in 1910–13) and a school of town planning and civic design.

Politics and honours Paradoxically for a plutocrat who created one of the world's largest combines, Lever all his life believed in self-help and free trade: W. E. Gladstone, who visited Port Sunlight on 28 November 1891, was his political hero. Lever contested Birkenhead as a Liberal without success in 1892, 1894, and 1895. In 1900 he failed again in the Wirral division of Cheshire, but in 1906 he was returned for that constituency, though he found parliamentary responsibilities too heavy and retired in December 1909. He unsuccessfully contested the Ormskirk division of Lancashire in January 1910. Although unsuited by temperament for party politics, he enjoyed electioneering and became a competent platform speaker. According to A. C. Menzies: 'Leverhulme speaks well, with a flow of language of a homely order, no great rhetoric, rather fatherly expoundings, mixed with endless anecdotes and not a few cryptic utterances' (Menzies, 147). One example of his speaking style was the observation: 'Every time a cloud appears in the sky it is not always going to rain cats and dogs. Our imagination is the architect of our fright.' Such sentiments led the Liberal journalist A. G. Gardiner to compare Lever to Benjamin Franklin: 'I can see him putting himself through the same hard moral discipline, taking himself in hand with a certain grim joy, and subduing himself to his own maxims with relentless firmness. He is a moral athlete who has trained himself down to the last ounce, and wins the race by first winning the victory over himself' (Gardiner, 195). On Liberal Party recommendation Lever was created a baronet in 1911 and was raised to the peerage in 1917 as Baron Leverhulme, his title combining his own and his wife's surnames. He was advanced to a viscountcy in 1922.

New business ventures Lever was always fearful of being held to ransom by monopolist suppliers of raw materials. He therefore became interested in bringing palm oil and palm-kernel oil from west Africa under his own control. In 1910 he established crushing mills in Nigeria, and to ensure continuity of supplies he obtained in the following year a concession of land and works in the Belgian Congo. There he planted forests of palm trees, erected a new town called Leverville, opened Lever hospitals, and put Lever steamers on the Congo River and Congolese children in Lever schools. His first mill opened at Leverville in 1911. He visited the Congo twice in great state, in 1912–13 and in 1924–5. His wife, who had accompanied him, died on her return from the first visit, and the second was swiftly followed by his own death. His aggrandizing African interests reached a disastrous climax in 1920 when Leverhulme committed his company to buying control of the Niger Company for over £8 million. This transaction was followed by a plummeting in values, and for a time his rashness threatened to ruin his life's achievement.

Leverhulme bought the Isle of Lewis in 1917, and the isles of North and South Harris in 1919. He set up a company called MacFisheries, and acquired several food companies, notably T. Wall & Sons, sausage makers, intending to develop the fishing industry and improve the conditions of the crofter population of these Scottish western isles. In 1923 he abandoned his plans for Lewis after encountering opposition, but his intentions were not repulsed on Harris, where the town of Obbe changed its name to Leverburgh. Leverhulme's great projects—Port Sunlight, the Congo plantations, the Hebridean venture, and the Niger fiasco—provided a necessary challenge for his creative, combative, and restless imagination. He had a passion for organizing, building, and regulating other people's lives.

Property Leverhulme relished architectural planning and was acquisitive of every sort of property: 'Sir William Lever of soap fame seems to have a passion for purchase and evidently thinks more of the buying than the thing bought,' Sir George Arthur commented in 1912 (284). He made a distinctive contribution to ecclesiastical architecture by building four Congregationalist churches and was an honorary fellow of the Royal Institute of British Architects from 1920. He rebuilt the house and village on his estate at Thornton Hough in Cheshire (bought in 1891), opening out an ambitious road system which, when the local authority would not take it over, he closed. He extended the outer ramparts of his great house at Hampstead (bought in 1904) until they dominated the most sylvan corner of the heath. In 1899 he bought the Rivington estate near Bolton, and after his home there was destroyed by a suffragette arsonist in 1913, he built a new bungalow. Lord Crawford noted after a visit: 'Leverhulme bought it years ago, kept extending it—only a year before his death he added a large ballroom—and now this preposterous accumulation of rooms and verandahs is perched in the middle of Rivington Moor … Here he was uncontrolled and one sees the odd potpourri of rubbish and good things he collected—a few really nice bits of tapestry hung between monstrous forgeries and a number of wretched canvases by RAs of the eighties' (Vincent, 527). He also lived at Lews Castle, Stornoway (1918–23), and Borve Lodge, Harris (1923–5). In his grounds he built belvederes, dug lakes, and employed hundreds of gardeners. After his death there was a sale lasting fifteen days of the purchases with which he had filled his houses.

In 1912 Lever bought Stafford House in St James's from the duke of Sutherland. His gift in 1914 of this ducal palace under its new name of Lancaster House to serve as the London Museum was interpreted sordidly as an attempt to ingratiate himself with the government. In 1919 Leverhulme bought Moor Park with 3000 acres in Hertfordshire from Lord Ebury and transformed it into a country club with three golf courses. From Ebury's cousin the duke of Westminster he bought Grosvenor House on Park Lane for £500,000 in 1924, with the intention of developing it as a national arts centre. Among other benefactions he donated an art gallery at Port Sunlight in memory of his wife.

Death and character Leverhulme was high sheriff of Lancashire in 1917, and mayor of Bolton and junior warden of the grand lodge of freemasons in 1918. Overwork, rather than his habit of sleeping outdoors in all weathers in a simple iron bed, caused his death from pneumonia on 7 May 1925, at The Hill, Hampstead. He was buried on 11 May 1925 at Port Sunlight.

Leverhulme's will, dated 11 September 1924, was brief but complex. It established a trust with four trustees. Though it mentioned 'research and education' as one of its objectives, it was the trustees rather than the benefactor who established the Leverhulme Trust which became the chief non-governmental funder of individual research in the second half of the twentieth century.

'Thickset in stature, with a sturdy body set on short legs and a massive head covered with thick, upstanding hair, he radiated force and energy', according to Sir Angus Watson. 'He had piercing, blue-grey eyes which, however, flashed with challenge when he was angry', and 'the short neck and closely-set ears of a prize-fighter' (Watson, 140–4). Leverhulme was often intensely troubled by his own fears, which he mastered courageously. He was both a tyrant and a sentimentalist, caring less for money than for the power it gave him. He never swerved from his sense that commercial efficiency was a service to humanity.

RICHARD DAVENPORT-HINES

Sources *Viscount Leverhulme, by his son* (1927) • W. P. Jolly, *Lord Leverhulme* (1976) • C. Wilson, *The history of Unilever: a study in economic growth and social change*, 1 (1954) • A. G. Gardiner, *Pillars of society* (1913) • A. C. B. Menzies, *Modern men of mark* (1921) • A. Watson, *My life: an autobiography* (1937), 140–41 • *The Crawford papers: the journals of David Lindsay, twenty-seventh earl of Crawford … 1892–1940*, ed. J. Vincent (1984) • [G. Arthur], *Some letters from a man of no importance, 1895–1914* (1928) • *The Times* (8 May 1925) • C. Binfield, 'Business paternalism and the Congregational ideal: a preliminary reconnoitre', *Business and religion in Britain*, ed. D. J. Jeremy (1988), 118–41 • A. Briggs, *The story of the Leverhulme Trust* (1991) • W. H. Lever, *Following the flag* (1893) • W. H. Lever, *The buildings erected at Port Sunlight and Thornton Hough* (1905) • W. H. Lever, *Art and beauty in the city* (1915) • GEC, *Peerage*

Archives Bolton Archive Service, Rivington estate papers • Lady Lever Art Gallery, Port Sunlight, Cheshire, papers relating to his art collections • NRA, business papers and transcripts of diary • Unilever Archives, London | BLPES, corresp. with E. D. Morel • HLRO, letters relating to portrait by Augustus John • U. Lpool L., corresp. with Leslie Patrick Abercrombie | FILM BFI NFTVA, actuality footage

Likenesses L. Fildes, oils, *c.*1898 • E. O. Ford, marble bust, 1900, Lady Lever Art Gallery, Port Sunlight • B. Stone, photograph, 1909, NPG • G. H. Heale, oils, 1916, Lady Lever Art Gallery, Port Sunlight • G. H. Heale, oils, 1917 • W. Strang, portrait, 1918, U. Lpool, art collections [*see illus.*] • W. Orpen, oils, 1919–21, Corporation of Bolton • A. John, oils, 1920 • photograph, 1920, repro. in Wilson, *A history of Unilever* • W. Stoneman, photographs, 1921–2, NPG • P. de Laszlo, oils, 1924, Lady Lever Art Gallery, Port Sunlight • W. G. John, bronze recumbent effigy, *c.*1926, Christ Church, Port Sunlight • photographs, repro. in *Viscount Leverhume, by his son* • photographs

Wealth at death £1,000,000: probate, 7 July 1925, *CGPLA Eng. & Wales*

Leverett, John (1616–1679), colonial governor, was born in Boston, Lincolnshire, the son of Thomas Leverett and Anne Fisher, and was baptized in St Botolph's parish on 7 July 1616. Thomas Leverett, a public supporter of the famed puritan preacher John Cotton, migrated with his family in 1633 to Boston, Massachusetts, where Cotton became minister. In 1639 John Leverett became a member of the Boston church and in 1640 a freeman able to vote in colonial elections. Also in 1639 he married Hannah Hudson (*d.* 1646), who bore him four children. After her death he married Sarah Sedgwick (*d.* 1680), the daughter of the prominent Charlestown merchant and militia officer Robert Sedgwick, in 1647. Fourteen children were born of this marriage, which ended with Leverett's death.

During the 1640s Leverett was a moderately successful merchant in the coastal and transatlantic trades, but his strongest interests were military and political. From 1639 to 1671 he was a member of Boston's artillery company. In 1642 the Massachusetts government put him on a vital commission to confer with the Narragansett Indians. He returned to England in 1644 to become a captain in the parliamentarian regiment of Thomas Rainborowe. After four years of service he returned to Boston. Resuming his political career, he was chosen a Boston selectman in 1651 and represented the town in the general court, the colony's legislature, from 1651 to 1653.

In the 1650s Leverett became more deeply involved in colonial diplomacy. In 1652 he was one of the agents sent to Maine to warn the French of Massachusetts's claim to the region. The next year he was in a delegation sent to Dutch New Netherland (later New York) to settle land and trade differences. Upon the failure of this mission Leverett, with his father-in-law Robert Sedgwick, went to England to gain aid against New Netherland during the First Anglo-Dutch War. Putting Sedgwick in command, Cromwell gave them four ships, 200 men, and a commission to raise local militia. Once back in New England, the expedition learned that the war was over. However, these and additional troops, commanded by Sedgwick, seized three French posts in Maine, thereby preventing further French penetration for the next thirteen years. Leverett organized the logistical and political support for the campaign.

At this triumph, the general court appointed him in 1655 colonial agent in England, where he remained until 1662, attempting to preserve the colony's autonomy during the delicate period of transition from protectorate to Restoration. Upon his return to Boston, he was again elected to the general court for 1663–5, serving as speaker during part of that time. In 1663 he was also made major-general of Massachusetts, a position he held until elected governor in 1673. Reputedly, he was one of the four entrusted with the colony's precious charter in 1664, when the first Restoration inspectors arrived to investigate New England's attitude towards the new regime and the emerging imperial system. From 1665 to 1670 he was annually elected to the court of assistants, the colonial upper house. Then from 1671 to 1673 he served as deputy governor prior to his first election as governor. He was annually re-elected governor from 1674 until his death.

Relations with England, the politics of internal reform, and American Indian warfare dominated Leverett's years as governor. A consistent defender of Massachusetts's autonomy, in 1676 he refused to take an oath to enforce the English Navigation Acts when pressed to do so by Edward Randolph, an agent of the newly formed lords of trade, and was reported to have claimed that English parliamentary legislation did not necessarily apply in Massachusetts. However, unlike some of the more isolationist of New England's leaders, he favoured religious toleration, the half-way covenant, and other inclusivist policies likely to encourage economic development, domestic peace, and imperial expansion. In that spirit, he resisted efforts by Increase Mather and other clerics to push internal moral and religious reforms he thought unnecessarily divisive.

At the outset of King Philip's War (1675–6), a massive conflict with Native Americans that embroiled all of New England, Leverett acted swiftly to support beleaguered Plymouth Colony, and throughout the struggle worked to maintain a united front among the area's colonial governments. Insisting on strong logistical and militia support from all the towns, he pursued an aggressive strategy of carrying the war to the Native American strongholds rather than using a static defence. Although he allowed the raising of troops from the Native American praying towns, he also favoured the condign policy of selling captives into slavery in the West Indies. The result of the war was the end of effective Native American resistance in southern New England.

John Leverett died in Boston on 16 March 1679. His career well illustrates the transatlantic character of the puritan movement and the tensions within the emerging empire of the seventeenth century.

RICHARD P. GILDRIE

Sources R. Middlekauff, 'Leverett, John', *ANB* • J. T. Adams, 'Leverett, John', *DAB* • N. B. Shurtleff, ed., *Records of the governor and company of the Massachusetts Bay in New England*, 5 vols. in 6 (1853–4); repr. (1968) • W. H. Whitmore, *The Massachusetts civil list for the colonial and provincial periods, 1630–1774* (1870) • D. E. Leach, *Flintlock and tomahawk: New England in King Philip's War* (1958) • S. S. Webb, *1676: the end of American independence* (1984) • R. P. Gildrie, *The profane, the civil and the godly* (1994) • R. S. Dunn, *Puritans and Yankees: the Winthrop dynasty of New England, 1630–1717* (1962) • F. J. Bremer, *Congregational communion: clerical friendship in the Anglo-American puritan community, 1610–1692* (1994) • K. H. Dacey, *In the shadow of the Great Blue Hill* (1995) • D. Staloff, *The making of an American thinking class* (1998)

Leverhulme. For this title name *see* Lever, William Hesketh, first Viscount Leverhulme (1851–1925).

Leveridge, Richard (1670–1758), singer and composer, was born in the parish of St Martin-in-the-Fields, London, on 19 July 1670, the son of Richard Leveridge and his wife, Mary, *née* Long. Although he sang on stage for more than fifty years and composed over 160 songs, many to his own words, nothing is known about his education.

In 1695 Leveridge became the leading bass in the company for which Henry Purcell composed music in the last few months of his life, creating the role of the magician Ismeron in the dramatic opera *The Indian Queen*, with the impressive incantation 'Ye twice ten hundred deities'. Purcell's music remained in his repertory for nearly fifty years. Leveridge also wrote vocal music for the theatre from 1696 and published handsomely engraved collections of his songs in 1697 and 1699. He joined Daniel Purcell and Jeremiah Clarke in composing music for *The Island Princess* (Drury Lane, February 1699); Peter Motteux, in his preface to the text, thanked Leveridge 'for gracing my words with his Composition, as much as for his celebrated singing' and for giving 'life to the whole Entertainment' in his comic dialogue with the tenor John Pate. By Christmas 1699 he had moved to Ireland: 'he Owes so much money he dare not come over, so for want of him we han't had one Opera play'd this Winter' (Vanbrugh, 4). Leveridge was at Smock Alley Theatre in Dublin as singer and composer for at least one season. Soon after his return to Drury Lane in November 1702 the company performed *Macbeth*, with 'Vocal and Instrumental Musick, all new Compos'd by Mr. *Leveridge*, and perform'd by him and others' (*Daily Courant*, 19 Nov 1702). His music became a regular part of the play until Henry Irving finally discarded it in 1875. In the late eighteenth century the *Macbeth* music was ascribed to Matthew Locke, but Leveridge's name is on the contemporary manuscript at the Fitzwilliam Museum, Cambridge. He wrote Hecate's music for himself, and continued to sing the role until 1750.

As one of London's star singers Leveridge also appeared in concerts, at court performances before Queen Anne, and at civic occasions such as the lord mayor's banquet for Marlborough and his generals in December 1706. Drury Lane mounted the first all-sung English opera in the Italian style, Thomas Clayton's *Arsinoe*, in January 1705 with Leveridge as the leading bass. He then created *buffo* roles in the extremely successful *Camilla* (30 March 1706), with music adapted from Bononcini, in the Clayton–Addison *Rosamond* (4 March 1707), and in the pasticcios *Thomyris* (1 April 1707) and *Love's Triumph* (26 February 1708). By 1708 opera had become dominated by Italian singers and the Italian language, and the English version of Scarlatti's *Didone delirante*, which Leveridge had prepared, was postponed and then abandoned. For a time music was banned from plays in an attempt to assist the now separate opera company. There was no place for Leveridge as a full-time member of a theatre company, but he sang in concerts, at London events such as the 1708 Post Office feast, and at Bath, Richmond Wells, and Greenwich. In November 1711 he registered his *New Book of Songs* at Stationers' Hall (it included two songs which he made by fitting his own words to opera arias by Handel), and in 1712–13 he appeared in the premières of Handel's operas *Il pastor fido* and *Teseo* and in a revival of *Rinaldo*, singing in Italian. In 1731 he was to sing Polyphemus in the first public performance of Handel's *Acis and Galatea*.

In December 1714 John Rich opened a new playhouse at Lincoln's Inn Fields and Leveridge returned to his old repertory of songs and comic dialogues, Purcell masques, *The*

Island Princess, and the *Macbeth* music. He also sang in new musical afterpieces, which were becoming a popular part of the evening's entertainment. For his benefit in 1716 he wrote *The Comick Masque of Pyramus and Thisbe*, adapting Shakespeare to produce a good-natured burlesque of Italian opera, with arias for Wall, Lion, and the Man in the Moon. He sang Pyramus to the Thisbe of the tenor George Pack. By summer 1720 the Lincoln's Inn Fields theatre was in financial difficulties and in the following three years Leveridge was advertised as singing there only once, at a benefit for John Rich. He had been running a coffee house at his home in Tavistock Street, Covent Garden, since at least April 1717. The diarist William Byrd of Virginia describes eating there after a play in November 1719: 'we had broiled chicken for supper and drank rack punch till 2 o'clock' (Byrd, 338). Leveridge composed music for *Jupiter and Europa* (March 1723), the first of John Rich's spectacular pantomime afterpieces, and returned to Lincoln's Inn Fields that autumn. On 20 December 1723 he sang Charon in Rich's hugely successful pantomime *The Necromancer* and it is Charon's song 'Ghosts of every Occupation' that he holds in his portrait by Thomas Frye. Leveridge made an imposing figure as the infernal god Pluto in three of the later pantomimes, as Morpheus and Silenus in *Apollo and Daphne*, and Merlin in *The Royal Chase*. The success of the pantomimes and of *The Beggar's Opera* enabled Rich to move to a new theatre in Covent Garden in 1732. In 1740 Leveridge undertook the naturalistic role of the father in Henry Carey's afterpiece *The Parting Lovers* and in 1741 had his last new part, as Dick Shamwell in John Lampe's *The Sham Conjuror*, for the benefit of Mrs Lampe and her sister. He enjoyed excellent health and only reduced the number of his appearances when he was in his mid-seventies.

Leveridge continued to compose and in 1727 published forty-three of his songs by subscription in an attractive pocket-sized two-volume set, with a frontispiece by William Hogarth, a member of the same masonic lodge as Leveridge. In 1728 a retrospective collection of seventy of his songs was issued by the music publisher John Walsh. Leveridge's songs appeared frequently in periodical publications and miscellaneous collections during his lifetime, from *Wit and Mirth* (1699) to the *Universal Magazine* (December 1753), and several continued to be republished many years after his death. The tune of his popular ballad 'A cobbler there was' was used for 'Ourselves Like the Great' in *The Beggar's Opera* and later ballad operas frequently adopted his tunes, but his only appearance in a ballad opera was in John Gay's posthumous *Achilles* (1733). Leveridge's most enduring song, 'The Roast Beef of Old England', was introduced at his benefit in 1735. As he grew older his annual benefits developed into very individual affairs, announced from the stage and in the newspapers by verses he wrote to sing to popular tunes and rounded off by a sung epilogue of thanks. In 1801 Mrs Thrale remembered that as a girl she sat in the pit at Leveridge's benefit and heard him twice encored: 'my Uncle who took Care of me, sayd Leveridge was fourscore years old' (Balderston, 1021). Leveridge's final appearance was at his benefit on 24 April 1751 and that October a subscription was organized, whereby ladies and gentlemen contributed a guinea a year 'for the support of honest Dick Leveridge, the Father of the English Stage' (*European Magazine*, 363).

On 16 October 1751 the *London Daily Advertiser* printed a rhyming appeal from Leveridge ('the Old Stager') for the return of his stolen watch, promising 'good Wine and a Song' if the watch was returned. In May 1752 he fell, hit his head, and was unconscious for a time, but recovered and 'would not accept of a Chair, but walked home supported by two Men' (*Daily Advertiser*, 22 May 1752). He died at his lodgings in High Holborn on 22 March 1758 and was buried at St Martin-in-the-Fields on the 30th, leaving everything to his widowed daughter, Mrs Mary Parratt. The *London Evening-Post* (21–3 March 1758) reported that he was sensible to the last, and concluded 'No Man lived more generally esteemed by his Acquaintance, nor more deservedly; being a most chearful Companion, and a strictly honest Man'.

OLIVE BALDWIN and THELMA WILSON

Sources W. Van Lennep and others, eds., *The London stage, 1660–1800*, 5 pts in 11 vols. (1960–68), pts 1–4 • *Muses Mercury* (Sept 1707–Jan 1708) • *Daily Courant* (2 April 1717) • *Daily Advertiser* [London] (16 Oct 1751) • *Daily Advertiser* [London] (21–2 May 1752) • *Public Advertiser* (23 March 1758) • *London Evening-Post* (23 March 1758) • R. Leveridge, *Complete songs (with the music in Macbeth)*, ed. O. Baldwin and T. Wilson (1997) • P. Motteux, *The island princess* (1985), ser. C, vol. 2 of *Music for London entertainment* [with introduction by C. A. Price and R. D. Hume] • M. Tilmouth, 'A calendar of references to music in newspapers published in London and the provinces (1660–1719)', *Royal Musical Association Research Chronicle*, 1 (1961) • P. Danchin, ed., *The prologues and epilogues of the eighteenth century: a complete edition* (1990–), vols. 1–5 • J. Milhous and R. D. Hume, eds., *Vice Chamberlain Coke's theatrical papers, 1706–1715* (1982) • 'An account of Richard Leveridge', *European Magazine and London Review*, 24 (1793), 243–4, 363–4 • *The complete works of Sir John Vanbrugh*, ed. G. Webb, 4: *The letters* (1928) • *The session of musicians* (1724) • H. Carey, *Poems on several occasions* (1720) • *Thraliana: the diary of Mrs. Hester Lynch Thrale (later Mrs. Piozzi), 1776–1809*, ed. K. C. Balderston, 2nd edn, 2 (1951) • Burney, *Hist. mus.*, vol. 4 • J. Hawkins, *A general history of the science and practice of music*, 5 (1776) • R. Leveridge, *The comick masque of Pyramus and Thisbe* (1716); facs. (1969) • W. Boyce, 'The man that say Dick Leveridge stinks', catch, Royal College of Music, MS 782, fol. 12v • W. Byrd, *The London diary (1717–1721)*, ed. L. B. Wright and M. Tinling (1958) • 'Musical anecdote', *Euterpeiad* [Boston] (21 July 1821) • O. Baldwin and T. Wilson, 'Richard Leveridge, 1670–1758', *MT*, 111 (1970), 592–4, 891–3, 988–90 • O. Baldwin and T. Wilson, '250 years of roast beef', *MT*, 126 (1985), 203–7 • O. Baldwin and T. Wilson, 'The music for Durfey's *Cinthia and Endimion*', *Theatre Notebook*, 41 (1987), 70–74 • parish register, St Martin-in-the-Fields, London, 1670 [baptism] • parish register, St Martin-in-the-Fields, London, 1758 [burial] • will, PRO, PROB 11/836

Likenesses formerly attrib. G. Kneller, oils, *c*.1710–1720 (young), NPG; repro. in Baldwin and Wilson, eds., *Complete songs* • A. van der Mijn, mezzotint, pubd 1753 (after oils by F. van der Mijn), BM, Harvard TC • T. Frye, oils (late middle age), Gerald Coke Handel collection; repro. in Baldwin and Wilson, eds., *Complete songs* • F. van der Mijn, oils (in old age), Garr. Club • W. Pether, mezzotint (after oils by T. Frye), BM, NPG, Harvard TC • J. Saunders, line engraving (after oils by T. Frye), repro. in *European Magazine* • double portrait, line engraving (with William Penkethman), BM; repro. in Baldwin and Wilson, eds., *Complete songs*

Wealth at death estate to widowed daughter; goods and chattels: will, PRO, PROB 11/836, sig. 80

Leverous, Thomas (*c.*1487–1577), bishop of Kildare, may have been born as early as 1487. Seventeenth-century accounts of his career, composed by Robert Ware and John Lynch, estimate that he was born ten years later, about 1497, but this is open to doubt. According to the earliest notice of his life and deeds, written by Richard Stanihurst—a chronicler who actually knew him—as a child Leverous was foster brother to the future ninth earl of Kildare, Gerald Fitzgerald. Gerald was born in 1487; to be a suitable foster brother Leverous must have been at least the same age, if not a little older. Other details of his early life and background remain stubbornly elusive. Nothing at all is known of his parentage, nor is it clear whether his family was of Anglo-Norman or Cambro-Norman origin. All that can be said with safety is that he was born in co. Kildare, and that his parents were of relatively moderate status.

Leverous was a creature of the Fitzgerald political system. After entering the priesthood early in the 1500s he was appointed vicar of Laraghbrine and Keroghe, co. Kildare, the advowson of which was in the gift of his former foster brother as earl of Kildare. It was, moreover, the parish church of Maynooth, the capital of the Kildare lordship, and it is reasonable to deduce that Leverous spent most of his time in the vicinity of Maynooth Castle ministering to the needs of the Kildare family. One of his functions was as family tutor. Some time after 1525 he began acting as tutor to the future eleventh earl, Gerald *Fitzgerald, the ninth earl's eldest son by his second marriage; if the comment of a hostile English observer is trustworthy, he inspired his charge with dread: '[Leverous] keepeth him so under that if he rebuke him never so little, he trembleth with fear' (*LP Henry VIII*, 3.211). It was as Gerald's tutor that Leverous first came to prominence in Irish affairs, following the outbreak of the ill-fated Kildare revolt in 1534, at which time (and after the ninth earl's death) he became the boy's governor and sole guardian.

With the collapse of the rising, the government of Henry VIII was anxious to lay its hands upon every member of the Fitzgerald bloodline, the better to extirpate their influence in Ireland. The surrender and imprisonment of the main rebel leaders between August 1535 and February 1536 had left Gerald Fitzgerald, just ten years of age, as heir presumptive to the earldom; accordingly it fell to Leverous to ensure the dynastic survival of the Fitzgeralds by keeping his ward free of the government's clutches. Throughout the remainder of 1536 he played hide-and-seek with the royal army, accompanying Gerald in his flight from Donore Castle, co. Kildare, taking him westwards to safe houses in Offaly, Iregan, and Thomond. Having crossed the Shannon and contacted regional lords hostile to Henry VIII, a major new rebel confederacy known as the Geraldine League was formed, its objective being to break the power in Ireland of the schismatic English king, defend the papacy, and restore Gerald to the outlawed Kildare earldom. The extent of Leverous's participation in the league is open to dispute. Catholic nationalist historians once claimed he was 'mainly instrumental in organising that confederacy' (Moran, *Archbishops*, 57); more recently scholars have tended to downplay his involvement—even to ignore it—conscious that the principal near contemporary account of the league, Stanihurst's *Historie* of 1577, had a vested interest in highlighting the role played in it by Leverous and others.

Whatever his political activities Leverous's primary concern remained the safety of his young charge. After 1536 he continued by Gerald's side, accompanying him from Kerry to Donegal, and when the league collapsed in 1540 he was one of a small company of servants to accompany the Fitzgerald lord on his voyage into exile in France. With government spies not far behind the Fitzgerald party was compelled to move from place to place, from St Malo to Paris and on to Liège, but eventually in 1543 they reached Rome, led there by Cardinal Reginald Pole. It was at this juncture that Leverous seems to have left his master's service—leaving Gerald to complete his education with new teachers—and he attached himself instead to Cardinal Pole's household. Through Pole's backing he secured a place in the English College of St Thomas in Rome, where he remained for some time.

It was while in Rome that Leverous's reputation as a leading Irish churchman was forged. His past involvement in the Geraldine League and his continuing identification with the Fitzgerald cause made him an emblem of Irish opposition to the English schism. Should political conditions in the British Isles change in the papacy's interest he might prove useful in securing papal control over the Irish church. Following the death of Henry VIII in 1547 he decided to return to Ireland, and he arrived in the country some time before October 1549, when he received a pardon from the government for his previous involvement in Geraldine conspiracy. The timing of his return is striking, coinciding as it did with Gerald Fitzgerald's initial attempt to recover his Irish inheritance from Edward VI through diplomacy.

Once home Leverous recommenced work as a cleric and gained notice through his preaching. The lord deputy of Ireland, Sir James Croft, was favourably impressed, reporting 'I heard him preach such a sermon as, in my simple opinion, I did not hear in many years'. In November 1551 he recommended Leverous for promotion to either of the vacant dioceses of Cashel or Ossory: 'for learning, discretion and (in outward appearance) good living, [he] is the meetest man in this realm, and best able to preach both in the English and the Irish tongue' (Shirley, no. 24). Good preachers were rare in Ireland, especially Gaelic speaking ones, yet Leverous was not appointed to either see. It should be noted that by this time his record of loyalty to the Geraldines was no longer a hindrance to advancement, as Gerald Fitzgerald had succeeded in making his peace with the royal government in London: one can only conclude he was bypassed because he had allowed his dislike of the religious policies of the Edwardian regime to become known.

Promotion eventually arrived with the accession of Mary I to the throne in 1553 and the dispatch of Cardinal

Pole as papal legate to England. In 1554 Leverous was appointed dean of St Patrick's Cathedral, Dublin, and Pole called on him to help restore full papal authority over the Irish clergy. Towards this end Leverous worked closely with two senior Catholic churchmen who were also close to Pole, the archbishop of Armagh, George Dowdall, and the future bishop of Meath, William Walsh. At his first annual synod Dowdall had Leverous, as archdeacon of Armagh, deliver a special sermon to the clergy of Armagh, hoping that his celebrated oratorical power would inspire the assembled priests to great efforts in the papal cause. Also in 1554 Leverous served with Dowdall and Walsh on a royal commission to deprive married clergy. As a direct consequence of this commission the Church of Ireland bishop of Kildare, Thomas Lancaster, was deposed; Leverous, by now an old man, was chosen to fill the vacancy, nominated by the crown on 1 March 1555 and confirmed by the pope on 3 August following. The bull of his appointment did not reach Ireland until 19 December, owing to the illness of the messenger who brought it from Rome. By special papal dispensation he was allowed to retain the deanery of Patrick's after his consecration as bishop.

Leverous stayed out of the limelight after gaining his bishopric. Despite his being made a full member of the Irish privy council, extant evidence indicates that his attendance at council meetings was at best infrequent. Unlike Walsh he took little part in the secular business of government, confining himself to church affairs. Hence the only major royal commission on which he was included after 1554 was that issued in December 1557 for the recovery of church chalices, vestments, and other regalia in counties Dublin and Kildare. An entry in the visitation book of the diocese of Dublin records that in 1557 he also presided over the trial and deprivation for matrimony of a Dublin cleric named James White (Mason, *History*, 162).

The death of Queen Mary and the succession of Elizabeth I shook Leverous out of his tranquillity and brought him once more onto the political stage. Early in 1559, shortly after the new regime was in place at Whitehall, the lord deputy of Ireland identified Leverous as a likely source of opposition should Elizabeth seek parliamentary approval in Dublin for a protestant religious settlement. To stifle Leverous's capacity for troublemaking the deputy suggested the prelate be summoned to London, ostensibly to treat of matters of state, in reality to be kept there for the duration of parliament. The suggestion went unheeded, and in the opening session of Elizabeth's first Irish parliament Leverous was to the fore among opposition elements. Early in 1560, on being asked to take the oath of supremacy identifying Elizabeth as head of the church, he refused, contending that as a woman she could not lead the church. An account of his opposition written early the following century represents his words thus:

> Since the Divine Founder of the church did not deem it fit to confer ecclesiastical authority even on the most privileged of women, His own blessed Mother, how could it be believed that supremacy and primacy of ecclesiastical authority should, in future ages, be delegated to anyone of that sex? (*Analecta of David Rothe*, 447–55)

If true, it was an interesting choice of strategy, one which managed to avoid a direct defence of the authority of the pope; successful, however, it was not. Fear of his influence proved greatly exaggerated. The majority of the Marian bishops offered no objection to the government's demands, so retaining their bishoprics while Leverous forfeited his. Allegedly when threatened by the lord deputy with the loss of his living he replied: 'What shall it profit a man to gain the whole world, if he lose his own soul?' (ibid.). Immediately his bishopric was seized, and a year later it was given to Alexander Craik, a protestant.

Despite the claims of some Catholic nationalist historians, Leverous was not the subject of protracted persecution. He was never imprisoned, but remained at large after his deprivation, much to the irritation of successive Church of Ireland bishops of Kildare. After a time he was persuaded to leave co. Kildare and (almost certainly through Geraldine patronage) he departed to take up a position as a schoolteacher at the former Dominican priory in Adare, co. Limerick. While there his name was forwarded to Rome as a prospective candidate for the vacant see of Armagh, recommended as one who had never wavered in his allegiance to the pope, but his advanced years counted against him, and he was passed over in favour of his Adare teaching assistant, Richard Creagh, who left for Rome in 1564. He did not stay at the Adare school long after Creagh's departure. By 1567 he was back in the pale, when he is known to have visited the Jesuit prisoner of conscience, David Wolfe, in Dublin Castle. According to Wolfe's own account, written in exile a few years later, the meeting came to nothing, with Leverous so overcome by the foulness of the conditions in the prison that he left before anything could be accomplished. Old age, not government action, restricted his movements, but early in 1569 he again involved himself in an Irish Catholic confederacy against English rule. In February that year he signed a petition to the pope and the king of Spain beseeching their aid against the heretical and schismatic government of Elizabeth I. He was fortunate that his part in this conspiracy—which gave rise to a series of abortive uprisings in the south of the country—went undetected by the royal authorities. He remained in co. Kildare long after the risings collapsed, ministering to his former flock, until October 1577, when he died at Naas having reached a very great age. He was buried there in the parish church of St David's, the burial place, it has been said, of his family. Seventeenth-century Catholic accounts state that his grave was a site of popular devotion and the reputed *locus* of several miracles.

DAVID EDWARDS

Sources *The analecta of David Rothe, bishop of Ossory*, ed. P. F. Moran (1884) · W. Mason, *History of the collegiate church of St Patrick near Dublin* (Dublin, 1819) [privately printed] · J. Linchaeo [J. Lynch], *De praesulibus Hiberniae*, ed. J. F. O'Doherty, 2 vols., IMC (1944) · R. Stanihurst, 'A history of the reign of Henry VIII [1577]', *Holinshed's Irish chronicle*, ed. L. Miller and E. Power (1979) · P. F. Moran, ed., *Spicilegium Ossoriense*, 3 vols. (1874–84) · P. F. Moran, *History of the Catholic archbishops of Dublin since the Reformation* (1864) · E. P. Shirley, ed., *Original letters and papers in illustration of the history of the church in Ireland during the reigns of Edward VI, Mary and Elizabeth* (1851) • *Calendar of the manuscripts of the most hon. the marquis of Salisbury*, 24 vols., HMC, 9 (1883–1976) • *The manuscripts of Charles Haliday … Acts of the privy council in Ireland, 1556–1571*, HMC, 40 (1897) • M. A. Lyons, 'Sidelights on the Kildare ascendancy', *Archivium Hibernicum*, 48 (1994), 73–87 • H. A. Jefferies, 'The Irish parliament of 1560: the Anglican reforms authorized', *Irish Historical Studies*, 26 (1988–9), 128–41 • H. A. Jefferies, *Priests and prelates of Armagh in the age of reformations, 1518–1558* (1997) • P. Wilson, *The beginnings of modern Ireland*, another edn (1914) • J. Begley, *The diocese of Limerick in the sixteenth and seventeenth centuries* (1927)

Leverson [*née* Beddington], **Ada Esther** (1862–1933), novelist, was born in London on 10 October 1862, the eldest child in the family of four daughters and four sons of Samuel Henry Beddington, a wool merchant resident in Hyde Park Square, London, and his wife, Zillah, daughter of Sir John *Simon, Liberal MP. Her mother was an outstanding amateur pianist. Educated at home, Ada became well read in English, French, and German literature and the classics. On 6 December 1881 she married Ernest David (1849/50–1921), son of George Bazett Colvin Leverson, a diamond merchant. Her parents had opposed the match; Leverson was twelve years her senior and it later transpired that his young 'ward', being educated in France, was in fact his illegitimate daughter. The Leversons had a son, who survived only twenty-one weeks, and a daughter.

From 1892 Ada Leverson published numerous stories and sketches in *Punch* and other magazines. Her Kensington home became a meeting-place for writers and artists, particularly those associated with the *Yellow Book*. Her friends included Aubrey Beardsley, H. Max Beerbohm, George Moore, and, most notably, Oscar Wilde. It was Wilde who christened her the Sphinx, the name by which she was thereafter known to her friends. When the Wilde scandal broke in 1895, Ada Leverson stood out against public opinion and took him into her home when he was released on bail, an act of courage and loyalty for which she has become justly renowned. She was one of the few people who rose early in the morning to greet him on his release from prison in 1897.

About 1902 the Leversons lost money through an unsound investment. Never happy together, they now agreed to separate, Ernest emigrating to Canada and Ada remaining in London. The publisher Grant Richards encouraged her to turn to novel writing, and between 1907 and 1916 she produced six books: *The Twelfth Hour* (1907), *Love's Shadow* (1908), *The Limit* (1911), *Tenterhooks* (1912), *Bird of Paradise* (1914), and *Love at Second Sight* (1916). These lightly plotted love stories represent the perfect expression of her personality: frivolous and witty, but with an underlying sense of melancholy. They are also important for their closely detailed depictions of the fashions and tastes of the Edwardian age—a picture made all the more vivid by Leverson's tendency towards playful exaggeration and the novels' inclusions of vignettes of eccentric personalities.

Ill health and the onset of deafness did little to diminish Ada Leverson's enjoyment of life. Shortly after the First World War she met F. Osbert Sitwell, Sacheverell Sitwell, and Edith Sitwell, who became close friends. During the 1920s she frequently stayed in Florence, where she befriended Harold Acton and Ronald Firbank. Though viewed by many as a relic of the 1890s, she never lost her enthusiasm for new artistic trends.

Ada Leverson was small but of striking appearance, with bright golden hair and a profile said to resemble that of Sarah Bernhardt. She was famous for her witty, outrageous remarks, which she delivered in a low, purring voice. When she heard, for instance, that Alfred Douglas's elder brother had produced a male heir, she is said to have remarked: 'For once I think Bosie would have preferred a girl' (*TLS*, 8 Oct 1993, 31). Her outwardly cynical manner concealed a warm heart, and she was devoted to those she loved. That her novels are not better known is due largely to her extreme modesty about her literary abilities; but there is no doubt that her concise, deceptively light prose style, reliance on dialogue to carry the plot, and delight in satirical exaggeration influenced both Firbank and Evelyn Waugh, and that she has thus left her mark on the development of the twentieth-century novel.

Ada Leverson died at her home, 8 Clarges Street, Mayfair, London, on 30 August 1933, having published her last book, *Letters to the Sphinx from Oscar Wilde, with Reminiscences of the Author*, in 1930. J. W. SPEEDIE, *rev.*

Sources J. Speedie, *Wonderful Sphinx: the biography of Ada Leverson* (1993) • V. Wyndham, *The Sphinx and her circle: a biographical sketch of Ada Leverson, 1862–1933* (1963) • O. Sitwell, 'Ada Leverson', *Noble essences or courteous revelations: being a book of characters and the fifth and last volume of 'Left hand, right hand!': an autobiography* (1950) • J. Speedie, '"Wonderful, witty, delightful sketches": Ada Leverson's periodical contributions to 1900, a checklist and an introduction', *Turn-of-the-Century Women*, 4 (1987), 11–22 • C. Burkhart, 'Ada Leverson and Oscar Wilde', *English Literature in Transition, 1880–1920*, 13 (1970), 193–200 • *CGPLA Eng. & Wales* (1933) • d. cert.

Wealth at death £248 4*s*. 10*d*.: administration with will, 7 Dec 1933, *CGPLA Eng. & Wales*

Leverton, Thomas (*bap.* 1743, *d.* 1824), architect, was born at Waltham Abbey, Essex, and was baptized there on 11 June 1743, the son of Lancelot Leverton, a builder. Little is known about his training and early career; after learning his father's business, he was able—through the generosity of influential patrons—to 'perfect himself in architecture' (Papworth, 70). In 1771 he showed the first of thirty-four designs at the Royal Academy, where he exhibited regularly until 1803.

Leverton built several town houses and villas in London and the country; although often credited with the planning and external form of Bedford Square, London, he was probably not responsible for it. He did, however, design the interiors of at least four of the houses: no. 1 (1778–82), for Sir Lionel Lyde; no. 6 (*c*.1782), for Alexander Wedderburn, first Baron Loughborough; no. 10 (*c*.1782), for Sir Samuel Lyde; and no. 13 (from 1782), for himself, in which he took up residence in late 1795. The elegant doorway of no. 1 is probably also his work, and also the interiors of nos. 14, 25, and 32.

Leverton's chief strength was in the brilliant handling of small-scale interiors, often incorporating simplified motifs which would be innovatory in the work of George

Dance junior, Thomas Harrison of Chester, and Sir John Soane, over a decade later. No. 1 Bedford Square has a remarkable entrance hall: a shallow dome rests on thin decorated bands, rather than cornices, and opens to lobbies in two directions. The Etruscan hall at Watton Wood Hall (now Woodhall Park), Hertfordshire, which he built in 1777–82 for Sir Thomas Rumbold, has a dome carried on flat segmental arches; a Leverton invention later reflected in the work of Harrison and Soane.

Leverton's early Plaistow Lodge (1780, for Peter Thellusson; now Quernmore School) at Bromley in Kent, incorporated various Adam motifs, while the domed Scampston Hall, Yorkshire (1803), remodelled for W. T. St Quintin, reflected the work of the Wyatts. Leverton's house plans followed the fashion of using interlocking curves to link a sequence of rooms. 'In a large house in the country' (Papworth, 70), however, he is said to have forgotten the staircase. Many of his buildings—including, for instance, Woodford Hall, Essex (1771, for William Hunt; dem. *c.*1900) and Riddlesworth Hall, Norfolk (1792, for Silvanus Bevan; des. 1892; rebuilt 1900)—have been demolished, hindering an overall assessment of his work.

Leverton was surveyor to the Grocers' Company, to the theatres royal in London, and to the Phoenix Fire Insurance Company, London, for whom he built (*c.*1787) offices in Lombard Street (dem.) and a fire engine house (dem. *c.*1830) at Charing Cross. He seems to have assisted John Marquand at the department of land revenue; on Marquand's retirement in 1809 Leverton and his pupil Thomas Chawner were appointed joint architects. In 1811, when Marylebone Park reverted to the crown, Leverton and Chawner submitted an unimaginative scheme for its development in which they extended the formal pattern of Bloomsbury squares northwards; John Nash's plan was preferred and partly executed.

Leverton was a JP for Westminster, Middlesex, Surrey, and Kent. He was married twice: about 1766, then in 1803, after his first wife's death on 21 August 1802, to Rebecca Craven of Blackheath. His only son died in 1789. Leverton's nephew William, son of his brother Andrew, had been a pupil but practised mainly as builder and surveyor. His niece Jane married his pupil James Donaldson; she was the mother of Thomas Leverton *Donaldson (1795–1885), professor of architecture at London University, and one of the founders of the RIBA. Leverton's other pupils included H. E. Kendall, J. Lotan, and R. Walker. Although he amassed a large fortune, Leverton was not singled out for praise during his lifetime. He died on 23 September 1824 at 13 Bedford Square, London, and was buried at Waltham Abbey. The pioneering nature of his work is not explained by his personal qualities of 'integrity, industry and true benevolence' cited in his epitaph.

MOIRA RUDOLF-HANLEY

Sources [W. Papworth], ed., *The dictionary of architecture*, 11 vols. (1853–92), vols. 5–6 • *DNB* • *GM*, 1st ser., 54 (1784), 237 • *GM*, 1st ser., 59 (1789), 182 • *GM*, 1st ser., 63 (1793), 424 • *GM*, 1st ser., 72 (1802), 879 • *GM*, 1st ser., 94/2 (1824), 469 • *VCH Essex*, 6.268n. • A. Byrne, *Bedford Square* (1990) • Colvin, *Archs.* • Graves, *RA exhibitors* • W. E. Riley, *The parish of St Giles-in-the-Fields*, ed. L. Gomme, 1, Survey of London, 3 (1912), 108 • W. E. Riley, *The parish of St Giles-in-the-Fields*, ed. L. Gomme, 2, Survey of London, 5 (1914), 150–51, 163

Archives BL, designs for new Exchequer Office, drawer 38, 5 • PRO, Land Revenue records, surveys, and drawings, Works 30/317 • RIBA

Likenesses J. Russell, portrait, Phoenix Insurance Company • oils, Church of St Giles-in-the-Fields, London

Wealth at death approx. £62,000: *GM* (1824), 469

Leveson, Sir John (1555–1615), landowner, was born on 21 March 1555 at Whornes Place, Cuxton, Kent, the eldest son of Thomas Leveson (1532–1576), landowner, and Ursula Gresham (1534–1574). The main family estates were in Kent and Essex, but the ancestral property in Wolverhampton was retained. On 10 January 1576 he matriculated at Queen's College, Oxford, and he also spent time at Gray's Inn. On 27 April 1579 he married Margaret, daughter of Sir Roger *Manwood, a leading member of the Kentish gentry. She died on 26 April 1585, and on 9 July the following year Leveson married Christian (*d.* 1627), daughter of Sir Walter *Mildmay and widow of Edward Barrett, a match which indicated Leveson's puritan sympathies. Leveson's letters also illustrate the faith which influenced his whole life.

Leveson was efficient in estate management, his family connections brought him into politics, and he became an excellent public servant. Later he traded in pearls and was a shareholder in the Virginia Company. First noted among the thirty-eight Kentish landowners petitioning the privy council against Archbishop Whitgift's attack on the puritans in 1584, he was appointed deputy lieutenant for Kent in 1590, and proved himself invaluable to the lord lieutenant, William, Lord Cobham, in both public and private affairs. Leveson first served him as a military commander in raising the trained bands, and later in the preparations against the Armada; the defence of Kent in 1588 can be followed in his papers. He served as a captain in Lord Willoughby's disastrous expedition to France in 1589 and protested at the hardships thus incurred. Knighted in 1589, he was active in raising volunteers for Norris's expedition of that year, for Cadiz in 1596, and for the Netherlands in 1601–2. With his cousin Sir Richard Leveson he shipped 2000 soldiers from Rochester for Ireland in 1601. Besides warning the government about the unpopularity of musters, he had earlier passed on a massive protest about taxation in 1593. He also served as captain of Upnor Castle from 1596, and advised the government about the placing of beacons.

Leveson was more directly linked with the court in the procurement of supplies for the royal household, and with the arrangements for Queen Elizabeth's Kent progress in 1596. During her last illness he informed the court about the security of the county, and later he reported treasonable talk against the new king, James I. The supervision of recusants, and the detection and apprehension of Jesuits and seminary priests, were also of concern to the government. Leveson entered parliament as MP for Bossiney in 1584, probably owing to Mildmay's influence, and later sat for Maidstone and Kent, being active also in the 1614 election there. He served on several parliamentary committees, most notably in 1601 when three of the four had particular reference to Kent. A Cecilite, he built up connections at court which were to prove invaluable. Executor to William, Lord Cobham, he was entrusted with the funds for Cobham College. Leveson was equally trusted by Henry, Lord Cobham, and helped him during his imprisonment.

On 8 February 1601, riding to his house in Blackfriars, Leveson suddenly became involved in Essex's revolt. The earl of Cumberland and the bishop of London had collected a large body of men on Ludgate Hill; Leveson was asked to take command. He stationed the halberdiers behind a chain drawn across the road, and armed the musketeers. Within half an hour Essex, coming from St Paul's Churchyard with a great company, was halted at the barrier. Recognizing Leveson, Essex sent two envoys to him asking for passage. He refused both persuasion and threats. Shots were fired when Essex's men tried to force their way through. Leveson's men gave no ground and returned the fire. Seeing that Sir Christopher Blount was injured, Essex called his men off and withdrew to Essex House.

When promoting the navigation of the Medway, Leveson had come into conflict with Thomas Sackville, later earl of Dorset and lord treasurer. The sudden death of his cousin Admiral Sir Richard Leveson in 1605 made Sir John's young son Richard (1598–1661) possessor of the great Leveson estate (over 30,000 acres) in Staffordshire and Shropshire. Sackville now showed himself Leveson's mortal enemy. In his official capacity he demanded £40,000 for treasure allegedly taken from the *St Valentine* carrack by Sir Richard. Then, with Sackville's support, a forged will was produced making Sir Richard's cousin Mary Curzon the heir; Mary was married to Sackville's younger grandson. Finally Sir John Leveson had to settle Sir Richard's debts. The carrack claim was settled for £5000, the forgery exposed, and much of the debt paid. But Sir John observed in his will that he had spent £18,000 more in clearing the estate than it had paid in income. Important for his public services, Leveson had survived in the harsh world of the Jacobean court. After a short illness, he died at Whornes Place on 14 November 1615, and was buried on 22 November at Cuxton parish church.

RICHARD WISKER

Sources Staffs. RO, Sutherland papers, D 593, S/4/1–70; S/4/20/12 · Staffs. RO, D 593, E 3/3/1; E/3/6/1–3; E 3/10/1–3 · J. N. McGurk, 'Armada preparations in Kent', *Archaeologia Cantiana*, 85 (1970), 71–93 · J. N. McGurk, 'Levies from Kent to the Elizabethan wars', *Archaeologia Cantiana*, 88 (1973), 60–70 · J. N. McGurk, 'A levy of seamen in the Cinque Ports, 1602', *Mariner's Mirror*, 66 (1980), 137–42 · J. N. McGurk, 'Rochester and the Irish levy of 1601', *Mariner's Mirror*, 74 (1988), 57–67 · P. Clark, *English provincial society from the Reformation to the revolution: religion, politics and society in Kent, 1500–1640* (1977), 131, 171, 256–7, 302, 310 · HoP, *Commons, 1558–1603* · *The letters of John Chamberlain*, ed. N. E. McClure, 1 (1939), 242, 279, 320 · Staffs. RO, D 868/1, 1/28, 29, 34, 38, 41, 43; 1/67 · P. Morant, *The history and antiquities of the county of Essex*, 2 (1768), 410, 480 · R. F. Wisker, 'The estates of James Leveson', *Staffordshire Archaeological and Historical Society*, 37 (1995–6), 126–9 · Staffs. RO, D 593, addnl 8.36, 164; addnl 8, 147 · Foster, *Alum. Oxon.* · parish register, Cuxton, Medway Archives and Local Studies Centre, Rochester, Kent

Archives CKS, Marsham of the Mote MSS, sale of Whornes Place 1630, U 1644 T 38 A · Essex RO, Barrett-Lennard Archive, D/DL TI 687, 742; D/DHT T 270/1, T 1/228 · Shrops. RRC, Sutherland MSS, Raby deeds, 2/3/4–5 · Staffs. RO, Sutherland MSS, letter-books, D 593, D 868 · Surrey HC, Leveson-Gower of Titsey

Likenesses oils, 1598, Dunrobin Castle, Sutherland · oils

Wealth at death £10,950 from sale of property: Kent Archives U1644 T 38 A; U 1515 T/43, T/45, T/105, T/108; *Archaeologia Cantiana* 73 (1959), 93

Leveson, Sir Richard (*c.*1570–1605), naval officer, was the son of Sir Walter Leveson (1551–1602) of Lilleshall, Shropshire, landowner and MP, and his first wife, Anne Corbett (*fl.* 1550–1576). Sir Walter engaged in privateering and was fined £2300 in 1587 for taking a Danish ship in Bergen harbour. On 13 December of this year Richard married Margaret Howard (*c.*1570–1641), daughter of Charles *Howard, Lord Howard of Effingham, the lord high admiral. Becoming a member of the Howard circle, he was a volunteer on board the *Ark Royal* against the Armada. During the next few years he and Margaret lived mostly in Shropshire, where he served as MP in 1589 and *custos rotulorum* in 1596. During the course of his naval career he suffered hostility on the family estate from his father, who was embittered by debts. Captain of the *Truelove* on the 1596 Cadiz expedition, with the *Lioness* (under Captain Sir Christopher Blount) he took three Hamburg ships carrying contraband. He was one of the sixty-six officers serving on the Cadiz campaign to be knighted by its commander, the earl of Essex. He served as vice-admiral on Lord Thomas Howard's voyage to the Azores Islands in 1597, and then gained his first independent command, of the winter guard in December 1598. His squadron captured ten Hamburg ships bound for Lisbon with valuable cargoes; the letter writer John Chamberlain's claim that they subsequently escaped is erroneous (Wernham, 262). On 26 August 1599, serving under Howard in the Downs, he was informed of a Spanish fleet approaching, which proved to be Frederico Spinola with six galleys. Leveson sailed to Calais with six warships and two armed hoys to confront him, but two days of gales damaged his ships, and forced him to put back on 30 August. As Spinola evaded the Dutch off Calais and reached Sluys safely Leveson was criticized for not stopping him, an unfair charge as he had insufficient seaworthy ships to detach any. In 1600 he was dispatched with a squadron to intercept either the East India carracks or the Mexican flota, but found only two Dutch ships.

In September 1601 a Spanish invasion force sent to Ireland under the command of Juan de Aguila landed at Kinsale, while Mountjoy, the lord lieutenant, contended with Irish insurgents. As part of the English reinforcements, Leveson embarked 2000 soldiers in his squadron of six galleons and some smaller ships at Chatham, assisted by his cousin Sir John Leveson, deputy lieutenant for Kent. Delayed by fog and hindered by severe gales, he reached Kinsale on 14 November, having left one damaged galleon at Plymouth. He arrived to find Mountjoy besieging Aguila. The guns of Leveson's ships soon forced the surrender of the outlying Castle Park fort. When it was learned that Pedro de Zubiaur was disembarking Spanish

Sir Richard Leveson (*c.*1570–1605), by Isaac Oliver, *c.*1595–1600

soldiers and equipment at nearby Castlehaven, Leveson led four galleons and three smaller ships to sea and on 6 December reached Castlehaven harbour. Though he was greeted by a hail of shot from an eight-gun battery and musketeers on the shore, he forced the Spanish to abandon all their ships, with their flagship forced onto the rocks, two ships driven ashore, a fourth sunk, and the remaining two beached by the Spanish. His own ship, the *Warspite*, was shot through a hundred times. He was then held in harbour by adverse winds for two days and bombarded from the shore, and the *Warspite* would have been lost 'had not sir R. Leveson played the man' (Corbett, 346). Finally, on the third night, he warped his ships out and regained Kinsale; thirteen of his men had been killed and thirty wounded. Leveson recommended to Sir Robert Cecil that a fleet be maintained on the north coast of Spain to prevent any further attempts at invasion and to attack Spanish shipping. He and Sir William Monson applied this strategy in 1602, sailing with eight galleons and some smaller ships. He was unable to attack the treasure fleet as he had only four galleons with him, but disrupted the coastal traffic. Later he learned of the arrival of the Portuguese carrack *St Valentine* (1700 tons) at Cezimbra. Volunteers had been rushed on board to reinforce a crew decimated by scurvy while Spinola brought eleven galleys to guard her during her unloading. On 3 June Leveson led the attack on the carrack anchored under the guns of Cezimbra. Although his own ship was carried out to sea leaving Monson in command, he returned as soon as possible. The fight began at ten o'clock, two galleys were burnt with their slaves escaping, the damaged remainder were withdrawn by Spinola, and the carrack surrendered at five o'clock. Next day Leveson took the carrack out of the bay and sailed back to Plymouth where her cargo realized £43,851. Rewarded by the queen with £3000, he commanded the channel squadron during the queen's last illness and after her death, to secure the country from invasion.

Leveson's private life was unhappy. His father had died in the Fleet prison leaving considerable debts, while his wife had become insane from 1602. He formed a liaison with Mary *Fitton (*bap.* 1578, *d.* 1641) and maintained her at Perton Manor House in Staffordshire. Their child, Anne, was born in 1603. James I made him vice-admiral of England in 1604, in which year he was again elected an MP for Shropshire. The 1608 commission of inquiry into the navy noted his correct behaviour both in not letting a private ship sail with the 1605 fleet and in not accepting bribes for appointments. Marshal to the 1605 embassy to Spain, he succumbed to the smallpox epidemic on his return to London, dying at the house of a Mr Bonelle in the Strand, on 2 August. He was buried in St Peter's, Wolverhampton, on 2 September. The lord treasurer, the earl of Dorset, demanded £40,000 from his estate for the treasure allegedly taken from the carrack at Cezimbra. Sir John Leveson, his executor, fought this demand fiercely, proved it to be unreasonable, and finally settled the claim for £5000. Sir Richard's tomb was inscribed 'Here lieth the body of Perfection's glory, Fame's own world wonder, and the ocean's story' (Clarke, 465). RICHARD WISKER

Sources *The naval tracts of Sir William Monson*, ed. M. Oppenheim, 1, Navy RS, 22 (1902), xvii–xxxi, 112–13, 358; 2, Navy RS, 23 (1902), 151–93, appx • J. Corbett, *The successors of Drake* (1900), 272–88, 291–3, 342–76, 399 • Staffs. RO, Sutherland papers, D 593, E/3/6/3/1–3; E 3/3/1, 2; C/9/3 • letter-books, Staffs. RO, Sutherland MS D 868/1 • *Fifth report*, HMC, 4 (1876) [incl. printed version of letter-books (Staffs. RO) but with some omissions] • R. B. Wernham, *The return of the armadas: the last years of the Elizabethan war against Spain, 1595–1603* (1994), 257–8, 262 • *The letters of John Chamberlain*, ed. N. E. McClure, 2 vols. (1939) • A. P. McGowan, ed., *The Jacobean commissions of enquiry, 1608 and 1618*, Navy RS, 116 (1971), 13, 16, 20, 207 • *CSP Ire., 1601–3*, 191, 199, 203–4, 258 • *CSP Venice, 1592–1603* • *CSP for.*, 1589–90 • A. E. Newdigate-Newdegate, *Gossip from a muniment room* (1897), 49, 67–70 • J. J. Silke, *Kinsale: the Spanish intervention in Ireland* (1970), 123, 135–7 • J. J. Clarke, 'Leveson, Richard', HoP, *Commons, 1558–1603* • parish register, 1605, Wolverhampton, St Peter

Archives Staffs. RO, Sutherland MSS, D 593 • Staffs. RO, letter-books, D 868/1–12 vol. 1

Likenesses I. Oliver, miniature, *c.*1595–1600, priv. coll. [*see illus.*] • H. Le Sueur, bronze statue, 1634, St Peter's, Wolverhampton • C. Vroem [H. C. Vroom?], oils, NMM • miniature, Wallace Collection, London • oils, Arbury Hall, Warwickshire

Wealth at death £3308 from sale of personal possessions; £16,880 debts past: Staffs. RO, Sutherland MSS, D 593, C/9/3; for rentals, P 595, E/3/3 1, 2

Levet [Levett], **Robert** (*bap.* **1705**, *d.* **1782**), surgeon and apothecary, was born in Kirk Ella, East Riding of Yorkshire, near Hull, and baptized there on 30 August 1705 (Boswell, *Life*, 4.137, n. 1). He was the first of ten children born to Thomas and Elizabeth Levitt. At the age of about twenty he left his parents' house and worked for Robert Bee, 'an Eminent Woolens Drapier att Hull' (Hyde MS). Having picked up a little medical knowledge from a friend of his master's, he went to London about 1727 intending to study medicine. After a brief period of service in the house of a lord, however, he travelled to Paris and Italy, where he planned again to pursue his studies. He returned to London with a valuable collection of books and enough money to help two brothers make their way in the world. Levet soon went back to Paris, which was then 'the pre-eminent medical centre of Europe' and provided public lectures and demonstrations of medicine (Wiltshire, 201–2). He worked as a waiter and studied medicine in Paris for five years before returning to London.

In 1746 Levet both met Samuel Johnson and began attending the medical lectures of William Hunter. In Paris and London, Levet had access to the most advanced medical knowledge of his day, although he was never licensed as a physician. Johnson's friends described Levet variously a 'Physician in ordinary', a surgeon, an apothecary, or a combination of the three together. His varied practice was almost exclusively among the lower classes or nearly poor people of London. However, as a member of Samuel Johnson's household from before 1756 (*Letters of Samuel Johnson*, 1.138) to 1782, he also gave medical assistance to the great writer, other occupants of the house, and, occasionally, Johnson's friends (ibid., 2.140–41).

On 17 April 1762 Levet married Margaret Wilbraham, whom Johnson described as a 'streetwalker' (*Letters of Samuel Johnson*, 2.214). The *Gentleman's Magazine* for March 1785 described her as:

> a woman of the town, who had persuaded him (notwithstanding their place of congress was a small coal shed in Fetter Lane), that she was nearly related to a man of fortune, but was injuriously kept by him out of large possessions. (*GM*, 55, 101)

She also had unrealistic expectations of Levet, and the marriage ended badly. Levet was indicted for debts his wife incurred; she ran away and was tried for petty larceny at the Old Bailey.

> Her husband was with difficulty prevented from attending the court, in the hope she would be hanged. She pleaded her own cause, and was acquitted; a separation between this ill-starred couple took place; and Dr. Johnson then took Levet home, where he continued till his death. (ibid., 101)

He is described by Johnson's contemporary biographers as uncouth and taciturn, but Johnson regarded him highly (Boswell, *Life*, 1.243 n. 3).

Levet died suddenly on the morning of 17 January 1782 in his room at Johnson's residence (8 Bolt Court) and was buried in Bridewell cemetery on 20 January. Writing of his death to Thomas Lawrence, Johnson concluded, 'So has ended the long life of a very useful, and very blameless man' (*Letters of Samuel Johnson*, 4.6). Johnson took it on himself to locate Levet's heirs (ibid., 4.10–12), and, as a result, received a long letter about Levet from a relative. This letter from John Thompson survives in the Hyde collection and provides (apparently) the only written evidence of Levet's parentage and his physical appearance: he was 5 feet 5 inches, 'thick sett, of rather dullish Complexion' with 'Blackish' hair. On 21 March Johnson recited to Boswell an early version of his very moving elegy 'On the Death of Dr Robert Levet' (Johnson, *Poems*, 313–15), which celebrates Levet's unpretentious medical work among the poor and dignifies him with the title he never attained in the medical establishment (Wiltshire, 206).

THOMAS SECCOMBE, *rev.* ROBERT DEMARIA, JUN.

Sources *GM*, 1st ser., 55 (1785), 101–2 · J. Hawkins, *The life of Samuel Johnson, LL.D.*, 2nd edn (1787) · Boswell, *Life* · J. Wiltshire, *Samuel Johnson in the medical world* (1991) · *The letters of Samuel Johnson*, ed. B. Redford, 5 vols. (1992–4) · S. Johnson, *Poems*, ed. E. L. McAdam jun. (1964) · John Thompson, letter to Samuel Johnson, 21 Feb 1782, Hyde Collection MSS · *DNB*

Wealth at death very little: *Letters of Samuel Johnson*, ed. Redford, vol. 4, p. 11

Levett, Henry (1668?–1725), physician, son of William Levett, of Swindon, Wiltshire, was sent to Charterhouse School, which he left in 1686, to enter Magdalen Hall, Oxford, on 12 June, aged eighteen. In the following month he was elected a demy of Magdalen College, and was present during the contest about the king's visitorial power in the autumn of 1687. He was probably expelled with most of the other demies during the winter, and on 30 June 1688 was elected a fellow of Exeter College. He graduated BA on 24 November 1692, MA on 7 July 1694, BM on 4 June 1695, and DM on 22 April 1699.

Levett settled in London, and was elected a fellow of the Royal College of Physicians on 23 December 1708. This was not his first encounter with the college, for in February 1701 it had prosecuted him for illicit practice. He had followed Thomas Wert's lead in claiming that his degree of MD gave him the right to practise: however, Sir John Holt, lord chief justice of the king's bench, rejected this claim in a decision important for the status and privileges of the Royal College of Physicians.

On 29 April 1707 Levett was elected physician to St Bartholomew's Hospital, in succession to Robert Pitt, and on 5 January 1713 he became physician to Charterhouse, his old school, where he lived until his death. Levett rebuilt at his own cost the physician's house by the great gate in Charterhouse Square. He was censor of the College of Physicians in 1717 and treasurer for five years. Among his friends were William Wagstaffe and John Freind, and he was throughout his life a supporter of the tory party.

On 10 June 1710 Levett wrote, at Freind's request, a letter on the treatment of smallpox. In this he describes two cases, and expresses an opinion in favour of the use of cathartics. The letter, which is in Latin, is printed in the Latin edition of Freind's collected works, published in 1733. It seems probable that Levett also wrote the short memoir of Wagstaffe prefixed to the first edition of the latter's *Miscellaneous Works* in 1725. In the second edition (1726) the author of Wagstaffe's 'character' is described as an 'eminent Physician, no less valued for his skill in his profession, which he shewed in several useful treatises, than admired for his Wit and Facetiousness in Conversation' (Wagstaffe, title-page).

Levett died in Charterhouse on 2 July 1725. Thomas Hearne wrote of him at the time of his death as 'a sweet tempered Man, a most excell^t Physician, well belov'd, very honest as a Complyer, and had an excellent Study of Books' (Hearne, 393). In his will he left £689 10*s.* to the

Royal College of Physicians. Levett's tomb, with an elegant Latin inscription commemorating his love for Charterhouse, is in the chapel of the brethren in the Charterhouse, London. In 1729 his widow married Andrew Tooke (1673–1732), headmaster of Charterhouse School. NORMAN MOORE, *rev.* PATRICK WALLIS

Sources Foster, *Alum. Oxon.* • Munk, *Roll* • V. C. Medvei and J. L. Thornton, eds., *The royal hospital of Saint Bartholomew, 1123–1973* (1974) • G. Clark and A. M. Cooke, *A history of the Royal College of Physicians of London*, 2 (1966) • Nichols, *Lit. anecdotes*, 9.187 • *Remarks and collections of Thomas Hearne*, ed. C. E. Doble and others, 8, OHS, 50 (1907) • W. Wagstaffe, *Miscellaneous works of Dr William Wagstaffe*, 2nd edn (1726) • C. W. Boase, ed., *Registrum Collegii Exoniensis*, new edn, OHS, 27 (1894)

Wealth at death £689 10s. 0d. left to Royal College of Physicians: Clark and Cooke, *History of the Royal College of Physicians*, 508

Levett, Robert. *See* Levet, Robert (*bap.* 1705, *d.* 1782).

Levett, William (*d.* 1554), Church of England clergyman and gun-founder, was the son of a substantial landowner in the Hollington area of Hastings, where he was born, and the brother of John Levett of Little Horsted, gentleman and ironmaster. He obtained an Oxford degree in canon law and was rector of Guestling in 1528 and of West Dean by 1529. He became rector of Buxted in April 1533, and the same year obtained the living of Stamford Ryvers in Essex. As deputy receiver of the king's revenue in Sussex in 1533, he would have had knowledge of Newbridge ironworks on the duchy of Lancaster estate in Ashdown Forest.

His executorship of the will of his brother John, proved in May 1535, involved Levett more closely in the iron trade. The executors were to lease John's iron mills and furnaces, the profits going, after payment of the debts and legacies, to John's son, who was not to occupy the ironworks himself. They included Stumbletts furnace, newly erected on the duchy estate in 1534, and it must be supposed that the executors leased these ironworks to William Levett himself. Levett's first supplies to the ordnance date from 1539 and in August 1540 he provided 15 tons of iron shot or 'gunstones'. In March 1541 he was appointed 'goonstone maker' to the king and received £200 towards the casting of shot.

Henry VIII urgently needed cannon for his new coastal forts, but casting these in bronze would have been a formidable expense. Cast iron had already been used in the Weald to manufacture ordnance, but with separate barrels and breeches, after the fashion of wrought-iron guns. The bulk of Levett's new guns were muzzle-loaders, cast in one piece on the pattern of the latest bronze ordnance. By 1543 falconets were being made. The cascabel pattern and dodecagonal barrel of the Padstow gun, a demi-culverin perhaps cast in 1544, indicate the correctness of the tradition that royal gun-founders assisted at Levett's Buxted furnace. However, circular-sectioned, strictly functional designs with few embellishments soon evolved and between July 1545 and 1553 over three hundred guns of up to demi-cannon in size were supplied. The new guns were too heavy to find favour with the navy, but bronze was ten times more costly, so in fortifications and for arming merchant ships iron guns were preferred. Gradually, owing to their 'toughness and validitie', an important export trade in wealden guns built up and they remained dominant on the Amsterdam market until displaced by Swedish guns around 1620.

Metallurgically Levett needed to cast culverins and demi-cannon of 1500 to 2000 kg, but contemporary furnace hearths produced only around 500 kg of metal at one tapping. A larger hearth was clearly needed, but when appointed to oversee the ironworks at Worth in December 1546, after the attainder of the duke of Norfolk, Levett soon had a double furnace built there, the first known example in the metallurgy of iron. How can the exceptional quality of wealden guns be accounted for? Like their bronze counterparts, they were cast vertically, breech downwards, in pits. But since vertical casting of iron guns was also practised on the continent, other factors, such as the phosphoric nature of some wealden ores and the use of loam rather than sand for the moulds, have been adduced.

The unlikely story that Levett was a recusant, that he was deprived of his benefices in 1545, and that he was not restored to Buxted until after the accession of Mary I, was based on the particular meaning which the word began to acquire only following the Elizabethan church settlement of 1563. In this instance a collector 'certified Levett recusant', possibly for the 'refusal' of a clerical subsidy, but the rector of the neighbouring parish of Rotherfield, Richard Collier, used this and Levett's frequent absence from home to induce the Canterbury authorities to declare the rectory vacant on 31 May 1545, and to install Collier in Levett's stead. This came exactly at a time when Levett was preparing his first major delivery of guns for the ordnance, and this expansion from being a simple supplier of wrought iron, iron artefacts, and cast-iron shot, into becoming England's first major manufacturer of cast-iron cannon, would have caused him the most severe financial pressure. The king's council at once made interventions on 3, 24, and 30 June, ordering Collier to desist and reprimanding the collector. Levett did indeed ultimately relinquish his distant rectory at Stamford Ryvers in Essex and some other preferments, but his continuing acceptability to the ecclesiastical authorities was shown in September when he was admitted to the rectory of Herstmonceaux, which lay nearer to his home. Levett's deprivation from Buxted probably lasted no more than a few weeks.

Levett continued as 'one of the Mynisters of the Kinges Majestyes ordynaunce' during Edward VI's reign, though the penury of the crown meant that the demand for guns declined. He died, unmarried, at some point between March and July 1554. His will provided for more than forty bequests, including £6 13*s.* 4*d.* to the poor of Buxted and 6 tons of cast iron to Levett's servant Ralph Hogge (*d.* 1585), who in 1559 succeeded him as royal gunstone founder.

BRIAN G. AWTY

Sources E. B. Teesdale, *Gunfounding in the Weald in the sixteenth century* (1991) • B. G. Awty, 'Parson Levett and English cannon founding', *Sussex Archaeological Collections*, 127 (1989), 133–45 • B. G. Awty,

'A cast-iron cannon of the 1540s', *Sussex Archaeological Collections*, 125 (1987), 115–23 • will, 6 March 1554, PRO, PROB 11/37/5 • 'Letters and papers', RS, 20 (1) nos. 856, 1019, 1071, 1275; (2) nos. 140, 496, 921
Wealth at death under £700: will, PRO, PROB 11/37/5

Levetus [*née* Moss], **Celia** (*c.*1819–1873), writer, was born in Portsmouth, the fourth of twelve children of Joseph Moss (*c.*1780–*c.*1840) and his wife, Amelia, *née* Davids (*c.*1780–*c.*1850). Amelia Moss was the granddaughter of the Portsmouth Jewish congregation's founder and the daughter of Sarah Davids, the first Jewish child born in Portsmouth in modern times.

Joseph Moss read widely—Lord Byron, Walter Scott, and Charlotte Brontë, among others—to his children, and as girls Celia and her younger sister Marion entertained the family with their own fairy tales. When their father discovered them writing these tales down, however, he decided that literary endeavour was unseemly for girls and threatened to burn their books. None the less, after an extended illness prevented Joseph Moss from supporting the family, Celia and Marion Moss wrote and secretly published their first book of poems, *Early Efforts* (1839). The volume was dedicated to Sir George Staunton MP and was subscribed to by Lord Palmerston, as well as by most of the prominent Jewish families in London.

The following year, encouraged by the success of *Early Efforts*, the Mosses published a collection of historical romances entitled *The Romance of Jewish History* (1840, 2nd edn, 1843). Dedicated by permission to Edward Bulwer Lytton, this book and its sequel, *Tales of Jewish History* (1843), adapted the Jewish romance genre—first established by Walter Scott in *Ivanhoe*—to Anglo-Jewish needs. By setting the tales at crucial moments during Jews' historical dispersion, the Moss sisters were able to reflect on their own experience of diaspora as Jews in Victorian England. Later Anglo-Jewish historians frequently dismissed these tales as simplistic and unimportant, but to the prominent Jews who sponsored them, they were entry tickets to social and political toleration among English Christians. Recent literary critics have begun to re-evaluate their significance, understanding them as direct adaptations of and confrontations with *Ivanhoe*. Among the first fiction ever published by Jewish women anywhere in the world, these tales are now understood to promote reform of English Jews' gender and religious practices as well as an early version of political Zionism. The tales implicitly argue for Jews' emancipation in the Victorian world, and women's emancipation in the Jewish world.

In the early 1840s, perhaps to oversee the publication of their romances, Celia and Marion Moss moved to London. Then in 1845 the sisters, along with Marion's new husband, the French Jewish scholar Alphonse Hartog, opened a boarding-school for girls at the home they shared on 68 Mansell Street, Goodman's Fields. While teaching, Celia Moss continued writing tales such as 'The Two Pictures', publishing them to acclaim in the American Jewish periodical *The Occident* and in her sister's short-lived periodical the *Jewish Sabbath Journal* (1854–5), the first Jewish women's periodical ever published. On 15 December 1847 the chief rabbi, Herman Adler, married Celia Moss to Edward Hyman Levetus (*d.* *c.*1880), the *shochet* (ritual slaughterer) of the New Synagogue in St Helen's. They moved shortly thereafter to Birmingham, where Celia Levetus would spend the rest of her life. There she turned her artistic skills to account by illustrating a collection of Turkish folk tales, and she collected her own stories in a volume entitled *The King's Physician and other Tales* (1865). The *Jewish Chronicle*'s reviewer praised the collection, saying it had the capacity 'to bring out the latent Jewish feeling, to foster and intensify it'. Celia Levetus died on 18 December 1873 at 59 Summer Hill in Birmingham, and was survived by her husband and her children, Hyman, Edward, George, Harry, and Emma.

MICHAEL GALCHINSKY

Sources M. Galchinsky, *The origin of the modern Jewish woman writer: romance and reform in Victorian England* (1996) • C. Moss and M. Moss, *Early efforts, a volume of poems by the Misses Moss, of the Hebrew nation, aged 18 and 16* (1839) • advertisement for school, *Jewish Chronicle* (12 Dec 1845) • C. Levetus, *The king's physician and other tales* (1865) • 'Marion Hartog: from a correspondent', *Jewish Chronicle* (23 Aug 1895) • 'Jewish women's work in philanthropy and education', *Jewish Chronicle* (13 June 1902) • m. cert. and Moss family tree (based on a diagram by Edward Lewis Levetus, *c.*1940), U. Southampton, Anglo-Jewish papers [priv. coll., on loan] • d. cert.
Archives Bodl. Oxf. • Portsmouth synagogue, archives • UCL, Jewish Studies Library | University of Pennsylvania, Philadelphia, Leeser MS collection, ARC MS 2
Likenesses photograph, priv. coll.

Levey. For this title name *see* Brophy, Brigid Antonia [Brigid Antonia Levey, Lady Levey] (1929–1995).

Levi, David (1742–1801), writer on Judaism, was born in London to poor immigrant parents who could not afford to educate him. With the distant help of his grandfather in Poland he learned Hebrew while working as a shoemaker, later as a hatter, and still later as a printer. He read voraciously in Jewish literature from ancient times to the present, as well as in Christian writings about Judaism and about the Bible. Seeing how little both Jews and Christians in England really knew about Judaism—its history, beliefs, and practices—and seeing inroads of Enlightenment scepticism emanating from the writings of Voltaire, David Hume, Tom Paine, and others affecting the Jewish community, Levi took upon himself the lifelong role of expositor and defender of his faith. Since the Jews in England did not know enough Hebrew, Levi wrote for them exclusively in English.

Levi's first published work, *A Succinct Account of the Rites and Ceremonies of the Jews* (1782), sought to explain Judaism to Jews and to correct Christian misconceptions about Jewish beliefs and practices. Levi then took on the task of translating the prayer books of both the Ashkenazi (German and Polish Jews) and those of the Sephardi (Spanish and Portuguese Jews). He supervised a translation of the Old Testament into English and published in weekly instalments *Lingua sacra* (1785–7), a Hebrew grammar and dictionary, and a guide to the Hebrew language.

Levi turned from expositor of Judaism to defender of the Jewish faith when Joseph Priestly published his *Letter to the Jews* (1786), urging them to convert. He published a lengthy answer which led to a many-sided controversy with several different Christian divines who were trying to convince the Jews that various biblical prophecies mandated their conversion. Levi carefully and studiously debunked such claims. This then led him to explain the Jewish understanding of biblical prophecy in his three-volume *Dissertation on the Prophecies of the Old Testament* (1793–1800); all three volumes were printed and published by himself, and the work was republished in London in 1817 in two volumes. He especially sought to counter Christian millenarian interpretations of various prophecies, principally those that concerned the punishment and later redemption of the Jews. He also sought to fortify belief in scripture, arguing that its prediction of Jewish survival in spite of all kinds of calamities still seemed to hold true. Thus the Bible, over two millennia earlier, had foreseen a state of affairs that people could witness even in their own time! On the other hand, Levi had grave doubts about the Christian millenarian interpretations that saw the American and French revolutions and Napoleon's Egyptian campaign as signs of the approaching providential climax of human history. Levi tried to be most cautious in evaluating biblical prophecies in terms of the news of the day, though he was impressed and even excited by the monumental events taking place at the end of the eighteenth century.

In his last years Levi published an answer to the messianic claims of Richard Brothers in his 1795 letter to Brothers's leading supporter, Nathaniel Brassey Halhed MP, showing the extreme implausibility of a non-Jewish English naval person being the Messiah. Levi also wrote a detailed answer to Tom Paine's deist critique of the Bible in part 2 of his *Age of Reason*. Levi's *Defence of the Old Testament* (1797) was published in New York as well as London. Here Levi stressed the catastrophic consequences for religious believers of taking seriously Paine's reading of scripture as fabulous and mythological, and not as a divinely given text. Levi insisted that if a Jew doubted that Moses was the author of the Pentateuch he would give up his faith entirely. Levi was uninterested in the historical and critical examination of the Bible. He was, however, much concerned to keep deist and sceptical tendencies coming from Spinoza, Hume, and Voltaire from eroding religious belief in his community.

Levi's work was well known in Christian circles, and his *Dissertation on the Prophecies* was accepted as authoritative by many scholars, both Jewish and Christian, well into the nineteenth century. His intellectual contacts included many persons outside the Jewish community. Though overworked from his many activities, he was an important intellectual force in the last decades of the eighteenth century. When he died in 1801, after much ill health, his protestant friend Henry Lemoine published a poetic eulogy in the *Gentleman's Magazine* (October 1801), 'He's Gone! the Pride of Israel's Busy Tribe', praising him as a great explainer and defender of Judaism against Christians and sceptics. RICHARD H. POPKIN

Sources H. Lemoine, *GM*, 1st ser., 71 (1801), 934–5 · J. Picciotto, *Sketches of Anglo-Jewish history*, rev. edn, rev. I. Finestein (1956) · R. H. Popkin, 'David Levi, Anglo-Jewish theologian', *Jewish Quarterly Review*, 87 (1996), 79–101 · S. Singer, 'Early translations and translators of the Jewish liturgy in England', *Transactions of the Jewish Historical Society of England*, 3 (1896–8), 36–71 · *DNB* · private information (2004)

Likenesses W. Bromley, line and stipple engraving (after S. Drummond), BM, NPG; repro. in *European Magazine* (1799)

Levi, Leone (1821–1888), jurist, political economist, and statistician, was born on 6 June 1821 in Ancona, later part of the kingdom of Italy. He came from a middle-class Jewish family. His father, Isaac, and his elder brother were both merchants. Leone received a practical, commercial education and began working for his brother at the age of fifteen. He travelled to Liverpool in 1844 to expand the business and became a naturalized British citizen in January 1847. The business suffered, however, following the commercial crisis of that year, so Levi later joined a Liverpool merchant house. Experiencing the day-to-day vagaries of commercial dealings, he regretted the absence of a local forum where common difficulties facing businessmen could be raised and solutions proposed. As a result, he outlined, in 1849, in the pages of the *Liverpool Albion* and later in a number of pamphlets, his ideas for commercial reform. First, he proposed reforms to the law of commercial arbitration; second, he advocated the creation of a local chamber of commerce (the first such body had in fact been created in Jersey in 1768); and third, he proposed the establishment of tribunals of commerce where adjudications on business disputes could be made efficiently by those with practical knowledge and understanding of the workings of the local or specialized commercial world.

Levi's plan for a local chamber of commerce received wide publicity, and after a public meeting in November 1849 the Liverpool chamber of commerce was founded, with Levi as its honorary secretary. He immediately set about sending circulars to foreign merchants, requesting information on matters facing similar institutions abroad. The answers he received drew attention to the legal anomalies existing between one country and another with respect to commercial practice. This encouraged him to address the idea of a treatise on the commercial laws of the world. The result was his *magnum opus* (if not necessarily his best remembered work), entitled *Commercial law: its principles and administration, or, The mercantile law of Great Britain compared with the codes and laws of commerce of [fifty-nine countries] and the Institutes of Justinian*, which was published between 1850 and 1852. The work was acclaimed nationally and internationally, and honours and prizes were heaped upon him. One immediate consequence was a meeting of the Law Amendment Society in November 1852, arranged through the good offices of Henry Brougham and of Lord Harrowby (formerly, as Lord Sandon, Liverpool's MP). The meeting discussed practical proposals for the harmonization of the mercantile laws of Scotland, England and Wales, and Ireland. It led to a royal commission in 1854, and eventually resulted in the enactment of the Mercantile Law Amendment Acts 1856 (19 and 20 Vict., cc. 60 and 97). These remained lasting

Leone Levi (1821–1888), by Elliott & Fry, 1873

memorials to Levi's influence and industry. Meanwhile, his previous proposals to reform the law of arbitration had borne fruit in the arbitration clauses of the Common Law Procedure Act 1854.

In 1852 Levi was appointed professor of the principles and practice of commerce and commercial law at King's College, London. His later books drew on his lectures there, and dealt with the economic context of international law and the role of international arbitration. In 1855, and anticipating the later work of Sir John MacDonnell (1845–1921), he read a paper before the Law Amendment Society on judicial statistics, thereby pointing suggestively to the need for proper national compilations, particularly of civil judicial statistics. Such a series did, in fact, commence in 1859 on an annual basis. Levi employed statistics imaginatively to analyse working-class living conditions. Some of his reports were submitted to M. T. Bass, the brewer and member of parliament, who was prominent in the campaign for the abolition of imprisonment for debt after the enactment of the Debtors Act 1869. Levi's most celebrated work is, undoubtedly, his *History of British Commerce* (1872). Though somewhat dry in style, and lacking the theoretical perspectives of the writings of contemporary lawyer–economists such as Henry Dunning MacLeod (1821–1902) and Sir Thomas Farrer (1819–1899), it is still occasionally cited in modern economic history texts.

Levi was a member and in some cases an office holder of various learned societies, including the Royal Statistical Society, the Society of Antiquaries, the Society of Arts, the Law Amendment Society, the National Association for the Promotion of Social Science, the Royal Geographical Society, and the International Statistical Institute, and honorary secretary of the metric committee of the British Association. He was called to the bar (Lincoln's Inn) in 1859 and received an honorary degree from the University of Tübingen in 1861. A friend and admirer of Richard Cobden, he was also a warm advocate of the channel tunnel.

Levi's work in relation to chambers of commerce and his advocacy of tribunals of commerce addressed a fundamental question: what significance did legal rules have for the development of trade and commerce in a nineteenth-century market economy? His experience of commercial difficulties in Liverpool in 1847–9 pointed to a reconsideration of the role of law in commercial transactions. He adopted a three-pronged approach. The first was to promote law reform with a view to removing obstacles in existing legal arrangements for business. The Mercantile Law Amendment Acts are examples of such reforms. Second, he embarked upon his enormous comparative study of international commercial law, and third (and somewhat contradictorily), he adopted the more radical approach of challenging whether law was itself an ideal framework for regulating business and commercial affairs. This last approach, which resulted in the advocacy of tribunals of commerce and of improved commercial arbitration arrangements, is premised on the view that the interests of commerce and trade are not necessarily consistent with the legal values of certainty, predictability, and the arms-length transactions to be found in contract and property law. Commercial sales, after all, do not involve the instant delivery of goods or securities or immediate payment. Instead, orders are taken and credit is extended. In other words, promises are made, and within commercial markets, honourable men honour them not because the law will impose sanctions for breach but because traders prefer to adhere to the values of the commercial community. Thus, a number of statutes regulating or even prohibiting the sales of certain securities were quietly ignored by exchange traders. Though the contracts entered into were unenforceable, the promises were honoured in spite of the law.

It is within this commercial climate in the second half of the nineteenth century that Levi's advocacy of tribunals of commerce should be understood, and where the drawbacks of legal procedure, and indeed of legal values, were to be circumvented. What were being promoted were the creation of the 'local state', in this case a local commercial state, and the advocacy of legal pluralism. It was favoured by many commercial traders but crucially (and decisively) rejected by the lawyers on the judicature commission in 1874. However, lawyers did go on to invent standard-form contracts which matched commercial needs, and commercial arbitration did become more popular among businessmen in the later nineteenth century (in some instances at the instigation of local law societies), developments in which Levi's influence in encouraging business autonomy (or semi-autonomy) from an insufficiently sensitive legal framework can yet be detected. Of his influence in fostering local chambers of commerce, in stimulating the reform of United Kingdom mercantile law, and in generating interest in comparative commercial law, there is no doubt.

Soon after his arrival in England, Levi abandoned Judaism and became an active member of the Presbyterian Church of England. His Italian roots remained strong, however. He dedicated a free scientific library and a lectureship on commercial laws to the Technical Institute at Ancona and he revisited Italy with a deputation from the Royal Statistical Society in 1887.

In 1856 Levi married Margaret, daughter of James Ritchie of Edinburgh. Thin and slightly gaunt in his late thirties, but described as 'little and bustling' towards the end of his life, he died on 7 May 1888 at his house, 31 Highbury Grove, London, after an illness lasting several months. He was buried five days later in Highgate cemetery. His wife survived him. G. R. RUBIN

Sources D. Sugarman and G. R. Rubin, 'Towards a new history of law and material society in England, 1750–1914', *Law, economy and society: essays in the history of English law, 1750–1914*, ed. D. Sugarman and G. R. Rubin (1984) • *Journal of the Royal Statistical Society*, 51 (1888), 340–42 • *The Times* (8 May 1888) • L. Levi, *The story of my life: the first ten years of my residence in England, 1845–1855* (1888) • *ILN* (30 June 1855), 653–4 • Holdsworth, *Eng. law*, 15.302–3 • W. Hug, 'History of comparative law', *Harvard Law Review*, 45 (1931–2), 1065–6 • Boase, *Mod. Eng. biog.* • *DNB* • M. W. Beresford, *The Leeds chamber of commerce* (1951) • A. R. Ilersic, *Parliament of commerce: the story of the Association of British Chambers of Commerce, 1860–1960* (1960) • R. B. Ferguson, 'Commercial expectations and the guarantee of the law: sales transactions in mid-19th century England', *Law, economy and society: essays in the history of English law, 1750–1914*, ed. D. Sugarman and G. R. Rubin (1984) • H. W. Arthurs, *Without the law* (1985) • I. Singer and others, eds., *The Jewish encyclopedia*, new edn, 12 vols. (1925) • I. Landman and L. Rittenburg, eds., *The universal Jewish encyclopedia*, 10 vols. (1939–43) • *CGPLA Eng. & Wales* (1888)

Archives NRA, papers | UCL, letters to Lord Brougham

Likenesses Elliott & Fry, cabinet photograph, 1873, NPG • Elliott & Fry, carte-de-visite, 1873, NPG [*see illus.*] • portrait, repro. in *London Figaro* (19 May 1888), 11 • wood-engraving (after a daguerreotype by Beard), NPG; repro. in *ILN*, 653

Wealth at death £10,847 12*s.* 7*d.*—effects in England: probate, 17 July 1888, *CGPLA Eng. & Wales*

Levick, (George) Murray (1876–1956), surgeon and explorer, was born at 12 Whitworth Place, Newcastle upon Tyne, on 3 July 1876, the son of George Levick, a civil engineer, and his wife, Jeannie Sowerby. Ruby Winifred *Levick (1871/2–1940) was his sister. He was educated at St Paul's School, and St Bartholomew's Hospital where he qualified MRCS LRCP in 1902. In the same year he was commissioned as a surgeon in the Royal Navy where he continued his long established interest in physical fitness, sport, and outdoor activities.

In 1910 Levick was selected by Robert Falcon Scott as surgeon and zoologist on his second and last expedition to the Antarctic, the *Terra Nova* expedition. He was assigned to what became the northern party (originally the eastern party) of six men who spent two years (1910–12) exploring the Victoria Land coast and the whole winter of 1911–12 living off seal and penguin in a snow cave at Evans Cove, an experience which remains an outstanding example of survival in the Antarctic if, in the view of some, also an example of the expedition's sometimes unsystematic preparations. During the period Levick was a tower of strength. As a doctor he was adequate though underemployed; he made a study of the Adélie penguin published as *Antarctic Penguins* (1914) and in the expedition's official reports as *The Natural History of the Adélie Penguin* (1915). His accounts, though very readable, were superseded by more rigorous and specialized studies. His photographs added significantly to the value of the expedition's scientific results. He was liked by all members of the expedition and was a loyal friend to Lieutenant Victor Campbell, leader of the northern party.

On his return Levick served in the First World War in the Grand Fleet, the North Sea, and at Gallipoli where he was in the last party to leave; he was promoted surgeon-commander in 1915 and retired in 1917. On 16 November 1918 at Christ Church, Broadway, in the parish of St Margaret's, Westminster, he married (Edith) Audrey Mayson (*b.* 1889/90), daughter of Mayson Moss Beeton. They had one son.

Returning to his interest in fostering physical fitness Levick was at various times electrologist and medical officer in charge at St Thomas's Hospital; consultant physiotherapist at the Victoria Hospital for Children; and a member of the London University advisory committee on physical education. In 1919 he was approached by the National Institute for the Blind about the feasibility of teaching blind students of massage some form of electrical treatment; through his untiring advocacy blind students were ultimately admitted to the examinations of the Chartered Society of Physiotherapy and a clinic was opened for and staffed by them. He was for thirty years medical director of the Heritage Craft School for Crippled Children, Chailey, founded by Dame Grace Kimmins.

Levick's best-known and, in some ways, his most rewarding and important work stemmed directly from his experiences with the Scott expedition. In 1932 he founded the Public Schools' Exploring Society (later the British Schools' Exploring Society, now BSES Expeditions). For the remainder of his life he was the society's head, at first chairman and later president; and was honorary chief leader of the first nine expeditions to some of the wilder parts of the world. His wife was also active in the society's affairs. The society encourages young people to go to remote, wilderness areas, to teach them to fend for themselves; to foster in them the spirit of adventure; to test their endurance and help them acquire physical fitness; and to give them a taste for, and elementary training in, exploration and field research. C. F. Spooner, who was assistant leader of the 1947 expedition and thereafter led several further expeditions, remarked of Levick:

> He was always so full of life and enthusiasm and he made everything such enormous fun; even a setback became the cause of greater enjoyment with him, as it simply offered a

> greater challenge. Coupled with this buoyant love of life was a quiet dogged persistence and a shrewd judgement which gave one great confidence. I cannot remember ever seeing him nonplussed and he was always the same whatever the circumstances, considerate and kindly to us all—one of those people whose gentleness emanates from their own great strength.

It is appropriate that the society's millennium expedition was to Antarctica. In 1942 the Royal Geographical Society recognized his services to exploration by the award of the Back grant.

During the Second World War Levick was recalled to the Royal Navy to assist in the training of commandos. Latterly Levick and his wife settled at Whitewater House, Ting Tong, Budleigh Salterton, and he died at Poltimore House Nursing Home, Poltimore, Devon, on 30 May 1956. He was survived by his wife.

RAYMOND PRIESTLEY, *rev.* ELIZABETH BAIGENT

Sources *The Times* (1 June 1956) • *WWW* • private information (1971) • personal knowledge (1971) • b. cert. • m. cert. • d. cert. • R. Huntford, *Scott and Amundsen* (1979) • R. F. Scott, *The diaries of Captain Robert Scott: a record of the second Antarctic expedition, 1910–1912*, 6 vols. (1968) • R. E. Priestley, *Antarctic adventure: Scott's northern party* (1914) • *GJ*, 122 (1956), 405–6

Archives RGS, BSES expeditions, MSS • Scott Polar RI, journals

Wealth at death £12,231 15*s.* 7*d.*: probate, 28 Aug 1956, *CGPLA Eng. & Wales*

Levick [*married name* Bailey], **Ruby Winifred** (**1871/2–1940**), sculptor, was born in Llandaff, Glamorgan, the eldest child of George Levick, a civil engineer born in Blaenau, Monmouthshire, and Jeannie Levick, *née* Sowerby, who was born in Gateshead, co. Durham. She had one sister, Lorna, born about 1873, and one brother, George Murray *Levick, born in 1876. Levick was a student at the National Art Training School (later the Royal College of Art), South Kensington, from about 1893 to 1897, under the tutelage of Professor Edward Lantéri. A new emphasis on modelling, as opposed to carving, as well as a resurgence of interest in small-scale sculpture, such as the statuette and the medal, meant that women artists were now in a position to make a significant contribution to the previously male-dominated field of sculpture. Thus Levick became one of a growing number of women entering the art schools at this time. Among her companions at the National Art Training School were Margaret Giles (1868–1949) and Gwendolen Williams (1871–1955), who both enjoyed notable success at the school and who, like Levick, went on to produce a significant body of work as professional women sculptors.

Recognition of Levick's potential began when she won a scholarship about a year after her admission to the National Art Training School. In 1893 she was awarded a bronze medal in the national art competition, and in 1896 she gained the British Institution scholarship for modelling. In 1897 she went on to receive the princess of Wales scholarship, and that same year she won critical acclaim and a gold medal for her statuette *Wrestlers*. This work was illustrated in the magazine *Studio* that year and was accompanied by a short but impressive account, in which the statuette is described as 'handled with something like mastery'. The group was exhibited at the Royal Academy in 1898.

Extant works by Ruby Levick provide some insight into the depth of her repertory, and a valuable assessment of her output, by Martin Wood, survives in *Studio* of 1905. The fact that such an article was written and published during the artist's lifetime provides an important comment on the significance of Levick's achievement. Like many of her contemporaries, she founded her reputation upon her ability to become proficient at a variety of different skills. Levick thus produced not only competent small-scale sculpture in the round, but also decorative relief work and stained-glass windows. Extant examples include the reredos of St Brelades, Jersey, which displays an appreciation of Sir George Frampton's foliage motif; the stained-glass windows of St Edmund and the Virgin Mary that decorate the Roman Catholic church of St Edmund at Hunstanton, Norfolk; and *Boys Fishing* in the Stirling Maxwell collection, Pollok House, Glasgow.

Levick's work was admired by, among others, Queen Alexandra, who is said to have purchased the statuette *Asleep in the Arms of the Slow Swinging Seas*. This echoes the languid and fluid style of many of Harry Bates's bronze reliefs, for example the *Aeneid* reliefs (1884) at the Glasgow Art Gallery; and it adopts something of the measured composure of Burne-Jones's *Briar Rose* series (1874–90; Buscot Park, Oxfordshire). While her interest in the expression of lyrical imagery is evident in this work, her passion was for its style and subject matter, traditionally the province of her male counterparts. Her vigorous studies of the adult male anatomy are among her most interesting work. In the statuettes *Fishermen Hauling in a Net* (1900) and *Rugby Football* (1901), and not least in her earlier group *Wrestlers* (1897), Levick displays a studied appreciation of the aesthetic philosophies of the new sculpture in her successful combination of the modern realism of Hamo Thornycroft's *The Mower* (1884) and the physicality of Sir Frederick Leighton's influential *Athlete Wrestling with a Python* (1877).

At the age of thirty-three Levick married an architect, Gervase Bailey (*b.* 1876/7), son of Alfred Bailey, a barrister, on 12 January 1905, while living and working at Leighton Lodge, Edwardes Square, London. The couple had a daughter and a son. Levick exhibited at the Royal Academy until 1919, but continued working until about 1930, more often using her married name from about 1914. She is known to have exhibited at the Society of Medallists (1898, 1901), the Arts and Crafts Exhibition Society (1899, 1903, 1916), the Walker Art Gallery, Liverpool, and the Ridley Art Club. In 1899 she exhibited a plaster bust of Leslie H. S. Matthews at the second exhibition of sculptors, painters, and engravers, and in 1902 the *Magazine of Art* noted an exhibition for the International Society at the Dutch gallery in Brook Street, where Levick exhibited work alongside Francis Derwent Wood, Edward Lantéri, and Alfred Drury. That same year she was among the exhibitors at the first Exhibition of Statuettes by the Sculptors of Today, British and French, at the Fine Art Society, London.

Ruby Levick died on 31 March 1940 at St George's Hospital, Hyde Park Corner, London, and was survived by her husband. FIONA DARLING-GLINSKI

Sources S. Beattie, *The New Sculpture* (1983) • T. M. Wood, 'A decorative sculptor: Miss Ruby Levick (Mrs Gervase Bailey)', *The Studio*, 34 (1905), 100–07 • M. H. Spielmann, *British sculpture and sculptors of to-day* (1901) • *The Studio*, 11 (1897), 260 • *Magazine of Art*, 24 (1901–2), 141 • m. cert. • *CGPLA Eng. & Wales* (1940) • private information (2004)

Wealth at death £246 11s. 11d.: administration, 11 July 1940, *CGPLA Eng. & Wales*

Lévignac, Abbé de. *See* MacCarthy, Nicholas Tuite (1769–1833).

Leving, William (*d*. 1667), parliamentarian army officer and spy, was a native of co. Durham, although his parentage and early life are very obscure. He served as a junior officer in the regiment of Sir Arthur Hesilrige in the course of the civil war. In 1659–60 he took the part of John Lambert in the divisions that arose in the army as the English republic began to falter, and as a consequence lost both his post, and any arrears of pay which might have been due to him. Dismissed from the army, he returned north at the Restoration, but he remained one of many unsettled former soldiers there under the new regime of Charles II.

Leving played a particularly prominent role in the northern plot of 1663. Alongside his father he was part of the plan to raise Durham for the rebels under Captain Roger Jones. In October 1663 any chance of a rebellion ignominiously collapsed, the conspiracy having been penetrated by government informers at an early stage. In the subsequent round-up of the participants Leving was imprisoned in York Castle. Sir Thomas Gower claimed to have 'two witnesses against him which will hang him upon a triall', but Leving's execution was averted by his turning king's evidence against his accomplices (PRO, SP 29/97, fol. 41*v*); he claimed that pangs of conscience rather than fear turned him round. Sir Roger Langley, the high sheriff of Yorkshire, suggested to the earl of Arlington in April 1664 that:

> if a way could be founde to gett … [Leving] … out of the gaole soe as he might not be suspected by his owne party he might be of greate use, for he assures me if hee were out he would not question to let you knowe some of the [names of the rebel] Councell now in London. (PRO, SP 29/97, fol. 41*v*; SP 29/98, fol. 132)

A relieved Leving accepted this offer and in May 1664 was transferred to the Tower of London. During his incarceration there he suggested that his use could be further extended by allowing him to escape and 'shift as a banished man' (*CSP dom., 1663–4*, 616). His escape was arranged that same year and he promptly went to ground in London.

Leving was supplied with funds, albeit irregularly, and a paper revealing his status as an agent to any officious government servants whom he might meet. During the difficult period as a double agent that followed he used various aliases, including that of Leonard Williams. While ostensibly playing a major role in the many schemes of his friends, he betrayed them, passing on his information by letter and meetings with 'Mr. Lee', the disguised Sir Joseph Williamson. Eventually Leving overplayed his hand and began to be suspected by his fellow plotters. In February 1665 they bundled him into an obscure house, where he was held for some days and threatened with pistols. That he managed to bluster his way out and pass the blame for the recent betrayals onto someone else shows his personal coolness in a situation of great danger.

Over the next year Leving, with various unreliable partners, turned to more criminal activities, becoming a highwayman in an attempt to supplement his already limited finances. His criminal activities soon led to his moral decline and made him less useful to his masters. He was arrested in Leicestershire in May 1665, but released on revealing his identity. The regime then insisted that he remain in London during the plague months and as a consequence he lost most of his family to the epidemic. Lacking funds he begged for a customs post to supplement his income and to provide an excuse to stay in London in order to remain close to his erstwhile friends and victims. The latter were now becoming suspicious of his loyalties once more and in late 1666 Leving was sent to Ireland to undertake espionage work on behalf of the government. After returning to England in December 1666 he once again resorted to highway robbery, this time in Yorkshire. Once more he was arrested and again released at the intercession of Williamson. In July 1667 he was placed in the company of the heavily guarded plotter Captain John Mason, who had escaped with him in 1664. Mason had been recaptured in June 1667 and under guard Leving was sent north with him, either to provide a witness against the prisoner at his trial at York or to try to inveigle more information out of Mason. In the event Thomas Blood and his friends, intent on freeing their colleague, ambushed the group in the town of Darrington on 25 July 1667. During the rather bloody action that followed Leving hid in a nearby house and observed from a safe distance, but he had finally been recognized as a spy.

In August 1667 Leving lay dead in the cells of York Castle, poisoned by his enemies according to his former highway companion William Freer. He had offended his rebel friends and finally revealed his identity as a spy, and this makes them obvious suspects in his death, but he had also become involved in another scheme of note: the duke of Buckingham had been dabbling in connections with the rebel party and in 1667 Arlington, using his many informants, tried to use these activities to bring the duke down; Leving's part was apparently to act as a witness against Buckingham. As this scheme collapsed Leving was left in a dangerous situation. Although Buckingham later denied any hand in his death, the fact that he went on record to do so seems to point the finger in his general direction.

Leving was fairly typical of the men that the regime of Charles II recruited for espionage. His background as a plotter gave him access to his former friends and as a spy he helped to scotch some of the many schemes bubbling under the surface of dissenting and rebel life in London, assisting the regime in maintaining its upper hand in the post-revolutionary situation. In the course of his work Leving himself undoubtedly suffered a degeneration of his character. He became motivated more by fear and greed than ideology after the collapse of the abortive rebellion of 1663 and spent his later years fearful of betrayal on both sides. In the end he was poorly rewarded for his efforts by his squalid death. He was buried in York.

ALAN MARSHALL

Sources PRO, SP 29, vols. 81–231 • *CSP dom.*, *1660–67* • Cumbria AS, D/Mus/Letters, Bundles • A. Pritchard, 'A defence of his private life by the second duke of Buckingham', *Huntington Library Quarterly*, 44 (1980–81), 157–77 • A. Marshall, *Intelligence and espionage in the reign of Charles II, 1660–1685* (1994) • H. Gee, 'A Durham and Newcastle plot in 1663', *Archaeologia Aeliana*, 3rd ser., 14 (1917), 145–56 • J. Walker, 'The Yorkshire plot, 1663', *Yorkshire Archaeological Journal*, 31 (1932–4), 348–59 • R. L. Greaves, *Deliver us from evil: the radical underground in Britain, 1660–1663* (1986)

Levinge, Sir Richard, first baronet (1656–1724), judge, was born on 2 May 1656, the second son of Richard Levinge (*d.* 1691) of Parwich, Ashborne, Derbyshire, and his wife, Anne, the daughter of George Parker of Park Hill, Staffordshire. He was educated at Audlem School, Derbyshire, St John's College, Cambridge (where he matriculated in 1671), and the Inner Temple (which he entered in September of the same year). He was called to the bar in November 1678. Two years later he married Mary, the daughter of Sir Gawen Corbyn. In 1686 he became recorder of Chester under the controversial new royal charter which restricted municipal voting rights. Showing his tory allegiance, he fulsomely welcomed James II to the city in August 1687. He and Sir Thomas Grosvenor won the Chester parliamentary election of 1690, their opponents' petition being defeated by one vote. They retained their seats unopposed in 1692.

Levinge was appointed solicitor-general for Ireland in 1690 and was knighted on 23 September 1692, in which year he was elected MP for both Belfast and Blessington; he chose to sit for the latter constituency in the Irish House of Commons. On 5 October of the same year he was unanimously chosen as speaker, an office which he tried to decline on account of 'the sense of my own imperfections'; he had 'ever studied rather to do than to speak or write well'. However, he accepted the post, and remained speaker throughout that parliament. In 1695 he was elected by Bangor and Longford, and sat for the latter.

Having been chosen by the English House of Commons in April 1699 as a commissioner to inquire into forfeited land in Ireland, Levinge queried the legality of including James II's private estates in the forfeiture for treason. As he disputed the majority's report, he was summoned before parliament on 16 January 1700 and accused fellow commissioners of admitting to pressure from Westminster. Parliament resolved that his accusations were 'groundless and scandalous', and committed him to the Tower until 13 April. A victim of whig politicking, he received only £500 for his services, while those commissioners who accepted the forfeiture of James's estates received £1000.

Levinge was re-elected MP for Longford in 1703, and on 13 April 1704 was created a baronet. He was again appointed solicitor-general for Ireland in 1704 but in 1709 was sacked by the whig lord lieutenant Thomas Wharton, suspected of passing information to Jonathan Swift, who believed that Levinge's reluctance to provide information against Wharton prevented the latter's impeachment. In 1710 he was elected MP for Derby in the English parliament, and in the following year was promoted to be attorney-general for Ireland. In 1713 he was elected for Gowran and Kilkenny and sat for the latter. He lost the contest for speaker to Alan Brodrick.

Despite being one of the few tories trusted by the new government, Levinge refused a judicial appointment in 1714, but in 1720 was made chief justice of the common pleas in Ireland through the influence of his friend Archbishop King of Dublin. In the same year his wife died.

In 1723 he married Mary Johnson, the daughter of a political colleague, Robert Johnson, baron of the Irish exchequer. He died on 13 July 1724. His first two sons with his first wife each held the baronetcy.

TIMOTHY VENNING

Sources R. Levinge, *History of the Levinge family* (1877) • J. G. Simms, *War and politics in Ireland, 1694–1730*, ed. D. W. Hayton and G. O'Brien (1986) • R. E. Burns, *Irish parliamentary politics in the eighteenth century*, 2 vols. (1989–90) • *VCH Cheshire*, vol. 2 • J. L. J. Hughes, ed., *Patentee officers in Ireland, 1173–1826, including high sheriffs, 1661–1684 and 1761–1816*, IMC (1960) • F. E. Ball, *The judges in Ireland, 1221–1921*, 2 vols. (1926) • W. A. Shaw, *The knights of England*, 2 (1906) • G. J. Armytage and W. H. Rylands, eds., *Staffordshire pedigrees*, Harleian Society, 63 (1912)

Archives BL, corresp., Add. MSS • NRA, priv. coll., corresp. • PRO NIre., corresp.

Likenesses portrait, Chester town hall, sessions courtroom

Wealth at death three homes (Parwich, Dublin, Westmeath) and estate at Mullalea, Westmeath; also some of Tyrconnel lands; left second wife £2000 and £300 p.a., grants to three sons: will, proved Nov 1724, PRO, PROB 11/600

Levinge, Sir Richard George Augustus, seventh baronet (1811–1884), army officer, born on 1 November 1811 in Hertford Street, London, was the eldest son of Sir Richard Levinge, sixth baronet (1765–1848), and Elizabeth Anne (*d.* 1853), eldest daughter of Thomas Boothby, first Lord Rancliffe. He entered the 43rd regiment as ensign on 25 November 1828, joined at Gibraltar, and returned to England in December 1830 because of disturbances in the manufacturing districts. In 1832 his regiment went to Ireland, and on 8 April 1834 he was promoted lieutenant. On 4 June 1835 he sailed with the left wing of the 43rd for St John's in Canada, and served in the suppression of the French Canadian uprising of 1837–8. He became captain unattached on 15 May 1840, and was appointed to the 5th dragoon guards on 27 January 1843; he retired, however, from the army on that day. On 3 January 1846 he was made lieutenant-colonel in the Westmeath militia.

On 12 September 1848 Levinge succeeded his father in the baronetcy, and in 1851 he was high sheriff for co. Westmeath. He married, on 20 March 1849, Caroline Jane (*d.* 1858), eldest daughter of Colonel Rolleston MP, of Watnall Hall, Nottinghamshire; they had no children. From 1857 to 1865 he was MP for the county of Westmeath. On 10 February 1870 he married Margaret Charlotte (*d.* 5 Nov 1871), widow of David Jones, MP, and daughter of Sir George Campbell; they had no children.

Levinge was an energetic sportsman, and took a keen interest in his old regiment and the Westmeath militia. His publications included *Echoes from the Backwoods* (2 vols., 1846), on his experiences in Canada, and *Historical Records of the Forty-Third Regiment, Monmouthshire Light Infantry* (1868). Levinge died in Brussels on 28 September 1884, and was succeeded by his brother, Vere Henry Levinge.

W. A. J. Archbold, *rev.* James Falkner

Sources *Army List* · *The Times* (30 Sept 1884) · *Hart's Army List* · Burke, *Peerage* (1959) · *WWBMP*

Wealth at death £10,425 9s. 6*d*.: probate, 10 Dec 1884, *CGPLA Eng. & Wales*

Levinstein, Herbert (1878–1956). *See under* Levinstein, Ivan (1845–1916).

Levinstein, Ivan (1845–1916), chemical manufacturer, was born on 4 July 1845 in Charlottenberg, Berlin, the eighth of seventeen children, eight boys and nine girls, of Levin Jacob Levinstein (1803–1865), and his wife, Bertha Liebermann. Levinstein senior was variously owner of a calico printing factory, political correspondent, and agent of the German branch of the Rothschild Bank. He fell out with Bismarck at the end of the 1850s, and subsequently encouraged his older sons to emigrate. Some of them became established in London as dye merchants, and started the manufacture of aniline dyes. Ivan was educated at the Royal Prussian Gymnasium, Berlin, and then at the Gewerbeinstitut, where he studied aniline dyes. By 1864 he was involved in a family dye-making business at Neu-Schöneberg, near Berlin. Later in 1864 he followed in the footsteps of his brothers, and arrived in Salford, Lancashire, where he began the manufacture of the aniline red known as magenta. When the original patent, owned by a London firm, was declared invalid in 1865, Levinstein took up its manufacture on a large scale at Blackley, Manchester, where he set up a works at Hulton House.

In the meantime, Levinstein's brother Hugo in London was sued for patent infringement over the magenta derivative known as aniline blue. Hugo lost the case, but Ivan circumvented the patent monopoly in 1869 by employing the intermediate known as toluidine. With these and similar products, an aniline salt used in aniline black printing on cotton, and the first of what were later known as azo dyes (derived from diazonium intermediates), Ivan Levinstein became a successful manufacturer. In 1871 he launched the trade journal *Chemical News*, which he edited for several years, and which was published until 1891. By 1874 his firm had offices and agencies in London, Birmingham, Glasgow, on mainland Europe, and in the United States. Expansion at Blackley continued with the acquisition of the adjacent Crumpsall Vale works, and by 1887 Levinstein's factory had been reconstructed. He employed several German chemists, though few appear to have remained for long periods.

In 1881 Levinstein became engaged in patent litigation with Badische Anilin- und Soda-Fabrik (BASF) over the azo dye fast red AV (Levinstein's version was known as roccelline), patented in London early in 1878 by Heinrich Caro, technical director of the German firm. Though judgement went against Levinstein in 1887, he subsequently developed a close business alliance with BASF, and friendship with Caro. By this time a class of novel azo dyes, the benzopurpurines, which attached directly to cotton without the aid of a mordant, was available. In 1889 Levinstein joined BASF against the powerful benzopurpurine convention of Agfa and Bayer. This failed, and Levinstein was forced into partnership with his adversaries. Agfa and Bayer controlled his firm from 1890 until 1895, during which time it traded as I. Levinstein & Co. Ltd. It came under Levinstein's control again from 1895, and the name changed to Levinstein Ltd. Other business interests included a partnership in the alkali manufacturers Murgatroyd Company Ltd, of Middlewich, and Ammonia Soda Company Ltd, of Northwich.

From about 1880 Levinstein became actively involved in public affairs, especially through the Manchester chamber of commerce. From 1885 he participated in management of the chemical and dyeing and printing departments of the Manchester Technical School, of which he was a councillor during 1888–91. He was also a member of Manchester city council's education committee, and chairman of the technical instruction committee of the Municipal School of Technology (later part of the University of Manchester Institute of Science and Technology). Subsequently Levinstein became a member of the court of the Victoria University and a governor of Owens College. He promoted utilitarian studies, and application of science to industrial problem-solving along German lines, which was opposed by some academics in Manchester. He was chairman of the 1887 Manchester Royal Jubilee Exhibition.

When the Society of Chemical Industry, founded in 1881, set up a Manchester section in 1883, Levinstein became a member of the committee. He was chairman of the section (1883–4 and 1889–94), vice-president of the society (1897–1900 and 1903–6) and president (1901–3), and vice-president of the Society of Dyers and Colourists (1884–1916).

From the end of the 1890s Levinstein lobbied for patent law reform and commercial protectionism. Following the introduction of German synthetic indigo in 1897 he implored dyers and printers of his adoptive country to support the colonial trade in the natural dyestuff. He was a member of Chamberlain's tariff commission and is given much credit for the steps leading to the Patent Act of 1907. Levinstein published widely in the chemical and dyeing trade literature, especially in the *Journal of the Society of Chemical Industry*, on matters relating to new industrial chemical developments, education, and patents. Early in the First World War he joined the Board of Trade's chemical supplies committee.

Levinstein became a British subject on 25 April 1873. About 1874 he married Hedwig Abeles of Vienna; they had three sons, Edgar (*b.* 1876), Herbert [*see below*], and Edward

Gerald (1887–1916). The first of six family homes was Hillside House, Prestwich Park, and Levinstein's final home was Parkfield, Hale Road, Hale, Cheshire, where he died on 15 March 1916. His wife, who suffered from poor health, had previously returned to her family in Austria, where she died in 1908.

Herbert Levinstein (1878–1956), who was born on 2 February 1878 at Prestwich Park, Prestwich, Lancashire, took over his father's business on the latter's retirement at the end of 1915. Herbert was educated at Rugby School, Owens College, Manchester, and Zürich Polytechnic, where in 1900 he received a PhD in organic chemistry. His name appeared on twenty-five patents, either jointly or alone. Under his direction the first British-made synthetic indigo was produced in 1916 at the sequestered Ellesmere Port factory of Hoechst, where novocain and the antiseptic acriflavine were also produced. During the First World War Levinstein's highly qualified technical team, led by Arthur G. Green, developed close links with academic institutions. The Blackley factory continued with the production of dyes and engaged in the manufacture of mustard gas. Levinstein was a member of the Chemical Warfare Committee, the Hartley mission to Germany, and the economic section of the Paris peace conference. In November 1918 Levinstein Ltd was merged, under government influence, with British Dyes Ltd to form the British Dyestuffs Corporation. Herbert Levinstein was joint managing director, and from 1921 sole managing director. Levinstein was highly critical of the Huddersfield division, his erstwhile rival, and in 1922 was voted off the board. Subsequently he became involved in the manufacture of viscose rayon, as founder director of Neura Art Silk Company Ltd (formed in December 1925) and, from 1928, technical director of Lansil Ltd. From the late 1920s he was closely involved with the successor to the Murgatroyd Company, in which his father had held an interest; in 1950 he was appointed life president of Murgatroyd Salt and Chemical Company Ltd. British Dyestuffs Corporation was one of four major British chemical corporations that merged in 1926 to create Imperial Chemical Industries (ICI). The Blackley site later became the regional headquarters of Zeneca plc.

Herbert Levinstein was at various times president of five institutions and societies, and published numerous articles concerning the chemical industry. In 1937 he endowed the Ivan Levinstein memorial lectures, the first two of which were given before the Manchester Chemical Club. The lectures were reintroduced after the Second World War under the aegis of the Society of Chemical Industry, and a further five were given until 1970. In 1949 Levinstein gave the inaugural George Douglas memorial lecture of the Society of Dyers and Colourists. In 1953 he received the Hinchley medal of the British Association of Chemists. His last home was Baddow, Pinkneys Green, Maidenhead. Herbert Levinstein was perhaps the only person to have attended both the 50th and the 100th anniversary celebrations of the discovery of William Perkin's mauve. He died on 3 August 1956 at King Edward VII Hospital, Windsor, Berkshire. ANTHONY S. TRAVIS

Sources M. R. Fox, *Dye-makers of Great Britain, 1856–1976: a history of chemists, companies, products, and changes* (1987) • A. S. Travis, *The rainbow makers: the origins of the synthetic dyestuffs industry in western Europe* (1993) • M. Wyler, 'Ivan Levinstein—what I know of him', *Journal of the Society of Dyers and Colourists*, 55 (1939), 142–6 • 'Mr. Ivan Levinstein', *Manchester Faces and Places*, 10 (1898–9), 21–3 • W. J. Reader, *Imperial Chemical Industries, a history*, 1 (1970) • C. Reinhardt and A. S. Travis, *Heinrich Caro and the creation of the modern chemical industry* (2000) • R. Brightman, 'Obituary notices: Herbert Levinstein', *Journal of the Society of Dyers and Colourists*, 72 (1956), 582–4 • P. Reed, 'The British chemical industry and the indigo trade', *British Journal for the History of Science*, 25 (1992), 113–25 • *Journal of the Society of Dyers and Colourists*, 32 (1916), 169–70 • M. Tordoff, *The servant of colour: a history of the Society of Dyers and Colourists, 1884–1984* (1984) • R. Brightman, 'Dr Herbert Levinstein', *Chemistry and Industry* (27 Oct 1956), 1194–5 • d. cert. • b. cert. [Herbert Levinstein] • d. cert. [Herbert Levinstein]

Archives Zeneca plc, Blackley, Manchester, MSS | Deutsches Museum, Munich, corresp. with Heinrich Caro, Caro Nachlass

Likenesses photograph, Zeneca plc, Blackley, Manchester • photograph, repro. in 'Mr Ivan Levinstein', *Manchester Faces and Places*, 22–3 • photograph (Herbert Levinstein), Zeneca plc

Wealth at death £113,884 1*s*. 3*d*.: probate, 27 May 1916, *CGPLA Eng. & Wales*

Levinz, Baptist (*c*.1644–1693), bishop of Sodor and Man, was the son of William Levinz of Evenley, Northamptonshire, and his wife, Mary Creswell. William *Levinz and Sir Creswell *Levinz were his brothers. He matriculated at Magdalen Hall, Oxford, on 11 April 1660 and was a demy of Magdalen College in 1663–4 (when his age was recorded as nineteen) and a fellow from 1664 to 1683. He graduated BA in 1663 and MA in 1666 and proceeded BD in 1677 and DD in 1683. From 1677 to 1682 he was White's professor of moral philosophy, a proctor of the university in 1676, and bursar of his college in 1677. From 1680 to 1682 he was curate of Horspath, Oxford, a position customarily filled by a resident member of Magdalen. On 3 July 1680 he married Mary (1663–1730), daughter of James Hyde, principal of Magdalen Hall, whom Thomas Hearne described in 1724 as 'a pretty woman, but not so now' (*Remarks*, 8.204); they had two children.

Levinz was a canon of Wells Cathedral from 1675 and rector of Tolland, Somerset from 1680 and of Christian Malford, Wiltshire, from 1682. He was consecrated bishop of Sodor and Man at Lambeth on 15 March 1685, taking possession of the see in August and subsequently visiting the island in 1688 and 1691, in which year he was additionally made a canon of Winchester. Levinz was unhappy with his diocese, which paid only £200 per annum, the same as his Wiltshire living, and much of it in kind. Archbishop Sancroft likened his position to St John's exile to Patmos (Clarke, 156) and Levinz was allowed to retain his existing preferments, also undertaking pastoral duties on Sancroft's behalf in the diocese of Canterbury. On the death of Henry Clark, president of Magdalen, in 1687 Levinz was nominated for the vacancy by the college's visitor, Peter Mews, bishop of Winchester, but withdrew when James II issued a mandamus requiring the election of Anthony Farmer. Levinz was a high Anglican, described by Hearne as 'a handsome but intolerably proud man'

(*Remarks*, 8.65), but was 'reckoned an ingenious Man and a good preacher' (ibid., 2.49). He died of a fever on 31 January 1693 and was buried in Winchester Cathedral.

JOHN STEPHENS

Sources Foster, *Alum. Oxon.*, 1500–1714, 2.905 • W. D. Macray, *A register of the members of St Mary Magdalen College, Oxford*, 4 (1904) • J. R. Bloxam, ed., *Magdalen College and James II, 1686–1688: a series of documents*, OHS, 6 (1886) • B. Willis, *A survey of the cathedrals of York, Durham, Carlisle … Bristol*, 2 vols. (1727) • A. W. Moore, *Sodor and Man*, Diocesan Histories (1893), 183–5 [diocesan history] • *Remarks and collections of Thomas Hearne*, ed. C. E. Doble and others, 11 vols., OHS, 2, 7, 13, 34, 42–3, 48, 50, 65, 67, 72 (1885–1921) • L. Brockliss, G. Harriss, and A. Macintyre, *Magdalen College and the crown: essays for the tercentenary of the restoration of the college, 1688* (1988) • *VCH Oxfordshire*, 5.186 • W. N. Clarke, ed., *A collection of letters … to Sancroft* (1848) • *DNB*

Archives Bodl. Oxf., letters to William Sancroft, MSS Rawl. • Bodl. Oxf., miscellaneous material

Levinz, Sir Creswell (1627–1701), judge, was the second son of William Levinz of Evenley, Northamptonshire, and of his wife, Mary, second daughter of Richard Creswell of Purston in the same county. His brothers, Baptist *Levinz and William *Levinz, are noticed separately. Robert *Levinz was his uncle. Born at Evenley, Levinz became in 1648 a sizar at Trinity College, Cambridge, but did not proceed to a degree. He entered Gray's Inn in November 1655 and was called to the bar in November 1661. He soon acquired a good practice, and became a bencher in 1678 and treasurer in 1679. On 2 October 1678 Levinz was knighted and on 25 October he was appointed king's counsel. As king's counsel he represented the crown in the Popish Plot trials of 1678–9 (Ireland, Pickering, Grove, Langhorn, Whitebread, and others), in which he appeared to have shared the popular belief in the supposed plot, but in which he seems to have conducted the prosecution with a certain decency and fairness. He was appointed attorney-general on 27 October 1679. Levinz married in 1670 Elizabeth, daughter of William Livesay, of Lancashire. They had two sons, William and Creswell, and one daughter, Catherine.

In December 1679 Levinz drafted (under protest) the royal proclamation against 'tumultuous petitioning' and the next year was called to account by the House of Commons. Finding himself under some threat of impeachment, he explained to the house (24 November 1680) that he had consented to draw up the proclamation on condition that Chief Justice North dictated its substance, and the threat of impeachment was dropped. Roger North in his biography of his brother says that the chief justice forgave Levinz as he 'knew him to be a mere lawyer and a timidous man' (North, *Lives*, 1.230). Thus Levinz's career was not interrupted, and on 12 February 1681 he was created serjeant-at-law and was simultaneously appointed a judge in the court of common pleas. He went on the Oxford circuit and sat with Chief Justice North on the trial at Oxford in August 1681 of Stephen Colledge. Later, in July 1683, he was a commissioner at the Old Bailey on the trial of Lord William Russell for his supposed part in the Rye House plot, and he delivered an opinion on the qualification of a juryman whom Russell had challenged for lack of freehold estate in the City. On the accession of James II he fell out of favour, having given the king the unwelcome advice that the farm of excise given by Charles II did not survive his death. Nevertheless Levinz was allowed to remain in office and he accompanied Chief Justice Jeffreys on the western circuit after Monmouth's rebellion, but he acted an entirely subordinate role to Jeffreys in the 'bloody assizes'. On 9 February 1686 his office was suddenly, but not unexpectedly, revoked by writ of *supersedeas*, 'whereunto', he records modestly in his reports, 'I humbly submit' (*Reports of Sir C. Levinz*, 3.257). Later, after the revolution of 1688, he was asked to explain to the House of Commons why he had been dismissed, and he said 'I thought my discharge was because I would not give judgment on the soldier who deserted his colours, and for being against the dispensing power' (Cobbett, *Parl. hist.*, 5.313).

Like some other judges who suffered dismissal at that time Levinz had no difficulty in returning to the bar. In 1688 he appeared as one of the counsel for the seven bishops and he nearly secured their early acquittal by taking the objection that there was no evidence of their petition being published in Middlesex. But an adjournment gave time for the lord president of the council, Sunderland, to come to Westminster Hall and supply the evidence of the presentation of the petition. Macaulay has conjectured that Levinz 'was induced to take a brief against the crown by a threat of the attorneys that if he refused it he should never hold another' (Macaulay, 1.512). A more likely explanation is that his brother Baptist, though not one of the seven defendants, was himself a bishop (of Sodor and Man). At the revolution of 1688 Levinz was appointed to advise the convention in matters of law, and, though not regaining judicial office, he continued to practise. In 1695, in the important habeas corpus case of *R.* v. *Kendall and Roe*, he argued successfully before Chief Justice Holt against the legality of imprisonment under general warrant of a secretary of state. His reports cease in 1696 and probably he ceased to practise then. Levinz died at Serjeants' Inn on 29 January 1701, and was buried at Evenley, where there are a monument and his standing effigy in robes.

Levinz's reports were published in the year after his death as a folio volume in three parts and were republished in 1722 in two volumes, when the law French was given English translations by Salkeld. A third edition in English only as revised by T. Vickers was published in Dublin (1793–7) and in London (1802) in three volumes. As a pleader Levinz also compiled a book of entries, published in 1702 in London as *A collection of select and modern entries of declarations, pleadings, issues, verdicts, judgments etc., referring to the cases in Sir Creswell Levinz's 'Reports', the judgment of the court being added to each president* [*sic*]. In the eighteenth century Lord Chancellor Hardwicke delivered a dictum that though Levinz was 'a good lawyer, he was sometimes a very careless reporter' (Foss, 407). There is no evidence that Levinz intended his private collection of reports and records to be published, and the collection generally does not deserve the adverse criticism that has sometimes been bestowed upon it. D. E. C. YALE

Sources E. Foss, *Biographia juridica: a biographical dictionary of the judges of England … 1066–1870* (1870), 406 • A. W. B. Simpson, ed., *Biographical dictionary of the common law* (1984), 311 • Baker, *Serjeants* • Holdsworth, *Eng. law*, vol. 6 • Sainty, *Judges* • *The reports of Sir C. Levinz* (1722) • R. North, *Examen, or, An enquiry into the credit and veracity of a pretended complete history* (1740) • R. North, *The lives of … Francis North … Dudley North … and … John North*, ed. A. Jessopp, 3 vols. (1890); repr. as *The lives of the Norths* (1972) • Cobbett, *Parl. hist.*, 5.312 • T. B. Macaulay, *The history of England from the accession of James II*, new edn, 2 vols. (1889)

Likenesses R. White, line engraving, 1702 (after G. Kneller), BM, NPG; repro. in *Reports* (1702) • J. Richardson, oils, Gray's Inn, London

Levinz, Robert (1614/15–1650), royalist agent, was the son of William Levinz (*d.* 1643), a brewer at Oxford and tenant of Lincoln College's farm at Botley, and his wife, Elizabeth (*d.* 1646), daughter of Anchor Brent of Little Wolford, Warwickshire, and sister of Sir Nathaniel Brent, warden of Merton College. Robert's grandfather William Levinz was an alderman of Oxford and served five terms as mayor in the late sixteenth century; he was buried at All Saints' Church, where he was commemorated by a recumbent effigy. Robert was uncle of the judge Sir Creswell Levinz, Baptist Levinz, bishop of Sodor and Man, and William Levinz, president of St John's College, Oxford; they were sons of his brother William.

Robert Levinz matriculated at Lincoln College as a gentleman's son on 21 June 1633 aged eighteen. He took a BA in 1634 and an MA in 1636. He was listed among MAs resident at the college in June 1637 and was noted as absent when the protestation oath was taken in February 1642. He was created DCL in November 1642. In 1640 he was commissary to the bishop of Norwich. He joined the royalist army and by 1645 was a captain in the King's regiment of foot. He was captured at the battle of Naseby. After the establishment of the Commonwealth, Robert became a royalist agent and in 1650 was in London entrusted with recruiting officers. Arrested, he was found to have blank commissions issued by Charles II. He was tried as a spy by a court martial. Although he acknowledged his role he refused to name his accomplices. Condemned to death, he was hanged outside the exchange in Cornhill on 18 July 1650.

Levinz had married a daughter of Sir Peregrine Bertie, son of the earl of Lindsey. A portrait of Levinz was included in William Winstanley's *Loyall Martyrology* of 1662. STEPHEN PORTER

Sources D. Lloyd, *Memoires of the lives … of those … personages that suffered … for the protestant religion* (1668), 560–61 • *The life and times of Anthony Wood*, ed. A. Clark, 1, OHS, 19 (1891), 104–5 • V. Green, *The commonwealth of Lincoln College, 1427–1977* (1979), 243 • P. Young, *Naseby 1645* (1985), 97–8 • J. Gibson, ed., *The Oxfordshire and North Berkshire protestation returns*, Banbury Historical Society, 24 (1994), 171 • Foster, *Alum. Oxon.* • *DNB*

Likenesses portrait, repro. in W. Winstanley, *Loyall martyrology* (1662)

Levinz, William (1625–1698), college head, was born on 25 July 1625, the son of William Levinz of Evenley, Northamptonshire, and his wife, Mary Creswell, and nephew of Robert *Levinz; Creswell *Levinz (1627–1701) and Baptist *Levinz (*c.*1644–1693) were his younger brothers. Educated at Merchant Taylors' School, London, from 1638 to 1641, Levinz was elected probationary fellow of St John's College, Oxford (matriculating on 23 July 1641), graduated BA on 21 April 1645, and proceeded MA on 8 May 1649. The parliamentary commissioners listed him for expulsion on 15 May 1648, but he must have submitted before 24 April 1651, when he signed the college register.

At the reception of the chancellor, the earl of Clarendon, on 9 September 1661 Levinz, 'though very sickly', made a speech (*Life and Times of Anthony Wood*, 1.414). He is credited with the *appendicula* on recent British history in the 1663 edition of Jean de Bussières's *Flosculi historici delibati, nunc deliberatiores redditi*. From 1665 he was professor of Greek, and on 19 June 1666 was made BM and DM. Chosen rector of Handborough, Oxfordshire, in 1673, on 10 October that year he was elected president of St John's, a promotion of which Wood disapproved as 'he beats the students there and fights' (ibid., 2.272). In the early and late years of his presidency the college did important building work. Levinz was made prebendary and subdean of Wells in 1679 and canon residentiary in 1682. 'Every one thought', Wood noted on 6 October 1685, that Levinz should have had the vice-chancellorship, 'but some say he is not fit because of infirmities, others that he will not be govern'd by Dr. Fell' (ibid., 3.165).

Levinz, who was unmarried, died suddenly while addressing a college meeting at St John's on 3 March 1698 and was buried in the college chapel, where his brother Sir Creswell Levinz erected a fine architectural tablet by Thomas Hill, master of the London Masons' Company. The inscription described Levinz as 'very well read, gentle, forebearing, righteous and loyal'. His estate was first subject to a grant by the chancellor's court at Oxford (29 October 1698), then letters of administration (PCC) were granted to Sir Creswell on 2 November 1698. His impressive library, which contained over 2400 books, of which 20 per cent were medical and scientific, was sold in 3478 lots, plus 200 more volumes of tracts and pamphlets.

H. E. D. BLAKISTON, *rev.* HUGH DE QUEHEN

Sources W. C. Costin, *The history of St John's College, Oxford, 1598–1860*, OHS, new ser., 12 (1958) • *The life and times of Anthony Wood*, ed. A. Clark, 5 vols., OHS, 19, 21, 26, 30, 40 (1891–1900) • Foster, *Alum. Oxon.* • Mrs E. P. Hart, ed., *Merchant Taylors' School register, 1561–1934*, 2 (1936) • R. H. Adams, ed., *Memorial inscriptions in St John's College Oxford* (1996) • *Fasti Angl., 1541–1857*, [Bath and Wells] • E. Millington, *Bibliotheca Levinziana* (1698) • *Hist. U. Oxf.* 4: *17th-cent. Oxf.*, 523–4, 537

Levis, Carroll Richard (1910–1968), talent spotter and broadcaster, was born on 15 March 1910 in Toronto, Canada, one of at least three children. Little is known of his family other than that his father, an Irishman from Cork, was a police detective. After leaving school at fifteen he had numerous jobs ranging from variety show compère to lumberjack, before joining Vancouver radio station

CKWX, where he was soon writing and presenting his own shows. To fill an unexpected gap in the programme he was presenting from Edmonton, Alberta, he invited an unknown singer from the audience to broadcast. This innovation proved so popular that it led to a regular programme introducing unknown artists to the microphone, which became the basis of his career for the next thirty years.

Despite Levis's popularity in his native Canada, he left for Britain in 1935, believing it offered greater opportunities. In 1939 he married his secretary, the lively Florence Mina Sumner (*d.* 1996). They had no children. Encouraged by Eric Maschwitz, the BBC's director of variety, he toured Britain, interviewing hundreds of unknown hopefuls. The best were invited to broadcast on *Carroll Levis and his Discoveries*, one of the broadcasting successes of 1936. He presented his shows with a heartiness and confidence that his audience found hugely attractive. Drawing over 20 million listeners in his heyday, he enthusiastically created the impression that a new star might emerge at any moment. Usually, the programme's formula was that of a conventional variety show with professional artists, within which was a regular discovery section. Constantly on the lookout for originality of material and presentation, plus a wide repertory, he never encouraged his discoveries to attempt a career in entertainment, unless they had exceptional talent.

Over the next decade Levis presented seven more series on the BBC and for Radio Luxemburg, as well as entertaining the troops overseas during the Second World War. An account of these travels appeared in *A Showman Goes East* (1945). In 1947 he suffered a mental breakdown and returned to Canada—his brother Cyril stepped in to present his 1948 show. By 1950 Levis was back in Britain, resuming his touring shows and returning to the airwaves in 1951. In 1955 the entertainer Hughie Green sued the BBC, Levis and his wife, and others, alleging a conspiracy to keep his own discoveries show *Opportunity Knocks* off the air. Green lost, yet it was Levis's career that went into decline. His last broadcast was on 4 November 1959 and despite successful shows on ITV his contracts were not renewed; in 1960 he again returned to Canada. After trying his luck in the United States and Paris, he fruitlessly tried to interest British broadcasters in plans for a new show in 1965. In the year of his death he realized that the days of the talent show were past and was considering instead the management of young artists.

Levis had a strong, round, fleshy face, blue eyes, and, from a young age, silver-grey hair, smoothed flat. Although grossly overweight he was dapper and elegant. Sometimes arrogant with a tendency to flamboyance, he was liable to be abusive and even aggressive during his periods of over-indulgence in alcohol. Yet there were times when he hardly drank at all, and beneath his often bumptious manner he was sensitive, caring, and trusting. Levis also had a minor film career, starring in *Discoveries* (1939) and appearing in *Brass Monkey* (1948) (retitled *Lucky Mascot*) and *The Depraved* (1957).

Levis died in obscurity in Charing Cross Hospital, London, on 17 October 1968 of cirrhosis of the liver, and was cremated on 24 October at Golders Green, London. During his career he had made three comebacks and had lost as many fortunes. He claimed to be a dollar millionaire by the time he was thirty, yet, according to press reports, left only a few hundred pounds on his death.

DAVID EVANS

Sources C. Levis, *A showman goes east* (1945) • C. Andrews, ed., *Radio who's who* (1947) • S. Heppner, 'All about Carroll Levis and his discoveries', *Radio Times* (19 Feb 1937), 11 • C. B. Rees, 'Discovering the discovery man', *Radio Times* (8 Oct 1937), 15 • B. Took, *A point of view* (1990) • *The Times* (18 Oct 1968) • *Daily Telegraph* (18 Oct 1968) •

Carroll Richard Levis (1910–1968), by unknown photographer, 1935 [holding a roof-top audition for the *Amateur Hour* show]

Daily Mail (18 Oct 1968) · *Daily Express* (18 Oct 1968) · G. Wood, 'The discovery man', *Sunday Times* (20 Dec 1970) [colour suppl.] · D. Gifford, *The golden age of radio* (1985) · D. Gifford, *The British film catalogue, 1895–1985: a reference guide*, [2nd edn] (1986) · C. G. Glover, 'Carroll carries on', *Radio Times* (19 Sept 1941), 5 · B. Took, *Laughter in the air: an informal history of British radio comedy* (1976) · *Evening News* (1 Jan 1968) · *Daily Telegraph* (26 Nov 1954) · *The Star* (23 Jan 1950) · *The Star* (9 Sept 1960) · J. Walker, ed., *Halliwell's film and video guide*, 12th edn (1997) · *Sunday Express* (19 March 1967) · *Radio Times* (1944) · *Radio Times* (5 March 1948) · *Radio Times* (20 April 1951) · records, BL NSA, BBC sound archive · records, BBC WAC · records, Golders Green crematorium · d. cert.

Archives FILM BFI NFTVA, 'Don't call us', BBC1, 13 Jan 1999 · BFI NFTVA, performance footage | SOUND BL NSA, BBC sound archive, 'Carroll Levis show', 8 Sept 1946

Likenesses photograph, 1935, Hult. Arch. [*see illus.*] · photographs, BBC WAC

Wealth at death a few hundred pounds: Wood, 'Discovery man'

Levison, Mordechai Gumpel Schnaber [*pseud.* George Levison] (**1741–1797**), physician and theologian, was born in Germany. He studied rabbinics in Berlin with the distinguished Talmudist David Fraenkel as a young man, before departing for London in 1771. He was drawn to England by the wonderful opportunity for a young foreign-born Jew to study at the medical course of the famous surgeon and physiologist John Hunter and his equally famous brother William. Upon completion of his medical apprenticeship in 1775, he was awarded a medical degree from Marischal College, Aberdeen. Levison never actually studied in Aberdeen, but the college was the first in the British Isles to award a Jew a medical degree. He was appointed a physician at the General Medical Asylum, London, in 1776. During this period he published his first major Hebrew work, *Ma'amar ha-Torah ve-ha-Hokhmah* ('Dissertation on Torah and wisdom') (1771) as well as two English medical texts where he used the name George Levison: *An Account of the Epidemical Sore Throat* (1778) and *An essay on the blood, in which the objections to Mr. Hunter's opinion concerning the blood are examined and removed* (1776).

Levison's professional success soon led him in a rather remarkable and bizarre direction. He met in London a young medical student from Sweden, August Nordenskjöld, who was soon to become a well-known physician in his own right. August's brother Carl Fredrik later published in Stockholm in 1783 a collection of hermetic and cabbalistic writings by Emanuel Swedenborg, the famous Christian mystical and messianic thinker. Levison shared a keen interest in alchemy and even assisted August in translating his *Plain System of Alchymy* into English. Through his contact with Nordenskjöld, in 1780 Levison was invited by Gustav III to Stockholm where he served as a professor of medicine and laid plans for an alchemical laboratory and an entire institute of medicine. Despite the non-mystical and more empiricist direction of his own published writing, Levison's contacts with Swedenborgians in London and Sweden during this entire period seem highly likely. His short-lived fame, however, soon came to an abrupt end with his sudden departure from Sweden for London probably after he lost the favour of the king. His relations with the English Jewish community deteriorated; he was accused of a moral crime that was never substantiated but a pamphlet damaged his reputation, forcing him to return to Sweden and then relocate to Hamburg where he re-established his medical practice.

In addition to his dissertation on the Torah and wisdom mentioned above, Levison's other important theological and scientific statements are found in two Hebrew works published in Germany: *Tokhahat megillah* ('Reproof of the scroll', published in Hamburg in 1784), a commentary meant to refute Moses Mendelssohn's Hebrew commentary on Ecclesiastes, and *Shelosh esrei yesodei ha-Torah* ('The thirteen principles of the Torah', published in 1792, probably in Altona), a commentary on Maimonides's thirteen principles of faith. Levison's primary theological concern in these writings is the relationship between science and religion. Levison's primary focus was the issue of faith in general, not necessarily of Judaism alone. Levison certainly did not hide his Jewish commitments; after all, he wrote in Hebrew, using a wide range of biblical, rabbinic, and even cabbalistic sources. But he was more interested in treating religion as a general cultural phenomenon in which belief in one God, providence, and prophecy constituted general categories of religious experience accessible to all humankind. Levison's two major sources in his discussion were the sensationalist epistemology of John Locke, on the one hand, and the physico-theology of Carl Linnaeus, on the other, reflecting respectively the formative intellectual environments—London and Stockholm—of his own professional career. Levison was also enamoured of Isaac Newton and was probably the first author to present a full exposition of the latter's laws of motion to a Hebrew readership.

For Levison, the disciple of Locke, Jewish faith rested on the single foundational principle of knowing God, a knowledge based solely on human sensation and cogitation as practised in the scientific laboratory. The primary evidence of God's existence was an intimate knowledge of how the world functions: specifically, the remarkable system of balance and compensation operating throughout the universe. Drawing freely from the writings of Linnaeus and the English tradition of physico-theology, Levison elaborated for his readers the great chain of being, a naturalistic understanding of divine providence based on the maintenance of equilibrium in nature, while virtually ignoring traditional notions of heaven and hell or revelation that fit uneasily into his universal understanding of religion and the cosmos.

The implications of Levison's conclusions were radical indeed. He offered flimsy support for ceremonial observance or for the particularity of Jewish existence. Despite his sharp denunciation of Spinozism, his arguments in favour of Mosaic chronology based on the well-known works of Martini and Bochart, or his defence of Hebrew as the original language, Levison's allegiance to traditional faith and praxis was tenuous at best. He had virtually transformed in his commentary a Maimonidean theology of the twelfth century into a conventional deism of the eighteenth. He died, presumably in Hamburg, in 1797.

DAVID B. RUDERMAN

Sources R. Ruderman, *Jewish thought and scientific discovery in early modern Europe* (1995) • D. B. Ruderman, *Jewish enlightenment in an English key: Anglo-Jewry's construction of modern Jewish thought* (2000) • H. M. Graupe, 'Mordechai Schnaber-Levinson: the life, works and thought of a Haskalah outsider', *Leo Baeck Institute Yearbook*, 41 (1996), 3–20 • D. Ruderman, 'Was there an English parallel to the German Haskalah?', *Two nations: British and German Jews in comparative perspective*, ed. M. Bienner, R. Liedtke, and D. Rechter (1999), 15–44 • H. J. Schoeps, 'Gumpetz Levison: Leben und Werk eines gelehrten Abenteurers des 18. Jahrhunderts', *Zeitschrift für Religions und Geistesgeschichte*, 4 (1952), 150–61 • C. Roth, 'The Haskalah in England', *Essays presented to … Israel Brodie*, ed. J. Zimmels, J. Rabbinowitz, and I. Finestein, 1 (1967), 368–72 • H. J. Schoeps, 'Läkaren och alkemisten Gumpertz Levison', *Lychnos* (1943), 189–229; 230–48 • M. K. Schuchard, 'The secret masonic history of Blake's Swedenborg Society', *Blake: an Illustrated Quarterly*, 26 (1992), 40–51 • K. E. Collins, 'Jewish medical students and graduates in Scotland', *Jewish Historical Studies*, 29 (1982–6), 75–96, esp. 79

Levizac, Jean Pons Victor. *See* Lecoutz de Lévizac, Jean Pons Victor (*c*.1750–1813).

Levy, Amy Judith (1861–1889), writer and poet, was born on 10 November 1861 at 16 Percy Place, London, the second of the seven children of Lewis Levy (1836–1895), a stockbroker, and Isabelle Levin (1840–1928). In 1872 the family moved to 11 Sussex Place, Regent's Park, London, where they lived until 1884. The Levys were Jewish, with roots in England that went back to the first half of the eighteenth century. The family observed the practices of their religion in a mild way and had strong ties to the native-born Anglo-Jewish community, but given the lack of religious belief in Levy's poems, Oscar Wilde was correct to say that 'as she grew up, [she] ceased to hold the orthodox doctrines of her nation, retaining, however, a strong race feeling' (Wilde, 3.52).

Early writings and education A precocious feminist, at thirteen Levy reviewed Elizabeth Barrett Browning's *Aurora Leigh* for a children's publication, and at seventeen wrote 'Xantippe', in which Socrates' maligned wife gives her perspective on their marriage. She attended Brighton High School for Girls, when it opened in 1876, and her letters from school show that she had a 'crush' on the young headmistress, Edith Creak, who became her model for a new kind of woman, autonomous and achievement-oriented. In a letter of 1878 to her sister Katie, she predicted that they would have divergent futures: 'You married, maternal, prudent … with a tendency to laugh at the plain High School Mistress sister who grinds, lodges with chums, and adores "without return"' (Beckman).

Levy became the second Jewish woman to attend Cambridge and the first at Newnham College, which she entered in 1879. She found the work both demanding and exhilarating, and left Newnham after two years: *Xantippe and other Verse* (1881) had been published, and she must have been eager to begin her career as a writer. Her story 'Leopold Leuniger: a study' (1880) also indicates that she found it difficult to deal with antisemitic attitudes (Amy Levy MSS), and an unpublished story ('Lallie: a Cambridge Sketch') expresses the strain of being a pioneering woman at Cambridge (Amy Levy MSS). She may have had unusual difficulty dealing with such stress because she struggled with what Richard Garnett calls 'constitutional melancholy' (*DNB*). In a letter of 1884 she referred to such bouts as 'the devil that lyeth ever in wait in the recesses of my heart'. Her story 'Sokratics in the Strand', her essay 'James Thomson: a minor poet', and her poem 'A Minor Poet' (all 1884) show her willingness to write about despondency and suicide.

Travel and writings After leaving Cambridge in 1881, Levy travelled in Germany and Switzerland, going back and forth between Europe and England until the end of 1884. Some of her letters from this period show that she had internalized the antisemitism of her time. Short and dark, she appears to have accepted Anglo-Saxon norms of beauty: in 1881 she reassured her mother about lack of chaperonage, writing: 'I regret to say that I am as safe as Grandma could be'. Those who did not know her well tended to be keenly aware of her Jewishness: Katharine Tynan, the Irish poet, described Levy's 'charming Eastern face' at the first meeting of a club for women writers in 1889 (Tynan, 330).

While in London, Levy lived with her parents but followed an independent life. With such friends as Clementina Black, Eleanor Marx, Dollie Radford, and Olive Schreiner she frequented the British Museum's reading-room, a former male bastion. The presence of women led to complaints by male scholars, a situation that Levy satirizes in 'The recent telepathic occurrence in the British Museum' (1888). The arrogance of male professors is also a theme in 'Between Two Stools' (1883) and 'At Prato' (1888).

Throughout her twenties Levy published poems and stories in London magazines, and between 1882 and 1885 belonged to a discussion club whose members were London intellectuals and social activists. Those of her friends also involved with the club were committed to a life of activism on behalf of the poor. Although her fiction shows concern about the ruthless individualism and competition of her age, she was not especially concerned with the problems of the working class: in 1887: 'Somehow these girls fr. the streets, with short & merry lives, don't excite my compassion half as much as small bourgeoisie shut up in stucco villas at Brondesbury or Islington. Their enforced "respectability" strikes me as really tragic' (Levy to V. Lee, 1887, Vernon Lee MSS).

In 1884 *A Minor Poet and other Verse* appeared, bringing before the public most of the poems she had been writing since her days at Cambridge. A group of these are about a failed romance with a woman who is associated with music. It is likely that she was writing about an actual relationship or infatuation since her letters from Germany indicate a disappointment in love. Nearly all the poems in *A Minor Poet* are sad, and many are about death, reflecting her own temperament and situation, but also the influence of the melancholy poetry of some Victorian women poets, and of the German pessimists, especially Heinrich Heine. Levy's lyrics and dramatic monologues are particularly striking for their philosophical questioning as to whether there is any essential order or meaning that can justify the anguish of her speakers.

In August 1885 Levy's sister Katie was married. In 'Out of

the World' (1886) Levy's narrator evokes what followed: 'When the wedding preparations was [*sic*] over … a great blankness fell over my soul' (*London Society*, 49, 1886, 53–6). The 'prudent' destiny which Levy had long ago predicted for Katie must have brought to the surface troubling questions about her own alternative path. Recovering from depression, she spent the winter of 1886 in Florence. Her father had arranged for her to write a series of articles for the *Jewish Chronicle*, and in these essays she reclaims her membership in what she calls the Jewish 'family'—on her own terms. Not religious, she emphasizes what Jews have in common culturally—particularly humour. In 'Jewish humour' (1886) she writes: 'The most hardened Agnostic deserter from the synagogue enjoys its pungency' (*Complete Novels and Selected Writings*). Nor does she refrain from criticism. 'Middle-class Jewish women of to-day' (1886) challenges the Jewish community's expectations of women: 'The assertion even of comparative freedom on the part of a Jewess often means the severance of the closest ties, both of family and of race' (*Complete Novels and Selected Writings*).

Friendship with Violet Paget and her circle Levy's visit to Florence in 1886 was pivotal because she met the novelist, scholar, and aesthetician Violet Paget (Vernon Lee). The love poems she sent to Lee ('To Vernon Lee' and 'New Love, New Life') reveal how important this meeting was, and in letters Levy expressed her admiration: 'You are something of an electric battery to me … & I am getting faint from lack of contact!' (Levy to V. Lee, 1887, Vernon Lee MSS). The friendship introduced Levy to Lee's circle of friends, particularly the poet Dorothy Blomfield, the novelist Bertha Thomas, and the historian Bella Duffy. Levy may have felt that she had more in common with these women than with her old friends (though she remained close to Black and Schreiner) because they were feminist writers and scholars rather than activists.

In 1886–7 and during much of 1888 Levy was in an unusually optimistic and energetic frame of mind. This is apparent from her activities on behalf of the University Women's Club, her vigorous lyrics about urban life, essays such as 'Women and club life' and 'The poetry of Christina Rossetti' (1888), and the burst of creative energy which produced two novels. *Romance of a Shop* (1888) is about four sisters who, in defiance of societal expectations, open a photography business and live on their own after their father dies. With her second novel, *Reuben Sachs*, about to be published, she revisited Florence in November 1888; her letters to Katie show her sadness about the end of a romantic relationship.

Reuben Sachs was a powerful novel about life in the affluent Anglo-Jewish community, telling of a rising lawyer who loves and then rejects his cousin Judith in favour of a more politically and socially advantageous marriage; Levy gives the novel a feminist focus by emphasizing Judith's predicament. It was perceived by the Jewish press as an attack on Jewish life, but Levy may have been more uncomfortable with the views of Gentile reviewers, who tended to read it as a corroboration of long-standing stereotypes about Jews. Few saw that its contradictory, multiple perspectives on Jewish character and life were far from wholly negative; that the longing Judith feels for her people when she is removed from them at the novel's end suggests the warmth and family love of the Jewish community; and that the novel's allusions to George Eliot's *Daniel Deronda* indicate that the Jewish world, materialistic and competitive, is a microcosm of the larger society.

In the winter of 1889 Levy threw herself into a whirlwind of social and professional activities, completing her third novel, *Miss Meredith*, in six weeks. After two Jewish newspapers excoriated *Reuben Sachs* her mood darkened, as those who saw her that spring and summer recalled. W. B. Yeats said: 'She was talkative, good-looking in a way and full of the restlessness of the unhappy' (Yeats, 87). In May, Levy published 'Cohen of Trinity' (1889). The story's Gentile narrator describes the growing despair of the Jewish protagonist who, having written a very popular book, comes to realize that he will none the less never be understood by the dominant culture.

Depression and death The controversy over *Reuben Sachs* probably triggered Levy's last episode of depression, as she retreated to her parents' home at 7 Endsleigh Gardens, Bloomsbury, five days after the *Jewish Chronicle* (which had previously shown restraint) attacked *Reuben Sachs* for the first time. While in seclusion that August she corrected the galleys for *A London Plane-Tree and other Verse*. (Its lyrics are marked by emotional integrity and condensed power.) A posthumous story, 'Wise in her generation' (1890), links the commodification of women to society's social Darwinism, more evidence that Levy did not believe the competitive ethos of the Jewish community to be an anomaly in British society.

Levy committed suicide by asphyxiation on 10 September 1889 at 7 Endsleigh Gardens. The controversy over *Reuben Sachs* was a factor, but her personal life was giving her pain, she was becoming increasingly deaf, and, according to Richard Garnett and Vernon Lee, she feared insanity (a groundless fear) (Lee to B. Duffy, 14 Oct 1889, Vernon Lee MSS). Garnett understood that Levy's final bout of depression had deep roots:

> She was indeed frequently gay and animated, but her cheerfulness was but a passing mood that merely gilded her habitual melancholy, without diminishing it by a particle, while sadness grew upon her steadily, in spite of flattering success and the sympathy of affectionate friends. (*DNB*)

Levy was the first Jewish woman in England to be cremated; her ashes were interred at Kingsbury Road Jewish cemetery, Dalston, London, on 15 September, in the presence of relatives and friends.

In the immediate wake of Levy's death, many spoke of their affection and of her gifts and promise. Yeats said: 'Had she cared to live, a future of some note awaited her' (Yeats, 87); Wilde praised both her poetry and her fiction: 'To write thus at six-and-twenty is given to very few' (Wilde, 3.52); and Garnett wrote: 'the sudden advance made in *Reuben Sachs* indicates a great reserve of undeveloped power' (*DNB*).

Levy's work received little attention after the 1890s, but

her obscurity should be seen as part of the larger neglect of women who wrote in the last two decades of the nineteenth century. *The Complete Novels and Selected Writings of Amy Levy, 1861–1889* appeared in 1993, sparking a revival of interest in her work, attention that is related to current scholarly investigations of the literature produced by British Jews and Victorian women.

LINDA HUNT BECKMAN

Sources L. H. Beckman, *Amy Levy: her life and letters* (2000) • *The complete novels and selected writings of Amy Levy, 1861–1889*, ed. M. New (1993) • O. Wilde, 'Amy Levy', *Woman's World*, 3 (1890), 52 • *DNB* • Colby College, Waterville, Maine, Miller Library, Vernon Lee MSS • *W. B. Yeats: letters to the new island*, ed. H. Reynolds (1934), 87 • A. Levy, 'Lallie: a Cambridge sketch', Camellia plc, Linton Park, Kent, Camellia Collection, Amy Levy Archive • K. Tynan, *Twenty-five years: reminiscences* (1913), 330 • d. cert.

Archives Linton Park, Kent, Camellia plc, Camellia Collection: Amy Levy Archive [manuscripts (published and unpublished), letters, Levy's daily calendar for 1889, sketches, photographs, juvenilia, books, other papers] | Colby College, Waterville, Maine, Miller Library, Vernon Lee Collection [letters to Lee]

Likenesses photographs, Camellia plc, Linton Park, Kent, Amy Levy Archive, Camellia collection • photographs, repro. in Beckman, *Amy Levy: her life and letters*

Wealth at death £174 6s.: probate, 18 Feb 1890, *CGPLA Eng. & Wales*

Levy, Benn Wolfe (1900–1973), playwright and theatre producer, was born in London on 7 March 1900, the younger child and only son of Octave George Levy, a prosperous wool broker of Hyde Park Gate, and his wife, Nannie Joseph. He was educated at Repton School and, after a period as a cadet in the RAF, in 1918 he went to University College, Oxford, which he left without a degree. He entered publishing in 1923, becoming managing director of Jarrolds. At this time he spelt his name Benn Wolf Levy. He then began to make a name as a witty, civilized, and incisive writer for the stage. His comedies and farces, fantasies and adaptations, melodramas and film scripts, including a libretto for the impresario C. B. Cochran, kept him in the public eye for over three decades. Although he started in 1924 with a West End comedy, *This Woman Business*, with Fay Compton and Leon Quartermaine, about an intruder in a house of professed misogynists, Levy brought an eye for character and a sense of fun to almost everything he wrote. An affable, popular, and chuckling personality, he worked in intelligence in the Second World War and entered parliament afterwards as a Labour MP, without ever losing sight of his craft as playwright. With his endearing habit of addressing all and sundry as 'ducky', Levy was popular wherever he went. Even when they misfired, his plays still possessed a quality and charm above the average in characterization, language, and intelligence. In their appeal to the best actors of the time they often met with success in the West End and on Broadway. Constance Cummings (*b.* 1910), the Hollywood actress and lawyer's daughter whom he married in 1933, appeared in most of his plays; and in 1937 he directed her in his New York adaptation of *Madame Bovary*.

After Levy's second success, *A Man with Red Hair*, adapted from a Hugh Walpole novel, came *Mud and Treacle* (1928). Among other plays that crossed the Atlantic were *Mrs Moonlight*; *Art and Mrs Bottle* (1929); *Topaze*, taken from a play by Marcel Pagnol; and *The Devil* (1930), which he also directed. What brought Levy into the London limelight was a C. B. Cochran musical comedy, *Ever-Green* (1930), headed by Jessie Matthews and Sonny Hale; at the time Levy was writing screenplays under contract to the German film company UFA, so Cochran had to send the composer Richard Rodgers and the lyricist Lorenz Hart to collaborate in Germany with Levy on what proved a great West End success.

The best known film on which Levy worked was Alfred Hitchcock's first 'talkie', *Blackmail* (1929), which he wrote with Hitchcock and Charles Brackett. Meanwhile his plays continued variously to please in London and New York, including two farces, *Springtime for Henry*, which he also directed, and *Hollywood Holiday* (1931), which he wrote with John van Druten. In 1936 he adapted from the German a melodrama, *Young Madame Conti* (1936), with Hubert Griffith, which James Agate, the critic, praised as 'rousing' and in which Miss Cummings, according to Agate, 'takes rank, even on the strength of one performance, as an incontestably fine emotional actress up to anything from pitch-and-toss to manslaughter' (Agate, 323). Cummings's acting and personality contributed to the success of many Levy plays.

Joining the navy in 1939, Levy rose from able-bodied seaman to lieutenant, and during service in intelligence in the Adriatic in 1944 he was wounded in cloak-and-dagger operations. He was appointed MBE. In the 1945 general election he won the new constituency of Eton and Slough for Labour, which he represented for five years. Resuming his West End career with *Clutterbuck* (1946), a sophisticated comedy set on a cruise liner with a good part for his wife, Levy followed it with *Return to Tyassi* (1950). Even though it failed at the highest level, this examination of human relationships was received as a characteristically elegant and wise insight into upper-middle-class family life. Its dialogue was praised for its 'hard, living and appropriate language' (Worsley, 182). One of Levy's last notable West End successes was *The Rape of the Belt* (1957; New York, 1960). This brought John Clements, Kay Hammond, and Cummings together in a comedy based on the ninth labour of Hercules. Among other Levy plays were *The Tumbler* (1960), which Laurence Olivier staged in New York, and *Public and Confidential* (Malvern and London, 1966).

As a post-war socialist MP Levy became a close friend of Aneurin Bevan and his wife, Jennie Lee. To them he exemplified good taste, not only in his Chelsea home—designed by the architect Walter Gropius—but also in the collection of pictures that he had bought from young artists. In the fight to abolish stage censorship, he introduced in 1949 a private member's bill. In the campaign to build a national theatre he took part in public debates, and when he decided to stand down as an MP in 1950 he joined the Arts Council (1953–61) and supported its policy of raising greater public subsidy for the arts. A contributor to left-wing publications such as the *New Statesman* and *The Tribune*, he supported the Council for Civil Liberties and the Fabian Society, and he urged unilateral nuclear disarmament in a pamphlet, *Britain and Bomb, the Fallacy of Nuclear Defence* (1959). After a serious heart attack in 1960 Levy withdrew more and more to his 600 acre farm, Cote House, Aston, Oxfordshire, where he established a well-known breed of Friesian cattle. He died at Oxford on 7 December 1973, and was survived by his wife and their son and daughter. ERIC SHORTER

Sources J. Parker, ed., *Who's who in the theatre*, 15th edn (1972) · J. Agate, *More first nights* (1937) · S. Morley, *Spread a little happiness* (1987) · C. Larkin, ed., *The Guinness who's who of stage musicals* (1994) · T. C. Worsley, *The fugitive art: dramatic commentaries, 1947–1951* (1952) · personal knowledge (2004) · *DNB* · *CGPLA Eng. & Wales* (1974)

Archives HLRO, corresp. and MSS · U. Sussex, corresp. and MSS | BL, corresp. with League of Dramatists, Add. MS 63409 · Bodl. Oxf., letters to Clement Attlee | SOUND BL NSA, performance recording

Wealth at death £129,245: probate, 30 Oct 1974, *CGPLA Eng. & Wales*

Levy, Hyman (1889–1975), mathematician and socialist activist, was born on 28 February 1889 in Edinburgh, the second of four sons and third of eight children of Marcus Levy, picture dealer of Edinburgh, and his wife, Minna Cohen. Their Zionist and socialist teachings were a strong formative influence. Levy was educated at George Heriot's School and then at the University of Edinburgh from which he received, in 1911, a first-class honours degree in mathematics and physics. As the winner of a Ferguson scholarship, an 1851 Exhibition scholarship, and a Carnegie research fellowship, Levy was advised to pursue further study at the University of Cambridge. This he declined to do, however, on the grounds that Cambridge was deeply complicit in Britain's class society; he chose instead to follow his research interests at the University of Göttingen. He returned to Britain on the outbreak of the First World War and, after a brief and not altogether happy period in the Royal Flying Corps, joined the National Physical Laboratory, where he stayed until 1920. He married Marion Aitken Fraser (a devout Presbyterian) in 1918; they had two sons and one daughter. In 1920 Levy went to the Royal College of Science (Imperial College) where he remained for the rest of his working life, becoming a professor in 1923, head of the mathematics department in 1946, dean, also in 1946, and professor emeritus on his retirement in 1954. Other honours included being made a fellow of the Royal Society of Edinburgh in 1916. He was a member of the council of the London Mathematical Society (1929–31) and its vice-president (1931–2).

Levy was a prolific author on both mathematical and social topics. His particular academic field was numerical methods, and among his early and late books were *Numerical Studies in Differential Equations* (1934) and *Finite Difference Equations* (1958). To understand Levy it is necessary to acknowledge the importance of his social philosophy. Appalled by the social and human consequences of the poverty of the Edinburgh working class among whom he grew up, and influenced by his parents, Levy was attracted from an early age to the doctrine of socialism. His perception of the class-divided nature of contemporary society was reinforced by his educational experiences, and he helped found a branch of the Fabian Society at Edinburgh University. Science, furthermore, was not for Levy separate from society, and scientific rationalism—in due course in his own case in the form of Marxism—was the tool which would liberate humanity from its present ills. This was specifically articulated in his *Modern Science*, published in 1939. Scientific rationalism also led Levy to be a lifelong member of the National Secular Society and, at one point, a director of the Rationalist Press Association.

It was directly in the field of politics that Levy sought to promote his vision of the role of science and scientific method. He was to remark in later life that he had been expelled from both the Labour Party and the Communist Party, and it was with the former that he first, in the 1920s, made an impact. By this time he had already gained practical political experience through his involvement with the National Union of Scientific Workers and as an election campaign speaker. Levy was instrumental in having the Labour Party create an advisory committee on science, and he served as its chairman from 1924 to 1930.

In common with other such committees, however, this had little real impact on Labour Party policy. By the late 1920s, as a result of his union activities, his involvement with the Central Labour College, and his lack of faith in the Labour Party leadership, Levy was increasingly moving in communist circles. From 1930 he was officially a Communist Party member, and for more than twenty years thereafter he was to be one of that organization's most prominent spokesmen on scientific matters. One important medium through which Levy was able to express his views on science and society in the 1930s was radio broadcasting. He was involved in a number of series—for example 'Scientific research and social needs', on which he collaborated with Julian Huxley. Levy also communicated his message to the labour movement and to the wider public through public speaking—at which he was especially adept—and newspaper and journal articles, and books.

When the Second World War broke out Levy supported the official Moscow and Communist Party line, that Germany and Britain were involved in an imperialist war. When the Soviet Union was invaded, Levy once again followed the party line, and so came to support the war effort. His loyalty to the Communist Party was, however, severely tested in the post-war era. Levy was deeply shocked by the revelations of antisemitism in the Soviet Union, and in late 1956 he was part of a British Communist delegation to that country charged with investigating the abuses associated with Stalin's regime. His findings and their subsequent publication—ultimately in *Jews and the National Question* (1958)—set in train the events which led to his expulsion from the Communist Party in 1958. Despite hopes on Levy's part of a political reconciliation this breach proved final and marked the effective end of his political career.

Levy's was in many respects a remarkable, and very twentieth-century, life. From his upbringing among the Edinburgh working class he went on to a distinguished academic career at London University while engaging wholeheartedly in a commitment to Marxist socialism. He was also, it would appear, greatly respected by his friends and colleagues for his warmth and kindness. Levy died on 27 February 1975 at his home, 25A Home Park Road, Wimbledon, Surrey. JOHN STEWART

Sources G. Werskey, *The visible college* (1978); repr. (1988) · *DNB* · W. McGucken, *Scientists, society and state: the social relations of science movement in Great Britain, 1931–1947* (1984) · *The Times* (1 March 1975) · D. S. Murray, 'Hyman Levy: man of action', *The Freethinker* (April 1975), 50, 52 · private information (2004) · d. cert.

Archives FILM BBC Film Library, interview with Esther Rantzen (1975)

Wealth at death £12,754: probate, 27 July 1975, *CGPLA Eng. & Wales*

Levy, Joseph (1906–1990), property developer and estate agent, was born on 27 January 1906 at 1 Mansell Road, Acton, Middlesex, the youngest of the five children of David Edward Levy, then a hotel waiter, and his wife, Ellen Kate Twine. David Levy was later described as a manufacturer's agent and as a bookmaker. Joe, as Levy was popularly known, spent his early life in Clapham and was educated at Emmanuel School, Wandsworth.

After working at a bookmaker's and as a stock exchange negotiator Levy entered the property world in 1924, when he and his older brother David went to work for the famous office developer and estate agent Jackie Phillips, whose contracts included the development of Broadcasting House in London. When in 1939 Phillips ran up heavy debts the brothers took over the ailing business, which became D. E. and J. Levy. A year earlier, on 29 December, Joe Levy had married Frances Ninot (*b*. 1912/13), daughter of Francis Charles Henwood, a hairdresser's assistant; they had two sons and a daughter.

During the Second World War Levy worked first as a civil defence warden and then with the National Fire Service. He was awarded the British Empire Medal in 1941 after entering a collapsing building and rescuing several people. Despite their war work the Levys were able to keep their estate agency open during the war years. They amassed a portfolio of well-located war-damaged properties which were to prove extremely valuable in the post-war property boom; as Levy later recalled, 'We were on the spot and we could see that if this country came out of the war, London would have to be rebuilt' (Marriott, 155). They entered the post-war property market with both substantial experience of the way market conditions had changed during the war and a substantial client base. They understood the complexities of war-damage regulations and arranged a number of 'lessor schemes' (by which developers built property for letting to government departments and thereby obtained the necessary building licences) on behalf of developers. During this period they became acquainted with some of the key figures of the property boom, including Harold Samuel, Charles Clore, Jack Cotton, Lew Hammerson, and Charles Forte.

Levy was a prime mover in the 1954–64 office development boom. In the mid-1960s D. E. and J. Levy claimed to have handled for clients some 9 million sq. ft of new London offices. However, the firm's most important role was as principal rather than agent. The brothers formed a partnership with Robert Clark, a shrewd Scottish solicitor whom they had met in 1937 when looking for finance for their first development, three depots for Dunlop. Joe Levy's relationship with Clark was said to be at times stormy, though Clark's cautious temperament, together with Levy's enthusiasm, provided a highly successful blend that was to make both men millionaires.

Joe Levy and his brother, together with Clark, initially established a separate company for each development, the three holding equal shares. However, in 1951 they acquired a small property company, Stock Conversion Investment Trust, to which they transferred their property assets. This was to become one of the most successful companies of the 'property boom' era.

David Levy died suddenly in 1952, aged forty-seven. In the same year Joe Levy came into contact with a project which was to form the basis of the largest single development in Britain initiated by the private sector during the first two post-war decades. D. E. and J. Levy were asked to handle the sale of a 1 acre corner site facing Euston Road and Stanhope Street. The vendor withdrew the property, for tax reasons, but resubmitted it to the practice four years later. Negotiations with the London county council revealed that in return for the use of some land for a road development the council would permit a large, co-ordinated development on a 13 acre site of which this property formed a part, it being left to the developer to acquire the remainder. Levy offered the project to Charles Clore, who was initially interested but later pulled out. Levy eventually decided to conduct the expanded project via Stock Conversion, but the estimated cost of development (£15–20 million) made it necessary for the firm to bring in two major contractors, George Wimpey & Co. and Wates, as partners; Wates later withdrew, leaving the others with 50 per cent each. The necessary land was acquired secretly (to prevent the price escalating) about 315 separate deals, and development commenced in the winter of 1963–4. The value of the development, which included 100 shops, 160,000 sq. ft of showrooms, a factory, luxury flats, and a huge volume of office space, was considerably boosted by the imposition of a ban on new office development in and around London imposed in November 1964 by the new Labour government. However, a later attempt to institute a similar development, in conjunction with a road development scheme, at Piccadilly Circus produced considerable delays and complications, leading Levy to sell off Stock Conversion's Piccadilly sites, including the Trocadero.

Levy retired from his surveying practice in September 1973 and subsequently devoted more of his time to Stock Conversion. He remained active with the company until the early 1980s, after which he suffered from increasing ill health. Levy had distributed much of his shareholding via a charitable foundation, together with various family trusts. In 1986 P. & O. took over Stock Conversion in a hostile bid; following this Levy's son Peter started another property company, Shaftesbury plc, of which the elder Levy became president, although he was by then too ill to take an active role.

Oliver Marriott described Levy as a jovial man with an uninhibited pleasure in the material results of great wealth (Marriott, 154), while his *Telegraph* obituary described him as an ebullient, likeable, and blunt cockney, who bubbled with enthusiasm and confidence. Levy was a keen footballer, enjoyed playing golf and tennis, and owned several racehorses and greyhounds. He was also heavily involved in charitable work, serving as founder trustee and chairman of the Cystic Fibrosis Research Trust, vice-president of the London Federation of Boys' Clubs, and a governor of Millfield School and chairman of its rebuilding fund. He was appointed MBE and CBE for his charity work. In 1972 Levy's charitable foundation bought Dickens's Old Curiosity Shop to ensure that it remained in British hands: this repeated history, as his mentor Jackie Phillips had purchased it for similar reasons in 1925, at which time Levy conducted the transaction.

Levy died on 18 December 1990 at his home, Goldsborough, 42 Ladbroke Road, Kensington, from Alzheimer's disease; he was buried at the Jewish cemetery in Golders Green on the 20th. Despite the trusts and the charitable foundation Levy's estate was valued at almost £9 million.

PETER SCOTT

Sources *Daily Telegraph* (24 Dec 1990), 23 · private information (2004) · O. Marriott, *The property boom* (1967) · E. L. Erdman, *People and property* (1982) · *Daily Telegraph* (20 Dec 1990), 22 [death notice] · C. Gordon, *The two tycoons* (1984) · B. P. Whitehouse, *Partners in property* (1964) · *Forte: the autobiography of Charles Forte* (1986) · b. cert. · m. cert. · d. cert.

Likenesses R. Goldman, photograph, *c.*1964, repro. in Whitehouse, *Partners in property*

Wealth at death £8,845,485: probate, 17 June 1991, *CGPLA Eng. & Wales*

Levy, Joseph Hiam (1838–1913), journalist and campaigner for individual rights, was born on 17 July 1838 at 7 Upper East Smithfield, Aldgate, London, son of Lawrence Levy, slop seller, and his wife, Maria Hiam. He was educated at the City of London School and City of London College.

In 1862 Levy was appointed inspector of accounts at the Department of Education, a position he retained until retirement in 1902. The post was believed by his colleagues to be 'far beneath his commercial opportunities' but he accepted it because it gave him sufficient leisure to pursue his developing interests as a journalist, lecturer, and participant in London intellectual life (*The Individualist*, 1913, 84). In journalism he first made his mark as a leader writer (1869–75) for *The Examiner*. In volunteer education work he gained a reputation among night students at Birkbeck College and at the City of London College for the incisiveness of his lectures in logic and political economy. In London intellectual life he was an early and prominent speaker at meetings of the London Dialectical Society, where an admiring young George Bernard Shaw identified him in the early 1870s as

> a champion debater … a young and vigorous man with bold prominent eyes, bold prominent round cheeks, and bold prominent lips, with black whiskers of the kind that used to be called bushy. He was of middle height, stoutly built, an unmistakable Jew and proud of it. (*The Individualist*, 1913, 83)

He married in the mid-1870s Emily Wheeler (1854–1894), with whom he had two daughters. At this stage of his career Levy was a close disciple of J. S. Mill, a supporter of sex equality and of land tenure reform.

In 1877 the Bradlaugh and Besant trial challenged Levy's belief in gender equality (which he owed to Mill) and in free enquiry, and led him further into the world of metropolitan liberal radicalism. Under the pseudonym 'D' he became a regular columnist in the freethinking journal the *National Reformer*. In 1877 he also joined the Vigilance Association for the Defence of Personal Rights (from 1885 the Personal Rights Association), a radical libertarian organization founded in 1871 by Josephine Butler and others to campaign for equality in individual citizen rights in the face of such challenges as the Contagious Diseases Acts. In 1879 Levy was invited to join its committee, a position which he held until his death; his wife became a member of the committee in 1890.

The 1880s saw Levy at the height of his public reputation as an advanced libertarian radical. He dominated the libertarian press through his editorship of the *Personal Rights Journal*. He was acknowledged to have played a major role in the successful parliamentary lobbying for repeal of the Contagious Diseases Acts in 1886. He was (partly as the result of the personal experience of one of his daughters) a leading campaigner against compulsory vaccination, and also an active anti-vivisectionist. His commitment to the cause of women's rights continued: in 1892 he chaired a notable public meeting of the Women's Franchise League at which Bernard Shaw clashed with the Pankhursts.

On other fronts, however, Levy's radical credentials were beginning to face challenge. He agreed with fellow radical libertarian James Stansfeld MP that the onset of adult male democracy in the mid-1880s posed a dilemma for libertarians, making English politics 'more democratic but less Liberal' (*The Individualist*, 1905, 50). He became particularly concerned to defend the view that 'personal liberty, without possession and free disposal of property, is like the liberty of a bird to fly in a vacuum' (*The Individualist*, 1913, 81). Such a view brought him into open conflict with Fabian socialists such as his debating friend Shaw, without reconciling him to the views of Conservative anti-collectivists. In compensation, he moved to convert the Personal Rights Association into a sounding board for his attacks on state injustices to individuals, and in 1888 launched the National Liberal Club political economy circle to combat 'new Liberal' enthusiasm for state intervention policies. Still sharing Mill's belief in reaching truth through public debate, he edited a series of symposia with prominent socialists, and also published several series of his own collected essays. The defeat of the Liberal government in 1895 gave him hope that 'John Bull has begun to realize what the "New Liberalism" means' (*Personal Rights Journal*, 1895, 61–2). The new century's drift toward militarism, clericalism, state regulation of citizen behaviour, and economic protectionism brought him close to despair, and a strain of Spencerian acceptance of arguments for the 'survival of the fittest' emerges more clearly from about this time. Pessimism was reinforced by the death of his wife in 1894 and the onset of deafness, which left him largely reliant on his younger daughter, Lorenza Garreau, for contact with public audiences. A workhorse to the end in the cause of personal rights, he died of influenza at his home, 11 Abbeville Road, Clapham, London, on 11 November 1913. He was buried, after a secularist funeral, at Brookwood cemetery on 14 November 1913, his death marking the effective dissolution of the Millite radical libertarian tradition that he had embodied. M. J. D. Roberts

Sources *The Individualist* (Nov–Dec 1913), 77–88 · *The Individualist* (July 1905), 50–51 · *Personal Rights* (15 Nov 1901), 79–80 · *Personal Rights Journal* (June 1892), 162–3; (Oct 1894), 62 · *Annual Report of the Vigilance Association for the Defence of Personal Rights*, 8 (1878); 9 (1880) · *National Reformer* (9 Sept 1877), 618–19 · M. W. Taylor, introduction, *Men versus the state: Herbert Spencer and late Victorian individualism* (1992) · *WWW* · b. cert. · d. cert. · census returns, 1881
Archives BLPES, letters to James Bonar
Likenesses F. C. Gould, sketch, 1897, repro. in J. L. Hammond and B. Hammond, *James Stansfeld: a Victorian champion of sex equality* (1932), 116 · photograph, *c*.1897, National Liberal Club, London · S. J. Solomon, oils, 1901, repro. in *The Individualist* (Nov–Dec 1913), 77
Wealth at death £2164 5*s*. 4*d*.: probate, 17 Dec 1913, *CGPLA Eng. & Wales*

Levy, Joseph Moses (1812–1888), newspaper proprietor, was born in Whitechapel in the East End of London on 15 December 1812, the son of Moses Lionel Levy and Helena, daughter of J. Moses. Like his father, he was an Orthodox Jew. After an unconventional education at Bruce Castle, Tottenham, a private school run by an eccentric schoolmaster, Thomas Wright Hill (1763–1851), brother of Sir Rowland Hill, the postal reformer, Levy left at the age of fourteen to start a seven-year apprenticeship as a printer in Germany. He was well liked by his employer and was given financial assistance to start his own printing business as soon as he had qualified. He married Esther, daughter of N. G. Cohen, in 1831. She died in 1883, leaving a large family. His eldest son, Edward Levy-*Lawson (1833–1916), became Baron Burnham, the first press peer, in 1903.

In his early twenties JML, as he came to be known, bought a small printing establishment at the Fleet Street end of Shoe Lane, London. In this way he also became the owner, as well as the printer, of the *Sunday Times* (founded in 1822), making himself chief proprietor in 1855. Later in the same year he took over the production of the *Daily Telegraph and Courier*, founded on 29 June 1855 by Colonel

Joseph Moses Levy (1812–1888), by Sir Hubert von Herkomer, exh. RA 1888

Arthur Burroughes Sleigh, a recently retired and slightly crazed army officer. Despite its quality appearance and low price of 2*d*., the newspaper was not successful. The first issues were printed by Aird and Tunstall of Essex Street, off the Strand, who threatened closure when their bills were not paid. In a chance meeting with Levy, Sleigh described his predicament. To Sleigh's relief Levy agreed to print his newspaper, but only on condition that if his bills remained unpaid beyond a certain date, its copyright and everything concerning it would pass to him in default.

Sleigh agreed, urging Levy to take over the failing business immediately; Levy was assisted by his 22-year-old son Edward, then drama critic of the *Sunday Times*. With issue no. 45 (published on 20 August 1855) father and son decided to drop the words 'and Courier' from the title, and on 16 September 1855 (issue no. 69) London was given its first double-sheet, eight-page morning newspaper at the sensationally low price of 1*d*. By January 1856 circulation had reached 27,000 copies per day. But Levy's ever-rising costs forced him to sell the *Sunday Times*. In a bold attempt to expand into profit Levy brought his prosperous financier brother, Lionel Levy-Lawson, into the family business. Together with his managing editor son Edward and experienced co-editor Thornton Leigh Hunt, they soon produced a circulation of 141,000. In 1860 they moved the steadily growing newspaper from its poky birthplace at 253 Strand to larger premises at 135 Fleet Street. In 1863, a royal wedding year, Levy saw his creation exceed 240,000. But only when the circulation had reached 300,000 did he consider further expansion. A palatial new building, spreading itself from 135 to 139 Fleet Street, was opened by the prince of Wales and his younger brother, the duke of Albany, on 28 June 1882. The *Daily Telegraph* continued as the leading daily newspaper until the appearance in 1896 of the *Daily Mail*, which overtook it early in 1897. Levy, who never officially retired, died at Florence Cottage, High Street, Ramsgate, his holiday home, on 12 October 1888. He was buried at Kingsbury Road Jewish cemetery, Dalston, London. During his lifetime Levy was praised publicly by Matthew Arnold for producing the first popular daily newspaper 'conducted with a high tone' and 'without Americanisms in lay-out or republicanism along American lines' (*Friendship's Garland*). RAY BOSTON

Sources *The Times* (13 Oct 1888) • *Daily Telegraph* (13 Oct 1888) • D. Griffiths, ed., *The encyclopedia of the British press, 1422–1992* (1992), 362–3 • D. Hart-Davis, *The house the Berrys built: inside the 'Telegraph', 1928–1986* (1990), 35–47 • Lord Burnham [E. F. L. Burnham], *Peterborough Court: the story of the Daily Telegraph* (1955) • *DNB* • private information (2004) • d. cert. • *ILN* (30 June 1882) • M. Arnold, *Friendship's garland* (1871)

Archives NRA, priv. coll., corresp. and papers

Likenesses double portrait, photograph, *c.*1882 (with eldest son), priv. coll.; taken for family archives • H. von Herkomer, oils, exh. RA 1888, NPG [*see illus.*] • line drawing, repro. in *The Graphic* (27 Oct 1888) • wood-engraving, NPG; repro. in *ILN* (27 Oct 1888)

Wealth at death £482,915 8*s.* 5*d.*: resworn probate, Feb 1889, *CGPLA Eng. & Wales* (1888)

Levy, Judith (1706–1803), benefactor, was born in London, the second of the six children of Moses *Hart (1675–1756) [*see under* Hart, Aaron], merchant and broker, and his wife, Prudence Heilbuth. Levy's father, the leading figure in the German Jewish community in Britain in the first half of the eighteenth century, was one of the twelve authorized 'Jew brokers' on the Royal Exchange. In 1727 she married a cousin, Elias Levy (1702–1750), a diamond merchant and army contractor. They lived first in Bishopsgate Street, London, and then in a large mansion in Wellclose Square, an area favoured by wealthy City merchants. As was common in Jewish mercantile families at the time, she took an active part in the family business, contributing, it is said, to its growing prosperity. When her husband died in 1750, and then her father in 1756, she was left a very wealthy woman, with an annual income of about £6000. Two of their children, Benjamin and Isabella, survived infancy, but the former died at age twenty-two, leaving his sister heir to a great fortune. Through the intervention of the duchess of Northumberland, a noted matchmaker with a reputation for procuring wealthy brides for well-born younger sons, Isabella married Lockhart Gordon, third son of the earl of Aboyne, in an Anglican ceremony in 1753. However, she did not enjoy her good fortune for long, dying within a year, possibly in childbirth.

In the wake of her daughter's tragic death, Levy abandoned her mansion in Wellclose Square and moved to the West End, to a house in Albemarle Street, Piccadilly, a district where few Jews lived at the time—a decision indicative of her growing distance from other Jews. She spent most of her time, however, at 4 Maids-of-Honour Row, near Richmond Green, with which she remained associated for the rest of her life, becoming known as the Queen of Richmond Green. In a break with her earlier habits of industry and frugality, she became a devotee of fashionable society, with which she had had some acquaintance from her youth. She entertained lavishly, set a Lucullan table, maintained a splendid equipage, frequented the best watering places, made the rounds of balls and masquerades, and played high-stakes card games with members of the nobility. An obituary in the *New Wonderful Museum, and Extraordinary Magazine* remarked that 'she preferred the company of female Gentiles to that of the Hebrew ladies, merely on account of the superior elegances and politeness of the former' (Granger, 400–01). Her self-indulgence, however, did not diminish her benevolence. She was reputed to distribute £1000 a year to her less fortunate relatives and was known for her kindness to her servants, allowing them, *inter alia*, the then luxuries of tea and coffee. Her most notable charitable act was a gift of £4000 in 1787 to the Ashkenazi synagogue in Duke's Place (later known as the Great Synagogue) to reconstruct and enlarge the building to accommodate its growing membership. Although no longer an observant Jew, Levy felt bound to the congregation by strong family ties. (Her father-in-law had been one of its founders and her father one of its chief supporters, having contributed £2000 to erect its first permanent building.) She died on 18 January 1803 at Albemarle Street, and was buried in the Jewish cemetery in Mile End Road, London, two days later. TODD M. ENDELMAN

Sources R. Daiches-Dubens, 'Eighteenth century Anglo-Jewry in and around Richmond, Surrey', *Transactions of the Jewish Historical Society of England*, 18 (1953–5), 143–69 • C. Roth, *The Great Synagogue, London, 1690–1940* (1950) • 'Authentic memoirs of Mrs Levy', W. Granger and others, *The new wonderful museum, and extraordinary magazine*, 1 (1803), 400–01 • J. Picciotto, *Sketches of Anglo-Jewish history*, rev. edn, rev. I. Finestein (1956) • T. M. Endelman, *The Jews of Georgian England, 1714–1830* (1979) • T. M. Endelman, *Radical assimilation in English Jewish history, 1656–1945* (1990)

Likenesses engraving, repro. in Daiches-Dubens, 'Eighteenth-century Anglo-Jewry'

Wealth at death approx. £125,000: Daiches-Dubens, 'Eighteenth century Anglo-Jewry'

Levy, Lewis (1785/6–1856), farmer of tolls, was probably born in 1786, but nothing else is known about his early life. Until 1864–5, tolls were levied on the major roads leading into London. The resulting revenue was used to repair and sometimes light the roads, and to service the debts incurred during construction and maintenance work. Collection of the tolls was generally not carried out by the turnpike authorities themselves, but was let by auction. Levy bid at these auctions, often with partners, sometimes as lessee or joint lessee, sometimes as surety. However, he was the dominant partner in these transactions and he was so successful that he became known as Turnpike Levy.

The earliest known record of Levy as a toll lessee dates from 1812. By 1825, he rented about three-quarters of the tolls in Middlesex and the neighbourhood of London, and in 1832 *The Times* referred to him as 'the master of nearly all the toll gates within 15 miles of London' (20 Aug 1832). In 1839, asked by the parliamentary select committee on turnpike roads whether he farmed them to a great extent, he responded 'Not so great an extent as I used to do. I used to farm £400,000 or £500,000 a year. I think I have had as much as £300,000 or £400,000 with Post Horse Duties' ('Select committee on the effect of the formation of railroads', qq. 204–7). He had not come prepared to say what the current amount was, but it was nothing like one fourth as much, he thought about £100,000. In 1854, however, he was again reported as leasing most of the tolls north of the Thames.

Levy also lent funds to turnpike trusts to finance road improvements, although his offer to lend £10,000 to the commissioners of the metropolitan roads had been turned down in 1827. He told the same select committee that he 'unfortunately' was a creditor on a great many turnpike roads, meaning that they had defaulted on interest or repayment and that he had had to exercise his right to collect the tolls to recover the money owed him ('Select committee … formation of railroads', q. 220).

Levy's name came before the public not only in newspaper reports of the auctions, but also in their reports of court cases, notably of one initiated by Cobbett in 1823, acting on behalf of 'several poor persons'. He claimed that Levy's toll-keepers were charging more than the law allowed for a one-horse cart. He was invited to sit on the bench. *The Times* reported Cobbett as saying to Levy 'You are a Jew I suppose,' to which Levy replied 'I am a Jew, it is true; but you are neither Jew, Christian or any other religion. You are an atheist as everybody knows' (17 Oct 1823). Cobbett then complained: 'I abstained from abuse … But he called me an atheist. This Jew-dog called me an atheist, this Jew-dog did' (21 Oct 1823). In another case, Levy had his claimed right to charge king's messengers confirmed. In 1830, he petitioned the House of Commons, saying that he did not desire the franchise but wanted a law removing doubts as to the ability of Jews to hold landed property.

Levy is known to have been married twice. His first wife was named Elizabeth, his second Rebecca. He died on 30 November 1856 at his home, 55 Tavistock Square, London. He had no children, but left half his fortune to his stepson Jonas, Elizabeth's son by her first marriage (to a Joseph Levy). Jonas, a lawyer, became vice-chairman of the London, Brighton, and South Coast Railway. The other half went to Levy's brother Nathaniel, who, like Jonas, had participated with Levy in turnpike contracting. The size of this fortune, amounting to approximately £250,000, testifies to the importance of Levy's business.

RALPH TURVEY

Sources 'Select committee on the effect of the formation of railroads on turnpike … trusts', *Parl. papers* (1839), 9.13, no. 295 • 'Select committee on … turnpike trusts within ten miles of London', *Parl. papers* (1825), 5.167, no. 355 • *The Times* (17 Oct 1823) • *The Times* (21 Oct 1823) • *The Times* (20 Aug 1832) • Levy's will, PRO, PROB 11 2244 pp. 297 ff. • 'Select committee … on communications in the metropolis', *Parl. papers* (1854–5), 10.1, no. 415; 10.297, no. 415-I • death duty register, PRO, PR 2103, no. 45 • W. Albert, *The turnpike road system in England, 1663–1840* (1972) • T. M. Endelman, *The Jews of Georgian England, 1714–1838* (1979) • W. J. Reader, *The Macadam family and the turnpike roads, 1798–1861* (1980) • d. cert.

Wealth at death approx. £250,000: PRO, death duty registers, PR 2103, no. 45

Lewenstein, (Silvion) Oscar (1917–1997), theatre and film producer, was born at a private nursing home at 2 Queens Down Road, Clapton, London, on 18 January 1917, the eldest among the four children of Arthur Solomon Lewenstein (1886/7–1944), merchant, and his wife, Mary, *née* Convisser (*b.* 1884/5). His father, a Russian Jew who had emigrated to Britain in 1907, became a successful businessman in the plywood industry. The family moved to Brighton in the middle of 1917, and some years later to Sandown on the Isle of Wight, before returning to London in 1932. Lewenstein was educated at Dunhurst (the junior school of Bedales), Ryde grammar school, and the Central School, Hackney, but when the family's fortunes declined he left school to take on a variety of menial clerical jobs. In 1936 he found work more to his taste, as an assistant at the Worker's Bookshop. Already a member of the Young Communist League, he became national organizer of the left-wing relief operation to supply food to the republicans in Spain and, after their defeat, to welcome and support refugees. On 19 February 1938 he married a fellow member of the Young Communist League, Clara Peissel (1918/19–1953), the daughter of Joshua Peissel, builder's foreman, of Hackney; there were no children of the marriage. In March 1940 he was called up and after basic training sent to the Pioneer Corps, where he edited a news-sheet, *Smoke*, for units specializing in putting up smokescreens over industrial cities. In 1943 he became an instructor at an army school for illiterates, and he ended the Second World War as a sergeant-instructor teaching classes in current affairs, economics, and politics.

After demobilization, and through his friendship with the left-wing writer and political activist Ted Willis, Lewenstein began working for the Unity Theatre, a co-operative of theatre groups that promoted popular socialist drama. At Unity, where he worked in a variety of capacities for five years, he learned the hard practicalities of putting on a play, but he was also enthused by the exciting new developments in the theatre of Europe and the USA. In 1951 he left Unity to work for the Embassy Theatre, Swiss Cottage, where he brought in Sandy Wilson's *The Boyfriend* before it was successfully launched in the West End. In 1952 he became artistic director of the newly reopened Royal Court Theatre, where his productions ranged from Jean Genet's *Les bonnes* ('The Maids') to a long-running revue, *Airs on a Shoestring*. Meanwhile, his first marriage having ended in divorce in 1946, on 27 June 1952 he married Eileen Edith Mawson (*b.* 1925/6), potter, daughter of Albert Henry Mawson, insurance manager. They had two sons, born in 1953 and 1956.

In 1954, in collaboration with the poet and playwright Ronald Duncan, Lewenstein founded the English Stage Company and approached George Devine to be its artistic director. Their intention was to break with the predominant West End tradition of lightweight plays built around smartly costumed stars in favour of a writer's theatre that brought to Britain the intellectually challenging work of playwrights like Arthur Miller, Bertolt Brecht, Eugene Ionesco, and Samuel Beckett, and encouraged British writers to emulate their achievements. The first season of English Stage Company plays at the Royal Court, in 1956, triumphantly vindicated the policy when John Osborne's *Look Back in Anger* became a critical and commercial success, setting in train a revolution in the English theatre. Lewenstein was a key figure in this revolution. He had staged the first British production of Brecht's *The Threepenny Opera* earlier in 1956, and in partnership with the writer Wolf Mankowitz he put on Eugene Ionesco's *Rhinoceros*, Willis Hall's *The Long and the Short and the Tall*, and *Billy Liar* by Hall and Keith Waterhouse; he also successfully transferred Joan Littlewood's Theatre Workshop productions of Shelagh Delaney's *A Taste of Honey* and Brendan Behan's *The Hostage* to the West End. Later in the 1960s it was Lewenstein who recognized the talents of Joe Orton and staged West End productions of *Loot* and *What the Butler Saw*.

Lewenstein also found himself drawn into the revival of British film production, working (uncredited) on *A Taste of Honey* (1961) and *The Loneliness of the Long Distance Runner* (1962), as associate producer on *Tom Jones* (1962), and as producer on *The Girl with Green Eyes* (1964) and *The Knack* (1965). *Tom Jones* was commercially one of the most successful films of the decade and its profits allowed its director, Tony Richardson, to work with Lewenstein on artistically ambitious projects such as *Mademoiselle* (1967), *The Sailor from Gibraltar* (1967), and *The Charge of the Light Brigade* (1968).

Film-making never supplanted theatre as Lewenstein's main concern, and in 1969 he opened the Roundhouse, a railway engine turning-shed on the edge of Camden Town, as a theatrical venue for the American anarchist collective, the Living Theatre. In 1971 he followed this with a stunning production of Théâtre du Soleil's *1789*. In 1972 he returned to the Royal Court, as artistic director, and for three years he maintained its reputation for radical drama with new plays from Athol Fugard, Brian Friel, Edward Bond, Caryl Churchill, Mustapha Matura, and Christopher Hampton, as well as from the two writers who had become stalwarts of the English Stage Company, John Osborne and David Storey. After 1975 he took more of a back seat, although the promise of working with talented new writers tempted him to produce Mary O'Malley's *Once a Catholic* in 1977 and to act as executive producer on the Channel 4 adaptation of Andrea Dunbar's *Rita, Sue and Bob too* (1987), directed by Alan Clarke.

Although he left the Communist Party in 1956 Lewenstein remained a committed socialist all his life. His passionate commitment to social justice, however, never seems to have narrowed his artistic vision. For him genuinely popular drama could encompass the avant-garde anarchism of the Living Theatre and the probing didacticism of Brecht. His memoirs, *Kicking Against the Pricks*, were published in 1994. He died of heart failure at his home, 11 Western Esplanade, Hove, Sussex, on 23 February 1997, and was survived by his second wife, Eileen, and their two sons. ROBERT MURPHY

Sources O. Lewenstein, *Kicking against the pricks: a theatre producer looks back* (1994) · R. Hayman, 'Oscar Lewenstein', *The Times* (30 Sept 1972) · *The Guardian* (28 Feb 1997) · *The Times* (1 March 1997) · *The Independent* (31 March 1997) · *The Stage* (13 March 1997) · *Variety* (31 March 1997) · *Variety* (6 April 1997) · b. cert. · m. certs. · d. cert.
Archives FILM interview on 'Last wave': episode of 'Hollywood UK – British cinema in the sixties', BBC2, 1993
Likenesses photograph, 1959, repro. in *The Guardian* · photograph, repro. in *The Independent* · photograph, repro. in *The Times*
Wealth at death under £180,000: probate, 29 May 1997, *CGPLA Eng. & Wales*

Lewes, Charles Lee (1740–1803), author and actor, was born on 19 November 1740 in New Bond Street, London. His father, according to Lewes's account in his *Memoirs*, was a classically educated Welsh hosier who was also a friend of the author Edward Young; his mother was the daughter of William Lewthwaite of Broadgate, Cumberland, and related to Sir John Gilford Lawson and Lady St Aubyn—presumably Catherine, *née* Morice, the wife of Sir John St Aubyn, third baronet. From the age of seven he was educated at a school in Ambleside, Westmorland, and when he was fourteen he returned to London to help his father with his work as a letter-carrier. Attendance at spouting clubs aroused in the young man an interest in the stage, leading, in 1760, to an amateur appearance (billed as C. Lewis) alongside Tate Wilkinson at the Haymarket, as Cash in Jonson's *Every Man in his Humour*. Lewes's early years as a performer were spent on the road, and included spells at Sheffield, Chesterfield, and Doncaster. In 1767 he was engaged at Covent Garden, and first appeared on 23 September as Prince Henry in *King John*. Perhaps in order to avoid confusion with the actor Philip Lewis (also at Covent Garden), he was now billed as Lewes. During the 1767–8 season he took on a range of supporting parts, among them a Recruit in George Farquhar's *The Recruiting Officer*, Burgundy in *King Lear*, and Harlequin in *Harlequin Skeleton, or, The Royal Chance*. He was in Bristol for the summer of 1768, but then returned to Covent Garden, where he remained for the next sixteen seasons. Honing his skills as a physical comedian, Lewes adopted the role of Harlequin, which he exhibited through the 1770–71 season in *The Rape of Prosperine*, *Harlequin's Jubilee*, and *Mother Shipton*, and later in a variety of entertainments. In March 1773 he took on Young Marlowe in the first performance of Oliver Goldsmith's *She Stoops to Conquer* and pleased the author enough for Goldsmith to add an epilogue for a benefit for Lewes on 7 May 1773, which gave voice to the actor's higher aspirations by presenting him 'in the character of Harlequin removing his mask and expressing his longing to act in Shakespeare' (Highfill, Burnim & Langhans, *BDA*, 9.271).

Success in this role brought Lewes to the attention of the public and secured him some better parts, although these rarely fulfilled his Shakespearian hopes (he played Prince Hal in *Henry IV* and Falstaff in *The Merry Wives of Windsor* in 1777, and Touchstone in *As You Like It* from 1783). A regular at Covent Garden during the winter season, Lewes spent the summers in York, Cambridge, Liverpool, Edinburgh, and elsewhere. From 1780 onwards he exploited his aptitude for virtuoso solo performance with his version of George Alexander Stevens's satirical monologue *Lecture upon Heads*, in which he impersonated a range of contemporary types, including 'the Heads of a Male and female President; a fashionable Foreigner; four national Characters, with the Heads of an English Sailor, a Spaniard, a Frenchman, and a Dutch Merchant; the Head of a Libeller' (Highfill, Burnim & Langhans, *BDA*, 9.273). This one-man *tour de force* was first given at Covent Garden and then at the Haymarket, at Bristol, and on tour in France and Ireland.

A quarrel with the Covent Garden manager Thomas Harris at the end of the 1783 season led to Lewes's engagement at Drury Lane, where Wingfield Palmer had already laid claim to many of Lewes's established roles. Lewes spent much of the next decade on tour, which included a brief and unsuccessful visit to India at the end of the 1780s, an excursion which provided the material for a posthumous publication, *Comic Sketches, or, The Comedian his Own Manager* (1804). Among Lewes's published output was *The London Songster* (1767), his version of the *Lecture upon Heads* (1784; reprinted in 1785, 1787, 1808, and 1821), *Hippisley's Drunken Man* (*c*.1787), and *The Stage and the Pulpit* (1794). In 1792 he was in Edinburgh in Stephen Kemble's company, and at Crow Street, Dublin; he spent the last decade of the century presenting monologues and comic sketches around Ireland while vainly attempting to secure a London engagement. On 24 June 1803 he gave his farewell benefit at Covent Garden, playing Lisardio in Susannah Centlivre's *The Wonder* and reciting Thomas John Dibdin's piece 'Lee Lewes's Ultimatum'. According to Dibdin, Lewes died two days later, although other sources record his date of death as 23 July 1803. He was buried at St James's, Pentonville.

Throughout the four decades of his professional life, Lewes was generally rated as an alert comedian and competent supporting player whose attempts at more substantial character parts were at best efficient and at worst inadequate. The details of his personal life are obscure. His first wife, Anne Hussey, an actress, died on 26 August 1772. One child is known to have survived from that marriage, Elizabeth Anne, baptized at Covent Garden on 31 March 1771. On 14 July 1775 he married Fanny Wrigley at St Nicholas's Church, Liverpool; she was probably the Fanny Rigley baptized there on 25 January 1751, the daughter of James Rigley. Their children included John Lee Lewes, baptized at St Pancras on 19 May 1776, and James Wrigley Lewes, born on 14 January 1781. Fanny died after giving birth to twins (who also died) on 27 March 1783. On 9 June 1787 Lewes married his third wife, Catherine Maria O'Neal, an actress, in Edinburgh; she died in Edinburgh in March 1796. Lewes's son John Lee Lewes, who appeared on provincial stages in the early part of the nineteenth century, edited his father's *Memoirs* (published in 1805) and was himself the father of the literary critic George Henry *Lewes. ROBERT SHAUGHNESSY

Sources Highfill, Burnim & Langhans, *BDA* · C. L. Lewes, *Memoirs* (1805)

Likenesses engraving, 1780 · engraving, 1784, Harvard TC · S. De Wilde, oils, 1790, Garr. Club · J. Kay, caricature, 1792 · S. De Wilde, watercolour (as Bobadil in *Every man in his humour*), Garr. Club · J. Hopwood, portrait, repro. in C. L. Lewes, *Comic sketches* (1804) · prints, BM, NPG

Lewes, George Henry (1817–1878), writer, was born in London on 18 April 1817, the youngest of the three sons of John Lee Lewes (1776–1831) and Elizabeth Ashweek (1786–1870), and grandson of the comic actor Charles Lee *Lewes (1740–1803), famous for playing the part of Bobadil in Ben Jonson's *Every Man in his Humour*.

Early years John Lee Lewes was a minor poet who lived in Liverpool in the early years of the nineteenth century and married Elizabeth Pownall, with whom he had six children, all born in Liverpool between 1803 and 1812. By then he had left his wife and set up house with Elizabeth Ashweek, a young woman born in 1786 of a Devon family, whom he appears never to have married. Together they had three sons: Edgar James (1807–1830), Edward Charles (1814?–1855), and George Henry.

When G. H. Lewes was about two years old, his father disappeared, emigrating to Bermuda to join a brother who was a customs officer there. He returned, ill, to his native Liverpool, where he died in 1831. There is no evidence that G. H. Lewes knew about his own illegitimacy or about the existence of his father's family in Liverpool.

Lewes and his brothers were brought up by their mother and a disliked stepfather, John Gurens Willim (1778?–1864), a retired captain in the army of the East India Company. Willim and Elizabeth Ashweek were married in St Pancras Old Church, London, on 29 November 1823. Lewes attended schools in London, France, and Jersey, and boarded for a time at Dr Burney's school in Greenwich. The family moved frequently, possibly because of money troubles. As Anthony Trollope remarked in his obituary of Lewes in the *Fortnightly Review* in January 1879, 'his education was desultory, but wonderfully efficacious for the purposes of his life' (Trollope, 15). Trollope had in mind Lewes's expert knowledge of the French language and literature, and his early career as a miscellaneous journalist trying to make a living in literary London without the benefit of a university education, orthodox religious affiliation, or financial support.

G. H. Lewes may have studied medicine briefly; his brother Edward was a doctor who travelled as a ship's medical officer until his death at sea in 1855. Lewes may also have been for a short time a clerk with pretensions to authorship, like the hero of his first novel, *Ranthorpe* (1847). In an article on Spinoza in the *Fortnightly Review* in 1866 he remembered attending, thirty years previously, a small club of students who met in a tavern in Red Lion Square, Holborn, to discuss philosophy. The group consisted of several self-educated men, including one who ran a secondhand bookstall, a journeyman watchmaker, and a bootmaker.

Youthful career and marriage Lewes's first literary venture was a proposed life of Shelley. He approached the poet and journalist Leigh Hunt, friend in his youth of Shelley and Byron, and now a useful contact with Shelley's widow,

George Henry Lewes (1817–1878), by John & Charles Watkins

Mary. Hunt lived in Chelsea, and was still known, as he had been as a young man, for his propensity to attach himself to, and borrow from, others. The biography of Shelley was never completed, but Lewes became friendly with the bohemian Hunt family; Leigh Hunt published his early articles, and Lewes formed a firm—and fateful—friendship with Hunt's eldest son, Thornton Leigh Hunt. Through the Hunts Lewes also got to know Carlyle and John Stuart Mill. When Lewes visited Berlin for an extended stay in 1838–9 Carlyle gave him a letter of introduction to the German man of letters Varnhagen von Ense. During this trip Lewes began his research for the biography of Goethe which he published to immediate and lasting acclaim in 1855.

In 1840 Lewes wrote the first of several long literary articles for the radical quarterly journal the *Westminster Review*, edited at that time by John Stuart Mill. Over the years he was to write about French, Spanish, and Italian drama, Shelley, Browning, Tennyson, Disraeli, Macaulay, Spinoza, Goethe, Lessing, Hegel, Balzac, Victor Hugo, and Alexandre Dumas, and to cover topics as diverse as drama, fiction, history, philosophy, and science in the *Westminster* and other periodicals. His articles appeared in almost every Victorian journal, including the *Edinburgh Review*, the *Foreign Quarterly Review*, the *British and Foreign Review*, *Fraser's Magazine*, *Blackwood's Magazine*, *The Leader*, the *Fortnightly Review*, the *Pall Mall Gazette*, and the *Cornhill Magazine*.

On 18 February 1841 at St Margaret's Church, Westminster, Lewes married Agnes Jervis (1822–1902), eldest daughter of Swynfen Stevens Jervis (1798–1867). The eccentric Swynfen Jervis, radical MP for Bridport in Dorset, had educated Agnes, aged eighteen at the time of her marriage, to a high enough standard to enable her to help her ambitious young husband with his literary journalism.

Living initially with Lewes's mother at 3 Pembroke Square, Kensington, Agnes and Lewes had five children: a girl, who died two days after her birth in December 1841; Charles Lee, born in November 1842; Thornton Arnott (Thornie), born in April 1844; Herbert Arthur (Bertie), born in July 1846; and St Vincent Arthy, born in May 1848, who died of measles in March 1850. Lewes was busy writing on a wide range of subjects, but his reviews of works by Dickens, Thackeray, and Charlotte Brontë led to correspondences with all three authors. It was fitting that Lewes, who was to become the encourager of George Eliot's fictional genius, should be such an accomplished critic of the fiction of her most famous predecessors and contemporaries in the genre.

One of Lewes's earliest articles was an appreciative review of Dickens's *Pickwick Papers*, *Oliver Twist*, and *Sketches by Boz*, in the *National Magazine and Monthly Critic* (1837). As a result of the article the two men met, and when Dickens formed his company of amateur actors in 1847, he asked Lewes to join it. Lewes spent the summer months touring provincial cities, acting comic roles in *The Merry Wives of Windsor* and—following in his grandfather's footsteps—*Every Man in his Humour* (though it was Dickens himself, not Lewes, who took the part of Bobadil).

The group was formed again the following year for a similar tour, and Lewes was so enamoured of the acting life that he made a brief attempt to act professionally in 1849, as the hero of his own pseudo-Jacobean play, *The Noble Heart*, and as Shylock in *The Merchant of Venice*. Although he was rather successful, especially in his unusually sympathetic rendering of Shylock, Lewes eventually gave up the idea of becoming a professional actor. Reviewers of his acting reported that his voice was not resonant enough and his physique too slight to carry conviction on the stage. However, he put his knowledge of the stage to good use in other respects, giving lectures on the history of philosophy at the Manchester Athenaeum in 1849, and taking on the persona of 'Vivian', the sharp-tongued theatre critic of *The Leader*, a weekly newspaper he co-founded and co-edited with Thornton Hunt in 1850.

Lewes's favourable review of *Jane Eyre* in *Fraser's Magazine* in December 1847 led to a correspondence with Charlotte Brontë. He advised her to read and learn verisimilitude from the novels of Jane Austen, to which she replied with a staunch defence of her own wilder imaginings.

Curious about her new correspondent, she read and commented on Lewes's own two novels, *Ranthorpe* (1847) and *Rose, Blanche, and Violet* (1848). Neither novel is very good, the first being a semi-autobiographical account of the struggles in love and literature of a young man of no means, and the second a confused tale of three sisters and their various vicissitudes in love. Jane Carlyle pronounced *Rose, Blanche, and Violet* 'execrable', and Carlyle annotated his copy with hilarious comments about the 'folly' of this book by a man the Carlyles called 'the Ape' on account of his ugliness (*Collected Letters*, 23, 18; Kaplan, 26–7).

By the time he met Marian *Evans (1819–1880) in October 1851, Lewes, then aged thirty-four, had, in addition to his acting and lecturing activities, written hundreds of articles and published several books. These included a hugely successful popular guide to philosophy from the Greeks to Kant, Hegel, and Auguste Comte, *A Biographical History of Philosophy* (four volumes in two, 1845–6), which sold nearly 10,000 copies in a year; *The Spanish Drama: Lope de Vega and Calderon* (1846); his two novels; his tragedy; a biography of Maximilien Robespierre (1849); and *The Game of Speculation*, an English adaptation of Balzac's *Mercadet* which had a successful run at the Lyceum Theatre in 1851.

Professionally, Lewes was, therefore, as Charlotte Brontë observed with astonishment, widely active and successful. Personally, however, he was despondent. His close friendship with Thornton Hunt had not only led to their joint founding of *The Leader* in 1850, with Hunt as political editor and Lewes as literary editor. So close were the two men that Lewes, who embraced the Shelleyan ideals of free thinking in religion and free living in sexual matters, condoned—and perhaps even encouraged—Hunt's adultery with Agnes.

Hunt and his wife lived with two other married couples in Bayswater; although it was rumoured that Lewes and Agnes also lived there, and that a comprehensive amount of wife-sharing went on, there is no evidence that the Leweses ever lived in Hunt's house, though they certainly lived in nearby Kensington. In 1843 they moved to 2 Campden Hill Terrace, and in 1846 to 26 Bedford Place, both in Kensington.

On 16 April 1850, two weeks after the launching of *The Leader*, Agnes gave birth to Edmund, the first of four children she was to have with Hunt, not Lewes. Lewes registered the child as his, making it impossible for himself ever to sue for divorce on grounds of adultery. Relations with Hunt continued to be warm; Agnes had a second child by Hunt—Rose—in October 1851, the very month in which Lewes was introduced to Marian Evans by John Chapman, the radical publisher and prospective owner and editor of the *Westminster Review*.

By the summer of 1852, however, Lewes had grown disillusioned with the domestic experiment. Having registered the births of Edmund and Rose, he did not register that of Ethel, born in October 1853, or Mildred, born in May 1857. Despite his continuing literary activities in 1852, this was, he later recalled, 'a very dreary *wasted* period of my life' (Ashton, 120). In late 1852 and early 1853 he had left Kensington and was living in Cork Street, Piccadilly, borrowing the rooms of his friend Frederick Oldfield Ward, who was in Brussels.

It was not initially the meeting with Marian Evans which changed things for Lewes. In 1852 she was in love with Herbert Spencer, writing impassioned letters to him that summer from Broadstairs; Lewes to her was only one of many radical men of literature and politics with whom she associated on her arrival in London in 1851 as a lodger at Chapman's house, 142 Strand, and as editorial assistant to Chapman on the *Westminster*.

It was Herbert Spencer himself whose friendship helped Lewes. Lewes wrote in his journal in January 1859 that he owed Spencer a debt of gratitude for helping him out of the despair he had felt about his marriage. Spencer's companionship in walking expeditions, during which 'the stimulus of his intellect roused my energy once more, and revived my dormant love of science', kept Lewes from complete desolation (Ashton, 120). The two men shared an interest in Auguste Comte's positivism, a philosophical system which rejected dogmatic Christianity in favour of the 'religion of humanity', offering a 'scientific' view of society as held together not by common religious beliefs but by social interaction between classes and professions. During 1852 Lewes published in *The Leader* a series of explanatory articles on Comte, which appeared as a book, *Comte's Philosophy of the Sciences*, in 1853.

Relationship with Marian Evans It was Spencer who provided the link between Lewes and Marian Evans. By early 1853 Spencer was taking Lewes with him when he went to visit her. He recalled later that on one occasion, 'when I rose to leave, he said he should stay'. To Spencer, who had been obliged to reject Marian's advances and make it clear that he was interested in friendship, not marriage, the new turn of affairs was 'an immense relief' (*George Eliot Letters*, 8.42–3n.).

It is probable that Lewes and Marian Evans became lovers some time in 1853. He had been planning for some months to go to Germany once more, in order to finish his research for the biography of Goethe; Marian agreed to go with him. In Germany she could help him with *The Life of Goethe*, and they could live together openly despite not being legally married. Lewes and Marian set off in July 1854 for an extended stay in Weimar and Berlin. In Weimar Lewes met people who had known Goethe; translated, with Marian's help, various passages from Goethe's works for inclusion in the biography; and continued to send regular articles to *The Leader*. The £20 a month he earned was given to Agnes to support her and the children. The couple's great happiness in Weimar, where they were accepted socially, was tempered by news from England about the unpleasant rumours at home about their relationship. Carlyle, who was at first supportive, accepting that Marian had not been the cause of the breakdown of Lewes's marriage, ceased to correspond with Lewes.

They spent the cold winter months in Berlin, where Lewes found Varnhagen von Ense once more helpful with materials on Goethe. In March 1855 they returned to England to face an uncertain future living in rented rooms—at first at 7 Clarence Row, East Sheen, then from October 1855 at 8 Park Shot, Richmond—and coping with the displeasure of their friends and acquaintances. Only Spencer, Chapman, and a few other friends, including two brave female friends, Bessie Rayner Parkes and Barbara Leigh Smith, visited the couple.

The *Life of Goethe* was published in November 1855, selling more than a thousand copies in the first three months, and going through several reprints over the years until long after Lewes's death. It is a fresh and fair account of Goethe's complicated and sexually rather scandalous life and of his extraordinarily wide range of writings. Lewes's interest in science made him an excellent appreciator of Goethe's scientific efforts, while his expertise in literary criticism and in European languages and culture qualified him to write authoritatively on the poetry, novels, drama, and essays. Moreover, with his own marital experience to draw on, Lewes was able to sympathize with Goethe's mistakes, without completely condoning them.

On his return to England, Lewes took up scientific studies in earnest. The summer of 1856 was spent away from London (partly to get away from prying eyes and scandalous tongues) in several coastal resorts in England and Wales, where Lewes, with Marian as his companion, undertook a study of marine life which bore fruit first in two series of articles in *Blackwood's Magazine* in 1856 and 1857, then in a popular illustrated book, *Sea-Side Studies*, in 1858. In late August 1856 Lewes set off with his two elder sons, Charles and Thornie, to Switzerland, where he settled them in a progressive boarding-school near Geneva. They knew nothing about either their father's relationship with Marian or their mother's with Thornton Hunt; one of the reasons for moving them to Switzerland may have been to protect them from London gossip as they grew up. Charles was nearly fourteen and Thornie twelve.

Once back in London, Lewes encouraged his brilliant but diffident companion to fulfil an ambition she had long harboured but never quite dared to put to the test: the writing of fiction. During 1855–6 she had written a number of wide-ranging, knowledgeable, and witty review articles in the *Westminster Review*, including her trenchant attack on religious intolerance in 'Evangelical teaching: Dr Cumming' (October 1855). Emboldened by Lewes's praise of her wit and narrative verve in these essays, as well as in a fictional sketch she had shown him in Germany, Marian began writing 'The Sad Fortunes of the Reverend Amos Barton', the first of three stories which would make up *Scenes of Clerical Life* (1858). Lewes sent the story to his publisher, John Blackwood, saying it was by a friend of his who was shy of revealing 'his' identity. This was the first of Lewes's acts of generosity towards his partner's career. From then until his death he would act unswervingly and energetically as her literary agent and encourager, the go-between between George Eliot and her publishers, her critics, and her readers.

Observers commented adversely at the time, and later, on Lewes's excessive defending of Marian from the outside world: he hid bad reviews from her, and frequently asked Blackwood and kind but frank friends like Barbara Leigh Smith to temper their expressions of criticism in their letters. The novelist Margaret Oliphant wrote about his keeping Marian in a 'mental greenhouse', suggesting that he was doing her a disservice and that her novels show the strains of her unnatural social situation (*Autobiography and Letters*, 5).

Whatever one's views on the latter point, there is little doubt that Lewes's patience, optimism, and sheer energetic delight in her genius created the enabling conditions for her writing. In March 1859 she dedicated the manuscript of her first full novel, *Adam Bede*, to 'my dear husband, George Henry Lewes', adding that the work 'would never have been written but for the happiness which his love has conferred on my life' (Haight, 278).

Lewes in turn was in no doubt about what their relationship had done for him. It was at this time, in January 1859, that he confided in his journal the remarks about Spencer's friendship, adding that Spencer had been the means of his getting to know Marian: 'To know her was to love her. To her I owe all my prosperity & all my happiness' (Haight, 272). Her tremendous success as a novelist brought him great pleasure, as well as rendering them both, in due course, rather comfortably off. In February 1859 they moved to larger accommodation at Holly Lodge, Southfields, near Wimbledon.

In the excitement which followed publication in February 1859 of *Adam Bede*, George Eliot had much need of Lewes's qualities of mind and temperament. All England was gossiping about the identity of the author. Joseph Liggins of Warwickshire was suspected; he omitted to deny the rumour, which rapidly got out of hand. Marian and Lewes were at first determined not to divulge the secret of authorship, but by the summer of 1859, with Liggins stories still appearing in *The Times* and other papers, and with London clubs buzzing with rumours, thanks to indiscretions by Spencer and Chapman, they bowed to the inevitable and let it be known that she was the author.

Lewes chose this time to tell his sons about the breakdown of his marriage and his partnership with Marian. Charles, now nearly seventeen, would be leaving school soon, and Lewes intended him to live not with Agnes and the younger children (fathered by Hunt), but with himself and Marian. He visited the boys—Bertie had now joined them—at their Swiss school at Hofwyl in July 1859 and, helped by the fact that the fame of *Adam Bede* had reached even that remote corner, told them the whole story.

Later career In November 1859 Lewes renewed his old friendship with Dickens, which had cooled in 1853 after Lewes had attacked Dickens's poor science in handling the spontaneous combustion of Mr Krook in *Bleak House*. Dickens now came to visit and to meet Marian, on whom he had his eye as a possible contributor of fiction to his journal *All the Year Round*. He also commissioned some natural history articles from Lewes. Blackwood published Lewes's *Physiology of Common Life* in 1859–60, a work which was translated into several languages and was to stimulate the great Russian scientist Pavlov to abandon a theological career for one in physiology.

George Smith, the publisher, also came to call, hoping to persuade both George Eliot and Lewes to contribute to his new journal, the *Cornhill Magazine*, of which Thackeray was the editor. Lewes wrote a series called Studies in Animal Life in 1860, in which he supported Darwin's groundbreaking hypothesis of natural selection in *Origin of Species* (1859).

Lewes also became friendly with Trollope at this time. When Charles Lewes came home from Hofwyl in the summer of 1860, Trollope gave useful advice on how to get him a job at the Post Office, where Trollope worked. Lewes and Marian moved from Holly Lodge to 10 Harewood Square, then to 16 Blandford Square in central London, to make it easier for Charles to get to work.

Lewes continued to write articles and reviews, mainly but not exclusively on scientific subjects; he also fitted in with Marian's needs, which included the desire to flee the country every time a new novel was about to be published. They established a pattern of going abroad for a few months when each work was finished, partly for her to recuperate from the exhaustion of completing her work, partly to escape the immediate critical response in England. Lewes's health began to deteriorate at this time, with headaches and nausea taking on the nature of a chronic complaint.

When Thackeray gave up the editorship of the *Cornhill Magazine* in March 1862, George Smith persuaded Lewes to take over at the princely salary of £600 a year. In 1863 the Leweses felt financially secure enough to buy a large house of their own, The Priory near Regent's Park, which Lewes's friend the designer Owen Jones furnished for them. Lewes's second son, Thornie, who had finished his schooling at Edinburgh and sat and failed the civil service examinations, went off to farm in Africa late in 1863. He was to be joined in Natal by his younger brother Bertie in 1866.

In January 1865 Lewes was asked by Trollope to be the editor of a new Liberal periodical, the *Fortnightly Review*. The periodical became a distinguished organ of liberal thought, devoted to literature, science, and culture as well as to airing political concerns in the months leading to the passing of the second Reform Act in 1867. Trollope, Huxley, Spencer, George Eliot, and Meredith were among the writers who contributed. Lewes himself wrote an influential series of essays, The Principles of Success in Literature, in which he advocated literary realism of an imaginative, rather than a 'coat-and-waistcoat' kind.

Lewes's health was so precarious that by the end of 1866 he had resigned the editorship, which was taken over by John Morley. For the rest of his life he worked tirelessly at an ambitious project to explain the connections between physiology and psychology, *Problems of Life and Mind*. After the publication of *Middlemarch* in 1871–2 he took to calling this work, self-mockingly, 'The key to all psychologies', in an echo of poor Mr Casaubon's unfinished work of scholarship, 'The key to all mythologies', in the novel. Life in the end imitated art. Although three volumes of the work were published between 1873 and 1877, the final two volumes had to be completed by George Eliot in the months after Lewes's death in November 1878.

Thornie and Bertie had little luck in Natal, either financially or in terms of their health. An extremely ill Thornie came home early in 1869, while George Eliot was writing *Middlemarch*. After months of excruciating pain, during which Lewes and Marian nursed him, he died of spinal tuberculosis in October 1869, aged twenty-five. Bertie stayed on in Natal, where he married a local girl, but in 1875 he too died young—aged twenty-nine—leaving behind a widow and two small children.

In 1877 the Leweses, through their friend John Walter Cross, found a large country house, The Heights, at Witley, near Godalming in Surrey. They spent only two summers there, during which Lewes got increasingly weaker from enteritis. On 21 November 1878 he performed his last act as Marian's literary agent, sending Blackwood part of her *Impressions of Theophrastus Such*; on 30 November he died at The Priory. He was buried on 4 December in the dissenters' part of Highgate cemetery.

Friends paid handsome tribute to this man of many parts in obituaries which gave résumés of Lewes's career, praising his versatility, his verve, his wit, the breadth of his knowledge, and the generosity of his spirit. His friend Robert Lytton wrote that Lewes 'had the most omnivorous appetite of any man I knew; a rare freedom from prejudice; soundness of judgment in criticism, and a singularly wide and quick sympathy in all departments of science and literature' (*Personal and Literary Letters*, 2.137). These qualities, together with his invaluable support of George Eliot, made him one of the most interesting and engaging men of letters of his time. ROSEMARY ASHTON

Sources R. Ashton, *G. H. Lewes: a life* (1991) • *Versatile Victorian: selected critical writings of George Henry Lewes*, ed. R. Ashton (1992) • *The George Eliot letters*, ed. G. S. Haight, 9 vols. (1954–78) • *The letters of George Henry Lewes*, ed. W. Baker, 2 vols. (1995) • G. S. Haight, *George Eliot: a biography* (1968) • *The collected letters of Thomas and Jane Welsh Carlyle*, ed. C. R. Sanders, K. J. Fielding, and others, [30 vols.] (1970–) • A. Trollope, 'George Henry Lewes', *Fortnightly Review*, 31 (1879), 15–24 • F. Kaplan, 'Carlyle's marginalia and George Henry Lewes's fiction', *Carlyle Newsletter*, 5 (1984) • T. J. Wise and J. A. Symington, eds., *The Brontës: their lives, friendships, and correspondence*, 4 vols. (1932) • *Personal and literary letters of Robert, first earl of Lytton*, ed. E. E. Balfour, 2 vols. (1906) • *The autobiography and letters of Mrs M. O. W. Oliphant*, ed. Mrs H. Coghill (1899) • J. Kaminsky, 'The empirical metaphysics of George Henry Lewes', *Journal of the History of Ideas*, 13 (1952) • H. Spencer, *An autobiography*, 2 vols. (1904) • Devon parish records [Elizabeth Ashweek] • Lpool RO • local record office, Oporto, Portugal

Archives BL, journals and diary, M/891 [microfilm] • Hunt. L., letters and literary MSS • Yale U., Beinecke L., corresp. and papers | BL, letters to C. Brontë, Add. MS 39763 • BL, letters to Richard Henry Horne, RP797 (2) [copies] • BL, letters to Macrey Napier, Add. MSS 34622–34626 • BL, letters to Elma Stuart, Add. MS 37952 • BL, letters to Mr Tingwell, RP3217 [copies] • BL OIOC, letters to earl of Lytton, MS Eur. E 218/50 • Co-operative Union, Holyoake House, Manchester, archive, letters to G. J. Holyoake • CUL, letters to C. Darwin • Harvard U., Houghton L., letters to Wathen Call and other MSS • Herts. ALS, letters to first Baron Lytton • Herts. ALS, letters to first earl of Lytton · Jagiellonian University, Cracow, Poland, Varnhagen von Ense collection · John Murray, London, archives, George Smith MSS · Maison d'Auguste Comte, Paris, letters to Auguste Comte · NL Scot., corresp. with Blackwoods · NL Scot., corresp. with George Combe · Trinity Cam., letters to Lord Houghton · UCL, corresp. with G. C. Robertson · UCL, letters to J. Sully

Likenesses A. Gliddon, pencil drawing, 1840, NPG · W. M. Thackery, group portrait, sketch, *c.*1848, NPG · T. Hunt, pen sketch, *c.*1849, Co-operative Union, Manchester, MS letter · Mayall, photograph, 1858, priv. coll. · R. Lehmann, drawing, 1867, BM · J. & C. Watkins, photograph, NPG [*see illus.*] · Swan Electric Engraving Co., photogravure (after Elliott & Fry), NPG · wood-engraving (after photograph by Elliott & Fry), NPG; repro. in *ILN* (14 Dec 1878)

Wealth at death under £2000: probate, 16 Dec 1878, *CGPLA Eng. & Wales*

Lewes, John Steel [Jock] (**1913–1941**), a founder of the Special Air Service (SAS), was born on 21 December 1913 in Calcutta, India, the first son and second of the three children of Arthur Harold Lewes (1869?–1962?), accountant, and his wife, Elsie Steel. He grew up in New South Wales, Australia, with his sister, Elizabeth, and brother, David, having moved there when he was two years old. Lewes was educated at Hayfield preparatory school, near Sydney, and then at the King's School, Paramatta, where he was awarded the divinity and Greek prizes. He also excelled at chemistry, and often experimented with chemicals with his brother, sometimes with dangerous results.

As early as 1924 Lewes developed an interest in a career in the armed forces, at this point notably in the navy. However, he left Australia for Oxford to read modern Greats at Christ Church (1933–7). He became president of the Oxford University boat club in 1936, and Oxford won the boat race in 1937, ending a Cambridge winning streak of fifteen years. This was after he had unselfishly given up his place in the Oxford boat for the greater good of the team. While still an Oxford undergraduate Lewes travelled in Europe, spending a reasonable amount of time in pre-war Berlin. He became favourably impressed with some of the policies of Nazism and, as he saw it, with the hard-working approach towards regeneration of the economy. He also fell in love with a German woman, a Nazi sympathizer, though this relationship, along with any lingering admiration for the Nazis, foundered with the events of the *Kristallnacht.*

Lewes graduated with a third-class honours degree, and pondered various careers in both England and Australia, failing the British Foreign Office exams in 1938. He eventually took up a position with the British Council, taking responsibility for its lectures sector abroad. However, late in 1938 Lewes became a territorial, joining the 1st battalion of the Tower Hamlet Rifles as an ensign, and transferring to the Welsh Guards in the autumn of 1939. Proving adept at weapons work, he was appointed training officer for the regiment. He attended his sister's wedding in August 1939, and there met Miriam Barford. Their friendship deepened, and Lewes corresponded with her throughout his active service. In October 1941, in a letter he never received, Miriam accepted his proposal of marriage. Lewes also became a friend of a fellow officer, the painter Rex Whistler. The latter painted a fine portrait of Lewes, Bren gun astride his knees, at the steps of the grandstand at Sandown Park (where they were billeted). Capturing his handsome auburn hair and moustache, the portrait also shows his somewhat detached, inward-looking nature.

In October 1940 Lewes was posted with 8th commando, and he underwent training in Scotland. On 31 January 1941 he sailed to the Middle East to begin active service. Lewes became impatient at the poor training arrangements available, and it was while here that he perceived the powerful advantage that could be gained by using smaller groups of men to raid behind enemy lines. He requested permission to assemble a small parachuting force, to train according to his methods.

In June 1941 Lewes had prepared no fewer than three parachute assaults, only to see them cancelled by Middle Eastern headquarters. He was posted to Tobruk, Libya, in July, although he felt that the work he had begun with his parachute detachment was unfinished. He quickly became disillusioned with his role in Tobruk, feeling that he had no sense of identity or of being part of a well-organized team. He was visited several times during this period by (Archibald) David *Stirling, who was attempting to persuade him to join a new parachute unit, based upon the very ideas the Lewes had formulated. Stirling had the contacts in the Middle Eastern headquarters to bring these to fruition. It took some time for Stirling to persuade Lewes to accept—he wanted to be sure that Stirling was fully committed to his ideas—but he did so at the end of August, and recruited some outstanding NCOs (who like Lewes had felt disillusioned over their use during the past year) to L detachment of the SAS.

Lewes carried on with the parachuting techniques he had pioneered earlier in the year and placed a great emphasis on training his men. He experimented with marching skills, which would enable the unit to disappear quickly after raids. An early setback occurred in October 1941 when two members of the detachment died in a practice parachute jump, owing to faulty clips. Morale was seriously affected, and in an effort to assuage this, and lead from the front, Lewes was the first person to jump the next day, once the fault had been corrected. He continued to develop his marches, constantly pushing himself, calculating the distances that could be covered with the most careful use of the rations available. He also developed the lightweight Lewes bomb, a forerunner of later plastic explosives. Its make-up was such that one person could carry a large number, and the time delay of detonation could be used to devastating effect.

After a mock raid the first operational task of the SAS took place on 17 November 1941. The objective of the parachutists was to destroy aircraft on the ground and so hinder the enemy's attacks on the following day. However, forty of the sixty-two men were lost, in treacherous conditions, and the raid had to be aborted. Later raids were much more successful—though Lewes did not live to see them. On Christmas day 1941 he left for Nofilia aerodrome to take part in an operation there. Six days later, on 31 December 1941, Jock Lewes was fatally wounded during an attack by a low-flying Messerschmitt; he was buried 20 miles inland, south-east of Nofilia. In a letter to his father, David Stirling paid tribute to him:

> There is no doubt that any success the unit has achieved up to the time of Jock's death and after it was, and is, almost wholly due to Jock's work. Our training programmes and methods are, and always will be, based on the syllabuses he produced for us. They must show the extent of his influences (Lewes, 247)

In a later interview Stirling argued that Lewes was 'the greatest training officer of the last war' (ibid., 195).

According to Field Marshal Rommel, SAS attacks deep inside Italian territory 'caused considerable havoc' (Lewes, 164). Although he did not live to see these successes considerable credit has to be given to the ethos and training instilled by Jock Lewes. FIONA MCPHERSON

Sources J. Lewes, *Jock Lewes, co-founder of the SAS* (2000) · '"Who dares … spins": the service that never was', BBC Radio 4 (22 Nov 2001) [programme on the foundation of the SAS] · *CGPLA Eng. & Wales* (1943)

Likenesses R. Whistler, portrait, 1940, priv. coll.

Wealth at death £341 1s. 1d.: probate, 11 March 1943, *CGPLA Eng. & Wales*

Lewes, Robert of (*d.* 1166), bishop of Bath, was of Flemish descent, though born in England apparently of noble parents. He had been a monk of the Cluniac priory of Lewes when he attracted the attention of Henry de Blois (*d.* 1171), who was to be his patron for the rest of his life. Of his pre-episcopal career little is known. Contemporaries comment that Henry de Blois secured for him first an administrative post at Glastonbury and then, at Easter 1136, promotion to the bishopric of Bath. It is possible that Robert had spent a brief period as prior of Winchester, but the evidence for this rests entirely on the appearance of a Robert, prior of Winchester, in the 1130 pipe roll and the comment of a fifteenth-century Wells historian.

Within his diocese, Bishop Robert's importance lies in his organizational work and above all in his establishment at Wells of a secular chapter. His period in office saw the appearance of three territorial archdeaconries, and it is evident from the frequency with which the archdeacons witnessed the bishop's charters that they were his closest companions and assistants. Of the six men who served in this capacity, three at some point used the title *magister*, revealing a new necessity for and emphasis on administrative competence. The greatly increased number of surviving *acta* from Robert's episcopate, as compared with those of his immediate predecessors, and the appearance for the first time in the diocese of an episcopal seal, similarly suggest a more bureaucratic approach towards his diocesan duties.

Closely related to this was Bishop Robert's work of rebuilding and reorganization at Wells, which enabled him to provide canonries for his clerical staff. Following the moving of the bishop's see to Bath under John of Tours (*d.* 1122), the canons of Wells had suffered the alienation of much of their revenue. In a document drawn up under the guidance of Henry de Blois, and almost certainly issued at Stephen's Easter court in 1136 (the occasion on which Robert was confirmed in the temporalities of his see), the bishop reorganized their existing estates and himself gave a number more. These were divided into prebends to endow a dean, precentor, subdean, and, initially, fifteen canons. A common fund was established to provide bread for those clergy attending the early morning office, and revenue was also set aside to maintain the fabric and ornaments of the church of Wells. The rebuilt church was dedicated within the period 1142–8.

As a Cluniac monk, Robert of Lewes's dealings with the religious houses of his diocese are clearly of some interest. He appears to have had entirely cordial relations with the cathedral priory at Bath, where he continued the rebuilding of the church begun by his predecessor, John of Tours, and gave generous gifts but nevertheless did not fully restore the priory's alienated properties. He showed no especial favour towards Montacute Priory, the one Cluniac house in the diocese, but does seem to have been keen to promote the Augustinian cause (as was Henry de Blois in the diocese of Winchester). Among his surviving *acta* the largest single beneficiary is the Augustinian house at Bruton. Robert was also involved with the economic development of the town of Wells, granting it borough status and conferring privileges on traders visiting for three annual fairs.

Beginning in 1962 R. H. C. Davis made a good case for Bishop Robert as the author of the *Gesta Stephani*. The issue is not one on which certainty is possible, but if the identification is correct, it shows the bishop to have been a scholar of some stature, adept at employing both biblical and, as one might expect of a Cluniac, classical idioms. Pastoral concerns are apparent in the humanity with which the suffering inflicted by the civil war is treated. The work also reveals a very high conception of the episcopal office, appropriate for one who was both a protégé of Henry de Blois and a supporter of priests, regular and secular, within his diocese. In political terms the author can be seen initially to have been an enthusiastic partisan of Stephen's, though subsequently a supporter of Duke Henry. From other sources the bishop is known to have been with the king at the siege of Bedford in 1138, present with his patron at the reception of the empress in Winchester in March 1141, and witness to a deed of Duke Henry's in April 1153. An elderly man when Stephen's reign ended in 1154, Bishop Robert was recorded as being ill in May 1163, and he died on 31 August 1166. He was buried before the high altar at Bath. FRANCES RAMSEY

Sources F. M. R. Ramsey, ed., *Bath and Wells, 1061–1205*, English Episcopal Acta, 10 (1995) · R. H. C. Davis, 'The authorship of the *Gesta Stephani*', *EngHR*, 77 (1962), 209–32 · K. R. Potter and R. H. C. Davis, eds., *Gesta Stephani*, OMT (1976) · F. M. R. Davies, 'The bishops of Wells and Bath and their *Acta*, 1061–1205', DPhil diss., U. Oxf., 1991 · 'A brief history of the bishoprick of Somerset from its foundation to the year 1174', *Ecclesiastical documents*, CS, 8 (1840) · *Reg. RAN*, vol. 3 · *Radulfi de Diceto … opera historica*, ed. W. Stubbs, 2 vols., Rolls Series, 68 (1876) · *The chronicle of John of Worcester, 1118–1140*, ed. J. R. H. Weaver (1908), 38

Lewgar, John (*d.* 1665), colonial administrator and writer, was born in London 'of genteel parents' and of long-established Suffolk stock: he may have been the John

Lugar, son of the scrivener Philip Lugar of Chancery Lane, who was baptized at St Dunstan-in-the-West, London, on 27 December 1601. He was admitted as a commoner to Trinity College, Oxford, where he matriculated on 13 December 1616 and took his BA on 13 November 1619; he graduated MA on 26 June 1622 and was incorporated at Cambridge in 1625. By 1632, when he was licensed to preach on 30 May and took his BD on 6 July, Lewgar was ordained and from 1627 held a fellowship of Trinity and the benefice of Laverton in Somerset.

Following several discussions of religion with the Oxford theologian William Chillingworth, however, who persuaded him that the Catholic church was the true church, Lewgar converted to Rome in 1634, and renounced his living in the Church of England, drawing up a brief memorandum of 'the chief reasons for which he doubteth of the protestant religion' (Anstruther, 2.189). In 1635 he co-authored *A Brief Relation of Maryland* with his wife, Ann, whom he married on 10 January of that year. Two years later at the invitation of Lewgar's Oxford student friend, the Catholic colonial proprietor Cecil Calvert, second Lord Baltimore, they migrated to Maryland along with their son, John, seven servants, and Baltimore himself. Lewgar was to act as provincial secretary and agent in the government of the colony for Baltimore—'a very serviceable and diligent man in his secretaries place' (Hall, 158). Lewgar also secured financial aid from a London linen draper. He sat in the Maryland assembly continuously from 1637 to 1642 and, on his return from a visit to England in 1645, in the upper house in 1647, and also served on the provincial council from 1637 to 1644 and from 1647 to 1648; the offices he held were collector of rents (1637–48), commissioner in causes testamentary (1638–48), and attorney-general (1644–8). While he served as surveyor-general between 1637 and 1642 Leonard Calvert, the governor of Maryland and Baltimore's brother, promised to use his services to parcel out lands for grant to the inhabitants of a part of the colony; Lewgar also acted as a justice in the county of St Mary's, where he lived and held the 200 acre St John's estate, operating as a planter and merchant. On 26 August 1644 Lewgar was dismissed for exceeding his authority in issuing a commission for dealing with the colony's Susquehannock Indians but by 6 September he was restored to office by Calvert. Following the death of his wife Lewgar applied, in 1647, to join the Jesuits and was refused, doubtless on account of his earlier direction of Lord Baltimore's efforts to limit the influence of the Society of Jesus in the colony; nevertheless, he became a secular Catholic priest about 1647 and served as Baltimore's chaplain.

Following the death of his patron, Leonard Calvert, in June 1647, Lewgar returned in October 1648 to England, where he lived in London in Baltimore's Wild Street property and began a new phase of his active career by turning to writing. The 1657 work by I. L., *The Only Way to Rest of Soule*, is attributed to him; he published *Erastus junior: a solid demonstration by principles, forms of ordination, common laws, acts of parliament, that no bishop, minister, nor presbyter hath any authority to preach, &c from Christ, but from the parliament* in 1659 and in 1662 *Erastus senior: scholastically demonstrating this conclusion, that admitting Lambeth records to be true, those called bishops here in England, are no bishops either in order or jurisdiction, or so much as legal*. A further work under his name, *A conference between him and Mr. Chillingworth, whether the Roman church be the Catholic church, and all out of communion heretics or schismatics*, was published posthumously in 1687. He died of the plague in the parish of St Giles-in-the-Fields in 1665 and was recorded in the following year as 'Mr. Lewgar, who looked after the infected persons' (Anstruther, 2.190).

Aside from their son, John and Ann Lewgar seem also to have had two daughters, Cecily and Ann.

MICHAEL MULLETT

Sources E. C. Papenfuse and others, eds., *A biographical dictionary of the Maryland legislature, 1635–1789*, 2 vols. (1979–85) • Gillow, *Lit. biog. hist.* • G. Anstruther, *The seminary priests*, 2 (1975) • Wood, *Ath. Oxon.*, new edn, vol. 3 • Foster, *Alum. Oxon.* • C. C. Hall, ed., *Narratives of early Maryland, 1633–1684* (1910); repr. (1967) [repr. 1967] • T. H. Clancy, *English Catholic books, 1641–1700: a bibliography*, rev. edn (1996)

Lewicke, Edward (*fl.* 1562), poet, is unknown except as the author of *The most wonderfull and pleasaunt history of Titus and Gisippus, whereby is fully declared the figure of perfect frendshyp, drawen into English metre* (1562). The tale was originally taken from Boccaccio by Sir Thomas Elyot, who introduced a prose version into his *Boke Named the Governour*. Lewicke's work, described by its twentieth-century editor as 'entirely devoid of any poetic quality' (Wright, *Early English Versions*, introduction, c), is little more than a rhymed paraphrase of Elyot's rendering.

G. B. DIBBLEE, *rev.* MATTHEW STEGGLE

Sources H. G. Wright, ed., *Early English versions of the tales of Guiscardo and Ghismonda and Titus and Gisippus from 'The Decameron'*, EETS, old ser., 205 (1937) • J. P. Collier, *The poetical Decameron*, 2 vols. (1820), 2.80–82 • T. Warton, *The history of English poetry*, 4 vols. (1774–81), vol. 3, p. 468 • H. G. Wright, *Boccacio in England from Chaucer to Tennyson* (1957), 136–7

Lewin, Hirsch. *See* Lyon, Hart (1721–1800).

Lewin, John William (1770–1819), naturalist and artist, was born on 28 March 1770 and baptized at St Dunstan and All Saints, Stepney, London, on 15 April 1770. He was the son (and one of at least six children) of the naturalist and artist William *Lewin (1747–1795) and his wife, Susanna. By 1794 the Lewin family was living at Hoxton, London. John William Lewin was probably still living at home and, with his brothers Thomas and Thomas William, helped his father compile the second edition of his book *The Birds of Great Britain* (1795–1801).

William Lewin died in 1795 but his patrons continued to provide assistance to John William Lewin. In 1798 he decided to travel to Australia. The third duke of Portland, then home secretary, recommended him (on 6 February 1798) to Governor John Hunter, introducing him as a 'painter and drawer in natural history' entitled to 'the usual Government rations in the settlement'. Portland granted Lewin a free passage to New South Wales; Lewin was also provided with financial assistance by the entomologist and goldsmith Dru Drury, who furnished him with instructions for specimen collection, a gun, and orders for insect engravings. The list of Lewin's distinguished and learned patrons also included the collector Lady Arden, Alexander McLeay, secretary of the Linnean Society, and the entomologist Thomas Marsham.

Lewin arrived at Sydney on 11 January 1800 in the *Minerva*, having missed the previous ship, the *Buffalo*, on which his wife, (Anna) Maria, had travelled (she arrived on 3 May 1799). Lewin was immediately engaged in a lawsuit to defend his wife over an accusation of misconduct with the second mate of the *Buffalo*. Lewin's wife was cleared and by September 1800 the couple were living in Parramatta. In the following March the governor of New South Wales, Captain Philip King, allowed Lewin to accompany Lieutenant James Grant on a survey of the Bass Strait. However, owing to bad weather Lewin's boat, *Bee*, was forced to turn back. He later proceeded with Colonel Paterson to explore the Hunter River. About November 1801 Lewin sailed to Tahiti on the *Norfolk*, which had been sent by Governor King to procure salt pork, although Lewin's prime objective was to find pearls for Drury. The ship was wrecked off Point Venus (near Papeete) and Lewin and the crew were subsequently stranded there for nine months, taking refuge with the London Missionary Society. Lewin and his fellow refugees returned to Sydney aboard the *Porpoise* on 19 December 1802.

Governor King granted Lewin 100 acres of farmland near Parramatta in 1804; a further 200 acres in the district of Mintos were given to him in 1809 by Colonel Paterson. A son, William Arden Lewin, was born possibly on 31 December 1805 in Parramatta, and was baptized later on 8 October 1806. The Lewins did have another child but it died before William Arden was born. The Parramatta farm was sold by Lewin in 1811 and in 1817 he mortgaged, and then sold, the 200 acres of farmland at Airds district, which had been granted by Governor Lachlan Macquarie in 1812. There is no evidence that Lewin ever found time to occupy these properties; instead he carried out trips to the Nattai River and the Cowpastures, and engraved plates for his books. Until his death in 1804 Drury continued to fund Lewin and yet, despite this help, Lewin struggled financially. Drury was also responsible for sponsoring Lewin's membership of the Linnean Society; he was elected an associate of the society in 1801.

Lewin spent many years forming collections of the birds and insects of his adopted country. In 1805 he published *Prodromus Entomology: Natural History of Lepidopterous Insects of New South Wales*. Between 1804 and 1808 Lewin's book *Birds of New Holland, with their Natural History* was produced in London. The London editions of his books were supervised and edited by his brother Thomas Lewin, who also wrote the prefaces and arranged contributions from scientific experts. His works were intended to raise sufficient funds to enable him to return to England. In 1808 Lewin described himself as a portrait painter and by November of that year he was living first at Chapel Row (Castlereagh Street, Sydney). He later moved to Brickfields, on the eastern side of George Street. Lewin's wife opened a succession of small shops or inns to help support the family. In 1813 he had a few copies of his book printed by George Howe in Sydney under the alternative title *Birds of New South Wales, with their Natural History*. It was the first illustrated natural history book to be published in Australia, and some of the copper plates (along with those from his *Prodromus entomology*) were probably the earliest engraved in New South Wales. A third edition of *Birds* was printed in 1822, with a fourth edition appearing in 1838.

Lewin also undertook commissions for landscape paintings, miniatures, and portraits in an attempt to raise some income; he drew and painted Aborigines, animals, birds, and plants at the request of Governor Macquarie, who became another of Lewin's patrons. In 1810 Macquarie appointed Lewin coroner for Sydney, and in 1812 Lewin and his wife set up the colony's first formal art school. Macquarie took Lewin on as artist for his expedition across the Blue Mountains to Bathurst in May 1815, and also attached him to record specimens brought back by surveyor-general John Oxley's explorations of 1817 and 1818. Lewin made the first drawing of a koala brought back from the expeditions across the new territory; he was also the first free artist to emigrate to New South Wales and attempt to earn a living as a professional painter.

Lewin died in Sydney on 27 August 1819 and was buried at the burying-ground there, the site on which Sydney town hall was later built. His remains were first removed to the Devonshire Street cemetery, and the tomb was later transferred to the Botany cemetery (La Perouse). He was survived by his wife, Maria, and their surviving child William Arden; the George Street property was granted to Maria Lewin following her husband's death. She and her son returned to England in 1820, from where Maria, herself a gifted botanical artist, arranged publication of the 1822 editions of her husband's books, and continued to promote his works. She was provided with a pension of £50 per annum by the New South Wales secretary of state which was paid from 1 January 1824 until 10 June 1850, when she died in the London Hospital.

YOLANDA FOOTE

Sources A. Wheeler and A. Thompson, 'John William Lewin's watercolour and line drawings in the Linnean Society of London archives', *Archives of Natural History*, 23 (1996), 369–84 · *AusDB* · H. M. Whittell, *The literature of Australian birds: a history and a bibliography of Australian ornithology* (1954) · J. Kerr, ed., *Dictionary of Australian artists* (1992) · C. E. Jackson, *Bird etchings: the illustrators and their books, 1655–1855* (1985) · P. Mander-Jones, 'Lewin, John William', *AusDB*, 2.111–12

Archives Art Gallery of South Australia, Adelaide, painting · Linn. Soc., watercolours/line drawings · Mitchell L., NSW, drawings · NHM, drawings · NL Aus., Rex Nan Kivell Collection, watercolours

Lewin, Sir Justinian (*bap.* **1613**, *d.* **1673**), civil lawyer, was baptized at St Bartholomew-the-Less, Smithfield, London, on 17 February 1613, the son of William Lewin, who was a clerk of the New River Company, of Smithfield, and his wife, Sarah. Although often referred to as the grandson of

William Lewin the ecclesiastical lawyer who died in 1598, the latter's three sons were called Thomas, Justinian (who died in 1620), and John, and his relationship to them remains unclear. He matriculated at Pembroke College, Oxford, in 1631, and graduated BCL in 1632. Appointed commissary for the archdeaconry of Norfolk in 1633, he resigned in the same year and proceeded DCL from Pembroke in 1637, when he was admitted to practise in the court of arches.

In 1639 Lewin was again appointed official of the archdeacon of Norwich. In the same year he joined the earl of Arundel's army as judge-martial in the Scottish expedition, deploring the 'ungodly and rebellious courses they took for the countenance and support of their ill cause' (*CSP dom.*, *1639*, 152). On his return from Scotland Lewin was rewarded for his services by the place of a master in chancery, the appointment dating from 22 July 1641, and in the same year he was granted honorific admission to Gray's Inn. A royalist during the civil war, Lewin was cited as a delinquent in paying parliamentary taxes in 1642, and subsequently 'quitted or lost his employments during the troubles' (ibid., *1660–61*, 220). He nevertheless promoted the interests of the future Charles II in Norfolk, and was temporarily imprisoned in 1655 for his share in a plot to gain control of Lynne, which he subsequently claimed 'might have been of eminent use but for the treachery of Hynderson, then governor of Norwich'.

At the Restoration Lewin was reinstated as commissary for the bishop in the archdeaconry of Norwich and as master in chancery. He was knighted for his loyalty in 1661. On 21 August 1634 Lewin was married to Mary (*d.* 1690), the daughter and heir of Rhees Wynn, serjeant-at-law, and niece and heir of Thomas Gwynne DCL. They had a son, John, who married Mary Kenrick. Although at the start of the civil war Lewin had a house at Heigham, a village just outside the walls of Norwich, by 1655 he is referred to as resident at Ludham. The only writings which have survived are a few letters to his friend John Hobart which afford interesting sidelights on Norwich during the civil war and after.

Lewin died on 1 January 1673 and was buried the next day near his parents in the church in which he had been baptized, St Bartholomew-the-Less, Smithfield, where his widow joined him on 21 April 1690. P. O. G. White

Sources B. P. Levack, *The civil lawyers in England, 1603–1641* (1973) • R. Waters, *Genealogical memoirs of the extinct family of Chester of Chicherley*, 2 (1887), 411 • R. W. Ketton-Cremer, *Norfolk in the civil war: a portrait of a society in conflict* (1969) • *CSP dom.*, *1639–40*; *1655*; *1660–61*; *1669* • F. Blomefield and C. Parkin, *An essay towards a topographical history of the county of Norfolk*, 5 vols. (1739–75), vol. 3 • Bodl. Oxf., MS Tanner 115, fols. 147, 149, 156, 160, 162, 171 • private information (2004) [C. Gwynn]

Archives Bodl. Oxf., Tanner MSS

Lewin, (George) Ronald (1914–1984), military historian and biographer, was born in Halifax, Yorkshire, on 11 October 1914, the eldest of four sons (there were no daughters) of Frank Lewin, patent agent, and his wife, Elizabeth, *née* Wingfield. He was educated at Heath grammar school in Halifax and the Queen's College, Oxford, where he was a Hastings scholar and a Goldsmiths' exhibitioner. His first class in classical honour moderations in 1934 was the best of its year and was followed by a first in *literae humaniores* (1936).

From Oxford, Lewin went in 1937 as an editorial assistant to the publishers Jonathan Cape. Having joined the Territorial Army as a gunner early in 1939, describing himself as 'probably the most inefficient civilian who ever put on uniform—and that includes the good soldier Schweik!', he was called up on the day war broke out and served in the Royal Artillery until 1945. He was in north Africa with the Eighth Army, was slightly wounded, and was mentioned in dispatches. In the winter of 1943 he was posted to England to train with a super-heavy regiment, and fought with Twenty-First Army group in north-west Europe from June 1944 until the end of the war, by which time he had become a captain.

Lewin returned to Cape briefly on being demobilized, but prospects seemed limited and in 1946 he joined the BBC as a talks producer in the Third Programme. In 1954 he became chief assistant, Home Service, its head from 1957, and its chief in 1963. He set up the Music programme and initiated the *Today* programme and other successful series. He was, however, not cut out for administration, and he retired ill in 1965. There followed some ten years of clinical depression, the strain of his work having brought on a delayed reaction to his wartime years.

Lewin returned to publishing, joining Hutchinson and specializing in works of military history and wartime experiences. But he also turned to writing his own books. Before the war he had written many book reviews and contributed poems and articles to various periodicals, and now he was commissioned to write *Rommel* in the Great Commander series. This appeared in 1968 and *Montgomery as Military Commander* followed in 1971. In 1969 he also edited the third volume of *Freedom's Battle: the War on Land, 1939–45*. In 1973 *Churchill as War Lord* was published, and in 1976 *Man of Armour*, about Lieutenant-General Vyvyan Pope. By now his reputation was well established and he was chosen to undertake the official biography of Field Marshal Viscount Slim. It was a difficult task, for Slim's autobiography had been justly acclaimed, but *Slim the Standard-Bearer* (1976) was a triumphant success, lucid, intelligent, and exceptionally readable. It won the W. H. Smith literary award in 1977. *The Life and Death of the Afrika Korps* followed in 1977.

Lewin was now accepted as one of the leading military historians but *Ultra Goes to War*, published in 1978, presented a new challenge. Though he lacked scientific or mechanical training, his mastery of the techniques by which the allied cryptographers broke the German ciphers was so complete that he was able to explain them in words that the least qualified could understand, and assess their significance with magisterial authority. He followed this with an account of cipher-breaking achievements in the USA, published as *American Magic* there and *The other Ultra* (1982) in Great Britain. For this he paid several visits to the United States and was the first to see many of the relevant papers in the National Archives. He moved on to *Hitler's Mistakes*, a study of Hitler's shortcomings as politician and general, but owing to a delay in publication this appeared only posthumously.

In 1982 Lewin was struck down by a recurrence of the cancer for which he had had an operation eight years earlier. From then on until he died he was undergoing treatment and in constant pain. He was kept going by his determination to finish the one-volume history of the Second World War which he had been asked to write by Oxford University Press. He achieved about a third of his objective, laying down his pen only on the day he went into hospital.

Lewin was appointed CBE for services to military history in the new year honours of 1983, but took even greater pleasure in receiving the Chesney gold medal of the Royal United Services Institute in the previous year for 'eminent work calculated to advance military science and knowledge'. His prodigious memory, clarity of mind, and immaculate prose style did indeed put him among the masters of his profession; his generosity to those less experienced who sought his help ensured that he was as well liked as he was respected. He was a fellow of the Royal Society of Literature and of the Royal Historical Society.

In 1938 Lewin married Sylvia Lloyd (*d.* 1988), daughter of Philip Maximilian Sturge, industrial print manufacturer, of a Quaker family in Birmingham. They had three sons and a daughter, and the death in a road accident of the youngest son in 1963 was a terrible blow. Lewin died on 6 January 1984 at St Luke's Hospital, Guildford, Surrey.

PHILIP ZIEGLER, *rev.*

Sources *WWW* · personal knowledge (1990) · private information (1990) · *CGPLA Eng. & Wales* (1984)

Archives CAC Cam., corresp. and papers · CAC Cam., corresp. relating to biography of Slim

Wealth at death £1,066,861: probate, 31 Oct 1984, *CGPLA Eng. & Wales*

Lewin, Terence Thornton, Baron Lewin (1920–1999), naval officer, was born in Dover, Kent, on 19 November 1920, the second son of Eric Lewin (*d.* 1963), civil servant, and his wife, Margaret (*d.* 1934), daughter of Frederick Falconer, draper, of Dover. He was educated at the Judd School, Tonbridge, where he became head boy and excelled at sports, particularly athletics and rugby football. In his final year at school, 1938, he joined a summer expedition of the Public Schools Exploring Society to Newfoundland. It was partly the confidence he gained in this unfamiliar milieu that led Lewin to seek to join the Royal Navy as a special entry cadet. He passed high in the January 1939 entry and after training in HMS *Frobisher* and HMS *Vindictive* passed out top, in July 1939.

War service After the outbreak of the Second World War Lewin was appointed to the new cruiser *Belfast*. The ship was mined some two months later and required extensive repair, and Lewin was reappointed to the battleship *Valiant*. There, with his lifelong friend Roderick Macdonald, he quickly made his mark, particularly in his action task, the direction of the ship's close-range anti-aircraft armament. His captain, Bernard Rawlings, taught the midshipmen much in the way of delegation and control. Lewin

Terence Thornton Lewin, Baron Lewin (1920–1999), by Franta Belsky, 1983

saw action in home waters and the Mediterranean and by the time he returned to Britain for sub-lieutenants' courses in April 1941 was a seasoned sea officer.

Lewin was then appointed to the destroyer *Highlander* in the Atlantic, but in December 1941 contracted diphtheria. After convalescence he was transferred to HMS *Ashanti*, a destroyer of the Tribal class. There, initially under the inspiring captaincy of Richard Onslow, he spent most of the remainder of the Second World War, at an exceptional level of operational activity. This included several Arctic convoys, the crucial operation Pedestal to relieve Malta in August 1942, and a number of brisk channel actions both before and after D-day in June 1944. Lewin, successively as gunnery control officer and first lieutenant, distinguished himself throughout, earning three mentions in dispatches and the Distinguished Service Cross, the latter mainly for his feats of endurance during the epic, though ultimately unsuccessful, tow of the destroyer *Somali*, torpedoed in Arctic waters in September 1942. In the spring of 1942, when *Ashanti* was under repair in Immingham, Lewin had met Jane Branch-Evans, daughter of the Revd Charles James Branch-Evans. She was then serving in the WRNS. Their romance continued, mostly by letter but with brief meetings, and they married on 14 February 1944. They had two sons, Timothy (*b.* 1947) and Jonathan (*b.* 1959), and a daughter, Susan (*b.* 1949).

Promotion After the war Lewin applied to specialize in gunnery and in 1945 joined the long course. His professional career followed conventional lines for the next few years, mainly in staff appointments ashore; during this time he played rugby for the navy as a wing three-quarter.

In 1949 he was appointed gunnery officer of the first destroyer flotilla in HMS *Chequers* on the Mediterranean station. His highly successful tenure of this post was brought to a somewhat sad end by the illness of his son Tim, who contracted poliomyelitis, a setback that in subsequent years was triumphantly overcome.

Selected for promotion to commander at the end of 1952, Lewin then passed the staff course and took up his first Admiralty post. This was on the staff of the naval assistant to the second sea lord, and dealt with officers' appointments. However, he quickly found himself involved in the wider field of officer structure, which was being studied by a high-level committee. With two commanders of other specializations he became a key adviser to the committee. This produced eventually the general list concept, which gave wider powers of command and decision-making to the engineer and supply branches, and in its essentials endured for the rest of the century. In the summer of 1955 Lewin was appointed to command the Battle-class destroyer *Corunna*. He quickly established himself as an outstanding operator and ship-handler on both the home and Mediterranean stations. During the Suez Crisis of 1956 his ship was in refit in Malta, and while not involved in the operation Lewin was exposed, as those at sea were not, to the controversy surrounding it.

Early in 1957 Lewin was informed that he was on the short list as a potential executive officer of the royal yacht *Britannia*. His first reaction was to decline the post as he did not regard himself as any sort of courtier. However, he was informed that the appointment would stand and he rapidly adapted to the yacht's ways while introducing a workmanlike, no-nonsense atmosphere. His relationship with Prince Philip had been established in HMS *Chequers* many years before, and all other members of the royal family soon recognized his worth. State visits to Denmark and the Netherlands, and a fleet gathering in the Moray Firth, were highlights of the years 1957 and 1958.

Promoted to captain on 30 June 1958, Lewin took up his next Admiralty appointment in November as deputy director of tactical and staff duties. This post, concerned with operational requirements for the navy, was heavily overlapped by others and during Lewin's time was rationalized, so that his vision for the future had greater scope. In consequence he was able to take a leading part in the inception of the Leander-class frigate, probably the most successful British ship design of the later twentieth century. A year at the Imperial Defence College followed in 1961. Lewin took part in the college's Far East tour, a mind-broadening episode that had a strong influence on his thinking. He then took command of the Dartmouth training squadron and for the years 1962 and 1963 was busy with the sea training of future officers in all branches of their profession. The squadron's cruises embraced the West Indies (twice), Scandinavia, the Mediterranean, and North America.

Lewin's next appointment was the onerous one of director of tactical and weapons policy at the Ministry of Defence. After coming into this at the beginning of 1964, he was almost at once involved in the defence review initiated by the incoming Labour government and its defence secretary, Denis Healey. This revolved, for the navy, round the struggle to keep alive the project for a new aircraft-carrier, CVA 01. Lewin's was not the leading division in this battle and it had many other projects to handle; however, he played a prominent part in the scheme, which eventually came to nothing, to buy one or more Essex-class carriers from the USA and adapt it for British use.

Nevertheless, when in February 1966 it was announced that no more fixed-wing carriers would be built for the Royal Navy, Lewin shared the trauma, particularly as he had by then been appointed to command the carrier *Hermes*, newly modernized and to come into service later in the year. His first task was to reassure the ship's company that they still had a worthwhile job to do, then as the ship approached operational status to work her and her squadrons up into a fully fighting unit. Despite the limitations of operating heavy aircraft from a small carrier, critical personnel changes, several early flying accidents, and constantly changing operational commitments—the commission was an outstanding success, with an immensely coherent and happy ship's company and air group. Lewin brought the ship home for Christmas 1967, as he had promised, by an inspired piece of engineering jugglery against pressure from shore staffs to keep her on the Far East station.

High office Lewin was promoted rear-admiral in January 1968 and took up the post of assistant chief of naval staff (policy) in the Ministry of Defence. The short history of this post had not been happy. Lewin had virtually to make what he could of it, and succeeded by instituting long-term administrative reforms, notably plan Constrain (the concentration of shore training in a smaller number of establishments). This, and a reorganization of the naval staff in the ministry, were his principal achievements, but he also established himself as a spokesman for the naval case.

Lewin next returned to the Far East as flag officer second in command of the fleet on that station. The run-down of forces east of Suez had begun and maintaining motivation was not easy, particularly as some of the ships were in poor material shape, but Lewin held the fleet together and, moreover, initiated the trials of the principal warfare officer system, which allowed ships to make a more rapid response to developing threats and was proved in action more than a decade later in the Falklands conflict. During this period, also, Lewin took a leading part in the celebrations of the bicentennial of the first British landings in New Zealand and Australia, and this stimulated an interest in the life and voyages of Captain Cook which endured for the rest of his life.

Promoted vice-admiral in January 1971, Lewin took up one of the heaviest loads of his career when he was appointed vice-chief of naval staff in the Ministry of Defence. The job embraced every aspect of naval policy, planning, and operations, and this at a singularly difficult time in many areas. While the Conservative government which had come into office in 1970 might be thought more sympathetic to defence than its predecessor, money was no less tight and the commitment to NATO, which had been made the keystone of the previous administration's defence policy, was still the overriding criterion for defence procurement. Moreover, relations between the services were strained, owing partly to personalities and partly to the struggle for resources, typified by the navy's desire to acquire the Sea Harrier short take-off / vertical landing aircraft, to operate from the new 'through-deck cruisers' of the Invincible class, and the Royal Air Force's opposition to this development.

Lewin's three years as vice-chief of naval staff were characterized by great skill, judgement, and humanity. He sponsored and carried through the concept of 'group deployments' for ships of the fleet to go to distant parts of the world, sometimes round it, for months at a time, thus maintaining operational autonomy, command expertise, and confidence. This needed careful negotiation with other Whitehall departments and with NATO. He initiated the idea of the 'offshore tapestry', drawing together the strands of management of Britain's offshore estate. He kept always in play the core capabilities of seaborne air power, amphibious shipping and forces, and nuclear-powered submarines. Both anti-submarine warfare and air defence were prime concerns. Finally, the question of inter-service relations was, at least on his level, greatly eased by his regular meetings with his RAF opposite number on the basis of 'let's talk about what we can agree on'.

Created KCB in the new year honours of 1973, Lewin assumed command of the fleet in December 1973. The headquarters were at Northwood, co-located with those of the air officer commanding 18 group (maritime patrol aircraft) and the NATO staffs of commander-in-chief eastern Atlantic and Channel, Lewin's NATO 'hats'. It was not easy for the commander-in-chief to get to sea, but in his twenty months in the job Lewin managed several fleet gatherings in places as far apart as the West Indies and the South China Sea, as well as a swing through the Indian Ocean, with a constant background of administration and high-level meetings both in Whitehall and overseas. The entertaining load at Admiralty House was heavy; Lady Lewin and a loyal staff were fully extended. In November 1975 the other commander-in-chief's post, that of the naval home command, fell to Lewin. This was at a somewhat slower tempo than the management of the fleet, but was still extremely busy; the implementation of plan Constrain, the reorganization of the reserves, and the introduction of the naval personal and family service all required careful and detailed attention.

It had long been clear that Lewin would eventually reach the pinnacle of the navy as first sea lord. However, this occurred somewhat sooner than planned early in 1977, owing to the untimely death of the chief of defence staff, marshal of the Royal Air Force Sir Andrew Humphrey. Lewin was now clearly a front-runner also for the latter post in due course, and it may have been for this reason that his time as first sea lord was not the most dazzling of his career. Consolidation was probably the chief objective, particularly in the light of the very difficult financial circumstances of the country. Principal concerns were the progress towards completion of HMS *Invincible*, the first carrier to fly the Sea Harrier, and of the 'Chevaline' modification to the Polaris strategic deterrent system, which had run seriously out of control. Over all loomed the question of service pay, which had fallen catastrophically behind that in the civilian sector.

These questions had been largely resolved when Lewin was promoted admiral of the fleet and assumed the position of chief of defence staff in September 1979. However, they were succeeded by even more critical ones. The financial position was viewed by the incoming Conservative administration as dire, and the correction of service pay which they had introduced meant there was even less money to pay for equipment. Against this background, up to the end of March 1982 three major developments occupied Lewin's main attention. The first was the replacement of Britain's strategic deterrent system, Polaris/Chevaline. Lewin held to the proposal that this should be the American Trident submarine-launched ballistic missile, resisting all suggestions for untried and assumption-sensitive alternatives, and carried this policy through. The second was the review of Britain's defences initiated by John Nott, defence secretary from January 1981. This resulted in a white paper adhering to rigid NATO-driven criteria, discounting the value of balanced sea power, and consequently diminishing plans for the surface fleet and amphibious forces. Lewin could not have found it easy to stomach what he clearly felt to be a distortion of strategic realities, but as chief of defence as a whole felt it his duty to continue in office. His experience in the Nott review, however, led to the third major preoccupation: the reorganization of the defence staff so that its chief should become the principal military adviser to the government, rather than simply the chairman of the chiefs of staff committee, and that he should have a substantial staff under his own control. This reform was introduced in February 1982.

The Falklands conflict On 2 April 1982 Argentine forces invaded the Falkland Islands and overwhelmed the small British garrison. Lewin at that time was in New Zealand on a planned official visit. He had known of some Argentine movements for the previous ten days, but all advice had been that he should proceed with his programme. He returned by air to the United Kingdom and within hours attended the first meeting of the 'war cabinet', the OD(SA) committee. At that meeting he presented ministers with an objective, not for the military alone but for the government: 'to bring about the withdrawal of Argentine forces from the Falkland Islands, and the re-establishment of British administration there, as quickly as possible'. It was adopted there and then, and was arguably Lewin's most important single contribution to the south Atlantic campaign.

During the remainder of the seventy days of the south Atlantic operations Lewin's achievements added up to a masterpiece of sound judgement, control, persuasion, and endurance. With his background of war experience he reminded ministers that losses were to be expected, but reassured them with his overall confidence of success. He maintained the closest touch with commanders afloat, in the field, and at headquarters, with the chiefs of staff, with senior officials, and with American counterparts, whose co-operation was essential. He paid great attention to the rules of engagement under which British forces operated, and initiated their relaxation by the prime minister on 2 May in order that the Argentine cruiser *General Belgrano* could be attacked and sunk, an action he unwaveringly defended in subsequent years. The choice of San Carlos Water for the British landings had his full approval and his presentation of the plan to OD(SA) was masterly. After the landings on 21 May there was hard fighting both at sea and ashore, with some reverses, including six ships sunk and a total of 255 British servicemen killed, but the operation was crowned with success when the Argentine forces surrendered on 14 June. Argentine casualties included about 750 killed and 13,000 taken prisoner.

Retirement Lewin was honoured with the Order of the Garter and a life peerage, as Baron Lewin of Greenwich. He left the office of chief of defence staff in October 1982 and settled at Carousel, Lower Ufford, near Woodbridge in Suffolk. He remained active in public life, most particularly as chairman of trustees of the National Maritime Museum from 1987 to 1995. There he was responsible for many reforms and far-reaching developments. He spoke but seldom in the House of Lords: his most important speech was a succinct description on 13 June 1984 of the 1982 higher defence reorganization, which had been so fully vindicated during the Falklands campaign. He also wrote and spoke widely on naval and defence matters, and on naval history. He became ill with cancer in the autumn of 1998 and died at home at Carousel on 22 January 1999. He was survived by his wife and their three children.

Lewin was for most who knew him the outstanding naval officer of his generation. A vibrant personality combined with great energy, warm humanity, a phenomenal memory, and impeccable judgement to make a character to whom all could respond and whom no one wanted to let down. He himself wished to be remembered as one who had achieved 'a real improvement of attitude and mutual respect between officer and rating' (Hill, 395); this, though undoubtedly true and at the core of his life of service, was only one of his many achievements in the defence and naval fields. RICHARD HILL

Sources R. Hill, *Lewin of Greenwich* (2000) • NMM, Lewin MSS • *The Times* (25 Jan 1999) • *Daily Telegraph* (25 Jan 1999) • *The Guardian* (25 Jan 1999) • *The Independent* (25 Jan 1999) • *WWW* • Burke, *Peerage* • private information (2004) • personal knowledge (2004) • d. cert.
Archives NMM, MSS
Likenesses photograph, 1973, repro. in *Daily Telegraph* • photograph, 1982, repro. in *The Independent* • F. Belsky, sculpture, 1983, NPG [*see illus.*] • M. Noakes, oils (in garter robes), Britannia Royal Naval College, Dartmouth • Wonnacott, portrait • photographs, repro. in *The Times*
Wealth at death under £200,000—gross; under £100,000—net: probate, 1999, *CGPLA Eng. & Wales*

Lewin, Thomas (1805–1877), legal writer and antiquary, was born on 19 April 1805, the fifth son of Spencer James Lewin, vicar of Ifield, Sussex, and rector of Crawley, in the same county. In March 1816 he went to Merchant Taylors' School, London, and from there to Oxford, matriculating from Worcester College on 29 November 1823. He transferred to Trinity College on obtaining a scholarship there in 1825, and took a first class in classical honours in 1827, graduating BA in 1828, and MA in 1831. On leaving Oxford he was admitted at Lincoln's Inn, and was called to the bar in 1833. His sound judgement and solid acquirements gradually secured for him an ample chancery practice. In 1852 Lord St Leonards (then lord chancellor), whom Lewin had assisted in framing measures of law reform, appointed him a conveyancing counsel to the court of chancery. He retained the post until his death.

Lewin's famous *Practical Treatise on the Law of Trusts and Trustees*, first published in 1837, became the standard treatise on the law of trusts and reached a fifteenth edition in 1950. Another work, *The Life and Epistles of St Paul* (1851), occupied him for forty years, during which he more than once visited all the principal scenes to which it relates. The later editions have abundant historical illustrations, many of them from sketches of his own.

Lewin was an active member of the Society of Antiquaries, of which he became a fellow on 19 March 1863. At the suggestion of the president, Lord Stanhope, the Admiralty in 1862 made a special series of tidal observations with a view to settling the place of Caesar's landing in Britain. Lewin believed it to be Hythe, a view strongly contested by Edward Cardwell, who claimed the distinction for Deal. In his paper 'Further observations on the landing of Caesar' in *Archaeologia* (39, 309–14), Lewin rightly said that the Admiralty favoured Hythe. He contributed several other papers to *Archaeologia* on issues including the origins of London and the topography of Jerusalem. He wrote several other works, on the New Testament and on classical subjects, particularly Roman Britain and Jerusalem.

Lewin married late in life. He died at his home, 6 Queen's Gate Place, South Kensington, London, on 5 January 1877, and was survived by his wife, Mary Emily.

GORDON GOODWIN, *rev.* CATHERINE PEASE-WATKIN

Sources C. J. Robinson, ed., *A register of the scholars admitted into Merchant Taylors' School, from AD 1562 to 1874*, 2 (1883), 202 • Foster, *Alum. Oxon.* • *Law Magazine*, 4th ser., 2 (1876–7), 272–3 • *Proceedings of the Society of Antiquaries of London*, 2nd ser., 7 (1876–8), 201–3 • Holdsworth, *Eng. law*, vol. 15 • *CGPLA Eng. & Wales* (1877)
Archives S. Antiquaries, Lond., corresp. and papers
Wealth at death under £60,000: probate, 30 Jan 1877, *CGPLA Eng. & Wales*

Lewin, William (*d.* 1598), ecclesiastical lawyer, was one of five known children of Edmund Lewin (son of John, of Cuffley, Hertfordshire), and his wife, Juliana, daughter of William Goche, feodary of Essex. He matriculated at Cambridge as a pensioner of Christ's College in November 1559, graduated BA in March 1562, and commenced MA in 1565. He was elected fellow of Christ's before midsummer 1562; he was appointed proctor in September 1568 and, on 10 July 1570, public orator (he resigned the following year).

When Elizabeth I visited Cambridge in 1564, Lewin

addressed her in Latin on behalf of the bachelors. His cousins Elizabeth and Thomas Lewin had served Elizabeth when princess, the former as a nurse. But Lewin's advancement was most directly assisted by William Cecil, chancellor of the university. In 1567 Lewin wrote to Cecil in Latin praising him for his patronage of learning and gratefully acknowledging his readiness to allow the members of the university access to him. Cecil possibly made Lewin tutor to his daughter Anne, whom Lewin later praised warmly to her father, writing that the goodness of her wit and nature derived from him. The earl of Oxford, who married her in 1571, made Lewin receiver of his revenues. Anne, when countess of Oxford, asked Burghley to recommend Lewin to the queen as translator of Jewel's works into Latin. In 1576, as Burghley's intermediary, Lewin corresponded with Johann Sturm of Strasbourg, an agent for the queen.

The College of Advocates admitted Lewin on 6 June 1572 at Lord Burghley's request, even though he was still only a student of civil law. After taking his LLD in 1576, Lewin was appointed on 16 March dean of the arches by Archbishop Grindal, under whom he held this office until 1583, and was admitted an advocate in May. He also became a judge of the prerogative court of Canterbury, commissary of the faculties, and, by November 1580, chancellor of Rochester diocese. He was reputed to be an honest and careful judge. In his will, after leaving legacies to the advocates and proctors of the arches, he asked them to impute any seeming strictness towards them on his part to his desire that cases might procced 'in a just orderlie and speedie course' (PRO, PROB 11/91, fol. 5*v*). In 1582 he was incorporated DCL at Oxford, and in 1584 he was in a commission to visit the diocese of St Asaph. As a member of the high commission for ecclesiastical causes he took part in some of its most controversial work. He was present when Robert Cawdry was deprived of his orders on 14 May 1590. When Thomas Cartwright was summoned before the commission in May 1591 for his refusal to take the *ex officio* oath (to which Cawdry had also objected) Lewin emphasized that it had been authorized by the crown. He was also involved in the investigation of the Marprelate tracts.

Lewin was returned to the parliaments of 1586, 1589, and 1593 as a member for Rochester. In 1586 he was appointed to the committees on Mary Stuart, for ensuring a learned ministry, and on the Low Countries. Speaking on the last named, on 24 February 1587, he urged that all the 'vayn charges of the land' should be bestowed on help to the Netherlands (Hartley, 2.389). He was on the subsidy committee in the parliaments of 1589 and 1593. Responding to James Morice's proposals for the reform of ecclesiastical jurisdiction *ex officio mero* on 27 February 1593, Lewin defended inquisitorial procedure, the subscription to three articles demanded by Archbishop Whitgift, and the oath to obey the ecclesiastical laws required of excommunicated persons before absolution. He was appointed to the committee on the bill against recusants (28 February), and speaking on 13 March agreed with some other members that protestant separatists should be dealt with as effectively as papists. In the parliament of 1597, Lewin was appointed a receiver of overseas petitions to the Lords.

Having obtained a dispensation to hold a benefice notwithstanding his being a layman, Lewin became a prebendary of Chichester Cathedral in 1581, and of St Asaph in 1587. By 1583 he was a justice of the quorum for Kent, where he joined with his colleague William Lambarde in some extra-sessional work. In June 1587 he was on a commission to visit hospitals and parish churches at Saltwood and Hythe in the same county. He was admitted a member of Gray's Inn, together with Richard Bancroft, on 27 February 1589, and appointed a master in chancery in January 1593.

About 1576 Lewin married Anne, daughter of Francis Goldsmith of London and Crayford, Kent, whose beauty and virtues Gabriel Harvey praised in the dedication to Lewin of his *Ciceronianus* in 1577 (Lewin wrote the Latin epistle to the printer which prefaces this work). He purchased his main estate of Otterden, in Kent, from Sir Humphrey Gilbert. His will, dated 15 November 1597, and proved on 23 May 1598, names three sons. Lewin envisaged that Thomas would succeed to most of his lands. He hoped that Justinian would study the civil law and that John, his third son and tenth child, would enter the church; he trusted Archbishop Whitgift, John's godfather, to judge his suitability for it. He named his wife, Anne, his sole executor, and Whitgift, his 'most singuler good Lord and Maister' his principal overseer, to be assisted by his friends Dr Byng, Dr Dunne, Thomas Hammon, and his brothers-in-law Anthony and Richard Luther. The will's many bequests include ones to Christ's College, to John Young, bishop of Rochester, to the earl of Oxford (Lewin's 'special good Lord'), and to Lord Burghley. He asked Whitgift to prefer his servant John Lear to a procuratorship in the arches.

Lewin died on 15 April 1598 in London and was buried at St Leonard, Shoreditch. A monument erected at Otterden in accordance with his will includes recumbent effigies of him and his wife, together with verses praising his skill and beneficence as a judge. His widow died before 31 March 1604. Of his three known daughters, Anne (*d.* 1645) married Sir Lawrence Washington (1579–1643), of Garsden, Wiltshire, registrar of the court of chancery; Catherine, James Paget of Northamptonshire; and Judith (*d.* 1625), in 1607, Sir John Isham, bt, of Lamport, near Northampton. Justinian, Lewin's second son and eventual heir, born in 1586, was admitted of Gray's Inn on 8 February 1603, became gentleman of the privy chamber to James I, and was knighted on 14 March 1604. He died on 28 June 1620. By his marriage on 14 May 1607 to Elizabeth, daughter of Arthur Capel of Little Hadham, Hertfordshire, he had an only daughter, Elizabeth. His widow married, second, on 18 March 1623, Ralph, Lord Hopton.

Ralph Houlbrooke

Sources will, PRO, PROB 11/91, sig. 1 • R. Hovenden, ed., *The visitation of Kent, taken in the years 1619–1621*, Harleian Society, 42 (1898) • HoP, *Commons, 1558–1603* • T. E. Hartley, ed., *Proceedings in the parliaments of Elizabeth I*, 3 vols. (1981–95) • J. Peile, *Biographical register of*

Christ's College, 1505–1905, and of the earlier foundation, God's House, 1448–1505, ed. [J. A. Venn], 1 (1910) • G. D. Squibb, *Doctors' Commons: a history of the College of Advocates and Doctors of Law* (1977) • register of Edmund Grindal, LPL • C. Read, 'William Lambarde's "Ephemeris", 1580–1588', *Huntington Library Quarterly*, 15 (1951–2), 123–58 • monument to William Lewin, Otterden church, Kent

Likenesses marble effigy on monument, Otterden church, Kent

Wealth at death wealthy; lands in Kent (specified in Otterden, Upchurch, and Iwade), incl. arable ground, meadow, woods, and marshes; lease of an estate at Holiwell(?) in Middlesex; tenement in Walbrook in the City of London; ready money and credits; a coach, coach horses, cattle, geldings, corn, and furniture; provided that each of his daughters who married with the advice and approval of his overseers, should receive 1000 marks (£666 13*s.* 4*d.*) on (or within six months of) day of marriage; eldest son was to have £200 at age of twenty-one to meet charges which would then 'grow upon him'; wife was to receive annuity of 400 marks on his eldest surviving son reaching his majority (provided she remained a widow), and was given the lease of Holiwell outright; provision for quite a substantial funeral and many other legacies: will, PRO, PROB 11/91, fols. 1–6

Lewin, William (1747–1795), naturalist and artist, was born on 10 February 1747, the son of William Lewin, a rate mariner, and his wife, Anne. He was baptized on 6 July 1748 at St Dunstan and All Saints, Stepney, where he grew up. Probably in 1768 or 1769, he married Susanna, with whom he had at least four sons and two daughters. Two sons were baptized at St Dunstan's in Stepney: John William (15 April 1770) and James (February 1776). John William *Lewin (1770–1819) became an artist and settled in Australia.

Lewin early became interested in art and natural history. He appears to have been a student of the painter Edward Hodgson (1719–1794) who exhibited work at the Free Society of Artists from 1763 to 1783; in 1764 Hodgson showed two drawings by Lewin. In 1770 Lewin was residing in the parish of Poplar. By 1776 he had moved to Mile End Old Town in London and was described as a pattern drawer. By 1783 Lewin was describing himself as a 'painter of Mile End Old Town' (Jackson, 158). In the previous year, he had exhibited work at the Free Society of Artists. His natural history paintings provided him with income, with some additional funding coming from book illustrating. Lewin and his family stayed in Mile End Old Town until 1786, when his daughter Sophia was baptized at St Dunstan's (another daughter, Ann, had been baptized there in 1783). Towards the end of the 1780s, Lewin moved to Darenth in Kent, also the home county of his friend the ornithologist John Latham (1740–1837). In 1790 Lewin found the water pipit in the Kent marshes, and was one of the first naturalists to mark it as a British bird.

In the late 1780s, after more than twenty years of study and preparation, Lewin began publishing *The Birds of Great Britain, with their eggs, accurately figured* (7 vols., 1789–94). It was dedicated to Latham, from whom, as well as from Parkinson and Thomas Pennant, Lewin had received material assistance. Subscribers for the first edition were limited to sixty, as Lewin painted every illustration by hand himself. His work featured plates of eggs from the collection of his patron the dowager duchess of Portland, and was probably the first such attempt to illustrate the eggs of British avifauna. In the descriptions of birds Lewin was helped by his sons. The second edition of the work, *The birds of Great Britain, systematically arranged, accurately figured, and painted from nature, with descriptions (in English and French), including the natural history of each bird; from observations the result of more than twenty years application to the subject, in the field of nature, … the figures engraved from the subjects themselves by the author and painted under his immediate direction*, appeared in eight volumes from 1795 to 1801. The drawings, 20,000 in all, included 267 plates. Lewin engraved plates for volumes one to three himself, while plates in volumes four to eight were contributed by his sons, signed as Thomas, Thomas William, and John William. (It was Lewin's sons who completed this work after his death.)

Lewin was elected a fellow of the Linnean Society on 20 December 1791. His membership was supported by his friend John Latham and the entomologists Thomas Marsham (secretary of the Linnean Society) and John Beckwith. He was still residing at Darenth in 1792, but by 1794 was living at Hoxton in London. Lewin issued a paper in 1793 on some rare British insects in the Linnean Society's *Transactions*, a work entitled *The Papilios of Great Britain* (1795), and a first volume only of *The insects of Great Britain: systematically arranged, accurately engraved, and painted from nature* (1795), with forty-six coloured plates. The plates in this latter work were engraved by Lewin, and the descriptions written in both French and English.

Lewin died at the end of 1795. His will was proved on 30 December 1795; his request 'to be buried in a decent manner in the parish burial ground of Edmonton or Tottenham' (Jackson, 159), was carried out by his widow, Susanna, who had him buried at Edmonton on 10 December 1795. Much material went to the McGill University Library: some 146 sketches of eggs by Lewin and many drawings by his sons. YOLANDA FOOTE

Sources L. Agassiz, *Bibliographia zoologiae et geologiae: a general catalogue of all books, tracts, and memoirs on zoology and geology*, ed. H. Strickland and W. Jardine, 4 vols. (1848–54), vol. 3, p. 465 • W. T. Lowndes, *The bibliographer's manual of English literature*, 4 vols. (1834) • private information (1892) [J. L. Harting] • C. E. Jackson, *Bird etchings: the illustrators and their books, 1655–1855* (1985) • A. Wheeler and A. Thompson, 'John William Lewin's watercolour and line drawings in the Linnean Society of London archives', *Archives of Natural History*, 23 (1996), 369–84

Archives CUL • McGill University Library

Lewins, Edward John (1756–1828), Irish nationalist, was born in Dublin, but nothing more is known of his early life and background. He was educated at a seminary in France, but returned to Ireland, where he practised as an attorney in Dublin. He was active in the campaigns for Catholic relief in Ireland during the early 1790s and was a member of the Catholic Convention in December 1792. In the same year he joined the Dublin Society of United Irishmen, and was a prominent radical within the organization as it moved in a more militant direction. In 1794 he introduced William Jackson, a French agent, to the jailed United Irish leader Archibald Hamilton Rowan.

By February 1797 Lewins was a member of the United Irish executive, which chose him as its agent to the French government, to continue negotiations for a French invasion force to support a United Irish insurrection. He arrived in Hamburg in late March 1797, where, using the pseudonym James Thomson, he held discussions with the French minister Reinhard, who was initially suspicious of Lewins's credentials. He later met the French general Lazare Hoche at Kassel in May 1797. He worked closely with the United Irish agent in Paris, Theobald Wolfe Tone, who had arrived from America the previous year. The pair travelled to the Netherlands, where preparations were under way for a Dutch-based attack on Ireland, but this did not come to fruition. Lewins and Tone returned to Paris, where they continued to work for French assistance for a projected United Irish rising. The hopes both men placed in Hoche were shattered by his death in September 1797. Lewins continued to work patiently for French military assistance throughout 1797–8. However, he gradually became increasingly removed from the reality of the situation in Ireland. Both he and Tone were openly confronted by other Irish radicals in Paris, centring on James Napper Tandy, in autumn 1797. Lewins and Tone appealed for immediate French assistance after the outbreak of an Irish rising in May 1798, but the result was small unsatisfactory expeditions.

After the departure of Tone and Tandy, the Directory increasingly placed its sole confidence in Lewins as the official spokesman of the United Irishmen in Paris. He continued to negotiate on the terms of his original brief throughout 1799, despite his lack of contact with United Irish leaders at home. Moreover he failed to recognize the severity of an increasing refugee crisis, as former Irish radicals escaped to France, and only belatedly negotiated financial relief for them. This opened another rift between Lewins and the United Irish committee in Paris, which submitted formal complaints about him in 1799 and 1800. Lewins gradually withdrew from his diplomatic role after about 1801, and after 1803 he had removed himself from radical Irish circles in Paris. Despite this he continued sometimes to help Irish exiles who were in difficult circumstances. His property in Ireland was confiscated under the terms of the Banishment Act, so he continued to reside in Paris as a naturalized Frenchman.

During the reign of Charles X Lewins was appointed inspector of studies at the University of Paris through the influence of his friend the abbé de Fraysinous, bishop of Hermopolis and minister of public instruction. Miles Byrne visited him two days before his death and found him 'reading Wolfe Tone's memoirs, in his sick bed, and repeating to me what a true Irishman Tone was!' (*Memoirs of Miles Byrne*, 3.21). Lewins died in Paris on 11 February 1828. His funeral was conducted by Fraysinous, and attended by members of the University of Paris and Irish exiles in the city. He was buried at Père Lachaise cemetery. He was almost certainly married, and his two known sons, Laurence and Hippolite, also settled in France.

LIAM CHAMBERS

Sources M. Elliott, *Partners in revolution: the United Irishmen and France* (1982) • W. T. W. Tone, *Life of Theobald Wolfe Tone*, ed. T. Bartlett (1998) • *Memoirs of Miles Byrne*, ed. F. Byrne, 3 vols. (1863); repr. in 1 vol. (1972) [repr. in 1 vol., 1972] • R. Hayes, *Biographical dictionary of Irishmen in France* (1949) • P. Weber, *On the road to rebellion: the United Irishmen and Hamburg, 1796–1803* (1998) • *DNB* • R. B. McDowell, 'The personnel of the Dublin Society of United Irishmen, 1791–4', *Irish Historical Studies*, 2 (1940–41), 12–53 • R. R. Madden, *The United Irishmen: their lives and times*, 2nd edn, 4 vols. (1857–60) • R. Hayes, *Ireland and Irishmen in the French Revolution* (1932)

Archives Archives du Ministère des Affaires Étrangères, Paris, correspondance politique, Angleterre, 590–95 • NL Ire., MS 705

Lewis. *See also* Lewes.

Lewis ab Owen. *See* Owen, Lewis (1522?–1555).

Lewis Glyn Cothi. *See* Lewys Glyn Cothi (*fl.* 1447–1489).

Lewis Morgannwg. *See* Llywelyn ap Rhisiart (*fl.* 1520–1565).

Lewis, Agnes Smith (1843–1926), Arabic and Syriac scholar and novelist, was born Agnes Smith on 16 April 1843 in Irvine, Ayrshire. She was the elder identical twin daughter of John Smith (*d.* 1866), writer to the signet of Irvine, and his wife, Margaret, *née* Dunlop (*d.* 1843). Her mother died three weeks after the twins' birth. Both parents were Scottish Presbyterians. Her father became wealthy after inheriting £200,000 from his distant cousin John Ferguson. Her life was closely linked with that of her twin sister, Margaret Dunlop *Gibson (1843–1920); almost indistinguishable, they were together nicknamed the Giblews (pronounced with a hard g). She was the dominant twin and leader. They were brought up by a nanny and governess, and were taught Latin, French, and German by their father. They attended Irvine Academy and fashionable boarding-schools in Birkenhead, Cheshire, and Kensington, London (1858–63). As a woman Smith was then unable to attend a British university, but she later received private tuition from distinguished university graduates. Her inheritance from her father left her wealthy. Later their fatherly mentor, the minister Dr William Robertson of Irvine, inspired her intellect and supported their desire to travel. The sisters' journey to Greece, Turkey, Egypt, and Palestine resulted in her travel book *Eastern Pilgrims* (1870). In the following years she acquired several languages (Greek, Spanish, Hebrew, Syriac, Arabic, and Persian). For several years she wrote novels: *Effie Maxwell* (1876), the partly autobiographical *Glenmavis* (1879), and *The Brides of Ardmore* (1880). Several journeys followed and resulted in two travel books, the pro-Greek *Glimpses of Greek Life and Scenery* (1884), and *Through Cyprus* (1887), and the translation of a Greek handbook *The Monuments of Athens* (1884) by P. G. Kastromenos. In 1883 her sister married James Young Gibson; he died suddenly on 2 October 1886. On 12 December 1887 Agnes Smith married the Revd Samuel Savage *Lewis (1836–1891), classicist, antiquary, and fellow and librarian of Corpus Christi College, Cambridge; they had no children. After his sudden death (31 March 1891) she published the *Life of the Rev. Samuel Savage Lewis* (1892). After their husbands' deaths she and her sister lived and travelled together. Their home was her large Gothic revival house, built in 1890, Castle-brae in Chesterton Lane, Cambridge. There they studied and entertained; at their garden parties a piper played on the lawn. Always loyal to Presbyterianism, they attended St Columba's

Church and assisted in its Sunday school and other activities. Forceful, they were considered eccentric. They dressed expensively if somewhat frumpishly, and wore white stockings. They had one of the first cars in Cambridge.

Agnes Smith Lewis's scholarly career began late. Persuaded by Dr James Rendel Harris, from 1892 until 1906 she and her sister made several journeys (1892, 1893, 1895, 1897, 1901, 1906) to Cairo, the monastery of St Catherine at Mount Sinai (where Harris and Tischendorf had discovered important manuscripts), the Coptic convent of St Mary Deipara at Deir al-Suriani in the Wadi al-Natrun, Egypt, and Palestine for research. Already in 1898 her *In the Shadow of Sinai: a Story of Travel and Research from 1895 to 1897* appeared. Her proficiency in modern Greek enabled her to gain permission to enter the Greek Orthodox monastery of St Catherine and to be on excellent terms with the monks. The first and second trip to St Catherine were the most successful. It was then that she discovered and photographed part of the Syriac Codex Sinaiticus (gospel palimpsest manuscript, fifth century AD), the second known manuscript of the Old Syriac version beside the incomplete 'Curetonianus' published by William Cureton (1858); this new discovery resulted in *A Translation of the Four Gospels from the Syriac of the Sinai Palimpsest* (1894), *The Old Syriac Gospels, or, Evangelion da-Mepharreshê* (1910), and the more general *Light on the Four Gospels from the Sinai Palimpsest* (1913). Her two letters dealing with the discovery of the gospel palimpsest and addressed to the editor of *The Times* were printed privately as *Two Unpublished Letters* (1893). During her succeeding trips to St Catherine she prepared manuscript descriptions which were published in *Catalogue of the Syriac MSS in the Convent of S. Catherine on Mount Sinai* (1894). She also copied three lectionaries of the gospels written in Christian Palestinian Aramaic (Palestinian Syriac) and published them together with another version from the Vatican as *The Palestinian Syriac Lectionary of the Gospels* (1899). Further Syriac text editions by her are *Select Narratives of Holy Women* (1900), *Apocrypha Syriaca: the protevangelium Jacobi and transitus Mariae* (1902), and *Acta mythologica apostolorum* (1904). Considered an authority on Syriac, she was asked to contribute her translation of the Syriac version of Ahikar which appeared as *The Story of Ahikar* (1898).

At the antiquities market in Cairo, Agnes Smith Lewis purchased manuscripts including unique palimpsests written in Christian Palestinian Aramaic (now in Westminster College, Cambridge). These not very legible palimpsests were edited and published as *A Palestinian Syriac Lectionary* (1897), the only non-palimpsest manuscript, *Codex climaci rescriptus* (1909), and *The Forty Martyrs of the Sinai Desert and the Story of Eulogios* (1912). Less successful was her edition, together with her sister, of palimpsest fragments from the Cairo genizah overwritten in Hebrew and Galilean Aramaic which were entrusted to her by S. Schechter, and four fragmentary pieces from their private collection. The fragments appeared in *Palestinian Syriac Texts from Palimpsest Fragments in the Taylor–Schechter Collection* (1900). An addition was published two years later as *An Appendix of Palestinian Syriac Texts*. One spectacular discovery among the sisters' acquisitions from the Cairo genizah in 1896 was a fragment in Hebrew of Jesus Ben Sira (Ecclesiasticus), a Jewish text composed in Hebrew about 180 BC, but only known until then from the Greek translation in the Septuagint. Her purchases in Cairo subsequently led Schechter to go to the Cairo genizah, once the Ben Sira fragment (39: 15–40: 8) had been identified. She and Alphonse Mingana edited the controversial *Leaves from Three Ancient Qurans, Possibly pre-Othomanic* (1914).

Agnes Smith Lewis's scholarly achievements were honoured with the Triennial gold medal of the Royal Asiatic Society—the blue riband of oriental research—in 1915, presented by Austen Chamberlain, secretary of state for India. She received honorary doctorates from Halle an der Saale (PhD, 1899), St Andrews (honorary DD, 1901), Heidelberg (honorary DD, 1904), and Dublin (LittD, 1911). She and her sister gave funds for the site and towards the buildings of the Presbyterian theological college, Westminster College, Cambridge. In May 1897 they laid the foundation stone. They also purchased the library of Eberhard Nestle, a renowned German New Testament scholar, containing valuable editions (later sold) for the college. In her last years she was entirely incapacitated by paralysis. Her sister died on 11 January 1920, and she died on 29 March 1926 at her home, Castle-brae, Chesterton Lane, Cambridge. She was buried in Cambridge. She left the residue of her estate to the English Presbyterian church, mainly for Westminster College. Castle-brae became a hostel for Clare College students. CHRISTA MÜLLER-KESSLER

Sources A. W. Price, 'The ladies of Castlebrae', *annual lecture to the Presbyterian Historical Society* (Oct 1964), 1–23 · A. Whigham Price, *The ladies of Castlebrae* (1985) · A. S. Lewis, *A translation of the four gospels from the Syriac of the Sinai palimpsest* (1894) · A. S. Lewis and M. D. Gibson, eds., *The Palestinian Syriac lectionary of the gospels* (1899) · A. S. Lewis, *Catalogue of the Syriac MSS in the convent of St Catherine on Mount Sinai* (1894) · A. S. Lewis and M. D. Gibson, eds., *A Palestinian Syriac lectionary* (1897) · A. Smith Lewis, *In the shadow of Sinai: a story of travel and research from 1895 to 1897* (1898) · A. S. Lewis, *Codex climaci rescriptus* (1909) · A. S. Lewis, *The forty martyrs of the Sinai desert and the story of Eulogios* (1912) · A. S. Lewis and M. D. Gibson, eds., *Palestinian Syriac texts from palimpsest fragments in the Taylor–Schechter collection* (1900) · P. E. Kahle, *The Cairo Geniza* (1947) · S. C. Reif, 'Memories of a momentous find', *Geniza fragments* (1996), 31

Archives Bodl. Oxf., old photographs and lantern slides · Westminster College, Cambridge, Cheshunt Foundation, papers and books

Likenesses J. P., oils, 1920, Westminster College, Cambridge · photograph, repro. in Price, *The ladies of Castlebrae* (1985), following p. 114 · photographs, Westminster College, Cambridge

Lewis [*née* Brereton], **Alethea** [*pseud.* Eugenia de Acton] (**1749–1827**), novelist, was born on 19 December 1749, at Acton, near Nantwich, Cheshire, the elder surviving child of the Revd James Brereton (*d.* 1787), and his first wife, whose first name was also Alethea (1727/8–1752). After her mother's death (when she was a little over two years of age) she was sent to live in Suffolk with her maternal grandfather, Samuel Kilderbee, a linen draper at Framlingham. Her father remarried and had another family; at his death in 1787 he left her 5 guineas, but his younger daughters £100 each.

Alethea attended a day school, and in her teens frequented reading circles and began to write, as a pastime and to earn money. As her works show, she read omnivorously. She introduced her close friend Sarah Elmy to George Crabbe, and the couple married; her own engagement to Crabbe's friend William Springal Levett (1752/3–1774) ended with Levett's death in October 1774. She corresponded with Crabbe for several years under the name of Stella; they resumed writing to each other on Sarah Crabbe's death.

On 19 June 1788 Alethea Brereton married Augustus Towle Lewis (*d.* 1819), a surgeon who had served a sentence of transportation. She reputedly met him on a stagecoach, and married him without knowing of his criminal record. He seems, however, to have been a good husband. Two months later they emigrated to Philadelphia; but they stayed in America only about a year. On their return they lived briefly in Lancashire, then settled at Preston Hill, Penkridge, Staffordshire, where Augustus Lewis practised surgery and farmed. In 1794 she published her first novel, *Vicissitudes in Genteel Life*. She went on to write five more books of which the attribution is unquestionable, while the authorship of five more remains in dispute.

Two doubtful novels, anonymous like Lewis's first, appeared from the Minerva Press in 1795 and 1797. A later title-page claim links them with other novels which may be hers; but they are not mentioned in her next undoubted work. This was *The Microcosm* (1801), 'by the author of Vicissitudes in Genteel Life', published by subscription and dedicated to her local member of parliament. Its critical preface claims the novel form as a vehicle for Christian instruction, and situates the author in a tradition of fiction reaching back through Fielding, Richardson, Fénelon, and Cervantes to Virgil.

In 1803 Alethea Lewis published with Minerva a moral work entitled *Essays on the Art of being Happy*. This launched the pseudonym by which she is often known: Eugenia de Acton, a humorous use of her birthplace. (She enjoyed playing with names: she gave three characters in *Vicissitudes* her own baptismal name, maiden name, and surname respectively.) The pseudonym recurs on *A Tale without a Title: Give it what you Please* (1804), *The Nuns of the Desert, or, The Woodland Witches* (1805), and *The Deserted Daughter* (1810).

The alternative claimant of the remaining doubtful works (*Things by their Right Names*, 1812, *Rhoda*, 1816, and *Isabella*, 1823) is Frances Margaretta Jacson, whose authorship was asserted both by her own family and by Maria Edgeworth. (Edgeworth mentions her as author of *Rhoda*; title-pages link *Rhoda* to the other novels claimed for both Jacson and Lewis.) Similarities of purpose and technique between the two groups are striking, but cannot be regarded as conclusive. Jane Austen's *Emma* was compared unfavourably with *Rhoda* by several readers at the time.

Whether or not the disputed titles are credited to Alethea Lewis, she is an interesting, even quirky writer. Her central plot lines (suffering virtue eventually rewarded) and her earnest Christian intent are conventional enough; but with these qualities go self-conscious and critical addresses to the reader, displays of erudition, use of incidents from her own life, play with titles and genres, and a vein of the fantastical. Alethea Lewis died in 1827, and was buried on 12 November 1827 in Penkridge, Staffordshire. ISOBEL GRUNDY

Sources N. Blackburne, *The restless ocean: the story of George Crabbe, the Aldeburgh poet, 1754–1832* (1972) • *George Crabbe: The complete poetical works*, ed. N. Dalrymple-Champneys and A. Pollard, 3 vols. (1988) • G. Crabbe, *Selected letters and journals*, ed. T. C. Faulkner and R. L. Blair (1985) • [A. Lewis], *Essays on the art of being happy* (1803) • E. P. Shippen, *Eugenia de Acton (1749–1827)* (1945) • A. B. Shteir, 'Botanical dialogues: Maria Jacson and women's popular science writing in England', *Eighteenth-Century Studies*, 23 (1989–90), 301–17 • D. Gilson, 'Jane Austen and *Rhoda*', *Persuasions*, 20 (1998), 21–30
Archives BL, corresp. with Crabbe, Egerton MS 3709A • Bodl. Oxf., corresp. with Crabbe

Lewis, Alun (1915–1944), poet and short-story writer, was born on 1 July 1915 in Cwmaman, Glamorgan, the eldest in the family of three sons and one daughter of Thomas John Lewis (1885–1964), a schoolmaster, and his wife, Gwladys Elizabeth (1884–1979), teacher, daughter of Melchizedec Evans, a Unitarian minister. He grew up in a depressed community and would never forget what he saw there:

> I used to watch the wheel of the pit spin round year after year, after school and Saturdays and Sundays; and then from 1926 on I watched it not turning at all, and I can't ever get that wheel out of my mind. (*Selected Poetry*, 9)

From Glynhafod elementary school, Aberdâr, he won a scholarship to Cowbridge grammar school, Glamorgan, a tough boarding establishment. He was unhappy there but, determined not to slip back into the pits where his grandfather had wielded a pick, worked hard and won scholarships both to Jesus College, Oxford, and the University College of Aberystwyth. Having to choose between being 'poor in Oxford or comfortable in Aber.', he chose Aberystwyth, where he worked on the university magazine, published his first poems and stories, and dabbled in left-wing politics. He left Aberystwyth in 1935 with a first-class degree in history, for Manchester, from which he returned a year later, with an MA, to take a teacher-training course at Aberystwyth.

In 1938 Lewis took a job in a Welsh secondary school, but could see the shadow of war approaching and worried over the problem of pacifism. In a letter to Richard Mills dated 30 May 1939 he wrote:

> I have a deep sort of fatalist feeling that I'll go. Partly because I want to experience life in as many phases as I'm capable of—i.e. I'm more a writer than a moralist, I suppose. But … I'm not going to kill. Be killed perhaps, instead. (*Selected Poetry*, 18)

He joined up in the spring of 1940 and spent the next two years moving from camp to camp around England with the Royal Engineers. During this period and against this background he wrote the poems of *Raiders Dawn* and the short stories of *The Last Inspection*, both published in 1942. Poems and stories alike reveal a compassionate concern for the victims of oppression and tyranny: Welsh miners, private soldiers, women, and children. Lewis never forgot that the military chain of command replicates the social scale, and the issues of the class war meant more to him than those of the fighting war.

In July 1941 Lewis married Gweno Ellis, a sailor's daughter, and that October was commissioned as a reluctant second lieutenant in the South Wales Borderers. A year later, taking leave of his wife with some piercing poems of separation, he set sail for India. There, troubled by the poverty of the peasants and his own involuntary role as a supporter of the imperial system, he became, as he wrote to Richard Mills on 3 March 1943, 'more and more engrossed with the single poetic theme of Life and Death' (*Selected Poetry*, 53).

On leave in the Nilgiri hills in July 1943, Lewis met—and fell instantly in love with—Freda Aykroyd, wife of a scientist eleven years her senior. Two months later, she and Lewis met in Bombay and became lovers. Their happiness was clouded, however, by the prospect of distress to their respective spouses. In November Lewis fell ill with malaria, which left him exhausted and increasingly prone to depression. His Indian writings reflect the turmoil of his emotional life in their recurrent images of sunlight and darkness. As in the work of his favourite poet, P. Edward Thomas, the darkness is often that of the forest. One of Lewis's more ambitious poems, 'The Jungle', ends with a question—

> does the will's long struggle end
> With the last kindness of a foe or friend?

—a question answered on 5 March 1944 when, hours before the start of his first patrol against the Japanese at Bawli Bazar on the north Burma coast, he did himself that kindness with a shot from his own revolver; his body was buried the same day in Bawli north military cemetery. He had no children. JON STALLWORTHY

Sources A. Lewis, *Ha! Ha! among the trumpets: poems in transit* (1945) • A. Lewis, *Letters from India* (1946) • A. Lewis, *In the green tree* (1948) • *Alun Lewis: selected poetry and prose*, ed. I. Hamilton (1966) • *Alun Lewis: a miscellany of his writings*, ed. J. Pikoulis (1982) • J. Pikoulis, *Alun Lewis: a life* (1984)

Archives NL Wales, corresp., literary MSS, and papers • NL Wales, typescript drafts of writings | NL Wales, letters to Brenda Chamberlain • NL Wales, letters to John Petts

Likenesses J. Petts, two engravings, repro. in Pikoulis, *Alun Lewis*

Wealth at death £390 19s. 7d.: probate, 12 Dec 1944, *CGPLA Eng. & Wales*

Lewis, Amelia. *See* Freund, Amelia Louisa (*b*. 1824/5, *d*. in or after 1881).

Lewis, Andrew (1720–1781), revolutionary army officer, was born on 9 October 1720 in co. Donegal, Ireland, the third of six children of John Lewis (1678–1762), farmer, and Margaret (1693–1773), daughter of William Lynn and his wife, Margaret. His parents went to America in 1732 and settled in Augusta county, Virginia. He grew up in frontier conditions, married Elizabeth Givens some time between 1744 and 1749, and moved to the upper Roanoke River near present-day Salem, Virginia. They had six children.

Lewis was agent and surveyor for a land company in 1745. Over the years he accumulated thousands of acres in Augusta and Botetourt counties. A prominent citizen and a physically imposing man, he served as county lieutenant of Augusta, and justice of the peace, county court member, coroner, legislative representative, and militia leader of Botetourt. In 1754 he was serving as an officer under George Washington when Washington surrendered to the French at Fort Necessity. A year later, as a colonel, he took part in Braddock's expedition but he was not present at the ambush near Fort Duquesne. In 1756 he commanded the Sandy Creek expedition that collapsed when food supplies ran out. He was captured with Major James Grant on 14 September 1758 in western Pennsylvania and spent a year as a guest of the French in Montreal. Developing a reputation as an authoritarian and status-conscious officer, he was unpopular with many militiamen.

In 1764 Lewis led a Virginia militia force against Indians on the frontier, and four years later he participated in negotiations that led to the treaty of Fort Stanwix. On 10 October 1774, during the campaign led by John Murray, fourth earl of Dunmore, governor of Virginia—a campaign known as 'Dunmore's War'—he commanded an army that decisively defeated the Shawnee Indians at Point Pleasant on the Ohio River and ended hostilities. His brother Charles was killed in the battle. Lewis served in Virginia's revolutionary conventions in 1775 and attended an Indian conference at Fort Pitt in September. On 1 March 1776 he was appointed a brigadier-general in the continental army and given command of troops at Williamsburg, Virginia. His primary concern was to defeat a loyalist army led by Dunmore, and compel that gentleman to withdraw from the province. On 9 July, after securing his base at Williamsburg, he attacked Dunmore on Gwynn's Island in the Chesapeake Bay and effected his purpose. Passed over for promotion to major-general in February 1777, he complained to General George Washington, who tried unsuccessfully to smooth down his ruffled feathers. He resigned his commission on 15 April, ostensibly because of ill health.

Lewis continued to serve in the Virginia militia and in 1778 conducted further Indian negotiations at Fort Pitt. He was appointed to the Virginia executive council and elected to the House of Delegates in 1780. He died on 25 September 1781 of 'bilious fever' (Johnson, 232–3) at the home of a Captain Talbot in Bedford county, Virginia, while returning home from a council meeting in Richmond. His body was carried to his estate of Richfield in Botetourt county, where he was buried on 27 September beside his youngest son, Charles, who had died as an infant. PAUL DAVID NELSON

Sources P. G. Johnson, *General Andrew Lewis of Roanoke and Greenbrier* (1980) • R. A. Brock, ed., *The official records of Robert Dinwiddie, lieutenant-governor of the colony of Virginia, 1751–1758*, 2 vols. (1883–4) • J. E. Selby, *The revolution in Virginia, 1775–1783* (1988) • H. M. Ward, *Major General Adam Stephen and the cause of American liberty* (1989) • P. D. Nelson, *General James Grant: Scottish soldier and royal governor of East Florida* (1993) • J. Stuart, 'Narrative by Captain John Stuart of General Andrew Lewis' expedition against the Indians in the year 1774, and the battle of Point Pleasant, Virginia', *Magazine of American History*, 1 (1877), 668–79, 740–50 • A. H. Tillotson jun., *Gentry and common folk: political culture on a Virginia frontier, 1740–1789*

(1991) • F. H. Hart, *The valley of Virginia in the American Revolution* (1942) • V. A. Lewis, *History of the battle of Point Pleasant* (1909) • R. D. Stoner, *A seed-bed of the republic: a study of the pioneers in the upper (southern) valley of Virginia* (1962) • A. H. Tillotson, 'Lewis, Andrew', *ANB*

Likenesses silhouette, Virginia State Library, Richmond; repro. in Johnson, *General Andrew Lewis*

Wealth at death substantial, especially in land (perhaps 3000 acres): Tillotson, 'Lewis, Andrew'

Lewis, Angelo John [*pseud.* Professor Hoffmann] (**1839–1919**), journalist and writer on magic, was born on 23 July 1839 at Crescent Place, St Pancras, London, the son of John Lewis, a coal merchant, and his wife, Victorie Josephine, *née* Calkin. He was educated at North London Collegiate School and Wadham College, Oxford, where he took a BA and an MA. He then went on to study law, and in 1861 was called to the bar at Lincoln's Inn, where he practised until 1876. He married Mary Ann Avery, the daughter of Joseph Avery, of Stollarks Crescent, St Pancras, on 12 May 1864 at St Mark's Church in the same parish; they had one daughter, Maud.

During his undergraduate years at Oxford, Lewis became interested in magic and witnessed the performances of the famous magician John Henry Anderson, the 'Great Wizard of the North'. Although he did little to develop this interest while at Oxford, his enthusiasm revived during the 1860s, apparently after seeing the 'very clever performance of a street conjurer' (Reynolds, vi). He then began to collect books and apparatus relating to magic and gave amateur performances. In 1876, the year in which he retired from the law, he published *Modern Magic* under the *nom de plume* of Professor Hoffmann. The book became a *cause célèbre* since it revealed closely guarded secrets of the conjuror's profession that had been handed down for generations, usually by word of mouth. In his introductory chapter, Lewis stated that 'there is a vast difference between telling how a trick is done and teaching how to do it' (p. vii), a comment which challenged previous approaches to teaching magic, excepting, of course, those techniques revealed by Jean Eugène Robert-Houdin's *Comment on devient sorcier: les secrets de la prestidigitation* (1878?), a volume which Professor Hoffmann went on to translate and publish in 1878. *Modern Magic* sparked further controversy for more general reasons relating to the precarious foundation upon which conjuring rested. *The Athenaeum* was moved to 'wonder whether this … sleight-of-hand is only valuable to conjurers and pickpockets!' (13 Oct 1877, 465). Regardless of the criticism, Professor Hoffmann wrote on 14 July 1877 to his uncle that 'the book has had the good fortune to be rather a hit'. In its first edition it sold 2000 copies, at the price of 7*s.* 6*d.*, 'in a little over six weeks' (Stott, 136). Raymond Toole Stott observed that Hoffmann's influence was such that 'the quantity and quality of trick and illusion has been most marked and conjurers have risen quickly in the estimation of the thinking portion of the public' (Stott, 13).

Using his real name, Lewis also wrote fiction for various journals, including *Belgravia* (1884–5), *Temple Bar* (1884), *Leisure Hour* (1884), *London Society* (1885–6), the *Cornhill Magazine* (1886–7), *Living Age* (1893), and the *Saturday Review*, where he was on the staff from about 1855 to 1866. Under his pseudonym he went on to write nearly forty articles and volumes on matters relating to magic, as well as his other hobbies, card games and chess. They included *More Magic* (1890), *Puzzles Old and New* (1894), 'Indian conjuring explained' (in *Chambers's Journal*, 1901), *Later Magic* (1904), *Hoyle's Games Modernized* (1907), and *Tricks with Handkerchiefs* (1911).

In 1903 Lewis moved from London to St Leonards, and then in 1915 to Bexhill, in order to live in semi-retirement. For reasons allegedly relating to financial necessity, he sold his magic library and apparatus for £25. Despite his physical decline, which led eventually to the loss of his eyesight, he wrote *Latest Magic* (1919), reportedly at Robert-Houdin's urging. On 23 December, in the year of this book's publication, Lewis died at the age of eighty at his home, Manningford, Upper Bolebrooke Road, Bexhill. The funeral service and cremation were held at Golders Green, Middlesex, on 29 December 1919, and his ashes were interred at Highgate cemetery.

Brenda Assael

Sources C. Reynolds, introduction, in *Hoffmann's modern magic*, ed. C. Reynolds, facs. edn (1978) • R. T. Stott, *A book of English conjuring, 1581–1876* (1976) • *The Times* (27 Dec 1919) • *The Magician* (Jan 1920) • *Bexhill Chronicle* (3 Jan 1920) • *The Athenaeum* (13 Oct 1877), 465 • *WWW* • *Poole's index to periodical literature*, 2 • *Poole's index to periodical literature*, 5 • C. E. Wall, ed., *Cumulative author index for Poole's index to periodical literature, 1802–1906* (1971) • *Wellesley index* • b. cert. • m. cert. • d. cert.

Wealth at death £2766 15*s.* 3*d.*: probate, 7 Feb 1920, *CGPLA Eng. & Wales*

Lewis, Sir Anthony Carey (**1915–1983**), musician and founder of Musica Britannica, was born on 2 March 1915 in Bermuda, the youngest of the three sons (there was no daughter) of Major (later Colonel) Leonard Carey Lewis (1880–1952) of the Lincolnshire regiment and Royal Army Ordnance Corps, then chief ordnance officer in Bermuda, afterwards of Hampton, Middlesex, and his wife, Katherine Barbara (1884–1965), only daughter of Colonel Henry George Sutton, Indian army, of Hartington, Derbyshire. At an early age Lewis revealed exceptional musical gifts. He went to Salisbury Cathedral choir school, and when he was eight was admitted a chorister at St George's Chapel, Windsor, where he sang under Sir Walter Parratt, Edmund Fellowes, and Sir Walford Davies.

In 1928, after several months at the Royal Academy of Music, where his composition professor was William Alwyn, Lewis entered Wellington College as the first music scholar. He became proficient at the oboe, achieved concerto standard as a pianist, and in 1932 won the Bernard Hale organ scholarship at Peterhouse, Cambridge. He studied composition and research with Professor Edward Dent, whose teaching and example influenced him profoundly. He won the John Stewart of Rannoch scholarship in sacred music in 1933, and the award of the Leith studentship enabled him to study composition in Paris with Nadia Boulanger during the summer of 1934. A year later he graduated BA and MusB, winning the Barclay Squire prize for musical palaeography.

In September 1935 Lewis joined the music staff of the BBC under Adrian Boult. Inspired by Dent's view that the standard classics should not be allowed to obscure other music of importance, Lewis brought before the public many revivals of unfamiliar pre-nineteenth century works. He produced the long-running series *Foundations of Music* and other similar programmes, and later became responsible for all broadcast chamber music. His composition *A Choral Overture*, in which an eight-part unaccompanied choir vocalizes to varying syllables, received its première in the 1938 season of Queen's Hall Promenade Concerts.

On the outbreak of war in 1939 Lewis joined the Royal Army Ordnance Corps. He was posted as a major to the Middle East in 1942, became deputy assistant director of ordnance services in 1943, and for a short period in 1945 was assistant director, with the rank of lieutenant-colonel, displaying administrative abilities which were to benefit music and musicians greatly in the years ahead. Under the auspices of the British Council and the Entertainments National Service Association he helped to organize the provision of music for the troops, himself conducting the Cairo Symphony and other orchestras.

Lewis returned to the BBC in February 1946, undertaking the planning and supervision of all music for the new Third Programme. The introduction of the network on 29 September 1946, under George Barnes, was soon recognized as the most important development for music since the beginning of broadcasting, and Lewis's contribution to laying its foundations was not the least of his achievements.

At the end of the year Lewis left the BBC, and in 1947 he succeeded Jack Westrup as professor of music in the University of Birmingham. It was from the Peyton and Barber chair that his greatest achievement as a musicologist was undertaken: the foundation of Musica Britannica as a national collection of the classics of British music. His proposals were submitted to the council of the Royal Musical Association in 1948. An editorial committee was appointed, with Lewis as general editor (which function he fulfilled for the rest of his life) and Thurston Dart as secretary. The first three volumes were published in 1951 as part of the Festival of Britain celebrations.

It was Lewis's constant aim to see that the fruits of scholarly research should be enjoyed through practical performance. During his time at Birmingham, where his compositions included concertos for trumpet, horn, and harpsichord, he conducted many revivals of baroque music, notably Handel operas, together with premier recordings of works by composers such as Lully, Rameau, Handel, and especially Henry Purcell. He served as honorary secretary of the Purcell Society (1950–76) and artistic director of the Festival of Britain's Purcell series (1951), and was chairman of the Arts Council's music panel (1954–65), the Purcell–Handel festival (1959), and the British Council's music committee (1967–73). He was also dean of the faculty of arts at Birmingham University (1961–4) and was president of the Royal Musical Association (1963–9). While he was at Birmingham he met his future wife, Lesley Lisle Smith (*b.* 1924), a physiotherapist who sang in the university music society choir. She was the daughter of Frank Lisle Smith, bank manager, of Northland, New Zealand. They were married on 10 September 1959. There were no children.

In 1968 Lewis succeeded Sir Thomas Armstrong as principal of the Royal Academy of Music. The balance between scholarly and artistic work which characterized his life was now demonstrated by the fact that for the next fourteen years he presided over many important developments in an institution where the emphasis was on performance and composition. This phase saw the publication of his contributions to *The New Oxford History of Music*—'English church music' for volume 5, *Opera and Church Music, 1630–1750* (1975), of which he was joint editor, and 'Choral music' for volume 8, *The Age of Beethoven, 1790–1830* (1982). During this period he was president of the Incorporated Society of Musicians (1968), a director of the English National Opera (1974–8), and chairman of the Purcell Society (1976–83).

Lewis was appointed CBE in 1967 and knighted in 1972. The honorary degree of DMus was conferred on him by Birmingham University in 1970. He was an honorary member of the Royal Academy of Music (1960) and the Guildhall School of Music and Drama (1969), an honorary fellow of Trinity College of Music (1948), and a fellow of the Royal College of Music (1971), the Royal Northern College of Music (1974), and the Royal Scottish Academy of Music and Drama (1980). He was a governor of Wellington College (1953–83). He died at his home, High Rising, Holdfast Lane, in Haslemere, Surrey, on 5 June 1983. His remains were cremated at Guildford crematorium on 10 June and his ashes were interred in the graveyard of All Saints parish church, Grayswood, Surrey. Just before his death he suggested the setting up of a prize competition for student performers using the repertory of Musica Britannica, and in 1987 the Sir Anthony Lewis memorial prize was inaugurated at the Royal Academy of Music.

Lewis was a musician of rare accomplishment, widely skilled in the science and practice of music. His knowledge as an editor, experience as a composer, insight as a conductor, and eloquence as a writer were all combined in solving the manifold problems surrounding practical performance, particularly of the neglected treasures of the national heritage. His appearance was imposing, his manner reserved; yet behind this lay a vigour which was essentially creative. He liked to see things grow. His chief recreation was gardening, a pastime which gave him much pleasure. He was genial and kindly, and had a lively sense of humour. Lewis's sustained vision, patient advocacy, and practical wisdom enabled him to blaze fresh trails. The foundation of Musica Britannica was an act of high imagination and courage; and, with over fifty volumes completed by the time of his death, this growing collection had achieved the early aim of ranging from

Dunstaple to Parry, and stood four-square as 'a living tribute to British musical achievement through the centuries'. MICHAEL POPE, *rev.*

Sources A. Lewis, 'Musica Britannica', *MT*, 91 (1951) · *Royal Academy of Music Magazine* (summer 1982) · D. Scott, 'Lewis, Sir Anthony (Carey)', *New Grove* · B. Trowell, *RAM Magazine* (autumn 1983) · J. L. Holmes, *Conductors on record* (1982) · family papers · personal knowledge (1990) · *CGPLA Eng. & Wales* (1983) · A. Lewis, 'Musica Britannica: past and future', *The Listener* (2 Feb 1956) · P. Cranmer, obituary, *Wellington Year Book*, 1983 · T. Dart, 'A background for Musica Britannica', *Music* 1952, ed. A. Robertson (1952) · N. Fortune, *Musical Times* (Aug 1983) · H. Carpenter, *The envy of the world: fifty years of the BBC Third Programme and Radio 3, 1946–1996* (1996) · d. cert.

Archives priv. coll., manuscripts and papers | SOUND BL NSA, documentary recording · BL NSA, performance recordings · BL NSA, recorded talk

Likenesses P. Thalben-Ball, portrait, 1976, Royal Academy of Music, London · photographs, Hult. Arch.

Wealth at death £67,495: probate, 15 Aug 1983, *CGPLA Eng. & Wales*

Lewis, Sir (William) Arthur (1915–1991), economist, was born on 23 January 1915 at Castries, St Lucia, the fourth son of George Ferdinand Lewis (*d. c.*1922) and his wife, Ida, both schoolteachers who had immigrated to St Lucia from Antigua. He later claimed that an illness that kept him from school furthered his education immensely and that his year spent in the civil service before he went to university taught him the importance of filing and method. After his time at St Mary's College, Castries, and in the civil service, he obtained a scholarship in 1932 and moved to Britain to study at the London School of Economics and Political Science (LSE). He gained BComm first-class, and obtained another scholarship to do his PhD there. In 1938 he was appointed to its faculty. He married in 1947 Gladys Jacobs, Grenadan by birth, a teacher. They had two daughters.

Lewis remained at LSE until 1948, by which time he was a reader, and in 1948 he took up a chair in economics at Manchester University. He stayed there until 1958, becoming the principal of the University College of the West Indies and then its vice chancellor when it became a fully-fledged university in 1962. He was a close spectator of the collapse of the West Indian Federation. After being knighted in 1963, he moved to Princeton University, where he remained until his retirement in 1983. From 1943, when he joined the Board of Trade, Lewis worked directly for governments or as a consultant for various governments or quasi-governmental organizations, the last of these being as president of the Caribbean development bank from 1970 to 1973.

Lewis's original research was on the problems of the industrialized world. In 1940 he produced his first substantial work, *Economic Problems of Today*, soon after the war *Monopoly in British Industry*, and in 1949 *Overhead Costs: some Essays in Economic Analysis* and *Economic Survey, 1919–1939*. In the last of these he had argued that the growing inter-war protectionism had exacerbated economic problems and prolonged the depression. In his last major purely economic work, *Growth and Fluctuations, 1870–1913* (1978), he returned to examine an earlier period when trade was much freer. He was, however, to become better known for his work in development economics, of which he was regarded as one of the founders and for which he received the Nobel prize in 1979 (shared with Theodore Schultz of the USA). The origins of this side of Lewis's work can be discerned in his early writings on the British West Indies. In 1936 he had written an analysis of the non-plantation sector of agriculture in those territories; in 1939 he published his discussion of the labour disturbances (*Labour in the West Indies: the Birth of a Workers' Movement*) and their economic causes and submitted a memorandum to the royal commission that was investigating those events.

Lewis's opportunity to do something practical came in 1944, when he moved from the Board of Trade to the Colonial Office. In 1945 he published a devastating critique of the proposals by another economist for the development of Jamaica. His own proposals grew out of his own earlier examination of the West Indies and his time as a consultant to the Caribbean commission, when he reflected upon the policies to develop Puerto Rico. In 1950 his *Industrialization of the British West Indies* built on those policies. Described somewhat inaccurately as industrialization by invitation, the main policies were adhered to by most of these governments but they failed to take sufficient note of Lewis's warning that a federation was the prerequisite for their success. At the University College of the West Indies his attempts to make the institution more relevant to the social and economic needs of the region were not always well received. He found the end of the federation disheartening. His continuing concern with the West Indies was demonstrated when he headed the Caribbean development bank, allegedly threatening to resign from Princeton University if he could not get an extra year's leave.

Lewis's major contributions to development economics were made in the early 1950s. By this time he had broadened his West Indian experience by working on the United Nations report *Measures for the Economic Development of Underdeveloped Countries* (1951), his membership of the board of the Colonial Development Corporation (1951–3), and as consultant to the Gold Coast and western Nigeria governments and for the United Nations in Asia and the Far East. He returned to Ghana from 1957 to 1958 as adviser to the prime minister, Kwame Nkrumah, though the relationship ended badly. His major, purely theoretical, statement of the major problems of development was 'Economic development with unlimited supplies of labour' (1954). Here he identified a capitalist sector of the economy that needed to expand if economic development was to be successful; it would do this by drawing labour from the stagnant traditional sector, thereby expanding and producing the investment needed for further economic growth. This article reintroduced the concerns for long-term growth and its effects on different sections of society that nineteenth-century classical economists maintained; it also served to demonstrate Lewis's recognition that neo-classical economics had severe limitations in dealing with the problems of developing countries. His summation of his experience appeared the next year as *The Theory of Economic Growth*. Here Lewis showed his knowledge that development was not a mere exercise in applied economic theory but had to take into account political, social, and cultural influences. In an appendix he even broached the topic of the links between growth and welfare. In 1966 he wrote *Development Planning: the Essentials of Economic Policy*, which displayed his usual humane good sense and returned to the ground that he had traversed in 1949, when dealing with developed economies. In *Politics in West Africa* (1965) he wrote about the problems of democracy in ethnically divided societies, a subject that has recently become more fashionable. In 1964, when most aid had a political agenda, he raised the issue of its effective use. In 1985 his lectures on *Racial Conflict and Economic Development* were published; there his concerns with the wider context of economic problems were once more clearly set out.

After his retirement from Princeton in 1983 Lewis moved to Barbados but continued to lecture. His last years were marred by illness and he died, in Bridgetown, Barbados, on 15 June 1991. He was buried on 22 June in the grounds of the Sir Arthur Lewis Community College in St Lucia. He is also commemorated by the Sir Arthur Lewis Institute of Social and Economic Studies (SALISES) on each of the three campuses of the University of the West Indies. PETER D. FRASER

Sources *The Times* (17 June 1991) • *The Independent* (18 June 1991) • *WWW* • Burke, *Peerage* • A. Lewis, www.nobel.se/economics/laureates [autobiographical notes for Nobel prize] • R. Lalljie, *Sir Arthur Lewis: Nobel laureate* (St Lucia, 1996) • B. Ingham, *The Manchester years, 1947–1958: a tribute to the work of Arthur Lewis* (1991) • C. W. King, *Summum Attingitus Nitendo: a tribute to Sir Arthur Lewis* (Castries, 1985)

Archives Princeton University Library, New Jersey, corresp. and papers | JRL, letters to *Manchester Guardian*

Likenesses photograph, repro. in *The Independent*

Lewis, Sir Aubrey Julian (1900–1975), psychiatrist, was born on 8 November 1900 in Adelaide, South Australia, the only child of George Solomon Lewis, a watchmaker, and Rachel Isaacs, a teacher. The family was a respected part of the local Jewish community. Lewis was an outstanding pupil at the Christian Brothers' College from 1911 to 1917, when he entered Adelaide University medical school. He graduated MB BCh from there in 1923, and remained at Adelaide Hospital until 1926 as resident medical officer, and then medical and, finally, surgical registrar. While there, Lewis took part in anthropological studies of Aborigines. He was awarded a Rockefeller fellowship to train as a psychologist with a view to further studies of Aborigines, but as the department of psychology in Adelaide then emphasized metaphysics over experimental research the fellowship was transferred to psychiatry; Lewis trained further first in the United States with Macfie Campbell in Boston and Adolf Meyer at Johns Hopkins, Baltimore, then with Gordon Holmes at the National Hospital for Nervous Diseases, Queen Square, London, and finally with Karl Beringer in Heidelberg and Karl Bonhoeffer in Berlin. When he returned to Australia in 1928 he was committed to psychiatry, but was unable to find suitable opportunities there. The same year he obtained the membership of the Royal College of Physicians and went to the Maudsley Hospital, London, first as a research fellow, and from 1929 as a member of the clinical staff. He remained there until his retirement.

Lewis's intellect and ability were quickly recognized, and in 1936 he was made clinical director of the hospital. In 1931 he took his MD (Adelaide) and in 1938 was elected FRCP (London). On 22 February 1934 he married Hilda North Stoessiger (1900/01–1966), a psychiatrist, the daughter of Alexander Goodwin Stoessiger, wholesale importer, and Emily Louisa North.

During the Second World War Lewis worked with a group of Maudsley psychiatrists who staffed the emergency hospital at Mill Hill. He came into contact with Sir Francis Fraser, then in charge of the Emergency Medical Service but later first director of the British Postgraduate Medical Federation, a relationship which was to bear fruit when after the war the Maudsley medical school became the Institute of Psychiatry and a member of the federation. In 1946 Lewis succeeded Edward Mapother (who had died prematurely in 1940) as professor of psychiatry at the University of London, an appointment which coincided with the designation of the Maudsley Hospital as the university teaching centre in the new British Postgraduate Medical Federation, with responsibility for research and postgraduate training being vested in the Institute of Psychiatry. Two years later the Maudsley was amalgamated with the Bethlem Royal Hospital, and under Lewis's guidance the institute steadily expanded. During the thirty years of Lewis's leadership the hospital and institute emerged as a postgraduate research and teaching centre of world rank, with a leading position in the United Kingdom. Around himself Lewis established a group of research workers who transformed British psychiatry from a clinically orientated study to a respected academic discipline with foundations in the empirical sciences, particularly epidemiology, psychology, neuroendocrinology, neuropathology, and biochemistry. Under him trained a generation of psychiatrists who later occupied many of the principal psychiatric posts in the United Kingdom and elsewhere, and his influence was so pervasive that it is perhaps no accident that, like Lewis's own, many units still held clinical meetings on Mondays long after Lewis's death. Many of Lewis's students recalled his severe and uncompromising style in which the highest intellectual standards of reasoning and evidence were combined with wide learning and critical scepticism. The sceptical aggressive challenge which he brought to debate could be painful to his opponents and students, but undoubtedly sharpened the quality of the research activity around him. He taught by threat, but those who survived learned much.

Although Lewis wrote no books he published numerous papers, notably on melancholia, neurosis, history, and biography. He was particularly interested in social and economic influences on mental illness. In 1942, for example, he was honorary secretary to the neurosis subcommittee of the Royal Medico-Psychological Association which examined the relevance to psychiatric disorders (such as neurosis) of poverty, occupation, unemployment, and housing.

In 1948 the Medical Research Council set up the occupational psychiatry research unit (later the social psychiatry unit), appointing him its honorary director. In 1952 he became the first psychiatrist to be a member of the Medical Research Council.

Lewis gave a number of important lectures: the Manson lecture (British Institute of Philosophy, 1949), the Maudsley lecture (Royal Medico-Psychological Association, 1951), the Bradshaw lecture (RCP, 1957), the Galton lecture (Eugenics Society, 1958), the Hobhouse lecture (University College, London, 1960), the Bertram Roberts lecture (Yale, 1960), the Maurice Bloch lecture (1962), the Harveian oration (RCP, 1963), the Linacre lecture (Cambridge, 1967), and the Mapother lecture (Institute of Psychiatry, 1969). In 1959 Lewis was knighted. He became a member of the American Philosophical Society (1961), and was elected FRCPsych (1972).

In 1966 Lewis retired, and in the same year his wife died. He died on 21 January 1975 at Charing Cross Hospital, London, and was survived by two sons and two daughters. Lewis's contribution to establishing psychiatry as a respected academic discipline in post-war Britain was outstanding. He is remembered primarily for his creation of an internationally recognized institute for psychiatric research and training. HUGH SERIES

Sources *The Times* (22 Jan 1975) • *The Lancet* (1 Feb 1975) • *BMJ* (1 Feb 1975) • M. Shepherd, 'Aubrey Lewis: the making of a psychiatrist', *British Journal of Psychiatry*, 131 (1977), 238–42 • M. Shepherd, 'Professor Sir Aubrey Lewis MD FRCP: a professional sketch', *Comparative epidemiology of the mental disorders*, ed. P. H. Hoch and J. Zubin (1961), ix–xiv • M. Shepherd, 'The legacies of Sir Aubrey Lewis', *Conceptual issues in psychological medicine* (1990), 219–37 • M. Shepherd, 'From social medicine to social psychiatry: the achievement of Sir Aubrey Lewis', *Healing and history: essays for George Rosen*, ed. C. Rosenberg (1979), 191–204 • R. Porter, 'The complacency of Sir Aubrey', *TLS* (25 Aug 1995) • J. G. Howells and M. L. Osborn, 'Lewis, Aubrey', *A reference companion to the history of abnormal psychology* (1984) • m. cert. • d. cert. • *DNB*

Likenesses R. Spear, portrait, repro. in A. Lewis, *Inquiries in psychiatry, clinical and social investigations* (1967)

Wealth at death £92,405: probate, 16 April 1975, *CGPLA Eng. & Wales*

Lewis, (Dominic) Bevan Wyndham (1891–1969), writer, was born Llewelyn Bevan Wyndham Lewis, on 9 March 1891 at 63 Seaforth Road, Seaforth, Litherland, Lancashire, the eldest son of David John Lewis, pharmaceutical chemist of Seaforth, and his wife, Cecelia Agnes, *née* Mayer. He was educated at Cardiff intermediate school, where he showed academic promise, winning four distinctions in the senior honours certificate of the Central Welsh Board at seventeen. His ambition to read law at Oxford, however, was never fulfilled. He enlisted as a private in the Welsh regiment on 1 September 1914, and served with the 11th battalion (the 'Cardiff pals') in France, where he was shell-shocked twice, and in Macedonia, where he caught malaria. He was invalided home in 1918, and demobilized, still a private, at the time of the armistice. On 29 October 1918 he married Winifred Mary (Jane) Holland (*b.* 1893/4), daughter of David Holland, marine surveyor, of Cardiff. They had one daughter, the actress Angela Wyndham Lewis.

(Dominic) Bevan Wyndham Lewis (1891–1969), by Howard Coster, 1935

In 1919 Lewis was offered a job by R. D. Blumenfeld, editor of the *Daily Express*. For six months he was a sub-editor, but then began to write a column for the paper called 'By the way'. He signed it Beachcomber. He thus pioneered in Britain the discursive, witty, exuberant, and surreal style of humour he bequeathed to his close friend J. B. Morton, who took the column over in 1924 and developed it through half a century into an art form. Lewis's marriage ended in 1926, and in the same year Jane married the writer J. B. Priestley. Lewis meanwhile moved on to the *Daily Mail*, where until 1930 he wrote a column called 'At the Sign of the Blue Moon'. His prolific imagination was never more happily displayed.

Lewis lived much in France, and immersed himself in its history and literature. After his first book, *A London Farrago*, appeared in 1921, he published almost annually a volume of satire or humour, but he had a parallel career as a biographer, writing vigorous and scholarly lives of writers like François Villon (1928), Pierre de Ronsard (1944), François Rabelais (1957), Molière (1959), and Cervantes (1962); studies of Louis XI (*King Spider*, 1930), and Charles V (*Emperor of the West*, 1932). His life of Boswell (*The Hooded Hawk*, 1946) vividly displayed his power of conjuring up the past. He had been received into the Roman Catholic church in 1921 (dropping his first name, Llewelyn, in favour of Dominic), and for all their drive and gusto, his books show a strong Catholic bias.

Lewis also wrote skits, burlesques, and film scenarios, and he was an inspired anthologist. Particularly amusing was *The Stuffed Owl* (1930), an anthology of bad verse he compiled with Charles Lee. On 22 July 1933 he married

Dorothy Anne (*b.* 1900/01), daughter of Bertie Henry Robertson, in a civil ceremony. They had two sons. He returned to the *Daily Mail* from 1933 to 1936, when he joined the *News Chronicle* as the columnist Timothy Shy. He also wrote the 'Mustard and the Cress' column in the *Sunday Referee* from 1930 and was a regular contributor to *The Tatler* from 1933. He was made a fellow of the Royal Society of Literature in 1947. He collaborated with the artist Ronald Searle by writing the text for *The Terror of St Trinian's* (1952). He published his last book, on Goya, in 1968.

Lewis was a leading member of an influential group of Catholic writers who flourished between the wars, including Hilaire Belloc, G. K. Chesterton, J. B. Morton, Compton Mackenzie, and Evelyn Waugh. Many of them used to meet regularly at Shirreff's wine bar under Ludgate Circus where, despite a lifelong stammer, Lewis more than held his own; he was indeed described by Belloc as the wittiest man he had ever known. He described himself as 'impulsive, lazy, easily imposed upon, distinctly Celt, full of strong loves and hates'. Among the former were wine, France, Spain, the Pyrenees, Elgar, and tradition; among the latter, financiers, socialists, bluestockings, officials, and novelty. He suffered with good humour the misfortune of sharing his name with Percy Wyndham Lewis, the Canadian artist. He was a gentle, courteous, convivial, slightly bemused romantic, born out of his time. He died in Altea, Spain, on 21 November 1969.

GODFREY SMITH, *rev.*

Sources *The Times* (24 Nov 1969) • *The Times* (27 Nov 1969) • M. Hoen, ed., *Catholic authors: contemporary biographical sketches, 1930–47* (1948) • S. J. Kunitz and H. Haycraft, eds., *Twentieth century authors: a biographical dictionary of modern literature* (1942) • personal knowledge (1993) • private information (1993) • b. cert. • m. certs. • d. cert. • *CGPLA Eng. & Wales* (1970)

Archives BL, corresp. with D. E. Collins, former secretary to G. K. Chesterton, and related papers, Add. MSS 73231 C, fols. 1–89*v*; 73232 B, fols. 77, 150; 73276 A; 73412, fol. 33; 733481 A, fols. 37, 46 • Cornell University, Ithaca, New York, papers • Westm. DA, letters to H. E. G. Rope

Likenesses H. Coster, photograph, 1935, NPG [*see illus.*] • H. Coster, photographs, NPG

Wealth at death £1996 effects in England: administration with will, 21 April 1970, *CGPLA Eng. & Wales*

Lewis, Bunnell (1824–1908), archaeologist, was born in London on 26 July 1824, the eldest of the twelve children of William Jones Lewis, a surgeon, of London, and his first wife, Mary Bunnell, a descendant of Philip Henry, the nonconformist divine. Samuel Savage *Lewis was his half-brother. Educated under John Jackson, afterwards bishop of London, at Islington proprietary school, Lewis went on to read classics with Charles Rann Kennedy at University College, London, and graduated BA in 1843 in the University of London, obtaining the university scholarship in classics. He became fellow of University College in 1847, and proceeded MA in classics in 1849, taking the gold medal, awarded for the first time that year. The same year he was appointed professor of Latin at Queen's College, Cork, an appointment which he held until 1905. He laboured to make archaeology an integral part of university education, and with that end in view collected objects of art and antiquity for the museum of his college. At the foundation of the Queen's University in Ireland he took an active part in its administration, and held the office of examiner in Latin for four years. He was twice married: first on 2 October 1855 to Jane (*d.* 31 Dec 1867), second daughter of the Revd John Whitley DD, chancellor of Killaloe; and second on 4 October 1871 to Louise Emily (*d.* November 1882), daughter of Admiral Bowes Watson of Cambridge. He left no children.

Lewis early devoted his attention to archaeology, being elected FSA on 2 February 1865, and was in 1883 appointed foreign corresponding associate of the National Society of Antiquaries of France. Having in 1869, in a *Letter to John Robson*, urged that part of the Slade bequest should be used to found a professorship of classical art or archaeology, he delivered in 1873–4 courses of lectures on classical archaeology at University College in connection with the Slade School of Art. The inaugural lecture was published. His special study was the survival of Roman antiquities in various parts of Europe, and his researches took him during the summer vacations to Norway, Sweden, Denmark, Germany, France, Switzerland, Italy, Sicily, and Turkey. His descriptions of Roman antiquities, in which he regularly attempted to shed new light on the interpretation of passages of Latin literature, were embodied in papers contributed between 1875 and 1907 to the *Archaeological Journal*.

Lewis died at his residence, 49 Sunday's Well Road, Cork, on 2 July 1908, and was buried at Cork. He bequeathed to University College, London, his classical and archaeological library and £1000 for a Bunnell Lewis prize for proficiency in original Latin verse and in translations from Latin and Greek.

Besides his archaeological papers and contributions to the second (revised) edition of Smith's Latin dictionary, he published *Remarks on Ivory Cabinets in the Possession of Wickham Flower, Esq.* (1871).

CHARLES WELCH, *rev.* RICHARD SMAIL

Sources *WWW* • *Men and women of the time* (1899) • *Summary of the life of the Rev. George Lewis* (1873) • *Q.C.C.: conducted by the students of Queen's College, Cork*, 2 (1906), 25–6 • *The Constitution* [Cork] (3 July 1908) • *Irish Times* (3 July 1908) • *CGPLA Eng. & Wales* (1908)

Archives UCL, notes on Juvenal

Likenesses portrait, repro. in *Q.C.C.*

Wealth at death £35,653 19*s*. 6*d*.: probate, 13 Aug 1908, *CGPLA Eng. & Wales*

Lewis, Cecil Arthur (1898–1997), airman and radio and television broadcaster, was born on 29 March 1898 at 11 Radnor Place, Birkenhead, Cheshire, the only child of Edward Williams Lewis, Congregational minister, and his wife, Alice, *née* Rigby. He was educated briefly at Dulwich College and at University College School before being sent to Oundle School. There he learned that his father—who, through forceful preaching, had been elevated from obscurity in Derbyshire to the most coveted living in London, Grosvenor Square—had eloped to Italy with a rich member of his flock. Lewis was to demonstrate a similar obedience to the dictates of his freest of spirits.

At seventeen, standing 6 feet 4 inches tall and equipped

with a precocious intelligence, Lewis lied about his age to join the Royal Flying Corps. He celebrated his eighteenth birthday in France, flying patrols over the western front at a time when the average life expectancy of a pilot was three weeks. On 1 July 1916 he flew the first patrol of the Somme offensive and witnessed the mile-high column of earth thrown up by the detonation of mines under the German positions. Later he duelled with the 'circus' of Manfred von Richthofen and was the last man to see the aircraft of Albert Ball VC, the allied ace who vanished in a bank of cloud. Lewis also hunted Gotha airships over London by moonlight, and in 1917 he was awarded the Military Cross for continuous bravery. His subsequent account of his wartime experiences, *Sagittarius Rising* (1936), remains the most vivid and poetic memoir of flight during the First World War.

In 1919 Lewis joined Vickers Aviation and was sent out to Peking (Beijing) to train Chinese pilots to fly, a task hampered by the absence of room in the cockpit for an interpreter. He married Yevdokia Dmitryevna (Duska) Horvath, the daughter of the White Russian leader, General Dmitry Horvath, in Peking in 1921; they had a son and a daughter. The next year Lewis was one of only five applicants for a post at the newly created BBC, in which Vickers had a stake. He was appointed deputy director of programmes, so becoming one of the four founders of the BBC and the youngest colleague of its new general manager, John Reith.

In its earliest days, the BBC operated out of a single room in the General Electric Building, Kingsway, London; at five in the afternoon, the company's entire staff would scamper down the road to an attic at the Gaiety Theatre from which the evening's radio broadcasts were transmitted. Lewis, like his fellow BBC pioneers, initially knew almost nothing about broadcasting, but he possessed imagination, vigour, and versatility. He mounted the first plays heard on the wireless, and later the first central transmission of the news to the regions, an event introduced by a drunk yet word-perfect F. E. Smith. Lewis also produced the BBC's earliest popular success, *Children's Hour*, for which he reluctantly took on the guise of Uncle Caractacus.

Lewis had a gift for being in at the start of important and potentially lucrative developments in technology, but he lacked the inclination, and perhaps the application, to see them through for long enough to reap the reward due him. Thus in 1926, irritated by the growth of bureaucracy at the BBC and by Reith's lack of interest in the arts, Lewis abruptly resigned his post, declaring that he would rather live by his wits. In this he would be greatly helped by the contacts he had made through the BBC, notably with Bernard Shaw, who in 1931 allowed him to adapt and direct the first of his plays for the screen, *How he Lied to her Husband*. Lewis wrote and directed several more films, including *Gypsy Blood*, a version of *Carmen*, before the expensive failure of Shaw's *Arms and the Man* drove him to retreat to a villa he had built on the shores of Lake Maggiore, Italy, where he wrote *Sagittarius Rising*. A favourable review by Shaw in the *New Statesman* ensured its success. Lewis returned to England in 1936 to become BBC television's first director of outside broadcasts, but within six months the success of *Sagittarius Rising* produced the offer of a rather better paid job in Hollywood as a screenwriter. Though there was little scope for genuine advancement there, in 1938 his slim contribution to the script of *Pygmalion* brought him a quarter share of an Oscar. This he celebrated with a prolonged bout of beachcombing in Tahiti.

Although Lewis himself seemed content, the second half of his life appeared to others something of an anticlimax. He served in the RAF throughout the Second World War, primarily as a flying instructor. Then, despairing of man's predilection for self-destruction, in the late 1940s he became deeply influenced by the ideas of the Russian mystic George Gurdjieff, and he set up a farming community in South Africa to preserve the philosopher's ideas against the expected Armageddon. When this venture failed, he worked first as a radio producer for the United Nations, then briefly for Associated Rediffusion during the launch of commercial television, and finally, from 1956, for the *Daily Mail*, principally as the organizer of its Ideal Home Exhibition. In 1969, aged seventy-one, he sailed a small boat to Corfu, where he spent the rest of his life, passing at ninety-five for a spry seventy. In old age Lewis continued to add to his output of more than twenty books and plays, although none matched the literary standard of *Sagittarius Rising*. The most readable of several volumes of autobiography was *Never Look Back* (1974), later filmed for television.

As a young man, Lewis displayed a prodigious appetite for seduction. He was divorced from his first wife in 1940. On 5 November 1942 he married his second wife, Olga Henrietta Burnett (*b.* 1911/12), a divorcée and daughter of Thet Herard, a barrister. She had changed her name to Lewis-Burnett by deed poll by the time of the marriage, which was childless; it ended in divorce in 1950. On 21 October 1960 Lewis married his third wife, Frances Olga Lowe (*b.* 1915/16), daughter of Ernest Lowe, a cotton merchant. He died, two months shy of ninety-nine, at the King Edward VII Hospital for Officers, London, on 27 January 1997. He was survived by his third wife, and by the two children of his first marriage. JAMES OWEN

Sources C. Lewis, *Never look back* (1974) · C. Lewis, *Sagittarius rising* (1936) · C. Lewis, *Broadcasting from within* (1924) · *Daily Telegraph* (29 Jan 1997) · *The Times* (29 Jan 1997) · *The Independent* (29 Jan 1997) · *WWW* [forthcoming] · b. cert. · m. cert. · d. cert. · *CGPLA Eng. & Wales* (1997)

Archives BBC WAC, corresp. with members of BBC staff | FILM BFI NFTVA | SOUND BL NSA · IWM SA, recording of his memories of aerial combat, First World War

Likenesses group portrait, photograph, 1917 (56 Squadron), IWM · C. Ricketts, bronze bust, 1928, probably priv. coll.; photograph, NPG · photograph, repro. in *The Times* · photograph, repro. in *The Independent* · photograph, repro. in *Daily Telegraph* · photographs, Hult. Arch.

Wealth at death under £180,000: probate, 21 May 1997, *CGPLA Eng. & Wales*

Lewis, Cecil Day- [*pseud.* Nicholas Blake] (**1904–1972**), poet and novelist, was born on 27 April 1904 at Ballintubbert, Queen's county, Ireland, the only child of Frank Cecil Day-

Lewis (1877–1937), Church of Ireland curate, and his wife, Kathleen Blake Squires (1878–1908), daughter of William Alfred Squires, civil servant. His mother died when he was four and he was brought up in London by his father and his selfless aunt Agnes Olive (Knos) Squires. Educated at Wilkie's preparatory school, London, and Sherborne School, he entered Wadham College, Oxford, in 1923 with a classics exhibition. He began writing verse as a schoolboy and, sure of his poetic vocation, he chose mainly literary friends and acquaintances at Oxford. During his third year there he met the undergraduate W. H. Auden, the major influence on his early work. Their collaboration continued through 1927–8 when Day-Lewis held a teaching post at Summer Fields preparatory school in Oxford. Together they edited *Oxford Poetry, 1927*. Day-Lewis obtained a second class in classical honour moderations in 1925 and a third in *literae humaniores* in 1927.

After his two early slim volumes of verse, more or less 'Georgian' in style, *Beechen Vigil* (1925) and *Country Comets* (1928), Day-Lewis (who dropped the hyphen from his surname for publication) became more rigorous with *Transitional Poem* (1929). This sequence was the first public manifestation of what was later to become known as the Auden gang or, as their unsympathetic contemporary Roy Campbell satirically put it, the MacSpaunday (Louis MacNeice, Stephen Spender, W. H. Auden, C. Day Lewis) beast. Though this poetic movement was really little more than a convenient pigeon-hole for critics, its supposed members were indeed contemporaries subject to the weather of the times and responding to it with a similar leftish stance. Day-Lewis in particular remained spellbound by Auden's work. Though private themes often provided a framework, they were used to question the social order and brimmed with Audenesque images and metaphors drawn from natural science. His early leftist sequences in *From Feathers to Iron* (1931), *The Magnetic Mountain* (1933), *A Time to Dance* (1935), and *Noah and the Waters* (1936) were exuberant, eclectic, and voguish enough to make him fashionable, but delayed the finding of his true voice as a lyric poet of nature and private emotion. At the same time Day-Lewis provided a critical manifesto for the young poets of his generation, *A Hope for Poetry* (1934), claiming Gerard Manley Hopkins, Wilfred Owen, and T. S. Eliot as their immediate ancestors.

Day-Lewis had married on 27 December 1928, when he took his second teaching post at Larchfield School, Helensburgh, near Glasgow. His wife was (Constance) Mary (1902–1975), daughter of one of his former Sherborne form-masters, Henry Robinson King. Two years later he moved to Cheltenham junior school in Gloucestershire. By 1934 he had two sons as well as a wife to support, and it was primarily to make money that he began to write detective novels under the pseudonym Nicholas Blake. His *A Question of Proof* (1935) was set at a preparatory school which featured aspects of those at which he had taught. It proved to be the first of twenty Blake novels mostly featuring the detective Nigel Strangeways, and its success was a factor in encouraging him to retire from teaching to become a full-time writer and political activist in December 1935. He joined the Communist Party three months later, and there followed two intense years when he wrote three straight novels, two detective novels, weekly book reviews, and many polemical pamphlets and essays. He was in demand as a speaker and lecturer and in organizing the tiny Gloucestershire branch of the party. By early 1938 he had decided he must make a choice between 'being an amateurish political worker or trying to make myself a better poet'. Poetry won.

In order to break with political and public life, Day-Lewis moved with his family to a secluded thatched cottage on an upper slope of Castle Hill above Musbury, a straggling east Devon village, in August 1938. It was a move crucial to his poetic development. In *Overtures to Death* (1938) the theme of the possibility of heroic action had been overshadowed by the theme of the inevitable disaster of war. As Auden sailed for the United States, Day-Lewis found his new and true home close to the Dorset border, and Thomas Hardy country. With his translation of Virgil's *Georgics* (1940) and his own verse collections *Word over All* (1943) and *Poems, 1943–1947* (1948) he achieved his full stature as a poet. The Hardy influence now predominated. He could parody his idol as in 'Singing Children: Luca della Robbia', part of the 'Florence: works of art' section of *An Italian Visit* (1953). He could make pastiche as in 'Birthday Poem for Thomas Hardy' in the collection of 1948. More importantly, he was able to absorb and transmute the influence into a voice unmistakably his own. His poetry in this period reflected his private concerns, his responses to war, his Devon neighbours and their landscape, and his divided emotional life.

After a hilarious period in command of Musbury's Home Guard platoon Day-Lewis went to London in spring 1941 to become an editor in the Ministry of Information's publications division. In 1946, soon after his release from the ministry, he became senior reader for the publishers Chatto and Windus, an association that lasted until the end of his life. Increasingly through this decade there was a conflict between the private Devon poet nourished by the countryside and the public London literary figure, the conscientious committee man.

This conflict was echoed in Day-Lewis's emotional life. In 1939–41 he took part in a volcanic love affair with the wife of a neighbouring Musbury farmer, dwelt upon in several poems and the final somewhat autobiographical Nicholas Blake story *The Private Wound* (1968). They had a son. From 1941 he began a more complete relationship with the novelist Rosamond Nina *Lehmann, commuting for the rest of the decade between her and his family at Musbury. She inspired some good poems, she broadened his personality, and she encouraged him to travel abroad and to take on such tasks as the Clark lectures at Cambridge in 1946. Such a divided life was a great strain on all concerned. At the end of 1949 he fell in love again, this time with the 24-year-old actress Jill Angela Henriette Balcon (*b.* 1925), daughter of Sir Michael *Balcon (1896–1977), film producer. The following year he left both Mary and Rosamond for a second marriage with Jill, which took place on 27 April 1951 after the dissolution of his first marriage. They had a daughter and a son (the Oscar-winning film actor Daniel Day-Lewis).

In the last two decades of his life Day-Lewis looked wistfully back towards Dorset, the county of his school-days as well as of Hardy, and to his Irish roots. But he decided against becoming the rural regional poet that he might have been, and opted permanently for London and the literary life. With every passing year the profile of his public honours and responsibilities moved upwards, while the profile indicating critical esteem curved downwards. In 1951, the year in which his translation of Virgil's *Aeneid* commissioned by the BBC was broadcast as part of the Festival of Britain, he was elected Oxford professor of poetry. His five-year term opened a period when he became more preoccupied with public poetry reading, mainly in partnership with his second wife; also with prestigious lectureships, and his public-spirited work for organizations like the Apollo Society, the Royal Society of Literature (which made him companion of literature in 1965), and the Arts Council. His taste for public honours was most gratified in 1968 when he was chosen to succeed John Masefield as poet laureate, the first Irish-born holder of that office since Nahum Tate (1652–1715). He also received honorary degrees from Exeter (1965), Trinity College, Dublin (1968), and Hull (1970). In 1968 he became an honorary fellow of his old Oxford College, Wadham, and was elected to the Irish Academy of Letters.

Though no longer fashionable and much diverted by this public activity, his work as a publisher, and the raising of a second family, Day-Lewis continued to regard the writing of poetry as the point of his life. His final volumes of verse, *Pegasus* (1957), *The Gate* (1962), *The Room* (1965), and *The Whispering Roots* (1970), were received with woundingly faint praise by reviewers. They nevertheless contain some of his best poems; their mature mastery of craftsmanship and fluency of technique delighted his discriminating band of admirers. His themes ranged from the public and prosaic to those private explorations of love and living that put him firmly in the poetic family of Hardy, Edward Thomas, and Robert Frost. His health declined after 1969 and he died of cancer on 22 May 1972 at Lemmons, Hadley Wood, Hertfordshire, the home of the novelists Elizabeth Jane Howard and Kingsley Amis. Appropriately he was buried at Stinsford in Dorset only a few feet from Hardy's grave, and less than 30 miles from the Devon border country where he found his voice.

In 2003 there was much debate in the national press over the exclusion of Day-Lewis from Poets' Corner in Westminster Abbey. Despite a petition organized by the Royal Society of Literature and signed by Seamus Heaney, P. D. James, A. S. Byatt, and Melvyn Bragg among others, the dean of Westminster argued that poets laureate are not 'automatically memorialized in the Abbey' (*TLS*, 7 Feb 2003).

Day-Lewis was a man of considerable generosity, charm, and elegance who laughed easily and was as stylish in his movements as in his dress. In his younger days he had a light lyric tenor voice very effective in the Irish songs of Tom Moore that he had learned at his aunt's knee, and good enough to be heard several times on BBC radio. If he loved women and was always vulnerable to them, he was also good at making and keeping friends of both sexes. He was a tireless advocate of English literature in general and poetry in particular and unsparing in his encouragement of younger writers in whom he found any glimmer of talent.

SEAN DAY-LEWIS

Sources C. Day-Lewis, *The buried day* (1960) · S. Day-Lewis, *C. Day-Lewis: an English literary life* (1980) · personal knowledge (2004) · m. certs. · d. cert. · *The Times* (23 May 1972) · V. Cunningham, *British writers of the thirties* (1988)

Archives BBC WAC, radio talks; corresp. with staff · Bodl. Oxf., corresp. · Harvard U., Houghton L., papers · Hunt. L., letters and literary papers · Ransom HRC, corresp. and literary papers · U. Lpool L., notebook · University of Bristol Library, editorial corresp. · Virginia Polytechnic Institute, Blacksburg, notes, poems, papers | BL, corresp. with Ernest Chapman, Add. MS 62949 · Tate collection, letters to Lord Clark · U. Durham L., letters to William Plomer · U. Leeds, Brotherton L., letters to Norah Smallwood · U. Oxf., faculty of English language and literature, letters to H. Owen · U. Reading L., letters to Jonathan Cape Ltd · U. Reading L., corresp. with Hogarth Press · U. Sussex, corresp. with Leonard Woolf · University of Bristol Library, corresp. relating to trial of *Lady Chatterley's Lover* · University of Exeter Library, letters to W. F. Jackson-Knight | SOUND BL NSA, recordings of readings from his own works, recordings of talks, etc.

Likenesses L. Gowing, oils, 1946, priv. coll. · photographs, Hult. Arch.

Wealth at death £57,866: probate, 29 Aug 1972, *CGPLA Eng. & Wales*

Lewis, Charles (1753–1795), still-life painter, was born at Gloucester. Apprenticed to a manufacturer at Birmingham, he established an early reputation for the decoration of japanned tea-trays. After turning to painting, he exhibited nine still lifes with the Society of Artists in 1772, giving his address as the Rainbow Coffee House, King Street, London. In 1776 he went to Dublin, but, not meeting with success as a painter, he took to the stage as a singer with Michael Arne's company at the Crow Street Theatre. Meeting with no better success on the stage, he returned to painting. In 1781 he visited the Netherlands, and shortly thereafter he settled in London, where he established himself as a talented painter of still lifes. He exhibited three pictures at the Royal Academy in 1786 and five at the Society of Artists in 1790. He exhibited for the last time in 1791, sending a fruit piece to the Royal Academy. On the invitation of Lord Gardenstone he moved to Edinburgh, but after the death of his patron his fortunes declined, and he died there on 12 July 1795. Lewis was married to a daughter of Mr *Pinto, a well-known violinist.

L. H. CUST, *rev.* MATTHEW HARGRAVES

Sources Graves, *Artists* · *GM*, 1st ser., 65 (1795), 704 · Graves, *RA exhibitors* · Redgrave, *Artists* · W. G. Strickland, *A dictionary of Irish artists*, 2 (1913), 19–20 · Waterhouse, *18c painters*

Lewis, Charles (1786–1836), bookbinder, was born in London, the fourth son of Johann Ludwig, a native of Hanover whose zeal in political matters caused him suffering and loss of friends, and who was one of the many German bookbinders who moved to England in the last quarter of the eighteenth century. Charles's two brothers, Frederick

Christian *Lewis (1779–1856) and George Robert *Lewis (1782–1871), were engravers. At the age of fourteen Charles was apprenticed to another German immigrant bookbinder, Henry Walther, and was freed by indentures in 1807. After working in several West End shops, he established himself 'up two pairs of stairs' at 4 Middle Scotland Yard. From there he moved to a third floor at 7 Denmark Court, Strand, and thence, not later than 1817, to 29 Duke Street, St James's. Lewis's Scotland Yard address is given on two of his binder's tickets but no binding definitely produced there has survived, while a green morocco binding on the second edition of Scott's *Lady of the Lake* (1810) has the ticket 'Bd by/C.L./7 D.C.' (BL, C.151.f.4). His earliest datable binding, of gold- and blind-tooled green straight-grain morocco on *Les œuvres de Virgile Maron* (Paris, 1582: BL, C.72.c.8), bears a note that the book was purchased at the duke of Roxburghe's sale in 1812 in its original vellum cover and was bound by C. Lewis for £2 in that year.

Once he had settled in the more stylish ground-floor premises in Duke Street, Lewis became unquestionably London's leading binder, patronized by all the great collectors of the day. Thomas Grenville, the duke of Devonshire, Sir Mark Masterman Sykes, Lord Grenville, and Mr Hibbert became his clients in addition to Sir Richard Colt Hoare, Lord Spencer, and Richard Heber, for whom he had been binding already. He built up a flourishing business and in 1823 employed twenty-one journeymen. Dibdin describes how he went about London sporting 'tassels to his half boots' (Dibdin, 520–24), a flamboyancy of style that some of his patrons evidently thought unbecoming in a mere tradesman.

Lewis's early bindings are more interesting than his later ones, but the fashion for bindings imitating earlier styles that took hold of most English collectors in the 1820s meant that very few opportunities for original design remained. A simple binding for Sir Mark Masterman Sykes (BL, G.9153), with doublures tooled in gold to a remarkably intricate and at the same time restrained design, clearly shows Lewis at his best, while an over-large copy of a Duodo binding (BL, C.151.f.3) shows the kind of pastiche to which he was reduced by his clients. Lewis's craftsmanship and the precision of his tooling are both admirable. He obviously controlled his large staff well as no binding of bad execution, although many of doubtful taste, left his workshop (at least not before 1830). According to Ramsden, from about 1830 Francis Bedford, then Lewis's foreman, was gaining control and, after Lewis died on 8 January 1836 in London, Bedford managed the shop for Lewis's widow, Maria, until 1841 (Ramsden, 16). The date of Lewis's marriage to Maria is unknown; the firm continued under her ownership at 35 Duke Street, St James's, until 1854. MIRJAM M. FOOT

Sources E. Howe, *A list of London bookbinders, 1648–1815* (1950), 58–9 • C. Ramsden, *London bookbinders, 1780–1840* (1956), 14–16, 36, 96 • T. F. Dibdin, *The bibliographical decameron*, 2 (1817), 520–24 • *GM*, 2nd ser., 6 (1836), 439–40 • H. M. Nixon, *Five centuries of English bookbinding* (1978), 192 • H. M. Nixon and M. M. Foot, *The history of decorated bookbinding in England* (1992), 99 • *The Bookbinder*, 2 (1889), 171 • *The Bookbinder*, 3 (1889), 187 • [G. Cowie], *Cowie's bookbinder's manual*, 2nd edn (1829); 7th edn [1852] • M. Packer, *Bookbinders of Victorian London* (1991), 92 • W. S. Brassington, *A history of the art of bookbinding* (1894), 246–8 • *The Post Office directory* [annuals]

Archives BL, bindings | BL, Ramsden collection

Likenesses G. R. Lewis, stipple, BM, NPG

Wealth at death see Dibdin, *The bibliographical decameron*; *GM*

Lewis, Charles George (1808–1880), engraver, was born in the Dower House, Forty Hill, Enfield, Middlesex, on 13 June 1808, the third child of Frederick Christian *Lewis senior (1779–1856), an engraver and landscape painter, and Elizabeth Exton (*fl.* 1800–1850). His elder brother was the painter John Frederick (Spanish) *Lewis (1804–1876), his elder sister was Mary Exton Lewis (*b.* 1806), his younger brother was the painter Frederick Christian (Indian) *Lewis junior (1813–1875), and his younger sister was Anne Lucy Lewis (1818–1864). Like his brothers and sisters, he was taught drawing and engraving by his father at an early age; having been enrolled in the family business as a skilled printmaker, he assisted his father in the production of etchings, engravings, and mezzotints. Although he was a good draughtsman, he used this skill only for printmaking and, unlike his brothers, did not become famous independently as a painter.

Lewis's father was a friend of the painter and engraver John Landseer, the father of Sir Edwin Landseer. The two families, both dynasties of painters and engravers, were further linked, as the young John Frederick Lewis became a friend of Edwin Landseer and a rival animal painter. As Landseer quickly became famous, and popular demand grew for reproductions of his paintings, the Lewis family engraved after many of his paintings. At this period a large part of a painter's earnings could come from reproduction fees, so it was essential for a successful artist or his publisher to employ the best engravers they could afford, and Charles George Lewis was quickly recognized to be in that category. The engravings he made after Landseer established his reputation. His engraving after *Shoeing the Horse* (1844), which in one version measures nearly 3 feet by 2, is typical of his large and detailed subjects.

Sometimes Lewis worked with his father on large plates after various other artists, and sometimes on his own, depending on demand. He went on to engrave works by Richard Bonington, Rosa Bonheur, David Wilkie, his brother John Frederick Lewis, and many others, including W. P. Frith, whose *Salon d'Or, Homburg* (1871) he engraved on a plate measuring nearly 4 feet across. Lewis did not marry, and lived with his family until late in life. Family tradition and a portrait, possibly by his brother John Frederick Lewis, depict him as a cheerful bachelor, continuing a long tradition of the highest quality reproductive engraving until just before it started to lose ground to photomechanical methods. He joined the Artists' Annuity Fund in 1834 and worked almost to the end of his life, retiring in 1877. He died (probably, like his father, of a heart attack) at his home, Cavendish Villa, Felpham, near Bognor Regis, Sussex, on 16 June 1880 and was buried in Felpham churchyard. Examples of his work are in the British Museum and the Victoria and Albert Museum, London. CHARLES NEWTON

Sources J. M. H. Lewis, *The Lewis family: art and travel* (privately printed, Old Woking, [1992]) · *Art Journal*, 42 (1880), 300 · *CGPLA Eng. & Wales* (1880)

Likenesses M. Claxton, watercolour, 1864, NPG · C. G. Lewis, stipple (after J. H. Lewis), BM · J. Watkins, carte-de-visite, NPG · portrait, repro. in Lewis, *The Lewis family: art and travel*

Wealth at death under £7000: probate, 28 July 1880, *CGPLA Eng. & Wales*

Lewis, Charles James (1830–1892), painter in oils and watercolours, was born in Chelsea. His father, Charles Thomas Lewis, gentleman, was of Welsh extraction; nothing further is known of his family or early life. Lewis began exhibiting in 1853 when he showed at the Royal Academy a portrait of Mary Ann Matilda Hammond Shelton (*b. c.*1831), the daughter of John Shelton, gentleman, whom he married on 31 August the following year. At that date he was living at Nelson Square, Peckham, although catalogues also give addresses (presumably of his studios) in Hunter Street, Brunswick Square, and Barnards Inn, Holborn. In 1857, however, Lewis returned to Chelsea where he lived for the rest of his life, firstly at Cheyne House and from 1884 at River View, 122 Cheyne Walk.

Lewis was a prolific painter. As well as exhibiting forty-nine pictures at the Royal Academy up to 1890, between 1853 and 1867 he showed forty-nine works at the British Institution, and between 1853 and 1884 forty-three works at the Society of British Artists in Suffolk Street. He also exhibited at the Dudley and Portland galleries. In 1882 Lewis was elected to the Institute of Painters in Water Colours where he exhibited seventy-two drawings; although more highly regarded for his watercolours, he was a member also of the associated Institute of Painters in Oil Colours. His pictures, usually signed C. J. Lewis, were priced from £5 up to 150 guineas. Lewis was an artist of landscapes, fishing, and rustic genre scenes such as *Our Picnic: New Lock, Berkshire* (exh. Society of British Artists 1872) and *On the Thames, Clifton-Hampden* (1891; Newport Art Gallery); nearly all his pictures have their settings in the south-east of England although some French, Scottish, and Welsh scenes are listed among his works. He appears to have fully exploited both the scope of his talents and the tastes of his middle-class market; if somewhat sentimental, Lewis's work was fluent and fresh. The *Art Journal* of 1869 reproduced *The Mill Door*, exhibited as *A Kentish Mill* at the Royal Academy in 1867, a scene depicting a mother and her children in a small village near Sevenoaks, Kent, and remarked that:

> as a rule, the occupations of rustic life offer so little of novelty to an artist's notice that we are pleased to meet something which breaks the monotony of what is ordinarily set before us in our exhibition rooms. Both in the subject and its treatment we have an attractive work. (p. 244)

According to the 1891 census return his household consisted of Lewis—who described himself as a 'painter in watercolours'—and his wife, four unmarried daughters between the ages of nineteen and thirty-five, and a maid. A portrait in *The Year's Art* of 1892 depicts Lewis as having a full dark beard. He continued painting until the end of his life; he died in his sixty-second year on 28 January 1892, at his home in Cheyne Walk following 'a long and painful illness' (*The Times*, 5 Feb 1892); he was buried at Brookwood cemetery in Woking. His wife survived him. A sale of remaining works and accessories held by Christie, Manson, and Wood on 4 and 6 March 1893 in 456 lots raised £2235 19*s.*; items included two sketching umbrellas, a lay figure, and a gas standard for a studio.

Simon Fenwick

Sources *DNB* · *The Times* (5 Feb 1892), 7 · 'The mill door', *Art Journal*, 31 (1869), 244 · census returns for Chelsea, 1891 · sale catalogue (1893) [Christies, 4 March 1893] · sale catalogue (1893) [Christies, 6 March 1893] · Bryan, *Painters* (1927) · m. cert.

Likenesses engraving (after a photograph), repro. in *The Year's Art* (1892)

Wealth at death £4905 8*s.* 3*d.*: resworn probate, May 1893, *CGPLA Eng. & Wales* (1892)

Lewis, Clive Staples (1898–1963), writer and scholar, was born in Belfast on 29 November 1898, the younger son of Albert James Lewis, a local solicitor, and his wife, Florence Augusta Flora, daughter of the Revd Thomas Hamilton. She had been a graduate of Queen's College in mathematics and logic. Lewis's mother died of cancer when he was nine, and within two weeks of her death he joined his older brother Warren at Wynyard House, a moribund preparatory school in Watford, Hertfordshire, which he later described as a 'concentration camp' (Wilson, 23). He briefly attended Campbell College, Belfast, in 1910, where his teacher J. A. McNeill introduced him to Matthew Arnold's poetry, but for health reasons Lewis was moved in 1911 to a preparatory school at Malvern. He entered Malvern College with a scholarship in 1913. His years at these schools were unhappy but at Malvern College he discovered an interest in Celtic and Norse literature and met Arthur Greeves, with whom he corresponded for nearly fifty years. In September 1914 he was sent for private tuition to W. T. Kirkpatrick (Kirk), a former headmaster of Lurgan College, then living at Great Bookham, Surrey; Kirk's fixed regimen and acutely logical mind exerted a lasting influence. It was Kirkpatrick who even at this early stage in Lewis's academic career recognized 'the maturity of [his pupil's] literary judgements which is so unusual and surprising' (ibid., 47). With him Lewis read Latin and Greek authors, but otherwise pursued his own academic interests, including works by William Morris and George Macdonald, whose influence can be traced in his own poems and romances. In December 1916 he won a classical scholarship to University College, Oxford, but had to re-sit the university examination, responsions. When he first arrived in Oxford, in April 1917, it was to train in the university Officers' Training Corps. Lewis experienced trench warfare when he was gazetted to the Somerset light infantry, crossing over to France in November 1917. He was wounded in the battle of Arras on 15 April 1918 and his convalescence lasted until the end of the war. In January 1919 he returned to Oxford to read for classical honour moderations. During his recovery he began an ambiguous relationship with Mrs J. K. (Janie) Moore (1871/2–1951), the mother of an Officers' Training Corps friend, Paddy Moore (1898–1918), who had been killed in the war. Lewis and

Clive Staples Lewis (1898–1963), by Arthur Strong, 1947

Paddy Moore had made a pact that in the event of either of their deaths, the other would look after the bereaved parent. As survivor, Lewis duly moved in with Mrs Moore and her daughter Maureen, first at 28 Warneford Road, Oxford, and from 1930 at The Kilns, Headington Quarry, on the outskirts of Oxford. They lived there until Mrs Moore's death in 1951, and Lewis continued to occupy the house until his own death over ten years later. The nature of their relationship remains a mystery, though in his biography A. N. Wilson makes a good case for its being a sexual one (Wilson, 58). They referred to each other as mother and son, and Lewis undertook the domestic tasks in their home. He remained loyal to Mrs Moore as she descended into senility prior to her death.

In Oxford a small college club, the Martlets, encouraged the literary and dialectical interests Lewis had been able to pursue while recovering from his wounds in hospital. He met W. B. Yeats and formed lasting links with Owen Barfield, who became his solicitor and philosopher-critic. He began a long narrative poem eventually published as *Dymer* (1926) under the pseudonym Clive Hamilton. In 1920 he obtained a first class in classical honour moderations, and in 1921 he won the chancellor's English essay prize with an essay on optimism. In 1922 he obtained a first in *literae humaniores*, and in 1923 achieved the same in English language and literature. Lewis's attempts at fellowships were initially unsuccessful, and he took a temporary post as lecturer in philosophy in his own college, but in 1925 Magdalen elected him as a fellow and tutor in English language and literature, a post he held for nearly thirty years. Throughout this period he had rooms in New Buildings, where initially he taught Anglo-Saxon, philosophy, and political theory as well as English literature. He was on the same staircase as J. A. Smith, which he remarked was a liberal education, and at Magdalen enjoyed the acquaintance of C. C. J. Webb and C. T. Onions. The main influences on his thinking at this time were the writings of Samuel Alexander and G. K. Chesterton. From agnosticism he moved, almost reluctantly, to theism and finally committed himself to the Christian position, after what Wilson describes as a mystical experience in 1929. This conversion is reflected in his first allegorical work, *The Pilgrim's Regress* (1933), written during a holiday in Northern Ireland in 1932. It was in his Magdalen rooms that a few friends, known as the Inklings, met weekly from 1936 to 1939. Among them were J. R. R. Tolkien—who was spurred on by Lewis to complete his epic *The Lord of the Rings*—H. V. D. Dyson, Nevill Coghill, and R. E. Havard, who became Lewis's doctor. They were joined in 1939 by Charles Williams.

Several years of wide reading in medieval literature bore fruit in *The Allegory of Love* (1936), which combined a study of medieval allegory with a new account of courtly love, and won Lewis the Hawthornden prize. He was soon in demand as a speaker and lecturer. *A Preface to 'Paradise Lost'* (1942) was based on lectures given at the University College of North Wales in 1941, and *The Abolition of Man* on the Riddell lectures given at Durham University in 1943; the former retains its value as an introduction to epic in general; the latter presented an indictment of some methods of teaching English that were then gaining ground. *The Screwtape Letters* (1942), an imaginary correspondence between an experienced devil and a subordinate, appealed to a different and far wider public, as did a series of broadcast talks on Christian topics which began in August 1941 and were published later. Among those influenced by them was the young Margaret Roberts, in whose memoirs Lewis features as the most formative influence on her religious outlook: 'the power of his broadcasts, sermons and essays came from a combination of simple language with theological depth' (Thatcher, 40). Lewis became internationally well known, and by 1963 his paperback sales alone had reached a million. But he continued to teach at Oxford, where in 1942 he founded the Socratic Club, a Christian discussion group of which he was president until 1954. By the end of the war he had completed a trilogy of allegorical science fiction with some scenes (such as the college meeting in the opening chapters of *That Hideous Strength*, 1945) set in the contemporary world. A fourth, unfinished, interplanetary story, *The Dark Tower*, was published posthumously in 1977. A retelling of the myth of Cupid and Psyche under the title *Till We Have Faces* (1956) was more subtle but less popular.

Of all Lewis's writings those that remain the most famous are *The Chronicles of Narnia*, seven works of fantasy written for children and published between 1950 and 1956. These books (in the order in which Lewis intended them to be read), *The Magician's Nephew* (1955), *The Lion, the Witch and the Wardrobe* (1950), *The Horse and his Boy* (1954), *Prince Caspian* (1951), *The Voyage of the 'Dawn Treader'* (1952), *The Silver Chair* (1953), and *The Last Battle* (1956), are often discussed by critics as Christian allegories or 'philosophical fairy tales' (Bingham, 357). They remain classics of children's literature and have been televised on a number of occasions, while *The Last Battle* won the Carnegie medal. Set in the imaginary land of Narnia, where animals speak and magic is everywhere, they describe the adventures of the children lucky enough to discover the entrance. Lewis wanted these books to answer the question: 'What might

Christ be like if there really were a world like Narnia and he chose to be incarnate and die and rise again in that world as he actually has done in ours?' Christ is characterized as a magnificent lion, Aslan, who oversees the rule of Narnia by the children, 'sons of Adam' and 'daughters of Eve'. Though the elements of Christian allegory are undeniable, Lewis disliked stories with morals, and the chronicles remain a favourite among children. They have inspired similar works of fantasy, such as Susan Cooper's *The Dark is Rising* sequence (1965–77) and Madeleine L'Engle's *A Wrinkle in Time* (1962). Katherine Patterson's Newbury medal winner, *Bridge to Terabitha* (1978) goes further, and tells the story of two children who are so influenced by the Narnia chronicles that they invent their own magic world. The novels also give amusing insight into Lewis's prejudices—the initially odious behaviour of Eustace Scrubb, who first appears in *The Voyage of the 'Dawn Treader'*, is explained by the fact that his parents are 'up to date and advanced people … vegetarians, non-smokers and teetotallers', three things Lewis emphatically was not.

Lewis's claim to the Merton chair of English literature was passed over in 1946, when his evangelical commitments were thought by some colleagues to be too pronounced. Similar considerations weighed against him when he stood for the chair of poetry in 1950, though his candidacy was strongly supported. In 1944 he had given the Clark lectures in Cambridge and these provided materials for his most substantial book, *English Literature in the Sixteenth Century* (1954), which included a reappraisal of humanism, and detailed his admiration for Hooker and Spenser. It made him the choice for the chair in English medieval and Renaissance literature established at Cambridge in that year, but he had to be persuaded to accept it. Even when he moved to Magdalene College in Cambridge, which had immediately offered him a fellowship, he regularly returned by train to Oxford for weekends and vacations. Magdalen (in 1956) and University College (in 1959) elected him to honorary fellowships but the Merton chair remained elusive, and it was for Cambridge audiences that he reshaped one of his standard Oxford courses on medieval thought and belief into *The Discarded Image* (1964). This, as with two collections of studies, was published posthumously. Freedom from teaching gave him time to complete two other critical works, and to produce a variety of papers and manuals on Christian topics until shortly before his death. He had resigned his chair a few months earlier when Magdalene College, Cambridge, made him an honorary fellow. He was elected Gollancz prizeman in 1937 and FBA in 1955 and among his honorary degrees were DD (St Andrews, 1946) and DLitt (Laval, Quebec, 1952). Lewis declined appointment as CBE.

On 10 January 1950 Lewis began to correspond with Mrs (Helen) Joy Gresham, a writer who lived in Westchester, New York. Leaving her adulterous and alcoholic husband, William Lindsay Gresham, she moved to England in 1952. She and Lewis became friends and on 23 April 1956 they married at the Oxford register office to avoid deportation for her and her two sons from her marriage to Gresham. In 1957 they repeated the ceremony in Anglican form in the Churchill Hospital, Oxford, where Joy was seriously ill with cancer. A year later she unexpectedly recovered and there was a halcyon interval before she succumbed to the disease in 1960. Under the pseudonym N. W. Clerk, Lewis poignantly set down his sense of loss in *A Grief Observed* (1961). Their relationship was explored in William Nicholson's drama *Shadowlands*, which was first aired on BBC television in 1985, starring Joss Ackland as Lewis and Claire Bloom as Gresham. Nigel Hawthorne portrayed Lewis in the London and Broadway stage productions (of 1990 and 1991 respectively), and Anthony Hopkins and Debra Winger took the lead roles in the 1993 film adaptation directed by Richard Attenborough.

Lewis's critical abilities, wit, and conviviality all made for his wide appeal. His critical work was compelling, but it invited criticism from other scholars. His powers as a disputant, which first showed themselves in *The Personal Heresy* (with E. M. W. Tillyard, 1939), and were spotted by his former tutor W. T. Kirkpatrick, made him a formidable defender of Christian values at a time when perplexities and ambiguities flourished. He had not only an imaginative understanding of morality but also, as a former pupil observed, a 'poet's gift for visual and even tactile splendours and a wickedly accurate and entertaining eye for human frailty' (*The Tablet*, 30 Nov 1963). *The Problem of Pain* (1940) reveals another side of his nature; and at least two of the later books, *The Four Loves* (1960) and *An Experiment in Criticism* (1961), show a perceptiveness and delicacy which some earlier readers had not expected to find. He lived more in the world of literature and the imagination than in the technological age; for diversion he preferred to read Kipling or Rider Haggard rather than modern poets or novelists. He showed little interest in college, university, or public affairs, and if he looked at *The Times* it was only to do the crossword. 'He was singularly unfitted for committee work; he detested compromise and was as incapable of negotiation as of intrigue' (*University College Record*, Dec 1963, 162). Impatient of political nostrums, he had a firm belief in ceremony and order, but he was no ritualist. The Ulster elements in his make-up showed in certain protestant and individualist attitudes which distinguished him from Chesterton, to whose role as lay apostle he succeeded. For the 'cult of culture' he felt a profound distaste. He was sometimes taken for a farmer, or a butcher. Fond of walking but not of travel, he only once crossed the channel after 1918, and that was when he took a brief holiday with his wife in Greece and the Aegean in 1960. Lewis died at The Kilns on 22 November 1963 and was buried at Holy Trinity Church, Headington, Oxford.

Assessments of Lewis's character and achievements were attempted by a varied group of friends and pupils in *Light on C. S. Lewis* (1966). In the United States admiration for his Christian writings attained the dimensions of a cult, and it is from America that anthologies and similar works (including several dissertations) have largely come. The most serious studies are by G. Kranz (Bonn, 1974, with a full bibliography) and A. N. Wilson, whose controversial biography (1990) included discussion of Lewis's sexuality and troubled relationship with his father.

J. A. W. BENNETT, *rev.* EMMA PLASKITT

Sources A. N. Wilson, *C. S. Lewis: a biography* (1990) • *The Times* (25 Nov 1963) • H. Gardner, 'Clive Staples Lewis, 1898–1963', *PBA*, 51 (1965) • J. Bingham, *Writers for children* (1988), 357–63 • H. Carpenter and M. Prichard, *The Oxford companion to children's literature*, pbk edn (1999), 309–10, 370 • *University College Record* (Dec 1963) • M. Thatcher, *The path to power* (1995) • C. S. Lewis, *Surprised by joy: the shape of my early life* (1955) • *Letters of C. S. Lewis*, ed. W. H. Lewis (1966) • C. S. Kilby and D. Gilbert, *Images of C. S. Lewis* (1973) • R. Lancelyn Green and W. Hooper, *C. S. Lewis: a biography* (1974) • H. Carpenter, *The Inklings* (1978) • *They stand together: the letters of C. S. Lewis to Arthur Greeves, 1914–1963*, ed. W. Hooper (1979) • personal knowledge (1981)

Archives Bodl. Oxf., corresp. • Bodl. Oxf., corresp. and literary MSS • NRA, corresp. and literary papers • Wheaton College, Illinois, Marion E. Wade Centre, corresp. and papers | BL, corresp. with Society of Authors, Add. MS 63282 • Bodl. Oxf., letters to Michael Edwards • Bodl. Oxf., letters to Arthur Greeves • Bodl. Oxf., letters to A. C. Laurence and Daphne Harwood • Bodl. Oxf., letters to W. H. Lewis • U. Birm. L., letters to C. T. Onions

Likenesses A. Strong, photograph, 1947, NPG [*see illus.*] • photographs, 1950, Hult. Arch. • W. Stoneman, photograph, 1955, repro. in Gardner, 'Clive Staples Lewis', pl. 42 • photograph, repro. in *The Guardian* (28 Nov 1998) • photographs, repro. in Wilson, *C. S. Lewis*

Wealth at death £55,869: probate, 1 April 1964, *CGPLA Eng. & Wales*

Lewis, David (*c.*1520–1584), civil lawyer and college head, was born at Abergavenny in Monmouthshire, the eldest son of Lewis Wallis, later vicar of Abergavenny, and his wife, Lucy, daughter of Llewelyn Thomas Lloyd of Bedwellte in the same county. The father, whose full Welsh name was Lewis ap John ap Gwilym ap Robert Wallis, was descended from a junior branch of the Wallis family of Treowen and Llan-arth Fawr. Another child, Maud, was the mother of David *Baker, the Benedictine monk.

Educated at All Souls College, Oxford, and graduating BCL on 12 July 1540, Lewis became both a notary public and a fellow of his college in 1541. He was appointed university scribe in 1546, early in which year (27 January or 1 February) he became principal of New Inn Hall; but he resigned that post on 27 August 1548, having taken his DCL degree in April, to become an advocate in the courts of civil law. He was admitted to the court of arches as an advocate on 8 August 1548 and to Doctors' Commons on 8 December 1549. He was a master in chancery from 1553 and a master of requests, holding also the 'officialty of Surrey'. During these years he also sat as an MP, for Steyning from 26 October until December 1553 and for his native county of Monmouthshire from 8 November 1554 until January 1555. Although said to have been a master of St Katharine's Hospital near the Tower of London, his name is not to be found in Stowe's list of masters.

With the foundation of Jesus College, Oxford, in 1571 Lewis was appointed first principal on 27 June, but he left the post in 1572, having already become a judge of the high court of admiralty in 1558. During his tenure of that office both it and the ecclesiastical courts found their jurisdiction being challenged by writs of prohibition issued by the courts of common law, which sought to remove cases to their jurisdiction. In 1573 and 1580 Lewis complained to the lord treasurer of the decay of his office and the consequent decline in his emoluments, but to no avail. In 1575 he exchanged his judgeship to become a joint commissioner of the admiralty with his fellow Welshman Sir John Herbert. An active judge, he was involved in cases concerning the maritime problems of Elizabeth I's reign. For instance, on 8 November 1564 he was a commissioner alongside Weston, the dean of the arches, and others inquiring into complaints of piracy against the king of Spain's subjects. In 1566 he conducted the examination of Martin Frobisher, suspected of having fitted out a ship to go to sea as a pirate, and in 1569 he made similar investigations regarding Hawkins's conduct in the West Indies. He was also one of the civil lawyers who signed the opinion dated 17 October 1571 to the effect that John Leslie, bishop of Ross and ambassador of Mary, queen of Scots, was punishable in England for intriguing against its queen.

Lewis retained his interests in south Wales and in 1573 he bought the Monmouthshire estate of Llanddewi Rhydderch. He also wrote to Walsingham on 3 January 1576 suggesting remedies for the troubled state of parts of Wales; in particular he highlighted the dangers involved in the custom of fosterage, and in the gatherings known as *comorthas*, which were liable to be turbulent. He became treasurer of Doctors' Commons and counted the famous civilian Sir Julius Caesar among his protégés. He died unmarried in London on 27 April 1584 and was buried on 24 May at Abergavenny in a tomb at the end of the north aisle of St Mary's Church in what has since become known as the Lewis chapel. The monument by John Gildon of Hereford, made from a single piece of stone and erected during Lewis's lifetime, inspired verses by his friend Thomas Churchyard in *The Worthines of Wales*.

T. G. WATKIN

Sources *DNB* • *DWB* • G. D. Squibb, *Doctors' Commons: a history of the College of Advocates and Doctors of Law* (1977) • Wood, *Ath. Oxon.* • Foster, *Alum. Oxon.* • C. O. S. Morgan, *Some accounts of the ancient monuments in the priory church, Abergavenny* (1872) • [C. Coote], *Sketches of the lives and characters of eminent English civilians, with an historical introduction relative to the College of Advocates* (1804) • HoP, *Commons, 1509–58*

Likenesses J. Gildon, monument, St Mary's Church, Abergavenny

Wealth at death see will, PRO, PROB 11/67/10

Lewis, David [St David Lewis; *alias* Charles Baker] (**1617–1679**), Jesuit and martyr, was born at Abergavenny in Monmouthshire in 1617. It has previously been argued that he was the son of Henry Baker and his wife, Anne (*née* Baskerville), of Herefordshire and thereby a great-nephew of Dom Augustine Baker OSB. However, there is more evidence to suggest that he was one of nine children born to the Revd Morgan Lewis (*d. c.*1638), the protestant principal of the Royal Grammar School, Abergavenny, and his wife, Margaret Pritchard (*d. c.*1638), a devout Catholic. He was certainly educated at the Royal Grammar School and in 1633 travelled to Paris with John Savage (later Earl Rivers).

David Lewis [St David Lewis; Charles Baker] (**1617–1679**), by Alexander Voet, pubd 1683

While in Paris he met Father William Talbot SJ and converted to Roman Catholicism.

Upon the outbreak of war in France Lewis returned to Wales in 1636 and 'engaged in the study of law' (Canning, 160) but two years later he was sent by John Pritchard, his uncle and a Jesuit priest, to the English College at Rome. He arrived there on 2 November 1638 and the following day was received at the English College. At the college he stated, 'My name is David Lewis, *alias* Charles Baker. My father was Morgan Lewis and my mother Margaret Pritchard, both Catholics who lately died of fever' (Canning, 160). In June 1641 he received minor orders and was ordained as a priest on 20 July 1642. On St Stephen's day in this year he gave a short Latin discourse entitled 'Corona Christi pro spinis gemmea' on the martyrdom of St Stephen before Urban VIII and on 19 April 1645 he entered the noviciate of St Andrew's in Rome. After two years probation he went to Wales to conduct missionary work, but he was recalled to Rome to act as confessor and spiritual director at the English College. In 1648 he was sent to Monmouthshire where he acted as a missionary priest for the disparate Roman Catholic population. He was twice superior of the south Wales district and rector of the Cwm Jesuit Seminary, Llanrothal, in Herefordshire, from 1667 to 1672, and again from 1674 to 1679. For thirty years he worked tirelessly visiting the persecuted Roman Catholic communities and, as a consequence of his charitable work, he was commonly known as Tad y Tlodion (Father of the Poor).

In November 1678 the government, alarmed by news of a popish plot, offered a reward of £20 for the capture of any Roman Catholic priest. This was supplemented by a further £200 by John Arnold, a local magistrate in Monmouthshire, for the conviction and execution of Catholic priests in the counties of Monmouthshire and Herefordshire. Lewis's popularity among Roman Catholics and his charitable deeds meant that he was sheltered from persecution for a brief period as none was 'willing to turn traitor to him, or give evidence against him, or in any way to conspire for his death' (Canning, 160). Nevertheless he soon fell victim to the mass hysteria whipped up by Titus Oates. He was arrested on Sunday 17 November 1678 at St Michael's, Llantarnam parish church, in Monmouthshire, where he was preparing to say mass. He was taken under armed guard to Abergavenny and thereafter committed to Monmouth gaol. He remained there until 13 January 1679 when he was transferred to Usk gaol. While imprisoned rumours spread that he had managed to escape from his captors as well as having poisoned his gaoler.

On 28 March 1679 Lewis was brought before Monmouth assizes on a charge of high treason and was condemned under the act of 27 Elizabeth as a traitor. During the trial there was evidence that one of his accusers, Dorothy James, sought revenge against him for an earlier failed chancery suit and sought to wash her hands in his blood and make 'porridge' of his head (Foley, 5.923). He was condemned to death the following day, but was reprieved until the following May by the judge, Sir Robert Atkins, on condition that he supply information to the privy council about the Popish Plot. At his arraignment in London Lord Shaftesbury suggested that Lewis renounce the Roman Catholic religion to save his life. Lewis, as a committed Roman Catholic, would not convert and was unable to offer any details about an alleged plot. He was sent back to Usk gaol, where he remained for a further three months before his execution at Usk on 27 August 1679. On the day of his execution he gave a speech in which he recorded that he had no knowledge of the plot and stated 'discover plot I could not, for I knew of none; and conform I would not for it was against my conscience' ('Speech of David Lewis', 2; O'Keefe, 121). Although he was sentenced to be hanged, drawn, and quartered, the assembled crowd took pity upon him and would not allow him to suffer. They thereby ensured that he died upon the scaffold and was not quartered. His disembowelled body was later that day buried in the churchyard of the priory church of St Mary at Usk. He was among the forty martyrs of England and Wales canonized by Paul VI on 25 October 1970.

RICHARD C. ALLEN

Sources 'The speech of David Lewis (Father Baker) at his place of execution at Usk, co. Mon. Envelope endorsed: original speech of Father Charles Baker written out by himself while in prison, and delivered from the scaffold at Usk', 27 Aug 1679, NL Wales, Baker-Gabb MSS 703–704 • 'A short narrative of the discovery of a college of Jesuits at a place called the Come, in the co. of Hereford, together with an account of the knavery of Father Lewis, the pretended Bishop of Llandaff', 1679, NL Wales, Baker-Gabb MS 723 [transcript copy] • 'A true narrative of the imprisonment and tryal of Mr David Lewis (Father Baker)', 1679, NL Wales, Baker-Gabb MS 724 [transcribed from the original manuscript preserved in the Old Clergy Chapter collection of MSS, London]; see *Fifth report*, HMC, 4 (1876), 467 • 'Notes on the trial of David Lewis otherwise Charles Baker, a Jesuit (pretended Bishop of Llandaff) at Monmouth assizes, for high treason', 28 March 1679, NL Wales, Baker-Gabb MS 726 • Oxford circuit, gaol files spring 1678 – Lent 1696/7, PRO, ASSI. 2/2 • J. Arnold and others, *An abstract of several examinations taken upon oath, in the counties of Monmouth and Hereford* (1680) • *The condemnation of the cheating popish priest ... Who lately cheated a poor woman of £15, and got a warrant against her for £15 more, on pretence of praying for her father's soul out of purgatory* (1679) • *Letter from a gentleman in the countrie to his friend in London, occasioned by a prophesie that was lately found in the place of retirement of Father Lewis, of Combe in Herefordshire* ... (1679) • J. H. Canning, 'The Titus Oates plot in south Wales and the marches', article 4: 'The Venerable David Lewis, S.J.', *St Peter's Magazine*, 3 (1923), 159–68, 189–97, 219–26 • J. M. Cronin, 'Ven. David Lewis, S.J.', *St Peter's Magazine*, 9 (1929), 265–9, 295–9, 328–33 • M. M. C. O'Keefe, 'The Popish Plot in south Wales and the marches of Gloucester and Hereford', MA diss., National University of Ireland (University College, Galway), 1970 • Gillow, *Lit. biog. hist.*, 4.205–9 • H. Foley, ed., *Records of the English province of the Society of Jesus*, 5 (1879), 912–31; 7 (1882–3), 456 • T. P. Ellis, *The Catholic martyrs of Wales, 1535–1680* (1933), 129–40 • R. P. Matthews, 'Roman Catholic recusancy in Monmouthshire, 1608–89. A demographic and morphological analysis', PhD diss., U. Wales, Cardiff, 1996 • D. A. Bellenger, ed., *English and Welsh priests, 1558–1800* (1984) • *The Catholic martyrs of England and Wales*, Catholic Truth Society, 2nd edn (1979) • R. Challoner, *Memoirs of missionary priests*, another edn, 2 vols. (1803), vol. 2, pp. 214–29 • R. Hodges, *Blessed David Lewis* (1931) • P. P. Murphy, 'Catholics in Monmouthshire, 1533–1689', *Presenting Monmouthshire*, 21 (1966), 33–8 • P. P. Murphy, 'The Jesuit College of the Cwm, Llanrothall', *Severn and Wye Review*, 1/6 (1970–72), 135–9 • J. H. Matthews, 'Mass in penal times', *St Peter's Magazine*, 9 (1929), 322–6 • J. B. Davies, *Blessed David Lewis* (1960) • E. T. Davies, 'Popish Plot in Monmouthshire', *Journal of the Historical Society of the Church in Wales*, 25 (1976), 32–45 • J. C. H. Aveling, *The handle and the axe: the Catholic recusants in England from Reformation to emancipation* (1976), chaps. 8–9 • J. Bossy, *The English Catholic community, 1570–1850* (1975) • P. Jenkins, 'Anti-popery on the Welsh marches in the seventeenth century', *HJ*, 23 (1980), 275–93 • G. Holt, *The English Jesuits, 1650–1829: a biographical dictionary*, Catholic RS, 70 (1984) • B. L. Norton, 'Recusancy in south Wales, 1600–1840', MA diss., U. Wales, Cardiff, 1996

Archives Newport Reference Library, Monmouthshire, Haines collection, speeches and accounts [transcript copy] • NL Wales, Baker-Gabb MSS, speeches and transcripts

Likenesses A. Voet, line engraving, pubd 1683, NPG [*see illus.*] • group portrait, lithograph, 1685 (*Titus Oates and Jesuits*), BM • Soldaticzat, engraving, Carmelite Convent, Lanherne, St Columb, Cornwall • A. Voet, portrait, repro. in Canning, 'The Titus Oates plot', 159

Lewis, David (1682–1760), poet, was probably born in Wales, the son of Roger Lewis of Llanddewi Felffre, Pembrokeshire. He was educated at Jesus College, Oxford, from where he matriculated on 4 January 1698, aged sixteen, and gained his BA on 20 March 1702. He moved to London and became usher or undermaster at Westminster School from 1726 to 1732.

Lewis also began to develop an interest in contemporary poetry, and this led to his first publication in 1726 of *Miscellaneous Poems by Several Hands*, published by J. Watts and dedicated to Lord Charles Noel Somerset, who had been his pupil at Westminster. The work has 320 pages of poems and inscriptions from a range of poets from Oxford and Cambridge who were living in London. It provides a pleasing mixture of occasional poems, ballads, songs, and translations, sad, happy, sincere, and frivolous. Some poems were by Lewis but are not identified. The collection is important for containing John Dyer's 'Grongar Hill' in its final form and the first draft of Alexander Pope's 'Vital spark of heavenly flame', written in 1712. Lewis began a literary contact with Pope, whose support is acknowledged in the introduction to his tragedy *Philip of Macedon, as it is Acted at the Theatre Royal in Lincoln's Inn Fields*, published in 1727. It presents the fortunes of Philip, king of Macedon, Olympias his daughter, Perses and Demetrius his sons, and Didas, captain of the guards and conspirator with Perses. It was first acted on 29 March 1727 and repeated three times. In 1729 it was played again at Drury Lane.

The good reception of his collection of poetry led Lewis to publish a second collection, *Miscellaneous Poems by Several Hands*, dedicated to the earl of Shaftesbury in 1730. Like its predecessor it contained verses on a range of topics, typical being 'To a Lady on the Death of her Only Child, an Infant' (p. 115), 'On the Picture of a Talkative Young Lady' (p. 304), 'The Dropsical Man' (pp. 116–17), and 'On the Late Order for Shooting the Geese in the Parks about St James' (p. 305). Lewis again included some of his poems but did not identify them. Pope's epigram 'On Certain Ladies' was included, as well as his epitaph for Mr Digby, Pope and Lewis discussing how it should be printed. Two years later Lewis contributed verses beginning 'While malice, Pope, denies thy page' to Richard Savage's *Collection of Pieces on Occasion of 'The Dunciad'* (1732). Pope appreciated the verses, as did Johnson later when he praised them highly on 13 June 1784 in conversation with Anna Seward.

Lewis married Mary (1683/1684–1774), fourth daughter of Newdigate Owsley, a merchant of Leyton, Essex, and later moved to Essex, where he died aged seventy-seven in April 1760 at Low Leyton. He was buried on 8 April in Leyton church, his inscription referring to his many excellent pieces of poetry. His wife died on 10 October 1774 aged ninety and was buried with him. F. D. A. Burns

Sources Foster, *Alum. Oxon.* • Boswell, *Johnson*, ed. G. B. Hill, [another edn], 4 (1887), 306–7 • *The correspondence of Alexander Pope*, ed. G. Sherburn, 3 (1956), 104–5, 123n • A. Pope, *The Dunciad*, ed. J. Sutherland (1943), vol. 5 of *The Twickenham edition of the poems of Alexander Pope*, ed. J. Butt (1939–69), 116 • A. Pope, *The Dunciad in four books*, ed. V. Rumbold (1999), 167–8 • *DNB*

Lewis [*formerly* Levy], **David** (1823–1885), department store owner, was born in London, the son of Wolfe Levy, a Jewish merchant. He had at least one brother, who emigrated to Australia in the 1840s. In 1839 Lewis went to Liverpool to work for Benjamin Hyam & Co., a firm of tailors and outfitters, and within eighteen months he was appointed manager of the Liverpool branch. In 1842 he was put in charge of opening new branches in Scotland and Ireland, and of supervising existing branches. On 6 September 1856 he married Bertha, daughter of Isaac Cohen, the rabbi in Dover.

Lewis started his own business at 44 Ranelagh Street,

Liverpool, in 1846, selling men's and boy's clothing. Most of the clothes were made in his own workshop, as was usual at the time, and he also designed new clothes—his speciality was knickerbocker suits. His customers were mainly working-class, and had not been able to afford tailoring before. From the beginning he established principles which were to guide his business throughout his life: he refused to haggle, setting a low price and sticking to it; he did not give credit; and he was always willing to exchange unsatisfactory goods. He never borrowed money, and he always ploughed his profits back into the business. In 1859 he opened premises in Bold Street, in a more fashionable area, and in 1864 began to sell London and Paris women's fashions. At the same time he was extending the Ranelagh Street shop, eventually buying five adjacent properties, and he built a clock tower, which became a Liverpool landmark. He continued to add departments, including women's shoes in 1874, and tobacco in 1879, and as the business expanded, he began to buy goods in from outside, making bulk purchases directly from the factories.

In 1877 Lewis opened a new shop, next door to George Henry Lee in Basnett Street, and called it Bon Marché, after the Paris store. As in Paris, all kinds of goods were displayed, with the emphasis on women's fashions and Paris 'nouveautés'. Lewis kept it completely separate from his main store, and its clientele was quite different. Its lavish attractions included a model of the Strasbourg Cathedral clock, and 'Christmas Fairyland'.

A large new store opened in Market Street, Manchester, in 1880, built in the French Renaissance style, with six departments. Other departments were soon added, including a grocery department with deliveries twice a day to the suburbs. In the early 1880s Lewis began to sell tea, in response to the rapid expansion of tea drinking in working-class families, and Lewis's two-shilling tea became famous nationally. Another well-known line was velveteen: the velveteen department was the largest in the Manchester store, and a large mail-order section was developed. Lewis built extensions on to the store, and by 1885 there were seven floors.

Two more branches were opened in the 1880s. In 1884 a small shop opened at 15 Waingate in Sheffield, selling tea, and soon expanded to sell such familiar Lewis lines as velveteen and cigars, but, with a depression in the cutlery trade, Sheffield was not prospering at this point and the shop closed down at the beginning of 1888. The huge Birmingham store, however, opened as a department store in 1885 in the newly built Corporation Street, on 850 square yards of land leased from the Birmingham corporation, and focusing on women customers, attracted 40,000 on the opening day.

Lewis was always aware of the importance of advertising. In 1869 he began publication of halfpenny memorandum books, with advertising on the cover and in eight special pages in the centre, and sold 20 million in the 1870s. In 1882 he launched a series of Penny Readings, and sold a quarter of a million in the first eleven weeks. In 1880 and 1881 he spent 10 per cent of the gross sales of the Manchester store on advertising. When rival Manchester shopkeepers took him to court in 1881 for blocking the market square, Lewis printed 100,000 copies of his story of the trial and offered one to every householder in Manchester. Shortly before he died he chartered the famous steamship the *Great Eastern* for a year, arranging for it to be anchored in the Mersey estuary as part of the Liverpool International Exhibition of 1886, to be used as a social centre. 20,000 went on board in the first four days, and over half a million visited it.

Lewis died on 4 December 1885 at his home in Liverpool, after a long illness, and was buried three days later in the Hebrew cemetery, Fairfield. Out of a small men's tailoring business he had created a large department store, the largest in Liverpool, catering for the working classes of the north of England, with branches in other cities. He had no children, but he had encouraged members of his family to join what he always regarded as a family business. Louis Cohen, Bertha Cohen's nephew, who was born in Australia, and who married Lewis's niece, Mary Levy, succeeded him as head of the business.

Lewis set up the David Lewis Trust, to be used for charitable purposes in Liverpool and Manchester. His executors developed the David Lewis Northern Hospital, and in 1906 the David Lewis Hotel and Club Association was founded, as a neighbourhood centre, in the Liverpool docklands.

ANNE PIMLOTT BAKER

Sources A. Briggs, *Friends of the people: the centenary history of Lewis's* (1956) • E. Midwinter, *Old Liverpool* (1971), 149–60 • A. Briggs, 'Lewis, David', *DBB* • B. Lancaster, *The department store: a social history* (1995) • C. M. King and H. King, *The two nations* (1938) • *Liverpool Courier* (5 Dec 1885) • *Liverpool Daily Albion* (5 Dec 1885) • *CGPLA Eng. & Wales* (1886) • m. cert. • d. cert.

Likenesses portrait, repro. in Briggs, *Friends of the people*, frontispiece

Wealth at death £125,081 9s. 7d.: probate, 12 April 1886, *CGPLA Eng. & Wales*

Lewis, David Malcolm (1928–1994), classical scholar, was born in Willesden, London, on 7 June 1928, the elder son of William Lewis, auctioneer, and his wife, Milly. His parents were both born in the United Kingdom; his grandparents were immigrants from Poland and Lithuania, part of the Jewish immigration in the last two decades of the nineteenth century. Lewis was educated at the City of London School and Corpus Christi College, Oxford, where he took a first in *literae humaniores* in 1949. After national service in the Royal Army Education Corps he went to Princeton University where he completed his PhD degree in 1952; he was also a member of the Institute for Advanced Study. He returned to Corpus Christi College, Oxford, as junior research fellow in 1954, and in the following year he became an official student (tutorial fellow) of Christ Church, in succession to R. H. Dundas, a post which he held until 1985 when the University of Oxford appointed him to a personal professorship. He was elected a fellow of the British Academy in 1973; other honours included corresponding membership of the German Archaeological Institute.

For the last two decades of his distinguished career

David Malcolm Lewis (1928–1994), by Jane Bown

Lewis was the world's leading expert in the study and interpretation of Greek (particularly Athenian) inscriptions on stone. This interest had been influenced at Princeton, which he himself regarded as the mecca of Greek epigraphy in the 1950s, by his contacts with A. E. Raubitschek and B. D. Meritt. It culminated in his re-edition in two volumes, under the auspices of the Berlin Academy, of the Athenian inscriptions prior to 403 BC (*Inscriptiones Graecae*). This labour on the standard corpus of Attic inscriptions occupied him, on and off, between 1962 and 1994. He also produced, in collaboration with Russell Meiggs, a revision of a much more accessible standard work, M. N. Tod's *Greek Historical Inscriptions to the End of the Fifth Century BC* (1969). He was, however, no mere technician. He understood that a document is both a physical object and a text with a specific historical context, and he constantly insisted on the importance of using a broad range of documents for the imaginative reconstruction of history. In doing so he went well beyond the confines of classical Greek inscriptions: he made an important contribution to the *Corpus papyrorum Judaicarum* III (ed. A. Fuks, V. Tcherikover, M. Stern, 1964) in the form of a section on the Jewish inscriptions of Egypt and he published authoritatively in his later years on the Persepolis Fortification Texts, written in Elamite and dating from the period 509–494 BC.

Lewis's rigour and breadth of vision in the central field of classical Greek history was demonstrated in his slim (but far from slight) book, *Sparta and Persia* (1977), which drew together the documentation and political history of the late fifth and early fourth centuries BC; and in an enormous amount of editorial and authorial work on volumes 4, 5, and 6 of the second edition of the *Cambridge Ancient History* (1988–94), covering the period from archaic times to Alexander the Great. His knowledge and authority ranged far beyond the conventional bounds of Greek history: he was also a considerable expert on (as well as a collector of) Greek coinage, and on Persian and Jewish history, and he was a formidable linguist with knowledge of Elamite, Aramaic, and Akkadian. He moved with ease across the conventional scholarly boundaries between classical antiquity and the ancient Near East. Underlying his scholarship was a passion for rational debate and a humanitarian vision far beyond the immediate historical context. He was fascinated by the ways in which different cultures, particularly Greek, Persian, and Jewish, interacted and communicated despite linguistic and cultural differences, and he was able to show that the complexities of particular societies and their relationships had a much wider relevance. These interests and qualities were also evident in a meticulously researched and authoritative book on a modern topic, *The Jews of Oxford* (1992). He was an active and leading member of the Oxford Hebrew congregation, a member for whom the continuity of the Jewish historical and cultural tradition was of paramount importance.

The range, size, and quality of Lewis's published output, great though it was, did not reflect the full measure of his influence. For four decades his unstinting generosity in offering advice and constructive criticism on ideas, drafts of articles, and books of other scholars, both established and postgraduate, was legendary, and crucially instrumental in shaping the progress of scholarship in Greek history in the second half of the twentieth century. On one occasion he was characterized by Keith Thomas, then a fellow of St John's College, as 'the man who writes other people's books for them' (Hornblower, 582). Much of this was done by written response, and it rested on the foundation of a prodigious and all but faultless memory. His criticism could be and often was very trenchant, but it was never mean or malicious. In conversation he was always enlightening and challenging, but his mode of discourse tended to be elliptical and could be disconcerting to those unfamiliar with it. Sometimes a train of thought in a conversation which had been interrupted was resumed hours, days, or even weeks later with little or no signposting. The quizzical look, the raised eyebrow, the mobility of the lips giving a clue to the internal scanning of the mind's hard disc, were all characteristic, with humour and the potential for self-mockery never far from the surface.

By the mid-1970s Lewis's international authority and reputation were such that he was a leading candidate (regarded by many as the leading candidate) for the Wykeham chair of ancient (Greek) history at Oxford, eventually vacated by his senior colleague and close friend A. Andrewes on 30 September 1977. In the event, W. G. Forrest of Wadham College was preferred. This was perhaps largely due to the influence of M. I. Finley, the Cambridge member of the electoral board, who appears to have considered Lewis more as a technical epigraphist than as a historian (a view which is comprehensively undermined by Lewis's published work, especially that subsequent to 1977). Nevertheless, Lewis's own superficial inscrutability and difficulty in communicating with those who did not know him well may have played a part; and, although first-class students found a mine of information in his lectures, the less able or erudite often found him difficult to follow. Lewis was disappointed to be passed over for the Wykeham chair, but not unduly so, nor to the detriment of relations with colleagues or pupils. He continued to tutor undergraduates at Christ Church and other colleges in Greek history until his elevation to a personal chair in 1985, and to lecture until the end of his life. The period from 1977 to 1994 was heavily occupied by work on the new edition of the *Cambridge Ancient History*, and he took on the challenge of understanding and using the resources of the new information technology with more understanding, vigour, and effect than most of his colleagues, senior and junior.

In 1958 Lewis had married Barbara Wright, daughter of the distinguished physiologist Professor Samson Wright. They had four daughters, Joanna, Isabel, Helen, and Eve. After a year-long struggle against cancer, during which his stoicism, good humour, and calm rationality were an inspiration to all around him, Lewis died at 1 Ferry Pool Road, Oxford, on 12 July 1994. He was buried in the Jewish section of the Oxford cemetery. He was survived by his wife. ALAN K. BOWMAN

Sources S. Hornblower, 'David Malcolm Lewis, 1928–1994', *PBA*, 94 (1997), 557–96 • A. K. Bowman, 'David Malcolm Lewis', *Christ Church* (1994) • *The Times* (18 July 1994) • *The Independent* (15 July 1994) • *The Guardian* (16 July 1994) • personal knowledge (2004) • private information (2004)

Likenesses J. Bown, photograph, British Academy, London [*see illus.*] • photograph, repro. in *The Independent*

Wealth at death £92,495: probate, 28 Oct 1994, *CGPLA Eng. & Wales*

Lewis, Edward (1701–1784), Church of England clergyman and writer, was born at Aldersey, near Chester, Cheshire, the son of John Lewis, a farmer. Educated at Wrexham under Mr Appleton he was admitted to St John's College, Cambridge, on 3 July 1719 on a sizar's scholarship; he graduated BA in 1722 and MA in 1726. On 23 September 1725 he was presented by Sir Henry Ashhurst to the rectory of Emmington, Oxfordshire, and on 18 July 1726 he became rector of Waterstock in the same county. In addition to these preferments, which he held until his death, he was chaplain to Earl Cadogan. He married at Waterstock, on 4 September 1725, Elinor Manby (*d.* 1766).

Lewis published several sermons and wrote repeatedly against Roman Catholicism; his works include the anti-Jacobite *The Invasion* (1744), *Peace to Britain, or, No Popish Pretender* (1745), and *The Patriot King Displayed in the Life and Reign of Henry VIII* (1769). He also published a translation of Chrysostom on St Paul, *Subjection to Higher Powers* (1777), and is thought to have been the author of a moral drama in verse, entitled *The Italian Husband, or, The Violated Bed Avenged* (1754). He died on 4 November 1784 and was buried with his wife in Waterstock church, where a tablet was erected to his memory in the chancel, according to the terms of his will.

W. A. J. ARCHBOLD, *rev.* EMMA MAJOR

Sources Venn, *Alum. Cant.* • *ESTC* • will, 1785, PRO, PROB 11/1134, sig. 473 • private information (1892)

Wealth at death £500; plus estate: will, 1785, PRO, PROB 11/1134, sig. 473

Lewis, Sir Edward George (1900–1980), record and gramophone company executive, was born at Allerton Mount, Duffield Road, Derby on 19 April 1900, the only son in the family of four children of Sir Alfred Edward Lewis (1868–1940), banker, and his wife, May Roberts. His father was an employee and later chief general manager of the National and Provincial Bank. Lewis was educated at Rugby School and Trinity College, Cambridge. Thereafter he entered the world of finance and at the age of twenty-five established his own stockbroking firm, E. G. Lewis & Co., which continued to trade in the late twentieth century. In 1923 he married Margaret Mary ('Masie'), daughter of the Revd George Dickson Hutton; they had two sons, one of whom died while still at Rugby School, attempting to rescue a drowning boy at the school's boys club summer camp. The other later became the senior partner in the stockbroking firm that Lewis founded.

Record production Through his stockbroking activities, Lewis became acquainted with the Decca Company, which manufactured recording and play-back equipment and developed the world's first portable gramophone. In the summer of 1928 Lewis's firm acted as brokers for Decca's stock market flotation, and the apparently excellent prospects of the firm, together with the boom then happening in the broader music industry, ensured that the share issue was oversubscribed some twenty fold. Lewis's interest in the company and music industry in general began to take up more and more of his time and he attempted to put his expertise to work in expanding Decca. His idea was for the company to build on its worldwide reputation and distribution network by expanding into the business of record production and manufacture, a far more lucrative branch of the industry than that of the manufacture of equipment to play records on.

However, when Lewis approached Decca's board of directors with his plans for establishing Decca's own catalogue of records, complete with a roster of artists, they were sceptical. They went as far as inspecting a possible factory site—the ailing Duophone Company's record factory at Shannon's Corner, Kingston—but turned Lewis down in January 1929. Undeterred, Lewis fell back on his own financial expertise and industry contacts, and set about forming a syndicate, the Malden Holding Company Ltd, with a view to establishing a record company of his own, based around the Duophone factory. In the event, Lewis and his colleagues decided to take over Decca, since it had an established name and network, and on 28 February 1929 a new Decca issue was made, shares this time being oversubscribed nearly twofold. The new business that began trading with such high hopes was soon engulfed in the great depression which began with the Wall Street crash later that year. As countless companies went to the wall, Lewis faced a titanic struggle to prevent Decca going under, a struggle that lasted a decade. Within a year of the 1929 issue, Decca's bankers were threatening foreclosure, and at its financial nadir some years later, the company even had its telephone cut off. It was not until 1945 that Decca's shareholders began to make even a small profit from their original investments.

Keeping Decca afloat As disaster loomed in 1931, Lewis argued for a change in the company's management, more rapid expansion, and, in an attempt to eat into the market share of the newly formed Electric and Musical Industries (EMI) conglomerate, substantial cuts in the retail price of Decca records. Lewis eventually got his way, but not without a series of managerial tussles, intense lobbying of shareholders, and even a nationwide tour on his own part (he never claimed for his travel expenses in all his years at Decca) to assess the company's performance in the market-place. By September Lewis had secured the departure of Decca's managing director, S. C. Newton, and *de facto* became his successor, although he took no official position other than becoming a member of the board. In practice, however, he had effective control of the company. It had been Lewis's intention for this state of affairs to last only a few months, but he was soon tied into the company's long-term prospects and was forced by the exigencies of the deepening great depression and attendant decline in the record industry (in Britain between 1929 and 1938 record sales fell by eighty-five per cent) to think of new ways of keeping Decca afloat. He signed new artists such as the singer Gertrude Lawrence and the best-selling dance band leader Jack Hylton, combining this with a policy of consistently lowering retail prices below those charged by EMI. In the early 1930s Lewis strengthened the Decca popular and classical record catalogues by accessing the recordings of two important overseas record companies. To achieve this, he first acquired the American Brunswick Record Company, then a subsidiary of Hollywood film-makers Warner Brothers, which marketed records by leading popular American artists such as Bing Crosby and Al Jolson. He then concluded a licensing agreement with the German Polydor Company giving him access to a whole range of classical recordings. Nevertheless, by 1933, as the record industry continued to disintegrate, Decca found itself in further difficulties, managing to raise only £23,000 on a share issue of £120,000. Despite the deep personal depression that Lewis experienced as a consequence of all this, he persevered, mobilizing his own resources and those of friends and family to take up the rest of the issue, though not without experiencing considerable hardship in the process of finding money to pay for it. At the same time, every available economy was made within the company and as part of this drive loyal staff accepted salary cuts. Lewis later recalled that without such selfless devotion the Decca enterprise could never have survived, but his own diplomatic skills and sheer determination were also important ingredients.

By 1934 Decca was breaking into the lucrative American market and the record division at least turned in its first profit. During this period, in order to supervise his growing transatlantic trade, Lewis travelled back and forth between Britain and the United States. Yet even this expansion proved a drain on the company's slender resources. However, through a combination of Lewis's adroitness, good luck, and a gradual upturn in the global economy, by the time the Second World War broke out in 1939, it appeared that Decca had weathered the storm. In the circumstances of war, demand for records began to rise: Lewis attributed this, in Britain at least, to the greater need for home entertainment as city centres closed down and blacked out in the face of much feared and expected air-raids. Furthermore, in 1940, Decca engineers began experiments in the field of radio navigation, a form of radar. Initial scepticism on the parts of both the British and United States military delayed its development somewhat, but, by 1944, entirely successful tests ensured that the 'Decca Navigator', as the final product was called, was crucial in the execution of the D-day landings at Normandy. Decca subsequently diversified into more specialized technical defence related fields, and its air and sea navigation equipment proved a cornerstone of the company's post-war development. Indeed, this area of the business continued to be profitable during the late 1970s, when the record division ran into serious trouble, and, in 1980, when the business was finally sold and broken up, the defence sector proved to be Decca's largest single asset.

Post-war surge in profits After the war, Decca came into its own and saw its profits surge. Lewis had an ear for popular and classical music, and gathered around him a strong team of artist and repertoire managers and classical record producers. He also had a great respect for (and a good grasp of) the ever changing tastes of the record buying public. His guiding principle was that it was no use arguing with the public about what it wanted. The only serious mistake Decca made was to audition and reject the Beatles, though they did sign the Rolling Stones and a host of other rock bands. That aside, Decca prospered under Lewis, who did not even assume the official title of chairman until 1957. He never claimed to be a technical or recording expert, but his great skill in co-ordinating and maximizing the efforts of the experts he worked with earned him the gold Albert medal of the Royal Society of Arts for services to the development of electronics in 1967. He was knighted in 1951.

Lewis was a man who combined a cheerful calm manner with incredible business acumen. A fervent believer in private enterprise, he was a vocal opponent of state intervention in the market-place after 1945, a view articulated most notably in his business memoirs, *No CIC*, first published in 1956 (the CIC in the title stands for 'Capital Issues Committee', the body established after the war to supervise capital issues and transfers). Lewis's point was that had its restrictive practices been in force during the 1930s, he would never have been able to build up Decca into the successful business it became. Like many who create, build, and retain close personal control over large enterprises, Lewis was unable to appoint a successor or relinquish control of the business. As a consequence, in 1980, days before his death, the business, then in the grip of a serious financial crisis, was sold.

Final years Lewis was not an extravagant man, despite his huge personal fortune. He donated large sums of money to Rugby School and the Middlesex Hospital, and he was more interested in watching a cricket match than living a life of obvious luxury. His first wife died in 1968 and in 1973 he married Jeanie Margaret, daughter of Thomas Henry Smith, a farmer. During the latter period of his life Lewis had a London home at 69A Cadogan Place, Chelsea, as well as one in the country at Bridge House Farm, Felsted, Essex. He died of cancer at his London home, on 29 January 1980. He was survived by his second wife. 'Leaving aside his successes in the field of electronics', noted his obituarist in *The Gramophone*, 'he will always be remembered as one of the great men of the record industry'.

PETER MARTLAND

Sources E. G. Lewis, *No CIC* (privately printed, London, 1956) • *The Times* (30 Jan 1980) • *The Gramophone*, 57/682 (March 1980), 1374 • *WWW* • b. cert. • d. cert. • m. cert. • *CGPLA Eng. & Wales* (1980)
Likenesses photograph, repro. in *The Gramophone*
Wealth at death £1,104,730: probate, 5 Feb 1980, *CGPLA Eng. & Wales*

Lewis, Elizabeth Anne (1843–1924), temperance activist, was born on 10 March 1843 at Market Drayton, Shropshire, the daughter of George Lewis and his wife (her name is not known), both total abstainers. As a child Elizabeth Anne helped her father at his outdoor temperance meetings. On 16 May 1867 she married her cousin Thomas Lewis (*d.* 1931), a coach builder of Sandbach, and the couple moved to Wigan. In 1868 they settled in Blackburn.

Adult active temperance work started in 1882 for Elizabeth Lewis when she assisted at a Blue Ribbon mission in Blackburn. When the mission was finished Mrs Lewis continued its work on her own. On 1 September 1883, supported by her husband, she opened her own mission and hired her own missionary workers. The following year she re-established her mission at Spinner's Rest in Blackburn and had temperance tracts printed and distributed. After a slow start she attracted a growing audience to Mrs Lewis's Teetotal Mission, as it became known, and in 1891 her husband built a new mission hall for his wife which was named Lees Hall, after the Leeds reformer Frederic R. Lees.

Known in Blackburn as the Drunkard's Friend, Mrs Lewis became a well-known temperance advocate throughout northern England, speaking at various missions as well as at many open-air meetings. In 1903 she started holding summertime temperance meetings on the sands at Blackpool. A strong moral suasionist, believing that the appetite for drink had to be eliminated by individual rejections and not by legal means, she strove to combat intemperance among the poorest working men, in Blackburn and other northern towns. Mrs Lewis and her assistants were personally involved in the individual drunkard's reform. She made many home visits and was reportedly so loved and respected by those she had 'saved' that her picture was often displayed in their homes alongside their pledge cards. She frequently accosted inebriated persons on the streets and sought to convert them to temperance. To promote the anti-drink message in Blackburn she held well-publicized public parades through its streets with reformed drunkards as the main attraction. These former drinkers also spoke at her meetings, telling how total abstinence had changed their lives. They were encouraged to run their own temperance meetings at her mission. The financial benefits of teetotalism were emphasized, bringing criticism from some religious leaders.

Not personally identified with any religious sect, Mrs Lewis encouraged those she pledged to attend their own churches. To avoid any conflict with the various churches she also had separate pledges for protestants and for Roman Catholics; the latter was called the Father Nugent pledge, after the Roman Catholic priest and temperance leader of that name. By such means she maintained good relations with most religious establishments in Blackburn. It was estimated that she was responsible for between 1000 and 2000 total abstinence pledges signed every year. Her mission also carried out other social aid programmes for the poor; for instance it supplied free clogs and free breakfasts to poor children in Blackburn.

As a counter-attraction to the entertainments of drinking facilities, Lees Hall was the scene of weekly Saturday evening musical entertainments as well as Sunday and Wednesday temperance meetings. Both Mr and Mrs Lewis were accomplished musicians and performed frequently. Lectures on phrenology, mesmerism, and the presentation of sacred dramas and magic lantern slides occurred during the regular Saturday presentations. The tickets to these entertainments cost 1*d.* each. They were very popular, attracting approximately 600 people every Saturday.

In 1889 a publican accused Mrs Lewis of sexual misconduct with her assistant. The following year, 'to save the reputation of her mission and herself', she sued her accuser for libel, winning her case. A public subscription raised £333 to pay her legal fees.

Mrs Lewis's work was supported by the local authorities. She was the first woman allowed to address prisoners in Lancaster gaol. Having become an important figure in the temperance reform movement, she was made a vice-president of the northern-based British Temperance League, the London Temperance Hospital, the Women's Total Abstinence Union, and the National British Temperance Association. In 1913, when the king and queen visited Blackburn, Mrs Lewis was presented to them.

Elizabeth Anne Lewis died on 14 March 1924 at her home, 4 St Andrew's Place, Blackburn, after a period of poor health. She was held in such high esteem by the publicans of Blackburn that when her funeral cortège passed by their drinking houses they closed their doors and lowered their blinds. Notice of her death was published in *The Times*.

LILIAN LEWIS SHIMAN

Sources W. E. Moss, *The life of Mrs Lewis — the Drunkard's Friend* (1926) • W. E. Moss, *Book of memories* (1951) • W. H. Burnett, *Sunlight in* *the slums* (1888) • E. H. Cherrington and others, eds., *Standard encyclopedia of the alcohol problem*, 6 vols. (1924–30), vol. 4, pp. 1536–7 • P. T. Winskill, *The temperance movement and its workers*, 4 vols. (1891–2), vol. 2, p. 178; vol. 4, pp. 153, 207 • m. cert. • d. cert.

Archives British Temperance League, Sheffield | Blackburn, Lees MSS

Wealth at death £4157 19*s*. 11*d*.: probate, 5 June 1924, *CGPLA Eng. & Wales*

Lewis, Erasmus (1670–1754), government official, was born in 1670 and baptized on 29 April 1671 probably at Abergwili, Carmarthen, the eldest child in the family of four sons and two daughters of the Revd George Lewis (1640?–1709), the vicar of Abergwili, and Margaret Stepney. (Lewis is often said to have been born at Abercothi, a house on the River Towy near Llanegwad, 6 miles east of Carmarthen; at the time of his birth, however, it was probably the home of George Jones, high sheriff of Carmarthenshire in 1664.) In 1686 Lewis was admitted to Westminster School as a king's scholar; from there he proceeded to Trinity College, Cambridge, being admitted pensioner on 28 June 1690, and elected a scholar on 24 May 1691. He took his BA in 1693–4.

After graduating Lewis travelled through Europe. In October 1698 he found himself in Berlin, where he wrote the first of a series of newsletters to John Ellis MP and under-secretary of state. There he also met George Stepney, the diplomat and poet, who prevailed on Ellis and Charles Montagu, fourth earl of Manchester, the lord great chamberlain, to help his cousin to find a government position (Lewis's mother and Stepney's father were sister and brother). In March 1699 Lewis went to Hamburg, and—after visiting Hanover, Brussels, and Lille, and other resorts—reached Paris in the summer. There, in 1700 or 1701, he became secretary to Manchester, who had become the English ambassador. When the peer was recalled in September 1701, Lewis remained to wind up affairs. That he later thanked Ellis for favours shown to him in London suggests that Lewis did not return to Wales immediately; by June 1702, however, he was again resident in Carmarthen, where he was probably employed as a schoolmaster.

In May 1704 Lewis found a generous patron whose family, from the Herefordshire marches, supported him throughout his career. Robert Harley, who became earl of Oxford and Earl Mortimer in 1711, brought Lewis back to the English capital as one of his secretaries. Lewis further became secretary to the embassy at Brussels in August 1708, and subsequently under-secretary of state to both William Legge, the second Lord Dartmouth (presently to be elevated to an earldom in the same style) and his successor, William Bromley. Working at the heart of the ministry, the Welshman prospered: 'This Lewis is an arrant shaver', Swift observed in his rendering of 'Horace, Epistle VII, Book I: Imitated and Addressed to the Earl of Oxford' (1713), 'And very much in Harley's favour' (ll. 17–18). Three years earlier, at the start of his second attempt to persuade the crown to remit the first fruits in favour of the Church of Ireland, Swift had been obliged to Lewis for introducing him to Harley. As the *Journal to Stella* elaborates, Swift soon found himself dining frequently, at times as often as once a week, with the minister's protégé. Swift consulted Lewis about the political pamphlets in which he was engaged during the protracted peace negotiations with France, and came to his defence when Lewis was wrongly rumoured to be corresponding with the Pretender, writing a paper for *The Examiner* (the issue of 30 Jan – 2 Feb 1713) reprinted in Swift's works as 'A complete refutation of the falsehoods alleged against Erasmus Lewis, esq.'.

Lewis's friendship with Swift, and his continuing association with Oxford, drew him into literary and political company, the acquaintance of Alexander Pope, John Gay, John Arbuthnot, and Matthew Prior, as well as a figure not associated with the Scriblerus Club, Sir Thomas Mansel, bt, later created Lord Mansel of Margam, a statesman intimate with both Harley and Swift who was also prominent in south Wales affairs, and with whom Lewis had corresponded since the turn of the century. In October 1712 Lewis was appointed provost-marshal general of Barbados, a position whose responsibilities he delegated to a deputy; and in September 1713 he was returned as the MP for Lostwithiel in Cornwall, a constituency he represented until January 1715. Lewis lost his under-secretaryship following Oxford's fall in July 1714, but continued to enjoy good relations with Pope, Gay, and Prior (a lifelong friend), and, according to Arbuthnot, was for several years a frequent guest to the great (he was particularly close to Allen, Lord Bathurst), 'princ-Governour in many familys', as the physician put it in October 1718 (*Correspondence of Jonathan Swift*, 2.299).

On 1 October 1724, at St Benet Paul's Wharf in London, Lewis married Anne Bateman, *née* Jennings, a widow of a similar age whose first husband, Thomas Bateman, of St Martin-in-the-Fields, had died in 1719. The couple, who had no children, lived in Cork Street, Burlington Gardens, where for a number of years they were near neighbours of Arbuthnot. In April 1727, Swift, writing under the guise of the imaginary Richard Sympson, Gulliver's cousin, directed his publisher Benjamin Motte to Lewis's house, saying that he had given Lewis the power to act for him, and there Motte and Lewis concluded the contract for the second edition of Gulliver's *Travels into Several Remote Nations of the World* (1727). In 1733 Lewis witnessed Arbuthnot's will; much of his time in these years was spent caring for his wife, who long suffered from ill health. After her death in November 1736, his unmarried sister Elizabeth lived with him, keeping house at Cork Street as his sight began to fail.

As early as 1711, in despair at the prospects for the tory ministry, Lewis had told Swift of his plans to retire to Wales. He owned several estates in the principality and, holding a number of lucrative posts, he acquired and disposed of a variety of further properties. Abercothi, for example, the old house which was long supposed his place of birth, he or his father bought soon after 1700 from the family of John Williams, high sheriff of the county in 1681. Indeed, as the eldest son, Lewis inherited substantial landholdings, including his father's properties in Newchurch, 3 miles north-west of Carmarthen, and the estate of Ynyswen, north of Llanegwad, acquired by the family in

1709, the year of his father's death. And as a result of his friendship with Mansel, from 1728 he and his sister Elizabeth began to buy up mortgages in Gower. Lewis's will, written in 1742, reveals that he disposed of his inheritance at Newchurch, but had retained some of the properties his father acquired in nearby parishes, and had added to them, including Allt-y-gog, 4 miles east of Carmarthen, bought ten years earlier from John Morgan of Carmarthen, high sheriff in 1704. This, and other property, he left to the trustees of James Morgan, his nephew, a successful barrister, and the treasurer and librarian of Lincoln's Inn. His immediate family were all provided for, and several of his friends, including Pope, Dr Mead, and Arbuthnot's daughter Anne. That he was able to leave handsome bequests (Elizabeth Lewis, for example, his executor, received £200 a year for life) shows his pessimistic caution and shrewd business sense; punctual, corpulent, fond of drinking water, and possessed of an easy charm—he 'wins the Ladys' money at ombre, & convinces them that they are highly oblig'd to him', Arbuthnot told Swift in November 1723 (*Correspondence of Jonathan Swift*, 2.470)—Lewis was admired by many as a loyal friend, and esteemed as a devoted spouse.

Lewis died on 10 January 1754. He was buried five days later, next to his wife and beneath a spare monument simply inscribed, in the east cloister of Westminster Abbey, as he had directed in his will. His age was recorded in the funeral book as eighty-three. JONATHAN PRITCHARD

Sources P. Morgan, 'George and Erasmus Lewis', *National Library of Wales Journal*, 17 (1971–2), [430]–32 • *Old Westminsters*, 2.575 • Venn, *Alum. Cant.*, 1/3.80 • *DNB* • G. R. Brigstocke, 'Abercothi and Cwmcothi, in Llanegwad parish', *Transactions of the Carmarthenshire Antiquarian Society*, 9 (1914), 64–5 • G. R. B., 'Rev. George Lewis, vicar of Abergwili, 1668–1709', *Transactions of the Carmarthenshire Antiquarian Society*, 11 (1916–17), 71, 79–80 • F. Jones, *Historic Carmarthenshire homes and their families* (1987), 1, 6, 199–200 • *DWB* • J. Spence, *Observations, anecdotes, and characters, of books and men*, ed. J. M. Osborn, new edn, 2 vols. (1966), item no. 213, 1.92–3 • *The correspondence of Jonathan Swift*, ed. H. Williams, 5 vols. (1963–5) • *The correspondence of Alexander Pope*, ed. G. Sherburn, 5 vols. (1956) • J. Swift, *Journal to Stella*, ed. H. Williams, 2 vols. (1948) • N. Luttrell, *A brief historical relation of state affairs from September 1678 to April 1714*, 5 (1857), 428 • *Swansea & Gower, Carmarthen*, Landranger 1:50,000 scale, Ordnance Survey, 2nd ser., no. 159 (1997)

Archives BL, corresp., Add. MSS 7058, 7077 | BL, letters to H. Davenant, Add. MS 9743 • BL, letters to J. Dayrolle, Add. MS 15866 • BL, letters to J. Ellis, Add. MSS 28888–28916 • BL, letters to Lord Oxford, Add. MS 70287 • BL, letters to Jonathan Swift, Add. MSS 4804–4805, *passim* • CKS, letters to Alexander Stanhope • NL Wales, letters to Thomas Mansell, MS 3521

Wealth at death several thousand pounds in cash and lands: will, PRO, PROB 11/806, sig. 18

Lewis, Essington (1881–1961), industrialist, was born on 13 January 1881 in Burra Burra, South Australia, the third son and third child in the family of four sons and two daughters of John Lewis (1844–1923), a partner in Bagot, Shakes, and Lewis Ltd, a stock and station agency, and later a member of the legislative council of South Australia, and his wife, Martha Ann Brook (*d.* 1894), daughter of an excise inspector. He was educated at the collegiate school of St Peter, Adelaide, and from 1901 to 1904 at the South Australian School of Mines and Industries, Adelaide, where he trained as a mining engineer.

In 1904 Lewis took a job as a miner with the Broken Hill Proprietary Company Ltd (BHP) at Broken Hill, New South Wales, founded in 1885 to mine the silver and lead deposits, a company which was to become one of the largest industrial concerns in Australia. In 1905, after gaining his diploma, he was transferred to the company's smelting works at Port Pirie, on the South Australian coast. On 12 April 1910 he married Gladys Rosalind (*d.* 1954), social worker, daughter of James Cowan, mining investor and grazier: they had two sons and three daughters. By 1913 Lewis had been promoted assistant manager, with the challenge of expanding the output of ironstone at the quarry at Iron Knob, across Spencer's Gulf from Port Pirie, ready for the opening of the steelworks at Newcastle, New South Wales. When the steelworks, a new venture for BHP, opened in 1915, it prospered owing to the increased demand for steel during the First World War. Lewis was then put in charge of the BHP contract to manufacture light artillery shells. His attempt to enlist in the army in 1916 was blocked by G. D. Delprat, general manager of BHP, and in 1919 he was promoted to the post of assistant general manager. In 1920, with Harold Darling, a director of BHP, who was to become one of his closest friends, he went on a tour of steelworks and iron mines in North America and Britain, his first overseas tour: his next world tour took him to South Africa in 1925, and from then on he made an overseas tour about every five years. The BHP steelworks were unable to compete in the early 1920s with the cheaper steel imported from Europe, and were forced to close from 1922 to 1923. General manager from 1921, in 1926 Lewis was appointed managing director by Harold Darling, then chairman of BHP, and was given a seat on the board.

After the economic depression of the early 1930s, with the reduced demand for steel, the fortunes of BHP began to revive at the end of 1932. By the mid-1930s the company was producing steel at prices comparable to those in Europe, despite having to pay higher wages because of the Australian labour laws, and output grew to twice that of before the depression. When, in 1935, BHP merged with Australian Iron and Steel Ltd, the other Australian steelworks, the new subsidiary company, with Lewis as manager and Darling as chairman, became the largest steel producer in the British Commonwealth.

In 1934 Lewis visited Japan on his tour of the Far East, and, although he was allowed to see only two steelworks, he became aware of the rapid expansion of the Japanese steel industry and saw that war with Japan was inevitable. Convinced that Australia would be unable to meet an armed attack, Lewis from then on organized BHP to prepare for war. The company began to stockpile coal and iron ore and raw materials, opened a new factory in Newcastle to manufacture shell cases, organized the manufacture of special steel needed to make machine tools, and in 1939 began to build a shipyard at Whyalla, which launched its first ship in 1941: this became the largest shipyard in Australia. Because Australia had few fighter aircraft, in 1938 Lewis formed a syndicate, the Commonwealth Aircraft Corporation, with BHP as the major shareholder, to build aircraft for the Australian government, and the first forty Wirraway fighter bombers went into production in 1938. It was Lewis more than anyone else who helped Australia prepare for the war against Japan.

Appointed chief general manager in 1938, Lewis was invited to chair the advisory panel on industrial reorganization, a panel of businessmen set up by the government to advise on the mobilization of industry for war. He was also business consultant to the department of defence. But it was not until the fall of France in May 1940 that the prime minister, Robert Menzies, realizing that Australia could no longer rely on Britain to supply munitions, set up a new department of munitions, and appointed Lewis director-general. With a seat on the defence committee, and very wide powers, he was able to control the production of all munitions and vehicles, and the tools with which to make them. From his headquarters in Melbourne he planned new factories and converted hundreds of existing factories to the manufacture of munitions, while recruiting leading industrialists to form a board of directors: within six months he had quadrupled the output of munitions. At the same time Lewis remained, throughout the war, chief general manager of BHP, refusing to be paid by the government, and because of this many politicians and union leaders called for his removal, on the suspicion that he was jeopardizing the Australian war effort for the sake of higher profits for BHP. This was despite the fact that BHP was supplying steel at a lower price than the American and British steelworks were charging their governments. With the fall of Menzies in August 1941, and the subsequent appointment of John Curtin as prime minister, Lewis was given even more power when in January 1942 he was appointed director-general of the department of aircraft production and was able to organize the manufacture of Boomerang fighter aircraft, capable of defending Australian cities from Japanese bombing attacks. By the time Japan entered the war in December 1941, Australia was largely self-sufficient in munitions and was in a position to supply munitions and aircraft to the allies in the fight against the Japanese in the Pacific. Lewis refused to be considered for a knighthood, but he was appointed a CH in 1943.

Lewis resigned his government positions in May 1945 to concentrate on BHP. He led the way in the mechanization of the coal industry, opened new ironstone quarries at Whyalla, and in 1948 began to build a new complex of mills at Port Kembla to produce tin plate. Elected chairman of BHP in 1950, he stepped down in 1952, remaining as deputy chairman.

Lewis held many public appointments, and was chairman of the Industrial Design Council of Australia. He helped to create the Australian Administrative Staff College at Mount Eliza, Victoria, and served as chairman from 1954 to 1959. He was instrumental in the establishment by BHP of chairs of mineralogy at the universities of Melbourne and Adelaide, and as an honorary fellow of the Australian Academy of Science he chaired the fifth Mining and Metallurgical Congress in 1953. Among his many awards were the Bessemer gold medal of the Iron and Steel Institute, London, awarded in 1944, and the gold medal of the Institution of Mining and Metallurgy, London, in 1954. He published three books about the Australian iron and steel industry, including *The Importance of the Iron and Steel Industry to Australia* (1948).

An excellent sportsman in his youth—star of Australian rules football and a celebrated polo player—Lewis remained energetic all his life, displaying great stamina during his frequent journeys to all the BHP plants, quarries, mines, and mills. He died on 2 October 1961 of a heart attack while riding round Landscape, his 3500 acre sheep station at Tallarook, Victoria, and was cremated on 4 October. ANNE PIMLOTT BAKER

Sources G. Blainey, *The steel master* (1971) • *AusDB* • *The Times* (3 Oct 1961); (6 Oct 1961); (14 Oct 1961) • *WW* • G. Perkin, 'Men of Australia', *The Age* (2 Sept 1959)
Archives University of Melbourne, papers
Likenesses A. Smith, photograph, repro. in Blainey, *The steel master*, facing p. 74
Wealth at death £98,483: *AusDB*

Lewis, Evan (1818–1901), dean of Bangor, born at Llanilar, Cardiganshire, on 16 November 1818, was the second (and posthumous) son of Evan Lewis and his wife, Mary, daughter of John Richards, both of Llanilar. His mother married, as her second husband, John Hughes of Tyn-y-beili, Llanrhystud. His elder brother, David Lewis (1814–1895), fellow (1839–46) and vice-principal (1845–6) of Jesus College, Oxford, served as curate of St Mary's, Oxford, under John Henry Newman, and joined the Roman Catholic church in 1846. Settling at Arundel in 1860, he devoted himself to the study of canon law and the lives of the saints. He translated from the Latin *The Rise and Growth of the Anglican Schism*, by Nicholas Sanders, with an elaborate introduction and notes (1877), and, among other works from the Spanish, the writings of St John of the Cross (1864).

Evan Lewis, after attending the Ystradmeurig and Aberystwyth grammar schools, went to a school at Twickenham run by his father's brother, David Lewis DD (1778–1859). Following his brother to Jesus College, Oxford, Lewis matriculated on 7 April 1838, and graduated BA in 1841 and MA in 1863. A powerful man, he rowed stroke in the college boat when it was head of the river, and in later life was a keen walker. Ordained deacon and priest in 1842 by Christopher Bethell, bishop of Bangor, he was successively curate of Llanddeusant (1842–3), Llan-faes with Penmon (1843–5), Llanfihangel Ysgeifiog (1845–6), all in Anglesey, and Llanllechid, Caernarvonshire (1847–59). He was vicar of Aberdâr, Glamorgan (1859–66), rector of Dolgellau, Merioneth, and rural dean of Ystumanner (1866–84), proctor in convocation for the diocese of Bangor (1868–80), chancellor of Bangor (1872–6), canon residentiary (1877–84), and dean from 1884.

On 11 October 1859 Lewis married Anne, youngest daughter of John Henry Cotton, dean of Bangor, at one time his vicar in Llanllechid; she died on 24 December 1860 at Aberdâr, leaving no children. On 15 June 1865

Lewis married Adelaide Owen, third daughter of the Revd Cyrus Morrall of Plas Iolyn, Shropshire; she survived him with three sons and three daughters.

While at Oxford, Lewis, like his brother David, was influenced by the Tractarians, and on returning to Wales he spread Tractarian doctrines widely. At Llanllechid he introduced choral services for the first time in Bangor diocese, and gradually adopted moderate ritualistic practices. These he supplemented by teaching a sacramental theology, being perhaps the first Anglican in the nineteenth century to preach in Wales the doctrines of apostolic succession and baptismal regeneration. Some of the younger clergy followed Lewis's lead, and the movement resulted in a latter-day Bangorian controversy (*Dadl Bangor*). The Revd John Phillips attacked the ritualist position in two famous lectures delivered at Bangor in November 1850 and January 1852 respectively, which were shortly afterwards published. Lewis replied to the first lecture in a series of Welsh letters in *Y Cymro*, signed Aelod o'r Eglwys ('a member of the church'), reprinted in 1852 in book form. His most important work was an elaborate treatise in Welsh on the apostolic succession, *Yr olyniaeth apostolaidd gan offeiriad Cymreig* (1851). He also wrote occasional papers on Welsh church questions, and on the Wesleyan succession (*Yr olyniaeth Wesleyaidd*), under the pseudonym of Amddiffynydd ('defender') in 1858. He was much interested in church music, co-operated in the production of the *Bangor Diocese Hymn Book*, and himself translated into Welsh F. W. Faber's 'Good Friday Hymns' and 'Adeste fideles'. Dean Lewis died at his home, the deanery, Bangor, on 24 November 1901, and was buried in the churchyard of Llandygái, Caernarvonshire, near Bishop Bethell, on 28 November.

D. L. THOMAS, *rev.* D. T. W. PRICE

Sources R. R. Hughes, 'Biographical epitomes of the bishops and clergy of the diocese of Bangor', 1932, U. Wales, Bangor • D. Jones, 'Y Deon Lewis', *Ceninen Gŵyl Dewi*, 21 (March 1903), 23–6 • H. L. James, 'Yr hen lwybrau', *Yr Haul*, 35 (Dec 1933), 354–9 • H. L. James, 'Yr hen lwybrau', *Yr Haul*, 36 (Jan 1934), 5–7 • H. L. James, *The life and work of the very rev. Evan Lewis MA* (1904) • *DWB* • M. Eryri, 'Y tra pharchedig Deon Lewis', *Ceninen Gŵyl Dewi*, 20 (March 1902), 37–8 • D. Evans, *Adgofion henafgwr* (1904), 35–6 • *Church Times* (29 Nov 1901) • T. R. Roberts, *Eminent Welshmen: a short biographical dictionary* (1908), 306 • D. E. Evans, 'Dylanwad mudiad rhydychen yng nghymru', *Journal of the Historical Society of the Church in Wales*, 6 (1956), 94–5 • D. E. Evans, 'Dylanwad mudiad rhydychen yng nghymru', *Journal of the Historical Society of the Church in Wales*, 10 (1960), 67–9 • private information (1912) • parish register (baptism), 28 Nov 1818, Llanilar parish, Cardiganshire • m. certs. • parish register (burials), 28 Nov 1901, Llandygai parish, Bangor, Caernarvonshire

Likenesses photograph, repro. in James, 'Yr hen lwybrau', 355 • portrait, repro. in *Yr Haul* (1902), 3

Wealth at death £1507 6*s*. 9*d*.: administration, 13 Sept 1901, *CGPLA Eng. & Wales*

Lewis, Evan (1828–1869), Congregational minister, was born at Cefn Bryn, near Newtown, Montgomeryshire, on 20 July 1828. His father was an architect, and Lewis was encouraged by his minister, Evan Jones, to preach. He determined to enter the ministry, and raised money for his studies at Airedale Independent college by undertaking lecture tours of south Wales. He graduated BA of London University in 1852 and served the Congregational churches at Barton upon Humber (1853–8); Rothwell, Northamptonshire (1858–63); Oak Street, Accrington (1863–6); Grimshaw Street, Preston (1866–8); and Offord Street, Islington (1868–9). Lewis was an effective preacher, and his educational and temperance work was complemented by his literary and scientific lectures for young men. He wrote, among other short works, *The Wines the Saviour Made and Sanctioned* (1856), *A Plea for the People* (1857), *The Two Twilights* (1860), the startlingly entitled *Independency: a Deduction from the Laws of the Universe* (1862), and *God's Week of Work, being an Examination of the Mosaic Six Days* (1865). At Preston he edited *The Grimshaw Street Chapel Pulpit*. An amiable and cheerful man, but never in good health, Lewis died of consumption on 19 February 1869; he was survived by his wife, Sarah Moulson Lewis.

GORDON GOODWIN, *rev.* IAN SELLERS

Sources B. Nightingale, *Lancashire nonconformity*, 6 vols. [1890–93], vol. 1 • *Congregational Year Book* (1870) • *Preston Guardian* (24 Feb 1869) • *Preston Guardian* (27 Feb 1869) • G. T. Streather, *Memorials of the Independent Chapel at Rothwell* (1994) • *Preston Chronicle* (27 Feb 1869) • *CGPLA Eng. & Wales* (1869)

Wealth at death under £450: probate, 8 June 1869, *CGPLA Eng. & Wales*

Lewis, Frederick Christian, senior (1779–1856), engraver and landscape painter, was born in London on 14 March 1779, the eldest son of Johan Ludwig (*b. c.*1740), an émigré miniature painter from Hanover who took the name of John Lewis, and his wife, Elizabeth. Frederick had two brothers who survived infancy: the bookbinder Charles *Lewis (1786–1836) and the landscape painter George Robert *Lewis (1782–1871). He was taught to draw by his father, and was apprenticed about 1794 to the engraver J. C. Stadler, who taught him aquatinting. He entered the Royal Academy Schools on 12 August 1797 and left about 1802. His first major printmaking project was the aquatinting of Thomas Girtin's *Twenty of the most Picturesque Views in Paris and its Environs*, published in 1803. About 1802 he married Elizabeth Exton. The couple first lived at 5 Rathbone Place, London, then in 1803 moved to 33 Queen Anne Street East, which they took over from Lewis's friend the engraver, John Landseer, father of the painter Sir Edwin Landseer. Here his son the orientalist painter John Frederick (Spanish) *Lewis (1804–1876) and his daughter Mary Exton Lewis were born.

In 1808 the Lewis family suddenly moved to Enfield, Middlesex, where they lived in the Dower House, Forty Hill. Here the engraver Charles George *Lewis (1808–1880) and the portrait painter, Frederick Christian (Indian) *Lewis junior (1813–1875), were born. A daughter, Elizabeth, was born in 1810 but died young. On the evidence of one of an extraordinary and affectionate series of informal pencil sketches of his wife and children, now in the Victoria and Albert Museum, London, Frederick encouraged his own young children to draw, as his father had taught him. As the children grew up they (including his daughter Mary, a skilled etcher) had to learn drawing,

Frederick Christian Lewis senior (1779–1856), by Charles George Lewis (after John Frederick Lewis, 1834)

painting, and printmaking, and eventually they formed a remarkable family business and a dynasty of artists. In 1814 the family moved back to central London, to Southampton Row. Another daughter, Anne Lucy Lewis (1818–1864), was born there. The family took drawing holidays in the country at Emery's Farm in Kempston Hardwick, Bedfordshire. Lewis exhibited landscapes in oil and watercolour at the Royal Academy from 1802 until 1853, and exhibited at the British Institution, the Society of British Artists, and the Old Watercolour Society.

Lewis developed into one of the most prolific, skilled, and versatile printmakers of his time. He was commissioned by William Young Otley to reproduce master drawings for the three-volume work *The Italian School of Design*, published between 1808 and 1823, and he engraved after works by such prominent contemporary artists as Sir Thomas Lawrence, Thomas Girtin, Franz Winterhalter, Sir Edwin Landseer, Richard Bonington, and J. M. W. Turner—though he did not engrave more than one plate of the *Liber Studiorum*, as he found Turner difficult to deal with. He normally signed his work 'F. C. Lewis'. His prints were more highly valued by his contemporaries than his watercolours: whereas the latter sold for around £1, a coloured engraving after a portrait by Sir Thomas Lawrence sold for about £2 and a set of eight sporting prints after Henry Alken cost £50, an enormous sum in the nineteenth century. Lewis's noted fidelity in interpreting drawings and paintings and rendering them either as engravings, etchings, aquatints, or mezzotints explains why he became engraver of drawings to Princess Charlotte, Prince Leopold, George IV, William IV, and Queen Victoria. He engraved after his own children's work as they came to maturity and fame, and they in turn engraved after his. He published various sets of etchings after his own landscape sketches, made on tours of Britain, France, the Netherlands, and the Rhineland, but remained in England after 1820. In 1813 he aquatinted a panorama in eight plates of Constantinople after the work of Henry Aston Barker, a view which may have stimulated the young John Frederick Lewis's curiosity about the East.

The family tradition is (and his sketches show) that Lewis was an affectionate father but of necessity a strict teacher: art was a precarious trade, and continual practice and self-discipline were necessary for the close and trying work of fine engraving. He was a good friend to various artists, particularly Sir Thomas Lawrence and John Landseer. A portrait shows him in late middle age as something of a dandy, with the aquiline features that seem to be hereditary for the males of the Lewis family. He joined the Artists' Annuity Fund in 1825 and continued working until 1855, and died, probably from a heart attack, at Bulls Cross, Enfield, Middlesex, on 18 December 1856. He was buried in Frimley churchyard in Surrey, where his son-in law Charles Stonhouse (who had married Anne Lucy) was rector. Collections of his work are held in the British Museum and the Victoria and Albert Museum, London.

CHARLES NEWTON

Sources J. M. Lewis, *John Frederick Lewis, R.A.* (1978) • J. M. H. Lewis, *The Lewis family: art and travel* (privately printed, Old Woking, [1992]) • *IGI* • S. C. Hutchison, 'The Royal Academy Schools, 1768–1830', *Walpole Society*, 38 (1960–62), 123–91, esp. 157 • *CGPLA Eng. & Wales* (1857)

Likenesses C. G. Lewis, drawing, 1834, V&A • A. E. Chalon, group portrait, pen-and-ink (*Study at the British Institution, 1806*), BM • C. G. Lewis, engraving (after drawing, 1834), V&A • C. G. Lewis, stipple (after J. F. Lewis, 1834), BM, NPG [*see illus.*] • J. F. Lewis, pencil drawing, V&A • C. Stonhouse, drawing, repro. in Lewis, *The Lewis family*

Lewis, Frederick Christian, junior [*called* Indian Lewis] (**1813–1875**), painter, was born on 16 November 1813 at the Dower House, Forty Hill, Enfield, Middlesex, and baptized at St Mary, St Marylebone, Middlesex, on 9 December 1813, the third son of Frederick Christian *Lewis senior (1779–1856), engraver and landscape painter, and his wife, Elizabeth, *née* Exton. The orientalist painter John Frederick (Spanish) *Lewis (1804–1876) and Charles George *Lewis (1808–1880), engraver, were his brothers. With his brothers and also his sisters—Mary, who later became a skilled etcher, and Anne Lucy—Lewis was taught to draw by his affectionate father; all five learnt from him the techniques of drawing, painting, and printmaking and together extended the family's artistic reputation. While the family were living at 3 Southampton Row, Marylebone Road, Lewis also studied under the celebrated portrait painter Sir Thomas Lawrence, many of whose portraits, including those of Lawrence's father and also his niece, Susan Bloxham, had been engraved by Lewis's father. 'At the age of fourteen [Lewis] painted a clever life-size self portrait' (Cotton, 53), formerly in the possession of his daughter, Mrs Musson.

From 1835 to 1836 Lewis travelled to Malta and Constantinople; of the drawings (priv. coll.) he made there, his brother J. F. Lewis published lithographs in 1837. His next journey was to Persia where he was the guest of the British minister at Tehran, Sir John McNeil, and painted a portrait of the shah. From Persia he went on to Baghdad, visited Mosul and Nineveh with Sir Austen Layard, and Babylon with Sir Henry Rawlinson. On his return he exhibited his drawings (priv. coll.), which received favourable notices in *The Athenaeum*, the *Literary Gazette*, and *The Examiner* and were purchased by Henry Petty, third marquess of Lansdowne, and John Rushout, second Baron Northwick.

On Lewis's arrival in India, the *Bombay Courier* announced on 16 November 1839 his intention to visit Poona, Ahmadnagar, and Aurangabad on his way to Delhi and Kashmir 'in case any parties should require the service of his pencil in portraiture' (quoted in Cotton, 55). At Hyderabad he painted a portrait of the resident, Colonel James Stuart Fraser, and for the nizam, the Raja Chandu Lal, *The Nautch*, a work that drew from Sir Edwin Landseer the comment, 'I think his pictures wonderfully clever … [He] possess[es] the power of rapidly seizing and as rapidly depicting character. I was astonished at some of his heads. They are like Velazquez' (ibid.). During this visit he met Eliza Bird, eldest daughter of Captain Joseph Andrews, whom he married in Secundarabad on 8 September 1841. According to a descendant this marriage, eight months after the birth of their eldest child—John Hardwicke (Swiss) Lewis (1841–1927), landscape painter, on 15 January 1841—was a more formal celebration of 'a form of marriage the year before at the Residency at Hyderabad conducted by the local chaplain' (Lewis, 77). They had five children in all. In the next ten years Lewis received many more lucrative commissions to paint glittering scenes of durbars and installations of Indian rulers and more subdued portraits of British officials.

In 1842 Lewis was at Madras where he restored and framed several paintings in the Government House collection—including portraits of Marquess Wellesley by Thomas Hickey; Sir Arthur Wellesley by John Hoppner; Lord Clive by Thomas Day (after Nathaniel Dance); and 'three nabobs', one of which was thought to be the large painting of Shuja ud-Daula, nawab wazir of Oudh, attributed to Tilly Kettle. His enormous painting (6 ft x 7½ ft) of the installation of the nawab of the Carnatic, Ghulam Muhammad Ghaus Khan, at Chenauk Palace by Lord Elphinstone on 25 August 1842, which includes between seventy and eighty portraits and took eighteen months to complete, is now in the Fort Museum, Madras. This work, for which Lewis was paid 5515 rupees, was exhibited at the Royal Academy and was engraved by Lewis's father and C. G. Lewis (impression, India Office Library, London; reproduced in Archer, 151, pl. 185; another impression, Victoria Memorial Hall, Calcutta, with key plate). From 1845 to 1846 he was in Mysore, where he painted a large picture of the Dasara durbar (exh. British Institution, 1849), which was engraved by his father (impression, BL OIOC). Of this *The Times* noted that it included 'an immense group of figures … producing a dazzling whole' (Cotton, 57). At Murshidabad in Bengal he painted the installation of the nawab nazim of Bengal, Behar, and Orissa, Syud Mansur Ali Faridun Jah, in 1847 (engraved by the elder F. C. Lewis; impression, BL OIOC), and a companion picture of the nawab in durbar. Both paintings were in the abandoned palace at Murshidabad in 1981. The former was described by *The Examiner* as 'a gorgeous work, resplendent with Eastern pomp and circumstance' (Cotton, 57). It was shown to Queen Victoria, who headed the list of subscribers for an engraving by the elder F. C. Lewis that was executed in 1854.

After a visit to England and Italy with his family from 1849 to 1850, Lewis returned to India in 1851. After spending a year in the Himalayas in 1855 he painted *The Durbar at Udaipur, Rajasthan* (India Office Library, London; reproduced in Archer, 134, pl. 133). Seated in the centre of the picture is the Maharana Sarup Singh, who gave protection to British subjects during the Indian mutiny. After completing this work Lewis's health broke down and he left India for a tour of Europe with his wife and family. In 1860 they embarked on a tour of America, New Zealand, Australia, Hong Kong, Singapore, and Siam, where he painted a portrait of Monghul IV (since destroyed by termites). From there Lewis travelled alone to China, where he made sketches of the dragon procession in Peking (Beijing) and visited the Great Wall. After a three-months journey by camel across the Gobi Desert he went on to Japan, rejoining his family in 1863 in Singapore, whence they sailed back to Calcutta. In November he was in Bombay, where he obtained many commissions from merchant princes. With many others, however, Lewis was financially ruined by the collapse of the Bank of Bombay in 1866; his health broke down again and he returned to England.

In 1868 Lewis set out for Cairo, where he painted for the khedive a large picture of his reception of the prince of Wales, for which he received £1000. At Wiesbaden he painted portraits of wealthy businessmen, including one of the Rothschild family. He returned to India in 1874, alone and in poor health, but within a year was advised by his doctor to leave. He died of exhaustion at Genoa on 26 May 1875 and was buried in a cemetery overlooking the harbour. His widow and his daughter Ellen had a marble memorial erected over his grave. His extensive library—which included over 3000 books, pictures and engravings—was bought by the government.

Mildred Archer observed that 'Lewis reacted to the splendid bejewelled figures who were his subjects with the same delight that his brother, J. F. Lewis, experienced in the sunlit harems of the middle east' (Archer and Lightbown, 107). Both brothers' compositions of thronged interiors were controlled by strongly defined architectural settings, but in contrast to the exquisitely rendered detail for which his brother's works became known, Frederick Christian Lewis's paintings are perhaps less static, retaining the impression of rapidly painted scenes full of movement. 'He *more than any other British painter* caught the splendour of these courts' (M. Archer, quoted in Lewis, 93).

ANNETTE PEACH

Sources E. Cotton, 'Frederick Christian Lewis', *Bengal Past and Present*, 44 (1932), 53–60 • J. M. H. Lewis, *The Lewis family art and travel*

(1992) • M. Archer and R. Lightbown, *India observed* (1982) [exhibition catalogue, V&A] • private information (2004) [BL OIOC] • private information (2004) [BL, prints and drawings] • *IGI*

Archives Worcs. RO, Churchill papers (Northwick papers), corresp. acc. no. 4221, boxes 8, 39

Likenesses self-portrait, oils, *c*.1855, repro. in Lewis, *Lewis family*, 71; priv. coll.

Lewis, George (1763–1822), Independent minister and theologian, was born at a farm called Y Fantais, in the parish of Tre-lech, Carmarthenshire, the only child of William and Rachel Lewis. He had an excellent elementary education under the tuition of four local ministers. In 1781 he was admitted to the Presbyterian college at Carmarthen, where he studied under Robert Gentleman. In 1785 he became pastor of the Independent church at Caernarfon. On 22 October 1787, at Bangor Cathedral, he married Jane, the second daughter of Thomas Jones, of Bodermid. They had three children; George, the eldest, was a surgeon in Wrexham; William J. Lewis, the second son, was also a doctor, and was the father of Bunnell Lewis (1824–1908), and of Samuel Savage Lewis (1836–1891); their daughter, Sara, married Edward Davies (1796–1857).

Lewis had republican sympathies and was minded to emigrate to America in 1794 but was dissuaded by Edward Williams (1750–1813) and others. In March 1794 he was called to Llanuwchllyn, Merioneth. Here he stayed seventeen years, immersed in theological studies, yet finding time to promote and sustain a powerful religious revival. In 1797 he issued his *Drych ysgrythyrol, neu, Gorph o dduwinyddiaeth*, a formidable volume of systematic theology which was much used in nonconformist academies. His greatest work was his New Testament commentary. Volume 1 appeared in 1802, and three further volumes were published by Lewis but the three remaining volumes were edited by his son-in-law, Edward Davies. It is a massive work which demonstrates the author's erudition. All Lewis's works were written in Welsh; in addition to his large theological volumes, he published some fourteen smaller works, some of them weighty sermons. One interesting aspect of these slighter works was their concern for children and young people.

On 13 January 1812 Lewis was appointed head of the Independent academy at Wrexham on a salary of £100 a year. In 1816 the ruling body of the academy, the Congregational Fund board, moved from Wrexham to Llanfyllin, Montgomeryshire, since the church there had invited Lewis to be its minister. His health was deteriorating; in February 1818 the board resolved to provide an assistant, and in May 1819 Edward Davies was appointed classical tutor. But in view of Lewis's increasing ill health it was thought advisable to move the academy to Newtown in the same county. But to no avail; some nine months after the move, on 5 June 1822, Lewis died at Newtown, and was buried in the New Chapel there, funeral sermons being preached in both English and Welsh.

George Lewis was an imposing personality. His preaching was substantial and undramatic, as he was more of a teacher than a prophet. And yet during his ministry at Llanuwchllyn in 1809 there was a highly emotional revival. Although considered a conservative in theology, his public attitude was liberal: his strict adherence to Calvinistic orthodoxy did not preclude a warm generosity towards those of different opinions. At a time when nonconformity, especially in north Wales, was looked upon with suspicion and often had to suffer petty persecution, Lewis gave it a dignity and self-assurance which its critics had to respect. R. TUDUR JONES

Sources R. T. Jenkins, *Hanes cynulleidfa hen gapel Llanuwchllyn* (1937), 117–30 • T. Rees and J. Thomas, *Hanes eglwysi annibynol Cymru*, 1 (1871), 388–9 • J. Peter and R. J. Pryse, eds., *Enwogion y ffydd*, 2 vols. (1878–84), vol. 2, pp. 397–9 • T. Stephens, ed., *Album Aberhonddu* (1898), 62–4 • *Yr Adolygydd*, 4 (1854), 40ff. • *Y Cofiadur*, 10 (1934), 3–26 • minutes of the Congregational Fund Board, DWL • A. N. Palmer, *A history of the town and parish of Wrexham*, 3: *A history of the older nonconformity of Wrexham* [1888] • T. Parry and T. Gee, eds., *The encyclopaedia Cambrensis, or, Y gwyddoniadur Cymreig*, 6 (1892), 561–5 • Bangor Cathedral records

Lewis, George (1803–1879), Free Church of Scotland minister and author, was born in May 1803 in Glasgow, the third son in the family of four sons and three daughters of George Lewis, grocer, of Glasgow, and his wife, Margaret Hardie. Educated in arts and divinity at the universities of Glasgow, St Andrews, and Edinburgh, he fell early under the spell of the eminent Scottish evangelical churchman, Dr Thomas Chalmers, during the latter's ministry at St John's, Glasgow, in 1819–23, and thereafter espoused his vision of social Christianity.

Lewis did not enter the ministry immediately, although licensed to preach by the Church of Scotland in 1828. Having lectured in economics at mechanics' institutes in central Scotland in the mid-1820s, he was in 1832–5 the first editor of the *Sottish Guardian*. This newspaper was founded to defend the established church against seceder attacks and to promote its evangelical party's programme of an extended state-supported church and parochial school system, based on a return to past Scottish tradition. Lewis was concurrently secretary of the Glasgow Educational Association (another body strongly identified with Glasgow presbytery's evangelicals) and published in 1834 a celebrated piece of partisan polemic, *Scotland a Half-Educated Nation*. Despite partial interpretation of available statistics, with patriotic allusions to an earlier idyll, his critique reflected genuine concern about educational inadequacy in expanding industrial communities, while arguing the unique contribution of establishment-influenced schooling to the underpinning of social stability in the post-Reform Act era. Amid proprietorial turmoil at the *Scottish Guardian* in 1835, as a rival organ gleefully reported, 'Mr Saint Louis … left in a pet' (*Reformers' Gazette*, 30 April 1836). An assistantship at Perth's Middle Church followed, then induction to St David's, Dundee, in 1839. There Lewis published several pamphlets, most notably *The State of St David's Parish, with Remarks on the Moral and Physical Statistics of Dundee* (1841), which graphically and compassionately depicted the poverty, deprivation, and squalor of that populous industrial parish.

In 1843, as schism in the established church loomed, Lewis's literary talents (always more consistent than his preaching skills) were deployed again for sectarian purposes: he published a series of *Tracts on Scottish Church Principles* which articulate evangelical claims. At the Disruption, Lewis led most of his congregation into the new Free Church and during 1843–4 participated in fund-raising missions to Ireland and North America. The latter, roving from Montreal to New Orleans, was financially successful, but acceptance of donations from southern slave owners provoked controversy; and denunciation of slavery in Lewis's published journal, *Impressions of America and the American Churches* (1845), failed to dispel it.

Lewis's vision of an extended national education system in Scotland based on a revived establishment was killed by the Disruption, and the demise of any religion-based system was sealed by the dominant educational sectarianism that soon emerged within the Free Church. Lewis took no significant part in this debate; indeed, education ceased to be his first priority, as he became increasingly depressed in the 1840s about the social cost of industrialization. In Scotland's overcrowded cities education in letters, he now held, was less urgent than education in cleanliness; increased exposure to English example, following improved rail communications, offered the best prospects of emulation and amelioration. Endorsement of Oastler's Ten Hours Bill agitation in 1846–7 reflected his concurrent loss of faith in the improvement of factory conditions through moral, rather than legal, restraint.

In 1849, at the age of forty-six, Lewis decided suddenly and controversially to quit industrial Dundee for Ormiston, East Lothian. In that essentially rural parish he devoted his energies to bringing up a family of five daughters from his marriage on 15 July 1845 to Mary Ann Elizabeth Miller, and to theological scholarship. He retired prematurely in 1865 with failing health and after years of declining mental powers, he died in Edinburgh from 'disease of the brain' (possibly Alzheimer's disease) on 27 January 1879 and was interred in Grange cemetery.

KENNETH J. CAMERON

Sources *Fasti Scot.*, 326–7 • *Free Church of Scotland Monthly Record* (1 May 1879), 120–22 • J. Smith, *Our Scottish clergy*, 2nd ser. (1849), 353–8 • D. J. Withrington, '"Scotland a half-educated nation" in 1834? reliable critique or persuasive polemic?', in W. M. Humes, *Scottish culture and Scottish education, 1800–1980* (1983), 55–74 • L. J. Saunders, *Scottish democracy, 1815–1840* (1950) • S. Mechie, *The church and Scottish social development, 1780–1870* (1960) • R. M. W. Cowan, *The newspaper in Scotland: a study of its first expansion, 1815–1860* (1946) • *CGPLA Eng. & Wales* (1879)

Archives U. Edin., New Coll. L., Thomas Chalmers MSS

Likenesses D. O. Hill, calotypes, 1843–6, Scot. NPG • D. O. Hill, group portrait, collage, 1843–67, Free Church of Scotland, Edinburgh • photograph, *c.*1863, NA Scot.

Wealth at death £4658 3*s.* 5*d.*: confirmation, 26 May 1879, *CCI*

Lewis, Sir George Cornewall, second baronet (1806–1863), politician and author, was born in London on 21 April 1806. He was the elder son of Sir Thomas Frankland *Lewis, first baronet (1780–1855), politician, of Harpton Court, Old Radnor, and his first wife, Harriet (*d.* 1838), fourth daughter of Sir George Cornewall, bt, of Moccas Court, Herefordshire. After Monsieur Clement's school at Chelsea, he attended Eton College from January 1819 until December 1823. He matriculated from Christ Church, Oxford, in February 1824 and took up residence in the following Michaelmas term, having spent the intervening months in foreign travel. In Trinity term 1828 he received first-class honours in classics and second-class honours in mathematics, and was elected in June to a studentship at Christ Church. Lewis shared his father's strong interest in political economy, and he left Oxford a convinced free-trader. He graduated BA in 1829 and proceeded MA in 1832.

Sir George Cornewall Lewis, second baronet (1806–1863), by Herbert Watkins, 1858

The law and the poor law Lewis entered the Middle Temple in June 1828. He attended John Austin's lectures in jurisprudence at London University in 1829 and 1830 and remained thereafter John and Sarah Austin's sympathetic yet not uncritical friend and supporter. The impress of Austin's thought is apparent in Lewis's *Remarks on the Use and Abuse of some Political Terms* (1832), which attracted the critical regard of another who had sat at Austin's feet, J. S. Mill.

Political economy and Austinian jurisprudence drew Lewis into the Society for the Diffusion of Useful Knowledge, of whose general committee he became an active member and to whose *Penny Cyclopaedia* and other publications he contributed. He acquired a reputation for expertise in both ancient and modern languages; he had translated German classical scholarship into English (notably, in 1828, a work by A. Boeckh, as *The Public Economy of Athens*) and had begun *An Essay on the Origin and Formation of the Romance Languages* (1835), a critique of the *provençaliste* philology of Raynouard. The *Essay* retains the respect of philologists for 'its readability and the lucidity and balance of its argumentation' (Posner, 349–50).

Lewis's industry and learning gained the attention of Nassau Senior, who in January 1832 recommended Lewis to Brougham for service on the momentous royal commission about to be appointed to inquire into the operation of the poor laws. Lewis did not receive this appointment, but he had developed a taste for the kind of public service that such appointments represented. Although he had joined the Oxford circuit in November 1831, he set aside plans for a legal career. Instead, the question of how materially and morally to improve the condition of the Irish claimed Lewis's interest and energies. In August 1833 he became an assistant commissioner of the inquiry into the condition of the poorer classes of Ireland, of which he conducted his portion early in 1834 among the Irish in the larger towns of the midlands, Lancashire, and Scotland. By December 1834, when he submitted his report for this inquiry, he was at work in Ireland on a commission to examine the state of Irish education. The knowledge he gained there, combined with his already formidable command of the existing literature on the land and the church questions, enabled him to become an authority of the first rank on the Irish problem in the 1830s.

This authority was manifest in the work Lewis published in 1836, *On Local Disturbances in Ireland; and on the Irish Church Question*. The first part of the book, still valuable to students of Irish history and of peasant movements, offered a thoroughgoing analysis of the widespread violence in rural Ireland. The second part offered 'concurrent endowment'—apparently the first public use of the phrase in British political discourse—as the remedy for Ireland's ecclesiastical problems. In suggesting a 'remedy' to the problem of rural violence, Lewis called for 'a legal provision for the poor': the introduction and implementation in Ireland of the principles of the 1834 English poor law. Lewis's remedy commended itself to the government of Lord Melbourne, eager in 1836 to throw over the recommendations of its own Irish poor commissioners. Officially invited to remark on those recommendations, Lewis did so scathingly and sarcastically. He denounced 'the principle that it is the duty of the state to find employment for the people', and called instead for the workhouse as 'an all-sufficient test of destitution' (*Parl. papers*, 1837, 51.260, 279). Lewis gave the government what it wanted; and when the Irish poor law was enacted, it was his and not the Irish commissioners' remedy which the law prescribed.

Soon after Lewis had completed his 'Remarks' for the government, he received from it an invitation to join John Austin on a commission to inquire into the troubled state of Malta. He and the Austins left Britain on 20 September 1836 and arrived in Valletta exactly a month later. The two commissioners made recommendations, accepted by the government, for the elimination of offices, for a much reduced expenditure on pensions, and for reforms of the fiscal system, government charities, the police, and education. They argued strongly for freedom of the press in Malta, but Lewis left for Britain in late April 1838, leaving Austin behind to draft a new law for the press.

Barely six months after Lewis returned from Malta in 1838, his father resigned from the poor-law commission. The son could now take his father's seat on the commission, and on 29 January 1839 he received it from Lord Normanby, the home secretary. The admiration Lewis had once expressed for Edwin Chadwick, the commission's secretary, had since been sorely tested by Chadwick's scarcely concealed contempt for T. F. Lewis as a commissioner. Chadwick also resented not having received a commissionership himself, resentment that deepened in November 1841, when the new Conservative home secretary, Sir James Graham, concurred in Normanby's recommendation that George Lewis's close friend Sir Edmund Head should fill the latest vacancy on the commission. With Graham, Lewis quickly developed a close rapport. Graham at first suspected Lewis as unsafe in his political opinions, but Lewis's administrative caution and willingness to defer to Graham's political judgement won Graham over. With Graham as home secretary and with Head as his colleague, Lewis's position at the poor-law commission looked safe and even formidable. Lewis, to Chadwick's indignation, continued to combine poor-law administration with his literary pursuits. Lewis had no stomach, Chadwick believed, for the demanding task of imposing upon the country the principles of the 1834 act, notably in the manufacturing districts; he yielded too easily to pressures from the government to economize. At the same time Lewis and Head bore the brunt of the intensifying agitation against the poor law expressed by uncooperative boards of guardians and magistrates, demonstrative working men, popular-radical and paternalistic tory MPs, and *The Times*.

Marriage, 1844 Lewis in 1844 successfully proposed marriage to Lady Theresa Lister (1803–1865), a widow with three young children from her first marriage. Theresa Lewis [*see* Lewis, Lady (Maria) Theresa] was attractive, intelligent, and well read, vivacious and high-spirited, a marked contrast to her grave and serious husband. She was exceedingly well connected: two of her brothers, the earl of Clarendon and Charles Villiers, were prominent Liberal politicians; a third, Montague Villiers, was an eminent London clergyman and bishop-to-be. The marriage, performed at Watford parish church on 26 October 1844, proved a success both personally and politically, although the child the Lewises hoped for was never born. After their marriage the Lewises lived in the Villiers residence in Knightsbridge, Kent House, and at Harpton Court.

The Andover workhouse scandal, 1845 Lewis needed all the political support he could muster and more, when the scandal of the Andover workhouse, involving allegations of noisome mistreatment of inmates, the appointment of an inhumane and unqualified master, and a bungled investigation thereof by the commission, broke in the late summer of 1845. Chadwick's hour of revenge had finally arrived. Working with aggrieved past and present assistant commissioners, and supplying critical testimony for

The Times and members of a Commons committee of inquiry eager to make use of it, Chadwick and his allies put Lewis, Head, and their defenders at a disadvantage impossible to overcome. That Lewis and Head mismanaged their original inquiry at the workhouse cannot be denied, nor that they sought to shift to others responsibility for the mismanagement which they might more worthily have accepted themselves. But the severity of censure in the committee's final report, issued in the autumn of 1846, was immoderate and excessive; as Graham put it, 'popular justice' prevailed. The adverse publicity which the Andover inquiry generated effectively meant the demise of the commission in 1847, when its five-year term ended. Lord John Russell, the new prime minister, refused to advocate its renewal.

Politics, and the *Edinburgh Review* Lewis accepted Russell's refusal as a political necessity, and he appreciated the case for a new poor-law board, whose officers sat in parliament. Lewis had already decided to seek a seat in the House of Commons in the general election of 1847. He secured the nomination for an unopposed return for Herefordshire in the Liberal interest and was elected on 4 August. He could now accept a political office with parliamentary responsibilities; at Lord Clarendon's behest, Russell at the beginning of November bestowed on Lewis one of the secretaryships of the Board of Control.

Advancement followed. In May 1848 Lewis moved to the Home Office as parliamentary under-secretary, and in July 1850 to the Treasury as financial secretary. He cultivated Russell's favour, as when, on the occasion of Russell's denunciation of 'papal aggression' in November 1850, he conveyed his warm approval to his chief. In September 1851 Lewis carried the prime minister's invitation to Graham to take office in the insecure Russell government. By the time Russell dissolved parliament in 1852, Lewis's prospects as a politician looked brighter than political observers five years earlier might have predicted. But the resurgent protectionists contested all three seats for Herefordshire at the general election in July, and Lewis finished fourth and last. A seemingly safe seat in the gift of Earl Fitzwilliam opened at Peterborough in the autumn, but on 4 December Lewis was defeated by a tory–radical coalition exploiting the issue of borough independence. For the moment he had had enough of politics. On 20 December he accepted the editorship of the *Edinburgh Review*.

The editorship of the *Edinburgh Review* confirmed Lewis's place at the centre of early Victorian Liberal politics and letters. To the latter in the 1840s and 1850s he contributed four ambitious studies, *An Essay on the Government of Dependencies* (1841), *An Essay on the Influence of Authority in Matters of Opinion* (1849), *A Treatise on the Methods of Observation and Reasoning in Politics* (2 vols., 1852), and *An Inquiry into the Credibility of the Early Roman History* (2 vols., 1855), a sustained attack upon the classical scholarship of Niebuhr. He numbered among his circle of friends George and Harriet Grote, T. B. Macaulay, H. H. Milman, Charles Greville, Anthony Panizzi, and Abraham Hayward. Sharp disagreement with John Stuart Mill over Irish policy led to an abortive debate in July 1848 at the Political Economy Club, but respectful, if distant, personal relations between the two remained unaffected. In August 1854 the Lewises, travelling in Germany, met Alexis de Tocqueville and his wife. The friendship flourished, and Lewis became Tocqueville's warm admirer and regular correspondent. The personal acquaintance of politicians of his father's generation, such as Henry Brougham and Lord Lansdowne, encouraged Lewis to undertake, from 1856, a series of carefully documented essays on the high politics of the era before the passage of the Reform Act. These first appeared in the *Edinburgh Review* and were posthumously published in one volume as *Essays on the Administrations of Great Britain from 1783 to 1830* (1864); they still repay the attention of students of Georgian political history.

Scholastic embarrassment Lewis maintained a conscientious interest in Oxford University and its reform in the 1850s: he examined for the Ireland scholarship in 1853 and assumed in Michaelmas term 1855 what he called the 'unpaid … troublesome, difficult and unpopular' duties of serving on the Oxford commission. The collections of the National Gallery and the British Museum often benefited from Lewis's attention; but in advising the British Museum in 1857 to acquire two collections of the *Fables of Babrius*, Lewis opened the way to having his own scholarly credentials called into question. Lewis, relying on a French edition of 1844, had edited the earlier of the two collections for English readers in 1846; ominously the work was poorly received by German philologists. Then in 1857 Constantin Minadi—otherwise known as Minoïde Mynas—the Greek antiquary and copyist who had collected the fables, offered his copies to the British Museum for sale. Lewis accepted the manuscripts as reliable transcripts of genuine originals and had the museum purchase them. He then edited and published the additional fables in 1859, only to have continental philologists—'to the eternal discredit of English scholarship'—reject them on linguistic and metrical grounds as fraudulent (W. G. Rutherford, *Babrius*, 1883, lxix). More recent investigation of the provenance of the manuscripts has suggested that in Minadi Lewis was dealing, not with a forger, but with a clumsy and amateurish collector who nevertheless performed genuine services for classical learning. At the time, of course, the distinction could not ameliorate the embarrassment suffered by Lewis's reputation as a classical scholar.

Chancellor of the exchequer, 1855–1858 On the death of Sir Thomas Frankland Lewis on 22 January 1855, George Lewis succeeded to his father's baronetcy. He succeeded also to his father's seat in the Commons for the Radnorshire boroughs: his return on 8 February (and thereafter until his own death) was unopposed. Sixteen days later Palmerston offered Lewis the chancellorship of the exchequer, vacant upon Gladstone's resignation. Lewis felt 'the strongest disinclination to accept the offer: I was to follow Gladstone, whose ability had dazzled the world;

and to produce a War Budget, with large additional taxation, in a few weeks'. But pressed by Clarendon at the Foreign Office and encouraged by an interview with Gladstone, Lewis accepted the seals of office and on 28 February was sworn of the privy council. He resigned the editorship of the *Edinburgh Review*.

Lewis remained chancellor until the government was defeated in February 1858. Gladstone at first was helpfulness incarnate to his successor, but Lewis deviated from Gladstone's canons of financial rectitude, especially with respect to the question of whether to finance the Crimean War by taxation or by loans. Lewis faced a severe crisis in the nation's finances, brought on by a war more prolonged and expensive than anyone had expected. His first budget, on 20 April 1855, had to meet a deficit of £23 million. Lewis raised £16 million by a loan, £3 million by exchequer bills (later increased to £7 million), and the remaining £4 million by raising income tax from the already high 14*d.* to 16*d.* in the pound and by raising indirect taxes. The £68 million thus raised was easily the largest sum raised up to this time by a British government. Lewis's budget set aside the Gladstonian view that war abroad should be met by corresponding taxation-pain at home but, in terms of practical politics, financing by loans (to which Lewis resorted again in his second budget of 19 May 1856) was probably unavoidable if Palmerston's government was to survive. In 1855 Lewis carried through the Commons the Newspaper Stamp Duties Bill, an inheritance from Gladstone and an important step in repealing the 'taxes on knowledge' (as the duties on newspapers and paper were called). Lewis's policy of loans meant excellent commissions and profits for the City of London, which greatly preferred him to Gladstone. These opinions became an invaluable asset to Lewis in the financial crisis of 1857, when he found it necessary to recommend that Peel's Bank Charter Act of 1844 be suspended. Lewis proposed in his third (and last) budget, on 13 February 1857 (his first in peacetime), to reduce income tax from 16*d.* to 7*d.* and only slightly to reduce the war duties, the more readily thereby to lower the debt charges increased by the war. In the Commons both Gladstone and Disraeli, demanding reduced taxation and a sharp reduction in 'extravagant' public spending, attacked Lewis's budget vigorously and, in the former's case, with bitter animosity. Lewis demanded and then received Gladstone's apology for language 'reflecting upon his personal honour' (Gladstone MSS, BL, Add. MS 44236, fol. 94).

Home secretary and war secretary, 1859–1863 On the fall of the second Derby ministry in June 1859, Palmerston intended Lewis again for the Treasury in his new government. But Gladstone, who continued to find Lewis's opinions on finance unsatisfactory, claimed the post; and Lewis accepted the home secretaryship. Two years later, in July 1861, at the prime minister's request, he moved reluctantly to the War Office. Palmerston acknowledged that Lewis was no 'pipeclay-and-patent-blacking man', but thought him 'methodical and clear headed, with great power of learning anything he wishes to know; … he has been Chancellor of the Exchequer, and is versed in finance' (A. I. Dasent, *John Thadeus Delane, Editor of 'The Times': his Life and Correspondence* 1908, 2.29). Lewis had learned his financial verses in a school different from Gladstone's, and his foreign policy verses in a school different from Palmerston's, Russell's, or Gladstone's. He shared Palmerston's scepticism of the prospective benefits to be gathered from Gladstone's proposal in 1860 to repeal the paper duties, but by May he was warning Palmerston of the necessity of 'submitting to our [fiscal] destiny' (Broadlands MSS, GC/LE/127). European politics in 1859 and 1860 found Lewis doubtful of the moral superiority of the Italian cause; he reflected on 'how this united Italy is to be governed … when the ordinary motives of selfishness, envy, rivalry, and discontent begin to tell upon it' (ibid., GC/LE/131).

In so far as the roots of late Victorian 'splendid isolationism' are to be found in the 1860s, Lewis can be accounted one of those who sowed its seeds. He advocated a 'less umbrageous' foreign policy, nowhere more effectively than in his leadership of the cabinet opposition to Russell's and Gladstone's pressure for British intervention in the American Civil War. Doubtful as Lewis was in 1861 that bellicose language in Washington implied a real threat to Canada, as secretary for war he presided over the reinforcement of the British position there. The greater threat, in Lewis's mind, to British interests came from Russell's and Gladstone's readiness in the early autumn of 1862 to intervene in the American conflict. Lewis, having opposed intervention within the cabinet, determined to contest the issue with Gladstone on the platform. On 14 October at Hereford he argued that the Confederacy had not vindicated its claim to be an independent state and that the time had not arrived for either British mediation or British recognition of the Confederacy. On 7 November he laid his case against intervention before the cabinet in a brief, written in collaboration with his stepson-in-law William Harcourt, with arguments grounded in law, precedent, and expediency. Russell could not match these arguments; Palmerston moved toward a policy of watchful waiting for a more decisive result on the battlefield; and the crisis of intervention passed. Lewis had achieved a notable victory among his colleagues. He had out-debated Gladstone, and he had liberated himself from the tutelage of both Palmerston and Russell.

Death, character, and reputation This victory was to be Lewis's last. The stresses of hard work had further taken their toll on a man dogged throughout his adult life by less than robust health. After a short illness affecting both his lungs and his liver, Lewis died at Harpton Court on 13 April 1863. Four days later he was buried in the Lewis family vault in Old Radnor parish church.

According to Disraeli, Lewis was 'rather above middle height. He had a remarkable countenance; massy features, antique but not classical' (Bodl. Oxf., MS Hughenden A/X/A/42). He lacked an effective speaking voice; thin and uninflected, it was often difficult to hear, even within the House of Commons. But he loved 'talk', when his companions marvelled at his erudition. Lucy Austin, in whose parents' salon the young Lewis often 'talked', saw him as then a 'downright and avowed infidel', and Disraeli marked him later a 'great Bayleist' (an allusion to the French philosopher Pierre Bayle). Nothing in Lewis's adult life suggests a belief in revealed religion, regular though his church attendance was. His friend George Ticknor thought that Lewis had 'the greatest respect for *facts* of any man I ever saw' (G. Ticknor, *Life, Letters, and Journals*, 1876, 2.462). If Lewis believed in anything, it was in a Baconian science of 'the facts'.

Erudite but wanting in imagination, conscientious, dispassionate, and cerebral, Lewis displayed both the strengths and the limitations of orthodox Liberalism in early Victorian politics and letters. After his death Sir Edmund Head described him as a whig in politics, but this was a somewhat misleading label used by a conservative Liberal writing in the 1860s. In 1845 Greville thought Lewis a 'moderate [man] not belonging to any party' (*Memoirs*, 1938, 5.211) and Lewis as a politician never called himself anything other than a Liberal. Youthful radical inclinations tempered by administrative trials at the poor-law commission metamorphosed into the official Liberalism of the 1850s which Lewis himself did much to shape. He came to accept the cases for further parliamentary reform and the repeal of church rates; he sympathized with the case for the ballot. There was something of the accidental in Lewis's career in politics, impelled as it was by his later marriage into a family ambitious for him and by the fortuitous conjuncture in 1855 of his father's death and Gladstone's resignation. These accidents made it possible for the hapless poor-law commissioner of 1846 to become what Bagehot called 'perhaps the best selective administrator of our time' (W. Bagehot, *Works*, 1974, 5.325). After 1855 Lewis's cool head, 'vegetable' temperament, and prosaic manner often appeared to welcome relief and advantage on the Liberal front bench in the House of Commons. Had he lived longer, he would have remained a prominent figure within the post-Palmerstonian party, yet speculation that he could have led it seems wide of the mark. Lacking the popular touch, he never won a contested election to the House of Commons. And his willingness to yield the exchequer to Gladstone in 1859 suggests that he should not have had the will to contest Gladstone's claim to lead the party once Palmerston and Russell had gone.

That Lewis is remembered more as a political than as a literary figure might have surprised those who knew him in the 1840s and early 1850s, when he was most productive as an author. But the big books of those years, on which his reputation as an author must depend, are prolix and over-supplied with illustrative examples: Lewis's respect for facts did not always serve him well. The deliberately flat prose of these works was that of one who disliked 'style' in writing. Nevertheless, Lewis's books and articles have never gone unread or even completely out of print, and they have attracted from time to time the appreciation of critics as different as Arnoldo Momigliano and Sir Kenneth Wheare.

Lewis's oft-quoted remark, 'Life would be tolerable were it not for its amusements' (*The Times*, 18 Sept 1872, 4), suggests something of the impression he often gave of a detached world-weariness. The same ironic sense of humour inspired and pervades his *Suggestions for the application of Egyptological method to modern history; illustrated by examples* (1862), which may still be read with amusement by anyone who has appreciated Richard Whately's *Historic Doubts Relative to Napoleon Bonaparte* (1819). By contrast, Lewis carried detachment to a perhaps unnecessary extreme in his final work, *A Dialogue on the Best Form of Government* (1863), at the end of which Crito, concluding a debate among Democritus, Aristocraticus, and Monarchicus, opines that 'it is the part of wisdom and prudence to acquiesce in any form of government, which is tolerably well administered, and affords tolerable security to person and property' (p. 116). Whatever Lewis's limitations, an excess of enthusiasm was not to be found among them. D. A. SMITH

Sources C. F. Mullett, 'Preface, introductory essay, and bibliography', in G. C. Lewis, *Remarks on the use and abuse of some political terms*, ed. C. F. Mullet (1970) • *Letters of the Right Hon. Sir George Cornewall Lewis to various friends*, ed. G. F. Lewis (1870) • W. Bagehot, 'Sir George Cornewall Lewis', *Works*, ed. N. St John Stevas, 3 (1968), 366–400 • K. C. Wheare, 'Sir George Cornewall Lewis as a political scientist', *Political Studies*, 20 (1972), 407–20 • R. Posner, 'Sir George Cornewall Lewis: statesman and "new philologist"', *Historiographia Linguistica*, 17 (1990), 339–56 • S. Buxton, *Finance and politics: an historical study, 1783–1885*, 2 (1888) • S. E. Finer, *The life and times of Sir Edwin Chadwick* (1952) • L. Hamburger and J. Hamburger, *Troubled lives: John and Sarah Austin* (1985) • H. Jones, *Union in peril: the crisis over British intervention in the civil war* (1992) • A. Dain, 'Un recueil byzantin des fables de Babrios', *Actes du IXe Congrès International d'Etudes Byzantines*, 9 (1958), 101–11 • *Wellesley index*

Archives NL Wales, corresp. and papers • NL Wales, corresp. and papers relating to his candidature in 1852 Herefordshire election | BL, corresp. with Lord Broughton, Add. MS 47229 • BL, corresp. with W. E. Gladstone, Add. MS 44236 • BL, letters to Macvey Napier, Add. MSS 34612–34626, *passim* • BL, letters to Sir Anthony Panizzi, Add. MSS 36716–36727, *passim* • BL, corresp. with Lord Ripon, Add. MS 43533 • BL, corresp. with Charles Wood, Add. MSS 49531, *passim* • Bodl. Oxf., corresp. with earl of Clarendon • Bodl. Oxf., Graham MSS [microfilm] • Bodl. Oxf., corresp. with Sir William Harcourt • Bodl. Oxf., corresp. with Sir Thomas Phillipps • Borth. Inst., corresp. with Sir Charles Wood • Bucks. RLSS, letters to duke of Somerset • CKS, letters to Lord Stanhope • Hergest Trust, Herefordshire, corresp. with Richard Banks • NL Wales, letters to W. E. Gladstone • NL Wales, corresp. with Nassau Senior • PRO, corresp. with Lord John Russell, PRO 30/22 • St Deiniol's Library, Hawarden, corresp. with duke of Newcastle • U. Newcastle, Robinson L., letters to Sir Charles Trevelyan • U. Nott. L., letters to duke of Newcastle • U. Southampton, Broadlands MSS • U. Southampton L., corresp. with Lord Palmerston • UCL, letters to Society for the Diffusion of Useful Knowledge

Likenesses G. Richmond, chalk drawing, 1857, NPG • H. Watkins, photograph, 1858, NPG [*see illus.*] • H. Weigall, oils, exh. RA 1863, NMG Wales • H. Weigall, portrait, 1863, NMG Wales • C. Marochetti, bronze statue, *c*.1864, opposite Shire Hall, Hereford • H. Weekes, bust, exh. RA 1864, Westminster Abbey, London • L. Caldesi, carte-de-visite, NPG • J. W. Gordon, oils, Somerset House, London • J. Phillip, group portrait, oils (*The House of Commons, 1860*), Palace of Westminster, London • D. J. Pound, stipple and line print (after a photograph by J. Watkins), NPG; repro. in D. J. Pound, *The drawing room portrait gallery of eminent personages* • J. Watkins, carte-de-visite, NPG • attrib. J. Watkins, photograph, NPG

Wealth at death under £20,000: probate, 5 June 1863, *CGPLA Eng. & Wales*

Lewis, Sir George Henry, first baronet (1833–1911), lawyer, was born on 21 April 1833, at 10 Ely Place, Holborn, London, one of eight children and second of four sons of James Graham Lewis (1804–1873) and his wife, Harriet Davis (*c.*1805–1869). He was educated at a private Jewish school at Edmonton and at University College, London (1847–50), before being articled to his father (1851) and admitted as a solicitor (1856). The firm of Lewis and Lewis, which he joined, then dealt chiefly in criminal cases, insolvency, and civil litigation arising from fraud (a prominent case being that of the banker Sir John Dean Paul).

On 29 March 1863 Lewis married Victorine (1840–1865), daughter of Philip Kann, of Frankfurt am Main; they had one daughter. After her death, he married on 10 February 1867 Elizabeth (1845–1931), daughter of Ferdinand Eberstadt, of Mannheim; they had one son, who succeeded Lewis as head of the firm, and two daughters. Lewis's second wife was a bold, ebullient, and astringent woman who created a salon of painters, writers, politicians, and lawyers; her ambition incited him.

Lewis's knowledge of the law was not profound, but he was cool, keen, and wily in court. He was meticulous in interviewing his witnesses before they testified and implacable in cross-examination. He reached national celebrity by his ruthless questioning on behalf of the deceased's parents at the inquest into the poisoning of Charles Bravo (1876). He acted as vigorously for malefactors as for the oppressed and innocent. In 1877 he was solicitor for Louis Staunton, who had starved his baby son and wife to death to obtain an inheritance. It was Lewis's plan to divide and discredit the expert witnesses who testified on the pathology of starvation. After Staunton and his coadjutors were convicted, Lewis helped to manipulate a press agitation which achieved the commutation of their death sentences.

Lewis was ingenious in exploiting Victorian sexual inhibitions to his clients' advantage. As solicitor of the transvestites Ernest Boulton and Frederick Park he devised their successful defence against a charge of conspiracy (1870–71). He had less success when acting for Valentine Baker who had been charged with indecent assault (1875). He secured Adelaide Bartlett's acquittal in the Pimlico poisoning case by preparing a defence that convinced the jury she had been victimized by a perverted husband (1886). Similarly, after the collapse of the marriage of John Francis Stanley Russell, second Earl Russell, the peer's grasping mother-in-law and siren wife consulted Lewis, who tried to intimidate Russell with imputations of homosexuality (1890). He was involved in other notorious matrimonial causes, notably representing the liar Virginia Crawford, who implicated Sir Charles *Dilke in her divorce (1885–6), and Lady Colin Campbell (1886).

Lewis's popularity with the Marlborough House set was crucial to his transformation from a police court hack. In 1869 he met the prince of Wales through Lord Marcus Beresford, whom he had represented after Beresford had beaten a moneylender. Having advised the prince during the divorce of Sir Charles Mordaunt (1870), Lewis was henceforth trusted to handle royal mistresses and *maris complaisants*. A quarrel between Frances Greville, Lady Brooke (afterwards countess of Warwick), her former lover Lord Charles Beresford, and the prince particularly taxed his resources (1889–90). The prince arranged for Lewis to represent the defendants in the unsuccessful slander action brought by Sir William Gordon-Cumming over the Tranby Croft baccarat scandal (1891). Lewis's study of Richard Pigott's forgeries had previously provided Sir Charles Russell with the materials for his devastating cross-examination on behalf of the nationalists at the Parnell commission (1888–9). His role in the Parnell and Gordon-Cumming affairs was rewarded with a knighthood in 1892. He obtained a baronetcy in 1902 at King Edward VII's coronation despite the reluctance of Balfour and Salisbury and was made CVO in 1905. Each year he was invited to Balmoral but he never accepted.

Everyone in society desired to be represented by Lewis. Professionally he was effective, discreet, and versatile (even advising Lord Durham in voluminous proceedings before the stewards of the Jockey Club, 1887–9). His advice and mediation kept most of his clients clear of public notoriety. At the request of Oscar Wilde, for example, he represented Lord Alfred Douglas, paying a blackmailer £100 to recover an incriminating letter (1893). His success was partly attributable to his audacity as a private enquiry agent: his narks and informants included convicted criminals such as William Meiklejohn, a detective inspector dismissed from Scotland Yard for corruption. Typically, after Gainsborough's portrait of Georgiana, duchess of Devonshire was stolen in 1876, Lewis was charged by William Agnew with its recovery, and tracked it to Antwerp from where he was still trying to secure it seventeen years later.

Lewis cared for rules only so far as not to be caught breaking them. He was a dangerous man to best. He so much resented the outcome of the prolonged libel litigation (1882–4) brought by the sculptor Richard Belt against his client Charles Lawes that he pursued and ruined Belt. He issued a writ for fraudulent representation after Belt had sold jewellery to Sir William Abdy, obtained Belt's bankruptcy, and initiated his prosecution for obtaining money under false pretences (1885–6). Lewis represented his friend Henry Labouchere in many libel actions launched against the magazine *Truth*. It was said that he knew 'enough to hang half-a-dozen of the biggest men in the City' (How, 'Lewis', 645): certainly he represented the swindler Whitaker Wright (1904). But he also appreciated the artistic *milieux* and was an early admirer of Lillie Langtry and an intimate of Edward Burne-Jones and adviser of James Whistler.

Lewis's experience in the case of Serafino Pelizzioni, wrongly convicted of murder, whose freedom he regained after a legal campaign of singular dexterity (1864–5), contributed to his long advocacy of the reforms finally embodied in the Prisoners' Evidence Act of 1898, by which prisoners and their wives were enabled to testify in criminal cases, and in the institution of a court of criminal appeal in 1908. In his last years he represented two famous victims of injustice, Adolph Beck (convicted on a wrongful identification) and the naval cadet George Archer-Shee, and campaigned against the racially motivated injustice inflicted on the Edalji family. He contributed to the movement which led to the Moneylenders Act of 1900 curbing usurious extortion. His enlightened testimony to the royal commission on the divorce laws (1910) urged equal rights for both sexes and cheaper divorce.

Strongly built with white Dundreary whiskers and penetrating eyes, Lewis wore a monocle and a fur coat even on hot days. He was a heavy cigar smoker. He bought the wooden Danish pavilion from the Paris Exhibition of 1900 and re-erected it on the cliffs at Overstrand, Norfolk, as his country house. Lewis died of leukaemia on 7 December 1911 at his home, 88 Portland Place, Marylebone, London, and was buried at the Jewish cemetery at Willesden on 10 December. RICHARD DAVENPORT-HINES

Sources *The Times* (8 Dec 1911) • *New York Daily Tribune* (31 Dec 1911) • J. Juxon, *Lewis and Lewis* (1983) • H. How, 'Sir George Lewis', *Strand Magazine*, 6 (1893), 645–57 • P. Magnus, *King Edward the Seventh* (1964) • *The letters of Oscar Wilde*, ed. R. Hart-Davis (1962) • R. S. Churchill, ed., *Winston S. Churchill*, companion vol. 1/2 (1967) • Earl Russell [J. F. S. Russell], *My life and adventures* (1923) • Lord Havers and others, *The royal baccarat scandal* (1988)

Archives Bodl. Oxf., corresp. and papers • Bodl. Oxf., family MSS • Holborn Library, Camden, London, Camden Local Studies and Archives Centre, letters and telegrams congratulating him on his knighthood | priv. coll., Lewis family MSS

Likenesses Elliott & Fry, photographs, 1893, repro. in *Strand Magazine*, 6 (1893), 645, 657 • M. Beerbohm, drawing, *c*.1896, Garr. Club • J. S. Sargent, oils, 1896, priv. coll. • Spy [L. Ward], cartoon, 1896, Mansell Collection, London • M. Beerbohm, drawing, *c*.1908, U. Texas • M. Beerbohm, cartoons, repro. in Juxon, *Lewis and Lewis*, facing p. 257 • P. Burne-Jones, oils, priv. coll. • S. P. Hall, pencil drawings, NPG • F. Pegram, pencil sketches, V&A • Spy [L. Ward], caricature, chromolithograph, NPG; repro. in *VF* (2 Sept 1876) • Walery, photograph, NPG

Wealth at death £224,110 5*s*.: resworn probate, 13 Feb 1912, *CGPLA Eng. & Wales*

Lewis, George Robert (1782–1871), painter and engraver, the second son of Johan Ludwig, reputedly a miniature painter and political refugee from Hanover, was born on 27 March 1782 in London. He came from a family of artists, his brothers being Frederick Christian *Lewis (1779–1856), engraver and watercolourist, William Lewis (*fl.* 1804–1838), amateur landscape painter, and Charles *Lewis (1786–1836), bookbinder. His nephew was John Frederick *Lewis (1804–1876), painter of oriental subjects, and his own son, Lennard Lewis (1826–1913), was a writer and painter of watercolour landscapes who exhibited from 1848 to 1898.

George Robert Lewis studied under Fuseli at the Royal Academy Schools, and exhibited landscapes at the academy from 1805 to 1807. With his brother Frederick, he executed aquatint plates for J. Chamberlaine's *Original Designs of the most Celebrated Masters* (1812), and W. Y. Ottley's *Italian School of Design* (1823). In 1813 he accompanied John Linnell on a visit to Wales, where the two artists made studies in the open air, relishing the chance to experience primitive landscape which reminded them of biblical times, and following a 'semi-Mosaic' diet in accordance with their religious beliefs (Linnell). Lewis exhibited a series of oil paintings at the Oil and Watercolour Society in 1816, presumably made in Herefordshire in the summer of 1815. They were all described in the catalogue as 'painted on the spot' and those which have survived show labourers harvesting in the fields around Haywood Lodge, near Hereford. Four of these are now in the Tate collection, including *Hereford, Dynedor and Malvern hills, from the Haywood Lodge, harvest scene, afternoon. Painted on the spot*. Lewis was thus one of a group of painters, including Constable and DeWint, who combined an interest in working landscape with an emphasis on painting everything from nature, which reached a peak in the closing years of the Napoleonic Wars. Two sketchbooks by Lewis in the British Museum from around this time contain many studies of farmworkers and gravel diggers. Lewis seems to have returned to the close study of landscape in the 1850s, when he made a visit to north Devon: three watercolours in the British Museum, whose precision of detail have been compared to the work of the Pre-Raphaelites, probably date from this period. Much of his work, however, was devoted to engraving. In 1818 he accompanied Dr Dibdin on his continental journey, illustrating his *Bibliographical, Antiquarian and Picturesque Tour in France and Germany*, published in 1821. From sketches made on this tour he etched a series of *Groups illustrating the physiognomy, manners, and character of the people of France and Germany*, which was issued in parts, and completed in 1823.

A man of strong and somewhat eccentric views, Lewis apparently chose his wife, whom he married in 1823, on account of her 'great show of the feelings' according to Spurzheim's phrenology (Lewis to Dawson Turner, Cambridge, Trinity College). He pursued the study of ecclesiastical architecture to show that early Norman architectural forms were designed in accordance with the law and the gospel. His publications reflect his interests in phrenology and physiognomy, and in ecclesiastical design. The most important of these are *Views of the Muscles of the Human Body* (1820); *Illustrations of Phrenology* (1841); *Illustrations of Kilpeck church, Herefordshire, with an essay on ecclesiastical design and a descriptive interpretation* (1842); *The Ancient Font of Little Walsingham Church* (1843); and *The Ancient Church of Shobden, Herefordshire, Illustrated and Described* (1852; reissued 1856). In 1838 Lewis printed at Hereford *An address on the subject of education as connected with design in every department of British manufacture, together with hints on the education of the poor generally*; this pamphlet advocated assessing the capabilities of the poor (using Spurzheim's phrenology) and framing their education accordingly. From 1820 to 1859 Lewis exhibited portraits, landscape, and figure subjects at the Royal Academy, the British Institution, and the Society of British Artists. He died at his home, 1 Haverstock Terrace, Hampstead, London, on 15 May 1871.

CHRISTIANA PAYNE

Sources *DNB* • J. Turner, ed., *The dictionary of art*, 34 vols. (1996) • *The Tate Gallery, 1980–82: illustrated catalogue of acquisitions* (1984) • C. Payne, *Toil and plenty: images of the agricultural landscape in England,*

1780–1890 (1993) [exhibition catalogue, U. Nott. Art Gallery, 7 Oct – 14 Nov 1993; Yale U. CBA, 15 Jan – 13 March 1994] • Trinity Cam., Dawson Turner MSS • J. Linnell, MS autobiography, priv. coll., Linnell Trust MSS • J. M. H. Lewis, *The Lewis family: art and travel* (privately printed, Old Woking, [1992]) • *CGPLA Eng. & Wales* (1871)
Archives Devon RO, letters to Thomas Dyke Acland • priv. coll., Linnell Trust MSS • Trinity Cam., Dawson Turner MSS
Wealth at death under £100: probate, 17 June 1871, *CGPLA Eng. & Wales*

Lewis, Griffith George (1784–1859), army officer, was born at Woolwich on 10 November 1784. He was educated privately and at the Royal Military Academy, Woolwich. He was then sent with the next two senior cadets to the west of England to be instructed in military surveying under Major W. Mudge, before obtaining his commission in the Royal Engineers. He was gazetted second lieutenant on 15 March 1803 and lieutenant on 2 July. After a year at Chatham he joined the Portsmouth command, and in May 1805 embarked for the Mediterranean under Sir James Craig. He served at Malta, and then in the campaign of Naples and Calabria. He was present at the battle of Maida on 4 July 1806, and after it joined Colonel Oswald's brigade in a projected attack on the castle of Scylla. They arrived on the night of 11 July, and Lewis with his engineers laboured unceasingly in the construction of the siege batteries, from which fire was opened on 21 July. So devastating was the effect that next day the garrison surrendered.

Lewis was promoted second captain on 18 November 1807. He served under Sir J. Stuart at the capture of Ischia and Procida in the Bay of Naples in August 1809, and in the Ionian Islands under Sir John Oswald at the siege of Santa Maura in 1810. In February 1811 he returned to England, stopping at Gibraltar on his way, and was stationed at Woolwich. On 10 July he embarked with the expedition for Sweden and the Danish island of Anholt, and returning in September was posted to the eastern district. In December 1812 he embarked for Portugal, and was employed in the construction of the defensive lines round Lisbon. In 1813 he served in the campaign in Spain under Wellington, and was promoted captain on 21 July 1813. At the siege of San Sebastián he was twice wounded, and in the forefront of the assault of the breach on 25 July was injured so severely that his leg was amputated above the knee. His gallant conduct was mentioned in Lord Lynedoch's dispatches, and he was promoted brevet major on 21 September. He returned to England in the same month. After some time on the sick list he joined the army of occupation in France, and in the autumn of 1817 was employed on special service.

On 18 January 1819 Lewis embarked for Newfoundland, where in St John's, on 6 March 1821, he married Fanny, *née* Bland; she survived him. On 29 July 1825 he was promoted lieutenant-colonel. He returned to England on 18 September 1827. On 1 April 1828 he embarked for Canada to serve on a commission on the Rideau Canal, and went home again on 6 September. He was commanding royal engineer at Jersey from December 1830 until January 1836, at the Cape from March 1836 until the autumn of 1842, in Ireland from January 1843 to January 1847, and at Portsmouth from January 1847 until 3 April 1851. On 20 June 1838 he was promoted brevet colonel, and on 23 November 1841 regimental colonel. On 19 July 1838 Lewis was made a CB for his war services. He also received a pension of £200 per annum for life for his wounds, and a distinguished service pension of £100 per annum. From April 1851 until July 1856 he was governor of the Royal Military Academy, Woolwich. He was promoted major-general on 11 November 1851 and lieutenant-general on 12 August 1858, and was made a colonel commandant of the corps of Royal Engineers on 23 November 1858.

Lewis was joint editor with Captain J. Williams of the *Professional Papers of the Corps of Royal Engineers* and of the *Corps Papers* (1847–54), and himself contributed papers to them on fortification and other subjects. Lewis died at Brighton on 24 October 1859.

R. H. Vetch, *rev.* James Falkner

Sources *Army List* • W. Porter, *History of the corps of royal engineers*, 2 vols. (1889) • *Hart's Army List*
Likenesses oils, Royal Engineers HQ Mess, Chatham, Kent
Wealth at death under £3000: probate, 3 Nov 1859, *CGPLA Eng. & Wales*

Lewis, Sir (John) Herbert (1858–1933), lawyer and politician, was born at Mostyn Quay, Whitford, Flintshire, on 27 December 1858, the only son of Enoch Lewis (1812–1885), merchant and shipowner (great-nephew of Thomas Jones of Denbigh, Methodist leader, 1756–1820), and his wife, Catherine Roberts (*d.* 1868), of Plas Llangwyfan, Denbighshire. He was educated at Denbigh grammar school, briefly at McGill University (Montreal), privately with Dr E. Pan Jones, and at Exeter College, Oxford, where he read jurisprudence and graduated with a fourth in 1879. He continued his legal training in Chester and London before he established the Liverpool practice of Herbert Lewis and Davies in 1885. His partner, Alfred Thomas Davies, became the first secretary of the Welsh department of the Board of Education. On 16 November 1886 he married, at the Welsh Presbyterian church, Toxteth, his cousin Adelaide Hughes (1862/3–1895), daughter of Charles Hughes JP, publisher, of Wrexham. After her death he married Ruth Caine (*b.* 1871/2), daughter of William Sproston *Caine, the Liberal MP and temperance advocate, on 8 July 1897. There was a son and a daughter of the second marriage.

Lewis was active in local politics from 1886 and was appointed treasurer of the North Wales Liberal federation. He was elected alderman and first chairman of Flintshire county council in 1889 and took part in implementing the provisions of the Welsh Intermediate Education Act of 1889 and the Technical Education Act of 1889 in the county. He remained chairman until 1893 and continued his involvement with the county council until 1913.

Lewis entered parliament in 1892 as a Liberal, representing Flint Boroughs until 1906 and Flintshire until 1918, when he was elected the first MP to represent the University of Wales, a seat for whose creation he had campaigned. He held it until his retirement in 1922. A close colleague of David Lloyd George and Tom Ellis, he practised a radical nonconformity which came early to the fore when in the 'Welsh revolt' of 1894 he joined Lloyd George, D. A.

Thomas (later Lord Rhondda), and Frank Edwards in refusing the Liberal whip over disestablishment of the Church in Wales. A leading figure in the Cymru Fydd (Young Wales) movement that flourished in the final decades of the nineteenth century, he was consistent in bringing a range of Welsh concerns to parliament's attention. His long and persistent campaign to obtain for Wales a share in the museum grants voted annually by parliament led to the establishment of a national museum in Cardiff and a national library in Aberystwyth, and his advocacy, with that of others, achieved status for the library as a place of deposit under the Copyright Act of 1911. He was a vice-president of the library from 1907 to 1926 and president from 1926 to 1927. He was also involved in the development of the university colleges in Wales and with others, notably Lord Rendel and Tom Ellis, succeeded in obtaining a royal charter establishing the University of Wales in 1893.

Lewis was appointed junior lord of the Treasury in 1906, parliamentary secretary to the Local Government Board in 1909, and parliamentary secretary to the Board of Education in 1915. At the Board of Education, with its president H. A. L. Fisher, he worked for educational reform, particularly the Education Act (1918), the Libraries Act (1919), and legislation concerning teachers' superannuation and educational grants for former servicemen. On leaving parliament in 1922 he was appointed GBE. In retirement he was able to indulge further his lifelong interest in travel, in 1924 revisiting India, where his daughter was involved in missionary work.

Lewis was sworn of the privy council in 1912 and was an alderman of Flintshire county council from 1889 to 1913; he was also constable of Flint Castle, a freeman of the boroughs of Flint and Aberystwyth, vice-president of University College of North Wales, Bangor, an honorary LLD of the University of Wales (1918), deputy lieutenant of Flintshire, and president of the Library Association of the United Kingdom (1920–21), and was awarded the gold medal of the Honourable Society of Cymmrodorion in 1927.

In June 1925, when visiting Aberystwyth, Lewis slipped and fell into a quarry, seriously injuring his spine. Thereafter he was confined to the family home at Penucha, Caerwys, Flintshire, where he died on 10 November 1933. He was buried at the Calvinistic Methodist cemetery of Ddol Chapel, near Caerwys, on 13 November. His widow, Lady Lewis, who was appointed OBE in 1918 and one of the first women JPs in 1921, survived him.

An obituarist writing in the *North Wales Times* (18 November 1933) noted that during his time in parliament Lewis did more constructive work for Welsh institutions than anybody else before or since. Throughout a long career in public service he was consistent and effective in his support of nonconformity, of the Welsh language, and of Wales. ROWLAND WILLIAMS

Sources B. Bowen Thomas, 'Sir John Herbert Lewis: centenary tribute', *Journal of the Flintshire Historical Society*, 18 (1960), 131–41 • W. H. Jones, 'Sir John Herbert Lewis: centenary tribute', *Journal of the Flintshire Historical Society*, 18 (1960), 142–55 • J. G. Williams, *The University College of North Wales: foundations 1884–1927* (1985) • W. L. Davies, *The National Library of Wales* (1937) • *DWB* • A. Mee, ed., *Who's who in Wales* (1921) • *North Wales Times* (18 Nov 1933) • *The personal papers of Lord Rendel containing his unpublished conversations with Mr Gladstone … and other famous statesmen*, ed. F. E. Hamer (1931) • b. cert. • m. certs. • d. cert. • *CGPLA Eng. & Wales* (1934)

Archives Flintshire RO, Hawarden, family corresp., deeds, political papers, photographs, and autobiographical notes • Flintshire RO, Hawarden, family, personal, and political corresp., papers incl. diaries • NL Wales, corresp., diaries, and papers | Flintshire RO, Hawarden, records of Flintshire county council • HLRO, letters to David Lloyd George • NL Wales, letters to D. R. Daniel • NL Wales, letters to Sir A. T. Davies • NL Wales, letters to T. E. Ellis • NL Wales, letters incl. to Thomas Iorwerth Ellis, Annie Hughes Griffiths, and Peter Hughes Griffiths • NL Wales, letters to David Lloyd George • NL Wales, letters to T. G. Jones • NL Wales, letters to Sir Daniel Lleufer Thomas

Likenesses L. Hughes, oils, 1892, Flintshire County Council, Mold, Flintshire, Civic Centre • M. Forbes, oils, presented 1938, NL Wales • F. Morris Brown, black chalk drawing, 1939 (after photograph), NL Wales • W. Goscombe John, marble bust, NL Wales

Wealth at death £76,585 13*s*. 2*d*.: resworn probate, 5 Jan 1934, *CGPLA Eng. & Wales*

Lewis, Howell Elvet [*pseud.* Elfed] (**1860–1953**), Congregational minister and devotional poet, was born on 14 April 1860 at Y Gangell, Blaen-y-coed, Cynwyl Elfed, Carmarthenshire, to Anna, *née* Davies (*b*. 1836/7), and James Lewis (*b*. 1834/5), an agricultural worker. He was educated at Blaen-y-coed British School, Newcastle Emlyn grammar school (1874–6), and the Presbyterian college, Carmarthen (1876–80). He is almost invariably referred to by his bardic name, Elfed.

Elfed was one of the best-known of the 'poet-preachers' who played a leading role in the cultural and religious life of Wales in the late nineteenth and early twentieth centuries. While his sphere of influence and public activity lay largely in Welsh-speaking Wales, there was a dichotomy in his life. His family life was conducted in English; his children knew no Welsh. This happened more by force of circumstance than by design. He began his ministry at Buckley, Flintshire, in an Anglicized area, and there he met the young woman of Scottish descent, Mary Taylor (1867–1918), who was to become his wife on 23 August 1887. His marriage set the seal on the cultural and linguistic duality which henceforth characterized his personal life and his work as a minister.

From Buckley (1880–84) Elfed moved to Fish Street Church, Hull (1884–91), but then returned to his native Carmarthenshire to serve the English-speaking Park Church, Llanelli (1891–8). Thence he moved to London to minister to the congregation of the historic Harecourt church (1898–1904), where Milton, Bunyan, and later Livingstone had all worshipped. In 1904 he was persuaded to become minister, for the first time, of a Welsh-speaking church (albeit in London). It was at Tabernacl, King's Cross, that he served the greater part of his ministry, remaining there until his retirement in 1940. During his time there, his wife died in the influenza epidemic of 1918. Five years later, on 22 March 1923, he married Elizabeth Lloyd (1870/71–1927), the widow of the Revd Emrys Lloyd and the daughter of Henry Harris, a farmer. She died after only four years of marriage, and on 24 February 1930 he married Mary Elizabeth (*b*. 1882/3), daughter of Jonah Davies, who proved to be a great support to him as, in succeeding years, blindness overtook him.

Elfed was much in demand as a preacher, in both languages. He attracted large congregations, particularly at the special preaching meetings which were an important feature of the nonconformist calendar. He was renowned for the clarity and directness of his sermons, which were lyrical and comforting in tone and delivered in a mellifluous voice. That same limpid lyricism can be seen in the style of his religious miscellanies, *Planu coed* ('Planting trees'; 1894) and *Lampau 'r hwyr* ('The lamps of evening'; 1945). It is also a noteworthy feature of his well-crafted hymns. These are often communitarian in spirit; one of the best-known, 'Cofia'n gwlad' ('Remember our country'), was for many years regarded in Wales as a kind of second national anthem. Elfed's hymns are largely devotional and supplicatory in content; they have been criticized for their lack of theological profundity, but they remain well loved. Among Elfed's many successful English hymns are 'The light of the morning is breaking' and 'Whom oceans part, O Lord, unite'. In *Sweet Singers of Wales* (*c*.1890) he sought to introduce Welsh hymn writers to an English audience. He was also a translator of hymns, particularly from English and German into Welsh. He was a prolific writer of religious verse in English, his main publications being *My Christ and other Poems* (1891), *Israel and other Poems* (1930), and *Songs of Assisi* (1938).

Elfed won the crown at the national eisteddfod in 1888 and 1891 and the chair in 1894. His eisteddfodic poems are largely in the nineteenth-century tradition, but show signs of the new Romanticism which was to become an important feature of early twentieth-century Welsh poetry. In his two volumes *Caniadau* ('Songs', 1895, 1901) the Romantic lyricist is well to the fore, with an emphasis on the beauties of nature and a benign spirituality. Such poems as 'Bethesda 1901', which casts striking quarrymen in a heroic light, are an expression of early socialism. Elfed's Romanticism was fuelled by his interest in German literature. His nature poetry was influenced by that of Goethe, whose work he translated into Welsh. His translation of Schiller's *Wilhelm Tell* appeared in 1924, but the influence of this portrait of a patriotic hero can be seen in Elfed's earlier heroic poem 'Llewelyn ein llyw olaf' ('Llewelyn our last leader', 1889).

Elfed's poetry, with the exception of a few short pieces which have a melodious beauty, is little regarded today. His critical writings, which include studies of Ceiriog (1899), Ann Griffiths (1903), and Morgan Rhys (1910), though they contain some valuable insights, share a similar fate. Elfed's writings on hymnology, including the materials for a full-scale study of the Welsh hymn which remain in manuscript, show evidence of a serious scholarly bent.

From later middle age, Elfed devoted himself increasingly to public life. He continued to travel extensively on preaching and lecturing tours, and took a leading part in the affairs of such bodies as the National Eisteddfod and the Congregationalist Unions in Wales and England. The University of Wales, *honoris causa*, conferred on him the degrees of MA (1906), DD (1933), and LLD (1948). In 1948 he was also made a CH and was presented with a national testimonial gift in Cardiff.

Elfed's personal life was not without sadness. In addition to the deaths of his first two wives, his son Wallace, youngest of his seven children, died at the age of five, another son, Duncan, having died when only few weeks old. In retirement Elfed lived in Penarth, near Cardiff, where he died at his home, 3 Erw'r Delyn, on 10 December 1953, at the age of ninety-three, survived by his wife. His ashes were interred at Blaen-y-coed.

BRANWEN JARVIS

Sources E. G. Jenkins, *Cofiant Elfed* (1957) • D. Owen, *Elfed a'i waith* [n.d.] • E. W. Parry, *Howell Elfed Lewis* (1958) • M. B. Davies and others, 'H. Elvet-Lewis (Elfed): a bibliography', *Journal of the Welsh Bibliographical Society*, 8 (1954–7), 7–23, 106 [English-language bibliography] • B. Jarvis, *Llinynnau* (1999), 121–51 • m. cert. [J. Lewis] • m. certs. [H. E. Lewis]

Archives NL Wales

Likenesses W. Stoneman, photograph, 1949, NPG

Wealth at death £3697 9*s*. 3*d*.: probate, 4 Feb 1954, *CGPLA Eng. & Wales*

Lewis, Hubert (1825–1884), jurist, was born on 23 March 1825, the second son of Walter Clapham Lewis of Upper Norland House, Kensington, London, and Ripon, Yorkshire. He was educated privately until December 1844 when he entered Emmanuel College, Cambridge, where he obtained a scholarship and graduated BA in 1848. He entered at the Middle Temple in May 1851, and after obtaining two certificates of honour was called to the bar in 1854. He practised conveyancing and equity, first at Bradford in Yorkshire (where he joined the northern circuit and attended the West Riding sessions), and subsequently in London. He died unmarried on 6 March 1884 at Margate, and was buried in the cemetery there.

Lewis was the author of legal works on the principles of conveyancing and of equity drafting, published in 1863 and 1865. The sixth edition of Goldsmith's *Equity* was almost entirely rewritten by him in 1870. His *Ancient Laws of Wales* was published posthumously in 1889 under the editorship of J. E. Lloyd. This work, which occupied almost all Lewis's leisure hours throughout his life, was designed to prove that the English constitution and the law of real property were largely based on or borrowed from early British institutions. These he reconstructed out of material found in the Welsh code of Howell the Good and in *The Record of Caernarvon*, or out of the evidence of place names, and some very inaccurate etymological reasoning based thereon. Lewis also left behind him in manuscript some works on local nomenclature and kindred subjects.

D. L. THOMAS, *rev.* CATHERINE PEASE-WATKIN

Sources private information (1892) • H. Lewis, 'Preface', *The ancient laws of Wales*, ed. J. E. Lloyd (1889) • Venn, *Alum. Cant.*

Lewis, Hywel David (1910–1992), theologian and philosopher, was born on 21 May 1910 at 5 Mostyn Crescent, Llandudno, the younger son of David John Lewis (1876–1947), a Calvinistic Methodist minister, first in Llandudno and then in Caernarfon, and his wife, Rebecca, *née* Davies

(1865–1953). His brother Alun Tudor Lewis (1905–1986) was a schoolmaster and an author of short stories in Welsh. Hywel was educated at Caernarfon grammar school and at the University College of North Wales, Bangor, where he developed his interest in philosophy. He graduated with a first-class degree in 1932. He returned to Bangor as a lecturer in philosophy after further studies at Jesus College, Oxford, from where he graduated with a BLitt in 1935. He became professor of philosophy at Bangor in 1947. Meanwhile, on 17 August 1943, he married a fellow university lecturer, Megan Jones (1909/10–1962), daughter of John Elias Jones, an inspector of schools.

Lewis's early books, *Morals and the New Theology* (1947) and *Morals and Revelation* (1951), provided a forceful critique of the Barthian claim that mankind is utterly dependent on divine revelation for a knowledge of God and of correct moral value, and in their trenchant anti-determinism they revealed the influence of C. A. (Charles Arthur) Campbell. Lewis held the view that awareness of the divine is a basic intuition rooted in normal human experience and can be articulated by reflection upon our awareness of value, particularly moral value. He developed these ideas in what came to be perhaps his most influential book, *Our Experience of God*, published in 1959, by which time he had been appointed (in 1955) to the chair of the history and philosophy of religion at the University of London, a position which he held until he retired in 1977.

Lewis's later, more developed work took two directions. He became increasingly interested in the subject of experience and the nature of the self (the influence of C. A. Campbell is also seen here), and the metaphysical and religious issues are energetically set out in *The Self and Immortality* (1973) and *Persons and Life after Death* (1978). The reverse side of this was an equally vigorous polemic against the 'linguistic turn' and the development of analytic philosophy, particularly A. J. Ayer's assault on the cognitive meaningfulness of theological language, but also on the reductionist and behaviourist account of the self which Lewis found in Gilbert Ryle's *The Concept of Mind* (1949). The nature of the mind in this broader polemical setting was the subject of his Gifford lectures delivered at Edinburgh in 1966–8 and published as *The Elusive Mind* (1969) and *The Elusive Self* (1982). At this period he developed an increasing interest in comparative religion and was the founding editor of *Religious Studies* in 1964, remaining editor until 1979. He published a number of titles in Welsh. A Festschrift, *Religion, Reason and the Self*, edited by S. R. Sutherland and T. A. Roberts, was published in 1990. He received honorary degrees from the universities of St Andrews and Emery, Atlanta, and from Geneva Theological College. He was president of the Mind Association (1948–9) and of the Aristotelian Society (1962–3), and chairman of the council of the Royal Institute of Philosophy (1965–88).

Lewis's editorship of the Muirhead Library of Philosophy (1947–78) provided him with another means of combating what he regarded as the narrowness of analytic philosophy. He edited *Clarity is not Enough* in 1962. During his editorship the Muirhead Library published titles by a wide range of philosophers, including those of a kindred spirit of Lewis's. Dom Illtud Trethowan's *The Absolute and the Atonement* was published in the library in 1971.

Lewis's first wife died in 1962, and he was married again on 17 July 1965, this time to (Kate Alice) Megan Pritchard (*b.* 1918/19), superintendent of a hospital X-ray department and daughter of Thomas Owen Pritchard, a businessman. Lewis, a small, fair-haired person, could be charming, but he was also an intense and doughty defender of whatever he believed was a matter of academic principle. Although residing near London for many years he retained a commitment to the principality of Wales, especially to its dissenting tradition, and to Welsh politics. He continued to be involved in academic work in retirement, though this period was marred by severe injuries sustained when he was hit by a car. He recovered and continued active for a further seven years. He died at his home, 1 Normandy Park, Normandy, Guildford, on 6 April 1992. He was buried in the St Tudno cemetery on the Great Orme. A memorial service was held in the chapel of King's College, London, on 3 June 1992. PAUL HELM

Sources *The Times* (14 April 1992) • *The Independent* (10 April 1992) • private information (2004) [Megan Lewis] • personal knowledge (2004) • *WWW, 1991–5* • b. cert. • m. certs.
Archives NL Wales
Likenesses photograph, repro. in *The Times* • photograph, repro. in *The Independent*
Wealth at death £566,977: probate, 2 June 1992, *CGPLA Eng. & Wales*

Lewis, James (1750/51–1820), architect, was probably born in Brecon in south Wales. In 1770, at the age of nineteen, he went to Italy, and a volume of drawings of friezes, urns, and classical ornaments which he made in Rome is preserved in the Paul Mellon collection. He later told the diarist Joseph Farington that he had become well acquainted with Piranesi, and that while abroad he had kept a journal written in Italian but had subsequently destroyed it because he was embarrassed by its poor linguistic quality. After returning to Britain in December 1772, he exhibited at the Society of Artists from 1774 to 1778 and his first recorded employment—minor work in London—belongs to this period; then in 1779–80 he published a volume of *Original Designs in Architecture, Consisting of Plans … for Villas, Mansions, Town Houses*, which was evidently intended as an advertisement for his talents, and thereafter he developed a modestly successful practice mainly as a country house architect in the south-east of England. In 1797 he published a second volume of designs which, in contrast to the first, included a significant proportion of executed projects, the product of this practice.

In 1792, however, Lewis was elected surveyor to Christ's Hospital and in the following year he was appointed to the corresponding post at the Bridewell and Bethlem hospitals: from then on these institutional responsibilities appear to have formed the principal element in his career. For Christ's Hospital he designed the new grammar school (1793; dem.)—receiving a gratuity of 100 guineas 'for his great attention during the building' because he had charged at a rate of only two and a half per cent instead of the usual five per cent—and additions to the school in Hertford (1800), and also made designs for various ambitious unexecuted schemes for redeveloping the main buildings.

Regarding the Bethlem Hospital, in 1810 a competition was held for designs for a new hospital in St George's Fields, Southwark; in the event none of the entries which gained the premiums was actually adopted, and instead Lewis was instructed to incorporate their best features in a new design of his own. The result, erected in 1812–15, was Lewis's largest undertaking. His best work, however, lies in the products of his private practice, in the series of houses such as Bletchingdon Park, Oxfordshire (1782), Eydon Hall, Northamptonshire (1788–9), Lavington Park, Sussex (1790–94), and Hackthorn Hall, Lincolnshire (1793–5), which are elegant neo-classical versions of the Palladian villa form, with interior decoration in the manner of Robert Adam.

Lewis was one of the fifteen original members of the Architects' Club, founded in 1791. Persistent ill health induced him to give up the surveyorship at Christ's Hospital in January 1816 and that of the Bethlem Hospital the following year. To his two sons and two daughters he left a 'good fortune', and he died in Powis Place, London, on 16 July 1820. PETER LEACH

Sources Colvin, *Archs.* • J. Gwilt, ed., *An encyclopaedia of architecture*, 2nd edn (1851); rev. edn, rev. W. Papworth (1867); new edn (1881); new edn (1888) • *The Farington diary*, ed. J. Greig, 8 vols. (1922–8)

Likenesses W. Daniell, soft-ground etching (after G. Dance), BM, NPG

Wealth at death a good fortune: *DNB*

Lewis, James Henry (1786–1853), stenographer, was born in the parish of King's Stanley, near Stroud, Gloucestershire, probably on 20 August 1786, the son of James Lewis, a cloth manufacturer and owner of oil mills, of Ebley, near Stroud, and his wife, Sarah. Little is known of his early years, but it is believed that he learned Samuel Taylor's shorthand system and, finding it deficient, developed a system of his own.

In 1812, at the age of twenty-six, Lewis published *The ready writer, or, Ne plus ultra of short hand, being the most easy, exact, lineal, speedy, and legible method ever yet discovered, whereby more may be written in forty minutes than in one hour, by any other system hitherto published*, a work sold by him at the 'Flying hand and pen, No. 55, Great Wild Street, Lincoln's Inn Fields, where he continues to teach his new method'. This work was issued in a ninety-seventh edition in the 1860s.

For many years Lewis taught shorthand at 104 High Holborn, and later at 113 Strand, London, but, for health reasons, he toured the provinces for some years, teaching and lecturing. Patronized by George IV, royal dukes, nobility, and gentry, Lewis was an energetic self-publicist. His enthusiastic self-promotion, which belied both the true sophistication and utility of his shorthand system, is evident in the title *Lewis's cranio-logical lecture on short-hand* [with the word 'hand' indicated by the representation of a hand], *which has been repeated upwards of four hundred times, to crowded audiences, in various parts of the United Kingdom, and met with the most enthusiastic and universal applause.* Lewis, who claimed to teach the 'Lewisian system' of shorthand in six easy lessons, composed doggerel verses both to entertain audiences and to serve as a memory aid for students. He employed the roughly sketched figure of a pugilist poised for competition to illustrate the sloping, curvilinear symbols used in his system.

Lewis was twice married. He had a son and four daughters with his first wife. With his second wife, Cecilia, *née* Richards, whom he had married on 26 December 1836, he had one son, Alfred Lionel Lewis, a London reporter, who edited his father's system in *The Lewisian System of Shorthand Displayed at a Glance* (1880).

One of the last of the great writing masters, Lewis believed that penmanship was a fine art and that a writer's pen should be individually suited to his hand and other physical requirements. He offered specific directions for holding the pen and invented a mechanical device to promote proper penmanship. On 10 July 1826 Sir Walter Scott wrote in his diary:

> This morning I was visited by a Mr. Lewis, a smart cockney, whose object is to amend the handwriting. He uses as a mechanical aid a sort of puzzle of wire and ivory which is put upon the fingers to keep them in the desired position like the muzzle on a dog's nose to make him bear himself right in the field. It is ingenious and may be useful. If the man come here [Edinburgh] as he proposes in winter I will take lessons. (*The Journal of Sir Walter Scott*, ed. W. E. K. Anderson, 1972, 170)

In addition to teaching elegant penmanship, Lewis endeavoured to increase writing speed and convenience. His invention of 'Lewis's patent fountain pens, with everlasting nibs' is described in *The Best Method of Pen-Making, Illustrated by Practical Observations on the Art of Writing* (1820?).

In 1816 Lewis published *An Historical Account of the Rise and Progress of Stenography*. The expanded version of a shorter work published the previous year, it contained discussions of eighty-seven shorthand writers from John Willis (1602) to Lewis himself (1815) and included the alphabets of most of them. The work was based on Lewis's extensive collection of shorthand books and manuscripts, many of which were unique copies. In a footnote Lewis claimed 'My collection has cost me more than fifteen years labour, and an expence of more than £500', but, he continued, 'I shall not regret, however, the occupation of my leisure, my money, or my humble talents, if they contribute, in a single instance, to facilitate the study and improvement of the art' (p. 211). Of his collection of 240 unduplicated shorthand books, 79 were purchased for the Birmingham Free Library, and were destroyed by fire in 1880; the rest were purchased by Cornelius Walford, the Bodleian Library, and the British Museum. Lewis, the most prolific shorthand writer of the early nineteenth century, died on 13 November 1853 at 49 Milton Road, Milton, Gravesend, and was buried at Kensal Green cemetery, Middlesex.

PAGE LIFE

Sources A. Paterson, 'James Henry Lewis, shorthand author and historian', *Phonetic Journal*, 60 (1901), 197–8, 213 • A. Heal, *The English writing-masters and their copy-books, 1570–1800* (1931); repr. (Hildesheim, 1962) • K. Brown and D. C. Haskell, *The shorthand collection in the New York Public Library* (1935); repr. (1971) • *DNB* • *IGI* • Boase, *Mod. Eng. biog.* • d. cert. • PRO, PROB 11/2191, sig. 379
Likenesses engraving (after a portrait) • oils; formerly in the possession of his son, Mr A. L. Lewis, 1892

Lewis, Jessie Elizabeth Penn- [*née* Jessie Elizabeth Jones] (**1861–1927**), missioner and revivalist, was born on 28 February 1861 in Victoria Terrace, Neath, Glamorgan, the eldest of the eight surviving children of Elias Jones (*d.* 1877), a civil engineer, and his wife, Heziah Hopkins. A sickly child, she was kept from school until the age of twelve out of fear that education would excite her overactive brain. Her home life was highly religious. In 1873 she was elected a member of the local Good Templar lodge and quickly went on to establish and organize the junior division of this temperance organization.

On 15 September 1880, at Neath parish church, Jessie married William Penn-Lewis (1859–1925), the auditor's clerk for Sussex county council; he was the son of William Lewis, a painter. She moved with him to Brighton where, blighted by ill health (the marriage was childless), she embarked upon a period of intense self-scrutiny and interior prayer. In August 1883 William Penn-Lewis was appointed accountant to Richmond borough council and the couple moved to Surrey. Jessie Penn-Lewis soon became involved in the religious life of her new community. She joined the Holy Trinity Church in Richmond and in 1886 helped establish a local branch of the YWCA. Despite her intense involvement in local mission and rescue work, Penn-Lewis remained convinced of her spiritual unworthiness and need for self-sanctification. On 18 March 1892 her long-prayed-for spiritual breakthrough arrived. At breakfast that day she was confronted by a vision of a fistful of dirty rags, which she interpreted as a sign of the emptiness of her previous life. Later that evening, in a railway carriage just outside Wimbledon, she finally experienced a sense of complete consecration.

Following her spiritual awakening, Penn-Lewis moved with her husband, who had become city treasurer for Leicester, to Great Glen, Leicester. There she developed her personal theology which stressed a life of continual self-denial in imitation of the self-sacrifice of the crucified Christ. Attendance at the annual Keswick conventions from 1892 similarly served to deepen her conviction that personal holiness could be achieved only through an ongoing process of self-renunciation. Her theology was clearly articulated in her essay *The Pathway to Life in God* (1895), the first of over fifty self-published pamphlets that issued from her home in Leicester.

In June 1896 Penn-Lewis travelled to Göteborg, Sweden, to attend the first Scandinavian conference of the YWCA. At this meeting she won the friendship of a group of Russian and Finnish aristocrats including Prince Oscar Bernardotte, who invited her to carry out mission work among the Russian nobility. She visited St Petersburg annually from 1897 to 1903, holding praise meetings and organizing experimental prayer groups. This experience confirmed her sense of spiritual guidance and established her international reputation as a missioner. In August 1900 she lectured in Canada and the USA as the guest of the Moody Bible Institute, and in January 1903 she embarked on a revivalist mission to India.

While in India, Penn-Lewis wrote and published her most popular work, *The Word of the Cross* (1903). This work, according to her biographer Mary Garrard, sold over a million copies and was translated into over 100 languages. Its charismatic message of spirit obedience and self-renunciation was echoed internationally in the theology of the emergent Pentecostal groups and most notably in the Welsh religious revival of 1904–5. Although Penn-Lewis probably overestimated her own contribution to the Welsh awakening, the revival did cement her friendship with the young evangelist Evan Roberts (1878–1951), who retired to her Leicester home after his spiritual breakdown in 1905.

Together with Roberts, Penn-Lewis devoted her later years to the development of a 'saving theology' which would allow believers to combat demonic interference and satanic deception. In 1907 she set up a monthly paper, *The Overcomer*, which hosted a 'spiritual clinic' dealing with cases of suspected possession. In 1912 she published *War on the Saints* (co-written with Roberts), a sort of spiritual combat manual containing tactics for vanquishing both Satan and the individual self. These tactics were further refined in a series of monthly meetings at Eccleston Hall in London and annual congresses in Derbyshire at Matlock (1912–14) and Swanwick (1919). Despite her growing ill health Penn-Lewis persisted in her evangelical activities until her death from pneumonia on 15 August 1927 at 4 Eccleston Place, Westminster, London, where she had lived following her husband's death. She was buried on 18 August alongside her husband in the Quaker burial-ground, Reigate, Surrey. RHODRI HAYWARD

Sources M. N. Garrard, *Mrs Penn-Lewis: a memoir* (1930) • J. Penn-Lewis, *The awakening in Wales* (1907) • R. Tudor Jones, *Ffydd ac Agyfwng Cenedl*, 2 (1982) • b. cert. • m. cert. • d. cert. • D. W. Bebbington, *Evangelism in modern Britain* (1989)
Archives NL Wales, corresp., papers
Wealth at death £6610 7s.: probate, 19 Sept 1927, *CGPLA Eng. & Wales*

Lewis, John (*d.* **1615/16**), historian, was born in Pencraig, Radnorshire, the son of Hugh Lewis and his wife, Sibyl, daughter of Roger ap Watcyn. He was admitted to Lincoln's Inn on 28 February 1563 and called to the bar after 4 June 1570. Lewis was the author of *The history of Great Britain, from the first inhabitants thereof, till the death of Cadwalader, last king of the Britains*, which he wrote at the encouragement of James I. He sent the king proposals for a history of Britain about 1605, in response to the great interest in British history occasioned by the succession of a Scottish monarch. The king, who was then promoting the fuller union of England and Scotland, encouraged Lewis, and by 1612 the author had submitted, probably through Henry, prince of Wales, some six books. The complete history was first published in 1729, over a century after its author's death, by the antiquary Hugh Thomas, perhaps using the text still extant in Harleian MS 4872 in the British Library. Like earlier Welsh historians, for instance Humphrey Llwyd (whose *Breviary of Britayne* is appended to the 1729 edition of Lewis's book), Lewis was reluctant to part with the much-criticized legends of ancient British kings, from Brutus the Trojan to King Arthur, as recorded by Geoffrey of Monmouth. Lewis's modern sources included a recent Roman Catholic historian, Richard White of Basingstoke, and he had also read Samuel Daniel's more critical history first published in 1612. He claims in the *History* (1.39) a personal acquaintance with the great antiquary William Camden, and a collection of manuscripts, largely in his hand, indicates that he was acquainted with other notable Elizabethan intellectual figures such as John Dee. The precise date of Lewis's death is unknown, but was some time between 14 February 1615, when he dated his will, and 12 February 1616, when it was proved. D. R. Woolf

Sources J. Lewis, *The history of Great Britain, from the first inhabitants thereof, till the death of Cadwalader, last king of the Britains*, ed. H. Thomas (1729) · D. R. Woolf, *The idea of history in early Stuart England* (1990) · Venn, *Alum. Cant.* · MS of Lewis's history, BL, MS Harl. 4872 · W. H. Cooke, ed., *Students admitted to the Inner Temple, 1547–1660* [1878] · *DWB*
Archives BL, MS Harl. 4872
Likenesses portrait

Lewis, John (1675–1747), Church of England clergyman and antiquary, was born in the parish of St Nicholas, Bristol, on 29 August 1675, and baptized in St Nicholas's Church on 16 September. He was the eldest child of John Lewis (*d.* 1679), wine cooper, of Bristol, and Mary, eldest daughter of John Eyre, merchant, of Poole, who had married on 6 November 1674. Following his father's death, Lewis was left to the care of his grandparents. After his paternal grandfather, Francis Lewis, vicar of Worth Matravers, Dorset, also died in 1679, he moved with his mother to his grandfather Eyre's house at Poole. There he began his education. On John Eyre's death in 1682 he received a legacy to enable him to learn a trade. However, by 1685, he had been taken under the wing of Samuel Conant, rector of Lytchett Matravers, with whom he resumed his education. From 1687 he attended Wimborne grammar school under John Moyle, but returned to Poole at Moyle's death. There, he entered the new grammar school established by John Russell. He acted as assistant to Russell who, after his removal to Wapping about 1690, obtained for Lewis admission to the free school of Ratcliff Cross, belonging to the Coopers' Company. On leaving school he was for two years tutor to the sons of Daniel Wigfall, a Turkey and lead merchant. On 30 March 1694 Lewis matriculated from Exeter College, Oxford, under the tuition of George Verman, a friend of Conant. Lewis's family still wished him to pursue a trade and recalled him to Dorset, where he became assistant in the free school of Poole in 1696, while keeping the university term. After graduating BA on 14 October 1697 he returned to his old friend Russell at Wapping, and shortly afterwards was ordained deacon. He applied to be sent to Maryland as a chaplain, but was refused since he was not a priest.

In April 1698 Lewis became curate of Acrise, Kent. He was collated to the rectory of the parish on 4 September 1699, and briefly set up a school there. Although he served for four months as domestic chaplain to the Foley family, his principal patrons at this time were Thomas and Philip Papillon. In 1702 Archbishop Tenison, having ordered the sequestration of the rectory of Hawkinge, near Dover, licensed Lewis to serve the cure, and in 1705 presented him to the vicarage of St John the Baptist, Margate for which he had earlier been recommended by a previous incumbent, John Johnson. The archbishop collated him to the rectory of Saltwood, with the chapel of Hythe, and the desolate rectory of Eastbridge in 1706. Lewis was reluctant to serve in these places, which he felt were too far from his home and where he worried that he would be expected to 'intermeddle with the civil or secular affairs of their parishioners' at the coming election (Bodl. Oxf., MS Eng. misc. c. 273, p. 21). Tenison subsequently removed him to the vicarage of Minster, to which he was instituted on 10 March 1709. Lewis was appointed to preach at the archiepiscopal visitation on 28 May 1712, when his whiggish and low-church views excited the open hostility of his hearers. He commenced MA in 1712 as a member of Corpus Christi College, Cambridge. In 1714 he attacked the high-church position on the eucharist of his former friend John Johnson, in his *Bread and Wine in the Holy Eucharist*. Although Tenison was disturbed by Lewis's quarrels with his clerical neighbours, others, such as Daniel Waterland and Samuel Bradford, approved his position. Lewis preached at Archbishop Wake's visitation on 19 June 1716 and again in Canterbury Cathedral on 30 January 1718. Wake rewarded him with the mastership of Eastbridge Hospital, Canterbury.

From the late 1710s Lewis was engaged in extensive antiquarian research on the history of the English Bible and liturgy. Encouraged by White Kennett and Daniel Waterland, Lewis wrote a succession of biographies of Wyclif (1720), Pecock (1744), and Fisher (eventually published in 1855), intended to show the state of the English church before the Reformation and to describe the antiquity of the tradition of vernacular worship in England. To these he added a history of the English liturgy, written in 1723 but never published, and an edition of Roper's *Life and Death of Sir Thomas More* (1731). These compilations were accompanied by editions of appropriate documentary material. The high point of Lewis's career as an editor, however, was the publication by subscription of Wyclif's translation of the New Testament (1731). Lewis's edition was based principally on two manuscripts of the later Wycliffite version, provided by Waterland and by the Dering family. For the introduction to his edition Lewis composed a substantial history of the translation of the Bible into English, which he revised and brought up to date in a separately published second edition, *A complete history of the several translations of the holy Bible and New Testament into English* (1739). He received considerable help with this work from Joseph Ames, Thomas Baker, and Peter Thompson, and had access to the collections of John Bagford and Humfrey Wanley, as well as to many manuscripts and printed books from Lambeth Palace. He also made good use of his own substantial library.

Lewis's interests in the history of printing and in the antiquities of Kent were combined in the collections that he made for *The Life of Wyllyam Caxton* (1737). In 1723 he published *The History and Antiquities, Ecclesiastical and Civil, of the Isle of Tenet*, which he continued to revise throughout the remainder of his life; he printed a second edition in 1736. *The History and Antiquities of the Abbey and Church of Favresham* appeared in 1727 and was followed by shorter studies of the ancient ports of Kent. He assisted Richard Rawlinson with antiquarian research on Kent and its inhabitants. He was also an enthusiastic correspondent of Archbishop Wake concerning the health of the diocese of Canterbury.

Lewis laid out considerable sums in the improvement of his parishes and in support of local charity. He was a regular correspondent of the Society for Promoting Christian Knowledge and wrote a succession of works of practical and controversial divinity, which drew on his Kent experiences. The most successful of these was *The Church Catechism Explain'd* (1700), frequently reprinted and also translated into Welsh and Irish. Lewis's local encounters with dissenters led to the writing of *A Brief History of the Rise and Progress of Anabaptism* (1738) as well as to letters condemning Methodism. For many years he conducted a dispute with Kentish nonjurors, in particular John Johnson and Thomas Brett, and he left a critical life of George Hickes in manuscript, as well as extensive corrections to Jeremy Collier's *Ecclesiastical History*, parts of which were published in 1724. His other controversial writings included a defence of the clergy against Matthew Tindal's *Rights of the Christian Church*, which he published in 1711, replies to the writings of Thomas Bisse, in which he argued in favour of the current liturgy of the church, and a manuscript life of Michael Servetus. He assisted John Walker with the research for *The Sufferings of the Clergy*, but claimed to be 'much scandalized' by the preface to the published work (Bodl. Oxf., MS J. Walker, c. 5, fol. 270*r*). Despite his loyalty to ecclesiastical traditions and institutions, Lewis was never tempted to deny the virtue of 'the principles and practices of certain *Moderate* Divines of the Church of England formerly call'd by their Enemies *Latitudinarians* and now *Low-Church men*' (JRL, MS 49, fol. 37*r*).

Lewis married Mary (1674/5–1719), the youngest daughter of Robert Knowler of Herne, Kent. They had no children and she died on 15 December 1719. Lewis rewrote many of his published works throughout his career and left extensive manuscript collections at his death. Among these was an autobiography, composed in 1738. He died in Minster on 16 January 1747 and was buried four days later, beside his wife in the chancel of the church at Minster. His library was sold at auction in three parts in 1748 and 1749. Many of the most important volumes from it were purchased by his friends Ames and Thompson.

SCOTT MANDELBROTE

Sources Bodl. Oxf., MS Eng. misc. c. 273 • R. Masters, *The history of the College of Corpus Christi and the B. Virgin Mary … in the University of Cambridge* (1753), pt. 2, pp. 337–41 • J. Lewis, *The history and antiquities, as well ecclesiastical as civil, of the Isle of Tenet, in Kent*, 2nd edn (1736) [annotated copy, Bodl. Oxf., Gough Kent 4] • Bodl. Oxf., MS J. Walker, c. 5 • JRL, MS 49 • J. Gregory, *Restoration, Reformation and reform, 1660–1828* (2000) • J. Shirley, 'John Lewis of Margate', *Archaeologia Cantiana*, 64 (1951), 39–56 • *DNB*

Archives BL, autobiography, life of Bishop Fisher and collections for a *History of Printing*, Add. MSS 20035, 28650–28651 • Bodl. Oxf., autobiography • Bodl. Oxf., collections • Bodl. Oxf., papers • CKS, collection • CUL, collection • JRL, papers, MSS 47, 49 • LPL, antiquarian collections • Wadham College, Oxford, collections | BL, Stowe MSS • Bodl. Oxf., annotated copy of Coker's *Survey of Dorset* • Bodl. Oxf., Gough MSS • Bodl. Oxf., MSS Rawl.

Likenesses G. White, mezzotint, *c*.1747, BM, NPG; repro. in J. Lewis, *History of Thanet* (1736)

Wealth at death probably meagre; over £100: will, PRO, PROB 11/752, sig. 44

Lewis, John (1836–1928), department store owner, was born at Town Street, Shepton Mallet, Somerset, on 24 February 1836, the fifth child (of nine) and first son of John Lewis (1798–1843), a cabinet-maker and baker of Town Street, and his wife, Elizabeth Speed. Orphaned when his father died, he was brought up by an unmarried aunt, Ann Speed, and educated at the local grammar school. Lewis was apprenticed at fourteen to a draper in Wells, and then worked for various firms before joining Peter Robinson of Oxford Street in 1856 as a buyer for silks and dress materials.

In 1864 Lewis began his own drapery business at a small leasehold shop at 132 (later 286) Oxford Street. Thus began twenty years of lonely bachelor life, which Lewis did not recollect with any fondness. The work was hard and dreary, but the location of the shop and Lewis's simple and honest trading policy—based on a wide assortment of good-value merchandise—proved successful. From silks, woollens, and cotton fabrics, he diversified into dress fabrics and clothing, then later furnishing fabrics and household supplies, such as china and ironmongery (though not food). Sales increased from £25,000 in 1870 to about £70,000 a decade later. By 1895 this expansion had allowed him to rebuild the original shop as a three-storey department store, with retail showrooms, warehouse space, and a customers' restaurant. He employed about 150 people, with 100 female staff housed in a hostel nearby, in Weymouth Street.

The business remained private, with Lewis continuing to build it up by working long hours. On 1 November 1884 he married Eliza Baker (*b*. *c*.1854), a schoolmistress from a west-country family who ran a drapery business. His wife was one of the first students at Girton College, Cambridge. Lewis took no one into partnership until his two sons, John Spedan *Lewis (1885–1963) and Oswald Lewis (1887–1966), came of age. His only attempt at expansion outside Oxford Street was the acquisition of Peter Jones Ltd, Chelsea, the control of which he had bought in 1906, when he walked from his store to Sloane Square with £20,000 in banknotes in his pocket. Spare capital from his business was invested quite randomly in various properties, some hundred of which were bought in his lifetime. Always an outspoken and colourful character, Lewis engaged in a running battle with his landlords (the Portland estate) to redress what he considered was an unfair balance of power between landlord and tenant; and he spent some weeks in Brixton prison in 1903 for contempt of court.

On his own terms, Lewis's life was a great success. By 1924 sales had reached £921,000. His customers had been served well by his department store and so had Lewis. For more than twenty years he lived in a large house on Hampstead Heath with his wife and family, and he drove a good pair of horses and later ran a Rolls Royce. He was appointed to St Marylebone vestry (later the borough council) between 1888 and 1919, and was the elected Liberal representative for the West Marylebone division of London county council between 1901 and 1904. On the other hand, he was a hard and arbitrary employer, with the persona of a Victorian curmudgeon. One staff member recalled that in the late 1920s, 'he still came down from Hampstead in the old Rolls Royce from time to time and would sweep round the place sacking anyone he didn't like the look of' (Macpherson, 23).

Lewis's son Spedan later wrote a withering portrait of his father's conservative business methods.

> His aims in life, his ideas and his methods were really quite ordinary but the ideas were held with a vigour and the methods were applied with an energy that was far indeed from being ordinary. With very little education and no friends he found himself in an occupation to which he was in many ways ill-suited. (Lewis, 5)

The result was that by the twentieth century John Lewis had 'got himself into the position of being the captain of a big ship much under-engined and with those engines much under-fuelled. As a whole the staff were not nearly good enough' (Lewis, 14). These comments were no doubt partial (Spedan and his father disagreed on business matters); however, evidence for their veracity can be found in John Lewis's business performance, which was far less dynamic than that of his rivals, such as William Whiteley, Frederick Gorringe, and Owen Owen. A staff strike in 1920, persistent mismanagement and losses at Peter Jones, and his reluctance to hand over control to his sons, which effectively prevented an infusion of fresh ideas, were other features of the founder's rule.

John Lewis died on 8 June 1928 at his home, Spedan Tower, Branch Hill, Hampstead, London. His death allowed his son Spedan to implement his more imaginative 'partnership' ideal, and so make the John Lewis department store nationally famous. However, the name was retained as a tribute to John Lewis's 'first-rate reputation for general trustworthiness' (Lewis, 15).

GEOFFREY TWEEDALE

Sources H. Macpherson, ed., *John Spedan Lewis, 1885–1963* (1985) · J. S. Lewis, *Partnership for all* (1948); repr. with appx (1952) · G. Tweedale, 'Lewis, John', *DBB* · B. Lancaster, *The department store: a social history* (1995) · *CGPLA Eng. & Wales* (1928) · d. cert.
Archives John Lewis plc, Cavendish Road, Stevenage
Likenesses photographs, John Lewis plc · photographs, repro. in Macpherson, ed., *John Spedan Lewis*
Wealth at death £84,661 5*s.* 6*d.*: probate, 19 Sept 1928, *CGPLA Eng. & Wales*

Lewis, John Delaware (1828–1884), writer, was born in St Petersburg, the only surviving son of John Delaware Lewis, a Russia merchant of Regent's Park, London, and his wife, Emma, daughter of James Hamilton Clewlow, naval officer. He was educated at Eton College and at Trinity College, Cambridge, where he matriculated in 1846 and graduated BA in 1850, proceeding MA in 1853. While at Cambridge in 1849, under the pseudonym 'John Smith of Smith Hall, gent.', he published a volume entitled *Sketches of Cantabs* which had considerable success and reached a third edition in 1858. Lewis was admitted to Lincoln's Inn in February 1850 and called to the bar there in Michaelmas 1858. He joined the south-eastern circuit. On 6 January 1868 he married Teresa, eldest daughter of Sir Jervoise Clarke-Jervoise; they had no children.

From 1868 to 1874 Lewis represented Devonport, Devon, as a Liberal in the House of Commons, unsuccessfully contesting the same constituency in February 1874 and in 1880, and Oxford in March 1874. He was a JP for Devon and Hampshire, and a lieutenant in the Pembrokeshire artillery militia. He spent much time at Arcachon, France. He died at his home, Westbury House, Petersfield, Hampshire, on 31 July 1884.

Lewis was a versatile scholar, who wrote as well in French as in English. Besides contributions to periodicals, he published *Science and Revelation* (1871), works on spiritualism, on legal subjects with reference to France and England, and on classical subjects. He translated Juvenal and Pliny (published 1873 and 1879), and at the time of his death was engaged on an edition of Seneca's works and an English–French dictionary.

W. A. J. ARCHBOLD, *rev.* CATHERINE PEASE-WATKIN

Sources private information (1892) · *The Times* (2 Aug 1884) · *The Academy* (9 Aug 1884), 94 · Venn, *Alum. Cant.* · *CGPLA Eng. & Wales* (1884)
Wealth at death £218,923 8*s.* 10*d.* in UK: probate, 24 Nov 1884, *CGPLA Eng. & Wales*

Lewis, John Frederick (1804–1876), painter of oriental subjects in watercolour and oil, was the eldest son of the engraver Frederick Christian *Lewis (1779–1856) and his wife, Elizabeth Exton. He was born at 33 Queen Anne Street East, London, on 14 July 1804; 1805 is incorrectly given as his birth year in most previous literature. He had two brothers and three sisters. His father's family was of German descent. Johann Ludwig, John Frederick's grandfather, went from Hanover to England in the second half of the eighteenth century.

Early career Lewis was trained as an artist by his father. As a youth he developed friendly ties to the Landseers and his early works, like those of Edwin Landseer, focused almost exclusively on animal life. He studied the menageries on exhibition in Exeter Change and Windsor Great Park, and his first exhibited work was *A Donkey's Head* at the British Institution in 1820. In the early 1820s Lewis worked as an assistant to Thomas Lawrence and probably depicted animals in the portraitist's works; he exhibited animal pictures at the British Institution and the Royal Academy throughout the decade. In addition to portraits of horses

John Frederick Lewis (1804–1876), by unknown photographer

and dogs and dramatic birds and lions, Lewis painted *Fatal Curiosity, or, The Broken Glass* (exh. RA, 1823), which illustrated a passage from Henry Fielding about a monkey and a mirror, and *Buck-Shooting in Windsor Great Park, with Portraits of his Majesty's Deer-Keepers* (exh. RA, 1826; Tate collection). He also published a set of six engravings of wild animals in 1825, and twelve etchings of animals and hunting scenes in 1826, dedicated to Mary, Countess Harcourt.

From 1827 Lewis made watercolour his primary medium, and exhibited for the first time that year at the Old Watercolour Society (OWCS; Society of Painters in Water Colours), showing his familiar subjects, both savage and domestic: *The Vanquished Lion*; *Dying Lioness*; *Mare and Foal*; *Gamekeepers Reposing—Scene in Windsor Forest*. He was elected an associate of the OWCS in 1827 and a full member in 1829. Lewis visited Flanders, Germany, Switzerland, the Tyrol, and Italy in 1827, stopping in Bruges, Antwerp, Venice, and Florence. Thereafter, genre scenes began gradually to replace animal subjects as his chief interest, and travel to picturesque sites became the basis of his career. Among the works he exhibited in 1828, for instance, were pictures of a chamois in the Tyrol (RA; formerly Sir John and Lady Witt collection), a praying Franciscan in the Black Forest (British Institution), Tyrolese hunters (OWCS), a Turkish home in Venice (OWCS); a Venetian gondolier (OWCS), and an Italian mountain vineyard (OWCS). As a watercolourist, Lewis added a robust note to his otherwise delicate and undramatic works through the liberal application of opaque body colour. This continued to be an essential feature of his art until he largely gave up watercolour for oil painting in 1858. His watercolour figures are more slight than his muscular animals; charming peasant types in pretty garb, they show Lewis's large debt to the art of David Wilkie.

Tours of Spain, Italy, and Turkey Lewis toured Devon in 1829 and Scotland in 1830 and 1831. *An Old Mill* (exh. OWCS, 1830; Blackburn Corporation Art Gallery) is one of his Devon products and *Highland Hospitality* (exh. OWCS, 1832; Yale Center for British Art, New Haven), *Interior of Crofter's Cottage in Arran* (1832; British Museum), and *Newhaven Fishwomen* (exh. OWCS, 1832; Manchester City Galleries) are among Lewis's quaint Scottish subjects. In Wilkie's footsteps, Lewis toured Spain from the summer of 1832 until late 1833, briefly travelling to Gibraltar and Tangier in the latter year; he stopped in Paris on his return trip to London and there visited the artist William Callow. During his Spanish tour Lewis stayed with the traveller Richard Ford and his wife in Seville, and corresponded with the artist David Roberts, who was also in Spain. Numerous watercolours based on Lewis's Spanish trip were exhibited at the Old Watercolour Society and the Royal Academy from 1833 to 1838, but the chief results of the tour were two albums of lithographs: *Lewis's Sketches and Drawings of the Alhambra* (1835), and *Lewis's Sketches of Spain and Spanish Character* (1836). The Spanish watercolours display many new characteristics and subjects: complex groups of active figures, bright colours, swaggering outlaws and bull fighters, Gothic and Islamic architectural monuments, scenes from the lives of the old masters, and dramatic representations of events from the Carlist Wars, which were only brewing while Lewis was in Spain. *A Spanish Fiesta* (exh. OWCS, 1836; Whitworth Art Gallery, University of Manchester), *A Spy of the Christino Army Brought before the Carlist General-in-Chief Zumalacarregui* (exh. OWCS, 1837), and *Murillo Painting the Virgin in the Franciscan Convent in Seville* (exh. OWCS, 1838; Minneapolis Institute of Art) are examples of Lewis's newly ambitious and exotic art; the latter two works are among Lewis's rare attempts at history painting. In Spain Lewis also made watercolour copies of oils by Murillo, Velázquez, and Zurburan. These copies and others of works by Titian, Rubens, Rembrandt, Veronese, Masaccio, Giorgione, Van Dyck, Watteau, and Delacroix, some of which were executed later in France and Italy, were acquired by the Royal Scottish Academy in 1853, and attest to his new seriousness.

In 1837 Lewis left Britain, and did not return until 1851. He spent the winter of 1837 in Paris, moved on to Italy in early 1838, visiting Venice and Pisa, and was in Florence in the spring, where he portrayed Lady Holland (ex Sothebys, 5 April 1973), the interior of the Tribuna of the Uffizi gallery (National Gallery of Scotland, Edinburgh) and the Palazzo Vecchio (Ashmolean Museum, Oxford). He spent the winter of 1838–9 in the vicinity of Naples, and travelled to Amalfi, Sorrento, and Capri. He became ill, produced little, and failed to exhibit anything in London in 1839 and 1840. He stayed in Rome in 1839–40 and there produced two large watercolours entitled *Easter day at Rome—pilgrims and peasants of the Neapolitan states awaiting the benediction of the Pope at St. Peter's*. One version is in the Sunderland Art Gallery, dated 1840, the other is in the Northampton

Art Gallery; one of these was exhibited at the Old Watercolour Society in 1841. Lewis left Rome early in 1840, and travelled to Constantinople via Albania, Corfu, Athens, and Smyrna. He visited Brussa and stayed in and around Constantinople for a year, where he met David Wilkie, who was *en route* for the Holy Land. In Turkey Lewis sketched harem-like subjects, and women and men in a variety of ethnic costumes of the Ottoman empire. He also sketched the mosques of Santa Sophia and Bajazet in Constantinople, and the Great Mosque of Brussa.

In Egypt Late in 1841 Lewis followed Wilkie's lead and sailed for Egypt, where he lived until 1851. He resided in Cairo, visited Sinai in 1842, Thebes, Edfu, and Aswan in 1850, and exhibited nothing in England until 1850, when *The Hhareem* was shown at the Old Watercolour Society. *The Hhareem* resurrected Lewis's reputation and established his role as England's chief orientalist artist. In Egypt he became well known. He executed a watercolour portrait of the Egyptian ruler Mehmet Ali (1844; V&A), and had contact with various Englishmen travelling in the East, notably Viscount Castlereagh, Lord Elphinstone, Sir Thomas Phillips, Richard Dadd, Joseph Bonomi, Sir John Gardiner Wilkinson, and William Makepeace Thackeray. After visiting Lewis in 1844, Thackeray published a humorous account of the artist living in oriental luxury 'like a languid lotus-eater' (W. M. Thackeray, *Notes of a Journey from Cornhill to Gran Cairo*, 1846, 282–91). The numerous sketches of colourful bazaars, mosques, streets, monuments, interiors, and people which Lewis made during his sojourn in the East provided his basic imagery for the remainder of his career.

On 8 May 1847, in Alexandria, Lewis married Marian Harper (*c.*1826–1906) of Hampton, Middlesex. A British chaplain officiated, and several prominent English business people, including A. C. Harris and Thomas and Hester Bell, were witnesses. The couple returned to England in the spring of 1851, welcomed by Lewis's father and three sisters, and settled first at 6 Upper Hornton Villas, Campden Hill, London. In 1854, they bought The Holme at Walton-on-Thames, Surrey, where they remained for the rest of Lewis's life. They had no children.

English career as orientalist painter Lewis exhibited regularly, although not every year, after his return from Egypt. He showed some of his continental watercolours and *The Hhareem* at the Royal Scottish Academy in 1853 (he was made an honorary member of the academy in 1855) and contributed five works to the Universal Exhibition in Paris in 1855. But the Old Watercolour Society and the Royal Academy were the centres of his professional life. He was elected president of the Old Watercolour Society in 1855, by ten votes to six, over the favoured candidate, Frederick Tayler. Apparently in need of money following the purchase of his house, Lewis sold about 140 of his sketches at auction on 5 July 1855, at Christies; at this time and later he also sold pictures through the London dealer William Vokins. Lewis's major work of 1856, exhibited at the OWCS, was *A Frank Encampment in the Desert of Mount Sinai* (Yale Center for British Art, New Haven), which depicts Viscount Castlereagh in Eastern garb with his entourage and Bedouin. John Ruskin in his *Academy Notes* of that year praised this large watercolour, likening it to masterworks of Titian and Veronese, and interpreting it as a meditation on East and West and antiquity and modernity. In a private letter to Lewis, Ruskin asked him to turn to oil instead of watercolour, and Lewis eventually did so, telling several artists that the superior remuneration of oil painting was the chief reason for his change of medium. Lewis resigned as president of the OWCS on 8 February 1858, and most of his exhibited works from that time onward were in oil. He was elected an associate of the Royal Academy in 1859, and a full Academician in 1864.

Lewis's oils display the same Eastern subject matter and smooth surface as his watercolours. *The Pipe Bearer* (1856; Birmingham City Art Gallery), *The Bouquet* (1857; Dunedin Public Art Gallery, New Zealand), *Edfou: Upper Egypt* (1860; Tate collection), *An Oriental Interior* (1863; Victoria and Albert Museum), *The Courtyard of the Coptic Patriarch's House in Cairo* (1864; Tate collection), and *In the Bey's Garden, Asia Minor* (1865; Harris Museum, Preston) are major examples of his works in public collections and represent the successful translation of his punctilious watercolour style into oil paint. In many cases there are watercolour replicas of oils, and vice versa, and Lewis habitually reused figures, interiors, costumes, camels, and groups, combining sections from various pictures in ever new variations of a few Near Eastern themes. Quiet, indolence, and lavish decoration mark his subjects, whether harems, markets, Bedouin camps, Islamic schools, or gardens. The near-microscopic minutiae of his works and the bright colours and brilliant light make his paintings seem similar to those of the Pre-Raphaelites at mid-century. But Lewis's pictures do not have the same theatrical intensity, and he portrayed standard, smiling types rather than irregular individuals. Also, there is no medievalism or primitive awkwardness in Lewis's art: his pictures of coffee drinkers, smokers, dozing women, and beautiful figures selecting carpets or flowers look forward, instead, to the languid, opulent images of Aestheticism in the 1870s and 1880s. Lewis had lived in the East, but his art is closer to fantasy than to reality. It is unlikely that he visited harems, especially ones where European women abounded, and the ceramic and metal objects in his interiors are often Chinese or Japanese, as well as Turkish and Persian. He played on familiar Western notions of oriental luxury and ethnic mingling in the East, rather than representing ordinary life in Egypt.

At the Royal Academy Lewis proved to be an ineffective teacher: an irritable perfectionist, he was unable to understand his pupils, according to W. R. Spanton, a student in the 1860s. Lewis had no true protégés, although he inevitably exercised a strong influence on any English artist who attempted to depict harems, Bedouin, or bazaars, such as Frederick Goodall. He was also not highly sociable: although he had been elected a member of the Athenaeum in 1856 (sponsored by Sir Charles Barry), corresponded regularly with Ruskin and others in the London art world, and conversed occasionally with J. E. Millais,

David Roberts, and Edward Lear, he generally lived in seclusion at Walton-on-Thames, where his wife would set out his brushes each morning.

Later works and death In the 1870s some changes in Lewis's art were discernible. The scale of his oils tended to increase: *Lilium auratum* (exh. RA, 1872; Birmingham City Art Gallery), for instance, is 54 inches by 34½, with very large figures of Eastern girls gathering flowers. There was also increased grandeur in the space and figural groupings in the work of Lewis's last decade. *The Reception* (exh. RA, 1874; Yale Center for British Art, New Haven) shows the same harem chamber that had appeared in dozens of earlier pictures, but the height of the room seems doubled, and Lewis's familiar figures stand and recline with more statuesque gravity than in previous works. *The Banks of the Nile* (exh. RA, 1876; Yale Center for British Art, New Haven) shows a group of camels with ornate saddlebags, similar to the animals in many of Lewis's earlier desert scenes, but the viewer now sees the camels from below, set against an immense sky, and the scene becomes monumental. Lewis's orientalism is less obviously erotic and violent than that of his continental contemporaries. Unlike Jean-Leon Gérôme and Eugène Delacroix, Lewis did not represent sensual nudes or barbarous warriors in his Eastern works. Indeed, his odalisques are always lavishly dressed, and Lewis's Bedouin were often interpreted by English critics not as tough savages, but as ancient-like figures who carried on the ways of life presented in the Bible. However, unlike William Holman Hunt, the other major English orientalist, Lewis did not directly represent religious subject matter.

Lewis's health began to decline severely in 1874, and he employed an assistant, W. Britten, to finish some of his works. He was very feeble in 1875, and became confined to a wheel chair in March 1876. He died at his home at Walton-on-Thames on 15 August of that year. He was buried at Frimley parish church, Surrey, on 20 August. His sister Anne's husband, Charles Stonhouse, was the rector at Frimley parish church and officiated at the funeral. His brother Frederick Christian *Lewis (1813–1875) was an artist active in India, and known as Indian Lewis. His brother Charles George *Lewis (1808–1880), known as Swiss Lewis, was an engraver, and Lewis's uncle George Robert *Lewis (1782–1871) was a painter. Sales of Lewis's works languished in the twentieth century until the general revival of interest in Victorian art in the 1960s and 1970s. The Lewis exhibition at the Laing Art Gallery, Newcastle upon Tyne, in 1971 particularly raised Lewis's reputation, and very high prices for his pictures were subsequently realized. KENNETH BENDINER

Sources M. Lewis, *John Frederick Lewis, RA, 1805–1876* (1978), 9–101 • R. Green, *John Frederick Lewis* (1971) [exhibition catalogue, Laing Art Gallery, Newcastle upon Tyne] • R. Davies, 'John Frederick Lewis, RA, 1805–76', *Old Water-Colour Society's Club*, 3 (1925–6), 31–50 • B. Ford, 'J. F. Lewis and Richard Ford in Seville, 1832–33', *Burlington Magazine*, 80 (1942), 124–9 • Graves, *RA exhibitors* • H. Stokes, 'John Frederick Lewis', *Walker's Quarterly* [whole issue], 28 (1929) • J. L. Roget, *A history of the 'Old Water-Colour' Society*, 2 vols. (1891) • R. Treble, ed., *Great Victorian pictures: their paths to fame* (1978) [exhibition catalogue, Leeds, Leicester, Bristol, and London, 28 Jan – Sept 1978] • K. Bendiner, 'Albert Moore and John Frederick Lewis', *Arts Magazine*, 54 (1980), 76–9 • N. Tromans, 'J. F. Lewis's Carlist subjects', *Burlington Magazine*, 139 (1997), 760–65 • W. S. Spanton, *An art student and his teachers in the sixties with other rigmaroles* (1927) • 'British artists, their style and character: no. XXXII, John Frederick Lewis', *Art Journal*, 20 (1858), 42 • B. Llewellyn, 'The Islamic inspiration: John Frederick Lewis, painter of Islamic Egypt', *Influences in Victorian art and architecture*, ed. S. Macready and F. H. Thompson (1985), 121–38

Archives Bodl. Oxf., corresp. • NRA, priv. coll., corresp. | Worcs. RO, Churchill papers, (Northwick papers), corresp. acc. no. 4221, boxes 8, 39

Likenesses S. J. Rochard, ivory miniature, *c*.1826, priv. coll.; repro. in Lewis, *John Frederick Lewis*, fig. 1 • W. Boxall, oils, 1832, NPG • J. W. Gordon, oils, *c*.1855, Scot. NPG; repro. in Lewis, *John Frederick Lewis*, fig. 2 • Elliott & Fry, photographs, NPG • C. G. Lewis, stipple and line engraving (after photograph by J. & C. Watkins), NPG • J. F. Lewis, self-portrait, pencil drawing, RA • Sem [G. Goursat], watercolour, caricature, AM Oxf. • photograph, NPG [*see illus.*] • portrait, St Mary's parish church, Walton-on-Thames, Surrey • wood-engraving, NPG; repro. in *ILN* (25 March 1865)

Wealth at death under £20,000: probate, 16 Oct 1876, *CGPLA Eng. & Wales*

Lewis, John Spedan (1885–1963), department store owner and industrial reformer, was born in Marylebone, London, on 22 September 1885, the elder son of John *Lewis (1836–1928), a Somerset draper who from 1864 built up a successful retail business in Oxford Street, and his wife, Eliza, daughter of Thomas Baker, draper, of Bridgwater. His mother was one of the earliest students at the college opened in Hitchin by Emily Davies, which later became Girton College, and before her marriage was a teacher at Bedford high school.

Educated as a day boy first at a preparatory school and then at Westminster, where he was a queen's scholar, Lewis regarded his upbringing as narrow. His father seldom entertained, and Lewis and his brother, Oswald (1887–1966), rarely stayed away from home. On his nineteenth birthday Lewis joined his father in the Oxford Street shop, in preference to going up to Oxford University. On their twenty-first birthdays, he and Oswald were taken into partnership and each given £50,000 capital. But Lewis's introduction into the business brought disillusion. He later wrote that his father's business was 'in fact no more than a second-rate success achieved in a first-rate opportunity' (Lewis, 3). He was also appalled by the glaring inequalities produced by his father's ruthless business methods. He sought an alternative.

Declining an invitation to stand for parliament as a Liberal in 1910, Lewis devoted the rest of his life to the department store business, but decided to use it as a vehicle for a far-sighted practical experiment in the reform of industrial organization. He believed that the rewards of capital should be limited and that the true profits of industry should go to the workers. Dividends on capital should be fixed and limited and working owners or senior employees should be content with professional earnings. But he was worried at the effect of distributing the profits to the workers on the capital needs of an expanding business. Apparently unaware of earlier experiments in profit-sharing and co-ownership, Lewis first conceived a solution to his problem in the autumn of 1910 when he was

John Spedan Lewis (1885–1963), by Elliott & Fry

recovering from a serious riding accident which left his health permanently impaired. His concept was that residual profits should be distributed annually to the employees in proportion to their pay in the form of non-voting shares carrying a fixed dividend which they would be free to sell without affecting the control of the business.

Lewis began putting these ideas into effect in 1914, when he took charge of the unsuccessful drapery business of Peter Jones Ltd in Chelsea which his father had acquired some years earlier. After disagreements with his father, he exchanged his profitable partnership in the Oxford Street shop for sole control of Peter Jones in 1916. To his father's trading principles of honesty, good value, and wide assortment, he added close control of merchandising and expenses together with energetic experiment. In 1920 he secured formal reconstruction of the company, whereby the few outside holders of ordinary capital accepted a fixed dividend, and he distributed some preference shares to the employees.

Owing to Lewis's ill health and difficult trading conditions, profit-sharing then lapsed until 1924 when Lewis was reconciled with his father and resumed his partnership at Oxford Street. He became the sole partner in this firm on his father's death in 1928, having by agreement acquired Oswald's share. His brother subsequently pursued a career in politics, serving as MP for Colchester from 1929 to 1945.

Lewis amalgamated the two shops to form a single business organized as an open partnership for the benefit of the employees, and in 1929 formed the public company, John Lewis Partnership Ltd, the two shops then having fewer than 2000 employees—or partners, as they were called—and annual sales under £2 million. He transferred all the equity capital of this company to trustees on behalf of the employees by means of an interest-free loan to the business of nearly a million pounds, to be repaid gradually out of profits.

Under Lewis's dynamic management the business expanded rapidly, while sharing its profits as he had planned. He achieved considerable improvements in efficiency: he established central buying and detailed budgetary control long before these techniques were generally used in retail distribution. In 1950 he completed a second and irrevocable trust settlement under which all the equity of the business was to be permanently held by trustees on behalf of the employees. When Lewis retired as chairman in 1955 the partnership had over 12,000 members and annual sales of more than £25 million.

Lewis aimed to share with his partners not only the profits but also the knowledge and power which go with ownership. He took pains to ensure good communications between workers at all levels. From 1918 he published weekly a house journal, *The Gazette*, which gave full information about the business and also provided an unusual additional means of communication by printing, with official comments, anonymous letters from readers. He did not aim to share the decision-making functions of management; he provided for democracy in industry by making management accountable to the managed, on the basis of a formal constitution specifying the rights and responsibilities of all members of the partnership. Largely by the force of his personality, he attracted to his partnership a wide variety of recruits from other occupations. He engaged five women graduates for senior positions. One of these became his wife in 1923. She was Sarah Beatrice Mary (1890–1953), daughter of Percy Hunter, of Teddington, Middlesex, an architect. A graduate of Somerville College, Oxford, she became deputy chairman of the company and was a director of the partnership between 1929 and 1951. They had two sons and a daughter.

Lewis was an emotional, combative, and outspoken man, whose actions demonstrated a mixture of autocracy and altruism. The preface to *Retail Trading* (1968), a privately published collection of his memoranda, admitted:

> He was vain and cantankerous, and it would not be hard to demonstrate that he was intolerant and sometimes cruel in the intellectual arrogance with which he treated individuals who were his mental inferiors. In some ways he was a humbug and he certainly sacrificed his family to his dream of partnership. (Macpherson, 13–14)

Yet Lewis retained the admiration and affection of most of his colleagues by his idealism, infectious enthusiasm, and sheer charm of manner. He had a deep sympathy with the underdog. His single-minded dedication to the development of a real sense of common interest among the ever-increasing number of workers of all kinds in his partnership carried it through the stresses of the early years when so many, inside and outside, were both sceptical and distrustful.

Lewis had wide-ranging interests and a versatile, sensitive, and unconventional mind. He had an abiding love of the classics and was president of the Classical Association in 1956–7. He was devoted to natural history, particularly entomology and botany, and served on the council of the Zoological Society. At his country estate, at Longstock Park, Stockbridge, Hampshire (which subsequently became the property of the John Lewis Partnership), he created beautiful water-gardens and an arboretum. He played chess and golf, enjoyed music and the arts, read voraciously, and, above all, loved to talk. He had a fine sense of the dramatic and was strikingly impressive as a public speaker, although he seldom spoke at gatherings of any importance outside the business. A prolific contributor to *The Gazette*, he also wrote *Partnership for All* (1948) and *Fairer Shares* (1954). Lewis died at The Burrow, Longstock Park, Hampshire, on 21 February 1963.

BERNARD MILLER, *rev.* GEOFFREY TWEEDALE

Sources H. Macpherson, ed., *John Spedan Lewis, 1885–1963* (1985) • A. Flanders, R. Pomeranz, and J. Woodward, *Experiments in industrial democracy: a study of the John Lewis Partnership* (1968) • *DBB* • *Gazette of the John Lewis Partnership* (2 March 1963) • *The Times* (23 Feb 1963) • *The Times* (25 Feb 1963) • J. S. Lewis, *Partnership for all* (1952) [with additional appx] • b. cert. • *CGPLA Eng. & Wales* (1964)

Archives John Lewis plc, Stevenage, business and personal records | Bodl. Oxf., corresp. with L. G. Curtis • Scott Bader Company Ltd, Wellingborough, corresp. with Ernest Bader • U. Sussex, corresp. with *New Statesman* magazine

Likenesses A. Devas, 1950–55, John Lewis Partnership, London; repro. in Macpherson, ed., *John Spedan Lewis* • B. Elkan, bronze, John Lewis Partnership, London • Elliott & Fry, photograph, NPG [*see illus.*]

Wealth at death £127,557: probate, 3 Feb 1964, *CGPLA Eng. & Wales*

Lewis, John Travers (1825–1901), archbishop of Ontario, was born on 20 June 1825 at Garrycloyne Castle, Cork, the son of John Lewis MA, curate of St Ann's, Shandon, Cork, and his wife, Rebecca Olivia, *née* Lawless. His father died suddenly of fever when he was eight. Educated at Hambin and Porter's School, Cork, he entered Trinity College, Dublin, where he won the first Hebrew prize; he graduated BA in 1847 as senior moderator and gold medallist in ethics and logic, and he passed his divinity testimonium in 1848. He was ordained deacon on 16 July 1848 and appointed curate at Newton Butler in co. Fermanagh. He was ordained a priest on 23 September 1849.

In 1848 Lewis's mother left Cork for Canada, and Lewis himself followed in November 1849, as a missionary of the Society for the Propagation of the Gospel. Joining the large migration of Irish clergy to the diocese of Toronto that had begun some twenty years earlier, Lewis was assigned by John Strachan, bishop of Toronto, to the mission at West Hawkesbury on the Ottawa River. In 1851 he married Anne (Annie) Sherwood of Brockville; they had six children before her death on 28 July 1886. Her father, Henry Sherwood QC, had extensive social, political, and economic connections throughout the region, and had served briefly as attorney-general and leader of the government in 1847. Through his father-in-law's influence Lewis was preferred in 1854 to the important rectory of St Peter's, Brockville.

Lewis soon became actively involved in colonial church politics. In 1861, after struggling for six years to raise an endowment, the clerical and lay representatives of the parishes in the eastern portion of the diocese of Toronto gathered in Kingston to elect a bishop for the new diocese of Ontario. Lewis, who had led the group opposing a British appointment, was selected on the first ballot, and at the age of thirty-seven the 'boy bishop' became the youngest prelate in the Anglican church. His elevation also marked an important transitional point in the constitutional history of the church. He was the last Canadian bishop to be appointed by royal letters patent, and the first to be consecrated in Canada.

Lewis's long episcopate was marked by a substantial increase in the number of missions, churches, and clergy. He was also instrumental in the formation of the Women's Auxiliary, a lay initiative that became one of the most important missionary organizations in the Canadian church. At the same time he faced several difficult problems. He was never able to establish good relations with the evangelical laity, and especially with the congregation of St George's Cathedral, Kingston: indeed, for most of his episcopate he resided in Ottawa. Divisions over ritualism and severe financial difficulties also plagued his diocese.

Lewis worked assiduously to maintain close links with the parent church in Britain. He was the first to advocate a national council of representatives for the whole of the Anglican church, which he hoped would address the doctrinal problems posed by the publication of *Essays and Reviews* in 1860 and by the Colenso case of the 1860s. His initiative played an important role in establishing the first Lambeth conference in 1867. He also returned frequently to Britain to raise money and to recruit clergy for his diocese. Through these visits he became one of the most well-known colonial bishops and was widely acknowledged in his later years as the senior statesman of the Anglican church in the British empire.

Lewis received many honours. In 1893 he was elected metropolitan of Canada and with the formation of the Anglican church in Canada became archbishop of Ontario. Trinity University in Toronto, Trinity College in Dublin, Oxford University, and Bishop's College in Lennoxville awarded him honorary degrees. In 1885 the governor-general of Canada presented him with the memorial medal in acknowledgement of his services to literature and science.

Three years after his first wife's death, on 20 February 1889, Lewis married Ada Maria Leigh, who was well known for her work in founding the British and American homes for young women and children in Paris. They had no children. Lewis died at sea on his way to England on 6 May 1901, and was buried at Hawkhurst, Kent.

W. S. JACKSON, *rev.* WILLIAM WESTFALL

Sources D. M. Schurman, *A bishop and his people: John Travers Lewis and the Anglican diocese of Ontario, 1862–1902* (1991) • P. Carrington, *The Anglican church in Canada* (1963) • C. Clapson, 'John Travers

Lewis', *Journal of the Canadian Church Historical Society* (Oct 1980), 17–31 • A. Lewis, *The life of John Travers Lewis, DD: first bishop of Ontario* [n.d.] • D. H. Akenson, *The Irish in Ontario: a study in rural history* (1984) • D. Swainson, ed., *St George's Cathedral: two hundred years of community* (1991) • *DCB*, vol. 13
Archives Archives of the Anglican Church of Canada, Toronto • Archives of the Diocese of Ontario, Kingston • Archives of the Diocese of Ottawa
Likenesses photograph, NPG

Lewis, Joseph (*fl.* 1750–1774), poet and ivory-turner, was born of untraced parentage, at an unknown date, possibly in Wales. By 1750 he was already living in London, but lines he wrote in praise of Sir John Philipps suggest that he may have spent his childhood in the neighbourhood of the Philipps family estate in Carmarthenshire. The poem acknowledges 'How good he's been to me in Infant Years' ('An Acrostick', Lewis, *Lucubrations*, 25), which might mean that Sir John, who was well known for his support of local schools, saw to Lewis's elementary education. Lewis worked throughout his career as an artisan; he was described in 1754 as 'an illiterate raw Lad … a mechanic' (Rizzo, *Bulletin of Research in the Humanities*, 83), later as 'a poor ivory-turner' (*GM*, 1758), and his poems frequently reflect the vicissitudes of a working man's life. Lewis's first traceable activity in London, however, is in 1750–51 as editor of the *Westminster Magazine*, under the pseudonym Lancelot Poverty-Struck. Most of its articles were reprinted from contemporary periodicals, but several poems can be identified as the work of Lewis himself.

Lewis's pseudonym represents both his public persona and his chronic condition. He lamented in 1773 that 'Poverty has stuck so close to me all my Life time: that Providence never trusted me with more Than Six Guineas at one period of Time' (Rizzo, 'Found: Joseph Lewis', 286). By 1752 he was married and living in the parish of Covent Garden, notorious then as a squalid, crime-ridden district. A son Joseph was baptized there on 17 December 1752. Lewis published two books of verse. The first, *Mother Midnight's Comical Pocket-Book* ([1753?]), appeared under the pseudonym Humphrey Humdrum, esq., but his authorship is attested by 'The Author's Epitaph', an acrostic spelling out the name 'Joseph Lewis', and confirmed by Ralph Griffiths in a handwritten note in the *Monthly Review*. His authorship of the second, *The Miscellaneous and Whimsical Lucubrations of Lancelot Poverty-Struck* (1758), follows from his assertion in it that he was author of the *Pocket-Book*. The second collection is said to have originated when, 'not having sufficient employment at his business to supply his family with bread', he thought of earning money by writing begging letters in verse. His success encouraged him to write other poems, until he had accumulated so many that 'he was advised and enabled by some of his friends to print them' (*GM*, 1758). Lewis's own account is somewhat different. He identifies himself in both books as 'Mother Midnight's merry grandson', alluding to the pseudonym Mrs Midnight adopted by Christopher Smart in *The Midwife* and for *Mrs Midnight's Oratory*, and he was apparently involved with Smart's ventures in the 1750s, but claims that he was 'abandoned by his antient and venerable Grandmother' for some misdemeanour, and was therefore 'oblig'd to commence Author for a small Livelihood' (Lewis, *Lucubrations*, 93).

While the *Pocket-Book* consists largely of *Oratory* material, Lewis's 'lucubrations' comment satirically on topical events and personalities, and depict with pungent realism and comic inventiveness the daily life of lower-class London. The struggles and humiliations of the author himself as he battles to keep his family from starvation are recounted with unquenchable humour. 'The Humble Petition of Lancelot Poverty-Struck' to David Garrick is typical: trade is bad, creditors are pressing, his wife Sarah is pregnant with a third child, while

Cold and Hunger closely pinches,
And kills his Family by Inches.

An effusive 'Acrostick' to Garrick which follows indicates that Lewis's plea was successful (Lewis, *Lucubrations*, 10–15). Although *Lucubrations* earned the commendation that there was 'in almost all of the pieces a strain of natural genius' (*GM*, 1758), the struggle against poverty continued. A street ballad of the 1760s shows 'Lancelot' desperate again but still clowning:

By my friends turn'd adrift,
I am at my last shift
('A Song on myself, by Lancelot Poverty-Struck', Madden Ballads, 3, CUL)

In 1768 Lewis tried a new method of soliciting help: he inserted a series of advertisements in the *Public Advertiser* (April–May) under the heading 'Real Calamity', describing in doggerel verse the hardships of 'the poor Poet' (now lame) and his 'distressed Family', and inviting donations. At that time he was living in Holborn, 'at Mr Jones's, a Baker in Field Lane' (Rizzo, *Bulletin of Research in the Humanities*, 81.86). He amassed over £10 in a few weeks by this device, but his troubles were not over. In a real letter sent in 1773 to Oliver Goldsmith from St Bride's workhouse, Hoxton, he explains how he and his family had been forced to take refuge in the workhouse. He had thirteen children by then but was unable to work because of swelling in his legs and lack of money to buy tools: 'I have got a Galloping consumption in my Pocket in this distressed Hotel: and have nothing to cheer my heart: or raise a Smile on the Countenance of my Wife and Children'. He was seeking money also to print a tract on the 'Oppressor of the poor', and planning to write a description of workhouse life, 'all Tragi Comic from Morning till Night' (Rizzo, 'Found: Joseph Lewis', 285–6). Apart from an acrostic by him praising a Dr Wolf Joseph Yonker, dated 1774 but sent to the *Gentleman's Magazine* by an anonymous contributor in 1785, that is the last heard of Lewis.

KARINA WILLIAMSON

Sources B. Rizzo, 'Found: Joseph Lewis, elusive author of *Mother Midnight's comical pocket-book*', *Bulletin of the New York Public Library*, 77 (1974), 281–7 [see also letter from Lewis to Goldsmith, BL, Add. MS 42515, fols. 129–30] • B. Rizzo, 'Joseph Lewis in REAL CALAMITY', *Bulletin of Research in the Humanities*, 81 (1978), 84–9 [for acrostics in *Public Advertiser* 16 April 1768 to 4 May 1768] • B. Rizzo, *Bulletin of Research in the Humanitites*, 83 (1980), 186 [reported in *Bulletin … for* *the Monthly Review* 10 (January 1754), 74 (Bodleian copy with annotations by Ralph Griffiths)] · parish register, St Paul's, Covent Garden, 17 Dec 1752 [baptism, son] · *GM*, 1st ser., 28 (1758), 135 · *GM*, 1st ser., 55 (1785), 779–80 · [J. Lewis], *The miscellaneous and whimsical lucubrations of Lancelot Poverty-Struck … author of the Westminster Magazine* (1758) · [J. Lewis], *Mother Midnight's comical pocket book*, 2nd edn (1754) · *The Westminster Magazine* (24 Nov 1750–23 Nov 1751) · K. Williamson, 'Joseph Lewis, "our Doggrel Author"', *Bulletin of Research in the Humanities*, 81 (1978), 74–83 · A. Sherbo, 'Can *Mother Midnight's comical pocket-book* be attributed to Christopher Smart?', *Bulletin of the New York Public Library*, 61 (1957), 373–82; repr. in *Evidence for authorship: essays on problems of attribution*, ed. D. V. Erdman and E. G. Fogel [1966], 283–93

Lewis [*née* Curzon], **Joyce** [Jocosa; *other married name* Joyce Appleby, Lady Appleby] (*d.* **1557**), protestant martyr, was the daughter of Thomas Curzon of Croxall, Staffordshire, and his wife, Anne Aston of Tixall. She married twice: her first husband was Sir George Appleby of Appleby, Leicestershire, with whom she had two sons; and then, after Appleby's death at the battle of Pinkie on 10 September 1547, she married Thomas Lewis (*d.* 1558), lord of part of the Warwickshire manor of Mancetter, as his second wife. Almost everything known of her is recorded by John Foxe—a partisan source, but thanks to his midlands connections a well-informed one. The martyrologist records that Joyce was orthodox in religion until moved by the burning of Lawrence Saunders at Coventry on 8 February 1555 first to question traditional Catholicism and then, under the influence of her neighbour John Glover, to reject it. Presumably she became one of a group of evangelicals headed by the Glover family which was centred upon Mancetter and nearby Baxterley. Compelled to come to church by her husband, her disrespectful conduct there led to her being cited before Bishop Ralph Baynes. Thomas Lewis, who had indignantly compelled the bishop's officer to eat the summons, was consequently cited too. He submitted whereas she did not, but Baynes treated her circumspectly as a gentlewoman and gave her a month to consider her position, binding her husband in £100 for Joyce's appearance. Thomas declined to connive at Joyce's escape and duly brought her back to the bishop, who examined and imprisoned her. After several further examinations she was finally condemned to burn, probably in late summer 1556, specifically for rejecting the real presence in the eucharist.

Joyce Lewis did not suffer at once, according to Foxe because the sheriff of Lichfield refused to put her to death during his term of office, and it was not until 10 September 1557 that she was finally executed. Having refused to make confession she spent her last night in prayer, reading, and discussion with her friends. Augustine Bernher accompanied her to the stake, where she drank to her fellow evangelicals, several of whom were present and drank with her. Her end was hastened by gunpowder supplied by the under-sheriff. Shortly afterwards eleven of her associates were summoned before the bishop for having supported Joyce Lewis at her death and for speaking well of her after it. John Glover's wife, Agnes, allegedly said that 'though her carcas suffered yet god receaved her soule' (BL, Harley MS 421, fol. 68). All eventually succumbed to pressure to recant.

Joyce Lewis clearly became a significant figure in an evangelical circle centred upon Lichfield, a position she owed to both her social standing and a striking personality. Her associates were mostly women, but also included the sheriff of Lichfield and one John Hurleston, who was said to have discussed religion with her. When she knew she was to suffer, she took counsel with her friends 'how she might behave herself, that her death might be more glorious to the name of God, comfortable to his people, and also most discomfortable to the enemies of God' (*Acts and Monuments*, 8.403). Both Foxe's account of her, and her commemoration at the beginning of Elizabeth's reign in Thomas Brice's *Compendious Regester* (1559) as one 'Continuing constant in the fier' (Farr, 171), suggest that she largely achieved her aim, as do the inscribed boards, commemorating her and Robert Glover, which were set up in Mancetter church in 1833. The support her death won for her cause, along with the circumstances of her own evangelical conversion, also illustrate how the Marian persecution was apt to defeat its own purposes.

Henry Summerson

Sources *The acts and monuments of John Foxe*, ed. S. R. Cattley, 8 vols. (1837–41), vol. 8 · BL, Harley MS 421 · E. Farr, ed., *Select poetry, chiefly devotional of the reign of Queen Elizabeth*, Parker Society, 25 (1845) · J. Nichols, *The history and antiquities of the county of Leicester*, 4/2 (1811); facs. edn (1971) · *VCH Warwickshire*, vol. 4 · J. W. Martin, *Religious radicals in Tudor England* (1989) · J. Fines, *A biographical register of early English protestants, 1525–1558*, 2 (1985) · *Warwickshire*, Pevsner (1966) · *DNB*

Lewis, Judith (*d.* 1781). *See under* Slaughter, Stephen (*bap.* 1697, *d.* 1765).

Lewis, Kid. *See* Lewis, Ted (1894–1970).

Lewis, Leopold David (1828–1890), playwright, was born in London on 19 November 1828, the eldest son of David Lewis, physician, of Middlesex, and his wife, Elizabeth. He was educated at King's College School, Wimbledon, was admitted a solicitor in 1850, and practised at 4 Skinner's Place, Sise Lane, London, until 1875. On 26 December 1868 he married Jane Williams.

A drama, *The Bells*, which Lewis had adapted from *Le juif polonais* by Emile Erckmann and Pierre-Alexandre Chatrian, was produced at the Lyceum Theatre in London on 25 November 1871. Henry Irving's performance in the leading role of Mathias, the conscience-stricken burgomaster, helped to make his reputation as an actor. The play ran for 151 performances with Irving in the lead. *The Bells* was published as no. 97 of Lacy's series of acting editions. Although he wrote three more dramas, produced between 1873 and 1881, *The Bells* was Lewis's only real success, and it cast a shadow over the rest of his career. Despite Irving's later generosity to him, Lewis 'believed that his adaptation of *The Bells* and not Irving's performance in it had made the fortune of the Lyceum' (Sims, 58).

From February to December 1868 Lewis and Alfred Thompson conducted a monthly periodical, *The Mask: a Humorous and Fantastic Review of the Month*. They wrote all the articles, and Thompson supplied the illustrations. *The Mask* featured parodies of current fiction, such as Wilkie Collins's *The Moonstone*, and satirical reviews of contemporary art by William Holman Hunt and John Everett Millais. However, it was not a popular success. Lewis also wrote a series of tales in three volumes entitled *A Peal of Merry Bells*, published in 1880. He died, after an epileptic seizure, in the Royal Free Hospital, Gray's Inn Road, London, on 23 February 1890, and was buried at Kensal Green cemetery on 28 February. He was survived by his wife.

MEGAN A. STEPHAN

Sources *The Times* (25 Feb 1890), 5 · *The Times* (27 Feb 1890), 9 · *St Stephen's Review* (1 March 1890), 8 · *St Stephen's Review* (8 March 1890), 18 · G. R. Sims, *Glances back* (1917), 53–8 · L. D. Lewis and A. Thompson, *The Mask: a Humorous and Fantastic Review of the Month* (Feb–Dec 1868) · F. R. Miles, ed., *King's College School: a register of pupils in the school … 1831–1866* (1974), 200 · D. Mayer, ed., *Henry Irving and 'The bells'* (1980), 4–5, 16 · *CGPLA Eng. & Wales* (1890) · *IGI*

Likenesses A. Bryan, caricature, drawing, 1883, repro. in Mayer, *Henry Irving and 'The bells'*, 16 · caricature, drawing, 1890, repro. in *St Stephen's Review* (8 March 1890) · A. Thompson, caricature, drawing, repro. in Lewis and Thompson, *The Mask*

Wealth at death £20 10s. 0d.: probate, 17 April 1890, *CGPLA Eng. & Wales*

Lewis, Lewis Jenkin [*called* Lewsyn yr Heliwr] (*bap.* **1793**, *d.* **1848**), radical leader in Wales, was baptized on 21 March 1793 in Penderyn near Merthyr Tudful, Wales, the son of Lewis Jenkin Lewis, a butcher, and his wife, Margaret. During his early life he broke in horses and found hunting dogs for local gentry. He was involved with Morgan Morgan of Bodwigiad, the local squire, who became his patron. He was literate and was fluent in both Welsh and English. Once a haulier between Llwydcoed pits and Penderyn lime-kilns, he acquired the nickname of yr Heliwr (the Huntsman). This may have been a corruption of the Welsh 'haulier', but in 1831, according to his petition for mercy after the Merthyr rising, he was a 38-year-old miner for Penydarren works, trying to keep a wife and four children on 8*s*. a week. From his first appearance in the records he was called the Huntsman in both languages.

Lewis came briefly to public prominence during the popular insurrection that occurred in depressed Merthyr Tudful in 1831, following the Reform Bill crisis. Agitation by Unitarian radicals, with the support of local ironmaster William Crawshay (1764–1834), coincided with a slump in Merthyr: wages were falling and hundreds going on poor relief. Miners began to hold torchlight meetings on the hillside during the election campaign of May, and popular leaders began to emerge: they included Lewis, who was blessed with a simple but powerful oratorical style.

In Merthyr franchise issues began to be linked to more local grievances, and in particular there was a wave of popular anger against the court of requests, the local court for the recovery of small debts. Amid mounting disorder, a crowd at Hirwaun rescued Lewis's trunk from the court (surety for a debt of £18 19*s*.) and hoisted him on it to make a speech.

The next morning (2 June) a mass insurrection broke out in Merthyr. Great crowds, primarily from Crawshay's works, mustered and turned into a 'natural justice' riot. They attacked over a hundred houses and shops, waving red flags and reform banners, restoring goods taken by the court of requests to the original owners, shouting down magistrates, and ignoring the Riot Act. The court went up in flames, as people all over Merthyr took an oath to the red flag and local officials sheltered in The Castle inn. Throughout, Lewis the Huntsman was the leader, making speeches from his trunk. With a painful sense of 'fair play' in the often complicated transactions which resulted, he rescued both magistrates and a hated parish constable from the wrath of the crowds.

Early on 3 June some eighty soldiers of the 93rd foot from Brecon marched through jeering crowds to The Castle inn to face a dramatic confrontation, a prolonged dialogue on reform between ironmasters and the crowd, and a futile reading of the Riot Act. When Crawshay inflamed them with a threatening speech, Lewis, who had been active throughout, urged the crowd to seize muskets and led them in the assault. After a prolonged struggle, the troops in the inn opened fire against repeated attacks. Some twenty-two civilians were killed and over seventy wounded.

Lewis rallied the survivors and on 4 June angry revolt spread. As ironmasters issued a proclamation singling Lewis out as a leader, and people in Hirwaun sacrificed a calf and washed a flag in its blood, the Huntsman helped to organize two armed camps, which drove off an ammunition train from Brecon and successfully ambushed the Swansea yeomanry, staging a triumphant demonstration at Cyfarthfa Castle. Sunday and Monday saw agonized efforts to mobilize support from both sides, with up to 1000 troops closing in, and the rising finally collapsed on Monday 6 June. Lewis was captured in Hendre-bolon near his home.

At the trials at the Glamorgan assizes, which opened on 13 July, twenty-eight scapegoats were punished, with four sentenced to transportation and two to death. Though there were hearings on all cases, Justice Bosanquet stopped the public trials after the fourth. This meant that many serious charges against Lewis were not heard. He was condemned to death on one count: for a riot outside a house during the 'natural justice' action, for which the jury recommended mercy; on another, with his young colleague Dic Penderyn (Richard *Lewis), of wounding a soldier outside The Castle inn, the jury found Richard guilty of murder, but Lewis guilty of urging the crowd to disarm the soldiers. A petition for mercy was organized by a Quaker ironmaster of Neath, Joseph Tregelles Price, which was signed by 11,000 people and, most remarkably, backed by Shoni Crydd (John the Shoemaker, John Thomas), the parish constable whose life Lewis had saved during the troubles, crying 'Honour! Honour! he's had enough!' (Williams, *The Merthyr Rising*, 183–4).

On 30 July, after much consultation and in highly mysterious circumstances, Bosanquet granted a reprieve to Lewis; and an order requiring his urgent transfer to the hulks was sent on 5 August. It had to be repeated on 16 August, so he was still in Cardiff gaol when Dic Penderyn was executed, an event which, like all these proceedings, aroused widespread disquiet, both at the time and thereafter. Lewis finally sailed for New South Wales on the convict ship *John* on 26 January 1832. On that ship he taught English fellow convicts to read and write their own language. The commander of the vessel thought well of him; so did the authorities in Australia. He was later pardoned and his wife and four children were permitted to join him in exile. His death was reported from Australia in 1848.

The sentence of death on Dic Penderyn (Richard Lewis) was not commuted, and in modern accounts of the Merthyr rising he has been depicted as an innocent martyr. His execution fuelled the legend that he was the leader and obliterated the well documented role of Lewis the Huntsman: yet it was the 'village Hampden' Lewis Lewis who was the nearest thing to a popular leader that the rising produced. Gwyn A. Williams

Sources G. A. Williams, *The Merthyr rising* (1978) • G. A. Williams, 'Dic Penderyn: myth, martyr and memory in the Welsh working class', *The Welsh in their history* (1982) • G. A. Williams, 'The Merthyr election of 1835', *The Welsh in their history* (1982) • D. J. V. Jones, *Before Rebecca* (1973) • M. Stephens, ed., *The Oxford companion to the literature of Wales* (1986) • C. Evans, *The labyrinth of flames: work and social conflict in early industrial Merthyr Tydfil* (1993) • parish register, Penderyn, Glamorgan, Wales; bishop's transcripts, NL Wales [baptism], 21 March 1793

Archives PRO, Home Office MSS | FILM MTV, Death and the Huntsman (1994), TV documentary

Lewis, Mark (1621/2–1681), Church of England clergyman and schoolmaster, was the son of William Lewis of Foxton, Leicestershire, clergyman. He matriculated from Lincoln College, Oxford, on 23 June 1637, aged fifteen, and graduated BA from New Inn Hall on 7 May 1641. On 11 June 1647 the Westminster assembly sequestered him to the rectory of Polstead, Suffolk. By 1648 he had married Anne (1625–1687), whose other name is unknown. They had at least three sons—**Mark Lewis** (1648–1714), born at Norwich, Abraham (*b.* 1650/51), and John (*b.* 1652/3)—all of whom were probably educated at a school kept by their father.

On 4 November 1656 Lewis was admitted as rector of Shipdham, Norfolk, but despite a House of Lords order of 1 September 1660 confirming his position he was ejected by April 1661. On 25 April that year he was licensed to teach grammar and preach in Norwich, but by 1670 he had moved to Tottenham High Cross. At private schools there and at Chancery Lane, London, he successfully taught an unusually wide curriculum, and through his method of teaching modern languages his pupils were 'perfected in the tongues by constant conversation' (*VCH Middlesex*, 243). His advanced, if derivative, ideas on education were cogently expressed in a number of short works, including *Institutio grammaticae puerilis, or, The Rudiments of the Latin and Greek Tongues* (1670), *An Essay to Facilitate the Education of Youth* (1674), and *A Model for a School for the Better Education of Youth* ([1675]). As an admirer of Comenius, he held that education should be based on an understanding of 'things' rather than an uncomprehending learning of words, and should proceed by 'syncrisis', meaning step-by-step progression from what is known to what is to be learned. For Lewis the traditional classical curriculum was sadly inadequate and in its place he suggested a somewhat optimistic programme which gave less time to Greek and Latin and included physical exercise, acting, and the study of a substantial list of cultural and scientific subjects. His advocacy of a thoroughly practical education for boys intended for the trades was perhaps better considered.

On 25 January 1676, as MA 'several years since' (*Calamy rev.*, 324), Lewis, who had evidently never been ordained, was granted permission to take deacon's and priest's orders. That year he became rector of Benefield, Northamptonshire, while his eldest son and namesake, who had graduated BA from Sidney Sussex College, Cambridge, in 1667, proceeded MA in 1670, and been ordained in London on 13 October 1672, became vicar of Stansted Mountfichet, Essex. It is not clear whether it was the father or the son who shortly after published *Proposals to the king and parliament how this tax of one hundred sixty thousand pounds per moneth, may be raised* (1677), *Proposals to Increase Trade and to Advance his Majesties Revenue* ([1677]), and *A Short Model of a Bank* ([1678]): although the style and outlook bear similarities to the father's works on education, the author of the last claimed a DD, a degree which has been attached to the son. The proposals for banking and monetary schemes were prompted, like those of numerous other writers, by the great expansion of English trade in the seventeenth century and the consequent need of a well-organized credit system. Following the work of such men as Francis Cradocke and Sir William Petty, the author argued for the establishment of a system of local banks of deposit and the use of transferable bills of credit as a form of money. He held that 'money in a nation, is like blood in the veins, if that circulates in all the parts of it, the whole body is in health' (*A Short Model of a Bank*, 3).

Lewis the elder died at Benefield on 30 July 1681 and was buried in the church there. He was succeeded as rector first by his son Mark, who died in 1714, and then by his grandson Mark (*d.* 1724). W. R. Meyer

Sources Foster, *Alum. Oxon.* • Venn, *Alum. Cant.* • *Calamy rev.*, 324 • H. I. Longden, *Northamptonshire and Rutland clergy from 1500*, ed. P. I. King and others, 16 vols. in 6, Northamptonshire RS (1938–52), vol. 8, p. 255 • *VCH Middlesex*, 1.243 • R. D. Richards, *The early history of banking in England* (1929), 102–3, 232 • J. K. Horsefield, *British monetary experiments, 1650–1710* (1960), 96–7, 239, 242, 281 • *ESTC*

Lewis, Mark (1648–1714). *See under* Lewis, Mark (1621/2–1681).

Lewis, Matthew Gregory [*called* Monk Lewis] (1775–1818), novelist and playwright, was born in London on 9 July 1775, the son of Matthew Lewis (1750–1812) and his wife, Frances Maria Sewell (*d.* in or after 1812).

Ancestry and early life Matthew Lewis's father held the two remunerative posts of chief clerk and deputy secretary at war in the war office, and owned slave plantations in Jamaica. In 1775 he married Frances Maria, the third daughter of Sir Thomas Sewell, master of the rolls, whose family (on the maternal side) were also Jamaican colonists, and whose brother Robert Sewell became attorney-general of Jamaica.

Matthew Gregory Lewis (1775–1818), by J. Hollis, pubd 1834 (after George Henry Harlow)

Frances, although badly educated, was musically talented and moved in artistic circles. The marriage was not a success: Frances separated from her husband in 1781 when Matthew was only six, having fallen in love with a music master named Harrison with whom she had an illegitimate child in July 1782. Matthew Gregory was the eldest of Frances's four legitimate children; the others were Maria (who later married Sir Henry Lushington); Barrington, who died young from a spinal injury; and Sophia Elizabeth (who later married Colonel Sheddon). Matthew, his mother's pet companion, was a precocious child and showed an early talent for music; after the separation he remained loyal to her despite the scandal which blighted her name, and his prolific literary activity at a young age was partly aimed at raising money for her support.

Lewis was educated at the Marylebone Seminary, a preparatory school run by Dr Fountain, dean of York, and Westminster School, which he entered in June 1783, aged almost eight; he distinguished himself as an actor in the Town Boys' play. He matriculated at Christ Church, Oxford, on 16 April 1790, and took his degree in the usual four years. He spent the summer vacation of 1791 in Paris, where he frequented the theatre, completed a farce, *The Epistolary Intrigue*, and, among other literary projects, burlesqued the fashionable novel in *The effusions of sensibility, or, Letters from Lady Honorina Harrow-Heart to Miss Sophonisba Simper* (the fragmentary text of which is published in the *Life and Correspondence* of 1839). By 1792 he had also completed his comedy *The East Indian*, based on Frances Sheridan's novel *Sidney Bidulph* (1761), although the play was not performed until 1799, at Drury Lane. In July 1792 Lewis travelled to Saxe-Weimar-Eisenach (where Sir Brooke Boothby was British ambassador to the court of Duke Karl August), in order to learn German and prepare himself, in obedience to his father's wishes, for a diplomatic career. Lewis however became more interested in Weimar's rich literary and dramatic culture, meeting Goethe and Wieland and developing that taste for the German *Schauerroman* ('spine-chiller') which he was so instrumental in transmitting to the British public.

Early in 1793 Lewis returned to Oxford, although in the Easter vacation he was off again to Scotland, staying with Lord Bothwell at Bothwell Castle and with the duke of Buccleuch at Dalkeith, and translating Schiller's tragedy *Kabale und Liebe*. In May 1794, after taking his bachelor's degree, he took up the post of attaché to Lord St Helens, British ambassador at The Hague, obtained through his father's political influence. Bored by Dutch society, he frequented the salon of Mme de Matignon, which was composed largely of French aristocratic émigrés, and witnessed at first hand the hazards of war.

***The Monk* (1795): publication and controversy** On 23 September 1794 Lewis wrote to his mother:

> What do you think of my having written, in the space of ten weeks, a Romance of between three and four hundred Pages Octavo? … It is called 'The Monk', and I am myself so pleased with it, that, if the Booksellers will not buy it, I shall publish it myself. (Peck, 213)

Lewis's modern biographer qualifies this claim by suggesting that 'passages in Lewis's letters … seem to deny this book the lustre of being a sudden inspiration' (Peck, 20). Two years earlier Lewis mentioned having begun a romance in the style of Horace Walpole's *Castle of Otranto* (1764), and a letter written shortly after he arrived in The Hague hints that he had been encouraged to persist in this plan by reading Anne Radcliffe's novel *The Mysteries of Udolpho* (1794). *The Monk*, perhaps the most celebrated of all English Gothic novels, nevertheless differs from Radcliffe's work in its use of German sources, its delight in the unexplained supernatural, sexual transgression, and an aesthetic of horror, as well as its (often misogynistic) burlesque elements. The monk Ambrosio's Faustian pact with the devil derives from French and English versions of a Persian tale entitled the *Santon Barsisa*.

Although there is some debate about the date of the first publication of *The Monk*, early March 1796 marked its appearance before the general public, in an edition published by Joseph Bell, its title-page carrying only Lewis's initials. Contrary to received opinion, early reviews were favourable, and the romance sold well enough to warrant a second edition in October 1796. Reassured by this warm reception, Lewis affixed his name to this new edition, as well as his new title of MP, having recently taken his seat for the rotten borough of Hindon, Wiltshire, recently vacated by William Beckford, author of *Vathek*. Lewis described himself, in the prefatory verses to *The Monk* (based on Horace's *corpus exigui*), as of 'graceless form and dwarfish stature', and Lady Holland described him in her journal in 1797 as 'little in person, rather ugly and short-sighted; upon the whole not engaging' (Peck, 50). Lewis paid dearly for the breach of anonymity. *The Monk* was widely attacked in the reviews for plagiarism, immorality, and extravagance, and Coleridge, writing in the *Critical Review* of February 1797, exclaimed, 'Yes! the author of the Monk signs himself a LEGISLATOR!—We stare and tremble' (Coleridge, *Shorter Works and Fragments*, 1.62). In the July 1797 edition of his satirical poem *The Pursuits of Literature*, T. J. Mathias, voice of the anti-jacobin backlash, attacked *The Monk* for diablerie, pornography, and blasphemy. His opinion that the romance was indictable at common law was supported in a long footnote by a list of obscene and blasphemous books which had been successfully prosecuted. Despite the statement in the biography of 1839 that 'the Attorney-general was actually instructed, by one of the societies for the suppression of vice, to move for an injunction to restrain its sale' (Cornwall-Baron-Wilson, *Life and Correspondence*, 1.13), there is no hard evidence that legal action was ever initiated against *The Monk*. Lewis did however comply with Mathias's suggestion that he should publish an expurgated edition, the fourth edition of 1798 (now entitled *Ambrosio, or, The Monk*), suppressing the more provocative and titillating passages. The scandal nevertheless contributed to the book's fame: by 1800 it had gone through five London and two Dublin editions and numerous chapbook versions, and had been adapted for the stage. Despite its practically unanimous condemnation by nineteenth-century critics, at least twenty more editions were published in Britain, as well as seven in the USA, four editions of the German translation by 1810, and seventeen of the French by 1883. *The Monk* was admired by Byron and Scott, and was emulated by E. T. Hoffmann in *Die Elixir des Teufels* (1816), by Charlotte Dacre in *Zofloya, or, The Moor* (1806), and by Charles Maturin in *Melmoth the Wanderer* (1824). The latter wrote in 1813 of his desire to 'out-Herod all the Herods of the German school, and get the possession of the Magic Lamp with all its slaves from the Conjuror Lewis himself' (letter to Walter Scott, 15 Feb 1813, *Correspondence of Scott and Maturin*, ed. F. E. Ratchford and W. H. McCarthy, Austin, Texas, 1937, 14).

Circle of friends and politics Lewis, now known by the sobriquet 'Monk', was lionized on account of the celebrity of his romance, which secured his place in fashionable Regency society. He befriended the unhappy princess of Wales, and became a frequent visitor to Inveraray Castle, seat of the fifth duke of Argyll, forming a warm attachment to the duke's daughter Lady Charlotte Campbell. He was often a guest of Lord Holland in the brilliant circle of Holland House, but Walter Scott echoed the opinion of many contemporaries when he later wrote that Lewis was:

> fonder of great people than he ought to have been, either as a man of talent or a man of fortune. He had always dukes and duchesses in his mouth, and was particularly fond of any one who had a title. (Peck, 45)

Lewis also frequented the company of writers like Tom Moore, Robert Southey, Theodore Hook, Thomas Campbell, Samuel Rogers, Walter Scott, and later Lord Byron. Early in 1801 Lewis took a cottage at Barnes which he furnished in rather precious taste, and in 1809 he moved into rooms at the Albany in Piccadilly, for which he paid 600 guineas. His six years (1796–1802) in the House of Commons were remarkably undistinguished, although he served on four select committees in 1796–7, and he appears to have made only one speech, in support of better treatment of debtors. In 1803 Lewis quarrelled with his father over the latter's insistence that he treat his mistress, Mrs Ricketts, with the respect due to a stepmother. Ever loyal to his mother, Lewis found that his refusal resulted in the reduction of his allowance. Although the breach was cleared up, mutual distrust soured the relationship between father and son until the former's death in 1812. Walter Scott wrote of Lewis, 'He did much good by stealth, and was a most generous creature' (ibid., 62); these characteristics were perhaps best exemplified in his charitable support of Mrs Isabella Kelly, a novelist and widow of Captain Robert Kelly of the Indian army. As well as granting an allowance to the mother, Lewis took charge of the education and upbringing of her son, William Kelly, who for many years drank, broke promises, and used Lewis's name to obtain credit from tradesmen. According to Montague Summers, Lewis's patronage of Kelly masked his homosexual obsession with the young man. While it is at least probable that Lewis (who never married) was homosexual, there is little firm evidence in this or any other case.

Dramatic writing, 1797–1811 In the wake of *The Monk*, Lewis's ambitions were literary and, especially, theatrical. His first and most popular drama, *Castle Spectre*, was performed at Drury Lane (despite the opposition of R. B. Sheridan) on 14 December 1797 with Kemble and Mrs Jordan in the leading roles. Although indebted—by Lewis's own admission—to the plot of Walpole's *Otranto*, Radcliffe's *Udolpho*, and Schiller's *Die Räuber*, *Castle Spectre* is perhaps the outstanding exemplar of British Gothic melodrama. Set in and around the atmospheric Castle Conway in the middle ages, it combines all the stock ingredients of the genre. An unusual touch lies in the anachronistic presence of Osmond's African servants Saib and Hassan, whose speeches attacking slavery, together with the play's critique of feudal tyranny, led to it being attacked for promoting radical politics. Coleridge, whose own play *Osorio* had recently been rejected by Drury Lane, described the serious passages as 'Schiller Lewis-ized—i.e. a flat, flabby, unimaginative Bombast oddly sprinkled with colloquialisms', and of the comic passages wrote, 'A very fat Friar, renowned for Gluttony & Lubricity, furnishes abundance of jokes … that would have stunk, had they been fresh' (*Collected Letters*, 1.378–9). Nevertheless, the play's masterful use of atmosphere and spectacle, its unflinching supernaturalism, and its sheer dramatic *éclat* (as Coleridge conceded, 'To admit pantomimic tricks the plot itself must be pantomimic'; ibid.) all contributed to its outstanding popular success; before the first three months of its run were over, it was said to have brought £18,000 into the Drury Lane treasury. It was presented over a dozen times over the next two seasons and became a reliable stock piece for years. Lewis's publisher Bell, who brought out the first printed edition in 1798, had published ten more by 1803.

Capitalizing on his success, Lewis embarked helter-skelter on his new dramaturgic career. In 1799 he supplied Drury Lane with two comedies, *The Twins* and *The East Indian*, and published *Rolla*, a translation of Kotzebue's historical melodrama *Die Spanier in Peru, oder, Rollas Tod*. *The Love of Gain*, a translation of Juvenal's thirteenth satire, was also published in the same year. In 1801 he published two plays, one of which, *Adelmorn the Outlaw*, was produced on 4 May, ploughing the same Gothic furrow as *Castle Spectre* and accordingly damned by the reviewers. After transferring his allegiance to Covent Garden, Lewis wrote the five-act tragedy *Alfonso, King of Castile*, set in fourteenth-century Burgos, which, in the opinion of Peck, 'is a serious attempt at tragedy and the closest Lewis came to writing good drama which can be called his own' (Peck, 86). First performed on 15 January 1802, *Alfonso* was well received by the reviewers and remained a standard for many years in a dramatic climate in which good tragedies were a rarity. Lewis's next offering to Covent Garden was a short monodrama entitled *The Captive*, performed on 22 March 1803. Mrs Litchfield's compelling performance of this speech of a mother on the verge of mental breakdown, imprisoned by her tyrannical husband, threw the audience into hysterical fits, and was subsequently withdrawn from performance by its author. (As Leslie Stephen quipped in the *Dictionary of National Biography* entry on Lewis, 'it may be read with impunity'). Two years later Lewis scored another success with *Rugantino, or, The Bravo of Venice*, presented on 18 October 1805, based on his translation of Zschokke's prose tale *Aballino der grosse Bandit* (1794). With his next production Lewis returned to Drury Lane; *The Wood Daemon, or, The Clock has Struck*, a two-act 'Grand Romantic Melo Drame', was first performed on 1 April 1807. Relying even more than *Castle Spectre* upon stage machinery and Gothic paraphernalia, *The Wood Daemon*'s treatment of the villainous Hardyknute's pact with Sangrida the wood daemon is partly based on *Faust*, and has in turn been regarded as a source for Byron's poem *The Deformed Transformed*. At the end of April 1807 *Adelgitha, or, The Fruits of a Single Error* was performed at Drury Lane, a five-act historical tragedy in blank verse set in late Byzantine Italy. Two further plays followed for the same company: *Venoni, or, The Novice of St Mark's*, a translation of Monvel's *Les victimes cloîtrées* (1 December 1808), and *Temper, or, The Domestic Tyrant* (1 May 1809), a rewriting of Sir Charles Sedley's *The Grumbler* (1702).

But perhaps Lewis's most excessive play was his last, *Timour the Tartar*, an equestrian spectacular first performed at Covent Garden on 29 April 1811. The escape of Agib, prince of Mingrelia, from Timour's fortress resembles that of Percy from Castle Conway in *Castle Spectre*, but the limelight was stolen by horses leaping barriers, plunging through the tide, and scudding up thunderous cataracts. 'The white horse which carried the heroine (Mrs H. Johnston) plays admirably', reported the *European Magazine* in a review which, Peck surmises, any horse would be proud to read. Despite the fact that *Timour* packed the house and was played forty-four times, purists of the English stage of course protested vehemently, and it was burlesqued in George Colman's *The quadrupeds of Quedlinburgh, or, The Rovers of Weimar*, played on 26 July 1811 at the Haymarket with basket-work horses parodying the final scene of *Timour*. Although Lewis wrote no new drama after *Timour*, he did adapt *The Wood Daemon* as a 'grand musical romance' for the English Opera House in August 1811, and in the following year refashioned *The East Indian* as a comic opera entitled *Rich and Poor*, which was performed twenty-seven times that season at the same theatre. The mediocrity and lack of development of much of Lewis's drama—with the exception of the tragedy *Alfonso*—may be attributed to the fact that all his published plays were conceived during his teens or twentieth year.

***Tales of Wonder* (1800)** In 1798 Lewis met William Erskine, friend of Walter Scott, who showed him some of the latter's translations and imitations of German ballads. Lewis's admiration for his writing represented an important opportunity for the as yet unknown Scott, whose subsequent poetry was greatly influenced by Lewis. In 1798 Lewis announced to Scott his plan to publish a collection of 'Tales of Terror', adding that 'a Ghost or a Witch is a sine-qua-non ingredient in all the dishes, of which I mean to compose my hobgoblin repast' (Peck, 118). This reveals Lewis's interest in fashionable Gothic horror rather than any scholarly concern for folkloric authenticity, a predilection which is evident in his subsequent publication. The collection appeared in late 1800 or early 1801 as *Tales of Wonder*, and, in addition to traditional material and nine original poems by Lewis (the best being 'Alonzo the Brave and Fair Imogine'), included five ballads by Scott, eight by Robert Southey, and one by John Leyden. Lewis's original poems display a remarkable variety of metrical feet, stanzaic form, and rhyme scheme, confirming Walter Scott's comment that Lewis 'had the finest ear for the rhythm of verse I have ever heard—finer than Byron's' (ibid., 123). Eight were Lewis's translations from the German, including five from Herder's *Volkslieder*, the main faults of which are overadornment and sentimentality. Of the sixty pieces included, about two-thirds had been published before in collections by Thomas Percy, David Herd, and other eighteenth-century compilers, a fact which contributed to the book's poor public reception and its popular appellation 'Tales of Plunder'. Of the many parodies elicited by *Tales of Wonder*, the most celebrated is the anonymous *Tales of Terror* (1801) on account of the fact that it was sold by Lewis's own publisher Bell, who issued it and the *Tales of Wonder* in uniform size and advertised the two works as companion volumes. The attribution of *Tales of Terror* to Lewis by his biographer of 1839 deepened the bibliographical confusion, and the work was thereafter taken to be Lewis's own, an attribution symptomatic of the fine line separating horror and parody in Lewis's opus. Although Lewis's energies were now largely taken up with writing for the theatre, he produced several translations from German literature, notably a rendering of Zschokke's *Aballino* (1805) (subsequently reworked as the two-act melodrama *Rugantino, or, The Bravo of Venice*; see above); *Feudal Tyranny, or, The Counts of Carlsheim and Sargans*

(1806), from C. B. E. Naubert's *Elisabeth, Erbin von Toggenburg, oder, Geschichte der Frauen in der Schweiz* (1789); and, most memorably, *Romantic Tales* (1808). This four-volume miscellany was composed of seven ballads, one long poem, and five prose stories, largely translated from Spanish, French, and German sources, particularly work by Oberon, von Kleist, and Klinger. Although it was more favourably reviewed than *Tales of Wonder*, no second edition of *Romantic Tales* appeared during Lewis's lifetime.

Final years, 1812–1818 Lewis's prolific literary career was suddenly ended by the death on 17 May 1812 of his father, who left his entire estate to his 36-year-old son; his *Poems*, appearing in the month his father died, was Lewis's last publication. After taking charge of the family's financial affairs, he settled generous allowances on his sisters and mother and decided to travel to Jamaica to oversee his plantations at Westmoreland and Hordley, and to ameliorate the condition of the 400-odd slaves employed there. He sailed from Gravesend on 10 November 1815, and after an eventful stay on the island returned to England on 31 March the following year, meeting William Wilberforce to discuss ways of 'securing the happiness of his slaves after his death' (Peck, 158). Lewis then departed on a continental tour which lasted for a year and a half, visiting Byron and the Shelley circle at the Villa Diodati in Geneva during August 1816. Here he made a translation for Byron (whom he had first met in 1813) of part 1 of Goethe's *Faust*, which influenced the latter's *Manfred* and other works. At nearby Coppet he argued with Mme de Staël about the slave trade, and drew up a codicil to his will insisting that future owners of his Jamaican estates visit their properties at least every three years on pain of forfeiture, to protect his slaves from abuse after his death. The document was signed by Byron, Shelley, and Polidori. He visited Florence, Rome, and Naples, and met up with Byron once again in July 1817 in Venice, where the two writers discussed the latter's *Marino Faliero* and the fourth canto of *Childe Harold*. Here Lewis engaged Byron's servant Tita, who accompanied him on his last voyage to Jamaica. Byron's final verdict on Lewis, whom he had lampooned in *English Bards and Scottish Reviewers* as 'Apollo's Sexton', was that he 'was a good man—a clever man—but a bore—a damned bore—one may say' ('Detached thoughts', in *Byron's Letters and Journals*, 18–19). After a brief stay in England, Lewis set off once again for Jamaica on 5 November 1817; the reforms which he implemented on his slave plantations, while antagonizing many of his fellow planters, foreshadowed general practice in Jamaica by nearly eighteen years. Lewis's transactions on these two Jamaican trips are vividly described in his journal, published posthumously in 1834 as *Journal of a West India Proprietor, Kept during a Residence in the Island of Jamaica*. This included several poems, notably the macabre *Isle of Devils: a Metrical Tale*, which had been published separately in Kingston, Jamaica, in 1827. In his *Table-Talk* for 20 March 1834, Coleridge praised the *Journal* as 'by far [Lewis's] best work, [which] will live and be popular' (Coleridge, *Table-Talk*, ed. C. Woodring, 1.470–71).

On his return voyage to England, on board the *Sir Geoffrey Webster* Lewis was struck down by yellow fever and insisted, against advice, upon taking an emetic. He died on the ship on 16 May 1818 after great suffering, and was buried at sea on the same day.

But Lewis had one 'final coup de theatre':

> As his coffin was sinking, the chains weighing it down slipped off and, like an apparition from one of his melodramas, the coffin popped up to the surface again. At their last sighting, his mortal remains were floating sedately back towards Jamaica. ('Simon Brett on Monk Lewis', *www.twbooks.co.uk/cwa/brettonlewis.html*)

Posthumous reputation The standard nineteenth-century biography of Lewis is *The Life and Correspondence of M. G. Lewis, with many Pieces in Prose and Verse* (1839), edited by Mrs Cornwell-Baron-Wilson. Montague Summers, in his *The Gothic Quest: a History of the Gothic Novel* (1938), speculates about Lewis's homosexuality, while many of the factual and biographical errors of the *Life and Letters*—and subsequent scholarship—were corrected by Louis F. Peck in his standard modern biography, *A Life of Matthew G. Lewis* (1961). A new critical biography by A. L. Macdonald appeared in 2000. Although *The Monk* never enjoyed the twentieth-century fame of Mary Shelley's *Frankenstein*, it has inspired some film adaptations, including a tepid version entitled *The Seduction of a Priest by Paco Lara* (1990), featuring Paul McGann as the Ambrosio character. By the beginning of the twenty-first century the novel was studied in university English departments all over the world.

NIGEL LEASK

Sources L. F. Peck, *A life of Matthew G. Lewis* (1961) • [Mrs Cornwall-Baron-Wilson], *Life and correspondence of M. G. Lewis, with many pieces in prose and verse*, 2 vols. (1839) • M. G. Lewis, *Journal of a West India proprietor* (1834) • M. Summers, *The Gothic quest: a history of the Gothic novel* (1938) • *Byron's letters and journals*, ed. L. A. Marchand, 12 vols. (1973–82), vol. 9 • *Collected letters of Samuel Taylor Coleridge*, ed. E. L. Griggs, 1 (1956) • S. T. Coleridge, *Shorter works and fragments*, ed. H. J. Jackson and J. R. de J. Jackson, 2 vols. (1995), vol. 1 • S. T. Coleridge, *Table-talk*, ed. C. Woodring, 2 vols. (1990), vol. 1, pp. 470–71

Archives Goethe- und Schiller-Archiv, Weimar, Germany • Harvard U. • Institute of Jamaica, letters • NL Scot. • V&A NAL, corresp. and papers | BL, corresp. with Lord Holland and Lady Holland, Add. MSS 51641–51642 • Hunt. L., MS notes in *Biographica dramatica* • NL Scot., letters to Sir Walter Scott

Likenesses J. Hollis, stipple (after G. H. Harlow), BM, NPG; repro. in *Life and works of Lord Byron* (1834) [*see illus.*] • H. W. Pickersgill, oils, NPG • W. Ridley, stipple (after S. Drummond), BM, NPG; repro. in *Monthly Mirror* (1796) • G. L. Saunders, miniature, NPG

Wealth at death 'very rich': Peck, *Life*, 176

Lewis, Mercy (*b.* 1672/3). *See under* Salem witches and their accusers (*act.* 1692).

Lewis, (Edward) Morland (1903–1943). *See under* Sickert, Walter, pupils (*act.* 1890–1939).

Lewis, Owen [Lewis Owen] (1533–1594), bishop of Cassano, Naples, was born on 27 December 1533 in the hamlet of Bodeon, Llangadwaladr, Anglesey, the son of a freeholder. He became a scholar at Winchester College in 1547 and a fellow of New College, Oxford, in 1554 and was admitted to the degree of bachelor in civil law on 21 February 1559. He taught civil law at Oxford until the change in religion forced his resignation. He matriculated in Louvain on 5 April 1563 and by 1566 was doctor of law and regius professor of canon law at the University of Douai, becoming rector on 5 April 1568.

In 1572 Lewis became archdeacon of Hainault and a member of the chapter of Cambrai Cathedral where he soon became provost. He was thus in a position to be of great help to Catholic exiles from England and Wales. In 1574 he was sent to Rome on diocesan business and for the next six years was agent for the diocese of Cambrai as well as acting on behalf of the college at Douai and Rheims. He was able to secure a pension for Douai from Pope Gregory XIII and also the papal licence to print the Douai Bible. He favoured the opening of a seminary in Rome to supplement the work at Douai and was involved in the change over from hospice to college. In 1579 he was invited by Charles Borromeo to become vicar-general in Milan and he spent the four years from 1580 to 1584 in that city, enjoying a close relationship with the reforming cardinal. Lewis granted hospitality to several English and Welsh exiles. Present at Borromeo's death, afterwards he returned to Rome and became secretary to the congregation of bishops. He also conducted the affairs of Rheims College and acted for Mary, queen of Scots.

In February 1588 Lewis was nominated bishop of Cassano in the kingdom of Naples and was consecrated in Rome on 14 February. Two years later he was summoned from his diocese for duties in Rome; these were to include visitations to various churches in Rome. Previously he had supported the expeditions of Stukeley and Fitzgerald to Ireland and now, at the time of the Armada, his name was put forward as a possible archbishop of York in the event of its success. Allen, however, considered a see such as St David's or Hereford or Worcester as being more suitable. On the death of Allen in 1594 there was a movement in favour of Lewis's elevation to the Sacred College, but neither he nor his rival Robert Persons was appointed.

Largely owing to some remarks by Cardinal Sega in his report on the troubles at the English College in Rome 1594–7, history has not been kind to Lewis's memory. The report blames him for the breakdown of discipline and the unrest at the college in the early days of its change from hospice to seminary. He was accused of inciting the conflict between the Welsh and English members of the community and also of making use of English government spies to further his own interests. However, it would seem that there is little or no evidence that Lewis fomented these troubles or that he was anti-Jesuit, although it can be admitted that he was sometimes lacking in discernment of the intentions of some of his associates. No one seriously disputes his learning, ability, or churchmanship. He was concerned to see the decrees of the Council of Trent enforced and the continuance of the Catholic faith in England and Wales assured. He died in Rome on 14 October 1594 and was buried in the church of the English College. MICHAEL E. WILLIAMS

Sources G. Anstruther, *The seminary priests 1: Elizabethan, 1558–1603* [1966], 209–10 · G. Anstruther, 'Owen Lewis', *The Venerable*, 21 (1962), 274–94 · J. H. Pollen, *The English Catholics in the reign of Queen Elizabeth* (1920), 272–83 · *DNB* · Gillow, *Lit. biog. hist.*, 4.211–16 · Wood, *Ath. Oxon.*, new edn, 2.837 · memorial tablet, church of the English College, Rome

Lewis, Paul (1739x41–1763), highwayman, was born either in Ireland or at Herstmonceaux, Sussex. He was one of ten children of an Anglican clergyman and appears to have come from a respectable family: Lewis himself drew attention to the good character of his ancestry in a plea against his death sentence, identifying a family line related to Archbishop William Laud and grandfathers who had served as chaplains at the Tower of London and to Lord Scarbrough.

When aged about six Lewis was sent to a 'good Foundation-school' where he remained for six or seven years but made no progress, 'such was his Incapacity, so impenetrable his Head to the Rudiments of Learning' (*Select Trials*, 4.271). On his removal from the school, Lewis fell among 'gay, idle young fellows' (ibid.) before he entered the army as a matross based at Woolwich. Rather than rescue him from his dissipation, military life heightened Lewis's sense of social ambition and love of sartorial display, resulting in substantial indebtedness to a tailor which 'obliged him to decamp and quit this genteel Support' (ibid.). Lewis next joined the navy, in which he became a lieutenant and saw action at the reduction of Cherbourg, the battle of St Cast (1758), and the capture of Guadeloupe (1759). Though commended for his bravery, in the West Indies he also gained a reputation for deception and robbery, having tricked fellow sailors out of money, for which he was forced to desert his ship.

On his return to England, Lewis took up as a highwayman, his first recorded crime being the robbery from a carriage travelling between Newington and Vauxhall, Surrey, in 1761. During the following year he was tried four times, and on each occasion acquitted, once at the county assizes and three times at the Old Bailey. On the evening of 12 March 1762 Lewis performed what proved to be his final assault when he attempted to rob, and then shot at, Joseph Brown, a farmer from Willesden, Middlesex. Lewis was subsequently apprehended by a witness and held captive by the more powerful Brown until, after protesting his gentlemanly status, he was released. Lewis then prepared to fire on Brown for a second time before he was once more overpowered and detained by a constable. Tried at the Old Bailey, Lewis was on this occasion found guilty of robbery and attempted murder and sentenced to death.

In the final days before his execution (4 May 1763) Lewis scandalized the Newgate authorities with his blasphemy and high living (funded by his father, whom he tricked out of money during a visit). Once more he assumed the character and habits of a young gentleman for which he was honoured with the title of Captain in a reference to a former fictional inmate of the gaol, the swaggering highwayman Captain Macheath from John Gay's *The Beggar's Opera* (1728). 'His Behaviour was such, as shocked every one who were Witnessed of it' (*Select Trials*, 4.273). To the young James Boswell, however, Lewis's conduct proved less clear-cut. On 3 May Boswell, denied a sight of John Wilkes at the Tower of London, had decided to visit the prisoners at Newgate where he met Lewis, to whom the impressionable young Scot was drawn by a display of gentlemanly bravado and fine dressing:

> Paul … was a genteel, spirited young fellow. He was just a Macheath … dressed in a white coat and blue silk vest and silver, with his hair neatly queued and a silver-laced hat, smartly cocked. Poor fellow! I really took a great concern for him, and wished to relieve him. (*Boswell's London Journal*, 251–2)

Lewis, together with the forger John Rice and the house burglar Hannah Dagoe, were led to Tyburn to be hanged on the following day. Despite his earlier contempt for the notion of redemption, Lewis now addressed the crowd from the scaffold, warning others not to follow his example and lamenting his untimely death at 'not twenty-three' (*Select Trials*, 4.271). One spectator who took Lewis's conduct to heart was Boswell, then attending the first of what became frequent visits to spectate at the gallows. As he wrote in his journal for 4 May, he had long been fascinated with the idea of Tyburn and the opportunity to witness the death of so beguiling an individual as Lewis proved irresistible. Historians now see Boswell's somewhat macabre interest as one example of a wider late eighteenth-century culture of sympathy or sensibility which prompted spectators to test their capacity for emotional sensitivity when faced with the plight of the condemned prisoner.

Deeply moved by what he saw at Tyburn, Boswell's desire to be thought a man of feeling instead plunged him into an intense period of melancholy and nightmares which continued to plague him, on and off, throughout his life. On the one hand Lewis's impact demonstrates the ease with which fashionable manners could degenerate to a debilitating pathology in the mind of hypochondriacs like Boswell. Equally, that it was the fate of a gentlemanly and gallant highwayman that proved so moving highlights the inherent snobbery of eighteenth-century sentimental culture; significantly Boswell felt no need to comment on, nor experienced lingering horrors for, Lewis's fellow victims, the sober John Rice and the plebeian Hannah Dagoe. PHILIP CARTER

Sources *Select trials … at the sessions house in the Old Bailey … from the year 1741 to the present year, 1764*, 4 (1764), 268–79 • *Boswell's London journal, 1762–63*, ed. F. A. Pottle (1950), vol. 1 of *The Yale editions of the private papers of James Boswell*, trade edn (1950–89) • *GM*, 1st ser., 33 (1763), 210–11, 254 • *A true, genuine and authentic account of the behaviour, conduct and transactions of John Rice and Paul Lewis* (1763) • M. Friedman, '"He was just a Macheath": Boswell and "The beggar's opera"', *Age of Johnson*, 4 (1991), 97–114 • V. A. C. Gatrell, *The hanging tree: execution and the English people, 1770–1868* (1994); repr. (1996)

Lewis, Richard [*known as* Dic Penderyn] (**1807/8–1831**), radical leader, was born in Aberafan parish, Pyle-Kenfig, south Wales, in a cottage named Penderyn, the son of Lewis Lewis, a cordwainer and later a miner of Cornelly near Pyle, and his wife, Margaret. The family were Methodists, and four Wesleyans later attended Lewis at his execution. His father's work as a miner brought him to Aberafan and Merthyr Tudful.

As a young man Dic worked as a haulier in Brecon timber, but broke a law on the handling of horses and fled to Penderyn in 1828 where he was associated with Lewis *Lewis ('the Huntsman'). Contemporary reports suggested the two were related, but nothing certain can be traced. By 1831 when he was twenty-three Dic was working as a miner in Merthyr. In October 1830 he married Mary Thomas and local tradition maintains a child was born to him, and died in its mother's arms at Lewis's execution. He was said, credibly, to have fought and won, as local champion, a battle with Shoni Crydd (John the Shoemaker or John Thomas), a parish constable notorious for blackmail. Another tradition maintains that Lewis was simple-minded, 'dim llawn llathen' ('not a full yard') in the vernacular.

Lewis could not fail to be affected by the popular disturbances prevalent in Merthyr Tudful in 1831 during the Reform Bill crisis. Demands for a wider franchise by Unitarian radicals were supported by the local ironmaster William Crawshay (1764–1834). A slump in industrial production, with falling wages and hundreds forced to seek poor relief, caused mass torchlight meetings on the hillside during the election campaign of May 1831.

In Merthyr, agitation for reform began to be linked to more local issues, and in particular there was a wave of popular anger against the court of requests, the local court for the recovery of small debts. Crowds set the court building alight on 2 June, as local officials sheltered in The Castle inn. The arrival of soldiers the following day sparked off further confrontations, which were only finally stamped out on 6 June.

Dic Penderyn (as he was later known) was arrested and put on trial as one of the leaders of the insurrection. However, he was widely believed to be innocent of the charges laid against him, and indeed to have played no role in the affray. He was put on trial jointly with Lewis Lewis, before Justice Bosanquet, on 14 July 1831. They were charged with wounding a soldier, Donald Black, outside The Castle inn and most of the evidence was against Lewis the Huntsman. The main accusation against Dic Penderyn came from James Abbott, a tory barber, with whom he had earlier clashed. Abbott was categorical against Dic, saying he saw him wound the soldier; he was backed by an associate called Drew, but neither the soldier nor a parish constable who had been present was able to identify Richard Lewis. Both he and Lewis Lewis were nevertheless condemned to death.

A petition for mercy organized by Joseph Tregelles Price, the Quaker ironmaster of Neath and supported by Shoni Crydd who apparently suffered a conversion, was at first directed to Lewis the Huntsman and secured his reprieve, which caused consternation and deep suspicion in Merthyr. Price was strenuous on Dic's behalf, organizing two petitions in which witnesses claimed that he was not even present and questioned the credibility of Abbott. Shoni Crydd had to be restrained by judicial action from harassing Abbott, and there was subsequently a riot at his house on the night of the execution and an attempt to boycott him out of Merthyr. Lord Melbourne rejected the petitions, however, and Dic Penderyn was hanged at Cardiff on 13 August 1831. At his execution Dic Penderyn said he was dying for thousands. His last words were 'O Arglwydd, dyna gamwedd' ('Oh God, what an injustice'; *Guardian*, 13 Aug 1996). There was widespread belief in his innocence, shared by a number of ironmasters and magistrates. Shops closed in protest and crowds followed Dic's coffin to Aberafan, where his brother-in-law, a Calvinistic minister, spoke and people said a white bird settled on the coffin.

The execution and associated anguish were driven from mind by the autumn surge of trade union formation under the National Association for the Protection of Labour and there was virtual silence about Dic Penderyn until 14 October 1874 when the *Western Mail* announced that, on his deathbed in Pennsylvania, a Welshman, Ianto Parker, had admitted that it was he who had wounded Donald Black the soldier. From the later nineteenth century there grew up a general belief that Dic was the victim of injustice, and this eventually made him into a Welsh national martyr. This view was fuelled by pamphlets written by Islwyn ap Nicolas, son of a well-known communist poet, and another by Harri Webb, a Welsh republican poet. Dic Penderyn was also the subject of several powerful novels. The Church in Wales raised a memorial to Dic at Aberafan, and in 1977 a plaque to him as a 'Martyr of the Welsh Working Class' was erected at Merthyr Public Library and unveiled by the then general secretary of the TUC. The ceremony was accompanied by readings from Alexander Cordell's stirring novel *The Fire People* (1973).

The cult of Dic Penderyn has unfortunately virtually effaced the major role of Lewis the Huntsman in the Merthyr rising, a leader if there was one. Although this distorts the import of the Merthyr rising, the fact that working people in south Wales should single out Dic Penderyn as a martyr representative of 160 years of industrial history speaks volumes in itself. GWYN A. WILLIAMS

Sources G. A. Williams, *The Merthyr rising* (1978); repr. (1988) · G. A. Williams, 'Dic Penderyn: myth, martyr and memory in the Welsh working class', *The Welsh in their history* (1982) · G. A. Williams, 'The Merthyr election of 1835', *The Welsh in their history* (1982) · D. J. V. Jones, *Before Rebecca* (1973) · 'The Merthyr rising', *The Oxford companion to the literature of Wales*, ed. M. Stephens (1986), 396–7 · G. Thomas, *All things betray thee* (1949) · A. Cordell, *The fire people* (1973) · R. Williams, *The angry vineyard* (1975) · C. Evans, *The labyrinth of flames: work and social conflict in early industrial Merthyr Tydfil* (1993) · *The Guardian* (13 Aug 1996) · bishop's transcripts of parish registers, Aberavon, Pyle-Kenfig, Merthyr Tydfil, NL Wales

Archives PRO

Likenesses plaque, in or before 1977, Merthyr Tudful Public Library

Lewis, Richard (1821–1905), bishop of Llandaff, was born on 27 March 1821 at Henllan in the parish of Llanddewi Felffre, Pembrokeshire, the second son of John Lewis, barrister, and his first wife, Eliza, daughter of Charles Poyer Callen of Grove, Narbeth. On the death of his elder brother, John Lennox Poyer Lewis, in 1886, Richard inherited the Henllan estate which, according to a survey made in 1873, comprised 2369 acres with an annual rental of £2229.

Richard Lewis (1821–1905), by Bassano, *c.*1897

After a year at Haverfordwest grammar school Lewis was sent to Bromsgrove School (1835–39). A scholar of Worcester College, Oxford, he matriculated on 18 June 1839. Due to illness he had to content himself with an ordinary degree in 1843, after which he and his brother set off on a grand tour of Europe and the Middle East. He returned in 1844 to be made deacon by the bishop of Oxford, Richard Bagot, but without a title, which was somewhat irregular even in those days. After more travelling he was ordained priest by Bagot's successor, Samuel Wilberforce, but still without a clerical office until, some six months later, he became curate of Denchworth, near Wantage. Nominated by his uncle to the family living of Amroth, Pembrokeshire, in 1847, he appointed a curate to serve the parish, remaining himself at Denchworth until he took another curacy at Flaxley in the Forest of Dean. In 1851 he was nominated by the lord chancellor to the parish of Llanbedr Felffre whereupon he resigned the parish of Amroth. The bishop of St David's, Connop Thirlwall, refused to institute him because his knowledge of Welsh was, to say the least, somewhat indifferent, but Lewis won an appeal to the archbishop of Canterbury and was instituted to his parish in June 1852. A dutiful parish priest, he contributed largely to the restoration of the parish church from 1860 to 1862.

On 6 April 1847 Lewis married Georgiana King, daughter of John Lewis of Swainswick, late of the East India Company. They had one son, Arthur Griffith Poyer Lewis (1848–1909), who rowed in the Oxford boat in 1870. Called to the bar in 1873, he was chancellor of the dioceses of Llandaff and St David's from 1908 to 1909. Georgiana Lewis died in Llandaff in 1875 and was buried in Llanddewi Felffre.

Rural dean of Lower Carmarthen from 1852, canon of St David's from 1867, Lewis was appointed archdeacon of St David's in 1875. Then in January 1883 came the offer of the see of Llandaff. The prime minister, W. E. Gladstone, was known to have stated that a vacancy in a Welsh diocese caused him more trouble than six English appointments. It was necessary for him to appoint a Welshman to succeed Ollivant at Llandaff, preferably one who could speak Welsh; but the choice was limited. Lewis had at least the social standing to grace the bench, so he was chosen. Lewis was hesitant. He was a countryman, known to be skilful with rod and gun and a good judge of horse and hound. He had no experience of industrial areas and was already sixty-two years old. His friends persuaded him to accept and he became a worthy and highly esteemed bishop. He took his seat in the House of Lords in 1885. On the few occasions that he attended, he voted on the Conservative side.

Lewis's episcopate coincided with the development of deep coalmining and the opening up of new areas in south Wales. The funds of Ollivant's Extension Society were nearly exhausted. Lewis inaugurated the Bishop of Llandaff's Fund for the erection of churches in populous districts which helped towards over 200 building projects, a good deal of money being raised locally. At the turn of the century he made an appeal which he called the Million Shilling Thank Offering Fund, but only a tenth of the hoped for sum was raised. He established an annual diocesan conference, bringing Llandaff into line with almost all the other dioceses.

A moderate high-churchman (one can detect the influence on him of the Tractarian William Palmer of Worcester College, who introduced a robed choir into his parish church long before it became fashionable), Lewis had more sympathy than his predecessor with the ritualist clergy of the Cardiff area and kept their obedience. He was a generous benefactor and supporter of the new theological college of St Michael's, founded in Aberdâr in 1892 and moved to Llandaff in 1907. He gave £1000 to the building fund and presided happily over a college council which was composed of men of advanced churchmanship. Concerned for the needs of Welsh-speaking parishes, there were two occasions when he refused to institute the patrons' nominees because they could not speak Welsh, and his decisions were upheld in law. After 1897 he was the senior Welsh bishop, often consulted by the primate on matters relating to the principality. Increasing age prevented him from playing any prominent part in the controversial matters in Wales in the early years of the twentieth century.

Lewis died at the bishop's palace, Llandaff, on 24 June 1905 and was buried at Llanddewi Felffre on 28 June. A life-size statue, in convocation robes, by Goscombe John, was placed on the wall of the presbytery of the cathedral in 1908, an indication of the high regard in which he was held in the diocese of Llandaff. O. W. JONES

Sources Foster, *Alum. Oxon.* • *Western Mail* [Cardiff] (25 June 1905) • F. Jones, 'A Victorian bishop', *National Library of Wales Journal*, 19 (1975–6), 14–56 • M. G. R. Morris, 'Bishop Richard Lewis: his life before Llandaff', *Journal of Welsh Ecclesiastical History*, 4 (1987), 57–92 • Dyfed Archives Service, The Castle, Haverfordwest, Henllan MSS • parish register (birth), Henllan, Pembrokeshire, 27 March 1821 • parish register (burial), Llanddewi Felffre, Pembrokeshire, 28 June 1905 • parish register (marriage), 6 April 1847

Archives Dyfed Archives Service, The Castle, Haverfordwest | LPL, corresp. with Archbishop Benson

Likenesses Bassano, photograph, *c.*1897, NPG [*see illus.*] • A. S. Cope, oils, 1904, Llys Esgob, Llandaff • photograph, *c.*1904 (after a portrait), St Michael's College, Llandaff • W. G. John, statue, 1908, Llandaff Cathedral • portrait (after A. S. Cope, 1904), Caer Maenau Fawr, Clunderwen, Pembrokeshire

Wealth at death £112,567 10*s.* 10*d.*: probate, 27 March 1906, *CGPLA Eng. & Wales*

Lewis, Richard [*real name* Thomas Thomas] **(1914–1990)**, singer, was born on 10 May 1914 at 69 Baden Street, Ardwick, Manchester, only son and the younger of the two children of Thomas Thomas (*d.* 1949) and his wife, Mary Hannah, *née* Lewis (*d.* 1963), who had moved to Manchester from Wales when Thomas was offered the job of coachman to the manager of the London, Midland, and Scottish Railway. They were Methodists, and he was brought up on Methodist hymns played on the harmonium by his mother. A boy soprano, he won gold medals at festivals all over the north of England until his voice broke when he was sixteen. He left Didsbury Central secondary school in 1930 to work as a clerk at the Calico Printers' Association, but he studied harmony and counterpoint in his spare time and continued to sing; after winning the gold medal of the Associated Board of the Royal Schools of Music in 1938, he won a scholarship to the Royal Manchester College of Music in 1939, to study with the bass Norman Allin.

In 1940 Thomas joined the Entertainments National Service Association, and in 1941 he made his début with the Carl Rosa Opera Company as Pinkerton in Puccini's *Madama Butterfly* and Almaviva in Rossini's *The Barber of Seville*. He was called up into the Royal Corps of Signals in 1941, but remained in England until 1944. In 1943 he married Mary, daughter of Joseph Lingard, first flute in the Hallé Orchestra and professor of flute at the Royal Manchester College of Music; they had one son. Thomas was posted to Normandy in 1944, and then to Brussels, where he was able to study at the Brussels conservatory and sang in Brussels, Antwerp, and Liège, including several performances of Benjamin Britten's *Les Illuminations*, the beginning of a close association with Britten's music. It was at this point that he took the name Richard Lewis. He sang Britten's *Serenade for Tenor, Horn, and Strings* in Copenhagen in 1945, and while stationed in Germany in 1946 took lessons from Pacho Kochen in Hamburg. After demobilization he enrolled in January 1947 at the Royal Academy of Music, where Norman Allin was now teaching, but his career was already taking off: he replaced Peter Pears in Britten's *Serenade* with the Southern Philharmonic Orchestra in Brighton in January, and after touring with the English Opera Group in Britten's *Albert Herring* in the summer of 1947 he made his début at the Royal Opera

House, Covent Garden, on 10 November 1947, as the Male Chorus in Britten's *The Rape of Lucretia* and took over the title role in *Peter Grimes* on 28 November 1947.

Richard Lewis sang in his first Glyndebourne season in 1950 as Ferrando in *Così fan tutte*, after singing Don Ottavio in *Don Giovanni* with the Glyndebourne Opera Company at the Edinburgh festival in 1948, and he sang there every year until 1967, except for 1957 and 1965, and returned in 1972 to sing Eumeaus with Janet Baker in Peter Hall's production of Monteverdi's *Il ritorno d'Ulisse*. During this period he sang in twelve different roles, most notably that of Tom Rakewell in Igor Stravinsky's *The Rake's Progress* (in which he sang in the British première at the Edinburgh festival in 1953), which became one of the most popular operas at Glyndebourne in the 1950s. He was the leading Mozart tenor at Glyndebourne for many years, singing in every *Idomeneo* from 1951 to 1974. He made his final appearance at Glyndebourne in 1979, in *Il ritorno d'Ulisse*. Lewis also sang regularly at Covent Garden, where he was particularly in demand as an interpreter of contemporary opera, including the role of Captain Vere in Britten's *Billy Budd*, which he first sang in 1949 and sang for the next thirty years, taking over at short notice in 1979, his final appearance at Covent Garden. He created Troilus in William Walton's *Troilus and Cressida* in 1954, and also the role of Mark in Michael Tippett's *The Midsummer Marriage* in 1955, when he sang opposite Joan Sutherland, and in 1962 he created Achilles in Tippett's *King Priam*. One of his most memorable performances was as Aaron in Schoenberg's *Moses and Aaron* in 1965.

The first British singer to be engaged by a major American opera company since before the war, Lewis made his American début in 1955 as Don José in *Carmen* in San Francisco, and he returned every autumn until 1968 to sing with the San Francisco Opera. He also sang regularly with the Metropolitan Opera in New York. In the United States he formed the Bach Aria Group, a group of singers and instrumentalists which performed in New York and toured the universities. He appeared in the major European opera houses, and created Amphitryon in Giselher Klebe's *Alkmene* in Berlin in 1961. In 1956 he sang the tenor solo in the first performance of Stravinsky's *Sacrum canticum* in St Mark's, Venice. As a singer of oratorio he was most renowned for his Gerontius in Sir Edward Elgar's *The Dream of Gerontius*, which he first performed with Sir Malcolm Sargent in 1949, and he was noted for his interpretations of Mahler's *Das Lied von der Erde*. He also sang regularly with the Handel Opera Society.

In 1963 Lewis was appointed CBE. In that year he was divorced from his first wife, and married Elizabeth, a singer, daughter of the television reporter (James) Fyfe *Robertson; they had one son. His widowed elder sister married Fyfe Robertson, by then a widower, in 1978. In 1967 Lewis accepted an appointment as professor of singing at the Curtis Institute in Philadelphia, and he taught there from 1968 to 1971, performing regularly with the Philadelphia Orchestra under its musical director, Eugene Ormandy; during this period he also had a home in Bermuda. He returned to England in 1972 and continued to perform until 1982, when he made his last appearance, in Britten's *Spring Symphony*, with the Concertgebouw Orchestra in Amsterdam. His most memorable recordings include Tippett's *A Child of our Time*, Mendelssohn's *Elijah* (recorded in 1969 with Eugene Ormandy and the Philadelphia Orchestra), and a series of Gilbert and Sullivan operas, including *The Gondoliers* and *The Mikado*, conducted by Sir Malcolm Sargent. He recorded *The Dream of Gerontius* twice, with Marjorie Thomas as the Angel in 1955, conducted by Sargent, and with Janet Baker and Sir John Barbirolli in 1965. Lewis was awarded the honorary degree of DMus by the universities of St Andrews in 1984 and Manchester in 1986. He died on 13 November 1990 at his home, Coombe House, 22 Church Street, Old Willingdon, Eastbourne, Sussex, and was cremated on 19 November.

ANNE PIMLOTT BAKER

Sources N. Ross-Russell, *There will I sing: the making of a tenor* (1996) • H. D. Rosenthal, 'Richard Lewis', *Opera*, 6/3 (March 1955), 144–8 • S. Hughes, *Glyndebourne: a history of the festival opera* (1965) • *The Times* (14 Nov 1990) • *Opera*, 42/1 (Jan 1991), 33–6 • *New Grove*, 2nd edn • *WW*

Likenesses photograph, repro. in *The Times* • photographs, repro. in Rosenthal, 'Richard Lewis', 144–8

Lewis, Roger Curzon (1909–1994), naval officer and torpedo specialist, was born at Killean, Russell Road, Buckhurst Hill, Essex, on 19 July 1909, the second son of Francis William Lewis, managing director of Boake Roberts, and his wife, Kathleen Mary, *née* Annesley. He went to the Royal Naval College, Dartmouth, as a cadet in 1923. His first ship as a midshipman was the old coal-burning battleship *Benbow*, which he joined in 1927. After service in the destroyers *Vivian* and *Valentine*, in 1934 he went to HMS *Vernon*, the torpedo and mining school in Portsmouth, and was torpedo officer of the cruiser *Enterprise* on the East India station from 1935 to 1937.

Lewis returned to *Vernon* on the staff in 1938. In 1939 he was in Sheerness, organizing blockships and demolition parties for an operation—never carried out—to block the harbours of Ostend and Zeebrugge, when it became clear in those early days of the war that the enemy was using a non-contact type of mine, immune to normal sweeping methods. In November 1939 twenty-seven merchant ships and two destroyers were sunk, the Port of London was effectively closed, and coastal shipping traffic was brought to a virtual standstill. Winston Churchill, then first lord of the Admiralty, ordered that an example of this new weapon be recovered 'at all costs'. On 22 November, off Shoeburyness in Essex, a German aircraft was seen to drop a parachute from which was suspended an object which 'looked like a sailor's kitbag'. Lieutenant-commanders John Ouvry and Lewis, Chief Petty Officer Baldwin, and Able Seaman Vearncombe, all from *Vernon*, set off to the scene. The party splashed across the mudflats in pouring rain, to find a 'dark menacing-looking object lying practically embedded in the sand' (personal knowledge). At first, Ouvry and Lewis thought it was an acoustic mine, sensitive to sound, and lowered their voices to a whisper. They also emptied their pockets of metal, such as coins and keys. By the light of Aldis lamps, they found 'two unpleasant-looking fittings near the fore end' (ibid.); Lewis took paper rubbings of them so that special non-ferrous tools could be made. The mine was photographed by flashlight and securely lashed down. They returned at midday on 23 November, when the mine was next uncovered by the tide. By then a second mine had been found and Ouvry decided that he and Baldwin would tackle the first. Lewis (who in fact had never disarmed a mine before in his life) and Vearncombe would then deal with the second. Lewis stood at a distance, taking notes for the benefit of their successors, should the mine explode. Ouvry removed one primer and detonator, and signalled to Lewis and Vearncombe to come and help him turn the mine over so that he could remove a second primer. After forty minutes of tense work, the mine was safe. The mine was taken to *Vernon*, where it was dismantled and its secret revealed: an electromagnetic device which detonated the mine when the magnetic influence of a ship's steel hull passed overhead. Within months, a solution had been found, by fitting all metal-hulled ships with 'degaussing coils'. On 19 December 1939, four days before the awards were actually gazetted, George VI came down to *Vernon* to invest Ouvry and Lewis as DSO, and Baldwin and Vearncombe with the DSM.

In June 1940 Lewis joined the battleship *Rodney* as torpedo officer and served in her during the chase and destruction of the German battleship *Bismarck* in May 1941. *Rodney* fired torpedoes from her submerged tubes during the final stages of the action, although one tube was jammed shut by a near miss from *Bismarck*. Lewis was mentioned in dispatches. In February 1943 he married Marguerite Christiane (*d.* 1971), daughter of Captain A. D. M. Cherry, naval officer; that year he was fleet torpedo officer in the Mediterranean, based at HMS *Hannibal* in Algiers, forming and training mine and bomb disposal teams to clear north African and Italian harbours as the allies advanced. In January 1944, off the beaches of Anzio, the allies captured a 'double torpedo'—the top one manned, with another slung underneath. Lewis organized evaluation trials in Malta. He was appointed OBE for his Mediterranean service in 1944. He then had his only sea command, the 11th minesweeper flotilla.

Lewis had an original mind and was bold enough to take an unusual initiative. In 1950 he was superintendent at the experimental establishment at Greenock when trials were being carried out on electric torpedoes. He knew that more silver would be needed for the batteries in the torpedoes and, as the stock exchange forecast that silver prices were going to rise, he bought £50,000 worth, on his own authority and in the teeth of Admiralty bureaucratic opposition. He was severely reprimanded for exceeding his annual budget, but the price of silver rocketed and the navy saved nearly all the £50,000. He was chief staff officer at HMS *Osiris* in the Suez Canal zone from 1953 to 1955 and his last appointment before retirement in 1959 was as captain superintendent and queen's harbour master, Chatham. He then worked with Reeds Paper Group and with a City stevedoring company until 1974. He was a member of the Medway Conservancy Board and a governor of the youth training ship *Arethusa*. He retired finally to Teignmouth, where he was a district councillor.

Bull Lewis, as he was known to his friends, of whom he had many, was a large, genial man, with great personal charm. His round cheerful face always seemed to bear a smile. He died of heart disease and carcinoma of the bladder on 9 August 1994, at Newton Abbot Hospital, Newton Abbot, Devon. He was survived by two sons, his wife having died in 1971. JOHN WINTON

Sources E. N. Poland, *The torpedomen: HMS Vernon's story, 1872–1986* (1993) • *Daily Telegraph* (16 Aug 1994) • *The Times* (13 Aug 1994) • R. C. Lewis, *The first magnetic mine*, [n.d.] • G. Thistleton-Smith, *The personal side of some Vernon mine recovery and investigation operations, September 1939 – December 1940*, [n.d.], HMS *Vernon* Archives • personal knowledge (2004) [including taped interview, 17 June 1982] • *WWW, 1991–5* • b. cert.

Likenesses photograph, repro. in *The Times*

Wealth at death £143,012: probate, 28 Nov 1994, *CGPLA Eng. & Wales*

Lewis [*née* Ovenden], **Rosa** (**1867–1952**), hotel proprietor, was born on 26 September 1867 at Leyton, Essex, the fifth of the nine children of William Edwin Ovenden (*d.* 1910), watchmaker and later undertaker, and his wife, Eliza, daughter of John Cannon, jeweller, and great-niece of Richard Cannon, military historian.

Rosa left the Leyton board school at the age of twelve to become a general servant for a shilling a week and her keep. At sixteen a fortunate recommendation took her to Sheen House, Mortlake, home of the exiled comte de Paris. No apprenticeship could have been more valuable. She worked her way up to head kitchen-maid, was lent to the duc d'Aumale at Chantilly, and took charge of the kitchen of the duc d'Orléans at Sandhurst. In 1887 she started going out to cook in private houses where a light style of cooking, such as Rosa had learned in her royal French houses, was now preferred to the interminable stodgy courses of the Mrs Beeton school. First to employ her was Lady Randolph Churchill; then followed the Saviles, the Asquiths, and Captain Charles Duff, a prominent member of the Marlborough House set.

In gossip, Rosa's name was often associated with Edward VII. He first saw her at Sheen House when the dinner so pleased him that he asked his host to send for the chef: he was no less pleased with Rosa, whose cockney wit amused him. For the next twenty years tactful hostesses entertaining him engaged the services of Rosa, whose cooking he liked best and who was careful to study his tastes.

In 1893 Rosa married, for business reasons, without enthusiasm (and in the process falsifying her father's identity on the church record), Excelsior Tyrel Chiney Lewis, a butler. They were set up in a house in Eaton Terrace where they were to provide discreet lodging for upper-class *liaisons amoureux*. Unfortunately her husband had little to do but drink as Rosa broadened her own business and social connections. In 1899 she briefly and not very successfully took on the catering at White's Club, but her popularity in private houses grew. She now took a team of cooks with her but she was always prepared to do anything herself which needed doing—even scrubbing the steps—to ensure that all was as it should be. She did the marketing and prepared much of the food beforehand. She also gave lessons at half a guinea a time to people such as W. W. Astor's cook.

In 1902 Rosa Lewis bought the Cavendish in Jermyn Street, already a fashionable private hotel. Such was her energy that this added responsibility did not restrict her outside cooking activities but merely gave scope to her flair for furnishing and decoration. Within a year she discovered that her husband was defrauding her; she was losing her suppliers' confidence and his drunken manner was driving away custom. Rosa had him declared bankrupt and sent him away, and then met all his debts herself.

A tall and elegant hostess, Rosa made the Cavendish so much like a private house that there seemed nothing odd about her favourite rebuke: 'You treat my house like an hotel'. Lord Ribblesdale had a permanent suite and Sir William Eden lived there for many years. In addition to distinguished English families—she preferred them distinguished—she welcomed presentable American millionaires. Before the First World War it was the height of chic for London hostesses to have Rosa to cook for them; and no hotel was more *comme il faut* than the Cavendish for those who lived in the country. With the war private entertaining on a grand scale ceased and Rosa had only the Cavendish to occupy her. Her immense good nature caused her to bring in impoverished young officers. They were never allowed to pay and Rosa embarked on the Robin Hood tactics of robbing the rich to pay for the poor which she continued until her death. Her companion for over thirty years, Edith Jeffrey, came after the First World War in answer to an advertisement for a seamstress to renovate the Cavendish's fabrics, and stayed on as Rosa's business and personal assistant and staunch friend.

Rosa's tolerance of the behaviour of others, her uninhibited language, the raffishness of some of the parties at the Cavendish, and the great names with which hers was linked gave her in later life a reputation which she had not earned. She accepted the legend with a chuckle rather than a denial. As Evelyn Waugh, who portrayed her in *Vile Bodies* (1930), put it, she was a warm hearted, comic, and totally original woman, whose beauty was still discernible even in old age. She continued to dress in Edwardian style and, aided by vast quantities of champagne, enjoyed a grandiose and majestic decline from 1918 to 1952.

Rosa Lewis maintained throughout her life an affectionate if intermittent connection with the Church of England and was confirmed shortly before her death at the Cavendish on 28 November 1952. Her life was used as the outline for the popular late 1970s television serial, *The Duchess of Duke Street*.

ROBIN MCDOUALL, *rev.* ANITA MCCONNELL

Sources A. Masters, *Rosa Lewis, an exceptional Victorian* (1977) • M. Harrison, *Rosa* (1962) • D. Fielding, *The duchess of Jermyn Street* (1964) • 'England's greatest woman chef', *Daily Mail* (25 Feb 1909) • personal knowledge (1971) • *The Times* (1 Dec 1952), 8d • *The Times* (4 Dec 1952), 10f • M. Hardwick, *The Duchess of Duke Street*, 3 vols. (1976–7)

Likenesses group portrait, photograph, 1890–95 (with the staff of Church Road School, Leyton), Leyton Public Library • C. Guevara, portrait, 1920–29, priv. coll. • N. Murray, drawing, 1922, repro. in Fielding, *The duchess of Jermyn Street*, facing p. 128 • D. Glass, photograph (aged eighty-three), repro. in Masters, *Rosa Lewis*, between pp. 116 and 117 • C. Guevara, black and white photograph, Hult. Arch. • C. Guevara, black and white photograph, BBC Picture Library • Swaebe, double portrait, photograph (with Edith Jeffrey), repro. in Harrison, *Rosa*, facing pp. 148, 149 • Swaebe, photograph (in later years), repro. in Harrison, *Rosa*, facing p. 148 • United Press International, photograph, repro. in Fielding, *The duchess of Jermyn Street*, facing p. 132 • photograph, Hult. Arch. • photographs, repro. in Masters, *Rosa Lewis, an exceptional Victorian* (1977), following p. 116 • photographs, repro. in Fielding, *The duchess of Jermyn Street*, facing pp. 16, 80, 108, 128, 140 • portraits, repro. in Harrison, *Rosa*, facing pp. 148–149

Wealth at death £122,924 15*s*. 1*d*.: probate, 12 March 1953, *CGPLA Eng. & Wales*

Lewis, Samuel (1782/3–1865), publisher, carried on business successively in Aldersgate Street, Hatton Garden, and Finsbury Place, London, under the style S. Lewis & Co. Although described by his former employee Thomas Parkin as 'a man of no education' (Parkin), he is remembered as the publisher of an impressive series of British topographical dictionaries and associated atlases. The series commenced with *A Topographical Dictionary of England with Maps and a Plan of London* (4 vols., 1831), which Lewis later claimed had taken six years to compile at an outlay of £48,000. Sales were harmed by imitations and Lewis was successful in an action brought in 1839 against Archibald Fullarton, whose *New and Comprehensive Gazetteer* (Glasgow, 1832–4) was found to be inherently plagiaristic. It was an important judgment in defining copyright in factual works of reference. Lewis's first dictionary ran to seven editions by 1849, and in the mean time the series had continued with similar dictionaries of Wales (2 vols., 1833), Ireland (2 vols., 1837), and Scotland (3 vols., 1846). These also ran into several editions. *A Topographical Dictionary of Ireland* caused considerable local furore when hostile notices in the *Dublin Evening Mail* and elsewhere led many subscribers to default. Lewis responded with a dignified pamphlet containing testimonials from Daniel O'Connell and others. The genuine merit of the work was eventually acknowledged and further legal action was discontinued. Little is known of Lewis's private life, although he was married and had at least one son, Samuel [*see below*], and one daughter, Eliza. Samuel Lewis died at his home, 19 Compton Terrace, Islington, London, on 28 February 1865, aged eighty-two.

His son, **Samuel Lewis** (1820/21–1862), topographer, first comes to notice as the draughtsman of the map of Wicklow for the Irish dictionary. He later wrote *The History and Topography of the Parish of St. Mary, Islington* (1842), *Islington as it was and as it is* (1854), and *The Book of English Rivers* (1855). On 20 September 1859 he married Jane Burn Suter, daughter of Edward Suter. He died of pneumonia at his home, 1 Priory Villas, Canonbury, Islington, London, on 4 May 1862, aged forty-one. LAURENCE WORMS

Sources *Nineteenth century short title catalogue* (1984–95) • S. Lewis, *A topographical dictionary of England*, 5th edn, 4 vols. (1842) • T. Parkin, *An exposé, touching Lewis & Co.'s Topographical dictionary* (c.1829) • S. Lewis, *Lewis's Topographical dictionary of Ireland, and atlas* (1838) • Boase, *Mod. Eng. biog.* • d. certs. • m. cert., 1859 [Samuel Lewis, son] • *CGPLA Eng. & Wales* (1863) • *CGPLA Eng. & Wales* (1865)

Wealth at death under £7000: probate, 23 March 1865, *CGPLA Eng. & Wales* • under £5000—Samuel Lewis: probate, 19 May 1863, *CGPLA Eng. & Wales*

Lewis, Samuel (1820/21–1862). *See under* Lewis, Samuel (1782/3–1865).

Lewis, Samuel (1838–1901), moneylender and philanthropist, was born on 14 May 1838 at 1 Lower Hurst Street, Birmingham, the elder of the two children of Frederick Lewis (*b. c.*1801), a dealer, and his wife, Sarah (*c.*1805–1872). They lived in impoverished slum conditions, and in 1841 his father was imprisoned for debt. On this, and on many other occasions, the family were rescued by benefits provided by the Birmingham Hebrew Philanthropic Society.

By 1851 Lewis's father had left his mother; Sam, as he was commonly known, became, at the age of thirteen, her sole support. Promising to send her £1 a week, he travelled around the Birmingham area as a pedlar, with a tray round his neck and a stock of cheap jewellery and steel pen nibs. After early struggles, he was well established as a travelling jeweller by 1867. In that year, on 14 August, he married Ada Davis (1844–1906) of Dublin, the third daughter (of ten children) of an Orthodox Jewish middle-class family, and the couple went to London, where Lewis hoped to advance his career as a jeweller. The marriage, which endured until Lewis's death, was happy but childless.

In 1869 Lewis changed his occupation: taking premises at 17 Cork Street, Mayfair, he became a moneylender. It was a propitious time to start, as the usury laws had been repealed in 1854 and were not restored until 1900. During the intervening years moneylenders had an almost free rein. Lewis sought the landed aristocracy as his clientele. The agricultural recession in the last quarter of the nineteenth century led to diminishing incomes from land, and the increasing cost of hunting, shooting, fishing, and servants, and particularly of the London season, combined to create a high demand for loans.

Lewis was intelligent, witty, and shrewd, a humorous raconteur, and, though short of stature, an imposing and engaging personality. He was a good judge of character, his mind having been well honed from his days on the road. He kept himself abreast of the latest political and social gossip, was a well-known figure in racing circles, and thoroughly researched the background of his potential clients. When they entered his office he knew almost as much about them and their finances as they did themselves, and was able accurately to gauge the risk of a loan.

From granting unsecured loans to prodigal sons at high rates of interest, Lewis rapidly progressed to entering into large transactions, on security, at rates competitive with the banks and insurance companies. With the unexpected backing of the Bank of England, he soon became recognized as the leading moneylender to the aristocracy of England. He took speedy decisions, was prepared to make higher advances on the security offered than banks would, was discreet, and his word was his bond. His terms were clearly stated, and he gained the respect, and even the friendship, of his clients, most of whom would have been astonished had they known his origins. He was fair with defaulters. 'I have never', he claimed, 'foreclosed upon an honest man' (R. D. Blumenfeld, *R. D. B.'s Diary 1887–1914*, 1930). But those able to pay, who sought to avoid payment, were pursued through the courts, and Lewis was involved in several colourful cases, both civil and criminal.

Samuel Lewis (1838–1901), by unknown artist

Lewis's clients included the eighth duke of Beaufort; several members of the exclusive Jockey Club; the second Viscount Esher, a power behind the throne and government and adviser to royalty and prime ministers, but none the less a frequent visitor to Cork Street; the fifth earl of Lonsdale, one of England's wealthiest men, but often short of cash; the fourth marquess of Ailesbury, whose financial depredations almost brought his family to ruins; and England's premier earl, the twentieth earl of Shrewsbury, who found it cheaper to borrow £367,000 from Lewis than from banks and insurance companies.

Moneylenders have rarely been popular; in the 1880s and 1890s they were increasingly reviled and attacked—in the courts, in the press, and in a select committee of the House of Commons which sat in 1897. As England's best-known moneylender, Lewis was a prime target. He attracted the relentless enmity—not reciprocated by him—of Sir George Lewis (1833–1911), England's foremost society solicitor, who believed that borrowing from moneylenders at high interest led to crime and disgrace, and who campaigned for the revival of the usury laws. He harried Sam Lewis relentlessly, but unsuccessfully, throughout the whole of the latter's career. In a letter to *The Times* of 22 March 1898 he branded him 'a curse to society and a danger to the community', and invited a writ for libel, an invitation Lewis declined. Sam Lewis not only survived, unscathed, all the attacks upon him, but, if anything, emerged with his reputation enhanced.

Society imposed boundaries beyond which a Jewish moneylender could not infiltrate, but, despite Sir George's efforts, Sam and Ada Lewis, with homes in Grosvenor Square, by Boulter's Lock in Maidenhead, and on the front at Brighton, mixed freely with their many high-placed friends, entertained generously, and were part of the daily parade in Hyde Park.

Within a few months of his retirement, Sam Lewis died, on 13 January 1901 at 23 Grosvenor Square. He was buried on 16 January 1901 at Golders Green Jewish cemetery. He left an estate of £2.6 million. Ada Lewis (who in 1904 married as her second husband an army officer more than thirty years her junior) left an estate of £1.1 million at her death in 1906. Between them, the Lewises bequeathed more than £3.4 million to fifty-one charities, mainly for cheap housing for the working classes, to voluntary hospitals in London, Brighton, and Maidenhead, and to trust funds established for the poor of Dublin and of the City of London. Asked what he would choose as a motto, Lewis, a latter-day Robin Hood, replied, 'I lend to the Lords; I give to the poor' (*Daily Telegraph*, 14 Jan 1901).

Gerry Black

Sources G. Black, *Lender to the lords: giver to the poor* (1992) · *Jewish Chronicle* (18 Jan 1901) · *Daily Express* (14 Jan 1901) · *Daily Mail* (14 Jan 1901) · C. S. C. Brudenell-Bruce, earl of Cardigan, *The wardens of Savernake forest* (1949) · G. Lambton, *Men and horses I have known* (1924) · E. Benzon, *How I lost £250,000 in two years* (1889) · W. B. N. [Lord William Nevill], *Penal servitude* (1903)

Likenesses H. Thaddeus, portrait · oils, Southern Housing Group, London [*see illus.*]

Wealth at death £2,572,658 17*s.* 0*d.*: resworn probate, Jan 1902, *CGPLA Eng. & Wales* (1901)

Lewis, Sir Samuel (1843–1903), lawyer and civic leader in Sierra Leone, was born on 13 November 1843 at Campbell Street, Freetown, Sierra Leone, the second of the seven children of William Lewis (*c.*1812–1901), a merchant, and his wife, Fanny Thorpe (*c.*1812–1903). Both his parents were liberated Africans, born in the Egba country of south-western Nigeria. He grew up at a time when successful west African traders of his parents' generation were investing the fruits of their enterprise in education for their children. His schooling in Freetown was completed at the Church Missionary Society's grammar school. From 1861 to 1866 he worked in his father's business, and was then sent to England for legal education. William Lewis wished to see a kinsman qualified to appear in the colonial courts and was encouraged by the Revd Benjamin Tregaskis, who hoped Samuel would 'stand up' in a sectarian spirit against the Anglican establishment. That hope was to remain unfulfilled; Lewis's devout Methodism was always tempered by an ecumenical spirit.

In January 1867 Lewis was admitted to the Middle Temple, and in 1868 he entered the chambers of S. D. Waddy, a Wesleyan barrister who later became a Liberal MP and a county court judge. In 1870 he won an inns of court exhibition for the study of real property and moved to the chambers of a chancery barrister called Everitt. After his call to the bar Lewis returned to Freetown in May 1872, the second Sierra Leonean barrister to practise there. During the next thirty years he enjoyed a successful professional career; African merchants who were building up considerable fortunes along the whole west African coast competed for the services of a countryman of legendary forensic ingenuity and a notable command of detail. In 1888 his retainer from a Cape Coast merchant, Jacob Sey, was estimated at 3000 guineas. Lewis's professional competence was recognized by several appointments to act as queen's advocate and once as chief justice; however, he preferred the independence, and the income, of private practice.

From 1882 to 1903 Lewis served as an unofficial member of the legislative council, one of up to four nominated Africans. He took his responsibility to scrutinize the government's legislation and financial proposals very seriously, and on several occasions was able to secure substantial modifications. While supporting official policy whenever conscientiously possible, he would criticize vigorously and effectively anything prejudicial to the interests or rights of those whom he had been appointed to represent. He sought to co-operate with all sections of the Freetown community for the common good; Europeans and Africans shared an interest in developing the port as a base for an expanding trade with substantial areas of the west African interior. During the early 1880s Lewis published three pamphlets which urged the government to encourage agriculture, moderate its taxation of commerce, and expand the influence of the British empire by a vigorous frontier policy, judiciously balancing diplomacy and force. He was also vigilant in council on issues affecting civil rights (including property rights). He was one of the architects of the Freetown municipality ordinance of 1893, and was three times elected as its mayor.

On 2 July 1874 Lewis married Christiana Horton (*c.*1856–1880); twelve years after her death, on 20 October 1892 he married her cousin Edith Grant (1874–1941). Each was a young educated Catholic, with whom Lewis shared a happily quiet domestic and social life in their home in Oxford Street . In all there were three children by the first and five by the second marriage, though three died in infancy. In 1882 Lewis bought a country estate called Christineville, though his hope of making this an exemplary agricultural enterprise had very limited success. Europeans admired his successful assimilation of Victorian values; in 1893 he was appointed CMG and in 1896 KCMG, thus becoming the first African to be knighted. Most Africans also applauded his achievements, although some may have thought him too remote from the popular Krio culture which was emerging in Freetown. He accepted briefs in controversial cases, which earned him some unpopularity, and many people resented paying rates in order to finance the municipality he had promoted.

The changing spirit of imperial policy during the 1890s brought Lewis's empire loyalism into conflict with his African patriotism. In 1895 his intervention in a Mende land dispute provoked a bitter conflict with the governor, Frederic Cardew, hitherto an admirer, over the form in which British jurisdiction was to be enforced in the interior. Although Lewis welcomed the establishment of a protectorate in 1896, Cardew resented his detailed criticisms of the powers conferred on the governor by ordinance. When in 1898 the collection of a house tax provoked a violent insurrection in Mende and Temne country, Cardew sought to blame Lewis, and the Freetown community in general, for encouraging disobedience. His assessment, though rejected by the commissioner, Sir David Chalmers, was substantially endorsed by Joseph Chamberlain, and this episode strengthened the reaction against granting increased responsibility to educated Africans in British west Africa. When Lewis died of cancer, at 22 Ulster Place, Marylebone, London, on 9 July 1903, he was disappointed by the evident retreat from those legal and political principles on which he had believed the British empire to be based. He was buried in Acton cemetery.

John D. Hargreaves

Sources J. D. Hargreaves, *A life of Sir Samuel Lewis* (1958) • C. Fyfe, *A history of Sierra Leone* (1962) • F. W. Hooke, *Life-story of a negro knight: Sir Samuel Lewis* [1915] • A. T. Porter, *Creoledom: a study of the development of Freetown society* (1963) • A. Wyse, *The Krio of Sierra Leone: an interpretive history* (1989) • J. D. Hargreaves, 'The establishment of the Sierra Leone protectorate and the insurrection of 1898', *Cambridge Historical Journal*, 12 (1956), 56–80

Archives PRO, occasional letters and references, incl. his three mayoral minutes, CO 267 • SOAS, Archive of Methodist Missionary Society

Likenesses photograph, repro. in Hargreaves, *Life*, 64

Lewis, Samuel Savage (1836–1891), librarian and antiquary, was born at Spital Square, London, on 13 July 1836. His father, William Jonas Lewis, youngest son of George Lewis (1763–1822), was a surgeon, and his mother, Elizabeth Bunnell, was descended from Philip Henry (1631–1696). Bunnel *Lewis was his half-brother. He entered the City of London School in 1844, won the Carpenter scholarship in 1847, and on 13 October 1854 entered St John's College, Cambridge as a pensioner. His eyesight failing, from 1857 to 1860 he lived and farmed in Canada. In 1861 he obtained a situation on the prince consort's model farm near Windsor. His eyesight improved after operations, and in December 1864 Lewis returned to Cambridge, migrating to Corpus Christi College at Easter 1865. He graduated BA as ninth classic in 1869, and proceeded MA in 1872. On 21 April 1869 he was elected fellow of Corpus Christi, and on 22 March 1872 he became FSA; in the same year he was ordained deacon at Ely, and in 1873 he became a priest. He was librarian of his college from 1870 to 1891, travelled widely, and was proficient in many languages. He had a reputation as an eccentric owing to his mannerisms and unconventional dress, and was generally known as Satan Lewis.

A keen antiquary, Lewis assiduously collected coins, gems, and seals, mostly linked to the classical world, forming a valuable museum in his college rooms. This collection, which he bequeathed to his college, is now on permanent loan to the Fitzwilliam Museum, Cambridge. Lewis wrote no books, but made numerous contributions to the *Transactions of the Society of Antiquaries*, to the *Journal of the Royal Society*, and to that of the Royal Archaeological Institute. On 12 December 1887 he married Agnes Smith (1843–1926), daughter of John Smith, of Irvine, Ayrshire. She was a writer who became better known under her married name of Agnes *Lewis as the discoverer of the Sinai Palimpsest. Lewis himself did not long survive his marriage, dying suddenly of heart failure in a train near Oxford, on 31 March 1891.

W. A. J. Archbold, *rev.* N. Wilkins

Sources A. Lewis, *Life of the Rev. Samuel Savage Lewis* (1892) • P. Bury, *The college of Corpus Christi and of the Blessed Virgin Mary: a history from 1822 to 1952* (1952), 218–20 • *Fitzwilliam Museum: classical heritage* (1978) • J. Spier and E. Vassilika, 'S. S. Lewis: notes on a Victorian antiquary and on contemporary collecting', *Journal of the History of Collections*, 7 (1995), 85–102

Archives CCC Cam., MSS • FM Cam., MSS

Likenesses C. E. Brock, portrait, 1894, CCC Cam.

Wealth at death £16,793 18*s*. 5*d*.: resworn probate, Dec 1891, *CGPLA Eng. & Wales*

Lewis, Sarah (*fl.* 1839–1848) was a writer on the status of women, about whom no biographical information has come to light apart from a comment by T. M. Rearden in the *Congregational Magazine* of 1840 that she was 'a lady known in Episcopalian circles'. *Woman's Mission*, published anonymously in 1839 and later attributed to Sarah Lewis, is her only work, apart from a short article on governesses 'by the author of *Woman's Mission*' which appeared in volume 37 of *Fraser's Magazine* (1848), and in which she argues for government-controlled qualification by examination for governesses in order to improve their status and pay.

The influential *Woman's Mission* is loosely based on Louis Aimé Martin's 1834 work *De l'éducation des mères de famille, ou, La civilisation du genre humain par les femmes*. The author emerges from this work as a firm advocate of 'separate spheres'; the book is aimed at middle-class women within the home, whose role she wishes to elevate but not extend in any public or political way. Indeed, since she views the qualities men bring to public life with distrust, and traces their selfishness and competitive temper to inadequate schooling, nothing would be gained, in her view, by allowing women to develop similar characteristics. Instead, she argues that while girls are trained in self-control, submission, and service to others, boys are given a predominantly intellectual training devoid of moral content, with the result that men become 'selfish husbands and tyrannical fathers'. The remedy for this lies in the moral influence of the Christian mother exerted within the home, which Lewis sees as balancing and ameliorating male power, and she wants boys to remain under the influence of such a mother for as long as possible. She also suggests that female moral influence will have its effect on the wider world, and will ultimately improve social and political attitudes. Her arguments both on influence and education are closely similar to those of Sarah Stickney Ellis, who comments approvingly on *Woman's Mission* in the last of her four books on conduct, *The Mothers of England, their Influence and Responsibility* (1843). Both these highly popular writers started from a belief in the moral equality of men and women, but Lewis directly argues against the advocates of 'women's rights', in the belief that women would only antagonize men by claiming the right to vote. Like Ellis, she also argues that women should be allowed to take paid employment without loss of caste, because marriage, as a moral enterprise, should not be entered into simply because a woman cannot afford to keep herself; hence the paradox that arguments elevating the role of the married woman also logically tended to support paid employment for the single.

The reassuringly moderate ideology of *Woman's Mission* was well received by reviewers for journals usually on opposite sides of the debates on the question of women, and stimulated considerable discussion, while on a more light-hearted note *Woman's Mission* pretensions, seen as manipulative self-promotion, were frequently burlesqued in *Punch* throughout the 1840s. Serious analysis of the weaknesses in Lewis's position began when Anna Jameson, in an article in *The Athenaeum* in 1843, pointed out the inapplicability of *Woman's Mission* ideology to the masses of labouring women, and in the same year Marion Reid published *A Plea for Woman*, in which, taking *Woman's Mission* as a starting point, she argued powerfully for women's right to the franchise. On education she also rejected Lewis's position, arguing that women should primarily be educated for their own benefit.

The very moderation of Lewis's position with regard to political rights for women seems to have helped the dissemination of her ideas, which stimulated debate, and explained how far the position of women could be improved without a more radical programme such as that advocated by Reid. H. S. Twycross-Martin

Sources S. Lewis, *Woman's mission* (1839) • [S. Lewis], 'On the social position of governesses, by the author of *Woman's mission*', *Fraser's Magazine*, 37 (1848) • M. Reid, *A plea for women* (1843) • T. M. Rearden, *Congregational Magazine*, new ser., 5 (1841) • A. Jameson, 'Condition of women and the female children', *The Athenaeum* (18 March 1843) • *Westminster Review*, 34 (1840) • *Westminster Review*, 52 (1849–50) • [T. H. Lester], 'Rights and conditions of women', *EdinR*, 73 (1841)

Lewis, (John) Saunders (1893–1985), writer and a founder of the Welsh Nationalist Party, was born on 15 October 1893 at 61 Falkland Road, Poulton-cum-Seacombe, Wallasey, Cheshire, the second of the three sons of the Revd Lodwig Lewis (1859–1933) and his wife, Mary Margaret, *née* Thomas (1862–1900). Though born and educated on Merseyside, his family on his mother's side consisted of a long line of Welsh Presbyterian (Calvinistic Methodist) preachers and ministers, with their roots in Anglesey.

Although Welsh was the language of the home and the chapel, Saunders Lewis was educated privately in English,

(John) Saunders Lewis (1893–1985), by Powys Evans

at home and then in Liscard High School for Boys, Wallasey. He entered Liverpool University in 1911 to read English and French, but volunteered for military service in 1914 and served as a lieutenant in the South Wales Borderers. He received commendations, was severely wounded in 1917, and had to convalesce for over a year. He was then sent to Athens to serve in British intelligence under Compton Mackenzie. He returned to the university in 1919, took a first in English under Oliver Elton, and carried out research for his MA. At first he seemed destined for a career as an English academic or writer. But he had been profoundly affected by his experiences in France during the war and by the Irish rising of 1916. At university he met Margaret Gilcriest (1891–1984), the daughter of Irish Wesleyan parents who had moved from Wicklow to Liverpool. She read geography and became a teacher, but she also espoused the cause of Irish nationalism, later turning her back on her parents' religion by becoming a Roman Catholic. Both she and Lewis steeped themselves in the works of the Irish literary renaissance and learned the Irish and Welsh languages.

Saunders Lewis had spent a deal of time in 1920 in Aberystwyth in research for his MA, but in 1921 he moved to 10 Hamilton Street, Canton, Cardiff, where he started attending mass at the nearby church of Our Lady of the Angels. He had a post as an assistant librarian in Pont-y-clun in Glamorgan. In 1922 he moved to 1 Ffynone Villas, Swansea, when he was appointed a lecturer in Welsh at the University College. As the correspondence between Lewis and

Margaret shows, their marriage was delayed not only by the war but also by the opposition in Wales at that time to Roman Catholicism. Soon after his appointment at Swansea he began looking for posts in English departments in England so that he could marry. There was also opposition from his family. His aunt, who had cared for him after his mother died when he was seven years old, intervened and persuaded Lewis's father to accept the inevitable and bless the marriage. Lewis and Margaret married in the Roman Catholic church of Our Lady and St Michael in Workington, Cumberland, on 31 July 1924 and settled in Swansea, at 9 St Peter's Road, Newton, Mumbles. They had one child, their daughter, Mair, born in 1926.

In moving to Wales, Lewis had made a choice; he had decided to become a Welshman, a Welsh-speaking man of letters, turning to Welsh literature with the mature mind of a distinguished graduate in English literature, who also had extensive knowledge of the literatures of France and Italy, and of the classical world. He became a provocative and inspiring figure. He was dynamic, small of stature, with piercing eyes; his concentrated, disciplined energy reminded one of Cocteau. He was suspected of Catholic leanings, was fond of wine and cigars, wore a bow tie: the epitome of all that was either proscribed or derided by nonconformists.

Having had no formal training in Welsh literature, Lewis's attitude to the work to which he now devoted himself was fresh and startling. In 1924 he published his MA thesis as *A School of Welsh Augustans*, which centred on the English influences on a number of eighteenth-century Welsh poets, such as Goronwy Owen.

Lewis was of a conservative cast of mind, and had been accused of espousing Maurras's Action Française; a suggestion he vehemently denied, though acknowledging a debt to Maurras as a literary figure. The issue was explored in a major exchange of open letters between him and an agnostic academic, W. J. Gruffydd, professor of Welsh in Cardiff, which is worth reading even today. The two protagonists managed to evoke a whole period, and the sheer presumptuousness of the two men is a delight. But the letters also show that, like most of their French counterparts, both saw literature as a total way of life.

As part of that commitment, and in a stance opposite to the *trahison des clercs*, Lewis had moved into politics, and in 1925 helped found the Welsh nationalist party Plaid Genedlaethol Cymru, later to become Plaid Cymru. He became its president in 1926. The scholar had come down to the market place, and this caused a split loyalty in his life from then on.

As a nationalist politician, as in his literary work, Lewis not only looked back to the medieval period when Wales had a degree of autonomy but also outward to continental Europe of his day. He eschewed the old romantic nationalism of most nation states, and in his inaugural lecture as party president in 1926 he asserted it was the rise of nationalism in Tudor times which had destroyed European nations such as Wales and Ireland. But his frequent allusions to Roman Catholic social teaching, such as the encyclicals *Rerum novarum* and *Quadragesimo anno*, led his opponents to use the Irish Unionist slogan, 'Home rule equals Rome rule.'

In 1927 Lewis published a controversial study of the writings of another eighteenth-century poet and hymn writer, *Williams Pantycelyn*, best known outside Wales as the author and co-translator of the hymn 'Guide me, oh, thou great Jehovah'. With the admonition of the poet Elfed in mind—'Shakespeare, follow his example; Dante, turn to his world, but remember Pantycelyn at the same time'—Lewis revealed the glories and importance of Pantycelyn's works. He made use of his knowledge of Étienne Gilson's study of *The Divine Comedy* and of that other underworld of the human consciousness mapped by Freud.

Almost at the same time Lewis produced a series of studies of individual writers from the nineteenth century. These were collectively titled The Artist in Philistia, and focused on the works of the poet Ceiriog, of the novelist Daniel Owen, and of the prose writer and poet Glasynys. Lewis castigated many of the writings after the Methodist Revival as being moralistic and sentimental, if not philistine: an attitude he found expressed in Daniel Owen's novels.

In all Lewis's writing there was the dramatic element which made him compulsive reading. The breadth of his learning and vision, his honesty and lack of cant, his interest in form as well as content, his ability to see Welsh works in the wider context of European literature and other arts forms, and his willingness to demolish myths and sacred cows and to elevate the importance of neglected authors made him an enigmatic figure, often reviled but also revered. There are few Welsh authors who have escaped his attention.

Lewis saw himself, too, as an 'Artist in Philistia'. In 1930, he published the first of his two novels, *Monica*, which, though somewhat moralistic, was akin in subject to *Madame Bovary*. He dedicated it to 'Pantycelyn … the sole initiator of this style of writing in Welsh'! That element of the moralistic was rare in his work. For all his abiding devotion to religion and politics, literature was always his delight, and in it he abhorred moralistic works, such as were so common in Welsh in the nineteenth century, and assiduously respected the autonomous roles of the various human disciplines.

In *Braslun o hanes llenyddiaeth Gymraeg* ('An outline of the history of Welsh literature' up to 1535), published in 1932, he attempted to reveal the glories of the literature of what he saw as the golden age: the period when Wales was Catholic and had a degree of political autonomy, before she was annexed by England in 1535–6 and her religion and language proscribed. He tried to elucidate the medieval mind for a mainly nonconformist audience, drawing on authors from Catholic and classical Europe, such as Francesco de Santis and Aquinas, Aristotle and Plato, to illustrate the background of scholastic philosophy and theology which was the patrimony of the poets and scholars of the period, and the basis of their poetic aesthetics.

Lewis also dealt with the earlier, heroic age when Wales,

as he insisted, had come into existence from a fusion of the Celtic substratum and the post-Roman elements. He made a few howlers, such as his suggestion that some of the very early epigrammatic short poems (*englynion*) from the ninth century or earlier were exercises by pupil poets in the bardic schools; a thesis which was totally refuted by Sir Ifor Williams. Usually, however, though he was often speculative, Lewis succeeded in casting new light on matters. For instance, he memorably compared medieval Welsh poetry to a great Gothic cathedral built, *pace* Newman, as a sinless edifice dedicated *Ad majorem Dei gloria* ('To the greater glory of God'). He also compared the whole corpus of Welsh literature to Hereford Cathedral which, though many of its parts were destroyed over the centuries—often by the Welsh—then rebuilt or added to, was yet a single building, containing many architectural styles in a remarkable unity.

In 1936 Lewis made a dramatic political challenge to his fellow countrymen which became a landmark in modern Welsh history and in the history of Welsh letters in the twentieth century. The Air Ministry acceded to objections by naturalists in England to the setting up of a bombing range in East Anglia and chose instead a location in the heartland of Welsh language and culture, Penyberth on the Llŷn peninsula in north-west Wales. The vast majority of Welsh public opinion vehemently opposed the proposal, but to no avail. Lewis decided to take direct action, and on the fourth centenary of the Act of Union, to challenge the constitutional legality of England to over-rule the wishes of the Welsh. Together with prominent Baptist minister Lewis Valentine, and teacher and short story writer D. J. Williams, he set fire to the bombing school and then gave himself up to the police. The three were tried at Caernarfon assizes for the arson attack—where Lewis made a speech described by A. J. P. Taylor as reaching rare heights of noble oratory. The jury failed to agree, and the trial was moved to the Old Bailey, where the three were sentenced to nine months' imprisonment. Lewis was dismissed from his post as a lecturer at University College Swansea. He subsequently sustained himself by writing poems and plays and supported his family with journalism, some teaching, inspecting of schools, and even some small farming. They were lean years, but full of the joy of rearing their daughter, Mair.

Believing his Catholicism inimical to the success of his party, Lewis resigned as president of Plaid Cymru in 1939, and returned to his literary work more or less full time. It was in the post-war period that he produced a body of truly great Christian poetry in which he manages to juxtapose what was viewed with the eye of faith with what was evident to the rational eye. For instance, in 'Y lleidr da' ('The good thief'), Christ is seen alternately as 'a sack of bones … nailed on a pole … like a scarecrow' and as the God-man who was transfigured before the eyes of some of his disciples, who had walked on the water and raised the dead; a God on a gibbet or a flea-ridden robber. In the poem to Saint Joseph, 'Y saer' ('The carpenter'), we are presented with the harrowing doubts which must have afflicted Joseph that the child Mary was carrying was begotten of no earthly father, but of the Holy Spirit. In the poem 'Emmäws' ('Emmaus'), about the spot where Christ was said to have appeared to his disciples after his death and reported resurrection, Lewis admits that possibly all that there is is the poet himself 'awaiting the dawn of the one brief hour of Emmaus, that is no more'.

Most of this poetry appeared first in a slim volume entitled *Byd a betws* ('The world and the church') in 1941. However, the main body of Lewis's work is his plays, and it can be asserted that he put into them much of what he had failed to accomplish as a politician. They certainly often deal with public issues, with public figures, with prelates and potentates, with issues of public rather than private morality. In *Siwan* ('The King's Daughter') (1956), we are made to wonder whether Llywelyn should put his love for his wife above the demands of statecraft. We are meant to face the predicament of those who tried to assassinate Hitler in July 1944 in *Brad* ('Treason') (1958), while *Esther* (1960) causes us to confront the possible wrath of the king of Persia. There are no clichés, no easy answers, and the most dramatic elements focus on the interface between faith and reason. In *Gymerwch chi sigaret?* ('Would you Like a Cigarette?') (1956), an atheist husband working for a communist regime in eastern Europe during the cold war has to face the fact that his pregnant wife has sacrificed herself to the torturers and killers of the secret police rather than allow him to become a professional assassin for them. Her love is awesome: 'She loves me as if eternity existed' her husband proclaims. Here we have that dimension which seems absurd without the candle of faith.

In 1951 Lewis received the medal of the Honorable Society of the Cymmrodorion and emerged from the academic wilderness with his appointment as lecturer in Welsh at Cardiff in 1952. He retired in 1957, but his one last venture into politics was to deliver the BBC Wales annual radio lecture in 1962. He predicted the demise of the Welsh language by the turn of the century unless direct action was undertaken. This led to the founding of the Welsh Language Society which, with its militant but non-violent campaigning, has revolutionized the position of the language, and played a major part in arresting its decline and promoting bilingualism in public life. In 1964 he published his second and last novel, *Merch Gwern Hywel* ('The Daughter of Gwern Hywel'), a historical romance, and was honoured by the Welsh Arts Council in 1970. Ecumenically minded, Lewis as a Catholic was more interested in the deposit of faith and tremendous mystery than in matters of church discipline. Though a loyal and devout adherent of his church, he was not uncritical, especially about the changes of the Second Vatican Council leading to vernacular liturgy rather than the Tridentine Latin mass which he felt was the perfect way for a human being to worship God. He also criticized the church for its lack of identification with Wales and its history and culture. Although Lewis was made a knight of St Gregory the Great in 1975 by Pope Paul VI, characteristically he forbade his family and his friend and confessor Bishop Daniel Mullins to reveal the award until his funeral. Twice nominated for the Nobel prize for literature, he also received an honorary doctorate from the University of Wales in 1983.

Saunders Lewis died on 1 September 1985 in St Winifred's Hospital, Cardiff, after a long period of failing health. The cause of death was pneumonia and exhaustion in advanced old age. He had received the last rites of his church, and was given what amounted to a national funeral, with a requiem mass at St David's Cathedral, Cardiff, on 5 September 1985. Prominent church leaders of all denominations as well as politicians and public figures from all walks of life were present. He was buried with Margaret, who had died the previous year, in Penarth public cemetery. He was, many would maintain, the greatest Welsh writer since Dafydd ap Gwilym and, as *The Guardian* said in its obituary, 'He ranks with W. B. Yeats in Ireland and T. S. Eliot in England.' HARRI PRITCHARD-JONES

Sources A. R. Jones and G. Thomas, eds., *Presenting Saunders Lewis* (1973) · D. Tewyn Lloyd, *John Saunders Lewis* (1988) · *Saunders Lewis: letters to Margaret Gilcriest*, ed. M. Saunders Jones, N. Thomas, and H. Pritchard Jones (1998) · M. Saunders, *Saunders Lewis* (1987) · d. cert. · m. cert. · b. cert. · personal knowledge (2004) · d. cert. [Margaret Lewis, wife]

Archives NL Wales, papers · NL Wales, MS of speech made to jury in the Bombing School trial | Georgetown University, Washington, DC, letters to Norman Grisewood · NL Wales, corresp. with Kate Roberts · NL Wales, corresp. with Moses Griffith and Ceridwen Griffith · NL Wales, letters to W. J. Gruffydd · NL Wales, literary MSS, papers, and letters to Lewis Valentine · NL Wales, letters to his wife, typescript articles, and MS poems · NL Wales, corresp. with Emyr Humphreys · U. Wales, Bangor, letters to Robert O. F. Wynne

Likenesses P. Evans, drawing, NMG Wales [*see illus.*] · K. Wojnarowski, bust, U. Wales, Cardiff

Lewis, Stuart (*c*.**1756–1818**), poet, was born at Ecclefechan, Dumfriesshire, the son of an innkeeper with Jacobite sympathies; he was named after Prince Charles Edward Stuart, the Young Pretender. Lewis's school career was shortened by his father's early death following bankruptcy. For a time he was in partnership as a merchant tailor in Chester, but being ruined by his partner, who absconded to America with the firm's money, he returned to Ecclefechan to carry on the same occupation. He read and wrote popular verses, besides establishing a village library and a debating club. But his business did not prosper, and he enlisted into the Hopetoun fencibles. Here he augmented his regulation pay by what he received for writing suitable lyrics for the officers. On the disbanding of the regiment in 1799, Lewis was employed as a travelling cloth merchant in the west of England, but he may have become an alcoholic, and from about his fiftieth year roamed over Scotland in the areas around Edinburgh, East Kilbride and Dumfriesshire as 'the mendicant bard', picking up a livelihood as 'beggar, ballad-vendor, and tinker' (Walker, 648).

While at Ecclefechan Lewis produced his poem, 'Fair Helen of Kirkconnell' (1796). The poem, a much more elaborate ballad of villainy and tragic love than that by the same name in Walter Scott's *Minstrelsy of the Scottish Border*, was afterwards published for the author at Edinburgh in 1815. The preface, in which he tries to settle the history of the famous legendary ballad published by Scott on the same theme, is intelligent and valuable. *Moranza, or, The African slave, an address to poverty, and an elegy on a young gentleman who died at Angola* was published at Edinburgh in 1816, the first of these poems having been published originally in 1796. 'Moranza' appeals to 'Britons / sons of sacred liberty' to contemplate the barbarity of slavery. Of his miscellaneous lyrics, 'O'er the Muir' is noteworthy both for its poetic skill and because it is either an anticipation or an expansion of 'O'er the muir amang the heather', by Jean Glover (1758–1801). Lewis averred that his piece was the earlier, but the precise relationship of the two cannot be determined and it is probable that both have their origins in much older pastoral folk-songs. Fever, induced by a fall into the Nith, ended in Lewis's death at Ruthwell, Dumfriesshire, on 22 September 1818. His wife, with whom he seems to have had at least ten children, died a year before. T. W. BAYNE, *rev.* GERARD CARRUTHERS

Sources A. Roger, ed., *The modern Scottish minstrel*, 3 (1866) · A. Whitelaw, ed., *The book of Scottish song* (1844); repr. (1875) · W. Scott, *Minstrelsy of the Scottish border*, ed. T. F. Henderson (1931) · W. Walker, *The bards of Bon-Accord, 1375–1860* (1887) · R. Burns and others, *The Scots musical museum*, ed. J. Johnson, 6 vols. (1787–1803) · J. Mactaggart, *The Scottish Gallovidian encyclopedia* (1824); 2nd edn (1876) [repr. (1876)]

Archives Broughton House, Kirkcudbright, Hornel Library, letters and poems

Lewis, Ted [*known as* Kid Lewis, Ted Kid Lewis] (**1894–1970**), boxer, was born Gershon Mendaloff at 56 Umberston Street, St George-in-the-East, Aldgate, London, on 28 October 1894, the third of eight children and eldest son of Harris Mendaloff (*d.* 1939), cabinet-maker, and his wife, Leah (*d.* 1938). He was educated at the Jewish Free School in Bell Lane, Spitalfields, and followed his father's trade. Shortly before his fifteenth birthday he began boxing professionally as Kid Lewis at the Judaean social and athletic club, Whitechapel, where he had nearly fifty contests, and when Premierland opened he boxed there thirty-five times in 1912. The largest boxing saloon in the East End, this was a Jewish institution for twenty years. In October 1913 he won the British featherweight championship at the national sporting club, and the European title four months later.

In 1914 an offer from Australia took Lewis and his trainer, Alec 'Zalig' Goodman, to Sydney and five matches in three months, from where they sailed to the USA on business which lasted five years. It was here that 'Ted' was added to his name. Boxing mostly on the east coast, Lewis had half his fights restricted by law to no-decision contests. He won the world welterweight championship in Boston in August 1915 from Jack Britton and lost the title to the same man eight months later. Lewis regained the title from the Irish-American in June 1917, and lost it back to him in March 1919. They had met nineteen times.

Lewis returned to Britain for a contest on Boxing day

1919 at the Royal Albert Hall. He won the British and European welterweight titles in March and June respectively of 1920, and the British middleweight championship a year later. In May 1922 he lost by a knockout in the first round to Georges Carpentier in his challenge for the world's light-heavyweight crown. Lewis lost all his boxing titles during 1923–4, and had his last contest in 1929. In over 270 boxing matches he lost only thirty times. He never refused to fight and earned money voraciously, spent it excessively, and gave hand-outs endlessly. He was sentimental and politically naïve, and the outstanding British boxer at the heavier weights in the first half of the twentieth century.

In January 1917 Lewis married Elsie Schneider (*d.* 1962) in New York; she was from a Jewish family. They had one child, a son. Lewis died on 20 October 1970 at 105 Nightingale Lane, Balham, London, and was buried five days later. STAN SHIPLEY

Sources M. Lewis, *Ted Kid Lewis: his life and times* (1990) • G. E. Odd, *Ring battles of the century* (1948) • J. Goodwin, *Myself and my boxers* (1924) • d. cert. • m. cert. [Bessie Mendaloff]

Archives FILM BFI NFTVA, documentary footage • BFI NFTVA, news footage • BFI NFTVA, sports footage

Likenesses photograph, 1911, repro. in Lewis, *Ted Kid Lewis*, facing p. 78 • G. Belcher, coloured etching, 1919, NPG • photographs, 1920–25, Hult. Arch.

Lewis [*née* Villiers; *other married name* Lister], **Lady (Maria) Theresa (1803–1865)**, author, was the only daughter of George Villiers (1759–1827), third son of Thomas *Villiers, first earl of Clarendon, and his wife, Theresa Parker (1775–1856), daughter of John Parker, first Lord Boringdon. She was born on 8 March 1803 at Upper Grosvenor Street, London. The only sister in a close-knit, high-spirited, and sharply opinionated family of five brothers, she was especially close to the second of these, George *Villiers, who in 1838 became fourth earl of Clarendon and soon a prominent whig politician. Upon her brother's accession to the earldom she was granted (February 1839) the precedence of an earl's daughter. She married first, on 6 November 1830, Thomas Henry *Lister (1800–1842); with him she had one son, (Thomas) Villiers (later KCMG), and two daughters, (Marie) Thérèse, who married William Harcourt, and Alice, who married Algernon Borthwick, first Baron Glenesk. She married second, on 26 October 1844, George Cornewall *Lewis (1806–1863); they had no children. 'Very beautiful in her youth', she retained 'in more advanced years … a charming smile and an expression in her blue eyes which in her earlier days might have been called "playful mischief"' (Boyle, 270). She was a 'most fascinating hostess, clever, agreeable, accomplished' (Redesdale, 2.52), and thus a considerable asset to George Cornewall Lewis in his political career, the advancement of which she and her politician brothers, Clarendon and Charles *Villiers, assiduously promoted.

In 1852 Lewis published, in three volumes, *The lives of the friends and contemporaries of Lord Chancellor Clarendon: illustrative of the portraits in his gallery*. The lives were those of Viscount Falkland, Lord Capel, and the marquess of Hertford, whose portraits hung in the Clarendon gallery at the

Lady (Maria) Theresa Lewis (1803–1865), by Sir Edwin Landseer, 1836 [*The Mantilla*]

Grove, Watford, the country residence of the Villiers family. Lewis's work remains 'equally valuable for its information and intelligence' (Ollard, 357). She edited for publication in 1859 the Hon. Emily Eden's novel, *The Semi-Detached House*, and, in 1865, *Extracts of the Journals and Correspondence of Miss [Mary] Berry from the Years 1783 to 1852*. Her taste, as might be inferred from her association with Eden and Berry and from her publications, had been formed early in the century: in 1857 she trusted 'to outlive the absurdity of the pre-Raphaelite School—the taste for Carlyle's writing and Tenison's [*sic*] poetry! We *are* getting over table turning and spirit rapping—that's some comfort' (Bodleian, MS Harcourt 615, fols. 100–01).

Lewis submitted to apparently successful surgery for the removal of a malignant tumour of the breast on 10 December 1862 (National Library of Wales, Harpton Court MS C2909). Soon thereafter she endured the deaths of her elder daughter (in childbirth) and, on 13 April 1863, of her husband. She herself died of cancer on 9 November 1865 in the lodgings of her relative, the principal of Brasenose College, Oxford. She was buried at her request beside her husband in Old Radnor parish church. D. A. SMITH

Sources H. E. Maxwell, *Life and letters of George William Frederick, fourth earl of Clarendon*, 2 vols. (1913) • *GM*, 3rd ser., 19 (1865), 802 • *A*

selection from the correspondence of Abraham Hayward, ed. H. E. Carlisle, 2 vols. (1886) • *Mary Boyle: her book*, ed. Sir C. Boyle (1901) • Lord Redesdale [A. B. Freeman-Mitford], *Memories*, 2 vols. (1915) • R. Ollard, *Clarendon and his friends* (1988) • Boase, *Mod. Eng. biog.*

Archives Bodl. Oxf., family corresp. | BL, letters to Lady Morley, Add. MS 48259 • Bodl. Oxf., Clarendon MSS • NL Wales, Harpton Court MSS

Likenesses R. J. Lane, lithograph, pubd 1828 (after a drawing by G. S. Newton, 1828), NPG • S. Cousins, mezzotint, pubd 1834 (after a drawing by G. S. Newton), BM, NPG • E. Landseer, oils on panel, 1836, priv. coll. [*see illus.*] • E. Landseer, sepia and wash sketch, 1836, Chatsworth House, Derbyshire • J. H. Robinson, line engraving, 1838 (after E. Landseer, 1836), BM, V&A • G. H. Phillips, mezzotint, 1842 (after drawing by G. S. Newton), BM, NPG; repro. in H. Murray, ed., *Gems of G. S. Newton* (1842) • Finden, stipple (after J. Hayter), BM, NPG • oils, Downton House, New Radnor

Wealth at death under £40,000: probate, 22 Jan 1866, *CGPLA Eng. & Wales*

Lewis, Thomas (*b.* 1689, *d.* in or after 1737), religious controversialist, was born at Kington, Herefordshire, on 14 March 1689, one of at least two sons of Stephen Lewis, vicar of Weobly and rector of Holgate, Shropshire, and Dorothy Spencer. He was educated at Hereford Free School under Mr Traherne and matriculated as a bible clerk from Corpus Christi College, Oxford, on 3 July 1704. He graduated BA on 6 February 1711 and was ordained priest at Worcester in 1713; it is not known when he proceeded MA. He had already made his high-church sympathies public in his first publication, *A Modest Vindication of the Church of England, from the Scandal of Popery* (1710). About this time his younger brother Stephen died while an undergraduate at Merton College, Oxford.

In February 1717 Lewis launched the first issue of a highly polemical periodical, *The Scourge, in Vindication of the Church of England*. Published every Monday it consisted of violent and abusive attacks on dissenters, Roman Catholics, and broad-churchmen alike. In the edition of 16 July 1717, at the height of the Bangorian controversy, Lewis roundly denounced the leading low-church bishop Benjamin Hoadly, taking as his biblical text 'Who is this uncircumcised Philistine that he should defie the Armes of the Living God?'. On 30 September he headed an attack on Scottish presbyterianism with the text 'Every beast loveth his like'. Such unrestrained high-church polemic successfully antagonized the ruling whig party, and *The Scourge* was presented by the grand jury of Westminster as the work of a libeller and an embroiler of the nation. Lewis, who promptly absconded, was ordered to stand trial for sedition at the king's bench. An anonymous response, *The Scourge Scourged, or, A Short Account of the Life of the Author of the Scourge*, appeared in 1718 full of obscene abuse of Lewis and his 'weekly excrement'.

From his hiding place Lewis defiantly published *The Danger of the Church Establishment of England from the insolence of the Protestant Dissenters* (1718), in which he accused the latitudinarian party of trying to destroy the Church of England by their tolerance towards dissenters. Though dissenters were his principal target, he saved his most bitter criticisms for Hoadly and like-minded Anglicans:

> those Latitudinarian Gentlemen, who nestle themselves, and grow fat by the Revenues of the Church, and yet with the most sanctified Ingratitude, are infinitely more severe in their Invectives upon her than the most *foul-mouth'd Dissenter*, or the *wildest* Libertine. (p. 65)

The pamphlet was rapidly reprinted, twice, and answered by a moderate anonymous pamphlet, *A Brief Answer to a Long Libel* (1718). When the doctrine of the Trinity was debated by leading dissenters at Salters' Hall in 1719, Lewis seized on their theological differences and portrayed them as both tyrannical and rebellious in *The Anatomy of the Heretical Synod of Dissenters at Salters-Hall* (1719).

For his next target Lewis turned to the writings of the freethinker John Toland, in particular the third part of his *Tetradymus* (1720). In *The History of Hypatia* (1721) Lewis championed St Cyril in his defence of orthodoxy against the Arian heretics and exonerated him from the charge of murdering Hypatia, the celebrated Neoplatonist philosopher of Alexandria. In refuting Toland's condemnation of Cyril he compared the high-church bishop Henry Sacheverell with Cyril, describing him as 'his faithful Successor in Zeal, against the Modern Novatians and the Arian Heresie' (p. 3). Lewis's other writings are mainly historical and include accounts of the Parthian empire and the antiquities of the Hebrew republic. His style remained combative and he courted further controversy by arguing in two pamphlets that the practice of burial in churches and churchyards was indecent and endangered public health.

About 1720 Lewis appears to have acted as curate at St Clement Danes, in London; this presumably was his only clerical appointment. After keeping a private boarding-school in Hampstead for several years, in 1737 he moved to Chelsea, from where he sent an account of his life to the bibliophile Thomas Rawlinson, in a letter dated 12 September 1737. His date and place of death are unknown. It is unlikely that he is the 'Rev. James Lewes' whose death at Chelsea on 8 September 1749 was reported in the *Gentleman's Magazine* (*GM*, 1st ser., 19, 1749, 429).

THOMAS SECCOMBE, *rev.* STEPHEN J. BARNETT

Sources Bodl. Oxf., MS Rawl. J, fol. 4, 33–6 • Foster, *Alum. Oxon.*, 1500–1714, vol. 3 • J. Darling, *Cyclopaedia Bibliographica* (1854) • Watt, *Bibl. Brit.* • Allibone, *Dict.* • W. T. Lowndes, *The bibliographer's manual of English literature*, ed. H. G. Bohn, [new edn], 6 vols. (1864) • private information (1892, 2004) • *IGI*

Lewis, Sir Thomas (1881–1945), physician, was born at Teigil House, Newport Road, Roath, Cardiff, on 26 December 1881, the third of the five children of Henry Lewis (1850–1916), a mining engineer, and his wife, Catherine Hannah, daughter of Owen Davies, of Cardiff, and his wife, Hannah. Apart from one year at Clifton College, Bristol, which he left owing to ill health, Lewis was educated entirely at home, at first by his mother, and for the last two years by a college tutor. Lewis said that, at the age of eleven, 'I decided to become a doctor for the curious reason that conjuring fascinated me and because two family doctors both conjured I fancied that doctoring was a prerequisite to sleight of hand.' (personal record, RS) At the age of sixteen he went to University College, Cardiff, for three years of preclinical work and graduated BSc with first-class honours. He was selected by his teacher,

Sir Thomas Lewis (1881–1945), by Evan John Walters, 1937

T. Swale Vincent, to undertake joint research work, and at the age of only twenty he wrote a 54-page article on the haemolymph glands, which became a standard work. This and other papers gained him the degree of DSc Wales at the age of twenty-three.

In 1902 Lewis entered University College Hospital, London, which became his medical home for the rest of his life, graduating MB BS with the gold medal in 1905. His lifelong interest in physiology was signalled by his election to the Physiological Society while he was still a student. He became house surgeon to Sir V. A. H. Horsley, and house physician to Sir Thomas Barlow. In 1907 he joined the staff of the Royal Naval Hospital and the City of London Hospital, took his MD by thesis, and was elected a fellow of University College, London. He took the MRCP exam in 1907 and was elected FRCP in 1913. In 1910 he was awarded the first Belt memorial fellowship. In 1911 he was appointed lecturer in cardiac pathology at University College Hospital, and assistant physician in 1913.

While still a house physician, Lewis did original work on the pulse and blood pressure and published seven papers. He then worked on the pulse and respiration, in the laboratory of E. H. Starling at University College, until in 1908 he met James Mackenzie, who stimulated him to undertake an analysis of irregular action of the heart beat. Lewis soon realized that the new invention by the Dutch physiologist, Willem Einthoven, of a string-galvanometer type of electrocardiograph was the only precise way to do this, so he went to Leiden to study the method. He and Einthoven became close collaborators and friends, and it was Lewis who became largely responsible for the clinical application of Einthoven's invention, a fact which Einthoven warmly acknowledged when he was awarded the Nobel Prize. Lewis's monograph in 1911, *The Mechanism of the Heart Beat*, established his worldwide reputation in this field. Having elucidated the mechanism of nearly every cardiac irregularity, he then undertook an original and technically demanding study of the spread of the excitation wave in the dog heart, which he described in papers to the Royal Society, which elected him a fellow in 1918. He became full physician to University College Hospital in 1919.

In 1916 Lewis married Alice Lorna Treharne James, daughter of Frank Treharne James. She was a handsome woman with much energy and charm, who gave him great support in his career. They had three children.

During the First World War Lewis became a physician at the Military Heart Hospital at Hampstead, London, and was appointed to the staff of the Medical Research Committee (later Council), which was the first full-time post in Britain for clinical research. He directed a study of the condition known as 'soldier's heart', and, having shown that it was not a cardiac condition, he renamed it the 'effort syndrome'. In 1918 he wrote the important monograph, *The Soldier's Heart and the Effort Syndrome*. By devising remedial exercises, he was able to return many soldiers to their duties, thus saving a huge loss of manpower; and for this he was appointed CBE in 1920 and was made a knight bachelor in 1921.

After the war Lewis, under the aegis of the Medical Research Council, established the department of clinical research at University College Hospital; there he continued his work on cardiac arrhythmias, which led to his famous hypothesis that a 'circus movement' was the mechanism of atrial flutter and fibrillation. In 1925 he declared that 'the cream is off' (Hollman, 1997) and changed from electrocardiographic work to a study of vascular reactions of the skin. In 1917 Lewis had been the first to show that the blood capillaries had independent contraction rather than being passive tubes, and he now investigated what he named the triple response of the skin to injury. He showed that this was due to the liberation of a chemical compound, similar or identical to histamine, which he labelled the 'H substance'. This work was summarized in 1927 in a monograph, *The Blood Vessels of the Human Skin and their Responses*.

Lewis then investigated peripheral vascular disease and was the first to show that Raynaud's disease was due to a local fault in the digital arteries. He studied the mechanism of muscle pain occurring with arterial disease of the legs, and showed it to be due to a chemical substance, the 'P factor'. This led to the third and last phase of his research career, which was research into the mechanism of pain. He was intrigued by the fact that injured skin becomes abnormally painful and postulated that this was mediated by a 'nocifensor system' of nerves. At the time there were few who believed in this hypothesis, but Lewis was later shown to have been correct. The hallmark of his work on the skin and on pain was the fact that it was done with the simplest of apparatus, yet with authoritative conclusions. He summarized his researches in this area in *Pain* (1942).

All Lewis's research had the common factor of applying the experimental method to clinical problems, and he named this type of work 'clinical science', a term he used as the title of his Harveian oration (1933) and his book, published in 1934. He had a passionate belief in the scientific validity of this discipline and with great zeal he set out in 1930 to promote the establishment of full-time and permanent posts in clinical research which at that time were few and far between in Britain. To help young research workers he founded, in 1930, the Medical Research Society, and in 1933 he changed the scope of his journal *Heart* (which he had founded with Mackenzie's help in 1909) and renamed it *Clinical Science*. He inspired young men such as George Pickering to enter the field of clinical science, and Sir Henry Dale wrote that they 'lived in the gleam of an eye—the eye of an eagle—which was always magnificent, indeed, but mild only on occasions when the mission was momentarily out of his mind' (Dale). Lewis's Harveian oration on clinical science, and other lectures, were republished in 1938 in *Research in Medicine and other Addresses*. Lewis had a tremendous output of work and personally wrote over 230 papers and 12 books.

Although Lewis's research work on the heart finished in 1925, he continued to practise in the speciality of cardiovascular disease (he disliked the term cardiology) for the rest of his life. He was an outstanding teacher at the bedside, where he emphasized the importance of accurate observation; and in 1933 he wrote a widely acclaimed book, *Diseases of the Heart*, for students and doctors.

Lewis was of medium height, bald from his twenties and slimly built. Everyone remarked on the penetrating look of his deep-set blue eyes, described by one American pupil as the '10,000-volt eyes' (Hollman, 1997). He was a stern taskmaster and he could be intimidating, but his zeal for the truth gained him the respect of all his associates and students. Lewis had amazing powers of concentration and drove himself relentlessly: 'the pace was terrific and it left his co-workers panting' (Drury and Grant, 146). He resented weekends and public holidays as interfering with his work, and he disliked light conversation when in his department. The daytime was reserved for experimental work in the laboratory, and he then worked late into the night at home, writing and reading. His reputation was especially high in the United States, where he made three lecture tours and gave important nominated lectures, such as the Harvey lecture in New York.

Lewis had a myocardial infarction (coronary thrombosis) when he was forty-five, and he then stopped smoking seventy cigarettes a day, being one of the first to realize that smoking injured the blood vessels. For two months of each year he stopped work and took up his hobbies of bird-watching and bird photography, and fishing. He had an outstanding collection of bird photographs and he gave as much attention to his hobbies as he did to his work. Lewis was a devoted father, and he and his wife constantly shared with their children their own interest in natural history.

Lewis received a royal medal from the Royal Society in 1927. In 1941 he was given their most prestigious award, the Copley medal, which in the previous 100 years had been given to only one other clinician, Lord Lister. He was honoured by many universities and foreign learned societies. He died from coronary heart disease on 17 March 1945 at his home, Clearburn, at Loudwater, Rickmansworth, Hertfordshire, and was buried in Llangasty churchyard by Llan-gors Lake, Brecknockshire, which from boyhood had been one of his favourite places to fish and to study nature. He was survived by his wife.

ARTHUR HOLLMAN

Sources A. N. Drury and R. T. Grant, *Obits. FRS*, 5 (1945–8), 179–202 • G. W. Pickering, 'Sir Thomas Lewis', *Clinical Science*, 6 (1946), 3–11 • H. H. Dale, 'Sir Thomas Lewis', *BMJ* (31 March 1945), 461–2 • A. Hollman, *Sir Thomas Lewis: pioneer cardiologist and clinical scientist* (1997) • A. Hollman, 'Sir Thomas Lewis: clinical scientist and cardiologist, 1881–1945', *Journal of Medical Biography*, 2 (1994), 63–70 • A. Hollman, 'Thomas Lewis — the early years', *British Heart Journal*, 46 (1981), 233–44 • H. B. Burchell, 'Sir Thomas Lewis: his impact on American cardiology', *British Heart Journal*, 46 (1981), 1–4 • personal record, RS • *WWW* • *CGPLA Eng. & Wales* (1945)

Archives Medical Research Council, London • UCL, diagrams, photographs, notes • Wellcome L., corresp. and papers | CAC Cam., corresp. with A. V. Hill • UCL, cardiographic and clinical research department files | FILM Wellcome L., 'The signs of venous congestion', PP/LEW

Likenesses photograph, 1920, repro. in Hollman, 'Sir Thomas Lewis: clinical scientist and cardiologist' • E. J. Walters, oils, 1937, NMG Wales [*see illus.*] • E. J. Walters, oils, 1938, Welsh National School of Medicine, Cardiff, Wales • photographs, Wellcome L.

Wealth at death £56,061 2*s*. 11*d*.: probate, 10 July 1945, *CGPLA Eng. & Wales*

Lewis, Sir Thomas Frankland, first baronet (1780–1855), politician, was born in Great Ormond Street, London, on 14 May 1780, the only son of John Lewis (1738–1797), barrister and landowner, of Harpton Court, Radnorshire, and his second wife, Ann (1753–1842), daughter of Admiral Sir Thomas *Frankland, bt, of Thirkleby Park, Yorkshire. He was educated at Eton College and at Christ Church, Oxford, but took no degree. His father having died during his minority, Lewis succeeded to the family's extensive Radnorshire estates in 1801 and immediately set about improving them by means of agricultural innovations, enclosure, and new purchases. Among his best tenants was Wordsworth's brother-in-law, Tom Hutchinson. The family seat at Harpton Court, Old Radnor, was completely refashioned by John Nash. On 11 March 1805 Lewis married Harriet, fourth daughter of Sir George Cornewall, bt, of Moccas Court, Herefordshire, with whom he had two sons, George Cornewall *Lewis (1806–1863) and Gilbert Frankland Lewis (*b*. 1808); she predeceased him, on 11 August 1838.

Ambitious to represent either his county or the Radnor boroughs in parliament, Lewis was unsuccessful in early attempts but was brought in for Beaumaris by its patron, Lord Bulkeley, in 1812. He held this seat until 1826, when

Sir Thomas Frankland Lewis, first baronet (1780–1855), by Richard James Lane, 1826 (after Joseph Slater)

he accepted Sir Edward O'Brien's offer of the Irish borough of Ennis. In parliament he followed Bulkeley in adhering to Lord Grenville's independent whig faction. Having 'quite from a boy turned his mind to political oeconomy', as his mother fondly recalled, he soon developed a reputation for mastery of difficult economic questions. He took a leading role in the 1817 Commons select committee on the poor laws, chaired by Sturges Bourne, and is said to have written its report; certainly he endorsed its condemnation of poor laws as conducive to low wages, low morals, and high population. The report was an important early marker in the drift towards the drastic restriction of poor relief, but it did not offer any immediate practical solutions. In 1819 he played a part in the movement to force the resumption of cash payments by the Bank of England and in 1820 blamed the corn laws for aggravating agricultural distress, though he had voted for the 1815 Corn Bill.

In all this Lewis shared Grenville's tendency towards a strict economic liberalism and a growing conservatism in constitutional matters (excepting the Catholic claims, with which he consistently sympathized). He voted for the suspension of habeas corpus in 1817 and, with Grenville's consent, joined the government's commission of inquiry into the Irish revenue in 1821. To his disappointment this and similar services (the revenue commission of 1822 and the Irish education commission of 1825–8) did not lead to government office.

Lewis's hopes revived with the ascendancy of Canning and Huskisson in 1827. In September of that year he was appointed financial secretary to the Treasury and in February 1828 became vice-president of the Board of Trade and was sworn of the privy council. In the same month a sudden vacancy in the representation of Radnorshire allowed him to attain this other long-desired position. Lewis enjoyed office, its status and emoluments, so it was with great reluctance that he resigned with Huskisson in May 1828, resisting the lure dangled before him by Wellington of the chief secretaryship of Ireland. He was able to return in February 1830 when Wellington appointed him treasurer of the navy, a sinecure which promptly came under radical attack.

After leaving office with Wellington in November 1830, Lewis maintained a mild but distinct opposition to the whig ministry and its Reform Bill. Among other reasons, he felt that a wider electorate would be too corruptible and sectional, heedless of public interests like free trade. The whigs, however, appointed him first chairman of the poor law commission for England and Wales in August 1834, as it was thought that the leadership of a tory country gentleman would lend authority to the new poor law. He did indeed work well with landlords of both parties in implementing the law, but not so well with the commission's secretary, Edwin Chadwick, whose personal and administrative ambitions he scorned. Poor health forced Lewis's retirement in January 1839, when he was succeeded on the commission by his son George.

Recruiting his health by continental travel and (on 15 October 1839) marrying a younger woman with an independent fortune of £40,000 (Marianne (1796–1868), daughter of Captain John Ashton), Lewis's interest in politics slowly returned, particularly after Peel's accession to power in 1841. He chaired the commission of inquiry into the Rebecca riots in Wales in 1843, showing sympathy with the rioters' cause; and in June 1846, just as the ministry was dissolving, Peel rewarded him with a baronetcy in recognition of 'the publick services of yourself and your son'. He successfully contested the Radnor boroughs in 1847, in part to preserve his interest there (with George's future in mind) and in part to support Peel. For eight years he rendered uneventful service to Peel and his political heirs, until his death at Harpton Court on 22 January 1855. He was buried in his parish church of Old Radnor.

Lewis was a rather preachy and officious but well-informed and industrious politician of the second rank, described by McCullagh Torrens as 'formal, verbose, and dull', but by Mrs Arbuthnot as 'a very agreeable clever man' with a 'farming mania'. He travelled widely, observing closely (and usually disapprovingly) the different social and political arrangements of other countries; and he collected art. He was a big fish in the small pond of Radnorshire—a leading light in agricultural, educational, and church affairs there. His brand of liberal-Conservatism—Grenvillite, Canningite, Peelite—did much to reconcile tory country gentlemen to changes (particularly in social and economic policy) that helped to forestall violent constitutional convulsions. PETER MANDLER

Sources NL Wales, Harpton Court papers • *The Times* (24 Jan 1855) • R. G. Thorne, 'Lewis, Thomas Frankland', HoP, *Commons* • G. F. Lewis, *Letters of the Rt. Hon. Sir George Cornewall Lewis, bt.* (1870) • S. E. Finer, *The life and times of Sir Edwin Chadwick* (1952) • W. Davies, *General view of the agriculture and domestic economy of south Wales*, 2 vols. (1814) · D. Williams, *The Rebecca riots* (1971) · J. J. Sack, *The Grenvillites, 1801–1829* (1979) · J. Williams and E. Davies, *A general history of the county of Radnor* (1905) · J. R. Poynter, *Society and pauperism: English ideas on poor relief, 1795–1834* (1969) · B. Hilton, *Corn, cash, commerce: the economic policies of the tory governments, 1815–1830* (1977) · R. C. B. Oliver, 'The (Wordsworth) Hutchinsons in Radnorshire', *Radnorshire Society Transactions*, 49 (1979), 24–46

Archives NL Wales, corresp. and papers | BL, corresp. with Sir Robert Peel, Add. MSS 40344–40595, *passim*

Likenesses T. Wright, stipple, pubd 1822 (after A. Wivell), BM, NPG · R. J. Lane, lithograph, 1826 (after J. Slater), BM, NPG [*see illus.*] · G. F. Watts, engraving, *c*.1845–1850, NL Wales · G. F. Watts, portrait, 1849, priv. coll. · J. Hoppner, oils, Eton · T. H. Maguire, lithograph (after G. F. Watts), BM, NPG

Wealth at death under £14,000; plus real estate, tithes and leasehold house at 31 Welbeck St, London; Lewis estates in Radnorshire valued at £7000 p.a.: will, Bateman, *The Great landowners of Great Britain and Ireland* (1876)

Lewis, Thomas Taylor (1799/1800–1858), geologist, was baptized on 26 January 1801 at Ludlow, Shropshire, the son of Edward Lewis (*d*. before 1838), a farmer, and his wife, Ann. He was educated at Cheam School, Surrey, under the Revd James Welchin, and was admitted to St John's College, Cambridge, on 5 October 1819, from where he graduated BA in 1825 and proceeded MA in 1828.

Lewis was appointed curate of Aymestrey, Herefordshire, in 1826, perpetual curate of Leinthall Earls on 17 March 1832, and vicar of Bridstow, near Ross, from 1841. On 24 April 1827 he married Eliza, eldest daughter of James Penfold of Cheam, Surrey. On 21 June 1838 he married Elizabeth Jane Woodhouse of Kensington, Middlesex, daughter of George Ferguson, a naval captain.

Lewis had attended Adam Sedgwick's lectures at Cambridge, and on becoming curate of Aymestrey:

> laboured zealously at the rocks and fossils, at a time when there were no ordnance maps of the district, and by the year 1829 he had traced the succession of the great groups of strata afterwards assigned to the Upper Silurian System. (Woodward, 94)

Lewis was a diligent local geologist, and formed a large collection of fossils in the neighbourhood of Aymestrey, paying particular attention to the Silurian period.

Lewis communicated the findings of his researches to the geologist Roderick Impey Murchison, whom he greatly assisted in the latter's work on the rocks and fossils of Caer Caradog, Ludlow, Aymestrey, and the Wenlock district. Murchison remarked that 'the application of his leisure hours to the cultivation of the natural history of his neighbourhood may one day enable Mr. Lewis to confer upon Aymestry the celebrity which White has bequeathed to Selborne' (R. I. Murchison, 'Silurian system', 201; *Proceedings of the Geological Society*, 1.449), while Fitton stated that Lewis was 'the only person who, previously to the author's inquiries, had determined the relations of any continuous portion of the stratigraphic series beneath the Old Red Sandstone, on the double evidence of superposition and of fossil contents' (Woodward, 94). On making Murchison's acquaintance Lewis 'cheerfully resigned' his subject to 'a geologist whose practical knowledge was much greater than his own' (*Edinburgh Review*, 33, 1841, 1–41), and reportedly resolved not to publish an account of the local geology. However, his memory was preserved in the names of local fossils, such as the *Lingula lewisii*, *Spirorbis lewisii*, and *Cephalapis lewisii*. He also edited the *Letters of Lady Brilliana Harley* in 1854, for the Camden Society. Lewis died, aged fifty-eight, from kidney disease on 28 October 1858 at the vicarage in Bridstow, and was survived by his second wife. YOLANDA FOOTE

Sources *GM*, 3rd ser., 6 (1859), 93 · J. Foster, ed., *Index ecclesiasticus, or, Alphabetical lists of all ecclesiastical dignitaries in England and Wales since the Reformation* (1890) · Venn, *Alum. Cant.* · Boase, *Mod. Eng. biog.* · H. B. Woodward, *The history of the Geological Society of London* (1907) · *DNB* · *CGPLA Eng. & Wales* (1859) · d. cert.

Archives GS Lond., letters to Roderick Impey Murchison

Wealth at death under £6000: probate, 19 Jan 1859, *CGPLA Eng. & Wales*

Lewis, Timothy Richards (1841–1886), pathologist and parasitologist, was born on 31 October 1841 in Llanboidy, Carmarthenshire, the eldest of eight children of William Lewis and his wife, Britannia Richards. Both parents came from established farming families, and Lewis's early years were spent at Crinow Farm, Narberth. Lewis left the grammar school in Narberth at fifteen to become apprenticed to a Narberth druggist. Four years later he was in London, first with a Mr Porter, an 'operative chemist' of Streatham, and next at the German Hospital in Dalston as an apothecary. As well as acquiring skills in chemistry and the German language, Lewis attended lectures at University College, London, and was awarded the Fellowes medal in 1866. His formal medical qualification (MB, 1867) was, however, gained from the University of Aberdeen. In February 1868 Lewis came first in the London examination for entry to the Army Medical School in Netley, and did equally well in the course. He was commissioned assistant surgeon on 31 March 1868, surgeon on 1 March 1873, and surgeon-major on 31 March 1880.

Lewis's career was decisively influenced by his being chosen in 1868 to study the current theories of cholera causation, first in Germany and then in India. His colleague on this officially sponsored mission was Douglas Cunningham of the Indian Medical Service, with whom Lewis was to collaborate for most of his career. While in Munich, Lewis made the acquaintance of another lifelong colleague, the epidemiologist Max von Pettenkofer. Lewis and Cunningham reached Calcutta in January 1869, and Lewis worked in India, with one interval, until 1883. In 1879 Lewis spent several months visiting European laboratories. His pathological researches and field studies appeared regularly in the form of official reports presented by Dr J. M. Cuningham, then sanitary commissioner with the government of India, and were concerned with such subjects as cholera, leprosy, 'oriental sore', enteric fever, relapsing fever, and prison dietaries.

Lewis's pre-eminence as a microscopist led in 1869 to his discovery in human urine of one stage of the filaria parasite, later known as *Wuchereria bancrofti*. Pursuing this finding, Lewis published in 1872 the first observation of nematode haematozoa in human blood, and coined the term *Filaria sanguinis hominis*. In 1877 he observed the adult male and female forms. In 1870 he gave the first authentic account of amoebae in the human intestine.

Lewis returned to England in March 1883 as assistant professor of pathology at the Army Medical School in Netley, where he introduced practical instruction in modern methods of bacteriological enquiry. From 1884 to his death Lewis was involved in critically evaluating Robert Koch's bacteriological explanation of cholera.

On 8 October 1879 Lewis married Emily Brown, daughter of James Brown of Lewisham. Lewis died childless on 7 May 1886 at his home, Bywood, in Woolston, near Southampton, from pneumonia, possibly aggravated by septicaemia. He gained only minimal official recognition for his work; his early death at forty-four prevented his election to the Royal Society. His name is associated with the first description (published 1878) of a mammalian trypanosome (*T. lewisi*). MARGARET PELLING, *rev.*

Sources *BMJ*, 1 (1886) • *The Lancet* (1886) • *In memoriam: physiological and pathological researches, being a reprint of the principal scientific writings of the late T. R. Lewis*, ed. W. Aitken, G. E. Dobson, and A. E. Brown (1888) • C. Dobell, *Parasitology*, 14 (1922), 413–16 • M. Walker, *Pioneers of public health* (1930) • L. Morton, *A medical bibliography* (1983) • *Western Mail and South Wales News* (12 Jan 1929)
Archives NL Wales, papers
Likenesses photograph, repro. in *Western Mail and South Wales News*
Wealth at death £3935 5*s.* 2*d.*: probate, 1886, *CGPLA Eng. & Wales*

Lewis, Titus (1773–1811), Particular Baptist preacher and author, was born on 21 February 1773 at Pentre, Cilgerran, Pembrokeshire, the second of three sons of Thomas Lewis (*d.* 1788) and Martha Evans, his wife. A shoemaker by profession, his father also served as a minister of the Baptist church at Cilfowyr, near Cardigan. Baptized by immersion on profession of faith on 1 July 1794 at Cilfowyr's daughter congregation of Blaenywaun, St Dogmaels, by Cardigan, Titus started preaching on 28 December 1794. Some time after Blaenywaun's constitution as a separate and autonomous church in March 1795, Lewis was invited to become its pastor and was ordained on 24 January 1798. Already a popular and effective preacher, he would henceforth exercise considerable influence within the dissenting community of south-west Wales.

Initially a shoemaker like his father, Lewis's marriage on 20 November 1800 to Elizabeth Havard (*d.* 1812), a prosperous member of the Dark Gate Baptist Church at Carmarthen, afforded him considerable financial independence. His connection with Blaenywaun was weakened by his removal, following his marriage, to his wife's home at Carmarthen, and from 1801 he combined his ministry there with oversight of the Dark Gate congregation in the town. Of his six children, two, Mary and John, died during their infancy while a third, Titus, survived until he was ten. A second Mary (1805–1841) eventually married the Revd H. W. Jones, one of Lewis's successors as minister of the Dark Gate church (by then called Tabernacle) at Carmarthen; Elizabeth (1807–1846) married John Jones, a Cardigan apothecary; while the youngest son, George, remained unmarried and practised as a lawyer in Carmarthen.

Like many Welsh dissenting ministers of his generation Lewis was virtually self-taught, but this did not prevent his contributing substantially to the religious culture of his day. He was an uncompromising Baptist and a zealous evangelical Calvinist; he was among the leaders chosen by the south-west Wales Baptist Association to preach on the Calvinist 'five points' in a meeting called at Carmarthen on 26 March 1799 to refute the charge of Arminianism. His Baptist principles were most readily expressed in his polemical tracts and in his much used catechism *Holwyddoreg y Bedyddwyr Neillduol* (numerous editions), while his doctrinal stance is evident from his manuscript sermons (deposited in the National Library of Wales), the notes appended to Christmas Evans's *Ffurf yr ymadroddion Iachus* (1803) and his other writings which include theological treatises, commentaries and hymns. Although Lewis's interests were predominantly religious they also extended to lexicography and history: he published *A Welsh-English Dictionary* (1805) and a 600-page history of Great Britain, *Hanes Prydain Fawr, yn wladol a chrefyddol* (1810).

Animated by the spirit of the evangelical revival, early nineteenth century dissent was poised to become a major force in the religious, social, and ultimately political life of Wales. Titus Lewis was typical of its most able and energetic leaders during that period. His death, of tuberculosis, at the height of his powers on 1 May 1811, at Carmarthen, was much lamented by the then dramatically expanding Welsh Baptist movement. He was the first to be interred in the burial-ground of Tabernacle Chapel, Carmarthen. D. DENSIL MORGAN

Sources E. T. Jones, 'Pennod o hanes Titus Lewis: ei lafur gweinidogaethol', *Trafodion Cymdeithas Hanes Bedyddwyr Cymru* (1908–9), 16–28 • R. T. Jenkins, 'Cwrdd chwarter Bedyddwyr glannau Teifi, 1794–1824', *Trafodion Cymdeithas Hanes Bedyddwyr Cymru* (1942), 5–32 • T. M. Bassett, *The Welsh Baptists* (1977) • E. T. Jones, 'Rhai o weinidogion cyntaf Cilfowyr', *Trafodion Cymdeithas Hanes Bedyddwyr Cymru* (1913–14), 15–22 • parish register (baptism), St Dogmael, Blaen-y-waun, Cardigan, 1 July 1794
Archives NL Wales • U. Wales, Bangor | NL Wales, MS 5395B • U. Wales, Bangor, MS 1511

Lewis, Wilfrid Bennett (1908–1987), physicist and civil servant, was born on 24 June 1908 in Castle Carrock, Cumberland, the second of four children of Arthur Wilfrid Lewis, a civil engineer, and his wife, Isoline Maud Steavenson. Lewis was a keen boyhood science experimenter and wireless enthusiast. After elementary education at Clare House Preparatory School, Beckenham, Kent, he attended Haileybury College (1922–6), followed by a year in industry. Entering Gonville and Caius College, Cambridge in 1927, he read physics at the Cavendish Laboratory (BA, 1930; MA, 1934; PhD, 1934). During postgraduate studies he worked with Lord Rutherford. Lewis was research fellow at Gonville and Caius College (1934–40), and demonstrator (1935–7) and lecturer (1937–9) in physics at Cambridge. Between 1935 and 1937 he joined J. D. Cockcroft in studying nuclear disintegration, then turned his electronic expertise to the construction of the Cambridge cyclotron. In 1939 he joined what became the Telecommunications Research Establishment (TRE) to work on radar development, quickly establishing a reputation as a scientific administrator. He ended his career with the TRE at Malvern (1945–6) as chief superintendent. His wartime work garnered him a CBE in 1946 and the American medal of freedom with silver palms in 1947.

Cockcroft had supervised the Canadian National Research Council's nuclear programme from April 1944. On his recall to England he nominated Lewis as his replacement. Lewis took up the post of director of its atomic energy division in September 1946. The division was just creating its new research centre at Chalk River, Ontario. He came with little knowledge of current nuclear physics and engineering, but with characteristic single-mindedness learned everything he could. His first task was to ensure completion of the national research experimental reactor, known as the NRX, which went critical in 1947. This was the world's finest high flux research reactor; it was also the first to have a nuclear accident in the same year, but Lewis responded coolly. The incident convinced him of the need for another research reactor, the NRU. Planning began in 1947 but it would not go critical until ten years later.

Lewis maintained regular scientific contact with Harwell, undertaking experimental work for Cockcroft in the 1950s, and exchanging scientific information with the British and American atomic energy agencies. When, in 1952, the government reorganized the division as a crown corporation, Atomic Energy of Canada Ltd (AECL), Lewis became vice-president, research and development. This allowed him to shed general administrative duties to concentrate on reactor design. As early as 1951 Lewis had championed the idea of a power reactor fuelled with natural uranium and moderated by heavy water. He persuaded the AECL board to support it and brought Ontario Hydro into the fold. Serious planning began in 1954. As a first step a nuclear power demonstration reactor (NPD) was built in Rolphton, Ontario. Its design and construction was a convoluted process, as AECL scientists and engineers grappled with conflicting technologies. Lewis acted as a stimulus and arbiter. When NPD began supplying power in 1962 it proved that the Canadian approach was feasible. By 1959 planning began for a power station employing the CANDU system, with horizontal pressure tubes, using natural uranium fuel and heavy water as both coolant and moderator. Lewis pushed the programme to successful completion of a full-scale commercial plant in 1971.

A key figure in international nuclear diplomacy, Lewis advised the World Bank, served on the United Nations scientific advisory committee, and helped to organize conferences on the peaceful uses of atomic energy. He sat on the scientific advisory committee of the International Atomic Energy Agency (1958–78). From 1963 until his retirement on 24 June 1973 he was senior vice-president, science, at AECL. Queen's University in Kingston, Ontario, then appointed him distinguished professor of science. He continued to lecture and to write in favour of nuclear power. A winner of the Fermi prize (1982) and a fellow of the royal societies of London (1945) and Canada (1952), Lewis garnered many awards and honorary degrees. A devout Anglican and community figure he remained unmarried. Diagnosed as having Alzheimer's disease in 1982 he spent his last five years in hospital, and died in Deep River, Ontario, on 10 January 1987, where he was buried.

RICHARD A. JARRELL

Sources R. Fawcett, *Nuclear pursuits: the scientific biography of Wilfrid Bennett Lewis* (1994) · R. Bothwell, *Nucleus: the history of Atomic Energy of Canada Limited* (1988) · A. J. Mooradian, 'Wilfrid Bennett Lewis, 1908–1987', *Proceedings and Transactions of the Royal Society of Canada*, 5th ser., 3 (1988), 165–7 · 'Lewis, W. Bennett', *McGraw-Hill modern scientists and engineers*, 2 (1980) · 'Lewis, Wilfrid Bennett', *Canadian Who's Who* (1986)

Archives CUL, notebooks · King's Lond., Liddell Hart C., papers · Queen's University, Kingston, Ontario | Atomic Energy of Canada Limited, Ottawa, Ontario records · Chalk River Nuclear Laboratories, Chalk River, Ontario, Ontario records · NA Canada, National Research Council records · PRO, United Kingdom Atomic Energy Authority records, AB6, AB19 · PRO, Telecommunications Research Establishment records, AVIA 7, 8, 15

Lewis, Sir Wilfrid Hubert Poyer (1881–1950), judge, was born in London on 9 February 1881, the eldest son of Arthur Griffith Poyer Lewis (1848–1909), a practising barrister and recorder of Carmarthen, of Henllan, Narberth, Pembrokeshire, and his wife, Annie Wilhelmine (*d.* 1930), daughter of James Ellison MD, surgeon to the household of Queen Victoria. His paternal grandfather, Richard Lewis (1821–1909), was bishop of Llandaff.

Tall, good-looking, and sociable, Lewis was educated at Eton College, where he played cricket, football, and fives, and University College, Oxford, where he took a third in modern history in 1903. From an early age he was well endowed with those social graces which he preserved throughout his life.

From heredity and temperament the church and the law provided the alternatives for his life's work. Lewis chose the law and read in the chambers of J. A. Simon, and John Sankey. In 1908 he was called to the bar by the Inner Temple, and began practice in Cardiff where family connections gave him a start and his own ability a rapidly expanding practice. On 29 July 1908 he married Margaret Annie (*d.* 1932), daughter of Sir John Eldon *Bankes, who became a lord justice of appeal. They had one son and four daughters. He married secondly, on 28 July 1934, Elizabeth Barty, daughter of David Barty King MD of London. There were two sons of the second marriage.

Lewis maintained his interest in church affairs throughout his life as a member of the provincial and special provincial courts of the Church in Wales, and of the joint and choir committees of the Temple Church, besides serving as chancellor of the dioceses of Llandaff, Monmouth, Manchester, Blackburn, and Worcester. In 1914 when war broke out, although he was the father of a young family, Lewis applied for and obtained a commission in the Glamorgan yeomanry. He served in France as aide-de-camp to Sir Charles Fergusson who commanded the 5th division and subsequently the II and XVII corps. Lewis was older and more mature than the usual run of aides-de-camp, and his relationship with the corps commander was one of close friendship. He was twice mentioned in dispatches and was awarded a military OBE.

After the war Lewis had to decide whether to resume his local practice at Cardiff or to accept an invitation to join T. W. H. Inskip, subsequently lord chancellor (as Viscount Caldecote) in the old chambers of his father-in-law at 3 Hare Court. His choice of London brought rapid success. He was regularly briefed for a leading London newspaper in actions for libel and for the Great Western Railway in their multifarious common-law litigation. The variety of his practice was remarkable and took him far outside the ordinary range of a common-law junior. His old clients in south Wales and elsewhere briefed him in commercial and admiralty cases, and he had almost a monopoly of the specialized prize-money cases arising from the war. He was an acknowledged authority on ecclesiastical law. Within seven years from the end of the war he had one of the largest and most varied practices in the Temple. In 1930, when the post of junior (common law) counsel to the Treasury ('Treasury devil') fell vacant, his appointment by the attorney-general (William Jowitt) was a foregone conclusion. A bencher in 1929, his appointment as a judge of the king's bench division, in succession to Horace Avory, followed with a knighthood in June 1935.

Lewis brought to the bench, besides great natural dignity and a fine presence, a wide experience of life and, although he was never an academic lawyer, a profound knowledge of the law and its practical application. The direct contact between judge and citizen he regarded as the highest judicial duty, and in this his inclinations tallied with his qualifications, pre-eminently those of a judge of first instance. On the bench he was courteous, patient, and detached. He never sought the limelight or to attract attention to himself. He was essentially a shy man, which in some quarters gave the impression that he was unsympathetic towards the Welsh view of life. This was not the case. While a separation between Wales and England was abhorrent to him, he was intensely proud of his long Welsh descent and valued the Welsh way of life which he did much to cherish and preserve.

Although his work occupied the greater part of his life, it was not his main object or interest. Lewis had inherited an estate in Pembrokeshire which had been in his family for many centuries. He was at heart a countryman, and his tastes were those of a Welsh squire. Although he gave ungrudgingly to the service of the law, this was a means to the end of keeping up his property and preserving it from passing into the hands of strangers. It was in Pembrokeshire during his short periods of leisure that he was happiest, managing his estates, visiting his farms, discharging the duties and enjoying the activities of a country gentleman. He was a deputy lieutenant for the county, chairman of quarter sessions, a trustee of Llandovery College, besides giving much time to the affairs of the Welsh church. He was a fellow of Eton (1940) and became an honorary fellow of his college (1943), two honours which gave him great pleasure. He was a keen shot, a fisherman, enjoyed a game of golf, and in particular gained much pleasure from deer stalking. He appreciated fine painting, a good play, but not the cinema, and was well read. He was a most hospitable man, a charming host, and attracted and held the warm affection of his many friends.

From 1946 to 1949 Lewis chaired a committee to inquire into the court martial system. In 1950 he would have completed fifteen years on the bench and might well have considered retiring and devoting the remainder of his life to his many interests and activities in south Wales, but the strain of the Second World War, during which he served in the Home Guard, left its mark. In January he was taken ill in the middle of a trial at the central criminal court and he died in the Middlesex Hospital, London, on 15 March 1950. He was survived by his wife.

Lewis was a fine judge. In private life he concealed great warmth of feeling beneath an unemotional exterior. He had an exacting sense of duty, and one who knew him well said that his chief characteristic was humility.

W. N. STABLE, *rev.* M. C. CURTHOYS

Sources *The Times* (16 March 1950), 9 • *The Times* (20 March 1950), 7d • *Law Times* (24 March 1950), 161–2 • Burke, *Gen. GB* (1952), Lewis of Henllan • private information (1959, 2004) • personal knowledge (1959, 2004) • Sainty, *Judges* • *CGPLA Eng. & Wales* (1950)
Likenesses W. Stoneman, two photographs, 1935, NPG
Wealth at death £23,574 5*s*. 3*d*. save and except settled land; £61,549 limited to settled land: probate, 27 June 1950, *CGPLA Eng. & Wales*

Lewis, William (1591/2–1667), Church of England clergyman, was a native of Merioneth, and probably the son of Dr Richard Lewis of Llanaber (the son of Lewis ap Tudur of Egrin) and his wife, a sister of Theodore *Price, then rector of Llanfair. He matriculated from Hart Hall, Oxford, and graduated BA on 20 April 1608. On 15 September 1609 he became a fellow of Oriel College, and he proceeded MA on 21 June 1612. One of those engaged to solicit contributions for the rebuilding of Oriel, begun in March 1613, he recalled in his will that he also laid the foundation stone. A series of vacant fellowships led him to gain seniority in the college very quickly, and on 10 January 1618, aged only twenty-six, and having recently become chaplain to the new lord chancellor, Sir Francis Bacon, he was elected dean. Five days later the provostship became vacant following the death of Anthony Blencowe. On 21 February—in the absence of the most senior fellow, Robert Cockram—Lewis presided over a college meeting attended by only eight of his seventeen colleagues, at which a bare majority of five elected him provost. The decision was confirmed by Bishop George Montaigne of Lincoln, and on 28 March Lewis was installed, but the affair aroused considerable protest and four fellows resigned. With dubious legality Bacon then claimed authority to settle the dispute in a letter of 11 July, which Lewis read out before the college. John Chamberlain reported that Bacon had secured his chaplain's appointment in the face of opposition from both Archbishop George Abbot and Bishop John King of London, who argued that 'the unfitness of his age was the way to bring the university into disrepute' (*Letters of John Chamberlain*, 2.139–40).

On 30 April 1621, just before Bacon's disgrace, Lewis secured a three-year pass for travel abroad. On 23 June,

Chamberlain reported that the chancellor's 'fine chaplain … is run away to Paris, some say for debt, some for a fouler fault' (*Letters of John Chamberlain*, 2.385). In his later attack on Archbishop William Laud and his protégés William Prynne was less restrained, alleging that Lewis 'fled hence for sodomy' (W. Prynne, *Canterburies Doome*, 1646, index *sub* Lewes). The sympathetic John Walker noted of Lewis's tenure as provost that, 'indulging himself in some things very unbecoming of it, he was in a manner forced to resign it' (Walker, 77). On 29 June 1621 the new dean of Oriel, John Taylor, recorded Lewis's resignation.

Lewis seems to have returned to Merioneth, but his career was by no means finished. At an unknown date he became secretary and chaplain to the duke of Buckingham, and a report of Walker suggests that he attended the duke on his visit to Paris in May 1625. Between March and December 1626 Lewis was certainly a paid servant of Charles I in Paris. In January 1627 he wrote to Buckingham of the need to counter the French maritime build-up in the channel now proceeding under Cardinal Richelieu's direction and of his perception of the cardinal's insecurity and consequent intention to lean for support on the *dévots*. On 26 February, however, Zorzi, the Venetian ambassador to Paris, reported that 'Secretary Lewis departed today without money and very ill-pleased' (*CSP Venice, 1626–8*, 132).

Compensation came almost immediately. The king presented Lewis, on 9 March 1627, to a canonry at Winchester and the same year to the mastership of the hospital of St Cross in the same diocese. Perhaps as a result of his marriage—if, as seems likely, he was the William Lewis who married Alice Ratcliffe on 10 June 1630 at St Vedast, Foster Lane, London—Lewis considered himself under some financial hardship. Writing on 10 September 1630 to secretary of state Dudley Carleton, Viscount Dorchester (who had been envoy to Paris in 1626), Lewis lamented that his income from the hospital, despite its great reputation, amounted to less than £300 per annum, and asked that the king be pressed to request Bishop Richard Neile of Winchester to grant him one of two vacant local livings in his gift. Three days later Charles complied, and although there was concern that the livings were already promised, Lewis seems to have succeeded: in 1631 he was instituted to the Hampshire rectory of East Woodhay. Thereafter his circumstances appear more comfortable. It was claimed in 1635 that he continued to preach regularly at the hospital and that he had spent £1000 of his own money on its maintenance. In 1636 he was able to contribute £100 to construction work at Oriel.

Lewis's good fortune probably stemmed partly from the favour of Archbishop Laud. On 25 June 1635 he was one of the archiepiscopal commissaries who imposed on Daniel Sauvage of the French church, Southampton, the new policy that foreigners should attend parish churches unless specifically exempted. In a letter received by Laud on 21 November 1639, Lewis reported on a copyhold dispute involving the dean and chapter of Winchester in the tone of a trusted confidant. A petition of 1653 reveals that he was the William Lewis who served in the February term as chaplain to the king from 1635 to 1641 and from 1641 to 1644.

During the civil war and interregnum Lewis was stripped of his preferments. In 1644 parliament granted the mastership of St Cross to the Winchester MP, John Lisle. Lewis was in Oxford during the final siege in the summer of 1646, and (according to his account in a 1653 petition) following the city's surrender obtained first a pass from General Sir Thomas Fairfax and then, in August, from the speaker of the Commons to go overseas. He lived for some time in France, although he was admitted to the University of Padua before the end of 1646, and then or earlier (as he reveals in his will) he lent Charles I £500 in gold and set aside £300 for the future Charles II. In spite of, or perhaps because of his generosity, his will complains of great impoverishment at this period. By 1651 he was back in England, fighting sequestration of various properties including an estate at 'Brynvoile', Merioneth, inherited from his mother after her death in 1646, land at Llanddwy and Llanenddwyn in the same county, and a house in Toxteth Park near Liverpool. On 15 July 1653 the minor properties were discharged and on 28 September Lewis was granted permission to compound for the main estate in Merioneth, paying a fine of £56 3s.

In 1660 Lewis was restored to his canonry of Winchester and to the mastership of St Cross, where 'he filled his place with becoming dignity, and maintained a generous hospitality' (Humbert, 44). By 5 October 1664 he had resigned his canonry. He died at the hospital on 7 July 1667 and was buried there. He was survived by his wife, Alice, sons Theodore (who had become a Jesuit in 1654) and John, daughter Alice, and niece Margaret, daughter of 'my brother Sir Alexander Radcliffe'. Among the bequests in his will, dated 16 July 1666, were a silver chalice and polyglot bibles, to be given to Oriel College.

STEPHEN WRIGHT

Sources *Walker rev.* • L. Humbert, *Memorials of St Cross* (1868) • G. C. Richards and H. E. Salter, eds., *The dean's register of Oriel, 1466–1661*, OHS, 84 (1926) • M. A. E. Green, ed., *Calendar of the proceedings of the committee for compounding … 1643–1660*, 4, PRO (1892), 2693–5 • will, PRO, PROB 11/325, fols. 310–311 • Foster, *Alum. Oxon.* • Wood, *Ath. Oxon.*, new edn • *CSP dom., 1625–56* • *CSP Venice, 1626–8* • *JHC*, 6 (1648–51) • *APC, 1619–21, 1625–6* • N. W. S. Cranfield, 'Chaplains in ordinary at the early Stuart court: the purple road', *Patronage and recruitment in the Tudor and early Stuart church*, ed. C. Cross (1996), 120–47, esp. 143, 145 • *IGI* [parish register, St Vedast, Foster Lane, London] • *The letters of John Chamberlain*, ed. N. E. McClure, 2 vols. (1939) • R. S. Bosher, *The making of the Restoration settlement: the influence of the Laudians, 1649–1662* (1951) • R. Lockyer, *Buckingham: the life and political career of George Villiers, first duke of Buckingham, 1592–1628* (1981); pbk edn (1984) • *Fasti Angl., 1541–1857*, [Canterbury] • J. Newman, 'The architectural setting', *Hist. U. Oxf.* 4: *17th-cent. Oxf.*, 135–77 • J. H. Stanning and J. Brownbill, eds., *The royalist composition papers*, 4, ed. J. H. Stanning, Lancashire and Cheshire RS, 36 (1898) • J. Walker, *An attempt towards recovering an account of the numbers and sufferings of the clergy of the Church of England*, 2 pts in 1 (1714)

Likenesses oils, Oriel College, Oxford

Lewis, William (*bap.* **1708**, *d.* **1781**), physician and experimental chemist, was baptized on 20 June 1708 in the church of St Mary Magdalene, Richmond, Surrey, the first of four children of William Lewis (*d.* 1736), a brewer of

Richmond, and his wife, Elizabeth (*d.* 1732) of whom little is known. Lewis matriculated at Christ Church, Oxford, on 14 October 1725 but appears not to have taken a degree. Five years later, on 15 April 1730 he was admitted a fellow-commoner at Emmanuel College, Cambridge, where in 1731 he again matriculated, taking the MB degree in the same year.

Some time in or before January 1737 Lewis began to give public lectures on chemistry and the improvement of pharmacy and manufacturing arts (*Daily Post*, 11 Jan 1737). With a growing reputation as a chemical experimentalist he was elected FRS on 31 October 1745; he was then living in Dover Street, London. In the following year he published *A Course of Practical Chemistry* as a revision of the *Complete Course of Chemistry* by George Wilson (*d.* 1711). This was immediately followed by an abridged version (in two volumes) of the Edinburgh *Medical Essays*. Soon afterwards Lewis began a translation of the Edinburgh *Pharmacopoeia* (4th edn), which he published in 1748, and he also rewrote Quincy's *Compleat English Dispensatory*, publishing it as *The New Dispensatory* in 1753.

In 1747 Lewis moved to Kingston, Surrey, where he set up a well-equipped laboratory and presumably continued in medical practice. It is believed that he gave the oration at the opening of Oxford's Radcliffe Library on 13 April 1749. From about 1750 until Lewis's death in 1781 Alexander Chisholm was employed as his assistant in chemical and literary matters, and Lewis's major chemical and pharmaceutical publications appeared during this period. *Commercium philosophico-technicum, or, The Philosophical Commerce of Arts* was published 1763–5, having been preceded in 1748 by a prospectus, *Proposals for printing, by subscription, Commercium philosophico-technicum, or, The philosophical commerce of arts*. Also important were *Chemical Works of Caspar Neumann* in 1759 and *An Experimental History of the Materia Medica* of 1761, which reached its fourth and final edition in 1791 (edited by J. Aikin).

Lewis is known to have acted as consultant to manufacturing concerns, including ironworks in the north and the midlands, but this activity has received little biographical recognition. However, he is well remembered as an author who improved the knowledge and practice of pharmacy. He was awarded the Copley medal by the Royal Society in 1754 for researches on platina (platinum), which he claimed was a distinct metal, and for devising methods of chemical identification. These results were published in the *Philosophical Transactions* in 1754 and 1757. His considerable, yet little recognized, contribution to quantitative chemical analysis is best seen in his work on American potashes in consultation with the Society for the Encouragement of Arts, Manufactures, and Commerce. The analytical methods he devised foreshadowed what later developed into titrimetric analysis and for this work Lewis was awarded the gold medal of the society in 1767. His comments regarding the use of hydrometers and other methods of determining specific gravity are noteworthy. Lewis died, probably at Kingston, on 21 January 1781 and was buried at Richmond parish church six days later.

FREDERICK G. PAGE

Sources F. W. Gibbs, 'William Lewis', *Annals of Science*, 8 (1952), 122–51 • N. Sivin, 'William Lewis, 1708–1781, as a chemist', *Chymia*, 8 (1962), 63–88 • Foster, *Alum. Oxon.* • Venn, *Alum. Cant.* • parish register (baptism), St Mary Magdalene, Richmond, 20 June 1708 • *Publications of the Surrey Parish Register Society*, 1 (1903) • *Daily Post* [London] (11 Jan 1737) • E. Kremers, 'William Lewis', *Journal of the American Pharmaceutical Association*, 20 (1931), 1204–9 • W. Lewis, 'Oratio in theatro Sheldoniano habita idibus Aprilis, mdccxlix. die dedicationis bibliothecae Radcl. ivanae', 1749, Bodl. Oxf. • 'William Lewis', society minutes, 25 Feb 1767, RSA

Archives RSA, 'Experiments and observations on American potashes'

Wealth at death £500 to brother; £100 to assistant: will, cited in Gibbs, 'William Lewis'

Lewis, William (1787–1870), chess player, born on 6 October 1787, apparently in Birmingham, was trained as a merchant's clerk, but learned chess under Jacob Henry Sarratt. In 1821 he played a match at Paris with Des Chapelles, the leading player in France before Labourdonnais, receiving the odds of the pawn and one move. Lewis won the first game in twenty-seven moves, the second and third being drawn. Labourdonnais, however, later beat him by five games to two. Lewis ran a well-known chess school at 5 Nassau Street, Soho, London; among his pupils was Alexander McDonnell. Some beautiful games, in which Lewis gave his pupil a pawn and move and generally won (though it is said that McDonnell could afterwards have given the same odds to him or any other English player), are given in George Walker's *Thousand Games* (1844, repr. 1893). Lewis, being a small man, also succeeded in 1819 to the position of inhabitant of William de Kempelen's celebrated chess-playing automaton the Terrible Turk, in which capacity he lost only 6 games out of 300 at odds of pawn and move. An unfortunate speculation in piano manufacture bankrupted him in 1827; from 1830, he largely abandoned chess to concentrate on work as an actuary for the Family Endowment Society and retrieve his fortunes. 'During the few last years of his life he employed his time chiefly in playing over the finest games of the day and in the graver study of his Greek Testament' (*ILN*, 555). Lewis died on 22 August 1870 at his home, 5 Brunswick Villas, St John's Wood, London, and was buried in Highgate cemetery.

Lewis was the author of numerous works on chess, mostly elementary in character and drawing on those of his teacher Sarratt. Some suggested that in his *Selection of Games at Chess* (1835) between Labourdonnais and McDonnell, he chose disproportionately those which his former pupil lost. 'The last and one of the best of the "old" writers' (Hooper and Whyld, 224–5), his output was superseded by that of authors such as Staunton, more willing to synthesize previous work—including Lewis's own—as a foundation for further analysis, and less inclined to reinvent the wheel for themselves.

THOMAS SECCOMBE, *rev.* JULIAN LOCK

Sources D. Hooper and K. Whyld, *The Oxford companion to chess*, 2nd edn (1992), 224–5 • Boase, *Mod. Eng. biog.* • K. Matthews, *British chess* (1948) • *ILN* (26 Nov 1870), 555 • G. Walker, 'Deschapelles the chess king', *Chess and chess Players* (1850), 38–60 • F. M. Edge, *The exploits and triumphs in Europe of Paul Morphy, the chess champion* (1859); repr. with introduction by D. Lawson (1873) • H. J. R. Murray,

'J. H. Sarratt', *British Chess Magazine*, 57 (1937), 353–9 • *Chess Players' Chronicle*, 1 (1841) • *CGPLA Eng. & Wales* (1870)

Likenesses group portrait, engraving, repro. in Edge, ed., *The exploits and triumphs in Europe*, facing p. 196 • lithograph, repro. in Matthews, *British chess*, 23

Wealth at death under £4000: resworn probate, March 1872, *CGPLA Eng. & Wales* (1870)

Lewis, William Cudmore McCullagh (1885–1956), physical chemist, was born in Belfast, co. Antrim, on 29 June 1885, the son of Edward Lewis, a linen merchant, and his wife, Frances Welsh McCullagh, daughter of the Revd William Cudmore McCullagh of Ballysillan Presbyterian Church, Belfast. Lewis was the only son in a family of five children. He was educated at Bangor grammar school, co. Down, and Queen's College, Belfast, which he entered as a medical student. Having developed an interest in the physical sciences Lewis changed his course and in 1905 obtained a first-class honours BA in physics and chemistry from the Royal University of Ireland. In 1906 he was awarded the MA and a university studentship in experimental science. After acting as a demonstrator in chemistry at the university for a year, he left northern Ireland to do research at the University of Liverpool under Professor F. G. Donnan, who had been appointed two years earlier to the new chair of physical chemistry. Donnan had recently studied with the great pioneers in physical chemistry, J. H. van't Hoff and W. Ostwald. The stimulating environment of Donnan's department shaped the directions of Lewis's interests and career. In 1908 he was awarded a scholarship which took him to Heidelberg to work for a year with Georg Bredig, an authority on colloid chemistry. In 1909 he returned to England and was appointed by Sir William Ramsay to a demonstratorship and later a lectureship at University College, London (UCL). Lewis's contributions to physical chemistry were already attracting attention and in 1913, when Donnan was appointed to Ramsay's chair at UCL, Lewis was invited to succeed him at Liverpool. He remained at Liverpool for the rest of his career, retiring in 1948 on grounds of ill health.

On 18 July 1914 Lewis married Jeanie Waterston Darroch (*b*. 1889/90), of a Scottish family who had settled in London; they had one son, Ian, who became a lecturer in physics at the University of Liverpool before joining the Atomic Energy Research Establishment at Harwell.

During his long association with Liverpool, Lewis gave devoted service to the university and directed one of the outstanding schools of chemistry in Britain. He is said to have been a friendly professor, always ready to give advice and listen to the difficulties of his students and colleagues. Many of his research assistants were later eminent in academic or industrial spheres. He was a man of wide learning and considerable breadth of outlook, an ardent student of Samuel Johnson, and also knowledgeable about early English architecture. Lewis was very retiring and hated publicity, but he had a keen sense of humour. Brought up in the Presbyterian tradition, he remained throughout his life a loyal churchman.

Lewis's earliest research work (with Donnan) was a highly successful experimental investigation of Willard Gibbs's theory of surface concentration. Later he studied various aspects of the colloidal and liquid states. He was also interested in reaction kinetics and mechanisms; between 1914 and 1922 he and his students published a long series of papers on catalysis, in which results of experimental or theoretical studies were presented for a wide range of systems. Although Lewis always felt that his work was hampered by insufficient mathematical training, he pioneered the application of statistical mechanics and quantum theory to reaction rates. Unfortunately he espoused the so-called radiation theory, in which infra-red radiation had a general role in governing reaction rates. This theory attracted considerable support in the period 1915 to 1925. Its ultimate downfall meant that various aspects of Lewis's work required reinterpretation, but his emphasis on the statistics of molecular collisions remained intact.

Between the wars Lewis became widely known to students of chemistry as the author of *A System of Physical Chemistry*, first published in two volumes in 1916, and in three volumes in 1918–19. It was the first original work in the English language to be devoted to physical chemistry for senior students. It was a standard work for two decades and went into four editions in ten years. The book was written at a time when the subject was growing rapidly, and it revealed that Lewis had a masterly grasp of the wide range of topics involved.

In the years after the First World War Lewis collaborated with the Liverpool Cancer Research Organization. This body had been formed by Professor William Blair-Bell, who enlisted many heads of university departments to apply appropriate expertise to various aspects of the cancer problem. His association with this body influenced Lewis's future work and he moved his research activities to the study of biological and physiological problems. He was interested in the physico-chemical processes which might underlie malignancy and he studied such properties as the electrical conductivity and ionic permeability of malignant tissue. Lewis believed that glycolysis was enhanced in cancerous cells and this led him to study the kinetics of acidic or enzymic hydrolysis of various glucosides and also the kinetics of the denaturation of proteins. The work also involved studies in the field of colloidal chemistry. Many of the projects were well conceived, but some were in advance of their time and before the techniques necessary for success had been developed.

Lewis was elected FRS in 1926, but was not prominent in the life of the society. However, he served on the council of the Faraday Society at various times between 1920 and 1941 (including a period as a vice-president). He was reluctant to attend scientific conferences. Some time after his retirement Lewis moved to Great Malvern. He died there at the Clanmere Nursing Home, Graham Road, on 11 February 1956. JOHN SHORTER

Sources C. E. H. Bawn, *Memoirs FRS*, 4 (1958), 193–203 • *DNB* • *Nature*, 177 (1956), 603–4 • m. cert. • d. cert.

Likenesses C. Pollard, photograph, RS; repro. in Bawn, *Memoirs FRS*
Wealth at death £11,145 6*s*. 2*d*.: probate, 23 April 1956, *CGPLA Eng. & Wales*

Lewis, William David (1823–1861), legal writer, was the eldest son of Revd George William Lewis (*d*. 1858), a curate of Ramsgate, Kent (where Lewis was born), and his wife, Caroline, daughter of Mathew Concanen of Dulwich, Surrey. His father had been admitted at Lincoln's Inn in 1819 before entering the church, and his grandfather, David Baxter Lewis of Rochester, was a solicitor.

At the age of fourteen Lewis began to read law books and, a year later, in 1838, he became a pupil of John Rudall, a well-known conveyancer. In response to both the rapid professional recognition of his ability, and his own worries about the capacity of his family to support him, he became at eighteen the youngest conveyancer on record. Before he was twenty he astonished the profession by finishing the manuscript of a book which concentrated on what is often regarded as the most complicated area of property law. Soon afterwards, in 1843, this was published as *A Practical Treatise on the Law of Perpetuity*. The book's 723 pages were supplemented by a substantial appendix, and an analysis of recent cases on the subject was added in 1849. The law of perpetuities, which determined the extent to which a current owner of land could provide for rights in the land at future dates, was of particular interest to lawyers advising clients on the ways in which property could be passed from one generation of a family to another without any particular individual (who might be extravagant) being given a power of sale, which could then lead to the loss of family land and wealth. For a book by a very young man the arguments in the text have a strikingly reflective and balanced quality, even if at times they are expressed at considerable length. There is much to be said for the judgement of John Chipman Gray, of Harvard, who mentions Lewis in his own book, *The Rule Against Perpetuities* (1886): 'I must acknowledge my great obligation to Mr. Lewis's classical treatise. He is prolix, and his prolixity makes him occasionally obscure; but no writer on the common law excels him in acuteness and candour' (J. C. Gray, *The Rule Against Perpetuities*, 1886, vi). In the context of English legal writing the study by Lewis stands comparison with that of Charles Fearne.

Lewis was called to the bar in 1844 and he soon established a practice. In the years which followed he continued to work with extreme dedication. He never visited the theatre and until 1859 his only holidays consisted of three tours of the Crystal Palace. He was made QC at the age of thirty-six. Despite the demands of his practice he became committed to the improvement of legal education and the reform of property law. Between 1847 and 1852 he gave sixty lectures a year at Gray's Inn, which (alongside those given by Sir Henry Maine) did much for the reputation of the new forms of voluntary education then being introduced for intending barristers. As early as 1844 he was a member of the Law Amendment Society, and later he sat on the royal commission on the registration of title (1854–7) and produced draft bills. In 1855 he founded the Juridical Society as a forum for discussion among barristers with an interest in historical and comparative arguments relating to law reform. His own papers for the society included such studies as 'Liberty of opinion in relation to blasphemous libels' and 'Peerages for life'.

In 1860 Lewis fell ill and was advised to cease practising. He continued to work and on 24 January 1861 he died in London of an aortal aneurism. He left a widow, Amelia Anne, whom he had married early in his career, and a son, William Arnold Lewis (*d*. 1877), who was also a barrister. Had he lived, his career had every prospect of comparing with those of other major Victorian property lawyers such as Edward Sugden, Joshua Williams, or Sir George Jessel. As it was, his most distinctive achievement lay in his remarkable and uniquely early book. R. C. J. Cocks

Sources *Solicitors' Journal*, 5 (1860–61), 242–4 · J. S. Anderson, *Lawyers and the making of English land law, 1832–1940* (1992) · Boase, *Mod. Eng. biog.* · Venn, *Alum. Cant.* · records of the Juridical Society, 1856–61 · R. Cocks, *Foundations of the modern bar* (1983) · *CGPLA Eng. & Wales* (1861)
Archives Lincoln's Inn, London
Wealth at death under £5000: probate, 12 March 1861, *CGPLA Eng. & Wales*

Lewis, William Garrett (1821–1885), Particular Baptist minister, was born on 5 August 1821 at Margate, the eldest son of William Garrett Lewis (1797–1865). Shortly after his birth, his father renounced his commercial employment and devoted himself to the Baptist ministry, being ordained in 1824 minister of Zion Chapel, Chatham, where he remained for eighteen years. An ardent opponent of slavery, the elder Lewis was the author of *Original Hymns and Poems on Spiritual Subjects* (1827).

His son was educated at Gillingham, Margate, and Uxbridge; from 1837 to 1840 he was articled to Dr Gray, a Brixton schoolmaster. In 1840 he obtained a clerkship in the Post Office, and joined the Baptist church at Mare Street, Hackney. There he was an active layman, participating in the church's mission to the East End of London and gaining valuable preaching experience. In 1847 he preached at the chapel in Silver Street, Kensington Gravel Pits, and in September of that year was ordained minister of the congregation there. On 7 December 1847 he married Susanna Mary, the youngest daughter of Daniel Katterns of the East India Company: they had a son and a daughter. In 1853 his congregation moved to a new, larger church in Westbourne Grove, and there Lewis continued to preach with great success until the end of 1880. A favourite theme for lectures was John Bunyan's *Pilgrim's Progress*; a volume of his sermons was published in 1872. The labour involved in maintaining a large London congregation proved a burden, and in 1881 he accepted the call of the small chapel in Dagnall Street, St Albans.

Lewis was one of the founders of the London Baptist Association, of which he was secretary from 1865 to 1869, and president in 1870. For nearly twenty years from 1861 he was editor of the *Baptist Magazine*, initially adopting a decidedly conservative theological stance. He died, having been diagnosed as having cancer of the oesophagus, on 16 January 1885 at his house in Victoria Street, St Albans, and was buried in Kensal Green cemetery.

W. A. J. Archbold, *rev.* L. E. Lauer

Sources E. C. Starr, ed., *A Baptist bibliography*, 14 (1969), 72 • L., 'Memoirs of deceased ministers', *Baptist Hand-Book* (1886), 124–6 • L., *Baptist Hand-Book* (1846), 129 • *Baptist Magazine*, 78 (1886), 83–4 • *The Freeman* (23 Jan 1885), 49 • *The Baptist* (23 Jan 1885) • *The Times* (23 Jan 1885) • m. cert.

Wealth at death £723 0s. 3*d*.: probate, 27 Feb 1885, *CGPLA Eng. & Wales*

Lewis, William Lillington (*bap.* **1743**, *d.* **1772**), translator, was baptized on 16 August 1743 at the church of St Michael, Gloucester, the son of William Lillington Lewis and his wife, Elizabeth. He matriculated at Pembroke College, Oxford, on 18 November 1760, graduated BA in 1764, and became a fellow and received an MA in 1767.

In his short life Lewis produced a single work: the first complete translation into English of P. Papinius Statius's late first-century epic the *Thebaid* (2 vols., 1767):

> I had long considered it as the most illustrious Work of *Roman* Antiquity after the *Aeneid*, and consequently was concerned, that it had never appeared in an *English* Dress. … With more Ambition therefore than Prudence, I begun it soon after I entered at the University, at the Age of eighteen, and must confess, that my chief Merit consists in having had the Patience to go through with it at a Time of Life, which is too often squandered away in a Circle of Follies and Amusements. (Lewis, preface, 1.xxi)

Various parts of the *Thebaid* had been translated before, and Lewis draws especially on Alexander Pope's version of the first book (1712) and Walter Harte's of the sixth (1727). In style of translation he is a follower of Pope, but, unlike him, Lewis is a zealous partisan of Statius, defending the Roman poet's art even when it may offend English Augustan taste. Statius's representation of cruel and monstrous behaviour on the battlefield exceeds the 'tolerable' in Pope's view, as when '*Tydeus* in the very Pangs of Death is represented as knawing the Head of his Enemy' at the end of *Thebaid*, book 8 (Pope, note on *Iliad*, book 22, line 437); but Lewis marshals an array of arguments to defend his author.

Lewis's work, which is among the best eighteenth-century translations, ably captures the sublimity, eeriness, and violence of the original. Statius's style is highly allusive, with constant reference to his epic predecessors, especially Homer, Virgil (his acknowledged master), and Lucan. To represent this allusive quality in English, Lewis draws on Pope's *Iliad*, Dryden's *Aeneid*, and Rowe's *Pharsalia*, among other works. His practice is to signal an allusion in Statius by adapting the language and expressions that his English predecessors used for the very passage to which Statius alludes. For instance, in book 3 Venus tries to prevent Mars, her erstwhile lover, from inciting the Argives to begin hostilities against Thebes. Lewis notes that 'This Speech of *Venus* is written in the Spirit of *Dido's* to *Aeneas*; and in many Places not only the Sentiment, but even the Diction is similar' (Lewis, 1.102); he translates:

> Go then; thy Flight no longer I detain;
> Go; bathe in kindred Blood the Theban Plain.
> (ibid., book 3, lines 393–4)

Dido speaks thus in Dryden's *Aeneid*:

> But go; thy flight no longer I detain;
> Go seek thy promis'd Kingdom through the Main.
> (Dryden, *Aeneid*, book 4, lines 548–9)

Although Lewis makes the allusion to the *Aeneid* more explicit than does Statius, his use of Dryden admirably reproduces the allusive texture of Roman epic. Lewis died in 1772.

Garth Tissol

Sources W. L. Lewis, *The Thebaid of Statius, translated into English verse, with notes and observations, and a dissertation upon the whole*, 2 vols. (1767) • Foster, *Alum. Oxon.* • *IGI* • *GM*, 1st ser., 42 (1772), 598 • S. Gillespie, 'Statius in English, 1648–1767', *Translation and Literature*, 8 (1999), 157–75

Lewis, William Thomas (**1746?–1812**), actor and theatre manager, was born in Ormskirk, Lancashire. There is disagreement about the date, but 1746 is widely accepted. His grandfather was a clergyman in Wales, and his father, William Lewis (*d.* 1753), was a linen draper in London until he decided instead to form a travelling theatre company, which eventually crossed to Ireland. The young William made early appearances in his father's company, but started to achieve prominence only when, after education at the grammar school in Armagh and more experience as a strolling player, he arrived in Dublin and joined the company at the Smock Alley Theatre, where he made his first appearance on 3 June 1761. In 1767–8 he performed at the Crow Street Theatre, and in 1771 he joined the company of his stepfather, William Dawson, at the Capel Street Theatre. There he made his first appearance as Belcour in Richard Cumberland's *The West Indian* (19 February 1771), in which part he 'vanquished Mossop' (Doran, 3.303–4). Cumberland saw his performance and commended Lewis as 'the VERY *Belcour* he had an idea of when he wrote the piece' (Haslewood, 2.5). It was on Cumberland's recommendation that Lewis made a move to Covent Garden, and he played Belcour there for the first time on 15 October 1773. Lewis's later appearances in Ireland were not restricted to Dublin: it was in Cork, playing Othello to her Desdemona, that he met a young actress, Henrietta Leeson [*see below*], whom he eventually married. Eight children (four daughters and four sons) were baptized, at St Martin-in-the-Fields and St Paul's, Covent Garden, between 1779 and 1789.

Lewis's later career was centred on Covent Garden, where he made almost all of his London appearances (*The London Stage* credits him with 799 between 15 October 1773 and 12 June 1800). Between his début and his retirement in 1808 he played some 194 parts and created at least 85 roles, including the original Faulkland in Sheridan's *The Rivals*. Among his (and his public's) favourite parts was Copper Captain in *Rule a Wife and have a Wife*, by Beaumont and Fletcher, and it was in this role that he made his final

William Thomas Lewis (**1746?–1812**), by Gainsborough Dupont, 1794 [as Mercutio in *Romeo and Juliet*]

appearance at Covent Garden. Haslewood wrote of him in this role (and as Mercutio): 'he is yet unrivalled; and it is doubtful whether he was ever excelled in those parts, which he represents in such perfection, that the most perfidious Critic cannot point out a single error or defect' (Haslewood, 2.6). Lewis's long career at Covent Garden was not solely as an actor: in 1782 he became deputy or acting manager of Covent Garden, and thereafter restricted most of the parts he played to comedy. Comedy seems to have been his forte. Haslewood obviously considered it so: '*Pert* or *outré* Comedy is his *chef d'oeuvre* … his proper sphere' (ibid.).

Nor were Lewis's appearances and activities limited to Covent Garden. In the early years he acted outside London, at Birmingham and Liverpool and for Tate Wilkinson's company at York, Leeds, Edinburgh, and Wakefield. Indeed, Wakefield appears to have been the only place where he did not attract an audience; on one occasion in 1780, on learning of the size of the house, he declined to appear. After giving up the management of Covent Garden (he sold his share to John Philip Kemble in 1803) he devoted much of his energy, with his colleague Thomas Knight, to the Liverpool theatre; their first season opened in November 1802. He also became involved with a theatre in neighbouring Manchester.

Lewis died at home at Westbourne Place, King's Road, Pimlico, London, on 13 January 1812, leaving his widow, two daughters, and three sons. He was buried at Christ Church, Liverpool. Two of the sons followed in their father's theatrical footsteps: Thomas became co-manager of the Liverpool theatre and Henry had a seemingly short and unsuccessful career as an actor. While Lewis was not as well known as some of his contemporaries, his unspectacular but steady career allowed him to leave a considerable fortune on his death. He was not recognized as a major figure of his age but is worthy of note, for he exemplifies not only the dominance of London through Covent Garden (and Drury Lane) but also important aspects of the theatre outside London—especially of Dublin, where the Licensing Act of 1737 did not apply—the role of the touring companies such as those of Dawson and Wilkinson, and the growth of provincial theatres in the last half of the eighteenth and the early years of the nineteenth century.

There is not a wealth of anecdote, as is the case with some of his contemporaries, to flesh out Lewis's life. His sobriquet Gentleman Lewis appears to have been well warranted: his farewell words to his audience at his final performance were that 'for the space of thirty years he had not once incurred their displeasure' (Russell, 209); and, of his management of Covent Garden, Haslewood commented: 'In this capacity it is, perhaps, impossible not to incur some dislike among the Performers, who regard his power with jealousy and envy; but his exertions for public entertainment have always been examined as they deserve, with approbation' (Haslewood, 2.6).

Lewis's wife, **Henrietta Amelia Leeson** (1751–1826), was born in London. Haslewood credits her with an early infatuation with the theatre, indulged by her father's inattention to his family and his business as a printer, and the encouragement of her friends. She was taken on by Charles Macklin as an apprentice and in 1771 went with him to Ireland, where she made her début at the Crow Street Theatre in Dublin. She accompanied Macklin to other towns, playing a number of roles, including Portia and Desdemona. After returning to Dublin she continued to act with Macklin until she obtained a release from her articles and joined the Dawson company at the Capel Street Theatre. She then lived with Lewis and in 1775 accompanied him to England, where they married about 1780. She also acted with the Covent Garden company, initially as Mrs Leeson, later as Mrs Lewis, and went with her husband on his visits to the provinces. Opinions differ about her abilities. Haslewood attributed her rare appearances on the stage (*The London Stage* lists 103 between 1775 and 1791) to her desire to provide for her large family rather than talent, although one critic said of her first appearance at Covent Garden that 'there was an ease and nature in her deportment and dialogue that entitles her to encouragement' (*Westminster Magazine*, November 1775) and Wilkinson described her as 'an amiable handsome woman, and a pleasing actress' (Wilkinson, 2.60). She died on 6 December 1826.

ROLAND METCALF

Sources Highfill, Burnim & Langhans, *BDA* • B. R. Schneider, *Index to 'The London stage, 1660–1800'* (1979) • G. W. Stone, ed., *The London stage, 1660–1800*, pt 4: 1747–1776 (1962) • C. B. Hogan, ed., *The London stage, 1660–1800*, pt 5: 1776–1800 (1968) • [J. Haslewood], *The secret history of the green rooms: containing authentic and entertaining memoirs of the actors and actresses in the three theatres royal*, 2 vols. (1790) • T. Wilkinson, *The wandering patentee, or, A history of the Yorkshire theatres from 1770 to the present time*, 4 vols. (1795) • J. Doran and R. W. Lowe,

'Their majesties' servants': annals of the English stage, rev. edn, 3 vols. (1888) • W. C. Russell, *Representative actors* [1888] • *IGI*

Likenesses S. De Wilde, engraving, 1791 (as Copper Captain), Harvard TC • M. A. Shee, oils, exh. RA 1792, National Gallery, London • G. Dupont, oils, 1794, NPG [*see illus.*] • J. Zoffany, group portrait, oils, *c*.1795–1796, Garr. Club • G. Dance, pencil, 1798, BM • S. De Wilde, pencil and watercolour, 1807 (as Jeremy Diddler in *Raising the wind*), Garr. Club; versions, Harvard TC • S. De Wilde, watercolour, 1809, Garr. Club • S. De Wilde, oils, Garr. Club • M. A. Shee, oils, Garr. Club • attrib. J. Stewart, oils, Garr. Club • prints, BM, NPG

Wealth at death over £22,500 in stocks and house in Westbourne Place and interest in Liverpool and Manchester theatres: Highfill, Burnim & Langhans, *BDA*

Lewis, William Thomas, first Baron Merthyr (1837–1914), mineral agent and colliery owner, was born at Merthyr Tudful on 5 August 1837, the second son of Mary Anne and Thomas William Lewis, engineer at the Plymouth ironworks, Merthyr. He was educated at a well-known local school run by Taliesin Williams until he was thirteen, and then he was apprenticed to his father as an engineer.

Lewis was appointed in 1855 as assistant to W. S. Clark, the chief mining engineer of the third marquess of Bute (1847–1890); and he succeeded him in 1864. He received an initial salary of £1000 and the occupancy of Mardy House, which was to be his long-term residence in Aberdâr. The same year he married Anne Rees (*d*. 1902), granddaughter of Lucy *Thomas, the legendary 'mother of the Welsh steam-coal trade'. They had two sons and six daughters. In 1880–81 Lewis was given control of all aspects of the Bute Welsh estates.

Lewis was a man of strong character, considerable talent and even more industry (it was said that, when travelling to Lord Bute in Scotland, he needed to dispatch secretaries, laden with shorthand notes, at stations on the way). None the less the foundation of his power and influence in south Wales undoubtedly stemmed from the Bute connection. The estate straddled the major coal measures of south-east Wales; several ironworks—notably Dowlais, for a time the world's largest—were on Bute land, as was much of Cardiff. The Bute family also owned the burgeoning docks at Cardiff and had holdings in some of the railways linking the pits to the port. Since the third Lord Bute chose a passive role in estate affairs, in sharp contrast to his entrepreneurial father, the active role fell to the officials and especially to Lewis once he was given overall management. Mineral and industrial developments, agricultural holdings, urban properties, docks, and railways were all under his control. This was an innovation for the estate and represented an enormous concentration of authority.

Lewis's stewardship was exercised energetically, shrewdly, and conscientiously. The upward trajectory of mineral and urban incomes was quickened both by the proving of viable new coal seams and by securing high ground-rents for residential properties through attractive layouts. The docks were more difficult. They were more effective in facilitating estate development than in giving

William Thomas Lewis, first Baron Merthyr (1837–1914), by unknown engraver, pubd 1891

a return on capital, but pressure of trade meant that additional, capital-hungry docks had to be provided, however reluctantly (the Roath Dock was added in 1887, followed by the vast Alexandra Dock in 1907). Lewis attempted to get the estate off this expensive escalator, but plans to sell the docks—to Cardiff Corporation, the Taff Vale Railway, or a harbour trust—all fell through, partly owing to Lewis's own obduracy in negotiation. He did reduce the direct family liability by incorporating the private undertaking into the Bute Dock company (with himself as general manager) in 1886, and he had some success in increasing imports of grain and meat to reduce the dependence on a one-way trade in coal. However, schemes to foster shipbuilding and to break into ocean-going passenger traffic failed to take off, and the hugely expensive, grandly named Cardiff Railway, built in the 1890s, turned out to be a short, defensive, feeder line, which rapidly became a white elephant.

Much of Lewis's authority was exercised in private, negotiating mineral leases, way-leaves, and building permissions. One public index of his status was the frequency of his appearances before parliamentary committees on bills for private railways and docks; another was his regular appointment to represent the district on royal commissions—on accidents in mines (1879–81); mining royalties (1890–91); coal dust in mines (1891–4); labour (1891–4); coal supplies (1901–5); trade disputes (1903–6); and shipping combination (1906–7). He was president of the Mining Association of Great Britain (1880), the Iron and Steel Institute (1910), and the University College at Cardiff (1911). He was also an active member of the South Wales Institute of Engineers, the Aberdâr board of health, and the Merthyr board of guardians. His services, his public standing, and his qualities were widely recognized: he was knighted in 1885, received a baronetcy in 1896, was elevated to the peerage as Baron Merthyr of Senghenydd in 1911, and was created a KCVO in 1912. He also received the freedom of Cardiff in 1905 and became the first freeman of Merthyr borough in 1908.

Perhaps the most eloquent expression of Lewis's authority was his domination for decades of the main institutions of the south Wales coal trade before he was himself a major colliery owner. He was chairman of the South Wales Coalowners' Association on seven occasions between 1879 and 1887; and for the eighteen years before 1898 he, as leader of the owners' side, monopolized the chair of the industry's central body, the joint sliding scale committee, which regulated wage changes. He had in the late 1860s (when he was in his early thirties) become part owner of a small house-coal colliery in the Lower Rhondda at Coedcae. He increased his Rhondda holdings by sinking the Lewis Merthyr colliery in the 1870s and by buying Hafod colliery in 1881. The firm of Lewis Merthyr Consolidated Collieries later sank the Rhondda Main pit in the Ogmore valley and the Universal colliery at Senghenydd. By 1913 the company owned seven collieries and employed 7000 men.

There were limits to Lewis's powers, however. Although he led the owners to victory in the six-month stoppage of 1898, the association then voted to admit the Bwllfa Company, which had worked throughout. Such an outcome, ignoring Lewis's incensed opposition, amounted to a vote of no confidence. He responded by withdrawing from active involvement and ended a bitter, emotive letter: 'my fellow-members … have a perfect right of selecting their own company, but I also claim the same privilege' (Williams, 257). Similarly, in the teeth of his opposition, a group of colliery owners promoted the Barry dock and railway (opened 1889). Politically also Lewis was rebuffed: he was rejected when he stood as independent Conservative for Merthyr in 1880. This last defeat was unsurprising. The lives of many working-class voters were frequently and directly affected by his actions, which his central position ensured would flavour social relations throughout the region for a whole generation. His influence was particularly stifling in relation to the collective aspirations of the workers. On the waterfront he defeated the dockers in 1891 with contemptuous ease, spurning all proposals for negotiations by blandly asserting that since the men had left and their places had now been filled there was nothing to negotiate (*South Wales Daily News*, 17 February 1891); he and Amon Beesley (of the Taff Vale Railway) were 'unscrupulous in their dealings with labour disputes' (Daunton, 195); and in 1897 Lewis was a founder member of the Free Labour Protection Association (Clegg, 173).

Lewis's long-time leadership of the owners' union did nothing to soften his total antagonism to mining trade unions, and his gifts to local charities did nothing to meet workers' aspirations. He was characterized by the Webbs as the most hated man in Wales, but fear increasingly gave way to grudging respect; and a fellow colliery owner's verdict was that he was a 'domineering old devil' (H. Williams, *Davies the Ocean*, 1991, 194). Eventually his imperious high-handedness—he 'carries the Coal Owners in his waistcoat-pocket' (*Western Mail*, 28 March 1898)—upset his tormentor and distant kinsman, D. A. Thomas, Viscount Rhondda, and alienated even the moderate miners' leaders like William Abraham (Mabon). During the 1898 coal strike, when the government sent Sir Edward Fry to arbitrate under the powers of the recent Conciliation Act, Lewis tersely declined 'to admit any intervention of the Conciliator whether appointed by the Government or otherwise' (*South Wales Daily News*, 14 July 1898). At the end of the strike, as the miners met to accept humiliating defeat, Lewis sent a telegram emphasizing that he would accept no variation from the dictated terms; this provoked a question from the floor, 'Oddiwrth bwy mae hwna, Mabon? Oddirwth yr Hollallnog?' ('Who's that from, Mabon? From the Almighty?'), and the response, 'Yn agos iawn' ('Very near it') (*South Wales Daily News*, 1 Sept 1898).

In his prime Lewis had an impressive head, an ample Santa Claus beard, and a bald pate with the remaining hair long, white and flowing. Such apparent benignity, even raffishness, belied the justifiably universal view of him as stern, strong, severe, though just (according to his lights): his multitudinous public pronouncements showed no traces of irony or humour. He died on 27 August 1914 at Oakhurst, Woodhay, Hampshire. JOHN WILLIAMS

Sources *South Wales Daily News* (14 July 1898) · *South Wales Daily News* (1 Sept 1898) · *South Wales Daily News* (17 Feb 1891) · *Western Mail* [Cardiff] (28 March 1898) · J. Davies, *Cardiff and the marquesses of Bute* (1981) · M. J. Daunton, *Coal metropolis: Cardiff, 1870–1914* (1977) · L. J. Williams, 'The Monmouthshire and South Wales Coalowners' Association', MA diss., 1957 · L. J. Williams, 'Lewis, William Thomas', *DBB* · L. J. Williams, 'The new unionism in south Wales', *Welsh History Review / Cylchgrawn Hanes Cymru*, 1 (1960–63), 413–29 · H. A. Clegg, A. Fox, and A. F. Thompson, *A history of British trade unions since 1889*, 1 (1964) · R. H. Walters, *The economic and business history of the south Wales steam coal industry, 1840–1914* (1977) · R. P. Arnot, *South Wales miners* (1949) · D. M. Richards, *Some episodes in the career of Sir William T. Lewis* (1908)

Archives Cardiff Central Library, Bute Collection · NL Wales, Coalowners' MSS · NL Wales, Bute MSS

Likenesses T. Brock, bronze statue, exh. RA 1899, Merthyr Tudful, S. Wales · photographs, repro. in Williams, 'Lewis, William Thomas' · wood-engraving, NPG; repro. in *ILN* (14 Feb 1891) [*see illus.*]

Wealth at death £615,522 8*s.* 2*d.*: probate, 14 Nov 1914, *CGPLA Eng. & Wales*

Lewis, Sir Willmott Harsant (1877–1950), journalist, was born in Cardiff on 18 June 1877, the son of James Oliver Lewis, coal shipper, and his wife, Marion Harsant Butler. He was educated at Eastbourne and at Heidelberg and the Sorbonne. After first working on a newspaper in Brighton he sought, but was unable to find, work on a London paper. He then went on the stage and drifted to Asia, travelling extensively in Japan and China and moving 'here and there, a brilliant, irresponsible, and adventurous young man' (*The Times*, 5 Jan 1950, 7). He became editor of the *North China Daily News*, and as correspondent for the *New York Herald* was in China during the Boxer uprising and in Korea during the Russo-Japanese War. He then went to San Francisco, engaging briefly in an unsuccessful commercial venture, before returning to Asia to edit the *Manila Times* from 1911 to 1917, when he made important contacts among the Americans then controlling the Philippines. At the request of one of these contacts, General Pershing, he went to France and handled American propaganda in Europe. He then attended the peace conference as representative of the *New York Tribune*. For his services in

France he was made a chevalier of the Légion d'honneur. Lewis was married three times: his first wife was Lina Jessie Ringer; then, on 8 June 1926, he married Ethel Stoddard, daughter of Frank Brett Noyes, president of the Associated Press; they had one son and two daughters; in 1939 he married Norma, daughter of Colonel T. F. Bowler, of Okemah, Oklahoma; she survived him.

The turning point in his career came when Lord Northcliffe, 'impressed by his familiarity with American journalism and his American methods' (*History of The Times*, 4.566), engaged Lewis in 1920 as Washington correspondent of *The Times*. This was a bold move, for all his journalistic experience had been gained in Asia; he knew nothing of the methods or spirit of *The Times*; and not a great deal about his native country. But in his thirty years as a correspondent in America, as the British ambassador, Sir Oliver Franks, commented in 1950, Lewis became 'a historic figure' (*The Times*, 5 Jan 1950, 4).

Lewis liked the Americans and they liked him. He was very far from being the standard British correspondent and was fond of saying that he owed his popularity and understanding of American ways to the fact that he was not English but a 'Celt'. Tall and handsome, Lewis preserved some of the manners of the stage on which he had served his apprenticeship. He was an admirable after-dinner speaker and a celebrated raconteur. In his office, in the Press Club, at scores of Washington dinner tables, he became a great social figure and this served him well in his professional work. He was soon a master of the complicated social and political life of Washington, especially well informed about the inner life of the senate, and he was recognized as a figure whom it was well worth informing and even consulting.

Lewis wrote forcefully and with a vast and detailed knowledge of the background and motivations in the gamut of issues affecting Britain's ties with the United States. His copious, unpublished, correspondence with editors on these matters was vital in formulating the approach of *The Times* towards many of the central military and foreign policy questions of the period. With this direct and indirect influence, his *Times* obituary was right to say that 'Few men have done more for Anglo-American relations' (5 Jan 1950, 7).

Lewis was 'for many years the unchallenged dean of the foreign press corps in Washington' (*History of The Times*, 5.151). He was appointed KBE in 1931. But he had weaknesses as a correspondent. Some news simply did not interest him. Particularly noted in Washington, and London, was his lack of interest in questions of social or political reform. The significance of the 'new deal' programme of the Roosevelt administration after 1933 was sadly under-reported, partly because Lewis had fewer contacts among the newcomers who then ran Washington. Although still the grand old man, Lewis's significance and influence faded over the years. He retired in 1948, but continued to live in Washington, where he died at his home, 3425 Prospect Street NW, on 4 January 1950. His funeral was held in Washington Cathedral three days later.

D. W. BROGAN, *rev.* MARC BRODIE

Sources *The Times* (5 Jan 1950) · *New York Times* (5 Jan 1950) · *New York Times* (6 Jan 1950) · [S. Morison and others], *The history of The Times*, 4 (1952) · I. McDonald, *The history of The Times*, 5 (1984) · *New York Herald Tribune* (5 Jan 1950) · personal knowledge (1959) · private information (1959) · *WWW* · Burke, *Peerage* · *CGPLA Eng. & Wales* (1951)

Archives News Int. RO, MSS

Likenesses B. Egeli, oils, repro. in *The history of The Times*, vol. 4 · photograph, repro. in *The Times*

Wealth at death £1172 14*s*. 7*d*. in England: administration, 2 April 1951, *CGPLA Eng. & Wales*

Lewis, (Percy) Wyndham (1882–1957), artist and writer, was born in his father's yacht off Amherst, Nova Scotia, on 18 November 1882. He was the son of Captain Charles Edward Lewis, a soldier who had been educated at West Point and had fought in the American Civil War, and Anne Stuart, a British-born woman with Irish and Scottish ancestors. Captain Lewis came from a wealthy family in New York state, and could have provided his son with a comfortable inheritance. But Lewis's parents separated about 1893, leaving him with his mother. She moved back to England and became largely responsible for his upbringing. They led a precarious life in London, but Lewis was sent to private schools and finally to Rugby School (1897–8). His growing passion for drawing and painting then led him to study at the Slade School of Fine Art in London between 1898 and 1901.

An experimental path Lewis spent the next eight years in an oddly indecisive state. His interest in writing both poetry and prose was developing, and it probably prevented him from committing himself full-time to art. He travelled restlessly, visiting Madrid with his friend Spencer Gore and spending time in Munich. Above all, though, he stayed in Paris for several years. Here he started to paint more seriously, and heard Henri Bergson lecture at the Collège de France. In 1907 his older friend and mentor Augustus John saw *Les demoiselles d'Avignon* in Picasso's studio. Lewis probably heard about the painting from John, but he was not yet ready to pursue a singlemindedly experimental path. John, already enjoying considerable acclaim in Britain, inhibited Lewis at this stage. He found more satisfaction in writing short stories about the itinerant acrobats and assorted eccentrics he encountered during his travels in Brittany.

Lewis's first success came in 1909, when he returned to London. Ford Madox Hueffer (later Ford) published several of his short stories in a new magazine called the *English Review*. They established his reputation as a promising young writer of fiction; but the drawings which survive from this period, like *The Theatre Manager* (1909; V&A), show that Lewis the artist was still caught uneasily between several disparate influences. A growing involvement with so-called primitive art and cubism was married, rather awkwardly, to his interest in Dürer and Leonardo da Vinci's grotesque heads.

By 1912, however, Lewis had decided to devote more of his energies to art. He had already appeared in two exhibitions of the *Camden Town Group (June and December 1911), where his interest in harsh distortions marked him out from the other members. But Lewis really began to

(Percy) **Wyndham Lewis** (1882–1957), by Alvin Langdon Coburn, 1916

define his own vision when Madame Strindberg commissioned him to make a monumental painting, a drop curtain, and other designs for her innovative Cabaret Club in London. The club became known as the Cave of the Golden Calf, and other decorations were provided by Jacob Epstein, Eric Gill, Charles Ginner, and Spencer Gore, who co-ordinated the scheme. Lewis's contributions were outstanding, especially a large painting called *Kermesse* (1912). Here his alert awareness of cubism, futurism, and expressionism was conveyed in an individual way—bleak, incisive, and charged with ferocious energy. With this arresting canvas of three dancing figures Lewis became a mature painter, and he fortified his reputation when Roger Fry included his illustrations for Shakespeare's *Timon of Athens* in the 'Second post-impressionist exhibition' (1912–13).

Like Timon, Lewis adopted an adversarial stance. Restless, satirical, and ceaselessly productive, he had no patience with most of the art then produced in Britain. His ability as a draughtsman was already outstanding, with a distinctive emphasis on whiplash line. At this stage he admired Filippo Marinetti's forceful advocacy of an art that would match the dynamism of a new century. He also respected Picasso and Matisse, as well as admiring the black harshness of the German expressionist woodcut.

Roger Fry enlisted Lewis's services when the Omega workshops opened in the summer of 1913. He executed a painted screen, some lampshade designs, and studies for rugs, but his dissatisfaction with the Omega soon erupted into antagonism. No longer willing to be dominated by Fry, Lewis abruptly left the Omega with Edward Wadsworth, Cuthbert Hamilton, and Frederick Etchells in October 1913. By the end of the year he had begun to define an alternative to Fry's exclusive concentration on modern French art. His essay for the cubist room section of 'The Camden Town group and others' exhibition in Brighton (1913–14) announced the emergence of a more volcanic group of artists, far more involved with the machine age than Fry would ever be. At the same time Lewis carried out a startling decorative scheme for Lady Drogheda's dining-room in Belgravia, shrouding the walls in black, mirrored panels and painting a semi-abstract frieze underneath the ceiling. Its fierce austerity challenged the more gentle mood of the Omega's interiors, and aroused a great deal of controversy.

Vorticism Lewis was fast becoming the most hotly debated young painter in Britain. He established a rival to the Omega when the Rebel Art Centre was founded in March 1914. Many of the artists who allied themselves with the vorticist movement [*see* Vorticists] attended the Rebel Art Centre, including Wadsworth, Hamilton, Henri Gaudier-Brzeska, Lawrence Atkinson, Jessica Dismorr, and Helen Saunders. Ezra Pound also supported it warmly, and he joined forces with Lewis to bring about the birth of vorticism. The movement finally emerged in the rumbustious magazine *Blast* (July 1914), which Lewis edited. He wrote many of the essays it contained, and illustrated a wide selection of work by himself and his friends in its large, boldly designed pages. Lewis had by now defined his opposition to Marinetti and the Italian futurists. He objected to the way futurism rhapsodized about the machine age, and he also disapproved of its emphasis on blurred movement. Lewis opted for hardness and clarity of definition in his own art. However explosive his vorticist designs may be, they are always enclosed by decisive contours. The skyscraper forms of the modern city may sway and induce vertiginous sensations, but Lewis insisted on structural lucidity. Vagueness and indistinct forms were abhorrent to him. He wanted his vorticist work to take on some of the character of the machines that fascinated him, and he hoped vorticism would be able to develop an art that made people more aware of the rapidly changing character of modern life.

War The advent of the First World War frustrated that hope. No sooner had *Blast* been published than hostilities were declared, and Lewis had very little time left to build on the vorticist initiative. He was able to pursue his interest in large-scale schemes, decorating the study of Ford Madox Ford's London house with blazing red murals, and then devising a complete vorticist room for the Restaurant de la Tour Eiffel in Percy Street (1915–16). He also organized London's only vorticist exhibition in June 1915, and produced a second issue of *Blast* (a 'war number') at the same time. But the entire country was being overtaken by the escalating war, and in 1916 Lewis joined the army as a gunner. His experiences in the war served him well as subjects for painting. After his appointment as an official war artist, he painted two enormous canvases based on his memories of life in a gun pit, and one of them, *A Battery Shelled* (1919; IWM), is among his finest achievements. But it revealed at the same time that Lewis was returning to a more representational style, and leaving his vorticist concerns behind. He subsequently came to regard his avant-garde period as 'a little narrow segment of time, on the far side of world war i. That first war, you have to regard, as far as I am concerned, as a black solid mass, cutting off all that went before it' (Lewis to James Thrall Soby, 9 April 1947, *The Letters of Wyndham Lewis*, 406).

The destructive power of a war dominated by terrible mechanical weapons altered Lewis's attitude towards the machine age. He also felt, in common with many other artists, that he needed to submit himself to the discipline of drawing from life again. His first one-man show, held at the Goupil Gallery in February 1919, contained many drawings of the war in a frankly figurative style. Lewis's move towards a more representational idiom was prompted, too, by his fast-developing interest in writing fiction. His first and most experimental novel, *Tarr*, was published in 1918, and from then on Lewis devoted an increasing amount of his formidable energy to writing. The exhibition called 'Group X', held at the Mansard Gallery in spring 1920, brought together many of the artists formerly associated with vorticism. But it was more of an end than a beginning, and they never again joined forces for group activities. From then on Lewis, the self-styled 'enemy', was a man alone.

A man alone Collectors as eminent as the New York patron John Quinn continued for a time to support Lewis on a generous scale, and he enjoyed travelling with friends to the continent. During a trip to Paris in 1920 he was introduced to James Joyce by T. S. Eliot, whose early poetry Lewis had published in the second issue of *Blast*. But these new contacts did not lead to a desire for the formation of another group. When he held the exhibition 'Tyros and portraits' at the Leicester Galleries in 1921, the sense of acid satire pervading the work belonged to Lewis alone. The most ambitious painting in the show, a carefully executed canvas called *A Reading of Ovid (Tyros)* (1920–21; Scottish National Gallery of Modern Art, Edinburgh), is animated by a strain of menacing absurdity. Lewis saw the tyros as elemental creatures, leering embodiments of his comic vision.

No one else in England was painting with this degree of peculiarly remorseless mirth. An unmistakable feeling of isolation and retrenchment pervades Lewis's *Portrait of the Artist as the Painter Raphael* (1921; City of Manchester Art Galleries), also included in the 1921 show. This is the redoubtable image of a thirty-eight-year-old artist who has decided to stand his ground and remain resolute in the face of any attempt to undermine his defences. The rim of his hat has a blade-like sharpness, signifying Lewis's willingness to wield it against adversaries who come too close. William Rothenstein recalled his astonishment when, meeting Lewis again after several years, he 'now discovered a formidable figure, armed and armoured, like a tank, ready to cross any country, however rough and hostile, to attack without formal declaration of war' (W. Rothenstein, *Men and Memories, 1900–22*, 1932, 378–9). There is a metallic quality about this portrait which recalls Tarr's declaration that 'the lines and masses of the statue are its soul. No restless, quick flame-like ego is imagined for the *inside* of it. It has no inside. This is another condition of art; *to have no inside*, nothing you cannot *see*' (W. Lewis, *Tarr*, 1918, 354).

Flesh and blood Lewis was ready, now, to engage with the physical world in a far more particularized way. He explained that:

> the geometrics which had interested me so exclusively before, I now felt were bleak and empty. They wanted filling. They were still as much present to my mind as ever, but submerged in the coloured vegetation, the flesh and blood, that is life. (Lewis, *Rude Assignment*, 129)

Portraiture presented an especially stimulating challenge to an artist impelled by this new-found appetite for close observation. Iris Barry, who lived with Lewis for a few years and bore him two children, became a forbidding presence in a large canvas called *Praxitella* (1920–21; Leeds City Art Gallery). Their relationship was continually riven by conflicts, and this steely painting reflects them. She was a quick-tempered individual who, according to Jeffrey Meyers, 'could be very amusing or quite truculent, always long on mockery and short on tact' (Meyers, *The Enemy*, 90).

With the Sitwells, Lewis enjoyed at first a mutually admiring friendship. Having contributed to the journal *Art and Letters*, for which Osbert worked, he soon met the brothers and contributed the frontispiece to Sacheverell's *Doctor Donne and Gargantua—First Canto* in 1921. Lewis was sufficiently interested in *Façade* to attend two performances, and for a while he regularly accepted Edith's invitations to her tea parties in Pembridge Mansions. When he began work on his celebrated portrait of her (Tate collection) Edith soon realized that she was dealing with a strangely unpredictable and multi-faceted personality, and described how 'this remarkable man had a habit of appearing in various roles, partly as a disguise … and partly in order to defy his own loneliness' (V. Glendinning, *Edith Sitwell: a Unicorn among Lions*, 1981, 83). But then she became upset by his behaviour. 'He was, unfortunately, seized with a kind of *schwärmerei* for me', she recalled. 'I did not respond. It did not get very far, but was a nuisance as he *would* follow me about' (E. Salter, *The Last Years of a Rebel*, 1967, 61). She was probably frightened by his advances, for her biographer Victoria Glendinning has pointed out that 'this is the only occasion on record when any man is alleged to have shown direct sexual interest in Edith' (Glendinning, 85). Her termination of their friendship did not, fortunately, prevent Lewis from completing the portrait in 1935. The antagonism which prompted him to lampoon Edith as Lady Harriet in his sprawling satirical novel *The Apes of God* (1930) did not impair the painting's imperturbable poise. Her trance-like appearance bears out Lewis's declaration, in his ambitious book *Time and Western Man* (1927), 'that creative art is a spell, a talisman, an incantation—that it is *magic*, in short' (W. Lewis, *Time and Western Man*, 1927, 198).

'The Man of the World' By this time Lewis's pictorial art had dwindled in quantity so much that he referred to his pictures as 'the fragments I amuse myself with in the intervals of my literary work' (W. Lewis, 'A world art and tradition', *Drawing and Design*, Feb 1929). After temporarily abandoning the Sitwell portrait in 1923 he did no oil painting for several years, and his production of graphic work also diminished as the decade proceeded. Although Lewis did not publish any books between 1919 and 1926, he was increasingly absorbed in the researching, planning, and execution of an enormous 'megalo-mastodonic masterwork' called 'The Man of the World'. The projected book proved far too ambitious, and he eventually split it up into half a dozen separate volumes: *The Art of being Ruled*, *The Lion and the Fox*, *Time and Western Man*, *The Childermass*, *Paleface*, and *The Apes of God*.

Lewis was permanently short of money, and he perpetually fell out with those most willing to be his patrons. But he managed to visit New York for the first time in 1927, and incorporated references to its vertically thrusting architecture in a painting called *Bagdad* (1927–8; Tate collection). He also travelled to Morocco and other parts of north Africa in 1931, a year after marrying Gladys Anne Hoskyns, a British art student whose father was a farmer. Her mother was German, and after visiting Germany in 1930 and the following year, Lewis published a disastrously admiring book called *Hitler* (1931). Although he repudiated his praise in *The Hitler Cult* (1939), the damage was done. Lewis made even more enemies than before, and when the Royal Academy rejected his portrait of Eliot (Durban Art Gallery, South Africa) in 1938 his notoriety increased. Augustus John resigned from the academy in protest at its hostility to Lewis's work, but Lewis remained a perpetual outsider in the eyes of the British art establishment. Illness dogged him in the 1930s as well, resulting from a gland infection contracted during the First World War. He had a number of serious operations and periods of convalescence, but they did not prevent him publishing one of his most outstanding novels, *Revenge for Love*, in 1937. Just before the Second World War was declared in 1939, Lewis and his wife left England for six years. They stayed in New York, Buffalo, and Toronto, where he remained until 1943. Then he accepted a year's lectureship at Assumption College, Windsor, Ontario. It proved an unexpectedly happy period, even though he was forced at times to produce mediocre, pot-boiling portraits. But he was in danger of being forgotten, and his reputation only revived after his return to London in 1945.

His appointment as *The Listener's* art critic the following year was felicitous, enabling Lewis to demonstrate his remarkable responsiveness to emergent artists as well as his contemporaries. He exerted a wide influence, and his *Listener* column was terminated only when blindness afflicted him in 1951. Visitors to his retrospective exhibition at the Redfern Gallery two years before knew how much of a loss he was to British art, but Lewis was awarded a civil-list pension and continued to write fiction with undiminished energy. *Self Condemned*, one of his finest novels, appeared in 1954, and in the same year he published *The Demon of Progress in the Arts*, a polemic which showed how far his attitude towards aesthetic extremism had altered since his early vorticist days. In the following year his trilogy *The Human Age* was broadcast on the BBC's Third Programme, uniting *The Childermass* (1928) with two succeeding parts commissioned by the BBC in 1951: *Monstre gai* and *Malign Fiesta*. They were his literary swansong, and his achievements as an artist were celebrated in 1956 by a large retrospective exhibition at the Tate Gallery called 'Wyndham Lewis and vorticism'. The show was staged just in time: he died in the Westminster Hospital, London, on 7 March 1957. RICHARD CORK

Sources W. Lewis, *Blasting and bombardiering* (1937) · W. Lewis, *Wyndham Lewis the artist, from 'Blast' to Burlington House* (1939) · W. Lewis, *Rude assignment: a narrative of my career up-to-date* (1950) · G. Grigson, *A master of our time: a study of Wyndham Lewis* (1951) · C. Handley-Read, *The art of Wyndham Lewis* (1951) · H. Kenner, *Wyndham Lewis* (1954) · E. W. F. Tomlin, *Wyndham Lewis* (1955) · G. Wagner, *Wyndham Lewis: a portrait of the artist as the enemy* (1957) · *The letters of Wyndham Lewis*, ed. W. K. Rose (1963) · W. Michel, *Wyndham Lewis: paintings and drawings* (1971) · D. G. Bridson, *The filibuster: a study of the political ideas of Wyndham Lewis* (1972) · R. T. Chapman, *Wyndham Lewis: fictions and satires* (1973) · R. Cork, *Vorticism and its allies* (1974) [exhibition catalogue, Hayward Gallery, London, 27 March – 2 June 1974] · R. Cork, *Vorticism and abstract art in the first machine age*, 2 vols. (1975–6) · A. Munton, *The politics of Wyndham Lewis* (1976) · T. Materer, *Wyndham Lewis the novelist* (1976) · F. Jameson, *Fables of aggression: Wyndham Lewis, the modernist as fascist* (1979) · J. Farrington, *Wyndham Lewis* (1980) · J. Meyers, *The enemy: a biography of Wyndham Lewis* (1980) · J. Meyers, ed., *Wyndham Lewis: a revaluation* (1980) · P. Edwards, *Wyndham Lewis: art and war* (1992) · C. M. Mastin, R. Stacey, and T. Dilworth, *The talented intruder: Wyndham Lewis in Canada, 1939–1945* (1993) · *CGPLA Eng. & Wales* (1957)

Archives Ransom HRC, MSS and letters | BL, letters to Sydney Schiff and Violet Schiff, Add. MS 52918 · BL, corresp. with Society of Authors, Add. MS 63282 · LUL, letters to Thomas Sturge Moore · Tate collection, letters to Sir William Rothenstein and Sir John Rothenstein [photocopies] · U. Reading L., letters to George Bell & Sons | FILM BFI NFTVA, news footage of Lewis in 1938, commenting on Royal Academy's rejection of his T. S. Eliot portrait | SOUND BBC sound archives, Lewis reading his own writings

Likenesses A. John, etching, *c*.1903, BM, NPG · A. John, etching and drypoint, *c*.1903, priv. coll. · A. John, oils, *c*.1905, priv. coll. · G. C. Beresford, photographs, 1913–29, NPG · photographs, 1914–38, Hult. Arch. · A. L. Coburn, photogravure photograph, 1916, NPG [*see illus.*] · photograph, *c*.1917, NPG · W. Lewis, self-portrait, drawing, 1920, State University of New York, Buffalo · W. Lewis, self-portrait, oils, *c*.1920–1921, Ferens Art Gallery, Hull · W. Lewis, self-portrait, oils, 1921, Man. City Gall. · W. Lewis, self-portrait, ink and wash drawing, 1932, NPG · W. Lewis, self-portrait, pencil drawing, 1938, State University of New York · M. Ayrton, pencil drawing, 1955, priv. coll. · M. Ayrton, portraits, 1955, NPG · W. Roberts, group portrait, oils, 1961–2 (*The Vorticists at the Restaurant de la Tour Eiffel, spring 1915*), Tate collection; *see illus. in* Vorticists (*act.* 1914–1919)

Wealth at death £1239 8*s*. 9*d*.: probate, 3 May 1957, *CGPLA Eng. & Wales*

Lewkenor, Sir Edward (1542–1605), politician and patron of puritans, was born in Hertfordshire, the eldest son of the ten children of Edward Lewkenor (1517–1556), groom-porter in the household of Edward VI and Mary I, and his wife, Dorothy (*c*.1525–1589), daughter of Robert Wroth of

Enfield. He was a scion of the illustrious Lewkenors of Sussex, and his parents were both staunchly protestant. His father, who had been Robert Wroth's ward, was implicated in the Dudley conspiracy and died a prisoner in the Tower. Through his mother he was related to the Rich family and to other leading Tudor families; Sir Francis Walsingham was named in her will. Lewkenor's uncle, Thomas Wroth, was Edward VI's favourite and, later, a Marian exile. In March 1559 Elizabeth's first parliament restored his family in blood. The Sussex estates were already back in Dorothy's possession.

Lewkenor matriculated at St John's College, Cambridge, in November 1559, proceeded BA in 1561, and was admitted a fellow on 27 March of the same year. He was admitted on 7 November 1562 to the Middle Temple, where from 1565 to 1567 he shared a room with James Morice, who in due course was to be a fellow puritan MP. His son's epitaph states that, after leaving Cambridge, Lewkenor obtained an appointment in the royal household. In 1569 he married Susan (1553–1605), the younger daughter and coheir of Thomas Heigham of Heigham Hall and Denham. He then settled at Denham Hall in Suffolk. About 1590 a modernization was added to the fairly modest early sixteenth-century hall, probably to accommodate their growing family. Edward and Susan worked with the widowed Martha Heigham, who also lived at the hall, in making Denham a place of evangelical enlightenment. They had nine children. Of their two sons, Edward, the elder, was to inherit the Suffolk estates, and Robert the manor of Kingston Bowsey in Sussex.

Lewkenor built up an estate of middling size in Suffolk: his lands were valued at the time of his death at a little under £100. In due course he owned the whole of the original manor of Denham and much of the surrounding area and was able to extend his domain into something like a private park. Denham Abbots, which included the church and its tithes, he held of the crown. Lewkenor arrived in west Suffolk shortly before a new generation of zealous and public-spirited Calvinistic gentry, headed by Sir John Heigham and Sir Robert Jermyn (to both of whom he was related), and a new and remarkable society of learned ministers, began to build up what has been called 'the primitive puritan commonwealth in Suffolk' (Collinson, 'Magistracy and ministry', 74). A JP for the county from 1593, Lewkenor became an important part of this 'aristocratic' first wave of puritanism. He was also influential in Sussex, filling one of the livings in his gift with Samuel Norden, who became the most militant of the puritan ministers in that county. He was recognized as an exemplary magistrate.

As impropriator of a donative cure Lewkenor was in the position of patron to the godly minister, Robert Oldmayne, alias Pricke, whom he brought to Denham in 1577 and with whom he established a close working partnership. Oldmayne, who was from the locality, received a stipend of £20 a year and an annuity from Mrs Heigham. He attested Lewkenor's love of the ministry of the word in the funeral sermon that he preached at Denham in 1606. The inscription on Lewkenor's tomb, while referring to his service at court and in parliament, says that he is to be praised 'chiefly' because 'by his means the preaching of the gospel was brought into this small and obscure village'.

It is as an MP that Lewkenor is chiefly renowned. He sat for every parliament from 1571 until his death, with the exception of the session of 1601. He represented Tamworth, New Shoreham, Newport (Cornwall), and, in five sessions, Maldon—in all but one case owing his election to patrons sympathetic to puritans. There can be no doubt that he was in parliament to advance the puritan cause; moreover, it was the radical presbyterian wing of the puritan movement that he sought to advance. He was a committee man rather than an orator, but much of his recorded activity is in matters of religion. Anthony Cope's bill and book of 1587, in support of which he spoke, was probably the most extreme proposal ever to be put before the House of Commons. It was a clerically inspired plan, with an accompanying revised edition of the Geneva prayer book, for an entirely presbyterian constitution for the Church of England. The queen's opposition quickly led to all the conspirators being imprisoned for a time in the Tower.

The collection of Lewkenor's papers, acquired by the British Museum in 1910 among the Townshend manuscripts, is now BL, Add. MS 38492. It comprises a unique file of the working parliamentary papers of an Elizabethan and Jacobean MP. All sixty-five items relate in some way to religion. Forty belong to the first two years of James's reign. They include matter relating to the issues of conformity and subscription as they impinged on James's first parliament, to the Hampton Court conference, and to the puritan 'surveys of the ministry' of which he was sponsor, as well as petitions and narratives of 'troubles'. All but thirteen are connected with the national campaign for further reformation.

As a militant member of the Elizabethan and early Jacobean puritan movement, Lewkenor was attempting by political means to complete the reformation of the Church of England from within. It was an attempt which stirred up the beginnings of the Anglican riposte. He was in parliament at a time when puritan aims, associated with a passionate protestant nationalism, were gaining ground and some puritan MPs were beginning to press for parliamentary liberty. Already, however, something of an archaic quality begins to be evident in him, as in his family in general. It is the archaic quality of aristocratic '*âmes d'élite*' who harken back to a distinguished past and to more ancient history. He was an interesting mixture of conservative and radical, with one foot in the old feudal order and one foot in the modern world. Religion is the key to his whole career. He was known to his contemporaries above all for his earnestness and piety. Despite the radical nature of his puritanism, he was probably in the last analysis more of a conservative. In presbyterianism he saw the form of the church's original apostolic order. He cared most for order and tradition. He was completely loyal to Queen Elizabeth and King James, and was knighted in May 1603. In his allegiance to the crown, however, he experienced an increasing frustration of his puritan aims.

Lewkenor died of smallpox at Denham Hall on 3 October 1605; his wife had died of the same disease the day before. The double tragedy made a profound local impression. He was buried at Denham church on 5 October. He left no will, his eldest son acting as his nuncupative executor. His obsequies were formally celebrated on 9 January 1606. A huge monument was provided in Denham church for his parents by their eldest son: a tomb chest with six Corinthian columns in mock porphyry bearing a canopy with tall superstructure and massive armorial achievements. Under the canopy on the tomb chest, in slightly less than life-size effigy, Sir Edward and Lady Susan kneel on cushions in attitudes of devotion, their eight surviving children in rows behind them. The monument is situated in the north side mortuary chapel which was purposely constructed for it, probably by Lewkenor or soon after his death. A threnodia of elegiac verse in Greek, Latin, Hebrew, and English, assembled by the eldest son in memory of his parents—to which many friends in Cambridge University contributed—was published in the year after they died. Among the contributors were two future and famous bishops, William Bedell and Joseph Hall. Adam Winthrop of Groton in Suffolk noted in an old almanac after Lewkenor's death:'Vir bonus et doctus fuit et patriae amans' ('He was a good and learned man, and devoted to his country'; Hervey, 212). JOHN WILLIAM BRIDGEN

Sources P. Collinson, 'Magistracy and ministry: a Suffolk miniature', *Reformation, conformity and dissent*, ed. R. B. Knox (1977), 70–91 • S. H. A. Hervey, *Denham parish registers, 1539–1850, with notes* (1904) • P. Collinson, *The Elizabethan puritan movement*, pbk edn (1990) • P. Collinson, *English puritanism* (1983) • HoP, *Commons, 1558–1603*, 2.472–3 • D. MacCulloch, *Suffolk and the Tudors: politics and religion in an English county, 1500–1600* (1986) • G. J. Armytage, ed., *Middlesex pedigrees*, Harleian Society, 65 (1914), 17 • *Threnodia in obitum D. Edwardi Lewkenor equitis & D. Susannae conjugis charissimae* (1606) • J. Neale, *Elizabeth I and her parliaments* (1953) • S. Clark [S. Clarke], *The lives of sundry eminent persons in this later age* (1683) • R. Oldmayne, *A very godly and learned sermon preached at the funeral of Sir Edward Lewkenor* (1608) • *VCH Oxfordshire*, Lewknor hundred • private information (2004) [librarian, Middle Temple] • private information (2004) [archivist, St John Cam.]

Archives BL, Add. MS 38492

Likenesses effigy on monument, 1605, Denham church, Suffolk

Wealth at death £96 2*s*. 0*d*.

Lewknor, Sir Lewes (*c*.**1560–1627**), courtier and translator, was the first surviving son of Thomas Lewknor (*c*.1538–1596), a politician, of Tangmere and Selsey, Sussex, and his first wife, Bridget, the daughter of John Lewes of Selsey. From Lyon's Inn, Lewknor entered the Middle Temple on 12 October 1579, bound with his uncle, Richard Lewknor (1542–1616), a distinguished lawyer. However, his Catholicism led him into voluntary exile in the Low Countries the following year. A captaincy in the Spanish service and marriage to Beatrice de Rota, the daughter of a Brabant merchant, soon followed, but a severe arm wound ended his military career. The loss of his pension, combined with litigation over his wife's dowry, brought severe financial difficulties, and in June 1590 Lewknor sought a safe conduct home through his relative Sir Robert Sidney. He reported in detail to Burghley on Englishmen in the Spanish service and was probably the anonymous author of *A Discourse of the Usage of the English Fugitives, by the Spaniard*, first published early in 1595; such co-operation gained protection from creditors. In 1591 Lewknor was in the suite of the embassy to France of his cousin Sir Henry Unton. His first acknowledged work, *The Resolved Gentleman*, an indirect translation (from Acuña's Spanish) of *Le chevalier délibéré* by Olivier de la Marche, appeared in 1594. It was dedicated to Anne, countess of Warwick, who was related to Lewknor through the Sidneys.

Following his father's death in 1596, Lewknor took possession of Selsey Park and the adjacent grange. (These were leased from the crown and surrendered in 1612.) Lewknor was returned to parliament in October 1597 for Midhurst, his father's old seat, probably through the interest of his uncle Richard.

In August 1598 Lewknor completed for Lady Warwick *The Commonwealth and Government of Venice*, largely a translation of Gasparo Contarini's *De magistratibus et republica Venetorum*. Commendatory poems in this and *The Resolved Gentleman* show him to have been an admired member of a literary circle that included John Harrington and, possibly, Edmund Spenser; and it has been argued that Lewknor provided source material for Shakespeare's *Merchant of Venice* and Ben Jonson's *Volpone*.

Lewknor claimed *The Commonwealth* was 'written at idle times when I had nothing els to doe, being at much more leysure then willingly I woulde bee' (sig. A3*v*), but its publication occurred as his various duties mounted. In 1599 he became a gentleman pensioner. The next year he was called on to supervise arrangements for hosting diplomats and other foreign dignitaries, his first recorded attendance on an ambassador being in February 1600. He also acted as an interpreter of Spanish. When still perfecting that language he had translated Antonio de Torquemada's *Jardín de flores curiosas*, and this was now brought into print by Ferdinando Walker as *The Spanish Mandevile of Miracles, or, The Garden of Curious Flowers*.

James I's succession in 1603 brought great benefits for Lewknor. On 22 April he was knighted; then on 21 May he was appointed master of the ceremonies, a newly created office that Sir Edmund Tilney had hoped for. This position formalized Lewknor's duties in respect of looking after diplomats and other important foreigners. Assisted by up to three deputies, he initiated the management of precedence and protocol that was so important in the seventeenth century and is still embodied in the office of marshal of the diplomatic corps. The following year he was again returned to parliament, this time for Bridgnorth (his uncle Richard being then justice of Chester).

Beatrice Lewknor died on 11 March 1605 after a long illness. Lewknor then married a young widow called Argall, but she died that October of smallpox. Such personal sorrow contrasted with public achievement. On 7 November 1605 Lewknor was granted for life his office of master of the ceremonies. His assistant master of ceremonies from

1612 was John Finet. The two were often on bad terms, Finet being very solicitous in his duties and Lewknor apparently feeling that his junior was encroaching on his prerogatives. Many of Lewknor's activities after October 1612 were recorded in Finet's notes, published posthumously in 1656 as *Finetti philoxenis: Som Choice Observations of Sir John Finet*. By 1613 Lewknor was a justice of the peace for Middlesex, and on 25 September 1614 he was appointed a commissioner for the musters in the same county.

If Lewknor ever shed his Spanish sympathies, they soon returned. In Spanish pay since at least July 1603, he was seen as among those 'that have Englishe tongues and Spanishe harts' (William Trumbull to Ralph Winwood, 14/24 Feb 1617, *Downshire MSS*, 6.112, no. 258). In 1615 Lewknor sent his younger son William over to Antwerp to supervise the litigation surrounding the estate of his first wife, Beatrice. By the following year William was serving in the Spanish garrison there. On 17 April 1618 Lewknor himself wrote to Diego de la Fuente, confessor to the Spanish ambassador Gondomar: 'Todo el consuelo que tengo en este mundo esta puesto en el fauor del Señor Conde y vuestra Paternidad' ('All the consolation that I have in this world rests in the favour of his lordship the count [Gondomar] and your [Fuente's] paternity'; Loomie, *Spain and the Jacobean Catholics*, 2.104). In 1623 Finet suggested that Lewknor 'leaned overmuch' to achieve the 'particular satisfaction' of the Spanish ambassador, and the following year he recorded Conway's comment that Lewknor 'would rather attend the Spanish ambassadors than the Dutch' (*Finetti philoxenis*, 118, 138). Such partiality had angered the less pecunious Venetian diplomats since 1606, and matters came to a head in 1625 when the Venetian ambassador Pesaro complained that Lewknor, whom he described as 'an utter Spaniard, and a pensioner' (Pesaro to doge and senate, 25 May 1625, *CSP Venice*, *1625–6*, 55), had slighted him by favouring his Spanish counterpart. The privy council accepted Lewknor's plea that sickness, rather than disrespect, was the cause, but found it politic to suspend him from office and put him under house arrest from October until December.

Lewknor died on 11 March 1627, survived by his third wife, Mary, the daughter of Richard Blount of Dedisham, Sussex, whom he had married some time after 1605, and by at least his first son, Thomas (1588–1645), a Jesuit who ministered in England from 1625 until his death. Lewknor was a man of varied talents and even Finet, his successor as master of the ceremonies, with whom he often quarrelled, could admit that, 'to say the truth, the gentleman him self for his many good partes deserve[s] respect, and should have more of me were he more patient and less jelous' (Finet to Trumbull, 12 Nov 1616, *Downshire MSS*, 6.43, no. 109). Lewknor's constituents in Bridgnorth bore witness to his 'honest and just dealing' with them (certain inhabitants of Bridgnorth to Salisbury, no date, *Salisbury MSS*, 24.197). Most tellingly, perhaps, the eulogies contained in his published works evince the esteem in which he was held by the literary coterie to which he belonged.

Roderick Clayton

Sources R. C. Gabriel, 'Lewknor, Lewis', HoP, *Commons, 1558–1603* • C. Whitfield, 'Sir Lewis Lewkenor and *The Merchant of Venice*: a suggested connection', *N&Q*, 209 (1964), 123–33 • *Report on the manuscripts of the marquis of Downshire*, 6 vols. in 7, HMC, 75 (1924–95), vols. 2–6 • *Calendar of the manuscripts of the most hon. the marquis of Salisbury*, 24 vols., HMC, 9 (1883–1976), vols. 10–11, 15–19, 21, 24 • *CSP dom., 1580–1626* • *CSP Venice, 1603–7; 1625–6* • *CSP for., 1579–80; 1589* • *APC, 1590–1625* • A. J. Loomie, *The Spanish Elizabethans* (1963) • A. J. Loomie, ed., *Spain and the Jacobean Catholics*, 2, Catholic RS, 68 (1978) • *Finetti philoxenis: som choice observations of Sir John Finet*, ed. J. Howell (1656) • H. Lonchay, J. Cuvelier, and J. Lefèvre, eds., *Correspondance de la cour d'Espagne sur les affaires des Pays-Bas au XVIIe siècle*, 1 (Brussels, 1923) • H. Sydney and others, *Letters and memorials of state*, ed. A. Collins, 2 (1746) • C. T. Martin, ed., *Minutes of parliament of the Middle Temple*, 4 vols. (1904–5), vol. 1 • 'The note-book of John Southcote, D.D., from 1623 to 1637', *Miscellanea, I*, Catholic RS, 1 (1905), 97–116 • *Calendar of the manuscripts of the marquis of Bath preserved at Longleat, Wiltshire*, 5 vols., HMC, 58 (1904–80), vol. 4 [Seymour papers, 1532–1686] • W. A. Shaw, *The knights of England*, 2 vols. (1906) • W. D. Cooper, 'Pedigree of the Lewknor family', *Sussex Archaeological Collections*, 3 (1850), 89–102 • *The letters of John Chamberlain*, ed. N. E. McClure, 1 (1939), 209

Lewkowitsch, Julius (1857–1913), industrial chemist, was born on 4 September 1857 at Ostrowo in Silesia. His father was Moritz Lewkowitsch, described as a general merchant. Julius studied chemistry at the University of Breslau, obtaining his PhD in 1879. During his time as a student, he supported himself and paid the expenses of his university education by undertaking private teaching. After graduation, he settled on an academic career of research and teaching in pure chemistry, first under Professor Victor von Richter at Breslau. Then he took a post under Professor Hans Landolt in the chemistry laboratory of the agricultural high school in Berlin. From there he moved to the University of Heidelberg, where he became assistant to Professor Victor von Meyer.

Had Lewkowitsch continued his academic career he would undoubtedly have achieved an eminent position, but in his late twenties he decided on a complete change of direction, into chemical technology. He first worked in the coal tar distilling industry, but at the age of thirty emigrated to England and turned to the soap industry, becoming a chemist and technical manager at Joseph Watson & Sons in Leeds. In 1895 he set up as a consulting chemist in Manchester, later moving to London. He became a naturalized British subject, and on 5 May 1902, at Hampstead register office, London, he married Katherine Julia Morris.

With his shift from pure to applied chemistry, Lewkowitsch embarked on the work that was to make him famous, the chemical technology of vegetable and animal oils, fats, and waxes. The development of this branch of the chemical industry owed much to his careful and thorough investigations, and at the time of his death *The Times* hailed him as the leading authority in this field. In 1895 he published the first edition of his monumental *Chemical Technology and Analysis of Oils, Fats and Waxes* in one volume. The work grew with successive editions and by the time the fifth edition appeared in 1913 it had expanded to three volumes. The final edition was brought out by his assistant in 1921. In addition the work was published in French and German.

Lewkowitsch was robust physically and intellectually and in spite of his investigative work and a busy consultancy, he placed his great knowledge and linguistic talents freely at the disposal of professional colleagues. He served on the councils of the Chemical Society and the Society of Chemical Industry, of which he was also a vice-president. He played an active part in several meetings of the International Union of Applied Chemistry.

Lewkowitsch was a keen mountaineer and possessed an intimate knowledge of the Alps. It was while on holiday at Chamonix that he contracted an acute respiratory infection; he died there after a short illness on 16 September 1913. He was survived by his widow, a son, and a daughter.

Apart from his published work consisting of his great treatise and scientific papers in several learned journals, listed in Poggendorf, Lewkowitsch left copious manuscript notes recording the development of his technological ideas. These are preserved in the library of Dr Carter Litchfield in the USA. A curious feature of these notes is that there are sentences in which English and German expressions are intermingled. L. R. DAY

Sources *The Times* (22 Sept 1913) • K. Berger, 'Julius Lewkowitsch and early palm oil technology', *Chemical Industry*, 17 (1989), 2445 • J. C. Poggendorff and others, eds., *Biographisch-literarisches Handwörterbuch zur Geschichte der exacten Wissenschaften*, 8 vols. (Leipzig, 1863–) • 'Joseph Watson and Sons Ltd', *Archives of British Chemical Industry, 1750–1914: a handlist*, 201–3 • *Journal of the Society of Chemical Industry*, 32 (1913), 931–2 • W. J. P., *JCS*, 105 (1914), 1217–19 • m. cert.
Wealth at death £21,410 5*s.* 2*d.*: administration, 15 Oct 1913, *CGPLA Eng. & Wales*

Lewson [*née* Vaughan], **Jane** [*known as* Lady Lewson] (**1699/1700?–1816**), eccentric and centenarian, is thought to have been born in Essex Street, Strand, London, her maiden name being Vaughan. Having been left in comfortable circumstances by the death in 1726 of her husband, a merchant named Lewson or Leveson, she refused several suitors, and as Lady Lewson, as she was known, lived reclusively in a large house in Coldbath Square, London.

To the end of her life, at which period she was attended by one old manservant, Lewson retained the dress and the manners of the time of George I. Her terror of taking cold led her to prohibit the use of water in her house, with the result that the windows and walls became in course of time completely encrusted with dirt. Although her house fell into disarray, her garden was always kept in good order. Her other eccentric habits included lubricating her face and hands with lard. Though she rigidly refused all drugs and doctors, she enjoyed excellent health, and, in a manner reminiscent of Katherine Fitzgerald, countess of Desmond (*d.* 1604), is said to have cut two new teeth at the age of eighty-seven. She had a retentive memory, and was fond of relating the events of 1715 and 1745. She died in Coldbath Square on 28 May 1816, at the reputed age of 116, and was buried on 3 June in Bunhill Fields, London. Lewson is one of the figures who may have provided the inspiration for Dickens's Miss Havisham in *Great Expectations*. THOMAS SECCOMBE, *rev.* DAVID TURNER

Jane Lewson (1699/1700?–1816), by R. Cooper, pubd 1821

Sources H. Wilson, *Wonderful characters*, 3 vols. (1821) • *GM*, 1st ser., 86/1 (1816), 633 • *A true and wonderful account of Mrs Jane Lewson* [n.d., 1816?]
Likenesses R. Cooper, engraving, NPG; repro. in Wilson, *Wonderful characters*, vol. 2 [*see illus.*] • stipple, BM, NPG

Lewsyn yr Heliwr. *See* Lewis, Lewis Jenkin (*bap.* 1793, *d.* 1848).

Lewy, Casimir (**1919–1991**), philosopher, was born in Warsaw, Poland, on 26 February 1919, the son of Ludwik Lewy (1887–1919) and his wife, Izabela, *née* Rybier (1892–1942). His father, who was a medical doctor, died when he was in infancy, so that he grew up in his mother's large and talented family. In 1927 he was sent to a fashionable private school in Warsaw owned by the Lutheran congregation, the Mikolaj Rej School, which was attended by a number of gifted people with whom he became friendly. At fifteen he read an article in a literary weekly by Tadeusz Kotarbiński, and his interest in philosophy was aroused. Characteristically he not only bought a copy of a book by Kotarbiński, but also started to attend lectures in philosophy at the University of Warsaw.

Lewy came to England in 1936 in order to improve his English but, concluding that this would be insufficiently stimulating, he matriculated at Cambridge and read philosophy as well. Although he had intended to return to

Warsaw after a year, he decided to continue with his studies in Cambridge under the supervision of John Wisdom at Trinity College. He graduated in 1939 with first-class honours, having already published four papers in the journal *Analysis*, a remarkable achievement for a man of twenty whose native language was Polish. The outbreak of war made a return to Poland impossible, and Lewy registered for a PhD on 'Some philosophical considerations about the survival of death' under the supervision of G. E. Moore. The degree was awarded in 1943, and from January 1943 to 1945 he lectured in Cambridge, taking as his theme an influential remark made by John Wisdom in his paper 'Metaphysics and verification' that the statements of philosophers are in a certain sense 'verbal'. Shortly after marrying Eleanor Ford (*b*. 1923/4), daughter of Percy Ford, a university professor, on 28 July 1945 Lewy took up a lectureship in Liverpool, where Eleanor also held a lectureship in economic history. They went on to have three sons: Nicholas, Sebastian, and John Dominic.

In 1952 Lewy returned to Cambridge as university lecturer in moral sciences. He was appointed Sidgwick lecturer in 1955, becoming a fellow of Trinity College in 1959. In 1972 he was appointed reader in philosophy, a post he held until his retirement in 1982. Lewy held visiting professorships at the University of Illinois in 1951–2, at the University of Texas at Austin in 1967, and at Yale in 1969. He was elected to an honorary fellowship of the Polish Society of Arts and Sciences Abroad in 1968, and to a fellowship of the British Academy in 1980. In 1985 *Exercises in Analysis*, which included papers by nine of his former pupils, was published as a token of gratitude for the passionate work that had gone into his supervisions.

During the first period at Cambridge, as well as attending many of Moore's lectures, Lewy attended all the lectures Wittgenstein gave between 1938 and 1945. He became friendly with both men, but it was Moore whom he chose as his PhD supervisor. His respect and affection for Moore were very great; in the preface to *Meaning and Modality* he says that he learned more from Moore's lectures on metaphysics in 1938–9 and in the preceding year than from any other course he attended. During the war he assisted Moore with the editorial work for the journal *Mind*, and after Moore's death he prepared two volumes of his papers for publication. The first, *Commonplace Book, 1919–1953*, was published in 1962, followed by *Lectures on Philosophy* in 1966. He also prepared for publication two books based on the lecture notes of C. D. Broad, Moore's successor at Cambridge, *Leibniz* (1975) and *Kant: an Introduction* (1978). The time devoted to meticulously preparing these volumes partly explains why he published so little after his return to Cambridge. However, his publications include *Meaning and Modality*, which though it was published in 1976 had grown out of the lectures he first gave in Cambridge during the war, for all that they were revised many times. Attacking reductive accounts of abstract entities, Lewy argues that many influential theories in the philosophy of language and logic—for example, that necessary truths are so by convention—are based on the mistaken supposition that such an account is possible. The book concludes with two dense chapters on entailment, the topic he wrote about most, concluding that any attempt to reconstruct an intuitive concept that avoids the paradoxes of strict implication will have aspects which are as anti-intuitive as the paradoxes themselves.

Lewy was an exceptionally able teacher, and many of his pupils went on to distinguished academic careers. To give of oneself as he did in lectures and tutorials must have been exhausting, and further explains why he published relatively little work of his own after 1952. His lectures and supervisions were devoted to a passionate and exhausting pursuit of the truth—the key point was invariably one of logic and meaning. It became apparent that it is easy to make mistakes, and difficult to live up to the standards set for one. But demanding though this was, supervisions could also be fun. Lewy had a superb dramatic talent, and loved telling stories delivered in a Polish accent with a strong vibrato and accompanying winks and gestures. Many concerned the extraordinary things other philosophers had said, culminating with such comments as 'If that's what his logic is like, I don't want to know about his moral philosophy' (personal knowledge). He died in Cambridge, of a heart attack, while being operated on for cancer of the colon, on 8 February 1991.

DAVID HOLDCROFT

Sources *The Guardian* (15 Feb 1991) • *The Times* (9 March 1991) • *The Times* (25 Nov 1991) • 'biographical note', *Exercises in analysis*, ed. I. M. Hacking (1985), 9–11 [essays by students of Casimir Levy] • Preface, C. Lewy, *Meaning and modality* (1976), 9 • personal knowledge (2004) • m. cert.
Archives CUL, letters to G. E. Moore
Likenesses photograph, repro. in Hacking, *Exercises in analysis*

Lewyn, John (*fl.* 1364–1398), master mason, is first recorded in 1364 working at Coldingham Priory, a Scottish dependency of Durham Cathedral priory. At Durham itself he had charge of building the kitchen serving the monks' refectory in 1367–74, during which period he was paid £13 6*s*. 8*d*. a year and a robe worth 13*s*. 4*d*. The kitchen is unique among Gothic structures of centralized plan in being covered by a masonry vault incorporating four pairs of intersecting parallel ribs. The small central octagon generated by these ribs carries the walls of the lantern and smoke louver. The inspiration behind this design is not obvious, although it is probably significant that a much less impressive square version of the same scheme was built over the kitchen of Raby Castle, co. Durham, also begun in 1367. An awareness of the timber vault over the octagonal crossing of Ely Cathedral (1334–41) is very likely, although the latter's solid geometry differs importantly from that at Durham. Whether Lewyn was acquainted with the much earlier Spanish Islamic and Romanesque vaults which provide the closest analogies for his vault cannot be known.

By 1368 Lewyn was described as 'the bishop's mason' and was granted lands by Bishop Thomas Hatfield (*d*. 1381); other grants by Hatfield were to follow in the 1370s. Also in 1368 Lewyn was appointed to repair the king's castle at Bamburgh. Some work had been done there by 1372, but in 1375 inquiry was made into allegations that Lewyn had received money for the work but had failed to carry out the repairs. In 1378, the same year as saw the reorganization of the king's works in southern England, Lewyn was appointed to carry out works at the royal castle of Carlisle and at Roxburgh Castle, the latter taken from the Scots in 1346. Lewyn's work at Carlisle, the still-extant main gatehouse, does not conform to the terms of the indenture for its building drawn up on 4 April 1378, perhaps because of the need to keep in continuous use the pre-existing and adjacent sheriff's office and prison.

By 1378 Lewyn may well have been regarded as the leading military architect in the north, for in that year he also contracted with Richard, Lord Scrope (*d.* 1403), for the first phase of Bolton Castle, Yorkshire. Work was completed *c.*1397, probably largely in accordance with the original scheme. Although unique in the intricacy of its internal planning, Bolton's quadrangular layout with bulky rectangular corner towers inspired imitations at Sheriff Hutton in the North Riding of Yorkshire (1382), Lumley in co. Durham, and Wressle in the East Riding of Yorkshire. The first two castles have several times been attributed to Lewyn. In their overall form, and in various points of detail, all the northern quadrangular castles are indebted to the greatest English castle-building project of the fourteenth century, Edward III's reconstruction of the upper ward at Windsor (1357–69).

In 1380 Lewyn contracted with John of Gaunt, duke of Lancaster (*d.* 1399), to build a new 'mantelet' against the inner face of the fourteenth-century gatehouse at Dunstanburgh Castle. Bishop John Fordham (*d.* 1425) in 1384 appointed Lewyn a commissioner of array for the city of Durham, and with several partners he was granted the borough of Durham to farm; he was also engaged in the export of wool overseas. In 1385–6 he was superintending building works for the crown at Berwick upon Tweed. For Ralph, sixth Lord Neville of Raby (*d.* 1425), Lewyn and his son Walter undertook in 1392 to renew all defective roads at Brancepeth, possibly the result of heavy wear during building operations at the castle there. Between 1390 and 1398 Lewyn was carrying out work at Finchale Priory, a dependency of Durham Priory. It has been plausibly suggested that around this time he was designing the unique cruciform donjon at Warkworth Castle for the earl of Northumberland. Even discounting this and the other major castles which have been attributed to him, Lewyn is clearly recognizable as the leading late fourteenth-century architect in the northernmost counties of England. JOHN HARVEY, *rev.* CHRISTOPHER WILSON

Sources J. Harvey and A. Oswald, *English mediaeval architects: a biographical dictionary down to 1550*, 2nd edn (1984), 181–4 · H. M. Colvin and others, eds., *The history of the king's works*, 6 vols. (1963–82), vol. 1, p. 186; vol. 2 · M. J. B. Hislop, 'John Lewyn and the architecture of the northern counties (1360–1400)', PhD diss., U. Nott., 1990 · M. J. B. Hislop, 'John of Gaunt's building works at Dunstanburgh Castle', *Archaeologia Aeliana*, 5th ser., 23 (1995), 139–44 · M. J. B. Hislop, 'Bolton Castle and the practice of architecture in the middle ages', *Journal, British Archaeological Association*, 149 (1996), 10–22 · M. R. McCarthy, H. R. T. Summerson, and R. G. Annis, *Carlisle Castle: a survey and documentary history* (1990), 146–8 · A. Emery, *Greater medieval houses of England and Wales, 1300–1500*, 1 (1996), 30–33, 303–12

Lewys ap Rhys ab Owain. *See* Dwnn, Lewys (*b. c.*1545, *d.* in or after 1616).

Lewys [Llywelyn] **Glyn Cothi** (*fl.* **1447–1489**), poet, was, as his cognomen indicates, a native of the region of the royal forest of Glyncothi in Carmarthenshire. Nothing is known of his family. According to local tradition his home was called Pwllcynbyd, which was in fact the name of a part of the forest in the parish of Llanybydder. Lewys was a familiar form of Llywelyn, both forms being used by the poet in his own work. There is evidence of a connection with the collegiate church of Abergwili near Carmarthen, and it may be that Lewys received some early education there, which would account for the element of Latin learning in his work, and perhaps also for his accomplishment as a scribe.

As many as 238 of Lewys's poems have survived, an unusually large corpus, which is explained by the fact that several of the poet's own manuscripts have been preserved, the most important being Peniarth MSS 70 and 109 in the National Library of Wales, both apparently completed in the late 1470s. The latter manuscript contains drawings of patrons' coats of arms above many of the poems, evidence of Lewys's detailed knowledge of heraldry. Lewys also copied some of his poems into manuscripts belonging to the relevant patrons, most notably the Red Book of Hergest when it was in the possession of the Tretower branch of the Vaughan family.

The number of Lewys's surviving poems, and the fact that he concentrated almost entirely on eulogy, means that his work provides invaluable evidence about the bardic circuits undertaken by fifteenth-century poets. He visited patrons in all parts of Wales, and the prosperous gentry of the border country of Gwent and Powys are especially well represented in his work. The heartland of his patronage was of course his own native region in the Tywi valley, where his principal patrons were the powerful family of Gruffudd ap Nicolas, his sons, and grandsons, most notably Sir Rhys ap Thomas. Lewys's career had only just begun when the Carmarthen eisteddfod was held under the auspices of Gruffudd ap Nicolas about 1451, but nevertheless it is surprising that there is no record of his part in it.

Lewys's political allegiance during the Wars of the Roses was probably determined initially by the influence of Gruffudd ap Nicolas's family, supporters of the Lancastrian cause. He went into hiding with Owain ap Gruffudd ap Nicolas in the mountains of north Wales after the Lancastrian defeat at the battle of Mortimer's Cross in 1461, and it was in that period that he composed several prophetic poems in support of the exiled Jasper Tudor. These probably gave rise to the unsubstantiated and inherently unlikely claim that he was an officer in Jasper's army. Lewys also enjoyed the patronage of prominent Yorkist noblemen during the reign of Edward IV, such as William Herbert of Raglan. Welsh interests seem to have been more important to him than the success of any of the English factions, and the defeat of the Yorkists at the battle of Banbury in 1469 is portrayed in his work as a national disaster. Towards the end of his life factional allegiance and nationalist sentiment converged when he enthusiastically welcomed the Welshman Henry Tudor as king in 1485, and it was with considerable justification that he declared then, 'Here is a long peace which is greatly deserved.'

There is evidence in several of Lewys's poems that he was maltreated by the citizens of Chester about 1465. He composed a virulent satire in response to the incident, and three request poems to Welsh gentry state that he was robbed of his possessions. The story that Lewys had married a widow of Chester, and was attacked by the citizens out of jealousy, is a late fabrication, and it is more likely that he was the victim of strict enforcement of the penal statutes which forbade Welshmen from settling in towns. Several of his other poems provide insights into his personal life, such as one thanking a nobleman and his wife for caring for him when he fell ill of a fever while on his way to celebrate the festival of St Padarn in the parish of Llanbadarn.

The style of Lewys Glyn Cothi's verse is typical of the golden age of classical Welsh poetry in its effortless artistry and genial celebration of the good life. He is outstanding for the naturalness of his versification, and his lines very often convey the rhythms of ordinary speech. This strength is the key to the popularity of his best-known poem, a heartfelt elegy on the death of his five-year-old son Siôn, in which he recalls the boy 'begging his mother for a little ball'. It seems that Siôn had already begun to learn his father's craft at that early age, and would have become a professional poet had he lived. It is not known whether Lewys had any other children.

Lewys's last poems are addressed to noblemen and clergymen in his own locality in the early years of the reign of Henry VII, and none can be dated later than 1489. He is believed to have been buried at Abergwili.

DAFYDD JOHNSTON

Sources *Gwaith Lewis Glyn Cothi*, ed. D. Johnston (1995) • *Lewys Glyn Cothi: (detholiad)*, ed. E. D. Jones (1984) • *Gwaith Lewis Glyn Cothi*, ed. E. D. Jones (1953) • E. D. Jones, 'A Welsh pencerdd's manuscripts', *Celtica*, 5 (1960), 17–27
Archives NL Wales, Peniarth MSS 70, 109

Lewys Môn (*d.* 1527), Welsh-language poet, was a native of Anglesey (Môn), and although his birthplace is unknown, references by other poets associate him with the commote of Llifon. The sixteenth-century genealogist Gruffudd Hiraethog names Lewys's parents as Gruffudd ap Dafydd ab Ieuan Finrwth and Angharad ferch Ieuan Goch ap Madog (NL Wales, Peniarth MS 139, ii). Gruffudd ap Dafydd ab Ieuan Finrwth, however, features as early as 1406 in a list of Anglesey submissions during the Glyndŵr uprising; this suggests that the Peniarth 139 genealogy has omitted a generation on the paternal side. It has been proposed (Wiliam) that Lewys may be identical with an Anglesey poet called Llywelyn ap Gruffudd ap Gwilym included in a late sixteenth-century list of poets (NL Wales, Cwrtmawr MS 3): no poem is ascribed to Llywelyn ap Gruffudd ap Gwilym, and the names Llywelyn and Lewys are commonly equated (Tudur Aled addresses Lewys Môn as Llywelyn). Significantly perhaps, a Llywelyn ap Gruffudd ap Gwilym appears as a party to a deed concerning land in Llanfair-yng-Nghornwy in the Anglesey commote of Talybolion which bordered on Lewys's commote of Llifon (University of Wales, Bangor, Bodorgan papers, 358). The years in which Llywelyn ap Gruffudd ap Gwilym flourished—the document is datable to the reign of either Henry VII or Henry VIII—are compatible with those of Lewys Môn. A Llywelyn ap Gruffudd ap Gwilym cited as a debtor in 1516 (University of Wales, Bangor, Porth yr Aur collection, 161, 166) may also be the Llywelyn ap Gruffudd ap Gwilym of Llanfair-yng-Nghornwy, possibly alias Lewys Môn.

Apart from the evidence of his poetry, which testifies to his travels among his patrons and to his bardic associates, very little is certainly known about Lewys Môn. He may have spent some time in London practising a craft other than poetry. A poem by Rhys Nanmor (*fl.* 1485–1513) requesting the gift of a buckler was addressed to a Lewys Môn who is described as a blacksmith then resident in Temple Bar, London. That Lewys Môn the poet was also the blacksmith of Temple Bar known to Rhys Nanmor may be indicated by an elegy which Lewys Môn wrote for Rhys Nanmor, which implies that the two poets were acquainted. A jocular reference in a poem by Tudur Aled also implies that Lewys was associated with smithcraft, although, in this instance, he is located as practising his craft in Anglesey. Of all his poetic contemporaries it was Tudur Aled who was most closely associated with Lewys. Satirical quatrains (*englynion*) in which they vilified each other were, in reality, jocular exchanges between friends: a highly complimentary verse which Tudur composed on meeting Lewys near Oswestry Castle and Lewys's powerful elegy for Tudur (*d.* 1526) are more reliable indicators of their relationship and of their mutual artistic regard. The two poets are generally acknowledged as the leading practitioners of their craft in early Tudor Wales.

Just over 100 poems by Lewys are extant, most of them praise poems and elegies composed in honour of gentry patrons. A poem addressed to Sir William Griffith of Penrhyn, Caernarvonshire, referring to Griffith's imprisonment by Richard III in 1485 may be his earliest surviving work. Another early poem is the elegy he composed in 1489 for Elisau ap Gruffudd of Plas-yn-Iâl, Bryneglwys, owner of the White Book of Rhydderch. He was evidently closely associated with the Griffith family of Penrhyn: he addressed praise poems to Sir William Griffith (*d.* 1505/6) and his son Sir William Griffith (*d.* 1531), and mourned the latter's wife, Jane Stradling, in an elegy. The Salisbury family of Lleweni, Denbighshire, also featured prominently as recipients of his poems. A clerical patron to whom he was much attracted was Robert ap Rhys of Ysbyty Ifan, chaplain to Cardinal Wolsey; other clerical patrons included Dafydd ab Owain, abbot of Aberconway, Siôn Llwyd, abbot of Valle Crucis, and Pirs Conwy, archdeacon of St Asaph. His patrons were largely concentrated in north Wales, his native Anglesey and the north-east march being favourite haunts; it appears that he rarely ventured to south Wales, although he found important patrons there in Sir Rhys ap Thomas and Sir William Herbert of Colebrook. An unusually high proportion of Lewys's extant poems consists of elegies; among them are poems commemorating his bardic contemporaries Dafydd ab Edmwnd, Rhys Nanmor, and Tudur Aled.

Lewys Môn was a learned, highly allusive poet and a skilled literary craftsman. He and Tudur Aled were masterly exponents of the art of *cynghanedd*: this mandatory feature of classical Welsh verse (involving consonance, sometimes combined with internal rhyme) is seen at its most complex in their work. Lewys, however, lacked Tudur's imaginative force and verbal fluency; his intricate *cynghanedd* is sometimes too intrusive, his verse too densely textured. Though not in the very front rank of medieval Welsh poets, he nevertheless composed some powerful individual poems.

An extract from the will, no longer extant, of a Lodowidus Mon, dated 12 April 1527 at Valle Crucis and proved on 28 June 1527, was published in *Archaeologia Cambrensis* in 1880. The testator was undoubtedly Lewys Môn: the legatees included his former patrons Abbot Siôn Llwyd and Robert ap Rhys; one of the witnesses was the Anglesey poet Wiliam Alaw, probably a kinsman of Dafydd Alaw, who commemorated Lewys as a 'chief poet' (*pencerdd*) in an elegy. Manuscripts record Valle Crucis Abbey, near Llangollen, as his burial place.

GRUFFYDD ALED WILLIAMS

Sources E. I. Rowlands, ed., *Gwaith Lewys Môn* (1975) • E. I. Rowlands, 'Lewys Môn', *Llên Cymru*, 4 (1956–7), 26–38 • E. I. Rowlands, 'Dadansoddiad o gynghanedd Lewys Môn', *Llên Cymru*, 4 (1956–7), 135–61 • D. W. Wiliam, 'Ach Lewys Môn', *Anglesey Antiquarian Society and Field Club Transactions* (1982), 137–9 • [D. R. Thomas], 'Extracts from old wills relating to Wales', *Archaeologia Cambrensis*, 4th ser., 11 (1880), 217–25

Wealth at death see [D. R. Thomas], 'Extracts from old wills relating to Wales', *Archaeologia Cambrensis*, 4th ser., 11 (1880), 218

Lexington. For this title name *see* Sutton, Robert, first Baron Lexington (1594–1668); Sutton, Robert, second Baron Lexington (1661–1723).

Lexinton, Henry of (*d.* **1258**). *See under* Lexinton, John of (*d.* 1257).

Lexinton [Laxton], **John of** (*d.* **1257**), administrator, was a younger son of Richard, son of Robert of Lexinton (Laxton), and his wife, Matilda. Like his brothers Robert of *Lexinton, Stephen of *Lexinton, Peter, and Henry [*see below*], John may have begun his career in the schools; it is difficult otherwise to see how he could have studied both canon and civil law, as the Burton annalist alleges that he did. By the late 1220s, however, he had become household knight to Ranulf (III) de Blundeville, earl of Chester. When Ranulf died in 1232, John went to Ireland as sheriff of Munster and constable of Limerick. He left Ireland in 1235 when he was appointed household knight to Henry III at a fee of £20 a year. He was promoted to knight marshal in 1238.

In 1240 John of Lexinton served the king as justiciar of Cheshire, duties for which his service under Earl Ranulf had equipped him well. In 1241 he went to Rome as one of King Henry's representatives to a general council summoned by Pope Gregory IX (*r.* 1227–41). Travelling with his brother Stephen, abbot of Savigny, John saved Stephen when many of the other clerical delegates to the council were captured at sea by Enzio, son of the emperor Frederick II (*r.* 1220–50). In late 1241 Lexinton was back in Cheshire, assisting in Henry III's campaign against Dafydd ap Llywelyn (*d.* 1246). In 1242 he went to France to negotiate with Louis IX (*r.* 1226–70) over truce violations alleged by King Henry. During 1242–3 Lexinton served in the latter's army in Gascony, and was unofficial keeper of the great seal during part of this time. He kept the seal again, in an official capacity, in 1247–8 and 1249–50, although he seems not to have been styled chancellor.

In early 1246 Lexinton was again in Cheshire, attempting to restore order in the wake of the military campaigns of the previous year. Having been appointed household steward between March and July 1246 Lexinton was also active as a justice of the court of *coram rege*. From November 1252, however, when he was appointed chief justice of the forests north of the Trent, Lexinton's activities were focused on the north, where he inherited extensive lands from his eldest brother, Robert, in 1250. In 1253 he was appointed keeper of Scarborough, Pickering, and Bamburgh castles and retired from the royal court.

Lexinton returned to court in 1255. Due to the absence of the three senior justices on vacation business he travelled with the king through Yorkshire and Lincolnshire as justice *coram rege* from August until October. It fell to Lexinton, therefore, to investigate reports that the Jews of Lincoln had crucified a Christian boy named Hugh. The confession he extracted from Copin of Lincoln led to the execution of nineteen Lincoln Jews, and the condemnation (and eventual pardon) of ninety-one others for their alleged involvement in the murder. Hugh's body was interred by Lexinton's brother, Bishop Henry of Lexinton, in Lincoln Cathedral, where it became an important pilgrimage shrine.

Between 1239 and 1243 John of Lexinton married Margery de Merlay, widow of Roger de Merlay, lord of Morpeth, Northumberland, and daughter of Richard de Umfraville, lord of Prudhoe, Northumberland. The marriage was childless. When Lexinton died, on or before 16 January 1257, his brother Henry was his heir.

Henry of Lexinton (*d.* 1258), bishop of Lincoln, was presented to the church at Stapleford, Nottinghamshire, between 1212 and 1214. By 1237 he had become canon of Southwell, Nottinghamshire, and in 1241 was appointed treasurer of Salisbury. In 1245 he resigned from Salisbury to become dean of Lincoln Cathedral, from which office he was elected bishop on 30 December 1253. He went to Gascony to obtain the king's assent; the election was confirmed on 28 March 1254 by Archbishop Boniface of Canterbury, who consecrated Lexinton on 17 May at Lambeth. The temporalities had been restored on 1 April. A dispute between Lexinton and the University of Oxford was referred to the mid-Lenten parliament of 1257 for discussion, but without known effect. He died at Nettleton, Lincolnshire, on 8 August 1258, and was buried in Lincoln Cathedral. His heirs were his nephews William of Sutton and Richard of Markham, the sons of his sisters Elizabeth and Cecily. ROBERT C. STACEY

Sources *Chancery records* • Paris, *Chron.* • *Ann. mon.* • *CIPM*, 1, no. 378 • private information (2004) • C. J. Holdsworth, ed., *Rufford charters*, 1, Thoroton Society Record Series, 29 (1972) • G. I. Langmuir, 'The knight's tale of young Hugh of Lincoln', *Speculum*, 47 (1972), 459–82 • L. B. Dibben, 'Chancellor and keeper of the seal under Henry III', *EngHR*, 27 (1912), 39–51 • *Fasti Angl., 1066–1300*, [Lincoln]

Wealth at death see *CIPM*

Lexinton, Robert of (*d.* 1250), justice and administrator, took his name from the Nottinghamshire village of Lexington, now called Laxton and famous for its open-field system of cultivation, the seat of the Caux family, hereditary keepers of the royal forest in Nottinghamshire and Derbyshire. He was probably the eldest of at least six sons and two daughters of Richard, son of Robert of Lexinton (and it has been suggested that Robert of Lexinton was an illegitimate son of the last male Caux, Robert (III), who died about 1167–8). Richard of Lexinton kept the manor of Laxton for King John for three years until 1207, when he was deprived of it for forest maladministration, but he regained royal favour a few years later. The family seems to have owed its position in the royal service to the patronage of Ralph fitz Stephen, chamberlain of Henry II, who married Maud de Caux and died as keeper of Laxton and the forest in 1202. Richard lived until at least 1229, still with property at Laxton, by which time Robert's own career was well established.

Lexinton began as clerk to Brian de Lisle, a prominent forest administrator and justice who had succeeded Richard as keeper of Laxton, between 1210 and 1215. He often accounted at the exchequer on behalf of his master. He received royal preferment to a prebend at Southwell Minster in 1214, in the same year becoming custodian of the archbishopric of York during a vacancy, as well as being in charge of a group of soldiers responsible for securing Nottinghamshire and Derbyshire for the king. In 1221, after the civil war that followed the issue of Magna Carta, he began his main career as a royal justice when he sat with a group appointed to hold eyres in counties in the west midlands. He still performed other important tasks, however; early in 1221, for instance, he shadowed the rebellious William, count of Aumale, on his flight north, reporting to Hubert de Burgh by letter. He served as a justice on eyre on sixty-four occasions between 1221 and 1244, on thirty-one of them, from 1234 onwards, as senior justice, as well as frequently sitting alone to deal with individual possessory assizes. In 1240 he was the leader of one of the two circuits of eyre justices accused by Matthew Paris of collecting money for the king under the pretext of justice. However, only one of his eyre rolls, from Middlesex in 1235, has survived. From 1227 to 1244 he was a justice of the bench at Westminster, and from 1236 to 1244 its senior justice, and therefore one of the leading justices in England; five of his bench plea rolls survive. On his retirement he secured the appointment of his clerk, Robert of Nottingham, as a justice of that court.

Lexinton attracted the anger of Bishop Grosseteste of Lincoln for his treatment of a rural dean who denounced him for hearing capital cases on Sundays; he nevertheless continued to acquire ecclesiastical preferment, including the church of Rotherham and a prebend at Wells, which he gave up in 1243 because he considered it was too far away for him to take an interest in it. He is said by the Dunstable annalist to have been elected in 1239 to the see of Lichfield, the right to elect being then in dispute between the canons of Lichfield and the monks of Coventry, but to have withdrawn; his candidature is not, however, mentioned by Matthew Paris. He also built up a considerable landed estate, mainly made up of property in Nottinghamshire and Derbyshire, but with estates in Northamptonshire and Oxfordshire as well. As a cleric he had no son, so some of his lands he disposed of to his brother John of *Lexinton, who inherited the rest of his estate after his death, and some of the rest to religious houses he chose to patronize. After deciding first to be buried at the Augustinian house at Newstead, in 1249 he changed his mind and, probably influenced by his brother Stephen of *Lexinton, a prominent Cistercian, chose Rufford Abbey instead. He also founded a chantry in the chapel of St Thomas the Martyr in the church of Southwell, between about 1241 and 1245. He died on 29 May 1250, after being stricken by paralysis. In his obituary, Paris described him as a long-serving justice whose office had brought him fame and ample possessions, and who ended his life laudably in alms-giving and prayer. DAVID CROOK

Sources C. J. Holdsworth, ed., *Rufford charters*, 4 vols., Thoroton Society Record Series, 29, 30, 32, 34 (1972–81) • D. Crook, *Records of the general eyre*, Public Record Office Handbooks, 20 (1982) • C. A. F. Meekings, 'Robert of Nottingham, justice of the bench, 1244–6', *BIHR*, 41 (1968), 132–8 • Paris, *Chron.*, vol. 4; vol. 5, p. 138 • *Ann. mon.*, vol. 3 • W. W. Shirley, ed., *Royal and other historical letters illustrative of the reign of Henry III*, 1, Rolls Series, 27 (1862) • *Roberti Grosseteste episcopi quondam Lincolniensis epistolae*, ed. H. R. Luard, Rolls Series, 25 (1861) • A. F. Leach, ed., *Visitations and memorials of Southwell Minster*, CS, new ser., 48 (1891) • *Chancery records* • court of common pleas, feet of fines, PRO, CP 25/1 • Bench and eyre plea rolls, PRO, KB 26, JUST 1 • Lord Treasurer's remembrancers, pipe rolls, PRO, E372

Lexinton, Stephen of (*c.*1198–1258), abbot of Clairvaux, was one of the four notable sons of Richard of Lexinton, whose name derived from the manor of Laxton, Nottinghamshire, of which he had been given custody by King John, and where Stephen was born. Stephen's eldest brother, Robert of *Lexinton, had a distinguished career as a royal judge; another brother, John of *Lexinton, became steward of the household to Henry III; and a third brother, Henry of *Lexinton [*see under* Lexinton, John of], ended his career as bishop of Lincoln (1253–8). Stephen studied arts at Paris. On 23 May 1215 he was presented by the crown to the prebend of 'Scrophul' and Oxton in Southwell Minster. He embarked upon the study of theology at Oxford in the school of Edmund of Abingdon (*d.* 1240) but, apparently with Edmund's encouragement, he abandoned his scholastic career in the company of six other students to enter the Cistercian order at Quarr Abbey on the Isle of Wight. According to the Dunstable annalist, Stephen's flight from the schools occurred in 1221.

In 1223 Stephen was elected abbot of Stanley, Wiltshire, a daughter house of Quarr and part of the great filiation of Savigny. In 1226, while abbot of Stanley, he was called upon to visit the Irish houses of the order on behalf of the general chapter, and to restore regular discipline which had lapsed badly in the abbey of Mellifont and its dependencies. It was probably to his success in this difficult and dangerous mission that he owed his election as abbot and head of the Savigny congregation in 1229. In the spring of 1241 he was involved in the catastrophe that overtook the prelates sailing to Rome to attend the general council summoned by Gregory IX (*r.* 1227–41). He was accompanied by his brother John, who was Henry III's proctor to the council, and with his help managed to escape the clutches of the imperialists after the Pisan fleet, acting on the orders of Frederick II (*r.* 1220–50), attacked the Genoese ships carrying the prelates to the council. In 1243 Stephen was elected abbot of Clairvaux in succession to Abbot William, who had died in Italy as a result of maltreatment by the emperor's gaolers. It was from his position as head of the most distinguished of the daughter houses of Cîteaux that he left his lasting mark on the order.

Stephen's academic training and his experiences in Ireland had convinced him of the need to organize a system of academic study in the order, to ensure that recruits were theologically informed and properly instructed in the principles and ideals of the Cistercian life. Accordingly he took up a plan adumbrated by a predecessor, Abbot Evrard, and obtained the agreement of the general chapter and the pope for the creation of a house of studies for white monks at Paris. The building of the college, initially called the Chardonnet after its site called Cardonetum ('place of thistles'), began in 1247, and student monks had taken up residence by 1250. The college remained under the jurisdiction of the abbot of Clairvaux, who appointed its head. The college was only the apex of Stephen's plan. He had persuaded the general chapter of 1245 to impose a co-ordinated system of studies on the order, modelled upon that of the Dominican Friars. It was decreed that every abbot who was able and willing to make such provision should create a school for his monks, and that every province should possess a specialized studium of theology, to which abler monks from elsewhere might be sent for more advanced study.

The plan to send monks to the schools encountered strong opposition from some sections of the order, and as a result Stephen was deposed from his abbacy by the general chapter in 1256, on the pretext that he had obtained a papal privilege contrary to the statutes of the order. But he had powerful friends at Rome, including the Cistercian cardinal John of Toledo, who supported his plans, and Abbot Guy of Cîteaux was sternly commanded by Pope Alexander IV (*r.* 1254–61) to reinstate him. But in order to avoid a damaging collision between the pope and the general chapter, and probably prompted by Stephen himself, Louis IX (*r.* 1226–70) intervened with the pope and urged that the sentence of deposition should stand. Stephen retired to the abbey of Ourscamp (Oise), where he died in 1258. His project, however, survived him. The Chardonnet continued to flourish, and before the end of the century the Cistercians had their own colleges at the universities of Oxford, Montpellier, and Toulouse, the constitution of which was modelled in each case upon that of the Paris college. Stephen also left a volume of letters, which constitutes a valuable source for the history of his order. C. H. LAWRENCE

Sources *Chancery records* · *Curia regis rolls preserved in the Public Record Office* (1922–), vol. 11 · Paris, *Chron.*, vols. 4, 5 · *Ann. mon.*, vol. 3 · 'E chronico savigniacensi', *Recueil des historiens des Gaules et de la France / Rerum Gallicarum et Francicarum scriptores*, ed. M. Bouquet and others, 23 (Paris, 1894), 584–7 · H. Denifle and A. Chatelain, eds., *Chartularium universitatis Parisiensis*, 1 (Paris, 1889) · *Les registres d'Alexandre IV*, ed. C. Bourel de la Roncière and others, 3 vols. (Paris, 1895–1959) · J. M. Canivez, ed., *Statuta capitulorum generalium ordinis Cisterciensis*, 1 (1933) · B. Griesser, ed., 'Stephen's letter-book', *Registrum Epistolarum Stephani de Lexinton*, *Analecta Sacri Ordinis Cisterciensis*, 2 (1946), 1–118 · B. Griesser, ed., 'Stephen's letter-book', *Registrum Epistolarum Stephani de Lexinton*, *Analecta Sacri Ordinis Cisterciensis*, 8 (1952), 181–378 · P. Pietresson de Saint Aubin, 'Le livre des sepultures: chronique inédite des abbés de Clairvaux', *Revue Mabillon*, 2nd ser., 36 (1929), 303–23 · C. H. Lawrence, 'Stephen of Lexington and Cistercian university studies in the thirteenth century', *Journal of Ecclesiastical History*, 11 (1960), 164–78 · P. Dautrey, 'Croissance et adaptation chez les Cisterciens: les débuts du collège des Bernardins de Paris', *Analecta Sacri Ordinis Cisterciensis*, 32 (1976), 122–98 · C. J. Holdsworth, ed., *Rufford charters*, 1, Thoroton Society Record Series, 29 (1972) · C. J. Holdsworth, ed., *Rufford charters*, 2, Thoroton Society Record Series, 30 (1974) · C. J. Holdsworth, ed., *Rufford charters*, 3, Thoroton Society Record Series, 32 (1980) · C. J. Holdsworth, ed., *Rufford charters*, 4, Thoroton Society Record Series, 34 (1981)

Ley, Sir Francis, first baronet (**1846–1916**), industrialist and promoter of sport, was born on 3 January 1846 in Burton upon Trent, the only surviving child of George Phillips Ley (1821–1886), for over forty years the high bailiff of the Burton upon Trent county court, and his wife, Sarah Potts (*d.* 1883). His education at Burton grammar school was interrupted by illness and he was privately tutored for a time in north Yorkshire. He spent several terms at the Royal Agricultural College in Cirencester with the intention of continuing the family tradition of gentleman farming but instead he joined the Derby engineering firm of Andrew Handyside & Co. He became a partner at the age of twenty-four in 1870. In that year he married Georgina Townsend (*d.* 1886), daughter of George Willis of Aislaby Hall, Whitby, Yorkshire, with whom he had a son and two daughters. He left Handyside in 1874 and built his own works at Litchurch in Derby, where he made malleable castings. The firm became the first European producers of blackheart malleable iron. In 1878 his firm infringed the patent of an American company making drive chain belts but he was soon the recipient of the sole manufacturing rights and was successful enough to be able to pull down the original works in 1880 and rebuild on a larger scale.

Ley, who moved to a country seat at Epperstone Manor, Nottinghamshire, was active in the public life of Derby and Nottinghamshire. He supported local hospitals and nursing institutions, contributed to the construction of St Christopher's Church next to the Derby works, and was a JP in both counties. Politically he was a 'staunch unionist', active for some years in the management of the South Derby Liberal Unionist association. He sat on Derby town council and was high sheriff of Nottingham in 1905; that year (27 December) he was created baronet for his public service.

Although he never enjoyed good health, Ley energetically promoted athletic sports in Derby. The source of his enthusiasm for sport is unclear. He was particularly keen on cricket and a committee member of the Derbyshire county club and later president of the Nottinghamshire county club. In 1888 he laid out a recreation ground for his workers. He was a patron of the Derbyshire Football Association for many years. He also attempted to establish baseball as a professional spectacle. He had first seen baseball on one of his visits to the United States, and he was among those contacted by the leading American sports goods entrepreneur and former baseball player, A. G. Spalding, in 1889 about the possibility of establishing a British professional league based on some of the clubs who had recently formed the English Football League. Only four teams began the inaugural season in the summer of 1890 and it was not a success. Ley had the best ground and the best team, strengthened by the inclusion of three Americans, one of whom became the league's most successful pitcher: so successful that the league decided he was too good for the rest and ought to be withdrawn. It is unclear whether Ley actually agreed to this. The star player was reintroduced and the Derby club was expelled. Although the league collapsed, recreational baseball remained a popular summer sport in several districts, including Derby. The Baseball Ground was leased to Derby County Football Club in 1895 and remained their ground until 1997, when they moved to a new stadium.

In his later years Ley spent a good deal of time in north Yorkshire enjoying the shooting and salmon fishing and developing a 1000 acre estate at Lealholm where, in 1901, he built Lealholm Lodge and its famous rock garden. Following the death of his first wife he married in 1888 Alison Catherine (*d.* 1940), third daughter of John Jobson JP, of Spondon, near Derby. Their two sons were both killed in the First World War. Sir Francis Ley died at Epperstone Manor on 17 January 1916 and was buried four days later in Lealholm churchyard. He was succeeded as second baronet by the son of his first marriage.

In spite of periods of poor health, Ley died in harness, still controlling what in 1916 was a major firm. As an employer he was strict but generous. His photographs suggest the hard and stern personality that contemporary obituaries attributed to him. Industrial relations in his business were claimed to be good. That Ley was conscious of the social responsibilities of wealth was suggested by his public benefactions, his remitting of half the rents of his Yorkshire tenants in bad years, and his payment of wartime bonuses to meet the increased cost of living. Perhaps he was 'an autocrat of the best type'.

TONY MASON

Sources biographical material, *c.*1908, Derby Local Studies Library, Acc. 3206, 84–7 · *Athletic News* (26 May 1890) · *Athletic News* (23 June 1890) · *Athletic News* (30 June 1890) · *Athletic News* (28 July 1890) · *Athletic News* (4 Aug 1890) · *Athletic News* (11 Aug 1890) · *Athletic News* (18 Aug 1890) · *Belper News* (11 May 1900) · *Derbyshire Daily Telegraph* (17–19 Jan 1916) · *Derbyshire Daily Telegraph* (22 Jan 1916) · *Whitby Gazette* (21 Jan 1916) · Burke, *Peerage*

Likenesses photographs, Derby Local Studies Library

Wealth at death £448,424 10*s.* 2*d.*: probate, 25 Aug 1916, *CGPLA Eng. & Wales*

Ley, Henry George (1887–1962), organist and composer, was born on 30 December 1887, at Chagford, near Moretonhampstead, Devon, the eldest child of the Revd Gerald Lewis Henry Ley (1856–1910x12), rector of Chagford, and his wife, Beatrice Emma Hayter-Hames. After his musical talent was recognized by Walter Parratt, he was admitted as a chorister at St George's Chapel, Windsor, in 1896. After two years at Uppingham School (1903–4) as a music scholar he gained an exhibition to the Royal College of Music, London. There he studied the organ under Walter Parratt, composition under Charles Stanford, and counterpoint with Charles Wood. An organ scholarship to Keble College, Oxford (1906), followed a brief period as organist at St Mary's, Farnham Royal (1905–6).

At Oxford, Ley's abilities as a musician soon became conspicuous, and in 1908 he became president of the Oxford University Musical Club. After Basil Harwood's untimely resignation as organist of Christ Church in 1909, Ley—who was young and relatively inexperienced and had not yet proceeded to any degrees—was appointed by the dean, Dr T. B. Strong, a decision openly criticized at the time. One of several distinguished pupils of Ernest Walker and Hugh Allen, he took the degrees of BMus in 1911 and BA two years later. He proceeded DMus in 1919. In addition to his duties at Christ Church (where he roundly confuted Strong's detractors), he assisted at St Peter's College, Radley, as precentor (1916–18) during the war and was appointed by Allen as a professor of the organ at the Royal College of Music in 1919, a position he retained until 1941. Ley married Evelyn Mary (1879/80–1946), daughter of the Revd Charles Abel Heurtley, vicar of Binsey, on 10 April 1917. A minor lyric poet, she was the source of several song texts set by her husband, including 'The Rose' (1920) and 'Up the Hillside' (1923), several children's songs, and music for an operetta (or 'fairy play'), *Savernake, or, The Professor's Dilemma* (1930).

After three years as choragus of Oxford University (1923–6), Ley decided to move on and was appointed precentor at Eton College in 1926. In December 1940 his home, Savile House, at Eton was destroyed by a bomb which nearly killed him and his wife. It was a severe shock which helped to precipitate his retirement to Devon in 1945. After the death of his first wife in 1946, Ley married Mary Elizabeth (*b.* 1899/1900), daughter of the Revd Charles Walford of Ascot under Wychwood, on 20 April 1949. Both marriages were childless.

Honorary fellowships of the Royal College of Organists (1920), the Royal College of Music (1920), Keble College, Oxford (1942), and the Royal Academy of Music (1942) endorsed Ley's national prominence as a recitalist, church musician, and teacher. He played at the coronations of George VI and Elizabeth II, was president of the Royal College of Organists (for which he did much examining) in 1933 and 1934, and was warden of the Music Masters' Association in 1936. During his retirement he was president of the Incorporated Association of Organists (1952–3). Ley's prowess as an organist was all the more extraordinary given his disability of a club foot. He possessed a brilliant pianistic technique—Alcock called him the 'Paderewski of the organ'—which strongly influenced the lively, exuberant character of his playing. Though not a born schoolmaster, he was immensely popular and respected at Eton, and did much to attract musical celebrities to concerts at the school—including Irene Scharrer, Harold Samuel, Jelly d'Aranyi, John Goss, Clive Carey, and Marcel Dupré—as well as giving numerous organ recitals himself. His most noted pupil was perhaps the young William Walton (then a chorister at Christ Church), whose talent he fostered during the years of the First World War.

Ley remained an active composer, editor, and arranger throughout his life. A violin sonata, a string quartet, and the orchestral *Variations on a Theme of Handel* (all unpublished), submitted as his DMus exercise, are rare examples of purely instrumental composition, and a few short pieces for organ were published, including the fantasia on the Welsh hymn tune 'Aberystwyth' (1928). Four albums of songs were written in his late twenties (1913–*c*.1917), the third of them devoted entirely to the poems of Mary Coleridge. These works drew approbation from Sir Hubert Parry, whose musical language informed Ley's own. Two settings of A. E. Housman, 'Far in a Western Brookland' and 'White in the moon the long road lies' (both 1921), are less distinguished. His output is dominated, however, by his church music, much of which has dropped out of the repertory in spite of its popularity during Ley's lifetime. Among those works that are still more regularly sung are the consciously archaic 'A Prayer of King Henry VI', an introit composed for the royal foundations of Henry VI at Eton College and King's College, Cambridge, in 1928, and the short anthem 'Pasture' (1944). Ley was also highly active as an editor of church music—including the *Church Anthem Book* with H. Walford Davies in 1933 and the *Oxford Chant Book No. 2* (1934) with Edgar S. Roper—organ music (which included editions of eighteenth-century English works), and numerous transcriptions. A warm-hearted, energetic, and generous man, he had many interests outside music including golf, chess, and motoring, though his greatest love was for steam railways and locomotives. He died of heart failure at Sidmouth Junction Station on 24 August 1962; he was survived by his second wife.

JEREMY DIBBLE

Sources H. W. Shaw, *The succession of organists of the Chapel Royal and the cathedrals of England and Wales from c.1538* (1991) • *The Times* (27 Aug 1962) • *The Times* (6 Sept 1962) • *MT*, 103 (1962), 705 • *DNB* • H. C. Colles, Grove, *Dict. mus.* (1927) • L. Ronald, ed., *Who's who in music* (1935) • b. cert. • m. certs. • d. cert. • *CGPLA Eng. & Wales* (1962)

Archives SOUND BL NSA, performance recordings

Likenesses group photograph, Royal College of Music, London • photograph, Royal College of Music, London • photograph, Eton

Wealth at death £18,682 18*s*.: probate, 13 Nov 1962, *CGPLA Eng. & Wales*

Ley, Hugh (1790–1837), physician, was born at Abingdon, Berkshire, where his father, Hugh Ley (1762–1826), a surgeon apothecary, was for a time in practice before settling at St Ives, Cornwall. Hugh was educated at John Lemprière's school in Abingdon, and he subsequently became a student of the then united medical schools of St Thomas's and Guy's hospitals in Southwark, London. He took the diploma of the Royal College of Surgeons, and then studied at Edinburgh, where he graduated MD on 24 June 1813 with a thesis on the pathology of phthisis.

Ley was admitted a licentiate of the Royal College of Physicians, London, on 30 September 1818, and he began to practise in London as a midwife. He was elected physician to the Westminster Lying-in Hospital, and soon afterwards he became lecturer on midwifery at the Middlesex Hospital, London. On 20 April 1835 he accepted the invitation of the staff of St Bartholomew's Hospital to become the professor of midwifery at the school, having delivered the lectures on midwifery there since the death of John Ashburner. His course was the first given in the summer; previously it had been the general custom of the London medical schools to have no regular classes except in the winter. In 1836 Ley published *An Essay on Laryngismus Stridulus, or, Crouplike Inspiration of Infants*, which was the first work to provide a full pathological discussion of the illness. He wrongly endeavoured to prove that the spasm of the larynx (the characteristic symptom of the disease) is caused by the pressure of enlarged lymphatic glands on the recurrent laryngeal nerve, and he appears to have confused cases of tubercular meningitis with those of laryngismus stridulus. Ley's publication shows much industry, but is too long and not clear.

Ley, who was married, lived in Half Moon Street, London; he had no children. He died from heart disease at Stilton, Huntingdonshire, on 24 January 1837.

NORMAN MOORE, *rev.* PATRICK WALLIS

Sources *Nomina eorum, qui gradum medicinae doctoris in academia Jacobi sexti Scotorum regis, quae Edinburgi est, adepti sunt, ab anno 1705 ad annum 1845*, University of Edinburgh (1846) • Munk, *Roll* • *GM*, 2nd ser., 7 (1837), 331 • V. C. Medvei and J. L. Thornton, eds., *The royal hospital of Saint Bartholomew, 1123–1973* (1974) • P. J. Wallis and R. V. Wallis, *Eighteenth century medics*, 2nd edn (1988)

Ley, James, first earl of Marlborough (1550–1629), judge and politician, was (according to a family pedigree of his own compiling) the fourth son of the soldier and landowner Henry Ley (*d.* 1574), of Teffont Evias, Wiltshire, formerly of Bere Ferrers, Devon, and his wife, Dionysia (*d.* 1589), daughter and coheir of Walter Seymour of Berwick St John, Wiltshire. Ley matriculated as a pensioner at Queens' College, Cambridge, in 1571, but migrated to Oxford, where he was 'brought up … in Balliol and Brassenos Colledges' (Ley, Wilts. & Swindon RO, 366/1), graduating BA from Brasenose in 1574. Ley later claimed that the

James Ley, first earl of Marlborough (1550–1629), by Daniel Mytens, 1627

death of his father cut short his academic studies, compelling his removal to an inn of chancery; if he could be identified with the James Ley installed as rector of Teffont Evias from 1569 to 1576, it may be that he was originally intended for a career in the church. While sufficiently proficient to be called to the bar at New Inn, Ley chose to enter Lincoln's Inn (rather than New Inn's parent inn of court, the Middle Temple) in February 1577. Here he 'applied the studie of the lawe' (ibid.), being again called utter barrister in 1584, and subsequently serving as reader of Furnival's Inn. In 1600 he joined the governing council of benchers, soon becoming one of four 'Censors or Visitors … for matter of religion and good liff' (Baildon, 2.66), while also successfully promoting a 'project for renewing of the Lybrarye' (Prest, *Inns of Court*, 166). Several sets of notes survive from his reading of 1602 on the Edwardian Statute of Tenures (1 Ed. VI c. 4).

By now Ley's marriage on 2 June 1590 to Mary Pettie, of Stoke Talmage, Oxfordshire, had brought him two sons and five daughters, including the poet Lady Hester *Pulter (1595/6–1678); another three girls (two surviving) arrived before their mother's death on 4 October 1613. Fortunately for this burgeoning family, Ley's considerable abilities were widely displayed: with his return to parliament in 1597 for the borough of Westbury, near the manor of Brembridge which he and his elder brother Matthew had held since 1578; with his service as justice of the peace since *c.*1593; and with his involvement from the late 1580s onwards as one of four founding members in the London-based Society of Antiquaries. Yet it may well have been the influence of his Lincoln's Inn colleague and fellow Brasenose alumnus Thomas Egerton that secured him in June 1603 a Welsh judge's place on the Carmarthen circuit. Egerton certainly figured as patron at Ley's call to serjeant in November 1603, alongside Charles Blount, earl of Devonshire, whom he had served as high steward since 1597, and with whose sword Ley was knighted by King James at Wilton House on 9 December 1603.

These honours were conferred preparatory to Ley's appointment as chief justice of king's bench in Ireland. He proved a committed and energetic member of the new administration, whether presiding in court and deliberating as a privy councillor at Dublin, or riding out on assize circuit. Besides having the English Book of Common Prayer translated into Irish, Ley was identified as author of a strategy designed to compel prominent individual Catholics to attend protestant church services, under threat of indictment in the court of castle chamber. Concerted protests at this exploitation of viceregal 'mandates' fell on deaf ears in both Dublin and London. James I indeed took Ley's zeal as evidence of 'his ability to do him service' (*CSP Ire.*, *1608–10*, 116), while some years later Francis Bacon would characterize his service in Ireland as marked by 'gravity, temper, and discretion' (*CSP Ire.*, *1615–25*, 166).

Back in England by royal command in October 1608, ostensibly to brief the privy council on the settlement of Ulster, Ley was rewarded with the lucrative office of attorney-general of wards, despite rival bids by Augustine Nicolls and Henry Yelverton. He moved quickly to exploit this influential quasi-judicial position, building up a mutually profitable working relationship with Henry Sherfield, an ambitious Lincoln's Inn barrister and Wiltshire neighbour whose dominance of court of wards practice reflected Ley's patronage. Although still formally a serjeant-at-law, Ley also resumed residence at Lincoln's Inn, where he busied himself with the affairs of the society, serving a term as treasurer (1609–10) and participating in several major building projects.

Given his abilities, age, and experience, Ley might well have regarded his attorneyship as no more than a temporary stopover *en route* for a Westminster Hall judgeship. Yet further advance proved elusive. In 1612, following the death of Robert Cecil, Ley was named among numerous suitors in contention to be master of the wards. Having sat briefly and unobtrusively as member for Westbury in the second session of James I's parliament (1609–10), he was returned for Bath in 1614, where although named to several committees he is not recorded as having spoken in the house. In 1617 he failed to win the post of attorney-general, despite offering £10,000 and enjoying Buckingham's support. Although made baronet in the summer of 1619, and appointed to the prince of Wales's council the following year, not until January 1621 was he at last raised to the eminence of lord chief justice of king's bench. This promotion undoubtedly anticipated the septuagenarian Ley's marriage on 4 July 1621 to Jane Boteler (*d.* 1672), Buckingham's seventeen-year-old niece, following the death in 1618 of Ley's second wife, Mary, widow of Sir William Bowyer, whom he had married earlier that year.

Returned once more for Westbury to James's fourth parliament, Ley found himself instead commissioned to preside over the House of Lords, after Bacon's withdrawal in mid-March. He therefore delivered formal sentences on Bacon and other prominent delinquents, without either participating in debate or seeking to lead the house from his chair. Despite its being said that Ley would move to the woolsack as lord keeper, by October 1624 an alternative rumour gained strength, that he would replace the disgraced Cranfield as lord treasurer, even if he might not hold office long, 'by reason of age or some other defect' (*Letters of John Chamberlain*, 2.583). Finally in mid-December Ley received the treasurer's staff and was sworn in as privy councillor, shortly after joining the peerage as Baron Ley of Ley, Devon. He nevertheless retained his judicial place, with attached profits, until the following Hilary term. Ley served as treasurer until July 1628, when he resigned in favour of his deputy, Sir Richard Weston, at least partly induced by payments of £10,000 and £5000 for his wife, and lateral preferment to the presidency of the council. The broadly unfavourable verdict of contemporaries and historians on his performance in high office possibly underestimates the scale of financial and political crisis that characterized the opening years of Charles I's reign. Marlborough (to use the title of the earldom to which he was raised in February 1626) may indeed deserve credit for resisting the more extreme courses being urged by some royal counsellors during the forced loans crisis of 1626–7. But it was precisely this attitude, together with the loss of Buckingham's support, which explains the king's readiness to dispense with his services.

In a sonnet addressed to Margaret Ley, John Milton depicted her father as an upright statesman, whose death at Lincoln's Inn on 14 March 1629 was hastened by news of the untimely dissolution of parliament (in the first session of which he had actively participated). This eulogy involves some poetical licence. According to Hutton, after resigning the presidency of the council in December 1628, Marlborough had retired to Lincoln's Inn, 'applied himself to divinity, heard prayers and sermons … and prepared himself to die' (*Diary*, 77). As for integrity, James Whitelocke, another contemporary judge, strongly endorsed Marlborough's reputation for deceit. Sherfield not only labelled him dishonest, but recalled his own part in transmitting a litigant's present of gilt plate to his patron. The balance of Hutton's delicately ambiguous epitaph bears repeating: 'he was a wise, discreet, sober man, of great patience, and profound ingenuity, and had good skill in antiquities and heraldry. And he loved old silver and gold coin of the Romans and others' (ibid.). He was buried at Westbury.

None of Ley's writings on law, heraldry, and miscellaneous antiquarian subjects was published during his lifetime. However, he bequeathed his collection of books, manuscripts, and works of art to his son and heir, Henry, whose own son James *Ley, third earl of Marlborough, may have facilitated the publication in 1642 of Ley's treatise on wardship (written *c.*1618–1621), and his collection of law reports, which concentrate on wardship matters, in 1659; both had previously enjoyed a wide circulation in manuscript. Four of Ley's papers originally delivered to the Society of Antiquaries were published by Thomas Hearne in his *Collection of Curious Discourses* (1720).

WILFRID PREST

Sources J. Ley, 'A declaration of the family of Ley', Wilts. & Swindon RO, 366/1 · *DNB* · HoP, *Commons*, *1558–1603* · W. R. Prest, *The rise of the barristers: a social history of the English bar, 1590–1640*, 2nd edn (1991) · W. P. Baildon, ed., *The records of the Honorable Society of Lincoln's Inn: the black books*, 2 (1898) · W. R. Williams, *The history of the great sessions in Wales, 1542–1830* (privately printed, Brecon, 1899) · *The letters of John Chamberlain*, ed. N. E. McClure, 2 vols. (1939) · M. Jansson, ed., *Proceedings in parliament, 1614 (House of Commons)* (1988) · *The diary of Sir Richard Hutton, 1614–1639*, ed. W. R. Prest, SeldS, suppl. ser., 9 (1991) · R. Lockyer, *Buckingham: the life and political career of George Villiers, first duke of Buckingham, 1592–1628* (1981) · R. P. Cust, *The forced loan and English politics, 1626–1628* (1987) · J. Ley, letters, Hants. RO, Jervoise of Herriard papers, 44M 69/XL · W. R. Prest, *The inns of court under Elizabeth I and the early Stuarts, 1590–1640* (1972) · PRO, PROB 11/155/217 · *CSP Ire., 1608–10; 1615–25* · G. E. Aylmer, *The king's servants: the civil service of Charles I, 1625–1642* (1961), 320

Archives Free Library of Philadelphia, MSS, MS LC 14.44 (1) · Yale U., Osborn Shelves, Tracts 1 (11) | CUL, MSS, MS Dd.5.50, fols.1r–21v; Dd.11.87, fols. 170r–180r · Hants. RO, corresp. with Henry Sherfield

Likenesses D. Mytens, oils, 1627, Harvard U., law school [*see illus.*] · tomb effigy, 1629 (with wife), All Saints' Church, Westbury, Wiltshire · oils, Lincoln's Inn, London · oils (after a portrait, *c.*1615), NPG

Wealth at death substantial; portions of £2000 for two daughters: will, PRO, PROB 11/155/217 · £130—twenty manors: G. S. Fry and E. A. Fry, eds., 'Abstracts of Wiltshire inquisitiones post mortem returned into the court of chancery in the reign of King Charles the first', *Index library*, 23 (1901)

Ley, James, third earl of Marlborough (1618/19–1665), naval officer, was the elder child of Henry Ley, second earl of Marlborough (1595–1638), and his wife, Mary (*bap.* 1597, *d.* 1670), daughter of Sir Arthur Capel of Little Hadham, Hertfordshire, and Rayne, Essex, and his wife, Margaret. His precise date and place of birth have not been traced. His grandfather was James *Ley, first earl of Marlborough (1550–1629), judge and lord high treasurer, who had extensive interests in the Caribbean. The family was well established in Wiltshire and the west. Henry Ley was on bad terms with his wife, perhaps because of her attachment to his steward, Thomas Wanklyn, whom she later married.

Unlike his father and grandfather, James Ley did not enter the inns of court. He showed an early interest in travel, visiting Massachusetts in 1637 where John Winthrop praised his wisdom and moderation. On 1 April 1638 the second earl died, leaving many debts, at least one of which was still unpaid when his son died. The new earl soon petitioned for payment of an annuity, long in arrears, and sold property in 1639–40. He pleaded poverty on 15 February 1639 as the reason for not accompanying the king to York. Marlborough was still a minor, and his wardship was granted to Sir John Danvers, the future regicide, who had been secretary to the first earl. On 2 March 1639 Marlborough was licensed to travel abroad for three years. Until 1642 the House of Lords records usually note 'extra regnum' to explain his absence, though he was at the Isle of Wight in September 1640. There was early involvement with ships and the sea: in September 1640 he planned to sell a great Spanish ship which he had recently bought in the Netherlands; one of his ships was captured by the Spaniards in the early 1640s; and in May 1642 the House of Lords gave him permission to go to sea.

By 1643 Marlborough was active in the cause of the king. He is said to have been in arms with his 'kinsman, lord Seymour of Troubridge' (*VCH Wiltshire*, 5.139). He took possession of a house at Fonthill, Wiltshire, in May 1643 in order to block Wardour Castle, became general of ordnance in the army of the west, and in July 1643 assisted his uncle Sir Ralph Hopton in the defence of Devizes. After Dartmouth and a small fleet of ships fell into royalist hands in October 1643, perhaps because of previous service at sea, he was appointed admiral of a royalist squadron which set out from Dartmouth. Before departing he joined other peers in signing a letter to the Scottish authorities, protesting against their planned invasion of England.

Marlborough's squadron was insufficient to engage in more than minor operations, though the earl of Warwick, lord high admiral, was fearful on 10 February 1645 of the threat to the American plantations. Marlborough operated initially in European waters, shipping munitions from St Malo, but was off Madeira in early 1645. Having been granted the Caribbean islands by Charles I in March 1645, he occupied Santa Cruz, but his party was soon driven out by the Spaniards.

Marlborough made his peace with parliament, his fine being set on 24 May 1649 at £113 6*s*. 8*d*. and later advanced to £200. He maintained an interest in maritime ventures and on 23 June 1649 obtained permission to go to sea, after entering bonds to do nothing prejudicial to England or the plantations, though evidently nothing came of the project. The only other reference to him in the interregnum is an unlikely story in 1655 that he was privy to conveying an heiress overseas.

After the Restoration Marlborough played little part in the House of Lords, but he became a commissioner of trade and counsellor for the colonies. He made proposals in November 1660 to encourage the plantation in Jamaica. Marlborough was no Restoration rake. Clarendon said that having no great estate he took more delight in all kinds of learning than in his title, but no foundation has been found for the statement that he was a distinguished mathematician. Pepys described him as a 'serious and worthy gentleman' (Pepys, 5.30). He was unmarried, although a poem on marriage has been attributed to him.

Marlborough was commander of the expedition sent in 1662 to take possession of Bombay, part of the dowry of Queen Catherine of Braganza. He reached Bombay on 18 September 1662, but the Portuguese governor refused to deliver it up, and Marlborough returned to England where he arrived in June 1663, having left the English garrison for Bombay on an island near Goa, where many perished. He was awarded an annuity of £500 payable out of the Caribbee Islands for his own life and that of his uncle William, but whether as a reward for services or as an equivalent for the payments due from the earl of Carlisle does not appear. Although nominated governor of Jamaica in 1664, at the outbreak of the Second Anglo-Dutch War he was appointed captain of the *Old James*. His correspondence at the time indicates that the prospect of battle turned his thoughts to religion, for which he confesses he had hitherto felt little interest. He was killed at the battle of Lowestoft on 3 June 1665, and was buried with ceremony in Westminster Abbey on 14 June.

G. G. Harris

Sources GEC, *Peerage*, new edn, 8.488–91 • *CSP dom.*, *1638–9*, 466, 527; *1640–41*, 40; *1649–50*, 204; *1655–6*, 152 • *JHL*, 4 (1628–42); 5 (1642–3), 58; 6 (1643–4), 420; 11 (1660–66) • high court of admiralty examinations, PRO, HCA 13, vol. 58, fol. 248; vol. 59, fols. 147–8; vol. 60, 25/8/1645 and 7/2/1646 • D. Warrand, ed., *Hertfordshire families* (1907), 91–2 • E. B. Sainsbury, ed., *A calendar of the court minutes … of the East India Company*, [6]: *1660–1663* (1922), xxiii, xxxviii, 321 • *CSP col.*, 1.281, 491–3; 5.nos. 236, 251, 637, 764, 1368 • *The journal of John Winthrop, 1630–1649*, ed. R. S. Dunn, J. Savage, and L. Yeandle (1996), 223–4, 573 • G. S. Fry and E. A. Fry, eds., *Abstracts of Wiltshire inquisitions post mortem … in the reign of King Charles the First*, British RS, 23 (1901), 235, 273 • M. A. E. Green, ed., *Calendar of the proceedings of the committee for compounding … 1643–1660*, 3, PRO (1891), 1783 • Pepys, *Diary*, 5.30; 6.122 • J. L. Chester, ed., *The marriage, baptismal, and burial registers of the collegiate church or abbey of St Peter, Westminster*, Harleian Society, 10 (1876), 162

Archives BL, corresp., Add. MS 46376 | NRA Scotland, priv. coll., letters to Sir Robert Atkyns

Wealth at death left £500 to his uncle; annuity of £500; left £160 to settle father's debt: will, PRO, PROB 11/317, fols. 58–9

Ley, John (1549?–1604), explorer, was the third of four sons who lived to adulthood of Henry Ley of Teffont Evias, Wiltshire (*d.* 1574), and his wife, Dionysia (*d.* 1589), the younger of the two daughters of Walter Seymour of Berwick St John, Wiltshire. He was educated at Winchester College, and attended Oxford University and Clement's Inn, but 'beinge nothing affected to Studie the lawe He betooke himself to marshiall Courses' (Wilts. & Swindon RO, 366/1, fol. 8*v*). He accompanied Martin Frobisher on two of his three voyages in search of a north-west passage (1576–8). He later served with the rebels in the Low Countries 'longe tyme', rising to the rank of captain. Ley also undertook several privateering voyages 'at his owne charge'. He was captain of the *John Young* of Southampton in 1590. In 1592 he commanded the *Alcedo* in Frobisher's fleet, dispatched by the earl of Cumberland to seek East Indies carracks. Although Ley went to Ireland in August 1594 with the new lord deputy, Sir William Russell, his contacts in the seafaring community appear to have kept him abreast of Sir Walter Ralegh's efforts to discover El Dorado in Guiana and to have inspired him to venture in search of it also.

Ley was among the earliest Englishmen to explore the coast of Guiana and the first to enter the Amazon. He sailed from Dartmouth with one ship on Shrove Tuesday 1597. He sighted what he called the 'westerne Cape' of the Amazon on 23 March before running up the coast to anchor in the Wiapoco (Oyapock). There he assembled a shallop and proceeded to explore the lower reaches of every river up to the Curratyne (Corantijn) for potential routes to El Dorado, making numerous contacts with Amerindian groups in the process. In the Curratyne Ley met up with Ralegh's *Watte*, commanded by Leonard Berry. The captains made for the Windward Islands and then parted company. Ley traded for tobacco with natives at St Lucia and took a Spanish frigate off Cumana. He returned to London with his prize on 24 August, his ship having arrived some time earlier.

In March 1598, when Cumberland's fleet set forth for Puerto Rico, Ley accompanied it as far as Lanzarote and then made off alone for Guiana in his prize frigate, now called the *Black Ley*. He reached the Amazon delta in June and spent about a month exploring 300 miles upriver, hoping to pick up news of an empire of Amazon women. He visited various native settlements, noting the long-house dwellings built on piles above the flood. He found their inhabitants less welcoming than the natives he had contacted a year earlier. From the Amazon, Ley stopped in all the rivers he had visited previously, before making for the Caribbean and thence for England.

It is not known why Ley delayed his third voyage to Guiana until October 1601. He dispatched an account of his two earlier voyages and of his progress to date in the third to his brother James *Ley, the future earl of Marlborough, in a letter from the Cape Verde Islands in December. John Ley's account, a response to his brother's plea for a record of his discoveries, also contained lists of the rivers between the Amazon and the Orinoco, and of the peoples who inhabited them. He included descriptions of their customs and local fauna, as well as tales of monstrous peoples such as those 'without heads, haveinge their Eies, nose and mouth in their breastes', or 'with two faces one behinde and thother before, fower Armes, fower legs … and they goe and come and shoote both waies'. Ley probably touched in the Amazon in 1602. He certainly visited the Wiapoco, leaving a man there whom Charles Leigh met when he entered the river later in the year. Having 'Referred the settinge downe' of his third voyage after his return, John Ley 'was prevented by death' (Wilts. & Swindon RO, 366/1, fol. 15*v*). He died in London on 7 June 1604, and was buried in the chancel of St Andrew by the Wardrobe.

Joyce Lorimer

Sources Wilts. & Swindon RO, 366/1 • T. Masham, 'The third voyage set forth by Sir Walter Ralegh to Guiana with a pinnesse called the *Watte*, in the yeere 1596', in R. Hakluyt, *The principal navigations, voyages, traffiques and discoveries of the English nation*, 11, Hakluyt Society, extra ser., 11 (1904), 1–15 • J. Layfield, 'A large relation of the Port Ricco voiage', in S. Purchas, *Hakluytus posthumus, or, Purchas his pilgrimes* (1625); repr. in Hakluyt Society, extra ser., 16 (1906) • 'A true report of such things as happened in the second voyage of Captaine Frobisher', R. Hakluyt, *The principal navigations, voyages, traffiques and discoveries of the English nation*, 7, Hakluyt Society, extra ser., 7 (1904) • PRO, HCA24/59, no. 191 • J. Lorimer, 'The reluctant go-between: John Ley's survey of aboriginal settlement on the Guayana coastline', *The European outthrust and encounter … essays in tribute to David Beers Quinn*, ed. C. H. Clough and P. E. H. Hair (1994), 190–223 • J. Lorimer, ed., *English and Irish settlement on the River Amazon, 1550–1646*, Hakluyt Society, 2nd ser., 171 (1989), 19–26, 132–6 • J. Stow, *The survey of London*, ed. A. M. [A. Munday] and others, rev. edn (1633), 407 • G. D. Squibb, ed., *Wiltshire visitation pedigrees, 1623*, Harleian Society, 105–6 (1954) • 'Captaine Charles Leighs letter to Sir Olave Leigh his brother', in S. Purchas, *Hakluytus posthumus, or, Purchas his pilgrimes* (1625); repr. in Hakluyt Society, extra ser., 29 (1906) • R. Robinson and others, 'A journall of the eleaventh and later voyage to the West India 1597 … Porto Rico', in G. C. Williamson, *George, third earl of Cumberland* (1920), 178 • *The naval tracts of Sir William Monson*, ed. M. Oppenheim, 1, Navy RS, 22 (1902), 1.281

Ley [Leigh], **John** (1584–1662), Church of England clergyman and religious controversialist, was born on 4 February 1584 at Warwick; his family was descended from the Leys of Cheshire. After attending the free school at Warwick, he matriculated at Christ Church, Oxford, on 12 February 1602, graduated BA on 23 October 1605, and proceeded MA on 30 May 1608. He was appointed vicar of Great Budworth, Cheshire, in 1616. He may have been the John Leigh who married Sarah Stockton there on 2 February 1617. He certainly married in or before 1620: a son, William, was born late in 1620 or early in 1621. When he engaged in a debate in 1619 with a prebend of Chester who opposed a morally binding sabbath, the bishop of Chester, John Bridgeman, ordered both men to cease preaching on the subject until he ruled, and in the meantime Ley sought the advice of Archbishop James Ussher. On 4 April 1627 Ley was appointed prebend of Chester Cathedral, where he also served as subdeacon, and he was the Friday lecturer at St Peter's, Chester. When he protested to Bridgeman in June 1635 that a recently erected monument to St Werburgh was regarded by some as an altar, the bishop ordered its removal; Ley subsequently published his protest as *A Letter (Against the Erection of an Altar)* (1641). He had ties to the Harley family, as reflected in the dedication of a funeral sermon, *A Pattern of Pietie* (1640), to Brilliana, Lady Harley, as well as to Alice, Lady Lucy, a member of the Warwickshire godly.

When the clergy who participated in the monthly exercises at Chester had doubts about the 'etcetera oath', they asked Ley to draft a statement, which he completed on 22 February 1641 and published as *Defensive Doubts, Hopes, and Reasons, for the Refusall of the Oath* (1641). Troubled by the oath's all-encompassing coverage, he argued against taking it on grounds of conscience. Two days later he put the finishing touches to a casuistic work, *A Case of Conscience, Concerning the Sacrament of the Lords Supper* (1641), explaining that a person who has difficulty partaking of an element can use a substitute or commune in a single substance. *Sunday a Sabbath* (1641), completed in March and dedicated to Archbishop Ussher, refuted John Pocklington's claim that Sunday was not the sabbath. Ley vividly depicted Sunday as 'the training day of military Discipline, by which the Church of Christ is unto the Synagogue of Satan … *terrible as an Army with Banners*' (c4r). In passing, he indicated his belief that the safety of England and Scotland depended on their union. He followed this work in September with *A Comparison of the Parliamentary Protestation with the Late Canonicall Oath* (1641), which he dedicated to Sir Robert Harley. He had no hesitation in endorsing the protestation to defend protestantism because it required a vow rather than an oath, allowed some freedom of interpretation, and was issued by the House of Commons, a free rather than a subordinate body. As the fissure between king and parliament widened, Ley sided with the latter. Consequently in 1642 the commissioners of array in Cheshire treated him harshly, prompting Sir William Brereton to complain to Oliver Cromwell on his behalf. *A Discourse Concerning Puritans* (1641) has occasionally been attributed to Ley, but Henry Parker, whose name is written on the title-page of George Thomason's copy, is the more likely author.

On at least two occasions Ley preached to the House of Commons (26 April 1643 and 2 October 1645), and a like number to the House of Lords (5 February 1646 and 12 May 1646). The most important of these sermons, *The Fury of Warre* (1643), was preached to the Commons at a monthly fast. Justifying the parliamentary war effort, he asserted that those who have been endangered have the right of self-defence, and he articulated six requirements for a just war: it must be authorized by a legal authority; be fought for a just and weighty cause; have valid aims; spare the innocent; be undertaken only after negotiations have failed; and bring a cessation of enmity at the conclusion of the fighting. He also warned that if the civil war continued, it could turn England into a 'seminary' of discord and a wilderness of want rather than a sanctuary of peace and a storehouse of plenty. The following month he completed funeral sermons, published as *A Monitor of Mortalitie* (1643), for the son of Sir Simon Archer of Warwickshire and the wife and daughter of the Chester merchant Henry Harpur.

On 27 April 1643 the House of Commons appointed Ley rector of St Mary-at-Hill, London, by which time the Westminster assembly had begun its work. Ley was the thirteenth person selected for membership, immediately following Thomas Goodwin. He played a major role in the assembly's activities, serving on the first committee (one of three standing committees to review the Thirty-Nine Articles), chairman of the printing committee, an examiner of ministerial candidates, and the administrator of applications for vacant livings. During the debates he opposed the institution of ruling as opposed to preaching elders, favoured sitting to receive the Lord's supper but would accept any posture, and supported dipping as a legitimate means of baptizing. In 1644 he obtained the rectory of Charlwood, Surrey, which he resigned to his son William in 1645, and in the latter year he was named president of Sion College, a centre for ministerial study and discussion.

Ley became embroiled in an extended debate with his friend John Saltmarsh when he responded to the latter's *A New Quaere* (1646), which opposed the establishment of a presbyterian state church. In *The New Quere, and Determination Upon It* (1646) Ley likened a church composed of independent gathered congregations to an army that comprised individual units without a central command structure. Instead he advocated a union of the state churches of England and Scotland. Replying in *The Smoke in the Temple* (1646), Saltmarsh espoused the need for liberty of conscience and rejected presbyterian polity because of its intimate relationship with civil government. Ley countered in *Light for Smoke* (1646) that Saltmarsh was an antinomian and an Anabaptist who accorded insufficient authority to civil authorities in religious matters.

> The Presbyteriall Government is more moderate, more subordinate to the Parliamentary Government then the Independent, because that is humbly submitted to the debate of the Parliament for approbation of it, and waiteth for their Civill establishment before any part of it is put into execution. (Ley, *Light for Smoke*, 54)

Weary of the dispute, Saltmarsh offered only a brief response, *An End of One Controversie* (1646), refusing to reply in kind to the perceived 'dirt' cast on him by Ley. The latter's surrogate, identifying himself as a divinity student in *An After-Reckoning* (1646), denounced Saltmarsh's response as abusive and inadequate. Because Ley had referred to the Baptist John Tombes in his controversy with Saltmarsh, Tombes briefly replied in *An Apology or Plea for the Two Treatises* (1646).

Citing Ley's service to the church and his suffering on behalf of the parliamentary cause, the committee for plundered ministers ordered on 3 June 1646 that he receive the profits of his prebend. On 2 September the assembly approved his appointment as rector of Astbury, Cheshire, but he did not take up his duties until 22 April 1647. He had trouble collecting some of his tithes at Astbury when a group of extruded ministers, citing a spurious declaration supposedly from General Sir Thomas Fairfax, encouraged parishioners not to pay. When London ministers issued a testimony against heretics and blasphemers, Ley drafted the *Attestation of the Ministers of Cheshire* (1648) supporting their position. By October 1649 he had been appointed rector of Brightwell, Berkshire, but he gave the sequestered minister, Edward Hyde, until 1 April 1650 to leave. Because of Hyde's ample estate and the losses sustained by Ley in support of parliament, on 19 October 1652 the county committee exempted Ley from having to pay Hyde the standard 20 per cent of the income. A protracted dispute ensued, which Ley recounted in *An Acquittance or Discharge* (1655; also published as *General Reasons, Grounded on Piety*, 1655) and *A Letter to Dr. E. Hyde* (1655).

Ley published annotations on the Pentateuch in 1651 and a defence of tithes, *Exceptions Many and Just* (1653), in response to two petitions submitted to parliament. Many godly people deemed it a privilege to pay tithes, he averred, because they are not burdensome, Jewish, or anti-Christian. He was appointed a trier for the approbation of ministers in 1653, and an assistant to the Berkshire commission for the ejection of scandalous ministers and schoolmasters the following year. By June 1656 he had become rector of Solihull, Warwickshire, a living obtained from Sir Simon Archer, and that year he published *A Debate Concerning the Liturgy*, recounting another controversy with Hyde, 'a *Seraphicall zealot* for the Service-book', since 1649. Ley was willing to use set forms of prayer, but not to the extent of excluding extempore utterances inspired by the Spirit. Following the death of Nathaniel Bryan, minister of St Mary's, Stafford, Ley wrote *A Consolatory Letter* (1658) to his father, John Bryan, minister at Coventry. When his own health began to fail, he resigned his living at Solihull and moved to Sutton Coldfield, Warwickshire, where he died on 16 May 1662 and was buried in the parish church.

RICHARD L. GREAVES

Sources Wood, *Ath. Oxon.*, new edn, 3.569–75 • *Walker rev.*, 3, 42, 69, 352 • Foster, *Alum. Oxon.* • J. F. Wilson, *Pulpit in parliament: puritanism during the English civil wars, 1640–1648* (1969) • R. S. Paul, *The assembly of the Lord: politics and religion in the Westminster assembly and the 'Grand debate'* (1985) • S. W. Carruthers, *The everyday work of the Westminster assembly* (1943) • *VCH Cheshire*, 3.32, 41, 102 • J. T. Cliffe, *Puritans in conflict: the puritan gentry during and after the civil wars* (1988) • K. L. Parker, *The English sabbath: a study of doctrine and discipline from the Reformation to the civil war* (1988) • L. J. Holley, 'The divines of the Westminster Assembly: a study of puritanism and parliament', PhD diss., Yale U., 1979

Archives BL, Add. MS 15671, fol. 182*v* • Bodl. Oxf., MS Rawl. 89, fol. 30

Ley, Roger (**1593/4–1668**), Church of England clergyman and author, was born at Crewe, Cheshire, of unknown parents. He matriculated at Jesus College, Cambridge, in Easter 1606, graduated BA in 1610, and proceeded MA in 1613. He was ordained deacon in Peterborough on 11 April 1614, and priest in London on 31 May 1618 (at the age of twenty-four). Shortly afterwards, he was appointed curate of St Leonard, Shoreditch, Middlesex, and he may also have been curate of Moulton, Northamptonshire, in 1619. On 19 February 1622 he married Anne, daughter of Thomas Norman of St Botolph without Bishopsgate, London, a leatherseller.

Ley's two Paul's Cross sermons, of 20 December 1618 and 9 September 1621, which were subsequently published as *The Scepter of Righteousness* and *The Bruising of the Serpent's Head* respectively, reveal a firm belief in the Calvinist doctrine of election to salvation, an early opposition to Arminianism, a preoccupation with the threat posed by the Antichrist, and an awareness of the danger of religion's being polluted by superstition and idolatry. Such views were to run counter to developments in the church under the growing influence of William Laud and his ecclesiastical allies. Ley was also the author of 'Gesta Britannica', a manuscript history in Latin of the church from the conversion of England to 1649 (BL, Stowe MS 76).

Ley's main claim to fame, however, was probably his outright denunciation of Paul Best for his anti-trinitarian views. Best and Ley had been fellow students and friends at Jesus College and in 1644 Best entrusted his first writings on the Trinity to Ley for his reactions and comments. Ley immediately betrayed Best to the authorities and was one of the divines who repeatedly visited him during his imprisonment to try and persuade him to renounce his heresy. In addition, Ley wrote an unpublished biographical memoir of his former friend in which he fully acknowledged Best's impressive intellect and abilities and explained how Best was drawn into his heretical opinions during his travels on the continent. The original manuscript appears not to have survived but notes were taken from it by the antiquary Joseph Hunter, its last custodian (BL, Add. MS 24482). These notes provide one of the main sources for Best's life and intellectual and theological development.

Ley ended his career as the rector of Brean, Somerset, from 1663 to his death in 1668. In his will made on 30 October 1667 he left an interest in a tenement called the Blue Anchor at Limehouse, Middlesex, a seven-year lease on a house in Phoenix Alley, off Long Acre, Westminster, a small library of books, and the contents of the house where he was accustomed to reside when at Wells. By this time his wife was dead, and there were apparently no surviving children. Isaac Saunderson, vicar of Plumstead, Kent, is identified as a 'loving friend' of Ley and his wife and was bequeathed five of Ley's books, including the 'Gesta Britannica', a folio volume entitled 'Tractatus theologicus', a collection of sermons containing Ley's two published Paul's Cross sermons, and a treatise entitled 'The peace of Jerusalem'. Saunderson was also named as joint executor with Ley's nephew, Timothy Ley. Dr Thomas Holt, the chancellor of Wells Cathedral, was appointed overseer of the will and was made responsible for the conduct of Ley's burial, which probably took place at Brean.

KEITH LINDLEY

Sources Venn, *Alum. Cant.* • will, PRO, PROB 11/326/49 • R. Ley, *The scepter of righteousness: a sermon preached at Paul's Cross, Dec. 20, 1618* (1619) • R. Ley, *The bruising of the serpent's head: a sermon preached at Paul's Cross, Sept 9, 1621* (1622) • J. Hunter, notes from Ley's MS on Paul Best, BL, Add. MS 24482 • J. L. Chester and J. Foster, eds., *London marriage licences, 1521–1869* (1887), 831 • 'Best, Paul', *DNB* • 'Best, Paul', Greaves & Zaller, *BDBR*, 1.60–61 • F. W. Weaver, ed., *Somerset incumbents* (privately printed, Bristol, 1889), 33 • K. Fincham, *Prelate as pastor: the episcopate of James I* (1990), 87, 265 • N. Tyacke, *Anti-Calvinists: the rise of English Arminianism, c.1590–1640* (1987), 258 • 'Gesta Britannica', BL, MS Stowe 76

Archives BL, 'Gesta Britannica to 1649', MS Stowe 76 [362 folios] • BL, notes taken by Joseph Hunter from Ley's MS biography of Paul Best, Add. MS 24482

Wealth at death modest interest in properties in Middlesex; small library: will, PRO, PROB 11/326/49

Leybourn, Thomas (*c.***1769–1840**), mathematician, was born about 1769 but nothing is known of his antecedents, childhood, or education. He probably had connections with Charles Hutton, since he dedicated to Hutton the first volume of a mathematical periodical, the *Mathematical and Philosophical Repository*, which he launched in 1795 and edited until 1835. In 1802 he was appointed mathematics master in the Royal Military College, then based near Marlow, Buckinghamshire, and after 1813 at Sandhurst. In 1803 and 1804 two other mathematicians, William Wallace and James Ivory, were taken on the staff and the college became an important centre of mathematical research. In 1804 Leybourn's periodical continued in a new series entitled the *Mathematical Repository*. This publication, especially its first three volumes, played a role in the reform of British calculus. Leybourn, Wallace, and Ivory contributed original papers to the *Mathematical Repository*, as did their colleagues at the college, John Lowry, James Cunliffe, and Mark Noble. Contributions also arrived from well-known mathematicians elsewhere, including Hutton, Babbage, John Herschel, George Peacock, and Mary Somerville.

Leybourn, like his colleagues Wallace and Ivory, was critical of the insularity of British mathematics. There is evidence that he was convinced that British mathematics was in a state of decadence and could not stand comparison with contemporary continental research. This interest in continental mathematics motivated the translations of memoirs by foreign mathematicians (most notably J. L. Lagrange and A. M. Legendre) which appeared in his *Repository*. In 1802 he published a textbook on trigonometry, and in 1817 he edited a volume of questions proposed in the *Ladies' Diary*. In 1835 he was elected FRS. He continued to teach at Sandhurst until November 1839, when he retired (on a pension) from the office of senior professor of mathematics. He died at Sandhurst on 1 March 1840. His library of nearly a thousand books was sold in June 1840. NICCOLÒ GUICCIARDINI

Sources *GM*, 2nd ser., 13 (1840), 442–3 • E. G. R. Taylor, *The mathematical practitioners of Hanoverian England, 1714–1840* (1966) • M. Panteki, 'William Wallace and the introduction of continental calculus to Britain: a letter to George Peacock', *Historia Mathematica*, 14 (1987), 119–32 • P. J. Anderson, 'Mathematical periodicals: Thomas Leybourn's *Mathematical Repository*', *N&Q*, 11th ser., 2 (1910), 466–7 • R. C. Archibald, 'Notes on some minor English mathematical serials', *Mathematical Gazette*, 14 (1928–9), 379–400 • T. W. Wilkinson, 'On Leybourn's *Mathematical Repository*', *Mechanics' Magazine*, 55 (1851); 56 (1852); 57 (1852) • *Complete guide to the junior and senior departments of the Royal Military College, Sandhurst* (1849) • N. Guicciardini, *The development of Newtonian calculus in Britain, 1700–1800* (1989) • G. Howson, *A history of mathematics education in England* (1982)

Leybourn, William (1626–1716), mathematician and land surveyor, started his career as a bookseller and printer; his address from 1645 was Monkswell Street, Cripplegate. From about 1651 he was in partnership with Robert Leybourn, possibly a brother. Together they printed scientific and mathematical books until 1665. In the following year Leybourn moved to Northcott, the northern part of Southall, Middlesex. He had a son, William, and perhaps a daughter as well, so was probably married although his spouse's name is not known.

Leybourn's reputation as an author grew from his first publication, *Urania practica*. This, the first substantial English compendium of astronomy, was written with Vincent Wing in 1648. Criticism by Jeremie Shakerley in 1649 was answered in the same year by the authors. In 1675 Leybourn wrote *An Introduction to Astronomy and Geography*, published by Robert Morden and William Berry, who were well known for their geographical works. His first contribution to surveying was a pamphlet, *Planometria, or, The Whole Art of Surveying of Land*, published in 1650 under the pseudonym of Oliver Wallinby. This was enlarged and published under his true name as *The Compleat Surveyor* in 1653. The success of the work led to the publication of four editions during Leybourn's lifetime; a fifth appeared in 1722, edited by Samuel Cunn.

In several of his works, Leybourn advertised as a teacher and land and building surveyor. In October 1666 he was appointed one of the six surveyors to measure the damage caused by the great fire of London. Leybourn's practice as a land surveyor continued and he mapped estates in London and many other English counties for several clients. He was also a quantity surveyor. His *Platform for Purchasers, Guide for Builders, Mate for Measurers* (1667–8) was an early work on the subject. He was employed in this capacity by the City of London and agreed the final cost of the building works of the Fleet Canal in 1674. His edition of Stephen Primatt's *City and Countrey Purchaser and Builder* was published in 1680. Later, in 1693, he published the most enduring of his works, a ready reckoner: *Panarithmologia, being a mirror for merchants, breviate for bankers, treasure for tradesmen, mate for mechanicks, and a sure guide for purchasers, sellers, or mortgagers of land, leases, annuities, rents, pensions, etc. … and a constant concomitant fitted for all mens occasions*. Well over twenty editions were issued and the work remained in print into the nineteenth century. To his fourth edition of Scamozzi's *The Mirror of Architecture* (1700), Leybourn added a 'Compendium of the art of building'.

Dialling and instrument making were other interests of Leybourn. He produced the second edition of *Horometria, or, The Compleat Diallist* by Thomas Stirrup in 1659. Leybourn's own work on the subject, *The Art of Dialling*, was first published in 1669. He erected sundials, too, and was paid for one on Basinghall steeple in 1676–7. Leybourn invented an instrument for 'performing all such conclusions geometrical and astronomical … usually wrought by … globes, spheres, sectors' and described it in *Panorganon, or, A Universal Instrument* (1672).

Leybourn was the author of several mathematical texts. His *Arithmetick: Vulgar, Decimal, Instrumental* was published in 1657. Leybourn's fourth edition of the *Works of Edmund Gunter* was published in 1662; a fifth edition followed in 1673 and a sixth in 1680. *The Line of Proportion or Numbers, Commonly called Gunter's Line, Made Easie*, published in 1667, was a theoretical guide to a logarithmic rule, dedicated to those who had been appointed to direct the survey of London after the fire. A treatise on Napier's computing rods, *The Art of Numbring by Speaking-Rods, Vulgarly Termed Nepeirs Bones* was also published in this year. The practical application of Gunter's line was described in *The Art of Measuring* (1669). All of these publications were reissued in later editions. In 1690 Leybourn published the substance of his former works in *Cursus mathematicus*, a folio volume of over nine hundred pages. It is noteworthy that the author discusses Kepler's discoveries, but says nothing of Newton's *Principia*, which had appeared three years previously.

Several of Leybourn's works reflect his role as a teacher and popularizer of mathematics. He first published *Arithmetical Recreations, or, Enchiridion of Arithmetical Questions both Delightful and Profitable* in 1667. Two years later appeared his *Nine Geometricall Exercises, for Young Sea-Men. Pleasure with Profit; Consisting of Recreations of Divers Kinds … to Recreate Ingenious Spirits* followed in 1694, and *Mathematical Institutions* in 1704.

Leybourn continued to live at Northcott until his death. He died in 1716, probably in September, and was buried in

St Mary the Virgin, Hanwell, on 12 September 1716. His heirs were Mary (probably his daughter) and Tabitha Morden, to whom he left the care of his son, W[illiam].

SARAH BENDALL

Sources C. E. Kenney, 'William Leybourn, 1626–1716', *The Library*, 5th ser., 5 (1950–51), 159–71 • F. W. Steer and others, *Dictionary of land surveyors and local map-makers of Great Britain and Ireland, 1530–1850*, ed. P. Eden, 2nd edn, ed. S. Bendall, 2 vols. (1997) • H. R. Plomer and others, *A dictionary of the booksellers and printers who were at work in England, Scotland, and Ireland from 1641 to 1667* (1907) • B. R. Masters, *The public markets of the City of London surveyed by William Leybourn in 1677* (1974) • will, PRO, PROB 11/556, sig. 12 • A. W. Richeson, *English land measuring to 1800: instruments and practices* (1966) • H. Bromley, *A catalogue of engraved British portraits* (1793) • parish register, Hanwell, St Mary the Virgin, 12 Sept 1716, LMA, DRO 25/A1/2 [burial] • W. Musgrave, *Obituary prior to 1800*, ed. G. J. Armytage, 6 vols., Harleian Society, 44–9 (1899–1901)

Archives Bodl. Oxf., maps • CLRO, maps • GL, maps • LMA, maps • Magd. Oxf., maps • PRO, maps • S. Antiquaries, Lond., maps

Likenesses R. Gaywood, etching (aged thirty), BM, NPG; repro. in W. Leybourn, *Arithmetick* (1657) • R. White, line engraving, BM, NPG; repro. in W. Leybourn, *Compleat surveyor* (1674) • R. White, line engraving, BM, NPG; repro. in W. Leybourn, *Cursus mathematicus* (1690) • R. White, line engraving, repro. in W. Leybourn, *Dialling* (1682) • engraving, repro. in W. Leybourn, *Art of dyalling* (1669) • engraving, repro. in W. Leybourn, *Arithmetick* (1678) • etching (aged twenty-seven), BM, NPG; repro. in W. Leybourn, *Compleat surveyor* (1674)

Leybourne, George [*performing name* Champagne Charlie] (**1842–1884**), music-hall entertainer, popularly known as Champagne Charlie, was born on 17 March 1842 in Stourbridge, Gateshead, the son of Joseph Leybourne, a currier and sometime theatre musician, and his wife, Isabella, *née* Bullerwell. Leybourne's early life remains obscure and misreported, but he is known to have moved to London with his family at the age of three. Poorly educated, he worked first as an engine fitter or engineer, and began his career as an entertainer in his late teens under the stage name Joe Saunders, playing the smaller music-halls and penny gaffs of London's East End and the provinces. He married Sarah Ann Fisher, a former dressmaker's apprentice, on 12 March 1865 in London. A versatile performer, he was by then appearing under his real name at the major metropolitan halls, singing and dancing in a variety of styles.

In 1866, already enjoying considerable popularity, Leybourne became a major star with the hit song 'Champagne Charlie', written in collaboration with Alfred Lee. Typical of a new genre of commercially produced music-hall songs and performed with a self-assertive comic realism, it celebrated the exploits of the swell, a lordly man about town of resplendent dress, confident air, and heroic appetite for champagne and admiring women. Leybourne was one of a new generation of young male stars in the same style—the *lions comiques*—but secured his prominence with a well-publicized contract with the music-hall proprietor William Holland at London's Canterbury Hall in 1868. In return for the sensational annual salary of £1500, Leybourne was obliged to play the swell off as well as on stage, appearing richly dressed at all times, driving to engagements in a carriage and four, and plying his public with champagne provided by the wine shippers. Tall, handsome, and with a 'curious faculty of filling the stage', Leybourne scandalized polite society with his vulgar appropriation of upper-class dress and manners, but offered a compelling model for young lower middle- and working-class male aspirants to gentility, who popularized the Champagne Charlie hat in his honour. (The Salvation Army paid homage by converting his hit into a hymn.) In 1869–70, in acknowledgement of his own working-class roots and in a rare political statement, Leybourne gave benefit performances in support of the Nine Hours Movement for a shorter working day. He did not, however, reduce his own work schedule. Widely employed in London, he also undertook frequent provincial tours, living out the same flamboyant and demanding persona and establishing himself as a national as well as a metropolitan favourite. He made his family home in London, though he moved several times; recorded addresses include Islington and Kennington (a music-hall artists' colony). There were allusions to a country estate. Leybourne was accused of sharp practice by fellow artists, and proprietors complained of his unpunctuality, but his public loved him. According to an oft-repeated story, in private he despaired of the emptiness of fame and the absence of true friendship amid the enthusiastic crowds, yet he remained the good fellow of his most successful stage role; dubbed 'honorary high almoner to the profession', he was notably generous with hand-outs as well as drink. Leybourne enjoyed success with other song hits—'The Daring Young Man on the Flying Trapeze' (1866), 'Up in a Balloon' (1868), 'If ever I cease to love' (1871)—but continued to style himself the Original Champagne Charlie. His later career is difficult to assess. He seems to have retained his popularity, but his health declined and his appearances became more sporadic. He ventured into management in minor London halls and experimented with a double act with his daughter, Florence. (Florence later married the music-hall star Albert *Chevalier; Leybourne's other child, George junior, became Chevalier's manager.) Reports of Leybourne's increasing indispositions attributed them to consumption, but his death certificate records exhaustion and abscess (perhaps cirrhosis) of the liver. Much indebted, he died on 15 September 1884 at his home, 136 Englefield Road, Islington, London, and was buried at Abney Park cemetery, Stoke Newington, on 20 September.

In keeping with music-hall's increasing pretensions to respectability, later spokesmen for the industry disavowed Leybourne and the *lions comiques* as 'the most vulgar and objectionable creatures' who 'gloried in sex and drink' and 'turned the music halls into veritable sinks'. More recent scholarly critics have not liked Leybourne and his kind any better, interpreting their songs in praise of the aristocratic style as a dilution of an older, more combative working-class consciousness and a damning example of music-hall's social conservatism. The upper-class swell and his variants have none the less proved a durable type in the popular repertory, and Leybourne himself underwent some rehabilitation in the 1944 film *Champagne Charlie* (featuring comedian Tommy Trinder in the name part), though this paid scant regard to historical accuracy.

Leybourne was a product of the music-halls' first great boom, and his career exemplified the opportunities and hazards of stardom in a prototype modern capitalist entertainment industry. Embodying traditional elements of male licence in carnivalesque pursuit of the good time, his characterizations also gave voice to the more culturally assertive mid-Victorian lower classes in an era of increased earnings, greater leisure time, more and cheaper consumer goods (including champagne), and the extension of the franchise. Leybourne's style of 'magnificent cheek' was that of the common man on the rise in a modern liberal democracy, though any delusions were undercut by a strong note of parody. PETER BAILEY

Sources Colindale, London, BL newspaper collection · Jones/Beeching George Leybourne collection · P. Bailey, 'Champagne Charlie: performance and ideology in the music-hall swell song', *Music hall: performance and style*, ed. J. S. Bratton (1986), 49–69 · b. cert. · m. cert. · d. cert.

Archives Hollings Farm, Heptonstall, Hebden Bridge, West Yorkshire, Jones/Beeching George Leybourne collection

Likenesses Crouch & Snowden, photograph, repro. in *Variety Theatre* (28 July 1905) · thirty prints, Harvard TC

Leybourne, Juliana, **countess of Huntingdon** (1303/4–1367), noblewoman, was the daughter of Thomas of Leybourne (*d.* 1307) and Alice Tosny (*d.* 1325) and the granddaughter and heir of William of *Leybourne, first Lord Leybourne, of Leybourne and Newington, Kent (*d.* 1309) [*see under* Leybourne, Sir Roger of]. After the death of her grandfather, Juliana became the ward of Aymer de *Valence, earl of Pembroke (*d.* 1324). She was married three times: before 4 May 1321 to her guardian's nephew, John *Hastings, second Lord Hastings (*d.* 20 January 1325) [*see under* Hastings, John, first Lord Hastings (1262–1313)]; in or before September 1325 to Sir Thomas Blount, later Baron Blount, steward of the king's household (*d.* 17 August 1328); and before 17 October 1328 to William *Clinton, later earl of Huntingdon (*d.* 1354). By her first marriage she was mother to Laurence *Hastings, earl of Pembroke (1320–1348). Although she had an heir in the latter's son, John, Juliana granted the reversion of almost all her extensive estates in Kent and Sussex to Edward III in 1362, retaining a life interest and reserving certain manors for pious benefactions. She died between 31 October and 2 November 1367 and was buried in St Anne's Chapel at St Augustine's Abbey, Canterbury, where she had also founded a chantry.

The inventory of her goods taken after her death reveals her to have lived in some estate. She was evidently a patron, and perhaps an exponent, of needlework: she owned a hanging depicting the legend of Bevis of Hampton, and there still survive some examples of fourteenth-century embroidery featuring the arms of Leybourne and the earl of Huntingdon. During her third husband's lifetime she spent much time at Maxstoke, Warwickshire, but her preferred residence on her own estates was at Preston, Kent. Edward III used the lands he acquired from Juliana chiefly to provide for his own religious foundations, and apparently intended to establish perpetual obits for her at the houses of Dominican friars at Kings Langley, Hertfordshire, and Dominican nuns at Dartford, Kent. However, Richard II's government for some time ignored the former king's directions and tried to reconstitute the Leybourne inheritance and to grant it, and the title of earl of Huntingdon, to Sir Simon Burley (*d.* 1388).

W. M. ORMROD

Sources GEC, *Peerage*, new edn · L. B. L. [L. B. Larking], 'The inventory of Juliana de Leyborne, countess of Huntingdon', *Archaeologia Cantiana*, 1 (1858), 1–8 · C. J. Given-Wilson, 'Richard II and his grandfather's will', *EngHR*, 93 (1978), 320–37 · *Chancery records* · *RotP* · *VCH Warwickshire*, vol. 2 · *Catalogue of English ecclesiastical embroideries of the XIII to XVI centuries*, V&A, 3rd edn (1916)

Leybourne [Leyburn], **Sir Roger of** (*c.*1215–1271), soldier and landowner, was the son of Sir Roger of Leybourne (*b.* 1182x90, *d.* before 1251), of Leybourne, Kent, and of Eleanor (*d.* 1219/20), daughter and coheir of Stephen of *Thornham (*d.* 1213/14), a Kentish landowner. Roger's father was a minor in 1199 when his wardship and marriage were sold to Thornham for 300 marks. He rebelled against King John in 1215, was taken prisoner at Rochester Castle in November, and had to pay 250 marks for his release in August 1216. By 1229 he had married his second wife, Agnes, widow of Henry de Miners, who outlived him. From his father the younger Roger inherited seven knights' fees in Kent and Oxfordshire held from Margery de Revières, heir of Warin fitz Gerold. This was supplemented by his mother's share of the Thornham inheritance. He was also heir to debts owed by his father both to Jewish moneylenders and to the crown. Roger remained liable for the latter until 1253, when the debt was cancelled by Henry III while Roger was in Gascony in the king's service.

Young courtier and rebel, 1252–1263 The younger Roger of Leybourne first came to public notice in 1252 when he killed one of the king's household knights, Arnulf de Munteny, during a tournament at Walden. According to Matthew Paris, he used a sharpened lance to revenge himself for an injury suffered at Arnulf's hands during a previous tournament. He took the cross to atone for Arnulf's death, and was subsequently pardoned by the king. In 1253 he was given the escheated lands of Roger Connell in Kent, and from then until his death in 1271 he added regularly to his estates in that county. In 1257 Leybourne served with the Lord Edward during his campaign in Wales against Llywelyn, and by 1259 had become part of an influential group that coalesced around Edward, whose steward he became around this time. In autumn 1259 he joined Edward in alliance with Simon de Montfort, and in November was appointed custodian of Bristol Castle. He took part in the attempt by Edward and the earl of Gloucester to enter London under arms in 1260. After the king and his son were reconciled Leybourne was pardoned for his actions. Edward rewarded him for his service with the grant of the manor of Elham, Kent, but in 1262 this grant was deemed to be against the terms of the king's original grant of the manor to his son, and Leybourne was accused of misappropriating funds from the latter. The sheriff of Kent was instructed to raise £1820 from Leybourne's lands to repay his debt to Edward, although his efforts were partially frustrated as Leybourne had already removed all his goods and chattels from Kent, Essex, and Sussex. The continuator of Gervase of Canterbury blamed the queen rather than Edward for the downfall of Leybourne, whose misfortunes none the less provoked a split between Edward and his former supporters.

In August 1262 the king's general prohibition of tournaments during his absence from the realm was supplemented by individual mandates forbidding Roger of Leybourne and other members of his circle to bear arms. The king's caution proved justified, for in 1263 Leybourne and other marcher lords arrested Bishop Aigueblanche of Hereford, took Hereford, Gloucester, and Bristol, and returned south to assault Windsor Castle. Joined by Simon de Montfort, they turned their attentions to Kent, where they harried Romsey and the Cinque Ports. By August Leybourne and the marcher lords were in negotiation with the king, and on the 18th of that month they made a formal agreement with Edward, with a clause saving their oath to the provisions of Oxford. There is no clear explanation for Leybourne's change of allegiance at this time. Two chroniclers suggest he and his associates were bribed by lands, but there is no evidence for this in Leybourne's case and the royalist Thomas Wykes says simply that Edward was persuasive. Michael Prestwich has suggested that the marcher lords found Simon de Montfort's plans for an alliance with Llywelyn unacceptable. Gervase of Canterbury, commenting on Leybourne's return to the king's cause, observes that 'Saul became Paul and the wolf was made a lamb' (*Works of Gervase of Canterbury*, 2.224).

Pillar of the crown, 1263–1267 From this point Leybourne's loyalty to the king was absolute. He was rapidly reinstated as a leading member of the royalist party and rewarded with various offices: by September he was steward of the king's household; he was given the keepership of Kent, Surrey, and Sussex; and in December he was appointed warden of the Cinque Ports and of the seven hundreds of the weald, and made sheriff of Kent. In October 1263 he was among the group of Edward's friends who sealed the king's side of agreement to the arbitration by Louis IX of France in the dispute between Henry III and the barons, and at the end of the year he accompanied the king to France. In 1264 Leybourne was present at the battle of Northampton and was badly wounded at the siege of Rochester Castle, where he was among the defenders. He fought for the king at Lewes, on 14 May, and after the battle was allowed to leave with the marcher lords on condition that they would return to stand trial at the next parliament. When they failed to do so Montfort sanctioned a military expedition against them, but they remained a thorn in the side of the baronial government, and throughout the last quarter of 1265 were active in the Welsh march on the king's behalf.

In January 1265 Leybourne and the marchers were granted a safe conduct to leave for Ireland, but they never did so, although the licence was renewed in March. Throughout this time Leybourne was able to keep in touch with the king and with Edward. In December 1264 he was given a safe conduct to visit the king, and in December 1264 and May 1265 he was allowed to confer with Edward, subsequently helping to mastermind his escape from Kenilworth Castle on 28 May. Leybourne fought at Evesham, and was credited with saving the king's life. In the two years after Evesham he acted as the Lord Edward's lieutenant during the pacification of England, with responsibilities primarily in the south-east and north-west of the country. In August 1265 he was appointed keeper of Westmorland and sheriff of Kent; in October he was given custody of Carlisle Castle and made sheriff of Cumberland, and was also entrusted with the task of subduing London on the king's behalf; in November he campaigned against the rebels in the weald of Kent and in January he captured the port of Sandwich. He served as Edward's deputy in the Cinque Ports and at Sandwich, and in March 1266 he again became warden of the seven hundreds of the weald. Together with Edward he besieged and took Winchelsea, and in May he launched an assault on rebels across the Thames in Essex. In September 1266 the king issued an order that 'his knight' Sir Roger of Leybourne should be received everywhere 'with due honour as the king's knight' (*CPR, 1258–66*, 636). He was appointed custodian of Nottingham Castle, he served as justice of the royal forests north of the Trent, and was also a member of the king's council.

During this time Leybourne was generously rewarded by the king with substantial estates in Kent, Cumberland, Westmorland, and elsewhere. These included the manor of Leeds, Kent, where Leybourne built a castle which became his main residence. Between 1264 and 1267 he married his second wife, Eleanor, daughter of William de Ferrers and coheir of the Marshal honours. A widow, she had previously been married to William de Vaux and Roger de Quincy, earl of Winchester, and held dower lands in Huntingdonshire and Leicestershire. Her marriage was probably another of Leybourne's rewards at this time. His first wife, the mother of his two sons William [*see below*] and Roger, has not been identified. In 1265 he was granted the wardship of Idonea, daughter and coheir of the rebel baron Robert de Vieuxpont of Westmorland, and married her to his younger son, Roger.

Death and descendants Roger of Leybourne took the cross for the second time in 1269, and was rewarded with a grant of 1000 marks from the papal legate Ottobuono. He did not go to the Holy Land, however, but to Gascony, where he had been appointed the Lord Edward's lieutenant on 29 November 1269. It may have been intended that he should raise men there for the crusade. His stay in the duchy was short, but still long enough for him to found, and give his name to, Libourne, perhaps the most successful of the English *bastides* founded in thirteenth-century Gascony. By December 1270 he was back in England, taking the part of the official of Christ Church, Canterbury, in a dispute with the prior of Dover. A transaction of 1271, in which Leybourne exchanged property in Huntingdonshire for Ashford and other manors in Kent, implies that in his later years he was exercising a deliberate policy of consolidation of his lands in the south-east. He also placed all his property in trust for his son, an unusual move at this early date, suggesting that he felt less than secure despite a series of pardons for his offences in 1260 and 1263. He was dead by 7 November 1271, leaving as his heir his eldest son, William. His heart was apparently buried in a shrine at Leybourne church where he had founded a chantry, granting lands in Leybourne to provide for the maintenance of two chaplains. He also endowed a light at Elham church, and was a benefactor of the priories of Bermondsey, Surrey, and Combwell, Kent.

William of Leybourne, first Lord Leybourne (*d.* 1310), soldier, was Roger of Leybourne's elder son from his first marriage. In 1266 he was left in command of Sandwich by his father, and joined the siege of Winchelsea. In 1275 he was involved in a dispute at the Jewish exchequer, claiming that a charter purporting to record an £800 loan made to his father had been fraudulently placed in the loan chest by the London chirographers. In 1278 he sold the manor and castle of Leeds to Queen Eleanor, who took over his Jewish debts, cancelled the arrears inherited from his father's many offices, and gave 500 marks to the former owner of Leeds. He may have been arranging his affairs to enable him to undertake a pilgrimage, as in 1280 he left for Santiago de Compostela. A household knight of Edward I, he took part in the conquest of Wales, where he served as constable of Cricieth Castle from 1284 until at least 1288. He also travelled to France several times on the king's service, and acted as escort to Edward I's daughter Eleanor when she crossed the channel in 1294; in the same year he was appointed custodian of Pevensey Castle. In 1295 he was described as admiral of the king's fleet, the first time the title was used, and two years later he became captain of the king's mariners. In 1299 he received his first personal summons to parliament. Leybourne took part in the war against Scotland, and was present at the siege of Caerlaverock, where he was described as a valiant man 'without but or if' (*Siege of Carlaverock*, 19). In 1306 he was pardoned all his debts to the crown in consideration of his services in Scotland and elsewhere. He married Juliana (*d. c.*1327), daughter of Henry of Sandwich and heir of her grandfather Simon, with whom he had at least two sons, Thomas and Henry, and two daughters, Idonea and Katherine. After his marriage Leybourne lived at his wife's manor of Preston, near Wingham, Kent. Some time before his elder son's death in 1307 he enfeoffed Thomas and his wife, Alice, sister of Guy de Beauchamp, earl of Warwick, with the manor of Leybourne. His younger son, Henry, fought for the earl of Lancaster at Boroughbridge, where he was taken prisoner; in 1329 he was recorded as having been outlawed. William of Leybourne died in 1310 leaving his young granddaughter Juliana *Leybourne (1303/4–1367) as his heir. KATHRYN FAULKNER

Sources A. Lewis, 'Roger Leyburn and the pacification of England, 1265–7', *EngHR*, 54 (1939), 193–214 • L. B. Larking, 'On the heart-shrine in Leybourne church', *Archaeologia Cantiana*, 5 (1863), 133–93 • L. B. Larking, 'On the heart-shrine in Leybourne church and the family of de Leybourne', *Archaeologia Cantiana*, 7 (1868), 329–41 • *Chancery records* • *The historical works of Gervase of Canterbury*, ed. W. Stubbs, 2 vols., Rolls Series, 73 (1879–80) • Paris, *Chron.* • W. Stubbs, ed., *Chronicles of the reigns of Edward I and Edward II*, 2 vols., Rolls Series, 76 (1882–3) • *Ann. mon.* • M. Prestwich, *Edward I* (1988) • GEC, *Peerage*, new edn, 7.631–7 • *Curia regis rolls preserved in the Public Record Office* (1922–), vols. 2, 6–7 • S. D. Lloyd, *English society and the crusade, 1216–1307* (1988) • F. M. Powicke, *The thirteenth century* (1962), vol. 4 of *The Oxford history of England*, ed. G. M. Clarke, 2nd edn, 275 • [Walter of Exeter?], *The siege of Carlaverock … with a translation, a history of the castle and memoirs of the personages commemorated by the poet*, ed. and trans. N. H. Nicolas (1828) • exchequer L. T. R. accounts, PRO, E101, bundle 3 [accounts for expenses while keeper of castles and in command of royal forces] • exchequer miscellaneous, PRO, 1/41 [royal writs to Roger de Leybourne] • *CPR*, 1258–66, 636

Archives PRO, E101, bundle 3

Leybourne, William of, first Lord Leybourne (*d.* **1310**). *See under* Leybourne, Sir Roger of (*c.*1215–1271).

Leyburn, George (1600–1677), Roman Catholic priest, was the fourth son of William Leyburn, esquire, of Cunswick in the parish of Beetham, Westmorland, and his wife, Jane Bradley, whose family also had an estate in the parish as well as at Bradley Hall in Lancashire. The Leyburns were a recusant family which had already suffered through the delinquency of James Leyburn, executed for maintaining the pope's supremacy in 1583. George Leyburn was sent to Douai for his education in 1613, while still a child, and entered the seminary under his mother's maiden name on 13 March 1617. He was ordained on 5 August 1625 at Cambrai, where he was chaplain to the English forces for a short time before moving to Arras College in Paris to complete his studies. On 29 August 1630 he set out for England on college business, with a travel permit in the name of John Good, but was immediately arrested on arrival at Dover. He concealed his identity from the lieutenant-governor, Sir Edward Dering, but, on its being discovered, the aristocratic connections of his family ensured him better treatment in prison.

Leyburn was always conscious of his gentle birth, which may have distanced him from some of his fellow priests in later years, and his connections brought him to the attention of Queen Henrietta Maria, who secured his release and made him one of her chaplains as *provisor* of her chapel on 9 August 1631. According to Leyburn's own account this made him her first English chaplain, and he subsequently exercised considerable influence on the queen's policy towards the position of English Catholics and Catholic affairs in general. Also in August 1631, as a result of the increasing hostility to the activities of the priests in England, Bishop Richard Smith thought it wise to leave the country, and Leyburn accompanied him to Paris. Leyburn was trusted by Smith, who was mistrusted by the Jesuits and whose position was becoming just as difficult within Catholic politics as with the English government, and Leyburn was commissioned by the bishop to raise funds for the mission, though he characteristically inflated this post to 'sole agent as to the outward management of all affairs pertaining to our bishop' (*The Memoirs*, 10). As he was not yet a member of the chapter this seems unlikely, but his standing with the queen no doubt assisted his authority. This did not, however, prevent a warrant for his arrest being issued on 17 September 1633, and this seems to have driven him underground, for little is known of his activities for the next five years, though letters by him to Smith using the pseudonyms Roberts and Fountain survive. Late in 1638 he arrived in Rome as clergy agent and secured a silver cross and a privileged altar for the college at Douai. In 1641 a group of staff at Douai petitioned for his appointment as president, but the post went to George Fisher.

Leyburn seems to have remained abroad in the early years of the civil wars, first at Tournai and then at Rheims, where he was awarded a DD, but he had returned by 1646 if a story about his meeting General Monk when both were prisoners in the Tower can be dated to that time. According to Thomas Grimble, Monk's biographer, Leyburn is alleged to have foretold the crucial role that Monk was later to play in the Restoration. On release Leyburn returned to the queen's court in France, but was sent to Ireland in March 1647, under the alias Winter Grant, to try and bring about a compromise between those armies, protestant and Catholic, loyal to the king, a task which unsurprisingly proved impossible. He returned to Queen Henrietta Maria in Paris, and composed an account of this mission which was published as *Memoirs of George Leyburn* in 1722, with an account of his life added. In 1648 he was appointed vicar-general, jointly with Mark Harrington, and elected to the chapter the following year. His relations with the chapter were mostly acrimonious, largely focused on his opposition to the eirenical views associated with Thomas White alias Blackloe, which he claimed dominated the chapter. The chapter retaliated with charges of high-handedness on Leyburn's part and the row finally came to public notice in an unedifying pamphlet war between 1657 and 1661, matters not settling down until 1667. During these years Leyburn was president of the college at Douai, being installed on 24 June 1652, and he remained there until 1670 when he resigned in favour of his nephew John Leyburn. He then went to Rome for a year and a half, returned to England for a short period, and retired to Chalons sur Mer in France, where he died on 29 December 1677, leaving a local reputation there for saintly behaviour which is somewhat at odds with the controversial character which emerges from his disputes with the English chapter. WILLIAM JOSEPH SHEILS

Sources *The memoirs of George Leyburn* (1722) • C. M. Hibbard, *Charles I and the Popish Plot* (1983) • G. Anstruther, *The seminary priests*, 2 (1975) • J. Miller, *Popery and politics in England, 1660–1668* (1973) • P. R. Harris, ed., *Douai College documents, 1639–1794*, Catholic RS, 63 (1972) • E. H. Burton and T. L. Williams, eds., *The Douay College diaries, third, fourth and fifth, 1598–1654*, 1–2, Catholic RS, 10–11 (1911)

Likenesses engraving, repro. in *Memoirs of George Leyburn*, frontispiece

Leyburn, John (1620–1702), vicar apostolic of the London district, was the fourth son of John Leyburn of Cunswick Hall, Beetham, Westmorland, where he was born, and his wife, Catherine Carus, and was nephew of Dr George Leyburn. He was educated in the English College at Douai, where he was admitted a student on 20 June 1633. During the time of the civil wars he was tutor to Francis Browne, eldest son of Viscount Montague, and made the tour of Europe with his pupil. He was ordained priest in Paris in December 1646 and was then secretary to Bishop Richard Smith in Paris. He was recommended to the authorities at Rome in 1657 as successor to Bishop Smith, vicar apostolic of England, but for about twelve years he lived in England as domestic chaplain in the family of Lord Montague. In 1668 he was appointed secretary to the chapter and in a list of persons deemed worthy of promotion to the projected episcopate in England in 1669 he is mentioned as an excellent Catholic, of great piety and prudence, but who had once been a heretic, and who had a brother who was a very great puritan. Unlike his uncle, he regarded the Catholic chapter in England as validly erected, and likewise confirmed by the Holy See, although he later seems to have temporized on this.

Leyburn was appointed president of the English College at Douai, succeeding his uncle Dr George Leyburn in May 1670. He resigned the presidency in 1676 and soon afterwards moved to Rome, when he became secretary and auditor to Cardinal Philip Thomas Howard. In a particular congregation for English affairs held in the Quirinal Palace on 6 August 1685, the Sacred Congregation of Propaganda Fide, on the instance of Cardinal Howard and at the request of James II, recommended Leyburn as vicar apostolic of all England, and the pope gave his approbation the same day. He was consecrated at Rome on 9 September with the title of bishop of Adrumetum, *in partibus*. In the following month he arrived in London, and the king lodged him in Lincoln's Inn Fields and allowed him a pension of £1000 per annum. With him came Archbishop Ferdinand d'Adda as papal nuncio. Some time afterwards Leyburn made a pastoral visitation throughout the whole kingdom, administering the sacrament of confirmation to great numbers of people, for there had been no Catholic bishop resident in England since 1629. During his residence at court he was on terms of friendship with Dr Thomas Cartwright, bishop of Chester, and when in Durham dined with the bishop there. In 1686 he published *A Reply to the Answer Made Upon the Three Royal Papers*, in answer to Bishop Stillingfleet.

Leyburn vainly endeavoured to moderate the imprudent zeal by which James II tried to advance the Catholic cause. He frequently sought to exercise a restraining influence, as did Cardinal Howard and even the pope himself, but the bishop's only success was to persuade the king to restore the protestant fellows of Magdalen College, Oxford, whom he had dispossessed in favour of a number of Catholics. Leyburn became the first vicar apostolic of the London district, when four new districts were created by letters apostolic of 20 January 1688.

When the revolution broke out bishops Leyburn and Bonaventure Giffard of the midland district were seized at Faversham on their way to Dover, and were actually under arrest when the king was brought into that town. Both bishops were committed to prison, Leyburn being sent to the Tower. On 9 July 1690 he and Giffard were liberated on bail by the court of queen's bench, on condition that they transported themselves beyond the sea before the last day of the following month. Both, however, remained quietly in England. Afterwards Leyburn was frequently alarmed and summoned when any disturbance happened in relation to the government, but eventually the government, being fully satisfied with his conduct, took no further notice of him, and desired only to be made acquainted from time to time with his place of abode. He died in London on 9 June 1702, and was succeeded as vicar apostolic of the London district by Giffard.

Dodd says that Leyburn was diminutive in stature, had acquired the character of being both wise and polite, and was a great master of style in the Latin tongue. He was not only a theologian, but also a good mathematician, and an intimate friend of Descartes and Hobbes.

THOMPSON COOPER, *rev.* G. BRADLEY

Sources G. Anstruther, *The seminary priests*, 2 (1975), 195–200 · B. Plumb, *Arundel to Zabi: a biographical dictionary of the Catholic bishops of England and Wales (deceased), 1623–1987* (privately printed, Warrington, [1987]) · W. M. Brady, *Annals of the Catholic hierarchy in England and Scotland* (1877) · W. M. Brady, *The episcopal succession in England, Scotland, and Ireland, AD 1400 to 1875*, 3 vols. (1876–7) · B. Hemphill, *The early vicars apostolic of England, 1685–1750* (1954) · J. A. Hilton and others, eds., *Bishop Leyburn's confirmation register of 1687* (1997) · J. Sergeant, *An account of the chapter erected by William, titular bishop of Chalcedon*, ed. W. Turnbull (1853) · Gillow, *Lit. biog. hist.*, vol. 4 · [J. Leyburn], *A reply to the answer made upon the three royal papers* (1686) · J. Leyburn, B. Giffard, P. Ellis, and J. Smith, 'A pastoral letter from the four Catholic bishops to the lay Catholics of England', 1688

Archives Ushaw College, Durham, corresp. and papers · Westm. DA, 'A' series

Likenesses oils, St Edmund's College, Old Hall Green, Ware, Hertfordshire · oils (of Leyburn?), Gilling Castle, North Yorkshire

Wealth at death approx. £1200: will, Westm. DA, 'A', vol. 38, nos. 11 & 12

Leycester, John (*b.* **1598/9**, *d.* in or after **1648**), writer, was born in Cheshire; his family may have been connected with Sir Peter Leycester, baronet, of that county. On 28 January 1620, aged twenty-one, he matriculated at Brasenose College, Oxford, where he graduated BA on 28 February 1622. He subsequently became a schoolmaster.

Leycester's first publication was a collection of proverbs and traditional sayings, which, surprisingly, were not derived from their most well-known exponent, Erasmus. It was titled *Enchiridion seu fasciculus adagiorum selectissimorum, or, A Manual of the Choicest Adagies* (Latin and English, 1623). His religious persuasion can be found in his translation from the Latin *An Excellent Oration of Dr. John Rainolds* (1638), a sermon by the celebrated puritan preacher. His political affiliation is evident in two poems, in single sheets folio, on aspects of the civil war: *An elegiacall epitaph upon the deplored death of that religious and valiant gentleman, Colonell John Hampden, esquire* (1643), in which Leycester extols the virtues of the moderate parliamentarian and patriot who was fatally wounded in a skirmish against Prince Rupert, and *England's miraculous preservation emblematically described, erected for a perpetuall monument to posterity* (1646). In 1648 he published an edition of Josiah Ricraft's *Survey of Englands Champions, and Truths Faithfull Patriots* (1647). Leycester gave it the new title of *The Civill Warres of England* and added a brief supplement, which brought the history up to 'this present', September 1648; this was republished the following year.

T. B. SAUNDERS, *rev.* JOANNA MOODY

Sources Watt, *Bibl. Brit.*, 2.604 · W. T. Lowndes, *The bibliographer's manual of English literature*, ed. H. G. Bohn, [new edn], 2 (1864), 1356 · *STC, 1475–1640*, no. 7681.3 · D. Hirst, *Authority and conflict: England, 1603–1658* (1986), 237 · Foster, *Alum. Oxon.*

Leycester, Sir Peter, first baronet (**1614–1678**), antiquary, was born on 3 March 1614 at Nether Tabley, Cheshire, the eldest son of Peter Leycester (1588–1647) of Nether Tabley and Elizabeth (1587–1647), daughter of Sir Randle Mainwaring, bt, of Over Peover, Cheshire. He entered Brasenose College, Oxford, on 13 October 1629 as a gentleman commoner. Like many contemporary gentlemen he took no degree, and on 20 August 1632 was admitted to Gray's Inn. At the outbreak of the civil war he was appointed as one of the king's commissioners of array for Cheshire, and consequently had to leave Nether Tabley at the close of 1642. On 6 November that year he married Elizabeth (1620–1679), third daughter of Gilbert Gerard, Lord Gerard, of Gerards Bromley, at Dutton, Cheshire; they had three sons and three daughters. In June 1646 he was at Oxford when the city surrendered to Fairfax and accordingly obtained the benefit of the articles then agreed. He subsequently compounded for his estates for £747 10*s*. His active interest in antiquarian research dates from this period, when he was excluded from other responsibilities. By 1648 he was being consulted about the Mainwaring family pedigree by William Dugdale. In the following year he collaborated with William Vernon on the purchase of a Domesday transcript for Cheshire, which he was at pains to ensure had been accurately copied.

Leycester's antiquarian studies were interrupted by a spell of imprisonment in 1655 and by his return to the bench as an active justice of the peace following the Restoration. His loyalty to the royalist cause was rewarded with a baronetcy on 10 August 1660. Within a few years he had resumed his antiquarian studies. In 1669 he sent a copy of his work to Oxford, where his son was at Brasenose, in order that those 'knowing in antiquities might peruse it' (Bailey, 28–9). Thus it came to the hands of Anthony Wood, who returned it with some corrections and additions. In 1673 this work appeared as *Historical antiquities in two books; the first treating in general of Great Brittain and Ireland; the second containing particular remarks concerning Cheshire, and chiefly of Bucklow hundred. Whereunto is annexed a transcript of Doomsday-Book, so far as it concerneth Cheshire*. The work reflects the methodical care and attention that Leycester applied to his antiquarian studies. It is possible that he contemplated undertaking a history of the whole county, but the majority of his antiquarian papers reflect his concentration on his own hundred. His antiquarian friends such as Dugdale, Simonds D'Ewes, and Sir John Crewe of Utkinton Hall undoubtedly hoped that he would take over the project abandoned by Vernon, and during Dugdale's regular visits to Tabley, Leycester presumably received similar encouragement to that which helped persuade Robert Thoroton to publish his history of Nottinghamshire.

In the *Historical Antiquities* Leycester gave the reasons for and against the argument that Amicia, wife of Ralph Mainwaring, was the lawful daughter of Earl Hugh Cyveliok (*d.* 1181) and noted that 'some are displeased' that he found against the legitimacy of his ancestress. Among those to take exception was Sir Thomas Mainwaring (1623–1689) of Peover, who was also descended from her. Mainwaring published a *Defence of Amicia* (1673) to which Leycester responded with *An Answer to the Book of Sir Thomas Manwaringe* (1673). The controversy generated a paper war of fifteen pamphlets, of which Leycester contributed a further four, and only closed with the latter's death. According to Wood, at the Chester assizes in 1675 the justices itinerant declared in favour of Amicia's legitimacy, a decision with which the editor of the tracts for the Chetham Society concurred. A contemporary humorist ridiculed the affair in some verses entitled *A New Ballad Made of a High and Mighty Controversy between Two Cheshire Knights* (1673). The feud, however, was not merely a dispute over genealogical and legal niceties, but reflected the division on the Cheshire bench between those like Leycester who sought a rigorous enforcement of the Act of Uniformity and the Conventicle Acts and those such as Mainwaring who opposed this policy.

The large collection of manuscripts left by Leycester evidences the breadth of his scholarly interests, as does the catalogue of 1332 books at Tabley he compiled in 1672, covering mathematics, astronomy, and theology as well as history and topography. Among the manuscripts is a treatise entitled 'Prolegomena historica de musica P. L.', which suggests that he was an accomplished musician. There is also a theological dissertation, 'On the soul of man', dated 1653, which is accompanied by a long correspondence upon the subject between Leycester and his old college tutor, Samuel Shipton, rector of Alderley, Cheshire. He also undertook major improvements at Nether Tabley, including the construction of a domestic chapel in the garden between 1675 and 1678. He died there on 11 October 1678 and was buried at Great Budworth, Cheshire. His wife died the following year. He was succeeded by his eldest son, Robert (1643–1684). JAN BROADWAY

Sources P. Leycester, *Historical antiquities in two books* (1673) · G. Ormerod, *The history of the county palatine and city of Chester*, 2nd edn, ed. T. Helsby, 1 (1882), xxxii–xxxiii, 29–32, 622–6 · P. Leycester and T. Mainwaring, *Tracts written in the controversy respecting the legitimacy of Amicia*, ed. W. Beaumont, 3 vols., Chetham Society, 78–80 (1869) · J. E. Bailey, *Sir Peter Leycester* (1878) · *First report*, HMC, 1/1 (1870); repr. (1874), appx, pp. 46–50 · A. T. Thacker, 'Cheshire', *A guide to English county histories*, ed. C. R. J. Currie and C. P. Lewis (1997), 75–6 · *The life, diary, and correspondence of Sir William Dugdale*, ed. W. Hamper (1827), 117, 119, 127–8, 132, 205, 215–16 · J. T. Cliffe, *The world of the country house in seventeenth-century England* (1999), 33–4, 161, 164, 166, 169, 201 · Wood, *Ath. Oxon.*, new edn, 3.1173–4 · *VCH Cheshire*, 2.115–16 · Foster, *Alum. Oxon.* · BL, Add. MS 6396, fol. 17 · BL, Harleian MS 2146, fol. 108

Archives Ches. & Chester ALSS, papers, mainly antiquarian

Likenesses engraving (after a miniature at Nether Tabley), repro. in Ormerod, *The history of … Chester*, 1.liv · engraving (after a portrait, possibly by Lely), repro. in Beaumont, ed., *Amicia tracts*, 1 · stipple, NPG

Wealth at death income between £500 and £1000 p.a.: Cliffe, *World of the country house*, 201

Leyden, John (1775–1811), linguist and poet, was born on 8 September 1775 at Denholm, in the parish of Cavers, near Hawick, Roxburghshire, the son of John Leyden and Isabella Scott. A year later his parents took over a farm 3 miles away in Henlawshiel; here Leyden grew up. Having been taught to read by his grandmother, he worked as a shepherd and attended (from the age of nine) the parish school at Kirktown. When twelve he became the student of the Reverend James Duncan, a covenanting pastor; from 1790 to 1797 he was a student at Edinburgh University (a hard day's journey from Henlawshiel). His 'rustic appearance and strong Teviotdale accent' made him an occasional object of laughter; none the less, he greatly distinguished himself as a scholar, reading very widely (Lockhart, 1.324). In the vacations he studied natural science and modern languages, besides Hebrew, Arabic, and Persian. His professional pursuits included both philosophy and theology, and he gave some attention to medicine. He practised public speaking at the university literary society. Among his associates were Henry Brougham, Sydney Smith, Francis Jeffrey, Francis Horner, and Thomas Brown. From 1796 to 1798 he was tutor to the sons of Mr Campbell, of Fairfield, Edinburgh, and accompanied them in 1797–8 to St Andrews, where he was licensed as a preacher. His pulpit appearances were not successful.

Leyden as a student had made the acquaintance of Robert Anderson, editor of the *British Poets* (1795), through whom he contributed to the *Edinburgh Literary Magazine*. He was one of the first to welcome Thomas Campbell's *Pleasures of Hope* (1799), though he and Campbell subsequently quarrelled. In 1799, while browsing in a bookshop owned by the young Archibald Campbell, later a central figure in Scottish publishing, Leyden met Richard Heber, then studying Scottish literature in Edinburgh. About the same time Leyden published *A historical and philosophical sketch of the discoveries and settlements of the Europeans in northern and western Africa at the close of the eighteenth century*. To Lewis's *Tales of Wonder* (1801) he contributed 'The Elf King', a ballad, and on the combined recommendation of Heber and Anderson he edited for Constable the *Complaynt of Scotland*, with an elaborate preliminary dissertation and an excellent glossary. Though not free from error, the work helped stimulate the study of earlier Scottish literature.

In 1801 Heber introduced Leyden to Walter Scott, whom he materially helped with the earlier volumes of the *Border Minstrelsy* (1802), contributing five poems to volume 1 and material for the learned disquisition on fairies to volume 2 (Lockhart, 1.326). He also got to know the eminent antiquary Joseph Ritson, but, on virtually every occasion when they were together, teased him mercilessly (often

John Leyden (1775–1811), by Captain Elliot, 1811

about his vegetarianism). In 1800 he accompanied a pair of German tourists to the Scottish highlands and the Hebrides, keeping a journal along the way (published 1903). While on this journey he investigated the Ossianic question, and recovered from James Beattie at Aberdeen the anonymous poem 'Albania', which he published along with John Wilson's 'Clyde' in his *Scottish Descriptive Poems* (1802). For six months in 1802 he edited the third series of the *Scots Magazine*, himself contributing both prose and verse. In several of his miscellaneous lyrics Leyden shows his best poetic quality.

In default of a church appointment, Leyden considered emulating Mungo Park's example as an African discoverer, under the aegis of the Sierra Leone Company. Worried about the perils of such a trip, his friends attempted to find him some safer post; eventually the Rt Hon. William Dundas secured for him the post of assistant surgeon at Madras. His previous medical studies enabled him in six months to take at St Andrews a nominal MD degree. For some months he zealously studied Eastern languages, passed a pleasant time in London with Heber and George Ellis, and prepared for publication his *Scenes of Infancy* (1803). The latter, perhaps his major poetical work, is notable for combining nostalgia about Scotland's past with anxiety about its future: Leyden worries that displaced peasants will leave the country altogether, settling new colonies and driving 'the displaced population there out of *its* traditionary homes' (Trumpener, 190). Meanwhile Leyden embarked on his own colonial adventure. After some delay—including his failure to board a ship that later sank, with many casualties—he reached Madras on 19 August 1803.

At first Leyden had charge of the Madras general hospital. In January 1805, as surgeon and naturalist, he accompanied the commissioners over the Mysore provinces taken from Tippoo Sultaun, and prepared a report on the geology, the diseases, the crops, and the languages of the districts traversed. He also used his medical skills, treating, for instance, a feverish military officer far away from any town; on this occasion he was stalked by a tiger. By November he had fallen ill himself; he stayed at Seringapatam, where he was befriended by Sir John Malcolm. When convalescent he studied Sanskrit, and translated from Persian and Hindustani. From May to September 1805 he travelled for his health through Malabar on to Cochin and Quilon, whence he sailed for Penang. While being chased on the voyage by a French privateer, Leyden characteristically composed a vigorous ode to his Malay kris, or dagger. In Penang he wrote a *Dissertation on the Languages and Literature of the Indo-Chinese Nations*, first published in Calcutta (1808). This essay affords a really remarkable survey of fourteen different languages and literatures geographically between India and China, treating, among other cultures, those of Malaysia, Java, the Philippines, Burma, Thailand, Cambodia, and Bali. Leyden also makes extensive historiographical comments on the development of European scholarship about these areas between the Renaissance and his own time.

Having returned to India in 1806, Leyden settled at Calcutta. His elaborate essay submitted to the government in 1807 on the Indo-Persian, Indo-Chinese, and Dekkan languages led to his election as a member of the Asiatic Society, and as professor of Hindustani in the Calcutta college. But he soon accepted Lord Minto's offer of the post of judge of the twenty-four *parganas* of Calcutta; one of his main tasks as judge was to direct troops engaged in pursuing 'freebooters' then circulating in Bengal, a task that he seems to have pursued with enthusiasm. At the beginning of 1809 he was appointed commissioner of the court of requests in Calcutta. While holding that office he undertook grammars of the Malay and Prakrit tongues, besides many translations. He also worked on translations of one or more of the gospels into Pashto, Maldivian, Baluch, Macassar, and Bugis. Some of his translations into English were published posthumously: his *Malay Annals* in 1821, and his *Commentaries of Baber*, completed by William Erskine in 1826.

Towards the end of 1810 Lord Minto appointed Leyden assay-master of the mint at Calcutta, and in 1811 he accompanied Lord Minto to Java, 'to assist', as he wrote to his father on the voyage, 'in settling the country when conquered, and as interpreter for the Malay language' (White, 103). When the expedition halted for some days at Malacca, Leyden journeyed inland, scrutinizing 'original Malays' and visiting sulphurous hot wells. Java was reached on 4 August, and as there was no opposition at Batavia, a leisurely possession was effected. Leyden's literary zeal took him into an unventilated native library: fever supervened, and he died at Cornelis, after three days' illness, on 28 August 1811.

Leyden did not always appreciate the cultures that he

studied. By his own account his early experiences of India filled him with nauseous confusion; moreover, in common with many other British observers of his time, he belittled the moral character of Hindus, finding their religion 'wicked, shameless, impudent, and obscene' (*Poetical Remains*, lxv). On the other hand, his Asian journeys also brought out his extraordinary intellectual vigour and curiosity—perhaps best matched, in his own generation, by the verve of other self-educated Scots, such as Alexander Murray (the scholar of Ethiopia). Leyden's strengths were much celebrated by those who marked his passing. Before the Literary Society of Bombay William Erskine read a eulogium, in which he claimed for Leyden that in eight years he had done almost as much for Asia as the combined scholarship of centuries had done for Europe—he had 'nearly effected a classification of its various languages and their kindred dialects' (White, 111). Scott, in addition to frequent references, embalmed his 'bright and brief career' in the *Lord of the Isles*, IV.xi. His 'Memoir of Leyden' first appeared in the *Edinburgh Annual Register* (1811). Lord Cockburn, after referring to his unconscious egotism and his uncouth aspect and uncompromising demeanour—characteristics also noted by Scott and John Lockhart—declares there was 'no walk in life, depending on ability, where Leyden could not have shone' (Cockburn, 179); James Hogg bewailed his loss of the poet's 'glowing measure'. A monument to Leyden's memory was erected by public subscription at Denholm in 1861, and there also in 1875 the centenary of his birth was celebrated under the presidency of Lord Neaves.

T. W. BAYNE, *rev.* RICHARD MAXWELL

Sources W. Beattie, *Life and letters of Thomas Campbell* (1849) • *Memorials of his time, by Henry Cockburn* (1856) • T. Constable, *Archibald Constable and his literary correspondents*, 3 vols. (1873) • *GM*, 1st ser., 82/1 (1812), 409, 420, 486 • D. Groves, 'James Hogg and John Leyden', *N&Q*, 233 (1988), 317–18 • J. Leyden, *Journal of a tour in the highlands and Western Islands of Scotland in 1800* (1903) [incl. comprehensive bibliography, pp. 285–318] • J. G. Lockhart, *Memoirs of the life of Sir Walter Scott*, 7 vols. (1837–8) • *The poetical remains of the late Dr John Leyden: with memoirs of his life by the Rev. James Morton*, ed. J. Morton (1819), incl. bibliography • J. Reith, *Life of Dr. John Leyden: poet and linguist* [n.d.] • W. Scott, 'John Leyden, M. D.', *Miscellaneous prose works*, 6 vols. (1827), 4.142–223 • J. Sinton, *Leydeniana, or, Gleanings from some unpublished documents regarding Dr. Leyden* (1912) • K. Trumpener, *Bardic nationalism: the romantic novel and the British empire* (Princeton, 1997) • R. White, *A supplement to Sir Walter Scott's biographical memoir of Dr. John Leyden* (1857)

Archives BL, corresp., literary MSS, and papers, Add. MSS 26555–26601 • BL OIOC, flora Indica and papers, MSS Eur. C 78, D 345, E 148 • Cumbria AS, Barrow, corresp. and papers • NL Scot., Advocates' Library • NL Scot., family corresp. and papers • University of Missouri Library, Columbia, travel journals and papers | Bodl. Oxf., letters to Richard Heber • NL Scot., letters, mostly to William Erskine • NL Scot., letters to Robert Lundie [transcript copies] • NL Scot., letters to first earl of Minto • NL Scot., corresp. with Sir Walter Scott

Likenesses Captain Elliot, photogravure of drawing, 1811, NPG [*see illus.*] • ink drawing, Scot. NPG

Leyds, Willem Johannes (1859–1940), politician in the Transvaal and diplomatist, was born on 1 May 1859 at Magelang, Java, the second son of Willem Johannes Leyds (1828–1865), a Dutch headmaster, and his wife, Tryntje, *née* van Beuningen van Helsdingen (1832–1914). Leyds was a musical child and also had a photographic memory. He won a scholarship to the Rijkskweekskool voor Onderwijzers in Haarlem where he trained as a teacher (1874–8); during teaching spells in Breda and Amsterdam he saved money to continue his education and also taught himself Latin and Greek. In 1880 he enrolled as a law student at the University of Amsterdam, where fellow students let him join an élite society without having to pay membership fees. He was awarded an LLD *cum laude* in 1884. In the same year, on 10 July, he married Louise Wilhelmina Susanna, *née* Roeff (1856–1907). They had three children: Willem Johannes, Louis Willem, and Wilhelmina Johanna. After being introduced to a delegation from the Transvaal (South African/Zuid-Afrikaansche Republic) by his university professors, Leyds was offered the post of state attorney of the republic by President Kruger. Leyds and his wife duly travelled to Pretoria where he was sworn in on 13 October 1884.

State attorney and secretary Leyds applied himself with great diligence to his new post. His reputation for incorruptibility was enhanced by the sensational trial of the tycoon A. H. Nellmapius in 1886: despite government pressure to drop the case, Leyds refused to do so and succeeded in getting Nellmapius convicted. The scope and complexity of Leyds's work as state prosecutor and supervisor of the police and prison services was increased by the rise in crime after the 1886 gold rush in the Witwatersrand, and he was involved in improving laws and introducing a secret police force. As the judicial adviser of the republic he was also involved in negotiations with the British government concerning Bechuanaland, St Lucia Bay, and the new republic.

Leyds's efficiency was tacitly recognized by several foreign orders which were conferred upon him, including a British knighthood which he politely declined. At only twenty-nine years of age he was elected state secretary of the South African Republic; on 2 May 1889, a day after he had reached the required minimum age of thirty, he was duly sworn in. As secretary, Leyds became Kruger's 'right hand', and they effectively ran the actual government of the republic together. Despite great differences in age, education, and cultural background, both strove to make the republic a strong, independent Afrikaner state and trusted and respected one another. Although they did clash at times, Kruger once told Leyds that he continued to trust him because 'you tell me everything to my face; you never do anything behind my back' (priv. coll.).

Leyds's tenure of office coincided with a difficult transitional period when the republic had to transform itself almost overnight into a modern industrial state. He was instrumental in modernizing the Transvaal, creating an efficient administrative system, helping to establish (in 1891) a national bank and a mint, and chairing a monetary conference in 1893 attended by representatives from the Cape, the Orange Free State, and Natal whose outcome was a treaty to create a uniform monetary system. Leyds was also largely responsible for the establishment of the Nederlandsch Zuid-Afrikaansche Spoorweg Maatschappij (NZASM) which obtained the sole right to construct and control the republic's railways and resulted in rail links with the Cape (1892), Mozambique (1894), and Natal (1895). His efforts to promote cultural ties with the Netherlands were strengthened by the appointment of N. Mansvelt as superintendent of education. Mansvelt improved existing education along Dutch lines and established a Staatsgimnasium, or Normal College, to train teachers, in 1893. Leyds promoted related projects, such as a botanic garden, a museum, and a bacteriological institute (later the Onderstepoort) in the Transvaal.

Leyds was also closely involved in the South African Republic's unsuccessful overt and covert attempts to obtain an outlet to the sea via St Lucia Bay, Kosi Bay, and Delagoa Bay—schemes which failed mainly owing to British opposition. Negotiations with France and Germany to construct an independent cable connection between Delagoa Bay and Europe also failed. Ever concerned about the security of the South African Republic, Leyds, although generally opposed to the republic's monopolistic concession policy, favoured the maintenance of the dynamite monopoly, since he felt state control of weapons and explosives was necessary. This stance made him unpopular with Rand capitalists but English press reports that the Kruger–Leyds government cared nothing for the mining interests were unfair. Leyds negotiated an agreement with the Mozambique government in 1897, for example, to recruit African workers for the mines. The republic's government saw the influx of foreigners after 1886 as a serious threat to the South African Republic's continuance as an independent Boer republic. Uitlanders were consequently subjected to discriminatory franchise qualifications and Johannesburg was denied a municipality. By not resolving Uitlander grievances the Kruger–Leyds government played into the hands of British imperialists who later used the problem as a *casus belli*. During the Jameson raid (1895–6) Leyds was on sick leave in Europe. He wanted to use the anti-British feeling aroused by the attempted coup to have the South African Republic's independence and neutrality guaranteed by the major European powers. However, in his absence his opponents in the Transvaal sowed distrust about his aims and about the possible outcome of the plans for the republic; the scheme was therefore aborted. Leyds was the chief target of 'Hollander hate' in the Transvaal, generated partly by the number of Hollanders whom Kruger had appointed to high posts. He was nevertheless re-elected as state secretary in 1892 and 1897 with increased majorities.

Leyds's able defence of the South African Republic against claims of British suzerainty and his efficient management of its affairs made British imperialists regard him as the chief obstacle to the overthrow of Kruger's government. Leyds was consequently largely demonized in the jingoistic British press. The British colonial secretary, Joseph Chamberlain, and the under-secretary, Lord Selborne, were therefore surprised when they met him in 1897 to find him 'distinctly agreeable', 'clever and good-looking', and possessed of an 'extraordinarily frank and conciliatory attitude'. Selborne warned Chamberlain not to praise Leyds in public, however, because 'all British South Africa, from Rosmead to Rhodes and from Hartley to Schreiner are united in believing him to be *the* enemy, and whether it is true or false, all that you say will be judged in the light of this prejudice' (Selborne to Milner, 24 May 1897, University of Oxford, MS Milner Dep. 204, fols. 67–8).

Ambassador during the Second South African War In 1898 Leyds was appointed ambassador-extraordinary and minister-plenipotentiary to the courts of France, Germany, the Netherlands, Belgium, Portugal, and Russia; despite British denial of the South African Republic's right to foreign representation, Leyds, whose fluency in five European languages made him eminently suitable for the post, gained accreditation at all six courts, and chose centrally located Brussels as his headquarters. He warned his government not to expect aid from any European government in the event of a South African war and, on a visit to the Transvaal in 1899, he was behind the 'great deal'—secret negotiations with Rand capitalists to resolve their grievances. The reconciliation attempt was, however, scuppered through a deliberate leak to the press by an agent of the war-mongering Lord Milner. After the outbreak of the Second South African War, Leyds tried to persuade one or more of the European powers to mediate and bring about an honourable peace for the Boers. A Russian mediation attempt in March 1900 floundered, however, partly owing to official German opposition. Leyds also launched a pro-Boer campaign, helped by press bureaux in Paris and Dordrecht, raising money for Second South African War victims, establishing an aid fund, advising pro-Boer groups abroad, and serving as a channel for protests against alleged British contraventions of international conventions, and for petitions for European intervention such as the 'Appeal to the nations for justice and peace'.

On 26 July 1900 the Transvaal executive adopted a secret resolution empowering Leyds to withdraw all the republic's considerable assets from European banks and place them under his personal control to be used at his discretion to further the Boer cause—a testimony to their confidence in him. Since Britain controlled the cable links between South Africa and Europe, Leyds made use of secret couriers and neutral shipping lines to maintain communications with the Transvaal. With the aid of secret agents he also purchased arms and ammunition which were smuggled to the Boers by the same means.

Final years When peace was finally declared, Chamberlain stated that Leyds would not be allowed to return to South Africa. He settled in Holland and resumed his former Dutch citizenship in 1905 but continued to act unofficially as a Boer representative. He declined offers of Dutch academic and diplomatic appointments, drawing on the South African Republic's government archives, which had been sent to him for safe keeping in 1900, to publish twelve books on the republic's struggle against British imperialism, from the British annexation of the Transvaal in 1877 to the end of the Second South African War. Leyds also composed Kruger's *Political Testament* of 1904 and, after Kruger's death, arranged for the return of his body to South Africa, personally accompanying the coffin to Cape Town.

Leyds refused to hand over the remainder of the South African Republic's secret funds to Britain after the Second South African War, as he wanted to use the money to promote the political, economic, and cultural resurrection of the former Boer republics. He purchased stock for the impoverished farms, provided funds for the Christian National Education schools, for the re-emergence of Afrikaans/Dutch newspapers, and for the establishment of the Het Volk and Orangia Union political parties. These projects went against Lord Milner's Anglicization programme and helped to create a spirit of Afrikaner solidarity. Leyds advised Boer leaders such as Botha and Smuts on political tactics to achieve self-government and secretly assisted Smuts in his negotiations with the Liberal government in Britain in 1907 which led to the restoration of self-government in the former Boer republics. In 1907 Leyds's wife died, leaving two children (Willem having died in infancy). He married a second time, on 8 October 1910, taking Anna Castens, *née* Grissee (1868–1942), as his wife.

Leyds visited South Africa in 1908–9 and in 1911 and continued to take a lively interest in South African affairs until his death, corresponding with leading political figures and voicing his opinion on matters such as the rebellion of 1914 and South African participation in the First World War. He was awarded honorary doctorates by the universities of Pretoria and Stellenbosch, in 1936 and 1939 respectively. His home in The Hague was at 237 Frankenslag, and he died in hospital in The Hague on 14 May 1940 during the German invasion of the Netherlands. He was buried alongside his first wife in the Eik en Duinen cemetery, The Hague. L. E. VAN NIEKERK

Sources L. E. van Niekerk, *Kruger se regterhand: biografie van dr. W. J. Leyds* (Pretoria, 1985) • State Archives, Pretoria, South Africa, Leydsargief • State Archives, Pretoria, South Africa, Leydshuisargief • Rijksarchief, The Hague, Netherlands, collectie Leyds • priv. coll., Leyds MSS • state attorney files, 1884–9, State Archives, Pretoria, South Africa • state secretary files, 1889–98, State Archives, Pretoria, South Africa • State Archives, Pretoria, Wijpkema versameling • L. W. S. Leyds-Roeff and W. J. Leyds, *Onze eerste jaren in Zuid-Afrika, 1884–1889* (1938) • W. J. Leyds, *Eenige correspondentie uit 1899* (1938) • W. J. Leyds, *Tweede verzameling: correspondentie, 1899–1900* (1930) • W. J. Leyds, *Derde verzameling: correspondentie, 1900* (1931) • W. J. Leyds, *Vierde verzameling: correspondentie, 1900–1902* (1934) • W. J. Leyds, *Het insluiten van de Boeren-republieken*, 2 vols. (Amsterdam, 1914) • H. van Hoek, *Kruger days: reminiscences of Dr W. J. Leyds* (1939) • Bureau of Genealogy, The Hague • U. Oxf., Milner MSS

Archives priv. coll. • Rijksarchief, The Hague, Netherlands • State Archives, Pretoria, South Africa • University of Stellenbosch, South Africa | PRO, Colonial Office records • State Archives, Pretoria, South Africa, Smuts collection • U. Birm., Chamberlain MSS • U. Oxf., Milner MSS

Likenesses photographs, 1884–98, State Archives, Pretoria, South Africa • photographs, 1884–1910, priv. coll. • B. Veth, drawing, 1895, priv. coll. • F. Wichgraff, oils, 1898, National Cultural History Museum, Pretoria, South Africa • Haveman, charcoal sketch, 1900, National Cultural History Museum, Pretoria, South Africa • F. Eloff, bust, 1936, University of Pretoria, South Africa

Wealth at death 490,973 Dutch guilders: Leyds MSS; 'Rekening en Verantwoording betreffende de nalatenschap van Dr. W. J. Leyds', H. Hartogh Heijs Notary, The Hague

Leyel [*née* Wauton], **Hilda Winifred Ivy** [*known as* Mrs C. F. Leyel] **(1880–1957)**, herbalist, was born in London on 6 December 1880, the daughter of Edward Brenton Wauton, from 1881 an assistant master at Uppingham School, and his wife, Elizabeth Anne Drewitt. She was educated, informally, at Uppingham School, where she developed a precocious interest in flowers and herbs; she also received some part of her education at Halliwick Manor. On leaving school she studied medicine. She then worked for a while with Frank Benson, the actor–manager. In 1900 she married Carl Frederick Leyel (*d.* 1925), a theatrical manager of Swedish descent, with whom she had two sons. The marriage was later dissolved. As a young society hostess in her flat in Lincoln's Inn, Mrs Leyel proved herself a connoisseur of food and wine, and made a number of influential friends, who rallied round her when in 1922 she was prosecuted for running the Golden Ballot which raised a large sum for the benefit of ex-servicemen and various hospitals. Her acquittal helped to establish the legality of such ballots. She was elected a life governor of St Mary's, the West London, and the Royal National Orthopaedic hospitals.

Soon, however, Leyel began to concentrate on the nearly forgotten craft of herbalism. Although she lacked a scientific training in botany, she acquired a profound and detailed knowledge of the work of the herbalist Nicholas Culpeper and his predecessors, and re-presented this vast knowledge of herbs, culinary, cosmetic, and healing. In 1926 she wrote *The Magic of Herbs* and in 1927 she opened Culpeper House in Baker Street, a shop selling herbal medicines, foods, and cosmetics, designed especially to appeal to women. Her imaginative and practical talents ensured the success of this and similar shops, which were decorated by Basil Ionides. Encouraged to apply her knowledge of herbs and their healing properties to the needs of patients dissatisfied with the drugs of orthodox medicine, she founded the Society of Herbalists, a non-profit-making organization for the study and application of the herbal art, and made available her own library, the nucleus of which was housed with the society. In 1941 the society's life was imperilled by the Pharmacy and Medicines Bill which, as drafted, would have destroyed the work of the herbalist in England. Again powerful friends rallied to her support and the bill was sufficiently modified to enable patients to obtain treatment on joining the society. She also co-operated with Sir Albert Howard in his campaign for compost versus artificial manure; and with those working for pure water and pure food of every kind.

In 1931 Leyel edited Mrs M. Grieve's *A Modern Herbal* in two volumes. She herself wrote a long series of works on herbs, including *Herbal Delights* (1937), *Compassionate Herbs* (1946), *Elixirs of Life* (1948), *Hearts-Ease* (1949), *Green Medicine* (1952), and *Cinquefoil* (1957), as well as others on cooking. She was honoured with the palme académique of France in 1924. She died in the Harley Street Nursing Home, 35 Weymouth Street, London, on 15 April 1957.

CHRISTMAS HUMPHREYS, *rev.* MICHAEL BEVAN

Sources private information (1971) • personal knowledge (1971) • Mrs C. F. Leyel [H. W. W. Leyel], *The truth about herbs* (1943) • *The Times* (18 May 1957), 14

Wealth at death £52,865 9*s.* 2*d.*: probate, 10 July 1957, *CGPLA Eng. & Wales*

Leyland, Frederick Richards (1831–1892), shipowner and art patron, was born on 30 September 1831 in Liverpool, the first of the three sons of John Leyland, a bookkeeper, and his wife, Ann Jane Leyland (*d.* 1877), both of Liverpool. Although Ann Leyland is reputed to have sold pies in the city streets after her husband died or deserted the family in the late 1830s, a contemporary records that she worked in a respectable eating-house near the offices of John Bibby & Sons, Liverpool's oldest independent shipping line. In 1844 she persuaded Bibby to apprentice her eldest son, educated at the mechanics' institute. Frederick Leyland's intellectual gifts and managerial talent quickly became apparent, and he is said to have been instrumental in Bibby's introduction of steamships into the Mediterranean trade in 1850. As the Bibby Line prospered, Leyland rose through the ranks from bookkeeper to clerk to merchant by 1859, and in 1861 he settled a dispute between Bibby and the Birkenhead corporation with such success that he was made a partner in the firm. When at the end of 1872 the partnership dissolved, he bought out his employers and changed the company name to his own. Under his direction the Leyland Line expanded into transatlantic trade and by 1882 comprised some twenty-five steamships. He retired from active business in 1888, leaving his son Frederick Dawson Leyland in charge of the shipping line.

On 23 March 1855 Leyland had married Frances, *née* Dawson (1836–1910), daughter of a master mariner, and by 1861 the Leylands were living with their four children in Falkner Square in Liverpool. His wealth and position were then on the rise, and in 1867 he leased a historic, half-timbered Tudor house, Speke Hall, 7 miles outside the city, where the family resided until 1877, when they moved to another mansion in the vicinity, Woolton Hall. With the advice of his closest friend, the artist Dante Gabriel Rossetti, whom he met through the Liverpool collector John Miller in 1866, Leyland restored much of Speke Hall and embellished it with the art which he had begun acquiring in the early 1860s. More of the paintings were installed at 23 Queen's Gate, Leyland's London home during his most active period of art collecting—from 1868 to 1875—and then, from 1876 until his death, at 49 Prince's Gate, a house remodelled to realize Leyland's 'dream of living the life of an old Venetian merchant in modern London' (Child, 82).

As a modern-day Medici, Leyland purchased Italian Renaissance paintings, including a Botticelli series illustrating Boccaccio's tale of Nastagio degli Onesti and mentioned in Vasari (now in the Cambó collection, Barcelona, and an Italian priv. coll.). He also became the leading patron of several living artists, primarily Rossetti, Edward Burne-Jones, and James McNeill Whistler. Whistler was commissioned to decorate the entrance hall at Prince's Gate, which featured a famous balustrade salvaged from Northumberland House. That project led to his redecoration of the adjacent dining room, which he gradually transformed into 'The Peacock Room', formally *Harmony in Blue and Gold* (1876–7, now in the Freer Gallery of Art, Washington, DC). The artist and his patron quarrelled over the price of the project, and Whistler immortalized the altercation in a mural of two peacocks poised for battle. He subsequently declared that Leyland would be remembered only as the owner of the work whose price he had refused to pay, and outside the annals of British shipping the prophecy mostly held true. Recent scholarship, however, has recognized Leyland's importance as a patron and supporter of the Victorian avant-garde.

In portraits by Whistler (Freer Gallery of Art) and Rossetti (Delaware Art Museum), Leyland appears aristocratic in demeanour and dressed like a dandy in ruffled shirts, which gradually became his attribute; he figures in Theodore Watts-Dunton's 1898 novel *Aylwin* as Symonds, 'an elegant-looking man in a peculiar kind of evening dress' (p. 230). Brooding and aloof, Leyland took solace in music, faithfully practising on his piano but never mastering the instrument to his satisfaction. According to contemporaries he was 'hated thoroughly by a very large circle of acquaintance' (White, 152), and his 'immorality and doings with women' are said to have been widely acknowledged (Stripe, 82). He and his wife officially separated in 1879, possibly because of Leyland's liaison with Rosa Laura Caldecott, *née* Gately (*d.* 1890), whom he had established in 1875 at Denham Lodge, Hammersmith, and who bore a son named Frederick Richards Leyland Caldecott in 1883. At about that time Leyland acquired Villette, near Broadstairs, Kent, a house he shared with Annie Ellen Wooster and her children, Fred Richards and Francis George Leyland Wooster, born in 1884 and 1890; they are noted in Leyland's will as his 'reputed sons'.

In his retirement Leyland was named president of the National Telephone Company (1889) and became deputy chairman of Edison & Sons United Electric Light Company. He died suddenly, from a heart attack, on 4 January 1892, while on a London underground train between Mansion House and Blackfriars stations. Leyland's estate was assessed at £732,770, from which his legitimate children each received substantial legacies. His will also made ample provision for Miss Wooster and her two children; to raise capital for these bequests, the art and furnishings of Prince's Gate were auctioned at Christie, Manson, and Woods on 26–27 May 1892, realizing £36,257; the house itself was sold in 1894. Leyland was buried on 8 January 1892 in Brompton cemetery, where his grave is marked by an impressive bronze monument designed by Edward Burne-Jones.

LINDA MERRILL

Sources H. E. Stripe, 'Sketch of the commercial life of H. E. Stripe', *c.*1893, Merseyside Maritime Museum Archives, Liverpool, DX/1744 • T. White, 'Albert Moore and the *DNB*', *N&Q*, 10th ser., 8 (1907), 152 • T. Child, 'A Pre-Raphaelite mansion', *Harper's New Monthly Magazine*, 82 (1890–91), 81–99 • Frederick Richards Leyland's will, 3 April 1889 [probate granted 4 Feb 1892] • M. S. Duval, 'F. R. Leyland: a Maecenas from Liverpool', *Apollo*, 124 (1986), 110–15 • L. Merrill, *The Peacock Room: a cultural biography* (1998) • D. S. Macleod, *Art and the Victorian middle class: money and the making of cultural identity* (1996) • B. G. Orchard, 'Victor Fumigus', *The second series of the Liverpool Exchange portrait gallery: being lively biographical sketches of some gentlemen known on the flags; sketched from memory, and filled in from fancy* (1884), 93–8 • P. Ferriday, 'Peacock Room', *ArchR*, 125 (1959), 407–14 • Boase, *Mod. Eng. biog.*, 6.51–2 • A. J. Tibbles, 'Speke Hall and Frederick Leyland: antiquarian refinements', *Apollo*, 139 (May 1994), 34–7 • E. R. Pennell and J. Pennell, *The Whistler journal* (1921) • B. Cousens, *Speke Hall: Merseyside* (1994) • *Liverpool Courier* (6 Jan 1892) • *Liverpool Mercury* (6 Jan 1892) • *Liverpool Daily Post* (6 Jan 1892) • 'Inquest on the late Mr F. Leyland', *Liverpool Courier* (8 Jan 1892) • 'Funeral of Mr F. R. Leyland', *Liverpool Mercury* (9 Jan 1892) • m. cert. • b. cert. [Frederick Dawson Leyland, 19 Jan 1856, Liverpool] • b. cert. [Fanny Leyland, 29 Oct 1857, Prescot] • b. cert. [Florence Leyland, 2 Sept 1859, Liverpool] • b. cert. [Elinor Leyland, 16 Oct 1861, Liverpool] • d. cert. • census returns, Liverpool, 1851, 1861, 1871

Archives U. Glas. L. | L. Cong., Pennell Whistler collection

Likenesses J. R. Parsons, photograph, *c.*1866, repro. in J. Maas, *The Victorian art world in photographs* (1984) • D. G. Rossetti, pastel drawing, 1870, Delaware Art Museum, Wilmington, Delaware • J. McN. Whistler, oils, *c.*1870, repro. in Merrill, *The Peacock Room* • J. McN. Whistler, oils, *c.*1870, repro. in Pennell and Pennell, *The Whistler journal* • J. McN. Whistler, oils, 1870–73, Smithsonian Institution, Washington, DC, Freer Gallery of Art • D. G. Rossetti, pastel drawings, 1870–79, repro. in Merrill, *The Peacock Room* • oils, 1880, Walker Art Gallery, Liverpool • photograph, 1880–1889?, repro. in W. B. Forwood, *Reminiscences of a Liverpool shipowner, 1850–1920* (1920) • V. Prinsep, oils, *c.*1891, repro. in V. Prinsep, 'The private art collections of London', *Art Journal* (1892) • Helsby, group portrait, photograph, 1932 (with the English cricket test team), Hult. Arch. • Smith, group portrait, photograph, 1934 (with the Middlesex County Cricket Club), Hult. Arch.

Wealth at death £732,770 19*s.* 4*d.*: resworn probate, June 1893, *CGPLA Eng. & Wales* (1892)

Leyland, Joseph Bentley (1811–1851), sculptor, was born on 31 March 1811 in Halifax, Yorkshire, and baptized there on 26 May 1811, the second son and one of five children of Roberts Leyland (1784–1847), a bookseller, publisher, and naturalist, and his wife, Susannah Bentley (1786–1850). Joseph went to the school kept by his grandfather and uncle in Wade Street, Halifax, and in his later teens he attended drawing classes at the Mechanics' Institute. At this time he also had the opportunity to study and make drawings from the collection of antique marbles belonging to Christopher Rawson at Hope Hall, Halifax.

In 1831 Leyland sent a model, *An Italian Greyhound*, to the exhibition of the Royal Manchester Institution and in 1832 he showed at the same venue a statue of Spartacus, which was said to have been the most striking work in the exhibition. Two years later he sent to the exhibition of the Royal Northern Society for the Encouragement of the Fine Arts in Leeds a colossal, 6 feet high, head of Satan, which also received much attention in the local press.

Encouraged by these successes, in 1834 Leyland moved to London, where he lodged with the Bradford engraver William Overend Geller, and worked in a studio in Queen Street, off Oxford Street. Through his friend and patron the portrait painter T. H. Illidge he met the sculptors Francis Chantrey and Richard Westmacott and he studied anatomy with the painter B. R. Haydon, who promoted his work. Leyland received consistently favourable notices in the London press for works such as *A Warrior Listening to a Prior Reading*, a subject from Maturin's tragedy *Bertram*, and *English Greyhounds*, which he exhibited at the Society of British Artists in 1834. His *African Bloodhounds* (1837), his most ambitious animal group, was considered by Landseer to be 'the noblest modern work of its kind' (*DNB*). This, together with the sculptor's *Thracian Falconer* (*c.*1838, plaster model), was presented following the sculptor's death to the museum at Peel Park, Salford, but they were subsequently destroyed. His figure of Kilmeny (1835), from James Hogg's poem 'The Queen's Wake', was purchased by the Halifax Literary and Philosophical Society and at one time displayed in the Bankfield Museum, Halifax, though it no longer survives.

Leyland returned to Halifax in 1838, a move which marked a change in the direction of his work. He abandoned for the most part the ambitious 'ideal' subjects of his early years, which had not been profitable, and turned his attention increasingly to church monuments and ornamental sculpture. His monuments include those to John Rawson (1838) in Holy Trinity Church, Halifax, Bishop Ferrar (1847) in the parish church, Halifax, and, his most important commission, the memorial to Stephen Beckwith (1849) in York Minster.

Leyland was a leading figure among a group of artists and writers who met regularly at the George Hotel in Bradford and other drinking-places in the area. The group, known for its sometimes unruly gatherings, included John Wilson Anderson the landscape painter, Skerrit the actor, John Nicholson the Airedale poet, and the writer and artist Patrick Branwell Brontë. Indeed it is Leyland's friendship with Brontë that has come to be his chief claim to fame. Branwell's surviving letters to the sculptor record the troubled Brontë brother's final years, and Leyland's medallion portrait of Branwell (1846, plaster) hangs at the parsonage at Haworth. Joseph's brother, Francis Alexander Leyland, was an early biographer of the Brontë family.

Leyland's own life followed an increasingly destructive course. Constantly in debt, given to heavy drinking, and subject to ill health, he had difficulties in completing commissions, which, combined with a tendency towards outspokenness, led to many disputes with clients. Mary Leyland described him as 'self-opinionated, sarcastic, and unreliable, scornful of religion and of anyone who disagreed with him, only working when the spirit moved him' (M. Leyland, 37), though others considered him to be a good-natured and generous friend with a remarkable, though largely unfulfilled, talent. He was arrested for debt in the autumn of 1850 and sent to Manor gaol where he remained, partly it seems through choice, until his death from dropsy on 28 January 1851. He was buried on 31 January in the Salem Chapel churchyard in Halifax. He never married. MARTIN GREENWOOD

Sources 'A Halifax sculptor', *Halifax Courier* (12 March–28 May 1927) • M. Leyland, 'The Leyland family', *Transactions of the Halifax Antiquarian Society* (1954), 29–48 • *Art Journal*, 13 (1851), 140 • R. Gunnis, *Dictionary of British sculptors, 1660–1851* (1953); new edn (1968) • *DNB* • Redgrave, *Artists* • P. B. Brontë, 'A complete transcript of the Leyland manuscripts showing the unpublished portions from the original documents in the collection of Col. Sir Edward A. Brotherton, Bt., LL.D.', ed. J. A. Symington and C. W. Hatfield, *Transactions and other Publications of the Brontë Society*, 6/35 (1925), 277–312 • F. A. Leyland, *The Brontë family, with special reference to Patrick Branwell Brontë*, 2 vols. (1886) • d. cert. • *IGI*

Archives U. Leeds, Brotherton L.

Likenesses group portrait, drawing, 1848, U. Leeds; repro. in W. Gerin, *Branwell Brontë* (1961), 275 • photograph, repro. in W. Gerin, *Branwell Brontë* (1961), 195

Wealth at death died in debt: Leyland, 'Leyland family'

Leyland, Maurice (1900–1967), cricketer, was born at 2 Wensley Terrace, Ripon Road, Bilton, Yorkshire, on 20 July 1900, the son of Edward (Ted) Leyland, a stonemason and groundsman, and his wife, Mercy Lambert. At birth his name was registered as Morris but he generally spelt it Maurice. His father, who played cricket professionally for Moorside (Lancashire), became a well-known groundsman at Harrogate, Headingley, and Edgbaston. Maurice appeared for Moorside when only twelve years old and then played for Harrogate from 1918 to 1923.

Leyland made his début for Yorkshire in 1920 and gained his county cap in 1923. In all he played 548 matches for Yorkshire until his retirement in 1946. He was a strongly built attacking batsman—perhaps the best left-handed batsman ever to play for the county—notable for his superb off-side stroke play, though his style was forceful rather than elegant. In every season between 1923 and 1939 he scored 1000 runs, his best score being 263 against Essex at Hull in 1936. He finished his career in first-class cricket with 33,660 runs at an average of 40.50. He also bowled slow left-arm, mainly chinamen and googlies, an art he learned from Roy Kilner, and took 466 wickets in his career at an average of 29.31.

Chosen for the MCC tour to India in 1926–7, Leyland made his test match début against the West Indies at the Oval in August 1928 (when he was out for nought). He subsequently went on three tours of Australia with success in 1928–9, 1932–3, and 1936–7. Always a thorn in the Australian side, he batted with the utmost confidence against Bill O'Reilly, who rarely got the better of him. In both his first appearance against the Australians, at Melbourne in March 1929, and his last, at the Oval in August 1938, he made centuries, the latter in a record-breaking partnership with Len Hutton. On that occasion, seeing Leyland come to the crease unexpectedly as number 3 in the batting order, O'Reilly exclaimed in exasperation, 'Good God, it's that Yorkshire bastard again' (Hutton, 26). He invariably wore his Yorkshire cap when batting for England. In all he played in 41 tests, hitting 2764 runs at an average of 46.06.

Leyland thrived on big, high-pressure occasions such as Yorkshire's roses matches against Lancashire or tests against Australia, when he displayed the serene, imperturbable outlook which made him popular with colleagues and opponents alike. He was unvaryingly cheerful even when his side faced a crisis. After his retirement as a county player he played for Harrogate from 1947 to 1950 before returning to Yorkshire as coach from 1951 to 1963, when Parkinson's disease brought his career to an end. His genial manner contrasted with the somewhat dour approach of his colleague Arthur Mitchell to make the ideal coaching partnership. In 1949 he was one of the retired professionals accorded the exceptional award of honorary life membership of MCC. The Leyland gates were erected at the St George's Road ground, Harrogate, in recognition of his services to cricket. Leyland died, unmarried, at Scotton Banks Hospital, Knaresborough, Yorkshire, on 1 January 1967.

ANTHONY WOODHOUSE

Sources *The Times* (3 Jan 1967) • P. Bailey, P. Thorn, and P. Wynne-Thomas, *Who's who of cricketers* (1984) • *Yorkshire County Cricket Club Year Book* • A. W. Pullin, *History of Yorkshire county cricket club, 1903–23* (1924) • J. M. Kilburn and J. H. Nash, *History of Yorkshire county cricket club, 1924–1949* (1950) • G. L. Greaves, *Over the summers again: a history of Harrogate cricket club* (1976) • L. Hutton, *Fifty years in cricket* (1984) • b. cert. • d. cert.

Archives FILM BFI NFTVA, news footage • BFI NFTVA, sports footage

Likenesses photograph, repro. in Kilburn and Nash, *History of Yorkshire county cricket club*, 176

Wealth at death £7257: probate, 11 April 1967, *CGPLA Eng. & Wales*

Leyland, Thomas (1752?–1827), merchant and banker, is thought to have been born in 1752, one of the two known children (he had a sister) of Richard Leyland of Knowsley, Lancashire. Nothing is known about his early life. By 1768, however, he was employed by Edward Bridge, cooper, of Liverpool. He then entered service with Gerald Dillon, an Irish trader, and by 1774 was his partner, having borrowed £500 to invest in the business. It was an inspired investment; in December 1776 they won £20,000 in the state lottery. Six months later Leyland married Ellen Bridge (*c*.1755–1839), daughter of his former employer, who had died in 1775. The marriage failed to produce children, but Leyland received one third of Ellen's mother's estate when she died in 1782.

By this time Leyland was in business on his own, having dissolved his partnership with Dillon in 1781. During the next twenty years his commercial affairs blossomed as he diversified from the Irish trade into the trades in olive oil, sherry, wine, and African slaves. The last was particularly important since its capital requirements encouraged him to form alliances with other local merchants. In March 1790 investment in slaving voyages by Thomas Leyland & Co. stood at over £36,000. Leyland remained active in the trade until its abolition in 1807. Some voyages yielded rich dividends and undoubtedly contributed to his growing fortune.

Seen as 'a man of amazing shrewdness, sagacity, and prudence' (Hughes, 177), Leyland remained appreciative of early good fortune, naming one of his ships *Lottery*. Others, appropriately, were named *Enterprise* and *Fortune*.

Thomas Leyland (**1752?–1827**), by unknown engraver

His growing wealth was accompanied by expanding business premises in Liverpool, and by 1800 he had offices and warehouses in Duke Street, Henry Street, York Street, and Nova Scotia. Two years later he purchased the 300 acre estate of Walton Hall, said to be 'a residence admirably suited for a commercial Gentleman of the first importance' (ibid., 172).

In 1802 Leyland became a partner in the banking firm of Clarkes and Roscoe of Dale Street. As William Roscoe had abolitionist sympathies, this was a strange alliance, but Leyland strongly supported Roscoe when he stood successfully as a whig at Liverpool in the election of November 1806. Within two months, however, Leyland had left Roscoe's firm to establish his own bank, taking his nephew Richard Bullin as partner, and in May 1807 strenuously opposed Roscoe's re-election, accusing him of a 'bitter mortification' (HoP, *Commons*). Interestingly, Roscoe finished bottom of the poll. In 1809 Richard's brother Christopher joined the new banking firm, now known as Leyland and Bullins. Based first in York Street and after 1816 in King Street, the bank prospered; between 1812 and 1827 customers' deposits doubled to £1.2 million, while loans to the public tripled to nearly £300,000. Following Leyland's death in 1827, it survived until 1901 under the guidance of the Bullins and, from 1849, the Naylors—Leyland's niece Dorothy having married in 1809 John Naylor of Hartford Hill, Cheshire.

Until the mid-1790s Leyland's interests were almost wholly centred on business, but his political standing in Liverpool rose in tandem with his wealth. In 1796 he was co-opted on to the Liverpool town council, and two years later was elected mayor. He was re-elected in 1814 and 1820. In addition to local office-holding, Leyland was also nominated in 1816 to challenge George Canning at a parliamentary by-election in Liverpool. Noted for his parsimonious nature, Leyland was a very reluctant candidate—Canning dubbed him 'a man of straw' (HoP, *Commons*)—and refused to campaign seriously; it was, Canning claimed, 'a struggle with an invisible phantom' (Hughes, 176). Despite his evident lack of interest, Leyland polled nearly 750 votes compared to his rival's 1260. He refused to be nominated for the 1818 parliamentary election, but in 1823 became a JP and deputy lieutenant for the county of Lancaster.

Said to be 'a fine-looking man, with what some thought a stern and forbidding, but what we should call a firm and decided, look' (Hughes, 177), Thomas Leyland died on 29 May 1827 at his home, Walton Hall, Liverpool. He was buried in the family vault at Walton church, Liverpool. He was survived by his wife, Ellen, who died in 1839. The main beneficiaries of his will were his wife and his nephews, Richard and Christopher Bullin, who subsequently adopted the name and arms of Leyland.

David Richardson

Sources J. Hughes, *Liverpool banks and bankers, 1760–1837* (1906), 169–81 • T. H. Naylor, *The family of Naylor from 1589* (1967), 21–34 • J. E. Inikori, 'Market structure and the profits of the British African trade in the late eighteenth century', *Journal of Economic History*, 41 (1981), 745–76 • *British Sessional Papers: Accounts and Papers*, 29 (1790) • L. S. Pressnell, *Country banking in the industrial revolution* (1956) • R. Craig and R. Jarvis, *Liverpool registry of merchant ships*, Chetham Society, 3rd ser., 15 (1967) • R. G. Thorne, HoP, *Commons*

Archives Lpool RO, accounts and letter-book | U. Lpool, Cohen Library, Dumbell MSS • U. Mich., Clements L., account books of Jenny and Hannah

Likenesses engraving, repro. in Hughes, *Liverpool banks and bankers*, 168 [*see illus.*] • portrait, repro. in Naylor, *The family of Naylor from 1589*, 13

Wealth at death under £600,000: Hughes, *Liverpool banks*, 177 • in December 1826 Leyland's private wealth was said to amount to £736,531, of which £384,000 was in government stock: Pressnell, *Country banking*, 419

Leylond [Leyland, Leland], **John** (*d.* **1428**), grammarian, was perhaps a native of Leyland, Lancashire. He has been called 'the elder' to distinguish him from his namesake, probably a relative, the antiquary John *Leland, who said of him, in words that may echo the grammarian's own publicity as well as substantial reputation: 'Ut rosa flos florum, sic Lelande grammaticorum' ('As the rose is the flower of flowers, so is Leland of grammarians'; *Commentarii*, 445). Six other similar laudatory tags survive, and no other late medieval English grammarian achieved such popular regard.

The earliest evidence for Leylond's teaching is a volume (CUL, MS Hh.1.5) containing many of his short treatises which was bequeathed to Worksop Priory *c.*1401, significantly earlier than other references. A further copy of his work, containing four of his Latin and one of his English treatises, notes him as having lectured at Oxford in 1414 (Lincoln Cathedral, MS 88); the earliest documentary record available is in the Queen's College long rolls noting payment of fees between 1415 and 1419 for the tuition of Thomas Eglesfield. Both Leland and J. Rowse have Leylond teaching at the merged Peckwater Inn and Vine Hall, now the site of Christ Church's Peckwater Quadrangle in Oxford.

Leylond was married and so taught outside the university in its developing fringe of lay education in grammar, French, law, accountancy, and administration. His success reinforced Oxford's 'faculty' of grammar and master of grammar degree as the yardsticks of their day. He and his wife, Margaret, prospered and acquired lands in Temple Cowley in 1422 which they later gave to the grammarian John Cobbow, who may have been their son-in-law.

Like other practical teachers of his day, Leylond produced no great grammatical *summa*. His fame rests rather on the development of a curriculum based on a graded series of shorter treatises, the more elementary of which were written in English and are the first post-conquest vernacular grammars to survive. The curriculum and texts he devised set a shape for elementary education that survived through the Renaissance period of John Stanbridge and William Lily into modern times. Embedded in his treatment of Latin grammar are some of the earliest essays at the grammar of English.

Leylond's English works include a version of the *Accedence* on parts of speech, the *Comparacio* on comparison, and *Informacio* on elementary syntax. Latin treatises attributed to him include *De declinationibus*, *De nominibus etheroclitis*, *De cognitione generum*, *De preteritis et supinis*, *De regimine casuum*, *De concordantiis gramatice*, together with a *Tractatus iuvenum pro dogmate factus*, *Distinctiones rhetorice*, and verses (for manuscript references see Thomson, *Catalogue*, 7–12).

Leylond died on 30 April 1428 and was buried in the lady chapel at St Frideswide's, Oxford. He bequeathed 20*s*. to Osney Abbey and was remembered in their obits. On 4 July 1435 the chancellor of the university ordered that cautions deposited by him for loans from a university chest be sold.

David Thomson

Sources *Commentarii de scriptoribus Britannicis, auctore Joanne Lelando*, ed. A. Hall, 2 (1709), 445 • J. Rowse, 'Catalogue of colleges and halls', in A. Wood, *Survey of the antiquities of the city of Oxford*, ed. A. Clark, 1, OHS, 15 (1889), 639; 2, OHS, 17 (1890), 174–5 • Emden, *Oxf.* [Cobbow Leland] • H. E. Salter, ed., *Cartulary of Oseney Abbey*, 1, OHS, 89 (1929), xxiii • H. E. Salter, ed., *Registrum cancellarii Oxoniensis, 1434–1469*, 1, OHS, 93 (1932), 16 • R. W. Hunt, 'Oxford grammar masters in the middle ages', *Collected papers* (1980), 167–97 • D. Thomson, 'The Oxford grammar masters revisited', *Mediaeval Studies*, 45 (1983), 298–310 • D. Thomson, *A descriptive catalogue of Middle English grammatical texts* (1979) [MS references] • D. Thomson, *An edition of the Middle English grammatical texts* (1984)
Archives CUL, MS Hh.1.5 • Lincoln Cathedral, MS 88

Leyser, Karl Joseph (1920–1992), historian, was born on 24 October 1920 in Düsseldorf, Nordrhein-Westfalen, son of Otto Leyser (1885–1945) and his wife, Emmy, *née* Hayum (1891–1987). He was educated at the Hindenburg Gymnasium, Düsseldorf. Otto was the head of a family firm which manufactured belts and braces, a scrupulous and successful businessman, but he and his wife were Jewish and suffered constant harassment after the National

Karl Joseph Leyser (1920–1992), by Deborah Elliott, 1984

Socialists came to power. Denounced by a discontented employee in 1937, Otto and Emmy moved to the Netherlands, but sent their two children, Karl and his sister, Dorothea, to England. There charitable organizations and family connections, including the distinguished medievalist Wilhelm Levison, enabled Karl to attend St Paul's School. At the school he studied history under Philip Whitting, who had a high regard for him, and made lasting friendships, including one with Christopher Lloyd, the younger son of Nathaniel Lloyd of Great Dixter, Sussex. In 1939 he matriculated as a demy of Magdalen College, Oxford, but in 1940 was interned with other refugees and sent to the Isle of Man.

Leyser's readiness to join the Pioneer Corps, the only branch of the armed forces open to internees, together with some pressure from his college, secured his release before the end of the year. He served until 1943, with the rank of corporal, when he was transferred to the Black Watch. Commissioned in 1944, he served with the 51st division in north-western Europe, and in 1945 had the great felicity of finding his parents alive, in hiding in Edam, Noord Holland. His father died in August that year, but Leyser brought his mother to England, where she lived until her death in 1987. Demobilized in 1945 with the rank of captain, and mentioned in dispatches, Leyser returned to Magdalen in 1946. He won the Gibbs scholarship in history that year and graduated BA with first-class honours in modern history in 1947.

Leyser then began work on the Good Parliament of 1376, but his time for research was soon curtailed by his election to an official fellowship and tutorship at Magdalen, followed by a university lectureship in 1950. By that time he had begun to lecture on the Saxon and Hohenstaufen periods. He also expressed an interest in the early years of the Empress Matilda and in Anglo-German relations in the late eleventh and early twelfth centuries. Those were long-laid plans. He later attributed his immensely productive concern with the empire, and particularly with the Ottonians, to an *obiter dictum* of Bruce McFarlane's that he should take advantage of his command of German and German sources. McFarlane's influence on him, beginning with his kindly concern during the war, in the bleak days of Leyser's internment, and subsequently for the rest of his own life, is hardly measurable, though much can be deduced from Leyser's perceptive notice of him in the *Proceedings of the British Academy* in 1976; but there was more to his momentous decision than that. One very powerful consequence of his commitment, however, came when Henrietta Bateman, an undergraduate at St Hilda's, came to hear him on the Ottonians; they were married in 1962 and family life with their four children provided an enriching stability in Leyser's life.

The 1960s and 1970s were certainly a remarkably prolific time, despite Leyser's commitment to teaching in Magdalen, an obligation to which he might have been supposed, from his pupils' recollection, to have devoted his entire energies. His only monograph, *Rule and Conflict in Early Medieval Society: Ottonian Saxony*, appeared in 1979, but it was supported by a long line of papers, beginning with his essays on the Lechfeld and on Henry I and the foundation of the Saxon empire, and was followed by a strong company of others extending down to his Raleigh lecture of 1983, published in 1984, entitled 'The crisis of medieval Germany'—that is, on the great Saxon revolt of 1073, which, together with the power of the reformed papacy, faced down the accomplishments of Ottonian kingship. Elected a fellow of the British Academy in 1983, he was also appointed to the Chichele chair of medieval history, and held the chair from 1984 to his retirement in 1988. After a severe stroke in spring 1992 he died in Oxford on 27 May 1992, and was buried in Islip churchyard.

Karl Leyser's eminence was based upon a unique blend of German and English scholarship. His own experiences as a refugee, an alien who found solace in his new identity and most particularly in his marriage, gave a special and productive intensity to his work. He drew sparingly and with great skill on his military experience in illuminating the past, though he also valued it as a means further to relish Englishness. Naturalized in 1946, he served after the war in the Territorial Army as captain and major, and was awarded the Territorial decoration in 1963. He died at a time when he seemed about to enter an even more impressive phase of his professional life, but a serious road accident in 1977 had made him particularly aware of mortality, and neither he nor his friends would have felt that his time, most especially in those later years, had been ill spent. G. H. MARTIN

Sources H. Mayr-Harting, *PBA*, 94 (1997), 599–624 • *WW* • K. B. McFarlane, *Letters to friends, 1940–66*, ed. G. Harriss (1997) • personal knowledge (2004)

Archives priv. coll., papers | SOUND priv. coll., a record of a conversation on German history with Dr John Gillingham

Likenesses D. Elliott, photograph, 1984, NPG [*see illus.*] • photograph, repro. in Mayr-Harting, *PBA*

Wealth at death under £125,000: probate, 2 Oct 1992, *CGPLA Eng. & Wales*

Leyson, Thomas (*b.* 1549, *d.* in or after 1608), Latin and Welsh poet and physician, was born at Neath in Glamorgan, and was probably the son of Dr Thomas Leyson, prebendary of Llandaff in 1535, and his wife, Mary, daughter of William Bennet of Beaupré (Phillips, 435). He was educated at Winchester College (scholar 1563) and New College, Oxford (scholar 1567, BA *c.*March 1571, MA 1 February 1576, MB 8 July 1583), where he was fellow from 1569 to 1586. In 1583 he was proctor of the university. At Oxford, Leyson was famed for his Latin verses and disputed in public. He later became a physician at Bath.

Leyson was a friend of the antiquary Sir Edward Stradling and a habitué of his seat, St Donat's Castle in Glamorgan. His Latin poem on the castle survives only in a Welsh translation by Siôn Dafydd Rhys (printed in G. J. Williams, *Iolo Morganwg a chywyddau'r ychwanegiad*, 226–9), who, in the preface to his *Cambrobrytannicae cymraecaeve linguae institutiones* (1592), describes Leyson as 'vir cum rei medicae, tum poetices peritissimus' ('an exceptionally gifted poet and physician'). The pair corresponded in Latin and Welsh verses that were admired and even plagiarized for their literary skill. Despite this, Leyson was a conservative, if not shy, man who did not relish entering eisteddfods (Williams, *Iolo Morganwg*, 56–67).

Anthony Wood says that much of Leyson's Latin poetry was printed, but it is now hard to find. Some elegant Latin elegiacs by him precede Sir John Stradling's *De vita et morte contemnenda* (1597) and others were inscribed on his grandparents' tomb at Monkton-Combe, Somerset (Clark). His Welsh poetry achieved a distinctive and original melding of classical ideas with Welsh forms (a *cywydd* by him is preserved in Williams, *Iolo Morganwg*, 223–4). A keen naturalist, he was famed for his thorough cataloguing of Neath flora.

Leyson died at Bath some time after 1607; he was buried there in St James's Church.

W. A. J. ARCHBOLD, *rev.* ROSS KENNEDY

Sources D. R. Phillips, *The history of the vale of Neath* (1925), 435 • G. T. Clark, *Limbus patrum Morganiae et Glamorganiae: being the genealogies of the older families of the lordship of Morgan and Glamorgan* (1886), 350 • G. J. Williams, *Iolo Morganwg a chywyddau'r ychwanegiad* (1926) • G. J. Williams, 'Sir John Stradling of St. Donat's (1563–1637)', *Glamorgan Historian*, 9 (1973), 11–28 • Wood, *Ath. Oxon.*, new edn, 2.27 • Wood, *Ath. Oxon.: Fasti* (1815), 187, 199, 223–4 • Foster, *Alum. Oxon.*, 1500–1714, 3.913 • T. F. Kirby, *Winchester scholars: a list of the wardens, fellows, and scholars of … Winchester College* (1888), 139 • R. Williams, *Enwogion Cymru: a biographical dictionary of eminent Welshmen* (1852), 272

Lhuyd [Lhwyd; *formerly* Lloyd], **Edward** (1659/60?–1709), naturalist and philologist, was born in the parish of Loppington, Shropshire, the illegitimate son of Edward Lloyd (1635–1681) of Llanforda, Oswestry, and Bridget Pryse of Glanfred, Tal-y-bont, Cardiganshire, the second daughter of Thomas Pryse of Gogerddan. Both his parents came from well-established gentry families and they were distantly related. His paternal grandfather was a sequestered royalist who, though he succeeded in recovering his land, never rebuilt his fortune. His father struggled to recoup his patrimony by engaging in market gardening and industrial ventures. He was actively interested in the new science, carried out chemical experiments, and corresponded on botanical matters with Robert Morison and Jacob Bobart. His attempt to set up a fishing business in the Dovey estuary is probably what first brought him into contact with the young Bridget Pryse, who belonged to one of the leading families of north Cardiganshire. They remained in contact with each other after the birth of their son.

Education, natural history, and linguistics Lhuyd, who adopted the Welsh form of the family surname Lloyd from about 1688 (he preferred the spelling Lhwyd but used Lhuyd or Luid[ius] in his published works), was first brought up by a nurse, Catherine Bowen, in Krew Green, and subsequently by his father at Llanforda. His earliest botanical training may have come from his father's gardener, Edward Morgan, who was highly respected in his craft and had contacts with John Evelyn (who described him as a skilful botanist) and John Ray. The milieu would have encouraged Lhuyd's scientific interests, and the earliest evidence for his botanical activities are some notes apparently taken during a journey from Llanforda to Cardiganshire. He may also have been a pupil at Oswestry grammar school.

Following his father's death Lhuyd went up to Jesus College, Oxford, in 1682, with the intention of acquiring a BCL. Though the college records state that he was eighteen at the time, he was probably older, for he was said to be forty-nine when he died. At Oxford he quickly became associated with the newly established Oxford Philosophical Society, a scientific group led by Robert Plot, who was appointed keeper of the Ashmolean Museum when it opened in the following year. In 1684 Lhuyd is noted as 'Register to the Chymical course at the Laboratory' situated in the museum's cellar; the course was being taught by Plot. From 1684 to 1687 Lhuyd regularly submitted papers to the Philosophical Society. His involvement with the Ashmolean and with the society is probably the reason that he did not take his degree, though he acquired the status of SCL.

The years between 1685 and 1690 were crucial for Lhuyd. Plot further encouraged him in his studies, appointing him his assistant in 1687, and he began to correspond with John Ray and Martin Lister, both of whom were generous in their support, advice, and encouragement. He reported to Plot and to the Philosophical Society in 1685 on plants that he discovered around Oxford and on expeditions to Snowdonia, and some of his later discoveries were warmly acknowledged in Ray's *Synopsis methodica stirpium Britannicarum* (1690). He also gave Lister information and drawings of the Ashmolean's shell collection. The preparation of a classified catalogue of the shell collection had been Lhuyd's first formal task at the museum, and he reported its completion to the Philosophical Society in January 1686.

Early signs of Lhuyd's linguistic interests appeared in the list of dialect words which he contributed to the second edition of Ray's *English Words not Generally Used* (1691). More innovative was his statistical analysis of the origins of the Welsh lexicon (divided into native, Latin, English), prepared as a criticism of some of Edward Barnard's statements in his epistle in George Hickes's *Institutiones grammaticae Anglo-Saxonicae et Moeso-Gothicae* (1689), and sent as a letter to Plot in 1690 under the name Mredydh Owen.

Lhuyd's circle of correspondents expanded in the 1690s when he began to discuss matters of natural history and antiquities with William Nicholson, Richard Richardson, and John Woodward, with whom he quarrelled over the theory of the earth and of the formation of fossils. Lhuyd's major undertaking in these years was the preparation of a catalogue of British fossils which was to be based on the museum's collections, augmented by his own fieldwork. This descriptive and illustrated catalogue was eagerly awaited by other naturalists. The task was, however, interrupted by Lhuyd's appointment as keeper after Plot's retirement in 1691, and by some large research projects.

In 1693 Lhuyd, though initially reluctant, was persuaded by William Nicholson to accept Edmund Gibson's invitation to revise the entries on the Welsh counties for his new edition and translation of Camden's *Britannia*. Within the strict and constrained timetable set by Gibson he found time to make a hurried tour of Wales, in the late summer and early autumn of 1693. He completed his revisions by October 1694. Though he grudged the time lost from his work on the fossil catalogue, *Britannia* whetted his appetite for Celtic antiquities, and it brought him to the notice of Welsh scholars in Oxford, as well as of some of the gentry in Wales who wished to see the natural history and antiquities of their country written up in a fashion similar to that which Plot had employed for Oxfordshire and Staffordshire.

The *Archaeologia* and travels through Britain Lhuyd responded enthusiastically to the suggestions put to him and in 1695 issued his proposal, *A design of a British dictionary, historical and geographical: with an essay entitl'd 'Archaeologia Britannica'; and a natural history of Wales*. This was a project which called for firm financial support and a carefully worked out strategy of information gathering, writing, and publication. Lhuyd envisaged a multi-volume work, the writing and publication of which, after four or five years of fieldwork, would extend over a period of five years for the dictionary, and a further two years for the *Archaeologia*. He set no time-scale for the *Natural History*. He was able to attract the support of powerful patrons such as Sir Thomas Mansel and Sir Roger Mostyn, as well as that of figures in the scientific fraternity, and he appointed a London barrister, Walter Thomas, to be his agent. A subscription scheme was devised which, it was hoped, would produce a regular income to support the fieldwork and to employ assistants.

In spite of fears that the time-scale of the work was too long, the initial response was sufficiently encouraging for Lhuyd to embark upon the project. In 1696 he produced 'Parochial queries in order to a geographical dictionary, a natural history, etc., of Wales', a detailed questionnaire of which four thousand copies were distributed, going to every parish in Wales. The questionnaire was to be returned to him, to serve as the primary material for a descriptive survey and the basis for further enquiries. He made a brief visit to Wales during April–October 1696, and he and assistants left Oxford for an extended journey in May 1697. They were to spend the next four years travelling through Wales, northern Ireland, the highlands of Scotland, and thence to Ireland, Wales again, Cornwall, and briefly to Brittany, where the party were arrested on the suspicion of being English spies. They gathered information on the natural history, landscapes, antiquities, languages, and human history of the 'Celtic lands', collecting examples of the flora and fauna, noting and describing historical and prehistoric monuments, acquiring and transcribing manuscripts, and compiling a mass of information on the local history, language, and culture of the places they visited. Throughout his journey Lhuyd discussed his findings with a number of correspondents; the resulting correspondence forms an important body of seventeenth-century views on palaeontology, natural history, early British history, and linguistics.

During his travels Lhuyd succeeded in completing his catalogue of fossils, and in writing six essays on related topics. The book was seen through the press by his friends Lister and Tancred Robinson, and published as *Lithophilacii Britannica ichnographia* (1699), in a limited edition of 120 copies sponsored by ten patrons. It contains descriptions of 1766 fossil types in thirteen classes, and twenty-two plates of hundreds of illustrative engravings. Another edition, probably pirated, appeared at Leipzig. Lhuyd's book contained a number of errors, and he planned a second revised edition which, however, he never completed. A new edition, based on his corrections, was published by William Huddersford in 1760. Lhuyd returned to Oxford in April 1701 to resume his role as the energetic keeper of the Ashmolean Museum, and began to plan the writing of the first volume of his project. *Glossography*, the first volume of *Archaeologia Britannica, giving some account additional to what has hitherto been publish'd, of the languages, histories, and customs of the original inhabitants of Great Britain: from collections and observations in travels through Wales, Cornwal, Bas-Bretagne, Ireland and Scotland*, went to the university press in 1703 and was published in 1707. It contains grammars of Irish, Cornish, and Breton; Irish, Breton, and Welsh vocabularies; catalogues of Irish and Welsh manuscripts; and sections on what would now be termed comparative etymology, describing rules of phonetic change.

Character and death Lhuyd was made an MA of the University of Oxford in 1701, and was elected a fellow of the Royal Society in 1708. In 1709 he was elected senior divinity bedel of the university. As keeper of the museum he was required to give lectures in natural history; his 1702 lecture, *De stellis marinis*, was published in Leipzig in 1719 by J. H. Linck, and was also included by Huddersford in the 1760 edition of the *Ichnographia*.

Lhuyd never married. He was praised by his friends for his modesty, good nature, and unusual industry; he was, nevertheless, single-minded, and did not suffer fools gladly. In an age when the acquisitiveness of natural historians and antiquaries was legendary, he was known by contemporaries as 'honest Lhuyd' (*DNB*). He had a sharp tongue, was astute in his observation and descriptions of phenomena, and was a thoughtful, restrained interpreter. Sir Hans Sloane described him as the best naturalist in Europe, and in his own day his work as a botanist and palaeontologist was what attracted most attention. For Lhuyd, fossils were natural products of the earth, to be collected and classified. He did not see them as offering any clues to the nature or time-scale of the forces which had eroded the landscapes through which he travelled. In this context, the first and only published volume of his *Archaeologia* caused some disappointment, since supporters were expecting a work of natural history. However, since then it has come to be recognized that his most innovative contributions were made in the area of linguistics. He 'discovered' Old Welsh, and was one of the pioneers of the comparative method in historical linguistics which placed the study of the Celtic languages on a sure foundation.

Lhuyd died in his room in the lower ground floor of the Ashmolean Museum, Oxford, on 30 June 1709. He was buried in the Welsh aisle of St Michael's Church, Oxford, the following day. He left no will, and his books and manuscripts were adjudged to the university on account of the debts he owed them, and to Lewis Thomas, the university printer, probably for the printing of *Archaeologia*. Some of his manuscripts, later purchased by private collectors, were lost in several fires. He is commemorated in *Loidia serotina*, the Snowdon lily, the alpine flower which he discovered. BRYNLEY F. ROBERTS

Sources R. T. Gunther, *Early science in Oxford*, 14: *Life and letters of Edward Lhwyd* (1945) • R. Ellis, 'Some incidents in the life of Edward Lhuyd', *Transactions of the Honourable Society of Cymmrodorion* (1906–7), 1–51 • F. Emery, *Edward Lhuyd, F.R.S., 1660–1709* (1971) • N. Owen, 'Memoirs of Edward Llwyd', *British remains* (1777), 131–84 • B. F. Roberts, *Edward Lhuyd: the making of a scientist* (1980) • G. J. Williams, 'Edward Lhuyd', *Llên Cymru*, 6 (1960–61), 122–37 • F. V. Emery, '"The best naturalist now in Europe": Edward Lhuyd, FRS, 1660–1709', *Transactions of the Honourable Society of Cymmrodorion* (1969), 54–69 • J. L. Campbell and D. Thomson, *Edward Lhuyd in the Scottish highlands, 1699–1700* (1963) • D. R. Williams, *Prying into every hole and corner: Edward Lhuyd in Cornwall in 1700* (1993) • P. W. Carter, 'Edward Lhuyd the scientist', *Transactions of the Honourable Society of Cymmrodorion* (1962), 48–56 • E. Rees and G. Walters, 'The dispersion of the manuscripts of Edward Lhuyd', *Welsh History Review / Cylchgrawn Hanes Cymru*, 7 (1974–5), 148–78 • R. H. Morris, ed., 'Parochialia', *Archaeologia Cambrensis*, suppl. (1909–11) • *DNB*

Archives BL, papers, Add. MSS 14941, 15053, 15065–15077 • Bodl. Oxf., corresp. and papers • Brighton and Hove Library Service, annotated book • NL Wales, corresp., notebook, and papers • RS • TCD, Sebright collection | BL, Sloane MSS, letters to J. Morton • BL, Sloane MSS, letters to Richard Richardson • BL, Sloane MSS, letters to Sir Hans Sloane • BL, Sloane MSS 3962, 4062, 4064, 3369, 4059, 4063 • Bodl. Oxf., letters to John Aubrey • Bodl. Oxf., letters to Martin Lister • Bodl. Oxf., Eng. Hist. c.11 • NL Wales, MS 6209E, Peniarth 120 • NL Wales, 309, 1565, Peniarth 427

Likenesses open link illuminated letter, *c.*1714, AM Oxf., MS 2, fol. 20 • engraving, repro. in *The donation book*, AM Oxf.

Wealth at death debts of approximately £78: B. F. Roberts, 'Edward Lhuyd's debts', *BBCS*, 26 (1975), 353–9

Liakhoff, Nicolai [Nikolay Liakhov] (**1897–1962**), pioneer of guide dog training, was born on 17 April 1897 in Odessa, Russia, one of the two sons of General Dmitry Liakhov, an army officer. He joined a Cossack regiment of the Russian imperial army, and was a member of the household guard of Tsar Nicholas II. He was awarded the order of St George for bravery during the First World War, and in 1920 he served as aide-de-camp to General Wrangel, leader of the anti-Bolshevik forces. When the White Russian army was forced to evacuate the Crimea in November 1920, Liakhoff escaped to Constantinople and from there found his way to Paris. In 1925 he married Princess Irina Urusova, another Russian refugee: they had two daughters. He worked in Paris as a taxi driver and waiter before moving in 1930 to Switzerland, where he became a driving instructor.

In 1932 Liakhoff became an apprentice trainer at L'Oeil qui Voit (the Seeing Eye) in Vevey, Switzerland, a centre for the training of guide dog instructors set up in 1928 by an American, Mrs Dorothy Eustis, after she had seen the work done in Potsdam to train dogs to act as guides for German soldiers blinded in the war. Interest in guide dogs was growing in Britain, and in 1931 she agreed to lend a trainer to run a trial scheme in Wallasey, Cheshire. When she decided to close the Swiss school she sent Liakhoff to Wallasey in October 1933 to take over as trainer. The Guide Dogs for the Blind Association, founded in 1934, rented a large house, The Cliff, and Liakhoff became the first permanent trainer.

Despite his lack of experience, Liakhoff was an excellent trainer. Adult dogs were trained for several months before being introduced to their new owners, who spent four weeks on a residential course, learning how to handle the dogs. One problem he faced was hostility to the idea of making dogs work, and trainers were often accosted in the street by members of the public, outraged at the sight of dogs in harnesses. However, as it became clear that the use of dogs meant that blind people could leave institutions and lead independent lives, attitudes changed. The association moved the centre to Edmondscote Manor, in Leamington Spa, at the end of 1940, and as most of the staff had been called up it was largely thanks to Liakhoff that it kept going. But although he was popular with the blind students, his relations with his colleagues were bad, and it became increasingly difficult for the staff to work with him and his wife, both of whom had become heavy drinkers. On Christmas eve 1949 all the training staff resigned, and the following year they started a second centre, Cleve House, in Exeter.

Despite operations in 1951 and 1952 for a duodenal ulcer, Liakhoff continued as director of training and controller of the Leamington Spa centre until 1953, when the general council decided to separate the two roles and relieved him of the day-to-day running of the training centre. Liakhoff continued to make innovations: for example, after the first fatal accident in 1951 he designed a white-painted harness to increase the dogs' visibility at night, which was adopted in 1953. That year he was appointed MBE. In 1954 the association bought him a house in Reading, so that he could more easily supervise training at the two centres, but his health was affecting his work, and in 1958 he was forced to retire, although he continued to act as a consultant to the association.

Liakhoff died on 30 April 1962 at his home, Stanwix, 31 Derby Road, Caversham, Reading, and was buried on 4 May in Gunnersbury cemetery. He was survived by his wife. ANNE PIMLOTT BAKER

Sources P. Ireson, *Another pair of eyes* (1991) • G. Carter, *Willing walkers: the story of guide dogs for the blind* (1965) • *The Times* (2 May 1962) • *CGPLA Eng. & Wales* (1963)
Archives Guide Dogs for the Blind Association, Reading, archives
Likenesses photographs, repro. in Ireson, *Another pair of eyes*
Wealth at death £3678: probate, 27 Aug 1963, *CGPLA Eng. & Wales*

Liaqat Ali Khan (1895–1951), prime minister of Pakistan, was born on 1 October 1895 at Karnal in the Punjab, the second son of Rukn ud-Daula, Shamsher Jang, Nawab Rustam Ali Khan, nawab of Karnal. This wealthy landowning family was of Iranian descent, and had been settled for some generations in the United Provinces. He was educated at Muhammadan Anglo-Oriental College, Aligarh, and at the University of Allahabad. He married a cousin, Nawabzadi Jahangir Begam, with whom he had a son. In 1921 he took the shortened honours course in jurisprudence at Exeter College, Oxford. He was called to the bar at the Inner Temple in 1922, and shortly after returning to India joined the All-India Muslim League, the party that two decades later campaigned for the establishment of Pakistan, an independent state for the Muslims of British India. In 1933 he married Irene Pant, whose Hindu family had become Christians; she converted to Islam, and was known as Begam Rana'a Liaqat Ali Khan. They had two sons.

Liaqat Ali Khan's connections with the different Muslim cultures of the rural Punjab and the urban United Provinces positioned him neatly to take a lead in the debates over Pakistan. Demands for an independent homeland for the Muslim community of British India were first articulated in areas, including the United Provinces, where Muslims were in the minority; but to gain broad political acceptance, support was needed from areas such as the Punjab where Muslims were in the majority. As most Punjabis were comfortable with the cross-community political equation that had been worked out by the landlord-dominated Unionist Party, Mohamed Ali Jinnah and the Muslim League had to look for support to the fringes of the Punjab, to areas like Karnal. This was to provide Liaqat Ali Khan's political constituency until 1947; ironically, the success of the calls for Pakistan led to the partition of his own region, and he migrated to Karachi.

Liaqat rose rapidly in the ranks of the Muslim League, and held several political offices in regional government. He was a member of the United Provinces legislative council in 1926–40 (serving as deputy president in 1931–3), general secretary of the All-India Muslim League in 1936–47, deputy leader of the Muslim League party in the central legislature of united India in 1941–7, and chairman of the Muslim League central parliamentary board in 1945. He joined Jinnah in all the important discussions that were held by the British to determine India's future as the British prepared to withdraw after the Second World War.

Liaqat Ali Khan (1895–1951), by Elliott & Fry, 1948

These included the Simla tripartite conferences of 1945 and 1946—called tripartite as they involved Muslim and non-Muslim communities and the British government—and the conference in London called in December 1946 by the British prime minister, Clement Attlee, to persuade the Indian political leaders to keep India united in the wake of their rejection of the cabinet mission plan.

In October 1946 Liaqat led the Muslim League into the interim government under Jawaharlal Nehru, and received the finance portfolio. In spring 1947 he presented the famous 'poor man's budget' to the legislative assembly and embarrassed the leadership of the Congress Party by directing several tax increases at the affluent Hindu business and industrial community. The budget was regarded as the last straw by the Congress, who had been reluctant to accept the loose federation vital to the Muslims because they wanted power for a strong centre; it convinced the Hindu leadership that sharing power with the Muslim leaders in an Indian union was not an attractive proposition after all. On 14 August 1947 Pakistan became a reality, and Liaqat Ali Khan was sworn in as the country's first prime minister. Even so, he remained in Jinnah's shadow. As governor-general, Jinnah wielded more power than had been assigned him under the Government of India Act of 1935 and the India Independence Act of 1947, the two documents that together served as the new countries' constitutions. Jinnah was very much a politician in office, rather than a non-elected official; his power flowed from the people, not from the crown as was usual in dominion practice. It was Jinnah, not the prime minister, for example, who selected the cabinet. Moreover, he kept the ministries of evacuation and refugee rehabilitation, and state and frontier regions, under his direct control. It was only after Jinnah's death in September 1948 that Liaqat emerged as the principal leader of Pakistan and as *de facto* head of the Pakistan government.

Liaqat's first task in September 1948 was to deal with the political trauma caused by Jinnah's death. Lacking Jinnah's personal authority, he knew he could not inherit his full political mantle, and that he had to arrive at a power-sharing arrangement with some of the more powerful political blocs. Three groups were especially important: the *mohajir* (or Urdu-speaking refugee) community of Karachi, the Muslim Leaguers of the Punjab, and the Muslim Leaguers of Bengal. He had the support of the *mohajirs*, but had problems dealing with both the Punjab and Bengal. His solution was to leave the management of Punjab politics to a group of bureaucrats-turned-politicians who included his finance minister, Ghulam Muhammad, and the most senior civil servant in the government of Pakistan, Chaudhri Muhammad Ali. He handled Bengal by throwing his weight behind the faction loyal to Khwaja Nazimuddin, a member of the family of the nawab of Dacca. This faction was conservative and loyal to the central government, and represented the interests of the Urdu-speaking élite. Of the three powerful positions Jinnah had held at the time of his death, Liaqat kept only one for himself, the presidency of the Muslim League. He invited Khwaja Nazimuddin to succeed Jinnah as governor-general, and Maulvi Tamizuddin, another Bengali politician, to become president of the constituent assembly.

Liaqat's next big task was to deal with the problems created by the arrival of Muslim refugees from all over India. Following widespread communal violence, the flood of incomers was far greater than had been expected. By the time Pakistan carried out its first population census, some 14 million people had moved across the frontier, 8 million into Pakistan and 6 million into India. In most cases the refugees arrived totally destitute, having left all their property in India when they fled. Caught totally unprepared by the avalanche of people that descended upon Pakistan, the Liaqat administration could only muddle through. The refugees had to wait until the advent of military rule in Pakistan before they were permanently settled. It is one of the surprising aspects of Pakistan's history that social and demographic upheaval of such magnitude did not have any immediate political consequences.

The creation of Pakistan had led to a major political realignment. Several established political parties and personalities lost power: the Unionists in the Punjab and the Khudai Khidmatgars in the North-West Frontier Province were thrown onto the dust-heap of history, because of their opposition to the Pakistan movement. The *mohajirs* emerged as a potent political force in Pakistan's eastern province, and the middle classes began to exert power in the urban areas of the Punjab. This state of political flux could not—and, in fact, did not—offer the right opportunity for Liaqat to design a new constitutional arrangement for Pakistan. Debates went on endlessly in the constituent assembly, but Liaqat failed to master the new political forces and was unable to develop a political consensus behind any constitutional formula.

Foreign affairs provided a similarly difficult arena. Liaqat concluded the war in Kashmir in January 1949 by signing a ceasefire agreement with the Indian prime minister, Jawaharlal Nehru, but he failed to get India to implement its terms. His effort to maintain neutrality in the cold war, while claiming to be India's equal in the international arena, resulted in both the USSR and the USA giving Pakistan the cold shoulder. Liaqat moved out of this difficult situation by tilting towards the United States and in 1950 he visited Washington and met President Truman.

By 1951 Liaqat Ali Khan had begun to lose ground in domestic politics. The Punjab and Bengal were restive under the control of the Muslim League, and Sind factions engaged in endless fighting with the Muslim League. It was only in the North-West Frontier Province that the Muslim League chief minister, Abdul Qayyum Khan, had succeeded in cultivating support for himself and his party. Liaqat decided to bypass the provincial political bosses and go directly to the people. It was while he was addressing a mammoth public meeting on 16 October 1951 in Rawalpindi's Company Bagh that he was shot from close range. He died on the spot. His assailant, Said Akbar, an unemployed youth from the North-West Frontier Province, was immediately shot dead; his motives remain the subject of intense speculation.

Despite his mild-mannered and retiring character, Liaqat Ali Khan tenaciously upheld his political principles. Although historians have accorded a mixed verdict to his premiership, he is widely revered in Pakistan, especially among the *mohajir* community, and was accorded the title Quaid-i-Millat (Leader of the People, or Leader of the Religious Community). His widow, Begam Rana'a Liaqat Ali Khan, was active in women's issues in Pakistan, and was the founding president of the All-Pakistan Women's Association in 1949. SHAHID JAVED BURKI

Sources S. J. Burki, *Pakistan: continuing search for nationhood* (1991) • L. Collins and D. LaPierre, *Freedom at midnight* (1975) • *WWW* • *DNB*
Archives FILM BFI NFTVA, news footage
Likenesses Elliott & Fry, photograph, 1948, NPG [*see illus.*]

Liardet, Francis (**1798–1863**), naval officer, second son of John Liardet and the Lady Perpétué Cathérine de Paul de Lamanon d'Albe, was born at Chelsea on 14 June 1798. He entered the navy in June 1809, on the frigate *Mercury* (Captain the Hon. Henry Duncan), in the Mediterranean. In March 1810 he was transferred to the frigate *Belvidera* (Captain Richard Byron), on the coast of Africa, and afterwards on the North American station, and was slightly wounded in her running fight with, and escape from, the United States squadron under Commodore Rodgers on 23 June 1812. The *Belvidera* was paid off in October 1814, and for the next two years Liardet served in the West Indies on the *Warrior* and the sloop *Forester*.

After the peace of 1814 Liardet studied mathematics and navigation, and in 1819 sailed to the East Indies as mate of a merchant ship. In May 1821 he was appointed to the *Hyperion* (42 guns), going out to the Cape of Good Hope, and afterwards to the West Indies, where he was moved into the schooner *Union* to suppress piracy. He was severely wounded on 25 July 1823. On 18 March 1824 he was promoted lieutenant, and appointed to command the schooner *Lion* on the same service. In her he destroyed several nests of pirates on the coast of Cuba, captured nine pirate vessels, some of their prizes, and a slaver. He was first lieutenant of the *Procris* (10 guns), attending on the duke of Clarence, then lord high admiral, in 1827–8, and of the *Jaseur* at the Cape of Good Hope from 1828 to 1832. He was three times officially reported for saving life by jumping overboard, once into a sea infested with sharks; he was awarded Royal Humane Society medals. From 1833 to 1835 he was first lieutenant of the *Snake* (16 guns), on the South American station, and from 1835 to 1838 of the frigate *Cleopatra* (26 guns, the Hon. Charles Grey). On 28 June 1838 he was promoted commander, and in the following January was appointed to the *Powerful* (84 guns), carrying the broad pennant of Commodore Napier, as second in command in the Mediterranean, on the Syrian coast, and notably at the bombardment of Acre. For his services then, when he was frequently in command of the *Powerful*, Napier being ashore, Liardet was promoted to post rank on 4 November 1840.

In 1841 Liardet was appointed agent for the New Zealand Company at Taranaki, arriving there in late September. On 29 November, in expectation of a Maori attack, he was trying to clear the vent of a rusty old 4-pounder when an explosion of the charge destroyed the sight of one eye and seriously injured the other. For several years he was almost totally blind. In February 1842 he left Taranaki for Sydney, from where he returned to England. On 11 October 1842 Liardet married Caroline Anne, sister of Sir Edmund Filmer and widow of Lieutenant John Jervis Gregory RN; they had two daughters and a son. During his enforced retirement and afterwards Liardet wrote or dictated three books on points of professional guidance for naval officers. In January 1856 he was appointed one of the captains of the Royal Naval Hospital, Greenwich. He died at the hospital on 1 March 1863, and was buried in the mausoleum of the old cemetery. His wife survived him.

J. K. LAUGHTON, *rev.* ROGER MORRISS

Sources private information (1892) • O'Byrne, *Naval biog. dict.* • E. J. Wakefield, *Adventure in New Zealand, from 1839 to 1844*, 2 (1845), 68, 163 • *GM*, 3rd ser., 14 (1863), 530 • W. James, *The naval history of Great Britain, from the declaration of war by France in 1793, to the accession of George IV*, [5th edn], 6 vols. (1859–60), vol. 5, p. 357 • Boase, *Mod. Eng. biog.* • T. Roosevelt, *The naval war of 1812* (1882), 74 • L. J. H. Young, *Acts of gallantry* (1872), 22, 35 • *CGPLA Eng. & Wales* (1863)
Likenesses T. Milnes, marble bust, NMM
Wealth at death under £800: administration with will, 1 May 1863, *CGPLA Eng. & Wales*

Liart, Matthew (*c.***1736**–*c.***1782**), engraver, was probably of French Huguenot descent. J. T. Smith held that he was the grandson of a peruke maker and barber and the son of a sausage maker. His birthplace, Hog Lane, Soho, London, and his parents, Matthew or Matthieu Liart (*d.* 1750), a peruke maker, and Eléonore Grignon, may possibly be identified from Huguenot records. He lived in Compton Street, Soho, where his father seems to have owned two houses, and was apprenticed to Simon Francis Ravenet the elder; he won a premium from the Society of Arts in 1764. According to Samuel Redgrave, he was also a student in the schools of the Society of Artists and the Royal Academy. He was awarded a silver medal for life drawing by the latter, and Smith reported Benjamin West's high opinion of his abilities in the drawing of the human figure.

Liart exhibited a proof of *The Convention between Jacob and Laban*, after Pietro da Cortona, and *The Sacrifice of Noah*, after Andrea Sacchi, at the Society of Artists in 1766 and 1767 respectively, and appears to have specialized in fine engravings after old masters; both prints were executed for the series of famous paintings in English collections published by John Boydell. For that series Liart also engraved a large tavern scene, *The Merry Companions*, after Adriaen van Ostade, then in the collection of Joshua Reynolds (1783). Redgrave, among others, particularly emphasized the quality of Liart's two engravings after his contemporary Benjamin West—*Venus Lamenting the Death of Adonis* and *Cephalus and Procris*—which the engraver published himself. Nineteenth-century critical opinion was unanimous in its praise for the elegance, neatness, and decorum of Liart's style of engraving. On a more modest level, Liart contributed five single figures in national dress to the publication by the painter Francesco Smith, *Eastern Costume* (1769), a set of twenty-six prints after Smith's paintings in Lord Baltimore's collection. For John Bell's *Edition of Shakespeare's Plays: as they are Now Performed at the Theatres Royal of London* (1774), Liart engraved five of the small-scale scenes from a variety of Shakespeare's plays; Bell's *Edition* consisted of illustrations only, each inscribed with a single identificatory line from the drama in question.

Several authorities have identified Matthew Liart with a Mathieu Liard, who engraved a *Recueil de différents meubles*, published in Paris in 1762. This set consists of four plates with designs for sofas in a rather restrained and graceful late rococo style; it was available from 'Liard décinateur [in] Rue de la Harpe' and another 'Liard [in] Rue Jacquelet'. Mathieu Liard was also responsible for a similar, though neo-classical, series, *Cahier de petits meubles* (1774), and a *Cahier de lits de diverses modes*, both published by Chereau, and several, probably earlier, sets of chairs and sofas. Given the fact that there seem to have been at least two Liards present in Paris at the time, and that there is no indication that Matthew Liart ever left England, the furniture designs cannot conclusively be attributed to the London-born engraver, who died about 1782, probably in Compton Street, Soho. ANNE PUETZ

Sources T. Murdoch, ed., *The quiet conquest: the Huguenots, 1685–1985* (1985), 168 [exhibition catalogue, Museum of London, 15 May – 31 Oct 1985] · Bryan, *Painters* (1886–9) · S. Jervis, *The Penguin dictionary of design and designers* (1984) · G. K. Nagler, ed., *Neues allgemeines Künstler-Lexikon*, 22 vols. (Munich, 1835–52), vol. 8 · Redgrave, *Artists* · Graves, *Soc. Artists* · *Katalog der Ornamentstichsammlung der staatlichen Kunstbibliothek Berlin*, Staatliche Kunstbibliothek, Berlin (Berlin, 1939), nos. 1260, 1265 · J. T. Smith, *Nollekens and his times*, 2 (1828), 54–5 · H. Wagner, 'Huguenot wills', 1926, Huguenot Society of London · *Engraved Brit. ports.*, vol. 3 · Thieme & Becker, *Allgemeines Lexikon* · Bénézit, *Dict.* · *The parish of St Anne, Soho*, 1 (1966), 195 · M. Huber and C. G. Martini, *Manuel des curieux et des amateurs de l'art*, 9 (Zürich, 1808), 266 · W. Minet and S. Minet, *Registers of the churches of the Tabernacle, Glasshouse Street, and Leicester Fields, London, 1688–1783* (1926)

Likenesses P. Audinet, mezzotint (as an engineer; after J. Liart), BM · P. Audinet, mezzotint (after J. Liart), BM

Liberton. For this title name *see* Winram, George, of Liberton, Lord Liberton (*d.* 1650).

Liberty, Sir Arthur Lasenby (1843–1917), fabric manufacturer and retailer, was born at Chesham, Buckinghamshire, on 13 August 1843, the eldest son of Arthur Liberty, draper and lace manufacturer, of Nottingham and Chesham, and his wife, Rebecca Lasenby. He was educated at University School, Nottingham. On leaving school at the age of sixteen he began work in a relative's lace warehouse before moving to London, where he was appointed joint manager of Farmer and Roger's oriental warehouse in Regent Street. This was the foremost depot in England for the sale of goods from the Far East. Liberty held this position until 1874 and during this time he came into close contact with artists interested in oriental and other crafts, who used to meet there, among them Leighton, Burne-Jones, Rossetti, Whistler, and William Morris.

In 1875 Liberty married Emma Louise, daughter of Henry Blackmore, of Exmouth, Devon, and went into business on his own account, with three employees, at 218a Regent Street, which he called East India House. Here the same coterie of friends continued to meet. By 1882 the business had expanded so greatly that separate shop premises were opened at 142–4 Regent Street for the sale of home furnishings. The original East India House, which continued to sell fabric and dresses, also expanded to occupy nos. 216, 218, and 222 Regent Street. This was to form the site of the Liberty department store.

Liberty acquired a genuine enthusiasm for handcrafted wares and, with the zeal of a reformer, sought to provide an antidote to the spread of mass-produced goods. He was also a shrewd business organizer, careful in the selection and treatment of his staff, many of whom remained in his service throughout their working lives. One of his principal designers was the architect Edward William Godwin. Liberty was a zealous promoter of better conditions for employees and an enthusiastic supporter of the early-closing movement. But his success was due mainly to his own thorough methods, his artistic perception, and his knack of anticipating the trend of public taste. As early as 1875 he realized that the industries of the East were influencing a much wider circle than a few connoisseurs; he therefore tried to satisfy the growing demand for oriental textiles and colours by marketing fine fabrics of softer texture and subtler tint than had hitherto been generally obtainable in the West.

Liberty's influence on the British silk and woollen industry of the 1870s was considerable. In conjunction with his friend Sir Thomas Wardle he succeeded in introducing fine dyes previously supposed to be the exclusive product of the East. His aims were closely parallel with those of William Morris, and it has been supposed that Liberty was largely guided by Morris's example. The suggestion is erroneous, for Liberty was in close touch with a large circle, and his artistic ideas were influenced by the East rather than by the medieval Western art to which Morris was devoted. But both men educated the artistic taste of the public, and stimulated manufacturers to higher standards of design and workmanship. In 1888–9 Liberty and his wife visited Japan in order to study Japanese arts and crafts and the details of their manufacture.

In 1913 Liberty was knighted in recognition of his services to applied and decorative arts. He was JP and deputy lieutenant for the county of Buckingham, and high sheriff in 1899, juror on several international exhibitions, member of council of the London chamber of commerce, and an officer of numerous commercial and artistic associations. He retired from business in 1914, and died at his home, Lee Manor, Buckinghamshire, on 11 May 1917. He was survived by his wife. Since there were no children of his marriage, his business empire was continued by his nephew and great-nephews.

G. D. Rawle, *rev.* Gareth Shaw

Sources J. W. Ferry, *A history of the department store* (1960) • A. Adburgham, *Shops and shopping, 1800–1914: where, and in what manner the well-dressed Englishwoman bought her clothes* (1964) • A. Adburgham, *Liberty's: a biography of a shop* (1975) • d. cert. • *CGPLA Eng. & Wales* (1917)

Archives City Westm. AC, corresp. and papers

Likenesses A. Hacker, oils, exh. RA 1913, Liberty & Co. Ltd, London • G. Frampton, marble bust, exh. RA 1914, Liberty & Co. Ltd, London • prints, Liberty & Co. Ltd, London

Wealth at death £343,505 18s. 10d.: probate, 14 Sept 1917, *CGPLA Eng. & Wales*

Libri, Guglielmo [Count Guglielmo Bruto Icilio Timoleone Libri-Carrucci dalla Sommaia] (**1802–1869**), scientist, book collector, and thief, was born on 2 January 1802 (or possibly 1803) in Florence, the son of Count Giorgio Libri-Carrucci dalla Sommaia (1781–1836) and Rosa del Rosso (*c.*1783–1849). His parents were legally separated in 1807 and his father spent much of the rest of his life in France, where he was convicted of forgery in 1816 and imprisoned until 1825.

In 1816 Libri entered the University of Pisa and after preliminary studies chose to specialize in law. He soon transferred to natural sciences, and took his doctorate in June 1820. In the same year he published a paper on the theory of numbers which later impressed Charles Babbage, and in 1823 he was appointed professor of mathematical physics at Pisa. In the following year, since he wished to travel to France to try to obtain his father's release from prison, he used the excuse of ill health to free himself from his teaching duties at Pisa. He retained his title and salary for the rest of his life.

In summer 1825 Libri returned from France to Florence, and during the next five years he published various scientific papers and developed an interest in the history of science which led in due course to his *Histoire des sciences mathématiques en Italie* (1838–41), his major published work. In 1830 he went back to France, where he apparently became involved in the July revolution. At the end of the year he returned to Tuscany where he participated in a coup which failed; he fled to France and settled in December 1831 in Paris, where he remained until 1848. He was naturalized in February 1833, in March was elected a member of the Académie des Sciences, and in November 1834 became professor in the calculus of probability at the Sorbonne. In 1837 he was appointed a chevalier of the Légion d'honneur and in 1843 he succeeded in becoming a professor at the Collège de France.

Libri had been a bibliophile since his youth, and his research into the history of science increased his interest in bibliography and palaeography. He became an ardent collector of books and manuscripts, and (though he denied it) a dealer in them. There were at least eleven auction sales of material from his collections between 1835 and 1846.

The provincial libraries of France contained rich collections including material confiscated by the state from religious institutions during the French Revolution, but these libraries were very badly managed. Libri had worked in a number of them and he drew attention to their unsatisfactory state, so when, in 1841, the government set up a commission to supervise the creation of a *Catalogue général des manuscrits des départements*, Libri was appointed its secretary. Between 1841 and 1846 he visited many of the libraries himself and took the opportunity to steal many items. Thefts by him have been traced at Dijon, Lyons, Grenoble, Carpentras, Montpellier, Poitiers, Tours, Orléans, and Autun. He also stole from the Bibliothèque Royale and the Bibliothèque Mazarine in Paris and the Archivio Mediceo in Florence. Sometimes he took whole volumes and sometimes leaves or quires; both manuscripts and printed books fell victim to him. He disguised the provenance of stolen material by altering inscriptions, erasing stamps, and rebinding volumes.

The first anonymous accusation that Libri was a thief was made in 1842, and in December 1845 the Paris prefect of police was told that his thefts were common knowledge. Libri decided that it was time to dispose of his collection and because of the dubious provenance of some of the material he thought it advisable not to sell it in France. So at the end of 1845 he wrote to Antonio Panizzi, the keeper of printed books at the British Museum, with whom he had been on friendly terms since the 1830s. Panizzi replied that most of the printed books offered for sale were already in the museum, but that he would refer the lists of manuscripts to his colleague Sir Frederic Madden, the keeper of manuscripts. Madden was excited by the descriptions sent, and in March 1846 the trustees of the British Museum agreed that Madden and his assistant keeper John Holmes should visit Paris to inspect the manuscripts. They were much impressed and Madden estimated that the collection was well worth £9000 (Libri was asking £10,000). On his return to London Madden was disconcerted when Thomas Rodd, a leading bookseller, warned him that Libri's probity was doubtful, and that he was suspected of having stolen some of the manuscripts which he possessed. Despite this Madden still wished to acquire the collection, and the trustees asked the Treasury for the necessary funds. At the end of August the Treasury refused a grant. Madden then tried to negotiate with Libri through the dealers Payne and Foss, but in 1847 the collection was bought by the fourth earl of Ashburnham for £8000. This saved the trustees of the British Museum from much embarrassment when it was later proved that many of the items were stolen property.

In February 1846 the Paris prefect of police received a further accusation that Libri had stolen from a number of libraries, and he referred the matter to Félix Boucly, the *procureur du roi*. In February 1848 Boucly sent a confidential report to the minister of justice, who communicated it to Guizot, the foreign (and chief) minister, a friend of Libri, who told him about the report but took no further action. Later in the same month revolution broke out again and Guizot fled to England. The report on Libri's activities was discovered in his office, and in March the new republican government began an investigation. Libri escaped to England on 29 February with eighteen crates of his most valuable books and manuscripts, and was welcomed by Panizzi and other supporters, including the mathematician Augustus De Morgan.

In August 1848 Libri printed his *Réponse … au rapport de M. Boucly*, the proofs of which were read by Panizzi and Guizot. Panizzi urged Libri to return to France to defend himself in court, but when the case came to trial in June 1850 Libri failed to appear, and as no defence was presented he was found guilty and sentenced to ten years' imprisonment. His name was erased from the rolls of the Légion d'honneur, the University of Paris, the Collège de France, and the Académie des Sciences. Libri refused to admit defeat and retained the support of his friends. Prosper Mérimée in particular campaigned on his behalf, but all attempts to rehabilitate him, including a petition submitted to the French senate in 1860, failed.

As soon as he arrived in London in 1848 Libri began to work in the reading-room of the British Museum. Madden's attempt to have him excluded failed when the trustees accepted Panizzi's testimony in favour of Libri. In 1850 Libri obtained British citizenship, and on 25 April he married Mélanie, *née* Double, the widow of Athénodore Collin; he had known her since 1832. Libri was a keen observer of British affairs, and knew people in many walks of life. He again became an active dealer in books and manuscripts, and Sothebys held ten auctions of his material between 1849 and 1865. He was skilled in enhancing the sale value of what he had to offer, and he developed the art of compiling what Bernard Quaritch described as 'puffing' catalogues to a high degree (Barker, 175). Despite this, and despite his thefts, Libri 'must be reckoned among the great collectors and manuscript scholars of his century' (Maccioni, 302).

Libri's wife, Mélanie, died in 1865 and two years later he married a young Englishwoman, Helen de la Motte. His financial problems were growing, and his declining health required a warmer climate, so in 1868 Libri left England for Florence. He settled in a villa at Fiesole, where he died on 28 September 1869. His widow erected a monument to him in the cemetery of San Miniato al Monte, where he was buried.

After his death Léopold Delisle, *administrateur général* of the Bibliothèque Nationale from 1874, proved conclusively that Libri had stolen many items from French libraries. The 166 items in this category which the fourth earl of Ashburnham had purchased from Libri in 1847 were in 1888 acquired by the Bibliothèque Nationale from Trübner, the Strasbourg bookseller, who had bought them from the fifth earl. P. R. Harris

Sources P. A. Maccioni and M. Mostert, *The life and times of Guglielmo Libri* (1995) · P. A. Maccioni, 'Guglielmo Libri and the British Museum: a case of scandal averted', *British Library Journal*, 17 (1991), 36–60 · A. N. L. Munby, '"The earl and the thief" and "The triumph of Delisle"', *Essays and papers*, ed. N. Barber (1977), 175–205 · G. Fumagalli, *Guglielmo Libri* (1963) · D. Varry, ed., *Les Bibliothèques de la Révolution et du XIXe siècle, 1789–1914*, Histoire des bibliothèques françaises (1991) · N. Barker, *Bibliotheca Lindesiana* (1978) · minutes of the trustees' general meeting, BM, CE 1/7, vol. 7 · minutes of the trustees' standing committee, BM, CE 3/22, vol. 22 · letters to Antonio Panizzi, BL, Add. MSS 36714–36736 · F. Madden, diary, Bodl. Oxf., MS Eng. hist. c. 159–161

Archives Bibliothèque Nationale, Paris, MSS | BL, corresp. with Panizzi, Add. MSS 36714–36736 · E. Sussex RO, Ashburnham MSS

Likenesses Martini, lithograph, repro. in Maccioni and Mostert, *Life and times* · A. N. Noël, lithograph, Bibliothèque Nationale, Paris; repro. in *British Library Journal*, 17 (1991), 39

Lichefeld, William (*d.* **1448**), preacher and author, was probably born in the 1380s, as suggested by the fact that, already a BA, he was admitted to a fellowship at Peterhouse, Cambridge, on 13 October 1404; by April 1416 he was a BTh, and he later became DTh. 'Lichefeld' may be a genuine toponym rather than a family name. He had vacated his fellowship by 1 November 1420, when he was admitted to the rectory of Carlton Curlieu, Leicestershire, which he resigned in 1423. He afterwards became rector of All Hallows-the-Great, London, and so remained until his death. While rector of All Hallows, he assisted William Bingham in the foundation of Godshouse (later Christ's College), Cambridge, in 1446–7, and was one of the four London rectors who petitioned parliament in 1446–7 for more grammar schools in London. When Bishop Reynold Pecok (*d. c.*1459) defended non-preaching bishops in 1447, belittling the importance of preaching, Lichefeld was one of the 'preachers of the word of God, famous doctors in theology' (Gascoigne, 188) who opposed him under Dr William Millington's leadership. In all these activities, Lichefeld was associated with a group of London rectors and Cambridge theologians.

Lichefeld was an active and esteemed preacher. Licensed to preach as early as 1416, he is said to have left 3083 sermons in his own handwriting at his death. He preached at court, and he was admired as a preacher by Dr Thomas Gascoigne. Copies of his sermons and of his collection of *Mille exempla* were in the library of Syon Monastery. His surviving works are two, both of which aim to move to repentance and amendment of life: the English verse 'Compleynt of God' (ed. Borgström, 508–24, from Cambridge, Gonville and Caius College, MS 174/95) and the English prose 'De quinque sensibus', a part of the

Ancrene Riwle adapted to suit a general audience, with some additional matter (BL, Royal MS 8 C.i, fols. 122*v*–143*v*). Lichefeld died in London on 24 or 26 October 1448. He was buried in All Hallows-the-Great, where he was formerly commemorated by a brass with a Latin verse epitaph. R. M. Ball

Sources Emden, *Cam.* • M. Archer, ed., *The register of Bishop Philip Repingdon, 1405–1419*, 3, Lincoln RS, 74 (1982), 143 • Flemyng register, Lincs. Arch., Bp. Reg. 16, fol. 88*v* • Fordham register, CUL, Ely diocesan records, G/I/3, fol. 88*a–b* • episcopal register of Robert Gilbert, GL, MS 9531/6, fol. 209*v* • T. Gascoigne, *Loci e libro veritatum*, ed. J. E. Thorold Rogers (1881), 188–9 • C. L. Kingsford, *English historical literature in the fifteenth century* (1913), 296 • M. Bateson, ed., *Catalogue of the library of Syon Monastery, Isleworth* (1898) • *CPR, 1441–52* • *RotP*, 5.137 • J. Stow, *A survay of London*, ed. A. M. [A. Munday], rev. edn (1618), 434–5 • PRO, exchequer accounts various, E 101/409/16 • W. Lichefield, 'Compleynt of God', ed. E. Borgström, *Anglia*, 34 (1911) • A. C. Baugh, ed., *The English text of the Ancrene riwle edited from British Museum MS Royal 8. C. I.*, EETS, original ser., 232 (1956) • C. Brown and R. H. Robbins, *The index of Middle English verse* (1943), 2714

Archives BL, Royal MS 8 C.i., fols. 122*v*–143*v* • Gon. & Caius Cam., MS 174/95

Lichfield. For this title name *see* Stuart, Lord Bernard, styled earl of Lichfield (1622–1645); Lee, George Henry, third earl of Lichfield (1718–1772).

Lichfield, Leonard (*bap.* **1604**, *d.* **1657**), printer, was baptized on 12 April 1604 in All Saints' Church, Oxford, the son of John Lichfield (*d.* 1635) and his wife, Margaret (*d.* 1639). John Lichfield was admitted as a tavern keeper by the University of Oxford in 1605 and was appointed printer to the university and inferior bedell of law in 1617. As printer he was variously in partnership with William Wrench, James Short, and William Turner, and was responsible for the first four editions of Robert Burton's *Anatomy of Melancholy*. Leonard Lichfield was made 'privilegiatus' and was one of the superior bedells in 1630. On the death of his father, who was buried in All Saints' Church on 14 May 1635, Leonard succeeded to the office of printer to the university. His output consisted largely of theological works (some of them controversial), the official publications of the university, and its volumes of congratulatory verse. Lichfield appended his own English verses, adulatory of the king and queen and the royal family, to most of these, but Cromwell was accorded the same treatment in *Musarum Oxoniensium elaiophoria* in 1654. At this time Lichfield was esquire bedell of divinity. He printed the English translation of Bacon's *Of the Advancement of Learning* in 1640.

Following King Charles's occupation of Oxford in 1642 Lichfield printed a large number of the king's declarations and proclamations, and his name was several times used in counterfeit (London) editions. His printing house in Butcher's Row was destroyed by fire in October 1644. This event apparently interrupted one of the few scholarly editions of this period, the *Epistolae* of Ignatius, Polycarp, and Barnabas, which was completed later, probably by Henry Hall. Although Lichfield resumed printing, the king's defeat meant that after 1644 he was not paid for the official work he had done. In 1649 the council of state ordered him to enter into heavy recognizances not to print any seditious or unlicensed books.

Lichfield died in 1657 and was survived by his wife, Anne; the university's convocation appointed her and her son Leonard [*see below*] as printers to the university on 17 September 1658, and their names appear jointly and separately in imprints after that date. Anne Lichfield succeeded in recovering some at least of the debts owed by the crown to her late husband.

By a will made in November 1665 Anne Lichfield divided her printing materials between her sons **Leonard Lichfield** (*bap.* 1637, *d.* 1686) and William; her copyrights in books printed or to be printed she left to her youngest son, St John Lichfield. She lived, however, until 1671. When the court removed to Oxford in November 1665 the younger Leonard Lichfield printed the first twenty-three numbers of the *Oxford Gazette*, which was continued on the court's return to London in 1666 as the *London Gazette*. Lichfield was buried on 25 February 1686 in All Saints' Church, Oxford. He was succeeded in his printing house by his son Leonard, the third of that name, who died in 1744; he does not seem to have been officially printer to the university. R. Julian Roberts

Sources F. Madan, *Oxford books: a bibliography of printed works*, 3 vols. (1895–1931); repr. (1964) • H. R. Plomer and others, *A dictionary of the booksellers and printers who were at work in England, Scotland, and Ireland, from 1641 to 1667* (1907); repr. (1968) • H. Carter, *A history of the Oxford University Press*, 1: *To the year 1780* (1975) • indexes to Oxford parish registers, Oxford Central Library, Centre for Oxfordshire Studies • register of convocation, Oxf. UA, T26 • will, Oxf. UA [Anne Lichfield] • *CSP dom., 1644; 1649–50; 1661–2* • J. Griffiths, *An index to wills proved in the court of the chancellor of the University of Oxford* (1862)

Lichfield, Leonard (*bap.* **1637**, *d.* **1686**). *See under* Lichfield, Leonard (*bap.* 1604, *d.* 1657).

Lichfield, William. *See* Lichefeld, William (*d.* 1448).

Lichfild, Henry (*fl.* **1613**), composer, is known almost exclusively through his single published volume, *The First Set of Madrigals of 5 Parts, Apt for both Viols and Voices* (1613), and through the biographical information that may be gleaned from its dedicatory preface to Lady Cheyney of Toddington House near Luton, Bedfordshire. Jane Cheyne or Cheyney, daughter of Thomas Wentworth, first Lord Wentworth, had inherited the estate from her late husband, Henry Cheyne or Cheyney, first Baron Cheney (*d.* 1587), and Lichfild was in her service, possibly as her household steward. But she also actively encouraged Lichfild's work as a composer, carried out during 'some hours of the night', and his preface also reveals that his madrigals were performed 'by the instruments and voices' of her family. Evidently Lichfild was a devoted and trusted servant, for his mistress, who died in 1614, left him £20 in her will.

Lichfild composed his twenty madrigals exclusively in the light canzonet style naturalized into English music by Thomas Morley in the 1590s. His chosen texts were largely amorous effusions from within the pastoral tradition (whether the Daphne who figures in seven of these masked some real-life individual is unknown) and were consistently untroubled by serious or tragic issues; Lichfild made no attempt ever to mine that darker, more substantial musical vein opened principally by Thomas Weelkes and John Wilbye during the preceding fifteen years. That said, it must be conceded he handled this undemanding, anachronistic style very well; his music is highly fluent and literate, the text is always decently set, and the effect gratifying, if anonymous.

DAVID BROWN

Sources H. Lichfild, *The first set of madrigals* (1613), preface • *New Grove*, 2nd edn • E. H. Fellowes, *The English madrigal composers*, 2nd edn (1950) • GEC, *Peerage*

Lichtenberg, Georg Christoph (1742–1799), natural scientist and author, was born on 1 July 1742 in Ober Ramstadt, near Darmstadt, Hesse-Darmstadt, the youngest of the seventeen children born to Johann Conrad Lichtenberg, a Lutheran priest, and his wife, Henriette Catherine, *née* Eckhardt, the daughter of a Lutheran priest. He was baptized on the day of his birth for fear he would die, and curvature of the spine left him a hunchback. After tuition in the natural sciences from his father and attendance at the elementary school at Darmstadt (1752–61) he was enabled by his patron, the landgrave of Hesse-Darmstadt, to attend the University of Göttingen between 1763 and 1767. There he met several English students, beginning the connections with England which dominated his life. Having completed his studies he was appointed professor of mathematics and English at the University of Giessen. At the same time (1767–90) his employment as tutor to English children, including Thomas Swanton and William Henry Irby, brought renewed contacts with England, although he wrote later that he had 'die zehn schönsten Jahre meines Lebens mit der Zähmung von Engländern verloren' ('wasted the ten best years of my life taming Englishmen'; letter of 6 June 1796 to Paul Christian Wattenbach).

In 1770 and 1774 Lichtenberg toured English cities, notably London, visiting theatres, coffee houses, and museums, as well as attending trials and executions. In 1770, as the guest of Lord Boston, the father of his charge William Irby, he was presented at court, and met scientists such as Joseph Priestley, the astronomer James Ferguson, and the horologist John Harrison.

George III's patronage lay behind Lichtenberg's appointment as professor of philosophy and mathematics at the University of Göttingen on 23 June 1770. There he pioneered the teaching of the natural sciences through experiments, using scientific instruments from England by such notable makers as Peter Dollond, whom he met at his first audience with George III in 1770. His contact with English scientists led to his election to the Royal Society in 1793. On 5 October 1789 he married Margarete Elisabeth, *née* Kellner (1768–1848), the daughter of a painter and decorator from Nikolausburg, near Göttingen. He died as a result of his lifelong weakness of the lungs and heart on 24 February 1799 in Göttingen and was buried there on 28 February. He was survived by six of his children and his widow. In his modest estate the most notable items were his library and scientific instruments.

Georg Christoph Lichtenberg (1742–1799), by unknown engraver

Lichtenberg's evocative descriptions of English life, on the streets and at court, in his 'Briefe aus England' published in the *Deutsches Museum* in 1776 and 1778, were the first such portrayals in German literature. In his *Göttingische Taschen-Calender*, published annually between 1776 and 1798, he introduced Hogarth to a German audience, and his satirical commentaries on the artist profoundly influenced contemporaries such as Jean Paul. Between 1764 and 1796 he published his nine *Sudelbücher*, in which he described his readings of such British philosophers as James Beattie and David Hartley the elder.

Lichtenberg's works were not translated into English until after his death, and his main audience lay among German intellectuals and *Bildungsbürgertum*, the rising middle classes, anxious to widen their intellectual horizons. In the nineteenth century he was recognized as the principal mediator of English culture during the Enlightenment. The impetus behind all his writings was English life, and his concise satirical style, most memorably employed in aphorisms, can also be traced to English roots. The epigram 'Ich bin eigentlich nach England gegangen, um deutsch schreiben zu lernen' ('I really went to England to learn to write German'; *Schriften und Briefe*, vol. 2, epigram 144) neatly epitomizes the way in which his experience of English life and culture shaped not only his own writing but that of many who followed him.

JOACHIM WEIHL

Sources H. Gumpert, ed., *Lichtenberg in England*, 2 vols. (1977) • *Georg Christoph Lichtenberg, 1742–1799, Wagnis der Aufklärung* (1992) • M. Maurer, *Aufklärung und Anglophile in Deutschland* (1987) • W. Promies, *Georg Christoph Lichtenberg in Selbstzeugnissen und Bilddokumenten* (1964) • G. C. Lichtenberg, *Ausführliche Erklärung der Hogarthschen Kupferstiche* (1991) • G. C. Lichtenberg, *Schriften*, 2 vols.

(1907) • G. C. Lichtenberg, *Schriften und Briefe*, ed. W. Promies, 2 vols. (1971–80) • J. Paul, *Gesammelte Werke*, ed. E. Bevend (1935)

Likenesses J. W. Hensche, bust, 1815, Ober Ramstadt, Germany • H. C. Schwenterley, copper engraving, Städtisches Museum, Göttingen, Germany • J. L. Strecher, copper engraving, 1781182, Ober Ramstadt, Germany • engraving, NPG [*see illus.*]

Wealth at death 3000 thaler; plus 1000 thaler (est. value of library)

Lichton [Leighton], **Henry** (1369x79–1440), bishop of Aberdeen, was originally from the diocese of Brechin. The son of Henry and Janet Lichton, he was also a kinsman of Robert Stewart, duke of Albany, though their exact relationship is not known. He was a student at Orléans in 1394, and obtained a licentiate in civil law and a bachelorate of canon law (by 1409) and doctorates in civil law (by 1415) and in both laws (by 1436), the last possibly from St Andrews University. He pursued his studies in conjunction with an ecclesiastical career which had begun with the vicariate of Markinch, Fife, by 1392. Significant advancement, however, lay in north-east Scotland. He was canon of Moray at an unknown date and of Aberdeen by 1394; in 1395 he became archdeacon of Aberdeen, but he subsequently resigned the latter position, perhaps in favour of his appointment as rector of Kinkell, Aberdeenshire. He was certainly rector of this wealthy parish between 1409 and 1414, and may have used its revenues to fund his studies.

Despite presumably lengthy absences for study, Lichton maintained cordial relations with the leading local magnate, Alexander Stewart, and was present at Kildrummy Castle on 10 December 1404, when Stewart married Isabella, countess of Mar, whose first husband he was (implausibly) alleged to have murdered, and so became earl of Mar. Thereafter Lichton sometimes witnessed Mar's charters and in 1415 he obtained an annulment of the earl's second marriage. It was probably with Mar's approval that he was elected bishop of Moray in 1414 and translated to Aberdeen in April 1422. Lichton visited Valencia for consecration by the Avignon pope Benedict XIII on 8 March 1415. On that occasion Benedict appointed him to enter into discussions with the Scottish government regarding the ending of the schism. A modicum of other diplomatic work followed. In 1428 Lichton led an embassy to France concerning the renewal of the Franco-Scottish alliance and on 31 March 1434 he was formally received at the Council of Basel, though nothing is known of his activities there.

Lichton spent most of his later life in north-east Scotland. Both at Elgin and Aberdeen he supervised extensive building work on the cathedrals, and he has also been credited with authorship of legal and devotional texts which do not survive. He appears to have fathered at least one illegitimate daughter, Janet, who received a papal dispensation for her marriage in 1432. In 1439 Lichton was reportedly an infirm sexagenarian, and he died in 1440, probably on either 12 or 14 December, when his obit was celebrated. He was buried at St Machar's Cathedral, Old Aberdeen. DAVID DITCHBURN

Sources D. E. R. Watt, *A biographical dictionary of Scottish graduates to AD 1410* (1977), 360–62 • C. Innes, ed., *Registrum episcopatus Aberdonensis*, 1, Spalding Club, 13 (1845) • E. R. Lindsay, A. I. Dunlop, and others, eds., *Calendar of Scottish supplications to Rome*, 1–2, Scottish History Society, 3rd ser., 23, 48 (1934–56); 3, Scottish History Society, 4th ser., 7 (1970); 4 (1983) • C. Innes, ed., *Registrum episcopatus Moraviensis*, Bannatyne Club, 58 (1837) • *Hectoris Boetii murthlacensium et aberdonensium episcoporum vitae*, ed. and trans. J. Moir, New Spalding Club, 12 (1894) • E. W. M. Balfour-Melville, *James I, king of Scots, 1406–1437* (1936) • J. Robertson, ed., *Illustrations of the topography and antiquities of the shires of Aberdeen and Banff*, 4, Spalding Club (1862) • J. H. Burns, *Scottish churchmen and the council of Basle* (1962) • *CEPR letters*, 8.447

Likenesses effigy on tombstone, St Machar's Cathedral, Old Aberdeen

Lickbarrow, Isabella (1784–1847), poet, was born on 5 November 1784 at Market Place, Kendal, Westmorland, the first of four daughters born to James Lickbarrow (1751–1805), schoolmaster, son of Henry and Isabel Lickbarrow of Cautley, in the parish of Sedbergh, and his wife, Mary (1756–1790), daughter of Samuel and Mary Bristo, of Howburn, in the parish of Caldbeck in Cumberland. Her sisters were Rachel (*b.* 1786), Hannah (*b.* 1787), and Margaret (*b.* 1789). The families were all members of the Society of Friends.

Lickbarrow was given an excellent Quaker education, probably at the Friends' school in Kendal where her relative (first cousin once removed) John Dalton, the eminent scientist, taught before going to Manchester. Her mother died when she was five years old, and her father when she was twenty. She states that her first volume of poetry entitled *Poetical Effusions* (1814) was published in order to create a fund 'to assist the humble labours of herself and her orphan sisters which would increase their family comforts and better their condition in life'. The list of subscribers to *Poetical Effusions* included Wordsworth, Southey, and De Quincey. John Dalton bought four copies.

From 1811 to 1815 Lickbarrow wrote prolifically for the *Westmorland Advertiser*, a weekly broadsheet published in Kendal first by Isaac Steele, then by M. and R. Branthwaite. The Branthwaites were responsible for arranging the publication of *Poetical Effusions*. In 1818 Lickbarrow appeared as the author of another volume of poetry called *Lament upon the Death of Princess Charlotte, and Alfred, a Vision*. She continued to write for the *Monthly Repository* (1818), the *Lonsdale Magazine* (1820), the *Westmorland Advertiser and Kendal Chronicle* (1820–23), and the *Kendal Mercury and Westmorland Advertiser* (1837–40). Her work shows not only a great appreciation of the beauties of nature in the local countryside, but also contains humanitarian reflections on the Napoleonic war, the slave trade, and contemporary domestic life.

For a time Lickbarrow kept a school in Kendal with her sisters Margaret and Rachel until 1820 when her sisters were admitted to Lancaster Lunatic Asylum, suffering from what was described as hereditary melancholia. Both were discharged as cured in 1822, but Rachel was admitted on a further three occasions over the period 1829–35, having twice attempted suicide. *Notes and Queries* (17 February

1866) suggested that Lickbarrow herself had been admitted to the same asylum, but it has not proved possible to confirm this. Later in their lives their poverty was alleviated; when he died in 1844 John Dalton left in his will one-eighth of his entire estate in trust to the three sisters, '£900 divided in third equal parts to my relations Isabella, Rachel and Margaret Lickbarrow'. It is possible that he helped them financially throughout his life, since there is evidence that the Kendal Society of Friends was supportive.

Lickbarrow lived with her sisters in Greenhow Yard, Highgate, in Kendal; J. F. Curwen's *Kirkbie-Kendal* (1900) lists her address as 95/99 Soutergate, the east side—which was later known as Highgate. Curwen wrote that Greenhow Yard 'has always been considered one of the nicest in Kendal, the houses not being too rank, and by reason of the tall poplars that used to flourish there' (pp. 105–6). After Isabella's death in 1847, the 1851 census recorded Rachel and Margaret Lickbarrow still living in Highgate, described as annuitants, and in the *Kendal Directory* (1849) they are found in the list comprising the addresses of 'Clergy, Gentry, Partners in Firms not arranged under the classifications of Trades and Professions', and so were not regarded as being 'working-class' as has been suggested.

Isabella Lickbarrow died on 10 February 1847 at Underbarrow, Kendal. Her death certificate states that she died of atrophy, which was the contemporary description of an emaciating illness such as tuberculosis. She was buried in Castle Street burial-ground, Kendal, on 15 February 1847. CONSTANCE PARRISH

Sources C. Parrish, 'Isabella Lickbarrow, Lakeland Quaker poet: more facts', *N&Q*, 243 (1998), 200–02 • C. Parrish, 'Postscript on Isabella Lickbarrow, the "unlettered poetess"', *Wordsworth Circle*, 28 (1997), 70–72 • C. Parrish, 'Isabella Lickbarrow's relationship to John Dalton', *N&Q*, 244 (1999), 34 • C. Parrish, 'Isabella Lickbarrow: an "unlettered poetess"', *Charles Lamb Bulletin*, n.s., 106 (April 1999), 66–77 [a short biography] • C. Parrish, 'Isabella Lickbarrow to Lord Lonsdale: a newly discovered letter', *N&Q*, 244 (1999), 448–9 • Society of Friends, Quarterly Meeting of Westmorland, Register of births, marriages and burials, Cumbria AS, Kendal • I. Lickbarrow, *Poetical effusions* (1814); repr. (1994) • *Westmorland Advertiser and Kendal Chronicle, Kendal Mercury and Westmorland Advertiser*, Kendal Library • casebooks, 1821–45, Lancs. RO, Lancaster lunatic asylum papers, HRL/1–13 • admissions and discharges book, 1816–24, Lancs. RO, Lancaster lunatic asylum papers • physicians' report books, 1816–40, Lancs. RO, Lancaster lunatic asylum papers, QAM.1/30/11–15 • *N&Q*, 3rd ser., 9 (1866), 145 • will, Cumbria AS [John Dalton] • J. F. Curwen, 'Kirkbie-Kendal', 1900, Cumbria AS, Kendal, 105–6 • d. cert. • Wellcome L. ['Atrophy' definition] • Castle Street burial-ground, plan: Kendal, 1843–1983, CEM/KC. register no. 5, portion A—graves 24/25 P.5.2/3 • F. Nicholson and E. Axon, *The older nonconformity in Kendal* (1915), 484–5

Wealth at death impoverished; interest in legacy of £900 in trust from John Dalton: will [John Dalton], Cumbria AS, Ref D/DA/1 (1841 and 1843) • under will of aunt, Frances Lickbarrow, Isabella received a third of half the residue to be shared with her two sisters, which amounted to about £30 for each sister: Lancs. RO, Ref. WRW/K (1834)

Lidbury, Sir Charles (1880–1978), banker, was born on 30 June 1880 at the School House, Middlewich, Cheshire, the elder son of Frank Albert Lidbury and his wife, Emily Harding, who were both schoolteachers. He left school when he was thirteen, and in October 1893 applied in Winsford, Cheshire, to Parr's Banking Company, which was growing rapidly in industrial areas by amalgamations. For the rest of his working life Lidbury was employed by Parr's and the London County and Westminster Bank, into which Parr's itself was merged in 1918. The bank was called the Westminster from 1923, and it and the National Provincial joined in 1970 to form the National Westminster Bank.

Lidbury's whole career was characterized by concentrated energy, speed of work, and attention to detail—virtues which he strongly recommended to young bank staff in later years. He progressed through junior posts in Winsford and Sandbach, accompanied by studies at night school, to a major branch in Leicester. He became involved in Parr's amalgamations, and in 1908 his shrewd assessment of figures led to his being in charge of an investigation of the Whitehaven Joint Stock Bank before it was absorbed by Parr's.

His studies completed, Lidbury spent some leisure time in the local yeomanry (he rose to lance-sergeant), but in 1909 ended membership on his marriage to Mary Moreton, the daughter of George Moreton of Kinderton Hall, Middlewich. They had two daughters, and Lidbury from then on had few interests outside the world of finance, his family, and their home, Winter Field, Melbury Abbas, Shaftesbury, Dorset, where he described himself as a part-time farmer and developed some enthusiasm for agriculture. After a spell on the inspection staff, at the age of thirty-four he was made joint branch manager of the bank's Iron Gate branch, Derby, becoming one of Parr's youngest branch managers. Its later merger with Westminster took Lidbury to London, where his shrewdness and skills were valued.

The Westminster in 1913 had created the Westminster Foreign Bank (WFB) and opened branches in Europe, which were loosely controlled through officers of its main bank. Lidbury was made inspector of foreign branches (1919), and in that capacity came to realize that WFB was an ill-devised scheme, embarked upon without real information or intelligent foresight. He restored some unwise lendings, but also curbed future activities. In 1923 he was made superintendent of foreign branches, and in 1924 general manager of WFB—a post he held until 1947. In Westminster Bank itself, after instituting a then novel costing exercise, he became joint general manager in 1927. He helped wind up the Banco Italo-Britannic in 1929, uncovering unsavoury dealings in the process, and in 1930 rescued the ailing Anglo-South-American Bank (he was made a knight commander of the order of Al Morito of Chile) and also became Westminster's chief general manager.

Lidbury had grown up in an industrial district, and was critical of speculative investment in industry. He was not convinced of the long-term wisdom of bank-financed rescue of ailing firms and industries as the 1929–32 depression took its toll, and believed that ideally British commercial banks should be providers of short-term finance only. However, he conceded that in the depression it was necessary to prolong temporarily unrepayable advances, if only because there was little demand for new lendings. He was chairman of the chief executive officers' committee of the Committee of London Clearing Bankers from 1936 to 1947 (after his tenure the chairmanship rotated): during the Second World War he saw the necessity of financial regulation, and was instrumental in keeping it to a minimum. He served as president of the Institute of Bankers (1939–45) and was awarded a knighthood (1941). Lidbury's wife died in 1939. After his London flat was bombed in 1941, he took up residence in the basement strongroom of the Westminster Bank head office for the duration of the war.

By 1943 all the 'big five' clearing banks, acutely aware of mounting criticism of their policies, had begun to consider initiatives for post-war finance for small firms. Despite his later opposition to the Industrial and Commercial Finance Corporation (ICFC), Lidbury himself, at a Liberal Party dinner held in February 1943, surprisingly and influentially called for the creation of an industrial bank to help finance the small businessman. However, he and others were unhappy with the idea that smaller, inherently more risky firms in special areas should get preferential interest rates on loans as the government suggested. Government-sponsored schemes would, it was argued, have banks lending to 'the incompetent, the thriftless and the indolent' (Coopey and Clarke, 21).

A committee of senior managers from the clearing banks was set up, under the auspices of the Bank of England, to draft a blueprint for what later became the ICFC. Lidbury, who was described by a Bank of England official as 'the boss-cat of the clearing bank managers' (Coopey and Clarke, 22), played a dominant role in its proceedings. Despite his opposition, he conceded that 'the present political ferments' (ibid.) called for some response, while attacking what he believed to be an 'indirect levy on the resources of the commercial banks for the subsidising of commercial and industrial "adventures" in the interests of the "full employment" campaign' (ibid.). Lidbury wanted a committee of clearing bankers to vet all applications and ensure that interest rates were not below those offered to their own customers.

In May 1944 Lord Catto replaced Montagu Norman as governor of the Bank of England. Catto stated that he 'should like the great ideal to be attempted' (Coopey and Clarke, 23). After he managed to reassure the chief executives of the banks about their commercial anxieties 'there was a cordial exchange of letters with Lidbury' (Fforde, 721), and detailed discussions about the final shape of the new finance corporation got under way. Later known as 3i, it proved to be Britain's most successful venture-capital entity.

Lidbury was a Liberal supporter, averse neither to Keynesian-style public works in times of failing demand nor to social reform within limits set by the ability to pay. His entirely realistic appraisal of Britain's post-war indebtedness and need for exports, set out in his delayed inaugural address to the Institute of Bankers in October 1945 ('The economic consequences of the war'), was reprinted in a number of journals. He was, however, opposed to any form of bank nationalization, or, mindful of the 1930s, to public disclosure of banks' true profits and reserves, and maintained that banks did not control the economy: they reflected it. At once genial and intolerant, he schooled three men who were to become successively chief general managers of his bank. Unusually, while still Westminster's chief general manager, he was made a board member, but was trenchant in defence of the separation of policy making from execution by its managers. The bank was his to run, and run it he did until his retirement as chief general manager in 1947. He continued as a director until 1962, and hoped to live to be a hundred. He died following an accident at the Harnham Croft Nursing Home, Salisbury, on 25 July 1978. Aged ninety-eight, he had been looked after by his two daughters, who never married. MARGARET ACKRILL

Sources *The Times* (27 July 1978) · R. Coopey and D. Clarke, *3i: fifty years investing in industry* (1995) · J. Fforde, *The Bank of England and public policy, 1941–1958* (1992) · National Westminster Bank archives, London · A. W. Tuke and R. J. H. Gillman, *Barclays Bank Limited, 1926–1969: some recollections* (1972) · *WWW* · *CGPLA Eng. & Wales* (1978) · b. cert. · d. cert.

Archives National Westminster Bank archives, London

Likenesses photographs, National Westminster Bank archives, London

Wealth at death £246,522: probate, 30 Oct 1978, *CGPLA Eng. & Wales*

Liddel, Duncan (1561–1613), astronomer and teacher of medicine, was born in Aberdeen, and received his early education there, perhaps including a spell at King's College then its sole university. In 1579 he travelled to Germany and enrolled in the University of Frankfurt an der Oder, where he came under the tutelage of a fellow Scot, John Craig, and studied mathematics, philosophy, and a little medicine with him. In 1582 Craig returned to Scotland and became physician to James VI, and Liddel moved for a while to Breslau, where he made the acquaintance of the famous humanist Andreas Dudith and the noted astronomer and mathematician Paul Wittich (1555?–1587). After another spell at Frankfurt he went on to Rostock, and acquired there the degree of master of philosophy. He also formed firm friendships with Henrich Brucaeus (professor of medicine), Johannes Caselius (professor of rhetoric), and Cornelius Martini (a young protégé of Caselius). In 1590 Caselius moved to the University of Helmstedt, established fairly recently by the duke of Brunswick, as professor of Greek and practical philosophy; after a further brief stay in Frankfurt, Liddel, in company with Martini and some noble Livonian pupils, followed him there. Quite soon both Liddel and Martini gained chairs—the former in mathematics and the latter in logic.

During his time at Rostock, Liddel had made the acquaintance of the great Danish astronomer Tycho Brahe, and at least twice visited him at his observatory on the island of Hven. Later the friendship thus established turned to enmity when Brahe came strongly to suspect Liddel of plagiarizing his astronomical system, in which the sun rotated annually around the earth but the moon and the other planets circuited the sun. Caselius reported that, so far as he knew, Liddel was the first in Germany to teach astronomy according not only to the theories of Ptolemy and Copernicus, but also to Brahe's outline. Liddel always claimed that he gave Brahe full credit for his system, but he clearly added his own mathematical details, which was probably the source of the confusion.

In Helmstedt, Liddel continued his study of medicine, a more lucrative occupation than mathematics, and in 1596 received the degree of doctor of medicine. Although he did not formally become a medical professor until 1600, he was teaching the subject and presiding over disputations in it from at least 1597. Theses for the disputations, which may be taken to be the work of Liddel himself, were printed, and were later to form the basis of his two principal medical works, the *Ars medica* of 1607 and the *De febribus* of 1610. Another medical work, the *Ars conservandi sanitatem* (1651), was completed after Liddel's death by Patrick Dun, a former pupil who became principal of Marischal College, Aberdeen. These works were highly regarded but do not appear markedly original, although the first two give quite a sympathetic hearing to the novel opinions of Paracelsus.

In 1598 a major dispute blew up at Helmstedt, with an anti-philosophical diatribe by the conservative theologian Daniel Hoffmann, aimed particularly at Caselius and his associates. Together with Cornelius Martini, Liddel was firmly in the Caselian camp, and in 1601 he found it expedient to produce a printed open letter to the duke of Brunswick, defending himself against the charge of having calumniated Luther. In general Liddel steered clear of theological controversy, and, especially since he held high administrative offices in the university, it seems safe to assume that he at least outwardly conformed to the usually tolerant Lutheran environment at Helmstedt.

In 1607 Liddel returned to Scotland but little more is known of his activities, except for the generous benefactions that he arranged for the newly founded Marischal College. He endowed six bursaries and a chair of mathematics, and also bequeathed to it his books and mathematical instruments. Many of the books are still preserved in the library of the combined University of Aberdeen. He died in Aberdeen on 17 December 1613 and was buried there.

CHARLES PLATTS, *rev.* GEORGE MOLLAND

Sources J. Caselius, 'Epistola … Dn. Joanni Cragio', in D. Liddel, *Ars medica, succincte et perspicue explicata* (1607) • J. Stuart, *A sketch of the life of Dr Duncan Liddel, of Aberdeen, professor of mathematics and of medicine in the University of Helmstadt* (1790) • G. Molland, 'Scottish-continental intellectual relations as mirrored in the career of Duncan Liddel (1561–1613)', *The universities of Aberdeen and Europe: the first three centuries*, ed. P. Dukes (1995), 79–101 • A. G. Molland, 'Duncan Liddell, 1561–1613: an early benefactor of Marischal College library', *Aberdeen University Review*, 51 (1985–6), 485–99 • P. J. Anderson, *Notes on academic theses with a bibliography of Duncan Liddel* (1912) • G. Gray, *In memoriam cl. viri Duncani Liddelii medicinae doctoris et mathematum professoris celeberrimi* (1614) • P. J. Anderson and J. F. K. Johnstone, eds., *Fasti academiae Mariscallanae Aberdonensis: selections from the records of the Marischal College and University, MDXCIII–MDCCCLX*, 3 vols., New Spalding Club, 4, 18–19 (1889–98) • P. Zimmermann, *Album academiae Helmstadiensis*, 1 (1926) • H. Haase, *Die Universität Helmstedt, 1576–1810: Bilder aus ihrer Geschichte* (1976) • F. Koldewey, *Geschichte der klassischen Philologie auf der Universität Helmstedt* (1895) • D. Liddel, *Epistola…in qua respondet ad illa quae ipsi a Reverendissimo et Illustrissimo Principe ac Domino, Dn. Henrico Iulio Postulato Episcopo Halberstadense, Duce Brunsvicense & Lunaeburgense proposita fuerunt* (1601) • M. R. Antognazza, '*Hofmann-Streit*: il dibattito sul rapporto tra filosofia e teologia all'Università di Helmstedt', *Rivista di Filosofia Neo-Scolastica*, 88 (1996), 389–420
Likenesses memorial brass, St Nicholas Church, Aberdeen
Wealth at death considerable benefactions: Anderson and Johnstone, eds., *Fasti academiae Mariscallanae Aberdonensis*

Liddell, Adolphus George Charles (1846–1920), society figure and lawyer, was born at Bramham House, near Tadcaster, on 29 June 1846, the elder of the two sons of the Hon. Sir Adolphus Frederick Octavius Liddell (1818–1885), under-secretary at the Home Office, eighth son of the first Baron Ravensworth, and Frederica Elizabeth Lane-Fox (*d.* 1867). He had four sisters. Educated at Eton College and Balliol College, Oxford, he was called to the bar in 1871 and practised on the north-eastern circuit. Through his father's influence he served as secretary to three royal commissions. He developed a profound distaste for the practice of the law and welcomed his appointment in 1886 as chief clerk to the crown office in chancery. He became assistant secretary in the Lord Chancellor's Department in 1888, which office he held until his retirement in 1919. He also served as private secretary to the lord chancellor from 1909 to 1915.

An unremarkable official career was enlivened by his social connections and a complex personal life. 'Doll' Liddell belonged to the set known as the Souls, through whom he met both of the women he hoped to marry, Laura Tennant (1862–1886) [*see under* Lyttelton, Alfred] and Edith Balfour (*d.* 1948), and the man who married them, Alfred Lyttelton (1857–1913). Captivated by Laura Tennant's 'mixture of innocence and mischief' (Liddell, 225), he enjoyed a passionate and physical (if unconsummated) affair with her from their first meeting in 1884 until some time after her engagement to Alfred Lyttelton was announced in January 1885. Three years later he became involved with Edith Balfour, a more conventional young woman, who also declined to marry him despite a shared physical attraction, and subsequently married Lyttelton, who had been widowed in 1886. Liddell, who remained unmarried, published a volume of closely observed recollections in 1911 under the title *Notes from the Life of an Ordinary Mortal*. He died on 12 August 1920, at his home, 6 Seville Street, Chelsea, London. K. D. REYNOLDS

Sources A. G. C. Liddell, *Notes from the life of an ordinary mortal* (1911) • P. Jalland, *Women, marriage and politics, 1860–1914* (1986) • J. Abdy and C. Gere, *The Souls* (1984) • R. F. V. Heuston, *Lives of the lord chancellors, 1885–1940* (1964) • Burke, *Peerage* • A. Lambert, *Unquiet Souls: the Indian summer of the British aristocracy, 1880–1918* (1984) • *WWW* • d. cert.
Archives U. Hull, Brynmor Jones L., corresp. with Lady Wenlock
Likenesses J. M. Cameron, photograph, 1864–7, NPG; repro. in Liddell, *Notes*, frontispiece • J. M. Cameron, photograph, 1865–9, repro. in Abdy and Gere, *The Souls* • J. M. Cameron, photograph,

Adolphus George Charles Liddell (1846–1920), by Julia Margaret Cameron, *c.*1867

*c.*1867, National Museum of Photography, Film and Television, Bradford [*see illus.*]

Wealth at death £23,784 6*s.* 9*d.*: probate, 27 Oct 1920, *CGPLA Eng. & Wales*

Liddell, Alice Pleasance. *See* Hargreaves, Alice Pleasance (1852–1934).

Liddell [*née* Clavering], **Ann** (*bap.* **1686**, *d.* in or after **1734**), political commentator, was baptized on 21 April 1686 at Chopwell, Ryton, co. Durham, the second of the three children of John Clavering (1655–1702), a landowner, of Chopwell, and his first wife, Ann (*b.* 1655), the daughter of Sir Henry Thompson, a merchant and MP, of York and Escrick, Yorkshire, and his first wife, Jane, the daughter and coheir of Richard Newton of York. John Clavering was married second to Elizabeth (*d.* 1703), the daughter and coheir of Thomas Hardwick of Potter Newton, Yorkshire; they had five children. Ann's elder sister, Mary Clavering (1685–1724) [*see* Cowper, Mary], later became a lady to the bedchamber of Caroline, princess of Wales, and married Lord Cowper in 1706. The family was in many ways typical of the lesser gentry in co. Durham at the end of the seventeenth century, deriving a modest but respectable income from a small estate on the Durham coalfield while cultivating an influential network of family and business connections that stretched from Tyneside to the inns of court in London. By marriage, the Claverings were connected with many of the leading families in north-east England, and Ann inherited a secure position within this charmed circle, confident that 'My Birth, Education, & Caract[er] make me Equal to the Best' (Ann Liddell to Mary Cowper, 19 Aug 1718, Herts. ALS, Panshanger MSS, D/EP F.195, fols. 6–7).

John Clavering's untimely death in 1702 not only left the Chopwell estate financially encumbered but also delivered it into the hands of the court of chancery until the heir, Ann's half-brother John Clavering (1698–1762), came of age in 1719. In the meantime responsibility for both the children and the estate devolved on their cousin James Clavering (1680–1748) of Lamesley and Greencroft, co. Durham, and on their two elder sisters. Ann, who was named as their legal guardian in 1706 on Mary's marriage, fought tooth and nail for the interests of 'my boy Jacky' and his sisters, scraping together the considerable sums that were spent on their upkeep and education while plunging headlong into the highly competitive business of the coal trade on which so much of the estate's income depended. Her sharp intelligence cut through the intricate web of disputed contracts and endlessly delayed accounts which had, she suspected, allowed unscrupulous dealers, factors, and tenants to divert the profits of Clavering-Stella colliery into their own pockets: 'A virago I know I shall be call'd, but I care not. I am conceited … and fancy I could understand my trade as well as many coal-owners' (Ann Clavering to James Clavering, 11 May 1711, *Correspondence of Sir James Clavering*, 122). She clearly thought that James Clavering in particular lacked resolution in dealing with the slippery and ruthless characters who operated in this notoriously risky industry, and never ceased to warn him of the need to account for every penny that passed through his hands as trustee of the estate. 'If this [advice] spurr you not', she wrote in 1712, 'the Guardian must sew the Trustees' (Ann Liddell to James Clavering, 25 Nov [1712], ibid., 124). It was probably little consolation that she proved all too accurate a prophet; the battle for control of Clavering-Stella raged on in the courts long after the colliery itself had gone out of production and long after John Clavering had reached his majority.

Ann's warnings, however, had a distinct benefit to the historian, since they prompted James Clavering to preserve an almost complete run of her letters from May 1708 until her marriage on 14 July 1711, after which she stood down as Jacky's guardian in favour of her husband, Henry Liddell (*c.*1673–1717), the third son of Sir Henry Liddell (*c.*1644–1723), of Ravenscroft Castle, co. Durham. During this time she lived in London with her aunt Alithea Thompson (*b.* 1666), the wife of Charles Allanson (*c.*1662–1729), of St Andrew's, Holborn, at the heart of an extensive and influential social network based mainly on family and business connections in north-eastern England but which also owed a great deal to her sister's marriage into the highest level of whig politics. Ann's own political convictions were passionate and outspoken: she gloried in her 'whigish phylosophical resolution' and 'daring spirit', despising every 'confounded Tory' but directing her fiercest insults against 'those Hell Hounds who stile themselves church-men' (Ann Clavering to James Clavering, 2

June 1709, 19 Sept, 3 and 31 Oct 1710, *Correspondence of Sir James Clavering*, 32, 97, 100–01). With complete indifference to the very real danger that her letters might fall into the hands of her political opponents, she regaled James Clavering with vivid accounts of the latest political intrigues, both at Westminster and at court, demanding in return news of fiercely contested election battles and lawsuits from the north-east. She cheered on the whig gentry of co. Durham in their battles with Nathaniel, Lord Crewe, bishop of Durham, and with the predominantly tory corporation of Newcastle upon Tyne—'a parsell of worthless fellows'—collecting the names of 'true and zealous friends' whom she hoped to promote through her interest with Lord Cowper (Ann Clavering to James Clavering, 10 and 26 June 1708, ibid., 7–8). Some of her letters, especially those on the Sacheverell trial of 1710, are of first-rate importance, since few other contemporary commentators combined her sharp observation, outspoken candour, and privileged access to the highest political circles. However, the correspondence as a whole should be valued as an insight into the close connections in this period between local and national politics, as the network of north-eastern whigs in London interacted with their friends and relatives at home on their estates and in the constituencies to pursue their common political interests.

The triumph of the whig cause with the succession in 1714 of 'the greatest prince in meritt, the universe can boast of' (Ann Liddell to James Clavering, 14 Aug 1714, *Correspondence of Sir James Clavering*, 128) should therefore have marked a turning-point in Ann Liddell's life, and so in a way it did. Unfortunately it seems to have been a downward turn. As her sister's fortunes rose, so Ann became increasingly resentful of her own comparatively modest wealth and status, accusing the Cowpers of failing to promote her husband to a sufficiently lucrative position, while they in turn accused her of ingratitude. Relations deteriorated still further after Henry Liddell's death in 1717 left her a childless and increasingly embittered widow, neglected by 'my son' John Clavering and his sisters, and forced to defend her husband's reputation against charges that he had mismanaged the estate's affairs. The sharpness and spirit which had seemed among her most attractive qualities in her youth were now more commonly ascribed to 'ill nature' (Margaret Clavering to Mary Cowper, 23 Aug 1718, Herts. ALS, Panshanger MSS, D/EP F.197, fol. 47) and, although she remained on good terms with her cousin James Clavering, by the 1720s she was embroiled in a bitter lawsuit against her husband's partner and closest friend, William Cotesworth of Gateshead, whom she had always disliked. The last known reference to her occurs in 1734 in a rather chilling estimate of the 'contingents' of the Ravenscroft estate, where it was assumed that her jointure of £190 a year would revert to her husband's family within ten years (Grand allies account book, 1727–38, North of England Institute of Mining and Mechanical Engineers, shelf 18, fols. 94–5). In one of her last surviving letters she described 'living upon dependance [as] to me great misery' (Ann Liddell to James Clavering, 29 Nov 1726, *Correspondence of Sir James Clavering*, 133), yet the flow of forthright commentary on her political and social world continues unabated in this final glimpse of her forceful personality.

J. M. Ellis

Sources *The correspondence of Sir James Clavering*, ed. H. T. Dickinson, SurtS, 178 (1967) • Herts. ALS, Panshanger MSS, D/EP F.193–197 • *The letters of Henry Liddell to William Cotesworth*, ed. J. M. Ellis, SurtS, 197 (1987) • Clavering letter-book, U. Newcastle, Robinson L., MM10 • E. Hughes, 'Some Clavering correspondence', *Archaeologia Aeliana*, 4th ser., 34 (1956), 14–26 • *Diary of Mary, Countess Cowper*, ed. [S. Cowper] (1864) • R. Surtees, *The history and antiquities of the county palatine of Durham*, 4 vols. (1816–40) • E. Hughes, *North country life in the eighteenth century*, 1 (1952)

Archives Herts. ALS, Panshanger MSS • Herts. ALS, Cowper MSS • U. Newcastle, Clavering correspondence

Liddell, Edward George Tandy (1895–1981), physiologist, was born on 25 March 1895 at Harrogate, Yorkshire, the second in the family of two sons of John Liddell, physician, of Harrogate, and his wife, Annie Louisa, *née* Tandy. His first three winters were marred by life-threatening bouts of pneumonia, which left him with a permanently damaged heart. As a result he had to limit his way of life and managed to escape further serious illnesses. Liddell was educated at two local dame-schools before being sent to Summer Fields, Oxford, in 1905. In 1909 he won a scholarship at Shrewsbury, but chose instead to go to Harrow, where he spent two years on the classical side before going over to science. He lived for six months in Germany before entering Trinity College, Oxford, in October 1914 to read medicine. He took a first-class degree in physiology in 1918, was elected to a senior demyship at Magdalen, and went for his clinical training to St Thomas's Hospital, qualifying BM, BCh (Oxon.) in 1921. A year before he qualified he had had a tentative offer of a research fellowship at Trinity, coupled with an assistantship to Charles Sherrington, then Waynflete professor of physiology. These appointments he took up in 1921. He married in 1923 Constance Joan Mitford, daughter of Bertram Mitford Heron Rogers, physician, of Bristol. They had three sons, one of whom died in 1978, and one daughter.

Already as an undergraduate Liddell had come under Sherrington's spell and had learned, unlike the majority of undergraduates, to derive inspired instruction from his notoriously difficult lectures.

Sherrington was president of the Royal Society from 1920 to 1925 and had to spend much time in London. Much, therefore, of the responsibility for their experiments necessarily devolved on Liddell, Sherrington's sole collaborator. As he was a beginner, and self-effacing almost to a fault, his contribution was inevitably overshadowed by Sherrington's: but his share in their classic researches went well beyond the level of consummate experimental skills. Their collaboration began at a turning-point in studies of reflex action, when Sherrington's interest was moving away from exteroceptive reflexes as items of animal behaviour and towards the cellular basis of synaptic excitation and inhibition, conceived as summing algebraically at the post-synaptic membrane. The exteroceptive reflexes were elicited by graded electrical stimulation of afferent nerves in spinal and decerebrate animals; the synaptic actions were detected by quantitative high-speed myography. The classical discovery of the proprioceptive stretch reflex was important because it could be elicited only by a pure physiological stimulus, minimal lengthening of a muscle; and because of its essential role in reflex posture. This work and its further development were summarized in the monograph *Reflex Activity of the Spinal Cord* (R. S. Creed, D. Denny-Brown, J. C. Eccles, E. G. T. Liddell, and C. S. Sherrington, 1932). The preface acknowledged Liddell's special editorial role. From 1930 onwards his experiments were concerned with the control of postural reflexes by impulses descending from different areas of the brain—work of special relevance to the understanding of 'spinal shock' in patients with lesions of the spinal cord.

Liddell was elected FRS in 1939 and Waynflete professor of physiology in 1940. In 1960 he published *The Discovery of Reflexes*. With the insights of an experienced neuroscientist combined with a scholarship equally at home in French, German, and eighteenth-century Latin, he traced the slow growth of knowledge and ideas about the nervous system that set in relief the revolution which Sherrington had brought about. In 1975 Liddell was awarded the Osler memorial medal for the science, art, or literature of medicine.

Liddell's college pupils held him in respectful awe. Those who penetrated his formidable reserve were rewarded by interesting tutorials and lifelong friendship. His university lectures lacked showmanship but those who stayed the course found that his reviews had been up to date and his laconic comments ahead of their time. As professor he had to run a shortened preclinical course that could be taught by the few demonstrators who remained in Oxford during the Second World War. After the war the old laboratory was overwhelmed by the resumption of honours work for unprecedented numbers of undergraduates. Liddell presided over the appointment of new demonstrators and the building of the new laboratory. As chairman of the organizing committee of the XVII International Congress of Physiologists which met in Oxford in July 1947 he coped with the many frustrations of the immediate post-war period. From 1930 to 1960, in spite of precarious health, he served on council and other university committees, served as external examiner, as member of the council of the Royal Society, and on the committee and the editorial board of the Physiological Society. He was chairman of the Oxford Eye Hospital.

Liddell died in a nursing home in Witney, Oxfordshire, on 17 August 1981. C. G. Phillips, *rev.*

Sources C. G. Phillips, *Memoirs FRS*, 29 (1983), 333–59 • personal knowledge (1990)

Archives RS, corresp. • U. Oxf., Centre for Cognitive Neuroscience, corresp. and papers, mainly relating to Sir C. S. Sherrington

Likenesses W. Stoneman, black and white photograph, 1946, RS archives, Box 3, no. Z 2296B • Vandyk, black and white photograph, before 1967, RS archives, Box 3, not numbered • P. Chandler, photograph, repro. in *Memoirs FRS* • A. C. Cooper, black and white photograph, RS archives, Box N101, not numbered

Wealth at death £104,516: probate, 6 Nov 1981, *CGPLA Eng. & Wales*

Liddell, Eric Henry (1902–1945), missionary and athlete, was born in Tientsin (Tianjin), China, on 16 January 1902, the second son in the family of two sons and a younger daughter of the Revd James Dunlop Liddell, a Congregational missionary from Drymen, Stirlingshire, and his wife, Mary Reddin, a trained nurse from Paxton in Berwickshire. His early childhood was spent at the mission station in the village of Siaokuan (Xiaoguan), southern Hebei. In 1907, at the age of five, he was brought back to Scotland, where he attended, first, the village school in Drymen, and, from 1908 to 1920, the School for the Sons of Missionaries in London (later Eltham College). At school both he and his elder brother (Robert Victor) excelled at sports; in 1919 Eric set a new (and still unbroken) school record of 10.2 seconds for the 100 yards. In 1920 he matriculated at Edinburgh University for a BSc degree in pure science. As a student he broke the Scottish records for the 100 and 200 yards, and set a new record for the inter-universities 440 yards (50.2 seconds). His electrifying speed earned him seven international rugby caps for Scotland as a wing three-quarter. He was selected to run in the 100 and 200 metres in the 1924 Olympics in Paris, but declined to run in the 100 metres on religious grounds, because the heats were to be run on a Sunday. He won the bronze medal in the 200 metres, and then had a spectacular and unexpected victory in the 400 metres to take the gold medal in a world record time of 47.6 seconds (10 July 1924).

Liddell graduated from Edinburgh University a few days later (17 July) and enrolled at the Scottish Congregational college in Edinburgh to read divinity for a year, for he had long since decided to devote his life to missionary work, like his parents. He spent the year immersed in student evangelical activities, speaking all over Scotland at weekends. In the summer of 1925 he took part in his last athletics meeting in Scotland, where he won the Scottish Amateur Athletics Association titles in the 100, 200, and 440 yards, before leaving to take up an appointment as a missionary teacher at the Anglo-Chinese College in Tientsin. He developed athletics at the college, and continued to run at meetings in China.

In 1931–2 Liddell returned to Scotland on furlough in order to be ordained as a Congregational minister. In 1934 he married Florence, who had trained in Canada as a nurse, the twenty-one-year-old daughter of Hugh McKenzie, a Canadian missionary at Tientsin. They had three daughters, but he never saw his third daughter; she was born in Canada after the upheavals of the civil war and the Japanese invasion of China had persuaded Liddell to send his pregnant wife and young children to safety in 1941.

Meanwhile, Liddell had been working as a field missionary in war-torn Siaokuan. He wrote *The Sermon on the Mount: for Sunday School Teachers* (1937), and back in Tientsin he worked on *A Manual of Christian Discipline*, to be translated into Chinese for the guidance of Chinese pastors, and published *Prayers for Daily Use* (1942). In 1943 he and his missionary colleagues were interned by the Japanese in a

Eric Henry Liddell (1902–1945), by unknown photographer, 1924

camp in Weihsien, Shantung. They were officially internees, rather than prisoners, and life, although monotonous and full of deprivation, was not brutal. Liddell was remembered by survivors for his modesty, his unfailing good humour, and his exemplary Christian conduct throughout their time there—and despite his strict sabbatarian principles he even refereed hockey matches on Sundays, for the sake of the youngsters with little else to do. He died in Weihsien on 21 February 1945 of a brain tumour. The story of his athletic triumphs was retold in the film *Chariots of Fire* (1981).

MAGNUS MAGNUSSON, *rev.*

Sources S. Magnusson, *The flying Scotsman* (1981) · D. P. Thomson, *Scotland's greatest athlete: the Eric Liddell story* (1970) · *CCI* (1946)
Archives FILM BFI NFTVA, sports footage
Likenesses photograph, 1924, Hult. Arch. [*see illus.*] · photographs, Hult. Arch.
Wealth at death £2415 8*s*.: confirmation, 17 Oct 1946, *CCI*

Liddell, Guy Maynard (1892–1958), intelligence officer, was born on 8 November 1892 at 64 Victoria Street, London, one of three sons of Augustus Frederick Liddell, a retired captain in the Royal Artillery, and his wife, Emily Shinner (*d.* 1901). At the time of his birth, Liddell's father worked in the royal household and was comptroller and treasurer to Prince and Princess Christian of Schleswig-Holstein. He studied in Germany, but then served in the Royal Field Artillery during the First World War and was awarded an MC. Having abandoned a promising career as a cellist, Liddell joined Scotland Yard's special branch in 1919 as a subordinate to Sir Basil Thompson in the directorate of intelligence. He was responsible for co-ordinating the police raid on the Arcos building in Moorgate in May 1927 (which also housed the Soviet trade delegation), in pursuit of a missing classified RAF document. Although the document was not recovered, more than enough evidence was found of Soviet espionage, which was enhanced by the unexpected defection of a terrified code clerk, Anton Miller, who had been detained while attempting to burn incriminating files.

In October 1931, following an amalgamation in Whitehall, Liddell moved with his small team of civilian analysts to the Security Service, MI5, and was appointed deputy director of counter-espionage under Brigadier Jasper Harker. His first great success came late in 1936 when he went to Washington, DC, to inform the Federal Bureau of Investigation (FBI) that a Dundee hairdresser, Mrs Jessie Jordan, was acting as a post-box for German intelligence and relaying letters to and from an address in New York. An immediate FBI investigation identified an immigrant, Gunther Rumrich, as a German spy, and allowed J. Edgar Hoover to take the credit for arresting an extensive transatlantic espionage network.

Following the success of this first example of co-operation with the FBI, Liddell supervised a brilliant coup in which a long-term MI5 agent, Olga Gray, penetrated the Communist Party of Great Britain and gained the confidence of its national organizer, Percy Glading. She accumulated proof that Glading had been recruiting sources inside the Woolwich arsenal, and when the spy ring was arrested in January 1938, three of its members pleaded guilty to stealing secret blueprints and were sentenced to long terms of imprisonment. The case demonstrated the value of cultivating deep-cover agents, and highlighted the threat of Soviet espionage, although it failed to link the spies with any Soviet officials.

Liddell was promoted to director of B division in June 1940 and played a key role in the appointment of his subordinates, including Dick White and Anthony Blunt, who were both to become close friends. His reliance on personal contacts led him to choose some impressive intellectual talent, and B division effectively took control of the enemy's entire espionage organization in Britain. This extraordinary achievement, documented by Sir John Masterman in *The Double Cross System* (1972), resulted in numerous future High Court judges and university dons running a large stable of double agents, thereby providing the deception planners with a reliable conduit into the German high command. Thus Liddell was closely associated with two of MI5's most spectacular accomplishments, the interception and decryption of German intelligence signals by the Radio Security Service, and the famous 'double cross system'. The Radio Security Service had grown, under Liddell's supervision, from an inter-service liaison committee known as the Wireless Board into a sophisticated cryptographic organization that operated in tandem with Bletchley Park, concentrating on *Abwehr* communications, and enabling MI5 case officers to monitor the progress made by their double agents through the reports submitted by their enemy controllers to Berlin.

Liddell had many Irish connections, having married

Guy Maynard Liddell (1892–1958), by unknown photographer [detail]

Lord Revelstoke's daughter, the Hon. Calypso Baring, in 1926, and he selected his brother Cecil to head MI5's highly successful Irish section. His marriage, however, was to cause him great unhappiness and it was dissolved in 1943 after Calypso had deserted him for her American half-brother, leaving Liddell to fight a long battle for custody of their son and three daughters.

In December 2002 Liddell's wartime diaries, typewritten in twelve volumes, were released at the Public Record Office. They provide 'an unrivalled account of the internal workings of MI5 from August 1939 to June 1945' (*Sunday Times*). The day-to-day workings of the Security Service are richly documented, including the unmasking of traitors such as John King, a Foreign Office clerk, who passed information to the Soviet Union. The diaries also record more lurid planning: a year before the war in Europe ended, Liddell was discussing a scheme to threaten Germany 'with the uranium bomb' (ibid.) if it fired V2 rockets.

After the war Liddell was appointed deputy director-general under the new Labour administration's choice of Sir Percy Sillitoe, and he remained in that post until 1953 when, embarrassed by the defection of his friend Guy Burgess, he took early retirement to become security adviser to the Atomic Energy Authority. After a remarkable career in counter-espionage, it was ironic that several of his closest friends were to be exposed as spies, among them the Welsh academic Goronwy Rees, for whose son he was godfather. Before Rees died in 1979 he denounced Liddell as a spy, and the disclosure that Liddell had failed to act against Anthony Blunt when Rees had first named him in 1951 created a furore that, together with his unwise friendships and his preference for homosexual company, posthumously wrecked his reputation as a shrewd intelligence professional. His principal legacy to the Security Service is a collection of diaries recording his daily activities during his career. Highly classified, and code-named Wallflowers, the document remains the most comprehensive historical account of MI5's clandestine operations.

Guy Liddell was appointed CBE in 1944 in recognition of his contribution to allied counter-intelligence and made a CB in 1953. He died on 2 December 1958 at his home, 18 Richmond Court, Sloane Street, London.

NIGEL WEST

Sources J. C. Masterman, *The double-cross system in the war of 1939 to 1945* (1972) · A. Masters, *The man who was M* (1984) · F. H. Hinsley and C. A. G. Simkins, *British intelligence in the Second World War*, 4: *Security and counter-intelligence* (1990) · C. Andrew, *Secret service: the making of the British intelligence community* (1985) · N. West, *MI5: British security service operations, 1900–1945* (1981) · J. Crossland, 'MI5 planned to threaten Hitler with A-bomb', *Sunday Times* (1 Dec 2002) · *CGPLA Eng. & Wales* (1959) · *WWW* · b. cert. · d. cert. · *The Times* (6 Dec 1958) · W. P. Coates and Z. K. Coates, *A history of Anglo-Soviet relations*, 2 vols. (1958) · R. Deacon, *The greatest treason: the bizarre story of Hollis, Liddell and Mountbatten*, rev. edn (1990)

Archives U. Leeds, Brotherton L., photograph and sketch albums

Likenesses photograph, Hult. Arch. [*see illus.*]

Wealth at death £28,258 4*s*. 6*d*.: probate, 5 Feb 1959, *CGPLA Eng. & Wales*

Liddell, Henry, **first Baron Ravensworth** (*bap.* **1708**, *d.* **1784**), politician and coal owner, was baptized on 1 August 1708 in Lamesley, co. Durham, the eldest son of Thomas Liddell (*c.*1680–1715) and his wife, Jane (1679–1774), the daughter of James Clavering of Greencroft, co. Durham. Both families were prominent north-eastern coal owners. Liddell succeeded his paternal grandfather, Sir Henry Liddell, as fourth baronet in 1723 and went to Peterhouse College, Cambridge, in 1725. Following a grand tour in the early 1730s, on 27 April 1735 he married Anne (1712–1794), the daughter of a former lord mayor of London, Sir Peter Delmé, and his first wife, Anne Macham.

In 1726 Liddell was one of the original signatories of the grand alliance, a cartel of Tyneside coal owners that came to dominate the production and sale of coal in the area. By 1750 the alliance was at the peak of its power, controlling sixteen of the twenty-seven Durham collieries that produced for the sea-going trade. Although it later declined in dominance, the alliance outlived its original organizers and remained a force in the industry into the nineteenth century.

Liddell pursued a parliamentary career that spanned nearly fifty years and included membership in both houses. He was first elected as a member for Morpeth in 1734, and was raised to the peerage as Baron Ravensworth in 1747. He was an active parliamentarian, attending regularly and speaking occasionally. While he was always solicitous of the interests of his fellow coal owners, he made his political reputation as an independent whig. He started out as a follower of Sir Robert Walpole and later supported the Pelhams, but often showed an independent streak. On occasion in the 1740s he clashed with William Pitt the elder on the issue of Hanoverian troops. Later, in

1778, he was one of a handful of peers to oppose the annuity bill for Pitt's heirs.

Ravensworth's best-known intervention in politics came in 1753, when, prompted by an anonymous memorial from Horace Walpole, he accused several of those in charge of the education of the prince of Wales—Andrew Stone and William Murray, together with James Johnson, the bishop of Gloucester—with having been Jacobites. The charge caused a sensation and was investigated by the cabinet. It was found to be groundless, and Ravensworth emerged as one who seemed both sincere and gullible. It did not, however, break him of the habit of raising politically awkward questions. In 1763 the duke of Newcastle characterized him as a 'Wild Man' when he moved for financial accounts of the war in Germany (BL, Add. MS 32947, fol. 164, 3 March 1763); he was ultimately dissuaded from dividing the upper house by the prospect of being a minority of one. By this time he was regarded as a political eccentric, respected for his honesty but viewed as erratic in his judgement. Shortly after his motion for the accounts, George III, in a letter to Lord Bute on 11 March 1763, used Ravensworth as an example of the sort of man he considered unfit for office.

At times Ravensworth espoused populist causes. He became a staunch early supporter of John Wilkes: Lord Ilchester described him on 3 May 1765 as 'so zealous for Wilkes that he is half mad' (BL, Add. MS 51421, fol. 41). In 1766 he pressed the Chatham administration for a bill to allow the import of rye and rye meal to alleviate the suffering of the common people of the north-east.

In 1756 Ravensworth's only child, Anne (*d*. 1804), married Augustus Henry Fitzroy, earl of Euston (1735–1811). During the 1760s the rise of his son-in-law, by then the duke of Grafton, to a position of importance gave Ravensworth closer connections to those at the highest level of politics. He, however, continued his independent course, voting both for and against Grafton's hard-pressed administration during the spring of 1767. His daughter later eloped with John Fitzpatrick, second earl of Upper Ossory (1745–1818), whom she married after her marriage to Grafton was dissolved in March 1769.

After 1770 Ravensworth increasingly inclined towards opposition. He often opposed the North administration's colonial policy and the resultant war in America. He was also strongly critical of the government's handling of the Gordon riots. He supported economical reform in 1782, and Shelburne listed him on 6 May 1782, in a letter to George III, as among 'the most independent people' who supported the Contractor's Bill (Shelburne to George III, *Correspondence of King George the Third*, 6.8–9).

Ravensworth died on 30 January 1784 and was buried on 8 February at Lamesley. His widow survived him by ten years, and died on 12 June 1794 at their house, 13 St James's Square, London. The peerage became extinct on Ravensworth's death, but the title was revived in 1821 in favour of the son of his nephew and heir.

WILLIAM C. LOWE

Sources H. Walpole, *Memoirs of the reign of King George the Second*, ed. Lord Holland, 2nd edn, 3 vols. (1847) • E. Hughes, *North country life in the eighteenth century*, 1 (1952) • M. W. Flinn and D. S. Stoker, *The industrial revolution: 1700–1830* (1984), vol. 2 of *The history of the British coal industry* (1984–93) • J. B. Owen, *The rise of the Pelhams* (1957) • T. S. Ashton and J. Sykes, *The coal industry of the eighteenth century*, 2nd edn (1964) • GEC, *Peerage* • Cobbett, *Parl. hist.* • *The correspondence of King George the Third from 1760 to December 1783*, ed. J. Fortescue, 6 vols. (1927–8) • HoP, *Commons, 1715–54* • *Letters from George III to Lord Bute, 1756–1766*, ed. R. Sedgwick (1939) • *IGI* • J. Ingamells, ed., *A dictionary of British and Irish travellers in Italy, 1701–1800* (1997) • *Political Magazine and Parliamentary, Naval, Military and Literary Journal*, 2 (1781), 589

Archives Durham RO, estate and legal MSS • Gateshead Central Library, family MSS • Tyne and Wear Archive Service, Newcastle upon Tyne, family letters and papers | BL, Holland House MSS, Add. MS 51421 • BL, corresp. with duke of Newcastle, Add. MSS 32695–32958, *passim* • North of England Institute of Mining and Mechanical Engineers, Newcastle, Grand Allies collection • Northumbd RO, Newcastle upon Tyne, letters to Matthew Ridley

Wealth at death £5000 (fourth largest estate in Durham): *Political Magazine*, 589

Liddell, Henry George (1811–1898), lexicographer and dean of Christ Church, Oxford, was born at Binchester, co. Durham, on 6 February 1811, the eldest son of the Revd Henry George Liddell (1787–1872), and his wife (and first cousin), Charlotte Lyon (*d*. 1871), niece of the ninth earl of Strathmore. The Liddells were a noble northern family, and had acquired their estates (nearly 14,000 acres in 1883) in Northumberland and Durham from the Gascoignes in 1607, and a baronetcy in 1642; their principal seats were Ravensworth Castle, Gateshead, and Eslington Park, near Alnwick. Liddell's uncle, his father's older brother, was the fifth baronet (created Baron Ravensworth in 1821). One of his own brothers was the noted railway engineer Charles Liddell (1813–1894).

Liddell was said by his biographer to have retained something of a northern accent throughout his life, (Thompson, *Liddell*, 103), although he spent almost all his life in the south. After an unhappy period (1815–23) at a private school, Bishopton Grove, near Ripon, he spent six years (equally detested) at Charterhouse (1823–9) under the headmastership of John Russell. He proceeded in 1829 to Christ Church, Oxford, becoming a student in December 1830 when the absentee canon, Dr Dowdeswell, gave his turn as nominator to Dean Samuel Smith.

Liddell's tutor was Robert Biscoe; his termly reports were among the best ever secured at Christ Church: his marks were almost always *optime*, *bene*, and *satis bene*, sinking only once to the mere *satis* with which lesser men had to be content (Christ Church archives, 11.b.4, 279). Liddell's immediate future was assured by his inevitable first classes in classics and mathematics in 1833; he considered applying for fellowships at Merton and Balliol colleges, but became a tutor of Christ Church in January 1836 and was ordained priest in June 1838.

The Greek–English Lexicon Liddell began the great work of his life in the 1830s: the first edition of the *Greek–English Lexicon* edited by him and Robert *Scott (1811–1887), who had gained his studentship and then his first class at the same time as Liddell, appeared in 1843. Various people are

Henry George Liddell (1811–1898), by Julia Margaret Cameron, 1865

credited with spurring the pair to embark on this daunting task: the Oxford bookseller D. A. Talboys, who apparently suggested a new lexicon based on that first compiled in 1819 by the German Franz Passow (*d.* 1833); William Sewell, fellow of Exeter College and later founder of Radley College, who had examined both Liddell and Scott; and Dean Gaisford who also offered vital stimulus. Details of the early editions tell a story of immediate success: the print run steadily increased from 3000 for the first edition to 15,000 for the sixth (1869), while the price fell from 42*s.* to 30*s.*

Passow's name was omitted from the title-page in the fourth edition (1855); the seventh (1883) was the first revised by Liddell alone; the eighth (1897) was the last by Liddell's own hand; these editions were reprinted twice and four times respectively; the ninth, extensively revised by Sir Henry Stuart-Jones and R. McKenzie 'with the cooperation of many scholars' was completed in 1940 and reprinted seven times. Liddell and Scott tried in successive revisions to take account of newly published texts; throughout many scholars provided information to improve the work (examples are in Christ Church Library MSS). The 1968 supplement took account of inscriptions and papyri, though it excluded material from the Linear B tablets. A second supplement (1996) was a revision of the supplement of 1968, and included the Linear B material. A tenth edition of the *Lexicon* itself is envisaged.

On Liddell's death, the novelist and poet Thomas Hardy (who had taught himself Greek and witnessed the conferment of Liddell's honorary DCL in 1893) wrote a poem, 'Liddell and Scott: on the Completion of their Lexicon', celebrating their feat. It begins:

> 'Well, though it seems
> Beyond our dreams,'
> Said Liddell to Scott,
> 'We've really got
> To the very end …'

Liddell and Scott had already been the subject of doggerel in their lifetimes:

> Two men wrote a lexicon, Liddell and Scott;
> Some parts were clever, but some parts were not.
> Hear, all ye learned, and read me this riddle,
> How the wrong part wrote Scott, and the right part wrote
> Liddell.

Whatever the shortcomings of particular editions, from the outset the *Lexicon* has been held in the highest repute throughout the world; no rival has appeared in any country, and schoolchildren have found the abridgements invaluable.

Liddell's early years at Christ Church also provided the first signs of his lifelong interest in art: Ruskin, who matriculated in 1837, wrote of him that 'he was the only man in Oxford among the masters of my day who knew anything of art' (*The Works of John Ruskin*, ed. E. T. Cook and A. Wedderburn, 39 vols., 1903–12, 35.204). Liddell was soon to serve on the delegacy which chose Cockerell as architect for what became the Taylor Institution and the Ashmolean Museum; Liddell's interest—and prejudices—in architecture dominated much of his work as dean, but his admiration for Ruskin waned in later years as he became increasingly irritated by Ruskin's behaviour. However, Ruskin's description of Liddell in *Praeterita* (chap. 11) as a 'nobly-presenced Englishman' was the first of many evoked by his friend's lifelong dignity of bearing.

In Christ Church, Liddell was reader in Greek from 1838 to 1845, and junior censor from December 1845 for less than a year. In the university he was appointed a select preacher in 1842 and 1847, and White's professor of moral philosophy in 1845–6; he was elected proctor for 1846–7. His reputation spread to London, where he was appointed Whitehall preacher (1845) and domestic chaplain to Prince Albert (1846). His marriage on 23 July 1846 to Lorina (*d.* 1910), daughter of James Reeve of Lowestoft, required the vacation of his studentship in 1847, and he gladly accepted the headmastership of Westminster School offered him by Dean Gaisford, who thus once again furthered Liddell's career.

Headmaster of Westminster School At Westminster (1846–55), Liddell suffered from the initial handicap of being a Carthusian; but the dignity of his bearing and the respect which he gained for his zeal as headmaster and lexicographer enabled him to raise the level of the school and improve its buildings within and without. The silver vase presented to him by the boys on his departure is shown in the *Illustrated London News* for 13 October 1855. His pupil H. L. Thompson, writing in 1899, and a recent historian of the school, John Field, agree in seeing a crisis in the development of Westminster in the early 1850s: a severe outbreak of typhoid which affected the Liddell family as well as the boys, and failure of the numbers seeking admission to rise thereafter, led for some years to serious discussion of the desirability of a move to a site in the country away from London, as Liddell was to advocate to the public schools commission in 1861–2. Liddell and Lord John Russell, sometimes with Prince Albert, inspected on horseback various possible sites, but in vain (Field, *The King's Nurseries*, 1987, 66).

Dean of Christ Church, Oxford Liddell was already known for his work on the history of Rome, to be published in two volumes in 1855, and was urged in 1849 to seek the Oxford regius chair of modern history, vacated by the death of J. A. Cramer. In 1850 he was appointed to the first Oxford University commission, and as a Liberal played a leading part—he missed only one of the eighty-seven meetings—in the compilation of its report. When Dean Gaisford died on 2 June 1855, Liddell's recent record made him the obvious successor, much desired by Oxford Liberals such as Jowett; Palmerston's announcement of Liddell's appointment in the House of Commons on 6 June was greeted with cheers.

A letter written on the same day by a Christ Church pupil and friend, Lord Elcho (later eighth earl of Wemyss), suggests that in his view the college faced a crisis in its relations with the class which had sent its young men there: 'I feel confident that in your hands Christ Church will hold out every possible inducement to us to send our sons there, in the full confidence that you will turn them out *gentlemen* and useful members of society'—a reference, no doubt, to Gaisford's notoriously bearish manners. (Elcho, however, sent none of his sons to Christ Church.) Another nobleman many years later was clear that the new reign had begun badly: according to Algernon Mitford (later Lord Redesdale), an undergraduate from 1855 to 1858, the new dean

> was a singularly handsome man, and a great figurehead. But he was not popular. The undergraduates resented his treatment of them as schoolboys; he could not quite shake off the schoolmaster attitude of his Westminster days, and this led to some follies, and worse than follies. Rebellion was rife, the lecture room was gutted, and the furniture destroyed; a kettle of gunpowder with a fuse attached to it was hung upon the door of the deanery, but was fortunately discovered in time. A subscription was got up to pay for the damage …, and the malefactors were rusticated; for the first year the condition of things was deplorable—after that they mended. But the Dean, in spite of his wife's judicious help, never in my time commanded the sympathy of 'the House'. (Lord Redesdale, *Memories*, 1915, 1.100)

There was clearly more here than the failure of a former headmaster to conform to the Oxford collegiate scene; according to one contemporary, H. A. Harvey, Liddell as a young tutor had by some been thought 'rude and haughty' (Thompson, *Liddell*, 47). Certainly he did sometimes evince an attitude of galling superiority: a telling example is recorded by P. W. Acland in his account of Liddell's condescension to Acland's own baronet father, who received it mildly (J. B. Atlay, *H. W. Acland*, 1903, 37). None the less, with contemporaries Liddell did form close friendships, notably with Acland himself, Ruskin, Halford Vaughan, and A. P. Stanley, of whom the first two had known him as undergraduates and the others were colleagues on the commission.

It was no easy task that Liddell assumed in 1855. There was no constitutional problem between bishop and dean at Oxford as there had been at Westminster between dean and headmaster; but Liddell's original canonical colleagues were strongly conservative in outlook, and only one canon, A. P. Stanley, who arrived in 1858, was in any way an ally of the new dean. Fortunately, Liddell himself did not hold violent opinions on the theological controversies then agitating Oxford (Thompson, *Liddell*, 45), or even on the British Association debate of 1860 in Oxford. On the other hand, Liddell's activities on the Oxford University commission meant that much remained to be done in reforming Christ Church itself in pursuance of the act which had resulted from that commission's report.

Liddell was seriously ill with pneumonia in 1856, and was forced to recuperate in Madeira; after his return he began a long programme of improvements in both cathedral and college, beginning with the cathedral and putting through in 1862–5 the construction of Meadow Buildings for which the dean and chapter had been accumulating funds since 1809. In 1862 he laid out the Broad Walk immediately to the south of Meadow Buildings. (The Long Walk followed in 1872.) In 1869 Liddell allowed the destruction in the college's New (1776) Library of delicate plasterwork by Henry Keene of Dublin which was less pleasing to him than the Rhenish Gothic of Meadow Buildings, built by T. N. Deane of Cork.

In the constitutional sphere the ordinances of 1858 applied to Christ Church some of the provisions of the Oxford Act of 1854. New tutors were appointed, some of them very successful ones, who broke the former near-monopoly of Christ Church tutorships held by men not always of outstanding merit who had gone from Westminster School to the House itself. Admissions rose from an average of fifty-five in each of Gaisford's five last years to one of sixty-two in Liddell's first ten. The improving standard of tutors had early results. Liddell's support for the institution of readerships in chemistry and physics and the appointments of A. G. V. Harcourt (1859) in chemistry, and A. W. Reinhold (1869) and R. E. Baynes (1872) in physics, initiated an era of growing success in scientific teaching and research. Liddell soon rationalized the arrangements at dinner in Christ Church hall: in November 1862 he banished from the high table the noblemen who had there occupied the place thenceforth assigned to their tutors, the Students (i.e. fellows).

As the work on Meadow Buildings finished Liddell was faced by a demand from the senior students for a share of power; this was led by T. J. Prout (1823–1909)—'the man who slew the Canons'—and backed by the two censors. For two years the energies of dean, canons, and students (meeting behind closed doors in the Great Quadrangle) were fastened on this one matter which was referred to five distinguished referees under the chairmanship of Archbishop C. T. Longley. Liddell's own attitude during this period was 'startlingly passive' (W. O. Chadwick, *EngHR*, 87, 1972, 646), and the main initiatives were not his. The solution was worked out by dean, canons, and students at meetings on four days of February 1867; here the dean's role was central, especially during meetings on 5 and 6 February, when the canons agreed to a loss of power which had been theirs for over three centuries and the students gained power which they had not previously had. The result was embodied in the Christ Church, Oxford, Act of 1867, which brought into being a unique educational institution in which the dean presided over a mixed governing body of canons most of whom were also professors and of students (the equivalent of fellows in other colleges), most of whom would soon cease to be in Anglican orders. The new body first met on 16 October, and from the outset Liddell had no difficulty in controlling it, quelling discussion, according to tradition, with a cough. He found leisure during meetings to make highly artistic sketches on pink blotting paper (collected afterwards by his biographer and others; examples are in Christ Church Library).

E. S. Talbot provides a somewhat critical glimpse of Christ Church and Liddell in the later 1860s: Christ Church

> was not then in very stimulating condition. Its government was in the hands, as Dean, of Henry George Liddell, a high-bred gentleman of lofty character, a man of unusual artistic sympathy and cultivation, certified to all of us as a great scholar by his work on the Lexicon; but too much aloof and temperamentally too reserved and distant to have much influence with the undergraduates, and not a man to put energy into the religious life of the place. (E. S. Talbot, *Memories of Early Life*, 1924, 31–2)

In 1870 Liddell was tested by 'the great Library riot'. On the night of 10 May 1870 members of Loder's Club gained entry to the New Library of Christ Church (truly new territory for many of them), found it full of statues, placed them in a circle in Peckwater Quadrangle outside, lit bonfires between them, and damaged them. Liddell rose to the occasion and the culprits were identified. The dean addressed the governing body in a speech the text of which has been preserved (printed in W. G. Hiscock, *A Christ Church Miscellany*, 1946, 99–101; copy in Christ Church archives): replete with historical allusion and social analysis, it confirms much of what Redesdale was to print in 1915, and does not touch on the discontents voiced by Talbot in 1924. The dean announced the punishments (eight expulsions, rustications, and gatings) all inflicted on well-born culprits.

In the early 1870s Liddell was at his most active. In Christ Church he turned his attention to the cathedral and to the adjacent corner of the Great Quadrangle. The former was restored by George Gilbert Scott, and the dean used a vacancy in a canonry to drive a twin-tunnel entrance to the cathedral from the quadrangle, thus creating two vertical stone surfaces which were to provide excellent locations for memorials of Christ Church men who died in two world wars. The cathedral bells were necessarily moved from their place above the crossing, first to a temporary structure (given various opprobrious names by critics) east of Christ Church hall and then to a new belfry tower built at that same point by G. F. Bodley. Liddell had the windows of Christ Church hall reglazed by a firm at Frome, removing the eighteenth-century glass installed by Dean Gregory; but the new glass was the least successful of Liddell's works, and lasted little longer than a century. The 'tunnel' and 'meat-safe' were satirized in pamphlets of 1872–3 by C. L. Dodgson, who ignored, however, the sickly green of the windows.

Liddell was increasingly seen as an important representative of Oxford opinion. Gladstone, who occasionally holidayed with Liddell in north Wales, consulted him on Oxonian and church appointments during his premierships. From 1870 to 1874 the dean was vice-chancellor, the first from Christ Church since the 1690s; his letters to the chancellor, Lord Salisbury, were succinct and pertinent, fully adequate for the business in hand. The experience left him still friendly to reform: he presided at the deanery on 1 February 1875 over a meeting of mostly liberal heads of houses and others which requested the appointment of a new commission to draw up statutes for the university and colleges. Salisbury offered him a place on this but eventually Liddell declined.

Two days before the meeting of 1 February 1875 Liddell was held up to derision in *Vanity Fair*: 'Jehu Junior', in a sarcastic comment on a somewhat cruel Spy cartoon of Liddell, thought him not unprepared for his high positions:

> he has discovered himself to be an amateur in art, and has produced sketches much admired by his friends. And finally he has so comprehended the relative importance of men and things as to believe most thoroughly in the necessity for maintaining the British Aristocracy as a superior and privileged race. His reign at Christ Church will be remembered as a pleasant one by all influential persons who have adorned 'the house' in his time. Dignified in appearance and with much superficial sternness of demeanour, he has yet never made his discipline uncomfortable, and has often tempered it with breakfasts and croquet-parties of much distinction. He is sixty-three years of age, fine-looking, and thoroughly domesticated. (*Vanity Fair*, 30 Jan 1875)

The last word probably echoed an unofficial version of a 'Balliol rhyme':

> I am the Dean, and this is Mrs Liddell;
> She is the first and I the second fiddle.

The above criticisms, though a mixture of journalistic spleen, undergraduate grievance, inter-collegiate rivalry, and mere jealousy, may suggest a not altogether happy reign, and there was tension even as late as the 1880s (in the matter of R. W. Macan); but Liddell remained at Christ Church, and turned down offers from Gladstone of the deanery of Durham in 1881 and of that of Westminster two years later. Lord Elcho's hopes were fulfilled, and Christ Church did indeed continue to recruit from the nobility and gentry, and received members of the royal family itself in the prince of Wales, his Danish brother-in-law, and his brother Leopold. The number of annual matriculations fluctuated but in the 1880s reached a peak of over eighty, about the same as in the 1650s, 1820s, 1890s, and later. In his last years as dean, Liddell devoted himself to his tasks as assiduously as ever. Despite other claims on his time he found an hour each evening for the *Lexicon*; not only that, as a delegate of the university press he furthered the publication of works of scholarship by Max Müller, York Powell and Gúdbrand Vigfússon, and James Murray. For thirty-three years (1858–91) he was a powerful member of hebdomadal council, and also a most active chairman of the university galleries where he secured a large programme of listing and repair of exhibits. Nor was his activity limited to university and college: in the city of Oxford he was among those who did much to improve the river and its banks. He paid one penalty for his preoccupation with the *Lexicon* and other matters. His ability to travel was much restricted: for instance, he visited Athens only once and Rome never (Thompson, *Liddell*, 85). In Britain, refuges available to him included Charlton Kings near Cheltenham, and a new house, Penmorfa, near Llandudno.

Liddell's Oxford career may occasion speculation about apparent inconsistencies in his character. Very high intellectual skills, a capacity for sustained hard work, and an ability to keep steadily in view long-term objectives, went with a frequent reluctance to take a public stand in theological or political controversy. For instance, though Dodgson in 1864 had chosen to dub him a 'relentless reformer', in university affairs Liddell was ultimately a disappointment to Oxford liberals. It may be that his preference, strengthened perhaps by some aristocratic aloofness, was rather to dominate others in conversation or in an assembly in which he had a defined place. He knew how to govern, and did not intend to be diverted from his cathedral-college and its complex artistic needs, the *Lexicon*, or his family.

In his eighty-first year, 'conscious of various infirmities incident to advancing years', Liddell announced in a dignified letter to the prime minister, Lord Salisbury, on 8 August 1891 his intention of resigning the deanery from the end of that year. He retired to Ascot Wood House, and after a serene retirement died there on 18 January 1898. He had been a member of Christ Church for over sixty years, and had served as dean for thirty-six, longer than any other man has ever done; he had helped, unobtrusively, to bring in a new, unique, and still enduring constitution, beautified the cathedral, built a major addition to the quadrangles, and furthered the cause of learning in disparate spheres. He became an honorary student of Christ Church in 1892, and a DCL of the university in 1893 (he was made an LLD of Edinburgh in 1884). He is commemorated at Westminster by a boarding-house (Liddell's) in Dean's Yard built in 1956, in Oxford by the Liddell Building completed by Christ Church and Corpus Christi College jointly in 1991, and in the learned world by the scholarship of the *Lexicon*.

The Liddells had five sons (two of whom died in infancy) and five daughters. In 1873 a pamphlet entitled *Cakeless* (by John H. Jenkins, an undergraduate at Christ Church during 1873–4) satirized the Liddells for their zeal in attempting to secure good marriages for their three eldest daughters, Lorina, Alice *Hargreaves (immortalized by Lewis Carroll), and Edith. Edith, however, died aged twenty-two in 1876. She and her father are buried outside the south wall of the sanctuary of the cathedral; he wrote the anguished inscription, 'Ave, dulcissima; dilectissima, ave', on a tablet in the south aisle which commemorates her.

J. F. A. Mason

Sources H. L. Thompson, *Henry George Liddell, D.D., dean of Christ Church, Oxford: a memoir* (1899) • H. L. Thompson, *Christ Church* (1900) • W. R. Ward, *Victorian Oxford* (1965) • E. G. W. Bill, *University reform in nineteenth-century Oxford: a study of Henry Halford Vaughan, 1811–1885* (1973) • E. G. W. Bill and J. F. A. Mason, *Christ Church and reform, 1850–1867* (1970) • H. C. Harley, 'Sir Henry Acland and his circle', *Oxford medicine: essays on the evolution of the Oxford Clinical School to commemorate the bicentary [sic] of the Radcliffe Infirmary*, ed. K. Dewhurst [1970], 63–75, esp. 73–5 • J. Gattegno, *Lewis Carroll: une vie* (1974), 127–36 • F. Max Müller, 'Dean Liddell: as I knew him', *Fortnightly Review*, 71 (1899), 10–24 • R. Hewison, *Ruskin and Oxford: the art of education* (1996), catalogue, no. 4 • Gladstone, *Diaries* • P. W. Kent, *Some scientists in the life of Christ Church, Oxford* (2001) • A. C. Amor, 'Dean Liddell and his family', *The Carrollian*, 2 (1998), 28–54 • S. H. Goodacre, 'The printed works of H. G. Liddell', *The Carrollian*, 2 (1998), 55–61 • *Hist. U. Oxf.* 7: *19th-cent. Oxf. pt 2*

Archives Christ Church Oxf., corresp. and papers • Christ Church Oxf., papers relating to affairs of governing body and tutors | Bodl. Oxf., letters to H. W. Acland and S. A. Acland • Bodl. Oxf., letters to Friedrich Max Müller • Bodl. Oxf., corresp. with H. H. Vaughan • LPL, letters to A. C. Tait • NL Scot., corresp. with Lord Rosebery • U. Nott. L., letters to J. E. Denison

Likenesses G. Cruikshank, portrait, 1839 • G. Richmond, crayon drawing, 1858 • attrib. Hills & Saunders, photograph, 1863, NPG • J. M. Cameron, photograph, 1865, NPG [*see illus.*] • G. F. Watts, oils, 1875, Christ Church Oxf. • H. R. Hope-Pinker, marble bust, 1888, NPG; version, Westminster Abbey, London • H. von Herkomer, oils, 1891, AM Oxf. • C. Dressler, stone statue, 1893, Christ Church Oxf., Deanery Tower • Ape [C. Pellegrini], caricature, chromolithograph, NPG; repro. in *VF* (30 Jan 1875) • Hills & Saunders, photograph, carte-de-visite, NPG • W. Holl, stipple (after G. Richmond), NPG • group photographs (with family), Christ Church Oxf.

Wealth at death £68,125 12*s*. 8*d*.: resworn probate, 22 Feb 1898, *CGPLA Eng. & Wales*

Liddell, Henry Thomas, **first earl of Ravensworth** (**1797–1878**), politician, was born at Ravensworth Castle on 10 March 1797, the eldest son of Sir Thomas Henry Liddell, sixth baronet (1775–1855), who was created Baron Ravensworth (of the second creation) on 17 July 1821, and Maria Susannah, daughter and coheir of John and Anne Simpson of Bradley. His father was a patron of George Stephenson, and rebuilt Ravensworth Castle in 1808 from designs by John Nash. Other sons were General George Augustus Liddell, a groom-in-waiting to the queen, and deputy ranger of Windsor Great Park; and Sir Adolphus Frederic Octavius Liddell (1818–1885), who was appointed permanent under-secretary of state for the Home department by Lord Derby in 1867. A son of Henry George Liddell, rector of Easington (the first baron's brother), was Henry George Liddell DD, dean of Christ Church. The first baron's father, Sir Henry St George Liddell (1749–1791), made an eccentric journey to northern Scandinavia in 1786—probably in consequence of a wager—of which an account, with plates by Thomas Bewick, was published in 1789 by Matthew Consett, one of his companions.

Henry Thomas Liddell was educated at Eton College and at St John's College, Cambridge, where, though he did not graduate, he became a good classical scholar. He married, on 9 November 1820, Isabella Horatia (1801–1856), eldest daughter of Lord George Seymour and his wife, Isabella; they had five sons and eight daughters. In February 1826 he unsuccessfully contested Northumberland as a tory. At the general election in June that year, after a poll of fifteen days, in which great sums of money were spent, Liddell and Matthew Bell were returned. He represented North Durham from 1837 to 1847, being unopposed in 1841. In 1852 he unsuccessfully contested South Shields, and from 1853 until 7 March 1855, when on the death of his father he succeeded to the peerage, he sat for Liverpool. On 21 November 1826 he moved the address in the House of Commons, and he frequently spoke on the tory side. Although he voted for Catholic emancipation, he steadily from 1829 opposed the movement for parliamentary reform; he voted with the protectionists in 1846, and he strongly disapproved of the disestablishment of the Irish church in 1869. On 2 April 1874 he was created earl of Ravensworth and Baron Eslington.

Ravensworth was very popular in Northumberland, although in later life he found himself out of sympathy with the contemporary developments of Conservatism. He published, in addition to speeches, *The Wizard of the North, and other Poems* (1833), *Poems* (1877), and several works on Horace and Virgil, and contributed papers to *Archaeologia Aeliana*. He died suddenly at Ravensworth Castle on 19 March 1878 and was buried at Lamesley.

W. A. J. ARCHBOLD, *rev.* H. C. G. MATTHEW

Sources GEC, *Peerage* · Boase, *Mod. Eng. biog.* · *The Times* (20 March 1878) · *Newcastle Daily Chronicle* (20 March 1878)

Archives BL, corresp. with Sir Robert Peel, MSS 40391–40600 · Bodl. Oxf., letters to Benjamin Disraeli · Durham RO, letters to Lord Londonderry and Lady Londonderry · Lpool RO, letters to fourteenth earl of Derby · NL Scot., letters to Blackwoods · W. Yorks. AS, Leeds, corresp. with George Canning

Wealth at death under £45,000: probate, 21 May 1878, *CGPLA Eng. & Wales*

Liddell, Sir John (1794–1868), naval medical officer, was born at Dunblane, Scotland, in 1794. After entering the navy as an assistant surgeon in 1812, he served in France, North America, Portugal, and the West Indies. He graduated MD at Edinburgh University in 1822 and became LCS (Edin.) in 1821.

Appointed surgeon of HMS *Asia* in 1826 Liddell served with distinction at the battle of Navarino in the following year. Around this time he became director of the hospital at Malta, where he remained for many years. In 1831 he was awarded the first Gilbert Blane medal for the journal which he kept at Malta but which remained unpublished. In 1837 he married Fanny, second daughter of Robert Clement Sconce; they had at least two sons. Fanny's sister Catherine was married to the naturalist Thomas Thomson.

In 1844 Liddell was appointed inspector of fleets and hospitals, and was afterwards deputy inspector-general of the Haslar Hospital and inspector-general of the Royal Naval Hospital at Greenwich. He was appointed director-general of the medical department of the Royal Navy in 1854 and held the appointment throughout the Crimean War; he retired in 1864.

Liddell held several foreign orders, including the Russian imperial order of St Anne, and the Greek order of the redeemer. He was elected FRS in 1846 and in 1859 became honorary physician to the queen. He was knighted in 1848 and made CB in 1850 and KCB in 1864. He died at his home at 72 Chester Square, London, on 28 May 1868, and was buried in the cemetery of the Royal Naval Hospital, Greenwich, on 2 June.

W. A. J. ARCHBOLD, *rev.* CLAIRE E. J. HERRICK

Sources J. J. Keevil, J. L. S. Coulter, and C. Lloyd, *Medicine and the navy, 1200–1900*, 4: *1815–1900* (1963), 6–7, 53–4, 56, 58, 257–8, 261–2 · J. Shepherd, *The Crimean doctors: a history of the British medical services in the Crimean War*, 1 (1991); 2 (1991), 23, 612, 624 · *The Lancet* (6 June 1868), 741 · *BMJ* (6 June 1868), 574 · *Medical Times and Gazette* (6 June 1868), 622 · *ILN* (6 June 1868) · *Navy List* · *CGPLA Eng. & Wales* (1868) · J. F. Waller, ed., *The imperial dictionary of universal biography*, 3 vols. (1857–63)

Wealth at death under £5000: probate, 13 June 1868, *CGPLA Eng. & Wales*

Lidderdale, William (1832–1902), merchant and banking official, was born on 16 July 1832 at St Petersburg, Russia, the second son of John Lidderdale (*d.* 1845), a Russia merchant, and his wife, Ann (1806–1844), the daughter of William Morgan, a merchant in St Petersburg. His father was ruined by a Scottish bank failure in 1837, and the large family of boys was orphaned by his death in 1845. Lidderdale's schooling at St Petersburg and at the academy in Birkenhead ended at the age of fifteen, when he entered Heath & Co., a Liverpool merchant house trading with Russia in which his guardian was a partner.

Lidderdale next joined the Liverpool merchant house of Rathbone & Co. as cashier. He worked at their New York agency (1857–63) before becoming the partner responsible for their London office (1864). Apart from finance, the London office's commercial speciality was the tea trade, but Lidderdale cultivated new, less seasonal lines of business. He understood that traditional merchanting, by buying through correspondents, was obsolete in the age of telegraphy, steamships, and the Suez Canal. As a general merchant he was not enamoured of bankers, and as a Liverpudlian outsider he had an entrenched mistrust of some City traditions.

In 1870 Lidderdale became a director of the Bank of England and in 1887, by rotation, deputy governor. He was by then widely recognized as shrewd, clear-sighted, and prudent. The early disasters which had befallen his family had impressed him with a sense of the fragility of banking credit. On becoming governor in March 1889 he took measures to strengthen the banking system, which he perceived as vulnerable because liabilities so far outran reserves. He persuaded public authorities and other bodies to deposit surplus reserves in the Bank of England to give it tighter control over credit. He tried to refine the central bank's influence over foreign exchanges, gold movements, and the bank rate. For the first time since 1858 bill brokers were readmitted to regular borrowing and rediscount facilities. He sought closer co-operation with private bankers and the Treasury. 'Lidderdale is considered in the City to be the best Governor the Bank has ever had', E. W. Hamilton recorded on 9 August 1890. 'He always knows his mind, & his judgment is very good' (diary, BL, Add. MS 48653). By September 1890 he had raised the bank's deposits to over £35 million.

In 1868 Lidderdale had married Mary Martha (1843–1924), the daughter of Wadsworth Dawson Busk, a Russia merchant, and his wife, Elizabeth, the daughter of Frederick Thielche, a St Petersburg merchant; the couple had four sons and three daughters. They constituted an affectionate and cultivated home circle: William enjoyed reading the great Victorian novelists, played the piano, and relished musical evenings at home or in concert halls. He was an intimate friend of his bank colleague Henry Hucks Gibbs, later Lord Aldenham, and other City figures.

The crisis which Lidderdale half anticipated occurred in 1890, when Baring Brothers overstretched themselves in the South American loan business and required a cash advance of about £9 million. Lidderdale was informed on Saturday 8 November. His initial response was noncommittal, and he spent Sunday with his son at London Zoo. Although other financiers panicked and dithered at the impending crash, Lidderdale kept his head. By 13 November he had borrowed £3 million in gold from the Bank of France and bought £1.5 million in gold from the Russian government to strengthen the bank's reserve. He pressed the government to support the bank in formulating a reserve, but was resisted by George Goschen, the chancellor of the exchequer, by whom he was unimpressed. On Friday 14 November he forced a long interview at Downing Street with Salisbury and W. H. Smith, at which he insisted that the government bear half the loss resulting from taking in Barings' bills over the next day. After returning to a conference at the Bank of England, he set up a guarantee fund to secure payment of Barings' liabilities. The bank contributed the first million pounds. By skill and force of character Lidderdale obtained subscriptions from other banks of £16 million by 16 November. It was 'mainly due to his courage, cool-headedness, and shrewdness that the arrangement has been carried through', Hamilton noted. 'Nine out of ten Governors would have lost their heads' (diary, BL, Add. MS 48654, 15 Nov 1890). Lidderdale's handling of this episode improved co-operation between bankers and the bank. Unprecedentedly, his governorship was extended 'for a third year, notwithstanding that it means a considerable private loss: he is wrapped up in the work at the Bank, and … fully alive … to the importance of the post' (ibid., 8 Jan 1891).

For some months Lidderdale was a hero. W. E. Gladstone consulted him when he was dining with Thomson Hankey MP (30 January 1891). He received the honorary freedom of the Grocers' Company (February 1891) and of the City of London (May 1891). Goschen recommended him to Salisbury (9 May 1891) for a GCB, believing that he was not rich enough for a baronetcy; a privy councillorship was gazetted on 30 May. Having vacated the governorship of the Bank of England in 1892, he became a commissioner of the Patriotic Fund (1893), which was repeatedly criticized for maladministration by Hudson Kearley, afterwards Viscount Devonport. Among other posts after 1892, Lidderdale was president of the council of the Corporation of Foreign Bondholders and chairman of the London finance committee of the Chicago Great Western Railway. Rathbone Brothers made serious losses during the 1890s, and Lidderdale retired as a partner on the closure of the London office in 1897. By that year he was in financial straits himself, having lost nearly all of his capital. Thereafter he was dependent on income from his wife's property, and also on the remuneration from three directorships in American railway companies. He died on 26 June 1902, at his home, 55 Montagu Square, Marylebone, and was buried at Winkfield, near Windsor, Berkshire.

RICHARD DAVENPORT-HINES

Sources Diaries of Sir Edward Walter Hamilton, BL, Add. MSS 48653, 48654 • D. Kynaston, *The City of London*, 4 vols. (1994–2001) • S. Marriner, *Rathbone's of Liverpool, 1845–1873* (1961) • J. Clapham, *The Bank of England: a history*, 2 (1944) • R. S. Sayers, *The Bank of England, 1891–1944*, 3 vols. (1976) • *The Times* (7 May 1891) • *The Times* (27 June 1902) • *The memoirs of Edwin Waterhouse*, ed. H. E. Jones (1988) • Gladstone, *Diaries* • A. D. Elliot, *The life of George Joachim Goschen, first Viscount Goschen, 1831–1907*, 2 (1911), 170–74, 283–4 • *The diary of Sir Edward Walter Hamilton, 1885–1906*, ed. D. W. R. Bahlman (1993) • *CGPLA Eng. & Wales* (1902)

Archives priv. coll., family papers

Likenesses photograph, 1880–89, repro. in S. Marriner, 'Lidderdale, William', *DBB*, 3 (1985), 786 • wood-engraving (after a photograph by Walery), NPG; repro. in *ILN* (9 May 1891)

Wealth at death £9337 17*s*. 5*d*.: resworn probate, July 1902, *CGPLA Eng. & Wales*

Liddesdale. For this title name *see* Bruce, Sir Robert, lord of Liddesdale (*c*.1293–1332); Douglas, Sir Archibald, lord of Liddesdale (1294?–1333); Douglas, Sir William, lord of Liddesdale (*c*.1310–1353).

Liddiard, William (1773–1841), travel writer and poet, was born in July 1773, the son of the Revd William Stratton Liddiard of Rockley House, Ogbourn St George, Wiltshire, and Jane Craven, sister of Lord Craven. On 26 February 1792, Liddiard matriculated at University College, Oxford, but did not take a degree, preferring instead, after two years of study, to join the 111th regiment of Loyal Birmingham Volunteers as a lieutenant, before becoming a captain a year later in the 54th (West Norfolk) regiment on 6 September 1795.

Liddiard left the army in 1796, and completed his degree at Trinity College, Dublin, in 1803. His services to the British cause during the French Revolutionary wars were not, however, forgotten. Having been ordained, Liddiard, on the recommendation of the duke of Bedford, was appointed chaplain to Charles, fourth duke of Richmond, the then lord lieutenant of Ireland, who subsequently placed him in the rectory of Knockmark, co. Meath.

Once the French wars were over, Liddiard's work as a clergyman gave him ample time to travel within Europe and to publish, first in Dublin and then in London, travel writing, Swiss legends which he had gathered on his travels, and verse, much of which was inspired by the mountainous landscape he witnessed in France and Switzerland.

Liddiard was twice married. His first wife, I. S. Anna Wilkinson, daughter of Sir Henry Wilkinson, was herself an accomplished and published writer of dramatic poems and masques. His second wife, Mary Ann, was the third daughter of John Tirel Morin of Weedon Lodge, Buckinghamshire. Both of Liddiard's marriages produced children: Liddiard and Mary had a daughter, while he and Anna had a son, to whom he resigned the rectory of Knockmark.

Liddiard, who was also an artist and musician, died at Clifton, Gloucestershire, where he had been living, on 11 October 1841. His work had a moderate reputation throughout the nineteenth century.

GORDON GOODWIN, *rev.* JASON EDWARDS

Sources *GM*, 2nd ser., 15 (1841), 659

Liddon, Henry Parry (1829–1890), Church of England clergyman and theologian, was born on 20 August 1829 at North Stoneham, Hampshire. He was the eldest son and second of the ten children of Matthew Liddon (1791–1869) and his wife, Ann (*d.* 1849), daughter of Samuel Bilke of Surrey. His father was a retired captain (RN) who had served under the command of Edward Parry in an expedition to find the north-west passage; Parry was Liddon's godfather and the source of his middle name. While he was still an infant the family moved to Colyton in Devon.

Education, ordination, and celibacy Liddon was educated locally, then at George Roberts's school in Lyme Regis. In 1844 he went to King's College School, London, where a contemporary recorded that his lifelong seriousness of character was already apparent. From there he went on to Christ Church, Oxford, in 1846, barely a year after Newman's secession to Roman Catholicism. No record has survived as to the origin of Liddon's interest in the Oxford Movement, although the curate at Colyton had tried to convince Liddon's parents that he should not go to Oxford in case he fell under the influence of the Tractarians. So bad was the reputation of the Tractarians in the mid-1840s that no cautious young man would have associated himself with them. However, Liddon was more interested in their perception of doctrinal truth than in worldly approbation, and soon got to know Pusey. He graduated in 1850 with a second class in classical honours, and won a theological scholarship in 1851. Despite the débâcle which had followed upon Newman's secession and the apparent defeat of the Tractarians in Oxford, the principles promoted by the Oxford Movement slowly gained ground, and Liddon was keen to assist the process.

Liddon enjoyed foreign travel and visited the continent most summers, often with one or more friends. In 1852, shortly before ordination, he visited Rome. It seems that his reputation as a high-churchman had gone before him, for he was befriended by the chamberlain to Pope Pius IX, George Talbot, who tried to convert him to Roman Catholicism. Talbot, himself a convert, used every weapon in his armoury, culminating in a private audience with the pontiff. Liddon was impressed but not won over: he recorded

Henry Parry Liddon (1829–1890), by George Richmond, 1866

his impressions of 'a wonderful day' and revealed his appreciation both of the honour and of what Talbot was trying to do.

Liddon believed that he was called to remain unmarried. He was ordained deacon by Bishop Wilberforce of Oxford on 19 December 1852 to curacy under W. J. Butler at Wantage and almost at once began to show promise as a preacher. However, his health was delicate and it became clear that he could not continue in parish work. Another curacy lasted only a few weeks, but he was ordained priest in 1853.

A priest in Oxford Wilberforce rescued him from idleness by appointing him vice-principal of the newly founded theological college at Cuddesdon in 1854. Alfred Pott, the principal, was an able man, but Liddon established the tone of the place with his considerable strength of character and deep commitment to Tractarian 'church principles'. This led to the criticism that his students were forced into a mould. Certainly his views were presented with a vigour which soon attracted opposition from those unhappy with the Anglo-Catholic revival. Even his appearance reinforced the accusation of Romanism: short of stature, he was described as 'Italian-looking' and 'glittering-eyed'. His custom of wearing a cassock outside chapel, unusual in those days, added to the effect. The bishop defended Liddon in the face of complaints about his churchmanship, but did not entirely agree with him, asking his archdeacons to investigate. They convinced

Wilberforce that changes were needed, and in 1859 he accepted Liddon's resignation as the price of keeping the college going.

Liddon's next post, until 1862, was vice-principal of St Edmund Hall, Oxford. During that time he established Sunday evening lectures there on the New Testament. Such large numbers attended that bigger premises had to be found, and they came to rest in Christ Church hall. The lectures were maintained until 1869 and recommenced in 1883. From 1862 Liddon occupied himself in accepting preaching appointments and lived on his private means, mostly in his rooms at Christ Church which he retained all his life. In 1864 the bishop of Salisbury, W. K. Hamilton, the first of the Tractarian disciples to become a diocesan bishop, appointed him an examining chaplain and made him a prebendary (honorary canon) of Salisbury. The two were friends, and Liddon assisted in the preparation of an important charge, which Hamilton delivered in 1867. After the bishop's death in 1869, Liddon published a short biography of him.

Another man who had a considerable influence on Liddon was John Keble, who became his confessor at the time of his appointment at Cuddesdon. (Perhaps with an inkling of possible trouble, Wilberforce had insisted, as a condition of his appointment, that Liddon gave up using Pusey as his spiritual director.) Liddon worried about how to tell Pusey. In the event he was gracious, and said that, in making the change, Liddon was 'giving up brass for gold' (O. Chadwick, *The Founding of Cuddesdon*, 1954, 26). Liddon kept in close and regular contact with Keble until the latter died in 1866, and he took a leading part in the discussions for a memorial to Keble in Oxford. His diary (5–6 April 1866) suggests that the founding of Keble College might have been Liddon's idea originally. It is a point of interest that he subsequently resisted Pusey's wish for him to be the first warden. Later he was also involved in founding Pusey House.

In 1866 Liddon was invited to give the annual Bampton lectures, a series established for the defence and exposition of the Christian faith. He delivered a full, masterly, but conservative exposition of traditional Christology, having been discouraged by Pusey from offering a more modern survey. The published version, which ran to fifteen editions, bore the title *The Divinity of our Lord and Saviour Jesus Christ*. It constitutes Liddon's most significant piece of sustained theological writing, and confirmed his reputation as a scholar and theologian. It attained almost the status of a theological textbook and was translated into German. Because of their thoroughness and scholarship, the lectures are a useful summary of basic orthodoxy, if not widely read.

Liddon visited Russia for two months in 1867 with Charles Dodgson, a friend of many years standing. Two impressions remained in his mind: the size and number of the monasteries, and the influence of the church over the ordinary people. They visited St Petersburg, where he was impressed by the liturgy. In Moscow he met a bishop named Leonide and found himself explaining the Colenso affair. They also met Archbishop Filaret, the metropolitan, and shared in the celebrations marking the jubilee of his consecration.

Canon of St Paul's: a famous preacher In April 1870 Liddon was appointed to a canonry at St Paul's Cathedral. In June of the same year he was also appointed Ireland professor of scripture at Oxford and served on the hebdomadal board between 1864 and 1875. He resigned the professorship shortly after Pusey's death in 1882, but he remained at St Paul's for the rest of his life. It was there that he obtained lasting and well-earned fame as a preacher, building upon a reputation already established through the Bampton lectures and another series of lengthy lectures delivered in Lent 1870 in St James's Church, Piccadilly. They had been remarkably well attended, and were published as *Some Elements of Religion* (1872). Crowds also gathered to hear him at St Paul's. After his first sermon there as a canon, it became necessary for the service to be moved out into the great space under the dome, and it was from the pulpit there that he preached for the whole of his twenty years at the cathedral. Liddon's sermons were long, but characterized by his fervour, firm orthodoxy, and the 'silvery' quality of his voice. Fourteen definitive volumes of sermons appeared in print, and these form the bulk of his published work. The titles of some of the collections bear witness to the periods when he was in residence at St Paul's—*Advent at St Paul's* (1888), *Christmastide at St Paul's* (1889), and two volumes entitled *Easter at St Paul's* (1885)—but the sermons contain a wide range of learning and theological perception. Other collections were published after his death: *Sermons on Old Testament Subjects* (1891), *Sermons on some Words of Christ* (1892), and *Sermons on some Words of St Paul* (1898). There were also two volumes entitled *University Sermons* and a volume of *Sermons Preached on Special Occasions* (1897). For the clergy, his posthumously published *Clerical Life and Work* (1894) long remained of value, if allowance were made for changed circumstances.

Ecclesiastical reform Shortly after Liddon's appointment, R. W. Church was made dean of St Paul's. Church, Liddon, and their colleagues formed one of the most dynamic cathedral chapters of the nineteenth century. But the reform of cathedrals progresses slowly: Liddon observed that 'an elephant may be taught to dance, but the process is not a quick one!' (Johnston, 140) He was probably more 'advanced' in his ritual practices than his colleagues, and more prepared to run risks for Anglo-Catholic freedom with regard to ritual. He used eucharistic vestments and faced east at the altar. In 1871 Liddon, with a brother canon, invited the bishop of London, John Jackson, to prosecute him, arguing that prominent churchmen, such as cathedral canons, were less vulnerable to episcopal heavy-handedness than isolated parish clergy. No action was taken. He was also outspoken in his opposition to the Public Worship Regulation Act of 1874, but he nevertheless urged moderation upon the more intransigent ritualists. Towards the end of his life Liddon followed closely the development of the trial of his friend and contemporary Bishop Edward King of Lincoln, but he died before the final judgment.

Religious controversies Liddon's commitment to the Church of England was seriously shaken only in 1871, when proposals were put forward to alter the use of the Athanasian creed. At Pusey's request, and in co-operation with other Oxford professors of theology, Liddon produced a rubric which was designed to explain the so-called 'warning clauses' of the creed. Archbishop Tait (whom Liddon regarded as a disastrous prelate) believed that the rubric was an implicit acceptance of what was proposed. In an effort to disabuse him, Liddon wrote that if the creed were 'mutilated', altered, or 'degraded', he would 'feel bound in conscience to resign my preferments, and to retire from the ministry of the Church of England' (Johnston, 161). In the event, nothing was changed. Whether this was due to the opposition of Liddon and Pusey is unclear, but it is apparent that Liddon was close to overreacting.

In 1873 Liddon once again entered the lists of theological controversy, when debate over the revival of sacramental confession by Anglo-Catholics was at its fiercest. He helped Pusey to compile a 'Declaration on confession and absolution, as set forth in the Church of England'—a response to a statement by the house of bishops, which was itself a reply to an earlier petition. This occupied much time in the summer of that year. It was published in *The Times* on 6 December 1873 over a token twenty-nine signatories, but had the support of many others.

At the end of 1874 Liddon was embarrassed by a controversy with a Roman Catholic priest, T. J. Capel, who alleged, in a letter to *The Times*, that Anglo-Catholics were disseminating Roman doctrines in their writings and thus increasing the numbers of converts to Rome. Liddon's denial was met by Capel with quotations from, and specific references to, other Anglican writers. Much correspondence followed in *The Times* and other newspapers. Liddon was able to answer satisfactorily the charges against his own teachings, but could not always defend those of other Anglo-Catholics. Consequently he was left looking rather foolish.

In 1874 and 1875 Liddon took part in conferences at Bonn which had originated as a reaction against the dogma of papal infallibility promulgated at the First Vatican Council in 1870. The participants sought a rapprochement between the emerging Old Catholics, some elements of Eastern Orthodoxy, and Anglicans. The conferences were completely unofficial, but represent an early attempt at ecumenical dialogue which has been largely unnoticed in the historical study of that movement. Subsequent plans were abandoned as a result of the Franco-Prussian War, and never revived.

Liddon was never afraid of controversy, but was not often publicly controversial in his sermons. However, in St Paul's on 13 August 1876, he was critical of the government's support for the repressive Turkish regime. In the October of that year he wrote to *The Times* criticizing the Turkish government for alleged atrocities in Bulgaria. He described how he and a friend had, a few months earlier, seen the impaled body of a Bulgarian prisoner on the banks of the River Save, while on a journey to visit Cardinal Strossmayer of Bosnia. The letter produced a strong reaction from the Foreign Office, which was sensitive to criticism of British government policy.

Travels and later career In 1886 Liddon undertook an extended tour of Egypt and Palestine with his widowed sister, Mrs King. While in the Holy Land he hoped to persuade eminent Orthodox ecclesiastics to support the opposition of Anglo-Catholic clergymen to the bishopric of Jerusalem, a plan which did not endear him to those in England who were trying to make the scheme work. (England and Prussia alternately nominated candidates from their established churches to the bishopric, which was created in 1841 to oversee English and German protestants in Palestine. High-churchmen regarded this as tantamount to union with another protestant body, without sufficient guarantees for church organization and doctrine.) In Jerusalem at Easter, Liddon met the patriarch of the Orthodox church, who unexpectedly showed him a photograph of the archbishop of Canterbury in convocation robes and one of the bishop of Aberdeen 'in a magnificent cope and mitre' and asked Liddon to explain why they were dressed differently (Johnston, 325).

During his tour Liddon heard that he had been elected bishop of Edinburgh. Mrs King recorded that he had a sleepless night, during which she heard him pacing the next room, before deciding to decline the appointment. Liddon's lack of preferment in the Church of England was for many years attributed to the opposition of the queen, who was said to have been annoyed by the style of his preaching during a visit to Windsor Castle in 1868. However, this was a baseless rumour: preferment was offered to Liddon from time to time, but he always declined. In the same year that he was offered the bishopric of Edinburgh he was also invited to accept the deanery of Worcester. Earlier, Lord Acton had urged Gladstone to secure his appointment to a bishopric. In 1885 there were three vacancies on the bench and Gladstone hoped that Liddon could be persuaded. In 1890, not long before his death, he was offered the see of St Albans, and commented '[I] felt as though I had been shot!' (Johnston, 376).

Final years and significance Although reluctant to be a leader, Liddon increasingly became the focus of the Oxford Movement as Pusey aged and became more reclusive. He was well placed to lead, having a professional and public position in both Oxford and London. In Oxford he had a considerable influence on generations of undergraduates, many of whom subsequently served in the Church of England ministry, and as a canon of St Paul's Cathedral he was renowned as an influential and popular preacher. He was also a select preacher at both Oxford and Cambridge on more than one occasion. His sermons, other writings, and university teaching, which were full of uncompromising dogma, presented a non-papal catholicism which was deeply penetrated by the traditions and learning of the Western church.

The final decades of Liddon's life were overshadowed by

his anxiety about Pusey. Fearful of offending the old man, he refused to serve on the memorial committee for Charles Darwin. After Pusey's death in 1882, Liddon undertook to write his biography, which involved collecting and compiling Pusey's voluminous correspondence. At the time of his own death, Liddon had completed only two of the four volumes, although the third was almost ready for publication and a considerable amount of material was assembled for the fourth. This work of devotion was rudely interrupted in 1889 by the publication of *Lux mundi*, a collection of essays by the younger generation of Anglo-Catholics. Liddon vehemently denounced the essay by Charles Gore, 'The Holy Spirit and inspiration', which, in its acceptance of new critical teaching on the Old Testament, rejected the conservative theology of Pusey and his contemporaries. At the time Liddon was already suffering from his last illness, having put on weight and gone 'very grey'. His immediate reaction to the essays would have been critical even if he had been well, but if he had survived their appearance by more than ten months, and had been able to formulate a more considered response, his subsequent reputation as a hidebound conservative might have been moderated. Liddon died on 9 September 1890 at 13 Claremont Crescent, Weston-super-Mare, Somerset, three weeks after his sixty-first birthday, following a long and painful illness. He was buried in the crypt of St Paul's on 16 September. The service was taken by an ailing Dean Church, who was himself terminally ill.

Liddon was an Anglo-Catholic whose contribution to modern Anglicanism has been consistently underestimated. He claimed no originality for himself, presenting his teaching as simply that of catholic Christianity, and thus obscuring the persuasive and masterly form which he gave to the doctrines he held: as his entry in the *Dictionary of National Biography* said, his thought was 'marked by an intense permanence' as he bent his mind to 'bringing everything into order', fighting shy of 'all that was vague in outline or paradoxical'. Moreover, he placed himself in almost uncritical subordination to Pusey: Francis Paget, bishop of Oxford, dismissed Liddon as 'always a henchman'. Surviving Pusey only eight years (during which he was immersed in his life and letters), he never threw off the mantle of the disciple. Consequently he has been seen as ineluctably and rigidly conservative (a conclusion which his tentative reflections on the compatibility of the theory of evolution with theism might disturb), and his reputation has never recovered. This assessment only gained strength when he responded so negatively to *Lux mundi*. Perhaps it would be more appropriate to see Liddon as a theologian in his own right, and not just as a weak link between the tract writers, many of whom he knew as older contemporaries, and the next generation of theologians, represented by the *Lux mundi* scholars.

MICHAEL CHANDLER

Sources J. O. Johnston, *Life and letters of Henry Parry Liddon* (1904) • G. W. E. Russell, *Leaders of the church: Dr Liddon* (1905) • Keble College, Oxford, Liddon MS • H. P. Liddon, diaries, Pusey Oxf. • M. Chandler, *The life and work of Henry Parry Liddon* (2000)

Archives Bodl. Oxf., letters • Bodl. Oxf., corresp. and papers, incl. diary, family letters, sermons • Keble College, Oxford, corresp. and papers • Pusey Oxf., corresp. and papers, incl. diaries • Ripon College, Cuddesdon, Oxford, corresp. and diaries | Birmingham Oratory, letters to J. H. Newman • BL, corresp. with Lord Carnarvon, Add. MS 60835 • BL, corresp. with W. E. Gladstone, Add. MS 44237 • BL, letters to Mrs W. E. Gladstone, Add. MSS 46227–46229 • BL, letters to Sir E. W. Hamilton, Add. MSS 48622–48625 • Bloxham School, near Banbury, letters to P. R. Egerton • Bodl. Oxf., letters to H. W. Acland and Sarah Acland • Bodl. Oxf., letters to William Bright • Bodl. Oxf., letters to Friedrich Max Müller • Bodl. Oxf., letters to Edwin Palmer • Bodl. Oxf., corresp. with Samuel Wilberforce • Borth. Inst., corresp. with second Viscount Halifax • Borth. Inst., Wood MSS • CAC Cam., letters to W. T. Stead • Durham Cath. CL, letters to J. B. Lightfoot • JRL, letters to E. A. Freeman • LPL, corresp. with A. C. Tait • LPL, letters to Benjamin Webb • LPL, letters to Christopher Wordsworth

Likenesses L. Carroll [C. L. Dodgson], photograph, *c.*1856, NPG • portrait, 1856 (after photograph), repro. in Johnston, *The life and letters of Henry Parry Liddon*, facing p. 36 • G. Richmond, chalk drawing, 1866, NPG [*see illus.*] • G. Richmond, oils, 1870–72, Keble College, Oxford • G. Richmond, portrait, 1878, repro. in Johnston, *The life and letters of Henry Parry Liddon*, facing p. 224 • H. M. Paget, portrait, 1885, repro. in Johnston, *The life and letters of Henry Parry Liddon*, facing p. 304 • engraving, 1890 (after a photograph, 1880), repro. in Johnston, *The life and letters of Henry Parry Liddon*, frontispiece • H. von Herkomer, oils, Christ Church Oxf. • Lock & Whitfield, woodburytype photograph, NPG; repro. in T. Cooper, *Men of mark: a gallery of contemporary portraits* (1881) • Spy [L. Ward], caricature, chromolithograph, NPG; repro. in *VF* (16 Sept 1876) • monument, probably St Paul's Cathedral • portrait, Liddon House, London

Wealth at death £47,226 0s. 10d.: probate, 7 Nov 1890, *CGPLA Eng. & Wales*

Lidell, (Tord) Alvar Quan (**1908–1981**), radio broadcaster, was born on 11 September 1908 at Wimbledon Park, Surrey, the third of three children and younger son of Swedish parents, John Adrian Lidell, timber importer, and his wife, Gertrud Lundström. He was educated at King's College School, Wimbledon, and Exeter College, Oxford, where he obtained a second class in classical honour moderations (1929). He studied piano, piccolo, and cello as a boy, and at seventeen began singing lessons. At Oxford he was an outstanding actor, notably in the production of *Comus* by Arthur Bryant.

After brief teaching jobs, and engagements as a singer with a puppet theatre company, Lidell joined the BBC as chief announcer at Birmingham; the following year he transferred to London, where he became deputy chief announcer in 1937. In 1938 he married Nancy Margaret, daughter of Thomas Henry Corfield, lawyer. They had two daughters and a son.

The task of reading the historic announcement of Edward VIII's abdication fell to Lidell; and on 3 September 1939 he read the ultimatum to Germany from a room at 10 Downing Street. He remained there to introduce the prime minister, Neville Chamberlain, who at 11 a.m. broke the news that Britain was from that moment at war. Lidell never forgot the experience of 'sitting there, behind this figure of terrible grief' (private information).

During the Second World War the BBC dispensed with the traditional anonymity of its newsreaders (to distinguish them from enemy propagandists) and Lidell was

(Tord) **Alvar Quan Lidell** (1908–1981), by Roger George Clark, 1975

one of the named readers who brought the war news to the nation. The phrase '… and this is Alvar Lidell reading it' was a guarantee of clarity, intelligence, and cool objectivity. Only once did Lidell break with this principle. When going on the air with news of the victory at El Alamein, he allowed himself to say: 'Here is the news, and cracking good news it is too' (private information). He was called up for war service in RAF intelligence in 1943, but a year later returned to his nationally important work at the BBC.

In 1946 Lidell was appointed chief announcer on the new Third Programme. He remained for six years in this post, for which he was admirably qualified by his command of languages and knowledge of music. Artists of the calibre of Clifford Curzon and members of the Amadeus Quartet insisted that Lidell should introduce their broadcasts, a state of affairs much appreciated by one who was always at his happiest with musical people. In his work for the Third Programme, he set and maintained the highest standards, taking infinite trouble over pronunciation and phrasing.

In 1952 Lidell returned to newsreading in a newly constituted team of specialists who, in 1954, added the presentation of television news to their other duties. Television work, however, did not appeal to Lidell, who devoted most of the remainder of his career to radio broadcasting. In 1964 he was appointed MBE and he retired in 1969. His influence, however, persisted. When, in 1979, *The Listener* published his article about deteriorating standards of speech at the BBC (it was headed 'Newsweeding'), the impact was considerable. As a result the BBC set up a panel of experts to report on the quality of spoken English on the air.

Lidell's talent as an exemplary stylist of the spoken word was not confined to announcing. He was in international demand as a narrator in such taxing works as Arnold Schoenberg's *Gurrelieder* and *A Survivor from Warsaw*, as well as *An Oxford Elegy* by Ralph Vaughan Williams and *Façade* by William Walton. Edith Sitwell admired his rhythmic perfection in *Façade*, and he performed it with a prologue he had written himself at a Downing Street party to mark the composer's seventieth birthday. He was a dedicated reader of Books for the Blind, recording a total of 237 volumes, including marathons such as *Anna Karenina*. As a baritone singer he also achieved distinction, giving lieder recitals during and after the war, and memorably recording English ballads with Gerald Moore at the piano.

In appearance Lidell was tall (6 feet 3½ inches), aristocratic, and perhaps a touch reserved. In private life he was a very loving and devoted husband and father. He was compassionate and generous not only to his family and friends but to all those he considered to be in great need. Despite being 'a notable exponent of spoken English … He never forgot his Swedish heritage' (*The Times*, 9 Jan 1981). By way of relaxation he enjoyed games. He played rugby, tennis, and cricket at school and later took up golf and darts; he could also solve the *Times* crossword in six minutes. After two years' illness he died of cancer on 7 January 1981 at Michael Sobell House, Mount Vernon Hospital, Northwood, Middlesex. RICHARD BAKER

Sources *The Times* (9 Jan 1981) • A. Briggs, *The history of broadcasting in the United Kingdom*, 4 vols. (1961–79) • private information (1990) • *CGPLA Eng. & Wales* (1981)

Archives FILM BFI NFTVA, 'Life is nothing without music', 1947 • BFI NFTVA, documentary footage • BFI NFTVA, performance footage | SOUND BL NSA, 'The BBC archive, the voice of Alvar Lidell', BBC Radio 3, 17 April 1998, H9869/2 • BL NSA, performance recordings • IWM SA, performance recordings

Likenesses R. G. Clark, photograph, 1975, NPG [*see illus.*] • photograph, Hult. Arch.

Wealth at death £17,977: probate, 25 March 1981, *CGPLA Eng. & Wales*

Lidgett, Elizabeth Sedman (1843–1919), poor-law guardian and suffragist, was born on 26 August 1843 at 20 Arbour Terrace, Mile End, London, the daughter of John Lidgett of Hull, a London shipowner, and his wife, Ann Jacob, *née* Hyett. Her elder sister was the women's activist Mary Hyett, who in 1869 married Percy William Bunting (editor of the *Contemporary Review*); John Scott Lidgett (warden of the Bermondsey settlement and nonconformist member of the London school board) was her nephew. However, nothing further is known of her early life and career.

In April 1881 Elizabeth was elected a poor-law guardian in St Pancras, where she served alongside Sarah Ward Andrews, who helped form the Society for Promoting the Return of Women as Poor Law Guardians in February that same year. Both women belonged to the Charity Organization Society, which organization was the formative influence in Lidgett's ideas of morally inspiring philanthropy:

in 1909 she declared 'We may devise schemes, we may appoint officials, but it is only the living human soul that can save a soul alive' (Hollis, 27–8). In 1883 they were joined by Florence Davenport Hill, who later served on the central committee of the National Society for Women's Suffrage. Overall, women were represented on committees dealing with the workhouse, visiting boarded-out children, and poor-law schools, and they were clearly encouraged to deal only with matters relating to female and child inmates. As a member of the Ladies' Reference Committee, Elizabeth was able to support the work of her sister on the Metropolitan Association for Befriending Young Servants, and the minutes for 19 April 1894 record that the male guardians welcomed women's contribution in finding employment for many female paupers. They also supported her active involvement in the emigration of pauper children to Canada in her capacity as member, and subsequently chair, of the boarding-out committee in 1894–1906, 1913, and 1916. On many occasions she was asked to represent the board on a variety of bodies, including the National Poor Law Conference in 1896 and the Distress Committee for St Pancras with Hilda Miall-Smith (a former member of the London school board) in 1905. She also spoke of her work as a female guardian at the annual conferences of the National Union of Women Workers.

Both Elizabeth Lidgett and her sister were prominent in the National Vigilance Association, and the first meeting 'to promote the return of Women as County Councillors' was held in the house of Mr and Mrs Percy Bunting on 17 November 1888. Although Elizabeth declined an invitation to stand for election to the London county council Mary Bunting was placed on the first general committee of the Women's Local Government Society (1893), and in the words of her obituarist 'ever continued a steadfast friend to the cause' (*Women's Local Government Society Report*, 29), as did Elizabeth.

Elizabeth Lidgett also took a keen interest in the work of the London school board. For instance, in 1889 she became a manager of the Gray's Inn Road group of schools, serving alongside Margaret Eve, who went on to represent Finsbury on the school board. In 1894 she campaigned on behalf of two Progressive candidates in Greenwich—Henry Gover and a nonconformist minister, Mr Wilson (school board for London; *Blackheath Gazette*). Finally, in 1912 she gave evidence to the royal commission on divorce.

Then living at 40 Gordon Square, Elizabeth Sedman Lidgett died at home of a pulmonary malignant disease and secondary abdominal growths on 8 April 1919. Aged seventy-five, she had been a member of the St Pancras board of guardians for nearly forty years. It is impossible to judge whether she was missed by the local poor, but in the opinion of the Women's Local Government Society 'Miss Lidgett was an ideal Guardian, and spared no effort to help young and old' (*Women's Local Government Society Report*, 29). JANE MARTIN

Sources St Pancras guardians' minutes, 1881–1919, LMA · *Women's Local Government Society Report* (1919–20) · *The Times* (9 April 1919) · *The Times* (9 Oct 1919) · *Englishwoman's Review* (15 April 1885) · school board for London, annual return of the managers of day schools, Sept 1889, LMA · *Blackheath Gazette* (9 Nov 1894) · P. Hollis, *Ladies elect: women in English local government, 1865–1914* (1987); pbk edn (1989) · J. Lewis, *Women in England, 1870–1950* (1984) · d. cert. · b. cert. · *IGI*

Archives LMA, minutes of St Pancras guardians · LMA, Women's Local Government Society papers

Wealth at death £14,300 7s. 1d.: probate, 3 July 1919, *CGPLA Eng. & Wales*

Lidgett, John Scott (1854–1953), Methodist minister and local politician, was born on 10 August 1854 at Kelso Cottage, Lewisham, the son of John Jacob Lidgett (1828–1869), shipowner and businessman, and Maria Elizabeth (1824–1911), daughter of the Revd John Scott and his wife, Maria. Scott, first principal of Westminster Teacher Training College and twice president of the Wesleyan Methodist conference, was an early and abiding influence on his grandson. The Lidgett–Scott cousinhood was steeped in Wesleyan Methodism: when Lidgett became president of conference in 1908, he claimed to have been personally acquainted with fifty of the ninety-one presidents who had held office since the death of John Wesley in 1791.

Following initial education at Blackheath proprietary school, Lidgett's plans for application to university were checked by his father's early death. After two years in a City firm of insurance and shipping brokers on the recommendation of his uncle George, however, he decided to pursue further study, and in 1873 entered University College, London, where he graduated BA in 1874 and MA in logic and philosophy in 1875. In 1876 Lidgett was accepted as a candidate for the Wesleyan Methodist ministry, and was sent, without further training, into circuit work, serving in Tunstall, Southport, Cardiff, Wolverhampton, and Cambridge. In his own reminiscences Lidgett acknowledged his theological debt to William Burt Pope and William Fiddian Moulton; an important, but understated, influence on his later thought was F. D. Maurice. Lidgett married, on 29 July 1884 at Abersychan church, Monmouthshire, Emmeline Martha (1857/8–1934), daughter of Andrew Davies, physician, of Newport, Monmouthshire. Their son, John Cuthbert Lidgett, born in 1885, was killed in action in March 1918. Their daughter, Lettice Mary Lidgett, was born in 1887.

While in Cambridge, Lidgett evolved the idea of establishing a Methodist presence for religious, social, and educational work in one of the poorer London districts, a project analagous to Samuel Barnett's Toynbee Hall (1884) and reflecting the ideas of the Oxford philosopher T. H. Green. Moulton's support helped to win official approval for the scheme from a Wesleyan establishment suspicious of social work without clear evangelistic goals, and the Bermondsey settlement was founded in 1891. It took Lidgett seven years to complete the building of the settlement and forty years to clear the debt, and he served as warden until 1949. Although he combined this role with pastoral work in Rotherhithe and Deptford, and with responses to the challenge of secularist lecturers in south London, Lidgett emphasized that the settlement's aims were not proselytism, but education, philanthropy, social reform,

John Scott Lidgett (1854–1953), by Elliott & Fry

and the provision of an unsectarian meeting-place for all classes.

A further dimension of Lidgett's educational and social work began the year after the opening of the Bermondsey Settlement, when he was invited by the Progressive Party to stand for election as a poor-law guardian. This inaugurated a long career in London local government, with a particular emphasis on education, inherited from his grandfather, which took Lidgett into national and ecumenical politics. He was a guardian from 1892 until 1906, an elected member of the London school board from 1897 until the board's responsibilities were taken over by the local education authority in 1904, a member (1905–28) and deputy chairman (1917–19) of the education committee of the London county council (LCC), an alderman of the LCC in 1905–10 and 1922–8, and leader of the Progressive Party on the council from 1918 to 1928. Lidgett took a moderate line in opposition to Balfour's Education Act (1902), and sought to steer the free churches away from official endorsement of the campaign for 'passive resistance' to the rates. His consultative role in Liberal attempts to revise Balfour's act brought increasing contact and friendship with Randall Davidson, archbishop of Canterbury from 1903. Nearly forty years later, Lidgett was one of the leaders of a deputation of Anglican and free church representatives to the president of the Board of Education which helped to lay the foundations for Butler's Education Act of 1944.

Lidgett took an active part in the affairs of the University of London. A member of convocation from 1875, he was elected to the senate in 1922 and continued to represent the arts graduates until he retired in 1946 at the age of ninety-two. He was a founder member of the court of the university, and served as deputy vice-chancellor (1929) and vice-chancellor (1930–32). Lidgett played a particular role in promoting university extension, in encouraging the women's colleges, and in developing relations between the university and the teacher training colleges, which led to the creation of the Institute of Education.

The social work and non-sectarian ethos of the Bermondsey settlement, combined with his growing political involvement on the LCC, made Lidgett a controversial figure in Wesleyan Methodism in the 1890s and early 1900s, but he gradually won a position of influence in the connexion, taking a more prominent role as a spokesman for progressive policies after the death of Hugh Price Hughes in 1902. Already secretary of the important committee of privileges, which monitored political issues, and a member of the legal conference, Lidgett made his mark as a conference speaker in 1903. He edited the *Methodist Times* from 1907 to 1918, sustaining the newspaper's tradition of liberty of thought. Designated president of conference in 1907 on a close vote, Lidgett's year of office (1908–9) was marked by his provocative intervention criticizing the House of Lords for its rejection of the 1908 Licensing Bill. A long-standing advocate of Methodist union, he was closely involved in the process of negotiation which culminated in the reunion of the Wesleyan, Primitive, and United Methodist churches in 1932, and was elected first president of the united church. His Wesleyan presidency of 1908 had brought with it the chairmanship of the then third London district, a post which he held for nearly forty years and from which he was only persuaded to retire with great reluctance.

Nurtured in a Wesleyan tradition which emphasized Methodism's debt to the Church of England and its distance from the dissenting denominations, Lidgett was actively involved in steps towards greater Christian unity. He attended the 1893 Grindelwald conference, organized by Henry Lunn, and joined the executive of the newly founded National Council of Evangelical Free Churches in 1897, later serving as president (1906) and honorary secretary (1914–40). After chairing the committee which produced a scheme for a Federal Council of the Evangelical Free Churches (1919), Lidgett held office as moderator of the council (1923–5) and represented it in responding to the 'Appeal' of the 1920 Lambeth conference. He enjoyed good relations with leading Anglicans, including Edward Stuart Talbot and Randall Davidson, and was a pallbearer at the latter's funeral. The archbishop, who sponsored Lidgett for membership of the Athenaeum, commented to him, 'You see, you understand us' (Davies, 151). Lidgett contributed towards the formation of the World Council of Churches as a member of the interim committee on faith and order (1914) and was a founder member of the British Council of Churches (1941).

Lidgett's first theological work was the 1897 Fernley lecture, published as *The Spiritual Principle of the Atonement*.

Building on divine fatherhood as the key to Christian doctrine, Lidgett's rejection of penal substitution in favour of a restored filial relationship, through the obedience of Christ as head and spiritual archetype of the human race, linked his theology to that of F. D. Maurice, and marked a Methodist example of the general late nineteenth-century shift of emphasis from the cross to the incarnation. The suspicion of Wesleyan conservatives was aroused, but Moulton's support, the availability of a more obvious target in the shape of J. Agar Beet, and the impenetrability of Lidgett's prose style enabled him to escape sustained opposition. A second substantial volume, *The Fatherhood of God* (1902), earned Lidgett an Aberdeen DD. In *The Christian Religion, its Meaning and Proof* (1907) he turned to apologetics. Expository volumes on Ephesians (*God in Christ Jesus*) and Hebrews (*Sonship and Salvation*) followed in 1915 and 1921. A somewhat belated recognition of his debt to Maurice was expressed in the Maurice lectures of 1934, published as *The Victorian Transformation of Theology*. Four years later, Lidgett set out his understanding of the connection between theology and social action in *The Idea of God and Social Ideals*.

Lidgett died on 16 June 1953 at Haley Nursing Home, Ashley Road, Epsom, at the age of ninety-eight, with memorial services following at Bermondsey and at Wesley's Chapel, London. The controversies of the 1890s and 1900s long outlived, he was hailed by obituarists and admirers as the greatest Methodist since John Wesley. The most immediately striking aspects of his life were his sheer longevity and his breadth of activity: simultaneously warden of the Bermondsey settlement, creative theologian, ecclesiastical statesman within and beyond Methodism, university vice-chancellor, London county councillor, and working editor (not only of the *Methodist Times* but also of the *Contemporary Review* from 1911 onwards). His contribution to many fields of religious, social, and political life had been acknowledged in 1933 when he became a Companion of Honour. Lidgett's capacity for hard work was legendary; the complementary characteristic was a disinclination to relax. More fluent and compelling in speech than in prose, he was also an able administrator and an effective and formidable chairman. An independent and austere personality made him a private man with few intimate friends. Assessments of his significance as a theologian have varied: his ideas were shaped in the nineteenth century, and he reiterated his great themes of divine fatherhood and the sonship of Christ without interaction with the later theologies of Schweitzer and Barth. Underpinning his life, however, was a theology and spirituality which might be characterized as Wesleyan catholicism: the 'church Methodism' of his boyhood, with the influence of Scott, Pope, and Moulton, leavened by Maurice and T. H. Green.

MARTIN WELLINGS

Sources R. E. Davies, ed., *John Scott Lidgett: a symposium* (1957) · J. S. Lidgett, *Reminiscences* (1928) · J. S. Lidgett, *My guided life* (1936) · *DNB* · A. Turberfield, 'A critical appraisal of the Rev. Dr John Scott Lidgett', DPhil diss., U. Oxf., 1998 · minutes of the Methodist Conference, 1953, JRL · *Methodist Recorder* (25 June 1953) · *Methodist Recorder* (2 July 1953) · *Methodist Recorder* (9 July 1953) · *South London Press* (19 June 1953) · *South London Press* (23 June 1953) · *South London Press* (30 June 1953) · b. cert. · m. cert. · d. cert.

Archives JRL, Methodist Church archives

Likenesses Russell & Sons, photograph, before 1928, repro. in Lidgett, *Reminiscences*, frontispiece · E. W. Tattersall, photograph, 1930, repro. in Davies, ed., *John Scott Lidgett*, frontispiece · photograph, 1952, repro. in *South London Press* (19 June 1953) · Elliott & Fry, photograph, NPG [*see illus.*]

Wealth at death £2609 13*s*. 10*d*.: probate, 19 Nov 1953, *CGPLA Eng. & Wales*

Lieberman, Aaron Samuel (1849?–1880), socialist activist, was probably born in 1849 in Lunna in Grodno province, then part of the Russian empire, son of Eliezer Dov Lieberman, a scholar of the Jewish enlightenment (haskalah). The family moved to Białystok and thence to Suwałki. Aaron Lieberman studied at the crown-controlled rabbinical seminary in Vilna, obtaining his teaching diploma in 1867. In 1870 he was also briefly enrolled as an external student at the Technological Institute of St Petersburg. He returned to Suwałki where he was appointed as a teacher and as secretary of the Jewish community, and is known to have worked for an insurance company in Vilna and as a draughtsman, having shown some talent in drawing.

By 1872 Lieberman was active in the local revolutionary circle based on ex-students of the Vilna seminary. He had been initiated by Aaron Zundelevich, a future leader of the Narodniki ('Popularists'), the forerunners of the Russian Social Revolutionary Party which advocated a form of peasant socialism in contrast to Marx's proletarian socialism. He was forced to flee abroad in June 1875, first to Berlin and then to London, where he arrived in August of that year. He found employment as a typesetter on the underground international socialist journal *Vperyod* ('Forward') (1872), then being published in London under the editorship of Pyotr Lavrov. Lieberman wrote under several English and Hebrew *noms de plume* including Arnold Lieberman and Arthur Freeman. From December 1875 he was sharing an address in north London with Lavrov and sub-editor V. N. Smirnov.

Through his old Vilna comrade Leib Weiner, Lieberman was introduced to the Jewish East End of London. Back in Russia, Lieberman had evinced attachment to the Hebrew language and interest in the specific plight of the Jewish working classes, in opposition to the assimilationism of mainstream Russian socialism. At Weiner's home, 40 Gun Street, Spitalfields, he founded the Hebrew Socialist Union in May 1876, claimed to be the first Jewish socialist organization in the world. The ten original members were all Russian political exiles working in the immigrant trades, especially tailoring, and the core membership never rose beyond forty. The union called a public meeting at the Zetland Hall, 51 Mansell Street, Goodman's Fields, on 26 August 1876, for which handbills were printed in Yiddish. Publication of a socialist appeal to Jewish workers in the native tongue of East European Jewry was itself unprecedented. At about the same time Lieberman published in *Vperyod* a 'Call to Jewish youth', the first socialist manifesto written in Hebrew. The London meeting was attended by several hundred, but broke up in disorder when Lieberman was accused of making anti-clerical statements against the chief rabbi and the synagogue establishment. Jewish immigrants in England may have shared Lieberman's views on the need to impose a ten-hour day in the sweated trades, but they were by and large traditionalist in matters of religion.

For their part, the leaders of Anglo-Jewry took steps to curb the Jewish socialists, by a mixture of economic pressure, the use of *agents provocateurs*, and rabbinical censure. The talents of the charismatic Rabbi Zvi Hirsch Dainov, the *maggid* (preacher) of Slutsk, were deployed to fulminate against the socialists while the *Jewish Chronicle* denounced them as missionaries. Lieberman's early attempt to create a Jewish Tailors' Union in London collapsed when the treasurer absconded with the funds. Tempers flared and he left London for Berlin in December 1876.

In 1877 in Vienna, Lieberman founded *HaEmet* ('The Truth'), significant as the first socialist propaganda periodical published in Hebrew, although it lasted for only three issues. He was arrested and expelled by both the Austrian and German authorities in turn and spent a total of two years behind bars. He appeared as a defendant in the so-called 'trial of the Russian nihilists' in Berlin in April 1879. He was finally deported to England and briefly returned to the East End, living at 21 Elder Street, Spitalfields. He worked with the young Morris Winchevsky (1856–1932) to set up an abortive Jewish Workingmen's Benefit and Educational Society, but eventually emigrated to the United States. In true Russian revolutionary style, in November 1880 Lieberman shot himself in a cheap lodging house in Syracuse, New York, after a failed love affair with Winchevsky's sister-in-law. (He is reputed to have left a wife in Russia.) In 1934 he was reinterred next to Winchevsky in the Workers' Circle cemetery in New York.

Lieberman never resolved the contradiction between international socialism and Jewish particularism. His position was attacked by anti-Jewish Russian intellectuals on the one hand and by traditionalist Jewish opinion on the other, a dilemma that was to face many Jewish socialists, both bundists and Labour Zionists, who came after him.

Sharman Kadish

Sources C. Roth, ed., *Encyclopaedia Judaica*, 16 vols. (Jerusalem, 1971–2) · P. Elman, 'The beginnings of the Jewish trade union movement in England', *Transactions of the Jewish Historical Society of England*, 17 (1951–2), 53–62 · W. J. Fishman, *East End Jewish radicals, 1875–1914* (1975) · *Aron Liebermans briv*, ed. K. Marmor (1951) [letters] · B. Sapir, 'Lieberman et le socialisme russe', *International Review for Social History*, 3 (1938), 25–88 · B. Sapir, 'Jewish socialists around *Vpered*', *International Review of Social History*, 10 (1965), 365–84 · E. Tcherikower, 'Der onheyb fun der yidisher sotsialistscher bavegung', *Historische Schriften*, 1 (Warsaw, 1909) · N. Weinstock, *Le pain de misère: histoire du mouvement ouvrier juif en Europe*, 3 vols. (Paris, 1984–6)

Archives Internationaal Instituut voor Sociale Geschiedenis, Amsterdam, V. N. Smirnov MSS · YIVO (Yiddish Scientific Institute), New York, minute book of the Hebrew Socialist Union · YIVO (Yiddish Scientific Institute), New York, Morris Vinchevsky collection

Likenesses photograph, BM; repro. in Fishman, *East End Jewish radicals* · photograph, Jewish National and University Library, Jerusalem, Schwadron collection; repro. in *Encyclopaedia Judaica*

Lienhardt, (Ronald) Godfrey (1921–1993), anthropologist, was born on 17 January 1921 at 19 Fernbank Road, Bradford, Yorkshire, the elder of the two sons of Godfrey Lienhardt, a textile merchant from Switzerland, and his Yorkshire wife, Jennie, *née* Benn. He was educated at Eastborough council school, Dewsbury, and Batley grammar school. In 1939 he went up to Downing College, Cambridge, on an open major scholarship to read English; his tutor there was F. R. Leavis, who was to have a lifetime influence on him. Having obtained a first in part 1 of the tripos, Lienhardt joined the Royal Army Ordnance Corps in 1941 and was appointed an army driving instructor (despite not being able to drive). In March 1943 he was commissioned as a lieutenant in the Royal Army Service Corps and posted to east Africa.

Lienhardt returned to Downing College in 1945 and read for the archaeological and anthropological tripos, in which he achieved first-class honours (with distinction) in 1947. Between 1947 and 1950 he carried out fieldwork among the Dinka of Sudan. In 1948 he migrated to Oxford, following his friend and colleague Edward Evans-Pritchard, to become a graduate student at Exeter College. The following year he was appointed research lecturer (later lecturer and then, in 1955, senior lecturer) in African sociology. He obtained his doctorate in 1952 and then conducted further research in Sudan among the Anuak in 1952–4. In the academic year 1955/6 he received leave from Oxford to help set up a department of sociology and social anthropology at the college of arts and sciences in Baghdad and in 1964 he was visiting professor at the University of Ghana in Accra. In 1967 he was elected to a governing body fellowship of the recently founded Wolfson College, of which he was vicegerent in 1973–5. In 1972 he was appointed to an *ad hominem* readership in social anthropology and in 1983 he received an honorary DLitt from Northwestern University, Illinois. He acted as external examiner for universities in both Britain and Africa, and between 1968 and 1976 was chief examiner in social anthropology for the international baccalaureate. He retired in 1988, when he became an emeritus reader of Oxford University and an emeritus fellow of Wolfson College.

Although Lienhardt published extensively, his anthropological reputation was above all made by *Divinity and Experience: the Religion of the Dinka* (1961). This book was immediately heralded as a masterful and outstanding contribution both to African ethnography and to the anthropological study of religion, and quickly took on the status of a classic work. He also wrote a highly successful textbook, *Social Anthropology* (1964), which was translated into Portuguese, Spanish, Japanese, Italian, and Greek. His earliest publications, dating back to 1941, were mainly literary in nature and were published in *Scrutiny*. From 1949, however, anthropology became the subject matter and his articles appeared in such academic journals as

Africa. As well as his scholarly publications he gave a number of radio talks, many of which were subsequently published in *The Listener.* He was also invited to give numerous public lectures, including the Malinowksi memorial lecture in 1961, the Spalding memorial lecture in 1969, and the Frazer lecture in Cambridge in 1992, the year before his death. This last was on Sir James Frazer himself, in whom he had had a long interest.

Lienhardt never married. However, his generous and sociable character was such as to attract a large circle of devoted friends. Many of these were present and former students, because for Lienhardt his tutorial duties were a lifetime commitment. Those who gathered round him for a drink came, however, from a much wider variety of backgrounds and countries, and people from all over the world came to visit him in Oxford. Indeed Lienhardt, who was of frail appearance, particularly during his last years, and by no means tall, was a memorable sight as he walked through Oxford surrounded by towering Dinka. He was a delightful and amusing raconteur but, as is often the case with such people, his wit was occasionally at other people's expense.

It is probable that Lienhardt was converted to Roman Catholicism while at Cambridge. If in his later life his practice fell away his faith did not, and one of his last requests was for a requiem mass. He died from bronchopneumonia at the John Radcliffe Hospital, Oxford, on 9 November 1993 and was cremated at Oxford crematorium on 16 November after a mass in St Aloysius's.

Peter Arnold Lienhardt (1928–1986), anthropologist, followed in his elder brother's footsteps. After taking a first in English and oriental languages at Downing College, Cambridge (1946–9), he did two years' national service (1950–52) in the Royal Air Force. He went up to Lincoln College, Oxford, as a graduate student in 1952, did fieldwork in the Gulf states, and obtained his doctorate in 1957. In 1957–60 he was senior research fellow at the East African Institute for Social Research at Makerere College, Uganda, during which time he carried out research in Zanzibar. During 1960–62 he was a research fellow at St Antony's College, Oxford (and briefly adviser to the ruler of Abu Dhabi, Sheikh Shakhbut bin Sultan), and in the latter year was appointed to a faculty lecturership in Middle Eastern sociology at Oxford's Institute of Social Anthropology. He undertook a further period of field research in Iran in 1965–6. He died, unmarried, on 17 March 1986.

Peter Rivière

Sources *Journal of the Anthropological Society of Oxford*, 28/1 (1997) [special issue in memory of Godfrey Lienhardt, with a full bibliography of his publications] · *The Independent* (17 Nov 1993) · *The Guardian* (19 Nov 1993) · private information (2004) · personal knowledge (2004) · A. Al-Shahi, 'Peter Lienhardt, 1928–1986: biographical notes and bibliography', *Journal of the Anthropological Society of Oxford*, 27/2 (1996), 107–12 · b. cert.

Likenesses J. Littlewood, bust, 1988, U. Oxf., Institute of Social and Cultural Anthropology · photographs, Wolfson College, Oxford · photographs, U. Oxf., Institute of Social and Cultural Anthropology

Wealth at death £193,058: probate, 15 March 1994, *CGPLA Eng. & Wales* · £318: further grant, 9 May 1994, *CGPLA Eng. & Wales*

Lienhardt, Peter Arnold (1928–1986). *See under* Lienhardt, (Ronald) Godfrey (1921–1993).

Liesching, Sir Percivale (1895–1973), civil servant, was born on 1 April 1895 at 1 Thurlestone Road, West Norwood, London, the son of Henry Selby Liesching, a Trinity House civil servant, and his wife, Elaine Frances Flint. A pupil at Bedford School, in 1913 Liesching was awarded a junior Hulme scholarship to read Greats at Brasenose College, Oxford. But before doing so he volunteered for war service, serving in Europe and east Africa. He was mentioned in dispatches and ended the war as a captain in the tank corps. In 1919 he proceeded to Brasenose, obtaining a distinction in the one-year Greats course for returning soldiers and playing rugby for his college and the university. He formally received his degree in 1921 (and took an MA in 1939).

In 1920 Liesching entered the Colonial Office but transferred to the newly created Dominions Office in 1925. In 1928 he joined the staff of Britain's first high commissioner in Canada where he made a good impression. 'Reserved, intelligent, efficient', he was sensitive to Canadian susceptibilities and 'as congenial in the drawing room as he was accomplished in the office' (Keenleyside, 1.251). He left Ottawa in 1932 to become political secretary (1933–5) and official secretary (1936–8) to the UK high commissioner in Australia. In 1939 he returned to London as an assistant under-secretary. However, he chafed at the confines of the rigidly run department and in 1942 transferred, as second secretary, to the Board of Trade. There he not only withstood the bullying of the board's president, Hugh Dalton, but won Dalton's grudging respect. Among other things, he skilfully negotiated the commercial side of the 1945 American loan. As permanent under-secretary at the Ministry of Food from 1946 to 1948, he again demonstrated considerable diplomatic prowess when, in 1947, he led a mission to tell Ottawa of drastic cuts in British food purchases.

Liesching became permanent under-secretary of the Commonwealth Relations Office in 1949. Being utterly different from Sir Eric Machtig, the previous permanent under-secretary whom the Commonwealth secretary, Noel-Baker, had determined to remove, Liesching seemed an admirable choice. He enjoyed exercising power and was decisive, shrewd, diplomatic, and clear-sighted. But to Noel-Baker's consternation, he could not work with Liesching. They disagreed on fundamentals. Liesching was a tough realist who had no time for his minister's idealism. Within less than a year Noel-Baker departed, suspecting Liesching had influenced his removal.

Liesching was a highly effective permanent under-secretary, not least in the way he reorganized the department. From 1955 until his retirement in 1958, he was high commissioner in South Africa and for Basutoland, the Bechuanaland protectorate, and Swaziland. He was appointed CMG in 1932, KCMG in 1944, KCB in 1947, GCMG in 1951, and KCVO in 1953. In retirement he was a director of the Rio Tinto Company, the Automatic Telephone and Electric Company, and W. J. Fraser & Co. As a member of the Plowden committee (1963), which led to the amalgamation of the Commonwealth Relations Office staff with those of the Foreign Office, Liesching safeguarded the interests of his former department.

On 26 March 1924 Liesching married a gentle and reserved woman, Ethel Georgina Nicol Williamson (*b.* 1900/01), the daughter of James Williamson, a gentleman of Bishops Down Grange, Tunbridge Wells, Kent. They had three daughters. Liesching was a lean man of average height, with dark hair, an upright bearing, and a very strong, sharp-featured, aquiline face. He had a military mien and was said to have applied a military ethos to his civilian work. Despite his charm, affability, conversational prowess, and skill in personal relations at all levels, he was respected rather than popular. He had practical rather than intellectual wisdom. In retrospect, he lacked vision on some issues (such as the Central African Federation and the exile of Seretse Khama) and, as was then common, had a touch of what would now be seen as racism. None the less, he was described as 'one of the outstanding public servants of his generation' (Garner, *The Times*). Liesching died of cancer at Holy Trinity vicarage, Hurst Road, Sidcup, Kent, on 4 November 1973.

LORNA LLOYD

Sources J. Garner, *The commonwealth office, 1925–1968* (1978) • private information (2004) [Kenneth East, Eleanor Emery] • Lord Garner, *The Times* (8 Nov 1973), 23 • *WW* (1962–73) • letters to H. Batterbee, 1939–45, Bodl. RH, MSS NZ.s.10, 13 • H. L. Keenleyside, *Memoirs of Hugh L. Keenleyside*, 1 (1981) • B. Pimlott, *Hugh Dalton* (1985) • N. Hillmer and D. Page, eds., *Documents on Canadian external relations, 1947* (1993), vol. 13 of *Documents on Canadian external relations* • Kelly, *Handbk* (1973) • b. cert. • m. cert. • d. cert. • *CGPLA Eng. & Wales* (1974)

Archives Bodl. RH, corresp. with Sir Harry Batterbee

Wealth at death £30,487: probate, 1 Feb 1974, *CGPLA Eng. & Wales*

Lieven [*née* Benckendorff], **Dorothea Khristoforovna, Princess Lieven in the Russian nobility** (1785–1857), political hostess, was born in Riga, Latvia, on 17 December 1785, the daughter of General Christoph von Benckendorff and his wife, Juliane (*née* Baroness Schilling von Canstatt). Her success in life owed much to her parents' powerful connections at the Russian court. Her father was governor of Riga, and enjoyed the full confidence of Emperor Paul I, while her mother was a childhood friend of the empress, Maria Feodorovna, whom she had accompanied to Russia on her marriage to Paul. It was thanks to the Empress Maria that Dorothea entered the Smolny Institute, Russia's leading school for noble girls, and became a lady-in-waiting at court a year before leaving the classroom.

Dorothea's marriage on 24 February 1800 to Count Khristofor Andreyevich Lieven (1774–1839) was also arranged by the empress: inevitably, it determined much of her subsequent life. Though a much older aristocratic family than the newly ennobled Benckendorffs, the Lievens were also Baltic protestants, with exceptionally strong connections at court. Lieven's mother, Charlotta, was governess of the imperial children and subsequently mistress of the robes. She was the Empress Maria's closest

Dorothea Khristoforovna Lieven, Princess Lieven in the Russian nobility (1785–1857), by George Frederic Watts, 1856

friend and confidante in Russia, and remained close to the younger generation of Romanovs, including the emperors Alexander I and Nicholas I. It was thanks to her influence that her son was an aide-de-camp general by 1798 and head of Paul's military campaign chancellery, the key post linking the monarch to the army. Subsequently he served as minister in Berlin, and then as minister and ambassador in London from 1812 to 1834. It was during this posting that his wife acquired her reputation as a hostess and intriguer.

Dorothea Lieven rapidly made her mark on London society, becoming one of the lady patronesses of the exclusive dances held at Almack's. In this capacity she formed a friendship with Emily, Countess Cowper, the mistress and eventual wife of Palmerston. Devoutly committed to the principle of autocratic government, Madame de Lieven (as she was generally known) was to use her social influence to promote the interests of Russia and the Holy Alliance for the next twenty years. Her extensive family connections at the Russian court—her brother, Alexander von Benckendorff, was the first chief of the so-called 'third section and gendarmerie', the state security police—enabled her to pass the unofficial information she garnered through her salon in London on to the Russian government. In 1818 at the congress of Aix-la-Chapelle she became the mistress of the Austrian chancellor, Metternich: although they met infrequently, they continued a regular political correspondence. Another regular correspondent, Lord Grey, was believed to have been her lover in the 1820s. She claimed to have used her influence with him to secure the foreign secretaryship for Palmerston in 1830, believing that he would provide a pro-Russian voice in the whig cabinet. Palmerston, however, proved a political disappointment to Princess Lieven (that title having been conferred in 1826), and in consequence of a diplomatic incident in 1832 he was held responsible by the princess for the recall of the Lievens to Russia in 1834. On their departure *The Times* observed that 'there never figured on the Courtly stage a female intriguer more restless, more urgent, more arrogant, more mischievous, more (politically, and therefore we mean it not offensively) odious than this supercilious Ambassadress'. Thereafter Dorothea Lieven was unremitting in her hostility to Palmerston, and after 1838, when she became the mistress of Guizot, derived satisfaction from thwarting his international plans.

Distress at the circumstances of her departure from London was exacerbated in 1835 by the deaths of Princess Lieven's two youngest sons from scarlet fever. Her own inability to adapt to the harsh Russian climate caused her health to deteriorate. She departed for Paris, where she eventually re-established her salon. The liaison with Guizot contributed to a breach with her husband, who died in January 1839. Living in Paris without any official position, she nevertheless remained a significant point of contact between the Russian and French governments, playing a role in the negotiations connected to both the outbreak and the conclusion of the Crimean War. Dorothea Lieven died at home in the rue St Florentin, Paris, on 26 January 1857, and was buried in the Lieven family cemetery at Mesothen, her nephew's estate near Mitrau in Courland.

Dorothea Lieven's sustained influence reflects not just her powerful international connections but also her native wit, charm, and intelligence, all of which were remarkable. Not a deep, still less a warm-hearted, woman, she lived for the world of high politics, and enjoyed to the full her influence and reputation. Her husband's recall to St Petersburg in 1834 was thus a devastating personal blow. Her role, unusual but not unique, was made possible by the context of aristocratic *ancien régime* Europe, and the intermingling of politics and social life in the diplomatic salons. Of these, none was more famous in the nineteenth century than Dorothea Lieven's, whether in London or Paris. Several of her voluminous correspondences—including those with Metternich, Guizot, Lady Holland, Lady Palmerston, Lord Aberdeen, and Lord Grey—have been published, and are a fine source for historians of early nineteenth-century diplomacy and London political society. DOMINIC LIEVEN

Sources H. M. Hyde, *Princess Lieven* (1938) • *The private letters of Princess Lieven to Prince Metternich, 1820–1826*, ed. P. Quennell (1937) • *The Lieven–Palmerston correspondence, 1828–1856*, ed. and trans. Lord Sudley [A. P. J. C. J. Gore] (1943) • *Correspondence of Princess Lieven and Earl Grey*, ed. and trans. G. Le Strange, 3 vols. (1890) • *The correspondence of Lord Aberdeen and Princess Lieven, 1832–1854*, ed. E. J. Parry, 2 vols., CS, 3rd ser., 60, 62 (1938–9) • A. A. Polovtsov, ed., *Russkii biograficheskii slovar'* [Russian biographical dictionary], 25 vols. (1896–1918)

Archives BL, corresp. and papers, Add. MSS 47341–47408, 47412–47419, 58121–58123 | Balliol Oxf., letters to Lady Alice Peel • Bedford estate office, London, Bedford MSS • BL, corresp. with Lord Aberdeen, Add. MSS 43052–43055, 43268, 43271–43272, 43278 • BL, corresp. with Lord Holland, Add. MS 51613 • BL, letters to Lady Palmerston, Add. MSS 45555–45556 • BL, corresp. with Sir Robert Peel, Add. MSS 40404–40600 • Chatsworth House, Derbyshire, letters to sixth duke of Devonshire • Lambton Park, Chester-le-Street, co. Durham, letters to first earl of Durham • Niedersächsisches Hauptstaatsarchiv Hannover, Hanover, letters to Ernest Augustus, duke of Cumberland • NL Scot., corresp. with Edward Ellice (senior) • PRO, letters to Countess Granville, PRO 30/29 • Staffs. RO, corresp. with second Earl Grey • Staffs. RO, Sutherland MSS • U. Southampton L., Broadlands MSS • U. Southampton L., corresp. with Lord Palmerston and Lady Cowper

Likenesses A. Robertson, watercolour on ivory, 1806, Scot. NPG • T. Lawrence, portrait, 1815, NPG • G. F. Watts, portrait, 1856, priv. coll. [*see illus.*] • J. Lucas, lithograph (after a drawing), BM • portraits, repro. in Hyde, *Princess Lieven*

Lifford. For this title name *see* Hewitt, James, first Viscount Lifford (1709x16–1789).

Liggins, Joseph (*c*.1806–1872), literary impostor, was born at Attleborough, a village near Nuneaton, Warwickshire, the only son of a baker, William Liggins, and his wife, Sarah. He matriculated at St Catharine's College, Cambridge, in 1824, but was rusticated and left without taking his degree. He travelled in Europe, and in 1830–33 was a tutor on the Isle of Man, subsequently returning to Warwickshire to a life of quiet poverty, until he was catapulted to fame by the assumption in and around Nuneaton that he was the new, unknown, author 'George Eliot'.

The real author of *Scenes of Clerical Life*, three stories of midland life published first in *Blackwood's Edinburgh Magazine* between January and November 1857, then in two volumes in January 1858, was Marian *Evans, a free-thinking 'strong-minded woman' (Thomas Carlyle's phrase). She and the writer and journalist G. H. Lewes lived together as man and wife from 1854 until Lewes's death in 1878, as he was unable to divorce his wife.

Marian Evans—or Mary Anne, as she was baptized in 1819 in Chilvers Coton church, near Attleborough—was brought up in and around Nuneaton, the setting of the three stories of *Scenes of Clerical Life*—'The Sad Fortunes of the Revd Amos Barton', 'Mr Gilfil's Love Story', and 'Janet's Repentance'. In them the author drew on personal memories and on hearsay about local clergymen and their families which she had picked up during her childhood and youth. So detailed and credible is her representation of the town and village life of the area that local people—including her own family, from whom she was estranged and who knew nothing of her literary life in London—began to speculate about the authorship. Liggins was first declared to be the author by the reviewer of 'Janet's Repentance' in the *Manx Sun* of 4 July 1857, who remembered this 'gentleman of our own acquaintance, an old Cantab, and well known in this island some five-and-twenty years or more ago'. The *Manx Sun* of 21 May 1859 added, in an article on *Adam Bede*, that Liggins had lived on the Isle of Man between 1830 and 1833. In the 1841 census he is recorded as being aged thirty-five and living in

Church Street, Attleborough, with his parents. No profession or trade is entered against his name.

Marian Evans was at first amused at the rumour, welcoming it as a smokescreen behind which she could hide, but when her first full-length novel, *Adam Bede*, was published to immediate acclaim in February 1859, the universal curiosity about the identity of the author became burdensome, especially as Liggins neglected to disclaim authorship. It became known that he was living in straitened circumstances, and various midlands clergymen and magistrates accused George Eliot's publisher, Blackwood & Sons, of cheating Liggins of his due financial reward. Letters appeared in *The Times* claiming Liggins's authorship. Elizabeth Gaskell, Harriet Martineau, and other well-known authors took up the claim, until in June 1859 Marian Evans and G. H. Lewes were obliged to reveal the true identity of George Eliot in order to put a stop to the wild Liggins stories. Dickens, who had been convinced on reading *Scenes of Clerical Life* and *Adam Bede* that the author was a woman, exulted to Lewes in August 1859, when the secret was at last out: 'I have a horrible and unnatural desire upon me to see Liggins, whom, I am proud to remember I contemptuously rejected' (*Letters of Charles Dickens*, 9.104).

After the Liggins myth had thus finally been scotched, the enigmatic supposed author settled back into obscurity in Nuneaton, dying destitute in the workhouse at Chilvers Coton in late May 1872. He was buried on 1 June at Attleborough. Joseph Liggins is perhaps the only person commemorated in the *Oxford Dictionary of National Biography* for having achieved nothing of importance or influence, except to have been a thorn in the side of a sensitive author. ROSEMARY ASHTON

Sources *The George Eliot letters*, ed. G. S. Haight, 3 (1954), 21n., 78n. • *The Times* (1 April 1859) • *The Times* (6 June 1859) • *Manx Sun* (4 July 1857) • *Manx Sun* (5 Sept 1857) • *Manx Sun* (21 May 1859) • census returns for Attleborough, Nuneaton, Warwickshire, 1841 • Attleborough parish records and register (residence, death, burial), 1872, Nuneaton Library • *The letters of Charles Dickens*, ed. M. House, G. Storey, and others, 9 (1997), 104

Wealth at death destitute: Attleborough parish register, 1872

Light, Edward (1746/7–1832), inventor of musical instruments and composer, was probably the man of that name who on 6 August 1774 married Elizabeth Hawkins at St Mary's, Marylebone Road, Middlesex. Nothing is known of his early life.

Light invented a number of instruments for ladies to play as an accompaniment to singing, at a time when the piano was not yet widely available. His first invention, about 1798, was the harp-guitar, which looked like a small pedal harp, but with seven gut strings, tuned like an English guitar, giving a more powerful tone than a guitar. This was followed by the harp-lute-guitar, with longer strings. He worked on the harp-lute between 1810 and 1813, adding five open strings off the fingerboard and a harp-like pillar to support the extra strings, with brass ring stops which could be used to raise their pitch by a semitone. He then went on to develop the British harp-lute, patented in 1816, with devices known as 'ditals' which when pressed by the fingers would change the pitch of the strings. This became known as the dital harp and although held like a guitar was in effect a small harp, played with both hands.

Light published a number of compositions and arrangements, including *The Ladies' Amusement* (1783), for voice and guitar; *A Collection of Songs* (c.1810), arranged for harp-lute, lyre, and guitar; *Preludes, Exercises, and Recreations* (c.1810), for harp-lute solo; and *A Collection of Psalms, Hymns, etc* (c.1814), arranged for harp-lute and lyre. On the title-page of the latter he describes himself as organist of Trinity chapel, St George's, Hanover Square, and 'Lyrist to H.R.H. the Princess of Wales'. He also brought out a number of instrument tutors, including *The Art of Playing the Guitar* (c.1785); *A Tutor for the Harp-Lute-Guitar* (c.1810); and *A New and Complete Directory to the Art of Playing on the Patent British Lute-Harp* (c.1816). Light died in 1832 at the age of eighty-five.

L. M. MIDDLETON, *rev.* ANNE PIMLOTT BAKER

Sources 'Non-keyboard instruments', *Victoria and Albert Museum catalogue of musical instruments*, 2 (1978), 63–9 • T. Busby, *Concert room and orchestra anecdotes of music and musicians, ancient and modern*, 2 (1825), 275–7 • *New Grove* • *New Grove*, 2nd edn • *IGI* • H. Mendel and A. Reissmann, eds., *Musikalisches Conversations-Lexikon: eine Encyklopädie der gesammten musikalischen Wissenschaften*, 12 vols. (Berlin, 1870–83), vol. 4, p. 529 • Edward Light, patents, 1816, no. 4041

Light, Francis (*bap.* 1740, *d.* 1794), colonist in Penang, Malaya, was baptized on 15 December 1740 in the parish church of Dallinghoo, near Woodbridge, in Suffolk, the natural younger son of William Negus, a prominent landowner of Melton, near Woodbridge, and Mary Light. He was educated at Seckford's Grammar School at Woodbridge and entered the Royal Navy in 1759 as a midshipman aboard the *Captain*. He transferred shortly afterwards to the *Dragon* as an able seaman, but in 1761 he joined the *Arrogant* as a midshipman. In 1763 he was paid off and two years later he embarked for India.

At Madras he obtained command of a country ship belonging to a syndicate of European merchants with interests in Sumatra and the northern regions of the Malay peninsula. He established trading connections with the sultan of Kedah, by whom he was offered in 1771 the port and the coast as far as the island of Penang in return for protection against the bugis of Selangor. He urged on his superiors in Madras the advantages of accepting this offer and on the East India Company the desirability of acquiring Penang as a commercial centre. Missions led by Edward Monckton and Charles Des Voeux were dispatched by the company in 1772 to north Sumatra and Kedah, but without results, because the East India Company refused to promise aid against Selangor.

Light continued to engage in private trade during the 1770s and early 1780s, notably in Salang, off the north-west coast of Siam. Growing Dutch power in the region led to new interest in establishing a British base in the Strait of Malacca, and in 1786 he obtained a renewal of the offer of Penang from the sultan of Kedah, on condition of a defensive alliance with the East India Company. This offer was accepted and Light was appointed superintendent of the island, which was formally acquired as a British possession on 11 August 1786 and called Prince of Wales Island.

From then on Light administered Penang with great skill and energy, and this led to a considerable growth in population and trade. He also successfully defended the island against an attempt by the sultan of Kedah in 1791 to reclaim it because of the East India Company's failure to observe the defensive clause in the treaty of cession.

Light lived with a Portuguese Eurasian woman, Martinha Rozells, and they had at least three children, including William *Light (1786–1839), the founder of Adelaide. Light died on 21 October 1794 in Penang.

JOHN BASTIN, *rev.*

Sources H. P. Clodd, *Malaya's first British pioneer: the life of Francis Light* (1948)
Archives BL, corresp. and papers, Add. MS 45271

Light, William (1786–1839), surveyor and founder of Adelaide, was born in Kuala Kedah, Malaya, on 27 April 1786, the second son of Captain Francis *Light, RN (*bap.* 1740, *d.* 1794), and Martinha Rozells, said to have been a Malay princess but who was most probably a Portuguese Eurasian. He had one brother and one sister. In 1786 his father had established the first British settlement at Penang and became its superintendent, and it was there that William spent his first six years before going to England to be educated by his father's friend George Doherty, of Theberton, Suffolk, where he became proficient in Spanish, French, and painting. In 1799, at the age of thirteen, he joined the navy, leaving two years later as a midshipman. In May 1804 he became a civil internee in France but escaped from Verdun nine months later. By 9 March 1805 he was present at his sister's wedding in Calcutta. Then, in a purely private capacity and for the sheer adventure of it, he accompanied his brother-in-law, Major Welsh of the Indian army, on various expeditions across southern India, helping to disarm Indian troops when a mutiny seemed likely.

Light returned to England, and in May 1808 purchased a commission in the cavalry and served in the Peninsular War, surviving over forty engagements with distinction and bravery. Because of his linguistic and artistic talents he was sent to negotiate with guerrilla groups, and served in Wellington's headquarters, mapping, sketching positions, and undertaking reconnaissance and reporting. He retired from the army on half pay and, ever restless, travelled extensively in Europe, but returned on full pay after 1814 and saw tours of duty in the Channel Islands, Scotland, and Ireland. In 1821 he sold his commission and married Miss E. Perois in Londonderry. In 1823 he became aide-de-camp to Sir Robert Wilson, who had raised an international force to assist the Spanish *Liberales* in their struggle against King Ferdinand. Light rose to lieutenant-colonel in the International Brigade, which was eventually defeated by superior French forces, and he was wounded and imprisoned in the battle of Corunna.

Light's first wife survived long enough to have three children with someone else, though her ultimate fate is not known. In 1824 Light married Mary Bennet, the natural daughter of Charles *Lennox, the third duke of Richmond. The marriage allowed Light to live well; the couple travelled in Europe for several years and in 1827 purchased a yacht and cruised around the Mediterranean for a further three years. These years of travel bore artistic fruit: Light's simple but charming water-colours and sketches were engraved and produced in 1823 as *Sicilian Scenery*, followed in 1828 by *Views of Pompeii*. While visiting Alexandria, Light won the friendship and trust of Mohammed Ali, the pasha of Egypt, and was allowed to cruise on the Nile for three months. Subsequently Light was commissioned by Ali Pasha to return to England to recruit British officers for the emerging Egyptian navy. During his absence his wife deserted him for another man and the couple separated in 1832.

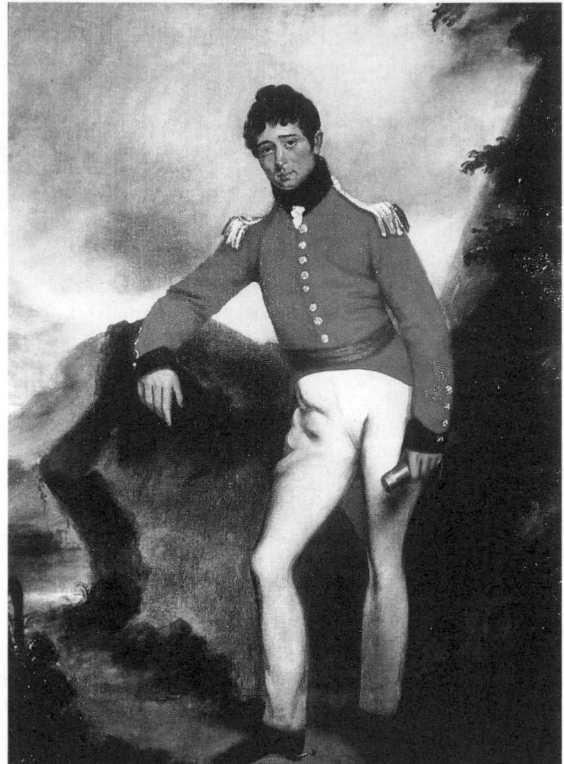

William Light (1786–1839), self-portrait, *c.*1815

In 1834 Light returned to Egypt as the captain of the paddle steamer *Nile*, meeting Captain John Hindmarsh, to whom he gave a letter of introduction to his friend Sir Charles Napier, who had just resigned as governor-designate of the newly founded colony of South Australia. Aided by the introduction Hindmarsh was appointed governor—although at the last minute Napier had recommended Light, who returned to England in January 1836 without a job, and, probably as some sort of compensation, was offered the surveyor-generalship of South Australia at a salary of £400. On 1 May he set sail in the *Rapid* for Australia.

The commissioners for colonization gave Light a series

of all but impossible tasks; he was to explore all the coasts of South Australia and select the site for the first settlement within about two months. With considerable skill he limited his search to five principal locations: the southern part of Eyre peninsula, Kangaroo Island, Encounter Bay, the mouth of the River Murray, and the east coast of St Vincent Gulf. He rejected the first four locations, for sound geographical reasons, in favour of the lightly wooded and well-watered plains of the eastern Gulf lands, which were central to the new colony.

Light also had to decide on the exact site for the capital and lay out 1000 acres of town lots. The coast was too swampy and lacked good drinking water so he planned the centre of Adelaide 6 miles inland. The location of the capital so far from the port was the subject of bitter criticism and at least three attempts were made in the first year to move it elsewhere. As if this were not enough, Light was given the task of surveying over 150,000 acres of land in the surrounding countryside where those who had paid cash in advance could request a 4000 acre special survey in any location. The strains of the unrealistic survey demands were exacerbated by insufficient staff, poor equipment, lack of transport, and low pay. Light himself was now in poor health. When asked to compromise trigonometrical accuracy by adopting the rough-and-ready 'running survey' in order to speed up apportionment, he resigned, in June 1838, and set up his own survey firm. Harassment by his enemies and detractors, increasing ill health, and the disappointment a few months later of losing a lifetime's accumulation of sketches, notebooks, and journals in a fire in his temporary home all took their toll. He moved into his new house, Thebarton, a broken and sick man, nursed by Maria Gandy, who had come out with him on the *Rapid*, eking out a living in his last few months by selling sketches. In October 1839 he died of tuberculosis, and was buried at Thebarton cemetery, Adelaide. Light died a poor man and, as far as is known, had no children with either wife or mistress.

Light was talented and had immense energy. In South Australia he displayed a remarkable vision and grasp of geography and was courteous to his enemies. In his *Brief Journal* (1839, 115) he wrote:

> The reasons that led me to fix Adelaide where it is I do not expect to be generally understood or calmly judged at present. My enemies, however, have done me the good service of fixing the whole of the responsibility on me. I am perfectly willing to bear it; and leave it to posterity, and not to them, to decide whether I am entitled to praise or blame.

Time has vindicated him entirely—his was an excellent site, and in the modern city of Adelaide the separation of port and industry from the central business and administrative district has proved a great advantage. The distinctive plan of Adelaide with its surrounding belt of parklands was most probably the idea of Matthew Davenport Hill, penal reformer, colonial activist, and brother of Rowland Hill, inventor of the penny postage. Light recognized its value and did not attempt to change it and the plan is now generally ascribed to him. Claims in the 1980s that the deputy surveyor-general George Strickland Kingston, and not Light, was the creator of the Adelaide town plan are based on conjecture and flimsy evidence and have been effectively rebutted.

Light's self-portrait in the Art Gallery of South Australia depicts a dashingly handsome but intelligent, even sensitive, face. One can speculate that his mixed ancestry, sallow complexion, alert and handsome face, and black curly hair must have caused him many difficult moments in early nineteenth-century Britain, but they may well have been the goad that prodded him into such furious activity in so many different spheres. MICHAEL WILLIAMS

Sources G. Dutton, *Founder of a city: the life of Colonel William Light* (1960) • D. F. Elder, 'William Light', *Dictionary of Australian artists*, ed. J. Kerr (1992) • D. F. Elder, 'Light, William', *AusDB*, vol. 2 • M. P. Mayo, *The life and letters of Col. William Light* (1937) • M. Williams, *The making of the South Australian landscape: a study in the historical geography of Australia* (1974) • A. F. Stewart, *A short sketch of the lives of Francis and William Light, the founders of Penang & Adelaide* (1901) • G. Dutton and D. F. Elder, *Colonel William Light* (1992) • D. L. Johnson and D. Langmead, *The Adelaide city plan: fiction and fact* (1986) • J. R. Porter, 'Who designed Adelaide? Light or Kingston?', *Building and Architecture* (Nov–Dec 1986), 9, 10, 27, 28 • D. Elder, review of Johnson and Langmead, *Journal of the Historical Society of South Australia*, 15 (1987), 179–83

Likenesses portrait, *c*.1808, priv. coll.; copy, Adelaide Town Hall, Adelaide, Australia • W. Light, self-portrait, *c*.1815, Art Gallery of South Australia, Adelaide, Australia [*see illus.*] • B. Rhind, bronze, 1906, Montefiore Hill, Adelaide, Australia • G. Jones, oils, NPG

Wealth at death owed £620 to Bank of South Australia after assets realized: Dutton, *Founder of a city*, 289

Lightfoot [*married name* Axford], **Hannah** (*b.* **1730**, *d.* in or after **1758**), supposed first wife of George III, was born in the parish of St John's, Wapping, London, on 12 October 1730, the daughter of Matthew Lightfoot (1690–1733), a cordwainer, and his second wife, Mary Wheeler (*d.* 1760). She was brought up by her mother and uncle, Henry Wheeler, a draper, at Wheeler's shop in St James's market. The family were Quakers.

On 11 December 1753, at Alexander Keith's marriage chapel in Curzon Street, Mayfair, Hannah married Isaac Axford (1731–1816), a grocer, originally from Erlestoke, Wiltshire, but apprenticed in Ludgate since 1747. Axford's family were Baptists, not Quakers; this, and the fact that the couple were married by a Church of England clergyman, was against Quaker rules. In 1755 the Westminster monthly meeting investigated the charge that Hannah had been married by a priest and that she had subsequently absconded from her husband. They established the fact of the marriage, but Hannah's mother told them that she knew neither whether Hannah had left her husband nor where she was. On 3 March 1756 the Westminster monthly meeting issued a testimony of denial against Hannah and suspended her. She may have been the Mrs Axford painted by Joshua Reynolds about this time. She was probably alive in early 1757, as Robert Pearne, a West Indies plantation owner living in Isleworth, left her an annuity of £40 per annum; she was described in the will as 'Mrs Hannah Axford formerly Lightfoot, the niece of the late John Jeffreys, watchmaker'. However, on 3 December 1759 Isaac Axford, described as a

Hannah Lightfoot (*b.* 1730, *d.* in or after 1758), by Sir Joshua Reynolds, *c.*1756

widower, married Mary Bartlett at Erlestoke. Axford may have known that Hannah was dead, but when Mary Lightfoot, Hannah's mother, made her will the next year she stated that she had not heard from her daughter in two years, suggesting that Hannah's fate was a mystery.

The disappearance of Hannah Lightfoot would probably have been forgotten, had it not been for a story that grew up around George, prince of Wales. On 10 December 1759 Lady Sophia Egerton wrote to her uncle, Count William Bentinck, that:

> it has often been buzz'd that H.R.H., in spite of his reserve, was not wholly insensible to the passion of Love: and I am assured that he kept a beautiful young Quaker for some years, that she is Dead, and that One Child was the produce of that intrigue. (BL, Egerton MS 1719, fol. 81; Storrar, 27)

The gossip was revived in the *Public Advertiser* for 7 September 1770, ten years after the prince had become George III, when it was stated that 'The defence of H.R.H. will speedily be followed by a new publication entitled, *The Letters of an Elder Brother to a Fair Quaker*.' The item appeared under the heading 'Intelligence Extraordinary', an irregular column which mixed derogatory gossip and fanciful stories about Henry Frederick, duke of Cumberland, the king's scandal-mired brother, and other easy targets. This might suggest that, while the *Public Advertiser* was aware of gossip suggesting that the king had fallen in love with a 'Fair Quaker', it was not expected to be taken very seriously. A few years later, on 26 February 1776, a paper called *The Citizen* explicitly connected Hannah with the king, promising in future editions 'The History and advances to Miss L—htf–t, (The Fair Quakeress), Wherein will be faithfully portrayed some striking pictures of female constancy and princely gratitude which terminated in the untimely death of a young lady' (Storrar, 28). William Combe included the story in his *R[oya]l Register*, alleging that, although 'many persons who live in the World' doubted that the king 'had a Mistress previous to his marriage', he had kept a Quaker, and that the story had been confirmed 'by the public proceedings of [the Quakers'] Meeting concerning it' (*R—l Register*, 141), suggesting that someone had seen or heard of the Westminster monthly meeting's investigations of 1755–6, and imagined that they provided circumstantial evidence to validate the legend. Sir Nathaniel William Wraxall, in his *Historical Memoirs of my Own Time* (1815), reported the story of the king's attachment to a Quaker; notes by Hester Piozzi appended to the 1836 edition stated that a son of George III and Hannah Lightfoot was alive in 1815.

The full flowering of the legend of the king's relationship to Hannah Lightfoot came only in 1821, after the king's death. A correspondent to the *Monthly Magazine* for April 1821 pronounced that 'All the world is acquainted with the attachment of the late King to a beautiful Quakeress of the name of Wheeler' (Thoms, 4), and sought further information. The responses offered varied in their details, but the *Monthly Magazine* claimed that it had verified the facts with a son of Axford's by his second wife:

> From him we learn that the lady lived six weeks with her husband, who was fondly attached to her, but one evening when he happened to be from home, a coach and four came to the door, when she was conveyed into it and carried off at a gallop, no one knew whither. It appears the husband was inconsolable at first, and at different times applied for information about his wife at Weymouth and other places, but died after sixty years in total ignorance of her fate. It has, however, been reported that she had three sons by her lover, since high in the army; that she was buried at Islington under another name, and even that she is still alive. (Thoms, 5)

Various correspondents embellished the story. 'Warminsteriensis' related how Axford's marriage to Hannah had been arranged by Elizabeth Chudleigh, with the help of 'Perryn of Knightsbridge' (a figure perhaps based on Hannah's benefactor Richard Pearne) with the intention of then spiriting her away to Prince George. Axford 'presented a petition at St James', which was not attended to' (Thoms, 6). 'An Inquirer' from Hertfordshire stated that 'a gentleman of the name of Dalton … married a daughter of this H. Lightfoot by the King' (Thoms, 8). When Axford family statements failed to make any allegations against George III, commentators none the less enthusiastically extrapolated confirmation of the king's involvement in Hannah's disappearance from their silence.

The story advanced in *An Historical Fragment Relative to Her Late Majesty Queen Caroline* (1824), where it was claimed that George IV's estranged wife had 'fully believed that his late Majesty, George III, was married to Miss Hannah Lightfoot' (Pendered and Mallett, 158). This pamphlet, along with *Authentic Records of the Court of England* (1832) and *The Secret History of the Court of England* (1832), may have been written by Olivia Serres, a miniature painter who had convinced herself and others that she was the daughter of Henry Frederick, duke of Cumberland, and thus a niece of George III. The legend continued to take up column inches in several periodicals, including in the 1850s and 1860s *Notes and Queries*, where it received the further embellishment that George Rex, a prominent landowner in Cape Colony, had been a son of George III and Hannah Lightfoot. In 1866 Lavinia Ryves, the daughter of Olivia Serres, while seeking a legal declaration that her mother was the duke of Cumberland's legitimate child, produced what purported to be marriage certificates between George, prince of Wales, and Hannah Lightfoot, dated 17 April and 27 May 1759 and witnessed by William Pitt the elder, as well as what she alleged was Hannah's will, dated 7 July 1762 and entrusting two sons and a daughter to the care of their father, George III. The documents were pronounced by the court to be forgeries. The next year William John Thoms, the founder of *Notes and Queries*, attempted to refute Hannah's existence in a pamphlet, but research by the historical writers John Heneage Jesse (a supporter of the marriage story) and Horace Bleackley established the facts of Hannah's origin, the details of the Quaker investigation, and that she was mentioned in Richard Pearne's will.

Interest in proving Hannah's marriage to George III continued. Several writers stated her marriage to the king as a fact, some with the intention of questioning the hereditary and moral right of Queen Victoria to the throne, such as Charles Bradlaugh in *The Impeachment of the House of Brunswick* (1872). Books continued to be published about her into the twentieth century, although the case rarely attracted the interest of academic historians. Mary Lucy Pendered's books *The Fair Quaker* (1910) and (with Justinian Mallet) *Princess or Pretender?* (1939) showed how the evidence had been confused by the extravagant claims of Olivia Serres and Lavinia Ryves, but still used the documentary evidence from the 1750s and the weight of hearsay to argue that there was a relationship between Hannah and George III. Pendered found seventeen families claiming descent from George and Hannah. In the period surrounding the abdication of Edward VIII in 1936, the marriage of George and Hannah Lightfoot was even cited as a precedent in the British royal family for a morganatic marriage, where neither the king's spouse nor his children would enjoy royal status.

Academic study of the early life of George III destroyed any credibility the story of his marriage to Hannah Lightfoot enjoyed. The publication of George's correspondence with John Stuart, third earl of Bute, revealed a prince acutely self-conscious of his moral responsibility as the head of society, to whom conducting a secret affair with any woman would have been inconceivable. The correspondence also confirmed that his passion for Lady Sarah Lennox in 1759 had been the first time he had fallen in love. Research by Ian Christie and Patricia Storrar into the origins of George Rex, the man most often claimed as the son of George and Hannah, showed that he was indisputably a son of John Rex, a distiller from Whitechapel. Christie speculated that the legend arose from gossip about the prince of Wales's character in the late 1750s:

> There must be a girl in his life—there always is. And, of course, the Quakers are splendid targets for malice, such ostentatiously virtuous people—all humbug, of course—two young humbugs together—I expect he's got a Quaker hidden in his closet. (Storrar, 28)

It would have been easy to identify this Quaker as the girl who had disappeared in St James's a few years before.

It is very unlikely that George, prince of Wales, secluded by his mother in Leicester House, knew Hannah Lightfoot. He did not have children with her, nor did he marry her. However, the story continues to attract family historians, romantics, anti-monarchists, and conspiracy theorists, and has been given a new lease of life by the growth of the internet. A television documentary by Kenneth Griffith in 1997 ignored Christie's and Storrar's work on George Rex and argued that the documents produced by Lavinia Ryves in 1866 were genuine. In December 2000 *British Archaeology* reported the discovery of the tomb of Charlotte Augusta Catherine Dalton (*d.* 1832) at St Peter's Church, Carmarthen, with the headline 'Forgotten "royal" graves found in Carmarthen church: George III's first marriage casts doubt on legitimacy of the Queen'. Charlotte Dalton was the daughter of the Dalton mentioned in the *Monthly Magazine* in 1821, but Pendered had shown that her mother was of the Ritzau or Ritso family, with a history of service to the house of Hanover in Germany and Britain, and there was no reason to connect the Daltons by blood to George III. The persistence of the Hannah Lightfoot legend owes more to the mystique that kinship with the British royal family continues to enjoy in the imagination of the worldwide public than to an interest in exploring the historical foundations of the story.

MATTHEW KILBURN

Sources P. Storrar, *George Rex: death of a legend* (1974) · I. R. Christie, 'The family origins of George Rex of Knysna', *N&Q*, 220 (1975), 18–23, 364 · M. L. Pendered, *The fair Quaker: Hanna Lightfoot, and her relations with George III* (1910) · M. L. Pendered and J. Mallett, *Princess or pretender?* (1939) · W. J. Thoms, *Hannah Lightfoot; Queen Charlotte and the Chevalier D'Éon: Dr Wilmot's Polish princess* (1867) · [W. Combe], *The r–l register, with annotations in another hand*, 3 (1779) · *Public Advertiser* (7 Sept 1770) · N. W. Wraxall, *Historical memoirs of my own time*, 2nd edn, 2 vols. (1815) · *The historical and the posthumous memoirs of Sir Nathaniel William Wraxall, 1772–1784*, ed. H. B. Wheatley, 5 vols. (1884), vol. 1 · www.britarch.ac.uk/ba/ba56/ba56news.html [*British Archaeology* 56 (Dec 2000)], 12 July 2002 · B. Wood-Holt, 'Hannah Lightfoot and Isaac Axford', *N&Q*, 229 (1984), 397–401 · S. Mitchell and W. I. Axford, 'Isaac Axford and Hannah Lightfoot', *N&Q*, 241 (1996), 304–5 · D. Mannings, *Sir Joshua Reynolds: a complete catalogue of his paintings*, 2 vols. (2000) · C. H. Price, *George Rex: king or esquire?* (1974) · *N&Q*, 178 (1940), 144 · S. Rex, 'Hannah Lightfoot—the fair Quaker', web.shockware.com/users/srex/hannah.html, 12 July 2002 · N. Greenway, 'Kenneth Griffith: the legend of George Rex', www.cix.co.uk/~nrgreenway/kg/doc_grex.htm, 12 July 2002

Likenesses J. Reynolds, oils, *c.*1756, priv. coll. [*see illus.*]

Lightfoot, John (1602–1675), Hebraist and biblical scholar, was born at home on 29 March 1602 in Stoke-on-Trent, the second son of Thomas Lightfoot (1577?–1658), vicar of

John Lightfoot (1602–1675), by Robert White, pubd 1684

Uttoxeter, Staffordshire, for thirty-six years, and Elizabeth Bagnall (1566?–1637). Both his parents had been born near by—his father at Shelton, his mother at Bagnall. Lightfoot had four brothers: Thomas (the eldest), a merchant; Peter, a physician; and Josiah and Samuel, both clergymen. When his father took up a living at Barthomley, John attended grammar school nearby at Moreton-Green, near Congleton, Cheshire, under Mr Thomas Whitehead. In July 1617 he matriculated from Christ's College, Cambridge, where one of his tutors, William Chappel, also the tutor of John Milton and Henry More, reportedly thought Lightfoot 'the best Orator of all the undergraduates in the Town' (Strype, 'Some account', 1.i–ii). About 1621 he graduated BA and in 1624 MA. From 1621 to 1623 he was briefly usher at Repton School, where Whitehead had become master, and he was ordained a deacon at Lichfield in 1622. In 1626 he became chaplain to Sir Rowland Cotton of Bellaport, Shropshire, who encouraged him to return to the study of Hebrew, which he had ceased at Cambridge. He went to London on the urging of Cotton's uncle, Sir Allen Cotton, who was lord mayor, but he did not stay long and even considered moving overseas. During his chaplaincy he acquired the rectory of Stone, Staffordshire, and on 21 May 1628 he married Joyce Copwood (*d. c.*1656), widow of Mr George Copwood of Dilverne, Staffordshire, and daughter of William Crompton of Stone-Park. Joyce already had two sons and a daughter from her first marriage; the union with Lightfoot brought more children—four sons and two daughters. After two years at Stone and about the time he married, Lightfoot moved to Hornsey, Middlesex, in order to work with the collections at Sion College. From his Hornsey study he 'penned for Recreation at Vacant Houres' a study of the Talmud and Jewish customs, *Erubhin, or, Miscellanies Christian and Judaicall* (1629), which he dedicated to Cotton.

A public life In 1630 Lightfoot returned to Staffordshire, when Cotton procured for him the rectory at Ashley, where he remained until 1642. He pursued biblical studies in this rural retreat (building a small study for the purpose in the middle of his garden), though a manuscript assize sermon of his from about 1633, in which he chastised 'our prophane wakes, maypoles, morises, shooting, danceing, leapeing, & what not upon the Sabbath day' (BL, Sloane MS 1926, fol. 65*v*), suggests a role in public debates.

In June 1642 Lightfoot returned to London, probably pressed into religious service by the new parliamentarian government. He preached a fast sermon before the Commons in March 1643 (his fast sermons of August 1645 and February 1647 were also published), and he praised members of the house for striving 'to preserve the State … [and] to serve the Temple' (Lightfoote, *Elias Redivivus*, sig. A2). He resigned his living at Ashley, upon being assured it would be presented to his younger brother, and took up that of St Bartholomew's behind the exchange. He was soon called upon to join the Westminster assembly of divines, probably because of his Hebraic knowledge. The assembly first met on 1 July 1643 and Lightfoot served uninterruptedly for about five months; in late January 1644 he took up the rectory of Much Munden, Hertfordshire (which living he held until his death). His journal from July 1643 to 31 December 1644 is a vital source for the assembly's activities, though Lightfoot's many contributions to debate are often found in Robert Baillie's *Letters and Journals* and other sources. His journal reveals a peripatetic existence: from February to December 1644 he travelled to Munden virtually every Saturday, held services on Sunday, and travelled back on Monday, as well as remaining in Munden for fast weeks in March, April, August, and November. In London he was living in Moor Lane in 1643 and in Little Britain in 1644. He moved his family to Munden in May 1644, but moved them back to London in September, and by 1650 was living in Old Jewry. Moreover, he occasionally missed a crucial vote as he was called into the City to advise ministers there or to dine with the Scots' commissioners. By September 1643 he was a regular member of an informal committee which heard and reported on a sermon before the start of each assembly from a ministerial candidate whom the Commons proposed to present to a living. He also mentions meeting in committee after dinner to consider what would be taken up at the next meeting. Given that Lightfoot was on the committee to consider Francis Rouse's metrical Psalms from December 1643 (he insisted that sung Psalms be kept in the *Directory*), and regularly held morning devotions with the Lords every Friday from mid-1644, the mid-1640s must have been the busiest period of his life.

In the assembly itself Lightfoot was outspoken. Despite holding marked Erastian views, he often sided with the presbyterians against the Independents. He was scandalized by blasphemies held by commoners and by Antinomian beliefs expressed by a few clergymen. His fast sermon of 1645 also attacked the 'erroneous' opinion of 'the Millenaries alate, which take this matter about the thousand years, strictly and exactly', which Lightfoot saw to be the result of 'when mechanicks, unlettered and ignorant men will take upon them to bee preachers' (Lightfoot, *A Sermon Preached*, dedication, 3, 31). But he resisted any hint of clerical superiority over the state, such as the attempt to have the assembly judge the Commons according to scripture, and in one debate dismissively referred to 'the Scots' Covenant' (Paul, 93). In 1643 he convinced Edmund Calamy and other presbyterians to preach on Christmas day, over their objections to that superstitious holiday, in order to prevent the London populace rising against parliament. Overall he supported the presbyterian directory, and presbyterians repeatedly latched on to his biblical exegesis—many congregations among early Christians in Jerusalem, but one church—to defend presbyterian church organization (of course, this same position could be used to defend episcopal diocesanal organization as well). Other times, however, Lightfoot appears to have been alone in his views: uniquely arguing, for example, that Christ had not given the disciplinary power of the keys directly to the apostles. And his annoyance grew with waiting on the spirit of God to achieve consensus with the Independent minority. As the military situation worsened in 1643–4, Lightfoot demanded a simple majority vote to establish doctrinal points.

Although the Westminster assembly ceased to meet regularly after 1649, Lightfoot continued to meet with a handful of divines until the triers began their work in March 1654. He also returned to biblical studies. In 1645 he had urged the Commons to commission a review and survey of the Bible, and he had already published volumes on Exodus (1643) and Acts (1645). He continued his four-part *Harmony of the Four Evangelists* (1644–58), in which he reconciled the life of Christ as revealed in the four gospels and linked it to the meaning of the Old Testament. And, in 1658, he published the first part of his most important biblical study, *Horae Hebraicae et Talmudicae*. (Further parts followed in 1663, 1664, 1671, 1674, and, posthumously prepared by Richard Kidder, 1678.)

Academic life at Cambridge Lightfoot returned to formal academic life and to the University of Cambridge when parliamentary visitors appointed him master of St Catharine's College in 1650. In 1651 he graduated DD, disputing 'against the Enthusiasts' and belief in contemporary prophecy by noting that in the book of Revelation 'even then men were directed to the written word' (Strype, 'Some account', 1.xiv). He preached frequently at the university, and the manuscript of a 1652 sermon preached at St Mary's, Cambridge, survives (BL, Lansdowne MS 122, fols. 114–137*v*). For a brief period in 1654 and 1655 he performed the office of vice-chancellor, the incumbent being very sick, and his 1655 commencement speech praised the first volumes of Brian Walton's polyglot Bible (1657) as well as Oliver Cromwell's patronage of it. Lightfoot assisted Walton's work throughout the 1650s, commenting on the Samaritan Pentateuch, providing manuscripts from the university library, helping draw a map of Judea, and providing notes from the Jerusalem Talmud. Lightfoot's own 'Chorographical observations' preface the Bible, and Drs Walton and Edmund Castel acknowledged his important assistance. 'The deserved repute of [Lightfoot's] name and worth amongst all the learned nation' (Castel to Lightfoot, BL, Lansdowne MS 1055, fol. 42, 2 Dec 1657) was highly valued by his circle of learned friends and correspondents: Walton, Castel (Arabic professor of Cambridge and author of *Lexicon heptaglotton*, 1669), the theologian Herbert Thorndike, Dr John Buxtorf of Basel (both the elder and his son, who succeeded him in the Hebrew professorship there), Frederick Mieg (counsellor to the elector palatine), Gisbertus Voetius (divinity professor of the Netherlands), Dr Edward Pocock (professor of Hebrew and Arabic at Oxford), and Samuel Clark (keeper of the library at Oxford), among others. He also assisted Matthew Poole with his *Synopsis criticorum* (1669).

Lightfoot's wife died about 1656. Soon thereafter he married Anne (*d*. in or before 1675), widow of Austin Brograve, uncle of Sir Thomas Brograve, baronet, Lightfoot's 'very worthy and learned friend and neighbor' (BL, Add. MS 22905, fol. 65*v*, 19 Aug 1667); there were no children of this marriage. His sons John (*d*. 1661) and Anastatius Cotton Jackson (named for Lightfoot's distinguished patron and his friend Sir John Jackson) received their BA degrees from St Catharine's in 1654; both became ministers and John was briefly chaplain to Walton, by then bishop of Chester.

Lightfoot continued to minister to Munden, where he often remained all Sunday at the church reading prayers and preaching morning and afternoon, as his parsonage house was a mile distant from the church. When he was elsewhere, he longed 'to be at home with his Russet-Coats, as he was wont to call his Country neighbours' (Strype, 'Some account', 1.v). Munden had been sequestered when Lightfoot obtained it in 1643, and he paid a regular contribution to the old incumbent, who died before the Restoration. At the Restoration Lightfoot was briefly ejected when a Cambridge fellow procured a grant for the living, but Archbishop Sheldon confirmed Lightfoot as rector and he was restored. He retained his love for Staffordshire, 'my dearly honoured and beloved Native Country' (Lightfoote, *Harmony*, sig. A2), and preached three sermons before the London feasts of the natives of that county in 1658, 1660, and 1663.

Also at the Restoration Lightfoot attempted to resign the mastership of St Catharine's and return it to the previous incumbent, Dr William Spurstow. But Spurstow refused and Lightfoot went to the king to get letters for the post. On his return from Westminster, the college fellows rode outside Cambridge to meet him and gave him a ceremonious reception. He dedicated one publication to St Catharine's and he continued to serve as master until his death. In addition he evidently encouraged the rebuilding of the main court there, which began in 1673.

In early 1661 Lightfoot was appointed one of the assistants to the Savoy conference, though he attended only once or twice, evidently disgusted by the acrimony. In any case, his interpretation of the Book of Common Prayer remained lax: he did not wear the surplice and selected only certain portions of the prescribed liturgy for worship. The lord keeper, Sir Orlando Bridgman, bestowed upon him a prebendary at Ely, where he was installed in February 1668. He preached a visitation sermon there in 1674.

Lightfoot's second wife, Anne, and his eldest and his youngest sons (John and Thomas) predeceased him, as did his youngest daughter, Sarah. Anastatius became a minister in Thundridge, Hertfordshire, and Athanasius, his third son, was brought up to trade in London. His daughters married: Joyce to Mr Duckfield, rector of Aspeden, Hertfordshire, and Sarah to Mr Coclough, a gentleman of Staffordshire. Lightfoot developed a fever during a cold spell, perhaps after travelling from Munden to take residence at Ely, and died after a fortnight's illness there on 6 December 1675. Gervase Fulwood, a former fellow of St Catharine's, preached his funeral sermon at Much Munden, where he was buried three days later.

Posthumous publications Lightfoot was unable to finish organizing his works so that a collection could be printed. Indeed he had complained that he could no longer find a publisher willing to finance printing his Latin works within England. Duckfield received many of his father-in-law's papers and gave them to John Strype, who wrote a memoir of Lightfoot's life which prefaced his *Works*, published in 1684. Other posthumous published collections of Lightfoot's studies are *Opera omnia* (1686, with a preface by John Texelius), and editions of his works by Jacob Rhenferd (1686), Campegius Vitringa the elder (1687), and Jacobus Lydius (1701), as well as Georg Henrich Goetze's *Syllogum observationum theolgicum J. Lightfooto* (1706), and *Observation Lightfootina de nomine Sethur cujus litterae faciunt numerum 666 ad Num. xiii* (1732). Strype also edited a miscellaneous collection in English, *Some genuine remains of the late pious and learned John Lightfoot, D.D. consisting of three tracts* (1700), and John Rogers Pitman edited a thirteen-volume *Whole Works* (1822–5). Lightfoot's *Horae Hebraicae*, four volumes translated into English, was edited by Robert Gardel as recently as 1859. Strype's collections and other Lightfoot manuscripts survive in the British Library, including his funeral sermon on Sir Rowland Cotton. He gave his many oriental books to Harvard College, but these burned in a fire in 1769. His portrait hangs in the hall of St Catharine's and is the frontispiece to his collected *Works* and to his *Opera omnia*. His chronological computations, for example that 'the creation of man had taken place at 9 a.m. on 23 October in the year 4004 B.C.' (Neil, 257), now seem dated. And Edward Gibbon thought Lightfoot had worked among the Hebrew texts for so long that he had become 'the Christian Rabbi' (E. Gibbon, 'Reign of Julian', chap. 23, n. 74). Lightfoot's work on Revelation has been adopted by contemporary preterists and placed on the internet, though he might be horrified to be associated with such prophetic enthusiasts. But modern Hebraic scholarship can be said to date from Lightfoot. His works such as *The Temple* (1649–50) display an archaeological, historical, philological, and even anthropological understanding of the biblical past.

NEWTON E. KEY

Sources J. Strype, 'Some account of the life of the Reverend and most learned John Lightfoot D.D.', *The works of the Reverend and learned John Lightfoot D.D.: … in two volumes: with the authors life*, rev. G. Bright (1684) · Venn, *Alum. Cant.* · A. Kippis and others, eds., *Biographia Britannica, or, The lives of the most eminent persons who have flourished in Great Britain and Ireland*, 2nd edn, 5 vols. (1778–93), 5.2931–6 · R. S. Paul, *The assembly of the Lord: politics and religion in the Westminster assembly and the 'Grand debate'* (1985) · J. Stryp[e], ed., *Some genuine remains of the late pious and learned John Lightfoot, D.D. consisting of three tracts* (1700) · *The whole works of Rev. John Lightfoot, D.D.*, ed. J. R. Pitman, *Journal of the Proceedings of the Assembly of Divines: from January [sic, July] 1, to December 31, 1644*, 13 (1824) · H. J. Rose, *A new general biographical dictionary*, ed. H. J. Rose and T. Wright, 12 vols. (1857), vol. 9 · A. Chalmers, ed., *The general biographical dictionary*, new edn, 20 (1815) · S. W. Carruthers, *The everyday work of the Westminster assembly* (1943) · J. Lightfoot, *A sermon preached before the honorable House of Commons … August 26, 1645* (1645) · J. Lightfoote, *Elias redivivus: a sermon preached before the honorable House of Commons … March 29, 1643* (1643) · J. Lightfoot, *A sermon preached before the honourable House of Commons … Febr. 24, 1646/47* (1647) · J. Lightfoote, *The harmony of the foure evangelists … the second part* (1647) [also first, third, and fourth pts consulted] · W. Neil, 'The criticism and theological use of the Bible, 1700–1750', *The Cambridge history of the Bible*, 3: *The west from the Reformation to the present day*, ed. S. L. Greenslade (1963), 238–93 · L. A. Weigle, 'English versions since 1611', *The Cambridge history of the Bible*, 3: *The west from the Reformation to the present day*, ed. S. L. Greenslade (1963), 361–82 · W. Haller, *Liberty and reformation in the puritan revolution* (1955) · G. G. Cunningham, ed., *Lives of eminent and illustrious Englishmen*, 3 (1835) · J. Granger, *A biographical history of England, from Egbert the Great to the revolution*, 4th edn, 4 vols. (1804), vol. 3, pp. 275–6 · J. Fletcher, *The history of the revival and progress of independency in England* (1849), vol. 4 · W. A. Shaw, *A history of the English church during the civil wars and under the Commonwealth, 1640–1660*, 1 (1900) · S. Maunder, *The biographical treasury* (1876) · philologos.org/_eb-jl/default.htm [where preterists have published parts of his *Horae Hebraicae et Talmudicae*], 18 Feb 2002 · www.preteristarchive.com/StudyArchive/l/lightfoot-john.html [where preterists have published parts of his *Horae Hebraicae et Talmudicae*], 18 Feb 2002

Archives BL, collections, Lansdowne MS 399 | BL, assize sermon, 1633, Sloane MS 1926, fols. 47–66*v* · BL, corresp. of Samuel Clarke, Add. MS 22905 · BL, corresp with and letters to J. Strype, Lansdowne MS 1055

Likenesses R. White, line engraving, BM, NPG; repro. in *Works of John Lightfoot*, 2 vols. (1684) [*see illus.*] · oils, St Catharine's College, Cambridge · portrait, repro. in J. Lightfoot, *Opera Omnia*, ed. [J. Texelius], repro. at www.kth-linz.ac.at/institute/at/lightfoot/, accessed 2 July 2002 · portrait, repro. in Strype, 'Some account of the life', frontispiece

Lightfoot, John (1735–1788), Church of England clergyman and naturalist, was born on 9 December 1735 at Newent in Gloucestershire, one of three children of Stephen Lightfoot (1707–1769), yeoman farmer, and his wife, Hester (1704–1769). He was married on 10 November 1780 to Matilda Raynes (*b.* 1759/60), daughter of a wealthy mill owner. They had six children in seven years, four girls, one of whom died in infancy, and two boys. A loving husband and father, Lightfoot was friendly, loyal, modest, and sensitive.

Lightfoot devoted his life to the study of natural history, focusing on the British flora, ornithology, and conchology. Educated at the Crypt School in Gloucester, he entered Pembroke College, Oxford, in 1753, as an exhibitioner, to study for the church. He obtained his BA in 1756, and his first appointment was as perpetual curate and lecturer at Colnbrook, Middlesex. He lived in the Lecturer's House in Uxbridge for the rest of his life. He also held the living of Shalden, near Alton, in Hampshire (1765–77), and became acquainted with the naturalist Gilbert White at nearby Selborne.

Lightfoot received his most important and personally fulfilling appointment, as chaplain to the dowager duchess of Portland, Margaret Cavendish-Bentinck, in 1767, soon after proceeding MA. The duchess gave him the livings of Gotham, Sutton in Lound, and Scrooby, Nottinghamshire, in 1777. Altogether he earned some £600 per annum, £500 from his ecclesiastical preferments and £100 from the duchess. He spent three days each week at Bulstrode Park, Beaconsfield, Buckinghamshire, the duchess's summer residence, mostly caring for her important collections of plants and shells. She shared his deep interest in natural history, and she and her great friend Mary Delany were devoted to him, enjoying deep discussions with him in the evenings—Mrs Delany called him 'the little philosopher'. Many famous naturalists and scientists visited the duchess, and Lightfoot was on good terms with Joseph Banks, William Curtis, Dryander, Samuel Goodenough, Thomas Pennant, and Solander, among others. Banks introduced him to Sir John Cullum, of Hardwick House, Bury St Edmunds, and they and their families became lifelong friends. Many of his letters to Cullum survive.

In 1772 the traveller and naturalist Thomas Pennant invited Lightfoot to accompany him on a tour of Scotland. They travelled on horseback and by sailing boat, from 18 May until 20 October. Lightfoot wrote his *Flora Scotica* (published 22 September 1777, at Pennant's expense) in English rather than Latin, and included information on habitats, synonymy, Scottish and Gaelic names, and the uses of plants. The work was arranged according to the Linnaean system. Pennant contributed an account on Scottish fauna, and Moses Griffiths, his servant, thirty-five drawings. Lightfoot consulted Sir Joseph Banks, Solander, Sibthorp, and Dr Hope of Edinburgh, among others, and acknowledged their help. Sir Robert Sibbald in 1684 had listed 500 Scottish species, mainly lowland plants; Lightfoot's *Flora* described 1250, including cryptogams.

In 1773 Lightfoot accompanied Joseph Banks on a botanical tour of Wales. He kept a journal (Riddelsdell, 290–307) and also wrote a long descriptive letter to Gilbert White on 13 September 1773. He completed his knowledge of the British flora by touring Devon and Cornwall in August and September 1774.

After the dowager duchess of Portland died in 1785 Lightfoot was commissioned to compile a catalogue of the Portland Museum, which was auctioned in 1786. A modest man, he declined the offer of a doctorate from Glasgow University, on the grounds that his position in the church did not merit it. The Natural History Society of Edinburgh sent him a parchment. Three genera of plants were named *Lightfootia* in his honour, by Schwartz, von Schreber, and L'Héritier (all now superseded). He was elected a fellow of the Royal Society in 1781, and accepted an invitation to be a founder member of the Linnean Society, but died before the first meeting.

Lightfoot was taken ill while shopping in Uxbridge and died at his home the following day, 21 February 1788, of what would now be called a coronary thrombosis. He was buried in Cowley churchyard near Uxbridge. His herbarium was bought by George III for Queen Charlotte, and is now at the Royal Botanic Gardens, Kew.

JEAN K. BOWDEN

Sources J. K. Bowden, *John Lightfoot, his work and travels* (1989) · T. Pennant, 'Account of the author', in J. Lightfoot, *Flora Scotica*, ed. T. Pennant, 2nd edn (1789) · *The autobiography and correspondence of Mary Granville, Mrs Delany*, ed. Lady Llanover, 2nd ser., 1 (1862) · T. Pennant, *A tour in Scotland and voyage to the Hebrides, 1772*, 1 (1774) · T. Pennant, *A tour in Scotland and voyage to the Hebrides, 1772*, 2 (1776) · H. J. Riddelsdell, 'Lightfoot's visit to Wales in 1773', *Journal of Botany, British and Foreign*, 43 (1905), 290–307 · R. Sibbald, *Scotia illustrata, sive, Prodromus historae naturalis* (1684) · [G. White], *The natural history and antiquities of Selborne*, ed. T. Bell, 2 vols. (1877) · A. Rees and others, *The cyclopaedia, or, Universal dictionary of arts, sciences, and literature*, 45 vols. (1819–20) · private information (2004) · J. Lightfoot, letters to Sir John Cullum, Suffolk RO · administration, PRO, PROB 6/164, fol. 207v

Archives NHM, journal [copy] · NL Scot., Flora Scotica · RBG Kew, specimens · RS, papers · U. Nott. L., notes and travel papers · U. Oxf., department of plant sciences, annotated books | Linn. Soc., corresp. with Richard Pulteney · Linn. Soc., letters to Dr J. E. Smith · NL Wales, letters to Thomas Pennant · NRA, letters to Sir Joseph Banks · Suffolk RO, Bury St Edmunds, letters to Sir John Cullum · U. Nott. L., letters to the duchess of Portland

Likenesses W. Curtis, silhouette, RBG Kew · portrait, Linn. Soc.

Wealth at death £600 p.a. from various ecclesiastical livings (falling to £500 in 1785): Pennant, 'Account of the author'

Lightfoot, Joseph Barber (1828–1889), biblical scholar and bishop of Durham, was born at 84 Duke Street, Liverpool, on 13 April 1828. His father, John Jackson Lightfoot (*d.* 1843), an accountant, was a member of a Yorkshire family. His mother was Ann Matilda, daughter of Joseph Barber of Birmingham, but originally of Newcastle upon Tyne; she was a sister of John Vincent Barber, the landscape artist. Lightfoot was a sickly child. Until he was thirteen he was educated by tutors at home, and then at Liverpool Royal Institution under Dr Iliff. In 1843 his father died, and in January 1844 the family left Liverpool for Birmingham; there Lightfoot was sent to King Edward's School, where he came under the influence of Dr James Prince Lee, to whose teaching he looked back with respect and gratitude. He was already an excellent classical scholar and a good mathematician. He delighted in work and rarely joined in games. He had a cheerful temper, with much dry humour, and a certain quaintness of manner, which seems to have persisted through life, together with a natural and unselfconscious piety. His closest friend at school was E. W. Benson, afterwards archbishop of Canterbury. They read Greek plays together and took long

Joseph Barber Lightfoot (1828–1889), by Sir William Blake Richmond, 1889 [detail]

walks, visiting churches and other places of interest. Their friendship remained unbroken in later life.

Cambridge In October 1847 Lightfoot went up to Trinity College, Cambridge, where his college tutor was W. H. Thompson, subsequently regius professor of Greek and master of Trinity. At the end of his first year he became a private pupil of B. F. Westcott, who had by three years preceded him from King Edward's to Trinity and later succeeded him as bishop of Durham. This was the beginning of another important and lifelong friendship. As an undergraduate Lightfoot is said to have matured slowly, but in 1851, already a wrangler, he became senior classic and chancellor's medallist. Legend had it that he wrote his tripos papers without a mistake. Not surprisingly he was elected fellow of Trinity in 1852, and the following years were spent in the routine usual for a young resident fellow—private study, instruction of private pupils, and college lectures.

In 1853 Lightfoot obtained the Norrisian prize with an essay which was long supposed, on the authority of F. J. A. Hort in the *Dictionary of National Biography*, to have been lost, apparently destroyed by Lightfoot. It has now been identified, with a high degree of probability, with a manuscript preserved in the Durham Chapter Library. The document is important as the earliest piece of Lightfoot's theological writing, on a subject that continued to be of great importance to him. The proposition to be discussed for the prize was 'The gospels could not have originated in any or all those forms of religious opinion which prevailed among the Jews at the time of our Saviour's incarnation'. Behind this could be traced D. F. Strauss's attack on the historical trustworthiness of the gospels in his *Life of Jesus*. It was fundamental to Lightfoot's understanding of Christianity that the gospel accounts were, in every sense, true, and to establish this he considered all the aspects of Judaism and Judaizing Christianity known to him.

Other early pieces by Lightfoot are contained in the *Journal of Classical and Sacred Philology*, which he helped to found and to edit, but which had a short life—from March 1854 to December 1859. It is indicative of Lightfoot's interests at this time that his contributions were made in both divisions, classical and sacred (biblical and patristic), of the journal's proposed scope. Most important in view of Lightfoot's subsequent career was a critical survey, 'Recent editions of St Paul's epistles', in which Lightfoot reviewed commentaries by C. J. Ellicott, A. P. Stanley, and Benjamin Jowett, and developed his own understanding of the commentator's task.

Lightfoot was ordained by Dr Prince Lee (by then bishop of Manchester) deacon in 1854 and priest in 1858. In 1857 he became one of the three tutors of Trinity and assumed greater responsibility in the life of the college. In college he lectured occasionally on the Greek New Testament, but mainly on classical texts, where he had a special interest in the Orestean trilogy of Aeschylus, of which he intended to bring out an edition—an intention that lingered for some time but which was never fulfilled. It seems that he did not find it easy to enter into close relations with his undergraduate pupils, but when his natural shyness was overcome they found him devoted to their interests, and in addition to work during term he was prepared to join vacation reading parties. At the same time he was deepening his knowledge of theology, and read for long hours not only in classical but in biblical and patristic texts.

> No man ever loitered so late in the Great Court that he did not see Lightfoot's lamp burning in his study window, though no man either was so regularly present in morning Chapel at seven o'clock that he did not find Lightfoot always there with him. (Eden and MacDonald, 5)

Lightfoot was soon to pass from tutorship to professorship. In 1860 he was a candidate for the Hulsean chair of divinity. He was not appointed, but after only one year the successful candidate, C. J. Ellicott, became bishop of Gloucester and Bristol, and Lightfoot took his place. He now lectured on the New Testament, especially Paul's epistles, and his lectures became so popular that no lecture room was large enough, and the hall of Trinity was brought into use. It was no doubt at this time that his commentaries began to take shape. He was also engaged in university administration. A new body, the council of the senate, had been established in 1856; of this Lightfoot was elected a member in 1860, and, with an interval of two years, he retained his place until 1878. He was an influential member of this influential council, which was responsible for the submission of graces to the senate. He played an important part in the institution of the local examinations. In 1861 he became one of the chaplains of the prince consort, then chancellor of the university; in the next year he became chaplain to the queen.

In 1870 the regius professorship of divinity fell vacant; it is most probable that, had he allowed his name to be considered, Lightfoot would have been elected; however, he refused to stand, and pressed the claims of his friend Westcott, who was appointed.

> He called me to Cambridge to occupy a place which was his own by right; and having done this he spared no pains to secure for his colleague favourable opportunities for action, while he himself withdrew from the position which he had long virtually occupied. (B. F. Westcott, Preface, in J. B. Lightfoot, *Clement of Rome*, 2nd edn, 1890, viii)

The two friends were soon joined in Cambridge by a third, F. J. A. Hort, who in 1872 became a fellow of Emmanuel College. Long before this, in 1859–60, the three (so closely associated that they were called the 'Cambridge triumvirate') had planned to collaborate in a commentary on the whole of the New Testament. Lightfoot began work without delay; his commentaries are noted below. Westcott and Hort were preoccupied with their work on the text of the New Testament and with other matters, but together the three, especially Lightfoot, exercised a strong personal influence in Cambridge. Lightfoot's great reputation as an outstanding biblical and patristic scholar, together with his generally tolerant and moderating influence, served both to maintain a stable atmosphere in Cambridge at a time of much instability and controversy in the Church of England and to inspire younger scholars to work on lines similar to his own. There is no doubt that he helped to assuage doubts that had been evoked by such publications as Darwin's *Origin of Species* (1859) and *Essays and Reviews* (1860). Hort was deeply interested in Darwin's work; Westcott found it hard to decide which he liked less—the liberalism of the essayists or the illiberalism of the episcopal reaction. Hort contemplated an essay on Darwinism, but he and Lightfoot were too busy to respond to *Essays and Reviews*.

Public duties Lightfoot continued to be a powerful influence in Cambridge but was more and more drawn away from the university. In 1871 he was appointed a canon of St Paul's, and he became widely known as a preacher. It was characteristic of him that in spite of some marked differences in theological and ecclesiastical opinion he lived on excellent terms with his fellow canons and especially perhaps with the dean (R. W. Church). He had advocated the revision of the familiar Authorized Version of the Bible, and was one of the original members of the New Testament Revision Company, whose revisers held sessions that occupied forty days a year, from 1870 to 1880. Lightfoot had argued that the *textus receptus*, the Greek text from which the older version was made, needed, as a result of the discovery of better and more ancient manuscripts, correction in many places, and that improved knowledge of Greek called for new renderings. He continued, after the publication of the Revised Version, to defend it.

Other public duties also took Lightfoot away from purely academic pursuits. In 1877 the Universities of Oxford and Cambridge Act nominated him one of the seven commissioners for Cambridge. In addition he argued, in an address at Liverpool and subsequently, that university colleges should be set up in all the great centres of population. There should, he thought, be a central university body charged with the power of conferring degrees. He also held that women should be admitted to these colleges.

Bishop of Durham The real break with Cambridge was still to come. In 1867 Lightfoot had declined Lord Derby's offer of the bishopric of Lichfield. He believed that he could do better and more useful work in Cambridge. The canonry at St Paul's may have encouraged him to feel that he was making a contribution to the life of the national church as well as to Cambridge. But Lord Beaconsfield's offer of the see of Durham he found in the end impossible to resist, backed as it was by the friends (including Benson, now bishop of Truro) whom he consulted. It was, however, a prospect that he dreaded. In a letter to his friend Henry Sidgwick he speaks of:

> this great trouble confronting me … this great trial of my life. How painful this uprooting of all the long associations and interests of more than twenty years will be to me, you will easily imagine. I dare not dwell on my Cambridge regrets for fear of unnerving myself. (J. B. Lightfoot to H. Sidgwick, 28 Jan 1879, Cambridge, Trinity College MSS)

But to Durham he went, writing to Westcott, 'Now that the answer is sent I intend to have no regrets about the past' (Eden and MacDonald, 20). He was consecrated in Westminster Abbey on 25 April 1879, when the sermon was preached by Westcott, and enthroned in Durham Cathedral on 15 May. The last ten years of his life were based in Durham.

The Durham diocese was large and the industrial revolution had greatly increased its population. Even had Lightfoot had the advantage of motor transport no bishop could have covered it pastorally and managed the administration; reorganization and division were immediately necessary tasks. Lightfoot's first action was to collect funds for a separate diocese to be carved out of the existing one. By 1881 sufficient money had been raised and on 25 July 1882 the first bishop of Newcastle was consecrated. Lightfoot also increased the number of rural deanships in the now smaller diocese of Durham, readjusted their boundaries (in July 1880), and divided the archdeaconry into two (in May 1882). A diocesan conference of clergy and laity assembled for the first time in September 1880, and met biennially thereafter. Lightfoot also called together a public meeting in the town hall of Durham in January 1884, to start a church building fund. In less than three years he was able to report that more than £40,000 had been subscribed and about the same amount promised; and that £224,000 had already been spent on churches, missions, schools, and the like. From 1886 a general diocesan fund was established at his suggestion; his own contributions to it totalled £500 a year (*DNB*).

The fund-raising and organizational changes that Lightfoot accomplished were in areas of which he had little or no previous experience. He accomplished his work willingly and efficiently, but it cannot have been the most congenial part of his episcopal duty. He found other tasks. Although the historical associations of Auckland Castle, where he refurbished the Early English hall which Bishop

Cosin at the Restoration had turned into a chapel, meant much to him, he had no love for a life of luxury and ease. It is recorded that before his consecration he visited the castle with his chaplains, and that:

> on passing the fine Gatehouse at the entrance to the Park from the market-place, the Bishop [the title is anticipated]—who had lived all his life alone in College rooms and dreaded the idea of a domestic establishment—looked up and said with genuine feeling, 'Ah if they would let you and me live there.' (Eden and MacDonald, 16f.)

In fact the castle became something like a college, for one of Lightfoot's first—and perhaps most important—steps as bishop was to gather about him a group of young men from Oxford and Cambridge who prepared for ordination under the guidance of Lightfoot himself and of his chaplains. They lived in the castle as a family—reading, hearing lectures, and gaining practical experience as they visited people in their homes; and they spoke in mission-rooms, and were active in clubs in the mining villages of the county. Many became incumbents in the diocese. Shy and silent as Lightfoot was apt to be, he engendered in these men an intense loyalty and affection which was shown in their readiness to accept at his request the hardest tasks in the diocese, knowing that he would show them no favour but would never fail to support them. The list of the eighty-six (thirty-two from Oxford, two from Dublin, one from Durham, and the rest from Cambridge), who in Lightfoot's time made up the Auckland brotherhood, is instructive (Eden and MacDonald, 166–9). There are eleven bishops, six deans (and one provost), and four archdeacons among them. Their fellowship was maintained by an annual gathering on St Peter's day.

Lightfoot took other steps to stimulate the life of the diocese, such as filling a vacant canonry by the appointment of a 'canon missioner'. He encouraged the work of missions and institutes for sailors, and set up a diocesan board of education. To ordinations he gave special care: candidates were no longer simply expected to present themselves at the place of ordination, and examinations were held some weeks beforehand so that they should know in good time whether or not they were accepted and to allow for preparation. All who were to be ordained were the bishop's guests for two quiet days before the ceremony. There are many testimonies to the impressiveness of Lightfoot's ordination addresses, which were given with deep feeling. Confirmations also were to him very important occasions. It was natural that he should show interest in Durham University, of which as bishop he was official visitor, but he gave encouragement also to other local and national bodies.

Illness and death As bishop, Lightfoot was more heavily engaged in the affairs of the Church of England as a whole than he had been in Cambridge. He spoke regularly in the convocation of York and took part in a number of church congresses. These tasks increased the strain placed upon him by local duties, and the Lambeth conference of 1888 'broke him down completely' as he himself said (*DNB*), though immediately after the conference he was able to invite sixty of his fellow bishops to attend the reopening of the restored chapel at Auckland Castle. Lightfoot spent the following winter at Bournemouth but was able to return to Durham by the end of May 1889. He was well enough to consecrate the church of St Ignatius the Martyr at Sunderland, which he had built at his own expense as a thank-offering for seven years of ministry in Durham. On 17 October he presided over the diocesan conference at Sunderland, and on 29 October he was publicly presented at Durham; but by 3 December he had left for Bournemouth where, on 17 December, he became seriously ill. He died there on 21 December 1889, of heart and lung troubles. His body was moved to Durham on 26 December and a memorial service was held in the cathedral the next morning. His body was finally buried at the chapel of Auckland Castle.

Lightfoot's work and influence may be considered under two headings, though related ones. He first became known as an outstanding biblical and patristic scholar; then, when he left Cambridge for Durham, it became clear that he was prepared to play a part in the life of the Church of England.

Biblical and patristic scholarship Lightfoot's work as a scholar rested on a wide and precise knowledge of Latin and Greek, to which he added other ancient languages as well as a number of modern ones. His survey 'Recent editions of St Paul's epistles', in the *Journal of Classical and Sacred Philology*, brought heavy linguistic criticism to bear on Stanley and expressed fundamental divergence from Jowett, who thought the Greek of the New Testament a debased and imprecise development of older Greek. Lightfoot, fully recognizing the differences, held that New Testament Greek was no less capable of exactness than Attic Greek, and that the first duty of a commentator was to elicit the precise meaning of the text before him. This he did, with clarity and economy of language, in his commentaries on Galatians (1865), on Philippians (1868), and on Colossians with Philemon (1875). After more than a hundred years, these demand the attention of every serious student of the New Testament; the exposition is supported by the use of patristic material and is set in its historical framework, which is brought out not only in the notes but in long appended dissertations. To these should be added the essays (most of them previously unpublished) in the posthumous *Biblical Essays* (1893), and to the commentaries the fragments collected after his death in *Notes on Epistles of St Paul from Unpublished Commentaries* (1895). One other volume should be mentioned here, though it spills over into the patristic field (as indeed do the commentaries and essays). In 1874 an anonymous book was published under the title *Supernatural Religion*. Its author (now known to have been W. R. Cassels) attacked both the idea of a supernatural revelation and the accuracy of the historical tradition of the origin of Christianity. It was a book that Lightfoot might well have ignored had not a rumour spread that its author was Bishop Thirlwall (who publicly had maintained a very different position and was thus implicitly accused of deceit) and had not the author attacked the scholarship and the integrity of Lightfoot's friend Westcott. Lightfoot answered the book step by step in a series of essays published first in *Contemporary Review*; these were subsequently collected and published as *Essays on the Work Entitled 'Supernatural Religion'*, a book of more than controversial importance.

Supernatural Religion embodied a number of the positions held by and often associated with F. C. Baur (1792–1860), professor at Tübingen, whose work on the early history of Christianity was the origin of the so-called Tübingen school. Lightfoot has often been depicted as the opponent of Baur and the destroyer of his 'school'. This view contains some truth but is frequently stated in an exaggerated form. Baur had told the story in terms of conflict between Judaistic Christianity, represented by James and others in Jerusalem, and Gentile Christianity, represented by Paul—a conflict finally settled by compromise in the development, towards the end of the second century, of catholic Christianity. Lightfoot was no less aware of the conflicts in early Christianity than Baur; he has been said, rightly, to have held a 'modified Baurian position' (W. G. Kümmel, *Das Neue Testament im 20. Jahrhundert*, 1970, 73). The difference between them lay primarily in their dating of the books of the New Testament and other early Christian literature. Much that Baur had placed in the second century Lightfoot placed in the first; on the whole, subsequent study has tended to confirm Lightfoot's dates. It remains, however, a vital question whether Lightfoot grasped the full significance of the fact that he was pressing sharp division back from the post-apostolic into the apostolic age.

Lightfoot's dating of the New Testament books turned to a great extent upon his work on the next Christian generation. His achievement here was even greater, if possible, than in his work on the New Testament itself. He published in 1869 an edition of the epistles of Clement of Rome; this was superseded by the discovery of the complete texts of these works, in Greek and in Syriac, and after adding in 1877 an appendix to his edition he set about editing the complete texts, a task that was not quite completed at the end of his life. The new edition of *Clement of Rome* was published in 1890. The texts are edited and provided with a commentary akin to those in the Pauline commentaries; there is an introduction dealing with the apostolic fathers and with Clement, and there are quotations and references, the letter, and the so-called second letter; also, of special importance, there is a long discussion of the early Roman succession, 145 pages of detailed evidence and argument which constitute an unsurpassed contribution to early Christian history.

Lightfoot's *Ignatius* (which includes the epistle and the martyrdom of Polycarp) intervened between the early and the later editions of *Clement*. It was first published in 1885 (2nd edn, 1889). This 'was the motive, and is the core, of the whole' (J. B. Lightfoot, *Ignatius*, 1.v) of Lightfoot's work on the apostolic fathers; and the core of *Ignatius* was the demonstration, worked out in great detail, of the originality not of the three-letter (Curetonian) or the thirteen-letter, but of the seven-letter (Vossian) recension. Lightfoot's argument is now all but universally accepted. The Polycarp texts are treated with equal thoroughness, though here there was not the same scope for controversy. The establishment of these texts as belonging to the early decades of the second century was seen by Lightfoot as establishing knowledge of the earliest period of church history and thus as disproving the historical scepticism of Baur and his colleagues, and supporting the traditional authorship (and thus, for Lightfoot, the historical trustworthiness) of John's gospel; hence its fundamental importance, importance which made it seem right to him to abandon 'the more congenial task of commenting on St Paul's Epistles' (ibid., xi). In doing this, however, he had thrust what had appeared to be second-hand, second-century, controversies into the time of the New Testament itself. It is right also to note the uninhibited historical criticism with which Lightfoot treated the post-apostolic literature and to compare it with the defensive attitude that he adopted, for example with regard to the historical intention and accuracy of the fourth gospel. A devout Christian, Lightfoot accepted the authority of scripture and understood this authority in such a way that it was for him incompatible with inaccuracy or disagreement within the New Testament texts. Work on non-biblical texts imposed no such restrictions upon him.

A further contribution of outstanding value to patristic study was Lightfoot's article (of the length of a small book) on Eusebius of Caesarea in William Smith's *Dictionary of Christian Biography*—a comprehensive and authoritative study based on intimate knowledge of the texts.

Churchmanship Lightfoot was a biblical scholar of the highest distinction; he was also an English churchman of—eventually—very great influence. Of his work within the diocese of Durham something has already been said. His canonry at St Paul's made him known, and his episcopate gave him a still wider ministry. He had a profound interest in the history and character of the Christian ministry. One of its expressions was a concern for the ministry of women. Phoebe (Romans 16: 1) must be recognized as being as much a deacon, a minister, as Stephen; and 1 Timothy 3: 11 refers not to the wives of deacons but to women who are deacons. In the commentary on Philippians he wrote a long dissertation on the Christian ministry, in which he argued that the episcopate was not devolved historically from the apostles but evolved upward out of the presbyterate. Out of a body of presbyters one was elevated to a monarchical position. This process went back, Lightfoot believed, to the time of the apostles, at least in the sense that it had the sanction of St John. It could therefore be claimed, in the words of the ordinal of the Church of England, 'that from the Apostles' time there have been these Orders of Ministers in Christ's Church: Bishops, Priests, and Deacons.' This position Lightfoot found historically and therefore ecclesiastically satisfying, but there were those in the Church of England who did not agree, and at the time of the Lambeth conference in 1881 Lightfoot issued not a withdrawal of his 'Christian ministry' but an elucidation. 'It would seem that partial and qualifying statements … have assumed undue proportions in the minds of some readers, who have emphasized them to the neglect of the general drift of the Essay' (*Philippians*, 6th ed, 1881, x). Lightfoot, however, though there were some things he no longer wished to emphasize, continued to maintain that in the apostles' time, and for some years afterwards, 'bishop' and 'priest' (presbyter) were synonymous terms, and that priests were to be understood in an entirely unsacerdotal sense.

Assessment Limited perhaps by an unsatisfactory view of biblical authority Lightfoot was nevertheless an outstanding figure in British New Testament scholarship, an example of learning, accuracy, and diligence to both his contemporaries and his successors. Compared with his accomplishments in philology and history, his achievements in theology were a weak spot; this was already recognized but perhaps exaggerated by Hort in his *Life and Letters* (2.35, 79). There is a hint of exaggerated modesty in Lightfoot's words, 'I brought to the task nothing more than ordinary sense' (J. B. Lightfoot, *Essays on … 'Supernatural Religion'*, 1889, 180), but it is true that speculative theology and reflection upon the philosophical problems involved in the assertions of the Christian faith were not his forte. He lacked Westcott's mysticism and Hort's feeling for the natural world and the post-biblical tradition, but in setting forth in plain speech (and this was his aim) the thoughts of men of ancient times—and since they were theologians this was a theological exercise—he has had few equals.

Lightfoot was not only a deeply learned man; he was also a cautious man, and especially as he grew older he felt himself responsible for the good order of the Church of England. As a historian he perceived the bitter conflicts reflected in the apostolic and post-apostolic writings, and pushed back the dates of these writings. This should have led to a more radical understanding of early Christian history than Baur's, but Lightfoot stopped short. As a churchman he saw that:

> an emergency may arise when the spirit and not the letter must decide. The Christian ideal will then interpose and interpret our duty. The higher ordinance of the universal priesthood will overrule all special limitations. The layman will assume functions which are otherwise restricted to the ordained minister. (J. B. Lightfoot, *Philippians*, 1894, 268)

But notwithstanding his use of lay evangelists on the Wesleyan model he did not allow these circumstances to change his ordering of the church.

Lightfoot was a man of complete integrity but his conception of biblical authority inhibited his application to scripture of the sharp criticism that he used elsewhere, and his loyalty to the church and to the church order of which he was part limited the liberty with which he was able to see and apply the historical results of his study of the ministry. These considerations are, however, better put positively. His understanding of scripture always served and determined his ecclesiastical position; conversely his churchmanship motivated and inspired, if it also to some extent limited, his understanding of scripture. C. K. Barrett

Sources *DNB* • review, *QR*, 176 (1893), 73–105 • G. R. Eden and F. C. Macdonald, *Lightfoot of Durham: memories and appreciations* (1932) • A. F. Hort, *Life and letters of F. J. A. Hort*, 2 vols. (1896) • A. C. Benson, *The life of Edward White Benson*, 2 vols. (1899) • A. Westcott, *Life and letters of Brooke Foss Westcott*, 2 vols. (1903) • J. D. G. Dunn, ed., *The Lightfoot centenary lectures* (1992) • A. C. Benson, *The leaves of the tree: studies in biography* (1911) • J. A. T. Robinson, *Joseph Barber Lightfoot* (1981) • G. R. Treloar and B. N. Kaye, 'J. B. Lightfoot on Strauss and Christian origins: an unpublished manuscript', *Durham University Journal*, 79 (1986–7), 165–200 • B. N. Kaye and G. R. Treloar, 'J. B. Lightfoot and New Testament interpretation: an unpublished manuscript of 1855', *Durham University Journal*, 82 (1990), 161–75 • B. N. Kaye, 'Lightfoot and Baur on early Christianity', *Novum Testamentum*, 26 (1984), 193–224

Archives Durham Cath. CL, corresp. and papers | BL, corresp. with W. E. Gladstone, Add. MSS 44424–44785, *passim* • BL, corresp. with Macmillans, Add. MS 55110 • LPL, corresp. with E. W. Benson • LPL, corresp. with A. C. Tait • Pembroke College, Oxford, letters to Peter Ranouf and Sir John Acton

Likenesses W. B. Richmond, portrait, 1889, Auckland Castle, Durham [*see illus.*] • L. Dickinson, chalk drawing, 1891 (after a photograph), Trinity Cam. • Lock & Whitfield, woodburytype photograph, NPG; repro. in T. Cooper, *Men of mark: a gallery of contemporary portraits* (1880) • W. B. Richmond, portrait, replica, Trinity Cam. • Rotary Photo, photograph on postcard, NPG • photograph, repro. in Eden and Macdonald, *Lightfoot of Durham* • photograph, repro. in Dunn, ed., *The Lightfoot centenary lectures* • photograph, repro. in Robinson, *Joseph Barber Lightfoot* • woodcut (after a photograph), BM; repro. in *The Graphic*

Lightfoot, Maxwell Gordon (1886–1911). *See under* Camden Town Group (*act.* 1911–1913).

Lighthill, Sir (Michael) James (1924–1998), applied mathematician and university administrator, was born on 23 January 1924 in the rue Puccini, Paris, the third and youngest child of Ernest Balzar (Bal) Lighthill (1868–1952), mining engineer, son of a Liverpool shipowner, and his wife, Marjorie (1887–1962), daughter of a Yorkshire engineer, L. W. Holmes. James's brother, Olaf, was seventeen years older than he, and his sister, Patricia, was nine years older. In 1917 James's father, Bal, had changed the family name from Lichtenberg to avoid anti-German sentiment. The name was probably of Alsatian origin. The family returned to England in 1927 when Bal retired.

Lighthill was a precocious child, showing especially great ability in mathematics, languages, and music, and revealing a prodigious memory. He was educated at first by his father and then at preparatory schools, until he won a scholarship to Winchester College in 1936. It was a wonderful coincidence that another twelve-year-old scholar at Winchester that year was Freeman Dyson (who for many years worked at the Princeton Institute of Advanced Study). Both pupils were passionate about mathematics and were so far ahead of their fellows that they were allowed to learn what they liked from original sources. At the age of fifteen they were both awarded major scholarships to Trinity College, Cambridge, but were not allowed to go up until 1941, when they were seventeen. At Cambridge the only lectures they attended were those for part three of the mathematical tripos, intended for graduates. Lighthill was particularly keen on the pure mathematics lectures of G. H. Hardy and J. E. Littlewood. He (like Dyson) graduated in 1943 with a first in part two and a distinction in part three.

As an undergraduate Lighthill enjoyed the musical life

Sir (Michael) James Lighthill (1924–1998), by Elliott & Fry, 1959

of Cambridge; during rehearsals for Mozart's G minor piano quartet he (the pianist) met Nancy Alice Dumaresq (*b.* 1921), cellist and also a mathematician, at Newnham College. They discovered that their families lived next door to each other in Highgate. They were married on 17 February 1945 and remained devoted to each other until Lighthill's death; they had four daughters and a son. Listening to opera and performing piano and chamber music (in both cases 'anything except Tchaikowsky') remained important parts of Lighthill's life—he performed regularly with the University College, London (UCL), chamber music society even when he was provost of UCL. After graduation in 1943 Lighthill was sent to work in the aerodynamics division of the National Physical Laboratory (NPL) at Teddington. Hitherto a pure mathematician, he was persuaded by Sydney Goldstein that the science of fluid mechanics (the study of the motions of liquids and gases and the forces that drive them) was a rich subject to which talented mathematicians could make an important contribution. Lighthill's work compellingly demonstrated the truth of that assertion and he became one of the world's greatest applied mathematicians.

During the Second World War, Lighthill made numerous contributions to supersonic aerodynamics. In those days numerical computation was laborious and time-consuming, involving extensive use of mechanical calculators and five-figure tables. It was essential, therefore, to analyse physical problems mathematically in order to develop formulae that could be used in design. Lighthill was a brilliant analyst, but under the guidance of Goldstein he also developed a deep physical insight which enabled him to explain the essence of his theories in words to the non-mathematical engineers and policymakers who had to use the results. (In later years he took this too far, writing enormously long sentences which, though grammatical and stylish, made too few concessions to those whose training in Victorian literature was less complete than his.)

After the war Lighthill was elected to a prize fellowship at Trinity College, Cambridge, where he was influenced by another great fluid dynamicist, G. I. Taylor. However, in 1946 Goldstein was elected to the Beyer chair of applied mathematics at the University of Manchester, and he took Lighthill with him as a senior lecturer (aged twenty-two). In 1950 Goldstein moved to Israel and Lighthill succeeded him in the chair, which he occupied until 1959. The thirteen years he spent at Manchester witnessed a tremendous outpouring of original, fundamental, and wide-ranging research, both by Lighthill himself and by his many research students. The subjects included the development, structure, and propagation of shock waves; the interaction of a shock wave with the thin 'boundary layers' of fluid adjacent to solid surfaces; the distortion of a complex flow (for example, in the wake of a moving body) encountering another body; non-linear wave motions, applied both to flood waves in rivers and to traffic flow on highways; and an early application of fluid mechanics to biology (the swimming of spermatozoa). Two pieces of work from this period were particularly influential. The first was a remarkable paper of 1952, 'On sound generated aerodynamically', published in the *Proceedings of the Royal Society of London* in two parts, in which Lighthill derived a formula for the acoustic power emitted by highly turbulent flows such as the wakes of jet engines. This paper, inaugurating the subject of aeroacoustics, neither contained nor needed any reference to prior work, but has itself been referred to thousands of times since. The second new subject was that of non-linear acoustics, which developed from Lighthill's 100 page article in *Surveys in Mechanics*, published to celebrate G. I. Taylor's seventieth birthday in 1956.

Lighthill epitomized applied mathematics: he immersed himself in the scientific or technological details of the phenomenon he was seeking to illuminate; he formulated a sequence of clear mathematical problems that encapsulated the essential features of that phenomenon; he attacked those problems with a formidable battery of mathematical techniques (often newly invented for the purpose: witness the method of strained co-ordinates and his splendid little book, *Fourier Analysis and Generalised Functions* in 1958); and finally he returned to the original problem with understanding, prediction, and advice. While he was at Manchester, Lighthill also played a leading role in the Aeronautical Research Council, developed a powerful interest in mathematical education, was in 1956 one of the founding associate editors of the *Journal of Fluid Mechanics* (which immediately became, and remained, the leading journal in the field), founded in

1959 a series of annual conferences called the British Theoretical Mechanics Colloquia (which rapidly became the leading forum for British applied mathematicians), and campaigned for the creation of the Institute of Mathematics and its Applications, which was eventually founded in 1964 with Lighthill as its first president.

In 1959, at the age of thirty-five, Lighthill was the unexpected choice as director of the Royal Aircraft Establishment (RAE), at Farnborough, which had a staff of 8000 on more than one site. Highlights of his directorship included major developments in vertical take-off and landing (leading to the Harrier jump jet); in supersonic transport (leading to Concorde); in weather-independent automatic landing; and in low-cost air transport. He also set up a powerful space department which was later run down through lack of government support. In hindsight, a weakness in the RAE and in Lighthill at that time was a failure to recognize the importance of computers in aerodynamic design. While he was at Farnborough, Lighthill continued to publish prolifically, but more reviews and didactic chapters than original research papers, though one exception was a brilliant 12 page article on the swimming of fish, published in the *Journal of Fluid Mechanics* in 1960.

People were rather afraid of Lighthill until they got to know him (and even after). He was tall, intimidatingly clever, had a loud, arrogant-sounding voice, and was impatient with the slow of comprehension, though very generous with his time and ideas to his students and colleagues. In later years he put on weight and mellowed considerably, willingly helpful to those who needed help (though still somewhat impatient with more senior colleagues). At all times he was a stimulating lecturer, accompanying his words with minutely written overhead transparencies and, whenever possible, acting out the phenomena being discussed; this became both easier and more memorable after he turned to biological applications of fluid dynamics in the 1960s and 1970s.

After five years at Farnborough, Lighthill returned to full-time research in 1964 as Royal Society research professor at Imperial College, London (he had been elected a fellow of the Royal Society in 1953 at the age of twenty-nine), where he remained for five years. He also served as secretary (physical sciences) and vice-president of the Royal Society (1965–9). At Imperial he wrote influential articles on the theories of wave motion and of rotating fluids, with application to the atmosphere and oceans. He also pioneered the application of fluid mechanics in biology, which remained his principal preoccupation for more than fifteen years. He wrote important surveys of undulatory fish-swimming (though all the main mechanisms had been foreshadowed in his 1960 paper), of undulatory micro-organism swimming (though the main feature was contained in a paper by his student Hancock in 1953), of animal flight, and of physiological fluid dynamics (blood flow, breathing, and so on). This work was all brought together in *Mathematical Biofluiddynamics* (1975). Administratively, Lighthill's main achievement while at Imperial was the formation in 1966 of the physiological flow studies unit, bringing together physiologists, physicians, and physical scientists, for interdisciplinary research.

In 1969 Lighthill was elected to the Lucasian chair of mathematics at Cambridge, in which he succeeded Paul Dirac (and, earlier, Isaac Newton) and preceded Stephen Hawking. Here his main research was in biology and waves (his advanced textbook *Waves in Fluids* appeared in 1978), and he contributed enthusiastically to teaching. He was also involved in many national and international committees, reporting on a variety of topics: postgraduate training in the UK, direct dialling for long-distance telephone calls, the future of telecommunications, control engineering, and artificial intelligence, which he notoriously declared (in 1973) to have no future. He became president of the International Commission on Mathematical Instruction (1971–4), president of the International Union of Theoretical and Applied Mechanics (1984–8), and chairman of the International Council of Scientific Unions committee on the international decade for natural disaster relief (1990–95). He had a strong influence in India, where he encouraged the study of monsoon dynamics, a branch of geophysical fluid dynamics with special relevance there.

Ten years in Cambridge were enough for Lighthill, who missed the wider influence he could exert as leader of a large organization, and in 1979 he was happy to be appointed as provost of University College, London, in succession to Noel Annan. Here his priority was to enhance UCL's already outstanding academic strength, not least by encouraging women academics to fulfil their high potential. He was also extremely popular. His formidable memory enabled him to come to know and to remember the interests of every professor and many other staff. He was unable to devote much time to research, but publications continued (for example, on the dynamics of the inner ear), including one undergraduate textbook, *An Informal Introduction to Theoretical Fluid Dynamics* (1986). After his retirement in 1989 he kept an office at UCL where he did some research, though most of his output consisted of long survey articles and lectures. He travelled widely. As well as his fellowship of the Royal Society, Lighthill received many honours, notably his knighthood in 1971 and the royal and Copley medals of the Royal Society, the former in 1964 and the latter posthumously in 1998. He was elected foreign associate or honorary member of nine national academies of science or engineering, including those of the USA (both), Russia, and France (he was fluent in French and Russian). He received twenty-four honorary doctorates around the world, having not taken a PhD in his younger days. His collected papers were published by Oxford University Press in four volumes in 1997.

No account of Lighthill's life would be complete without reference to his principal form of physical recreation: swimming. He could cover long distances using his 'old English backstroke'. On holiday every year, after detailed study of tides and currents, he would embark on an 'adventure swim', preferably round an island. There were many anecdotes: once he swam round Stromboli while it was erupting, and once he was accompanied for several minutes by a basking shark as he swam round Lundy. His favourite island was Sark. He was the first person to swim round it, in 1973, and he successfully repeated the feat five times (the distance was about 10 miles, and on a calm day it would take six hours). On 17 July 1998 he had almost completed the swim once more, having been in the water for nine hours, when his mitral valve ruptured and he died. Following cremation at St Marylebone crematorium, in Finchley, London, on 27 July, his ashes were scattered on Hampstead Heath. He was survived by his wife and five children. T. J. PEDLEY

Sources *Collected papers of Sir James Lighthill*, ed. M. Yousuff Hussaini, 4 vols. (1997) • autobiographical notes, RS • *Recollections of Sir James Lighthill* (1999) • *The Independent* (22 July 1998) • *The Independent* (1 Aug 1998) • *The Times* (20 July 1998) • *Daily Telegraph* (20 July 1998) • *The Guardian* (21 July 1998) • *WWW* • *CGPLA Eng. & Wales* (1998) • *Yearbook of the Royal Society*

Archives Bodl. Oxf., corresp. with Torkel Weis-Fogh • CAC Cam., corresp. with Sir Edward Bullard | FILM *Aerodynamically generated sound*, film made by US National Committee for Fluid Mechanics Films

Likenesses Elliott & Fry, photograph, 1959, NPG [*see illus.*] • photograph, repro. in *The Times* • photograph, repro. in *Daily Telegraph* • photograph, repro. in *The Guardian* • photograph, repro. in *The Independent* (22 July 1998) • photographs, repro. in *Recollections of Sir James Lighthill*

Wealth at death £33,113: probate, 6 Nov 1998, *CGPLA Eng. & Wales*

Lightowler [*née* Butler], **Miriam** (1875–1958), local politician, was born on 29 June 1875 at 11 Preston Place, Francis Street, Halifax, the youngest daughter of James Ryder Butler (1842–1917), master machine maker, and his wife, Elizabeth, *née* Mitchell (1841–1932). She was educated at Holy Trinity School, Halifax, and Cliff House, Harrogate, and had a lifelong association with Hanover Street Methodist Church, Halifax, serving for twenty years as a member of the leaders' meeting, which helped to prepare her for a life of public service. Her earliest experience of politics was in campaigning in local government elections for her father, a leading Halifax engineer and founder of the Butler Machine Tool Company Ltd, who represented the Liberals on Halifax county borough council between 1892 and 1895, but later defected to the Unionists on the issue of tariff reform. Her husband was Henry Charles Lightowler (1871–1918), a carpet dealer and church furnisher, and son of Joseph Lightowler, carpet dealer, whom she married on 2 July 1896; she also campaigned for him when he was returned for the Conservatives on Halifax county borough council in 1912. He served until his death on 11 February 1918.

Lightowler's own public life began in 1913 when she was elected a member of the Halifax poor-law union board of guardians, the first Conservative woman to be elected to the board. During the First World War she contributed to the day-to-day operation of the union as treasurer of a sewing committee of thirty ladies who undertook to repair all the clothes that were used at the union hospital. She later became the first woman chair of the board of guardians in April 1928 and made such an impression that a new public clock at the institution on Gibbet Street was named in her honour in 1929, when she set the clock in motion. When the board of guardians was superseded by the public assistance committee in 1929, she was appointed first chair of the new body. She became well known for her concern for the welfare of children and mentally handicapped people, visiting children boarded out in homes or in institutions, and becoming in 1926 chair of the mid-Yorkshire Joint Board for the Mentally Defective and chair of the Menston Mental Hospital board. She also served on the children's hospital and probation committees.

The experience which Lightowler gained in this work led to her appointment as the first woman magistrate for Halifax in 1920, and in January 1924 she became the first woman Halifax councillor, when she was returned unopposed for South Ward. The *Halifax Courier* commented:

> It has … taken seventeen years [since women were allowed to sit on municipal bodies in 1907] for a progressive town such as Halifax … to overcome that innate conservatism which regards the entry of women into public life as something to be tolerated with extreme caution. (*Halifax Courier*, 23 June 1998)

However, she remained the sole woman councillor in Halifax for another decade, combining her public life with running the family business of Lightowler & Co. Ltd, church furnishers, as co-director with her son. Following her election to the council she became only the third woman in England to be appointed a member of a watch committee, and again made such an impression that the fire brigade chose to name a new turntable ladder in her honour. In 1934 she accepted the unanimous invitation of the council to become the first woman mayor of Halifax, but throughout her year of office was addressed in the council chamber as 'Mr Mayor'. In the speech inaugurating her mayoralty, she declared: 'The real purpose of life is not the accumulation of wealth, nor the gaining of power, but service to the community' (*Halifax Courier*, 9 Nov 1934). During her mayoral year she launched a major fund-raising appeal for a new children's holiday home in a rural location close to the town, raising over £3000 for the appeal in eight weeks, the highest sum raised locally by a public appeal during the inter-war years. She even travelled to Leeds to broadcast an appeal on the BBC radio 'week's good cause'. She was awarded the King George silver jubilee medal and appointed an alderman in 1935. As chair of the finance committee she became the first woman to present a council budget statement in 1936, and in the 1938 birthday honours she was made OBE for her public services. In 1948 she was appointed to the new hospital management committee for Halifax and district, serving on the committee until March 1956. She was a supporter of the Halifax and District Nursing Association and the Halifax Council of Social Service. She was also chair of the Halifax Women's Conservative Association and a founder of the Halifax branch of the National Council of Women, serving as branch president in 1935.

New regulations compelled Lightowler's retirement from the bench in June 1950 at the age of seventy-five, and she subsequently also retired as an alderman in May 1952 and as president of the Halifax Women's Conservative Association in March 1953. In newspaper cartoons in the 1930s she was affectionately portrayed with neatly permed, short dark hair, light spectacles, and a beaming rotund face with a pronounced double chin, features still recognizable in photographs taken to mark her retirement from public life in the early 1950s. She declared in 1952 that she remained 'a real Tory' and attributed her success in politics to sheer hard work (*Halifax Courier*, 6 May 1952). Outside politics she loved choral singing and was president of the Halifax Madrigal Society from 1937 to 1939. In failing health for several years, she spent the last year of her life in the Halifax General Hospital and died of bronchopneumonia, following cerebral degeneration due to arteriosclerosis, on 19 June 1958 at the St John's Hospital, Halifax, which housed the clock that bore her name in the building where she had cut her political teeth at the meetings of the Halifax poor-law union board of guardians. She was buried at the Halifax borough cemetery following a civic funeral on 23 June 1958 at Halifax parish church, where the turntable ladder of the Halifax fire brigade which had been named in her honour in 1936 was stationed as a final mark of respect during the service.

JOHN A. HARGREAVES

Sources J. A. Hargreaves, *Halifax* (1999) • *Halifax Courier* (9 Nov 1934) • *Halifax Courier* (6 May 1952) • *Halifax Courier* (20 June 1958) • *Halifax Courier* (24 June 1958) • *Halifax Courier* (23 June 1998) • *Halifax Guardian* (4 July 1896) • *Halifax Guardian* (12 Feb 1918) • b. cert. • m. cert. • d. cert. • b. cert. [Elizabeth Butler] • d. cert. [Elizabeth Butler] • b. cert. [Henry Lightowler]

Likenesses group portrait, photograph, *c.*1934, Calderdale Central Library, cuttings file • J. J. Mulroy, sketch, *c.*1935, repro. in *Halifax Courier* • photograph, 1936, repro. in *Halifax Courier* (16 Feb 1999) • cartoon (*Halifax Courier* (11 June 1938)), Halifax Courier Library • photograph, Halifax town hall

Wealth at death £3360 8*s.* 11*d.*: probate, 17 July 1958, *CGPLA Eng. & Wales*

Lightowller, Thomas (*fl.* **1741–1769**), coiner, was the eldest son of Thomas Lightowller, joiner, and his wife, Mary, of Walton-le-Dale, near Preston, Lancashire. His date and place of birth are uncertain but the parish registers of Walton-le-Dale record the marriage of his parents in 1721 and the baptism of their second son, Timothy Lightoler, in 1727. The brothers trained as joiners and carvers with their father but Thomas turned early to coining. In 1745 he was acquitted in Cardiff on a charge of coining. About five years later, when Thomas and Timothy went to Warwick to work on the interior of the castle, the former settled in Warwickshire. By 1751 he was married and two years later he rented a house in Coventry with his wife, Margaret (*née* Gill); a son, John, was baptized at Holy Trinity Church, Coventry, on 12 May 1755.

Overtly Lightowller traded as a carver, snuff-box maker, and 'engine turner' but secretly he soon developed a thriving operation in the counterfeiting of gold and silver coins from mixed or base metals. Lightowller's contacts were extensive. His known customers for false coin, often food dealers whose trades were heavily dependent on cash transactions, included names from London, Banbury in Oxfordshire, and Stone in Staffordshire; in January 1755 Lightowller himself visited the Isle of Man to dispose of counterfeit coin. Both in the west midlands and Lancashire, furthermore, he trained others in the art of coining. Thus, when Abraham Healy the elder and Abraham Healy the younger were convicted of coining at Lancaster Lent assizes in 1756, the evidence given in court proved that Lightowller had not only counterfeited coin in the presence of the Healys but had supplied their equipment and instructed them in its use. Lightowller was apprehended in Coventry in May 1756 but he betrayed his accomplices and procured his youngest brother, Henry, to be admitted as an evidence against them. Partly on the strength of Henry's testimony Jonathan Tilley, a Coventry plumber, and Joseph Leigh of Bedworth were convicted of coining at Coventry summer assizes in 1756 and executed. Lightowller himself was tried at Lancaster summer assizes the same year on the indictment previously lodged against the Healys and, to the amazement of William Chamberlayne, the mint solicitor, acquitted. After being returned to Coventry to stand trial for coining there, he was discharged in 1757 because the attorney-general opined that 'the discoveries at Coventry having been made by means of Thomas Lightowller he ought not to be prosecuted' (mint solicitor's account, 1757, PRO, Tl/387/54). Lightowller subsequently went to Yorkshire, where he assisted his brother Timothy in the redecoration of Burton Constable Hall in the East Riding and then resumed his coining activities in the West Riding. In 1768, when several of his associates (notably Joseph Stell, executed at York) were apprehended, Lightowller fled the country and entered the service of Maria Theresa in Austria. There, by 1769, he had been granted 6 florins per day and a house in Vienna to set up flatting mills for the production of copper and iron plates and establish a variety of manufactures.

Lightowller's subsequent activities, and the circumstances of his death, are unknown. Alderman John Hewitt, who investigated the Coventry coiners, considered Lightowller the 'greatest mechanical genius' of his time. He was, indeed, a fine carver and metalworker, but his talents were misapplied and his dissolute lifestyle and unscrupulous character rendered him untrustworthy even in his dealings with his business associates and accomplices.

PHILIP SUGDEN

Sources J. Hewitt, *The proceedings of J. Hewitt, alderman … in the year 1756 … being a particular account of the gang of coiners … pursued by the author* (1783) • mint solicitor's accounts for 1756 and 1757, PRO, T1/387/53–4 • B. Langlois to earl of Rochford, 23 May 1769, PRO, SP 80/206 • J. Styles, 'Our traitorous money makers', *An ungovernable people*, ed. J. Brewer and J. Styles (1980), 172–249 • D. Hay, 'Crime, authority and the criminal law: Staffordshire, 1750–1800', PhD diss., University of Warwick, 1975 • Colvin, *Archs.* • G. E. C. Clayton, ed., *The registers of the parish of Walton-le-Dale in the county of Lancaster* (1910) • parish registers (baptism), Holy Trinity, Coventry, Coventry RO, 12 May 1755 • I. Hall, *An exhibition of paintings … collected … by William Constable* (1970) [exhibition catalogue, Ferens Art Gallery, Kingston upon Hull, 27 Jan – 22 Feb 1970] • M. L. Baumber, *From revival to regency: a history of Keighley and Haworth, 1740–1820*, 1 (1983) • G. Otruba, *Die Wirtschaftspolitik Maria Theresias* (1963)

Lightwood, John Mason (1852–1947), barrister and legal writer, was born on 6 July 1852 at King's Norton, Birmingham, the second son of Edward Lightwood, a Methodist minister, and his wife, Elizabeth, daughter of William Wild of Milford Haven. He was educated at Kingswood School, Bath, before entering Trinity Hall, Cambridge, where he was elected a scholar in 1871. He graduated BA in 1874. In the same year he became a fellow of his college and obtained a first class in mathematics at London University. Lightwood entered Lincoln's Inn on 25 January 1875. Until 1878 he was an assistant master at Mill Hill School. He was called to the bar on 7 May 1879. From then onwards he practised continuously as a conveyancer and draftsman, and in 1932 he was appointed conveyancing counsel to the court. At the time of his death he was senior conveyancing counsel.

Lightwood combined learning in the field of real-property law with sound historical insight and a gift of lucid exposition. His initial contribution to legal literature, however, was in the field of jurisprudence, and his essay entitled *The Nature of Positive Law* (1883), a work in the tradition of John Austin, temporarily directed his attention to law teaching; he was runner-up to Frederick Pollock when the latter was appointed to the chair of jurisprudence at University College, London, in 1882. Thereafter he did not apply for any university appointment. In common with other eminent conveyancers, Lightwood made relatively infrequent appearances in court, but he was very well regarded by the profession, and his practice was very wide. He none the less published substantial works in the field of property law and was later responsible for editing several of its major texts. He was one of the small band of eminent conveyancers who assisted Lord Birkenhead and Sir Leslie Scott at the time when the property legislation of 1922–4 was in preparation. He had advocated for a long time many of the more important changes then achieved.

Lightwood produced a stream of articles for various legal journals, and in addition he reviewed many of the most important works of contemporaries in the field of property law. In 1925, when already over seventy, he became legal editor of the *Law Journal*, a position which he retained until after the outbreak of war in 1939. From 1925 onwards, until shortly before his death over twenty years later, few weeks passed without an article, under the general title 'A Conveyancer's Letter', appearing over the initials J. M. L.

Many of the most important titles on real property and conveyancing were contributed by Lightwood to Halsbury's *Laws of England*, and he was one of the editors of the second edition of the *Encyclopaedia of Forms and Precedents* which was prepared to incorporate the great changes introduced by the property statutes of 1925. Of the third edition he was editor-in-chief. His work enabled lawyers, especially solicitors, to become familiar with the scope and purpose of the new property law which changing social conditions had made necessary.

In 1884 Lightwood married Gertrude, daughter of Henry Clench, who worked for a London firm of silk merchants; they had three sons and three daughters. He died at his home, Greenleys, 3 Briton Hill Road, Sanderstead, Surrey, on 4 April 1947. G. W. Keeton, *rev.* Eric Metcalfe

Sources J. Foster, *Men-at-the-bar: a biographical hand-list of the members of the various inns of court*, 2nd edn (1885) · *The Times* (16 April 1947) · *Law Journal* (11 April 1947) · *Law Journal* (18 April 1947) · private information (1959) · personal knowledge (1959) · *CGPLA Eng. & Wales* (1947)

Wealth at death £3943 11s.: probate, 18 Sept 1947, *CGPLA Eng. & Wales*

Ligon, Richard (*c.*1585–1662), business agent and natural science writer, was the son of Thomas Ligon of Elstone in Wiltshire and his wife, Frances, daughter of Hugh Dennis of Pucklechurch, Gloucestershire. His life before the 1630s is poorly documented, although he was apparently active at court. Ligon may have been what contemporaries called a 'man of business', a kind of attorney or 'friend' who looked after the interests of wealthy relatives and friends. He was executor of at least four wills, those of Giovanni or John Coperario (*d.* 1626), Sir Robert Killigrew (*d.* 1633), Henry Killigrew (*d.* 1646?), and his sister-in-law, Elizabeth Liggon, *née* Pratt. He often assumed responsibility for debts of the will-maker in return for payment or property that would come to him in his role as executor.

Ligon also apparently acted for Sir Robert Killigrew, who held the farm of the seal office, in setting and collecting fees. Through the Killigrews Ligon acquired fenland in Lincolnshire, and he entered into a scheme in the mid-1630s led by the earl of Lindsey and Sir Robert's son, the playwright Sir William Killigrew, to drain the fens, known as the Lindsey level. The investors testified that they had lost £60,000 in the early 1640s when the local people rose up and drove the drainers away. Ligon adhered to the royalist side in the English civil war and left England after being present at the surrender of Exeter. Identified as of London or Westminster, he also testified before the committee on compounding that he had 'no estate but lands in the fens' (*Calendar of the … Committee for Compounding*, 2, 1536).

Ligon wrote that he was over sixty when he set out in June 1647 on Thomas Modyford's expedition to the Caribbean. In his *True and Exact Historie of the Island of Barbadoes* (1657) he wrote vividly of the environment, economy, and society of the newly successful English colony. He witnessed the sugar revolution and the transition to African slavery as the principal labour system. He offered detailed and illustrated descriptions of the growing and processing of sugar and of the plants and animals of the island. He also provided vivid portraits of the island's inhabitants—English, African, and Indian. Ligon's presentation of Barbados was designed to show his own accomplishments as musician, chef, mathematician, and classical scholar. He took his theorbo with him to Barbados, and tried to raise the cultural tone of the colony. Ligon's exact role on Barbados is unclear. He was a gentleman, as he stated on his title-page, but he clearly worked as an overseer or plantation manager. He wrote that he was employed sometimes 'upon publick works'.

Ligon wrote his *True and Exact Historie of the Island of Barbadoes* in the Upper Bench prison where he was imprisoned for debt after his return to England in 1650. He believed he had been defrauded by his former partner: 'I am now cast in Prison, by the subtle practices of some, whom I have formerly called Friends'. He wrote a pamphlet accusing those he held responsible, *Severall circumstances to prove that Mistris Jane Berkeley and Sir William Killigrew have combined together to defraud me of an estate left unto me by Henry Killigrew, Esq; for payment of his debts, for which I lye now in prison* (1653). Sir Henry Killigrew had deeded two properties in Cornwall to Ligon in return for Ligon's standing surety for Killigrew's debts, but the civil war had swept away these careful arrangements. Ligon was released from prison under an act for the relief of 'Creditors and Poor Prisoners' passed in October 1653; one goal of the act was to help those imprisoned for the debts of another. When he made his will on 10 July 1659 he was living at Pill, Somerset. He left the estate he still hoped to reclaim in the Lincolnshire fens to Edward Berkeley, also of Pill, the cousin who cared for him during his final illness. He died in 1662, and his will was proved on 22 August that year.

KAREN ORDAHL KUPPERMAN

Sources J. B. Boddie, 'Lygon of Madresfield, Worcester, England and Henrico, Virginia', *William and Mary College Quarterly*, 2nd ser., 16 (1936), 289–315 • M. A. E. Green, ed., *Calendar of the proceedings of the committee for compounding … 1643–1660*, 5 vols., PRO (1889–92) • P. F. Campbell, 'Richard Ligon', *Journal of the Barbados Museum and Historical Society*, 37 (1985) • W. D. Ligon, *The Ligon family and connections* (New York, 1947) • K. Lindley, *Fenland riots and the English revolution* (1982) • J. Smyth, *Lives of the Berkeleys* (1883), vol. 2 of *The Berkeley manuscripts*, ed. J. Maclean (1883–5), 178, 183–4 • N. D. Thompson, 'Further observations on the ancestry of Colonel Thomas Ligon of Henrico county', *Virginia Genealogist*, 38 (1994), 48–52 • M. J. Wood and G. B. Roberts, 'Four Thomas Lygons (Ligons): an abstract of new findings', *Virginia Genealogist*, 22 (1978), 247–52 • will, PRO, PROB 11/308, sig. 105
Archives PRO, letter to Killigrew, SP 16/452, 27

Ligonier, Edward [Francis Edward], **Earl Ligonier of Clonmell (1740?–1782)**, army officer, was the only son of Colonel Francis Augustus *Ligonier (1693–1746) [*see under* Ligonier, John, Earl Ligonier], a Huguenot émigré, and Mrs Anne Murray, *née* Freeman, a widow. His parents were not married, and this has probably contributed to the uncertainty surrounding his date of birth, some writers giving 1729, others 1740, and whether his name was Edward or Francis Edward. On the basis of his career progress a later birth date seems more likely. Ligonier's father became colonel of the 13th dragoons and died shortly after the battle of Falkirk (1746), during the Jacobite rising, leaving his family in straitened circumstances. The young Edward was taken under the patronage of an uncle, General John *Ligonier. His younger sister, Frances Ligonier, was similarly provided for; she married Thomas Balfour at St James's, Westminster, on 18 September 1775.

Ligonier entered the army in 1752 as cornet in the 2nd dragoon guards (Queen's Bays). In 1757 he exchanged into the 7th dragoons (hussars). While on service in Germany during the Seven Years' War (1756–63) he was appointed aide-de-camp to John Manners, marquess of Granby, and then, as a result of his uncle's influence, to the same post with Prince Ferdinand of Brunswick. He served in this capacity at the battle of Minden (1 August 1759), and during the latter stages of the battle he was the second of three aides-de-camp sent to Lord George Sackville, who commanded the allied cavalry on the right wing, with orders to advance against the disordered French squadrons. Sackville found the breathless messages contradictory and confusing, and the resulting delay allowed the opportunity to pursue the French cavalry to pass. Ligonier appeared as one of the witnesses at the subsequent court martial in London of Sackville, on charges of disobedience to orders. Ligonier's evidence, like that of the other aides, may be seen as highly unsympathetic to Sackville, as an acquittal would have reflected very badly upon his ability to deliver a vital message in the heat of battle.

Ligonier took back to London the dispatches after Minden. He received, in addition to the customary purse of £500, advancement on 15 August 1759 to captain and lieutenant-colonel in the 1st foot guards. From 1760 he continued to serve in Germany until appointed aide-de-camp to George II in 1763; he was advanced to colonel on 21 April of that year. A plan for Ligonier to succeed his uncle as MP for Bath on the latter's elevation to the peerage came to nothing, as both Pitt the elder, the other member for Bath, and the corporation preferred another of his uncle's protégés, Sir John Sebright, who had shown more political interest in the borough. He continued to rely upon his uncle for financial support.

In 1763 Ligonier was made confidential secretary to the special embassy to the Spanish court in Madrid led by William Nassau de Zuylestein, fourth earl of Rochford. He succeeded to his uncle's Irish viscountcy on the latter's death on 28 April 1770, and on 8 August 1771 he became colonel of the 9th foot. He was made major-general on 29 September 1775, was created Earl Ligonier of Clonmell on 4 July 1776, became lieutenant-general on 29 August 1777, and was appointed KB on 17 December 1781.

Ligonier was a tall, slim man of handsome military appearance, with fine features and a high forehead. He married twice: firstly, on 16 December 1766, at the British embassy in Paris, Penelope (*b.* 1749), the eldest daughter of George *Pitt, Baron Rivers. Within five years of the marriage she had began an affair with the Italian poet Count Vittorio Amadeo Alfieri. A duel was fought in Hyde Park in 1771 between Ligonier and his wife's paramour. The Italian had little skill with the small-sword, and Ligonier gallantly declined to take advantage of his opponent's clumsiness. The affair was sensationalized in a popular novella entitled *Lord Lelius and the Fair Emelia, or, The Generous Husband* (1771). The couple were divorced on 7 November 1771. Penelope, Viscountess Ligonier, subsequently remarried, though reports differ as to whether her husband was a trooper in the Royal Horse Guards or a Captain Smith. Ligonier married, secondly, on 14 December 1773, Lady Mary Henley (*d.* 1814), the second daughter of Robert Henley, earl of Northington. There were no children of either marriage, and, accordingly, Ligonier's titles became extinct on his death, on 14 June 1782. Mary, Countess

Ligonier, married Thomas Noel, second Viscount Wentworth, on 2 February 1788 and died on 29 June 1814 at Kirkby Mallory, Leicestershire. JAMES FALKNER

Sources *DNB* • *Army List* (1752–72) • *GM*, 1st ser., 41 (1771) • *GM*, 1st ser., 44 (1774) • B. Burke, *A genealogical history of the dormant, abeyant, forfeited and extinct peerages of the British empire*, new edn (1866) • N. B. Leslie, *The succession of colonels of the British army from 1660 to the present day* (1974) • R. Whitworth, *Lord Ligonier* (1958) • H. N. Cole, *Minden* (1972) • P. Mackesy, *The coward of Minden: the affair of Lord George Sackville* (1979) • *Journal of the Society for Army Historical Research*, 32 (1954) • GEC, *Peerage*, new edn

Likenesses T. Gainsborough, oils, 1770, Hunt. L.

Wealth at death limited: will, PRO, PROB 11/1093, sig. 364

Ligonier, Francis Augustus [François-Auguste de Ligonier] (**1693–1746**). *See under* Ligonier, John, Earl Ligonier (1680–1770).

Ligonier, John [*formerly* Jean-Louis de Ligonier], **Earl Ligonier** (**1680–1770**), army officer, was born on 17 October 1680 at Castres, near Toulouse, France, the son of Louis de Ligonier, sieur de Montcuquet (1640–1693), and his wife, Louise du Poncet (*b.* 1652). The Ligoniers, a landowning Huguenot family, had been settled at Castres since at least the sixteenth century. Six of the children of Louis de Ligonier and Louise du Poncet survived to adulthood, and three became officers in the British army. Following the revocation of the edict of Nantes in 1685, several of Ligonier's adult protestant relatives fled France to havens in the United Provinces, Switzerland, and Britain; at least one obtained a commission in a Huguenot regiment raised and sent to Ireland by William III in 1689.

Early military career Following an education said to have been in France and Switzerland, in 1698 Ligonier escaped from France and travelled via Utrecht and England to Ireland to seek sanctuary with his relatives there. On 22 February 1702 he obtained naturalization as an Englishman and took service in Flanders as a volunteer in the British force commanded by John Cutts, Baron Cutts. He served with such distinction at the storming of Liège that he was allowed to purchase a captaincy in the 10th regiment of foot (Lord North and Grey's) in 1703.

Having served with his regiment at the battles of the Schellenberg and Blenheim in 1704, Ligonier fought with it at Ramillies in 1706 and later in the same year led an assault column in an attack on the fortress of Menin, after the fall of which his bravery was rewarded with the brevet rank of major. He returned briefly to Britain in 1708, when it was feared that a Jacobite rising was imminent, then was present at the battles of Oudenarde and Wynandael and at the siege of Tournai in 1709 before coming close to death at the battle of Malplaquet. During an assault by a brigade containing his regiment on the well-defended French position in the wood of Taisnieres, Ligonier is said to have had his clothes virtually shredded by musket balls—none of which (variously estimated in number at between twenty and twenty-three) wounded him.

The year 1711 brought a change of theatre for Ligonier and he was appointed to serve on the staff in Spain, initially in the post of major of brigade and subsequently as assistant adjutant-general. Late in 1711 he was promoted

John Ligonier, Earl Ligonier (1680–1770), by Sir Joshua Reynolds, 1760

lieutenant-colonel in the 12th regiment of foot (Phillips's) and almost immediately secured for his youngest brother, Francis, an ensign's commission in that regiment. **Francis Augustus Ligonier** [*formerly* François-Auguste de Ligonier] (1693–1746) had been born in Castres and had moved to England in 1710. Although their brother, Anthony, was also an officer in the British army, the careers of John and Francis were to be especially closely linked until Francis's death. In 1712 John Ligonier received the brevet of colonel and the appointment of adjutant-general in Spain; the war in the Iberian peninsula drawing to a close, in 1713 he was appointed to the lieutenant-governorship of the newly acquired island of Minorca.

Between the wars Minorca constituted an important Mediterranean base for Britain. Its large, deep-water anchorage of Port Mahon provided shelter for a fleet able to threaten France's naval base of Toulon. During his three-year posting to the island Ligonier oversaw enormous improvements in its fortifications and armaments. In 1716 he and his brother Francis returned to England and transferred regiments, Ligonier to the position of lieutenant-colonel of the 4th regiment of horse (Lord Windsor's) and his brother to that of cornet in the Royal Regiment of Horse Guards (the Blues). In 1719 Ligonier was able to rediscover his skills as a staff officer in the post of adjutant-general to the expedition to Vigo Bay led by Richard Temple, first Viscount Cobham, and commanded the assault on the arsenal at Ponte Vedras.

In 1720 Ligonier received the first of his many regimental colonelcies, perhaps the one with which he has been most associated: that of the 8th regiment of horse (later the 7th dragoon guards). He retained this colonelcy for twenty-nine years, and the regiment maintained its association with him for two centuries by using his crest on its appointments and as its cap badge. He was remarkable for his diligence as the regiment's colonel, maintaining an additional surgeon at his own expense and transforming the regiment into one of the finest of the British cavalry. In 1720, too, Francis Ligonier obtained his lieutenancy in the blues, and in 1722 he transferred to the 9th regiment of dragoons (Wynne's) with the rank of captain; in 1729 he was promoted to his elder brother's regiment as its major and subsequently to executive command as its lieutenant-colonel. During this period John Ligonier had a sexual relationship with Penelope Miller, of Southwark; they had a daughter, also called Penelope (*b. c.*1727). Ligonier's regiment remained on the Irish establishment until 1742, forming part of the cavalry garrison of the island, but Ligonier himself was often absent in England, where his position at court gradually grew in importance: he was appointed a gentleman of the privy chamber to George I in 1724 and aide-de-camp to George II in 1729. He was also active in the court of the lord lieutenant when in Ireland, becoming a governor of Kilmainham veterans' hospital and from 1736 sharing the sinecure of chief ranger of Ireland with his brother Francis and Lord John Sackville. Ligonier managed, unusually, to combine a friendship with Frederick, prince of Wales, with the retention of the confidence of the prince's father, George II, who had him promoted brigadier-general in 1736 and major-general in 1739, on the outbreak of war with Spain.

Return to European conflict The War of Jenkins's Ear necessitated Ligonier's return to active duty in Ireland, where he became governor of the Charles Fort at Kinsale and commander of the forces in south-west Ireland with responsibility for making preparations against a possible invasion. Once the invasion scare lessened, in 1741, Ligonier was ordered to accompany George II to Hanover, initially as commander of Danish troops hired for the protection of the electorate against a Franco-Prussian invasion, and later as commander of a Hessian force hired for the same purpose.

As the War of the Austrian Succession began, so Britain's Hanoverian interests and network of alliances and rivalries with the continental European powers gradually drew her into the growing conflict. Initially, Ligonier's role was that of a senior staff liaison officer between the king, John Dalrymple, second earl of Stair, the commander-in-chief, and John Carteret, second Baron Carteret, the secretary of state for the northern department. By 1743 he had secured a field command—that of the 2nd division—in the army in Germany, with which came his temporary promotion to the rank of lieutenant-general. His command comprised an infantry regiment of a single battalion, a composite grenadier battalion—formed for use as assault troops—and a regiment of dragoons; he also had deputy command of the British cavalry force. In this role Ligonier participated in the battle of Dettingen on 27 June 1743, the last battle at which a British sovereign took the field, and after the battle he was one of four generals created KB (12 July 1743). Set against the honour of knighthood was the fact that his brother Francis had been badly wounded at the battle while in executive command of Ligonier's regiment of horse, which distinguished itself in the action and suffered in consequence. The regiment remained in Flanders until 1747, although Francis Ligonier left it in 1745 to become colonel of the newly raised 59th regiment of foot. During its five years on active service, thirty-seven of the non-commissioned officers and troopers of Ligonier's horse received commissions for distinguished service: such a record is without parallel for the period and reflects not only the care taken in the selection of recruits by the Ligonier brothers but also the *esprit de corps* of the regiment itself. For the campaign of 1745 Ligonier was given the command of the infantry with the title general of foot. As such he commanded the British, Hanoverian, and Hessian infantry at the battle of Fontenoy in that year, carefully controlling the withdrawal of the defeated army from the battlefield. After the start of the Jacobite rising in Scotland in 1745, Ligonier was sent back to Britain in command of ten infantry battalions which were withdrawn from the fighting on the continent in order to confront the crisis at home. His brother Francis was appointed to the colonelcy of the 13th dragoons, following the death of the regiment's previous colonel at the battle of Prestonpans, and was thus in the rare position of holding two regimental colonelcies simultaneously. Ligonier himself was given command of a force of fourteen regiments, the role of which was to concentrate in the midlands of England and form a 'stop-line' beyond which the rebels could not pass. Ceding his command late in November 1745 to William Augustus, duke of Cumberland, the second son of George II, shortly before the rebels evaded the stop-line and advanced to Derby, Ligonier remained in command of the reserve forces in England while the action moved to Scotland. During the time he was away from the scene of events, Ligonier received the news that Francis, while serving as commander of the dragoon brigade at the battle of Falkirk early in 1746, had exacerbated a chest infection. Francis died in Edinburgh on 25 January 1746 and was buried there about five days later, leaving his two natural children, Edward *Ligonier (1740?–1782) and Frances, from his relationship with Anne Murray, *née* Freeman, a widow, to the care of their uncle.

In 1746, with the rebels on their way to defeat at Culloden, Ligonier returned to the continent as commander-in-chief of the British forces and their mercenary allies. His rank as a lieutenant-general was confirmed by the king in mid-1746 in order to give him standing among the allies, and later in the year he was promoted to the rank of general of horse. In October 1746 he commanded the British forces at the battle of Rocoux, where the allies were defeated by the French army commanded by Marshal Maurice de Saxe.

In 1747 Ligonier's campaigning continued and, at Laffeldt in July, this 66-year-old Anglicized Frenchman, in his last battle, commanded a cavalry charge which saved the hard-pressed British infantry at a critical moment. Bold and necessary though this action was, it resulted in Ligonier's capture, an event which made him fear summary execution for treason. Instead, however, he was kindly treated by Louis XV, who entertained him, rewarded his two *carabinier* captors with battlefield commissions, and used Ligonier as a paroled intermediary to investigate the possibilities of peace. He was exchanged before the end of the year, was appointed lieutenant-general of the ordnance in March 1748, and took little part in the last year of the War of the Austrian Succession.

Politics and the ordnance The next eight years of peace in Europe were years of social consolidation and reward for Ligonier. In 1748 he was appointed governor of the French protestant hospital, La Providence, in London, and, without canvassing, he was elected MP for Bath in succession to Field Marshal George Wade; he secured a suitable marriage for his natural daughter, to Lieutenant-Colonel Arthur Graham of the 1st foot guards, in the same year. In 1749 he was promoted to the colonelcy of the 2nd dragoon guards, received the sinecure post of governor of Guernsey, was sworn of the privy council, and was elected a fellow of the Royal Society. In 1750 he bought the estate of Cobham Place in Surrey, in 1752 he exchanged the governorship of Guernsey for that of Plymouth, and in 1753 he was appointed colonel of the Royal Horse Guards Blue—a rank and position reflective not only of great prestige but also of considerable royal favour.

Since the vacant post of master-general was not filled until 1756, Ligonier's role as lieutenant-general of the ordnance put him in control of the *matériel* of the Royal Navy and the army, as well as the logistic support of the latter: for eight years he held the most senior professional military post in the realm. As Britain drifted, through escalating skirmishes in America and India in 1754 and 1755, towards the outbreak of the Seven Years' War in 1756, Ligonier confronted the last great military test of his long and distinguished career. His military position as effective head of the ordnance brought him increasingly into the cockpit of political intrigue, the ramifications of which led to the appointment of Charles Spencer, third duke of Marlborough, as master-general of the ordnance in 1756. In the same year Ligonier was promoted to the substantive rank of general on the duke of Cumberland's staff, retaining his ordnance duties since Marlborough had few pretensions to military professionalism. Ligonier's promotion was in the gift of George II, who consulted him over military matters in preference to Cumberland, a favouritism which did not help relations between the duke and Ligonier.

The Seven Years' War 1757 saw Cumberland posted to Germany to defend Hanover and Ligonier left in effective command of the army at home and in America. Ligonier's post meant that he had direct access to both the king and his ministers and was thus in a very strong position to influence administrative and strategic decisions at a time of escalating crises. The corps of engineers received military status, and the first of several assaults, albeit abortive, was launched on the French coast: both these acts bore Ligonier's stamp. The capitulation of Cumberland at Klosterzeven in September 1757 destroyed his credibility with his father—necessitating his resignation from all his military offices—and left a vacuum at the head of the army. As the only senior soldier to command the confidence of both George II and the government, Ligonier was the obvious choice to succeed Cumberland, which he did late in the year with the title of general and commander-in-chief. Ligonier was also promoted to the colonelcy of the 1st regiment of foot guards, a prized post vacated by Cumberland, elevated to the Irish peerage with the title Viscount Ligonier of Enniskillen, and created a field marshal.

Ligonier's leadership of the army, together with the command of the navy of Admiral George Anson, Baron Anson, and the ability as a speaker in the Commons and as a war minister of William Pitt the elder, made a great contribution to Britain's decisive victory in 1763. Ligonier's personality made him easy to work with, his extensive experience and battlefield bravery commanded natural respect, and his network of social connections, built up over a long life, opened doors and smoothed paths. He had an acute eye for military talent, and many deserving officers owed their advancement to his patronage; this was especially so in the American theatre of the war, in which his protégés Jeffrey Amherst, James Wolfe, and William Howe distinguished themselves. His physical robustness and undiminished mental powers had been a matter of remark by contemporaries, but the strain imposed by the war inevitably took a periodic toll upon a man in his late seventies. Despite occasional bouts of illness, including an especially serious one in late 1760, Ligonier maintained a tight grip on the army's administration and activities, actively contributing to strategic decisions and pursuing policies which had far-reaching consequences for the army, such as the establishment of regiments of light horse and the embodiment and training of the long-neglected English militia. His commitment and activity were rewarded in 1759 by his appointment as master-general of the ordnance, an appointment which, when combined with that of commander-in-chief, gave him undisputed political and military control of Britain's land forces at a time when the threat of a French invasion was all too real. This combination of posts had previously been held only by the first duke of Marlborough; it would later be held by the first duke of Wellington.

The ending of the war in 1763 resulted in the wholesale reduction in the size of the army and in Ligonier's removal from the post of master-general. Although he nominally remained as commander-in-chief, he lost both the staff support and the salary of that office. In recognition of his services, on 27 April 1763 he was created Baron Ligonier in the peerage of Great Britain, by which he exchanged his seat in the House of Commons for one in the House of Lords, but he received no financial compensation for the resultant and sudden drop in his income. On 20 May 1762 he had been given a further Irish viscountcy, with remainder to his nephew Edward.

Final years Ligonier's powers were clearly gradually failing during the final five years of his life, and his age was given as the reason for his removal from the post of commander-in-chief in 1766. His retirement from the post to which he had contributed so much was marked by his elevation in the British peerage to the title of Earl Ligonier. Retaining his colonelcy of the 1st regiment of foot guards to the end, Ligonier died on 28 April 1770, probably at his London home in North Audley Street, and was buried at Cobham parish church a few days afterwards.

Ligonier made few enemies during his long life, achieved lasting friendships with both sexes, and maintained a justified reputation as both lover and soldier. Widely respected and just as sincerely mourned by contemporaries, he combined, in Horace Walpole's words, the 'gallant gaiety of his nation' (GEC, *Peerage*, 7.656) with a robust single-mindedness thought characteristic of Britain, a country which he served so long and so loyally as one of the most distinguished British army officers of the eighteenth century. STEPHEN WOOD

Sources R. Whitworth, *Field Marshal Lord Ligonier: a story of the British army, 1702–1770* (1958) • J. A. Houlding, *Fit for service: the training of the British army, 1715–1795* (1981) • GEC, *Peerage* • R. R. Sedgwick, 'Ligonier, John Louis', HoP, *Commons, 1754–90* • R. R. Sedgwick, 'Ligonier, John Louis', HoP, *Commons, 1715–54* • *DNB*

Archives BL, military memoranda, Add. MS 22537 • U. Mich., Clements L., letter-book | BL, letters to C. Frederick, Add. MS 57318 • BL, corresp. with duke of Newcastle, Add. MSS 32714–32975, *passim* • CKS, corresp. with J. Amherst • TCD, papers mainly referring to Seven Years' War • U. Hull, Brynmor Jones L., letters to C. Hotham-Thompson

Likenesses P. Mercier, oils, 1738, French Protestant Hospital, Rochester • D. Morier, group portrait, oils, *c.*1749 (with the duke of Cumberland), Royal Collection • B. Dandridge, oils, 1752, French Protestant Hospital, Rochester • G. Bockman, mezzotint, 1756 (after J. Worsdale), BM • attrib. H. Morland, oils, 1757–70, Officer's House, Hyde Park Barracks, London • attrib. D. Morier, oils, 1758?, Lloyds Bank, Cox and King's Branch, London • D. Morier, oils, *c.*1759–1762, Anglesey Abbey and Garden, Cambridgeshire • J. Reynolds, oils, 1760, Fort Ligonier, Pennsylvania [*see illus.*] • D. Morier, group portrait, oils, *c.*1760–1765 (with George III), Royal Collection • L. F. Roubiliac, terracotta bust, probably *c.*1761, NPG • L. F. Roubiliac, marble bust, *c.*1761–1762, Royal Collection • J. F. Moore, medallion on monument, 1773, Westminster Abbey • J. Brooks, mezzotint (after J. Latham), BM • J. Reynolds, oils, Tate collection • J. Reynolds, oils, Royal Armouries, Leeds • J. Reynolds, oils, NAM • engraving (after J. Reynolds)

Ligulf (*d.* 1080), nobleman, was an Anglo-Danish landowner with substantial hereditary landholdings in Yorkshire. It has been suggested that he may also be that Ligulf, lawman of York, who gave evidence on the archbishop's liberty in 1080. During the Norman occupation of the north of England he seems to have been displaced in the aftermath of the rebellion in Yorkshire against William I, *c.*1068–1070. He made his way north with his family and his Yorkshire estates may have passed to Robert, count of Mortain. Ligulf is described as a devotee of St Cuthbert and John of Worcester's chronicle says that he would recount to Ealdred, archbishop of York, his visions of the saint; but his decision to settle in the area to the north of the Tees was probably more influenced by his marriage to Ealdgyth, the daughter of Ealdred, earl of Northumbria. With the death of Earl *Osulf, the exile of Earl *Gospatric, and the execution in 1076 of Earl *Waltheof, Ligulf may have become the most senior representative of the comital house of Bamburgh, and therein lies his importance in northern English politics at this period. It was probably in this capacity that he became one of the closest advisers of Walcher, bishop of Durham (*d.* 1080), who had assumed the role of earl of Northumbria after Waltheof's execution. Ligulf is described as a 'noble and good thegn' by the author of the Durham compilation the *Historia regum Anglorum* and it is said that Bishop Walcher would not conduct any secular matters without his advice, indicating a close working relationship between the Norman-appointed bishop and the representative of the native aristocracy.

The administration was, however, undermined by the antagonism towards Ligulf of two members of Walcher's entourage, his chaplain Leobwin and the bishop's kinsman, Gilbert. Leobwin had been elevated to a high position within Walcher's *familia* with general oversight of the administration of the bishopric and county of Durham, possibly indicative of archidiaconal status. Leobwin opposed Ligulf's counsel and quarrelled with him often in the bishop's presence. In one meeting of the episcopal council Ligulf seems to have won the day, prompting Leobwin to plot Ligulf's death with Gilbert, who had been appointed governor of the earldom under the bishop. One night in April or May 1080, Gilbert and Leobwin, together with their own men and soldiers of the bishop, marched to Ligulf's residence and slew him and almost all of his family. Learning of Ligulf's murder, Bishop Walcher retired to Durham Castle and sent out messengers dissociating himself from the act, offering to banish Gilbert from the bishopric and submit himself to the judgment of the pope. At this point Walcher may have also tried to conciliate Ligulf's wife with a gift of land. A meeting was arranged between the two sides at Gateshead on 14 May 1080 where, despite Walcher's protestation of innocence, the Northumbrians slaughtered the bishop and his men.

Ligulf had two recorded sons with Ealdgyth, Morcar and Uhtred. By 1074–5 Morcar had been given as a boy to the monastery at Jarrow through the intervention of his uncle Earl Waltheof. He may also be the Morcar, son of Ligulf, who appears as a lawman of York in the early twelfth century. Uhtred may have succeeded his father in some of his Yorkshire lands as Domesday Book records an Uhtred as tenant of the king in the manor of Rudston in Yorkshire in 1086. It is just possible that Ligulf had a daughter, since a Ragnald, daughter of Ligulf and wife of Robert de Sarz, appears making a series of grants to Fountains Abbey, probably in the 1130s. WILLIAM M. AIRD

Sources Symeon of Durham, *Opera*, vol. 2 • John of Worcester, *Chron.* • W. Farrer and others, eds., *Early Yorkshire charters*, 12 vols. (1914–65), vols. 1–3 • A. Farley, ed., *Domesday Book*, 2 vols. (1783) • W. M. Aird, 'St Cuthbert, the Scots and the Normans', *Anglo-Norman Studies*, 16 (1993), 1–20 • A. Williams, *The English and the Norman conquest* (1995) • H. S. Offler, ed., *Durham episcopal charters, 1071–1152*, SurtS, 179 (1968) • R. C. van Caenegem, ed., *English lawsuits from William I to Richard I*, SeldS, 1, 106 (1990)

Lilburne [*née* Dewell], **Elizabeth** (*fl.* 1641–1660), Leveller, was the daughter of Henry Dewell (*d.* in or after 1655), a London merchant. Nothing is known of her early life but in or before September 1641 she married the future Leveller leader John *Lilburne (1615?–1657), who had recently been released from the imprisonment imposed on him in 1638 for circulating subversive religious literature. She was already involved in London separatist circles, and was among the thirteen women and sixteen men arrested in September 1641 for attending John Spilsbury's Baptist congregation in Stepney. Her life was dominated by the political activism of her husband which brought him frequent imprisonment and a long period of exile, and meant for Elizabeth tireless lobbying, shared prisons, and much hardship. When John, a captain in Lord Brooke's regiment, was captured by royalists at Brentford and sentenced to death it was Elizabeth's determined petitioning that persuaded parliament to threaten retaliation on royalist prisoners if Lilburne was hanged. It was a pregnant Elizabeth who carried to Oxford the life-saving letter from the speaker of the Commons.

After Lilburne's release Elizabeth spent some quieter months in Boston, Lincolnshire, during John's service in the army of the eastern association, but her tranquil existence was shattered by her husband's increasing disaffection from the dominant parliamentary factions. When John was imprisoned in August 1645 for an attack on Speaker Lenthall, a heavily pregnant Elizabeth joined him in Newgate. Their daughter Elizabeth was born in prison and was baptized, perhaps against her parents' wishes. In their absence parliament's officers searching for 'dangerous Bookes' in the Lilburnes' London home stole Elizabeth's childbed linen. Later, during John's two-year imprisonment for his attacks on presbyterian and parliamentarian authoritarianism from the summer of 1646, Elizabeth was herself arrested and examined by a Commons committee for circulating John's books in February 1647.

John, along with other Leveller leaders, was imprisoned again in March 1649 for his opposition to the new Commonwealth regime, but he was bailed in July because Elizabeth and her three children were all dangerously ill with smallpox. Their two sons died but Elizabeth and her daughter recovered. In all some ten children were born during the Lilburnes' stormy marriage, of whom only three reached adulthood. In October 1649 Elizabeth, ill and distressed, was absent when John was famously acquitted of treason by a London jury. An uncharacteristically peaceful eighteen months followed for the Lilburnes, supported in part from the proceeds of confiscated Durham church lands granted in recompense for the 1630s punishments. But John's ill-judged attack on Sir Arthur Hesilrige's administration of sequestered estates in the north-east brought ruin to his family. He was convicted of libel by parliament, heavily fined, and banished in January 1652, leaving his wife to the protection of the prominent Baptist William Kiffin, an old friend, though no longer a political ally.

John Lilburne's exile writings are full of bitter complaints against his wife for her 'mournfull arguments' urging him to make peace with Cromwell for the sake of his impoverished family. Elizabeth is portrayed as a weak, irrational woman, 'my poor credulous wife', 'perfectly distracted' by the recent death of another baby. She had pressed John to compromise on 'such sneaking terms as my soul abhorres'. A bitter meeting at Bruges did nothing to persuade Lilburne to give in, although he did come back to England in June 1653 and was promptly returned to prison, where he remained, with various paroles, for the rest of his life. Two further children were born in these years. In July 1655 Elizabeth and her father-in-law petitioned unsuccessfully for John's release from prison out of pity for herself and her children, promising implausibly that her husband would be 'quiet and thankful'. John Lilburne was, however, moved from Jersey to Dover, and died while on bail at Eltham, Kent, following Elizabeth's last confinement. He had become a Quaker, but his writings suggest that Elizabeth did not share his stance.

Elizabeth's assessment of her family's best interests was to be vindicated. After John's death on 29 August 1657 she petitioned the protector for the lifting of the swingeing £7000 fine imposed on Lilburne's estate in 1652 following his attack on Hesilrige, for renewal of a pension of 40s. per week for herself and her children, and for help in settling disputes over the Durham property. All these requests were granted in subsequent months, and her pension was still being paid in March 1660. Throughout the 1650s Hesilrige's attempts to sort out with Elizabeth the Lilburnes' complicated property disputes in Durham had been blocked by John's intransigence but now agreement was reached, and in February 1659 Hesilrige himself recommended Elizabeth's situation to parliament's consideration. In return Elizabeth delivered up all the papers concerned with the original dispute. Information for Elizabeth's later life is scarce but the Restoration in 1660 presumably meant that any significant improvement in her circumstances was short-lived.

Almost everything known about Elizabeth Lilburne comes from the writings of her self-regarding husband—and his presentations of his suffering wife may well owe as much to the demands of particular polemical situations as they do to the reality of her personality or their life together. The impression is left of a brave and realistic radical woman, determined to preserve herself and her children in the most difficult public circumstances.

ANN HUGHES

Sources P. Gregg, *Free-born John: a biography of John Lilburne* (1961) • K. Lindley, *Popular politics and religion in civil war London* (1997), 80–81 • *JHC* • *CSP dom.* • *Diary of Thomas Burton*, ed. J. T. Rutt, 4 vols. (1828) • J. Lilburne, *Englands birthright justified* (1645) • J. Lilburne, *An impeachment of high treason against Oliver Cromwel and his son-in-law Henry Ireton* (1649) • J. Lilburne, *As you were* (1652) • J. Lilburne, *L. Colonel John Lilburne revived, shewing the cause of his late long silence* (1653) [Thomason tract E 689(32)] • J. Lilburne, *The upright mans vindication* (1653) • *The resurrection of John Lilburne, now a prisoner in Dover-castle … in these following lines, penned by himself*, 2nd edn (1656) [with added appendix]

Lilburne, John (1615?–1657), Leveller, was probably born at Sunderland in 1615. His father was Richard Lilburne (1583–1667), heir to a modest manorial holding at Thickley Punchardon near Bishop Auckland. His mother was Margaret (*d.* 1619), daughter of Thomas Hixon (*d.* 1619), who

Gaze not vpon this shaddow that is vaine,
But rather raise thy thoughts a higher straine,
To GOD (I meane) who set this young-man free,
And in like straits can eke deliuer thee.

John Lilburne (1615?–1657), by George Glover, 1641

was master of the standing wardrobe at Greenwich Palace under Charles I. He was one of four children, and the second of three sons: his elder brother, Robert *Lilburne (*bap.* 1614, *d.* 1665), was a Cromwellian army officer, regicide, protectoral MP, and deputy major-general; his younger brother, Henry (1618–1648), was a parliamentarian during the first civil war who defected in 1648 to the royalists. The extended Lilburne family was well known in Northumberland and Durham and in his generation John was the most famous of them all. He founded no lasting family, however. In or before September 1641 he married Elizabeth [*see* Lilburne, Elizabeth], daughter of Henry Dewell, a London merchant. They had ten children. Seven were to die young, the others childless.

Early life to 1637 In 1616 the infant Lilburne went to Greenwich with his parents to stay with his maternal grandparents but in 1620, soon after the deaths of his mother and grandfather, he was taken back north. There he attended the school in Bishop Auckland and the Royal Grammar School in Newcastle upon Tyne. He was to acquire a reputation for intellectual acuity—he said of himself that he was not one of the 'dronnesest' of schoolboys (Lilburne, *Innocency and Truth*, 8)—but he attended neither university nor inn of court, knew no Greek, and claimed to know little Latin although he was able later in life to read Milton's *Defensio secunda*. In 1630 he was apprenticed to the puritan Thomas Hewson, a wholesale clothier of Londonstone, Candlewick Street, in the heart of London. The young apprentice engrossed himself in reading the Bible, was a member of Edmund Rosier's separatist congregation, and attended sermons in a wide range of the city's anti-episcopal churches. He read widely in puritan divines, and admired especially John Foxe's book of martyrs, which recounted the sufferings and martyrdoms of protestant reformers under Queen Mary. His apprenticeship is likely to have ended in 1636 and probably in the same year he underwent a conversion experience, learning to know 'God as my loving and reconciled father, that had particularly washed and cleansed my soul with the precious bloud of Jesus Christ' (Lilburne, *Legall Fundamentall Liberties*, 20). Certainly it was in the course of that year that he was introduced to Dr John Bastwick, the presbyterian divine who was in prison for writing scandalous books against the bishops. Lilburne became a frequent and admiring visitor and for his part, Bastwick, impressed by Lilburne's energy and intellect (though not by his lack of wealth and his country manners), instructed him in points of religious controversy and in matters of deportment, so as to make him 'fit for all Gentlemans and Noblemen's society' (Gregg, 48).

On 30 June 1637 Lilburne witnessed with sympathy the sufferings of Bastwick and his fellow presbyterian William Prynne. Sharing their fate of having his ears cropped was the more Independent Henry Burton, who is said to have looked down from the pillory and asked the young man: 'Sonne, Sonne, what is the matter you look so pale?' (Gregg, 51). If indeed he was afraid at that time, Lilburne showed no further signs of fear in the face of danger: as his life became increasingly public he confronted a continually widening array of enemies with a courage often amounting to foolhardiness, and in most of his rather more than sixty pamphlets, dramatized and publicized what he did and suffered as of the utmost concern to all Englishmen, clearly picturing himself in the mould of those martyrs in the protestant cause whose lives had been recorded by Foxe.

The clash with Star Chamber, 1637–1640 From late 1636 or early 1637 Lilburne had been involved in printing and distributing Burton's satirical anti-episcopal pamphlet, *A Letany*. The printing had had to be carried out in the Netherlands to avoid the censorship of the Stationers' Company—Lilburne had probably travelled there—and distributing the book in England was dangerous, but his commitment to the puritan cause was absolute and with his apprenticeship over he may well have entered the enterprise with profit in mind. In the early winter of 1637 he went to the Netherlands to arrange further printings of other books. Soon after his return he was arrested and imprisoned for importing 'scandalous' and 'factious' books. From 14 January to 13 February 1638 he was given the opportunity to defend himself, first to the chief clerk of the attorney-general, then to the attorney-general, Sir John Bankes, himself, and finally to the infamous prerogative court, the Star Chamber. Defying all lawful procedure, he refused to take the oath to tell the truth as to all matters he might be asked about. Presenting the subversive face of separatist Christianity, he insisted that oaths could not be required of Christians and that, in any case, he was unsure whether the particular oath in question was legal. He also refused to answer his examiner's direct questions 'upon interrogatories'. He (wrongly) argued that according to common law he should not be condemned out of his own mouth in answering his judges. Such was the outrage that these arguments generated among his triers that the crime of 'insufferable disobedience and contempt' was added to the crimes of illegal printing for which he was initially arraigned. He was condemned by Star Chamber on 13 February to be whipped from the Fleet prison to the New Palace Yard in Westminster, there to be pilloried, thence returned to the Fleet, to remain until he should 'conform'. The sentence was carried out on 18 April 1638, and was immediately publicized by Lilburne in his second pamphlet, *A Worke of the Beast*. (His first, *The Christian Mans Triall*, had already been published in March.) *A Worke* related how he was tied to a 'cart's arse' and whipped with a knotted rope from the Fleet to the pillory. From the pillory, until silenced, he inveighed against the illegality of his treatment at the hands of Star Chamber and the bishops—minions of the popish Antichrist in Rome. Eventually gagged by officials, he distributed pamphlets to the crowd. Imprisoned, he was for a time bound in shackles and was refused the company of his friends (including, apparently, his future wife). His bravery commended him to the London anti-episcopal movement, and the experience toughened him and gave him assurance of his election to salvation:

> I assuredly know that all the power in Earth, yea and the gates of Hell itselfe shall never be able to move me or prevaile against me, for the Lord who is the worker of all my workes in and for me, hath founded and built me upon that sure & unmoveable foundation the Lord *Jesus Christ*. (Lilburne, *Come out of her my People*, 5)

Until he was freed Lilburne never ceased, in pamphlets and petitions, to publicize the injustice of his condemnation and the continuing barbarous illegalities of his gaolers. He also laid down his separatist ecclesiological principles. A true church was:

> a company of believers who are washed in the blood of Christ by a free and voluntary Consent or willingnesse to enter into that … holy State, City or Kingdome … and by the power of Christ to become a constituted or Politique body or Corporation … uniting & joyning themselves together each to other & so unto the Lord, promising to walk in his waies and to yeild obedience to all his Laws and commands. (J. Lilburne, *An Answer to Nine Arguments*, 1645, 28)

The prelatical church was thus not a true church. It was, moreover, both idolatrous and—because its hierarchy was authorized by the pope—antichristian. The English must, in the phrase from Revelation, 'Come out of her' (Lilburne, *Come out of her my People*).

Parliamentarian and soldier, 1640–1645 As a result of Oliver Cromwell's pleading for him in the newly called House of Commons of the Long Parliament, Lilburne was released from the Fleet on 13 November 1640. His portrait was engraved by George Glover—evidence that he was now a man of some standing and popularity—but domestic matters demanded his attention. His uncle, George Lilburne of Sunderland, helped him with capital to set up as a brewer, and in or before September 1641 he married. His wife, Elizabeth, had been 'an object deare in my affections severall yeares before from me she knew anything of it' (Lilburne, *L. Colonel John Lilburne Revived*, 1). Lilburne may have been further encouraged in his domestic ambitions when the Commons resolved on 4 May 1641 that the Star Chamber sentence against him had been 'bloody, wicked, cruel, barbarous, and tyrannical', and voted him monetary reparations, though without specifying how much or a means of delivery (Gregg, 87). However, whatever his personal concerns, he was by now addicted to public affairs, and was active in following and furthering parliament's quarrel with Charles I. He frequented Westminster Hall and there on 3 May 1641, demonstrating against the earl of Strafford, he told an acquaintance that were justice not done, 'they would pull the King out of Whitehall' (Gregg, 86). Discharged from consequent accusations of treason, on 12 May he was involved in a fracas with constables when attending Strafford's execution. On 27 December 1641 he was wounded in the New Palace Yard by musket fire when demonstrating (as he admitted) 'with my sword in my hand' against bishops and 'popish lords' (Frank, 26; Gregg, 89), and when in July 1642 parliament voted to raise an army he eagerly enlisted as a captain of foot in the puritan Lord Brooke's troop.

Lilburne fought at Edgehill on 23 October. On 12 November he defended Brentford with distinction, was captured, and sent to the royalist headquarters in Oxford as a prisoner. The royalists planned that he and other prisoners should be tried for treason, but they were saved from trial when the House of Commons declared on 17 December 1642 that it would administer *lex talionis* on parliament's prisoners should those in Oxford be sentenced. Elizabeth Lilburne bravely delivered the message from London to Oxford, and in May 1643 her husband was exchanged by the royalists for prisoners in parliament's hands.

When he returned home Lilburne sold his brewery at a loss and returned to war. On 7 October 1643, at the instigation of his friend Cromwell (now a lieutenant-general), he took a commission in the earl of Manchester's eastern association army as a major of foot in the regiment of Colonel Edward King which was stationed in Lincolnshire. Elizabeth went with him (as she had to Edgehill), quartering with their child in Boston. Lilburne probably fought with the army when it relieved Lincoln on 20 October and in May 1644 he found promotion as a lieutenant-colonel of dragoons in Manchester's own regiment. On 2 July he fought at Marston Moor and later that month negotiated the royalist surrender of Tickhill Castle in Yorkshire. However, membership of the New Model Army, which was instituted in army reorganizations of early 1645, would have required him to take the solemn league and covenant. That instrument, besides requiring adherence by oath, pointed strongly to a presbyterian and Scots-dictated church settlement: Lilburne could not stomach an oath, the Scots, or presbyterianism, so he left the army on 30 April. By mid-May he and Elizabeth had set up house in Petty France, Westminster. He contemplated a career in the cloth export trade but found himself excluded by the monopoly of the Merchant Adventurers' Company.

First clashes with presbyterians, 1643–1646 A series of events set Lilburne on a collision course with the powerful presbyterian divines of London, with 'political' as well as 'religious' presbyterian members of the House of Commons, and with almost all the members of the House of Lords. Colonel King was a rabid presbyterian, and it is likely that Cromwell sent Lilburne to King's regiment on a watching brief for that and other reasons. In December 1643 Lilburne found that the colonel had imprisoned several officers and townspeople of Lincoln for meeting in a conventicle and, after observing behaviour still more unsavoury, he joined the committee of Lincolnshire in preferring charges against King to the House of Lords—most notably that the colonel had misappropriated public property meant for the army and had traitorously betrayed the towns of Crowland and Grantham to the enemy. Soon after, Lilburne also fell out with Manchester, who was not only his general, but a presbyterian and a leading figure in the Lords. This was partly because the earl, having strongly discouraged him from taking Tickhill Castle and then reprimanding him for doing so, had the effrontery in reporting the victory to parliament to take the credit to himself. Lilburne also evidently shared with Cromwell an aversion to the earl's lukewarmness in bringing the war to a rapid and victorious conclusion, and when Cromwell charged the earl in the Commons with crimes attendant on that lukewarmness, Lilburne gave evidence against him, on 25 November 1644. Soon after, on 7 January 1645, he attacked an old ally when, in *A Copie of a Letter … to … Prynne*, he complained of the influential Prynne's bitterness of language and intolerance, defended the freedom of the press against presbyterian calls for censorship, and spelt out his own position on a national church government: a 'state-government' of the church was permissible, only if 'they leave my Conscience free to the Law and Will of my Lord and King' (Lilburne, *Copie of a Letter … to … Prinne*, 7). Independent congregations remained his ideal: nobody should be forced to join a national church.

Lilburne thus joined a war of pamphlet and political manoeuvre between Independents and presbyterians. He had maintained his connections with the underground press and during winter 1644–5 had probably met and co-operated with Richard Overton, a General Baptist who was heavily implicated in illegal printing. By May 1645 Lilburne was also associated with a group of radical political Independents who met both at the Windmill tavern in Lothbury and at the Salters' Hall, the headquarters of a subcommittee to raise volunteer forces in London, and he began to frequent meetings at the Windmill. Like other Independents and sectarians he was now attacked not only by Prynne and the heresiarch Thomas Edwards, but by his old mentor and friend, Bastwick. Prynne drew attention to Lilburne's energetic proselytizing and dissemination of Independent literature as he had moved around Lincolnshire on military duties. All three dwelt on his sectarian London connections, Edwards calling him 'the darling of the sectaries' (T. Edwards, *Gangraena*, 3 pts., 1646, 3.153) and Bastwick speaking of the 'Rabble rout, tagragge and bobtaile' of his London following (J. Bastwick, *A Just Defence … Against the Calumnies of John Lilburne*, 1645, 16–17). It was to be a characteristic of Lilburne's life henceforth that he would quarrel with almost all his friends. One of his favourite observations was to be that the wounds suffered at the hands of friends were the worst. Its scriptural lesson (which by 1647 he had quoted against his old Independent parliamentarian friends) was Micah 7: 5—'Trust ye not in a friend, put ye not confidence in a guide' (Lilburne, *Jonah's Cry*, title-page).

Quarrels with the presbyterians were not restricted to verbal ones. From January 1645 Lilburne was entangled by Prynne in proceedings before the Commons' committee for examinations for the illegal publishing of *A Copie of a Letter*. The proceedings were eventually dismissed, not because of Lilburne's modest silence in the face of attack—he published continuously—but probably because he had powerful Independent friends in parliament including Miles Corbett, Cromwell, and William Bradshaw. Even so he could not succeed in persuading the Commons to complete the arrangements for the reparations they had voted for in May 1641. Nor did Prynne rest. He next organized a false charge to the committee of examinations that Lilburne was author of certain Marpriest pamphlets, and though the charge was dismissed on 19 July, on that same day Lilburne was legally enmired again—this time by Bastwick and King. They alleged that he had slandered the speaker, William Lenthall, in the course of some too-public plotting with William Walwyn (a member of the Salters' Hall group, though a conforming parishioner), Henry Ireton, and others. His Independent friends sought to protect Lilburne and help him out of Newgate prison where he was sent in the interim, but on 11 August the Commons irrevocably committed him until he should be tried by an ordinary court. Not for the last time, Elizabeth joined him in prison.

Although in the event a trial was avoided, Lilburne was not freed until 14 October, after he had produced *The Copie of a Letter … to … a Freind* (25 July), in which he articulated a hitherto unheard-of doctrine of supreme authority. Until then pamphleteers had contended that supreme authority was vested either in the king, or the two houses of parliament, or in king and parliament combined, and had argued, if not for a continuous and uncontrolled authority in whichever of those places they favoured, at least for an arbitrary power in times of emergency. Now Lilburne argued that the Commons alone was:

> the supreame power of England, who have residing in them that power that is inherent in the people, who are yet not to act according to their own wills and pleasure, but according to the fundamentall Constitutions and Customes of the Land, which I conceive provides for the safety and preservation of the people. (Lilburne, *Copie of a Letter … to … a Freind*, 14)

Lilburne would have supremacy vested in an elected legislature, but far from being an arbitrary power, it would be a severely limited supremacy.

In *The Copie of a Letter … to … a Freind*, and at much more length in *Englands Birthright Justified* (10 October 1645), Lilburne demonstrated a greatly enlarged political education from the time he had first entered politics in 1636. He had added much legal knowledge and many legal texts to his arsenal (especially Edward Coke's 1642 *Second Institutes* on Magna Carta). He had become expert in the royalist–parliamentarian literature of declaration and response which was consolidated in the *Exact Collection* published by parliament in 1643. He was an eager student also of the pamphlet literature that built on the primary documents of the 'paper war', especially on the parliamentarian tracts of Henry Parker and the Prynne of 1643. By the time of *Englands Birthright* he had developed clear ideas of parliamentary reform: he wanted the Commons elected and meeting annually, the enforcement of the self-denying ordinance (which called for no army officers in parliament), no other placemen or lawyers as members, and the payment of poor members. He added to these demands a series of typical radical Independent and sectarian ones: an end to the solemn league and covenant and persecuting presbyterianism, to monopolies and monopolists (especially the Merchant Adventurers), to the tithes that supported a national church unchosen by congregations, to the excise which penalized the small manufacturer and trader, to the barbarous technicalities of a law written in foreign tongues, and to the oligarchical structure of the City's government.

The quarrel with the House of Lords and Leveller writing, 1646–1649 Set free and back in Petty France in October 1645, Lilburne reapplied to parliament to settle his long-standing claim to compensation for his whipping and incarceration by Star Chamber. The Commons got only as far as discharging him from his Star Chamber fine in November, at which the Lords concurred, but delays as to his 'reparations' continued; then Colonel King—still awaiting trial for high treason at the Lords' bar—charged him at the court of common pleas with slander. As a result of going public during the consequent proceedings Lilburne was called to the Lords on 11 June 1646 to answer for a libel he had made against Manchester in a pamphlet, *The Just Mans Justification*. Responding at the Lords' bar, he told his story against King and proceeded to deny utterly the Lords' right to try a commoner, for which he was yet again sent to Newgate. Unimpeded by close confinement, on 16 June he published *The Freemans Freedome Vindicated* which recorded all this, and added on the last page that Manchester was so 'glu'd in interest' to the cavalier party and to Colonel King that his 'head hath stood too long upon his shoulders'. He also smeared the earl of Stamford as a closet royalist, concluding: 'the free People of *England* … scorn to be made slaves & vassals, by the meer Creatures of their Creature *the King*'. In 'an appeal' appended to the work he addressed the Commons as the 'formal and legal supreme power of England', asking for their help. Unsurprisingly, by 11 July he was at the Lords' bar yet again, answering charges of scandal and illegal printing: he was fined £2000 and imprisoned in the Tower of London during the Lords' pleasure; *The Just Mans Justification* and *The Freemans Freedome Vindicated* were ordered to be burned; and he was disqualified from holding any office in Commonwealth or army whatsoever. He was not allowed visitors until later in the year, and he was not allowed out on bail until 9 November 1647. He had to wait until 2 August 1648, in the middle of the second civil war, to be freed.

During his long imprisonment Lilburne parted company with his most powerful independent allies in parliament, city, and army, and emerged as a leader of the Levellers—so named by Cromwell or Ireton (who was by then Cromwell's son-in-law) in early November 1647. He never forgave the Lords, was to write a series of attacks on their very right to existence, and was to demand henceforth that all should be equal before the law, whatever their social or political rank. During his prison years he also developed further his habit of demanding trial by a jury of his peers, on a specified and known charge brought by known accusers, in a court of common law, and 'according to the known and declared laws of the land' as specified especially in the petition of right and Magna Carta. These were the rights of 'freeborn Englishmen'. The royalist judge, David Jenkins, strengthened his legalism with his friendship and example.

On 26 August 1645 a petition supporting Lilburne and signed by two or three thousand citizens had been presented to the Commons. Pamphleteers—Overton and Walwyn prominent among them—began to defend him in print, and by June the next year his name was regularly invoked by radical Independents. As the Leveller movement was forged it was (both at the time and by later historians) significantly defined by its supporters' sympathy with and admiration for him. His main contribution consisted in providing a barrage of nearly forty pamphlets from the spring of 1646 until the fragile coalition between London and New Model radicals petered out in mutiny in September 1649. In these writings he insisted that the unjust dealings he found at the hands of established authorities epitomized the actions of the arbitrary and lawless powers which had ruled England ever since his first sufferings in 1637. He named the Lords, the Commons (both pre- and post-purge), Commons' committees, court officials, judges, gaolers and prison officers, the officers of the New Model, and the council of state as acting 'exorbitantly' and 'tyrannically'. Each ruling group, intent on pursuing 'particular interests', used unnecessary emergency powers to govern. They all persisted with excise, customs, monopolies, and forced loans to raise money not only for their wars but for the enrichment of committeemen and war profiteers. The Long Parliament insisted on free quarter for soldiers, would not guarantee them indemnity from war crimes, kept them permanently in arrears of pay, and proposed to send them to Ireland or disband them. Both houses persecuted the well-affected for religion, and the Commons, 'the supreme power', refused to hear (and burned) the petitions of the people, especially the 'large' petition of March 1647. No better were the 'grandees' of the New Model who, led by Cromwell, were to overawe parliament. They had from the beginning undermined the solemn engagement of the army of 5 June 1647 which had proclaimed that the army would be governed by a general council, made up not only of the general officers but of two soldiers from every regiment. They had soon after been seduced by the promise of royal favours into dealing with King Charles. When disappointed in him (as earlier with parliament) they had decided during 1648 to purge the parliament and kill the king without due process of law. Having done that, they—and their 'creatures' in the council of state erected with the Commonwealth in 1649—proceeded to rule tyrannically. Lilburne's *Legall Fundamentall Liberties* of 1649 best summarized and heightened his writings in this vein, and paid full attention to the author's own part in the welter of affairs which he thus characterized.

In torrents of rough prose Lilburne thus made himself a commanding presence in the minds of his contemporaries. Sometimes he wrote with others, Overton, Walwyn, and Thomas Prince in particular, but mostly he wrote alone. His writings were full of ambiguous and self-serving accounts of his own doings and sufferings, and of invective against the weakness or ambition of his targets. At times he spoke in his own voice, but as often he loaded his texts and margins with holy scripture and legal texts, and with quotations from the declarations of parliament or the New Model 'in the dayes of their virginity'. A selection of titles show the man: *Liberty Vindicated Against Slavery* (1646); *Jonah's Cry out of the Whale's Belly* and *The Juglers Discovered* (1647); *A Whip for the Present House of Lords* and *The Prisoners Mournful Cry* (1648); and *An Impeachment of High Treason Against Oliver Cromwell* and *Strength out of Weakness* (1649).

The movement of Lilburne's thought through time was as complex as his own interests were variously at stake and as public events unfolded, but the foundations of his thinking were clear enough, if not easily seen to be consistent. They lay in covenant theology, in a general commitment to 'lawful' institutions and actions, and in a personal psychology marked by acute distrust of others' motives as centring on desires for unlimited power or slothful ease. All men and women since Adam and Eve, he held:

> are … by nature all equal and alike in power, dignity, authority, and majesty none of them having (by nature) any authority, dominion or magisterial power one over or above another; neither have they nor can they exercise any, but merely by institution or donation, that is to say by mutual agreement or consent, given, derived, or assumed by mutual consent or agreement, for the good benefit and comfort each of other. (Lilburne, *Freemans Freedome Vindicated*, postscript)

Thus constituted, all power ought to be limited by 'law', and people should obey the 'law'. 'God the supreme King, never created any man whatsoever lawless'; 'He that is not God but mere man', cannot 'make his will a rule and law unto himself and others'. But the law which limited governments and demanded obedience was not the law of the land as it actually was. Actual law should be purged of its Norman and prerogative monstrosities imposed by conquest, and written in plain English. Limits to government and the duty of obedience were set by the natural law of *salus populi* which bound all human beings, forbidding them to destroy themselves and commanding them to do what was reasonable to pursue their welfare and safety. In England, such general injunctions found expression—when they did—in biblical injunction, in reasonable customs which had been approved by the people, and in statutes, similarly reasonable and made in parliament. From mid-1647 Lilburne was often (but not consistently) to claim that all power in England was 'broken' by corruption or the sword and 'dissolved into the originall law of nature', and that the great challenge was for people and soldiers to come together to reconstitute government anew.

Lilburne came to support both a process by which a new form of government might be instituted by 'the people', and a specifically representative form of government which he and other Levellers urged upon those 'people' to choose. Both of these (the process and the representative form) would embody the consent of 'the people' and be legitimate for that reason. In a number of only slightly differing formulations he advocated an 'agreement of the people' in which, by mutual consent, the people should adopt a written constitution which would both define the form and powers of government and limit those powers by reserving to the people a set of inalienable rights. Lilburne demanded a supreme 'representative of the people', elected annually or biennially on a more extensive, though far from universal, franchise and one geographically more representative, unhindered by a veto in king or Lords. The representative would exercise all the traditional powers of government at home and abroad, except where it was restricted by powers 'reserved' to 'the people'. The people would retain freedom of religion, assembly, and trade, and there were to be no legal privileges granted any particular class of person. These were main provisions in the famous agreements of the people of 1647–9 in which Lilburne had a hand and which he supported.

Throughout 1647 and 1648, however, the Levellers also petitioned the Commons. The petitions—by contrast with the proposals for *An Agreement of the People*—were presented on the assumption that England was not in an original state of nature, and begged the Commons as the current 'supreme power' to deliver either an agreement, or (more often) the substance of the reforms they desired. Lilburne, never consistent in all matters, supported the petitions as well as the agreements.

Imprisonment in the Tower, 1646–1648 Lilburne had a more limited active involvement in Leveller organization and activity while he was in prison than he doubtless would have wished. It is difficult to gauge his influence at a time of secrecy and intrigue both in the New Model and in the Tower, where he became friendly with the royalist Sir Lewis Dyve as well as Judge Jenkins, but leaving aside the personal matters of reparations and arrears which he continued unsuccessfully to pursue via a Commons' committee under his republican friend Henry Marten, it is clear that he was politically active and influential, even in prison. From September to November 1646 he concerned himself with writing on the democratic reform of London politics, urging universal suffrage for all adult males in elections to the common council. In January 1647 he was questioned by the Lords with Overton concerning *Regall Tyranny Discovered*, a vigorous attack on kings, kingship, and the House of Lords. In February he was before the Commons' committee of examinations for *The Oppressed Mans Oppressions Declared*, in which the authors complained of a tyrannical Commons crushing their friends and throwing the people into 'the originall law of nature', where 'every man' must 'preserve and defend himselfe as best he can' (Lilburne, *Oppressed Mans Oppressions*, 14).

Lilburne was associated too with the forging of the alliance between London and New Model radicals, and with advocating in some detail the appropriate actions of the soldiers and people against all who would oppose them. On the London front, in March 1647 he 'underhand' (Lilburne, *Juglers Discovered*, 3) supported friends (including Walwyn, Nicholas Tew, William Brown, and Major Alexander Tulidah) in the matter of the 'Large' Leveller petition, and he unsuccessfully tried to persuade the defecting John Goodwin and his Independent congregation to continue to aid those gathering petitions on his behalf. As to the New Model, possibly also in March, Lilburne wrote to Cromwell arguing that tyranny was resistible 'in a Parliament as well as a King', advising him not to allow the army to lay down its arms before its own petitions were heard by parliament, and accusing him of frustrating the soldiers' plans to petition (Woolrych, *Soldiers and Statesmen*, 36). When the army revolted soon after, he gave counsel and encouragement via prison visitors such as Tulidah, Edward Sexby, William Allen and Captain John White. In April and May he supported the selection of 'agitators' from the regiments, and in June he applauded the solemn engagement which made them part of the army's governing general council. From then on he supported the agitators through his contacts, though from September he advocated their constant renewal: 'lest they become corrupted by bribes of offices, or places of preferment' (ibid., 192). By late July, in *Jonah's Cry*, he was publicly scathingly suspicious of Cromwell and Ireton's intentions to override the general council and govern the army without it. He became the close friend of John Wildman, who was with Sexby the most prominent conduit between the city and army Levellers.

Despite Elizabeth's constant pleading to the army leaders, Lilburne was not granted bail when the army took control of London from the presbyterians on 7 August. Nor was Walwyn's proposal that 'well-affected inhabitants' (Leveller and London Independents) be put at the head of the city militia accepted by General Fairfax. Lilburne's rejection of his Independent allies in parliament was now complete, and he began to alienate such agitator-soldiers as Allen by bitterly opposing the army leadership. A prison meeting with Cromwell on 7 September did no good. He would not promise to be quiet. He might go overseas, but only if the Lords admitted they had no jurisdiction over him. He would appeal to the 'private souldiers'—that is, try to replace the agitators with new agents—and the 'Hobnayles and the clouted Shooes' of London (Woolrych, *Soldiers and Statesmen*, 191–2). By late September his initiative had to some degree succeeded. There were some new agents in the army councils; Wildman and Petty seem to have been meeting with them almost daily into early October, and Lilburne was informed of their proceedings. He probably also played some part in the writing of *An Agreement of the People for a Firm and Present Peace* (28 October), but it was never true that the New Model was, as a contemporary claimed, 'one Lilburne throughout' (ibid., 63). There were great divisions between Leveller and soldier, which he soon experienced personally. Released on bail on 9 November, Lilburne travelled to Ware to lend aid to the mutineers of Corkbush Field on 15 November. Finding the mutiny crushed and the *Agreement* ripped from the hats of the soldiers, he, 'sick, sick of the sullens' (Gregg, 385), returned to London to join Wildman and the London Levellers in organizing a campaign of petitioning. On 17 January 1648 the two leaders attended a meeting (one of a series) in Wapping, where the outline of a Leveller organization in London, Southwark, Kent, Hertfordshire, Buckinghamshire, Oxfordshire, and Cambridgeshire was described. Doubters were assured that the petition on hand, partly drawn up by Lilburne, was intended to bolster the Commons against all contending powers and not to provide an occasion for rebelling against it. However, the meeting was betrayed and next day Lilburne's bail was withdrawn. He was remanded back to the Tower on a charge of treasonable practices, and remained there until 2 August 1648.

It was not his own efforts that finally secured Lilburne's release. John Maynard, a presbyterian leader in the Commons who had also been imprisoned in the Tower by the Lords, was instrumental in having his fine and sentence remitted and new arrangements made for his reparations. Some thought Lilburne's release a presbyterian plot to embarrass an embattled Cromwell, on duty in Wales, by having the chief Leveller join Major Robert Huntingdon in charging him with treason. Moreover, those who engineered it may have thought that Lilburne was not so antimonarchical as he seemed, having heard that in October 1647 he had engaged, through the royalist Dyve and via his Baptist friends, in clandestine negotiations with the king. But Lilburne would have nothing to do with furthering 'a Scotch interest' by aiding the royalists and their allies during the second civil war, and would not 'strike Cromwell when he was low' (Frank, 164). Parliament in any case, on 5 September, at last awarded him £300 subsistence and £3000 reparations from as yet unspecified sequestered royalist land in the north. The favour did not stop his joining on 10 September 1648 the petitioners against a personal treaty with the king, and he was energetic in promoting the Leveller petition of 11 September. Thenceforth he would publicly stand for the *Agreement of the People* and the petition of 11 September.

Betrayal by the officers, 1648–1649 It was such a settlement that Lilburne and the Levellers urged Cromwell to support as the second civil war drew to a close. Probably with Cromwell's agreement, Lilburne, Wildman, and Walwyn met in late November 1648 with Independents and soldiers at the Independents' meeting place, the Nag's Head near Blackwell Hall. There, Lilburne alleged, Ireton told the Levellers of the officers' plans: 'first to cut off the Kings Head … and force, if not dissolve the Parliament' (Gregg, 251). This horrified Lilburne as providing no guarantee of an agreement. There followed four weeks of negotiation at Windsor, St Albans, and Whitehall among representatives of Levellers, city religious Independents, army officers, and—of the 'honest members' of parliament who were invited—Henry Marten alone. A compromise agreement was hammered out. Ireton insisted on taking it to the council of officers, much to the chagrin of the Levellers, who had understood that it would be tendered directly to the people for subscription. They attended the council anyway, but remained divided from the officers on religious liberty and the right of the government to punish where no law existed. In mid-December Lilburne took his 'leave of them as a pack of dissembling juggling knaves', and reported back to those he 'represented'. Overton, Wildman, and Walwyn remained a little longer (Lilburne, *Legall Fundamentall Liberties*, 29–42). On the 15th Lilburne published a slightly doctored version of the compromise agreement so that the public could see what changes the officers might make. On the 28th he and thirteen others, including Overton, published *A Plea for Common Right and Freedom*, insisting on the role of soldiers in the political decisions of the army, and supporting the new agreement and the petition of 11 September. Two or three days later he left London for Newcastle to lay the groundwork for collecting his reparations. He had already objected to the trial of Charles, saying it would have been justifiable had due process occurred under a regime based on an agreement, but that it would have been better as things stood to keep the king to provide a balance of power whereby that tyrant might stand against the other—the army. Nevertheless he was made an offer that he should be on the high court, perhaps in the belief that his anti-monarchicism was so strong as to overcome what might have been thought to be a merely tactical revulsion. He refused (and did not return to London until shortly after Charles's execution). His analysis of the negotiations was that the officers had talked with the Levellers 'meerly to quiet and please us (*like children with rattles*) till they had done their main work'. Certainly the Levellers were silent during the revolutionary days which began in December 1648.

When Lilburne returned from the north his family took up lodgings in Winchester House, Southwark. He made an unsuccessful attempt to remain silent, then with *Englands New Chains* (26 February 1649), entered his last phase of Leveller activity. He appealed to the army and the provinces as well as Londoners to join him in rejecting the rule of the military junta, the council of state, and their 'puppet' parliament. Leveller agitation, inspired by his example, revived. He was soon in the Tower again for the suspected authorship of a book which parliament had declared treasonable: *The Second Part of Englands New Chains* (24 March). He and his fellow prisoners, Overton, Thomas Prince, and the guiltless Walwyn, produced a final *Agreement of the Free People of England* and a defence of those 'commonly (though unjustly) styled Levellers' (*A Manifestation from Lieut. Col. J. Lilburne*, 30 April), but by March the Baptist and Independent backbone of their London following had declared allegiance to the Rump, and their New Model friends were deserting them. Mutinies of March to May were ill co-ordinated, unsuccessful, and only in a few cases inspired by the Leveller call for an agreement. Lilburne continued to goad the authorities, however. In June he published his *Legall Fundamentall Liberties*, which, besides providing a long self-justifying account of his life, insisted that the Commonwealth regime was one without a title. Though he was allowed on bail in July to attend his family who were gravely ill with smallpox (two children died), on 4 August he published an enlarged edition of *Legall Fundamental Liberties* and on the 10th published *An Impeachment of High Treason Against Oliver Cromwell … and Ireton*. His last Leveller piece, which he helped circulate, was *The Outcryes of the Youngmen and Apprentices* (29 August), which mixed apocalyptic calls to armed resistance with hopeless attempts to revive the project of an agreement, and found an echo in a minor mutiny at Oxford on 8 September.

Treason trials, exile, and last days, 1649–1657 Lilburne's denial of the revolutionary regime's legitimacy, his calls to armed resistance, and suspicions of a royalist–Leveller alliance persuaded the authorities to bring him to trial for treason at the Guildhall on 24–5 October. It had been expected that he would follow the lead of King Charles and the royalist peers who had been tried in January and February and would deny the competence of a revolutionary tribunal to try him. Instead, however, he brought a barrage of objections against the details of the proceedings and against the evidence that his prosecutors provided of his authorship. Having successfully persuaded the jury—to the proper outrage of the judges—that they were judges of law as well as fact, he was pronounced guiltless. The legalities were hardly the issue. Popular enthusiasm was all, expressed in a packed court with open doors and swirling crowds outside, and his acquittal was marked with bonfires. A medal was struck in his honour, inscribed with the words: 'John Lilburne saved by the power of the Lord and the integrity of the jury who are judge of law as wel of fact. Oct 26. 1649' (Gregg, 301–2). On 8 November all four Levellers were freed to great applause, though the Leveller movement was effectively at an end. On the wave of enthusiasm, directed not at the Levellers as a whole but at Lilburne himself, Lilburne was elected to the common council of London on 21 December 1649. He brought himself (though with clearly fatal reservations) to take the engagement to be 'faithful to the commonwealth … without king and Lords', but his election was quashed.

Lilburne now attempted to eschew politics and settle down in a new house to the trade of soap-boiler, to craft a career in law, and to attend to the matter of the reparations voted to him by parliament in late 1648. His career as a soap-boiler was apparently successful enough, but has left no records except of his petitioning the Rump in

March 1650 for £1583 outstanding reparation payments so that he could pursue a quiet, remunerative life, and of his joining soap-boiler petitioners in November 1651 in complaining against excise on barrels of soap. His mixing with law was less successful though, and in the end embroiled him once more with the authorities. Though the Inner Temple repulsed his efforts to join the profession, he nevertheless busied himself giving legal advice to the many who approached him. Most notably, from autumn 1650 until late 1651, he and Wildman—probably invited by Lilburne's old contacts from his army days in Lincolnshire—acted for the tenants of the manor of Epworth on the Isle of Axholme, who had a long-standing claim as fenmen to common lands which had been drained by projectors and were now partially under projector control. Legal action, riot, and arson characterized the commoners' actions, while Lilburne acted for them as a legal agent, advocate at Westminster, and local organizer. His enemies in Lincolnshire, the courts, and parliament—and some modern historians—have characterized the episode as part of an attempt by him to spread Leveller doctrines and organization. For his own part, Lilburne condemned the disorder, concentrated as much as was in him on the legalities and political realities of the issue, and was in any case otherwise inactive in the moribund Leveller cause (J. Lilburne, *The Case of the Tenants of the Manuor of Epworth*, 1651). This did not save him, though, from falling foul of the parliamentary élite with whom he was in any case embroiled because of his support, as legal adviser, for his uncle George against Sir Arthur Hesilrige, the Durham notable and leading Rumper. Heselrige, with whom John Lilburne had been at odds since late 1648 over sequestered lands set aside for him by parliament in Durham, had now quarrelled with George Lilburne over similar issues of ownership and control of sequestered lands, and was backed by the central sequestrations committee at Haberdashers' Hall. John soon burst into print with *A Just Reproof to Haberdashers Hall* (2 August 1651) and a petition of 23 December. The attacks contained therein on Hesilrige were taken by parliament to be treasonous. The house assumed judicial powers and without hearing him ordered him to pay a fine and damages of £7000. To complete the atrocity, by an act of banishment they sent him into exile to be condemned as a traitor should he return.

Except for his last few months when he was on parole, Lilburne spent the rest of his life in exile or prison. By 8 February 1652 he was in Amsterdam. On the outbreak of war between the Dutch and English in May, he went to meet Elizabeth in Bruges, where he planned to settle. After all her tribulations she was in need of comfort, but Lilburne was more interested in finding materials for proposed defences of himself, insisting that she should send him the necessary books when she returned. She would not comply, advising silence so that she and other friends might help him back to England, and they quarrelled. Lilburne's grip on political practicality, never strong, further weakened. He became acquainted with exiled royalists, bragged to them of his powers to bring about a restoration, and was accused of being—and denied being—a royalist. He alternately threatened and cajoled the Commonwealth regime, at times, for instance, seeking Cromwell's friendship and promising perfect submission to government, at others denouncing him as 'the grandest Tyrant and Traytor that ever England bredd', and the council of state as corrupt and illegal (Woolrych, *Commonwealth*, 250). Unable to obtain a pass to return to England, he nevertheless did so in June 1653, soon after the dissolution of the Rump, and was promptly sent to Newgate to await trial for treason.

Lilburne was active in writing in his own defence. The Leveller movement for a time revived, swamping the authorities—the council of state, the mayor of London, and later Barebone's Parliament—with petitions and remonstrances. Lilburne's argument was that the Rump had been an illegal parliament, and that therefore its decrees, including that which banished him, were void. Cromwell and the army junta, who had expelled it for tyranny and oppression, could hardly deny it. Alternatively, appealing to due process, Lilburne argued that he had not been tried, or even heard, before he was banished. His trial, at which he repeated these arguments and added many more legal ones both serious and quibbling, was held from 13 July to 20 August at the Old Bailey. Public support for him was, as at his first treason trial, very obvious, and ominous for the continued existence of the regime. A broadsheet asked:

> And what, shall then honest John Lilburne die?
> Three score thousand will know the reason why.
> (Woolrych, *Commonwealth*, 255)

Public order was at serious risk. The legal point at issue was whether or not the act of banishment was on the statute book; the issue of fact was whether Lilburne, having been forbidden by that act to return, had come back. The jury, convinced again that they were judges of 'law as well as of fact', found him 'not guilty of any crime worthy of death'. The council of state found it unwise to discipline the jurymen but after long debate the new parliament ordered Lilburne's imprisonment to be continued 'for the Peace of this Nation' (ibid., 258).

Lilburne was accordingly held in the Tower until March 1654. He was then moved to Castle Orgueil on Jersey until October 1655, when, tired and ill, he was brought back to the mainland, to Dover Castle. The problem from the point of view of Cromwell, Lilburne's wife, and his father-in-law—all of whom, with others, had tried to persuade him—was that he would not, until the very end, promise to lay down the 'temporal sword'. A process of conversion, however, seems to have begun to quieten him. On parole in Dover, about October 1655 he met Luke Howard, a Quaker, and asked of him: 'I pray, sir, of what Opinion are you?' To Lilburne's astonishment and admiration, Howard answered, 'none'. Thus began a change whereby Lilburne became 'dead to the world', regretted the hurly-burly of his previous life, and swore to 'never thereafter be a user of a temporall sword more' (Gregg, 343–4; *Resurrection of John Lilburne*). Henceforth, tired after a life of conflict and imprisonment, he was more frequently allowed out on parole to be with his family. He died in Eltham,

Kent, on 29 August 1657. Even his obsequies were to be marked by turmoil and conflict. There was a scuffle at his funeral service on 31 August over whether a velvet pall should be thrown over his coffin, and another over the same question as the body was taken for burial in the Quaker burial-ground at Bethlehem churchyard by Bishopsgate.

The man and his reputation Lilburne was a man of powerful, undisciplined, and narrow intelligence; of personal charm based on his face, form, dress, and conversation; and of impressive bearing and energy in public places. In his twenties he was thin-faced and soulful, with a high forehead, aquiline nose, neat moustache, and hair curled back from his ears. In the 1640s he dressed in a somewhat dandyish fashion, sporting the short red coat of the dragoon even after he left the army. An accidental pike-wound to an eye in January 1645 caused a slight disfigurement and he began to wear glasses. A portrait of 1649 shows him to have thickened round the waist. His hair, hanging now to his shoulders, was somewhat 'grizzled and unkept' (Gregg, 301), the nose somewhat more pronounced. His face had lost its youthful optimistic set but still he dressed for show: a doublet to the hips with lace at the neck and cuffs, trousers slashed and decorated, long boots with spurs.

Of a restless and humourless disposition, Lilburne was changeable in his relationships. He was capable of generously forgiving his many enemies but he was more characteristically a man of vengeful malignity who distrusted everyone and was not easy even on himself. He spent the bulk of his life proclaiming his belief in salvation but, at the end, admitted his insecurity. A tradition, effectively originating in the words of Judge Jenkins but more likely coined by the wittier Henry Marten, has it that: 'if the World was emptied of all but John Lilburne, Lilburne would quarrel with John, and John with Lilburne' (Frank, 237 and n.). His oppositional politics were marked by a powerful sense of injustice and a remarkable capacity to describe and exaggerate it in the current arrangements of his society; his proposals for reform showed an equally remarkable capacity to sketch plans for reformation so radical as to astound and frighten his contemporaries. Conservatives thought democracy simply meant anarchy and levelling; his friends came to think it would lead to rule by the Godless majority.

While royalist versus parliamentarian and whig versus tory sensibilities remained, such judgements on Lilburne prevailed. Later in his century Anthony Wood thought of him as a quarrelsome fanatic. The tory author of *The History of King-Killers* (1707) added that 'his only Aim was to be above all others himself, the universal design of the Rebell'. Less obsessed with the old politics, the author of *The Biographical Dictionary* (1798) had him as a 'remarkable enthusiast' of 'prompt genius', who was too hot-headed for his own good. Goodwin in his *History of the Commonwealth* (1827) admitted his evident intelligence and courage, but unfavourably compared his lack of self-doubt, hatred of others, rigidity, and thinly disguised self-seeking with Cromwell's broad and wise view of humankind and the good of his country. Lilburne's Quaker biographer (*The life of John Lilburne*, 1854) recorded how the truth released him from inner and outer tumult. Since then Lilburne's character has been judged in the light of the broadening interests of historians, the dying of the partisan fires of his own century, and the growth of the historical profession in the later nineteenth century. Most sympathetic to him have been those—Marxist, Christian Democrat, liberal democrat, American constitutionalist (Brailsford, Pease, Gibb, Haller, Frank, Gregg, Manning)—who have found contemporary political and ethical reason to admire, if not his successes, at least his vision and that of his fellow 'levellers'. They have tended to extenuate his faults and remember his virtues. He has appeared as a spokesman for the 'hobnails and clouted shoes' and (more often) for the 'middling sort' of tradespeople, lower professionals and farmers. He was one who, 'before his time', made a case for a written constitution, a democratically elected legislature bound by law, and something like a bill of rights.

Lilburne's politics and his constitutionalism were built on distrust, most of all on a distrust of any power lodged in any member of a fallen species. His friends called him Freeborn John. He would rather that all were subject to God's law, but saw that most were not and tried to come to terms with such a world by way of human lawmaking.

ANDREW SHARP

Sources P. Gregg, *Free-born John: a biography of John Lilburne* (1961) • J. Frank, *The Levellers* (1955) [incl. bibliography of Lilburne's writings] • M. Tolmie, *The triumph of the saints: the separate churches of London, 1616–1649* (1977) • A. Woolrych, *Soldiers and statesmen: the general council of the army and its debates, 1647–1648* (1987) • A. Woolrych, *Commonwealth to protectorate* (1982) • M. A. Gibb, *John Lilburne the Leveller* (1947) • H. N. Brailsford, *The Levellers and the English revolution* (1976) • D. Wootton, 'Leveller democracy and the puritan revolution', *The Cambridge history of political thought, 1450–1700*, ed. J. H. Burns (1991), 412–42 • W. Haller, *Liberty and reformation in the puritan revolution* (1955) • W. Haller, *The rise of puritanism: … the New Jerusalem as set forth in pulpit and press from Thomas Cartwright to John Lilburne and John Milton, 1570–1643* (1938) • W. Haller and G. Davies, eds., *The Leveller tracts, 1647–1653* (1944) • D. M. Wolfe, ed., *Leveller manifestoes of the puritan revolution* (1944) • W. Haller, *Tracts on liberty*, 3 vols. (1933–4) • S. R. Gardiner, *History of the Commonwealth and protectorate, 1649–1660*, 3rd edn, 4 vols. (1901) • T. C. Pease, *The Leveller movement* (1916) • B. Manning, *1649: the crisis of the English revolution* (1992) • A. Sharp, *The English Levellers* (1998) • A. Sharp, 'John Lilburne and the parliament's *Book of declarations*', *History of Political Thought*, 9 (1988), 19–44 • A. Sharp, 'John Lilburne's discourse of law', *Political Science*, 40/1 (1988), 18–33 • R. B. Seaberg, 'The Norman conquest and the common law', *HJ*, 24 (1981), 791–806 • V. Pearl, 'London's counter-revolution', *The interregnum: the quest for settlement, 1646–1660*, ed. G. Aylmer (1972), 29–56 • K. Lindley, *Popular politics and religion in civil war London* (1997) • K. Lindley, *Fenland riots and the English revolution* (1982) • C. Holmes, *Seventeenth-century Lincolnshire*, History of Lincolnshire, 7 (1980) • C. Holmes, 'Drainers and fenmen: the problem of popular political consciousness in the seventeenth century', *Order and disorder in early modern England*, ed. A. Fletcher and J. Stevenson (1985), 166–95 • *DNB* • A. S. P. Woodhouse, ed., *Puritanism and liberty: being the army debates (1647–9) from the Clarke manuscripts, with supplementary documents*, new edn (1951) • Wood, *Ath. Oxon.*, 1st edn, 2.101–2 • *The history of king-killers*, 2 vols. (1720), 2.72–6 • *A new and general biographical dictionary*, 9 (1798) • *The* *life of John Lilburne*, Friends' Tracts, 105 (1854) • E. Bernstein, *Cromwell and communism* (1930) • B. Manning, *The English people and the English revolution, 1640–1649* (1976) • G. L. Craik, *Pictorial history of England*, 10 vols. (1855), vol. 3, pt xvi • J. Lilburne, *Innocency and truth justified*, 2 pts (1645–6) [Thomason tracts E 314(21), E 314(22)] • J. Lilburne, *The legall fundamentall liberties of the people of England*, 2nd edn (1649) [Thomason tract E 567(1)] • J. Lilburne, *The Christian mans triall*, 2nd edn (1641) [Thomason tract; incl. *A worke of the beast*] • J. Lilburne, *Come out of her my people* (1639) • J. Lilburne, *L. Colonel John Lilburne revived, shewing the cause of his late long silence* (1653) [Thomason tract E 689(32)] • J. Lilburne, *A copie of a letter, written by John Lilburne … to Mr William Prinne* (1645) [Thomason tract E 24(22)] • J. Lilburne, *The copie of a letter from Lieutenant Colonell John Lilburne, to a freind* (1645) [Thomason tract E 296(5)] • J. Lilburne, *The freemans freedome vindicated, or, A true relation of the cause and manner of Lieut. Col. John Lilburns present imprisonment in Newgate … by the house of peeres* (1646) [Thomason tract E 341(12)] • *The oppressed mans oppressions declared, or, An epistle written by Lieut. Col. Iohn Lilburne … in which the … cruelty of all the gaolers of England is declared* [1647] • J. Lilburne, *The juglers discovered* [1647] [Thomason tract E 409(22)] • *The resurrection of John Lilburne, now a prisoner in Dover-castle … in these following lines, penned by himself*, 2nd edn (1656) [with added appendix] • J. Lilburne, *Jonah's cry out of the whale's belly* [1647] [Thomason tract E 400(5)]

Likenesses G. Glover, line engraving, 1641, NPG, BM; repro. in *Christian mans triall* (1641) [*see illus.*] • W. Hollar, etching, *c.*1641, NPG, BM • T. Simon, silver medal, 1649, NPG • line engraving, pubd 1659, NPG • line engraving, pubd 1713 (after M. Vandergucht), NPG, BM • engraving, BM; repro. in *England and Irelands sad theatre* (1645) • print, NPG, BM; repro. in *The triall of Lieut. Collonell John Lilburne* (1641)

Lilburne, Robert (*bap.* **1614**, *d.* **1665**), regicide and deputy major-general, was baptized in St Andrew's Church, Auckland, co. Durham, on 2 February 1614. His parents were Richard Lilburne (1583–1667), of Thickley Punchardon, co. Durham, and Margaret Hixon (*d.* 1619), the daughter of Thomas Hixon of Greenwich. Robert married Margaret Beke, daughter of Henry Beke of Haddenham, Buckinghamshire.

Lilburne rose to prominence as a parliamentarian soldier after the outbreak of the civil war in 1642, before which little is known about him. He served in the earl of Essex's army in southern England in 1642–3, after which he raised a regiment of horse in his native co. Durham, serving in the northern association army in 1644. In 1646 Fairfax appointed him to command the Kentish New Model Army regiment of Sir Ralph Weldon on the latter's appointment as governor of Plymouth. Resentment at being passed over for the command of the regiment partly accounts for the efforts of Lilburne's second-in-command, Lieutenant-Colonel Nicholas Kempson, in the spring of 1647 to persuade the soldiers in the regiment to accept the House of Commons' offer of service in Ireland, which Lilburne successfully resisted. By this time Lilburne had emerged as a leading figure in the opposition within the New Model Army to the campaign of conservative MPs to get rid of the New Model Army by sending it to Ireland or by disbanding it without paying it its wage arrears or giving it any guarantees of legal indemnity against prosecution. In March 1647 Lilburne helped draft an army petition urging parliament not to send the army to Ireland before its wage arrears were paid and only with its own officers. He was elected by the officers to act as one of their spokesmen when parliamentarian commissioners came to the army at Saffron Walden on 15 April 1647. He signed the army's *Vindication of the Officers* (27 April 1647) and was appointed to a committee to draft the army's response to the Commons' order of 25 May 1647 to disband the army. On 1 April 1647 he had appeared before the Commons to answer charges that he was a promoter of the army petitioning movement and on 27 April 1647 he was ordered to appear again for turning soldiers against service in Ireland. He remained with the army as it marched towards London until at least 11 June 1647, when he was the signatory of a letter sent to the municipal authorities in London explaining the army's case. But his prominence in the revolt of the New Model Army ended before the army reached London in August.

Lilburne had by this time been appointed governor of Newcastle (the earliest reference in the town records to him in this office is 11 August 1647). Consequently, he was not with his regiment when it mutinied in October and November against the army high command. On 23 October 1647, just north of Dunstable, his regiment refused to continue its march to Newcastle. Instead, prompted by Leveller agents who had recently emerged in some New Model Army regiments in and around London, the regiment moved back to a rendezvous at Dunstable, using the Leveller slogan, 'England's freedom, soldiers' rights', to defy their senior officers' orders. The mutiny was firmly suppressed at Corkbush Field near Ware on 15 May 1647 by Fairfax and Cromwell, and the regiment presented Fairfax with a formal submission of its loyalty.

Historical opinion is divided about the depth of army commitment to Leveller ideas. Nor is there any certainty about Robert Lilburne's support for the Leveller ideas of his brother, John *Lilburne. That he may have given them tacit support is suggested by the fact that he allowed his brother to receive over £500 of the arrears owed to his regiment in August 1647 (PRO, SP 28/47, fol. 298). This, though (like his attendance at the second day of John Lilburne's trial on 25 October 1649), may be accounted for by concern for his brother's welfare rather than his ideas. Another possible source of Lilburne's political radicalism is his religious beliefs. There is ample evidence for Lilburne's commitment to Baptism other than hostile sources like Thomas Edward's *Gangraena* (1646) and Thomas Gumble's 1671 biography of General Monck. With Major Paul Hobson, Lilburne founded the first Baptist congregation in Newcastle when he was governor there in 1647. Later in his career as commander-in-chief in Scotland and deputy major-general in Yorkshire and co. Durham he proved a consistent champion of the cause of toleration of religious separatist groups like the Baptists.

In the later 1640s Lilburne remained a committed opponent of the king. On 1 July 1648 he defeated a force of northern royalists, before joining Lambert and Cromwell in their defeat of an invading Scottish army near Preston in August and subsequent march into Scotland. When Cromwell returned to England in October Lambert and Lilburne stayed behind for another month. Lilburne then took part in one of the last military engagements of the second civil war, the siege of Pontefract Castle, which ended on 27 March 1649. For a time in January 1649 he left Pontefract to carry out his duties as one of the commissioners appointed by parliament to try the king. Although he did not attend all the meetings of the commissioners he was present when the court delivered its final verdict, and he signed the king's death warrant [*see also* Regicides].

Lilburne served on Oliver Cromwell's military expedition against the Scots in 1650–1. When Cromwell followed the royalist–Scottish armies into England before the decisive battle of Worcester (3 September 1651), Lilburne marched only as far south as Lancashire, where on 25 August 1651 he defeated the forces of James Stanley, seventh earl of Derby, near Wigan, effectively putting paid to royalist hopes in northern England. In November 1651 he returned to Scotland, joining English troops attempting to suppress Glencairn's rising in the Scottish highlands, and in December 1652 he replaced General Richard Deane as commander-in-chief of the army in Scotland. The competition for English resources to fight the war against the Dutch, together with the outbreak of the Scottish uprising in the highlands, made Lilburne's military task in Scotland far from easy. His letters to Cromwell and Thurloe asking for more men and money often fell on deaf ears, unlike those of his successor, General George Monck, a fact which in part accounts for Monck's superior military record in Scotland. Lilburne's expulsion in July 1653 of the general assembly of the Scottish church, motivated by his antipathy for the religious intolerance of many Scottish churchmen, caused disaffection in Scotland. But in general he had some success in winning over the hearts and minds of the Scots by his concerted efforts to relieve their grievances. The best recent historical assessment of Lilburne's rule in Scotland is that 'in his analysis of the fundamental ills of the body politic, he was cooler and more realistic than in his appraisal of the military situation, and in his desire for conciliation he showed many statesmanlike qualities' (Dow, 99).

For most of the 1650s Lilburne remained a loyal supporter of the protectorate in England as well as in Scotland. He was elected MP for co. Durham in the first protectorate parliament (1654–55) and, after he was replaced as commander-in-chief in Scotland in May 1654, he was made governor of York, acting effectively as second-in-command to General Lambert of the English forces in northern England. He helped suppress an attempted royalist uprising in the north in March 1655. After Lambert was appointed major-general of the north-eastern counties Lilburne was made his deputy in Yorkshire and co. Durham. His correspondence with Thurloe and others during this time reveals that he shared the aspirations of many of the major-generals in other parts of England and Wales: to take firm action against royalist activists (what should he do with 'such kind of cattle', he asked Thurloe in 1655) and to rid the magistracy and ministry of men 'too much addicted to tippling, and that which is called good-fellowship' (Thurloe, *State papers*, 3.587; 4.397). He was also appointed to the committee charged with founding a new university at Durham.

Lilburne's commitment to the protectorate was shaken in 1657. As MP for the East Riding of Yorkshire in the second protectorate parliament (1656–8) he opposed the offer of the crown to Oliver Cromwell in 1657, and, even though Cromwell rejected the offer, Lilburne remained (as he was described by one of the backers of the kingship scheme) 'a malcontent' (Thurloe, *State papers*, 7.85). These views, together with his zeal for toleration for religious separatists, made him not only a natural opponent of the protectorate of Richard Cromwell, who succeeded his father in September 1658; they also made him a target for the anti-militarism of his fellow MPs in the third protectorate parliament in 1659 who decreed that his election as MP for Malton was irregular. In April 1659 he made a temporary alliance with Commonwealth republicans and enthusiastically supported the restoration of the Rump Parliament. In August 1659 he helped arrest supporters of Sir George Booth's ill-fated uprising in Cheshire. By this time he had become disillusioned with the Rump and when the army expelled it in October 1659 he was appointed a member of the army's committee of safety. During the next few months he followed General Lambert's lead. Although he allowed emissaries from General Monck to go to London, for a time he and Lambert used their military control of the north to threaten the safe passage of General Monck's army southwards from Scotland. As elsewhere in England, though, support for the army dwindled and Lilburne's regiment deserted him and he had to surrender York. When the Rump was restored again in December 1659 it relieved Lilburne of his command in the north.

After the monarchy was restored Lilburne surrendered and, as a regicide excluded from the Act of Indemnity, he was tried for treason before a high court of justice on 16 October 1660. His only defence was that he had acted 'ignorantly' and 'in Obedience to the Command over me' (*State trials*, 2.381, 390). He was found guilty, but, perhaps because he had surrendered voluntarily, his death sentence was commuted to life imprisonment. On 31 October he was ordered to be sent to either Plymouth Castle or St Nicholas Island. He died in the latter prison in August 1665. BARRY COWARD

Sources R. Howell, 'The army and the English revolution: the case of Robert Lilburne', *Archaeologia Aeliana*, 5th ser., 9 (1981), 299–315 · C. H. Firth and G. Davies, *The regimental history of Cromwell's army*, 2 vols. (1940) · Thurloe, *State papers* · C. H. Firth, ed., *Scotland and the Commonwealth: letters and papers relating to the military government of Scotland, from August 1651 to December 1653*, Scottish History Society, 18 (1895) · A. Woolrych, *Soldiers and statesmen: the general council of the army and its debates, 1647–1648* (1987) · I. Gentles, *The New Model Army in England, Ireland, and Scotland, 1645–1653* (1992) · F. D. Dow, *Cromwellian Scotland, 1651–1660* (1979) · *The Clarke papers*, ed. C. H. Firth, 4 vols., CS, new ser., 49, 54, 61–2 (1891–1901) · *CSP dom.* · J. Rushworth, *Historical collections*, 5 pts in 8 vols. (1659–1701) · parish register, Auckland, St Andrew, Durham RO · A. Woolrych, introduction, in *Complete prose works of John Milton*, ed. D. M. Wolfe, 7, ed. R. W. Ayers (1980), 1–228 · P. Gregg, *Free-born John: a biography of John Lilburne* (1961); pbk edn (1986) · M. A. Kishlansky, *The rise of the New Model Army* (1979) · *A true copy of the Journal of the High Court of*

Justice for the tryall of Charles I … taken by J. Nalson (1731) • *The writings and speeches of Oliver Cromwell*, ed. W. C. Abbott and C. D. Crane, 4 vols. (1937–47) • M. H. Dodds, ed., *Extracts from the Newcastle upon Tyne minute book, 1639–1656*, Newcastle upon Tyne Records Committee, 1 (1920) • *JHC*, 5 (1646–8) • *JHL*, 9 (1646–7) • *State trials*, vol. 2 • *A catalogue of the names of the knights, citizens, and burgesses, that have served in the last four parlaments* (1656) [Thomason tract E 1602(3)] • T. Gumble, *The life of General Monck, duke of Albemarle* (1671) • T. Edwards, *Gangraena, or, A catalogue and discovery of many of the errours, heresies, blasphemies and pernicious practices of the sectaries of this time*, 3 vols. in 1 (1646) • *Diary of Thomas Burton*, ed. J. T. Rutt, 4 vols. (1828), vol. 4 • G. Ormerod, ed., *Tracts relating to military proceedings in Lancashire during the great civil war*, Chetham Society, 2 (1844) • W. H. Rylands, ed., *The visitation of the county of Buckingham made in 1634*, Harleian Society, 58 (1909)

Archives Worcester College, Oxford, corresp. | BL, corresp. with Captain Baynes, Add. MSS 21417–21425

Likenesses S. Cooper, miniature, 1650, V&A • S. Cooper, watercolour miniature, 1650, FM Cam.

Lilford. For this title name *see* Powys, Thomas Littleton, fourth Baron Lilford (1833–1896).

Lille, Alain de (1116/17–1202?), theologian and Cistercian monk, was a native of Lille in Flanders (now in northern France). However, the fact that his name was commonly Latinized as de Insulis, combined with the ill-documented course of his career, subsequently licensed speculation that his origins were literally insular, and he was at various times claimed not just for France, Germany, and Spain, but also for Sicily and Britain. A late medieval epitome of his *Anticlaudianus* put in a bid for England—'ex proprio nomine dictus vir erat nacione Anglicus' (BL, Cotton MS Titus D.xx, fol. 140)—as Thomas Tanner recorded in 1748. The Scottish bio-bibliographer Thomas Dempster, writing in the early seventeenth century, was equally emphatic that Alain was born on the Isle of Man, before proceeding to confuse him with Alan, fifteenth-century abbot of the *Schottenkloster* of Sankt Jakob near Würzburg, who was described as a Scot on his tombstone.

In spite of these conflicting claims, there can be no doubt of Alain's Flemish birth, nor is there any evidence that he ever crossed the boundaries of present-day France. He spent many years at Paris, first as a student and later as a celebrated teacher in the schools, before moving to Languedoc, where he probably taught at Montpellier. He also wrote numerous theological works which enjoyed a wide circulation, inside and outside France. While in the Midi he made the acquaintance of Cistercians combating heresy in the region, and he eventually retired to Cîteaux, where he became a monk. Alain de Lille died there between 14 April 1202 and 5 April 1203, but probably on 29 December 1202, and was buried in the monastery. His remains were exhumed in 1960.

Henry Summerson

Sources Alan of Lille, *Anticlaudianus*, ed. J. J. Sheridan (1973) • Alain de Lille, *Textes inédits*, ed. M. T. d'Alverny, Études de Philosophie Médiévale, 52 (1965) • A. Dupuis, *Alain de Lille: études de philosophie scholastique* (1859) • BL, Cotton MS Titus D.xx, fol. 140 • Tanner, *Bibl. Brit.-Hib.*, 16 • *Thomae Dempsteri Historia ecclesiastica gentis Scotorum, sive, De scriptoribus Scotis*, ed. D. Irving, rev. edn, 1, Bannatyne Club, 21 (1829), 45–6 • G. R. Evans, *Alan of Lille: the frontiers of theology in the later twelfth century* (1983)

Archives BL, Cotton MS Titus D.xx, fol. 140

Likenesses manuscript painting, *c*.1250, BL, Add. MS 19767, fol. 217

Lillicrap, Sir Charles Swift (1887–1966), naval constructor, was born at Ford, Devonport, on 12 November 1887, the eldest of the five sons of Charles Lillicrap, of Hastings, naval constructor in the Royal Dockyard, Devonport, and his wife, Selina Jane Chapman. He received his early education at Stoke School, Devonport, and entered HM dockyard school, Devonport, as a shipwright apprentice at the age of fourteen. After four years he was awarded a cadetship in naval construction in 1906. After one year at the Royal Naval Engineering College, Keyham, he completed the three-year course in naval architecture and ship construction at the Royal Naval College, Greenwich, passing out in 1910 with a first-class professional certificate.

Lillicrap's first appointment in the Royal Corps of Naval Constructors in 1910 was to Devonport Dockyard and in February 1913 to the *Superb* for a year's sea service. In 1911 he married (Harriet) Minnie (1881/2–1961), a schoolteacher, the daughter of Richard Shears, of Plymouth. They had two sons and one daughter.

In March 1914 Lillicrap was appointed to the naval construction department of the Admiralty, where he was engaged on the design of the Royal Sovereign class of battleships and subsequently on a group of large monitors, mine-sweepers, and other craft. It was during this period that he served as secretary to the landship committee under the chairmanship of the director of naval construction, Eustace Tennyson-d'Eyncourt; it was from the work of this committee that the first tanks were produced for the army. For this Lillicrap was appointed MBE in 1918.

In 1917 Lillicrap assumed responsibility for cruiser design on promotion to constructor and in 1921 was responsible for the design of the cruiser-minelayer *Adventure*. In the same year he was appointed lecturer in naval architecture at the Royal Naval College, Greenwich. This was the time of the Washington treaty (1922), which imposed rigorous limitations of tonnage and gun calibre, and Lillicrap was responsible for the design of the 10,000 ton 8 inch gun cruisers of the Kent class. He received the Board of Admiralty's commendation for his work on this design. He was responsible for subsequent designs of variants of the County class, including the *Surrey* and *Northumberland*, the construction of which was cancelled in 1928 when the London naval treaty was implemented.

Although naval construction activity was low at this time, design work and research and development continued and among this the development of electric welding occupied an important place. Lillicrap made a special survey of welding in 1930 and cultivated an interest that was the subject of several papers in journals and before learned societies and which was to colour his entire career and lead to the presidency of the Institute of Welding (1956–8). Lillicrap's next design, the Arethusa class, featured an extensively welded forward end.

In 1936 Lillicrap was promoted to assistant director of naval construction and took responsibility also for the design of submarines. The rearmament programme and the outbreak of the Second World War vastly increased naval design and construction and by 1941 Lillicrap was the senior officer in the naval construction department, Bath, where he played the major part in adapting the organization to the wartime pattern of work. In 1944 he was promoted director of naval construction, the year in which he was appointed CB; he held this post until his retirement in 1951. In January 1944 he also became head of the Royal Corps of Naval Constructors. In 1947 he was appointed KCB. He was also made an officer of the Légion d'honneur by the French government and a grand officer of the order of Orange Nassau by the Dutch.

Lillicrap was always active in the work of the learned societies connected with his profession. He was a member of the council of the Royal Institution of Naval Architects from 1937 until his death, becoming vice-president in 1945, and an honorary vice-president in 1955. He was a member of the council of the Institute of Welding and of the British Welding Research Association and was president of each body. He presented papers on 'The uses of electric arc welding in warship construction' to the Naval Architects in 1933, and 'Welding as applied to shipbuilding' to the Institute of Welding in 1935, and the literature of these institutions is rich with other contributions from his pen.

Lillicrap was a liveryman of the Worshipful Company of Shipwrights and was its prime warden in 1958. He took an active interest in the education and welfare of shipyard apprentices and was for many years chairman of the Worshipful Company's committee for awards to apprentices. He was a member of the board of governors of the Imperial College of Science and Technology for nearly twenty years and in 1964 was elected to a fellowship in recognition of his valuable service. He was awarded the honorary degree of DSc (Eng.) by Bristol University in 1951.

Lillicrap's retirement from Admiralty service marked a change in emphasis rather than a cessation of work. In addition to his work for the institutions, he became a director of J. Samuel White & Co., the Island Transport Company, Henry Bannister Ltd, and Marinite Ltd.

In earlier years Lillicrap's recreations included walking. His major diversion was, however, books, and he became a collector of first editions which reflected his scholarship and erudition. A notable admirer of Dr Samuel Johnson, he was president of the Johnson Society in 1955–6. He was by nature and inclination a student with broad sympathies and wide interests. He was a man of great energy, directness of purpose, and charm, who enjoyed being with people and made friends readily. He died at the Bromhead Nursing Home, Lincoln, on 17 June 1966.

R. J. DANIEL, *rev.*

Sources *The Times* (20 June 1966) • personal knowledge (1981) • *WWW* • *CGPLA Eng. & Wales* (1966) • d. cert. [Harriet Minnie Lillicrap]

Archives NMM, corresp. and papers

Likenesses W. Stoneman, photograph, 1948, NPG

Wealth at death £29,098: probate, 16 Aug 1966, *CGPLA Eng. & Wales*

Lillie, Beatrice Gladys [*married name* Beatrice Gladys Peel, Lady Peel] (**1894–1989**), actress and singer, was born on 29 May 1894 in Toronto, the younger daughter (there were no sons) of John Lillie, cigar seller, of Lisburn in Ireland, and his wife, Lucie Ann, eldest daughter of John Shaw, a Manchester draper. Following her parents' emigration to Toronto, the family grew up there and Bea, as she was known, was educated at St Agnes' College in Belleville, Ontario; she began to appear in amateur concerts there with her mother and sister as the Lillie Trio. At the outbreak of the First World War they all returned to London, and it was at the Chatham Music Hall in 1914 that she made her professional stage début.

Already it was clear that the Lillie Trio was not much of a success, and that if Beatrice Lillie was to succeed in the theatre it would have to be as a solo act. Almost immediately after her London début she formed an alliance with the leading First World War producer of intimate revues, André Charlot, who saw in her not the serious singer she had set out to become, but a comedian of considerable if zany qualities. Charlot at this time was also fostering the very early careers of Gertrude Lawrence (who for a time was Lillie's understudy), W. J. ('Jack') Buchanan, and Noël Coward. During the First World War, Lillie became a favourite of troops on leave from the front, relying on spontaneity and an improvised response to her audiences, which Charlot had to restrain when it threatened to go too far. Lillie's great talents were the arched eyebrow, the curled lip, the fluttering eyelid, the tilted chin, the ability to suggest, even in apparently innocent material, the possible *double entendre*.

On 5 January 1920 Lillie married Robert Peel (1898–1934), son of Robert Peel, and great-grandson of Sir Robert *Peel, prime minister. He succeeded his father as fifth baronet in 1925. He died in 1934, leaving his wife with one beloved son, Robert, sixth baronet, the last of the senior line of the Peel family, who was killed in the Second World War, in April 1942. The loss of her husband and then her son comparatively early in her life (she never married again) left Lillie with a constant private sadness that she seemed able to overcome only on stage. Her career encompassed some fifty stage shows in the West End and Broadway as well as a dozen films, but she excelled in live performance, demolishing scripts and songs alike with her own particular brand of solo eccentricity. Charles Cochran, Coward, and Florenz Ziegfeld all employed her in their revues, but in 1932 American audiences saw her as the Nurse in the New York première of *Too Good to be True* by Bernard Shaw, one of the comparatively few 'straight' roles she undertook: others were in Robert Morley's first play, *Staff Dance* (1944), and the non-musical version of *Auntie Mame*, which she brought to London after the war.

Lillie made her cabaret début at the Café de Paris in 1933, worked in revue and troop concerts throughout the war, and made her own television series, based on her cabaret routines, as early as 1951. She then developed, and toured for many years around the world, a solo show called simply *An Evening with Beatrice Lillie*, which ranked alongside those of Joyce Grenfell and Ruth Draper. Her

Beatrice Gladys Lillie (1894–1989), by Sir Cecil Beaton, 1920s

career in films began with the silent film *Exit Smiling*, in 1927 and continued intermittently right through to *Around the World in Eighty Days* (1956) and *Thoroughly Modern Millie* (her last, in 1967). But in films as on radio something was missing: the live audience to which she could respond and which she often made part of the act. She was excellent as the mad Auntie Mame, or as Madame Arcati in *High Spirits* (1964), a Broadway musical version of Coward's *Blithe Spirit*. Coward called her 'the perfect comedienne' and wrote his 'Marvellous Party' for her to sing, while Cole Porter wrote her 'Mrs Lowsborough-Goodby'. Her entire career was a sustained monument to anarchic alternative comedy before those terms had ever been invented, and hers was a triumph of manic high spirits. With her long face, tall brow, lively eyes, natural poise, and radiant personality, she was one of the great female clowns.

Lillie's last years were overshadowed by illness; she lived at Peel Fold, Mill Lane, Henley-on-Thames, a virtual recluse had it not been for her devoted manager John Philip, who shared the house with her for twenty years and who died of a stroke only a matter of hours after her death. She died on 20 January 1989 in Henley.

SHERIDAN MORLEY, *rev.*

Sources B. Lillie, *Every other inch a lady* (1973) • *The Times* (21 Jan 1989) • *CGPLA Eng. & Wales* (1991) • private information (1996)
Likenesses C. Beaton, photograph, 1920–29, NPG [*see illus.*]
Wealth at death £949,203: probate, 21 Aug 1991, *CGPLA Eng. & Wales*

Lillingstone [Lillingston], **Luke** (1653–1713), army officer, was the son of Colonel Henry Lillingstone (1620–1676) and his second wife, Elizabeth, daughter of Marmaduke Dolman of Bottesford, Lincolnshire, and sister of Colonel Thomas Dolman of the Anglo-Dutch brigade. Henry Lillingstone served in the Dutch army but returned to England during the 1640s and was a major in Edmund Syler's regiment in George Monck's army in Scotland by the 1650s. On the expedition to Dunkirk and Mardyke in 1657 he commanded a foot regiment, but this was disbanded soon after the Restoration. He re-entered Dutch service in 1661, coming back to England early in 1673 to take the lieutenant-colonelcy of the earl of Mulgrave's foot. This regiment was demobilized in 1674 and Lillingstone returned to the United Provinces as colonel of an English regiment in the Anglo-Dutch brigade, a post which he held until his death in 1676.

Luke Lillingstone received an ensign's commission in Mulgrave's foot in 1673 and accompanied his father to the United Provinces in 1674 to take up a similar post in his new regiment. By 1688 he was a captain in Sir Henry Bellasise's Anglo-Dutch regiment and sailed to England with William of Orange's expedition. Between 1689 and 1691 he fought in Ireland before promotion to the lieutenant-colonelcy of John Foulkes's foot (1 October 1692). His brother Jarvis, or Gervais, another Anglo-Dutch officer, was a captain in Foulkes's battalion. The battalion departed for the West Indies on 9 January 1693 with Sir Charles Wheeler's expedition. Apart from an abortive attack on Martinique, Wheeler achieved nothing and sailed home via New York and Newfoundland. On arrival in England in October Lillingstone was advanced to the colonelcy of Foulkes's battalion, the latter having died from disease while in the Caribbean. Gervais was major and among the ensigns was William Lillingstone, presumably a nephew.

Lillingstone's battalion took part in Robert Wilmot's expedition to Jamaica in 1695, sent in response to alarmist reports that the island had fallen to France. In reality, French forces under Du Casse, based in Hispaniola, had simply raided Jamaica, although much property had been destroyed. Wilmot and Lillingstone attacked the French-held section of Hispaniola in ill-conceived and poorly co-ordinated operations, failing to dislodge Du Casse from the south of the island. Wilmot died late in 1695 but, when Lillingstone returned to England in 1696, he submitted to the council of trade and plantations a scathing indictment of Wilmot's conduct. At the root of the problem was a clash of personalities resulting in a failure of army–navy co-operation. Lillingstone's weakened battalion was disbanded in 1697 and he was reduced to half-pay until 1705, although he was compensated by the retrospective grant of a pension of £200 by Queen Anne on 9 March 1702. In 1702 Lillingstone published an account of the Hispaniola operations and his reputation was further damaged by the rejoinder of Josiah Burchett, secretary of the Admiralty. Accordingly, Lillingstone failed to secure employment on the outbreak of the War of the Spanish Succession in 1702, having to wait until 25 March 1705 before receiving a commission to raise a regiment of foot. His battalion was ordered to the West Indies in 1707, but Lillingstone, with most of his officers, stayed in London. When his battalion arrived in Antigua, Governor Daniel Parke complained to London about the absence of officers. Lillingstone was ordered to repair to his command but refused and was dismissed on 2 June 1708 even though he had been promoted to brigadier-general on 22 April as a bribe to persuade him to attend to his duties. Even worse, he was forbidden to sell his battalion, which was given, gratis, to his lieutenant-colonel, James Jones.

During the 1690s Lillingstone had purchased an estate at North Ferriby, near Hull, on which he built a mansion of 'six rooms on a floor'. The investment in his regiment being forfeit, he advertised in the *London Gazette* offering to sell his house 'for a pennyworth' (*Letters and Dispatches of John Churchill*, 4.67). Lillingstone was twice married: first to Elizabeth, only daughter of Robert Sanderson of Bonnel, Guelderland. Following her death on 18 October 1699, he married, in 1699 or 1700, Catherine, daughter and heir of Colonel Thomas Hassall of Kirby Grindlayth, Yorkshire, and widow of Colonel Towey. Lillingstone died on 6 April 1713, and a monument was erected to him in North Ferriby church. He was survived by his second wife. He had no sons by either marriage and so his estates at North Ferriby and Kirby Grindlayth passed to his sister's son Luke Bowden, who took the name Lillingstone, and whose granddaughter married, in 1797, Abraham Spooner of Elmdon, Warwickshire, who also assumed the name Lillingstone. JOHN CHILDS

Sources *The letters and dispatches of John Churchill, first duke of Marlborough, from 1702 to 1712*, ed. G. Murray, 5 vols. (1845) • *The Marlborough–Godolphin correspondence*, ed. H. L. Snyder, 3 vols. (1975) • C. Dalton, ed., *English army lists and commission registers, 1661–1714*, 6 vols. (1892–1904) • J. Ferguson, ed., *Papers illustrating the history of the Scots brigade in the service of the United Netherlands, 1572–1782*, 1, Scottish History Society, 32 (1899) • R. E. Scouller, *The armies of Queen Anne* (1966) • C. H. Firth and G. Davies, *The regimental history of Cromwell's army*, 2 vols. (1940) • J. Burchett, *Memoirs of transactions at sea during the war with France* (1703) • *DNB*

Likenesses monument, North Ferriby church, Yorkshire

Lillo, George (1691/1693–1739), playwright, was born in February 1691 or 1693 in Moorgate or Moorfields, London. The registers of the Dutch Reformed church known as Austin Friars record the baptism on 8 February 1691 of Joris van Lillo, the youngest of the four children of Jacobus van Lillo and his wife, Elisabeth Whitehorn. Mention in Lillo's will of 'my cousin Ann Whitehorn' supports the identification of Jacobus and Elisabeth as the playwright's parents and Joris as George himself. The baptism record, in turn, supports the reports of early biographers that Lillo's father was Dutch and his mother English. A difficulty is raised by the report in Cibber's *Lives*, and later in Thomas Davies's brief account of the playwright's life included in his edition of Lillo's works, that he was born on 4 February 1693, not 1691, a date supported by the register of burials at St Leonard's Church, Shoreditch, which includes an entry for 6 September 1739: 'George Lillo from Rotherhith. Aged 46 years' (Pallette, 263). No further evidence verifies either date of birth.

Lillo spent his life in London, his childhood probably in or near Moorgate or Moorfields, his later years in Rotherhithe, where he was resident by November 1735, when he assigned the copyright of *The London Merchant* to his friend the bookseller John Gray. Davies reports that Lillo was, like his father, a goldsmith or jeweller. There is no record of his having a wife or children; the principal legatee named in his will is a nephew, John Underwood. In politics he sympathized with constitutional monarchy as propounded by the 'patriot' opposition to Walpole and the whig establishment. In religion he was a dissenter, and an essentially Calvinist point of view informs his plays, though his burial in the vault of St Leonard's Church, Shoreditch, suggests that ultimately he became a member of the Church of England.

Thomas Davies, a member of Henry Fielding's company at the Haymarket who had acted in Lillo's *Fatal Curiosity* in 1736, describes the playwright as 'Plain and simple … in his address, his manner … modest, affable, and engaging. … In his person … lusty, but not tall, of a pleasing aspect, though unhappily deprived of the sight of one eye' (Davies, xvi, xlviii). Fielding eulogized Lillo's honest manner and lack of worldly ambition, his 'Contempt for all base Means of Application'. He had, said Fielding, 'the Spirit of an old Roman, join'd to the Innocence of a primitive Christian' (*Dramatic Works*, xix).

Early plays In 1730, at the age of thirty-seven (or thirty-nine), Lillo launched a career as a playwright. Although he was neither a professional man of the theatre nor at home in literary circles, he was not the naive artist he is sometimes described as having been. His writing for the stage reveals not only a sharp awareness of the current theatrical repertory but also familiarity with earlier types of drama. His tragedies contain allusions to Elizabethan and Jacobean dramas long neglected by London's acting companies. The catalogue of the books auctioned off after his death may also indicate his considerable interest in old as well as the most recent plays, though his library was sold intermixed with the books of 'Another Gentleman … lately Deceased' (McBurney, 276). The books offered for sale included a remarkably comprehensive collection of Greek, Renaissance, and Restoration plays.

Lillo's first play, *Silvia, or, The Country Burial*, is curiously at odds with those that he would later bring to London's stages. One of the many ballad operas attempted after the success of *The Beggar's Opera* in 1728, it was a singular mixture of bawdy comedy and morally edifying romance. Performed three times at Lincoln's Inn Fields in November 1730, it was acted again only in March 1738, when, reduced to two acts, it was performed once at Covent Garden.

The London Merchant In 1731 Lillo offered a new drama to Theophilus Cibber, the manager of the summer company of young actors at Drury Lane. He requested an out-of-season production for this piece, choosing 'rather … that it should take its fate in the summer, than run the more hazardous fate of encountering the winter critics'. *The London Merchant, or, The History of George Barnwell* was unusual theatrical fare, 'almost a new species of tragedy, wrote on an uncommon subject' (Cibber, 5.388–9). Lillo admired the tragedies in 'humbler dress' of Thomas Otway, Thomas Southerne, and Nicholas Rowe, but sought to appeal even more effectively to the emotions of his audience by writing in prose and choosing as his hero a London apprentice. Basing his play on the old ballad of George Barnwell, known at least by the early seventeenth century, Lillo dramatized the downfall of the promising London youth, led by the temptress Millwood into debauchery, theft, and murder, until both arrive at the gallows. The pathos that Lillo intended for his play arose from the remorse of the unlikely tragic hero, Barnwell, and the torrent of feeling that his distress elicits from his friends. With the character of Millwood, Lillo created a complex and finally tragic figure who strikes a strong feminist note unexpected in this era. As her counterpart he developed the character of Barnwell's master, the merchant Thorowgood, whose 'Methods of Business … founded in Reason, and the Nature of Things' define the rational shield against passionate appetite and confusion. The defence of his own class and of commerce—'by mutual Benefits diffusing mutual Love from Pole to Pole' and rightly rewarding its honest practitioners—is one of the strikingly original elements of the play. Equally important is the insistence on the relationship between the assertions of mercantile values and a protestant moral system.

The London Merchant was first performed at Drury Lane on 22 June 1731. Theophilus Cibber himself played Barnwell, with Millwood acted by Mrs Elizabeth Butler, later a notable Gertrude and Lady Macbeth. The old ballad had been reprinted, copies were sold around the town, and 'many gaily-dispos'd spirits brought the ballad with them to the play, intending to make their pleasant remarks … and ludicrous comparisons between the ancient ditty and modern play' (Cibber, 5.339). But those who came to scoff stayed 'to drop their ballads and pull out their handkerchiefs'. An immediate success, the play was acted at Drury Lane seventeen times during the summer and eleven times during the regular season which followed. Queen Caroline requested that a manuscript copy be carried to her at Hampton Court, and on 28 October 1731 *The London Merchant* was acted in the presence of the king and queen. When printed copies of the play became available in mid-July it was staged by other managements. By 1 June 1732 *The London Merchant* had been acted at every theatre in London then offering plays. Performances at two theatres on 27 December 1731—a holiday for apprentices—began a tradition that persisted long into the nineteenth century. During its first months at Drury Lane performances frequently were 'bespoke' by 'eminent merchants and citizens who much approved its moral tendency' (Cibber, 5.339). In following seasons such sponsorship recurred only occasionally; more often actors selected the play for their benefit nights. Respected literary judgement supported the City's high opinion of Lillo's tragedy. It is reported that Pope was much pleased by it, though he noted occasional inadvertent 'poetical luxuriancy' (ibid., 5.139). Lady Mary Wortley Montagu was among its admirers and expressed her tart opinion 'that whoever did not cry at George Barnwell must deserve to be hanged' (Lord Wharncliffe, 1.92).

Lillo entrusted publication of his tragedy and all of his later plays to the bookseller John Gray, a friend, later one of three executors of the playwright's will, and a fellow dissenter, who by Davies's account became a dissenting minister and later a clergyman of the Church of England. Demand for copies of the play was such that, by February 1732, Gray was advertising a fourth edition. His fifth edition (February 1735) included a powerful scene at the place of execution, never before printed or acted, and an author's advertisement explaining that the scene, omitted from production on the advice of friends, was now published 'to distinguish this Edition from the incorrect, pyrated ones which the Town swarms [*sic*], to the great Prejudice of the Proprietors of the Copy'. On 25 November Lillo signed an agreement formally granting, for the sum of £105, exclusive copyright to Gray.

Later plays Late in 1733 or early in 1734 Lillo wrote a short masque to celebrate the marriage of Anne, the eldest daughter of George II, to the prince of Orange. *Britannia and Batavia* was never performed, though at times it has been confused with *Britannia, or, The Royal Lovers*, a masque first staged at Goodman's Fields in February 1734. It did not appear in print until included in Gray's posthumous nonce collection of Lillo's work (1740).

The Christian Hero, first acted at Drury Lane on 13 January 1735, is modelled on heroic drama. Its language is verse, its setting the exotic medieval East, and its subject the triumphs of Scanderbeg, the fifteenth-century Albanian liberator George Castriot, 'A Pious Hero and a Patriot King'. Lillo's primary source was *Scanderbeg the Great*, the English translation of a late seventeenth-century novel by Anne de la Roche Guilhem. The play was performed for four nights, then permanently disappeared. In attempting a heroic style, Lillo produced a rhetoric that was more hollow than resonant.

On 6 May 1736 *Fatal Curiosity* was produced by Fielding's company at the theatre in the Haymarket. Although it was written in verse, the play was another realistic domestic drama, the oft-told tale of the impoverished old couple who kill and rob a young stranger only to discover that he is their long-lost son. While this version of the story probably originated in a black-letter pamphlet, *Newes from Perin in Cornwall* (1618), the playwright's source was an abbreviated account given in *Sanderson's Annals* (1656) and reprinted in *Frankland's Annals* (1681). Lillo's action is spare, his dramatic model classical tragedy: the parents, too ready to yield to despair, and the son, too eager to experience the extremes of their grief and later joy, are brought together to play out swiftly the inexorable consequences of their fatal combination. Lillo is indebted also to Shakespeare, in particular in his handling of the wife, who recalls Lady Macbeth as she urges, then observes, the murder. Davies, cast as the son, reports that Fielding 'himself took on the management of the play', instructing 'the actors how to do their parts' (Davies, xvi), perhaps having a hand in revising the script. He also wrote a prologue and warmly recommended the play to his friends and to the public. Despite his efforts, *Fatal Curiosity* was not greatly successful, being acted only five times after its initial performance. Fielding did his best to revive the play in the following season, billing it with the first ten performances of his own *Historical Register for the Year 1736*. In June the Licensing Act brought an abrupt end to his season, his company, and any current interest in Lillo's domestic tragedy. Fielding's continued belief in the play is attested by a piece he printed in *The Champion* in 1740: *Fatal Curiosity*, he wrote, 'is a Master-Piece in its Kind, and inferior to only Shakespeare's best pieces [and] gives [its author] a Title to be called the best Tragick Poet of his Age' (*Dramatic Works*, xix).

Lillo's *Marina*, an adaptation of acts IV and V of Shakespeare's *Pericles*, appears to have been written and acted through the influence of the Shakespeare Ladies' Club, a group formed in 1736, whose purpose was to persuade the managers of the theatres to offer more performances of Shakespeare's plays and fewer harlequinades and similar light entertainments. Offered at Covent Garden on 1 August 1738 and played three times, the piece did not succeed.

Lillo lived to complete the tragedy of *Elmerick, or, Justice Triumphant*. A brief moral anecdote of the honest regent and righteous king, set into the history of Andrew II of Hungary, provided well for his most political play, a heroic tragedy asserting 'Liberty and Justice' (a minimally disguised critique of the Walpole government) while offering opportunities to develop romantic intrigue and pathos. The result, in Genest's judgement, 'is a good play of its kind' (Genest, *Eng. stage*, 3.608), though marred by an ill-handled act of violence. Lillo left the play in the care of Gray with the request that it be dedicated to Frederick, prince of Wales, whose 'protection', Gray reports, the prince 'was graciously pleas'd to afford this piece during the Performance of it'. A member of the prince's circle, James Hammond, composed the prologue, while another, Lord Lyttleton, probably provided the epilogue. Staged at Drury Lane on 23 February 1740, with Quin in a role particularly well suited to him, *Elmerick* was acted six times, but not scheduled again. The prologue to the tragedy, which was posthumously presented, describes the playwright as dying 'Deprest by want, afflicted by Disease'. However, Lillo's will indicates that he was prosperous, able to make bequests of money and personal property to a number of relatives as well as houses and holdings of land in and out of the City. He died at Rotherhithe on 3 September 1739, and was buried on 6 September at St Leonard's Church, Shoreditch.

Legacy The adaptation of the Elizabethan domestic tragedy *Arden of Feversham*, long accepted as left unfinished by Lillo and completed or revised by John Hoadly, first appeared in 1759. Given once at Drury Lane (the theatre's only summer performance that year), it was advertised as 'written by the late Mr Lillo, Author of *George Barnwell*'. Evidence of the actual authorship of the piece is inconclusive. No author is identified in the manuscript of the play submitted for licensing nor is the piece included or mentioned in the posthumous collection issued by Gray. In 1762 Davies published the play as Lillo's, and later he included it in his collection of Lillo's works, reporting that the actor John Roberts (*d.* 1748) told him that the play 'was written before the year 1736' (Davies, xliii). In December 1762 the *Monthly Review* had noted that 'the manuscript … was long in the possession of Theophilus Cibber' (*d.* 1758). John Hoadly became associated with the adaptation in 1782, when the updated edition of the *Biographica dramatica* reported that the play 'was left imperfect by Mr. Lillo, and finished by Dr. Hoadly' (Baker, 2.20). Hoadly, chaplain to the prince of Wales, was a friend of Garrick, with whom he corresponded about revising old plays. The lack of a fully articulated didactic framework, characteristic of Lillo's plays, and discontinuities between ideas introduced early in the play and its resolution indicate that, to the extent (if any) Lillo had a hand in the adaptation, his work required substantial 'completion', apparently by Hoadly.

The London Merchant did more than any other English eighteenth-century play to popularize domestic drama. In the dedication printed with the play Lillo described the elements he intended to define a new sort of tragedy—the strong moral view and the appeal to pathos that, when combined with domestic subject matter, could both move and instruct contemporary audiences. Continental playwrights found in these aspects of the play possibilities for alternatives to the increasingly moribund conventions of French tragedy. The Abbé Prévost, having seen performances at Drury Lane in 1733, published translations of substantial portions of *The London Merchant* that created interest in Paris. French admirers, among them Diderot, explored the new style and evolved a middle-class drama, passionate, didactic, but with happy endings. In 1754 the first of a series of German translations of French variations on Lillo's play (*Der Kaufman von London*, 1752) was acted in Hamburg. Almost immediately it achieved a popularity among German-speaking theatres that continued until the 1770s, and thereafter it turned up as a work for the wandering troupes that played in smaller towns. Lessing's *Miss Sara Sampson* appeared in 1755, his first published comments about Lillo in 1756, then and later citing *The London Merchant* for its power to elicit pity—in Lessing's view the essential tragic emotion. It is highly improbable, however, that he knew Lillo's play before writing his own famous tragedy.

In Britain *The London Merchant* had several successors—notably Edward Moore's *The Gamesters* (1753) and the plays of Richard Cumberland—but the new style was not long-lived on the stage. Its enduring influence was in the novel. But the play itself persisted in English-speaking theatres far into the nineteenth century. Cycles of performance often reflected the ambitions and needs of leading actors. In 1765 Garrick chose *The London Merchant* as a suitable vehicle with which to inaugurate the adult career of his protégé Samuel Cautherley. In 1796 Sarah Siddons scored a triumph as Millwood in a new production of the play intended to show to good advantage her brother Charles Kemble. The play was in the repertory of the first company of actors to travel to the American colonies in the

1750s, and for more than a century *The London Merchant* was acted as a 'stock play' in American theatres. It has never been out of print, and, if London theatres came to ignore it, provincial audiences remembered. Henry Irving frequently played Barnwell at the Theatre Royal, Manchester, early in his career and Dickens counted on his readers' knowledge of the play to the extent that he four times made it a subject for parody—in *The Pickwick Papers*, *Martin Chuzzlewit*, *Barnaby Rudge*, and *Great Expectations*.

Fatal Curiosity achieved long-delayed recognition when James Harris published his *Philological Enquiries* (1781), in which he singled out the play as the one modern drama which matched in power the tragedies of ancient Greece. A pair of new productions followed: an adaptation (primarily deletions) offered at the Haymarket by George Colman the elder in the summer of 1783, and at Covent Garden the following year Henry MacKenzie's successful expanded adaptation, *The Shipwreck*. Neither came near achieving the triumph of Sarah Siddons's production of Lillo's original play, revived for her end-of-season benefit for 1797. As the new century began the play was taken as a significant model for the German theatre's heavily ironic *Schicksalstragödie*, or fate tragedy. The most effective of Lillo's tragedies, *Fatal Curiosity* has come to be identified as one of the few theatrical masterpieces of the first half of the eighteenth century. JAMES L. STEFFENSEN

Sources E. L. Avery, 'The Shakespeare Ladies Club', *Shakespeare Quarterly*, 7 (1956), 153–8 • D. E. Baker, *Biographia dramatica, or, A companion to the playhouse*, rev. I. Reed, new edn, 1 (1782), 283–5 • R. Shiels, *The lives of the poets of Great Britain and Ireland*, ed. T. Cibber, 5 (1753), 338–40 • T. Davies, 'Some account of the life of Mr. George Lillo', *The works of Mr. George Lillo*, ed. T. Davies, 2 vols. (1775), vol. 1, pp. ix–lviii • Genest, *Eng. stage* • C. B. Hogan, ed., *The London stage, 1660–1800*, pt 5: 1776–1800 (1968) • J. Harris, *Philological enquiries in three parts*, 2 vols. (1781), 1.154–83 • F. J. Lamport, *Lessing and the drama* (1981) • *The dramatic works of George Lillo*, ed. J. L. Steffensen (1993) • G. Lillo, '*The London merchant, or, The history of George Barnwell*' and '*Fatal curiosity*', ed. A. W. Ward (1906), v–x • W. McBurney, 'What George Lillo read: a speculation', *Huntington Library Quarterly*, 29 (1965–6), 275–86 • D. B. Pallette, 'Notes for a biography of George Lillo', *Philological Quarterly*, 19 (1940), 261–7 • A. F. Prévost and others, *Le pour et contre*, ed. S. Larkin, 2 vols. (1993), nos. 1–60 • L. M. Price, 'George Barnwell abroad', *Comparative Literature*, 2 (1950), 126–56 • A. H. Scouten, ed., *The London stage, 1660–1800*, pt 3: 1729–1747 (1961) • G. W. Stone, ed., *The London stage, 1660–1800*, pt 4: 1747–1776 (1962) • Lord Wharncliffe [J. A. Stuart-Wortley-Mackenzie], 'Introductory anecdotes', in *The letters and works of Lady Mary Wortley Montagu*, ed. Lord Wharncliffe, 3 vols. (1837), vol. 1, p. 92

Archives Hunt. L., Larpent MSS [Larpent MS 9, *Marina*, Larpent MS 19, *Elmerick*, Larpent MS 160, *Arden of Feversham*]

Wealth at death heir received £60–£600 p.a.; properties in Ealing; leaseholds of two houses in the City of London; mortgage on a third London house; bequests of approximately £360: will, PRO, PROB 11/698, fols. 72r–73v; will, Bodl. Oxf., MS Rawl. J, fol. 43; Davies, 'Some account'

Lilly, Christian (*d.* 1738), military engineer, was born in Hamburg, Germany, the son of Thomas Lilly and his wife, Mary. He began his military career in the service of Georg Wilhelm, duke of Celle, and Ernst August, duke of Hanover, in 1685, and was under the command of Prince Friedrich August (the second son of the duke of Hanover and brother of the future George I of Great Britain) and of Lieutenant-General Chauvet. Having served in several campaigns against the Turks in Hungary, when he was present at the battle of Grau and the sieges of Neuhausel, Caschaw, Polack, and Buda (1683–6), in 1688 he entered the service of William III, and he was naturalized as English in April 1700. He served in Scotland in 1689 and in Ireland for most of the war. Posted to King William's Dutch train of artillery, he served under Count Hendrik Trajectinus van Solms-Braunfels at the battle of the Boyne on 1 July 1690, then under General Godart van Reede-Ginckel at the first siege of Athlone and the first siege of Limerick, raised on 27 August. On 3 September 1690 he was appointed ensign in Lieutenant-General Douglas's regiment and quartermaster-general to the grand detachment of the army commanded by Douglas. He again served under Ginckel at Ballymore in June 1691, was director of the approaches in the second siege of Athlone that month, took part in the battle of Aughrim on 11 July, and was engineer at the short siege of Galway which followed, and during August and September at the second siege of Limerick, which ended the war.

On 1 May 1692 Lilly was appointed engineer of the Office of Ordnance, and was sent with the ordnance train on the duke of Leinster's expedition with the Channel Fleet to attack the French coast; when this proved unsuccessful, a descent was made upon Flanders instead. By royal warrant of 4 August 1692 he was appointed engineer at 10s. a day to accompany an ordnance train with guns and mortars to the West Indies. The following year he was sent with Sir Francis Wheeler's expedition to Barbados, Martinique, the Leeward Islands, New England, and Newfoundland, where, besides his post of engineer, he had chief command of the artillery train and was captain of a company of foot. On his return home he was appointed, on 30 October 1693, captain in Colonel Luke Lillingstone's regiment of foot and was sent into garrison at Plymouth.

On 12 October 1694 Henry Sidney, earl of Romney, master-general of the ordnance, appointed Lilly engineer and to command the artillery train for the West Indies. He went out with Lillingstone in 1695, and served at the sieges of Cap François and Port à Paix in Hispaniola, which were captured from the French. He was afterwards stationed at Jamaica. Kingston was built to Lilly's plans after Port Royal had been destroyed by earthquake in June 1692. On 19 May 1696 Lilly was appointed fireworker to the artillery train, and that same year he was sent to report on Havana, after which he returned to England. On 17 November he was appointed chief engineer of Jamaica at 20s. a day. He repaired the Port Royal fortifications and strengthened other fortifications under the lieutenant-governor, Sir William Beeston. In accordance with a warrant of the lieutenant-governor, dated 1 May 1698, Lilly went with Admiral Benbow's squadron to investigate the Spanish ports on the coast of Peru. He visited Portobello, Carthagena, and the Scottish settlements, and following his return to England reported on their defence capabilities.

When in May 1698 the artillery trains employed in Flanders and at sea were dismissed and a reduced peace train ordered to be formed, Lilly was appointed one of the six engineers at £100 per annum from 1 May 1698. Following Colonel Jacob Richards's death, on 28 June 1701 Lilly was appointed third engineer of England, his commission to date from 1 July, with a salary of £150 per annum.

On 14 August 1701 Lilly was again appointed chief engineer at Jamaica, and he accompanied Brigadier-General Selwyn to the West Indies. He made surveys of Port Royal and other Jamaican harbours, and repaired and improved the fortifications. On 10 November 1703 the acting governor, Handasyde, appointed him lieutenant-colonel of artillery in Jamaica. On 4 May 1704 the Board of Ordnance appointed him chief engineer in the West Indies and instructed him to fortify Barbados under General Sir Bevil Granville, the governor. On 29 January 1705 Granville appointed him colonel of artillery at Barbados. In 1707 he was sent to Antigua, Nevis, and St Kitts to investigate under the governor of the Leeward Islands, Daniel Parke, their military condition and report home on their defence. He then returned to Barbados and resumed superintending the construction of defence works. On 12 May 1709 the Board of Ordnance appointed him keeper of the naval ordnance stores at Barbados.

In the summer of 1711, under a warrant of the Board of Ordnance dated 6 March, Lilly went to Newfoundland to report on the harbours of St John and Ferryland and settle controversies on their security and fortification. His reports were sent to the Board of Ordnance and the Board of Trade and Plantations. He returned to England in 1712, but, his whig friends having left office, he remained unemployed, paid only as third engineer of Great Britain.

On George I's accession, by royal warrant of 2 March 1715, Lilly was continued in the post of third engineer of Great Britain (paid £150 per annum, plus travelling allowances of 13*s.* 4*d.* a day), and by a warrant of the Board of Ordnance, dated 22 March, he was appointed to examine the fortifications of Portland, Dartmouth, Plymouth, Falmouth, and the Isles of Scilly, and to survey, repair, and propose improvements to their defences. His reports were approved by the Board of Ordnance, and their form was considered so good that it was adopted for general use. Lilly was then appointed engineer in charge of the Plymouth division, from Portland to the Isles of Scilly. He continued in this post until 1719, when he was called to London. In 1720 the Board of Ordnance ordered him to Port Mahon, Minorca, as engineer, but he did not comply, 'excusing himself by letter, as he did when ordered on the late expedition to Vigo' (Ordnance minutes, WO 47/33, p. 298, 18 Nov 1720). Such unacceptable behaviour presumably put him in a precarious position; that the board again employed him was probably because he was too good an engineer to discard.

From 1701 Lilly was concerned with the firing of shells from mortars and howitzers, and he experimented intermittently to determine rules for charges and elevations for specific ranges. In 1722 he obtained metal from the Board of Ordnance to construct a small experimental howitzer for systematic trials. That year he petitioned unsuccessfully for promotion; he blamed his failure on his foreign origin, although he spoke English so well that he was said to be mistaken for a born Englishman. In an unsuccessful petition in 1726 for preferment he described himself as the oldest engineer in the service, and stated that he had been present at fifteen battles and sieges.

On George II's accession Lilly's appointment as third engineer of Great Britain was renewed by royal warrant of 23 December 1727, and his salary was increased from £150 to £200 per annum, plus pay for special service. In Barbados he drew in addition £365 as chief engineer, West Indies, £319 7*s.* 6*d.* as colonel of artillery, and £146 as keeper of naval ordnance stores.

In November 1728, after much negotiation, Lilly went to Jamaica as chief engineer to superintend the fortifications and the proposed new settlement at Port Antonio. He arrived at Jamaica on 5 April 1729, and on 4 May he accompanied Governor Robert Hunter in HMS *Plymouth* to Port Antonio, which was exposed to Spanish raids from Cuba. Lilly remained at Port Antonio for nearly a year, planning the defences and suffering much from fever and ague. He was so ill that it was reported home by the masters of ships from Jamaica that he was dead, and so he was struck off the books for salary for March quarter 1730. However, he continued in Jamaica, constructing Fort George at Port Antonio and superintending the other defence works and barracks. Disagreement on their respective fortification designs between himself and the governor culminated in Lilly's suspension on 20 August 1733, but apparently he was soon reinstated, as he continued his reports to the Board of Ordnance. On 31 March 1734 Governor Hunter died, and was succeeded the following month by John Ayscough, who appointed Lilly captain of Fort Charles. Lilly died in 1738. Several of his plans are in the British Library.

R. H. Vetch, *rev.* Roger T. Stearn

Sources royal engineers' records, Archives of the Institution of Royal Engineers, Chatham · BL, Add. MS 12427 · ordnance minutes, 1720, PRO, WO 47/33 · W. A. Shaw, ed., *Letters of denization and acts of naturalization for aliens in England and Ireland, 1603–1700*, Huguenot Society of London, 18 (1911) · W. Porter, *History of the corps of royal engineers*, 1 (1889) · M. C. Tomlinson, *Guns and government: the ordnance office under the later Stuarts* (1979) · R. E. Scouller, *The armies of Queen Anne* (1966) · J. C. R. Childs, *The British army of William III, 1689–1702* (1987) · D. Chandler, *The art of warfare in the age of Marlborough* (1976) · private information (2004) [P. Latcham]

Archives BL, letter-book incl. details of fortification at Port Antonio, Jamaica, Add. MS 12427 · BL, reports on coastal defences in the Plymouth district, King MS 45 · Bodl. Oxf., another report on the Plymouth division drawings, plans, and views · NA Canada, report on Newfoundland

Lilly, Edmond (*d.* 1716), portrait painter, was probably of Norfolk origin. He is known to have painted some history pieces and still lifes, though none of his work in these genres appears to have survived. As a portraitist, Lilly was extensively patronized by Queen Anne, who seems to have preferred his style to that of his more renowned contemporaries Sir Godfrey Kneller and Michael Dahl. Many of his portraits of the queen were reproduced for leading members of the nobility, especially a full-length state portrait, of which a version painted in 1703 still hangs at Blenheim Palace, Oxfordshire. His portrait of Jeremy Collier was engraved in mezzotint by William Faithorne junior. Lilly was buried at Richmond, Surrey, on 25 May 1716, and was survived by his wife, Katherine Hindley. In his will, proved 11 July 1716, Lilly left property to relatives including 'my sister Lilly', 'my neice Barbara Lilly', 'my neice Katherine Hindley', and 'my cousin William Storer of Norwich'. To his nephew, Edward Lilly, he bequeathed several of his paintings. The will carefully records both his titles of these works and their unusually large dimensions and includes 'the Originalle Picture of the Blessed Virgin and the Angel commonly called the Salutation about 5 foot in breadth and 7 and a half in length', 'the goddess Minerva about 5 foot in breadth and about 8 foot in heighth', and a 'whole length picture of Queen Ann of or over the size of the said picture of Minerva', 'Also a picture of a devout Virgin 3 foot 4 Inches by 4 foot 2 Inches' and 'one whole length Picture of the Dutchess of Richmond copydd after Vandike 5 foot and half in heighth and about 4 foot in breadth marked on the back with letter (L) and likewise the Picture of Grapes' (will).

GORDON GOODWIN, *rev.* SUSAN COOPER MORGAN

Sources will, PRO, PROB 11/553, fols. 128r–130r • J. Turner, ed., *The dictionary of art*, 34 vols. (1996) • Redgrave, *Artists* • J. C. Smith, *British mezzotinto portraits*, 4 vols. in 5 (1878–84) • Bénézit, *Dict.*, 4th edn • M. Whinney and O. Millar, *English art, 1625–1714* (1957) • E. Einberg, *Manners and morals: Hogarth and British painting, 1700–1760* (1987) [exhibition catalogue, Tate Gallery, London, 15 Oct 1987 – 3 Jan 1988]

Archives Courtauld Inst., Witt Library, MSS, photographs, cuttings

Wealth at death bequeathed approx. £185 cash; paintings; library; widow became executrix: will, PRO, PROB 11/553, fols. 128r–130r; *DNB*

Lilly, Henry (1588/9–1638), herald painter, the second of two sons of John Lilly (*d.* 1590) of London, joiner, and his wife, Mary, daughter and coheir of John Gabbett, merchant tailor of London, was born in Worcestershire. He was admitted to Christ's Hospital on 12 April 1595 aged six, being then a poor orphan, according to his will. On 16 July 1605 he was apprenticed to Robert Goodman and in 1607 to Ralph Treswell the elder, citizen and painter-stainer of London. By 1610 he was apparently producing pedigrees under his own name. On 1 June 1616 he married by licence at St Botolph, Aldersgate, Elizabeth Flint (*d.* 1635). Both were said to be of the parish but she is identified in the 1634 London visitation pedigree as daughter of Gregory Flint of Salisbury, Wiltshire.

Lilly was a central figure in the long-running dispute between the painter-stainers and the heralds over the monopoly claimed by the kings of arms and their deputies the heralds over the production of artwork for heraldic funerals. Lilly's work was of such outstanding quality that it was difficult for the heralds to exclude him. On 20 April 1620 the College of Arms agreed that eight painter-stainers including Lilly would be employed on heraldic painting and in return they would not canvass for heraldic funeral work without reference to the heralds. On 29 November 1628 he was one of four painter-stainers to whom the chapter of the College of Arms resolved that no painting work should be put out as they had been refractory to the orders of the office. On 19 February 1631, on demanding details of the crest and descent of someone named Bishop from the heralds, Lilly stated that 'he kept a shop of paintinge and wold do such paynting work as was brought to him to do and wold not loose the custom of his shop' (Bodl. Oxf., MS Ashmole 836, fol. 619). Despite this, on 5 July 1631 he was readmitted to be one of the eight painters to the Office of Arms. In 1632 he produced a fine pedigree of the families of Weston and Cave now in the British Library (BL, Add. MS 18667). On 1 April 1633 Lilly was committed to the Marshalsea prison for doing work for the funeral of Robert Wilkinson of Nottinghamshire without reference to Norroy king of arms, acknowledging his wrong in a signed statement of 8 April.

Less than a year later, on 4 January 1634, Lilly was appointed Rouge Rose pursuivant-extraordinary and deputed by Clarenceux and Norroy, to whom a joint visitation commission had been issued, to visit with the York herald Worcestershire, Bedfordshire, and Essex. In the same year Lilly was paid £1200 by Sir Kenelm Digby for producing a great pedigree giving Digby a Saxon descent. In 1635 William Dugdale on coming to London was introduced to Lilly as a person of note 'having been employed by divers persons of honour and quality in framing theire pedigrees out of originall Evidences and other warrantable authorities' (Hamper, 11) and in a letter of 1647 Dugdale refers to Lilly as 'my old freind' (ibid., 212).

A case in the court of chivalry in 1640 (Duck *v.* Woodall) referred to Lilly's activities in 1635 and showed that he was assisted by apprentices. William Sedgwick, who was subsequently the distinguished herald painter responsible for the Hatton–Dugdale Facsimiles and the Book of Monuments, deposed that in 1635 he was Lilly's servant when the arms on a painting certified by Robert Cooke, Clarenceux, had been erased and arms for Woodall substituted. Henry Manning, a painter-stainer aged twenty-seven in 1640, stated that he had served Lilly for seven years and that:

> Mr. Lillie was not in that tyme ever detected or accused for forgeinge of Armes but was reputed to bee an honest man yet this deponent saith that hee for his part did suspect the sayd Mr. Lillie to bee guilty of alteringe of Armes.
> (Squibb, 41)

In August 1635 a dispute between Henry Lilly and his servant Henry Manning was referred by the City chamberlain to the court of the Painter-Stainers' Company so this may have influenced Manning's evidence against Lilly. In 1635 Lilly produced a Sandys pedigree and in 1637 one of Villiers.

On 18 January 1638 Lilly was forced to acknowledge the right of the kings of arms to regulate the price of all heraldic artwork. Shortly afterwards, by patent dated 1 February 1638, he was appointed Rouge Dragon pursuivant and in 1638 produced a Howard pedigree of which J. H. Round, who described it as 'that grossly fabulous pedigree', but admitted its magnificence, wrote 'A finer heraldic volume than this need not be wished for; the drawings and their colourings are of the first class' (Round, 76). Lilly's daughter Elizabeth sold the book to Lord Northampton for £100. By 1910 it was in the possession of the duke of Norfolk. It contains facsimiles of deeds, portraits, and monuments on 271 vellum leaves and like the Digby pedigree records a Saxon descent.

In his will dated 24 July 1638 Lilly admitted to suffering from many infirmities of body. According to records of a memorial inscription at Farnham, Essex, he died on 29 August 1638 and was buried on 4 September at Farnham where the incumbent was the puritan mystic William Sedgwick. Lilly's will leaves his second book of ordinaries to his servant William Sedgwick and to another servant, Thomas Proctor, he left all his surveying instruments. On the pedigree recorded at the 1634 heralds' visitation of London, which he signed 'Henry Lily, R. Rose', he is shown with a son, Henry, and four daughters, Elizabeth, Hannah, Mary, and Dorothy. In his will he mentions only three children, all daughters: Elizabeth, his executor and residuary beneficiary; Mary, who received £240 and the lease of the tithes of Langley, Essex; and Dorothy, who received £300.

Lilly was unusual but not unique in being a herald painter who became an officer of arms. He was distinguished for the remarkable quality of his artistic work. In the words of Noble 'the manuscript pedigrees he left of the nobility, so justly prized, evince he was a person of great merit in his profession' (Noble, 249).

THOMAS WOODCOCK

Sources W. H. Godfrey, A. Wagner, and H. Stanford London, *The College of Arms, Queen Victoria Street* (1963), 221–2 · 'Heralds' visitation of London, 1634', Coll. Arms, MS C 24, 538 · J. H. Parker Oxspring, 'The painter-stainers and their dispute with the heralds' (typescript), 3 vols., Coll. Arms, vol. 1, pp. 43–4, 50, 54, 63–5, 69, 88–9, 95, 102–12, 116, 118 · *The life, diary, and correspondence of Sir William Dugdale*, ed. W. Hamper (1827), 11, 174, 212, 268 · M. Noble, *A history of the College of Arms* (1804), 249–50 · J. H. Round, *Peerage and pedigree: studies in peerage law and family history*, 2 (1910), 15, 39 · G. D. Squibb, ed., *Reports of heraldic cases in the court of chivalry*, Harleian Society, 107 (1955), 40–41 · W. P. W. Phillimore, *The visitation of the county of Worcester, 1569* (1888), 87–8 · J. L. Chester and J. Foster, eds., *London marriage licences, 1521–1869* (1887), 846 · parish register, Farnham, Essex, 4 Sept 1638, Essex RO [burial] · *Surrey Archaeological Collections*, 6 (1874), 228 · Coll. Arms, MSS CB vol. 1, 18, 40, 42; ICB 82(i), fol. 100 · Society of Antiquaries, MS 664, 1–9 · BL, Add. MS 71474 · private information (2004) · T. C. Dale, ed., *The inhabitants of London in 1638*, 1 (1931)

Archives BL, heraldic and genealogical collections, Add. MSS 47185–47187 | Arundel Castle, Sussex, Howard pedigree 1638, duke of Norfolk · BL, Weston and Cave pedigree, 1632, Add. MS 18667 · BL, pedigrees of Worcestershire families, 1634, Add. MS 19816, fols. 100–24

Wealth at death over £557: will, PRO, PROB 11/177/106

Lilly, William (1602–1681), astrologer, was born on 1 May 1602, in the village of Diseworth, Leicestershire, near Derby, the son of William Lilly and Alice Barham (*d.* 1619). His family were of long-standing yeoman stock. A different date of birth, 30 April 1602 at 2.08 p.m. was given by his rival, the astrologer John Gadbury; 1 May, given in Lilly's own account, is, however, to be preferred. When he was eleven, Lilly was sent to the town of Ashby-de-la-Zouch to be instructed in the grammar school there by John Brinsley, an eminent puritan schoolmaster who taught him grammar, rhetoric, Latin and some Greek, and Hebrew. He remained there until 1620, when his father's poverty obliged him to return home. The same misfortune prevented him, despite some aptitude, from entering university.

William Lilly (1602–1681), by unknown artist, 1646

First marriages and early astrology Lilly did not stay long in Diseworth. On 9 April 1620 he arrived in London to enter the service of Gilbert Wright and his wife. Wright was a salt merchant known to Lilly's father's attorney; his wife, who died of breast cancer, was nursed by Lilly in her final illness in 1624. They lived 'at the corner house in the Strand' (by Strand Bridge). Wright being illiterate, Lilly also helped with the accounts. After a second marriage, to Ellen Whitehaire, Wright died on 22 May 1627, leaving an annual income of £20 for Lilly. Later that year, Lilly and Wright's elderly widow secretly married, and in an arrangement that apparently suited them both lived together until her death in 1633. He then inherited nearly £1000, a considerable sum.

Recent research has considerably increased knowledge of Lilly's astrology. In 1632 he heard about one John Evans, a wise- or cunning-man living and plying his trade in Gunpowder Alley. After visiting Evans, Lilly became interested in his craft and paid him for instruction in judicial astrology for seven or eight weeks, during which time he learned to 'set figures' and picked up some rudiments of interpretation (Evans owned only one book, apart from an ephemeris—Haly's *De judiciis astrorum*) and a little knowledge of primitive ceremonial magic, chiefly conjuring spirits. Evans was apparently a competent astrologer, but he had a serious drinking habit to support and would supply judgements calculated to please the client even when (as Lilly became sufficiently skilled to notice) the astrological significations were quite to the contrary. Lilly's pointing this out was the occasion of their break, and he then applied himself diligently to studying the subject himself, having bought some old books in a sale.

Lilly also continued with his study of the magical arts and according to his autobiography was partner, in 1632, to a bizarre search for buried treasure in the cloisters of Westminster Abbey. It was interrupted by a sudden, fierce, and inexplicable wind that, although apparently quelled by Lilly's dismissal of the disturbed demons, badly scared the participants. Some time in 1634–5 Lilly was engaged to teach John Hegenius the use of dowsing rods and talismans, but he claims that he burnt his magic books a couple of years later, having grown 'very much afflicted with the Hypocondraik Melancholly' (Lilly, 33).

Although he apparently dropped practical magic, Lilly continued with astrology, noting in his autobiography that 'in this time, *viz.* in 1633, [it] was very rare in London, few professing it that understood any thing thereof' (Lilly, 23). However, he succeeded in making the acquaintance of Nicholas Fiske, later John Gadbury's tutor, who gave him invaluable assistance with astronomy and mathematics as well as with astrology.

Lilly now acquired a patron, William Pennington MP, of Muncaster, Cumberland. He purchased a number of houses in the Strand, and on 18 November 1634, following the death of Ellen in the previous year, married Jane Rowley; this was less happy than his first marriage as 'she was of the Nature of Mars' (Lilly, 31) (that is, bad-tempered). His melancholy continuing, he decided in the spring of 1636 to move to the country, and settled in the village of Hersham, in the parish of Walton-on-Thames, Surrey. He lived there quietly and simply, except for trips to London to extricate Pennington from various scrapes. These included a paternity suit and an accusation of immorality by a disaffected divine, Isaac Antrobus. Lilly performed his tasks ably by resorting to means of discrediting the accusers that show a firm grasp of political infighting, if somewhat flexible ethics.

In September 1641, as he recorded:

> Having now in part recovered my Health, being weary of the Country, and perceiving there was Money to be got in London, and thinking my self to be as sufficiently enabled in Astrology as any I could meet with, I made it my Business to repair thither. (Lilly, 35)

He continued studying, now Valentine Naibod's commentary on Alcabitius, but also commenced writing his own thoughts upon an approaching great conjunction of Jupiter and Saturn—a concern that reveals his interest in mundane astrology and in the broader social and political implications of the stars.

Lilly and the English revolution The events which began in 1642 certainly offered Lilly plenty of scope. His sympathies were already on the side of parliament and puritanism (broadly defined), when in 1643 he was consulted as an astrological physician in an illness of the parliamentarian politician Sir Bulstrode Whitelocke. Whitelocke credited Lilly's intervention, brought about by John Lisle's wife, with saving his life, and he became a powerful ally.

In April 1644 Lilly published his first almanac, *Merlinus Anglicus Junior*, and sold out the first edition within a week. He then complained to some MPs that parliament's licenser, the astrologer John Booker, had insisted on 'many impertinent Obliterations' (Lilly, 41), and was rewarded with permission for a second, unadulterated edition.

His almanac for the following year, 1645, entitled *Anglicus, Peace or No Peace*, made his name by suggesting for June—based on an unfortunate aspect from Mars to the king's Ascendant—that 'If now we fight, a Victory stealeth upon us' (ibid., 43). The outcome of the battle of Naseby that month spectacularly confirmed Lilly's pre-eminence over the unfortunate royalist almanac-writer, now his chief rival, Sir George Wharton.

After *Anglicus, or, An Ephemeris* (1646), Lilly produced an almanac annually under the title *Merlini Anglici Ephemeris*, beginning with that for 1647, until his death. Written in a vivid style that mixed eschatological prophecy, judicial astrology, and gritty politics, it was an immediate success. His sales reached undreamt of heights. The royal monopoly of the Company of Stationers, and censorship by appointed ecclesiastical and university authorities, had broken down at the start of the civil war and both licensed and unlicensed publications burgeoned. His almanacs sold 13,500 copies in 1646, 17,000 the next year, and 18,500 in 1648. The following year this leaped up to nearly 30,000 copies. In the 1650s they were translated into Dutch, German, Swedish, and Danish.

Lilly also published a number of popular pamphlets which, to varying degrees, materially influenced events. One of these, *A Prophecy of the White Kings Dreadfull Dead-Man Explaned* (1644), drew upon traditional forms of popular prophecy. Two others, *England's Propheticall Merline* (1644) and *The Starry Messenger* (1645), were more explicitly astrological. The former was a masterful exposition of the recent conjunction of Saturn and Jupiter, various eclipses, the comet of 1618, and the nativities of English kings. Carefully but relentlessly piling detail upon detail, Lilly inferred the end of the Stuart monarchy, indicted Charles for engaging in 'an uncivill and unnatural war against his own Subjects' (Geneva, 212), and strongly implied, to an astrologically literate audience, the violent death of the king himself.

The Starry Messenger, published on the day of the battle of Naseby, drew the same conclusions from the appearance in London on 19 November 1644 of a divine but ominous portent, namely three suns (known in astronomical parlance as parhelia)—especially as this occurred at 8° of Sagittarius, the point of the 1603 great conjunction that had ushered in the Stuart succession and, to top it all, Charles's own birthday. Lilly then used the forthcoming solar eclipse of 11 August 1645 to issue his most explicit prediction of the king's fate.

Lilly's astral republicanism was thus both early and consistent, despite the rhetorical red herrings resulting from his natural caution, such as assertions that Charles was 'not the Worst, but the most unfortunate of kings' (Geneva, 234), and claims that he had affection for the king personally. There can also be no doubting the sincerity of his astrological (as distinct from political) conviction that unless Charles acceded to parliament's authority—'Fac hoc & vives' ('Do this and live'), as he urged in a pamphlet of 1645—he was doomed.

Despite this, Lilly still had enemies on his own side, particularly the Presbyterians, who (he later recalled) 'were, in their Pulpits, as merciless as the Cavaliers in their Pamphlets' (Lilly, 53). He was closely examined by one parliamentary committee in 1645, and nearly again shortly after, but both times powerful personal and political friends interceded on his behalf. They were keenly aware of his value as a propagandist—that of more than half a dozen regiments, as one contemporary put it—and on one occasion cavaliers tried to kidnap Lilly from his house; he wasn't at home.

Two things should be noted here. One is that Lilly himself drew the line at the more extreme sects of his time, such as the Fifth Monarchists and 'that monstrous people called Ranters' (Lilly, 64). The second is that political differences of opinion, although serious, were not necessarily insuperable. In 1646 Lilly was introduced by Jonas Moore, a royalist, to Elias Ashmole, a staunch supporter of the king who became Windsor herald and comptroller of the excise after the Restoration. The two men became the closest friends, in a relationship that ended only with Lilly's death.

***Christian Astrology* and political troubles** In 1647 Lilly published *Christian Astrology*, the first major astrological textbook in the English language. His decision to publish a specialized work in this manner was deliberate, part of the demotic-democratic programme he shared with other astrologers on the side of parliament and the army, especially Nicholas Culpeper, to make astrology and physic available to as many people as possible in the vernacular. There was a second edition in 1659 (and a facsimile reprint in 1985, Lilly's textbook still being in use more than three centuries later). *Christian Astrology* was based on Lilly's reading of the 228 earlier titles listed in his bibliography, among whose authors Claude Dariot (1523–1594) seems to have been particularly influential, plus his own innovations. It covers both nativities and horaries, and besides specific techniques reveals Lilly's commitment to an openly divinatory and occasionally prophetic astrology, in which the stars are divine signs, not physical causes, and 'the more holy thou art, and more neer to God, the purer judgement thou shalt give' (*Christian Astrology*, 1647, 13).

In the summer of 1647 Lilly was approached by Lady Jane Whorewood, acting as an emissary of Charles I (then a prisoner in Hampton Court) and with his consent, for his advice as to where the king might safely hide upon escaping; Lilly advised Essex, but the king chose, or had already chosen, to try the Isle of Wight. There, at Carisbrooke Castle, Lilly was again apparently instrumental through Lady Whorewood in supplying Charles with a metal saw and further astrological advice, but again to no avail.

At about the same time, Lilly was granted £50 and an annual pension of £100 (paid only for 1648–9) by parliament, probably for intelligence services. In January 1649, after attending the king's trial, Lilly had the satisfaction, although he evinced no enjoyment from it, of seeing his prophecies regarding the fate of Charles fulfilled, and also of magnanimously procuring the release of his old antagonist George Wharton.

In 1651 Lilly and Booker were sent for by the parliamentary besiegers of Colchester to cheer on their soldiery. The following year, however, tiring of the fray, Lilly purchased Hurst Wood, a house with some grounds, probably on Thrupps Lane, in Hersham, Surrey. But the quiet life was not yet to be. In 1653 he made bold to criticize parliament in his almanac of that year, and he was again arraigned before a committee. He had advance notice from the speaker, however, and quickly arranged with his printer for another edition with the most dangerous passages left out. Then he disowned the former one before the committee; despite the disarray this produced he was imprisoned for thirteen days before being released on bail, after which the matter was quietly dropped.

Lilly breathed more freely after Cromwell's dissolution of parliament in April 1653, but Presbyterian divines continued to harry him with their 'malevolent barking' (Lilly, 50). In particular, beginning in 1651, Lilly carried on an acrimonious exchange with Thomas Gataker that only ended with the latter's death in 1654. Matters were probably not helped by the fact that in *Christian Astrology* Lilly had considered a horary enquiry by Sir Thomas Myddelton as to 'if Presbytery should prevail, or not, in England?' Lilly's reply was that 'the Commonalty will defraud the expectation of the Clergy, and so strongly oppose them, that the end hereof shall wholely delude the expectation of the Clergy' (*Christian Astrology*, 1647, 439).

Third marriage and the business of astrology On 16 February 1654 Lilly's second wife died, unregretted. In October of the same year he married Ruth Needham, in what was evidently a happy match. In 1659 he received a gold chain and medallion from the king of Sweden, whose nativity he had praised in his almanac the preceding year.

All this time Lilly kept up a thriving business as a practising astrologer in his house on the Strand. His surviving (though incomplete) casebooks for 1644–66 reveal a clientele of nearly 2000 a year. Although about a third of his clients were female servants, the remainder included many members of the gentry and aristocracy, and in all, nearly as many men as women. His clients included Major-General John Lambert; Anthony Ashley Cooper, future first earl of Shaftesbury; and the leading Leveller Richard Overton, who sought Lilly's opinion in April 1648 as to 'whether, by joining with the agents of the private soldiery of the Army for the redemption of common right and freedom to the land and removal of oppressions from the people, my endeavors shall be prosperous or no' (Bodl. Oxf., MS Ashmole 420, attached to fol. 267). Unfortunately Lilly's reply is not recorded.

Usually questions were more mundane, though no less practical and vital to those concerned: the uncertainties of love-life and children, lost or stolen property, medical problems, and military service in a time of turmoil. The commonest question was 'Quid agendum?' ('What is to be done?'). For this service, Lilly normally charged about a half-crown, but it could be as much as £40 for the well-off. He also taught astrology for a fee, to a considerable number of students. By 1662 he was earning as much as £500 a year—unquestionably a high income.

By now Lilly's reputation was considerable. In a glowing letter of 4 April 1651 he was hailed by Abraham Whelock, head librarian at Cambridge University, as the chief 'promotor of these admired studies' (Bodl. Oxf., MS Ashmole 423, fol. 173); at the other end of the political spectrum, John Webster's ambitious attack on the universities in *Academiarum examen* (1654) recommended astrology as an art 'high, noble, excellent, and useful', and praised Lilly and his colleagues (Ashmole, Culpeper, Saunders, and Booker) for 'unwearied pains for the resuscitation, and promotion of this noble Science' (J. Webster, *Academiarum Examen*, 1654, 51). The respected astronomer (and, incidentally, royalist) Vincent Wing wrote to Lilly in 1650 politely seeking his astrological judgements, and asking for 'a line of Comendacion' for his new book (Bodl. Oxf., MS Ashmole 423), while Lilly's correspondents wrote to him with observations and queries from everywhere in the British Isles, and from continental Europe. As for the popular influence of his almanac, John Evelyn recalled in 1699 that during the solar eclipse of 29 March 1652, 'many were so terrified by Lilly that they durst not go out of their houses' (*Diary of John Evelyn*, 3.144), and an anonymous pamphlet complained that people put more confidence in Lilly than they did in God.

Lilly also seems to have been recognized as an authority on more recondite questions of angels, spirits, and fairies. Among other consultations, Aubrey records that 'Anno 1670, not far from Cyrencester, was an Apparition: Being demanded, whether a good Spirit, or a bad? returned no answer, but disappeared with a curious Perfume and most melodious Twang. Mr W. Lilley believes it was a Fairie' (J. Aubrey, *Brief Lives*, ed. O. L. Dick, 1949, 297).

During the years 1649–58 Lilly was the leading figure in an extraordinary group, the Society of Astrologers. A letter in George Wharton's florid handwriting, dated 24 April 1650, thanks Whitelocke for his patronage, and acknowledges 'the dextirous Scrutiny and Pains of Mr. Lilly' (G. Wharton to B. Whitelocke, 24 April 1650, Bodl. Oxf., MS Ashmole 423, fol. 168*v*). The society met once a year for a feast and sermon from a sympathetic divine; its members numbered about forty, and by common agreement matters of politics or religion were set aside for the evening. The tide, however, was already turning. The society did not survive the Restoration; on 22 June 1677, Ashmole nostalgically 'summoned the remainder of our old Club about Strand Bridge that are left alive' (*Elias Ashmole*, 1485). The last two reconvened feasts took place in 1682–3, after Lilly's death.

The Restoration and after The Restoration presented Lilly with obvious difficulties. However, he kept his head down, swore loyalty to Charles II, and was greatly helped by Ashmole and (in his turn) Wharton. In June 1660 he was examined by another parliamentary committee as to the identity of the regicide. Providence had not entirely deserted Lilly, it seems, for Richard Pennington, the son of his old patron William, appeared in time to whip up support behind the scenes and convinced one of Lilly's three examiners, Richard Weston, to take his side. Lilly described the circumstances of the king's death, named Lieutenant-Colonel George Joyce, and was let go at that.

Pepys describes a convivial evening spent at Lilly's house on the Strand, together with Ashmole and Booker, on 24 October 1660, so evidently something like a normal life continued. However, Lilly was again arrested in January 1661, and roughly treated before being released at the insistence of Sir Edward Walker.

Apart from a protracted and tedious civil suit over a property dispute, Lilly spent more time in Hersham, where he was made churchwarden of Walton-on-Thames parish for 1663–4. With the plague ravaging London, he and his wife withdrew to Hersham for good in June 1665. On 2 September 1666 the great fire of London broke out, devastating the old city. In the aftermath, it was recalled that in his *Monarchy or No Monarchy* (1651) Lilly had included some mysterious hieroglyphics, including one a pair of twins (symbolizing Gemini, the sign held to rule London) suspended over a fierce conflagration. People also noticed that the date of the fire fell on that chosen by the former parliamentary conspirators led by Colonel Rathbone, executed in April, for their attempted coup—and chosen for its anti-royal auspiciousness, so they claimed, from Lilly's almanac for 1666. There is in fact no such encouragement in his almanac, but suspicion fell on Lilly and he was summoned to appear before yet another parliamentary committee on 25 October, chaired by Sir Robert Brooke. Lilly was accompanied by Ashmole, who also did some lobbying on his behalf. This time, Lilly was gently treated. He admitted to having foreseen a plague and a fire for London, but pressed on whether he had also foreseen the dates, he replied, 'I did not, [n]or was desirous; of that I made no scrutiny' (Lilly, 90). In typically tantalizing fashion Lilly's own copy of the hieroglyphic of the fire carries his scribbled note, '*forsan* [perhaps] 1666 *vel* [or] 1667' (Bodl. Oxf., MS Ashmole 553, fol. 1137), but there is no way of knowing whether that was written before or after the event. Only one thing seems sure: even if Lilly had anticipated the date, he would not have admitted it to his examiners.

Despite this backhanded compliment to his powers, Lilly must have found the intellectual and social atmosphere of the Restoration uncongenial. Astrology was becoming firmly identified as 'enthusiastic' and vulgar: Lilly was parodied by Samuel Butler as the astrologer Sidrophel in *Hudibras* (1662–3); Pepys records how he and his friends laughed at Lilly's prophecies in 1667; and by 1664 sales of his now unfashionable almanac had plummeted to about 8000 copies a year.

In Hersham, Lilly continued his practice, consulted by many local people—whom he charged little or nothing—for advice regarding their personal and medical problems. Every Sunday he rode to Kingston for the day, as Ashmole recalls, 'where the poorer sort flockt to him from several Parts' (Lilly, 102). He also renewed his study of physic, and asked Ashmole to use his influence with Gilbert Sheldon, the archbishop of Canterbury, to obtain a licence for its practice. This, signed by two physicians from the college, was duly forthcoming on 8 October 1670. Ashmole and his wife were the mainstays of the Lillys' social life, and their letters reveal a touchingly close relationship among the four of them.

In November 1675 Lilly fell ill. Although he slowly recovered, he began to use the London astrologer Henry *Coley (1633–1704) as an amanuensis in preparing the next year's almanac; Coley would come down to Hersham at the beginning of every summer and stay until it had been dispatched to the press. Coley received Lilly's permission to continue his almanac, under the same title, after his death.

Seized by a 'palsy' on 30 May, Lilly died, in the company of his wife and Ashmole, at about 3 a.m. on 9 June 1681 at his home, Hurst Wood, Hersham. He was buried in the chancel of St Mary's parish church, Hersham, the next day. His black marble tombstone, paid for by Ashmole and still in place, bears a Latin inscription which identifies him as 'a most learned astrologer'. George Smalridge, a future bishop of Bristol, then a scholar at Westminster sponsored by Ashmole, composed an elegy which lamented that

> Our Prophet's gone … the Stars had so decreed;
> As he of them, so they of him, had need.
> (Lilly, 105–6)

Lilly had no children, though he regarded his protégé Henry Coley as his adopted son. His will divided his extensive property and land (over 60 acres) between his wife, Ruth, and Carlton, the son of Bulstrode Whitelocke, and left legacies to his six servants and the parish poor. He had already arranged for Ashmole to purchase his books, papers, and letters from his widow for £50; they were later deposited in the Bodleian Library.

Lilly's place in history William Lilly, scourge of Charles I and prophet of a world turned upside down, thus died covered in respectability if not exactly glory. His interest, as recent research has shown, lies in his astrology: a pre-Enlightenment unity of what was already, during his lifetime, fast becoming more sharply divided into natural philosophical knowledge, divinatory or 'magical' astrology, and religious prophecy. Lilly flourished at the last historical moment when such a thing was unselfconsciously possible. His undoubted powers of sagacity and survival, in this context, were not so much a contradiction as an adjunct—in his own words, 'Discretion, together with art' (*Christian Astrology*, 1647, 397). Probably divination has always worked in such a way. However, his successors, chiefly Gadbury and Partridge, were obliged to embark upon drastic programmes of differing but explicitly 'rational' reforms, something with which Lilly was never overly concerned. Overtly magical astrology was now virtually confined to the village cunning-man and -woman, with whom it remained until the time of Ebenezer Sibly.

The historiographical problem Lilly presents is simply stated: he was virtually a genius at something—judicial astrology—which modern mainstream opinion fails to recognize as even something that it is possible to do, let alone do well or badly. That opinion largely has its own historical origins in the very period spanned by Lilly's life. He therefore constitutes a valuable challenge and test of historians' ability to transcend the assumptions and prejudices of their own times. PATRICK CURRY

Sources P. Curry, *Prophecy and power: astrology in early modern England* (1989) • A. Geneva, *Astrology and the seventeenth century mind: William Lilly and the language of the stars* (1995) • K. Thomas, *Religion and the decline of magic* (1971) • B. S. Capp, *Astrology and the popular press: English almanacs, 1500–1800* (1979) • W. Lilly, *Mr William Lilly's history of his life and times: from the year 1602, to 1681*, 2nd edn (1715); repr. with introduction by K. M. Briggs (1974) • D. Parker, *Familiar to all: William Lilly and astrology in the seventeenth century* (1975) • *DNB* • Bodl. Oxf., MSS Ashmole 420, 423, 553 • *Elias Ashmole (1617–1692): his autobiographical and historical notes*, ed. C. H. Josten, 5 vols. (1966 [i.e. 1967]) • *Diary of John Evelyn*, ed. W. Bray, new edn, ed. H. B. Wheatley, 4 vols. (1879) • J. Gadbury, *Collectio geniturarum, or, A collection of nativities* (1662)

Archives BL, collection of astrological observations, SI MS 3856 • Bodl. Oxf., astrological collections | BL, corresp. with Elias Ashmole and Elizabeth Ashmole, Add. MS 4293

Likenesses oils, 1646, AM Oxf. [*see illus.*] • T. Cross, line engraving, NPG; repro. in W. Lilly, *Almanack* (1678) • Hollar, engraving, repro. in W. Lilly, *Almanack* • W. Marshall, line engraving (after oils, 1646), BM, NPG; repro. in W. Lilly, *Christian astrology* (1647) • Vaughan, engraving, repro. in W. Lilly, *Almanack* • line engraving, BM; repro. in W. Lilly, *Merlini Anglici Ephemeris* (1667) • line engraving, NPG

Wealth at death property and land; personal possessions; also small legacy: *DNB*

Lillywhite, (Frederick) William (1792–1854), cricketer, was born at West Hampnett, near Goodwood, Sussex, on 13 June 1792, the elder child and son of James Lillywhite, a brick-field manager in the duke of Richmond's service, and his wife, Martha Lillywhite. He established himself in trade as a bricklayer and brick-maker and in 1822 moved to Brighton; shortly afterwards he settled in Hove as the manager of a brick-making gang. This was already a busy cricket area, and, as was the case with many putative cricket professionals, his working routine was flexible enough to allow him opportunities to improve his cricket. None the less, he was over thirty before he made a serious mark, and did not play his first game at Lord's until June 1827. Thereafter he never looked back, and became known as the Nonpareil Bowler, a model of consistency for another twenty years. The round-arm method of bowling that he used was not legalized by the MCC until 1828, and this may have accounted in part for the stuttering beginning to his career. Indeed, Lillywhite was the first eminent and distinctive bowler of this type, and was much involved in the experimental matches of 1827 which led to the legalization of round-arm bowling.

Lillywhite's slow deliveries masked sharpness off the pitch, but, above all, they needled batsmen by their uncommon accuracy of line and length: it is said that he bowled fewer than a dozen wide balls throughout his lengthy career. 'I bowls the best ball in England', he mused, 'I suppose if I was to think every ball, they'd never get a run'. In the 245 major matches in which he participated, often in lethal partnership with another round-

(**Frederick**) **William Lillywhite** (1792–1854), by John Corbet Anderson

arm bowler, Jem Broadbridge, he had the phenomenal haul of 1570 wickets, and in those important games for which bowling analyses are available he produced a bowling average of just under 11. It is said that his bowling average in all cricket was no more than 7. His best summer was in 1844, when he took 115 wickets, but perhaps his best single performance was at Lord's in 1837, when he took ten wickets for the Players against a Gentlemen's team of eighteen. He was less accomplished as a batsman, but could defend sturdily, and ended his career with 2350 runs in major matches to his name. He also took 140 catches, but he was notorious for concentrating on bowling and leaving to others what he regarded as the servile chores of batting and fielding. He coined a definition of cricketing perfection well known in his time, 'me bowling, Pilch batting, and Box keeping wicket'.

In 1837, following the example of several leading professional cricketers, Lillywhite became a landlord: he took the Royal Sovereign inn, Brighton, and next to it he laid out a cricket ground. He played seventy matches for Sussex (1825–53) and in an era less fussed about residential qualification he also played a handful of games for Middlesex, Surrey, and Hampshire. From 1844 to his death he was engaged as a bowler by the MCC, who granted him a benefit in 1853. In the seasons 1851–3 he was coach at Winchester School, another example of how older and respected 'pros' added to their income. A further source of income was the cricket outfitters store which he opened in Islington.

Again like many cricketers, Lillywhite produced a cricketing family. He married Charlotte Parker on 15 July 1822, and they had three sons who came to be noted in the game. James Lillywhite senior (1825–1882), an occasional Sussex cricketer and cricket coach at Cheltenham College, was instrumental in founding in 1863 the popular Lillywhites store of London, the longest-established sports emporium in the country. John Lillywhite (1826–1874) played a hundred matches for Sussex and was a useful all-rounder; he was a member of the first overseas cricket tour by an England team, to North America in 1859. He also edited the *Cricketer's Companion* journal (1865–85), and, as an umpire, he brought to a head the overarm bowling controversy in 1862 by constantly no-balling the chief exponent of the new method, Edgar Willsher. Frederick Lillywhite (1829–1866) was well known as a cricket reporter: he helped produce the early tomes of *Scores and Biographies* and the somewhat caustic annual *Guide to Cricketers* from 1849 to 1866. Another cricket-playing relative was William's nephew James Lillywhite junior (1842–1929), the Sussex and England left-arm bowler, who took 1210 wickets in his career and captained England in the first two test matches ever played, in 1877. He gave his name to the famous *Red Lillywhite* cricket annual (edited by Charles Alcock, and a distinctive rival of *Wisden*) that was published between 1872 and 1900.

'Lilly' was only 5 feet 4 inches tall but his stocky build and ruddy countenance, together with his tall hat, black braces, and stiff collar made his rustic presence a characteristic part of the cricketing scene. He died of cholera at his home, 10 Prince's Terrace, Caledonian Road, Islington, London on 21 August 1854, and was buried in Highgate cemetery, Middlesex. The MCC erected a monument above his grave, simply inscribed Lillywhite, for, perhaps in death as in life, only amateurs were allowed the use of initials. ERIC MIDWINTER

Sources A. Haygarth, *Arthur Haygarth's cricket scores and biographies*, 15 vols. (1862–1925), vols. 1, 4 · P. Bailey, P. Thorn, and P. Wynne-Thomas, *Who's who of cricketers* (1984) · privately compiled family tree, Sussex County Cricket Club Library · G. D. Martineau, *They made cricket* (1956) · Boase, *Mod. Eng. biog.*

Likenesses W. H. March, sketch, *c*.1835, Mansell collection, London · J. C. Anderson, lithograph, Marylebone Cricket Club, Lord's, London [*see illus.*]

Lily, George (*d.* 1559), Roman Catholic ecclesiastic and cosmographer, was born in London, the eldest son of William *Lily (1468?–1522/3) and his wife, Agnes. Probably privately educated by his father, a scholar and teacher, Lily may have become a commoner of Magdalen College, Oxford, in 1528. Perhaps in 1529 he entered Reginald Pole's service. By 1535 Pole had given him a prebend in Wimborne Minster, and Lily had begun to study in Padua under Giovanni Battista Egnazio, Lazzaro Bonamico, and Fausto da Longiano in Greek. About the same time he expressed the wish to become a Theatine. In 1538–9 he lived in the English Hospice in Rome, and then accompanied Pole to Viterbo. Before 1543 he was outlawed for treason, presumably for his association with Pole, and his property was transferred to his brother Peter.

In the 1540s George Lily collaborated with Paolo Giovio on the *Descriptio Britanniae, Scotiae, Hyberniae et Orchadum* (printed in Venice by Michele Tramezzin in 1548) which also contained four works by Lily: 'Virorum aliquot in Britannia qui nostro seculo eruditione & doctrina clari, memorabilesque fuerunt elogia'; 'A Bruto … omnium in quos variante fortuna Britanniae imperium translatum brevis enumeratio'; 'Lancastrii et Eboracensis de regno contentiones'; and 'Regum genealogia'. The 'Elogia' attempted a kind of biography new in England since its subjects were neither royal nor saints. The model may have been Erasmus's capsule life of John Colet which served as one of Lily's major sources. The work served the end of defending traditional religion. The sketch of John Fisher in the 'Elogia' probably led to Henry Wharton's claim that Lily had written a full-length biography, which was mistakenly identified in the *Dictionary of National Biography* as BL, Arundel MS 152, no. 2, but this work postdates Lily's death. At the same time as his co-operation with Giovio, Lily drew the first map of the British Isles to be printed (1546); the copperplate-engraving was descended from the Gough map of *c.*1360.

In 1546 George Lily mediated between Pole and Vittoria Colonna. In the second half of 1549 he served as warden of the English Hospice, Rome, as Pole's deputy, and he held the same position in 1551 and finally in 1554. When Pole left Rome in 1553, Lily stayed behind translating various newsletters, and taking a hand in the composition and dissemination of the report of the duke of Northumberland's speech from the scaffold. The following year, having joined Pole in Brussels, he acted as proxy for at least two English bishops supplicating for absolution for schism. In 1555 he drew up an inventory of Pole's books. John Bale credited him with 'De vita, moribus et fine Thomae Cranmeri', otherwise known as 'Cranmer's recantacyons' of which Lily probably had a manuscript. It is really by Nicholas Harpsfield. In February 1556 Lily was ordained subdeacon on the title of Santa in Cosmedin, Pole's titular church in Rome. By then he had an important role in Pole's administration, as is indicated by his letter to Cuthbert Scot about the visitation of Cambridge. Late in the year he gained the prebend of Cantlers in St Paul's Cathedral and probably on 10 March 1558 the first prebend of Canterbury Cathedral when he was described as Pole's domestic chaplain. Lily almost immediately took up residence. A letter of 27 April 1558 to Pole's close friend Alvise Priuli makes it obvious that Lily missed Pole's household. He probably gave a funeral oration for Pole.

George Lily died on 14 July 1559 in Canterbury, possibly of influenza. His books were left to his nephew Polydore Jacob, and rings to his brother Peter and sister Dionisia for her first married daughter. Lily also disposed of three substantial sums of money: 300 crowns on deposit in a *monte* (approximately 'bank') in Rome went to his brother for his children; 200 more as a dowry for his daughters; and £10 with a merchant in London to Lily's servant George Morbrede. Pole's general receiver Henry Pyning handled the arrangements for the first two transfers. Lily's household goods went to his brother, and he left small remembrances to Robert Collins and also to John Friar, another old inmate of Pole's household. T. F. MAYER

Sources Bale, *Index*, 723 • *LP Henry VIII*, 8, no. 581; 9, nos. 292, 673, 1034; 10, nos. 503, 971; 18/1, p. 365 • *CSP Venice*, 1534–54, 171–2, no. 409 • Emden, *Oxf.*, 4.357 • E. L. Hirsh, 'The life and works of George Lily', PhD diss., Yale U., 1935 • G. Manzoni, ed., 'Il processo Carnesecchi', *Miscellanea di Storia Italiana*, 10 (1870), 189–573, esp. 254 • R. Shirley, 'General maps of Great Britain and the British Isles', *Historians' guide to early British maps: a guide to the location of pre-1900 maps of the British Isles preserved in the United Kingdom and Ireland*, ed. H. Wallis and A. McConnell (1994), 10–12 • H. Wharton, *A specimen of some errors and defects in the History of the Reformation of the Church of England; wrote by Gilbert Burnet* (1693), 61 • Archivio di Stato, Viterbo, Archivio notarile distrettuale di Viterbo, vol. 1451, Giov. Malvicini, Sr., pt. 2, fol. 86*v* • Biblioteca Civica 'Angelo Mai', Bergamo, Archivio Stella in Archivio Silvestri, 40/88, 40/96, 40/133 • Bibliothèque Municipale de Douai, MS 922, vol. 1, fols. 11*r*–12*v* and 14*r*–15*v* • Bodl. Oxf., MS Broxbourne 84.11 • BL, Add. MS 25425, fol. 50*r*–*v* • BL, Add. MS 35830, fol. 24*r* • BL, Add. MS 48029, fols. 58*r*–59*v* • BL, Harley MS 6989, fol. 40*r* • BL, Cotton MS Nero B.vi, fols. 158*r*–*v*; 163*r*–*v*; 165*r*–166*r*; 167*r*–*v* • Canterbury Cathedral Archives, Dean and Chapter, register V1, fols. 43*r* and 44*v* • LPL, Pole's register, fol. 76*v* • GL, MS 9535/1, fol. 55*v* • PRO, PROB 11/42B, fols. 280*v*–281*r* • PRO, SP 1/55, fol. 194*r* • PRO, SP 1/104, fol. 281*r* • CUL, Collect. Admin. 5, fol. 136*v*

Archives Biblioteca Apostolica Vaticana, Vatican City, MS Vat. lat. 5967, fols. 494*r*–500*v* • BL, Add. MS 35830, fol. 24*r* • BL, Cotton MS Nero B.vi, fols. 158*r*–*v*; 163*r*–*v*; 165*r*–166*r*; 167*r*–*v* • BL, Harley MS 6989, fol. 40*r* • PRO, SP 1/104, fol. 281*r*

Wealth at death approx. £200: will, PRO, PROB 11/42B, fols. 280*v*–281*r*; Biblioteca Civica 'Angelo Mai', Bergamo, Archivio Stella in Archivio Silvestri, 40/133

Lily [Lilly], **Peter** (**1562/3–1615**), Church of England clergyman, was probably a grandson of William *Lily, the grammarian, and nephew of the George *Lily who died in 1559 as a prebendary of Canterbury. Although he was certainly born in the latter city he was not, as previously believed, the son of 'Peter Lily, prebendary of Canterbury', no such man being found in the chapter records. At Michaelmas 1579 he matriculated pensioner at Jesus College, Cambridge, graduating BA in 1583 and MA in 1587. On 21 December 1588, aged twenty-five, he was ordained deacon, and on 24 November 1590, priest, both in the diocese of London and on each occasion at the commendation of Richard Bancroft. Having continued his studies at Jesus, he proceeded BTh in 1595 and DD in 1608.

Lily was a notable pluralist. Between 1590 and 1601 he was rector of St Nicholas Olave, London, and he is recorded as a chaplain of the Savoy Hospital, London, in April 1591. On 18 May 1594 he was installed in the Salisbury prebend of Hurstbourne and Burbage, but his tenure was for some reason short-lived, a successor being instituted on 13 March 1595. On 2 December 1594 Lord Hunsdon, writing to Bishop Hutton of Durham, described 'Dr Lillie' as competing with Richard Edes for the office of dean of Christ Church, Oxford, but Hunsdon seems to have been misinformed—the deanery was not vacant at this time, and when it became so two years later Thomas Ravis was the successful candidate against Edes. If this meant disappointment for Lily he would receive ample consolation. On 17 March 1599 he was instituted in the vicarage of Fulham, while on 16 April the same year Bancroft, now bishop of London, collated him to the prebend of Caddington Major in St Paul's. On 24 February 1604 William Young of Ogbourne St George presented him to the prebend of Highworth in Salisbury Cathedral, and in 1610 added the rectory of Hornsey in Middlesex to his collection; in 1614 he was chided by Hornsey manor court for failing to maintain a ditch by the highway. On 15 November 1613 he was installed in the archdeaconry of Taunton in a final, albeit posthumous, demonstration of Bancroft's good will. In 1606 the bishop of Bath and Wells had granted the next presentation to the archdeaconry to Bancroft, now archbishop of Canterbury, and the primate had then conveyed it to his executors, so that they could present Lily when the office next became vacant. Three years after Bancroft's death it duly came to Lily together with its attached prebend of Milverton. All these benefices Lily retained until his death.

Lily enjoyed royal favour as well, enabling him to become one of the seventeen founding fellows of Chelsea Hospital on 8 May 1610. He made a brief will on 22 February 1615 and had died by 11 March that year, when his successor was collated to Highworth. He was buried in the chapel of the Savoy. In his will he described his wife, Dorothy, as 'lovinge and faythfull' (PRO, PROB 11/125, fol. 508*r*), and according to Wood it was she who arranged for the publication in 1619 of two volumes of his sermons, Latin addresses in one book and English in the other. They were prefaced by English verses by Lily's daughter Mary, and dedicated, respectively, to James I and to Barbara, wife of Sir Edward Villiers, brother of the earl (later duke) of Buckingham. STEPHEN WRIGHT

Sources R. Somerville, *The Savoy: manor, hospital, chapel* (1960) · Wood, *Ath. Oxon.*, new edn, 1.34–5 · Venn, *Alum. Cant.*, 1/3.85 · *Fasti Angl., 1541–1857*, [St Paul's, London] · *Fasti Angl., 1541–1857*, [Bath and Wells] · *Fasti Angl., 1541–1857*, [Salisbury] · R. Newcourt, *Repertorium ecclesiasticum parochiale Londinense*, 1 (1708) · will, PRO, PROB 11/125, sig. 64 · *The correspondence of Dr Matthew Hutton, archbishop of York*, ed. [J. Raine], SurtS, 17 (1843) · W. Marcham and F. Marcham, eds., *Court rolls of the manor of Hornsey, 1603–1701* (1929) · W. H. Loomie, *Memorials of the Savoy* (1878) · GL, MS 9535/2 [ordination as deacon, then priest], fols. 44, 51

Wealth at death see will, PRO, PROB 11/125, sig. 64

Lily, William (1468?–1522/3), grammarian and schoolmaster, was born at Odiham in Hampshire. Nothing is known of his parents, and the estimate of the date of his birth is based on his age at death, recorded as fifty-four on his memorial tablet in the old St Paul's, and on the statement that he was eighteen in 1486, when he seems to have been elected as a semi-commoner at Magdalen College, Oxford.

Education and learning It is commonly believed that Lily went to Magdalen because his godfather, William Grocyn, was a reader in divinity there. In 1488 he became a pupil of John Stanbridge, author of a Latin/English vocabulary, *Vulgaria* (1508), when Stanbridge succeeded John Anwykyll as informator or schoolmaster at the college. On graduating from Oxford, about 1490 Lily made a pilgrimage to Jerusalem. On the return journey he spent some time at Rhodes, where he learned Greek, probably from refugees from the Turkish conquest of Constantinople: Rhodes was seen to be a haven for western Christians on account of the garrison of the knights of St John there.

Nevertheless, his study at Rhodes is surprising since the island was not seen as a centre of academic excellence; Thomas Fuller, in his later biographical sketch of Lily, claimed that, in late fifteenth-century Rhodes, 'to find one Elegant in Modern Greek (sowred with long continuance) is as impossible as to draw good wine from a vessel of Vinegar' (Fuller, *Worthies*, 1662, 'Hantshire', 11). From Rhodes, Lily travelled to Italy, where he spent the next few years. It was probably at the English Hospice in Rome, where he registered his name on 4 November 1490, that Lily met several of the patrons and scholars who were later associated with humanist learning in England—men such as John Colet, Thomas Linacre, Christopher Bainbridge, Giovanni Gigli, and William Warham. In Rome he studied Latin under the renowned Renaissance scholars Johannes Sulpizio Verolano and Pomponio Leto.

Lily's connection with Rhodes may explain the presentation of one 'Wilhelmus Lilye, scholaris', to the rectory of Holcot in Northamptonshire on 24 May 1492 (BL, Lansdowne MS 979, fol. 32) by John Kendall, prior in England of the knights of St John. However, it is unlikely that he progressed beyond minor orders, as according to the *Dictionary of National Biography* he gave up the benefice in 1495, and subsequently taught grammar, poetry, and rhetoric privately. Possibly about this time he married Agnes, with whom he had six children, four boys (the eldest being George *Lily, the cleric and cosmographer) and two girls. John *Lyly the dramatist was a grandson, as was probably the clergyman Peter *Lily.

St Paul's School Some time after 1510, presumably acting on their previous acquaintance and Lily's reputation as a scholar, Colet selected him to be first master of the newly formed St Paul's School in London, which Colet had endowed as 'one of the centers of humanist-inspired teaching in England' (Enkvist, 577). The post was made official in 1512 after the completion of the building. The choice was felicitous as the school flourished, attracting praise from Erasmus and others; among the pupils during Lily's tenure were the antiquary John Leland, the physician John Clement, the statesman William Paget, and Edward North, privy councillor and father of the translator of Plutarch. Rumours of Lily's severity while at St Paul's appear unfounded; it seems he was an upright man concerned with the moral rectitude of his pupils. It is also clear that, at the time of his death, he had had a longstanding involvement with the local St Faith's parish church, its fraternity, and the needs of its poor.

It is possible that Lily met Sir Thomas More in Oxford: according to Flynn, as a young man Lily had discussed the possibility of entering the priesthood with More, his close friend. More's letter to Colet describing Lily as his dearest friend is dated October 1504. We know that their friendship and friendly rivalry were consolidated in London, where they competed in writing Latin verse translations from Greek epigrams. These were published in 1518 in Basel under the title *Progymnasmata*. In lighter vein, Lily also translated for More Lorenzo Spirito's *Il sorte* (about a parlour game which tells fortunes on the basis of thrown dice) from the Italian.

As befits a Renaissance humanist, Lily also wrote occasional Latin verse, ranging from the 'Carmen de moribus'—a pedagogically inspired poem in elegiac couplets containing advice to the schoolboys of St Paul's (included in the 1548–9 edition of 'Lily's grammar')—to a share in the vituperative *Antibossicon*, in which the grammarian Robert Whittington was attacked. Both were published in London by Pynson in 1521. Other poetry included a set of congratulatory verses on the landing of Philip the Fair on 15 January 1506, and a panegyric to be read by one of his scholars when the emperor Charles V rode past St Paul's School in the summer of 1522.

Lily's grammar Lily's fame, however, rests on what is known as 'Lily's grammar' or *The Royal Grammar*, a work published some years after his death. It is a composite piece, most of which Lily didn't write, but he did make considerable valuable contributions to it. The history of the grammar is rather fragmented, complex, and obscure. None the less, in light of the work of V. J. Flynn and R. C. Alston, the following account can be constructed.

At Colet's request Lily wrote a short syntax in Latin, the *Absolutissimus de octo orationis partium constructione libellus*. This work was supervised by Erasmus, who also wrote a preface to the text; his international reputation no doubt contributed to its popularity. For the best part of a century afterwards, it was published under slightly varying titles by printers all over Europe—sometimes ascribed to Lily, sometimes to Erasmus, and occasionally anonymously. The first edition seems to have appeared about 1513, but the earliest surviving edition is dated 1533.

Another grammar, the *Rudimenta grammatices*, a very short syntax written by Lily in English, adapted from Donatus and Priscian, was usually published with Colet's own *Aeditio*, a rather longer accidence. No copy of either work survives from Lily's or Colet's lifetime, though the Bodleian Library holds a fragment of Lily's syntax (Vet A 1 a 4(1)) which may have been printed before his death. The earliest extant edition dates from 1527 and was printed at Antwerp. It seems likely that the earlier editions were produced in small numbers for internal school use, and that fame only gradually accrued. In 1529 the book, with the addition of new prefatory material relating to teaching, was adopted by Cardinal Wolsey for his school at Ipswich. The title-page of the 1529 edition contains the information that it was 'prescribed for all English schools'. As Wolsey died in the following year after being arrested for treason, it perhaps should not be surprising that few traces of this particular edition remain. It is interesting, however, that the idea of Lily's grammar survived, chameleon though it was.

Lily's two Latin grammatical poems, *De generibus nominum ac verborum praeteritis et supinus regulae*, written independently from the two grammars already mentioned, are in the humanist tradition, though their verse form awakens memories of the medieval grammars in verse by Alexander de Villa Dei and Evrard de Bethune. Once again the earliest extant edition (1525) was posthumous.

A revised compilation of all three grammars mentioned above, Lily–Erasmus, Lily–Colet, and Lily's poems, was circulating by 1542, the date of the earliest extant edition. In essence it represents two complete grammars, one in English for beginners and one in Latin. Both parts have title-pages proclaiming the royal prerogative from Henry VIII. In the next extant edition (1548–9) the title-pages have changed, and it is this edition that may be considered the definitive form of 'Lily's grammar'. The respective titles for each grammar were *A shorte introduction of grammar generally to be used in the kynges maiesties dominions, for the bryngynge up of all those that entende to atteyne the knowledge of the Latine tongue* (1548) and *Brevissima institutio, seu, Ratio grammatices cognoscendae, ad omnium puerorum utilitatem praescripta, quam solam regia maiestas in omnibus scholis profitendam praecipit* (1549).

The canonical nature of the grammar was underlined by a proclamation of 1543. It was repeated in injunctions by Edward VI in 1547 and Elizabeth I in 1559, and was subsequently endorsed in the ecclesiastical canons of 1571 and 1604, which meant that Lily's grammar was the only authorized one in the kingdom. Edward VI's order that no other grammars were to be used in schools, reprinted in the prefatory material of the 1548–9 edition, justifies the use of 'one kynd of grammar' since 'the tendernes of youth' could not 'suffre the endles diversitee of sundry schoolemaisters'—a verdict with which modern scholars can sympathize (Lily and Colet, sig. A1*v*). Although subjected to subsequent slight modifications by practising schoolmasters during the sixteenth century, the grammar's basic structure remained intact, and it 'reigned supreme from 1515 to 1758', when a more extensively revised edition, originally proposed to John Ward in 1732, was adopted as *The Eton Latin Grammar* (Padley, 25). However, this further renewed its influence, which extended into the nineteenth century and beyond. As Enkvist writes: 'As the categories of [Latin] were taken to be universals of lang[uage] and even thought, "Lily" was the formative influence on Englishmen's views of lang[uage]s, not least their own' (Enkvist, 577). The effect of Lily's grammar on English literature was equally great: Shakespeare's characters quote it verbatim, the dramatist John Lyly repeated lines from it, Ben Jonson adapted it, and Thomas Fuller complained of being beaten because of it, while in the nineteenth century George Borrow recorded being made to memorize it, Charles Lamb played with it, and Edgar Allan Poe mentioned Lily in his 'Rationale of verse'.

Padley even suggests that Lily's grammar may have been a lost opportunity for linguistics. Although he recognizes Lily's dependence on Donatus and Priscian for, among other things, the eight parts of speech and the five-way division into tenses, he continues:

> Lily's most interesting contribution to grammatical theory lies in his system of *signs*, with its structural implications. But the time was not ripe for the development of such a system, and the widespread use of his grammar ensured in fact the continuation of the more semantic elements of his approach to the end of the century and beyond. (Padley, 26)

This was a reference to the contrast between Latin and English, where in Latin an inflection is the sign of a case, while in English a preposition is used.

Lily himself was modest about his own contribution in that he claimed only to have made grammar 'a lytle more easy to yonge wyttes' (Flynn, 88). Be that as it may, Lily gave at least one piece of advice which does stand the test of time and remains as useful to the would-be translator or second-language learner as it was then: 'When I have an englysshe to be tourned into latin, I shall reherse it twyes or thryes and loke out the verbe' (Flynn, 90).

Death and burial Lily died in London, but sources vary as to the cause and date of his death. Most claim that he died of the plague, but it has also been said that he developed a boil or carbuncle on his hip which became inflamed, and was operated on against the advice of his friend Linacre, and that Lily died from complications. Given the obscurity surrounding the date itself, the second hypothesis would seem more plausible, especially as it does not wholly preclude the accuracy of the first. The exact month of his death is difficult to assess. He appears to have died by 10 December 1522, when a successor at St Paul's was appointed; however, a codicil was added to his will in late February 1523, and the memorial stone, placed by his son George, was dated 25 February, which suggests that he may have been alive in December but with little or no hope for his survival. Nevertheless, the probate date for his original will, 9 March 1523, provides a definite *terminus ante quem*.

Lily's first will (2 September 1522) made provision for his estate to pass to the eldest of his sister's children if his own children should 'fail to remain' (PRO, PROB 11/21, sig. 4*r*). He was a widower when he died, and only two of his children are known to have survived him. It has been suggested that Agnes and his other children died of the plague in 1517, but Lily's epitaph for his wife, who died on 11 August after seventeen years of marriage, gives neither cause nor year. The second will with codicil appended was granted probate on 21 May 1523. The codicil is itself a little curious, since it appears to halve to 20 marks the amount of money his elder daughter, Denyse, should receive if she remained unmarried and agreed to obey those who inherited the estate. Denyse, however, seems to have taken the point for she married Lily's successor at St Paul's, John Rightwise, and, after Rightwise's death, another surmaster of St Paul's, John Jacob. Lily was buried, as he requested, next to his wife, in Pardon churchyard, Poplar.

R. D. Smith

Sources W. Lily and J. Colet, *A shorte introduction of grammar* (1549); facs. edn, ed. R. C. Alston (1970) • *DNB* • W. Lily, J. Colet, and T. Robertson, *A shorte introduction of grammar* (1567); facs. edn, ed. V. J. Flynn (1945) • V. J. Flynn, 'The grammatical writings of William Lily, ?1468–?1523', *Papers of the Bibliographical Society of America*, 37 (1943), 85–113 • Emden, *Oxf.* • Wood, *Ath. Oxon.*, 2nd edn • N. E. Enkvist, 'William Lily', *Lexicon grammaticorum: who's who in the history of world linguistics*, ed. H. Stammerjohann (1996) • will, PRO, PROB 11/21, sigs. 4 and 8 • Fuller, *Worthies* (1662) • J. Hackett, *Select and remarkable epitaphs on illustrious and other persons in several parts of Europe*, 2 vols. (1757) • I. Michael, *English grammatical categories and the tradition to 1800* (1970) • G. A. Padley, *Grammatical theory in western Europe, 1500–1700: the Latin tradition* (1976) • T. Stapleton, *Tres Thomae, seu, Res gestae S. Thomae apostoli: S. Thomae archepiscopi Cantuariensis & martyris, Thomae Mori Anglice quondam cancellarii* (1588) • *The correspondence of Sir Thomas More*, ed. E. F. Rogers (1947) • E. Vorlat, *The development of English grammatical theory, 1586–1737* (1975) • A. P. R. Howatt, *A history of English language teaching* (1984) • BL, Lansdowne MS 979, fol. 32

Likenesses Edwards, engraving, 1510 (after lost portrait?) • line engraving, BM, NPG • stained-glass window (after Edwards)

Wealth at death 'londes'; money; clothing; books: will, PRO, PROB 11/21, sigs. 4 and 8

Limerick. For this title name *see* Dongan, Thomas, second earl of Limerick (1634–1715); Pery, Edmond Henry, first earl of Limerick (1758–1845); Pery, Angela Olivia, countess of Limerick (1897–1981).

Limner, Luke. *See* Leighton, John (1822–1912).

Limpus, Richard Davidge (1824–1875), organist, was born at Isleworth, Middlesex, on 10 September 1824, the son of Richard Limpus (*d.* 1868), organist of Isleworth Old Church. He studied at the Royal Academy of Music and became organist successively at Brentford, and at St Andrew Undershaft and St Michael, Cornhill, London. He was a highly educated musician, and composed some minor sacred and secular music. He became best known, however, as the founder, in 1864, of the College of Organists (which became the Royal College of Organists in 1893). This institution, of which he was secretary until his death, was established to provide a central organization for professional organists, together with a system of examinations and certificates of proficiency. It became perhaps the most influential body of British organists. Limpus died at his home, 41 Queen Square, Bloomsbury, on 15 March 1875, and was survived by his wife, Tabitha Ann.

J. C. Hadden, *rev.* Nilanjana Banerji

Sources Grove, *Dict. mus.* • Brown & Stratton, *Brit. mus.* • *MT*, 17 (1875–6), 52 • *CGPLA Eng. & Wales* (1875)

Wealth at death under £600: probate, 26 April 1875, *CGPLA Eng. & Wales*

Linacre, Thomas (*c.*1460–1524), humanist scholar and physician, is of unknown origins. Of his early life nothing definite is known although a connection with Kent and Canterbury is possible. He was in Oxford by 1481, but the earliest certain record of him is his election in 1484 to a fellowship at All Souls. In 1487 he left for Italy, probably in the company of William Sellyng, prior of Christ Church, Canterbury, and other envoys sent from Henry VII to Rome. Whether he reached Rome then is unclear, for he spent two years around 1489 in Florence studying Greek (which he had begun in Oxford) with Politian and Demetrius Chalcondylas. Certainly in November 1490 he was in Rome, and he was named a *custos* of the English Hospice there in May 1491. In 1492 or 1493 he left for Venice and for Padua, where he took a degree in medicine in 1496, although he still remained on the books of All Souls. While in northern Italy he became closely involved with Aldus and his circle, the *Neakadēmia* at Venice, a group of humanists keen to promote the study of Greek in all its aspects. Later assertions of friendships with Barbaro and Leoniceno, however, while possible, lack contemporary proof. It was as part of a collection of Greek astronomical writings published by Aldus that Linacre's first book appeared, a Latin translation of the *De sphaera* of Proclus (fifth century AD). While in Italy, Linacre purchased books and, in particular, Greek manuscripts which he brought back with him to England and from which he was to make the Galenic translations that gave him a European reputation.

By 27 August 1499 Linacre was back in London, and was soon given the charge of educating Prince Arthur; a generation later, about 1523, he also acted as tutor briefly to the future Queen Mary. He was also a leading member of the group of humanists that included John Colet (to whom he offered a Latin grammar for St Paul's School, and was turned down), Sir Thomas More (to whom he taught Greek), and William Grocyn (whose executor he became in 1520), and he was also a close friend of Erasmus. He published three works on Latin grammar, the *Progymnasmata grammatices vulgaria* (London, *c.*1515), *Rudimenta grammatices* (London, 1523?), both written in English, and *De emendata structura Latini sermonis* (London, 1524; 2nd edn, London, 1525?), a far more elaborate grammar in Latin for those already beyond the mere rudiments. None is entirely satisfactory. Although Linacre displays much learning there are several careless errors, and his close adherence to the precedents of the classical Latin grammarians and his scrupulous recording of ancient grammatical debates, although useful to the advanced student, were liable to confuse as much as to enlighten. But they did inform their audience as to the latest developments in new humanist Latin.

Royal physician It was not until 1509 that Linacre was appointed a royal physician, and five years later he accompanied Princess Mary as personal physician to Paris, where he met the French humanist Guillaume Budé. His royal services were rewarded by, among other things, presentation to a variety of ecclesiastical livings from at least 1509 onwards, including Mersham and Hawkhurst, Kent; Freshwater, Isle of Wight; Holsworthy, Devon; and Wigan, Lancashire, as well as prebends at St Stephen, Westminster, and York Minster, although he was not actually ordained until late in life, subdeacon in 1515, and deacon in 1520. His friendship with Erasmus might indicate some sympathy for the Dutchman's reforming views, but there is nothing to demonstrate any interest in either side of contemporary religious debates.

Translator of Galen Of Linacre's actual work as a physician little is known; he seems to have favoured his humanist friends Budé and Longolius with cramp-rings; his advice to the hypochondriac Erasmus is as much moral in content as medical, and that to William Lily, high master of St Paul's School, warning against an operation, may have proved all too accurate. His prime importance as a physician lies in his abilities as a translator of Galen from Greek into Latin. Apart from (unpublished) parts of Aristotle's *Meteorology*, small portions of the seventh-century Byzantine author Paul of Aegina, *De victus ratione* (Cologne, 1526), and *De crisi* and *De diebus criticis*, published along with some reprinted Galenica (Paris, 1528), Galen occupied his attention exclusively. Linacre translated the following works: *De sanitate tuenda* (Paris, 1517); *Methodus medendi* (Paris, 1519); *De temperamentis* and *De inaequali intemperie* (Cambridge, 1521); *De naturalibus facultatibus* (London, 1523); *De usu pulsuum* (London, 1523–4); *De symptomatum differentiis*, and *De symptomatum causis* (London, 1524).

Three points need stressing about this selection. With the exception of *Methodus medendi* none of these writings was available in print before 1525; Linacre thus worked from Greek manuscripts, probably in his own library, and he appears to have used a manuscript of the *Methodus medendi* as well as the printed text (Venice, 1500). Second, none of these works formed part of the standard university syllabus, and even when medieval Latin versions were available in print they were translations made from Arabic intermediaries, not from Greek. Third, this selection included some of Galen's largest and most important texts for the practical physician. *De sanitate tuenda* is a text on the preservation of health, the *Methodus medendi* Galen's major treatise on the principles and practice of therapeutics. *De naturalibus facultatibus* was a detailed investigation into the ruling principles of the human body. All of them, in Linacre's versions, challenged the orthodox interpretation of Galenic medicine by providing in effect new information on what the great Greek physician had believed. This fitted well with the views of other humanist physicians that medicine could be reformed by a return to a more accurate understanding of what the ancient physicians had written, unencumbered by Arabic or medieval error.

As translations from Greek into Latin they are almost impeccable. Linacre employs a wide vocabulary and understands well the nuances of the Greek. He avoids the literal word for word translation of medieval interpreters and provides instead an elegant humanist Latin. At times he emends his text, with the result that in the standard nineteenth-century edition of Galen, by C. G. Kühn (Leipzig, 1821–32), Linacre's Latin version of the *Methodus medendi* often represents Galen's words more accurately than the Greek text that is printed above it. These versions attracted the admiration of Linacre's fellow scholars around Europe; they were often reprinted, even into the nineteenth century, and they gave to the physician without Greek access to some of the most important medical texts from the past. No longer could the medical humanists be reproached for trumpeting the merits of the ancient Greeks without making it possible for those who knew only Latin to follow them, except at a very great distance.

Reformer of medical education In 1518 Linacre, along with five other physicians and Wolsey, successfully petitioned Henry VIII for the creation of a college of physicians in London which would be responsible for the inspection and control of all physicians within the city of London and the surrounding area, up to a 7 mile limit. This fulfilled a long held aspiration of the physicians; an earlier attempt in 1423 had lasted for a few years at most, and although the barbers and surgeons had their own companies, there was no such organization specifically for physicians. By contrast, in Italy medical practice was regularly controlled in all its aspects by local colleges of physicians, bringing together those who had graduated in medicine and often working together with the civil authorities to regulate all matters of health. The humanist physicians, especially those trained in Italy, like Linacre and many of the early members of the college, also believed that the new learning gave them added academic reasons for superiority; many medieval doctrines had been shown to rest on misinterpretations of classical antiquity. A new college could set new standards for physicians who, by virtue of their superiority to other healers, would bring about a general improvement in them too, and, perhaps, not only in London.

That, at least, was the theory. Linacre's college, however, whose statutes show links with both Italy and the new humanist inspired Corpus Christi College, Oxford, faced greater problems than a similar continental college. Its numbers were small; by Linacre's death, its original six members had increased to twelve, and numbered only eighteen in 1537. London was far more populous than most other cities, and there was an abundance of those offering healing services. The college also faced competition from those who wished to assert their own rights or those of others to heal; parliament, which ratified the charter in 1523 and gave it authority to govern medical practice throughout England, was notoriously loath to allow the physicians unfettered control, and barbers, barber-surgeons, and surgeons, to say nothing of the two universities, all had their own reasons for non-co-operation. Only rarely in the sixteenth century, in alliance with the royal authorities, did the College of Physicians succeed in achieving even a small percentage of Linacre's aims.

That Linacre was its leading light in its first years is clear. He was its first president; he was responsible for its first statutes, and its first meetings were held in his house, which he subsequently made over to the college for its meeting place and for its library. He recruited to it men like himself, with humanist ideals, and looked for it to have national authority. It was perhaps his successors who, by subtle modifications of the statutes, made it even more parochial, rigid, and authoritarian.

Linacre's humanist intentions were further manifest in a plan, already known in 1523, to establish lectureships in medicine at Oxford and Cambridge. A man of considerable wealth, obtained partly through a series of ecclesiastical appointments, Linacre spent the last few months of his life (he died on 20 October 1524 and was buried in St Paul's) acquiring and disposing of property, including the manor of Traces (for £216) and other smaller properties in Kent, and houses and land in London, including Frognal (costing £130) and his own house in Knightrider Street (for £46 13*s.* 4*d*). Most of this was to serve as the basis for his lectureships, which were to be established at Oxford and Cambridge as soon as his executors, including More and Cuthbert Tunstall, thought appropriate. Oxford was to have two, read by MAs at least, and devoted to the exposition of Galenic medicine, largely based on Linacre's own versions. The lectures were to provide a course of medical theory lasting from two and a half to three years. Responsibility for the lectures was in future to rest with the Mercers' Company, who already had control of that prime humanistic foundation, St Paul's School. Cambridge was to have one lecture, at St John's College, on the model of the senior of the two Oxford lectureships. In their content and plan these lectureships broke with the traditional syllabus of medicine; there was no reference to Arabic authorities and the choice of Galenic texts left out such standard fare as the *Ars medica*. While the lecturer was to explain the meaning of words, he was specifically forbidden to pursue logical questions, common in academic medical lectures.

In Cambridge the implementation of Linacre's plans followed quickly, and the first lecturer may well have been appointed within a year of his death. At Oxford there were many difficulties and delays. The Mercers refused to act, and negotiations involving Brasenose and All Souls in 1540 broke down. Not until December 1549 was Cuthbert Tunstall, by then the sole executor in England, able to conclude an agreement with Merton for the establishment of two lectureships, and not for another decade were lecturers appointed. The impact of their teaching was not as great as Linacre had hoped, in part because the medical humanism he had espoused was becoming outdated, but the holders of the lectureships at both universities were, for the first century at least, competent. But from the mid-seventeenth century onwards the posts came to be used to augment the revenues of college fellows, and it was no surprise when the Victorian reformers took exception to such a use. By the end of the century the lectureships and their revenue had been transformed, at Oxford into the Linacre professorship of comparative anatomy, and at Cambridge into a single annual lecture, given by a 'man of mark'.

The first Cambridge Linacre lecture, delivered in 1908 by William Osler on the theme of Thomas Linacre, established what came to be the image of Linacre as a humanist within medicine. Osler rightly drew attention to the affection felt for Linacre by his friends and associates and to the way in which he could be said to bridge the gap between arts and sciences. But such a formulation obscures the fact that, for Linacre, and for his fellow medical humanists, this reversion to classical precedent was at the same time the way forward within medicine, and was as progressive in 1515 as anatomy was to be in the 1540s.

Assessment The influence of Linacre on English medicine is hard to assess. Despite some vigorous efforts in the 1550s his London college did not secure for three centuries the pre-eminence within medicine that he had hoped for it, and it was more often viewed as a home of reaction rather than progress. While his lectureships may have helped to keep medicine as an active subject within the English universities, they too, after initial success, became seen as outmoded in what they were intended to do. None the less, Linacre did encourage the leading physicians of London for almost a century to follow his example of buying, editing, collating, and translating Greek books and manuscripts as a means of improving understanding of the traditional principles of medical practice. The first edition (Venice, 1525) of the collected works of Galen in Greek was owed in large part to his English followers, John Clement, Edward Wotton, and Thomas Lupset, and one can trace a Linacre tradition through scholars like John Caius and Theodore Goulston at least down to William Harvey, a doughty defender of the Galenism of the London College of Physicians.

Linacre may have had, like so many humanists, botanical interests, for Hakluyt in 1582 made the plausible, though far from proven, claim that he had introduced the damask rose into England. Of Linacre's own library, with its fine collection of Greek books and manuscripts, hardly more than twenty volumes remain, remarkably few of them in England. Some, like Eustratius' *Commentary on Aristotle's 'Ethics'* (Oxford, New College, 240–41, later owned by Cardinal Pole), may have been passed on to friends. John Clement, one of his executors, certainly had in his own library several volumes of medicine that were once Linacre's, and some details of them were taken down by John Caius around 1555. When Clement and the rest of Thomas More's household went into exile in Flanders under Elizabeth, some of Linacre's books and manuscripts went with them, only to be dispersed again after the sacking of Malines in 1572 and again in 1580. What remains shows the wide range of Linacre's interests in Greek philosophy, history, and medicine, as well as in patristic theology. It bears out the opinion of his contemporaries that Linacre was a scholar of the highest quality, to be ranked alongside Erasmus and Budé as one of the leaders of the Northern Renaissance.

Linacre House, Oxford, was established by the university in 1962. Its name was changed to Linacre College in 1965. It admits only graduate students, and has expanded notably since its foundation. VIVIAN NUTTON

Sources Munk, *Roll* • W. Osler, *Thomas Linacre* (1908) • R. Weiss, 'Notes on Thomas Linacre', *Miscellanea Giovanni Mercati* (1946) • G. Clark and A. M. Cooke, *A history of the Royal College of Physicians of London*, 1 (1964) • C. D. O'Malley, *English medical humanists: Thomas Linacre and John Caius* (1965) • F. Maddison, M. Pelling, and C. Webster, eds., *Essays on the life and works of Thomas Linacre, c.1460–1524* (1977) • C. Webster, ed., *Health, medicine and mortality in the sixteenth century* (1979) • I. Hutter, 'Cardinal Pole's Greek manuscripts in Oxford', *Manuscripts in Oxford: an exhibition in memory of Richard William Hunt (1908–1979)*, ed. A. C. de la Mare and B. C. Barker-Benfield (1980), 108–14 [exhibition catalogue, Bodl. Oxf.] • V. Nutton, *John Caius and the manuscripts of Galen* (1987) • *Oxford University Calendar* (1997)

Archives Bibliotheek der Rijksuniversiteit, Leiden • Merton Oxf. • St John Cam.

Likenesses oils, 1521–37, Royal Collection; copies, RCP Lond., All Souls Oxf. • oils, *c.*1535, NPG • drawing, *c.*1590, BM • etching, *c.*1700, Royal Collection, Raphael Collection • H. Cheere, bust, *c.*1749, All Souls Oxf. • H. Weekes, statue, 1876 • woodcut, repro. in *Galeni de sanitate tuenda libri sex*, trans. T. Linacre (Paris, 1517), title-page • woodcut, repro. in A. Clarmundus, *Vitae clarissimorum … virorum*, new edn, 4 vols. (Wittenberg, 1704–5)

Wealth at death over £250: Maddison, Pelling, and Webster, eds., *Essays*

Linche, Richard (*fl.* 1596–1601), poet and translator, was the author of two translations from Italian printed by Adam Islip in London in 1599 and 1601. An entry in the Stationers' register reports that Islip was fined for printing the first of the two, *The Fountain of Fiction*, before entering it into the register. *The Fountain* was dedicated to 'the right virtuous and well-disposed Gentleman, M. Peter Davison, Esquire' and *An Historical Treatise of the Travels of Noah* to 'the worshipful my very good friend Master Peter Manwood, Esquire'. Similarities in style and the unusual use of Italian tags and mottoes have led critics to identify the initials R. L. on the title-page of *Diella, Certain Sonnets* (1596) with Linche. The sonnet sequence was reprinted several times in the nineteenth century and was included in Sidney Lee's *An English Garner: Elizabethan Sonnets* (1904). An entry in the registers of St Vedast-alias-Foster, Foster Lane, and of St Michael-le-Querne, London, records the baptism of Thomas Lynche's son, Richard, on 4 October 1574. The significance of this entry, according to which Linche would probably have been twenty-two years old by the time he published *Diella* in 1596, is substantiated by the internal evidence provided by Sonnet 9, where the poet refers to his 'budding prime'. The only other contemporary reference to Linche, if it is to Linche, occurs in the dedication of Richard Barnfield's sonnet 'If music and sweet poetry agree' to his 'friend, Maister R. L.'. The identification of Barnfield's dedicatee with Linche was endorsed by A. B. Grosart in 1877. However, Grosart's argument rested on internal evidence and this identification cannot be definitively established. Although this identification remains hypothetical, an interesting piece of indirect but substantiating evidence can be found in a short note dated 1598 and addressed by Sir Robert Sidney to the earl of Essex. It reads as follows: 'Sir Robert Sydney … renews his suit on behalf of Lieutenant Linch for a company to be bestowed upon him' (*Salisbury MSS*, vol. 14, 176.26). There is reason to believe that Linche might be the lieutenant mentioned by Robert Sidney in this note. In his sonnet Barnfield claims that Spenser and Dowland shared a patron, a certain 'knight', whose identity remains unknown. If the unnamed knight in Barnfield's sonnet dedicated to R. L. is Sir Robert Sidney, the most likely candidate given his strong personal connection with Spenser and Dowland, it would be reasonable to assume that Richard Linche, poet and translator, and Lieutenant Linch are the same person. Although the identification of

Barnfield's 'R. L.' with Linche remains doubtful, it allows for intriguing and far from improbable conjectures about Linche's literary and social affiliations.

Sonia Massai

Sources *STC, 1475–1640* • D. Poulton, *John Dowland* (1972), 314 • *Calendar of the manuscripts of the most hon. the marquis of Salisbury*, 14, HMC, 9 (1923) • *Richard Barnfield: the complete poems*, ed. G. Klawitter (1990) • H. C. Morris, *Richard Barnfield, Colin's child* (1963) • E. Brydges, *Restituta, or, Titles, extracts, and characters of old books in English literature*, 4 vols. (1814–16) • J. Ritson, *Bibliographia poetica* (1802) • T. Warton, *The history of English poetry*, 4 vols. (1774–81) • Harleian Society, 24 (1902) [christenings]

Lincoln. For this title name *see* Roumare, William de, first earl of Lincoln (*c*.1096–1155x61); Gant, Gilbert de, earl of Lincoln (*c*.1123–1155/6); Ranulf (III), sixth earl of Chester and first earl of Lincoln (1170–1232); Lacy, John de, third earl of Lincoln (*c*.1192–1240); Lacy, Margaret de, countess of Lincoln (*d*. 1266); Lacy, Henry de, fifth earl of Lincoln (1249–1311); Thomas of Lancaster, second earl of Lancaster, second earl of Leicester, and earl of Lincoln (*c*.1278–1322); Lacy, Alice, *suo jure* countess of Lincoln, and countess of Lancaster and Leicester (1281–1348) [*see under* Thomas of Lancaster, second earl of Lancaster, second earl of Leicester, and earl of Lincoln (*c*.1278–1322)]; Pole, John de la, earl of Lincoln (*c*.1460–1487); Clinton, Edward Fiennes de, first earl of Lincoln (1512–1585); Clinton, Elizabeth Fiennes de, countess of Lincoln (1528?–1589); Clinton, Elizabeth, countess of Lincoln (1574?–1630?); Clinton, Henry Fiennes Pelham-, ninth earl of Lincoln and second duke of Newcastle under Lyme (1720–1794); Opdebeck, Lady Susan Harriet Catherine [Susan Harriet Catherine Pelham-Clinton, countess of Lincoln] (1814–1889).

Lincoln family (*per. c*.**1100**–*c*.**1280**), gentry, held extensive lands in Dorset and neighbouring counties in the twelfth and thirteenth centuries. The family may have been descended from **Alfred** [i] **of Lincoln** (*d*. in or before 1110). In 1086 this man, possibly of Breton origin, held land in Thoresway, Lincolnshire, and it was probably the same man who then claimed half a hide of land in Wymington, Bedfordshire. The first member of the Dorset branch of the family was **Alfred** [ii] **of Lincoln** (*d*. in or after 1130). He was also known as Alfred de Nichol, that name being an old French form of Lincoln. He seems to have been the second husband of a Domesday tenant, the widow of Hugh fitz Grip, a former sheriff of Dorset, and he acquired nearly all his wife's lands in the county; these lands were mostly located in the eastern hundreds of Dorset and included land held from Glastonbury Abbey. The feodary of the abbey includes a list of the lands, which in 1086 were held by the widow and then later by the Lincolns and included Duntish and 'Hermyngswell' in Buckland (Buckland Newton), Woodyates and Okeford Fitzpaine in Dorset, and Damerham in Hampshire. The Lincolns also held Colway, probably the manor of Lym, on the border of Devon and Dorset, and Sturminster Newton in Dorset from Glastonbury Abbey at a later date. It may have been Alfred [ii] who witnessed a charter of William II in 1091, and he served as a county justice in Dorset in the reign of Henry I. He witnessed over a dozen royal charters in the period *c*.1100–22 although he may not have been a member of the royal court. He was a patron of Montacute Priory in Somerset to which he gave 'Brigam' near Weymouth (part of his wife's estate in 1086). He was still living in 1130 when he paid 60 marks to have Pulham manor for his lifetime.

Alfred's son **Robert of Lincoln** (*d*. in or before 1156) presumably succeeded to all his father's estates. His possessions are recorded as including land at Worth Matravers, Langton (either Langton Herring or Langton Matravers), Cheselbourne, and probably Winterborne St Martin. Robert founded the Cluniac priory of Holme as a cell of Montacute Priory in the mid-twelfth century. His foundation grant included land at Holme which his father had bought from Grimbald the Physician before 1107. The endowment also comprised three virgates in Worth Matravers, the tithes of Langton (Herring) and Okeford Fitzpaine, and one tribute of salt from the salt-cotes at Langton (probably Langton Matravers). Robert was married to a certain Beuza and their son **Alfred** [iii] **of Lincoln** (*d*. 1198) confirmed his father's grant to Holme. In addition he also gave to the priory the church of Warmwell, a garden near Bradle, and land at Plush with the right to pasture 10 oxen, 1 heifer, and 250 sheep with the abbot of Glastonbury's cattle. Alfred [iii] was married to Albereda and is first mentioned in the early years of Henry II's reign. In 1166 he returned a *carta* which recorded that he held twenty-five fees of the old enfeoffment and four fees and eighty parts of fees of the new enfeoffment. Following the inquest of sheriffs in 1170 he was appointed sheriff of Dorset.

In the early thirteenth century Alfred [iii]'s son **Alfred** [iv] **of Lincoln** (*d*. 1240) was recorded as holding twenty-four and a half fees in Dorset and Somerset. These included lands at Langton (Herring or Matravers), Tatton, Lyme, and Buckland Newton. Alfred acted as a royal justice in Dorset in the 1220s and early 1230s, and in 1230 he was granted protection while he was overseas on the king's service. He married Maud and was succeeded by his son **Alfred** [v] **of Lincoln** (*d*. 1264), who was charged a relief of £100 in 1240. This Alfred was also active in the service of Henry III. In the mid-thirteenth century he was acting as a royal justice in Dorset and Wiltshire. He was commissioned with others to investigate the condition of royal castles in Somerset and Dorset, and also to inquire into 'excesses, trespasses and injuries' in Dorset. In 1242 he was granted protection while on the king's service overseas, and between 1258 and 1263 he was summoned to take part in several royal expeditions to Wales. Alfred [v] died without a male heir and his estates were divided between his sisters Beatrice de Gouiz (*d*. before 1278) and Aubreye of Lincoln (*d*. *c*.1277), and Robert Fitzpain (*d*. 1281), the son of his eldest sister, Margery (*d*. after 1245), who married Roger Fitzpain. Beatrice and her son William inherited four fees and one-fifth of a knight's fee in Dorset and land at Norton in Somerset; Aubrey's share included over three knights' fees in Dorset at Warmwell, 'Muleburn', 'Lollebrook', and 'Stafford'; Robert's share included livery of the manor and advowson of Winterbourne St

Martin, the manor of Langton (probably Langton Herring), and the manors and advowsons of Akeford and Duntish chapel. Alfred's widow, Joan, held almost six knights' fees in dower including land in 'Ringstead', 'Frome Wytefield', and Watercombe. She later married William de Molum, a king's yeoman, the marriage being his reward for service to Henry III and Queen Eleanor.

JOHN WALKER

Sources J. Hutchins, *The history and antiquities of the county of Dorset*, 3rd edn, ed. W. Shipp and J. W. Hodson, 4 vols. (1861–74) • *VCH Dorset*, vol. 2–3 • I. J. Sanders, *English baronies: a study of their origin and descent, 1086–1327* (1960) • *Two cartularies of the Augustinian priory of Bruton and the Cluniac priory of Montacute*, Somerset RS, 8 (1894) • F. M. Stenton, *The first century of English feudalism*, 2nd edn (1961) • *Reg. RAN*, vol. 2 • J. Morris, ed., *Domesday Book: a survey of the counties of England*, 38 vols. (1983–92), vol. 31 [Lincolnshire; in 2 pts] • J. Morris, ed., *Domesday Book: a survey of the counties of England*, 38 vols. (1983–92), vol. 7 [Dorset] • *CIPM*, vol. 1

Lincoln, Aaron of (*d.* 1186), financier, was the greatest Jewish moneylender in twelfth-century England. Of his life before 1165 nothing is known. He was probably born before 1130, and if so, the place of his birth was probably London, with which he also had close associations in the last twenty years of his life. But the centre of his business enterprises was clearly Lincoln, then the major city in the north and east of England.

A Jewish community was flourishing in Lincoln by 1159, when its existence is first recorded. A loan to Robert de Chesney, bishop of Lincoln from 1148 to 1166, could conceivably date Aaron's residence in the city somewhat earlier, in the 1140s; he was clearly well established there by 1165, when Henry II's repayment of a loan to him marks Aaron's first securely dated appearance in the records. Aaron lent modest sums to the crown over the next ten years, but took no part in the London-based consortia of Jewish moneylenders from whom the crown borrowed so heavily and disastrously in 1177. Loans to the crown never constituted a major part of Aaron's business, however, and after 1169 he ceased to be a primary crown lender, concentrating instead on building up his own vast financial network of agents and clients from his Lincoln base.

It was during Aaron's lifetime that Jewish moneylending developed in England on a large scale, an achievement to which Aaron's own extraordinary success must have contributed greatly. Credit systems in England were already highly sophisticated by the 1160s, as the surviving records of the Christian William Cade attest. Aaron's operations, however, were much more extensive than those of any previous lender, Christian or Jewish. By the 1180s his network of financial agents reached into almost every shire in England; his clients ranged from the king of Scots and the great religious houses to the local parish priests of Lincoln; and his business interests involved not only mortgages, but also the purchase and sale of discounted bonds, pawnbroking, property development, and commodity brokering. He was also instrumental in establishing a new Jewish community at York.

Upon Aaron's death in London, early in April 1186, the king confiscated his entire estate. Most of his treasure was lost in the channel on its way to the king in France, but his bonds were sent to the exchequer, where a special committee, known as the Scaccarium Aaronis, was charged with their collection. Five years later, when the remaining bonds were transferred to the regular exchequer rolls for collection, they amounted to £15,000 in face value, owed by more than 430 debtors. The total value of Aaron's estate on his death is unknown, but it may have amounted to as much as £100,000 in cash, treasure, and bonds.

Aaron had at least three sons, Elijah (Elias), Haim (Vives), and Isaac, and perhaps a fourth son, Abraham. His brother Baruch (Benedict), his sister's husband, Jacob, and their son, Baruch, also participated in Aaron's business dealings, as did his own sons. All continued to live in Lincoln after 1186 except perhaps Isaac, whose house in London was in the king's hands by 1213. None, however, approached the eminence of Aaron of Lincoln.

ROBERT C. STACEY, *rev.*

Sources J. Jacobs, 'Aaron of Lincoln', *Transactions of the Jewish Historical Society of England*, 3 (1896–8), 157–79 • J. W. F. Hill, *Medieval Lincoln* (1948) • H. G. Richardson, *The English Jewry under Angevin kings* (1960)

Wealth at death possibly £100,000: *Pipe rolls*

Lincoln, Alfred of (*d.* in or before **1110**). *See under* Lincoln family (*per. c.*1100–*c.*1280).

Lincoln, Alfred of (*d.* in or after **1130**). *See under* Lincoln family (*per. c.*1100–*c.*1280).

Lincoln, Alfred of (*d.* **1198**). *See under* Lincoln family (*per. c.*1100–*c.*1280).

Lincoln, Alfred of (*d.* **1240**). *See under* Lincoln family (*per. c.*1100–*c.*1280).

Lincoln, Alfred of (*d.* **1264**). *See under* Lincoln family (*per. c.*1100–*c.*1280).

Lincoln, Benjamin (1733–1810), revolutionary army officer and politician in America, was born on 29 January 1733 in Hingham, Massachusetts, the sixth of eight children of Colonel Benjamin Lincoln (1699–1771), farmer and maltster, and his wife, Elizabeth Thaxter, a widow. Although his father was moderately wealthy and a member of the governor's council, Lincoln was allowed to secure only a common school education in Hingham. In 1754 he was elected town constable of Hingham and a year later was appointed adjutant in his father's militia regiment, the 3rd regiment of Suffolk county. He was promoted major of the 3rd Suffolk in 1763 and lieutenant-colonel in 1772. On 15 January 1756 he married Mary Cushing (*b.* 1734); they had eleven children. Over the next twenty years Lincoln farmed in Hingham while holding the offices of clerk and justice of the peace. As political difficulties mounted between America and Britain in the 1770s, he was elected to a term in the legislature and membership on the Hingham committee of safety. In 1774 he attended the provincial congress, serving as secretary and on the committees of supplies and correspondence.

In April 1775, at the commencement of the American War of Independence, Lincoln marched with the 3rd Suffolk to the siege of Boston. He was promoted brigadier-general of Suffolk county militia on 30 January 1776 and in

Benjamin Lincoln (1733–1810), by Henry Sargent, 1806

September was appointed major-general of Massachusetts militia. He fought in the battle of White Plains on 28 October, winning the good opinion of General George Washington. He was promoted major-general in the continental army on 19 February 1777, and on 13 April at Bound Brook barely escaped capture when the enemy caught him by surprise in camp. In the summer he organized militia in Vermont to oppose the advance of General John Burgoyne into upstate New York. He commanded the American right wing in the battle of Bemis Heights on 7 October, and a day later was shot in his right ankle. After recuperating at home he rejoined Washington's army, and on 25 September 1778 was appointed commander of the southern department. In Charles Town, South Carolina, he organized his forces, then marched against the enemy in Georgia. Outmanoeuvred, he fell back to Charles Town, where he was captured with his entire army on 12 May 1780. He was exchanged in November 1780, and rejoined Washington's army in New York the following summer. In August 1781 he marched southward to Yorktown, Virginia, and on 19 October was allowed by Washington to receive the sword of surrender from Charles, Lord Cornwallis. On 31 October he was appointed secretary of war by congress. Having held this office until October 1783, he resigned and returned to Hingham, where he was elected president of the Massachusetts Society of the Cincinnati.

In the next few years Lincoln speculated in Maine lands and almost fell into financial ruin. In early 1787 he was given command of Massachusetts militia to suppress Shays's rebellion in the western part of the state. Having marched to Springfield, he defeated the insurgents in a battle on 27 January, then dealt moderately with the rebels in order to lure them into submission. He resigned his militia command on 10 June and later that year was elected lieutenant-governor of Massachusetts. In 1788 he was elected a member of the state convention to consider the new constitution. In 1789 he was appointed collector of the port of Boston, a well-paid position that helped him alleviate some of his financial difficulties. That year, and in 1793, he served on commissions to make peace with Creek Indians in the south, and north-west Indians in Ohio. As a member of the American Academy of Arts and Sciences and of the Massachusetts Historical Society, he also wrote a number of scientific papers on various topics. In 1809 he was compelled by his political foes to resign the office of collector. He died in Hingham on 9 May 1810, in the house of his birth, and was buried in the town on 11 May, probably at the First Congregational Church. His wife survived him. PAUL DAVID NELSON

Sources D. B. Mattern, *Benjamin Lincoln and the American Revolution* (1995) · C. K. Shipton, 'Benjamin Lincoln: Old Reliable', *George Washington's generals*, ed. G. A. Billias (1964) · J. C. Cavanagh, 'The military career of Major General Benjamin Lincoln in the war of the American Revolution, 1775–1781', PhD diss., Duke U., 1969 · J. C. Cavanagh, 'American military leadership in the southern campaign: Benjamin Lincoln', *The revolutionary war in the south: power, conflict and leadership*, ed. W. R. Higgins (1979) · P. D. Nelson, 'Lincoln, Benjamin', *ANB* · F. Bowen, 'Life of Benjamin Lincoln, major-general in the army of the revolution', *The library of American biography*, ed. J. Sparks, 23 (1847), 207–434 · *Boston Gazette* [Boston, MA] (10 May 1810)

Archives Boston PL · Mass. Hist. Soc. | L. Cong., Washington MSS · National Archives and Records Administration, Washington, DC, papers of the continental congress, nos. 149, 158

Likenesses C. W. Peale, oils, *c.*1781, Independence National Historical Park, Philadelphia · H. Sargent, oils, 1806, Mass. Hist. Soc. [*see illus.*] · J. R. Smith, oils, priv. coll.

Wealth at death land: Mattern, *Benjamin Lincoln*, 187–8

Lincoln, Hugh of. *See* Hugh of Lincoln (1140?–1200); Hugh of Lincoln (*c.*1246–1255).

Lincoln, Ignatius Timotheus Trebitsch [*formerly* Ignácz Trebitsch; *name in religion* Chao Kung] **(1879–1943)**, political adventurer, was born in Paks, Hungary, on 4 April 1879, the second son of Nathan Trebitsch (*d.* 1899), a merchant, and his wife, Julia, *née* Freund (*fl.* 1870–1920). He was educated in the Jewish elementary school in Paks and at a secondary school in Budapest. In 1895–6 he enrolled in the Royal Hungarian Academy of Dramatic Art but left Hungary before completing his course after being accused of stealing a gold watch. He travelled to England and Germany where he fell in with missionaries and, in 1899, was converted from his native Judaism to Christianity, being baptized Ignatius Timotheus Trebitsch. After studying at a Lutheran seminary at Breklum in Schleswig-Holstein, in 1900 he moved to Montreal where he worked as a missionary to the Jews, initially for the Presbyterian church, later for the Anglican Church of Canada. In July 1901 he married Margarethe Kahlor (*b. c.*1877, *d.* after 1948), daughter of a German sea captain, with whom he had four sons.

In 1903 Trebitsch returned to England and served briefly

as a curate in Appledore, Kent. After failing an examination for the priesthood in April 1904, and squandering his wife's inheritance, he was engaged early in 1906 by the philanthropist Benjamin Seebohm Rowntree as an assistant. He gathered sociological information for Rowntree's book *Land and Labour: Lessons from Belgium* (1911), which involved numerous visits to the continent. He quickly ingratiated himself with Rowntree who, being much impressed, deployed his influence in the Liberal Party to secure Trebitsch's nomination as candidate for the parliamentary seat of Darlington. Meanwhile Trebitsch took the surname Lincoln by deed poll on 11 October 1904 (and was known as Tribich Lincoln or I. T. T. Lincoln) and speedily secured British naturalization, on 5 May 1909. In the general election of January 1910 he campaigned on a platform of free trade and won an upset victory by a majority of twenty-nine votes. His first speech in the House of Commons, on 23 February 1910, earned him only ridicule, and his parliamentary career was short and undistinguished. In the election of December 1910 he was compelled to withdraw his candidacy, owing to financial difficulties. The following month he admitted to a creditors' meeting in York that he was insolvent.

With large subventions from Rowntree he nevertheless embarked on a business career, floating a series of public companies to exploit Galician and Romanian oil. He raised large sums on the London stock exchange to finance these enterprises. One after another, they collapsed and by the summer of 1914 he was down and out in London. Upon the outbreak of the First World War he offered his services as a double agent to the British naval intelligence bureau, headed by Captain Reginald Hall. Rejected by the British, he turned to the Germans who engaged him to send reports on shipping activity in British ports. In 1915, fearing arrest, he abandoned his family and fled to the USA where he published embroidered accounts of his exploits as an 'international spy'. He was arrested, escaped, was recaptured and, after failing in an appeal to the US supreme court, was extradited to Britain in 1916. Tried for fraud at the central criminal court in July 1916, he was found guilty and sentenced to three years in prison.

Released in August 1919, Lincoln was deported and his British naturalization rescinded. He quickly insinuated himself into German nationalist circles in Berlin, and in March 1920 served as 'director of foreign press affairs' in the short-lived militarist government of Wolfgang Kapp. After the collapse of the Kapp *Putsch* he fled to Munich and devoted the next two years to complex intrigues with right-wingers in Budapest, Prague, and Vienna. He was indicted for high treason in Vienna but the charge was dropped. Deported from Austria in 1921, he wandered to China, where he spent most of the rest of his life.

From 1923 to 1925 he acted as an arms dealer and political adviser to several warlords in northern China. In 1925 he converted to Buddhism, took the Chinese name Chao Kung, adopted oriental garb, shaved his head, and after six years of meditation and religious study was ordained a monk and raised to the rank of Bodhisattva. He established his own monastery in Shanghai to which he attracted a small flock of European Buddhist monks and nuns. During the Second World War he earned a meagre living as a low-level agent for Japanese and German intelligence agencies in Shanghai. He died at the general hospital in Shanghai on 6 October 1943, ostensibly as a result of a stomach ailment. Some evidence suggests that he was murdered by the Shanghai Gestapo. His wife, from whom he had separated in 1925, outlived him.

Endowed with considerable linguistic facility and personal magnetism, Lincoln was an unscrupulous confidence trickster who ruined the lives of many of those with whom he came into close contact. Subject to swift changes of mood, he exhibited symptoms of manic depression. He was the only person ever to have been formally adopted by a major British political party as a parliamentary candidate while still a Hungarian citizen; he was also the only former British MP ever to serve as a member of a German government. A shameless self-promoter, he wrote a readable but unreliable account of his early life, *Autobiography of an Adventurer* (1932), as well as several other books, mainly on Buddhist themes. He was buried in the Buddhist section of a municipal cemetery in Shanghai. BERNARD WASSERSTEIN

Sources B. Wasserstein, *The secret lives of Trebitsch Lincoln*, rev. edn (1989) [incl. bibliographical material]

Likenesses photograph, 1901, McGill University, Montreal, Canada, Notman Photo Archive • photograph, 1910, Darlington Public Library • photographs, 1915–38, US National Archives; repro. in Wasserstein, *The secret lives of Trebitsch Lincoln* • photograph, 1919, Hult. Arch.; repro. in Wasserstein, *The secret lives of Trebitsch Lincoln* • photograph, 1931, Prip-Møller Collection, Copenhagen, Denmark; repro. in Wasserstein, *The secret lives of Trebitsch Lincoln* • photograph, 1934, Pacific Press, Vancouver, Canada; repro. in Wasserstein, *The secret lives of Trebitsch Lincoln* • photograph, 1934, repro. in *Liverpool Post and Echo* (1934) • photograph, 1943, repro. in *Buddhist China*, 1/2 (winter 1943)

Wealth at death Buddhist habiliments and three trunks of books, papers, and press cuttings about himself

Lincoln, Robert of (*d.* in or before **1156**). *See under* Lincoln family (*per. c.*1100–*c.*1280).

Lincolnshire. For this title name *see* Carrington, Charles Robert Wynn-, marquess of Lincolnshire (1843–1928).

Lind, James (1716–1794), naval surgeon and physician, was born in Edinburgh on 4 October 1716, the son of James Lind, a merchant, and his wife, Margaret Smelholme (Smellum), a member of an Edinburgh medical family. (He is not to be confused with his cousin James Lind (1736–1812), also an Edinburgh-born naval surgeon, and later physician to the household of George III.) After attending grammar school in Edinburgh, in 1731 Lind was apprenticed to George Langlands, an Edinburgh surgeon. Lind is also recorded as having attended, in 1734, a course of anatomy lectures in the medical faculty of Edinburgh University given by Alexander Monro *primus*. With no formal qualification beyond his apprenticeship, Lind became a royal naval surgeon in 1738, serving until 1748. Most of his service was spent aboard ships in the English Channel during the War of the Austrian Succession (1740–48).

James Lind (1716–1794), by John Wright (after Sir George Chalmers, 1783)

These nine years at sea opened up for Lind the two areas of enquiry and concern that were to be his life's work, namely, the general welfare of seamen, and the nature and treatment of scurvy.

On leaving the navy Lind returned to Edinburgh, where, in 1748, he graduated MD from the university, with a thesis on venereal disease. His precise activities for the next ten years are unknown, but it is likely that he engaged in private medical practice in Edinburgh while participating in the professional medical life of the city. He was elected a fellow of the Royal College of Physicians of Edinburgh in 1750 and became its treasurer in 1756. He was also a member of the Philosophical and Medical Society of Edinburgh, and was elected a fellow of the Royal Society of Edinburgh in 1783. Lind's most notable work, *A Treatise of the Scurvy*, was published in Edinburgh in 1753. This was followed in 1757 by *An Essay on the Most Effectual Means of Preserving the Health of Seamen in the Royal Navy*. In 1758 he moved south to Gosport to take up the post of physician in charge at Haslar Royal Naval Hospital. Lind had dedicated *A Treatise of the Scurvy* to Lord Anson, first lord of the Admiralty, and it is believed that Anson helped obtain the position at Haslar for Lind. Lind held the post until 1783, when he was succeeded by his son John. While at Haslar, Lind published revised editions of both his *Treatise* and his *Essay*. He published a new work, *An Essay on Diseases Incidental to Europeans in Hot Climates*, in 1768, and papers on fevers.

Scurvy, the disorder tackled in Lind's first book, was a pressing matter for a nation whose maritime horizons were steadily expanding. The disorder regularly disabled ships' crews. The symptoms of scurvy had, for centuries, been widely recognized and carefully recorded. In the early stages of the disorder sufferers complain of stiff joints, loose teeth, and lassitude. In later stages, old wounds re-open and subcutaneous bleeding starts. Eventually, if conditions on board do not change, and the ship remains at sea, the sufferer dies. However, no clear consensus on a sure cure for the disorder had emerged, although several authorities, and many seamen, believed that fresh fruit and vegetables were potent remedies. A vivid demonstration of the ravages of what Lind was to call 'this foul and fatal mischief' (*Treatise of the Scurvy*, 85) was provided by the four-year voyage of a small squadron under Anson, between 1740 and 1744. From a complement of 1400 men, very nearly 1000 died from scurvy. It was against the backgrounds both of Anson's disastrous voyage, and of his own first-hand observations of the disorder, made during his years at sea as a naval surgeon, that Lind wrote his *Treatise of the Scurvy*.

The book opens with Lind's critical review of earlier writers on scurvy. This review establishes two features of the long-standing consensus concerning the nature of the disorder. First, diet seems to be a key feature both in the onset of, and recovery from, scurvy, and second, outbreaks seem often to be associated with cold and wet weather. Lind then goes on to set out his own theory of the disease. Scurvy is, he says, essentially a disease of faulty digestion and excretion. The digestive system, according to Lind, operates optimally when people live in generally warm and dry conditions, and eat a reasonably varied diet. Under such conditions, he asserts, the digestive system breaks down food into the small particles necessary for the renovation of the body, and, eventually, for excretion. The mode of excretion is important. Lind was impressed by the work of the Paduan physician Sanctorius, who had calculated that over half of the body's waste products are evacuated by what Lind calls 'insensible perspiration' through the pores of the skin. On this theory, if food is imperfectly digested, and cannot, as a consequence, be insensibly perspired, it is likely to acquire 'the most poisonous and noxious qualities, and a very high degree of putrefaction' (*Treatise of the Scurvy*, 203). Lind goes on to apply this theory to outbreaks of scurvy at sea. On long voyages, and especially when the weather is wet and close, the digestive system of an otherwise perfectly healthy seaman is hard-pressed to cope with the sea diet of unleavened bread and heavily salted meat. The stomach cannot break the sea diet down into small, digestible particles. At the same time, the pores of the skin are tending to close up in response to the poor weather, thus further jeopardizing healthy excretion by perspiration. The symptoms of scurvy then appear: the imperfectly digested, unexcretable food is starting to putrefy the body.

Lind then moves to his proposed cure. Broadly, he recommends the reversal of the conditions that produced the symptoms: a warm and dry atmosphere, coupled with a more readily digestible diet, must be provided. But plainly, such restorative conditions cannot be managed in a ship at sea, especially if it is on a naval blockade and is obliged to maintain its station for months at a time, in fair weather or foul. Medicines, rather than the re-establishment of a generally healthful environment, must then be prescribed by the ship's surgeon. It is in this context that Lind presents the results of what he called his 'experiments' with twelve scurvied seamen on HMS *Salisbury* conducted in May 1747, when he was in service as the ship's surgeon. Lind divided the twelve seamen into pairs, and prescribed for each pair a different potential remedy (1, cider; 2, elixir of vitriol; 3, vinegar; 4, sea water; 5, oranges and lemons; 6, a purge prepared from garlic, mustard seed, and other substances). The pair who were prescribed the oranges and lemons quickly recovered. The others did not. To the modern reader, these experiments seem conclusive. They are perfectly in line with modern knowledge both of the cause of the disease (vitamin C deficiency), and of the vitamin C richness of fresh oranges and lemons. But Lind had no conception of what would today be called vitamin deficiency, or of a single constituent, present in most fruit and green stuff, which is uniquely efficacious in the treatment of scurvy. His experiments, therefore, did not have the significance for him that they are likely to have for the modern reader. Lind gave the *Salisbury* experiments no decisive place in the *Treatise*: they take their modest place in a chapter which is devoted to a wide-ranging set of recommendations for the amelioration of shipboard life. The *Treatise* notably does not end with a ringing declaration to the Admiralty that seamen must regularly be issued with orange or lemon juice, even though the book, in common with most other books on seamen's health written during the eighteenth century, contained plenty of examples, along with the *Salisbury* experiments, of the efficacy of oranges and lemons in curing scurvy. But the *Treatise* as a whole did not deliver a single, clear, weighty recommendation.

In medical and naval circles, the potential force of Lind's work was further weakened by the extraordinary success of Captain James Cook, who, while ascribing no indispensable properties to oranges and lemons, and being unconcerned to provision his ships with them, managed to keep his crews free of scurvy during three celebrated circumnavigations of the globe between 1768 and 1780. Prevention of scurvy was easier for Cook than for captains of ships on station, for he had only small crews and could put into land whenever he needed to. Cook knew the curative potential of green stuff: he regularly foraged ashore for it whenever his ships were at anchor.

Lind's own practice, as physician at Haslar Hospital, indicates further that he did not regard his own *Salisbury* experiments as having been conclusive, for, while the range of treatments he prescribed to the thousands of patients who came under his care certainly did include oranges and lemons, these fruits were not seen by him as a routine, sovereign cure. In the third edition of the *Treatise* (1772), which recorded his experience at Haslar, he ruefully conceded that 'though a few partial facts and observations may, for a little, flatter our hopes of greater success, yet more enlarged experience must ever evince the fallacy of all positive assertions in the healing art' (*Treatise on the Scurvy*, v–vi). It was not until 1795 that the Admiralty was persuaded, by Gilbert Blane (who freely acknowledged Lind's pioneering work), to issue seamen with a regular ration of orange, lemon, or lime juice.

In his *Essay on the Most Effectual Means of Preserving the Health of Seamen in the Royal Navy* (1757, 3rd edn 1779), Lind argued for better hygiene on ships and for more humane, but efficient, treatment of seamen. Lind's tone is paternalistic. Ships should be regularly fumigated and ventilated. Seamen should be obliged to take baths. They should be issued with uniforms rather than having to clothe themselves. 'Such idle fellows as are picked from the streets or prisons' should not be included in ships' crews, for they bring contagious diseases and low morale on board with them (*Essay*, 28). Diet should be improved. Pickled vegetables and 'rob'—extract of—oranges and lemons should be carried. Shallots and garlic should be included in 'the surgeon's necessaries' (ibid., 34). Ships on station should be regularly supplied by small boats bearing fresh vegetables. The drinking of spirits, rather than beer, should be discouraged. Wholesome drinking water can be manufactured by distillation. Lind's book is highly practical and plainly written.

Lind's final book, his *Essay on Diseases Incidental to Europeans in Hot Climates* (1768), was conceived as a sequel to his book on the health of seamen. Having made recommendations for the improvement of the seaman's lot, he wanted to go further and 'draw the attention of all the commercial nations of Europe towards the important object of preserving the health of their countrymen, whose business carries them beyond seas' (*Essay on Diseases*, 8). In his habitual sober and painstaking way, Lind reviewed everything that had been written on the subject, and surveyed the tropics, port by port, discussing the diseases peculiar to each locality. He identified 'fevers' as the commonest and most dangerous hazards and attempted to classify them. He had no clear general theory as to the causes of fevers, but associated them, time and again, with hot, swampy conditions which give rise to pestilential vapours. Violent changes in temperature, hot dry winds (which, he thought, tend to close up the pores), and certain types of sandy soil are presented as further signs of an unhealthy country. Lind's recommendations are unsurprising: he suggests that settlements should be built as far away as possible from low-lying, swampy regions. Ideally, they should be on breezy headlands, cleared of undergrowth. The work of clearing woods, draining swamps, and carrying water to higher, healthier ground can, he suggests, be undertaken by slaves. The book can be seen chiefly as a set of environmental, public health recommendations, rather than as a series of specific cures for precisely identified tropical diseases. The book was translated into German, Dutch, and French, and an American edition appeared in 1811. There were also

French, Italian, and German editions of *A Treatise of the Scurvy* and a Dutch translation of the earlier *Essay*.

Lind seems to have had no taste for lobbying and politicking at the Admiralty or at metropolitan scientific and medical societies. This reticence, coupled with the unrhetorical, sometimes rather tentative nature of his writing, meant that he made no immediate and decisive impact on naval and medical practice. But his books were widely translated and quoted, and the regimes he established at Haslar, one of the largest hospitals in Europe, were respected. His influence on the health and welfare of seamen, though diffuse, is indisputable.

Lind died at Gosport on 18 July 1794 and was buried at St Mary's Church, Portchester, Hampshire, where a tablet was erected to his memory. The tablet also commemorates his wife, Isabel Dickie (*d.* 1797).

MICHAEL BARTHOLOMEW

Sources *Lind's treatise on scurvy*, ed. C. P. Stewart and D. Guthrie (1953) • R. Stockman, 'James Lind and scurvy', *Edinburgh Medical Journal*, 3rd ser., 33 (1926), 329–50 • K. J. Carpenter, *The history of scurvy and vitamin C* (1986) • J. J. Keevil, J. L. S. Coulter, and C. Lloyd, *Medicine and the navy, 1200–1900*, 3: *1714–1815* (1961) • *The health of seamen: selections from the works of Dr. James Lind, Sir Gilbert Blane and Dr. Thomas Trotter*, ed. C. Lloyd, Navy RS, 107 (1965) • *GM*, 1st ser., 64 (1794), 767 • W. S. Craig, *History of the Royal College of Physicians of Edinburgh* (1976) • V. L. Bullough, 'Lind, James', *DSB* • tablet, St Mary's Church, Portchester, Hampshire

Likenesses J. Wright, stipple (after G. Chalmers, 1783), Wellcome L. [*see illus.*]

Lind, James (**1736–1812**), physician, was born in Scotland, probably Edinburgh, on 17 May 1736, the son of William Lind and Ann Allan. He went out as surgeon in an East Indiaman in 1766 and visited China. In 1768 he graduated MD at Edinburgh, and his inaugural dissertation, on a fever in Bengal in 1762, was published at Edinburgh in 1768. In 1769 he observed the transit of Venus at Hawkhill, near Edinburgh, and sent an account of his observations to the Royal Society, in whose *Transactions* it is printed, with remarks by Nevil Maskelyne, the astronomer royal (*PTRS*, 59, 1769, 339–41). His account, in a letter to Maskelyne of 14 December 1769, of an observation of an eclipse of the moon made by him at Hawkhill, was also read before the Royal Society (ibid., 363–5). On 6 November 1770 Lind was admitted a fellow of the Royal College of Physicians of Edinburgh. Thomas Pennant was indebted to Lind for the true latitude of Islay, and for a beautiful map of the isle, from which he derived his measurements (*Tour to the Hebrides*, 1790, 262). Lind accompanied Joseph Banks on his voyage to Iceland, in 1772. He reported several astronomical observations to the Royal Society, London, and a paper by him was read there in 1775. He was elected a fellow of the Royal Society on 18 December 1777, and on 3 November 1783 was elected a fellow of the Royal Society of Edinburgh.

About the same time Lind apparently settled at Windsor, where he afterwards became physician-in-ordinary to the royal household. Whether he obtained much of a private practice is doubtful. 'With his taste for tricks, conundrums, and queer things', commented Fanny Burney, people were 'fearful of his trying experiments with their constitutions, and think him a better conjuror than physician'. In 1792 Joseph Banks recommended Lind as a useful member of Lord Macartney's embassy to the emperor of China. Banks said that Lind 'is a man accustomed to Obedience & well acquainted with the Station of an inferior' (Gascoigne, 38).

When the coffin of Edward IV was opened and examined at Windsor in 1789, Lind made an analysis of the liquid found in it. In 1795 he printed at his private press at Windsor *The genealogy of the families of Lind and the Montgomeries of Smithson, written by Sir Robert Douglas, baronet, author of the 'History of Scotland'*. Charles Knight mentions mysterious little books which Lind printed from characters which he called 'Lindian Ogham', cut by himself into strange fashions from battered printing types given to him by Knight's father.

Charles Burney described Lind as extremely thin—'a mere lath'; and in her *Diary* Fanny Burney refers to his collection of Eastern curiosities, and to his 'fat handsome wife', Ann Elizabeth Mealy, 'who is as tall as himself, and about six times as big'. Lind had married her at St Anne, Soho, London, on 7 November 1778. Lind's good nature was generally acknowledged. Shelley, when at Eton, became friends with Lind, of whom he said, 'I owe to that man far, ah! far more than I owe to my father; he loved me, and I shall never forget our long talks, where he breathed the spirit of the kindest tolerance, and the purest wisdom.' On one occasion Lind, according to Thomas Hogg, prevented Shelley from being consigned by his father to a private madhouse. Hogg's further statement that Lind was Shelley's 'Mentor in the art of execrating' his father and George III can probably be dismissed, since Lind was devotedly loyal to the king. He lives in Shelley's verse as the old hermit in 'The Revolt of Islam' and as Zonoras in the fragment 'Prince Athanase'. He died at the house of his son-in-law, William Burnie, in Russell Square, London, on 17 October 1812.

THOMPSON COOPER, *rev.* PATRICK WALLIS

Sources T. J. Hogg and others, *The life of Percy Bysshe Shelley*, 1 (1933) [introduction by H. Wolfe] • N. I. White, *Shelley*, [2nd edn], 2 vols. (1947) • *Diaries and letters of Madame D'Arblay*, ed. C. Barrett (1876) • C. Knight, *Passages of a working life during half a century*, 3 vols. (1864–5) • Nichols, *Illustrations* • Edinburgh University, *Doctors of medicine, 1705–1845* (1846) • *GM*, 1st ser., 82/2 (1812) • J. Gascoigne, *Joseph Banks and the English Enlightenment* (1994) • *IGI*

Archives NHM, botanical catalogues • University of British Columbia Library, Woodward Biomedical Library, corresp. | Birm. CA, corresp. with James Watt and Dr Alexander Wilson • BL, letters from T. Cavello and notes relating to lectures of William Cullen, Add. MSS 22897–22898; 71229, 71230 • FM Cam., letters to Joseph Banks • NRA, priv. coll., letters to Sir Joseph Banks

Likenesses engraved silhouettes, BM

Lind [*married name* Lind-Goldschmidt], **Jenny** [Johanna Maria] (**1820–1887**), singer, was born on 6 October 1820 at 40 Mästersamuelsgränd, Stockholm, the daughter of Niclas Jonas Lind (1798–1858), a bookkeeper, and Anne-Marie Fellborg (1793–1856), a schoolmistress. Her mother had divorced her first husband for infidelity but refused on religious grounds to remarry during his lifetime. Jenny's birth was not legitimized until she was fourteen,

Jenny Lind (1820–1887), by William Edward Kilburn, 1848

when her mother married Niclas Lind, the feckless father from whom she inherited her musical gifts. The happiest years of her impoverished childhood were spent with her grandmother in an almshouse for widows, where she would sit at the window overlooking the narrow Stockholm street, singing to her cat with a voice of amazing agility and heart-rending beauty. She was overheard by a lady's maid employed by Mademoiselle Lundberg, the principal dancer at the Royal Swedish Opera House, who persuaded the mother to allow Jenny to be taught singing. She was awarded a scholarship to the Royal Opera School, where she made her stage début in a dancing and singing role at the age of ten.

On 7 March 1838 Lind created a sensation as Agathe in *Der Freischütz*, and throughout her life she celebrated that date as the beginning of her phenomenal adult operatic career. She was equally successful in the full range of vocally taxing coloratura soprano roles, including Donna Anna, Euryanthe, Pamina, Lucia di Lammermoor, Norma, and Alice in Meyerbeer's *Robert le diable*. She was appointed court singer and made a member of the Royal Swedish Academy of Music, but by the time she was twenty her voice was seriously impaired through overwork and faulty technique. Her career was saved from extinction by a gruelling year's tuition in Paris with Manuel García. Initially he informed her: 'It would be useless to teach you, Mademoiselle. You no longer have a voice' (Holland and Rockstro, 1.110). His prescription was two months of complete silence, after which her abused vocal cords had recovered sufficient elasticity for him to commence rebuilding her technique. From García she also learned an iron discipline and perfect breath control.

Meyerbeer had originally wished to launch Lind in Paris at the Théâtre des Italiens, but she hated the artificiality and immorality of the French operatic world. 'What I, with my potato nose?' she is reputed to have said. 'No, it would never have done' (Bulman, 54). She lacked both the beauty and the sophistication of the conventional prima donna. Instead she returned to Stockholm to lead the Royal Opera for a further two seasons. She was also highly acclaimed in neighbouring Copenhagen, where she captivated Hans Christian Andersen with her sincerity and fine grey eyes. She inspired at least partly two of his best-known children's stories, *The Ugly Duckling* and *The Emperor's Nightingale*, but when she rejected him as a suitor she became the Snow Queen, whose heart was made of ice.

On 15 December 1844 Lind made her début in Berlin. Meyerbeer had written the principal role in *Ein Feldlager in Schlesien* (later refashioned as *L'étoile du nord*) for her to open the rebuilt Berlin opera house, but the première was awarded to an established German singer, Leopoldine Tuczek, though Lind sang the part several days later. She also sang in the first Vienna performance of the work (as *Vielka*) in 1847. The aria for soprano and two flutes in which Meyerbeer exploited the technical brilliance of Lind's coloratura and the precision of her trills remained one of the favourite showpieces of her repertory.

The year 1845 marked Lind's triumphant débuts in Hamburg, Hanover, Frankfurt, and Darmstadt; in August she was summoned by the king and queen of Prussia to sing for the visit of Queen Victoria and Prince Albert at Schloss Stolzenfels on the Rhine. She returned to Berlin for the winter season to entrance the public with her singing of Donna Anna, Agathe, Julia in *La vestale*, and Valentine in *Les Huguenots*. On 4 December 1845 she sang for the first time at the Gewandhaus in Leipzig under the baton of Felix Mendelssohn, who had become a close friend and musical mentor. Such was the demand for tickets that privileges normally enjoyed by Music Academy students were withdrawn, resulting in a student protest led by a red-headed youth from Hamburg, Otto Moritz David *Goldschmidt, later to become her husband. The following day Lind gave her services for a charity concert in aid of the Orchestra Widows' Fund. Her generosity in devoting substantial proceeds of her concerts towards the poor and the sick was to become a pattern in her career, which ensured her enduring popularity and fame among a far wider public than merely those who heard her sing. In April 1846 Lind appeared for the first time before a Viennese audience, as Norma at the Theater an der Wien; such was the public enthusiasm that she had to be rescued by a troop of mounted police from the crowds waiting for her to leave the theatre.

Lind's London début was delayed on account of contractual difficulties. She had made the mistake of signing contracts with two rival impresarios, promising first to sing for Alfred Bunn at Covent Garden and then preferring to appear under Benjamin Lumley's management at Her Majesty's Theatre. When she finally sang as Alice in

Roberto il diavolo on 7 May 1847, the Haymarket was packed from early afternoon with a solid line of carriages and the colonnade of the theatre thronged with society figures in full evening dress waiting for unreserved seats in the pit. The performance was the most overwhelming operatic success London had ever experienced. At its conclusion, the apogee of public appreciation was reached when Queen Victoria threw her bouquet down from the royal box to land on stage at Lind's feet. Enthusiasm for Jenny Lind increased to fever pitch when Lind sang two more of her favourite roles: Amina in *La sonnambula* and Marie in *La figlia del reggimento*. Her portrait was on snuff-boxes, matchboxes, and pocket handkerchiefs; there was Jenny Lind soap, Jenny Lind scent, and Jenny Lind candle snuffers in the shape of the singer's body topped with the head of a nightingale. The duke of Wellington sat in a stage box for all her performances, and on three occasions the House of Commons had no quorum to vote as so many members had gone to hear 'the Swedish Nightingale', as she was known.

Lumley had rashly promised to crown the season with an opera specially composed by Mendelssohn: *The Tempest* with Lind as Miranda and the bass Lablache as Prospero, but the composer was too exhausted and overburdened to fulfil the project. Instead Lumley secured the première of Verdi's *I masnadieri*, based on Schiller's drama *Die Räuber*. The role of Amalia was written for Lind but failed to exploit the full scope of her voice. Verdi travelled to London to supervise rehearsals and conduct the first two performances. The heroine was rapturously received, but the opera soon fell into neglect.

In February 1848 the suit of *Bunn* v. *Lind* was heard in the Queen's Bench Division. Lind's plea of not being able to learn English in time to fulfil her contract was dismissed and damages of £2500 were awarded to the plaintiff. Lumley assumed full financial responsibility, but the moral stain, singularly bitter for someone of Lind's high moral principles, remained hers alone. Lumley persuaded her to return to London for a second operatic season, which was to prove even more successful than the first. She confided in Queen Victoria that it would be her last: although she was only twenty-seven, she was increasingly physically and emotionally exhausted from the intensity of her performances. As she became more deeply religious, she found the artificiality of the operatic world ever more distasteful and wished to dedicate what she saw as her God-given musical gifts to singing sacred oratorios and raising money for worthy causes. She had been encouraged in these aims by her friendship with Edward Stanley, the bishop of Norwich, and his family. Lind had been devastated by the premature death of Mendelssohn in November 1847 and waited more than a year before she felt able to sing for the first time the soprano part in *Elijah*, which he had written specially for her. The performance in the Exeter Hall raised £1000 to fund a Mendelssohn scholarship, the first holder of which was Arthur Sullivan.

After a third triumphant London season ending as she had begun with Alice in *Roberto il diavolo*, Lind accepted a contract with the American impresario Phineas Barnum for 150 concerts in America and Cuba. He promised these would earn her enough money to provide for the rest of her days and for all her charitable concerns; 30,000 people lined the streets of New York to welcome her arrival, the first great European singer to be heard there in her prime. After ninety-three concerts she decided to dispense with the self-styled 'Greatest Showman on Earth' and complete the tour under her own management. When her music director, Julius Benedict, had to return to London, she invited the young Otto Goldschmidt (1829–1907), Mendelssohn's pupil and the son of a wealthy Jewish banking family in Hamburg, to travel to America as her accompanist. On 5 February 1852 they married quietly in Boston, shortly after Goldschmidt had been baptized an Episcopalian. On their return to Europe they settled in Dresden, and despite all blandishments Lind refused to return to the operatic stage. Although only in her early thirties, she appeared middle-aged; her voice had already lost its bloom, as the excessive strain of the earlier years had taken its toll, and the top notes no longer had their brilliance and freedom. However, she still excelled all other singers in her spiritual qualities, which evoked a unique emotional response in the hearts of her listeners.

When Lady Westmorland heard that Jenny Lind-Goldschmidt had lost her voice, she retorted: 'If she has still got her soul, she is better worth hearing than all the other singers in the world' (Bulman, 291). When in Handel's *Messiah* she sang 'I know that my redeemer liveth', the emphasis she placed on the second word was a radiant testimony of her religious faith. She continued to raise enormous sums of money by singing without fee for the benefit of hospitals throughout Great Britain, including £1872 to help Florence Nightingale's Nursing Fund at the end of the Crimean War.

In 1858 the Goldschmidts decided to make their permanent home in England, where they enjoyed a tranquil family life in Surrey with their two sons, Walter Otto and Ernest, and their daughter, Jenny, first in Roehampton and then in Wimbledon. On Otto's appointment as professor of piano and vice-principal of the Royal Academy of Music under their friend Sir William Sterndale Bennett, the Goldschmidts moved to 1 Moreton Gardens, South Kensington. When Otto formed the amateur Bach Choir, Jenny coached the sopranos in their drawing-room for the first English performance of Bach's B minor mass, on 26 April 1876 in St James's Hall. The last significant event of Jenny Lind-Goldsmidt's professional life was her appointment by the prince of Wales as the first professor of singing at the newly founded Royal College of Music in 1883. Her pupils included Liza Lehmann and Amanda Aldridge, the daughter of the American actor Ira Aldridge, known as the Black Othello. Her final public appearance was at a concert given for the Railway Servants' Benevolent Fund, at the Spa Hall, Malvern Hills, in 1883. She and her husband spent their last years together there at Wynd's Point, where she died of an inoperable cancer on 2 November 1887. Otto Goldschmidt lived until 1907; they were buried together under a simple stone of Swedish granite in Great Malvern cemetery, Worcestershire.

Jenny Lind is honoured in Poets' Corner, Westminster Abbey, with a plaque placed under the statue of Handel. Round her head are the words inextricably associated with her legendary purity of voice, generosity of spirit, and unwavering religious conviction: 'I know that my redeemer liveth'. Perhaps the best summation of her life and career was given by Oskar II to the Musical Academy of Stockholm: 'She was like a meteor, blazing its trail above the heads of a wondering world' (Bulman, 318).

CAROLE ROSEN

Sources H. S. Holland and W. S. Rockstro, *Memoir of Madame Jenny Lind-Goldschmidt*, 2 vols. (1891) • J. Bulman, *Jenny Lind* (1956) • Grove, *Dict. mus.* • J. M. C. Maude, *The life of Jenny Lind* (1926)
Archives Royal Library, Stockholm • University of the South, Sewanee, Tennessee • Westervelt and Hildebrand Collection, New York | BL, letters, MS VI.1985 [index] • CKS, letters
Likenesses E. Magnus, oils, 1846, Staatliche Museen zu Berlin; replica, NPG • Count D'Orsay, oils, 1847, NPG • W. E. Kilburn, daguerreotype, 1848, Royal Collection [*see illus.*] • E. Bieber, carte-de-visite, NPG • D. Maclise, drawing, V&A • H. Murray, photograph (with her husband), NPG • K. Radinitsky, medal, Barcelona Museum, Spain • daguerreotype, Royal Collection • prints, BM, Harvard TC, NPG • prints, NPG
Wealth at death £40,630 13*s.* 8*d.*: probate, 9 Feb 1888, *CGPLA Eng. & Wales*

Lind, John (1737–1781), political writer, was born on 13 August 1737, the only son of Charles Lind (*d.* 1771), vicar of West Mersea and rector of Wivenhoe and Paglesham, Essex, and his wife, *née* Porter, originally from Winchester. Lind's father died on 6 March 1771, leaving his livings sequestrated and his family penniless; two of John's sisters, Mary and Laetitia, attempted to keep themselves by means of a boarding-school for girls at Colchester. John matriculated on 22 May 1753 at Balliol College, Oxford, graduating BA (1757) and MA (1761).

About 1758 Lind took deacon's orders in the Church of England, and a few years later accompanied John Murray on his embassy to Constantinople in the capacity of chaplain, but 'being too agreeable to his Excellency's mistress' (Bowring, 10.247) was dismissed from his post. Lind then travelled to Warsaw, where he dropped his clerical title and became tutor to Prince Stanislaus Poniatowski. He was soon noticed by King Stanislaus, who promoted him to be governor of an institution for educating 400 cadets, and gave him the title of privy councillor.

In 1773 Lind, accompanied by his illegitimate daughter, returned to England with a pension from the king but remained financially constrained by his need to repay his father's debt and by his sisters' hardship. He added to his income by reading to Prince Czartoriski, the king's uncle, and continued to send news to the king almost daily until his death. At this time he was well received by the prime minister, Lord North, and was a familiar figure at the card parties of Henrietta Maria North, wife of Brownlow North, bishop of Winchester. Through the king of Poland, Lind also gained an introduction to Lord Mansfield, who employed him to promote his political views, and through whose management he was admitted at Lincoln's Inn on 23 June 1773, and called to the bar in 1776. Already a fellow of the Society of Arts, in 1773 he was elected FRS.

Lind's style of writing was much praised by Lord Grenville, Bishop Lowth, and Samuel Parr, but through 'a want of accuracy' did not satisfy his close friend Jeremy Bentham. His first and most famous publication was the anonymous *Letters Concerning the Present State of Poland* (1773), in which he condemned the injustice of the partition of that country. Of his other works his *Remarks on the Principal Acts of the Thirteenth Parliament of Great Britain*, which justified the American War of Independence, was probably the best known, and is said to have resulted in his two sisters receiving a pension of £50 p.a.

Lind died in Lamb's Conduit Street, London, on 12 January 1781 and was buried in the churchyard of Long Ditton, Surrey. A pension was paid thereafter to his widow, of whom no details are known, other than that the couple were married in London at St Andrew's, Holborn. Difficulties over the provision of the pension in 1794 were solved by the intervention of Bentham, who entered into a long correspondence with the tsar of Russia on the subject.

W. P. COURTNEY, *rev.* M. E. CLAYTON

Sources J. Bowring, 'Memoirs of Jeremy Bentham', in *The works of Jeremy Bentham*, ed. J. Bowring, [new edn], 1 (1843) • C. M. Atkinson, *Jeremy Bentham: his life and work* (1905) • Walpole, *Corr.* • O. Manning and W. Bray, *The history and antiquities of the county of Surrey*, 3 (1814) • Foster, *Alum. Oxon.* • *GM*, 1st ser., 41 (1771), 143 • *GM*, 1st ser., 51 (1781), 47, 72, 162–3 • *IGI*

Lind-af-Hageby, (Emilie Augusta) Louise (1878–1963), animal welfare campaigner, was born in Sweden on 20 September 1878, the daughter of Emil Lind-af-Hageby, a lawyer, and granddaughter of a chamberlain to the king of Sweden. She attended Cheltenham Ladies' College for a short period from 1896 and made her main home in England from 1902 until her death, becoming a British citizen in 1912.

In 1900 Lind-af-Hageby went to Paris with her friend Liesa Schartau; a visit to the Pasteur Institute there allegedly led directly to her crusade against animal experimentation. She succeeded Frances Power Cobbe (1822–1904) as doyenne of the British anti-vivisectionist movement. Like Cobbe, she used vigorous journalism and public speaking to pursue her campaigns, especially under the auspices of the Animals Defence and Anti-Vivisection Society (later the Animal Defence Society) which she founded in 1906, and as founder-owner, editor, and main columnist of the *Anti-Vivisection Review* for forty years from its establishment in 1909. In her voluminous writings and many speeches she, like Cobbe, linked the case for opposition to animal experiments to the cause of animals generally, to opposition to authoritarian public health, and, especially, before 1914, to the cause of women's emancipation.

Lind-af-Hageby's public career as an anti-vivisectionist in England began in 1903 with the publication, with Liesa Schartau, of *The Shambles of Science*. This purported to be an eye-witness account by the two young women of their experience in physiology classes which they had attended in 1902–3 while enrolled as visiting students at the London School of Medicine for Women. Their claims to have witnessed a conscious dog at a demonstration in University

College, London, were widely publicized by Stephen Coleridge (1854–1936), secretary of the National Anti-Vivisection Society. When Coleridge was successfully sued for libel by Professor W. M. Bayliss (1860–1924), the physiologist leading the demonstration, Lind-af-Hageby was a key witness for the defence at the much publicized trial. Afterwards, a chapter entitled 'Fun', depicting the jocularity with which students and teachers allegedly regarded a conscious dog's suffering, was withdrawn from subsequent editions of *The Shambles of Science*.

The allegations made in Louise Lind-af-Hageby's book and at the trial were central concerns of the second royal commission on vivisection (1906–12), to which she gave extensive evidence. In 1906 anti-vivisectionists erected a statue of the Brown Dog in Battersea, which became a focus of contention between anti-vivisectionists and medical students and among local residents and politicians until it was removed in 1910. Lind-af-Hageby's regular public speaking and writing in favour of both the Brown Dog and women's suffrage during this period reinforced the association between anti-vivisection and the cause of women. She attacked animal experimentation as morally and scientifically wrong, urging the development of an alternative 'science of anti-vivisection' with which to criticize an erroneous biological method (*Anti-Vivisection Review*, 1, 1909, 23) She attributed growing support for the cause of animals and the enfranchisement of women to 'a general undercurrent of rising humanity', and saw these as stepping stones towards a new humanitarian morality 'which consciously or unconsciously is coveted in all efforts to help the down-trodden and suffering' (ibid., 91).

Lind-af-Hageby was the main instigator of the first of two international anti-vivisectionist congresses held in London in July 1909. Her congress promoted gradualist tactics as the best means of ending animal experimentation whereas the other brought together those unwilling to contemplate compromise. In 1913 she was a central figure in another much publicized libel case, this time as unsuccessful plaintiff against Dr C. W. Saleeby (1878–1940), a prominent eugenicist and temperance campaigner who, she alleged, had accused her of being 'a systematic liar' in her campaign against vivisection.

In the First World War, Louise Lind-af-Hageby founded the Purple Cross Service, authorized by the French war office, for sick and wounded warhorses. She continued to promote the welfare of animals affected by war during the 1920s, 1930s, and the Second World War, leading an animal protection deputation to the disarmament conference of the League of Nations in Geneva in 1932. Although public support for the anti-vivisectionist cause declined after the end of the war, her own implacable opposition to scientific use of animals continued, often in close association with her great friend Nina, duchess of Hamilton (1878–1951), in whose memory she established the Ferne Animal Sanctuary in Dorset in 1954. She died at her home, 7 St Edmunds Terrace, Regent's Park, London, on 26 December 1963. M. A. Elston

Sources E. A. L. Lind-af-Hageby and E. L. Schartau, *The shambles of science: extracts from the diary of two students of physiology* (1903) • E. Douglas-Hume, *The mind-changers* (1939) • E. Westacott, *A century of vivisection and anti-vivisection* (1949) • J. Vyvyan, *The dark face of science* (1971) • *The Anti-Vivisection Review* (1909–20) • C. Lansbury, *The Old Brown Dog: women, workers and vivisection in Victorian England* (1985) • *WWW* • *CGPLA Eng. & Wales* (1964) • d. cert.

Archives Wellcome L., Research Defence Society MSS

Likenesses photograph (after portrait), repro. in Vyvyan, *The dark face of science*

Wealth at death £91,739: administration with will, 6 May 1964, *CGPLA Eng. & Wales*

Lindehleim, Joanna Maria [*performing name* the Baroness] (*d.* **1724**), singer, was the 'Italian Gentlewoman that was never heard in this Kingdom before' (*LondG*, 2 Nov 1702) who sang at York Buildings on 3 November 1702 and again on 3 December. Charles Burney believed that she was a German who had learned to sing in Italy. On 20 January 1703 the *Daily Courant* advertised her as 'Signiora Joanna Maria Lindehleim', but the surname was omitted in later announcements. The spelling Johanna Maria Lindelheim was a conjecture by Alfred Loewenberg in the 1954 edition of *Grove's Dictionary*. She may have been a relative of the Locker von Lindenheim family, who were ennobled in 1705, about the time that she began to use the style Baroness, but this is unverified. She sang in Italian and French at Drury Lane in January and February 1703, accompanied by Gasparo Visconti, who had performed with her at York Buildings. John Evelyn wrote in his diary for 28 February 1703 that she had sung with modesty, grace, and skill and left for the Prussian court with 'above 1000 pounds, every body coveting to heare her at their privat houses, especialy the noble men' (Evelyn, 5.531).

Signora Joanna Maria returned to England to sing in the Italian pastoral *Gli amori di Ergasto* at the opening of Vanbrugh's new theatre in the Haymarket in April 1705. The cellist and composer Nicola Francesco *Haym (1678–1729) became her teacher and manager and she was to live with him for the rest of her life. He arranged her contract of 100 guineas for ten performances and handled negotiations when the pastoral flopped and the management prevaricated over fulfilling the terms of the agreement. On 30 March 1706 she sang the second soprano role of Lavinia in the première of *Camilla* at Drury Lane, with Catherine Tofts in the title role. Haym had adapted the music for this extremely successful English version of Giovanni Bononcini's opera. She was referred to as 'the Barroness' in the published songs from *Camilla* (April 1706), and from this time seems to have used no other name. She sang in the pasticcio opera *Love's Triumph* in February and March 1708 and that April took over the title role in another pasticcio, *Thomyris*, newly revised by Haym. From March 1707, when the castrato Valentini sang in *Camilla*, operas in London became dual-language affairs and the Baroness sang in Italian in her scenes with Italian singers. However, her operatic career was in decline and in spring 1708 she was being paid £3 a performance when Valentini, Mrs Tofts, and Margherita de l'Epine were each receiving £7 10*s*. In December 1708 she created Deidamia in *Pyrrhus and Demetrius*, adapted by Haym from Alessandro Scarlatti's opera, and her last stage appearance was as Deidamia on 12 May

1711. Her benefit concerts at Hickford's Room were advertised each year from 1713 to 1717. She also taught singing; Anastasia Robinson was one of her pupils.

The Baroness was ill during much of 1724, when an Italian doctor, Antonio Cocchi, recorded visits to the 'Baronessa d'Haym' in his diary. Cocchi gave Latin lessons to 'Giovannino dell'Haym' or 'Jack d'Haym' (Lindgren, 282–3), who was perhaps her son with Haym. She was buried at St Anne's, Soho, on 20 December 1724, as 'The Right Hon[ble] Mary, Baroness of Linchenham'.

OLIVE BALDWIN and THELMA WILSON

Sources L. Lindgren, 'The accomplishments of the learned and ingenious Nicola Francesco Haym', *Studi Musicale*, 16 (1987), 247–380 • E. L. Avery, ed., *The London stage, 1660–1800*, pt 2: *1700–1729* (1960) • *Daily Courant* (20 Jan 1703) • *Daily Courant* (21 Jan 1703) • *Daily Courant* (29 Jan 1703) • *Daily Courant* (17 Nov 1705) • *Daily Courant* (6 Dec 1707) • *LondG* (2–5 Nov 1702) • J. Milhous and R. D. Hume, eds., *Vice Chamberlain Coke's theatrical papers, 1706–1715* (1982) • Evelyn, *Diary*, vol. 5 • Burney, *Hist. mus.*, vol. 4 • J. Hawkins, *A general history of the science and practice of music*, 5 (1776) • J. Milhous and R. D. Hume, eds., *A register of English theatrical documents, 1660–1737*, 1 (1991) • D. Hunter, *Opera and song books published in England, 1703–1726* (1997) • parish register, Soho, St Anne [burial] • Grove, *Dict. mus.* (1954)

Likenesses M. Ricci, group portrait, oils (*The rehearsal of an opera*), repro. in Lindgren, 'Accomplishments'

Lindemann, Frederick Alexander, Viscount Cherwell (**1886–1957**), scientist and politician, was born on 5 April 1886 at Baden-Baden, where his mother was taking the cure. He resented all his life the accident of his birthplace being in Germany. He was the second of three sons of Adolphus Frederick Lindemann (1846–1927), whose family was of Catholic (not, as was often stated, Jewish) French Alsatian origin, and his wife, Olga Noble, American daughter of a successful British-born engineer and widow of a rich banker called Davidson. She was a protestant and insisted on her four children being brought up as Anglicans. Lindemann's father, born in 1846, emigrated to Britain in his twenties and later became naturalized. He was a wealthy man, and his and his wife's combined income was about £20,000 a year. He was also a scientist and astronomer of distinction, and built a private laboratory at his home near Sidmouth.

Early life Lindemann and his elder brother, Charles, were educated at Blair Lodge, Polmont, in Scotland, a school now extinct, and from 1902 first at the *Realgymnasium* then the *Hochschule* in Darmstadt. They both distinguished themselves sufficiently in science to be accepted as PhD students by Professor Nernst, the celebrated head of the Physikalisch-Chemisches Institut in Berlin. Lindemann gained his doctorate, although oddly not with the highest honours, in 1910. He must have been an unusual student. His comfortable allowance of £600 a year enabled him to live in the luxury of the Adlon Hotel. Somewhat incongruously he was a vegetarian—a temporary fad of his mother having left a permanent influence on him. Moreover, all his life he neither smoked nor drank alcohol except upon the rare occasions when, at Winston Churchill's insistence, he would take a carefully measured glass of brandy. He was fond of music and an excellent pianist, but he was indifferent to the visual arts, and to the end of his days had a 'lowbrow' taste in literature. Lindemann and his elder brother were first-class tennis players, and won many prizes. Later Lindemann achieved the probably unique distinction of competing at Wimbledon after he had become a professor. Lindemann had a playboy younger brother nicknamed Seppi. He lived in Paris and owned two Rolls-Royces—a white one with a black chauffeur, and a second with the colours reversed. Lindemann did not approve.

Frederick Alexander Lindemann, Viscount Cherwell (1886–1957), by unknown photographer

Lindemann was playing tennis in Germany just before war broke out in 1914, but left in time to avoid being interned. In March 1915, after vainly seeking a commission, he joined the Royal Aircraft Factory at Farnborough, the chief centre of experimental aviation in England. His most notable contribution was his solution to the problem of 'spin' in aircraft. According to official records he learned to fly in the autumn of 1916, invariably—to the surprise of his colleagues—appearing at the station with the bowler hat, black Melton coat, and furled umbrella which were to be his characteristic uniform all his life. During June and July 1917 he tested empirically the theory that he had worked out to explain the nature of a spin and the way to get out of it. He was not the first person to extricate himself from a spin, but he was the first to establish the correct scientific principle—an achievement which not only entailed great courage, but the remarkable power of memorizing in nerve-wracking conditions no fewer than eight different sets of simultaneous instrument readings. The theory has been advanced that he performed this feat in June or July of the previous year, but the weight of the evidence is against it.

In 1919, thanks partly to Henry Tizard, who was a colleague of his Berlin days, Lindemann was elected Dr Lee's professor of experimental philosophy (that is, physics) in the University of Oxford. The chair was attached to Wadham College, where he remained a fellow until his retirement. But in 1921 Lindemann was also elected, as was legally possible in those days, to a 'studentship not on the governing body' at Christ Church, which had provided the endowment for the chair. This entitled him to rooms more spacious than Wadham could provide, and from 1922 for the rest of his life he lived in Christ Church.

Scientific career Lindemann's most important personal contributions to physics were made between 1910 and 1924. His first papers under Nernst's influence were concerned with low-temperature physics, and his doctoral thesis on the law of Dulong and Petit was a criticism of Einstein's formula for explaining the startling decrease in the specific heat of diamond at the temperature of liquid hydrogen. He and Nernst devised a formula which gave a better explanation, but it was later caught up and replaced by the Debye formula, the superiority of which Lindemann at once recognized. At the same time he was working on the connection between the characteristic frequency and the melting-point of a solid, and produced a theory relating melting to the amplitude of oscillation of atoms. He was exceedingly versatile while in Berlin. He invented, along with his brother Charles, a glass transparent to X-rays, which he patented. He endeavoured to improve the electronic theory of metallic conduction. He contributed to the theory of solids and was probably the first person to notice the paradox that their breaking stress is nothing like as great as theoretical considerations would suggest. He wrote papers on astronomical problems including one in conjunction with his father on the use of photo-electric cells in astronomical photometry. In the same paper he gave the first account of his 'Lindemann fibre electrometer' which, with modification, became a standard instrument and was his main contribution to experimental techniques. In 1919 he collaborated with F. W. Aston in a paper on the possibility of separating isotopes. He did some valuable work on certain geophysical problems and in 1923 with G. M. B. Dobson produced a paper which, although some of its suggestions are not now accepted, was the beginning of the modern theory of meteorites. In 1920 and 1922 he made important contributions to the theory of the mechanism of chemical reactions.

Lindemann's strength as a physicist rested on his remarkable capacity for simplifying problems and in his very wide range. His relative weakness was in mathematics, and this was reflected in the limitations of his *Physical Significance of the Quantum Theory* (1932). He was a man of intuition and flair in widely diverse fields, but he never pursued any one subject long enough to become its complete master. Much of his brilliance was shown in discussion at scientific conferences, and has not survived in published form. For this reason later generations have not found it easy to understand the high esteem in which he was held by such persons as Albert Einstein, Max Planck, Max Born, Ernest Rutherford, and Henri Poincaré. He was elected a fellow of the Royal Society in 1920.

The chair at Wadham gave Lindemann the headship of the Clarendon Laboratory, whose prestige had sunk to a very low ebb. It had no research staff, and no mains electricity. Its principal contents were packing cases full of unused optical instruments. Although Lindemann's career is in many respects controversial, no one has disputed his massive achievement in turning this museum piece into a great laboratory. He was adept at extracting money from the university and from outside sources. Long before he retired, the new Clarendon which he had persuaded the university to build was one of the foremost physics departments in Britain. Lindemann did not concentrate on any one line, although there was a slight bias towards the nucleus. Among the earlier research workers whom he picked were T. R. Merton, A. C. G. Egerton, G. M. B. Dobson, and Derek Jackson. In the 1930s he was active in recruiting to posts in Oxford Jewish refugee scientists from Hitler's Germany. The most prominent of these was Francis Simon, who became one of Lindemann's closest friends and in 1956 succeeded him as Dr Lee's professor.

Lindemann's academic career was not without friction and he had more than one clash with the university authorities. He was apt to make wounding and sarcastic remarks. He was both prickly and aggressive in the cause of natural science, which he regarded with some justice as a slighted subject in Oxford. He did not readily suffer fools. His wealth—his father, who died in 1927, had handed on a large sum to each of his sons—allowed him to move in circles very different from those of the academic middle class. He preferred ducal houses to north Oxford. In 1919 he was introduced by J. C. Masterman to Lord Birkenhead—tennis being the link—and it was at Birkenhead's house that he received the nickname of the Prof, by which he came to be almost universally known. In 1921 through the duke of Westminster he met Winston Churchill—the beginning of a lifelong friendship.

Air defence Lindemann's political views were well to the right. He was an out-and-out inequalitarian who believed in hierarchy, order, a ruling class, inherited wealth, hereditary titles, and white supremacy (the passing of which he regarded as the most significant change in the twentieth century). It was fully in keeping with this attitude that he should have mobilized some of the personnel (not wholly willing) of the Clarendon to help produce Churchill's *British Gazette* during the general strike of 1926. Exceptionally for a person of these views, Lindemann was one of the first to recognize the danger of Hitler. His pre-war sojourn in Germany had given him an acute awareness of that country's formidable strength and aggressive potential. Filled with these apprehensions, he became gravely perturbed at the inadequacy of British air defence, and at the seeming fatalism of the government.

In 1934, both independently and through Churchill, he pressed for the creation of a high-level committee to consider the problem urgently. In fact, the Air Ministry had decided towards the end of the year to set up a departmental committee of its own, the committee for the scientific survey of air defence under Tizard's chairmanship, with Dr. A. V. Hill, H. E. Wimperis, and P. M. S. Blackett as members. The Tizard committee was to be responsible for one of the most important achievements in British defence: the effective application of radar to the interception of enemy bombers. But Churchill and Lindemann were convinced that a mere advisory departmental committee would not carry enough weight. In the spring of 1935 the government partly gave way and agreed to set up the air defence research sub-committee of the committee of imperial defence, with Sir Philip Cunliffe-Lister as chairman. Both Tizard and Churchill were members, but the sub-committee's functions were limited and in practice it seems to have been regarded as little more than a sop to Churchill. There was, however, one important by-product. Churchill insisted that Lindemann should be put on the Tizard committee.

Lindemann, who joined the sub-committee at the end of June 1935, treated his colleagues from the start in a spirit of criticism bordering upon hostility. Relations between him and Tizard—which had previously seemed friendly enough, at least on the surface—deteriorated rapidly, to the consternation of their many mutual friends, and the breach was never healed. A year later the committee broke up with the resignation of Hill, Blackett, and Tizard in protest at Lindemann's tactics. It was promptly reconstituted in October, but without Lindemann.

The conflict has been wrongly presented by Lord Snow and others as a dispute about the priority to be given to radar. The evidence of its inventor, Sir Robert Watson-Watt, is conclusive that Lindemann very strongly backed radar, although he was more apprehensive than the others about the possibility of enemy jamming. It is true too that Lindemann favoured the simultaneous exploration of various other defence devices which turned out to be impracticable, such as aerial mines. But the real conflict was over the status of the committee. Lindemann with his grand social and political contacts was prepared to go to almost any lengths, including publicity and political lobbying, to obtain real executive powers for it. His objective was sound, but his methods difficult to defend, and Tizard and his colleagues found it intolerable that Lindemann should report behind their backs to Churchill on the air defence research committee. With their service background and orthodox approach, they considered that it was not for them to try to change the terms of reference laid down by the Air Ministry.

Their doubts about Lindemann cannot have been allayed by his efforts to enter parliament for Oxford University on a programme of revitalizing British air defence. He failed to secure the second Conservative nomination at the general election of 1935, when he was defeated by C. R. M. F. Cruttwell, principal of Hertford College, who to Lindemann's glee subsequently lost his deposit. In 1937 there was a by-election. Lindemann resolved to fight with or without the official nomination, which in the event went to Sir Farquhar Buzzard. They were both easily beaten by Sir Arthur Salter, standing as an independent.

Churchill's personal assistant The next few years were a period of frustration for Lindemann, but with the outbreak of war in 1939 he moved at once to the centre of affairs as personal assistant to Churchill at the Admiralty and head of his statistical section. He continued the same work when Churchill became prime minister in May 1940.

Lindemann was made a peer in 1941 with the title of Baron Cherwell of Oxford. In 1942 he became paymaster-general, in 1943 a privy councillor. Although never a member of the war cabinet, he frequently attended its meetings. His loyalty to Churchill was absolute, his influence on him profound.

Cherwell was a master at the art of lucidly presenting highly complicated matters with the greatest economy of words. He wrote about 2000 minutes to Churchill during the war on a vast range of topics. The prime minister greatly admired this gift, and would often pass on bloated memoranda from other departments with the request, 'Prof. 10 lines please'. Cherwell's advice was by no means only on scientific matters. He had a staff of economists, headed by Donald MacDougall, one of whose tasks was to produce charts and graphs for Churchill so that he could visualize changes in such areas as weapon production, food imports, and shipping losses. Another task—and a very unpopular one—was the critical scrutiny of departmental statistics. For example, Lindemann correctly discovered that the German front-line strength in bombers in 1940 was grossly exaggerated, and after an inquiry by a High Court judge into the rival statistics Lindemann's became the basis of policy. He also came to the less agreeable, but no less correct, conclusion that British night bombing at that time was less than one-third as accurate as the Air Ministry claimed. Navigational aids were at once improved. Another result of his quantitative analysis was to cut by a factor of more than two the ships going to the Middle East and America in the summer of 1942.

Lindemann actively supported experiments in new weapons of every sort. Hollow charge bombs and proximity fuses were among those whose development he pressed. One of his major contributions was the 'bending' of the wireless beam on which in 1940 German night bombers were relying for finding their targets. R. V. Jones, a former pupil then employed at the Air Ministry, was the first to suspect that the Germans possessed this device. Tizard appears to have been sceptical. If Lindemann had not pressed for counter-measures with all his weight, the consequences might have been disastrous. Cherwell also strongly backed the researches of his old pupil Derek Jackson into microwave radar. One of many important results was the invention of H_2S, the name of the device which gave a radar picture of the country to the navigators of the Pathfinder night bombers. It is probably fair to say that what Tizard did for Fighter Command Cherwell did for Bomber Command.

Cherwell's judgement, like that of most persons in high places during the war, sometimes went astray. He greatly overestimated the damage that could be done to war production by the massive area bombing of German towns, and was rightly criticized by Tizard and Blackett. But it seems unlikely that his famous minute in 1942 to Churchill on this theme was the determining factor in a decision which had its roots far back in recommendations of the chiefs of staff in 1940. Area bombing did not stop German war production. It rose until the winter of 1944–5, by when German air defence had been pulverized. But Cherwell's calculations were based on a bomber front-line strength of 4000, never remotely attained. And critics have seldom taken account—nor did Cherwell himself—of what is now known to be the huge diversion of resources from the eastern front in order to defend German towns. Cherwell accompanied Churchill to Potsdam in 1945. They surveyed the scene of destruction in the city where Lindemann had spent his happy formative years. Whatever his feeling, Cherwell did not say a word.

Cherwell was wrong, too, to advise postponing for nearly a year the use of 'Window', the technique of confusing enemy radar by dropping strips of tinfoil. Although he had encouraged its development he feared lest the enemy would be alerted to use it too, and it should be said in justice to him that many radar experts took the same view. Another error was his excessive scepticism about the German rocket bomb, or V2. He was right in ridiculing the danger of its possessing a 10 ton warhead, but he was characteristically extremist in maintaining that it did not exist at all. Still, when all criticisms have been made, the value of his war work must be regarded as immense. Churchill, and through Churchill the whole country, owed him a great debt of gratitude.

Return to Oxford With the fall of the Churchill administration in 1945 Cherwell returned to Oxford and the Clarendon. He was at the same time a member of the shadow cabinet, and principal opposition spokesman in the House of Lords on economic affairs. He was also prominent in discussion of the atomic bomb, and had nothing but contempt for the arguments of those who wished to ban tests. In October 1951 he reluctantly joined Churchill's cabinet, again as paymaster-general. His main achievements were to defeat the Treasury proposals to bring in immediate sterling convertibility together with a floating rate of exchange and to prise the control of atomic energy out of the Ministry of Supply and into the hands of an independent authority. He had a great dislike of Whitehall 'bureaucracy', though happy relations with many individual civil servants. One of Cherwell's 'causes' after the war was the creation of a new technological university on the lines of the Massachusetts Institute. He failed to overcome Treasury objections, and although he welcomed the foundation of Churchill College, Cambridge, it met his objectives only in part. There is still no British MIT.

In 1953 Cherwell's leave of absence from Oxford ran out and he resigned his government post. He was made a CH, and three years later was created a viscount. Although he possessed life tenure of his chair, he retired in 1956 but was allowed to reside in college, for, whatever friction there might have been in the past, he was now regarded as the most interesting and entertaining of companions. His last important speech in the House of Lords was an acid analysis of the United Nations in December 1956. For some time his heart had been giving him trouble, and he died in his sleep at Christ Church on the morning of 3 July 1957, and was buried in the North Oxford cemetery. He never married and his titles became extinct. Two-thirds of his estate was left to Christ Church, one-third to Wadham, with a wish but not a legal obligation that it should be used for 'Lindemann scholarships' in physics.

Lindemann was on any view a remarkable person. Reinforcing with his scientific expertise and his clarity of mind his personal friendship with one of the greatest statesmen in British history, he exercised more influence in public life than any scientist before him. He had a brilliant mind, 'one of the cleverest men I ever met, as clever as Rutherford', to quote Tizard's generous judgement. He was a man of extremes: passionate loyalty to friends, implacable detestation of enemies. And he inspired correspondingly extreme sentiments, deep devotion on the one hand and something near to hatred on the other. There were curious apparent contradictions about him. He was an ascetic who deeply distrusted asceticism in others. It came as a surprise to many to learn how vigorously he campaigned in the war for the plain man against austerity and meagre rations. Yet he knew singularly little about how the vast majority of his fellow countrymen lived—even the middle classes, let alone the masses. He was reputed never to have been on a London bus or tube train. He believed that most people were stupid and needed to be governed for their own good by an élite. He was a most amusing, indeed fascinating, conversationalist, but he could utter sentiments so cynical and sardonic as to shock his hearers, especially the young. 'One shouldn't kick a man when he's down', said a guest in the Christ Church common room. Lindemann replied, 'Why not? It's the best time to do it because then he can't kick you back'. Yet he was kind-hearted and secretly most generous to those in need. The sinister picture of him drawn by Rolf Hochhuth in his play *The Soldiers* was to anyone who knew Cherwell an absurd travesty.

Lindemann's voice was curiously frail, and his rather mumbling mode of delivery somewhat marred his lectures and speeches, which read better than they sounded. In appearance he was a big man with broad shoulders, and an aquiline countenance. He dressed conventionally and immaculately, but he was a striking figure in any company. Few who met him ever forgot him.

Robert Blake

Sources G. Thomson, *Memoirs FRS*, 4 (1958), 45–71 • R. Harrod, *The Prof* (1954) • C. P. Snow, *Science and government* (1961) • C. P. Snow, *A postscript to 'Science and government'* (1962) • Earl of Birkenhead, *The Prof in two worlds: the official life of Viscount Cherwell* (1961) • R. W. Clark, *Tizard* (1965) • C. M. Bowra, *Memories* (1966) • Lord Moran, *Winston Churchill: the struggle for survival, 1940–65* (1966) • personal knowledge (2004) • R. V. Jones, *Most secret war* (1978) • T. Wilson, *Churchill and the Prof* (1995) • Lord Blake and R. Lewis, eds., *Churchill* (1995) • *CGPLA Eng. & Wales* (1957)

Archives IWM, corresp. and papers • Nuffield Oxf., corresp. and papers • PRO, papers, CAB 127/194–203 | Bodl. Oxf., corresp. relating to Society for Protection of Science and Learning • CAC Cam., corresp. with R. V. Jones
Likenesses H. Carr, oils, 1946, IWM • photograph, RS [*see illus.*]
Wealth at death £101,390 18*s*. 7*d*.: probate, 25 July 1957, *CGPLA Eng. & Wales*

Lindesay, Thomas. *See* Lindsay, Thomas (1656–1724).

Lindgren, Ernest Henry (1910–1973), film archivist, was born on 3 October 1910 at 15 Westwick Gardens, Hammersmith, London, the eldest child of Ernst Wilhelm Lindgren (1878–1935), a master tailor from Sweden, and his wife, Charlotte Elvery (1877–1971). He was educated in London: at Minchenden School, Southgate, at King's College, and then at Birkbeck College, where he read English. It was at Birkbeck that he met his future wife, Rose Rachael (1907–2001), daughter of Henry Stephen Taylor, a gas fitter. Rose, whom he married on 4 September 1937, was at that time a fellow English student who also worked for J. W. Brown, secretary of the British Institute of Adult Education. This body had been central to the Commission on Educational and Cultural Films, which in 1932 published *The Film in National Life*. This report led to the formation of the British Film Institute (BFI) in 1933 and it inspired Lindgren, already an enthusiastic film-goer, to devote himself to the art of film, its preservation, and its dissemination. He became the BFI's information officer and in 1935 was invited to draft a memorandum on the possible organization of a national repository of films (as recommended in the BFI's articles of association); in May 1935 the National Film Library (NFL) was created, with Lindgren in charge. For some years the NFL had a staff of only two, the other being Harold Brown, who became its long-standing preservation officer and pioneered many of the standard practices of film preservation. The NFL had no equipment, no money, and no films. Patiently Lindgren began acquiring films and establishing links with a suspicious film industry. At the same time he was developing fundamental policies of film preservation, whereby the original copy of a film acquired by the NFL became its inviolate master, with access granted only to a second or duplicate copy.

By the end of the 1930s the NFL had 2 million feet of film in preservation, with a growing loan section. Libraries of books and stills were established, as well as viewing facilities, a lecture service and annual summer school, and links with local film societies. The war saw the NFL adopting temporary accommodation for its nitrate film holdings in a Sussex stables, but in November 1939 Lindgren had acquired premises for preservation vaults at Aston Clinton, in Buckinghamshire; these were augmented by a second site at Berkhamsted in the mid-1960s.

In the 1940s the NFL developed its pioneering artificial ageing test (recommended by experts from Kodak) for determining when a nitrate film was likely to start decomposing, and initiated a programme of copying films onto acetate (safety) stock. Films were selected for the NFL by a number of committees (general, science, and history, with television added in 1962). These had to justify the selection of each title, which Lindgren would then endeavour to acquire. The NFL had little or no funds for acquisition and was wholly dependent on the good offices of the film industry (the principled Lindgren generally refused to deal with private film collectors) to supply films, which too often were worn ex-distribution prints. Lindgren lobbied tirelessly for a system of statutory deposit for film all his working life. It never came about in his lifetime; it has not been implemented yet.

In 1955 the NFL became the National Film Archive (NFA), having ceased its original loan service, and by its change of name emphasized that film preservation was its core activity. The BFI had developed around it with the successful establishment of the National Film Theatre, but the NFA struggled to maintain its targets and its principles in the face of chronic underfunding. Lindgren wrote and argued and pleaded year after year for adequate funds to maintain a satisfactory level of acquisition, copying, and cataloguing. A fortress mentality set in at the NFA, which began to gather a reputation for parsimony, supposedly denying access to any of its film holdings. The growing body of film scholars and enthusiasts felt that it contrasted badly with the open, adventurous policy adopted by Henri Langlois, Lindgren's spiritual opposite, at the Cinémathèque Française.

Lindgren's death occurred on 22 July 1973 at his home, 57 Ventnor Drive, Totteridge, London; he was cremated at Hendon on 27 July. He died before his time, with the NFA an established, if sometimes grudgingly accepted national organization, a collection of over 32 million feet of film, and dreams still unfulfilled. He remains the unsung hero of film archiving. The long-held belief that the puritanical Lindgren and the romantic Langlois represented two opposing philosophies of film archiving is false. Lindgren's steady, conscientious, and protective policies have proven to be the only proper path for a film archive, and long after Langlois's flame blew out Lindgren's vision led to one of the major national film collections and the inspiration for film archives the world over, most of them members of FIAF, the international federation of film archives, to which Lindgren contributed greatly from its inception in 1938. Lindgren was ahead of his time in his insistence on collecting non-fiction film as a medium of historical record, and again pioneered the acquisition of television alongside film. His reputation as one who denied access to films needs to be overturned; the National Film Theatre from the outset benefited greatly from its access to NFA viewing prints, and Lindgren was as committed to access as anyone—but not by breaking the rules of film preservation and always within the harsh limits of meagre resources. In his latter years he became beset by battles with the BFI over budgets and by further battles with the Langlois faction within FIAF, and some thought that the force that had driven him over the pioneering years had become dogmatic and unyielding. Lindgren was bureaucratic, reserved, and possessive. But equally he was tenacious, canny, kindly, a fine teacher (his book *The Art of the Film*, published in 1948, was a film-study classic for over twenty years), and a man of unimpeachable integrity, with a dry, too-often overlooked sense of humour. He was appointed OBE in 1962. The NFA became the National Film and Television Archive in 1993. The British national film heritage owes everything to Lindgren and will lose much if it ever forgets the sound principles upon which it was built. LUKE MCKERNAN

Sources private information (2004) [family, colleagues] • P. Houston, *Keepers of the frame* (1994) • I. Butler, *To encourage the art of film* (1971) • BFI, papers, special collections department • R. Roud, *A passion for films* (1983) • R. Borde, *Les cinémathèques* (1984) • E. Lindgren, 'The importance of film archives', *Penguin Film Review*, 5 (1948) • R. Low, *Documentary and educational films of the 1930s* (1979) • *Sight and Sound*, 42 (1972–3), 270–71 • b. cert. • m. cert. • d. cert.

Archives BFI, papers relating to formation and operation of British Film Institute and National Film Archive | FILM BFI NFTVA, documentary footage

Likenesses photographs, BFI

Wealth at death £25,608: probate, 16 Nov 1973, *CGPLA Eng. & Wales*

Lindley, Sir Francis Oswald (1872–1950), diplomatist, was born on 12 June 1872 at The Lodge, East Carleton, Norwich, the youngest child in a family of five sons and four daughters of Nathaniel *Lindley, Baron Lindley (1828–1921), who became a lord of appeal in ordinary, and his wife, Sarah Katharine (*d.* 1912), daughter of Edward John Teale, solicitor, of Leeds. He was educated at Winchester College and at Magdalen College, Oxford, where his great friend was Simon Joseph Fraser, fourteenth Baron Lovat, whose brother-in-law and biographer he later became. He obtained a third-class degree in jurisprudence in 1893 but, choosing the career which his father had rejected, he entered the diplomatic service as an attaché in October 1896, passing a competitive examination the following year when he was promoted to Foreign Office clerk. From 1899 to 1901 he was a third secretary in Vienna and Tehran. The year 1902 saw him in Cairo, first as an official under the Egyptian government, and then as second secretary under Lord Cromer. From Cairo he went to Tokyo, from November 1905 to June 1908, then back to the Foreign Office until October 1909, and then, as first secretary, to Sofia, until October 1911. He was then posted to Norway, from January 1912 until July 1915; in the latter month he became counsellor of embassy in Petrograd. He was appointed CBE in 1917. After the withdrawal of the ambassador, Sir George William Buchanan, in January 1918 he was left in charge of the mission. In May he was transferred to Archangel as commissioner, and in June became consul-general for Russia. He was appointed CB in 1919 and transferred to Vienna in October that year as high commissioner, becoming envoy-extraordinary and minister-plenipotentiary in July the following year. In November 1921 he went to Athens in a similar capacity. He had only been there twelve months when the revolution broke out which resulted in the second banishment of King Constantine and the judicial murder of the royalist ministers, whose lives, had Lindley's advice been taken in time, might have been saved. Diplomatic relations with Greece were broken off and he was recalled home whence, after some months *en disponibilité*, he was sent as minister to Norway in November 1923. There he remained for nearly six years, being appointed KCMG in 1926, until his promotion in September 1929 as ambassador at Lisbon, when he was sworn of the privy council. In Portugal he spent two highly successful years.

In May 1931 Lindley was promoted GCMG and went to the Far East as ambassador to Japan. Within two months of his arrival in Tokyo in July, he became involved in a world crisis connected with Japan's expansion in north-east China, the so-called Manchurian crisis. Lindley reported the high level of anti-British feeling he found and urged that Britain should not be pushed into positive action, as for example by imposing sanctions on Japan at the behest of the League of Nations. Supported by his embassy staff, he questioned the policies being followed by London, which he regarded as provocative. By April 1934 when he left Japan—and the diplomatic service—relations had greatly improved.

Lindley was the embodiment of British common sense, and in this lay the secret of his success as a representative of his country abroad. He never attempted to conceal the fact that he considered his own country to be the finest on earth and the British empire the greatest instrument for good in the world, and he took it for granted that foreigners were equally patriotic. This attitude, added to an invariably friendly and welcoming manner to high and low, enabled him on many occasions to gain his ends without any rancour left behind, where subtler and more calculated methods would in all probability have failed. He was fond of quoting the remark that the only thing worse than a military defeat was a diplomatic victory.

Lindley sought his relaxation out of doors and his book *A Diplomat Off Duty*, first published in 1928, ranges from ski-running in Norway to tiger-hunting in Korea; further, he was once golf champion of Portugal. He was a keen and untiring sportsman, with both rod and gun, and after his retirement he bought a small property at Alresford in Hampshire, where he was able to continue these pursuits. He was chairman of the Test and Itchen Fishing Association, a member of the council and honorary treasurer of the Zoological Society, and from 1943 an official verderer of the New forest. Local and business interests also occupied his time, for he was a county alderman and held a number of directorships; and in addition to his biography of Lord Lovat published in 1935 he was a frequent correspondent to *The Times*. He was also chairman of the council of the Japan Society of London from 1935 to 1949 and of the executive committee of the Anglo-Portuguese Society over an extended and difficult period. In 1937 he stood as Conservative candidate for the combined English Universities at a by-election, but was defeated.

On 12 January 1903 Lindley married (Etheldreda) Mary (1872–1949), third daughter of Simon Fraser, thirteenth Baron Lovat. There were four daughters, Bridget Mary (*b.* 1904), Alice Elizabeth (*b.* 1905), Sarah Katharine (*b.* 1907), and Mary Etheldreda (*b.* 1911). Lindley survived his wife by ten months, dying at his home, the Weir House, Alresford, Hampshire, on 17 August 1950. He was buried in Old Alresford churchyard. J. H. F. MCEWEN, *rev.* IAN NISH

Sources H. Cortazzi, 'The Japan Society: a hundred-year history', *Britain and Japan, 1859–1991*, ed. H. Cortazzi and G. Daniels (1991) · I. H. Nish, 'Jousting with authority: the Tokyo embassy of Sir Francis Lindley, 1931–4', *Proceedings of the Japan Society*, 105 (1986), 9–19 · F. Lindley, 'Preface', in Y. Yoshida, *Whispering leaves in Grosvenor Square, 1936–7* (1938) · K. Sansom, *Sir G. Sansom and Japan: a memoir* (1972) · I. H. Nish, *Japan's struggle with internationalism, 1931–3* (1993) · W. N. Medlicott and others, eds., *Documents on British foreign policy, 1919–1939* · *WWW* · Burke, *Peerage* · L. H. Lamb, ed., *Winchester College: a register for the years 1915 to 1960* (1974) · *CGPLA Eng. & Wales* (1950) · *FO List* (1926?)

Archives priv. coll. | Bodl. Oxf., Dawson MSS · Bodl. Oxf., Sir Horace Rumbold MSS · CUL, Hardinge MSS · Mitchell L., Glas., Glasgow City Archives, Sir John Stirling-Maxwell MSS

Likenesses W. Stoneman, photograph, 1943, NPG · H. von Angeli, portrait, priv. coll.; formerly in possession of the family, 1959 · photograph (in youth), NPG

Wealth at death £33,423 2*s*. 4*d*.: probate, 17 Oct 1950, *CGPLA Eng. & Wales*

Lindley, John (1799–1865), botanist and horticulturist, was born on 5 February 1799 at Catton, near Norwich, the first of the four children of George Lindley (*c*.1769–1835), a nurseryman of Yorkshire extraction, and his wife, Mary (*née* Moore). He was educated under Dr Valpy at Norwich grammar school, where he collected wild plants for pleasure. He had wanted to seek a military career but his father could not afford to buy him a commission. Instead, in 1815, he travelled to Belgium as the agent of Wrench, a Camberwell seed merchant. By 1817 he was befriended by William Jackson Hooker, in whose Suffolk home Lindley completed his first botanical publication, *Observations on the Structure of Fruits and Seeds* (1819), a translation of Louis-Claude Richard's *Demonstrations botaniques, ou, L'analyse du fruit*. Hooker introduced Lindley to Charles Lyell (1769–1849) of Kinnordy and to Robert Brown, through whom Lindley met Sir Joseph Banks. Banks promised Lindley that he might be sent overseas as a naturalist, either to succeed the late Joseph Arnold in Sumatra, or to Madagascar. However, in 1819 Banks instead decided to employ Lindley in his library and herbarium at Soho Square as an assistant to Robert Brown. Lindley grasped this opportunity with both hands, and by Banks's death had completed important work on roses, *Digitalis*, and apples. The acuity of his taxonomical judgement may be gauged by the survival of many genera which he defined when he was barely twenty-one. Lyell, to whom Lindley had dedicated his monograph on roses, presented him with £100, which Lindley used to purchase a microscope and to begin the herbarium, which at his death contained some 58,000 sheets. He was elected to the Linnean and the Geological societies in 1820, to the Imperial Academy of Natural History in Bonn in 1821, and to the Royal Society in 1828, and his work was honoured in the genus *Lindleya* (1824) by Humboldt, Bonpland, and Kunth. In 1829 Lindley became the first professor of botany in the University of London, a post he held until 1860. In 1832 the University of Munich conferred on him an honorary DPhil.

On 1 November 1823 Lindley married Sarah Freestone (1791–1869), of South Elmham, Suffolk, the only daughter of Anthony George Freestone and Sarah, *née* Doggett, his wife. They had five children, of whom three grew to adulthood, including Nathaniel *Lindley, Baron Lindley, and Sarah, the future Lady Crease. He was not perhaps a close husband, arranging to be away for most of each week, and while at their home, 5 The Terrace, Acton Green, he tended to retire to his study or garden. There he was often accompanied by Sarah Drake, his botanical artist, one of the greatest of all orchid painters, whom he installed in the family home from 1835 until her marriage in 1853. He was adored by his children and, in later years, it was his daughter Sarah, rather than his wife, who accompanied him on social engagements.

Lindley was an early and enthusiastic partisan of Jussieu's 'natural system'. In his 1829 inaugural lecture at London and his lecture to the British Association for the Advancement of Science (1833) he declared that botany should become a philosophical subject, using every aspect of anatomy and physiology to order plants in their natural families. From this commitment came his *Synopsis of the British Flora* (1829) and the *Introduction to the Natural System* (1830), of which Asa Gray, reviewer of the 1831 American edition, exulted, 'No book, since printed bibles were sold in Paris by Dr Faustus, ever excited so much surprise and wonder' (quoted in Stafleu and Cowan, 3.54). It was expanded and revised into *A Natural System of Botany* (1836) and his monumental *The Vegetable Kingdom* (1846). Lindley, in the former, was responsible for an enduring reform of botanical nomenclature, arguing that taxonomical divisions of the same hierarchical standing should wear names which shared a common suffix. The subsequent practice of ending the names of all families with '-acae', or of all orders with '-ales', for example, derives from this initiative. Of one family, the *Orchidacae*, Lindley remains considered the most distinguished of all students. In the *Genera and Species of Orchidaceous Plants* (1830–40), *Sertum Orchidaceum: a Wreath of the most Beautiful Orchidaceous Flowers* (1838), *Orchidacae Lindenianae* (1846), and *Folia orchidacea* (1852–9), he laid the foundations of modern orchidology, establishing some 120 genera. At that time increasingly rapid transportation and the development of artificially heated greenhouses led to orchid-collecting crazes in Britain. Both transport and heating depended on coalmining, and it was finds in the coal measures which, in part, urged Lindley, with Hutton, to prepare the pioneering *Fossil Flora of Great Britain* (3 vols., 1831–7). By the time of his retirement from University College he had more than two hundred publications to his credit. In 1853 the Institut de France elected him a corresponding member, and in 1857 the Royal Society awarded him its royal medal.

Lindley was forthright to the point of appearing brusque. He was fearless when he felt in the right, entering into public disputes with powerful figures such as Sir James Smith (over Linnaeus), Lord Brougham (for the right of professors to choose the books used in the University of London), and Brown (over the natural history collections of the British Museum). His energy and drive were famous: his working day often began at dawn and continued into the evening, and he could give as many as nineteen different lectures a week while also undertaking a range of extra-curricular responsibilities. His regular diet of overwork may well explain his sometimes difficult manner.

Lindley's material circumstances led him to take on this punishing schedule. He had, to his lasting regret, agreed in 1822 to stand as a guarantor of his father's liabilities. He himself was respectable enough to have to keep up appearances, but too poor to do so without borrowing. Lindley thus lived his life under the shadow of debt to both bankers and such friends as Sir Joseph Paxton. Money was a preoccupation of his correspondence, and it is under its pressure that Lindley, accepting duty after duty, became an ubiquitous administrator and lecturer, and a prolific author and editor for an amateur audience, perhaps the most important figure in the public life of Victorian horticulture.

In 1821 Lindley agreed to superintend the construction of the Chiswick garden of the Horticultural Society, and from 1822 was its garden assistant secretary, rising in 1826 to full assistant secretary, and in 1841 to vice-secretary. In 1830, with George Bentham, he rescued the society from bankruptcy, organizing at Chiswick the first annual flower show in Britain. He was at its centre from 1841 until 1858, when he retired to the council and the title of honorary secretary, ending his association only in 1862. His rich collection of botanical works forms today the core of the Royal Horticultural Society's Lindley Library. From 1836 he was also lecturer on botany to the Apothecaries' Company, and *praefectus* of the Chelsea Physic Garden.

Lindley's sumptuously illustrated works, such as *Victoria regia* (1837), of which only twenty-five were printed, and his studies on orchids, were available only to wealthy subscribers. But Lindley wrote vastly more for a popular readership, preparing descriptions for 16,712 plants for John Loudon's *Encyclopaedia of Plants* (1829), and many entries for the *Penny Cyclopaedia*, the *Dictionary of Science, Literature and Art* (1837), and Paxton's *Pocket Botanical Dictionary* (1838). He became the principal botanical author for the Society for the Diffusion of Useful Knowledge, at about £30 a volume. His *Ladies Botany* (2 vols., 1837–8) sold well, but his most successful work was *Elements of Botany* (1841), a textbook, which went through seven English editions within his lifetime, and was translated into German, French, Italian, Portuguese, Russian, and Swedish. He was an untiring editor, responsible for the *Botanical Register* (1826–1847), the *Journal of the Horticultural Society* (1846–55), and the *Gardeners' Chronicle*, which he had founded with Charles Wentworth Dilke and Joseph Paxton. He was editor of the last from 1841 until his death.

By the 1830s official bodies had begun to seek Lindley's counsel. He advised the Board of Ordnance on vegetable sources of carbon for gunpowder, the Hudson's Bay Company on botanical exploration, the Colonial Office on appointments to botanic gardens, the Admiralty on the cultivation and reforestation of Ascension Island, and the Inland Revenue on coffee and its adulterants. In 1838 he prepared for the Treasury the influential report on Kew Gardens which recommended that it should become a national centre for botany, and an instrument for the management of colonial economies. Peel sent Lindley to Ireland to report on the potato blight, entertained him at Drayton Manor, and used information from him to stage a prime minister's question in the House of Commons in February 1846. In 1858 Lindley became adviser on botanical matters to the India Office. He played a key role in organizing the agricultural aspects of the 1851 Great Exhibition, and the colonial department of the 1862 Paris Universal Exhibition.

All his life Lindley took the greatest interest in military matters, following with enthusiasm the fate of British wars in India and the Crimea. He helped organize and drill an armed body of loyal gardeners to oppose Chartist crowds in 1848. His only leisure pursuits, apart from gardening, and the popular novels he devoured on the Acton omnibus, were archery and rifle shooting, and at the heart of his garden was a 100 yard range. He was reputed a good shot, despite having lost the sight in one eye as a child, although on one occasion he missed and hit his servant in the thigh. (Harrington later returned the compliment, striking Lindley on the head, accidentally, with an axe handle.) Lindley was formally an Anglican, and wrote of nature as bearing 'the living Hieroglyphics of the Almighty', but he disliked the church, and refused all discussion of religious matters. He was equally reticent on politics, although during the 1830s he had canvassed in Middlesex on behalf of Joseph Hume, the radical politician.

During his last few years, possibly due to accumulated effects of the mercury preparation he had used to preserve his specimens, Lindley had fainting fits, and lost both his memory and his power of work. He died of apoplexy on 1 November 1865 at home in Acton Green, and was buried in Acton cemetery five days later.

RICHARD DRAYTON

Sources RBG Kew, Lindley letters, A–K, L–Z · RBG Kew, Dr Lindley's official correspondence, 1832–1854 · private information (2004) [R. M. Hamilton] · RBG Kew, W. J. Hooker MSS · American Philosophical Society, W. J. Hooker MSS · BL, W. J. Hooker MSS · J. Lindley, *An introductory lecture delivered in the University of London* (1829) · J. Lindley, *On the principal questions at present debated in the philosophy of botany* (1833) · W. T. Stearn, 'Lindley, John', *DSB* · *Gardeners' Chronicle* (11 Nov 1865), 1058–9 · *Gardeners' Chronicle* (18 Nov 1865), 1082–3 · R. Drayton, 'Imperial science and a scientific Europe', PhD diss., Yale U., 1993, 207–11, 234–40 · W. Gardener, 'John Lindley', *Gardeners' Chronicle*, 3rd ser., 158 (1965), 386–526 · J. Reynolds Green, *A history of botany in the United Kingdom* (1914) · UCL, SDUK MSS · F. A. Stafleu and R. S. Cowan, *Taxonomic literature: a selective guide*, 2nd edn, 3, Regnum Vegetabile, 105 (1981) · d. cert. · W. T. Stearn, ed., *John Lindley, 1799–1865: gardener, botanist, and pioneer orchidologist* (1998)

Archives Carnegie Mellon University, Pittsburgh, Hunt Institute for Botanical Documentation, papers · NHM, corresp. and papers · RBG Kew, corresp. and papers · RBG Kew, letters · RBG Kew, official corresp. · Royal Horticultural Society, London, description of plants · U. Cam., department of plant sciences, notes on *Quercus* · U. Newcastle, Hancock Museum, corresp. and papers · UCL, lecture notes | Archives of British Columbia, Vancouver, Crease collection · BL, corresp. with Sir Robert Peel, Add. MSS 40576–40602 · NHM, letters to the Sowerby family · RBG Kew, letters to Sir William Hooker · RS, letters to Sir John Herschel · U. Newcastle,

Robinson L., letters to Sir Walter Trevelyan • UCL, SDUK, MSS, letters

Likenesses engraving, *c*.1830, BL • sketch, *c*.1848, repro. in *Gardeners' Chronicle* • E. Edwards, sepia photograph, *c*.1860, RBG Kew • Maull & Polyblank, photograph, *c*.1860, RBG Kew • E. U. Eddis, oils, 1862, Royal Horticultural Society, London • engraving, *c*.1865, repro. in *Gardeners' Chronicle* • C. Fox, oils, British Columbia Archives and Record Service, Crease Collection • S. Lindley, etching (after C. Fox), BM • T. H. Maguire, lithograph, BM, NPG; repro. in T. H. Maguire, *Portraits of honorary members of the Ipswich Museum* (1852) • Turner, lithograph (after E. U. Eddis), BM • pencil drawing, Royal Horticultural Society Gardens, Ripley, Surrey • photograph (after an engraving), RBG Kew; repro. in F. W. Oliver, *Makers of British botany* (1848), pl. XIV • photograph (after sketch by his daughter), RBG Kew • photograph (aged fifty; after lithograph), RBG Kew; repro. in T. H. Maguire, *Portraits of honorary members of the Ipswich Museum* (1852) • photograph (aged early thirties; after lithograph), RBG Kew; repro. in *The Naturalist* (4 May 1839) • photograph (after line drawing, repro. in De Puydt, *Les orchidées*, fig. 19), RBG Kew • portraits, British Columbia Archives and Record Service, Crease Collection

Wealth at death under £3000: resworn probate, Oct 1866, *CGPLA Eng. & Wales* (1865)

Lindley, Nathaniel, Baron Lindley (1828–1921), judge, was born at Chiswick on 29 November 1828. He was the younger son of John *Lindley FRS (1799–1865), professor of botany at University College, London, and Sarah (1791–1869), daughter of Anthony George Freestone of South Elmham, Suffolk. She was a descendant, through the female line, of the chief justice Sir Edward Coke. Lindley's only brother died in childhood, but he and his two sisters survived to a great age. Educated in London at University College School and then, like Jessel, at University College, he does not appear to have had a distinguished academic career. After two years at the college, when he was about eighteen, his father sent him to France to learn the language with a view to his entering the Foreign Office. However, he rejected the possibility of a diplomatic career, and on the advice of a solicitor uncle decided to read for the bar, entering the Middle Temple in 1847. From November 1848 he read in various chambers and finally, with an interlude of a few months in Bonn studying Roman law, in those of the future lord justice of appeal Charles Jasper Selwyn. These pupillages lasted for four and a half years. During this time he had sufficient leisure to abridge fifty-seven of the leading legal texts.

At the bar Lindley was called to the bar in 1850 and his first clients were solicitors to the Horticultural Society, which was run until 1858 by his father, its vice-secretary. In May 1854 he painted up his name at 16 Old Square, Lincoln's Inn, and by 1858, with an income at the bar of £300, he felt sufficiently secure to marry Sarah (*d*. 1912), daughter of Edward John Teale, solicitor, of Leeds, to whom he had been engaged for some years. They married on 5 August 1858, and went on to have nine children. The youngest child, Sir Francis *Lindley, became British ambassador to Japan.

For the first year or two, however, Lindley's practice remained slack. By 1856 he was prominent enough to be led in the Court of Appeal by James Bacon, the future vice-chancellor, who left him alone to argue before the formidable duo of lords justices Knight-Bruce and Turner. The publication of his *Treatise on the Law of Partnership, Including its Application to Companies* in 1860, a work which he had begun five years earlier, may have brought him greater prominence for it was publicly noticed by the judges. The treatise became the authoritative treatment of the law of partnership. This was not his first foray into print. In 1855 he published a translation with notes of the first part of Thibaut's *System des Pandektenrechts*, under the title of an *Introduction to the Study of Jurisprudence*, which made him favourably known to students of that subject. In comparison, his second treatise on company law, published in 1867, never received the same acclaim as these works.

But by that time Lindley's practice was passing from a safe to a formidable junior practice. Among his pupils were Francis Maclean, later chief justice of Bengal (Inner Temple, 1866) and Frederick Pollock (Lincoln's Inn, 1871), legal historian and jurist; indeed it was Lindley's example which taught Pollock that 'the law is neither a trade nor a solemn jugglery but a science'. He never took more than two pupils at a time, and was known to be a meticulous pupil master, sitting with his pupils as he went through their drafts. His was a typical Lincoln's Inn successful practice. For example, in 1866 he acted for the old established house of Overend, Gurney & Co. whose failure produced a financial crisis in the City; but he wisely refused to take briefs in the arbitrations which followed for he wished to consolidate his chancery work. He subsequently appeared in a number of well-known partnership disputes and in actions for breach of copyright.

Among Lindley's many theatrical clients was the well-known impresario Frederick Gye the younger. In *Knox* v. *Gye* (1872) George Jessel QC and Lindley were his counsel. One of the questions before the House of Lords was whether letters between Gye and Knox constituted a contract of partnership in the profits of the Italian Opera at both the old and new Covent Garden and the Lyceum. It was held that the agreement, which was not a partnership agreement, was confined to the old Covent Garden, which had been burnt to the ground; Knox's bill for an account of profits when the Italian Opera was held elsewhere was therefore refused. The more contentious point of law concerned the running of the Statute of Limitations; a third party had advanced money to Gye and in his will left half of that loan to Knox. Knox's claim was held to be barred, for time ran from the death of the third party (Lindley had the satisfaction of hearing counsel for Knox, Sir Roundell Palmer QC, citing *Lindley on Partnership*; so in 1872 a living author could be cited in court, a practice which was soon to be discouraged).

In more colourful litigation Lindley represented the defendants in an action for breach of copyright brought by the authors, Meilhac and Halévy, of the French play *Frou-frou*. Lindley's successful defence to their claim, based on a close reading of the French text, was that the English play was an adaptation not a translation of it, and was moreover altered to suit English tastes. The court was crowded and when it was explained to the many French and Belgian theatrical performers that the defendants had succeeded, the tall Belgian actress who played the central character, Frou-frou, embraced Lindley, exclaiming 'Mon sauveur! Mon sauveur!'

By 1872 Lindley was making £4500 a year and was overworked. On the advice of Jessel, then solicitor-general, he took silk in that year and attached himself to the court of Vice-Chancellor Wickens. At this time one of Wickens's leaders, James Dickinson, was seriously ill, and this helped Lindley to establish his silk's practice. In his first year as silk he made a larger income than in his last junior year.

Judge of common pleas Only three years later, by 1875, such was Lindley's reputation that Lord Chancellor Cairns, to the surprise of Lindley and the profession, offered him a judgeship in the court of common pleas. The Judicature Acts (1872–5), which were to fuse the administration of the courts of common law and equity, also contained the provision that where the rules of common law and equity conflicted, those in equity should prevail. Lindley's appointment to a common-law judgeship was perceived to be a preference of the chancery over the common-law bar, for neither Lord Cairns nor Lord Selborne, lord chancellors during this period, had appointed a common lawyer to a chancery judgeship. Lindley naturally hesitated. His common-law experience was very limited; it was confined to the office of revising barrister for Middlesex (1866) and he held that modest appointment only for one turn. Lindley was encouraged to accept the post by the offer of Mr Justice Denman, then a stranger, 'to go' the coming circuit for him, thus giving him time to prepare for criminal work. Lindley accepted the post, was sworn in, knighted, made a serjeant-at-law, and took his seat in the exchequer chamber. From the moment of his appointment he worked from 6 a.m. every day to study the criminal law; and by his second circuit his conduct of a criminal trial was praised by a former chief justice of his court, Sir William Erle. Such became his standing with his brethren that not infrequently he was asked to write the judgment of the court *in banco*.

After six years as a puisne judge, in 1881 Lindley began his eighteen and a half years in the Court of Appeal; for half of that time he normally presided in one court or the other. According to *The Times*, his judgments in that court were 'informed with the scientific spirit, clear and concise'. In 1897 he succeeded Lord Esher as the master of the rolls. His spare time during these years was largely given to drafting rules and orders and consolidating statutes; some were used by the chancellor who had requested them, some were pigeon-holed.

In 1900 Lindley succeeded Lord Morris and Killanin as a lord of appeal and was created a life peer, having refused a hereditary peerage. With his departure from the Court of Appeal the coif (the serjeant's black patch, sitting on the wig) was never seen again in an English court. He was then aged seventy-two, hence his predecessor's witticism: 'a worn-out old man of 73 has been succeeded by a lad of 72'! At first he sat more frequently in the privy council than in the appellate committee of the house. In both tribunals he showed characteristic independence of judgment, though he was, on occasions, overshadowed, indeed overborne, by Macnaghten's forceful personality and penetrating intellect. But there were notable speeches, including his dissent in the litigation arising from the union of the Free Church of Scotland and the United Presbyterian church in 1900 (1904), and his concurring speech in *Quinn* v. *Leathem* (1901) which established the parameters of the tort of conspiracy.

Old age and death In 1905 Lindley fell on the steps of the duke of York's column and was concussed. Soon afterwards, on his seventy-seventh birthday, he was persuaded to resign to make way for Atkinson. His judicial career had lasted thirty years. In sum, it may be fairly said of him that he was a conservative lawyer who, unlike Jessel, was not prepared to sacrifice established precedent for principle. Sound and careful, impeccably impartial, he was the lawyer's lawyer, devoted to the law, never tempted by political ambition, and never the creature of any politician or party. Lindley had none of the élan of Henry James, the brilliance of Charles Bowen, or the refulgent rhetoric of Edward Macnaghten. 'His rubicund features, grizzled whiskers and cheery face betokened rather the vigorous country farmer than the accomplished judge' (*Solicitors' Journal*, 9 Dec 1905). As his career as a puisne judge in the common pleas demonstrated, he was more versatile than any of his contemporaries; he was as comfortable, legally speaking, dealing with an easement of light as with a group of picketers.

Lindley retired to his country home in East Carleton, near Norwich. It had been left to him by the uncle and friend who suggested that he should go to the bar and who had died in 1874, also leaving him a considerable sum of money. His main literary activity consisted of occasional letters to *The Times*. He died at East Carleton on 9 December 1921, two days before Lord Halsbury, who had been called in the same year (1850). Lindley was ninety-three, Halsbury ninety-eight.

Lindley received many honours including FRS (1897) and FBA (1903), and honorary doctorates from Oxford, Cambridge, and Edinburgh. An unusual tribute was Captain Scott's naming after him an Antarctic mountain, Mount Lindley (81°46′ S, 159°05′ E), 'discovered' during the expedition of 1901–4; Lindley had been a member of the committee that drew up the instructions for the expedition. GARETH H. JONES and VIVIENNE JONES

Sources *The Times* (12 Dec 1921) • unpublished autobiography [location unknown by contributor] • *Solicitors' Journal*, 50 (1905–6), 88 • *Solicitors' Journal*, 66 (1921–2), 131–2, 147–8 • *Knox* v. *Gye*, L.R. (1872), 656 • *Quinn* v. *Leathem*, A.C. (1901), 495 • Scottish Free Church case, A.C. (1904), 513 • F. Pollock, *Law Quarterly Review*, 22 (1906), 3 • F. Pollock, *Law Quarterly Review*, 38 (1922), 1 • *Men and women of the time* (1899) • F. G. Alberts, ed., *Geographic names of the Antarctic* (1981) • A. Davies and E. Kilmurray, *Dictionary of British portraiture*, 4 vols. (1979–81)

Archives Middle Temple, London, memoirs [copy]

Likenesses G. Reid, oils, 1907, Middle Temple, London • W. W. Ouless, bust, repro. in *Royal Academy pictures* (1897) • Spy [L. Ward], caricature, chromolithograph, NPG; repro. in *VF* (8 Feb 1890) • W. Strang, etching, BM

Wealth at death £23,718 0s. 4*d*.: probate, 14 Feb 1922, *CGPLA Eng. & Wales*

Lindley, Robert (1776–1855), cellist, was born on 4 March 1776, and baptized on 12 April, at Rotherham, Yorkshire, the son, according to the parish register, of Shirley Linley of Masbrough. His father was a proficient performer on the cello who began to teach his son the violin when he was five, and his own instrument at the age of nine. In 1792 Lindley became a pupil of James Cervetto, the outstanding cellist of his day, who, after hearing him play, gave him free tuition. He then moved to the south of England and subsequently deputized for a soloist at the Brighton Theatre. As Rees (*New Grove*) states, his performance 'caused a sensation and he was engaged by the theatre, where he frequently played before the Prince Regent'.

In 1794 Lindley succeeded Sperati as principal cello at the Italian Opera in London, a post he held until 1851, and at all the major concerts. Domenico Dragonetti, the great double bass virtuoso, joined the opera orchestra in the same year as Lindley, and a close friendship developed between the two, lasting for fifty-two years (see Palmer). In addition to the opera, they played at the same desk at every orchestral concert of importance, establishing long-term associations with the Philharmonic Concerts, the Concerts of Ancient Music, and the principal provincial and other festivals.

Lindley was generally considered to be the greatest English cellist of his time, perhaps his most celebrated achievement being his elaborate and ornamental accompaniment of recitative. His exceptional technique, using a firm hand and brilliant full tone complemented by deep artistic feeling, was widely recognized. Apparently the cellist Bernhard Heinrich Romberg, hearing him in London, told Salomon, 'He is the devil' (Rees). It is also reported that Lindley would occasionally in private play the first violin part of a quartet, or of a Beethoven trio, on his cello (a Carlo Giuseppe Testore, made in 1690). As a composer he was less distinguished, but made a significant contribution to the repertory of his instrument. His four concertos are described by a contemporary critic as 'peculiar, and … suited to every species of audience' (*Quarterly Musical Magazine*, 6, 1824, 480). Other works include some thirty-five solos and duets for the cello; duets for violin and cello; a trio for bassoon, viola, and cello, or two cellos and viola, op. 7 (1810?); a trio for violin, viola, and cello, op. 13 (1820?); a *Caprice bohème* for piano; and a *Handbook for the Violoncello*, published in the year of his death.

In 1822, on the formation of the Royal Academy of Music, Lindley was appointed one of the first professors. Perhaps his most distinguished pupil was Charles Lucas (who succeeded him in the opera orchestra and Cipriani Potter as principal of the academy). He remained very active into his sixties (he and Dragonetti were the only principals who refused to accept 10 guinea cuts in pay for the 1841 Philharmonic season), and finally retired in 1851. He died on 13 June 1855. His daughter married the composer John Barnett in 1837, and his son, William Lindley (1802–1869), was a cellist of much promise with 'a position in all the best London orchestras' (Rees). However, he was unable to achieve prominence as a soloist owing to extreme nervousness and delicate health, and he subsequently withdrew from public performance.

DAVID J. GOLBY

Sources *Musical World* (23 June 1855), 393 · F. M. Palmer, *Domenico Dragonetti in England (1794–1846): the career of a double bass virtuoso* (1997) · C. Ehrlich, *First philharmonic: a history of the Royal Philharmonic Society* (1995) · C. Ehrlich, *The music profession in Britain since the eighteenth century: a social history* (1985) · *Quarterly Musical Magazine and Review*, 6 (1824), 479–80, 482 · *Quarterly Musical Magazine and Review*, 7 (1825), 12 · *Quarterly Musical Magazine and Review*, 8 (1826), 164–5 · *Quarterly Musical Magazine and Review*, 9 (1827), 501 · *Musical World* (21 July 1855), 475 · L. L. Rees, 'Lindley, Robert', *New Grove* · [J. S. Sainsbury], ed., *A dictionary of musicians*, 2 vols. (1824) · E. van der Straeten, *History of the violoncello*, rev. edn (1971) · B. W. Harvey, *The violin family and its makers in the British Isles: an illustrated history and directory* (1995)

Likenesses A. E. Chalon, pen and watercolour drawing, NPG · W. Davison, oils, NPG; repro. in P. A. Scholes, *The mirror of music, 1844–1944* (1947), vol. 1, pl. 48 · M. Hart, engraving (with Dragonetti; after a sketch by Landseer), Royal College of Music, London

Lindley [Lyndeley], **William** (1739–1819), architect, was born on 4 June 1739, possibly at Heath, near Wakefield, the eldest of five children. About 1754 he joined the office of the important provincial architect John Carr of York, as draughtsman; he engraved Carr's stables at Harewood House, Yorkshire, in 1758.

A neo-classical architect, Lindley derived his simplified and unadventurous style from James Paine, Robert Adam, and Carr himself. After twenty years with Carr he advertised his architectural skills in the *York Chronicle* on 18 October 1773. As a result, the corporation of Doncaster appointed him to design a new theatre in 1774, which he completed in 1774–5 (dem.); soon afterwards he moved to Doncaster and was made a freeman in 1783. For the corporation Lindley undertook whatever was required in the way of public architecture: he enlarged Paine's mansion house (1800–01, 1805) and Carr's racecourse grandstand (1804; dem. 1969), improved the town hall (1784–6; dem. 1846), and designed a gaol (1779; dem.) and a dispensary (1793–4; dem. 1969). He was also responsible for civic architecture in Sheffield, where he designed the market (1784–6; dem. 1851) and the Ecclesall court house and gaol (1791; dem.).

Lindley also built domestic architecture, lining the streets of Doncaster with handsome late Georgian houses; one, his own, provided lodging for the prince of Wales when he was attending the races. He designed others at Sheffield, Bawtry, Knaresborough, and Leeds. Wakefield gave him the opportunity to design a 'new' town of stately terraces centred on a classical church (1791–5; with Charles Watson). His grandest town house was undoubtedly Denison Hall (1786–8), built for John Denison, one of Leeds's wealthiest merchants. Lindley went on to design alterations to Denison's country house, Ossington Hall, Nottinghamshire (1788–90, 1805–6; dem. 1963). Lindley's letters to Bryan Cooke of Owston, Yorkshire, in which he constantly pressed Cooke to build a new house by reference to his work for others, enable a number of other country houses to be attributed to him. These include: Ferham House, Rotherham (1781), for Jonathan Walker; Thundercliffe Grange (Grange Hall), near Ecclesfield (1794–5), for the fourth earl of Effingham; and Newhill Hall, Wath-on-Dearne (1784–5; dem.), for John Payne.

A bachelor uncle, whose sister, nephews, and nieces inherited his estate, Lindley never sought office. He paid 'as a gentleman' in guineas (Stapleton, 37) and, sure of his worth, was direct with patrons. His mortification at receiving a dismissal at the hands of a workman was sharply expressed in a letter to St Andrew Warde of July 1798. Lindley had several pupils: in 1790 Charles Watson, the son of an architect, entered his office, before becoming a partner in 1792. John Woodhead became Lindley's partner about 1810, and William Hurst, another partner, was articled *c.*1815. William Lindley died on 28 February 1819, probably at his home, 20 South Parade, Doncaster, and was buried in the parish church on 1 March.

ANGUS C. TAYLOR

Sources A. Taylor, 'William Lindley of Doncaster', *Georgian Group Journal*, [4] (1994), 30–42 · Colvin, *Archs.* · records of the borough of Doncaster, Central Library, Doncaster Archives · J. Tomlinson, *Doncaster* (1887) · H. E. C. Stapleton, ed., *A skilful masterbuilder: the continuing story of a Yorkshire family business, craftsmen for seven generations* (1975) · A. C. Taylor, 'Denison Hall, Leeds: a postscript to Richard Hewlings', *Yorkshire Archaeological Journal*, 63 (1991), 220–21 · *Doncaster, Nottingham and Lincoln Gazette* (5 March 1819) · parish registers, Warmfield, W. Yorks. AS, Wakefield · will, Borth. Inst. · R. Hewlings, 'Denison Hall, Little Woodhouse, Leeds', *Yorkshire Archaeological Journal*, 61 (1989), 173–80 · P. Leach, 'Doncaster Mansion House', *Country Life*, 164 (1978), 18–21 · H. A. Johnson, 'Ossington Hall', *Transactions of the Thoroton Society*, 84 (1980), 48–58 · Doncaster Central Library, Doncaster Archives, Baxter MSS, 61925–61926 · Wakefield City Art Gallery, Gott Collection · U. Nott. L., Denman MSS · Central Library, Doncaster Archives, Cooke of Owston MSS · *Yorkshire Journal* (17 July 1790) · *York Courant* (27 March 1792) · *York Chronicle* (18 Oct 1773)

Archives RIBA BAL | Borth. Inst. · Bucks. RLSS, Drake MSS · Derbys. RO, Turbutt MSS · Doncaster Central Library, Doncaster Archives, Baxter MSS · Doncaster Central Library, Doncaster Archives, Campsmount MSS · Doncaster Central Library, Doncaster Archives, Cooke MSS · Leeds Central Library, Gascoigne MSS · Sheffield Central Library, Arundel MSS · Sheffield Central Library, Fitzwilliam MSS · U. Hull, Thorpe Hall MSS · U. Leeds, Beaumart MSS · U. Nott. L., Denison MSS · U. Nott. L., Galway MSS · W. Yorks. AS, Leeds · Wakefield City Art Gallery, Gott Collection · Wakefield Reference and Information Library, Goodchild loan MSS · York Minster Library, Hailstone Collection

Wealth at death under £2000; some bequests: will, Borth. Inst.; Doncaster Central Library, Doncaster Archives, Baxter MSS

Lindley, William (1808–1900), civil engineer, was born on 7 September 1808 at 1 Surrey Square, Old Kent Road, London, the youngest of four children of Joseph Lindley (1756–1808), of Heath, Yorkshire, a topographical writer, and his wife, Catherine (1772–1845), the eldest daughter of Michael Searles, architect. He was educated at Croydon and at Wandsbeck, near Hamburg (1824–5). In 1827 he became a pupil of Francis Giles and assisted him in the design of the Newcastle and Carlisle Railway and the London and Southampton Railway. In 1836–8 he worked on the regulation of the River Mersey and on the Thames Tunnel with Isambard Kingdom Brunel.

On Brunel's recommendation Lindley was in 1839 appointed engineer-in-chief to the Hamburg and Bergedorf Railway, and subsequently was responsible for a number of projects in Hamburg. In 1840 he designed the drainage and reclamation of the low-lying Hammerbrook district. However, Lindley's great reputation as an engineer largely stemmed from his role in halting the disastrous fire which raged in Hamburg in May 1842. Under his direction controlled explosions of threatened buildings retarded the conflagration and eventually extinguished the fire. He was thanked for his services to the city and a special committee of the senate and town council appointed him consulting engineer to the Hamburg water board and the board of works. Lindley subsequently proposed a trigonometrical survey of the city and suburbs and drew up plans for the complete rebuilding of Hamburg. In the years 1848–60 he supervised that great spate of urban reconstruction. He also designed, executed, and supervised the construction of the Hamburg sewage system and water supply, with later extensions, and the gas works on the Grasbrook. These engineering works transformed the ancient Hanseatic city into one of Europe's most advanced seaports. The water supply and sewerage arrangements constituted one of the most complete systems adopted on the continent up to that time.

William Lindley (1808–1900), by unknown photographer, 1879

In 1850 the three Hanseatic cities (Hamburg, Bremen, and Lübeck) entrusted Lindley with the negotiation of the sale of a large wharf on the banks of the Thames. The sale was successfully concluded, and the site was later used as the location for Cannon Street railway station. In the same year he carried out works on the great retaining wall on the island of Heligoland. In 1855 Lindley supervised the Altona gas and water works that had been designed by Thomas Hawksley. Although principally employed in Hamburg, he carried out consultancy work for a number of other cities, including Berlin, Bremen, Kiel, Stralsund, Stettin, and Leipzig.

On 6 April 1852 Lindley married Jeanne Julie Heerlein (1828–1862); they had four children. However, his wife's ill health caused Lindley to leave Hamburg in 1860, and she died two years later. In 1863 he was invited by the city authorities of Frankfurt am Main to report on its drainage and two years later he was appointed its consulting engineer. In 1868 he submitted a report to the city of Pest on its water supply. Construction of new waterworks began the following year and Lindley was assisted by his eldest son, William Heerlein *Lindley. The latter was just beginning his engineering career, but later took over the running of the family business.

In later years Lindley senior was consulted on water supply systems by the authorities of Düsseldorf, Chemnitz, Basel, Galatz, Brăila, and Jassy and on sewage systems by Düsseldorf, Basel, Krefeld, and Sydney. His last, extensive design was sewerage and water supply for the cities of St Petersburg and Warsaw. The latter was carried out by his three sons, William, Robert, and Joseph.

Lindley retired from active work in 1879. He was elected a member of the Institution of Civil Engineers in 1842 and the Smeatonian Society of Engineers in 1844, serving as its president in 1864. As one of the most important civil engineers working on the continent, he was responsible for the design and construction of water supply systems and sewerage networks in many of the great cities of Europe in the second half of the nineteenth century. He died at his home outside London, 74 Shooter's Hill Road, Blackheath, on 22 May 1900, in his ninety-second year, and was buried at Charlton cemetery, Greenwich, on 25 May.

RYSZARD ŻELICHOWSKI

Sources G. H. Leo, *William Lindley: ein Pionier der technischen Hygiene* (1969) • J. Spallek, 'Alexis de Chateauneuf und William Lindley: ihre gemeinsam erichtete Bauwerke', PhD diss., University of Hamburg, 1978 • R. J. Evans, *Death in Hamburg: society and politics in the cholera years, 1830–1910* (1987) • *Six generations of civil engineers: notes on Lindley family history, 1640–1953* (1953) • *PICE*, 142 (1899–1900), 363–70 • *Neues deutsche Biographie* (1985) • *Wielka encyklopedia powszechna ilustrowana* (1919) • Lindley family MSS, W. Yorks. AS, Leeds, Yorkshire Archaeological Society • *DNB* • d. cert. • R. Żelichowski, *Lindleyowie-dzieje inżynierskiego rodu* (Warszawa, 2003)
Archives W. Yorks. AS, Leeds, Yorkshire Archaeological Society, family papers | Deutsches Museum, Munich, Archive, Plan Sammlung, Stiftung Lindley Handschriften 1981–2 • Inst. CE, letters and the records concerning William Lindley and the Hamburg fire of 1842 and engineering works in the same city, 1842–92 • Staatsarchiv, Hamburg, St AH 321-1, 62-1, etc. • UCL, corresp. with Edwin Chadwick • W. Yorks. AS, Leeds, Yorkshire Archaeological Society, MD 280
Likenesses H. W. Soltau, watercolour drawing, 1852; copy at Inst. CE • photograph, 1853, Inst. CE • engraving, 1869, repro. in *Die Fackel* (3 Oct 1869) • photographs, 1879, Stadtarchiv, Frankfurt am Main; copyprints, Inst. CE [*see illus.*] • photograph, 1888, Archiwum PAN, Warsaw, Poland • H. Wagner, sculpture, unveiled 1993, Baumwall, Hamburg, Germany • photographs, priv. coll.
Wealth at death £142,157 10*s.* 4*d.*: resworn probate, June 1900, *CGPLA Eng. & Wales*

Lindley, Sir William Heerlein (1853–1917), civil engineer, was born on 30 January 1853 at 50 Ferdinand Strasse, Hamburg, Germany, the eldest son in a family of four children of William *Lindley (1808–1900), an English civil engineer, and his wife, Jeanne Julie (1828–1862), daughter of Martin Edward Heerlein, a Hamburg merchant. He was educated in London at private schools in Greenwich and Blackheath and matriculated at London University in 1869.

In 1870 Lindley began his practical training as a pupil of his father, who was working on the construction of new waterworks at Budapest. During his father's absence he was left in charge of the work. In 1873 he became his father's assistant at Frankfurt am Main in Germany, and from 1874 to 1879 he acted as his father's representative and as resident engineer there. His father retired in 1879 and Lindley became chief engineer of the sewerage works in the city. On 24 March of that year he married Fanny Henriette Getz (1858–1923), the daughter of a well-established physician in Frankfurt; their three children, two daughters and a son, were all born in the city. In 1882 the direction of Frankfurt's water supply was also entrusted to Lindley and later in the same year his appointment as the city's chief engineer meant that all its engineering works came under his direction.

During twenty-two years in this post Lindley carried out numerous works: these included construction work on the harbour, new quay walls along the river and embankments with storehouses, and also the conversion of the old stone Main–Neckar railway bridge into a road bridge (the Wilhelmsbrücke). In the course of the latter project he developed a system of boring numerous small tube wells down into fine sand in a long row and coupling them to a suction pipe, and this was subsequently widely copied. Lastly, in 1889, he designed a new electrical supply works. In 1891 he served as a member of the commission of experts, and also as president of the jury at the great Frankfurt Electro-Technical Exhibition.

At the end of 1879 Lindley had also taken over his father's civil engineering practice outside Frankfurt and abroad, extending to at least forty-eight cities. In this capacity he was responsible for the design of waterworks for Moscow, Tiflis, Trieste, Jassy, Bucharest, Craiova, Ploesti, Pitesti, and Warsaw, but only the last four were actually built. He was also consulted as to the water supply of Vienna, Amsterdam, Dorpat, Kovno (Kaunas), Łódź, and St Petersburg. Designs for drainage systems were also prepared and executed in Prague, Würzburg, Mannheim, Tölz, Hanau, Homburg, Elberfeld, Samara, Ploesti, and Włocławek.

Lindley was a prominent figure in the engineering profession. President of the German commission on electric stray currents and of the standardization committee of the German Gas and Water Engineers, he also represented Germany in the international pipe-threads standardization committee. Other bodies on which he served

Sir William Heerlein Lindley (1853–1917), by Eckert, pubd 1912

included the commission for the regulation of the Danube and the German commission of the government board of health. Appreciation of the value of his work was shown by the presentation to him of diplomas at technological exhibitions in Turin (1890), Dijon (1893), Chicago (1893), and Lwów (Lemberg) (1894). In 1893 he was made a knight of the iron crown of Austria, and in 1894 the order of the Corona d'Italia was conferred on him. His professional expertise was also recognized in Britain. He served on the royal commission on canals and waterways in 1906, and was honoured with a knighthood in 1911.

Lindley became a member of thirty-two prestigious organizations, including the Institution of Civil Engineers (1878), the French Society of Sanitary Engineers (1897), and the Society of German Gas and Water Engineers. In 1914 the University of Darmstadt presented him with the honorary degree of doctor of engineering. Lindley's last great undertaking was the construction of a water supply system in the city of Baku in the Caucasus. These works were completed in February 1917, just before the outbreak of the Russian revolution, and led to his being presented with the freedom of Baku. In July 1917 he returned to London. He died at his home, 74 Hazlewell Road, Putney, on 30 December 1917. He was buried at Putney Vale cemetery, on 2 January 1918. RYSZARD ŻELICHOWSKI

Sources F. Lerner, 'William Heerlein Lindley, 1853–1917. Umriss seines Lebens von…', *Archiv für Frankfurts Geschichte und Kunst*, 49 (1965), 123–33 · 'In memoriam, Sir William H. Lindley, Mem. Inst. C.E., F.G.S., 30 Jan 1853–30 Dec 1917', 1917, Stadtarchiv, Frankfurt am Main, Germany, Nachlässe S1/186.12, 1–5 · E. Sokal, 'Dr Inż Sir William Heerlein Lindley', *Wodociągi i Kanalizacja m.st.Warszawy, 1886–1936*, ed. W. Rabczewski and S. Rutkowski (1937), 5–10 · *Engineering* (4 Jan 1918) · 'Water for a great oil-city: building the longest conduit in Europe', *ILN* (25 May 1912), suppl. · d. cert. · *CGPLA Eng. & Wales* (1918) · *WWW* · family MSS, W. Yorks. AS, Leeds, Yorkshire Archaeological Society · *The Times* (2 Jan 1918) · R. Żelichowski, *Lindleyowie-dzieje inżynierskiego rodu* (Warszawa, 2003)

Archives W. Yorks. AS, Leeds, Yorkshire Archaeological Society, family papers | Deutsches Museum, Munich, Archive, Plan Sammlung, Stiftung Lindley Handschriften 1981–2 · Inst. CE, reports and lectures · Stadtarchiv, Frankfurt am Main, Germany, Nachlässe

Likenesses engraving, 1891, repro. in *Elektrizität* (10 May 1891), 103 · photograph, 1911, repro. in A. Grotowski, *Kanalizacja, wodociągi i pomiary* (1911) · photograph, 1915, Muzeum Techniki NOT, Warsaw, Poland · Elliott & Fry, photograph, 1918, repro. in *Engineering* · Z. Wendrowska-Sobolt, stone bas-relief, 1936, Warsaw, Poland · Eckert, photograph, NPG; repro. in 'Water for a great oil-city', xxviii [*see illus.*] · photograph, repro. in *Narodni Listy* (14 June 1929) · photographs, priv. coll.

Wealth at death £15,088 9*s*. 7*d*.: probate, 22 Jan 1918, *CGPLA Eng. & Wales*

Lindo, Abigail (1803–1848), lexicographer, was born in London on 3 August 1803, the third daughter and fifth child of the eighteen children of David Abarbanel Lindo (1772–1852), a prominent Jewish communal worker, and his wife, Sarah (1777–1852), the daughter of Abraham Mocatta and his wife, Esther. Her parents were Sephardi Jews belonging to leading families established in London since the early years of the community in the seventeenth century. She was closely related to the best-known Sephardi Jewish families of the time; Sir Moses Montefiore (1784–1885) was a cousin, and her uncle Ephraim Lindo was a brother-in-law of Disraeli's mother, Maria Basevi. (Her father performed Disraeli's circumcision on 28 December 1804.) Her family home was in Whitechapel, London: first at 15 Leman Street and later at 37 Mansell Street, Goodmanfields, not far from Bevis Marks Synagogue, of which her father was an influential and strictly Orthodox member. Intellectual pursuits were highly regarded in the family circle. Her uncle Moses Mocatta (1768–1857) was a writer and patron of Jewish scholars, and one of her cousins, Elias Haim Lindo (1783–1857), was a pioneer Anglo-Jewish historian.

A studious girl, Abigail benefited from her father's keen interest in Jewish education and also from the tuition of her uncle Moses Mocatta. She became thoroughly proficient in Hebrew and unusually well versed in biblical studies, reaching a level sufficient to be respected by the religious head of the Sephardi community from 1828, Rabbi (Dayan) David Meldola (1797–1853). In the course of her studies she compiled a Hebrew and English vocabulary, which also included brief Hebrew and English dialogues, exchanges amusingly reflecting the polite middle-class society in which she lived. The volume was intended for her own use, but, encouraged by friends, she sanctioned its publication (1837). The value of the work was soon recognized, and it was recommended for use in the community's Hebrew schools. A second edition (1842) incorporated a list of Hebrew abbreviations in ordinary use, the fruit of her extensive reading and a valuable study aid of a kind not then readily available. In 1846 came her main work, a Hebrew–English dictionary, which was intended to assist students towards the works of the most eminent Hebrew lexicographers.

Abigail Lindo was the only woman involved in the early nineteenth-century expansion of biblical philological research and to have publications to her name. She was presumably unacquainted with the cognate languages Aramaic and Arabic, and her work has therefore to be judged by amateur standards. Though overshadowed by subsequent developments in Hebrew philology, her achievement is remarkable for a young English Jewish woman of the time. A later age might well have provided a wider field for her talents. Her writings reveal her as a devout and dutiful daughter, not given to emphasizing her independence; the title-pages of all her works describe her as the third daughter of David Abarbanel Lindo, and his portrait prefaces her dictionary. Valuing what she had achieved by protracted study, she was concerned to inspire others to pursue the same course.

Abigail Lindo did not enjoy robust health. She died at home on 28 August 1848, aged forty-five, following an attack of phlegmasia dolens—a condition described as 'white leg'—which lasted for five weeks; she had suffered from growths in the uterus for fifteen years. She was buried two days later in the Novo (new) cemetery of the Sephardi congregation in Mile End Road, Stepney, in the first of the three graves her father had reserved in 1844 for his unmarried daughters then aged over thirty-five, next to the two he reserved for himself and his wife. He presented £50 in stock (consols) to the congregation in remembrance of her. Her epitaph, in Hebrew, with a poem in Hebrew and English praising her character and achievements, was compiled by Dayan Meldola and printed and circulated to her relatives and friends.

MIRIAM RODRIGUES-PEREIRA

Sources A. Lindo, dedication to Moses Mocatta, *A Hebrew and English and English and Hebrew vocabulary* (1837) • A. Lindo, foreword, *A Hebrew and English and English and Hebrew vocabulary*, 2nd edn (1842) • A. Lindo, preface, *A Hebrew and English and English and Hebrew dictionary*, new edn (1846) • M. Gaster, *History of the ancient synagogue of the Spanish and Portuguese Jews* (1901), 172–4 • M. Rodrigues-Pereira and C. Loewe, eds., *Bevis Marks records*, 5: *The birth register, 1767–1881, of the Spanish and Portuguese Jews' congregation, London* (1993) • M. Rodrigues-Pereira and C. Loewe, eds., *Bevis Marks records*, 6: *The burial register (1733–1918) of the Novo (New) Cemetery of the Spanish and Portuguese Jews' Congregation, London* (1997) • mahamad (wardens') minute books, 1794–1857, Spanish and Portuguese Jews' congregation, London, MSS 108–114 • S. Scharfstein, 'Abigail the lexicographer', *Leshoneinu la-am*, 116–17 (1961), 83–90 [in Hebrew] • d. cert.

Lindon, Patrick. *See* Mac Giolla Fhiondáin, Pádraig (*c*.1665–1733).

Lindores, Lawrence (*d.* 1437), natural philosopher and university principal, is first recorded as a Scottish student in Paris, taking his MA in 1393 under the nominalist Aegidius Jutfaes. Parisian records are wanting for the ten years before this, and nothing records his precise date or place of birth. As a master he presented pupils in arts up to 1401 at least; at the same time he was also studying in theology, in which he was a *scholaris* by 13 October 1394, BTh by 8 August 1403, and LTh by 1406. Playing only a modest part in the wider life of the ('English') nation and university, he did successfully argue that members of his nation should not—through the vagaries of end-of-schism politics—lose their rights to supplicate for benefices under the aegis of the university.

Lindores is last attested at Paris on 7 August 1403, though still technically 'present' in the university on 9 November 1403. He is next recorded—for the first time in Scotland—on 10 May 1408, when he is styled rector of Criech, near St Andrews. The appointment had been his from no later than 1407, by which year he was also an ordained priest, and Criech was to remain his only benefice until his death in 1437. He had earlier been styled *dominus* (April 1393), 'cleric of St Andrews diocese' (October 1394), and by August 1403 had done everything needed to take up a benefice, with or without cure. He is not to be confounded with a namesake who became abbot of the Cistercian house of Culross, who outlived him by some years.

Two strands stand out in Lindores's work in Scotland: his distinguished part in the foundation of St Andrews University, and his career as inquisitor-general. Named first among the university's first teachers—he was the only theologian listed—he lectured for a time on the four books of *Sentences*, but taught regularly in arts, as his status as examiner implied. He was rector twice: at the beginning, and in the crucial town-and-gown delegation which persuaded James I to confirm the university's privileges, and abandon the project of transferring it to Perth. He was more often dean of arts, consciously strengthening the relatively powerful faculty both in symbols of status, and in its possessions. Master for life of the college of St John from 1418, he became in addition principal of the faculty's pedagogy (regulated hall), which was founded on an adjacent site in 1430, and ran them increasingly as one institution, formally recognized as the faculty's possession on Lawrence's death.

The 'Roman' inquisition operated for at least some sixty years in Scotland. Lindores was not the only inquisitor-general recorded, but he was the first, acting under Avignon and post-schismatic papal jurisdictions successively from 1408 until his death. Two trials ended in burning. At Perth in 1408 one James Resby, an English Wycliffite priest (and arguably not, *pace* some, a Franciscan) was burnt. The inquisitor's arguments against two of the forty or more tenets found objectionable were recorded by the chronicler Walter Bower (*d.* 1449). They are commonplace enough, but show that the inquisitor was taking Resby not as a simple enthusiast, but as someone who had been arguing a case (on papal authority) that would have to be met. The second burning, at St Andrews on 23 July 1433, was that of Pavel Kravar, who is now thought to have been a Bohemian (as Knox indeed said), rather than from Kravaře in Silesia. An academic turned Hussite propagandist, Kravar had used a medical cover in Poland, and was apparently set to do the same in Scotland, to win support for the Hussite cause at the Council of Basel. Against a third accused, the Franciscan Robert Harding, Lindores showed himself reluctant to act. Harding, an English theologian, had been invited by the duke of Albany (*d.* 1420), regent of Scotland during the captivity of James I, to put the case against the measures taken by the Council of Constance to end the papal schism. Arguing on broadly conciliarist lines, Harding was vigorously opposed by Scottish churchmen, who also pressed Lindores to act. Despite further pressure from Martin V (*r.* 1417–31) too, Lindores delayed still, and Harding died a natural death in 1419. The Avignon pope Benedict XIII (*r.* 1394–1417) under whose jurisdiction the inquisitor had earlier worked, was still alive, and Lindores (who had been significantly absent from crucial steps in transferring allegiance) is not recorded as acting again as inquisitor until after the deaths of both Benedict and Martin V. The two remaining cases known ended in recantations at an early stage. John Fogo, abbot of Melrose, one of those who had pressed Lindores to act against Harding, later exposed himself to the inquisition through loosely stated views on oath-bound obligations. Summoned to St Andrews, Fogo recanted. In 1435 one Robert Gardiner extolled canon law and disparaged arts in a lecture to St Andrews canonists. Before a significantly solemn assembly (27 October) Gardiner recanted the propositions that had been found objectionable.

From Lindores's arts teaching at Paris come the surviving commentaries on Aristotle's *Physics* and *De anima* which migrated with 'Parisian' nominalism itself to Prague (by 1406), Cracow, Leipzig, Erfurt, Vienna, Freiburg, and elsewhere, and kept his name alive among philosophers for over a century. A commentary on the *Perihermeneias* was last recorded in sixteenth-century Alcalá, and a *De caelo* commentary and a question *De reflexionibus* have also been attributed to him. No theological works are known to survive, though he did lecture on Peter Lombard's *Sentences* at St Andrews. Later attributions of works in canon law are more dubious.

What of the thought in the surviving works? By the time of Lindores, nominalists were concerned to show in detail how the abstract terms needed in a scientific language could be grounded in a world of concrete particulars, and without appeal to the abstract entities of some earlier metaphysicians. Thus in Aristotelian psychology (*scientia de anima*) Lindores set himself to explain how the term *anima*, taken as connoting a capacity for certain observable, vital operations, might be made sense of in relation to the operations: much as dispositional terms generally (for example 'soluble', 'fragile') have to be made sense of, he appears to have thought. This may not be particularly easy for a nominalist of Lawrence's stripe, and how far his programme succeeds either in this, or in his treatment of impetus in physics (which attracted some attention, but no known followers), or in his treatment of universals generally, cannot yet be safely assessed.

Little is known of Lindores's family, and even his name need not tie him to Lindores, or to its abbey. The most intimate insight into the man comes from a charter of 1434, founding a chaplaincy in the parish church of St Andrews to celebrate mass 'for the salvation of the souls of … the present bishop of St Andrews, of my father and mother; also for the salvation of my own soul, and of the souls of my brothers and sisters and benefactors … living or dead … and of all the faithful' (Fleming, 578–87). No children are known, and no suggestion of interest in the romantic or the prurient was made in his lifetime. The chaplaincy was fulfilled into Reformation times, monitored by the provost and council.

Poor enough in Paris, Lindores passed for a man of property in St Andrews: he put up the money, jointly with the earl of Douglas, for the faculty's mace, and owned houses in fashionable South Street. Named material beneficiaries of the chaplaincy were the bishop of St Andrews (10s. annually), the abbot and convent of Balmerino (10s.), the (Augustinian) 'monastery of St Andrews' (2s.), and Agnes Fryslae and her heirs (6s.).

Lindores's inquisitorial work was followed by a couple of generations of (perhaps merely specious) calm. At St Andrews his institutions endured, and in the Scottish universities generally it became something of a custom for theologians to teach in arts, as John Mair (*d.* 1550) was to note. But from the complexities made easier to appreciate by the publication of the arts faculty's *acta*, he should not—in view of his opportunities—be ascribed quite such a masterful personality, or quite the dominance in the university, that historians used sometimes to attribute to him. And his management of people left recurring conflicts, independently of the waning of nominalism at St Andrews, which in any case came neither from intellectual revolution nor active suppression (or release), but rather because academic contacts proved easier with realist-favouring Louvain and Cologne, than with the nominalist-favouring universities of central Europe. His natural philosophy, apparently unavailable at Paris when George Lokert (*d.* 1547) and others were printing nominalist texts there in the early sixteenth century, fell into oblivion, until Michalski and other Polish scholars reported on it from the 1920s. Editions of the *Physics* and *De anima* commentaries are in progress, but a systematic and comprehensive exposition of his thought is not yet available.

Neither the place of Lindores's death nor that of his burial is known, but the arts masters' haste to secure his muniments and assume his funeral costs—before the theology faculty could be formally constituted (and hence succeed to the college of St John)—makes the early hours of 16 September 1437, in or near St Andrews, the likeliest time and place of his death. LAWRENCE MOONAN

Sources D. H. Fleming, *The Reformation in Scotland: causes, characteristics, consequences* (1910), 578–87 • L. Moonan, 'The scientific writings of Lawrence of Lindores (d. 1437)', *Classica et Mediaevalia*, 38 (1987), 217–66 • L. Moonan, 'The scientific writings of Lawrence of Lindores (d. 1437)', *Classica et Mediaevalia*, 39 (1988), 273–317 • H. Denifle and A. Chatelain, eds., *Auctarium chartularii universitatis Parisiensis*, 1 (Paris, 1894); repr. (Paris, 1937) • H. Denifle and A. Chatelain, eds., *Chartularium universitatis Parisiensis*, 4 (Paris, 1897) • A. I. Dunlop, ed., *Acta facultatis artium universitatis Sanctiandree, 1413–1588*, 2 vols., Scottish History Society, 3rd ser., 54–5 (1964) • W. Bower, *Scotichronicon*, ed. D. E. R. Watt and others, new edn, 9 vols. (1987–98), vol. 8 • W. H. Bliss, ed., *Calendar of entries in the papal registers relating to Great Britain and Ireland: petitions to the pope* (1896) • *CEPR letters*, vols. 8–9 • Robert of Montrose, 'Charter', *University of St Andrews* (1837), vol. 3 of *Evidence, oral and documentary, taken and received by the commissioners … for visiting the universities of Scotland*, 350 • [J. Haldenston], *Copiale prioratus Sanctiandree: the letter-book of James Haldenstone, prior of St Andrews, 1418–1443*, ed. J. H. Baxter, St Andrews University Publications, 31 (1930), 3–4 • F. McGurk, ed., *Calendar of papal letters to Scotland of Benedict XIII of Avignon, 1394–1419*, Scottish History Society, 4th ser., 13 (1976) • L. Moonan, 'Lawrence of Lindores (d. 1437) on "Life in the living being"', diss., University of Louvain, 1966, 359ff. [copy in St Andrews Library and comments in S. Wzodek, 'Wawrzyniec z Lindores—zycie, dziela i poglady', *Studia Mediewistyczne*, 19 (1978) 95–108] • D. E. R. Watt, *A biographical dictionary of Scottish graduates to* AD

1410 (1977), xlii, 607ff. • J. M. Anderson, 'The beginnings of St Andrews University', *SHR*, 8 (1910–11), 225–46, 333–58 • K. Michalski, *La philosophie au XIVe siècle*, ed. K. Flasch (Frankfurt am Main, 1969), xv, 415ff. • T. Dewender and O. Pluta, 'Lawrence of Lindores on immortality. An edition with analysis of four of his *Quaestiones in Aristotelis libras de anima*', *Bochumer Philosophisches Jahrbuch für Antike und Mittelalter*, 2 (1997), 187–242

Archives NA Scot., St Andrews charters

Wealth at death £1 8*s*. p.a. in annual bequests: charter of mortification

Lindow Man (*fl.* **1st cent.**?), victim of ritual sacrifice, colloquially named Pete Marsh or the Body in the Bog, was found in Lindow Moss, near Wilmslow, Cheshire, in August 1984. A Celt, probably of the Brigantes tribe, he was a ritual sacrifice whose remains were deposited in a peat bog. The skin, hair, fingernails, bone collagen, and some internal organs had been preserved by the tannins of the sphagnum moss.

Lindow Man died aged twenty to twenty-five years old. He stood about 5 feet 5 inches tall and was of average build. His hair and beard were neatly trimmed, and he was buried face down, naked except for a fox-fur band around his left arm. His unscarred body, smooth fingernails, and possible traces of blue body paint, imply that he was a priest, bard, or prisoner, prepared—perhaps willingly—to act as a sacrifice. The remarkable preservation of the body allows an accurate picture of his last hours to be drawn. Lindow Man's final meal consisted of a coarse wheat and barley griddle bread and he had drunk peaty water. His stomach also contained four pollen grains of mistletoe and he had a bad case of worms. He was killed in a particularly savage way: he received two severe blows to the top of the head, fracturing his skull; an animal sinew was tied tightly around his neck and twisted until his neck broke; his throat was cut and he must have bled forcibly. The body was then carried 200 yards across a treacherous peat bog, stripped nearly naked, and put into the bottom of a peaty pool or under a carpet of moss.

No datable artefacts were found with the body, so the dating of this discovery relies upon the radiocarbon method. For Lindow Man, three date ranges have emerged. His stratigraphic position belonged to the middle Iron Age. Dates taken on samples from the body at Oxford University produced a mean uncalibrated date of 1940 ± 25 bp (which converts to 2 BC–AD 119), while those undertaken at the Harwell laboratory produced a mean of 1575 ± 30 bp (converting to AD 410–500). Reconciliation of these dates is problematic. Since the body was buried below the surface of the bog, this stratigraphic position must be older than the corpse itself. The difference between the date ranges for the body must arise from an instrumentation error. Taking these factors into account, a first century AD date for Lindow Man is favoured.

Taken individually, Lindow Man might be explained as the victim of a brutal murder. However, Lindow Moss has produced at least one other bog body. A well-preserved head, Lindow I, was found in May 1983 (and, bizarrely, led to the solving of a modern murder). Most of the body of a naked adult male, Lindow III, was recovered in pieces in February 1987. These two, buried separately, probably belong to the same body, dating to the period AD 25–230. The Lindow bodies can also be compared with other famous bog bodies: Tollund Man and Grauballe Man from Denmark, Damendorf Man from Germany, Zweeloo Man and Yde Girl from Holland, and Gallagh Man from Ireland, all late prehistoric in date and suffering violent deaths. Well-preserved bog bodies have also been found in small numbers, since the seventeenth century, elsewhere in northern England and in Wales. Celtic people were known to venerate peat bogs and other watery places. As well as bodies, these sites have often produced valuable single objects or hoards of tools and weapons from the late Bronze Age into the Roman period. Classical authors, Celtic myths, and English folktales all describe ritual sacrifice and burial in peat bogs. It is these many strands of evidence which confirm that Lindow Man was a religious ritual sacrifice, a special act of propitiation or even divination.

The torso and right foot of Lindow Man have been conserved and are displayed in the British Museum. His buttocks and thighs, recovered in 1988, and the remains of Lindow III, are stored unconserved in the museum.

RICK TURNER

Sources I. M. Stead, J. B. Bourke, and D. Brothwell, eds., *Lindow Man, the body in the bog* (1986) • R. C. Turner and R. G. Scaife, eds., *Bog bodies: new discoveries and new perspectives* (1995) • J. A. J. Gowlett, R. E. M. Hedges, and I. A. Law, 'Radiocarbon accelerator (AMS) dating of Lindow Man', *Antiquity*, 63 (1989), 71–9 • P. V. Glob, *The bog people* (1969) • M. Green, *The gods of the Celts* (1986)

Likenesses photographs, 1984, BM • R. Neave, wax and bronze medical reconstruction, 1986, BM • hologram, 1988, BM

Lindrum, Walter Albert (**1898–1960**), billiards player, was born on 29 August 1898 at Bourke, near Kalgoorlie, a Western Australian goldmining town, the youngest of four children and the second of the two sons of Frederick William Lindrum II (1865–1943), billiard-hall proprietor and bookmaker, and his wife, Harriett Atkins (1864–1951). His grandfather Frederick William Lindrum I (*d.* 1880) emigrated as a child from Britain in 1838, and eventually established himself in South Australia as a hotelier and billiard-hall proprietor. Walter's father and grandfather were both outstanding billiards players, so the next generation of Lindrum men were expected to follow suit. The elder boy, Frederick William III (1888–1958), was tutored by an obsessional father, whose aim was to produce a world billiards champion. Fred III showed considerable talent, even flamboyance, in becoming champion of Australia in 1908, but his reign was tenuous after a poor tour of England in 1911–12; thereafter young Walter Lindrum began to capture the billiards spotlight.

Walter Albert, whose name was chosen to match the initials of the colony where he was born, was educated mainly in Sydney, where he attended St Francis's Boys' School, Darlinghurst, and Albion Street School, Paddington. He was an avid sports player: in addition to a passion for billiards he was particularly able at cricket. But Walter's father insisted that he specialize, so when he left school at fifteen he became, like his older brother, a professional billiards player. Walter had grown up in the shadow of Fred III but was now expected to outshine him. He was, none the less, somewhat reticent about upstaging his brother, and allowed Fred III to retain the title of champion of Australia, despite having defeated him during a three-way tussle with New Zealand champion Clark McConachy. By the age of eighteen, however, Walter was clearly the outstanding billiards player in Australia, regularly giving competitors a healthy start and a sound beating. Intriguingly, both the Lindrum boys played with their 'unnatural' hand: Fred III, though a left-hander, was trained for the convenience of his father's instruction as a right-hand player, while Walter changed to the left-hand grip because part of the index finger on his right hand was removed after a childhood accident.

The war delayed Walter Lindrum's rise to world prominence in billiards, though during the 1920s he defeated several distinguished visiting English players, including W. H. Stevenson (1922) and Claude Falkiner (1924). He soon received numerous cash offers to play in Britain but mysteriously declined them all. His reluctance to tour England, the hub of the billiards world, suggests a rather puzzling lack of purpose in seeking to become world champion. It was not until after he had defeated the great English player Willie Smith, who toured Australia in 1928, that Lindrum conceived a plan to compete in Britain. He convinced John Wren, a prominent gambler in Victoria, to organize a betting plunge with English bookmakers: now that Lindrum had conquered Smith he was convinced he could beat all-comers. But the idea went awry: Lindrum's long-time girlfriend Nellie (Rosie) Coates (*b.* 1908) died on 23 August 1929 after injuries sustained in a car accident. Tragically, he married Rosie on her deathbed. Though mortified, Lindrum still went to England, but under these dire circumstances the plan with Wren was never pursued.

Upon Lindrum's arrival in England in October 1929 there was great anticipation among billiards players and audiences. They were not disappointed, except to see their local stars dominated by a player who compiled the greatest breaks the game has ever seen. He broke seventeen billiards world records on this tour, and returned three more times to England either to match or to eclipse these startling performances. Lindrum's exploits even captured the interest of royalty: on 1 February 1931 he accepted an invitation from George V to put on an exhibition game at Buckingham Palace. In his third visit to England he made a world record break of 4137 in 2 hours 55 minutes against Joe Davis at Thurstan's Hall on 19 and 20 January 1932. Such was Lindrum's mastery of nursery cannons (shots where the balls barely moved but still counted as a score) that billiards authorities disallowed that technique from September 1932. Lindrum was, however, not the only player to use this strategy to great effect, and when he was obliged to change his game-plan he did so with ease. He made his final visit to England in October 1932, and during that season he finally had the opportunity to compete for the title of world champion. His defeat of the English billiards champion Joe Davis in May 1933 and his defence of the title the following year confirmed his status as the greatest player of his era. Yet Lindrum invited hostility from the English billiards establishment by insisting that he take the championship trophy to Australia and defend the title there, which he did successfully against Davis and the New Zealander Clark McConachy in 1934.

It is not clear why Lindrum never again returned to England. He continued to break world billiards records in Australia, so a decline in form does not seem to be a factor. For instance, during 1940–41 Lindrum made four breaks over 3000—each of them under the new baulk-line rule—so the game's 'reformers' had hardly eroded the champion's scoring capacity. Some commentators have suggested

Walter Albert Lindrum (1898–1960), by Edward G. Malindine, 1929 [lining up a shot, watched by Willie Smith]

that because Lindrum had taken all before him, he was no longer as keen to travel and to compete abroad. In 1950 Lindrum refused a challenge from McConachy and returned the championship trophy to England, though its importance was by this time diminished as snooker had taken prominence over billiards.

Lindrum was appointed MBE in 1951 and OBE in 1958. These awards acknowledged the champion's billiards talent, but they also recognized his drive and initiative in raising huge sums for charity. After the death of his first wife, Lindrum married Alicia (Pat) Hoskin (1906–1977) on 9 April 1933, but this alliance ended in divorce on 1 April 1954. He then married (on 21 July 1956) Beryl Elaine Russell (*née* Carr), with whom he stayed until his death. Lindrum died on 30 July 1960 while holidaying at Surfers' Paradise, Queensland. Awarded the honour of a state funeral, he was buried at Melbourne general cemetery on 3 August 1960. DARYL ADAIR

Sources A. Ricketts, *Walter Lindrum: billiards phenomenon* (1982) · *DNB* · *AusDB* · *Daily Examiner* (3 Aug 1960)

Archives FILM BFI NFTVA, documentary footage · BFI NFTVA, sports footage

Likenesses E. G. Malindine, photograph, 1929, Hult. Arch. [*see illus.*]

Lindsay. For this title name *see* individual entries under Lindsay; *see also* Bethune, Sir Henry, first baronet and *de jure* ninth earl of Lindsay (1787–1851).

Lindsay family, **earls of Crawford** (*per.* *c.*1380–1495), nobility, became important in the history of north-east Scotland, and especially Angus, in the fourteenth century.

The basis for an earldom Originating in the twelfth century, the family rose through service to the crown and a series of profitable marriages. Two other branches had died out, but the Lindsays of Crawford, Lanarkshire, still flourished in the mid-fourteenth century. **David Lindsay**, first earl of Crawford (*d.* 1407), was the elder son of Sir Alexander *Lindsay of Glenesk, third son of Sir David *Lindsay of Crawford [*see under* Lindsay family (*per.* *c.*1250–*c.*1400)], and his first wife, Katherine, daughter of Sir John Stirling of Glenesk. Alexander died in Crete, probably early in 1382, while undertaking a pilgrimage to the Holy Land. Yet it was not before Martinmas 1382, and in some instances not until 1384, that Sir David (who seems to have been knighted by the early 1380s) gained title to his father's legacy. This was composed of various heritable annuities (drawn from the burgh fermes of Aberdeen, Crail, and Forfar) and a disparate collection of lands: Glenesk and Finavon in Angus; Newdosk in Kincardineshire; Cambo in Fife; and possibly also Balindoch and Earl's Ruthven in Perthshire and Inverarity and Ethiebeton in Angus, lands which were certainly in David's possession before his death. By 1381 he also held nominal title to the barony of Strathnairn, Inverness-shire, which may have constituted the dowry of his wife, Elizabeth Stewart, a daughter of King Robert II. The date of their marriage is unknown, though a papal dispensation for it was granted on 22 February 1375. It underlines the extent to which the Lindsays, already influential under David II, were able to consolidate their position in the reign of Robert II. In 1381/2 the income from Strathnairn was granted by the crown to Elizabeth's brother Alexander, earl of Buchan, but Lindsay was compensated from the customs revenues of Dundee.

Lindsay's income from paternal and perhaps marital sources was substantially augmented following the deaths first of his cousin Sir James *Lindsay of Crawford [*see under* Lindsay family (*per.* *c.*1250–*c.*1400)] between 5 April 1395 and 6 March 1396, and then of his brother, Alexander, between June 1397 and May 1398. From James, in accordance with the terms of an entail confirmed by Robert II in 1384 or 1385, Sir David acquired Crawford in Lanarkshire and Kirkmichael and perhaps also Ewesdale, both in Dumfriesshire. From his brother he probably obtained Baltrody in Perthshire and Downie in Angus, which had both belonged to his father; Alyth in Perthshire, which had previously belonged to his cousin; and Urie in Kincardineshire, which Alexander had obtained in 1390. These multifariously acquired lands and pensions were to form the basis of the earldom of Crawford, to which Sir David was elevated on 21 April 1398. In subsequent years further lands and pensions were to come his way. In 1403 he acquired Megginch in Perthshire and Clova in Angus from the countess of Mar, and the following year William Megill resigned his Perthshire barony of Meigle to the earl. At an unknown date he also obtained Kineff in Kincardineshire, which, although regranted to his half-brother Walter, reverted to the comital line on the death of Walter's son Walter some time after 1438. While the income from the earl's lands remains unquantifiable, annuities which he drew from various towns ensured that he was a wealthy man. These included £66 13*s.* 8*d.*, drawn from the Aberdeen customs, in return for service to David, duke of Rothesay, from 1391/2; a further £44 8*s.* 11*d.*, drawn from the Dundee customs, inherited from his cousin James from 1396/7, which rose to £66 13*s.* 4*d.* from 1403/4, following the death of the latter's wife; and £26 13*s.* 4*d.* from 1397/8, drawn from the Montrose customs.

Domestic and foreign affairs As the leading magnate in north-east Scotland and also, it would seem, a responsible and diligent nobleman, David Lindsay played a prominent part in regional and local politics. He worked in collaboration with the dukes of both Rothesay (of whose council he was a member) and Albany, guardians of the realm for most of the period between 1388 and 1420, to curtail the recalcitrant earl of Buchan's influence. In 1391 he participated in the highland campaign led by Albany which was directed against Buchan. On or about 18 January 1392 he took part in a skirmish at either Glen Brerachan or Glasclune; his adversaries are variously reported as Buchan's illegitimate sons and members of clan Donnchaidh. During this encounter Walter Ogilvy, sheriff of Angus, was killed and Lindsay was wounded. Further encounters with highland caterans and Buchan's family were to follow. Lindsay was involved in arranging the famous judicial combat between members of clan Quhele and clan Kay which was staged before King Robert III at Perth on 28 September 1396. His promotion to the rank of earl in 1398 should probably be regarded as part of the crown's programme of strengthening its position in the north at this time. By November 1400 he had aligned himself with the Erskine family in its claim to the earldom of Mar, advanced in anticipation of the death of Countess Isabella. In 1402, following the death of Isabella's second husband, Sir Malcolm Drummond, Crawford became a member of the countess's council, but his plans for an Erskine succession were thwarted two years later by Isabella's unexpected third marriage to Buchan's son Alexander. Crawford was, however, instrumental in brokering a deal between the new earl and Erskine's principal supporter, Albany, at Kildrummy on 1 December 1404, which left Alexander in possession of Mar for life.

Well before he became an earl Lindsay had acquired an international reputation, one secured during a visit in 1390 to London, where on 4 or 6 May he defeated Lord Welles in a tournament, to be rewarded with gifts from Richard II. Chivalric interests and a family tradition of crusading probably explain why he and his brother, Alexander, enrolled in the order of the Passion, a crusading order established by Philippe de Mézières in 1395, though neither is known to have engaged the infidel. Instead Lindsay became increasingly involved in governmental matters. Although he was appointed deputy chamberlain north of the Forth in 1405, his chief responsibility concerned foreign affairs. In March 1394 he was named a conservator of the Anglo-Scottish truce and he participated in further Anglo-Scottish truce negotiations between 1397 and 1400. Probably in 1401 and certainly by 1403 he had been made admiral. In December 1401, in the hope of winning French military assistance for Scottish campaigns against England, Crawford arrived in Paris, apparently spreading the falsehood that the by now deposed Richard II was alive and well in Scotland, and on 3 January 1402 he entered the service of Louis, duc d'Orléans, the leader of the French war party. By 22 March Crawford was at Harfleur, in command of a predominantly French fleet, which in the subsequent four months captured at least twenty-five English merchant vessels in the channel. Some of the spoils were taken to Corunna in Spain, where Crawford donated an anchor and a boat to Jean de Béthencourt, seigneur de Grainville, in furtherance of the latter's attempt to conquer the Canary Islands. As the fleet reached Scotland only late in July, Crawford was absent during the time of the removal from power and subsequent death of Rothesay, his former patron, though his half-brother Sir William Lindsay of Rossie had been one of the duke's captors. Nor is he recorded as having fought at Homildon Hill on 14 September following.

Political doldrums Crawford died in 1407, probably in February, and was reportedly buried in the Franciscan church in Dundee. He was succeeded by his eldest son, **Alexander Lindsay**, second earl of Crawford (*d.* 1438/9), who was much less prominent in public life than his father. In part this was the result of two spells in captivity, in 1406–7 as a hostage for the fourth earl of Douglas and in 1424–7 as a hostage for James I. In 1407 Henry IV of England granted him a safe conduct for travel to Amiens, an early indication of a long-standing family devotion to St John the Baptist, whose head was venerated there. He received a safe conduct for travel to England in 1416 and again in 1421, when he was one of the commissioners appointed to negotiate the release of James I from English captivity. In December of the same year he arranged a male entail for the Crawford lands. In 1424 he met James at Durham with hostages for the king's release. Although Crawford is said to have been knighted at James's coronation on 21 May 1424, on 25 March he had taken oath as a hostage for the king, his own ransom set at 1000 merks. During this second period of captivity he was imprisoned in the Tower of London, York, and finally Pontefract. Two years after his release in 1427 he endowed a chaplaincy in the parish church of Dundee with an annual grant of 12 merks. He received another safe conduct in January 1430, to meet English envoys at Hawdenstank, and in January 1431 he was again nominated as an ambassador to England. In 1438 he was appointed a commissioner of the Anglo-Scottish truce. Little else is known of Crawford, but he was said to have been active in the capture of James I's assassins. He and his wife Marjory, whose identity is unrecorded, had five sons and two daughters. When the second earl died, between 31 March 1438 and 8 September 1439, he was succeeded by his eldest son, David.

David Lindsay, third earl of Crawford (*d.* 1446), had been knighted by 17 September 1425 and witnessed a royal charter as earl on 1 February 1440. During the minority of James II he was associated politically with the Douglas family and he was among those who ravaged the lands of James Kennedy, bishop of St Andrews, in 1445. As a result he was excommunicated; according to a later source, this did not bother him greatly. He died at Finavon Castle on 17 January 1446, having been mortally wounded while attempting to prevent a battle at Arbroath between Lindsay kinsmen and the Ogilvy family, to which his wife, Marjory, belonged. Friction between the two families had arisen after the earl's son Alexander was replaced as justiciar of Arbroath Abbey by Alexander Ogilvy of Inverquharity. Countess Marjory, the daughter of Alexander Ogilvy of Auchterhouse, outlived her husband and endowed a mass on his behalf in the Franciscan church at Dundee. Later chroniclers stated that she smothered her wounded cousin Alexander *Ogilvy as revenge for the death of her husband. He had died excommunicate and was not buried until his erstwhile foe Bishop Kennedy lifted the sentence. The couple had two sons, of whom the elder, Alexander, succeeded as fourth earl. The younger, Walter of the Aird and Beaufort, Inverness-shire, possessed estates at Edzell and Kynblethmont in Angus. They also had at least one daughter, Johanna, who married Sir Alexander Seton of Tullibody.

The tiger earl **Alexander Lindsay**, fourth earl of Crawford (*d.* 1453), who had been knighted during his father's lifetime, was nicknamed both the Tiger (because of his fierce character) and Beardie (for obvious facial reasons). He had been appointed sheriff of Aberdeenshire by 1450 and as an envoy to England and commissioner of the truce the following year. From 1453 he was also a guardian of the march. Despite his border interests he was also active in the north-east, and probably in the early 1450s entered into a bond with the eighth earl of Douglas and John Macdonald, lord of the Isles. Its terms do not survive, but it was most likely intended to resolve tensions in the region while securing the interests of the subscribers. This alliance of three of the most powerful magnates in the kingdom aroused the suspicion of James II, however, and was the immediate cause of his slaying of Douglas on 22 February 1452. Shortly afterwards, on 18 May, Crawford was defeated by the earl of Huntly at Brechin and fled to Finavon. Although Huntly is said to have 'displayit the kingis banere' (McGladdery, 173), the battle may have been as much an extension of a private feud (Huntly had been involved in the hostilities at Arbroath in which Crawford's father was fatally wounded) as a consequence of James's hostility to Crawford. Crawford was forfeited in the parliament which assembled at Edinburgh on 12 June, but he subsequently reconciled his differences with Huntly and his father's foe Bishop Kennedy and, helped by their intercession on his behalf, had been restored to the king's favour by 23 May 1453, when he was made a conservator of a truce with England.

Crawford married Margaret (*d.* 1498x1500), daughter and heir of Sir David Dunbar. James II had granted the lands of Auchtermonzie and Cairnie to Dunbar. These estates passed to Margaret and then to her second son, also named Alexander, who ultimately became seventh earl of Crawford. The fourth earl's other children included a daughter, Elizabeth (who married John, first Lord Drummond), and an illegitimate son, yet another Alexander, who became rector of Belhelvie and a canon of Aberdeen Cathedral. The earl died in September 1453 and was buried at the Greyfriars church in Dundee, the resting place of his predecessors. After his death Margaret married Sir William Wallace of Craigie.

Earl and duke The fourth earl's eldest son, **David Lindsay**, fifth earl of Crawford and duke of Montrose (1440–1495), was still a minor at the time of his father's death. His great-uncle Walter, the third earl's brother, was appointed as his tutor and also acted, along with John *Lindsay, Lord Lindsay of the Byres [*see under* Lindsay family of the Byres], as sheriff of Aberdeenshire. David's ward and marriage were granted to James, Lord Hamilton, in 1459. Perhaps aged about eighteen, David married Hamilton's daughter, Elizabeth. His minority came to an end in 1462. In January 1464 he granted his mother the barony of Kirkmichael for life and in 1466 he became hereditary sheriff of Angus, following the resignation from that position of Alexander Ogilvy of Auchterhouse, nephew of the third earl's wife.

Politically the fifth earl was closely associated with James III. He may have been in England on diplomatic business in 1466, when members of the Boyd family abducted the king. He remained aloof from the Boyd regime and in 1469 headed the assize which sentenced Sir Alexander Boyd to death for his role in the royal kidnapping. Thereafter he was a regular witness of royal charters and frequently attended parliament. The earl's attachment to James III was further demonstrated by his endowment in 1474 of a perpetual chaplaincy for the king's soul, and that of Queen Margaret, at the church of Meigle. By then the king had already shown him considerable favour. In 1473 he was granted the lordship of Brechin and made keeper of Berwick, a position which he held for three years. In 1474 he was involved in the unsuccessful negotiations for the king's marriage to Cecilia, daughter of Edward IV of England. By 1482 Crawford was master of the royal household and the following year he was appointed royal chamberlain and, together with the second earl of Huntly, justiciar of the north. Loyal service to the crown was rewarded on 18 May 1488, when he was created duke of Montrose. This was the first instance of ducal rank accorded to a man who was not a member of the royal family and it was accompanied by the award of additional lands, including the castle and burgh of Montrose and the lordship of Kinclaven in Perthshire, to be held in full regality. The new duke's fortunes declined temporarily after the defeat of James III at the battle of Sauchieburn on 11 June; he was imprisoned and removed from public office, resigning the sheriffdom of Angus. He was not, however, charged with treason and was soon pardoned by the new king, James IV. His ducal title was confirmed, but only for life, by royal charter of 19 September 1489. Appointment to the privy council in 1490 appeared to confirm his rehabilitation.

Crawford and his first wife, Elizabeth, who was the only child of James, first Lord Hamilton, and his first wife, Euphemia, daughter of Patrick Graham, earl of Strathearn, had four children. The elder son, Alexander, quarrelled with and was killed by the younger son, John (*d.* 1513), who succeeded as sixth earl. One daughter, Margaret, was married to John Blair of Balmyle, while the other, Elizabeth, married David Lyon of Baky. By 1484 the earl's first marriage had been dissolved on the grounds of consanguinity, and he then married Margaret Carmichael of Meadowflat, who was later styled duchess of Montrose. In 1488 she was granted the lands of Cockburn in Berwickshire, previously held by James III's brother Alexander, duke of Albany. The duke of Montrose died at Finavon Castle on Christmas day 1495 and was buried in the church of the Dundee Greyfriars. The dowager duchess later endowed a mass for her husband's soul at Brechin Cathedral; she died in 1534.

ALISON CATHCART and DAVID DITCHBURN

Sources J. M. Thomson and others, eds., *Registrum magni sigilli regum Scotorum / The register of the great seal of Scotland*, 11 vols. (1882–1914), vols. 1–2 • *CDS*, vol. 4 • G. Burnett and others, eds., *The exchequer rolls of Scotland*, 23 vols. (1878–1908), vols. 2–10 • *RotS*, vol. 2 • *APS, 1124–1567* • P. Chalmers, J. I. Chalmers, and C. Innes, eds., *Registrum episcopatus Brechinensis*, 2 vols., Bannatyne Club, 102 (1856) • H. Maule, *Registrum de Panmure*, ed. J. Stuart, 2 vols. (1874) • C. Innes, ed., *Registrum episcopatus Moraviensis*, Bannatyne Club, 58 (1837) • W. Bower, *Scotichronicon*, ed. D. E. R. Watt and others, new edn, 9 vols. (1987–98) • W. B. D. D. Turnbull, ed., *Extracta e variis cronicis Scocie*, Abbotsford Club, 23 (1842) • C. McGladdery, *James II* (1990) • Lord Lindsay [A. W. C. Lindsay, earl of Crawford], *Lives of the Lindsays*, [new edn], 3 vols. (1849) • *Scots peerage*, 3.15–24 • *Miscellany of the Maitland Club*, 4 vols., Maitland Club, 25, 51, 57, 67 (1833–47) •

Archives Nationales, Paris, K57; J645B · J. de Béthencourt, *The Canarian, or, The book of the conquest and conversion of the Canarians*, ed. R. H. Major, Hakluyt Society, 1st ser., 46 (1872) · GEC, *Peerage*, 3.507–13 · S. I. Boardman, *The early Stewart kings: Robert II and Robert III, 1371–1406* (1996)

Archives NA Scot., deeds; legal and estate MSS | Archives Nationales, Paris, K57/9/12; J645B/36; J645B/48 · NA Scot., GD/124

Lindsay family of Barnweill, Crawford, and Glenesk (*per. c.*1250–*c.*1400), nobility, took their name from Lindsey, Lincolnshire. They arrived in Scotland early in the twelfth century, as tenants of the future King David's honour of Huntingdon, and established a territorial base in Haddingtonshire where they held Byres, Luffness, and Ballencrief, as well as Barnweill in Ayrshire and the large barony of Crawford in Lanarkshire. Three main lines developed in the thirteenth century, but the two senior ones finished in heiresses who married into families which took the English side in the wars of independence. What became the main Scottish line descended from Sir David Lindsay of the Byres, who enjoyed a distinguished career in the mid-thirteenth century, during which he was a regent in 1255 and chamberlain the following year, and who died on crusade in Egypt in 1279. The son of his marriage, **Sir Alexander Lindsay of Barnweill** (*d.* 1309x14), must have been a minor when his father died, for his ward was granted to John Comyn of Badenoch in 1279. His lands were valued at 43 merks yearly. Of age by 1290, when he attended the parliament of Birgham, Lindsay is said to have been knighted by Edward I, and in August 1296 did homage for his Scottish lands to the English king. He is also recorded in that year as holding Luffness and Ballencrief from Henry de Pinkney, the English heir to those Lindsay estates and possibly also to Crawford.

Despite his early links with Comyn and Edward I, after 1296 Alexander Lindsay is usually found among the adherents of the younger Robert Bruce; his wife was probably a sister of James the Steward, a prominent Bruce supporter. Lindsay refused to participate in Edward I's expedition to Flanders in 1297, and with his younger brother John instead joined Wallace and Bruce in their short-lived rising against the English king in July 1297. Following the Scottish capitulation, Lindsay stood surety for Bruce's handing over of hostages. Lindsay appears to have been briefly in Edward's peace after the battle of Falkirk (22 July 1298), but was forfeited again later that year, and presumably continued to fight against the English until the general surrender of 1304. Recognized as a prominent figure in the Scottish resistance, Lindsay was exiled from Scotland for half a year by Edward's ordinance of September 1305, but he seems to have returned early, in time to be present in Bruce's company when the latter killed John Comyn of Badenoch on 10 February 1306 and declared himself king. Lindsay then remained with King Robert during the difficult months which followed, until he was himself captured at Kildrummy in September and his lands forfeited. However, Lindsay was free again by the summer of 1308, when he was one of the leaders of that year's Galloway campaign. As a prominent Bruce supporter he was a signatory of the letter sent to Philippe IV of France from the St Andrews parliament of 1309. He may have witnessed a royal charter in 1312, but was certainly dead by 10 December 1314.

Sir David Lindsay (*d.* in or before 1357), normally styled 'of Crawford', Sir Alexander's eldest son, had earlier been captured by the English with his brothers Alexander and Reginald, and he remained in prison until late in 1314, when he was probably exchanged for an Englishman taken at Bannockburn. Already a knight by that date, he was a witness to several important documents, notably the declaration of Arbroath in 1320, the truce with England of 1323, and the treaty of Edinburgh of 17 March 1328. Lindsay obtained various grants of land in Annandale from Robert I, and is recorded as keeper of Berwick in 1329. After the renewal of Anglo-Scottish hostilities, he was forfeited by Edward III in 1337 of his lands of Byres and of tenements at Chamberlain-Newton in Roxburghshire. He was never close to David II, but rather was an associate of Robert the Steward, his likely kinsman, who as guardian of Scotland appointed him constable of Edinburgh Castle in 1346, after the king's capture at Nevilles Cross. Lindsay was, however, granted several safe conducts to visit England to negotiate for David's release.

About 1324 David Lindsay married Mary Abernethy (*d.* 1355), daughter and coheir (with her sister Margaret, countess of Angus) of Alexander Abernethy, and widow of Andrew Leslie. This important marriage was the foundation of later Lindsay influence north of Forth, eventually raising the family from the ranks of the middling baronage into the peerage. David Lindsay had four sons, of whom David, the eldest, was killed at Nevilles Cross. In 1327 Lindsay gave land in Lanarkshire to Newbattle Abbey for the souls of himself and his wife, and he also established a mass for his wife at Lindores Abbey in Fife, where she was buried. Lindsay himself was dead by 13 October 1357, when his son James is referred to as lord of Crawford. **Sir James Lindsay of Crawford** (*d.* 1358), David's second son, inherited only his father's possessions, raising the possibility that he was the son of an earlier marriage. He maintained his family's links with the stewards, in 1346 marrying Egidia Stuart, the daughter of Walter the Steward and half-sister to the future Robert II. He attended the king's parliament of September 1357, and later that year was appointed ambassador to England. He died in the following year. It seems clear that he was not the James Lindsay executed in 1358 for killing Roger Kirkpatrick near Dumfries. His estates went to his son without further ado, and the fact that on 1 October 1358 David II confirmed the grant of the Byres which James Lindsay had earlier made to his brother Alexander would also appear to clear James of suspicion.

Sir Alexander Lindsay of Glenesk (*d.* 1382), the beneficiary of his elder brother's grant, served in his youth as squire to his cousin Thomas Stewart, earl of Angus. He had inherited his mother's lands north of Tay, and also received grants from his aunt Margaret, countess of Angus, which effectively reconstituted the Abernethy inheritance. About 1358, moreover, he married Catherine Stirling (*d.* by 1378), daughter and coheir of John Stirling of

Glenesk, whose estates in the sheriffdoms of Forfar and Inverness were entailed on him and their joint heirs. His lands of Byres he entailed to his younger brother William in January 1367 [*see* Lindsay family of the Byres (*per.* 1367–1526)]. Active as a crusader and jouster, Sir Alexander was high in David II's favour, while after 1371 he was equally close to Robert II, whose niece Marjory Stewart he married, probably about the time of Robert's accession. He attended Robert's coronation, together with his nephew James Lindsay of Crawford [*see below*] (the son of Sir James and Egidia), and became a regular charter witness for the new king, as he had been for David II. It may also have been in 1371 that he was made justiciar north of Forth jointly with his nephew; they were certainly acting in this capacity by 1373, though from 1374 Alexander Lindsay held this office on his own. In 1375 he arranged for his son and heir, David, to marry the king's daughter Elizabeth. He retained royal favour and the justiciarship until 1381, when he set off on pilgrimage to the Holy Land. Granted a safe conduct on 4 December to travel through England, he died on Crete some time before March 1382.

Like his uncle Sir Alexander, **Sir James Lindsay of Crawford** (*d.* 1395/6) was a charter witness for Robert II, but his closest links were with John Stewart, earl of Carrick, the heir to the throne. He acquired the barony of Kirkmichael in Dumfriesshire in 1377 and received royal patronage elsewhere, including the old thanage of Alyth in Perthshire. Thanks to his connection with Carrick, and with the first earl of Douglas, he was prominent in Anglo-Scottish diplomacy, receiving numerous English safe conducts between 1374 and 1395. He helped to shelter John of Gaunt in Scotland during the peasants' revolt, took part in a raid into England in 1384, and in August 1388 was captured by the bishop of Durham while pursuing an English knight from the battlefield of Otterburn, though he was released in the following summer. In 1373–4 he acted as justiciar north of Forth with his uncle, and from 1378 is recorded as sheriff of Lanark. Following Alexander Lindsay's death in 1382, James Lindsay failed to secure the justiciarship for himself. In the same year the title of earl of Buchan, to which James had a remote claim, was given to Alexander Stewart, the king's youngest son. Possibly it was his failure to secure these dignities which on 4 November 1382 caused Lindsay to assassinate Sir John Lyon, the king's son-in-law and chamberlain. Lindsay had perhaps befriended Lyon (one chronicler asserts that he had concealed Lyon's liaison with Robert II's daughter Jean, whom he subsequently married), and he may have been disappointed that Lyon, who could also have been a territorial rival, did not sufficiently use his influence with the king to promote Lindsay's claims.

Following the death of his uncle in 1382, Sir James Lindsay (as lord of Crawford head of the senior line of the family) became the effective leader of a powerful Lindsay–Leslie northern affinity which had probably originated in the marriage of his grandfather, Sir David Lindsay. After the murder of Lyon he withdrew briefly to England, but had returned by November 1384, when he used his affinity to support Carrick when the latter grasped power and marginalized Robert II. He then litigated for Buchan, and styled himself 'lord of Crawford and Buchan' for the rest of his life. His hopes of restricting Alexander Stewart's power were not realized, but he remained loyal to Carrick, supporting his accession as Robert III in 1390. He then became a close associate of the new king's eldest son, David, earl of Carrick, and was probably the leading member of the latter's household. He was also much involved in government. An exchequer auditor in 1391, he stood surety for an extension of the truce of Leulighem in 1392, and was a conservator of the Anglo-Scottish truce in 1394, when he was also one of the commissioners appointed to negotiate a permanent peace with England.

Sir James Lindsay married Margaret, daughter of Sir William Keith, a union which did not prevent Lindsay from becoming embroiled in a serious inheritance dispute with his wife's family in 1395. They had two daughters, Margaret and Euphemia, but lacking male heirs he obtained mutual charters of entail with his cousin, David *Lindsay of Glenesk [*see under* Lindsay family, earls of Crawford (*per.* c.1380–1495)], the son of Alexander, about 1384. Consequently the bulk of his estates (but not Barnweill) passed to the collateral line when Sir James died, between 5 April 1395 and 6 March 1396. The steady rise of the Lindsays, which was made possible by marriages and royal patronage for both the main branches of the family, achieved its appropriate culmination when David Lindsay, who united in his person the Crawford and Glenesk inheritances, was created earl of Crawford in 1398.

SONJA CAMERON

Sources J. M. Thomson and others, eds., *Registrum magni sigilli regum Scotorum / The register of the great seal of Scotland*, 11 vols. (1882–1914), vol. 1 • *CDS*, vols. 1–3, 5 • Rymer, *Foedera*, new edn, vols. 1–3 • G. W. S. Barrow and others, eds., *Regesta regum Scottorum*, 5–6, ed. A. A. M. Duncan and B. Webster (1982–8) • *Scots peerage*, 3.1–15 • G. Burnett and others, eds., *The exchequer rolls of Scotland*, 1–3 (1878–80) • S. I. Boardman, *The early Stewart kings: Robert II and Robert III, 1371–1406* (1996) • W. Bower, *Scotichronicon*, ed. D. E. R. Watt and others, new edn, 9 vols. (1987–98), vol. 7 • G. W. S. Barrow, *Robert Bruce*, 3rd edn (1988) • *RotS*, vol. 1 • W. B. D. D. Turnbull, ed., *Extracta e variis cronicis Scocie*, Abbotsford Club, 23 (1842) • J. Stevenson, ed., *Documents illustrative of the history of Scotland*, 2 vols. (1870) • *CEPR letters*, vol. 2 • *APS*, *1124–1423*

Lindsay family of the Byres (*per.* **1367–1526**), landowners, were members of the extended Lindsay family which had first settled in Scotland in the twelfth century and whose estates included Byres in Haddingtonshire no later than 1241. The Lindsays were prominent in the entourage of David II, and on 17 January 1367 Sir William Lindsay, the youngest son of David *Lindsay of Crawford [*see under* Lindsay family of Barnweill, Crawford, and Glenesk (*per.* c.1250–c.1400)], received from the king a grant entailing upon himself and his male heirs the land of the Byres, which had been resigned for the purpose by William's elder brother, Sir Alexander *Lindsay of Glenesk [*see under* Lindsay family of Barnweill, Crawford, and Glenesk (*per.* c.1250–c.1400)]. Sir William married Christiana, daughter of Sir William Mure of Abercorn, and thereby obtained the barony of Abercorn in Linlithgowshire. He became a retainer of the earl of Douglas after the death of David II, but may have returned to the king's affinity by the time of his own death, before 1 July 1393.

Sir William's son and heir, another **Sir William Lindsay of the Byres** (*d.* 1414), married Christian, daughter of Sir William *Keith, the marischal [*see under* Keith family], receiving through her the barony and castle of Dunnottar, although in 1392 he exchanged these properties with the Keiths for the lands of Crawford Priory in Fife. He received a pension from Robert III in 1394 in recognition of his services to the crown, and in 1413 he founded a chapel dedicated to the Holy Trinity in St Andrews Cathedral. He died in 1414 and was succeeded by his son.

John Lindsay, first Lord Lindsay of the Byres (*d.* 1482), received a safe conduct to go to James I at Durham in 1423, and he was one of the original hostages sent to England in 1424 as pledges for the payment of the king's ransom. He returned to Scotland in the first exchange of hostages the following year, but his subsequent career is obscure until he appears once more in active royal service by January 1440, serving the king from his Lothian base which, as it included the barony of Abercorn, would have connected him with the Black Douglases who held the castle of Abercorn. He witnessed a Douglas indenture on 26 August 1447, but, in the crisis between the king and the Black Douglases in the 1450s, he stood with James II at the crucial time just after the killing of the earl of Douglas on 22 February 1452, witnessing charters granted by the king at Lochmaben and Jedburgh on 2 March, and he remained with him throughout that year's summer campaign, acting thereafter as a regular witness to royal charters.

The exact date at which John Lindsay was created a lord of parliament is uncertain. He appears in a list, appended to Walter Bower's *Scotichronicon*, of men said to hold Scottish peerages by 1445. However, his title in the witness lists in the register of the great seal changes from John Lindsay of Byres on 2 March 1452, to John, Lord Lindsay of Byres, on 12 May 1452, indicating that official royal sanction was given at that time, specifically, it would seem, for support during the crisis with the Black Douglases. It may have been diplomatic services connected with the downfall of the Douglases that led to Lindsay travelling abroad, for, according to the exchequer accounts, he was in Flanders between 13 September 1455 and 7 July 1456. In 1457 he was appointed justiciar north of Forth, becoming a lord of session on 6 March 1458, and was appointed to hear petitions in parliament in 1466 and from 1468 to 1479. He married a daughter of Robert Stewart of Lorne and died on 6 February 1482, being succeeded by his son.

David Lindsay, second Lord Lindsay of the Byres (*d.* 1490), was a staunch supporter of James III. He was present with the king in Edinburgh in May 1488, and is alleged to have brought 1000 horse and 3000 infantry to the king's assistance at Sauchieburn, and to have presented James III with the large grey horse on which the king fled from the battlefield. However, beyond the fact that Lindsay was at the battle, the details are exaggerations by Robert Lindsay of Pitscottie, a descendant of David Lindsay's youngest brother, Patrick. David Lindsay married Janet, daughter of Walter Ramsay of Pitcruvie, but died childless in 1490. He was consequently succeeded by his brother John, third Lord Lindsay of the Byres, who was infeft as heir on 25 January 1492. John married Marion, daughter of Sir William Baillie of Lamington, but he also died childless, between 29 September and 5 November 1497, being succeeded by his younger brother.

Patrick Lindsay, fourth Lord Lindsay of the Byres (*d.* 1526), was styled Patrick Lindsay of Kirkforthar before succeeding to his brother's title and estates. The story of his appearing as advocate in defence of his brother David when the latter was tried for treason after Sauchieburn, causing him to cry out in pain by standing on his sore foot, appears to be another of Pitscottie's embellishments of his ancestors' exploits. On 28 October 1497 Patrick Lindsay received a charter confirming him in the lands and barony of Byres, in addition to a precept infefting him in the barony of Abercorn. He survived Flodden (where he is said to have urged James IV not to fight in person), and on 1 December 1513 was one of the four lords appointed to advise the queen, while in July 1525 he received the office of sheriff of Fife. He married Isabella, daughter of Henry Pitcairn of that ilk, and died in 1526, his burial taking place at St Andrews. He was succeeded in quick succession by his son and grandson, both named John.

C. A. McGladdery

Sources Lord Lindsay [A. W. C. Lindsay, earl of Crawford], *Lives of the Lindsays*, [new edn], 3 vols. (1849) • J. M. Thomson and others, eds., *Registrum magni sigilli regum Scotorum / The register of the great seal of Scotland*, 11 vols. (1882–1914), vol. 1 • G. Burnett and others, eds., *The exchequer rolls of Scotland*, 23 vols. (1878–1908), vol. 6 • *APS*, 1424–1567 • *Scots peerage*, vol. 4 • *The historie and cronicles of Scotland … by Robert Lindesay of Pitscottie*, ed. A. J. G. Mackay, 3 vols., STS, 42–3, 60 (1899–1911) • GEC, *Peerage*, 8.6–8 • S. I. Boardman, *The early Stewart kings: Robert II and Robert III, 1371–1406* (1996) • W. Bower, *Scotichronicon*, ed. D. E. R. Watt and others, new edn, 9 vols. (1987–98), vol. 9, p. 31

Lindsay, Sir Alexander, of Barnweill (*d.* **1309x14**). *See under* Lindsay family of Barnweill, Crawford, and Glenesk (*per.* *c.*1250–*c.*1400).

Lindsay, Sir Alexander, of Glenesk (*d.* **1382**). *See under* Lindsay family of Barnweill, Crawford, and Glenesk (*per.* *c.*1250–*c.*1400).

Lindsay, Alexander, second earl of Crawford (*d.* **1438/9**). *See under* Lindsay family, earls of Crawford (*per.* *c.*1380–1495).

Lindsay, Alexander, fourth earl of Crawford (*d.* **1453**). *See under* Lindsay family, earls of Crawford (*per.* *c.*1380–1495).

Lindsay, Alexander, of Evelick (*c.***1561–1639**), bishop of Dunkeld, was the second son of John Lindsay of Evelick, in Kilspindie, Perthshire, and inherited Evelick as his elder brother was ousted from the succession. After studying at the University of St Andrews and teaching as a regent at St Leonard's College there he was ordained minister of St Madoes, Perthshire, on 1 October 1591. At an unknown date he married Barbara Bruce, who died in or before 1626, after which he married Nicholas Dundas.

In 1606 Lindsay was made constant moderator of the

presbytery of Perth, but faced strong opposition in the presbytery from those opposed in principal to a permanent appointment. When he was appointed bishop of Dunkeld on 21 December 1607 he retained his parish ministry and he was evidently not consecrated until 1611. He sat in eleven general assemblies up to 1618, and was a member of the new Scottish court of high commission established in 1610. Admittance to the Scottish privy council came on 27 January 1624.

However, though Lindsay accepted royal policy in the church, and benefited from it, he favoured a limited role for bishops. An enemy conceded that 'that Bishop wes not verie proud', though adding that he was 'much given to conques[t]'—the buying of land (Row, 327). Although he participated in Charles's coronation in 1633, he was rumoured to have been opposed to the new prayer book imposed by the king in Scotland in 1637, and when the covenanters overthrew royal religious policies he was prepared to submit to presbyterianism. As he was 'lying under a long sicknesse' (Gordon, 1.145) he gave a statement to the general assembly in Glasgow in December 1638 accepting its authority. 'Many spake for him That he did not approve the late courses of the Bishops' (R. Baillie, *Letters and Journals*, 3 vols., 1841–2, 1.154), the earl of Argyll giving him 'the testimoney of a modest and peaceably disposed man' (Gordon, 2.95). Some argued that he should be excommunicated, but it was agreed that he should only be deposed from office, and that if he repented publicly he should be allowed to remain a parish minister.

Lindsay signed a demission of office at St Madoes on 24 January 1639, and did public penance in the parish church of Kilspindie on 30 January. He died in October, when he is said to have been aged about seventy-eight.

Alexander Lindsay was one of those Scottish bishops who went along with the religious innovations of James VI and Charles I, but with increasing unease. His continuance in the parish ministry after losing his bishopric was a rare piece of generosity by the covenanters to a very old man who had done little positive to support the discredited innovations—and to have a bishop submit and return to a parish made good propaganda.

DAVID STEVENSON

Sources *Fasti Scot.*, new edn • *DNB* • J. Gordon, *History of Scots affairs from 1637–1641*, ed. J. Robertson and G. Grub, 3 vols., Spalding Club, 1, 3, 5 (1841) • J. Row, *The history of the Kirk of Scotland, from the year 1558 to August 1637*, ed. D. Laing, Wodrow Society, 4 (1842) • Lord Lindsay [A. W. C. Lindsay, earl of Crawford], *Lives of the Lindsays*, [new edn], 3 vols. (1849) • *Recantation and humble submission of two ancient prelates* (1641) • GEC, *Baronetage*, 4.249n.

Archives NA Scot., letters to George Stewart of Airntully and John Stewart of Airntully, GD 38 • NRA Scotland, Lindsay of Evelick muniments, survey 0133 • NRA Scotland, priv. coll., contributions to College of Justice, discharges for taxation

Lindsay, Alexander, first Lord Spynie (*c*.1563–1607), landowner and courtier, was the fourth son of David *Lindsay, tenth earl of Crawford (1526/7–1574) [*see under* Lindsay, David, eleventh earl of Crawford], and Margaret, an illegitimate daughter of Cardinal David Beaton, archbishop of St Andrews. First mentioned in an entail of March 1564, Alexander was the younger brother of David *Lindsay, eleventh earl of Crawford (*d.* 1607), and like the rest of his family was well educated. Styled 'of Sandiford' in Angus (Forfarshire), from 1588 Alexander was also consistently styled 'master', though where he graduated is uncertain. Moysie describes him as 'ane great courtier' (Moysie, 71), but to Lord Home he was much more: 'the King's only minion and conceit … esteemed of the King most of any man in Scotland … and his nightly bed-fellow' (*CSP Scot.*, 1586–8, 558). On 2 November 1588 Lindsay was unexpectedly placed in command of the king's guard, and though political pressure soon forced him to surrender the post he was within a year appointed to the household office of vice-chamberlain.

In October 1589 Lindsay accompanied James VI on his marital expedition to Norway and Denmark (when he fell ill). He had lent several thousand crowns to the king to help defray the cost of the voyage, and in return James promised him a lordship. On 6 May 1590, therefore, Lindsay received a charter for Spynie, near Elgin, and other lands and patronage in the counties of Elgin and Forfar that had previously belonged to the bishopric of Moray. The grant was confirmed on 4 November 1590, when Lindsay was also knighted and created Lord Spynie. (He nevertheless neglected his northern estate to the extent that at the turn of the century its low-lying land flooded.) About the same time as his ennoblement, King James persuaded Jean Lyon (*d.* 1608x10), daughter of Lord Glamis (and widow successively of Robert Douglas the younger, of Lochleven, and Archibald Douglas, eighth earl of Angus) to marry Spynie. After the marriage the couple took up residence in Aberdour Castle, where they lived in great splendour; they had two sons and two daughters.

Despite his prominence at court, where he was also a favourite of Queen Anna, Spynie exerted little direct influence in the political arena. Although he attended parliament in 1591 and was frequently present at meetings of the privy council, he tended to ally himself with the interests of the more powerful earls of Huntly and Bothwell and was consequently regularly at odds with Chancellor Maitland. He suffered personally when his allies fell from favour and so rumours of his advancement, for instance that he was to be made treasurer of the realm, in 1591, remained unfulfilled. Then on 15 August 1592 Spynie was accused of treason by Colonel William Stewart for harbouring Francis Stewart, first earl of Bothwell. Spynie offered to fight his accuser in single combat, but instead the case went to trial. Stewart declined to proceed in the case and Spynie was released from custody in Stirling Castle, but after this accusation he never fully regained James's confidence, and in October 1592 he lost his place as gentleman of the bedchamber, regaining it only in 1601. However, on 24 July 1593, when the newly forfeited Bothwell made a penitential appearance before the king at Holyroodhouse, Spynie was one of those who interceded for him. His close association with Bothwell led to Spynie being denounced for treasonable practices twice within the next twelve months. It was intended that he should be forfeited in the parliament of 1594, but James's residual goodwill ensured that his name was removed from the summons. Not long afterwards, Spynie made his peace with the king and returned to administrative and household business. Although considered a protestant in the late 1580s, in the mid-1590s he was ordered to satisfy the presbytery of Edinburgh as to his religion after he had been in the company of Walter Lindsay of Balgavie, a papal emissary (Spynie's brother, the earl of Crawford, was a staunch Catholic).

Spynie's main interests centred on the Crawford comital lands of Forfarshire. He took part in the long running feud between the Lindsays and the Lyons, even against his own father-in-law, Lord Glamis; in 1600 a similar dispute broke out between Spynie himself and the Ogilvies. Although the council did its utmost to settle the feud, it ultimately resulted on 30 January 1603 in a night attack by the master of Ogilvie and his brother on Spynie's house at Kinblethmont. After blowing up the principal gate with a petard, the assailants searched the house for Spynie and his wife in order to murder them. Finding that they had escaped, the Ogilvies ransacked the mansion. Late in 1605, on the revival of the ancient bishopric of Moray, Spynie resigned the temporalities at the request of the king (retaining liferent); James had already compensated him with the grant of Boysack and other lands in Forfarshire. On 5 June 1607, in the High Street of Edinburgh between nine and ten in the evening, Spynie witnessed a surprise attack on his nephew David, master of Crawford, by ten armed men led by David Lindsay the younger of Edzell. Along with the laird of Drumlanrig, Spynie endeavoured to prevent bloodshed, but as the result of 'a pitiful mistake' (Pitcairn, 3.62) he was shot several times and attacked with a sword to the head. He died from his injuries eleven days later. His heir was his eldest son, Alexander *Lindsay; his widow died early in 1610.

ROB MACPHERSON

Sources *CSP Scot.*, *1547–1603* • R. Pitcairn, ed., *Ancient criminal trials in Scotland*, 7 pts in 3, Bannatyne Club, 42 (1833) • *Scots peerage*, 8.95–101 • Lord Lindsay [A. W. C. Lindsay, earl of Crawford], *Lives of the Lindsays*, 2nd edn, 3 vols (1858) • J. G. Dalyell, ed., *Fragments of Scottish history* (1798) • D. Calderwood, *The history of the Kirk of Scotland*, ed. T. Thomson and D. Laing, 8 vols., Wodrow Society, 7 (1842–9) • [T. Thomson], ed., *The historie and life of King James the Sext*, Bannatyne Club, 13 (1825) • *Reg. PCS*, 1st ser. • D. Moysie, *Memoirs of the affairs of Scotland*, *1577–1603*, ed. J. Dennistoun, Bannatyne Club, 39 (1830) • J. Spottiswood, *The history of the Church of Scotland*, ed. M. Napier and M. Russell, 3 vols., Bannatyne Club, 93 (1850) • GEC, *Peerage*, new edn, 12/1.161–4

Lindsay, Alexander, **second Lord Spynie** (*c.*1597–1646), army officer, was the eldest son of Alexander *Lindsay, first Lord Spynie (*d.* 1607), and his wife, Jean (*d.* 1608x10), widow of Archibald Douglas, earl of Angus (*d.* 4 Aug 1588), and Robert Douglas the younger of Lochleven (*d.* March 1585), and daughter of John *Lyon, eighth Lord Glamis. He was still a minor at the time of his father's murder in June 1607: when in 1609 the trial of his father's murderer did not proceed owing to the absence of a prosecutor, a protest was entered on his behalf and that of his siblings that their right of prosecution should not be invalidated. After he entered his majority, Spynie waived his right of prosecution against David Lindsay the younger of Edzell, who swore the death was accidental and promised payment of 8000 merks and the lands of Garlobank, Perthshire, to Spynie and his sister. On 7 March 1617 Edzell received a remission for the murder under the great seal. Spynie received a licence to travel abroad from the privy council on 3 April. Spynie married Lady Margaret, only daughter of George *Hay, first earl of Kinnoul, on 19 August 1620.

Spynie's public service began in 1621. He attended the convention of estates in January. On 3 March he was served heir to his father. The crown erected the new barony of Spynie from the land of Ballysak, Moray, on 16 July. Spynie was one of the Scottish lords in attendance at James VI and I's funeral at Westminster Abbey in 1625. In January and June 1626 the king appointed him, due to his 'martiall and generose mynd and dispositioun' (*Reg. PCS*, 2nd ser., 2.293–4), general muster-master and colonel of all the militia in Scotland in an attempt to create an inexpensive standing royal army. He became a member of the Scottish council of war on 12 July. In April 1627 he protested against the appointment of Colonel Harie Bruce as master of weaponshowings (military training). Earlier, on 8 March, he had received a royal commission to levy 3000 foot for the king of Denmark; subsequently the crown granted him £2000 for that purpose.

The regiment departed Scotland in October. Spynie served under Christian IV through May 1628. In that year he placed his regiment in Stralsund and Wolgast, then held by Sir Alexander Leslie (the future earl of Leven) against Wallenstein. Spynie's regiment played a major role in defending the towns when it sallied against an attacking force and drove it back into the siege lines. The regiment ceased to exist in 1629, but Spynie had already returned to Scotland in September 1628. In 1629–31 he attempted to purchase the title of the earldom of Crawford from George, the fourteenth earl, a fellow mercenary, but the king allowed him to buy only the barony of Finavon and the family burial-ground in Dundee. By November 1631 Spynie was again fighting in the German wars. He attended parliament in 1633 during Charles I's visit. Complaints by the lairds and burghs against the attempt to establish a free standing army led to a meeting in March 1634 with the burghs and privy council. The former opposed the taxes necessary to make the militia system work, which effectively deprived the operation of funds. Recognizing that he would gain neither profit nor military power by the office of general muster-master, Spynie resigned it by October 1636. (Sir Patrick Ruthven replaced him.)

Meanwhile other matters had occupied Spynie. In September 1634 he became a JP for Forfarshire. From June 1634 to February 1637 he was at feud with Robert Fletcher of Ballinsho, Fletcher's wife, Elizabeth Lindsay, and Sir Andrew Fletcher of Innerpeffer over sums of money. James Lyon of Auldbar, a relative of Lady Spynie, acted as his cautioner in the affair.

In the political strife after July 1637 Spynie took the king's side. He joined Montrose at Perth after the battle of Tippermuir in September 1644. He entered Aberdeen with him on 14 September, but when Montrose evacuated the burgh Archibald Campbell, first marquess and eighth earl of Argyll, took him prisoner. Spynie was sent south to Edinburgh. In October 1645 he was allowed the freedom of Dundee on 2000 merks caution. He died there in March 1646. His contemporary, the lawyer John Scot of Scotstarvit labelled Spynie 'a noble spendthrift and exquisite in all manner of debauchery' (Scott, 48).

Spynie and his wife had two sons—Alexander, master of Kinnoul (who predeceased his father) and George *Lindsay, who succeeded him as third Lord Spynie—and two daughters—Margaret, married to William Fullarton of Fullarton, and Anne, who died unmarried. Lady Spynie died before 16 August 1650. EDWARD M. FURGOL

Sources *APS* • *Reg. PCS*, 1st ser. • *Reg. PCS*, 2nd ser. • *Scots peerage* • J. Balfour, *Works*, 4 vols. (1823–5) • R. Monro, *Monro his expedition with the worthy Scots regiment (called Mac-Keyes regiment) levied in August 1626* (1637); new edn, with introduction by W. S. Brockington (1999) • J. Scot, *The staggering state of the Scots statesmen* (1754) • J. Spalding, *Memorialls of the trubles in Scotland and in England, AD 1624 – AD 1645*, ed. J. Stuart, 2 vols., Spalding Club, [21, 23] (1850–51) • A. I. Macinnes, *Charles I and the making of the covenanting movement, 1625–1641* (1991) • J. R. Young, *The Scottish parliament, 1639–1661: a political and constitutional analysis* (1996) • M. Lee, *The road to revolution: Scotland under Charles I, 1625–1637* (1985) • GEC, *Peerage*

Lindsay, Alexander, **first earl of Balcarres** (1618–1659), royalist army officer, eldest son of David, first Lord Lindsay of Balcarres (*d.* 1641) and Sophia Seton, daughter of the first earl of Dunfermline, was born on 6 July 1618 at Balcarres in Fife. He attended Haddington School (from 1627) and St Andrews University, and in April 1640 he married Lady Anna *Mackenzie (*d.* 1707), daughter of the first earl of Seaforth. After inheriting his title on his father's death in March 1641 Balcarres was active in the covenanting cause. He commanded a regiment of cavalry which served in the Scottish army in England in 1644, taking part in the battle of Marston Moor (2 July) and the sieges of York and Newcastle. Withdrawn to Scotland to face the royalist rising of the marquess of Montrose, he commanded the horse in Major-General William Baillie's army at the battle of Alford on 2 July 1645. By some accounts Balcarres's over-eagerness to attack played a major part in the covenanters' defeat, but eight days later the Scottish parliament praised him as 'ane nobleman Who in all the trust and military chairges committed to him hath behaved himselfe as ane gallant and generous patriote' (*APS*, 6.1.438–9). On 15 August Baillie and Balcarres again met with defeat at Montrose's hands, at the battle of Kilsyth, after Baillie had agreed, in the face of political pressure which only Balcarres opposed, to a disastrous change to the position of his army.

In December 1645 Balcarres was among the Scots who negotiated unsuccessfully with Charles I, then a prisoner of the Scottish army in Newcastle, in the hope of reaching a compromise settlement. He was one of the covenanting nobles who became concerned, after Charles was handed over to the English in January 1647, that the concessions being demanded of him for a settlement were too extensive, and who believed that, instead of continuing their alliance with the English parliament, the Scots should try to help the king. These emerging sympathies were rewarded on 20 July 1647 by the king's appointing him keeper and captain of Edinburgh Castle. In 1648 when the engagers urged the necessity of invading England to help the king, Balcarres favoured the principle, but eventually decided that the policies being pursued were too royalist and breached the solemn league and covenant. He therefore failed to take his seat on the engagers' committee of estates, and though he raised a regiment of horse he then resigned his command—cautiously citing ill health as his motive. After the failure of the engagers the new kirk party regime investigated his conduct, but he was spared the humiliation of doing public penance as a supporter of the engagement on offering to the presbytery of St Andrews in January 1649 apologies for any offence caused by his failure to denounce it publicly. Thereafter he took an active part in the work of the new regime.

After Cromwell's invasion of Scotland Balcarres was appointed in December 1650 colonel of a regiment raised to oppose him, and on 9 January 1651 Charles II created him earl of Balcarres. When the general assembly of the Church of Scotland met at St Andrews on 16 July 1651, Balcarres attended as king's commissioner—the first royal representative to attend an assembly since 1643. On 20 July news arrived of the English victory at Inverkeithing. At a midnight meeting the assembly agreed to retreat to Dundee, and there Balcarres presided over a dispirited rump. When Charles II led the Scots army into England in August 1651 it was hoped that this would force the withdrawal of sufficient English forces from Scotland for the Scots to regain control of the country, and Balcarres was one of those commissioned to raise forces to drive out the enemy and maintain a government within Scotland. Most members of the committee of estates were, however, surprised and captured at Alyth on 28 August. Balcarres escaped, and tried to maintain resistance in the north-east with local levies led by the third marquess of Huntly, but he was eventually forced to capitulate at Elgin on 3 December 1651. This marked the end of any organized resistance to the English conquerors in lowland Scotland.

Balcarres settled in St Andrews, but he maintained contact with the exiled king, who in March 1653 wrote regretting that Balcarres's reported illness would deprive him of his services for the present, but urging him to co-operate with the earl of Glencairn in a rising against the English. By June Balcarres had joined Glencairn in the highlands, complaining that the English were breaking the terms of his 1651 capitulation. Despite 'the extreame indisposicion of my body for travell', he explained, he had fled to maintain his freedom and perhaps escape death (Firth, *Scotland and the Commonwealth*, 146). Though a loyal supporter of the king, Balcarres remained staunchly presbyterian, and he was reluctant to serve under Glencairn, who had supported the engagement of 1648 and was no friend to presbyterianism. He therefore proposed that the royalist forces should have no commander but be governed by a committee. Moreover, the committee's members and all military commanders should declare their support for the solemn league and covenant. When Glencairn reacted to this by revealing that he already had a commission from the king authorizing him to take command, Balcarres wrote to Charles to complain, but his letters were intercepted and given to Glencairn. Balcarres then withdrew from the rising, travelling in disguise through England to France, to present the presbyterian–royalist case to the king. His wife, Anna, accompanied him, she having 'through dearness of Affection, marched with him, and lay out of doors with him in the Mountains' during his months in the highlands. He arrived in Paris in April or May 1654, but his strong antipathy to Glencairn soon alienated the king. In November 1654 Balcarres sought to persuade his supporters among the royalists in arms in the highlands to demand that the king declare support for the covenant. When this was discovered in April 1657 Balcarres was banished from the exiled court. A visit to London a few months later brought suspicions that he was betraying the king's cause, and in August 1658 Charles II was still expressing his bitterness at what he regarded as Balcarres's malice and dishonesty. The earl died at Breda on 30 August 1659, and his wife had him buried at Balcarres on 12 June 1660.

Balcarres's efforts to reconcile royalism with presbyterianism and the covenant were, in his eyes, in the best interests of the crown, and he was greatly saddened by Charles's hostility. In the early 1650s he had raised large sums for the royalist cause from his lands and goods, and he was impoverished in his later years. To Robert Baillie he was 'sweet Balcarres', one of the most brave men of the nation, but 'not the most able' (Baillie, 3.437), while Gilbert Burnet thought him 'a virtuous and knowing man, but somewhat morose in his humour' (*Bishop Burnet's History of his Own Time*, 6 vols., 1823, 1.108). A poem on his death by Abraham Cowley was more indiscriminate in its praise, including wisdom as well as piety among his virtues (A. Cowley, *Complete Works*, 2 vols., 1881, 1.157). Balcarres's widow, Anna Mackenzie, shared his religious beliefs, and subsequently became a friend of Richard Baxter, who commended her as 'a woman of very strong love and friendship, with extraordinary entireness swallowed up in her husband's love'. Baxter went so far as to accept that she had 'solid understanding of religion for her sex' (*Reliquiae Baxterianae*, 1.120–21). Countess Anna remarried in 1671, her second husband being the ninth earl of Argyll; he was executed in 1685, and she died in May 1707. DAVID STEVENSON

Sources *DNB* • *Scots peerage*, vol. 1 • GEC, *Peerage* • Lord Lindsay [A. W. C. Lindsay, earl of Crawford], *Lives of the Lindsays*, [new edn], 3 vols. (1849) • J. Maidment, ed., *Historical fragments, relative to Scotish affairs* (1833) • *APS* • *Calendar of the Clarendon state papers preserved in the Bodleian Library*, ed. O. Ogle and others, 5 vols. (1869–1970) • *The letters and journals of Robert Baillie*, ed. D. Laing, 3 vols. (1841–2) • C. H. Firth, ed., *Scotland and the Commonwealth: letters and papers relating to the military government of Scotland, from August 1651 to December 1653*, Scottish History Society, 18 (1895) • C. H. Firth, ed., *Scotland and the protectorate: letters and papers relating to the military government of Scotland from January 1654 to June 1659*, Scottish History Society, 31 (1899) • D. Stevenson, *Revolution and counter-revolution in Scotland, 1644–1651*, Royal Historical Society Studies in History, 4 (1977) • G. Wishart, *Memoirs of James, marquis of Montrose* (1893) • *Reliquiae Baxterianae, or, Mr Richard Baxter's narrative of the most memorable passages of his life and times*, ed. M. Sylvester, 1 vol. in 3 pts (1696)
Archives NL Scot., corresp., papers, Adv. MSS 29.2.9
Likenesses portraits, priv. coll.; registered with Scot. NPG

Lindsay, Alexander, sixth earl of Balcarres and *de jure* twenty-third earl of Crawford (1752–1825), army officer and colonial governor, was born on 18 January 1752 at Kilconquhar, Fife; he was the eldest son of James Lindsay, fifth earl of Balcarres (1691–1768), and his wife, Anne (1727–1820), youngest daughter of Sir Robert Dalrymple of Castletown. His father, the son of Colin *Lindsay, third earl of Balcarres, commanded a troop of gentlemen on the side of James Francis Edward, the Pretender, at Sheriffmuir but, having been pardoned by the government on account of his youth, he obtained a commission in the army. Although he specially distinguished himself at the battle of Dettingen on 10 June 1743 George II refused him promotion, owing to his previous support of the Stuart cause. He thereupon left the army, and in his retirement, besides devoting much attention to the science of agriculture, he compiled a family history that was used by Sir Robert Douglas in the compilation of his *Scots Peerage* and by Alexander Lindsay, twenty-fifth earl of Crawford and eighth earl of Balcarres, for his *Lives of the Lindsays*.

At the age of fifteen Alexander Lindsay entered the army as ensign in the 15th foot, then stationed at Gibraltar. Having succeeded to the peerage on the death of his father, on 20 February 1768, he went to Germany, where he studied for two years at the University of Göttingen. In 1771 he was appointed by purchase captain in the 42nd highlanders and, in 1775, major of the 53rd foot, then under orders to sail for Canada on the outbreak of the American War of Independence. In the following year he obtained the command of a battalion of light infantry. At the battle of Ticonderoga on 7 July 1777 thirteen bullets passed through his clothing and he was fortunate to receive only a slight wound in the left thigh. At the head of his battalion he stormed the heights of Huberton. On 7 October, while commanding an advance corps during the British defeat at Saratoga, he was promoted brigadier-general, following the death of Simon Fraser in that rank. He strongly fortified his battalion's position and received within his entrenchments other routed battalions, thus frustrating the American attack under Benedict Arnold. He was compelled to surrender with Burgoyne however and did not regain his liberty until 1779. Following his return to England he married his first cousin Elizabeth (1759–1816), daughter of Charles Dalrymple of North Berwick, at St Marylebone, Middlesex, on 1 June 1780.

While a prisoner in America Balcarres had been appointed lieutenant-colonel of the 24th regiment; in February 1782 he was raised to the rank of colonel, and made lieutenant-colonel, commanding the 2nd battalion of the 71st foot. In 1784 he was chosen representative peer for Scotland and in the same year he made a forcible speech supporting the bill for the restoration of forfeited estates, which passed on 18 August. He was chosen a representative peer at succeeding elections (excepting the period 1796–1802) until his death. On 27 August 1789 he was made colonel of the 63rd foot, a command that he retained for the rest of his life, and in 1793 he was gazetted major-general. On the outbreak of war in 1793 he was appointed commander of the forces in Jersey, and in the following year he was appointed lieutenant-governor of Jamaica, Britain's main colony in the West Indies, where he served from April 1795 to August 1801. This was a period of crisis and widespread rebellion in Caribbean slave societies. Soon after his arrival Balcarres faced an insurrection in Jamaica's mountainous interior by several hundred Maroons—freed descendants of fugitive slaves—which he blamed on French revolutionary agents. Critics have claimed that his heavy-handed over-reaction turned a minor local incident into a six-month war. His use of hunting dogs in the conflict also proved controversial and his deportation of the Maroons after they had surrendered caused a breach with his military commander, Major-General George Walpole. The colonial assembly, however, praised the governor's energetic prosecution of the war and presented him with a sword. Maria Nugent described him in 1801 as a man of unclean habits and a 'profligate and disgusting' (*Lady Nugent's Journal*, 38) domestic life, who kept a pet pig in Government House. His wife had remained in England.

In 1798 Balcarres was made lieutenant-general and in 1803 was raised to the full rank of general. After his return to England he resided chiefly at Haigh Hall, near Wigan, Lancashire, which his wife had inherited from her mother, Elizabeth, *née* Edwin. On being introduced by George III to the American General Arnold he is said to have exclaimed 'What, the traitor Arnold?' A duel resulted. After Arnold had fired Balcarres walked away. 'Why don't you fire, my lord?' exclaimed Arnold. 'Sir', replied Balcarres over his shoulder, 'I leave you to the executioner' (Lindsay, 2.353). On the death of George Lindsay-Crawford, twenty-second earl of Crawford, in 1808 Balcarres became *de jure* twenty-third earl of Crawford but did not claim the title, which by decision of the House of Lords was adjudicated to his eldest son, James Lindsay, seventh earl of Balcarres, on 11 August 1848. His other children included three sons—Charles Robert, collector of taxes at Agra, in India, and Richard and Edwin, who died young—and two daughters: Elizabeth Keith, who married R. E. Heathcote of Longton Hall, Staffordshire; and Anne, who married Robert W. Ramsey of Balgarvie, Fife.

The sixth earl of Balcarres completed the 'Memoirs of the Lindsays' begun by his father. He also left in manuscript 'Anecdotes of a soldier's life'. A selection from his correspondence during the Maroon war was published in the appendix to *Lives of the Lindsays* by his grandson, the twenty-fifth earl of Crawford. He died at Haigh Hall on 27 March 1825 and was buried alongside his wife (who had died on 10 August 1816) at All Saints', Wigan.

T. F. HENDERSON, *rev.* DAVID P. GEGGUS

Sources *DNB* • Lord Lindsay [A. W. C. Lindsay, earl of Crawford], *Lives of the Lindsays*, [new edn], 3 vols. (1849) • *Lady Nugent's journal of her residence in Jamaica from 1801 to 1805*, ed. P. Wright, new edn (1966) • B. Edwards, *The proceedings of the governor and assembly of Jamaica in regard to the Maroon negroes* (1796) • PRO, CO 137/95–100, CO 140/85–89; WO 1/70 • council minutes, 1795–9, archives, Spanish Town, Jamaica • A. E. Furness, 'The Maroon war of 1795', *Jamaican Historical Review*, 5/2 (1965), 30–49 • GEC, *Peerage* • Burke, *Peerage* (1959) • R. Dallas, *The history of the Maroons*, 2 vols. (1803) • *Journals of the Assembly of Jamaica*, ed. Assembly of Jamaica, 14 vols. (1811–29), vol. 9 • W. J. Gardner, *A history of Jamaica* (1873) • *IGI*

Archives Jersey Archive, St Helier, corresp. relating to his command in Jersey • JRL, corresp. and papers relating to his administration of Jamaica during the Maroon War • NL Scot., Crawford muniments, corresp. and papers • PRO, official corresp., CO 137/95–100 | BL, letters to Lord Hardwicke, Add. MSS 35395–35916 • NAM, corresp. with Sir George Nugent and papers relating to Jamaica

Likenesses oils, priv. coll.; repro. in P. Wright, ed., *Lady Nugent's journal* (1966), 106–7

Lindsay, Sir Alexander (1785–1872), army officer in the East India Company, second son of James Smyth Lindsay (1751–1837) and his wife, Ann, was born on 14 January 1785, and at the age of nine received an ensigncy in the 104th (Royal Manchester volunteers) regiment of foot, in which he became lieutenant in 1795. The regiment was disbanded in the same year, and Lindsay remained on half pay to the end of his life. He entered the Royal Military Academy, Woolwich, in January 1800 and passed out in February 1804, as a cadet for the Bengal artillery, and received his first Indian commission as first-lieutenant on 14 August 1804. He became captain on 26 March 1813, brevet major on 12 August 1819, lieutenant-colonel on 1 May 1824, and colonel and colonel-commandant on 2 July 1835. He served with the Bengal foot artillery at the siege of Gohad in 1806, at the sieges of Komanur and Gunnowrie, and in Bundelkhand in 1807–8. While with the Dinapore division of Ochterlony's army in the Nepal campaigns of 1814–16 he was severely wounded at the siege of Harriharpur in 1816, a musket ball shattering the forefinger and thumb of the right hand and entering the right hip joint. He took part in the siege of Hathras in March 1817 and in the operations against the Pindaris in 1817–18. He was subsequently superintendent of telegraphs between Calcutta and Chunar, and agent for the manufacture of gunpowder at Allahabad. He married at Government House, Calcutta, on 1 January 1820 Flora Loudon, daughter of Captain Donald Mackenzie of Hartfield, Applecross, Ross-shire; she died in 1863. He commanded the artillery of General Morrison's division engaged in Arakan during the First Anglo-Burmese War 1825–6. Lindsay became a major-general in 1838, lieutenant-general in 1851, general in 1859, was transferred to the royal army as a colonel-commandant with the Bengal artillery in 1860, and was made KCB in 1862. Lindsay died of bronchitis at his home at Earlybank, Perth, on 22 January 1872, aged eighty-seven.

H. M. CHICHESTER, *rev.* JAMES FALKNER

Sources *Army List* • *Indian Army List* • F. W. Stubbs, ed., *History of the organization, equipment, and war services of the regiment of Bengal artillery*, 3 vols. (1877–95) • *Hart's Army List* • Boase, *Mod. Eng. biog.* • V. C. P. Hodson, *List of officers of the Bengal army, 1758–1834*, 3 (1946)

Wealth at death £3973 16*s.* 4*d.*: confirmation, 18 July 1872, NA Scot., SC 49/31/94/84

Lindsay, Alexander Dunlop, first Baron Lindsay of Birker (1879–1952), educationist, was born at 37 Westbourne Gardens, Glasgow, on 14 May 1879, the third of five

Alexander Dunlop Lindsay, first Baron Lindsay of Birker (1879–1952), by Howard Coster, 1938

children (with two older sisters and two younger brothers) of the Revd Thomas Martin *Lindsay (1843–1914) and his wife, Anna Dunlop (1845–1903) [*see* Lindsay, Anna]. Lindsay's grandfather, the Revd Alexander Lindsay, had been a minister in the Free Church of Scotland which broke away from the established church in the Disruption of 1843. His father, Thomas Lindsay, was principal of the United Free Church College in Glasgow as well as a notable historian of the Reformation. Anna Dunlop, his mother, was an active campaigner on behalf of women's higher education and for a wide range of social and political causes. Lindsay carried on this characteristic family tradition of educational idealism, reforming passion, and unconventional politics throughout his distinguished career.

Lindsay showed high academic promise from an early age. After entering Glasgow Academy at the age of eight in 1887 he was soon awarded the top prize in his class in English, history, geography, arithmetic, Bible, and writing. He later received the Academical Club prize which was awarded to the dux of the classical section of the school for excellence in Latin, Greek, mathematics, French, and English. Before leaving in 1895 he was dux of the academy, and in the Glasgow University bursary competition of 1895 he gained fourth place and was awarded a Clark bursary. After proceeding to Glasgow University he gained an MA degree in 1899, with second-class honours in classics, having been second prizeman in the classes of logic and moral philosophy. Although he failed to win a scholarship to Balliol College, Oxford, as he had hoped, he was a scholar of University College, Oxford, from 1898 to 1902, and became president of the Oxford Union Society in 1902. He took a first class in honour moderations (classical) in 1900 and in Greats in 1902. In 1901 he was awarded the Ferguson scholarship in mental philosophy, and in 1902 he obtained the George Clark fellowship in philosophy at Glasgow University.

College tutor, marriage, and First World War Lindsay had expected to go into the church, and studied Hebrew at Corsock Inn in Galloway to prepare for training at the Glasgow United Free Church College, but he decided instead on an academic career. In the following year, 1903, he won the Shaw fellowship in moral philosophy at Edinburgh University, emulating the achievement of his father, who had been the first recipient of this award. In this capacity Lindsay gave the Shaw lectures on the philosophy of Kant, viewed from the standpoint of the critique of judgement. He was assistant lecturer in philosophy at the Victoria University of Manchester from 1904 until 1906, when he was elected a fellow and tutor in philosophy at Balliol College, Oxford. In December 1907 he married Erica Violet Storr (*d.* 1962), a student at Somerville College. Erica, artistic and devoted to poetry, was the third daughter of Francis Storr, a schoolmaster with strong Church of England connections and editor of the *Journal of Education*. The Lindsays settled in north Oxford and had three children: Michael, born in 1909, Anna in 1911, and Thomas in 1915. In his early thirties, with a young family, Lindsay was tall and broad-shouldered, with a large head, high forehead, and blue-grey eyes, and was regarded by a pupil and later colleague, Alice Cameron of Somerville College, as being simple and unworldly in his approach to life (Scott, 53–4).

In 1914 Lindsay contributed to the series of pamphlets *Why we are at War*, arguing for the importance of upholding international law. He volunteered for commissioned service in the army. He served in France, was mentioned twice in dispatches, and rose to the rank of lieutenant-colonel. He also had an opportunity to discover his skills in administration and the exercise of power, becoming deputy controller of labour. In 1919 he was appointed CBE. After returning to Oxford after the war, he took a new interest in the business of the university. He was one of a group of twenty college tutors who drafted proposals for reform and submitted them to the royal commission on Oxford and Cambridge universities which reported in 1922. He was also involved in the successful campaign for an honours school of modern humanities—philosophy, politics, and economics, or modern Greats, as it was known—created in 1920, and himself taught and lectured for the new school. Also in 1920 he seconded the preamble for the statute which admitted women to full membership of the university and in particular opened its degrees to them. He was drawn into the major developments taking place in Ireland, and in 1921 he visited Dublin as a member of a small group of observers, staying at the house of the president of the Irish Dominion League, Horace Plunkett. In 1922 his growing reputation was recognized when he was appointed to the chair of moral philosophy at Glasgow University. Only two years later, however, he was attracted back to Oxford after the death of A. L. Smith to become master of Balliol College at the early age of forty-five. He held this prominent position for a quarter of a century.

Master of Balliol and university vice-chancellor As master of Balliol, Lindsay's qualities of leadership began to come to the fore. He established remarkably close relations with undergraduates, delivering 'lay sermons' after dinner in hall and holding more informal gatherings in his lodgings, where he inculcated through wide-ranging discussion a faith in democracy, a distrust of ideology, and an ideal of meritocracy. Among those who acknowledged his influence were Denis Healey, Edward Heath, and Roy Jenkins. Lindsay's relations were not so easy with some of the fellows, who regarded his beliefs as a form of anti-intellectualism: he 'could not believe that it was possible for a man to have convictions on which he did not act', and regarded research 'as a form of self-indulgence' (*DNB*).

There were many even in Lindsay's own college who were suspicious of his unpredictable and unconventional approach to solving problems, as also of his left-leaning political views. He urged conciliation during the general strike of 1926, and was sympathetic to the Labour Party during inter-war political conflicts. In October 1938, following the Munich agreement, he stood as an Independent Progressive candidate (albeit still a member of the Labour Party) in a famous by-election in Oxford City, representing the 'stage army of the good'—the popular front of all progressive forces opposed to the appeasement of fascism. The Labour and Liberal parties did not field rival candidates, and so the Conservative Party provided his only opponent in the election, Quintin Hogg, a fellow of All Souls College and son of Lord Hailsham, then the lord president of the council. Following a short but passionate campaign that attracted widespread attention, Hogg emerged as the winner but Lindsay performed creditably, gaining 12,363 votes to Hogg's 15,797. He shared the plight of progressive intellectuals in the period when Labour superseded the Liberals. Speaking at a Liberal summer school in August 1939, he regarded Labour on its own as 'a party with no leaders worth mentioning' and the Liberals as 'leaders with no party worth mentioning', and urged that doctrinaire attitudes needed to be avoided if anti-Conservative forces were to be marshalled with maximum effect (*Manchester Guardian*, 7 Aug 1939).

Lindsay involved himself in the reform of the university's governmental structure and institutions. In 1929 he was a member of a group of prominent Oxford teachers and administrators which set out a detailed exposition of the government of the university for a broad readership (*The Government of Oxford*, 1931). In 1935 it was Lindsay's turn as a senior head of college to become vice-chancellor of the university for a three-year period, and this proved to be highly significant for Oxford's further development. He forged a strong partnership with the university registrar, Douglas Veale, to pursue new facilities for the university with an appeal for funds and the aid of outside sponsors. The most striking progress at this time was made through Lord Nuffield, the motor manufacturer and philanthropist, who offered some £1 million to the university for a college of engineering and accountancy. Lindsay and Veale controversially prevailed on Nuffield to fund instead a new physical chemistry laboratory and a postgraduate college for social studies, Nuffield College. The establishment of Nuffield College, indeed, was a practical realization of Lindsay's long-held ambitions on behalf of the systematic study of society, although Nuffield came to feel that he had been misled as to the true nature of the project. Nuffield and Lindsay did successfully collaborate to bring doctors and scientists together in order to get clinical medicine properly launched in Oxford.

Adult education Lindsay's broader educational ideals were vividly reflected in his active support for adult education. He had known William Temple and R. H. Tawney when they were all undergraduates at Oxford, and he was imbued with the same zeal on behalf of the higher education of working people. He became closely involved in tutorial classes and the Workers' Educational Association, and especially after the First World War he took part in their work assiduously. Alice Cameron of Somerville College admired his contribution to the Balliol summer school of 1920, and especially 'the *respect* for the workers which marked his attitude in all he said and did', which she felt was rooted in his respect for the skill and craftsmanship of the artisan. According to Cameron 'Lindsay's respect seemed to have a personal quality which made his style of approach infinitely winning to the shy and awkward men who filled the Balliol Common Room those summer days' (Cameron, undated, Lindsay papers, Keele University, L113). Lindsay's enthusiasm for university extension was also noted, if a little sourly, in John Betjeman's *Summoned by Bells* (1960):

> While Sandy Lindsay from his lodge looks down
> Dreaming of Adult Education where
> The pottery chimneys flare
> On lost potential firsts in some less favoured town.

During his Glasgow professorship he lectured to the Clydesiders and helped to set up a joint committee of the university and labour along the lines of the Oxford tutorial classes committee; he was also a founder of the Scottish Institute of Adult Education.

On returning to Oxford Lindsay became a leading figure in the adult education movement as a whole, his significance later emphasized by Sir Charles Morris, who saw him as inspirational and, 'except of course for Tawney, its greatest philosopher' (Morris). One event helps to evoke the importance that Lindsay himself attached to this area of his work. John Elkin, a miner at Longton, had joined the Longton tutorial class in 1909 and was still an active member in 1930. Lindsay's class decided to present Lindsay with a portrait of Elkin, painted by a local artist, J. A. Lovatt. According to another colleague, Lindsay 'came down to receive it and spent all the night travelling back to Oxford with Mrs Lindsay through the fog, both of them proud of the honour which had been done them' (H. P. Smith, *A Tutorial Class Celebrates*, [1958]). Elkin's portrait hung for many years in the master's lodgings at Balliol College.

Lindsay's other outside activities included the National Council of Social Service, through which he was involved in co-ordinating voluntary work for the unemployed. He was connected with the running of clubs for the unemployed and with the survey sponsored by the Pilgrim Trust which produced the report *Men without Work* (1938). He was adviser to the Labour Party and Trades Union Congress on educational matters. In 1930 he visited India as chairman of a committee set up by the International Missionary Council to survey the work of protestant colleges in India. He met Gandhi, who stayed with him in Balliol while taking part in the second Round Table conference.

Philosophy and political thought As a philosopher Lindsay was perhaps more successful as an expositor of ideas rather than as an original thinker. He lectured frequently on Plato and Kant, and his early publications especially reflected their influence on him. In 1907 he published a translation and introduction of Plato's *Republic* for an Everyman edition; this was followed by further introductions to works by other philosophers including Berkeley, Descartes, T. H. Green, Hobbes, Hume, and Kant. In 1911 he produced a substantial study of the philosophy of Bergson which his father greeted with the accolade that he had his 'mother's gift' of 'putting profound things in simple plain language' (Scott, 51). Between the wars he tried to use this gift to make sense of contemporary global dilemmas, for example concerning the role of the state, the problems of international relations, the future of Christianity, solutions to unemployment, and the nature of democracy. Although he produced a substantial volume of scholarly work, his output was summed up as that of 'a fully-occupied teacher and administrator who read widely and assimilated new materials, but who did not depend on sustained critical study for his motive power' (*Oxford Magazine*, 304).

Lindsay's best known work, *The Modern Democratic State* (1943), traced the guiding ideals of the modern democratic state in the development of Western civilization, and discussed the social and political implications of democracy. The modern democratic state, he claimed, came into being in western Europe, North America, and the British dominions during the nineteenth century; Bolshevism, fascism, and national socialism were conscious reactions against it. This view had obvious contemporary resonance, especially in the middle of the Second World War. He was also suspicious of the potential power of the state to undermine democracy, and emphasized the countervailing role provided by voluntary associations of individuals. The puritan congregation with which he was deeply familiar gave him his model of a democratic group-association (Maddox, 'The Christian democracy of A. D. Lindsay' and 'Skirmishes in advance'). He intended to write a second volume of *The Modern Democratic State* to discuss the problem of democratic control and how a democratic government could make a community 'more truly a community' (A. D. Lindsay, *The Modern Democratic State*, 1943, 286), but this second volume never materialized.

Peerage and Keele During the Second World War Lindsay took up the cause of education in the army, while also helping to organize supplies of books and courses of study to prisoner-of-war camps. In 1940 he became director of the educational books section of the Red Cross and St John's Ambulance Association. He also supported the idea of education for citizenship, and stressed the need to avoid returning to high unemployment in a post-war society. After the war, he led a commission in Germany on the reform of the universities in the British zone, seeking to reinvigorate the spirit of a university in a democratic community. In November 1945 he was rewarded for his continuing efforts with the award of a peerage by the incoming Labour prime minister, Clement Attlee, who had been two years his junior as an undergraduate at Oxford. He took the title of Lord Lindsay of Birker, after Birker Moor in the Lake District where he and Erica had bought a house, Low Ground, in 1926, and which had become a favoured retreat.

In 1949 Lindsay, who was approaching retirement from the mastership of Balliol at the age of seventy, agreed to become the first principal of the new University College of North Staffordshire, later the University of Keele. He knew the location for this new institution well from his extramural work, and was attracted to it as a way of realizing his educational ideals. It was designed to offer a new kind of curriculum, bridging the arts and the humanities, based on a tutorial system in a democratic residential college for both sexes. He envisaged a constitution that would enable the university college to take control over its own degree examinations, but with a guarantee of standards through the academic council which would have a majority of representatives from the older universities. Overall, as he declared, this promised 'a fulfilment of hopes that go back a long way, as far as Tawney's original Longton class at any rate' (A. D. Lindsay, 'The University College of North Staffordshire', *The Highway*, 42, 1951, 102). But his health had already begun to fail, and in summer 1950 he suffered a cerebral thrombosis. Although he recovered to take charge of the opening of the college in October 1950, and continued to be active in its leadership, he died suddenly at Keele from a blood clot in the brain on 18 March 1952. He was buried in Cumberland, and was succeeded as second baron by his elder son, Michael Francis Morris *Lindsay (1909–1994).

In his long educational career, Lindsay never lost the religious and social faith with which he had been imbued from his childhood. Yet he found his true vocation outside the church to which his father had devoted himself. He learned to adapt to the great changes of the time so as to become one of the outstanding educators of his generation. In the end his contribution to public life was as substantial as it was paradoxical. Unworldly and wily in equal measure, comfortable with both abstract ideas and pragmatic calculation, he could converse with leaders but always retained and cherished a common touch, and as a public intellectual he had few peers.

GARY MCCULLOCH

Sources D. Scott, *A. D. Lindsay: a biography* (1971) • *DNB* • *The Times* (19 March 1952) • G. Maddox, 'The Christian democracy of A. D. Lindsay', *Political Studies*, 34 (1986), 441–55 • G. Maddox, 'Skirmishes in advance: A. D. Lindsay and modern democratic theory', *Balliol College Record* (1997), 11–18 • W. B. Gallie, *A new university: A. D. Lindsay and the Keele experiment* (1960) • *Hist. U. Oxf.* 8: *20th cent.* • *Oxford Magazine* (8 May 1952) • C. Morris, 'Lindsay of Balliol', *Rewley House Papers*, 3 (1953) • L. Goldman, *Dons and workers: Oxford and adult education since 1850* (1995) • J. Campbell, *Edward Heath: a biography* (1993)

Archives Keele University Library, personal and family corresp. and papers | Bodl. Oxf., corresp. with Lionel Curtis • Bodl. Oxf., corresp. with Gilbert Murray • Bodl. Oxf., corresp. relating to the Round Table • Bodl. Oxf., corresp. relating to the Society for Protection of Science and Learning • JRL, letters to the *Manchester Guardian* • NL Wales, corresp. with Thomas Jones • Nuffield Oxf., corresp. with Lord Cherwell • TCD, corresp. with Mary Alden Childers

Likenesses H. Coster, photograph, 1938, NPG [*see illus.*] • J. Epstein, bronze bust, Balliol Oxf. • R. Goodwin, oils, Keele University • L. Gowing, oils, Balliol Oxf.

Wealth at death £5362 1s.: probate, 23 July 1952, *CGPLA Eng. & Wales*

Lindsay, Alexander William Crawford, twenty-fifth earl of Crawford and eighth earl of Balcarres (1812–1880), book collector and writer on art, was born at Muncaster Castle, Cumberland, on 16 October 1812. He was the eldest son of James Lindsay, twenty-fourth earl of Crawford and seventh earl of Balcarres (1783–1869), and Maria Frances Margaret (*bap.* 1783, *d.* 1850), daughter of John Pennington, first Baron Muncaster. He was educated at Eton College and at Trinity College, Cambridge, where he graduated in 1833. A substantial legacy from Lady Mary, sister of George Lindsay-Crawford, twenty-second earl of Crawford, combined with his family's vast incomes derived from coalfields in Lancashire, was more than sufficient to give him financial independence. By 1840, following the publication of *Letters on Egypt, Edom and the Holy Land* in 1838, based on a journey to the Near East in 1836–7, and the completion of *Lives of the Lindsays* in 1840 (which led in due course to his father's successful claim in 1848 to the earldom of Crawford), he had firmly resolved to resist any family pressures to participate in public life or stand for election to parliament. 'The cultivation of the intellect requires a private life', he confided to his cousin Anne Lindsay (*née* Trotter), on 23 January 1840, and went on to outline his ambitions:

> I have many schemes, grand noble schemes, floating before me … the Providential history of Man which I told you I planned at Thebes sitting on the broken obelisk, a Poem … a Work on Art to lead men to the true moral religious dignity and object. (Brigstocke, 'Lord Lindsay and the *Sketches*', 35)

Christian art Lindsay travelled widely in Italy in 1829–30, 1839, and again in 1840, and became profoundly interested in early Christian art, both from an art-historical viewpoint and as a potential source of inspiration for contemporary artists. He also visited Germany, where he was moved by the work of the Nazarene painters in Munich.

Alexander William Crawford Lindsay, twenty-fifth earl of Crawford and eighth earl of Balcarres (1812–1880), by Camille Silvy, 1863

This led to his most important published work, *Sketches of the History of Christian Art* (3 vols., 1847), the first serious survey of early Italian sculpture and painting by an English writer. It followed extensive travel from Naples to Venice and Milan in 1841–2, well documented in a remarkable sequence of letters addressed to his muse, Anne Lindsay. He had been fired initially by reading A. F. Rio's *De la poésie chrétienne* (1836), an account of early Italian art to which Anne had introduced him while they were travelling together from Rome to Assisi in 1839.

Rio, a Roman Catholic, denounced the paganism associated with high Renaissance painting and concentrated his attention on the *école mystique* which preceded it. Like Rio, Lindsay brought a strong moral and philosophical bias to his study of art, but he also established his own independence through a scholarly interest in medieval iconography, symbolism, and legends of the saints. In 1839 he also read Charles, comte de Montalembert's *Histoire de Sainte Elisabeth* (1836), which began a vogue for medieval hagiography in France; and perhaps under this influence he anticipated Anna Jameson in his recognition that medieval religious art was a reflection of the legendary literature of previous ages. He was well acquainted with popular Romance literature of the middle ages and recognized the origin of some Christian beliefs in ancient pre-

Christian Eastern cultures. He relied especially on the *Catalogus sanctorum* of Petrus de Natalibus, a Venetian compilation of the lives of the saints, originating from the late fourteenth century and published in 1493, which he bought in Rome in 1841 and thereafter carried around with him for daily use during his travels. He showed particular art-historical insight in his appreciation of the seminal importance of Byzantine art in the revival of Christian painting in the West, whereas Rio's sectarian bias against schismatic Byzantium had blinded him to this connection. However, Lindsay shared with his French mentor empathy with the pure religious spirit of fourteenth- and fifteenth-century Italian artists, including Nicola Pisano, Giotto, Duccio, Orcagna, Fra Angelico, and Botticelli, although as a protestant, anxious to dissociate himself from the Puseyites and the Oxford Movement, he could not follow their Catholic faith, nor as a critic could he bring himself entirely to overlook their technical limitations. Equally he was unwilling to renounce all classical art because it was pagan.

To resolve this internal conflict Lindsay devised a determinist historical and philosophical system, published as *Progression by Antagonism* in 1846, by which man advances towards the truth by a dialectical process, involving sense, intellect, and spirit. He then applied this system to the opening section of the *Sketches* under the heading 'The ideal and the character and dignity of Christian art'. The architecture of Egypt thus expressed 'the ideal of Sense or Matter', the sculpture of Greece was 'the voice of Intellect and Thought, communing with itself in solitude, feeding on beauty and yearning after Truth', while 'the Painting of Christendom … is that of an immortal Spirit, conversing with its God'. Lindsay's thesis was clearly inspired directly and indirectly by earlier German writers, including Friedrich Schiller, Friedrich Wilhelm von Schelling, A. W. Schlegel, and his brother Friedrich von Schlegel, all of whom saw the artist as a prophet and art as truth revealed through the unconscious medium of the artist. Lindsay went on to express his hope for a second regeneration of Christian art in England—and pointedly dedicated the *Sketches* to his cousin Sir Coutts Lindsay (1824–1913), founder of the Grosvenor Gallery, London, with whom he had travelled extensively in Italy in 1841–2.

Picture and book collecting *Sketches of the History of Christian Art* was written in the magnificent library Lindsay created at the family home, Haigh Hall, Lancashire. However, following his marriage on 23 July 1846 to his second cousin Margaret (1824–1909), eldest daughter of Lieutenant-General James Lindsay (1793–1855) and Anne Lindsay, of Balcarres, Fife, Lord Lindsay and his wife settled into a newly acquired estate at Dunecht, Aberdeenshire; they had one son and five daughters. The Lindsays later commissioned an extension with library and chapel at Dunecht, from G. E. Street (completed 1881). Lindsay continued to build up his library at Haigh and also began to collect early Italian paintings for display at Dunecht. The picture collection, which was acquired both from the London salerooms and from dealers in Florence, reflected above all Lindsay's interest in the early Christian legends and the lives of saints and martyrs in distant locations, from the Egyptian desert to southern India. Pictures such as Grifo di Tancredi's *Triptych with the Death of St. Ephraim and Scenes from the Lives of the Thebaid Saints*, Giuliano Amedei's *Death of St. Ephraim and Scenes from the Lives of Hermits*, and Luca di Tommè's predella panels, *Scenes from the Life of St. Thomas*, all enrich Lindsay's writings concerning Eastern and Byzantine influences on the mythology and iconography of early Christian art in western Europe.

The *Bibliotheca Lindesiana*, containing over 30,000 books, ostensibly was conceived on the strict principle of utility and the pursuit of knowledge, but Lindsay's capacity for self-deception enabled him to succumb sufficiently to the 'charms of the bibliomaniacal Circe' (Barker, 224) to allow himself to buy a small but choice collection of illuminated manuscripts which added a further dimension to his art collection. His acquisitions, mainly achieved *c.*1859–1872, later than pioneer connoisseurs such as W. Y. Ottley and James Dennistoun, included a ninth-century Carolingian gospels, Nicolas de Lyra's *Commentary on the Complete Text of the Bible*, written at Pesaro in 1402 for Pandolfo III Malatesta and illuminated throughout, and the missal of Cardinal Pompeo Colonna, in Renaissance classical style, where the illustration to the mass of St John exhibits a panoply of Egyptian motifs.

These specialist collections were conceived as part of Lindsay's much wider plan to form a private museum and library which would represent all branches of science, literature, and art, and all stages in the development of human intellectual progress. As he recorded in his library report (1861–5) addressed to his heir:

> I had, in fact, in my earliest youth determined to assemble together the wisest and most graceful thinkers of all countries, ages and pursuits as agreeable companions, instructive teachers, and honoured guests, under the symbolical pavilion of the Lindsays, who, with their friends, might thus converse hereafter, as in the School of Athens, with congenial associates in whatever branches of literature, art or science, their genius or taste should severally direct them to. (Brigstocke, 'Lord Lindsay as a collector', 287)

As a Victorian nobleman who had 'spent his life dreaming dreams of art and learning' (Lightbown, 31), on the basis of wealth derived from the sweat of Lancashire coalminers, he went on, without any apparent sense of irony, to draw a romantic parallel between the intellectual and artistic achievements of Cosimo and Lorenzo de' Medici and his own ambitions for the Lindsays:

> the growth of trade and commerce has … afforded us, through the possession of coalfields in England, the means of doing that which our more powerful ancestors, the contemporaries of Cosimo, could not have compassed—of building up our old Library after the example of the Medici, and in the mode they would themselves have acted upon had they been now living. (ibid., 327–8)

Earl of Crawford On 15 September 1869 Lindsay succeeded to the earldoms of Crawford and Balcarres. Although obliged now to concentrate on the demands of the Wigan Coal and Iron Company and other practical concerns, he continued to exercise his mind, speculating for instance on the origins of the Indo-Aryan race, exploring the nature of Etruscan civilization and language—culminating in his *Etruscan Inscriptions Analysed* of 1872—and going on to explore the primal roots of language in his *Creed of Japhet*, which was never completed. He also composed the epic poem *Argo* (1876) with a long autobiographical prelude. He died in Florence on 13 December 1880 at the Villa Palmieri, which he had acquired in 1872, and was succeeded by his only son, James Ludovic *Lindsay (1847–1913), who continued to develop the library. He was first buried at Dunecht in the family vault under the chapel, but after the tomb was raided was re-interred at Haigh Hall in 1882. HUGH BRIGSTOCKE

Sources J. Steegman, 'Lord Lindsay's *History of Christian art*', *Journal of the Warburg and Courtauld Institutes*, 10 (1947), 123–31 • N. Barker, *Bibliotheca Lindesiana* (1977) • H. Brigstocke, 'Lord Lindsay and the *Sketches of the history of Christian art*', *Bulletin of the John Rylands University Library of Manchester*, 64/1 (1981), 27–60 • H. Brigstocke, 'Lord Lindsay as a collector', *Bulletin of the John Rylands University Library of Manchester*, 64/2 (1982), 287–333 • R. Lightbown, 'The inspiration of Christian art', *Influences in Victorian art and architecture*, ed. S. Macready and F. H. Thompson (1985), 3–40 • N. Barker, H. Brigstocke, and others, *'A Poet in Paradise': Lord Lindsay and Christian art* (2000) [exhibition catalogue, National Gallery of Scotland, Edinburgh, 2000] • *CGPLA Eng. & Wales* (1881) • GEC, *Peerage* • H. Brigstocke, 'Lord Lindsay: travel in Italy and northern Europe for *Sketches of the history of Christian art*', *Walpole Society*, 65 (2003)
Archives NL Scot., Crawford papers, Acc. 9769 | NL Scot., corresp. with John Riddell • U. Edin. L., letters to David Laing
Likenesses C. Silvy, photograph, 1863, NPG [*see illus.*] • T. Rodger, photograph, NPG
Wealth at death under £300,000: probate, 28 March 1881, *CGPLA Eng. & Wales* • under £275,244 2*s*. 3*d*.: double probate, 27 Oct 1881, *CGPLA Eng. & Wales*

Lindsay, Ann. *See* Davies, Ann Lorraine (1914–1954).

Lindsay [*née* Dunlop], **Anna** (1845–1903), women's activist, was born at 38 Melville Street, Edinburgh, on 24 June 1845, the elder daughter of Alexander Colquhoun Stirling Murray *Dunlop (1798–1870), Free Church lawyer and MP, and his wife, Eliza Esther, *née* Murray (*c*.1818–1902). Educated at home in a liberal political atmosphere, she added a study of literature and philosophy to her early training, and was one of the earliest members of the University Classes for Women in Edinburgh, where her work was much praised by professors Tait and Campbell Fraser. On 8 October 1872 she married Thomas Martin *Lindsay (1843–1914), who had just been appointed professor of divinity and church history at the Free Church college in Glasgow: she was to pass the rest of her life in that city.

In 1877 Anna Lindsay was one of the founders of the Glasgow Association for the Higher Education of Women, acting as one of the organization's honorary secretaries until 1883, when the association became Queen Margaret's College; she remained on the college council for some years. Anna Lindsay's wide range of work on behalf of women sprang from her Christianity; engaged in the home mission work of the Free Church at Broomielaw, her contact with poor women led her to consider other means, beyond the strictly religious, for improving their lot. She was actively involved in a number of philanthropic organizations for the benefit of working-class women and girls, including the Partick division of the Scottish Girls' Friendly Society, which she managed from 1881; the Ladies' Union for the Care and Help of Women, a preventive and reformatory association of which she was vice-president from 1885 until her death; the Training School and Temporary Home for Friendless Servant Girls; and the Mothers' Prayer Meeting (which evolved into the Scottish Mothers' Union).

From the 1880s onwards, however, the main focus of Mrs Lindsay's attention was women in industry. Margaret Irwin of the Scottish Council for Women's Trades (SCWT) commented of her that 'It is not possible to give any definite account of her work here, as the history of this would practically be the history of the Women's Industrial Movement itself' (*Anna Lindsay*, 6). She was one of the founder members of the Women's Protective and Provident League, which later merged with the SCWT, and chaired the executive committee of the latter for a number of years. Again according to Irwin, she was 'the mainspring of the whole movement. … Whoever might grow tired of committee work and drop away from time to time, Mrs Lindsay never failed, but was to be found standing loyally at the helm' (ibid., 7). From her desire to promote legislation in the interests of women workers, Mrs Lindsay was led into party politics. In 1889 she was one of the committee which formed the Glasgow and West of Scotland Women's Liberal Association, and was vice-chair until its merger with the Scottish Women's Liberal Federation (SWLF) in 1891. She chaired the SWLF from 1891 until 1899, when her health gave out.

Unswerving in her attachment to her church (she was an influential member and vice-president of the Glasgow branch of the Women's Foreign Missionary Society, and from 1892 to 1899 vice-president of the executive committee of the Free Church of Scotland), Anna Lindsay was valued for her capacity for seeing her opponents' points of view, for the catholicity of her sympathies, and for her great tact and judgement. The countess of Aberdeen observed that her domestic life was 'as ideal as her public life, and remains a testimony to the possibility of a mother's duties to the family and to the wider community outside the home being combined without clashing on one another' (*Anna Lindsay*, 17). The Lindsays had three sons and two daughters; their eldest son, Alexander Dunlop *Lindsay, first Baron Lindsay of Birker, was to become master of Balliol College, Oxford, and their daughter Susan married Sir Frederick Maurice Powicke.

Anna Lindsay's health failed in 1899, and after suffering from Bright's disease for some three years she died early in the morning of 1 March 1903 at 37 Westbourne Gardens, Kelvinside, Glasgow; her death was certified by Dr Alice McLaren, her support for working women evident to the last. K. D. REYNOLDS

Sources *Anna Lindsay, nata 1845, revixit 1903* (1903) • *Englishwoman's Review*, 34 (1903), 210–11 • D. Scott, *A. D. Lindsay: a biography* (1971) • b. cert. • m. cert. • d. cert. • *CCI* (1903)
Likenesses photograph, repro. in *Anna Lindsay*
Wealth at death £185 19*s*. 8*d*.: confirmation, 8 June 1903, *CCI*

Lindsay, Colin, third earl of Balcarres (1652–1721), politician and Jacobite sympathizer, was baptized at Kilconquhar, Fife, on 23 August 1652, the fourth and youngest (but second surviving) son of Alexander *Lindsay, first earl of Balcarres (1618–1659), and his wife, Anna *Mackenzie (*c.*1621–1707), daughter and coheir of Colin *Mackenzie, first earl of Seaforth.

Early years In the 1650s Lindsay and his brother Charles lived in Scotland, assigned £10 a year from the sequestrated family estates and educated by the local minister.

On Charles's unexpected death aged eleven Colin succeeded, on 15 October 1662, as third earl of Balcarres, Lord Lindsay and Balneil, under his mother's guardianship. About 1663 she sent him to St Andrews University. The loans his father had contracted in supporting the covenanting, royalist, and national causes hopelessly burdened his Fife estates. 'I know, were I a man, I must take my sword in my hand, ane beggar', he wrote in 1665 (A. W. C. Lindsay, *Lady Anna Mackenzie*, 76). A £1000 pension granted during Lady Balcarres's and her sons' lives for surrendering the hereditary governorship of Edinburgh Castle was seldom paid. Secretary John Maitland, earl of Lauderdale, for years ignored his cousin and close friend's widow and children, and took offence when she married, on 28 January 1670, Archibald *Campbell, ninth earl of Argyll. She paid off the most dangerous debts, but, as she evidently feared, Colin later increasingly failed to economize and master his affairs.

Colin was presented at court about 1670, and his characteristic charm captivated everybody. Charles II also remembered his father's services. He was rapidly married to Mauritia Margareta van Nassau, daughter of Louis van Nassau, heer van Beverwaert (illegitimate son of Maurice, prince of Orange) and sister of Lady Arlington and Lady Ossory, with a £16,000 portion; but she died in childbirth in August 1671. No official record supports his claim that he became captain of a troop of old cavaliers. He served under James, duke of York, at the naval battle of Solebay on 28 May 1672. However, in late 1672 or early 1673 he impulsively married Lady Jean Carnegie (*d.* 1681), eldest daughter of David Carnegie, second earl of Northesk, who had refused him before, and, since Charles had now committed his honour in arranging a match with a London heiress, Balcarres was banished from court. Retiring to his estates, he spent much time in study. If he was ever, as John Macky later claimed, 'a very good Countryman [opposition supporter]' (*Memoirs of the Secret Services*, 245), it was then. Before his wife died, shortly before 26 October 1681, they had seven children.

Politics and family, c.1680–1688 In 1679 Balcarres commanded the Fife heritors during the Bothwell Bridge rising, and on 3 June 1680 he was appointed a privy councillor. Of his sisters, Lady Sophia had married their stepfather Argyll's son Charles Campbell, and Lady Henrietta his chief Campbell henchman. Lady Sophia rescued Argyll from Edinburgh Castle in 1681. Balcarres was wrongly suspected of complicity in Argyll's 1683 plots, and both his brothers-in-law played leading parts in the

Colin Lindsay, third earl of Balcarres (1652–1721), by John Riley

earl's 1685 rising. Need to prove his loyalty to the regime, and friendship with James Drummond, fourth earl of Perth, helped bring him into active politics. He won friends at James's Edinburgh court, including John Churchill, the future duke of Marlborough. He married as his third wife, possibly in early 1682, Lady Jean Kerr (*d.* 1686), daughter of William Kerr, second earl of Roxburghe (Perth's uncle). They had a son, Colin Lindsay, Lord Cummerland (*d.* 1708), and a daughter, Margaret.

In 1682 Balcarres was appointed sheriff of Fife and on 28 December captain in John Grahame of Claverhouse's regiment of horse (though his lieutenant generally commanded the troop). There was much covenanting support in Fife, where Archbishop James Sharp had been assassinated. Balcarres and his deputy, Alexander Malcolm of Lochore, soon enforced the laws there vigorously. In late 1684, when four committees of council and justiciary dispersed to the south and west, punishing covenanters and obliging the shires to raise extra-parliamentary taxation, he was on that for the borders. He would not risk pushing Fife so far; but in January 1685 he and Claverhouse, sitting there as a justiciary court, proposed that all persons over sixteen should be obliged to abjure the recent Cameronian declaration of war. Balcarres again commanded the Fife forces during Argyll's rebellion. James II in 1687 imposed him on Kirkcaldy as provost. Though he was not associated with particular killings, the presbyterians after the revolution named him among the five men they wanted permanently incapacitated from office.

However, Balcarres showed his amiability towards individual presbyterians. He restrained proceedings against Sir John Dalrymple. He persuaded James to relieve his impoverished stepbrother, Archibald Campbell, future tenth earl of Argyll. His fourth marriage, about 1687, was to Lady Margaret Campbell (*d.* 1747), daughter of James Campbell, second earl of Loudoun, of another covenanting family then in low water. Granted William Denholm of Westshields's forfeited estate, he agreed with the family to sell it back cheaply and obtained his pardon; but they ignored the bargain after 1688.

Balcarres assisted Perth and his brother, secretary of state John Drummond, Viscount Melfort, in overthrowing William Douglas, first duke of Queensberry, in 1685–6. His support for James's catholicizing policies gained him appointment to the Scottish Treasury commission on 19 November 1686, and later to the secret committee controlling the privy council. He had Lochore, his main follower, made a lord of session, justiciary and council, and his former parish minister made bishop of Moray. He received lodgings in Holyroodhouse Palace. His pension, although reduced, was paid, and he was granted Fife covenanters' fines. By buying up the late Argyll's debts he eventually obtained from his estate Sunart and Ardnamurchan, which the crown then bought for Cameron of Lochiel. He began rebuilding Balcarres House, possibly to Sir William Bruce's design, but only a wing was completed by 1688. He assembled 'a great Bibliotheck' (Sibbald, 137) and, perhaps later, Dutch paintings. In 1682 he founded nearby Colinsburgh, informally a burgh of barony from 1686 (though formally only from 1707).

Revolution and plots, 1688–1691 When invasion threatened, in late 1688, and James summoned the Scottish army south, Balcarres played a leading part in the secret committee's proposal to supplement it instead with militia and highlanders to overawe Scotland and northern England. Melfort overrode this, largely from jealousy that other ministers might gain credit. On 24 October 1688 James appointed Balcarres lord lieutenant of Fife. He was needed in too many places. After William's invasion, as a nobleman who was neither a Catholic nor seeking advantage by changing sides, he was the mainstay of the Edinburgh government, and worked to win back Queensberry to strengthen it. He was commissioned to prevent the presbyterian interception of the mail. Finally, in early December, with communications totally cut by the risings in northern England, he rode to London to inform James of events and to serve as the Scottish government's representative at any compromise negotiations. That government swiftly disintegrated behind him as leading figures hoping for power tricked Perth into retreating (only to be seized by the Fife mob) and encouraged presbyterian riots.

Balcarres reached London just after James's first flight. His later tale of a meeting during the king's brief return where he gave him civil authority in Scotland and Claverhouse, now Viscount Dundee, military command, is untrue. In the confused period after James's final escape Balcarres several times waited on William, his relation and acquaintance through his first marriage, and on 31 January 1689 obliquely applied for an English peerage. However, on hearing from James in February that he was going to Ireland, Balcarres and Dundee began organizing Scottish support for him. They drafted a conciliatory letter for him to send to the forthcoming convention, and warned him that general hostility made it necessary to dismiss Melfort. Parting coldly from William they returned to Scotland, prevented the duke of Gordon from surrendering Edinburgh Castle, and organized James's supporters for the convention. They had electoral hopes from Balcarres's influence in Fife and two burghs there. However, Melfort for selfish reasons suppressed all their letters and advice, and instead drafted a threatening letter from James to the convention, which, when read on 16 March 1689, shattered his infant party. After their plans for a rival convention at Stirling failed Balcarres retreated home almost immediately.

In early April Balcarres (with Lochore) was arrested at Balcarres after a messenger was captured carrying important instructions, letters, and military commissions (including a regiment each of horse and foot for him). An intercepted letter from Melfort to him was read out on 18 April in the convention: 'Experience has Convinced Our Master that some folks Most be Made Gibeonites ["hewers of wood and drawers of water" Joshua, 9: 21–7] And that ther are Greatmen Most be Made Examples of Which you and I hav thought long to Deserv it' ([Melfort] to B[alcarres], 30 March [1689], NA Scot., GD406/1/9138). The convention's leaders, hysterically supposing themselves among the 'Examples', ordered Balcarres's close imprisonment in Edinburgh tolbooth, and came close to trying him for treason. He believed, implausibly, that Melfort had intended this, and became his enemy for life.

William declined to overrule the convention's decision and Balcarres remained imprisoned, despite dangerous sicknesses and his offer to retire to England. After a month's milder house arrest he was transferred to the captured Edinburgh Castle in early July and remained there until 14 March 1690. He could play no part in Dundee's Jacobite rising.

Meanwhile Sir James Montgomery, a leader of the presbyterian opposition 'club', was driven into Jacobite plotting by public and private discontent with William and hopes that James, having recently dismissed Melfort, had reformed. He organized the Montgomery plot, an alliance between club extremists and Jacobite peers to restore James by a parliamentary majority. Montgomery delayed Balcarres's release on bail until he was brought into the plot. Balcarres hoped that the alliance could at least destroy William's Scottish army by refusing supplies. He was therefore among the Jacobite nobles who took the oaths on 22 April 1690 for the new parliamentary session. However, prudent government concessions soon diminished the opposition's numbers. A secret meeting of conspirators, including Balcarres, on 3 May to hear James's reply to the club plotters' proposals exposed their disregard for their allies. The plot fell apart; and Balcarres, hearing that the club leaders were hurrying to betray it, was among those seeking William's pardon who rode to Chester in early June.

Balcarres is known for his detailed memoir of events

from 1688 to mid-1690, composed for James's information. He may have sent him a version in late 1690, but did not, as generally supposed, carry it to his court at St Germain; after considering the possibility he remained in Scotland. Halting his narrative at that point avoided the admission that Sir John Dalrymple thereafter successfully tempted Balcarres's pre-1688 colleagues towards taking office under William. Balcarres, the most scrupulous, took part, reporting on Scottish affairs to William in December 1690, only because he needed a pardon after the Montgomery plot (granted on 22 December), and because Dalrymple had secretly assured him that he was bringing the episcopalians into office merely to restore James. Naïvely Balcarres communicated this story not only to James but to his stepbrother Argyll, hoping to win him over; Argyll instead informed the government, endangering Dalrymple's negotiations. Balcarres finally ceased political activity and broke with Dalrymple in July 1691 when he belatedly realized his insincerity. Contact with St Germain was barred as an alternative after Melfort became chief minister there in December 1691.

Exile Balcarres benefited little when his episcopalian friends took office in early 1692, but his continued personal links with them encouraged their presbyterian opponents to attack them through him. In May 1693 he was summoned to take the oaths of allegiance and assurance, so that his refusal would discredit them. Instead, he and his protégé James Malcolm (the late Lochore's brother) retreated abroad, to Denmark, Hamburg for several months from August 1693, and twice to the Low Countries, where he was captured by robbers and ransomed by the Douai Jesuits, and renewed his friendship with Perth, then at odds with his brother Melfort.

Finally, in May 1694, just before Melfort's fall and departure, the protestant secretary of state, his old friend Charles Middleton, second earl of Middleton, asked French permission for Balcarres to come to St Germain. On his arrival, which provoked rumours that he would be secretary for Scotland, he presumably presented his 'Account of the revolution' personally to James. He remained in favour there until late 1696, when he was suddenly disgraced for having concealed from James how forged letters from Scottish Jacobites had helped overthrow Melfort in 1694. Malcolm had been involved. Balcarres had informally reported to Middleton the chief culprit's boast that Middleton's own under-secretary was implicated. Now, however, Middleton, to save himself, denied this, used against him their jocular private correspondence and conversations, and turned him groundlessly against Perth. The actual culprit was pardoned, but about December 1696 Balcarres, having submitted a final memorial on Scottish affairs, left St Germain and retreated slowly via Basel to Montpellier.

Melfort returned to St Germain in May 1697, and Balcarres found James reluctant to invite him back. He apparently returned notwithstanding—James perhaps relented—but finding Middleton still obstructive, had left France finally for the Netherlands by October 1697. After calling over his family he settled at Utrecht and met the Huguenot intellectuals Pierre Bayle and Jean le Clerc. His repeated applications for permission to return to Scotland to avert his total ruin, made via William's favourite, the earl of Albemarle, and chaplain, William Carstares, finally gained William's permission on 3 October 1700. The second duke of Queensberry hoped he would be 'an instance of the folly of Jacobitism' (M'Cormick, 630).

Political eclipse and personal decline During Anne's reign Balcarres at first politically followed George Mackenzie, Viscount Tarbat. In the 1703 parliament he was initially active in the cavalier faction. However, George Lockhart of Carnwath wrote in his *Memoirs* (largely inspired, ironically, by Balcarres's own memoir), that after lord commissioner Queensberry broke with them Balcarres and the earl of Dunmore (another former Jacobite) switched their allegiance 'to the Court, and went along with all their measures; wretches of the greatest ingratitude! they ow'd all they had, and much they had squander'd away, to King Charles and King James'. The betrayal was the greater because 'Till now they claim'd more merit than others … [Balcarres] had some pretence for what he did, having a numerous family and little to subsist them on but what the Court bestow'd' (Lockhart, 1.64–5) but it profited neither them nor their new allies, since they simply acquired money to get drunk regularly. Balcarres indeed nearly died as a result of a 1705 drinking bout. After James's ill treatment of him, and his death, he presumably saw his allegiance as now owed to Anne. Late in 1703 he hoped that exposure of the supposed Jacobite Scots plot would strengthen Queensberry.

Before 1688 Balcarres had been a significant politician: now, although he was reappointed to the privy council in December 1704, and there were occasional rumours that he would receive office, he remained a government dependant. He transferred loyalties to the squadrone during their brief 1704–5 ministry—though voting in council to reprieve the officers of the *Worcester*—then back to Queensberry, denouncing conspicuously in the 1705 session the squadrone's proposed limitations on the prerogative. He voted for the union and received £500 of the notorious £20,000 sent from England. His closest political friend and frequent guest was John Paterson, archbishop of Glasgow, whom some similarly considered to have betrayed the Scottish episcopalian church politically and financially.

Balcarres petitioned Anne to restore his pension. Marlborough's influence led her, on 29 May 1704, to grant one for £500, backdated to 1701, but the Treasury could not pay it. On 18 February 1707 he was granted a further £500 for ten years, but his difficulties made him sell it. Meanwhile, Balcarres's Edinburgh writer despairingly accused him of drunkenness, extravagance, and failure to pay creditors' interest. His hopes for his sons' military careers further tied him to the court. Colin became a captain of dragoons and an (unsatisfactory) aide-de-camp to Marlborough, but died in early 1708. Balcarres unsuccessfully requested Marlborough until 1711 to promote Alexander (*d.* 1736), his elder son from his fourth marriage, beyond an infantry captain.

Balcarres showed his continuing scholarly interests in late 1712 by giving to the (crypto-Jacobite) Advocates' Library, Edinburgh, a collection of important state papers gathered by his ancestors, including Mary of Guise's correspondence.

On George I's accession Balcarres petitioned to have his pension continued. His slight hopes were swiftly shattered. His memoir of Scottish events in 1688–90 had been influential. William Dicconson's Jacobite official biography of King James (published in 1816) summarized large sections. Colonel Nathaniel Hooke was given a copy to help in his Scottish missions. In November 1714 a version was published in London—either brought from France by lord justice clerk Adam Cockburn of Ormiston, or taken from one of the copies circulating in Britain. Its publication, with that of Lockhart's *Memoirs* shortly before, formed the most devastating and legitimate whig propaganda coup of 1714.

According to John Sinclair, master of Sinclair, Balcarres joined the 1715 rebellion because his former protégé James Malcolm of Grange, now one of Mar's busiest intriguers in Fife, assured him that it could not fail. Since Balcarres had no armed following, and was not invited on to Mar's council, it seemed ungrateful advice. His son Lord James Lindsay (1691–1768), then a half-pay naval lieutenant, who followed him out of filial duty, had the opposite view: he was a violent anti-union Jacobite, but was convinced that the rising was hopeless. He fought bravely in Sinclair's cavalry at Sheriffmuir. Afterwards Marlborough and the second duke of Argyll intervened to protect Balcarres, who was not financially worth forfeiting. He was allowed to remain under house arrest (with one dragoon) at Balcarres until the 1717 indemnity. James had temporarily to abscond; and Alexander (who had served in a government regiment in Ireland throughout) and he had their military careers long blighted by the family's involvement—in James's case, despite fighting at Dettingen, permanently.

Balcarres died, presumably at Balcarres House, in early October 1721, and was buried at the chapel there, probably on 27 October. His widow died in May 1747. His sons Alexander and James successively became fourth and fifth earls of Balcarres.

Balcarres was, Macky wrote, 'handsome in his person, very fair' (with the family's face and reddish hair), 'a gentleman of very good natural parts', with 'abundance of application' (*Memoirs of the Secret Services*, 245). Circumstances, particularly inherited debts, were adverse to the useful employment of his abilities; but had James and Melfort shown more wisdom in late 1688, or even early 1689, he and Dundee might possibly have maintained Jacobite control over Scotland. His abandonment of Jacobitism, after further damaging his family fortunes and then suffering dismissal from St Germain, did not merit Lockhart's denunciation. Yet, Jacobitism apart, his active obedience to three Stuart monarchs' differing policies contrasts with his father's struggles to reconcile loyalty and other principles, and his generalized charm with his mother's deep passion in marital love and friendship.

Balcarres's memoir was first published as *An Account of the Affairs of Scotland* in 1714 (an accompanying *Key* appeared just afterwards explaining its abbreviations), and its popularity generated many manuscript copies. A 1754 edition included the names in full. Balcarres himself and others protested, however, that the pamphlet contained many interpolations by others. In his 1814 edition (published in *Scarce and Valuable Tracts … Lord Somers*) Sir Walter Scott, ignorant of the *Key*, expanded most initials into the wrong names. The version published in 1841 as *Memoirs Touching the Revolution in Scotland* has always since been accepted as the authentic text; yet it is based on a transcript by Balcarres's son James, with more genteel language (changing the term 'fanatic', for instance) and possible omission of a few embarrassing charges against individuals. Where the summary in King James's official biography is most detailed, it resembles more the text printed in 1714. Most of the differences suggest two authors' drafts rather than purposeful interpolations; they may possibly, despite later alterations, represent versions presented to James at different times (the 1714 one in 1694).

PAUL HOPKINS

Sources *Scots peerage* · Lord Lindsay [A. W. C. Lindsay, earl of Crawford], *Lives of the Lindsays*, 2nd edn, 3 vols (1858) · NL Scot., Crawford and Balcarres MS, Acc. 9769 · C. Lindsay [earl of Balcarres], *Memoirs touching the revolution in Scotland*, ed. A. W. C. Lindsay [earl of Crawford and Balcarres], Bannatyne Club (1841) · *Reg. PCS*, 3rd ser. · P. A. Hopkins, *Glencoe and the end of the highland war*, rev. edn (1998) · R. Dick, *Annals of Colinsburgh* (1896) · A. W. C. Lindsay, Lord Lindsay, *A memoir of Lady Anna Mackenzie, countess of Balcarres and afterwards of Argyll, 1621–1706* (1868) · *Historical notices of Scotish affairs, selected from the manuscripts of Sir John Lauder of Fountainhall*, ed. D. Laing, 2 vols., Bannatyne Club, 87 (1848) · G. Lockhart of Carnwath, *The Lockhart papers*, ed. A. Aufrere, 2 vols. (1817) · NA Scot., dukes of Hamilton papers, GD406 · D. Nairne, diary, NL Scot., MS 14266 · J. Sinclair, *Memoirs of the insurrection in Scotland in 1715*, ed. W. Scott (1858) · GEC, *Peerage*, new edn · duke of Buccleuch and Queensberry's papers, Drumlanrig Castle, Scotland · *The manuscripts of his grace the duke of Buccleuch and Queensberry … preserved at Drumlanrig Castle*, 2 vols., HMC, 44 (1897–1903) · NA Scot., Mar and Kellie papers, GD124 · [C. Lindsay, earl of Balcarres], *An account of the affairs of Scotland* (1714) · *State papers and letters addressed to William Carstares*, ed. J. M'Cormick (1774) · R. Sibbald, *The history, ancient and modern, of the sheriffdom of Fife and Kinross* (1710) · *The life of James the Second, king of England*, ed. J. S. Clarke, 2 vols. (1816) · BL, Marlborough papers, Add. MS 61291 · C. Huygens, *Journaal*, 2 vols. (1876), 1.78–9 · T. Thorpe, *Catalogue of the Southwell manuscripts* (1834), 51, 469 · *Memoirs of the secret services of John Macky*, ed. A. R. (1733) · W. Scott, ed., *A collection of scarce and valuable tracts … Lord Somers*, 2nd edn, 13 vols. (1809–15), vol. 11

Archives BL, Memoirs of the late revolution, Add. MS 69396 · Drumlanrig Castle · Mitchell L., Glas., 'An account of the affairs of Scotland' [transcript, with contemporary notes] · NL Scot., Crawford and Balcarres papers | BL, Marlborough papers · Hunt. L., letters to the earl of Loudon

Likenesses J. Riley, oils, *c.*1670, Scot. NPG · G. Kneller?, oils, *c.*1680–1689, priv. coll.; registered with Scot. NPG, SP III 153-4 · miniature, oils, *c.*1700, repro. in T. B. Macaulay, *History of England*, ed. C. Firth, 6 vols. (1915), vol. 4, p. 1555 · oils, *c.*1700, priv. coll. · J. Riley, portrait, priv. coll. [*see illus.*]

Wealth at death estates in Fife, so burdened with debt that full interest was not paid

Lindsay, Colin (1819–1892), founder of the English Church Union and Roman Catholic convert, born at Muncaster

Castle, Cumberland, on 6 December 1819, was the fourth son of James Lindsay, twenty-fourth earl of Crawford and seventh earl of Balcarres (1783–1869), and his wife, Margaret Maria Frances (1783–1850), daughter of John Pennington, first baron Muncaster. After some private tuition he matriculated at Trinity College, Cambridge, in 1839. There he came under the influence of the high-church movement. He did not graduate, and on 29 July 1845 married Lady Frances, daughter and coheir of William Howard, fourth earl of Wicklow.

Lindsay's early married life was passed on his father's estate near Wigan, and as a magistrate he took an active part in local affairs. As churchwarden of All Saints', Wigan, he was largely responsible for the careful restoration of that church. His adherence to Tractarian views led him to found the Manchester Church Society which, through his exertions as president, amalgamated with other local associations in 1860 to form the English Church Union. Lindsay was president of this predominantly lay body from 1860 to 1867, and he devoted himself enthusiastically to the work of the society, attacking Erastianism and upholding the rights of Anglican clergymen to teach Catholic doctrine and use elaborate ceremonial. As well as being a frequent platform speaker, he wrote various controversial works, of which the most important was *The Royal Supremacy and Church Emancipation* (1865), in which he defined the view taken of the establishment by the English Church Union. During these years he lived at Brighton, but in 1870 he moved to London.

Meanwhile Lindsay's researches on the Reformation in England convinced him of the impossibility of maintaining a Catholic position within the Church of England. Influenced also by his wife, who had joined the Roman Catholic church on 13 September 1866, Lindsay was received into that church on 28 November 1868 by J. H. Newman at the Birmingham Oratory. He gave an account of the reasons for his conversion in the introductory epistle to his *Evidence for the Papacy* (1870) and showed himself a staunch champion of extreme papal claims. He further expounded these views in his *De ecclesia et cathedra, or, The Empire Church of Jesus Christ* (2 vols., 1877), but was forced by illness to leave this work incomplete. He also defended Mary Queen of Scots in *Mary Queen of Scots and her Marriage with Bothwell* (1883 reprinted from *The Tablet*).

In 1877 Lindsay retired to Deer Park, Honiton, which his wife had inherited in 1856. Pope Pius IX granted him the rare privilege of having mass celebrated there or in whatever house he might be living. He died of bronchitis in London at 22 Elvaston Place, Queen's Gate, on 28 January 1892. He and his wife, who died on 20 August 1897, aged seventy-nine, were buried at St Thomas's Church, Fulham. He left five sons and three daughters, of whom the eldest son, William Alexander Lindsay KC, became Windsor herald. A. F. Pollard, *rev.* P. Kitchenham

Sources *The Times* (30 Jan 1892), 7 • *The Tablet* (6 Feb 1892), 233 • Gillow, *Lit. biog. hist.* • G. B. Roberts, *The history of the English Church Union, 1859–1894* (1895) • Venn, *Alum. Cant.*

Archives BL, Gladstone MSS • BL, J. W. Jones MSS • LPL, English Church Union MSS • NL Scot., Crawford and Balcarres MSS

Wealth at death £5099 18*s.* 3*d.*: probate, 3 June 1892, *CGPLA Eng. & Wales*

Lindsay, Sir David. *See* Lyndsay, Sir David (*c.*1486–1555).

Lindsay, Sir David (*d.* in or before **1357**). *See under* Lindsay family of Barnweill, Crawford, and Glenesk (*per. c.*1250–*c.*1400).

Lindsay, David, first earl of Crawford (*d.* **1407**). *See under* Lindsay family, earls of Crawford (*per. c.*1380–1495).

Lindsay, David, third earl of Crawford (*d.* **1446**). *See under* Lindsay family, earls of Crawford (*per. c.*1380–1495).

Lindsay, David, second Lord Lindsay of the Byres (*d.* **1490**). *See under* Lindsay family of the Byres (*per.* 1367–1526).

Lindsay, David, fifth earl of Crawford and duke of Montrose (**1440–1495**). *See under* Lindsay family, earls of Crawford (*per. c.*1380–1495).

Lindsay, David, tenth earl of Crawford (**1526/7–1574**). *See under* Lindsay, David, eleventh earl of Crawford (*d.* 1607).

Lindsay, David (**1531–1613**), bishop of Ross, belonged to the family of Lindsay of Edzell and was a nephew of David Lindsay, ninth earl of Crawford. His pedigree is not well authenticated and he has been identified as son variously of Robert Lindsay of Kirkton and of Alexander Lindsay of Haltoun and Rachael Barclay of Mathers. He is said to have been a student at St Andrews University, though his name does not appear in the matriculation and graduation lists, and to have travelled in France and Switzerland. Certainly the name David Lindsay occurs at Geneva associated with the congregation to which John Knox ministered. Lindsay became minister in Leith by 1560, a strategic town as the port of Edinburgh where reforming opinions had spread in the decades before the Reformation. His services were sought by the general assembly, which frequently appointed him its commissioner and temporary visitor to oversee such areas as Kyle, Carrick and Cunningham, Moray, Lothian, Galloway, Teviotdale, Tweeddale, Angus (Forfarshire), and Clydesdale.

Nominated by the assembly in 1562 to preach in churches lacking ministers in the Merse (Berwickshire), Lindsay rose to prominence in the work of the assembly's committees and in discussions with government. On six occasions he was elected moderator of the general assembly: February 1569, October 1577, October 1582, May 1586 (when the king, voting first, chose him), April 1593, and March 1597. Earlier, he had been appointed to the convention of Leith in 1572 which secured a compromise between church and crown on the thorny subject of ecclesiastical endowment leading to the introduction of protestant bishops. When John Knox refused to inaugurate John Douglas as archbishop of St Andrews, Lindsay was one of three ministers who laid hands on the new archbishop and embraced him as a sign of his admission. He visited Knox on his deathbed in November 1572 and at Knox's request, though he 'thought the message hard', went to Edinburgh Castle to warn William Kirkcaldy of

Grange that unless he surrendered the castle, which he held for Mary, he would 'be brought down over the walls of it with shame and hang against the sun' (Calderwood, 3.234; *Works of John Knox*, 6.657). Lindsay visited Kirkcaldy after his condemnation and was sent by him to the Regent Morton to intercede for his life, being empowered to offer Kirkcaldy's whole estate as a ransom. But his intercession failed and Lindsay, at Kirkcaldy's request, attended his execution in 1573.

Lindsay participated in the preparation of the *Second Book of Discipline*, completed in 1578 with its endorsement of a presbyterian constitution for the church, and in 1580 helped prepare a plan for establishing presbyteries. Yet Lindsay himself was ever inclined to moderation. He was apt to be dubbed a 'court minister', though as late as 1592 he reiterated the opinion he held with other ministers that King James was not exempt from the censure of excommunication if he disobeyed God's will. That 'not a little offended' the king (Calderwood, 5.162). Even when elevated to the episcopate, he spoke out in the privy council against the king's treatment of the presbyterian ministers banished for defying the king's wishes in 1605 by holding a general assembly at Aberdeen—a punishment which he considered harsher than that accorded to Jesuits or murderers. Much earlier, in 1579, he was selected to instruct King James's French cousin, Esmé Stewart, who professed a willingness to convert to protestantism but whose arrival at court had aroused fears that he was the agent of a Catholic plot. Distrustful of Esmé's influence, he welcomed the Ruthven lords' palace revolution in 1582. At the same time, he sought to reduce antagonisms among political factions: not only had he tried to mediate between the Regent Morton and earls of Atholl and Argyll who had dislodged him from power in 1578, but in 1583 he sought to enlist the support of the English ambassador as mediator between the ultra-protestant Ruthven lords, who fled to England, and the earl of Arran, who headed a conservative, anti-presbyterian administration. When he attempted to delay the application of the reactionary 'Black acts' passed by parliament in 1584, he found himself imprisoned in Blackness Castle for forty-seven weeks.

Lindsay's moderate counsels gradually gained the king's support. He stood out as the only minister—with the exception of the king's own minister—who was willing to comply with James's request that ministers pray for his mother before her execution in 1587. He accompanied James as chaplain in October 1589 when the king set sail for Norway to bring home his bride, Anne of Denmark, and married James and Anne at Oslo on 23 November, conducting the ceremony in French. Thereafter, on their return to Edinburgh, he officiated at the queen's coronation at Holyrood in May. He was present, too, at the baptisms of Prince Henry in the Chapel Royal at Stirling in August 1594, when he delivered an address in French, of Princess Margaret in April 1599, and of Prince Charles in November 1600. He went to Edinburgh from Falkland Palace in an effort to persuade ministers of the veracity of the king's version of the Gowrie conspiracy in August 1600, and when they declined to approve a general service of thanksgiving for the king's safety, he conducted a service at the market cross, and preached a sermon in his own church in the king's presence. As James began the task in 1597 of reviving episcopacy by approving 'parliamentary bishops' who would sit and vote as bishops in parliament but were not then accorded any special jurisdiction within the church, Lindsay was one of the first three ministers selected for appointment. He became titular bishop of Ross in November 1600 when almost seventy years old and by 1609 was accounted infirm through age. After episcopal succession was restored in 1610 when three Scottish bishops were consecrated in England, Lindsay duly received consecration in Scotland on 24 February 1611.

Although Lindsay survived until his eighty-third year, when he died at Leith on 14 August 1613, there is little sign of his activity in his northern diocese. For the most part his continuing work as parish minister in Leith, his attendance at parliament and general assembly, and his seat on the privy council kept him outside his diocese. His son-in-law, Archbishop John Spottiswoode, depicted him as a man 'of a peaceable nature, and greatly favoured of the king, to whom he performed divers good services, especially in the troubles he had with the Church: a man universally beloved and well-esteemed of by all wise men'. He was buried in Leith (at South Leith parish church) 'by his own direction, as desiring to rest with the people on whom he had taken great pains in his life' (*History of the Church*, 3.220). His first wife was Janet or Jonet Ramsay, daughter of George Ramsay of Clattie; his second, Helen Harrison. His elder son became Sir Jerome Lindsay of Annatland, Lyon king of arms; his second son, David *Lindsay, served as rector of St Olave's, Southwark, and then succeeded his father in the ministry at South Leith; his daughter, Rachel, married Archbishop Spottiswoode.

JAMES KIRK

Sources T. Thomson, ed., *Acts and proceedings of the general assemblies of the Kirk of Scotland*, 3 pts, Bannatyne Club, 81 (1839–45) • D. Calderwood, *The history of the Kirk of Scotland*, ed. T. Thomson and D. Laing, 8 vols., Wodrow Society, 7 (1842–9) • J. Spottiswood, *The history of the Church of Scotland*, ed. M. Napier and M. Russell, 3 vols., Bannatyne Club, 93 (1850) • [T. Thomson], ed., *The historie and life of King James the Sext*, Bannatyne Club, 13 (1825) • *The works of John Knox*, ed. D. Laing, 6 vols., Wodrow Society, 12 (1846–64) • *Reg. PCS*, 1st ser., vols. 1–10 • D. E. R. Watt, ed., *Fasti ecclesiae Scoticanae medii aevi ad annum 1638*, [2nd edn], Scottish RS, new ser., 1 (1969) • *Fasti Scot.*, new edn, 1. 160–61 • D. Stevenson, *Scotland's last royal wedding* (1997) • J. Kirk, *Patterns of reform: continuity and change in the Reformation kirk* (1989) • J. Kirk, *The Second Book of Discipline* (1980) • *Livre des habitants de Genève* (1957) • C. Martin, *Les protestants anglais* (1915) • *The autobiography and diary of Mr James Melvill*, ed. R. Pitcairn, Wodrow Society (1842)

Lindsay, David, eleventh earl of Crawford (*d.* 1607), nobleman, was the eldest son of **David Lindsay**, tenth earl of Crawford (1526/7–1574), and Margaret (*d.* in or after 1574), eldest daughter of David *Beaton (1494?–1546), cardinal and archbishop of St Andrews, and Marion *Ogilvy (*d.* 1575); his parents married at Finavon in April 1546, his mother bringing a substantial dowry. His paternal grandfather, Alexander Lindsay (*d.* 1542), usually known as 'the wicked master', had forfeited the Crawford title following his murder of a servant of Lord Glamis; this began a feud with the Lyon family that was to erupt at intervals for the remainder of the century. However, his first marriage being childless, David Lindsay of Edzell (*d.* 1558), who had become ninth earl of Crawford, adopted as his heir David son of Alexander, who in due course became tenth earl. This earl acted as cupbearer to Queen Mary at her marriage to Lord Darnley in July 1565 and took his seat as a privy councillor the following October. He supported the queen at the battle of Langside in 1568, but submitted to the new regime in 1570. He died at Finavon or Cairnie, Fife, shortly before 1 November 1574, when his son David was recorded as eleventh earl; the tenth earl was buried at Dundee.

The eleventh earl had married at Perth on 12 February 1573 Lilias, daughter of David Drummond, second Lord Drummond, and his wife, Lilias Ruthven. Lilias brought a portion of 10,000 marks, but the couple soon separated. Crawford continued the conservative political and religious traditions of the family, being regarded as a 'convert' of the Jesuit William Crichton, and he was a supporter of the imprisoned Queen Mary. He is recorded as a member of the privy council in 1575, but in March 1578 an encounter in School House Wynd in Stirling between John Lyon, eighth Lord Glamis, the chancellor, and Crawford, together with their respective retinues, culminated in the shooting of the chancellor. Glamis had been a prominent member of King James's party and a supporter of the recently deposed regent, James Douglas, fourth earl of Morton. Crawford, who had a reputation as a marksman, was held responsible for the murder and was temporarily imprisoned in Edinburgh Castle before being allowed to return to his house at Cairnie. Further trouble followed with the master of Glamis and the Lyon family. In September 1579 Crawford was summoned to answer on 3 November for various crimes in the Tolbooth of Edinburgh. Lord Lindsay of the Byres and David Lindsay of Edzell stood caution for him. On 7 November Crawford signed a bond valid until 1 May 1579 undertaking not to molest the master of Glamis any further. In December he was given licence to go abroad for three years, with a group of Lindsays and Gordons standing surety for him.

The arrival in September 1579, at the invitation of James VI, of Esmé Stewart, later duke of Lennox, prompted a resurgence of the minority pro-Marian interest within the country and the final eclipse of the earl of Morton, along with the increase in power and influence of a Stewart faction. A distinct, but secret, foreign policy developed, Francophile in character, sympathetic to the exiled Queen Mary, and with vague and half-hearted aspirations for the restoration of Roman Catholicism. Contacts were fostered between James VI, Lennox, Catholic exiles in France, English and Scottish Jesuits, and seminary priests. Crawford was part of this network. He was at the French court in February 1580, and was reported to have left in May for Orléans with a view to travelling to Italy. By October he had apparently departed Orléans for Rome, with David Graham of Fintry, an important Marian and member of the Catholic party. On 22 July 1581 Crawford returned from France with George Gordon, sixth earl of Huntly, a prominent conservative who had been in exile at Orléans, and from this time was to be associated with him and with the policies of Lennox, especially in his confrontation with the presbyterian party in the reformed kirk. Having divorced his first wife, in December Crawford married Lady Grizel Stewart, daughter of John *Stewart, fourth earl of Atholl (*d.* 1579), and his wife, Margaret Fleming.

In August 1582 an Anglophile party of disaffected nobles and lairds united around a platform of militant protestantism, and seized the king in a coup—the Ruthven raid—which forced the exile of Lennox. During the king's captivity Crawford several times asked for leave to go to France, but was not granted a safe conduct by the English. In June 1583, when James escaped from the government of the Ruthven raiders, Crawford and the conservative, Francophile, and Marian party rallied to his support. A new favourite emerged, James Stewart, fifth earl of Arran, who consolidated his authority by intruding royal agents into positions of power. In September 1583 Crawford was made provost of Dundee, against the will of the burgesses. James demonstrated his favour by spending two days with the earl at Cairnie, continuing to urge reconciliation between Crawford and the master of Glamis. James displayed his confidence in Crawford and cultivated the Catholic party, which was useful to him for its cosmopolitan contacts and as an alternative to an increasingly aggressive kirk. Crawford was a consistent opponent of the Melvillian party in the kirk; he was a lord of the articles at the parliament of May 1584, which drew up the 'black acts' and which reasserted the authority of bishops and denounced the new presbyteries. In 1587 he protested against an act of parliament appropriating ecclesiastical revenues to the crown, displaying his innate religious conservatism but also arguing for the right of noble patronage and the continuance of the manipulation of ecclesiastical revenues which had been customary for centuries.

During the ascendancy of Arran the English government worked with Scottish dissidents to undermine his position. Arran's fall in November 1587, engineered by a coalition of nobles including some Ruthven raiders, caused a reversal of Crawford's fortunes. Crawford continued to manoeuvre to regain access to the king and to promote pro-Marian and anti-English policies. He was imprisoned from November 1585 to March 1586 by the new government because of his French and Catholic sympathies. On his release he joined his former confederate the earl of Huntly. The emergence of John Maitland of Thirlestane as chancellor in 1587 signalled for Crawford another unwelcome development in Scottish politics. As well as sealing an alliance with England, Maitland promoted greater participation by the lairds in parliament as shire commissioners, and co-operated with the radical presbyterians in the general assembly of the kirk, using them as a counterweight to the influence of the Catholic earls. Crawford rightly saw this as a challenge to the traditional privileges of the nobility and opposed it.

Scottish political society became increasingly polarized in the late 1580s, reflecting the unresolved tensions of the

Lennox years. Each faction attempted to increase its power at home through winning foreign support. Throughout 1588 the earls conspired to destabilize the king's government by ejecting Maitland from the chancellorship and Crawford's old enemy, the master of Glamis, from the treasurership. The king retained his chancellor while urging reconciliation between Crawford and Glamis and showing personal favour and patronage to Huntly. A precarious balance between the factions was thus maintained. Although Crawford was suspected of disaffection and of links with Spain he was still given charge of the defence of Forfarshire and the neighbouring coast against the threat of the Spanish Armada.

Despite its defeat, the Armada showed that Spain retained considerable power. Huntly, Crawford, and their confederates, advised by the duke of Guise, had been trying to tap into this source of power since 1586. The nature of their correspondence with Spain was revealed to James VI by the English ambassador in February 1589. It is likely that James had been aware of these contacts for some time and may even have encouraged them. Huntly, the emerging leader of the Roman Catholic anti-Maitland and pro-Spanish party, was imprisoned for a week on easy terms in Edinburgh Castle. On his release he made for the north-east, where he began an insurrection designed to win the king to his cause and eradicate Maitland; he was joined by Francis Hay, ninth earl of Erroll, and Crawford, and later by Francis Stewart, fifth earl of Bothwell.

On 10 April Crawford, with Huntly and Erroll, captured the master of Glamis in Perth, thereby striking at a reported plot against them by Maitland, John Stewart, twenty-fourth earl of Atholl, and Morton. The Catholic earls declared that their grievance was solely against Maitland, while religious concerns were added to their manifesto to encourage further support from Spain, whose considerable subsidies enabled them to maintain their forces in the field. The earls took possession of Aberdeen, from where they issued proclamations in the king's name stating that he was held captive and forced against his will to treat the nobles with more rigour than he desired. The king adhered to Maitland and the English alliance and marched north to confront the earls at the Brig O'Dee outside Aberdeen in April 1589. Despite their superior force, 3000 men to the king's 1000, the earls did not give battle but surrendered. Crawford confessed his crime and was imprisoned briefly in Edinburgh before being warded in St Andrews, nearer his own power base. He was released in September 1589.

Crawford's public involvement with the Catholic party diminished after 1589. He attended the privy council in 1591, and his religious opinions were still causing concern in 1593 when the provincial synod of Fife advised Andrew Melville to confer with him and the earl of Rothes. He maintained his attachment to the Huntly faction since in October 1593 he was on the assize which acquitted Huntly, Erroll, and Angus for the murder of the earl of Moray. Crawford was present at the parliament of May 1594 but did not play a prominent role. By 1595 he was observed attending protestant sermons and religious exercises. In 1596 the king was still trying to achieve the final reconciliation of Crawford and the master of Glamis. In March that year Crawford sought a safe conduct to go abroad; it was also reported that he was a possible ambassador to France. In April a further opportunity arose for him to serve as envoy, to Denmark. The safe conduct was granted since the English government believed that careful handling might win Crawford to their cause but already he was politically a spent force. He found himself more isolated, with his own former allies on the defensive.

Crawford's last years were marked by the resurgence of a feud. In October 1605 his eldest son, **David Lindsay**, master of Crawford (*bap.* 1576, *d.* 1620), baptized at Perth on 8 March 1576, murdered and mutilated David Lindsay of Balgavie, a Roman Catholic convert of William Crichton and deeply implicated in traffic with Spain and Rome. Despite his conviction and outlawry the master remained at large and appeared in Edinburgh in June 1607. On 5 June David Lindsay of Edzell, son of Walter Lindsay of Balgavie, lay in wait for the master, and in the resulting ambush the master's uncle and the earl of Crawford's brother, Alexander *Lindsay, Lord Spynie, were killed. Spynie was a friend of Walter and his murder split the Lindsay family more deeply. Crawford himself died either early in October that year or on 22 November, at Cupar, Fife. He was buried at Dundee. His son David, who succeeded as twelfth earl, married some time between 4 March 1606 and 16 April 1610 Lady Jane (Joan) Kerr, daughter of Mark Kerr, first earl of Lothian and widow of Robert Boyd, master of Boyd (*d.* 1597); the couple later divorced. The twelfth earl died in June 1620 at Edinburgh Castle and was buried in the Canongate. His former countess had married before 16 February 1618 Thomas Hamilton of Robertoun; she died before 1633. ALLAN WHITE

Sources *Scots peerage*, 4.539–40 • GEC, *Peerage* • Lord Lindsay, *Lives of the Lindsays, or, A memoir of the house of Crawford and Balcarres* (1844), vol. 1 • *CSP Scot.*, 1574–1603 • *Reg. PCS*, 1st ser., vols. 3, 4, 7 • *CSP Scot. ser.*, 1509–1603 • J. Leslie, *The historie of Scotland*, ed. E. G. Cody and W. Murison, trans. J. Dalrymple, 2 vols. in 4 pts, STS, 5, 14, 19, 34 (1888–95) [1596 trans. of *De origine moribus, et rebus gestis Scotorum libri decem* (Rome, 1578)] • D. Calderwood, *The history of the Kirk of Scotland*, ed. T. Thomson and D. Laing, 8 vols., Wodrow Society, 7 (1842–9), vols. 3–4 • D. Moyses, *Memoirs of the affairs of Scotland* (1755) • *The correspondence of Robert Bowes, of Aske, esquire, the ambassador of Queen Elizabeth in the court of Scotland*, ed. [J. Stevenson], SurtS, 14 (1842), 588 • W. Scott and D. Laing, eds., *The Bannatyne miscellany*, 1, Bannatyne Club, 19 (1827), 58 • R. Pitcairn, *Criminal trials in Scotland from 1488 to 1624* (1833), vol. 1, pt 2, 85 • J. Goodare, 'Scottish politics in the reign of James VI', *The reign of James VI*, ed. J. Goodare and M. Lynch (2000), 32–54 • R. Grant, 'The Brig O'Dee affair, the sixth earl of Huntly and the politics of the Counter-Reformation', *The reign of James VI*, ed. J. Goodare and M. Lynch (2000), 93–109 • M. H. B. Sanderson, *Cardinal of Scotland: David Beaton, c.1494–1546* (1986), 221–2

Lindsay, David, Lord Edzell (1551?–1610), judge, was the eldest son of David Lindsay, ninth earl of Crawford, and his second wife, Katherine (*d.* 1578), daughter of Sir John Campbell of Calder. His father had become ninth earl of Crawford in 1542 as a result of the disinheritance five years earlier of the eighth earl's only son. But when the ninth earl died on 20 September 1558 the earldom passed to the grandson of the eighth earl, another David Lindsay, while the latter's cousin and namesake inherited the Edzell estates. His mother was responsible for bringing up and educating her children and for managing the family estates. Together with his younger brother, John *Lindsay, later Lord Menmuir, David Lindsay of Edzell was educated on the continent and at Cambridge by James Lawson, a future colleague at St Giles, Edinburgh, of John Knox. On a contract dated 1 and 2 March 1570 Edzell married Lady Helen Lindsay (*d.* 1579), daughter of David Lindsay, tenth earl of Crawford. They had four children, David, who succeeded to Edzell, John, Alexander of Canterland, and Margaret, who married David Carnegie, first earl of Southesk. Edzell was among those who, on 3 May 1578, signed a band in favour of the earl of Mar as guardian of James VI, and he was knighted when Esmé Stewart was created duke of Lennox on 5 August 1581. In 1586 Edzell was appointed an extraordinary lord of session. His participation in national affairs increased considerably after his brother, Lord Menmuir, became incapacitated and then died. Shortly before his death Menmuir had resigned his position as an ordinary lord of session to Edzell, who successfully passed the trial of his abilities and was admitted a judge on 2 March 1598 under the title of Lord Edzell. He also stepped into two other of his brother's offices, that of privy councillor (his first appearance was on 16 November 1598), and master of the metals. Between 13 May 1597 and 7 June 1605 Lord Edzell attended six conventions of the estates, a more informal, less authoritative alternative to a parliament. He was also a commissioner for the summoning of parliament.

Edzell combined a wide variety of talents and interests. '[H]e was learned and accomplished—the sword, the pen, and pruninghook were equally familiar to him; he even anticipated the geologist's hammer, and had at least a taste for architecture and design' (Crawford, 1.339). He devoted much attention to the utilization of the minerals on his estate, agricultural improvements, building, and planting trees. The walled garden which he built at Edzell is the finest surviving example of its kind produced by the Scottish Renaissance. It is decorated on three sides with relief panels on which are carved the liberal arts, the planetary gods, and the cardinal virtues, and its walls are also pierced with small rectangular holes arranged to represent the fess chequy of his family's arms. At his death he had a library of 144 books. Edzell and his family were, however, both victims of, and participants in, the endemic violence that plagued Scottish society at this time. Two of his brothers, Robert Lindsay of Balhall and Sir Walter *Lindsay of Balgavie, were murdered. On 27 October 1583 Edzell and twenty-one others were granted a remission for the murder of John Campbell of Lundie. For his negligence in failing to prevent a fray between his son Alexander and the young laird of Pitarrow in the high street of Edinburgh on 17 June 1605 he was briefly warded first in Dumbarton, then in Stirling Castle. On 5 June 1607 his eldest son and heir, David, mortally wounded Alexander Lindsay, Lord Spynie, in Edinburgh in a quarrel arising from the murder of his uncle, Sir Walter. The earl of Crawford blamed Lord Edzell himself for this act, but did not appear to prosecute on 19 September 1609, the date set for his trial. Edzell's second marriage, to Isobel Forbes, on a contract dated 1 December 1585, was childless, and she survived him. He had an illegitimate son, Thomas Lindsay, who was also implicated in Lord Spynie's death. Lord Edzell died on 15 December 1610 at Edzell Castle.

MICHAEL WASSER

Sources *Scots peerage*, vols. 1, 3 • Lord Lindsay [A. W. C. Lindsay, earl of Crawford], *Lives of the Lindsays*, [new edn], 1 (1849) • J. H. Burton and D. Masson, eds., *The register of the privy council of Scotland*, 1st ser., 14 vols. (1877–98), vols. 2–8 • NL Scot., Crawford and Balcarres MS, Acc. 9769, personal papers § 4/1/80–145 • R. Pitcairn, ed., *Ancient criminal trials in Scotland*, 7 pts in 3, Bannatyne Club, 42 (1833) • G. Brunton and D. Haig, *An historical account of the senators of the college of justice, from its institution in MDXXXII* (1832) • *APS*, 1593–1625 • F. D. Bardgett, *Scotland reformed: the Reformation in Angus and the Mearns* (1989) • J. M. Thomson and others, eds., *Registrum magni sigilli regum Scotorum / The register of the great seal of Scotland*, 11 vols. (1882–1914), vol. 6 • *CSP Scot.*, 1593–7 • R. Douglas, *The peerage of Scotland*, 2nd edn, ed. J. P. Wood, 1 (1813) • M. Livingstone, D. Hay Fleming, and others, eds., *Registrum secreti sigilli regum Scotorum / The register of the privy seal of Scotland*, 8 (1982) • D. Howard, *Scottish architecture: Reformation to Restoration, 1560–1660* (1995), vol. 2 of *The architectural history of Scotland* • GEC, *Peerage*, 3.510–15
Archives NL Scot., corresp. and papers • NL Scot., Crawford and Balcarres MSS, acc. 9769, personal papers § 4/1/80–145
Wealth at death £24,097 13*s.* 4*d.* Scots—excl. land: testament dative, 30 Oct 1612, NL Scot., Crawford and Balcarres MSS, acc. 9769, personal papers § 4/1/104

Lindsay, David (*c.*1566–1627), Church of Scotland minister and religious writer, was probably the son of David *Lindsay (1531–1613), later bishop of Ross, and his first wife, Janet or Jonet Ramsay. He graduated MA from St Andrews University in 1586 and entered the ministry at Forfar in 1590. In August 1597 he was translated to St Andrews by the crown to replace Robert Wallace, removed for opposition to the crown's ecclesiastical policies. Between 1606 and 1609 he served the parish of Forgan in Fife and in 1609 he was translated to the second charge at South Leith near Edinburgh, where he replaced John Moray, deposed from the ministry for having preached against bishops. Lindsay's appointment was on the recommendation of Archbishop Spottiswoode, who had described him to James VI as a minister 'for whom the people is earnest' (Laing, 1068), although Calderwood suggested that he was appointed 'notwistanding of the protestation of the parochiners made in contrare' (Calderwood, 7.20). Lindsay thereby seems to have become assistant to his ageing father and, in 1613 on the death of Bishop Lindsay, he succeeded to the first charge. Three years later he too received the help of an assistant because of failing health, but in the event he lived another decade and published two devotional works, *The Heavenly Chariot Laid Open* (St Andrews, 1622) and *The Godly Man's Journey to Heaven* (London, 1625). He died in Leith in January 1627 and was survived by his wife, Margaret Hepburn (*d.* 1635); he is believed to have been married previously. In all, he is known to have had two sons and five daughters, two of whom married ministers. ALAN R. MACDONALD

Sources *Fasti Scot.*, new edn, vol. 1 • D. Calderwood, *The history of the Kirk of Scotland*, ed. T. Thomson and D. Laing, 8 vols., Wodrow Society, 7 (1842–9), vol. 7 • D. Laing, ed., *Acts and proceedings of the general assembly of the Kirk of Scotland* (1846) • A. R. Macdonald, *The Jacobean kirk, 1567–1625: sovereignty, polity and liturgy* (1998)

Wealth at death approx. £1500 Scots: NA Scot., Commissary of Edinburgh, Register of Testaments, CC8/8/54, fols. 61*v*–62*r*

Lindsay, David (*c.*1575–1639/40), bishop of Edinburgh, was the son of John Lindsay of Edzell, and graduated as master of arts at St Andrews University in 1593. He became master of the grammar school of Montrose before moving to be master at Dundee in 1597. He was minister of Dundee from about 1604 to 1618, a parish conveniently close to the estate he owned at Dunkenny in Forfarshire. By 1603 he was married to Christian Rutherford, widow of the former master of Dundee School, and after her death he married Katherine, daughter of Gilbert Ramsay of Banff.

Lindsay was appointed to the Scottish court of high commission in 1616. On 12 July 1617 he proposed and defended theses on the power of princes in a public disputation in St Andrews before James VI. His theses, published as *De potestate principis aphorisme* (1617), argued that the king was *summus gubernator* (supreme governor) of the kirk, able to command all things that were 'not repugnant to the will of God', his powers including the right to determine forms of worship (Mullan, 121). He followed this up by supporting the reforms that became known as the five articles of Perth in the 1618 general assembly, and he was elected bishop of Brechin on 10 April 1619 (consecrated on 23 November).

Pamphlets of 1619 on communion, and of 1621 defending the articles, confirmed Lindsay as one of the most active supporters of royal policy in the kirk, and he crowned Charles I at his Scottish coronation on 18 June 1633 after a sermon 'wherein he had some good exhortations to his Majestie', an opponent admitted, though they were 'general and ambiguous' (Row, 362–3). On 31 July 1634 he was admitted to the Scottish privy council, and in the same year became a justice of the peace and a commissioner of the exchequer.

Lindsay was transferred to the bishopric of Edinburgh on 16 September 1634, and in his capacity as bishop was present in St Giles on 23 July 1637 when the dean began to read the new prayer book introduced by Charles I. In the rioting by protesters that followed Lindsay became a prime target as protesters 'beganne to throw at him stooles and ther very bybles … And it is reported, that he hardly escaped the blow of a stoole' (Gordon, 1.7–8). Order was restored and he managed to preach his sermon, though he was assaulted in the streets afterwards and was unable to get into his lodgings, but was rescued by servants of the earl of Wemyss. He ventured out in the afternoon to hold a second service in the church, from which women (who had led the disorders) were excluded. Afterwards he had to be protected by footmen with drawn swords as he drove to Holyroodhouse with the earl of Roxburghe in the latter's coach, harassed by a stone-throwing mob shouting 'Kill the traitour' (Lippe, 174). Hostile accounts of his absurd 'crying to the people, That he had no wyt [knowledge] of the matter' (Row, 409) and that 'his greatnesse' displayed physical symptoms of extreme terror (J. Leslie, *True Relation*, 1830, 199–200) are doubtless exaggerated propaganda.

After refusing to submit to the authority of the covenanters' general assembly in 1638 Lindsay prepared for the dangers ahead by making his will, on 2 December. He was deprived of office and excommunicated on 13 December. Like the other Scottish bishops he then fled to England, where he died in 1639 or 1640. The date of the death of his wife, who was alive in December 1638, is unknown.

Lindsay had proved 'A tough opponent' (Mullan, 155) in debate with those resisting James VI's reforms of worship. His resolutions in favour of the Perth articles earned him—from an opponent—the nickname Dr Resolutus (Calderwood, 7.396). He took little part in the formulation of religious policies under Charles I, and the rumour that he tried to get some of the 'trashe' of the English liturgy left out of the new Scottish prayer book (*The Letters and Journals of Robert Baillie*, ed. D. Laing, 3 vols., 1841–2, 1.4) may indicate that he was not entirely happy with the king's reforms, though his obedience remained unswerving.

David Stevenson

Sources *Fasti Scot.*, new edn • R. Lippe, ed., *Selections from Wodrow's biographical collections: divines of the north-east of Scotland*, New Spalding Club, 5 (1890) • D. G. Mullan, *Episcopacy in Scotland: the history of an idea, 1560–1608* (1986) • *Reg. PCS*, 2nd ser., vols. 5–6 • D. Calderwood, *The history of the Kirk of Scotland*, ed. T. Thomson and D. Laing, 8 vols., Wodrow Society, 7 (1842–9) • J. Row, *The history of the Kirk of Scotland, from the year 1558 to August 1637*, ed. D. Laing, Wodrow Society, 4 (1842) • A. Jervise, *History and traditions of the lands of the Lindsays*, 2nd edn (1882) • J. Gordon, *History of Scots affairs from 1637–1641*, ed. J. Robertson and G. Grub, 3 vols., Spalding Club, 1, 3, 5 (1841) • Lord Lindsay [A. W. C. Lindsay, earl of Crawford], *Lives of the Lindsays*, [new edn], 3 vols. (1849) • R. Keith and J. Spottiswoode, *An historical catalogue of the Scottish bishops, down to the year 1688*, new edn, ed. M. Russel [M. Russell] (1824)

Likenesses portrait, probably priv. coll.; in possession of Thomas Carnegie of Craigie, Perthshire, in mid-19th century

Lindsay, David, twelfth earl of Crawford (*bap.* **1576**, *d.* **1620**). *See under* Lindsay, David, eleventh earl of Crawford (*d.* 1607).

Lindsay, David (**1856–1922**), explorer and entrepreneur, was born at Goolwa, South Australia, on 20 June 1856, the younger son of John Scott Lindsay, master mariner, of Dundee and of Goolwa, and his wife, Catherine Reid. His father had gone to Australia two years before Lindsay's birth, in command of a schooner destined for the coasting trade. Lindsay was educated privately at Port Elliott, near Goolwa, and in 1873 entered the South Australian survey department, where he remained until 1882. He held the post of junior surveyor in the land office of the department of the Northern Territory from 1878 to 1882. On 10 March 1881 he married Annie Theresa Stuart, daughter of Arthur Lindsay, civil servant, of Adelaide; they had four sons and one daughter. In 1882 Lindsay resigned his government post and set up as a private surveyor in Palmerston.

In 1883 Lindsay led a government expedition across the north of Arnhem Land from Palmerston (as Darwin was then known) to Blue Mud Bay on its east coast and discovered land which subsequently became an extensive Aboriginal reserve. In 1885–6 he continued his explorations in central Australia between the Georgina River in western Queensland and the Hay and Finke rivers to the east of the Macdonnell ranges and (mistakenly) reported deposits of rubies in the Macdonnell ranges. Two years later he rode across Australia from north to south, a journey of some 1400 miles which he made with just one Aborigine companion. His report threw some light on unknown geographical features of the interior and he was elected fellow of the Royal Geographical Society.

When in 1891 Sir Thomas Elder, of Adelaide, provided funds for a scientific exploration of the interior of Western Australia, Lindsay was chosen to command the expedition. The projected route was from Peake, on the railway, to the west of Lake Eyre, across the Great Victoria Desert to Lake Barlee, 100 miles north-east of the then unknown Kalgoorlie, and from there to the Murchison River and the west coast; the return journey was to be across the western desert to the Kimberley district of the north-west and from there to Tennant Creek (Northern Territory) on the overland telegraph line. The expedition was organized by the Royal Geographical Society of Australasia and its patron spared no expense. The results, however, fell far short of this ambitious programme. With the help of camels, the expedition, starting in May 1891, crossed the north of the Great Victoria Desert, traversing 550 miles in thirty-five days to Lake Lefroy; from there it proceeded north-west to Geraldton. But in January 1893 Lindsay was ordered home to face an enquiry into his leadership by four of his men who had rebelled. Their criticism proved groundless and Lindsay was completely exonerated. A typical bushman, somewhat autocratic and bombastic, he was a 'booster' for the Northern Territory, though he did not find much good country there, nor in the centre. His journey had, however, revealed the existence of the west Australian goldfield, which he later was active in developing as a surveyor, publicist, broker, and manager of mines.

In 1913 Lindsay served on the commonwealth (that is, federal) royal commission, which advised on the development of ports and railways in the Northern Territory, and in 1914 he attempted to set up a cattle ranching and meat freezing operation in the Northern Territory. In 1920 he started investigating the possibilities of cotton growing in the north, but while busy with this he died of a heart attack at Port Darwin on 17 December 1922; he was survived by his wife.

R. N. RUDMOSE BROWN, *rev.* ELIZABETH BAIGENT

Sources *The Times* (19 Dec 1922) · *Journal of the Elder scientific exploring expedition, 1891–2* (1893) · *GJ*, 1 (1893), 552–3 · *South Australian Register* (11 July 1878) · private information (1937) · *AusDB*
Archives Mitchell L., NSW, Daniel Lindsay MSS

Lindsay, David (1876–1945), writer, was born on 3 March 1876 at 5 Llanberis Terrace, Lewisham, London, the third of the three children of Alexander Lindsay (*b.* 1839), bookkeeper, and his wife, Elizabeth (1841–1925), *née* Bellamy, of a farming family from Leamington Spa, Warwickshire. Alexander Lindsay was a borders Scot, and David spent holidays in Scotland until he was forty; he placed his roots in Scotland and traced his ancestry back to the poet Sir David Lindsay and further to a Nordic prince, Ivar. Educated at Colfe's Grammar School, Lewisham (1885–December 1890), Lindsay excelled in English, winning the school prize; but the desertion of the family by his father about 1889 forced him to leave school at fourteen and start work as an office boy with the London firm of insurance brokers Price Forbes, probably in 1891. He remained there until 1918, advancing to accountant and then confidential clerk, absent only for war service in London with the Grenadier Guards (1916–18).

On 21 December 1916 Lindsay married the young Jacqueline Silver (1898–1965), with whom he had two daughters, in 1919 and 1922. In 1918 he resigned from Price Forbes (although he had been offered the post of office manager), and committed himself, as he had long planned, to the untried life of a novelist, settling in 1919 at St Columb Minor, Cornwall. There he wrote the interplanetary romance *A Voyage to Arcturus* (1920), the supernatural fictions *The Haunted Woman* (1922), *Sphinx* (1923), and what became *Devil's Tor* (1932), and the historical novel *The Adventures of Monsieur de Mailly* (1926). Two other fantastic works, *The Violet Apple* (1924–6) and *The Witch* (1932–45) remained unpublished, the latter being unfinished at Lindsay's death.

Most of Lindsay's novels had difficulty finding publishers, were poorly reviewed, and sold badly, despite attempts by him to accommodate his vision to contemporary taste. Only the sturdy asceticism and otherworldliness of the author, which most of his novels expound, kept him at work through long years of self-isolation and poverty and the growing restiveness of his wife. In 1928 the Lindsays moved to a rural bungalow at Ferring, near Worthing, in Sussex; and in 1938 to a town house in Hove where Jacqueline Lindsay took in lodgers, and where Lindsay became increasingly reclusive and distant.

Lindsay's novels seem more metaphysically inspired than personal: they are full of an intense vision of a sublime reality beyond all human desires, utterly alien, cold, and solitary, and yet apprehended, particularly through great music and through spiritual pain, as the soul's home. While this philosophy has a unique, if restricted, power which was buttressed by Lindsay's reading in Schopenhauer, Nietzsche, and mystics of the 'negative way', it was in part the expression of his own frustrated experience of the world. Lindsay is best known for *A Voyage to Arcturus*. This long-gestated book is Lindsay's gnostic outlook at its fiercest, describing a journey to an imaginary planet of violently contrastive landscapes and creatures, where the hero Maskull is continually tempted by various forms of pleasure or self-denial, and by rejecting them all learns the sublimity of the god Muspel. Stylistically the book works superbly by constantly subverting the reader's expectations in parallel with those of the protagonist.

Lindsay's other books are set in the 1920s English society

he had contemptuously encountered; they reject superficiality, and feature a passionate love which mutates into spiritual awakening and sometimes death. *The Haunted Woman* is a striking picture of a conventional relationship transformed intermittently by a vision of another world seen from an ancient house. In Lindsay's longest novel, the Jamesian *Devil's Tor*, the central characters realize that they are the last representatives of an ancient spiritual force which must renew itself through their marriage. Lindsay here subverts the reader's novelistic expectations by revealing all apparently human thoughts and conversations as actually the workings of a transcendent destinal agency. Lindsay's last book, the overwritten *The Witch*, returns us to the world-renouncing vision of *A Voyage*, a journey of the alone towards the Alone.

In the scant photographs available of Lindsay, he looks the quintessential man of his times. Calm and good-humoured with his family, if shy and cold with others, he was always inwardly frustrated, tormented, and spiritually stricken. Lindsay died of vascular disease and cancer at 193 Upper Shoreham Road, Kingston by Sea, Shoreham, Sussex, on 16 July 1945. He was buried in an unmarked grave in nearby Lancing. Some fame then ironically came to him, through the enthusiasm of influential individuals and a public increasingly more receptive to visionary fantasy. COLIN MANLOVE

Sources B. Sellin, *The life and works of David Lindsay* (1981) • C. Wilson, E. H. Visiak, and J. B. Pick, *The strange genius of David Lindsay* (1970) • C. Manlove, *Scottish fantasy literature: a critical survey* (1994) • private information (2004) [Diana Moon; J. Coulter, Lewisham local studies committee; P. M. Heinecke, Information Officer, Colfe's School] • b. cert. • m. cert. • d. cert.
Archives NL Scot., MSS
Likenesses photograph, *c.*1914, priv. coll. • photograph, repro. in D. Lindsay, *Devil's tor* (1932)

Lindsay, David Alexander Edward, twenty-seventh earl of Crawford and tenth earl of Balcarres (1871–1940), politician and art connoisseur, was born on 10 October 1871 at Dunecht House, Aberdeen, the eldest of the six sons of James Ludovic *Lindsay, twenty-sixth earl of Crawford and ninth earl of Balcarres (1847–1913), an astronomer, collector, and bibliophile, and his wife, Emily Florence (1848–1934), second daughter of Colonel Edward Bootle-Wilbraham and his wife, Emily Ramsbottom. The Lindsays were an ancient family from Fife, but their home had been at Haigh, Wigan, since the 1790s, when Alexander Lindsay, sixth earl of Balcarres, sold his land in Fife and moved south to repair his tattered fortunes by developing his wife's Lancashire estate.

Until succeeding his father in 1913 David Lindsay held the courtesy title of earl of Balcarres (and was known as Bal). Heir to his father as chairman of the family firm, the Wigan Coal and Iron Company, he also inherited the valuable collections built up out of its profits by his father and grandfather—the Bibliotheca Lindesiana was the last great private library in Britain. He was educated at Eton College (1886–90) and at Magdalen College, Oxford (1890–94), where he took a third in history. He was secretary, treasurer, and president (1894) of the Oxford Union and secretary of the Canning Club; after completing his studies he undertook social work at the Oxford House university settlement in Bethnal Green under the auspices of the Charity Organization Society. At Oxford, he began to write a diary, which he kept in unbroken sequence, filling fifty volumes from 1892 until 1940.

At a by-election in June 1895, at only twenty-three, Balcarres was elected unopposed as Conservative MP for the Chorley division of Lancashire, in which Haigh Hall, then the family seat, was situated. He held the seat until his succession to the peerage in 1913. He became private secretary to Gerald Balfour, gravitating towards the circle of A. J. Balfour. He took an early interest in the administration of the arts; his attack on the muddle and maladministration of the South Kensington Museum led to the creation of the Victoria and Albert Museum in 1899. In 1900 he introduced an Ancient Monuments Protection Act. He became a fellow of the Society of Antiquaries in 1901 and a trustee of the National Portrait Gallery. He was chairman (1903–21) of the National Art Collections Fund, established to prevent America buying up Britain's treasures. He published a study of Donatello (1903) and a book entitled *The Evolution of Italian Sculpture* (1909), also contributing an article, 'Museums of art', to the eleventh edition of the *Encyclopaedia Britannica* (1911).

On 25 January 1900 Balcarres married Constance Lilian (*d.* 1947), younger daughter and coheir of Sir Henry Pelly, third baronet. They had two sons and six daughters. At coal-blackened, smoky Haigh, Bal lived among his father's collections, which were serviced by a staff of six librarians; locally, he enjoyed the prestige of a Victorian grandee, and thousands turned out to see him on public occasions. In 1903 he became a party whip in the House of Commons, and for the next ten years Westminster was his world. His political diaries reveal a keen eye for detail and for the frailties of his fellows; he watched the disintegration of the Balfour government with shrewd detachment. As he moved closer to Balfour and the Conservative ruling clique, the diary becomes a unique insider account of Edwardian high politics.

Bal was promoted chief whip in July 1911, and he handled the bitter party divisions over the Parliament Bill and the succession of Bonar Law with skill and diplomacy. His habit of writing detailed notes within minutes of political conversations makes his diary an unrivalled historical source for these events. He was fortunate that the work of constituency organization had been devolved to the newly created post of party chairman, allowing the chief whip to concentrate on the Commons. Essentially a parliamentary creature, Bal (who drank very little) flourished in the all-male world of lobby gossip and political cabals. Under Bonar Law, to whom he was as loyal as he had been to Balfour, he reformed the organization of the party in the Commons, setting back-bench MPs to work. These were probably the happiest years of his life.

In January 1913 Bal's father died unexpectedly and he succeeded as twenty-seventh earl of Crawford and tenth earl of Balcarres. Heavy succession duties of £107,000 on his father's estate of £321,500 forced him to rationalize the collections at Haigh; he kept the core of the Bibliotheca Lindesiana but dismissed the librarians, sold the manuscript and stamp collections, and dispatched 53 tons of books to Quaritch. In 1915, at the age of forty-three, Crawford joined up as a private in the Royal Army Medical Corps, giving a false age and declaring himself a bachelor. Months later, in July 1916, he was summoned from France to become president of the board of agriculture and a cabinet minister. No admirer of Asquith, he watched the prime minister's fall with grim satisfaction. In December 1916 he was appointed lord privy seal outside the cabinet, with responsibility for the wheat commission—an inconspicuous but vital administrative job, saving the bread situation in Europe. After the war, as chancellor of the duchy of Lancaster (January 1919–April 1921), he brought bread supplies back to normal, while acting as deputy leader in the House of Lords. He was appointed first commissioner of works in 1921, adding the portfolio of minister of transport (unpaid) in 1922, when he was promoted to the cabinet. Since he was a supporter of Lloyd George, the fall of the coalition found him out of office for the first time in six years; he regretted the change, reluctantly retiring from front-bench politics at fifty-two.

Crawford turned to the world of art, where he made a second career. He became chancellor of Manchester University (1923) and a trustee of the British Museum. He was chairman of the Royal Fine Arts Commission (1924), a body set up to approve public works. In 1925 he chaired the Crawford committee on broadcasting, which recommended the formation of the BBC as a public monopoly. Though he continued to observe politics close-up, dining with political colleagues, he was by now the 'uncrowned king of British art'. He chaired the Royal Literary Fund, sat as a trustee of the National Gallery and chairman of the Council for the Preservation of Rural England, and was president of the Society of Antiquaries (1924–9) and of the Roxburghe Club (1936). Meanwhile, the family business, the Wigan Coal and Iron Company, reported bigger and bigger losses. In 1931, after the company was 'rationalized' and forced to amalgamate, Crawford was asked to step down as chairman. He died suddenly at Haigh Hall on 8 March 1940.

Crawford was burly and bucolic-looking, but he neither hunted nor shot. A dedicated public servant, he never really questioned his order, but with the flexibility of a man whose laird ancestors had reinvented themselves as coal merchants, he moved from politics, where a hereditary peer had nowhere to go beyond junior office, to an art world where he had a real contribution to make. But his greatest claim to historical reputation is his diary, which was published in 1984, and which gives an indispensable account of pre-1914 tory politics. JANE RIDLEY

Sources *The Crawford papers: the journals of David Lindsay, twenty-seventh earl of Crawford … 1892–1940*, ed. J. Vincent (1984) • N. Barker, *Bibliotheca Lindesiana*, Roxburghe Club (1977) • *The Times* (9 March 1940) • *DNB*

Archives NL Scot., corresp. and papers • NRA, priv. coll., papers, incl. diaries | BL, Balfour MSS • BL, corresp. relating to binding of Codex Sinaiticus, Add. MS 68932 • Bodl. Oxf., corresp. relating to Society for the Protection of Science and Learning • Herts. ALS, letters to Lady Desborough • HLRO, corresp. with Andrew Bonar Law • HLRO, letters to David Lloyd George • NL Aus., corresp. with first Viscount Stonehaven • U. Glas. L., letters to D. S. MacColl • U. Leeds, Brotherton L., letters to Edmund Gosse

Likenesses G. C. Beresford, photographs, 1903, NPG • J. Russell & Sons, photographs, 1921, NPG • F. May, gouache caricature, 1936, NPG • W. Rothenstein, chalk drawing, *c.*1938, NPG • J. Gunn, oils, 1939, NPG

Wealth at death £389,064 8*s.*—save and except settled land: probate, 24 June 1940, *CGPLA Eng. & Wales*

Lindsay, David Alexander Robert, twenty-eighth earl of Crawford and eleventh earl of Balcarres (1900–1975), connoisseur of the arts and politician, was born on 20 November 1900 at 49 Moray Place, Edinburgh, the son of David Alexander Edward *Lindsay, twenty-seventh earl of Crawford and tenth earl of Balcarres (1871–1940), and his wife, Constance Lilian (*d.* 1947), daughter of Sir Henry Carstairs Pelly MP, third baronet. He was the elder son, and eldest of six children, the heir both to an ancient Scottish house with substantial property in Lancashire, and to a long line of learned collectors in which the twenty-fifth earl (Alexander William Crawford *Lindsay) was especially prominent. Hereditary taste is most uncommon, but Crawford, brought up amid the treasures of the family homes at Haigh Hall, Wigan, 7 Audley Square, London, and Balcarres, Fife, was a worthy upholder of the learning and sensitivity that had marked his family for several generations. Administrative shrewdness and personal charm enabled him throughout his life to place his knowledge unreservedly at the service of the arts in Great Britain.

Lindsay was educated at Eton College (where he gained much from the informal encouragement of A. S. F. Gow, who became a lifelong friend) and, from 1919, at Magdalen College, Oxford, where he obtained a second class in French in 1922. On 9 December 1925 he married Mary Katharine (1903–1994), daughter of Lord Richard Frederick Cavendish, of Holker Hall, Cartmel. A period as honorary attaché at the British embassy in Rome gave him opportunities for developing his knowledge of Italian Renaissance painting; he remained a dedicated and well-informed traveller in Italy. In 1930 he shared in the active organization of the Burlington House exhibition of Italian art, 1200–1900, with Kenneth Clark, and was joint editor of the enormous commemorative catalogue (1931).

As Lord Balniel, he had entered the House of Commons as Conservative member for the Lonsdale division of Lancashire in 1924, and sat until he succeeded to the earldom in 1940, whereupon he sat in the House of Lords as Baron Wigan. Although he enjoyed life in the Commons, his main contribution to public life lay elsewhere. In October 1935 he was appointed to the board of trustees of the National Gallery, and (with short intermissions) remained a trustee until June 1960. He served as chairman in 1938–9 and 1946–8; his first tenure was particularly important in defusing unpleasant tensions between the director and

David Alexander Robert Lindsay, twenty-eighth earl of Crawford and eleventh earl of Balcarres (1900–1975), by unknown photographer

his staff, and in making preparations for the evacuation of the collections from Trafalgar Square at the outbreak of war.

The National Gallery was but the first of a demanding range of distinguished trusteeships concerned with the national heritage. Crawford served on the board of the British Museum from 1940 to 1973; as chairman of the Royal Fine Arts Commission from 1943 to 1957, of the National Library of Scotland from 1944 to 1974, of the National Trust from 1945 to 1965, and of the National Gallery of Scotland from 1952 to 1975. He was chairman of the national art collections fund from 1945 until 1970, when he became its president; and he was a Pilgrim trustee from 1949. His prolonged tenures of these and other appointments made him uniquely influential, and he applied himself energetically to each with wide-ranging knowledge, unobtrusive forcefulness, and a charm of manner that communicated itself to junior officials as well as to the senior directing staff. He was unsparing of himself, conducted a vast correspondence in a minute and idiosyncratic hand, and travelled constantly from Fife (Haigh was given up in favour of Balcarres after the war) to meetings in London, or on National Trust business throughout England and Wales. Perhaps his most celebrated effort was on behalf of the National Art Collections Fund (of which his father had been a founder), when in 1962 he personally supervised the special appeal to secure for the National Gallery the Leonardo da Vinci cartoon of the Virgin and St Anne, to be sold by the Royal Academy; £800,000 was asked, and Crawford's energetic, but personally exhausting, efforts succeeded in raising the essential £450,000 in four months, the balance being found by the government.

Constant voluntary work took its toll on Crawford's health, but even in his last years he vigorously opposed entrance charges for national museums and galleries, and later the Labour government's wealth tax proposals, which threatened the existence of the great private collections of Britain. His opposition was the reverse of self-interested, but he had seen the great Crawford family holdings much reduced by death duties, and he cherished the more keenly the still marvellous collections that remained. Among them his taste was firmly directed towards the gold-ground and Renaissance periods of Italian art, and the *Crucifixion* formerly attributed to Duccio (now in the Manchester City Galleries) was a particular favourite. He was deeply versed in the history of the family and its possessions, and in the reduced public activity of his last years he gave urgent and learned encouragement to several younger scholars working on his family papers. Nicolas Barker's *Bibliotheca Lindesiana* (Crawford's own presentation volume to the Roxburghe Club, issued in 1977) was the principal result of this activity; Crawford was working on the typescript at the time of his death at Balcarres on 13 December 1975. He was buried at the family chapel there.

Crawford was created GBE in 1951 and KT in 1955. He received many honours, academic and artistic, including the Oxford DCL (1951) and the Cambridge LLD (1955). He was rector of St Andrews University in 1952–5 and became an honorary fellow of Magdalen in 1975. He was succeeded in his peerages by his eldest son, Robert Alexander (*b.* 1927); his younger sons also continued the family interest in the fine arts, Patrick (*d.* 1986) as a senior director of Christies, Thomas as a specialist restorer of paintings.

ALAN BELL, *rev.*

Sources *The Times* (16 Dec 1975) • *The Times* (24 Dec 1975) • *The Times* (29 Dec 1975) • *Burlington Magazine* (April 1976) • K. Clark, *Another part of the wood* (1974) • private information (1986) • personal knowledge (1986) • GEC, *Peerage*

Archives Harvard University Center for Italian Renaissance Studies, near Florence, Italy, letters to Bernard Berenson • Tate collection, corresp. with Lord Clark • U. Glas., letters to D. S. MacColl

Likenesses W. Stoneman, photograph, 1950, NPG • photograph, NPG [*see illus.*]

Wealth at death £1,432,317.50: confirmation, 23 March 1976, *CCI*

Lindsay, Eric Mervyn (1907–1974), astronomer, was born on 26 January 1907 at Hannavale House, near Portadown, co. Armagh, Ireland, the youngest of the thirteen children of Richard and Susan Lindsay. After attending the King's Hospital school in Dublin, he took a BSc in physics at Queen's University, Belfast, in 1928, and an MSc on a research topic in astrophysics the following year. Having been awarded a Musgrave studentship from Queen's University, in September 1929 he went to Harvard. There he met and came to know the director of Harvard College observatory, Harlow Shapley, and Bart Bok, recently arrived at Harvard from the Netherlands, became his research supervisor. Lindsay worked on the distribution of stars between magnitudes 10 and 13.5, which involved examining photographic plates from the observatory's stations in the southern hemisphere, and after taking his PhD in 1934 he was appointed chief assistant at Harvard's Boyden station at Bloemfontein in South Africa. There in 1937 he married Sylvia Mussells, who had been an assistant astronomer at Harvard. They had one son, Derek Michael, born in 1944.

Lindsay returned to Northern Ireland in 1937 as director of the Armagh observatory. He was the only member of staff in a hopelessly underfunded institution that had been in decline for many years. It was an unexpected and unpromising move, one that Shapley judged ruinous for Lindsay's career, but he went to Armagh with an ambition to make it a significant centre of astronomical work and with the determination to carry this through. He began by negotiating a threefold increase in the annual grant from the Northern Ireland government. It was an indication of Lindsay's political acumen and persuasive skills, something that would be important to the future of the observatory.

Lindsay became head of the new department of astronomy at Queen's University, a post he held until 1953 alongside his Armagh position, and he maintained his Harvard connections. He began to promote a scheme that would involve the observatories of Armagh and Dunsink, near Dublin, collaborating in the installation of a new reflecting telescope at Boyden. In September 1941 war work took him to the Admiralty in London as principal scientific officer to P. M. S. Blackett, and there he was able to contribute more directly to plans for how astronomy might develop in the United Kingdom after the war.

Lindsay's Admiralty work took him to Washington in August 1945 as British liaison officer, and his stay there enabled him to work out with Shapley detailed proposals for what would become the Armagh-Dunsink-Harvard or 'ADH' telescope at Boyden. Lindsay was particularly adroit in persuading the government of the Republic of Ireland to provide its share of the funding, and then challenging the government of Northern Ireland to match it. He had developed a good relationship with Eamon De Valera, and both he and Lindsay were pleased that the arrangement to co-operate over the telescope was the first formal agreement between the two administrations in Ireland. For Lindsay it was a concrete instance of his belief that astronomy could play a role in improving understanding in a divided Ireland. The telescope was completed in 1950.

Meanwhile, in Armagh Lindsay had re-established the Irish Astronomical Society in 1946, negotiated a settled and adequate funding arrangement for the observatory with the Northern Ireland government, enlarged the staff, and installed a large Schmidt telescope. In 1947 he persuaded the distinguished Estonian theoretical astronomer Ernst Öpik, who had been one of Lindsay's PhD examiners and was now a displaced person after the war, to move to Armagh, and raised special funding for him from the Northern Ireland government.

Lindsay maintained his observing work in South Africa, and spent long periods there in 1951 and 1952. When in 1953 Harvard announced its intention to withdraw support from the Boyden station, Lindsay was much involved in the extensive negotiations to set up an international observatory there, which reached a satisfactory conclusion in June 1955. At the same time he was also seeking to realize a long-held ambition to establish a public planetarium in Armagh, with a strong educational role for people on both sides of the border. He often discussed his plans with both De Valera and Lord Brookeborough, and relished his unusual position of being on terms of personal friendship with both of Ireland's prime ministers. Eventually his efforts bore fruit with the appointment of Patrick Moore as director of the planetarium and its opening by Terrence O'Neil, prime minister of Northern Ireland, in May 1968. Lindsay had been appointed OBE in 1961.

Lindsay died suddenly at the observatory on 27 July 1974. Until the end of his career he had been promoting cross-border astronomical ventures, the final, unsuccessful, one being a refurbishment of the ADH telescope as a scheme appropriate to the climate of the ill-fated Sunningdale agreement of 1973. His lasting achievement was the reputation and viability of Armagh observatory, together with the success of the nearby planetarium. It was an outcome that could scarcely have been imagined when he took over a near-derelict observatory thirty-seven years previously. J. A. Bennett

Sources J. A. Bennett, *Church, state, and astronomy in Ireland: 200 years of Armagh observatory* (1990) · *Irish Astronomical Journal*, 12 (1975–6) · P. A. Wayman, *Quarterly Journal of the Royal Astronomical Society*, 16 (1975), 215–17 · private information (2004)
Archives Armagh observatory archives
Likenesses photographs, Armagh observatory
Wealth at death £8523.38: administration, 20 Sept 1974, *CGPLA NIre.*

Lindsay, George, third Lord Spynie (*d.* 1671), nobleman, was the second child, and second son, of Alexander *Lindsay, second Lord Spynie (*d.* 1646), and his second wife, Lady Margaret, only daughter of George Hay, first earl of Kinnoull and lord chancellor of Scotland (1622–34). He was served heir to his father in 1646. Like his father he was a staunch supporter of Charles I. He opposed the surrender of the king to the English parliament in 1647 and, as colonel of the Stirling and Clackmannan horse, supported the engagement negotiated with him in December 1647. In December 1650 the Scottish parliament, then reconciling a number of former engagers, appointed him colonel of foot for Angus (Forfarshire), though he did not make his peace with the kirk until early 1651. He was among the former engagers admitted to the committee for regulating the army in March 1651, and led his regiment into England in Charles II's 1651 campaign. Captured at the battle of Worcester, he was imprisoned in the Tower of London on 16 September 1651. His estates were forfeited on the proclamation of the Cromwellian act of grace and pardon, from which he was excepted, at the Mercat Cross of Edinburgh on 5 May 1654. The forfeiture was later changed to a heavy fine which, with other financial obligations apparently incurred in the royal cause, left him greatly in debt. With the death of Ludovic Lindsay, sixteenth earl of Crawford, in November 1652, he was served his heir, although he did not inherit the earldom.

Following the Restoration Spynie's losses were placed before a commission of enquiry, in 1661, and he secured royal protection from arrest for debt. He sat in parliament in 1663, 1669 and 1670. He died insolvent and without heirs in January 1671, and was buried in Holyrood on 21 January. T. F. HENDERSON, *rev.* ALISON G. MUIR

Sources *Scots peerage* · *APS, 1648–69* · Burke, *Peerage* (1970) · J. Nicoll, *A diary of public transactions and other occurrences, chiefly in Scotland, from January 1650 to June 1667*, ed. D. Laing, Bannatyne Club, 52 (1836), 59, 68, 125 · *CSP dom.*, 1651, 432 · R. Douglas, *The peerage of Scotland*, 2nd edn, ed. J. P. Wood, 2 (1813), 518 · GEC, *Peerage* · E. M. Furgol, *A regimental history of the covenanting armies, 1639–1651* (1990)

Archives NA Scot., Lindsay of Edzell?

Wealth at death died insolvent; estates valued *c.*1654 at £462 0s. 4*d*.: Paul, *Peerage*, 8 (1911), 107

Lindsay, George Mackintosh (1880–1956), army officer, was born in Cardiff on 3 July 1880, the sixth son of Lieutenant-Colonel Henry Gore Lindsay (1830–1914) of Glasnevin House, Dublin, and his wife, Ellen Sarah (*d.* 1912), daughter of Charles Morgan, first Baron Tredegar. Having been educated at Sandroyd and Radley College, Lindsay was commissioned into the Royal Monmouthshire Royal Engineers, a militia unit, shortly before his eighteenth birthday. In 1900 he gained a regular commission in the rifle brigade with which he served in Natal and the Transvaal during the Second South African War, earning a mention in dispatches.

In 1906 Lindsay became the adjutant of a volunteer regiment, and from 1908 to 1911 he served the 17th (county of London) battalion of the London regiment of the Territorial Force (the organization which succeeded the volunteers) in the same capacity. On 9 February 1907 he married Constance Elizabeth, daughter of George Stewart Hamilton. The first of their two daughters died at birth in 1910. At the outbreak of the First World War Lindsay was serving at the School of Musketry at Hythe where he was a machine-gun specialist. He went to France as a machine-gun officer in 1915 and was selected as instructor to the newly formed general headquarters machine-gun school. Later in 1915 he returned to England as general staff officer, grade 2, of the machine-gun corps training centre at Grantham. After returning to France in June 1916 he served as brigade major of the 99th brigade in the battles of the Somme and Arras. He was awarded the DSO in 1917. In March 1918 he became machine-gun officer at the headquarters of the First Army with the rank of colonel.

During the First World War George Lindsay's professional advancement had been steady rather than spectacular. The most remarkable aspect of his career in this period was his passionate advocacy of the importance of the machine-gun and of the creation of a specialist machine-gun corps. The obvious use of heavy, belt-fed machine-guns like the British .303 inch Vickers gun was defensive, engaging with direct-fire targets the gunners could actually see. But machine-guns could also be used in an indirect-fire role, the curved trajectory of their bullets being exploited to allow the bombardment of targets not visible to those firing. Machine-guns could thus support attacking infantry by firing at targets over their heads, rather like artillery. Given that the allies had substantial numerical superiority on the western front for most of the war and did most of the attacking, the offensive use of machine-guns in the indirect-fire role was of particular importance. Achieving the best possible results with machine-guns in this more technically sophisticated fashion required, Lindsay believed, the creation of a specialist corps to take charge of them. During the course of 1915 machine-guns were taken out of British infantry battalions on the western front, concentrated at brigade level, and manned by members of the new corps. This reorganization was bitterly controversial. Infantry officers generally resented the loss of the Vickers gun as an infantry weapon and had difficulty in establishing good relations with the new corps, tending to think that the tactical awareness of its officers did not match their supposed technical expertise. Significant tactical innovations were, however, made by the machine-gun specialists, the most important being the machine-gun barrage as a supplement to the field artillery barrage, first used by the Canadian machine-gun corps but universally adopted in the British expeditionary force by the final campaign of the war. The machine-gun corps as an institution separate from the infantry may have been desirable in the special circumstances of the western front in the First World War, but the decision to terminate its existence early in the post-war period was the correct one. Since the First World War machine-guns in all important armies have been regarded as weapons integral to and inseparable from the infantry. The tank corps, however, another wartime creation based on advanced military technology, survived into the peace. Much of Lindsay's subsequent military career was to be associated with that institution.

After the First World War Lindsay attended and passed the Staff College, and in June 1921 he was given command of 1 armoured car group stationed in Iraq. There he carried out experiments in the use of a mechanized force in combination with aircraft, keeping the force supplied by air. Lindsay became fascinated by possibilities of armoured, mechanized mobility and came to believe that it could transform warfare. He preached this idea vigorously to fellow officers and from about 1923 to about 1934 he appears to have been the intellectual leader of those in the Royal Tank Corps (RTC) and the wider army who adopted it. J. F. C. Fuller, who had been the principal staff officer of the tank corps for much of the First World War, had been advocating the same sort of idea for considerably longer, but Fuller was a deeply eccentric individual who found it rather difficult to work harmoniously with others. Lindsay, on the other hand, was widely liked by equals and subordinates and generally enjoyed much better relations with his superiors.

Lindsay returned to England in 1923 and took up an appointment as chief instructor of the RTC, taking charge of its central schools at Bovington and Lulworth. In 1926 he became inspector RTC, a War Office post. He had for some years been advocating a series of practical experiments with a mechanized force centred around tanks but also comprising several other arms, the whole receiving close co-operation from aircraft. This concept was approved by the new chief of the Imperial General Staff, Sir George Milne, under the influence of J. F. C. Fuller, his military assistant. Initially known as the experimental mechanical force, the formation held exercises on Salisbury Plain in 1927 and 1928 which attracted international military attention and are still regarded as a landmark in the history of mechanized warfare. Lindsay subsequently played a very important role in the development of radical ideas on the future of armoured warfare, which were incorporated in two general staff pamphlets, one published in 1929 and the other in 1931.

Between 1929 and 1932 Lindsay served as a brigadier on the general staff in Egypt. On his return he took command of the 7th infantry brigade, a motorized brigade based at Tidworth. Earlier his views on the future of land warfare had been too tank-centred, but by 1934 he was pressing for the development of an armoured division which would be a well-balanced all-arms mechanized formation. He was actually given command of a rudimentary, improvised armoured division for an exercise held on Salisbury Plain at the end of the training season of 1934. In order to test the formation the directing staff deliberately made Lindsay's task rather difficult. Lindsay was impeded in meeting the challenge this provided in two important respects. His wife was suffering from a form of mental illness and this was preying on his mind. Secondly the commander of the tank brigade, P. C. S. Hobart, whose views on armoured warfare had now diverged from those of Lindsay, proved an unruly and difficult subordinate. Lindsay's performance was considered weak by the exercise director and his career henceforth fell under something of a cloud. The British general staff did not, as has sometimes been alleged, lose faith in armoured forces as a result of this exercise, but Lindsay's influence on the development of British military thought and organization virtually ceased. This was most unfortunate as, by 1934, Lindsay's ideas on the future of armoured warfare were the most balanced and sophisticated of any British officer.

Lindsay, who had become a major-general in 1934, went to Calcutta in 1935 as commander of the presidency and Assam district. There he remained until his retirement in 1939. On the outbreak of war later that year, however, he was given command of the 9th Highland division. In 1940 he was appointed deputy regional commissioner for civil defence in the south-west of England, where he showed untiring activity during air raids. In 1944 he was appointed commissioner for the British Red Cross and order of St John in north-west Europe; he held that post for two years, and was colonel-commandant of the Royal Tank regiment from 1938 to 1947.

Lindsay was appointed CMG in 1919, CB in 1936, and CBE in 1946. He died at 49 Dorking Road, Epsom, Surrey, on 28 November 1956, survived by his wife and daughter.

J. P. Harris

Sources *DNB* • J. P. Harris, *Men, ideas and tanks: British military thought and amoured forces, 1903–1939* (1995) • K. Macksey, *The tank pioneers* (1981) • H. R. Winton, *To change an army: General Sir John Burnett-Stuart and British armoured doctrine, 1927–1938* (1988) • R. H. Larson, *The British army and the theory of armored warfare, 1918–1940* (1984) • B. H. Liddell Hart, *The tanks: the history of the royal tank regiment and its predecessors*, 1 (1959) • P. Griffith, *Battle tactics of the western front: the British army's art of attack, 1916–1918* (1994) • Burke, *Peerage* (1967) • *CGPLA Eng. & Wales* (1957) • m. cert.

Archives King's Lond., Liddell Hart C., corresp. and papers • Tank Museum, Bovington, Dorset, official papers | King's Lond., Liddell Hart C., papers • King's Lond., Liddell Hart C., corresp. with Sir B. H. Liddell Hart

Likenesses photograph, 1947 (after a sketch by S. Morse-Brown), Tank Museum, Bovington

Wealth at death £13,201 9*s*. 6*d*.: probate, 15 April 1957, *CGPLA Eng. & Wales*

Lindsay, Harriet Sarah Loyd-, Lady Wantage (1837–1920), benefactor, was born at Norfolk Street, Park Lane, London, on 30 June 1837, the only surviving child (a son had earlier died in infancy) of Samuel Jones *Loyd, later first Baron Overstone (1796–1883), a banker, and his wife, Harriet (1799–1864), daughter of Ichabod Wright, a Nottingham banker. She was educated at home by governesses under her father's close supervision. Long treated as a child, being made to wear washed muslin dresses, she grew up shy and reserved, but in time learnt to write and talk with ease and fluency.

Harriet Loyd first met her future husband at the age of fourteen during a tour of Italy in 1851–2. He was Robert James Lindsay (1832–1901) [*see* Lindsay, Robert James Loyd-], tall, bearded, and highly personable, of Scottish aristocratic lineage, a Scots guards officer who later served with distinction in the Crimean War, being awarded the Victoria Cross. On 17 November 1858 they were married at St Martin-in-the-Fields, London. They had no children. The marriage discomposed her possessive father; he took some time to develop a rapport with Robert, who had changed his name to Loyd-Lindsay before his marriage and soon had to give up the army. Her father settled on the young couple Lockinge House, near Wantage, and 20,000 acres of land in Berkshire.

In his subsequent activities, which included the volunteer movement, the Red Cross, and many business and agricultural schemes, Robert Loyd-Lindsay involved his wife as far as he could. He commanded the Berkshire volunteer force and then the home counties volunteers. A fearless horse rider, in 1870 Harriet broke her leg while out hunting, but a year later spent six hours in the saddle while accompanying her husband on army manoeuvres (which he still undertook), even joining in one of the heavy cavalry brigade's charges. Partly because of her injury, she grew lame with advancing years.

After her husband was appointed chairman of the British Red Cross Society in 1870, Harriet Loyd-Lindsay played an influential part on the ladies' committee. In

1883 she was one of the first to be awarded Queen Victoria's Royal Red Cross order. Until Baron Overstone died in 1883, she was his amanuensis and virtually constant companion. The fortune which she then inherited probably helped to finance her husband's business ventures, such as the London Electricity Supply Corporation Ltd of 1887, of social value but yielding only meagre returns. She likewise interested herself in his farming and estate management projects. Her close studies of documents and architects' plans proved very useful when discussing and seeing through subsequent benefactions.

Like her father, Lady Wantage and her husband, Baron Wantage (he was ennobled in 1885), were art connoisseurs, and she handsomely supported the National Art Collections Fund. She fully collaborated with her husband in his work for Reading University College, of which he was the first president; after his death in 1901 she was appointed vice-president and life governor. She made two outstanding gifts to the college, to which she donated nearly £150,000 in all: she built and endowed a men's hall of residence, Wantage Hall (1908), and in 1911 gave £50,000 towards an endowment fund. The Royal Berkshire Hospital also benefited from her generosity. In 1907 she was the first woman to receive the freedom of the borough of Reading.

Lady Wantage kept her good looks—marred only by a beaky nose—and dignified bearing into old age, as well as a love of foreign travel. In 1908 she published a readable if reticent memoir of her husband. Adopting her father's inflexible belief that women had a separate role from men in Britain's social system (he had resigned from London University's senate over the awarding of degrees to women), she worked hard for the Anti-Suffrage League, while shrewdly acknowledging the difficulties of fighting for a negative cause.

In 1914 the death of her cousin and lifelong close friend, Madeleine Shaw-Lefevre, caused Lady Wantage much grief, as did the outbreak of the First World War; she then fitted up a country house as a convalescent home for wounded and shell-shocked soldiers. She died of senility and heart failure at Lockinge House on 9 August 1920, and was buried in Ardington churchyard, near Wantage, on 13 August. T. A. B. Corley

Sources H. S. Loyd-Lindsay [Baroness Wantage], *Lord Wantage … a memoir*, 2nd edn (1908) • *The correspondence of Lord Overstone*, ed. D. P. O'Brien, 3 vols. (1971) • W. M. Childs, *Making a university: an account of the university movement at Reading* (1933) • W. M. Childs, diary, 1903–1920, U. Reading • *The Times* (1 July 1837) • *The Times* (10 Aug 1920) • *The Times* (19 Aug 1920) • *Reading Chronicle* (13 Aug 1920) • *Reading Observer* (21 Aug 1920) • GEC, *Peerage* • B. Harrison, *Separate spheres: the opposition to women's suffrage in Britain* (1978) • *Anti-Suffrage Review*, 26 (Jan 1911), 1 • *EdinR*, 195 (1902), 29–57 • *WWW* • *Reading Mercury* (5 Dec 1908) • m. cert. • d. cert.

Archives British Red Cross Museum and Archives, Wonersh, Surrey, corresp. and papers • LUL, corresp. • NL Scot., papers • U. Reading • Yale U., Beinecke L., diary

Likenesses J. M. Cameron, photograph, *c*.1865, NPG; *see illus. in* Lindsay, Robert James Loyd-, Baron Wantage (1832–1901) • W. Richmond, oils, 1885, repro. in Loyd-Lindsay, *Lord Wantage, VC, KCB* • oils (after P. A. L. de Lomdos, 1909), U. Reading, Wantage Hall • oils, U. Reading, Wantage Hall

Wealth at death £768,587 5*s*. 5*d*.: probate, 14 Jan 1921, *CGPLA Eng. & Wales*

Lindsay, Sir James, of Crawford (*d*. 1358). *See under* Lindsay family of Barnweill, Crawford, and Glenesk (*per. c*.1250–*c*.1400).

Lindsay, Sir James, of Crawford (*d*. 1395/6). *See under* Lindsay family of Barnweill, Crawford, and Glenesk (*per. c*.1250–*c*.1400).

Lindsay, James, seventh Lord Lindsay of the Byres (1554–1601). *See under* Lindsay, Patrick, sixth Lord Lindsay of the Byres (1521?–1589).

Lindsay, James Bowman (1799–1862), experimenter with electricity and writer on theology, was born on 8 September 1799 at Cotton of West Hills, Carmyllie, Arbroath, the eldest son of John Lindsay, tailor then farmer, and his wife, Elizabeth Bowman. He was apprenticed as a weaver but, persuaded by his love of learning, his parents sent him to St Andrews University in 1821. After completing the general curriculum he read theology, possibly intending to be ordained, but in 1829 he was appointed science and mathematics lecturer at the Watt Institute, Dundee. He also taught private classes. After a period of teaching abroad he settled in Dundee in 1834 and resumed his science classes.

Electrical technology was in its infancy, but in his classes Lindsay demonstrated its possibilities, including telegraphy and power from batteries. In an advertisement in the *Dundee Advertiser* of 11 April 1834, he proclaimed that 'houses and towns will in a short time be lit by electricity instead of gas, and heated by it instead of coal; and machinery will be worked by it instead of steam'. He claimed in 1835 to have developed a continuously burning electric light, probably based on Humphry Davy's observations of the electric arc. Few details survive, and its potential was almost certainly exaggerated. In 1845 he sent a proposal to the *Dundee Advertiser* for an autograph telegraph, which used vibrating needles to etch messages into pith balls. When the *Dundee Advertiser* carried a suggestion for a submarine Atlantic telegraph cable, Lindsay responded with a letter detailing how a cable might be constructed, using uninsulated copper wire with joints welded by electricity. This was probably the first suggestion of the use of electricity for welding. Also in 1845 he proposed a telegraphic dictionary—combinations of signals to represent words.

1853 saw the first demonstration of Lindsay's underwater wireless telegraph. This involved instruments and batteries connected to metal plates submerged in the water. Lindsay persevered in publicizing his system through several demonstrations in Scotland and England between 1853 and 1860. He took out a patent in 1854 and demonstrated it to the Electric Telegraph Company in London. He also presented a paper and demonstrations to the British Association in 1859. That such a method could send signals through water had already been observed, most notably by Samuel Morse, but it had not been adopted practically, and, while Lindsay's telegraph drew some favourable comment, it was never taken up, since there was no use for it over short distances, and over long distances it was unworkable.

Theological research, using philology and astronomy to investigate the historical accuracy of the Bible, was Lindsay's overriding passion. In 1828 he had begun his *Pentecontaglossal Dictionary*, a comparison of fifty languages. Through this he hoped to shed light on human origins, and prove the Bible's accuracy. He never completed this massive work, but in 1846 he published the *Pentecontaglossal Paternoster*, a comparison of the Lord's prayer in fifty languages, as an introduction. *The Chrono-Astrolabe* (1858) had the same aim. Through study of astronomy and careful dating of phenomena such as eclipses mentioned in ancient Greek, Roman, Hebrew, and Chinese texts, he hoped to establish an accurate chronology of ancient history, including the Bible. This painstaking project was begun in 1849. A devout Christian, he was a member of the Presbyterian church until 1843 when that movement disrupted, and he joined the new St Paul's Free Church. In 1861 he became a Baptist, arguing from his studies of early Christian history and the use of the term 'bapto' in ancient Greek that adult immersion was the apostolic form of baptism, and that infant baptism and sprinkling were human inventions. He published these arguments in his *Treatise on the Mode and Subjects of Baptism* (1861).

Lindsay never married, and spent most of his earnings on books and apparatus, which he crammed into his house at 11 Union Street. He reputedly had little mechanical skill, so commissioned apparatus from a local instrument maker, George Lowdon. In 1841 he was appointed as a teacher in Dundee prison, a post he held until 1858, when the award of an annual civil-list pension of £100 allowed him to resign.

Lindsay was entirely devoted to his research. His theological work was as important to him as electricity, but it was in the latter that he displayed striking foresight. He realized that electricity could be applied to lighting, heating, power, and communication, and he experimented with it as much as possible, on limited resources, away from the mainstream of the scientific world. He pursued his research to the detriment of his health, which began to fail in 1860. He died at his home, Beach Land, Blackness Road, Dundee, on 30 June 1862, after a prolonged attack of diarrhoea. He was buried on 2 July in Dundee's western cemetery; in 1901 a monument, paid for by public subscription, was erected by his grave. TIM PROCTER

Sources A. H. Millar, *James Bowman Lindsay and other pioneers of invention* (1925) • J. J. Fahie, 'James Bowman Lindsay, electrician, astronomer, linguist', *Electrical Engineer* (6 Jan 1899) • J. J. Fahie, 'James Bowman Lindsay, electrician, astronomer, linguist', *Electrical Engineer* (13 Jan 1899) • J. J. Fahie, *A history of wireless telegraphy, 1838–1899* (1899) • W. Norrie, *Dundee celebrities of the nineteenth century* (1873) • 'Dundee's eccentric scientist', *Glasgow Herald* (29 June 1962) • Lord Lindsay [A. W. C. Lindsay, earl of Crawford], *Lives of the Lindsays*, 2nd edn, 2 (1858) • A. H. Millar, 'James Bowman Lindsay, the pioneer of electrical lighting and wireless telegraphy', *People's Friend* (9 Sept 1901) • 'James Bowman Lindsay', *Dundee Advertiser* (16 Sept 1901) • 'James Bowman Lindsay: memorial celebration in Dundee', *Dundee Yearbook* (1901), 186–95 • A. H. Millar, 'James Bowman Lindsay, scientist and philologer', *British Association handbook and guide to Dundee and Forfarshire*, ed. A. W. Paton and A. H. Millar (1912), 491–514 • E. C. Baker, *Sir William Henry Preece FRS, Victorian engineer extraordinary* (1976) • NA Scot., Carmyllie parish records (birth, baptism), September 1799 [microfilm; originals are at SRO] • Dundee register of deaths

Archives Dundee City Library, MSS relating to electrical experiments, mathematical and astronomical calculations, and dictionaries • University of Dundee, archives, papers | Inst. EE, Fahie MSS

Likenesses G. Webster, marble bust, *c.*1899, Dundee Arts and Heritage, Mills Observatory, Balgay Park, Dundee, Australia • Valentine & Co., photograph, Dundee Central Library, Dundee, Australia • G. Webster, marble sculpture, Dundee City Art Gallery, Dundee, Australia • line sketch (after a photograph? by Valentine & Co.?), repro. in A. H. Millar, *The Dundee Year Book* (1901) • painting (after a photograph? by Valentine & Co.?), repro. in Millar, *James Bowman Lindsay* • photograph, Dundee City Library, rare books collection, 'Notebook of experiments on wireless telegraphy'

Wealth at death £471 1*s.* 4*d.*: recording, 5 Aug 1862, NA Scot., SC45/31/17, 134–6

Lindsay, James Gavin (1835–1903), army officer, born on 21 October 1835, was the younger son of Colonel Martin Lindsay CB, of Dowhill, Londonderry, who commanded the 78th highlanders. Educated at Addiscombe College from 1852 to 1854, he obtained a commission in the Madras engineers, becoming second-lieutenant on 9 December 1854 and lieutenant on 27 April 1858. He served in the Indian mutiny in 1858–9 under Sir George Whitlock, and was at the actions at Jheegung and Kabrai, the battle of Banda, and the relief of Karwi. He was in the reserve at the storming of the heights of Punwarree. He was made second captain on 29 June 1863, and subsequently entered the railway department as deputy consulting engineer.

In April 1870 Lindsay was appointed executive engineer of the first grade for the railway survey of Mysore. In 1872 he undertook as engineer-in-chief the construction of the Northern Bengal Railway. A capable administrator, during the Bengal famine of 1873–4 he employed on public works many who were out of work because of crop failure. He was promoted captain on 30 July 1871, major on 5 July 1872, lieutenant-colonel on 31 December 1878, and colonel on 31 December 1882.

During the Second Anglo-Afghan War in 1879–80 Lindsay was engineer-in-chief of the Sukkur–Sibi Railway. It was constructed, for military purposes, in three months and opened to traffic on 27 January 1880. He also started the Harnai and Gulistan–Karez sections of the Kandahar Railway. Afterwards he took part in the march from Quetta to the relief of Kandahar with the force under Major-General Sir Robert Phayre and in the destruction of the towers of Abu Saiad Khan's fort.

In 1881 Lindsay became chief engineer of the Southern Mahratta Railway, and by his organizing powers and by obtaining the devoted services of his staff he finished the railway in 1891. The line proved effective in relieving distress during subsequent famines. Meanwhile in 1885, when there was unrest on the north-west frontier, he as engineer-in-chief made arrangements for continuing the railway from Sibi up the Bolan towards Quetta. Incapacitated by injury, he retired from the service in 1891 before the completion of this line. On returning home he became deputy chairman of the Southern Mahratta Railway and in 1896 chairman.

Lindsay was a leader of railway work in India, identified with the establishment of the North Bengal State Railway, and the Southern Mahratta, the Ruk–Sibi, and Bolan railways. His influence over those who worked with him enabled him to carry out fine work rapidly. He was twice married, but both his wives predeceased him and there were no children. Lindsay died on board the P. & O. steamship *Caledonia* near Aden on 19 December 1903 on his way to Bombay, where he had intended to visit railway works with which he was associated.

H. M. Vibart, *rev.* James Falkner

Sources *The Times* (23 Dec 1903) • *Hart's Army List* • *Indian Army List* • *Army List* • *Royal Engineers Journal*, 34 (1904) • H. B. Hanna, *The Second Afghan War*, 3 (1910)

Wealth at death £2252 3*s.* 4*d.*: probate, 2 May 1904, *CGPLA Eng. & Wales*

Lindsay, James Ludovic, twenty-sixth earl of Crawford and ninth earl of Balcarres (1847–1913), astronomer and book collector, the only son of Alexander William Crawford *Lindsay, twenty-fifth earl of Crawford and eighth earl of Balcarres (1812–1880), and his wife, Margaret, the eldest daughter of Lieutenant-General James Lindsay, of Balcarres, Fife, was born at St Germain-en-Laye, Seine-et-Oise, France, on 28 July 1847. He was educated at Eton College and later, briefly, at Trinity College, Cambridge. He originally lived at Haigh Hall in Wigan, but after his marriage on 22 July 1869 to Emily Florence (*d.* 1934), the second daughter of Edward Bootle-Wilbraham, took up residence in London. The couple had a daughter and six sons. Lindsay entered the Grenadier Guards, but resigned his commission after being elected (1874) MP for Wigan, a seat that he held until he succeeded to his father's earldom in 1880 (after which he sat in the upper house as Lord Wigan).

Attracted to astronomy, Lindsay organized a station at Cadiz in 1870 for observing the eclipse of the sun. In 1872 he moved to Dun Echt, near Aberdeen, where he erected an observatory whose modern equipment, including a 15 inch refractor, was second only to Greenwich in the United Kingdom and the envy of professional astronomers. He became acquainted with David Gill, who became his distinguished assistant. In 1874, with Gill and Ralph Copeland, he went to Mauritius to observe the transit of Venus. He was elected president of the Royal Astronomical Society in 1878 and 1879, fellow of the Royal Society in 1878, and honorary associate of the Royal Prussian Academy of Sciences in 1883.

In 1886 Lord Crawford purchased the old family estate at Balcarres (where he had been a frequent visitor in his youth), but he continued to maintain the family library at Haigh Hall and a residence in London as well. He was an enthusiastic bibliophile, and added greatly to the splendid library inherited from his father, making it perhaps the finest private library assembled in the nineteenth century. However, the principal source of his fortune, the Wigan Coal and Iron Company, suffered in the depression in the 1880s, and to maintain the great houses he was obliged in 1888 to auction most of the extraordinary collection of bibles, including a Gutenberg Bible. In 1888 he presented to the Scottish nation all his telescopes, instruments, and remarkable astronomical library, both to establish an improved observatory at Edinburgh and to maintain the position of astronomer royal for Scotland. Ralph Copeland, who had directed the observatory at Dun Echt since 1876, was in 1889 appointed astronomer royal for Scotland, and the new Royal Observatory on Blackford Hill was opened by Crawford in 1896. The Crawford collection of rare astronomical books, particularly rich in comet tracts, remains a jewel of that institution.

During the rest of his life Crawford made large collections of proclamations, broadsides, and documents of the French Revolution, areas of collecting that, unlike the bibles, still held bibliographical challenges. Most of the manuscripts were sent to the John Rylands Library, Manchester. However, he presented a series of English and oriental manuscripts illustrating the progress of handwriting to the Wigan Free Library, of which he was chairman for thirty-five years. He issued a number of catalogues and handlists, and also collations and notes of the rarer books in a valuable series of volumes entitled Bibliotheca Lindesiana (1883–1913).

In 1898 Crawford purchased the yacht *Consuelo*, and soon convinced himself that he felt well only at sea. In 1901 he acquired the *Valhalla*, a three-masted, coal-fired yacht with a crew of sixty-five, which he took on three long voyages in 1902–5 around Africa, to the West Indies, and around the world. He had become a trustee of the British Museum in 1885, and his sea journeys aided in the collection of scientific and natural history specimens for the museum. It was the most important such British enterprise since the *Challenger* expedition.

An old enthusiasm returned in 1899 when at a sale of manuscripts Crawford acquired some rare postage stamps; his collection of British empire stamps forms the foundation of the British Museum's holdings, and he also bequeathed a philatelic library to the museum. He presided over the Royal Philatelic Society, as well as over the Royal Photographic Society and the Camden Society. He was invested knight of the Thistle in 1896 and held the volunteer decoration. In January 1913, at a meeting of the trustees of the British Museum, Crawford collapsed. He died the following day, 31 January, at 2 Cavendish Square, and was buried at the old chapel of Balcarres House on 4 February 1913. He was succeeded as twenty-seventh earl by his eldest son, David Alexander Edward *Lindsay (*b.* 1871).

Owen Gingerich

Sources *Monthly Notices of the Royal Astronomical Society*, 74 (1913–14), 271–3 • D. Gill, *Nature*, 90 (1912–13), 652–3 • N. Barker, *Bibliotheca Lindesiana* (1978) • G. Forbes, *David Gill, man and astronomer* (1916) • M. J. Nicoll, *Three voyages of a naturalist* (1908) • private information (2004)

Archives Royal Observatory, Edinburgh, corresp. and papers | NL Scot., Lord Crawford MSS • RAS, letters to Royal Astronomical Society

Likenesses W. Orchardson, oils, 1898, repro. in Barker, *Bibliotheca Lindesiana*; priv. coll. • Spy [L. Ward], caricature, Henschel-colourtype, NPG; repro. in Barker, *Bibliotheca Lindesiana*, 364 • Spy [L. Ward], caricature, watercolour study, NPG; repro. in *VF* (11 May 1878) • photograph (after an original?; priv. coll.), Royal Observatory, Edinburgh, Crawford collection

Wealth at death £436,279 19*s*. 8*d*.: probate, 26 April 1913, *CGPLA Eng. & Wales*

Lindsay [*née* McLachlan], **Jean Olivia** (1910–1996), historian and educationist, was born on 10 December 1910 in Bangalore, India, the only child of Major-General James Douglas McLachlan (1869–1937), of the Cameron Highlanders, and his wife, Gwendolen Mabel, *née* White (1880–1959). She was very much a daughter of the regiment, growing up in the world of public events, and her education followed her father's distinguished military postings. She attended at least eight schools, in Scotland, Gibraltar, Germany, and England. Her last was in London, Queen's College, Harley Street, which she attended from 1925 until she went up to Girton College, Cambridge, in 1929. This was her father's choice for her. As she could not go into the regiment, and perhaps unaware of her desire to go to Oxford, he took the advice of an academic acquaintance that 'Girton would be a good place for your daughter' (Perry). She was interviewed for a history place by Mary Gwladys (MG) Jones, who became an important influence in her life. Asked what she intended to do after Cambridge, on the spur of the moment she said that she wanted to write a book on Spanish history. She was given a place among the last on the list—her wandering education perhaps had left its mark. 'I wasn't very bright, and not considered equal to political theory' (ibid.). Nearly three years later, after brilliant achievement in part one of the tripos, she was taken aback to be asked by MG which particular aspect of Spanish history she was going to tackle for her thesis. After her first class with distinction in part two of the tripos—the first woman to achieve this in history—she was awarded a Cairnes studentship for research. Harold Temperley supervised her thesis, and her research included months in chaotic archives in Madrid, Seville, and Simancas, where her mother insisted that she had a chaperone—'wise, I think' as she later said (ibid.). Her thesis, later published as *Trade and Peace with Old Spain, 1617–1750* (1940), carried off a share in the Prince Consort prize (again, a first for a woman) and a Seeley medal. Two years working for the New Commonwealth Society gave a pause from academic life, but in 1937 she returned to Girton with a Pfeiffer research fellowship. She began research on the Boxer uprising but the world situation frustrated this and her research was never resumed. These achievements during her student years were due to her brilliant mind, her immense zest for learning and living, her very hard and ungrudging work, and her ability to accept situations and persons with enjoyment or, if necessary, tolerance, affection, and good humour. Her effortless elegance and handsome presence were no disservice.

The Second World War brought dramatic changes of scene and occupation, but for Jean McLachlan it also returned her to her native territory, service life. She worked first, however, in the Ministry of Information and then was invited to join Arnold Toynbee's intelligence unit, first in the Spanish and then in the German department. She was soon longing for work close to the conduct of the war, and when she was headhunted for a hush-hush unit she was glad to leave work which could be done by 'an old gentleman of seventy' (Perry). In May 1943 she joined the First Aid Nursing Yeomanry (FANYs), and found herself working for the Special Operations Executive (SOE). She was sent on a course in motor mechanics, a cover for her real work in signals intelligence. Her first posting was in Algiers as liaison officer with Polish forces, which she then accompanied to Italy. She was 'in her element' (Chibnall): she knew how to look after her troops, how to use her initiative, and how to deal with emergencies and get authorization afterwards. 'One spent one's time not knowing things', in case one might say something (Perry). Her experiences showed that 'nothing in even the most fantastic of Evelyn Waugh's war novels should be treated as impossible' (Chibnall). Her more serious covert work in signals took her in December to Cairo, where SOE had its principal intelligence-gathering centre for the Balkans. She also had an enjoyable interlude in Athens. When the war ended in Europe and the FANYs were sent to the Far East, she returned to Girton, where a job awaited her, but she continued also with war work and did not resign from the FANYs until 1953.

Jean McLachlan's return to Girton with an assistant college lectureship in 1945 was not the beginning of her teaching career, which had been at the Girton village Sunday school and had continued in teaching singing games to the small children of Simancas. When MG Jones retired in 1946 she was made director of studies in history and in the following year university lecturer in the history faculty, an appointment then very rare for a woman. On 21 August 1947 she married Humphrey David Richard Pelham Lindsay (1901–1990), headmaster of a preparatory school in Hertfordshire, and together they brought up three children; the 'regiment' rallied round and one of the Girton domestic staff, Gladys Crane, came as nanny.

Jean Lindsay's scholarly interest was resumed in editing volume 7 of the New Cambridge Modern History, *The Old Regime, 1713–1763* (1957). She contributed four articles as well as the Introduction: 'The social classes and the foundations of the states', 'Monarchy and administration', 'International relations', and 'The western Mediterranean and Italy'. Her personal and academic experience prepared her for the comparative method needed, and her writing significantly revealed her eye for concrete detail, the mark of an effective teacher of all ages. At Girton she was a notable teacher. For fifteen years she selected the ten or so entrants for history places from the two or three hundred applicants, with an eye for intellectual potential and character. She cared for her students, both academically and socially. 'I always treated pupils as though they were part of the regiment' (Perry). She wanted them to enjoy themselves. In the somewhat restricted arena for women at Cambridge in the post-war world her parties became famous. She wrote a light-hearted 'Manual of university etiquette for young ladies'. Many undergraduates owed her a debt for her sociability and kindness, and her help in seeking opportunities for further training and careers. These sympathies led to her founding the 'Coffee-Pot clubs', where informal and undemanding hospitality was open to young people beginning professional careers. The first were in London, but with the help of the YMCA and the YWCA they were opened all over England and Scotland, and met a real need, linking young people to a network of opportunities.

In Cambridge Jean Lindsay was active in civic affairs, as a magistrate and on the parish council of Girton village, where she lived and continued to teach in the Sunday school. In the university she was, in her own words, always 'looking to see the way history was going and then giving things a little push in that direction' (Perry). She did not undertake further major research but was concerned with the development of the tripos and discussed with Herbert Butterfield the possibility of a tripos in the history of science. She worked with the group aiming at founding a third college for women, eventually established as New Hall in 1954.

At the height of all this, in 1960, Jean Lindsay accepted an invitation to become headmistress of St George's School in Edinburgh. 'The headhunters were out again' and the old network of girls' schools and university colleges was still strong (Perry). But it is necessary to ask why she accepted the Edinburgh post. Perhaps it was because it was in her character to do so; almost certainly it was not because the position of women at Cambridge was still unsatisfactory. Her heart was more in education than in academic research, and the post was a return to her Scottish roots and an exciting challenge. MG Jones had recently died, and a bond which had kept her at Girton had snapped. A new stage of her life had begun.

Jean Lindsay was headmistress of St George's from 1960 until 1975 and gave it 'dedicated and brilliant' service (McClure). At first she suspected that her colleagues might be wary of a don who spoke with an English accent ('but my maiden name was McLachlan, hang it'; Perry), but careful and continuous consultation won their trust and affection. She won co-operation from parents, children, and governors. The school grew from 450 to 750 pupils and its academic standards rose. A development plan was drawn up, a new primary department and library were built, an appeal target for £25,000 was reached and raised to £40,000. Advanced level examinations were introduced as well as 'Highers', to give leavers the maximum choice of universities and careers. She taught history to the youngest children with vigour and inventiveness, enlivened by 'ruthless rhymes'. The older girls felt that she treated each as an individual. At a time of great educational change, she 'presided over the modernisation of the school' (Shepley).

Jean Lindsay retired on grounds of health a little early, in 1975, and proceeded with zest to exploit the possibilities of leisured life in Edinburgh. She 'was almost the person who invented the third age' (McClure). After putting up her feet and reading a lot of Latin she increased her involvement with the Saltire Society as chair of its council. She set up a children's holiday club for the society to encourage interest in Scottish history and traditional games and rhymes. She wrote the life of Elizabeth B. Mitchell (1993), one of the society's former secretaries and a town planner involved in the creation of East Kilbride. She helped to prepare a history of the Murrayfield district and a short history of Edinburgh's West End for the West End Community Council. She continued her relationship with St George's and its past pupils and with Girton College. When she was eighty she was made a fellow of her old school, Queen's College, Harley Street. Her husband died on 30 August 1990. She herself died at the Royal Infirmary, Edinburgh, on 2 June 1996, following a stroke. She was cremated at Warriston crematorium on 7 June, and her ashes were scattered over her parents' graves in St Marylebone cemetery, East Finchley. Girton established a Jean Lindsay memorial fund. In all the changing scenes of her life she had 'fought her own corner with her own fists', but when she ended her recorded reminiscences by saying 'I owe the whole of my career and existence to Girton and to MG Jones' (Perry), she spoke as a historian placing herself in context.

MARGARET BRYANT

Sources K. Perry, interview with Mrs Lindsay, Girton Cam., GCOH 2/3/9 · *Girton Newsletter* (1997) · M. Chibnall, address at memorial service, 1 March 1997, Girton Cam. · J. Roskill, memorial service reading, 1 March 1997, Girton Cam. · J. McClure, address at memorial service at Church of St John the Evangelist, Edinburgh, 21 June 1996 · N. Shepley, *Women of independent mind: St George's School, Edinburgh, and the campaign for women's education, 1888–1988* (1988) · R. Murray, *The making of New Hall, 1954–1972* (1980) · M. Funnell, 'The coffee pot book', typescript history · MSS [in possession of family] · personal knowledge (2004) · private information (2004) · baptism cert. · m. cert. · d. cert.

Archives priv. coll. | Girton Cam. · Saltire Society, Edinburgh, archives · St George's School, Edinburgh, archives | SOUND Girton Cam., GCOH 2/3/9

Likenesses photograph, repro. in McClure, memorial address, p. 117

Wealth at death £1,399,349.76: resworn confirmation, 5 Feb 1997, NA Scot., SC/CO 933/1 (1996)

Lindsay, John (*d.* 1334x6), bishop of Glasgow, may have been the youngest son of John Lindsay, chamberlain of Alexander III. He was certainly closely related to that family, for he inherited the barony of Staplegordon, Dumfriesshire, as heir of Philip Lindsay, who was probably his elder brother. John held the church of Ratho in the diocese of St Andrews by early in the fourteenth century and, having received a university education before 1309, was also a canon of Glasgow for an unknown period of time. Although while he served in the St Andrews diocese Lindsay was used by Bishop William Lamberton for diplomatic and other duties, it seems that he probably supported the

English king against Robert I before Bannockburn, suggesting that he had belonged to the Balliol–Comyn faction. His brother Simon was captured by the Scots at Bannockburn, and John came to Scotland with an English safe conduct to arrange Simon's ransom.

Lindsay must have changed his allegiance soon afterwards, since King Robert chose him for the vacant see of Glasgow after the death of Stephen Dunnideer in 1317. The choice of Lindsay may represent Robert I's wish to indicate his willingness to promote such members of this influential family as would come to his peace. Lindsay's election was not approved by the pope, however, and his journey to the curia for consecration was futile. The papal choice of John Eglescliffe, an Englishman, was designed to satisfy Edward II. But Eglescliffe never gained possession of the see, and in 1323 was translated first to Connor in Ireland and then to Llandaff. (It seems that the Scottish king regarded the Glasgow see as being in his own hands during this period—in effect vacant, if not technically so.) Thereafter Lindsay was accepted by the pope and was consecrated during the summer or autumn of that year. His canonry was then given to Walter Twynham, a favourite clerk of the king, who later became chancellor.

Lindsay's name is found regularly in the witness lists of the later acts of Robert I and, as a senior bishop, he appears at significant state events, such as the signing of the treaty of Edinburgh in 1328. Yet after Robert I's death he supported the kingship of Edward Balliol, and is last recorded as attending the parliament held by Balliol in February 1334. Lindsay's see was vacant by February 1336 and he must therefore have died before that date. There is no evidence to substantiate claims either that his allegiance reverted to the Bruce kingship before his death or that he died as a result of an attack by English pirates on the ship that was bringing him back to Scotland from Flanders. It was his successor at Glasgow, John Wishart, who perished thus in 1337. According to John Spotswood, Bishop Lindsay was buried in the lower church of his cathedral. NORMAN H. REID

Sources D. E. R. Watt, *A biographical dictionary of Scottish graduates to AD 1410* (1977), 351–3 • J. Dowden, *The bishops of Scotland … prior to the Reformation*, ed. J. M. Thomson (1912), 311–13 • *CDS*, vol. 3 • G. W. S. Barrow and others, eds., *Regesta regum Scottorum*, 5, ed. A. A. M. Duncan (1988) • C. Innes, ed., *Registrum episcopatus Glasguensis*, 2 vols., Bannatyne Club, 75 (1843), no. 286 • *RotS*, 1.132 • *APS*, *1124–1423*, 542 • Rymer, *Foedera*, new edn, 2.876–8 • J. Spottiswood, *History of the church and state in Scotland*, 4th edn (1677), 114

Lindsay, John, first Lord Lindsay of the Byres (*d.* 1482). *See under* Lindsay family of the Byres (*per.* 1367–1526).

Lindsay, John, fifth Lord Lindsay of the Byres (*d.* 1563), nobleman, was the eldest son of John, master of Lindsay (styled Sir John Lindsay of Pitcruvie), and Elizabeth Lundie, eldest daughter of Sir John Lundie of Balgonie. He had a charter in liferent from his grandfather Patrick, fourth Lord Lindsay, to the lordship and barony of Byres on 30 March 1524, and on 8 March 1526 was served heir to his father, who had died the previous year. On the death of his grandfather shortly afterwards, John was entered fifth Lord Lindsay of the Byres. In addition to the lands and title, he inherited the sheriffship of Fife, granted to his grandfather by parliament in July 1525. He married Helen, second daughter of John Stewart, second earl of Atholl, and they had ten children—three sons and seven daughters, their eldest child being born in 1521.

In September 1526 Lord Lindsay was among those lords who attempted to rescue the young King James V from the Douglases. As a result he found himself imprisoned and his goods forfeited and gifted to Archibald Douglas. When King James escaped in 1528 Lord Lindsay was among those whom he summoned to support him as he established his personal rule.

In June 1529, following allegations that he had been negligent and abusive in the exercise of the office, Lindsay lost his position as sheriff of Fife to the fourth earl of Rothes. In June 1538 King James considered reappointing Lindsay and even drew up a letter to that effect, but it was never acted on, and in 1540 Rothes and his heirs were confirmed in the office. Lindsay resented the loss, which for some time remained a bone of contention between his family and the Leslies. When the master of Rothes was forfeited in 1563, Queen Mary reinstated Lindsay in the sheriffship. The dispute was finally settled in 1573, when the sixth Lord Lindsay was bought out by the fifth earl of Rothes.

Lindsay was made an extraordinary lord of session in 1532, and in 1540 sat on the assizes that tried and condemned Sir James Hamilton of Finnart for treason, and Sir John Borthwick for heresy. He may have hoped that service on these assizes would help him to recover the sheriffship of Fife.

Pitscottie reports that Lindsay was present at the death of James V at Falkland on 14 December 1542. On account of his presumed neutrality between the competing factions, Lindsay was appointed one of the custodians of the infant Queen Mary. However, the English ambassador Sir Ralph Sadler recorded that Lindsay would gladly have left the queen's household for the party of the earl of Arran, the governor of Scotland, in August 1543, but that the queen mother, Mary of Guise, halted the removal of his baggage in order to stay his departure. He was one of the commanders of the Scottish army which defeated the English at Ancrum Moor on 27 February 1545, and about that time was acting as curator to David Lindsay, master and later tenth earl of Crawford (the so-called 'wicked master's' son).

In June 1545 Lord Lindsay sat with the privy council. He served regularly until May 1547, but then his attendance ended abruptly, and his career in public life seems to have ceased. Perhaps because he 'favoured religious reform from an early date' (Lord Lindsay, 1.267), he found it safer to maintain a low profile. His daughter Isobel had married Norman Leslie, master of Rothes, in 1541, and the latter's association with other known advocates of protestantism, not to mention his part in the murder of Cardinal David Beaton in 1546, may have brought Lindsay under suspicion at court.

Although no longer active in public life, Lindsay continued to take part in litigation, pursuing his adversaries and ensuring the maintenance of his children. By June 1559 he was described as being 'a very aged man' (Lord Lindsay, 1.269), but despite his age it was he who negotiated a compromise between the regent, as Mary of Guise now was, and the lords of the congregation, which averted a pitched battle at Cupar Muir.

Lindsay was present at the Reformation Parliament in August 1560 and gave his approval to the change of religion. A sympathetic eyewitness, who described him as 'as grave and goodly a man as ever I sawe' recorded his speech:

> I have lyved maynie yeres, I am the eldest in thys compagnie of my sorte, nowe that yt hathe pleased God to lett me see thys daye wher so maynie nobles and other have allowed so worthie a work, I will say with Simion, *Nunc dimittis*. (*CSP Scot. ser.*, 1509–89, 467)

Lindsay also served as a lord of the articles, but although Knox claims that the fifth lord was present to subscribe the Book of Discipline in January 1561, he does not appear among the signatories.

Lord Lindsay's last public act, early in 1562, was to sign a letter to Queen Elizabeth requesting safe passage through England for Lord James Stewart, going to meet his half-sister Queen Mary in France. Randolph noted in a letter to Cecil of 21 December 1563 that Lord Lindsay had died within the last four days, while the precept of *clare constat* recognizing his eldest son Patrick *Lindsay as his father's heir, dated 13 March 1564, records that the fifth lord had died three months previously. He is reported to have died at Struthers in Fife. His widow lived until May 1577.

MARY BLACK VERSCHUUR

Sources Lord Lindsay [A. W. C. Lindsay, earl of Crawford], *Lives of the Lindsays*, 2nd edn, 3 vols (1858), vol. 1 • *The historie and cronicles of Scotland … by Robert Lindesay of Pitscottie*, ed. A. J. G. Mackay, 2, STS, 43 (1899) • *Scots peerage*, 5.397–9 • *LP Henry VIII*, vols. 4, 16 • *CSP for.*, 1560–61 • M. Livingstone, D. Hay Fleming, and others, eds., *Registrum secreti sigilli regum Scotorum / The register of the privy seal of Scotland*, 1–5 (1908–57) • *Reg. PCS*, 1st ser. • J. M. Thomson and others, eds., *Registrum magni sigilli regum Scotorum / The register of the great seal of Scotland*, 11 vols. (1882–1914), vols. 3–4 • J. Cameron, *James V: the personal rule, 1528–1542*, ed. N. Macdougall (1998) • M. H. B. Sanderson, *Cardinal of Scotland: David Beaton, c.1494–1546* (1986) • W. Fraser, ed., *The Douglas book*, 4 vols. (1885) • W. Fraser, *The Lennox*, 2 vols. (1874), vol. 1 • *CSP Scot. ser.*, 1509–89

Lindsay, John, of Balcarres, Lord Menmuir (1552–1598), administrator, was the second son of David Lindsay of Edzell (*d.* 1558), ninth earl of Crawford, and his wife, Katherine Campbell (*d.* 1578). When John was a child his father gave him the benefices of Menmuir, Lethnot, and Lochlee in Angus (Forfarshire), of which he was patron. John Lindsay was thus commonly known as 'Parson of Menmuir', though he was never ordained. On 29 November 1581 he married Marion Guthrie (*d.* 1592), widow of David Borthwick of Lochhill and daughter of a burgess of Edinburgh. She was to be the mother of all seven of his children.

John Lindsay's early years were spent being privately educated at the family seat at Edzell. About the year 1570, however, he and his elder brother David *Lindsay (1551?–1610) went to the continent to be educated under the care of James Lawson, later minister of Edinburgh. They took up residence in Paris but fled to England because of trouble between Huguenots and Roman Catholics in the French capital. The brothers proceeded to Cambridge; David soon returned home but John, 'able to come to great understanding of letters', according to Lawson, stayed on (Lindsay, 1.332). On his return to Scotland he devoted himself to legal studies and became an advocate. Perhaps with the help of his kinsman the earl of Argyll, he was presented to the lords of session by the king on 5 July 1581 as John Lindsay of Drumcairne. He was recommended as 'a man that fears God, of good literature, practice, judgement and understanding of the lawes, of good fame, haiffing sufficient leiving of his awin, and quha can mak gud expedition and despatche of materis tueching the leiges' (Brunton and Haig, 177). Lindsay thus became an ordinary lord of session, taking the title Lord Menmuir, and began a relatively short but influential career as a statesman.

Menmuir's involvement in parliamentary affairs began in October 1583 when he was recorded as one of the king's commissioners for holding parliament. From 1587 onwards he was appointed to numerous parliamentary commissions concerning such matters as taxation, coinage, the publication of statutes, and ecclesiastical finance. He was also involved in drafting a number of significant acts, most notably that of 1587 for the representation of the shires in parliament (though his draft of this was not used). In the later 1580s he was appointed to two privy council commissions for visitation of the University of St Andrews, of which he was to be appointed chancellor in 1587. As Menmuir his name is found on privy council sederunts after November 1589 and he attended frequently for the next eight years. In 1586 he bought Balcarres and other lands in eastern Fife, all of which in June 1592 were united and erected into the barony of Balcarres in a great seal charter. These lands would form the basis of the estates of his successors. Menmuir made his principal residence there, and in 1595 embellished the existing tower house with the addition of a substantial stair tower on the east and further accommodation on the south.

Menmuir's accumulation of public offices continued in May 1592 with his appointment as master of the metals, with responsibility for regulating all mining of ore and manufacture of metals. In January 1594 he acted in this capacity when approving a tack of mines to Thomas Foulis, an Edinburgh goldsmith. He also attempted to use this position to his own advantage, and in partnership with his brother David attempted to mine lead ore on the family estates in Angus. They imported German and Dutch expert labour but it is unclear how successful the venture proved.

Menmuir became prominent in financial affairs when in July 1593 he was appointed to a council for managing the income from the property of Queen Anne. The council was so successful that the queen is said to have goaded her husband about the greater ease with which she could obtain cash. James reacted almost immediately, in January 1596 appointing her financial commissioners and four others to an exchequer commission which became known as the *Octavians. They took over all responsibility for royal finance, while the treasurer, comptroller, and collector lost their positions, Menmuir being appointed to the two latter posts. No alienation of royal property was to take place, nor any disbursement of money even by the king, without the consent of five commissioners. Menmuir was also appointed keeper of the privy seal in March and secretary in May 1596. The power of the Octavians was immense and caused widespread resentment. Coupled with their lack of success in rectifying the dire financial situation of the crown, this was enough to force them to demit office after a year.

The Octavians were particularly unpopular with the kirk, largely because of the Roman Catholicism, or suspected Roman Catholic sympathies, of some of them. Menmuir seems initially, however, to have had honourable intentions for the kirk. In the summer of 1596 he drafted a putative act of parliament presenting a sensible solution to two long-standing problems. His own Act of Annexation of 1587 had taken the revenues of the prelacies into crown hands and dealt what seemed at the time a death blow to episcopacy. Nine years later he suggested a permanent financial settlement for the kirk from these revenues; each of Scotland's fifty presbyteries would also send a commissioner to parliament. James Melville described this scheme as 'the best and maist exact that ever was devysit … and wald, sum litle things amendit, haiff bein glaidlie receavit be the breithring of the best judgment' (*The Autobiography and Diary*, 345). It was never implemented, however, for a breakdown in relations between James VI and the kirk in the later months of 1596 caused the plans to be scrapped. At the beginning of 1597 James decided to assert royal supremacy over the kirk, and he enlisted the forensic mind of Menmuir to draw up a list of fifty-five penetrating questions concerning ecclesiastical polity and authority to be presented to the general assembly. This apparent volte-face by Menmuir led to a serious clash with the presbytery of St Andrews when he was sent by the king to complain about the political content of a minister's sermons. Things became very personal; the royal secretary was described as 'a plaine mocker of religioun' (Calderwood, 548), and the lavishness of his recently built house was cast up against him.

By this time, however, Menmuir was gravely ill, having suffered for some time from 'the stone'. His attendances at meetings of the privy council became less frequent and he planned in March 1597 to go to Paris for surgery, combining the visit with an embassy to the French court. He did not leave Scotland, however. In June his 'lang absence fra court' (Lindsay, 1.371) was commented upon, and in December he made his final appearance on the privy council and resigned as a lord of session and as secretary, comptroller, and collector. In the spring of 1598 he again planned to travel to France but again did not go. He died on 3 September at Balcarres House and was buried in the nearby parish church of Kilconquhar. He was survived by his second wife, Jane Lauder, who had already been twice widowed after marriages to Sir James Forrester of Corstorphine and John Campbell of Cawdor, and who went on to marry for a fourth time. His heir was his eldest surviving son, David, through whom he was the ancestor of the earls of Balcarres. ALAN R. MACDONALD

Sources Lord Lindsay [A. W. C. Lindsay, earl of Crawford], *Lives of the Lindsays*, [new edn], 3 vols. (1849) • *Scots peerage*, 1.516–18; vol. 3 • G. Brunton and D. Haig, *An historical account of the senators of the college of justice, from its institution in MDXXXII* (1832) • *APS*, 1567–1625 • J. H. Burton and D. Masson, eds., *The register of the privy council of Scotland*, 1st ser., 14 vols. (1877–98), vols. 8–9 • *The autobiography and diary of Mr James Melvill*, ed. R. Pitcairn, Wodrow Society (1842) • D. Calderwood, *The history of the Kirk of Scotland*, ed. T. Thomson and D. Laing, 8 vols., Wodrow Society, 7 (1842–9), vol. 5 • NL Scot., Adv. MS 29.2.8, fols. 56–103 [relating to incidents in spring of 1597] • *Fife*, Pevsner (1988) • Edinburgh commissary court, register of testaments, NA Scot., CC 8/8/35

Archives NL Scot., corresp. and papers

Wealth at death £5382 2*s*. 8*d*. Scots—moveables: NA Scot., CC 8/8/35, 11 Aug 1601

Lindsay, John, seventeenth earl of Crawford and first earl of Lindsay [*known as* earl of Crawford-Lindsay] (**1596–1678**), politician, was the son of Robert, ninth Lord Lindsay of the Byres (*d.* 1616), and Lady Christian Hamilton (*d.* 1646), eldest daughter of Thomas, first earl of Haddington. He is said to have received 'a noble education both at home and in foreign parts' (Lindsay). He was served heir to his father on 1 October 1616. By 1630 he had married Lady Margaret Hamilton, daughter of James *Hamilton, second marquess of Hamilton. Their first daughter was baptized on 1 September 1631; they had four other daughters and five sons.

Opposition peer and the bishops' wars On 8 May 1633 Lindsay was created earl of Lindsay and Lord Parbroath, but the patent was held back until 1641 due to his opposition to the policies of the Caroline administration of Scotland. He made his objections to the king's ecclesiastical policy clear as early as in the 1633 parliament, and he was prominent in the opposition to the introduction of the Scottish prayer book in 1637, being one of the noblemen who protected the conventicles that had sprung up in Fife. In the 1638 parliament he became a member of the Tables, the provisional government in Edinburgh, and was one of only four nobles appointed to decide on the measures to be taken against the prayer book; at that time he was described as one of the 'cheife Covenanter lords' (Gordon, 1.68) and of the 'professed Covenanters' (ibid., 1.109). On 24 September 1638 he was appointed a commissioner to oversee the subscription in Fife of the 1580 confession and the 1589 general band. On 3 October 1638 he presented a complaint of the presbyterian nobles to James Hamilton, third marquess of Hamilton, which protested against the attempts to force the people to subscribe the king's covenant. His high-profile role at the 1638 general assembly in Glasgow was reflected in his appointment on 27 November to the committee which met beforehand in private with the moderator, Alexander Henderson, to discuss the order of proceedings. He was also involved in an assembly committee which discussed the rivalry between the towns of Ayr and St Andrews for the appointment of Robert Blair as minister.

Lindsay attended the 1639 parliament and on 31 August

John Lindsay, seventeenth earl of Crawford and first earl of Lindsay (1596–1678), by unknown artist, 1663

he was elected to be one of the lords of the articles. On 28 September he was appointed to a subcommittee which was to inquire about the condition of the University of St Andrews and then report back to the articles; four weeks later he was made responsible for drafting an act of visitation. In the June 1640 parliamentary session Lindsay was a member of the session committee for furnishing provisions for the army (3 June) and the committee of estates (8 June). Meanwhile he witnessed military action in the first and second bishops' wars. He raised a regiment in 1639 and his foot regiment of 1000 men took part in the battle of Newburn in August 1640.

Lindsay maintained a high parliamentary profile throughout 1640–41. In April and May 1641 he was a member of the delegation of the committee of estates which was to consider the continuation and prorogation of parliament. He was appointed to several important committees in the session of 15 July – 17 November 1641. On 28 August he was selected to be one of the Scottish diplomatic commissioners to negotiate with representatives of the English parliament concerning the ratification of the articles of the peace treaty following the second bishops' war. On 8 October he was included on the committee to consider the petition of General Major Monro and his regiment, who were seeking approval of their military service. He was also involved in the parliamentary investigation into the 'Incident', the plot by royalists to murder the leading proponents of the new order, Argyll, Hamilton, and Lanark, and was instructed on 30 October to attend the king to hear the reading of a letter from the earl of Montrose concerning these events. On 11 November he was a member of the session committee to consider which acts were to be passed in parliament, while on 13 November he was appointed a treasury commissioner and was included on the new privy council, as well as being appointed as an extraordinary lord of session. He was placed on interval committees for the plantation of kirks and valuation of teinds, for the visitation of St Andrews University, and (the most important for the conduct of covenanting diplomacy) the committee anent the articles referred to consideration by the treaty and the committee for conserving the articles of the treaty (conservators of the peace). It was as part of the king's attempt to conciliate leading covenanters that he received the grant of his earldom from Charles I during the king's visit to Scotland.

Parliamentary negotiator and army officer, 1641–1644 At the first meeting of the new privy council on 18 November 1641 Lindsay was commissioned with the earl of Lothian to proceed to London to discuss the recent Irish rising with the English parliament, and the decision of the covenanters to offer 10,000 men to help suppress it. They were also instructed to act as peacemakers between the king and the English parliament. On 11 March 1642 Lindsay was given the command of a regiment in the covenanting army which was being sent to serve in Ulster, although he never took up the commission personally. Early in March 1643 he contributed two sums of £500 Scots (3 March) and £6000 Scots (7 March) for the maintenance of the Scottish army in Ulster. As a privy councillor he was appointed on 5 July 1642 to be a commissioner for Fife for the apprehension of Jesuits, priests, and those undertaking pilgrimages to chapels and wells, and on 8 June 1643 to be one of the commissioners to take depositions concerning the murder of one Alexander Stuart, a former student of St Andrews University.

Lindsay played an important role in the 1643 convention of estates (22 June – 26 August) and the securing of the solemn league and covenant. He was a member of a number of committees, including those concerned with the trial of the earls of Traquair and Carnwath, remedies of the dangers of religion (11 July), and the army (4 August), meeting with the English commissioners (9 and 10 August), and he was at the heart of the negotiations which led to the solemn league and covenant, not only as a parliamentary representative, but also as a ruling elder of the general assembly. Indeed, he was a member of the general assembly's commission of the kirk in 1643, 1644, 1645, and 1647. On 17 August Lindsay produced the solemn league and covenant before the assembled convention. On 26 August he was appointed to the new committee of estates and was a member of the shire committee of war for Fife and Kinross. He signed the treaty of military assistance with the English parliament as one of the Scottish diplomatic representatives on 29 November 1643. On 1 December Lindsay was included in the section of the committee of estates which was to accompany the covenanting army into England in January, although he stayed in Edinburgh to attend the opening diets of the convention between 3 and 11 January.

The presbyteries of Cupar and St Andrews raised ten

companies of men for Lindsay in the army. He distinguished himself in action at the battle of Marston Moor on 2 July 1644. According to Robert Baillie, he incurred 'the greatest hazard of any' (*Letters and Journals of Robert Baillie*, 2.204) when he charged and dislodged four brigades of royalist troops. In the aftermath of the battle he wrote to the estates suggesting a general thanksgiving for the victory.

On the expiry of the Scottish Treasury commission, Lindsay was on 23 July appointed treasurer by parliament and the next day he was included on the renewed commission for the plantation of kirks and valuation of teinds. Following the forfeiture of Ludovic, earl of Crawford, on 26 July, the titles and dignities of the earl of Crawford were ratified to Lindsay and he became known as the earl of Crawford-Lindsay. That day he was also included on the army section of the committee of estates.

Managing war, 1645–1648 Owing to the ill health of the president of parliament, John Maitland, earl of Lauderdale, on 11 January 1645 Crawford-Lindsay was appointed vice-president and then on 20 January, following Lauderdale's death, president. Since as president he had access to and an entitlement to preside over all parliamentary committees, he played a key constitutional and political role; in the event he presided in all the remaining sessions of the first triennial parliament until it concluded its business on 27 March 1647. He was a member of the committee appointed on 10 January for managing the war within and without the country, which dealt with the Montrose rebellion and covenanting military commitments outside Scotland, and of similar committees established in 1645–6, such as those for managing the war (8 July), for the prosecution of the war (29 July), for dispatches (1 December 1645), and for common burdens (10 November 1646). On 8 March 1645 he was included on the section of the committee of estates which was to accompany the covenanting army in Scotland against Montrose and, in the absence of Chancellor Loudoun, he was to preside over it. He was also involved in the ensuing military operations and was a member of the covenanting committee advising General Baillie on strategy. In this capacity he must bear the partial burden of responsibility for the covenanting defeat at Kilsyth on 17 August 1645 when he, and other leading covenanters, persuaded a reluctant General Baillie to abandon his superior position and attack Montrose's forces. Crawford-Lindsay's own regiment suffered heavily at Kilsyth and according to Robert Blair the 'whole regiment was cut off almost wholly' (Lindsay, 2.73). Indeed, it was one of the few regular units of the army of the solemn league and covenant to be destroyed in battle.

In May 1646 Crawford-Lindsay was appointed temporary president of the privy council in the absence of Chancellor Loudoun. On 10 December he received a formal ratification from the king of his previous appointment as treasurer and he was one of the Scottish deputies sent to England following the capture of the king to try and persuade Charles to agree to the Newcastle propositions. He protested against the parliamentary decision of 16 January 1647 to withdraw the covenanting army from England and hand Charles over to the jurisdiction of the English parliament in return for arrears of pay. He did sign the act for the surrender of the king, but he only agreed to do so in the constitutional capacity of president and not of his own personal accord. On 19 January an act was passed in his favour for reimbursement of £23,799 14*s*. Scots which he had previously lent for the public service.

Crawford-Lindsay was closely involved with the engagement following the king's imprisonment at Carisbrooke. He was present in the Engagement Parliament of 1648, although Chancellor Loudoun was elected as president. He served on committees for the garrisoning of Berwick and Carlisle and for war in Fife and Kinross, as well as those of estates on 11 May and 9 June. In March he became involved in a dispute in parliament with Archibald Campbell, eighth earl of Argyll, over whether or not Crawford-Lindsay had said that he was a 'better man' than Argyll, and over the former's response that he 'would not make accompt to Argyle what he said; but whatever it was, he would make it good with his sword' (*Letters and Journals of Robert Baillie*, 3.36). A duel was arranged for seven o'clock on a Sunday morning at Musselburgh Links. Both parties kept the appointment, but the duel did not take place. According to Henry Guthrie this was due to the reluctance of both men to fight, despite being at the scene for over an hour 'so that they had leisure enough to have fought if they had been willing' (*The Memoirs*, 261), but Baillie's explanation focused on the intervention of outside parties; 'by God's providence, before they began their pley, some fell on them, and made them part without a stroke' (*Letters and Journals of Robert Baillie*, 3.36). Furthermore, the privy council, 'with much adoe, gott them to a professed coldryse friendship' (ibid.). Both men faced the wrath of the commission of the kirk and on 22 March they 'professed their sorrow for any scandall they had given by the late combat' (Mitchell and Christie, 1646–7, 405–6). Argyll adhered to repentance before the commission, but Crawford-Lindsay refused to do so and the commission was still urging him to repent for the combat as late as 8 June.

Interregnum, royalism, and Restoration retirement Following the battle of Preston in August 1648 and the installation of a political regime of radical covenanters in Edinburgh, backed by Oliver Cromwell, Crawford-Lindsay was deprived of his offices, including on 13 February 1649 that of treasurer, because of his involvement with the engagement. He also came under the scope of the 1649 Act of Classes. In December that year he refused to subscribe a band acknowledging the legality of the current parliament and he was apprehended at Elie, Fife, on the point of departure for the Netherlands. He was returned to his own home, although no further action was taken against him. In January 1650, however, he subscribed a band for the peace of the country. As events unfolded in Scotland in 1650–51 he returned to political life, joining the patriotic accommodation against the Cromwellian advance. In December 1650 he was appointed as a colonel of foot in Fife and he carried the sceptre at the coronation of Charles II at Scone on 1 January 1651. He also entertained the king at his house of the Struthers between 15 and 17 February 1651. He was a member of the committee for managing the affairs of the army of 28 March, playing an important role liaising with the commission of the kirk, and of the committee of estates of 3 June.

When the king marched into England in the summer of 1651, Crawford-Lindsay was appointed lieutenant-general under the earl of Leven. By 18 July 1651 his regiment of foot consisted of 1045 men, and following Charles II's invasion of England by the army of the kingdom Crawford-Lindsay became 'the effective commander-in-chief of forces in Scotland' (Furgol, 367). He was later captured along with other members of the committee of estates at Alyth on 28 August. He was initially imprisoned in the Tower of London and then Sandown Castle, but on 27 November 1656 he was transferred to Windsor Castle, where he was to remain until the end of his captivity. He was excepted from Cromwell's Act of Grace and he was forfeited at Edinburgh Cross on 5 May 1654.

At the Restoration Crawford-Lindsay was freed from imprisonment and in December 1660 he returned to Scotland. He was present at the parliament in Scotland which met on 1 January 1661, and he was included in the membership of commissions to the lords of articles and processes (8 January), for trade and complaints (8 January), and for plantation of kirks and valuation of teinds (6 March). On 29 January parliament confirmed a patent issued by the king making Crawford-Lindsay treasurer for life and an act of 13 February exonerated his role in the decision of 16 January 1647 to leave Charles I in England. He was appointed on 29 March an excise commissioner for Fife and Kinross and on 5 April an extraordinary lord of session. Nevertheless, he opposed the rescissory act of 28 March and was against the restoration of episcopacy in Scotland. He was a member of the new privy council, over which he was to preside in the absence of Chancellor Glencairn. He did not attend the parliamentary sessions of 1662 and 1663 and he resigned all his offices in 1663 and withdrew from public life rather than accept the revival of episcopacy. As a committed presbyterian, he is often mentioned in the parish register of Ceres. Although on 20 May 1663 he became one of the original members of the Royal Society, he took up residence at his estate of Struthers and died at Tynninghame there in 1678. His wife was living in 1666, but the date of her death is unknown. William *Lindsay (1644–1698), their eldest surviving son, succeeded to the earldom. JOHN R. YOUNG

Sources *Scots peerage*, vols. 3, 5 • *APS, 1625–41; 1643–51; 1660–69* • *Reg. PCS*, 2nd ser., vols. 8–9 • *Reg. PCS*, 3rd ser., vol. 1 • *The memoirs of Henry Guthry, late bishop*, 2nd edn (1747) • A. Peterkin, ed., *Records of the Kirk of Scotland* (1838) • Lord Lindsay [A. W. C. Lindsay, earl of Crawford], *Lives of the Lindsays*, [new edn], 3 vols. (1849) • *The letters and journals of Robert Baillie*, ed. D. Laing, 3 vols. (1841–2) • A. F. Mitchell and J. Christie, eds., *The records of the commissions of the general assemblies of the Church of Scotland*, 1, Scottish History Society, 11 (1892) • A. F. Mitchell and J. Christie, eds., *The records of the commissions of the general assemblies of the Church of Scotland*, 3, Scottish History Society, 58 (1909) • J. Gordon, *History of Scots affairs from 1637–1641*, ed. J. Robertson and G. Grub, 3 vols., Spalding Club, 1, 3, 5 (1841) • J. Nicoll, *A diary of public transactions and other occurrences, chiefly in Scotland, from January 1650 to June 1667*, ed. D. Laing, Bannatyne Club, 52 (1836) • E. M. Furgol, *A regimental history of the covenanting armies, 1639–1651* (1990)

Archives BL, letters to Lord Lauderdale, Add. MSS 23114–23135 • Buckminster Park, Grantham, corresp. with duke of Lauderdale

Likenesses oils, 1663, Scot. NPG [*see illus.*]

Lindsay, John (1685/6–1768), nonjuring Church of England clergyman and writer, was probably a kinsman of Robert Lindsey, father of the Unitarian minister Theophilus Lindsey of Middlewich in Cheshire. Although he is described in his epitaph as an alumnus of Oxford, his name does not appear in the records of the university. After acting as attorney-at-law in Cheshire, he was admitted into holy orders among the nonjurors, although the date of his admission is unknown. In 1727 he was living in Islington, and appears to have acted as chaplain to Lady Fanshaw at her house in Little Ormond Street, about 1728. In 1741 he moved to Pear Tree Street, near St Luke's, Old Street, where he lived quietly, dividing his time between study and gardening. He officiated in London for many years as minister of the nonjuring society in Trinity Chapel, Aldersgate Street, and was reputedly their last minister, and among the last of the nonjurors. He is also said to have acted as corrector of the press for the printer William Bowyer the younger. Lindsay was married, although the date of his marriage is unknown. His wife's name was Mary, and she predeceased him by over forty years, dying in 1727 at the age of forty-three.

As a nonjuror Lindsay was involved in controversy with the mainstream Church of England, and his various works tend to reflect this, dealing with subjects such as episcopal and royal succession. Also typical of nonjuring sympathies was his account of the character of the 'Royal Martyr' Charles I, in reply to attacks on that monarch made in the *Monthly Review* (February 1758). Like most nonjurors Lindsay was often accused of being partial to Catholicism, but his *Seasonable Anecdote Against Apostasy* (1758), which is strongly anti-Catholic, seems to disprove this.

Lindsay's translation of Thomas Mason's *Vindicatio ecclesiae Anglicanae* (1728) was valued for the preface he added, which contains a comprehensive account of the episcopal succession in all the English bishoprics, as well as an early sermon by Mason. Other works by Lindsay include a history of England, two parallel dialogues in support of the nonjuring position, and works of biblical commentary. Lindsay died on 21 June 1768, aged eighty-two, and was buried in St Mary's churchyard, Islington, alongside his wife; they were together commemorated in a Latin epitaph.

The *Dictionary of National Biography* article on John Lindsay concluded with a brief memoir of his namesake, but apparently no relation, **John Lindsay** (*fl.* 1758–1759), naval chaplain and writer, who served as the chaplain in the *Forgueux* during Augustus Keppel's attack on Goree in September 1758. In the following year he published *A Voyage to the Coast of Africa* with details of this engagement; other works attributed to him are *A Voyage to Senegal* and

'Sir John Tostle, a Poem'. This John Lindsay's brother, William, served as a brigade major in Lord Ancrum's dragoons and was killed in action during the Seven Years' War. ALEXANDER DU TOIT

Sources Nichols, *Lit. anecdotes*, 1.373–6 • T. Lathbury, *A history of the nonjurors* (1845), 396–403 • Wood, *Ath. Oxon.*, new edn, 2.307 • *DNB*
Archives Bodl. Oxf., Brett MSS

Lindsay, John, twentieth earl of Crawford and fourth earl of Lindsay (1702–1749), army officer and politician, was born on 4 October 1702, the son of John, nineteenth earl of Crawford (*d.* 1713/14), and his wife, Emilia (*d.* 1711), daughter of James Stewart, Lord Doune, and widow of Alexander Fraser of Strichen. After the death of his mother he was placed under the care of his great-aunt Elizabeth, dowager duchess of Argyll. He attended the University of Glasgow and later (1721–3) the military academy of Vaudeuil, Paris. Crawford inherited an encumbered estate and was financially insecure throughout his life, receiving a pension from 1714. Like his father he sought a military career; he entered the army in 1726 and was a captain in the 3rd foot guards by the end of 1734.

During the 1730s Crawford also began to play a visible part in public life. Having been elected a fellow of the Royal Society in 1732, the next year he was made a gentleman of the bedchamber to Frederick, prince of Wales. Also in 1732, he was elected a representative peer. In parliament Crawford took his cue from Archibald Campbell, earl of Ilay, and proved a loyal supporter of Sir Robert Walpole. He was one of the seven representative peers who stuck by Walpole during the excise crisis in 1733, and he helped to frustrate an attempt to elect an opposition slate of Scottish peers in 1734. In the upper house Crawford was a fairly attentive member when in London, though he made no reputation as a speaker; in the debates over Edinburgh's handling of the Porteous riots Lord Hervey commented that Crawford and Lord Findlater made 'so many long, dull, absurd speeches in broad Scotch … that they fretted everybody who was of their side' (Hervey, 3.712).

Crawford began to establish a reputation for military prowess and bravery after joining the Austrian army under Prince Eugène as a volunteer in 1735 and distinguishing himself at the battle of Claussen (17 October 1735). He embarked on a lengthier tour of foreign service in 1738 when he arrived in St Petersburg. After declining the Empress Anna's offer of a regiment of horse and the rank of lieutenant-general he joined the army of Marshal Münnich on its march to the Dniester and saw action against the Turks and Tartars. His skilled horsemanship and his prowess with the sword won him great admiration. Crawford then rejoined the Austrians, serving under Marshal Wallis at the battle of Krotzka (22 July 1739), where he was severely wounded in the left thigh. In 1741, after a lengthy convalescence, he returned to England. The wound proved a constant source of pain and difficulty. According to the *Gentleman's Magazine* it opened twenty-nine times before complications from it eventually proved fatal in 1749.

Meanwhile Crawford had been made in October 1739 colonel of the highland regiment that became the Black Watch, and in December 1740 colonel of the horse Grenadier Guards. In May 1743 he joined the Pragmatic army under John Dalrymple, second earl of Stair, in Germany. At the battle of Dettingen (16 June) he commanded a brigade of cavalry with credit, and after the battle he was one of sixteen officers created knights banneret by George II. Promoted brigadier-general in 1744 he next served under William, duke of Cumberland, in the Southern Netherlands. At the battle of Fontenoy (30 April 1745) he unsuccessfully urged on Cumberland the need to occupy the strategic wood of Barry, and later covered the army's retreat with skill and coolness. On 30 May 1745 Crawford was made a major-general. After the Jacobite rising in Scotland he was appointed to the command of 6000 Hessian troops brought from the continent. He occupied Perth as Cumberland's army proceeded northwards.

However, when the Jacobites captured a series of posts in Perthshire, Crawford and the Hessians began a retreat to Stirling, threatening Cumberland's communications with Edinburgh. The duke curtly ordered them to move in the opposite direction and raise the siege of Blair Castle. When Crawford joined others in urging more lenient treatment towards the highlanders after Culloden, the duke described them as 'arrant Highland mad' (Yorke, 1.534). Both men agreed that Crawford would be better posted outside Scotland.

After rejoining the army in the Southern Netherlands Crawford fought at Roucoux (5 October 1746), where he evaded capture by impersonating a French general. Colonelcies and promotion followed: the 25th foot (December 1746), the Scots Greys (May 1747), and on 20 September 1747 he was made lieutenant-general. On service in Scotland, Crawford had met Lady Jane Murray (1730–1747), sixteen-year-old daughter of James, second duke of Atholl. The couple eloped and were married on 3 March 1747. The countess accompanied Crawford back to the continent but was seized with fever and died on 10 October 1747 at Aix-la-Chapelle.

Crawford remained on active service until the conclusion of peace in 1748. In 1749 he returned to his home at Upper Brook Street, London, where he died on 24 December 1749. His body was brought to Scotland, and buried on 18 January 1750 by the side of that of his wife in the family vault at Ceres, Fife.

Horace Walpole told the story that Crawford died from taking 'a large quantity of laudanum, under impatience at the badness of his circumstances, and at the seventeenth opening of the wound' (Walpole to Horace Mann, 10 Jan 1750, Walpole, *Corr.*, 20.109–10). He left his estate of Struthers in Fife heavily indebted, and administration was granted to a creditor. He had no children, and was succeeded as earl of Crawford and Lindsay by his kinsman George Lindsay, fourth Viscount Garnock.

Undoubted bravery, far-flung service, generosity of spirit, and courageous persistence in living with a painful wound made 'the gallant earl' a hero to his contemporaries. Crawford's posthumous reputation was further enhanced by Richard Rolt's celebratory biography, published in 1753 and reprinted in 1769. Although his one independent command provoked a sharp rebuke from Cumberland, the duke also remarked: 'If his head was as good as his heart, His Majesty would not have a better officer in his whole army' (Charteris, 258).

WILLIAM C. LOWE

Sources R. Rolt, *Memoirs of the life of the late right honourable John, earl of Crawford* (1769) • F. H. Skrine, *Fontenoy and Great Britain's share in the War of Austrian Succession* (1906) • E. Charteris, *William Augustus, duke of Cumberland* (1913) • *GM*, 1st ser., 19 (1749), 572–3 • P. C. Yorke, *The life and correspondence of Philip Yorke, earl of Hardwicke*, 3 vols. (1913) • John, Lord Hervey, *Some materials towards memoirs of the reign of King George II*, ed. R. Sedgwick, 3 vols. (1931) • J. Black, *Culloden and the '45* (1990) • W. A. Speck, *The Butcher: the duke of Cumberland and the suppression of the 45* (1981) • GEC, *Peerage*, new edn • *Scots peerage* • J. Redington, ed., *Calendar of Treasury papers*, 5, PRO (1883) • W. A. Shaw, ed., *Calendar of treasury books and papers*, 4, PRO (1901) • C. Grant, *The battle of Fontenoy* (1975)

Archives NL Scot., letter-book, corresp., and papers • NL Scot., papers | BL, letters to Sir Thomas Robinson, Add. MSS 23803–23827

Likenesses T. Worlidge, etching, BM, NPG; repro. in R. Rolt, *Memoirs of the life of the right honourable John Lindesay, earl of Craufurd* (1753)

Wealth at death £500 p.a. pension; heavily in debt; estate administered to creditor: GEC, 3.521–2

Lindsay, John (*fl.* **1758**). *See under* Lindsay, John (1685/6–1768).

Lindsay, Sir John (**1737–1788**), naval officer, was the younger son of Sir Alexander Lindsay of Evelix, near Dorloch in Easter Ross, and Emilia, daughter of David Murray, fifth Viscount Stormont, and sister of William Murray, first earl of Mansfield. Lindsay was made a lieutenant in 1756 commanding the fireship *Pluto*, which in 1757 was attached to the fleet under Sir Edward Hawke in the Rochefort expedition. On 29 September 1757 he was posted to the frigate *Trent*, in which he served during the war, on the home and West Indian stations.

In 1762 the *Trent* was part of the fleet under Sir George Pocock in the expedition against Havana; and on the death of Captain Goostrey of the *Cambridge* in action with the Moro Fort on 1 July, Lindsay was sent to fill his place, in which he 'gave many strong proofs of his valour' (Beatson, 2.550). Pocock afterwards offered him the command of the *Cambridge* or one of the other ships of the line, but he was still in the *Trent* in December 1763. On returning to England he was knighted on 10 February 1764 in reward for his gallantry; Lindsay went to the West Indies again in the *Tartar*, and returned in 1765. He married on 19 September 1768 Mary, daughter of Sir William Milner, and was MP for Aberdeen burghs from 1767 to 1768. His illegitimate daughter Dido Elizabeth *Belle (*b. c.*1763), whose mother was a black slave captured from a Spanish ship, became a protégée of his uncle, William Murray.

From August 1769 to March 1772 Lindsay was commodore and commander-in-chief in the East Indies, with his broad pennant in the frigate *Stag*. He was appointed a knight of the Bath (28 June 1770), a remarkable honour for a not very senior sea officer. He was later recalled from the East Indies apparently due to the hostility of the East India Company. In March 1778 he was appointed to the *Victory*, but on Admiral Keppel's selecting her for his flagship he was moved to the *Prince George* (90 guns), which he commanded in the engagement off Ushant on 27 July. His evidence before the subsequent courts martial was adverse to Sir Hugh Palliser; and on Keppel's resignation of the command, Lindsay also resigned, and refused all employment under Lord Sandwich, who none the less thought highly of Lindsay's ability. He was an Admiralty commissioner between April and December 1783, and then commodore and commander-in-chief in the Mediterranean.

With his broad pennant in the *Trusty* Lindsay was at Naples in June 1784; and on June 24 he had the honour of entertaining the king and queen on his ship. Not long afterwards his health broke down, and he was obliged to return to England. He was promoted rear-admiral on 24 September 1787, and died at Marlborough, on his way from Bath, on 4 June 1788, aged fifty-one. His body was brought to London and buried in Westminster Abbey.

J. K. LAUGHTON, *rev.* CLIVE WILKINSON

Sources R. Beatson, *Naval and military memoirs of Great Britain*, 3 vols. (1790) • J. Charnock, ed., *Biographia navalis*, 6 (1798) • E. Haden-Guest, 'Lindsay, John', HoP, *Commons, 1754–90*, 3.44

Archives BL, appointment and corresp. with East India Company, Add. MS 18020 • NRA, priv. coll., corresp. with East India Company

Likenesses A. Ramsay, oils, Glasgow Art Gallery and Museum • plaster medallion (after J. Tassie, 1779), Scot. NPG

Lindsay, John [Jack] (**1900–1990**), writer, was born on 20 October 1900 in Melbourne, Australia, the son of the artist and author Norman Lindsay (1879–1969) and his wife, Catharine, *née* Parkinson (1879–1949). Norman Lindsay's work spanned several fields and was filled with 'lush imagery of ribald satyrs and fleshly nymphs … generally in a Rococo style, executed with great technical skill' (*Dictionary of Art*, 19.143), although he is best remembered as the author of a children's classic *The Magic Pudding* (1918). Having failed to induce a miscarriage when Katie Parkinson became pregnant, Norman had married her reluctantly on 23 May 1900. Jack Lindsay was born two months premature and was named after his uncle, Jack Elkington, the attending physician and a progressive sanitary reformer. By the time Katie had her second child, Ray, in 1903 Norman was shuttling between her and a model called Rose Soady.

Tumultuous early years and education When Jack was five, Norman left his wife, who repeatedly feigned drowning in response; she desperately attempted to save the marriage by becoming pregnant again, giving birth to a third son, Philip, in 1906. Three years later Norman abandoned his family in order to travel to England to promote his illustrated edition of Casanova's *Memoirs*; bereft, Katie moved to Brisbane. Norman later returned to Australia but refused to be reconciled with his wife.

Elkington became an occasional father-substitute and enrolled Jack at Bowen House, a school in Sydney. Despite a late start Jack advanced from the infants' class to the lower sixth within a year. From 1913 his mother began drinking heavily, and his childless Aunt Mary took charge, leaving Jack doubly mothered but scarred by resentment. Distressed by his mother's decline into mental illness, he sought refuge in verse. He won scholarships to Brisbane grammar school (1914–17), and Queensland University (1918–21), where he studied classics under Professor James Michie and developed a lifelong interest in the ancient world. He also worked independently with the socialist V. Gordon Childe. The influences upon him were numerous and diverse: the major English poets, socialist thinkers, Plato, Jack London, Jane Harrison, Freud, Whitehead, Bergson, Croce, Gentile, and Hegel.

Rebelling point-for-point against his aunt, Lindsay became active in several social causes, including the anti-war movement and the promotion of aboriginal rights. He also taught for the Workers' Educational Association. It was at this time that his father, who had divorced Katie in 1920, re-established contact with him, sending him his aesthetic gospel, *Creative Effort* (1920), a book which significantly influenced Jack Lindsay's intellectual and aesthetic development. He endured several thwarted platonic affairs (one girl thought him about to explode), but earned a double first in 1921. He was outraged to lose Queensland's Rhodes scholarship to Eric Partridge and was censured when in retaliation he submitted poems attacking academics as 'dead and sexless eunuchs' to *Galmahra*, a magazine edited by his university contemporary P. R. Stephensen. He subsequently allied himself with his fascist-leaning father, who expected his son to bear his moral aesthetic into all cultural realms. Norman drew a portrait of Jack as an exultant faun astride Pegasus.

First marriage, literary projects, and move to England In 1921 Lindsay was befriended by the statuesque Janet Beaton (1898–1973), granddaughter of William Dalley, a conservative Catholic and former premier of New South Wales. Over her mother's objections they married in October 1922 and lived in Bondi on Janet's slender income. Lindsay worked with his father and Alfred Beutler on a Wagnerian music drama about Atlantis and Australia, and although the project collapsed, Lindsay learned much about composition from it. He consequently became a critic on the *Bulletin*, writing under the pseudonyms Panurge and (Miss) Jean Andrade. He went on to collaborate with Ken Slessor and Frank Johnson in publishing the anti-modernist *Vision* (1923–4), which included contributions from Chris Brennan and R. D. Fitzgerald, among others, and was Australia's first 'little magazine'. Lindsay and Slessor also edited *Poetry in Australia* (1923). Lindsay's own *Faun and Ladies*, heavily influenced by Hugh McCrae, was published by John Kirtley in 1923, and two years later his translation of Aristophanes' *Lysistrata* was published by Fanfrolico, as Kirtley's hand-press had been renamed.

The state of Lindsay's marriage, marked by mutual infidelities, was reflected in his joyless 'Joy's confessional' (September 1925), and he left his wife in February 1926, travelling with Kirtley to England, where the two men hoped to promote Norman Lindsay's notion of a sexually utopian Australian renaissance. They based themselves at 5 Bloomsbury Square, London, and during the general strike Lindsay hectored printers about overthrowing the system. Among the first titles published by the re-established Fanfrolico Press were a reprint of *Lysistrata* (1926), Lindsay's *William Blake* (1927), and *Loving Mad Tom: Bedlamite Verse* (1927), which had annotations by Peter Warlock and a foreword by Robert Graves. P. R. Stephensen took over from Kirtley in September 1927, publishing his own translation of Nietzsche's *Antichrist* and *Homage to Sappho* (a collaboration between Norman and Jack Lindsay) in the following year. Jack Lindsay's admirer Brian Penton took Stephensen's place as co-publisher of the Fanfrolico Press in April 1929.

Lindsay's bohemian coterie in London included the shy,

John Lindsay (1900–1990), by Alec T. Bolton, 1985

Pre-Raphaelitish former wife of Gordon Craig, Elza de Locre, who caused him to contemplate divorcing Janet. Behind Elza's back, however, Lindsay also tangled briefly with a former associate of Aleister Crowley called Betty May, who soon left Lindsay for his fellow poet Edgell Rickword.

Lindsay and Stephensen promoted the 'third millennium' in the brash *London Aphrodite*, which ran from August 1928 to July 1929, and published many former contributors to *Vision*. The 'modern consciousness' espoused by Lindsay combined many facets of his father's philosophy with Spengler, Croce, and Marx and attacked conservatives such as J. C. Squire, Wyndham Lewis, and T. S. Eliot for surrendering to post-war futility. Lindsay extolled lyricism and colour imagery like that of de la Mare, W. H. Davies, and the Sitwells, the painting of Delacroix, Cézanne, and Turner, and the music of Beethoven and Wagner. His egotistical manifesto *Dionysus* (1928) demonstrated the early influences of Plato and Nietzsche while also displaying the growing importance of Bergson, Freud, and Wagner. He called for man's 'forcible civilisation' (p. 22), condemned chastity, and extolled 'Zarathustra, with … Siegfried as our New Testament' (p. 242). Aldous Huxley lampooned the 4 feet 9 inches Lindsay in *Point Counter-Point* as little 'Willy Weaver … bubbling with good humour and inexhaustible verbiage' (p. 121).

Lindsay was forced to liquidate Fanfrolico in 1930 when he became bankrupt. Of the press's forty-one volumes he had written six, translated ten, edited many, and hand-printed the last seven. Editions like those of John Eliot and Tourneur contained unique matter; notable figures such as Edmund Gosse added distinction to the list, but Fanfrolico's ultimate legacy was scholarly literary erotica.

Politics and writing During the depression Lindsay took Elza (whose mental health was becoming precarious) to Cornwall, where they became vegans. Seeking some kind of rebirth, Lindsay fasted during the winter of 1930 and burnt manuscripts and letters. He contemplated suicide when letters he had written to his father chastising him for cutting his mother's allowance went unanswered. During this period he nevertheless collaborated with Elza on the novel *Time—Please!* (1931) about Essex locals grousing in a pub rebuilt from an old ship and, more crucially, made his own transition to fiction with *Rome for Sale* (1934), the first of a historical trilogy that also included *Caesar is Dead* (1934) and *Last Days with Cleopatra* (1935). These novels sold well and virtually saved his life. He went on to produce two lively translations, *Medieval Latin Poets* (1934) and *I am a Roman* (1934), which, like his novel *Storm at Sea* (1935) and the non-fictional *The Romans* (1935), emphasized civilizing order. Lindsay admired Mussolini and had sent him a copy of *Rome for Sale*, but subsequently repudiated his previously held views and wrote the quasi-Marxist study *Mark Antony* (1936), which opposed the fascism of the Caesars. Under the pseudonym Richard Preston he sifted his Cornish experience in *Shadow and Flame* (1936), and jumbled Lawrencian romance, murder mystery, and Marxism in *End of Cornwall* (1937).

As the popular front coalesced, Lindsay wavered about converting to communism, although his pioneering agit-prop declamation *Who are the English?* (1936) supported the party's co-option of England's diverse traditions of revolt with a litany of rebels from John Ball to the general strikers. Lindsay also promoted 'mass-declamation poems' during this period, once appearing before a crowd of several thousand in Trafalgar Square. When in April 1937 the Unity Theatre players performed *On Guard for Spain*, the *Daily Worker* ignored Lindsay's authorship and Stephen Spender skewered the play's falsity. Other works of this period, such as *Adam of a New World* (1936) and its spin-off *Anatomy of Spirit* (1937) demonstrate an attempt to synthesize Marx with Freud.

During the phoney war, at Rickword's request, Lindsay wrote *England, my England* (1939), surveying the country's heterogeneous radicalism, and both men gathered documentation for *Handbook of Freedom* (1939). Lindsay's other works of both fiction and non-fiction at this time demonstrate a constant concern with radical and revolutionary movements.

When Germany invaded Russia in 1941, Lindsay was drafted to the signals corps, but, tone-deaf, was recalled to the barracks at Trowbridge, Wiltshire, where he illegally joined the Communist Party. In that same year the schizophrenic Elza, who had been placed in medical care, died of cancer. Distraught, Lindsay nevertheless became absorbed in work, writing the epic poem *Into Action: the Battle of Dieppe* (1942) and the novels *We Shall Return* (1942), which viewed Dunkirk through the eyes of a communist would-be hero, and *Beyond Terror* (1943), which described British resistance to the airborne invasion of Crete. In 1943 he was reassigned to the War Office in London as a scriptwriter for the Army Bureau of Current Affairs theatre. Here he met Ann Lorraine *Davies (1914–1954), who became his common-law wife. He went on to produce *Second Front* (1944), which propagandized for the relief of Russia, and *Hullo Stranger* (1945), about women in the aircraft industry. Overall, he felt that the war years marked a 'cultural upsurge', a thesis developed in his *British Achievement in Art and Music* (1945).

The period from 1945 to 1956 can best be viewed in the light of Lindsay's attempts to sustain this upsurge. His immediate post-war work included editing (with Maurice Carpenter and Honor Arundel) *New Lyrical Ballads* (1945), a stage production of his novel *The Subtle Knot* (1945), and a revised *Men of Forty-Eight* (1948). The latter concluded a trilogy on radical movements (*1649* and *Lost Birthright*). His ambitious symbolist poem *Clue of Darkness* (1949) tried, unsuccessfully, to surpass *The Waste Land*. His heretical updating of Marx–Engels dialectic led to his *Marxism and Contemporary Science* (1949) being condemned, and almost resulted in his expulsion from the Communist Party for deviationism.

Three Letters to Nikolai Tikhonov (1950) overlooked the starvation resulting from the 'Lysenkoist transformation' of Ukraine, but Lindsay was a visionary who consistently failed to penetrate Stalinist fronts. His Marxist psychobiography *Dickens* was criticized for discussing Ellen Ternan.

Byzantium into Europe (1952) attempted to summarize the cultural influences that nearly united East and West, but defined feudalism as expropriation, ignoring mutuality, and was panned in the *Times Literary Supplement* as Soviet propaganda.

Lindsay would not give up his political agenda, however, and in his next project turned his attention to contemporary British troubles in a trilogy of propagandistic 'novels of the British way'. *Betrayed Spring* (1953), *Rising Tide* (1953), and *Moment of Choice* (1955) dramatized the consequences of Labour's inaction between September 1946 and March 1947 and dealt with such topics as London squatters, Lancashire miners during the nationalization of the coal industry, the dockers' strike of 1949, and the problems caused by Yorkshire's antiquated textile mills. These novels were followed by *Civil War in England* in 1954 and a study of George Meredith in 1956.

Ann Davies died of cancer in 1954, and was mourned alongside Dylan Thomas and Alexander Fadayev in Lindsay's *Three Elegies* (1956). Visiting Amsterdam in 1955, Lindsay became the lover of Meta Waterdrinker (*b*. 1921), a potter and a communist member of the Dutch resistance, daughter of Peter Waterdrinker, a farmer, and his wife, Tryntge Slik. They confirmed the relationship at an informal ceremony in June 1958. They had two children, and the marriage was legally certified in 1974, a year after the death of Janet Lindsay. Living in straitened circumstances and dealing with Lindsay's obsessions created strains within the marriage, but the family was held together by Meta's steadfast, caring character.

Lindsay's critical look at the novel in Britain, *After the Thirties* (1956), advocated socialist realism, while his novel *A Local Habitation* (1957), set in the East End and Essex, expressed a less doctrinaire view of getting by. Jack's alcoholic brother Phil, a novelist and screenwriter, with whom he had an off-and-on creative rivalry, died just as Jack's multi-volume autobiography was published. The first volume, *Life Rarely Tells*, appeared in 1958; *Roaring Twenties* (1960) disclosed Norman Lindsay's spiritualism and led to a much-regretted breach between father and son; *Fanfrolico and After* (1962) memorialized Elza. Lindsay was awarded the gold medal of the Australian Society of Literature in 1960 and was proclaimed by his old friend Stephensen 'the finest classical scholar and the most accomplished and versatile author Australia has produced' (Chaplin, 75).

Lindsay continued to analyse the Communist Party's contemporary problems with several more 'British way' novels, of which *All on the Never Never* (1961) was filmed as *Live Now, Pay Later* (1962) from a script by Jack Trevor Story. Lindsay continued to work with classical elements and themes in *Death of the Hero*, about the painter Jacques David; *Writing on the Wall* (1960), an evocation of Pompeii; and *Ribaldry of Ancient Greece* (1961) and *Ribaldry of Ancient Rome* (1961). *Thunder Underground* (1965) examined Neronian Rome; *The Clashing Rocks* psychoanalysed an Argonaut castration rite; and Roman Egypt was dissected in two studies of the period's daily life and leisure habits. His *Short History of Culture* (1962) and *Ancient World* (1968) were fine condensations of such interests. Personally most significant, however, was his publication of *J. M. W. Turner: his Life and Work* (1966), as it resulted in a reconciliation with his father; Norman Lindsay had admired Turner and resumed a correspondence with Lindsay about the biography.

Later years and reputation *Meetings with Poets* (1968) amplified his relationships with Dylan Thomas, Edith Sitwell, and various poet-partisans. The Soviets awarded Lindsay the order of Znak Pocheta in 1968, an honour of which he was proud until they invaded Czechoslovakia shortly afterwards; this led him to move politically slightly to the right, as is evident in his literary output from 1968 to 1982. He produced further books about the ancient world and began a critique of science with *Origins of Alchemy* (1970) and *Origins of Astrology* (1971). In 1973 he was awarded an honorary DLitt degree by his alma mater, Queensland University. In the following year his *Blast Power and Ballistics*, intended as a *summa* of his opposition to violence, occasionally slipped into pseudoscience.

The Normans and their World (1974) was Lindsay's most even-handed work of history. He now accepted that class struggle could be balanced by social concord, and went on to investigate Norman musical culture in *The Troubadors* (1976). His multifaceted biographies *William Morris* (1975) and *William Blake* (1978) proved politically unexpectedly tame, while he displayed an excellent understanding of the artist in *Hogarth: his Art and his World* (1977), to which *Monster City: Defoe's London* (1978) provided an interesting background.

Crisis in Marxism (1981) is a key to understanding the shift in Lindsay's political beliefs. He felt that Lévi-Straussian structuralism had to be overcome, but that a kind of Althusserian idealism was not the answer. The theorists that he found most useful were Whyte, Gramsci, and (as always) Lukács, but he also found Ernest Bloch's hopeful utopianism inspiring. Convinced of the ultimate worth of Marxism, but disillusioned by communist leadership, Lindsay now described himself as a social democrat.

A Garland for Jack Lindsay was published in 1980, with contributions from novelists such as Doris Lessing and Naomi Mitchison and poets such as Roy Fuller and David Holbrook. Lindsay was awarded the Order of Australia in 1981, the year in which his *Collected Poems* appeared. *Life Rarely Tells* was republished in 1982 in three volumes, with significant annotation. A heftier volume of essays in Lindsay's honour, edited by Bernard Smith and including contributions from Christopher Hill and Bernard Miles, was published in 1984 as *Culture and History*.

By now Lindsay's health was declining and he withdrew into himself, occasionally fretting about his children or the demise of communism. He transferred his archive to Canberra, and he and Meta moved to Maid's Causeway, Cambridge, where he died on 8 March 1990, partly as a result of excessive fasting.

Jack Lindsay has been described as English-speaking communism's 'most distinguished man of letters and scholar' (private information, Jack Beeching), and was recognized as such during his lifetime, but his works (of which a good number remain unpublished) are little read now. This neglect can be attributed to Lindsay's uprooted cosmopolitanism, variety, fugitive imprints, and idiosyncratic politics. As an imagist he wrote opalescent, rhythmic, technically accomplished verse. His translations retain vitality, although the same cannot really be said of his verse dramas such as *Hereward* (1929). Characterized by both breadth and density, his erudite historical fiction, histories, and biographies re-examined social crises, but also suffered spasmodically from projections, jejune emotions, data manipulation, reprehensible footnoting practices, and ideological blinkering. Overall he created fascinating syntheses throughout his works, but left a magnificent ruin. Doris Lessing found him 'perhaps the purest example I know of a good writer done in by the Party' (D. Lessing, *Walking in the Shade*, 92). Nevertheless, the contributions of this prolific polymath to the field of literature remain highly significant. JAMES M. BORG

Sources J. Lindsay, *Life rarely tells* (1982) · personal knowledge (2004) · private information (2004) [Helen Lindsay, daughter; Jack Beeching] · B. Smith, ed., *Culture and history: essays presented to Jack Lindsay* (Sydney, 1984) · N. Lindsay, *My mask: an autobiography* (Sydney, 1970) · H. F. Chaplin, *The Fanfrolico press: a survey* (Sydney, 1976) · O. Anderson, 'Jack Lindsay', *Dictionary of literary biography yearbook*, ed. J. W. Ross (1984), 294–307 · *Letters of Norman Lindsay*, ed. R. G. Howarth and A. W. Barker (Sydney, 1979) · L. Bloomfield, ed., *The world of Norman Lindsay* (Sydney, 1995) · P. Lindsay, *I'd live the same life over* (1941) · R. Lindsay, *Model wife: my life with Norman Lindsay* (Sydney, 1967) · E. Rickword and J. Lindsay, *Nothing is lost: Ann Lindsay, 1914–1954*, London: Writers Group of the Communist Party (1954) · J. Arnold, ed., *Ray Lindsay: a letter from Sydney* (Melbourne, 1983) · A. West, *Mountain in the sunlight* (1958) · O. Anderson, 'The more perfect hunt: Jack Lindsay unchained', 1980 · D. Lessing, E. Rickword, and others, *A garland for Jack Lindsay* (1980) · L. Lindsay, *Comedy of life: an autobiography* (Sydney, 1967) · D. Lindsay, *The leafy tree: my family* (Melbourne, 1965) · J. Lindsay, *Portrait of PA: Norman Lindsay at Springwood* (1973) · J. Turner, ed., *The dictionary of art*, 34 vols. (1996)

Archives NL Aus., papers, MS 7168 · priv. coll., books, letters, film · Ransom HRC, letters and MSS | priv. coll. · U. Leeds, Brotherton L., letters to Sir E. W. Gosse · U. Reading L., letters to Bodley Head Ltd · University of Victoria, British Columbia, McPherson Library, letters to F. Muller | FILM priv. coll., 'A day in the life of Jack Lindsay', James Borg, 1981 | SOUND James Borg audio, 'A day in the life of Jack Lindsay'

Likenesses K. Hutton and H. Magee, photograph, 1949, Hult. Arch. · J. Borg, photographs, 1980–89, priv. coll. · A. T. Bolton, photograph, 1985, NL Aus. [*see illus.*] · photographs, priv. coll. · photographs, priv. coll. · studies, priv. coll.

Wealth at death Cambridge townhouse

Lindsay [*née* Murray], **Lilian** (1871–1960), dentist, was born on 24 July 1871 at 29 Hungerford Road, London, the third of the eleven surviving children of James Robertson Murray (*d.* 1885), professional organist, and his wife, Margaret Amelia Bennett (*b.* 1841). She attended Camden School for Girls and the North London Collegiate School (1887–9) and considered the headmistress, Miss Buss, to have deprived her of a scholarship in 1888 when she refused to envisage a career in teaching. On 3 August 1889 Murray registered as a dental student with the General Medical Council, having begun a three-year apprenticeship to a dentist. This choice of career owed much to a family friend, Olga von Oertzen (DDS Philadelphia, 1881), then in unregistered

Lilian Lindsay (1871–1960), by unknown photographer

dental practice in London. On 1 October 1892, refused admission in London, Murray entered Edinburgh Dental School. She thoroughly enjoyed her student days, despite being charged double fees by Sophia Jex-Blake for lectures in surgery. Murray had committed the unforgivable sin of attending classes in anatomy and physiology at the rival Medical College for Women. Murray graduated licentiate of dental surgery, Royal College of Surgeons of Edinburgh on 3 May 1895, thus becoming the first woman with a British qualification in dentistry.

Despite an attachment to a fellow dental student, Robert Lindsay (1864–1930), Murray returned to London in 1895 (both of them had to support dependent relatives). There she set up practice at 69 Hornsey Rise, Islington. Murray and Lindsay were finally married on 26 July 1905 in West Holloway and she joined her husband in practice at 2 Brandon Street, Edinburgh. Here they remained until Robert Lindsay became first dental secretary of the British Dental Association (BDA) in 1920 and they moved into a flat at headquarters in Russell Square, London. While her husband was immersed in the negotiations that surrounded the 1921 Dentists Act, Lilian Lindsay was charged by the BDA with building up a specialist library. This she did so effectively that the 361 books of 1921 had grown to 10,000 by 1951. She remained honorary librarian until 1946.

After the death of her husband in 1930, Lilian Lindsay involved herself even more in professional concerns, and with a success which brought her universal recognition. She became sub-editor of the *British Dental Journal* (1931–51), the first woman branch president (1933) and the first woman president of the association (in 1946, the year she was appointed CBE). She was elected a fellow in dental surgery of the Royal College of Surgeons of England (1947), was awarded their Colyer gold medal (1959), and received the HDD and an honorary fellowship in dental surgery (1959) from the Royal College of Surgeons of Edinburgh. The University of Durham conferred on her an MDS (1939), that of Edinburgh an honorary LLD (1946). She was president or honorary member of numerous prestigious professional societies, as well as becoming vice-president of the Johnson Society (1950). After her death, the BDA library bore her name for many years and the Lindsay Club (later the Lindsay Society for the History of Dentistry) was founded in her memory (1962).

In addition to more than sixty papers (twenty-eight of them on historical aspects of dentistry), Lindsay's publications included a *Short History of Dentistry* (1933), the introduction to the reprint of Charles Allen's *Curious Observations on the Teeth* of 1687 (1924), and the first translation into English of the second edition of Pierre Fauchard's *Le chirurgien dentiste* of 1746 (1946). Unpublished were translations, mainly from German, of two books and 112 scientific papers. Lindsay's historical writing reflects the priority she placed on original research based on primary sources and her unshakeable faith in dentistry as a learned profession, with the BDA (to which she had initially been admitted on condition that she did not attend meetings) firmly at its centre. She was the first to write seriously and at length on the development of dentistry in Britain.

During her lifetime Lindsay was highly esteemed for her intellect, wide-ranging achievements, and her 'goodness, graciousness and gentleness' (*British Dental Journal*, 205). She nevertheless possessed strong views (she was adamantly opposed to the admission of academically unqualified dentists to the BDA in 1921) and was possessed of shrewdness and great tenacity of purpose. This is amply borne out by pictures of this diminutive, bespectacled lady, her hair in an increasingly wispy bun, and a sweet but enigmatically determined smile on her lips. Towards the end of her life, she was universally seen as the matriarch of the association, a last link between the legendary figures of the early days and the changed world of the present. Subsequently she was remembered chiefly for her historical writing, and was occasionally cast in the role of heroic feminist pioneer, a perspective she would likely have scorned.

Lindsay lived the last years of her life in Orford, Suffolk. She died at 26 Wolverton Avenue, Kingston upon Thames, Surrey, on 31 January 1960 and was cremated at Golders Green on 5 February. She bequeathed the residue of her estate to the BDA benevolent fund.

CHRISTINE HILLAM

Sources E. M. Cohen and R. A. Cohen, 'The autobiography of Dr Lilian Lindsay', *British Dental Journal*, 171 (1991), 325–8 · H. A. Cuffin, 'A bibliography of Lilian Lindsay (1871–1960)', typescript, 1962, British Dental Association, 64 Wimpole Street, London, Library · C. Hillam, 'The remarkable career of an accidental heroine: Lilian Lindsay (1871–1960)', *Dental Historian*, 32 (1997), 28–46 · E. M. Cohen, 'The historical writings of Lilian Lindsay', *Dental Historian*, 15 (1988), 16–31 · *British Dental Journal*, 108 (1960), 167–9, 205, 308 · *The Times* (2 Feb 1960) · register of dental students, U. Edin. · papers relating to registration (and renewal) for dentists' register, General Medical Council · d. cert. · private information (2004) · *CGPLA Eng. & Wales* (1960)

Archives priv. coll.

Likenesses photographs, 1905?–1946, repro. in *British Dental Journal*, 171, pp. 217, 328 · K. Williams, oils, 1942, British Dental Association, London · A. E. Baker, pencil drawing, 1946?, repro. in *Dental Record*, 67 (1947), 58 · Fayer, photograph, 1946, repro. in *British Dental Journal* · photograph, 1950?–1959, repro. in *British Dental Journal*, 108, p. 167 · T. C. Dugdale, oils, 1951, British Dental Association, London · portrait, in or before 1961; formerly in British Dental Association headquarters, Hill Street, London, 1961 · photograph, British Dental Association, London [*see illus.*] · photographs, priv. coll.

Wealth at death £9618 9*s*. 7*d*.: probate, 22 April 1960, *CGPLA Eng. & Wales*

Lindsay, Ludovic, sixteenth earl of Crawford (*d.* **1652**), royalist army officer, was the third son of Henry Lindsay, thirteenth earl of Crawford (*d.* 1620x23), and Margaret, sister of Sir James Schaw of Sauchie. Ludovic Lindsay sought a career as a mercenary officer, and is said to have 'gained honour abroad in the Swedish, Austrian, and Spanish services' (G. Wishart, *Memoirs of James, Marquis of Montrose*, 1893, 132). He was a colonel in Swedish employment in 1632, and later in the 1630s he levied a regiment of 3000 for the Spanish service through a commission from the Spanish ambassador in Vienna. After two years' service the regiment, then reduced to about 300 men, was disbanded in Burgundy. Lindsay subsequently spent six months in Madrid in an unsuccessful effort to get payment of his arrears. On 4 January 1639 he was in Vienna and, having newly inherited the earldom of Crawford from his elder brother, was intending to return to Britain and seek employment from Charles I. He took his seat in the Scottish parliament on 31 August 1639, but spent most of the bishops' wars of 1639–40 in England, and evidently commanded a unit of Scots who had enlisted to fight for the king.

Crawford was with Charles I in Edinburgh when the king sought a compromise settlement with the covenanters in 1641, being one of a group of ardently royalist but ill disciplined and loud-mouthed nobles and officers whose threats of violence seriously embarrassed the king. They were convinced that the marquess of Hamilton, the king's leading adviser, was betraying his interests, and in September Lord Kerr, when drunk, dispatched Crawford, 'his no less furious and drunken second' (*Letters and Journals of Robert Baillie*, 1.391), to accuse Hamilton of being a traitor. In October he attained further notoriety for his part in the obscure plot against Hamilton and the earl of Argyll known as 'the Incident'. Crawford confessed that he had said of Hamilton 'if he wes ane traittor, I wish he hed the reward of ane traittor' (*Fourth Report*, HMC, appx, 167) and other witnesses attested that while it was planned to arrest the two nobles, Crawford favoured their assassination. Apart from a few days under arrest Crawford escaped punishment for his follies, both king and covenanters deeming it inexpedient that the Incident be investigated too closely for fear that evidence revealed might disrupt the settlement being negotiated.

At this point Crawford decided that there was no future for him in Scotland. His title of earl had brought him no lands or other property, and he may have planned to return to the life of a mercenary officer on the continent. Whatever his motivation he agreed to a regrant of his earldom (15 January 1642) on new terms, whereby if he died without leaving a legitimate son to succeed him the title earl of Crawford would pass to John *Lindsay, first earl of

Lindsay, a distant kinsman. John Lindsay coveted the title of Crawford as it was the senior title of the Lindsay kin, of which he was the most prosperous and powerful member, and Crawford was willing to give him (perhaps in return for financial help) a chance of gaining it. That Lindsay thought the deal worthwhile strongly suggests that Crawford was unmarried at this point and appeared unlikely to have a son, but in or before October 1643 Crawford married Margaret Graham, daughter of the earl of Airth and Menteith and widow of Alexander Stewart, Lord Garlies. Moreover Crawford remained in Britain, for the English civil war brought him opportunities for employment and a chance to redeem his reputation. He fought for the king at the battle of Edgehill (23 October 1642), and served under Sir Ralph Hopton against Sir William Waller in central southern England in 1643. He contributed to Waller's defeat at Lansdown (5 July), but on 13 December he was surprised by Waller at Alton, near Farnham, and escaped with only a few men, nearly 1000 being captured.

In April 1644 Crawford took part in Montrose's attempt to provoke a royalist rising in Scotland, and with him was forced back into England after the initial capture of Dumfries. He was with Montrose at the siege of Morpeth in May, but was captured in Newcastle when it fell to the Scottish army on 19 October. Crawford was sent to Edinburgh and imprisoned, having already been excommunicated by the church and forfaulted (deprived of his title and property) by the Scottish parliament (26 July). In royalist eyes he remained earl of Crawford until his death, but the covenanters declared that the title had passed to the earl of Lindsay (now Crawford-Lindsay). The sixteenth earl and other royalists were freed after Montrose's victory at Kilsyth on 15 August 1645 had temporarily destroyed the covenanting regime. When Montrose was routed at Philiphaugh on 13 September and forced to flee to the highlands, Crawford took command of his remaining cavalry, and in the months that followed aided his efforts to rebuild a royalist army. On 3 June 1646 he wrote to Charles I of his determination to fight on with Montrose: 'I could wish that the litell drops of blood which remains in my bodie unspent might be shede to make your Majestie a glorious and happie prince' (*Hamilton MSS*, 1.110), but in August he, like Montrose, was forced to flee abroad. He reached Paris by way of Ireland, and there on 9 October he laid before Queen Henrietta Maria a plan by Montrose to raise 30,000 men to conquer Scotland, invade England, and free Charles I from imprisonment. The grandiose scheme came to nothing, but Crawford did not give up. In May 1647 he was in Ireland, and converted to Roman Catholicism before leaving to make another attempt to get help to revive the war in Scotland (*Commentarius Rinuccinianus*, ed. S. Kavanagh, 1932–49, 2.753). However, by April 1648 he was in the service of Spain, and landed in Ireland to seek to recruit troops for the Spanish service. He is said subsequently to have commanded an Irish regiment in Spain, and at the end of 1649 a report reached Scotland that he was living in Spain, being 'in great honor and credit', and having a 'very great deall of money' (*Various Collections*, 5.250). However, he is said to have left Spain in poverty in 1651—though, mysteriously, also to have had a frigate operating from St Malo which had taken one or two prizes (*CSP dom.*, *1651–2*, 3). The following year he led fifty Scottish officers who had served under Montrose in guarding the cardinal de Retz during the Fronde. He died in October or November 1652 in The Hague 'of an ague and fever' (*Nicholas Papers*, 319).

Virtually nothing is recorded of Crawford's character or personal life. In seeking to serve Charles I his intemperate antics in 1641 were damaging, but his services in the English civil war, his tenacity in adversity alongside Montrose in 1645–6, and his efforts to renew the war thereafter reveal more solid military virtues. His wife, Margaret, joined him in exile, and was with him in Spain in 1649, when she 'also turned Catholicke Romane' (*Various Collections*, 5.250). Their only known child, Henry, was aged twelve in 1657 when he was expelled from the Scots College at Douai since (for reasons unknown) he was deemed illegitimate. DAVID STEVENSON

Sources *DNB* · *Scots peerage*, 3.34–5 · GEC, *Peerage*, new edn, 3.518–19 · *Calendar of the Clarendon state papers preserved in the Bodleian Library*, ed. O. Ogle and others, 5 vols. (1869–1970) · P. Gordon, *A short abridgement of Britane's distemper*, ed. J. Dunn, Spalding Club, 10 (1844) · *The memoirs of Henry Guthry, late bishop*, ed. G. Crawford, 2nd edn (1748) · *The historical works of Sir James Balfour*, ed. J. Haig, 4 vols. (1824–5) · S. R. Gardiner, *History of the great civil war, 1642–1649*, new edn, 4 vols. (1893) · *APS* · R. Monro, *Monro his expedition with the worthy Scots regiment (called Mac-Keyes regiment) levied in August 1626* (1637) · *CSP dom.*, *1651–2*, 3 · Lord Lindsay [A. W. C. Lindsay, earl of Crawford], *Lives of the Lindsays*, 2nd edn, 3 vols (1858) · *The Nicholas papers*, ed. G. F. Warner, 1, CS, new ser., 40 (1886) · *The letters and journals of Robert Baillie*, ed. D. Laing, 3 vols. (1841–2) · *Fourth report*, HMC, 3 (1874) · *Report on manuscripts in various collections*, 8 vols., HMC, 55 (1901–14), vol. 5 · *The manuscripts of the duke of Hamilton*, HMC, 21 (1887)

Lindsay, Sir Martin Alexander, of Dowhill, first baronet (1905–1981), explorer and politician, was born in London on 22 August 1905, the only son and elder child of Lieutenant-Colonel Alexander Bertram Lindsay, 2nd KEO Gurkhas, and his wife, Gladys, widow of Lieutenant Maurice Cay RN, and daughter of William Hutton, of Beetham House, Milnthorpe, Westmorland. Lindsay came of a military family and traced his descent, as twenty-second feudal baron of Dowhill, from Sir William Lindsay (*b. c.*1350). His father died when he was fourteen and his only sister at the age of twenty-five. He was educated at Wellington College (where he won English essay prizes) and at the Royal Military College, Sandhurst, which he left without distinction, blaming his own idleness. In 1925 he was commissioned in the Royal Scots Fusiliers. He was a keen horseman and rode in steeplechases as an amateur.

In 1927 he was seconded to the 4th battalion of the Nigeria regiment at Ibadan. In 1929 he travelled across Africa through the Ituri Forest in the Belgian Congo, unaccompanied save by porters and enduring considerable hardship, collecting pygmy artefacts for the British Museum.

On his return to England, Lindsay volunteered for the expedition to Greenland which H. G. (Gino) Watkins was to lead and whose aim was to survey south-east Greenland with a view to establishing an Arctic air route to Canada.

Watkins accepted Lindsay on condition that he learned surveying. Such was Lindsay's enthusiasm that he fulfilled the condition and overcame the objections of his commanding officer. During this expedition (1930–31) Lindsay acquitted himself with distinction and gained invaluable experience. He was awarded the king's polar medal and wrote an account of the expedition in *Those Greenland Days* (1932). In 1932 he married Joyce Emily, daughter of Robert Hamilton Lindsay, of the Royal Scots Greys, son of the twenty-sixth earl of Crawford. They had two sons and one daughter.

Lindsay was now fired with ambition to lead his own expedition to the east coast mountains of Greenland and complement the work of Watkins. Access from the east coast being difficult, he planned to approach his objective from the west, across the ice cap. He had difficulty in getting backing, but finally won the approval of the Foreign Office, the consent of the Danish government, and the patronage of the prince of Wales. He was accompanied by Andrew Croft and Lieutenant A. S. T. Godfrey of the Royal Engineers (killed in action, 1942). Lindsay dispatched Croft in advance to train dogs for sledging, and, with Godfrey, joined him in May 1934. Thanks to careful planning and the courage and resource of all three, the expedition was a success. They sledged 1050 miles in 103 days over the ice cap from Jakobshavn to Angmagssalik, carrying their equipment with them, and mapped 350 miles of mountains between Scoresby Sound and Mount Forel. With the approval of the Danish government Lindsay named two mountain ranges after Prince Frederick of Denmark and the prince of Wales respectively. Lindsay received medals from the French, Belgian, and Swedish geographical societies. He described the expedition in *Sledge* (1935).

In 1936 Lindsay left the army and was adopted as prospective Conservative parliamentary candidate for the Brigg division of Lincolnshire, but war intervened. Lindsay saw active service in Norway and trained airborne troops in Britain and India. In 1944 he was appointed to command the 1st battalion, Gordon Highlanders, whom he led in sixteen operations in north-west Europe. He was wounded, twice mentioned in dispatches, and appointed DSO (1945). He described his experiences in *So Few Got Through* (1946).

Lindsay was elected Conservative MP for Solihull in 1945 and held the seat until 1964. He was a loyal tory but did not fear to take an independent line. He conscientiously represented his constituency, greatly helped by his wife, and took a special interest in the motor industry. He was always quick to defend the interests of the armed forces and of former soldiers and their families. From 1949 to 1952 he was chairman of the West Midlands Conservative Party and his services were in demand to advise new parliamentary candidates.

He was appointed CBE in 1952 and created a baronet in 1962. His first marriage was dissolved in 1967. On 1 August 1969 he married Loelia Mary, formerly wife of Hugh Richard Arthur Grosvenor, second duke of Westminster, and daughter of Frederick Edward Grey *Ponsonby, first Baron Sysonby, treasurer to George V. There were no children of this marriage. He was a gold staff officer at the coronation of Queen Elizabeth II and a member of the queen's bodyguard for Scotland (Royal Company of Archers). From 1977 to 1979 he was vice-chairman of the standing council of the baronetage, of which he wrote a history in 1979.

A man of action, Lindsay gained an assured place in the annals of Arctic exploration. He had considerable presence and charm as well as drive, energy, and organizing ability. Sometimes impulsive and frequently outspoken, he was not universally popular, but he enjoyed the affection and respect of many friends. Lindsay died at Send, where he lived near Woking, on 5 May 1981. He was succeeded in the baronetcy by his elder son, Ronald Alexander (*b.* 1933). W. P. GRIEVE, *rev.*

Sources M. Lindsay, *Sledge* (1935) · M. Lindsay, *Those Greenland days* (1932) · M. Lindsay, *So few got through* (1946) · *The Times* (7 May 1981) · *GJ*, 147 (1981) · *CGPLA Eng. & Wales* (1981)

Archives HLRO, corresp. with Lord Beaverbrook · NA Scot., corresp. and papers

Wealth at death £13,704: probate, 28 May 1981, *CGPLA Eng. & Wales*

Lindsay, Michael Francis Morris, second Baron Lindsay of Birker (1909–1994), university teacher and writer, was born at 40 Mecklenburg Square, St Pancras, London, on 24 February 1909, the elder son and first of the three children of Alexander Dunlop *Lindsay, first Baron Lindsay of Birker (1879–1952), and his wife, Erica Violet Storr (1877/8–1962).

Michael Lindsay was educated at Gresham's School, Holt, and at Balliol College, Oxford, of which his father was master. After graduating in 1931 with second-class honours in philosophy, politics, and economics, he undertook two spells of social work in south Wales (1931–2, 1935–7) and was briefly (1933) engaged in accountancy. In 1937 he was offered a teaching post at Yenching (Yanjing) University, Peking (Beijing), to introduce the Oxford tutorial system as an experiment and compare it with the American system. Yenching was a protestant foundation set up in 1926 by American missionaries to provide an education in English for Chinese students: Lindsay knew little about China at that time, but he felt interested in the project and accepted the position, arriving in Peking in January 1938.

Japan had invaded China in July 1937, and when Lindsay arrived Japanese military units were fighting for control of the whole of north China; most of the Chinese soldiers in northern China were communist guerrilla forces. Peking was under Japanese control, but Yenching University, a few miles outside the city, had extra-territorial status and Lindsay, as a foreigner, was free to enter or leave Peking without being searched. During his vacations he used to take his bicycle on the train and then ride into the countryside where he met the Chinese communist soldiers. He brought them radio parts and medical supplies, writing Chinese labels for them with the help of one of his students, Li Hsiao-li, the daughter of Li Wen-chi, a retired colonel in the Chinese army. On 25 June 1941 he and Hsiao-li were married. Later that year, on 8 December, he heard a

German radio bulletin reporting the Japanese attack on Pearl Harbor, so he fled immediately with his wife to join the troops he had been supplying, and later heard that the Japanese secret police had arrived at Yenching to arrest him only ten minutes after his departure.

Lindsay spent the next two and a half years with the communist guerrillas on the Shansi (Shanxi) border, working as a radio technician and teaching radio engineering to the troops. In 1942 the Lindsays' first child, Erica Susan, was born. In 1943 they made a difficult journey across mountainous country to reach the main force of the communists in Yenan (Yan'nan), where Lindsay was appointed adviser to the Eighteenth Army group communications department. He succeeded in building a transmitter powerful enough to reach the USA, and became adviser to the English language service of the New China News Agency.

In January 1945 the Lindsays' son, James Francis, was born in the Bethune International Hospital at Yenan, but after the Japanese surrender in August Michael Lindsay decided to leave China: although the communists offered him an interesting administrative post, he did not wish to remain in China with two small children and the prospect of a civil war. In November the family returned to England and to Balliol College.

From 1946 to 1974 Lindsay held a series of academic posts: in England as lecturer in economics at University College, Hull, 1948–51 (in 1951 the Lindsays' third and last child, Mary Muriel, was born); as senior research fellow then reader in international relations at the Australian National University, Canberra, 1951–9; and finally as professor of Far Eastern studies at the American University, Washington, DC, 1959–74. Although he succeeded to his father's peerage in 1952 and visited England from time to time, occasionally speaking in the House of Lords, Lindsay's home until the end of his life remained the house in Maryland to which the family had moved for his final appointment. He died in Washington, DC, on 13 February 1994. He donated his body to the George Washington University Hospital.

Lindsay wrote a number of books and articles based on his experiences. His most valuable book is his account of his wartime life in China, *The Unknown War: North China, 1937–1945*, published in London in 1975 and illustrated with many photographs which he took at the time. From the time of his arrival in China he had been critical of the Chinese Communist Party's emphasis on Marxist–Leninist doctrine: as he wrote in *The Unknown War*, 'Communists have been willing to use common sense, to take the advice of technical experts … with very good results. Where Marxist–Leninist doctrine applies, common sense vanishes'. Such comments made him unpopular in China during the 1960s and 1970s, but in later years—following political changes in China and the emergence of Deng Xiaoping as leader—Lindsay became reconciled to Chinese communism and the Chinese welcomed him again. *The Unknown War* was published in China in 1987 in a Chinese translation, and Michael Lindsay himself, once observed in Yenan as a 'tall, baldish and bespectacled figure' (H. Forman, *Report from Red China*, 1946, 47), remains a part of the history of that period; in China he is remembered with gratitude as one of the sympathetic foreigners who supported the Chinese during the war of resistance against Japan. Radio had always been his hobby, and he is remembered especially for his contribution of radio equipment and for his invaluable help in the setting up and supervising of radio communications systems.

ANN GOLD

Sources M. Lindsay, *The unknown war: north China, 1937–1945* (1975) · M. Lindsay, *China and the cold war* (1955) · *The Times* (14 Feb 1994) · M. Lindsay, *Educational problems in communist China* (1950) · E. Lemon, ed., *The Balliol College register, 1916–1967*, 4th edn (privately printed, Oxford, 1969) · Burke, *Peerage* (2000) · *WWW* [forthcoming] · b. cert. · d. cert. [E. V. Lindsay]

Likenesses group photographs, 1938–43, repro. in Lindsay, *Unknown war*

Wealth at death £16,761—in England and Wales: administration with will, 13 July 1995, *CGPLA Eng. & Wales*

Lindsay [*née* Bourke], **Norah Mary Madeleine** (1873–1948), gardener, the second child of Major the Hon. Edward Roden Bourke (1835–1907), and his wife, Emma Mary Augusta Hatch (1853–1935), was born in India in April 1873. The family, with three children under three years, returned to London in the following year, to live in a house in Montagu Square, and then at 25 Great Cumberland Place. Here Norah Bourke was educated by governesses and made her début in society, becoming celebrated for her beauty and her musical skill, especially her piano-playing. On 27 April 1895 she married a dashing soldier, Henry Edith Arthur Lindsay, the 29-year-old grandson of the twenty-fifth earl of Crawford and the younger brother of Violet Lindsay (1856–1937) [*see* Manners, (Marion Margaret) Violet, duchess of Rutland], a talented artist and the 'angel of the Souls'. The Lindsays were given, as a wedding present from a family friend, Lord Wantage, the manor house at Sutton Courtenay, on the banks of the Thames in Oxfordshire. Their children, Nancy Robina Winifred and David Ludovic Peter, were born in 1896 and 1900 respectively; soon after Norah Lindsay became interested in her garden. She was a romantic figure in enormous hats tied with chiffon and long pale dresses draped with lovely pearls, but she was also a seriously knowledgeable gardener, learning from practical work pruning, planting, and tying. The long, low, and romantic old manor house looked out onto two large garden 'rooms', the Long Garden and the Persian (or Jewel) Garden, side by side but screened from each other by high walls, covered in luxuriant roses, jasmines, and clematis. In a gardening society enthralled by Gertrude Jekyll's long drifts of single kinds of plants, Norah Lindsay led a revolt: allowing self-set seedlings to stay, she created bounteous jungles of mixed flowers, all contained and controlled by elephantine but low box hedges and carefully clipped yew sentinels.

During the First World War Colonel Lindsay worked with the Red Cross; subsequently he used his taste and knowledge of antique furniture to become a peripatetic dealer and adviser, apparently returning to the manor house only on rare occasions. Mrs Lindsay refined her garden in the 1920s, adding a wild garden beside the river. It was described in detail in *Country Life* magazine on 16 May 1931, in a piece which she herself wrote, a privilege rarely accorded to owners. Advised by her friend Nancy Astor, she began to charge for garden consultancy among rich friends: she inaugurated this professional career by 'dressing' the Astors' gardens at Cliveden for Ascot house parties, and arranging planting schemes for country house owners including Philip Sassoon at Port Lympne and Trent Park, Philip Lothian at Blickling Hall, and the Russells at Mottisfont Abbey. Her skill became legendary, and was admired by Christopher Hussey and jealously regarded by Vita Sackville West. In particular, her use of colour, including one-colour gardens or strident contrasts, and her way of constructing a mounded or pyramidal form on perfectly flat land, commanded applause. Her greatest gardening friendship was during the 1930s with Lawrence Johnston: their shared gardening tastes brought the planting of Johnston's garden at Hidcote Manor to its best just at the beginning of the Second World War. By the end of the war Johnston wished to retire to his garden in France and leave Hidcote Manor to Mrs Lindsay, who was now forced to sell the manor house at Sutton Courtenay, following her husband's death in 1939. When Norah Lindsay died suddenly on 20 June 1948, at her London home, Flat 410, Carrington House, Hertford Street, Westminster, Hidcote Manor was taken over by the National Trust; Sutton Courtenay was purchased by David Astor.

JANE BROWN

Sources M. Whitbread, memoir, priv. coll. [typed MS, by sister] · N. Lindsay, 'The Manor House, Sutton Courtenay', *Country Life*, 69 (1931), 610–16 · J. Brown, *Eminent gardeners* (1990), 60–76 · GEC, *Peerage* · A. Pavord, *Hidcote Manor garden* (1993) · m. cert. · d. cert.

Likenesses double portrait, 1904 (with Colonel Lindsay), repro. in *Country Life* · Violet, duchess of Rutland, sketch · photograph, repro. in *Country Life* (1903)

Wealth at death £3856 5s.: administration, 16 Dec 1948, *CGPLA Eng. & Wales*

Lindsay, Patrick, fourth Lord Lindsay of the Byres (*d.* 1526). *See under* Lindsay family of the Byres (*per.* 1367–1526).

Lindsay, Patrick, sixth Lord Lindsay of the Byres (1521?–1589), nobleman, was the eldest son of John *Lindsay, fifth Lord Lindsay of the Byres (*d.* 1563), and his wife, Helen, daughter of John Stewart, third earl of Atholl. By a dispensation dated May 1545 he married his kinswoman Euphemia (*d.* 1580), eldest daughter of Sir Robert Douglas of Lochleven, Fife, and half-sister of James Stewart, earl of Mar and later earl of Moray. In February 1546 he received a charter of the lands of Drem, and in November following his father resigned to him the lands and barony of Byres, Haddingtonshire. However, despite or perhaps because of his father's prominence, Patrick Lindsay was slow to appear on the political scene.

Protestant activist A supporter of the Reformation, Lindsay joined the lords of the congregation. He was among those who fortified Perth in May 1559 following the town's declaration of its commitment to protestantism, and he answered to the regent, Mary of Guise, for this defiant action. In January 1560, along with Sir William Kirkcaldy of Grange, Lindsay was active in Fife in resisting the French troops called in by the regent. They laid siege to the house of Glamis, which had been fortified by an officer in the French forces named La Bastie, whom Lindsay killed in hand-to-hand combat. It was said that 'if we had lost Lyndsay and Grange, it would have been more hurt to us than 1000 to the French' (*CSP Scot., 1547–63*, 192–3). One of the commissioners who in February 1560 negotiated the treaty of Berwick, thereby securing English aid against the French in Scotland, on 27 April Lindsay was a signatory of the band of Leith, which committed the signatories to advance the reformation of religion, expel the French from Scotland, and support the English alliance. According to John Knox, Lindsay subscribed the first Book of Discipline in December 1560. He was a member of the 1561 general assembly and directed a petition from the assembly to the privy council.

According to Knox, Lindsay was one of the protesters against the first mass celebrated following Queen Mary's return to Scotland in August 1561. Nevertheless, his relations with the queen were initially cordial. He took part in the campaign against George Gordon, fourth earl of Huntly, in 1562, and was with the queen's forces when they defeated the earl at Corrichie on 28 October 1562. He is recorded in that year as partnering Mary in an archery match against his brother-in-law Mar and one of the queen's ladies.

Dealings with Queen Mary Although not a member of Mary's privy council, Lindsay was present on three occasions as one of the additional members of the augmented council which met in the summer of 1565. Said to be a favourer of the Darnley marriage, Lindsay broke from James Stewart, now earl of Moray, as the latter became increasingly hostile to the queen's matrimonial plans and eventually engaged in the overt rebellion known as the chaseabout raid. When the fifth Lord Lindsay died in 1563 his son inherited from him a long-running dispute with Andrew Leslie, fifth earl of Rothes, over the office of sheriff of Fife. This was resolved in Rothes's favour on 13 January 1565 with the proviso that Lindsay and his family were exempted from Rothes's jurisdiction. By October, however, the disturbances of the times had led to Lindsay's being made lieutenant of Fife, and it was alleged that Mary secured Lindsay's loyalty by playing on his resentment towards Rothes, who was a supporter of Moray. Lindsay was present at the meeting of the privy council on 10 October when the order of battle against Moray was laid down, and it was agreed that he was to accompany Darnley's forces in leading the battle. This did not denote any change in his religious position—he had been one of the nobles who offered to stand surety for the leaders of the Edinburgh protestant activists caught drilling in July 1565 when they were brought before the court of justiciary, and he was a member of that year's general assembly.

Following Moray's exile in England, Lindsay was said to be one of those friendly to the banished lords. He refused Mary's invitation to attend mass on Candlemas day, 2 February 1566, and shortly afterwards he was one of the leading participants in the murder of David Riccio on 9 March.

He then fled from Edinburgh, initially perhaps to Fife, then to England. Summoned with others by the Scottish privy council to appear on 19 March to answer for Riccio's murder, Lindsay was denounced rebel on 1 June, but pardoned in December.

On 1 May 1567 Lindsay subscribed the Stirling bond undertaking to defend Prince James, the son of Mary and Darnley, against the latter's murderers. Consequently he was discharged from his lieutenancy of Fife eight days later. He was with the confederate lords who opposed the queen at Carberry on 15 June, and when James Hepburn, fourth earl of Bothwell, offered to settle the issue by single combat, Lindsay volunteered to take up the challenge. James Douglas, fourth earl of Morton, lent Lindsay the broadsword which had belonged to his famous ancestor, Archibald Douglas, fifth earl of Angus. However, Mary intervened, refusing to give permission for the encounter and surrendering herself to the confederate lords.

Having been a signatory of the order committing Mary to Lochleven, Lindsay conveyed her there and was one of her guardians during her imprisonment. On 20 July he subscribed the acts of the general assembly. With William, fourth Lord Ruthven, he was charged with securing the queen's abdication, which they achieved on the 24th. According to the *Memoirs* of Sir James Melville, it was Lindsay who persuaded Mary to resign the crown, and Mary's supporters later claimed that 'the Lord Lyndsay, he menassit hir grace, that, gif scho wald not subscryve, he had command to putt hir presently in the towre' (*CSP Scot.*, 1563–9, 532). Historians have generally accepted the truthfulness of this charge. On 29 July 1567, ostensibly acting on the queen's behalf, Lindsay and Ruthven publicly presented documents declaring that she had abdicated and appointed Moray as regent, and claimed that she had done so voluntarily. Lindsay was present at James's coronation later that day.

A member of the privy council following Mary's deposition, Lindsay was one of the councillors who witnessed Moray's acceptance of the regency on 22 August 1567, having been present at Lochleven a week earlier when Mary was induced to confirm Moray's appointment. Following Mary's escape from captivity, on 13 May 1568 Lindsay was with the regent's forces at Langside, where he was credited with reinforcing the right wing as it was about to give way. Lindsay accompanied Moray to the conferences held at York and Westminster between October and December 1568 to investigate the charges against Mary, and testified to the authenticity of Mary's handwriting in the casket letters. When John Maxwell, fourth Lord Herries, one of Mary's leading supporters, claimed at Westminster on 1 December that the real murderers of Darnley were the regent and his associates, Lindsay challenged him to maintain the accusation in single combat. In reply, Herries specifically excepted Lindsay from this charge. Lindsay voted against Mary's petition to divorce Bothwell on 30 June 1569.

Political malcontent In April 1569, after Lord Herries had had an audience with Moray to discuss a possible peace between the supporters of James and Mary, Lindsay and Ruthven took him to be imprisoned in Edinburgh Castle. Following Moray's assassination on 21 January 1570 Lindsay was one of the bearers of the regent's body at his funeral. During the ensuing civil war Lindsay was active on behalf of the king's party, both politically and militarily. In June 1571 forces led by Lindsay and the earl of Morton killed Gavin Hamilton, commendator of Kilwinning, and captured Alexander, fifth Lord Home, and others. Later that month Lindsay intercepted at Wemyss a quantity of gold sent on Mary's orders to the defenders of Edinburgh Castle. In September Lindsay captured George, fifth Lord Seton after a skirmish in the High Street of Edinburgh. That month the house of Byres, with Lindsay's wife inside, was surrounded by Marian troops from Edinburgh Castle, and cattle were taken from his estates by the queen's supporters. In the following year Lindsay was with the king's men at Leith, and as lieutenant repelled an attack by Marian forces. At this time he was said to be one of those most opposed to a peace, at least one on terms the queen's supporters would accept. In October 1572 he was elected provost of Edinburgh, a position which he held until 1576, and on 24 November he voted for Morton at the convention which chose the latter as regent. Lindsay became sheriff of Fife in February 1574, following Rothes's resignation. In September 1575 he was one of the Scottish signatories to an agreement reached at Foulden, Berwickshire, formally resolving the dispute over a fray which had erupted at an Anglo-Scottish day of truce on 7 July, in which Sir George Heron, the deputy warden of the English middle march, along with several other Englishmen, had been killed.

By 1577 Lindsay's support for Morton was waning—in July that year Robert Bowes reported that John Stewart, fourth earl of Atholl, Ruthven, Lindsay, and others had confederated themselves by oath for maintenance of the king—and a year later Lindsay was seen as having 'become colonel of the malcontents' (*CSP Scot.*, 1574–81, 295). He was an active supporter of Morton's removal from power, and attended the convention in March 1578 which accepted the latter's resignation as regent. A member of the council appointed to manage affairs until parliament could meet, he signed the order of 3 May 1578 that James should remain in Stirling under the care of the second earl of Mar. On 17 June he opposed the sending of an embassy to England to negotiate an amity and league for mutual defence. In July he protested against Morton's holding of a parliament at Stirling, on the grounds that it was not a free parliament; for this he was warded in Stirling. He was invited to attend the meeting in October of the general assembly, which was unhappy with Morton's handling of ecclesiastical policy. On 1 December 1579 he was appointed a commissioner for the reformation of the University of St Andrews, and on the 9th he was appointed heritable bailie of the regality of the archbishopric.

During Morton's temporary return to power, Lindsay initially adhered to the opposing faction surrounding the royal favourite Esmé Stewart, seigneur d'Aubigny, who was granted the dukedom of Lennox in March 1580. After Morton's arrest that December on charges of complicity in Darnley's murder, and his subsequent execution on 2 June 1581, Lindsay was no happier with the regime which succeeded. In September 1581 he left court, allegedly saying that 'but yet this sworde and buckler hath helped to dryve the Frenche men furthe of Scotland, and I fear yt muste be imployed to that use agagne' (*CSP Scot.*, *1581–3*, 52). He signed the bond that resulted in the Ruthven raid, the ultra-protestant coup which culminated in the seizure of the king's person in August 1582, and he was part of the administration which followed. On 26 October he was formally nominated a member of the privy council, in place of the eleventh earl of Crawford. After the king's escape from the Ruthven raiders in June 1583, Lindsay fled to England. Subsequently he returned to Scotland and took part in the plotting whereby William Ruthven, now earl of Gowrie, hoped to recover power. Arrested in April 1584 and warded in Blackness Castle, it was rumoured that he would follow Gowrie to the block, but he was released following a further change of regime in November.

Lindsay died on 11 December 1589 at Struthers Castle, three miles south of Cupar, Fife. His wife had died in June 1580. Their son **James Lindsay** (1554–1601), courtier and royal administrator, succeeded as seventh Lord Lindsay of the Byres, and by a contract dated 9 May 1573 had married Euphemia (*d.* in or after 1605), daughter of Andrew Leslie, fifth earl of Rothes. No doubt the union was intended to help resolve the dispute between their two families over the sheriffdom of Fife. They had two sons and four daughters. James Lindsay was appointed a gentleman of the bedchamber in September 1580, during his father's period in Lennox's circle. On 18 January 1594 he was made a privy councillor. He died on 5 November 1601, when his heir was his elder son, John. SHARON ADAMS

Sources GEC, *Peerage* • *Scots peerage* • G. Hewitt, *Scotland under Morton, 1572–1580* (1982) • G. Donaldson, *All the queen's men: power and politics in Mary Stewart's Scotland* (1983) • M. Lynch, *Edinburgh and the Reformation* (1981) • *Memoirs of his own life by Sir James Melville of Halhill*, ed. T. Thomson, Bannatyne Club, 18 (1827) • *CSP Scot.* • *Reg. PCS*, 1st ser., vols. 1–6

Lindsay, Patrick (1566–1644), archbishop of Glasgow, was the son of Alexander Lindsay, portioner of Monikie, Forfarshire, and Jean, daughter of Alexander Guthrie the younger of that ilk. After graduating MA from St Andrews University in 1587 he was appointed minister of Guthrie in 1588. He was translated to St Vigeans in the same county in the early 1590s, and although he was appointed bishop of Ross in 1613 (consecrated 1 December) he remained minister of St Vigeans until 1618, and thereafter joint minister of the parish until 1630. At some point early in his career he married Helen, daughter of Patrick Whitelaw of Newgrange.

Lindsay, who is said to have been 'a very fervent preacher' (Keith and Spottiswoode, 265), had been appointed a member of the new Scottish court of high commission in 1610, and on 31 March 1615 he was admitted to the Scottish privy council. He sat in many general assemblies, actively supporting the five articles of Perth in 1618. On 13 August 1633 he was translated to the archbishopric of Glasgow, and in 1637 appears to have been diligent in trying to gain acceptance for the new Scottish prayer book, contradicting the later report that he had been 'much against the liturgy' (ibid., 265). After open opposition to the new book emerged charges were raised against him in his own presbytery of Glasgow and were referred to the general assembly that sat there in 1638.

By this time Lindsay was not only demoralized by the collapse of royal authority in church and state in face of the opposition of the covenanters, but was disillusioned by bitter financial disputes with the bullying earl of Traquair, the treasurer: 'Glasgow he abuses pitifullie at his pleasure' it had been reported in 1637 (*Letters and Journals of Robert Baillie*, 1.7–8). He therefore wavered, considering escaping the threat of excommunication by accepting the authority of the assembly over him: 'He seemed oft not farre from this course' (*Letters and Journals of Robert Baillie*, 1.157). Though living in his house next to the cathedral in which the assembly was being held, he refused to appear before it, but was said to be 'contented verbally' to accept its authority, but would not do so in writing (Gordon, 2.140). The assembly ordered his deprivation from office on 11 December, but allowed him the chance of escaping excommunication if he submitted without reservation by 13 December, the day on which the sentences on all the bishops were formally pronounced. When he failed to do so he was both deprived and excommunicated.

'Since that time he hes lived verie privatelie, miskent [despised] by all', it was noted late in 1639 (*Letters and Journals of Robert Baillie*, 1.157). He was said to have fled to England in January 1639, 'in great seiknes' (J. Spalding, *Memorialls of the Trubles*, 2 vols., 1850–51, 1.244–5). In December 1640 he was one of a number of deposed Scottish bishops in London 'in great povertie' (*Letters and Journals of Robert Baillie*, 1.188). He was buried on 2 July 1644 in York, being left 'to be put in the earth by some few poor men' (*Letters and Journals of Robert Baillie*, 2.213), the rest of those attending the funeral having departed hastily on news of the battle being fought at Marston Moor.

DAVID STEVENSON

Sources *Fasti Scot.*, new edn • *DNB* • *The letters and journals of Robert Baillie*, ed. D. Laing, 3 vols. (1841–2) • J. Gordon, *History of Scots affairs from 1637–1641*, ed. J. Robertson and G. Grub, 3 vols., Spalding Club, 1, 3, 5 (1841) • R. Keith and J. Spottiswoode, *An historical catalogue of the Scottish bishops, down to the year 1688*, new edn, ed. M. Russel [M. Russell] (1824) • Lord Lindsay [A. W. C. Lindsay, earl of Crawford], *Lives of the Lindsays*, [new edn], 3 vols. (1849)

Wealth at death 'in great povertie': *Letters and journals*, ed. Laing, vol. 1, p. 188

Lindsay, Patrick (*bap.* **1686**, *d.* **1753**), politician, was baptized on 10 March 1686. He was descended from a younger branch of the Lindsays of Kirkforthar, Fife, and was the only surviving son of Patrick Lindsay, rector of St Andrews grammar school, and Janet, only daughter of John Lindsay of Newton. He served with Sir Robert Riche's infantry regiment in Spain until the treaty of Utrecht in 1713. On 22 June 1715 he married Margaret, daughter of David Monteir, an Edinburgh merchant. They had three sons and two daughters: Patrick, appointed deputy secretary at war in

1741; John, a lieutenant-colonel in the army; James, a merchant navy officer; Mary, who was unmarried; and Janet, who married James Anderson of Monthrieve, Fife.

Lindsay appears to have learned the same trade as his grandfather, a joiner in St Andrews, for after leaving the army he became an upholsterer in Edinburgh. He prospered in his business, and was granted the freedom of the city of St Andrews (10 September 1722) and chosen a magistrate of Edinburgh. He became successively dean of guild and lord provost, holding the latter office twice (1729–31 and 1733–5). During his first term he tried (26 October 1730) and hanged two men who had murdered his apprentice during a burglary at his upholstery shop (15 August 1728). At this time he published *The Interest of Scotland … with Reference to its Police, Agriculture, Trade, Manufacture and Fishery* (1733). In 1734 he was elected MP for Edinburgh under the patronage of Lord Ilay, and held his seat until 1741.

During the Porteous riots in 1736 he was charged with passing a request for assistance from the Edinburgh magistrates to the commander of the troops, General Moyle. The request was not met because, in Moyle's opinion, Lindsay was drunk at their meeting. In May 1737 Lindsay spoke against a bill to disfranchise Edinburgh as a result of the riot, but his attack on the local clergy for their part in the disturbances won him few friends in the city.

In November 1739 Lindsay's second wife, Janet, daughter of James Murray of Polton, died, and on 7 May 1741 he married Lady Catherine Lindsay, daughter of William, eighteenth earl of Crawford; neither marriage produced children. After retiring from the representation of the city he was in 1747 appointed governor of the Isle of Man by the duke of Atholl. On account of indisposition Lindsay resigned the office some time before his death, which took place at the Canongate, Edinburgh, on 20 February 1753. JANET SORENSEN

Sources R. R. Sedgwick, 'Lindsay, Patrick', HoP, *Commons* • M. Wood and T. B. Whitson, *The lord provosts of Edinburgh, 1296 to 1932* (1932) • *GM*, 1st ser., 23 (1753) • *DNB*

Archives NA Scot., letters to John Clerk • NL Scot., letters to John Clerk

Lindsay, Robert, of Pitscottie (*c*.1532–*c*.1586), historian, was a younger son of William Lindsay of Pyotstoun and Isabella Logan (married 1529), and a cousin of Patrick Lindsay, sixth Lord Lindsay of the Byres (1521?–1589). His date of birth has to be deduced from his first public appearance, in December 1553, when he was granted the escheated goods of Andrew Lindsay, a burgess of Edinburgh and probably a kinsman. In December 1560 he was styled 'of Pitscottie' when he was a member of an assize at Cupar, Fife, and he was associated with it again two years later. He may have held Pitscottie as a tenant. There is no evidence of his education and his date of death is unknown. It was certainly before 1592, when his son Christopher was styled 'of Pitscottie'. His *History* ends on 1 January 1576; the preface may arguably be no later than 24 April 1579 when one dedicatee, John, fourth earl of Atholl, died, and must certainly be earlier than 29 August 1586 when the other dedicatee, Robert Stewart, bishop of Caithness, died.

Pitscottie's *History* is a continuation, from the death of James I in 1437, of John Bellenden's Scots adaptation of Hector Boece's Latin history of Scotland. For events before *c*.1555 his sources were a mixture of borrowings from Boece, family traditions, personal recollections of Fife men, and general knowledge. An unnamed but likely source is his kinsman the Lyon herald, Sir David Lindsay of the Mount (1486?–1555); some of the latter's verses appear as epigraphs in Pitscottie's work and he is the best candidate for providing information about the reigns of James IV and V and the earliest years of Queen Mary.

After about 1555 Pitscottie uses contemporary material and his personal bias becomes clearer. His story becomes a protestant chronicle, telling a tale of protestant martyrs (much as John Knox did, but it is highly unlikely that Pitscottie knew Knox's history, which was not printed until 1586–7), of the struggles of the lords of the congregation for their faith, and, later, of the regents for the infant James VI against Queen Mary's men. This latter part is by far the most original and spirited, and Pitscottie clearly sees it as a critical, almost apocalyptic, struggle.

The climax of the *History* comes with the attempts of the regents to defeat the queen's men tenaciously holding out in Edinburgh Castle in the early 1570s. Pitscottie never reveals whether he took part in these raids, counter-raids, and artillery duels. If he did not, he nevertheless had excellent sources—one was probably his kinsman Lindsay of the Byres, a leader of the regent's forces—and he has left a vivid picture of the changing fortunes of the battle, to say nothing of demands for men and money which must have severely strained the resources of Fife, Forfarshire, and the Lothians. This part ends with the surrender of Edinburgh Castle in 1573—thanks largely to the help of English gunners—and peace between the two main Scottish factions.

Pitscottie's attention then turns to Scottish soldiers being shipped to the Baltic; he notes other religious struggles in mainland Europe and a series of domestic problems as James Douglas, earl of Morton, tried as regent to restore order. He is now dutifully recording plague, dearth, and high taxation; some of the earlier verve has gone—except at the end, when he records the happy wedding at Cupar on 25 December 1575 (significantly, he calls it neither Yule nor Christmas) of the earl of Angus and a lady from Fife.

Although only one manuscript (formerly in the collection of John Scott of Halkshill) preserves the text as Pitscottie probably intended it, much of his work must have soon become known, since at least sixteen manuscripts (and possibly four more) have survived and there are scrappy continuations to 1603. The *History* was first published, by subscription, at Edinburgh in 1728 by Robert Freebairn, a well-known printer, bookseller, and ardent Jacobite; later editions appeared at Glasgow in 1749, and again at Edinburgh in 1778 and 1814. All were superseded when a full text, based on two of the oldest manuscripts, with extensive introduction, notes, and glossary, was published in three volumes by A. J. G. Mackay for the Scottish Text Society between 1899 and 1911.

Sir Walter Scott read Pitscottie as a teenager and was carried away by his telling phrases and vivacity; parts of Pitscottie turn up little altered in *Marmion* and *Tales of a Grandfather*, and shorter quotations appear in the Waverley novels. The mature Scott knew very well that Pitscottie was historically unreliable in the earlier part of his work but recommended him for his language, anecdotes, and knack of presenting a scene—and as a relief from contemporary dry-as-dust writing, especially John Pinkerton's *History of Scotland* (1797). Freebairn and Scott together put Pitscottie on the map, and he has been there ever since.

Modern studies have gone much further than Scott in showing just how garbled, inventive, and biased Pitscottie can be. He is not only pro-protestant; anti-Hamilton and anti-Douglas strains are also evident—the latter may explain why the work was not printed during the regency of Morton (1572–80) and so confined to manuscript circulation then and, as it turned out, for some 150 years. Whatever the critical historians may say, the romantic view of Scottish history never dies and so the influence of Pitscottie's colourful episodes, such as the death of James III's favourite at Lauder, the same king's fate after the battle of Sauchieburn, the doings of James IV before and at Flodden, and the deathbed of James V, is certain to persist. Yet there may often be a substratum of fact or probability in what he says, usually when the tale can be plausibly traced to one of his known informants, and in the last fifteen years of the narrative what he says is often confirmed elsewhere.

Like other contemporary diarists, Pitscottie wrote in Scots. Otherwise, his techniques are those of medieval chroniclers; he took material as and when he could find it and is no less episodic and unreflective in the way he uses it. His focus is usually regional, centred especially on the east half of Fife and the Lothians. But he also drew on a unique reservoir of family tradition. Throughout there are stories of Lindsays behaving honourably and loyally. The stories may not always be true, but they entertain at the same time as they record traditional family themes and oral lore. No earlier Scot had written quite like this about his own blood relatives or left such a lively personal view of events. The best verdict on Pitscottie (it is rather like Scott's) was given by W. C. Dickinson in 1949: he is 'to be used with the greatest caution, but to be read with the greatest pleasure' (*Knox's History*, 2.347). W. W. SCOTT

Sources *The historie and cronicles of Scotland … by Robert Lindesay of Pitscottie*, ed. A. J. G. Mackay, 3 vols., STS, 42–3, 60 (1899–1911) • *The letters of Sir Walter Scott*, ed. H. J. C. Grierson and others, centenary edn, 12 vols. (1932–79) • J. C. Corson, *Notes and index to Sir Herbert Grierson's edition of the letters of Sir Walter Scott* (1979) • C. McGladdery, *James II* (1990) • N. Macdougall, *James III: a political study* (1982) • N. Macdougall, *James IV* (1989) • *John Knox's History of the Reformation in Scotland*, ed. W. C. Dickinson, 2 vols. (1949)

Lindsay, Robert James Loyd-, Baron Wantage (1832–1901), army officer and agriculturalist, born of Scottish descent in London on 16 April 1832, was the youngest child

Robert James Loyd-Lindsay, Baron Wantage (1832–1901), by Julia Margaret Cameron, *c.*1865 [with his wife, Harriet Sarah Loyd-Lindsay, Lady Wantage]

of Lieutenant-General James Lindsay (1793–1855), Grenadier Guards, of Balcarres, Fife—paternal grandson of James Lindsay, fifth earl of Balcarres—tory MP for Wigan (1825–31) and for Fife (1831–2), and of his second wife, Anne (*c.*1803–1894), eldest daughter and coheir of Sir Coutts Trotter, first baronet, banker. Robert Lindsay's elder brother Coutts Lindsay (1824–1913) in 1837 inherited his maternal grandfather's baronetcy. His elder sister Margaret married her cousin Alexander William Crawford Lindsay, twenty-fifth earl of Crawford.

Lindsay was educated at a private school—its master was 'about the only man Lindsay ever thoroughly hated' (Loyd-Lindsay, 11)—and at Eton College (1846–50); he was handsome, blue-eyed, and golden-haired. He was intended and tutored for Haileybury and the East India Company's civil service. However, through the influence of his younger sister's admirer, in December 1850 he received a commission (by purchase) in the Scots Fusilier Guards. In February 1854 they left for the Crimean War. Lindsay escaped cholera but nearly died of dysentery. At the battle of the Alma he carried the queen's colour and helped rally the regiment, confused by a mistaken order to retire. He also distinguished himself at Inkerman. In November he was promoted lieutenant and captain without purchase. His indignant letters home on British logistic bungling and the resultant suffering of the soldiers were shown by Samuel Jones Loyd, first Baron Overstone, a family friend, to the duke of Newcastle, secretary of state for war. From March 1855 Lindsay was aide-de-camp to General Sir James Simpson, a friend of his father, until

August, when he became adjutant of his regiment. After the troops' return from the Crimea in July 1856 he was promoted brevet major. He was awarded the Légion d'honneur and the Mejidiye, and in 1857 the Victoria Cross (24 February) for the Alma and Inkerman.

A devout Anglican, Lindsay became an evangelical, was influenced by Catherine Marsh, and held Bible classes for soldiers. According to his wife, his 'religious convictions and serious views of duty remained with him through life, but the Evangelical phase proved a passing one' (Loyd-Lindsay, 138). Carefully chosen by Prince Albert—who described him as 'studious in his habits' (Martin, 4.206)—in early 1858 Lindsay was appointed equerry in the new household of the young prince of Wales at White Lodge, Richmond Park; the appointment ended in 1859 following Lindsay's marriage. On 23 October 1858 Lindsay, in anticipation of his marriage, assumed the name Loyd-Lindsay. On 17 November he married Harriet Sarah [*see* Lindsay, Harriet Sarah Loyd- (1837–1920)], only surviving child and heir of Samuel Jones *Loyd, first Baron Overstone (1796–1883), millionaire banker and landowner, one of the richest men in England. Overstone endowed his daughter and son-in-law with a considerable fortune and land in Berkshire, and later made them further gifts.

In September 1859 Loyd-Lindsay retired from the army with the rank of captain and lieutenant-colonel, and thereafter largely devoted himself to the Lockinge estate near Wantage, Berkshire, settled on him and his wife by Overstone. Their Lockinge estate was no ancient feudal relic, but a Victorian capitalist *nouveau riche* construct. Its nucleus, the East Lockinge estate, was bought as an investment in 1854 by Overstone's father, Lewis Loyd (1768–1858); following Loyd-Lindsay's marriage continued purchases gradually extended and consolidated the estate. By the 1874 'New Domesday' it was the largest in Berkshire, but had not yet reached its maximum. Well before the agricultural depression Loyd-Lindsay began incorporating previously tenanted farms with the home farm: from 1854 to 1891 fourteen farms were amalgamated into one. Prominent and influential within the county, Loyd-Lindsay was Conservative MP for Berkshire from 1865 to 1885.

Loyd-Lindsay was a pioneer and continued as the leading advocate of the volunteer movement. He helped raise volunteers in Berkshire, and was from 1860 lieutenant-colonel and from 1872 to 1895 colonel of the Berkshire rifle volunteers. In 1859 he raised at Overstone the 1st Northamptonshire light horse volunteers, and he continued to advocate mounted infantry. In October 1866 he led over 1100 volunteers on a visit to Brussels. At the request of the prince of Wales, its captain-general, he also commanded from 1866 to 1881 the Honourable Artillery Company and attempted, with limited success, to modernize that ancient and idiosyncratic unit. He encouraged closer relations between regulars and volunteers, and the holding of large-scale manoeuvres. In May 1881 he was made KCB (civil) for services to the volunteers. He was brigadier-general, home counties brigade, volunteer force, from 1888 to 1895. A good shot and an enthusiast for rifle shooting, he was a prominent member of the National Rifle Association, which was closely associated with the volunteers, and was its chairman from 1887 to 1891. He presided over its move from Wimbledon to Bisley, where the new range was opened in July 1890.

In 1870, partly responding to the Franco-Prussian War, Loyd-Lindsay was a founder, and from 1870 until his death the first chairman, of the National Society for Aid to the Sick and Wounded, later the British Red Cross Society. On its behalf he went to the Franco-Prussian War, and in 1876 to the Turco-Serbian War. He criticized and offended the Serbs—whose government he considered 'cunning rascals'—established a British Red Cross hospital, the Katharine Hospital, at Belgrade, and later also helped the Turkish army. Following his return home—greeted enthusiastically at Wantage with bands playing and crowds singing 'See the conquering hero comes'—he was criticized for his pro-Turkish, anti-Serbian speeches. Archibald Forbes, in the Liberal *Daily News*, alleged he had confused his two roles as Conservative MP and chairman of a neutral organization, and had used 'for party and political purposes' opportunities offered him as National Aid Society representative. Loyd-Lindsay, however, saw no incompatibility.

As an MP Loyd-Lindsay was a member of the volunteer interest, and also spoke on other military issues. He opposed abolition of purchase of commissions, but favoured other Cardwell reforms. During Disraeli's ministry, from August 1877 to April 1880 he was financial secretary to the War Office, and worked on preparations for possible war with Russia. His War Office experience confirmed his support for the Cardwell system. In 1885 Salisbury offered him the post of surveyor-general at the War Office but, because of serious illness the previous year, he declined it.

Overstone's death in November 1883 placed a princely fortune at the disposal of Loyd-Lindsay and his wife. In July 1885, nominated by Salisbury, the incoming prime minister, he was created Baron Wantage of Lockinge. From 1886 he was lord lieutenant of Berkshire, and from 1898 provincial grand master of the Berkshire freemasons.

Following Overstone's death Loyd-Lindsay and his wife owned large estates in Berkshire, Northamptonshire, and elsewhere, totalling about 52,000 acres, and also had large non-agricultural investments. Loyd-Lindsay was an innovative, improving agriculturalist, and a paternalist landlord and employer. He bought the latest machinery, experimented with irrigation and ranching, and planted woods. A leading shire-horse breeder, in 1889 he became president of the Shire Horse Society. He built picturesque model housing—himself designing cottages—improved the pay of his agricultural labourers, provided allotments, and introduced a bonus scheme, co-operative stores 'upon the Rochdale System', and a savings bank paying 5 per cent interest.

During the agricultural depression, cushioned by his non-agricultural income, Loyd-Lindsay attempted when possible to 'keep tenants on their legs' (Perry, 73) with heavy rent remission. Unable to obtain suitable tenants for some farms, he farmed them himself, ultimately farming some 13,000 acres—probably the largest farmer in Britain—using economies of scale and management, and investing heavily despite poor returns. He opposed agricultural trade unionism and 'Red Van' propaganda, and was criticized by the *Daily News* for his tory paternalist control over his villagers. He advocated smallholdings, partly for the Conservative political benefits from increasing 'the body of men interested in maintaining the rights of property' (Loyd-Lindsay, 402). In 1885 he was a founder, and soon became chairman, of the Small Farm and Labourers' Land Company, intended to facilitate the purchase of smallholdings but which, despite his subsidy, failed. He gave evidence to the 1889 parliamentary committee on smallholdings, was invited in 1893 to be chairman of the royal commission on agriculture but declined, and in 1894 gave evidence to it.

In 1891 Edward Stanhope (Conservative secretary of state for war) chose Wantage to be chairman of the committee on terms and conditions of service in the army (the Wantage committee). Its report (1892), largely drafted by Wantage, endorsed the Cardwell system and recommended improved pay and conditions for soldiers. Arthur Haliburton (assistant under-secretary, the War Office civilian representative) was hostile and largely dissented. The report was favourably received by the press and MPs but, to economize, the government did not then implement its recommendations, though some were later introduced, including slightly improved pay.

Wantage purchased the advowsons of local livings, ending neglect by absentee Oxford-don clergy, and was a generous benefactor of the established church, local schools, and the town of Wantage. He was a founder and supporter of the ultimately unsuccessful Oxford Military College (1876–96) at Cowley, became chairman of its council, and in 1893 temporarily subsidized it. He was a founder, generous benefactor, and from 1892 president of Reading University College, and especially encouraged its agricultural studies. He was also an art collector. The artist Louis William Desanges had painted pictures of VC heroes which for years were exhibited at the Crystal Palace, then offered for sale. Wantage presented them to the town of Wantage, where they were exhibited in the Victoria Cross Gallery, opened in November 1900 (the collection was dispersed after the Second World War).

Devout, brave, earnest, and philanthropic, Wantage personified the Victorian chivalric ideal. He believed in duty: 'I must do something to justify my existence' (Loyd-Lindsay, 427). Tall, soldierly, and handsome, his appearance was much admired by contemporaries. Julia Margaret Cameron said he was the nearest to her ideal of King Arthur, and he was painted by Sir William Richmond, Lady Butler, Walter Ouless, and Louis Desanges. After a long illness Wantage died on 10 June 1901 at his residence, Lockinge House, Berkshire, and was buried on 13 June at Ardington churchyard, Berkshire; his peerage became extinct. His widow erected a memorial cross on the downs. After her death on 9 August 1920 the Lockinge estate was inherited by her distant cousin Arthur Thomas Loyd (1882–1944), Conservative MP for the Abingdon division of Berkshire (1921–3). Florence Nightingale wrote of Lord Wantage, 'he had been a great gain. … *All* are better than if he had not lived' (ibid., 430).

ROGER T. STEARN

Sources H. S. Loyd-Lindsay, *Lord Wantage, V.C., K.C.B.: a memoir* (1907) • GEC, *Peerage* • Burke, *Peerage* (1959) • M. A. Havinden, D. S. Thornton, and P. D. Wood, *Estate villages: a study of the Berkshire villages of Ardington and Lockinge* (1966) • *EdinR*, 195 (1902), 29–57 • *The Spectator* (4 Jan 1908), 20–22 • private information (1912) • A. P. Humphry and T. F. Fremantle, *History of the National Rifle Association* (1914) • D. Anderson, *The Balkan volunteers* (1968) • T. Martin, *The life of … the prince consort*, 4 (1879) • S. Lee, *King Edward VII*, 1 (1925) • I. F. W. Beckett, *Riflemen form: a study of the rifle volunteer movement, 1859–1908* (1982) • I. F. W. Beckett, *The amateur military tradition, 1558–1945* (1991) • E. M. Spiers, *The late Victorian army, 1868–1902* (1992) • H. Cunningham, *The volunteer force: a social and political history, 1859–1908* (1975) • R. C. Michie, 'Income, expenditure and investment of a Victorian millionaire: Lord Overstone, 1823–83', *BIHR*, 58 (1985), 59–77 • R. T. Stearn, 'Oxford Military College, 1876–1896', *Soldiers of the Queen*, 83 (1995), 6–15 • P. J. Perry, *British farming in the great depression, 1870–1914: an historical geography* (1974) • G. E. Mingay, ed., *The Victorian countryside*, 2 (1981) • *WWBMP*

Archives LUL, misc. corresp. • NL Scot., corresp. and MSS | priv. coll., corresp. and MSS rel. to Red Cross • letters to Edward Stanhope

Likenesses J. M. Cameron, photograph, c.1865, NPG [*see illus.*] • H. J. Brooks, group portrait, oils, 1888 (*Private view of the old masters exhibition, Royal Academy*), NPG • Violet, duchess of Rutland, lithograph, 1891, NPG • oils, 1895?, U. Reading • Spy [L. Ward], chromolithograph caricature, NPG; repro. in *VF* (4 Nov 1876) • print, NPG

Wealth at death £21,671 1s. 7d.: probate, 9 July 1901, *CGPLA Eng. & Wales*

Lindsay, Sir Ronald Charles (1877–1945), diplomatist, was born in London on 3 May 1877, the fifth of the six sons and sixth of the seven children of James Ludovic *Lindsay, Lord Lindsay, later the twenty-sixth earl of Crawford and ninth earl of Balcarres (1847–1913), astronomer and bibliophile, and his wife, Emily Florence (*d.* 1934), second surviving daughter of Colonel Edward Bootle-Wilbraham. His eldest brother was David Alexander Edward *Lindsay, twenty-seventh earl of Crawford (1871–1940), Conservative politician.

Lindsay was educated at Winchester College and, after studying foreign languages abroad, passed the competitive examination for the diplomatic service in January 1899. After nine months at the Foreign Office in London, he went as an attaché to the St Petersburg embassy. During his time there he was promoted third secretary, learned Russian, and passed a public law examination. In July 1903 he was transferred to Tehran. Learning the intricacies of Near Eastern politics—already grasping its Russian dimension—he added Persian to his quiver of languages, and was promoted second secretary in December 1904. Marked as a man on the rise who needed professional breadth and depth, he served in Washington from April 1905 to June 1907, and in Paris from July 1907 to November 1908. While in America he met Martha Cameron (*d.* 1918), daughter of Senator James Donald Cameron, of Pennsylvania. They married on 18 March 1909. His American appointment also had importance because the ambassador, Sir Mortimer Durand, antagonized President

Theodore Roosevelt, who engineered Durand's recall in late 1906. This unfortunate situation schooled Lindsay in the partisan side of the diplomatic profession. At Paris he received grounding in the complexities of European statecraft that devolved from the Anglo-French and Anglo-Russian ententes. Like many of the British diplomatic generation beginning careers after the mid-1890s, he came to distrust German ambitions and to favour the balance of power as safeguard for Britain's continental interests.

In November 1908 Lindsay's record led to his appointment as assistant private secretary to the foreign secretary, Sir Edward Grey. From this central position he was exposed to two crises, Bosnia in 1908–9 and Morocco in 1911, that underscored the lessons garnered at Paris. His anti-Germanism intensified, and he understood more poignantly the importance of maintaining the balance. His administrative abilities were also reinforced. In September 1911 he was transferred to The Hague, where he was promoted first secretary in December that year. Most of his sixteen months at the Dutch capital saw him assist British delegates to an international opium conference. Although the conference achieved little, Lindsay gained practice in conducting multilateral negotiations. In January 1913 he was seconded to the Egyptian government as under-secretary in the ministry of finance—Egypt then coming under the remit of the Foreign Office (and not the Colonial Office). His work had little connection with big diplomatic questions; but, partly because of his administrative competence, and partly because of the outbreak of the First World War and the pressures it brought, his transfer back to the diplomatic service was delayed until March 1919. None the less Lindsay did his duty, helping to ensure that the British presence in Egypt, tied to the Suez Canal, remained firm.

Upon reverting to the diplomatic service Lindsay was unexpectedly returned to Washington in May 1919. The ambassador, Lord Reading, was rarely in the United States. The Foreign Office needed competent professional diplomats to run the embassy. After September 1919, as counsellor there, Lindsay served essentially as Britain's chief representative in the United States until a new ambassador, Sir Auckland Geddes, succeeded Reading in March 1920. In winter 1919–20 Lindsay assisted his former chief, now Viscount Grey of Fallodon, on an unsuccessful mission to convince President Woodrow Wilson to accept changes to the League of Nations covenant demanded by his congressional opponents. As occurred with Durand, Grey's mission reinforced for Lindsay the important place of political in-fighting in foreign policy making, especially in the United States. He was made a CVO in December 1919.

Following four brief months as minister at Paris from August to December 1920, where he deputized for the ambassador, Lord Hardinge, Lindsay relocated to the Foreign Office as assistant under-secretary responsible for Near Eastern affairs. In this position he assisted the foreign secretary, Lord Curzon, in negotiating a new peace treaty with Turkey. The original agreement, the treaty of Sèvres, had collapsed as a result of the overthrow of the sultan by Mustafa Kemal and the outbreak of the Graeco-Turkish war. To preserve Britain's Near Eastern position, essential to India's defence, Curzon had to deal with France. In labyrinthine diplomacy marked by personal bitterness between Curzon and his French opposite number and a need to maintain an eastern Mediterranean balance, Lindsay proved an able deputy—his earlier time in Tehran and Cairo guiding his advice. The treaty of Lausanne (July 1923) marked a high point of Curzon's career; and in February 1924 he designated Lindsay his majesty's representative, with the rank of minister, in Turkey, a position converted into an ambassadorship in March 1925. Curzon wanted a diplomat in this important post who understood the Near East. Lindsay did not disappoint. Indeed, in 1925–6 he proved crucial in resolving a post-treaty territorial dispute over Mosul between Turkey and Britain's client, Iraq. Thanks to Lindsay's careful diplomacy Kemal relented, and renewed crisis in the Near East evaporated. Lindsay (who had been made a CB in June 1922) was appointed KCMG in January 1925, sworn of the privy council in July 1925, and promoted GCMG in June 1926. Meanwhile, his first wife having died in April 1918, on 14 July 1924 he married Elizabeth Sherman Hoyt, the daughter of Colgate Hoyt, of New York.

In October 1926 a new Conservative foreign secretary, Sir Austen Chamberlain, appointed Lindsay ambassador at Berlin. For nearly two years Lindsay played a central role in 'Locarno diplomacy', endeavouring to support Chamberlain's role as 'honest broker' between France and Germany, made difficult by German disfavour about reparations payments and protracted league disarmament talks. Burying his German animus Lindsay represented Chamberlain fairly and forthrightly; part of the credit for the improvement of Franco-German differences in this period goes to him. In July 1928 Chamberlain demonstrated his faith in Lindsay by appointing him permanent under-secretary, the civil service head of the Foreign Office. Lindsay's diplomatic skills and his administrative talents accounted for his selection. He continued to support the honest-broker approach to the continental balance; but when a Labour government took office in June 1929 his relationship with his new political masters quickly soured, chiefly over policy relating to European security.

In March 1930 Lindsay was relieved to be allowed to move to Washington as ambassador to the United States. He served there for almost ten years. He took the embassy at a high point in Anglo-American relations—naval differences were resolved; and war debts and reparations had ceased to be emotive. But the onset of the great depression played havoc with the international stability established by the late 1920s. As the war debts–reparations agreements splintered (Britain defaulted in 1934), as Japanese ambitions destroyed the naval agreements, and as Europe's horizons darkened through Adolf Hitler's rise to power and the crises in Abyssinia, Spain, Austria, and eastern Europe, Lindsay's diplomatic talents faced their greatest test. His earlier American experiences helped him after Franklin Roosevelt became president in March 1933.

Concerned more with domestic economic reconstruction than foreign policy until early 1939, Roosevelt genuflected to American isolationists to avoid confronting the dictators. Nevertheless Lindsay deftly kept Anglo-American relations on an even keel. In summer 1939 his efforts to foster closer relations were reinforced by a visit by George VI to the United States. Although Lindsay left Washington in August 1939, on the eve of the Second World War, the basis for trans-Atlantic co-operation thereafter remained in part his legacy. He was made GCB on retirement, having been made KCB in June 1929.

In many respects Lindsay was the last of what Hardinge called 'old' diplomats: schooled in the balance of power, supportive of military and economic power to underpin diplomatic strategy, and willing to use that power to protect and extend national and imperial interests. Moreover, he combined decided charm and grace with the sang-froid of *realpolitik*. Like others of his generation, he believed that Britain had no permanent friends or enemies, only permanent interests.

In retirement Lindsay lived at Stepleton House, Blandford, Dorset. He died at 14 West Cliff Road, Bournemouth, on 21 August 1945. His wife died two weeks later. There were no children of either marriage.

B. J. C. McKercher

Sources *DNB* • *WWW* • Burke, *Peerage* • *FO lists* (–1940) • PRO, FO series 371 • J. Jacobson, *Locarno diplomacy: Germany and the west, 1925–29* (1972) • B. J. C. McKercher, *Transition of power: Britain's loss of global pre-eminence to the United States, 1930–1945* (1999) • 'The permanent under-secretary of state: a brief history of the office and its holders', *History Notes*, 15 [forthcoming] • P. Kinross, *Atatürk: the birth of a nation* (1964) • *CGPLA Eng. & Wales* (1946)

Archives Bodl. Oxf., corresp. with Sir Horace Rumbold • CUL, corresp. with Lord Hardinge • Cumbria AS, Carlisle, letters to Lord Howard of Penrith • NA Scot., eleventh marquess of Lothian MSS • PRO, FO 371 | FILM BFI NFTVA, news footage

Likenesses W. Stoneman, photograph, 1925, NPG • W. Stoneman, photograph, 1936, NPG • J. S. Sargent, portrait, priv. coll.

Wealth at death £134,147 10s. 5d.: probate, 13 March 1946, *CGPLA Eng. & Wales*

Lindsay, (John) Seymour (1882–1966), designer and metalworker, was born in London on 16 May 1882, the fourth son and youngest surviving child of William Henry Lindsay, iron merchant and proprietor of Lindsay's Paddington ironworks, and his wife, Alice Charlotte Garman. His mother died in 1892, leaving Seymour and a brother to be brought up by a maiden Garman aunt in their father's house. Lindsay was educated at home, and early showed talent for drawing and painting, a characteristic he shared with many of his family. At the age of seventeen he was apprenticed to Leonard Ashford, designer and draughtsman, of 5 John Street, Adelphi, and later joined the firm of Higgins and Griffiths, electrical engineers, of 21 Orchard Street, London W1, as a designer of electrical fittings and lamps.

On the outbreak of war in 1914 Lindsay joined the London rifle brigade as a private and served in France. He was awarded the Distinguished Conduct Medal and promoted to officer rank in the field. He was wounded in September 1916, and invalided home. In 1915 he had married Mildred Ethel Williams (*d.* 1948), with whom he had one daughter.

After the war Lindsay rejoined Higgins and Griffiths, and extended his range of designs to gates, balustrades, and other ironwork. In the early 1930s he started his own business, employing a blacksmith in Suffolk. He did much work for the architects Sir Herbert Baker, Sir Edwin Lutyens, and Albert Richardson. This included, for Baker, ironwork in the Bank of England (1921–37), wrought-iron altar rails, vestry stairs balustrade, and lectern at the Church House chapel, Westminster (1937–40), and ironwork in branches of Barclays Bank throughout London; for Baker and Lutyens the designing of light fittings and ironwork in the government buildings in New Delhi; for Lutyens the gates for Roehampton Hospital, and the ironwork in the Midland Bank, Poultry, London (1929–37); and for Richardson, in London, the iron staircase and weathervane of Trinity House, Tower Hill, and the restoration of ironwork at St James's, Piccadilly, and St Alfege, Greenwich.

On his own account Lindsay made, for the chapel of St George and the English Martyrs in Westminster Cathedral, the bronze screen (designed by L. H. Shattock in 1930) which was erected only after the Second World War. In 1946 he designed the silver altar rails, and plate for the altar (a pair of candlesticks, a pair of candelabra, and a cross) of the Battle of Britain memorial chapel (dedicated in 1947) in Westminster Abbey, which were made by Garrards, and the wrought-iron lectern for the roll of honour.

During the Second World War Lindsay was appointed to the ancient monuments department (Ministry of Works) to advise on what ironwork should be preserved, and what melted for munitions. During this time and until his retirement in 1952, he made a comprehensive record of ironwork in and on public buildings and palaces, and ironwork of especial interest (National Monuments Record Centre, Swindon). On retirement he joined Messrs Grundy, Arnatt Ltd, metalworkers, who carried out his designs for numerous architects.

In 1914 Lindsay published in *The Architect* a series of articles, illustrated by himself, on domestic ironwork, which were a prelude to his later works, *Iron and Brass Implements of the English House* (1927, rev. 1964), and *An Anatomy of English Wrought Iron* (1964), both illustrated by himself. His skill as a draughtsman, able to suggest the substance and surface texture of metal, vied with a very considerable technical and historical knowledge of ancient and obsolete domestic implements and ironwork. Such knowledge led him to favour the historicist in his designs. Between 1914 and 1933 he gave, and occasionally sold, to the Victoria and Albert Museum items of domestic ironwork, pewter, glass, and paintings.

Lindsay joined the Art-Workers' Guild in 1930, was made a fellow of the Society of Antiquaries in 1942, and a fellow of the Royal Society of Arts in 1949. He was a perfectionist, sometimes irascibly so, a man of charm and modesty, of whom it might be said that collaboration was the thief of fame. He was scarcely ever seen without his huge-brimmed black felt artist's hat, and his recreations were, appropriately, sketching and painting in watercolour and oil. He was a member of the Langham sketching club. He was also a skilful maker of toys and models, and a collector of ancient domestic ironwork. Like so many ironwork designers and craftsmen of the past, anonymity bedevils a fair assessment of Seymour Lindsay's creative work. His contribution has been submerged beneath the reputations of his famous architectural patrons—Baker, Lutyens, and Richardson. Commentators on their architectural *œuvre* generally accept the metalwork as theirs, although it is likely that some, perhaps much, was designed by Lindsay. For example, the Lutyens house at Little Thakenham, Suffolk, has distinctive iron door-latches which are remarkably like those drawn by Lindsay in his *Anatomy of Wrought Iron* (figs. 80, 81); see *Lutyens*, the catalogue of the exhibition at the Hayward Gallery, London, 1981 (no. 134 and plate). Lindsay's published work concentrated on English domestic metalwork—especially brass and iron—of the seventeenth and eighteenth centuries, which were exactly the periods admired and evoked by his architectural patrons. Lindsay died at the Stud Farm, Sulhampstead Abbots, Berkshire, on 8 January 1966, and was survived by his widow Iris Elizabeth Godwyn, daughter of Alfred Bennett, whom he had married in 1959. MARIAN CAMPBELL

Sources H. Baker, *Architecture and personalities* (1944) • *London: except the cities of London and Westminster*, Pevsner (1952) • *London: the cities of London and Westminster*, Pevsner (1957) • private information (1981) • personal knowledge (2004) • *CGPLA Eng. & Wales* (1966) • *The Times* (11 Jan 1966)

Archives V&A, archives, nominal file

Wealth at death £989: administration, 7 April 1966, *CGPLA Eng. & Wales*

Lindsay, Thomas (1656–1724), Church of Ireland archbishop of Armagh, was born in Blandford Forum, Dorset, on 28 March 1656, the son of John Lindsey (*d.* 1680), Church of England clergyman, and Mary Clark (*c.*1616–1680). He came of Scottish stock; his father was a nephew of John Young, the former royal tutor brought to England by James VI and I to be dean of Winchester. Through his uncle's influence John Lindsey was installed in 1638 as vicar of Blandford Forum. On his mother's side Thomas was a second cousin of Francis Atterbury. He was educated at Blandford grammar school, where William Wake, a future archbishop of Canterbury, was among his schoolfellows. In 1673 he went up to Wadham College, Oxford, where he was made a fellow in 1679, dean in 1684, and bursar in 1689. According to an anonymous panegyrist he was 'eminent' in the university 'for strict discipline, singular attainment in oratory and theology, for a public spirit, and invincible firmness of mind' (Boyer, 28.103). Thomas Hearne, however, had a different memory of him: 'a man of good parts but little or no learning, spending his time in … tippling and (as some say) in wenching too' (*Remarks*, 1.187).

Although Lindsay acquired the rectory of Woolwich in Surrey in 1684, allegedly through the patronage of Bishop Sprat of Rochester, he did not make much of a name for himself as a preacher, publishing only one sermon, which had been delivered at a 'Dorsetshire feast' in London. Somehow he came to the notice of Henry, Lord Capell, whom he accompanied to Ireland in 1693 as a chaplain when Capell took up a place on the commission of lords justices in Dublin. Soon Capell was lord deputy and able to secure Lindsay's preferment, first to the deanery of St Patrick's, Dublin, and then, in 1695, to the bishopric of Killaloe. This was by no means a plum, since it was remote and relatively poor (conferring an income of less than £1000 p.a.). Lindsay worked hard for the material improvement of the diocese with a programme of rebuilding. Since, as even his fiercest critics accepted, he 'despised money' (BL, Add. MS 47087, fol. 57) much of this was happily paid for out of his own pocket. He also made his presence felt on the episcopal bench and in 1702 was dispatched to London by his colleagues, together with Bishop Ashe of Clogher, to solicit Queen Anne to remit to the Church of Ireland the produce of the first-fruits and tenths; he was also to pursue some legislative improvement to the clause in the English parliament's Forfeitures Resumption Act of 1700 that had reserved impropriate livings and tithes seized from rebels in Ireland to establish a fund for church building but which was hampered in its execution by the fact that the forfeitures were often encumbered with debt.

Despite his early attachment to Capell, which persuaded some commentators to believe that he had started his career as a whig, Lindsay's real political sympathies lay with tories and high-churchmen, as he soon showed in the Irish parliament through his resistance to statutory relief for protestant dissenters and open hostility towards the whig ministers who succeeded Capell. It may well be that on his visit to England he renewed contacts with English high-churchmen for on his return he began a correspondence with his cousin Atterbury. He was one of the keenest clerical agitators for the recall of the Irish convocation in 1704 and, once convocation met, took a prominent part in its proceedings. As early as the first session he was identified as one of the 'incendiaries of the upper house' (TCD, MS 668/1), leading the tory or high-church side in attacks on their whig or low-church opponents. He does not seem to have taken much interest in schemes for reform but threw himself wholeheartedly into personal quarrels and party political conflicts. In the House of Lords, too, he was one of the most aggressive and vociferous of tory partisans and effectively led the opposition in the Lords to the whig viceroyalty of Lord Wharton in 1709–10. He rejoiced in the ministerial revolution of 1710 which saw the return of the tory duke of Ormond to Dublin Castle. He was admitted to the inner counsels of the viceroy, and in both parliament and convocation threw his considerable political weight into the war against what he called 'the cant of moderation' (Lindsay to Arthur Charlett, 14 June 1711, MS Ballard 8, fol. 94). In 1712 he was appointed to the Irish privy council, where he vowed to exercise his 'zeal for [the queen's] and the church's service' (ibid., fol. 106, 10 May 1712), but despite his undoubted political value to the ministry and his many English connections, his promotion in the episcopate, when it came the following year, represented no very great advance. He was sent to the north-western diocese of Raphoe, which was as remote as Killaloe, little better endowed, and, what was worse, largely populated by Presbyterians. The very vehemence of his toryism had presumably worked against him.

It was only after the failure of the duke of Shrewsbury's viceroyalty in the autumn of 1713, with its ill-judged project of 'moderation', that Lindsay secured what he felt were his deserts, on his nomination to the vacant primatial see of Armagh in December 1713, partly through the influence of Swift, whose good offices he was quick to acknowledge. In this new capacity he was also named a lord justice in Shrewsbury's absence in February 1714. The death of Queen Anne the following July was thus a cruel blow. He immediately lost his position on the commission of lords justices and in the years to come was consistently ignored by government, not even consulted for form's sake on ecclesiastical promotions. Naturally he took up the cudgels of opposition in the Irish House of Lords, where he gained something of a reputation as a 'patriot' for his defence of Irish interests, in particular against the claim of the British House of Lords to exercise a superior appellate jurisdiction over Irish cases. In this new-found Irish patriotism there was at least an element of political opportunism. When it came to advancing the interests of the church through legislative action a certain lack of vitality was remarked on by his critics but he continued his impressive record as a diocesan; he was responsible for much repair and reconstruction in Armagh Cathedral and took a special interest in musical provision, donating a new organ and bells, and establishing a choir, partly at his own expense.

In 1720 Lindsay suffered a paralytic attack of such severity that his life was despaired of. Although he recovered his constitution was weakened, and after struggling with chronic ill health for some years he died on 13 July 1724. His funeral, at Christ Church in Dublin, was appropriately lavish. Swift was among the pallbearers. Lindsay never married and his will was notable for its charitable bequests, including £1000 to the 'oeconomy' of Armagh (Boyer, 28.105). His services to his party had moderated the asperity of Hearne's opinion, who, on hearing of his death, lamented him as 'an honest Tory bishop'. But perhaps the sharpest appreciation came from the first earl of Egmont: 'He was no scholar, but a man for business, was bold, had a working head, drank hard, and spoke well at the Council board and in the House of Lords' (BL, Add. MS 47025, fol. 118). D. W. Hayton

Sources *Walker rev.*, 130, 134 • R. Mant, *History of the Church of Ireland, from the revolution to the union* (1840) • R. B. Gardiner, ed., *The registers of Wadham College, Oxford*, 1 (1889), 296 • A. Boyer, *The political state of Great Britain*, 28 (1724), 103–5 • Bodl. Oxf., MS Ballard 8, fols. 61–118 • *The epistolary correspondence, visitation charges, speeches, and miscellanies of Francis Atterbury*, ed. J. Nichols, 5 vols. (1783–90), vol. 3, pp. 104–61 • papers, TCD, King MSS, MSS 750/1–8, 1995–2008; 2531–2537 • *Journals of the [Irish] House of Lords*, 5 vols. (1779–86), vols. 1–2 • journals of the upper house of the Irish convocation, 1704–11, PRO NIre., Armagh diocesan registry MSS, DIO/4/10/3/2–3 • BL, Blenheim MSS, Add. MSS 61633–61634 • BL, Egmont MSS, Add. MSS 47025, 47087 • *Remarks and collections of Thomas Hearne*, ed. C. E. Doble and others, 11 vols., OHS, 2, 7, 13, 34, 42–3, 48, 50, 65, 67, 72 (1885–1921), vol. 1, p. 187; vol. 2, p. 49 • J. Hutchins, *The history and antiquities of the county of Dorset*, 4 vols. (1861–74), 1.278
Archives BL, Portland MSS, Add. MS 70247 • Bodl. Oxf., Ballard MSS, 8

Lindsay, Thomas Martin (1843–1914), historian, the eldest son of Alexander Lindsay (1807/8–1864) and his wife, Susan Irvine Martin, was born on 18 October 1843 at Lesmahagow, Lanarkshire, where his father was minister of the Relief church. He was educated at the universities of Glasgow and Edinburgh; at the latter, which he entered in 1861, his brilliance in philosophy was rewarded by the Ferguson scholarship and the Shaw fellowship, both open to graduates of the Scottish universities. He became assistant to Professor Alexander Campbell Fraser, but abandoned the career of a university teacher to study for the ministry of the Free Church of Scotland. After completing his course at New College, Edinburgh, in 1869, he acted as assistant to R. S. Candlish, minister of St George's Free Church, Edinburgh.

In 1872 the general assembly of the Free Church of Scotland elected Lindsay to the chair of church history in its theological college at Glasgow; in 1902 he also became principal of the college. This appointment, which he held until his death, diverted his studies from philosophy to history, and his 1871 translation of Friedrich Ueberweg's *System der Logik* (1857), to which he appended some original dissertations, remained his only publication in philosophy. He was at once recognized as an able and inspiring teacher of church history, but his enthusiasm for social work, and especially for foreign missions, at first restricted his literary output, though he found time for wide and varied reading. He reorganized the administration of the important missions supported by the Free Church, acquiring a mastery of their complicated financial arrangements, and was convener of the foreign missions committee from 1886 to 1900. He visited the mission fields in Syria and spent a year in India. Apart from brief but well-constructed textbooks on the gospels of St Mark and St Luke, the Acts of the Apostles, and the Reformation, the literary fruits of his earlier professional years are to be found in articles (including 'Christianity') for the ninth edition of the *Encyclopaedia Britannica* (1875–88). The contributions of his friend William Robertson Smith to the *Encyclopaedia* led to the famous heresy prosecution, and in the courts of the Free Church Lindsay defended Smith with courage and ability from 1877 to 1881.

Lindsay's first historical work to attract widespread attention was his *Luther and the German Reformation*, published in 1900. It was followed by his remarkable chapter on Luther in the second volume of the *Cambridge Modern History* (1903) and, in 1906–7, by his largest and most important book, *A History of the Reformation in Europe* (2 vols.). He intended this work to be the description of 'a great religious movement amid its social environment', and he broke fresh ground in his investigations into popular and family religious life in Germany in the decades

Thomas Martin Lindsay (1843–1914), by Olive Edis, *c.*1910

immediately preceding the Reformation, and in his exposition of 'the continuity in the religious life of the period'. This insistence on the significance of the records of social and cultural life was Lindsay's characteristic approach to any period of history. That sensitivity was apparent too in his awareness that the Reformation was set in a framework of political, intellectual, and economic change from which it ought not to be divorced. His work on the Reformation remains one of the most substantial Scottish accounts, with six chapters devoted to the Counter-Reformation and two on Anabaptism and Socinianism.

While Lindsay is best remembered as a historian of the Reformation, the literary activity of his later life, when he published the reflections of many years of reading and study, is illustrated by his Cunningham lectures on *The Church and the Ministry in the Early Centuries* (1903), by his *Revivals* (1909), by chapters in the first volume (1911) of the *Cambridge Medieval History* and in the third volume (1909) of the *Cambridge History of English Literature*, and by his estimate of the personality and the achievement of George Buchanan in *Glasgow Quatercentenary Studies* (1906). These were marked by breadth of interest and sympathy, and clarity of exposition. He wrote vigorously and often picturesquely, and had a remarkable power of visualizing both individuals and events.

Throughout his life Lindsay was deeply interested in social problems. He organized the efforts of his students in poorly equipped Glasgow parishes, and he took part in the crofter agitation in the west highlands and islands; he was associated with the early political career of Joseph Chamberlain, and was the friend of such labour leaders as Ben Tillett, Tom Mann, and Cunninghame Graham. He married on 8 October 1872 Anna (1845–1903) [*see* Lindsay, Anna], elder daughter of Alexander Colquhoun Stirling Murray *Dunlop (1798–1870), of Edinbarnet and Corsock, and his wife, Eliza Esther Murray. The couple had three sons and two daughters; their eldest son, Alexander Dunlop *Lindsay, first Baron Lindsay of Birker, is separately noticed. Lindsay shared his wife's enthusiasm for the education of women. His advice was sought by many religious and social workers, who benefited from his sympathy and his robust, penetrating common sense. Lindsay was a DD of Glasgow University and LLD of St Andrews. He died in Glasgow on 6 December 1914.

R. S. Rait, *rev.* James Kirk

Sources *Glasgow Herald* (8 Dec 1914) • J. A. Lamb, ed., *The fasti of the United Free Church of Scotland, 1900–1929* (1956) • *Letters of principal T. M. Lindsay to Janet Ross* (1923) • W. Ewing, ed., *Annals of the Free Church of Scotland, 1843–1900*, 2 vols. (1914) • *Acts of the general assembly of the Free Church of Scotland*, 12 vols. (1852–1900) • R. Small, *History of the congregations of the United Presbyterian church from 1733 to 1900*, 2 vols. (1904) • *CCI* (1915)

Likenesses O. Edis, photograph, *c.*1910, NPG [*see illus.*] • O. Edis, photographs, 1914, NPG • photograph, repro. in *Glasgow Herald*

Wealth at death £2358 11*s.* 2*d.*: confirmation, 27 Jan 1915, *CCI*

Lindsay, Wallace Martin (1858–1937), classical scholar, was born at Pittenweem, Fife, on 12 February 1858, the fourth and youngest son of Alexander Lindsay, Free Church minister there, and his wife, Susan Irvine, *née* Martin, and brother of Thomas Martin *Lindsay (1843–1914). From Edinburgh Academy he entered Glasgow University as first bursar, aged sixteen. In 1877 he graduated with first-class honours in classics and second-class honours in philosophy and went, as Snell exhibitioner, to Balliol College, Oxford. There he obtained a first class in classical moderations (1878) and in *literae humaniores* (1881). He studied for a year in Germany at Leipzig University; on his return he was elected fellow of Jesus College, Oxford, and, after two years as assistant in humanity at Edinburgh University, in 1884 took up tutorial duty at Jesus, where he remained fifteen years. From 1899 he was professor of humanity at St Andrews University until his death.

His critical acumen and untiring industry made Lindsay one of the greatest of British Latinists; in philology and in palaeography he was the outstanding figure of his time, and his position was recognized by election to membership of learned societies in Europe and America. The most striking characteristic of his work was method. He was an accomplished literary scholar of elegance and taste, but, although he valued these things, he devoted his life to the austere work of scientific scholarship. He confined himself to the course which was marked out for him as one inquiry led to another as its preliminary or its complement, shirking no labour, however tedious, in the determination to make each step of his advance secure.

Lindsay's philological studies in Germany had brought him into contact with the new comparative methods, and the first task which he set himself was a scientific treatment of Latin philology. *The Latin Language* (1894) was immediately accepted as a standard work and established his reputation. He had broken new ground in using Celtic to illustrate Latin, and in order to find new early Irish material he made a search for glosses in the Latin manuscripts in Italian libraries. These researches led to two large undertakings, critical editions of Martial (1903) and Plautus (1904–5), and to several ancillary studies. Plautus involved the preparation of editions of the lexicographers Nonius (1902) and Festus (1912), and of Isidore's *Etymologiae* (1911).

Study of manuscripts had shown Lindsay that much detailed work in palaeography remained to be done, and in a series of monographs, culminating in *Notae Latinae* (1915), which collected the abbreviation-symbols of early Latin manuscripts, he continued the work of Traube and recorded the fruits of investigations in most of the continental libraries. Festus had suggested a new study, that of the medieval glossaries as a source for supplementing the text; pursuing this with characteristic thoroughness, he exposed the origin and nature of the glossaries and, with collaborators, produced the five volumes of *Glossaria Latina* (1926–32). In the midst of this vast labour he found time to return not only to the dramatists, producing *Early Latin Verse* (1922) and an edition of Terence (1926), but also to palaeography, conducting from 1922 to 1929 a new journal, *Palaeographia Latina* (6 vols.), mostly written by himself, and in 1928 becoming co-editor of the Italian *Monumenti Palaeografici Veronesi*, of which part 2 (1934) was almost wholly his work. He contributed a steady stream of articles and notes to British and foreign journals.

Lindsay was always ready to help an interested student, but, although he sometimes knew more about his pupils than they imagined, he had little patience with routine teaching, and university business did not appeal to him. He loved the countryside and in vacation, when not abroad, was always in the highlands, taking long walks on the hills. He knew his own abilities, but never paraded them; he made no pretence to omniscience and was generous in appreciation of others' work. He was witty and in his young days a lively companion; after he left Oxford deafness cut him off more and more from society and from the pleasures of golf and music, but he continued vigorous, gay, and debonair.

Lindsay was elected an honorary fellow of Jesus College, Oxford, in 1928, and a fellow of the British Academy in 1905. He received honorary degrees from Glasgow, Heidelberg, Dublin, and Groningen. Lindsay was unmarried, and lived at Sandyford, St Andrews, with his sister Elizabeth Lindsay. He died at St Andrews, following a road accident, on 21 February 1937.

C. J. Fordyce, *rev.* Roger T. Stearn

Sources *The Times* (22 Feb 1937) • H. J. Ross, 'Wallace Martin Lindsay, 1858–1937', *PBA*, 23 (1937), 487–512 • personal knowledge (1949) • *WWW*, 1929–40 • *CGPLA Eng. & Wales* (1937)

Archives BL, lectures on palaeography, Add. MS 38095 • Bodl. Oxf., corresp. and papers | BL, letters to J. P. Gilson, Add. MS 47686

Likenesses W. Stoneman, photograph, 1919, NPG

Wealth at death £1677 3*s.* 2*d.*: confirmation, 24 March 1937, *CCI*

Lindsay, Sir Walter, of Balgavie (*d.* 1605), Roman Catholic conspirator, was the third son of Sir David Lindsay of Edzell, afterwards ninth earl of Crawford (*d.* 1558), and his second wife, Katherine (*d.* 1578), daughter of Sir John Campbell of Lorn and Calder. Walter married Margaret, sister of David Campbell of Kethnott; they had a son, David, and a daughter, Margaret, who married Adam Menzies of Boltoquhan. Lindsay became a gentleman of the bedchamber to James VI in 1580 and together with other young men entered into an obligation to serve the king in time of war at his own expense. On 20 February 1584 he acquired the property of Balgavie, Forfarshire.

In 1583 Lindsay was regarded as an unconvinced protestant, and at some point before 1589 he became a Catholic under the influence of William Crichton and James Gordon, Jesuits working on the Scottish mission. Lindsay claimed that he was one of the first of their converts. He maintained John Ingram—an English Jesuit martyred at Newcastle upon Tyne on 25 July 1594—as his domestic chaplain, and his house became a centre of Catholic life, worship, and intrigue against the protestant party in the country. Lindsay boasted of influencing the earls of Huntly, Erroll, and Angus in their profession of Catholicism, and said that it was at his suggestion that they opened negotiations with Spain in an attempt to secure foreign intervention in Scotland and a possible invasion of England. In subsequent years his fortunes were to be tied to theirs.

In 1589 Lindsay was imprisoned in Edinburgh Castle, but was conditionally released on 29 November. Francis Stewart, first earl of Bothwell, stood caution for him in the sum of £1000 Scots, that he would on ten days' notice return to custody. At this time Lindsay was acting as an intermediary between the northern Catholic earls and the protestant Bothwell, enlisting his temporary support in their enterprise against the king. Lindsay failed to appear for his trial and on 19 May was proclaimed a rebel. On 11 January 1593 he was ordered to appear before the king on charges of acting against the religious polity of Scotland and in defiance of royal authority. King James marched against the northern earls and their supporters in February, but did not press matters to a conclusion. In May it was reported that Angus, Huntly, and Erroll were meeting in Lindsay's house and attending mass celebrated by an English priest. Lindsay was seen by the English ambassador in Scotland as the 'chief instrument and counsellor' of the earls (*CSP Scot.*, 1593–5, 419). After the excommunication and forfeiture of the Catholic earls, the king made an autumn march to the north. On 30 September 1594 Lindsay was denounced as a rebel for his association with the earls and for his religious dissent and in October his house was razed by the king's army.

The earls again declined to meet the king in the field and in March 1595 Huntly and Erroll agreed to go abroad.

Meanwhile Lindsay was understood to have gone to Rome, as an emissary of the Catholic party in Scotland, in search of a subsidy and military support. He was variously reported in different parts of Europe, including the Low Countries, and it was claimed in 1595 that he had been knighted by the king of Spain. In 1596 Spanish sources speak of Lindsay as being in Spain, negotiating with the government under the pseudonym of Don Balthasar. While abroad he composed his *Account of the present state of the Catholic religion in the realm of Scotland in the year of Our Lord one thousand five hundred and ninety-four*. It was published by Forbes-Leith in 1885.

Huntly and Erroll returned to Scotland in June 1596 and sought terms with the king and the kirk. In June 1597 they were formally reconciled with the reformed church and their forfeitures were revoked. A month later Lindsay too sought to return to Scotland, promising to reveal to the government various items of secret information relating to Spanish policies. On 27 November Sir Robert Cecil was asked for a passport for Lindsay to return home by way of England where, much to King James's displeasure, he was given a polite reception. On his return to Scotland, Lindsay agreed to a conference with the ministers of the kirk, and to remain within the presbytery of Brechin until he had satisfied them as to his orthodoxy. Alexander Lindsay, Lord Spynie, stood cautioner on 24 May 1599 that Lindsay would satisfy the kirk within forty days or else go into exile. There is no record of his submission, however. He may have been under the king's protection, since it was alleged that his contacts were used by James as a secret channel of communication with foreign powers. George Nicholson, the English agent in Scotland, certainly suspected James of double-dealing with Lindsay.

As late as 1601 Lindsay was described as 'deep in Papist courses' and of being privy to the earl of Tyrone's rebellion in Ireland (*CSP Scot.*, *1600–03*, 843). In the last years of his life he also maintained an aggressive local campaign of defence of the Lindsay interests. On 25 October 1605 he was murdered as he rode from Brechin to the Place of Edzell, by a small group of men led by David, master of Crawford and later twelfth earl. The master was a notoriously irresponsible and violent young man, as he showed on this occasion, he and his company giving Sir Walter 'ma nor twenty bludie woundis' and cutting his throat for good measure. He was denounced by the king's advocate as having 'consavit ane lurkand haitrent causeles' against his victim, to whom, indeed, he was 'particularie obleist for his grite kyndnes and beneficiall help … in his distres' (*Reg. PCS*, *1604–7*, 143–4). The ferocity of the crime may well have reflected the killer's personality, but it also had a wider context, that of the powerful tensions within the Lindsay kindred, and especially between the family of the earls of Crawford and the Lindsays of Edzell, arising from their competition for local power. Sir Walter was succeeded by his son David. ALLAN WHITE

Sources Lord Lindsay [A. W. C. Lindsay, earl of Crawford], *Lives of the Lindsays*, [new edn], 3 vols. (1849), vol. 1, pp. 312, 324, 327, 336, 429, 476; vol. 2, p. 280 • W. Lindsay, 'An account of the present state of the Catholic religion in the realm of Scotland, in the year of our lord 1594', *Narratives of Scottish Catholics under Mary Stuart and James VI*, ed. W. Forbes-Leith (1885), pp. 351–60 • *Scots peerage*, 3.28–9 • *Reg. PCS*, 1st ser., vol. 5, vol. 7 • J. M. Thomson and others, eds., *Registrum magni sigilli regum Scotorum / The register of the great seal of Scotland*, 11 vols. (1882–1914), vol. 4 • *CSP Scot.*, *1593–1603* • A. Jervise, *The history and traditions of the land of the Lindsays in Angus and Mearns with notices of Alyth and Meigle* (1853) • D. Calderwood, *The history of the Kirk of Scotland*, ed. T. Thomson and D. Laing, 8 vols., Wodrow Society, 7 (1842–9), vol. 5, p. 314 • R. Pitcairn, ed., *Ancient criminal trials in Scotland*, 3, Bannatyne Club, 42 (1833), 65, 248

Lindsay, Sir William, of the Byres (*d.* **1414**). *See under* Lindsay family of the Byres (*per.* 1367–1526).

Lindsay, William, eighteenth earl of Crawford and second earl of Lindsay (**1644–1698**), nobleman, was born in April 1644, the eldest surviving son of John *Lindsay, seventeenth earl of Crawford and first earl of Lindsay (1596–1678), and Lady Margaret, second daughter of James Hamilton, second marquess of Hamilton. William succeeded to the earldoms on the death of his father in 1678. Described by Burnet as 'passionate in his temper, and … out of measure zealous in his principles' (Burnet, 4.52), Crawford's inflexible presbyterian beliefs largely determined the course of his political career. In the years before the revolution of 1688 his religious nonconformity made him an obvious target for government persecution, and it would appear he had little choice but to live in profound retirement. His problems were compounded by his obvious financial difficulties, resulting from his father's extravagance, and through having made his non-entailed property responsible for payment of the former earl's debts. These circumstances were certainly instrumental in Crawford's decision to leave the country—even before the death of Charles II—although ultimately he could not obtain the requisite permission.

It is hardly surprising that Crawford took a more active role in politics and public life following the accession of William III. He was sworn of the privy council, and regularly attended both council and parliament from 1689, being employed in a number of different capacities. In March he subscribed both the act declaring the Convention a lawful meeting of the estates and the letter of congratulation to King William. The following month he was nominated a commissioner to treat for union with England, and appointed a member of the committee of estates. In June 1689 Crawford was named president of parliament, a position he held in the first four sessions of 1689–93. In a letter to Lord Melville on 22 July 1689 Sir William Lockhart claimed of Crawford 'he means well; but he is not capable to doe the Kings bussines' (Melville, 183). However, on 15 April 1690 he was appointed a commissioner of the treasury, and on 9 May one of the commissioners for settling the government of the church. Clearly this had serious repercussions for the episcopal clergy. Crawford himself affirmed that:

> no Episcopal since the late happy Revolution, whether laic or of the clergy, hath suffered by the council upon account of his opinion in church matters, but allenarly [solely] for their disowning the civil authority and setting up for a cross interest. (ibid., 376)

However, although he may have acknowledged the virtue

of moderation, his zeal against the episcopalians was unquestionably excessive. He has subsequently been described as providing 'the personification of official integrity whilst in fact erecting a screen behind which zealous Presbyterians, with his connivance and even active co-operation, purged the Scottish Church' (Riley, 36). But these measures must be moderated by some appreciation of the extremities inflicted on Crawford and his allies by the episcopalians after the Restoration.

Lindsay had married first, on 8 March 1670 at Leith, Lady Mary (1652–1681), daughter of James Johnstone, earl of Annandale and Hartfell, who died in April 1681. They had three sons—John, nineteenth earl of Crawford, Colonel James, who was killed in 1707 at the battle of Almanza in Spain, and Patrick, baptized at Ceres in July 1677—and two daughters—Henrietta and Margaret. He married, second, Lady Henrietta, daughter of Charles Seton, earl of Dunfermline, and widow of William Fleming, earl of Wigtown. They had a son, Thomas, and six daughters—Anne, Christian, Margaret, Helen, Susanna, and Catherine. Crawford died on 6 March 1698, his testament being confirmed at St Andrews in September.

T. F. Henderson, *rev.* Derek John Patrick

Sources *Scots peerage* • Lord Lindsay [A. W. C. Lindsay, earl of Crawford], *Lives of the Lindsays*, [new edn], 3 vols. (1849) • *APS*, *1689–1701* • *Reg. PCS*, 3rd ser., vol. 13 • W. H. L. Melville, ed., *Leven and Melville papers: letters and state papers chiefly addressed to George, earl of Melville … 1689–1691*, Bannatyne Club, 77 (1843) • Anderson, *Scot. nat.* • *Bishop Burnet's History* • P. W. J. Riley, *King William and the Scottish politicians* (1979) • GEC, *Peerage*

Archives NRA, priv. coll., financial papers | NA Scot., corresp. with Lord Melville • NRA, priv. coll., corresp. and papers

Lindsay, William (1802–1866), minister of the United Presbyterian church, was born in Irvine, Ayrshire. He studied at Glasgow University and attended the Relief Theological Hall in Paisley from its opening in 1824, before he was ordained minister of the new East Church, Johnstone, Renfrewshire, on 27 April 1830. He was translated to Dovehill Relief Church, Glasgow, on 22 November 1832, where he served as colleague and successor to John Barr (*d.* 1839), though he was effectively in sole charge from the outset due to Barr's incapacity. At the Relief Synod of 1841 Lindsay was appointed to his church's chair of exegetical theology and biblical criticism. He was honoured with the degree of DD from Glasgow University in 1844 and in December of that year he transferred, with his congregation, to a new building in Cathedral Street, Glasgow. Though seldom prominent in public matters, Lindsay delivered a memorable address at the union of the Relief and United Secession churches in 1847. He became professor of biblical criticism and sacred languages in the new denomination, his duties overlapping with those of John Eadie. After the death of John Brown in 1858 Lindsay held the chair of exegetical theology.

A contemporary described Lindsay as 'about the middle size and habit. His countenance is fresh and ruddy, and indicates placidity, benevolence and kindness. His small, dark eyes look from beneath a prominent brow, surmounted by a plentiful supply of greyish hair' (Smith, 111). By nature he was sensitive and retiring, living very much in his study. As a professor he was popular, esteemed for his exemplary character and soundness rather than for any brilliance. As a preacher, his sermons were edifying without ever attracting crowds. He published a number of works, including a life of Thomas Gillespie and a small volume on relationships which bar marriage. His most substantial work, *Lectures on the Epistle to the Hebrews* (1867), was edited by George Brooks, in two volumes, after his death.

Lindsay appeared to be in normal health, and had preached twice earlier in the day, when he collapsed and died of heart disease at his home, 33 Monteith Row, Glasgow, on 3 June 1866. He was buried in a family grave at Irvine on 7 June.

Lionel Alexander Ritchie

Sources *Glasgow Herald* (6 June 1866) • 'The late Dr Lindsay and his lectures', *United Presbyterian Magazine*, new ser., 11 (1867), 351–6 • W. Mackelvie, *Annals and statistics of the United Presbyterian church*, ed. W. Blair and D. Young (1873), 298 • R. Small, *History of the congregations of the United Presbyterian church from 1733 to 1900*, 2 (1904), 34–5, 537 • J. Smith, *Our Scottish clergy*, 1st ser. (1848), 108–12 • *DSCHT* • private information (1892) • *DNB* • wills, 9 July 1866, NA Scot., SC 36/51/50, 327–9

Wealth at death £2994 3*s.* 8*d.*: inventory, 9 July 1866, NA Scot., SC 36/48/55/740

Lindsay, William Lauder (1829–1880), physician and botanist, was born on 19 December 1829 in Edinburgh, the eldest son of James Lindsay of the sasine office, General Register House, Edinburgh, and his wife, Helen, daughter of Captain Lauder. He was educated at the Royal High School, Edinburgh, where he was dux in 1844 and 1845. He then entered the University of Edinburgh, where he studied medicine. His interest in botany was fostered by John Hutton Balfour (1808–1884), who suggested he study lichens, then greatly neglected. Although he worked as a clerk in the register house during the whole of his medical course, Lindsay obtained several university prizes, including the medal and first prizes in botany, and on graduating MD in 1852 he obtained the highest honours (three stars) for his thesis, 'Anatomy, morphology, and physiology of the lichens'.

In 1854, after serving for a year as resident physician of the City Cholera Hospital, Edinburgh, and subsequently as assistant physician in the Crichton Royal Institution, Dumfries, Lindsay was appointed medical officer to Murray's Royal Institution for the Insane at Perth. There he combined geological with botanical researches, but continued to specialize in lichens, publishing, in 1856, *A Popular History of British Lichens*. The work contained numerous coloured plates, and was a readable and stimulating account of lichens, which did much to popularize the subject. For his work in this department of botany he received in 1859 the first Neill gold medal from the Royal Society of Edinburgh. In the same year, he had married, on 26 April, Elizabeth, the only daughter of William Paterson Reid, solicitor, of Demerara. They had at least one daughter.

In 1861–2 Lindsay visited the Otago province, New Zealand, making many observations on the botany and geology of the region, collecting specimens, and later publishing many papers on his work there. He received from the

New Zealand Exhibition of 1865 a silver medal in recognition of his botanical researches, which were published in 1868 as *Contributions to New Zealand Botany*. He also travelled to north Germany, Norway, and Iceland and published on the flora of those countries. In 1870 he published his important *Memoir on the Spermogones and Pycnides of Lichens*, to which is appended a list of his thirty-three contributions to lichenology, which appeared either in the *Journal of Microscopical Science* or in the transactions of the Linnean and Royal (Edinburgh) societies. Lindsay studied chemical variation in lichens and pioneered new areas of study, including the diversity of lichenicolous fungi, and conidiomata in lichens. He published profusely, illustrating his monographs and papers with his own fine anatomical drawings.

Besides these botanical papers Lindsay published many pamphlets on mental disease and other medical subjects, on education, and on the place of natural history in colonization. His last work, *Mind in the Lower Animals in Health and Disease* (1879), which aimed at showing the similarity of mental processes in man and the lower animals, broke new ground. Lindsay was a great and omnivorous reader, and a most energetic worker. He died at his home, 3 Hartington Gardens, Edinburgh, on 24 November 1880. He is commemorated by the fungal genus *Lauder lindsaya*.

THOMAS SECCOMBE, *rev.* D. J. GALLOWAY

Sources D. L. Hawksworth and M. R. D. Seaward, *Lichenology in the British Isles, 1568–1975* (1977) · *Transactions of the Botanical Society* [Edinburgh], 14 (1883), 163–4 · *Gardeners' Chronicle*, new ser., 14 (1880), 734 · *The Lancet* (4 Dec 1880), 916 · *Proceedings of the Linnean Society of London* (1880–82), 18–19 · *Nature*, 23 (1880–81), 131 · F. A. Stafleu and R. S. Cowan, *Taxonomic literature: a selective guide*, 2nd edn, 3, Regnum Vegetabile, 105 (1981) · D. L. Hawksworth, P. M. Kirk, B. C. Sutton, and D. A. Pegler, *Ainsworth and Bisby's dictionary of the fungi*, 8th edn (1995)

Archives NHM, lichen collections in lichen herbarium · Royal Botanic Garden, Edinburgh, lichen herbarium · Royal Botanic Garden, Edinburgh · University of Helsinki, Nylander herbarium | U. Newcastle, Robinson L., letters to Sir Walter Trevelyan

Likenesses photograph, repro. in Hawksworth and Seaward, *Lichenology in the British Isles*

Lindsay, William Schaw (1816–1877), shipowner and politician, was born at Ayr. His family details are sketchy, but he was probably the third son of Joseph Lindsay, and his mother's maiden name was Schaw. His will names two sisters, one of whom was married to the prominent United Presbyterian clergyman, John McKerrow. Orphaned early in life Lindsay came under the guardianship of his uncle, William Schaw (*d.* 1847), of Ayr, a minister of the Secession church. After early schooling, at the age of fifteen he ran off to Liverpool, determined to pursue life as a seafarer. After some weeks of destitution he secured a berth as a cabin-boy in the *Isabella*, a West Indiaman, and after three years he became second mate. Shortly afterwards he was shipwrecked, in the course of which he broke both legs and an arm. He recovered to become the chief mate of the *Olive Branch*, owned by a Mr Greenwell of Sunderland, and a year later he was master, at the age of twenty. In 1839 he received a sabre wound from a pirate, whom he then shot dead, in the Persian Gulf.

In 1840 Lindsay left the sea and Greenwell secured his appointment as fitter for the Castle Eden Coal Company at Hartlepool—the beginning of Lindsay's career in business. In 1842 he married Helen Stewart of Glasgow; the couple had at least one son. Through his wife Lindsay became connected to the family firm of iron-founders, and when he went to London in 1845 he acted as agent for his brother-in-law, in addition to his coal-fitting and shipbroking activities. W. S. Lindsay & Co., of Austin Friars, in the City of London, rapidly became one of the largest shipowners in the world with, at one stage, 220 vessels in its fleet. The Crimean War offered Lindsay the opportunity to charter steamers to the French government on particularly remunerative terms.

Lindsay also pursued parliamentary ambitions and, after unsuccessful attempts at Monmouth and Dartmouth in 1852, he was returned as MP for Tynemouth and South Shields in March 1854. At the general election of 1859 he withdrew from the contest in this constituency and was returned instead for Sunderland. As an MP he championed the shipping interest, naturally enough, and took an interest in naval as well as commercial matters. He took an active part in the Administrative Reform Association. However, his support for the Confederate states in the American Civil War, together with other maverick tendencies, caused some consternation among his supporters.

Lindsay's political and business careers ended in 1864 when he lost the use of his legs. Retiring to the seclusion of his home, Shepperton Manor, Shepperton, Middlesex, he turned his energy to writing. He had already published various pamphlets, as well as more substantial works such as *Our Navigation and Mercantile Marine Laws* (1853) and *Our Merchant Shipping* (1860). He fictionalized many of his experiences for the anonymously published *Log of my Leisure Hours* and the unfinished *Recollections of a Sailor*. However, his monument as a writer is his authoritative four-volume *History of Merchant Shipping and Ancient Commerce* (1874–6). He died at Shepperton Manor on 28 August 1877, and was survived by his wife.

Lindsay's energy and driven personality were evident in all that he undertook. His remarkable career took him from cabin-boy to MP, by way of merchant prince, and when he was incapacitated he was still only in the prime of life. That he provoked strong feelings was inevitable, but the combination of admiration and unease he aroused was best expressed by another shipowner, Alfred Holt, who wrote of him as being 'a strange mixture of energy, industry, self-reliance, egotism and pretence' (Jones, 2.132).

GORDON GOODWIN, *rev.* LIONEL ALEXANDER RITCHIE

Sources W. Brockie, *Sunderland notables: natives, residents, and visitors* (1894) · *Sunderland Times* (31 Aug 1877), 6 · *The Times* (30 Aug 1877) · *Glasgow Herald* (29 Aug 1877), 5 · *Shipping and Mercantile Gazette* (30 Aug 1877) · Boase, *Mod. Eng. biog.* · C. W. Jones, *Pioneer shipowners*, 2 [1938], 132 · W. Mackelvie, *Annals and statistics of the United Presbyterian church*, ed. W. Blair and D. Young (1873), 407 [William Schaw] · *WWBMP* · d. cert. · *CGPLA Eng. & Wales* (1877)

Archives NMM, papers | BL, corresp. with Sir A. H. Layard, Add. MSS 38988, 39101–39118 · Bodl. Oxf., letters to Disraeli · PRO,

corresp. with Lord John Russell, PRO 30/22 • William Patrick Library, Kirkintilloch, letters to Peter Mackenzie
Wealth at death under £45,000: probate, 29 Sept 1877, *CGPLA Eng. & Wales*

Lindsell, Augustine (*d.* 1634), bishop of Hereford, was born at Steeple Bumpstead, Essex. On 14 April 1592 he was admitted a pensioner of Emmanuel College, Cambridge, but it was from Clare College that he graduated BA in 1596 and proceeded MA in 1599, and where he became a fellow. An Oxford MA by incorporation was bestowed upon him in July 1614. He was instituted rector of Molesworth, Huntingdonshire, in 1606, rector of Wickford, Essex, in March 1610, and granted a prebend of Lincoln Cathedral by Bishop William Barlow in November 1612, a position that he held until 1624. On the appointment of Bishop Richard Neile to Lincoln in 1614, Lindsell acquired a more powerful patron. He followed Neile to Durham and in March 1619 was collated to the tenth stall of that cathedral, which he resigned for the second stall in August 1620. He proceeded DD in 1621 and became a firm—and resident—member of the 'Durham House group' located at Neile's diocesan house in the Strand, London. Close friends with other intellectuals of the group like John Cosin and Richard Mountague, Lindsell was one of Neile's chaplains closely involved in the publication of Mountague's controversial *A New Gagg for an Old Goose* in 1624. He was strongly associated with the ceremonial changes for which Durham Cathedral became infamous in parliamentary circles in 1628–9, when Peter Smart described him as 'the oracle of our Arminian sectaryes' (*Correspondence of John Cosin*, 175).

Lindsell was an unsuccessful candidate for the regius professorship of Greek at Cambridge, vacant by the death of Andrew Downes in 1627, but his clerical career was enhanced when he was installed dean of Lichfield on 15 October 1628. His relatively high profile at Durham ensured that he came under attack when Peter Smart's allegations about ceremonial changes became public, and Neile and William Laud had to intervene to protect Lindsell and Cosin when Durham was presided over by a less sympathetic Bishop John Howson after 1628 [*see* Durham House group]. Fortunately for Lindsell, Neile and Laud quite clearly had the ear of King Charles by this date. On 10 February 1633 Lindsell was consecrated bishop of Peterborough (to which was attached the rectory of Castor, Northamptonshire), where he sought to effect greater respect for baptism, greater conformity to the rites of the Book of Common Prayer, and to suppress nonconformist lecturers. His articles of visitation which survive for 1633 were firmly based on a set devised for Norwich diocese in 1619 by the prominent proto-Arminian Bishop John Overall, and he believed in them so firmly that he applied the same set when he was translated to Hereford in March 1634. According to William Prynne, Lindsell was:

> an earnest promoter of the book of pastimes on the Lord's day, a great champion for the Arminians, and all the late innovations in doctrine, ceremony or worship introduced among us, a bitter enemy to preaching, lecturers, lectures and godly people. (Prynne, chapter 6)

The health of Lindsell, a leading intellectual of the Arminian party, had often been a cause of concern to his friends. If Prynne is to be believed, however, Lindsell died quite suddenly on 6 November 1634 as a result of the stress induced by quarrels with the dean and chapter of Hereford over the position of the altar. He died unmarried and was buried in Hereford Cathedral. In his will he bequeathed Greek books and manuscripts to Clare College; to Sir Robert Cotton he gave a manuscript history in Latin of Ely Cathedral. To his old patron Richard Neile he gave books, and in recognition of the part played by Neile's family in his life he gave Richard's wife, Dorothy, a piece of plate, and his son Paul a copy of John Speed's *Chronicles*. Laud was also a beneficiary of books from a library which was said at the time to have been worth about £800—a rather significant collection. Other gifts went to Sir William Paddy, fellow Durham clergyman Daniel Birkhead, the civil lawyer Edward Lively, and his old pupil from Clare, Nicholas Ferrar. Apart from visitation articles produced for both of his dioceses, together with a set for Hereford Cathedral, Lindsell worked on an edition of Theophylact's commentaries on the epistles of St Paul, which was published by his associate in the work, Dr Thomas Baily, subdean of Wells, in 1636; it was aptly dedicated to William Laud. Together with Giles Thompson, Lindsell is one of only two bishops of the period 1559–1660 who does not appear to have been granted a coat of arms.

ANDREW FOSTER

Sources W. Prynne, *The antipathie of the English lordly prelacie*, 2 vols. (1641), vol. 2 • P. Heylyn, *Cyprianus Anglicus* (1668) • N. Tyacke, *Anti-Calvinists: the rise of English Arminianism, c.1590–1640* (1987) • K. Fincham, *Prelate as pastor: the episcopate of James I* (1990) • K. Fincham, ed., *Visitation articles and injunctions of the early Stuart church*, 2 (1998) • J. Davies, *The Caroline captivity of the church: Charles I and the remoulding of Anglicanism, 1625–1641* (1992) • A. Milton, *Catholic and Reformed: the Roman and protestant churches in English protestant thought, 1600–1640* (1995) • J. Fielding, 'Arminianism in the localities: Peterborough diocese, 1603–1642', *The early Stuart church, 1603–1642*, ed. K. Fincham (1993), 93–113 • *The correspondence of John Cosin D.D., lord bishop of Durham*, ed. [G. Ornsby], 1, SurtS, 52 (1869) • D. Pearson, 'The libraries of English bishops, 1600–40', *The Library*, 6th ser., 14 (1992), 221–57, esp. 246–7 • Venn, *Alum. Cant.*

Lindsell, Sir Wilfrid Gordon (1884–1973), army officer, was born at Portsmouth on 29 September 1884, the younger son and second child in the family of two sons and three daughters of Colonel Robert Frederick Lindsell (1856–1914) of the Gloucester regiment, from Holme, Biggleswade, and his wife, Kathleen, daughter of Richard Eaton, advocate, of Mitchelstown, Ireland. Educated at Birkenhead School, Victoria College in Jersey, and the Royal Military Academy, Woolwich, Lindsell showed from an early age an unusual capacity for wrestling problems through to a logical conclusion which was to stand him in good stead later in his chosen career. He was commissioned into the Royal Garrison Artillery in 1903.

After gunnery school at Shoeburyness, Lindsell went to Malta in the garrison regiment. There his administrative talents were noted by Major-General Sir Harry Barron, who on appointment as governor-general of Tasmania in 1909 took Lindsell with him as aide-de-camp. Four years later when Barron became governor of Western Australia, Lindsell accompanied him in the same capacity.

In 1914 Lindsell returned to England and became aide-de-camp to the general officer commanding, 7th division, with whom he went to France with the British expeditionary force (BEF). A succession of wartime regimental and staff appointments followed, notably with 8th corps and the French cavalry corps. The armistice found Lindsell as a major, his having been awarded the MC in 1916 and the Croix de Guerre (1918), and appointed to the DSO in 1918; in addition he had been mentioned in dispatches four times and was to become an OBE in 1919. In 1916 he had married Marjorie Ellis (*d.* 1957) (OBE 1946), daughter of Admiral Swinton Colthurst Holland, of Langley House, Chichester; they had a son, who died in infancy, and two daughters.

Lindsell was selected to attend the first post-war course at Staff College, Camberley. In 1920 he was appointed to the adjutant-general's staff at the War Office and from 1921 to 1923 he was instructor at the school of military administration. Here he began to realize his true métier and produced the first edition of *Military Organization and Administration* (1923), which was to prove a fund of knowledge for successive generations of officers in passing their promotion examinations and studying for the Staff College. By 1944, when the twenty-sixth edition had gone out of print, this work had become a standard military publication; when rewritten it was renamed *Lindsell's Military Organization and Administration* (1948).

Lindsell was instructor at the Staff College from 1925 to 1928, becoming brevet lieutenant-colonel in 1927. During his service in the War Office (1930–33) he became colonel (1931) and attended one of the early courses at the newly established Institute of Defence Studies. A brigadier in 1937, he was appointed major-general in charge of administration in southern command in 1938.

On the outbreak of the Second World War, as temporary lieutenant-general Lindsell was appointed quartermaster-general of the BEF. After being evacuated from Dunkirk he returned to England to help reconstruct the British army. Establishing his headquarters at Kneller Hall, Twickenham, he set about his task with vigour. After a year's work he was selected by H. D. R. Margesson the secretary of state for war, for secondment to the Ministry of Supply under Sir Andrew Duncan and Lord Beaverbrook. His post was that of senior military adviser for the re-equipment of the army. He performed his task with such marked success that less than a year afterwards Britain had thirteen fully trained and equipped divisions in readiness to defend the country against a German invasion. In 1942 Lindsell was appointed lieutenant-general in charge of administration in the middle east, as one of General Montgomery's team to revitalize the Eighth Army.

Following the successful desert campaign, Lindsell was selected in 1943 to be principal administration officer to the Fourteenth Army in India in preparation for the attack against the Japanese in Burma led by General W. J. Slim. In 1945 Lindsell, or Tommy, as he was affectionately known, returned to England for attachment to the Board of Trade to co-ordinate the clearing of factories used for wartime storage, so that peacetime production could begin.

Lindsell finally retired from the active list in December 1945, after which he lived at The Haymersh, Britford, Salisbury, Wiltshire. He was governor and commandant of the Church Lads' Brigade (1948–54) and also a church commissioner (1948–59). From 1946 to 1955 he was chairman of the board of Ely Breweries (later Watney Mann), and was active in the affairs of the Royal Artillery Institution, for whose journal he wrote a series of articles on his wartime experiences entitled 'Reminiscences on four fronts'.

Lindsell was appointed KBE (1940), CB (1942), KCB (1943), and GBE (1946). The Second World War also brought him the US Legion of Merit (degree of commander) and three mentions in dispatches. He was made an honorary LLD by Aberdeen University.

The death of his first wife in 1957 marked the beginning of Lindsell's gradual withdrawal from public life. In 1958 he married, secondly, Evelyn Nairn, daughter of Gamaliel Henry Butler, of Hobart, Tasmania, formerly premier of Tasmania. In 1970 he moved to Flat 6, 169 Queen's Gate, London, where he died on 2 May 1973. His wife returned to her native Tasmania, where she died in 1982.

RICHARD WORSLEY, *rev.*

Sources *The Times* (3 May 1973) · private information (1986) · *WWW* · *CGPLA Eng. & Wales* (1973) · *Gunner*, 32 (July 1973)

Archives King's Lond., Liddell Hart C., corresp. and papers | IWM, corresp. with Sir Thomas Riddell-Webster

Wealth at death £60,484: probate, 2 July 1973, *CGPLA Eng. & Wales*

Lindsey. For this title name *see* Bertie, Robert, first earl of Lindsey (1582–1642); Bertie, Montague, second earl of Lindsey (1607/8–1666).

Lindsey, Theophilus (1723–1808), Unitarian minister and theologian, was born at Middlewich, Cheshire, on 20 June 1723, the youngest son of Robert Lindsey (*d.* 1742) and his second wife (*d.* 1747). His father was a mercer who also had interests in the salt trade. His mother, whose maiden name was Spencer, had resided for many years with Frances, countess of Huntingdon, whose son, Theophilus, earl of Huntingdon, was the boy's godfather.

Lindsey was educated at Middlewich grammar school and at the free grammar school at Leeds, under its celebrated headmaster Thomas Barnard. In 1741 he matriculated at St John's College, Cambridge, and after graduating BA in 1744 was in 1747 elected a fellow of his college. He was ordained deacon in 1746 and priest a year later. He was then presented to a chapel in Spital Square, London on the recommendation of Lady Ann Hastings, who, like her sister, Lady Betty Hastings, had from his earliest years shown him many kindnesses, as did their niece by marriage, the evangelical countess of Huntingdon. Shortly afterwards he became domestic chaplain to Algernon Seymour, seventh duke of Somerset, and after the duke's death in 1750 became tutor to his grandson, Hugh Smithson, afterwards second duke of Northumberland. He accompanied his pupil on a continental tour between 1751 and 1753. On relinquishing this post in the latter year he was presented by the earl of Northumberland (subsequently the first duke) to the valuable rectory of Kirby Wiske, Yorkshire, but he resigned this living in 1756 for that of Piddletown, Dorset, which was in the gift of the earl of Huntingdon.

On 29 September 1760 Lindsey married Hannah Elsworth (1740–1812), the stepdaughter of his friend Archdeacon Francis *Blackburne, and soon afterwards adopted Blackburne's latitudinarian views on subscription to the Thirty-Nine Articles. He declined in 1762 the offer of the chaplaincy made by the duke of Northumberland when appointed lord lieutenant of Ireland. In 1763 he left Piddletown for the rectory of Catterick in Yorkshire, which though of less value enabled him to see more of Archdeacon Blackburne and other friends. In the controversy that arose on the publication of Blackburne's *The Confessional* in 1766, Lindsey strongly supported the latitudinarians and advocated a relaxation of the system of clerical subscription to the Thirty-Nine Articles. His own views had become Unitarian, and he helped to organize the Feathers tavern petition in 1771–2, signed by over 200 persons, which was designed to change the laws on subscription. On the rejection of the petition by the House of Commons (6 February 1772) he resigned his living, and on 28 November 1773 he preached his farewell sermon at Catterick. Lindsey had generously assisted his poor parishioners, and he was obliged to sell his plate and part of his library to maintain himself after leaving his rectory.

Lindsey and his wife arrived in London in the spring of 1774, and with the help of Joseph Priestley, Richard Price, and other prominent Unitarian friends a room was engaged in Essex House, Essex Street, which was fitted as a temporary chapel and opened for public worship in April of that year. He published for his congregation *A Liturgy, Altered from that of the Church of England, to Suit Unitarian Doctrine*, which he amended in later editions. His friends built a chapel for him in Essex Street, which opened on 29 March 1778, and this became the first Unitarian congregation.

Meanwhile Lindsey had issued an *Apology* (1774), giving his reasons for leaving the Church of England, and a history of the doctrine of the Trinity and Unitarianism. It reached a fourth edition by 1775, arousing both hostile and friendly criticism, to which he replied in the preface to his next work, *A Sequel to the 'Apology'* (1776), which was the most elaborate, and in many respects the most valuable, of his contributions to dogmatic theology. Lindsey's Unitarianism was firmly Socinian, involving belief in the divine unity, and the humanity of Christ, together with a denial of Christ's pre-existence and atonement.

Early in 1783 it was arranged that John Disney, who, like Lindsey, had seceded from the Church of England, and had married Mrs Lindsey's stepsister, should serve as Lindsey's colleague at Essex Street Chapel. He was thus enabled to devote more time to theological writing and to campaigning for dissenting civil liberties. He reported on the moves for the repeal of the Test and Corporation Acts in 1787–90 and organized an unsuccessful petition for the legal toleration of Unitarian worship in 1792. Lindsey was at first a reluctant dissenter: he had hoped to reform the Church of England from within. But subsequently his associates were drawn increasingly from the nonconformist sects. His closest colleague and friend was Priestley, whom he defended in *Vindiciae Priestleyanae, addressed to the students of Oxford and Cambridge, by a late member of the University of Cambridge* (1784); a second part appeared in 1790. In another work, *Conversations on Christian Idolatry*, issued in the following year, he once more vindicated his theological views.

In July 1793 Lindsey retired from his ministry at Essex Street, although he continued to reside in the minister's house. He responded to the Priestley riots and the travails of Unitarians in the wake of the French Revolution by reprinting Joseph Priestley's *Reply to Paine's 'Age of Reason'*, with a preface of his own. In 1802 he published *Conversations on the Divine Government*. In 1800 he inherited considerable property from a member of his congregation, Elizabeth Rayner, and his last years were spent in comparative affluence. He died at his house in Essex Street on 3 November 1808, and was buried in the cemetery at Bunhill Fields, London, on 11 November.

Lindsey published many occasional sermons and pamphlets. A collection of his sermons, in two volumes, appeared in 1810. He was also a voluminous letter writer, and his correspondence is a valuable source of information for the religious history of the period.

ALBERT NICHOLSON, *rev.* G. M. DITCHFIELD

Sources T. Belsham, *Memoirs of the late Reverend Theophilus Lindsey*, new edn (1873) • H. McLachlan, *Letters of Theophilus Lindsey* (1920) • H. McLachlan, 'More letters of Theophilus Lindsey', *Transactions of the Unitarian Historical Society*, 3/4 (1923–6), 361–77 • G. M. Ditchfield, *Theophilus Lindsey (1723–1808): from Anglican to Unitarian* (1998) • W. Turner, *Lives of eminent Unitarians*, 2 (1843), 25–81 • *Life and correspondence of Joseph Priestley*, ed. J. T. Rutt, 2 vols. (1831–2) • G. M. Ditchfield, 'Some aspects of Unitarianism and radicalism, 1760–1810', PhD diss., U. Cam., 1968 • G. M. Ditchfield, 'Anti-trinitarianism and toleration in late eighteenth century British politics: the Unitarian petition of 1792', *Journal of Ecclesiastical History*, 42 (1991), 39–67 • R. Aspland, *A sermon … on the occasion of the death of the Rev. Theophilus Lindsey* (1808) • G. M. Ditchfield, 'The Lindsey–Wyvill correspondence', *Transactions of the Unitarian Historical Society*, 20 (1991–4), 161–76 • R. F. Scott, ed., *Admissions to the College of St John the Evangelist in the University of Cambridge*, 3: *July 1715 – November 1767* (1903), 101, 516–18 • *Report on the manuscripts of the late Reginald Rawdon Hastings*, 4 vols., HMC, 78 (1928–47), vol. 3, pp. 70–77, 93–5, 98–9, 104–6, 111–14, 117–18, 149–50 • J. McLachlan, 'The Scott collection: letters of Theophilus Lindsey and others to Russell Scott', *Transactions of the Unitarian Historical Society*, 19/2 (1987–90), 113–29 • will, PRO, PROB 11/1488, fol. 213 • will, PRO, PROB 11/1529 [Hannah Lindsey], fols. 235–6

Archives DWL, corresp. and papers • Harris Man. Oxf., sermons • Hunt. L., letters • Literary and Philosophical Society of Newcastle upon Tyne, letters to William Turner | CUL, William Trad MSS • Drew University, Madison, New Jersey, countess of Huntingdon MSS • DWL, letters to William Turner • JRL, corresp. with William Tayleur • N. Yorks. CRO, Wyvill of Constable Burton MSS • priv. coll. • Westminster College, Cambridge, Cheshunt Foundation, corresp. of Lady Huntingdon

Likenesses stipple, pubd 1809 (after Vandrimini), NPG; repro. in McLachlan, *Letters of Theophilus Lindsey*, frontispiece; copy DWL • Neele, engraved silhouette, NPG • silhouette, DWL

Wealth at death several thousand pounds: will, PRO, PROB 11/1488, fol. 213; PRO, PROB, 11/1529 fols. 235–6 [Hannah Lindsey]

Line, Anne [St Anne Line] (*d.* **1601**), Roman Catholic martyr, was the daughter of John or William Heigham, a protestant and an Essex landowner. According to Henry Garnett she was educated at court. Anne and her brother William converted to Catholicism and were disinherited by their father after she married a fellow convert, Roger Line (*c.*1568–1594), the heir to large estates. In January 1585 William and Roger were arrested when attending mass and imprisoned. While in prison Roger was disinherited when he refused the entreaty of his dying uncle to attend a protestant service. He was described as a recusant gentleman under the age of nineteen when both men were banished in December 1586 (William went to Spain, Roger to study in Douai). Anne was left destitute.

Until his death in 1594, Roger Line sent his wife part of his small pension, but her own family refused to help. John Gerard found her lodgings with the Wiseman family, who had sheltered him. She reciprocated by teaching their children and embroidering gifts, including two chalice palls for Garnett. Believing her to be 'possessed of such prudence as I have not seen in many women', Gerard and Garnett appointed her housekeeper of the refuge in London they established for priests, particularly those just arrived in England, and the young men and women travelling to seminaries and convents in Flanders, naming her 'Mistress Martha' to protect her identity. Gerard paid for everything with contributions from English Catholics and lived there whenever he was in London. According to him, Line 'was able to manage the finances, do all the housekeeping, look after the guests, and deal with the inquiries of strangers. She was full of kindness, very discreet and possessed her soul in great peace' (*Autobiography*, 84). About this time she took a vow of chastity and poverty.

The house became a centre for priests and for lay Catholics who went there to do the Jesuit spiritual exercises and attend mass. After Gerard's capture and imprisonment in 1594, Line continued to run the establishment but, despite her caution, it began to attract the attention of pursuivants and when Gerard escaped from the Tower of London in 1597 he visited the house only to arrange new accommodation. This proved timely; just two days after Line left, the house was surrounded and searched. She had moved to an apartment, also in London, which included space to lodge visiting priests, a room to instruct young girls, and a separate room for a resident priest to minister to Catholics. Garnett was practical about the dangers and Line frequently told Gerard 'I naturally want more than anything to die for Christ, but it is too much to hope that it will be by the executioner's hand' (*Autobiography*, 84).

Line remained at the centre of London Catholic life. In summer 1599 she was arrested and fined after she helped stall the magistrates, while Gerard hid in the roof-gable, when they burst into a house where he was holding a retreat. She continued to shelter priests in her apartment. On 2 February 1601 she admitted an unusually large number of people to hear mass, and this alerted her neighbours, who called the constables. Although the priest retreated into a hiding place the altar was prepared for mass so the constables knew that he was present. The apartment was searched but they failed to find him. Even so, Line was arrested and imprisoned.

Line was the last woman to be hanged in England as a felon for harbouring priests. Her behaviour during her imprisonment, trial, and execution inspired at least three Catholic eyewitness accounts. Thomas Jollett, a protégé of William Byrd, described how Line remained bedridden throughout most of her incarceration and how, on 23 February, she had a premonition of martyrdom. On the day of her trial, 25 February, Line had to be carried to the courthouse in a chair and remained sitting throughout, but when accused of sheltering priests she replied: 'my Lords, nothing grieves me more but that I could not receive a thousand more'. She was sentenced to death and spent her final day disposing of her few possessions, leaving Gerard a finely wrought cross of gold that had belonged to her husband. On 27 February, unable to walk, she was driven in a cart to Tyburn. Ignoring the protestant minister's words she gave her handkerchief and other small mementoes to her friends. Line was hanged, rather than beheaded, but she retained her dignity, 'bynding her garments beneth about her knees and putting a handkerchief about her face, pynning it fast she meekly kissed the gallows tree' (Bodl. Oxf., MS Eng. th. b 2, fols. 117–118). 'Before and after her private prayers blessing herself, the carte was drawn awaye, and she made the signe of the crosse uppon her, and after that never moved' (*Rutland MSS*, 1.370). That night, hearing that Line's friends were determined to retrieve her body from the common grave, Anne Howard, dowager countess of Arundel, sent her coach to convey it to her house so that it could be decently buried in secret. Line bequeathed her bed to Gerard, but it was stolen from her cell by the gaolers. Gerard managed to buy back her coverlet, which he used thereafter when he was in London 'and felt safer under its protection' (*Autobiography*, 85). Line was canonized in 1970.

CHRISTINE J. KELLY

Sources T. Jollett, 'Authoritates', 1601, Bodl. Oxf., MS Eng. th. b. 2, fols. 117–18 • *John Gerard: the autobiography of an Elizabethan*, trans. P. Caraman, 2nd edn (1956) • *The manuscripts of his grace the duke of Rutland*, 4 vols., HMC, 24 (1888–1905), 1.370 • *Miscellanea, II*, Catholic RS, 2 (1906) • T. F. Knox and others, eds., *The first and second diaries of the English College, Douay* (1878)

Line [*alias* Hall]**, Francis** (**1595–1675**), Roman Catholic priest and natural philosopher, was born in London or Buckinghamshire, probably to a recusant family. It is not known where he received his boyhood education; he was already a young man when he arrived at the college of the English Jesuits at St Omer, in Flanders, where, in 1622, he was listed among the top six pupils in the senior class. The following year he entered the noviciate and transferred first to the English Jesuit college at Liège, then to nearby Watten. Having been ordained priest he was appointed professor of mathematics and of Hebrew at Liège by 1632.

The cosmology taught at Liège broadly followed Aristotle in describing a geocentric universe; this was at odds with the Copernican system, which put the sun at the centre, a system which gained more support with the publication of Galileo's observations. Line was among those who read Galileo's works. Although some Jesuit astronomers were sympathetic to the Copernican system, Galileo was condemned to house arrest in 1633. This event brought to light one of Line's inventions, which was thought by one of Galileo's friends to offer a possible support for the Copernican system. In a book published in 1634 a Jesuit visiting Liège had mentioned Line's water-clock, which consisted of a glass globe filled with water, within which rotated a metal globe, carrying round with it a small 'fish' which pointed to the hours of the day marked on the outer globe. Such a device might, it was proposed, demonstrate the rotation of the earth on its own axis. Although Line never disclosed the secret of his clock, it was probably the same as those previously contrived elsewhere, the inner globe containing clockwork, rotating an arm and magnet to which the 'fish' was attracted.

The various types of sundial for which Line later became famous show his ingenuity and mathematical competence. When the future Charles II visited Liège he was shown in the college garden a great pyramidal structure bearing several dials, which so impressed him that twenty years later he invited Line to construct a similar one at Whitehall. Line, meanwhile, joined with other famous mathematicians of the day in the debate on squaring the circle. Proponents were searching for an algebraic formula to yield the dimensions of a square which would have the equivalent area to a given circle; opponents, of whom Line was one, denied that such a formula could exist.

In late 1657 or early 1658 Line left Liège and crossed to England, possibly by the petition of a nobleman who could offer protection. It has been suggested that this was Henry Pierrepoint, marquess of Dorchester and earl of Kingston. Line's first ministry may have been at the College of the Immaculate Conception, Derbyshire. By 1659 he was in London, then, by 1665, in Lancashire. His *De pseudo-quadratura circuli Dom. Thomas Viti*, attacking the proposals of the English secular priest Thomas White, was published in London in 1659, followed the next year by its English translation, *Refutation of the Attempt to Square the Circle*. He soon became embroiled in other arguments, notably with Robert Boyle. Boyle published in 1660 his *New Experiments Physico-Mechanical Touching the Spring of Air*, which had led him to conclude that the void over the mercury in the closed end of a barometer tube was indeed a vacuum, and that the mercury column was supported by the spring of air—in modern terms, atmospheric pressure—bearing down on the open end. This idea was anathema to Line, who responded with *Tractatus de corporum inseparabilitate in quo experimenta de vacuo* (1661), in which he defended Aristotle's teaching. Irritated by what he saw as a confusion of theological and scientific ideas, Boyle issued his *Defence Against Franciscus Linus* as an appendix to the second edition of his *New Experiments*. In addressing 'the learned author, who ever he may be', Boyle may have known Line as Francis Hall, the alias he seems to have used in England. The *Defence* obliged Boyle to clarify his arguments and to expound the principle now known as Boyle's law; whether or not Line was convinced, he published nothing further on this matter.

The sundial which had been erected in the privy gardens of Whitehall Palace by the prince of Wales, later Charles I, having been defaced, Charles II decided to replace it and invited Line to design the new dial, a task he undertook 'at my lodging in the country' (F. Line, *Explication of the Diall Sett up in the King's Garden at London*, 1673, 1). Unveiled on 24 July 1669, Line's 'Grande pyramidical multiform diall' (Line, *Explication*) was a large and elaborate structure rising tree-like from its stone pedestal. Comprising altogether more than 250 units, there were six main pieces of the dial in the form of stacked circular tables and large globes supported by iron branches, decreasing in size as they approached the pinnacle, an orb surmounted by a cross. Round the tables were dials showing time according to various historical and foreign forms of reckoning, above them glass plates bearing portraits of the royal family. Three dials consisted of water-filled globes which focused the sun's rays in various ways. One of these was Line's sundial for blind people, an example of which had been installed at Liège in 1635, and was seen there by an English visitor in 1699. It consisted of a 3 inch glass globe filled with water inside a 6 inch sphere consisting of several iron rings representing the hour circles. The sun's rays were brought to a focus on the rings, where it could be felt by hand. Unfortunately no one thought to protect Line's grandiose structure from winter's frost, and it suffered considerable damage. Line wrote his *Explication of the Diall Sett up in the King's Garden at London*, but had returned to Liège before its publication there, in Latin and English versions, with an engraving, in 1673. The structure was still standing in 1674 when the earl of Rochester and his friends passed through the garden in a mood of drunken exuberance and smashed its glass spheres. By 1681 it seems to have been dismantled and taken out of the garden.

Back in his post as professor of mathematics, Line continued with his earlier experiments in optics, and unwisely took up an argument between the Jesuit Ignace Gaston Pardies and Isaac Newton over the theory of colours as demonstrated with prisms and lenses. Pardies had realized his misunderstanding of Newton's work when he died in 1674, but Line decided to commence battle afresh, which he did in a series of letters to Henry Oldenburg, secretary to the Royal Society. His letters were passed to Newton, and Newton's increasingly exasperated replies were modulated by Oldenburg and sent to Line. Both sides made their experiments again, and still could not agree on the shape of the spectrum displayed by light passing through a prism; it later transpired that the disparity of their results arose largely because they were using prisms of differing density. But amid the argument Line succumbed to an epidemic and died at Liège on 15 November 1675. ANITA MCCONNELL

Sources C. Reilly, *Francis Line S. J., an exiled English scientist, 1595–1675*, *Bibliotheca Instituti Historici S. J.*, 29 (1969) • J. de Graeve, 'Francis

Hall's sundial for the blind', *Making instruments count*, ed. R. G. W. Anderson, J. A. Bennett, and W. F. Ryan (1993), 216–17 · J. MacDonnell, *Jesuit geometers* (1989) · H. Foley, ed., *Records of the English province of the Society of Jesus*, 4 (1878) · *The correspondence of Henry Oldenburg*, ed. and trans. A. R. Hall and M. B. Hall, 2 (1965); 11–13 (1977–86) · *The correspondence of Isaac Newton*, ed. H. W. Turnbull and others, 1 (1959) · T. M. McCoog, *English and Welsh Jesuits, 1555–1650*, 2 vols., Catholic RS, 74–5 (1994–5)

Archives RS · Stonyhurst College, Lancashire · University Library, Liège

Lines, Samuel (1778–1863), designer and art teacher, was born at Allesley, near Coventry, where his mother was mistress of a boarding-school. On his mother's death in his boyhood he was placed in the charge of an uncle, a farmer, who employed him in agricultural work. Lines, however, managed to teach himself the rudiments of drawing and painting, and in 1794 he was apprenticed to Mr Keeling, a clock-dial enameller and decorator of Birmingham, for whom he worked as designer. He was employed in a similar capacity by Mr Clay, a papier mâché maker, and also by the die-engravers Wyon and Halliday. Among other objects he was frequently employed to design presentation shovels and swords of state, manufactured by Mr Gunby of Birmingham, a great amateur of art, with a fine private collection, and Gunby's gallery was freely open to Lines, as well as to his contemporary David Cox the elder. In 1807 Lines began to teach drawing in Birmingham, using casts to draw from; he set up a school in Newhall Street, met with success, and was able to build himself a house in Temple Row West, where he resided for the remainder of his life. In 1809 Lines, with Moses Haughton the elder, Charles Barber, John Vincent Barber, and other artists established a life academy in Peck Lane, New Street, which moved in 1814 to larger premises in Union Passage. It was in this room that the first exhibition of the works of Birmingham artists was held in 1814. Lines took a large share in the foundation of the Birmingham School of Art in 1821, and on the subsequent foundation of the Birmingham Society of Artists he was elected treasurer and curator, holding those offices until he reached the age of eighty, when he resigned, and was elected an honorary member. Nearly all the artists of the neighbourhood and many from other parts of the country received instruction in drawing at Lines's academy. A good landscape painter himself, he possessed a gift for teaching others, and many of his pupils attained much excellence. He died at his home in Temple Row West, Birmingham, on 22 November 1863, leaving three sons, Henry Harris Lines of Worcester, artist; Frederick Thomas Lines of Heathfield Road, Handsworth, Staffordshire; and Samuel Restell Lines [*see below*]. An oil portrait of him by W. T. Roden and his drawing *Llyn Idwal*, are in Birmingham Museum and Art Gallery. He very rarely exhibited out of Birmingham.

Samuel Restell Lines (1804–1833), painter, third son of Samuel Lines, was born at Birmingham on 15 January 1804, and was taught drawing and painting by his father. He showed some skill in sketching trees, and was employed to make lithographed drawings for drawing books. He also specialized in views of picturesque buildings such as Haddon Hall. He was an occasional exhibitor at the Royal Academy and with the New Society of Painters in Water Colours and showed much promise. He died at his father's house in Birmingham on 9 November 1833, aged twenty-nine. Examples of his work are in the Victoria and Albert Museum, London, and Maidstone Museum, Kent. Birmingham Museum and Art Gallery holds a small collection of his pencil drawings of regional landscapes. L. H. CUST, *rev.* ANNETTE PEACH

Sources *CGPLA Eng. & Wales* (1864) · Mallalieu, *Watercolour artists* · private information (2004) [Birmingham Museum and Art Gallery]

Likenesses W. T. Roden, oils, Birmingham Museums and Art Gallery

Wealth at death under £1500: resworn probate, May 1864, *CGPLA Eng. & Wales*

Lines, Samuel Restell (1804–1833). *See under* Lines, Samuel (1778–1863).

Lines, Walter (1882–1972), toy manufacturer, was born on 10 March 1882 in London, one of the four sons of Joseph Lines, a rocking-horse maker, and his wife, Jane, *née* Fitzhenry. After education at Owens School until 1896, he joined the family firm of G. and J. Lines, taking evening classes in woodworking and design at the Camden School of Art and the Northern Polytechnic. In 1908 he became the company's managing director. Demobilized after the First World War, in 1922 he married Henriette Hendrey (*d.* 1970); they had four children.

In 1920 Lines launched his own toy and pram business in partnership with his brothers, William and Arthur. When asked for security against the required bank loan, he simply showed his hands to the bank manager; and there is no doubt that he was a talented toy designer with a good eye for a novelty. His brothers took specific responsibilities for running the firm's purpose-built factory, designed to facilitate mass production, and for selling the products under the famous Triang trade mark. Lines himself had special responsibility for the design department, and was also managing director. His was the public face of Lines Brothers, a vigorous, relatively small man, whose occasionally prickly exterior hid a generous and warm-hearted spirit, not least towards his workforce. In 1933 Lines Brothers, by now the biggest toy manufacturer in Britain with some 1600 employees, became a public company. Numerous acquisitions during this decade, including Hamleys, London's famous toy store, further strengthened the company's prominence in the contemporary toy trade. Lines enjoyed an equally high personal profile. A member of the board of the British Industries fair, he played a major part in creating the Toy and Fancy Goods Federation in 1922, and was chairman of the manufacturers' representatives on the toy trade board. During the Second World War he successfully represented the toy manufacturers in negotiations with the Board of Trade. He took the lead in establishing the new British Toy Manufacturers' Association in 1944, remaining chairman for a decade.

Lines's resignation from the association in 1955 was prompted by a policy disagreement. Thereafter he devoted himself largely to his own company which by the

1950s claimed to be the world's largest toy producer, responsible for 40 per cent of British production and a third of the industry's exports. In the post-war years Lines ensured Triang's continued dominance by opening new manufacturing facilities all over the world, modernizing existing plants, and developing a stream of new products. When he finally retired as chairman in 1962, company profits stood at an all-time record level.

In the longer run, however, Lines's legacy was perhaps less beneficial, and there is some truth in the claim that he was a toy maker first and a businessman second. It was said that he could rarely resist a new idea, and his group was certainly permeated by an ethos which emphasized play value and children's enjoyment, sometimes at the expense of hard economic logic. This did not matter too much in the immediate post-war years but in the later 1960s as the international toy business became increasingly competitive, and as the tariffs protecting the home market were progressively dismantled, Lines Brothers' profits came under pressure. Even as he formally stepped down, commentators were suggesting that the group's business empire was over-extended, its toys increasingly derivative and imitative, and its senior management too inbred (seven of the ten members of the board in the 1950s were family members, including Lines's own two sons). In 1971 the family enterprise which he had made virtually synonymous with the British toy trade went into liquidation. Lines's own enthusiasm for toys remained unabated, however. Restless and still energetic, even in his eighties, he set up a small manufacturing business in his garden shed, which as Good-Wood Toys eventually became a thriving business in its own right. He died at Leigh Place, Godstone, his Surrey home, on 23 November 1972. KENNETH D. BROWN

Sources *British Toys* (Dec 1972) • *Toy Trader and Exporter*, 88 (March 1952) • private information (2004) • W. Lines, *Looking backwards and looking forwards: Lines Brothers Limited and its subsidiary group of companies* (1958) • *The Times* (24 Nov 1972) • d. cert.
Likenesses photograph, repro. in *The Times*
Wealth at death £86,092: probate, 28 March 1973, *CGPLA Eng. & Wales*

Lingard, Frederick (1811–1847), organist and composer, was born in Manchester, the fifth and youngest son of Thomas Lingard (*d. c.*1844), principal agent for the Mersey and Irwell Navigation Company (also known as the Old Quay Company). He was educated at Manchester grammar school and was intended for the bar, but decided instead to enter the musical profession. He later studied vocal and instrumental church music with Harris, organist of the collegiate church of Manchester. Lingard was for two years organist and choirmaster at St George's Church, Hulme, Lancashire, of which his brother, Joshua Lingard, was at that time incumbent. About 1835 Lingard became a lay vicar of Durham Cathedral, a post he held until his death. He was also a teacher of music and a composer, and published *Antiphonal Chants for the Psalter* (1842), in the style of Palestrina and Byrd; a *Series of Anthems* consisting of a compilation from various sources, including the sacred works of Mozart, Haydn, and Beethoven; many anthems and chants, issued individually and frequently used at Durham Cathedral; and many separately published secular songs and duets. He is said to have possessed a melodious and effective bass voice, and was active in the promotion of ecclesiastical music, particularly antiphonal chanting. He died at Durham on 4 July 1847, and was buried there in St Giles's churchyard.

L. M. MIDDLETON, *rev.* DAVID J. GOLBY

Sources *GM*, 2nd ser., 28 (1847), 215–16 • J. F. Smith, ed., *The admission register of the Manchester School, with some notes of the more distinguished scholars*, 3/2, Chetham Society, 94 (1874), 111, 195–6 • Brown & Stratton, *Brit. mus.*

Lingard, John (1771–1851), Roman Catholic priest and historian, only son of John Lingard (*c.*1738–1804), a carpenter and builder, and his wife, Elizabeth Reynolds (*c.*1733–1824), was born in Winchester on 5 February 1771. He was one of the last students to study at the English College, Douai, in northern France, caught up as it was in events following the French Revolution. Lingard arrived there at the age of eleven in 1782 and left for Britain a few days after the French *commissaires* had taken possession of the college in 1793. Eventually he joined the handful of northern exiles which settled at Crook Hall, near Durham. Lingard was ordained deacon there in December 1794, and priest at the Bar Convent in York on 18 April 1795. At Crook he took on various administrative and academic tasks and moved with the community to the new buildings at Ushaw, Durham, in 1808. In 1810 he became acting president but a year of 'anxiety and misery' (Lingard to Bishop Poynter, 26 Feb 1817, CUL, Add. MS 9418), peppered by unnecessary interference from Bishop Gibson, convinced him that college life was not for him; he refused invitations to St Edmund's College, Ware, and to Maynooth. He was grateful for the chance of moving in 1811 to the small Catholic mission in Hornby, Lancashire, where he remained until his death in 1851.

Here Lingard not only wrote his major *History of England* (London, 1819–30), a study of English history from the Roman invasion to 1688, but a host of smaller works of history and theology, including a collection of English prayers for the use of his parishioners (1833), an English translation of the gospels (1836), and a volume of catechetical instruction (1840). Lingard's version of the *Ave maris stella*, 'Hail queen of heaven', remains a popular hymn among Roman Catholics. In 1820, out of the profits of the first volumes of his *History*, Lingard built a simple Catholic chapel, adjoining the priest's house in Hornby. He preferred liturgy to be intelligible and attractive both to the Catholic community and to protestant visitors, disliking repetitious litanies and over-fanciful metaphor. He wanted his congregation to understand and follow the priest's prayers at the altar and, in Holy Week, for example, had someone read the Passion clearly in English while he continued quietly in Latin. Above all, he wanted simplicity, and disdained both the medievalism of Pugin's Gothic revival and the unwarranted pomp that often accompanied the opening of churches, with the church being 'turned into an opera house' and 'the bishop performing as the first dancer in the ballet' (Lingard to John

John Lingard (1771–1851), by Thomas Skaife, 1848

Walker, 16 Nov 1843, Ushaw, LL 1361). His vast and delightfully unbuttoned correspondence reveals him as an important commentator on Catholic life during the first half of the nineteenth century. He was a valued adviser to vicars apostolic as well as to laity; his work represented an important contribution to the political programme of the English Catholics petitioning for emancipation.

To strangers Lingard could be somewhat off-putting but he delighted in his friends. A regular visitor to Hornby in the last years of Lingard's life described him as

> a thin, spare, light-figured, sallow, dark complexioned man, about 5ft 9in, or 5ft 10in in height, with remarkably small feet and small hands, and apparently of delicate constitution … [looking] quite as old at 65 as he did at eighty, with the exception of the whitening ring often seen in the eyes of old people. (Mrs Thomas Lomax, unpublished memoir, priv. coll.)

Everything in the house was 'small and of the neatest' (ibid.). Lingard was a keen gardener, 'a great grafter of pear trees' (ibid.), and was proud of the oaks he grew from acorns gathered once in Italy. He boasted a series of pets, including a tortoise and a guinea fowl. To Mrs Lomax, he was, above all, friend and scholar, 'his sacerdotal character never particularly present[ing] itself to me, unless I happened to be there on a Sunday' (ibid.).

Lingard rarely travelled, though he went to Rome in 1817, both in search of manuscripts and to assist in negotiations for the reopening of the English College after the devastations of Napoleon. In 1821 Pius VII conferred on him the triple degrees of doctor of divinity and of civil and canon law and gradually he achieved European acclaim, his *History of England* being published in French, German, and Italian editions. He became an associate of the Royal Society of Literature and in 1839 was elected a corresponding member of the Académie Française. Leo XII presented him with a gold medal on a return visit to Rome in 1825, and invited him to stay in the city, but Lingard preferred to return to his historical studies in the seclusion of Hornby. It was rumoured that Leo had created Lingard a cardinal *in petto* in the consistory of October 1826. This is a secret which died with the pope but, in the more expansive mood of old age, Lingard considered it to have been the case. The issue was raised again after Lingard's death by Mark Tierney (historian and priest of the Southwark diocese, who was Lingard's first memoirist) in a sharp exchange with Cardinal Wiseman, who, though acknowledging himself to be close to Lingard, his old teacher, was anxious to scotch the idea. The same official unease pervades a guarded obituary of Lingard in *The Tablet* (26 July 1851), written from a decidedly ultramontanist perspective. This is fighting new battles on old ground: Wiseman was not prepared to concede additional ammunition to Tierney's championing of the Cisalpine tradition, for which Tierney claimed Lingard as a leading representative.

Like many Catholics, Lingard had contact with whig circles, for the whigs had for long espoused the cause of Catholic emancipation. It was Lord Holland who had encouraged Joseph Mawman to publish the first edition of the *History of England*, and Henry Brougham was a welcome visitor to Hornby, when travelling north for the Lancaster assizes. Lord Melbourne made him a grant from the public purse in 1839 of £300, and Lingard forwarded Ullathorne's *The Catholic Mission in Australia* to a select committee on transportation, resulting in Ullathorne's call to give useful evidence before the committee in 1838. Lingard was no whig, however. The volumes of his *History* dealing with the Reformation provided material for the blatant anti-Anglican polemic of William Cobbett's *The Protestant Reformation* (1824–7), which betrays Lingard's subtle undermining of the prevailing protestant interpretation. John Allen, a close associate of the Holland House circle, could only alight on a footnote regarding the St Bartholomew's day massacre as grounds for a vigorous attack on Lingard in the pages of the *Edinburgh Review*, an attack which provoked Lingard to one of his very few public responses, *A Vindication of Certain Passages in the Fourth and Fifth Volumes of the History of England* (1826).

Correspondence reveals that Lingard thought little of the whig historians, and described Macaulay's work as 'abound[ing] in claptrap of every description' (Lingard to John Walker, 27 Dec 1848, Ushaw, LL 1296). Lingard set out his programme in the preface to his *Antiquities of the Anglo-Saxon Church*, clearly distancing himself from whig history: 'my object is truth; and in the pursuit of truth I have made it a religious duty to consult the original historians. Who would draw from the troubled stream, when he may drink at the fountainhead?' (*The Antiquities of the Anglo-Saxon Church*, 1806, 1.vi). It was a programme he stuck to, searching out manuscripts and relying on colleagues to do the same. Lingard was the first English historian to make serious use of rare printed material and manuscript sources in the Vatican and other Italian libraries, as well as French dispatches, and material from the state papers of Ferdinand and Isabella and Philip II of Spain preserved in an almost inaccessible state in the Spanish castle of Simancas. The pioneering use of such material enabled him to move away from a tendency towards parochialism in English political history, placing it in a more broadly European context. The five editions of the *History* published during his lifetime allowed him to include new collections of sources as they were brought to his notice and set out a more explicit statement of Catholic revisionism than he had felt to be appropriate in the pre-emancipation years of the 1820s.

Lingard professed to acknowledge no interpretative scheme of history but sought to let the facts speak for themselves. His was a revisionist history: he considered this dry clarity, with its appearance of impartiality, to be the best way of serving the Catholic cause. This was not always accepted as the case: Bishop Milner, strident ultramontanist and vicar apostolic for the midland district since 1803, was particularly outspoken in his attacks. The pages of the *Orthodox Journal* chart the progress of this debate, although Rome intervened in April 1820 to demand that Milner sever his connection with the journal. Milner, and Lingard's other Catholic critics, objected to his eirenic approach to non-Catholics: Lingard numbered non-Catholics among his friends and correspondents, and struck up a close friendship with the local Anglican incumbent at Hornby, who, on his death, bequeathed his pets to Lingard's care, and rather unusually the Anglican church at Hornby has a memorial to the Catholic priest whose chapel was across the road.

Lingard, however, was not averse to formal controversy and published a series of pamphlets initiated by an attack made on Catholicism by Shute Barrington, bishop of Durham (*A collection of tracts on several subjects connected with the civil and religious principles of Catholics*, 1826). As in his historical work, Lingard felt the Catholic cause best served by a calm and conscientious statement of facts which would serve to disabuse opponents of misapprehensions. This almost naive, Enlightenment, belief in the power of fact, it must be conceded, was more a matter of Catholic apologetic than ecumenical intent. Lingard never warmed to the Oxford Movement, always remaining suspicious of its converts to Catholicism, and, in a long review of works by William Palmer of Worcester and of the early Tracts for the Times, disputed the continuities claimed by these authors, praising the Catholic martyrs who had preserved the tradition handed on by Augustine and his companions (*Dublin Review*, May 1842).

Accusations regarding the illiberality of Roman Catholicism were addressed by Lingard in his first work, *The Antiquities of the Anglo-Saxon Church* (1806), a work which reveals him to be a moderate upholder of the Catholic cisalpine and Gallican tradition of historical scholarship. In this work he sought to oppose the errors of a generation of protestant Anglo-Saxon scholars who argued for an English church, which was from the beginning independent from Rome. Against these writers Lingard asserts the catholicity of the Anglo-Saxon church, presenting a picture of a national church, guided by regular diocesan and provincial synods, but always absolutely loyal to the representative of St Peter. Lingard was anxious to show how Christianity brings culture and civilization, together with its promise of salvation, and was keen, quietly and subtly, to undermine arguments which suggest an aggressive approach to the English church on the part of Rome.

Impervious to the wiles of romanticism, Lingard's work belongs to the Enlightenment; his style is akin to that of Gibbon, though his irony is more gentle. As the nineteenth century progressed, Lingard appeared increasingly old-fashioned, though his *History* remained a standard English text for Catholics into the twentieth century. He disliked innovation, and looked askance at nineteenth-century theories of doctrinal development, and was always to emphasize the permanence and unchanging nature of the doctrine received from Christ by the apostolic community. Lingard's is a political history, cool towards the miraculous, cool towards heroes: his treatment of Thomas Becket was as irritating to Milner as was his treatment of William Wallace to his Scottish critics. His uncomplimentary characterizations of Henry VIII and Elizabeth emerge from the unfolding of events and Mary Tudor is equally disdained, though he does not dwell on her persecutions. Lingard's work looks back to the great tradition of historical scholarship and source criticism established by the Bollandists and Maurists and is consonant with the marked revival of historical study in late eighteenth- and early nineteenth-century Britain. There is nothing more revealing of Lingard's somewhat tetchy eighteenth-century rationalism than a comment on Sharon Turner (1768–1847), perhaps his closest contemporary among the British historians:

> To my surprise he has written to me a congratulatory letter … and has sent me as a present a poem which he has just published. Unfortunately that detracts from the compliment. For he is seventy-seven, and a man who publishes a poem in his seventy-seventh year must be on the high road to a second childhood. (Lingard to John Coulston, 10 June 1845, Ushaw, LL 290)

Lingard outlived Turner, although troubled by worsening eyesight and increasing bouts of ill health. He walked in his garden for the last time on Easter Sunday 1851 and the following day took to his bed. Severe bouts of asthma in the last few weeks of his life made it more convenient to spend his days and nights propped up on the sofa in his library, and there he died just before midnight on 17 July 1851. At Lingard's own request his body was taken to Ushaw College, where he was buried on 22 July.

PETER PHILLIPS

Sources M. Haile [M. Halle] and E. Bonney, *Life and letters of John Lingard, 1771–1851* (1911) • J. P. Chinnici, *The English Catholic Enlightenment: John Lingard and the Cisalpine movement, 1780–1850* (1980) • D. F. Shea, *The English Ranke: John Lingard* (1969) • G. Culkin, 'The making of Lingard's *History*', *The Month*, new ser., 6 (1951), 7–18 • P. Hughes, 'Lingard and the St Bartholomew', *From the Renaissance to the Counter-Reformation: essays in honour of Garrett Mattingly*, ed. C. H. Carter (1966), 179–204 • E. Jones, 'John Lingard and the Simancas archives', *HJ*, 10 (1967), 57–76 • S. Gilley, 'John Lingard and the Catholic revival', *Renaissance and renewal in Christian history*, ed. D. Baker, SCH, 14 (1977), 313–27 • L. Gooch, 'Lingard *v.* Barrington, et al: ecclesiastical politics in Durham, 1805–29', *Durham University Journal*, 85 (Jan 1993), 7–27 • P. Phillips, 'John Lingard and *The Anglo-Saxon church*', *Recusant History*, 23 (1996–7), 178–89 • *The Tablet* (26 July 1851) • Ushaw College, Durham, L1–4, LL 290, 1296, 1361 [correspondence, journals and MSS] • E. Jones, *John Lingard and the pursuit of historical truth* (2001) • P. Phillips, ed., *John Lingard remembered* (2003) • P. Cattermole, 'John Lingard: the historian as apologist', PhD diss., University of Kent at Canterbury, 1984 • *The letters of Dr John Lingard to Mrs Thomas Lomax (1835-51)*, ed. J. Trappes-Lomax, Catholic RS, 77 (2000)

Archives Archives of the British Province of the Society of Jesus, London, corresp. and copy corresp. • CUL, corresp. and papers • Lancs. RO, corresp. and papers; letters • Leeds Diocesan Archives • Ushaw College, Durham, corresp., journals, and papers • Westm. DA, letters | CUL, Hengrave MSS, corresp. with Gage • Harris Man. Oxf., corresp. with Joyce • Harris Man. Oxf., letters to William Shepherd • NRA, priv. coll., letters to Henry Howard • priv. coll., corresp. with Mrs Thomas Lomax

Likenesses C. Fox, line print, pubd 1823 (after J. Ramsay), BM, NPG • J. Lonsdale, oils, *c.*1834, Ushaw College, Durham; repro. in Haile and Bonney, *Life and letters*, frontispiece • H. Cousins, mezzotint, pubd 1836 (after J. Lonsdale), BM, NPG • T. Skaife, miniature, 1848, NPG [*see illus.*] • S. Lover, portrait • J. Ramsay, oils, Ushaw College, Durham; repro. in Chinnici, *The English Catholic Enlightenment*, frontispiece • L. Stocks, line print (after S. Lover), NPG; repro. in J. Lingard, *A history of England* (1837), frontispiece

Wealth at death £2000—residue, apart from minor benefactions: will, PRO, PROB 8/244

Lingard, Richard (*d.* 1655). *See under* Lingard, Richard (1633/4–1670).

Lingard, Richard (1633/4–1670), dean of Lismore, was probably the son of **Richard Lingard** (*d.* 1655), Church of Ireland clergyman, with whom he has often been confused. The elder Lingard is said to have been educated at Cambridge University 'about the year 1620, or during the reign of King James' (Stokes, *Worthies*, 4) and proceeded to Ireland, where he was ordained deacon on 22 October 1621 and priest on 22 October 1622 by Thomas Ram, bishop of Ferns and Leighlin. He became vicar of Killaire on 5 November 1630 and by September 1633 had been collated to the vicarage of St Mary's, Athlone, and later to that of Killcleagh and the curacy of Ballyloughloe. In March 1639 he was appointed archdeacon of Clonmacnoise and was granted the rectorial tithes of his Athlone benefice as an augmentation by Charles I, the tithes of Ratoath, co. Meath, being added.

There is uncertainty regarding the elder Lingard's movements after 1641. Some authorities claim he left Ireland in 1645, others that he remained at Athlone until it fell to Ireton in 1651, and it is this uncertainty that has led to the confusion between him and his likely son. Nevertheless, strict contemporaries distinguished between the two men, and it seems probable that the elder Lingard did indeed leave Ireland at some point after 1641 to become the minister of Workington in Cumberland. It was there that he died in 1655, naming a son, Richard, in his will.

It seems likely that it was the younger Lingard who was admitted, aged fifteen, to Pembroke College, Cambridge, in 1649, graduating BA in 1653. Elected one of five senior fellows of Trinity College, Dublin, and lecturer in divinity in 1661, in the same year he was appointed to recover the library of James Ussher for the college, alongside the vice-chancellor, Jeremy Taylor, and the provost, Thomas Steele. On 4 June 1662 he was made vice-provost, and in the following November became public professor of divinity. On 25 January 1666 the grace of the house was passed for his degree of Doctor of Divinity. Shortly afterwards he was appointed dean of Lismore and designated vicar of the parish of St Andrew's, Dublin. For this reason he resigned his college positions as senior fellow, vice-provost, and senior dean on 6 April 1666.

Lingard's *Sermon Preached before the King at Whitehall July 26 1668: in Defence of the Liturgy* (1668) was his first published work. His only other publication, *A letter of advice to a young gentleman leaving the university concerning the behaviour and conversation in the world* (1670), was written for the benefit of his friend James Lane at the request of the latter's father, Viscount Lanesborough. Lingard may have visited Oxford as a grace of convocation on 15 July 1670, and was passed there for a DD in 1670, though it is not known whether he actually took the degree. A letter from Charles II to the lord lieutenant of Ireland on 3 August 1669 proposed that he be advanced to the bishopric of Raphoe, but he died before this came to pass, on 11 November 1670. He was buried in the college chapel on 13 November. The fact that he left in his will rent from land in Cumberland provides a further telling link of his likely parentage. *An elegy and funeral oration on the death of the Rev. Dr. R. Lingard, dean of Lismore and public professor of divinity* was published in Dublin in 1671. ELIZABETHANNE BORAN

Sources G. T. Stokes, *Some worthies of the Irish church* (1900), 3–31 • J. B. Leslie, ed., 'Biographical succession list of the clergy of Meath diocese', vol. 1 (revised up to 1947), Representative Church Body Library, Dublin, pp. 60–61 • J. B. Leslie, ed., 'Dublin clergy succession list', Representative Church Body Library, Dublin, 274 • *The whole works of Sir James Ware concerning Ireland*, ed. and trans. W. Harris, 3 (1746), 348 • Venn, *Alum. Cant.*, 1/3.87 • S. Dunelm, 'Will of Richard Lingard', *N&Q*, 2nd ser., 2 (1856), 104–5 • *CSP Ire., 1666–9*, 674–7, 737; *1669–70*, 1–3, 52, 175, 205, 208, 300, 305, 428 • H. Cotton, *Fasti ecclesiae Hibernicae*, [another edn], 5 vols. (1851–60), vol. 1, p. 169; vol. 3, p. 147; vol. 5, p. 25 • A. Vicars, ed., *Index to the prerogative wills of Ireland, 1536–1810* (1897), 287 • Betham's abstracts of wills, NA Ire., MS 2/434/3, pp. 75, 84 • H. L. Murphy, *A history of Trinity College, Dublin from its foundation to 1702* (1951), 126–8 • register books, TCD, MUN V/5/2 pp. 49, 54, 55, 61, 86, 87, 89, 143; MUN P/1/423; MUN P/1/461 • Foster, *Alum. Oxon.*, *1500–1714*, 3.916 • G. T. Stokes, 'The parish of Athlone', *Meath Diocesan Magazine*, 3 (1887), iv • W. Urwick, *The early history of Trinity College, Dublin 1591–1660* (1892), 74 • *Report on the manuscripts of the earl of Egmont*, 2 vols. in 3, HMC, 63 (1905–9), vol. 2, pp. 22–3 • S. Lewis, *A topographical dictionary of Ireland*, 1 (1837), 88 • F. R. Bolton, *The Caroline tradition of the Church of Ireland with particular reference to Bishop James Taylor* (1958), 189 • Burtchaell & Sadleir, *Alum. Dubl.*, 2nd edn, 503

Wealth at death £451: Dunelm, 'Will of Richard Lingard'

Lingen, Sir Henry (1612–1661/2), royalist army officer, born at Rotherwas, near Hereford, on 23 October 1612, was the eldest son of Edward Lingen (*d.* 1635), of Freen's Court, in the parish of Sutton St Michael, Herefordshire, and his wife, Blanch Bodenham, daughter of Sir Roger Bodenham of Rotherwas. Lingen's father was twice imprisoned by the council of the marches—once for refusing to pay alimony to his estranged wife and then on the grounds of insanity—but he was restored to his property by the privy council. Edward Lingen was a Catholic, but Henry was brought up an Anglican by John Scudamore, first Viscount Scudamore. On 3 April 1626 he married Alice Pye (*d.* 1684), daughter of Sir Walter Pye of the Mynde, Herefordshire, who brought with her a marriage portion of £1000. They had eight daughters and one son, Henry, who was to outlive his father but died a minor in 1670. In 1635 Lingen inherited large estates from his father in Herefordshire, Shropshire, and Gloucestershire. In 1638 he was appointed sheriff of Herefordshire and reported to the privy council the opposition in the county to ship money.

In April 1642 Lingen was one of the Herefordshire justices who signed a letter defending the Church of England, directed to the county's MPs, declaring their resistance to parliament's orders because they were not sanctioned by the king. In 1643 he was again sheriff and in June he was one of the commissioners of array ordered by the king to assist the local commander, Sir William Vavasour, in raising forces in Herefordshire. He had soon collected 1200 foot and 200 horse and had agreed to raise £1200 per month from the county in local taxes. In July 1643 with Vavasour he was engaged in the siege of Brampton Bryan Castle, Herefordshire, held by Lady Brilliana Harley, and he took sole command when Vavasour was summoned to the siege of Gloucester. News of the royalist defeat there and a lack of ordnance compelled Lingen to raise the siege and he retired to Knighton where he was attacked by Lady Brilliana's forces. Subsequently he withdrew to Hereford, which was garrisoned with 700 troops, and occupied the earl of Kent's property, Goodrich Castle, in order to strengthen the line of the Wye against the parliamentarian forces at Gloucester.

Early in 1644 Lingen, with the other senior officers at Hereford, wrote to Prince Rupert, saying that he could no longer serve under Vavasour because his command had been incorrectly drawn up. In December Rupert appointed Barnabus Scudamore governor of Hereford and to consolidate his position made him sheriff in Lingen's place. The 'able Lingen' was left in command of Goodrich but he warned Rupert that Herefordshire was 'much ruined by plunder and quarter' through the passing of troops from north Wales to Bristol (Hutton, 136; Herefs. RO, M70). In March 1645 Herefordshire was paralysed by the rising of the Clubmen who resisted the demands made upon them by the royalist garrisons. Lingen's home at Freen's Court was attacked and he was forced to promise £1000 in compensation for the injuries he had inflicted on the county. With Rupert's arrival the rising was suppressed.

In July 1645 Lingen was knighted when the king visited Hereford and relieved it of the Scottish siege. Lingen was in Hereford when the city was surprised by Colonel Birch on the morning of 18 December 1645. He escaped across the frozen river and shut himself up in Goodrich Castle with 200 'cavaliers' and 'bold riders' (Hutchinson, 72). Birch was granted a pension of £50 by parliament from Sir Henry's estate. The latter maintained his forces by forcibly requisitioning supplies from his neighbours. During the two years in which Lingen garrisoned Goodrich nearly £300 of damage was done to Kent's estate. Birch made an effort to storm Goodrich Castle on the night of 9 March 1646, but succeeded only in burning down the stables and outhouses. During the temporary absence of Birch, Lingen, with a mere handful of comrades, attempted the recovery of Hereford. Finding little support in the city, he returned to Goodrich which was reinvested by Birch. 'The last of the royalist warlords' surrendered on 31 July 1646 only after the walls of the castle had been battered down by a large cannon called Roaring Meg which Birch had had made in the Forest of Dean (Hutton, 199). According to tradition the garrison marched out to a lively tune called, after their leader, 'Sir Harry Lingen's Fancy' or 'Delight', which was 'long used in the neighbourhood in the dances of the peasantry' (Webb, 2.280).

Lingen spent two months in prison at Hereford, but petitioned on 1 October 1646 to compound for his estate, which was valued at £936 per annum. He was still popular in Hereford and when he reappeared in the city—contrary to his parole, wearing his sword—he caused a riot but was considered too dangerous to arrest. In November Lingen was obliged to take the covenant and a few days later the negative oath restraining him from any further attempt against parliament.

In August 1648, with the outbreak of the second civil war, Lingen received a commission from the prince of Wales to foment a rising in Shropshire, Staffordshire, Worcestershire, and Herefordshire. Several strongholds were to have been seized, but the plot was detected by Andrew Yarranton, governor of Hartlebury in Worcestershire, and measures were taken to suppress it. However, Lingen drew together 400 men and surprised a group of horse under Sir Edward Harley near Leominster in September, taking eighty prisoners, but two or three days later he was overthrown between Radnor and Montgomeryshire by the forces of Harley and Sir Richard Hopton, and all the captives were recovered. Lingen himself, seriously wounded, was captured and confined in Powis Castle, Montgomeryshire. The House of Commons ordered him to be banished on 10 November 1648, but the sentence was revoked on 13 December following. He was ultimately obliged to sell a portion of his estates. The fine levied by parliament upon his property amounted to £6350, and it had been heavily taxed by the maintenance of a regiment of horse. Sir Robert Harley was authorized to recompense himself for his losses out of Lingen's property, but through his son Edward he generously returned the schedule, waiving all right or title to the estates which it had conferred upon him.

Lingen retired to Stoke Edith, Herefordshire, which became his principal home. He was elected MP for Hereford on 20 November 1660 and again in April 1661. The second election was subject to an inquiry by the committee on elections and privileges, which quashed it, but Lingen was returned again. He was an inactive MP, but in 1661 was appointed to the committees on bills for confirming public acts and restoring advowsons.

Lingen died of smallpox at Gloucester on his way home from London, and was buried at Stoke Edith on 22 January

1662. In consideration of Lingen's heavy losses his widow was authorized by a royal warrant of November 1663 to receive £10,000, but little of this seems to have materialized. In 1670 Stoke Edith was sold to Paul Foley and the rest of Sir Henry's estate was divided among his daughters and their husbands.

GORDON GOODWIN, *rev.* DAVID WHITEHEAD

Sources C. J. Robinson, *A history of the mansions and manors of Herefordshire* (1872) • J. Hutchinson, *Herefordshire biographies* (1840) • J. Duncumb and others, *Collections towards the history and antiquities of the county of Hereford*, 2 (1812), 184–5 • J. Webb, *Memorials of the civil war … as it affected Herefordshire*, ed. T. W. Webb, 2 vols. (1879) • Roe, *Military memoir of Colonel John Birch*, ed. J. Webb and T. W. Webb, CS, new ser., 7 (1873) • R. Hutton, *The royalist war effort, 1642–1646* (1982) • J. Eales, *Puritans and roundheads: the Harleys of Brampton Bryan and the outbreak of the English civil war* (1990) • E. Heath-Agnew, *Roundhead to royalist: a biography of Colonel John Birch, 1615–1691* (1977) • I. J. Atherton, *Barnabas Scudamore's defence* (1992) • C. Hopkinson, *Herefordshire under arms* (1985) • G. Marshall, 'A short account of Freen's Court', *Transactions of the Woolhope Naturalists' Field Club* (1914–17), 211–18 • D. Whitehead, 'The purchase and building of Stoke Edith Park, Herefordshire', *Transactions of the Woolhope Naturalists' Field Club*, 43 (1979–81), 181–202, esp. 181–4 • P. Gladwich, 'The Herefordshire clubmen', *Midland History*, 10 (1985), 62–71 • *Diary of the marches of the royal army during the great civil war, kept by Richard Symonds*, ed. C. E. Long, CS, old ser., 74 (1859) • *CSP dom.* • misc. sources, Herefs. RO, esp. M70 • HoP, *Commons, 1660–90*

Likenesses portrait, repro. in Webb, *Memorials of the civil war*, 4.258

Lingen, Ralph Robert Wheeler, **Baron Lingen** (**1819–1905**), civil servant, was born in Birmingham on 19 February 1819, the only son (and probably only child) of Thomas Lingen (1771–1848), businessman, and his wife, Ann Palmer, daughter of Robert Wheeler of Birmingham. From 1831 to 1837 he was a pupil at Bridgnorth grammar school, where his schoolfellows included Osborne Gordon and James Fraser. In 1837 he won a scholarship to Trinity College, Oxford. An accomplished classical scholar—and an inveterate versifier in Greek—Lingen thrived in the competitive atmosphere then developing within Oxford. He won the Ireland scholarship in 1838, the Hertford scholarship in 1839, a first class in final schools in 1840, a Balliol fellowship in 1841, the chancellor's Latin essay prize in 1843, and the Eldon scholarship in 1846. At Balliol, Benjamin Jowett was embarking on his project to place men of talent in the service of the state and Lingen, with whom he formed a lifelong friendship, was one of his earliest and greatest successes. Without great enthusiasm Lingen had begun in 1844 to read for the bar at Lincoln's Inn, being called in May 1847. However, already in October 1846 he had been appointed by the marquess of Lansdowne, lord president of the council, to serve on a commission of inquiry into Welsh education; and when that was complete in July 1847 Lansdowne appointed him to a chief examinership, a new administrative post, in the education department, which formed part of the privy council office. In December 1849 he succeeded James Kay-Shuttleworth as permanent secretary to the education department. On 4 December 1852 he married Emma, second daughter of Robert Hutton, at one time MP for Dublin. They had no children.

Kay-Shuttleworth, the first permanent secretary, had been a zealous missionary, determined to bring education and all its benefits to the industrial working class. Lingen's approach was very different. He was profoundly uninterested in elementary education and associated schemes for social regeneration, and was disdainful of the passions generated by religious denominations competing to provide this. His zeal was instead for orderly, rigorous, and economical administration, and he set exacting standards not only for his official colleagues but also for his political masters. Lingen was among those consulted by Sir Stafford Henry Northcote and Sir Charles Edward Trevelyan as they prepared their report on the reorganization of the civil service in 1853, and was a firm supporter of their proposals both for departmental restructuring and for recruitment through competition rather than patronage. In 1856 he carried through a reorganization of the education department, separating it from the privy council office proper and grouping its staff into distinct administrative and clerical grades. Successive lords president were steered into appointing only honours graduates, among whom Balliol men figured largely, to both administrative posts and the schools' inspectorate. Lingen played a part, too, in curbing the independence of her majesty's inspectors of schools. Between 1864 and 1866 he and Robert Lowe, then vice-president of the committee of council on education, mounted a vigorous and eventually successful defence of the department's right to edit the reports of the inspectorate before their publication. The *Saturday Review* remarked on 16 April 1864, 'If rumour does not much belie him, Mr Lingen is quite as powerful as Mr Lowe and a good deal more offensive. It is from Mr Lingen that all the sharp snubbing replies proceed'.

Lingen and Lowe shared not only an aggressive personal style but also a commitment to the principles of the free market, which they saw as underpinning competition. They had already worked closely together on a major reconstruction of grant provision for elementary education. The system, built up in higgledy-piggledy fashion since 1833, was essentially one of incentives: grants were available to aid a range of activities from building to the employment and training of pupil teachers, and local school promoters who fulfilled certain conditions could claim them. The inspectorate assessed these schools and could recommend the reduction or withholding of grants if work was unsatisfactory, but very seldom did so, and grant expenditure rose steadily. In their revised code of grant regulations, first promulgated in the summer of 1861, Lowe and Lingen set out to replace all but the building grants with capitation grants. A portion of these depended on the child's regular attendance, and the remainder on his or her performance each year in examinations in the three Rs conducted by the inspectorate. The examinations were arranged in a series of 'standards' and the child was expected to move up one each year. Outcry from school managers, teachers, and several inspectors greeted this system of payment by results. However, Lowe, supported by Lingen, stood firm, and their code, with minor amendments, was finally introduced in 1863.

Grant levels fell sharply and did not recover to the level of 1861 again until 1869. Matthew Arnold suspected that Lingen would have been content to intervene no further: 'the schools might now be trusted to go alone' (Ward, 2.258). Certainly he was profoundly out of sympathy with larger schemes for providing elementary schools nationally, on which W. E. Forster began work when he became vice-president late in 1868. From this Lingen was rescued at the end of 1869, when the permanent secretaryship to the Treasury fell vacant. Lowe, who was chancellor of the exchequer in Gladstone's first government (1868–74), pressed strongly and ultimately successfully for his promotion.

At the Treasury from 1870, Lingen, with Lowe, set the tone for Treasury control in the last third of the century, and worked to extend its grip on civil service departmental organization and recruitment. Lingen contributed to and enthusiastically supported the order in council of May 1870 that made open competition the general rule for recruitment to the civil service. He set about the work of bringing individual departments within its operation with a vigour that dismayed a number of Lowe's cabinet colleagues, who had been prepared to assent to the principle but planned to hold their own departments aloof from its operation. More generally, Lingen brought an abrasive, often hectoring, ultimately negative tone to Treasury scrutiny of all expenditure proposals, whether on establishment or policy, which made interdepartmental negotiations increasingly resemble guerrilla warfare. Inevitably the education department was subjected to a mercilessly detailed interrogation as it struggled to construct something approaching a national system of elementary education in the years following Forster's 1870 act. Lingen was one of the first to recognize that grants designed as incentives to local school promoters were ill-adapted to such a purpose, but he was less than patient with the denominational conflicts that made reconstruction so politically difficult. Similar interrogative tactics, although backed by less intimate knowledge, were deployed against other government departments, especially the high spending defence ones. These tactics were rooted not simply in personal style but also in the belief Lingen shared with Lowe, and which they both expounded to the 1873 select committee on civil service expenditure, that the Treasury was not strong enough, and that since it could not impose a financial strategy on other departments it had to try to shape patterns of expenditure by continuous critical scrutiny. R. E. Welby, who was to succeed Lingen, and W. E. Baxter, the parliamentary financial secretary of the day, were more optimistic about what could be achieved by guidance and negotiation. Nevertheless the issue was a real one, and it shaped the relations of the Treasury with other departments for the remainder of the century. Lowe's successors as chancellor did not all share his combative approach, and several felt that Lingen's tone needlessly exacerbated already difficult interdepartmental relations. Although Gladstone praised Lingen's 'unsleeping vigilance for the public interests' (Gladstone to Lingen, 27 Jan 1885, BL, Add. MS 44546, fol. 170) there was a certain relief when, in June 1885, on the fall of Gladstone's second government, Lingen resigned his Treasury post.

Lingen collected honours in his public life rather as he had collected prizes and scholarships at Oxford. At the end of 1869 he was made CB and in 1878 KCB. In 1881 Oxford made him an honorary DCL, and he was raised to the peerage on his retirement in 1885 as Baron Lingen of Lingen. He served as an alderman of the London county council 1889–92 and as chairman of its finance committee. He died at his house, 13 Wetherby Gardens, South Kensington, London, on 22 July 1905, and was buried at Brompton cemetery. Lady Lingen died on 27 January 1908. GILLIAN SUTHERLAND

Sources *The Times* (24 July 1905), 8 • Burke, *Peerage* (1900) • H. Roseveare, *The treasury: the evolution of a British institution* (1969) • M. Wright, *Treasury control of the civil service, 1854–1874* (1969) • R. Johnson, 'Administrators in education before 1870: patronage, social position, and role', *Studies in the growth of nineteenth-century government*, ed. G. Sutherland (1972), 110–38 • G. Sutherland, *Policy-making in elementary education, 1870–1895* (1973) • 'Mr Lowe and the inspectors', *Saturday Review*, 17 (1864), 464–5 • T. H. Ward, ed., *The reign of Queen Victoria: a survey of fifty years of progress*, 2 vols. (1887) • Gladstone, *Diaries* • *DNB*

Archives Balliol Oxf., letters to B. Jowett • BL, memoranda and corresp. with W. E. Gladstone, Add. MSS 44132–44788, *passim* • priv. coll., Hutton MSS • PRO, letters to Lord Granville, PRO 30/29 • PRO, Treasury MSS

Likenesses G. P. Jacomb-Hood, oils, 1896, Trinity College, Oxford

Wealth at death £50,832 2*s*. 8*d*.: probate, 9 Sept 1905, *CGPLA Eng. & Wales*

Lingstrom, Freda Violet (1893–1989), television producer and writer, was born on 23 July 1893 at 3 Pond Place, Chelsea, London, the daughter of George Louis Lingstrom, a copperplate-engraver, and his wife, Alice Clarey Amiss. She went to school in London and then to the Central School of Arts and Crafts. Her skills in painting and design were combined with organizing ability and a talent for writing. She held her first one-woman show in 1936, arranged exhibitions, worked as a publicity officer, as private secretary and play reader to the actress Edith Evans, and painted mural decorations for Norway House. Her parents were born in England, but her paternal grandparents were Swedish and she travelled in Scandinavia. Her first book, *This is Norway* (1933), a survey on its culture and history, was followed by two novels, *The Seventh Sister* (1938) and *A Flower in his Hand* (1939) which was published in England, the USA, and Sweden.

Lingstrom first applied to the BBC in 1940 at the suggestion of the broadcaster Olive Shapley, and was eventually given a post in the staff pool of the home and empire talks department. This involved some reporting, script writing, and monitoring until, in 1947, she became a radio producer in the schools department. She originated a new series, *Looking at Things*, which was accompanied by publications for use in schools and, later, an illustrated book, *The Seeing Eye*, which was designed to attract children to the pleasures of form, design, and colour in everyday objects.

A tall, rather masculine looking woman, with a direct air of authority, Lingstrom forged good relationships with educationists and BBC mandarins, and in 1951 she was asked to become head of the recently formed children's department in television. Her output expanded rapidly and built on earlier successes such as Annette Mills's *Muffin the Mule* and the Sunday afternoon magazine *For the Children*. The new head achieved a more systematic daily output of a variety of programmes for different age groups and encouraged her new producers who had come from radio or the theatre to stimulate the growing audience. New characters were introduced, including Mr Turnip in *Whirlygig* and Harry Corbett's *Sooty*, and many exciting drama serials and comedies were transmitted live from a small studio in Lime Grove.

Lingstrom's own interest in young children inspired her to create new puppet programmes with her colleague Maria Bird in a new strand called *Watch with Mother*. Each day's short programme reflected the interests of children under five. *Andy Pandy* invited the audience to join in simple actions and songs; *The Flowerpot Men* explored the fantasy world and language of Bill and Ben; *The Woodentops* depicted family life; *Rag, Tag and Bobtail* introduced natural history; *Picture Book* foreshadowed many further storytelling programmes. Production techniques were primitive, but the ideas they embodied are still evident in today's output for this age group. String or rod puppets were followed by stop frame animations in Gordon Murray's *Trumpton* and other inventions, all made in a tin shed in a back yard in Lime Grove, which was known as 'the puppet studio'.

In the 1950s the suspicion that children could be corrupted by television was robustly dismissed by Lingstrom. She affirmed that children would watch anyway and they deserved programmes of the highest standards which they could understand, and she fought for her producers to have resources that were as good as those for adult programmes. In her annual report for 1956 the controller of television programmes wrote: 'She abhors the cheap and flashy and will accept no second rate thought or standards. She is human and warm and these qualities in addition to her integrity have gained the respect of her staff' (F. Lingstrom file, BBC WAC). Her producers referred to her as Mum, though none would call her that to her face.

Lingstrom was particularly careful about drama and knew how powerful its visual and emotional images could be. The former head of BBC drama, Shaun Sutton, who, like other distinguished directors and designers, started his career under her guidance, explained:

> For a Cavalier to pierce a Roundhead with his sword was alright. That was years ago and in costume and couldn't happen today. But for a child to threaten Granny with a fork in a modern play was totally forbidden. That could be imitated. (private information)

Alongside the plaudits for *Billy Bunter* or the dramatic narratives of *The Silver Sword*, *Huckleberry Finn*, and *The Moonstone*, arguments surrounded the Bible series *Jesus of Nazareth* (directed by Joy Harrington) which involved diplomatic and theological negotiations. Lingstrom's success and leadership as the first influential head of children's television were recognized by appointment as an OBE in 1955. She continued her freelance work long after retirement and, at the age of seventy-four, remade *Andy Pandy* in colour. The programmes she produced are now regarded as classics of children's television and today's computer-literate audiences still respond to her understanding of the way children think and feel.

Lingstrom was unmarried but had an adopted daughter, and lived for many years with her friend Maria Bird near Westerham in Kent. She died on 15 April 1989 at her house, Chartwell Cottage, Mapleton Lane, Chartwell, near Westerham, at the age of ninety-five. MONICA SIMS

Sources staff files, BBC WAC · private information (2004) · A. Home, *Into the box of delights: a history of children's television* (1993) · *The Independent* (22 May 1989) · b. cert. · d. cert.
Archives BBC WAC
Likenesses photograph, repro. in *The Independent*
Wealth at death £182,169: probate, 24 Aug 1989, *CGPLA Eng. & Wales*

Linklater, Eric Robert Russell (1899–1974), writer, was born on 8 March 1899 at Penarth, Glamorgan, the only son and elder child of Robert Baikie Linklater (*d.* 1916), master mariner, of Dounby, Orkney, and his wife, (Mary) Elizabeth (*c.*1867–1957), daughter of James Young, master mariner. Though herself no Scot, Elizabeth Linklater was passionately Scottish and Orcadian in her loyalties. She insisted on maintaining a holiday house in Orkney, where the Linklaters had lived for many generations, and once it became possible she transferred the family home from Cardiff to Aberdeen. Eric Linklater, who would also see himself as both Scottish and Orcadian, attended Aberdeen grammar school from 1913 to 1916.

In 1914 Linklater enlisted in a territorial battalion of the Gordon Highlanders, but when war broke out he was rejected for service because of his poor eyesight. In 1917, however, by which time his father had died in Ceylon after an engagement with a German U-boat, he contrived to get himself accepted by the army and then posted to France. He served with the Black Watch in late 1917 and early 1918, until wounded in the course of the German spring offensive. Ironically, given the basis of his previous rejection, he became a sniper. In spite of grudgingly admitting to terror of the mud, the bullying, and the sudden slaughter of the western front, he was exalted. The war was for him a deep and intense emotional experience, as he recorded in *Fanfare for a Tin Hat* (1970):

> My few weeks as a sniper gave my life an excitement, an intensity which I have never known since. I have, on the whole, had a happy life, and I have known much pleasure. But in my nineteenth year I lived at a high pitch of purpose, a continuous physical and mental alertness, that has never again suffused my brain and body. (Linklater, *Fanfare*, 67)

His head wound was near fatal; he was saved only by the legendary tin hat.

From 1918 to 1925 Linklater was a student at Aberdeen University, first, unsuccessfully, in medicine, a course of study which he had begun in 1916 and which provided material for his first novel, *White Maa's Saga* (1929). This was only the first example of his use of his own life experience as material for fiction. He subsequently studied English, and graduated MA in 1925, with first-class honours,

Eric Robert Russell Linklater (1899–1974), by Howard Coster, 1954

being awarded the Seafield medal, the Minto memorial prize, and the Senatus prize in English. The unforgotten intensity of the eighteen-year-old, however, would leave the mature writer liable to search for novelty, change, and action, and ensured that travel would be a central feature of Linklater's life and writing. He spent the years 1925 to 1927 in Bombay, as an assistant editor of the *Times of India*. There followed a year in Aberdeen (1927–8) as assistant to the professor of English, and two years (1928–30) in the USA as a Commonwealth fellow, based first at Cornell and then at Berkeley.

Linklater's literary career proper began in 1929, and his output was both varied and prolific. He published twenty-three novels, three volumes of short stories, two children's books, two books of verse, ten plays (including several 'conversations' for radio during the Second World War), three fine autobiographies, and another twenty-three books of miscellaneous essays and histories. His greatest popularity was in the earlier part of his career. His reputation was effectively established by his third novel, *Juan in America* (1931), a richly comic, picaresque extravaganza rather in the manner of Byron's *Don Juan*, but based on his observation of the United States, then in the grip of the extreme absurdities of prohibition and the resultant gangsterism.

But, characteristically, Linklater hated to repeat himself, and he deliberately dashed the expectations of the vast readership of *Juan in America* by following it with *The Men of Ness: the Saga of Thorlief Coalbiter's Sons* (1932), a spare, laconic viking adventure in which traditional heroism is defeated, and the survivor, Gauk, is a small, comic figure, in some ways a precursor of the eponymous hero of *Private Angelo* (1946). This is only the most obvious example of Linklater's preoccupation with Orkney life and Old Norse literature and culture. He wrote in a letter to a friend that he wanted 'to make Scotland "Viking-conscious"' (Parnell, 126), and he had a personal belief in an aesthetic evaluation of action behind the viking way of life. In *The Ultimate Viking* (1955), he wrote:

> They were unabashed by social obligation, undeterred by moral prohibition, and they could be quite contemptuous of economic advantage and the safety of their own skins. But they saw clearly a difference between right and wrong, and the difference was aesthetic. If what they did became a story that would please the ear, then it was right and beautiful. (E. Linklater, *The Ultimate Viking*, 8)

Linklater's son Andro has recognized fatalism as a major element in his father's life and work, and sees Linklater as 'a convinced, unwavering pagan', perceiving a major preoccupation in his father's stories as 'the proper way to confront an inevitable fate' (A. Linklater, 'Introduction', to E. Linklater, *The Goose Girl*, vii, x). Julian D'Arcy, who has devoted a book to the influence of Old Norse literature on Scottish writers, details Linklater's studies in the sagas, and, although he finds Linklater's interpretation of viking saga and ethos a trifle slanted, concludes that he 'was so steeped in Old Norse lore and literature in both his personal and literary life, that it would be perhaps appropriate to give him the epitaph of the "Ultimate Viking" of modern Scottish literature' (D'Arcy, 238).

In 1933 Linklater experimented with the world of the 'Scottish Renaissance' in literature and politics, and stood as the Scottish nationalist candidate in a parliamentary by-election in East Fife. This resulted in *Magnus Merriman* (1934), a light-hearted and thinly fictionalized account of his disastrous campaign, including much fairly affectionate satire on contemporary Scotland, and a parodic representation of C. M. Grieve (Hugh MacDiarmid) in the poet-leader Hugh Skene. On 1 June 1933 he had married Marjorie MacIntyre [*see below*], and after a period in Italy the couple settled at Dounby in Orkney; they had two daughters and two sons.

Linklater's experiences in the First World War had made him particularly sensitive to the paradox of the horrors of war on the one hand, and its broadening of experience on the other. He repeatedly illustrated this paradox in his writing, and also continually expressed his unfailing admiration and love for the soldiers who carried on the war. He wrote a great deal about combat, in military histories and pamphlets as well as fiction. Between the wars he saw communism as just as dangerous as fascism, and was emotionally disabled by the Spanish Civil War, finding it impossible to support either side wholeheartedly. His fictional response took the form of *The Impregnable Women* (1938), a loose adaptation of the *Lysistrata* of Aristophanes, inspired by angry revulsion against the prospect of the war's renewal. *Judas* (1939), however, with its themes of loyalty and treachery, was inspired by the way in which Britain and France in particular had deserted the cause of Czechoslovakia in the name of appeasement.

From 1939 to 1941 Linklater commanded the Orkney fortress company, Royal Engineers. He was then posted to the directorate of public relations in the War Office, where he wrote pamphlets on several aspects of the army at war; he also produced at this time, in his personal capacity, a number of conversation pieces on war aims. From 1944 to 1945 Linklater served in Italy, and it was there that he had the experiences central to his most successful war novel, *Private Angelo* (1946), a work dedicated to the Eighth Army. Linklater described his love affair with Italy as 'a state of idealistic adultery'. '[T]he subject of my novel was not only war and its capacity for destruction, but Italy and its genius for survival' (Linklater, *Fanfare*, 316). The work's protagonist, Angelo, has led a rout of Italians fleeing from battle, and is dismissed in the first sentence as lacking the gift of courage. But the novel goes on to re-examine the idea of courage, and to stress the importance of understanding. By the end Angelo has served in three armies (Italian, German, and British) and has become the father of children, three of them illegitimate, one English, one Polish, and one Moroccan. The tenor of the book is against nationalism, and Linklater prefigures Heller and Waugh, and even Henry Kissinger, when he has the innocent Angelo say: 'I hope you will not liberate us out of existence'. As armies bomb their own troops, and Angelo repeatedly deserts, the reader is shown the essential folly of war. But the wandering refugees, and the rapes of both Angelo and his fiancée, keep the serious horror in the forefront, and serve to maintain Linklater's conviction that, despite everything, this is a just and necessary war.

In 1945 Linklater was elected rector of Aberdeen University, which awarded him an honorary degree in 1946. In 1947 the Linklaters left Orkney, where conditions had changed greatly during the war, for Pitcalzean House in Ross-shire. Here they lived until 1972 when, faced with oil-related developments in the locality, they moved to Aberdeenshire. In 1951 he published a semi-official history, *The Campaign in Italy*, and visited Korea with the temporary rank of lieutenant-colonel. In 1954 he was appointed CBE; from 1968 to 1973 he was deputy lieutenant of Ross and Cromarty; and in 1971 he was elected a fellow of the Royal Society of Edinburgh.

Linklater's novels in this later period are well written and ingenious, but to an extent lack the comic energy of their predecessors; and finding himself less in rapport with the public, he turned more to history as time went on. At the end of the twentieth century, however, they had yet to receive serious critical evaluation, which some certainly deserve. Linklater's best fiction often uses myth as a central structuring device, as with his use of Byron in *Juan in America*. *A Man over Forty* (1963) repeats that appropriateness by juxtaposing the worlds of twentieth-century television and ancient Greek myth: Edward Balintore is a television personality who unconcernedly submits to a gruelling interview on air, only to collapse suddenly and dramatically after confessing he is afraid of being found out. The book charts his comic journey in search of peace, his gradual self-discovery, and the exorcizing of his guilt. The basic myth is that of Orestes, and Balintore's buried memory of matricide and his pursuit by twentieth-century Furies forms the sober centre of a comic novel which combines all of Linklater's best ingredients.

Linklater was notable for his craftsmanship, his sense of style, his love of wit, and his zest for life, all of which are apparent in his autobiographies. As a novelist he excels mainly in providing civilized entertainment for intelligent middlebrow readers. Although he travelled widely his roots were deep in Scottish rural life: he loved fishing, walking, and boating, and once described himself as 'an old peasant with a pen' (Linklater, *Fanfare*, 326), although his lifestyle was in fact more that of a country gentleman. His manner tended to the brusque and military. In appearance, his most striking features were a high domed forehead, prematurely bald head with a deeply indented skull due to his war wound, rimless spectacles, and a moustache. He died in St John's Nursing Home, Aberdeen, on 7 November 1974 after a thrombosis, and was buried in the Harray churchyard in Orkney on 11 November.

Linklater's wife, **Marjorie Linklater** (1909–1997), campaigner for the arts and the environment, was born on 19 March 1909 at 19 Northumberland Street, Edinburgh, the daughter of Ian MacIntyre (1869–1946), writer to the signet, Scottish rugby international, and later Unionist MP for West Edinburgh, and his first wife, Ida (*d*. 1942), daughter of Charles Van der Gucht. Educated at St George's School, Edinburgh, Downe House, Berkshire, and the Royal Academy of Dramatic Art, London, and considered a great beauty, she acted in small West End parts, then returned to Scotland. She met her future husband while campaigning for a Scottish national theatre. One of their sons described their marriage as 'turbulent and ultimately consoling' (*The Guardian*, 5 July 1997). Following the family's move to Ross-shire in 1947 she was a member of Ross and Cromarty county council (1953–69), involved in conservation and education issues. She was also a member of the Scottish Arts Council (1957–63). After her husband's death she moved back to Orkney, to which she was devoted. She was active in local heritage, arts, environment, and politics, successfully opposed uranium mining and off-shore nuclear-waste dumping, was chairman of the Orkney Heritage Society (1977–81), helped establish the St Magnus festival, and campaigned for the Scottish National Party. She died on 29 June 1997 at 20 Main Street, Kirkwall, Orkney, and was survived by her four children, one of whom, Magnus (*b*. 1942), was editor of *The Scotsman* (1988–94) and chairman of the Scottish Arts Council (1996–2001).

ANDREW RUTHERFORD, *rev*. ISOBEL MURRAY

Sources E. Linklater, *The man on my back* (1941) • E. Linklater, *A year of space* (1953) • E. Linklater, *Fanfare for a tin hat* (1970) • M. Parnell, *Eric Linklater* (1984) • I. Murray, 'Novelists of the Renaissance', *The history of Scottish literature*, 4: *Twentieth century*, ed. C. Craig (1987), 103–17 • A. Linklater, introduction, in E. Linklater, *The goose girl and other stories*, ed. A. Linklater (1991), vii–xi • J. M. D'Arcy, *Scottish skalds and sagamen: Old Norse influence on modern Scottish literature* (1996) • *The Scotsman* (4 July 1997) • *The Independent* (4 July 1997) • *The Times* (5

July 1997) • *The Guardian* (5 July 1997) • *WWW* • m. cert. • b. cert. [Marjorie Linklater] • d. cert. [Marjorie Linklater] • *CCI* (1975)
Archives BBC WAC, corresp. • NL Scot., MSS and literary MSS • U. Reading, corresp. | NL Scot., letters to Neil M. Gunn • NL Scot., letters to Rachel Annand Taylor • NL Scot., letters to Isobel H. Walker • U. Reading, corresp. with Jonathan Cape • U. Reading, corresp. with Chatto & Windus Press and Hogarth Press | SOUND BL NSA, BBC Radio 4, recording of a talk about Aberdeen
Likenesses S. Cursiter, group portrait, oils, 1950 (*Authors in session*), Glasgow Art Gallery and Museum • H. Coster, photographs, 1954, NPG [*see illus.*] • S. Cursiter, portrait, U. Aberdeen • photographs, Hult. Arch.
Wealth at death £38,779.41: confirmation, 28 May 1975, *CCI*

Linklater, Marjorie (1909–1997). *See under* Linklater, Eric Robert Russell (1899–1974).

Linley [*married name* Sheridan], **Elizabeth Ann** (1754–1792), singer and writer, was born on 5 September (some sources give 4 or 7 September) 1754, probably in her parents' house on Abbey Green, Bath, Somerset, the eldest daughter of the musician Thomas *Linley (1733–1795) and his wife, Mary Johnson (1729–1820). She probably sang in Bath concerts from 1763, and sold tickets for concerts from an early age. After a short stint at a boarding-school in Bristol (Bor and Clelland, 26) or Wells (Black, 15), Elizabeth probably made her stage début with her brother Thomas *Linley the younger [*see under* Linley, Thomas] in Thomas Hull's *The Fairy Favour* at Covent Garden, London, in 1767. Thomas Linley fully exploited his children's talents: in 1768 Mary Dewes noted that Elizabeth sang in Bath's weekly concerts and that 'she has a sweet voice; but he makes her sing *too much* and *too hard* songs, for she is very young' (Delany, 2nd ser., 1.133). Thomas Linley retained tight control over his children's performances in Oxford and London and at the Three Choirs festival: in 1770 he accepted George Colman's contract for a daughter (probably Elizabeth) to sing in the Covent Garden oratorios, but would not let her act there, as he did not 'relish giving the prime of my Daughters performance to support the schemes of others' (Colman, 151).

In 1773, when Elizabeth was at the height of her fame, Frances Burney commented that her voice was:

> soft, sweet, clear & affecting, she sings with good Expression, & has great Fancy & even taste in her Cadences, though perhaps, a finished singer would give less way to the former, & prefer few & select Notes. She has an exceeding good shake, & the best & most critical Judges pronounce her to be infinitely superiour to *all* other English singers. (*Early Journals and Letters*, 1.249–50)

Burney's sister Susan, however, noted that she was 'without the soul or refinement of a great Italian singer' (Black, 94–5). Elizabeth's voice, enhanced by her beauty, intelligence, and modesty, fostered the cult that surrounded her throughout her life. David Garrick affectionately named her 'the Saint' (*Letters of David Garrick*, 3.1163). Joshua Reynolds painted her as Saint Cecilia, as Charity for the window of New College, Oxford, and as the Virgin in the nativity. She was also a frequent subject for Thomas Gainsborough, and Richard Samuel painted her as Terpsichore in *The Nine Living Muses of Great Britain*. Charles Burney called her a:

Elizabeth Ann Linley [Sheridan] (**1754–1792**), by Thomas Gainsborough, *c*.1785–7

> 'Sancta Caecilia rediviva' … The tone of her voice and expressive manner of singing were as enchanting as her countenance and conversation … she was possessed of the double power of delighting an audience equally in pathetic strains, and songs of brilliant execution, which is allowed to very few singers.

He said that her range extended 'a fourth above the highest note of the harpsichord' (which was *f'''*) (Rees, 5.21).

This 'saint' had certainly had her trials. In December 1770 the wealthy, elderly Walter Long became engaged to Elizabeth, indemnifying her parents against their loss of her earnings. He resigned his claim in 1771—apparently abruptly, shortly before the intended wedding—avoiding a lawsuit by paying her £3000 and leaving her about £1000 of jewellery and clothing already gifted (*Bath Chronicle*, 27 June and 1 Aug 1771). The reason for his actions are uncertain: Elizabeth may have refused to retire from public life, or may have begged him to release her from the match, or he may have been scared off by Samuel Foote's popular play *The Maid of Bath* (premiered 27 June 1771), which dealt with her relationship difficulties. These difficulties also included an importunate married suitor, 'Captain' (in fact, Ensign) Thomas Mathews, a friend of her father's. Mathews's pursuit became so overbearing that she ran away to France in 1772. She was escorted by the young Richard Brinsley *Sheridan (1751–1816), brother to her confidant, Alicia Sheridan (later Alicia Le Fanu). According to Alicia's report, Elizabeth intended to board in a convent, but once in France Sheridan persuaded her that, given appearances, she should marry him (Moore, 50). The 'marriage', putatively in March 1772, went unrecorded, was kept secret, and is unlikely to have been valid. On their return to Bath, Sheridan fought two duels with Mathews, and Elizabeth was kept under strict parental surveillance. When Sheridan's father sent him to Waltham Abbey, forbidding him contact with Elizabeth, and when Sheridan consequently began dalliances with other women, their relationship cooled.

In 1773 Thomas Linley took his family to London for the oratorio season. Elizabeth took principal parts in the oratorios, and at two performances the *London Chronicle* reported that 'their Majesties paid great attention both night's to Miss Linley's singing, and seemed much pleased' (11–13 March 1773). Horace Walpole said that the king 'ogles her as much as he dares to do in so holy a place as an oratorio' (Walpole, *Corr.*, 32.106). Frances Burney exclaimed: 'The whole Town seem distracted about her. Every other Diversion is forsaken—Miss Linley Alone engrosses all Eyes, Ears, Hearts' (*Early Journals and Letters*, 1.249). Meanwhile, Elizabeth resigned herself to accept her father's choice of London suitor (who had agreed to leave her fortune with her father). Sheridan's interest was rekindled, however, and he somehow won her and her father round, perhaps partly through promising she could sing again (for Garrick) if the family were in need. Their widely anticipated marriage occurred on 13 April 1773 at St Marylebone.

Once married, Sheridan ended Elizabeth's public career, explaining to her aggrieved father that 'your daughter's marriage [marked] … quite as natural a period to your rights over her as her death' (*Letters of Richard Brinsley Sheridan*, 1.80). The *Bath Chronicle* of 19 April 1773 estimated that her father had made nearly £10,000 from her voice. Sheridan certainly declined large sums for various appearances—some say £3200 (Sichel, 1.425), others £2000 per annum for seven years (Watkins, 1.143). On 4 February 1774, however, he advertised a twice-weekly series of exclusive 'private' subscription concerts (*Letters*, 1.84). Elizabeth's feelings about her career are unclear: her father apparently had promised her a lighter workload on returning from France, and her constantly delicate state of health must have made the strenuous schedule of concert and oratorio tours all the more daunting. She had joked of fainting during a performance of *Samson* in Cambridge in June 1772, causing 'no small bustle among the Cantabs' (Rae, 1.195). Sheridan's refusal to let her sing for family and friends on their first Christmas cannot have pleased her, however. After the initial failure of his play *The Rivals* (1775), she wrote to him:

> My dear Dick, I am delighted. I always knew that it was impossible you could make anything by writing plays; so now there is nothing for it but my beginning to sing publickly again, and we shall have as much money as we like. (Sichel, 1.500–01)

Amid family concerns and poor health—she had one son, Thomas (Tom) *Sheridan, and several miscarriages—Elizabeth devoted herself to furthering Sheridan's career. When Sheridan, Thomas Linley, and Dr Ford bought Garrick's share in Drury Lane Theatre in 1776, Elizabeth kept accounts, auditioned singers, and read and advised Sheridan on play manuscripts. Michael Kelly stated that she adapted *Richard Coeur de Lion* for the English stage—this was presumably the version of which the libretto is usually credited to John Burgoyne—and wrote English words to a Gluck song that he performed. Sheridan's letters regarding *The Duenna* (1775) demonstrate Elizabeth's hand in the music, and according to Watkins she composed for Sheridan's *Robinson Crusoe*. When Sheridan and Thomas Harris took over management of the King's Theatre opera house in 1778, Elizabeth was apparently also engaged in selecting music for that venture. Elizabeth had a bent for verse (much of her output—particularly her courtship and elegiac poetry—became public), and Sheridan said of their early married life that 'Mrs. Sheridan and myself were often obliged to keep writing for our daily leg or shoulder of mutton' (Watkins, 1.144). While the couple's courtship furnished the material for Sheridan's plays, Elizabeth may also have had an active role in their creation. In 1775 her sister Mary *Linley [*see under* Linley, Thomas] speculated that Elizabeth had written the 'much admired' epilogue to *The Rivals* (Moore, 101), and Watkins said that *The School for Scandal* was 'by some … attributed to the pen of Mrs. Sheridan' (Watkins, 1.159).

As Sheridan turned from the theatre to politics, winning the seat of Stafford with Edward Monckton in 1780, his wife assisted him, and became one of the leading politically active whig women. In 1784 and 1790 she electioneered for Charles James Fox, her 'passionate admirer' (Sichel, 1.186); in 1789, during the Regency crisis, she wrote out the letter from George, prince of Wales, to the ministry, accepting the Regency, and jokingly said to her friend Mehetabel Canning that 'I intend when he is Regent to claim something good for myself for *Secret Service*' (Gillaspie, 201). Elizabeth continued her own writing; in December 1782 she told Alicia Sheridan, 'I have begun my book and you cannot think what a respectable figure it cuts already' (Sichel, 2.392). William Linley apparently told Thomas Moore that she had written 'an entertainment called the "Haunted Village", which she gave Sheridan to add some touches to', but which he never returned, suppressing it (so Linley thought) out of jealousy (Bor and Clelland, 109).

Although in 1779 Frances Burney noted that Sheridan 'evidently adores her,—and she as evidently idolizes him' (*Early Journals and Letters*, 3.230), their marriage did not continue happily. Burney also noted that 'Mrs. Sheridan's Beauty is unequaled by any I *ever* saw except Mrs. Crewes' (ibid., 3.226), and indeed Sheridan's first notable affair, beginning as early as 1775, was with Frances Anne Crewe, a prominent whig hostess. Over his later liaison with Harriet Ponsonby (*née* Cavendish), Lady Duncannon, Elizabeth wrote to Canning proposing 'an amiable separation', as 'we have been sometime separated *in fact* as Man and Wife … the duplicity of his Conduct to me, has hurt me more than any thing else, and I confess to you that my Heart is entirely Alienated from him' (Gillaspie, 324).

Elizabeth suffered depression not only from Sheridan's alienation, but also from the death of several of her siblings, particularly her beloved sister Mary in 1787. Caring for Mary's children distracted her, and the eldest, her namesake, was made her ward: 'the Legacy of her ever Dear and lamented Mother … constitutes all my Happiness', she wrote (*A Nest of Nightingales*, 80). Distraction also came in the form of a dalliance with the infatuated duke of Clarence (later William IV). She claimed to Canning that:

> tho' I own to you I am not indifferent to his devoted Attachment for Me, and have thought more favourably of him still, since I have had reason to make Comparisons between his Conduct and S—' … you may rely on the propriety of my Conduct in regard to him for many sakes—but I will in future live by myself, and to my own Tastes. (Gillaspie, 324)

By the end of 1790 Elizabeth had all but separated from Sheridan. Only pressure from her friends, including Fox, had prevented her from making the break obvious, and she continued to accompany Sheridan at Foxite whig social events. About that time she began a sexual relationship with Lord Edward *Fitzgerald (1763–1798), then a Foxite nobleman with leanings towards the radicalism of Thomas Paine. In Fitzgerald's words, 'She managed me' (Tillyard, 124). She became pregnant with his child in summer 1791, but was soon obviously ill with tuberculosis, and the pregnancy probably hastened her own death. Her daughter, Mary, was born on 30 March 1792. Elizabeth died at Bristol Hotwells in Clifton, Gloucestershire, on 28 June 1792. Her dying wish was that Sheridan should recognize Mary as his own child, but that Canning should have charge of her. Elizabeth's independence of mind extended to religious matters: she told Canning, 'there is nobody has more true Religion *at Heart* than I have, tho' I profess to think less seriously of forms and Ceremonies than some do' (Gillaspie, 190). None the less, she was buried on 7 July in Wells Cathedral next to her sister, in front of a great crowd of onlookers. SUZANNE ASPDEN

Sources J. A. Gillaspie, ed., *The catalogue of music in the Bath Reference Library to 1985* (1986) • W. S. Sichel, *Sheridan, from new and original material, including a manuscript diary by Georgiana duchess of Devonshire*, 2 vols. (1909) • T. Moore, *Memoirs of the life of the Right Honourable Richard Brinsley Sheridan* (1825) • *A nest of nightingales: Thomas Gainsborough, the Linley sisters* (1988) [exhibition catalogue, Dulwich Picture Gallery, 21 Sept–30 Dec 1988] • M. Bor and L. Clelland, *Still the lark: a biography of Elizabeth Linley* (1962) • J. Watkins, *Memoir of the public and private life of … Richard Brinsley Sheridan, with a particular account of his family and connexions*, 2 vols. (1817) • *The early journals and letters of Fanny Burney*, ed. L. E. Troide, 3 vols. (1988–94) • *The letters of Richard Brinsley Sheridan*, ed. C. Price, 3 vols. (1966) • C. B. Hogan, ed., *The London stage, 1660–1800*, pt 5: *1776–1800* (1968) • C. Black, *The Linleys of Bath*, rev. edn (1971) • A. Rees, *Cyclopædia*, 45 vols. (1802–20), 5.21 • *The autobiography and correspondence of Mary Granville, Mrs Delany*, ed. Lady Llanover, 1st ser., 3 vols. (1861); 2nd ser., 3 vols. (1862) • W. F. Rae, *Sheridan, a biography*, 2 vols. (1896) • F. Colman, *Posthumous letters, from various celebrated men; addressed to Francis Colman, and George Colman, the elder: with annotations, and occasional remarks, by G. Colman, the younger* (1820) • H. Angelo, *Reminiscences of Henry Angelo, with memoirs of his late father and friends*, 2 vols. (1828) • *The letters of David Garrick*, ed. D. M. Little and G. M. Kahrl, 3 vols. (1963) • M. Kelly, *Reminiscences*, 2nd edn, 2 vols. (1826); repr., R. Fiske, ed. (1975) • Walpole, *Corr.* • Boswell, *Life* • Highfill, Burnim & Langhans, *BDA* • S. Foote, *The maid of Bath* (1771) • *London Chronicle* (11–13 March 1773); (30 July–1 Aug 1775) • *Bath Chronicle* (27 June 1771); (1 Aug 1771); (19 April 1773) • S. Tillyard, *Citizen lord* (1997) • I. Woodfield, *Opera and drama in eighteenth-century London* (2001), 154

Archives Harvard TC, autograph letters • Harvard U., Widener Library, letters • priv. coll., letters • priv. coll., papers [typescripts] • PRO NIre., letters and papers, D1071 | Bath Central Library, letters to Mehetabel Stratford Canning, ALB.1535–ALB.1571, ALB.2289–MSB.2308 • Harvard TC • King's Cam., letters to Alicia Le Fanu

Likenesses T. Gainsborough, double portrait, oils, c.1768 (*Miss Linley and her brother*), Sterling and Francine Clark Art Institute, Williamstown, Massachusetts • T. Gainsborough, double portrait, oils, c.1771–1772 (with her sister Mary; *The Linley Sisters*), Dulwich Picture Gallery, London • T. Gainsborough, oils, c.1775, Philadelphia Museum of Art, George Elkin collection • J. Reynolds, oils, 1775 (as St Cecilia), Waddesdon Manor • J. Reynolds, oils, c.1777 (for the window at New College, Oxford, painted by Thomas Jervais and installed in 1783) • B. West, oils, c.1778 (*The Sheridan family*), Trustees of the National Museums and Galleries on Merseyside • J. Ogbourne, engraving, 1779 (after O. Humphry) • R. Samuel, group portrait, oils, 1779 (*The nine living muses of Great Britain*), NPG • T. Gainsborough, oils, c.1785–1787, National Gallery of Art, Washington, DC [*see illus.*] • H. H. Meyer, stipple, pubd 1816 (after O. Humphry), NPG • C. Middlemist, stipple and line engraving, pubd 1816 (after J. Reynolds), BM, NPG • O. Humphry, crayon, 1911; formerly at Frampton Court • O. Humphry, pastel on paper on canvas, Victoria Art Gallery, Bath • line engraving (after unknown artist), NPG

Linley, Francis (1770/71–1800), composer and music-seller, was born in Doncaster. Although he was blind from birth, he received a good education, and studied music under Edward Miller, organist of Doncaster parish church from 1756 to 1807. About 1790 Linley held the post of organist at St James's Chapel, Pentonville, London, and about the same time he married a wealthy blind lady. In 1796 they bought the business of Bland, a music-seller in Holborn, but their commercial and domestic affairs did not prosper. His wife left him, and Linley went to America, where he remained for several years; he returned to Doncaster in 1799.

Linley's compositions and compilations include *Three Sonatas for Pianoforte and Flute*, op. 1; *Thirty Familiar Airs for Two German Flutes*, with prefatory remarks (1791); *Three Solos for the German Flute, with Accompaniment for Violoncello*; 'Through groves and flowery fields' (1796?), 'When angry nations' (1796?), and other songs; and *A Practical Introduction to the Organ, in Five Parts*, of which the twelfth edition appeared about 1810. The last contained a description of the organ, fifteen preludes, eight voluntaries, eight full pieces, eight fugues, and psalms.

Linley died at his mother's house in Doncaster on 13 September 1800. Beechey reports that an obituary appeared in the *Doncaster, Nottingham and Lincoln Gazette* on 19 September 1800 stating that Linley was twenty-nine at the time of his death and a freemason.

L. M. MIDDLETON, *rev.* DAVID J. GOLBY

Sources G. Beechey, 'Linley, Francis', *New Grove* • [Clarke], *The Georgian era: memoirs of the most eminent persons*, 4 (1834), 548 • *GM*, 1st ser., 70 (1800), 1006 • *Doncaster, Nottingham and Lincoln Gazette* (19 Sept 1800)

Linley, George (1798–1865), poet and songwriter, was born at Briggate, Leeds, and baptized on 7 February 1798, at St Peter's Church, Leeds, a younger son of James Linley (1764–1812), a tin plate worker, and his wife, Ann (1769–1839), whose maiden name was possibly Townsley. He was educated first by Joshua Eastburn, a Quaker, then at Leeds grammar school; by the age of sixteen he was an ensign in the 3rd West Yorkshire militia. His service took him to Doncaster and Dublin. He had stirred up antagonistic feelings in Leeds by attacking local dignitaries in lampooning verses in the *Leeds Intelligencer*, and 'bolted to London in a huff' (Spark, 'God bless'). On 4 April 1824, at St Cuthbert's Church in Edinburgh, he married Violet, the youngest daughter of the orientalist Dr John Borthwick *Gilchrist (1759–1841). About 1826 he was reported to be a partner in a mercantile firm in Leith, but he soon returned to London. He and his wife had at least four children, three of whom were christened there: Julia (*bap.* 1832), Mary Ann (*bap.* 1834), and Violet Olivia (*bap.* 1837). He also had at least one son, George [*see below*].

Once established in London, Linley proved that he was, in his own words, 'addicted to poetry' (Spark, 'God bless'), by his prolific outpouring of song lyrics, hymns, ballads, musical arrangements of nursery rhymes and folk songs, and more ambitiously, operatic works, for which he sometimes wrote both words and music. He wrote the lyrics and/or music of several hundred songs between 1830 and 1865. Many of these had considerable contemporary popularity: his obituarist in the *Leeds Mercury* (29 September 1865) gives particular mention to 'Thou art gone from my gaze', 'Ever of thee', and 'Little Nell'. These works are marked by a pronounced sentimentality, somewhat at odds with the aggressively satirical tone of Linley's other poetical works, *Musical Cynics of London* (1862; reprinted 1862) and *The Modern Hudibras* (1864; enlarged edn, 1864). In the former work he interpolates prose passages among the heroic couplets; a main target of his satire is Henry Fothergill Chorley, music critic of *The Athenaeum*. Linley was unrepentant that some people had 'hinted at an undue severity' towards Chorley: he refers to the 'malignant ravings' of Chorley, defending his poem as 'retributive justice' (Preface, 2nd edn). *The Modern Hudibras* is more wide-ranging in its satirical attacks—including references to his native Yorkshire. Both poems are characterized by awkward rhymes and laboured movement, and Linley's attempts at grander musical forms were no more successful. His first such undertaking was to write the music and songs for *Francesca Doria* which was produced on 3 March 1849 at the Princess's Theatre, London. This was followed by *The Toymaker* (1861), an adaptation of Adams' *La poupée de Nuremberg*, performed at Covent Garden Theatre on 19 November. *Law versus Love*, a one-act comedietta, was performed at the Princess's Theatre on 6 December 1862. Linley also wrote a number of librettos, including that for Balfe's *Catherine Grey*, the first English opera without spoken dialogue. Most of this material, however, has been relegated to the realms of musical history. Perhaps the most enduring of Linley's compositions was the song 'God Bless the Prince of Wales'; he is said to have suggested ideas for the musical setting to its composer, Henry Brinley Richards. Richards earned £100 for the composition, from which sum £10 was given to Linley. Linley appears to have had no musical training and thus the limited nature of his achievements may be viewed with greater tolerance.

Linley died at his home, Alfred Cottage, Victoria Road, Kensington, after prolonged illness, on 10 September 1865 and was buried on 15 September at Kensal Green cemetery. He was survived by his wife. His son **George Linley** (*bap.* 1834, *d.* 1869), poet, was baptized on 29 September 1834 at St Phillip's, Birmingham. He followed in his father's footsteps as an aspiring poet. He published *The Goldseeker and other Poems* (1860), based on his travels in Australia, and dedicated to the duke of Argyll, and *Old Saws Newly Set* (1864), a collection of fables. On 4 October 1862 he married Emma, the younger sister of Sims Reeves, singer. He died on 28 April 1869, aged thirty-three.

ROSEMARY SCOTT

Sources Summersgill collection of newspaper cuttings, Leeds Local Studies Library • *Leeds Mercury* (29 Sept 1865) • *Monumental inscriptions of St. John the Evangelist, Leeds*, Publications of the Thoresby Society, vol. 35 • W. Spark, 'God bless the prince of Wales', *Local Notes and Queries* [*Leeds Mercury* supplement], 331 (May 1885) • G. Hauger, 'Linley of Leeds', *Yorkshire Illustrated* (May 1949), 9 • W. Spark, *Musical memories*, 2nd edn (1888) • *GM*, 3rd ser., 19 (1865), 654 • *The Times* (25 Sept 1865) • L. J. De Bekker, *Black's dictionary of music and musicians* (1924) • *New Grove* • Brown & Stratton, *Brit. mus.* • Boase, *Mod. Eng. biog.* • *IGI*

Archives Bodl. Oxf., assignments of copyright, MS Eng. misc. c. 669

Likenesses C. H. Schwanfelder, oils, 1820–29, Leeds City Art Gallery

Wealth at death under £450: probate, 18 Oct 1865, *CGPLA Eng. & Wales*

Linley, George (*bap.* 1834, *d.* 1869). *See under* Linley, George (1798–1865).

Linley, Maria (*bap.* 1763, *d.* 1784). *See under* Linley, Thomas (1733–1795).

Linley, Mary (1758–1787). *See under* Linley, Thomas (1733–1795).

Linley, Ozias Thurstan (*bap.* 1765, *d.* 1831). *See under* Linley, Thomas (1733–1795).

Linley, Thomas (1733–1795), impresario and composer, was born at Badminton, Gloucestershire, on 17 January 1733 and baptized at Badminton parish church on 20 January, the eldest child of the carpenter William Linley (*bap.* 1704, *d.* 1792) and his wife, Maria (1701–1792). He was evidently musically precocious, as on the family's move to Bath in 1744 he was apprenticed to the organist of Bath Abbey, Thomas Chilcot. As a child he may have studied in London with Domenico Paradies.

Linley sang—in a 'particular natural stile' (*Letters of Richard Brinsley Sheridan*, 1.20)—and played the harpsichord in Bath's Assembly Rooms concerts, directed by Chilcot, from 1755; after Chilcot's death in 1766 he ran the concerts. Linley's income must initially have derived chiefly

Thomas Linley (1733–1795), by Thomas Gainsborough, *c.*1771

from his numerous students, either visitors to Bath (such as Frances Sheridan) or young apprentices such as his own children. On 11 May 1752 Linley married Mary Johnson (1729–1820), whose 'natural talents for musick were nearly equal to his own' (*A Nest of Nightingales*, 50), according to their lodger, Ozias Humphry.

The growth of the Linley family All eight Linley children who survived infancy (four did not) proved musically talented, and the three eldest in particular were greatly admired, Thomas (Tom) [*see below*], as a violinist and later a composer, Elizabeth Ann *Linley and Mary [*see below*] as singers. The children regularly appeared in Linley's benefit concerts, and he boasted in 1767 that 'to merit their future Favour, it shall be his constant Study, by every Effort in his Power, to promote their Improvement' (*Bath Chronicle*, 14 May 1767). Linley was both praised for nurturing his children's abilities and criticized for working them too hard; the flight of his eldest daughter, Elizabeth, to a French convent in 1772 may partly have stemmed from overwork, and on returning to England she spoke of Linley's 'promise' (Rae, 1.191) of fewer engagements. In 1772 Richard Brinsley Sheridan told his father that 'Mr. Linley and his whole family, down to the seven year olds are to support one set [of oratorios] at the new [Assembly] Rooms, and a band and Singers from London another at the old' (*Letters of Richard Brinsley Sheridan*, 1.23).

Other Bath musicians resented Linley's success: in 1771 Francis Fleming wrote that 'by dint of congé's and scrapes, and the plea of a young family to maintain, [Linley] excited the pity and compassion of the company so compleatly, that it became a customary phrase among them to say "Let us go to poor L—y's concert;" by this means he *never failed* filling the concert room' (Fleming, 3.98), while others were effectively put out of business. Linley's appointment in 1771 as director of music at the New Assembly Rooms attracted particular resentment, both as the new rooms openly rivalled the old, and as Linley excluded four of his seven Pump Room players (including Fleming) from the new ten-strong band. Within months, the new band member William Herschel quarrelled with Linley and left the band, ostensibly over the lack of music stands, but actually because Linley refused to allow Elizabeth to sing in Herschel's benefit concert. Herschel, a composer and oboist from Hanover, had gone to Bath in 1767 to act as organist to the newly opened Octagon Chapel, and Linley responded with his own proprietary chapel, St Margaret's, in 1772. Linley was also director for the Long Room at Bristol Hotwells, and the Bath rivalry continued during Bristol's oratorio seasons of 1772–4. Linley eventually triumphed in 1775, winning a monopoly of the oratorio seasons at both the old and the new rooms, his band alternating between the two.

As the family travelled farther afield—to perform in Oxford, at the Three Choirs festivals, and in London oratorios—Linley could use demand for his children, particularly the now famous Elizabeth, to his advantage. In his letter of October 1770 to the Covent Garden theatre manager, George Colman, Linley agreed that a daughter (probably Elizabeth) could sing in the 1771 oratorios (for the very high fee of '200 Guineas, and a clear Benefit'), but:

> It is contrary to my Inclination that my Daughter should sing at either House for the Oratorio's, or anywhere else in London, where I am not myself a Principal in the Undertaking—for were I properly settled in London, I think I could conduct the Business of Oratorios myself, whenever an opportunity offered for me to attempt it … In regard to engaging her as an Actress, I shall never do that, unless it were to ensure myself and Family a solid Settlement, by being admitted to purchase a share in the Patent on reasonable Terms … w[ch] I perceive no probability of obtaining—and I shall never lay myself at the mercy of my Children, especially when their very power of being service to me depends so entirely upon Chance. (Colman, 150–1)

In 1773 John Christopher Smith and John Stanley contracted Elizabeth, Mary, and Tom for the Drury Lane season of Lenten oratorios; the *Bath Chronicle* for 1 April reported that 'The two Linleys carry all before them', estimating receipts at over £500 a night. The sisters' fee for the Foundling Hospital concert that year was an unprecedented £80. The *Bath Chronicle* for 19 April estimated that Linley had made nearly £10,000 by Elizabeth's voice; Elizabeth, however, had just married Richard Brinsley *Sheridan, and he had terminated her singing career. In November 1773 Linley declined the Pantheon's request for Mary to sing (Sheridan having had first refusal for Elizabeth), but told Sheridan that he would have liked to 'make the People here [Bath], sensible, that I am not absolutely dependent upon them, which they seem mightily inclined to believe, as Your Wife is no more to appear in Publick' (Gillaspie, 226).

Linley at Drury Lane In 1774, when Smith retired from co-managing the Drury Lane oratorios, George III recommended Sheridan to succeed him (evidently hoping Elizabeth would sing again); Sheridan declined, but proposed Linley instead, who, he said, had 'twenty Mrs. Sheridans more' (*Letters of Richard Brinsley Sheridan*, 1.86). Garrick offered Linley a seven- or fourteen-year contract to co-manage the Drury Lane oratorios, as part of which his daughters Mary and Maria [*see below*] would join the Drury Lane company. Linley rejected this offer, but negotiations were renewed and from 1776 he ran the oratorios with Stanley. The latter retired in 1784; Linley's subsequent colleagues were Samuel Arnold until 1793 and Stephen Storace in 1794. The eleven-night season was generally profitable, and if in 1779 it cleared about £500, in 1794, in a new Drury Lane theatre which opened on the first oratorio night, profits were over £4000.

On retiring in 1776 David Garrick sold his share of Drury Lane's patent to Linley and Sheridan. Linley was praised as 'an Example of great Merit & Industry' (*Letters*, 3.1114), who 'will be of great Service—Sing Song is much the Fashion, & his knowledge of Musick & preparing fit Subjects for the Stage, will be a Strength, that the Proprietors may depend upon, when the Heroines are prankish' (ibid., 3.1063). Linley for his part wrote to Garrick that he wished to 'remove myself from the place I am in, where I do not see the least chance of being any other than a Servant to ye [Assembly] Rooms' (Highfill, Burnim & Langhans, *BDA*, 9.312). When the contract was signed, Linley and Sheridan paid £10,000 each and Dr Ford, court physician, paid £15,000; Linley's share came from mortgages on his Bath properties and on his share in the theatre. The Linleys moved to Norfolk Street in London, leaving their three youngest children, Ozias Thurstan [*see below*], Jane Nash (1768–1806), and William *Linley, in Bath, and when Sheridan took over from Garrick as manager of Drury Lane, Linley became musical director for £500 per annum, and his wife became wardrobe mistress for £1 10*s*. a week, in which capacity her parsimony grew legendary.

Insecurity may have played its part in preventing Linley from taking up Garrick's first offer: in 1775 he claimed he had 'great reason to be diffident of my own abilities and genius' (*Private Correspondence*, 2.101). His first venture in theatrical composition, for Thomas Hull's *The Royal Merchant* at Covent Garden, in 1767, had failed. One diarist noted that 'The music may be good, but the piece is trifling and childish' (*The London Stage, 1660–1800*, pt 4, 3.1299). While in the Drury Lane post, Linley composed the music for several dialogue operas, pantomimes, and other pieces. Several of these were works written by his sons-in-law: he composed seven songs for Sheridan's *The Duenna* (Covent Garden, 1775); wrote one song for Sheridan's *The School for Scandal* (1777); wrote the music for *The Camp* (1778, attributed to Sheridan and Richard Tickell), and for Sheridan's *Monody on the Death of Garrick* (1779); added songs for Sheridan's revision of Henry Woodward's *Fortunatus* (1780); wrote for Sheridan's *Robinson Crusoe* (1781), though Watkins attributes the music to Elizabeth Sheridan (Watkins, 2.93); and wrote for Tickell's *The Carnival of Venice* (1781). He wrote occasional music—particularly songs—for a variety of other pieces.

His post also required him to arrange others' music. Linley arranged, for example, choruses and accompaniments for Matthew Locke's music for *Macbeth* (1776), for Purcell's and Arne's music for Dryden's *King Arthur* in John Philip Kemble's 1784 production, *Arthur and Emmeline*, and for Kemble's version of *The Tempest* (1789). He adapted André Grétry's music for Sir George Collier's *Selima and Azor* (1776) and for John Burgoyne's *Richard Coeur de Lion* (1786). He compiled and wrote for several of James Cobb's pieces, *The Strangers at Home* (1785), *Hurly-Burley* (1785), *Love in the East* (1788), and *The Haunted Tower* (1789). Charles Burney said that in his theatrical duties Linley 'gave more satisfaction, and escaped censure, public and private, by his probity and steady conduct, more than is often allowed to the governor of such a numerous and froward family' (Rees), no doubt intending a contrast with Linley's wayward son-in-law Sheridan. Linley was admitted to the Royal Society of Musicians in 1780.

Linley's forte was vocal music, and the Drury Lane débuts of his singing students, such as Anna Maria Crouch, Ann Field, and Charles Dignum, regularly featured his songs. As well as individual songs, Linley published *Elegies for Three Voices* (*c*.1770) and *Twelve Ballads* (1780). In 1800 his widow published *The posthumous vocal works of Mr. Linley and Mr. T. Linley, consisting of songs, duetts, cantatas, madrigals and glees*. Linley also published a series of letters 'On music' (in fact, on singing) in the *European Magazine* (1792). Of the *Elegies*—of which Linley was so proud that he was painted with a copy—Burney said that Linley had 'stedfastly adhered to a style of [his] own, which seems to have been formed upon the melodies of our best old English masters, and those of the last age, that were most worthy of being preserved' (Burney, *Hist. mus.*, 2.1016–17).

Linley was widely respected as a singing teacher. Michael Kelly praised his 'masterly instructions' (Kelly, 164), while William Thomas Parke described his teaching abilities as 'almost unrivalled in England' (Parke, 1.203). No doubt his 'grave' manner contributed to his success: Anna Maria Crouch described him as 'dark, stern, and gigantic; I tremble sometimes when I look at him' (Young, 1.84). At least some of Linley's gravity was due to the deaths of his children, particularly Tom in 1778, Samuel (a talented oboist, who died from a fever caught at sea) in 1781, Maria in 1784, Mary in 1787, and Elizabeth in 1792. Mary Young said that, at a play rehearsal after Tom's death, when one of the characters:

> gave an impressive description of a promising young man … the feelings of Mr. Linley could not be repressed, the tears of mental agony rolled down his cheeks; nor did he weep alone, the cause of his distress was too well known not to obtain the tears of sympathy from many who beheld *his* flow so fast. (Young, 1.79)

Linley became increasingly melancholy and unwell (suffering from giddiness and loss of memory) in his latter years. He died on 19 November 1795 at 11 Southampton Street, Westminster, and was buried with his daughters

Elizabeth and Mary on 29 November 1795 in Wells Cathedral.

It was reported that Linley left a fortune of £25,000 on his death (Boswell, *Life*, 2.521). In his will, made in 1788, he left to his 'Dear Wife' most of his household possessions and £300 per annum, also making lesser annual financial provision for his surviving children (Elizabeth, Ozias, William, and Jane), and for his grandsons Richard and Samuel Tickell. Elizabeth was left his harpsichord, music books, and manuscripts; his sons Ozias and William his other musical instruments; his estate at Didmarton, Gloucestershire, was left to Ozias; bequests of £100 were made to his grandson Thomas Sheridan, his granddaughter Elizabeth Tickell, and his daughter Jane. The *Gentleman's Magazine's* obituary gave measured praise:

> His works are not distinguished by any striking marks of original genius, but they uniformly manifest taste, feeling, and a full knowledge of his art. The publick are indebted to him for many beautiful airs; he has harmonized with great judgement the melodies of former writers; and, if it was not in his power to astonish by sublime effects, his compositions always soothe and charm by delicacy, simplicity and tenderness. (*GM*, 1st ser., 65/2, 1795, 973)

Linley's eldest son, **Thomas Linley junior** (1756–1778), violinist and composer, was born on 5 May 1756, probably at Linley's house on Abbey Green, Bath. Known to his family and friends as Tom, according to Matthew Cooke he had an 'early and strong passion for Music' (Highfill, Burnim & Langhans, *BDA*, 9.316). He was taught the violin by David Richards, of the Bath assembly rooms band, and was already singing and playing the violin in public in 1763. He then went to London to study with William Boyce for five years. In 1767 he made a much praised London stage début at Covent Garden in Thomas Hull's *The Fairy Favour*. In 1768 Tom went to Florence to spend three years under Pietro Nardini. There he met and befriended the young Mozart, and Burney said that the two were 'talked of all over Italy, as the most promising geniusses of this age' (*Musical Tour*, ed. Scholes, 184). Tom returned to England to act as soloist and leader in his father's concerts, both on the oratorio circuit and, from 1776, in London. His compositions also excited attention: by 1776 about twenty violin concertos were added to six sonatas written in 1768 under Boyce's tutelage. His first anthem, 'Let God arise', written for the 1773 Three Choirs festival in Worcester, achieved particular praise for its technical sophistication. For *The Duenna* he wrote the overture and several songs, and arranged two-thirds of the music. Once attached to Drury Lane he wrote a *Lyric Ode* on Shakespeare's supernatural creatures (1776), incidental music for *The Tempest* (1777), and a comic opera *The Cady of Bagdad* with a libretto by Abraham Portal (1778). His short oratorio *The Song of Moses* (1777) was described as one of the 'finest specimens of the Simple, Affecting, Grand and Sublime styles that ever was produced by the pen of a Musician' (Highfill, Burnim & Langhans, *BDA*, 9.317). W. T. Parke nominated Tom Linley to the Royal Society of Musicians in 1777. He seemed to be in the early stages of a brilliant career; but his life was to be dramatically and tragically cut short. In summer 1778 he accepted a position as music teacher to the daughter of Peregrine Bertie, third duke of Ancaster, at Ancaster's country estate of Grimsthorpe in Lincolnshire. On 5 August 1778 he fell in the lake at Grimsthorpe while boating and was drowned. He was buried in the Ancaster family vault at Edenham parish church, Lincolnshire. He was unmarried.

Mary Linley [*married name* Tickell] (1758–1787), known as Polly, made her first London stage appearance at Covent Garden in 1769 as Sally in George Colman's *Man and Wife*, playing her part 'with great humour and vivacity' (*Freeholder's Magazine*, Oct 1769, quoted in *A Nest of Nightingales*, 79). She was principally a singer, however, and after a brief period at a boarding-school in Bristol or Wells toured with her family, appearing in a variety of oratorios and concerts from 1771. Mary was always overshadowed by Elizabeth: even in looks, Frances Burney exclaimed, she was 'handsome, but *nothing* near her sister' (*Early Journals and Letters*, 3.226). Garrick tried to contract Mary and Maria for Drury Lane theatre in 1775, in exchange for a seven- or fourteen-year contract co-managing the theatre oratorios for Linley: he wrote to Colman from Bath of a secret to 'make your hairs stand on End!—I believe I may engage the blood of the Linleys!' (*Letters*, 3.1003). Although Sheridan agreed with Linley that Mary's 'Talents for the Stage … are undoubted' (*Letters of Richard Brinsley Sheridan*, 3.305), he persuaded Linley that acting careers would be improper, especially given his daughters' musical abilities: 'Polly is certainly at present considered *here* as the best *Oratorio* Singer there now is, and tho' her Sister Maria may come to surpass her in some things—She will always be respectable and in the first Line' (ibid., 3.303). Mary sang in her father's Drury Lane oratorios until 1779. The *Morning Chronicle* for 24 February 1776 reported that

> Miss Linley, last night, in Acis and Galatea, gave every delight that the ear, the heart, or understanding could receive from music … Miss Linley's manner of delivering Recitative is peculiarly distinct and sensible … Her voice is clear and melodious, and capable of the truest expression.

She ceased her singing career when she married, at St Clement Danes on 26 July 1780, Richard *Tickell (1751–1793), a sometime playwright and political pamphleteer, and a practical joker suited to her own witty temperament. The Tickells initially lived at Wells, but when Tickell was made a commissioner of the stamp office they moved to rooms in Hampton Court, although they also kept a house in Brook Street and then Queen Anne Street, Westminster. If Tickell and Sheridan were close friends (Mary jokingly accused her husband of 'Sheridanisms'; *A Nest of Nightingales*, 79), Mary and Elizabeth were closer, and supported each other against their husbands' thoughtlessness and irresponsibility. The Tickells had three children, Elizabeth Ann (Betty; 1781–1860), Richard Brinsley (1783–1805), and Samuel (1785–1817). When Mary died from tuberculosis at Bristol Hotwells, Gloucestershire, on 27 July 1787, the children were entrusted to Elizabeth's care; Betty became her ward. Mary was buried in Wells Cathedral.

Maria Linley (*bap.* 1763, *d.* 1784), singer, was the eighth child of Thomas and Mary Linley, baptized on 10 October

1763 at St James's, Bath. She was evidently prodigiously talented, if Garrick was attempting to engage her at twelve. Sheridan wrote to Linley that Garrick was 'particularly stimulated by the Reputation of what Maria promises to be, in whom He hopes to forestall at least another Mrs. S.' (*Letters of Richard Brinsley Sheridan*, 3.295), adding that 'whatever you *did* get by Betsey—and what more you *might* have got … you *may* get and if you rely only on yourself, certainly *will* get by Maria' (ibid., 3.303). Maria's sexual orientation is uncertain; Mary's letters seem to suggest that her headstrong sister may have had an affair with 'the well-timber'd [Miss] Troward' (Black, 133), and she occasionally dressed in men's clothing. Maria sang in the Drury Lane oratorios from 1776 to 1783, but in 1784 contracted a fever that led to her death at Bath on 5 September 1784. Her brother William told Michael Kelly that 'After one of the severest paroxysms of the dreadful complaint, she suddenly rose up in her bed, and began the song of "I know that my Redeemer liveth" in as full and clear a tone as when in perfect health' (Kelly, 238). The *Gentleman's Magazine*'s obituary stated: 'Her death is a loss almost irreparable to the musical world … The union of a sweet voice, correct judgement, extensive compass, and, above all, beauty of mind and person distinguished this much-lamented maid' (*GM*, 1st ser., 54/2, 1784, 717).

Ozias Thurstan Linley (*bap.* 1765, *d.* 1831), composer and Church of England clergyman, was baptized at Bath Abbey on 22 August 1765, the ninth child of Thomas and Mary Linley. He was left in Bath when the Linleys moved to London, as were William and Jane (the only Linley daughter not trained as a professional singer, though she sang very well). He lodged with his paternal grandparents, and was taught music and mathematics by William Herschel. Ozias demonstrated early 'Traits of a strong understanding', though his father was 'apprehensive of his being very deficient in common sense' (Lubbock, 43), and indeed he was later known for his absentmindedness and eccentricity. Although he composed some liturgical pieces (some surviving in the Royal College of Music, London, with work by his brother William), Ozias preferred theoretical to practical music. He matriculated at Corpus Christi College, Oxford, on 19 March 1785 and proceeded BA in 1789. He was made a minor canon of Norwich Cathedral in 1790 through the offices of his beloved sister Elizabeth. In 1807 and 1815 he received two livings from the cathedral, those of Stoke Holy Cross, Norfolk, and Trowse with Lakenham, Norfolk, respectively, but in 1816 moved to Dulwich College, Dulwich, Surrey, where he became junior fellow and organist. He died at Dulwich College on 6 March 1831, and was buried in the college chapel. He was unmarried.

SUZANNE ASPDEN

Sources *The letters of Richard Brinsley Sheridan*, ed. C. Price, 3 vols. (1966) • *A nest of nightingales: Thomas Gainsborough, the Linley sisters* (1988) [exhibition catalogue, Dulwich Picture Gallery, 1 Sept – 30 Dec 1988] • M. Bor and L. Clelland, *Still the lark: a biography of Elizabeth Linley* (1962) • *The letters of David Garrick*, ed. D. M. Little and G. M. Kahrl, 3 vols. (1963) • Highfill, Burnim & Langhans, *BDA* • I. Woodfield, *The celebrated quarrel between Thomas Linley (senior) and William Herschel: an episode in the musical of 18th century [sic] Bath*, Holborne of Menstrie Museum, University of Bath Music Monographs, 1 (1977) • J. A. Gillaspie, ed., *The catalogue of music in the Bath Reference Library to 1985* (1986) • S. McVeigh, *Concert life in London from Mozart to Haydn* (1993) • *The early journals and letters of Fanny Burney*, ed. L. E. Troide, 3 vols. (1988–94) • C. B. Hogan, ed., *The London stage, 1660–1800*, pt 5: *1776–1800* (1968) • Burney, *Hist. mus.*, new edn • *An eighteenth-century musical tour in France and Italy: being Dr Charles Burney's account of his musical experiences as it appears in his published volume, with which are incorporated his travel experiences according to his original intention*, ed. P. A. Scholes (1959) • F. Fleming, *The life and extraordinary adventures, the perils and critical escapes, of Timothy Ginnadrake, that child of chequer'd fortune*, 3 vols. (1771) • M. J. Young, *Memoirs of Mrs Crouch*, 2 vols. (1806) • W. T. Parke, *Musical memoirs*, 2 vols. (1830) • A. Rees and others, *The cyclopaedia, or, Universal dictionary of arts, sciences, and literature*, 45 vols. (1819–20), vol. 5, p. 21 • W. S. Sichel, *Sheridan, from new and original material, including a manuscript diary by Georgiana duchess of Devonshire*, 2 vols. (1909) • J. Watkins, *Memoir of the public and private life of … Richard Brinsley Sheridan, with a particular account of his family and connexions*, 2 vols. (1817) • *The private correspondence of David Garrick*, ed. J. Boaden, 2 vols. (1831–2) • G. Colman, ed., *Posthumous letters, from various celebrated men: addressed to Francis Colman, and George Colman, the elder, with annotations … by George Colman, the younger* (1820) • W. F. Rae, *Sheridan: a biography* (1896) • Boswell, *Life* • T. Moore, *Memoirs of the life of the Right Honourable Richard Brinsley Sheridan* (1825) • E. Sheridan Le Fanu, *Betsy Sheridan's journal: letters from Sheridan's* (1960) • E. Green, *Richard Brinsley Sheridan and Thomas Linley, their residences at Bath, with a notice of the Sheridan grotto* (1904) • *European Magazine and London Review*, 23 (1793) • *The autobiography and correspondence of Mary Granville, Mrs Delany*, ed. Lady Llanover, 1st ser., 3 vols. (1861); 2nd ser., 3 vols. (1862) • C. Black, *The Linleys of Bath*, rev. edn (1971) • H. Angelo, *Reminiscences*, 1 (1828) • M. Kelly, *Reminiscences*, 2nd edn, 2 vols. (1826); repr., R. Fiske, ed. (1975) • Walpole, *Corr.* • T. Moore, *Memoirs of the life of the Right Honourable Richard Brinsley Sheridan* (1825) • C. A. Lubbock, *The Herschel chronicle* (1933) • *Pope's Bath Chronicle* (14 May 1767) • *Bath Chronicle* (1 April 1773) • *Bath Chronicle* (19 April 1773) • *GM*, 1st ser., 54 (1784), 717 • *GM*, 1st ser., 65 (1795), 973, 1052 • Foster, *Alum. Oxon., 1500–1714*, 3.854 • *Morning Chronicle* (24 Feb 1776)

Archives Bath Central Library, autograph letters | Folger, autograph letters of Mary Linley [Mary Linley] • Harvard TC, autograph letters of Mary Linley [Mary Linley] • Harvard U., Harry Elkins Widener collection, autograph letters of Mary Linley [Mary Linley]

Likenesses T. Gainsborough, oils, 1766–1769? (Thomas Linley junior), Dulwich Picture Gallery • T. Gainsborough, oils, *c.*1768 (Thomas Linley junior; *Miss Linley and her brother*), Sterling and Francine Clark Institute, Williamstown, Massachusetts • T. Gainsborough, oils, *c.*1771, Dulwich Picture Gallery [*see illus.*] • T. Gainsborough, oils, *c.*1771–1772 (Mary Linley; *The Linley Sisters*), Dulwich Picture Gallery • attrib. O. Humphry, miniature watercolour on paper, *c.*1777–*c.*1778 (Maria Linley), Bath City Council, Victoria Art Gallery • attrib. O. Humphry, watercolour and body colour on white paper, *c.*1777–*c.*1778 (Thomas Linley junior), Bath City Council, Victoria Art Gallery • T. Ryder, stipple, pubd 1785 (after R. Westall), BM, NPG • A. J. Oliver, oils, 1805–1810? (Ozias Linley), Dulwich Picture Gallery • J. Condé, stipple (Mary Linley; after R. Cosway), NPG • R. Cosway, miniature (Mary Linley); formerly in possession of Kenwood House Lumsden Property • T. Gainsborough, oils (Mary Linley after marriage?; the 'Kenwood Gainsborough') • T. Gainsborough, oils (Thomas Linley junior), Greenwich, Connecticut • O. Humphry, portrait (Mary Linley; *Mrs Tickell, when a child*) • T. Lawrence, pastels on paper (Maria Linley), Dulwich Picture Gallery • attrib. T. Lawrence, pastels on paper laid down on canvas (Ozias Linley; aged fourteen), Dulwich Picture Gallery

Wealth at death £25,000: Boswell, *Life*, ed. Hill and Powell, 2.521

Linley, Thomas, junior (1756–1778). *See under* Linley, Thomas (1733–1795).

Linley, William (1771–1835), composer and author, youngest son of Thomas *Linley the elder (1733–1795) and his wife, Mary Johnson (or Johnston), was born on 27 January 1771 in Bath. Five years later his parents moved to London. In 1780 William was sent to school at Harrow (where his sister Elizabeth [*see* Linley, Elizabeth Ann] and her husband, Richard Brinsley Sheridan, were then living). In February 1785 he was transferred to St Paul's School, and later was sent to C. F. Abel for counterpoint lessons; he also studied, so he himself said, with J. B. Cramer. His father taught him singing, however, and Coleridge, hearing him in a song of Purcell's in 1797, promptly made him the subject of a sonnet. In 1790 (and with the backing, it is said, of Charles James Fox), Linley gained a place as a writer in the East India Company and sailed for Madras, where, in 1791, he was appointed assistant under the collector of Madura and Dindigul, and, two years later, deputy secretary to the military board. His health soon gave way, however, and he was obliged to return to England, where he arrived just in time to witness his father's death in November 1795.

On 18 January 1796, a pantomime, *Harlequin Captive, or, The Magick Fire*, was successfully produced at Drury Lane, and in April Linley also contributed some incidental music to W. H. Ireland's Shakespearian hoax *Vortigern*. It was no doubt on the strength of his performance so far that Sheridan made him composer at Drury Lane later that year. But everything else Linley attempted over the next four seasons failed miserably. Among these were a comic opera, *The Honeymoon* (1797), and an entertainment, *The Pavilion* (1799) (in which Michael Kelly had a leading role), for both of which Linley wrote not only the music but also the words. Though Sheridan had apparently agreed that he should be paid £7 a week together with 2 per cent of the net profits, it seems that Linley saw very little of this; by 1800 his circumstances were so much reduced that he was more or less forced to return to India.

Earlier that year Linley's first novel, *Forbidden Apartments* (in two volumes), had appeared, and shortly after his arrival in Madras he began another, *The Adventures of Ralph Reybridge*, which came out in four volumes in 1809. In 1801 he became paymaster at Vellore, and in 1805 sub-treasurer and mint-master to the presidency at Fort St George—two posts which were evidently sufficiently lucrative to enable him only a year or so later to return to London, where, with his inherited interest in the Drury Lane Theatre (and other properties left to him by his father), he was able, as a gentleman amateur, to devote himself to writing and composition. During this second spell of Indian service he wrote a fair amount of music, and also a number of 'Sonnets and odes, elegies, ballads, and sketches' which later (in 1819) found their way into print (together with an account of the life and writings of Charles Leftley, a school friend at St Paul's).

Linley's musical output is almost entirely vocal, and consists mainly of songs and glees, only a relatively small number of which were ever published. Some are settings of his own words, and some of words by Thomas Moore (whose friendship over many years he also enjoyed). First to appear were six glees to words by Leftley, issued under the title *Flights of Fancy* in 1797, four of which were reprinted in his final set of *Eight Glees* (1832). A two-volume anthology of Shakespearian songs by Linley and various other composers (1815–16) is by far his most important publication. A good many songs and glees, most of them individually dated, survive in manuscript. His church music was nearly all written for St Margaret's Chapel, Bath (of which he was a proprietor). A proposed book of critical observations on music offered to the publishers Cadell and Davies in 1811 never materialized.

On his return to London, Linley evidently became a good friend of Samuel Wesley, who later dedicated an organ work to him, although their friendship eventually soured. He resumed his membership of the Concentores Sodales, a vocal club at whose second meeting (on 23 June 1798) he had been present; a mason of several years' standing, he also joined the Catch and Glee clubs, and from 1809 until his death he was a member of the Madrigal Society and the Noblemen and Gentlemen's Catch Club as well. In February 1810 he was elected to the Sublime Society of Beefsteaks. The last of his line, he died unmarried at his chambers at 3 Furnival's Inn, Holborn, London, on 6 May 1835, and was buried in the family vault at St Paul's, Covent Garden. A memorial tablet to him was erected in the church. His property he left to the only daughter of his sister, Mrs Mary Tickell, and several family portraits by Lawrence, Gainsborough, and others he bequeathed to Dulwich College, of which his clergyman brother Ozias had been organist-fellow. H. Diack Johnstone

Sources W. Linley, preface, *Eight glees* (1832) · Grove, *Dict. mus.* · *New Grove* · [J. S. Sainsbury], ed., *A dictionary of musicians*, 2 vols. (1824) · C. Black, *The Linleys of Bath*, 2nd edn (1926) · Highfill, Burnim & Langhans, *BDA* · W. L. Bowles, 'Recollections of the late William Linley', *GM*, 2nd ser., 3 (1835), 574–6 · J. A. Gillaspie, ed., *The catalogue of music in the Bath Reference Library to 1985* (1986) · R. Fiske, *English theatre music in the eighteenth century* (1973) · [J. Watkins and F. Shoberl], *A biographical dictionary of the living authors of Great Britain and Ireland* (1816) · C. B. Hogan, ed., *The London stage, 1660–1800*, pt 5: 1776–1800 (1968) · Brown & Stratton, *Brit. mus.* · D. Baptie, *A handbook of musical biography* (1883) · M. Kelly, *Reminiscences*, 2nd edn, 2 vols. (1826); repr., R. Fiske, ed. (1975) · C. Price, 'Sheridan–Linley documents', *Theatre Notebook*, 21 (1966–7), 165–7 · *Memoirs, journal and correspondence of Thomas Moore*, ed. J. Russell, 8 vols. (1853–6) · letter from S. Wesley to Mr Bridgetower, 24 Jan 1814?, BL, Add. MS 56411 · private information (2004) [P. Olleson]

Archives Bath Central Library · GL · Royal College of Music, London · Theatre Museum, London | Bath Central Library, letters to George Brook and others · BL, letters to William Ayrton, Add. MS 52342

Likenesses T. Lawrence, oils, exh. RA 1789, Dulwich College, London; copy, Royal College of Music · J. Oliver, portrait, 1810 · T. G. Lupton, mezzotint, pubd 1840 (after T. Lawrence), BM, NPG · W. P. Sherlock, stipple, 1840 (after J. Lonsdale), NPG; repro. in Linley, *Eight glees*, frontispiece · J. Lonsdale, portrait

Linlithgow. For this title name *see* Livingstone, Alexander, first earl of Linlithgow (*d.* 1621); Livingstone, Helen, countess of Linlithgow (*d.* 1627); Livingstone, George, third earl of Linlithgow (1616–1690); Livingstone, George, fourth earl of Linlithgow (*c.*1652–1695); Hope, John Adrian Louis, seventh earl of Hopetoun and first marquess of Linlithgow (1860–1908); Hope, Victor Alexander John, second marquess of Linlithgow (1887–1952).

Linnaeus, Carl [*later* Carl von Linné] **(1707–1778)**, naturalist and taxonomist, was born on 13 May 1707 in a turf-roofed homestead at Råsult, near Stenbrohult, in the province of Småland in southern Sweden, the eldest of five children of the pastor, Nils Nicolaus Linnaeus (1674–1748), and his wife, Christina Broderzonia (1688–1733). After schooling at Växjö, a nearby town, he began medical studies at the University of Lund, transferring in August 1728 to Uppsala University. Befriended by the theologian and naturalist Olof Celsius (1670–1756), who appointed him demonstrator in botany in 1730, he travelled to 'Lappland', as it was then known, in summer 1732, reporting to the Vetenskapsakademien (Swedish Royal Society of Sciences) on its natural history and economy. In 1734 he met his future wife, Sara Elisabeth Moraea (1716–1806), daughter of Johan Moraeus, the town physician of Falun, and Elizabeth Hausdotter; they were engaged in January 1735 with an agreement to delay marriage for three years.

Linnaeus left Sweden for the Netherlands in April 1735, travelling via Hamburg to Harderwijk, a Dutch university town specializing in issuing 'instant' degrees. He registered as a student on 18 June and gained his medical doctorate on 23 June within a week of his arrival. He then moved to Leiden and met and impressed the medical doctor and botanist Johan Gronovius (1690–1760). Gronovius and Isaac Lawson, a young Scottish doctor, agreed to fund the printing of Linnaeus's first published work, the *Systema naturae* of 1735, which classified the three kingdoms of nature and outlined the sexual system for the classification of plants. Gronovius was also instrumental in introducing Linnaeus to the wealthy but hypochondriac Anglo-Dutch financier and director of the Dutch East India Company, George Clifford (1685–1760), owner of a magnificent garden at Hartecamp, suggesting that he employ Linnaeus as house physician and garden superintendent. Linnaeus moved to Hartecamp in September with a salary of 1000 florins a year and free board and lodging. His own and contemporary accounts give a picture of a methodical and sensual observer of nature 'little, flurried, rushed, nimble' (Linnaeus, 97) and Lindroth concludes that his success in the Netherlands was due to 'his personal attractiveness, his capacity for captivating grizzled authorities' (Frängsmyr, 54).

After almost a year in Clifford's employment Linnaeus travelled to England, arriving at the end of July 1736 and returning to the Netherlands in late August. His *Systema naturae* of 1735 had been sent ahead by Gronovius and Lawson to Sir Hans Sloane, president of the Royal Society. Despite a fulsome letter of introduction he met with a cool reception from Sloane, although he was shown Sloane's museum. He also met Philip Miller, superintendent of the Society of Apothecaries' garden at Chelsea. Both were unhappy initially about Linnaeus's new system of classification but Miller was won over by Linnaeus's

Carl Linnaeus (1707–1778), by Lorenz Pasch, before 1805 (after Alexandre Roslin, 1774)

botanical knowledge and was then generous with plants for Clifford. Other London acquaintances included the Quaker naturalist and merchant Peter Collinson, whom he visited and with whom he maintained a lifelong correspondence. He travelled to Oxford to meet the Sherardian professor of botany, Johan Jakob Dillenius, who initially disagreed with him, also giving him a cold reception. This changed just as Linnaeus was about to return to London when, after discussing what Dillenius had marked as errors in advance pages of *Genera plantarum* (which was not published until the following year), it was demonstrated by dissection of plants that Linnaeus was correct. They remained lifelong friends and correspondents, Dillenius telling him to 'write as one friend ought to address another' (Smith, 2.107). Linnaeus also records meeting John Martyn, professor of botany at Cambridge, and Georg Ehret, whom he knew from the Netherlands. The majority of the forty-plus British correspondents of Linnaeus first wrote to him later on, when he had established his reputation.

These contacts were important as being among the earliest to promote both Linnaeus's binomial nomenclature for living organisms and to publish floras using his sexual system for the classification of plants. The rules for this were explained in Linnaeus's *Fundamenta botanica* (1736) and expounded in his *Classes plantarum* of 1738, based on the tabular key published in the *Systema naturae* of 1735. This system used the flower and the number and arrangements of its sexual organs of stamens and pistils to group plants into twenty-four classes, which in turn are divided into orders, genera, and species. Amateur botanists and gardeners in England, such as Peter Collinson and John Ellis, were quick to adopt his methods. The binomial system that Linnaeus used for genus and species names supplied short names ideal for quick reference. The accompanying diagnostic phrase names give the fuller description of the plant. Among the earliest to use Linnaean concepts in a published work were the naturalist and apothecary John Hill, who described the system in his publications as early as 1751, and the Irish naturalist Patrick Browne, who used phrase names in his *Civic and Natural History of Jamaica* of 1756. The apothecary William Hudson published his *Flora Anglica* in 1762, one of the first floras to use the binomial system, and its acceptance in British circles was shown when Philip Miller adopted it in the eighth edition of his *Gardener's Dictionary* of 1768. Its adoption became widespread in Britain and its overseas colonies, and was reinforced when Sir Joseph Banks employed one of Linnaeus's pupils, Daniel Solander, as his curator and librarian. These British contacts formed the start of what later became the almost universal acceptance of the Linnaean system, and were further reinforced in the 1780s when Linnaeus's botanical collections, purchased by J. E. Smith, went to Britain and the Linnean Society of London was founded. Linnaeus himself was elected to the Royal Society of London in 1753.

Returning to the Netherlands, Linnaeus took back new plants for Clifford's garden and remained in Clifford's employment until autumn 1738; using Dutch printing facilities he published in 1737 *Genera plantarum*, *Flora Lapponica*, *Critica botanica*, and *Hortus Cliffortianus*. A brief visit to Paris was followed by his return to Sweden in the autumn of 1738, to establish a medical practice in Stockholm.

Practical advice on treatment of venereal disease from a French medical doctor helped to establish Linnaeus's reputation and, through a successful prescription for a friend of the queen and contact with Count Carl Tessin (1695–1770), leader of the ruling Hat party, he was appointed physician to the admiralty, also becoming first president of the newly established Academy of Science of Stockholm. His long-awaited marriage to Sara Lisa Moraea took place on 26 June 1739 and in January 1741, a son, Carl, was born. Later that year the medical professorship at Uppsala University was offered to Linnaeus, and in making the move he was able to arrange to exchange positions with E. Rosén (1714–1796), botanical professor and a rival of long standing, each then teaching the subjects best suited to him. Linnaeus took charge of the botanical garden and revived it, adding a small menagerie. He was an incomparable academic teacher, inspiring his disciples, and his lectures were often crowded.

In 1744 Linnaeus wrote in his autobiography that he had achieved his desires. He continued to publish prolifically but increasingly suffered from brooding despair, despite the increasing international fame which followed publication of the *Species plantarum* of 1753, now recognized as the starting point of modern botanical nomenclature, and the tenth edition in 1758 of the *Systema naturae*, which is the equivalent for zoological nomenclature. Today's international codes which govern the use of scientific names for all living organisms recognize Linnaeus as the starting point of modern taxonomy: about 12,000 of these names have the abbreviation 'L' appended to them, indicating their origin in a published Linnaean description.

An increasing family included four surviving daughters (a daughter and a son dying in infancy). In 1758 Linnaeus bought a country estate at Hammarby, and was made a knight of the Polar Star; further honours followed in 1761 when he was ennobled, taking the title Carl von Linné in 1762. At this time he arranged to hand over his teaching duties to his son, Carl von Linné the younger (1741–1783), for reasons of ill health; he continued to live mostly at Hammarby, where he built a museum to hold his collections safe from fire. In his last years his health declined, after he suffered two strokes. He died on 10 January 1778 in Uppsala from an ulcerated bladder. His funeral and burial were at Uppsala Cathedral on 22 January 1778.

GINA DOUGLAS

Sources Th. M. Fries, *Linné, Lefnadsteckning*, 2 vols. (1903) • C. Linnaeus, *Vita Caroli Linnaei*, ed. E. Malmström and A. H. Uggla (1957) • W. Blunt, *The compleat naturalist: a life of Linnaeus* (1971) • J. E. Smith, ed., *A selection of the correspondence of Linnaeus and other naturalists*, 2 vols. (1821) • W. T. Stearn and G. Bridson, *Carl Linnaeus, 1701–1778: a bicentenary guide to the career and achievements of Linnaeus and the collections of the Linnean Society* (1978) • T. Frängsmyr, ed., *Linnaeus, the man and his work*, rev. edn (1994) • F. A. Stafleu and R. S. Cowan, *Taxonomic literature: a selective guide*, 2nd edn, 3, Regnum Vegetabile, 105 (1981) • F. A. Stafleu, *Linnaeus and the Linnaeans: the spreading of their ideas in systematic botany* (1971) • B. D. Jackson, *Linnaeus (afterwards Carl von Linné) the story of his life* (1923) • B. D. Jackson, 'The visit of Carl Linnaeus to England in 1736', *Svenska Linné sälskapets Årgang*, 9 (1926), 1–11 • B. H. Soulsby, ed., *A catalogue of the works of Linnaeus … preserved in the libraries of the British Museum (Bloomsbury) and the British Museum (Natural History)*, 2nd edn (1933) • *Svenskt biografiskt lexikon*

Archives BL, corresp. and papers, Egerton MSS 2037–2041 • BL, letters • Carnegie Mellon University, Pittsburgh, Hunt Institute for Botanical Documentation, papers • Linn. Soc., corresp. and papers • NHM, lecture notes and papers • NHM, plant specimens and printed works • Riksmuseum, Stockholm, Linnaean herbarium • Uppsala University, Museum of Evolution, Linnaean zoological specimens • Uppsala University Library, Linnaean collections | BL, letters to Antoine Govan, Add. MS 22935 • Carnegie Mellon University, Pittsburgh, Hunt Institute for Botanical Documentation, Strandell collection • Linn. Soc., corresp. with John Ellis

Likenesses L. Pasch, portrait, before 1805 (after A. Roslin, 1774), Linn. Soc. [*see illus.*]

Wealth at death 1000 guineas in collections of natural history specimens, books, and MSS; also house and land: will, Linnaean collections, 1778

Linnecar, Richard (1722–1800), writer, was born at Wakefield and was for some time postmaster there. In 1763 he was elected one of the coroners for the West Riding of Yorkshire. For many years he was a prominent freemason. Linnecar was initiated into the order at Gibraltar in 1743 and then later held the office of master of the lodge of unanimity at Wakefield for twenty-six years. In 1787 his portrait was painted for the lodge by Singleton. It was later engraved by T. Barrow and reproduced on a masonic banner that remains at the Wakefield lodge.

Richard Linnecar (1722–1800), by Thomas Barrow, pubd 1800 (after Henry Singleton)

Linnecar published by subscription in 1789 *Miscellaneous Works*, containing two comedies, *The Lucky Escape* and *The Plotting Wives*, the latter of which was performed at York on 6 February 1769; a tragedy, *The Generous Moor*, 'founded upon a true story' which Linnecar apparently heard in Gibraltar (Linnecar, 105); some prose *Strictures on Freemasonry* and numerous songs and other trifles in verse. The work was dedicated to John Berkenhout and the author's other 'generous subscribers' (ibid., unpaginated dedication). Linnecar's substantial list of subscribers induced his unenthusiastic anonymous reviewer in the *Critical Review* 'to suppose that Mr. Linnecar has some other claim on public favour than his literary abilities' (1792, 229).

Linnecar died while holding an inquest at Swillington, Yorkshire, on 14 March 1800, aged seventy-eight (*GM*, 1800, 391). GORDON GOODWIN, *rev.* JEFFREY HERRLE

Sources *GM*, 1st ser., 70 (1800), 391 • N. B. Cryer, *Masonic halls of England: the north* (1989) • R. Linnecar, *The miscellaneous works of Richard Linnecar* (1789) • review of *The miscellaneous works of Richard Linnecar*, *Critical Review*, [new ser.], 6 (1792), 229–30

Likenesses H. Singleton, portrait, 1787, Wakefield Masonic Lodge, Yorkshire; repro. in Cryer, *Masonic halls*, 107 • T. Barrow, stipple, pubd 1800 (after H. Singleton), NPG [*see illus.*] • portrait on banner (after H. Singleton), Wakefield Masonic Lodge, Yorkshire

Linnell, John (**1792–1882**), landscape and portrait painter, was born on 16 June 1792 in Plum Tree Street, Bloomsbury, London, the fourth and youngest child of James Linnell (1759–1836), woodcarver, framemaker, and picture dealer, and his wife, Mary Susannah, *née* Welshman (*d.* 1825). Linnell had a long and very successful career as an artist, but modern assessments of his importance centre on his early work, and on his relationships with his fellow artists William Blake and Samuel Palmer, who became his son-in-law in 1837.

Early years, 1792–1811 Linnell claimed that he had no formal education, but learned to paint by copying works by George Morland for his father. He was introduced to artists by the latter, and *c.*1804 made visits to Benjamin West, who looked at his sketches and offered advice. In his diary entries for 9 and 14 November 1806 Farington mentioned that his small-scale oil studies had attracted the attention of David Wilkie, Benjamin Haydon, and Sir George Beaumont. In 1805 Linnell entered the Royal Academy Schools, and at about this time he became a pupil of John Varley. With William Mulready and William Henry Hunt, also pupils of Varley, he made oil sketches from nature along the banks of the Thames, for example, *Study of Buildings: Sketch from Nature* (1806; Tate collection). He was especially close to Mulready, with whom he was to share lodgings between 1809 and 1811. In the evenings, at this early period, *c.*1805–6, Linnell copied drawings in the house of the art patron Dr Thomas Monro. From 1807 to 1811 he exhibited oil paintings at the Royal Academy and at the British Institution, mainly genre scenes and landscapes which show the influence of seventeenth-century Dutch art, for example, *The Quoit Players*, 1810, which was bought by Sir Thomas Baring for 75 guineas. At the British Institution Linnell won a premium of 50 guineas in 1809 for *Removing Timber in Autumn*.

During this period Linnell was apprenticed to his father, having signed an indenture for seven years in 1806.

Early landscapes, 1811–1818 In 1811 Linnell left the Academy Schools. His friendship with Cornelius Varley, brother of John, seems to have stimulated both a religious conversion and a new approach to landscape painting in this year. He joined the Baptist church in January 1812, becoming a member of the chapel at Keppel Street, Bloomsbury, and bought drawing instruments which would enable him to transcribe what he saw with scientific accuracy. He read the writings of William Paley, whose natural theology encouraged Linnell, like many other artists of his time, to regard the study of landscape as a valuable response to the work of God. In his subject matter a new interest in working figures is evident, especially in *Kensington Gravel Pits* (1812; Tate collection). Many of his watercolour studies in this decade adopt unconventional compositions, suggesting a self-consciously haphazard, informal method of constructing landscape, such as *Brick Kiln, Kensington, 1811–12* (priv. coll.). When the Society of Painters in Water Colours changed its name to the Society of Painters in Oil and Water Colours in 1813, Linnell was a founding member, and contributed fifty-two works (probably all oils) to its exhibitions between 1813 and 1820. Many of these were based on sketching trips made in 1813, 1814, and 1815. In 1813, with George Robert Lewis, he visited north Wales, where he was impressed by the wild scenery, writing many years later, 'I could almost fancy myself living in the times of Jacob and Esau and might expect to meet their flocks' (Linnell, autobiography, 45–6).

John Linnell (1792–1882), self-portrait, *c.*1860

In 1814 he was in Derbyshire, making drawings for an edition of I. Walton and C. Cotton's *Compleat Angler*, commissioned by the Baptist publisher Samuel Bagster; in 1815 he went to Southampton and the Isle of Wight. The watercolour sketches of this period are remarkably fresh and have been the basis for the reassessment of Linnell's work from the 1970s onwards. Linnell himself, however, seems not to have exhibited them, regarding them as raw material for landscapes in oil. Exhibited landscapes of this time, such as *The River Kennet Near Newbury* (1815; FM Cam.), follow the sketches closely, implying a commitment to naturalism on Linnell's part. In 1818 he exhibited his first religious painting, *St John Preaching in the Wilderness*.

This period of Linnell's life came to an end with his marriage to Mary Ann Palmer (1796–1865, no relation to the artist Samuel Palmer) in 1817. The couple travelled to Scotland for a civil ceremony, Linnell believing that the Church of England one was blasphemous. He had taught himself Greek and Hebrew so that he could read the Bible in the original, since he held that the Authorized Version was corrupt. Just as he went to the fountainhead of nature in his landscape studies, so he felt that he should go to the works of God rather than man in his religious studies.

Friend and patron of Blake and Palmer, 1818–1829 In 1818 Linnell was introduced, by George Cumberland junior, to William Blake. Their shared attitudes to art and religion brought about a strong rapport, and Linnell played an important role in Blake's last years. He commissioned the engravings for the *Book of Job* (1825) in 1823 and the watercolour illustrations to Dante's *Divine Comedy* (1827) in 1824. He gave Blake, who was often unable to work through illness, a regular income, and arranged his funeral when he died in 1827. Both men were part of a circle of collectors, artists, and writers, which included Mr and Mrs Charles Aders and Henry Crabb Robinson, who were interested in early Renaissance art. Linnell himself bought early paintings in this period of his life, including one attributed to Lucas van Leyden in 1822. Linnell also introduced Blake to Dr Thornton, the Linnell family doctor, in 1819; it was Thornton who commissioned the woodcut illustrations for his translation of Virgil's *Eclogues*, which were to be so much admired by Samuel Palmer.

Linnell met Palmer in 1822 and introduced him to Blake in 1824. In his notebooks Palmer recorded the advice of both men, which led him away from the conventional watercolour style of his day into a more intense and visionary engagement with landscape. It was Palmer's opinion at this time that 'it pleased God to send Mr Linnell as a good angel from Heaven to pluck me from the pit of modern art' (Palmer, *Life and Letters*, 14). After Blake's death, Linnell made visits to Palmer at Shoreham (August and September 1828 and June 1829) and encouraged him to make studies from nature. Surviving correspondence reveals a stimulating relationship, not without its tensions as Palmer feared naturalism was a diversion from his real mission, which was to paint his inner visions in keeping with the ideas of Blake. However, Linnell commissioned studies from Palmer, thus helping to support him when the younger artist was selling very few pictures. Religious beliefs were to be a growing source of disagreement: Palmer was drawn to high Anglicanism, while Linnell became increasingly low church, breaking with the Baptists in the 1820s, considering membership of the Society of Friends in 1830, and eventually joining the Plymouth Brethren in 1843. In 1848 he left the Plymouth Brethren when his son John was accused by them of heresy, and henceforth belonged to no established religious group. His faith remained strong, however, grounded in his conviction of the necessity of going directly to the source of divine revelation. In later life he published pamphlets expounding his views on the corrupt nature of existing translations of the Bible: *Diatheekee, Covenant not Testament* (1856) and *Burnt offering not in the Hebrew Bible: shown by a revised version of the first part of Leviticus* (1864).

Society portrait painter, 1821–1846 Following his marriage in 1817, Linnell's first child, Hannah (who married Samuel Palmer), was born in 1818; by 1835 he had nine children. The need to earn a steady income led him to concentrate on portrait commissions. In 1820, when the Society of Painters in Oil and Water Colours resumed its original title and reverted to showing watercolours only, Linnell resigned and began exhibiting once again at the Royal Academy, where he had pictures almost every year from 1821 to 1881. Between 1824 and 1846 nearly all his exhibits were portraits. His first portrait had been of John Martin, pastor of the Keppel Street Chapel, in 1812: Linnell made and published an engraving, copies of which found a ready market among members of the Baptist church. In the 1820s, however, he acquired royal and aristocratic patronage and painted miniatures, including one of Princess Sophia Matilda (1821; Royal Collection), the daughter of William Henry, duke of Gloucester. Other sitters included the earl of Denbigh (1823), Lady Lyndhurst (1830), the Revd Thomas Malthus (1833), the marquess of Bristol (1835), the marquess of Lansdowne (1840), and Thomas Carlyle (1844). His portraits of William Mulready (1833) and Sir Robert Peel (1838) are in the National Portrait Gallery, London, which also holds a *Self-Portrait* (*c.*1860). Linnell's portraits show the influence of Renaissance prototypes, as well as that of contemporaries such as Sir Thomas Lawrence: a notable example is the group portrait of *Lady Torrens and her Family* (1820; Elvehjem Museum of Art, University of Wisconsin, Madison, USA). In addition to commissioned portraits, Linnell made many informal studies of his friends, family, and fellow artists, including Blake and Palmer. There are also portraits of obscure sitters, made in part payment to the craftsmen who worked on the house he had built at 38 Porchester Terrace, Bayswater, in the late 1820s and early 1830s.

In addition to his work in portraiture and landscape, Linnell was an accomplished copyist and printmaker. Between 1828 and 1834 he executed watercolour drawings of pictures in the National Gallery which were engraved by John Pye and published in *The British Gallery*. He made several finished copies in oil of works by the old masters, including Titian, Rembrandt, and Raphael, some for his own use, others on commission. In 1834 he published *Michelangelo's Frescoes in the Sistine Chapel*, a series of mezzotints made from drawings in Samuel Rogers's collection which Linnell considered to be Michelangelo's working drawings for the chapel. He also made etchings, engravings, and mezzotints after his own portraits, and mezzotints after paintings by his friends William Collins and John Varley. Linnell acquired a large collection of old master prints, including works by Dürer, Holbein, Marcantonio Raimondi, Bonasone, Rembrandt, and Claude.

In 1821 Linnell put his name down for an associateship of the Royal Academy, and continued trying to get elected until 1842, when he withdrew his name. He suspected that malicious gossip, for which he held John Constable partly to blame, had prevented his election: Linnell and his family had stayed with Constable's friend D. C. Read at Southampton in 1819, Read had accused Linnell of meanness, and Linnell believed that Constable had talked about the matter to academicians. Much later on, in 1867 Linnell was asked if he would agree to his name being put down for an associateship, but refused. By this time Linnell's continued exclusion from membership of the academy was perceived as scandalous: Millais and Eastlake had cited him as an artist who should have been elected, at a government inquiry into the Royal Academy in 1863. Following a further dispute with the academy over their failure to hang a painting in 1867, Linnell wrote a pamphlet, *The Royal Academy, a National Institution* (1869), which was highly critical of the exclusiveness of the main body of academicians.

Linnell claimed that he painted portraits to live, but he lived to paint poetical landscapes (Linnell, autobiography, 16); thus, as soon as his finances permitted he moved out into the country and concentrated on landscape painting.

Pastoral landscapes, 1847–1882 From 1847 onwards almost all Linnell's exhibits at the Royal Academy were landscapes. Like other successful Victorian artists, he was able to buy land and have a substantial house built: the site he chose was at Redstone Wood, Redhill, in Surrey. Here he painted landscapes which were sold to north of England merchants and industrialists, often through the London dealers Agnews who also had a saleroom in Manchester. His professed ambition was to paint biblical scenes, such as *The Eve of the Deluge* (1848; Cleveland Museum of Art), which was bought by Joseph Gillott, Birmingham pen manufacturer, for £1000. But most of his patrons preferred pastoral landscapes, especially the harvest scenes, peopled by cheerful, ruddy-cheeked, smock-frocked labourers, which he made his speciality, such as *Harvest Home, Sunset, the Last Load* (1854; Tate collection). Linnell owned arable fields around his house, which he let out to farmers, and he appreciated the paradox that by painting a scene in one of these fields he could make more money than the farmer would get for his crop (Story, 2.33). As well as being accessible, the subject of harvest was full of symbolic meaning for Linnell, as a demonstration of divine benevolence.

While Linnell continued to sketch from nature, and to use sketches as the basis for his exhibited pictures, such as *The Noonday Rest* (1865; Tate collection), his later landscapes are more conventional and idealized than his earlier work. Their Claudian compositions and sketchy handling were somewhat out of step with the tastes of the 1850s, influenced by the Pre-Raphaelites, and dealers repeatedly urged him to give more finish to his paintings. However, his works sold so readily that he had little incentive to change his style: his landscape sketchbook (BM) records that his last landscape was sold 'off the easel' (that is, before being sent to exhibition) for £1000 in 1879, when he was eighty-seven.

At Redstone Wood, Linnell lived like a patriarch, surrounded by his large family, all of whom painted, James (1823–1905) and William (1826–1906) being important artists in their own right. Linnell baked his own bread and brewed his own beer, and educated the children himself, teaching them to read and write, draw and paint, grind corn and bake bread. In 1865 his first wife died and in 1866 he married Mary Ann (Marion) Budden (*d.* 1886), who survived him.

Linnell's reputation In his lifetime Linnell was a successful and much admired artist. However, his strongly held views and his legalistic approach to business and family transactions caused difficulties with some of his relatives and acquaintances. He operated strict business terms, requesting deposits in advance and payment in full on delivery, and insisted on decisions being recorded in writing and signed by all the relevant parties. His relationship with Samuel Palmer, who married his daughter Hannah in 1837, cooled during their Italian honeymoon, and remained problematic. Initially there were tensions because the Palmers stayed away longer than they had planned, and because of the pressures induced by Linnell's commission for them to colour his set of mezzotints of the Sistine Chapel frescoes. Later on, their religious disagreements surfaced, and Palmer came to resent Linnell's interference in the lives of the couple, which was exacerbated by Palmer's failure to earn much through his art. In their lifetimes it was Palmer who struggled while Linnell enjoyed success; in their posthumous reputations, positions have been reversed, and Palmer is now seen as the more original and important of the two artists.

Like that of many successful Victorian artists, Linnell's reputation has suffered because of new developments in the art of the late nineteenth and early twentieth centuries, and because of his tendency to repeat a selling formula in his landscapes, the style of which remained very similar from the 1840s to the 1880s. Reassessment of his work since the 1970s has centred on his early landscapes, and especially on the studies from nature shown at the exhibition at Colnaghis in 1973.

In the literature on Palmer, Linnell often appears as a villain rather than 'a good angel'. Palmer's son, A. H. Palmer, compiled his father's *Life and Letters* in 1892, and also copied out Linnell's journals, with the intention of writing a biography of Linnell. However, his judgement of Linnell, whom he blamed for his own father's lack of worldly success, became increasingly bitter and has affected subsequent writers on Palmer. In recent years writers on both artists have tried to correct this imbalance and reach a fairer assessment of Linnell's character and achievement.

John Linnell died at Redstone Wood on 20 January 1882 and was buried at Redhill, Surrey.

CHRISTIANA PAYNE

Sources A. T. Story, *The life of John Linnell*, 2 vols. (1892) • E. R. Firestone, 'John Linnell, English artist: works, patrons, and dealers', PhD diss., University of Wisconsin, 1971 • K. Crouan, *John Linnell: a centennial exhibition* (1982) [exhibition catalogue, FM Cam., 5 Oct – 12 Dec 1982, and Yale U. CBA, 26 Jan – 20 March 1983] • D. Linnell, *Blake, Palmer, Linnell and Co: the life of John Linnell* (1994) • J. Turner, ed., *The dictionary of art*, 34 vols. (1996) • *A loan exhibition of drawings, watercolours and paintings by John Linnell and his circle* (1973) [exhibition catalogue, Colnaghis, London, 10 Jan – 2 Feb 1973] • E. R. Firestone, 'John Linnell and the picture merchants', *The Connoisseur*, 182 (1973), 124–31 • landscape and portrait sketchbooks, BM, 1976-1-31-6/7 [containing a record of most of his paintings] • J. Linnell, unfinished autobiography, 1863–4, FM Cam., Linnell MSS • J. Linnell, journals, 1811, FM Cam., Linnell MSS • J. Linnell, journals, 1817–79, FM Cam., Linnell MSS • account books and letters, FM Cam., Linnell MSS • C. Payne, 'John Linnell and Samuel Palmer in the 1820s', *Burlington Magazine*, 124 (1982), 131–6 • K. Crouan, *John Linnell: truth to nature* (1982) [exhibition catalogue, Martyn Gregory Gallery, London, 8–20 Nov 1982, and Davis and Langdale and Co., New York, Feb, 1983] • *DNB* • E. R. Firestone, 'John Linnell: *The eve of the deluge*', *Bulletin of the Cleveland Museum of Art*, 62/4 (1975), 131–9 • C. Knowles, 'John Linnell: his early landscapes, to 1830', MA diss., Courtauld Inst., 1980 • A. H. Palmer, *The life and letters of Samuel Palmer* (1892) • R. Lister, *Samuel Palmer: a biography* (1974) • *The letters of Samuel Palmer*, ed. R. Lister, 2 vols. (1974) • *Winter exhibition* (1883) [exhibition catalogue, RA]

Archives BM, landscape and portrait sketchbooks, 1976-1-31-6/7 • FM Cam., MSS

Likenesses C. H. Lear, pencil drawing, *c*.1845, NPG • J. Linnell, self-portrait, oils, *c*.1860, NPG [*see illus.*] • A. E. Chalon, group portrait, watercolour (*students at the British Association, 1807*), BM • Elliott & Fry, carte-de-visite, NPG • Maull & Co., carte-de-visite, NPG

Linnett, John Wilfrid [Jack] **(1913–1975)**, chemist and university administrator, was born on 3 August 1913 at 4 Earlsdon Avenue North, Coventry, the only child of Alfred Thirlby Linnett, works accountant in the Rover car company, and his wife, Ethel Mary, typist, daughter of William Ward, ribbon weaver, of Coventry. He was educated at King Henry VIII School, Coventry (1919–31), from where he won the Sir Thomas White scholarship to St John's College, Oxford. He graduated in 1935 with first-class honours in chemistry. He spent two further years in Oxford, doing research on spectroscopy and photochemistry of metal alkyls under Harold W. Thompson, and was awarded a DPhil in 1938.

In 1937–8 Linnett, who was known as Jack, was a Henry fellow at Harvard University where he worked under G. B. Kistiakowsky and E. Bright Wilson on infra-red and Raman spectroscopy and on the quantum theory of molecular vibrations. In September 1938 he returned to Oxford, where he was to remain for twenty-seven years. He held a junior research fellowship at Balliol College from 1939 to 1945 and was engaged on wartime research. In 1944 he was appointed university demonstrator (having previously been departmental demonstrator) in the inorganic chemistry laboratory and in 1945 was elected official fellow and praelector in chemistry at Queen's College, Oxford. He was dean of Queen's in 1945–8. On 20 December 1947 he married Rae Ellen Fanny, daughter of Lawrence John Libgott, a schoolmaster, of Birmingham. They had a son and a daughter. In 1948 and in 1950 Linnett visited the University of Wisconsin where he worked with Professor J. O. Hirschfelder. In 1960 he made the first of several visits to the University of California in Berkeley.

Linnett's research in Oxford was concentrated on molecular force fields, on the measurement and interpretation of burning velocities in gases, on recombination of atoms at surfaces, and on theories of chemical bonding. His undergraduate textbook *Wave Mechanics and Valency* (1960) was widely read. He was elected a fellow of the Royal Society in 1955 in recognition of his distinguished work 'on molecular structure and on the physical chemistry of combustion and flame propagation'. Oxford University appointed him to a readership in 1962, and in 1964 he was made a JP.

In 1965 Linnett was elected to succeed R. G. W. Norrish as professor of physical chemistry in Cambridge, and to a professorial fellowship at Emmanuel College. The Cambridge department of physical chemistry enjoyed a fine reputation in gas-phase chemical kinetics and in photochemistry. Linnett preserved and fostered this strength and introduced research on surface chemistry. His own investigations were mainly devoted to quantum chemistry and to the development of simple and practical models of chemical bonds.

In 1970 Linnett was elected master of Sidney Sussex College, and after only three years in that office he became vice-chancellor of the university. This was an especially difficult time for vice-chancellors because of student unrest, and Cambridge was not immune from this challenge. Linnett served with high distinction in the post, his qualities as scholar, teacher, and man winning him the respect and affection of all sections of the university. He was concerned that its growth had strained internal communications, so he strove to keep people informed.

Linnett played a vital part in the foundation of Robinson College; his personality and approach enabled him to revitalize an offer of a remarkable benefaction to found a college at Cambridge, which had been made by the businessman David Robinson. Having been somewhat disappointed by the attitude of the established university administrators, Robinson found in Linnett a man who appreciated his intentions and knew how to implement them in a Cambridge setting. Moreover (according to Lord Lewis, warden of Robinson College) Linnett played a major role in the choice of the architects, and his experience of college life was paramount in influencing the general design of the buildings. He chaired the trustees' meetings and provided a strong base from which Robinson College was able to proceed to full college status in a minimum period of time.

During the period Linnett was vice-chancellor there was growing parliamentary and public criticism of the universities, and there was a fear that this could lead to more government control than had so far been considered compatible with academic freedom. Linnett believed that there was a need to inform the public about the role of universities and in 1975 he produced a survey of 'useful' research in progress in Cambridge.

Linnett consistently displayed those qualities which a university looks for in its head: a thorough knowledge of the business; an ability to see the issues which matter most; wisdom and judgement in guiding debates; and dignity and assurance on public occasions. Despite the heavy demands on him from his department, college, and university, he found time for individuals and gave them his full, courteous, and good-humoured attention.

Linnett was president of the Faraday Society (1971–3). He received an honorary DSc from Warwick University (1973) and the Coventry award of merit (1966). He was made an honorary fellow of St John's College, Oxford, in 1968, and a fellow of the New York Academy of Sciences in 1965. On 7 November 1975 Linnett died suddenly of a cerebral haemorrhage at his club, the Athenaeum.

DAVID BUCKINGHAM

Sources A. D. Buckingham, *Memoirs FRS*, 23 (1977), 311–43 · private information (1986) [Lord Lewis, warden of Robinson College, Cambridge; relatives] · personal knowledge (2004) · C. N. L. Brooke, *A history of the University of Cambridge*, 4: *1870–1990*, ed. C. N. L. Brooke and others (1993)

Likenesses photograph, *c.*1970, repro. in Buckingham, *Memoirs FRS*, facing p. 311 · W. E. Narraway, portrait, 1978, Sidney Sussex College, Cambridge

Linskill, Mary Jane (1840–1891), novelist, born in Blackburns Yard, Whitby, Yorkshire, on 13 December 1840, was the eldest child of Thomas Henry Linskill (1809–1874), watchmaker and constable of the town, and his wife, Mary Ann Tireman (1814–1903). Mary Linskill attended a private school in Bagdale, Whitby. She was apprenticed to a milliner and later worked in shops in the midlands. She then became a governess, and while so employed in Leeds her first work, *Tales of the North Riding* (1871), written under the pseudonym Stephen Yorke, was published. On the death of her father she returned to Whitby and tried to establish herself as a writer in order to maintain her mother and younger siblings who had been left impoverished. By her own efforts she raised herself out of the unproductive, non-creative, inarticulate majority which surrounded her. The noisy ebb and flow of communal life in a Whitby yard was torture to her sensitive nature, and only in the very early hours of the day would the isolation and peace of silence envelop and enrich her. But if the life of the yard gave no support to the creative mood, it did supply the turbulent background against which her spirit enacted its essential creative role. Unsupported by a husband or a father, she managed to produce three major novels (*Between the Heather and the Northern Sea* in 1884, *The Haven under the Hill* in 1886, and *In Exchange for a Soul* in 1887) and a score of lesser tales over a period of twenty years. Mary Linskill was deeply religious and her writing reflects the monastic and maritime influence of the old seaport of Whitby. Much of her fiction was published by the SPCK. She made short-lived efforts to get away from the yard, moving to nearby Ruswarp and Newholm, but was forced by poverty to return to Whitby. Eventually she and her mother moved to a pleasant house in Spring Vale, in the town, a few years before she died, of apoplexy, on 9 April 1891 at the age of fifty. She was buried in Whitby cemetery. The greater part of Mary Linskill's writing was published in *Good Words*, and it was one of its sub-editors, John Hutton, who wrote a eulogistic, if inaccurate, memoir in the 1891 edition, on which the *Dictionary of National Biography* entry was based. CORDELIA STAMP

Sources C. Stamp, *Mary Linskill* (1980) · *Good Words* (June 1891) · b. cert. · d. cert.

Archives Whitby Museum, Whitby Literary and Philosophical Society, notes and MSS

Likenesses F. M. Sutcliffe, photograph, 1880

Linstead, Sir (Reginald) Patrick (1902–1966), organic chemist and educationist, was born in London on 28 August 1902, the second son of Edward Flatman Linstead, pharmaceutical chemist, of London, and his wife, Florence Evelyn Hester. His elder brother was Hugh Linstead, who became MP for Putney (1942–64) and secretary and registrar of the Pharmaceutical Society. Linstead was educated at the City of London School and, from 1920, at Imperial College, South Kensington, where he began his study of chemistry. On graduating with first-class honours in 1923, Linstead commenced research with Thorpe and

Sir (Reginald) Patrick Linstead (1902–1966), by Walter Stoneman, 1945

G. A. R. Kon and obtained his PhD in 1926. After continued studies as one of Thorpe's research assistants, he worked for a year with the Anglo-Persian Oil Company, before returning to Imperial College in 1929 as a demonstrator in organic chemistry; he later became a lecturer. In 1930, Linstead married Aileen Edith Ellis Rowland, daughter of J. Abbott, a fellow research worker at Imperial College. In 1938 the couple moved to Sheffield, where Linstead had been appointed as Firth professor of chemistry at the university. However, his stay there was short; following the death of his wife in childbirth that year Linstead accepted a chair of organic chemistry at Harvard University.

At the outbreak of war in 1939 Linstead was drawn into the joint British and American government research programme into RDX (the explosive cyclonite). In 1942, on extended leave from Harvard, he returned to the United Kingdom as deputy director of scientific research at the Ministry of Supply. In the same year he married again; his second wife was Marjorie, daughter of W. D. Walters of Aberdâr. She had an Oxford doctorate and subsequently became principal of Lady Spencer Churchill College of Further Education at Wheatley in Oxfordshire.

Linstead resigned the Harvard chair in 1945 and was appointed director of the government Chemical Research Laboratory at Teddington. After four years he returned to Imperial College as professor of organic chemistry; subsequently he became head of the reintegrated chemistry department when Professor H. V. A. Briscoe retired in 1954. In 1953 he was appointed dean of the Royal College of Science. In October 1954 the rector of Imperial College Sir Roderic Hill died suddenly and Linstead was appointed as his successor. During his term of office, which began in 1955, Imperial College expanded greatly and facilities for teaching, research, and student welfare were improved by new buildings and equipment.

Linstead investigated the synthesis, tautomerism, and cyclization of unsaturated mono- and dicarboxylic acids. During these studies, he extended the Kolbe electrochemical reaction to the synthesis of natural products. Linstead's study of hydrogen transfer from donor to acceptor molecules using quinones, olefins, or dihydroaromatic compounds is classic. His greatest contributions were in the chemistry of the phthalocyanin, porphyrin, and chlorin pigments and their metal derivatives. These studies led naturally to an investigation of photosynthesis and the verification of the structures of chlorophyll and bacteriochlorophyll. During the Second World War, Linstead completed significant studies relating to the chromatographic characterization of metals including uranium. He wrote *A Course in Modern Techniques of Organic Chemistry* (with J. A. Elvidge and M. Whalley, 1955) and *A Guide to qualitative Organic Chemical Analysis* (with B. C. L. Weedon, 1956), both notable treatises.

Linstead possessed insight and sound judgement and was masterly in both discussion and organization. His enthusiasm for chemistry was infective and he was popular with research collaborators and students alike. His diplomacy and administrative skills ensured he was enthusiastically followed. Always interested in art and literature, he encouraged students to pursue diverse interests and sponsored the establishment of an arts and music library at Imperial College. His great chemical reputation and popularity ensured him excellent research collaborators. An innovative teacher, Linstead established an undergraduate tutorial system at Imperial College and introduced specialization and research projects for third-year chemistry undergraduates.

Linstead was awarded the Harrison memorial prize (1929), the Meldola medal (1930), and the Hofmann medal of the German Chemical Society (1939). He became DSc London, 1930, and received honorary degrees from Harvard and Exeter universities. He was appointed CBE in 1946 and knighted in 1959. He was elected to the fellowship of the Royal Society in 1940 and became its vice-president (1959–65) and foreign secretary (1960–65). He also served as vice-president of the Chemical Society three times between 1946 and 1957, and of the Royal Institute of Chemistry in 1949–51. Linstead's diverse accomplishments were recognized by his appointment as a governor of Charterhouse, the London School of Economics and Political Science, and the London Graduate School of Business Studies, and as a trustee of the National Gallery from 1962. He was twice president of the Science Masters' Association, and a member of the council of the Royal Albert

Hall. Linstead was frequently consulted by the government about science policy, and his influence was also significant in educational forward planning: he was a member of both the Central Advisory Council for Education chaired by Sir Geoffrey Crowther (1956–60) and the committee on higher education, chaired by Lord Robbins (1961–4).

On 22 September 1966 Linstead, whose London home was at 170 Queens Gate, suddenly died at St George's Hospital, London, having suffered a heart attack. He was survived by his wife and daughter.

A. G. M. Barrett and D. H. R. Barton, *rev.*

Sources D. H. R. Barton, H. N. Rydon, and J. A. Elvidge, *Memoirs FRS*, 14 (1968), 309–47
Archives ICL, corresp. and papers • RS, papers relating to Royal Society | ICL, letters to Marjorie Walters
Likenesses W. Stoneman, photograph, 1945, NPG [*see illus.*] • W. Stoneman, photograph, 1946, RS • *The Times*, photograph, *c*.1960, RS • Associated Press, photograph, *c*.1960, RS • W. Bird, photograph, *c*.1960, RS • E. Halliday, portrait, ICL, rector's house
Wealth at death £8077: probate, 17 Nov 1966, *CGPLA Eng. & Wales*

Linton, David Leslie (1906–1971), geographer and geomorphologist, was born on 12 July 1906 at 883 Old Kent Road, London, the second of three children of Samuel James Linton, master grocer, and Elizabeth Baird Kennedy. His parents were immigrants from northern Ireland. He was educated at Haberdashers' Aske's Hatcham School and then went up to King's College, University of London, on a scholarship to read for a general honours degree in chemistry, physics, and geology. He was awarded a first class in 1926 and then proceeded to a special honours degree in which he obtained a first class in geography in 1927. He stayed on at King's, where he succeeded S. W. Wooldridge as demonstrator. In 1929 he moved to Edinburgh University and remained there until 1945, although during the Second World War he was on photo-reconnaissance duties with the Royal Air Force Volunteer Reserve, where he held the rank of squadron leader.

In 1945 Linton was appointed professor of geography at Sheffield University, and then in 1958 professor of geography at Birmingham University, where he remained until his sudden death in 1971. Linton held a range of national positions including the editorship of *Geography* (from 1947 to 1965), the presidency of section E of the British Association for the Advancement of Science (1957), the presidency of the Institute of British Geographers (1962), and the presidency of the Geographical Association (1964). In 1942 he received the Murchison award from the Royal Geographical Society, while in 1971 he was appointed honorary fellow of King's College, London. He was the first chairman of the newly formed British Geomorphological Research Group (1961), a body that rapidly grew in stature and influence.

Linton's personality was seen as complex by his contemporaries. Though shy and sometimes appearing aloof and distant he was a gifted lecturer and fluent writer. Though capable of charm, fairness, and kindness, he could also appear obdurate, brusque, arrogant, and disinclined to accept opposition to his ideas. He worked long hours and suffered from repeated bouts of insomnia and migraine, yet he was also a devoted family man with four children (three sons and a daughter), having married Vera Cicely (*b*. 1903/4), daughter of William Tebbs, manager, on 13 August 1929. He was an able artist and gifted musician.

Linton was a geographer with wide interests, though he is most remembered for his work in geomorphology. Under the influence of Sidney Wooldridge, with whom he wrote the classic *Structure, Surface and Drainage in South East England* (1939, second edition 1955), he became a leading exponent of denudation chronology—the attempt to reconstruct long-term landform evolution on the basis of the identification of erosional remnants. Although in the 1980s some of the major findings of this work were challenged, it remains as an enduring monument to one of the most distinctive phases of British geomorphology.

Another area where Linton made a major impact was in the study of tors (upstanding rock features, often of granite, characteristic of Devon and Cornwall). He regarded tors as ancient features that were the product of warm climate weathering. He distrusted those who regarded them as relict periglacial features and this involved him in a less than edifying debate with those who opposed his ideas. He also held firm views about the extent of the impact that glaciation had had on the British landscape, and championed the importance of preglacial events and forms. Above all Linton was a fieldworker in the era before process studies and quantification came into vogue.

In addition to his work as a geomorphologist Linton also made some contributions to the study of landscape value assessment, and to the geography of development and energy. In his last years he had developed an interest in the landscapes of the moon, but his premature death stopped these and other new ventures. Suffering from carcinoma of the colon he died on 11 April 1971 at the Queen Elizabeth Hospital, Edgbaston, Birmingham.

Andrew S. Goudie

Sources J. R. Gold, M. J. Haigh, and G. T. Warwick, 'David Leslie Linton, 1906–1971', *Geographers Bibliographical Studies*, 7 (1983), 75–83 [incl. bibliography] • J. A. Steers, 'Professor David Leslie Linton', *Geographical Magazine*, 43 (1970–71), 658–9 • A. Garnett, 'David Leslie Linton, 1906–1971', *Geography*, 56 (1971), 341–3 • 'David Leslie Linton', *Transactions of the Institute of British Geographers*, 55 (1972), 171–8 [incl. bibliography] • R. S. Waters, 'David L. Linton', *GJ*, 137 (1971), 432–3 • *WWW* • b. cert. • d. cert. • m. cert. • *CGPLA Eng. & Wales* (1971)
Likenesses photograph, repro. in Steers, 'Professor David Leslie Linton', 658
Wealth at death £13,829: probate, 30 June 1971, *CGPLA Eng. & Wales*

Linton, Elizabeth [Eliza] **Lynn** (1822–1898), writer, was born on 10 February 1822 at Crosthwaite vicarage in Keswick, Cumberland, the twelfth and youngest child of the Revd James Lynn (1776–1855), vicar of Crosthwaite, and his first wife, Charlotte Alicia (1782/3–1822), daughter of the Revd Samuel *Goodenough, bishop of Carlisle. Eliza Lynn's mother died shortly after her birth. Raised in the

Lake District and in Kent, she received no formal schooling but pursued a course of rigorous self-education. She later recounted the unhappiness of her motherless childhood, accentuated by her conflicts with her tory clergyman father over her radical political views and loss of faith in Christianity. Eager for attention and approval, she determined early in her youth to achieve fame as an author.

At the age of twenty-three, encouraged by the publication of two of her poems in *Ainsworth's Magazine*, Eliza Lynn left her family home in Keswick and went to London to make her way as a writer. Describing herself as 'one of the vanguard of independent women' (Linton, *Christopher Kirkland*, 1.253), she succeeded in publishing two well-reviewed historical novels, *Azeth, the Egyptian* (1847) and *Amymone: A Romance in the Days of Pericles* (1848), the latter a passionate appeal for women's rights. She also joined the staff of the whig newspaper the *Morning Chronicle* in 1848, becoming the first woman journalist in England to draw a fixed salary.

Seeking fame, Eliza Lynn instead achieved notoriety with the publication in 1851 of her third novel, *Realities*, which was a fiery attack on Victorian respectability. Even with the expurgation of certain sexually suggestive passages the novel received damning reviews, and it established the young Eliza Lynn's reputation as a person of questionable moral character. Also in 1851 she argued with John Douglas Cook, her employer on the *Morning Chronicle*, and for three years (1851–4) worked as a foreign correspondent in Paris. She did not publish another novel for fourteen years after *Realities*, concentrating instead on contributions to such respectable periodicals as Charles Dickens's *Household Words*. Dickens valued her work and considered her 'good for anything, and thoroughly reliable', though he did caution his sub-editor that she 'gets so near the sexual side of things as to be a little dangerous to us at times' (Anderson, 66).

On 24 March 1858 the 36-year-old Eliza Lynn married the engraver and radical republican William James *Linton (1812–1897), a widower with seven young children. Described by a colleague as 'a tall, stately, handsome young woman' (Layard, 91), always wearing spectacles because of her severe near-sightedness, she attributed her decision to marry Linton to her desire to help his motherless children. A union of two discordant personalities, the marriage was a disaster. The increasingly conservative Eliza, hoping to make their London home a social and literary centre, was frustrated by her husband's lack of personal ambition and his preoccupation with continental revolutionary causes. She also had the responsibility of supporting the family with her writings. Styling herself E. Lynn Linton, thereby keeping her birth-name in equal prominence with her married name as a means, she said, of maintaining 'cherished individualism' (Anderson, 86), she published mainly potboiler articles in popular periodicals such as the *Literary Gazette* and the *National Magazine*, as well as continuing her contributions to *Household Words* and its successor, *All the Year Round*.

In 1864, recognizing that the marriage was a failure, William James Linton moved with his children back to Brantwood, his house in the Lake District. Although spending the summers at Brantwood, Eliza Lynn Linton lived the rest of the year in London, concentrating, as she told the publisher John Blackwood, on fulfilling her ambition to 'get out of periodical literature and to succeed as a writer of good novels' (Anderson, 99). Ever one to achieve her goals, she did publish during that time three reasonably successful novels, *Grasp your Nettle* (1865), *Lizzie Lorton of Greyrigg* (1866), and *Sowing the Wind* (1867). The marriage reached a final end in 1867 when William moved to the United States, where he was joined by his children. Although he returned several times to England, they did not see each other again. They never divorced, perhaps because there were no legal grounds.

Despite her concern to succeed as a novelist, it was Linton's sensational articles in the conservative and prestigious *Saturday Review* in the late 1860s and the 1870s that made her reputation in Victorian England. Taking on the role of critic of women, the once-impassioned defender of women's rights became its most ardent opponent. She damned the 'shrieking sisterhood' (*Saturday Review*, 12 May 1870) who sought the right to vote, even as she criticized the 'modern mother' (*Saturday Review*, 29 Feb 1868) whose aspirations for ladyhood caused her to neglect her maternal duties. Her most controversial article was 'The girl of the period', published on 14 March 1868, in which Linton shockingly accused young women who flirted and wore make-up of envying and imitating the *demi-monde*. Called 'perhaps the most sensational middle article the *Saturday Review* ever published' (Bevington, 110), this anonymous essay was soon identified as authored by Linton, and thereafter she was usually described with reference to it. In 1883 her articles in the *Saturday Review* were collected and published in two volumes as *'The Girl of the Period' and other Social Essays*.

Linton became an even more controversial figure when she, a self-styled agnostic, published in 1872 the novel *The True History of Joshua Davidson, Christian and Communist*, in which she severely criticized the Church of England for what she saw as its hypocrisies and abuses. Creating the fantasy of Jesus (Joshua Davidson) returning to Victorian England, she argued that he would be a communist who would advocate the sharing of wealth and the end of class inequalities. The novel ends with Joshua Davidson kicked to death by the leaders of the Church of England. An immediate best-seller, *Joshua Davidson* was Linton's most widely sold book.

Hard-working and rigorously self-disciplined, Linton enjoyed a profitable, even though controversial, literary career. Continuing the success of her *Saturday Review* articles, she wrote primarily on women's role in society, with her arguments becoming increasingly strident as women gained more rights and freedoms in late Victorian England. Although criticized for what many saw as her exaggerated and hysterical views, she found a forum in a wide range of respected Victorian periodicals, including the *National Review*, *Belgravia*, the *New Review*, *Temple Bar*, and *The Queen*. Her many novels published in the 1870s and

1880s were generally successful. Her later novels, however, most notably *The One too Many* (1894) and *In Haste and at Leisure* (1895), which were harsh though ambiguous denunciations of the 'new woman', received bad reviews and had poor sales. In 1885 she published her psychologically revealing but financially unsuccessful fictionalized autobiography, *The Autobiography of Christopher Kirkland*, in which she wrote of herself in the persona of a male.

Ridiculed by many, Eliza Lynn Linton remained a respected woman of letters who counted among her friends and admirers such diverse persons as Walter Savage Landor, Algernon Charles Swinburne, Herbert Spencer, and Thomas Hardy. She detailed many of these friendships in *My Literary Life*, published posthumously in 1899. In her older years a stout, bespectacled woman with grey hair, usually photographed wearing a severe black gown and a white lace cap, she was fierce to her enemies and loving to her friends. She was especially supportive of aspiring young authors, including, anomalously, the progressive author Beatrice Harraden. Linton also travelled a great deal, particularly between 1876 and 1884, when she often visited Italy. She moved to Malvern in 1895, and it was during a London visit to a friend that she died at her former residence, Queen Anne's Mansions, Westminster, London, of bronchial pneumonia on 14 July 1898, aged seventy-six. She was cremated, and her ashes were buried on 30 September in the cemetery of Crosthwaite church in Cumberland. She left to her relatives and friends an estate of £16,574, which was the fruit of her labour and a testament to her hard-won success.

NANCY FIX ANDERSON

Sources G. S. Layard, *Mrs Lynn Linton: her life, letters and opinions* (1901) • N. F. Anderson, *Woman against women in Victorian England: a life of Eliza Lynn Linton* (1987) • E. L. Linton, *The autobiography of Christopher Kirkland*, 3 vols. (1885) • E. L. Linton, *My literary life* (1899) • M. M. Bevington, *The Saturday Review, 1855–1868: representative educated opinion in Victorian England* (1941) • E. L. Linton, 'A retrospect', *Fortnightly Review*, 44 (1885), 614–29 • *CGPLA Eng. & Wales* (1898) • F. B. Smith, *Radical artisan: William James Linton, 1812–1897* (1973)

Archives Fitzpark Museum, Keswick, Cumbria, small collection of youthful writings • Hunt. L., letters | Duke U., letters to Sir Thomas Wardle • NL Scot., Blackwood MSS • University of Illinois Library, Urbana, Illinois, Bentley Collection • Yale U., Beinecke L.

Likenesses S. Lawrence, oils?, *c*.1840, repro. in Layard, *Mrs Lynn Linton*, 31 • photograph, 1858, repro. in Layard, *Mrs Lynn Linton*, 98 • W. & D. Downey, woodburytype, 1880–89, NPG; repro. in Layard, *Mrs Lynn Linton*, frontispiece • Elliott & Fry, photograph, *c*.1880–1889, repro. in Layard, *Mrs Lynn Linton*, 320 • photograph, *c*.1880–1889, Hult. Arch. • C. O'Neill, photograph, *c*.1890–1899, repro. in *Women at Home*, 5 (Dec 1897), 181 • J. Collier, oils, 1900–04, Fitzpark Museum and Art Gallery, Keswick, Cumbria • Barraud, photograph, NPG; repro. in *Men and Women of the Day*, 8 (1890)

Wealth at death £16,574 4*s*. 0*d*.: probate, 13 Aug 1898, *CGPLA Eng. & Wales*

Linton, William (1791–1876), landscape painter, was born at Liverpool on 22 April 1791, the son of William Linton and Sarah Brockbank, and was probably the child baptized on 6 May at Benn's Garden Unitarian Chapel, the son of William Linton, mariner, and his wife, Sarah, of Park Lane. His mother married Thomas Eskrigge in Lancaster on 11 August 1796. Linton grew up at Lancaster and Cartmel. After schooling at Windermere, he went on to Rochdale, Lancashire, where he spent six years studying the classics, mathematics, and drawing. Holidays were spent in Windermere, where his mother's family had an estate, and his days rambling and drawing in the mountains made him long to be a landscape painter. There, he came under the influence of the self-taught landscape painter William Havell (1872–1857).

However, at sixteen, Linton's artistic aspirations were thwarted when his family placed him in a merchant's office at Liverpool, where he was articled for five years. He still managed to make truant visits to the Lake District, where he painted landscapes and carried out some hasty commissions of local views, and nourished his love of painting by visiting at Mold the tomb of Richard Wilson, whose Italianate classical landscapes he saw and copied at Ince Blundell Hall and at Wynnstay. His enthusiasm for the genre was strengthened by the Claudes he saw at Holker Hall, near Windermere. Yet it was not until he had completed four more years of classical and mathematical study at Windermere that, aged about twenty-four, he was finally allowed to attempt life as a painter in London.

Despite early disappointments, Linton soon made his mark. He began sketching in oils from nature during visits to Hampstead Heath and the countryside around London. In 1817, living at 34 Duke Street, Manchester Square, he first succeeded in getting his work exhibited, showing three landscapes at the Royal Academy, and another at the British Institution. At these two venues, he continued to exhibit annually for more than forty years, sending fifty-seven works to the former and seventy-eight to the latter. From 1830 to 1865 he also exhibited regularly at the Liverpool Academy, though he continued to live in London, by 1822 at 19 Blenheim Street.

Morning after a Storm (exh. British Institution, 1823), painted near Lynton, Devon, was his first work to obtain notice. *Delos* (exh. Society of British Artists (SBA), 1825; possibly the version in Wolverhampton Art Gallery) was purchased on the advice of Turner and led to the sixth duke of Bedford's commissioning *An Italian Scene, Evening* (exh. British Institution, 1826) for Woburn Abbey. Linton was among the artists and art-lovers who met regularly at the Bull and Bush tavern at North End. Their discussions led in 1823 to the founding of the Society of British Artists, to provide greater possibility for artists to exhibit their work. Its first secretary, Linton became its vice-president in 1836 and its president in 1837. In 1824 he sent eleven British landscapes, including *The Vale of Lonsdale*, to its opening exhibition, and a seascape to the Paris Salon. Between 1824 and 1869 he exhibited over a hundred works at the society's galleries in Suffolk Street.

As well as painting all over England, Scotland, and Wales and particularly in his native Lancashire, Linton produced large idealized classical paintings, like *Aeneas and Achates* (exh. SBA, 1828) and *Caius Marius amid Ruins of Carthage* (exh. SBA, 1834). These were done from his imagination, and from his wide knowledge of classical literature and archaeology, without his ever having left England. With these works, considered his greatest achievements by his contemporaries, Linton's reputation was established. In 1828 he embarked on a tour of France, Belgium, Germany, Switzerland, and Italy, when he made over 500 sketches from nature. Many of these formed the basis of later studio paintings, but even these more realistic landscapes were often chosen for their classical or literary associations. His catalogue descriptions of his paintings were heavily annotated with quotations from the classics or the works of classical scholars. His British landscapes were also often annotated from literary sources. On this trip Linton spent fifteen months in Italy and the winter of 1828 in Rome, where he daily met other English artists, including Turner. For his two-volume *Sketches in Italy*, published in 1832, Linton wrote the descriptive texts and supplied lithographs based on his work. After returning to England he married Julia Adeline, daughter of the Revd Thomas Swettenham, rector of Swettenham, and of Anna Antonia Hayes, at Shillinglee, Sussex, on 27 October 1831. On marrying, he acquired a second address, Downshire Hill Cottage, Hampstead.

Linton's large *Ancient Jerusalem, during the approach of the miraculous darkness which attended the crucifixion* (exh. SBA, 1836) was awarded a case of silver medals by Pope Gregory XVI; when it was reproduced in a mezzotint by Thomas Lupton, the first subscriber was the archbishop of Canterbury. One of his most celebrated paintings, *Embarkation of the Greeks for the Trojan War* (exh. SBA, 1839), was another large imaginative construction. After a fifteen-month tour of Greece, Sicily, and Calabria, he exhibited nearly 300 sketches from his trip at the New Society of Painters in Water Colours in 1842, and held further exhibitions at his home at 7 Lodge Place, Hanover Gate, where he had moved by 1837, and at Lancaster, Manchester, and Liverpool. These sketches formed the basis of his *The Scenery of Greece and its Islands*, published privately in 1856, with fifty steel engravings by himself; a second commercial edition followed in 1869. His last European trip, a twelve-month exploration of the Mediterranean coast from Nice to Spezia, was made in 1843–4. His large *Temple of Paestum* (Tate Collection), shown at the Westminster exhibition in 1847 and, as he noted in his will, 'reputed my best work', was bequeathed by him to the National Gallery, London. Another Italian scene, *A Festa Day at Venice—the Grand Canal* (exh. RA, 1851), was awarded a 50 guinea prize at the Royal Institute of Manchester. Despite his large output of Greek and Italian subjects, Linton continued to paint his beloved native countryside. One of several depictions of his home town of Lancaster (on loan to Lancaster City Museum) was lithographed and dedicated (by permission) to Queen Victoria in honour of the royal visit to the city in 1851.

Linton's interest in the technical and archaeological basis of his painting resulted in two more publications. In 1851 Prince Albert presented him with two bronze medals for being an associate juror in the chemical class at the Great Exhibition. He soon published *Ancient and Modern Colours* (1852), which records his studies of the artistic and chemical properties of pigments used by ancient and modern painters. This was later published privately in tabular form (*c.*1859). His last publication, *Colossal Vestiges of the Older Nations* (1862), which surveys ruins throughout the world, reflects his interest in archaeology and the scholarship that underlay his landscapes.

In his last years Linton's work fell out of fashion. It had always been eclipsed by that of Turner, who had influenced some of his paintings. Yet, after Turner, he was the best practitioner of landscape in the classical tradition of his day. Large two-day sales of the 'Entire collection' of his works were held at Christies in 1860 and 1865, as well as a posthumous studio sale in 1877. He died at his house at 7 Lodge Place on 18 August 1876, his wife having predeceased him. In his will—written on 15 September 1874 and proved on 21 August 1877—his principal heirs were his sister, Frances Eskrigge of Morecambe, and his Eskrigge nephews. Examples of his paintings are held in Lancaster City Museum and Wolverhampton Art Gallery.

J. G. P. Delaney

Sources 'William Linton', *Art Journal*, 20 (1858), 9–11 · 'William Linton', *Art Journal*, 12 (1850), 252 · *Records of several of Mr Linton's works which have appeared in the London exhibitions in the course of half a century with opinions of the public journals* (1872) · *Catalogue of the entire collection of the beautiful and truly classical works of William Linton, Esq.* (1860) [sale catalogue, Christies, 1860] · *Catalogue of the entire collection of the beautiful works of William Linton, Esq (retired from the profession)* (1865) [sale catalogue, Christies, 1865] · J. Johnson, ed., *Works exhibited at the Royal Society of British Artists, 1824–1893, and the New English Art Club, 1888–1917*, 2 vols. (1975) · Graves, *Brit. Inst.* · Graves, *RA exhibitors* · *DNB* · M. H. Grant, *A chronological history of the old English landscape painters*, rev. edn, 8 vols. (1957–61) · 'The salon of 1824', *The Connoisseur*, 68 (1924), 66–76 · C. Fleury, *Time-honoured Lancaster* (1891), 313–14 · H. Hubbard, *An outline history of the Royal Society of British Artists* (1937) · *CGPLA Eng. & Wales* (1877) · *IGI* · register of births, PRO, RG.4/1042 · d. cert.

Archives Man. CL, Manchester Archives and Local Studies, letters to Royal Manchester Institution

Likenesses portrait, *c.*1821 · E. H. Baily, bust · C. K. Childs, woodcut, BM, NPG; repro. in *Art Journal* (1850) · Nyall, photograph

Wealth at death under £5000: probate, 21 Aug 1877, *CGPLA Eng. & Wales*

Linton, Sir William (1801–1880), military physician, eldest son of Jabez Linton of Hardrigg Lodge, Dumfriesshire, and Jane, daughter of William Crocket of Grahamshill in the same county, was born at Kirkpatrick Fleming, Dumfriesshire. He was educated at Edinburgh University, and became LCS in 1826. While at university he spent four of his summer vacations working as a surgeon on a whaling ship in the Arctic regions. He entered the army medical department in 1826, and graduated MD at Glasgow University in 1834. He became staff surgeon of the first class in 1848.

After serving in Canada, the Mediterranean, and the West Indies, Linton was appointed deputy inspector-general of hospitals of the first division of the army in the Crimea. He was present at every action until the fall of Sevastopol and had care of the barrack hospital in Scutari shortly after its establishment in 1854 until the British forces came home. On his return in 1856 he was created CB. In 1857 he was appointed inspector-general of hospitals, and shortly afterwards he proceeded to India to assume the post of principal medical officer of the European army. He held these offices throughout the Indian mutiny.

In 1859, as a reward for his services, Linton was appointed an honorary physician to Queen Victoria. He retired from active service in 1863, and was advanced to KCB in 1865. Linton never married, and after a short illness he died of apoplexy, on 9 October 1880, at his home in Skairfield, near Lockerbie, Dumfriesshire.

THOMAS SECCOMBE, *rev.* CLAIRE E. J. HERRICK

Sources *BMJ* (16 Oct 1880), 644 · *The Lancet* (16 Oct 1880), 639 · *The Times* (12 Oct 1880) · *Annual Register* (1880), 205 · *Medical Directory* (1880), 1257
Archives Wellcome L.
Likenesses J. Barrett, oils, 1857, NPG · J. Barrett, group portrait, sketch (for *Florence Nightingale at Scutari*), NPG
Wealth at death £47,381 4*s*. 7*d*.: confirmation, 31 Jan 1881, *CGPLA Eng. & Wales*

Linton, William James (1812–1897), wood-engraver, polemicist, and poet, was born on 7 December 1812 in Ireland's Row at Mile End in London, probably the second among four children of William Linton, a provision broker in the London docks, and his second wife, Mary (*née* Stephenson), apparently of a 'superior' shopkeeping background. The family moved to the village of Stratford, Essex, in 1818, and the young William was sent to the grammar school in Chigwell, a distinguished early seventeenth-century foundation attended by sons of the Essex and City of London middle classes. With the advantage of a rounded education, William seemed destined for the world of London commerce, but persuaded his father to pay for drawing lessons, and in 1828 was bound apprentice to the engraver George Wilmot Bonner (1796–1836) in Kennington in south London. With this declaration of Romantic belief in the superiority of a life of art over that of the counting-house, Linton signalled the future direction of his whole career: a life driven by the conviction that he had much to tell the world, yet held back by his unworldliness. Not that the decision to become an engraver was itself unworldly: engraving was the principal means of mass visual communication in the early nineteenth century and, for a young man without capital, could promise good wages and the possibility of an independent establishment in a market certain to expand. This was doubtless why William Linton senior allowed his younger son, Henry Duff Linton (1816–1899), to enter the same trade—and Henry, less prudent even than his brother, also found the mobility of his trade a valuable resource in later life.

On 21 October 1837 Linton married Laura Wade (1809–1838), who was well educated and freethinking and belonged to a family of independent (though insufficient) means. Fulfilling another Romantic stereotype, she had been a governess, and died of consumption six months after her marriage. Linton never ceased to mourn for her, and some of his late poems (*Love-lore*, 1887) look back to this tragic moment. By about 1839 he was living with Laura's sister Emily, and a child registered later as William Wade Linton (*d.* 1892), known as Willie, was evidently born soon afterwards. At this time Linton publicly advocated an end to all state interference in marriage, with partners associating as consenting equals, free if they wished to use contraception. Since 1835 the biblical prohibition against marrying a deceased wife's sister had been incorporated into English law, so there was never a formal marriage, and Emily simply assumed the name Linton, bearing some seven children: three boys (Willie, Lancelot, who died in December 1863, and Edmund) and four girls (Emily, Margaret, Ellen, and Eliza, who died in December 1857), the youngest of whom was born in July 1854. Emily died, also of consumption, in December 1856. On 24 March 1858 at St Pancras Church, Linton married Eliza Lynn (1822–1898) [*see* Linton, Elizabeth Lynn], the writer and moralist. His marriage to Eliza was childless and unhappy. She soon began to dislike his distinctive clothing, the peculiar cut of his long-waisted coat, which lacked the two buttons at the junction of the skirts at the back—Linton seeing these, according to Walter Crane, as 'superfluous reminders of gentlemanly, militaristic dress' (Smith, 142). She found him 'ungraceful—careless in the matter of dress and generally unkempt—with unstarched collars and long hair', adding:

William James Linton (1812–1897), by Sir Emery Walker

> I could not convince him of the need of method, regularity, foresight, or any other economic virtue. He was sweet in word and acquiescent in manner; smiled, promised compliance—and indeed did much that I wished because I wished it. But I never touched the core. (Layard, 97–8)

The couple grew steadily apart during the early 1860s, separating informally but finally in 1867 when he emigrated to the United States.

The craft that Linton learned from George Bonner was not that of the woodcut, which had been historically the cheapest means of image-making and the mainstay of popular religious and topical publications well into the eighteenth century. Linton was a wood-engraver, and his was the craft which, more than any other nineteenth-century printmaking technique, pushed forward the illustration of books, periodicals, newspapers, and ephemeral publications, and transformed visual awareness in all advanced societies. Wood-engraving was the first of the major printmaking media to exploit photography, and it was partly as a reaction against the effects of lithography and photo-mechanical printing that the so-called original printmaking media of etching and engraving were re-invented in the second half of the nineteenth century as a major vehicle of artistic expression. Linton's career spans these developments, in craft terms linking Thomas Bewick (1753–1828) to Walter Crane (1845)–1915—Crane being Linton's apprentice from 1858 to 1862—and linking the world of art to that of the *Illustrated London News* and the pictorial advertisement boom of the last quarter of the century. In his own practice Linton increasingly found the personal independence and control over the means of production associated with the ideology of the arts and crafts movement by operating his own small private press.

No one was more aware than Linton of the large professional and social issues involved in these developments. He wrote extensively on the technical aspects of his craft (*Specimens of a New Process of Engraving for Surface Printing*, 1861), on the inherent tension between the artistic and the artisanal aspects of printmaking ('Art in engraving on wood', *Atlantic Monthly*, 43, June 1879), on the history of the craft in Britain and America (*History of Wood Engraving in America*, 1882; *Masters of Wood Engraving*, 1889), and on his own life (*Three Score and Ten Years?*, New York, 1894; published in London as *Memories*, 1895). As a reproductive engraver he participated in many of the most important publishing projects of the epoch, including Moxon's edition of Tennyson and George Eliot's *Romola*, on which he and his brother worked after designs by Frederic Leighton. Beyond his vast output of relatively ephemeral material, Linton's most important works are the botanical studies for his own *Ferns of the Lake District* (1864), and the views and other subjects for Eliza Lynn Linton's *The Lake Country* (1864) and for Harriet Martineau's *The English Lakes* (1858). A considerable group of his flower drawings, probably intended for another botanical work on the Lake District, was presented by Kineton Parkes to the Victoria and Albert Museum in 1938. They are of beautiful quality.

Linton 'discovered' the Lake District during a walking tour of 1846. He acquired the lease of a house at Miteside in Eskdale, where he installed his family in April 1849. In March 1852 they moved to Brantwood, on Coniston, which Linton then managed to buy outright by means of mortgages. At Brantwood he set up his first private press, using it with help from a group of intense young radical printers to produce a stream of pamphlets on English and European politics, mostly written by himself. (A small collection of Linton's publications and wood-engraving materials is held at Brantwood.)

From his earliest years in London, Linton had been heavily involved in fringe republican and Liberal nationalist circles, becoming acquainted with Giuseppe Mazzini about 1842, and regarding himself as the leading English agent and interpreter of the master's views. Within the Chartist movement Linton tended to take his own line. He strongly opposed O'Connor and in 1848 backed the People's Charter Union, which favoured collaboration between middle and working classes. In the 1840s he had regularly composed anti-odes on royal birthdays, and he now proposed the sovereignty of a single legislative chamber, elected by universal adult suffrage, its laws subject to referendum. At the general election of 1852, however, he toyed with the idea of standing as a Chartist candidate at Carlisle, but found that he lacked adequate support.

The Chartist failure in 1848 led Linton and other radicals increasingly to find their inspiration in European nationalism:

> for true civilization, for the free growth of national peculiarities of character; for the unlimited development of the boundless resources of varied clime and country … that every man may have the opportunity of placing himself in that sphere to which his energies may be turned in the best account for the public service … We claim for every People the right to choose their own constitutions, to determine their own way of life. (Mazzini, partly re-drafted by Linton, address published by the People's International League, 1848, quoted in Smith, 60–61)

Italy, Poland, Switzerland, France, and Ireland successively and simultaneously aroused Linton's journalistic intervention during the 1850s and 1860s, and it was in this cause that he launched his own most important contribution to this ferment of constitutionalist debate in early January 1851. This was the *English Republic*, published weekly and monthly until April 1855, virtually all of whose copy and illustrations Linton himself supplied. The *English Republic*'s programme involved individual self-realization under the law providing 'opportunity for growth even for the least and weakest'. A leading function of the state was to provide education for all, to cultivate the 'perceptive faculties' of children, and to teach the 'broad facts of Nature and God in relation to [their] position in the Universe' (Smith, 103). Later the curriculum would include geology and botany, with gardening as the principal out-of-school activity. This was the curriculum experienced by his own children at Brantwood, the family being packed into the house together with Emily's mother, four bachelor printing assistants, the Polish carbonaro Karl Stolzman (1793–1854) and his wife, and Agnes, the servant. The children were all dressed in shifts of blue flannel, and all had shoulder-length hair and wide hats. Their food was home-grown by Linton, and in winter consisted largely of porridge.

Emily's death at the end of 1856 signalled the beginning of the difficult but, in terms of literary stimulus, not unfruitful relationship with Eliza Lynn. In 1865 Linton published *Claribel and other Poems*, illustrated with engravings after his own designs. They reflect his stoical acceptance of private adversity, and their lyrical style shows the influence of Tennyson's *In Memoriam*. But his financial circumstances reached a decisive crisis, and in November 1866 he set off to reconnoitre prospects in New York. Armed with introductions from Mazzini to the American enthusiasts for European national self-determination, he quickly made contact with the Cooper Union and the Society of Wood Engravers of New York, and secured a salaried appointment as artistic director of the local equivalent of the *Illustrated London News*. This enabled him briefly to return early in 1867 to London, where he began collecting material for his history of wood-engraving, gathered up his younger son Edmund, and (his wife having declined to accompany him) set sail again for the New World. Linton's old Micawberish life of financial deficits now achieved an equally Micawberish transformation into one of surplus and social acceptance in the liberal republic of the United States. His artistic and literary reputation secured election to the Century Club, the self-electing élite of artistic New York, and he was honoured by the high-minded liberal intellectuals of New England society as an authentic voice of European radicalism. Not that this stopped him, as a journalist, from castigating various aspects of American life, social organization, and foreign policy—including the sentimental Fenianism of the New England Irish and the Monroe doctrine's implementation in Spanish America—nor from maintaining his voice in European affairs with a passionate but un-American advocacy of the Paris communards in 1870–71.

In 1870 Linton moved out of New York and acquired a farmstead at Hamden, near New Haven, Connecticut, which became his home for the rest of his life. Threatened with bankruptcy proceedings in the English courts, he suggested to Willie, who was looking after the house at Brantwood, that he should contact Ruskin and offer him the property at a nominal discount, for £1500. The sale was completed in May 1871, and was in many ways a serendipitous event, for the characteristic Ruskin works of the Brantwood years, apart from his own increasing interest in fine printing and book illustration, were the radical *Fors Clavigera* addressed to the workmen of Britain, *Deucalion*, and *Proserpina*, the last two respectively his reformulations of field geology and botany for the education of the young. Linton invested proceeds from the Brantwood sale in a new press for the house at Hamden, named Appledore, and again the tireless voice rang out, identifying significant long-term issues such as the corruptions of Tammany Hall politics and the anti-competitive practices of big business and finance. The family was now more or less gathered round him at Appledore, with the exception of his wife, Willie—who worked as a printer in London—and his eldest daughter, Emily, who was partially paralysed and was looked after in an asylum in Dumfries, Scotland. Margaret, the second daughter, was married locally to an engineer at Yale, Thomas Mather, and Ellen helped her father as amanuensis and typesetter. Edmund, who was simple, helped his father in growing vegetables for the house and, again as at Brantwood, in botanizing.

Proximity to Yale's libraries as well as his literary acquaintances encouraged Linton to publish in 1878 a volume of selected American verse, *Poetry of America*, followed by a limited edition of an anthology of English verses showing an exceptional knowledge for this period of the metaphysical poets, *The Golden Apples of Hesperus* (1882); another limited edition, *Rare Poems of the Seventeenth Century* (1882); and, with R. H. Stoddard, the five volumes of *English Verse* (1884). Alongside his genuine editorializing of early seventeenth-century verse, there is evidence that he flirted with producing forged pamphlets—probably, like some art forgers, to mock the scholarship of 'experts'. But he himself was now an increasingly respected figure in the English-speaking world of art and letters. In 1882 he was elected to the American National Academy of Arts, and on his occasional trips to England he became a figure more familiar in the libraries and print rooms of London than on the radical fringes of politics. He particularly loathed W. E. Gladstone, however, regarding him as the betrayer of the old radical vision of land reform and universal suffrage, and he backed Disraeli during the Bulgarian atrocities controversy of 1876. On the last of his English trips in 1889 he brought his *magnum opus*—*Masters of Wood Engraving*, printed by hand at Appledore in only three copies—for reproduction in two limited folio editions at the Chiswick Press. In 1891 he was awarded an honorary MA degree of Yale University. Linton's late books are mostly memoirs: *European Republicans: Recollections of Mazzini and his Friends* (1893), a *Life of Whittier* (1893), and his own *Memories* (1895). A further volume of his own verses, *Poems*, was published in the same year.

During the 1890s Linton's prodigious energies declined, and by autumn 1897 he was unable to continue to operate the press at Appledore. He died at his daughter's house in New Haven on 29 December 1897, and was survived briefly by Eliza Lynn, who died in July 1898. His papers, the basis for F. B. Smith's scholarly biography *Radical Artisan: William James Linton, 1812–97* (1973), are preserved in three main collections: the Istituto Giangiacomo Feltrinelli in Milan, the National Library of Australia in Canberra, and the Beinecke Rare Book and Manuscript Library at Yale University. Smith reproduces photographs of him in his forties as international agitator with long brown hair, and in his eighties as the benign Morrisite patriarch, with a cloud of white hair and deep smile-lines around his eyes. The modern view, largely influenced by Smith, is increasingly to see Linton as a significant figure in the non-socialist tradition of European radicalism. He has benefited also from art historians' changed valuation of 'reproductive' printmaking, and from the recognition of his own 'original' work as a designer of images, illustrator, and poet. His integrity, courage, and moral stature are beyond doubt. JOHN MURDOCH

Sources G. White, *English illustrators of the sixties* (1897) · W. Linton, *Specimens of a new process of engraving for surface printing* (1861) · W. Linton, *Three score and ten years?* (New York, 1894) [published in

London as *Memories*, 1895] • J. Murdoch, *The discovery of the Lake District: a northern Arcadia and its uses* (1984) • F. B. Smith, *Radical artisan: William James Linton, 1812–97* (1973) • *IGI* • G. S. Layard, *Mrs Lynn Linton* (1901)

Archives Instituto Giangiacomo Feltrinelli, Milan, corresp. and papers • NL Aus., papers • Yale U., Beinecke L., corresp., notebooks, journals, literary MSS | Bishopsgate Institute, London, corresp. with Charles Bradlaugh and J. G. Crawford • Co-operative Union, Holyoake House, Manchester, Co-operative Union archive, letters, mostly to G. J. Holyoake • Harvard U., Houghton L., letters to W. E. Adams • JRL, letters to J. H. Nodal

Likenesses Dalziel, woodcut (after W. Linton), BM; repro. in *Frank Leslie's Illustrated Newspaper* (1867) • E. Walker, photograph, NPG [*see illus.*] • photograph, Brantwood, Cumbria • photographs, repro. in Smith, *Radical artisan* • wood-engraving, NPG; repro. in *ILN* (14 May 1892)

Lintot [Lintott], **(Barnaby) Bernard** (1675–1736), bookseller, was born on 1 December 1675 at Southwater, near Horsham, Sussex, the son of John Lintott, yeoman. He was bound apprentice to the bookseller Thomas Lingard on 1 December 1690, but was turned over to John Harding before being freed on 18 March 1700. At this time he usually spelt his name with a double *t* (the decided preference for only one dates from around 1716), but he may have been related to Joshua Lintot, printer to the House of Commons between 1708 and 1710, whose son John he took as his apprentice on 4 February 1724. Bernard began to trade independently, at the Cross Keys in St Martin's Lane, London, before the official end of his apprenticeship, his name appearing on the title-pages of six plays in 1698. He married Catherine Langley (1664–1748), widow, at St Bartholomew's, Smithfield, on 13 October 1700, and that same year he moved premises, to the Post Office or Post House in the Middle Temple Gate in Fleet Street, where he remained until 1705. He then moved to the Cross Keys (sometimes 'and Crown' or 'Cushion'), between the two Temple Gates in Fleet Street or next to Nandy's Coffee House at Temple Bar, the first house east of Inner Temple Lane.

Lintot, in conscious rivalry with Jacob Tonson, rapidly became the premier literary bookseller of the first third of the eighteenth century. By investing first in plays and later in translations and poetry he secured a significant role in the development of English literature. In the first decade of the century his name is found in the imprints of plays by Farquhar, Dryden, Congreve, Steele, Baker, Centlivre, Cibber, and lesser figures. Between 1705 and 1712 he regularly published the plays performed at Drury Lane, and on 16 February 1718 he agreed with Tonson that they should in future share all the plays they purchased. Publications also included practical, especially legal, guides, Dennis's criticism, and works by the deists Toland and Wollaston. The major playwrights were regularly reprinted, with editions continuing to be issued well into the 1750s.

In 1712 Lintot published *Miscellaneous Poems and Translations*, which contained the first version of Pope's *Rape of the Lock*. The collection was designed to rival Tonson's series of *Poetical Miscellanies*, edited by Dryden, with Pope taking Dryden's role. Pope and Gay humorously compared Lintot to the great humanist printers of the Renaissance, with Pope exalting Lintot over his great predecessors:

> Others with *Aldus* would besot us;
> I, for my part, admire *Lintottus*.
> (*Twickenham Edition*, 6.83)

In the following two decades Lintot published first editions of important works by Pope, Gay, and their friend Rowe: *Windsor Forest*, *Temple of Fame*, *Eloisa to Abelard*, *Three Hours after Marriage*, *Trivia*, *The What d'ye Call it*, *Jane Shore*, and *Lady Jane Grey*, as well as Pope's *Works* (1717), Gay's *Poems on Several Occasions* (1720), and Rowe's posthumous *Works* (1728).

Nichols's extracts from Lintot's accounts show he was generous to successful authors. Farquhar received £15 for the *Twin Rivals*, but £30 for the *Beaux' Stratagem*; Rowe was paid £50 15*s*. for *Jane Shore* and £75 for *Jane Grey*; Gay earned £43 from the copyright of *Trivia* and £75 from the 'Revival of the Wife of Bath'. For Urry's Chaucer, Lintot agreed to pay all the cost of publication but to take only one-third of the subscription. Shrewdly he paid Cibber £105 for the *Nonjuror*; inexplicably he paid the same to James Moore Smythe for *The Rival Modes*. But the contracts with Pope were the most generous. For his six-volume translation of the *Iliad* (issued in instalments, 1715–20) Pope was given £2201 by Lintot: £1275 in copy money and £926 in books. Lintot hoped to make a complementary profit of £2200 himself by selling 250 illustrated large folios and 1750 plain small ones to the public, but he miscalculated and for the second volume reduced his print run of small folios to 1000. Moreover, a Dutch duodecimo piracy in 1720 undercut his folios and forced him immediately into his own duodecimo edition. Nevertheless, he probably made over £600 profit on the first edition, and over £2000 on the duodecimos in 1720. For the *Odyssey* translation that followed, Pope tried to win Tonson as publisher by agreeing to edit an edition of Shakespeare for only £100; but he failed. Fenton reported to Broome, on 9 January 1724, 'Tonson does not care to contract for the copy, and application has been made to Lintot, upon which he exerts the true spirit of a scoundrel, believing that he has Pope entirely at his mercy' (*Correspondence of Alexander Pope*, 2.214). The terms of the contract were less generous than for the *Iliad*. For five volumes, Pope was given £367 10*s*. in copy money and £673 14*s*. 7½ *d*. in books (worth, as it turned out, £5,549 5*s*. in subscriptions). Lintot's profits again amounted to over £600 on the folios, with about £1500 from the duodecimos, but this time the poet and bookseller quarrelled. When Tonson advertised the Shakespeare subscription for his own benefit (23 January 1725), Lintot became infuriated at the contrast between his own position and Tonson's and retaliated with 'Proposals by Bernard Lintot, for his own Benefit' offering the equivalent folios for a guinea less than Pope's quartos. Pope declared Lintot a scoundrel and resolved never to employ him again, but Lintot held the copyright to the majority of Pope's early poems and continued to reprint them at regular intervals.

Lintot figures as a minor character in Pope's *Narrative of Dr Norris* and *Full and True Account* of the poisoning of Curll, and he laments his treatment by Pope in Oldmixon's *The Catholick Poet*. In the *Dunciad* Pope mocks Lintot's fondness for the red and black title-pages he liked to post outside his shop, and then compares him to a dabchick in his race against Curll. Lintot was large, clumsy, and choleric; Young described him to Spence as 'a great sputtering fellow' (Spence, 848). Pope comically describes a ride in Lintot's company, marked by the bookseller's profanity and callousness but revealing his ingenuity in using gentlemen to check the work of his translators. Lintot had better relations with the trade than with Pope; his accounts list many arrangements with other booksellers, including thirteen agreements with the Tonsons. He was also a pioneer in book advertising, and established the *Monthy Catalogue* (1714–16), the first regular listing of books. After the accession of George I he became one of the printers of the parliamentary votes and retained the office until 1727. In 1708 he was called to the livery of the Stationers' Company, in 1715 he was renter warden, in 1722–3 he joined the court of assistants, and in 1729 and 1730 he was under-warden.

From 1730 Bernard Lintot shared the business with his son Henry [*see below*], buying land near his father's holding in Sussex and becoming semi-retired. In November 1735 he was nominated high sheriff for Sussex, but did not live to enjoy the office. Pope reported him ill of an asthma on 12 January 1736 and he died in London on 3 February. He was buried in St Dunstan-in-the-West, Fleet Street, London, on 9 February. His will, made on 17 December 1730, was proved on 14 February 1736 by his son Henry.

Henry Lintot (*bap.* 1703, *d.* 1758), bookseller, son of Bernard and Catherine Lintot, was baptized at St Clement Danes, London, on 6 August 1703. He was educated at Westminster School. In 1730 he married Elizabeth (*d.* 1734), daughter of Sir John Aubrey, bt, of Llantrithyd House, Glamorgan, and Boarstall, Buckinghamshire, and his father made a settlement, providing for an estate in land of £200 a year. Henry became a freeman of the Stationers' Company by patrimony on 1 September 1730, and joined his father in business. He inherited the business and estates in 1736, when he was also appointed high sheriff for Sussex in place of his father. Humfrey Wanley reports a visit by Lintot to the Harleian Library on 31 January 1726 in search of family arms, and Bugden's unofficial heraldic visitation of Sussex, 1724, lists the arms of Henry Lintot of Southwater, who must be either the bookseller or a near relation. Lintot also had a town house, Broome House, Fulham.

Henry Lintot retained his father's literary copyrights and issued regular editions of major writers, but he made little attempt to develop that side of the firm's list. He did, however, buy the copyright to the *Dunciad* when it became available, resisted Pope's threats of litigation, and secured his share of profits in editions of Pope's works. He built up the firm's interest in law books and became law printer to the king on 10 March 1749. Lintot's first wife died on 21 January 1734 and he married his second wife, Philadelphia, daughter of John Gurr of Fulham (and possibly the sister of two of his apprentices) on 29 December 1752. They had no children. Henry Lintot died on 10 December 1758 and was buried at the Temple Church on 17 December. Philadelphia Lintot died in 1763.

Catherine Fletcher [*née* Lintot], Lady Fletcher (1733–1816), printer, was the only survivor of the four children of Henry and Elizabeth Lintot; according to the family Bible, she was born by Temple Bar, London, in 1733. She succeeded to her father's business on his death in 1758, but quickly withdrew from active management. Much of the literary property she had inherited was sold at a trade sale on 26 April 1759, and on 24 June 1760 she sold half her patent as king's law printer to Samuel Richardson. Richardson removed her printing house from the Savoy to join his own in White Lyon Court, Fleet Street. On Richardson's death in 1761 she continued the business for a year with his widow, Elizabeth, but they then sold the patent to Henry Woodfall and William Strahan. On 20 October 1768 she married Captain Henry *Fletcher (1727?–1807) of Ashley Park, Walton-on-Thames, bringing with her a fortune of £45,000; together they had a son and a daughter. On 20 May 1782 her husband received a baronetcy. Lady Fletcher died on 17 October 1816 at Ashley Park; a monument was raised to her and her husband in the church of Walton-on-Thames.

JAMES MCLAVERTY

Sources *ESTC* • Nichols, *Lit. anecdotes* • M. W. Barnes, 'The firm of Lintot', MA diss., U. Lond., 1943 • D. F. Foxon, *Pope and the early eighteenth-century book trade* (1991) • *The correspondence of Alexander Pope*, ed. G. Sherburn, 5 vols. (1956) • J. Spence, *Observations, anecdotes, and characters, of books and men*, ed. J. M. Osborn, new edn, 2 vols. (1966) • *The Twickenham edition of the poems of Alexander Pope*, ed. J. Butt and others, 11 vols. in 12 (1939–69) • J. P. Fletcher, 'Bernard Lintot, bookseller', *N&Q*, 6th ser., 2 (1880), 293 • M. A. Lower, 'Family of Lintot', *Sussex Archaeological Collections*, 8 (1856), 275–6 • W. S. Ellis, 'Bugden's unofficial heraldic visitation of Sussex, 1724', *Sussex Archaeological Collections*, 25 (1873), 85–100 • *The diary of Humfrey Wanley, 1715–1726*, ed. C. E. Wright and R. C. Wright, 2 vols. (1966) • J. Thorne, *Handbook to the environs of London* (1876) • D. F. McKenzie, ed., *Stationers' Company apprentices*, [3]: *1701–1800* (1978) • G. Creed, 'Bernard Lintot', *N&Q*, 2nd ser., 4 (1857), 149 • *VCH Sussex* • *Old Westminsters* • Stationers' Company records, Stationers' Hall, London • private information (2004) [M. Treadwell, Trent University, Canada] • W. M. Sale, *Samuel Richardson: master printer* (1950) • *GM*, 1st ser., 38 (1768), 494 • *GM*, 1st ser., 86/2 (1816), 468

Archives BL, Add. MS 4809 • BL, Egerton MS 1951 • BL, Egerton Charters MS 128–130

Lintot, Henry (*bap.* **1703**, *d.* **1758**). *See under* Lintot, (Barnaby) Bernard (1675–1736).

Linwood, Mary (**1755–1845**), artist in needlework, was born in Birmingham, where she was baptized at St Martin's on 18 July 1755, the daughter of Matthew Linwood and his wife, Hannah, *née* Turner (*d.* 1804), who had married at St Philip's, Birmingham, on 19 March 1753. Following her father's bankruptcy in 1764, the family moved to Leicester where her mother opened a boarding-school for young ladies at Belgrave Gate. By the age of twenty Mary was working in needlework, for both she and her mother exhibited needlework pictures with the Society of Artists in London in 1776. Mary Linwood exhibited with the society again, a *Landscape in Needlework*, in 1778. An example of her work in that medium was sent to Catherine the Great of Russia in 1783. A series of puffs in the *Morning Post* (April–June 1787) records her introduction to Queen Charlotte and the opening of a temporary exhibition of her work in the Pantheon, Oxford Street. In 1789 she copied the *Salvator mundi* by Carlo Dolci in the collection of the ninth earl of Exeter, and was reputedly offered 3000 guineas for the work. In 1794 she designed and executed an embroidered banner for the Leicestershire volunteer cavalry, said to be the first instance of such a patriotic act.

By the end of 1796 Linwood was preparing a large exhibition of her needlework pictures; Farington noted that she 'is preparing an Exhibition of needlework as an extraordinary instance of industry. It is calculated that she has worked 1500 square feet of needlework' (Farington, *Diary*, 9 Dec 1796). Having hired rooms in Hanover Square for three years, the exhibition opened in April 1798, to immediate public applause. With the death of her mother in 1804, Linwood took over the boarding-school in Leicester. The exhibition continued, however, now in Leicester Square, and between 1804 and 1809 the collection went on tour, being shown in Edinburgh, Glasgow, Belfast, Limerick, and Cork. In March 1809 it reopened in Leicester Square, where it was to remain for more than forty years.

Although her art has been slighted by modern commentators, Mary Linwood was considered 'one of the most gifted and remarkable women of the age' (*The Times*). Moreover, in an era of great commercial exhibitions, Linwood's deserved to be distinguished for its longevity. A watercolour of *c.*1820 in the Victoria and Albert Museum, London, records the appearance of the interior of the gallery, which was richly attired in red and furnished in the latest fashions. Her needlework was executed on tammy cloth specially woven for her, with woollen 'crewels' dyed to her specifications; by abandoning conventional needleworking techniques and using a wide range of stitch lengths she achieved eminently painterly effects. Examples of her work are to be found in the Royal Collection, Leicestershire museums, and at the Victoria and Albert Museum.

From 1818 until her death Mary Linwood was implicated (apparently unjustly) in a complex chancery suit regarding her rooms in Leicester Square. She offered her collection of needlework pictures to the British Museum and to the House of Lords, but these offers were refused. By 1830 her health had declined and she was forced to give up needlework. However, the exhibition remained open, and it was on a visit to her London gallery in 1844 that she fell terminally ill. On 27 September 1844 she returned to Belgrave Gate, where she died, unmarried, on 2 March 1845. She was buried with her parents in St Margaret's Church, Leicester. The exhibition in Leicester Square stayed open for a short period, before her collection was sold for less than £1000. By the terms of her will her copy of Dolci's *Salvator mundi* was left to Queen Victoria. The gallery continued to bear her name for some years and served as an exhibition hall.

In modern times Mary Linwood has often been confused with her niece, also Mary Linwood, who was a musical composer and author of *Leicestershire Tales* (1808) and other works of literature. MARTIN MYRONE

Sources *GM*, 2nd ser., 23 (1845), 555 • *The Times* (11 March 1845) • 'Miss Linwood', *The Lady's Monthly Museum*, 5 (1800), 1–4 • Countess of Wilton, *A history of needlework* (1847) • J. Nichols, *The history and antiquities of the county of Leicester*, 3/1 (1800) • Farington, *Diary* • M. Swain, *Embroidered Georgian pictures* (1994) • N. R. Whitcomb, *Mary Linwood* (1951) • M. Jourdain, *History of English secular embroidery* (1910) • C. P. Ingram, 'Miss Mary Linwood', *The Connoisseur*, 48 (1917), 145–8 • *IGI*

Archives Leics. RO, MSS | Birm. CA, letters to Boulton family

Likenesses J. Hoppner, oils, V&A • W. Ridley, stipple (after W. Beechey), BM, NPG; repro. in *Monthly Mirror* (1800) • W. Ridley, stipple (after Rivers), BM, NPG; repro. in *Lady's Monthly Museum* (1800) • P. W. Tomkins, engraving, Leicestershire Museums

Wealth at death £45,000: will, PRO, PROB 11/2019; *The Times*

Linwood, William (1817–1878), classical scholar, was born in Birmingham, and baptized there on 29 December 1818, the only son of William Linwood and his wife, Mary Iliffe. He was a nephew of the needlework artist Mary *Linwood. Educated at King Edward's School, Birmingham, during the headmasterships of John Cooke and Francis Jeune, he was admitted to Trinity College, Cambridge, in 1834, but matriculated at Oxford in December 1835 as a member of Christ Church, where he was nominated by Thomas Gaisford to a studentship in 1837. His university career was remarkable. In 1836 he gained the Hertford, Ireland, and Craven scholarships, and in 1839 obtained the Boden Sanskrit scholarship. Graduating BA in 1839 with first-class honours in classics, he proceeded MA in 1842. He was briefly a master at Shrewsbury School in 1841, and he also took private pupils at Oxford on the strength of his achievements as an undergraduate, but he never held an official tutorial position in the university. Two contemporaries, William Gregory and William Tuckwell, left unfavourable accounts of his shabby appearance and uncouth manner, which perhaps explain his failure to gain further advancement as a teacher. He did, however, serve as an examiner in classics at Oxford during 1850–51, scandalizing his fellow examiners by proposing that in deciding the candidates' merits they should 'throw into the fire all that other rubbish, and go by the Greek Prose' (Tuckwell, 150).

Sermons delivered by Linwood as assistant curate at St Chad's, Shrewsbury, on the Catholic church (1841) and baptismal regeneration (1842) indicated a sympathy with the Tractarian movement. He took deacon's orders in 1843 but never proceeded to the priesthood, and on his failure to do so was obliged to relinquish his studentship at Christ Church in June 1851. He appears thereafter to have lived on private means.

Linwood was described as using ancient Greek like a vernacular tongue, and as showing an extraordinary readiness at Greek versification. His scholarship was hardly reflected in his publications, which were more or less intended for elementary students. His *Lexicon to Aeschylus* (1843) was regarded as clearly arranged and serviceable. Although his edition of Sophocles (1846; 4th edn, 1877) was widely used in schools, two later editors, F. H. M.

Blaydes and F. A. Paley, had occasion to comment on his notes as being hurriedly compiled. He became best known as editor and contributor to *Anthologia Oxoniensis* (1845), a collection of verse in Greek, Latin, and English which became a model for subsequent compilations. Latterly, he turned his attention to conjectural emendation of the New Testament. Linwood, whose achievements never lived up to his promise as a student, died unmarried at his home, Birchfield, Handsworth, Staffordshire, on 7 September 1878. He is to be distinguished from William Linwood, the former Unitarian minister from Brixton, who, in 1850, edited the *Eclectic Review* (*Victorian Periodicals Review*, 27, 1994, 183).

W. W. WROTH, *rev.* M. C. CURTHOYS

Sources *The Academy* (28 Sept 1878), 515 • *The Athenaeum* (21 Sept 1878), 371 • Boase, *Mod. Eng. biog.* • *Sir William Gregory*, ed. I. A. Gregory (1894) • W. Tuckwell, *Reminiscences of Oxford*, 2nd edn (1907) • Foster, *Alum. Oxon.*

Wealth at death under £20,000: probate, 26 Oct 1878, *CGPLA Eng. & Wales*

Lionel [Lionel of Antwerp], **duke of Clarence** (**1338–1368**), prince, was the third (but second surviving) son of *Edward III (1312–1377) and *Philippa of Hainault (1310?–1369). He was born at St Michael's Abbey, Antwerp, on 29 November 1338 during his parents' period of residence in the Low Countries at the start of the Hundred Years' War. Master Giles de Monte, a physician from Hainault, was later given £15 as a gift for the thirteen weeks during which he cared for the infant prince. The unusual name given to the child is often supposed to have been a reference to the lion of Brabant, the duke of Brabant being one of Edward III's allies at the time of the prince's birth. But Edward had already specifically identified himself with the mythological and chivalric figure of Lionel—one of the knights of Arthur's round table and cousin of Lancelot—in a tournament held at Dunstable in 1334. Furthermore, the name carried obvious associations with the heraldic lions (more properly leopards) on the royal arms of England. The prince's personal heraldic repertoire was expanded in 1339 when William Montagu, first earl of Salisbury, to whom the king had earlier granted the right to bear the royal crest of an eagle, passed on the privilege to Lionel in his capacity as the child's godfather.

On 9 September 1342, at the Tower of London, Lionel was married to Elizabeth de Burgh (*b.* 6 July 1332), the daughter and sole heir of the deceased William de Burgh, third earl of Ulster. The marriage was consummated in 1352 and produced only one recorded child, Philippa Lionel, who married Edmund (III) Mortimer, earl of March: the house of York descended from this union. Lionel was recognized as earl of Ulster in the right of his wife at the latest by 26 January 1347. In organizing the marriage to Elizabeth de Burgh, Edward III evidently intended to set up Prince Lionel as the principal magnate in Ireland. However, the increasing power of the Gaelic tribal chiefs and the competing claims of the heirs male to the earldom of Ulster meant that Lionel's agents had effective control over only a comparatively small part of the landed estate associated with the title. In order to rectify this situation, a marriage was arranged between Lionel's widowed mother-in-law, Maud, daughter of Henry, earl of Lancaster, and Ralph Ufford, younger brother of the king's friend Robert Ufford, earl of Suffolk; Ralph was then appointed justiciar of Ireland in 1345 and given the task of re-establishing the earldom of Ulster. In fact, these plans came to little since Ufford died in 1346, and Lionel's destined career in Ireland was put off for some fifteen years.

Not the least of the reasons for this delay was the king's preoccupation with the wars in France. Lionel was appointed regent of England during his father's absence in Flanders from 3 to 26 July 1345, and again from 11 July 1346 to 12 October 1347 during the lengthy Crécy–Calais campaign. The prince was obviously not old enough to exercise authority in person, and the task of government was fulfilled by the council; nevertheless, on the latter occasion the regent was provided, at the king's expense, with a personal seal in order to authorize the limited range of administrative responsibilities technically reserved to him. The surviving warrants under this seal indicate that during 1346–7 Lionel's household was based successively at the Tower of London, Windsor, Reading (for much of 1347), and Bristol.

Lionel's own military career began in 1355 when he was knighted and he accompanied the king to Calais to take part in an inconclusive foray into enemy territory. He also participated in the invasion of Scotland in the winter of 1355–6 and headed the list of witnesses to the official instrument by which Edward Balliol renounced his claim to the Scottish throne in favour of Edward III. In May 1359 he took part in a tournament at Smithfield, London, and was in France from October 1359 to May 1360, being present both at the siege of Rheims and at the peace negotiations held at Brétigny. He was nominated a knight of the Garter to fill the stall vacated by John, Lord Beauchamp of Warwick, who had died on 2 December 1360, and first received robes from the king for the Garter ceremonies of April 1361.

The Anglo-French peace of 1360–69 offered an opportunity for Lionel to take up his long-awaited role in Ireland. In July 1360 the Anglo-Irish political community had begged the king to send them a leader with the authority and resources necessary to re-establish order in the troubled lordship. Late in 1360, furthermore, the Countess Elizabeth's grandmother, Elizabeth de Clare, died, and Lionel came into possession not only of her share of the Clare estates in England and Wales but also of the Irish lands of the earldom of Ulster in which she had enjoyed a life interest. Edward III announced his intention to dispatch Prince Lionel to the lordship on 15 March 1361 and on 1 July created him royal lieutenant in Ireland. Lionel's elevation to the title of duke of Clarence (meaning the town, castle, and honour of Clare) in parliament on 13 November 1362 also had the effect of making him the senior Irish peer.

In the mid-fourteenth century the English colony in Ireland was on the defensive. Theoretically Edward III claimed lordship of the whole island, but in practice the native clans enjoyed a great deal of independence. Beyond the Bann and the Shannon there lay large areas in which English lordship was exercised only fleetingly and with difficulty, and even the heart of the English colony immediately around Dublin was threatened from time to time by Gaelic Irishmen such as the Ó Broin, Ó Tuathail, and Mac Murchadha tribes. Within the areas controlled by the English, royal authority was only ultimately effective if it met with the acquiescence of the resident aristocracy, in particular the earls of Desmond, Ormond, Louth, and Kildare. These and other members of the colonial aristocracy were highly critical of Edward III's neglect of the lordship: in 1346 it was alleged that the earl of Desmond had even sent messengers to the pope asking the latter to take Ireland under his special jurisdiction and appoint Desmond his vicar there. Consequently, although they regularly demanded royal intervention in the lordship, it was apparent even before Clarence's arrival that the 'English born in Ireland' (as the resident Anglo-Norman lords were often called) had a very different political perspective from the 'English born in England' (the description used for viceroys and other ministers sent into Ireland by the Westminster government). This was to be the great dilemma of Clarence's lieutenancy.

Lionel's task was to repair the ruinous state of the English colony by a demonstration of military might: he was equipped with a force of approximately 50 knights, 300 men-at-arms, and 540 mounted archers, and provided with ample financial resources to raise additional troops within Ireland (the original scheme to raise 800 foot archers in Wales and the west of England appears to have foundered). Almost as soon as he landed, the prince made a foray into Wicklow against the Gaelic forces that were challenging the English settlements around Dublin. In order to provide a more effective base for a military-style administration, some of the government was moved to Carlow, although Lionel himself continued to use Dublin as his personal headquarters and had the royal castle there renovated. He appears to have been diligent in his duties: early in 1362 he was at Drogheda and later that year he campaigned in Meath. On 22 April 1364 the earl of Ormond was appointed keeper of the lordship and Clarence returned to England to consult with the king and council; but Lionel was reappointed lieutenant on 24 September 1364 and took up residence in Ireland again in December, when he began a progress which took him from Cork via Trim to Drogheda. After a further visit to England in 1365, he held a parliament at Kilkenny in February 1366 which produced the most lasting of his legacies to Irish government. The statute of Kilkenny aimed to prevent the process of political and cultural 'degeneracy' among the English born in Ireland by forbidding the subjects of the king from using the Irish tongue, marrying Irish wives, or observing Irish law. There was little that was new about these rules, but their codification in 1366 meant that the statute of Kilkenny became regarded as the definitive statement on the subject down to the early seventeenth century.

Lionel was replaced as lieutenant on 7 November 1366 and left Ireland, vowing (according to the author of the *Eulogium historiarum*) never to return. His contribution to the English regime in the lordship was mixed. On the one hand, his period as lieutenant witnessed the first sustained attempt to force absentee landholders to contribute to the defence of the colony. Nor was it devoid of military success: the capture of Art Mór Mac Murchadha and the latter's subsequent death while in Lionel's custody removed the most troublesome of the Gaelic chieftains. On the other hand, Clarence's lieutenancy demonstrated that the colony was no longer self-supporting and that English authority could only be maintained with regular support, both military and financial, from the English government at Westminster; when the crown's interest and determination waned, such resources could all too easily disappear. The political rhetoric of the Irish parliaments of this period certainly does not suggest that the resident aristocracy perceived any appreciable improvement in the state of the Plantagenet regime. Above all, the statute of Kilkenny demonstrated the conflict between official government policy and the reality of Anglo-Irish political culture.

Even before Lionel left Ireland, the king appears to have had a new career marked out for him. Clarence's first wife had died in Dublin in 1363; her body had been transported back to England, at the crown's expense, and buried in her family mausoleum at Clare Priory in Suffolk. On 30 July 1366 a diplomatic mission was sent to Italy to discuss the possibility of a marriage between Violante Visconti, daughter of Galeazzo Visconti, lord of Pavia, and either Prince Lionel or his younger brother *Edmund of Langley. Lionel quickly emerged as the preferred candidate. The initiative for this alliance came from Violante's uncle, Bernabò Visconti, lord of Milan, who was prepared to pay dearly for the prestige of a Plantagenet alliance. It also complemented the anti-papal stance adopted by the English crown in the mid-1360s. Otherwise, it is difficult to see how the marriage offered any particular advantages to Edward III, whose dynastic strategy was focused very much on the British Isles and France. The terms were settled at Westminster in May 1367 and the prince and his entourage began to make plans for their departure in February 1368. Lionel was accompanied across the channel by an entourage of 457 men, together with no fewer than 1280 horses. The wedding took place before the door of Milan Cathedral on 28 May or 5 June 1368 and was celebrated with great pomp; the aged poet Petrarch was said to have dined with the wedding party during the sumptuous celebrations that followed.

Violante brought with her a marriage portion of 2 million gold florins and a string of towns and castles in Piedmont; English chroniclers, playing on the apparent success of Edward III's family policy in the 1360s, believed that Galeazzo had surrendered half his lands to his new son-in-law. In the event, the marriage was brief and fruitless: Clarence died at Alba, in Piedmont, on 17 October 1368 and was initially buried at Pavia. By his will, dated at Alba on 3 October 1368 and proved at Lambeth on 8 June 1369, he expressed the wish to be buried at Clare, and his body was later removed to England and interred with that of his first wife. Violante subsequently married Ottone Palaeologo, marquess of Monferrato (*d.* 1378), and finally Ludovico Visconti, lord of Lodi (*d.* 1381); she died in 1382.

In contrast to his brothers, *Edward, prince of Wales (the Black Prince), *John of Gaunt, and *Thomas of Woodstock, Lionel of Antwerp had only a minor role to play in English political life and made very little impression upon contemporary chroniclers and commentators. Perhaps, like his other brother, Edmund of Langley, he was not instinctively drawn to the world of high politics; more likely, his careers in Ireland and Italy and his early death, shortly before his thirtieth birthday, deprived his English contemporaries of any real knowledge of the prince's personal attributes and worth. In the fifteenth century, however, he achieved posthumous fame as one of the two sons of Edward III through whom the house of York claimed its right to the throne of England: this dynastic link undoubtedly explains, for instance, why the chronicler John Hardyng not only concocted an idealized physical description of the duke but also speculated that the Visconti marriage might, in the fullness of time, have made Clarence king of Italy and even emperor. W. M. ORMROD

Sources GEC, *Peerage* • E. B. Fryde and others, eds., *Handbook of British chronology*, 3rd edn, Royal Historical Society Guides and Handbooks, 2 (1986) • J. A. Watt, 'The Anglo-Norman colony under strain, 1327–99', *A new history of Ireland*, ed. T. W. Moody and others, 2: *Medieval Ireland, 1169–1534* (1987), 352–96 • T. W. Moody and others, eds., *A new history of Ireland*, 9: *Maps, genealogies, lists* (1984) • PRO • *Chancery records* • J. de Mussis, 'Chronicon Placentinum', *Rerum Italicarum scriptores*, ed. L. A. Muratori, 16 (1730), columns 448–633 • 'Annales Mediolanenses', *Rerum Italicarum scriptores*, ed. L. A. Muratori, 16 (1730), columns 642–840 • [J. Nichols], ed., *A collection of … wills … of … every branch of the blood royal* (1780) • W. M. Ormrod, 'Edward III's government of England, *c.*1346–1356', DPhil diss., U. Oxf., 1984 • J. Vale, *Edward III and chivalry: chivalric society and its context, 1270–1350* (1982) • A. Goodman, *John of Gaunt: the exercise of princely power in fourteenth-century Europe* (1992) • *The wardrobe book of William de Norwell*, ed. M. Lyon and others (1983) • F. S. Haydon, ed., *Eulogium historiarum sive temporis*, 3 vols., Rolls Series, 9 (1858) • [T. Walsingham], *Chronicon Angliae, ab anno Domini 1328 usque ad annum 1388*, ed. E. M. Thompson, Rolls Series, 64 (1874) • *The chronicle of John Hardyng*, ed. H. Ellis (1812)

Likenesses effigy (stylized as miniature 'weeper'), Westminster Abbey, tomb of Edward III

Liotard, Jean-Étienne (1702–1789), painter, born with his twin, Jean-Michel, on 22 December 1702 in Geneva, was among the seven children to survive infancy of Antoine Liotard (1661–1740) and his wife, Anne Sauvage (1659–1731), Huguenots who had left Montélimar following the revocation of the edict of Nantes (1685) and settled in Geneva. There Antoine, a jeweller, had been admitted to the bourgeoisie in 1701. Following a brief apprenticeship about 1721 to the miniaturist Daniel Gardelle (1673–1753), Liotard left in 1723 for Paris, where he was apprenticed for three years to Jean-Baptiste Massé (1687–1767), a portraitist, miniaturist, and engraver. Although he is said to have learned little from Massé, it was these three activities which Liotard undertook after his apprenticeship. The earliest known of his many self-portraits, painted about

Jean-Étienne Liotard (1702–1789), self-portrait, *c.*1744–5

1727 (priv. coll.), shows a mastery of a genre which was to be the mainstay of Liotard's career. His sitters during this stay in Paris included Voltaire.

In 1735 Liotard was invited by the French ambassador to accompany him to Naples, which he did before going to Rome in 1736. There his sitters included Pope Clement XII and the Pretender, James Stuart. In Rome he met William Ponsonby, later earl of Bessborough, who invited Liotard to join him and Lord Sandwich on their journey to Constantinople in 1738. During the four years that Liotard spent in Constantinople he adopted Turkish costume, and grew the long beard seen in numerous self-portraits, including one of *c.*1744–1745 in the Staatliche Kunstsammlungen, Dresden. This, like much of his work, was executed in pastel. During his Turkish period Liotard made some portraits of great presence including life-size oils of Richard Pococke (Musée d'Art et d'Histoire, Geneva) and William Ponsonby (Stansted Park, Hampshire), smaller pastels and drawings of members of the resident French and British communities, and pastel and drawn genre scenes. These last were often of young women in oriental costume, and their popularity is evidenced by some existing in several autograph versions.

In 1742–6 Liotard went first to Moldavia at the invitation of the reigning prince Constantin Mavrocordato, then to Vienna, where he made a lifelong friend of the empress Maria Theresa, and then to Frankfurt, Venice, Karlsruhe, Geneva, and Lyons (where he had relatives), before returning to Paris in 1746. In Paris his companion, Mlle Nicolle, gave birth to a daughter whom he later adopted. A child born from his relationship with Mlle de L'Isle during his first stay in Paris had died young. Despite his professional success, Liotard failed to gain admittance to the Académie Royale. Instead he joined the Académie de St Luc, exhibiting at its salon in 1751, 1752, and 1753. At the 1752 salon he exhibited *The Chocolate Drinker* (Stansted Park, Hampshire), later bought in London in 1774 by Lord Bessborough. In 1749 or 1750 Liotard made a series of pastels of the French royal family and about 1750 he made his celebrated pastel *Young Woman in Turkish Costume Seated on a Divan* (Musée d'Art et d'Histoire, Geneva). This was a reprise of a drawing made some ten years earlier and was itself repeated about 1752–4 in his portrait *Mary Gunning, Countess of Coventry* (Rijksmuseum, Amsterdam). The Geneva pastel uses a highly original composition and a limited palette of the three primary colours to suggest a story of disappointed romance with a directness and lack of theatricality unusual in genre painting of the period. Liotard's appeal to an English clientele, which in Paris had included David Garrick and Lord Augustus John Hervey, was reinforced by a visit to London in 1753–5 when his sitters included Lady Maria Beauclerk (later Lady Spencer), Henry Fox (later the first Lord Holland), and, in oriental costume, Simon Luttrell. Horace Walpole noted Liotard's long beard, his high prices, and his great talent, a talent acknowledged by his being commissioned to portray each of the prince and princess of Wales and their nine children, and in *The Gentleman's and Connoisseur's Dictionary of Painters* (1770) Matthew Pilkington wrote of Liotard's 'astonishing force, and beauty of tint; [the] striking resemblance of his models; a remarkable roundness and relief; and an exact imitation of life and nature' (p. 351).

There followed stays in the Netherlands (1755–6), where Liotard married Marie Fargues (1728–1782), daughter of a French businessman, having shaved off his beard for the occasion. Their eldest son, Jean-Étienne, was born in 1758. The couple had one other son and four daughters, one of whom died in infancy. For a period from 1757 Liotard settled in Geneva. In 1763, however, he recommenced his travels, going to Vienna (1763); Turin (1766); Lyons (1770), where he made a portrait of Rousseau; Paris (1771); London (1773–4), where he exhibited at the Royal Academy in successive years and organized a sale of his works at his lodgings in Great Marlborough Street in 1773 and another through Christies the following year; then on to Nice (1776) at the invitation of Augustus Hervey, by then third earl of Bristol; Vienna (1777–8); and Lyons again (1781). It was in Lyons that Liotard had printed his *Traité des principes et des règles de la peinture* (1781). Here he emphasized the importance of drawing which, he wrote, 'should be clear, without being dry; firm, without being hard or stiff; flowing, without being flabby; delicate and true, without being mannered'.

The works of Liotard's later years in Geneva include self-portraits, portraits of his family and of the Genevan bourgeoisie, but also his only landscape, *A View from the Artist's House with Self-Portrait* (Rijksmuseum, Amsterdam), and some still lifes. These he invested with the same directness and intensity of vision that he had brought to bear on his portraits. Liotard died in Geneva on 12 June 1789, leaving his art collection to his five children, the eldest of whom, Jean-Étienne (*d.* 1822), later wrote a life of his father (published 1933). HUMPHREY WINE

Sources [J.-É. Liotard], *Traité des principes et des règles de la peinture: par M. J. E. Liotard, peintre, citoyen de Genève* (Geneva, 1781) [preface by P. Courthion, Geneva, 1947] • R. Loche and M. Roethlisberger, eds., *L'opera completa di Liotard* (Milan, 1978) • A. de Herdt, *Dessins de Liotard* (1992) [exhibition catalogue, Musée d'Art et d'Histoire, Geneva, and Louvre, Paris]

Likenesses J.-É. Liotard, self-portrait, pastels, *c.*1744–1745, Staatliche Kunstsammlungen, Dresden, Gemäldergalerie Alte Meister [*see illus.*] • J.-É. Liotard, self-portrait (*A view from the artist's house with self-portrait*), Rijksmuseum, Amsterdam

Lipscomb, Christopher (1781–1843). *See under* Lipscomb, William (1754–1842).

Lipscomb, George (1773–1846), antiquary, was born on 4 January 1773 at Quainton, Buckinghamshire, the son of James Lipscomb (1730–1794), a former naval surgeon from Hampshire, and his wife, Mary (1745–1828), daughter of Jonathan George, farmer, of Grendon Underwood, Buckinghamshire. After attending schools at Quainton and Aylesbury and receiving some medical instruction from his father, he studied surgery in London under Sir James Earle. In 1792 he was appointed house surgeon of St Bartholomew's Hospital and became a member of the Lyceum Medicum Londinense. He obtained the degree of MD from Marischal College, Aberdeen, in 1806.

In 1794 Lipscomb became lieutenant of the North Hampshire militia and in 1798 captain commandant of the Warwickshire volunteer infantry, for whom he wrote an *Address to the Volunteers on their Duty to their King and Country*. Also in 1798 he was chosen deputy recorder of Warwick. At this period Lipscomb was practising as a surgeon in Warwick and he drew on his experience there in *An Essay on the Nature and Treatment of a Putrid Malignant Fever which Prevailed at Warwick* (1799). Later he moved to Birmingham, where he practised as a chemist and surgeon, and then to Coleshill, Warwickshire. He was declared bankrupt in 1805, but reached agreement with his creditors. In the same year he left Warwickshire for London and afterwards moved to Whitchurch, Buckinghamshire, where he was practising medicine by 1819. After leaving Whitchurch in 1832, he spent the rest of his life at various addresses in London.

As an author, Lipscomb displayed a wide range of interests. In addition to medical writings on subjects including asthma, hydrophobia, and vaccination, of which he was a staunch opponent, he published five topographical works between 1799 and 1823, one of which, *A Journey into South Wales* (1802), contains a section on Buckinghamshire. He wrote three novels published between 1809 and 1812, two of them anonymously and one under the pseudonym John English. He contributed numerous articles to the *Gentleman's Magazine*, usually signed Viator, and various essays on subjects connected with political economy, statistics, and general literature to the *Literary Panorama* and other periodicals. He suggested in an essay the plan of the Society for the Encouragement of Agricultural Industry.

In 1832 Lipscomb delivered in London a series of lectures on cholera, which he afterwards published in the form of a treatise, accompanied by his correspondence on the subject with Lord Melbourne. Lipscomb also published sermons, edited the *Clerical Guide* for 1821, and composed hymns and anthems for charity schools.

On 16 January 1803 at St Martin's, Birmingham, Lipscomb married Elizabeth (1760–1834), the widow of Richard Hopkins of Stratford upon Avon, Warwickshire, and third daughter of Thomas Wells, also of Stratford. They had no children. On his wife's death in 1834 her whole fortune, on which he chiefly depended, passed to her own family.

Lipscomb's great work, *The History and Antiquities of the County of Buckingham*, was based chiefly on his own collections, which he spent over twenty-five years in acquiring, and on those which he received on the death of the Revd Edward Cooke (1772–1824), rector of Haversham, Buckinghamshire, of whose will he was executor. The first part of the *History* was published in 1831 by John Bowyer Nichols, but despite extensive subscriptions it created such financial difficulties for Lipscomb that publication of the succeeding parts had to be suspended. He expected to acquire considerable property from Cooke's estate, but the inheritance was contested and after many years in chancery the case was decided against him in 1831.

The remainder of the work was published between 1838 and 1847 by J. and W. Robins, and before Lipscomb died he had the satisfaction of knowing that the eighth and final part was in the press. The complete *History* filled four quarto volumes with title-pages dated 1847. The book, considering the difficulties of its publication, is very creditable, although Lipscomb lacked the means to make full use of his materials. *The Victoria History of the County of Buckingham* (1905), in its preface, described Lipscomb's *History* as 'the only serious attempt to compile a complete history of the county' and gave the opinion that 'Perhaps not quite equal to our best county histories, it is yet a work of great value' (1.xxiii). Lipscomb died at home at 1 Merrow Street, Walworth, London, on 9 November 1846 and, as his wife had been, was buried in the graveyard of St George the Martyr, Southwark. ROGER BETTRIDGE

Sources *GM*, 2nd ser., 27 (1847), 88–90 · G. H. Wyatt, 'Lipscomb and his history of Bucks.', *Records of Buckinghamshire*, 19 (1971–4), 272–97 · C. R. J. Currie and C. P. Lewis, eds., *English county histories: a guide* (1994), 55–6 · parish register (baptism), Quainton, 29 Jan 1773 · d. cert. · P. Garside and R. Schöwerling, *The English novel, 1770–1829: a bibliographical survey of prose fiction published in the British Isles*, 2: *1800–1829* (2000)

Archives BL, corresp., Add. MSS 34188, 40595, 41859 · Buckinghamshire County Museum, Aylesbury, Buckinghamshire Archaeological Society, corresp. and papers relating to his history of Buckinghamshire · Bucks. RLSS, corresp. and papers | BL, letters to Stacey Grimaldi, Add. MS 34188 · Bodl. Oxf., letters to Sir Thomas Phillipps

Wealth at death under £100: PRO, death duty registers, IR 26/1778, fol. 312

Lipscomb, William (1754–1842), writer, was baptized on 9 July 1754 at St Thomas, Winchester, the son of Thomas Lipscomb, surgeon, of Winchester, and his wife, Sarah. He entered Winchester College in 1765, and matriculated at Oxford as a scholar of Corpus Christi College on 6 July 1770. In 1772 he won the prize for English verse, the subject being the beneficial effects of inoculation, and the poem appeared as a pamphlet that year. It was reprinted in 1793, and in the *Oxford Prize Poems* in 1807 and 1810. He graduated BA in 1774, and MA in 1784. On 19 August 1780 he married Margaret, second daughter of Francis Cooke of Gower Street, cashier of the navy; they had a large family. For some years he was private tutor and subsequently chaplain to the earl of Darlington at Raby Castle, Durham. From 1789 to 1832 he was the rector of Welbury in the north riding of Yorkshire, which he was allowed to hand over to his son Francis in 1832. He was also master of St John's Hospital, Barnard Castle, Durham.

Lipscomb, a frequent contributor to the *Gentleman's Magazine*, wrote: *Poems … to which are Added Translations of Select Italian Sonnets* (1784) and *The Canterbury Tales of Chaucer Completed in a Modern Version* (3 vols., 1795). This publication was a compilation of the work of several translators, with which Lipscomb combined his own. George Lipscomb MD was his cousin.

Lipscomb died at Brompton, London, on 25 May 1842. He was survived by ten of his children, including **Christopher Lipscomb** (1781–1843), who was baptized on 20 November 1781 at Staindrop, Durham. He matriculated at New College, Oxford, on 12 July 1800 at the age of eighteen. He graduated BA in 1804, MA in 1811, and BD and DD in 1825. He was vicar of Sutton Benger, Wiltshire, from 1818, and was appointed the first bishop of Jamaica in 1824, a post which he took up in 1825, and the duties of which he pursued with vigour, 'always bearing in mind that the object, as he said, of his mission was to improve the spiritual condition of the slave population' (Ellis, 65). He was the author of *Church Societies a Blessing to the Colonies* (1840). He died on 4 April 1843, and was buried at St Andrew's Church, in Jamaica. He was survived by at least three sons, Cyril William (*b.* 1831), Edward Webber (*b.* 1832), and Arthur Morton (*b.* 1841).

GORDON GOODWIN, *rev.* REBECCA MILLS

Sources *IGI* · Foster, *Alum. Oxon.* · *GM*, 2nd ser., 18 (1842), 100–01 · T. F. Kirby, *Winchester scholars: a list of the wardens, fellows, and scholars of … Winchester College* (1888), 260 · [J. Watkins and F. Shoberl], *A biographical dictionary of the living authors of Great Britain and Ireland* (1816) · [D. Rivers], *Literary memoirs of living authors of Great Britain*, 1 (1798), 376–7 · W. Lipscomb, *The Canterbury tales of Chaucer*, 3 vols. (1795), 1.v–xi · Watt, *Bibl. Brit.*, 2.609 · Allibone, *Dict.* · PRO, PROB 11/1962, fol. 356 · J. B. Ellis, *The diocese of Jamaica* (1913)

Wealth at death exact sum unknown: will, PRO, PROB 11/1962, fol. 356

Lipson, Ephraim (1888–1960), economic historian, was born in Sheffield on 1 September 1888, the son of Hyman Lipson, furniture dealer, and his wife, Eve, daughter of Michael Jacobs. His elder brother, Daniel Leopold Lipson (1886–1963), a schoolmaster, was independent member of parliament for Cheltenham from 1937 until 1950. Lipson had been dropped as a small child, and was left with grievous deformities. He was extremely sensitive about his appearance, and he was resentful of any criticism, longing to live a normal life which was never possible. Academically, he was successful and he obtained scholarships which took him to Sheffield Royal Grammar School and Trinity College, Cambridge, where he obtained first class honours in both parts of the historical tripos in 1909 and 1910. Since Cambridge offered no opportunity for remunerative work he moved to Oxford, where he became a private tutor and was prominent in the Oxford Hebrew congregation.

Lipson resolved to produce a new survey of English economic history based on 'both the older sources of evidence and the new material' (*DNB*). The first volume, *An Introduction to the Economic History of England, 1: the Middle Ages*, appeared in 1915. It was praised by J. H. Clapham as 'a work of considerable, even in parts of great learning', based on the 'mastery … of pretty well all the very abundant new material—primary and secondary—which has appeared in English in the last 15 years or so'. But this initially favourable assessment was soon dissipated by Clapham's cutting comments. In Clapham's view, Lipson managed to produce thorough and scholarly discussions of certain themes which were serious contributions to the subject, but the book was let down by a lifeless style and odd arrangement, by his capacity to 'infallibly take up each of the well-worn topics', and his inclusion of dull material of little consequence. As Clapham remarked, Lipson was 'learned, independent, and often conclusive in discussion, but he never starts a fresh hare … If he had thrown overboard a few bales of old controversy he might have found room for more valuable cargo' (J. H. Clapham, review, *Economic Journal*, 25, 1915, 570–72). Although the same faults were apparent in his survey of nineteenth-century Europe in 1916, and his study of the woollen and worsted industries in 1921, his strengths were enough to secure his appointment to the readership in economic history and a fellowship of New College, Oxford, in 1922.

Economics and economic history were not in a healthy position at Oxford in the 1920s, and Lipson's position was more difficult than Clapham's at Cambridge. To the institutional difficulties should be added his own personality. When his parents died in 1919, he bought a plot of land for himself and a wife who never materialized; in his house he installed a nursery for a child who was never born. One student recalled attending classes given by the 'austere, forbidding' Lipson:

> one entered this rather gloomy building … I remember going into a room which was painted green and it was November time when the mists were about … It was very cold and we sat on chairs which had been covered with dust-sheets, and Lipson sat in the middle of a ring of us and fired questions at us and then made sarcastic remarks. (F. E. Hyde, quoted in Barker, 11)

His lectures were recalled as 'very useful … He said everything twice very slowly so that you could take it all down' (J. de L. Mann, ibid., 10).

Lipson's major contribution to the subject was the creation of the *Economic History Review*. In 1924 he approached his publisher—A. and C. Black—with the idea of a new journal on the lines of the *English Historical Review*. The proposal was accepted and terms suggested, but Lipson did not take any action until the Royal Economic Society in 1925 announced its intention of publishing an economic history supplement to the *Economic Journal*. Lipson was prompted into action, signing a contract with Blacks in 1926 to be joint editor of the new review with R. H. Tawney. This was an interim arrangement until the Economic History Society was created a few months later, and it took over responsibility for the journal. It remained under Lipson's editorship until 1934.

Meanwhile, Lipson pressed on with his economic history of England, and by late 1930 he had finished the second and third volumes covering the period from Elizabeth to the industrial revolution, which he subtitled 'The age of mercantilism'. When he learned that Oxford was to establish a professorship of economic history, he urged his publisher to get the volumes out before the electors met in June 1931. The publisher set seventeen indexers to work, and had copies with the electors by May. The effort was to no avail, for Lipson was not selected. The decision was not entirely surprising, for Lipson was not a popular man in Oxford or the profession. M. M. Postan recalled that his approach to the subject was 'extraordinarily moderate', based on the belief that 'the right solution would always be found half-way between two wrong solutions'. At the same time he always claimed that he had anticipated anyone who suggested a new idea or argument. In his personal relations he was 'extraordinarily immoderate' (M. M. Postan, quoted in Barker, 10), with a clear divide between those whom he believed to love and hate him. Nor was it surprising that Lipson was deeply affected by his failure to obtain the chair. His formal academic career came to an end. Hurt and angry, he left Oxford, rarely to return; he sold his house and disposed of his library. Invitations to lecture in North America led to a leisurely tour around the world in 1932–4. Thereafter his life was divided between summer residence at the National Liberal Club in London and escape from bronchial problems by wintering abroad in warmer climates. The war drove him out of London and restrictions on travel limited his range of refuge to south-west England.

In such circumstances, the old life of sustained research and writing was no longer possible. There could be no volume 4, but an attempt was made to keep the other three up to date. The third edition of 1943 added a long introduction in which Lipson reiterated the theme that had run through the first edition: 'There is no hiatus in economic development, but always a constant tide of progress and change in which the old is blended almost imperceptibly with the new' (*DNB*). In particular, his study of organization and ideas before 1750 had convinced him that there was no industrial revolution, no violent breach with the past in the eighteenth century, or any other. To that central motif he added another conviction that the tide of human affairs was governed by the law of ebb and flow, with pendulum-like or cyclical alternating periods of co-operative or corporate control and of free enterprise.

Medieval society was co-operative and corporate; after a full turn of the wheel, mercantilism emerged as 'England's first planned economy'; and by the 1940s the wheel was again coming full circle 'to the spirit of an older regime based on co-operation' (*DNB*).

It was easier to philosophize than to keep up with the rapid advances of research. Two minor works, published in 1950 and 1953, made no attempt to do so. Lipson died at King's College Hospital, Denmark Hill, London, on 22 April 1960. His will directed that his letters, papers, and manuscripts should be burned, that he should be buried next to his mother at Willesden Jewish cemetery, and that his mother's wedding ring was not to be removed from his finger.

MARTIN DAUNTON

Sources *DNB* • T. C. Barker, 'The beginnings of the Economic History Society', *Economic History Review*, 2nd ser., 30 (1977), 1–19 • D. M. Lewis, *The Jews of Oxford* (1992) • *CGPLA Eng. & Wales* (1960)

Wealth at death £7862 7s. 4d.: probate, 29 July 1960, *CGPLA Eng. & Wales*

Lipson, Henry Solomon (1910–1991), physicist, was born on 11 March 1910 at 107 Wavertree Road, West Derby, Liverpool, the third and last child of Israel Lipson, shopkeeper, and his wife, Sarah, *née* Friedlander. All his grandparents were Polish Jewish emigrés who settled in Liverpool at the end of the nineteenth century. Shortly after his birth his father's business failed and, to support his family, Israel used his only asset, his considerable physical strength, and became a steelworker at Shotton, Flintshire. Lipson's mother managed the home well and also encouraged her children to become educated. From 1921 to 1927 Lipson attended Hawarden grammar school where he developed his lifelong interest in physics. At the age of seventeen he was awarded the Henry Neville Gladstone scholarship and a Flintshire county exhibition, and began studying physics at Liverpool University, eventually obtaining a first-class honours degree and the Oliver Lodge prize in 1930. The award of a demonstratorship enabled him to stay in Liverpool to do research. Lipson teamed up with another research student, one year his senior, C. A. Beevers. They were set the task of solving crystal structures from X-ray diffraction data and they had to make all their own equipment. Since they had no idea how to use their data they sought advice from Professor Lawrence Bragg, who had set up a world centre for crystallography in Manchester. With his help they solved a number of structures, including that of copper sulphate. This required extensive calculations, and Beevers and Lipson invented an aid to calculation, the Beevers–Lipson strips, which were widely used and immortalized their names in crystallography.

As a demonstrator Lipson continued to do research in Liverpool, together with some teaching, until 1936 when Bragg invited him to work in Manchester with Dr J. A. Bradley on the structure of metals. However, in 1937 Bragg became director of the National Physical Laboratory in Teddington and just one year later he replaced Lord Rutherford as the Cavendish professor at Cambridge. Bradley and Lipson accompanied him on each of these moves. It was while at Teddington that, on 12 December 1937, Lipson married Jane (Jenny; *b.* 1909/10), an invoice clerk, and daughter of Samuel Rosenthal, master tailor.

Lipson was, *de facto*, in charge of the crystallography group in Cambridge. Many young researchers—for example Max Perutz (later a Nobel laureate)—benefited from the care and effort he lavished on them. Lipson also tried to instil in them a sense of serving the needs of other scientists and of society at large. In his turn Lipson was influenced by others at the Cavendish. In particular, contact with P. P. Ewald made him realize the importance of the Fourier transform in relation to X-ray crystallography—something that influenced all his subsequent research. Lipson's stay in Cambridge was scientifically successful but he was never fully integrated into the life of the university. He was awarded a Cambridge MA in 1942, adding to the DSc awarded by Liverpool in 1939, but he never became a member of a college.

In 1945 W. H. Taylor became head of the crystallography group at the Cavendish and Lipson moved with his family to take over Taylor's vacant post at the Manchester College of Technology (later the University of Manchester Institute of Science and Technology). The post to which Lipson moved, head of the physics department, carried with it little status and no title. Lipson built up crystallographic research so that within a few years the college became an important world centre. He began a new optical approach to solving crystal structures, based on ideas first suggested by Bragg and exploiting the Fourier transform theory he had learned from Ewald. Initially the physics department was wholly involved in service teaching but in 1951 Lipson established an applied physics degree course. He believed in establishing a sound foundation to the learning process and he particularly enjoyed giving first-year courses. In 1954 he was given the title of professor and in 1957 he became a fellow of the Royal Society. By 1967 the character of the department began to change and new areas of research, such as meteorology and plasma physics, had been introduced. By the time he retired, in 1977, the department was established as a centre of high quality and varied research.

Lipson was active, in different ways, in both the international and local spheres. He served as the British co-editor of *Acta crystallographica* for twenty years, and he served two terms as president of the Manchester Literary and Philosophical Society, the only person to have done so in the twentieth century. He was also an enthusiastic voluntary worker at the local Withington Hospital. He strongly believed that science should be used for the benefit of mankind and he was a supporter of Pugwash (the movement among scientists to promote the peaceful application of scientific discoveries) and of SANA (Scientists Against Nuclear Arms). For his many services to society he was appointed CBE in 1976. His many activities did not detract from his central interest in life—his family. His three children, Ann (*b.* 1938), Stephen (*b.* 1941), and Judith (*b.* 1943) all became scientists, although he did not coerce them in any way. The death of his younger daughter from leukaemia in 1990 devastated both Henry and Jenny Lipson.

In 1991 the Lipsons were visiting their son, Stephen, a professor of physics at the Technion in Haifa, Israel. After a happy family day with grandchildren, Lipson went to bed and shortly after suffered a heart attack from which he died the same night, on 26 April. He was buried the next day in Haifa, close to his son's home.

M. M. WOOLFSON

Sources M. M. Woolfson, *Memoirs FRS*, 39 (1994), 229–44 · personal knowledge (2004) · private information (2004) · *WWW* [forthcoming] · b. cert. · m. cert. · *CGPLA Eng. & Wales* (1993)
Archives Bodl. Oxf., letters to Dorothy Hodgkin · ICL, archives, corresp. with J. D. McGee
Likenesses photograph, *c.*1975, repro. in Woolfson, *Memoirs FRS*, p. 228
Wealth at death under £125,000: probate, 23 Aug 1993, *CGPLA Eng. & Wales*

Lipton, Sir Thomas Johnstone, baronet (1850–1931), grocer and yachtsman, was born in a tenement house in Crown Street, Glasgow, on 10 May 1850, the only surviving son of Thomas Lipton and his wife, Frances, daughter of Frank Johnstone, of Kilrid, Clones. His father was a poor labourer from Shannock Green Mills, near Clones, co. Monaghan, who left Ireland with his wife because of the potato famine. After working in Glasgow in a warehouse and as timekeeper in a cotton mill, his father subsequently opened a small grocer's shop at 13 Crown Street, Glasgow. In this enterprise he was aided by his wife, a shrewd and kindly woman, whose salutary example was frequently praised by her son in the days of his prosperity.

At the age of nine Lipton started work as an errand-boy in his father's shop. Two years later he was employed by A. and W. Kennedy, stationers, and then briefly with the shirtmakers Tilley and Henderson at a wage of 4*s.* per week. After a brief spell as a cabin-boy on the Belfast-based steamships, he took passage on a Burns liner for the United States in the autumn of 1865, landing with little more than 30*s.* He secured employment first as a labourer on a Virginia tobacco plantation, then for a few months as a bookkeeper in the rice fields of South Carolina. These diverse jobs typified the young Lipton's abilities, for apart from his physical strength he was highly literate and had a natural aptitude for figures. He eventually stowed away in a ship from Charleston to New York, revealing his presence *en route* with an offer to work. Once in New York he did well as an employee in a large grocery store, an experience that was to serve well for his future. The efficiency of the store impressed Lipton and it was the only employment that had really appealed to him. However, at the age of twenty he became homesick and returned to Glasgow having saved 500 dollars. In keeping with a penchant for publicity which was later to contribute so much towards the foundation of his fortunes, he timed his return for a Saturday afternoon when the neighbours were at home. He ordered the cab to process slowly down the street so as to give maximum exposure to the presents for his

Sir Thomas Johnstone Lipton, baronet (1850–1931), by Howard Coster, 1930

mother—a rocking chair and barrel of flour—ostentatiously displayed on the roof.

Lipton again worked in his father's shop, but his quest for a larger trade and expansion conflicted with his father's cautious attitude. These differences led to them parting company, on friendly terms, and they remained a close family. At the age of twenty-one with savings of £100 Lipton opened his first shop in Stobcross Street, Glasgow. By obtaining supplies of butter, bacon, and eggs from Ireland direct, he eliminated middlemen's profits and was able to undersell his rivals. By the age of twenty-four he opened his second shop in High Street, a mile away from the Stobcross store. Others followed in rapid succession and all were on a larger scale: the Paisley store in 1879, for instance, boasted a large counter served by twelve assistants. Called 'Irish markets' to emphasize their trade, with their smart, clean style his shops brought a new quality to the ordinary housewife. Lipton was the hardest working and smartest salesman of all, setting a strong example to his staff. He was also a pioneer in the art of publicity, devising advertising schemes that amused the public and spread his name. He would stage an elaborate procession for the opening of a new shop, for instance, by publicly parading through the streets of Glasgow a monster cheese, which when cut was found to contain gold coins.

This publicity was reinforced by sound stock and fair prices, leading to a massive expansion of his shops to England and Wales during the 1880s. The first London shop was opened in 1888 and by 1889 Lipton had transferred his headquarters there. By the age of thirty he was a millionaire controlling an empire of shops and related activities. He ran his own printing and paper bag works, and in Chicago established a meat-packing factory, which was followed by a much larger plant in South Omaha, Nebraska. In 1889 Lipton moved into the tea trade in a dramatic fashion by purchasing his own tea plantations in Ceylon.

Until 1897 Lipton devoted the whole of his energies to business and had virtually no outside interests. Thereafter he began to dispense some of his great wealth in munificent charity, and to show that keenness for yacht-racing which was to win him an international reputation in sporting circles.

In 1897 the princess of Wales had a scheme for the provision of meals for poor people, but was £25,000 short of the £30,000 which she needed. Lipton provided it, and a few years later when she sponsored a poor people's restaurant, he funded the whole cost of £100,000. The year 1898 brought him a knighthood and saw the formation of the limited liability company Lipton Ltd, and the purchase of the steam yacht *Erin*, on board which Lipton entertained many distinguished people, including Edward VII.

In 1899 Lipton issued his first challenge for the America's Cup with the yacht *Shamrock I*. He was defeated then, and again year after year, but yacht-racing became an all-absorbing passion on which he lavished a fortune. His attempts on the cup over thirty years cost him around £1 million. He did not take the helm personally, but employed professional skippers (notably Sycamore and Heard) and was represented on board by his friend Colonel Duncan Neill. Although Lipton never won the cup he earned from the Americans the reputation of being 'the world's best loser'; and in 1930, after his fifth challenge, they presented him with a gold cup and an album of signatures in appreciation of his sportsmanship. During his yacht-racing period, which embraced the remaining thirty years of his life, he became known as a lavish and genial host, whose lifelong abstention from alcohol and tobacco in no way impaired his hospitality.

Lipton was appointed KCVO in 1901 and created a baronet in 1902. He was a member of the City lieutenancy and was for a time honorary colonel of the 6th volunteer battalion, Highland light infantry. During the First World War he plied the *Erin* between Marseilles and Salonica with medical supplies until she was sunk by a submarine. He kept up his connection with Lipton Ltd until 1927, when he retired, retaining the title of life president. He died at his home, Osidge, Southgate, East Barnet, London, on 2 October 1931. Unmarried, he bequeathed most of his fortune to charitable institutions in Glasgow.

Lipton kept all policy-making in his own hands and this inability to decentralize management was to create long-term problems for the company. However, he is remembered as one of the most successful businessmen of his time, and a devotee of the great sport of yachting, whose splendid hospitality, good humour, and inability to accept defeat made him virtually an ambassador of goodwill from Great Britain to America. In business Lipton was shrewd, hard-working, and honest, but he owed his success to an association of those qualities with a perception of the power of advertising which far outstripped that of most of his contemporaries.

H. B. GRIMSDITCH, *rev.* GARETH SHAW

Sources P. Mathias, *Retailing revolution: a history of multiple retailing in the food trades based upon the Allied Suppliers group of companies* [1967] • *The Times* (3 Oct 1931) • T. C. Bridges and H. H. Tiltman, *Kings of commerce* [1928] • T. J. Lipton, *Leaves from the Lipton logs* (1931) • *Literary Digest* (17 Oct 1931) • *Allied Staff Magazine* (Dec 1931) • private information (1949) • J. Mackay, *The man who invented himself: a life of Sir Thomas Lipton* (1998) • *DNB* • d. cert.

Archives Mitchell L., Glas., papers | FILM BFI NFTVA, actuality footage

Likenesses H. von Herkomer, oils, 1896, Art Gallery and Museum, Glasgow • T. Robinson, pencil drawing, 1898, NPG • H. Coster, photographs, 1930, NPG [*see illus.*] • E. Pizella, drawing, Lipton Ltd, London • A. P. F. Ritchie, print on cigarette card, NPG • Spy [L. Ward], caricature, chromolithograph, NPG; repro. in *VF* (19 Sept 1901)

Wealth at death £566,068 18*s.* 6*d.*: probate, 18 Feb 1932, *CGPLA Eng. & Wales*

Lisgar. For this title name *see* Young, John, Baron Lisgar (1807–1876).

Lisieux, Thomas (*d.* 1456), administrator and dean of St Paul's, is of unknown origins, though it was stated in a papal dispensation of 1437 that he was of noble birth. An Oxford graduate, he was senior proctor of the university in 1426–7. On 23 October 1430 he was presented to the rectory of Murston near Hollingbourne, Kent, by William Cromer, citizen of London and lord of that manor, and in 1433 he became rector of St Michael Cornhill, London. On 12 May 1435 he was granted a prebend in St George's Chapel in Windsor Castle, and in 1436 described as a clerk and chaplain of Henry VI, the prebend of Rugmere in St Paul's Cathedral. He had resigned Windsor by 22 February 1442, and he exchanged Rugmere for the prebend of Tottenhall in the same cathedral in 1452. From 1443 he also held the prebend of Henfield in the diocese of Chichester, from 1447 the treasurership of Abergwili in Carmarthenshire, and from 1449 a prebend in the king's free chapel of Bridgnorth. Meanwhile on 12 December 1441 he was elected dean of St Paul's, London, an office that he probably owed to the influence of Thomas Kemp, then bishop of London, and that proved to be the final reward for his services to the crown. In February 1449, following the death of Robert Gilbert, bishop of London, he was appointed to administer the spiritualities of the see.

On 12 May 1452 Lisieux was appointed keeper of the privy seal, and was subsequently granted an annuity of £365 from the customs for as long as he held that post. His promotion to one of the great offices of state seems unexpected, even in a man who had been a royal clerk for over fifteen years, and may have been due to the support of Thomas Kemp as well as to royal favour. Unlike his predecessor but one, Adam Moleyns, who had been so closely associated with the duke of Suffolk's highly unpopular regime that he was murdered in 1450, Lisieux does not appear to have been a powerful figure in the administration, a consideration which, quite as much as his own ability and adaptability, probably explains how he was able to retain his office for over four years of continuous political crisis. He was as efficient as circumstances permitted, but he did not attend all the meetings of the king's council, and during the early months of 1454 it appears to have been the deliberate policy of the chancellor, Cardinal John Kemp, to keep Lisieux away from council sessions. Lisieux remained in office during and after the duke of York's protectorate, but his association with the duke probably led to his dismissal by a regime headed by Queen Margaret, for on 24 September 1456 he was replaced as keeper by Lawrence Booth. It is possible, however, that ill health, or even death, lay behind his replacement, for he was dead by 13 October—his will, dated 29 November 1450, was proved on 17 October 1456. In it he desired to be buried in the south side of the crypt of St Paul's Cathedral, in the chapel of Our Saviour. Arrangements for his funeral, to be conducted in St Paul's, St Michael Cornhill, and Kentish churches including Murston and Kingsnorth, for a chantry, and for his anniversaries, were elaborated. Small sums of money were left to the staff of St Paul's, including canons, vicars, and bell-ringers, to the prisoners in Ludgate, and all other London prisons, to the friars and other religious of London, the nuns of Markyate, Hertfordshire, and the London hospital of Elsing Spital, as well as to his own household, his cook, steward, serjeant-at-arms, and other named servants. To his otherwise unknown brother, John, he left 20 marks. J. L. KIRBY

Sources *Chancery records* • Emden, *Oxf.*, 2.1197 • R. A. Griffiths, *The reign of King Henry VI: the exercise of royal authority, 1422–1461* (1981) • E. F. Jacob, ed., *The register of Henry Chichele, archbishop of Canterbury, 1414–1443*, 1, CYS, 45 (1943), 267 • *Fasti Angl., 1300–1541*, [St Paul's, London] • *Fasti Angl., 1300–1541*, [Chichester] • E. B. Fryde and others, eds., *Handbook of British chronology*, 3rd edn, Royal Historical Society Guides and Handbooks, 2 (1986) • C. N. L. Brooke, 'The deans of St Paul's, *c.*1090–1499', *BIHR*, 29 (1956), 231–44 • *CEPR letters*, 8.595 • will, PRO, PROB 11/4, sig. 8 • H. Anstey, ed., *Epistolae academicae Oxon.*, 1, OHS, 35 (1898), 18n., 276–7 • G. Hennessy, *Novum repertorium ecclesiasticum parochiale Londinense, or, London diocesan clergy succession from the earliest time to the year 1898* (1898), 5, 48, 51, 332 • C. Deedes, ed., 'Extracts from the episcopal register of Richard Praty, … 1438–1445', *Miscellaneous records*, Sussex RS, 4 (1904), 128–9 • *Ninth report*, 1, HMC, 8 (1883), 45a, 48b • A. T. Bannister and others, eds., *Registrum Ricardi Beauchamp, episcopi Herefordensis*, 1, CYS, 25 (1919), 9 • I. J. Churchill, *Canterbury administration: the administrative machinery of the archbishopric of Canterbury*, 2 vols. (1933), vol. 2, p. 248 • P. A. Johnson, *Duke Richard of York, 1411–1460* (1988)

Wealth at death approx. £100 in legacies: will, PRO, PROB 11/4, sig. 8

Lisle. For this title name *see* individual entries under Lisle; *see also* Talbot, Thomas, second Viscount Lisle (*c.*1449–1470); Plantagenet, Arthur, Viscount Lisle (*b.* before 1472, *d.* 1542).

L'Isle, de. For this title name *see* Sidney, William Philip, first Viscount de L'Isle (1909–1991).

Lisle [de Lisle] **family** (*per. c.*1277–1542), gentry, was the principal family on the Isle of Wight, one of the leading Hampshire county families, and received individual summonses to parliament between 1302 and 1314, which in modern doctrine supposedly created a barony. They took their name of Lisle, or de Insula, or de Insula Vecta, from the island itself, like several other families from whom it is often difficult to distinguish them until they died out early in the fourteenth century. They were the principal tenants of the Revières earls of Devon and Isabella, countess of Aumale, lords of the isle until it passed to the crown on the countess's death in 1293. This particular line of Lisles has been traced back to Jordan and Hawise (*c.*1130), whose grandson Walter (*d.* in or before 1224) was bailiff of the island and whose great-grandson Geoffrey was sheriff of Hampshire in 1236–9 and had died in or before 1252, when his son William swore fealty. This William was the father of **Sir John** [i] **de Lisle** (*d.* 1304), the first member of the family recorded as active outside the island and Hampshire itself. John [i] served in Wales in 1277, again in 1282, and in Gascony in 1295. He served in the garrison of Blays in the Gironde, received protections against seizures and exemption from taxation during his absence, and £200 was still owing in 1306. He was the first Lisle to be knighted in 1282 and the first to be summoned to parliament in 1299. His son **Sir John** [ii] **Lisle** (*d.* 1331) was no longer summoned after 1314. Only John [iv] (*d.* 1408) [*see below*] seems of comparable national importance. The ward of his stepfather, Sir Richard Stury, an influential household knight of Richard II and the servant of John of Gaunt, duke of Lancaster, John [iv] was knighted at the coronation of Henry IV, to whom he was a king's knight and annuitant and who twice summoned him to great councils.

Inquisitions in 1252 and 1263 reveal the Lisles as almost exclusively an island family. Apart from two half-virgates, their entire estate consisted of seven and a half fees held of the earl of Devon as of the castle of Carisbrooke by knight's service, castleguard, and suit at the knights' court. The *Nomina villarum* of 1316 and a feudal aid of 1346 reveal the Lisles as lords of four places in the hundred of East Medina and one in West Medina. In 1304 John [i] died seised of the grange of Bridlesford, the manor and fishery of Wootton and seven other manors on the Isle of Wight, the manor of Mansbridge in Swaythling, and La Rugge Hall; he was also lord of Woodhouse and 30 acres in the forest of Chute, and hereditary bailiff of the east walk of Chute, which had been settled on him on his marriage to Nichola de Columbiers. The estate was extended at a total of £79, of which £71 13*s.* 6½*d.* was on the Isle of Wight. In 1306 John [ii] was granted free warren on the whole estate. Wootton, of which John [i] styled himself lord in 1301, was apparently his principal seat, but was not the sole one: John [iii] was born at Mansbridge. Thereafter the family made only modest additions to this estate. In 1345 **Sir Bartholomew Lisle** (*d.* 1345) died seised of the manor of Welton in Northamptonshire and Maiden Newton in Dorset. The marriage of his son **Sir John** [iii] **Lisle** (*d.* 1370) to Maud Edington, a relative of Bishop William *Edington (*d.* 1366), somehow produced the manors of Kingston, Thruxton in north-west Hampshire, and South Baddesley in Boldre in the New Forest. **Sir John** [iv] **Lisle** (*d.* 1408) also acquired property in Crookham, Berkshire. In 1412 the estate was assessed for taxation at £187, about £33 in Dorset, about £40 (Chute) in Wiltshire, and about £112 in Hampshire, two-thirds being held by **John** [v] **Lisle** (*d.* 1429) and a third in dower by the dowager Elizabeth. **Sir John** [vi] **Lisle** (*d.* 1471) married the heiress Anne Botreaux, niece of William, Lord Botreaux, who brought Briston in Devon, Holt in Wiltshire, and two Hampshire manors to the family. Altogether by 1471 there were fifteen manors and two advowsons in Hampshire, four manors in Dorset, and two each in Wiltshire and Devon. The estate was appropriate for a leading family of gentry, but insufficient as endowment for a peer. Yet within Hampshire, a county dominated by ecclesiastical landlords, this was one of the largest secular estates.

Several times the Lisles intermarried with important families. Bartholomew married Elizabeth Courtenay, daughter of the earl of Devon. His son John [iii] married into the Edingtons. But most Lisle consorts were unidentifiable or from gentry families like Bremshott and Botreaux that did not expand their inheritance. It was nevertheless an indication of their importance among county gentry not only that almost all the heads of family were knighted, but that they were knighted on such important state occasions as the knighting of Prince Edward in 1306, the coronation of Henry IV, the coronation of Elizabeth of York in 1487, and the creation of Henry, prince of Wales, in 1503. The only head of the family who was not knighted was John [v], who was a nonentity—he was never even a JP and lost the lease of the herbage of the Wiltshire forest of Savernake granted to his father.

Most of the Lisles were active in local government, as justices of the peace, commissioners of array and oyer and terminer, John [i] and John [ii], Bartholomew, and John [vi] being especially active. John [ii], John [v], John [vi], **Sir John** [vii] **Lisle** (*d.* 1523), and **Sir Thomas Lisle** (*d.* 1542) were sheriffs of Hampshire, John [iv] and John [vi] of Wiltshire. All served on Hampshire commissions, and John [iv] (1401, 1404), John [v] (1417, 1422), and John [vi] (1433, 1439) were elected as knights of the shire for Hampshire. The commissions on which they served often related to maritime defence as befitted an island family. Bartholomew was joint keeper of the island in 1339 and John [iv] was made responsible for the defence of Winchester and Southampton against invasion in 1403. Indeed John [iv] was appointed governor of Guernsey in 1405 and probably spent his last two years there. His service in Brittany, that of his father John [iii] in France in 1370, where he died, and his grandson John [vi]'s participation in Somerset's expedition in 1443 and the disastrous Aquitaine campaign of 1453 do not constitute a distinguished military record.

Actually the identification of the family with the defence of the Isle of Wight diminishes, perhaps because the Lisles increasingly resided from preference on the mainland. There are several pointers. The shrievalty of Wiltshire strictly implied residence in Wiltshire. It is striking how frequently John [iv], John [v], and John [vi] attended the Hampshire county elections. Early Lisles patronized Quarr Abbey, co-founded Barton oratory in 1275, gave lords to Godsfield preceptory, and were presumably buried at Wootton, all on the Isle of Wight, but their fifteenth-century successors were different. John [v] chose in 1429 to be buried at Chute. John [iv] in 1408, John [vii] in 1523, and at least one other were interred at Thruxton, where their tombs remain and where John [vii] apparently intended to build an ambulatory. The will of John [vi] (*d.* 1471) mentions his daughter Anne and that of **Sir Nicholas Lisle** (*d.* 1506) a kinswoman Joan, both nuns of Amesbury in Wiltshire. Other bequests to Edington and Mottisfont priories suggest a focus on the mainland.

The Lisles were a fertile but not, apparently, a long-lived family. For fourteen generations from Jordan to John [vii] the estate descended from father to son. There are occasional glimpses of younger children and cousins, such as the six sons and three daughters of John [v], but only one of these established a lasting line. Lands settled on younger sons by John [iv] and Nicholas soon reverted to the main line. Both John [iii] and John [iv] succeeded as minors. They and John [v] found their inheritance encumbered for long periods by dowagers. The continuation of the family for a further generation was assured before John [vii] died in 1523 by the marriage of his great-niece Mary Kingston (*d.* 1539), the heir general, to her distant cousin and heir male Sir Thomas Lisle (*d.* 1542). When this match proved childless, the estate devolved on three distant cousins descended from two of John [v]'s daughters. The association of the Lisles with Wootton was perpetuated a little longer as John [vii] conveyed it to Thomas's brother Lancelot (*d.* 1544), whence it descended within the Lisle family into the seventeenth century.

MICHAEL HICKS

Sources GEC, *Peerage* • *VCH Hampshire and the Isle of Wight* • *Inquisitions and assessments relating to feudal aids*, 6 vols., PRO (1899–1921) • J. C. Wedgwood and A. D. Holt, *History of parliament … 1439–1509*, 2 vols. (1936–8) • HoP, *Commons, 1386–1421* • *Chancery records* • wills, PRO, PROB 11/3, sig. 10 [John (v) Lisle]; PROB 11/6, sig. 3 [John (vi) Lisle]; PROB 11/21, sig. 19 [John (vii) Lisle]; PROB 11/29, sig. 10 [Thomas Lisle]; PROB 11/15, sig. 7 [Nicholas Lisle]; PROB 11/16, sig. 1 [John (iv) Lisle] • *LP Henry VIII*

Likenesses brass, 1408 (John (iv) Lisle), Thruxton church, Hampshire • effigy, 1523 (John (vii) Lisle), Thruxton church, Hampshire

Wealth at death £79 p.a.—John (i) Lisle: 1304, *Feudal aids* C133/114/5 • £187 p.a.—John (v) Lisle

Lisle, Lady Alice [*née* Alice Beconsawe] (*c.*1614–1685), supposed traitor, was born at Moyles Court, Ellingham, Hampshire, the second daughter of Sir White Beconshaw (or Beconsawe; *d.* 1638), a local landowner and ship money sheriff for Hampshire. Her mother's identity is unknown. Alice was reared and educated in Hampshire. In 1636 she became the second wife of John *Lisle (1609/10–1664), MP for Winchester in the Short and Long parliaments, and a regicide who was elevated to Cromwell's upper house in 1657. From that point until her death she was usually referred to as Lady Alice.

Little is known of Alice Lisle's roles as wife and mother. She was in exile with her husband at Lausanne in 1664 when two Irish royalists, Thomas MacDonnell and James Cotter, murdered him. John Lisle had fled to Switzerland after the Restoration with Edmund Ludlow and other regicides rather than stand trial in England. He was on his way to church when he was spotted and shot at such close range that all three bullets passed through his body and powder burns covered his clothing (Marshall, 296). After her husband's burial in Lausanne, Alice returned to Moyles Court, on the outskirts of the New Forest, a property she had inherited from her father. She was a pious woman who sympathized with dissenters but was not an active sectarian (Bruce, 124). For the next twenty years, her peaceful Hampshire lifestyle was interrupted only by occasional trips to London. She had three children: a son, William, a royalist, who married Lady Katherine Hyde; and two daughters, Triphena Lloyd and Bridget Usher. Both daughters married twice: nothing is known of Triphena's husbands; however, Bridget married Leonard Hoar, president of Harvard University, and after his death wed Hezekiah Usher of Boston.

Alice Lisle's quiet life ended abruptly with Monmouth's rebellion. On 25 July 1685 James Dunne, a nonconformist baker from Warminster, came to Moyles Court bearing a note from John Hicks, who was seeking shelter for himself and Richard Nelthorp. Dunne had been hiding the fugitives since the battle of Sedgemoor and seems to have been part of a network of dissenters across the region. Lisle knew Hicks as a presbyterian minister and readily consented to his plea for sanctuary. Hicks and Nelthorp dined with her, then hid in the malt house. Alerted by John Barter, a local labourer, that rebels had taken refuge at Moyles Court, Colonel Thomas Penruddock and his men searched the property and arrested Hicks and Nelthorp on the morning of the 26th. Lady Alice was also taken into custody, transferred to Winchester, and charged with treason for harbouring Hicks.

Brought before a special commission at Winchester on 27 August 1685, Lady Alice was the first person tried before Lord Chief Justice George Jeffreys in what was subsequently labelled the 'bloody assizes'. To drive home the serious consequences of harbouring fugitives, the government clearly wished to make an example of her (Earle, 169–71). Aged, infirm, and nearly deaf, she asked that a friend, Matthew Brown, be designated to stand by her in court and repeat all that was said to her. Throughout the ordeal she proclaimed her innocence. A version of the trial record survives (*State trials*, 11.298–382); however, according to Muddiman, its veracity is open to question. First printed in 1719, long after all who could check the transcript for accuracy were deceased, the proceedings seem to have been prepared from trial notes (Muddiman, 27–8). What makes the document suspect is the vitriolic language and court demeanour attributed to Jeffreys. Its excessiveness differs from any other extant trial record involving the chief justice (Keeton, 314).

The case against Alice Lisle hinged on proving that she knew Hicks and Nelthorp were fugitive rebels. As the trial progressed, with Jeffreys apparently badgering witnesses sympathetic to Alice Lisle, Dunne, the key witness, found his testimony contradicted by Barter. Under blistering examination, and fearing that he might also be charged, he recanted and implicated her. Lady Lisle acknowledged hiding Hicks but steadfastly rejected the charge of treason. Replying directly to Jeffreys, she stated, 'And I beseech your lordship to believe I had no intention to harbour him but as a Nonconformist; and that, I knew, was no treason' (Bruce, 136). Because of her age and deafness, Alice Lisle proved no match for her determined accuser. After a gruelling six-hour trial, she was convicted and condemned by a reluctant jury to be burned alive. According to Jeffreys, 'I would have condemned her had she been my mother' (Chenevix Trench, 237). Her appeal to King James for clemency modified the sentence only slightly, and she was beheaded in the Market Square, Winchester, on 2 September 1685. In her dying speech, she reiterated that her only crime was 'Entertaining a Non-Conformist Minister' ('Last Speech'). The body was returned to her family for burial at Ellingham, and her small estate was transferred to Louis Duras, second earl of Feversham. Her attainder was reversed in 1689 after a petition from her daughters.

Popular opinion overwhelmingly supported Alice Lisle, portraying her as a protestant martyr, a victim of royal vindictiveness. Many were shocked that a woman of her age and social standing should be executed, while others, more fully implicated in the actual rising, received lesser sentences or pardons. Only one contemporary elegy suggested her guilt and sanctioned the punishment. Penning her epitaph, its misogynist author wrote:

> Here Lies Madam Lisle Dead,
> Which for Treason lost her Head,
> She Patroniz'd the Cause, The Cause,
> Against the Church and stablish'd Laws,
> Let all her sex both Great and small,
> Take here Example by her Fall,
> And henceforth ever shun to be
> Entangled by Presbi ery.
> (*Elegy on Mrs. Alicia Lisle*)

While Jeffreys was probably technically correct in his decision, the excessive sentence cast a pall over the remaining trials and lent credence to the charge that she was the victim of judicial murder. MICHAEL J. GALGANO

Sources *An elegy on Mrs. Alicia Lisle which for high-treason was beheaded at Winchester September the 2(n)d 1685* (1685) • 'The last speech of Madam Lisle, beheaded at Winchester, in September, 1685', *The dying speeches of several excellent persons, who suffered for their zeal against popery, and arbitrary government* (1689) • *State trials*, vol. 11 • G. W. Keeton, *Lord Chancellor Jeffreys and the Stuart cause* (1965) • J. G. Muddiman, ed., *The bloody assizes* (1929) • C. Bruce, ed., *The book of noble Englishwomen: lives made illustrious by heroism, goodness, and great attainments* (1875) • C. Chenevix Trench, *The western rising: an account of the rebellion of James Scott, duke of Monmouth* (1969) • A. Marshall, *Intelligence and espionage in the reign of Charles II, 1660–1685* (1994) • P. Earle, *Monmouth's rebels: the road to Sedgemoor 1685* (1977) • R. Clifton, *The last popular rebellion: the western rising of 1685* (1984) • H. Montgomery Hyde, *Judge Jeffreys* (1948) • J. Webb, N. Yates, and S. Peacock, eds., *Hampshire studies presented to Dorothy Dymond* (1981) • *DNB*

Lisle, Ambrose Lisle March Phillipps de (1809–1878), Roman Catholic layman and ecumenist, eldest son of Charles March Phillipps (1779–1862), of Garendon Park,

Leicestershire, was born at Garendon, the home of his grandparents, on 17 March 1809. His mother, Harriet (1790–1813), youngest daughter of Gerald Gustavus Ducarel of Walford, Somerset, died when her son was five years old. In youth he was delicate and solitary. The choice of Maisemore Court School, near Gloucester (it was later moved to Edgbaston), was not a happy one, but was crucial to the rest of his life. Phillipps's unhappiness there was aggravated by religious questions to which the answers he was given seemed contradictory. The French master, Abbé Giraud, an emigré priest exiled by the revolution in France, treated him kindly and lent him books. Without the knowledge of his family, Phillipps at the age of sixteen was received as a Roman Catholic at the church of St Peter, Birmingham.

After tuition at home, Phillipps matriculated at Trinity College, Cambridge, in 1826. His religious affiliation was reinforced by his friendship with Kenelm Digby, a recent convert and the author of books which extolled the holiness of the medieval period and the principles of chivalry. Phillipps began to emphasize his descent from a knight who had accompanied Duke William to England and was rewarded by land on the Isle of Wight, from which the family name Lisle derived. He changed his name to de Lisle in 1862, on the death of his father and his inheritance of the Garendon estates.

Each Sunday, Phillipps, with Digby, rode to St Edmund's, Ware, 25 miles from Cambridge to attend mass. In the spring of 1828 the exertion overpowered him and his lungs were affected. He left Cambridge and was taken by his father to winter in Rome. Here he met John, sixteenth earl of Shrewsbury, a Roman Catholic peer, who was later to provide substantial sums for church building in England, often at Phillipps's prompting. He also met Hugh Clifford, later seventh baron, whose ward Laura was to become Phillipps's wife. During this and a subsequent visit to Rome a year later, he was received by two popes, Leo XII and Pius VIII, and made the acquaintance of Luigi Gentili and his superior, Antonio Rosmini, and Dominic Barberi.

Phillipps visited a hermit who predicted that he would father a large family, and that he would not die until he had seen the reunion of the churches, in which process he would play a part. This incident became the justification for many later initiatives. Phillipps married Laura Mary Clifford on 25 July 1833; she bore sixteen children, to whom he was devoted. They set up house in 1835 at Grace Dieu Manor, Whitwick, with adjoining acres and tenants provided from his father's estates nearby. This became the focus of his social and religious programme. A. W. N. Pugin, architect and a friend of Phillipps's, designed extensions to the house several times, and also to the Gothic chapel where an elaborate liturgy, with plainchant sung by a choir, was provided on feast days. Phillipps refused to accept nomination to parliament, but took on local appointments as magistrate, deputy lieutenant, and, in 1868, high sheriff, of Leicestershire.

The conversion to Roman Catholicism in 1830 of George Spencer, son of the second Earl Spencer, was at least partly owing to Phillipps's influence; it was the catalyst that encouraged him to act to bring about what he called 'the return of England to Catholic unity'. This was to be achieved in two ways: by the conversion of individuals and, more importantly, by the corporate absorption of whole groups into the Roman Catholic communion. He built chapels in the Gothic style in his neighbourhood and brought priests to minister in them. The proportion of Roman Catholics increased substantially. In 1835 he bought 230 acres of land to found a Cistercian monastery, with buildings designed by Pugin and largely paid for by Lord Shrewsbury. Two major attempts were made by him to secure corporate reunion. The first, in 1841, was the subject of a lengthy correspondence with J. R. Bloxam of Magdalen College, Oxford, and other Tractarians, but was short-lived. The second, in 1856, in collaboration with F. G. Lee, led to the founding of the Association for the Promotion of Christian Unity. At its peak in 1862 there were 8000 members, of whom 1000 were Roman Catholics. A ban from the Holy Office required them to withdraw in 1864, which they did. But de Lisle continued his ecumenical efforts with greater discretion, by correspondence and exchanges of hospitality with friends and acquaintances in England and abroad. Grace Dieu became a meeting place across denominational boundaries. Portrayal of de Lisle, faintly disguised as Eustace Lyle, a Roman Catholic philanthropist, in the novel *Coningsby* by Benjamin Disraeli was the result of meeting members of the Young England movement.

Although a life-long Conservative, in 1868 de Lisle established a friendship with William Gladstone, who made a visit to Garendon in 1873 while prime minister. When Gladstone asked de Lisle, an 'opportunist' over the impending definition of papal infallibility in 1870, for help in drafting pamphlets in reaction to the Vatican decrees, de Lisle was able to see that J. H. Newman, whom he had known since 1841, received a proof copy. It owed much to his insistence that Newman was persuaded to write his *Letter to the Duke of Norfolk*. It was a type of covert activity typical of de Lisle, who incurred accusations of meddling in the church's business. But from the perspective of the late twentieth century, with its emphasis on the participation of lay people, he can be seen as something of a prophet. He was also unusual for a Roman Catholic in taking an important part with Gladstone in the campaign against the Bulgarian atrocities in 1876. De Lisle was small and slight in appearance; he weighed 9 stone in 1844, and was described, in 1856, as delicate with a 'trifle melancholy look'. His writings were not well received in his lifetime, due partly to their verbosity. He died on 5 March 1878 and was buried in the abbey church of Mount St Bernard, which he had founded.

His eighth son, **Rudolph Edward March Phillipps de Lisle** (1853–1885), was born at Grace Dieu on 23 November 1853 and entered the training ship *Britannia* on 2 May 1867. In August 1884 he was appointed to the naval brigade attached to the upper Nile expedition sent to relieve Gordon at Khartoum. He was killed at the battle of Abu Klea on 17 January 1885 and buried on the battlefield. His letters to his family, which survive in the de Lisle archives, contain descriptions of scenes he witnessed during his naval career, particularly in South America.

MARGARET PAWLEY

Sources E. S. Purcell, *Life and letters of Ambrose Phillipps de Lisle*, 2 vols. (1900) • M. Pawley, *Faith and family: the life and circle of Ambrose Phillipps de Lisle* (1993) • *The Tablet* (16 March 1878), 328–30 • Gladstone, *Diaries*

Archives Centro Internazionale di Studio Rosminiani, Stresa, Italy • NRA, priv. coll., corresp. and papers • Quenby Hall, Leicestershire • Rosminian English Province Archives, Wonersh, Surrey • Sacra Congregazione di Propaganda Fide • Stockerston Hall, Oakham, Rutland | Birmingham Oratory, letters to John Newman • BL, correspondence with W. E. Gladstone, Add. MSS 44444–44785, *passim* • Magd. Oxf., letters to J. R. Bloxam • NL Ire., letters to William Monsell, Lord Emly, MSS 8318, 20680 • Pembroke College, Oxford, letters to Sir Peter Le Page Renouf

Likenesses A. Stokes, oils, 1879 (posthumous), Quenby Hall, Hungarton, Leicestershire

Wealth at death under £20,000: probate, 21 June 1878, *CGPLA Eng. & Wales*

Lisle, Aubrey Edwin Orchard- (1908–1989), commercial estate agent, was born on 12 March 1908, at Crediton, Devon, the second of four sons of Edwin Orchard-Lisle and his wife, Lucy Ellen Lock. He was educated at West Buckland School, north Devon, and later attended the College of Estate Management in London. He left school at the age of sixteen following the death of his father, and started work with the Hampstead-based estate agents Ernest Owers. He passed the Auctioneers' and Estate Agents' Institute examination when he was twenty-one, achieving the highest mark for the London area. In 1926 he moved to Healey and Baker, an old-established surveying firm which was just beginning to move into commercial property. In 1929 he transferred to the firm's new West End office in St George Street, where he managed the development of the practice's commercial side (which was eventually to replace its residential business) together with Arthur Hemens, who had joined Healey and Baker in 1926. In 1930 his brother Mervyn also joined the practice. The two brothers, together with Arthur Hemens and, later, Douglas Tovey, were the guiding forces behind the firm's development as one of Britain's largest and most successful commercial estate agencies.

Early deals with shop developers led Orchard-Lisle to concentrate his activities on the lucrative shops sector. A highly successful strategy was adopted of developing strong links with rapidly expanding multiple retailing chains such as Montague Burton, Marks and Spencer, and Woolworth's. Close relationships with these retailers enabled the practice to gain a key position as the presence of one of the major multiples could determine the success or failure of a development.

Orchard-Lisle was also instrumental in forging links between retailers, property developers, and institutional investors such as the Prudential and Norwich Union. He put together deals which allowed retailers and developers to raise considerable finance on the strength of their property portfolios by selling stores to financial institutions, and simultaneously taking long (99- or 999-year) leases on them at fixed rents. Healey and Baker's success in this field led to rapid expansion; between 1930 and 1939 the number of its employees grew from fifteen to more than a hundred. In 1934 Orchard-Lisle became a partner, and in the same year he married Phyllis Muriel Viall (*d.* 1981); they had one son.

Shortly after the outbreak of war in 1939 Orchard-Lisle recruited Douglas Tovey, a surveyor who had worked for the Great Western Railway, and the shopping parade developer Edward Lotery; the partnership of Orchard-Lisle and Tovey was to provide the cornerstone of Healey and Baker's success in the post-war property boom. After the war ended they took over the firm's investment and West End business. Orchard-Lisle began to advise large City institutions such as the Prudential and the Pearl insurance companies, helping them to acquire investment property at a time when cheap money and government controls on capital issues greatly reduced the supply of alternative assets. He also advised some of the first pension funds to invest in property, including the National Coal Board's superannuation scheme (to which he was appointed as property consultant in 1953) and the National Bus Company pension fund.

Orchard-Lisle worked with some of the most famous property entrepreneurs of the 1950s, including Jack Cotton, whose main property adviser he became, often setting up entire deals for him. 'If Jack Cotton said yes to Aubrey Orchard-Lisle … [he was] saying yes to a full package which included acquisition, letting and funding' (Gordon, 31). He and Cotton became close friends; the Orchard-Lisles bought a house in Marlow from one of the Cotton trusts, located across the Thames from Cotton's home.

Orchard-Lisle was known for his single-minded devotion to business. His brother Mervyn recalled a time when they had been invited to lunch at the House of Commons; they were walking through the Great Hall of Westminster when Mervyn paused to stop and said: 'You know Aubrey, this is where Warren Hastings was impeached.' Aubrey replied: 'No, but by the way you did complete the deal with Montague Burton's at Woolwich?' (private information). However, while he listed his main recreation in *Who's Who* as work, Orchard-Lisle was also a good all-round sportsman and was particularly keen on cricket. His business activities outside Healey and Baker included serving on the board of the General Practice Finance Corporation, as chairman of the advisory panel for institutional finance in new towns, and as a member of the board of the National Bus Company. He also applied his organizational abilities to the benefit of the National Health Service, as a governor of Guy's Hospital medical school, chairman of the special trustees of Guy's Hospital, and a member of the Lambeth, Southwark, and Lewisham Area Health Authority (teaching). He was a fellow of the Royal Institution of Chartered Surveyors and was appointed CBE in 1973.

Orchard-Lisle became a senior partner at Healey and Baker in 1972 and continued to work for the practice as a consultant partner until he was eighty-three. He died on 5 August 1989 from cancer at the London Bridge Hospital, Tooley Street, London. PETER SCOTT

Sources C. Gordon, *The two tycoons* (1984) • O. Marriott, *The property boom* (1967) • E. L. Erdman, *People and property* (1982) • Healey & Baker, *Healey & Baker, 1820–1970* (1970) • private information (2004) • *WWW* • d. cert.

Wealth at death £6,334,391: probate, 15 Dec 1989, *CGPLA Eng. & Wales*

Lisle, Sir Bartholomew (*d.* 1345). *See under* Lisle family (*per.* *c.*1277–1542).

Lisle, Sir (Henry de) Beauvoir De (1864–1955), army officer, was born on 27 July 1864 on Guernsey, one of five sons of Richard Francis Valpy De Lisle MRCS, honorary deputy inspector general, and his wife, C. E. de Lisle. His father had served as an assistant surgeon of the 96th foot (1841–51), and of the 1st (Royal) Dragoons (1851–2), and as surgeon of the 4th (King's Own) foot (1852–9) including service in the Crimean War.

Beauvoir De Lisle was educated on Jersey, possibly privately, and in 1882 at the Royal Military College, Sandhurst, and was commissioned into the 2nd battalion, the Durham light infantry in 1883, joining the battalion at Gibraltar. He served in Egypt in 1885–6 with the mounted infantry of the frontier force, was awarded the DSO (after recommendation for the VC) for his part in the rescue of the garrison of Ambigole Wells Fort in August 1885, and took part in the battle of Giniss in December 1885.

De Lisle rejoined his battalion in India in 1887, and was promoted captain in 1891. An excellent horseman and enthusiastic amateur jockey, he was also a natural all-round athlete and an accomplished big-game hunter. He was the captain of his battalion polo team (1888–98), and has been described as 'the inventor of modern polo' (McGregor, 89) for introducing team training and tactics into the sport. His team regularly won major competitions in India, including the infantry cup (1894–8), the all-India inter-regimental cup (1896–8) and the championship of India (British and Native) (1898), an unprecedented achievement for an infantry regiment.

After attending the Staff College, Camberley, from 1898 to 1899, De Lisle saw active service in the Second South African War. He first commanded the 6th mounted infantry, and then held various brigade-sized mounted commands far above his substantive rank. He was severely wounded near Venterskroon in August 1900, and was promoted major in 1902. On 16 July 1902 he married, at Stoke Poges church, Leila Annette (*d.* 1938), eldest daughter and heir of Wilberforce Bryant of Stoke Park, Stoke Poges, Buckinghamshire. They had one son, Christian de Beauvoir. Recognizing De Lisle's abilities as a leader of mounted troops, Field Marshal Lord Roberts arranged his transfer to the cavalry. In 1902 he joined the 5th dragoon guards, and in 1903 the 1st (Royal) Dragoons, which he saw as the family regiment, wrongly believing that his father had served with it in the Crimea. He accompanied the regiment to India in 1903, and was promoted lieutenant-colonel commanding in 1906. He returned to Britain in 1910 to become general staff officer, grade 1 (GSO1) of the 2nd division at Aldershot, and in 1911 was promoted brigadier-general commanding the 2nd cavalry brigade.

At the start of the First World War, De Lisle took his brigade into action in France as part of the British expeditionary force. He performed well in the retreat from Mons, being promoted to command the 1st cavalry division in October 1914 as a major-general. In June 1915 he was sent to Gallipoli to take the command of the 29th division, and in July was appointed to temporary command of the 9th corps. After the evacuation from Gallipoli he reverted to the command of his division, which under his leadership became known as 'The Incomparable 29th'. In early 1916 the division was sent to the western front to take part in the battle of the Somme. It also fought in all the major British battles on the western front in 1917. In March 1918 De Lisle was promoted as an acting lieutenant-general to command the 13th corps, followed by the 15th corps in April, taking part in the battle of the Lys and the Last Hundred Days campaign. Twice he was briefly in acting command of an army.

Following the war Field Marshal Sir Douglas Haig obtained De Lisle's final appointment as a substantive lieutenant general and general officer commanding-in-chief, western command (1919–23), and in 1926 he retired from the army with the rank of full general. He remained much in demand for his polo skills, and spent 1929–30 in India training polo teams for the maharaja of Kashmir.

Despite his very active life De Lisle was also a prolific writer. In addition to his memoirs and two semi-autobiographical books on polo, he also wrote numerous articles on warfare and sport. His unpublished works include detailed accounts of his service in Egypt, the Second South African War, the First World War, and a semi-autobiographical novel, all preserved in his papers.

De Lisle passed staff college in 1899, was made CB in 1900, KCB in 1917, and KCMG in 1919, and was awarded various foreign decorations. He was colonel of the Durham light infantry (1928–34) and president of the 29th Division Association from 1919 until his death. During his last years De Lisle was virtually confined to his mansion at 34 Hertford Street, Mayfair, London, having gone blind. He died of old age at home on 16 July 1955, and a memorial service was held on 21 July at Christ Church, Down Street, London.

Personally fearless and a devout Christian, De Lisle was regarded by contemporaries as perhaps the best example of the 'thruster' or 'fighting general' of the First World War. He summed up his own beliefs in 1939 as 'Sport and War are closely allied. The man who excels in sport always excels in war. To me both are great games and the greater is War' (De Lisle, *Reminiscences of Sport and War*, 272).

STEPHEN BADSEY

Sources B. De Lisle, *Reminiscences of sport and war* (1939) • E. D. Miller, *Modern polo* • W. L. Vane, *The Durham light infantry* (1914) • C. T. Atkinson, *History of the royal dragoons, 1661–1934* (1934) • M. McGregor, *Officers of the Durham light infantry, 1758–1968*, 1 (1989) [privately printed] • King's Lond., Liddell Hart C., De Lisle MSS • Durham light infantry museum, De Lisle MSS • *Durham Light Infantry Journal* [especially 1955] • *The Times* (18 July 1955) • *WWW* • *CGPLA Eng. & Wales* (1955)

Archives Durham light infantry museum, MSS, incl. medals · King's Lond., Liddell Hart C., memoirs, papers relating to cavalry, unpublished novel based on his experiences · PRO, divisional war diaries, 29th division | FILM IWM FVA, actuality footage · IWM FVA, documentary footage
Likenesses Elliott & Fry, photogravure, 1890–99, NPG · photographs, 1914–18, IWM · W. Stoneman, photograph, 1918, NPG · portrait, 1954, Durham light infantry museum · photograph, repro. in De Lisle, *Reminiscences*, frontispiece
Wealth at death £21,548 11*s*. 3*d*.: probate, 6 Sept 1955, *CGPLA Eng. & Wales*

Lisle [Insula], **Sir Brian de** (*d.* 1234), soldier and administrator, was the son of Robert de Lisle, seneschal of the honour of Eye for William de Longchamp (*d.* 1197), bishop of Ely. His family came from Mottistone, Isle of Wight, where it had been since at least the 1130s. Lisle was in the service of King John by April 1200, and was first described as a household knight in November 1204. He appears to have become a close intimate and even a gambling partner of the king. His status raised by his marriage in January 1205 to Grace, widow of Norman of the Chamber, and daughter and heir of Thomas fitz William of Saleby, Lisle took his place among the king's *familiares*. In the same year he became one of the custodians of William de Stuteville's lands, and when these were redeemed, retained control of the major northern strongholds of Knaresborough and Boroughbridge. He came to hold a number of other custodies and offices in the north midlands and Yorkshire, helped to organize John's continental campaigns, and himself served in France and Poitou. In 1213 he became a royal steward. When civil war broke out in England, his position in the north, based on his command of the castles of the Peak and Bolsover in Derbyshire as well as of Knaresborough and Boroughbridge, was vital to John's cause.

In the meantime Lisle had begun a long-lasting association with the royal forest. In May 1207 he was appointed chief forester for Nottinghamshire and Derbyshire under Hugh de Neville, a position that he held until November 1217, after which he went on crusade. In February 1221 he was made chief justice of the forest for the whole of England and although he lost this office to Hugh de Neville in January 1224, he continued to act as one of Hugh's deputy foresters, before returning in October 1229 as chief forester for the counties in the north and east of England. During these years Lisle's position fluctuated according to the state of English politics. Although he joined the king's forces besieging Bedford Castle in 1224, and witnessed the 1225 reissue of Magna Carta, he was often found in opposition to the justiciar, Hubert de Burgh, and in 1232 supported the regime of the justiciar's victorious enemy Peter des Roches, which once more entrusted him with the custody of Knaresborough Castle. He died between 15 and 18 August 1234.

Lisle was evidently an extremely valuable, if sometimes difficult, royal servant. In 1205, for example, the sheriff of York was ordered to inquire into complaints that Lisle and others of the king's *fideles* had been improperly operating the York mint, and this was only the first of many occasions on which his conduct was questioned by the king. During the civil war John repeatedly ordered Lisle to hand over custody of the Peak Castle, first to Ranulf (III), earl of Chester, and then to William de Ferrers, earl of Derby, but he steadfastly refused to comply, and in the end Derby and Lisle went to war. When Lisle's activities as constable of Knaresborough during the civil war came under scrutiny in the mid-1220s, it became clear that he had frequently acted arbitrarily and to his own profit.

But there is another view of him, for it seems that Lisle was a close friend and supporter of St Robert of Knaresborough (*d.* 1218). According to the metrical life of the saint, it was Lisle who introduced King John to St Robert and induced the king to offer the saint land in Knaresborough Forest for himself and his followers. For his pains St Robert foretold the time of Lisle's death, causing him to leave 'wyth drery mod'. Nevertheless, the author had one crumb of comfort for those who might have felt sorry for him:

And to Northe Cuntre he rayd,
And thair he dyed als Robertt sayd;
His saule passed unto paradyse
For in this warld Bryan was wyse
(*Life of St Robert of Knaresborough*, 68)

His heirs were his sister Alice (wife of Thomas le Bret), William of Glamorgan (son of his sister Constance), and Ralph de Slopham (son of his sister Annabel).

S. D. Church

Sources *Pipe rolls* · *Chancery records* · F. Palgrave, ed., *Rotuli curiae regis: rolls and records of the court held before the king's justiciars or justices*, 2 vols., RC, 27 (1835) · J. Bazire, ed., *The metrical life of St Robert of Knaresborough together with the other Middle English pieces in British Museum MS Egerton 3143*, EETS, old ser., 228 (1953) · S. F. Hockey, ed., *The charters of Quarr abbey* (1991) · V. Brown, ed., *Eye Priory cartulary and charters*, 2 vols., Suffolk RS, Suffolk Charters, 12–13 (1992–4) · J. C. Holt, *The northerners: a study in the reign of King John*, new edn (1992) · H. C. M. Lyte and others, eds., *Liber feodorum: the book of fees*, 3 vols. (1920–31) · Paris, *Chron.* · D. A. Carpenter, *The minority of Henry III* (1990)

Lisle, Sir George (*d.* 1648), royalist army officer, was the son of Lawrence Lisle, who had the monopoly of viewing and repairing arms in England and a lease of the right to collect the imposts on tobacco and tobacco pipes; he married a near relation of George Villiers, duke of Buckingham, and was said to have lost £12,000 in the royalist cause.

George Lisle had his military training in the Netherlands, and was a captain in the army against the Scots of 1640. After joining the royalist cause early in the civil war, he served in Lord Grandison's regiment of foot, and, already a lieutenant-colonel of dragoons, at Edgehill (23 October 1642) he cleared the hedges on the royalist left. After fighting at Chalgrove (18 June 1643), Lisle bravely led a 'forlorn hope' of musketeers at the first battle of Newbury (20 September), and was wounded. He was commissioned to raise a foot regiment in November, and on the death of Colonel Richard Bolles at Alton, Hampshire, in December, Lisle took over the latter's much depleted regiment in Reading. On the eve of the battle of Cheriton (29 March 1644) Lisle was posted with 1000 musketeers and 500 horse on an eminence between the two battle-lines, close enough to hear the chatter of the enemy's sentinels;

Sir George Lisle (*d.* 1648), circle of John Michael Wright

but next day, the parliamentarian capture of Cheriton Wood forced him to retire.

After participating in the relief of Dudley Castle in June 1644 and the drawn battle of Cropredy Bridge, Lisle commanded one of the three royalist infantry divisions in the king's campaign in Devon and Cornwall in July and August. He signed the letter to the parliamentarian commander the earl of Essex on 8 August, in which Charles I offered somewhat hazy peace terms in return for an understanding. At the second battle of Newbury on 27 October Lisle commanded the second tertia of foot under Sir Jacob Astley which bore the brunt of the earl of Manchester's attack. Holding the royalist centre at Shaw House, he led three gallant charges and 'did all things with so much courage, cheerfulness, and present dispatch, as had special influence on every common soldier, taking particular care of all except himself' (*Mercurius Aulicus*, 28 Oct 1644). His troops scattered Manchester's infantry 'like spray before some storm-driven ship' (ibid.), and, as the twilight deepened, Lisle, who seldom wore defensive armour, threw off his buff coat, so that the white glimmer of his holland shirt was distinguishable to his men:

> From whence the frighted Rebels gave it out
> That a white witch was seen to fly about
> The Royal Army scouring to and fro,
> Where'er the Contest did the hottest grow.
> (Money, 173)

Sir Samuel Luke, the parliamentarian scoutmaster-general, reported on 10 November that at a rendezvous near Oxford the previous month the king, who had closely witnessed Lisle's bravery at Newbury, intended to knight him. But Lisle declined, saying 'he would not be knighted or receive any honour till he was sure to keep it and then doubted not but he should as well deserve to be a Lord as many that were near his Majesty' (Newman, *Royalist Officers*, 235). If accurately reported, Lisle's disclaimer may have arisen from his fear of becoming entangled in the disgrace of his superior Henry Wilmot, Baron Wilmot, earlier in 1644, on suspicion of treating with parliament.

During the winter of 1644–5 Lisle became governor of Faringdon, Berkshire, and complained to Prince Rupert that it was only one-third fortified and entirely unprovisioned. On 16 April 1645 he was created an honorary DCL by Oxford University. He commanded a tertia of foot at the storming of Leicester on 30 May, and on 1 June he was appointed lieutenant-general in Leicestershire under Lord Loughborough. At Naseby on 14 June 1645 the tertia of foot he commanded in the left centre bore the brunt of Cromwell's charge; Joshua Sprigg, Sir Thomas Fairfax's retainer, said they fought 'with incredible courage and resolution' (Young, 268). Although wounded, Lisle escaped to Leicester. He seems already to have been replaced as governor of Faringdon, and Loughborough recommended him for the post of deputy governor of Lichfield. He was knighted by the king at Oxford on 21 December 1645, when he was, apparently, master of the royal household.

In the winter of 1647 Lisle was in London, compounding for his estate. But he was soon busily occupied in getting together troops for a new rising. He was a ringleader of the insurrection in Kent in May 1648, which Fairfax suppressed after bitter street fighting in Maidstone. Lisle led the survivors to join the earl of Norwich's forces, which crossed the Thames into Essex, made a rendezvous with Sir Charles Lucas at Chelmsford, and, after a circuitous march, occupied Colchester. During the ensuing siege Lisle commanded the foot. On 6 July he and Lucas led a large raiding party across the River Colne, to recapture the parliamentarian stronghold at East Mill. Sallying forth 'as if it had been a sporting skirmish amongst tame soldiers in a general muster' (Carlton, 322), they pitched the two enemy cannon into the river before withdrawing with dignity. Lisle, captured during the raid, was soon rescued. But the garrison and citizens were reduced to a diet of horse, dog, and cat, occasionally sweetened with prunes; when even this food supply ran out, the royalists accepted Fairfax's terms of surrender on 27 August.

Senior officers were put at the lord-general's mercy: peers were reserved for the judgment of parliament, but Lisle, considered a mere soldier of fortune, was dealt with by a council of war. By 2 p.m. on 28 August he and Lucas had been condemned to death, probably through the influence of Henry Ireton, appointed commissioner for the surrender of Colchester, and to make a vindictive example of the leaders of such a lengthy and obstinate siege. Lisle was refused time to write to his parents, and at 7 p.m., with Lucas and Sir Bernard Gascoigne (a Florentine who was reprieved), he was brought out to the castle courtyard to face three files of musketeers. As Lucas's body fell, Lisle ran forward to catch it and tenderly kissed his face. When his turn came, he extracted from his pocket a gold piece for the executioners and four others for friends in London, and suggested the dragoons came nearer. One said, 'I'll warrant you, sir, we'll hit you'; Lisle replied, 'Friends, I have been nearer you when you have missed me' (Clarendon, *Hist. rebellion*, 4.388).

The pair quickly became martyrs; it was said that the grass on the spot where they fell never grew again, and within a few days eight pamphlets appeared condemning this 'most barbarous, unsoldierly murder' (Carlton, 228). Lisle and Lucas were buried obscurely, but in 1661 were reinterred in the Lucas family vault in St Giles's Church, Colchester. Above their tomb a black marble slab inscription said they had been 'in cold blood barbarously murdered' (Warburton, 3.407) at the command of Fairfax. There is a tradition that when, after the Restoration, the second duke of Buckingham, who married Fairfax's daughter, asked for the inscription to be erased, Charles II had it cut more deeply. In January 1662 Lisle's sister Mary petitioned the king for a pension (she had also lost another brother, Francis, at Marston Moor); she was granted £2000 on 31 January but seven years later had only received £1100 and was destitute.

Lisle was one of the more attractive commanders thrown up by the civil war. Clarendon's relatively succinct panegyric remarks that he led his men into battle:

> with such an alacrity that no man was ever better followed, his soldiers never forsaking him; and the tertia which he commanded never left anything undone which he had led them upon. But … to this fierceness of courage, he had the softest and most gentle nature imaginable; loved all, and beloved of all, and without a capacity to have an enemy. (Clarendon, *Hist. rebellion*, 4.389)

Basil Morgan

Sources *DNB* • P. R. Newman, *Royalist officers in England and Wales, 1642–1660: a biographical dictionary* (1981) • G. R. Smith and M. Toynbee, *Leaders of the civil wars, 1642–48* (1977) • P. Young and R. Holmes, *The English civil war* (1974) • P. R. Newman, *The old service: royalist regimental colonels and the civil war, 1642–1646* (1993) • J. H. Round, 'The case of Lucas and Lisle', *TRHS*, new ser., 8 (1894), 157–80 • P. Young, *Naseby, 1645* (1985) • C. Carlton, *Going to the wars* (1992) • W. Money, *The first and second battles of Newbury*, 2nd edn (1884) • Clarendon, *Hist. rebellion*, vol. 4 • *Memoirs of Prince Rupert and the cavaliers including their private correspondence*, ed. E. Warburton, 3 vols. (1849), vol. 3 • M. Bence-Jones, *The cavaliers* (1976) • F. T. R. Edgar, *Sir Ralph Hopton* (1968) • J. Adair, *Cheriton, 1644* (1973)

Likenesses M. Vandergucht, line engraving, BM, NPG; repro. in Ward, *History of Rebellion* (1713) • G. Vertue, double portrait, line engraving (with Sir C. Lucas), BM, NPG; repro. in *Loyalists* • circle of J. M. Wright, portrait; Sothebys, 11 July 1990, lot 20 [*see illus.*] • portrait (unfinished; after A. Van Dyck), repro. in Smith and Toynbee, *Leaders of the civil wars*, pl. 58

Lisle, Sir John de (*d.* 1304). *See under* Lisle family (*per. c.*1277–1542).

Lisle, Sir John (*d.* 1331). *See under* Lisle family (*per. c.*1277–1542).

Lisle, Sir John (*d.* 1370). *See under* Lisle family (*per. c.*1277–1542).

Lisle, Sir John (*d.* 1408). *See under* Lisle family (*per. c.*1277–1542).

Lisle, John (*d.* 1429). *See under* Lisle family (*per. c.*1277–1542).

Lisle, Sir John (*d.* 1471). *See under* Lisle family (*per. c.*1277–1542).

Lisle, Sir John (*d.* 1523). *See under* Lisle family (*per. c.*1277–1542).

Lisle, John, appointed Lord Lisle under the protectorate (**1609/10–1664**), regicide, was the second, but eldest surviving, son of Sir William Lisle (*d.* 1648) of Wootton, Isle of Wight, and Bridget, daughter of Sir John Hungerford of Down Ampney, Gloucestershire. On 25 January 1626 he matriculated at Magdalen Hall, Oxford, graduated BA in February, and proceeded to the Middle Temple in May, aged sixteen. He was called to the bar in 1633, becoming a bencher of the Middle Temple in 1649. On 15 February 1632 he married Elizabeth Mary Hobart (*d.* 1633), daughter of Sir Henry *Hobart, lord chief justice, with a massive dowry of £4000. An anonymous poet wrote that Elizabeth was:

> Neither well-proportioned, fair nor wise
> All these defects four thousand pounds supplies.

The dowry, said to have been the largest ever in the Isle of Wight, helped to offset Sir William's feckless extravagance, and after Elizabeth died in childbirth Lisle acquired another heiress, Alice Beconshaw (*c.*1614–1685) [*see* Lisle, Lady Alice], daughter of Sir White Beconshaw of Moyle's Court near Fordingbridge, whom he married in 1636. According to the arrangements Lisle took over his father's estate at this juncture, giving him £150 p.a. allowance; on Beconshaw's death Alice brought him Moyle's Court and half the estate of Ellingham.

Lisle was chosen as MP for Winchester in March and October 1640, and as an energetic civil war parliamentarian took a leading role on county committees to fund the war effort and defend Hampshire, Portsmouth, and Wight. On the eviction of Dr William Lewis in November 1644 he was made master of St Cross Hospital, Winchester. In parliament he chaired the committee investigating Cromwell's allegations against the earl of Manchester in December 1644, and that in January 1645 appointed to frame the ordinance creating the New Model Army. He displayed hostility to the king right from 1642, condemning him in a 1645 speech to the lord mayor and citizens of London after the capture of royal correspondence at the battle of Naseby. He was one of the parliamentary commissioners chosen to take Charles the four bills, parliament's latest terms for a settlement, in December 1647. His growing national prominence was offset by local concern at his niggardly treatment of his father. Lisle's godfather, Sir John Oglander, who claimed that Lisle had grown up with maternal neglect and paternal alcoholic excess, complained that Sir William was allowed but 'one nasty chamber' for all his possessions and animals. Sir William's extravagance may have made his son over concerned to protect his inheritance. When Sir William died in 1648, refusing to see his children, Lisle arranged a cheap evening funeral.

Voting against negotiations with Charles in November to December 1648, Lisle was selected as a commissioner for his trial and took a leading role, sitting next to the president to advise him on legal matters. He helped to draw up the sentence, along with the new republican form of the constitution and legal procedure, and had his reward with his appointment as commissioner of the great seal from 8 February 1649 at a salary of £1000 p.a [*see also* Regicides]. He was one of the committee of five trusted to select councillors of state and vet MPs, and pressed for legal reform particularly of chancery. He was, however, keen to acquire the fruits of office, leasing Beaufort House, Chelsea, and persuading his fellow commissioner Bulstrode Whitelocke to join him there to seem less ostentatious. Whitelocke accused him of fixing their lots for which lodgings to occupy to avoid those needing repair, further indication of miserliness. When the commissioners borrowed Sion House in August 1649 Lisle invited the earl of Mulgrave to move in without asking Whitelocke.

Despite his republicanism Lisle had no hesitation in retaining office under Cromwell, to whom he administered the oath of office. Elected to parliament on 12 July 1654 for Southampton, where he was recorder from 1651–9, and the Isle of Wight, he chose to sit for the former. He presided over the high court trying royalist plotters in 1654, 1655, and 1658, became a commissioner of the exchequer in 1655, and was retained as commissioner of the great seal when his colleagues were dismissed on 15 June 1655. He supported Cromwell's becoming king, and took a seat in the other house in December 1657. He was eventually dismissed by the restored Rump on 14 May 1659, but unlike most Cromwellians he was sufficiently trusted to become a commissioner for the admiralty and navy in January 1660 and a local militia commissioner.

Lisle was a prime target at the Restoration for his role in the king's trial, and fled abroad just before a parliamentary vote on 6 June 1660 exempting him from pardon and requiring his surrender. His lands were seized. His exiled younger brother, Sir William, a royalist, regained Wootton; Alice retained Moyle's Court but not Ellingham. Lisle's younger son William's mother-in-law, Lady Katherine Hyde, petitioned for land to support William, disinherited for his royalist sympathies. Lisle settled by May 1663 in Lausanne with other republicans including Ludlow, Whalley, and Goffe, and was said to 'much charm' the Swiss with his religious devotion. Already fearing assassination, he was shot at a church door in Lausanne by an Irish royalist known as Thomas Macdonnell (allegedly shouting 'Vive le roi') on 11 August 1664 and was buried in the church; the murder was greeted with pleasure in London. His fellow exile Edmund Ludlow incorporated some of his papers into his MS, 'Voyce from the watch tower'.

Lisle's second wife, Alice, was executed by Judge Jeffreys in 1685. As well as two sons, John (*d.* 1709) of Dibden, Hampshire, and William, he had at least three daughters. An efficient constitutional lawyer and genuine reformer capable of putting principle above safety, he cannot be dismissed as just a Cromwellian timeserver. But his ability was countered by acquisitiveness, a reputation for intrigue, a personal harshness, and resort to sharp practice. Loathed by royalists, as the events of 1664 showed, harsh criticism came too from among family and friends.

TIMOTHY VENNING

Sources *A royalist's notebook: the commonplace book of Sir John Oglander*, ed. F. Bamford (1936) · C. H. Firth and R. S. Rait, eds., *Acts and ordinances of the interregnum, 1642–1660*, 3 vols. (1911) · *The diary of Bulstrode Whitelocke, 1605–1675*, ed. R. Spalding, British Academy, Records of Social and Economic History, new ser., 13 (1990) · *The memoirs of Edmund Ludlow*, ed. C. H. Firth, 2 vols. (1894) · E. Ludlow, *A voyce from the watch tower*, ed. A. B. Worden, CS, 4th ser., 21 (1978) · *VCH Hampshire and the Isle of Wight*, vols. 2–4 · J. B. Williamson, ed., *The Middle Temple bench book*, 2nd edn, 1 (1937) · G. N. Godwin, *The civil war in Hampshire, 1642–45, and the story of Basing House*, new edn (1904) · *CSP dom.*, 1650; 1655–7; 1660–61; 1663–4 · J. S. Davies, *A history of Southampton* (1883) · Keeler, *Long Parliament* · G. D. Squibb, ed., *The visitation of Hampshire and the Isle of Wight, 1686*, Harleian Society, new ser., 10 (1991) · J. Maclean and W. C. Heane, eds., *The visitation of the county of Gloucester taken in the year 1623*, Harleian Society, 21 (1885) · R. Zaller, 'Lisle, John', Greaves & Zaller, *BDBR*, 191–2 · *DNB* · GEC, *Peerage*

Archives BL, register of ecclesiastical preferments, Add. MS 36792 · University of Kansas, Kenneth Spencer Research Library, legal commonplace book | Bodl. Oxf., Ludlow papers, MS C.487 [contains Lisle MSS at pp.1082–6]

Likenesses mezzotint, BM, NPG

Wealth at death property confiscated 1660 as excluded from act of indemnity; wife retained one estate and presumably supplied money: *CSP dom., 1660–61*; *Memoirs*, ed. Firth, vol. 2

Lisle, Sir Nicholas (*d.* **1506**). *See under* Lisle family (*per. c.*1277–1542).

Lisle, Rudolph Edward March Phillipps de (**1853–1885**). *See under* Lisle, Ambrose Lisle March Phillipps de (1809–1878).

Lisle, Samuel (**1683–1749**), bishop of St Asaph and of Norwich, was born in Blandford, Dorset, the son of Richard Lisle, a landowner. He was educated first at the grammar school in Blandford, which he entered about 1688, and then at Salisbury grammar school under the eminent teacher Edward Hardwick. On 4 March 1700 he entered Wadham College, Oxford. Having been elected to a scholarship in 1701, he graduated BA in 1703 and proceeded MA in 1706. He was elected to a Goodridge scholarship and a fellowship of Wadham in 1707. In 1710 he became chaplain to the Levant Company in Smyrna, and in 1716 he accepted a similar chaplaincy at Aleppo, Syria. During this time he visited Constantinople and much of Asia Minor and mastered a number of oriental languages. In 1728 Lisle was to contribute some inscriptions to Edmund Chishull's *Antiquitates Asiaticae*. After returning to England in 1719 he was appointed bursar of Wadham. In 1720 he was appointed chaplain to Lord Onslow and thereafter he quickly accumulated the rectories of Holwell in Bedfordshire, Tooting in Surrey, and St Mary le Bow, London. Technically he held the last position while an incumbent also of the ancient London livings of St Pancras, Soper Lane, and All Hallows, Honey Lane.

In 1721 Lisle was created a Lambeth DD by Archbishop Wake, who also appointed him his domestic chaplain. Lisle attracted much patronage from Wake: in 1724 he was appointed archdeacon of Canterbury; in 1726 he became rector of Fetcham, Surrey; in 1728 he was appointed to a canonry of Canterbury; and in 1729 he became vicar of Northolt. Although he was among those members of the chapter censured for poor residence at the cathedral, he was also a member of a corps of able and energetic administrators who helped Archbishop Wake superintend his diocese. His high standing among the clergy was affirmed by his election as deputy prolocutor in the lower house of convocation in 1726 and as prolocutor in 1734. As prolocutor he preached a sermon entitled *Concio ad synodum* at the commencement of the convocation.

Lisle's character and integrity were such that he was chosen to succeed Robert Thistlethwayte in 1738 when the latter fled the country and abandoned the wardenship of Wadham in the wake of a homosexual scandal. Lisle, it was felt, would repair the college's reputation; by way of reward he was awarded a BD and DD by diploma on 10 April 1739.

In 1737 Lisle had refused the poorly endowed bishopric of Oxford, having been denied commendams which would have enabled him to have sufficient income. In 1744 he accepted appointment to the see of St Asaph, and on 1 April he was consecrated at Lambeth; he retained the archdeaconry of Canterbury and vicarage of Northolt *in commendam* with the bishopric. When, in 1748, he asked to be translated to the vacant see of Norwich, he was permitted it on the grounds of his age and labours in north Wales. He was to hold the bishopric for just eighteen months.

Though he was a regular attender in the House of Lords Lisle was not an actively political bishop; he rarely spoke or voted. In 1748 he was, however, active, with Bishop Sherlock and Archbishop Herring, in discussions with Samuel Chandler to achieve a comprehension of dissenters within the Church of England, and while they reached agreements over matters of doctrine, their divisions over oaths and reordination prevented any union.

Lisle died, apparently unmarried, in Lisle Street, Leicester Fields, London, on 3 October 1749, and was buried in the churchyard of his former parish of Northolt. His will directed that his papers, including his manuscript notes of his journeys in Asia Minor, be burnt by his executor.

WILLIAM GIBSON

Sources Foster, *Alum. Oxon.* • *The autobiography of Thomas Secker, archbishop of Canterbury*, ed. J. S. Macauley and R. W. Greaves (1988) • *GM*, 3rd ser., 16 (1864), 636–7 • BL, Add. MSS 35,590, fol. 7 • N. Sykes, *William Wake, archbishop of Canterbury*, 2 vols. (1957) • E. Hasted, *The history and topographical survey of the county of Kent*, 2nd edn, 12 (1801) • BL, Egerton MSS, 7.786

Archives Wadham College, Oxford, Bauchery MSS • Wadham College, Oxford, letters to Revd Mr Lewis

Likenesses oils, Wadham College, Oxford

Lisle, Thomas (*c*.1298–1361), bishop of Ely, probably came from Kent. He may have been a kinsman of the Thomas Lisle (Thomas de Insula) associated with collectors of customs at Sandwich in 1292, while his nephews Thomas, Robert, and William Michel came from Canterbury diocese. According to the antiquary William Cole (*d.* 1782), the coat of arms adopted by the future bishop was 'a chevron between three trefoils slipped', suggesting that he claimed a relationship with a branch of the Hampshire Lisles. It has been assumed since the sixteenth century that Lisle studied at Cambridge (of which he was to become a notable benefactor), entering the Dominican house there and incepting as doctor of theology. Closer investigation of the evidence has cast doubt on these claims, and it is possible that Lisle was not even a graduate; it is certainly hard, if not impossible, to find a reference to him as *magister*.

Probably born about 1298, Lisle was ordained priest on 18 December 1322 by Rigaud d'Assier, bishop of Winchester. He was then a member of the Dominican convent at Winchester. By 1340 he was prior—an office he probably held until his promotion as bishop. In that year he was at Avignon on royal business, seeking a dispensation for the marriage of Hugh Despenser and Elizabeth, daughter of William Montagu, earl of Salisbury (*d.* 1344). The bull was issued on 27 April 1341, but already in March the same envoys had been deputed to oppose William Zouche's election as archbishop of York and to press the claims of William Kilsby (*d.* 1346), the king's secretary, who at the time was in conflict with Archbishop John Stratford (*d.* 1348) in his royal master's interest. Ironically—in view of Lisle's subsequent misfortunes—they were also ordered to protest to the pope about the archbishop's conduct.

Following the unexpected death of Simon Montagu in 1345 the prior of Ely, Alan Walsingham, was elected bishop. Lisle was conveniently at the curia, where he had been appointed a penitentiary. He was provided to the see on 15 July and consecrated at Avignon on the 24th. To meet his expenses he was granted a faculty to raise a loan of 12,000 florins and permission to levy a charitable subsidy from his diocese. His profession to Canterbury followed on 9 September and the day after, having performed fealty, his temporalities were restored, which suggests that Edward III was not averse to the appointment even if he disliked the method. Lisle was solemnly enthroned on 27 November, following which, alleges his Ely biographer, he acted with extravagant splendour.

Lisle's episcopal register suggests diligence. He performed all recorded ordination ceremonies in person except for one in 1349, when the bishop of Leighlin acted for him during his absence abroad. He held a visitation of his cathedral priory in 1346, and in that year and the following one is stated to have visited seven religious houses, for some of which injunctions are recorded. Of parochial visitation nothing is discoverable. Under the year 1352 the register lists his dedication of thirteen parochial and conventual churches, and his consecration of the high altars of six other churches. In 1349 he had papal licence to appropriate Leverington church, valued at £85, to the bishop's *mensa*, or general fund for his support, on the grounds that his possessions were held of the king *in capite*, and could therefore be confiscated. Administration was complicated by the fact that, although Pope Clement VI (*r.* 1342–52) had provided Cardinal Gaillard de la Mothe to the archdeaconry of Ely, there were two other claimants, one of whom—unnamed but presumably in *de facto* possession—was, so the bishop alleged, publicly defamed of adultery and fornication in the diocese and guilty of failing to exercise his office in accordance with the canons. The king, who for reasons of his own had confiscated the fruits of the archdeaconry, issued a prohibition against interference with the archdeacon's jurisdiction. Lisle, however, explained the situation and secured a writ of consultation, which enabled him to continue proceedings. The outcome is unknown.

The black death took a heavy toll of incumbents. Between the beginning of April 1349 and the end of January 1350 eighty-one institutions are recorded, as against a total of fourteen for the years 1345–8 inclusive. By March 1349 Lisle himself was at Avignon, but on 1 October 1348, before his departure, he had appointed no fewer than five vicars-general—an unprecedented number. So great was the mortality, however, that emergency arrangements were called for, and on 9 April 1349, still at Avignon, Lisle appointed three supplementary vicars-general, and on account of its impracticability cancelled the clause in the earlier commissions requiring two persons for certain types of business. Lisle was back in his diocese by the end of 1350, and the following year appropriated Whaddon and Caxton rectories to St George's Chapel, Windsor. On 1 January 1352 at his manor of Hatfield he confirmed the refoundation by the Norwich diocesan, William Bateman (*d.* 1355), of the Hall of the Annunciation, as Gonville Hall was called following its founder's death, and on 3 February 1353 licensed the founding of another college under the name of the Guild of Corpus Christi. The establishment of a third Cambridge college, Pembroke, had been confirmed (23 November 1349) in his absence by Chancellor John Hoo as vicar-general. It was alleged that in 1358 the bishop appropriated the manors of West Wratting and Swaffham Prior to Peterhouse without licence.

The anonymous *Historia Eliensis* considered Lisle a good pastor and an excellent preacher, but felt that although he advocated mercy he himself preferred justice. He kept a good table and maintained a fine retinue. The ill omen of the fracture of a glass flagon full of wine at his consecration need not be taken too seriously—it follows the recitation of two other miracles. His quarrel with the prior and convent over their right to dig gravel and clay from the episcopal demesne for the cathedral's repair temporarily impaired their relationship. On the evidence of commissions of oyer and terminer it has been claimed that Lisle was prone to violence. Early in his episcopate commissions were appointed to examine complaints against him, and the final years of the episcopate saw a bitter quarrel with the king. Previously he had been been on good terms with Edward. Thus, in 1346 he had added a forty days' indulgence to that of Archbishop Stratford for those praying for the king's safe return from the continent, and in the following year he had given rather than loaned him six sacks of wool. He was among those who in August 1354 sealed the 'procuration' for persuading the pope to act as arbiter in his quarrel with the French king.

The damaging dispute that erupted between Lisle and Blanche, daughter of Henry of Lancaster (*d.* 1345) (hence kinswoman of the king), widow of Thomas, Lord Wake of Liddell (*d.* 1349), precipitated a fracas at Colne near Somersham, Huntingdonshire, in the summer of 1354. Following Blanche's complaint two commissions of oyer and terminer were appointed, and on an indictment that the bishop was an accessory to trespass (a wide-ranging term) the case was taken before king's bench but not actually tried. Meanwhile, the second commission found the bishop and others guilty of trespass and awarded damages against him of £900. This verdict was upheld in king's bench by Sir William Shareshull (*d.* 1370). There was doubt as to whether a writ of *elegit* could be issued against a bishop, but Shareshull and his fellow justices ruled in favour and Lisle was forced to pay the fine. In the summer of 1355 Lisle was again indicted, this time for incitement to murder one of Blanche's retainers and for having harboured the murderers. The bishop, having irritated Edward by claiming that his justice was perverted in Blanche's favour, planned to escape abroad, but the king issued a prohibition and summoned Lisle to answer in the parliament of November 1355 where, incensed by the bishop's conduct, he adopted Blanche's quarrel and demanded confiscation of the bishop's temporalities. The doubtful legality of this step was overcome by a coroner's indictment brought into king's bench in 1356, the holding of an inquest in which the jury found Lisle guilty as an accessory, and his subsequent surrender as a clerk to Archbishop Simon Islip (*d.* 1366). Refusing to submit to the king, as the archbishop advised, Lisle, who had previously unsuccessfully demanded trial by his peers, now sought purgation. Either this was denied on the grounds that he was a convicted clerk, or possibly Islip was too afraid to publish the outcome, since no one testified against the bishop. He fled to Avignon in November 1356. On the 18th his temporalities were confiscated and in February 1357 farmed to the Lynn merchant John Wesenham, for 3740 marks—3000 in successive years—payable to the royal wardrobe. In 1357 the archdeacon of Richmond, Henry Walton, was under sentence of excommunication for contumacy in failing to appear in the case brought against him by Lisle in the curia for injuries alleged to total 10,000 marks, the archbishop and the bishops of Lincoln and London having failed to take action.

Clement VI responded to Lisle's appeal by citing to Avignon three of the justices (including Shareshull), the commissioners, and the coroner. On their failure to appear, he excommunicated them, entrusting the execution of the sentence to Bishop John Gynwell of Lincoln. Archbishop Islip—castigated by the pope in 1357 as a dumb dog who had not acted as the successor of St Thomas—had been prevented from securing transcripts of the English court proceedings. The affair possibly complicated the negotiations for peace with France, which hung fire until 1360. Wesenham was still in possession of the temporalities at Lisle's death on 23 June 1361, perhaps from a fresh outbreak of plague.

Lisle was buried at Avignon in the church of St Praxedes,

a house of Dominican nuns. Aspects of his case bear a resemblance to those of Adam Orleton (*d.* 1345), John Stratford, and even Simon Mepham (*d.* 1333), who were likewise accused of provoking violence, but he might have argued, as they certainly did, that he was defending clerical immunity against secular power. His anonymous biographer, a monk of Ely, doubtless mindful of the reputation of the see, defended the bishop against any complicity in the crimes and regarded his accusers as malicious. By contrast, the most recent analyst of his career attempts to prove that, like some lay magnates of the period, 'he was the leader of a criminal gang that operated in East Anglia', whose crimes involved arson, theft, abduction, extortion, and even murder (Aberth, *Criminal Churchmen*, 203). This 'gang' was allegedly comprised principally of relatives, notably his brother John, his nephews, and his manorial servants. Certainly the most damning evidence against the bishop is the number of violent incidents and his failure to disown those of his familiars implicated in them. However if, as suggested, the purpose of such conduct was to support an extravagant way of life, it proved counter-productive.

To Peterhouse, for which college he secured papal authority to appropriate Hinton church, thus implementing a plan of his predecessor Hugh of Balsham (*d.* 1286), Lisle gave a number of manuscripts: a Bible, a commentary of Thomas Aquinas on the *Sentences*, and a glossed version of St John's gospel, in which he noted the meaning of *logos*. To his cathedral priory he left vestments, a chalice, and other silver vessels. ROY MARTIN HAINES

Sources register of Thomas de Lisle, CUL, EDR G/1/1 • F. J. Baigent, ed., *The registers of John de Sandale and Rigaud d'Asserio, bishops of Winchester*, Hampshire RS, 8 (1897) • [H. Wharton], ed., *Anglia sacra*, 2 vols. (1691) [incl. *Stephani Birchingtoni … de vitis Archiepiscoporum Cantuariensium* and *Monachi Eliensis continuatio historiae Eliensis*] • F. Godwin, *A catalogue of the bishops of England, since the first planting of Christian religion in this island*, [2nd edn] (1615); enl. edn and Latin trans. as *De praesulibus Angliae commentarius* (1616) • *Chronica Johannis de Reading et anonymi Cantuariensis, 1346–1367*, ed. J. Tait (1914) • *Adae Murimuth continuatio chronicarum. Robertus de Avesbury de gestis mirabilibus regis Edwardi tertii*, ed. E. M. Thompson, Rolls Series, 93 (1889) • *Chancery records* • *RotP*, vol. 2 • M. R. James and J. W. Clark, *A descriptive catalogue of the manuscripts in the library of Peterhouse* (1899) • B. H. Putman, *The place in legal history of Sir William de Shareshull* (1950) • R. W. Kaeuper, 'Law and order in fourteenth century England: the evidence of special commissions of oyer and terminer', *Speculum*, 54 (1979), 734–84 • J. Aberth, *Criminal churchmen in the age of Edward III* (1996) • J. Aberth, 'The black death in the diocese of Ely: the evidence of the bishop's register', *Journal of Medieval History*, 21 (1995), 275–87 • Tout, *Admin. hist.*, vols. 3–4 • R. M. Haines, *Archbishop John Stratford: political revolutionary and champion of the liberties of the English church*, Pontifical Institute of Medieval Studies: Texts and Studies, 76 (1986) • C. R. Cheney, 'The punishment of felonous clerks', *EngHR*, 51 (1936), 215–36 • *Fasti Angl., 1300–1541*, [Monastic cathedrals] • Emden, *Cam.* • D. M. Smith, *Guide to bishops' registers of England and Wales: a survey from the middle ages to the abolition of the episcopacy in 1646*, Royal Historical Society Guides and Handbooks, 11 (1981)

Archives CUL, register MS, EDR G/1/1

Lisle, Sir Thomas (*d.* **1542**). *See under* Lisle family (*per. c.*1277–1542).

Lisle [L'Isle], **William** (*c.*1569–1637), translator and Anglo-Saxon scholar, was one of numerous children of Edmond Lisle of Tandridge, Surrey, and Dorothy Rudston, daughter of Thomas Rudston of Cambridgeshire. About 1580 Lisle went to school at Eton College, from where, in 1584, he went on to King's College, Cambridge. He took bachelor's and master's degrees there, and in 1593 is recorded supplicating for incorporation at Oxford. He became a fellow of his Cambridge college, and seems to have stayed in this post until 1608.

While Lisle's most enduring reputation derives from his work on Anglo-Saxon, he worked too on several other languages, and his first translations were from French. In 1595 he published *Babilon: a part of the seconde weeke of Guillaume de Saluste Seigneur du Bartas, with the commentarie, and marginall notes of S. G. S.* The translation was dedicated to the lord admiral, Thomas Howard of Effingham. Three years later appeared another translation, *The colonies of Bartas: with the commentarie of S. G. S. in diverse places corrected and enlarged by the translatour.* He has also been conjecturally identified as the 'W. L.' who wrote, in 1603, the verse pamphlet *Nothing for a New Year's Gift*.

In 1608 there took place a 'bloody quarrel' at the notoriously rowdy King's College, in which Roger Goad, the vice-chancellor of Cambridge University, was wounded. Goad involved Lord Salisbury, the chancellor of the university, and Lisle wrote submitting to Salisbury's jurisdiction and begging not to be sacked for his offence. It is unclear whether or not any action was taken against him on this occasion, and very little else is known about his life.

During these years, Lisle became a pioneer in the study of Anglo-Saxon. In the preface to his edition of the *Saxon Treatise*, he describes his methods in teaching himself this unfamiliar tongue: he studied whatever Old English materials he could find collected by previous antiquaries, as well as other tangentially relevant material such as the Dutch language, and then, having learned 'as it were to swimme without bladders', embarked upon independent studies (*Saxon Treatise*, sig. d1r). Lisle worked in collaboration with other antiquaries such as his kinsman Henry Spelman, and also Robert Cotton, in recovering Old English. His motives were both political and religious, as may be seen by the extended title of his print publication, *Saxon treatise concerning the Old and New Testament: written about the time of King Edgar (700 yeares agoe) by Ælfricus Aebas, thought to be the same that was afterward archbishop of Canterburie, whereby appeares what was the canon of holy scripture here then received, and that the Church of England had it so long agoe in her mother tongue* (1623). Lisle edited this work from a manuscript belonging to Cotton, and as the title also shows, he suspected the incorrect identification of Ælfric Grammaticus with Ælfric, archbishop of Canterbury. Appendices contain homilies and epistles of Ælfric. The volume is almost in itself an Anglo-Saxon primer, containing as it does additional material such as the Lord's prayer, the creed, and the ten commandments in Anglo-Saxon with interlinear translation.

The *Saxon Treatise* was Lisle's only work of Anglo-Saxon

scholarship to be printed in his lifetime, and it was also reissued in 1638 under the title *Divers Ancient Monuments*. However, he contributed much other work to the revival of Anglo-Saxon studies. Letters exchanged with Robert Cotton mention a lexicon prepared by Lisle of Anglo-Saxon vocabulary, which Lisle was seeking to have printed, but this work has not survived. Two manuscripts now in the Bodleian (MS Laud misc. 201, MS Laud misc. 381) represent substantial projects by Lisle. The first of these is entitled, in the manuscript, 'The Saxon-English psalter, to preserve the memory of our mother churche and language'. Based on the Eadwine psalter and completed by Lisle in 1630, this is the first modern edition and translation of an Old English psalter. A similar search for national identity informs the other manuscript, a collection of largely Old Testament material in Old English, designed to illustrate 'the Roots & grounds of our mother toong' (Pulsiano, 183). Lisle also worked on the *Ancrene Wisse* and on Anglo-Saxon law.

Lisle appears to have had access to some manuscripts that are now lost, and his work is the sole source for subsequent knowledge of, for instance, Ælfric's homily on Esther. While his all-round achievements are remarkable, recent scholarship has discovered that he occasionally distorts the texts he transcribes, most notably through deliberate archaizings and silent omissions. He certainly had the facility to compose in Old English if he chose to.

Alongside his Anglo-Saxon career, Lisle continued to produce verse translations from other languages. In 1625 and 1637 appeared more work by him on Du Bartas: in 1628 he printed *Virgil's Eclogues, Translated into English by W. L., Gent.*, with the accompanying commentary of Vives. In 1631 Lisle printed *The Faire Aethiopian*, a verse translation of Heliodorus dedicated to the king and queen. This was reissued in 1638 under the title, *The Famous Historie of Heliodorus*. In addition, Lisle wrote Latin hexameter verses which appeared in the preface to the second edition of his neighbour Michael Dalton's book *The Countrey Justice* (1619); a verse inscription on the tomb of William Benson in St Olave's, Southwark; and he has been credited with English verses signed 'W. L.', beginning 'When stout Achilles heard of Helens rape', that appeared prefixed to the 1590 *Faerie Queene*. However, this last identification is far from certain.

Lisle died in September 1637 at the family estate at Wilbraham, Cambridge. He was buried in Walmer, Kent, where a monument commemorates him.

MATTHEW STEGGLE

Sources T. Graham, ed., *The recovery of Old English* (2000) • P. Pulsiano, 'William L'Isle and the editing of Old English', *The recovery of Old English*, ed. T. Graham (2000), 173–206 • S. Lee, 'Oxford, Bodleian Library, MS Laud misc. 381: William L'Isle, Ælfric, and the *Ancrene Wisse*', *The recovery of Old English*, ed. T. Graham (2000), 207–42 • W. Sterry, ed., *The Eton College register, 1441–1698* (1943) • Venn, *Alum. Cant.* • *CSP dom.*, 1603–9 • will, PRO, PROB 11/175/132

Lister, Anne (1671–1695×1704). *See under* Lister, Susanna (*bap.* 1670, *d.* 1738).

Lister, Anne (1791–1840), diarist and traveller, was born on 3 April 1791, probably in Halifax, Yorkshire, although some accounts suggest Welton, South Cave, Yorkshire. She was the daughter of Captain Jeremy Lister (*d.* 1836) and his wife, Rebecca Battle (*d.* 1817), of North Cave, Yorkshire. Her father, youngest son of the Lister family of Shibden Hall, Halifax, one of the chief landowning families of the area, was of a restless disposition and spent his youth in the army. Anne was never very attached to him and wished him more gentlemanly. Two of her brothers died very young; John, the younger of the two surviving boys, died in 1810, and Samuel, the elder (whom Anne loved), died in 1813, leaving Anne one sister, Marian, of whom she was not fond. She was educated at private schools in Ripon and York where, at the age of fifteen, she began her diaries which were partly encoded in a cipher which became more complex with time and which she used to record all private matters, particularly financial and sexual. At school she had her first lesbian experiences with a schoolfriend Eliza Raine who calls Anne her 'husband' in writings which use Anne's code.

In 1815, to escape her parental home where she was unhappy, Lister moved to Shibden Hall to live with her uncle James and aunt Anne, unmarried siblings. She was fiercely independent in running the estate and conducting her own affairs. She dressed in a masculine style: being much concerned with her appearance, she decided early that she would wear only black. She was intelligent and, helped by the scholarly Reverend Samuel Knight, later vicar of Halifax, taught herself Latin, Greek, algebra, geometry, and other subjects in which she read widely. She also enjoyed music and played the flute. She took an active interest in local schools and was the first woman to be elected to the Halifax Literary and Philosophical Society. She was keenly interested in all details of estate business which she directed personally even when abroad, not least because lack of money was a constant embarrassment to her. She developed a hotel and sold and leased land for building, coal mines, and stone quarries, using and indeed exceeding her income on ambitious alterations to the hall (carried out with the help of the architect John Harper), on landscaping the park, and on travelling. She was an old-fashioned tory and Anglican, disdaining tradesmen, set against dissent, and using her power over tenants and her limited means unsuccessfully to fight the radicalism sweeping the area. Her lesbianism caused her no mental anguish since she explicitly stated it to be a pure form of love, and she was very largely protected from gossip by her discretion and dominant social position. Mary (Marianna) Belcombe was her lover from 1814, and the affair continued after Mary's marriage in 1816 to Charles Lawton. After some other relationships, Lister took as a lover Ann Walker (1803–1854) of Lightcliffe, near Halifax—a shy malleable girl whom Lister pursued, at least partly, for her wealth, and who lived at Shibden Hall with Lister from 1834.

In 1826, on the death of her uncle, Lister became sole executor of his will and owner of the Shibden estate. When in 1836 her aunt and father—who had drawn some

Anne Lister (1791–1840), by unknown artist

of the income of the estate—died, Lister became completely financially independent. Her increasing wealth gave her scope for travel. Her first journeys, in the 1820s and 1830s, took her to Europe. She spent three years in Paris, where she lived with her aunt and studied anatomy under Baron Georges Cuvier. Medical matters had always interested her and are an important part of her diaries; she now combined interest with practical experiment. She went on to Switzerland, the Netherlands, Denmark, Germany, Italy, and Spain. There she visited not only sights of historical and cultural interest, but also factories, prisons, orphanages, farms, and mines and climbed high mountains, making the first recorded ascent of Vignemarle (10,821 feet) in the Pyrenees.

In 1839, with her partner Miss Walker, Lister travelled through Belgium, Germany, Sweden, Finland, Russia, the Caucasus, and Persia. Her adventures ranged from galloping across the frozen Volga to visiting a Tartar harem. She reached the Black Sea but became ill with what is variously described as a fever, the plague, and poisoning from an insect bite. She was carried back to Kutaisi, the capital of West Georgia, where she died on 22 September 1840. Her remains and her diaries were brought back to England by Miss Walker and her remains interred in Halifax parish church. Lister bequeathed Miss Walker a lifetime interest in Shibden Hall, from which she was forcibly removed after becoming insane. After Miss Walker's death the house and estate passed to Anne Lister's Welsh male cousins, notably John Lister (1845–1933), an important local benefactor and the first national treasurer of the Independent Labour Party.

Anne Lister was remembered in her locality long after her death and was the model for Maud in Rosa Kettle's *The Mistress of Langdale Hall* (1872). She later became known through her diaries which, in twenty-seven volumes and 4 million words (about one sixth in cipher), chronicle in minute detail her daily life at Shibden, her travels, and her personal life. Her cousin John was the first to bring them to public view, choosing extracts of local social and economic interest for the *Halifax Guardian* (1887–92). He did not publish any of the secret parts, although he had deciphered them. Later authors were also reluctant to publish the coded sections, explained away by one as 'sentimental exchanges with her friends, excruciatingly tedious to the modern mind' (Ramsden, 4). Since the 1980s, however, the diaries have been fully accessible to scholars, and they and about 900 surviving letters have attracted very considerable interest, not least from women's historians because of the commanding position which Lister occupied in her locality and because of her lesbianism. While her diaries and letters are a testimony to her private life, Lister's alterations to Shibden Hall (now a folk museum) and park remain a lasting memorial to her public figure. ELIZABETH BAIGENT

Sources J. Liddington, 'Anne Lister of Shibden Hall, Halifax: her diaries and the historians', *History Workshop Journal*, 35 (1993), 45–77 • H. Whitbread, ed., *I know my own heart: the diaries of Anne Lister, 1791–1840* (1988) • P. M. Ramsden, 'Anne Lister's Journal, 1817–1840', *Transactions of the Halifax Antiquarian Society* (1970), 1–13 • V. Ingham, 'Anne Lister in the Pyrenees', *Transactions of the Halifax Antiquarian Society* (1969), 55–70 • J. Liddington, 'Anne Lister and Shibden Hall, Halifax (1791–1840)', *Transactions of the Halifax Antiquarian Society*, new ser., 1 (1993), 62–78 • M. Green, *Miss Lister of Shibden Hall: selected letters (1800–1840)* (1992) • H. Whitbread, *No priest but love: excerpts from the diaries of Anne Lister* (1992) • P. Brears, 'A Gothic lady and her Victorian architect', *The York Historian* (1971)

Archives Calderdale District Archives, Halifax, West Yorkshire

Likenesses J. Horner, oils, after 1840, Shibden Hall, Halifax, West Yorkshire • oils, Shibden Hall, Halifax, West Yorkshire [*see illus.*] • watercolours, Calderdale District Archives, Halifax, West Yorkshire

Wealth at death under £4000—personal estate: private information

Lister, Arthur (1830–1908), botanist, was born at Upton House, Upton, Essex, on 17 April 1830, the youngest son in the family of four sons and three daughters of Joseph Jackson *Lister (1786–1869). Joseph *Lister (later first Baron Lister of Lyme Regis) was his elder brother. A lifelong member of the Society of Friends, Lister was educated at Hitchin. He left school at sixteen and joined as a partner at the firm of Lister and Beck, wine merchants, in the City of London. On 2 May 1855 he married Susanna, daughter of William Tindall of East Dulwich. The couple later had three sons and four daughters; their eldest son was Joseph Jackson Lister FRS. Lister retired from the business in 1888 with sufficient money to support his activities as an amateur scientist.

Lister's name is specially identified with his painstaking researches on the Mycetozoa, on which, from 1888 onwards, he published many articles in the *Annals of Botany*, the *Journal of the Linnean Society*, and the *Proceedings of the Essex Field Club*. His principal work, *A Monograph of the Mycetozoa*, the seventy-eight plates for which were produced by his daughter Gulielma *Lister, was issued by the trustees of the British Museum in 1894 and is an exhaustive catalogue of the species in the national herbarium. He was also the compiler of the museum's *Guide to the British Mycetozoa* (1895).

Lister was elected a fellow of the Linnean Society on 3 April 1873, served on the council (1891–6), and was vice-president (1895–6). He was elected FRS on 9 June 1898, and was president of the Mycological Society in 1906–7. He was a JP for Essex. He died at Highcliff, Lyme Regis, on 19 July 1908, and was buried at Leytonstone, Essex where he had lived for much of his life.

T. E. JAMES, *rev.* ALEXANDER GOLDBLOOM

Sources Desmond, *Botanists*, rev. edn, 431 • *Proceedings of the Linnean Society of London*, 121st session (1908–9), 46–7 • *Bradford Scientific Journal*, 2 (1909) • *Stratford Express* (25 July 1908) • *Nature*, 78 (1908), 325 • *The Times* (23 July 1908) • *The Times* (1 Sept 1908)
Archives NHM
Likenesses portrait, repro. in *Proceedings of the Dorset Natural History and Archaeology Society*, 83 (1961), 79–81
Wealth at death £147,130 11*s*. 5*d*.: probate, 28 Aug 1908, *CGPLA Eng. & Wales*

Lister, Sir (Robert) Ashton (1845–1929), industrialist, was born on 4 February 1845 in Dursley, Gloucestershire, the third of four sons and the sixth of eight children of George Lister, tanner and wire card maker of Dursley, and his second wife, Louisa Richards, who came from a Dursley family of maltsters. He was educated at Dursley Agricultural and Commercial Grammar School and then at schools in Banbury, Düsseldorf, and Versailles, before joining his father's business.

Lister became estranged from his father and in 1867 set up on his own as a repairer of farm machinery, thus beginning the firm of R. A. Lister & Co. Soon he began manufacturing a range of agricultural and dairy equipment, much of which was exported. Lister travelled widely, promoting trade vigorously, and by 1911 had visited North America fifteen times. His company was not afraid to diversify, and from 1905 to 1914 it produced Dursley-Pedersen bicycles. In 1901 production of woodware began, which by 1909 included teak garden seats, and in 1908 came petrol engines, developed in 1929 into the famous range of diesels. Also in 1908 production began of the equally renowned sheep-shears.

As an employer, Lister was paternalistic and somewhat autocratic, but benevolent. He drove himself hard, expecting his workforce to do the same, but he was quick to provide them with social benefits—housing in 1901 and 1908, a hospital and benefit scheme in 1917, holidays with pay, and a consultative board of directors and workers' representatives in 1927. The greatest benefit was to the local community as a whole: as Listers grew so the area climbed to prosperity from the depression that followed the collapse of the woollen trade.

Lister's activities extended into the community. In 1883 he was elected bailiff of Dursley and in 1893 was appointed a JP. In 1889 he was elected as first county councillor for Dursley, a position he held for thirty years and which was followed by nine years as county alderman. He supported a great variety of movements both by his presence and financially, including temperance, welfare, council housing, and education. The mainsprings of his activity were his religious and political convictions. Brought up by an agnostic father, he was introduced to church life by his wife and by 1899 he was a trustee of Dursley Congregational Church and a keen supporter of nonconformity in general. In recognition of his public work he was knighted in the 1911 new year's honours and in 1919 appointed CBE.

Apart from his council work, Lister found time to address with technical skill and lucidity trade problems such as marketing and exporting agricultural produce, the new techniques of refrigeration and of drying milk, food adulteration, and the wartime rationalization of flour and bread movements to prevent price rises. Politically he was a Liberal and a strong supporter of free trade and of the social reforms of David Lloyd George. He made three attempts to enter parliament (for Tewkesbury) before succeeding in 1918, when he stood for Stroud as a coalition candidate. He held the seat until 1922.

Lister was a man of large, spare frame, standing 6 feet tall, with a keen eye and forceful presence. He had a highly retentive memory and was an accomplished and lively speaker. He was a good judge of character, hated hypocrisy, and had no time for conceit. Discussing a sermon with a workman was as pleasurable to him as dining with his friend the prime minister H. H. Asquith.

In 1866 Lister married Frances Ann (*d.* 1911), daughter of John Box of Dursley, a watchmaker. They had four sons, the eldest of whom died in 1895; from the family of the second, Charles, came the five grandsons who as a team continued the family firm until it was sold in 1965 to the Hawker Siddeley Group. Lister died at his home, The Towers, Dursley, on 6 December 1929, and was buried in the cemetery of the Dursley Tabernacle United Reformed Church.

DAVID E. EVANS, *rev.*

Sources D. E. Evans, *Listers: the first hundred years* (1979) • C. More, 'Lister, Sir Charles Percy', *DBB* • *CGPLA Eng. & Wales* (1930)
Archives Glos. RO • Gloucester Public Library
Likenesses photograph, *c*.1885, Stroud Library, Gloucestershire • photograph, *c*.1915, Stroud Library, Gloucestershire
Wealth at death £303,512 6*s*. 0*d*.: probate, 18 Feb 1930, *CGPLA Eng. & Wales*

Lister, Edward (1557–1620), physician, son of William Lister and brother of Sir Matthew *Lister, was born at Wakefield, Yorkshire, and educated at Eton College. In 1575 he was elected a scholar of King's College, Cambridge, where he graduated BA in 1580, MA in 1583, and MD in 1590. He was elected a fellow of the College of Physicians on 30 September 1594, was chosen as censor six times, and was treasurer from 1612 to 1618. He was physician-in-ordinary to Queen Elizabeth and to James I.

Lister lived in the parish of St Mary Aldermanbury, London, and married Anne (*d.* 1613), widow of his fellow collegian, John Farmery, on 27 February 1593 in the parish church. Lister died on 27 March 1620 in Aldermanbury, and was buried in the same church.

NORMAN MOORE, *rev.* RACHEL E. DAVIES

Sources Munk, *Roll* • Venn, *Alum. Cant.*

Lister [Litster], **Geoffrey** (*d.* 1381), rebel, has been the subject of much confusion over his identity. Walsingham wrongly states that he was called John and that he was a Norwich dyer, while Froissart says that his name was William and that he came from Stafford. He was in fact a dyer from Felmingham, near North Walsham, Norfolk. He paid 6*d.* in the poll tax of 1379, and is described in the tax records as a 'lestere' or dyer. He had a wife called Agnes. He possessed at the time of his death goods and chattels worth 33*s.* 9*d.*, and held half an acre of land from the duchy of Lancaster. He was the most prominent rebel leader in Norfolk during the rising of 1381, when his actions displayed a political and tactical acumen comparable to that of the better-known rebel leader in Kent, Wat Tyler.

The first outbreaks of insurgency in Norfolk in 1381 occurred in west Norfolk, beginning with the appearance of Suffolk rebels at Thetford on 14 June 1381 and culminating in the sack of houses belonging to John Reed, a poll tax collector, at Rougham on 18 June. During this time proclamations were made in Lister's name urging people to rise in east Norfolk, but there is no record of any major incident there before 17 June, when a great force of rebels assembled on Mousehold Heath outside Norwich. Lister was already established as the leader of this band. His lieutenants included two disaffected members of the local gentry, Sir Roger Bacon and Thomas, son of Sir Thomas Gissing. While they were at Mousehold, the rebels killed three men they had captured: Reginald Eccles, a local justice of the peace, Sir Robert Salle, a notable military leader, and John Newlyn, a serf of John of Gaunt, duke of Lancaster (*d.* 1399). The insurgents burst into Norwich and sacked houses there. On 18 June Lister led his force to Yarmouth, where they forced the burgesses to hand over a charter that gave the town a monopoly over the local herring trade and control of the port of Kirkley Road. Lister and his followers cut the charter in two, sending one part to their fellow rebels in Suffolk. Houses belonging to William Ellis and Hugh Fastolf, the most powerful of the Yarmouth burgesses and the customs collectors there, were attacked and records destroyed. A proclamation was made in the name of Lister and Bacon at Kirkley Road against the collection of customs in the port. On 19 June, perhaps after Lister had left the town, the gaol was attacked, and three Flemings held there were killed. Lister returned towards North Walsham, attacking the manor of John of Gaunt at Gimingham. Lister appears to have assumed some kind of judicial authority. Thomas Soppe was arrested for attacking property of the abbot of Dereham at Holkham, but was released because Lister said he approved the act. Then on 21 June, at Thorpe Market, Lister received a bill naming the parson of Thursford and others as traitors, and also heard an appeal for help in destroying the records of the prior of Binham.

These actions support stories told by Walsingham and repeated, many years later, by John Capgrave. Walsingham claims that Lister tried to capture William Ufford, earl of Suffolk (*d.* 1382), to give authority to his actions. Ufford escaped, disguised as a groom, but five other members of the local gentry—Roger Scales, William Morley, John Brewes, Stephen Hales, and Robert Salle—were forced to ride with the rebels. Walsingham states that Lister called himself 'the king of the commons', and compelled the captive knights to taste his food and drink and to kneel to him in deference. Salle was supposedly killed because he was disobedient. Eventually Lister decided to send Morley and Brewes to try and purchase a charter of manumission from the king with money looted in Norwich. The two knights were accompanied by three of Lister's most trusted men. But when they reached Icklingham near Newmarket they met the bishop of Norwich, Henry Despenser (*d.* 1406), 'a man ideally suited for fighting and armed to the teeth' (*Historia Anglicana*, 2.6). He urged the knights to give up any traitors among them. Emboldened by the bishop's forceful manner, they told him the story of their mission. The bishop seized the three rebels and killed them, and then headed for North Walsham, where Lister was awaiting the return of his envoys. Despenser probably arrived at North Walsham on 26 June. The rebels had fortified their camp outside the town by surrounding it with a ditch filled with stakes. The bishop and his retinue nevertheless overwhelmed the rebels. Despenser—who seems to have been acting without due legal authority—sentenced Lister to be hanged, drawn, and beheaded. He accompanied Lister to the gallows, 'thereby performing despite his victory a work of mercy and piety. He held up the rebel's head to prevent it knocking on the ground while he was being dragged to the place of his hanging' (*Historia Anglicana*, 2.8). Two medieval stone crosses outside North Walsham are said to be associated with Despenser's victory over the rebels. ANDREW PRESCOTT

Sources *Thomae Walsingham, quondam monachi S. Albani, historia Anglicana*, ed. H. T. Riley, 2 vols., pt 1 of *Chronica monasterii S. Albani*, Rolls Series, 28 (1863–4) · *Chroniques de J. Froissart*, ed. S. Luce and others, 10 (Paris, 1897) · *Johannis Capgrave Liber de illustribus Henricis*, ed. F. C. Hingeston, Rolls Series, 7 (1858) · court of king's bench, ancient indictments, PRO, RB 9/166/1 · exchequer, king's remembrancer, PRO, E 153 · exchequer, king's remembrancer, PRO, E 159 · exchequer, king's remembrancer, PRO, E 179 · H. Eiden, *'In der Knechtschaft werdet ihr verharren …': Ursachen und Verlauf des englischen Bauernaufstandes von 1381* (Trier, 1995) · A. Réville, *Le soulèvement des travailleurs d'Angleterre en 1381*, ed. C. Petit-Dutaillis (1898) · E. Powell, *The rising in East Anglia* (1896) · B. Cozens-Hardy, 'Norfolk crosses', *Norfolk Archaeology*, 25 (1933–5), 297–336, esp. 327–8 · S. Walker, *The Lancastrian affinity, 1361–1399* (1990) · C. Hoare, *The history of an East Anglian soke: studies in original documents* (1914)

Wealth at death approx. 33*s.* 9*d.*: PRO, E 159/160

Lister, Gulielma (1860–1949), mycologist and naturalist, was born on 28 October 1860 at Sycamore House, 871 High Road, Leytonstone, Essex, one of seven children and the third of four daughters of Arthur *Lister (1830–1908), a London wine merchant and naturalist, and his wife, Susanna, daughter of William Tindall of East Dulwich. The Listers were a Quaker family of distinction: one of Gulielma's uncles was the surgeon Lord Joseph *Lister (1827–1912), and two of her brothers had outstanding careers in zoology and medicine respectively. Gulielma was educated at home except for a year spent at Bedford College for Women, about 1876, where she acquired a grounding in systematic and structural botany.

Long her father's companion and helper in his natural history studies, in the late 1880s Gulielma joined him in investigations of the Myxomycetes, or slime moulds, a group whose classification was then somewhat confused. Together they worked over collections in the British Museum (Natural History), Kew Gardens, the Paris Natural History Museum, and De Bary's collection at the University of Strasbourg, Gulielma making notes and drawings. The result of their labours was Arthur Lister's *Monograph of the Mycetozoa* (1894). A work of widespread interest, both in Britain and abroad, it brought a great influx of new material to the British Museum which in turn led to the recognition of new forms and extended knowledge of geographical distributions. After her father's death Gulielma brought out an expanded second edition (1911); a third, further enlarged and illustrated with coloured plates (an impressive collection of her own outstanding watercolours), followed in 1925. The latter remains a classic—a key work on the taxonomy and nomenclature of the Myxomycetes.

The Listers' investigations, pursued without interruption over a period of sixty years, over the last forty by Gulielma Lister alone, were recorded in a remarkable collection of seventy-four research notebooks bequeathed to the British Mycological Society, and later deposited in the British Museum (Natural History). They contain a wealth of material, including the results of the Listers' early classification studies of historical collections, accounts of their own collections and research (which included some early life history studies), notes on materials submitted to them from collectors worldwide, and many fine watercolour illustrations. A long succession of their papers published in the botanical journals includes a number of reports on Myxomycetes from Switzerland where Gulielma Lister and her father especially enjoyed collecting, although Gulielma's real hunting-grounds were Epping Forest and the region around Lyme Regis. Of special interest was her 1912 presidential address to the British Mycological Society, 'Past students of the Mycetozoa and their work'. Painstaking and accurate in her observations, free from bias and preconception, she kept abreast of studies by others in the field, even learning Polish to follow the work of Josef Rostafinsky. She was widely acknowledged as a world authority on the Myxomycetes.

Gulielma Lister's close association with the British Museum lasted from the late 1880s until 1939, when wartime conditions prevented her travelling to London. For many years she was virtually honorary curator of the Myxomycetes, a collection she had helped to make the most important and complete then in existence, and greatly enriched with her watercolours giving magnified views. At the museum she and her close friend lichenologist Annie Lorrain Smith were remembered particularly for their interest and understanding patience in teaching younger workers. A gentle, kindly, generous woman of attractive personality, she had a wide circle of friends and numerous correspondents in many countries (including the emperor of Japan, in whose honour she named a specimen from the palace gardens and whose gift of a pair of porcelain vases she greatly cherished).

A foundation member of the British Mycological Society, Gulielma Lister gave it considerable help in its early years; she was an influential council member and served twice as president (1912 and 1932). She became a member of the Essex Field Club in 1907, was its first woman president (1916), and thereafter a permanent vice-president. Long one of the club's leading spirits, participating regularly in its forays, she was especially active in the work of its Stratford museum, to which she donated both myxomycete and botanical collections. She was one of the first women fellows of the Linnean Society (elected 1904), served on the council (1915, 1927), and became a vice-president in 1929.

A distinguished naturalist with detailed field knowledge of both plants and animals, Gulielma Lister had particularly strong interests in birds and conifers. For many years she worked with quiet enthusiasm with the London School Nature Study Union, providing sound advice and for a time serving as chair. Her artistic skills often brought requests for help; she prepared the illustrations for both her cousin F. J. Hanbury's *Illustrated Monograph of British Hieracia* (1889) and Dallimore and Jackson's *Handbook of Coniferae* (1923).

Gulielma Lister died, unmarried, following a stroke, at her home, Sycamore House, 871 High Road, Leytonstone, Essex, on 18 May 1949. Her ashes were scattered over her mother's grave in Wanstead Friends' meeting-house burial-grounds. MARY R. S. CREESE

Sources *Nature*, 164 (1949), 94 · *Transactions of the British Mycological Society*, 33 (1950), 165–6 · *The Times* (6 June 1949) · *Essex Naturalist*, 28 (1950), 214 · G. C. Ainsworth and F. L. Balfour-Browne, 'Gulielma Lister centenary', *Nature*, 188 (1960), 362–3 · J. J. L. [J. J. Lister], *PRS*, 88B (1914–15), i–xi [obit. of Arthur Lister] · G. C. Ainsworth, 'The Lister notebooks', *Transactions of the British Mycological Society*, 35 (1952), 188–9 · L. E. Hawker, 'The Lister memorial lecture: the physiology of *Myxomycetes*', *Transactions of the British Mycological Society*, 35 (1952), 177–87 · Desmond, *Botanists* · A. Lister and G. Lister, *A monograph of the Mycetozoa*, rev. 2nd edn (1911), preface · 'Lister, Arthur', *DNB* · J. Webster and D. Moore, *Brief biographies of British mycologists*, ed. G. C. Ainsworth (British Mycological Society, Stourbridge, 1996) · private information (2004) [Steven Moss, secretary, British Mycological Society]

Archives Commonwealth Mycological Institute, Kew, London, notebooks · NHM, notebooks and drawings · RBG Kew, archives, corresp., notes, and papers | New York Botanical Garden, letters to William Codman Sturgis

Likenesses J. Barkus, photograph, repro. in *Essex Naturalist*, facing p. 214 · photograph, British Mycological Society, Surrey · photograph, repro. in *Transactions of the British Mycological Society* (1950), 165

Wealth at death £37,448 13*s*. 5*d*.: probate, 29 Sept 1949, *CGPLA Eng. & Wales*

Lister, Sir John (*bap.* **1587**, *d.* **1640**), merchant and politician, was baptized on 7 June 1587, the only son (there was one daughter) of John Lister (*d.* 1617), merchant and member of parliament, of the High Street, Kingston upon Hull, and his wife, Anne (*d.* 1621), daughter of Robert Geyton, of

Hull. Lister's father was born in Halifax, but settled in Hull and made his fortune there; in 1614 he was the largest exporter of lead from Hull. Lister matriculated from University College, Oxford, in 1604 and was admitted to the Middle Temple in 1606. He was never called to the bar. By 1609, when his first son was born, he had married Elizabeth (*c.*1589–1656), daughter and sole heir of Hugh Armin (*d.* 1606), draper, of Hull. Eight sons and four daughters survived him.

After his father died, Lister came to be identified closely with the town of Hull. On 12 March 1617 he was admitted a freeman and the very next day he took his father's seat on the governing bench of aldermen. In September 1618 he was elected mayor, and in that capacity travelled to London on behalf of the Hull Society of Merchants to argue for an unfettered trade in lead. After some delay the privy council ruled in the town's favour.

Lister's hard work pleased his fellow burgesses and in 1620 they chose him as their MP. Re-elected six times, he represented the borough of Hull in every parliament until his death and was the only local man to serve more than once during these years (although in 1624 he had to wait for a by-election). He was active both in the House of Commons and in committee, and made a notable contribution in 1621 to the debate on England's trading position. Even during the 1630s, when parliament did not sit, he travelled several times to London, especially in connection with a long-running dispute over the management of Hull Castle. His instructions from the corporation mostly survive, as do many of his letters in reply. Meanwhile the government employed him as one of its agents in the town. In 1627, for instance, he helped to organize the shipment of soldiers to the continent; he was knighted on 23 May 1628, perhaps as a token of thanks.

Like much of the town Lister had puritan sympathies. This is suggested both by his circle of friends (they included the elder Andrew Marvell, lecturer at Holy Trinity Church), and by the vigorous campaign against wickedness and vice, in particular the haunters of alehouses, which characterized his second term as mayor in 1629. Little however can be seen of his personal reaction to the burning political issues of the day. (He died barely a year before the outbreak of civil war.) He was interested in the arguments about the liberties of the subject aired during the 1628 parliamentary session and brought copies of the debates back with him to Hull. Yet it was during this session that he was knighted. Again, he was elected by his fellow burgesses to the Short and Long parliaments in 1640, but was chosen by Strafford that same summer to be lieutenant-colonel of the town's trained bands. His loyalty to the government was clearly in no doubt. Indeed, on 30 September 1640 (often misdated 1639), King Charles himself was entertained at Lister's magnificent house in Hull, which later became the Wilberforce Museum.

Lister died in London on 23 December 1640 and was buried in Holy Trinity Church, Hull, on 19 January 1641. A merchant of great wealth (he lent the corporation £620 in 1639), who had property in Lincolnshire and Derbyshire as well as in Hull and the East Riding, he provided generously for his numerous offspring. He also left cash and land to build and endow an almshouse for twelve poor men and women. M. J. SHORT

Sources Hull corporation MSS, Hull City RO, BRB 3; BRL 168–73, 178–80, 197, 199–201, 202a, 212, 221, 223, 226, 234–5, 249, 255–6, 289, 299, 1434 • will, 21 Dec 1640, Borth. Inst., wills, bundle for Feb 1641 • F. W. Brooks, ed., *The first order book of the Hull Trinity House, 1632–65*, Yorkshire Archaeological Society Record Series, 105 (1942) • *APC*, *1618–19*, 351–2, 482–3; *1619–21*, 90–91 • W. Notestein, F. H. Relf, and H. Simpson, eds., *Commons debates, 1621*, 2 (1935), 176, 365, 386; 3 (1935), 169, 194, 298; 4 (1935), 339; 6 (1935), 60, 81 • R. C. Johnson and others, eds., *Commons debates, 1628*, 6 vols. (1977–83), vol. 2, p. 550; vol. 3, pp. 308, 310; vol. 4, p. 474 • H. L. L. Denny, *Memorials of an ancient house* (1913), 271–5 • Keeler, *Long Parliament*, 252–4 • T. Gent, *Annales regioduni Hullini, or, The history of Kingston-upon-Hull*, facs. edn (1869) • L. M. Stanewell, ed., *City and county of Kingston upon Hull: calendar of the ancient deeds, letters, miscellaneous old documents, &c. in the archives of the corporation* (1951)

Archives Hull City RO, Hull Corporation MSS

Likenesses oils, Wilberforce Museum, Hull

Wealth at death very wealthy; numerous properties in Hull and estates in Yorkshire, Lincolnshire, and Derbyshire; also a half share in smelting mill

Lister, John (1847–1933), philanthropist and politician, was born on 8 March 1847 at 55 Beaumont Street, Cavendish Square, Marylebone, Middlesex, the eldest of the three children of John Lister (1802–1867), physician, and his wife, Louisa Ann, *née* Grant (1815–1892). His maternal forebears were from a well-to-do military family and his paternal ancestors had links with Halifax dating back to the early fourteenth century. A delicate child of slender build, Lister inherited his mother's reflectiveness and emotional passivity and his father's energetic imagination and mental agility. He spent his early childhood at Sandown on the Isle of Wight, but moved to Halifax in 1855 when his father inherited the 40 acre, freehold Shibden estate, with its extensive mineral rights. He was tutored privately by a Halifax clergyman, John H. Warneford, before proceeding to Winchester College in 1861, where he distinguished himself in the composition of Latin verse, and then Brasenose College, Oxford, where he became influenced by the Tractarian movement. He qualified as a barrister of the Inner Temple in 1877 but never practised, returning to Halifax to manage the estate which he inherited on attaining his majority in 1868, following the sudden death of his father in the previous year. He remained a bachelor and outlived his younger siblings, Charles, who died of malaria in 1889 while on a scientific expedition to South America, and Anne, who lived with her elder brother until her death in 1929.

As the heir of a prominent Anglican landowning family, Lister's reception into the Roman Catholic church at St Mary of the Angels, Bayswater, London, in 1871, following an interview with Cardinal Manning, created a 'mild sensation' (Drake, xiv). Shortly afterwards he provided the site and laid the foundation-stone for the new St Joseph's Catholic School in Halifax and accepted nomination as Catholic candidate for the Halifax school board, serving in that capacity for nine years. It was on his initiative that the first and only Roman Catholic reformatory school in the diocese of Leeds was founded in 1877, on his estate. The Shibden Industrial School provided training in a range of useful trades and occupations for initially sixty and eventually as many as 150 Catholic boys from deprived social backgrounds. Lister retained an active personal interest in the management of the school, securing donations from influential friends and acquaintances, including the duke of Norfolk, and contributing generously himself towards extensions.

Lister's subsequent spasmodic involvement in politics included representation of the Liberals on Halifax town council from 1873 to 1876 and of Labour from 1892 to 1894, and a term on the West Riding county council. He also founded the Catholic Registration Society in 1875, and was the founding secretary of the Catholic Working Men's Association in 1882. A former progressive Liberal, he emerged in the 1890s as a prominent ethical socialist, campaigning against the economic and social inequalities of capitalist society. At Oxford, he had been deeply influenced by the writings of John Ruskin and William Morris, and he became a fully-fledged member of the Fabian Society in June 1891. He offered hospitality to visiting Fabian speakers at Shibden Hall, and read a wide range of socialist literature, including 'that exhilarating work by Karl Marx entitled *Das Kapital*' (Laybourn, 29). He was a founder member of the Halifax Labour Union in July 1892, and became the first national treasurer and a generous financial supporter of the Independent Labour Party at its inaugural conference in Bradford in January 1893, a post which he retained until he left the party in 1895.

In 1893 Lister contested Halifax for the Independent Labour Party in a by-election in which, although he came bottom of the poll, he obtained over 25 per cent of the vote, exceeding the 'wildest expectations' of contemporaries (Laybourn and Reynolds, 69). During the campaign he had emphasized his links with Gladstonian Liberalism, pledging his commitment to home rule for Ireland, his support for the Newcastle programme, and his determination 'to make the pathway to Westminster as smooth and easy as possible' for working men (election address, *Halifax Courier*, 23 Jan 1893). His announcement of his intention to quit municipal politics in 1894 after disputes with the party caucus, however, revealed a sharp divergence between his own moral individualism and the collectivist attitudes of other local Labour activists. He survived a move to censure him and strip him of his parliamentary candidature with support from his friend Keir Hardie. The differences were patched up and Lister contested Halifax again in the general election of 1895, polling a decreased share of the vote. He subsequently contested the municipal elections in November 1895, but then quickly drifted out of local and national labour politics, disillusioned by the divisions within the labour movement.

Lister retained, however, a close personal friendship with the Leeds socialist engineer Alf Mattison, and their correspondence reveals Lister's increasingly depressed state of mind after 1900 as he struggled to deal with intractable financial problems arising from the management of his estate, with its exhausted coal seams honeycombing potential development land and thereby diminishing its market value. In March 1918, confiding his anxieties about the future to Mattison, he declared that he was 'sick of having nothing on my brain now but miserable pounds, shillings and pence' (Drake, xiii). During this period his only consolation was his continuing interest in historical research. He served as president of the Halifax Antiquarian Society from its foundation in 1900 until his death, wrote voluminously on the history of Halifax and the West Riding of Yorkshire, and campaigned vigorously for the preservation of local historic buildings threatened by urban redevelopment. He appears in later photographs weary but determined, with deep-set eyes peering out from under heavy lids, a greying head of hair, and a drooping moustache. He died at Shibden Hall on 12 October 1933 from heart failure after suffering a severe stroke three months earlier, the last of his line and 'the last survivor of the old gentry of Halifax' (Kendall, ii). Following a requiem mass at St Mary's Roman Catholic Church, Halifax, where the celebrant paid tribute to his selfless public service, a hearse, drawn by black horses, carried his body through the town whose freedom he had declined in 1925 for interment in the family tomb at St Anne's Church, Southowram, Halifax. JOHN A. HARGREAVES

Sources J. Wilson, 'Pedigree of Lister of the Shibden Hall', *Transactions of the Halifax Antiquarian Society* (1956), 15 • *Halifax Courier* (13 Oct 1933) • H. P. Kendall, 'John Lister, 1847–1933', *Transactions of the Halifax Antiquarian Society* (1933) • K. Laybourn, *The labour party, 1881–1951* (1988) • K. Laybourn and J. Reynolds, *Liberalism and the rise of labour, 1890–1918* (1984) • J. Lister, 'The independent labour party in Halifax', W. Yorks. AS, Calderdale, SH 7 JH/B/45 • file of newspaper cuttings, Leeds Roman Catholic Diocesan Archives • H. J. O'H. Drake, 'John Lister of Shibden Hall (1847–1933)', PhD diss., University of Bradford, 1972 • K. Laybourn and D. James, eds., *"The rising sun of socialism": the independent labour party in the textile district of the West Riding of Yorkshire between 1890 and 1914* (1991) • P. A. Dawson, 'The early labour movement in Halifax, 1891–1906', MA diss., Huddersfield Polytechnic (CNAA), 1984 • P. A. Dawson, 'Halifax politics, 1890–1914', PhD diss., Huddersfield Polytechnic, 1987 • J. A. Hargreaves, *Halifax* (1999) • J. A. Hargreaves, 'Catholic communities in Calderdale in the eighteenth and nineteenth centuries', *Transactions of the Halifax Antiquarian Society*, new ser., 3 (1995), 63–5 • b. cert. • d. cert.

Archives W. Yorks. AS, Calderdale, corresp., diary, notebooks | BLPES, Independent Labour Party archives • U. Leeds, Brotherton L., Alfred Mattison MSS • W. Yorks. AS, Calderdale, Horsfall Turner collection

Likenesses group portrait, photograph, 1893, repro. in *Independent labour party, 1893–1943: Jubilee souvenir* (1943) • photograph, repro. in Kendall, 'John Lister, 1847–1933', frontispiece • photograph (in old age), repro. in *Halifax Courier*

Wealth at death £1622 3*s*. 3*d*.: probate, 18 Dec 1933, *CGPLA Eng. & Wales*

Lister, Joseph (1627–1709), nonconformist autobiographer, was born on 7 June 1627 at Bradford, Yorkshire, to 'godly religious parents'. His father died when Joseph was about six and, after a period at the free grammar school, he was apprenticed by his mother to John Sharp, a godly clothier of the town, about 1641. At this time Joseph attended 'many funeral sermons, lectures and monthly exercises and constantly repeated what I had heard' (*Autobiography*, 7), and his autobiography describes his puritan upbringing, conveying effectively the influence of the preachers on the religious temper of that part of the West Riding on the eve of the civil wars. The panic which passed through the population of the area following the Irish rising in 1641 is described graphically and, after the outbreak of war, Joseph also compiled a full account of the siege and relief of Bradford in 1643. As a result of the siege his master withdrew from the town and Lister moved to another master at Sowerby in Halifax parish, where he completed his apprenticeship and set up in trade for a short time. In the early 1650s, possibly following an ill-judged engagement to his former master's daughter, Lister moved to London, where he joined the presbyterian congregation of Edmund Calamy at St Mary Aldermanbury, and where, as he was later to acknowledge, he was influenced by the preaching of Simeon Ashe. Lister remained in London for about three years, finding employment as a servant in various godly households.

In 1655 Lister returned north, to Greatham, co. Durham, as steward to Captain Askwith, and stayed there for two years, commenting on the poor quality of preaching in that region. Following a period of illness he returned to his mother's house at Bradford and in 1657 he married Sarah Denton, of a local family, in a civil ceremony which was followed later by a church service conducted by his uncle Edward Hill of Crofton, later a nonconformist minister. Soon after his marriage he inherited from his wife's uncle a farm at Bailey Fold, Allerton, in the parish of Bradford, and farmed there. His puritan convictions were out of sympathy with the established church after the Restoration, and he joined the dissenting congregation at Kipping nearby, playing a prominent part in its activities. The early years of the church there were characterized by faction and schism involving radical Fifth Monarchist elements, and these engaged the attention of other leading dissenters, such as Oliver Heywood, who tried to act as peace makers. In the absence of a settled pastor, Lister sometimes exercised ministerial functions during these disturbances. He intended his two sons for the ministry and sent the elder, David, to Richard Frankland's academy at Kendal, where he died in 1677. The second son, Accepted, became a minister and preached at Kipping, being called by the congregation, but he did not settle there, and in 1695 moved to the congregation at Bingley. Accepted had been partially disabled following a fall from a horse and was joined at Bingley by Lister and his wife, the latter dying there about 1697. Lister remained there, but returned to the farm at Allerton when his son returned to the church at Kipping in 1702 as 'a repairer of breaches'.

Joseph Lister remained at Allerton until his death on 11 March 1709, a fortnight after that of his son. He was buried on 13 March in the chapel yard at Horton, Bradford, and his funeral sermon was preached by Thomas Whitaker of Leeds. By his will Lister left his estate at Allerton to his nephew Joshua Dawson of Leeds, with legacies of £100 to each of his four remaining nephews and nieces, along with other small bequests. His autobiography, which is typical of other puritan texts in its emphasis on the workings of God's providence at critical moments of the subject's life, remained unpublished until 1842, though his account of the siege of Bradford was published earlier, in 1810. WILLIAM JOSEPH SHEILS

Sources *The autobiography of Joseph Lister of Bradford, 1627–1709*, ed. A. Holroyd (1860) • original will, March 1709/10, Borth. Inst. • T. Whitaker, *Sermons on several occasions* (1712) • Bradford Library, Ts. MI list

Wealth at death over £600: will, Borth. Inst.

Lister, Joseph, Baron Lister (**1827–1912**), surgeon and founder of a system of antiseptic surgery, the second son and fourth child of seven of Joseph Jackson *Lister FRS (1786–1869), wine merchant and microscopist, and his wife, Isabella, *née* Harris (1794?–1864), daughter of Anthony Harris of Maryport, Cumberland, was born at Upton House, Upton, Essex, on 5 April 1827. His younger brother, Arthur *Lister, became a botanist.

Early life and education Lister's ancestors had been members of the Society of Friends since the early part of the eighteenth century. Great deference was paid to learning in the comfortably off Lister household, and several members of the family were talented artists. Joseph had a stammer and possibly for this reason he was educated at home until he was eleven, when he was sent to the local school at Hitchin. At the age of thirteen he was sent to Grove House School, Tottenham. At school he was apparently a precocious child and enjoyed natural history, collecting, dissecting, and preparing and drawing specimens of various kinds. In later life he frequently spoke of the great influence on him of his father (of whose life he wrote the account for the *Dictionary of National Biography*) and of how much he was indebted to him for encouraging him in scientific pursuits and especially the study of natural history. According to his nephew, Rickman John *Godlee, in his biography of Lister, Joseph determined to be a surgeon while still at school (Godlee, 14). None of his near relatives was in the medical profession, and it seems that this desire was entirely spontaneous.

Lister entered University College, London, in 1844, aged seventeen. While a student in the faculty of arts he was present at the first operation under ether in Great Britain, performed by Robert Liston in the theatre of University College Hospital in December 1846. Lister took his BA degree at the University of London in 1847. There then followed an attack of smallpox and, more importantly, a religious crisis, in which he seems to have doubted whether medicine was his true vocation. Following this in 1848 he had some form of mental breakdown, and he spent time in Ireland recuperating. Lister, who all of his life was said to be aloof, reportedly had no close friends at University College (Fisher, 39). He did not resume his medical studies until the autumn of 1849.

University College, founded in 1828, had a small medical school at this time. It was unusual in London, however, for it was here, rather than at any other metropolitan school, that a student would come in contact with the view that the basic sciences, particularly the experimental sciences

Joseph Lister, Baron Lister (1827–1912), by unknown photographer, 1850s

and especially physiology, should be the foundation of all medical education, practice, and progress. This was an opinion Lister adopted early in his career and it can be seen to have informed not only his reforms of surgical practice but his views of where and how medicine should be taught and practised, and of who should be the leaders of the medical profession. Two teachers at University College seem to have been particularly important to Lister in this respect. One was Wharton Jones, who had formerly been a lecturer in physiology at Charing Cross Hospital, and who was professor of ophthalmic medicine and surgery; he was keenly interested in microscopy and Lister's early microscopical investigations were very similar to work carried out by Jones. The other was William Sharpey, professor of physiology, who was a central figure in the creation of the British school of experimental physiology, which flourished from the early 1870s. Sharpey liked and admired Lister and directed his early researches. Lister won gold medals in comparative and pathological anatomy and silver medals in surgery and medicine. He was also an accomplished artist and many drawings of his dissections during this period survived. In 1852 he became president of the students' medical society of University College. During his student career Lister served as house physician to Dr Walter Hayle Walshe and as house surgeon to John Eric Erichsen. In 1852 he took his MB degree and became a fellow of the Royal College of Surgeons.

Edinburgh, 1853–1860 In September 1853 Lister visited Edinburgh to witness the surgical practice of James *Syme, professor of clinical surgery. Syme was an old friend of Sharpey, who had advised Lister to make the journey and had given him a letter of introduction. Syme was at this time fifty-four years of age, a surgeon of acknowledged eminence, a bold, skilful operator, and an inspiring teacher. He was a man of decided views, who seems to have enjoyed controversy. Lister found Syme to have 'a very original mind' (Fisher, 60). He soon became Syme's dresser and familiarized himself with his methods, and he subsequently acted as his house surgeon for one year. Lister then decided to settle in Edinburgh. He took an active part in teaching in the extramural school, and in 1856 he became assistant surgeon to the Royal Infirmary.

During these years Lister was also pursuing microscopical and physiological researches in his spare time. In his first published work, on the structure of the iris, he endorsed and extended the view of the German physiologist R. A. von Kölliker that this structure was muscular. This paper and another on the involuntary muscular fibres of the skin were published in 1853 in the *Quarterly Journal of Microscopical Science*. During the same year he also carried out experimental work on the flow of chyle, and during the years 1853–8 he published a series of papers dealing with physiological problems. In 1857 he read before the Royal Society a paper published in the *Transactions* of 1858, 'The early stages of inflammation', in which he made detailed observations on blood clotting. For this paper Lister used a camera lucida to draw the microscopic changes he observed in the blood flow in the frog's web and the bat's wing. The coagulation of the blood was central to the physiological issues that preoccupied Lister throughout his scientific life. Various other papers on physiological and pathophysiological questions were published in these years, during which time he received a great deal of intellectual and financial support from his father.

On 23 April 1856 Lister married Agnes Syme (1834–1893), the eldest daughter of the surgeon. The Symes were Episcopalians and Lister, confessing a preference for Church of England services, left the Society of Friends. The wedding was followed by a three-month tour of the continent, including visits to the most celebrated medical schools. Throughout their married life Agnes Lister took a great part in assisting her husband in research work, the notebooks of his experiments being largely written by her. They had no children.

Antiseptic surgery In 1860 Lister was appointed to the chair of surgery at Glasgow University. The same year he became a fellow of the Royal Society. A year later he became surgeon to the Glasgow Infirmary, at that time a hospital with 572 beds. From this time onward Lister's laboratory studies were mainly concerned with inflammation and suppuration, and his clinical research centred on the management of injuries and wounds. During his tenure of the chair of surgery at Glasgow, Lister was an unsuccessful candidate for the chair of surgery at Edinburgh in 1864, and for a similar chair at his old medical school at University College, London, in 1866. In 1869 he was appointed professor of clinical surgery at Edinburgh, and he remained there until 1877.

During the late 1860s and throughout the 1870s Lister published papers which brought him to prominence in the medical profession and also projected him to the centre of scientific and surgical controversy. Eighteenth-century voluntary hospitals were small institutions and their wards had not been noted as breeding grounds of septic diseases. However, the enlarged wards, particularly the surgical wards, of the great Victorian hospitals, often situated at the centre of vast insanitary cities, were a different matter. In these hospitals, perhaps encouraged by the availability of anaesthetics, surgery was performed that was much more ambitious than that of the previous century and it was widely recognized that septic febrile diseases, such as erysipelas and hospital gangrene, could break out and very rapidly wreak havoc in terms of morbidity and mortality among the surgical patients. Fever in a surgical ward often began with sepsis in a wound. These phenomena, christened 'hospitalism' by the Edinburgh obstetrician James Young Simpson in 1869, were addressed in various ways. Sanitary reformers such as Edwin Chadwick and Florence Nightingale proposed the redesigning and resiting of hospitals. Lister, whose Glasgow wards were subject to the menace of hospitalism, proposed a method of wound treatment, based, he said, on scientific principles, which would ensure uncomplicated healing and thus obviate fevers. At stake therefore were not only patients' lives but experimental science and the future of the urban hospital-university complex as the centre of medical practice and education—to all of which Lister was committed.

In 1867 Lister published a number of papers in *The Lancet* which announced his system of antiseptic surgery. These papers describe the management of various cases of compound fracture (in which the broken bone pierces the skin), a condition recognized as having great likelihood of becoming septic. Lister claimed a high degree of success in the healing of these wounds following the setting of the fractures. A key feature of these papers was Lister's claim that his antiseptic treatment was based upon scientific principles discovered by microscopy and experimental physiology, notably principles arrived at through his own work on inflammation.

Central to much thinking in the public health sphere and also to medical ideas about fever at this time was the issue of decomposition, decay, or putrefaction. Decaying organic materials in the wrong place (the street, for example) were implicated as the causes of the epidemic and endemic fever of towns, just as the putrefaction of dead blood and other tissue was seen as the source of mischief in wounds. The causal mechanisms by which this occurred, however, were subjects of much dispute. Many held that putrefaction was a fermentation caused by chemicals, oxygen being implicated by some. In 1865 Lister's attention had been directed by his colleague Thomas Anderson, professor of chemistry at the university, to the work of Louis Pasteur. On the basis of experimental work Pasteur claimed that fermentation and putrefaction were caused by minute living organisms, 'germs', suspended in the atmosphere.

In the light of this knowledge, Lister said, he devised the idea of a chemical barrier interposed between the wound and the air to prevent the ingress of germs. Within the protected wound, he predicted, healthy healing by what was known as granulation could occur in a blood clot. His choice of chemical barrier was carbolic acid, which was known to him as a disinfectant used at Carlisle for the treatment of sewage. He first used carbolic acid in the treatment of compound fracture in the spring of 1865 and in his earliest cases he used liquefied German creosote, an impure carbolic acid; this he introduced into the wound and then he covered the part with a layer of lint soaked in carbolic acid. He used a similar method in the treatment of abscesses. In the first series of *Lancet* papers Lister described eleven cases of compound fracture, of which nine recovered, an excellent result which has to some extent obscured the historical context in which it occurred.

Lister's views at this time about the causes of wound sepsis were very different from those which he was to hold twenty years later. In 1867 Lister did not regard pus formation in wounds as the central problem of healing; pus had appeared in eight of the cases of compound fracture described in *The Lancet*, and Lister took the common surgical view that pus was not ominous unless it were malodorous, signifying putrefaction. Similarly Lister's 'germs' of those years were not like the germs described in later germ theory. They were more like seeds of disease, highly plastic agents (not specific causal entities) whose pathogenic qualities depended on the local environment in which they developed. In this respect Lister shared the assumptions of many Victorian sanitary reformers who regarded fever as the product of local miasmata. In Lister's early theory germs were the intermediary through which miasmata acted. Indeed at one point Lister claimed his method had succeeded in spite of the fact that the Glasgow Infirmary had beneath it the coffins of the cholera victims of 1849 and was next to the cathedral churchyard where paupers were once buried in pits.

Lister's achievement is also complicated by the fact that many other surgeons of this period were experimenting with chemicals and with cleanliness and also claiming equivalent success. In 1868 the Birmingham surgeon Lawson Tait reported that of twelve cases of compound fracture he had managed, all healed without suppuration except the two he treated using Lister's methods. The next fifteen years saw intense debate over the method and the 'principles' of Lister's antiseptic surgery. Those surgeons not convinced by Lister complained that carbolic acid irritated the skin and that simple dressings and cleanliness produced equally good results. Time and again Lister's critics iterated the view that in many environments wounds exposed to the air healed by the most desirable of all mechanisms: first intention. One of Lister's most hostile opponents was the Birmingham surgeon Sampson Gamgee, a former old friend. No controlled trial, in a modern sense, of Lister's methods was possible and many surgeons produced retrospective statistics showing how morbidity and mortality had fallen on their wards using their own techniques. Surgical mortality undoubtedly did fall in this period, but other factors played a part in the decline too: for example, hospitals installed new sanitation systems, nursing and dressings improved, and the diet of patients got better. Lister, by contrast, at times seemed to revel in the 'dirty' conditions of his wards and the 'cleanliness' of his patients' wounds.

From 1867 Lister constantly revised his principles, which were always based on claims about experimental evidence. His practice was continually modified too, the published modifications nearly always being referred to new scientific evidence, usually the result of his own researches. In particular the irritation of crude carbolic acid was a problem he struggled to circumvent. Thus he introduced carbolic oil and carbolized putty, and later he employed carbolized shellac and watery solutions of carbolic acid. From the first he insisted on the necessity of immersing instruments and everything else that came into contact with the wound in carbolic acid, and he also carried out a thorough chemical cleansing of the patient's skin in the vicinity of the wound. Further, he devoted much time and thought to devising dressings, such as gauze impregnated with resin and paraffin and then dipped in a watery solution of carbolic acid. He also introduced the carbolic spray apparatus for disinfecting the air in the field of the operation, being at the time impressed with the belief that the air was the most important factor in the causation of sepsis, owing, he said, to the presence of germs in its dust. Later the spray was dispensed with, when Lister acknowledged that the air did not play as important a part in sepsis as infection derived from the skin, instruments, and dressings, for example. Nevertheless, the introduction of the spray showed his single-mindedness in devising means to counteract septic agencies where he considered them most malign: at the surface of the wound. He also experimented with other chemical antiseptics.

Besides his antiseptic work Lister modified the technique of many operations and invented new methods of treatment. He revived an earlier form of lithotomy, modified the operation for varicose veins, and increasingly chose to open elbow and knee joints to make repairs, though he was by no means the first to do the last. He introduced the use of absorbable ligatures and of drainage tubes in the treatment of wounds; surgeons opposing drainage tubes did so on the grounds that they were only necessary because it was the carbolic acid that produced the fluid which had to be drained off. Lister studied experimentally in animals the changes undergone by ligatures in wounds, and on this basis he introduced catgut for ligatures as it was ultimately absorbed. Raw catgut, however, proved unsuitable, and Lister devoted many years to experiments on catgut in order to prepare it in such a manner that it should retain its firmness and at the same time be aseptic. He also introduced many other techniques, such as the expedient of elevating a limb prior to an operation on it and so rendering it bloodless before the application of a tourniquet, thus saving the patient an unnecessary loss of blood.

London and the impact of germ theory In 1877, before leaving Edinburgh to succeed Sir William Fergusson as professor of surgery at King's College, London, Lister antagonized many London surgeons, and those of King's College Hospital in particular, by criticizing the teaching of clinical surgery in London. Such antagonisms were grounded in the Listerian experimentalist approach to surgery versus the tradition of practical empirical innovation, which was favoured by some London surgeons. Lister withdrew his remarks eleven months later. On accepting the professorship at King's College he made it a condition that he should bring with him his house surgeon, William Watson Cheyne, a senior assistant, John Stewart, and two dressers, W. M. Dobie and James Altham, in order that his antiseptic methods might be carried out to his satisfaction. The Listers moved to a John Nash house at 12 Park Crescent, Portland Place. Little seems to have been known of Lister's methods at King's and there were conflicts, especially with the nursing staff. Cheyne reported that the nursing staff 'hampered him as much as they could' (Fisher, 238). Lister complained about the small number of students attending both his rounds and the operating theatre. The King's medical faculty were split in their views of Lister and his techniques. Lister gradually gained converts among surgeons, notably among younger men who, like him, were proponents of the cause of experimental science in medicine. The most significant of these was Cheyne, his house surgeon.

Lister also gained a considerable reputation in Germany. At the end of the 1870s and in the 1880s a new germ theory, mainly formulated by the German Robert Koch, began to be adopted in Britain. This theory was quite different from Lister's putrefaction theory: it posited specific disease-causing micro-organisms which invaded the body. The Listerians acknowledged this theory but still for a while adhered to their putrefaction theory of wound decay. Cheyne noted in his *Antiseptic Surgery* (1882) that 'antiseptic surgery is simply a struggle with the causes of putrefaction. I have not mentioned the germ theory of infective disease at all. That has no essential bearing on the *principles* of antiseptic surgery', and he chastised surgeons for 'confusing together the two germ theories' (Cheyne, 287–8). Gradually, however, Lister, Cheyne, and other disciples adopted Koch's views and as they did so they modified their practice and theories to take account of them, even though they maintained that their modifications were a development of Lister's earliest opinions. They also took the view that any surgeon achieving good results was practising Listerian antiseptic surgery whatever method was employed. By the late 1880s German germ theory and aseptic surgery (which placed much more stress on the sterility of the whole surgical environment rather than just the wound) were dominant. In 1882 Cheyne took the view that aseptic surgery was 'introduced by Mr. Lister' (Cheyne, 123).

Lister's achievement Any assessment now of how much more successful Lister's antiseptic surgery was (if at all) than that of the practices of other surgeons who were endeavouring to reduce mortality seems impossible.

Equally it is hard to assess how far aseptic surgery was the outcome of antiseptic practices or of the cleanliness tradition. Successful pioneers of abdominal surgery in women, Spencer Wells and Lawson Tait, either gave up Listerian methods or aggressively opposed them. But whatever the merits of the case, the revolution in surgery—for revolution there was—was perceived to be largely Lister's achievement. Lister was of that party which triumphed in late nineteenth-century medicine, indeed triumphed in late nineteenth-century society at large: the party of so-called scientific naturalism. Those identifying with this cause usually embraced Darwinism and campaigned for a greater place for science in education, policy, and industry. They called for the introduction of experimental scientific disciplines into the universities, and in medicine they advocated the large university hospital as the apex of patient treatment, medical education, and research. Lister was one of the heroes of the party. Soon after his move to London two of the foremost scientific naturalists, Thomas Huxley and John Tyndall, proposed Lister for membership of the Athenaeum. The Royal Society was the stronghold of the scientific naturalists and it is testimony to Lister's place within that circle that he was elected president in 1895.

Lister filled the chair of clinical surgery at King's College for fifteen years. During the whole of this time he was actively engaged in operating and teaching and in pursuing his researches in his laboratory at Park Crescent. He had a modest private practice but reportedly this never became extensive because of his unpunctuality. Convinced as he was of the necessity of experimental science for the progress of medicine he took a major part in promoting it. He testified in favour of animal experimentation to the royal commission which reported in 1876. He took an active part in the founding in 1891 of the British Institute of Preventive Medicine on the lines of the Pasteur Institute in Paris, and he became its first chairman. In 1897 its name was changed to the Jenner Institute and again in 1903 it was renamed the Lister Institute of Preventive Medicine. In 1880 he was elected to the council of the Royal College of Surgeons and he served for the usual period of eight years. He was unwilling to serve for a further period and thus was never president. In 1883 a baronetcy was conferred on him, and in 1897 he was raised to the peerage as Baron Lister of Lyme Regis. In 1899 the neurologist Henry Head recorded in a letter:

> The Chinese minister paid Lister the most colossal compliment that it has ever been my lot to hear from any man's mouth—but this is the Chinese way. He stated that he was writing the lives of the hundred greatest men of the world for the perusal of my Imperial master. England furnished him with the names, William Shakespeare, William Harvey 'and you, my Lord are the third', bowing low to Lister in the President's chair. As we cheered I almost expected to see poor Lister fall together in internal agony like Herod the Tetrarch. (Wellcome L.)

Character and final years Lister was regarded by his enemies as distant and even his friends agreed he was not greatly given to laughter. In Glasgow, Edinburgh, and then London, the Listers held dinner parties, of which there are conflicting accounts. John Dobie reported that his chief was full of fun at the dinners and that he had called wine 'the milk of old age' (Fisher, 241). But the surgeon John Leeson observed of one of these occasions that the 'dinner was perfectly correct, verging a little on the side of plainness, as became a Puritan household. There was no smoking, and the wine was partaken sparingly' (Fisher, 241). Politically Lister was a Conservative. In 1902 Lister was one of the twelve original members of the newly constituted Order of Merit. On the occasion of his eightieth birthday in 1907 he received the freedom of the City of London. He remained, however, more fond of Edinburgh. In 1908 Lister left 12 Park Crescent, Portland Place, where he had lived ever since he went to London in 1877, and moved to Park House, Walmer, Kent, where he died on 10 February 1912. Burial in Westminster Abbey was offered, but he had left instructions to be buried by the side of his wife. The funeral service was held in Westminster Abbey on 16 February 1912, and the burial took place at the Hampstead cemetery.

CHRISTOPHER LAWRENCE

Sources R. J. Godlee, *Lord Lister* (1917) • R. B. Fisher, *Joseph Lister, 1827–1912* (1977) • C. Lawrence and R. Dixey, 'Practising on principle: Joseph Lister and the germ theories of disease', *Medical theory, surgical practice*, ed. C. Lawrence (1992), 153–215 • L. Granshaw, '"Upon this principle I have based a practice": the development and reception of antisepsis in Britain, 1867–90', *Medical innovations in historical perspective*, ed. J. V. Pickstone (1992), 17–46 • W. W. Cheyne, *Antiseptic surgery: its principles, practice, history and results* (1882) • *DNB* • *WWW* • G. T. Wrench, *Lord Lister: his life and work* (1913) • Wellcome L., PP HEA D4/5

Archives Commonwealth Mycological Institute, Kew, London, notebooks • Edinburgh Royal Infirmary, minute books • King's College Hospital, London, minute books • NRA, casebooks • Passmore Edwards Museum, London • RCP Lond., letters • RCS Eng., corresp. and papers • Royal College of Physicians and Surgeons of Glasgow, corresp. and papers • Royal Medical Society, Edinburgh, dissertation • Suffolk RO, Ipswich, corresp. and papers • U. Birm. L., letters • U. Glas. L. • Wellcome L., corresp., diary, notebooks, papers, and sketch book | Bodl. Oxf., letters to Sir Henry Acland • Bodl. Oxf., corresp. with Sir Henry Burdett • RCP Lond., corresp. with Sir Thomas Barlow • RCS Eng., corresp. with John Chiene • U. Edin. L., letters to Albert Wilson • W. Sussex RO, letters to Sir Alfred Kempe • Wellcome L., letters to Sir Thomas Barlow • Wellcome L., letters to Lister Institute • Wellcome L., corresp. with Sir Edward Sharpey-Shafer

Likenesses photograph, 1850–59, NPG [*see illus.*] • E. B. Stephens, bust, 1873, St Thomas's Hospital, London • J. H. Lorimer, oils, 1895, U. Edin. • W. W. Ouless, oils, exh. RA 1897, RCS Eng. • M. M. Jenkin, wax medallion, 1898, NPG • C. E. Ritchie, portrait, 1908 • T. Brock, marble bust, 1913, RCS Eng.; related plaster cast in NPG • T. Brock, bronze bust, *c.*1922, Portland Place, London • Barraud, cabinet photograph, NPG • S. Begg, process print, NPG; repro. in *ILN* (9 Jan 1897) • T. Brock, marble medallion, Westminster Abbey, London • H. J. Brooks, group portrait, oils (*Council of the Royal College of Surgeons of England of 1884–5*), RCS Eng. • H. M. Paget, process print (after sketches by A. Cox), NPG; repro. in *The Graphic* (26 Sept 1896) • J. H. Thomas, memorial medallions, UCL; also University College Hospital, London • E. Walker, photogravure photograph (after Moffat), NPG • Walker & Boutall, photogravure photograph (after Barraud), NPG • glass positive photograph, NPG • photographs, Wellcome L.

Wealth at death £67,996 4s. 6d.: resworn probate, 1912, *CGPLA Eng. & Wales*

Lister, Joseph Jackson (1786–1869), wine merchant and microscopist, was born on 11 January 1786 in Lothbury, City of London, the only son of John Lister, a wine merchant, and his wife, Mary Jackson (*d.* 1808). His parents were members of the Society of Friends; his father's family, originally from Yorkshire, had settled in London, and both parents were part of the close-knit Quaker business community of the City. Mary Lister's father, Stephen Jackson, was a wine merchant and on their marriage John Lister left his trade as a watchmaker and took over his father-in-law's business in Lothbury. The Listers had two daughters before their son, Joseph Jackson, was born after a gap of seventeen years. His birth was greeted with rejoicing, and he was given a name commemorating his two grandfathers. He was a gifted child, and was educated from 1792 to 1796 at a Friends' school in Hitchin, and then for a year at Rochester School. At the age of twelve in 1798, he was sent as a boarder to one of the best private schools open to members of the Society of Friends, run by Thomas Thompson at Little Compton in Dorset. The school encouraged general reading and the pupils were allowed some discretion in the employment of their time. That was good for Lister, who had great mental curiosity and was well able to follow his own paths to knowledge. He was said to be the only boy at the school who owned a telescope.

Joseph Jackson Lister (1786–1869), by Maull & Co.

At the age of fourteen Lister left school to work in the family wine business, living above the premises in Lothbury with his parents until the death of his mother in 1808. His father then moved to Stoke Newington, where he lived with his unmarried daughter, taking an annuity out of the business. Joseph Jackson Lister was now a wine merchant, and about 1812 he transferred to a new address nearby at 5 Tokenhouse Yard, where, on 14 July 1818, he brought Isabella Harris (*c.*1795–1864), a schoolteacher, as his bride. Four years later they moved to Stoke Newington, and then in 1826 Lister bought Upton House, West Ham, where he lived for the rest of his life. The property was large enough to provide space for a growing family of three daughters and four sons, of whom Joseph *Lister became Baron Lister of Lyme Regis, the famous surgeon, and Arthur *Lister became a botanist. These moves were made possible by the addition to the staff of Lister's nephew, Richard Low Beck, who became a resident partner.

Alongside the family man with a successful business and an energetic younger associate, was the meticulous inventor, who, in his spare time, and for no remuneration, carried out the research in the design of lenses that transformed the microscope into the most ubiquitous and practically useful of all scientific instruments. The development and use of the microscope, from its invention in 1608 until the early years of the nineteenth century, were hampered by the quality of glass available for the lenses, and by aberrations of the image. Chromatic aberration was the name given to the coloured edge to the image caused by unequal refraction of light rays. This was corrected for the telescope by John Dollond in 1758, and for the microscope by the Amsterdam instrument maker, Harmanus van Deijl, who published in 1807. The other serious source of aberration resulted from the spherical curvature of the lenses, which produced a blurred image, and this problem was still unsolved in the early 1800s. Lister described how, in his thirty-eighth year, he became involved in the design of microscope lenses. about 1824 he saw at William Tulley's, the instrument maker, an achromatic object glass of two convex lenses of plate glass sandwiching a concave lens of flint glass. By a tracing made from a camera lucida with his own microscope he showed Tulley that his objective was clumsy. Lister's suggestions resulted in '"Tulley's 9/10" which became *the* microscopic object-glass of the time' (J. Lister, 141).

Further researches resulted in Lister's important discovery announced in the paper 'On the improvement of compound microscopes' read before the Royal Society on 21 January 1830. There he stated that an achromatic combination of a negative flint glass lens with a positive crown glass lens has two aplanatic focal points. The spherical aberration is overcorrected for all points between these foci, and is undercorrected for all points outside. So if a doublet objective is made that is composed of two sets of achromatic lens combinations, spherical aberration can be avoided if the object to be viewed is at the shorter aplanatic focus of the first lens pair, which then passes the rays on to the longer aplanatic focus of the second pair. Lister's design of the first aberration corrected object glass for the microscope thus brought to an end the trial and error efforts of instrument makers and scientists alike by establishing a scientific principle for the making of microscope objectives. These could now be free of both achromatic and spherical aberration, and also of the effect known as coma, which caused a spot of light to appear elongated and fuzzy, like a comet. The design of low-power objectives for the optical microscope even at the end of the twentieth century was based on Lister's discovery. Its importance was recognized by the election of Lister to fellowship of the Royal Society in February 1832.

Having made a highly significant contribution to microscope design Lister was eager to continue his research but found that Tulley could not spare the time to make lenses to his specification. Therefore Lister began, in late 1830, to do his own grinding and polishing. As he explained:

> Without having ever before cut brass or ground more than a single surface of a piece of glass, I managed to make the tools and to manufacture a combination of three double object-glasses, without spoiling a lens or altering a curve. (J. Lister, 140)

The optical instrument makers did not immediately adopt Lister's designs, since there is always inertia in economic production. He had hoped that his improvements would be followed up by the opticians, but the object glasses produced by the makers continued to be of the usual simple design of two or three plano-convex compound lenses until the beginning of 1837. It was then that Andrew Ross, a leading maker, made a one-eighth inch objective to Lister's design, and in 1840 James Smith constructed quarter inch objectives that became popular with microscopists. Over the next four decades, with Lister's designs commercially available, the microscope became a serious scientific instrument in many fields, notably in medicine and public health, and it reached its limit of resolution in the 1880s.

James Smith's association with Lister was a long and important one. In 1826 he made a new form of microscope stand to Lister's design, intended to provide the greater stability demanded by the increased magnification that could be achieved. This innovation was also gradually adopted by microscopists. Richard Beck, the son of Lister's nephew and partner, Richard Low Beck, was apprenticed to Smith and went into partnership with him in 1847. Richard Beck was joined in the firm by his brother Joseph in 1851 and the latter was made a partner in 1857. The firm of R. and J. Beck was established on Smith's retirement in 1865. The optical factory of the firm was opened at Holloway in 1853, appropriately named the Lister Works, and it clearly followed the Quaker tradition. The microscopist Thomas Hudson recorded in his diary a visit to the works in May 1854, finding it 'a model optical manufactory having a Steam Engine working Lathes &c this is a most complete establishment having a Library and Reading and Refreshment Room' (Turner, 'Frederick Thomas Hudson's microscopical diary', 198).

Lister was not only a designer, but also throughout his life a skilled microscopist. He published in 1827 a paper with Thomas Hodgkin that described for the first time the true form and most accurate measure of the diameter of red blood cells. His observations of zoophytes and ascidians were reported to the Royal Society in 1834. He did considerable research into the resolving power of the human eye and of the microscope, anticipating some of the findings of Abbe and Helmholtz, but did not publish the paper, which existed ready for press, during his lifetime. Lister's manuscripts include designs and draft papers, and these, together with a case of tools, lenses, and microscope objectives made by Joseph Jackson Lister were presented to the Royal Microscopical Society on 15 May 1912 by the executors of Lord Lister.

Lister's greatest work was his paper on the theory of the microscopic image drafted during 1842–3, although it was not published in his lifetime; it represented over ten years' work. On receiving Lord Lister's bequest, the council of the Royal Microscopical Society asked Alexander Eugen Conrady, a lens designer who became, in 1917, the first professor of optical design at Imperial College, London, to examine the Lister archive. He transcribed (not always accurately) for publication in the *Journal of the Royal Microscopical Society*, 33 (1913), 27–55, Lister's memorandum to Andrew Ross dated 1837, some correspondence, and the draft paper 'On the limit to defining-power, in vision with the unassisted eye, the telescope, and the microscope', dated 1842–3; it occupies pp. 34–55. Conrady commented that the paper is the first proof that J. J. Lister knew in 1832 that the resolving-power of microscope objectives grows not with the angle itself, as was thought for many years after that date, but with the chord of an angle, later called numerical aperture (Conrady, 52). The paper is evidence that Lister, having provided the original impetus to developing the scientific microscope, derived the law of image formation three decades before Ernest Abbe of Jena University. The development of the instrument would have been even more rapid had he published this paper. It also seems curious that his son, Lord Lister, when writing his father's obituary in 1869, did not see fit to publish it, for he was in possession of the archive.

Lister lived during the golden age of the light microscope, and was admired by many of its leading users. He was one of the group of microscopists who met in September 1839 and agreed to form a society to promote microscopical investigation, the Microscopical Society of London, later to receive a royal charter. John Quekett, the first secretary of the society, dedicated to Lister his best-selling *Practical Treatise on the Use of the Microscope* (1848), with the words: 'To Joseph Jackson Lister Esq. FRS, to whose labours in perfecting the achromatic compound microscope science in England is so deeply indebted'. Lister died at his home, Upton House, on 24 October 1869, of old age and pneumonia. G. L'E. TURNER

Sources J. J. Lister, 'On some properties in achromatic object-glasses applicable to the improvement of the microscope', *PTRS*, 120 (1830), 187–200 • MHS Oxf., Lister papers, Royal Microscopical Society archive • B. Bracegirdle, 'Famous microscopists: Joseph Jackson Lister, 1786–1869', *Proceedings of the Royal Microscopical Society*, 22 (1987), 273–97 • A. E. Conrady, 'The unpublished papers of J. J. Lister', *Journal of the Royal Microscopical Society* (1913), 27–55 • W. Beck, *Family fragments respecting the ancestry, acquaintance and* *marriage of Richard Low Beck and Rachel Lucas* (1897) [privately printed] • J. Lister, 'Obituary notice of the late Joseph Jackson Lister, F.R.S., Z.S., with special reference to his labours in the improvement of the achromatic microscope', *Monthly Microscopical Journal*, 3 (1870), 134–43 • J. C. Deiman, 'Microscope optics and J. J. Lister's influence on the development of the achromatic objective, 1750–1850', PhD diss., ICL, 1992 • G. L'E. Turner, 'Frederick Thomas Hudson's microscopical diary, 1849–1864', *The Quekett Journal of Microscopy*, 37/3 (spring 1994), 191–206 • G. L'E. Turner, 'The microscope as a technical frontier in science', *Proceedings of the Royal Microscopical Society*, 2 (1967), 175–99 • G. L'E. Turner, *The great age of the microscope: the collection of the Royal Microscopical Society through 150 years* (1989), 309–10, no. 382 [experimental lenses by J. J. Lister] • R. B. Fisher, *Joseph Lister, 1827–1912* (1977) • *Lister centenary exhibition at the Wellcome Historical Medical Museum, handbook, 1927* (1927) • J. J. Lister, account books, 1807–69, American Philosophical Society Library, Philadelphia [7 vols.] • T. Hodgkin and J. J. Lister, 'Notice of some microscopic observations of the blood and animal tissues', *Philosophical Magazine*, new ser., 2 (1827), 130–38 • J. J. Lister, 'Some observations on the structure and functions of tubular and cellular polypi, and of ascidiae', *PTRS*, 124 (1834), 365–88 • d. cert.

Archives MHS, technical material and MSS • Sci. Mus., four microscopes [incl. the first made in 1826 to his design by James Smith] • Wellcome L., account books and MSS • Wellcome L., microscope collection

Likenesses Maull & Polyblank, photograph, *c.*1860, repro. in Beck, *Family fragments* • J. J. Lister, self-portrait, repro. in Fisher, *Joseph Lister* • Maull & Co., photograph, Sci. Mus. [*see illus.*]

Wealth at death under £80,000: probate, 29 Nov 1869, *CGPLA Eng. & Wales*

Lister, Martin (*bap.* **1639**, *d.* **1712**), physician and naturalist, was baptized on 11 April 1639 at Radclive, Buckinghamshire, fourth of the ten children of Sir Martin Lister (1602–1670), farmer and MP for Brackley, and his second wife, Susanna (1604?–1669), widow of Sir Gifford Thornhurst (*d.* 1627), and daughter of Sir Alexander Temple of St Mary's Hoo, Kent, and his first wife, Mary. In 1646 Sir Martin moved with his family to the manor of Thorpe Arnold, Leicestershire. Young Martin is said, by Anthony Wood, to have been educated under the care of his great-uncle, Sir Matthew *Lister MD, who was childless. He attended Melton Mowbray School and was admitted as a pensioner to St John's College, Cambridge, in 1655. The following year Sir Matthew died and the family moved to his old home, the manor of Burwell, Lincolnshire, to which Martin returned after graduating BA in 1659. At the Restoration he was appointed fellow of St John's College by royal mandate. It is probable that he owed this to his great-uncle's service as physician to the king's father and grandfather.

In 1663 Lister travelled to France, joining other English scholars at Montpellier. Protestants could not enrol at the university, but Lister was able to join an academy through which he studied medicine, anatomy, and botany. He travelled a lot, notably for a few months in 1665–6 with John Ray and Philip Skippon, when they made observations on the natural history of the countryside, and when they travelled back to England.

Lister and Ray became firm friends and began a correspondence on scientific matters that lasted more than ten years. Meanwhile Lister did a little teaching at St John's College, but he secured some financial independence through a settlement of land by his father. In the summer of 1669 he resigned his fellowship and married, in York, Hannah (1645–1695), daughter of Thomas Parkinson of Carleton Hall in Craven, Yorkshire.

The Listers moved to Hannah's home for the birth of her first child, Susanna *Lister, while Lister explored the natural history of Craven. In 1670 he established a medical practice at York. Here were born other children: Anne *Lister [*see under* Lister, Susanna], Michael, Frances, Dorothy, Alexander, and Barbara. He gathered around him a club of virtuosi, including the artists Francis Place and William Lodge, who illustrated some of Lister's works. Lister continued his correspondence with John Ray, and with Henry Oldenburg, secretary of the Royal Society. Several of his letters were published in the *Philosophical Transactions*, and in 1671 Lister was admitted as fellow of the Royal Society. He continued to publish there and wrote his first book, the *Historia animalium Angliae tres tractatus* (1678–81), of which the first part was a systematic description of English spiders and their habits, while the others were about terrestrial and marine molluscs. Other books followed, on insects (translation of work by the Dutch entomologist Goedart), mineral waters, and Lister's collected papers from the *Philosophical Transactions*.

In September 1683 the Lister family moved to London, where their last child, Jane, was born. Martin Lister began to participate regularly in meetings of the Royal Society and was elected to its council. However, lacking a medical degree he would not have been permitted by the Royal College of Physicians to practise medicine in London. Perhaps it was to win goodwill at Oxford that, in 1682, shortly after the opening of the Ashmolean Museum, he had made substantial donations to it of books, manuscripts, antiquities, and other specimens. In March 1684 he was granted a DM by the University of Oxford. Two months later he was accepted by the Royal College of Physicians, and began to practise medicine among the highest levels of society, including attending the post-mortem of Charles II. When James II renewed the charter of the Royal College in 1687 Lister was named a fellow; in 1694 he was elected censor.

In January 1685 Lister was elected vice-president of the Royal Society. Since the president, Samuel Pepys, was often absent, Lister chaired most of the meetings that year. But his attendance ended abruptly, early in 1686, although he continued to contribute to the *Transactions*. He frequently attended the weekly meetings of the Temple Coffee House club of naturalists in the 1690s. His chief activity in natural history at this time was the preparation of a classified set of copperplate-engravings of all known shells, largely executed by his eldest children, Susanna and Anne. The work is divided into four sections, the first of which (on land snails) was issued in 1685 under the title *De cochleis*, the others following in successive years. Sets were sent to friends for review and each was continually revised: the final version, *Historia sive synopsis methodica conchyliorum*, with over a thousand plates, was not completed until 1697. He also published, in three parts, descriptions of the internal anatomy of Mollusca: *Exercitatio anatomica* (1694–6). He published a set of essays on common diseases, *Sex exercitationes medicinales de quibusdam morbis chronicis* (1694), in order 'to stop the censorious mouthes who thinke and say a man that writes on Insects can be but a trifler in Physic' (BL, MS Ashmole 1816, fol. 113).

Two of the Listers' children died as infants. A tablet in Westminster Abbey bears the simple but eloquent statement 'Jane Lister, dear Childe, died Oct 7th, 1688'. Hannah Lister died in 1695 and was buried at St Paul's Church, Clapham. The only surviving son, Alexander, matriculated at Balliol College, Oxford, in the same year, but in 1697 earned his father's displeasure by an imprudent marriage. In October 1698 Martin Lister married Jane (*d.* 1736), daughter of Peter Cullen.

Late in 1697 William Bentinck, Lord Portland, was sent on a diplomatic mission to Paris, and Lister accompanied him as physician. His duties left him ample time to meet and talk with other intellectuals, to see their collections and gardens, and to explore the city. He was there for six months and shortly after his return published *A Journey to Paris in the Year 1698* (1699). The book ran to three editions within a year, but was lampooned by William King for its supposed triviality. In fact it is a unique first-hand account of Parisian scientific society, and a useful description of the city and its life.

Lister was asthmatic: he enjoyed the dry air of France, but not the 'choakie air of London' (BL, MS Ashmole 1816, fol. 126). In 1699 he and Jane moved from London, taking lodgings at Leatherhead, and in 1702 they moved to Epsom, though he still travelled to London when necessary. He had a useful connection at court: Sarah, duchess of Marlborough, was Lister's niece by his mother's first marriage, and a close friend of Queen Anne. In 1702 he became fourth physician to the queen. At Epsom he spent much time in his garden, but continued to write. He translated the aphorisms of Sanctorius and Hippocrates (1702), and a Roman cookery book in *De arte coquinaria* (1705). His last works were published in 1709: an essay on body fluids, *Dissertatio de humoribus*, and an account of British beetles appended to John Ray's *Historia insectorum*. In 1710 he was appointed second physician to the queen, but he died at Epsom on 2 February 1712, and was buried beside his first wife at Clapham, where there was formerly a monument to his memory. He was commemorated by Robert Brown in the genus *Listeria* among orchids.

Martin Lister was a successful and respected physician who had the gift of 'hitting distempers' (Gunther, 288) but is better remembered for his work in natural history. In both fields he was initially a keen observer and had some good ideas, but later became more conservative. He was reluctant to use a microscope because, by revealing details of tiny creatures, it seemed to be disrespectful to the ancients. His advice to a prospective medical student in 1698 was to study 'the ancients … he will find that all the rest have added little' (BL, MS Ashmole 1818, fol. 124). His career was marked by contentious relations with other physicians, with fellows of the Royal Society, and with two of his children. In natural history he was the first to study spiders, making detailed observations on their structure and behaviour. He was the first to suggest that rocks might be characterized by their fossil contents, and to propose the creation of geological maps. A painstaking observer, he was well aware of the differences between fossils and modern shells and was therefore prepared to accept that they were 'formed stones' (like crystals). 'If otherwise, the animals they so exactly represent have become extinct' (Stearns, xlvi). He was the first to attempt a comparative anatomy of the Mollusca, and his *Historia conchyliorum* was the bible of conchologists for over a hundred years. It is for that work that he is chiefly remembered. J. D. WOODLEY

Sources J. Carr, 'The biological work of Martin Lister (1639–1712)', PhD diss., U. Leeds, 1974 • W. Goulding, 'Martin Lister, M.D., F.R.S.', *Associated Architectural Societies' Reports and Papers*, 25 (1900), 329–70 • R. P. Stearns, ed., *A journey to Paris in the year 1698, by Martin Lister* (1967) • R. Davies, 'A memoir of Martin Lister', *Yorkshire Archaeological and Topographical Journal*, 2 (1871–2), 297–320 • G. L. Wilkins, 'Notes on the *Historia conchyliorum* of Martin Lister, 1638–1712', *Journal of the Society of the Bibliography of Natural History*, 3 (1953–60), 196–205 • J. D. Woodley, 'Anne Lister, illustrator of Martin Lister's *Historiae conchyliorum*, 1685–1692', *Archives of Natural History*, 21 (1994), 225–9 • J. Parker and B. Hadley, eds., *Martin Lister's English spiders 1678* (1992) • C. R. Markham, *Life of Robert Fairfax of Steeton* (1885) • *Further correspondence of John Ray*, ed. R. W. T. Gunther, Ray Society, 114 (1928) • Venn, *Alum. Cant.* • Munk, *Roll* • parish register, Radclive, Buckinghamshire

Archives Bodl. Oxf., Radcliffe Science Library, notes • Bodl. Oxf., corresp. and papers • Linn. Soc., notes • NHM, papers • NHM, plants at Oxford • RCP Lond., commentary on St Sanctorius • RS, papers | BL, Sloane MSS, letters to Sir Hans Sloane, etc. • Bodl. Oxf., letters to Edward Lhuyd • RS, letters to Henry Oldenburg

Likenesses oils, repro. in Wilkins, 'Notes on the *Historia conchyliorum*'

Wealth at death property in York; provided for £1400 bond

Lister, Sir Matthew (*bap.* 1571, *d.* 1656), physician, son of William Lister, and younger brother of Edward *Lister, was born at Thornton, Yorkshire, and baptized on 7 April 1571 at Gisburn, Yorkshire. He entered Oriel College, Oxford, on 23 February 1588, graduated BA in 1591, became a fellow of his college, and proceeded MA in 1595. He graduated MD at Basel about 1603 and was incorporated at Oxford in 1605, and at Cambridge in 1608. He was elected a fellow of the College of Physicians, London, in 1607 along with William Harvey, serving as censor in 1608, and as an elect in 1625. On 4 October 1614 Lister and Sir William Paddy were sent to persuade the lord mayor, Sir Thomas Middleton, that the City had no right to force the college to bear arms, and succeeded in establishing this immunity. Soon after his election to the college, Lister began a successful court practice, serving as physician to James I and Queen Anne, and treating William Cecil during his final illness in 1612. Lister later became physician to Mary, countess of Pembroke, and there were rumours that they were married shortly before her death. However, in Lister's will made on 18 August 1656, he refers to 'my loving wife the Ladie Anne Lister' (PRO, PROB 11/261).

The medical faculty at Basel was known for its support of chemical and Paracelsian remedies, and Lister associated with other chemical physicians at court, such as Sir Theodore Turquet de Mayerne, whose manuscripts contain a number of Lister's remedies. At the request of the

Sir Matthew Lister (*bap.* 1571, *d.* 1656), by Paul van Somer, 1646

privy council, Lister also assisted Mayerne in drawing up plans for a board of health for the City of London and for the construction of a pest house to control epidemics of the plagues. Their proposal would have removed the responsibility of public health from the City and placed it more directly under the crown and the privy council, but Charles I allowed the project to die. In May 1644 Lister and Mayerne made an emergency trip to Exeter, responding to Charles's panicky letter from Oxford concerning Queen Henrietta's health. Pregnant and past due, the queen was successfully delivered after the two aged physicians made the seven days' journey in her chariot. Lister was knighted at Oatlands, Surrey, on 11 October 1636. He retired to Burwell, Lincolnshire, and died there on 14 December 1656.

BRIAN NANCE

Sources B. Hamey, Bustorum aliquot reliquae, BL, Sloane MS 2149, fol. 69 • annals, RCP Lond. • T. Turquet de Mayerne, Recipes from Lister, BL, Sloane MS 3426, fols. 29–72v • T. Turquet de Mayerne, Recipes from Lister, BL, Sloane MS 3505, fols. 25–42, 57–67 • *CSP dom.* • Foster, *Alum. Oxon.* • Munk, *Roll* • C. Goodall, *The College of Physicians vindicated* (1676) • H. Cook, 'Policing the health of London: the College of Physicians and the early Stuart monarchy', *Social History of Medicine*, 2 (1989), 1–34 • W. J. Birkin, 'The fellows of the Royal College of Physicians of London, 1603–1643: a social study', PhD diss., University of North Carolina at Chapel Hill, 1977 • will, PRO, PROB 11/261, sig. 9

Likenesses P. van Somer, line engraving, 1646, BM, NPG [*see illus.*]

Wealth at death property in Strand and Covent Garden, London; also property in Thorpe Arnold, Leicestershire: will, PRO, PROB 11/261, sig. 9

Lister, Philip Cunliffe- [*formerly* Philip Lloyd-Greame], **first earl of Swinton (1884–1972)**, politician, was born on 1 May 1884 at East Ayton, near Scarborough, the third son of Yarburgh George Lloyd-Greame (1840–1928), later of Sewerby House, near Bridlington, and his wife, Dora Letitia O'Brien (*d.* 1922), daughter of James Thomas *O'Brien, the Irish Anglican bishop of Ossory. He took the name Cunliffe-Lister in 1924.

Early years and career: marriage and family Lloyd-Greame was at school at Winchester College and read law at University College, Oxford, in which subject he obtained a second class in 1906. Rejecting the diplomatic career which had been mooted, he was admitted at the Inner Temple in 1908 and set up chambers in Lincoln's Inn two years later. He specialized in mining law. In 1911 he was adopted as Conservative candidate for his local constituency of Buckrose, though in the event he was never to contest it.

On 5 September 1912 Lloyd-Greame married Mary Constance (Mollie), daughter of the Revd Charles Ingram Boynton of Barmston, near Sewerby. Her mother was the second and only married daughter of Samuel Cunliffe-Lister, first Earl Masham of Swinton, mill owner and industrialist, to whose estate of more than 20,000 acres near Ripon she fell heir, though not until 1924. It was in connection with this inheritance that Philip changed his surname. Although it was not certain in 1912 that Mary Boynton would inherit, there was at least the prospect that Philip would have substantial independent means to underpin the political career on which he had early settled. Their marriage lasted for sixty years (Mollie died in 1974) but both their sons predeceased them. The elder, John, born in 1913, died of wounds received in north Africa in 1943. The younger, Philip, born in 1918, won the DSC while serving as a meteorological reconnaissance pilot, but was then a prisoner of war in Germany for two years. He found it difficult to adjust to the post-war world and took his own life in 1956. The earldom passed to their grandson, David Yarburgh (*b.* 1937), whose wife received a life peerage as Lady Masham of Ilton in 1970.

Lloyd-Greame's career took unexpected turns with the advent of the First World War. He enlisted immediately in August 1914, though it was not until May 1916, having until then been engaged in various training activities, that he saw action in France, and in the event only briefly. Serving as a brigade-major, he won the MC for gallantry on the Somme in September 1916, but had to be invalided home in the following month. In July 1917, having recovered, he began working for Sir Auckland Geddes, then director of recruiting at the War Office. When Geddes became minister of national service, Lloyd-Greame occupied a senior administrative position in that ministry. In this role, as a temporary civil servant working on manpower priorities, he came into frequent contact with Lloyd George, Bonar

Philip Cunliffe-Lister, first earl of Swinton (1884–1972), by Sir Oswald Birley, 1933

Law, and Smuts. In 1920 he was created KBE in recognition of his services.

The Board of Trade In December 1918 Lloyd-Greame was elected as Conservative MP for Hendon—and remained as its member until he accepted a peerage in 1935. He played a prominent part in the newly founded British Commonwealth Union, which sought to promote the interests of business in the political arena. He was a committed tariff reformer and supporter of imperial preference. With such a background it is not surprising that he became parliamentary secretary to the Board of Trade in August 1920. In 1921 he was appointed director of the department of overseas trade. His work centred upon protective measures designed to 'safeguard' British industry. He gained insight into another political world as a member of the British delegation to the Genoa conference in April 1922. He thought Lloyd George too sanguine in supposing that an accommodation with the new Soviet state would be possible—and said so. Nevertheless, both men respected each other. In June 1922 Lloyd-Greame was effectively the leader of the UK delegation to another international conference, this time at The Hague, but it also failed to resolve the complex issues of private property, debts, and credit which dominated the discussion.

In the early months of 1922 Lloyd-Greame was still proclaiming himself in the press as an 'unrepentant Coalitionist' but by October he was voting with the majority of Conservative MPs in wishing to end their party's continuing support for the coalition. Helped by the fact that some senior party figures held aloof from the Conservative administration which Bonar Law then formed, Lloyd-Greame came into the cabinet at the early age of thirty-eight, after just four years in the Commons, as president of the Board of Trade. His relationship with the prime minister was close, though since Bonar Law survived his electoral victory by only six months, it could not constitute a basis for further political advancement. In his new post Lloyd-Greame continued to push for the implementation of duties to protect various British industries from 'unfair competition'. The possibility of financial co-operation between different parts of the empire and the mother country excited his enthusiasm. He was naturally disappointed by the outcome of the general election of December 1923, which produced a minority Labour administration and threatened the commercial policies to which he was so much committed. A year later, however, with the demise of that government, he was back at his old post, having used the summer to concern himself in Argentina with the pressing business of the Anglo-Argentine Tramway Company. The year out of office had also allowed him to move into the great house on the magnificent Swinton estate. Its attractions henceforth tempted him away from London, at weekends and during recesses, with impressive regularity.

Cunliffe-Lister, as he had now become, remained at the Board of Trade under Baldwin until the government was defeated in the general election of 1929. The central issue throughout his term in that office remained that of 'safeguarding'. Argument among colleagues revolved around the scope of such protection and the timing of any possible extension beyond the existing provision. His own commitment remained strong but was somewhat tempered by what he judged to be political practicalities. He forged a good working relationship with Neville Chamberlain, less so with his prime minister. There were particular matters on which he left his mark. He was instrumental in the passage of the Cinematograph Films Act (1927), designed to ensure that a British industry survived the American onslaught and that a larger and increasing proportion of films exhibited throughout the empire should be made within it. His support for what became the Empire Marketing Board (1926) was another reflection of the imperial emphasis in his thinking. The responsibilities of his department naturally gave him a position of importance both leading up to and during the general strike. He had been prepared for the government to impose a solution if the coal owners and the miners could not come to an agreement on the issues that separated them. However, he was a 'hardliner' in May 1926. His wife had become a coal owner and this fact had earlier led him to offer his resignation, though it was not accepted. The reputation he acquired during these years was that of an effective minister, somewhat abrasive in style, but personally very interested in and knowledgeable about the topics with which he dealt on a daily basis.

The Colonial Office On the formation of the National Government in August 1931 Cunliffe-Lister was one of the four Conservatives included in the new cabinet, again as president of the Board of Trade. He pressed strongly for the adoption of the 'full tariff': the time for compromises had passed and the political circumstances were now favourable. However, when changes were made in November 1931, after the election which massively endorsed the

National Government, he moved to the Colonial Office. A possibility that he might have become foreign secretary had apparently received a royal frown. It was thought that his rather caustic wit and direct approach rendered Cunliffe-Lister unsuitable for the diplomatic world.

In fact the Colonial Office suited his interests and convictions very well. Immediately, it enabled him to make a significant contribution to the Import Duties Bill and to the preparations, through the first half of 1932, for the Imperial Economic Conference to be held in Ottawa in July. His actual role in the conference, however, was secondary—and as a representative of the colonies rather than the United Kingdom itself; nevertheless he took satisfaction at its outcome. The colonial secretary had ceased, since 1925, to have responsibility for relations with the self-governing dominions. These were handled by a separate ministry. Even so, the exclusion of the dominions still left him with an extraordinary portfolio of responsibilities in different parts of the world. His zeal for facts and detail soon found expression in the compilation of *An Economic Survey of the Colonial Empire* (1932), and his enthusiasm for the potential it disclosed was very apparent. Although he had the safeguarding of British interests very much in mind, he was not insensitive to the issues of under-development and poverty which he encountered in the empire. A hallmark of his tenure of the post was an emphasis on thinking about the colonies as a whole, very diverse though they were. When later he left the Colonial Office, one admirer went so far as to suppose that Cunliffe-Lister had hammered out a single colonial empire from a scattered collection of colonies. The changes in recruitment to a now unified colonial service, which he implemented, were a means to this end. Men should move around. It could not be said that the colonial secretary himself did not move around. Attracted by air travel, he visited the Middle East and heard at first hand about the problems in the mandated territories of Iraq and Palestine, about Cyprus and about east Africa. He set a fierce pace and expected those who worked with him to fall in behind. His stature in the government was considerable but even so he was not at its heart. Still only fifty, and the fourth-youngest member of the cabinet, his time might yet come.

Secretary of state for air In June 1935, in succession to Lord Londonderry, who had become an electoral liability, Cunliffe-Lister was made secretary of state for air. The defence white paper in March 1935 had set out the government's rearmament plans and at the end of April Cunliffe-Lister rather than Londonderry had been asked by Baldwin to chair a small sub-committee to produce a programme for restoring air parity with Germany, which Hitler himself encouraged British visitors to believe had already been lost. In this capacity he lost no time in trying to establish the facts and identifying how an accelerated programme could be put in train. He treated with some contempt estimates of the number of trained German pilots who were available—and doubled the number. The central dilemma before the committee was whether to proceed as a matter of urgency with bulk orders before prototypes had been fully tested: how to balance quality and quantity. After much debate the cabinet in May accepted a new expansion plan (scheme C), which identified numbers and types of aircraft, in all amounting to 3800 aircraft, to be ready by April 1937. It was this plan, which he had already had such a major part in formulating, which was the basis of Cunliffe-Lister's work when he moved to the Air Ministry.

An argument for dropping Londonderry, among a number available, had been that the new minister should sit in the Commons at this particularly sensitive juncture. Strangely, however, in November 1935, a few days after the general election which had confirmed the government in office, it was announced that Cunliffe-Lister had accepted a peerage as Viscount Swinton. It seems unlikely that Baldwin pressed this upon him. The assumption must be, though it cannot be proved, that it reflected Swinton's own wishes. If so, while it may have been gratifying to attach his own name to a property which was his wife's, the reason is likely to reflect his own conception of his prospects and of the immediate task before him. He had never found the House of Commons or constituency work very congenial. He had contemplated leaving politics altogether on several occasions. He had an executive temperament and now had a major job, possibly a vital one, which he could better concentrate upon if he were free from the time-consuming pressures of the Commons. If such reasoning may be assumed, it is not an exaggeration to say that it was a serious error of judgement, as he himself came to recognize. The rearmament programme, as far as it concerned the Air Ministry, was not simply a technical operation requiring the 'hustling' capacity that Swinton undoubtedly possessed. Public speculation and anxiety swirled around air power at this time and, far from being an advantage, his removal from the Commons made it impossible for him directly to engage with the questions and criticisms which were raised there. His junior ministerial colleagues who did sit in the Commons were no substitute. The role he played as a minister was unusual in the extent to which he was a kind of managing director, a term used by Neville Chamberlain, then still chancellor of the exchequer, to describe him at this time.

In cabinet and in his own ministry, Swinton proved a forceful figure who forged an effective working relationship with Lord Weir, his unofficial industrial adviser, who had himself been president of the Air Council in 1918. He was not overawed by his chiefs of the air staff, or indeed by any of the service members of the Air Council. He did not expect a civil servant secretary to the Air Council, however experienced, to have an enlarged concept of his responsibilities. Sir Christopher Bullock did have such a conception and Swinton may well not have been sorry—to put it no more strongly—when Bullock was dismissed on other grounds in July 1936. In short, no one with whom he worked had any doubt that Swinton was his own man. Together with Weir he immersed himself energetically in the complex task of assessing both the merits of particular aircraft types, at a time of rapid changes in design and capability, and the capacity of the 'approved firms' in the aircraft industry, which was believed to be able to deliver the necessary production. As time passed, however, and as the international situation worsened, scheme C had to be replaced by others with more ambitious targets. There was running debate on the subject of German air power, with various figures being tossed about—one unusual source of information being directly from the state secretary of the German ministry of aviation. The further expansion entailed bringing forward the 'shadow' armament factories, which had been designed to exist alongside industries—notably the motor vehicle industry—which were still engaged in normal production and trade. In the complex negotiations that followed Swinton's manner was frequently brusque and there was a public row with Lord Nuffield. Since the government remained opposed to taking statutory powers to direct industry, throughout Swinton's tenure at the Air Ministry the burden of negotiating voluntary agreements was extremely heavy. Another demanding task was the chairmanship of the air defence research sub-committee, one not made any easier by Churchill's joining the committee and the battle of the scientists F. A. Lindemann and Sir Henry Tizard, which then raged. The minister gave very firm backing to the development of radar. Speaking more generally of Swinton's support for the work of scientists, Tizard commented in 1940 that he was the only air minister with whom he had had to deal who could understand their recommendations and take action on them. In March 1937, as a result of over-taxing his strength, Swinton had to take a month's sick leave.

A complication for Swinton, as for all the service ministers—for it entailed some circumscription of their roles—was the appointment in February 1936 of Sir Thomas Inskip as minister for the co-ordination of defence. In fact the prime minister had initially considered Swinton for the post but he was reluctant to dislodge him from the Air Ministry, and his being in the Lords was a disadvantage. Inskip's somewhat ill-defined role necessarily affected the way business was done and gave the new minister a pivotal position in allocating resources between the services. It was inevitable, given the expansion of the air force, that the costs gave rise to inter-service arguments over priorities and the overall strategy. Inevitably, in this situation, alliances and alignments shifted. In some circumstances Inskip was an ally and in others an opponent. Swinton reluctantly had to accept Inskip's settlement in July 1937 of the long-running dispute between the Air Ministry and the Admiralty concerning the control of naval aviation. Dialogue with Inskip on costs and priorities was almost constant in the context of overall cabinet policy, and Swinton increasingly found that where Inskip was backed on a number of issues by Neville Chamberlain, now prime minister, he could not carry the day. Additionally, in the early months of 1938 critics in the press and in the Commons itself pressed strongly that a secretary of state should be in the Commons. Both the way in which an inquiry into civil aviation under Lord Cadman was set up and its critical report also added to Swinton's difficulties. Chamberlain felt it necessary to defend him publicly on several occasions in spring 1938. By 16 May 1938, however, the prime minister felt that he could do so no longer in the wake of a critical Commons motion a few days earlier on which many of the government's own supporters abstained. Swinton had already indicated his willingness to step down and acknowledged the handicap which his presence in the Lords now constituted. He declined the offer of another office and indeed indicated that he might never come back into political life. The resignation did not result in a breach with Chamberlain, whom he continued to support in the Munich crisis of September 1938 and beyond. The further expansion of rearmament, agreed after the German invasion of Austria, gave Swinton some satisfaction. Nevertheless, he understandably found it hard that his resignation could be interpreted as a confession of failure. It was only in 1940, with the battle of Britain, fought by the Hurricanes and Spitfires he had ordered under an operational system he had backed, that his achievements in office began to be recognized, even by Churchill, one of his strongest critics at the time.

Later career At the time of his resignation Swinton was only fifty-four, but he had reached the summit of his career. He held a variety of posts of varying significance thereafter, but none matched in importance that which he held as secretary of state for air at this critical time. From September 1939 until June 1942 he worked variously on behalf of the Ministry of Economic Warfare and had a co-ordinating role in relation to internal security matters in the new security executive. In June 1942 he was sent to west Africa as resident minister at a time when the region, and its raw materials, was of increasing strategic importance. It was a task which enabled him to bring together various aspects of his previous ministerial experience as he tackled a range of commercial, military, and administrative issues. His determination to see the region as a whole disconcerted the four governors of the particular British territories involved. Believing that the pace of political change would be slow, he thought that what he called a sound progressive policy would not be upset by ephemeral African agitation. Although far removed from the centre of decision-making in London, it seems clear that Swinton relished his role and perhaps, of all the tasks in government which he undertook, it was the one from which he gained pleasure as well as satisfaction. In August 1943 he was made a Companion of Honour.

In October 1944 another aspect of his earlier career was drawn upon when Swinton returned to London to become the first minister of civil aviation, a topic on which it was increasingly important to formulate a clear post-war policy. It was also one on which there were divergencies of interest and policy between the United Kingdom and the United States. A conference between the parties at Chicago in November 1944 degenerated into a personal battle, in which their mutual dislike was very evident, between Swinton and the American representative, Adolf Berle. This ministerial post came to an end with the Labour victory in 1945—a victory which also meant the abandonment of Swinton's plans for post-war British civil aviation.

In opposition Swinton was a member of the Conservative shadow cabinet and played an active role at the Conservative central office. He made possible the creation of a Conservative College at Swinton. In 1951 he became chancellor of the duchy of Lancaster, with a variety of particular duties, a post he combined with being deputy leader of the House of Lords. In the following year he became secretary of state for Commonwealth relations. Independence for India, Pakistan, and Ceylon in 1947–8 had changed the nature of the Commonwealth club. It no longer consisted entirely of the 'old dominions' and, although Swinton travelled widely in his new capacity, it was not a new world which was altogether congenial to him. The emerging issue of immigration caused him some problems. If the government legislated on immigration, he wrote in 1954, though it could do so in non-discriminatory terms, it would not be possible to conceal the fact that the object would be to keep out coloured people.

Swinton found no place in the cabinet formed in 1955 by Sir Anthony Eden. On retirement from public office he was raised to an earldom. However, he remained active in the House of Lords and in the confidence of senior Conservative figures. In 1948 he had published a book of reminiscences with the title *I Remember* and in 1966, in collaboration with James D. Margach, he published *Sixty Years of Power*, largely reminiscences of prime ministers from Balfour to Douglas-Home. Although not without interest, neither volume constitutes a rounded assessment of his life in politics. Perhaps this was because he could not himself come to a satisfactory assessment of his own contribution. Despite the length of his public service and his central role in important matters, he had never been a name to conjure with in the country at large—and indeed his changes of name virtually precluded easy public identification with his career in all its phases. His indifference to public relations was not shared, for example, by his colleague as a service minister in 1937, the secretary of state for war, Hore-Belisha. He also seemed indifferent to popularity, and was no more than a modest performer on a public platform. In meetings he often appeared to have little regard for the effect of his remarks or for the manner in which he made them. What he prized was concentrated effort, rapid assimilation of detail, and economy of presentation. He was quintessentially a man of business in politics, and there were not infrequent moments when he wished that he had in fact been a businessman. He had no pretensions to being a political thinker and his outlook was essentially pragmatic. He had his place in the engine-room of government and, where possible, left to others the public presentation of policy. Swinton realized, probably quite early on, that there were pinnacles of power which were beyond his reach, and was content to make his mark at a lower but none the less essential level of government. He died of a heart attack at his home, Swinton, Masham, Yorkshire, on 27 July 1972, and was buried in Masham churchyard. KEITH ROBBINS

Sources J. A. Cross, *Lord Swinton* (1982) • H. M. Hyde, *British air policy between the wars, 1918–1939* (1976) • M. Smith, *British air strategy between the wars* (1984) • R. Higham, 'Quality vs quantity: the impact of changing demand on the British aircraft industry, 1900–1960', *Business History Review*, 42 (1968) • J. D. Hargreaves, *The end of colonial rule in west Africa* (1979) • R. J. Overy, *William Morris, Viscount Nuffield* (1976) • R. P. Shay, *British rearmament in the thirties: politics and profits* (1977) • G. C. Peden, *British rearmament and the treasury, 1932–1939* (1979) • K. Middlemas, 'The party, industry and the city', *Conservative century: the conservative party since 1900*, ed. A. Seldon and S. Ball (1994)

Archives CAC Cam., corresp. and papers • PRO, papers relating to air ministry, AIR 19/23–24 | Bodl. RH, corresp. with Lord Lugard • HLRO, corresp. with Viscount Davidson • HLRO, corresp. with David Lloyd George • HLRO, corresp. with Viscount Samuel relating to article on 1931 crisis • IWM, corresp. with Sir Henry Tizard • NA Scot., corresp. with Lord Lothian • Nuffield Oxf., corresp. with Lord Cherwell • PRO, corresp. with Sir Edward Bridges, CAB 127/60 • PRO, corresp. relating to West Africa, CO 967/110–111

Likenesses H. Coster, photographs, 1930–39, NPG • W. Stoneman, three photographs, 1931–55, NPG • O. Birley, portrait, 1933, priv. coll. [*see illus.*] • J. Gunn, portrait, priv. coll.

Wealth at death £454,430: probate, 24 Oct 1972, *CGPLA Eng. & Wales*

Lister, Samuel Cunliffe, first Baron Masham (**1815–1906**), inventor of textile machinery, born at Calverly Hall, near Bradford, on 1 January 1815, was the fourth son in the large family of Ellis Cunliffe Lister-Kay (*d.* 1854) of Manningham and Farfield, and his second wife, Mary, daughter of William Kay of Cottingham. The original family name was Cunliffe; the father, Ellis Cunliffe, a wealthy manufacturer and the first MP for Bradford after the Reform Bill of 1832, assumed the name of Lister by the will of a cousin, Samuel Lister of Manningham, and the name Kay on the death of William Kay, father of his second wife.

In 1834 Samuel's paternal grandmother, Mary, daughter of William Thompson, bequeathed him Addingham rectory in Yorkshire on condition that he took orders; but, after education at a private school at Balham Hill, Surrey, he chose to join Sands, Turner & Co., merchants, of Liverpool, for whom, while still young, he made repeated visits to America, gaining an insight into American business methods. In 1837 his father built for him and his elder brother John a worsted mill at Manningham, near Bradford, opened in 1838 under the style J. and S. C. Lister. The partnership lasted until 1845, when John retired, having inherited the family estate on the death of the eldest brother, William. From 1845 to 1864 Samuel was successively in partnership with J. Ambler and J. Warburton. He carried on the business alone from 1864 until 1889, when the Manningham Mills became a limited company, of which he remained the chief shareholder and chairman.

Lister devoted a great part of his long career to invention, taking out over 150 patents, apart from early inventions not patented. The first invention, in 1841, was a swivel shuttle for inserting a silk figure on a plain ground; his earliest patent, in 1844, was a method for fringing shawls. Also in 1841, he first turned his attention to mechanical wool combing, the object of which is to separate the long fibres from the short, the long making worsted cloth, the short being used in the woollen branch of the textile industry. Wool combing was the last of the main processes of the industry to be mechanized. In 1842 Lister bought from George Edmund Donnisthorpe a wool-

Samuel Cunliffe Lister, first Baron Masham (1815–1906), by Frank Holl, 1882

combing machine, which, like earlier machines patented by Edmund Cartwright in 1789 and 1790, proved unsatisfactory. Unable to resell it, he determined to improve it, and evolved by 1845 the Lister–Cartwright machine, with which he produced the first pound of Australian wool combed in England. Improvements in the machine itself, and in subsidiary processes, led in 1848 to the 'square-motion' comb in the invention of which Isaac Holden had an undoubted input. Lister started working with Holden, subsequently joining him in an uneasy partnership and helping to finance the setting up of three wool-combing factories in France, run by Holden. The partnership ended in 1858 with Holden purchasing Lister's share of the business for £74,000. There was acrimony between Lister and Holden for the rest of their lives over the invention of the square-motion comb. Holden maintained that he had invented the principle before meeting Lister. The argument was exacerbated by the publication of James Burnley's *The History of Wool and Woolcombing* (1889), financed by Holden and extolling Holden's inventive genius. Lister retaliated by publishing his own claim to the invention. Lister was also involved in legal proceedings with the representatives of a French inventor named Heilmann over patent rights to other combing machinery. When the verdict went against him, Lister assured his position by purchasing the English rights to Heilmann's patent. He made little use of it himself and prevented its use elsewhere in England. In 1853 he acquired the Noble comb, an improved type invented by one of his own mechanics.

For some years Lister dominated the wool-combing industry, but ultimately Sir Isaac Holden gained a greater influence. Through his control over inventions and their patents, Lister determined the technical direction of the industry in England. But his personal role in technological development remains unclear. His influence may have been primarily in the way he utilized and developed the ideas of others and kept control of the whole patent position of wool combing. He ferociously fought intricate and expensive legal actions over patents. By 1853 he controlled twenty-three English wool-combing patents, effectively determining the course of English wool-combing technology. By that stage he believed his patents to be unassailable. Lister married on 6 September 1854 Annie (*d.* 1875), eldest daughter of John Dearden of Hollin's Hall, Halifax. They had two sons and five daughters.

From 1853 Lister devoted himself to further inventions with what seems to have been reckless zeal. In that year he took out nine patents, in 1855 twelve, all for textile processes. Also in 1855, he first thought of utilizing silk waste, produced when the fibre was reeled off the cocoon, and then purchasable at a halfpenny a pound. In 1859 Lister, though ignorant of the silk industry, invented a machine which answered his purpose; yet for years, despite continual improvements, spinners would not consider it. Bad business followed, and costly experiments brought him face to face with ruin. In 1864 his partner, Warburton, fearing bankruptcy, left him, and his loss on the machine reached a total of £250,000. At last, in the latter half of that year, his machine established confidence, and he regained his financial standing. Silk waste, shipped from China, India, Italy, and Japan, and bought at 6*d.* a pound, was converted into silk velvets, carpets, imitation sealskin, poplins, and other silk products. A second fortune was made. This was increased in 1878, when a velvet loom, bought in Spain in 1867, and developed through eleven years by experiments costing £29,000, at last began to pay. The old Manningham Mills, burnt down in 1871, were replaced on a far larger scale by the new Manningham Mills, which covered 27 acres and employed 5000 people by 1893. By 1889 Lister's annual profit was £250,000. In that year the business was converted into a limited liability company with a share capital of £1,550,000, Lister remaining as chairman. The business suffered from trading restrictions to the United States following the McKinley tariff. Profits declined. His attempts to cut costs by reducing wages led to labour disputes and, as a result, he became an early advocate of tariff retaliation.

In 1848 Lister had invented a compressed-air brake for railways (though he made no commercial use of it), anticipating by twenty-one years the Westinghouse patent (1869) in America. His last invention was a process for compressing corn so that it could be stored for wartime use.

In later life Lister used his enormous wealth to buy, for nearly £1 million, three adjoining estates in north Yorkshire—Swinton Park, Jervaulx, and Middleham Castle. He also purchased Ackton colliery at Featherstone, Yorkshire. Here, during the coal strike of 1893, some of the colliery works were destroyed and the military fired on the rioters, causing loss of life. Under Lister's ownership the mine's coal output multiplied twelve times. Although a hard man of business, Lister was a generous benefactor to

Bradford, selling the Manningham estate to the city for the relatively nominal sum of £40,000, for its conversion into Lister Park. He also readily acknowledged the claims of all who in any way anticipated or helped in his inventions, contributing £47,500 to the Cartwright Memorial Hall and the statue of Cartwright erected in Lister Park, and also commissioning the sculptor Matthew Noble in 1875 to make two busts of Donnisthorpe, one for his widow, the other to be placed at the entrance to Manningham Mills.

Lister owned pictures by Reynolds, Romney, Gainsborough, and other great painters. He was fond of every kind of sport, was a good shot, and devoted to coursing (he was a member of the Altcar Club from 1857). Although an ambition to win the Waterloo cup was never gratified, he owned, among other successful greyhounds, Liverpool, which in 1863 shared the Croxteth Stakes with N. B. Jones's Julia Mainwaring; he also owned Chameleon, which, out of seventy-nine courses in public, lost only twelve, winning the Altcar cup in its fourth season, and beating J. Lawton's Liberty for the Waterloo purse in 1872.

Lister's great gifts received public recognition during his lifetime. In 1886 he was awarded the Albert medal of the Society of Arts. In 1887 he was offered, but refused, a baronetcy; and on 15 July 1891 he was made first Baron Masham. He was an honorary LLD of Leeds University, deputy lieutenant and justice of the peace in the North and West Ridings, high sheriff of Yorkshire in 1887, and at one time colonel of the West Riding Volunteers. On two occasions he unsuccessfully fought parliamentary elections.

In old age Lister remained active, and in 1905 he published *Lord Masham's Inventions*, an account of his main labours. He died at his home, Swinton Park, Masham, Yorkshire, on 2 February 1906. His son, Samuel, succeeded him as second Baron Masham.

S. E. Fryer, *rev.* D. T. Jenkins

Sources K. Honeyman and J. Goodman, *Technology and enterprise: Isaac Holden and the mechanisation of woolcombing in France, 1848–1914* (1986) • J. Burnley, *The history of wool and woolcombing* (1889) • S. C. Lister, *Lord Masham's inventions, written by himself* (1905) • H. Priestman, *Principles of wool-combing* (1921) • *Industries of Yorkshire* (1888) • [J. Hogg], ed., *Fortunes made in business: a series of original sketches*, 3 vols. (1884–7) • D. T. Jenkins and K. G. Ponting, *The British wool textile industry, 1770–1914* (1987) • J. A. Iredale and J. M. Trickett, 'Lister, Samuel Cunliffe', *DBB* • d. cert.

Archives N. Yorks. CRO, papers • U. Leeds, Brotherton L., Lister and Co. Ltd, business records • W. Yorks. AS, Bradford, corresp. and papers | University of Bradford Library, J. B. Priestley Library, corresp. with Isaac Holden and related papers

Likenesses M. Noble, statue, 1873, Lister Park, Bradford • F. Holl, portrait, 1882, priv. coll. [*see illus.*] • J. Collier, oils, 1901, Bradford Museum and Art Gallery • A. Drury, marble bust, *c.*1904, Bradford Museum and Art Gallery • H. Carter, portrait, priv. coll.; formerly in family possession, 1912 • H. C. Fehr, marble bust, Bradford Museum and Art Gallery • portrait, repro. in *The Engineer* (9 Feb 1906)

Wealth at death £648,558 8*s.* 3*d.*: probate, 15 Aug 1906, *CGPLA Eng. & Wales*

Lister [*married name* Knowler], **Susanna** (*bap.* **1670**, *d.* **1738**), natural history illustrator, and her sister **Anne Lister** (1671–1695x1704), who worked with her, were the first and second of the eight children of Martin *Lister (*bap.* 1639, *d.* 1712), physician and naturalist, and his wife, Hannah (1645–1695), daughter of Thomas Parkinson (1607–1671) of Carleton in Craven and his wife, Anne. Susanna was born at Carleton Hall and baptized on 9 June 1670, while Anne (Nancy to her family) was born on 13 October 1671 at her father's house 'without Micklegate Bar' at York. The sisters began to draw and paint as children. On his way to France in July 1681, Lister wrote to his wife:

> I did send home a box of colour in oil for Susan and Nancy to paint with. As for the pencils sent with them, and the colours in shells, which are for limning, I would have thee lock them carefully up, till I return, for they know not yet the use of them. (Goulding, 342)

Susan and Nancy were then eleven and nine years old. Before long, they were drawing and painting pictures of their father's growing shell collection.

In 1684 the family moved to London and, in the following year, Lister published a collection of plates depicting exotic land shells (*De cochleis*, 1685). Monograms (SL and AL 'pni.') on the title page indicate that the pictures were painted by Susanna and Anne, although the plates were probably engraved by William Lodge (1649–1689), who had illustrated Lister's first book, on spiders and molluscs (Keynes, 28). None the less, plates published that year in the *Philosophical Transactions* are signed 'SL sculp.', indicating that fifteen-year-old Susanna was already mastering the craft. Meanwhile, the family embarked on a project, to prepare an illustrated catalogue of all known shells, that was to occupy them for another ten years. Martin Lister amassed a collection, borrowed from others, and prepared a classification system. The two sisters drew and painted illustrations and engraved them on copper plates, with their father's terse Latin descriptions. The *Historia conchyliorum* was divided into four sections, the title-pages of which bear the consecutive dates 1685 to 1688, and the footnote 'Susanna et Anna Lister figuras delinearunt' (or variations of the same). Each was continually revised and reissued, and the final version, with 1062 plates, was not complete until 1697. In 1692 Edward Lhwyd wrote to Lister 'I do not wonder your workw[omen] begin to be tired, you have held them so long to it' (Gunther, 155).

Many of the sisters' original pencil and watercolour drawings exist (Bodl. Oxf., MS Lister 9) and some are signed, as are a few of their engravings. Their styles differ, especially in the representation of cast shadows; Anne (whether painting or engraving) used bold parallel lines of graduated thickness, while Susanna used washes or cross-hatching. 'The plates are executed with great fidelity and spirit, and bear testimony to the extraordinary talents and industry of the artists' (Davies, 308). Their father published no further descriptive works, and no later work of either woman is known.

In 1706 or 1707 Susanna married Gilbert Knowler (1663–1730) of Herne, to become his third wife and mother of Susanna (1708–1768), her only child, who was married at Canterbury Cathedral in 1730 to William Bedford (1702–

1783), rector of Bekesbourne. Susanna died at Bekesbourne on 8 March 1738, and was buried beside her husband at Herne on 15 March. Nothing more is known about Anne Lister. Only two of her brothers and sisters had died by 1695, so she was still alive when her mother's memorial tablet recorded 'six children in teares'. However, when her father made his will in 1704 he named only five, and she was not among them.

The *Historia conchyliorum*, reprinted in 1770 and 1830, was a major reference work for which Martin Lister was renowned as 'the father of British testaceology' (Maton and Rackett, 138). These authors also bear testimony to the part played by Susanna and Anne Lister, 'whose names deserve to descend to posterity with their father's, and whose truly meritorious industry and ingenuity are patterns for their sex' (ibid., 141). J. D. WOODLEY

Sources J. D. Woodley, 'Anne Lister, illustrator of Martin Lister's *Historiae conchyliorum*, 1685–1692', *Archives of Natural History*, 21 (1994), 225–9 • G. Keynes, *Dr Martin Lister: a bibliography* (1981) • R. Davies, 'A memoir of Martin Lister', *Yorkshire Archaeological and Topographical Journal*, 2 (1871–2), 297–320 • R. W. Goulding, 'Martin Lister, M.D., F.R.S.', *Associated Architectural Societies' Reports and Papers*, 25/2 (1900), 329–70 • W. G. Maton and T. Rackett, 'An historical account of testaceological writers', *Transactions of the Linnean Society of London*, 7 (1804), 119–244 • G. L. Wilkins, 'Notes on the *Historia conchyliorum* of Martin Lister, 1638–1712', *Journal of the Society of the Bibliography of Natural History*, 3 (1953–60), 196–205 • G. L. Wilkins, 'The shell collections of Sir Hans Sloane, bart., 1660–1753', *Journal of Conchology*, 23 (1952), 247–59 • R. T. Gunther, *Early science in Oxford*, 14: *Life and letters of Edward Lhwyd* (1945) • M. Lister, *De cochleis* (1685) • M. Lister, *Historia sive synopsis methodicae conchyliorum* (1685–97) • parish register, Leeds, 9 June 1670, W. Yorks. AS, Leeds, P18/3 [baptism] • parish register (burial), 15 Mar 1738, Herne, Kent • parish register (baptism), 24 Oct 1671, York, Holy Trinity Micklegate [Anne Lister] • will, PRO, PROB 11/689, sig. 122

Archives Bodl. Oxf., MS Lister 9 | Radcliffe Science Library, Lister 1770, RR y 56 [1770 edn of *Historia conchyliorum*, with some of original paintings pasted in]

Lister, Thomas (*c*.1559–1628), Jesuit, was apparently a younger son of Christopher Lister of Midhope, Yorkshire, and Ellen, daughter and coheir of John Clayton of Clayton Hall, Leyland, Lancashire, where he may have been born. He entered the English College at Rome on 15 September 1579, joined the Society of Jesus on 20 February 1583, being fellow novice with Vitelleschi, afterwards general of the society, and graduated DTh at Pont-à-Mousson in 1592. Lister was sent to England, and worked with Edward Oldcorne in the Worcestershire district, based at Hindlip, the home of Thomas Habington. He apparently used the surname Butler as an alias. Because of Lister's claustrophobia and fear of priest's holes, the Jesuit superior, Henry Garnet, employed him as a socius. But Lister's nervous energy, violent headaches, excitability, and neuroses made him a difficult companion, unsuited to the clandestine English mission. He spent some time in Flanders, but was once again in England at the turn of the century. Garnet wrote that Lister's troubles stemmed not so much from 'weakness of character' as from 'a disturbed mind and lack of responsibility' (Caraman, 233). On 3 June 1610 Lister was professed of the four vows. In 1621 he was superior of the Oxford district.

Lister was the author of 'Treatise of schism', in which he maintained that the appellant priests who refused to acknowledge the archpriest's jurisdiction were *ipso facto* deprived of their ecclesiastical powers, and ought to be treated as schismatics. This work, which caused much disquiet among the secular clergy, was extensively circulated in manuscript. It was first published in Christopher Bagshaw's *Relatio compendiosa* of 1601.

Lister died at Liège on 19 February 1628, and was buried there. THOMPSON COOPER, *rev.* MARK NICHOLLS

Sources T. M. McCoog, *English and Welsh Jesuits, 1555–1650*, 2 vols., Catholic RS, 74–5 (1994–5) • Gillow, *Lit. biog. hist.* • P. Caraman, *Henry Garnet, 1555–1606, and the Gunpowder Plot* (1964) • M. Hodgetts, 'Elizabethan priest holes III: East Anglia, Baddesley Clinton, Hindlip', *Recusant History*, 12 (1973–4), 171–97 • J. Morris, ed., *The troubles of our Catholic forefathers related by themselves*, 3 vols. (1872–7) • H. Foley, ed., *Records of the English province of the Society of Jesus*, 7 vols. in 8 (1875–83) • *Dodd's Church history of England*, ed. M. A. Tierney, 5 vols. (1839–43) • *The memoirs of Gregorio Panzani*, ed. and trans. J. Berington (1793) • G. Oliver, *Collections towards illustrating the biographies of the Scotch, English and Irish members of the Society of Jesus*, 2nd edn (1845)

Lister, Thomas (1597–1668), politician, was the eldest son of William Lister (*d.* 1641) of Coleby Hall, Lincolnshire, and his wife, Grisell (*d.* 1642) daughter of William Rivett of Rowston in the same county. On 1 November 1616 he was admitted of Gray's Inn. He married Margaret Armyn or Armine (*d.* 1661), daughter of Sir William Armine of Osgodby, Lincolnshire, on 6 February 1622 at Lenton, Lincolnshire. Robert, earl of Lindsey, gave him a commission on 5 July 1629 as captain of foot in the Lincolnshire militia (Sleaford session). At the outbreak of civil war in August 1642 royalist troopers broke into Coleby Hall and carried him prisoner before the king's council. After his release he became a lieutenant-colonel in the parliamentary army and deputy governor of Lincoln. In 1644 he served as high sheriff of Lincolnshire and also served as a member of the parliamentarian county committee. He was elected MP for Lincoln on 24 May 1647, and was one of the MPs who fled to the army in July 1647. He survived Pride's Purge and continued as an MP until the dissolution of the Rump Parliament in 1653. On being appointed one of the commissioners to try the king he attended for a short time, after which he declined to act. He was nominated a member of the council of state on 13 February 1651, and served on several committees. He represented Lincolnshire in Cromwell's parliaments from 1653 until 1656, and again from May 1659 until the overthrow of the Commonwealth, his name frequently occurring as one of the tellers in division. He was included in the exceptions to the Act of Oblivion, but on 24 June 1660 he petitioned the House of Lords that he might receive the benefit of the indemnity, claiming that he had not been present when the king was tried and sentenced. Accordingly, on 29 August he was merely incapacitated for life from holding any office.

Lister died at his house in Lincoln's Inn Fields, and was buried in the church of St Paul's, Covent Garden, on 10 November 1668. His wife had been buried at St Paul's, Covent Garden, on 14 November 1661. He left no children, and his estates of Coleby Hall Manor, Downehall in Rippingale, Lincolnshire, and others, descended to his nephew, William Lister (1632–1687).

GORDON GOODWIN, *rev.* ANDREW J. HOPPER

Sources private information (1892) [Mrs A. Tempest] • R. Howell, 'Lister, Thomas', Greaves & Zaller, *BDBR*, 2.192–3 • A. R. Maddison, ed., *Lincolnshire pedigrees*, 4 vols., Harleian Society, 50–52, 55 (1902–6), vols. 3–4 • C. Holmes, *Seventeenth-century Lincolnshire*, History of Lincolnshire, 7 (1980) • C. Holmes, 'Colonel King and Lincolnshire politics, 1642–1646', *HJ*, 16 (1973), 451–84 • will, PRO, PROB 11/328, sig. 142 • J. Foster, *The register of admissions to Gray's Inn, 1521–1889, together with the register of marriages in Gray's Inn chapel, 1695–1754* (privately printed, London, 1889) • *JHL*, 11 (1660–66), 118 • *Seventh report*, HMC, 6 (1879), 1–182, esp. 121 [House of Lords] • *CSP dom.*, 1651, 44

Archives BL, Add. MS 22546, fol. 39 • BL, Add. MS 37682, fols. 26, 80 • BL, Sloane MS 645, fol. 46

Wealth at death landed estates at Coleby Hall Manor and Downehall in Rippingale, Lincolnshire; £134 10s. in gifts distributed; £15 in pensions distributed p.a.: will, PRO, PROB 11/328, sig. 142; *DNB*

Lister, Thomas (1810–1888), poet and naturalist, was born at Old Mill, Barnsley, Yorkshire, on 11 February 1810, the youngest of the fourteen children of Joseph Lister, a Quaker gardener and small farmer. From 1821 until 1824 he attended Ackworth School, and afterwards was an assistant to his father until 1832, when he began work in a linen warehouse in Barnsley. During the parliamentary election of 1832 Lister worked actively for the return of Lord Morpeth (afterwards earl of Carlisle) for the West Riding of Yorkshire, and wrote several effective verse squibs in his support. Lord Morpeth offered to obtain for him the postmastership of Barnsley, but, as a Quaker, Lister was unwilling to take the requisite oath.

In 1834 Lister published *Rustic Wreath*, a collection of his verses. It was very popular; an edition of 3000 copies was quickly sold. It was followed by *Temperance Rhymes* in 1837. In that same year, after visiting Spencer T. Hall at Nottingham, and forming an acquaintance with Ebenezer Elliott, Lister made a walking tour of the Lake District, and journeyed into Scotland, where he met Professor John Wilson (Christopher North), William and Robert Chambers, and William Miller the artist. In 1838 he visited France, Italy, Switzerland, and the Netherlands. He forwarded many of the poems, sonnets, and translations which he wrote during this tour to Elliott, and they were published in *Tait's Magazine*. In 1839, when the office of postmaster at Barnsley again became vacant, Lister was appointed to it, as a simple affirmation had been substituted for the oath, and he held the post until 31 March 1870. The new security of this position permitted him to marry, on 12 March 1841, Hannah Schofield (1812–1882); they had no children.

An enthusiastic naturalist, Lister regularly contributed meteorological observations and notes on birds to the *Barnsley Chronicle*. He was to combine his literary and scientific interests in 1862, with the publication of his *Rhymes of Progress*. For many years he was president of the Barnsley Naturalists' Society, and contributed to its collections, and he was a constant attendant and contributor of papers at the annual meetings of the British Association. Accompanying the association to Montreal in 1884, he visited the principal towns in Canada and the United States.

Lister died at Barnsley on 25 March 1888, and was buried on 29 March in the Friends' meeting-house ground in Cockerham Road, Barnsley.

GORDON GOODWIN, *rev.* MEGAN A. STEPHAN

Sources *The Athenaeum* (7 April 1888), 439 • S. T. Hall, *Biographical sketches of remarkable people* (1873), 36 • W. C. Newsam, *The poets of Yorkshire* (1845), 163–5 • W. Grainge, *The poets and poetry of Yorkshire*, 2 vols. (1868), 2.444–6 • J. Searle [G. Searle Phillips], *The life, character and genius of Ebenezer Elliott* (1856), appx • W. Andrews, ed., *Modern Yorkshire poets* (1885) • *Barnsley Chronicle* (31 March 1888), 8 • *Barnsley Independent* (31 March 1888), 6 • J. H. Nodal, *Bibliography of Ackworth School* (1889), 22 • Boase, *Mod. Eng. biog.*

Wealth at death £1740 12s. 11d.: probate, 19 April 1888, *CGPLA Eng. & Wales*

Lister, Thomas, fourth Baron Ribblesdale (1854–1925), politician and huntsman, was born at the Hôtel de France, Fontainebleau, on 29 October 1854, the eldest son of Thomas Lister, third Baron Ribblesdale (1828–1876), and his wife, Emma (*d.* 1911), youngest daughter of Colonel William Mure of Caldwell, Ayrshire. His father had been a devotee of the turf, and in straitened circumstances had taken his young family to live in France. Ribblesdale later observed that a spell abroad was 'a method of reconstruction often adopted in those days by families and single gentlemen who had outrun the constable, or, in Burton's phrase, had galloped themselves out of their fortunes' (Lister, 22). Lister's formal education was, however, in England, where he attended a preparatory school, Winton House, in Winchester and Harrow School (1868–72).

In 1873 Lister joined the army. Initially with the 64th regiment, he later transferred to the rifle brigade, from which he retired in 1886 with the rank of major. He succeeded his father, who committed suicide, in 1876, and took his seat in the Lords the following year, but seldom attended the house. He later confessed that army life induced in him political apathy. By the time that he was appointed a lord-in-waiting to the queen in 1880 he had 'lost, if not forgotten' the whig principles that he had imbibed in youth from his step-grandfather, Lord John Russell (Lister, 155). Ribblesdale found life at the royal court agreeable without always being stimulating, and he was conscious of the peculiar atmosphere that prevailed. News came practically first-hand to Windsor, but 'at the Household dinner … it was seldom mentioned and never discussed' (ibid., 107). He left court in 1885, with the fall of the Liberal government, but returned in 1892 as master of the buckhounds. Gladstone's intimation that this office might lead to greater things spurred Ribblesdale to be more active on behalf of the government. He was its spokesman in the Lords on agriculture and, later, Ireland, and with the fall of the ministry in 1895 he became chief Liberal whip, continuing until 1911. This office proved to be the acme of his political career, but by his own admission it carried little influence.

It was riding, rather than politics, that dominated Ribblesdale's life. He had been successively a soldier, a

Thomas Lister, fourth Baron Ribblesdale (1854–1925), by John Singer Sargent, 1902

courtier, and a politician, but was best known to his contemporaries as a great huntsman, and is best known to posterity as the subject of a great painting. John Singer Sargent's magnificent portrait of Ribblesdale (1902) captures the spirit of an age, as much as the image of one man. The subject's casual elegance exudes the confidence of the English aristocracy in its heyday before the First World War. He is depicted by Sargent wearing his favourite hunting clothes. These were not the dark green gala coat and white leathers of the master of the buckhounds: though more striking than the chosen mufti, this uniform would have been less apt. Ribblesdale's life was one of understated grandeur, and did not need the imprimatur of a uniform. An expert horseman, in 1897 he published a substantial history, *The Queen's Hounds*. His love of hunting was shared by his first wife, Charlotte (Charty) Monckton Tennant (1858–1911), daughter of the industrialist Sir Charles *Tennant, first baronet, whom he married on 7 April 1877. She was one of the celebrated sisters who took London society by storm (the others being Laura Lyttelton, Lucy Graham Smith, and Margot Asquith) and formed the nucleus of the aristocratic set the Souls. She died after a three-year fight against tuberculosis in 1911. They had five children; both their sons died on active service—the elder in Somaliland in 1904, the younger after the Gallipoli campaign in 1915. It was in their memory, as well as their mother's, that Ribblesdale gave his Sargent portrait to the National Gallery (of which he had been a trustee since 1909) in 1916. He spent his widowhood at Rosa Lewis's Cavendish Hotel, and in 1919 married an American, Ava, widow of John Jacob Astor and daughter of Edward Willing. He died at 18 Grosvenor Square, London, on 21 October 1925; his widow renounced her title and resumed her American citizenship. His autobiographical *Impressions and Memories*, both interesting and well written, was posthumously published in 1927, with an introduction by his eldest daughter. MARK POTTLE

Sources *WWW*, 1916–28 • T. Lister, *Impressions and memories* (1927) • M. Asquith, *The autobiography of Margot Asquith*, 2 vols. (1920–22); repr. in 1 vol. with introduction by M. Bonham Carter (1962) • A. Forbes, *Memories and base details* (1922) • GEC, *Peerage* • J. Abdy and C. Gere, *The Souls* (1984)

Likenesses J. S. Sargent, oils, 1902, National Gallery, London [*see illus.*]

Wealth at death £42,332 9*s*. 2*d*.: probate, 26 Nov 1925, *CGPLA Eng. & Wales*

Lister, Thomas Henry (1800–1842), writer and civil servant, was the eldest son of Thomas Lister of Armitage Park, near Lichfield, Staffordshire, and his first wife, Harriet Anne, the daughter of John Seale of Mountboone, Devon. His father was a cousin of the first Baron Ribblesdale (1752–1826). Lister was educated at Westminster School, London, to which he was admitted on 25 March 1814, and he entered Trinity College, Cambridge, in May 1819. Although he matriculated in 1820, he left the university without taking a degree.

Lister was a refined and accomplished man who moved in aristocratic circles. In 1826 he published *Granby*, a novel set in English high society. It tells the story of its eponymous young hero's love for Miss Jermyn, whose parents disapprove of the relationship. But when Granby turns out to be the heir of Lord Malton, all is well. It is often regarded as the first full example of the 'fashionable' or 'silver-fork' novel, a genre also associated with Theodore Hook, Disraeli, Bulwer-Lytton, Mrs Gore, and Lady Blessington, among others. It was well received, with Sidney Smith in the *Edinburgh Review* of February 1826 going so far as to praise it as 'a very easy and natural picture of manners, as they really exist among the upper classes' (p. 396). When it was republished in 1838 as volume 11 of Henry Colburn's Modern Novelists, Lister was compelled to deny an assertion in the *Quarterly Review* of March 1826 that it owed much to Lord Normanby's *Matilda* (1825); it had, in fact, been completed four months previously. Two years later he published *Herbert Lacy* (1828), another 'fashionable' novel. He wrote a tragedy, *Epicharis*, based on the history of Piso's conspiracy; this was successfully staged at the Theatre Royal, Drury Lane, London, on 14 October 1829.

Lister married Lady Maria Theresa Villiers (1803–1865), the only daughter of the Hon. George Villiers, on 6 November 1830 [*see* Lewis, Lady (Maria) Theresa]. They had a son, Thomas Villiers (1832–1902), who became an assistant under-secretary for foreign affairs in 1873 and was made a KCMG in 1885. They also had two daughters, of whom the elder, Marie Thérèse Lister (1835–1863), married in 1859 Sir William G. G. V. Harcourt, and the younger, Alice Beatrice Lister (1841–1898), married in 1870 Sir Algernon Borthwick (later Lord Glenesk). In 1832 Lister published *Arlington*, the third and last of his 'fashionable' novels.

Lister held a number of official administrative posts. On

4 June 1834 he was nominated a commissioner for inquiring into the state of religious and other instruction which then existed in Ireland. He was given a similar responsibility on 19 July 1835, when he was one of those commissioned to investigate the opportunities for religious worship and the means of religious instruction in Scotland. On 19 August 1836 he was appointed the first registrar-general of births, marriages, and deaths of England and Wales. It was suggested that he owed this last appointment to the patronage of Lord John Russell, who was his brother-in-law. Nevertheless, he carried out his duties thoroughly and systematically, issuing his first annual report in 1839.

Meanwhile Lister continued his literary work. Between 1830 and 1841 he made twenty-one contributions to the *Edinburgh Review*. Dickens was delighted with his appreciative review in October 1838 of *Sketches by Boz*, *Pickwick Papers*, and the first instalments of *Oliver Twist*, in which Lister compared the young writer to Hogarth. He published *The Life and Administration of Edward, First Earl of Clarendon* (1837–8), which had a hostile reception in the *Quarterly Review* of October 1838 from John Wilson Croker, who thought that it was unjust in its judgements and inaccurate, but the biography was welcomed by others as a valuable contribution to historical knowledge. Lister issued *An Answer to the Misrepresentations* [in Croker's article] in 1839.

Lister died of lung disease on 5 June 1842 at Kent House, Knightsbridge, London, the mansion of his relative the earl of Morley, and was buried in Kensal Green cemetery, Middlesex.

Thomas Henry Lister's half-sister, **Harriet Cradock** [*née* Lister] (1809–1884), novelist, was born on 18 June 1809 at Armitage, near Lichfield, the daughter of Thomas Lister and his second wife, Mary, daughter of William Grove of Honileigh, Warwickshire. Harriet Lister was a maid of honour to Queen Victoria for six years, from 1 July 1837, and was the only one to hold the post who was not the daughter or granddaughter of a peer. She left the queen's service to marry her cousin, the Revd Edward Hartopp Grove DD (1810–1886), on 9 July 1844. He took the surname Cradock in 1849, and was the rector of Tedstone Delamere in Herefordshire, canon of Worcester, and afterwards principal of Brasenose College, Oxford.

Harriet Cradock's first novel, *Anne Grey, a Novel, Edited by the Author of 'Granby'*, appeared in 1834. It was sometimes attributed to Lister, despite (or perhaps because of) the fact that its anonymity was reinforced by Lister's statement in the preface that 'the writer is pleased to remain unknown'. The novel is not a 'fashionable' one, but a lively and unexaggerated tale of personal relationships in upper-middle-class English society. Harriet Cradock's other novels include *Hulse House* (1860), *John Smith* (1878), and *Rose* (1881). Among her miscellaneous works are *The Calendar of Nature, or, The Seasons of England* (1849), edited by her kinsman, Lord John Russell, and the letterpress for *Views of Elf Land* (1878), designed and executed by William Weird. She died on 16 June 1884 at her home, Cowley Grange, near Oxford.

DONALD HAWES

Sources *DNB* • Allibone, *Dict.* • *GM*, 2nd ser., 2 (1834), 207 • *GM*, 2nd ser., 4 (1835), 199 • *GM*, 2nd ser., 18 (1842), 323 • M. W. Rosa, *The silver-fork school: novels of fashion preceding Vanity Fair* (1936) • W. A. Lindsay, *The royal household* (1898) [H. Cradock] • Boase, *Mod. Eng. biog.* [Harriet Cradock] • W. Hughes, 'Silver fork writers and readers', *Novel*, 25 (1991), 328–47 • S. Smith, review of T. H. Lister, *Granby*, *EdinR*, 43 (1826), 395–406 • review, *QR*, 33 (1825–6), 474–90 • [J. W. Croker], review of T. H. Lister, *The life and administration of Edward, first earl of Clarendon*, *QR*, 62 (1838), 505–66 • *Old Westminsters*, vols. 1–2 • W. W. Rouse Ball and J. A. Venn, eds., *Admissions to Trinity College, Cambridge*, 4 (1911) • *BL cat.* • *Wellesley index*, vol. 1 • 'Lewis, Lady Maria Theresa', *DNB* • d. cert.

Archives Bodl. Oxf., family corresp. | BL, letters to Macvey Napier, Add. MSS 34614–34622, *passim* • PRO, letters to Lord John Russell, PRO 30/22 • Staffs. RO, letters to Lord Hatherton • V&A NAL, letters to Henry Colburn

Likenesses I. W. Slater, lithograph, pubd 1834 (after J. Slater), BM • Finden, stipple, 1836 (after Wright), BM; repro. in T. H. Lister, *Granby* (1836) • Wright, engraving (after Finden), repro. in T. H. Lister, *Granby* (1838), vol. 11 of H. Colburn, *Modern Novelists Series*, frontispiece

Wealth at death £6981 16*s.* 9*d.*—Harriet Cradock: probate, 16 July 1884, *CGPLA Eng. & Wales*

PICTURE CREDITS

Leavis, Frank Raymond (1895–1978)—© Paul Joyce / National Portrait Gallery, London

Le Blanc, Sir Simon (1748/9–1816)—photograph by courtesy Sotheby's Picture Library, London

Le Blond, Elizabeth Alice Frances (1860–1934)—Alpine Club Photo Library, London

Lecky, (William) Edward Hartpole (1838–1903)—© National Portrait Gallery, London

Lecky, Squire Thornton Stratford (1838–1902)—© National Maritime Museum, London

Leclercq, Carlotta (1838–1893)—© National Portrait Gallery, London

Le Courayer, Pierre-François (1681–1776)—© National Portrait Gallery, London

Lee, Arthur Stanley Gould (1894–1975)—© National Portrait Gallery, London

Lee, Sir Frank Godbould (1903–1971)—© National Portrait Gallery, London

Lee, George Henry, third earl of Lichfield (1718–1772)—© Bodleian Library, University of Oxford

Lee, Sir Henry (1533–1611)—© National Portrait Gallery, London

Lee, James Prince (1804–1869)—© National Portrait Gallery, London

Lee, Janet [Jennie], Baroness Lee of Asheridge (1904–1988)—© Jorge Lewinski; collection National Portrait Gallery, London

Lee, John (1783–1866)—© National Portrait Gallery, London

Lee, Laurence Edward Alan (1914–1997)—© National Portrait Gallery, London

Lee, Richard Henry (1733–1794)—Independence National Historical Park

Lee, Robert (1793–1877)—Wellcome Library, London

Lee, Robert (1804–1868)—Scottish National Portrait Gallery

Lee, Sir Sidney (1859–1926)—V&A Images, The Victoria and Albert Museum

Lee, Thomas (1551/2–1601)—© Tate, London, 2004

Leech, John (1817–1864)—© National Portrait Gallery, London

Leeson, Spencer Stottesbery Gwatkin (1892–1956)—© National Portrait Gallery, London

Le Fanu, (Joseph Thomas) Sheridan (1814–1873)—© National Portrait Gallery, London

Lefevre, Charles Shaw-, Viscount Eversley (1794–1888)—private collection; photograph: Photographic Survey, Courtauld Institute of Art, London

Lefevre, George John Shaw-, Baron Eversley (1831–1928)—© National Portrait Gallery, London

Lefroy, George Alfred (1854–1919)—© National Portrait Gallery, London

Lefroy, Sir John Henry (1817–1890)—private collection; photograph National Portrait Gallery, London

Le Gallienne, Richard Thomas (1866–1947)—© National Portrait Gallery, London

Legge, George, first Baron Dartmouth (*c.*1647–1691)—© National Portrait Gallery, London

Legge, (Harry) Walter (1906–1979)—© EMI Records UK

Legge, William (1607/8–1670)—private collection

Legge, William, second earl of Dartmouth (1731–1801)—private collection; photograph National Portrait Gallery, London

Lehmann, Elizabeth Nina Mary Frederica (1862–1918)—© National Portrait Gallery, London

Lehmann, Rosamond Nina (1901–1990)—© National Portrait Gallery, London

Lehzen, (Johanna Clara) Louise, Baroness Lehzen in the Hanoverian nobility (1784–1870)—The Royal Collection © 2004 HM Queen Elizabeth II

Leicester, John Fleming, first Baron de Tabley (1762–1827)—private collection; © reserved in the photograph

Leigh, Anthony (*d.* 1692)—© National Portrait Gallery, London

Leigh, Evan (1810–1876)—© National Portrait Gallery, London

Leigh, Sir Thomas (*d.* 1571)—© reserved

Leigh, Vivien (1913–1967)—© Laszlo Willinger / The John Kobal Foundation; collection National Portrait Gallery, London

Leighton, Alexander (*c.*1570–1649)—© National Portrait Gallery, London

Leighton, Clara Ellaline Hope (1898–1989)—© Estate of Powys Evans; collection National Portrait Gallery, London

Leighton, Frederic, Baron Leighton (1830–1896)—photograph by courtesy Sotheby's Picture Library, London

Leighton, John [Luke Limner] (1822–1912)—© National Portrait Gallery, London

Leighton, Margaret (1922–1976)—© Tom Hustler / National Portrait Gallery, London

Leighton, Robert (*bap.* 1612, *d.* 1684)—© National Portrait Gallery, London

Leiper, Robert Thomson (1881–1969)—Wellcome Library, London

Leitch, Charlotte Cecilia Pitcairn [Cecil] (1891–1977)—Getty Images - Hulton Archive

Leitch, William Leighton (1804–1883)—© Scottish National Photography Collection, Scottish National Portrait Gallery

Le Jeune, Henry (1819–1904)—© National Portrait Gallery, London

Lely, Sir Peter (1618–1680)—© National Portrait Gallery, London

Leman, Sir John (1544–1632)—The Royal Collection © 2004 HM Queen Elizabeth II

Le Marchant, John Gaspard (1766–1812)—Le Marchant Family collection / Geoffrey Shakerley

Lemass, Seán Francis (1899–1971)—Getty Images - Hulton Archive

Le Masurier, Sir Robert Hugh (1913–1996)—Universal Pictorial Press

Lemon, Denis Edward (1945–1994)—Getty Images - Hulton Archive

Lemon, Margaret (*b. c.*1614)—The Royal Collection © 2004 HM Queen Elizabeth II

Lemon, Mark (1809–1870)—© National Portrait Gallery, London

Lennon, John Ono (1940–1980)—© Annie Leibovitz; collection National Portrait Gallery, London

Lennox, Charles, first duke of Richmond, first duke of Lennox, and duke of Aubigny in the French nobility (1672–1723)—© National Portrait Gallery, London

Lennox, Charles, second duke of Richmond, second duke of Lennox, and duke of Aubigny in the French nobility (1701–1750)—photograph by courtesy Sotheby's Picture Library, London

Lennox, Charles, third duke of Richmond, third duke of Lennox, and duke of Aubigny in the French nobility (1735–1806)—© National Portrait Gallery, London

Lennox, Charles Gordon-, fifth duke of Richmond and fifth duke of Lennox (1791–1860)—© National Portrait Gallery, London

Lennox, Lord George Henry (1737–1805)—photograph courtesy of Spink-Leger

Lenthall, William, appointed Lord Lenthall under the protectorate (1591–1662)—© National Portrait Gallery, London

Leo, Alan (1860–1917)—Heritage Images Partnership

Leonowens, Anna Harriette (1831–1915)—Kenneth and Margaret Landon Collection (SC-38) Special Collections, Wheaton College, Illinois, USA

Leopold, Prince, first duke of Albany (1853–1884)—The Royal Collection © 2004 HM Queen Elizabeth II

Leopold I (1790–1865)—© Photo RMN

Le Patourel, (Herbert) Wallace (1916–1979)—© National Portrait Gallery, London

Le Queux, William Tufnell (1864–1927)—© National Portrait Gallery, London

Lesley, John (1527–1596)—Marischal Museum, University of Aberdeen

Leslie, Sir Bradford (1831–1926)—© reserved

Leslie, Charles (1650–1722)—© National Portrait Gallery, London

Leslie, Charles Robert (1794–1859)—© National Portrait Gallery, London

Leslie, David, first Lord Newark (1601–1682)—in a private Scottish collection; on loan to the Scottish National Portrait Gallery

Leslie, George (*d.* 1637?)—© National Portrait Gallery, London

Leslie, John, sixth earl of Rothes (*c.*1600–1641)—private collection; © reserved in the photograph

Leslie, John, duke of Rothes (*c.*1630–1681)—private collection; © reserved in the photograph

Leslie, John, ninth earl of Rothes (1679–1722)—Christie's Images Ltd. (2004)

Leslie, Sir John (1766–1832)—Scottish National Portrait Gallery

Leslie, Sir John Randolph, third baronet (1885–1971)—© National Portrait Gallery, London

Lessore de Saint-Foix, Helen [Helen Lessore] (1907–1994)—© Michael Ward / National Portrait Gallery, London

Lestor, Joan, Baroness Lestor of Eccles (1927–1998)—© National Portrait Gallery, London

L'Estrange, Sir Roger (1616–1704)—© National Portrait Gallery, London

Lestrange, Sir Thomas (*c.*1490–1545)—Kimbell Art Museum, Fort Worth, Texas. Photographer Michael Bodycomb

Lethaby, William Richard (1857–1931)—RIBA Library Photographs Collection

Letheby, Henry (1816–1876)—© National Portrait Gallery, London

Lettsom, John Coakley (1744–1815)—by permission of the Royal College of Physicians, London

Lever, Charles James (1806–1872)—© National Portrait Gallery, London

Lever, William Hesketh, first Viscount Leverhulme (1851–1925)—University of Liverpool Art Gallery and Collections

Leveson, Sir Richard (*c.*1570–1605)—private collection

Levi, Leone (1821–1888)—© National Portrait Gallery, London

Levis, Carroll Richard (1910–1968)—Getty Images - Hulton Archive

Levy, Joseph Moses (1812–1888)—© National Portrait Gallery, London

Lewes, George Henry (1817–1878)—© National Portrait Gallery, London

Lewin, Terence Thornton, Baron Lewin (1920–1999)—© Estate of Franta Belsky; photograph National Portrait Gallery, London

Lewis, (Dominic) Bevan Wyndham (1891–1969)—© National Portrait Gallery, London

Lewis, Clive Staples (1898–1963)—© Arthur Strong / National Portrait Gallery, London

Lewis, David [St David Lewis; Charles Baker] (1617–1679)—© National Portrait Gallery, London

Lewis, David Malcolm (1928–1994)—photograph reproduced by courtesy of The British Academy

Lewis, Frederick Christian, senior (1779–1856)—© National Portrait Gallery, London

Lewis, Sir George Cornewall, second baronet (1806–1863)—© National Portrait Gallery, London

Lewis, John Frederick (1804–1876)—The Maas Gallery Ltd

Lewis, John Spedan (1885–1963)—© National Portrait Gallery, London

Lewis, Matthew Gregory (1775–1818)—© National Portrait Gallery, London

Lewis, Richard (1821–1905)—© National Portrait Gallery, London

Lewis, Samuel (1838–1901)—reproduced by permission of Southern Housing Group Limited

Lewis, (John) Saunders (1893–1985)—© National Museums and Galleries of Wales

Lewis, Lady (Maria) Theresa (1803–1865)—private collection

Lewis, Sir Thomas (1881–1945)—© National Museums and Galleries of Wales

Lewis, Sir Thomas Frankland, first baronet (1780–1855)—by courtesy of the National Library of Wales

Lewis, William Thomas (1746?–1812)—© National Portrait Gallery, London

Lewis, William Thomas, first Baron Merthyr (1837–1914)—© National Portrait Gallery, London

Lewis, (Percy) Wyndham (1882–1957)—© National Portrait Gallery, London

Lewson, Jane (1699/1700?–1816)—© National Portrait Gallery, London

Ley, James, first earl of Marlborough (1550–1629)—Collection Harvard University Law School, Cambridge, Massachusetts; © reserved in the photograph

Leyden, John (1775–1811)—© National Portrait Gallery, London

Leyland, Thomas (1752?–1827)—© National Portrait Gallery, London

Leyser, Karl Joseph (1920–1992)—© reserved; collection National Portrait Gallery, London

Liaqat Ali Khan (1895–1951)—© National Portrait Gallery, London

Lichtenberg, Georg Christoph (1742–1799)—© National Portrait Gallery, London

Liddell, Adolphus George Charles (1846–1920)—NMPFT / Science & Society Picture Library

Liddell, Eric Henry (1902–1945)—Getty Images - Hulton Archive

Liddell, Guy Maynard (1892–1958)—Getty Images - Hulton Archive; photograph National Portrait Gallery, London

Liddell, Henry George (1811–1898)—© National Portrait Gallery, London

Liddon, Henry Parry (1829–1890)—© National Portrait Gallery, London

Lidell, (Tord) Alvar Quan (1908–1981)—© Roger George Clark; collection National Portrait Gallery, London

Lidgett, John Scott (1854–1953)—© National Portrait Gallery, London

Lieven, Dorothea Khristoforovna, Princess Lieven in the Russian nobility (1785–1857)—private collection; photograph National Portrait Gallery, London

Light, William (1786–1839)—Art Gallery of South Australia, Adelaide

Lightfoot, Hannah (*b.* 1730, *d.* in or after 1758)—private collection

Lightfoot, John (1602–1675)—© National Portrait Gallery, London

Lightfoot, Joseph Barber (1828–1889)—Chapter of Durham Cathedral

Lighthill, Sir (Michael) James (1924–1998)—© National Portrait Gallery, London

Ligonier, John, Earl Ligonier (1680–1770)—Fort Ligonier, Pennsylvania, USA

Lilburne, John (1615?–1657)—© National Portrait Gallery, London

Lillie, Beatrice Gladys (1894–1989)—© Cecil Beaton Archive, Sotheby's; collection National Portrait Gallery, London

Lilly, William (1602–1681)—Ashmolean Museum, Oxford

Lillywhite, (Frederick) William (1792–1854)—Marylebone Cricket Club, London / Bridgeman Art Library

Lincoln, Benjamin (1733–1810)—courtesy of the Massachusetts Historical Society

Lind, James (1716–1794)—Wellcome Library, London

Lind, Jenny (1820–1887)—The Royal Collection © 2004 HM Queen Elizabeth II

Lindemann, Frederick Alexander, Viscount Cherwell (1886–1957)—© The Royal Society

Lindley, William (1808–1900)—courtesy of the Institution of Civil Engineers Archives

Lindley, Sir William Heerlein (1853–1917)—© National Portrait Gallery, London

Lindrum, Walter Albert (1898–1960)—Getty Images - Edward G. Malindine

Lindsay, Alexander Dunlop, first Baron Lindsay of Birker (1879–1952)—© National Portrait Gallery, London

Lindsay, Alexander William Crawford, twenty-fifth earl of Crawford and eighth earl of Balcarres (1812–1880)—© National Portrait Gallery, London

Lindsay, Colin, third earl of Balcarres (1652–1721)—private collection; photograph © National Galleries of Scotland

Lindsay, David Alexander Robert, twenty-eighth earl of Crawford and eleventh earl of Balcarres (1900–1975)—© National Portrait Gallery, London

Lindsay, John, seventeenth earl of Crawford and first earl of Lindsay (1596–1678)—Scottish National Portrait Gallery

Lindsay, John (1900–1990)—by permission of the National Library of Australia / The Alec Bolton Portrait Collection

Lindsay, Lilian (1871–1960)—image courtesy of BDA Museum

Lindsay, Robert James Loyd-, Baron Wantage (1832–1901)—© National Portrait Gallery, London

Lindsay, Thomas Martin (1843–1914)—© National Portrait Gallery, London

Lingard, John (1771–1851)—© National Portrait Gallery, London

Linklater, Eric Robert Russell (1899–1974)—© National Portrait Gallery, London

Linley [Sheridan], Elizabeth Ann (1754–1792)—Andrew W. Mellon Collection, Photograph © 2004 Board of Trustees, National Gallery of Art, Washington

Linley, Thomas (1733–1795)—by permission of the Trustees of Dulwich Picture Gallery

Linnaeus, Carl (1707–1778)—by permission of the Linnean Society of London

Linnecar, Richard (1722–1800)—© National Portrait Gallery, London

Linnell, John (1792–1882)—© National Portrait Gallery, London

Linstead, Sir (Reginald) Patrick (1902–1966)—© National Portrait Gallery, London

Linton, William James (1812–1897)—© National Portrait Gallery, London

Liotard, Jean-Étienne (1702–1789)—Gemäldegalerie Alte Meister, Staatliche Kunstsammlungen Dresden

Lipton, Sir Thomas Johnstone, baronet (1850–1931)—© National Portrait Gallery, London

Lisle, Sir George (*d.* 1648)—photograph by courtesy Sotheby's Picture Library, London

Lister, Anne (1791–1840)—Calderdale M.B.C., Museums & Arts (Shibden Hall)

Lister, Joseph, Baron Lister (1827–1912)—© National Portrait Gallery, London

Lister, Joseph Jackson (1786–1869)—Heritage Images Partnership

Lister, Sir Matthew (*bap.* 1571, *d.* 1656)—© National Portrait Gallery, London

Lister, Philip Cunliffe-, first earl of Swinton (1884–1972)—Estate of the Artist; private collection. Photograph: Photographic Survey, Courtauld Institute of Art, London

Lister, Samuel Cunliffe, first Baron Masham (1815–1906)—private collection. Photograph: Photographic Survey, Courtauld Institute of Art, London

Lister, Thomas, fourth Baron Ribblesdale (1854–1925)—© The National Gallery, London